Collins Complete

World Atlas

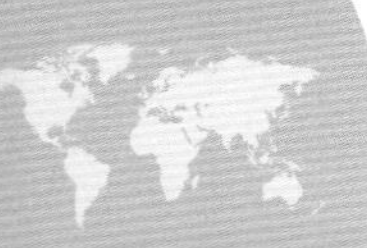

Introduction to the atlas

The atlas is arranged into a world thematic section and continental sections. As indicated on the contents list below, each section is distinctively colour-coded to allow easy identification. The continental sections contain detailed, comprehensive reference maps which are preceded by introductory pages consisting of a mixture of statistical and thematic maps, geographical statistics and photographs illustrating various topics. These topics aim to show the character of the continent and to highlight current issues of concern and interest. Each map and thematic spread contains a 'Want to know more?' box indicating links to other atlas pages with related information. The world and continental thematic pages also contain links to useful internet sites and a selection of facts relevent to the topics covered. The world section covers topics at a global level to allow a broader perspective to be gained.

Contents

Map symbols

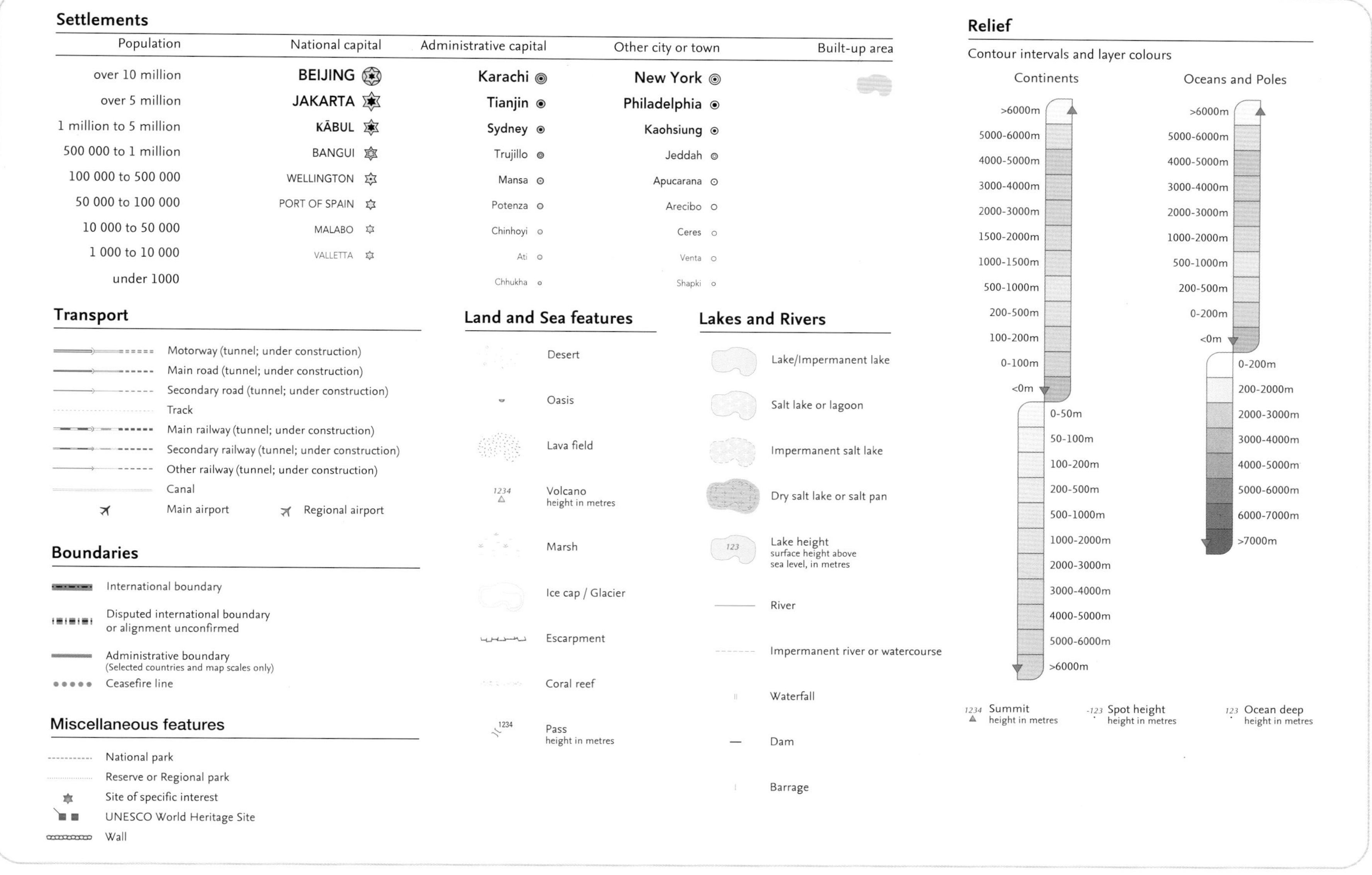

Reference Maps

Symbols and generalization

Maps show information by using symbols which are designed to reflect the features on the Earth which they represent. Symbols can be in the form of **points**, **lines**, or **areas** and variations in their **size**, **shape** and **colour** allow a great range of information to be shown. The symbols used on the reference maps are explained above.

Not all features on the ground can be shown, nor can all characteristics of a feature be depicted. Much detail has to be generalized to be clearly shown on the maps, the degree of generalization being determined largely by the scale of the map. As map scale decreases, fewer features can be shown, and their depiction becomes less detailed. The most common generalization techniques are **selection** and **simplification**. Selection is the inclusion of some features and the omission of others of less importance. Simplification is the process of smoothing lines, combining areas, or slightly displacing symbols to add clarity. These techniques are carried out in such a way that the overall character of the area mapped is retained.

Scale

The amount of detail shown on a map is determined by its scale – the relationship between the size of an area or a distance on the map and the actual size of the area or distance on the ground. **Larger scales** show more detail, **smaller scales** require more generalization and show less. Scales used for the reference maps range from 1:3 000 000 (large scale) to 1:48 000 000 (small scale). The scale of each map is indicated by a **scale bar**, which allows distances to be measured, and a **scale statement** – for example 1: 8 000 000, which means that one unit on the map (1 millimetre, for example) represents eight million of those units on the ground (in this case 8 million millimetres, or 8 kilometres).

Map projections

The 'projection' of the three-dimensional globe onto a two-dimensional map is always a problem for cartographers. All map projections introduce distortions to either **shape**, **area** or **distance**. Projections for the maps in this atlas have been specifically selected to minimize these distortions.

Geographical names

There is no single standard way of spelling names or of converting them from one alphabet, or symbol set, to another. Instead, conventional ways of spelling have evolved, and the results often differ significantly from the original name in the local language. Familiar examples in English include Munich (München in German), Florence (Firenze in Italian) and Moscow (Moskva from Russian). A further complication is that in many countries different languages are in use in different regions.

These factors, and any changes in official languages, have to be taken into account when creating maps. The policy in this atlas is generally to use **local name forms** which are officially recognized by the governments of the countries concerned. Standard rules are applied to the conversion of **non-roman** alphabet names, for example in the Russian Federation, into the roman alphabet used in English.

However, **English conventional name forms** are used for the most well-known places for which such a form is in common use. In these cases, the local form is included in brackets on the map and appears as a cross-reference in the index. Other alternative names, such as well-known historical names, may also be included in brackets. All country names and those for international physical features also appear in their English forms. The language and meaning of important non-English **geographical terms** appearing within place names on the maps are explained on page 335.

All names appearing on the reference maps are included in the **index** and can be easily found from the information included in the index entries. Full details of index policies and content can be found in the Introduction to the Index on page 225.

Boundaries

The status of nations and their boundaries, and the names associated with them, are shown in this atlas as they are in reality at the time of going to press, as far as can be ascertained. All recent changes of the status of nations and their boundaries have been taken into account. Where international boundaries are the subject of dispute, the aim is to take a strictly **neutral** viewpoint and every reasonable attempt is made to show where an active territorial dispute exists. Generally, prominence is given to the situation as it currently exists on the ground (the **de facto** situation).

International boundaries are shown on all the reference maps, and those of a large enough scale also include internal administrative boundaries of selected countries. Boundaries in the sea are generally only shown where they are required to clarify the ownership of specific islands or island groups.

UNESCO World Heritage Sites

The locations of places or features designated as UNESCO World Heritage Sites are shown on the maps by a distinctive symbol. However, limitations of map scale mean that not all individual sites can be mapped and named. Where this is the case, the symbols indicate the presence of one or more sites within a city, town or region.

The earth's physical features, both on land and on the sea bed, closely reflect its geological structure. The current shapes of the continents and oceans have evolved over millions of years. Movements of the tectonic plates which make up the earth's crust have created some of the best-known and most spectacular features. The processes which have shaped the earth continue today with earthquakes, volcanoes, erosion, climatic variations and man's activities all affecting the earth's landscapes.

The total topographic range of the earth's surface is nearly 20 000 metres (12 miles), from the highest point Mount Everest, to the lowest point in the Mariana Trench. Major mountain ranges include the Himalaya, the Andes and the Rocky Mountains, each of which give rise to some of the world's greatest rivers. In contrast the deserts of the Sahara, Australia, the Arabian Peninsula and the Gobi cover vast areas and each provide unique landscapes.

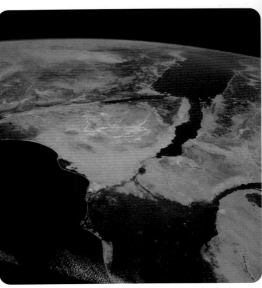

This oblique Space Shuttle photograph looks southeast from above the Mediterranean Sea over the **Sinai peninsula**, which marks the join of the continents Asia and Africa. The arid landscape is dramatically changed by the Nile delta, shown as the dark triangle in the foreground.

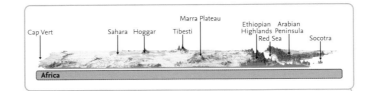

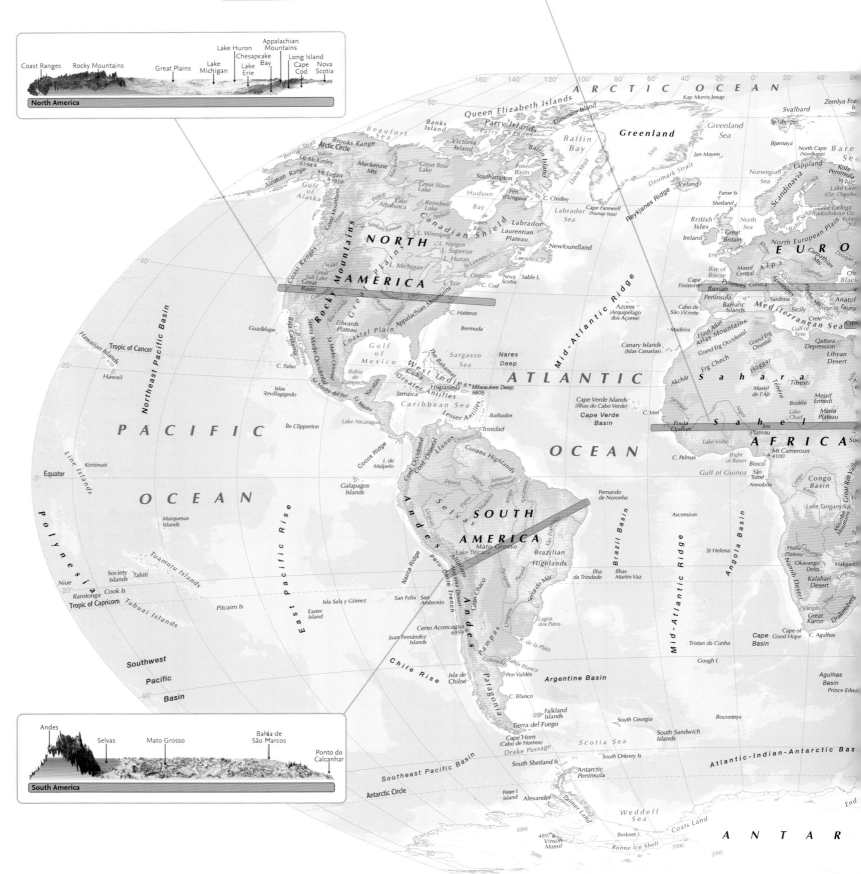

Earth's dimensions

Earth's dimensions	
Equatorial diameter	12 756 km (7 926 miles)
Polar diameter	12 714 km (7 900 miles)
Equatorial circumference	40 075 km (24 903 miles)
Meridonial circumference	40 008 km (24 861 miles)
Mass	5.974×10^{21} tonnes
Total area	509 450 000 sq km 196 672 000 sq miles
Land area	149 450 000 sq km 57 688 000 sq miles
Water area	360 000 000 sq km 138 984 000 sq miles
Volume	$1\ 083\ 207 \times 10^{6}$ cubic km $259\ 875 \times 10^{6}$ cubic miles

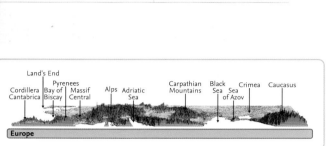

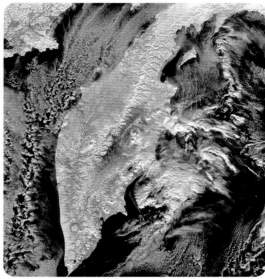

The **Kamchatka Peninsula** in the Russian Federation, is a sparsely populated region which contains over sixty active volcanoes. One of these, Sopka Klyuchevskaya (4 750 metres/ 15 584 feet), is the highest point of the central mountain range, Sredinnyy Khrebet.

Want to know more?

Distribution of earthquakes and volcanoes	10–11
Perspective view and images of Europe	28–29
Perspective view and images of Asia	60–61
Perspective view and images of Africa	110–111
Perspective view and images of Oceania	134–135
Perspective view and images of North America	154–155
Perspective view and images of South America	188–189

Internet links

Observing the earth	earthobservatory.nasa.gov
The earth's environment	www.unep.org
International conservation	www.iucn.org
Earth Resource Observation System	edc.usgs.gov

Facts

52 per cent of the earth's land surface is below 500 metres (1 640 feet).

Lake Baikal is the world's deepest lake with a maximum depth of 1 637 metres (5 371 feet).

The Pacific Ocean is larger than all the continents' land areas combined.

The Maldives in the Indian Ocean consist of approximately 1 200 low-lying islands, all under two metres (7 feet) in height.

Permanent ice covers approximately 10 per cent of the earth's land surface.

Highest mountains	metres	feet	location
Mt Everest	8 848	29 028	China/Nepal
K2	8 611	28 251	China/J and K*
Kangchenjunga	8 586	28 169	India/Nepal
Lhotse	8 516	27 939	China/Nepal
Makalu	8 463	27 765	China/Nepal
Cho Oyu	8 201	26 906	China/Nepal
Dhaulagiri	8 167	26 794	Nepal
Manaslu	8 163	26 781	Nepal
Nanga Parbat	8 126	26 660	J and K*
Annapurna I	8 091	26 545	Nepal

*Jammu and Kashmir

Longest rivers	km	miles	continent
Nile	6 695	4 160	Africa
Amazon	6 516	4 049	South America
Yangtze	6 380	3 964	Asia
Mississipi-Missouri	5 969	3 709	North America
Ob'-Irtysh	5 568	3 459	Asia
Yenisey-Angara-Selenga	5 550	3 448	Asia
Yellow	5 464	3 395	Asia
Congo	4 667	2 900	Africa
Río de la Plata - Paraná	4 500	2 796	South America
Irtysh	4 440	2 759	Asia

Largest islands	sq km	sq miles	location
Greenland	2 175 600	840 004	North America
New Guinea	808 510	312 167	Oceania
Borneo	745 561	287 863	Asia
Madagascar	587 040	266 657	Africa
Baffin Island	507 451	195 927	North America
Sumatra	473 606	182 860	Asia
Honshū	227 414	87 805	Asia
Great Britain	218 476	84 354	Europe
Victoria Island	217 291	83 897	North America
Ellesmere Island	196 236	75 767	North America

Largest lakes	sq km	sq miles	continent
Caspian Sea	371 000	143 243	Asia / Europe
Lake Superior	82 100	31 698	North America
Lake Victoria	68 800	26 563	Africa
Lake Huron	59 600	23 011	North America
Lake Michigan	57 800	22 316	North America
Lake Tanganyika	32 900	12 702	Africa
Great Bear Lake	31 328	12 095	North America
Lake Baikal	30 500	11 776	Asia
Lake Nyasa	30 044	11 600	Africa
Great Slave Lake	28 568	11 030	North America

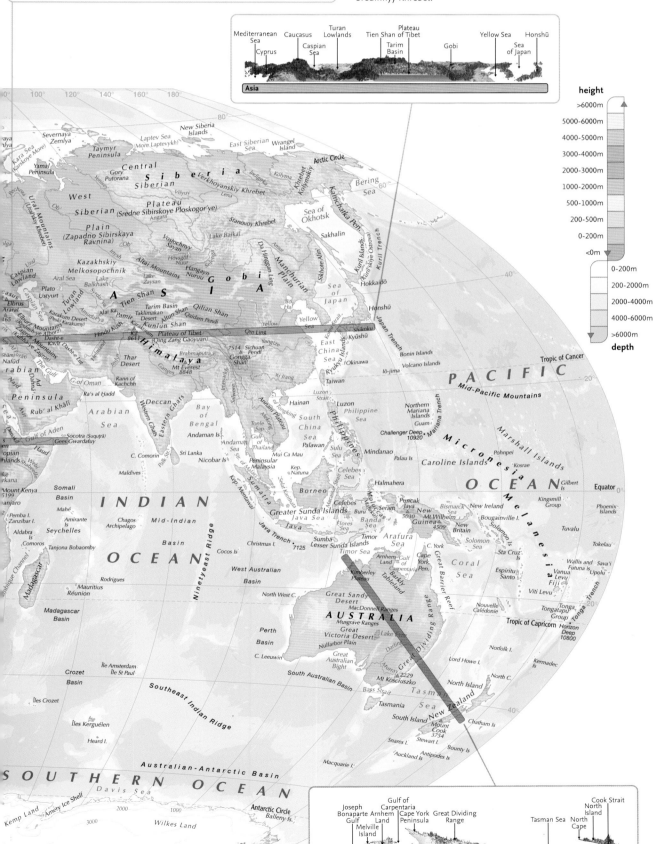

The current pattern of the world's countries and territories is a result of a long history of exploration, colonialism, conflict and politics. The fact that there are currently 193 independent countries in the world – the most recent, East Timor, only being created in May 2002 – illustrates the significant political changes which have occurred since 1950 when there were only eighty-two. There has been a steady progression away from colonial influences over the last fifty years, although many dependent overseas territories remain.

The shapes of countries and the pattern of international boundaries reflect both physical and political processes. Some borders follow natural features – rivers, mountain ranges, etc – others are defined according to political agreement or as a result of war. Many are still subject to dispute between two or more countries, and many remain undefined on the ground.

The capital of the United States, **Washington, D.C.**, is situated on the confluence of the Potomac and Anacostia rivers, seen here to the left and bottom respectively. The Capitol, the White House and Union Station can all be seen in the centre of this infrared aerial photograph.

Country abbreviations

A.	ANDORRA	**HUN.**	HUNGARY	**ROM.**	ROMANIA		
AL.	ALBANIA	**ISR.**	ISRAEL	**S.**	SWAZILAND		
ARM.	ARMENIA	**JOR.**	JORDAN	**SL.**	SLOVENIA		
AUST.	AUSTRIA	**L.**	LUXEMBOURG	**SLA.**	SLOVAKIA		
AZER.	AZERBAIJAN	**LAT.**	LATVIA	**S.M.**	SERBIA AND MONTENEGRO		
B.	BURUNDI	**LEB.**	LEBANON	**SUR.**	SURINAME		
BEL.	BELGIUM	**LITH.**	LITHUANIA	**SW.**	SWITZERLAND		
B.H.	BOSNIA-HERZEGOVINA	**M.**	MACEDONIA	**TAJIK.**	TAJIKISTAN		
BULG.	BULGARIA	**MOL.**	MOLDOVA	**TURKM.**	TURKMENISTAN		
CR.	CROATIA	**NETH.**	NETHERLANDS	**U.A.E.**	UNITED ARAB EMIRATES		
CZ.R.	CZECH REPUBLIC	**N.Z.**	NEW ZEALAND	**U.K.**	UNITED KINGDOM		
EST.	ESTONIA	**R.**	RWANDA	**U.S.A.**	UNITED STATES OF AMERICA		
GEOR.	GEORGIA	**R.F.**	RUSSIAN FEDERATION	**UZBEK.**	UZBEKISTAN		

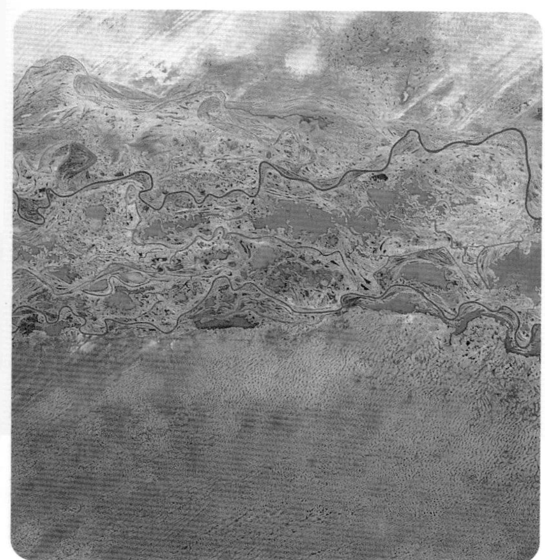

The **Senegal river** forms the border between Mauritania and Senegal. At the top of this infrared satellite image the southern edge of the Sahara desert in Mauritania becomes semi-desert, the Sahel, which stretches east to Chad. The lower half of the image shows mixed scrubland in Senegal.

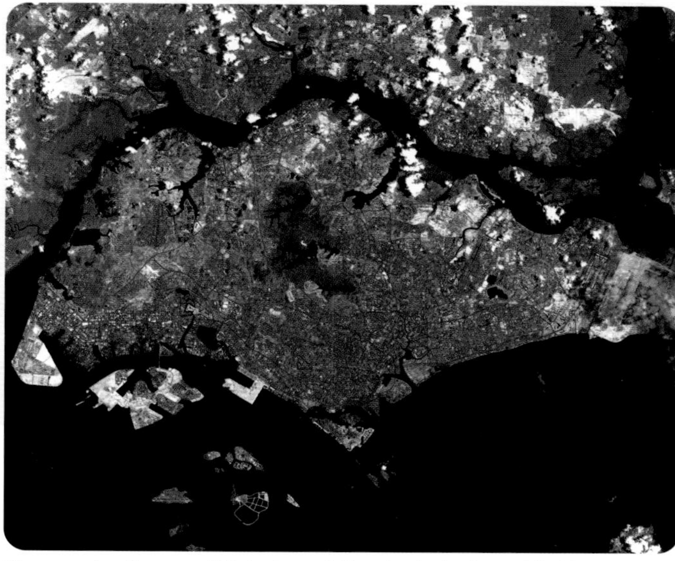

Singapore has the second highest population density in the world with over 6 500 people living per square kilometre (2 510 people per square mile). This island city state helps overcome this problem by land reclamation as can be seen by the light regular shaped areas to the southwest of the island. The airport at the far east of the island was also built on reclaimed land.

Internet links

United Nations	www.un.org
International boundaries	www.ibru.dur.ac.uk
European Union	europa.eu.int
US Board on Geographic Names	geonames.usgs.gov
Permanent Committee on Geographic Names	www.pcgn.org.uk
Foreign and Commonwealth Office	www.fco.gov.uk

Facts

Canada and the USA share the longest single continuous land border which stretches for 6 416 kilometres (3 987 miles).

Both China and the Russian Federation have borders with fourteen different countries.

The break up of the U.S.S.R. (Union of Soviet Socialist Republics) in 1991 resulted in fifteen new independent countries including the Russian Federation.

East Timor is the world's newest independent country, gaining independence from Indonesia on 20 May 2002.

Taiwan and the Vatican City are the only countries in the world who do not belong to the United Nations.

Largest countries by area

		sq km	sq miles
1	**Russian Federation**	17 075 400	6 592 849
2	**Canada**	9 970 610	3 849 674
3	**United States of America**	9 809 378	3 787 422
4	**China**	9 584 492	3 700 593
5	**Brazil**	8 547 379	3 300 161
6	**Australia**	7 682 395	2 966 189
7	**India**	3 065 027	1 183 414
8	**Argentina**	2 766 889	1 068 302
9	**Kazakhstan**	2 717 300	1 049 155
10	**Sudan**	2 505 813	967 500

Smallest countries by area

		sq km	sq miles
1	**Vatican City**	0.5	0.2
2	**Monaco**	2	1
3	**Nauru**	21	8
4	**Tuvalu**	25	10
5	**San Marino**	61	24
6	**Liechtenstein**	160	62
7	**St Kitts and Nevis**	261	101
8	**Maldives**	298	115
9	**Grenada**	378	146
10	**St Vincent and the Grenadines**	389	150

Capital city extremes

Most populous	Tōkyō, Japan	26 444 000
Least populous	Yaren, Nauru	600
Highest	La Paz, Bolivia	3 636m / 11 910ft
Lowest	Manama, Bahrain and Male, Maldives	0.9m / 3ft
Furthest north	Nuuk, Greenland	64° 11'N
Furthest south	Stanley, Falkland Islands	51° 43'S
Furthest east	Vaiaku, Tuvalu	179° 13'E
Furthest west	Nuku'alofa, Tonga	175° 12'W

Joint capitals		country
Amsterdam/The Hague		Netherlands
Kuala Lumpur/Putrajaya		Malaysia
La Paz/Sucre		Bolivia
Pretoria/Cape Town		South Africa

Earthquakes and volcanoes hold a fascination because of their destructive power, their beauty, and the fact that they cannot be controlled or accurately predicted. Our understanding of these phenomena relies on the theory of plate tectonics. This defines the earth's surface as a series of 'plates' which are constantly moving. The distribution of earthquakes and volcanoes relates closely to plate boundaries. Enormous pressure builds up between plates, causing the rock to fracture and energy to be released as earthquakes. The pressures involved can also melt the rock to form magma which then rises to the earth's surface to form a volcano. Whilst potentially very destructive, the energy generated by these processes can also be exploited by man – geo-thermal energy is becoming an increasingly important renewable energy source.

Richter Scale

The scale measures the energy released by an earthquake. The scale is logarithmic – a quake measuring 5 is ten times more powerful as one measuring 4.

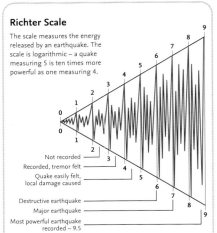

Not recorded
Recorded, tremor felt
Quake easily felt, local damage caused
Destructive earthquake
Major earthquake
Most powerful earthquake recorded – 9.5

Earthquakes

Most earthquakes are caused by movement of the earth's crust along tectonic plate boundaries. There are three types of plate boundary: constructive boundaries where plates are moving apart; destructive boundaries where two or more plates collide; conservative boundaries where plates slide past each other. The size, or magnitude, of an earthquake is generally measured on the Richter Scale.

If earthquakes occur below the ocean floor, they can cause tsunamis – very powerful waves which can travel enormous distances at great speed. The great tsunami of December 2004 caused over 250 000 deaths and widespread destruction in eleven countries around the Indian Ocean.

Distribution of earthquakes and volcanoes

- ⊙ Deadliest earthquake
- ● Earthquake of magnitude >= 7.5
- ∘ Earthquake of magnitude 5.5–7.5
- ▲ Major volcano
- ▲ Other volcano

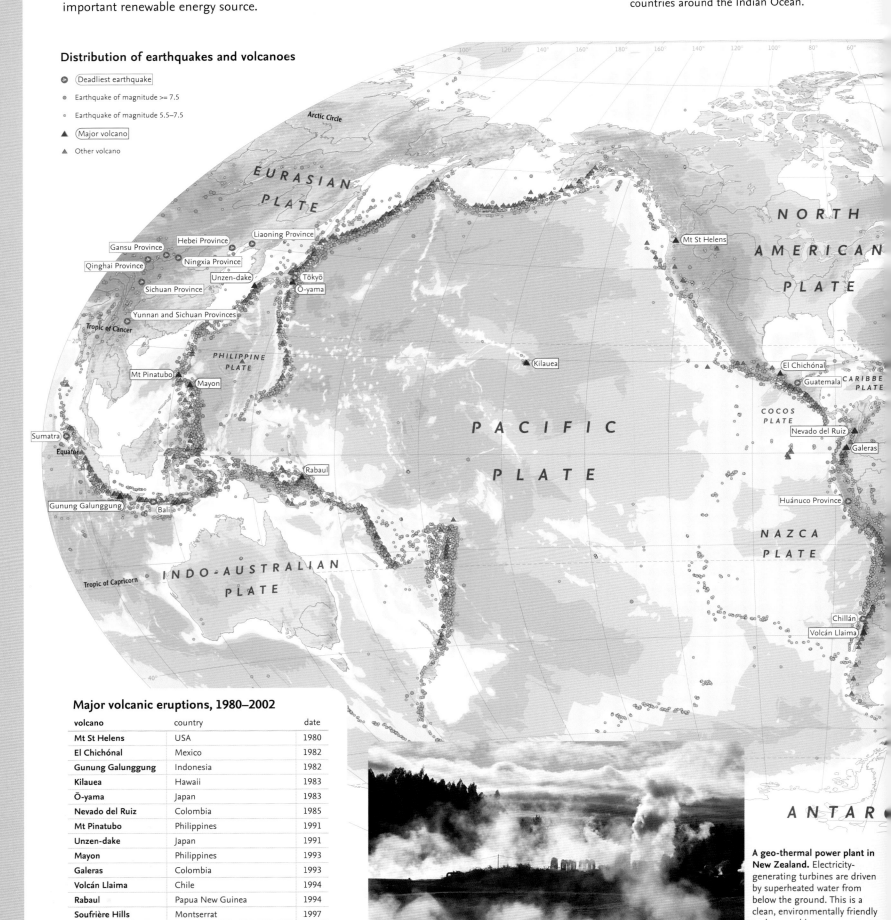

Major volcanic eruptions, 1980–2002

volcano	country	date
Mt St Helens	USA	1980
El Chichónal	Mexico	1982
Gunung Galunggung	Indonesia	1982
Kilauea	Hawaii	1983
Ō-yama	Japan	1983
Nevado del Ruiz	Colombia	1985
Mt Pinatubo	Philippines	1991
Unzen-dake	Japan	1991
Mayon	Philippines	1993
Galeras	Colombia	1993
Volcán Llaima	Chile	1994
Rabaul	Papua New Guinea	1994
Soufrière Hills	Montserrat	1997
Hekla	Iceland	2000
Mt Etna	Italy	2001
Nyiragongo	Democratic Republic of the Congo	2002

A geo-thermal power plant in New Zealand. Electricity-generating turbines are driven by superheated water from below the ground. This is a clean, environmentally friendly and renewable energy source concentrated in areas of volcanic activity. It is used widely in New Zealand, Iceland, Japan, Italy and the USA.

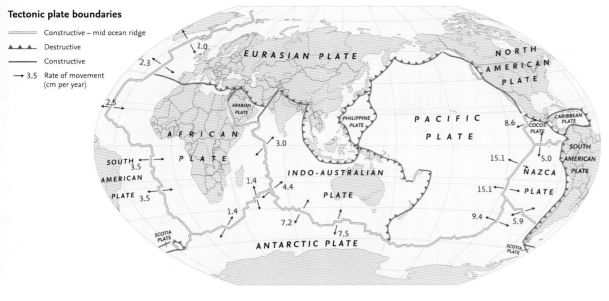

Tectonic plate boundaries

- Constructive – mid ocean ridge
- ▲▲▲ Destructive
- Constructive
- → 3.5 Rate of movement (cm per year)

Want to know more?	
➤ Map of the world's physical features	6–7
➤ Image of Mt St Helens	14–15
➤ Indian Ocean tsunami	66–67
➤ Maps of ocean features	206–209

Internet links	
USGS National Earthquake Information Center	neic.usgs.gov
USGS Volcano Information	volcanoes.usgs.gov
British Geological Survey	www.bgs.ac.uk
NASA Natural Hazards	earthobservatory.nasa.gov/NaturalHazards
Volcano World	volcano.und.nodak.edu

Facts

Over 900 earthquakes of magnitude 5.0 or greater occur every year.

Indonesia has more than 120 volcanoes and over 30 per cent of the world's active volcanoes.

Volcanoes can produce very fertile soil and important industrial materials and chemicals.

The Indian Ocean tsunami of December 2004 was recorded on tide gauges throughout the world.

Deadliest earthquakes, 1900–2005

year	location	deaths
1905	**Kangra**, India	19 000
1907	west of **Dushanbe**, Tajikistan	12 000
1908	**Messina**, Italy	110 000
1915	**Abruzzo**, Italy	35 000
1917	**Bali**, Indonesia	15 000
1920	**Ningxia Province**, China	200 000
1923	**Tōkyō**, Japan	142 807
1927	**Qinghai Province**, China	200 000
1932	**Gansu Province**, China	70 000
1933	**Sichuan Province**, China	10 000
1934	**Nepal/India**	10 700
1935	**Quetta**, Pakistan	30 000
1939	**Chillán**, Chile	28 000
1939	**Erzincan**, Turkey	32 700
1948	**Ashgabat**, Turkmenistan	19 800
1962	**Northwest Iran**	12 225
1970	**Huánuco Province**, Peru	66 794
1974	**Yunnan and Sichuan Provinces**, China	20 000
1975	**Liaoning Province**, China	10 000
1976	central **Guatemala**	22 778
1976	**Hebei Province**, China	255 000
1978	**Khorāsan Province**, Iran	20 000
1980	**Ech Chélif**, Algeria	11 000
1988	**Spitak**, Armenia	25 000
1990	**Manjil**, Iran	50 000
1999	**Kocaeli (İzmit)**, Turkey	17 000
2001	**Gujarat**, India	20 000
2003	**Bam**, Iran	26 271
2004	off **Sumatra**, Indian Ocean	>250 000

Extensive damage caused by a major earthquake of magnitude 6.6 centred on **Bam**, southeast Iran, in December 2003. The quake killed over 30 000 people and 85 per cent of buildings in the area were destroyed.

Volcanoes

The majority of volcanoes occur along destructive plate boundaries in the 'subduction zone' where one plate passes under another. Friction and pressure cause rock to melt and to form magma which is forced upwards to the earth's surface where it erupts as molten rock (lava) or as particles of ash or cinder. This process created the numerous volcanoes in the Andes, where the Nazca Plate is passing under the South American Plate. Volcanoes can be defined by the nature of the material they emit. 'Shield' volcanoes have extensive, gentle slopes formed from free-flowing lava, while steep-sided 'continental' volcanoes are created from thicker, slow-flowing lava and ash.

The climate of a region is defined by its long-term prevailing weather conditions. Classification of climate types is based on the relationship between temperature and humidity and how these factors are affected by latitude, altitude, ocean currents and winds. Weather is the specific short term condition which occurs locally and consists of events such as thunderstorms, hurricanes, blizzards and heat waves. Temperature and rainfall data recorded at weather stations can be plotted graphically and the graphs shown here, typical of each climate region, illustrate the various combinations of temperature and rainfall which exist worldwide for each month of the year. Data used for climate graphs are based on average monthly figures recorded over a minimum period of thirty years.

World climate changes in the future

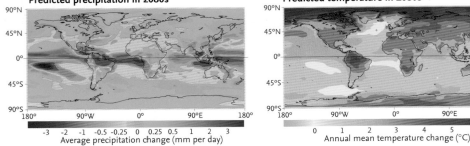

Predicted precipitation in 2080s

Average precipitation change (mm per day)

Predicted temperature in 2080s

Annual mean temperature change (°C)

World average annual precipitation

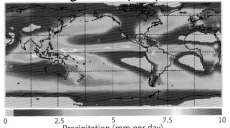

Precipitation (mm per day)

Prediction of climate change

Climate modelling has produced predictions of temperature and precipitation change. These suggest that there will be significant impacts on sea level, which could rise by as much as 500 millimetres (19.7 inches) over the next century.

World major climate regions, ocean currents and sea surface temperature

Weather extremes

Highest recorded temperature	57.8°C/136°F Al ʿAzīzīyah, Libya (13th September 1922)
Hottest place — annual mean	34.4°C/93.9°F Dalol, Ethiopia
Lowest recorded temperature	-89.2°C/-128.6°F Vostok Station, Antarctica (21st July 1983)
Coldest place — annual mean	-56.6°C/-69.9°F Plateau Station, Antarctica
Driest place — annual mean	0.1 mm/0.004 inches Atacama Desert, Chile
Wettest place — annual mean	11 873 mm/467.4 inches Meghalaya, India
Most rainy days	Up to 350 per year Mount Waialeale, Hawaii, USA
Most sunshine — annual mean	90% Yuma, Arizona, USA (over 4 000 hours)
Least sunshine	Nil for 182 days each year, South Pole
Windiest place	322 km per hour/200 miles per hour in gales, Commonwealth Bay, Antarctica

Weather stations

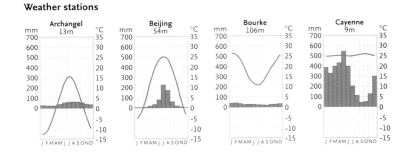

Climate regions

- Ice cap
- Tundra
- Subarctic
- Continental cool summer
- Continental warm summer
- Temperate
- Humid subtropical
- Mediterranean
- Steppe
- Desert
- Savanna
- Rain forest

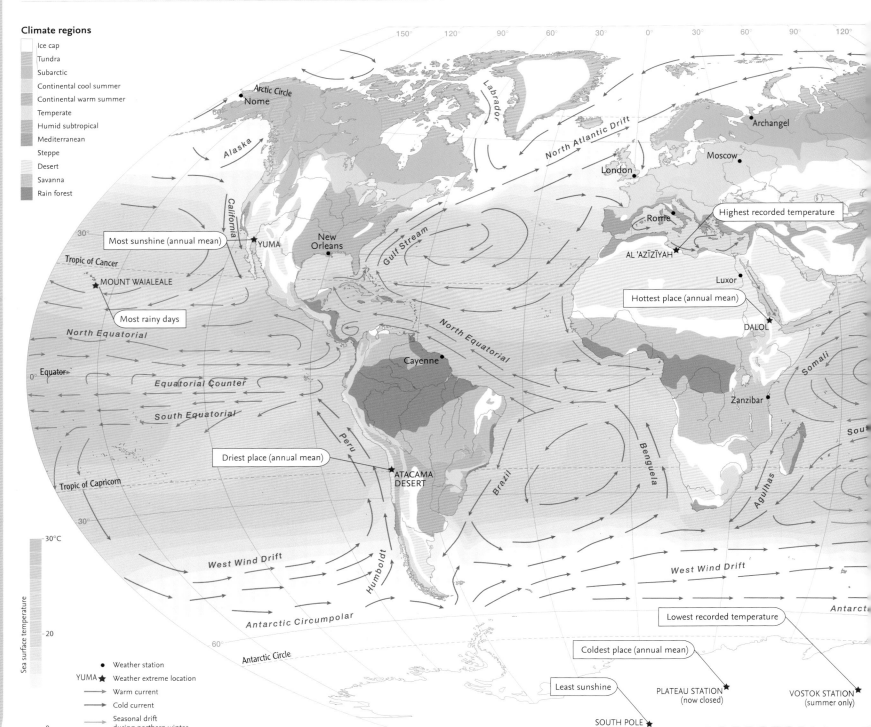

- Weather station
- YUMA ★ Weather extreme location
- → Warm current
- → Cold current
- → Seasonal drift during northern winter

Sea surface temperature

World temperature

January

July

32°C
16
0
-16
-32

Want to know more?	
▸ Asia water resources	68–69
▸ Sea level rise in Oceania	140–141
▸ Hurricanes in North America	160–161
▸ Image of hurricane Ivan	160–161
▸ Antarctic ozone hole	212–213

Internet links	
BBC Weather Centre	www.bbc.co.uk/weather
Met Office	www.met-office.gov.uk
National Climate and Data Center	www.ncdc.noaa.gov
National Oceanic and Atmospheric Administration	www.noaa.gov
United Nations World Meteorological Organization	www.wmo.ch
University of East Anglia Climatic Research Unit	www.cru.uea.ac.uk

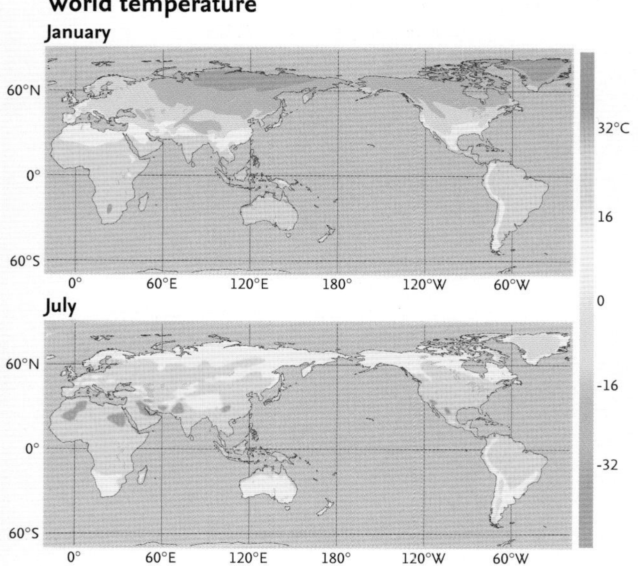

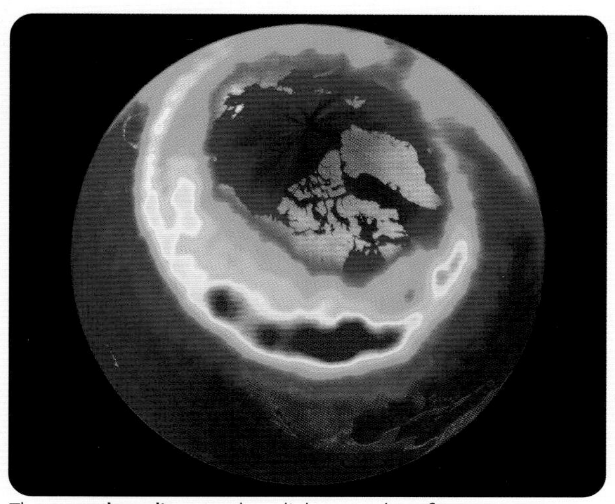

The **aurora borealis** or northern lights, seen here from space, are caused by particles from the sun interacting with the earth's atmosphere. The earth's magnetic field channels the charged particles to the poles where they collide with gas molecules in the upper atmosphere, causing them to glow.

Facts

Arctic Sea ice thickness has declined 4 per cent in the last 40 years.

2001 marked the end of the La Niña episode.

Sea levels are rising by 10 millimetres (0.4 inches) per decade.

Precipitation in the northern hemisphere is increasing.

Droughts have increased in frequency and intensity in parts of Asia and Africa.

Climate graphs for London (24m), Luxor (82m), Moscow (156m), New Orleans (1m), Nome (11m), Rome (2m), Zanzibar (15m).

⌒ Average monthly temperature
▪ Average monthly rainfall
13m Height above sea level

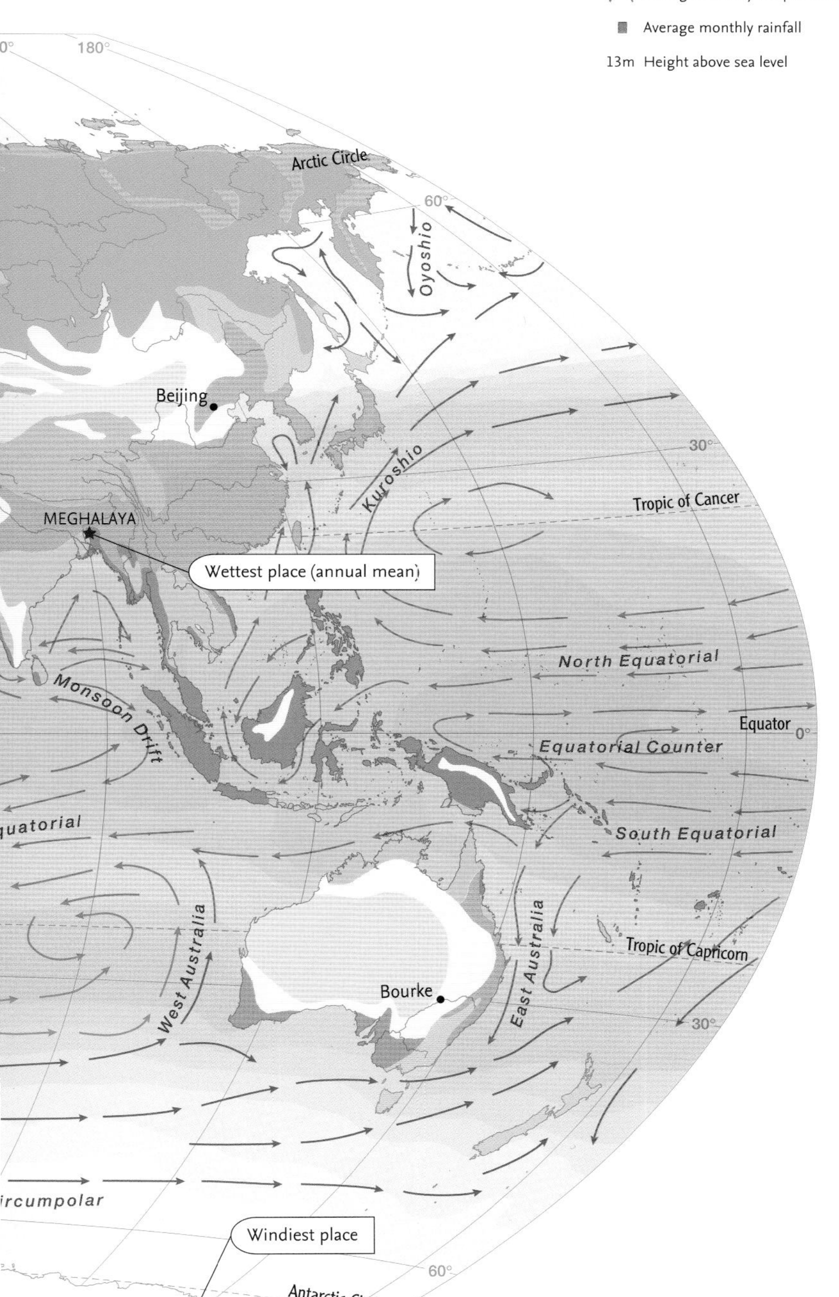

Evidence of climate change

In 2001 the global mean temperature was 0.63°C higher than that at the end of the 19th century. Most of this warming is caused by human activities which result in a build-up of greenhouse gases, mainly carbon dioxide, allowing heat to be trapped within the atmosphere. Carbon dioxide emissions have increased since the beginning of the industrial revolution due to burning of fossil fuels, increased urbanization, population growth, deforestation and industrial pollution. Annual climate indicators such as number of frost-free days, length of growing season, heatwave frequency, number of wet days, length of dry spells and frequency of weather extremes are used to monitor climate change. The map highlights some events which indicate climate change. Until carbon dioxide emissions are reduced it is likely that this trend will continue.

1. Warmest winter recorded in **Alaska and Yukon**.
2. Third warmest year on record in **Canada**.
3. Severe rainfall deficit in **northwest USA**.
4. Costliest storm in US history was tropical storm **Alison**.
5. Extreme summer drought in **Central America**.
6. Strongest hurricane to hit Cuba since 1952 was **Michelle**.
7. End of **La Niña** episode.
8. Severe flooding in **Bolivia**.
9. Normal rainy season hit by drought in **Brazil**.
10. Longer lasting ozone hole than previous years in **Antarctica**.
11. Worst flooding since 1997 in **southwest Poland and Czech Republic**.
12. Temperatures 1°–2°C above average for 2001 in **Europe and Middle East**.
13. Severe November flooding in **Algeria**.
14. Continued drought in area around **Horn of Africa**.
15. Widespread minimum winter temperatures near -60°C in **Siberia and Mongolia**.
16. 1998 drought continues in **Southern Asia**.
17. Severe drought and water shortages in **Northern China, Korean Peninsula and Japan**.
18. Extensive flooding in September caused by Typhoon **Nari**.
19. Severe flooding August to October in **Vietnam and Cambodia**.
20. Severe flooding causes more than 400 deaths when four tropical cyclones, **Durian, Yutu, Ulor and Toraji** made landfall in July.
21. Major flooding in February on **Java**.
22. Driest summer on record in **Perth**.
23. Cooler and wetter than normal in **Western Australia**.
24. One of the driest summers recorded in **New Zealand**.
25. Severe flooding February to April in **Mozambique, Zambia, Malawi and Zimbabwe**.

Temperature above average
Temperature below average
Rainfall above average
Rainfall below average
⌒ Paths of storms
㉕ Indicator of climate change

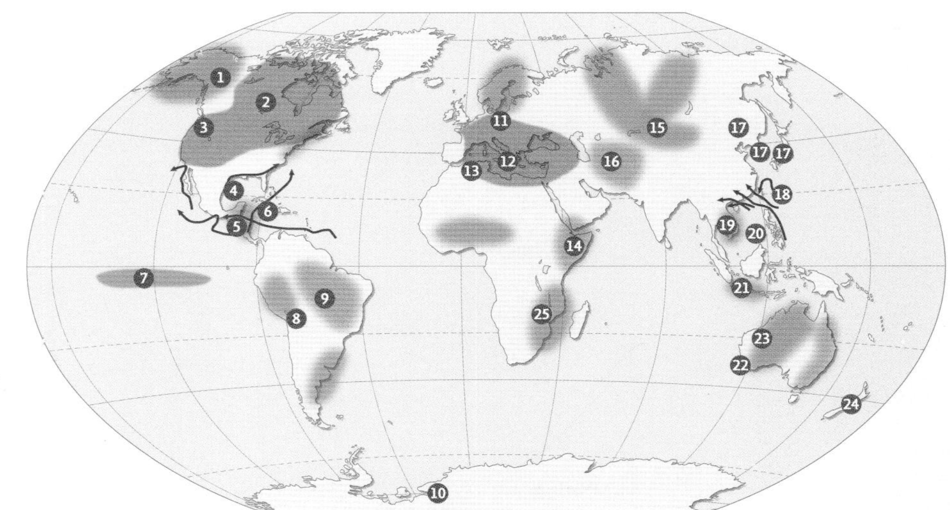

The earth has a rich and diverse environment. Forests and woodland form the predominant natural land cover with tropical rain forests believed to be home to the majority of animal and plant species. Grassland and scrub tend to have a lower natural species diversity but have suffered the most impact from man's intervention through conversion to agriculture, burning and the introduction of livestock. Wherever man interferes with existing biological and environmental processes, degradation of that environment commonly occurs, to varying degrees. This interference also affects inland water and oceans where pollution, over-exploitation of marine resources and the need for fresh water have had major consequences to terrestrial and marine environments.

The **Yellowstone National Park** in Wyoming, U.S.A., was the world's first national park, established in 1872. It is also a World Heritage Site. As well as being home to threatened species, the park sits on a volcanic basin which is evident by its hot springs and geysers.

Environmental impacts

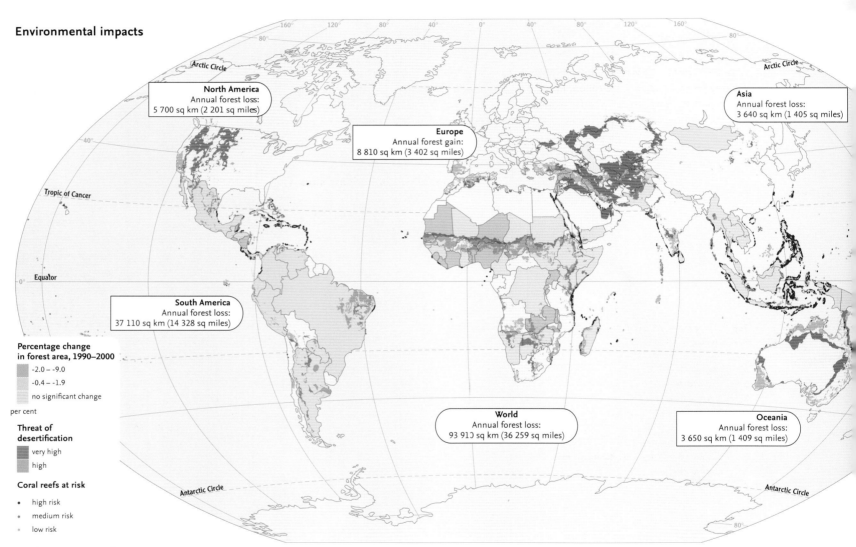

North America
Annual forest loss:
5 700 sq km (2 201 sq miles)

Europe
Annual forest gain:
8 810 sq km (3 402 sq miles)

Asia
Annual forest loss:
3 640 sq km (1 405 sq miles)

South America
Annual forest loss:
37 110 sq km (14 328 sq miles)

World
Annual forest loss:
93 910 sq km (36 259 sq miles)

Oceania
Annual forest loss:
3 650 sq km (1 409 sq miles)

Percentage change
in forest area, 1990–2000

-2.0 – -9.0
-0.4 – -1.9
no significant change
per cent

Threat of
desertification
very high
high

Coral reefs at risk
· high risk
· medium risk
· low risk

Man's impact on the environment

Almost half of the world's post-glacial forest has been cleared or degraded and old-growth forest continues to decline. Desertification caused by climate change and the impact of man can turn marginal grassland areas back to arid desert. The northern edge of the Sahel region, south of the Sahara, sees this creep of the desert areas southwards whereas in the southern parts of the region, rainforest is being cleared to provide more grassland. Water is precious to the natural environment and to man, but polluted water can be devastating to both.

The Ganges river is sacred to the Hindu religion but it is polluted by **industrial and domestic effluent.** People still come daily to wash and bathe in it.

Livestock feeding on and uprooting sparse vegetation in arid areas can increase the risk of **desertification.** Replanting these areas with specific species can hold the dunes in place and help slow the process.

Deforestation can take place on a large scale by organized logging teams or on a small scale by migrant farmers clearing an area to create pasture and crops. The slash-and-burn technique, used here in Madagascar, creates ash which acts as a short term fertiliser.

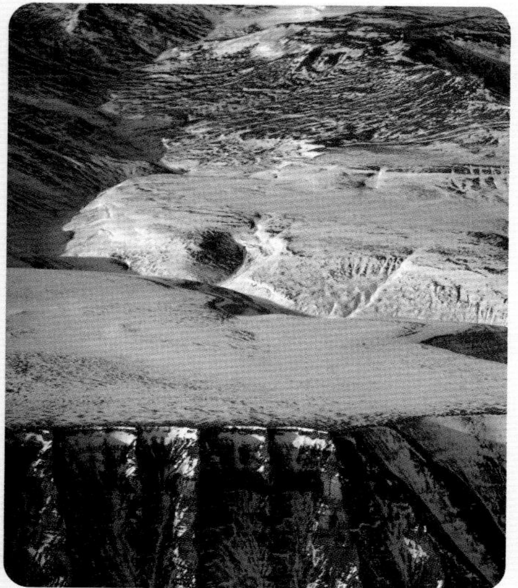

The **Northeast Greenland National Park** is the world's largest area of protected land and is extremely remote. Because of this it is an ideal place to study the effects of climate change.

Top 20 protected areas by size

	protected area	country	size (sq km)	designation
1	Greenland	Greenland	972 000	National Park
2	Rub' al Khālī	Saudi Arabia	640 000	Wildlife Management Area
3	Great Barrier Reef Marine Park	Australia	344 360	Marine Park
4	Northwestern Hawaiian Islands	United States	341 362	Coral Reef Ecosystem Reserve
5	Amazonia	Colombia	326 329	Forest Reserve
6	Qiangtang	China	298 000	Nature Reserve
7	Macquarie Island	Australia	162 060	Marine Park
8	Sanjiangyuan	China	152 300	Nature Reserve
9	Cape Churchill	Canada	137 072	Wildlife Management Area
10	Galapagos Islands	Ecuador	133 000	Marine Reserve
11	Northern Wildlife Management Zone	Saudi Arabia	100 875	Wildlife Management Area
12	Ngaanyatjarra Lands	Australia	98 129	Indigenous Protected Area
13	Alto Orinoco-Casiquiare	Venezuela	84 000	Biosphere Reserve
14	Vale do Javari	Brazil	83 380	Indigenous Area
15	Ouadi Rimé-Ouadi Achim	Chad	80 000	Faunal Reserve
16	Arctic	United States	78 049	National Wildlife Refuge
17	Yanomami	Brazil	77 519	Indigenous Park
18	Yukon Delta	United States	77 425	National Wildlife Refuge
19	Aïr and Ténéré	Niger	77 360	National Nature Reserve
20	Pacifico	Colombia	73 981	Forest Reserve

Want to know more?

▸ Map of the world's physical features	6–7
▸ Distribution of earthquakes and volcanoes	10–11
▸ Map of availability of safe water	20–21
▸ Pollution in the Mediterranean Sea	34–35
▸ Oceania's coral reefs at risk	140–141
▸ Deforestation in South America	194–195

Internet links

UN Environment Programme	www.unep.org
UNESCO World Heritage Sites	whc.unesco.org
IUCN World Conservation Union	www.iucn.org
World Resources Institute	www.iucn.org

Facts

There are an estimated 44 000 parks and protected areas covering about 10 per cent of the earth's surface.

Degraded soils have lowered global agricultural yields by 13 per cent since 1945.

Rennell Island in the Solomon Islands is the largest coral atoll in the world measuring 86 kilometres (53 miles) by 15 kilometres (9 miles).

The Sundarbans stretching across the Ganges delta is the largest area of mangrove forest covering 10 000 square kilometres (3 861 square miles) forming an important ecological area, home to 260 species of birds, the Bengal tiger and other threatened species.

World heritage sites

UNESCO adopted an international treaty in 1972 to recognize sites, cultural and natural, of worldwide significance. Such places would be unique irreplaceable sites of inspiration demonstrating either man's achievement or nature's creation. Presently there are 788 official sites, the 154 natural and 23 mixed sites are plotted on the map. The atlas reference pages show their exact locations and names. 35 of the 788 sites are cited as 'in danger' either due to civil conflicts or war, such as those in the Democratic Republic of the Congo, or through pressure from agriculture and logging as in Honduras.

Distribution of world heritage sites

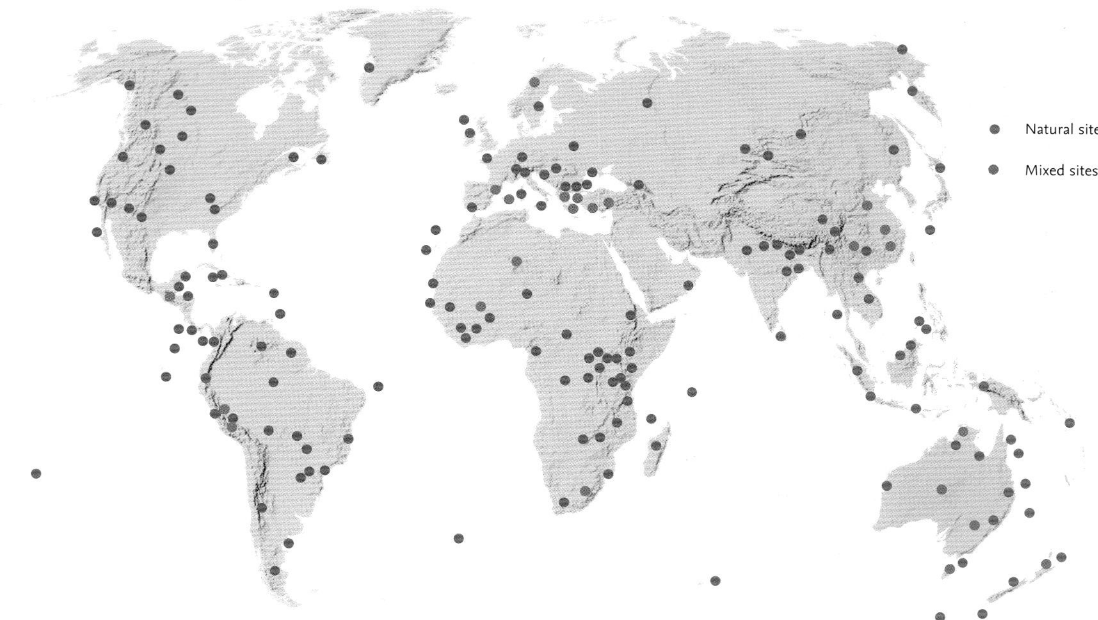

- Natural sites
- Mixed sites

Top 10 coral reef 'hot spots'
Ranked by degree of threat

	location
1	Philippines
2	Gulf of Guinea
3	Sunda Islands
4	Southern Mascarene Islands
5	Eastern South Africa
6	Northern Indian Ocean
7	Southern Japan, Taiwan and Southern China
8	Cape Verde Islands
9	Western Caribbean
10	Red Sea and Gulf of Aden

Natural environmental hazards

Natural changes to the planet's equilibrium impact on the surrounding environment and on man's use of the land. Volcanoes such as Mt St Helens can leave deep layers of ash and lava covering large areas. Surrounding vegetation and woodland can be severely damaged as a result of such events. Dust storms can travel great distances, polluting the atmosphere while the failure of seasonal rains or a sudden excess of water in floods can devastate crops and food resources for man and wildlife.

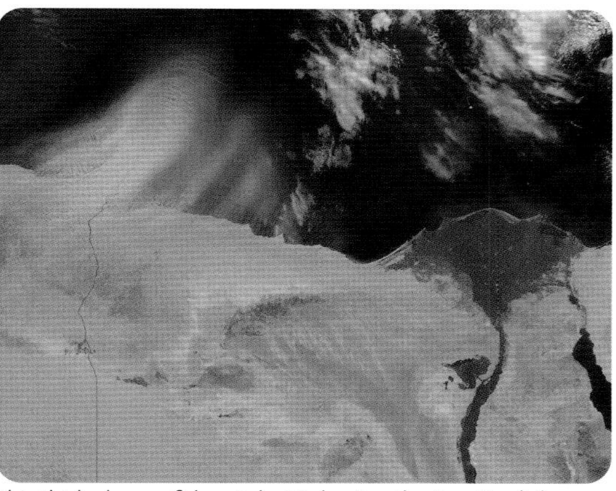

This thick plume of desert dust is leaving the Egyptian/Libyan coast heading into the Mediterranean Sea. Such events can result in **air pollution** as far away as mainland Greece. Inland, soil structure can be degraded by the addition of sand and any 'alien' spores or viruses.

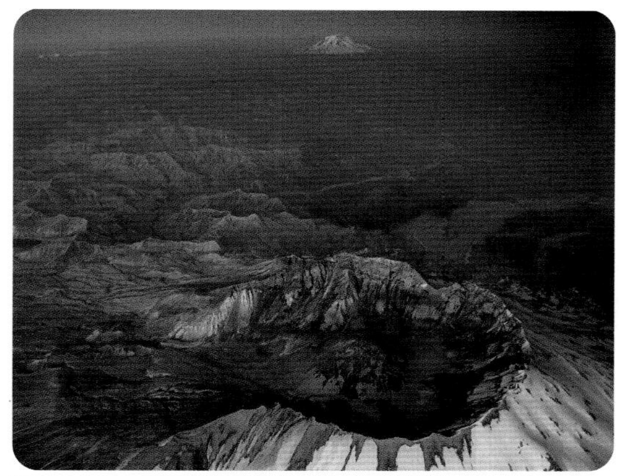

The picturesque Mt St Helens erupted in 1980 reducing its height by 400 metres (1 312 feet). Lava, pumice and ash produced by **volcanoes** covers the surrounding area. Some plants are adapted to rejuvenate after such events whilst in other areas the land can lie barren for many years.

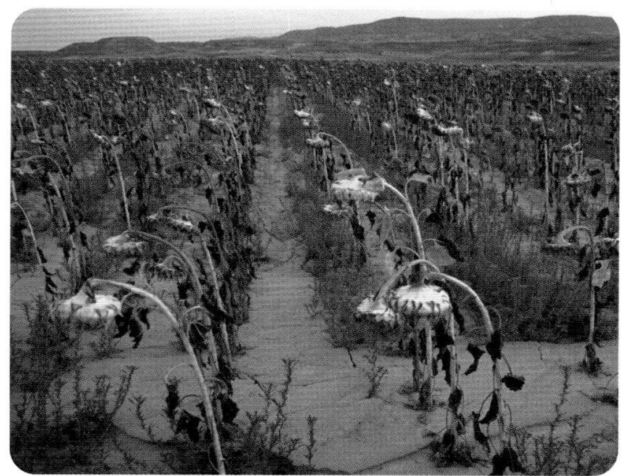

This field of sunflowers in Spain shows the effect of one season's **drought.** However damaging this may be here, in the Third World whole regions can be devastated by similar events.

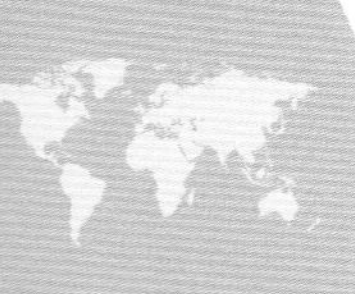

After growing very slowly for most of human history, world population more than doubled in the last half century. World population passed the one billion mark in 1804 and 123 years later reached two billion in 1927. It then added the third billion in 33 years, the fourth in 14 years and the fifth in 13 years. Just twelve years later on October 12, 1999 the United Nations announced that the global population had reached six billion. It is expected that another three billion people will have been added to the world's population by 2050.

Over half the world's people live in six countries: China, India, USA, Indonesia, Brazil and Pakistan and over 80 per cent of the total population live in less developed regions. As shown on the population distribution map below, over a quarter of the land area is uninhabited or has extremely low population density. Barely a quarter of the land area is occupied at densities of 25 or more persons per square kilometre, with the three largest concentrations in east Asia, the Indian subcontinent and Europe accounting for over half the world total.

Less developed countries

More developed countries

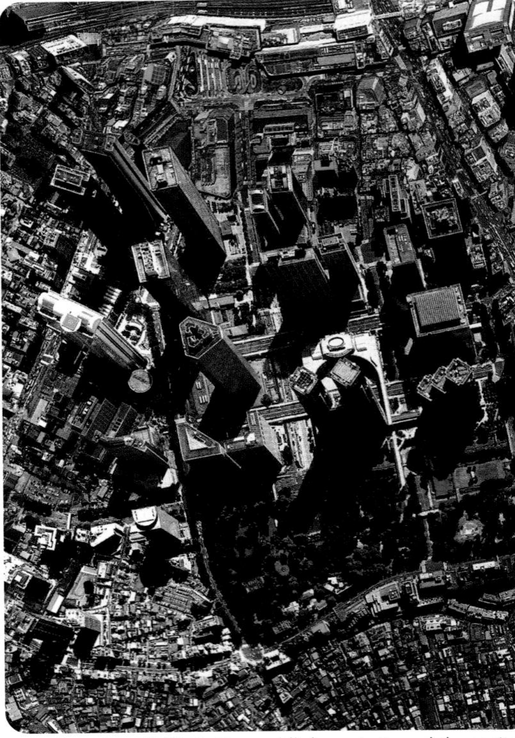

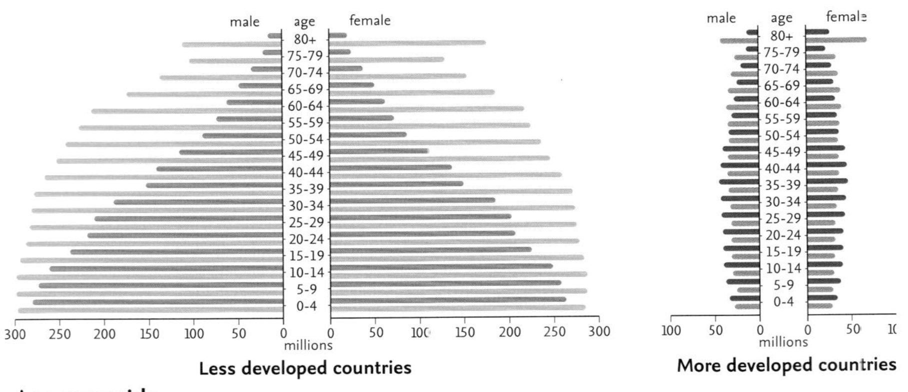

Age pyramids
Structure of population within less developed countries and more developed countries, by age

less developed countries
— 1998
— 2050

more developed countries
— 1998
— 2050

A small section of **Tōkyō**, the world's largest city and the capital of Japan, is shown in this aerial photograph mosaic. The contrasting pattern of high-rise development and densely packed low-rise buildings is typical of many major Asian cities. For a modern city, it has retained much of its cultural and historical identity.

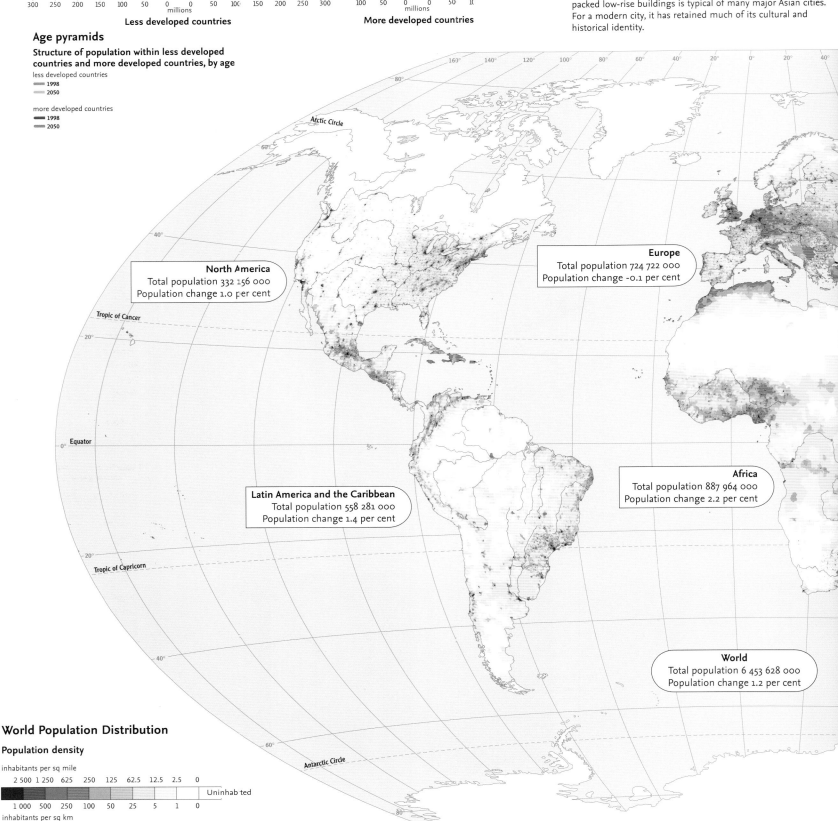

North America
Total population 332 156 000
Population change 1.0 per cent

Europe
Total population 724 722 000
Population change -0.1 per cent

Latin America and the Caribbean
Total population 558 281 000
Population change 1.4 per cent

Africa
Total population 887 964 000
Population change 2.2 per cent

World
Total population 6 453 628 000
Population change 1.2 per cent

World Population Distribution

Population density

inhabitants per sq mile
2 500 1 250 625 250 125 62.5 12.5 2.5 0
Uninhabited
1 000 500 250 100 50 25 5 1 0
inhabitants per sq km

Population change

While the world's population has been growing rapidly since 1950, a massive 89 per cent increase has taken place in the less developed regions. In contrast, Europe's population level has been almost stationary and is now decreasing. There are also marked differences between the age structures within developed and less developed regions, with the former much better placed to support generally ageing populations. India and China alone are responsible for over one-third of current growth – although China's rate of growth has slowed recently, its population still grows by over 9 million each year. Most of the highest growth rates are found in Sub-Saharan Africa and until population growth is brought under tighter control, such regions will continue to face enormous problems in supporting a rising population.

The Kalahari Desert stretches across the southwest and central part of **Botswana** and into Namibia and South Africa. Here, a small village settlement is very isolated in a sparsely populated region. Such villages are usually temporary with the area's people living nomadic lives, moving on when food sources run low.

World population growth by continent 1750-2050

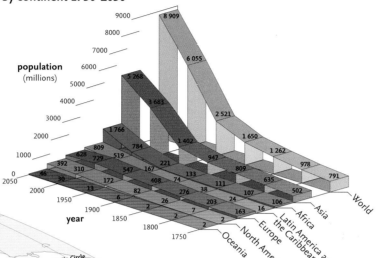

Want to know more?	
▶ Map of the world's major cities	18–19
▶ Map of child mortality	20–21
▶ World's richest and poorest countries	22–23
▶ Major refugee populations	24–25
▶ Map of population living with HIV/AIDS	116–117
▶ Colonization of North America	162–163
▶ Peoples of the Arctic	214–215

Internet links	
UN Population Information Network	www.un.org/popin
US Census Bureau	www.census.gov
UK Census	www.statistics.gov.uk/census2001
Socioeconomic Data and Applications Center	sedac.ciesin.columbia.edu
Population Reference Bureau	www.prb.gov

Facts

The world's population is growing each year by 77 million.

In August 1999 the population of India passed 1 billion.

Today's population is only 5.7 per cent of the total number of people who have ever lived on the earth.

Estimates suggest that in 2050 there will be more people over sixty than children under fourteen.

It is estimated that by 2007 more people will be living in urban areas than rural areas.

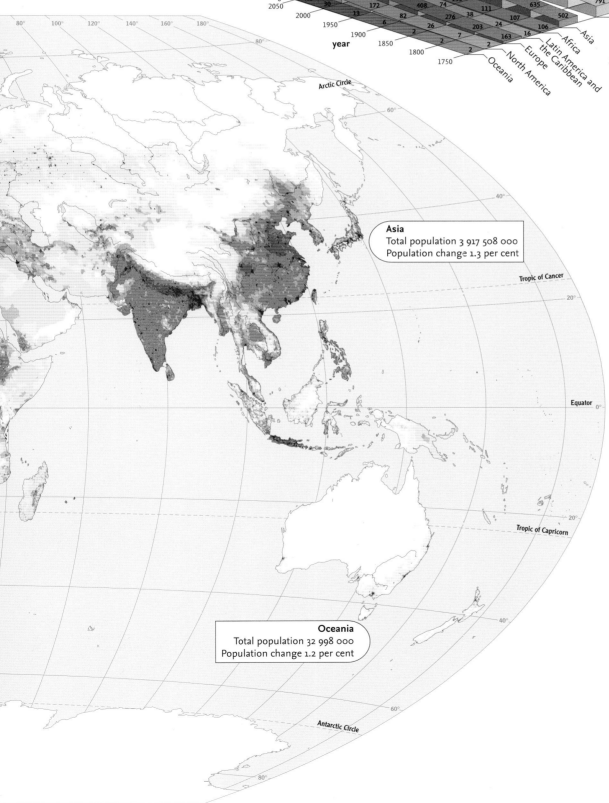

Asia
Total population 3 917 508 000
Population change 1.3 per cent

Oceania
Total population 32 998 000
Population change 1.2 per cent

Top 20 countries by population, 2005

	country	population
1	China	1 323 345 000
2	India	1 103 371 000
3	United States of America	298 213 000
4	Indonesia	222 781 000
5	Brazil	186 405 000
6	Pakistan	157 935 000
7	Russian Federation	143 202 000
8	Bangladesh	141 822 000
9	Nigeria	131 530 000
10	Japan	128 085 000
11	Mexico	107 029 000
12	Vietnam	84 238 000
13	Philippines	83 054 000
14	Germany	82 689 000
15	Ethiopia	77 431 000
16	Egypt	74 033 000
17	Turkey	73 193 000
18	Iran	69 515 000
19	Thailand	64 233 000
20	France	60 496 000

Top 20 countries by population density, 2005
(people per square kilometre)

	country	population density
1	Monaco	17 500
2	Singapore	6 770
3	Malta	1 272
4	Maldives	1 104
5	Vatican City	1 104
6	Bahrain	1 052
7	Bangladesh	985
8	Nauru	667
9	Taiwan	632
10	Barbados	628
11	Mauritius	610
12	South Korea	482
13	San Marino	459
14	Comoros	429
15	Tuvalu	400
16	Netherlands	393
17	India	360
18	Rwanda	343
19	Marshall Islands	343
20	Lebanon	342

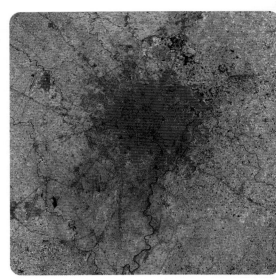

The world's population is becoming increasingly urban based. But levels of urbanization vary greatly between and within continents. The first half of the 20th century saw an increase from 14 to 30 per cent in the world's urban population. In more developed regions and Latin America and the Caribbean, 70 per cent of the population is urban, while in Asia and Africa the figure is less than 40 per cent. It is the developing regions where the increase is greatest and estimates suggest by 2030 over half the urban dwellers worldwide will live in Asia. Migration from the countryside due to famine, feuds or just for better job opportunities is the main factor in urban growth.

Although London was the first city to reach a population of 5 million, **Paris** has overtaken London to be the largest city in western Europe.

Level of urbanization
Percentage of population living in urban areas

- 80–100
- 60–80
- 40–60
- 20–40
- 0–20
- no data

Urban agglomerations
Cities with over 1 million inhabitants

- 1 million–2.5 million
- 2.5 million–5 million
- 5 million–10 million
- 10 million–20 million
- over 20 million

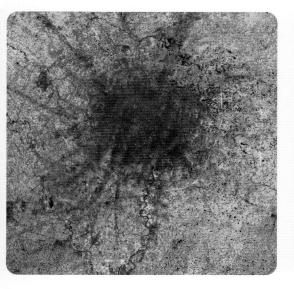

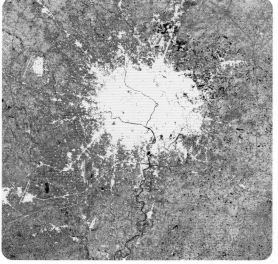

Urban growth

Chengdu currently has a population of 3.5 million. The image on the far left shows the city in 1990 and the central image was taken ten years later. By superimposing one on top of the other the urban growth can be clearly seen on the right hand image where the red areas show the growth in buildings and infrastructure.

Want to know more?

Countries of the world	8–9
World population	16–17
World's richest and poorest countries	22–23
Image of Istanbul	32–33
Asia statistics	70–71

Internet links

United Nations Population Division	**www.un.org/esa/population/unpop.htm**
United Nations Population Information Network	**www.un.org/popin**
The World Bank - Urban Development	**www.worldbank.org/urban/**
City Populations	**www.citypopulation.de**

Facts

- Cities occupy less than 2 per cent of the earth's land surface but house almost half of the human population.
- Urban growth rates in Africa are the highest in the world.
- Antarctica is uninhabited and most settlements in the Arctic regions have less than 5 000 inhabitants.
- India has thirtytwo cities with over one million inhabitants; by 2015 there will be fifty.
- London was the first city to reach a population of over 5 million.

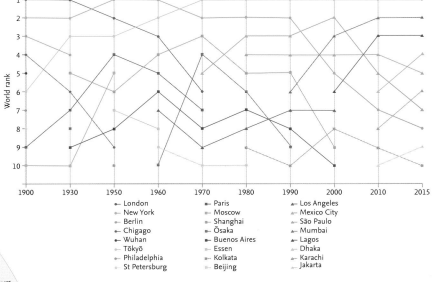

1. Peshawar
2. Amritsar
3. Gujranwala
4. Ludhiana
5. Faridabad
6. Varanasi
7. Allahabad
8. Bhopal
9. Jabalpur
10. Dhanbad
11. Vadodara
12. Indore
13. Asansol
14. Rajkot
15. Jamshedpur
16. Nagpur

World top 10 cities 1950-2015

World's largest cities

	city	country	population
1	**Tōkyō**	Japan	35 327 000
2	**Mexico City**	Mexico	19 013 000
3	**New York**	USA	18 498 000
4	**Mumbai**	India	18 336 000
5	**São Paulo**	Brazil	18 333 000
6	**Delhi**	India	15 334 000
7	**Kolkata**	India	14 299 000
8	**Buenos Aires**	Argentina	13 349 000
9	**Jakarta**	Indonesia	13 194 000
10	**Shanghai**	China	12 665 000

10 million cities

Dates at which cities attained 10 million population 1950-2015

Bangkok
Hyderabad
Tianjin
Istanbul
Moscow
Cairo
Rio de Janeiro
Manila
Jakarta
Delhi
Karachi
Dhaka
Lagos
Seoul
Beijing
Kolkata
Buenos Aires
Los Angeles
Mumbai
Ōsaka
São Paulo
Mexico City
Shanghai
Tōkyō
New York

Population over 10 million

1950 1960 1970 1980 1990 2000 2010 2015

While nations strive to improve their economies, other indicators need to be considered to assess a country's level of development, such as their provision of health care, education and clean water. The United Nation's Millennium Development Goals have highlighted problem areas to target. Child mortality figures are a clear indicator highlighting less-developed countries disadvantaged by a lack of health services and little access to safe water or sanitation. The situation is reflected by the comparison of countries' health spending – developed countries can afford to invest more in their health services and personnel. Variations in the availability of health care, access to safe water and contrasting lifestyles in the developed and less-developed regions result in differing health problems and causes of death.

A **field hospital** in Burkina, west Africa. The provision of even the most basic healthcare is lacking in many of the world's poorest countries. Availability of trained personnel, and education of the local population about health issues, are important factors in reducing the number of deaths from preventable diseases.

Causes of death

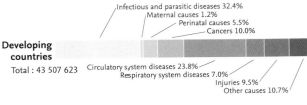

Developing countries
Total : 43 507 623

Infectious and parasitic diseases 32.4%
Maternal causes 1.2%
Perinatal causes 5.5%
Cancers 10.0%
Circulatory system diseases 23.8%
Respiratory system diseases 7.0%
Injuries 9.5%
Other causes 10.7%

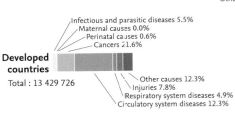

Developed countries
Total : 13 429 726

Infectious and parasitic diseases 5.5%
Maternal causes 0.0%
Perinatal causes 0.6%
Cancers 21.6%
Other causes 12.3%
Injuries 7.8%
Respiratory system diseases 4.9%
Circulatory system diseases 12.3%

World

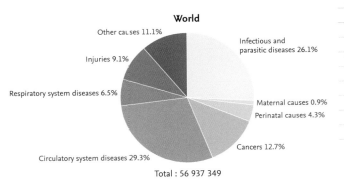

Other causes 11.1%
Injuries 9.1%
Respiratory system diseases 6.5%
Circulatory system diseases 29.3%
Cancers 12.7%
Perinatal causes 4.3%
Maternal causes 0.9%
Infectious and parasitic diseases 26.1%

Total : 56 937 349

Health spending as a percentage of GDP

	highest	per cent
1	United States of America	13.9
2	Lebanon	12.2
3	Cambodia	11.8
4	Switzerland	11.0
5	Uruguay	10.9
6	Germany	10.8
7	East Timor	9.8
8	Marshall Islands	9.8
9	France	9.6
10	Jordan	9.5

	lowest	per cent
183	Somalia	2.6
184	Chad	2.6
185	North Korea	2.5
186	Indonesia	2.4
187	São Tomé and Príncipe	2.3
188	Myanmar	2.1
189	Congo	2.1
190	Madagascar	2.0
191	Equatorial Guinea	2.0
192	Azerbaijan	1.6

Under-five mortality rate, 2003 and life expectancy by continent, 2000–2005

Deaths of children under five per 1 000 live births

- over 250
- 151–250
- 91–150
- 51–90
- 34–50
- 0–33
- no data

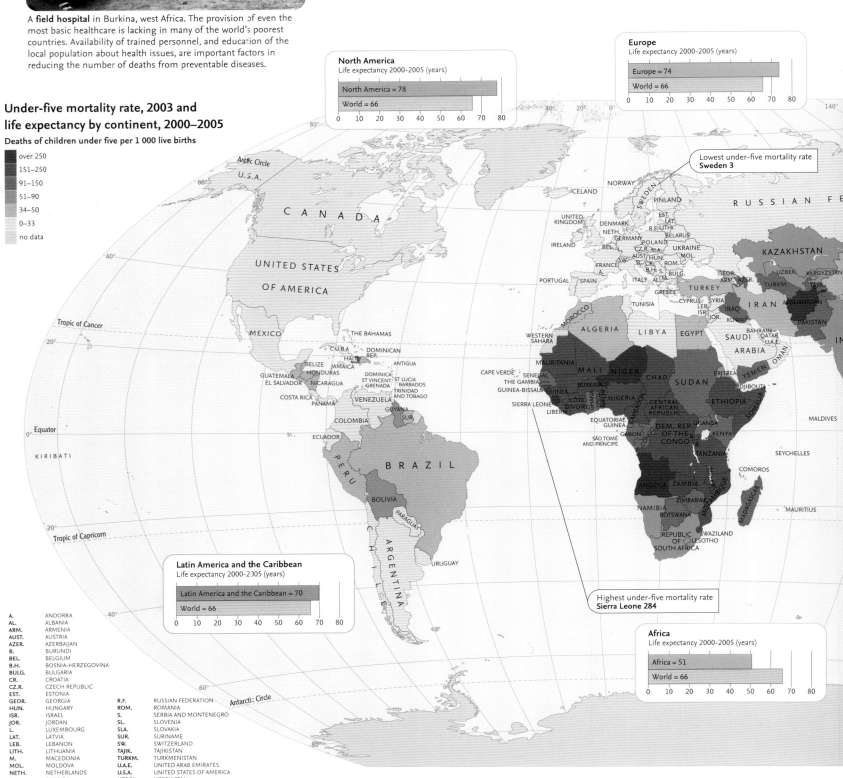

North America
Life expectancy 2000-2005 (years)
North America = 78
World = 66
0 10 20 30 40 50 60 70 80

Europe
Life expectancy 2000-2005 (years)
Europe = 74
World = 66
0 10 20 30 40 50 60 70 80

Latin America and the Caribbean
Life expectancy 2000-2005 (years)
Latin America and the Caribbean = 70
World = 66
0 10 20 30 40 50 60 70 80

Africa
Life expectancy 2000-2005 (years)
Africa = 51
World = 66
0 10 20 30 40 50 60 70 80

Lowest under-five mortality rate
Sweden 3

Highest under-five mortality rate
Sierra Leone 284

A.	ANDORRA
AL.	ALBANIA
ARM.	ARMENIA
AUST.	AUSTRIA
AZER.	AZERBAIJAN
B.	BURUNDI
BEL.	BELGIUM
B.H.	BOSNIA-HERZEGOVINA
BULG.	BULGARIA
CR.	CROATIA
CZ.R.	CZECH REPUBLIC
EST.	ESTONIA
GEOR.	GEORGIA
HUN.	HUNGARY
ISR.	ISRAEL
JOR.	JORDAN
L.	LUXEMBOURG
LAT.	LATVIA
LEB.	LEBANON
LITH.	LITHUANIA
M.	MACEDONIA
MOL.	MOLDOVA
NETH.	NETHERLANDS
R.	RWANDA

R.F.	RUSSIAN FEDERATION
ROM.	ROMANIA
S.	SERBIA AND MONTENEGRO
SL.	SLOVENIA
SLA.	SLOVAKIA
SUR.	SURINAME
SW.	SWITZERLAND
TAJIK.	TAJIKISTAN
TURKM.	TURKMENISTAN
U.A.E.	UNITED ARAB EMIRATES
U.S.A.	UNITED STATES OF AMERICA
UZBEK.	UZBEKISTAN

Doctors per 100 000 people
Number of trained doctors per 100 000 people

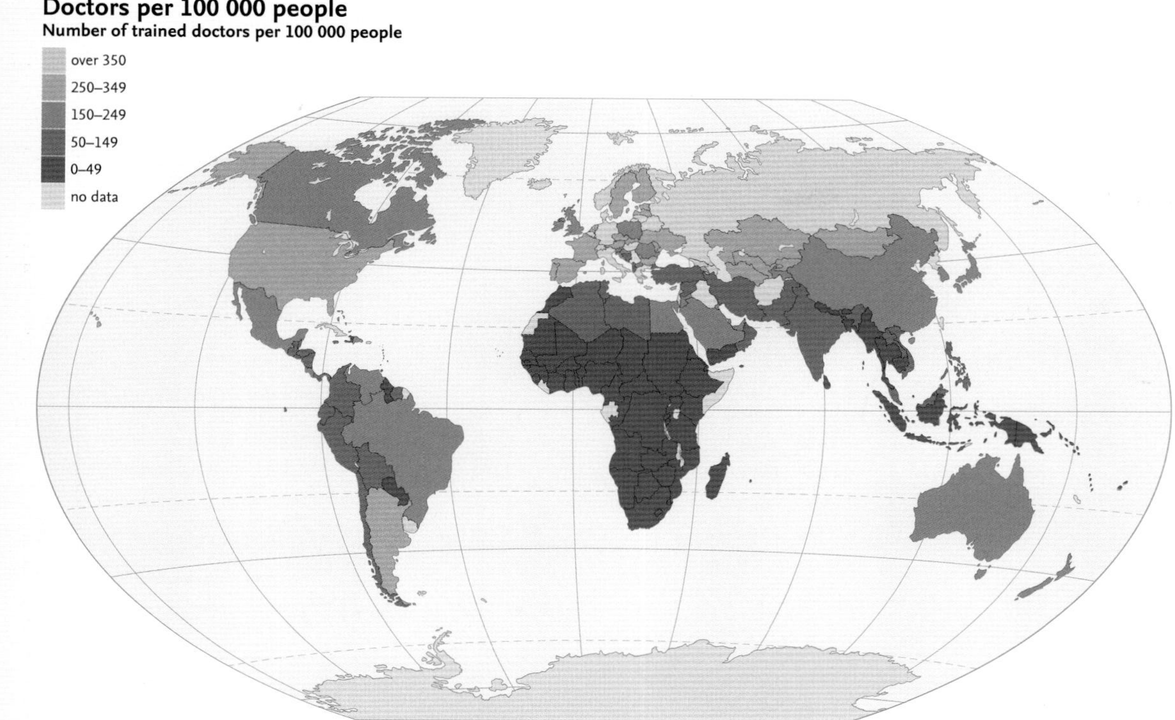

- over 350
- 250–349
- 150–249
- 50–149
- 0–49
- no data

Want to know more?	
▶ Map of world population distribution	16–17
▶ UN Millennium Development Goals	22–23
▶ World's poorest countries	22–23
▶ Water resource issues in Asia	68–69
▶ AIDS/HIV in Africa	116–117
▶ Drugs trade	194–195

Internet links	
United Nation Development Programme	www.undp.org
World Health Organization	www.who.int
United Nations Statistics Division	unstats.un.org
United Nations Millennium Development Goals	millenniumindicators.un.org

Facts

Of the fifteen countries with under-5 mortality rates of more than 200, fourteen of them are in Africa.

One in five developing nations will face water shortages by 2030.

Over five million people die each year from water-related diseases such as cholera and dysentery.

There is only a 12 per cent chance that the birth of a baby in Nepal will be attended by skilled heath personnel.

Life expectancy, 1950–2030

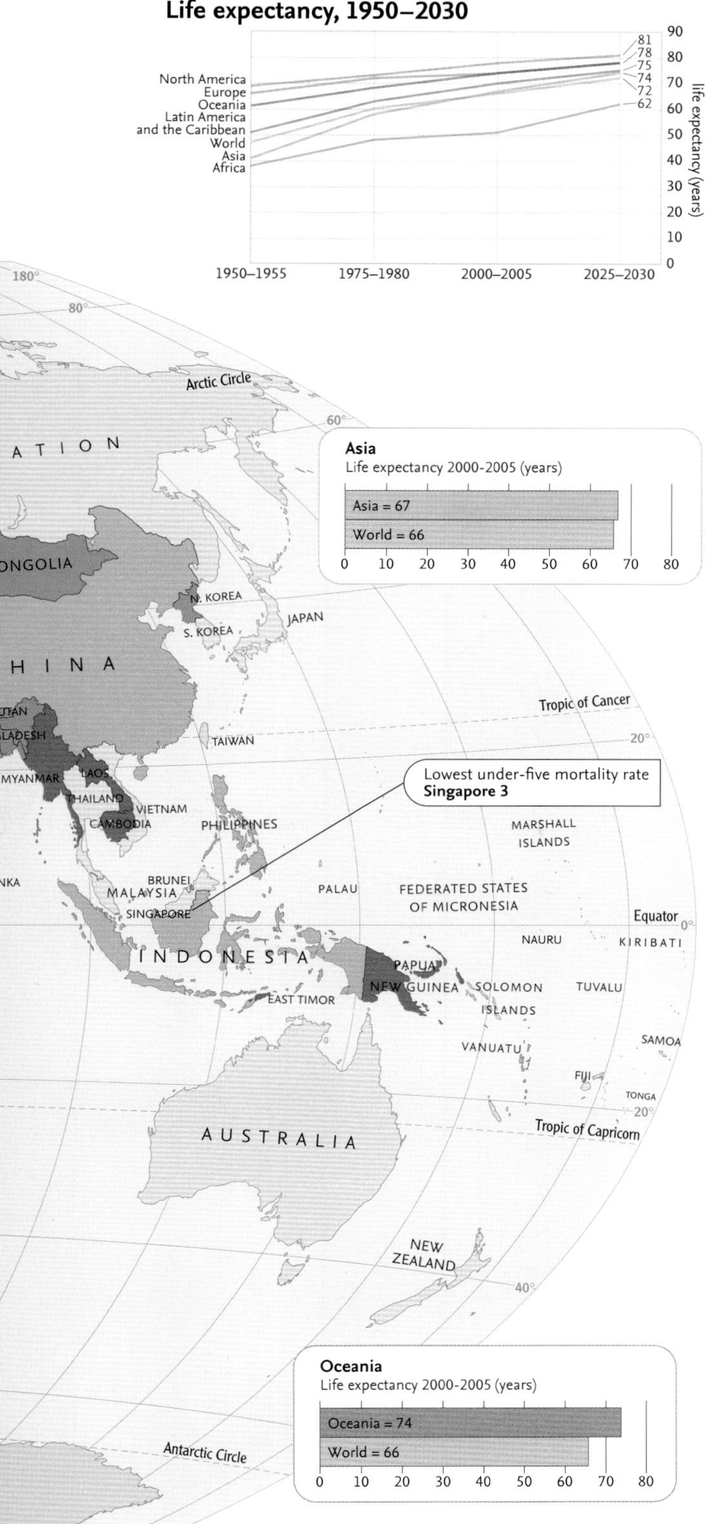

North America — 81
Europe — 78
Oceania — 75
Latin America and the Caribbean — 74
World — 72
Asia — 72
Africa — 62

life expectancy (years)

1950–1955   1975–1980   2000–2005   2025–2030

Asia
Life expectancy 2000-2005 (years)

Asia = 67
World = 66

0 10 20 30 40 50 60 70 80

Lowest under-five mortality rate
Singapore 3

Oceania
Life expectancy 2000-2005 (years)

Oceania = 74
World = 66

0 10 20 30 40 50 60 70 80

Availability of water

Water is one of the fundamental requirements of life, but increasing population and climate change means it is becoming scarce in some countries. Approximately eighty countries, with 40 per cent of the global population suffer from severe water shortages. Over one billion people have to drink unclean water and thus expose themselves to serious health risks. Water can be contaminated when extracted from deeper and deeper wells or when flooding overruns an area. But it is agriculture which uses the majority of freshwater withdrawn for irrigation.

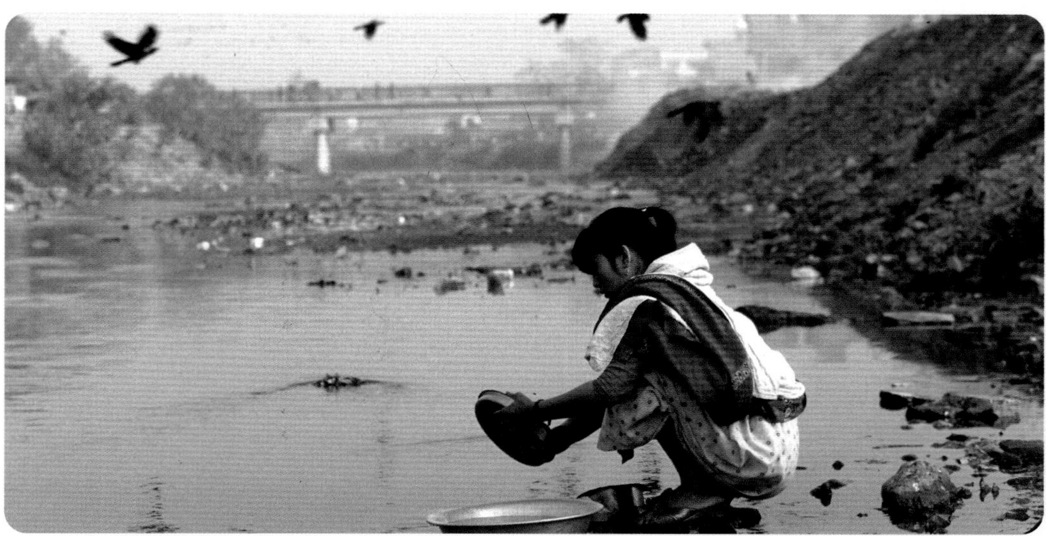

Domestic use of **untreated water** in Kathmandu, Nepal. Access to safe water and adequate sanitation is vital in preventing disease. Lack of such provision, which is worst in Africa and Asia, currently results in hundreds of millions of cases of water-borne diseases, and over five million deaths around the world each year.

Access to safe water
Percentage of population with access to improved drinking water

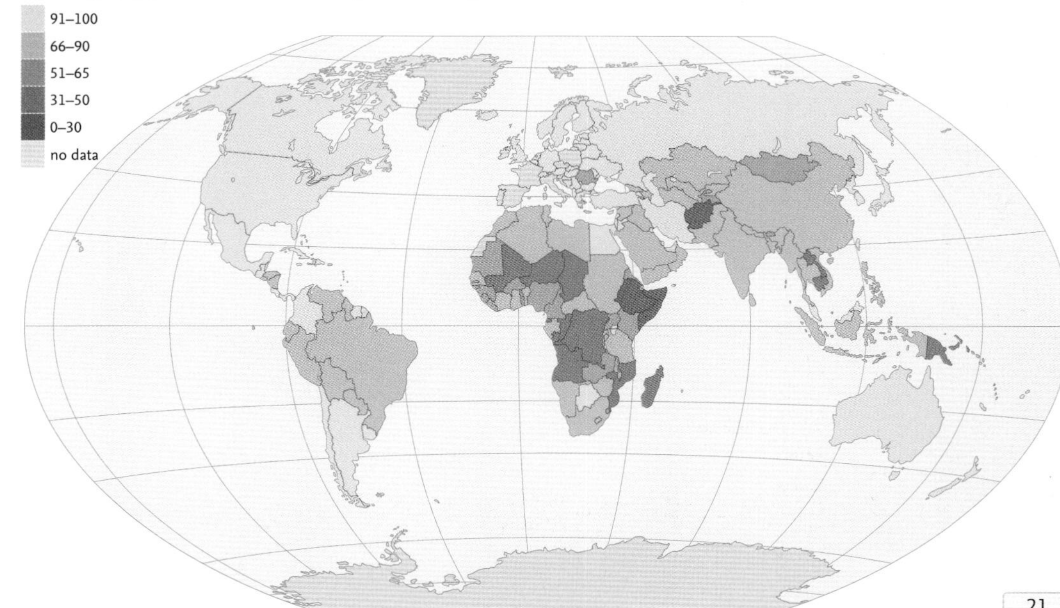

- 91–100
- 66–90
- 51–65
- 31–50
- 0–30
- no data

The globalization of the economy is making the world appear a smaller place but countries are being included and excluded from this global economy to differing degrees. Wealthy nations in the developed world have market-led economies, access to international markets and new technology and so can dominate the world economic system. But wealth is not always spread evenly within countries due to social or ethnic divisions. Low-income countries suffer from weak economies with debts which need to be repaid and some are dependent on external aid to survive. In 2000 the United Nations identified eight Millennium Development Goals to address such development issues and poverty.

The City, London, the world's largest financial centre.

Gross National Income per capita

	highest	US$
1	Luxembourg	43 940
2	Norway	43 350
3	Switzerland	39 880
4	United States	37 610
5	Japan	34 510
6	Denmark	33 750
7	Iceland	30 810
8	Sweden	28 840
9	United Kingdom	28 350
10	Finland	27 020

	lowest	US$
142	Niger	200
143=	Eritrea	190
143=	Tajikistan	190
144	Malawi	170
145	Sierra Leone	150
146	Guinea-Bissau	140
147	Liberia	130
148=	Burundi	100
148=	Congo, Dem. Rep.	100
149	Ethiopia	90

The world's biggest companies

	company	Sales (US$ millions)
1	Wal-Mart Stores	256 330
2	BP	232 570
3	ExxonMobil	222 880
4	General Motors	185 520
5	Ford Motor	164 200
6	DaimlerChrysler	157 130
7	Toyota Motor	135 820
8	General Electric	134 190
9	Royal Dutch/Shell Group	133 500
10	Total	131 640

UN Millennium Development Goals
From the Millennium Declaration, 2000

Goal 1	Eradicate extreme poverty and hunger
Goal 2	Achieve universal primary education
Goal 3	Promote gender equality and empower women
Goal 4	Reduce child mortality
Goal 5	Improve maternal health
Goal 6	Combat HIV/AIDS, malaria and other diseases
Goal 7	Ensure environmental sustainability
Goal 8	Develop a global partnership for development

The UN Millennium Development Goals were issued in September 2000. Forty-eight indicators were identified to measure the progress of countries trying to combat the development issues being addressed by the eight goals. These issues include those of poverty, hunger and environmental degradation – problems experienced in areas such as this in **Freetown,** capital of Sierra Leone, one of the world's poorest countries.

Gross National Income

An indicator of a country's wealth is its Gross National Income (GNI). This is assessed by the value of final output of goods and services produced by a country plus net income from non-resident sources. The total GNI figure can then be divided by the country's population to give an average figure of GNI per capita. The map shows the dominance of developed countries but China is rapidly increasing its GNI of and has a relatively high GNI per capita of $1 100 given the size of its population.

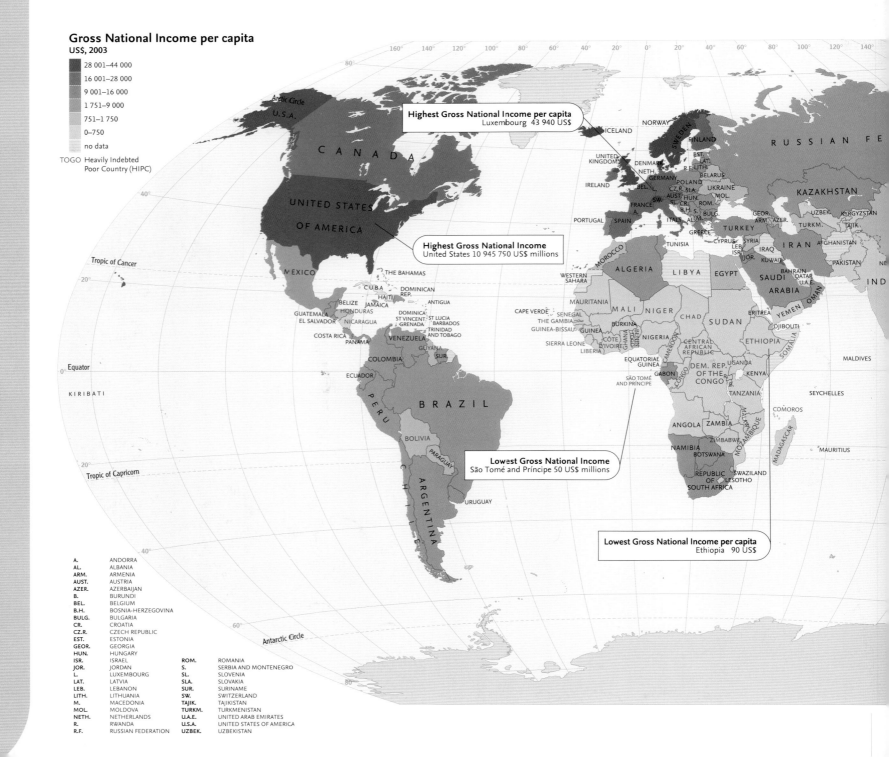

Gross National Income per capita
US$, 2003

- 28 001–44 000
- 16 001–28 000
- 9 001–16 000
- 1 751–9 000
- 751–1 750
- 0–750
- no data

TOGO Heavily Indebted Poor Country (HIPC)

Highest Gross National Income per capita
Luxembourg 43 940 US$

Highest Gross National Income
United States 10 945 790 US$ millions

Lowest Gross National Income
São Tomé and Príncipe 50 US$ millions

Lowest Gross National Income per capita
Ethiopia 90 US$

A.	ANDORRA		
AL.	ALBANIA		
ARM.	ARMENIA		
AUST.	AUSTRIA		
AZER.	AZERBAIJAN		
B.	BURUNDI		
BEL.	BELGIUM		
B.H.	BOSNIA-HERZEGOVINA		
BULG.	BULGARIA		
CR.	CROATIA		
CZ.R.	CZECH REPUBLIC		
EST.	ESTONIA		
GEOR.	GEORGIA		
HUN.	HUNGARY		
ISR.	ISRAEL	ROM.	ROMANIA
JOR.	JORDAN	S.	SERBIA AND MONTENEGRO
L.	LUXEMBOURG	SL.	SLOVENIA
LAT.	LATVIA	SLA.	SLOVAKIA
LEB.	LEBANON	SUR.	SURINAME
LITH.	LITHUANIA	SW.	SWITZERLAND
M.	MACEDONIA	TAJIK.	TAJIKISTAN
MOL.	MOLDOVA	TURKM.	TURKMENISTAN
NETH.	NETHERLANDS	U.A.E.	UNITED ARAB EMIRATES
R.	RWANDA	U.S.A.	UNITED STATES OF AMERICA
R.F.	RUSSIAN FEDERATION	UZBEK.	UZBEKISTAN

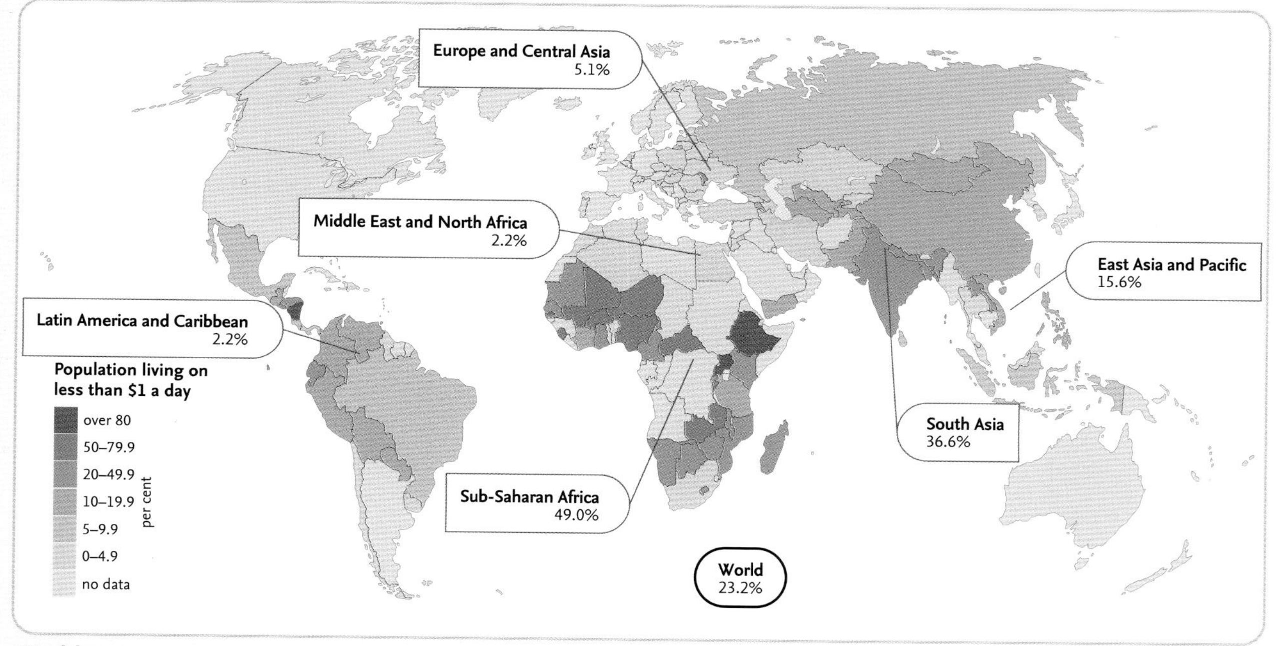

World poverty

An income of $1 a day is the accepted definition of extreme poverty. An estimated 1.2 billion people live below this poverty line. Over 80 per cent of the total population of Ethiopia, Uganda and Nicaragua live on less than $1 a day.

Population living on less than $1 a day (per cent)
- over 80
- 50–79.9
- 20–49.9
- 10–19.9
- 5–9.9
- 0–4.9
- no data

Europe and Central Asia 5.1%
Middle East and North Africa 2.2%
Latin America and Caribbean 2.2%
East Asia and Pacific 15.6%
South Asia 36.6%
Sub-Saharan Africa 49.0%
World 23.2%

Want to know more?

World's largest countries	8–9
The European Union	34–35
Energy consumption in North America	160–161
The drugs trade in South America	194–195

Internet links

United Nations Statistics Division	unstats.un.org
The World Bank	www.worldbank.org
International Monetary Fund	www.imf.org
Organization for Economic Co-operation and Development	www.oecd.org

Facts

Half the world's population earns only 5 per cent of the world's wealth.

During the second half of the 20th century rich countries gave over US$1 trillion in aid.

For every US$1 in grant aid to developing countries, more than US$13 comes back in debt repayments.

On average, The World Bank distributes US$30 billion each year between 100 countries.

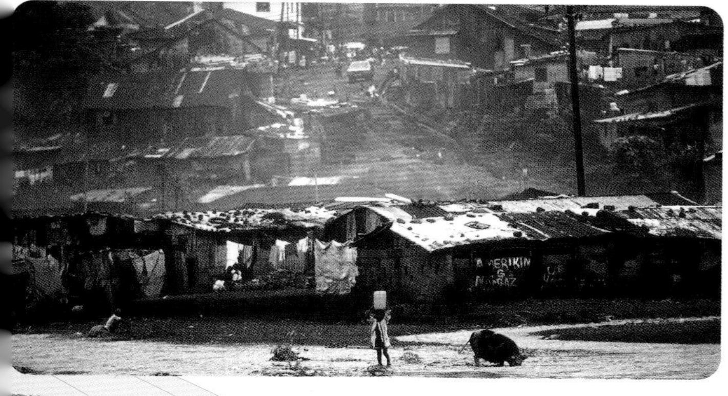

Overseas aid and debt

Globalization means the poorest countries find it particularly hard to develop and attract economic activity, resulting in an inability to repay loans or stimulate their own economies. Therefore their debts become greater and more loans are taken out to cover them. International efforts are ongoing in trying to suspend or write off some of these debts but meanwhile overseas aid is essential for the survival of some of the poorest countries.

Overseas aid
Donations as a percentage of GNI, 2002
- Recipient: 15.1–100
- Recipient: 4.1–15
- Recipient: 0–4
- Donor: over 0.7
- Donor: 0–0.7
- no data

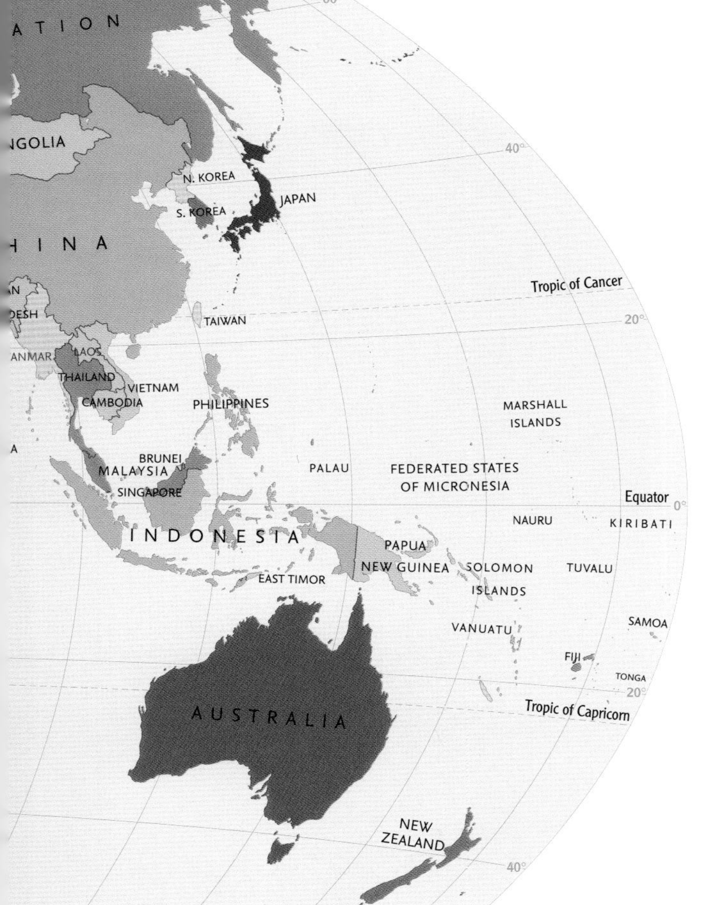

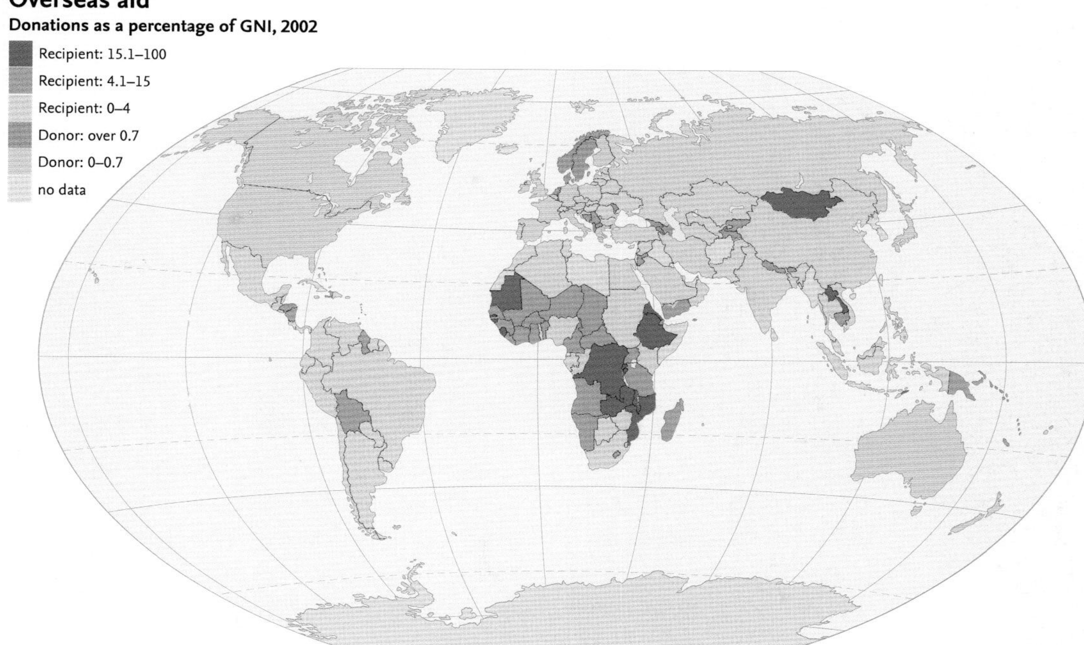

Debt
Debt as a percentage of GNI and top 5 total debt service, 2002
- 15.5–100
- 11.5–15.4
- 7.5–11.4
- 5.5–7.4
- 3.5–5.4
- 0–3.4
- no data

China US$ 30 615 799 808
Thailand US$ 19 737 800 704
Turkey US$ 27 604 400 128
Mexico US$ 43 535 499 264
Brazil US$ 51 631 599 616

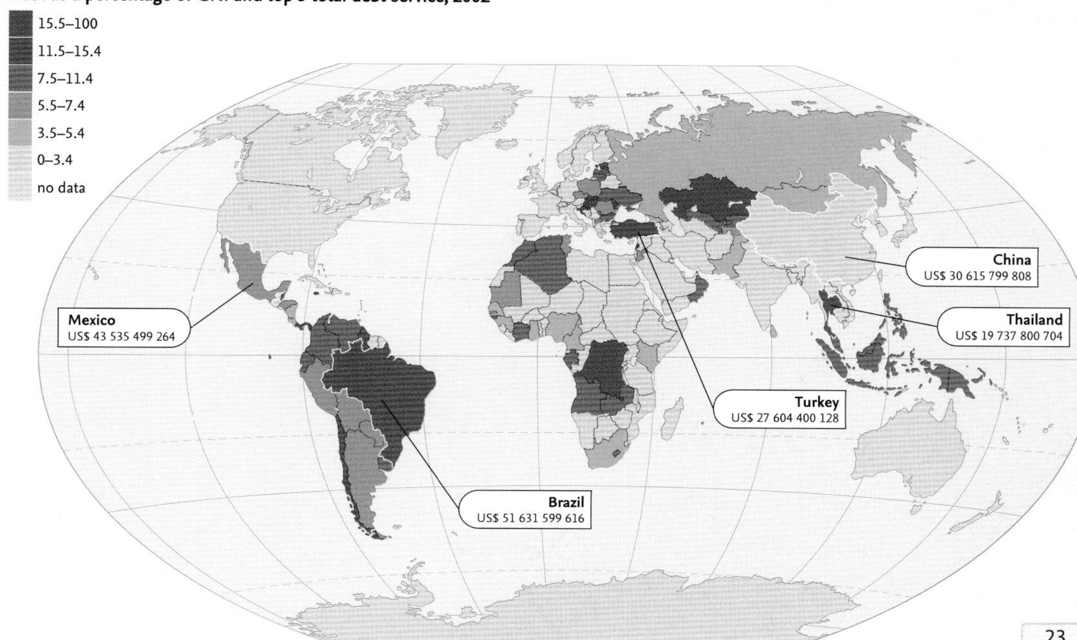

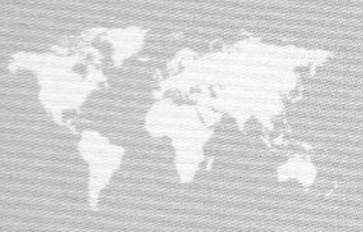
Geo-political issues shape the countries of the world and the current political situation in many parts of the world reflects a long history of armed conflict. Since the Second World War conflicts have been fairly localized, but there are numerous 'flash points' where factors such as territorial claims, ideology, religion, ethnicity and access to resources can cause friction between two or more countries. Such factors also lie behind the recent growth in global terrorism.

Military expenditure can take up a disproportionate amount of a country's wealth. Many poor developing countries spend a relatively large amount on their military resources. Recently there have been some significant drops in the highest spending levels and there is an encouraging trend towards wider international cooperation, mainly through the United Nations (UN) and the North Atlantic Treaty Organization (NATO), to prevent escalation of conflicts and on peacekeeping missions.

Highest and lowest military spending countries 2002

	top 5	% GDP
1	Oman	13.0
2	Saudi Arabia	11.3
3	Kuwait	11.2
4	Bosnia-Herzegovina	9.5
5	Israel	8.6

	bottom 5	
189	Zambia	0.6
190	Mexico	0.5
191	Moldova	0.3
192	Mauritius	0.2
193	Iceland	0.0

Location of international wars, wars of independence and civil or internal wars since 1946

AFGHANISTAN — International war
Angola — War of independence
Angola — Civil or internal wars

Military spending, 2002 and conflicts since 1946

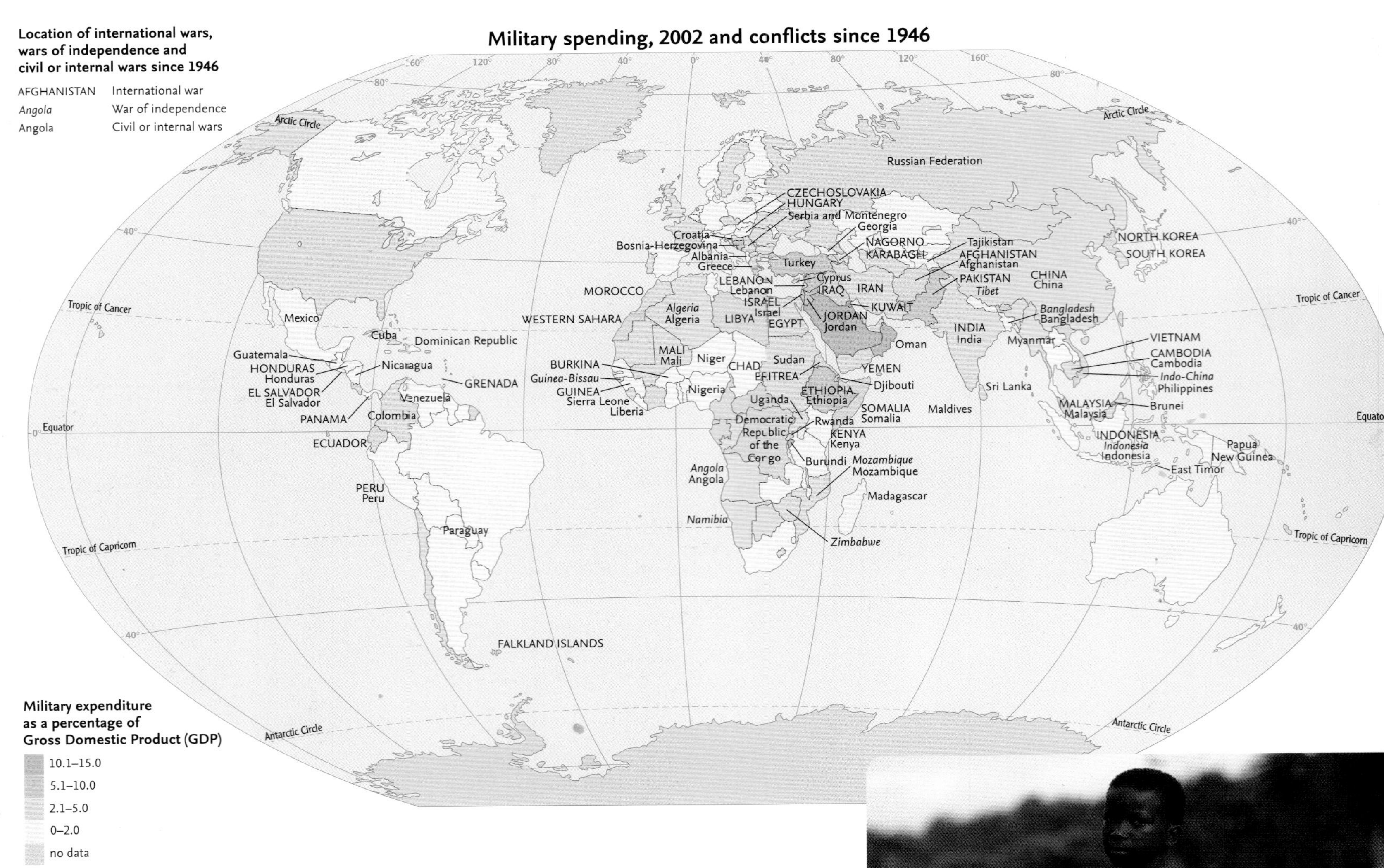

Military expenditure as a percentage of Gross Domestic Product (GDP)

- 10.1–15.0
- 5.1–10.0
- 2.1–5.0
- 0–2.0
- no data

Refugees

A refugee is defined by the United Nations Geneva Convention as 'someone with a well-founded fear of persecution on the basis of his or her race, religion, nationality, membership of a particular social group or political opinion, who is outside of his or her country of nationality and unable or unwilling to return'. Refugees are forced from their countries by war, civil conflict, political strife or gross human rights abuses. There were an estimated 17 million refugees in the world in January 2004 – people who had crossed at least one international border to seek safety. The global refugee crisis affects every continent and almost every country. Palestinians are the world's most long-standing and largest refugee population, and make up more than one quarter of the world's refugees.

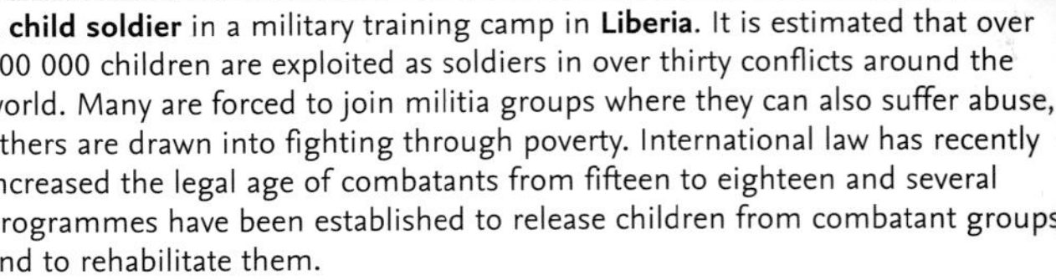

A **child soldier** in a military training camp in **Liberia**. It is estimated that over 300 000 children are exploited as soldiers in over thirty conflicts around the world. Many are forced to join militia groups where they can also suffer abuse, others are drawn into fighting through poverty. International law has recently increased the legal age of combatants from fifteen to eighteen and several programmes have been established to release children from combatant groups and to rehabilitate them.

Origin of major refugee populations 2003

area of origin[1]	main countries of asylum	total
Afghanistan[2]	Pakistan / Iran	2 136 000
Sudan	Uganda/Chad/Ethiopia/ Kenya/D.R. Congo/Central African Rep.	606 200
Burundi	Tanzania / D.R. Congo / Zambia / South Africa / Rwanda	531 600
Democratic Republic of the Congo	Tanzania / Congo / Zambia / Burundi / Rwanda / Angola / Uganda	453 400
Palestine[3]	Saudi Arabia / Iraq[4] / Egypt / Libya / Algeria	427 900
Somalia	Kenya / Yemen / United Kingdom / Ethiopia / Djibouti / USA	402 200
Iraq	Iran / Germany / Netherlands / Sweden / United Kingdom	368 500
Vietnam	China / Germany / USA / France	363 200
Liberia	Guinea / Côte d'Ivoire / Sierra Leone / Ghana / USA	353 300
Angola	Zambia / D.R. Congo / Namibia / South Africa	329 600

1 This table includes UNHCR estimates for nationalities in industrialized countries on the basis of recent refugee arrivals and asylum seeker recognition.
2 This is a UNHCR estimate. In 2004, this figure is subject to revision in consultation with the governments of Iran and Pakistan.
3 This figure excludes some 4 million Palestinians who are covered by a separate mandate of the U.N. Relief and Works Agency for Palestine Refugees in the Near East (UNRWA).
4 Figure refers to end 2002.

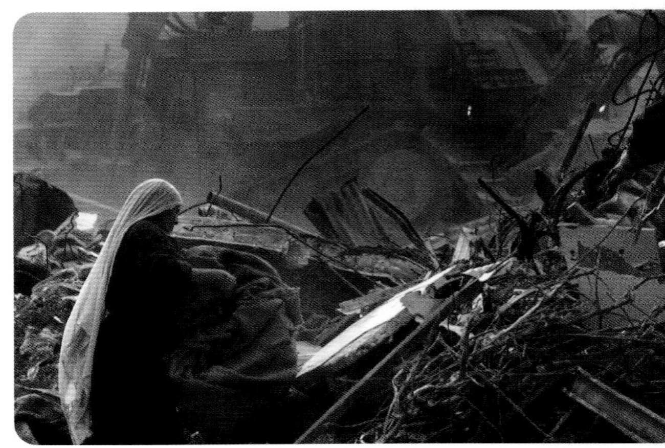

A Palestinian woman searches the rubble of her home in the **Rafah refugee camp** in southern **Gaza** after Israeli forces demolished it with tank shells and armoured bulldozers.

The aftermath of a **terrorist** car bomb in **Baghdād**, Iraq. Often carried out as suicide missions, such attacks are commonly used by insurgents aiming to destabilize Iraq. Terrorist incidents have resulted in hundreds of deaths since the end of the US-led war on Iraq and have continued since the Iraqi elections in January 2004.

Want to know more?	
▷ World Countries	**8–9**
▷ Conflict in the Middle East	**68–69**
▷ Conflict in Africa	**116–117**

Internet links	
United Nations Peace and Security	**www.un.org/peace**
NATO	**www.nato.int**
United Nations Refugee Agency	**www.unhcr.ch**
BBC News	**www.bbc.co.uk**

Facts
The Iran-Iraq war in the 1980s is estimated to have cost half a million lives.
There have been around seventy civil or internal wars throughout the world since 1945.
The UN is currently involved with sixteen peacekeeping operations making a total of fifty nine since 1946.
There have been nearly 2 000 fatalities in UN peacekeeping operations since 1948.

International terrorism

Terrorism is defined by the United Nations as, 'All criminal acts directed against a State and intended or calculated to create a state of terror in the minds of particular persons or a group of persons or the general public'. The world has become increasingly concerned about terrorism and the possibility that terrorists could acquire and use nuclear, chemical and biological weapons. One common form of terrorist attack is suicide bombing. Pioneered by Tamil secessionists in Sri Lanka, it has been widely used by Palestinian groups fighting against Israeli occupation of the West Bank and Gaza. In recent years it has also been used by the Al Qaida network in its attacks on the western world.

Global terrorism

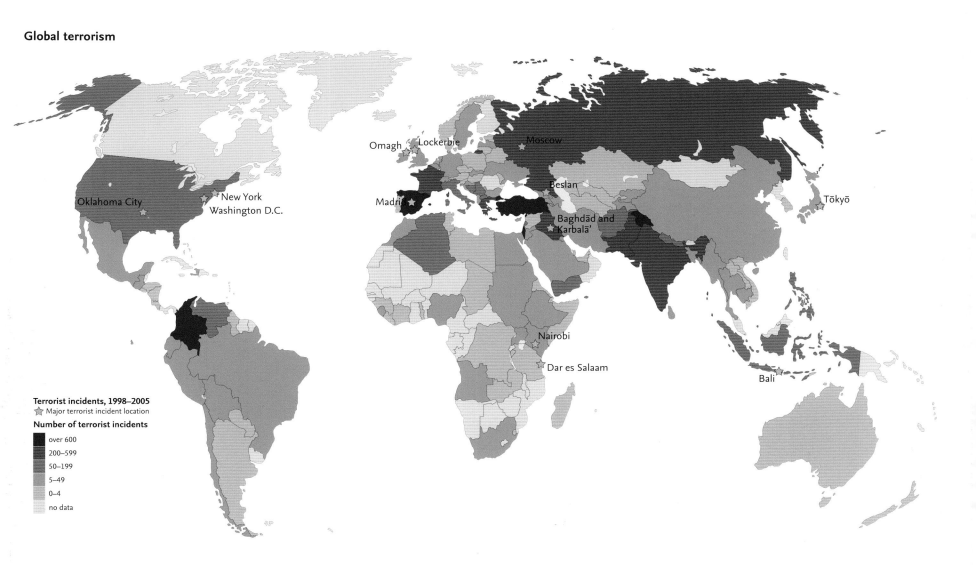

Terrorist incidents, 1998–2005
☆ Major terrorist incident location

Number of terrorist incidents
- over 600
- 200–599
- 50–199
- 5–49
- 0–4
- no data

Major terrorist incidents

location	date	summary	killed	injured
Lockerbie, Scotland	December 1988	Airline bombing	270	5
Tōkyō, Japan	March 1995	Sarin gas attack on subway	12	5 700
Oklahoma City, USA	April 1995	Bomb in the Federal building	168	over 500
Nairobi, Kenya and Dar es Salaam, Tanzania	August 1998	US Embassy bombings	257	over 4 000
Omagh, Northern Ireland	August 1998	Town centre bombing	29	330
New York and Washington D.C., USA	September 2001	Airline hijacking and crashing	2 752	4 300
Bali, Indonesia	October 2002	Car bomb outside nightclub	202	300
Moscow, Russian Federation	October 2002	Theatre siege	170	over 600
Baghdād and Karbalā', Iraq	March 2004	Suicide bombing of pilgrims	181	over 400
Madrid, Spain	March 2004	Train bombings	191	1 800
Beslan, Russian Federation	September 2004	School siege	330	700

Terrorist incidents by region 1998–2005

region	incidents	killed	injured
Middle East / The Gulf	4 355	5 385	12 814
Western Europe	2 672	336	1 463
South Asia	2 541	4 173	10 404
Latin America	1 461	1 341	2095
Eastern Europe	1 035	1 808	4 664
Southeast Asia and Oceania	431	918	3 138
Africa	311	2 127	7 249
North America	103	2 994	30
East and Central Asia	83	134	151

The nature and origin of the planets and the universe has been the subject of much speculation since humans first inhabited the earth and began to look up at the sky. However, it was only in the twentieth century that humankind began to achieve the bulk of its understanding of our cosmos, aided by the rapid development of technology. We are now equipped with an advanced arsenal of instrumentation to begin to answer questions that have been unanswered for a long time.

With a growing knowledge of space, and an increasing ability to explore it, has come the possibility of 'exploiting' it, particularly through satellites. Today, satellites are vital for observing the earth, exploring outer space, weather forecasting, communications and navigation. Images from earth-observing satellites, which allow detailed monitoring of the environment and the detection of change, are increasingly important tools in managing the earth's resources.

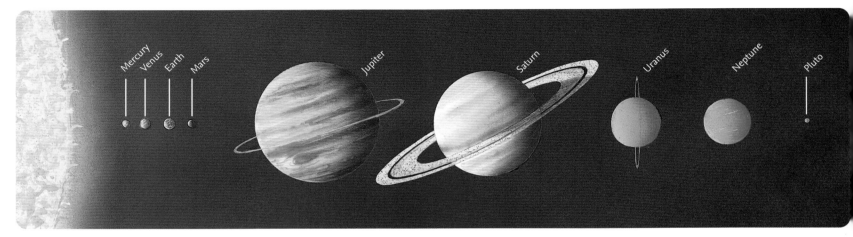

1968 First spacecraft to orbit the Moon (Zond 5, USSR)
1968 First manned orbiting of the Moon (Apollo 8, US)
1957 First artificial satellite (Sputnik 1, USSR)
1957 Laika (dog) orbits Earth in Sputnik 2
1959 First spacecraft to attain solar orbit (Luna 1, USSR)
1959 First artificial object to crash-land on the Moon (Luna 2)
1959 First photographs of the far side of the Moon (Luna 3)
1966 First lunar lander (Luna 9)
1966 First photographs from the Moon's surface (Surveyor 1, US)
1965 First 'space walk' (by Leonov, USSR)
1965 First photographs of the surface of Mars (Mariner 4, US)
1962 First American in orbit (John Glenn)

1958 | 1960 | 1962 | 1964 | 1966 | 1968

1967 First spacecraft to pass Venus (Venera 4, USSR)
1963 First woman in space (Valentina Tereshkova, USSR)
1961 First person in space (Yuri Gagarin, USSR, in Vostok 1)
1961 First American in space (Alan Shepard)
1960 First weather observation satellite (Tiros 1, US)
1958 First US satellites (Explorer 1 and Vanguard)
1969 First people on the Moon (Armstrong and Aldrin, Apollo 11)

Mercury Venus Earth Mars Jupiter Saturn Uranus Neptune Pluto

Exploration of the solar system

Exploration of the solar system began in the 1950s and was in its prime through the 1970s and 1980s. Missions reached several planets during this period, notably Pioneer (Jupiter), Voyager (Saturn), Mariner 10 (Mercury and Venus) and the Viking missions (Mars landings). Perhaps the most successful mission is that of Voyager 2 which, since 1977, has visited all four of the gas giants – Jupiter, Saturn, Uranus and Neptune. Such journeys provide vast amounts of information about the solar system and its origins. Exploration of the planets continues today, as does 'exploration' of the universe through the use of astronomical satellites – such as the highly successful Hubble Space Telescope – which allow observation of the stars from beyond the earth's distorting and turbulent atmosphere.

The planets	Sun	Mercury	Venus	Earth	Mars	Jupiter	Saturn	Uranus	Neptune	Pluto
Mean orbital distance from Sun (million km/*million miles*)	-	57.9/ 36.0	108.2/ 67.2	149.6/ 93.0	227.9/ 141.6	778.4/ 483.7	1 426.7/ 886.6	2 871.0/ 1 784.0	4 498.3/ 2 795.2	5 906.4/ 3 670.2
Equatorial diameter (km/*miles*)	1 392 000/ 864 988.8	4 879.4/ 3 032.1	12 103.6/ 7 521.2	12 756.3/ 7 925.8	6 794/ 4 221.8	142 984/ 88 850.3	120 536/ 7 4901.1	51 118/ 31 764.7	49 528/ 30 776.7	2 390/ 1 485.2
Rotation period (earth days)	25–36	58.65	-243	23hr 56m 4s	1.03	0.41	0.44	-0.72	0.67	-6.39
Year (earth days/years)	-	88 days	224.7 days	365.24 days	687 days	11.86 years	29.42 years	83.8 years	163.8 years	248 years
Mean orbital velocity (km/s/*miles/s*)	-	47.87/29.75	35.02/21.76	29.79/18.51	24.13/14.99	13.07/8.12	9.67/6.01	6.84/4.25	5.48/3.41	4.75/2.95
Mean surface temperature (°C)	5 700	167	457	15–20	-90– -5	-108	-139	-197	-200	-215.2
Mass (Earth=1)	332 830	0.055	0.815	1 (6 x 1024)	0.107	317.82	95.161	14.371	17.147	0.002
Density (Water=1)	1.41	5.43	5.24	5.52	3.94	1.33	0.70	1.30	1.76	1.10
Surface gravity (Earth=1)	27.5	0.38	0.91	1	0.38	2.53	1.07	0.90	1.14	0.06
Total number of known moons	-	0	0	1	2	63	30	21	8	1

Satellite remote sensing

Satellite remote sensing – the acquisition, processing and interpretation of images captured by satellites – is an invaluable tool in observing and monitoring the Earth, and in exploring outer space. Sensors carried by satellites or space probes can capture electromagnetic radiation in a variety of wavelengths, including those visible to the eye (colours), infrared wavelengths and microwave and radio radiation detected by radar sensors. Data received can be processed to allow detailed interpretation of planetary and stellar phenomena, landscapes, and environmental and atmospheric conditions. The level of detail discernible on satellite images – effectively the size of the smallest feature which can be detected – is known as image resolution, and is usually expressed in metres.

Landsat

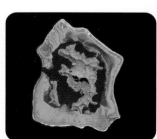
SPOT

Main earth-observing satellites/sensors

Satellite/Sensor name	launch dates	aims and applications
Landsat 4, 5,	July 1972-April 1999	The first satellite to be designed specifically for observing the Earth's surface. Originally to produce images of use for agriculture and geology. Today images are used for numerous environmental and scientific applications.
SPOT 1, 2, 3, 4, 5	February 1986-May 2002	Particularly useful for monitoring land use and water resources, coastal studies and cartography.
Space Shuttle	Regular launches 1981-	Each shuttle mission has separate aims. Astronauts take photographs with high specification hand-held cameras. The Shuttle Radar Topography Mission (SRTM) in 2000 obtained near-global high-resolution data of the earth's topography.
IKONOS	September 1999	First commercial high-resolution satellite. Useful for a variety of applications mainly cartography, defence, urban planning, agriculture, forestry and insurance.

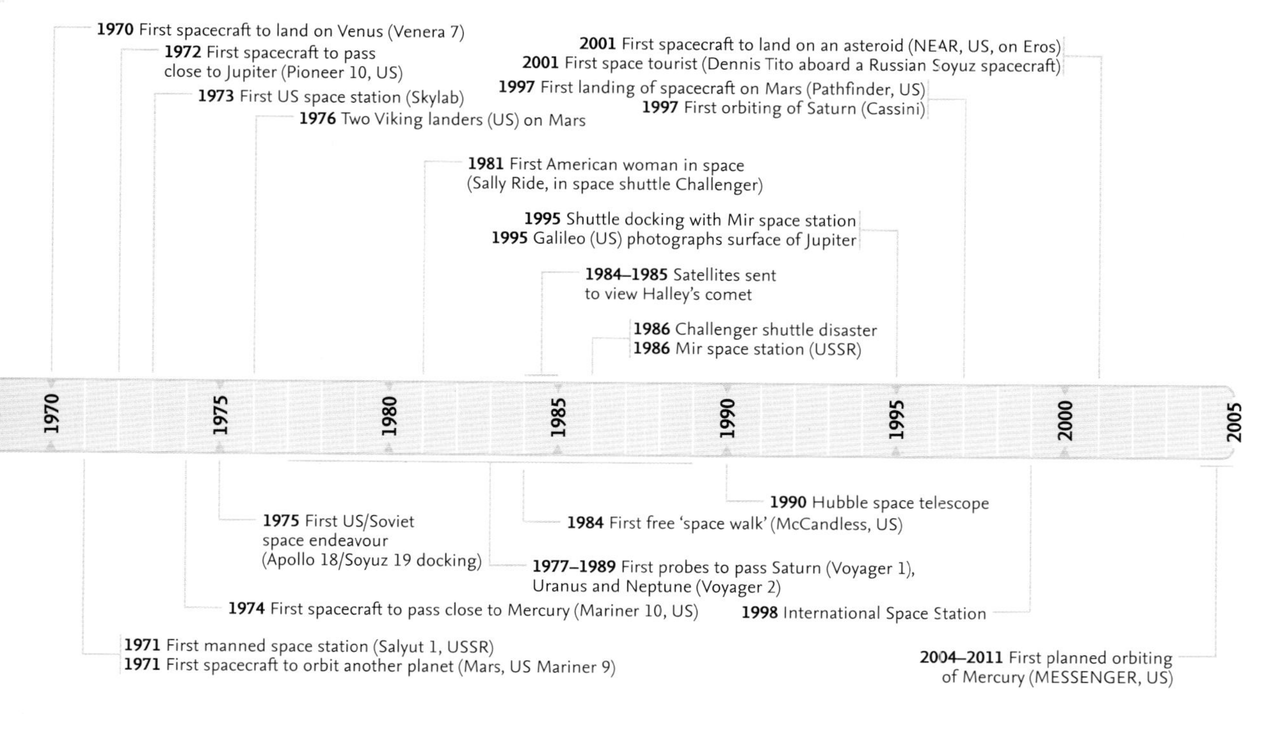

1970 First spacecraft to land on Venus (Venera 7)
1972 First spacecraft to pass close to Jupiter (Pioneer 10, US)
1973 First US space station (Skylab)
1976 Two Viking landers (US) on Mars

2001 First spacecraft to land on an asteroid (NEAR, US, on Eros)
2001 First space tourist (Dennis Tito aboard a Russian Soyuz spacecraft)
1997 First landing of spacecraft on Mars (Pathfinder, US)
1997 First orbiting of Saturn (Cassini)

1981 First American woman in space (Sally Ride, in space shuttle Challenger)

1995 Shuttle docking with Mir space station
1995 Galileo (US) photographs surface of Jupiter

1984–1985 Satellites sent to view Halley's comet

1986 Challenger shuttle disaster
1986 Mir space station (USSR)

1970   1975   1980   1985   1990   1995   2000   2005

1975 First US/Soviet space endeavour (Apollo 18/Soyuz 19 docking)
1984 First free 'space walk' (McCandless, US)
1990 Hubble space telescope
1977–1989 First probes to pass Saturn (Voyager 1), Uranus and Neptune (Voyager 2)
1974 First spacecraft to pass close to Mercury (Mariner 10, US)
1998 International Space Station
1971 First manned space station (Salyut 1, USSR)
1971 First spacecraft to orbit another planet (Mars, US Mariner 9)
2004–2011 First planned orbiting of Mercury (MESSENGER, US)

Internet links

NASA	www.nasa.gov
Exploring the solar system	www.jpl.nasa.gov/solar_system
Observing the earth	visibleearth.nasa.gov
Global Positioning System	www.garmin.com/aboutGPS

Facts

The first GPS satellites were launched in 1978 with the full constellation of twenty four satellites being completed in 1994.

Voyager 2 took twelve years to reach Neptune, using the gravitational pull of other planets to increase its speed.

Commercial earth-observing satellites can now provide images of less than 1 metre (3 feet) resolution.

Radar sensors on board satellites can observe the earth through clouds and at night.

Geostatellite communications satellites

Geostationary communications satellites

Status of satellite
- In service
- Inclined orbit
- Planned

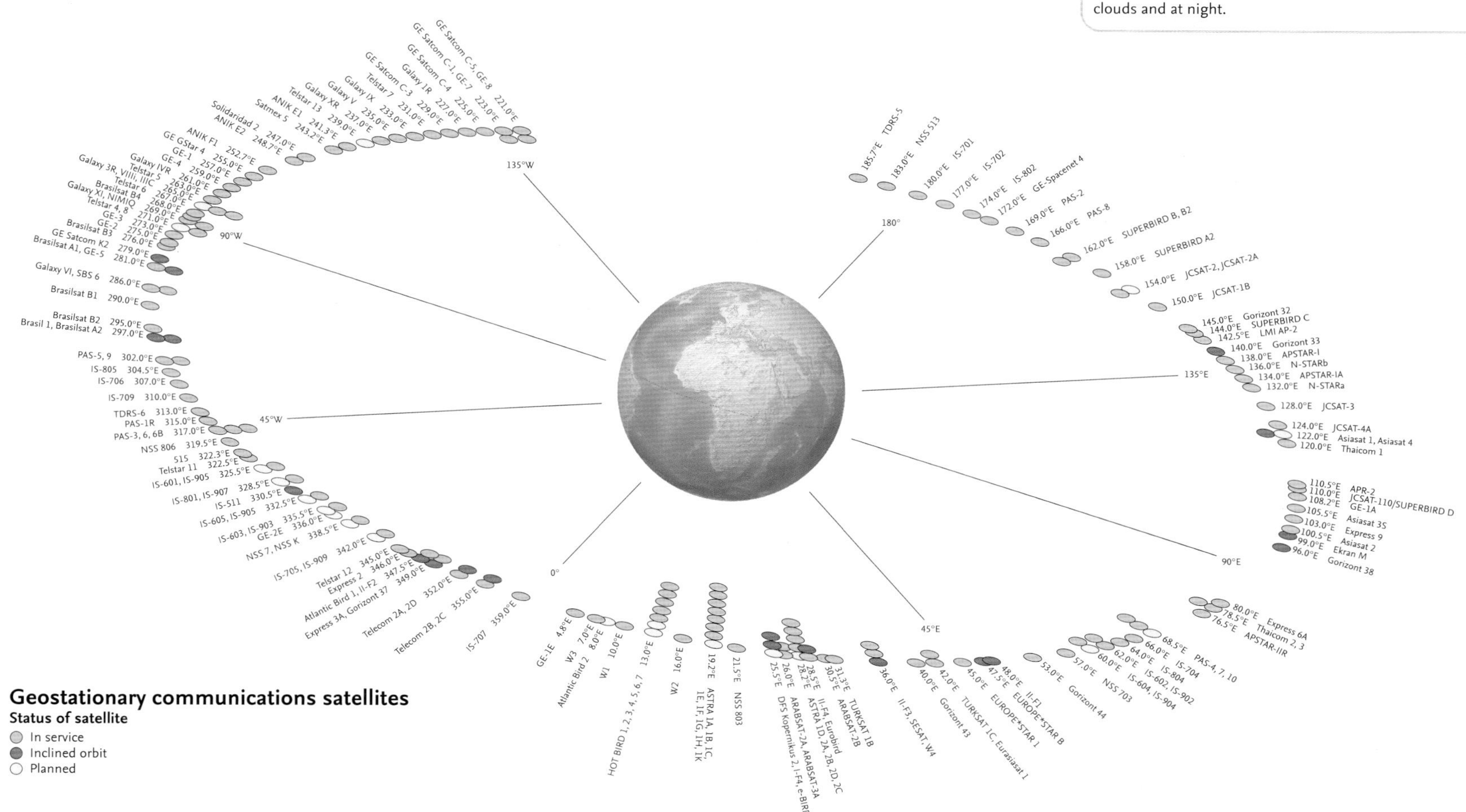

Satellite communications

International telecommunications use either fibre-optic cables or satellites as transmission media. Although cables carry the vast majority of traffic around the world, communications satellites are important for person-to-person communication, including mobile telephones, and for broadcasting. The positions of communications satellites are critical to their use, and reflect the demand for such communications in each part of the world. Such satellites are placed in 'geostationary' orbit 36 000 kilometres (22 370 miles) above the equator. This means that they move at the same speed as the earth and remain fixed above a single point on the earth's surface.

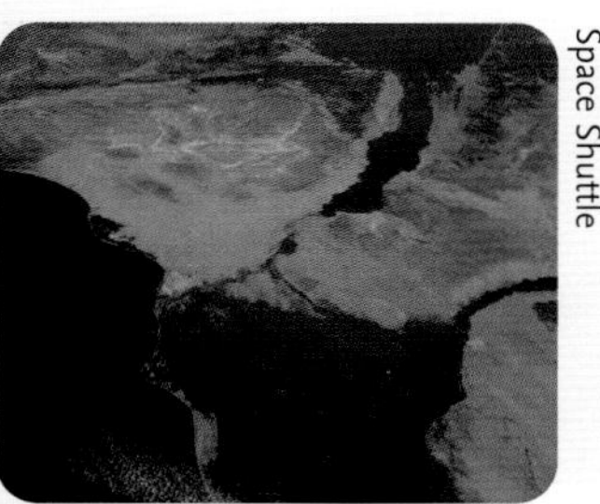

Space Shuttle

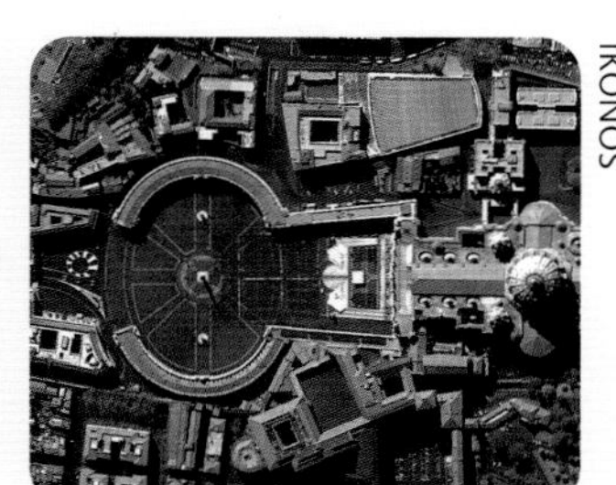

IKONOS

resolution	web address
15m in the panchromatic band (only on Landsat 7), 30m in the six visible, near and short-wave infrared bands and 60m in the thermal infrared band.	geo.arc.nasa.gov ls7pm3.gsfc.nasa.gov
Panchromatic 10m. Multispectral 20m.	www.cnes.fr www.spotimage.fr
SRTM: 30m for US and 90m for rest of the world.	science.ksc.nasa.gov/ shuttle/countdown www.jpl.nasa.gov/srtm
Panchromatic 1m. Multispectral 4m.	www.spaceimaging.com

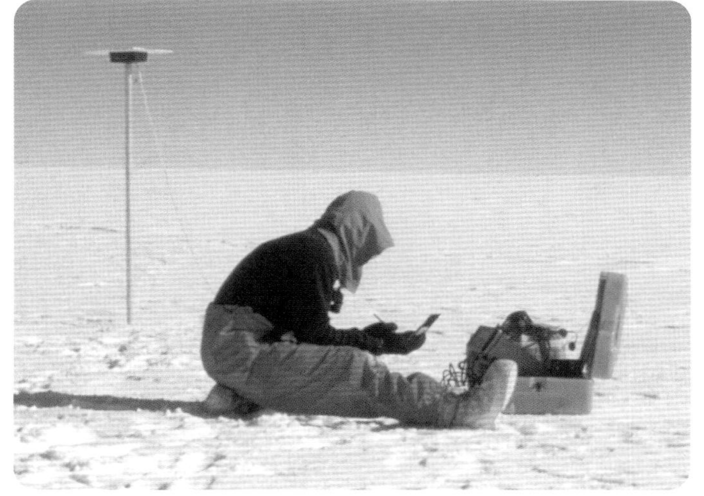

Consisting of twenty-four satellites, the **Global Positioning System** (GPS) – seen in use here in Antarctica for monitoring glacier movement – allows accurate position fixing and navigation. Originally developed by the US military, the signals from the satellites now serve hand-held personal and in-car navigation uses, as well as more sophisticated surveying and mapping applications.

Europe, the world's second smallest continent, is located on the western tip of the vast Eurasian landmass. The curve of mountain ranges, which includes the Alps, the Pyrenees and the Carpathians divides the north of the continent from the south. The highest peak in Europe, Mount El'brus lies in the Caucasus, the mountain range between the Black Sea and the Caspian Sea. North of these mountains, the rolling plains of the Ukraine and European

Russia extend to the Ural Mountains which, together with the Caucasus and the Bosporus in Turkey, form the physical boundary between Europe and Asia. The Mediterranean Sea, in the south, is a large inland sea which is enclosed by mainland Europe to the north and west, Africa to the south, and Asia to the east. The Strait of Gibraltar connects the Mediterranean to the Atlantic Ocean in the west and in the southeast the Suez Canal is the seaway to the Red Sea.

Iceland, seen here in winter, is Europe's second largest is and. It is physically isolated from mainland Europe, being much closer to Greenland. Iceland has great volcanic activity and geothermal hot water heats more than half the country's homes.

Spitsbergen

Lappland

Norwegian Sea

Scandinavia

Gulf of Bothnia

Baltic Sea

Vistula River

Faroe Islands

Largest island Great Britain

North Sea

Elbe River

Rhine River

Ireland

Great Britain

Seine River

English Channel

Alps

Po Ri

Loire River

Massif Central

Bay of Biscay

Corsica

Pyrenees

Sardinia

Atlantic
Ocean

Balearic Islands

Iberian Peninsula

Tagus River

Strait of Gibraltar

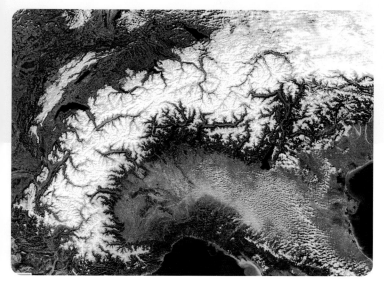

The snow-capped crescent-shaped **Alps**, seen here in early spring, separate Italy from the rest of central Europe. The valley in the lower centre of the image is that of the river Po and also visible are Lake Garda, right of centre, and Lake Geneva left of the snow covered area. The Alps are the source of several major European rivers including the Danube, Rhine and Rhône.

Want to know more?

▶ Cross-section of Europe		6–7
▶ Major volcanic eruptions		10–11
▶ Land cover map of Europe		30–31
▶ Map of Mediterranean issues		34–35
▶ Maps of Europe		38–59

Internet links

European Centre for Nature Conservation NGO	www.ecnc.nl
European Environment Agency	www.eea.eu.int
Alpine Mountaineering	www.alpine-club.org.uk
European Space Agency	www.esa.int

Facts

The Danube flows through 7 countries and has 7 different names. The name Danube is the English language conventional form.

All the seas on this map are branches of the Atlantic Ocean even as far as the Black Sea. The Caspian Sea is isolated in its own drainage basin.

The Strait of Gibraltar, which separates Europe from Africa, is only 13 kilometres (8 miles) wide at the narrowest point. The Bosporus in Turkey, separating Europe from Asia, is only 0.5 kilometres (0.3 miles) wide.

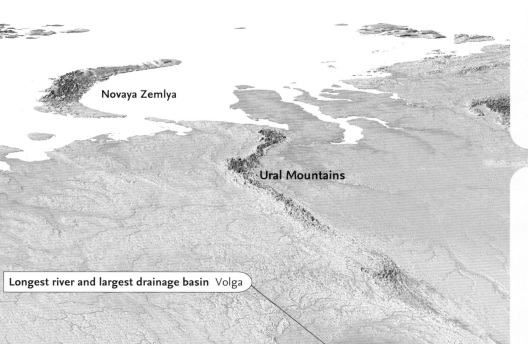

Barents Sea

Novaya Zemlya

Ural Mountains

Lake Ladoga

orth European Plain

Longest river and largest drainage basin Volga

Volga River

Don River

El'brus

Caspian Sea

Dnieper River

Carpathian Mountains

Caucasus

Crimea

Danube River

Black Sea

Bosporus

Dalmatia

Adriatic Sea

ennines

Highest point El'brus

Sicily

Crete

Mediterranean Sea

Largest lake and lowest point Caspian Sea

Highest mountains

	metres	feet	map
El'brus *Russian Federation*	5 642	18 510	107 E2
Gora Dykh-Tau *Russian Fed.*	5 204	17 073	107 E2
Shkhara *Georgia/Russian Fed.*	5 201	17 063	107 E2
Kazbek *Georgia/Russian Fed.*	5 047	16 558	107 F2
Mont Blanc *France/Italy*	4 808	15 774	51 M7
Dufourspitze *Italy/Switzerland*	4 634	15 203	51 N7

Longest rivers

	km	miles	map
Volga	3 688	2 291	41 I7
Danube	2 850	1 770	58 K3
Dnieper	2 285	1 419	41 E7
Kama	2 028	1 260	40 J4
Don	1 931	1 199	41 F7
Pechora	1 802	1 199	40 J1

Largest islands

	sq km	sq miles	map
Great Britain	218 476	84 354	47 J9
Iceland	102 820	39 699	44 inset
Novaya Zemlya	90 650	35 000	38 T2
Ireland	83 045	32 064	47 D11
Spitsbergen	37 814	14 600	38 B2
Sicily	25 426	9 817	57 F11

Largest lakes

	sq km	sq miles	map
Caspian Sea	371 000	143 243	102 B4
Lake Ladoga	18 390	7 100	40 D3
Lake Onega	9 600	3 706	40 E3
Vänern	5 585	2 156	45 K4
Rybinskoye Vodokhranilishche	5 180	2 000	43 T3

Land area

		map
Total land area 9 908 599 sq km/3 825 731 sq miles		
Most northerly point	**Ostrov Rudol'fa** *Russian Fed.*	38 F1
Most southerly point	**Gavdos, Crete** *Greece*	59 F14
Most westerly point	**Bjargtangar** *Iceland*	44 A2
Most easterly point	**Mys Flissingskiy** *Russian Fed.*	39 G2
Lowest point	**Caspian Sea**	102 B4

Cultivated fields and nearby mountains in the Consuegra area of central **Spain**, south-east of Toledo. This is an agricultural centre for cereals, grapes, saffron and olives. There is also sheep rearing, a hydroelectric plant and quarries for jasper and marble.

Europe has the highest percentage of cultivated land of all the continents – almost 40 per cent. With a generally high population density there are relatively few areas which remain truly wild making most habitats managed to some degree. Cultivation is difficult in the northern latitudes of Scandinavia, due to climate conditions, the mountainous terrain and a deeply incised coastline. The major mountain ranges in the south, mainly the Alps and the Pyrenees, although high, are easily accessible in both summer and winter for leisure activities. Demand for food and for land has led to some countries reclaiming land from the sea or draining lakes to create more farmland.

This landscape east of **Kuopio** is typical of the lakelands of Finland where the low-lying area is covered with marsh and about 60 000 lakes are connected by short rivers and canals.

Europe land cover

Tree cover, broadleaved, evergreen
Tree cover, broadleaved, deciduous, closed
Tree cover, broadleaved, deciduous, open
Tree cover, needle-leaved, evergreen
Tree cover, needle-leaved, deciduous
Tree cover, mixed leaf type
Tree cover, regularly flooded, fresh water
Tree cover, regularly flooded, saline water
Mosaic: Tree cover/Other natural vegetation
Tree cover, burnt
Shrub cover, closed-open, evergreen
Shrub cover, closed-open, deciduous
Herbaceous cover, closed-open

Sparse herbaceous or sparse shrub cover
Regularly flooded shrub and/or herbaceous cover
Cultivated and managed areas
Mosaic: Cropland/Tree cover/Other natural vegetation
Mosaic: Cropland/Shrub and/or grass cover
Bare areas, sandy
Bare areas, gravel
Bare areas, rocky
Water bodies
Snow and Ice
Artificial surfaces and associated areas
No data

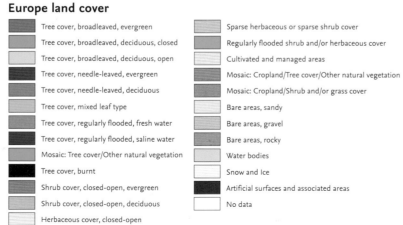

Land cover composition (percentage)

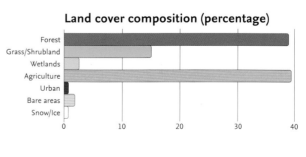

Forest
Grass/Shrubland
Wetlands
Agriculture
Urban
Bare areas
Snow/Ice

0   10   20   30   40

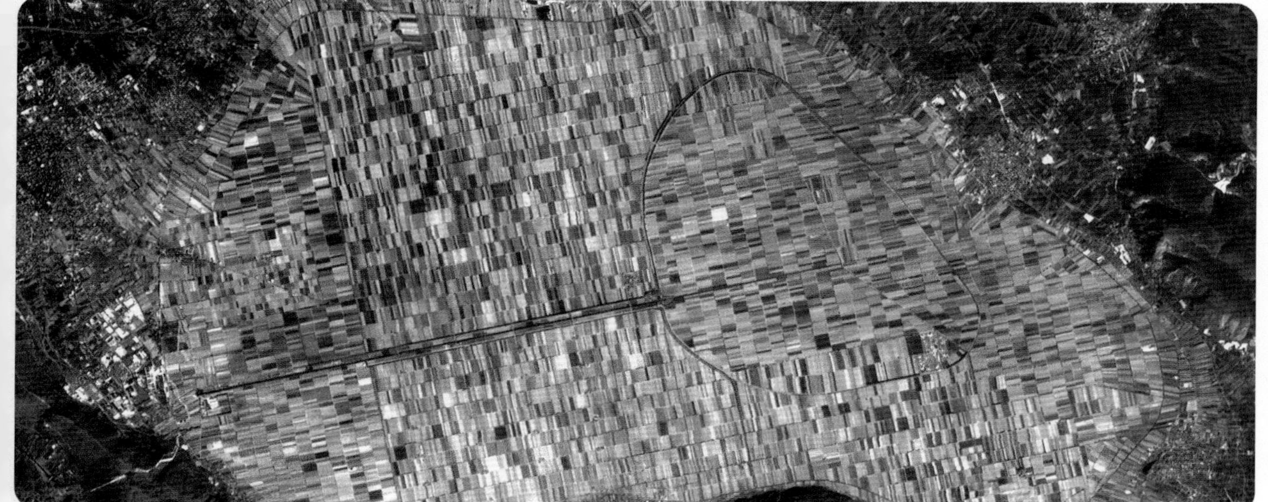
The **Fucino plain** to the east of Avezzino, Italy was once a lake but was drained in the 19th century. It is now intensively cultivated into a patchwork of fields. Wheat produced here is used to make flour especially suited to pizza dough.

Want to know more?

►	World climate and weather	12–13
►	World environmental threats	14–15
►	Perspective view of Europe	28–29
►	Mediterranean Sea pollution	34–35

Internet links

European Centre for Nature Conservation	www.ecnc.nl
Red List of Threatened Species	www.redlist.org
UN Environment Programme	www.unep.org
IUCN the World Conservation Union	www.iucn.org
Images of Europe	earthobservatory.nasa.gov

Facts

Without the existing dykes and dunes, 65 per cent of the Netherlands would be under water.

Lakes cover almost 10 per cent of the total land area of Finland.

Loggerhead sea turtles, found in the eastern Mediterranean, only lay eggs every two or three years.

Due to Iceland sitting at the junction of two of the earth's tectonic plates, it grows by about the length of a car in a lifetime.

Top 10 protected land by country

	country	percentage land protected
1	Austria	36.4
2	Germany	31.7
3	Switzerland	28.8
4	Netherlands	26.2
5	Denmark	25.6
6	Poland	23.5
7	Slovakia	22.5
8	Estonia	19.6
9	Czech Republic	16.0
10	Latvia	15.1

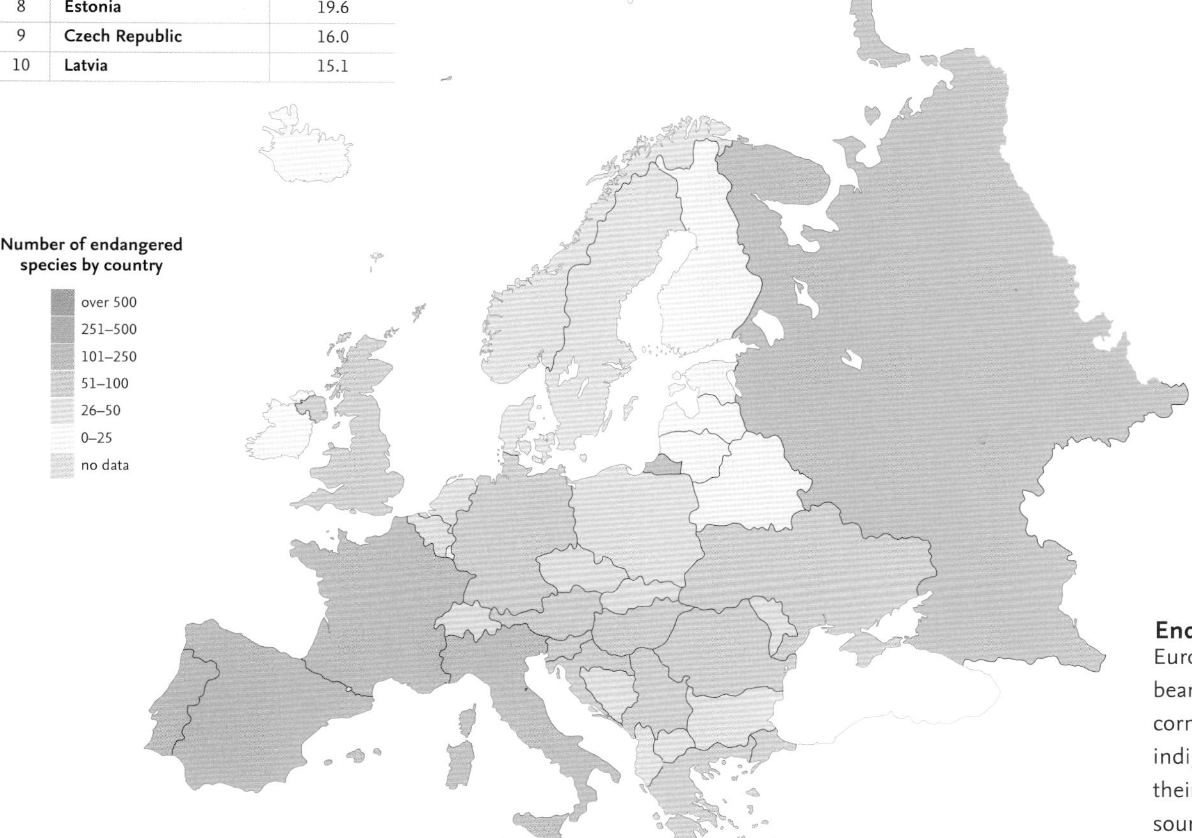

Number of endangered species by country

- over 500
- 251–500
- 101–250
- 51–100
- 26–50
- 0–25
- no data

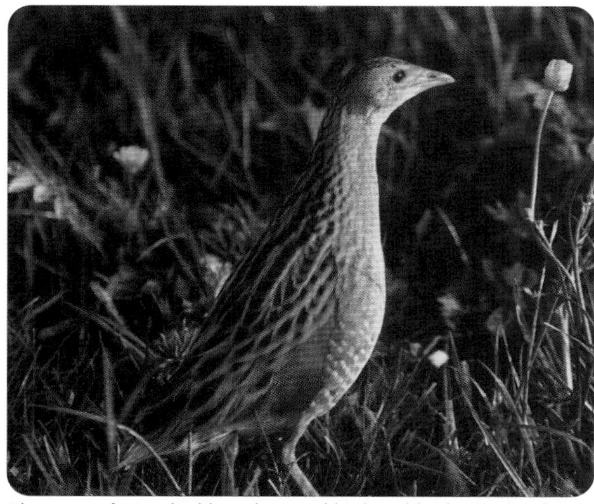
The **corncrake** is a highly endangered bird worldwide. On **South Uist**, in the Outer Hebrides of Scotland, it is one of several species – others affected are the redshank, dunlin, plover and snipe – at risk from the hedgehog. Hedgehogs were introduced in the 1970s to control slugs.

Endangered species

European species under threat include the Iberian lynx, brown bear, loggerhead sea turtle, monk seal, Atlantic salmon, corncrake and freshwater mussel. There are only a few indigenous wild mammals in Europe but a shrinking habitat is their main threat. The seas around Europe provide a great food source but, as on land, demand outstrips supply and the use of synthetic pesticides to increase yield can have a detrimental affect on the sealife.

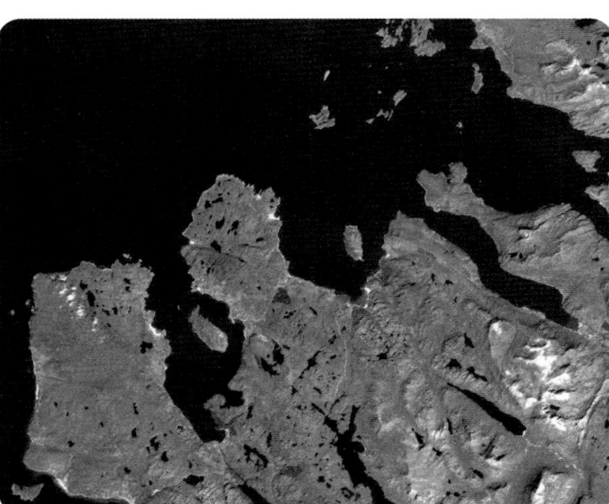
The ice age has shaped the west coast of **Scotland**. Retreating glaciers have left barren mountains with deep valleys and a rugged, indented coastline. Population is sparse and cultivation is generally restricted to sheep farming.

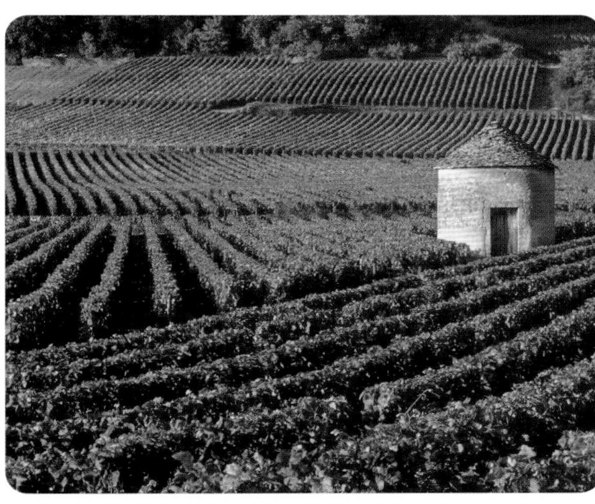
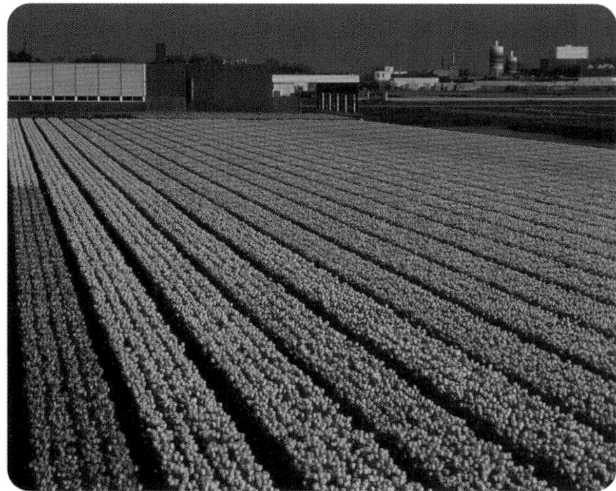
In parts of southern Europe south facing slopes are dominated by **vineyards** for the production of wine. These traditional areas are now competing with an increasing supply from the southern hemisphere. In the Netherlands, reclaimed or drained land is used for the mass production of **flowering bulbs**. In the 17th century rare tulip bulbs were valuable commodities.

Countries capital		sq·km sq miles	population	languages	religions	currency	official website	map
Albania Tirana (Tiranë)		28 748 11 100	3 130 000	Albanian, Greek	Sunni Muslim, Albanian Orthodox, Roman Catholic	Lek	www.keshilliministrave.al	58–59
Andorra Andorra la Vella		465 180	67 000	Spanish, Catalan, French	Roman Catholic	Euro	www.andorra.ad	55
Austria Vienna (Wien)		83 855 32 377	8 189 000	German, Croatian, Turkish	Roman Catholic, Protestant	Euro	www.oesterrich.at	48–49
Belarus Minsk		207 600 80 155	9 755 000	Belorussian, Russian	Belorussian Orthodox, Roman Catholic	Belarus rouble	www.government.by	42-43
Belgium Brussels (Bruxelles)		30 520 11 784	10 419 000	Dutch (Flemish), French (Walloon), German	Roman Catholic, Protestant	Euro	www.belgium.be	51
Bosnia-Herzegovina Sarajevo		51 130 19 741	3 907 000	Bosnian, Serbian, Croatian	Sunni Muslim, Serbian Orthodox, Roman Catholic, Protestant	Marka	www.fbihvlada.gov.ba	56
Bulgaria Sofia (Sofiya)		110 994 42 855	7 726 000	Bulgarian, Turkish, Romany, Macedonian	Bulgarian Orthodox, Sunni Muslim	Lev	www.government.bg	58
Croatia Zagreb		56 538 21 829	4 551 000	Croatian, Serbian	Roman Catholic, Serbian Orthodox, Sunni Muslim	Kuna	www.vlada.hr	56
Czech Republic Prague (Praha)		78 864 30 450	10 220 000	Czech, Moravian, Slovak	Roman Catholic, Protestant	Czech koruna	www.czech.cz	49
Denmark Copenhagen (København)		43 075 16 631	5 431 000	Danish	Protestant	Danish krone	www.denmark.dk	45
Estonia Tallinn		45 200 17 452	1 330 000	Estonian, Russian	Protestant, Estonian and Russian Orthodox	Kroon	www.riik.ee	42
Finland Helsinki (Helsingfors)		338 145 130 559	5 249 000	Finnish, Swedish	Protestant, Greek Orthodox	Euro	www.valtioneuvosto.fi	44–45
France Paris		543 965 210 026	60 496 000	French, Arabic	Roman Catholic, Protestant, Sunni Muslim	Euro	www.premier-ministre.gouv.fr	50–51
Germany Berlin		357 022 137 849	82 689 000	German, Turkish	Protestant, Roman Catholic	Euro	www.bundesregierung.de	48–49
Greece Athens (Athina)		131 957 50 949	11 120 000	Greek	Greek Orthodox, Sunni Muslim	Euro	www.greece.gov.gr	58–59
Hungary Budapest		93 030 35 919	10 098 000	Hungarian	Roman Catholic, Protestant	Forint	www.magyarorszag.hu	49
Iceland Reykjavík		102 820 39 699	295 000	Icelandic	Protestant	Icelandic króna	www.eng.stjornarrad.is	44
Ireland Dublin (Baile Átha Cliath)		70 282 27 136	4 148 000	English, Irish	Roman Catholic, Protestant	Euro	www.irlgov.ie	46–47
Italy Rome (Roma)		301 245 116 311	58 093 000	Italian	Roman Catholic	Euro	www.governo.it	56–57
Latvia Rīga		63 700 24 595	2 307 000	Latvian, Russian	Protestant, Roman Catholic, Russian Orthodox	Lats	www.saeima.lv	42
Liechtenstein Vaduz		160 62	35 000	German	Roman Catholic, Protestant	Swiss franc	www.liechtenstein.li	51
Lithuania Vilnius		65 200 25 174	3 431 000	Lithuanian, Russian, Polish	Roman Catholic, Protestant, Russian Orthodox	Litas	www.lrv.lt	42
Luxembourg Luxembourg		2 586 998	465 000	Letzeburgish, German, French	Roman Catholic	Euro	www.gouvernement.lu	51
Macedonia (F.Y.R.O.M.) Skopje		25 713 9 928	2 034 000	Macedonian, Albanian, Turkish	Macedonian Orthodox, Sunni Muslim	Macedonian denar	www.gov.mk	58

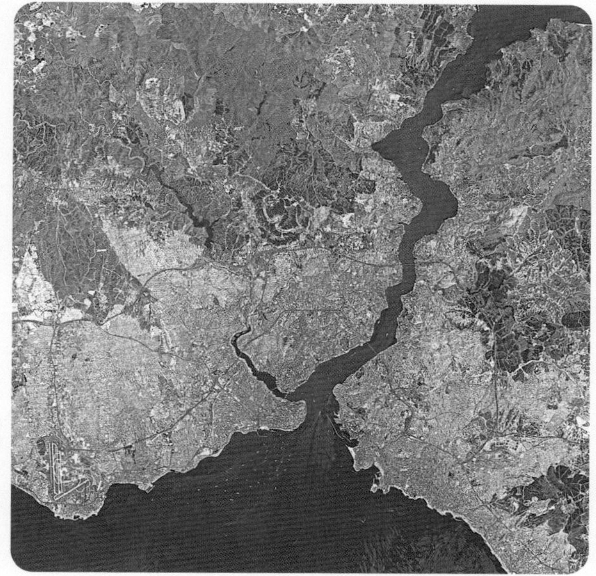

The continents of Europe and Asia are physically separated by a narrow strait of water, **the Bosporus**, in Turkey. The strait, which at its narrowest point is less than 1 kilometre (0.6 mile) wide, is 31 kilometres (19 miles) long and connects the Sea of Marmara in the south to the Black Sea in the north. It is straddled by the city of Istanbul.

Top 10 countries by area

		sq km	sq miles	world rank
1	**Russian Federation**	17 075 400	6 592 849	1
2	Ukraine	603 700	233 090	44
3	France	543 965	210 026	48
4	Spain	504 782	194 897	51
5	Sweden	449 964	173 732	55
6	Germany	357 028	137 849	62
7	Finland	338 145	130 559	64
8	Norway	323 878	125 050	67
9	Poland	312 683	120 728	69
10	Italy	301 245	116 311	71

Top 10 countries By population

		population	world rank
1	**Russian Federation**	143 202 000	7
2	Germany	82 689 000	14
3	France	60 496 000	20
4	United Kingdom	59 668 000	21
5	Italy	58 093 000	22
6	Ukraine	46 481 000	27
7	Spain	43 064 000	29
8	Poland	38 530 000	31
9	Romania	21 711 000	50
10	Netherlands	16 299 000	59

Want to know more?

▶ Political map of the world	8–9
▶ Map of Mediterranean issues	34–35
▶ Map of the European Union	34–35
▶ Detailed maps of Europe	38–59

Internet links

European Union	europa.eu.int
European Parliament	www.europarl.eu.int
UK Foreign and Commonwealth Office	www.fco.gov.uk
Visit Europe	www.visiteurope.com

Facts

Europe has two of the smallest countries in the world. Monaco, between France and Italy, and the Vatican City which is wholly within the city of Rome and is the centre of the Roman Catholic church.

In 2004 the European Union membership grew from fifteen to twenty-five.

Iceland is isolated in the North Atlantic and is closer to Greenland, part of the North American continent, than to Europe. Its capital Reykjavik is the world's most northerly capital city.

Countries

Countries / capital		sq km / sq miles	population	languages	religions	currency	official website	map
Malta Valletta		316 / 122	402 000	Maltese, English	Roman Catholic	Maltese lira	www.gov.mt	57
Moldova Chişinău (Kishinev)		33 700 / 13 012	4 206 000	Romanian, Ukrainian, Gagauz, Russian,	Romanian Orthodox, Russian Orthodox	Moldovan leu	www.moldova.md	41
Monaco Monaco-Ville		2 / 1	35 000	French, Monegasque, Italian	Roman Catholic	Euro	www.monaco.gouv.mc	51
Netherlands Amsterdam/The Hague ('s–Gravenhage)		41 526 / 16 033	16 299 000	Dutch, Frisian	Roman Catholic, Protestant, Sunni Muslim	Euro	www.overheid.nl	48
Norway Oslo		323 878 / 125 050	4 620 000	Norwegian	Protestant, Roman Catholic	Norwegian krone	www.norway.no	44–45
Poland Warsaw (Warszawa)		312 683 / 120 728	38 530 000	Polish, German	Roman Catholic, Polish Orthodox	Złoty	www.gov.mt	49
Portugal Lisbon (Lisboa)		88 940 / 34 340	10 495 000	Portuguese	Roman Catholic, Protestant	Euro	www.portugal.gov.pt	54
Romania Bucharest (Bucureşti)		237 500 / 91 699	21 711 000	Romanian, Hungarian	Romanian Orthodox, Protestant, Roman Catholic	Romanian leu	www.guv.ro	58
Russian Federation Moscow (Moskva)		17 075 400 / 6 592 849	143 202 000	Russian, Tatar, Ukrainian, local languages	Russian Orthodox, Sunni Muslim, Protestant	Russian rouble	www.gov.ru	38–39
San Marino San Marino		61 / 24	28 000	Italian	Roman Catholic	Euro	www.consigliograndeegenerale.sm	56
Serbia and Montenegro Belgrade (Beograd)		102 173 / 39 449	10 503 000	Serbian, Albanian, Hungarian	Serbian Orthodox, Montenegrin Orthodox, Sunni Muslim	Serbian dinar, Euro	www.gov.yu	58
Slovakia Bratislava		49 035 / 18 933	5 401 000	Slovak, Hungarian, Czech	Roman Catholic, Protestant, Orthodox	Slovakian koruna	www.government.gov.sk	49
Slovenia Ljubljana		20 251 / 7 819	1 967 000	Slovene, Croatian, Serbian	Roman Catholic, Protestant	Tólar	www.sigov.si	56
Spain Madrid		504 782 / 194 897	43 064 000	Castilian, Catalan, Galician, Basque	Roman Catholic	Euro	www.a-moncloa.es	54–55
Sweden Stockholm		449 964 / 173 732	9 041 000	Swedish	Protestant, Roman Catholic	Swedish krona	www.sweden.se	44–45
Switzerland Bern (Berne)		41 293 / 15 943	7 252 000	German, French, Italian, Romansch	Roman Catholic, Protestant	Swiss franc	www.admin.ch	51
Ukraine Kiev (Kyiv)		603 700 / 233 090	46 481 000	Ukrainian, Russian	Ukrainian Orthodox, Ukrainian Catholic, Roman Catholic	Hryvnia	www.kmu.gov.ua	41
United Kingdom London		243 609 / 94 058	59 668 000	English, Welsh, Gaelic	Protestant, Roman Catholic, Muslim	Pound sterling	www.ukonline.gov.uk	46–47
Vatican City Vatican City		0.5 / 0.2	552	Italian	Roman Catholic	Euro	www.vatican.va	56

Dependencies

Dependencies / capital		territorial status	sq km / sq miles	population	languages	religions	currency	official website	map
Azores (Arquipélago dos Açores) Ponta Delgada		Autonomous Region of Portugal	2 300 / 888	241 762	Portuguese	Roman Catholic, Protestant	Euro	www.azores.gov.pt	216
Faroe Islands Tóshavn (Thorshavn)		Self-governing Danish Territory	1 399 / 540	47 000	Faroese, Danish	Protestant	Danish krone	www.tinganes.fo	46
Gibraltar Gibraltar		United Kingdom Overseas Territory	7 / 3	28 000	English, Spanish	Roman Catholic, Protestant, Sunni Muslim	Gibraltar pound	www.gibraltar.gov.gi	54
Guernsey St Peter Port		United Kingdom Crown Dependency	78 / 30	62 692	English, French	Protestant, Roman Catholic	Pound sterling	www.gov.gg	50
Isle of Man Douglas		United Kingdom Crown Dependency	572 / 221	77 000	English	Protestant, Roman Catholic	Pound sterling	www.gov.im	47
Jersey St Helier		United Kingdom Crown Dependency	116 / 45	87 500	English, French	Protestant, Roman Catholic	Pound sterling	www.gov.je	50

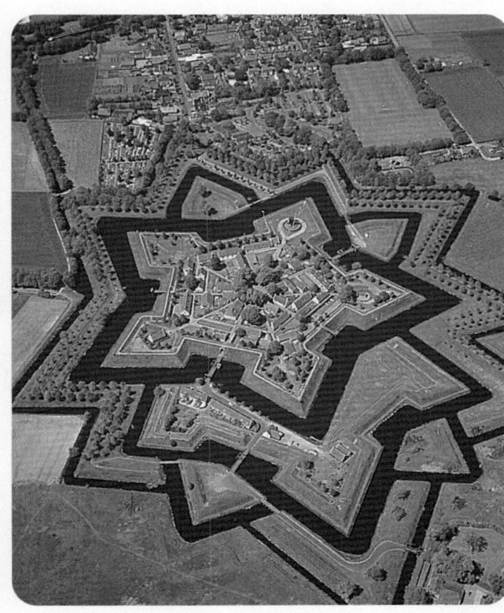

The village of **Bourtange** is located in the Groningen province in the Netherlands. The star-shaped fortress dates back to the late sixteenth century. The old core of the village was restored in 1967 and has since been protected as a national monument.

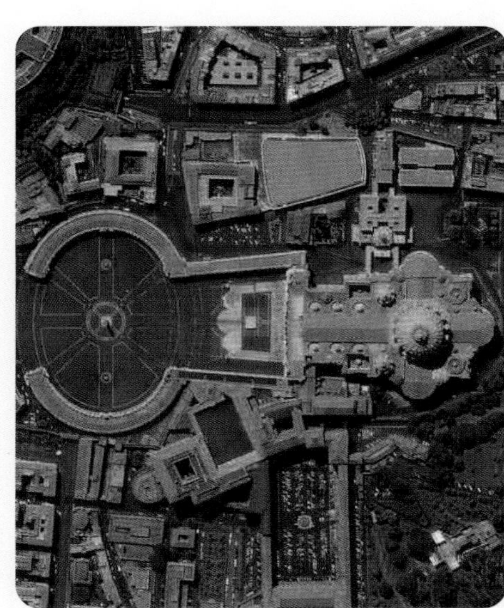

Satellite image of St Peter's Basilica in the Vatican City. The Vatican is the world's smallest independent country in terms of both area and population. It was formed from part of central Rome by agreement with the Italian government in the 1920s.

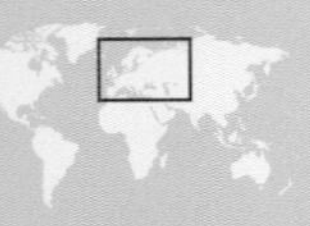

Europe was the first continent to industrialise and it has seen many changes over the last few centuries. Europeans are a continent of relatively small nations and by becoming more integrated they can compete on the world stage as well as help each other. Not all countries developed at the same speed or to the same level and there are continuing inequalities to be addressed.

Industrialisation and urbanisation create their own problems. Europe now averages a 69.9 per cent urban population which is around 409 million people. Europeans with leisure time to spare flock to Mediterranean beach resorts, a short journey from home, to enjoy the natural and cultural attractions. However, this increases the coastal development of new and historic areas resulting in intense pressure all round the Mediterranean basin coastline.

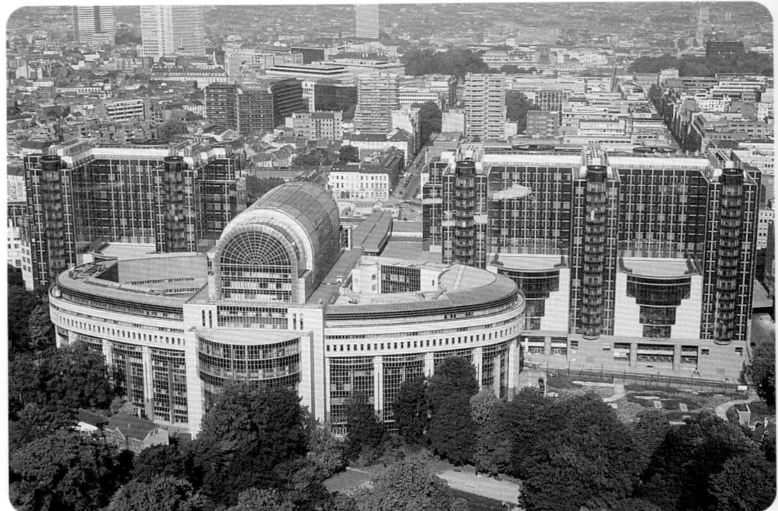

The European Union has it's headquarters in **Brussels** which is the captial of Belgium. The headquarters building shown in the photograph is known as the Hémicylce Européen and it has a distinctive curved glass roof.

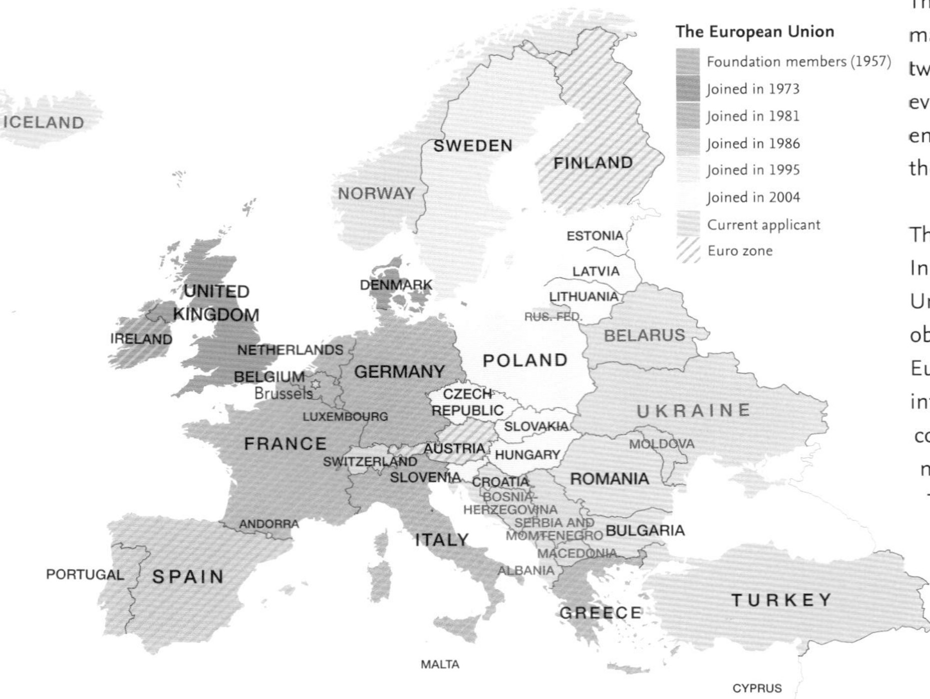

The European Union

- Foundation members (1957)
- Joined in 1973
- Joined in 1981
- Joined in 1986
- Joined in 1995
- Joined in 2004
- Current applicant
- Euro zone

The European Union has grown from six founder members in 1957 – who mainly cooperated over trade and the economy – to an amalgamation of twenty four countries who deal together with many subjects of importance in everyday life including regional development, security and justice, and environmental protection. Twelve member states also share a single currency, the euro.

The EU has developed from an economic community into a political union. In 1984, while known as the EEC, it adopted a draft treaty on European Union, following this with the 1987 Single European Act which had the objective of completing the single market by 1992. In 1992 the Treaty on European Union was signed in Maastricht, establishing the EU and introducing a common foreign and security policy. The treaty also allowed for cooperation in the field of justice and home affairs, for economic and monetary union and for the establishment of a single European currency. The 1997 treaty of Amsterdam intensified European integration and allowed for reform of the European institutions. This happened with the Treaty of Nice in 2001 and paved the way for the EU enlargement of 2004 when ten new members joined.

The EU is currently embarking on the ratification of a new constitution. All member states will have to ratify this by parliament or referendum. The Constitution is planned to enter into force on 1 November 2006.

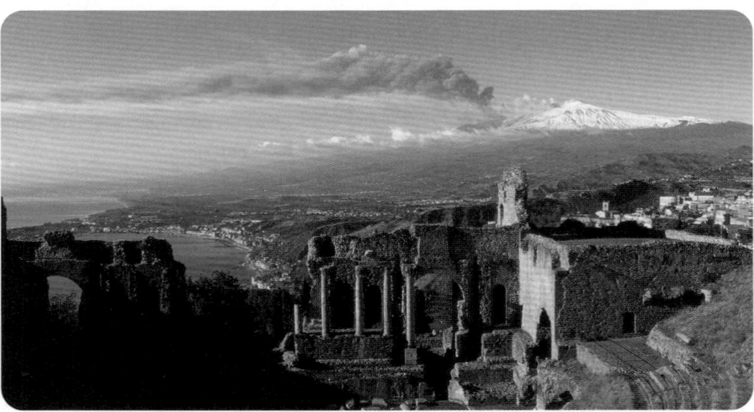

Sicily, situated at the toe of Italy has long been a popular destination for visitors to the Mediterranean. The name conjures up images such as this one at **Taormina** of the ruins of a Greek Amphitheatre and the gently smoking volcano of Mount Etna.

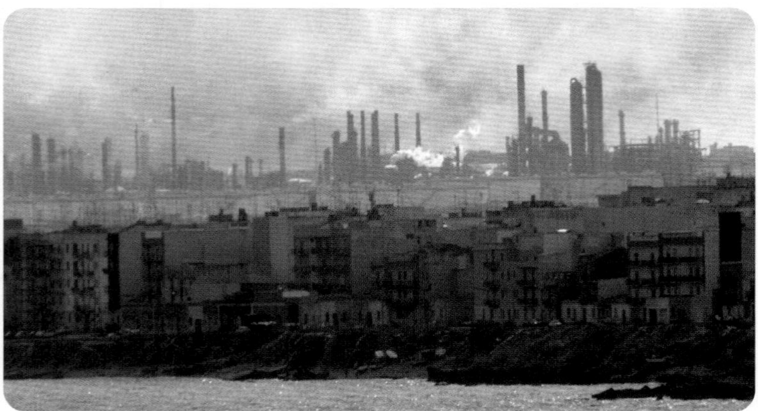

For those who live just to the south of Taormina in **Augusta** the view is not quite so scenic. Much of the Italian coastline in this area is built up and industrial pollution has become inescapable. This view shows the Augusta oil refinery. There is another refinery just down the coast at Priolo Gargallo.

The Mediterranean

Total coastline length	46 267 kilometres/28 750 miles
Islands coastline length	19 274 kilometres/11 977 miles
Area	2.5 million square kilometres/ 1 million square miles
Volume	3.7 million square kilometres/ 0.9 million cubic miles
Average depth	1 500 metres/4 921 feet
Average temperature (W-E)	15–21°C/59–70°F
Average salinity (W-E)	36.2–39 parts per thousand
Mediterranean as % of total marine surface	0.7 per cent
Seawater renewal rate	80–90 years
Wastewater disposed into sea untreated	80 per cent
Countries round the coast	22
Mediterranean land coastal area	1 025 348 square kilometres/ 395 887 square miles
Mediterranean land population	150 million
Population density average for Mediterranean countries	45 inhabitants per square kilometre/117 per square mile
Mediterranean land population density	132 inhabitants per square kilometre/342 per square mile
Coastline urbanized	65 per cent
Tourist visitors annually	220 million
Tourist visitors to the Mediterranean as a percentage of total international tourists	30 per cent

Mediterranean region
Population and tourist arrivals

- North countries population
- South countries population
- Total population
- Urban population (cities of 10 000 plus)
- Tourist arrivals

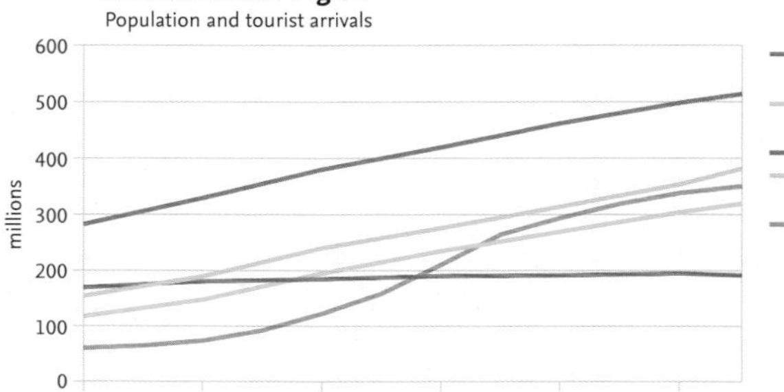

The **euro** is now the currency for twelve European Union member states (see map). One euro is made up of 100 cents. Coins range from 1 cent to 2 euros and notes from 5 to 500 euros.

The euro in August 2004	banknotes	coins
Total cash in circulation (number)	8.89 billion notes	54.16 billion coins
Total cash in circulation (value)	460.21 billion	14.95 billion
Total value as a share of GDP	6.10 per cent	0.20 per cent
Most popular note/coin (total number)	50 euro note	1 cent coin
Most popular note/coin (total value)	50 euro note	2 euro coin

Internet links

United Nations Environment Programme Mediterranean Action Plan	www.unemap.gr
European Environment Agency	www.eea.eu.int
European Union	www.europa.eu.int
CIA World Factbook	www.cia.gov/cia/publications/factbook

Facts

The Mediterranean Sea covers more than 2.5 million square kilometres (1 million square miles), but represents only 0.7 per cent of the world's salt water.

In recent years around 60 per cent of tourism income has returned to fewer than ten tour operators from northern Europe.

The European Union has twenty languages and annual translation costs are around 800 million euros – 2.55 euros per EU citizen.

There are currently 732 Members of the European Parliament (MEPs). This will rise to 786 in 2007.

The 5 European Institutions

European Parliament	Elected by the peoples of the Member States
Council of the European Union	Representing the governments of the Member States
European Commission	The driving force and executive body
Court of Justice	Ensures compliance with the law
Court of Auditors	Controlling sound and lawful management of the EU budget

The top 5 other important EU bodies

European Economic and Social Committee	Expresses opinions of organized civil society on economic and social issues
Committee of the Regions	Expresses opinions of regional and local authorities
European Central Bank	Responsible for monetary policy and managing the euro
European Ombudsman	Deals with citizens' complaints about mal-administration by any EU institution or body
European Investment Bank	Helps achieve EU objectives by financing investment projects

Mediterranean Sea

The Mediterranean coast is an increasingly busy area as the coastal population expands and becomes more urbanized. One of the main reasons for this is the great growth in tourism since the introduction of package holidays in the 1970s. Tourist arrivals are rising every year putting the very environment and culture that attracts the visitors at risk.

Mass tourism degrades landscapes, increases waste discharge into the sea, destroys natural habitats and puts higher pressure on endangered species. It also creates a huge strain on water resources and can lead to the disruption of local cultures. This pressure is only going to increase with the estimate that tourism-related development will double in the next twenty years. However, recently, tourism has provided a strong incentive to protect the landscape and to improve the quality of the environment. This should prevent more areas becoming damaged beyond repair.

84 per cent of Mediterranean tourists come from Europe. Germany is the largest single source.

Urbanization has effectively created a 25 000 kilometre/15 500 mile concrete barrier which is approximately 53 per cent of the Mediterranean coastline.

The average Spaniard uses 250 litres/55 gallons of water per day. A tourist will average 440 litres/97 gallons but can use up to 880 litres/194 gallons.

Tourism provides economic benefits, but adversely affects the physical and human environment that attracts visitors.

Pollution can affect water quality in beach areas and drinking water supplies.

The monk seal habitat has been destroyed by tourist development.

In Zakynthos, sea turtles have had nesting grounds disturbed and destroyed.

43 per cent of Italy's coast is urbanized, mainly due to tourist development.

Tourism contributes 24 per cent of Malta's GNI.

The Mediterranean Sea receives up to 10 billion tonnes of waste water annually. Only about 20 per cent of this is treated.

Northern Mediterranean countries
Southern Mediterranean countries

Population	Pollution
over 840 000	severe
480 000–40 000	heavy
290 000–480 000	light or
150 000–290 000	moderate
0–150 000	

3500 BC Megalithic monument period, including building of Stonehenge

1500 Start of the Renaissance in Italy (Michelangelo, Raphael, Botticelli, Machiavelli)

54 BC Julius Caesar invades Britain

1453 Turks conquer Constantinople (İstanbul)

1215 Magna Carta (England)

863 Cyrillic alphabet invented (Russia)

1896 First wireless telegraphy (radio transmitter) by Marconi (Italy)

1863 First underground railway (London)

1853–1855 Crimean War

1822 Invention of photography by Niépce (France)

1804 Napoleon becomes emperor of France

1582 Gregorian calendar first used instead of Julian calendar

1709 Iron smelter invented by Abraham Darby (England): start of Industrial Revolution

| 3500 | 3000 | 2500 | 2000 | 1500 | 1000 | 500 | BC | AD | 800 | 900 | 1000 | 1100 | 1200 | 1300 | 1400 | 1500 | 1600 | 1650 | 1700 | 1750 | 1800 | 1850 | 1900 |

1066 Norman conquest of England

1337–1453 Hundred Years' War (England - France)

1455 Book printing pioneered by Gutenberg (Germany)

1517 Martin Luther's '95 Theses': start of the Reformation

1543 Operation of the solar system described by Copernicus (Poland)

31 BC – AD 14 Classical Roman literature (Virgil, Horace, Ovid, Livy)

1588 Spanish Armada

479–338 BC Greek classical culture (Sophocles, Herodotus, Hippocrates, Socrates, Aristotle etc.)

1618–1648 Thirty Years' War

776 BC Traditional date for first Olympic Games (Greece)

2000 BC Sails first used on sea-going vessels (Aegean Sea)

1789–1799 French Revolution

1707 Act of Union, joining Scotland with England

1683 Turkish siege of Vienna

1825 First steam railway (Stockton and Darlington, UK; Stephenson's 'Locomotion No. 1')

1848 The Communist Manifesto by Marx and Engels (Germany); The 'Year of Revolutions' across central Europe

1859 Darwin's 'Origin of Species' published (UK)

1861 Pasteur's germ theory of disease (France)

1885 Invention of the motor car (Daimler and Benz, Germany)

1898 Radioactivity research by the Curies (France)

	Population							Economy					
	total population	population change (%)	urban population (%)	total fertility	population by age 0-14 (%)	population by age 60+ (%)	2050 projected population	total Gross National Income (GNI) (US$M)	Gross National Income (GNI) per capita (US$)	debt service ratio (% GNI)	total debt service (US$)	aid receipts (% GNI)	military spending (% GDP)
World	**6 464 750 000**	**1.2**	**48.3**	**2.7**	**28.2**	**10.4**	**9 075 903 000**	**34 491 458**	**5 500**	**...**	**...**	**...**	**2.4**
Albania	3 130 000	0.4	43.8	2.3	27.0	12.0	3 458 000	5 517	1 740	1.2	58 400 000	6.2	1.2
Andorra	67 000	0.4	91.7	...	...	...	58 000	...	...	...	...	...	...
Austria	8 189 000	0.2	65.8	1.4	15.5	22.7	8 073 000	215 372	26 720	...	...	...	0.8
Belarus	9 755 000	-0.6	70.9	1.2	15.2	18.6	7 017 000	15 700	1 590	1.4	197 400 000	...	1.4
Belgium	10 419 000	0.2	97.2	1.7	16.8	22.4	10 302 000	267 227	25 820	...	...	...	1.3
Bosnia-Herzegovina	3 907 000	0.3	44.3	1.3	16.5	19.2	3 170 000	6 386	1 540	2.7	158 100 000	9.6	9.5
Bulgaria	7 726 000	-0.7	69.8	1.2	13.8	22.4	5 065 000	16 639	2 130	8.9	1 368 000 000	...	2.7
Croatia	4 551 000	0.2	59.0	1.4	15.5	22.1	3 686 000	23 839	5 350	13.6	3 018 400 000	0.6	2.5
Czech Republic	10 220 000	-0.1	74.3	1.2	14.6	20.0	8 452 000	68 711	6 740	6.9	4 534 400 000	...	2.1
Denmark	5 431 000	0.3	85.3	1.8	18.8	21.1	5 851 000	181 825	33 750	...	...	...	1.6
Estonia	1 330 000	-0.6	69.4	1.4	15.2	21.6	1 119 000	6 699	4 960	12.7	782 899 968	...	1.9
Finland	5 249 000	0.3	60.9	1.7	17.3	21.3	5 329 000	140 755	27 020	...	...	...	1.2
France	60 496 000	0.4	76.3	1.9	18.2	21.1	63 116 000	1 523 025	24 770	...	...	...	2.5
Germany	82 689 000	0.1	88.1	1.3	14.3	25.1	78 765 000	2 084 631	25 250	...	...	...	1.5
Greece	11 120 000	0.3	60.8	1.3	14.3	23.0	10 742 000	146 563	13 720	...	...	...	4.3
Hungary	10 098 000	-0.3	65.1	1.3	15.7	20.8	8 262 000	64 028	6 330	24.3	14 869 900 288	...	1.8
Iceland	295 000	0.9	92.8	2.0	22.0	15.8	370 000	8 813	30 810	...	...	...	0.0
Ireland	4 148 000	1.8	59.9	1.9	20.2	15.1	5 762 000	106 417	26 960	...	...	...	0.7
Italy	58 093 000	0.1	67.4	1.3	14.0	25.6	50 912 000	1 242 978	21 560	...	...	...	1.9
Latvia	2 307 000	-0.6	66.2	1.3	14.7	22.5	1 678 000	9 441	4 070	7.7	650 000 000	...	1.8
Liechtenstein	35 000	1.0	21.6	...	...	...	44 000	...	...	...	...	...	...
Lithuania	3 431 000	-0.4	66.7	1.3	16.7	20.7	2 565 000	15 509	4 490	9.2	1 281 400 064	...	2.0
Luxembourg	465 000	1.3	91.9	1.7	18.9	18.3	721 000	19 683	43 940	...	...	...	0.9
Macedonia (F.Y.R.O.M.)	2 034 000	0.2	59.5	1.5	19.6	15.5	1 884 000	4 058	1 980	6.3	237 900 000	7.3	2.8
Malta	402 000	0.5	91.7	1.5	17.6	18.8	428 000	3 678	9 260	...	...	0.3	0.8
Moldova	4 206 000	-0.3	46.0	1.2	18.3	13.7	3 312 000	2 137	590	12.6	228 500 000	7.8	0.3
Monaco	35 000	1.1	100.0	...	...	...	55 000	...	...	...	...	...	...
Netherlands	16 299 000	0.5	65.8	1.7	18.2	19.2	17 139 000	426 641	26 310	...	...	...	1.6
Norway	4 620 000	0.5	78.6	1.8	19.6	20.0	5 435 000	197 658	43 350	...	...	...	1.8
Poland	38 530 000	-0.1	61.9	1.3	16.3	16.8	31 916 000	201 389	5 270	7.1	13 488 799 744	...	1.8
Portugal	10 495 000	0.5	54.6	1.5	15.9	22.3	10 723 000	123 664	12 130	...	...	...	2.3
Romania	21 711 000	-0.4	54.5	1.3	15.4	19.3	16 757 000	51 194	2 310	6.8	3 088 199 936	...	2.3
San Marino	28 000	0.9	88.7	...	...	...	30 000	...	...	...	...	...	...
Serbia and Montenegro	10 503 000	-0.1	52.0	1.7	18.3	18.5	9 426 000	15 512	1 910	1.0	150 200 000	12.4	4.9
Slovakia	5 401 000	0.0	57.4	1.2	16.7	16.2	4 612 000	26 483	4 920	14.2	3 376 999 936	...	1.9
Slovenia	1 967 000	0.0	50.8	1.2	13.9	20.5	1 630 000	23 230	11 830	...	...	0.2	1.5
Spain	43 064 000	1.1	76.5	1.3	14.3	21.4	42 541 000	698 208	16 990	...	...	...	1.2
Sweden	9 041 000	0.4	83.4	1.6	17.5	23.4	10 054 000	258 319	28 840	...	...	...	1.9
Switzerland	7 252 000	0.2	67.5	1.4	16.5	21.8	7 252 000	292 892	39 880	...	...	...	1.1
Ukraine	46 481 000	-1.1	67.2	1.1	14.9	20.9	26 393 000	46 739	970	7.8	3 242 899 968	...	2.8
United Kingdom	59 668 000	0.3	89.1	1.7	17.9	21.2	67 143 000	1 680 300	28 350	...	...	...	2.4
Vatican City	552	-0.1	100.0	...	...	...	1 000	...	...	...	...	...	...

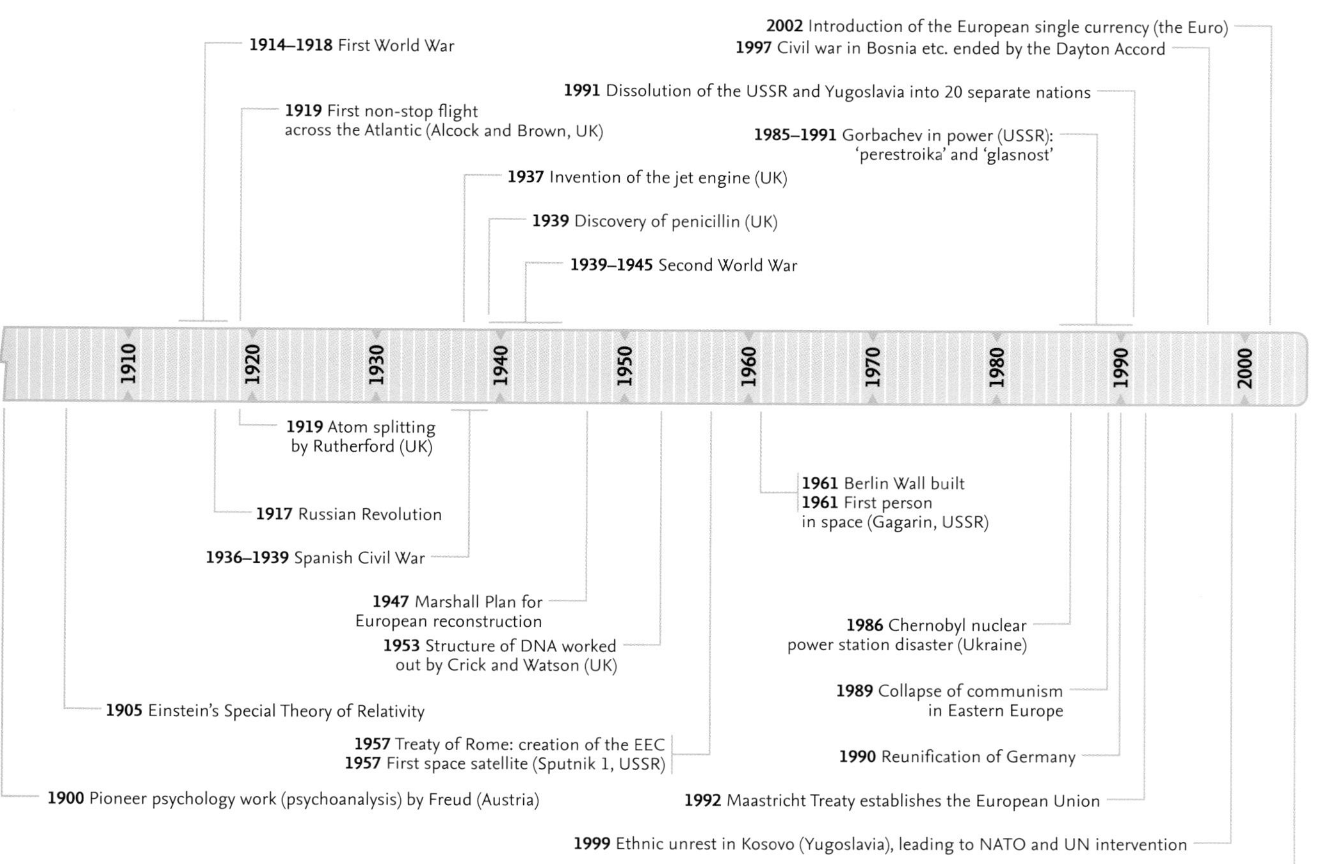

1914–1918 First World War
1919 First non-stop flight across the Atlantic (Alcock and Brown, UK)
1937 Invention of the jet engine (UK)
1939 Discovery of penicillin (UK)
1939–1945 Second World War
2002 Introduction of the European single currency (the Euro)
1997 Civil war in Bosnia etc. ended by the Dayton Accord
1991 Dissolution of the USSR and Yugoslavia into 20 separate nations
1985–1991 Gorbachev in power (USSR): 'perestroika' and 'glasnost'

1910　1920　1930　1940　1950　1960　1970　1980　1990　2000

1919 Atom splitting by Rutherford (UK)
1917 Russian Revolution
1936–1939 Spanish Civil War
1947 Marshall Plan for European reconstruction
1953 Structure of DNA worked out by Crick and Watson (UK)
1905 Einstein's Special Theory of Relativity
1957 Treaty of Rome: creation of the EEC
1957 First space satellite (Sputnik 1, USSR)
1900 Pioneer psychology work (psychoanalysis) by Freud (Austria)
1961 Berlin Wall built
1961 First person in space (Gagarin, USSR)
1986 Chernobyl nuclear power station disaster (Ukraine)
1989 Collapse of communism in Eastern Europe
1990 Reunification of Germany
1992 Maastricht Treaty establishes the European Union
1999 Ethnic unrest in Kosovo (Yugoslavia), leading to NATO and UN intervention
2004 European Union enlarged from 15 to 25 members

Want to know more?	
▶ World's smallest countries	8–9
▶ Highest population densities	16–17
▶ Terrorist incidents	24–25
▶ Space exploration	26–27
▶ Guide to Europe's countries	32–33

Internet links	
European Union	www.europa.eu.int
European Parliament	www.europarl.eu.int
Council of Europe	www.coe.int
European Environment Agency	www.eea.eu.int

Facts

Catholic countries adopted Pope Gregory's calendar in 1582 but Britain didn't follow until 1752, by which time eleven days had to be lost to catch up.

The first London underground line was the Metropolitan line. It carried 38 000 people on its first day.

Alcock and Brown's non-stop trans-Atlantic flight in 1919 took 16 hours 27 minutes. 50 years later Concorde could do the same journey in less than 3 hours.

Social indicators					Environment				Communications					See page 335 for explanatory table and sources
child mortality rate	life expectancy male	female	literacy rate (%)	access to safe water (%)	doctors per 100 000 people	forest area (%)	annual change in forest area (%)	protected land area (%)	CO₂ emissions (metric tons per capita)	main telephone lines per 100 people	cellular mobile subscribers per 100 people	internet users per 10 000 people	international dialling code	time zone	
80	63.3	67.6	87.3	83	...	29.6	-0.2	11.4	3.8	18.8	21.9	1 125	...	...	World
21	70.9	76.7	98.2	97	137	36.2	-0.8	2.6	0.9	8.3	35.8	98	355	+1	Albania
7	...	...	...	100	...	...	...	6.4	...	43.8	30.2	900	376	+1	Andorra
5	75.4	81.5	...	100	323	47.0	0.2	28.0	7.6	48.1	87.9	4 620	43	+1	Austria
17	64.9	75.3	99.8	100	450	45.3	3.2	6.4	5.9	31.1	11.3	1 410	375	+2	Belarus
5	75.7	81.9	...	...	419	22.2	-0.2	3.4	10.0	49.4	78.6	3 283	32	+1	Belgium
17	71.3	76.7	...	98	145	44.6	...	0.5	4.8	24.5	27.4	262	387	+1	Bosnia-Herzegovina
15	67.4	74.6	99.7	100	344	33.4	0.6	10.1	5.2	36.8	33.3	2 058	359	+2	Bulgaria
7	70.3	78.1	99.8	...	238	31.9	0.1	6.4	4.4	41.7	58.4	2 318	385	+1	Croatia
4	72.1	78.7	...	...	342	34.1	...	18.3	11.6	36.0	96.5	2 683	420	+1	Czech Republic
4	74.2	79.1	...	100	366	10.7	0.2	25.5	8.4	66.9	88.7	5 128	45	+1	Denmark
9	66.5	76.8	99.8	...	313	48.7	0.6	19.6	11.7	35.1	65.0	3 277	372	+2	Estonia
5	74.4	81.5	...	100	311	72.0	...	8.8	10.3	48.8	90.1	5 089	358	+2	Finland
5	75.2	82.8	...	...	330	27.9	0.4	3.0	6.2	56.6	69.6	3 656	33	+1	France
5	75.2	81.2	...	100	363	30.7	...	31.3	9.6	65.9	78.5	4 727	49	+1	Germany
5	75.7	80.9	99.8	...	438	27.9	0.9	3.2	8.5	45.4	78.0	1 500	30	+2	Greece
8	67.7	76.0	99.8	99	355	19.9	0.4	8.9	5.4	36.1	67.6	2 322	36	+1	Hungary
4	77.6	81.9	...	100	352	0.3	2.2	4.7	7.7	66.0	96.6	6 747	354	GMT	Iceland
6	74.4	79.6	...	...	239	9.6	3.0	1.1	11.1	48.6	84.5	3 130	353	GMT	Ireland
4	75.5	81.9	99.8	...	607	34.0	0.3	10.8	7.4	48.4	101.8	3 367	39	+1	Italy
12	65.6	76.2	99.8	...	291	47.1	0.4	15.1	2.5	28.3	52.9	4 057	371	+2	Latvia
11	...	...	...	...	...	46.7	1.2	35.4	...	58.3	33.3	5 850	423	+1	Liechtenstein
11	67.5	77.6	99.8	...	403	31.9	0.2	9.2	3.4	25.3	66.6	2 136	370	+2	Lithuania
5	75.1	81.4	...	100	254	...	...	17.1	19.4	79.7	106.1	3 765	352	+1	Luxembourg
11	71.4	75.8	...	...	219	35.6	...	7.9	5.5	27.1	17.7	485	389	+1	Macedonia (F.Y.R.O.M.)
6	75.9	80.7	98.7	100	291	n.s.	...	13.5	7.2	52.1	72.5	3 030	356	+1	Malta
32	65.5	72.2	99.8	92	271	9.9	0.2	1.4	1.5	16.1	7.7	653	373	+2	Moldova
4	...	...	...	100	...	...	...	0.0	...	104.0	59.6	4 940	377	+1	Monaco
5	75.6	81.0	98.3	100	328	11.1	0.3	26.7	8.7	61.4	76.8	5 219	31	+1	Netherlands
4	76.0	81.9	...	100	367	28.9	0.4	6.2	11.1	73.4	90.9	3 457	47	+1	Norway
7	69.8	78.0	99.8	...	220	29.7	0.2	22.7	7.8	31.9	45.1	2 325	48	+1	Poland
5	72.6	79.6	99.8	...	318	40.1	1.7	5.2	5.9	41.4	90.4	1 935	351	GMT	Portugal
20	67.0	74.2	99.7	57	189	28.0	0.2	2.5	3.8	20.5	32.9	1 905	40	+2	Romania
5	...	...	...	...	...	...	...	...	...	76.3	62.1	5 310	378	+1	San Marino
14	70.9	75.6	...	93	...	28.3	-0.1	3.7	3.7	24.3	33.8	787	381	+1	Serbia and Montenegro
8	69.8	77.6	...	100	326	45.3	0.9	22.5	6.6	24.1	68.4	2 559	421	+1	Slovakia
4	72.6	79.8	99.8	100	219	55.0	0.2	14.4	7.3	40.7	87.1	3 758	386	+1	Slovenia
4	75.9	82.8	99.8	...	329	28.8	0.6	9.1	7.0	42.9	91.6	2 391	34	+1	Spain
3	77.6	82.6	...	100	287	65.9	...	10.1	5.3	73.6	88.9	5 731	46	+1	Sweden
5	75.9	82.3	...	100	350	30.3	0.4	28.7	5.4	74.4	84.3	3 510	41	+1	Switzerland
20	64.7	74.7	99.9	98	299	16.5	0.3	3.3	6.9	21.6	8.4	180	380	+2	Ukraine
6	75.7	80.7	...	100	164	11.6	0.6	24.8	9.6	59.1	84.1	4 231	44	GMT	United Kingdom
...	...	...	...	...	...	...	...	...	...	...	...	...	39	+1	Vatican City

Want to know more?

Elevation scale:

>6000m
5000-6000m
4000-5000m
3000-4000m
2000-3000m
1000-2000m
500-1000m
200-500m
0-200m
<0m

0-200m
200-500m
500-1000m
1000-2000m
2000-3000m
3000-4000m
4000-5000m
5000-6000m
>6000m

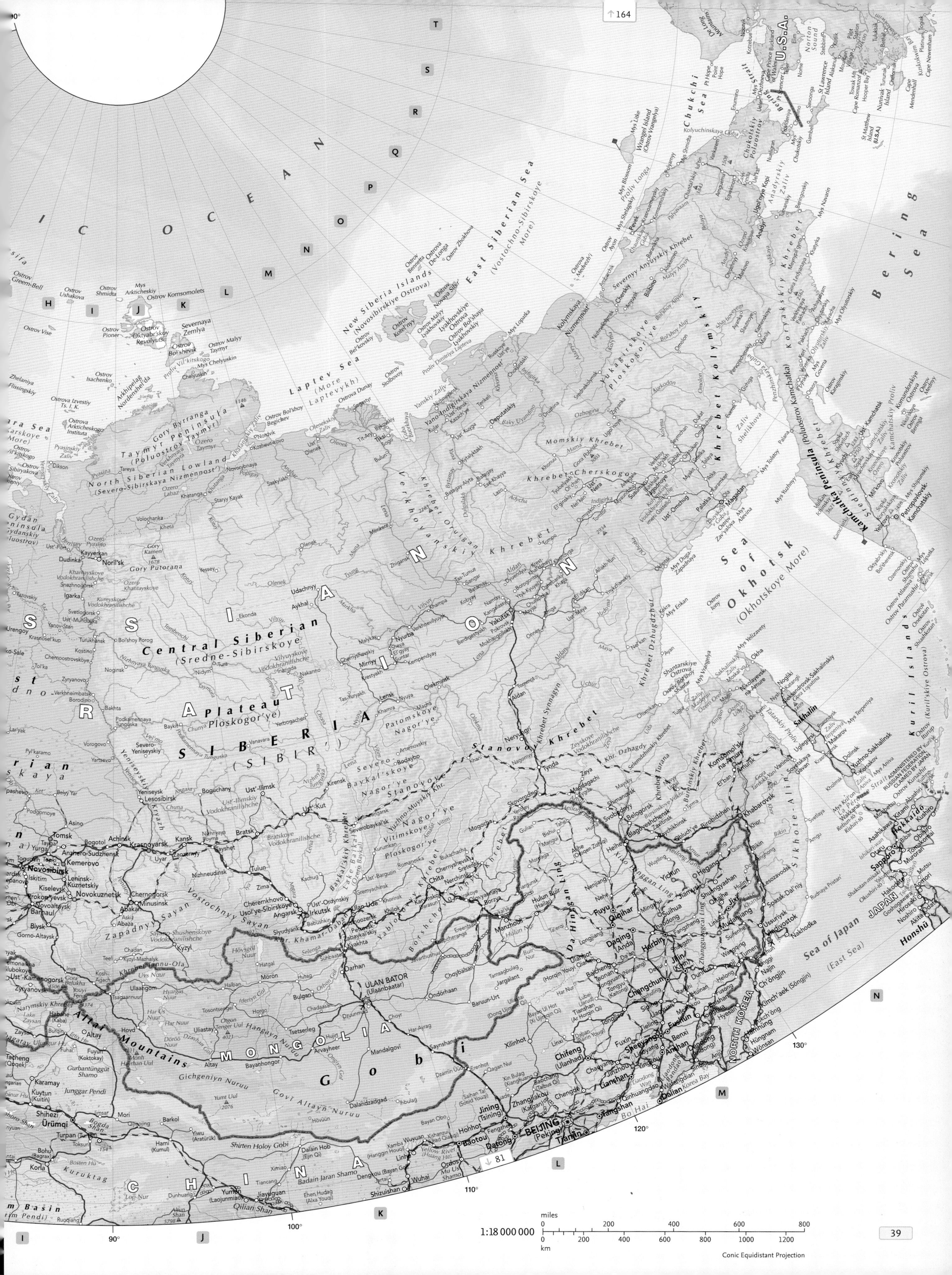
164
81
East Siberian Sea
(Vostochno-Sibirskoye More)
New Siberia Islands
(Novosibirskiye Ostrova)
Laptev Sea
(More Laptevykh)
Severnaya Zemlya
Taymyr Peninsula
(Poluostrov Taymyr)
North Siberian Lowland
(Severo-Sibirskaya Nizmennost')
Central Siberian Plateau
(Sredne-Sibirskoye Ploskogor'ye)
SIBERIA
(SIBIR')
Verkhoyanskiy Khrebet
Khrebet Cherskogo
Khrebet Kolymskiy
Chukchi Sea
Bering Sea
Sea of Okhotsk
(Okhotskoye More)
Kamchatka Peninsula
(Poluostrov Kamchatka)
Kuril Islands
(Kuril'skiye Ostrova)
Sakhalin
Sea of Japan
(East Sea)
JAPAN
Hokkaidō
Honshū
NORTH KOREA
U.S.A.
Stanovoy Khrebet
Lake Baykal
Altai Mountains
MONGOLIA
Gobi
ULAN BATOR
(Ulaanbaatar)
BEIJING
(Peking)
Tianjin
Bo Hai
Korea Bay
Da Hinggan Ling
CHINA
Novosibirsk
Krasnoyarsk
Irkutsk
Yakutsk
Magadan
Khabarovsk
Vladivostok
Harbin
Shenyang
Dalian
Ürümqi
Qilian Shan
1:18 000 000
miles
0 200 400 600 800
km
0 200 400 600 800 1000 1200
Conic Equidistant Projection
90°
100°
110°
120°
130°

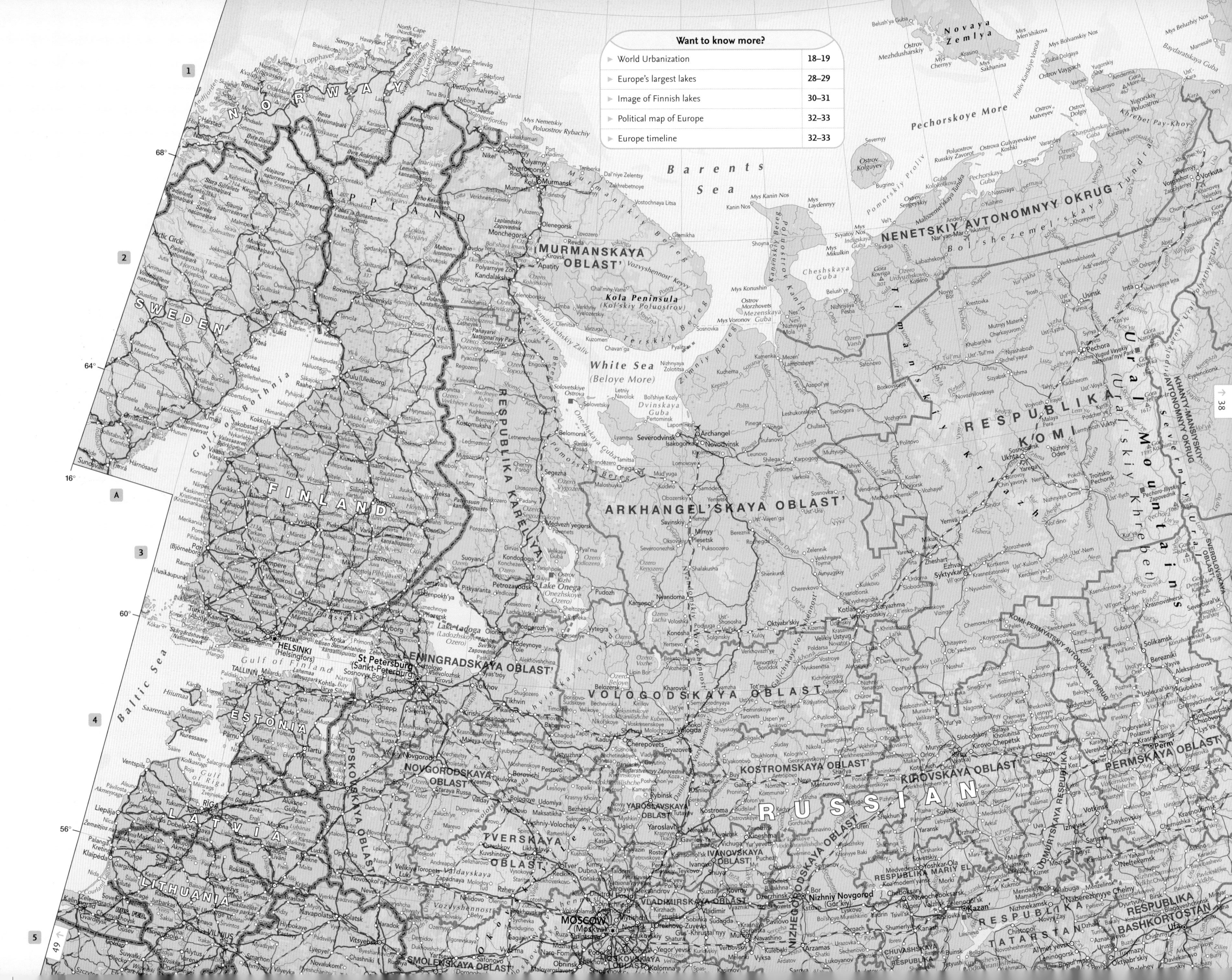

Want to know more?

▲ World Urbanization	18–19
▲ Europe's largest lakes	28–29
▲ Image of Finnish lakes	30–31
▲ Political map of Europe	32–33
▲ Europe timeline	32–33

↓ 49

Europe Western Russian Federation

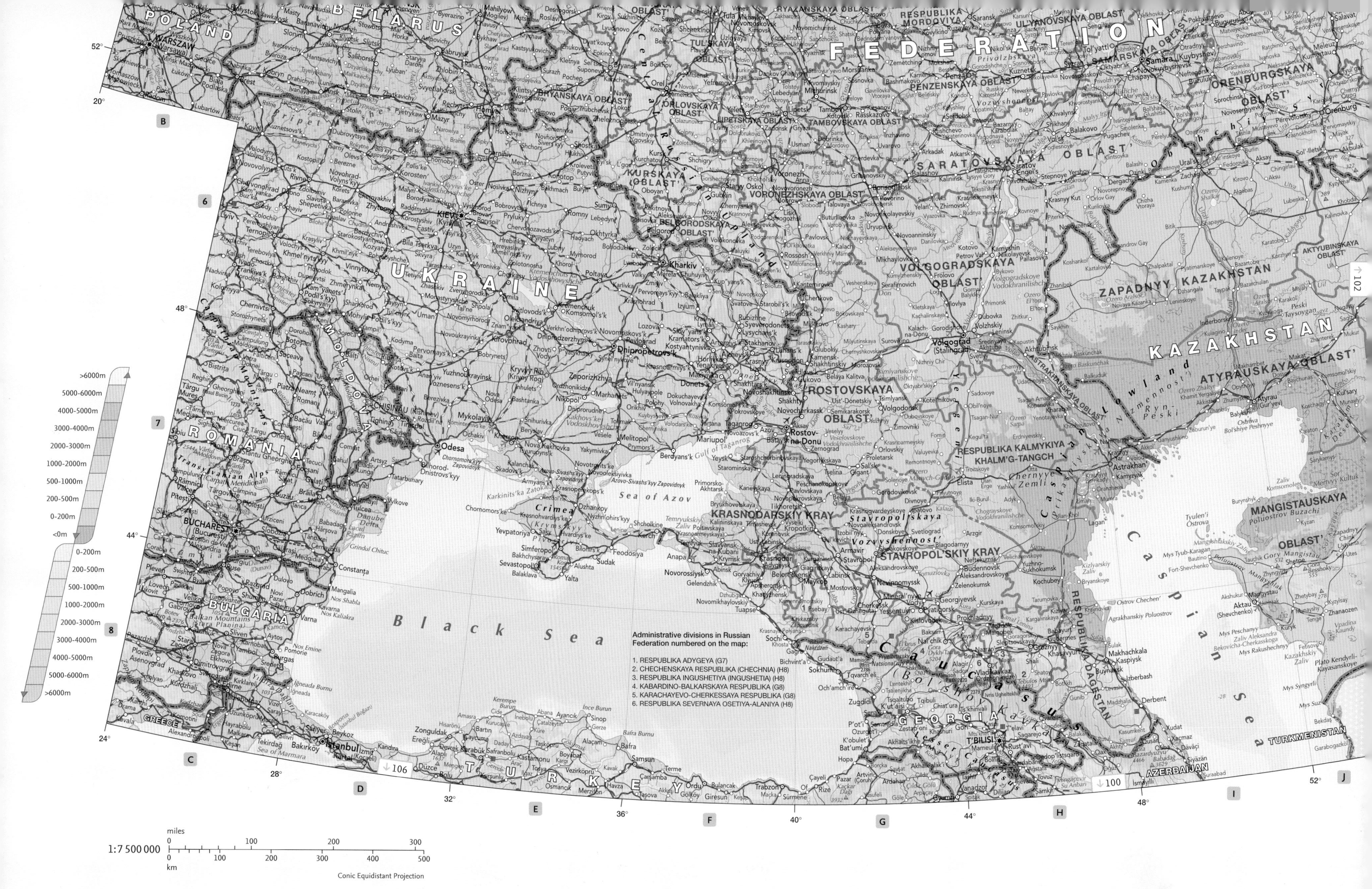

RUSSIAN FEDERATION

KAZAKHSTAN

ZAPADNYY KAZAKHSTAN

ATYRAUSKAYA OBLAST

MANGISTAUSKAYA OBLAST

UKRAINE

BELARUS

POLAND

MOLDOVA

ROMANIA

BULGARIA

TURKEY

GEORGIA

AZERBAIJAN

TURKMENISTAN

GREECE

Caspian Sea

Black Sea

Sea of Azov

ORENBURGSKAYA OBLAST'
RYAZANSKAYA OBLAST'
ULYANOVSKAYA OBLAST'
RESPUBLIKA MORDOVIYA
PENZENSKAYA OBLAST'
TAMBOVSKAYA OBLAST'
SARATOVSKAYA OBLAST
VOLGOGRADSKAYA OBLAST'
ASTRAKHANSKAYA OBLAST'
RESPUBLIKA KALMYKIYA-KHALMG-TANGCH
ROSTOVSKAYA OBLAST
KRASNODARSKIY KRAY
STAVROPOL'SKIY KRAY
RESPUBLIKA DAGESTAN
VORONEZHSKAYA OBLAST'
BELGORODSKAYA OBLAST'
KURSKAYA OBLAST'
OREL'OVSKAYA OBLAST'
TUL'SKAYA OBLAST'
LIPETSKAYA OBLAST'

Central Russian Upland

Caucasus

Bol'shoy Kavkaz

Carpathian Mountains

Transylvanian Alps

Balkan Mountains

Administrative divisions in Russian Federation numbered on the map:

1. RESPUBLIKA ADYGEYA (G7)
2. CHECHENSKAYA RESPUBLIKA (CHECHNJA) (H8)
3. RESPUBLIKA INGUSHETIYA (INGUSHETIA) (H8)
4. KABARDINO-BALKARSKAYA RESPUBLIKA (G8)
5. KARACHAYEVO-CHERKESSKAYA RESPUBLIKA (G8)
6. RESPUBLIKA SEVERNAYA OSETIYA-ALANIYA (H8)

Kyiv
Odesa
Kharkiv
Rostov-na-Donu
Volgograd (Stalingrad)
Astrakhan'
Saratov
Samara (Kuybyshev)
TBILISI
BUCHAREST (București)
Istanbul
Simferopol'
Sevastopol'
Yalta
Sochi
Constanța
Varna

Crimea

Zaliv Kara-Bogaz-Gol

1:7 500 000

Conic Equidistant Projection

miles 0 100 200 300
km 0 100 200 300 400 500

>6000m
5000-6000m
4000-5000m
3000-4000m
2000-3000m
1000-2000m
500-1000m
200-500m
0-200m
<0m

0-200m
200-500m
500-1000m
1000-2000m
2000-3000m
3000-4000m
4000-5000m
5000-6000m
>6000m

↓100
↓106

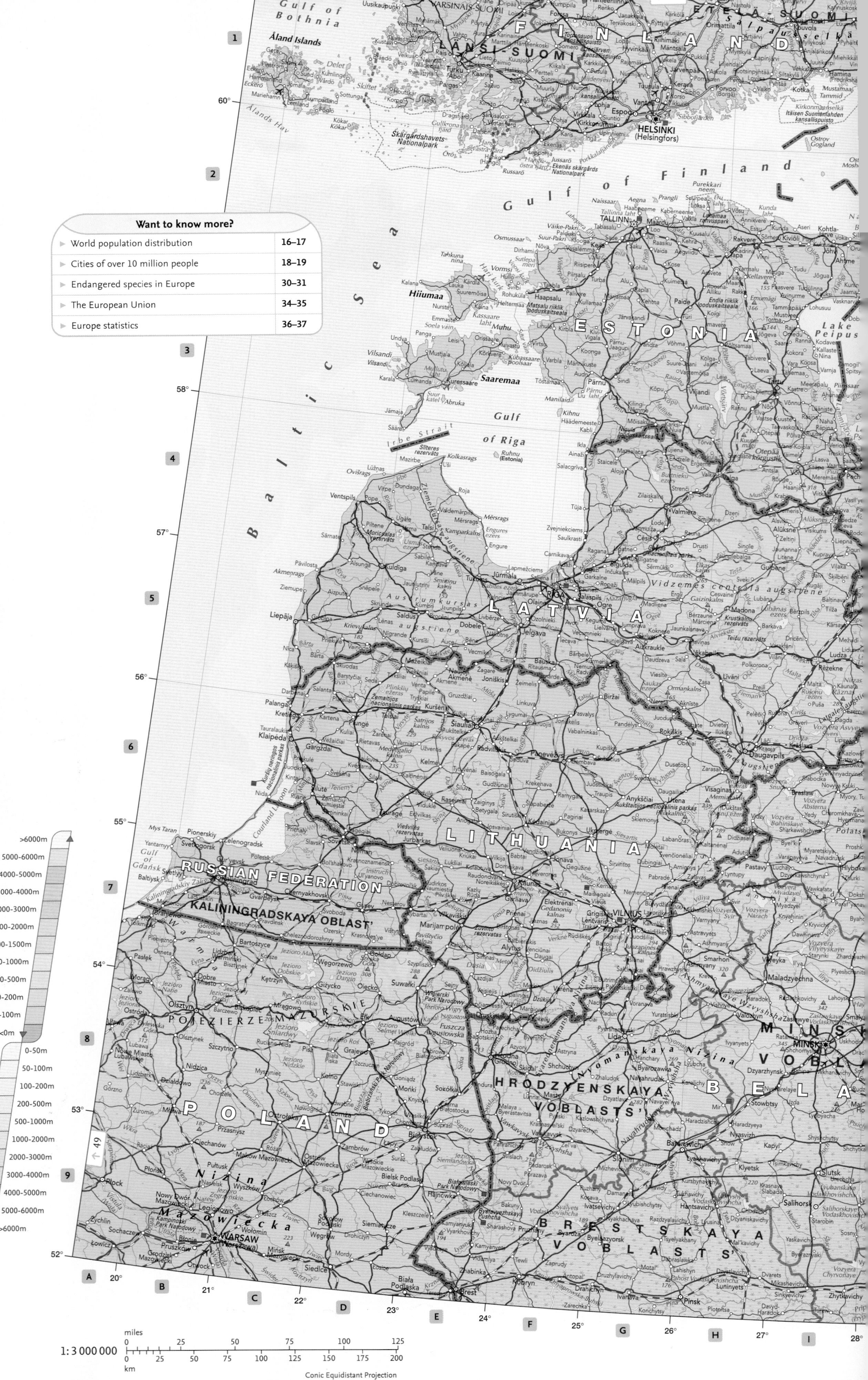

Europe Baltic States and Moscow Region

>6000m
5000-6000m
4000-5000m
3000-4000m
2000-3000m
1500-2000m
1000-1500m
500-1000m
200-500m
100-200m
0-100m
<0m

0-50m
50-100m
100-200m
200-500m
500-1000m
1000-2000m
2000-3000m
3000-4000m
4000-5000m
5000-6000m
>6000m

miles
0 25 50 75 100 125
1 : 3 000 000
km
0 25 50 75 100 125 150 175 200

Conic Equidistant Projection

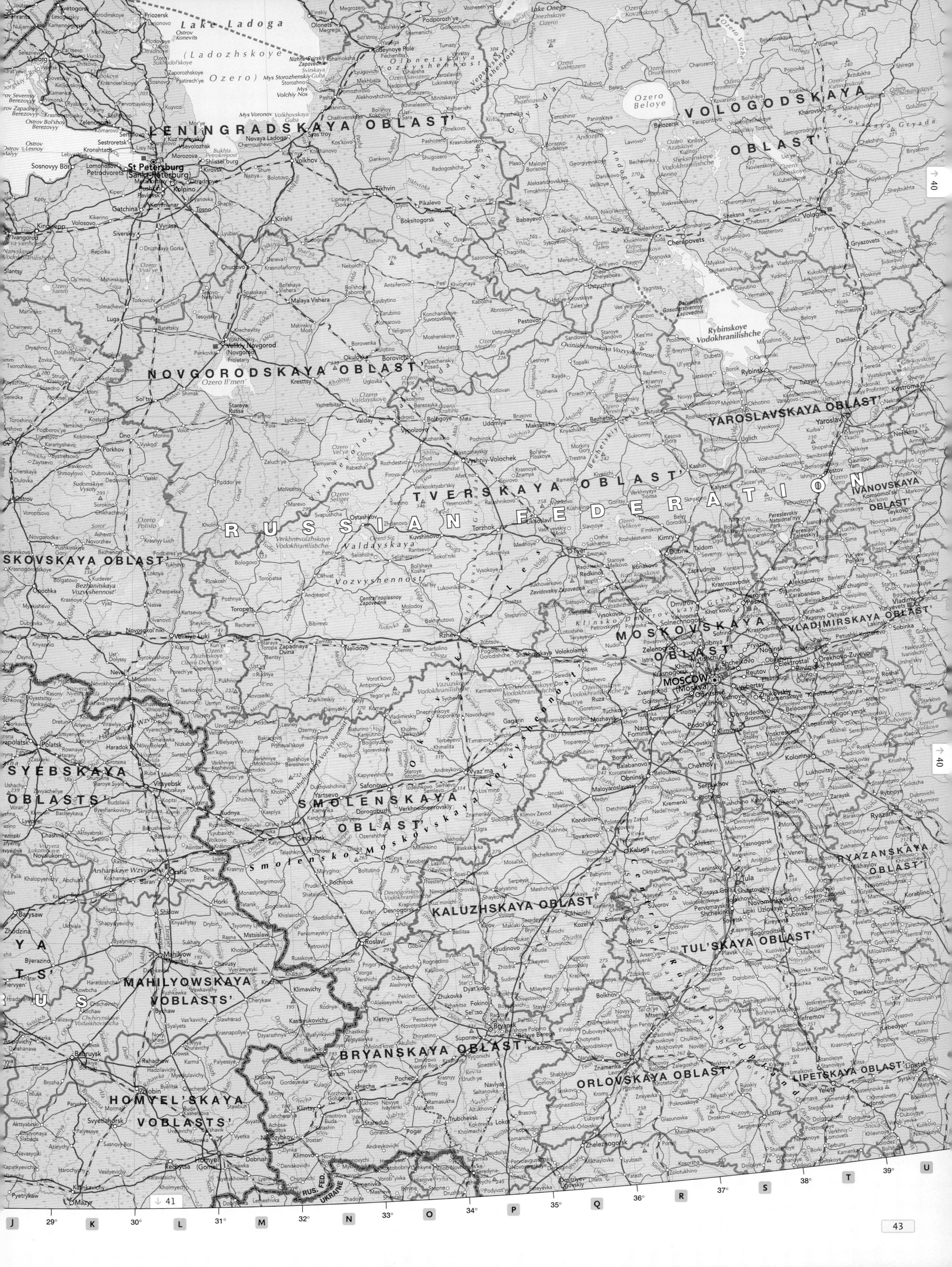

RUSSIAN FEDERATION
LENINGRADSKAYA OBLAST'
VOLOGODSKAYA OBLAST'
NOVGORODSKAYA OBLAST'
YAROSLAVSKAYA OBLAST'
TVERSKAYA OBLAST'
IVANOVSKAYA OBLAST'
SKOVSKAYA OBLAST
MOSKOVSKAYA OBLAST'
VLADIMIRSKAYA OBLAST'
SYEBSKAYA OBLASTS'
SMOLENSKAYA OBLAST'
RYAZANSKAYA OBLAST'
KALUZHSKAYA OBLAST'
TUL'SKAYA OBLAST'
MAHILYOWSKAYA VOBLASTS'
BRYANSKAYA OBLAST'
ORLOVSKAYA OBLAST'
LIPETSKAYA OBLAST'
HOMYEL'SKAYA VOBLASTS'
RUS. FED.
UKRAINE
Lake Ladoga (Ladozhskoye Ozero)
Lake Onega Onezhskoye Ozero
Ozero Beloye
Rybinskoye Vodokhranilishche
Ozero Il'men'
Ozero Seliger
Valdayskaya Vozvyshennost'
Smolensko-Moskovskaya Vozvyshennost'
St Petersburg (Sankt-Peterburg)
MOSCOW (Moskva)
Velikiy Novgorod (Novgorod)
Vologda
Yaroslavl'
Tver'
Kostroma
Vladimir
Ryazan'
Tula
Kaluga
Smolensk
Bryansk
Orel
Lipetsk
Vitsyebsk
Mahilyow (Mogilev)
Homyel' (Gomel')
Pskov
Cherepovets
Rybinsk
Tikhvin
Vyborg
Velikiye Luki
Vyaz'ma
Rzhev
Obninsk
Serpukhov
Kolomna
Novomoskovsk
Yelets
Bobruysk
Orsha
Roslavl'
Klintsy
Zhlobin
Mazyr
J 29° K 30° L 31° M 32° N 33° O 34° P 35° Q 36° R 37° S 38° T 39° U
→ 40
→ 40
↓ 41

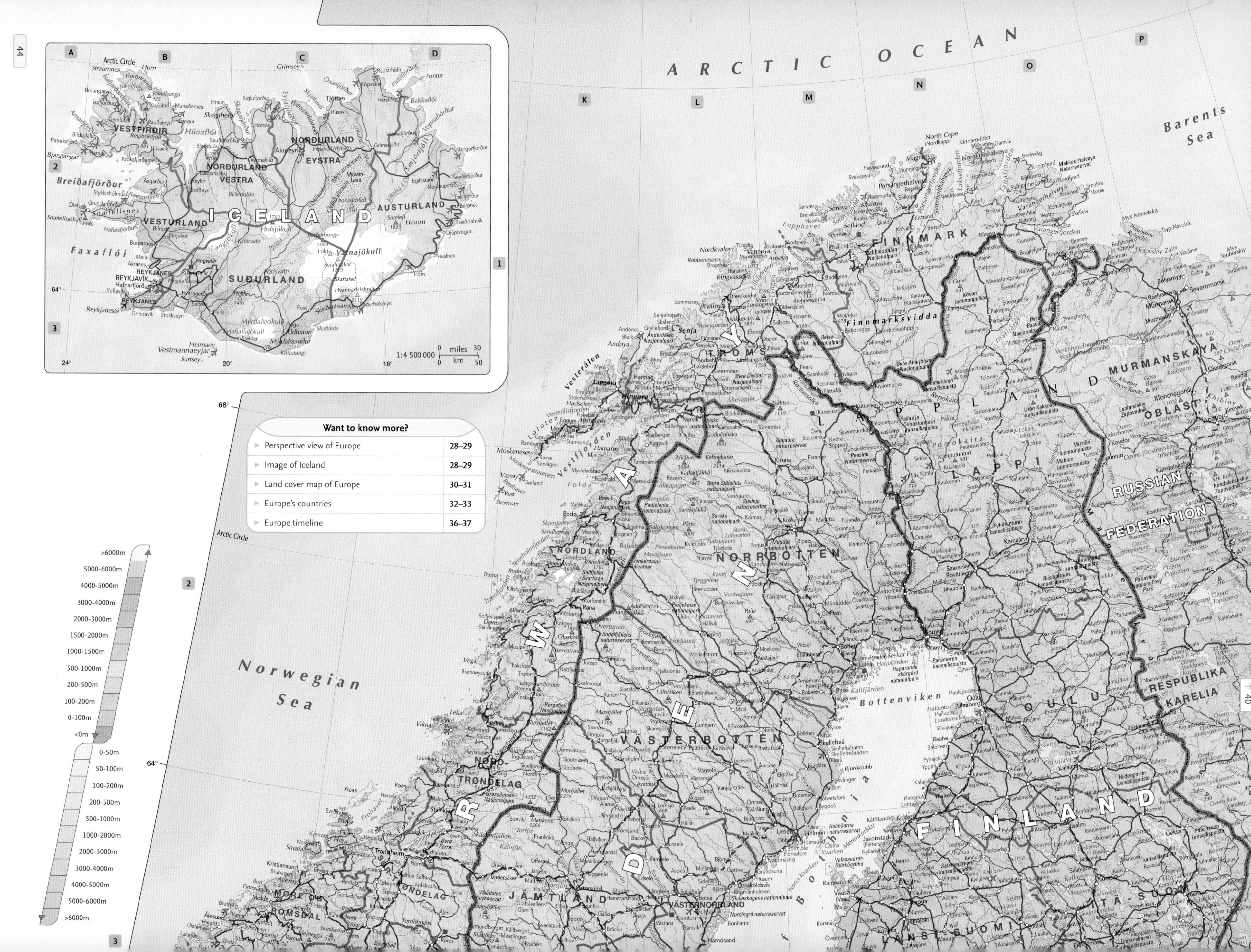

ARCTIC OCEAN

Barents Sea

Norwegian Sea

RUSSIAN FEDERATION

MURMANSKAYA OBLAST

RESPUBLIKA KARELIA

FINLAND

SUOMI

LAPPI

FINNMARK

TROMS

NORDLAND

NORRBOTTEN

VÄSTERBOTTEN

JÄMTLAND

NORD-TRØNDELAG

SØR-TRØNDELAG

ROMSDAL

ICELAND

NORDURLAND EYSTRA

NORDURLAND VESTRA

VESTURLAND

VESTFIRDIR

AUSTURLAND

SUDURLAND

REYKJAVIK

Want to know more?

Perspective view of Europe	28–29
Image of Iceland	28–29
Land cover map of Europe	30–31
Europe's countries	32–33
Europe timeline	36–37

1 : 4 500 000

0   miles   30
0   km   50

>6000m
5000–6000m
4000–5000m
3000–4000m
2000–3000m
1500–2000m
1000–1500m
500–1000m
200–500m
100–200m
0–100m
<0m

0–50m
50–100m
100–200m
200–500m
500–1000m
1000–2000m
2000–3000m
3000–4000m
4000–5000m
5000–6000m
>6000m

Europe Scandinavia and Iceland

↓ 49

1:4 500 000

Conic Equidistant Projection

miles

km

0   50   100   150   200

0   50   100   150   200   250   300

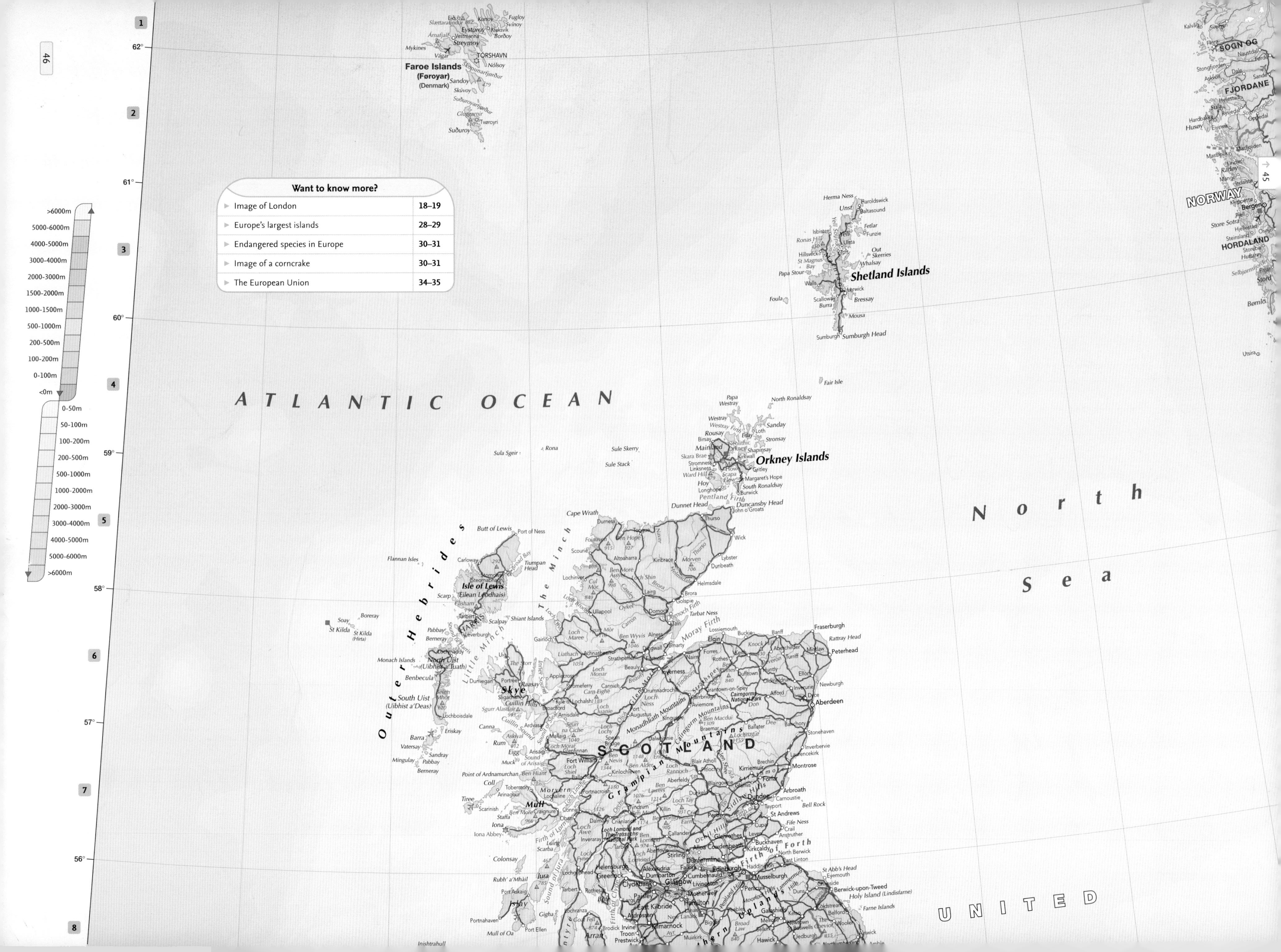

Want to know more?
Image of London 18–19
Europe's largest islands 28–29
Endangered species in Europe 30–31
Image of a corncrake 30–31
The European Union 34–35
ATLANTIC OCEAN
North Sea
UNITED
SCOTLAND
NORWAY
SOGN OG FJORDANE
HORDALAND
Faroe Islands (Føroyar) (Denmark)
TÓRSHAVN
Shetland Islands
Orkney Islands
Outer Hebrides
Isle of Lewis (Eilean Leòdhais)
Skye
Mull
Islay
Jura
Grampian Mountains
Southern Uplands
The Minch
Little Minch
Moray Firth
Firth of Forth
Pentland Firth
Aberdeen
Dundee
Edinburgh
Glasgow
Inverness
Perth
Stirling
Fort William
St Andrews
Peterhead
Fraserburgh
Wick
Thurso
Kirkwall
Lerwick
Bergen
Cape Wrath
Butt of Lewis
Dunnet Head
Duncansby Head
Sumburgh Head
Fair Isle
Foula
Sula Sgeir
Rona
Sule Skerry
Sule Stack
St Kilda
Flannan Isles
Monach Islands
North Uist (Uibhist a Tuath)
South Uist (Uibhist a'Deas)
Benbecula
Barra
Tiree
Coll
Colonsay
Iona
Arran
Bute
>6000m
5000-6000m
4000-5000m
3000-4000m
2000-3000m
1500-2000m
1000-1500m
500-1000m
200-500m
100-200m
0-100m
<0m
0-50m
50-100m
100-200m
200-500m
500-1000m
1000-2000m
2000-3000m
3000-4000m
4000-5000m
5000-6000m
>6000m
62°
61°
60°
59°
58°
57°
56°
1
2
3
4
5
6
7
8

45

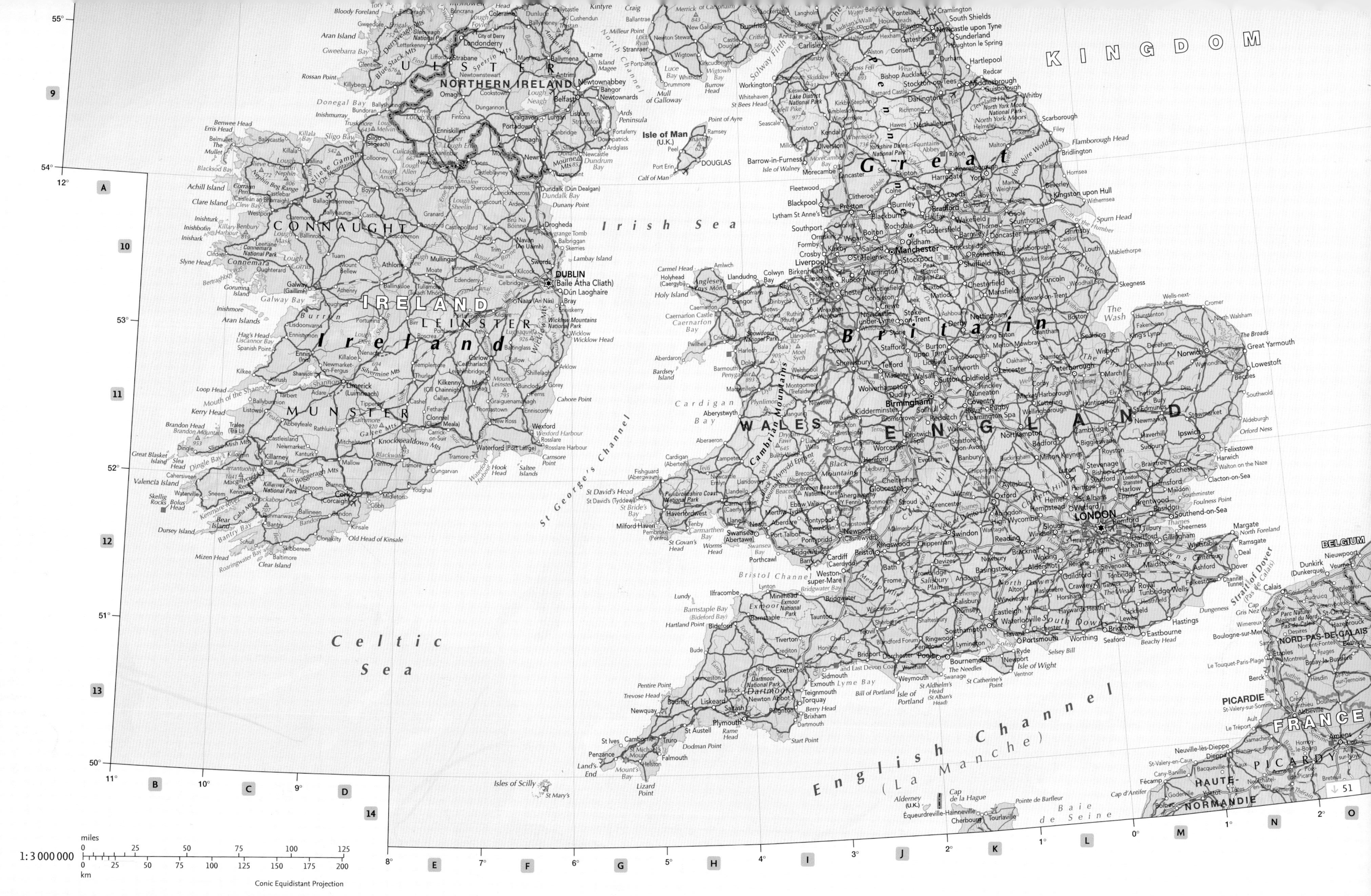

1 : 3 000 000

Conic Equidistant Projection

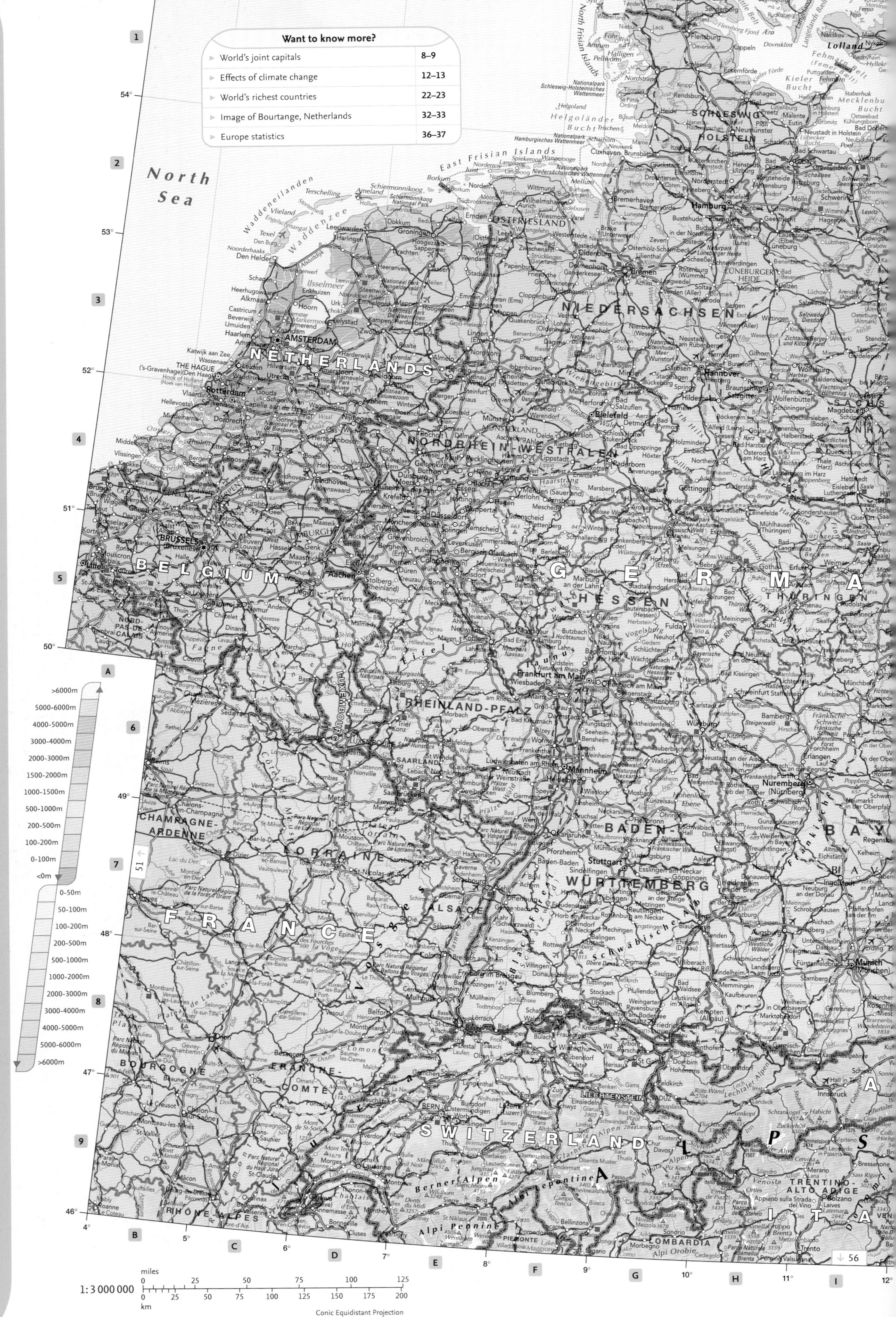

North Sea

Want to know more?

>6000m
5000-6000m
4000-5000m
3000-4000m
2000-3000m
1500-2000m
1000-1500m
500-1000m
200-500m
100-200m
0-100m
<0m

0-50m
50-100m
100-200m
200-500m
500-1000m
1000-2000m
2000-3000m
3000-4000m
4000-5000m
5000-6000m
>6000m

miles
1:3 000 000
km
Conic Equidistant Projection

↑ 45
→ 40
→ 41
↓ 58

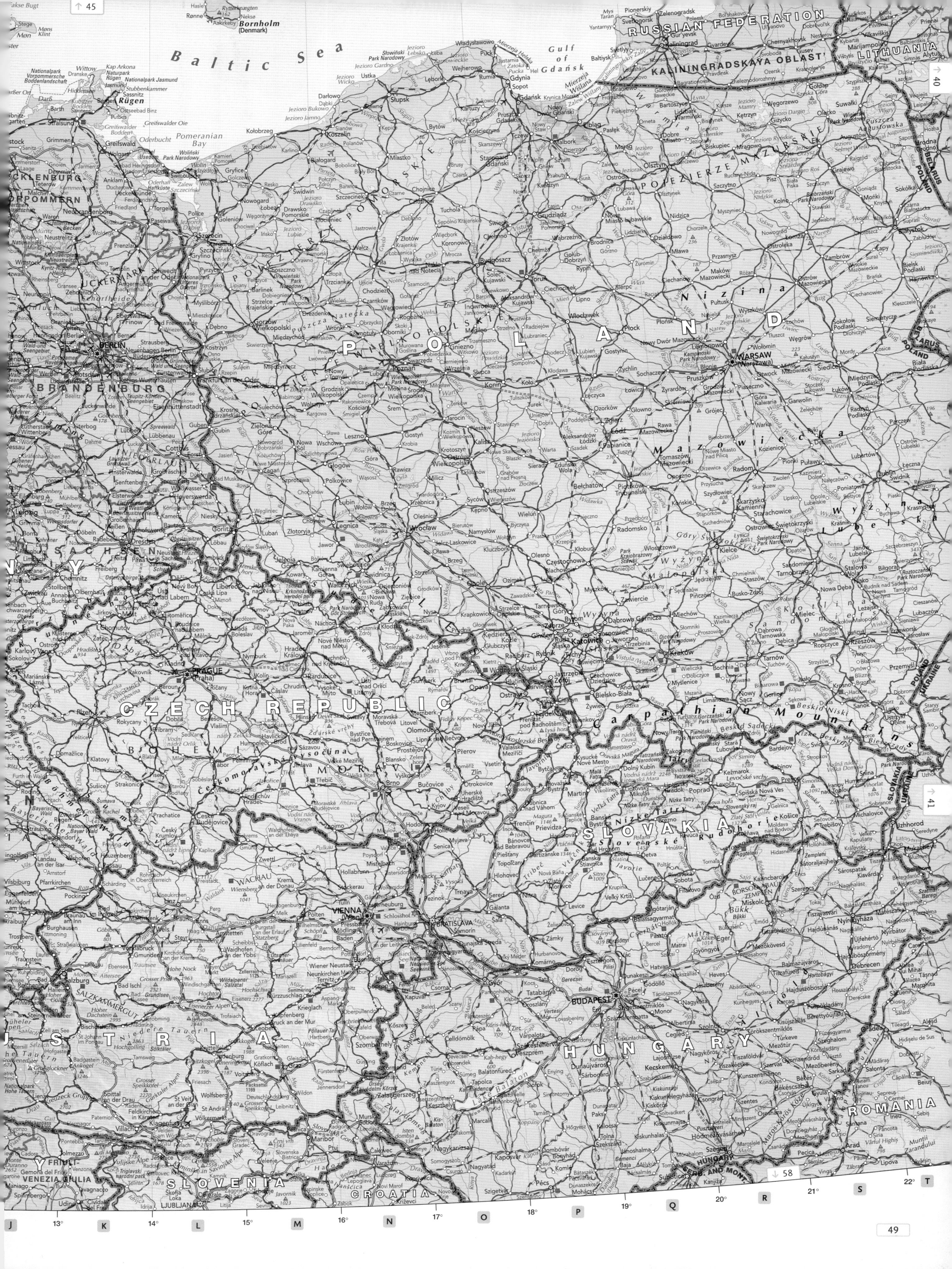

Baltic Sea
Bornholm (Denmark)
Gulf of Gdańsk
RUSSIAN FEDERATION
KALININGRADSKAYA OBLAST'
Kaliningrad
LITHUANIA
BELARUS
POLAND
UKRAINE
ROMANIA
P O L A N D
WARSAW (Warszawa)
Gdańsk
Szczecin
Poznań
Wrocław
Łódź
Kraków
Katowice
Lublin
Białystok
Rzeszów
Toruń
Bydgoszcz
Pomerania Bay
Pojezierze Pomorskie
Pojezierze Mazurskie
Pojezierze Wielkopolskie
Nizina Mazowiecka
Wyżyna Lubelska
Wyżyna Małopolska
Kotlina Sandomierska
Carpathian Mountains
BERLIN
BRANDENBURG
MECKLENBURG
VORPOMMERN
SACHSEN
Rügen
Dresden
Leipzig
CZECH REPUBLIC
PRAGUE (Praha)
BOHEMIA
MORAVIA
Brno
Ostrava
Plzeň
SLOVAKIA
BRATISLAVA
Košice
Nízke Tatry
AUSTRIA
VIENNA (Wien)
Salzburg
Graz
Linz
SALZKAMMERGUT
HUNGARY
BUDAPEST
Debrecen
Szeged
Miskolc
Lake Balaton
SLOVENIA
LJUBLJANA
CROATIA
FRIULI-VENEZIA GIULIA
SERB. AND MONT.
13° 14° 15° 16° 17° 18° 19° 20° 21° 22°
J K L M N O P Q R S T

Europe France and Switzerland

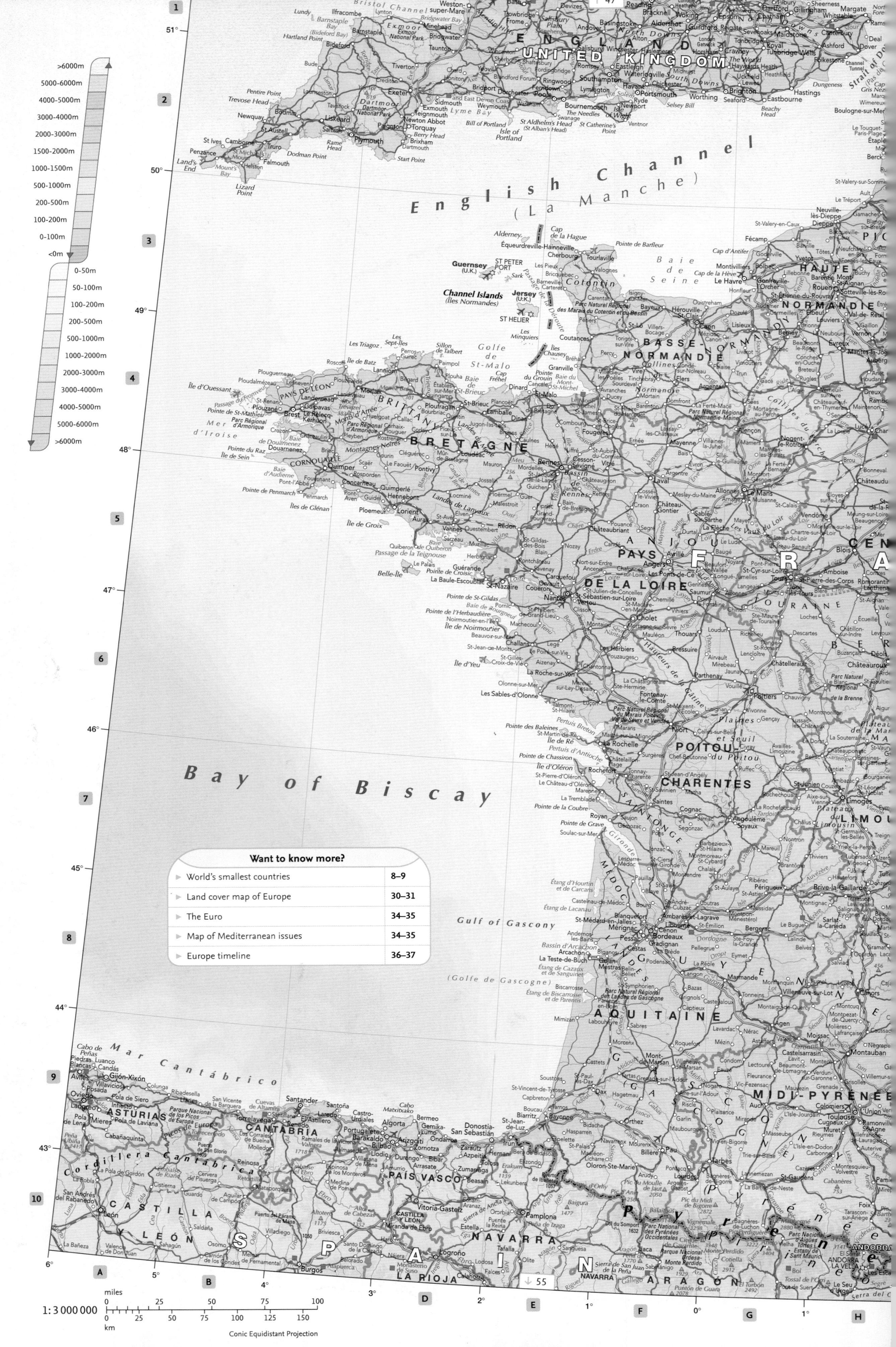

Want to know more?

↑ 47

↓ 55

48

49

56

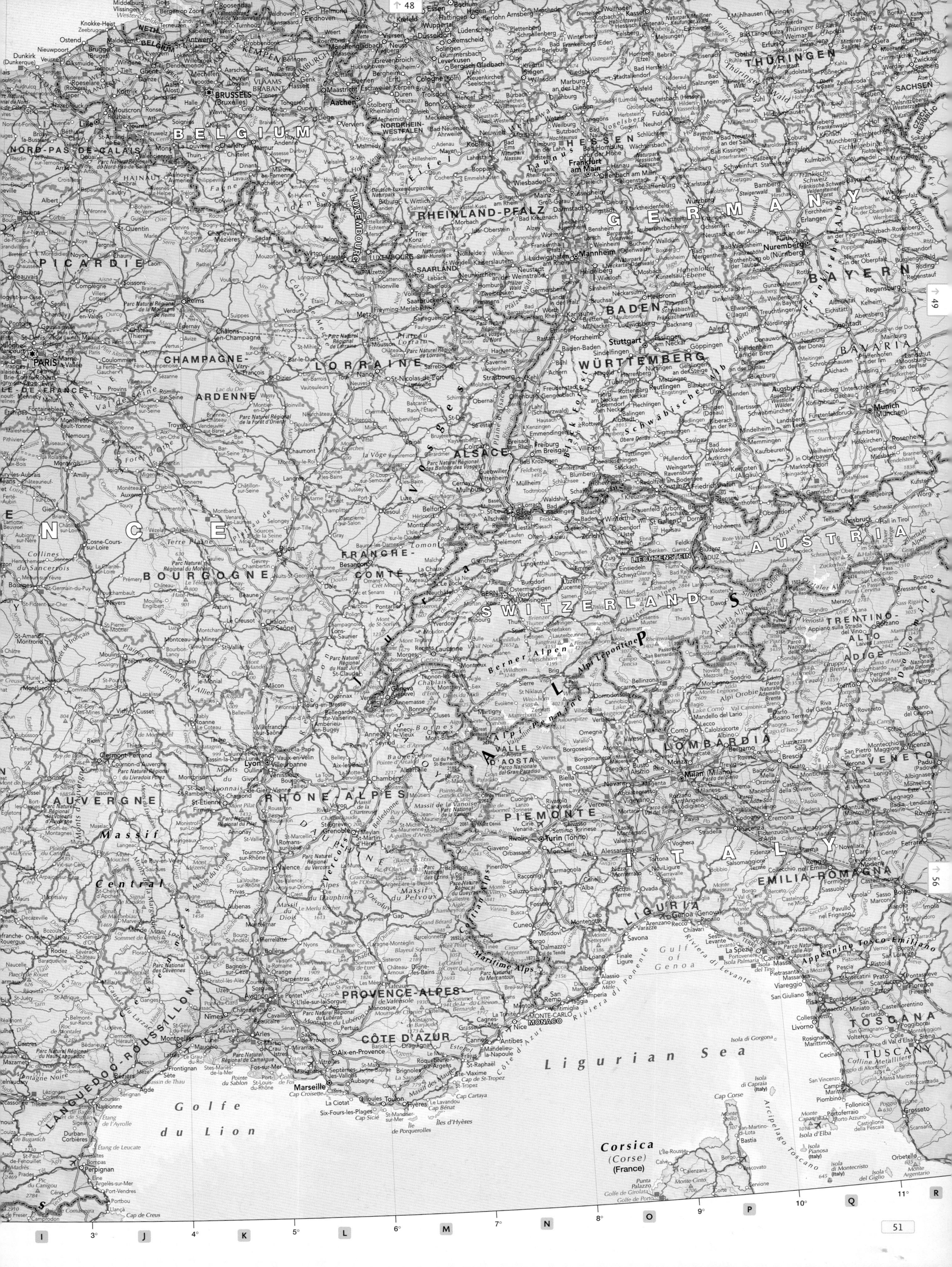

BELGIUM
GERMANY
LUXEMBOURG
NETH.
FRANCE
SWITZERLAND
AUSTRIA
ITALY
LIECHTENSTEIN
MONACO
NORD-PAS-DE-CALAIS
PICARDIE
CHAMPAGNE-ARDENNE
LORRAINE
ALSACE
FRANCHE-COMTÉ
BOURGOGNE
AUVERGNE
RHÔNE-ALPES
PROVENCE-ALPES-CÔTE D'AZUR
LANGUEDOC-ROUSSILLON
RHEINLAND-PFALZ
SAARLAND
HESSEN
THÜRINGEN
SACHSEN
BAYERN
BAVARIA
BADEN-WÜRTTEMBERG
NORDRHEIN-WESTFALEN
TRENTINO-ALTO ADIGE
LOMBARDIA
PIEMONTE
VALLE D'AOSTA
VENETO
EMILIA-ROMAGNA
LIGURIA
TOSCANA
TUSCANY
Massif Central
Ligurian Sea
Golfe du Lion
Gulf of Genoa
Corsica
(Corse)
(France)
PARIS
BRUSSELS
LUXEMBOURG
BERN
VADUZ
Lyon
Marseille
Nice
Milan (Milano)
Turin (Torino)
Genoa (Genova)
Munich (München)
Stuttgart
Frankfurt am Main
Nuremberg
Strasbourg
Zürich
Genève (Geneva)
Dijon
Reims
Lille
Metz
Grenoble
Montpellier
Nîmes
Avignon
Toulon
Clermont-Ferrand
Saint-Étienne
Mannheim
Karlsruhe
Freiburg im Breisgau
Basel
Luzern
Lausanne
Bolzano
Trento
Verona
Bergamo
Brescia
Parma
Modena
Bologna
Firenze
Pisa
Livorno
La Spezia
Cannes
Antibes
Aachen
Köln
Düsseldorf
Antwerp
Gent
Brugge
Namur
Liège
3°
4°
5°
6°
7°
8°
9°
10°
11°
I
J
K
L
M
N
O
P
Q
R

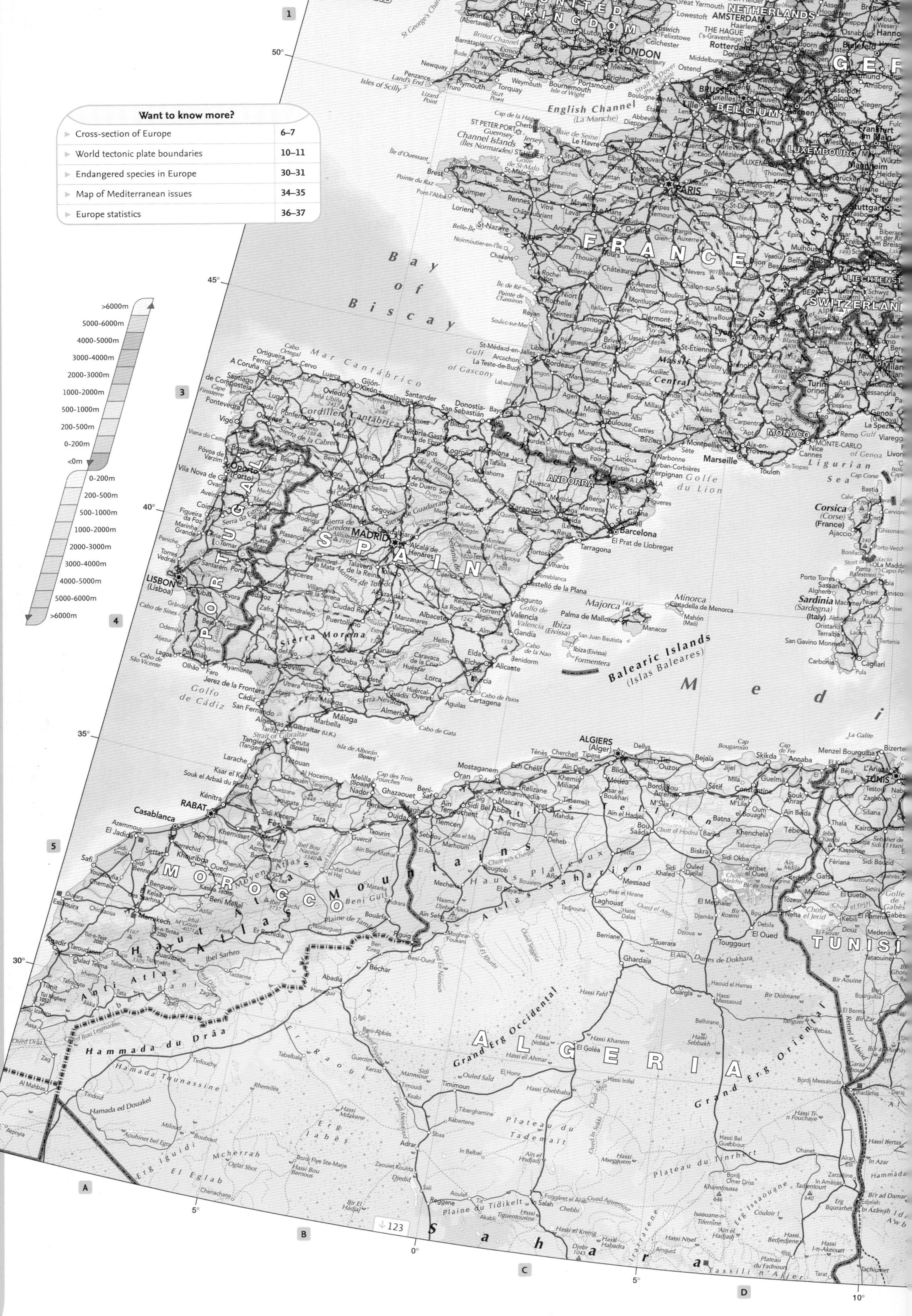

Want to know more?

>6000m
5000-6000m
4000-5000m
3000-4000m
2000-3000m
1000-2000m
500-1000m
200-500m
0-200m
<0m

0-200m
200-500m
500-1000m
1000-2000m
2000-3000m
3000-4000m
4000-5000m
5000-6000m
>6000m

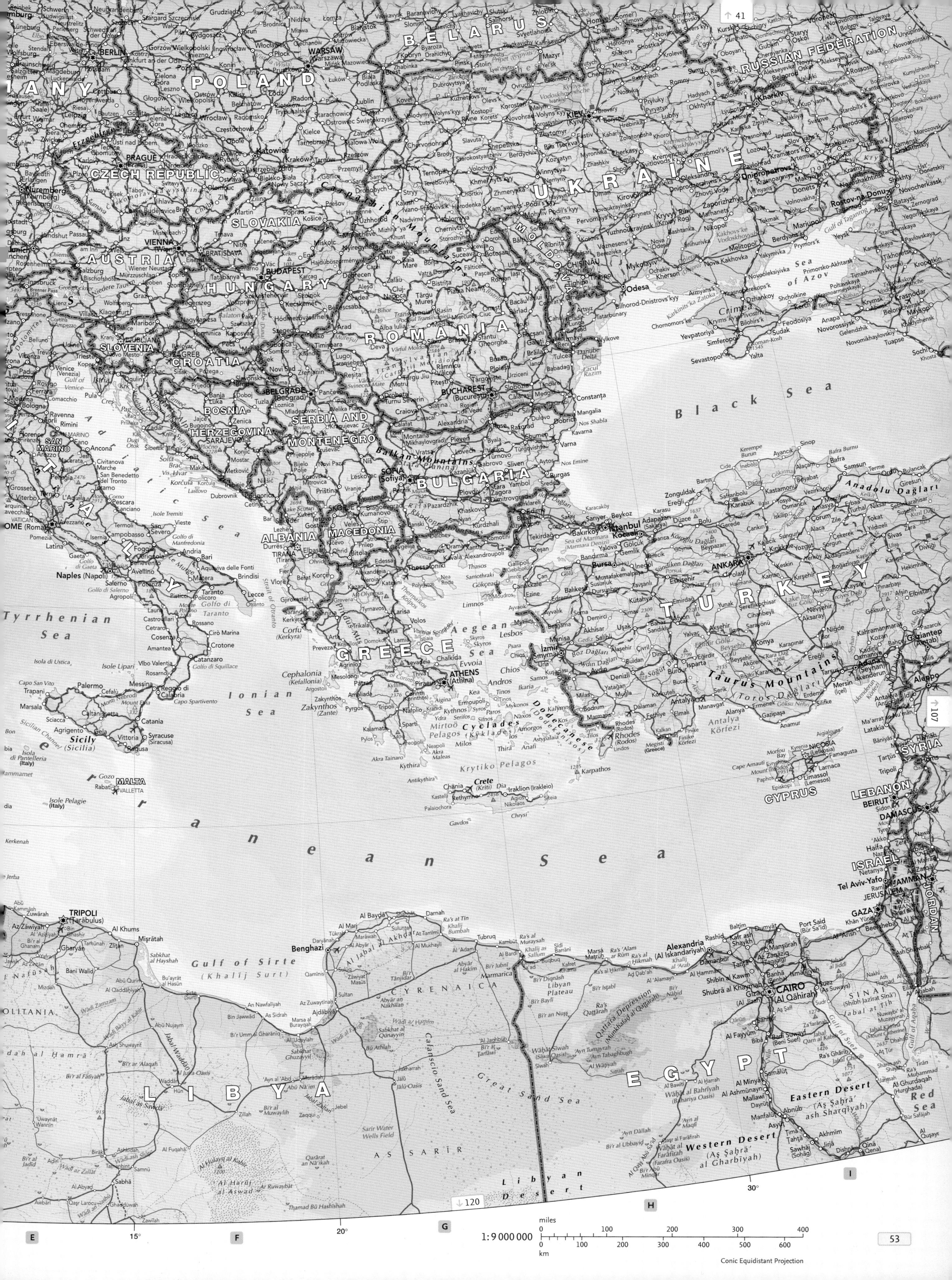
BELARUS
POLAND
RUSSIAN FEDERATION
UKRAINE
CZECH REPUBLIC
SLOVAKIA
AUSTRIA
HUNGARY
MOLDOVA
ROMANIA
SLOVENIA
CROATIA
BOSNIA-HERZEGOVINA
SERBIA AND MONTENEGRO
BULGARIA
ALBANIA
MACEDONIA
GREECE
TURKEY
CYPRUS
SYRIA
LEBANON
ISRAEL
JORDAN
MALTA
LIBYA
EGYPT
Black Sea
Sea of Azov
Aegean Sea
Ionian Sea
Tyrrhenian Sea
Adriatic Sea
Mediterranean Sea
Gulf of Sirte
Red Sea
Libyan Desert
Western Desert
Eastern Desert
Great Sand Sea
Taurus Mountains
Balkan Mountains
Carpathian Mountains
Crete
Cyclades
Dodecanese
Sicily
BERLIN
WARSAW
PRAGUE
VIENNA
BRATISLAVA
BUDAPEST
KIEV
CHIŞINĂU
BUCHAREST
BELGRADE
SARAJEVO
ZAGREB
LJUBLJANA
SOFIA
SKOPJE
TIRANA
ATHENS
ANKARA
NICOSIA
BEIRUT
DAMASCUS
AMMAN
JERUSALEM
CAIRO
TRIPOLI
VALLETTA
ROME
İstanbul
Alexandria
Benghazi
Odesa
Naples
Thessaloniki
Izmir
Adana
Aleppo
Gaza
Port Said
CYRENAICA
AS SARĪR
↑ 41
↑ 107
↓ 120
E
F
G
H
I
15°
20°
30°
1:9 000 000
miles
0
100
200
300
400
km
0
100
200
300
400
500
600
Conic Equidistant Projection

Europe Spain and Portugal

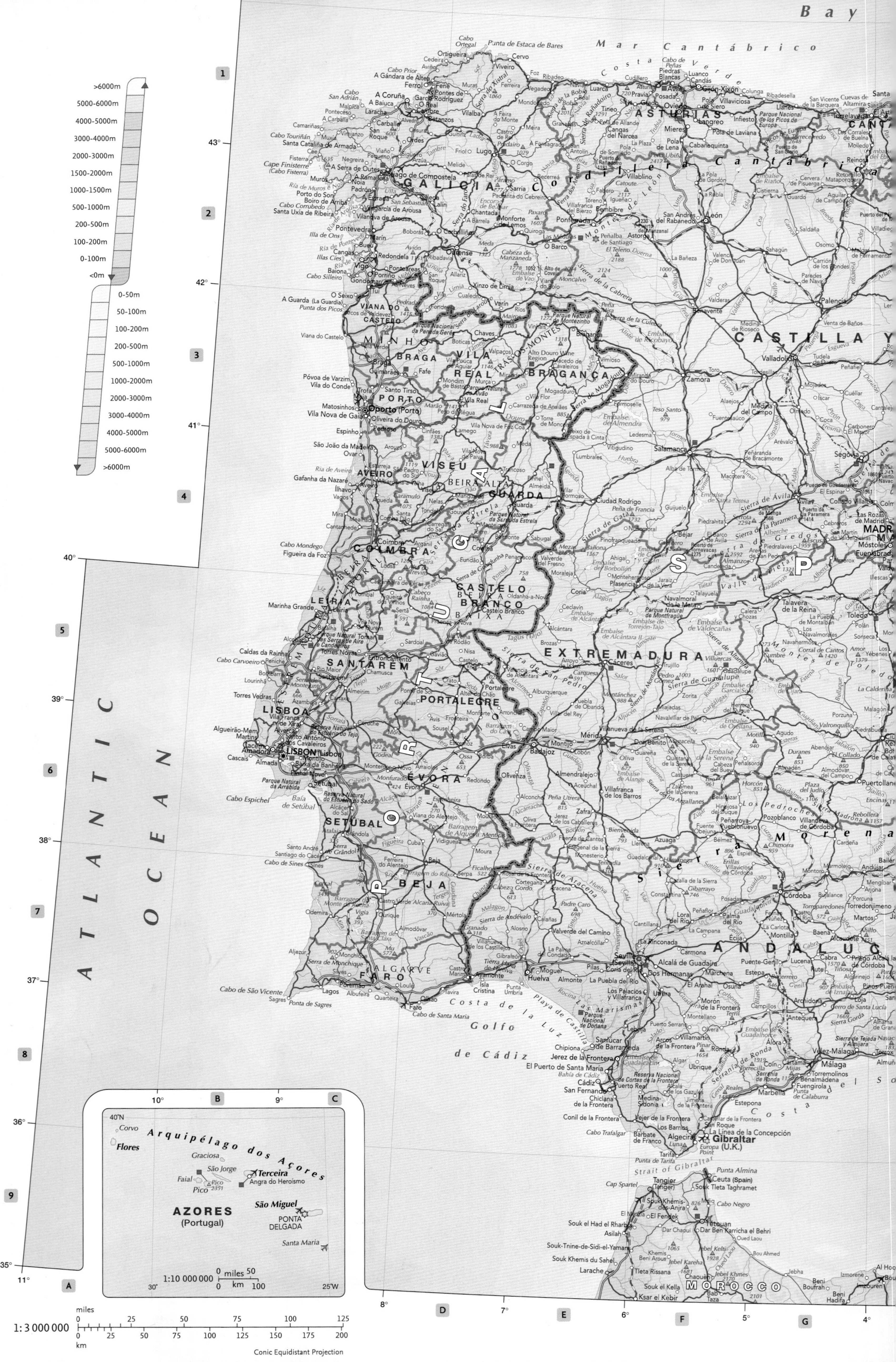

1: 3 000 000 — miles 0 25 50 75 100 125; km 0 25 50 75 100 125 150 175 200

Conic Equidistant Projection

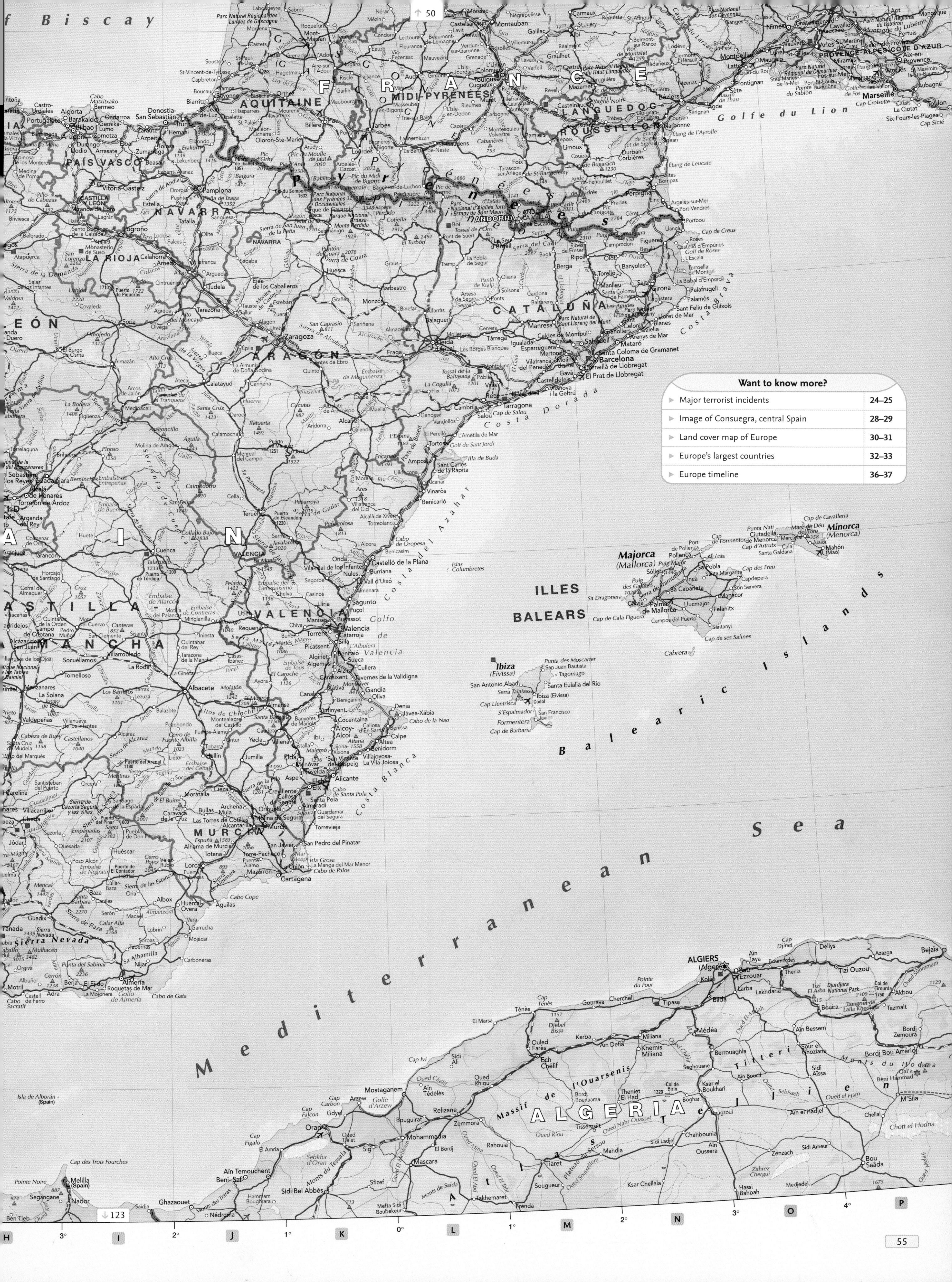

Want to know more?

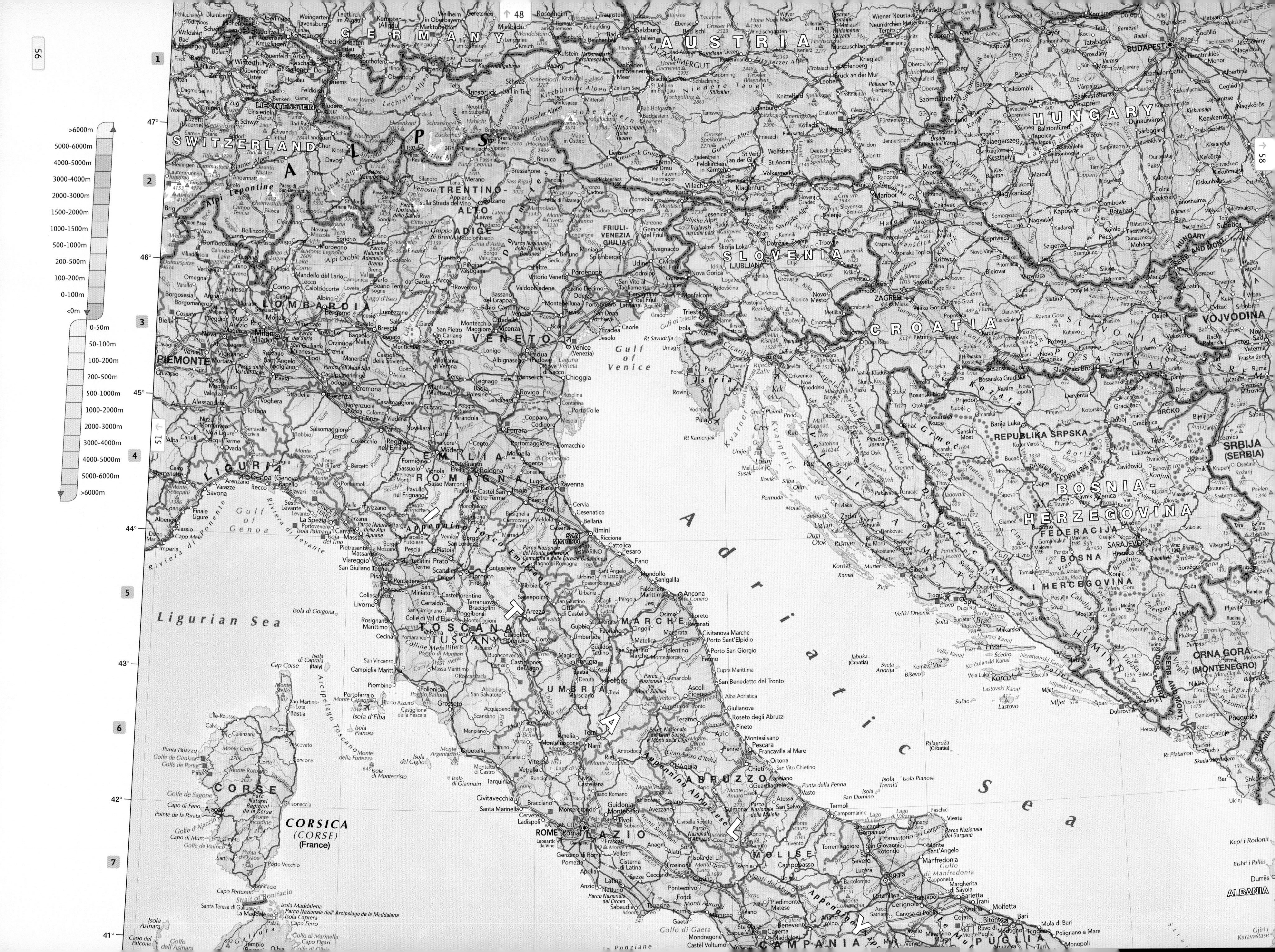

GERMANY
AUSTRIA
HUNGARY
SWITZERLAND
LIECHTENSTEIN
ALPS
SLOVENIA
CROATIA
BOSNIA-HERZEGOVINA
REPUBLIKA SRPSKA
FEDERACIJA BOSNA I HERCEGOVINA
SRBIJA (SERBIA)
CRNA GORA (MONTENEGRO)
SERB. AND MONT.
VOJVODINA
ALBANIA
ITALY
SAN MARINO
TRENTINO-ALTO ADIGE
FRIULI-VENEZIA GIULIA
LOMBARDIA
PIEMONTE
LIGURIA
VENETO
EMILIA-ROMAGNA
TOSCANA TUSCANY
MARCHE
UMBRIA
LAZIO
ABRUZZO
MOLISE
CAMPANIA
PUGLIA
CORSICA (CORSE) (France)
CORSE
Adriatic Sea
Ligurian Sea
Gulf of Venice
Gulf of Genoa
Gulf of Trieste
Arcipelago Toscano
Appennino Tosco-Emiliano
Appennino Abruzzese
Riviera di Levante
Riviera di Ponente
Isola d'Elba
BUDAPEST
LJUBLJANA
ZAGREB
SARAJEVO
ROME (Roma)
Milan (Milano)
Venice (Venezia)
Trieste
Bologna
Florence (Firenze)
Ancona
Pescara
Split
Rijeka
Pula
Zadar
Dubrovnik
Mostar
Podgorica
Bastia
Ajaccio
Bari
47°
46°
45°
44°
43°
42°
41°
1
2
3
4
5
6
7
>6000m
5000-6000m
4000-5000m
3000-4000m
2000-3000m
1500-2000m
1000-1500m
500-1000m
200-500m
100-200m
0-100m
<0m
0-50m
50-100m
100-200m
200-500m
500-1000m
1000-2000m
2000-3000m
3000-4000m
4000-5000m
5000-6000m
>6000m

48
58
51

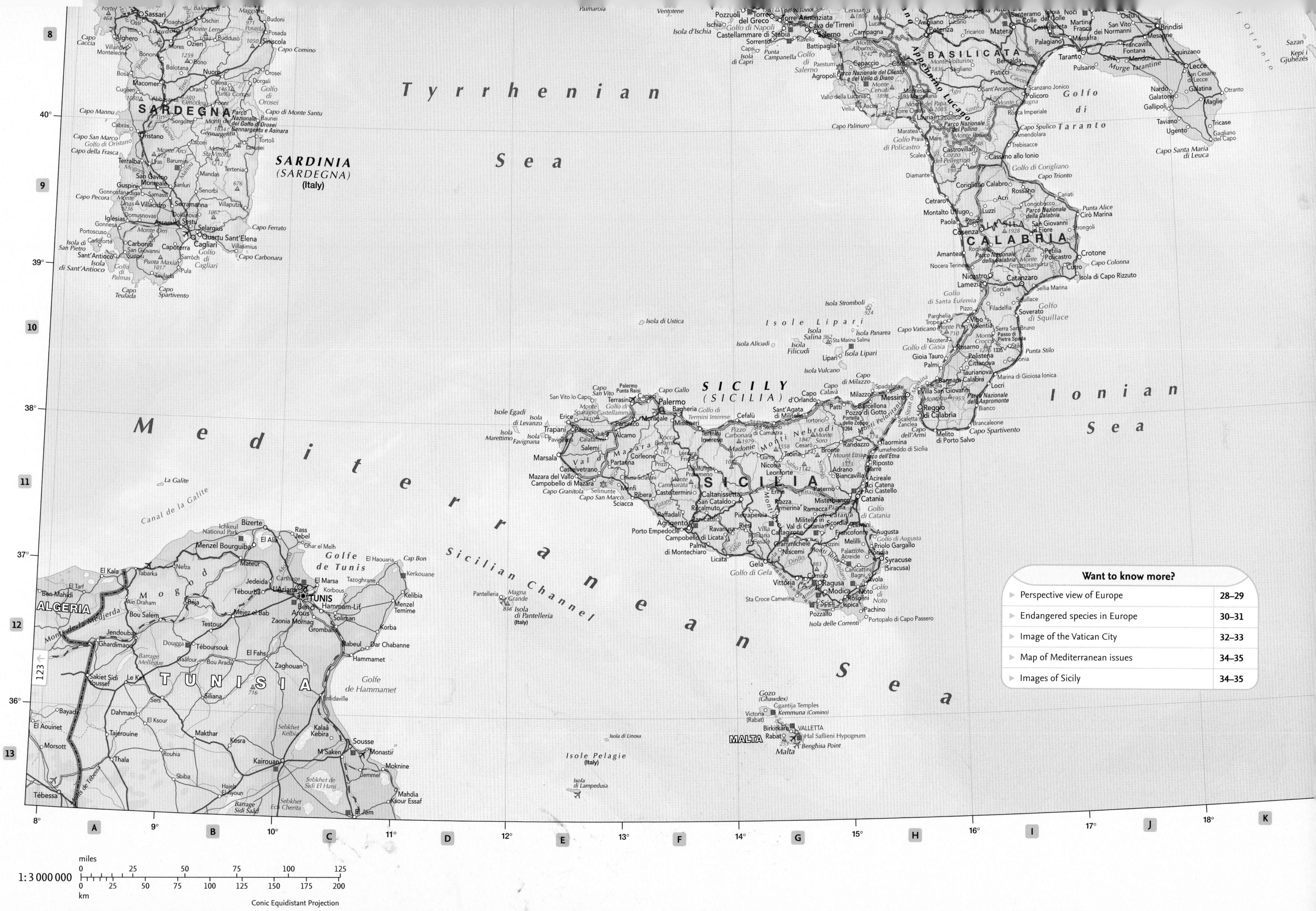

Europe Italy, Slovenia, Croatia and Bosnia-Herzegovina

Want to know more?

▲ Perspective view of Europe	28–29
▲ Endangered species in Europe	30–31
▲ Image of the Vatican City	32–33
▲ Map of Mediterranean issues	34–35
▲ Images of Sicily	34–35

Tyrrhenian Sea

Ionian Sea

Mediterranean Sea

SARDINIA (SARDEGNA) (Italy)

BASILICATA

CALABRIA

SICILY (SICILIA)

MALTA

VALLETTA

TUNISIA

ALGERIA

Golfo di Taranto

Golfo di Squillace

Sicilian Channel

Isole Lipari

Golfe de Tunis

Golfe de Hammamet

1:3 000 000

Conic Equidistant Projection

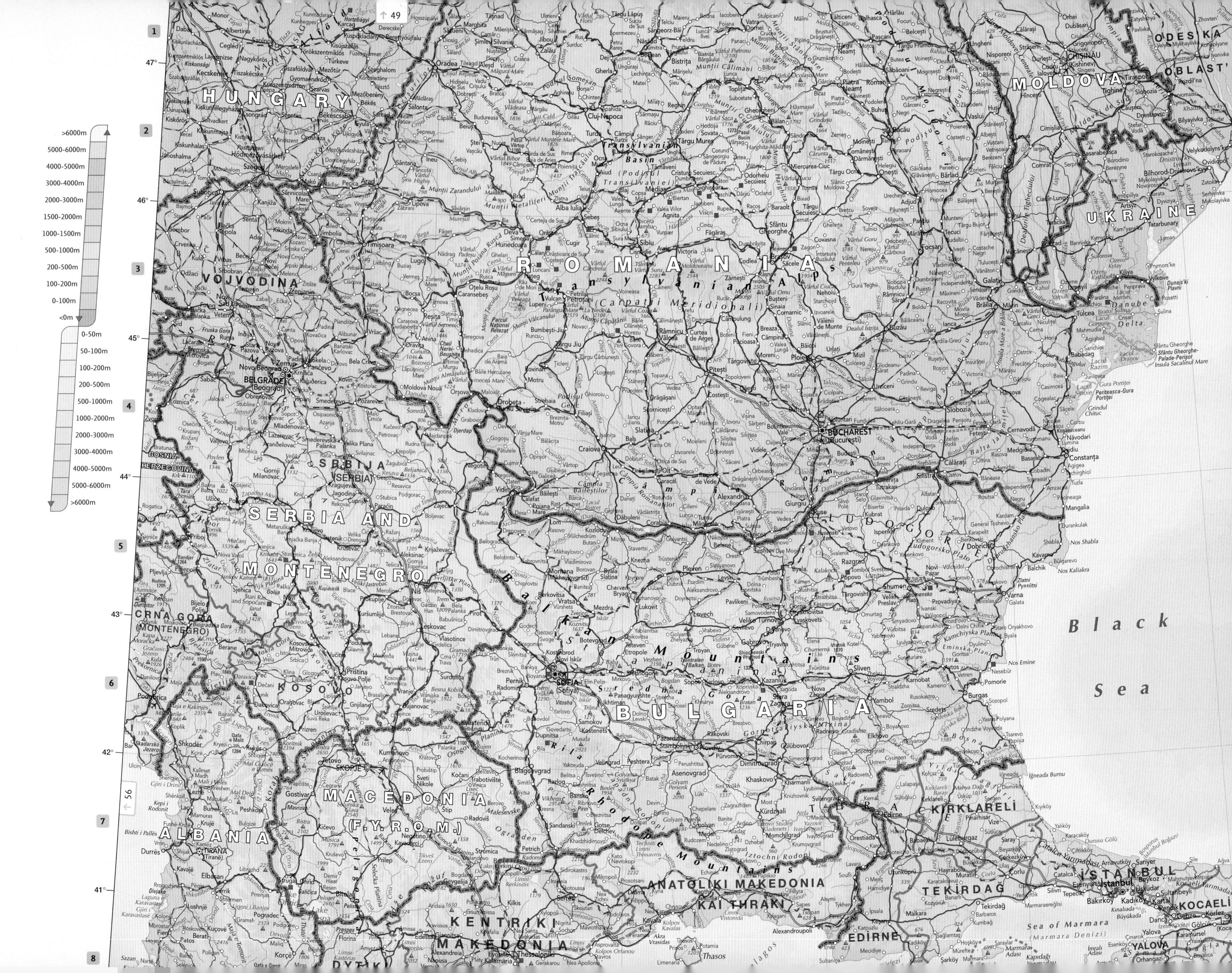
HUNGARY
ROMANIA
BULGARIA
MOLDOVA
UKRAINE
ODESKA OBLAST'
VOJVODINA
SRBIJA (SERBIA)
SERBIA AND MONTENEGRO
CRNA GORA (MONTENEGRO)
KOSOVO
MACEDONIA (F.Y.R.O.M.)
ALBANIA
BOSNIA-HERZEGOVINA
ANATOLIKI MAKEDONIA KAI THRAKI
KENTRIKI MAKEDONIA
KIRKLARELI
TEKIRDAĞ
EDIRNE
İSTANBUL
KOCAELİ
YALOVA
Transylvanian Alps
Balkan Mountains
Rhodope Mountains
Black Sea
Sea of Marmara
BUCHAREST (Bucureşti)
SOFIA (Sofiya)
BELGRADE (Beograd)
SKOPJE
TIRANA (Tiranë)
CHIŞINĂU (Kishinev)
İstanbul
49
56
47°
46°
45°
44°
43°
42°
41°
1
2
3
4
5
6
7
8
>6000m
5000-6000m
4000-5000m
3000-4000m
2000-3000m
1500-2000m
1000-1500m
500-1000m
200-500m
100-200m
0-100m
<0m
0-50m
50-100m
100-200m
200-500m
500-1000m
1000-2000m
2000-3000m
3000-4000m
4000-5000m
5000-6000m
>6000m

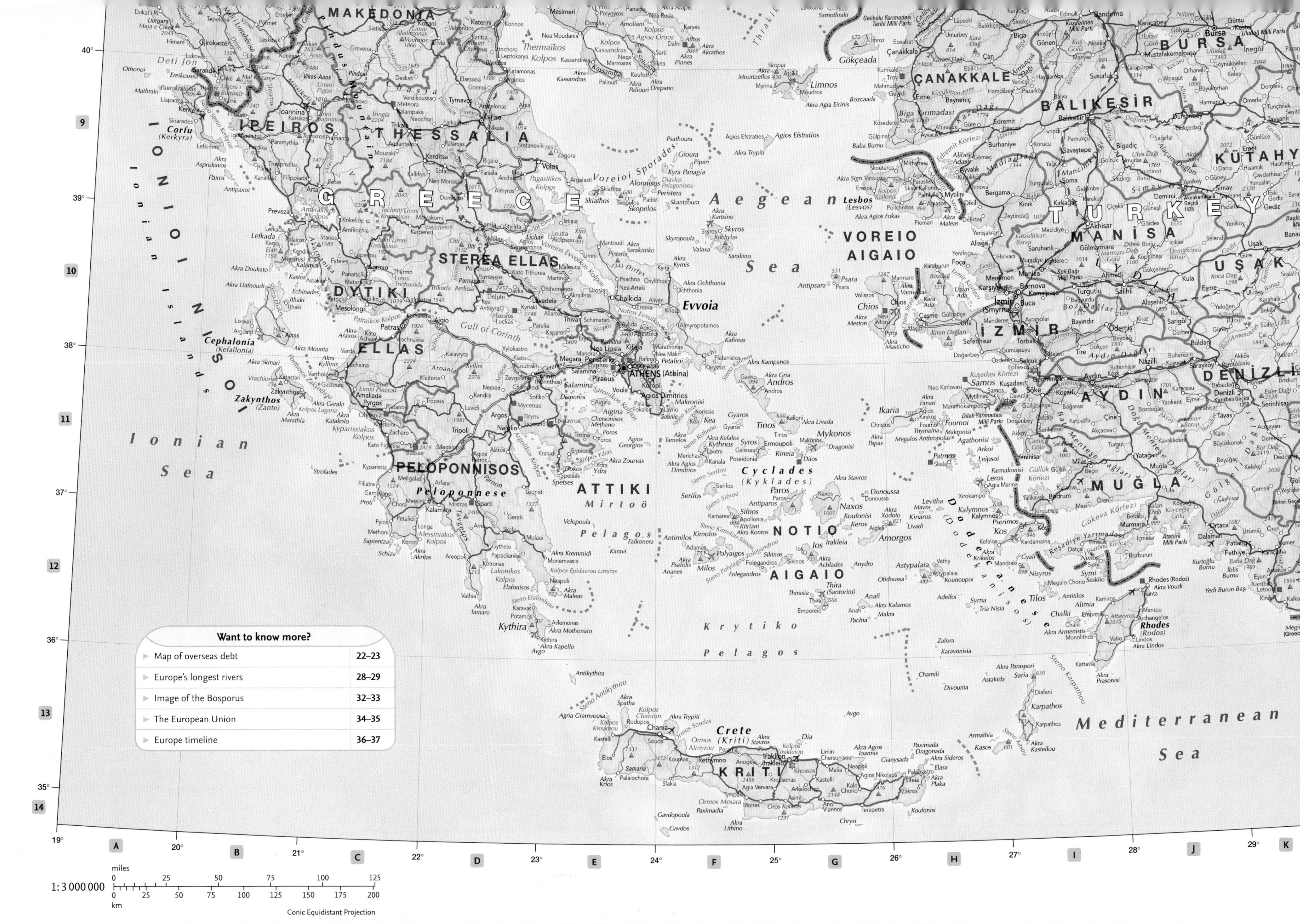

Europe Southeast Europe

Want to know more?

1:3 000 000

Conic Equidistant Projection

Map of overseas debt	22–23
Europe's longest rivers	28–29
Image of the Bosporus	32–33
The European Union	34–35
Europe timeline	36–37

Asia Landscapes

Asia is the world's largest continent and its huge range of physical features is evident in this perspective view from the southeast. These include, in southwest Asia the Arabian Peninsula; in southern Asia the Indian subcontinent; in southest Asia the vast Indonesian archipelago; in central Asia the Plateau of Tibet and the Gobi Desert and in east Asia the volcanic islands of Japan and the Kamchatka Peninsula.

North to south, the continent extends over 76 degrees of latitude from the Arctic Ocean in the north to the southern tip of Indonesia in the south. The Ural Mountains and the Caucasus in the west form the boundary with Europe. Asia's most impressive mountain range is the Himalaya, which contains the world's highest peaks. The continent is drained by some of the world's longest rivers and the Caspian Sea is the world's largest lake or inland sea.

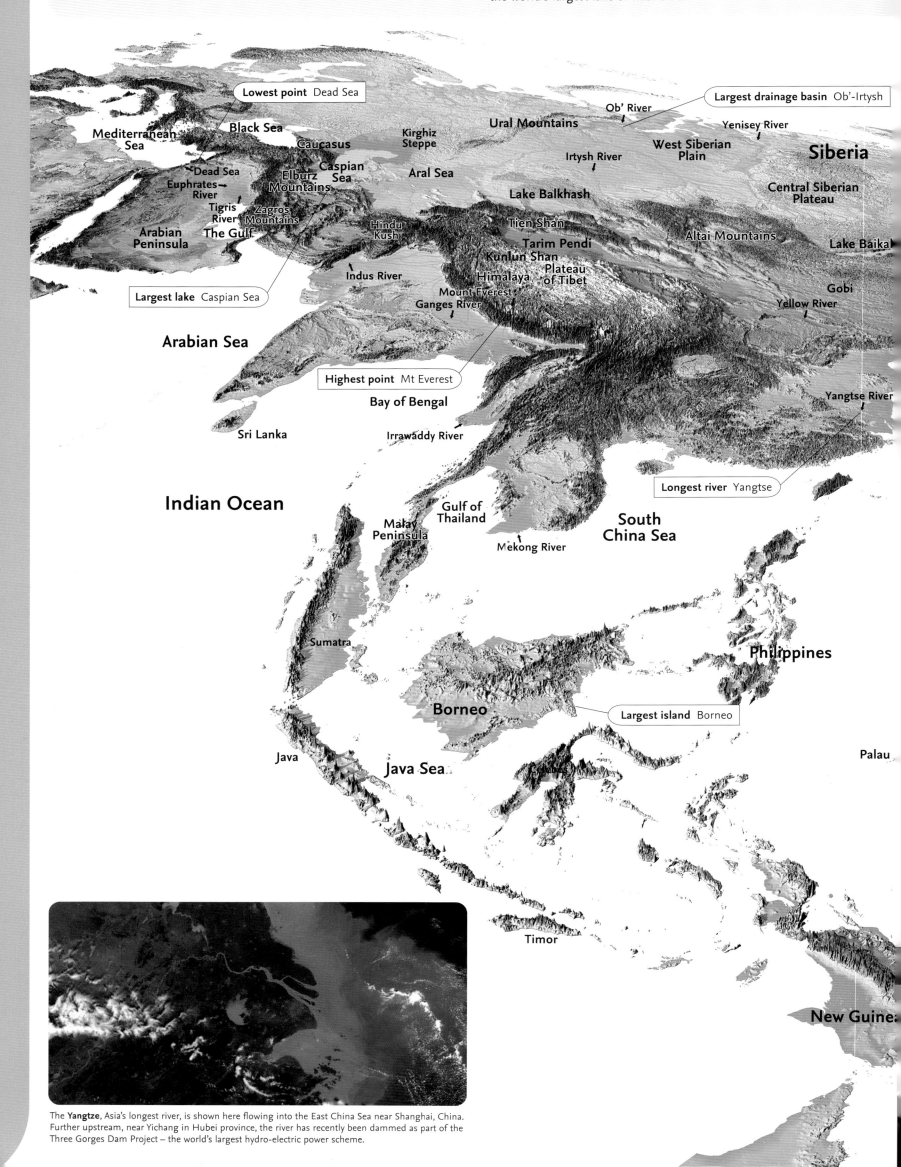

Lowest point Dead Sea

Largest drainage basin Ob'-Irtysh

Mediterranean Sea

Black Sea

Caucasus

Kirghiz Steppe

Ural Mountains

Ob' River

Yenisey River

Dead Sea

Euphrates→ River

Elburz Mountains

Caspian Sea

Aral Sea

Irtysh River

West Siberian Plain

Siberia

Tigris River

Zagros Mountains

Lake Balkhash

Central Siberian Plateau

Arabian Peninsula

The Gulf

Hindu Kush

Tien Shan

Altai Mountains

Lake Baikal

Indus River

Tarim Pendi

Kunlun Shan

Plateau of Tibet

Gobi

Yellow River

Largest lake Caspian Sea

Himalaya

Mount Everest

Ganges River

Arabian Sea

Highest point Mt Everest

Yangtse River

Bay of Bengal

Sri Lanka

Irrawaddy River

Longest river Yangtse

Indian Ocean

Gulf of Thailand

South China Sea

Malay Peninsula

Mekong River

Philippines

Sumatra

Borneo

Largest island Borneo

Palau

Java

Java Sea

Celebes

Timor

New Guinea

The **Yangtze**, Asia's longest river, is shown here flowing into the East China Sea near Shanghai, China. Further upstream, near Yichang in Hubei province, the river has recently been dammed as part of the Three Gorges Dam Project – the world's largest hydro-electric power scheme.

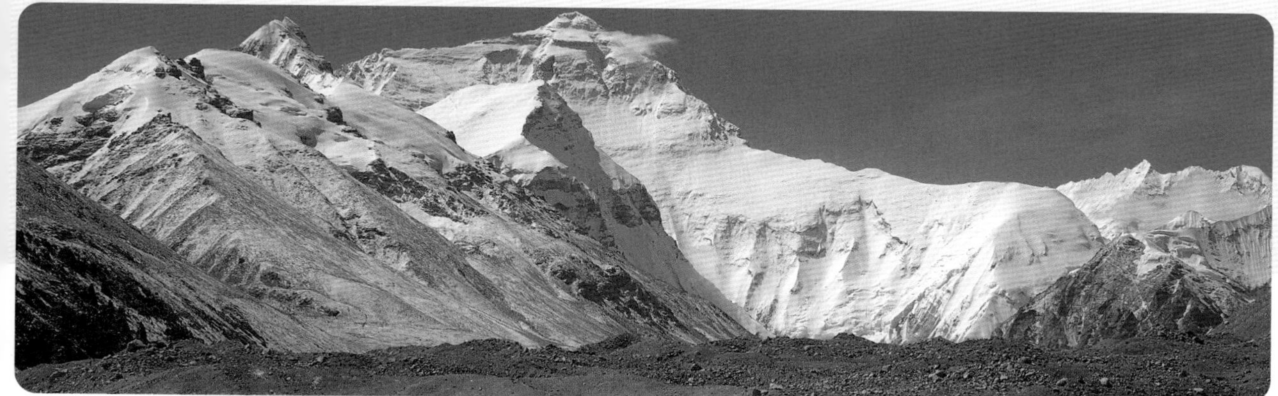

This view of the Himalayas shows **Mount Everest**, at 8 848 metres (29 028 feet) the world's highest mountain. The photograph looks south from the Plateau of Tibet, with its typical barren landscape in the foreground. The plateau lies at a height of over 4 000 metres (13 123 feet). The Himalayas mark the southern limit of the plateau and stretch for over 2 000 kilometres (1 242 miles), forming the northern limit of the Indian sub-continent.

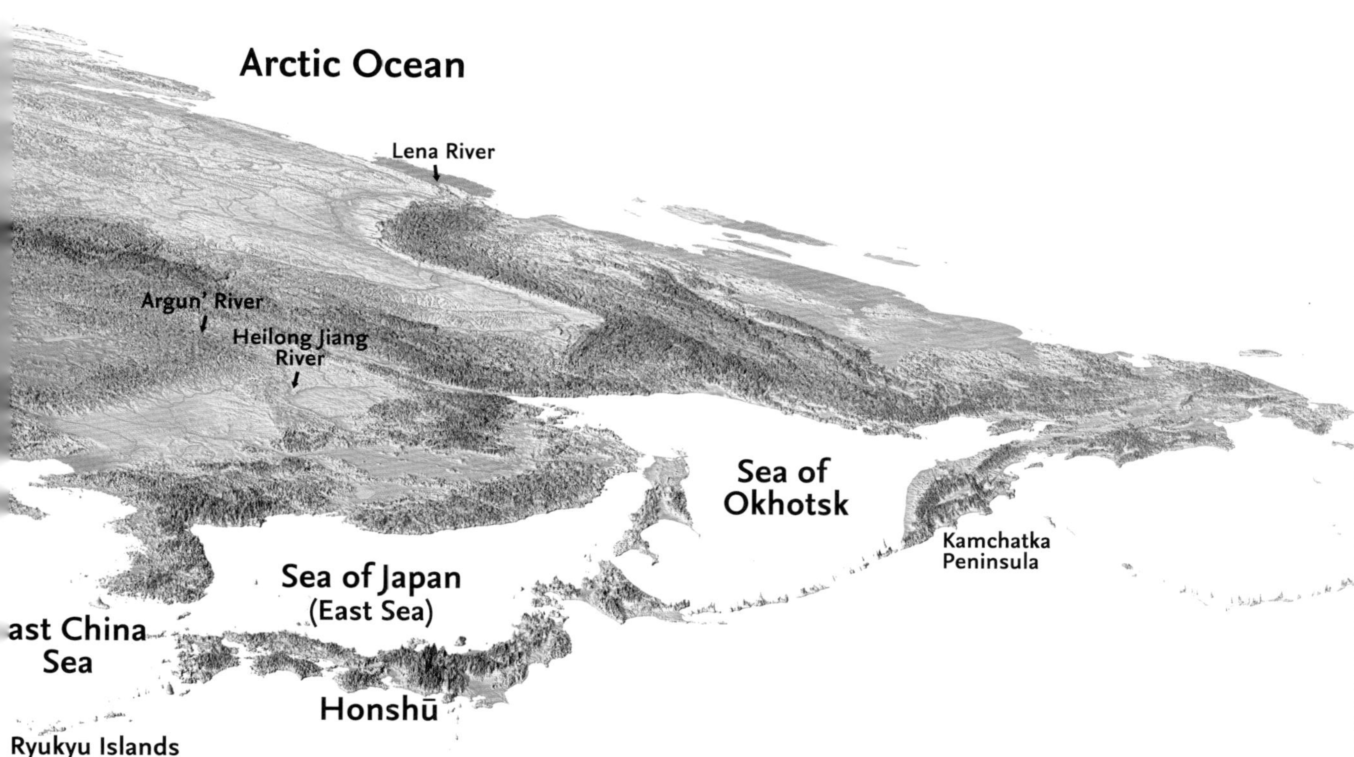

Arctic Ocean

Lena River

Argun' River

Heilong Jiang River

Sea of Okhotsk

Kamchatka Peninsula

Sea of Japan (East Sea)

ast China Sea

Honshū

Ryukyu Islands

Pacific Ocean

Northern Mariana Islands

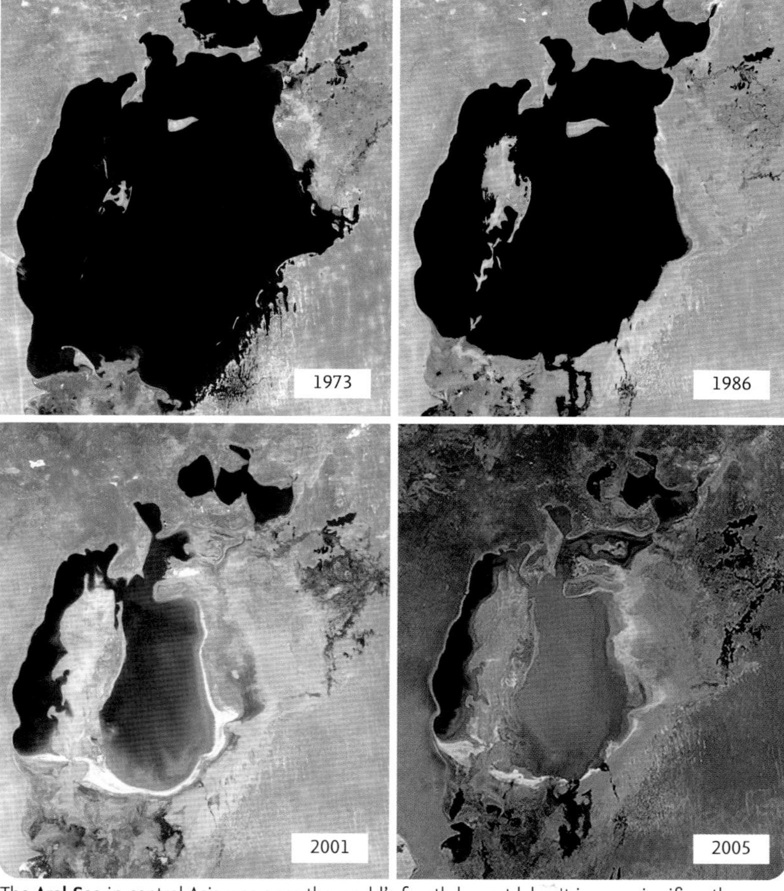

1973

1986

2001

2005

The **Aral Sea** in central Asia was once the world's fourth largest lake. It is now significantly smaller and shrinking rapidly due to climatic change and the diversion of water, for farming purposes, from the rivers which feed the lake. The change has had a devastating effect on the local fishing industry and has caused health problems for the local population.

Want to know more?

▸ Cross-section of Asia	6–7
▸ World's highest mountains	6–7
▸ Maps of Asia	38–59
▸ Land cover map of Asia	62–63
▸ Indian Ocean tsunami	66–67
▸ Three Gorges Dam Project	68–69

Internet links

NASA Visible Earth	visibleearth.nasa.gov
NASA Earth Observatory	earthobservatory.nasa.gov
Peakware World Mountain Encyclopedia	www.peakware.com
The Himalaya	himalaya.alpine-club.org.uk

Facts

90 of the world's 100 highest mountains are in Asia.

The Indonesian archipelago is made up of over 13 500 islands.

The height of the land in Nepal ranges from 60 metres (197 feet) to 8 848 metres (29 028 feet).

The deepest lake in the world is Lake Baikal, Russian Federation which is over 1 600 metres (5 249 feet) deep.

Highest mountains	metres	feet	map
Mt Everest *China/Nepal*	8 848	29 028	97 E4
K2 *China/Jammu and Kashmir*	8 611	28 251	96 C2
Kangchenjunga *India/Nepal*	8 586	28 169	97 F4
Lhotse *China/Nepal*	8 516	27 939	97 E4
Makalu *China/Nepal*	8 463	27 765	97 E4
Cho Oyu *China/Nepal*	8 201	26 906	97 E3
Dhaulagiri *Nepal*	8 167	26 794	97 D3
Manaslu *Nepal*	8 163	26 781	97 E3
Nanga Parbat *Jammu and Kashmir*	8 126	26 660	96 B2
Annapurna I *Nepal*	8 091	26 545	97 D3

Longest rivers	km	miles	map
Yangtze	6 380	3 964	87 G2
Ob'-Irtysh	5 568	3 459	38 G3-39 I5
Yenisey-Angara-Selenga	5 550	3 448	39 I2-K4
Yellow	5 464	3 395	85 H4
Irtysh	4 440	2 759	38 G3
Mekong	4 425	2 749	79 D6
Heilong Jiang-Argun'	4 416	2 744	81 M3
Lena-Kirenga	4 400	2 734	39 M2-K4
Yenisey	4 090	2 541	39 I2
Ob'	3 701	2 300	38 G3

Largest islands	sq km	sq miles	map
Borneo	745 561	287 863	77 F2
Sumatra	473 606	182 860	76 C3
Honshū	227 414	87 805	91 F6
Celebes	189 216	73 057	75 B3
Java	132 188	51 038	77 E4
Luzon	104 690	40 421	74 B2
Mindanao	94 630	36 537	74 C5
Hokkaidō	78 073	30 144	90 H3
Sakhalin	76 400	29 498	82 F2
Sri Lanka	65 610	25 332	94 D5

Largest lakes	sq km	sq miles	map
Caspian Sea	371 000	143 243	102 B4
Lake Baikal	30 500	11 776	88 A2
Lake Balkhash	17 400	6 718	103 H3
Aral Sea	17 158	6 625	102 D3

Land area		map
Total land area 45 036 492 sq km/17 388 686 sq mls		
Most northerly point	**Mys Arkticheskiy** *Russian Fed.*	39 J1
Most southerly point	**Pamana** *Indonesia*	75 B5
Most westerly point	**Bozcaada** *Turkey*	59 H9
Most easterly point	**Mys Dezhneva** *Russian Fed.*	39 T3
Lowest point	**Dead Sea**	108 G6

Asia Ecology

The continent of Asia includes most land cover types as it stretches from the tropical rain forests of Indonesia through the verdant vegetation of southeast Asia up onto the high mountain plateau beyond the Himalaya mountain range. This gives it a diverse range of habitats and a huge variety of species. Although on the same latitude as the Mediterranean Sea, the Plateau of Tibet stretches over a vast area at an elevation range of 4 000–6 000 metres (13 123–19 685 feet). It is susceptible to extreme climate conditions making it a difficult habitat. Further north at lower levels, mixed forests and grassland give way to wetland and scrubby vegetation areas which become completely frozen during the winter months.

The brackish waters of Tso Moraki lake sit among the **Zaskar Mountains**, at the western edge of the Himalayas. The lake is over 4 000 metres (13 123 feet) above sea level.

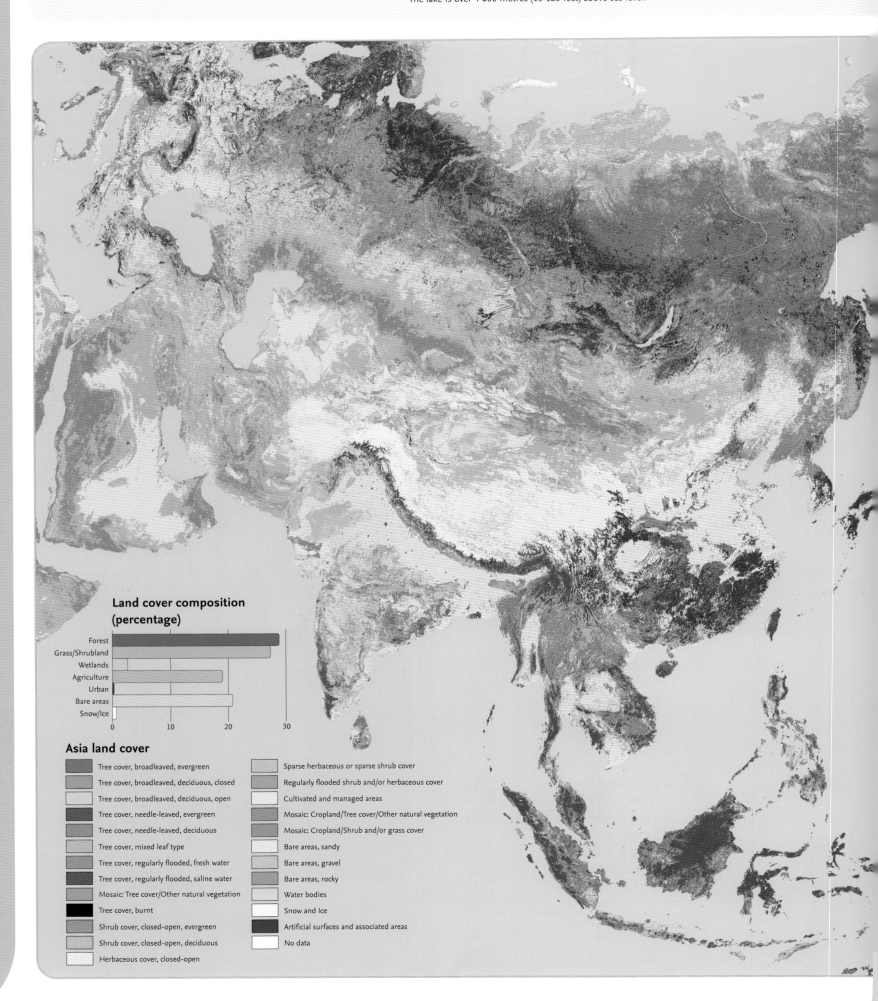

Land cover composition (percentage)

Forest
Grass/Shrubland
Wetlands
Agriculture
Urban
Bare areas
Snow/Ice

0   10   20   30

Asia land cover

- Tree cover, broadleaved, evergreen
- Tree cover, broadleaved, deciduous, closed
- Tree cover, broadleaved, deciduous, open
- Tree cover, needle-leaved, evergreen
- Tree cover, needle-leaved, deciduous
- Tree cover, mixed leaf type
- Tree cover, regularly flooded, fresh water
- Tree cover, regularly flooded, saline water
- Mosaic: Tree cover/Other natural vegetation
- Tree cover, burnt
- Shrub cover, closed-open, evergreen
- Shrub cover, closed-open, deciduous
- Herbaceous cover, closed-open

- Sparse herbaceous or sparse shrub cover
- Regularly flooded shrub and/or herbaceous cover
- Cultivated and managed areas
- Mosaic: Cropland/Tree cover/Other natural vegetation
- Mosaic: Cropland/Shrub and/or grass cover
- Bare areas, sandy
- Bare areas, gravel
- Bare areas, rocky
- Water bodies
- Snow and Ice
- Artificial surfaces and associated areas
- No data

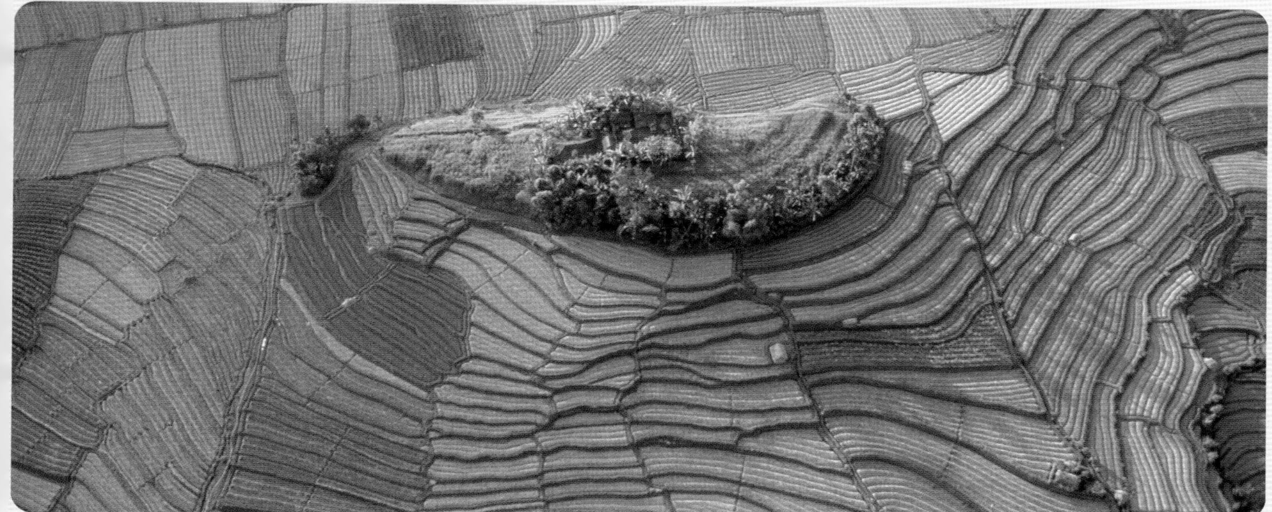

Agricultural land is precious on **Bali** so hillsides are terraced to retain water and to get maximum use from the land. The Balinese grow their main crop of rice with the aid of elaborate irrigation systems.

Internet links	
Red List of Threatened Species	www.redlist.org
UN Environment Programme	www.unep.org
IUCN the World Conservation Union	www.iucn.org
Images of Asia	earthobservatory.nasa.gov

Facts

Mongolia can have temperatures of 35°C in summer and −35°C in winter.

Lake Balkhash is split by a sandspit; half is salt water, half is freshwater.

Only 15 per cent of Brunei is cultivated.

Approximately two-thirds of Bangladesh is fertile arable land served by the Ganges and Brahmaputra rivers but during the monsoon these rivers can seriously flood the area.

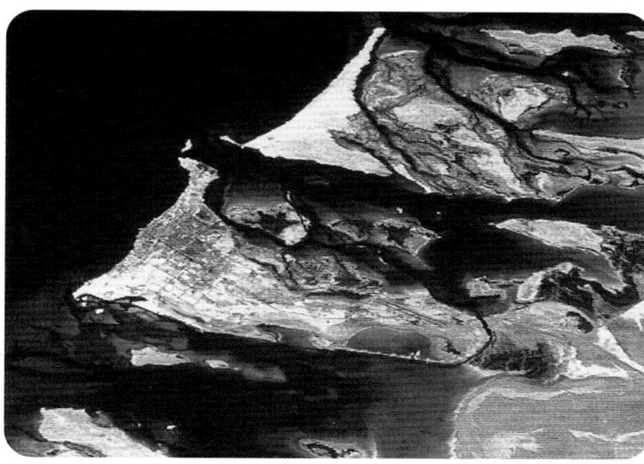

Abu Dhabi, once a small fishing village, has developed its infrastructure, altered land use and extended its area by extensive **reclamation**. Much of this was to accommodate growth after the discovery of offshore oil in the 1960s.

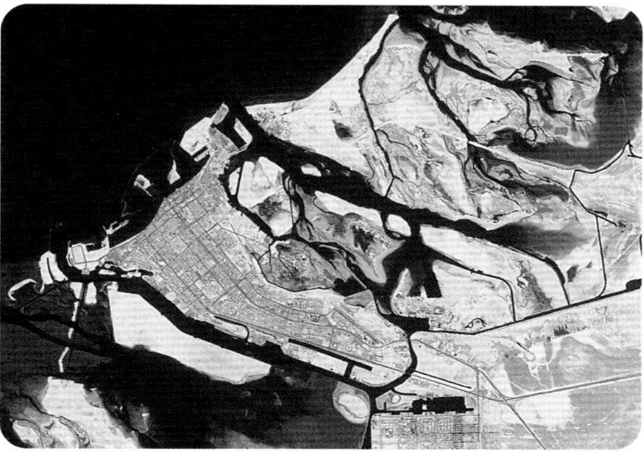

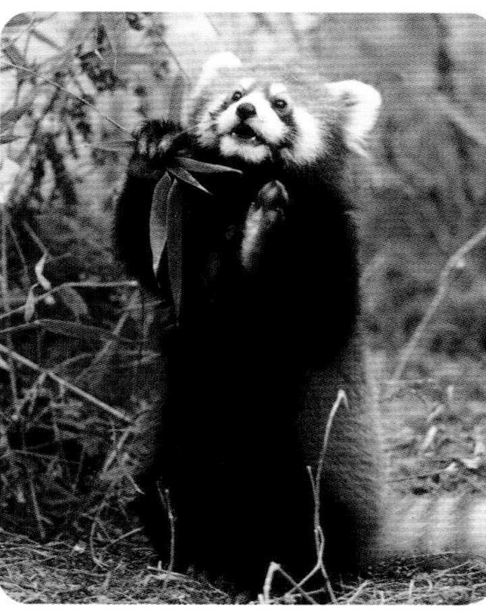

The **red panda** is found in the mountains of China, north-east India and Nepal. It is a solitary, nocturnal animal feeding mainly on bamboo leaves. It is under threat from agriculture, logging and other native species.

Top 10 protected land by country

	country	percentage land protected
1	Saudi Arabia	41.8
2	Malaysia	30.6
3	Bhutan	30.2
4	Sri Lanka	26.5
5	Cambodia	23.7
6	Israel	19.1
7	Laos	18.8
8	Tajikistan	18.3
9	Nepal	18.1
10	Thailand	15.7

Endangered species

The ecosystem of a tropical rain forest is thought to be home to the majority of the earth's animal and plant species. Countries such as the Philippines, Indonesia and India which have growing populations and relatively low Gross National Incomes do not have the resources to encourage conservation. The extensive clearing of rain forests on some Indonesian islands is driven by the need to disperse people and relieve the high population density of Java. Animals such as the Sumatran tiger are under serious threat as their habitat disappears.

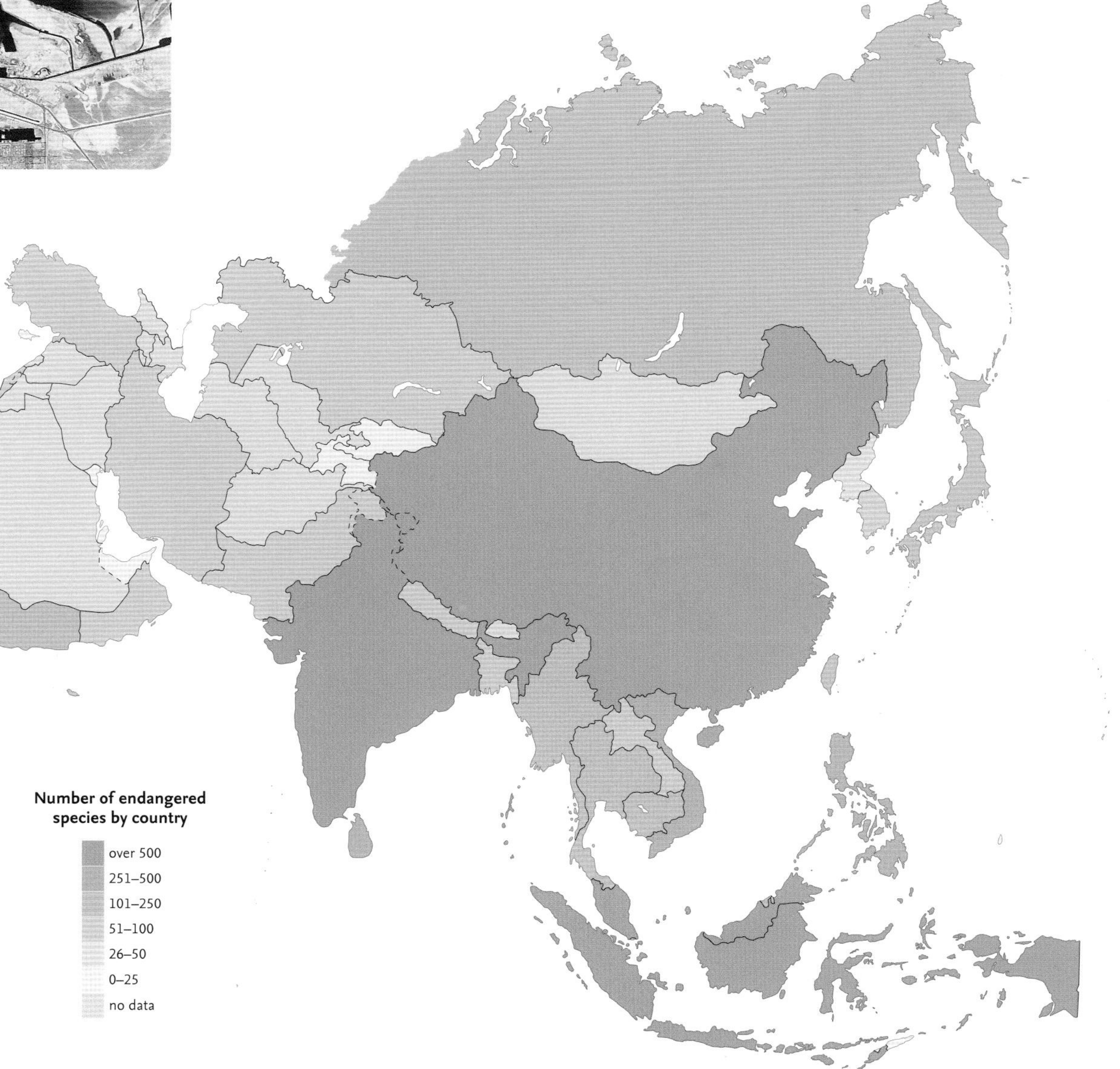

Number of endangered species by country

- over 500
- 251–500
- 101–250
- 51–100
- 26–50
- 0–25
- no data

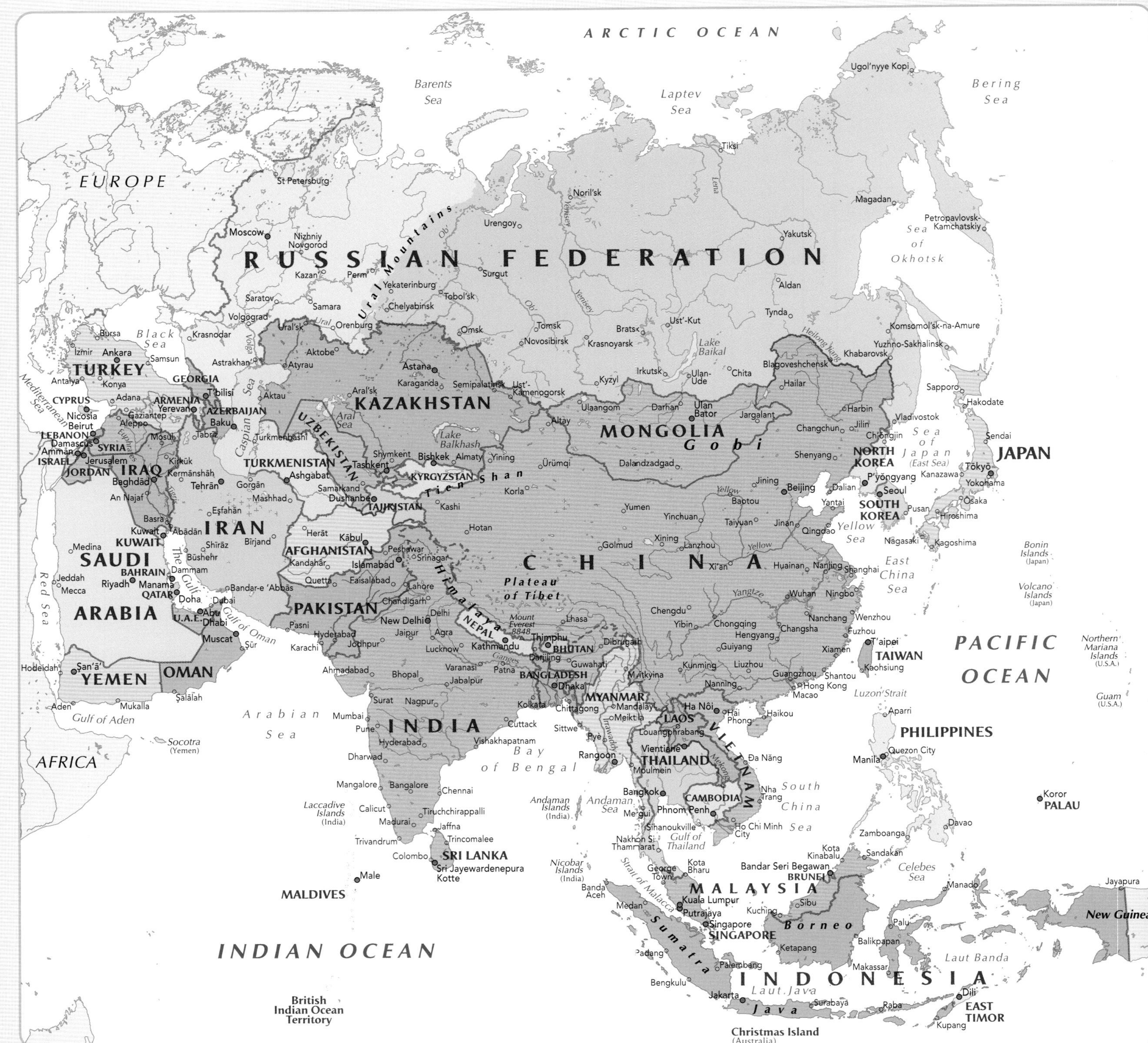

Countries capital		sq km sq miles	population	languages	religions	currency	official website	map
Afghanistan Kābul		652 225 251 825	29 863 000	Dari, Pushtu, Uzbek, Turkmen	Sunni Muslim, Shi'a Muslim	Afghani	www.afghanistan-mfa.net	101
Armenia Yerevan (Erevan)		29 800 11 506	3 016 000	Armenian, Azeri	Armenian Orthodox	Dram	www.gov.am	107
Azerbaijan Baku		86 600 33 436	8 411 000	Azeri, Armenian, Russian, Lezgian	Shi'a Muslim, Sunni Muslim, Russian and Armenian Orthodox	Azerbaijani manat	www.president.az	107
Bahrain Manama (Al Manāmah)		691 267	727 000	Arabic, English	Shi'a Muslim, Sunni Muslim, Christian	Bahraini dinar	www.bahrain.gov.bh	105
Bangladesh Dhaka (Dacca)		143 998 55 598	141 822 000	Bengali, English	Sunni Muslim, Hindu	Taka	www.bangladesh.gov.bd	97
Bhutan Thimphu		46 620 18 000	2 163 000	Dzongkha, Nepali, Assamese	Buddhist, Hindu	Ngultrum, Indian rupee	www.bhutan.gov.bt	97
Brunei Bandar Seri Begawan		5 765 2 226	374 000	Malay, English, Chinese	Sunni Muslim, Buddhist, Christian	Brunei dollar	www.brunei.gov.bn	77
Cambodia Phnom Penh		181 035 69 884	14 071 000	Khmer, Vietnamese	Buddhist, Roman Catholic, Sunni Muslim	Riel	www.cambodia.gov.kh	79
China Beijing (Peking)		9 584 492 3 700 593	1 323 345 000	Mandarin, Wu, Cantonese, Hsiang, regional languages	Confucian, Taoist, Buddhist, Christian, Sunni Muslim	Yuan, HK dollar, Macau pataca	www.china.org.cn	80–81
Cyprus Nicosia (Lefkosia)		9 251 3 572	835 000	Greek, Turkish, English	Greek Orthodox, Sunni Muslim	Cyprus pound	www.cyprus.gov.cy	107
East Timor Dili		14 874 5 743	947 000	Portuguese, Tetun, English	Roman Catholic	US dollar	www.gov.east-timor.org	75
Georgia T'bilisi		69 700 26 911	4 474 000	Georgian, Russian, Armenian, Azeri, Ossetian, Abkhaz	Georgian Orthodox, Russian Orthodox, Sunni Muslim	Lari	www.parliament.ge	107
India New Delhi		3 064 898 1 183 364	1 103 371 000	Hindi, English, many regional languages	Hindu, Sunni Muslim, Shi'a Muslim, Sikh, Christian	Indian rupee	www.goidirectory.nic.in	92–93
Indonesia Jakarta		1 919 445 741 102	222 781 000	Indonesian, local languages	Sunni Muslim, Protestant, Roman Catholic, Hindu, Buddhist	Rupiah	www.indonesia.go.id	72–73
Iran Tehrān		1 648 000 636 296	69 515 000	Farsi, Azeri, Kurdish, regional languages	Shi'a Muslim, Sunni Muslim	Iranian rial	www.president.ir	100–101
Iraq Baghdād		438 317 169 235	28 807 000	Arabic, Kurdish, Turkmen	Shi'a Muslim, Sunni Muslim, Christian	Iraqi dinar	www.iraqmofa.net	107
Israel *Jerusalem (Yerushalayim) (El Quds)		20 770 8 019	6 725 000	Hebrew, Arabic	Jewish, Sunni Muslim, Christian, Druze	Shekel	www.index.gov.il/FirstGov	108
Japan Tōkyō		377 727 145 841	128 085 000	Japanese	Shintoist, Buddhist, Christian	Yen	www.web-japan.org	90–91
Jordan 'Ammān		89 206 34 443	5 703 000	Arabic	Sunni Muslim, Christian	Jordanian dinar	www.nic.gov.jo	108–109
Kazakhstan Astana (Akmola)		2 717 300 1 049 155	14 825 000	Kazakh, Russian, Ukrainian, German, Uzbek, Tatar	Sunni Muslim, Russian Orthodox, Protestant	Tenge	www.president.kz	102–103
Kuwait Kuwait (Al Kuwayt)		17 818 6 880	2 687 000	Arabic	Sunni Muslim, Shi'a Muslim, Christian, Hindu	Kuwaiti dinar	www.kuwaitmission.com	107
Kyrgyzstan Bishkek (Frunze)		198 500 76 641	5 264 000	Kyrgyz, Russian, Uzbek	Sunni Muslim, Russian Orthodox	Kyrgyz som	www.gov.kg	103

*De facto capital. Disputed.

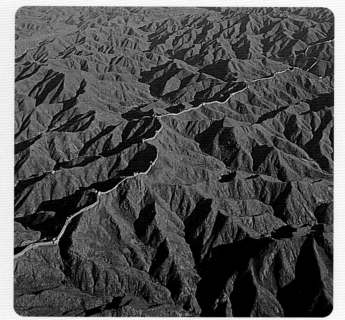

The **Great Wall of China** was built in various stages over a period of 1 000 years from the 3rd century BC. It is one of China's most distinctive and spectacular features. Stretching a total length of over 2 400 kilometres (1 490 miles) from the coast east of Beijing, to the Gobi desert, the wall was first built to protect China from the Mongols and nomadic peoples to the north of the country.

Top 10 countries by area		sq km	sq miles	world rank
1	**Russian Federation**	17 075 400	6 592 849	1
2	**China**	9 584 492	3 700 593	4
3	**India**	3 065 027	1 183 414	7
4	**Kazakhstan**	2 717 300	1 049 155	9
5	**Saudi Arabia**	2 200 000	849 425	13
6	**Indonesia**	1 919 445	741 102	16
7	**Iran**	1 648 000	636 296	18
8	**Mongolia**	1 565 000	604 250	19
9	**Pakistan**	803 940	310 403	35
10	**Turkey**	779 452	300 948	37

Top 10 countries by population		population	world rank
1	**China**	1 323 345 000	1
2	**India**	1 103 371 000	2
3	**Indonesia**	222 781 000	4
4	**Pakistan**	157 935 000	6
5	**Russian Federation**	143 202 000	7
6	**Bangladesh**	141 822 000	8
7	**Japan**	128 085 000	10
8	**Vietnam**	84 238 000	12
9	**Philippines**	83 054 000	13
10	**Turkey**	73 193 000	17

Want to know more?

World Landscapes	**6–7**
Political map of the World	**8–9**
Indian Ocean tsunami	**66–67**
Middle East crisis	**68–69**
Detailed maps of Asia	**72–109**

Internet links

Asian Development Bank	**www.adb.org**
Asia-Pacific Economic Cooperation	**www.apecsec.org.sg**
Association of Southeast Asian Nations	**www.aseansec.org**
International Boundaries Research Unit	**www-ibru.dur.ac.uk**

Facts

Over 60 per cent of the world's population live in Asia, with Indonesia having the fourth largest population in the world after China, India and the USA. Java is one of the most densely populated parts of the globe.

Taiwan, or the Republic of China, has been claimed by China ever since the People's Republic was established in 1949. It is not a member of the United Nations which makes it the only de facto independent country in the world apart from the Vatican City not to be so.

The Russian Federation and China both have borders with fourteen different countries.

Mongolia's location results in some extreme temperatures. In winter temperatures fall below -40°C and rise to over 35°C during the short summer.

Countries capital		sq km *sq miles*	population	languages	religions	currency	official website	map
Laos Vientiane (Viangchan)		236 800 *91 429*	5 924 000	Lao, local languages	Buddhist, traditional beliefs	Kip	www.un.int/lao	78–79
Lebanon Beirut (Beyrouth)		10 452 *4 036*	3 577 000	Arabic, Armenian, French	Shi'a Muslim, Sunni Muslim, Christian	Lebanese pound	www.presidency.gov.lb	108–109
Malaysia Kuala Lumpur/Putrajaya		332 965 *128 559*	25 347 000	Malay, English, Chinese, Tamil, local languages	Sunni Muslim, Buddhist, Hindu, Christian, traditional beliefs	Ringgit	www.mcsl.mampu.gov.my	76–77
Maldives Male		298 *115*	329 000	Divehi (Maldivian)	Sunni Muslim	Rufiyaa	www.maldivesinfo.gov.mv	93
Mongolia Ulan Bator (Ulaanbaatar)		1 565 000 *604 250*	2 646 000	Khalka (Mongolian), Kazakh, local languages	Buddhist, Sunni Muslim	Tugrik (tögrög)	www.pmis.gov.mn	84–85
Myanmar Rangoon (Yangôn)		676 577 *261 228*	50 519 000	Burmese, Shan, Karen, local languages	Buddhist, Christian, Sunni Muslim	Kyat	www.myanmar.com	78–79
Nepal Kathmandu		147 181 *56 827*	27 133 000	Nepali, Maithili, Bhojpuri, English, local languages	Hindu, Buddhist, Sunni Muslim	Nepalese rupee	www.nepalhmg.gov.np	96–97
North Korea P'yŏngyang		120 538 *46 540*	22 488 000	Korean	Traditional beliefs, Chondoist, Buddhist	North Korean won	www.korea-dpr.com	82–83
Oman Muscat (Masqaţ)		309 500 *119 499*	2 567 000	Arabic, Baluchi, Indian languages	Ibadhi Muslim, Sunni Muslim	Omani riyal	www.moneoman.gov.om	105
Pakistan Islamabad		803 940 *310 403*	157 935 000	Urdu, Punjabi, Sindhi, Pushtu, English	Sunni Muslim, Shi'a Muslim, Christian, Hindu	Pakistani rupee	www.infopak.gov.pk	101
Palau Koror		497 *192*	20 000	Palauan, English	Roman Catholic, Protestant, traditional beliefs	US dollar	www.palauembassy.com	73
Philippines Manila		300 000 *115 831*	83 054 000	English, Pilipino, Cebuano, local languages	Roman Catholic, Protestant, Sunni Muslim, Aglipayan	Philippine peso	www.gov.ph	74
Qatar Doha (Ad Dawḩah)		11 437 *4 416*	813 000	Arabic	Sunni Muslim	Qatari riyal	www.english.mofa.gov.qa	105
Russian Federation Moscow (Moskva)		17 075 400 *6 592 849*	143 202 000	Russian, Tatar, Ukrainian, local languages	Russian Orthodox, Sunni Muslim, Protestant	Russian rouble	www.gov.ru	38–39
Saudi Arabia Riyadh (Ar Riyāḍ)		2 200 000 *849 425*	24 573 000	Arabic	Sunni Muslim, Shi'a Muslim	Saudi Arabian riyal	www.saudinf.com	104–105
Singapore Singapore		639 *247*	4 326 000	Chinese, English, Malay, Tamil	Buddhist, Taoist, Sunni Muslim, Christian, Hindu	Singapore dollar	www.gov.sg	76
South Korea Seoul (Sŏul)		99 274 *38 330*	47 817 000	Korean	Buddhist, Protestant, Roman Catholic	South Korean won	www.korea.net	83
Sri Lanka Sri Jayewardenepura Kotte		65 610 *25 332*	20 743 000	Sinhalese, Tamil, English	Buddhist, Hindu, Sunni Muslim, Roman Catholic	Sri Lankan rupee	www.priu.gov.lk	94
Syria Damascus (Dimashq)		185 180 *71 498*	19 043 000	Arabic, Kurdish, Armenian	Sunni Muslim, Shi'a Muslim, Christian	Syrian pound	www.moi-syria.com	108–109
Taiwan T'aipei		36 179 *13 969*	22 858 000	Mandarin, Min, Hakka, local languages	Buddhist, Taoist, Confucian, Christian	Taiwan dollar	www.gov.tw	87
Tajikistan Dushanbe		143 100 *55 251*	6 507 000	Tajik, Uzbek, Russian	Sunni Muslim	Somoni	www.tgus.org	101
Thailand Bangkok (Krung Thep)		513 115 *198 115*	64 233 000	Thai, Lao, Chinese, Malay, Mon-Khmer languages	Buddhist, Sunni Muslim	Baht	www.thaigov.go.th	78–79
Turkey Ankara		779 452 *300 948*	73 193 000	Turkish, Kurdish	Sunni Muslim, Shi'a Muslim	Turkish lira	www.mfa.gov.tr	106–107
Turkmenistan Aşgabat (Ashkhabad)		488 100 *188 456*	4 833 000	Turkmen, Uzbek, Russian	Sunni Muslim, Russian Orthodox	Turkmen manat	www.turkmenistanembassy.org	102–103
United Arab Emirates Abu Dhabi (Abū Ẓabī)		77 700 *30 000*	4 496 000	Arabic, English	Sunni Muslim, Shi'a Muslim	UAE dirham	www.uae.gov.ae	105
Uzbekistan Toshkent		447 400 *172 742*	26 593 000	Uzbek, Russian, Tajik, Kazakh	Sunni Muslim, Russian Orthodox	Uzbek som	www.gov.uz	102–103
Vietnam Ha Nôi		329 565 *127 246*	84 238 000	Vietnamese, Thai, Khmer, Chinese, local languages	Buddhist, Taoist, Roman Catholic, Cao Dai, Hoa Hao	Dong	www.na.gov.vn	78–79
Yemen Şan'ā'		527 968 *203 850*	20 975 000	Arabic	Sunni Muslim, Shi'a Muslim	Yemeni riyal	www.nic.gov.ye	104–105

Dependencies capital		territorial status	sq km *sq miles*	population	languages	religions	currency	official website	map
British Indian Ocean Territory		United Kingdom Overseas Territory	60 *23*	uninhabited					219
Christmas Island The Settlement		Australian External Territory	135 *52*	1 508	English	Buddhist, Sunni Muslim, Protestant, Roman Catholic	Australian dollar		72
Cocos Islands (Keeling Islands) West Island		Australian External Territory	14 *5*	621	English	Sunni Muslim, Christian	Australian dollar		218
French Southern and Antarctic Lands		French Overseas Territory	439 580 *169 723*	uninhabited					219
Gaza Gaza		Semi-autonomous region	363 *140*	1 406 423	Arabic	Sunni Muslim, Shi'a Muslim	Israeli shekel	www.pna.gov.ps	108
Heard and McDonald Islands		Australian External Territory	412 *159*	uninhabited					219
Jammu and Kashmir Srinagar		Disputed territory (India/Pakistan)	222 236 *85 806*	13 000 000					96-97
West Bank		Disputed territory	5 860 *2 263*	2 421 491	Arabic, Hebrew	Sunni Muslim, Jewish, Shi'a Muslim, Christian	Jordanian dinar, Israeli shekel	www.pna.gov.ps	108

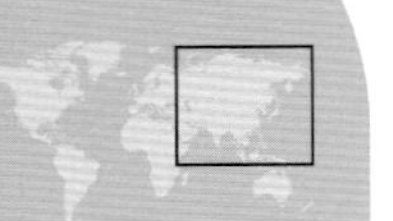

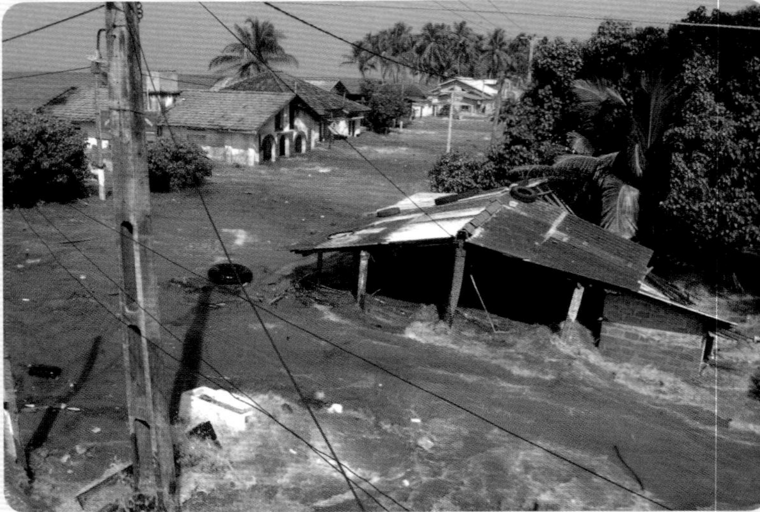

The caption for the first photograph:

The tsunami of 26 December 2004 engulfs the town of Maddampegama, south of Colombo in **Sri Lanka**. The tsunami hit the coast of Sri Lanka, without warning, two hours after the earthquake occurred, causing widespread destruction and 31 000 deaths.

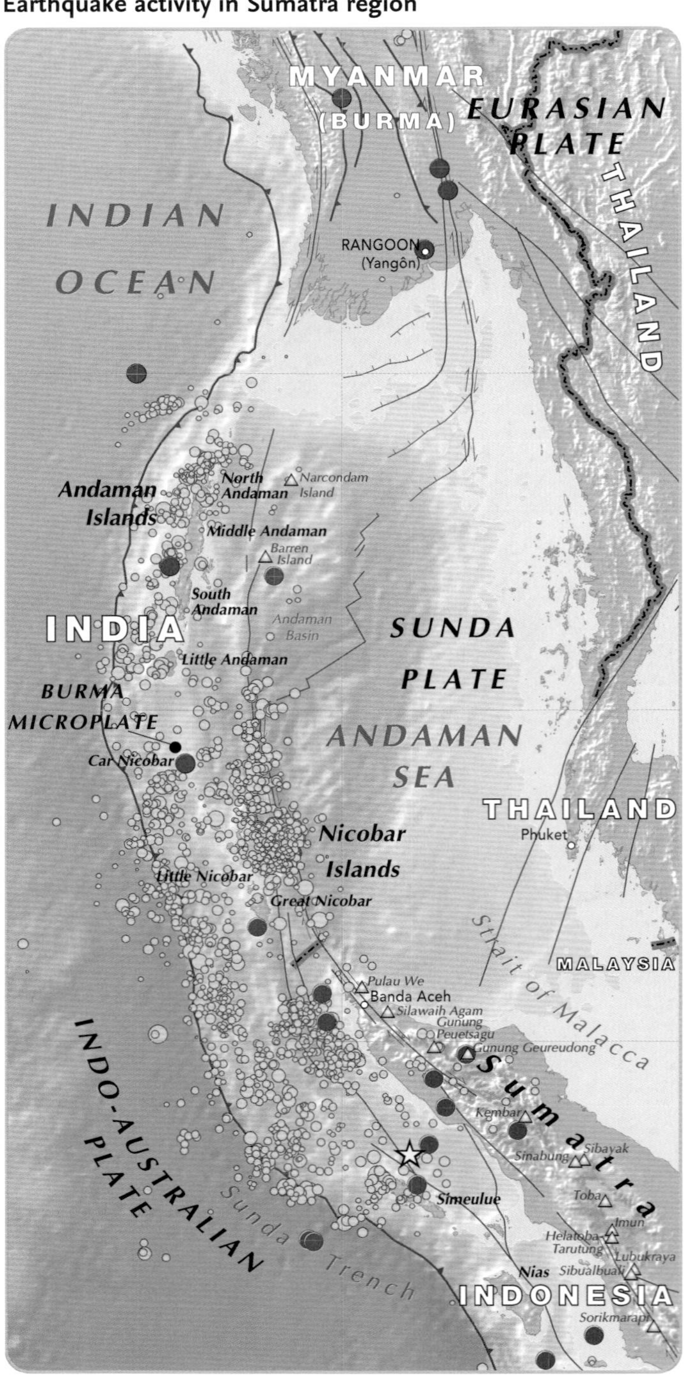

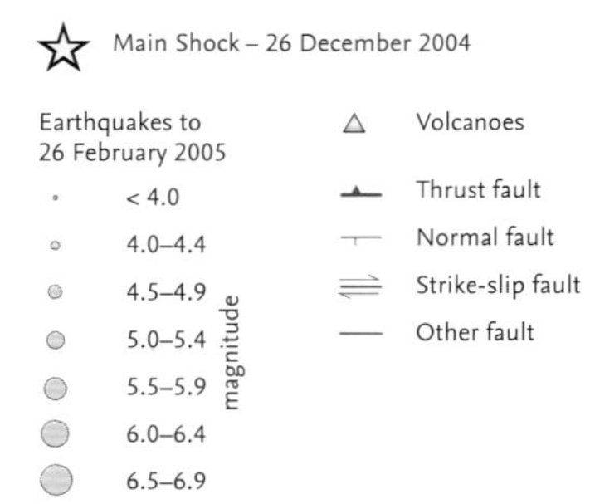

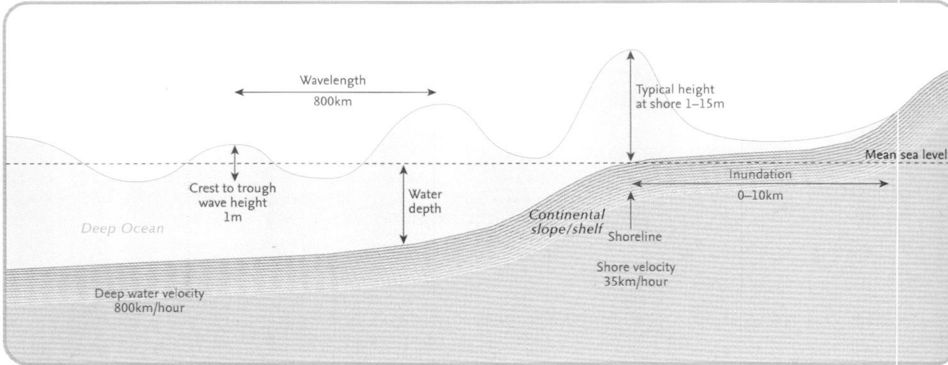

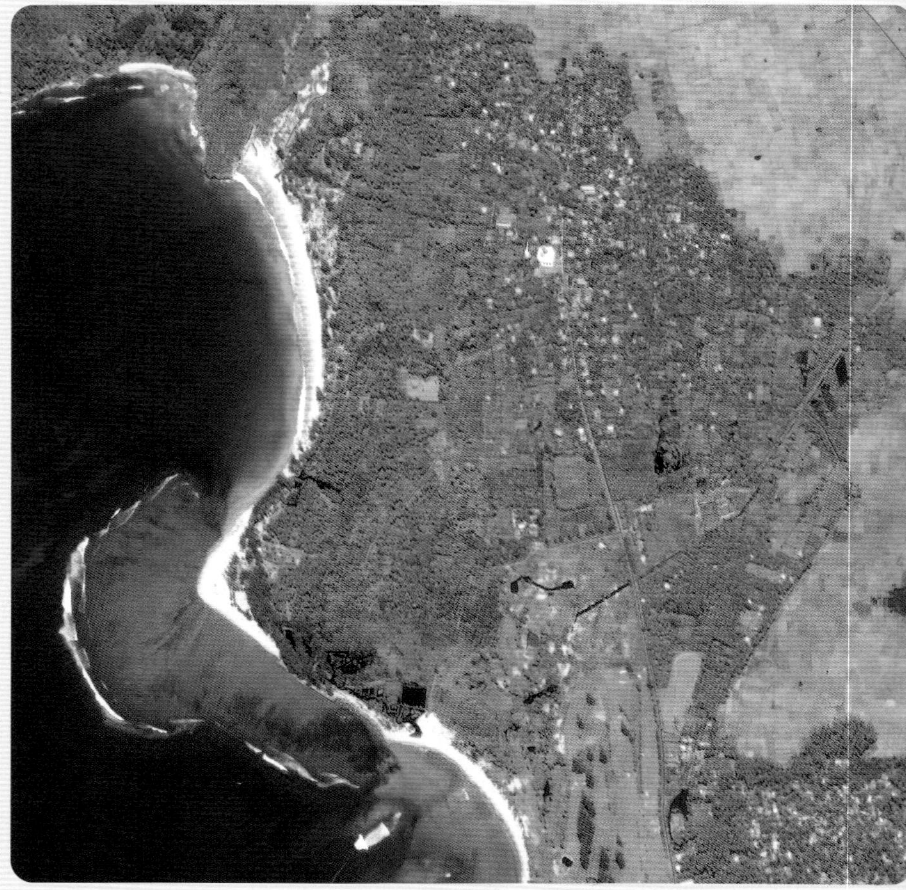

The Indian Ocean tsunami of 26 December 2004, caused by a major earthquake – the world's fourth largest since 1900 – off the coast of Sumatra, Indonesia, was one of the world's most dramatic and devastating natural disasters. With a final death toll likely to be over 250 000 across twelve countries, and billions of dollars worth of damage in coastal areas around the Indian Ocean, it had a major global impact.

Earthquakes are common in this region. The Sunda Trench is an active geological fault zone marking the boundary between two of the earth's major tectonic plates - the Indo-Australian Plate and the Eurasian Plate (and smaller sub-divisions of it). Although earthquakes are frequent, tsunamis resulting from them are relatively rare. It was the magnitude of this earthquake (measured as 9.0 on the Richter Scale) and the specific movement of the seafloor which it caused, which led to this being such a destructive event. Numerous communities were destroyed and it will take many years for the areas affected to recover.

Earthquake activity in Sumatra region

Map labels: MYANMAR (BURMA), EURASIAN PLATE, THAILAND, INDIAN OCEAN, RANGOON (Yangôn), Andaman Islands, North Andaman, Narcondam Island, Middle Andaman, Barren Island, South Andaman, Andaman Basin, INDIA, SUNDA PLATE, Little Andaman, BURMA MICROPLATE, ANDAMAN SEA, Car Nicobar, THAILAND, Phuket, Nicobar Islands, Little Nicobar, Great Nicobar, Strait of Malacca, MALAYSIA, Pulau We, Banda Aceh, Silawaih Agam, Gunung Peuetsagu, Gunung Geureudong, INDO-AUSTRALIAN PLATE, Sumatra, Kembar, Sibayak, Smahung, Simeulue, Toba, Amun, Helatoba-Tarutung, Lubukraya, Sunda Trench, Nias, Sibualbuali, INDONESIA, Sorikmarapi

☆ Main Shock – 26 December 2004

Earthquakes to 26 February 2005
- · < 4.0
- ○ 4.0–4.4
- ○ 4.5–4.9
- ○ 5.0–5.4
- ○ 5.5–5.9
- ○ 6.0–6.4
- ○ 6.5–6.9
- ● ≥ 7.0

magnitude

△ Volcanoes
⊥ Thrust fault
⊣ Normal fault
≡ Strike-slip fault
— Other fault

Causes of the tsunami

The most dangerous types of boundary between tectonic plates are those along subduction zones, where one plate (in this case the Indo-Australian Plate) is forced under another (here the Burma microplate, part of the larger Eurasian Plate). Great pressure builds up over centuries as the plates converge. This pressure is released by the overlying plate slipping back into position when the rocks can no longer bear the pressure. In the Sumatran earthquake, it is estimated that the overriding Burma microplate shifted vertically by up to 13 metres (43 feet), along a distance of over 500 kilometres (310 miles). This vertical movement caused the sea to rise above the fault line, triggering the tsunami which then rapidly spread across the whole width of the Indian Ocean, reaching the coast of Somalia, over 5 000 kilometres (3 100 miles) away, seven hours after the earthquake.

Cross-section of the tsunami

Diagram labels: Wavelength 800km, Typical height at shore 1–15m, Mean sea level, Crest to trough wave height 1m, Water depth, Continental slope/shelf, Shoreline, Inundation 0–10km, Deep Ocean, Deep water velocity 800km/hour, Shore velocity 35km/hour

This satellite image captured in January 2003 shows the town of Lhoknga, in **Aceh Province**, near the provincial capital of Banda Aceh, on the Indonesian island of Sumatra. The surrounding area appears lush and well cultivated, with pristine beaches either side of the central headland.

Tsunami travel times
Time taken for tsunami to travel across Indian Ocean (hours)

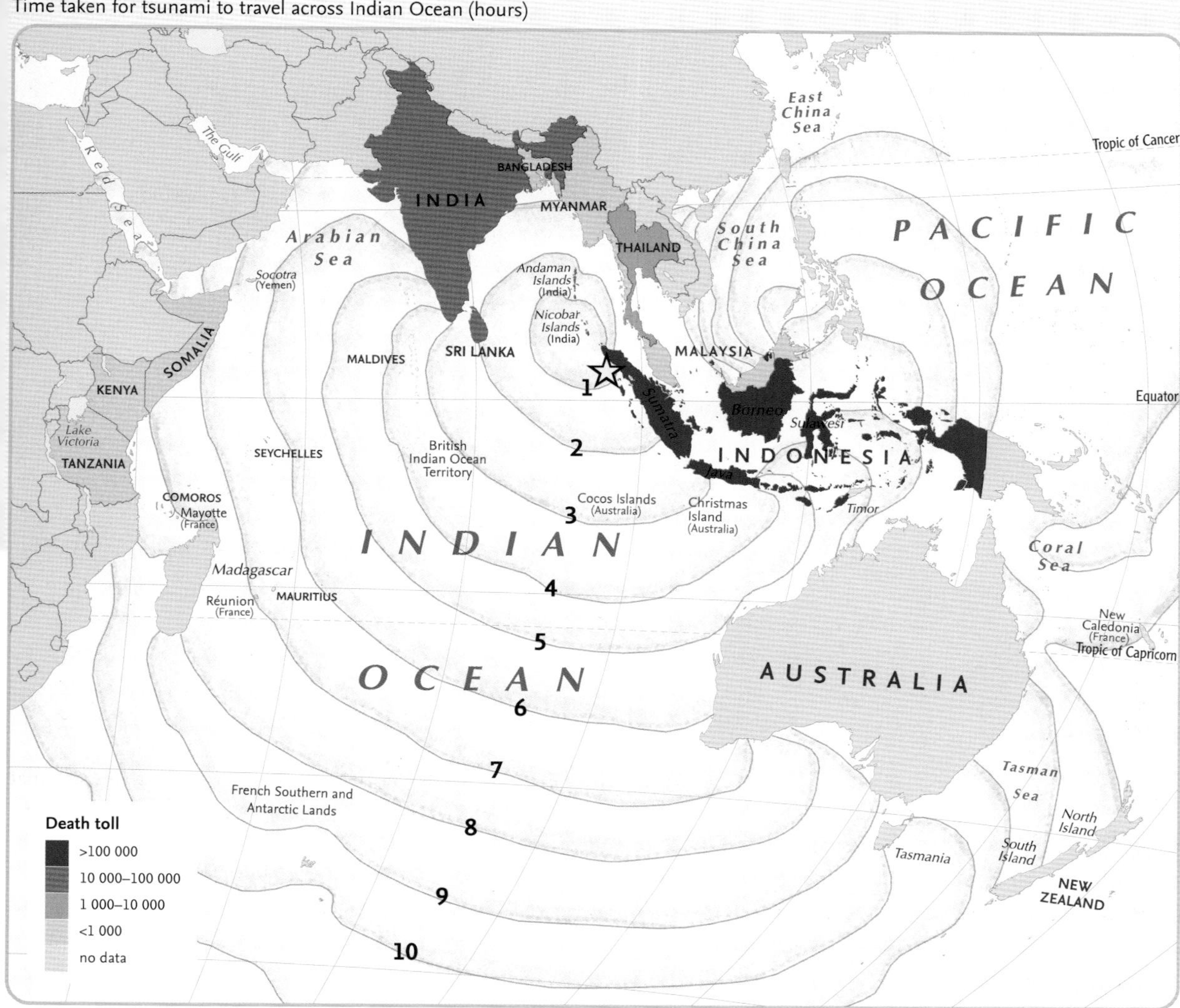

Death toll
- >100 000
- 10 000–100 000
- 1 000–10 000
- <1 000
- no data

Want to know more?

►	World earthquakes and volcanoes	10–11
►	Asia landscapes	60–61
►	Map of Sumatra	76–77
►	The oceans – image of the ocean floor	210–211
►	Map of the Indian Ocean	218–219

Internet links

News on the tsunami aftermath	news.bbc.co.uk
National (US) Earthquake Information Center	neic.usgs.gov
International Tsunami Information Center	www.prh.noaa.gov/itic
Tsunami research	walrus.wr.usgs.gov/tsunami
Asian Regional Information Center	aric.adb.org/asiantsunami

Facts

Citizens of 55 different countries were killed by the tsunami.

Subsequent analyses of the earthquake data suggest that the magnitude of the earthquake causing the tsunami was 9.3, which would make it the second most powerful quake since 1900.

Earthquakes are not the only cause of tsunamis – they can also be triggered by underwater landslides and volcanic activity.

The Indo-Australian Plate is moving towards the Eurasian Plate at an average rate of approximately 68 millimetres (2.5 inches) per year.

The Tsunami Warning System in the Pacific monitors seismological and tidal stations throughout the Pacific Basin. World leaders have pledged to set up an Indian Ocean early warning system.

When Krakatau erupted in 1883 the resultant tsunami claimed around 33 000 lives, around 90 per cent of the total death toll from the eruption.

Effects of the tsunami

Tsunami of this size travel at great speed in the open ocean, in this case at over 800 kilometres (500 miles) per hour. In deep ocean water, the wave itself may seem small and insignificant, with wave heights of only 1 metre (3 feet) greater than normal. However, as such waves reach shallower water their speed decreases but their height increases dramatically to create highly destructive waves which can be over 15 metres (50 feet) high.

The local coastal topography, and shape of the sea bed influences the final effect, but the forces involved are enormous and it was the force of the water over vast areas – stretching many kilometres inland in some areas, and washing completely over smaller islands in others – which caused such widespread destruction and tragic loss of life.

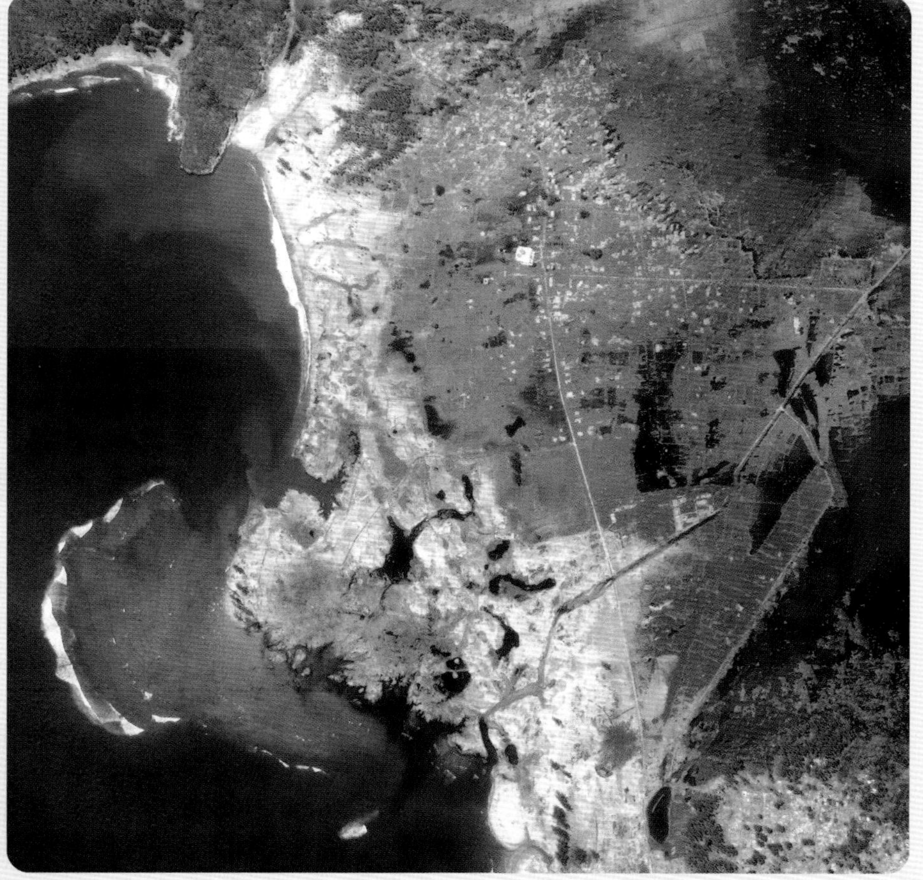

This equivalent image, captured three days after the tsunami shows the **extent of the destruction** in this region. The town has been completely destroyed, apart from the mosque in its centre. Beaches have been washed away, as has most of the areas vegetation. Water still stands inland on low-lying agricultural land.

Tsunami death tolls
Estimated death tolls by country (April 2005)

1	Indonesia	126 915
2	Sri Lanka	31 000
3	India	10 629
4	Thailand	5 300
5	Somalia	200
6	Maldives	82
7	Malaysia	68
8	Myanmar	61
9	Tanzania	10
10	Bangladesh	2
11	Kenya	1
12	Seychelles	1

Official aid donations
Top 10 donors of tsunami aid (US$)

1	Australia	764 000 000 (over 5 years)
2	Germany	647 000 000 (over 3 years)
3	Japan	500 000 000
4	USA	350 000 000
5	Canada	343 000 000
6	Norway	183 000 000
7	UK	96 000 000
8	Italy	95 000 000
9	China	83 000 000
10	Sweden	80 000 000

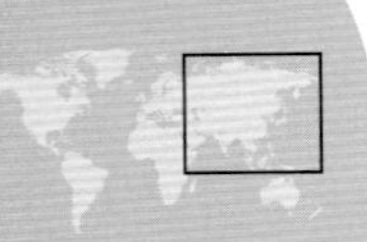

Many parts of Asia have a long history of instability. As well as the current high profile conflict in Iraq, many areas across the continent are witnessing disputes over territory, ideology, religion, political control and independence, ethnicity or resources. Afghanistan, China-Japan, China-Taiwan, Japan-South Korea, the Caucasus region, Indonesia and the South China Sea are all areas experiencing active disputes. One of the most complex, long-running, and seemingly intractable conflicts is that between Israel and the Palestinians. This involves several of the factors mentioned above and has affected millions of people in Israel, Palestine and the surrounding countries. Wealth and resources are often underlying causes of tension. One of the most contentious resources, and one which is increasingly likely to cause conflict, is water. The scarcity of water in generally arid regions can directly cause disputes or, in already unstable regions, can fuel existing conflicts and animosities.

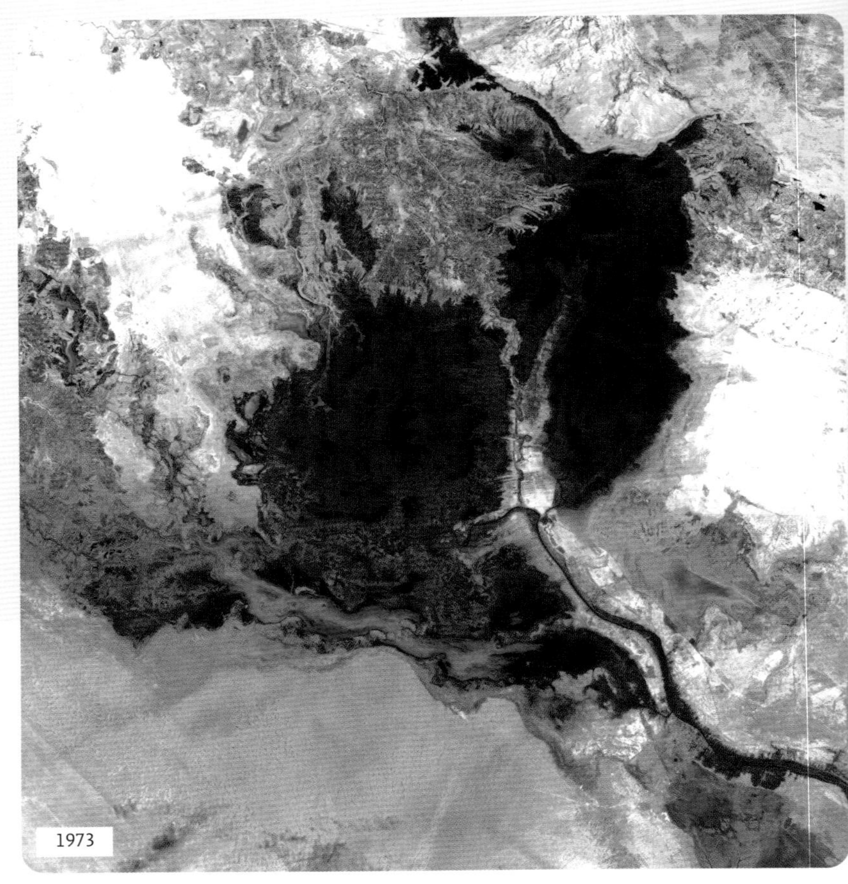

1973

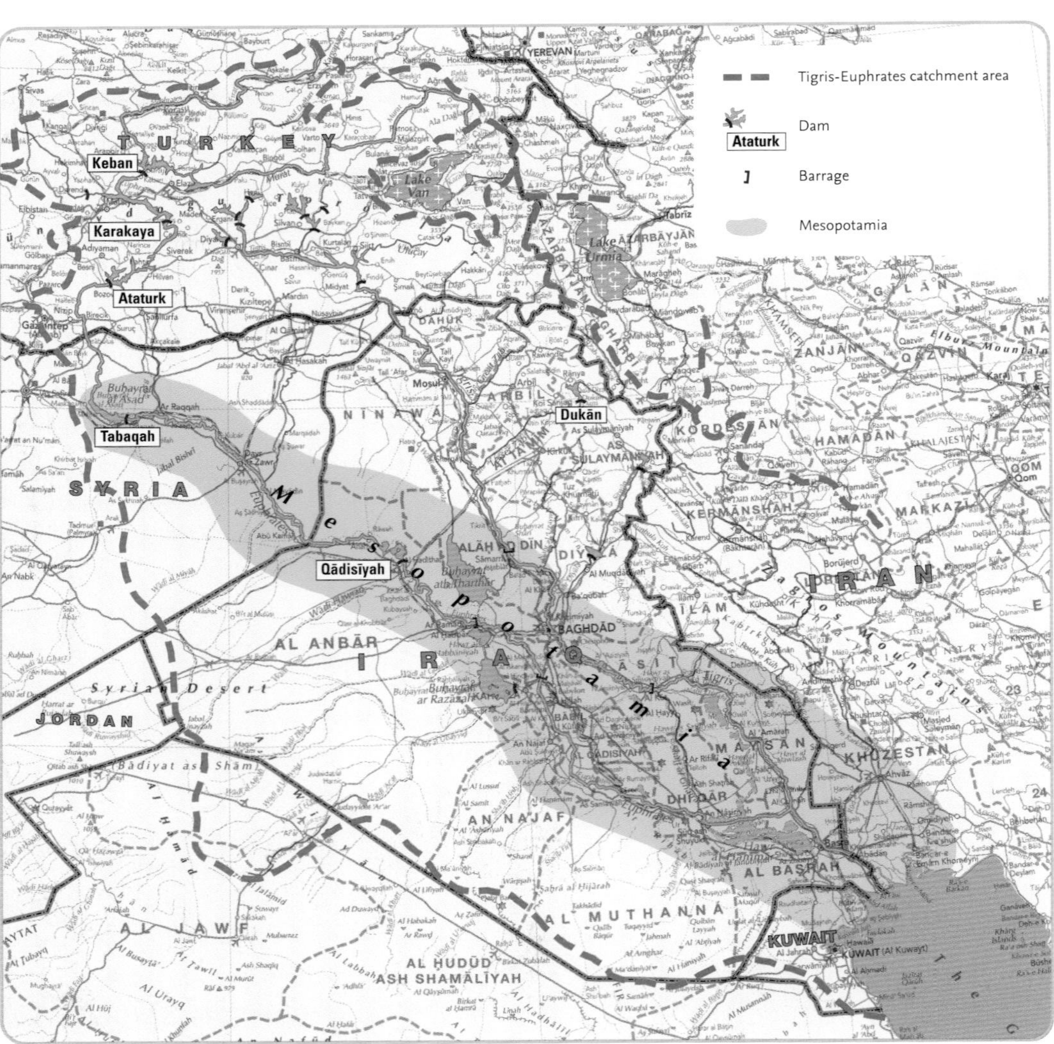

Water resources

As demand for water steadily increases, the potential for international disputes over its use also rises. Irrigation and extraction of water for power and industry put great strain on limited resources and immediately affect the areas further downstream. The flow in several major Asian rivers, including the Yellow river and the Jordan, has been severely reduced in recent years, The Tigris and Euphrates rivers, which originate in Turkey, have been important sources of water since the times of the ancient civilizations of Mesopotamia. They continue to be vital for Iraq and the countries where the majority of their water is generated – Turkey and Syria. Numerous dams have been built along these rivers, particularly in Turkey, which affect the volume and flow of water through Syria and Iraq. Many attempts have been made to formulate treaties between these nations but the issue remains a source of tension. The problems of water supply in Iraq have been complicated by major irrigation schemes which have drained large areas of environmentally sensitive marshland.

Top 20 water withdrawals
Annual water usage as a percentage of renewable water resources

	country	per cent
1	Kuwait	3 097
2	United Arab Emirates	1 614
3	Saudi Arabia	955
4	Libya	801
5	Oman	181
6	Jordan	151
7	Uzbekistan	132
8	Egypt	127
9	Yemen	123
10	Turkmenistan	116
11	Israel	108
12	Pakistan	100
13	Tajikistan	81
14	Iraq	80
15	Afghanistan	72
16	Iran	59
17	Azerbaijan	58
18	Bulgaria	58
19	Syria	55
20	Kyrgyzstan	55

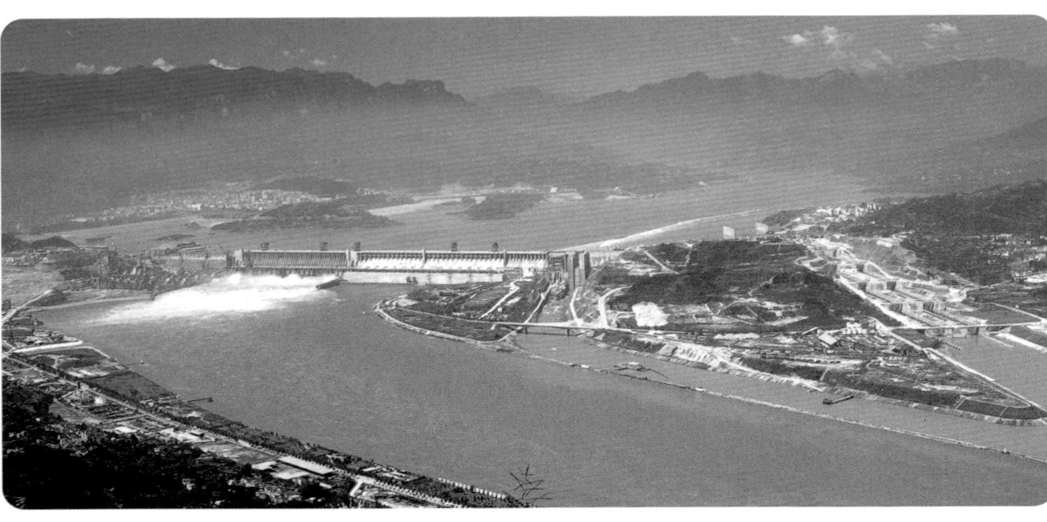

Aerial view of the **Three Gorges Dam** on the Yangtze river in China. This project, due for final completion in 2009, is the world's largest hydro-electric power scheme. The reservoir created is over 600 kilometres (373 miles) long. The project has raised many environmental and political issues, including the forced relocation of between 1–2 million people.

2000

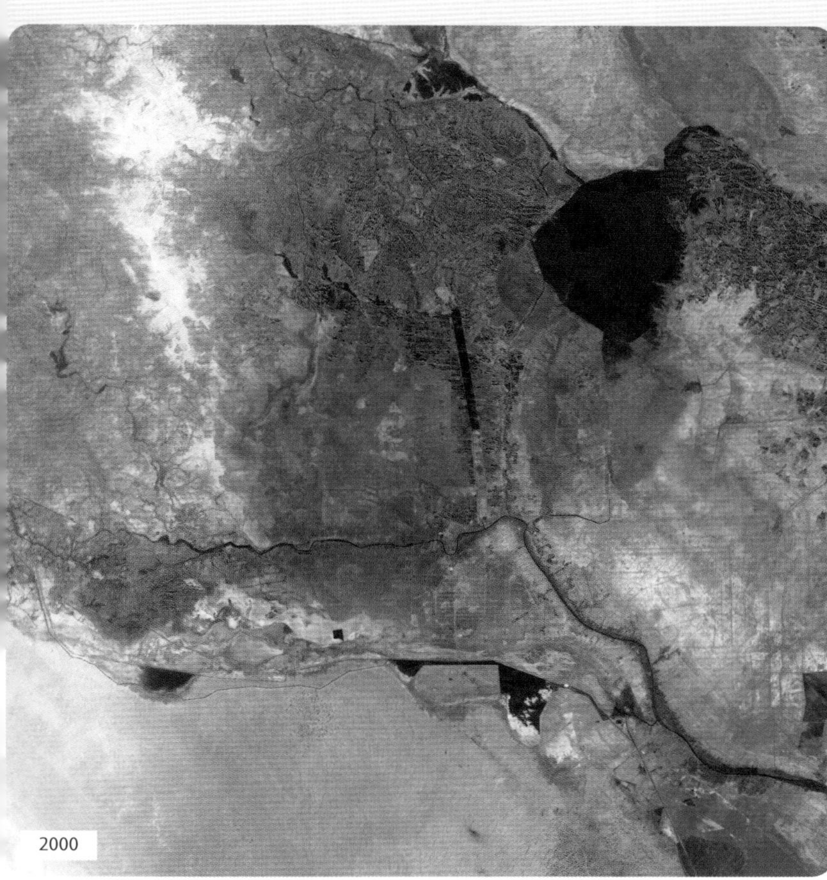

These two satellite images of the Mesopotamian marshes, are centred on the confluence of the **Tigris** and **Euphrates** rivers in south-eastern Iraq. In the left image, from 1973, are large areas of dense marsh vegetation (red) and areas of standing water (blue).

In the later image, from 2000, vast areas of former marshland now appear as grey – identifying them as areas of sparse vegetation or bare ground. It is estimated that only 7 per cent of these valuable wetlands remain after systematic drainage of the area and upstream diversion of the Tigris and Euphrates.

Want to know more?	
▶ World political map	8–9
▶ World conflicts	26–27
▶ Map of Iraq	106–107
▶ Map of the Middle East	108–109
▶ Images of the shrinking Lake Chad	112–113

Internet links	
Palestinian refugees	www.un.org/unrwa
International boundary information	www-ibru.dur.ac.ac
Wateraid	www.wateraid.org.uk
Three Gorges Dam Project	civcal.media.hku.hk/ threegorges

Facts
The unemployment rate in Gaza is estimated to be nearly 50 per cent, compared to a rate of 9 per cent in Israel.
Immigration of Jews into Israel, and the building of new Jewish settlements in the occupied territories, have been actively encouraged by the Israeli government.
The level of the Dead Sea has dropped by over 16 metres (53 feet) in the last 30 years through extraction of water for agriculture and industry.
The UN have estimated that 7 billion people could be short of water by the year 2050.

The Middle East conflict

The Israeli/Palestinian conflict reflects decades of unrest in Palestine which, after the First World War, was under British control. In 1947 the United Nations (UN) proposed the creation of separate Jewish and Arab states – a plan which was rejected by the Palestinians and the Arab states in the region. When Britain withdrew in 1948, Israel declared its independence. This led to a war in which Israel gained more territory, and during which hundreds of thousands of Palestinians were forced out of their homeland and became refugees. In the Six Day War in 1967, Israel took possession of Sinai and Gaza from Egypt, West Bank from Jordan, and the Golan Heights from Syria. These territories (except Sinai) remain occupied by Israel – one of the main reasons for the Palestinian uprising or 'Intifada'. The situation remains complex, and it remains to be seen whether mutually acceptable independent states can be established.

Middle East politics

Changing international boundaries in Israel and Palestine since 1922.

West Bank
Security
18 per cent of land under Palestinian control
23 per cent of land under Palestinian civil control and joint security control
59 per cent of land under Israeli control

West Bank
Population
97 per cent Palestinian Arab
610 000 refugees

Gaza
Security
60 per cent of land under Palestinian control
40 per cent of land under Israeli control or settlement

Gaza
Population
98 per cent Palestinian Arab
865 000 refugees

-·-·- International boundary
-×-×- Disputed International boundary
········ Ceasefire line
━━━ British Mandate Boundary 1922-1948
━━━ Israel Boundary 1948

▨ Land occupied by Israel 1967

Jenin □ Main Palestinian towns

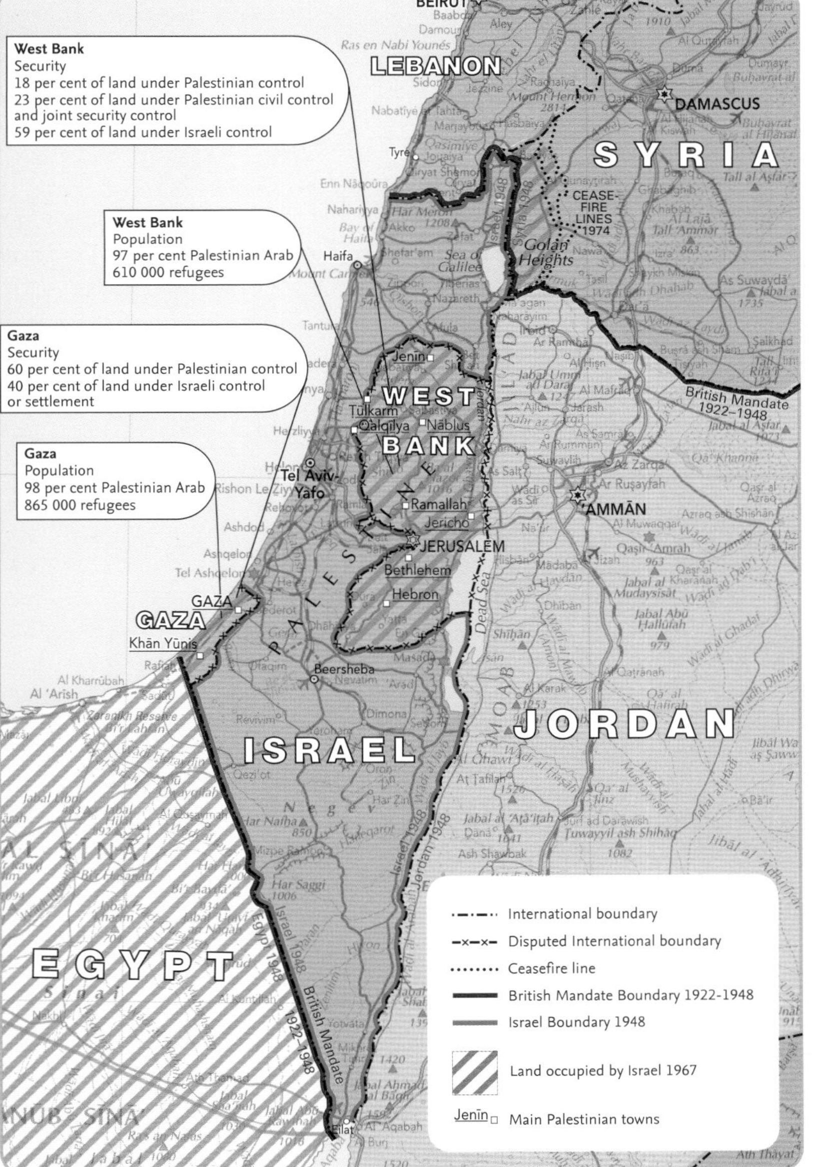

Israel-Palestine comparisons	Israel	Palestinian Occupied Territories
Population	6 725 000	3 837 914
Projected population 2050	10 403 000	10 058 000
Total fertility (number of children per woman)	2.9	5.6
Total GNI (Million US$)	105 160	3 582
GNI per capita (US$)	16 020	1 110
Child (under-5) mortality rate (per 1000 live births)	6	24
Doctors per 100 000 people	375	84
Unemployment (per cent)	10.7	25.6

Palestinian refugees in the Middle East country	number of refugees
West Bank	683 000
Gaza	952 000
Lebanon	399 000
Syria	422 000
Jordan	1 777 000

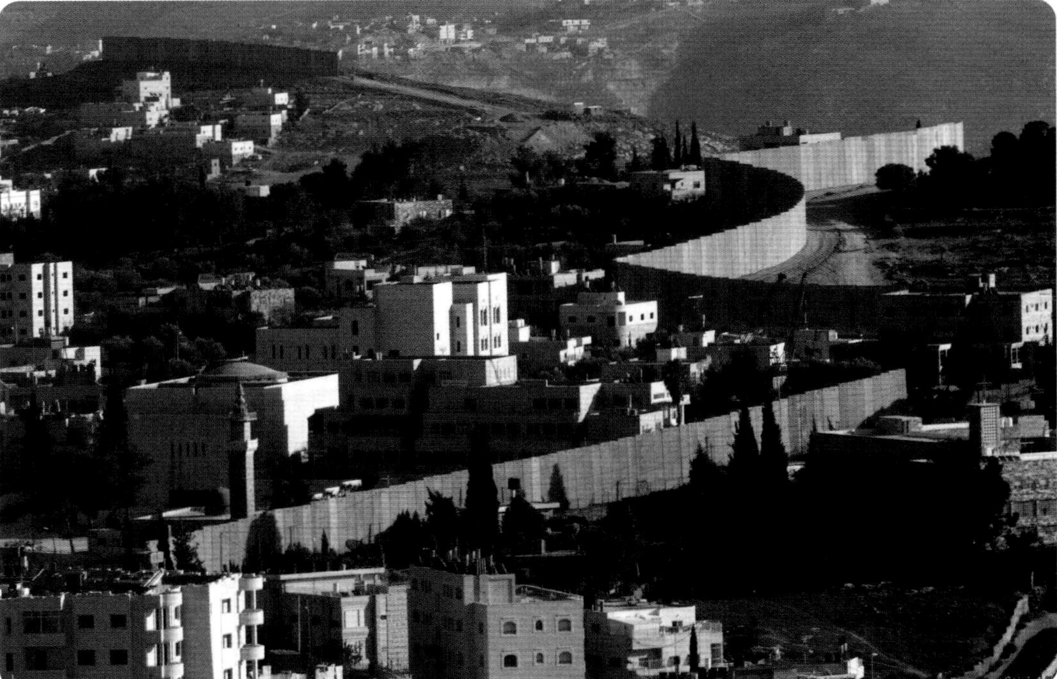

A section of the highly controversial **security barrier** being built by Israel around the West Bank. Ruled illegal by the International Court of Justice, the wall often separates Palestinians from their own land, greatly restricts movement, and in some areas encroaches into the West Bank beyond its boundary with Israel.

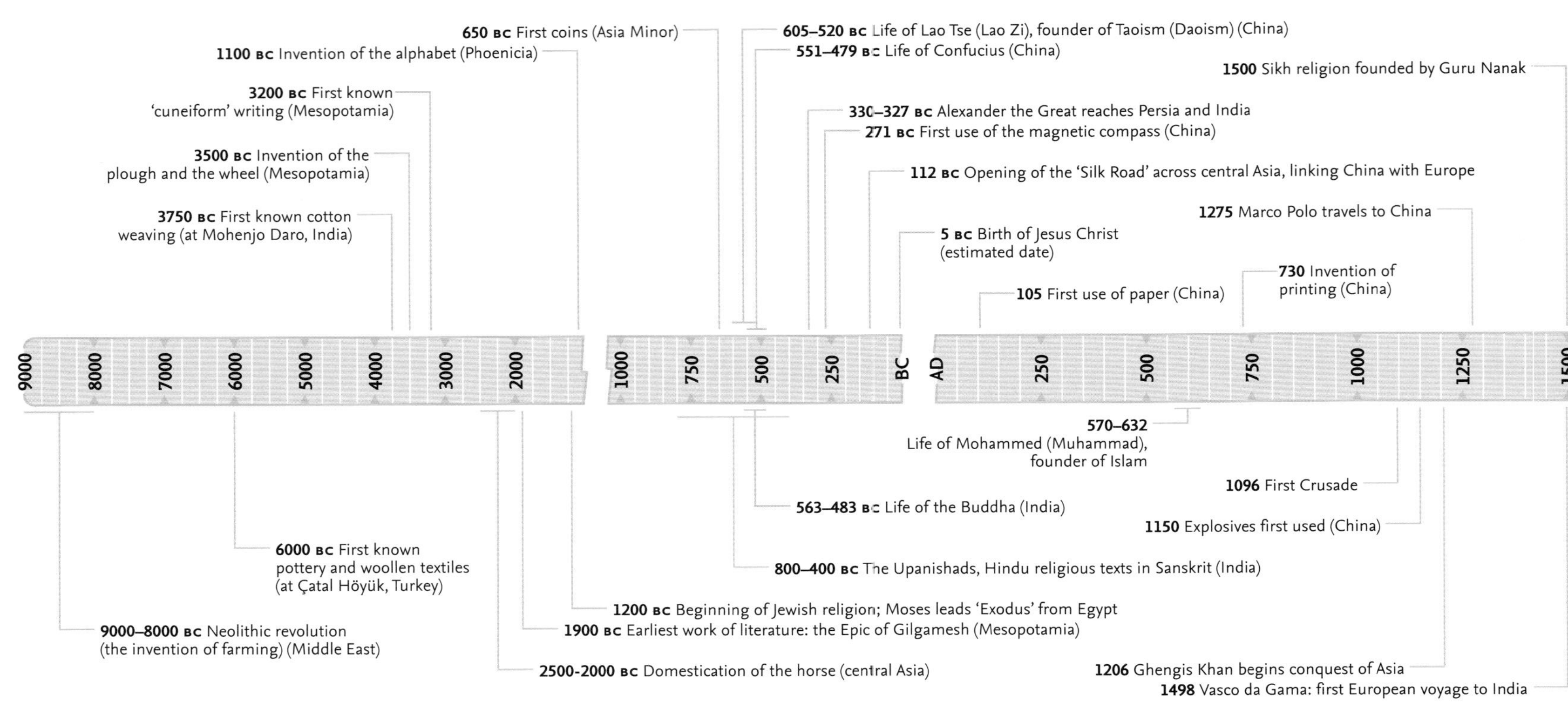

9000 BC Invention of farming

Timeline labels:
- 3750 BC First known cotton weaving (at Mohenjo Daro, India)
- 3500 BC Invention of the plough and the wheel (Mesopotamia)
- 3200 BC First known 'cuneiform' writing (Mesopotamia)
- 1100 BC Invention of the alphabet (Phoenicia)
- 650 BC First coins (Asia Minor)
- 605–520 BC Life of Lao Tse (Lao Zi), founder of Taoism (Daoism) (China)
- 551–479 BC Life of Confucius (China)
- 1500 Sikh religion founded by Guru Nanak
- 330–327 BC Alexander the Great reaches Persia and India
- 271 BC First use of the magnetic compass (China)
- 112 BC Opening of the 'Silk Road' across central Asia, linking China with Europe
- 1275 Marco Polo travels to China
- 5 BC Birth of Jesus Christ (estimated date)
- 730 Invention of printing (China)
- 105 First use of paper (China)
- 6000 BC First known pottery and woollen textiles (at Çatal Höyük, Turkey)
- 570–632 Life of Mohammed (Muhammad), founder of Islam
- 1096 First Crusade
- 563–483 BC Life of the Buddha (India)
- 1150 Explosives first used (China)
- 800–400 BC The Upanishads, Hindu religious texts in Sanskrit (India)
- 9000–8000 BC Neolithic revolution (the invention of farming) (Middle East)
- 1200 BC Beginning of Jewish religion; Moses leads 'Exodus' from Egypt
- 1900 BC Earliest work of literature: the Epic of Gilgamesh (Mesopotamia)
- 2500-2000 BC Domestication of the horse (central Asia)
- 1206 Ghengis Khan begins conquest of Asia
- 1498 Vasco da Gama: first European voyage to India

	Population							Economy					
	total population	population change (%)	urban population (%)	total fertility	population by age 0-14 (%)	60+ (%)	2050 projected population	total Gross National Income (GNI) (US$M)	Gross National Income (GNI) per capita (US$)	debt service ratio (% GNI)	total debt service (US$)	aid receipts (% GNI)	military spending (% GDP)
World	**6 464 750 000**	1.2	48.3	2.7	28.2	10.4	9 075 903 000	34 491 458	5 500	...	...	...	2.4
Afghanistan	29 863 000	4.6	23.3	7.5	46.5	4.4	97 324 000	...	...	...	...	...	...
Armenia	3 016 000	-0.4	64.4	1.3	20.8	14.5	2 506 000	2 910	950	3.0	74 200 000	12.0	2.7
Azerbaijan	8 411 000	0.7	50.0	1.9	25.8	9.2	9 631 000	6 709	810	3.2	186 700 000	6.0	2.1
Bahrain	727 000	1.6	90.0	2.5	27.1	4.5	1 155 000	7 569	11 260	...	...	1.0	3.9
Bangladesh	141 822 000	1.9	24.2	3.3	35.5	5.7	242 937 000	54 587	400	1.5	722 200 000	1.8	1.1
Bhutan	2 163 000	2.2	8.5	4.4	38.4	7.0	4 393 000	578	660	1.2	6 400 000	13.7	...
Brunei	374 000	2.3	76.2	2.5	29.6	4.7	681 000	...	...	...	...	...	7.0
Cambodia	14 071 000	2.0	18.6	4.1	37.1	5.6	25 972 000	4 105	310	0.5	21 000 000	12.7	2.7
China	1 323 345 000	0.7	38.6	1.7	21.4	10.9	1 402 062 000	1 417 301	1 100	2.4	30 615 799 808	0.1	2.5
Cyprus	835 000	1.2	69.2	1.6	19.9	16.8	1 174 000	9 373	12 320	...	...	...	2.1
East Timor	947 000	5.4	7.6	7.8	41.1	5.0	3 265 000	351	430	...	...	58.3	...
Georgia	4 474 000	-1.1	51.9	1.5	18.9	17.9	2 985 000	3 780	830	3.9	128 800 000	9.4	0.6
India	1 103 371 000	1.6	28.3	3.1	32.1	7.9	1 592 704 000	567 605	530	2.6	13 127 600 128	0.3	2.6
Indonesia	222 781 000	1.3	45.6	2.4	28.3	8.4	284 640 000	172 733	810	10.3	16 971 100 160	0.8	1.1
Iran	69 515 000	0.9	66.7	2.1	28.7	6.4	101 944 000	132 896	2 000	1.3	1 460 400 000	0.1	4.8
Iraq	28 807 000	2.8	67.2	4.8	41.0	4.5	63 693 000	...	...	...	...	...	...
Israel	6 725 000	2.0	91.6	2.9	27.8	13.3	10 403 000	105 160	16 020	...	...	...	8.6
Japan	128 085 000	0.2	65.4	1.3	14.0	26.3	112 198 000	4 389 791	34 510	...	...	...	1.0
Jordan	5 703 000	2.7	79.0	3.5	37.2	5.1	10 225 000	9 800	1 850	6.3	584 899 968	5.6	8.4
Kazakhstan	14 825 000	-0.3	55.8	2.0	23.1	11.3	13 086 000	26 535	1 780	17.4	4 115 300 096	0.8	0.9
Kuwait	2 687 000	3.7	96.3	2.4	24.3	3.1	5 279 000	38 037	16 340	...	...	...	11.2
Kyrgyzstan	5 264 000	1.2	33.9	2.7	31.5	7.6	6 664 000	1 649	330	11.2	172 800 000	12.0	1.7
Laos	5 924 000	2.3	20.7	4.8	40.9	5.3	11 586 000	1 821	320	2.6	44 600 000	16.2	2.1
Lebanon	3 577 000	1.0	87.5	2.3	28.6	10.3	4 702 000	18 187	4 040	12.2	2 187 699 968	2.5	4.7
Malaysia	25 347 000	2.0	63.9	2.9	32.4	7.0	38 924 000	93 683	3 780	9.1	8 081 999 872	0.1	2.1
Maldives	329 000	2.5	28.8	4.3	40.7	5.1	682 000	674	2 300	3.7	22 100 000	4.6	...
Mongolia	2 646 000	1.2	56.7	2.5	30.5	5.7	3 625 000	1 188	480	4.7	52 400 000	18.6	2.3
Myanmar	50 519 000	1.1	29.4	2.5	29.5	7.5	63 657 000	...	...	...	113 300 000	...	2.3
Nepal	27 133 000	2.1	15.0	3.7	39.0	5.8	51 172 000	5 824	240	1.8	98 000 000	6.7	1.4
North Korea	22 488 000	0.6	61.1	2.0	25.0	11.2	24 192 000	...	...	...	...	...	...
Oman	2 567 000	1.0	77.6	3.8	34.5	4.2	4 958 000	19 877	7 830	8.8	1 748 099 968	0.2	13.0
Pakistan	157 935 000	2.0	34.1	4.3	38.3	5.8	304 700 000	69 236	470	4.8	2 844 100 096	3.6	4.5
Palau	20 000	0.7	68.6	...	...	...	21 000	150	7 500	...	...	21.2	...
Philippines	83 054 000	1.8	61.0	3.2	35.1	6.1	127 068 000	87 771	1 080	11.1	9 191 999 488	0.7	1.0
Qatar	813 000	5.9	92.0	3.0	21.7	2.6	1 330 000	...	...	...	...	...	...
Russian Federation	143 202 000	-0.5	73.3	1.3	15.3	17.1	111 752 000	374 937	2 610	4.2	14 330 099 712	...	4.0
Saudi Arabia	24 573 000	2.7	87.7	4.1	37.3	4.6	49 464 000	186 776	8 530	...	...	0.0	11.3
Singapore	4 326 000	1.5	100.0	1.4	19.5	12.2	5 213 000	90 229	21 230	...	...	...	5.2
South Korea	47 817 000	0.4	80.3	1.2	18.6	13.7	44 629 000	576 426	12 020	...	...	...	2.7
Sri Lanka	20 743 000	0.9	21.0	2.0	24.1	10.7	23 554 000	17 846	930	4.4	715 900 032	2.1	3.9
Syria	19 043 000	2.5	50.1	3.5	36.9	4.7	35 935 000	20 211	1 160	1.4	258 200 000	0.4	6.1
Taiwan	22 858 000	0.4	...	...	19.8	9.2	...	...	...	...	...	...	...
Tajikistan	6 507 000	1.1	24.7	3.8	39.0	5.1	10 423 000	1 221	190	7.0	79 200 000	14.8	1.2
Thailand	64 233 000	0.9	31.9	1.9	23.8	10.5	74 594 000	136 063	2 190	15.8	19 737 800 704	0.2	1.4
Turkey	73 193 000	1.4	66.3	2.5	29.2	8.0	101 208 000	197 220	2 790	15.2	27 604 400 128	0.2	5.0
Turkmenistan	4 833 000	1.4	45.3	2.8	31.8	6.2	6 780 000	5 426	1 120	...	...	0.9	3.8
United Arab Emirates	4 496 000	6.5	85.1	2.5	22.0	1.6	9 056 000	...	...	...	...	...	2.5
Uzbekistan	26 593 000	1.5	36.6	2.7	33.2	6.2	38 665 000	10 779	420	7.7	733 000 000	2.0	1.1
Vietnam	84 238 000	1.4	25.7	2.3	29.5	7.5	116 654 000	38 786	480	3.4	1 180 999 936	3.6	...
Yemen	20 975 000	3.1	25.6	6.2	46.4	3.6	59 454 000	9 894	520	1.9	171 200 000	6.3	4.5

Want to know more?

▶ World's largest countries	8–9
▶ Cities of over 10 million people	18–19
▶ Guide to Asia's countries	64–65
▶ The Middle East conflict	68–69

Internet links

Asian Development Bank	www.adb.org
Asia-Pacific Economic Cooperation	www.apecsec.org.sg
Association of Southeast Asian Nations	www.aseansec.org
International Boundaries Research Unit	www.ibru.dur.ac.uk

Facts

The world's largest statue of a sitting Buddha is in the Sichuan province of China. It is carved in stone and is 72 metres (236 feet) high.

The Trans-Siberian railway, between Moscow and Vladivostok, is the longest continuous railway line in the world at 9 288 kilometres (5 772 miles) long.

Erech (Uruk) in modern-day Iraq, which is mentioned in the Epic of Gilgamesh, thought to have been written about 1900 BC, is thought to be the world's first city.

Timeline (1890–2000)

- **1891–1905** Trans-Siberian Railway crosses Asia
- **1911** Chinese revolution under Sun Yat-sen
- **1917** Balfour Declaration promises a Jewish homeland in Palestine
- **1920** Gandhi starts non-cooperation movement in India
- **1947** Partition of India and creation of Pakistan
- **2003** Invasion of Iraq by US-led coalition
- **1997** Kyoto global warming agreement
- **1980–1988** Iran-Iraq War
- **1979** Fall of the Shah of Iran and establishment of Islamic republic
- **1976** Tangshan earthquake (China), worst of the 20th century, over 250 000 killed
- **1974** Turkish invasion of northern Cyprus
- **1959–1975** Vietnam War
- **1949** Communist victory in China
- **1941** Japan enters Second World War
- **1945** Atom bombs dropped on Hiroshima and Nagasaki
- **1948** Britain withdraws from Palestine. Foundation of Israel
- **1950–1953** Korean War, leading to partition
- **1966** The 'Cultural Revolution' in China
- **1967** 'Six-Day War' between Israel and Egypt
- **1971** Bangladesh splits from Pakistan
- **1975–1978** Khmer Rouge atrocities in Cambodia
- **1990–1991** Iraqi invasion of Kuwait
- **1997** Hong Kong returned to China
- **2001** Overthrow of the Taliban government in Afghanistan
- **2004** Indian Ocean tsunami, most lethal earthquake since the 16th century, over 250 000 killed

	Social indicators						Environment				Communications					
child mortality rate	life expectancy male	life expectancy female	literacy rate (%)	access to safe water (%)	doctors per 100 000 people	forest area (%)	annual change in forest area (%)	protected land area (%)	CO₂ emissions (metric tons per capita)	main telephone lines per 100 people	cellular mobile subscribers per 100 people	internet users per 10 000 people	international dialling code	time zone	
80	63.3	67.6	...	83	...	29.6	-0.2	11.4	3.8	18.8	21.9	1 125	...	...	World
257	43.0	43.3	...	13	...	2.1	...	0.3	0.0	0.1	0.1	...	93	+4.5	Afghanistan
33	69.0	75.6	99.8	92	287	12.4	1.3	10.1	1.1	14.8	3.0	526	374	+4	Armenia
91	68.7	75.5	...	77	359	13.1	1.3	4.6	3.6	11.4	10.7	369	994	+4	Azerbaijan
15	72.5	75.9	98.6	...	169	...	14.9	1.4	29.1	26.8	63.8	2 819	973	+3	Bahrain
69	61.0	61.8	52.1	75	23	10.2	1.3	0.5	0.2	0.6	1.0	18	880	+6	Bangladesh
85	62.0	64.5	...	62	5	64.2	...	30.2	0.5	3.6	1.1	204	975	+6	Bhutan
6	74.2	78.9	99.5	...	99	83.9	-0.2	56.2	14.1	25.6	40.1	1 023	673	+8	Brunei
140	55.2	59.5	80.1	34	16	52.9	-0.6	22.7	0.0	0.3	2.8	25	855	+7	Cambodia
37	68.9	73.3	98.2	77	164	17.5	1.2	11.8	2.2	20.9	21.4	632	86	+8	China
5	76.0	80.5	99.8	100	269	18.6	3.7	8.4	8.5	68.8	58.4	3 371	357	+2	Cyprus
124	48.7	50.4	...	52	...	34.3	-0.6	...	...	...	...	...	670	+9	East Timor
45	69.5	77.6	...	76	463	43.7	...	4.3	1.2	13.3	10.7	308	995	+3	Georgia
87	63.2	64.6	74.1	86	51	21.6	0.1	5.1	1.1	4.6	2.5	175	91	+5.5	India
41	64.8	68.8	98.0	78	16	58.0	-1.2	13.6	1.3	3.7	5.5	376	62	+7 to +9	Indonesia
39	68.9	71.9	94.8	93	110	4.5	...	6.5	4.9	22.0	5.1	724	98	+3.5	Iran
125	59.2	62.3	45.3	81	...	1.8	...	0.0	3.3	2.8	0.1	10	964	+3	Iraq
6	77.1	81.0	99.5	100	375	6.4	4.9	22.3	10.0	45.3	95.5	3 014	972	+2	Israel
4	77.9	85.1	...	100	202	64.0	...	14.0	9.3	55.8	68.0	4 827	81	+9	Japan
28	69.7	72.5	99.5	91	205	1.0	...	10.9	3.2	11.4	24.2	834	962	+2	Jordan
73	60.9	71.9	...	86	345	4.5	2.2	2.9	8.1	13.0	6.4	157	7	+4 to +6	Kazakhstan
9	74.9	79.0	93.1	...	160	0.3	3.5	0.0	21.9	19.8	57.8	2 308	965	+3	Kuwait
68	64.8	72.3	...	76	272	5.2	2.6	3.6	0.9	7.8	1.0	298	996	+5	Kyrgyzstan
91	53.3	55.8	73.3	43	61	54.4	-0.4	16.2	0.1	1.1	1.0	27	856	+7	Laos
31	71.9	75.1	95.6	100	274	3.5	-0.4	0.7	3.5	19.9	22.7	1 171	961	+2	Lebanon
7	70.8	75.7	97.9	95	68	58.7	-1.2	30.5	6.2	18.2	44.2	3 441	60	+8	Malaysia
72	67.8	67.0	99.2	84	78	3.3	...	...	1.8	10.2	14.9	534	960	+5	Maldives
68	61.9	65.9	99.6	62	278	6.8	-0.5	14.0	3.1	5.3	8.9	581	976	+8	Mongolia
107	54.6	60.2	91.4	80	30	52.3	-1.4	5.3	0.2	0.7	0.1	5	95	+6.5	Myanmar
82	60.1	59.6	62.8	84	5	27.3	-1.8	18.1	0.1	1.6	0.2	34	977	+5.75	Nepal
55	60.5	66.0	...	100	...	68.2	...	2.6	8.5	...	...	...	850	+9	North Korea
12	71.0	74.4	98.5	79	137	0.0	5.3	0.1	8.2	9.2	18.3	709	968	+4	Oman
103	61.2	60.9	58.7	90	68	3.1	-1.5	8.3	0.8	2.7	1.8	103	92	+5	Pakistan
28	...	...	...	84	...	76.1	...	0.0	12.7	...	...	...	680	+9	Palau
36	68.0	72.0	98.8	85	115	19.4	-1.4	8.2	1.0	4.2	19.1	440	63	+8	Philippines
15	70.5	75.4	95.3	100	220	0.1	9.6	0.0	69.5	28.9	59.0	1 974	974	+3	Qatar
21	60.8	73.1	99.8	96	420	50.4	...	7.6	9.9	24.2	12.0	409	7	+2 to +12	Russian Federation
26	71.1	73.7	93.6	90	153	0.7	...	41.8	18.1	15.5	32.1	666	966	+3	Saudi Arabia
3	75.9	80.3	99.8	100	140	3.3	...	5.2	14.7	46.3	79.6	5 088	65	+8	Singapore
5	71.8	79.3	99.8	92	180	63.3	-0.1	3.6	9.1	47.2	69.4	6 097	82	+9	South Korea
15	69.9	75.9	97.1	78	43	30.0	-1.6	26.5	0.6	4.7	4.9	117	94	+6	Sri Lanka
18	70.6	73.1	88.3	79	142	2.5	...	1.4	3.3	12.3	2.4	129	963	+2	Syria
...	73.4	79.1	...	...	...	58.1	...	8.2	...	59.0	110.8	3 906	886	+8	Taiwan
118	66.2	71.4	99.8	58	212	2.8	0.5	18.3	0.6	3.7	0.7	6	992	+5	Tajikistan
26	65.3	73.5	99.0	85	30	28.9	-0.7	15.6	3.3	10.6	26.0	1 105	66	+7	Thailand
39	68.0	73.2	96.9	93	123	13.3	0.2	2.6	3.3	27.7	40.8	805	90	+2	Turkey
102	63.9	70.4	...	71	300	8.0	...	4.2	7.5	7.7	0.2	17	993	+5	Turkmenistan
8	73.3	77.4	91.5	...	177	3.8	2.8	0.2	18.1	28.1	73.6	2 748	971	+4	United Arab Emirates
69	66.8	72.5	99.7	89	293	4.8	0.2	4.6	4.8	6.7	1.3	192	998	+5	Uzbekistan
23	66.9	71.6	97.3	73	54	30.2	0.5	4.2	0.7	5.4	3.4	430	84	+7	Vietnam
113	58.9	61.1	67.8	69	22	0.9	-1.9	0.0	0.5	2.8	2.1	51	967	+3	Yemen

See page 335 for explanatory table and sources

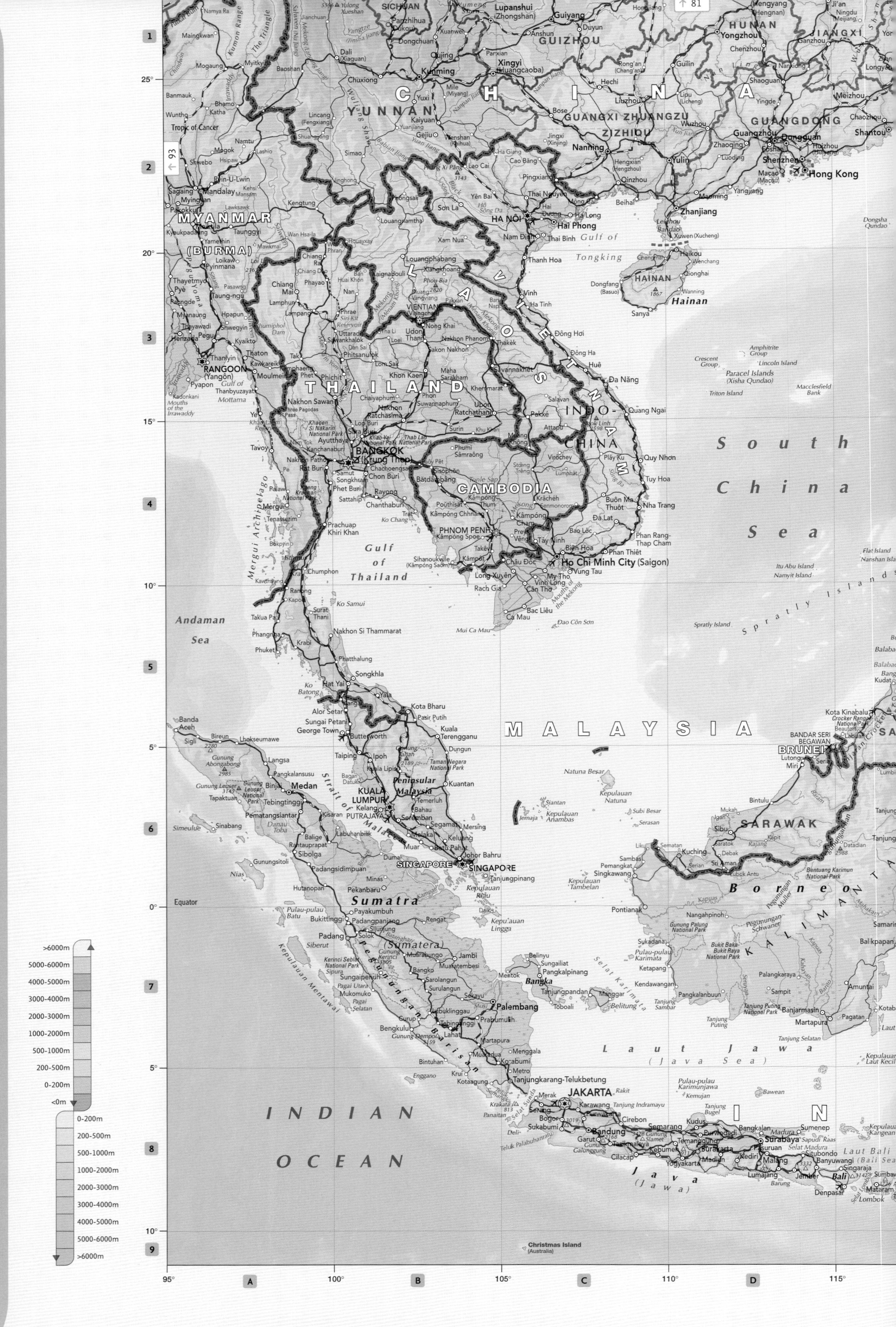

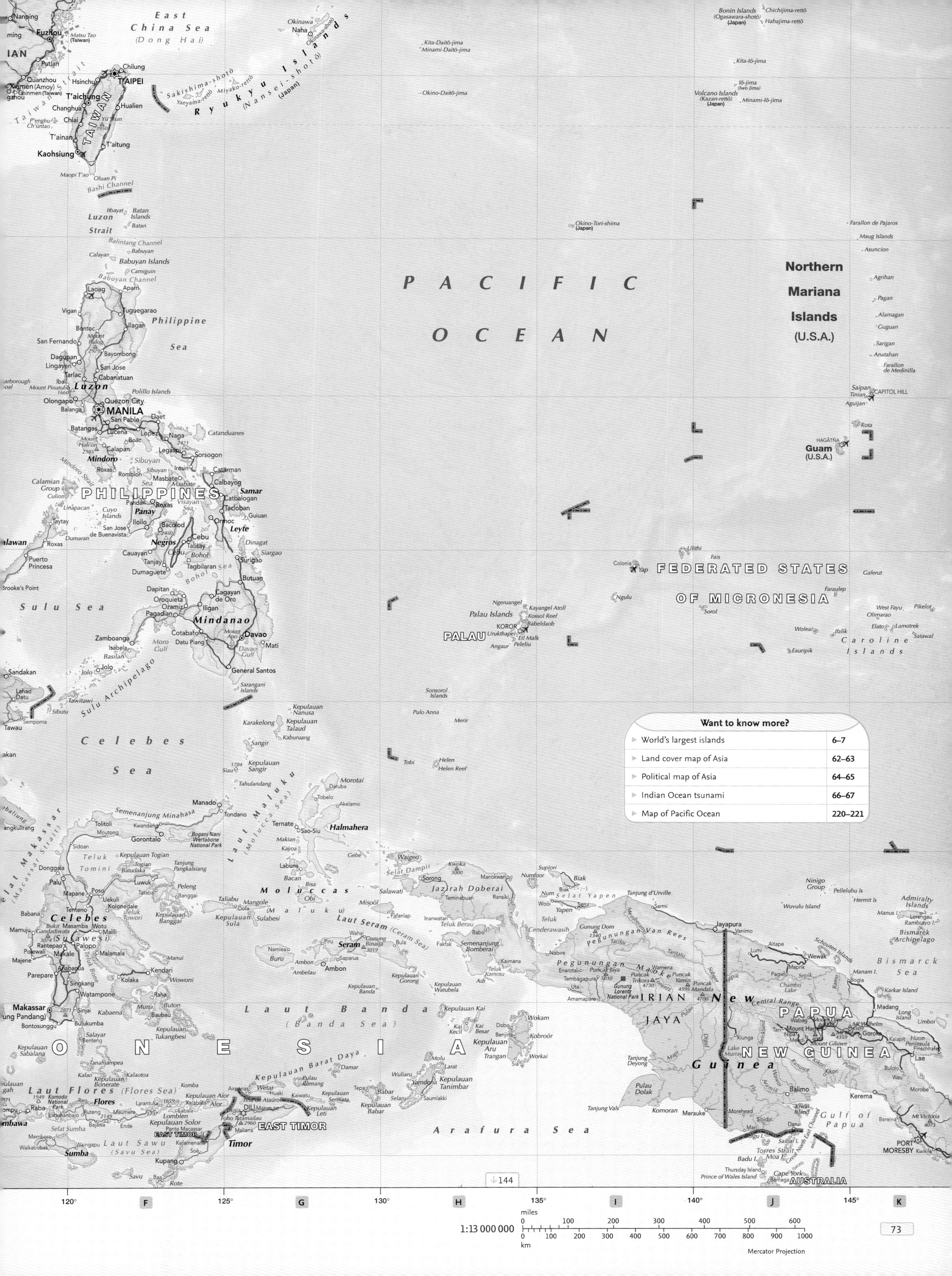

East
China Sea
(Dong Hai)

Bonin Islands Chichijima-rettō
(Ogasawara-shotō) Hahajima-rettō
(Japan) (Japan)

PACIFIC
OCEAN

Northern
Mariana
Islands
(U.S.A.)

Guam
(U.S.A.)

HAGÅTÑA

FEDERATED STATES
OF MICRONESIA

PALAU
KOROR

Caroline
Islands

PHILIPPINES

Luzon

MANILA

Mindanao
Davao

Celebes
Sea

Sulu Sea

Moluccas
(Maluku)

Halmahera

Celebes
(Sulawesi)

Laut Seram (Ceram Sea)

Seram

Laut Banda
(Banda Sea)

I N D O N E S I A

IRIAN
JAYA

New

Guinea

NEW GUINEA

PAPUA

PORT
MORESBY

East
Timor

EAST TIMOR

Timor

Arafura Sea

Gulf of
Papua

AUSTRALIA

Bismarck
Sea

Admiralty
Islands

↓144

Want to know more?

120° F 125° G 130° H 135° I 140° J 145° K

miles
0   100   200   300   400   500   600

1:13 000 000

km
0 100 200 300 400 500 600 700 800 900 1000

Mercator Projection

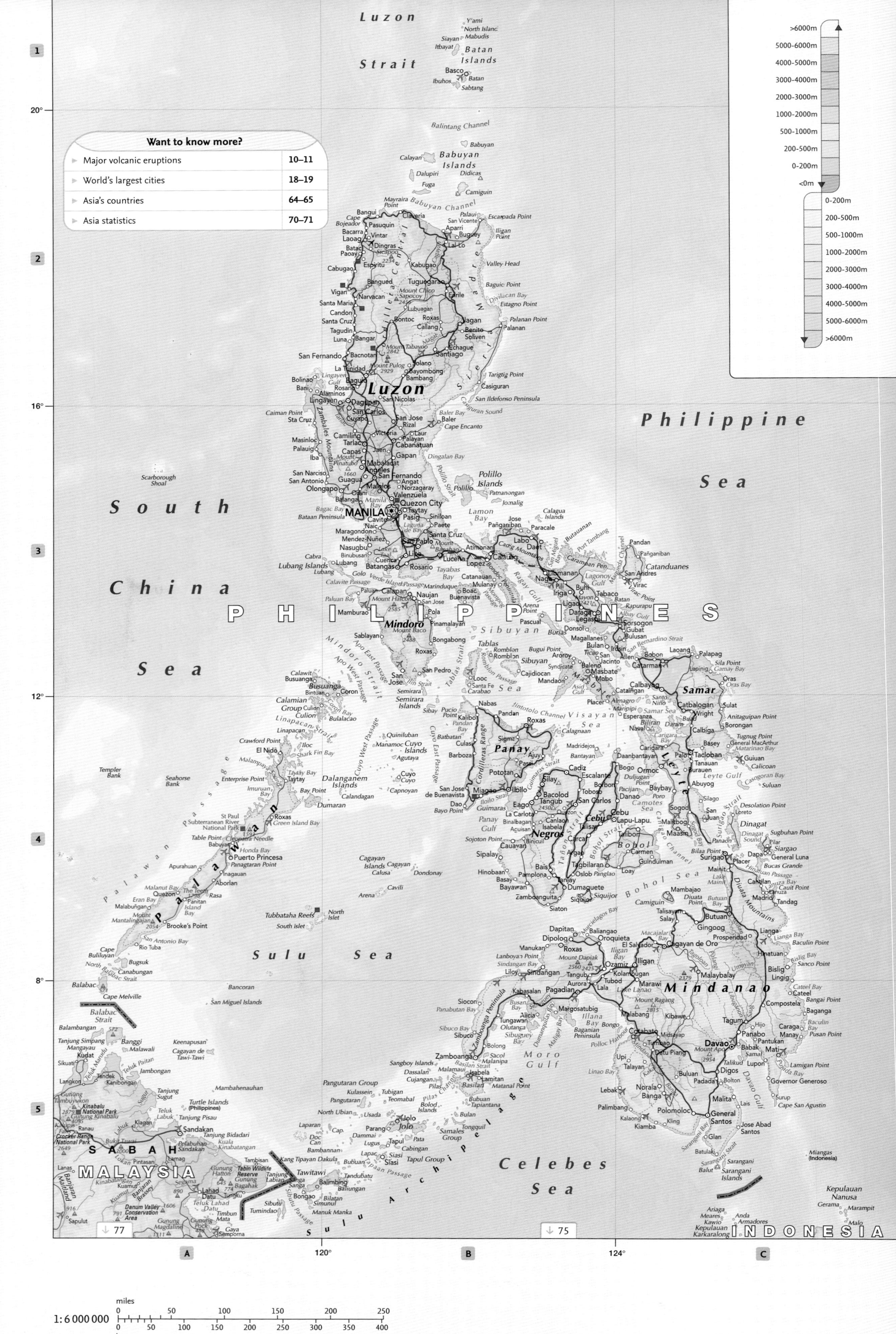

>6000m
5000-6000m
4000-5000m
3000-4000m
2000-3000m
1000-2000m
500-1000m
200-500m
0-200m
<0m

0-200m
200-500m
500-1000m
1000-2000m
2000-3000m
3000-4000m
4000-5000m
5000-6000m
>6000m

Luzon

Strait

Philippine

Sea

Luzon

South

China

Sea

P H I L I P P I N E S

Philippine

Sea

MANILA

Mindoro

Panay

Samar

Negros

Cebu

Visayan
Sea

Bohol

Dinagat

Sulu   Sea

Palawan

Mindanao

Davao

Celebes

Sea

MALAYSIA

SABAH

I N D O N E S I A

miles
0   50   100   150   200   250

1:6 000 000

km
0   50   100   150   200   250   300   350   400

Mercator Projection

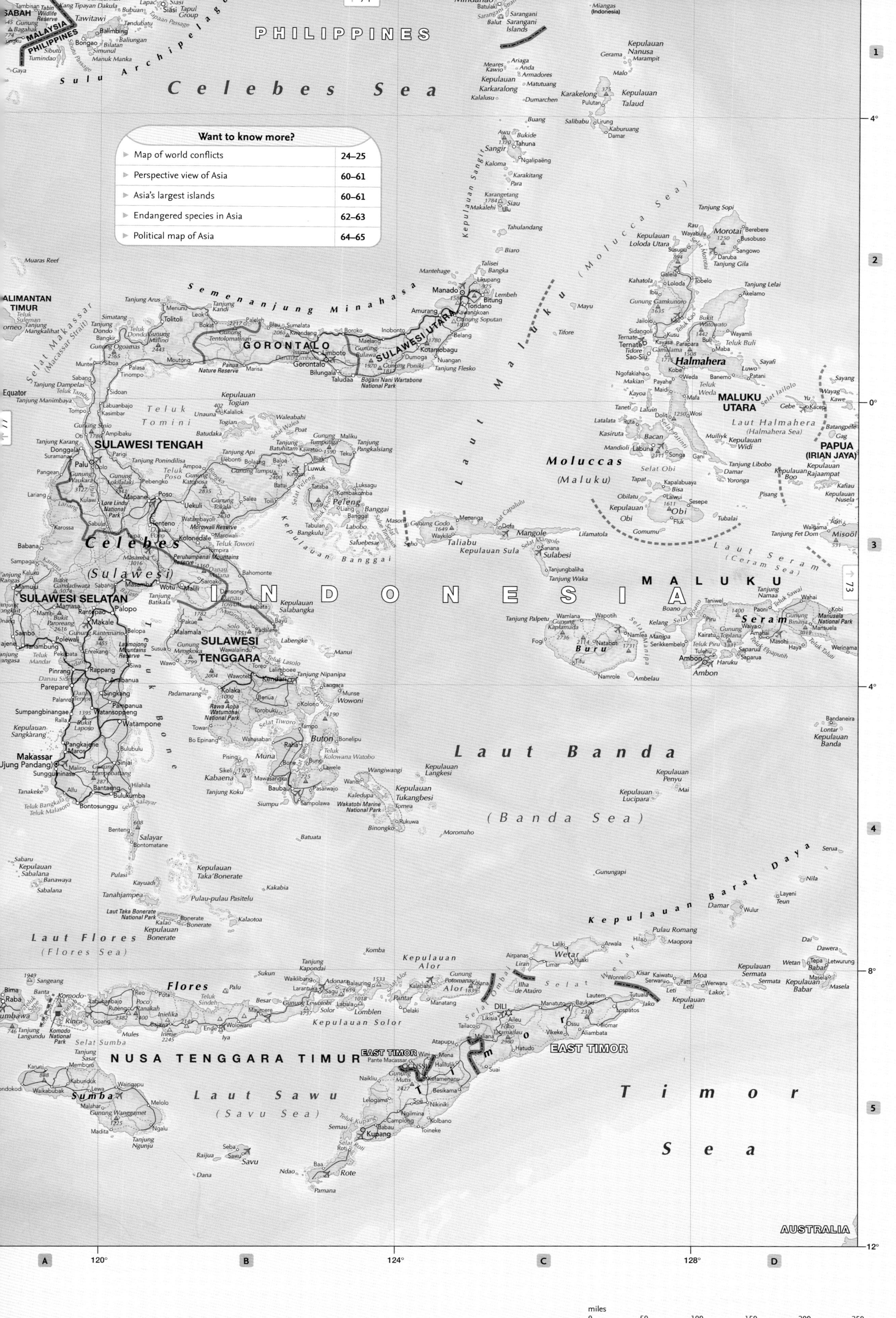

Want to know more?

→ 73

1 : 6 000 000

miles
0   50   100   150   200   250

km
0 50 100 150 200 250 300 350 400

Mercator Projection

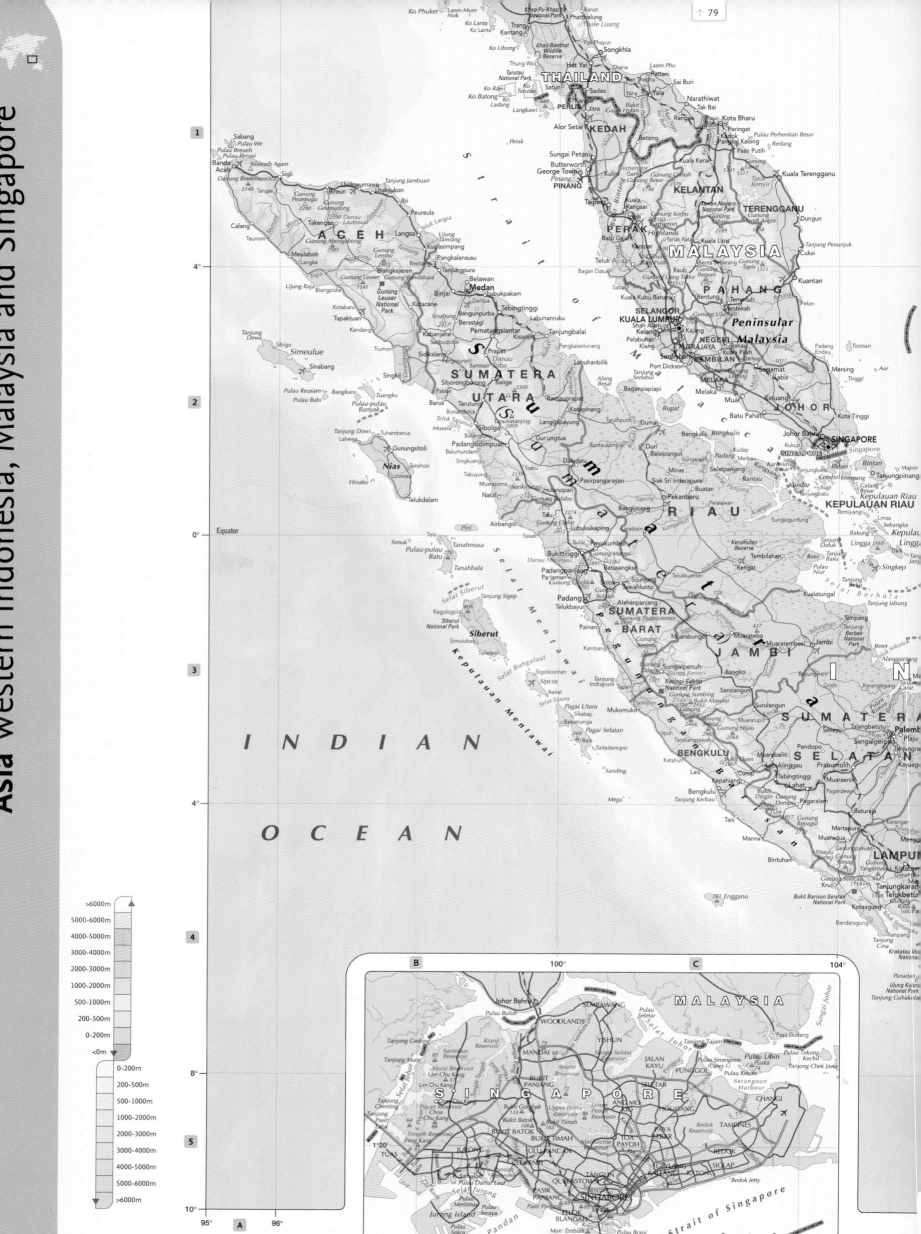

Asia Western Indonesia, Malaysia and Singapore

THAILAND

Ko Phuket · Laem Mum Nok · Khao Pu-Khao Ya Nasional Park · Kanot · Phattalung · Thale Luang
Ko Lanta · Ko Lanta · Chao Banthat Wildlife Reserve · Pha Phayun · Songkhla
Ko Libong · Kantang · Thung Wa · Trang · Chana · Laem Pho
Ko Rawi · Tarutao National Park · Ko Tarutao · Sadao · Hat Yai · Sai Buri
Ko Batong · Satun · Ban Thepha · Yaha · Pattani · Narathiwat
Ko Batong · Langkawi · Betong · Yala · Tak Bai

PERLIS · Alor Setar · Jitra · Gunung · Kota Bharu
KEDAH · Sungai Petani · Kulim · Peringat · Pulau Perhentian Besar · Redang
Butterworth · George Town · Pinang · **PINANG** · Kuala Kerai · Pasir Putih
Taiping · Kuala Kangsar · Taman Negara National Park · **TERENGGANU** · Kuala Terengganu
PERAK · Batu Gajah · Cameron Highlands · Gunung Korbu 2182 · Gunung Mandi Angin 1558 · Dungun
Kampar · Raub · Benta Seberang · Gunung Benum · **MALAYSIA** · Tanjung Penunjuk · Cukai
Teluk Anson · Bentung · Temerloh · **PAHANG** · Gunung Tapis 1511 · Kuantan
Bagan Datuk · Kuala Kubu Baharu · Mentekab · Pekan
SELANGOR · **KUALA LUMPUR** · Shah Alam · Kajang · **Peninsular**
PUTRAJAYA · Kelang · Bahau · **Malaysia**
Pelabuhan Klang · Port Dickson · **NEGERI SEMBILAN** · Gemas · Segamat · Labis · Mersing · Tioman
Melaka · **MELAKA** · Muar · Batu Pahat · Kluang · **JOHOR** · Aur
Johor Bahru · **SINGAPORE** · Kota Tinggi

INDIAN OCEAN

Sabang · Pulau We · Pulau Breueh · Pulau Penasi · Banda Aceh · Sigli · Silawaih Agam
Gunung Bateemeucica 2140 · Lhokseumawe · Tanjung Jambuair
Tangse · Gunung Peuetsagu 2280 · Bireun · Lhoksukon · Ibi
Calang · Gunung Geureudong 2590 · **ACEH** · Peureula
Teunom · Gunung Abongabong 2985 · Langsa · Teluk Langsa
Meulaboh · Langka · Gunung Lembu · Besitang · Kualasimpang · Ujung Tamiang
Blangkejeren · Gunung Bandahara · Pangkalansusu · Tanjungpura · Belawan
Ujung Raja · Blangpidio · Gunung Leuser 3145 · Gunung Leuser National Park · **Medan** · Lubukpakam
Kotabaru · Kutacane · Delitua · Tebingtinggi · Labuanruku
Tapaktuan · Kandang · Sinabung 2417 · Bangunpurba · **SUMATERA** · Pematangsiantar · Kisaran · Tanjungbalai
Tanjung Dewa · Sibigo · **Simeulue** · Sinabang · Kabanjahe · Serbudolok · Berastagi · **UTARA** · Pangkalanlunang
Sibolga · Samosir · **Danau Toba** · Prapat · Rantauprapat
Pulau Reusam · Bangkaru · Tuangku · Barus · Balige · Bandolok · Tarutung · Kotapinang · Tanahputih · Dumai
Pulau-pulau Banyak · Pulau Babi · Batangtoru · Tapulonanjing 2009 · Sibolga · Gur ungtua · Langgapayung
Tanjung Dowi · Lahewa · Tuhemberua · Musala · Padangsidimpuan · Bengkalis · Bengkalis · Kudap · **RIAU**
Gunungsitoli · Balumundam · Singkuang · Siabu · Minas · Daludalu · Rantaukampat · Duri · Siak Sri Inderapura · Buatan
Nias · Tetehosi · Lolowau · Tabuyung · Sarikmarad 2139 · Natal · Pasirpangarayan · Bangkinang · Pekanbaru · Pelalawan
Hinako · Telukdalam · Muarasoma · Gunung Ophir 2911 · Talu 2274 · Lubuksikaping · Cipatkan
Tanahmasa · Pini · Airbangis · Gunung Malintang · Ipatkan · Buntiang · Kampar
Pulau-pulau Batu · Tanahbala · Suliki · Payakumbuh · Tembilahan · Rengat
Simuk · Bukittinggi · Gunung Marapi · **Kerumutan Reserve**

Selat Siberut · Tanjung Sigep · Danau Maninjau · Batusangkar · Telukkuantan
Kagologlo · Siberut National Park · Padangpanjang · Solok · Sijunjung · Sarolangun
Muarasome · Sipura · Pariaman · Gunung Landa 2707 · Sawahlunto · Surulangun
Kepulauan Mentawai · Selat Mentawai · Padang · Gunung Panticermin · **SUMATERA** · Muaratebo · Jambi
Siberut · Simulube · Telukbayur · Painan · **BARAT** · Kerinci Seblat National Park
Taileleo · Kambang · Gunung Kerinci · **JAMBI** · Bangko · Betet
Selat Bungalaut · Sigoisooinan · Tanjung Indrapura · Gunung Sumbing 2753 · Sungaipenuh · Bukit National Park
Sipora · Kaliet · Gunung Masurai 2931 · Muaratembesi
Pagai Utara · Selat Sipura · Sikakap · Mukomuko · Bukit Masurai
Sikabaluan · Gunung Hijau · Surulangun · **INDONESIA**
Pagai Selatan · Bale · Gunung Dingin 2020 · Gunung Hijau · **SUMATERA**
Taitaitanopo · Ketahun · Muarabeliti · Gunung Besar 2068 · Palembang
Sanding · Lubuklinggau · Muaraenim · Plaju · **SELATAN**
Bengkulu · Curup · Tebingtinggi · Kayuagung
Bengkulu · Kepahiang · Lahat · Pendopo · Sangaigerong
Tais · Bukit Dingin 1916 · Gunung Dempo 3159 · Pagaralam · Pagardewa · Baturaja · Martapura · **LAMPUNG**
Manna · Muaradua · Gedungpakuan

INDIAN OCEAN · Bintuhan · Tanjung Kerbau · Bukit Barisan Selatan National Park · Krui · Kotaagung · Telukbetung · Tanjungkarang
Enggano · 781 Enggano · Bandaragung · Krakatau · Tanjung Cina · Teluk Semangka

Elevation scale:
>6000m
5000-6000m
4000-5000m
3000-4000m
2000-3000m
1000-2000m
500-1000m
200-500m
0-200m
<0m

0-200m
200-500m
500-1000m
1000-2000m
2000-3000m
3000-4000m
4000-5000m
5000-6000m
>6000m

INSET MAP — SINGAPORE

95° · A · 96° · B · 100° · C · 104°

MALAYSIA

Johor Bahru · Pulau Buloh · SEMBAWANG · Pulau Seletar · Sungai Johor
Pulau Buloh · WOODLANDS · YISHUN · Pasir Gudang
Tanjong Gedong · Kranji Reservoir · Selat Johor · Tanjung Tajam · Pulau Serangoon (Coney I.) · Pulau Ubin · Tanjung Chek Jawa
Tanjong Murai · Sarimbun Reservoir · MANDAI · 68 · Sungei Seletar Reservoir · Pulau Tekong Kechil · Puaka
Murai Reservoir · Lim Chu Kang · JALAN KAYU · Pulau Tekong
Lim Chu Kang · PUNGGOL · Serangoon Harbour
Tanjong Choa Chu Kang · Poyan Reservoir · BUKIT PANJANG · Upper Seletar Reservoir · SELETAR · HOUGANG
Peng Kang · BUKIT GOMBAK · Upper Peirce Reservoir · ANG MO KIO · CHANGI
Tengeh Reservoir · BUKIT BATOK · Bukit Timah · TAMPINES
SINGAPORE · CLEMENTI · MacRitchie Reservoir · TOA PAYOH · Bedok Reservoir · BEDOK
JURONG · ULU PANDAN · TANGLIN · GEYLANG · SIGLAP
TUAS · Pulau Damar Laut · PASIR PANJANG · QUEENSTOWN · KATONG · Bedok Jetty
Jurong Island · Pulau Merlimau · Pulau Seraya · TELOK BLANGAH · **SINGAPORE**
Pulau Busing · Pulau Sakra · Mount Imbiah · Pulau Brani · Pulau Serapong · Buran Darat · **Strait of Singapore**
Pulau Bukum · **Sentosa** · Selat Pandan

Selat Johor · **Selat of Singapore**
1 : 360 000 · 0 miles 3 · 0 km 5
103°40' · 103°50' · 104°00'
1°20'

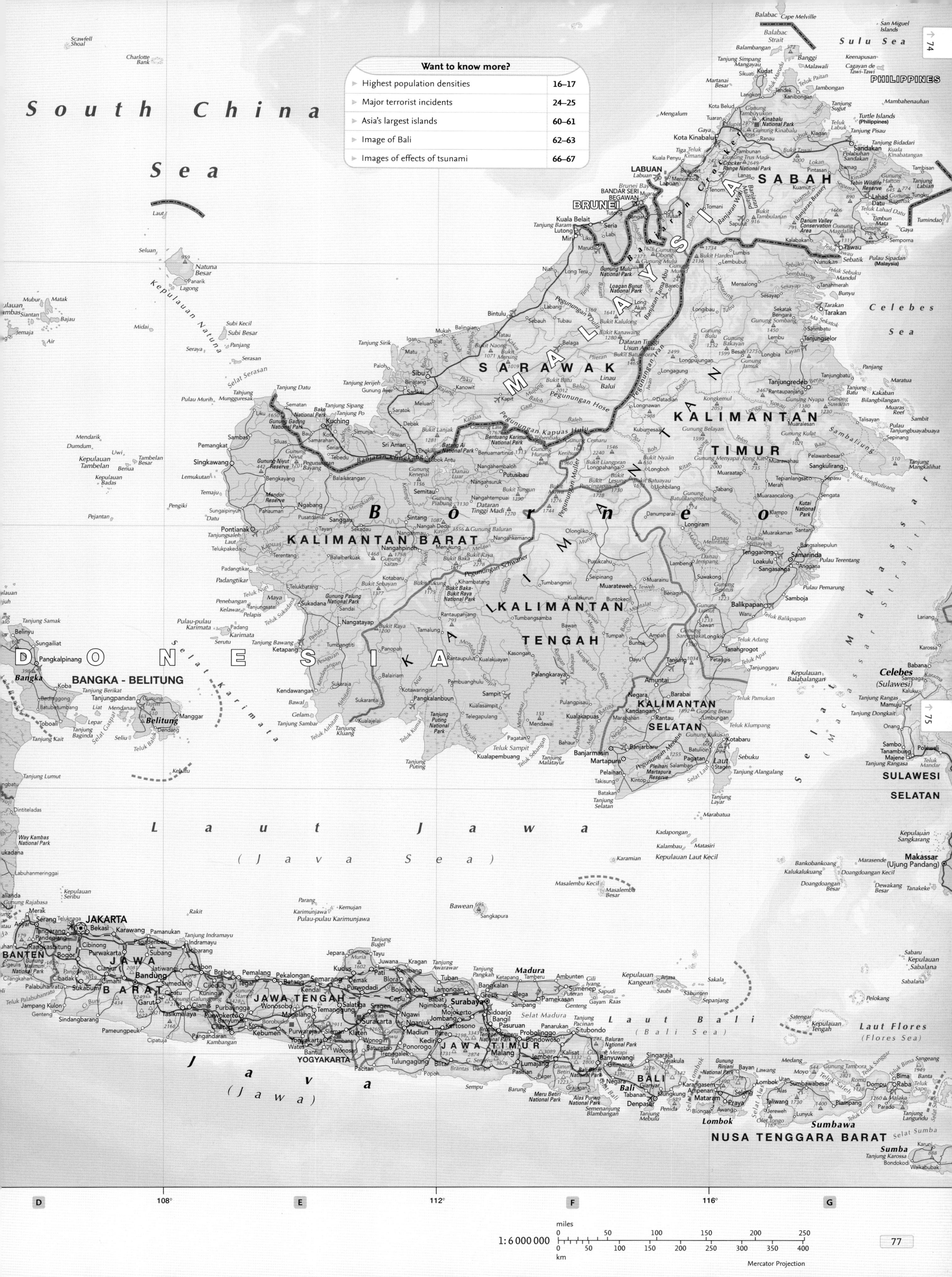

Want to know more?
Highest population densities 16–17
Major terrorist incidents 24–25
Asia's largest islands 60–61
Image of Bali 62–63
Images of effects of tsunami 66–67
South China Sea
Sulu Sea
Celebes Sea
PHILIPPINES
MALAYSIA
BRUNEI
BANDAR SERI BEGAWAN
LABUAN
SABAH
SARAWAK
Kota Kinabalu
Sandakan
Tawau
Miri
Bintulu
Sibu
Kuching
Borneo
INDONESIA
KALIMANTAN BARAT
KALIMANTAN TENGAH
KALIMANTAN TIMUR
KALIMANTAN SELATAN
Pontianak
Samarinda
Balikpapan
Banjarmasin
Palangkaraya
Tarakan
BANGKA - BELITUNG
Pangkalpinang
Bangka
Belitung
Selat Karimata
Kepulauan Natuna
Natuna Besar
Selat Makassar
Laut Jawa
(Java Sea)
Celebes (Sulawesi)
SULAWESI SELATAN
Makassar (Ujung Pandang)
JAKARTA
BANTEN
JAWA BARAT
JAWA TENGAH
JAWA TIMUR
YOGYAKARTA
Bandung
Semarang
Surabaya
Malang
Madura
Java (Jawa)
Laut Bali (Bali Sea)
BALI
Denpasar
Lombok
Mataram
Sumbawa
NUSA TENGGARA BARAT
Laut Flores (Flores Sea)
Sumba
108°
112°
116°
D
E
F
G
1:6 000 000
miles
km
Mercator Projection

74
75

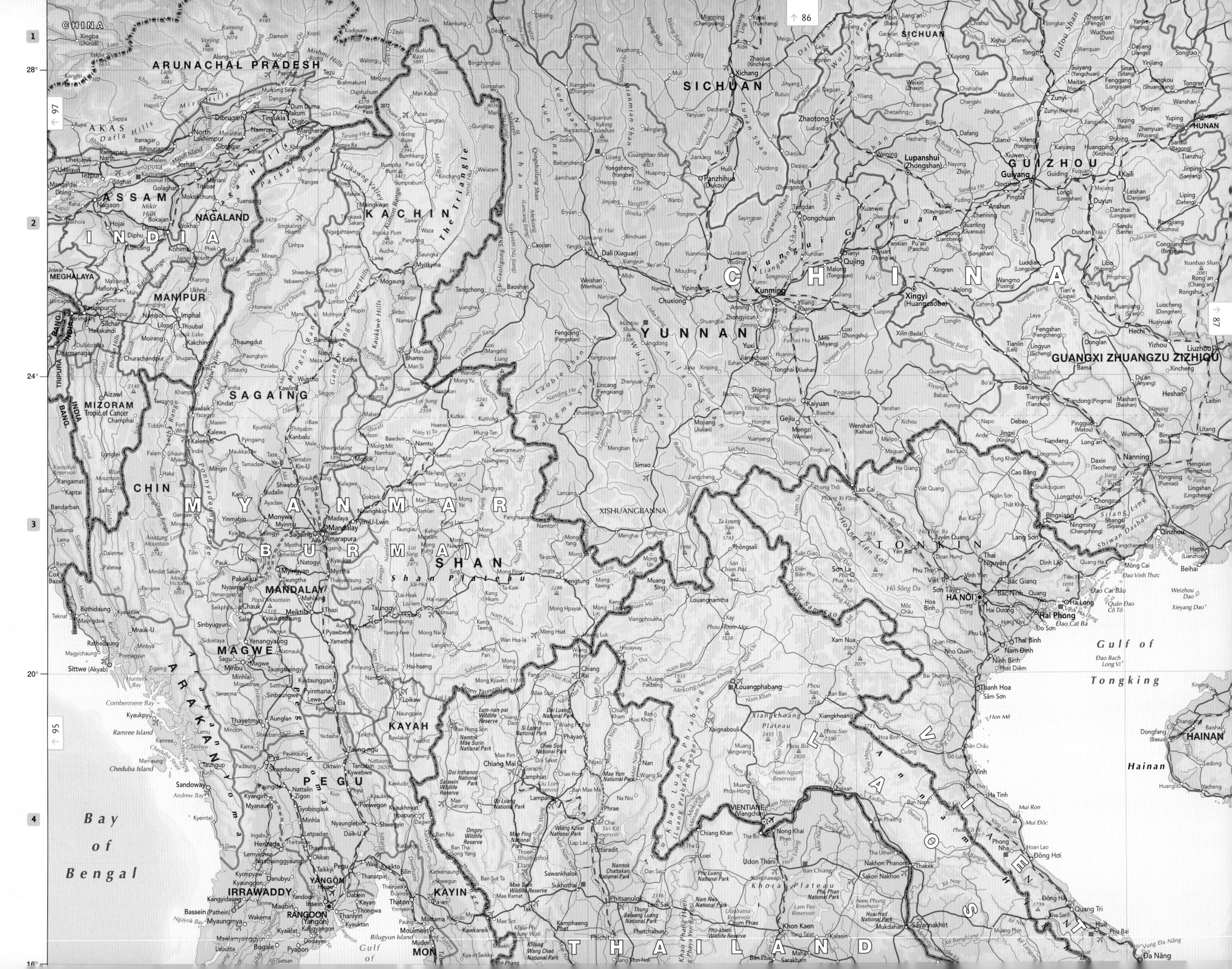

CHINA
SICHUAN
GUIZHOU
YUNNAN
GUANGXI ZHUANGZU ZIZHIQU
HAINAN
INDIA
ARUNACHAL PRADESH
ASSAM
NAGALAND
MANIPUR
MIZORAM
MEGHALAYA
MYANMAR (BURMA)
KACHIN
SAGAING
SHAN
Shan Plateau
MANDALAY
MAGWE
CHIN
ARAKAN
PEGU
YANGON
IRRAWADDY
KAYIN
KAYAH
MON
THAILAND
LAOS
VIETNAM
TONKIN
Gulf of Tongking
Bay of Bengal
Hainan

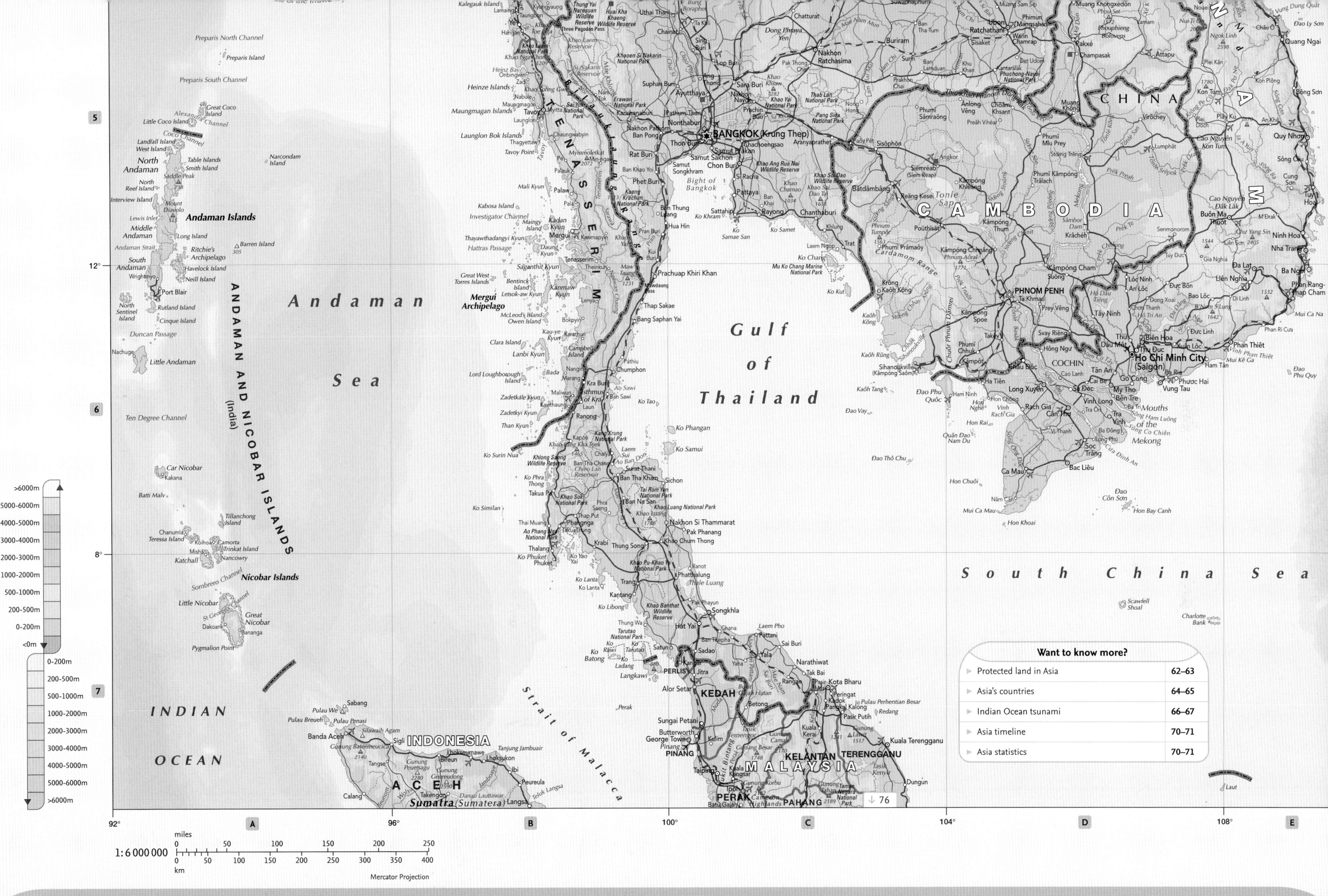

Asia Myanmar, Thailand, Laos, Cambodia and Vietnam

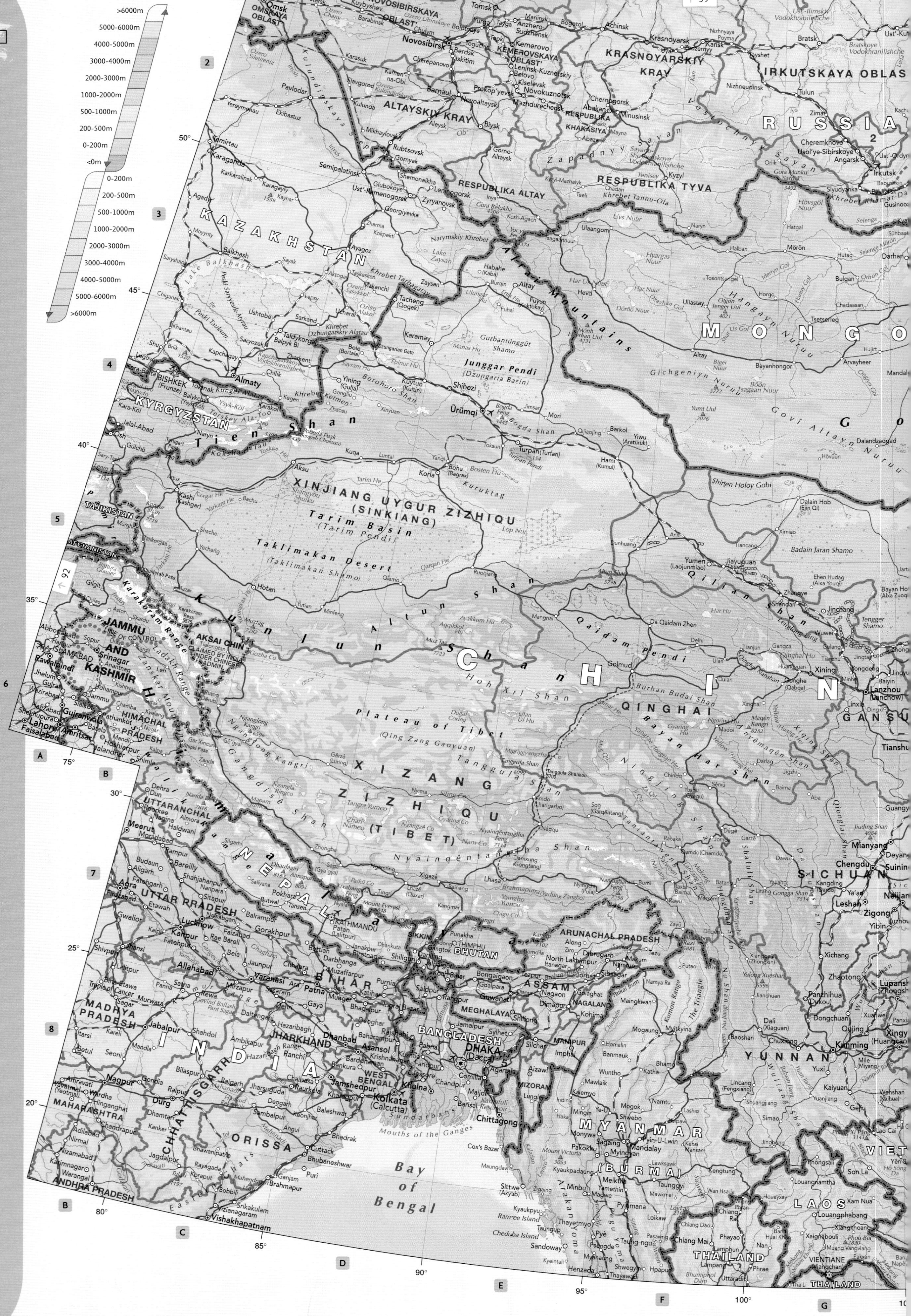

Asia Eastern Asia

>6000m
5000-6000m
4000-5000m
3000-4000m
2000-3000m
1000-2000m
500-1000m
200-500m
0-200m
<0m
0-200m
200-500m
500-1000m
1000-2000m
2000-3000m
3000-4000m
4000-5000m
5000-6000m
>6000m
↑ 39
↑ 92
RUSSIA
KAZAKHSTAN
KYRGYZSTAN
TAJIKISTAN
AFGHANISTAN
MONGOLIA
CHINA
XINJIANG UYGUR ZIZHIQU (SINKIANG)
XIZANG ZIZHIQU (TIBET)
QINGHAI
GANSU
SICHUAN
YUNNAN
JAMMU AND KASHMIR
AKSAI CHIN
HIMACHAL PRADESH
UTTARANCHAL
UTTAR PRADESH
MADHYA PRADESH
MAHARASHTRA
CHHATTISGARH
JHARKHAND
BIHAR
WEST BENGAL
ORISSA
ANDHRA PRADESH
INDIA
NEPAL
SIKKIM
BHUTAN
ARUNACHAL PRADESH
ASSAM
NAGALAND
MEGHALAYA
MANIPUR
MIZORAM
BANGLADESH
MYANMAR (BURMA)
THAILAND
LAOS
NOVOSIBIRSKAYA OBLAST'
OMSKAYA OBLAST
KEMEROVSKAYA OBLAST'
ALTAYSKIY KRAY
KRASNOYARSKIY KRAY
IRKUTSKAYA OBLAST
RESPUBLIKA KHAKASIYA
RESPUBLIKA ALTAY
RESPUBLIKA TYVA
Tien Shan
Altai Mountains
Kunlun Shan
Altun Shan
Qilian Shan
Tarim Basin (Tarim Pendi)
Taklimakan Desert (Taklimakan Shamo)
Junggar Pendi (Dzungaria Basin)
Qaidam Pendi
Plateau of Tibet (Qing Zang Gaoyuan)
Karakoram Range
Himalaya
Gobi
Bay of Bengal
Mouths of the Ganges
Novosibirsk
Omsk
Tomsk
Krasnoyarsk
Irkutsk
Barnaul
Novokuznetsk
Kemerovo
Karaganda
Semipalatinsk
Almaty
BISHKEK (Frunze)
Ürümqi
Kashi (Kashgar)
Hotan
Lanzhou
Xining
Chengdu
Kunming
Lhasa
KATHMANDU
THIMPHU
DHAKA (Dacca)
Kolkata (Calcutta)
Patna
Varanasi
Lucknow
Kanpur
Nagpur
Chittagong
Mandalay
Srinagar
Lahore
Amritsar
Rawalpindi
Vishakhapatnam
VIENTIANE
1
2
3
4
5
6
7
8
B
C
D
F
G
55°
50°
45°
40°
35°
30°
25°
20°
75°
80°
85°
90°
95°
100°

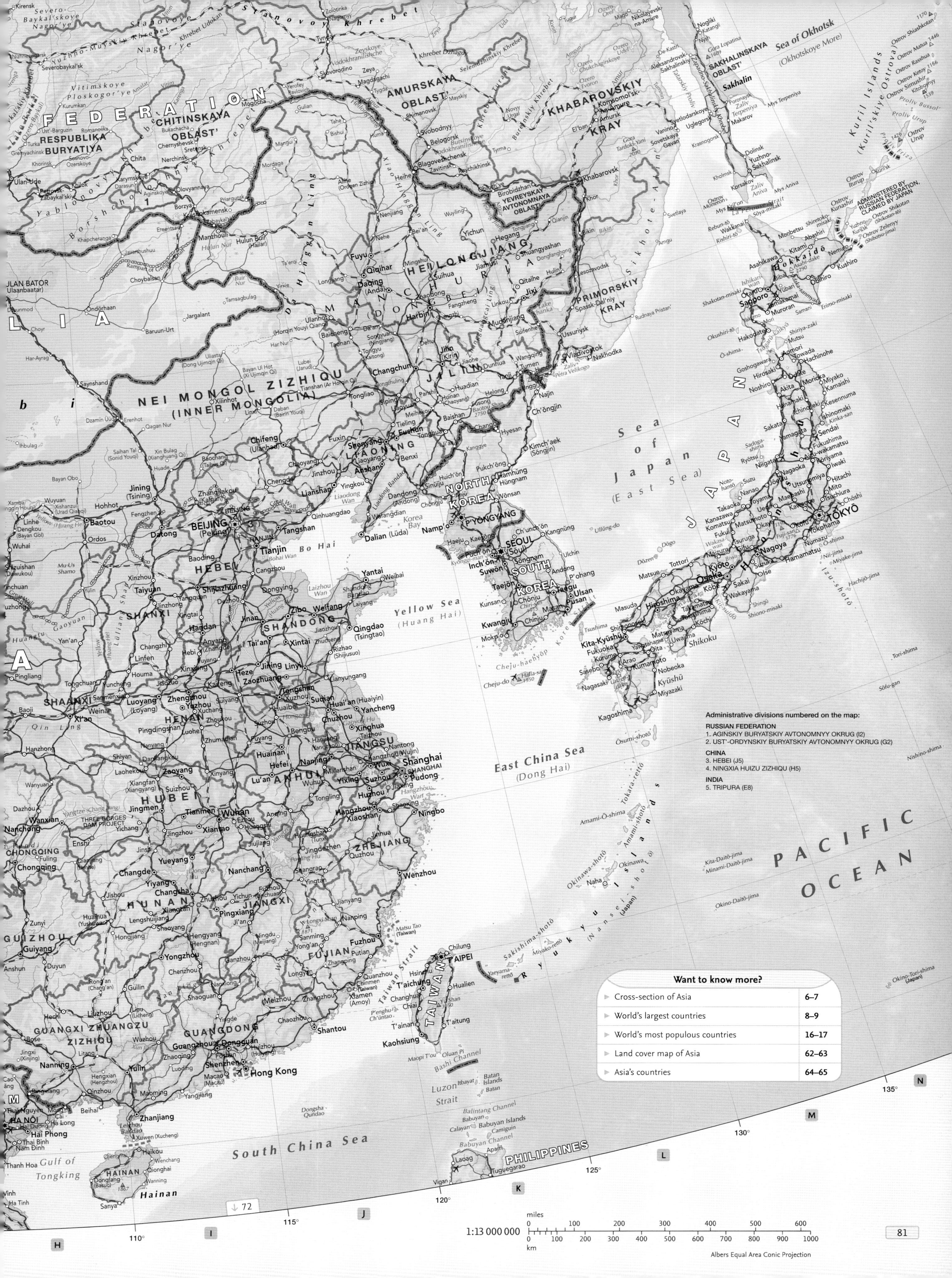

Labels and place names on the map:

Severo-Baykal'skoye Nagor'ye, Stanovoy khrebet, Sea of Okhotsk (Okhotskoye More), Kuril Islands (Kuril'skiye Ostrova)

FEDERATION, CHITINSKAYA OBLAST', RESPUBLIKA BURYATIYA, AMURSKAYA OBLAST', KHABAROVSKIY KRAY, SAKHALINSKAYA OBLAST', Sakhalin

JLAN BATOR (Ulaanbaatar), MONGOLIA

HEILONGJIANG, MANCHURIA (DONGBEI), NEI MONGOL ZIZHIQU (INNER MONGOLIA), JILIN, LIAONING, HEBEI, SHANXI, SHANDONG, SHAANXI, HENAN, JIANGSU, ANHUI, HUBEI, ZHEJIANG, HUNAN, JIANGXI, FUJIAN, GUANGDONG, GUANGXI ZHUANGZU ZIZHIQU, GUIZHOU, CHONGQING, HAINAN

NORTH KOREA, P'YONGYANG, SOUTH KOREA, SEOUL

JAPAN, Hokkaidō, Sapporo, TOKYO, Kyōto, Ōsaka, Kyūshū, Shikoku

TAIWAN, TAIPEI, PHILIPPINES

Sea of Japan (East Sea), Yellow Sea (Huang Hai), East China Sea (Dong Hai), PACIFIC OCEAN, South China Sea, Bo Hai, Korea Bay, Gulf of Tongking

Beijing (Peking), Tianjin, Shanghai, Hong Kong, Macao (Macau), HA NÔI

Major cities: Qiqihar, Daqing, Harbin, Changchun, Jilin, Shenyang, Fushun, Anshan, Dalian, Chifeng, Hohhot, Baotou, Datong, Taiyuan, Shijiazhuang, Jinan, Qingdao, Zhengzhou, Xi'an, Wuhan, Nanjing, Hangzhou, Ningbo, Wenzhou, Nanchang, Changsha, Fuzhou, Xiamen, Guangzhou, Shenzhen, Nanning, Chongqing, Guiyang, Kunming

↓ 72

Administrative divisions numbered on the map:

RUSSIAN FEDERATION
1. AGINSKIY BURYATSKIY AVTONOMNYY OKRUG (I2)
2. UST'-ORDYNSKIY BURYATSKIY AVTONOMNYY OKRUG (G2)

CHINA
3. HEBEI (J5)
4. NINGXIA HUIZU ZIZHIQU (H5)

INDIA
5. TRIPURA (E8)

miles: 0 100 200 300 400 500 600
1:13 000 000
km: 0 100 200 300 400 500 600 700 800 900 1000

Albers Equal Area Conic Projection

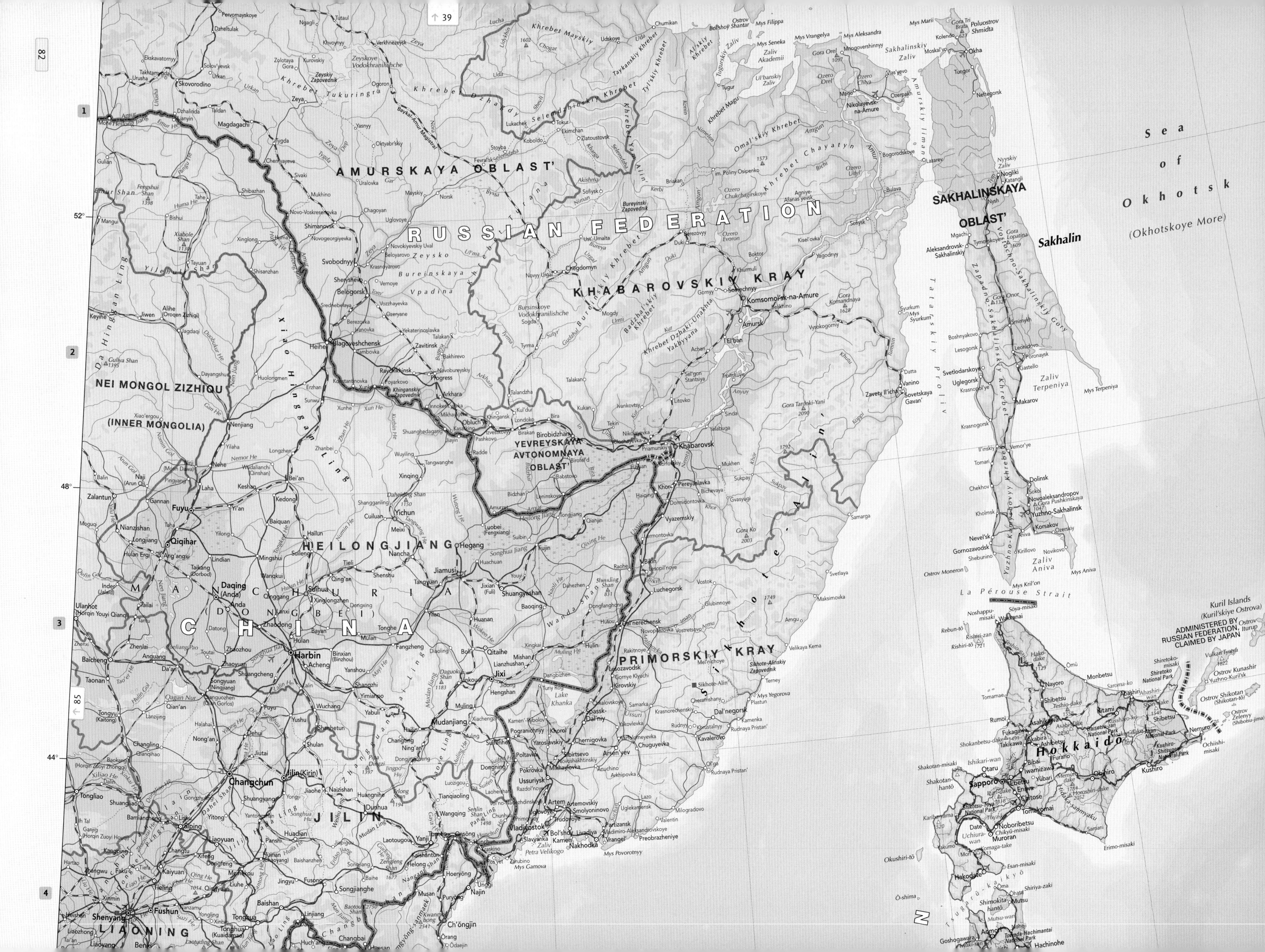

Sea of Okhotsk
(Okhotskoye More)
Sakhalin
SAKHALINSKAYA OBLAST'
RUSSIAN FEDERATION
AMURSKAYA OBLAST'
KHABAROVSKIY KRAY
YEVREYSKAYA AVTONOMNAYA OBLAST'
PRIMORSKIY KRAY
Tatarskiy Proliv
La Pérouse Strait
Hokkaidō
Kuril Islands (Kuril'skiye Ostrova)
ADMINISTERED BY RUSSIAN FEDERATION, CLAIMED BY JAPAN
CHINA
HEILONGJIANG
JILIN
LIAONING
NEI MONGOL ZIZHIQU
(INNER MONGOLIA)
MANCHURIA
(DONGBEI)
Xiao Hinggan Ling
Harbin
Changchun
Shenyang
Khabarovsk
Vladivostok
Sapporo
Lake Khanka
52°
48°
44°
1
2
3
4
39
85

Asia Northeast Asia

PACIFIC OCEAN

Sea of Japan (East Sea)

Yellow Sea (Huang Hai)

East China Sea (Dong Hai)

Korea Bay

NORTH KOREA

PYŎNGYANG

SOUTH KOREA

SEOUL (Sŏul)

HONSHŪ

TŌKYŌ

SHIKOKU

KYŪSHŪ

Conic Equidistant Projection

1 : 6 000 000

Want to know more?	
World's largest islands	6–7
Map of world conflicts	24–25
Perspective view of Asia	60–61
Asia's countries	64–65
Asia statistics	70–71

miles
0   50   100   150   200   250
km
0   100   200   300   400

Elevation legend:
>6000m
5000–6000m
4000–5000m
3000–4000m
2000–3000m
1000–2000m
500–1000m
200–500m
0–200m
<0m

Major cities and places labelled on map include: Pusan, Taegu, Taejŏn, Kwangju, Inch'ŏn, Suwŏn, Ulsan, Namp'o, Hamhŭng, Wŏnsan, Kaesŏng, Osaka, Kyōto, Nagoya, Hiroshima, Fukuoka, Nagasaki, Kumamoto, Kagoshima, Matsuyama, Kōchi, Sendai, Niigata, Kanazawa, Shizuoka, Yokohama, Chiba, Cheju, Tsushima.

Elevation legend:

>6000m
5000-6000m
4000-5000m
3000-4000m
2000-3000m
1000-2000m
500-1000m
200-500m
0-200m
<0m

0-200m
200-500m
500-1000m
1000-2000m
2000-3000m
3000-4000m
4000-5000m
5000-6000m
>6000m

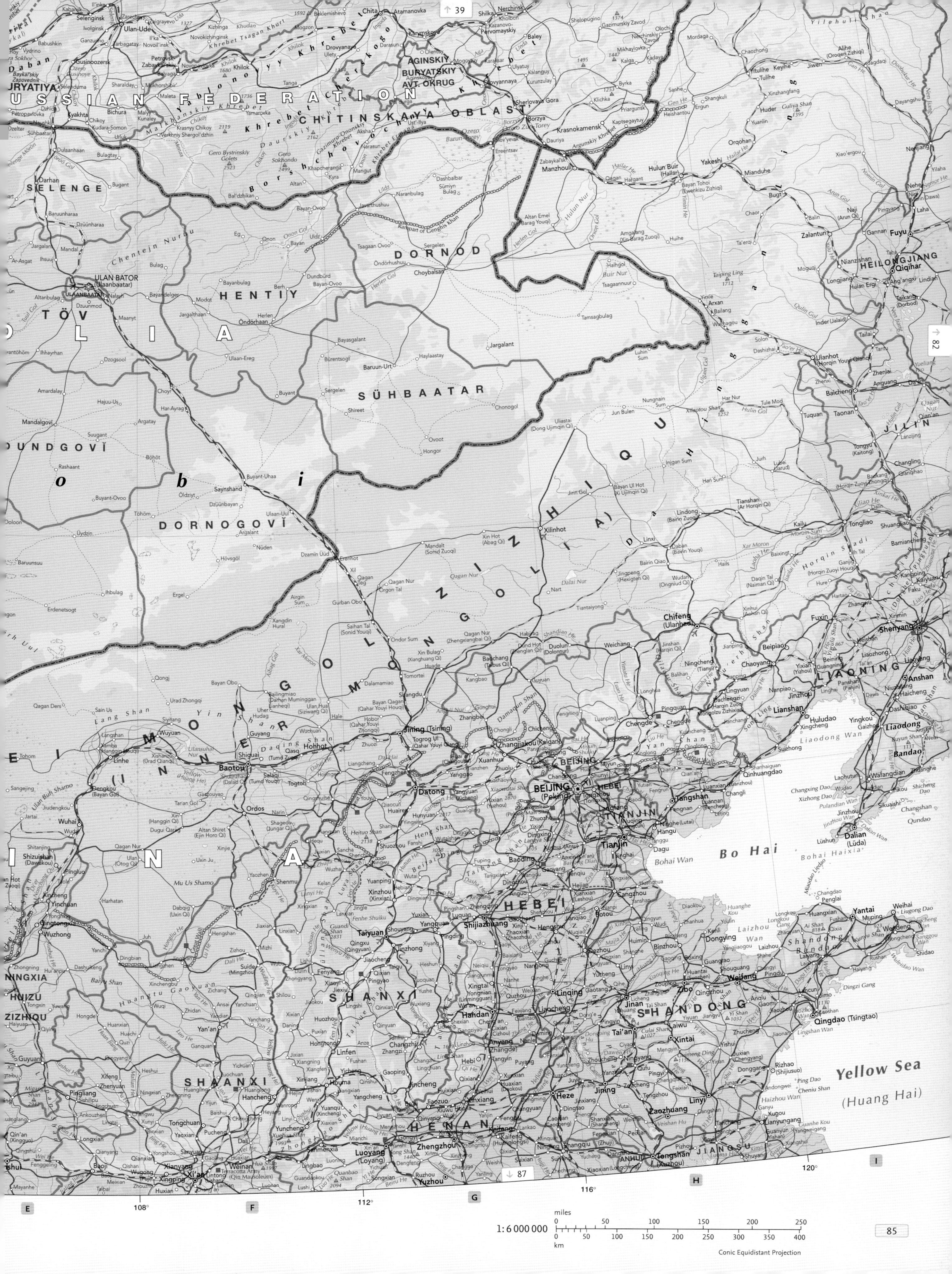

1:6 000 000

Conic Equidistant Projection

miles
0   50   100   150   200   250

km
0   50   100   150   200   250   300   350   400

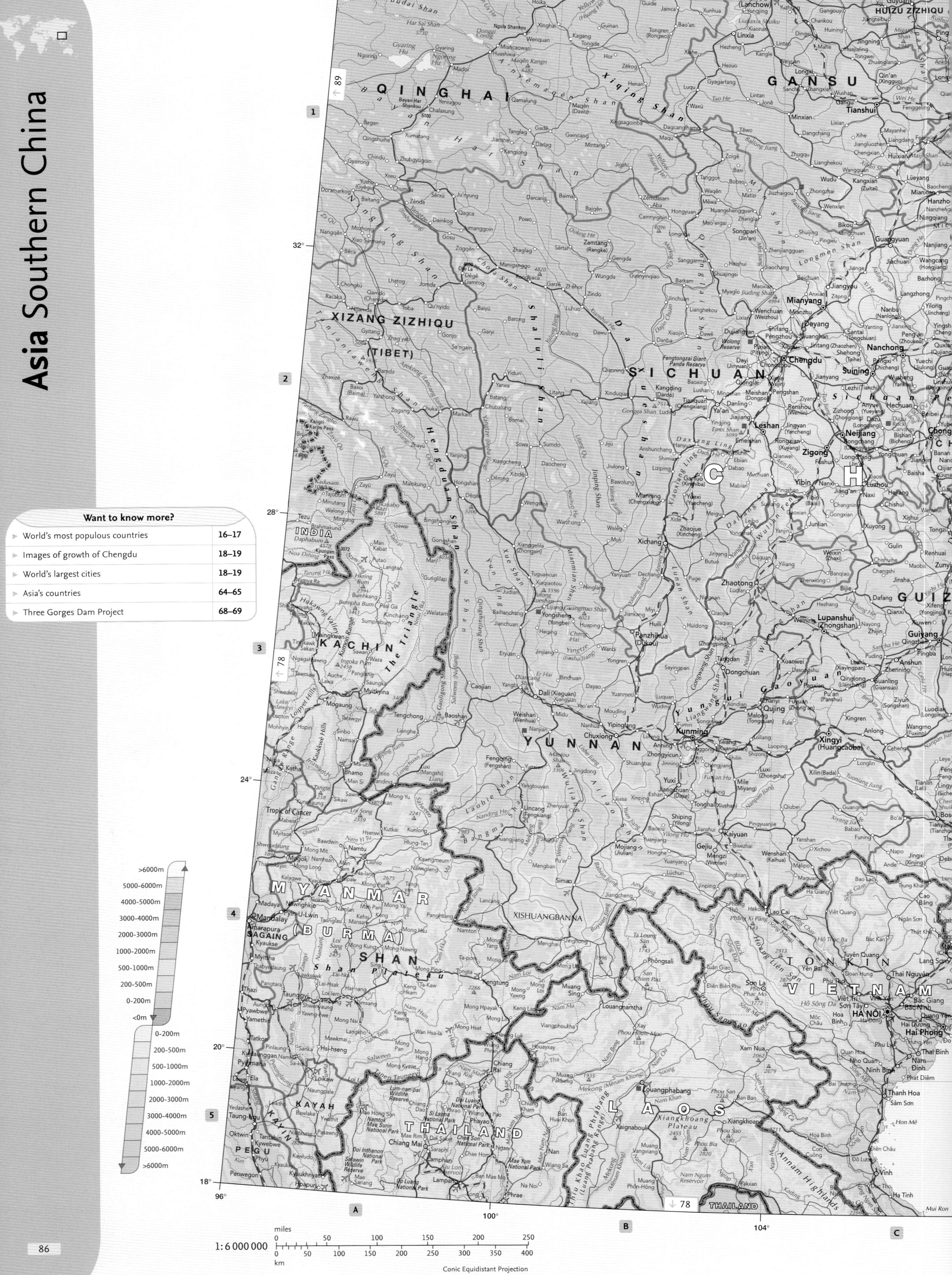

1:6 000 000

miles
0   50   100   150   200   250

km
0   50 100 150 200 250 300 350 400

Conic Equidistant Projection

85

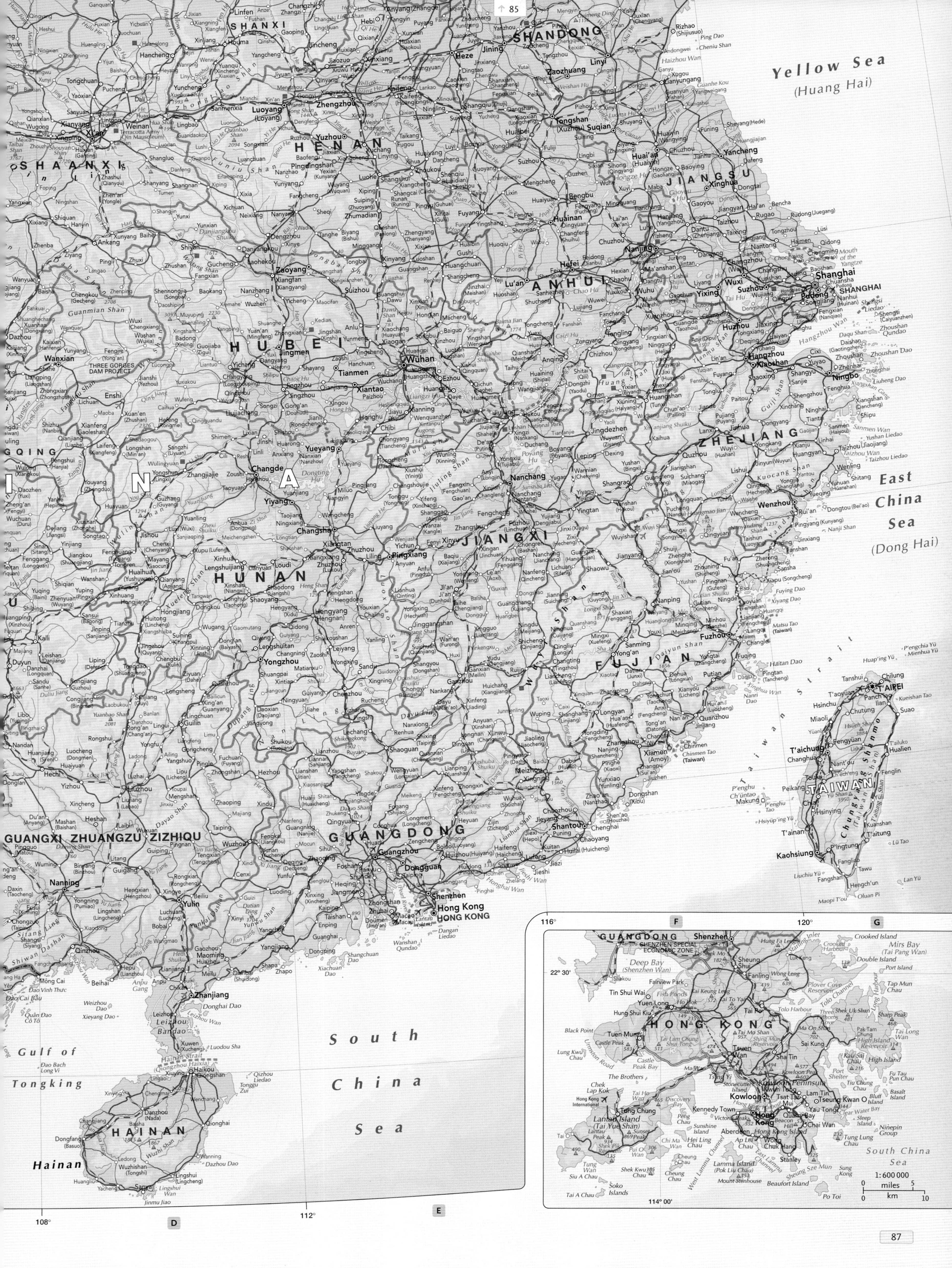
SHANXI
SHANDONG
Yellow Sea
(Huang Hai)
HENAN
JIANGSU
SHAANXI
ANHUI
Shanghai
SHANGHAI
HUBEI
Wuhan
Nanjing
Hangzhou
ZHEJIANG
East
China
Sea
(Dong Hai)
Changsha
HUNAN
JIANGXI
Nanchang
FUJIAN
Fuzhou
TAIWAN
T'AIPEI
Taiwan Strait
GUANGXI ZHUANGZU ZIZHIQU
GUANGDONG
Guangzhou
Nanning
Shenzhen
Hong Kong
HONG KONG
Macao
South
China
Sea
Gulf of
Tongking
HAINAN
Hainan
Haikou
HONG KONG
Kowloon
Lantau Island
Hong Kong Island
1:600 000
miles
km
108°
112°
116°
120°
114° 00'
22° 30'
D
E
F
G

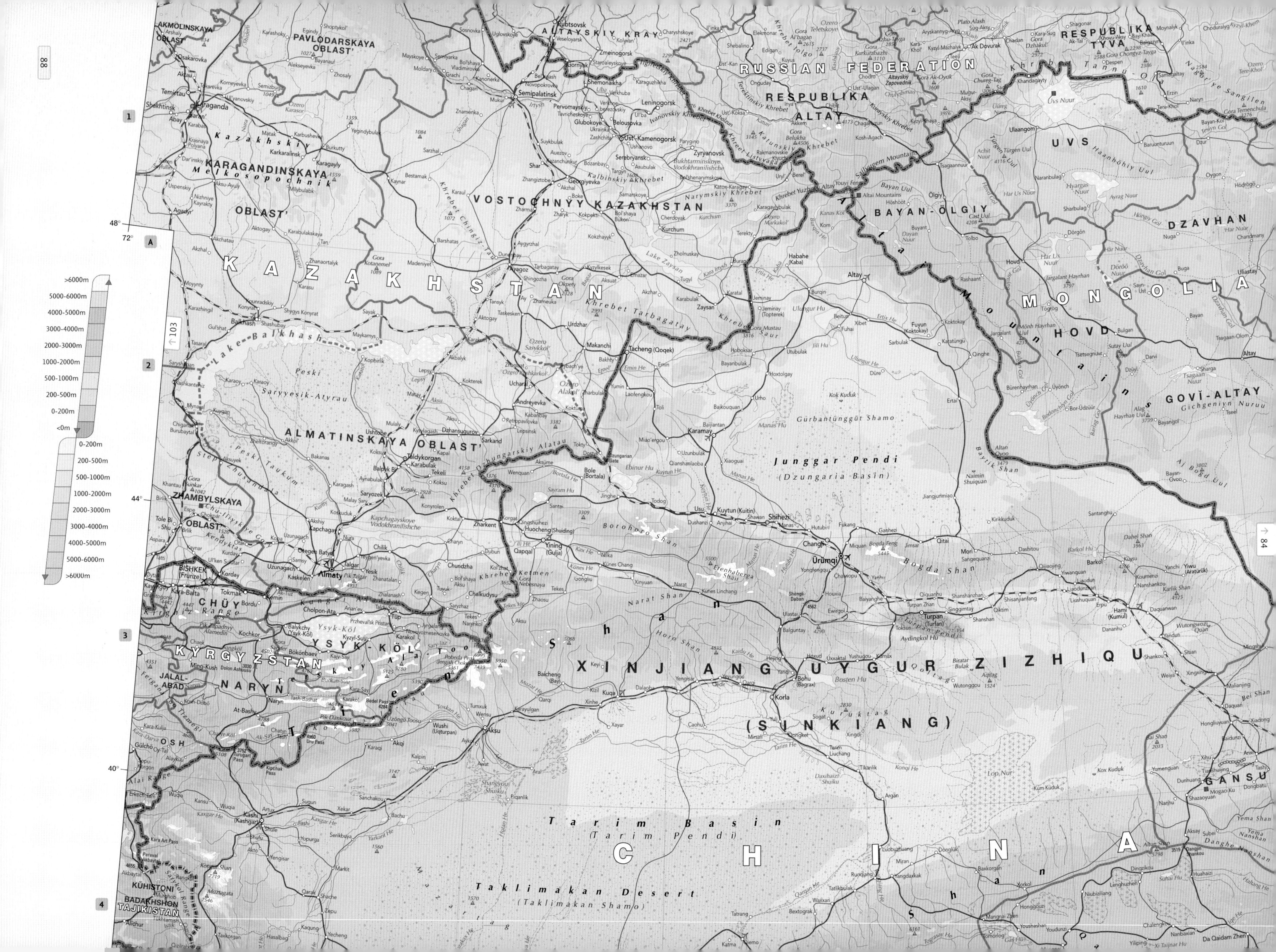

RUSSIAN FEDERATION
RESPUBLIKA ALTAY
RESPUBLIKA TYVA
ALTAYSKIY KRAY
MONGOLIA
UVS
DZAVHAN
HOVD
BAYAN-ÖLGIY
GOVĬ-ALTAY
KAZAKHSTAN
VOSTOCHNYY KAZAKHSTAN
PAVLODARSKAYA OBLAST'
KARAGANDINSKAYA OBLAST'
ALMATINSKAYA OBLAST'
ZHAMBYLSKAYA OBLAST'
AKMOLINSKAYA OBLAST'
KYRGYZSTAN
CHÜY
YSYK-KÖL
NARYN
JALAL-ABAD
OSH
KÜHISTONI BADAKHSHON
TAJIKISTAN
CHINA
XINJIANG UYGUR ZIZHIQU
(SINKIANG)
GANSU
Junggar Pendi
(Dzungaria Basin)
Tarim Basin
(Tarim Pendi)
Taklimakan Desert
(Taklimakan Shamo)
Lake Balkhash
Ozero Alakol'
Lake Zaysan
Ysyk-Köl
Altai Mountains
Tian Shan
Ürümqi
Almaty
Bishkek (Frunze)
Semipalatinsk
Karaganda
Kashi (Kashgar)
Aksu
Turpan (Turfan)
Hami (Kumul)
Korla
Karamay
Yining (Gulja)
Taldykorgan
Ust'-Kamenogorsk
Hovd
Ölgiy
Altay
↑ 84
↑ 103
72°
48°
44°
40°
1
2
3
4
A
>6000m
5000-6000m
4000-5000m
3000-4000m
2000-3000m
1000-2000m
500-1000m
200-500m
0-200m
<0m

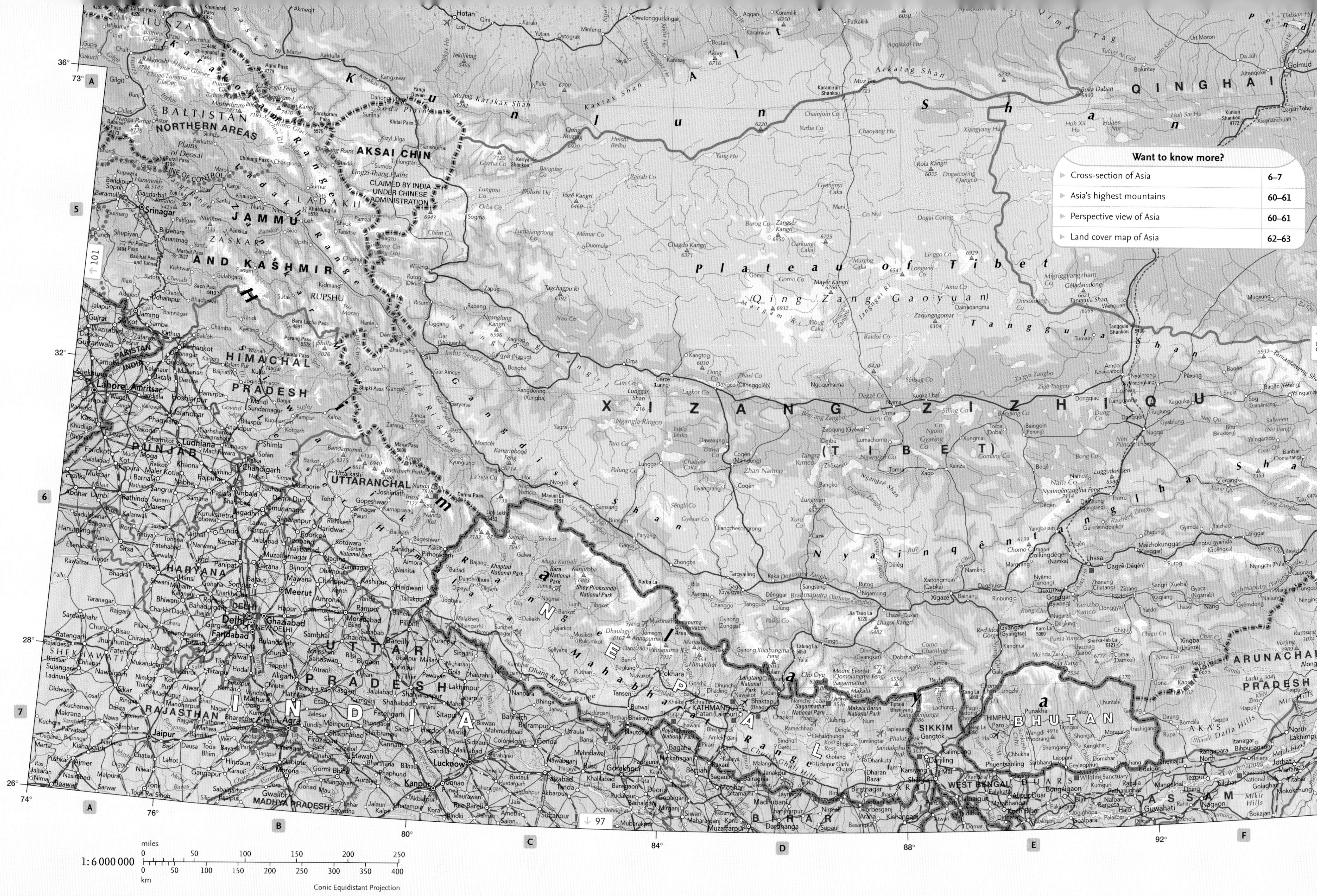

Want to know more?

▲ Cross-section of Asia	6–7
▲ Asia's highest mountains	60–61
▲ Perspective view of Asia	60–61
▲ Land cover map of Asia	62–63

Asia Western China

↓ 97

↓ 101

1:6 000 000

Conic Equidistant Projection

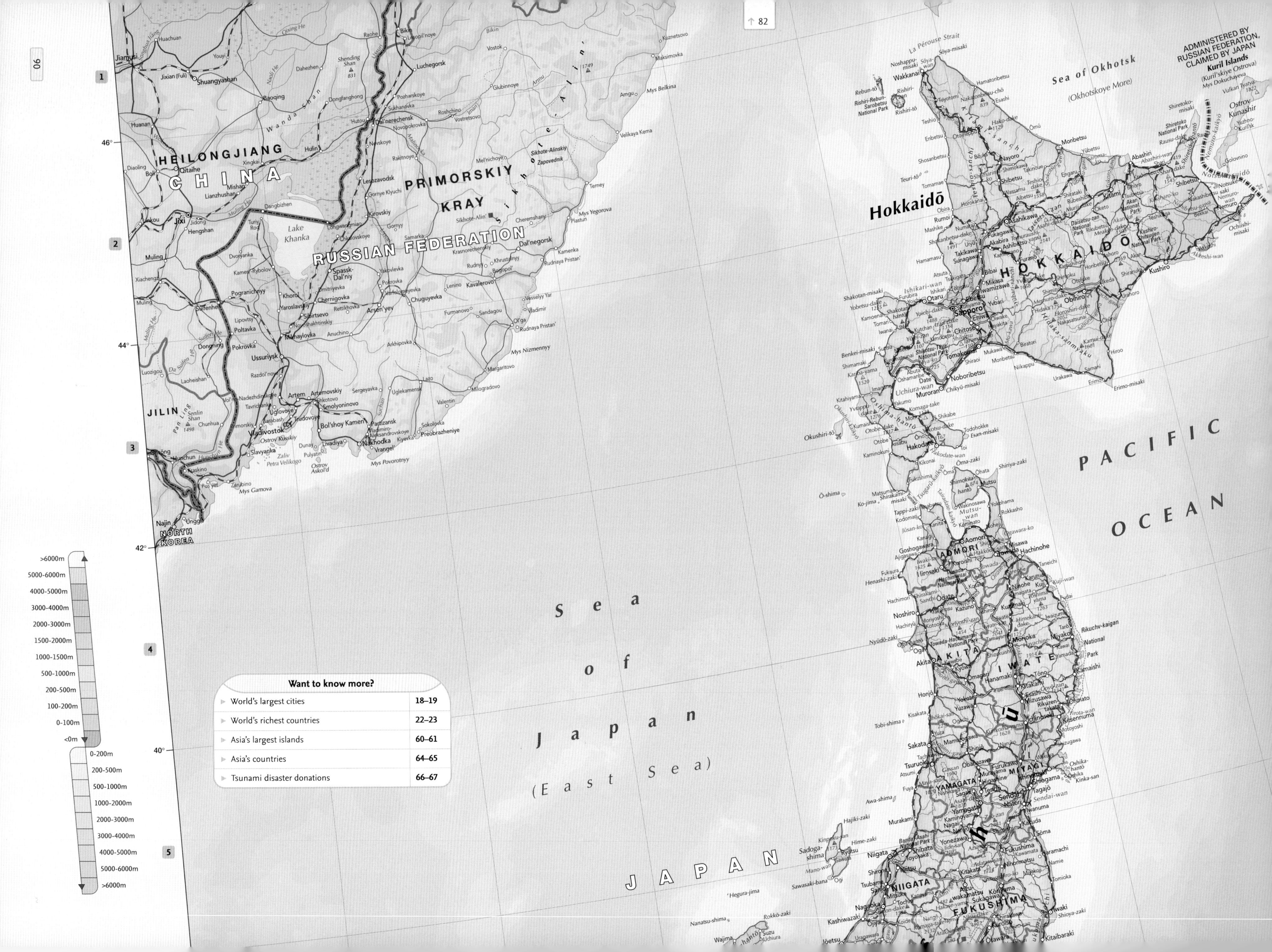

Want to know more?

World's largest cities	18–19
World's richest countries	22–23
Asia's largest islands	60–61
Asia's countries	64–65
Tsunami disaster donations	66–67

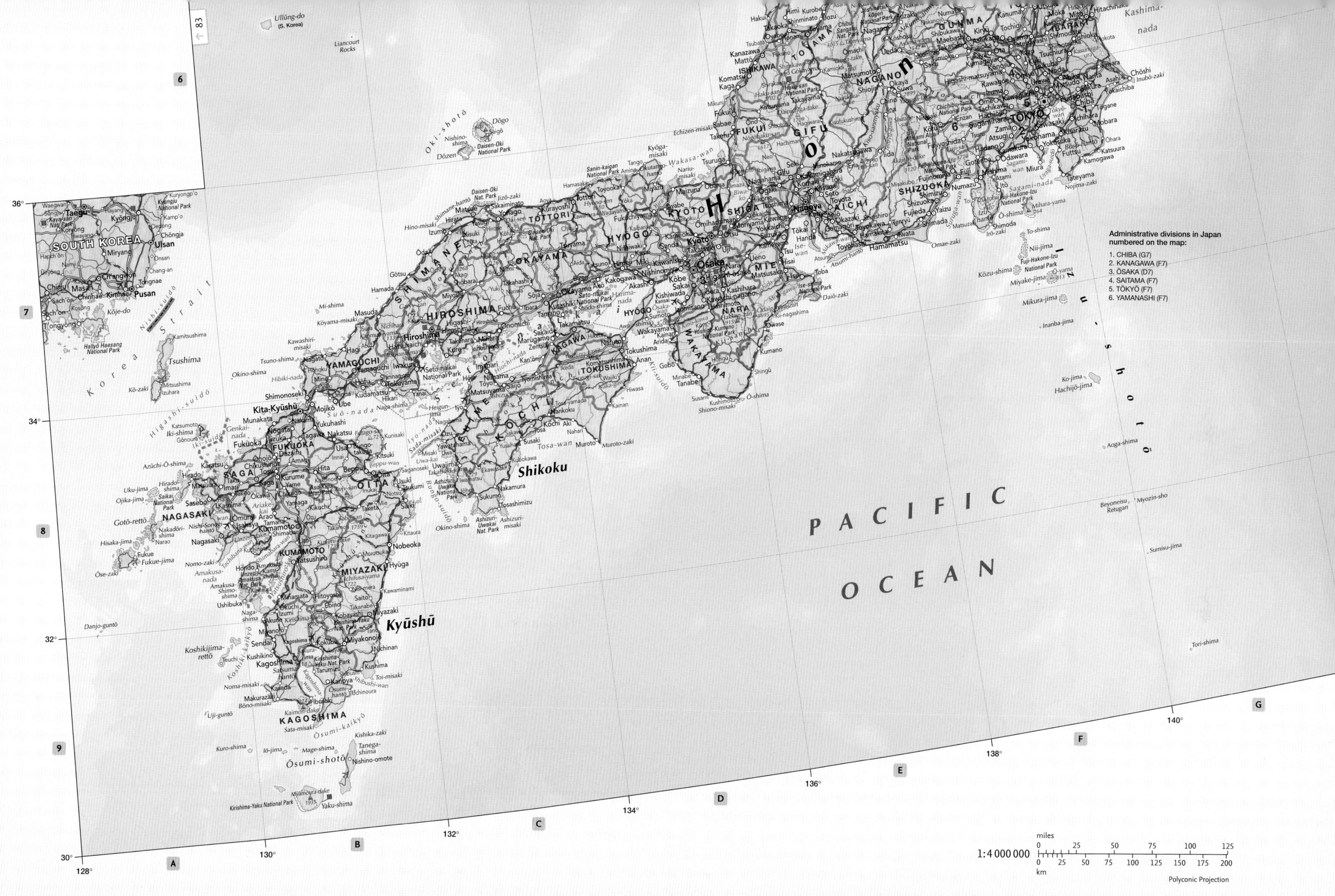

Administrative divisions in Japan numbered on the map:
1. CHIBA (G7)
2. KANAGAWA (F7)
3. ŌSAKA (D7)
4. SAITAMA (F7)
5. TŌKYŌ (F7)
6. YAMANASHI (F7)

1:4 000 000

Polyconic Projection

PACIFIC OCEAN

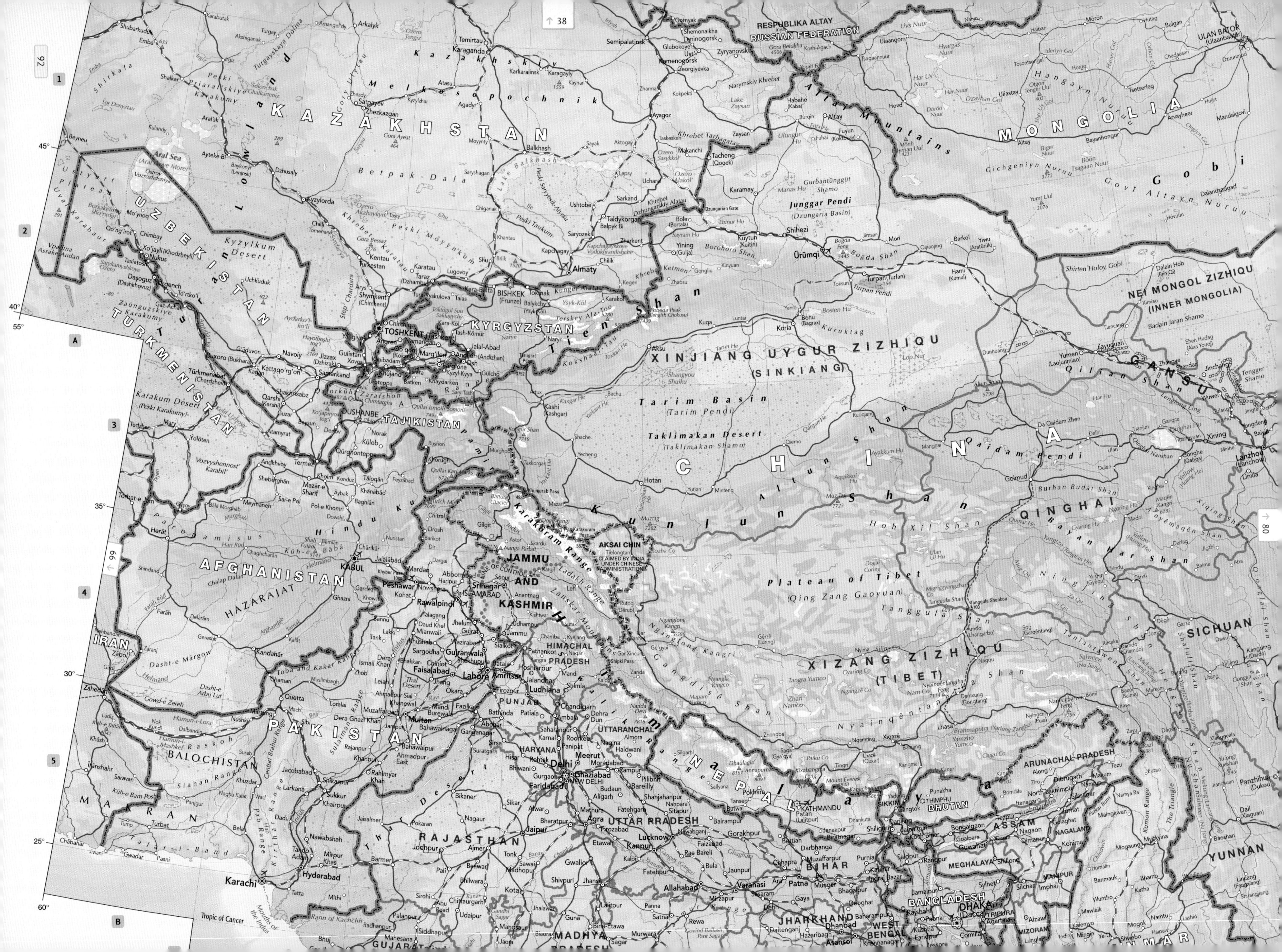
38
80
66
KAZAKHSTAN
UZBEKISTAN
TURKMENISTAN
KYRGYZSTAN
TAJIKISTAN
AFGHANISTAN
PAKISTAN
IRAN
MONGOLIA
CHINA
NEPAL
BHUTAN
BANGLADESH
RUSSIAN FEDERATION
RESPUBLIKA ALTAY
NEI MONGOL ZIZHIQU (INNER MONGOLIA)
GANSU
QINGHAI
SICHUAN
YUNNAN
XINJIANG UYGUR ZIZHIQU (SINKIANG)
XIZANG ZIZHIQU (TIBET)
AKSAI CHIN
JAMMU AND KASHMIR
HIMACHAL PRADESH
PUNJAB
HARYANA
UTTARANCHAL
UTTAR PRADESH
RAJASTHAN
BIHAR
JHARKHAND
WEST BENGAL
SIKKIM
ARUNACHAL PRADESH
ASSAM
MEGHALAYA
NAGALAND
MANIPUR
MIZORAM
TRIPURA
BALOCHISTAN
HAZARAJAT
ULAN BATOR
BISHKEK
TOSHKENT
DUSHANBE
KABUL
ISLAMABAD
KATHMANDU
THIMPHU
DHAKA
NEW DELHI
Almaty
Karachi
Altay Mountains
Gobi
Tien Shan
Kunlun Shan
Himalaya
Plateau of Tibet
Tarim Basin
Taklimakan Desert
Junggar Pendi
Qaidam Pendi
Karakoram Range
Hindu Kush
Aral Sea
Kyzylkum Desert
Karakum Desert
Lake Balkhash
Tropic of Cancer
Mouths of the Indus
1
2
3
4
5
A
B
45°
40°
35°
30°
25°
55°
60°

Asia Central and Southern Asia

Administrative divisions in India numbered on the map:
1. DADRA AND NAGAR HAVELI (D6)
2. DAMAN AND DIU (D6)

Want to know more?

► Cross-section of Asia	6–7
► Perspective view of Asia	60–61
► Political map of Asia	64–65
► Asia statistics	70–71
► Map of Indian Ocean	218–219

1:12 000 000

miles
0   100   200   300   400   500

km
0   100   200   300   400   500   600   700   800

Albers Equal Area Conic Projection

>6000m
5000-6000m
4000-5000m
3000-4000m
2000-3000m
1000-2000m
500-1000m
200-500m
0-200m
<0m

0-200m
200-500m
500-1000m
1000-2000m
2000-3000m
3000-4000m
4000-5000m
5000-6000m
>6000m

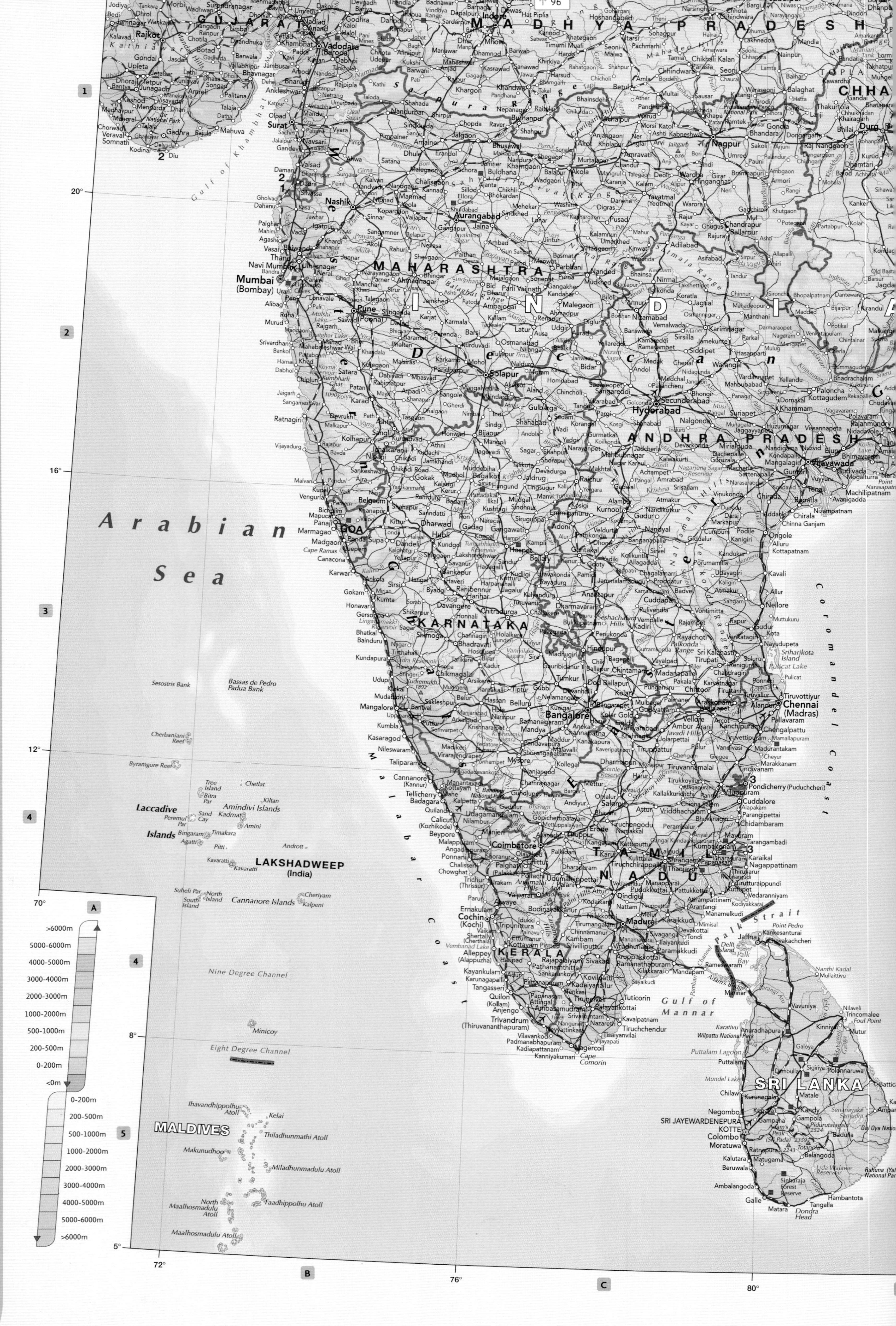

Asia Southern India and Sri Lanka

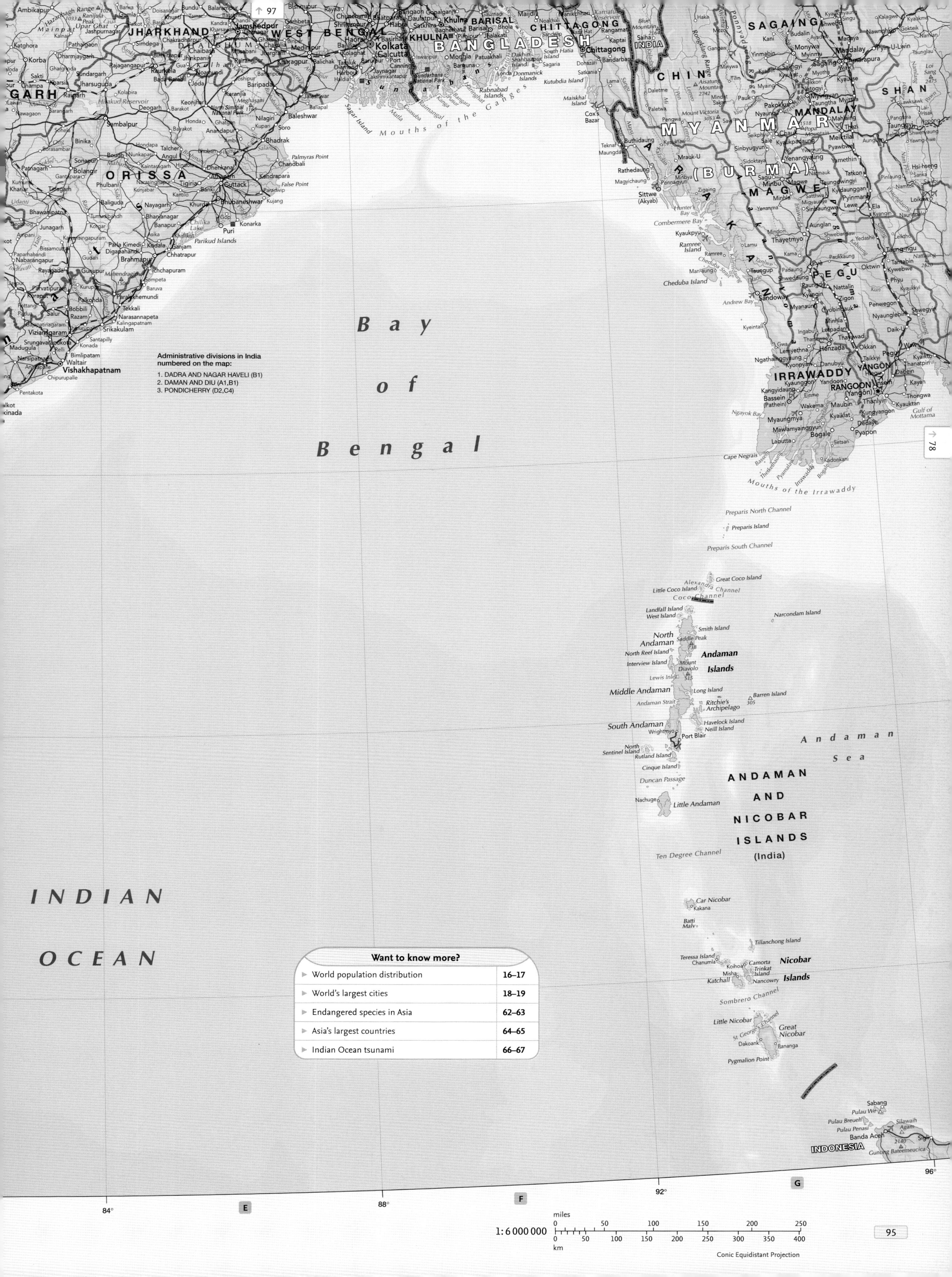

Want to know more?

World population distribution	16–17
World's largest cities	18–19
Endangered species in Asia	62–63
Asia's largest countries	64–65
Indian Ocean tsunami	66–67

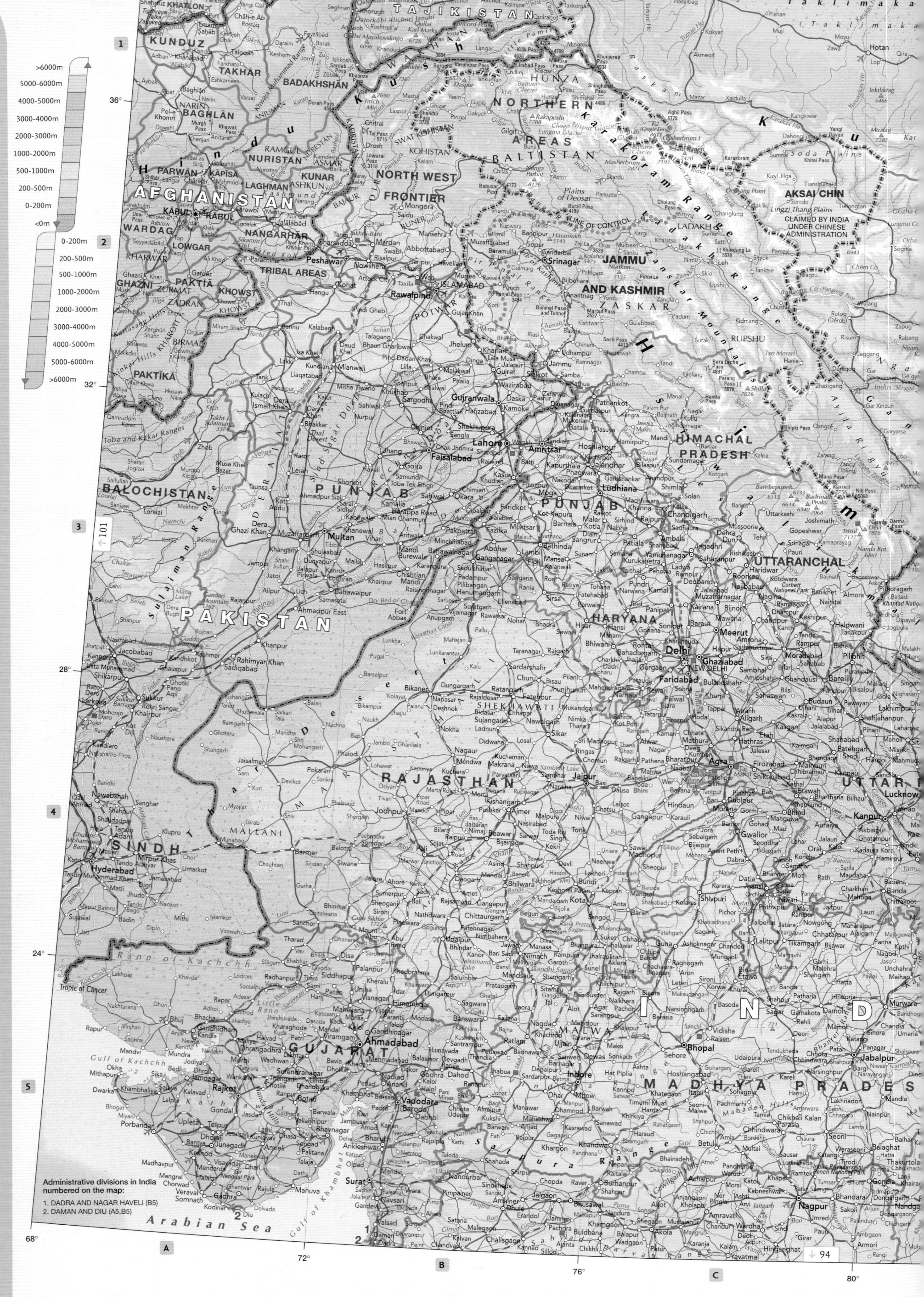

Administrative divisions in India
numbered on the map:

1. DADRA AND NAGAR HAVELI (B5)
2. DAMAN AND DIU (A5,B5)

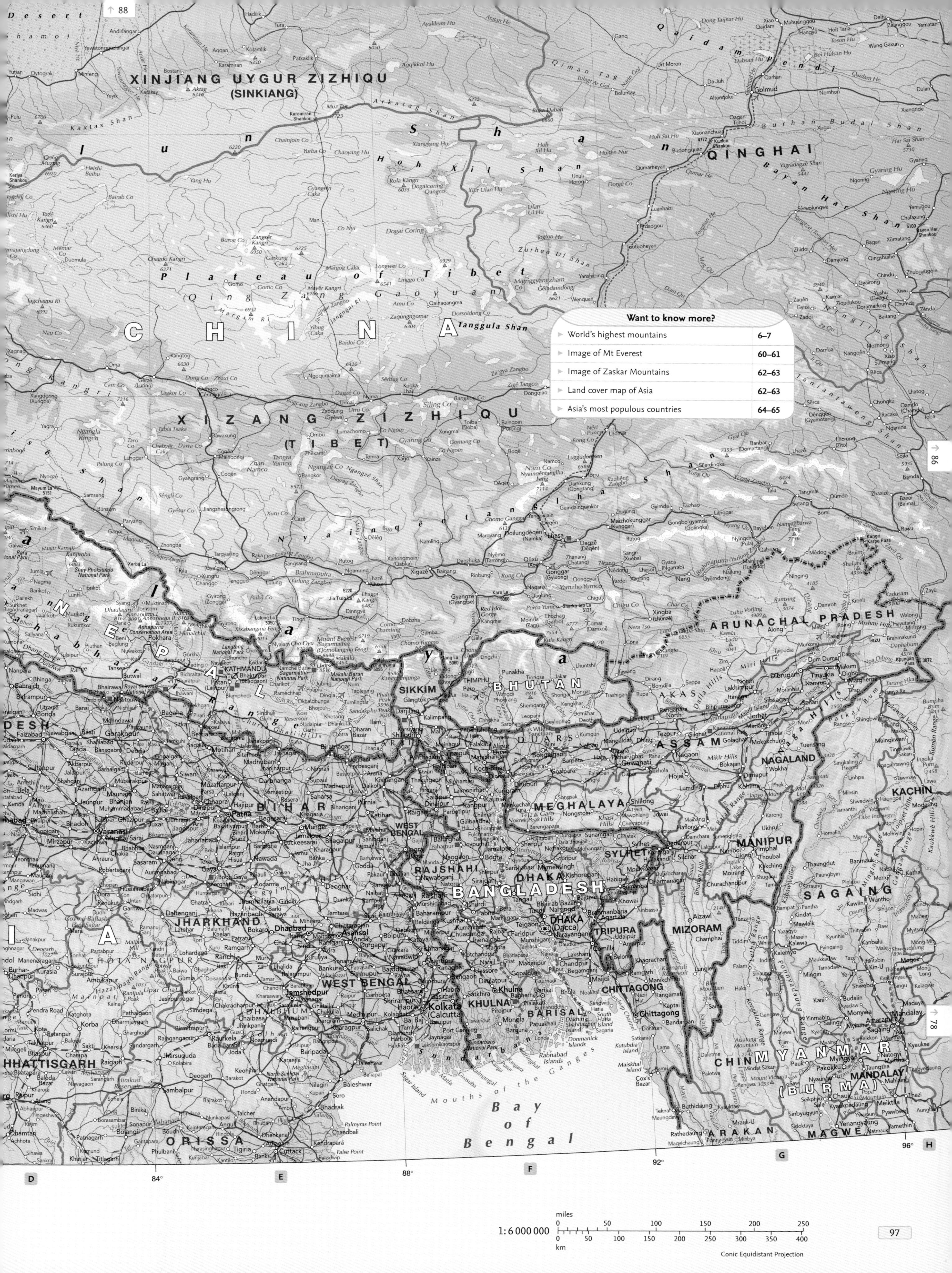

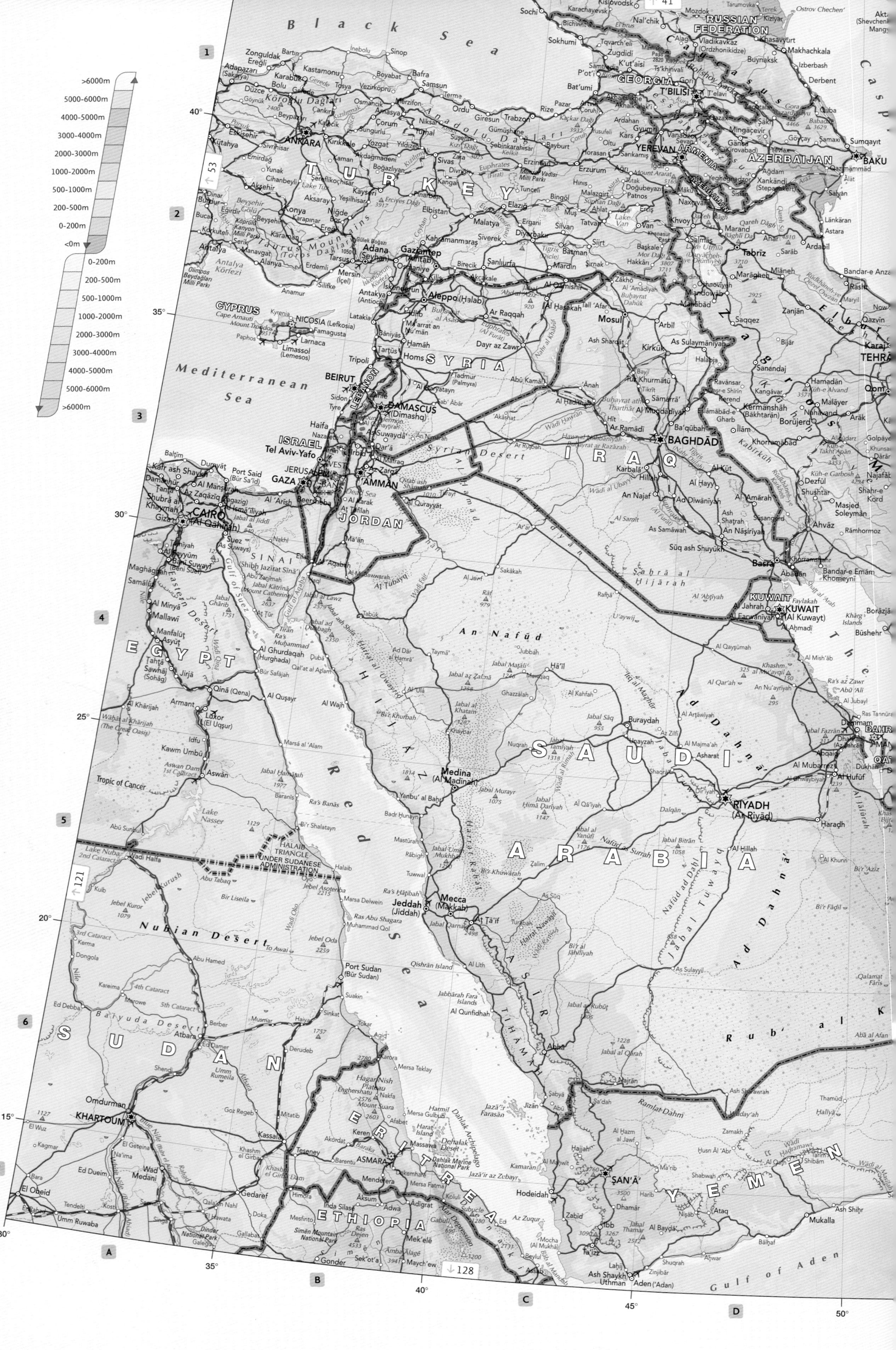
>6000m
5000-6000m
4000-5000m
3000-4000m
2000-3000m
1000-2000m
500-1000m
200-500m
0-200m
<0m
0-200m
200-500m
500-1000m
1000-2000m
2000-3000m
3000-4000m
4000-5000m
5000-6000m
>6000m
Black Sea
Mediterranean Sea
Red Sea
Gulf of Aden
RUSSIAN FEDERATION
GEORGIA
T'BILISI
ARMENIA
YEREVAN
AZERBAIJAN
BAKU
TURKEY
ANKARA
CYPRUS
NICOSIA (Lefkosia)
SYRIA
DAMASCUS (Dimashq)
LEBANON
BEIRUT
ISRAEL
JERUSALEM
Tel Aviv-Yafo
GAZA
JORDAN
'AMMAN
IRAQ
BAGHDĀD
KUWAIT
KUWAIT (Al Kuwayt)
SAUDI ARABIA
RIYADH (Ar Riyāḍ)
Mecca (Makkah)
Medina (Al Madīnah)
Jeddah (Jiddah)
EGYPT
CAIRO (Al Qāhirah)
SINAI
SUDAN
KHARTOUM
Omdurman
ERITREA
ASMARA
ETHIOPIA
YEMEN
ṢAN'Ā'
HALAIB TRIANGLE UNDER SUDANESE ADMINISTRATION
Syrian Desert
An Nafūd
Nubian Desert
Rub' al Khali
Tropic of Cancer
Lake Nasser
Aden ('Adan)
Port Sudan (Būr Sudan)
Aleppo (Ḥalab)
Mosul
Basra
Tabrīz
↑ 41
↑ 53
↑ 121
↓ 128
40°
35°
30°
25°
20°
15°
45°
50°
1
2
3
4
5
6
7
A
B
C
D

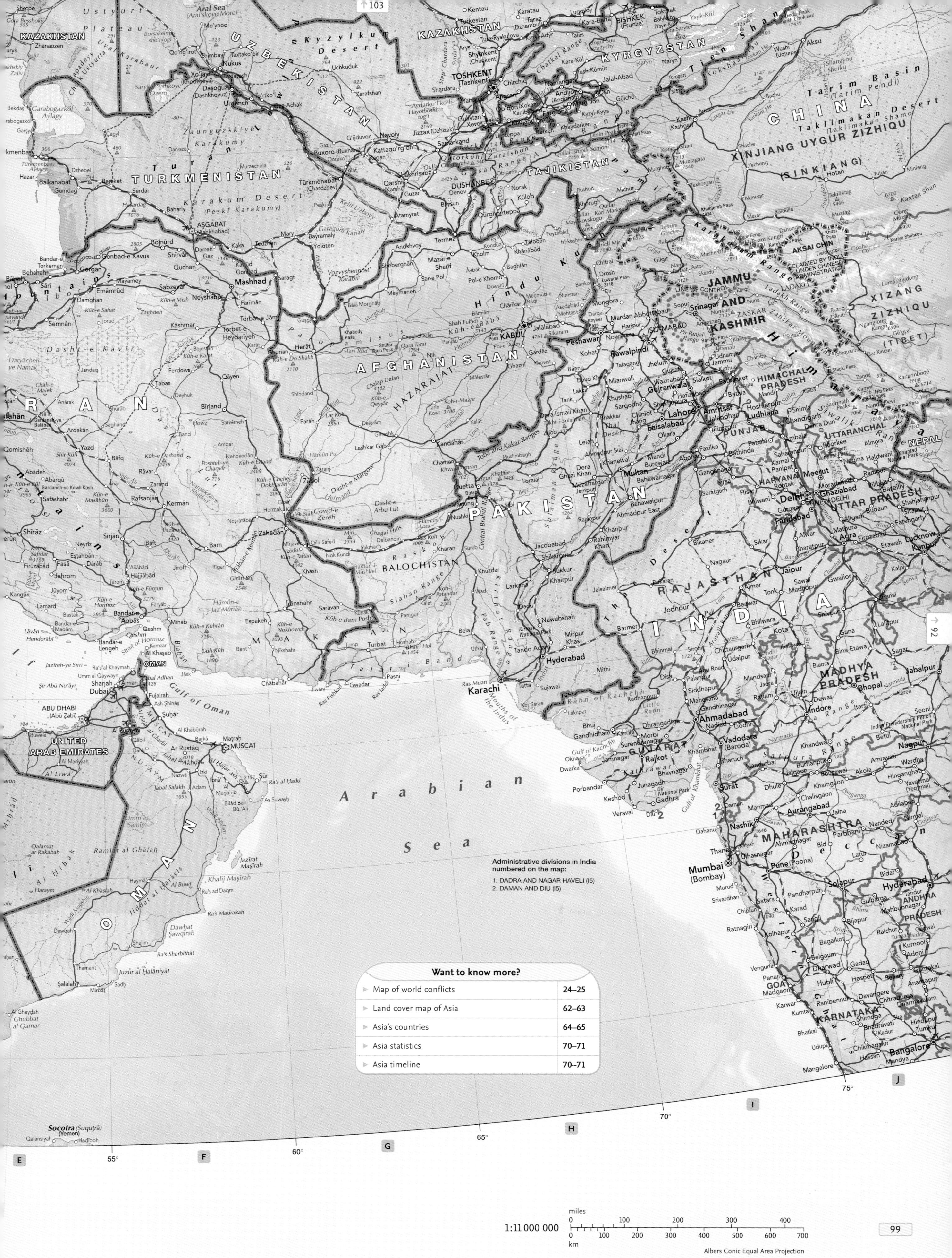

→ 92

Want to know more?

▷ Map of world conflicts	24–25
▷ Land cover map of Asia	62–63
▷ Asia's countries	64–65
▷ Asia statistics	70–71
▷ Asia timeline	70–71

Administrative divisions in India numbered on the map:
1. DADRA AND NAGAR HAVELI (I5)
2. DAMAN AND DIU (I5)

1:11 000 000

miles
0   100   200   300   400

0 100 200 300 400 500 600 700
km

Albers Conic Equal Area Projection

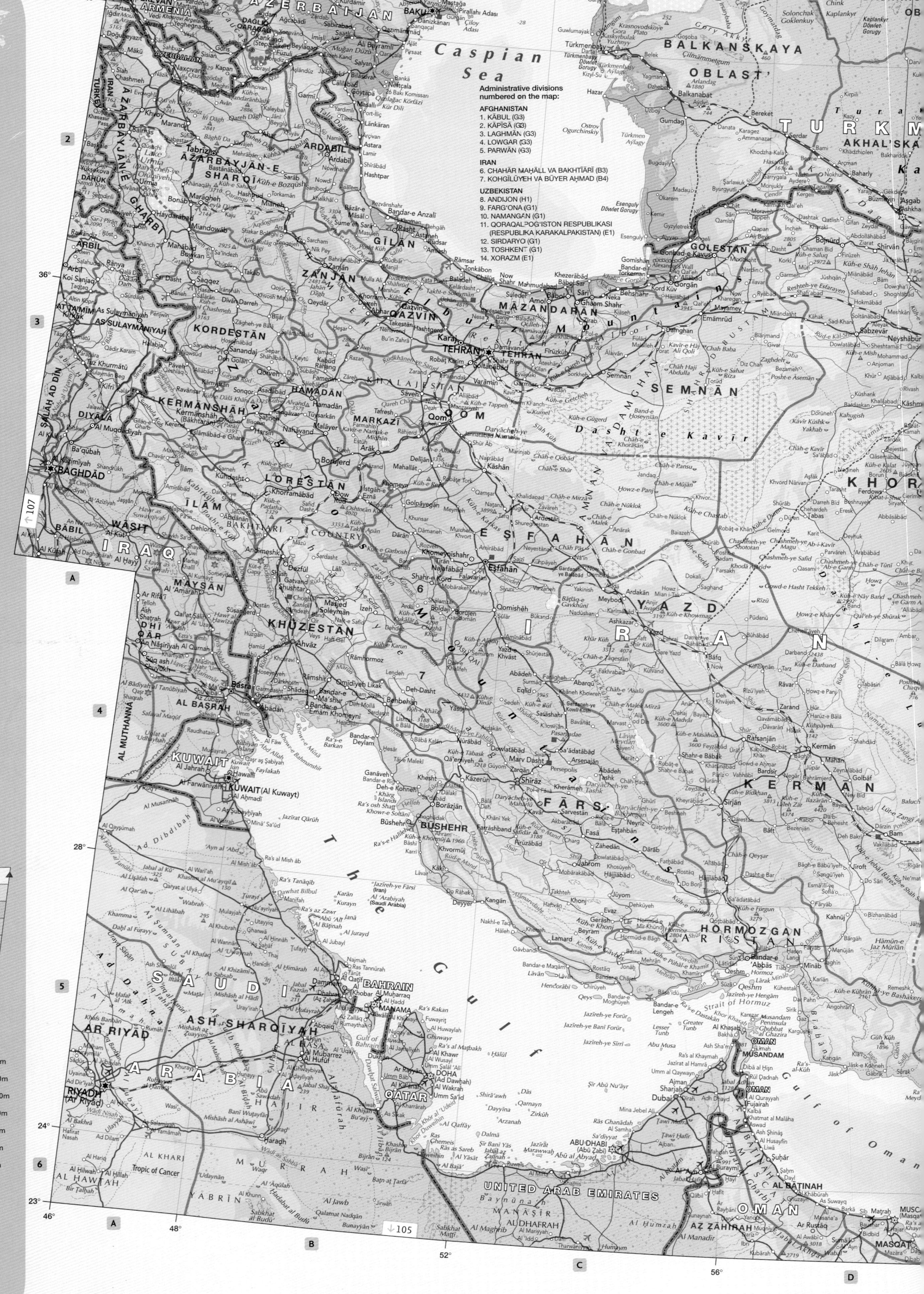

↑ 102
↑ 107
↓ 105

Administrative divisions
numbered on the map:

AFGHANISTAN
1. KĀBUL (G3)
2. KĀPĪSĀ (G3)
3. LAGHMĀN (G3)
4. LOWGAR (G3)
5. PARWĀN (G3)

IRAN
6. CHAHĀR MAḤALL VA BAKHTĪĀRĪ (B3)
7. KOHGĪLŪYEH VA BŪYER AḤMAD (B4)

UZBEKISTAN
8. ANDIJON (H1)
9. FARG'ONA (G1)
10. NAMANGAN (G1)
11. QORAQALPOG'ISTON RESPUBLIKASI
(RESPUBLIKA KARAKALPAKISTAN) (E1)
12. SIRDARYO (G1)
13. TOSHKENT (G1)
14. XORAZM (E1)

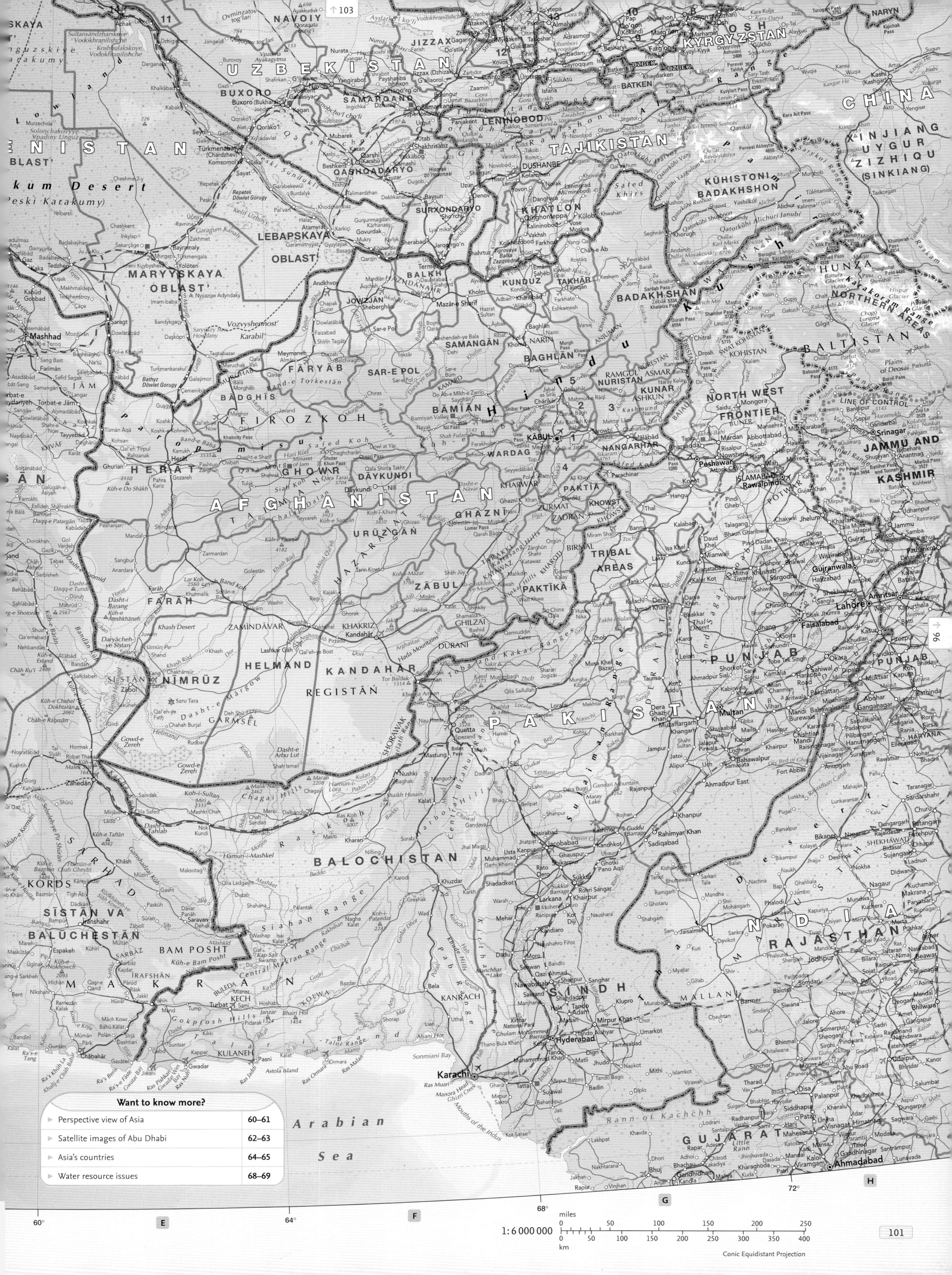

1:6 000 000

miles

Conic Equidistant Projection

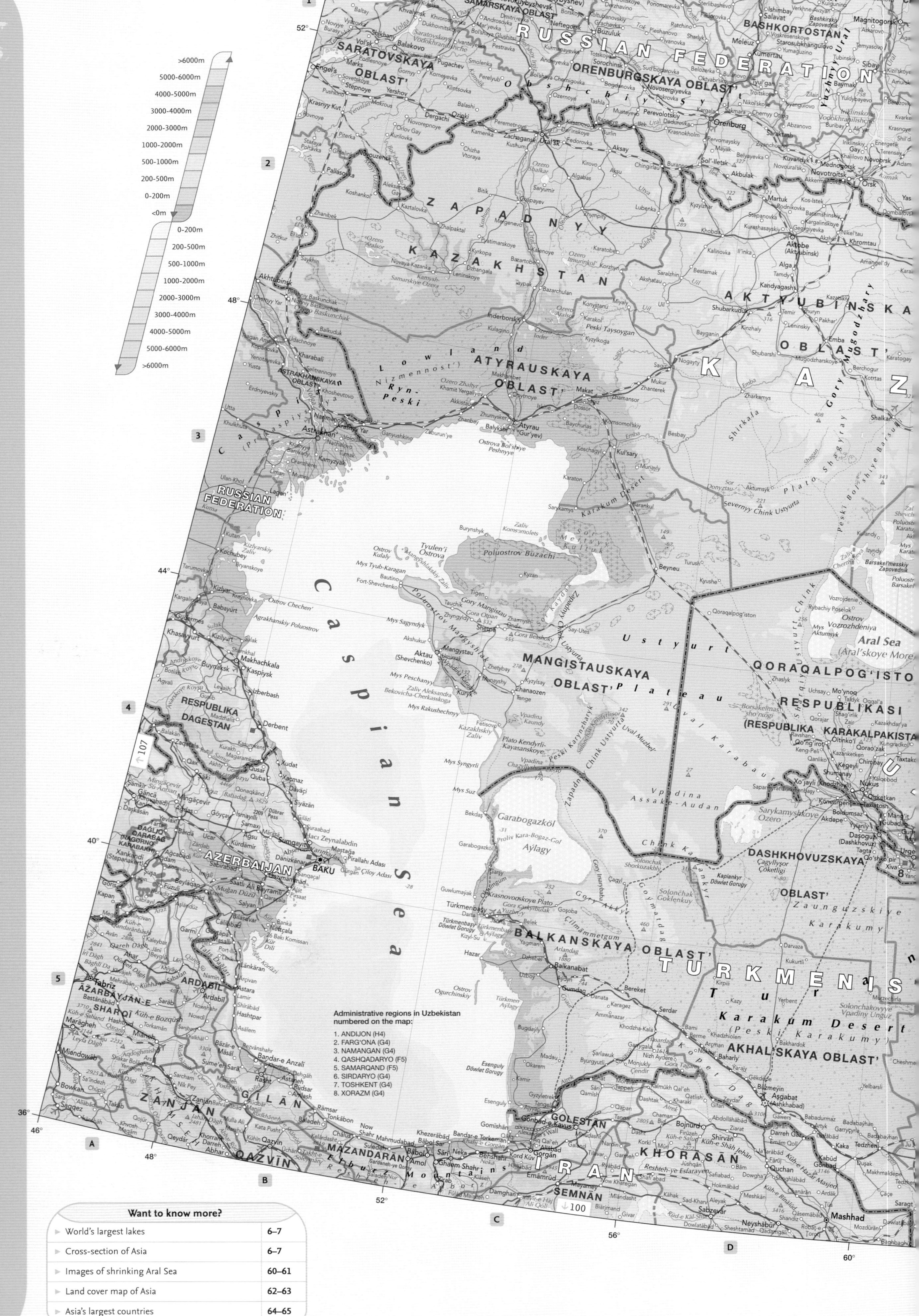

Administrative regions in Uzbekistan
numbered on the map:

1. ANDIJON (H4)
2. FARG'ONA (G4)
3. NAMANGAN (G4)
4. QASHQADARYO (F5)
5. SAMARQAND (F5)
6. SIRDARYO (G4)
7. TOSHKENT (G4)
8. XORAZM (G4)

Want to know more?

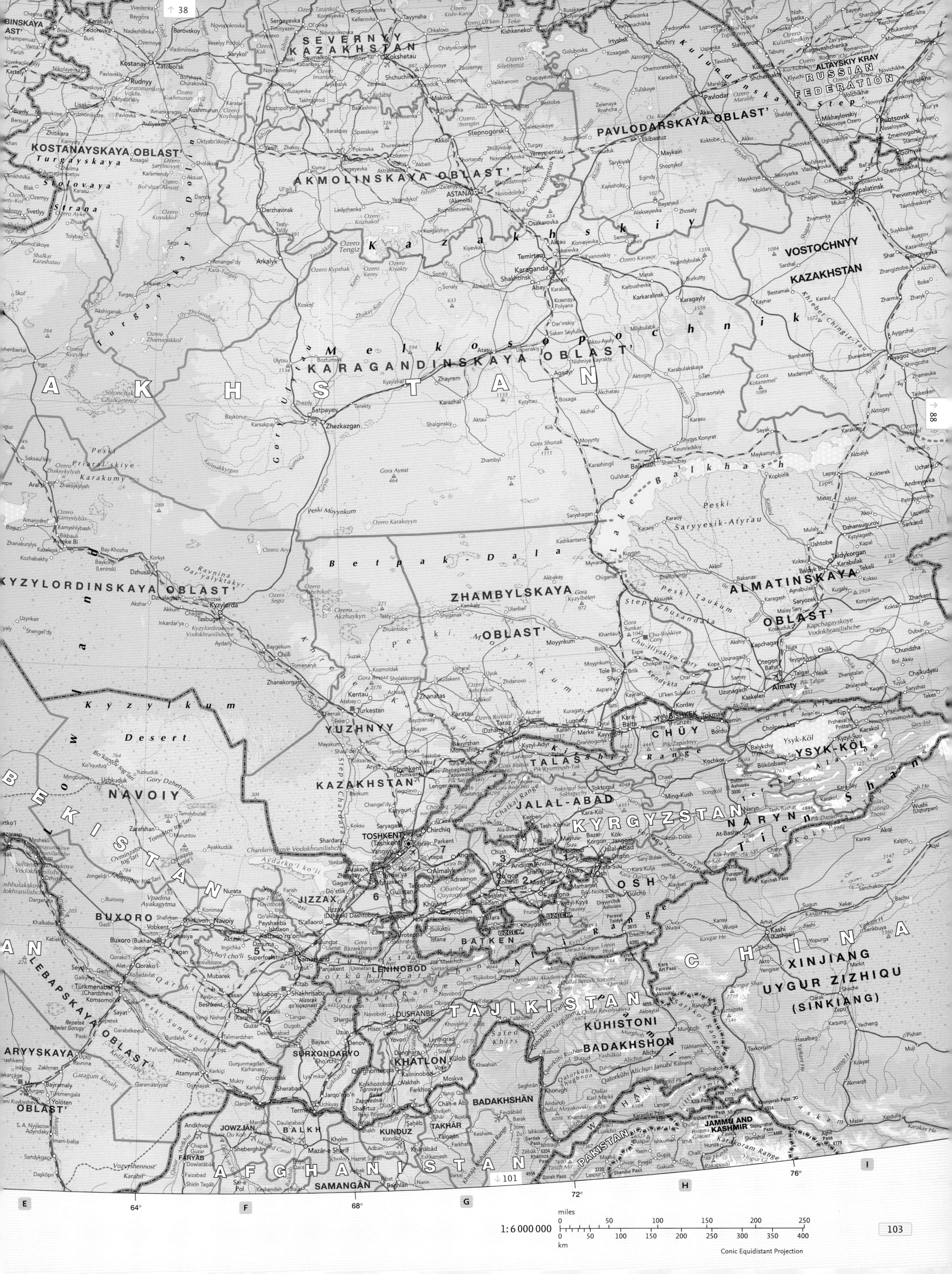

↑ 38
SEVERNYY KAZAKHSTAN
KOSTANAYSKAYA OBLAST'
AKMOLINSKAYA OBLAST'
PAVLODARSKAYA OBLAST'
ALTAYSKIY KRAY
RUSSIAN FEDERATION
Kulundinskaya Step'
Turgayskaya Stolovaya Strana
Kazakhskiy Melkosopochnik
KARAGANDINSKAYA OBLAST'
VOSTOCHNYY KAZAKHSTAN
ASTANA (Akmola)
Karaganda
Kostanay
Pavlodar
Semipalatinsk
Kokshetau
Zhezkazgan
Balkhash
Lake Balkhash
Peski Priaral'skiye Karakumy
Betpak-Dala
KYZYLORDINSKAYA OBLAST'
Kyzylorda
ZHAMBYLSKAYA OBLAST'
ALMATINSKAYA OBLAST'
Almaty
Taldykorgan
Kyzylkum Desert
YUZHNYY KAZAKHSTAN
Shymkent (Chimkent)
Taraz (Dzhambul)
BISHKEK (Frunze)
CHÜY
TALAS
YSYK-KÖL
Ysyk-Köl
NARYN
JALAL-ABAD
KYRGYZSTAN
OSH
BATKEN
Tien Shan
Alai Range
NAVOIY
BUXORO
JIZZAX
TOSHKENT (Tashkent)
UZBEKISTAN
LEBAPSKAYA OBLAST'
MARYYSKAYA OBLAST'
SURXONDARYO
Samarkand
Qarshi
LENINOBOD
TAJIKISTAN
DUSHANBE
KHATLON
KŪHISTONI BADAKHSHON
BADAKHSHĀN
JOWZJĀN
BALKH
KUNDUZ
TAKHĀR
SAMANGĀN
AFGHANISTAN
PAKISTAN
JAMMU AND KASHMIR
CHINA
XINJIANG UYGUR ZIZHIQU (SINKIANG)
Kashi (Kashgar)
88 →
↓ 101
E
F
G
H
I
64°
68°
72°
76°
1:6 000 000
miles
0 50 100 150 200 250
0 50 100 150 200 250 300 350 400
km
Conic Equidistant Projection

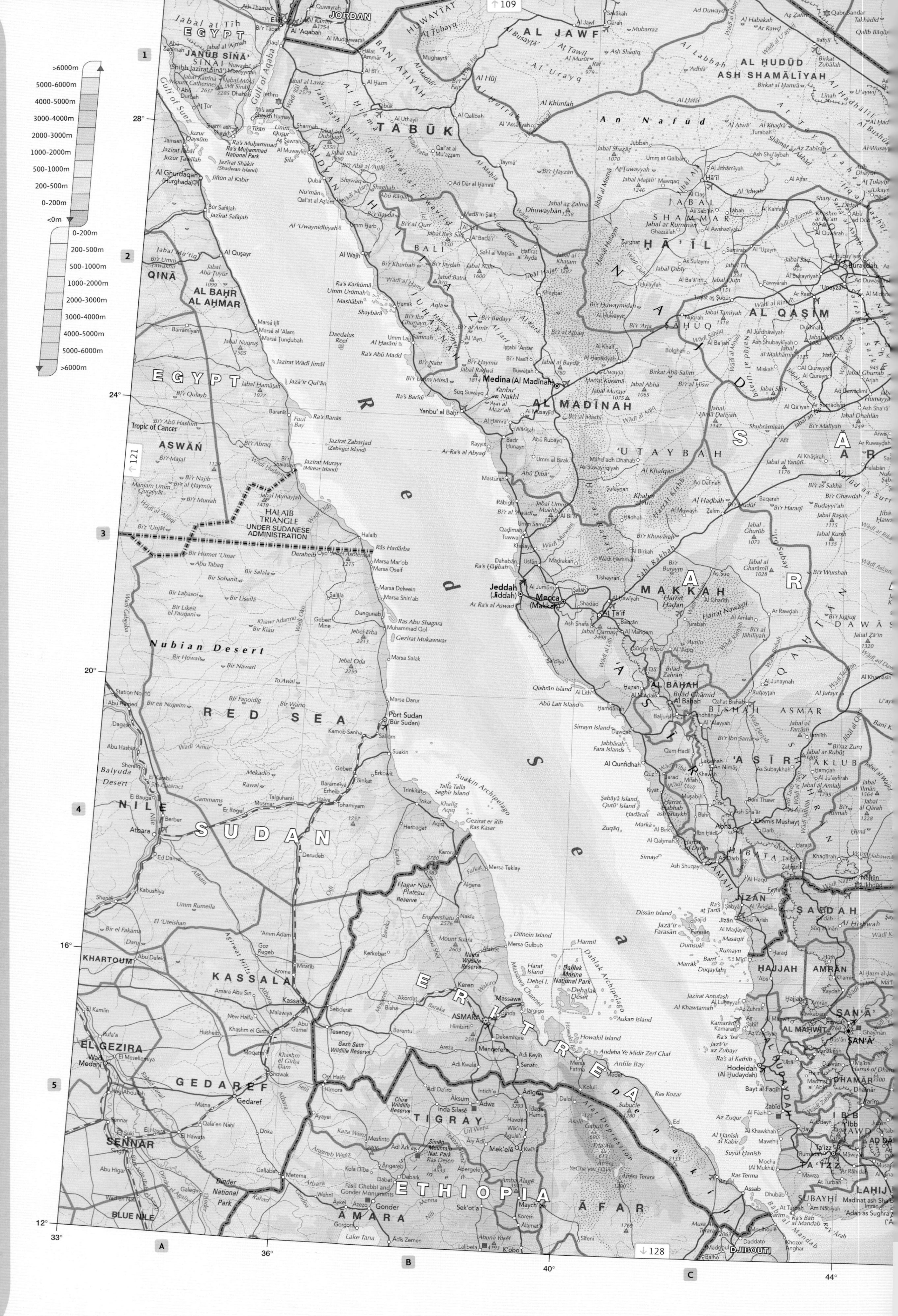

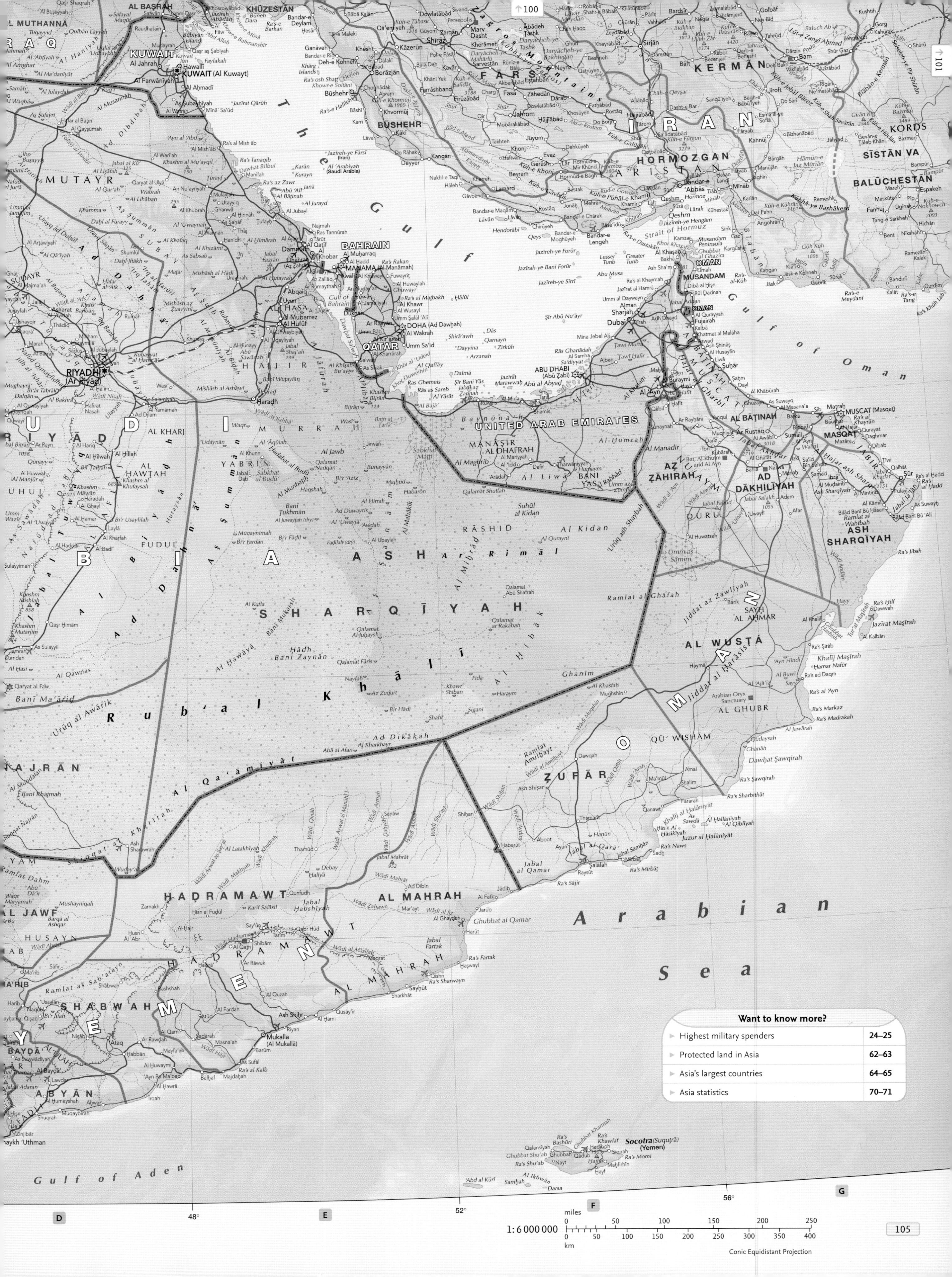

1:6 000 000

miles
0   50   100   150   200   250
0 50 100 150 200 250 300 350 400
km

Conic Equidistant Projection

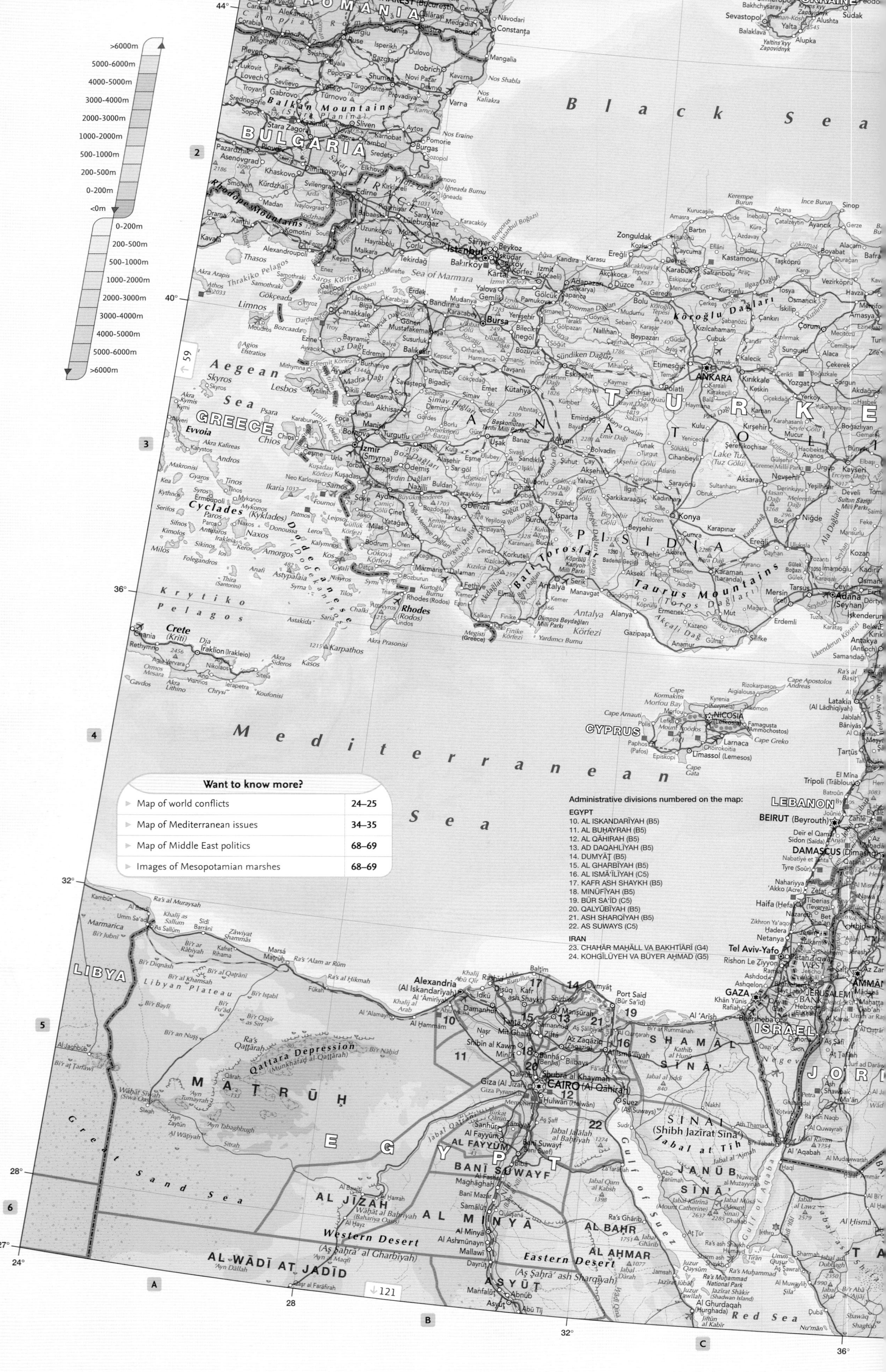

Elevation scale:
- >6000m
- 5000-6000m
- 4000-5000m
- 3000-4000m
- 2000-3000m
- 1000-2000m
- 500-1000m
- 200-500m
- 0-200m
- <0m

Depth scale:
- 0-200m
- 200-500m
- 500-1000m
- 1000-2000m
- 2000-3000m
- 3000-4000m
- 4000-5000m
- 5000-6000m
- >6000m

Want to know more?

Administrative divisions numbered on the map:

EGYPT
10. AL ISKANDARĪYAH (B5)
11. AL BUḤAYRAH (B5)
12. AL QĀHIRAH (B5)
13. AD DAQAHLĪYAH (B5)
14. DUMYĀṬ (B5)
15. AL GHARBĪYAH (B5)
16. AL ISMĀ'ĪLĪYAH (C5)
17. KAFR ASH SHAYKH (B5)
18. MINŪFĪYAH (B5)
19. BŪR SA'ĪD (C5)
20. QALYŪBĪYAH (B5)
21. ASH SHARQĪYAH (B5)
22. AS SUWAYS (C5)

IRAN
23. CHAHĀR MAḤALL VA BAKHTĪĀRĪ (G4)
24. KOHGĪLŪYEH VA BŪYER AḤMAD (G5)

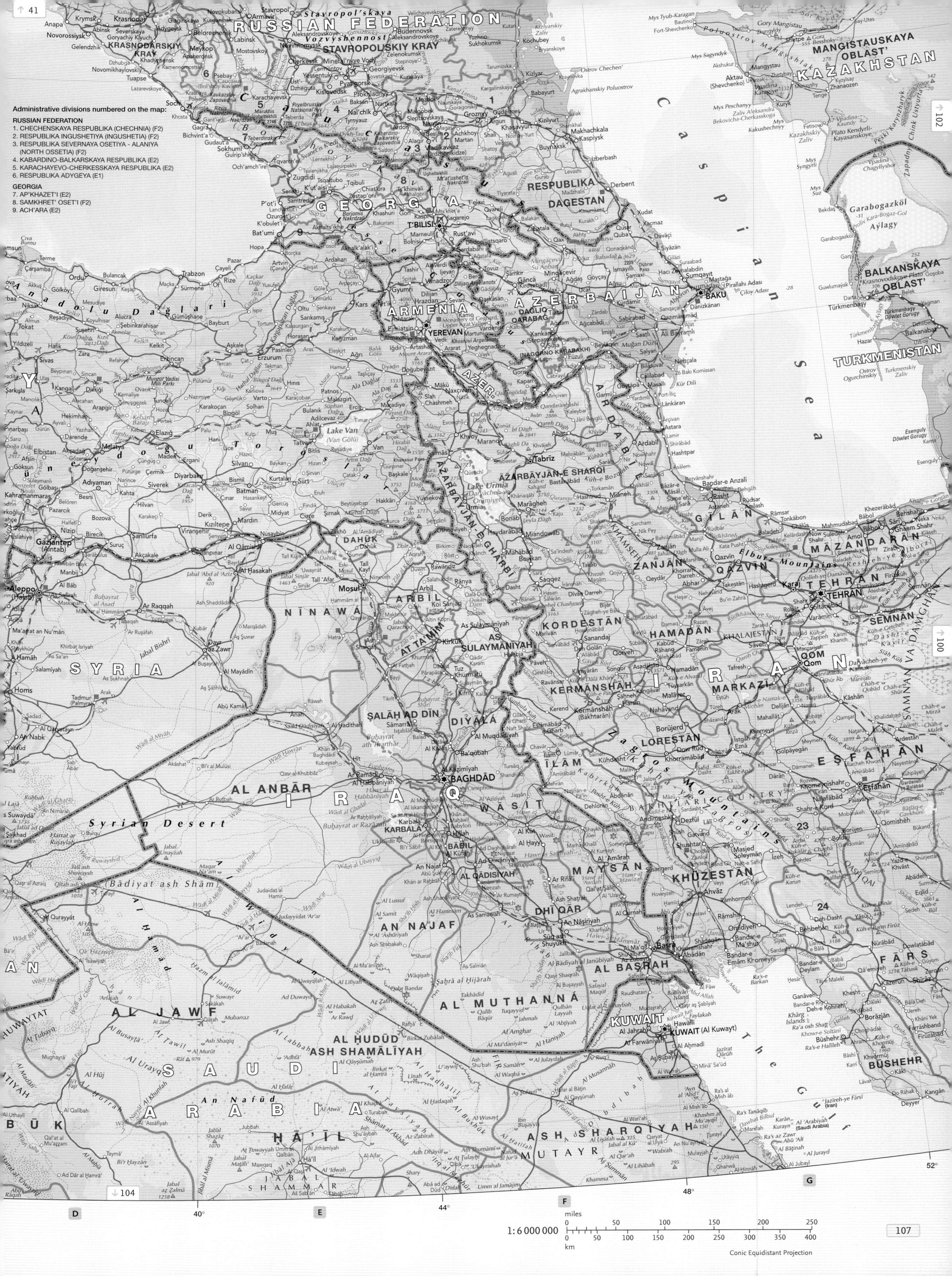
Administrative divisions numbered on the map:
RUSSIAN FEDERATION
1. CHECHENSKAYA RESPUBLIKA (CHECHNIA) (F2)
2. RESPUBLIKA INGUSHETIYA (INGUSHETIA) (F2)
3. RESPUBLIKA SEVERNAYA OSETIYA - ALANIYA (NORTH OSSETIA) (F2)
4. KABARDINO-BALKARSKAYA RESPUBLIKA (E2)
5. KARACHAYEVO-CHERKESSKAYA RESPUBLIKA (E2)
6. RESPUBLIKA ADYGEYA (E1)
GEORGIA
7. AP'KHAZET'I (E2)
8. SAMKHRET' OSET'I (F2)
9. ACH'ARA (E2)
RUSSIAN FEDERATION
STAVROPOL'SKIY KRAY
KRASNODARSKIY KRAY
RESPUBLIKA DAGESTAN
GEORGIA
T'BILISI
ARMENIA
YEREVAN
AZERBAIJAN
BAKU
Caspian Sea
KAZAKHSTAN
MANGISTAUSKAYA OBLAST'
BALKANSKAYA OBLAST'
TURKMENISTAN
SYRIA
IRAQ
BAGHDAD
IRAN
TEHRAN
KUWAIT
KUWAIT (Al Kuwayt)
SAUDI ARABIA
The Gulf
Lake Van
Lake Urmia
Syrian Desert
Zagros Mountains
Elburz Mountains
1: 6 000 000
miles
0 50 100 150 200 250
0 50 100 150 200 250 300 350 400
km
Conic Equidistant Projection
40°
44°
48°
52°
D
E
F
G

→ 102
→ 100
↓ 104

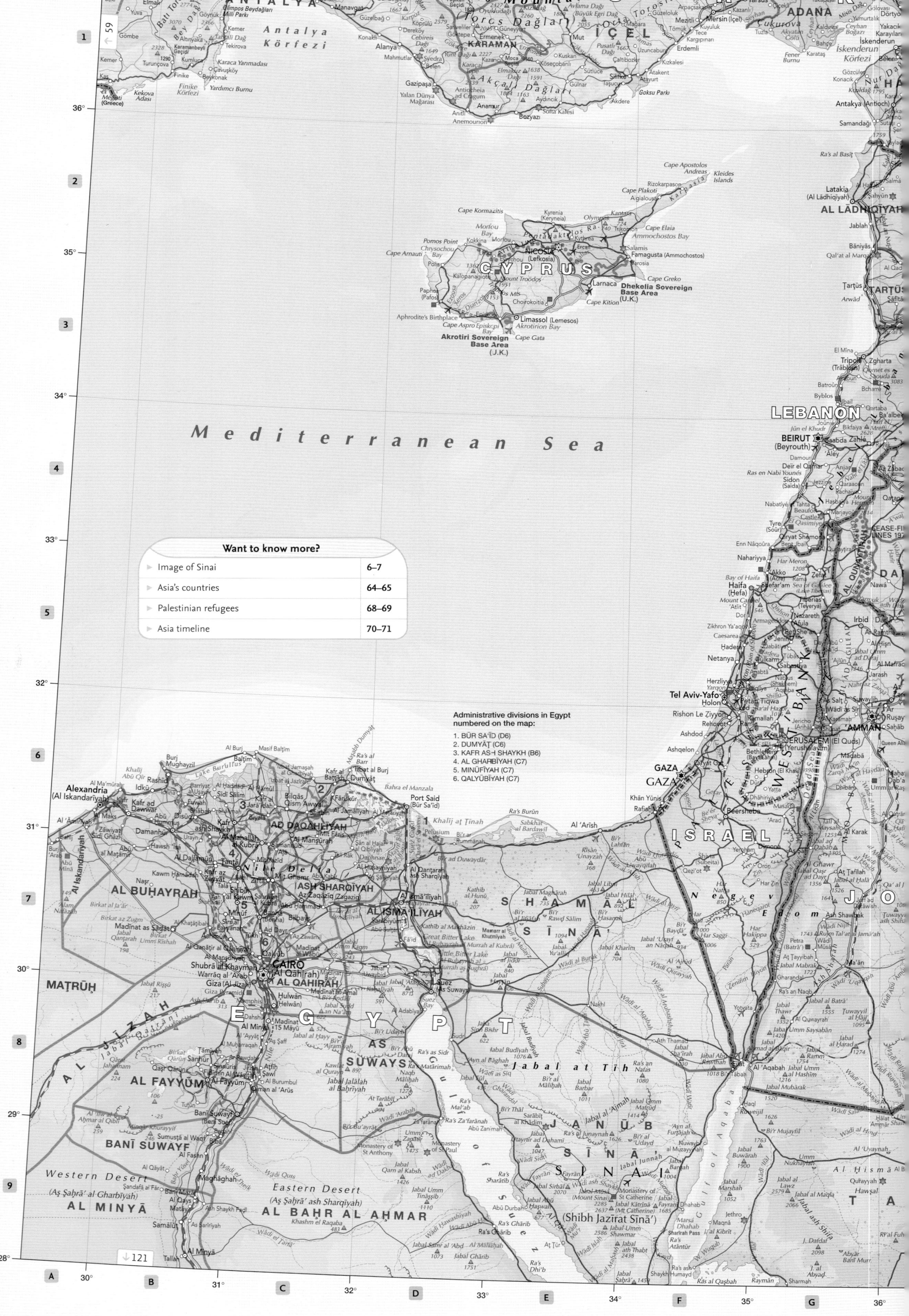

← 59
↓ 121

Want to know more?

Administrative divisions in Egypt
numbered on the map:

1. BŪR SA'ĪD (D6)
2. DUMYĀṬ (C6)
3. KAFR ASH SHAYKH (B6)
4. AL GHARBĪYAH (C7)
5. MINŪFĪYAH (C7)
6. QALYŪBĪYAH (C7)

>6000m
5000–6000m
4000–5000m
3000–4000m
2000–3000m
1500–2000m
1000–1500m
500–1000m
200–500m
100–200m
0–100m
<0m

0–200m
200–500m
500–1000m
1000–2000m
2000–3000m
3000–4000m
4000–5000m
5000–6000m
>6000m

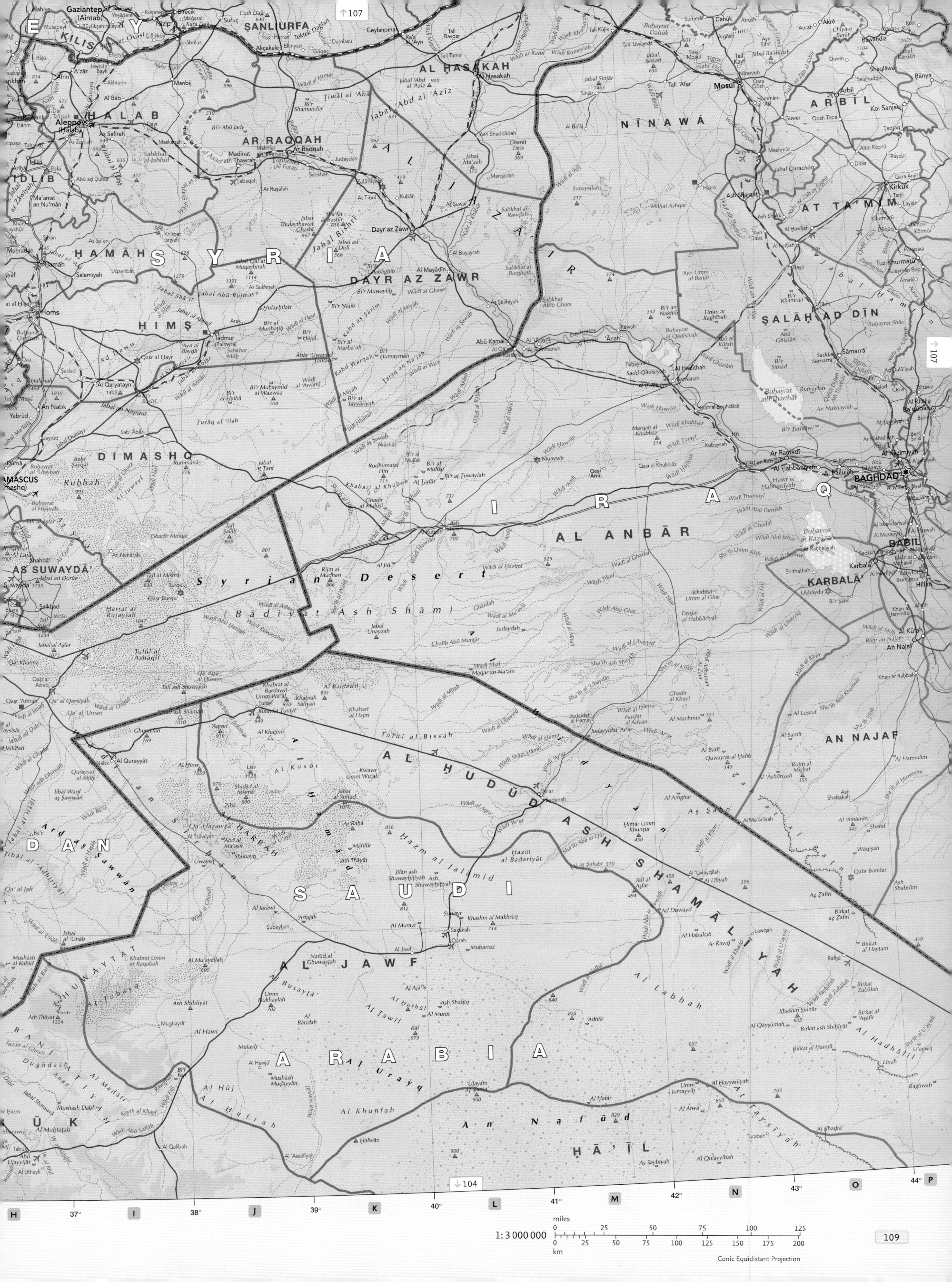

SYRIA
IRAQ
SAUDI ARABIA
Syrian Desert
(Bādiyat Ash Shām)
AL JAZĪRAH
ḤALAB
AR RAQQAH
AL ḤASAKAH
DAYR AZ ZAWR
ḤAMĀH
ḤIMṢ
DIMASHQ
AS SUWAYDĀ'
IDLIB
NĪNAWÁ
ARBĪL
AT TA'MĪM
ṢALĀḤ AD DĪN
AL ANBĀR
BĀBIL
KARBALĀ'
AN NAJAF
AL ḤUDŪD ASH SHAMĀLĪYAH
AL JAWF
ḤĀ'ĪL
An Nafūd
Al Ḥamād
Aleppo (Ḥalab)
Homs
Ḥamāh
Tadmur (Palmyra)
Ar Raqqah
Dayr az Zawr
Al Ḥasakah
Mosul
Arbīl
Kirkuk
Sāmarrā'
BAGHDAD
Ar Ramādī
Al Fallūjah
Karbalā'
Al Ḥillah
Al Kūfah
An Najaf
Ar Ruṭbah
Abū Kamāl
Ḥadīthah
Hīt
Gaziantep (Aintab)
ŞANLIURFA
Euphrates
Tigris
Buḥayrat ath Tharthār
Buḥayrat ar Razāzah
Sakākah
Ṭurayf
'Ar'ar
Rafḥā'
1:3 000 000
miles
0 25 50 75 100 125
0 25 50 75 100 125 150 175 200
km
Conic Equidistant Projection

↑107
↑107
↓104

Africa, viewed here from above the southern Indian Ocean, is dominated by several striking physical features. The Sahara desert extends over most of the north and in the east the geological feature known as the Great Rift Valley, extends from the valley of the river Jordan in southwest Asia to Mozambique. The valley contains a string of major lakes including Lake Turkana, Lake Tanganyika and Lake Nyasa. The river basin of the Congo, in central Africa draining into the Atlantic Ocean, is the second largest river basin in the world.

The land south of the equator is higher than in the north and forms a massive plateau dissected by several large rivers which flow east to the Indian Ocean or west to the Atlantic. The most distinctive feature in the south is the Drakensberg, a range of mountains which run southwest to northeast through Lesotho and South Africa. The large island separated from Africa by the Mozambique Channel is Madagascar, the fourth largest island in the world.

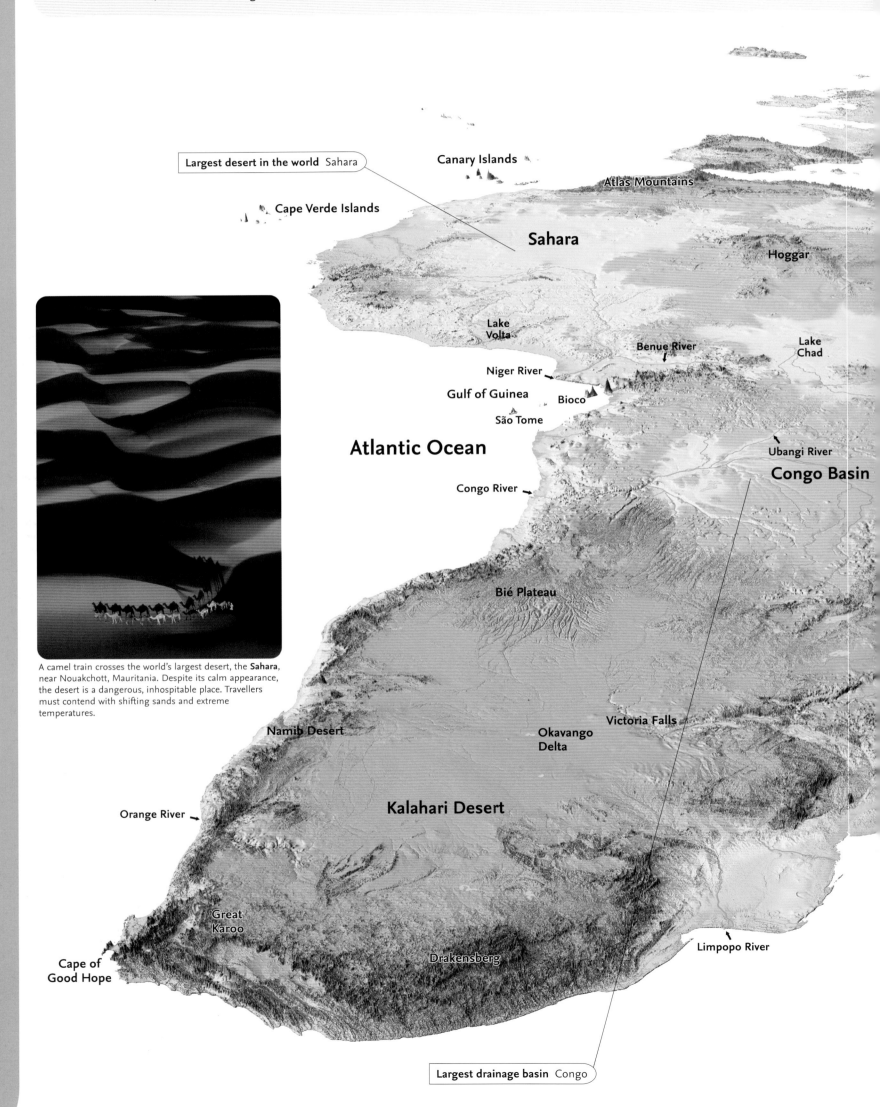

A camel train crosses the world's largest desert, the **Sahara**, near Nouakchott, Mauritania. Despite its calm appearance, the desert is a dangerous, inhospitable place. Travellers must contend with shifting sands and extreme temperatures.

Largest desert in the world Sahara

Canary Islands

Atlas Mountains

Cape Verde Islands

Sahara

Hoggar

Lake Volta

Benue River

Lake Chad

Niger River

Gulf of Guinea

Bioco

São Tome

Atlantic Ocean

Ubangi River

Congo Basin

Congo River

Bié Plateau

Namib Desert

Victoria Falls

Okavango Delta

Orange River

Kalahari Desert

Great Karoo

Drakensberg

Limpopo River

Cape of Good Hope

Largest drainage basin Congo

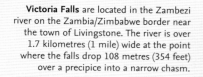

Victoria Falls are located in the Zambezi river on the Zambia/Zimbabwe border near the town of Livingstone. The river is over 1.7 kilometres (1 mile) wide at the point where the falls drop 108 metres (354 feet) over a precipice into a narrow chasm.

Want to know more?	
▶ Cross-section of Africa	6–7
▶ World's longest rivers	6–7
▶ World weather extremes	12–13
▶ Images of shrinking Lake Chad	112–113
▶ Maps of Africa	120–133

Internet links	
The African Union	www.africa-union.org
UN Convention to combat desertification	www.unccd.int
Foreign and Commonwealth Office	www.fco.gov.uk
UNESCO World Heritage sites	whc.unesco.org

Facts

Lake Chad was once the fourth largest lake in Africa but has shrunk by almost 95 per cent in the last 40 years.

The Suez Canal linking the Mediterranean Sea to the Red Sea was built in 1869 and is 163 kilometres (101 miles) long.

The Sahara Desert covers 9 million square kilometres (3.5 million square miles) which is approximately 30 per cent of Africa's total land area.

Lake Assal in Djibouti is the saltiest lake in the world and the lowest point in Africa at 152 metres (499 feet) below sea level.

Longest river Nile

Mediterranean Sea

Tibesti

Nile River

Suez Canal

Qattara Depression

Sinai

Lake Nasser

Red Sea

Arabian Peninsula

Blue Nile River

White Nile River

Lake Tana

Sudd

Ethiopian Highlands

Lake Assal

Gulf of Aden

Lake Turkana

Lake Victoria

Great Rift Valley

ake anganyika

Kilimanjaro

Webi Shabeelle River

Lowest point Lake Assal

Highest point Kilimanjaro

Lake Nyasa

Aldabra Islands

Indian Ocean

Comoro Islands

Largest lake Lake Victoria

Zambezi River

Mozambique Channel

Madagascar

Highest mountains	metres	feet	map
Kilimanjaro *Tanzania*	5 892	19 331	128 C5
Mt Kenya *Kenya*	5 199	17 057	128 C5
Margherita Peak *Dem. Rep. Congo/Uganda*	5 110	16 765	126 F4
Meru *Tanzania*	4 565	14 977	128 C5
Ras Dashen *Ethiopia*	4 533	14 872	128 C1
Mont Karisimbi *Rwanda*	4 510	14 796	126 F5

Longest rivers	km	miles	map
Nile	6 695	4 160	121 F2
Congo	4 667	2 900	127 B6
Niger	4 184	2 599	125 G5
Zambezi	2 736	1 700	131 H2
Webi Shabeelle	2 490	1 547	128 D5
Ubangi	2 250	1 398	126 C5

Largest islands	sq km	sq miles	map
Madagascar	587 040	226 657	131 J3

Largest lakes	sq km	sq miles	map
Lake Victoria	68 800	26 563	128 B5
Lake Tanganyika	32 900	12 702	129 A6
Lake Nyasa	30 044	11 600	129 B7
Lake Volta	8 485	3 276	124 F5
Lake Turkana	6 475	2 500	128 C4
Lake Albert	5 345	2 064	128 A4

Land area

Total land area 30 343 578 sq km/11 715 721 sq mls		map
Most northerly point	**La Galite** *Tunisia*	123 H1
Most southerly point	**Cape Agulhas** *South Africa*	130 C7
Most westerly point	**Santo Antao** *Cape Verde*	124 inset
Most easterly point	**Raas Xaafuun** *Somalia*	128 F2
Lowest point	**Lake Assal** *Djibouti*	128 D2

The heavily braided **Congo** river shows here through broken clouds on its way to the Atlantic Ocean. In this remote, tropical area the river acts as a highway between communities where roads do not exist.

Sitting between 40°N and 40°S, Africa may not suffer the extreme desolate environments of the far northern latitudes but over 30 per cent of the continent is barren. Africa is dominated by the harsh environment of the Sahara desert stretching east to west across the northern third of the continent. The Kalahari and Namib deserts in the south may be smaller but they are still significant features. The Great Rift Valley in eastern Africa contains large lakes which are vital to the wildlife and human population of the area. The continent also has a rich variety of other habitats, including grasslands which make up 25 per cent of Africa's land cover, and the rich tropical rainforest of the Congo basin in the heart of the continent.

A classic view of a sandy desert. The **Namib** desert on the south west of Africa stretches for 1 900 kilometres (1 200 miles) giving way to barren hills which are rich in minerals. The desert has little rain but the coastal region is often foggy.

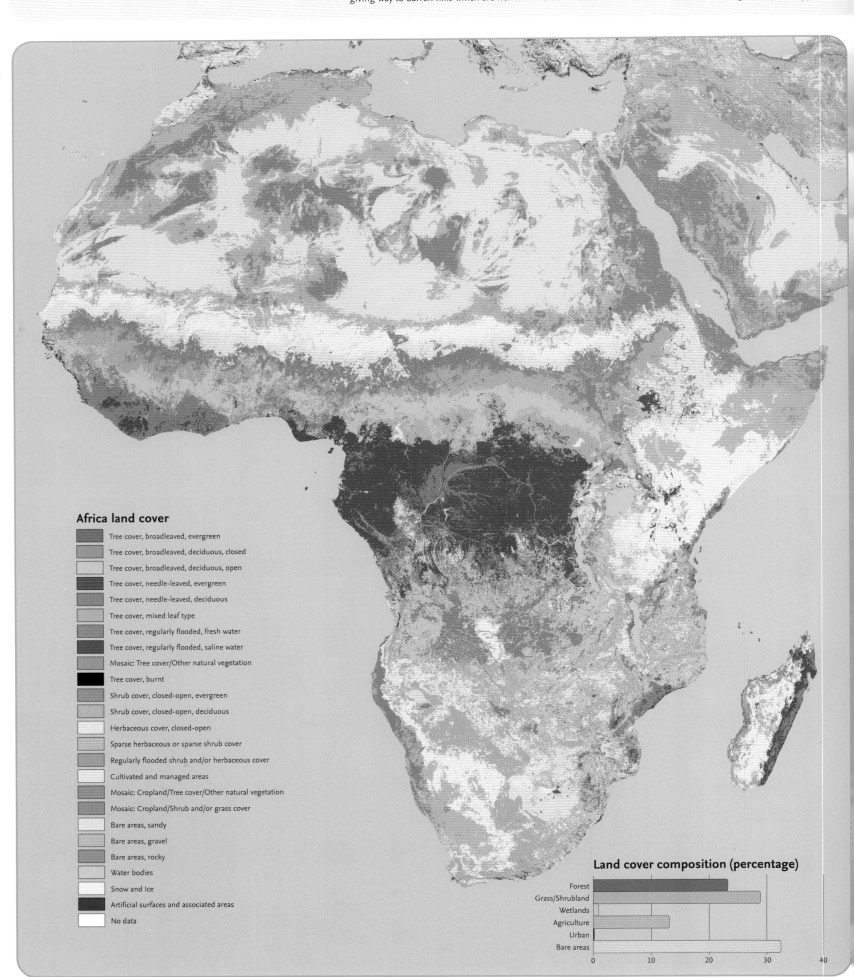

Africa land cover

- Tree cover, broadleaved, evergreen
- Tree cover, broadleaved, deciduous, closed
- Tree cover, broadleaved, deciduous, open
- Tree cover, needle-leaved, evergreen
- Tree cover, needle-leaved, deciduous
- Tree cover, mixed leaf type
- Tree cover, regularly flooded, fresh water
- Tree cover, regularly flooded, saline water
- Mosaic: Tree cover/Other natural vegetation
- Tree cover, burnt
- Shrub cover, closed-open, evergreen
- Shrub cover, closed-open, deciduous
- Herbaceous cover, closed-open
- Sparse herbaceous or sparse shrub cover
- Regularly flooded shrub and/or herbaceous cover
- Cultivated and managed areas
- Mosaic: Cropland/Tree cover/Other natural vegetation
- Mosaic: Cropland/Shrub and/or grass cover
- Bare areas, sandy
- Bare areas, gravel
- Bare areas, rocky
- Water bodies
- Snow and Ice
- Artificial surfaces and associated areas
- No data

Land cover composition (percentage)

Forest
Grass/Shrubland
Wetlands
Agriculture
Urban
Bare areas

0   10   20   30   40

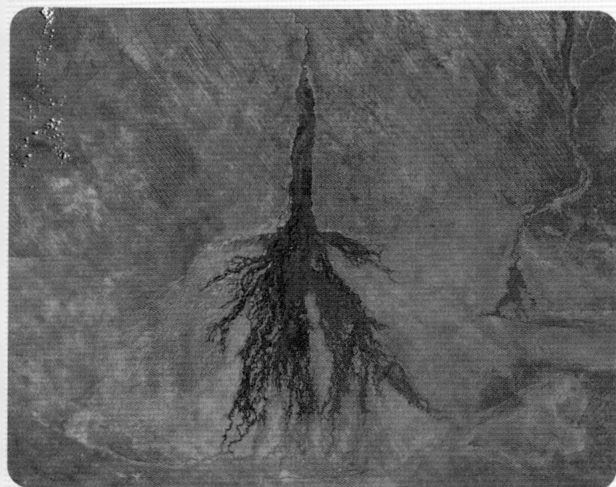

The **Okavango** delta is the world's largest inland delta and one of its most ecologically sensitive areas. The Okavango river, boosted by rains from October to March, has created a rich alluvial plain covering 10 000 square kilometres (3 860 square miles), which is essential to migrating wildlife.

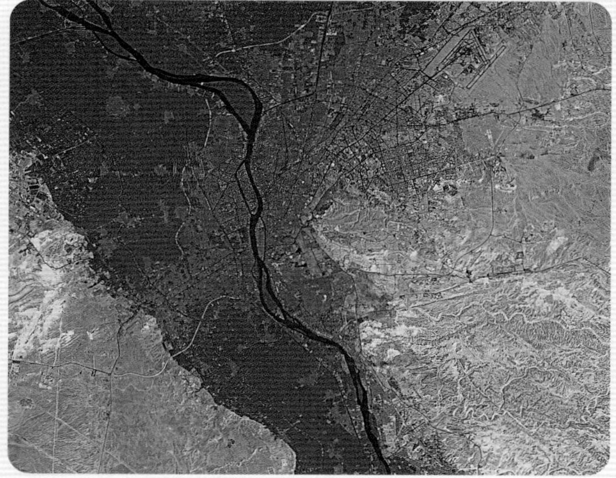

The **Nile** and its delta which forms to the north of Cairo, shown here, is essential to life in the region. The red areas show cultivation, possible because of irrigation channels from the river. Produce from here and water from the Nile serve the city (in dark grey).

Want to know more?	
▶ World climate and weather	12–13
▶ Global environmental threats	14–15
▶ Mediterranean Sea issues	34–35
▶ Image of the Sahara	110–111
▶ South American deforestation	194–195

Internet links	
RedList of Threatened Species	www.redlist.org
World Wildlife Fund for Nature	www.wwf.org.uk
UN Environment Programme	www.unep.org
IUCN World Conservation Union	www.iucn.org
Images of Africa	earthobservatory.nasa.gov

Facts

6 per cent of the total population of African grey parrots are exported each year.

The World Health Organisation estimates that 60 per cent of the world's population rely on plants for primary healthcare.

Conservation efforts have helped increase the population of mountain gorillas to over 700.

Only 15 per cent of the original natural forest remains in Madagascar.

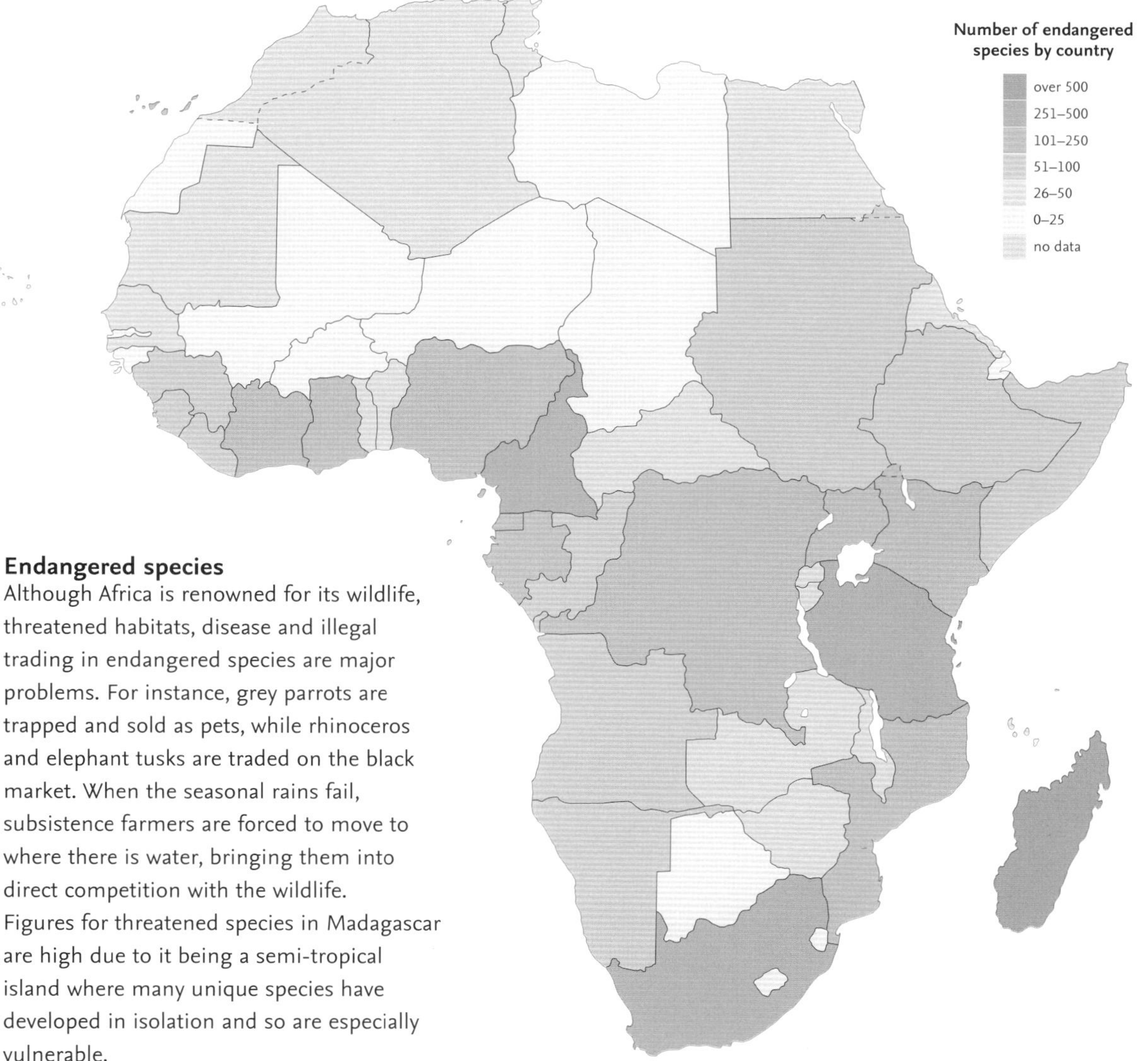

Number of endangered species by country

- over 500
- 251–500
- 101–250
- 51–100
- 26–50
- 0–25
- no data

Endangered species

Although Africa is renowned for its wildlife, threatened habitats, disease and illegal trading in endangered species are major problems. For instance, grey parrots are trapped and sold as pets, while rhinoceros and elephant tusks are traded on the black market. When the seasonal rains fail, subsistence farmers are forced to move to where there is water, bringing them into direct competition with the wildlife. Figures for threatened species in Madagascar are high due to it being a semi-tropical island where many unique species have developed in isolation and so are especially vulnerable.

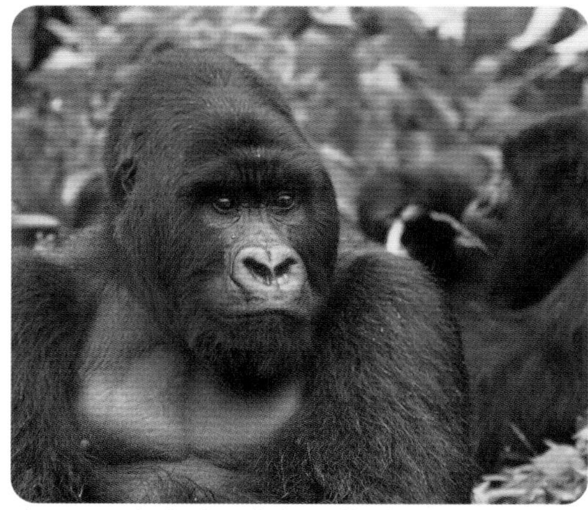

The **western lowland gorilla** has suffered a 56 per cent decrease in its numbers due to the ebola disease and also their habitat is under threat as rainforest is cleared for timber to be exported.

Top 10 protected land by country

	country	percentage land protected
1	Zambia	41.4
2	Tanzania	39.6
3	Botswana	30.2
4	Uganda	26.4
5	Benin	22.7
6	Côte d'Ivoire	16.9
7	Equatorial Guinea	16.8
8	Central African Republic	16.6
9	Ethiopia	16.4
10	Malawi	16.3

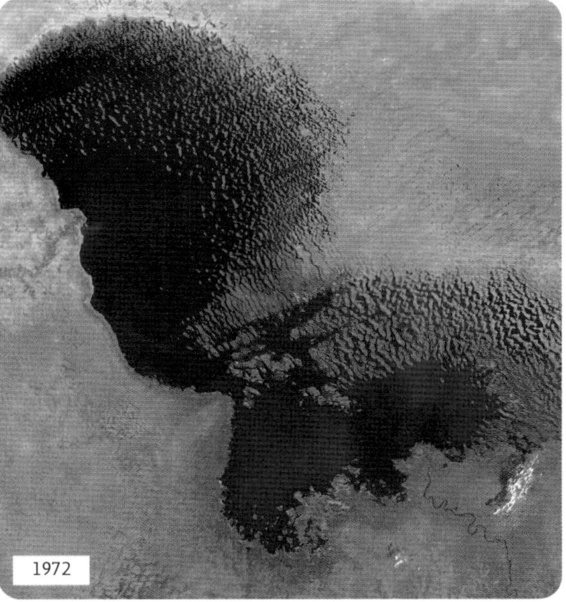

1972

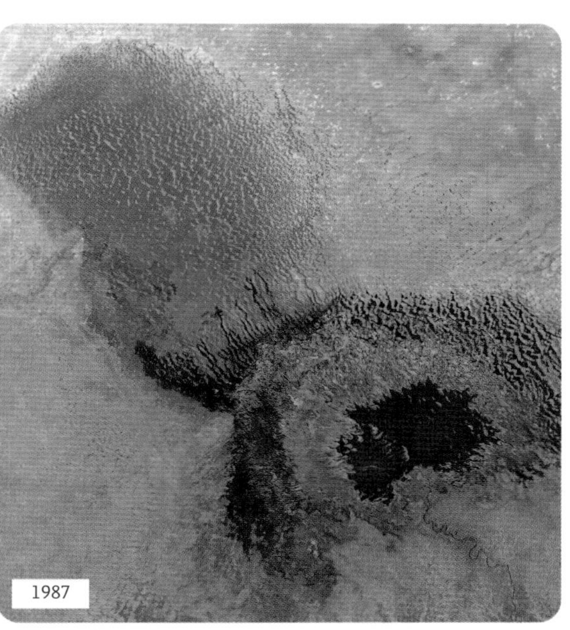

1987

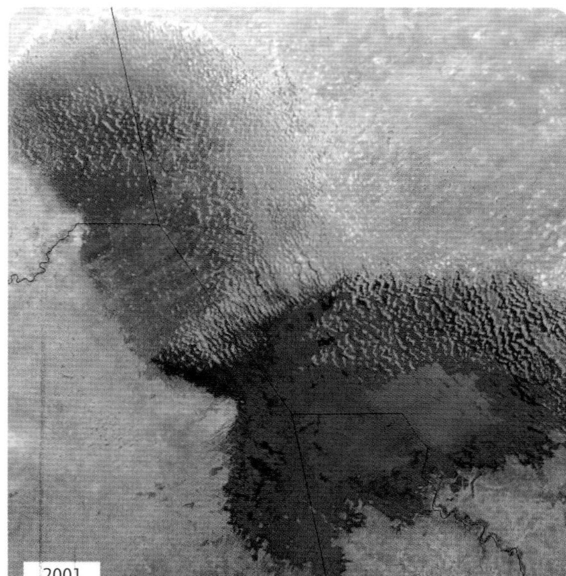

2001

Lake Chad was once one of the largest lakes in Africa but due to extensive irrigation projects, the encroaching desert and an increasingly drier climate, the lake is a tenth of its former size. These images were taken over a period of thirty years and show the diminishing water area.

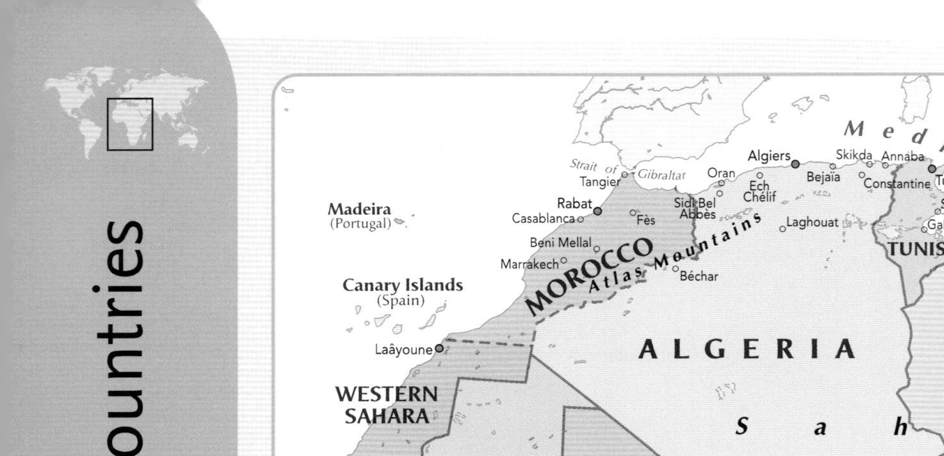

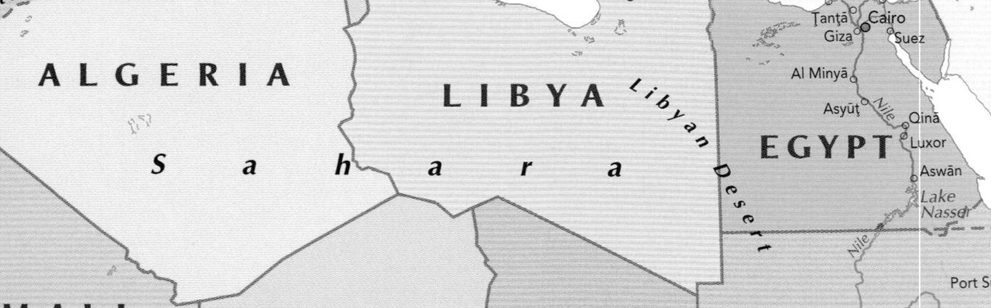

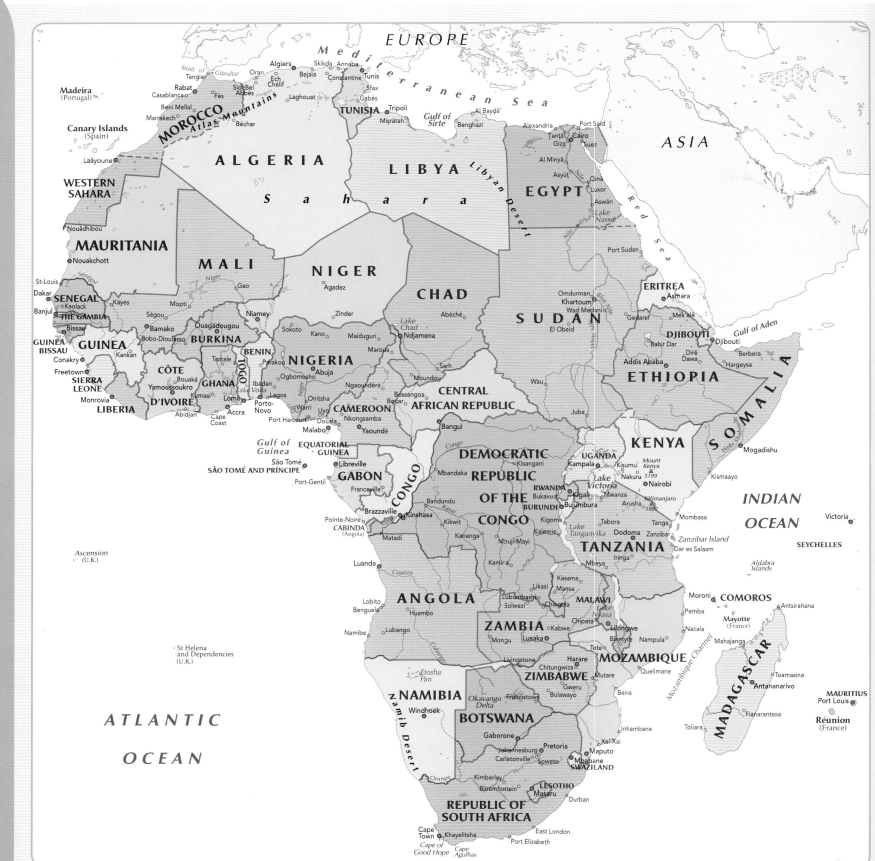

Countries		sq km						
capital		**sq miles**	**population**	**languages**	**religions**	**currency**	**official website**	**map**
Algeria Algiers (Alger)		2 381 741 919 595	32 854 000	Arabic, French, Berber	Sunni Muslim	Algerian dinar	www.el-mouradia.dz	122–123
Angola Luanda		1 246 700 481 354	15 941 000	Portuguese, Bantu, local languages	Roman Catholic, Protestant, traditional beliefs	Kwanza	www.angola.org	127
Benin Porto-Novo		112 620 43 483	8 439 000	French, Fon, Yoruba, Adja, local languages	Traditional beliefs, Roman Catholic, Sunni Muslim	CFA franc	www.gouv.bj	125
Botswana Gaborone		581 370 224 468	1 765 000	English, Setswana, Shona, local languages	Traditional beliefs, Protestant, Roman Catholic	Pula	www.gov.bw	130–131
Burkina Ouagadougou		274 200 105 869	13 228 000	French, Moore (Mossi), Fulani, local languages	Sunni Muslim, traditional beliefs, Roman Catholic	CFA franc	www.primature.gov.bf	124–125
Burundi Bujumbura		27 835 10 747	7 548 000	Kirundi (Hutu, Tutsi), French	Roman Catholic, traditional beliefs, Protestant	Burundian franc	www.burundi.gov.bi	126
Cameroon Yaoundé		475 442 183 569	16 322 000	French, English, Fang, Bamileke, local languages	Roman Catholic, traditional beliefs, Sunni Muslim, Protestant	CFA franc	www.spm.gov.cm	126
Cape Verde Praia		4 033 1 557	507 000	Portuguese, creole	Roman Catholic, Protestant	Cape Verde escudo	www.governo.cv	124
Central African Republic Bangui		622 436 240 324	4 038 000	French, Sango, Banda, Baya, local languages	Protestant, Roman Catholic, traditional beliefs, Sunni Muslim	CFA franc		126
Chad Ndjamena		1 284 000 495 755	9 749 000	Arabic, French, Sara, local languages	Sunni Muslim, Roman Catholic, Protestant, traditional beliefs	CFA franc	www.tit.td	120
Comoros Moroni		1 862 719	798 000	Comorian, French, Arabic	Sunni Muslim, Roman Catholic	Comoros franc	www.presidence-uniondescomores.com	129
Congo Brazzaville		342 000 132 047	3 999 000	French, Kongo, Monokutuba, local languages	Roman Catholic, Protestant, traditional beliefs, Sunni Muslim	CFA franc	www.congo-site.com	126–127
Congo, Dem. Rep. of the Kinshasa		2 345 410 905 568	57 549 000	French, Lingala, Swahili, Kongo, local languages	Christian, Sunni Muslim	Congolese franc	www.un.int/drcongo	126–127
Côte d'Ivoire Yamoussoukro		322 463 124 504	18 154 000	French, creole, Akan, local languages	Sunni Muslim, Roman Catholic, traditional beliefs, Protestant	CFA franc	www.pr.ci	124
Djibouti Djibouti		23 200 8 958	793 000	Somali, Afar, French, Arabic	Sunni Muslim, Christian	Djibouti franc		128
Egypt Cairo (Al Qāhirah)		1 000 250 386 199	74 033 000	Arabic	Sunni Muslim, Coptic Christian	Egyptian pound	www.sis.gov.eg	120–121
Equatorial Guinea Malabo		28 051 10 831	504 000	Spanish, French, Fang	Roman Catholic, traditional beliefs	CFA franc	www.ceiba-equatorial-guinea.org	125
Eritrea Asmara		117 400 45 328	4 401 000	Tigrinya, Tigre	Sunni Muslim, Coptic Christian	Nakfa	shabait.com	121
Ethiopia Addis Ababa (Ādīs Ābeba)		1 133 880 437 794	77 431 000	Oromo, Amharic, Tigrinya, local languages	Ethiopian Orthodox, Sunni Muslim, traditional beliefs	Birr	www.ethiopar.net	128

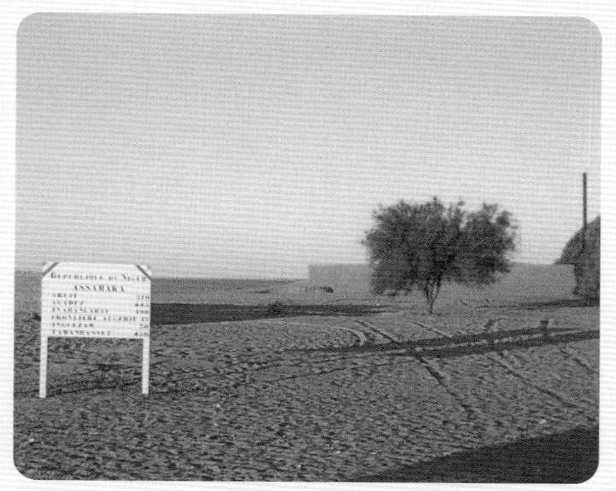

The border between Algeria and Niger lies in the Sahara Desert. Both countries have largely straight borders in a relatively featureless landscape which offers no obvious physical boundaries. As a result, a simple marker is the only feature which advises of the passage from one country to the other.

Top 10 countries by area

		sq km	sq miles	world rank
1	Sudan	2 505 813	967 500	10
2	Algeria	2 381 741	919 595	11
3	Congo, Dem. Rep. of the	2 345 410	905 568	12
4	Libya	1 759 540	679 362	17
5	Chad	1 284 000	495 755	21
6	Niger	1 267 000	489 191	22
7	Angola	1 246 700	481 354	23
8	Mali	1 240 140	478 821	24
9	South Africa, Republic of	1 219 090	470 693	25
10	Ethiopia	1 133 880	437 794	27

Top 10 countries by population

		population	world rank
1	Nigeria	131 530 000	9
2	Ethiopia	77 431 000	15
3	Egypt	74 033 000	16
4	Congo, Dem. Rep. of the	57 549 000	23
5	South Africa, Republic of	47 432 000	26
6	Tanzania	38 329 000	32
7	Sudan	36 233 000	33
8	Kenya	34 256 000	34
9	Algeria	32 854 000	35
10	Morocco	31 478 000	37

Want to know more?

▶	Political map of the world	8–9
▶	Land cover map of Africa	112–113
▶	Conflicts in Africa	116–117
▶	Detailed maps of Africa	120–133

Internet links

Southern African Development Community	www.sadc.int
UN Economic Commission for Africa	www.uneca.org
UN Regional Commission for Peace and Disarmament in Africa	www.unrec.org
International Boundaries Research Unit	www.ibru.dur.ac.uk

Facts

The continent of Africa has over 1 000 linguistic and cultural groups. Across northern Africa, Arabic is the dominant language and in most other areas the language of the former colonial power remains in common use.

The people of Madagascar, isolated by some distance from the African continent, speak a unique language called Malagasy.

Nine of the ten poorest countries in the world are in Africa.

Countries

Countries / capital		sq km / sq miles	population	languages	religions	currency	official website	map
Gabon / Libreville		267 667 / 103 347	1 384 000	French, Fang, local languages	Roman Catholic, Protestant, traditional beliefs	CFA franc	www.un.int/gabon	126
The Gambia / Banjul		11 295 / 4 361	1 517 000	English, Malinke, Fulani, Wolof	Sunni Muslim, Protestant	Dalasi	www.statehouse.gm	124
Ghana / Accra		238 537 / 92 100	22 113 000	English, Hausa, Akan, local languages	Christian, Sunni Muslim, traditional beliefs	Cedi	www.ghana.gov.gh	124–125
Guinea / Conakry		245 857 / 94 926	9 402 000	French, Fulani, Malinke, local languages	Sunni Muslim, traditional beliefs, Christian	Guinea franc	www.guinee.gov.gn	124
Guinea-Bissau / Bissau		36 125 / 13 948	1 586 000	Portuguese, crioulo, local languages	Traditional beliefs, Sunni Muslim, Christian	CFA franc		124
Kenya / Nairobi		582 646 / 224 961	34 256 000	Swahili, English, local languages	Christian, traditional beliefs	Kenyan shilling	www.kenya.go.ke	128–129
Lesotho / Maseru		30 355 / 11 720	1 795 000	Sesotho, English, Zulu	Christian, traditional beliefs	Loti, S. African rand	www.lesotho.gov.ls	133
Liberia / Monrovia		111 369 / 43 000	3 283 000	English, creole, local languages	Traditional beliefs, Christian, Sunni Muslim	Liberian dollar	www.liberiaemb.org	124
Libya / Tripoli (Ṭarābulus)		1 759 540 / 679 362	5 853 000	Arabic, Berber	Sunni Muslim	Libyan dinar	www.libya-un.org	120
Madagascar / Antananarivo		587 041 / 226 658	18 606 000	Malagasy, French	Traditional beliefs, Christian, Sunni Muslim	Malagasy ariary, Malagasy franc	www.madagascar-diplomatie.ch	131
Malawi / Lilongwe		118 484 / 45 747	12 884 000	Chichewa, English, local languages	Christian, traditional beliefs, Sunni Muslim	Malawian kwacha	www.malawi.gov.mw	129
Mali / Bamako		1 240 140 / 478 821	13 518 000	French, Bambara, local languages	Sunni Muslim, traditional beliefs, Christian	CFA franc	www.maliensdelexterieur.gov.ml	124–125
Mauritania / Nouakchott		1 030 700 / 397 955	3 069 000	Arabic, French, local languages	Sunni Muslim	Ouguiya	www.mauritania.mr	122
Mauritius / Port Louis		2 040 / 788	1 245 000	English, creole, Hindi, Bhojpurī, French	Hindu, Roman Catholic, Sunni Muslim	Mauritius rupee	www.gov.mu	218
Morocco / Rabat		446 550 / 172 414	31 478 000	Arabic, Berber, French	Sunni Muslim	Moroccan dirham	www.mincom.gov.ma	122–123
Mozambique / Maputo		799 380 / 308 642	19 792 000	Portuguese, Makua, Tsonga, local languages	Traditional beliefs, Roman Catholic, Sunni Muslim	Metical	www.mozambique.mz	131
Namibia / Windhoek		824 292 / 318 261	2 031 000	English, Afrikaans, German, Ovambo, local languages	Protestant, Roman Catholic	Namibian dollar	www.grnnet.gov.na	130
Niger / Niamey		1 267 000 / 489 191	13 957 000	French, Hausa, Fulani, local languages	Sunni Muslim, traditional beliefs	CFA franc	www.delgi.ne/presidence	125
Nigeria / Abuja		923 768 / 356 669	131 530 000	English, Hausa, Yoruba, Ibo, Fulani, local languages	Sunni Muslim, Christian, traditional beliefs	Naira	www.nigeria.gov.ng	125
Rwanda / Kigali		26 338 / 10 169	9 038 000	Kinyarwanda, French, English	Roman Catholic, traditional beliefs, Protestant	Rwandan franc	www.rwanda1.com	126
São Tomé and Príncipe / São Tomé		964 / 372	157 000	Portuguese, creole	Roman Catholic, Protestant	Dobra	www.uns.st	125
Senegal / Dakar		196 720 / 75 954	11 658 000	French, Wolof, Fulani, local languages	Sunni Muslim, Roman Catholic, traditional beliefs	CFA franc	www.gouv.sn	124
Seychelles / Victoria		455 / 176	81 000	English, French, creole	Roman Catholic, Protestant	Seychelles rupee	www.virtualseychelles.sc	218
Sierra Leone / Freetown		71 740 / 27 699	5 525 000	English, creole, Mende, Temne, local languages	Sunni Muslim, traditional beliefs	Leone	www.statehouse-sl.org	124
Somalia / Mogadishu (Muqdisho)		637 657 / 246 201	8 228 000	Somali, Arabic	Sunni Muslim	Somali shilling		128
South Africa, Republic of / Pretoria (Tshwane)/Cape Town		1 219 090 / 470 693	47 432 000	Afrikaans, English, nine official local languages	Protestant, Roman Catholic, Sunni Muslim, Hindu	Rand	www.gov.za	130–131
Sudan / Khartoum		2 505 813 / 967 500	36 233 000	Arabic, Dinka, Nubian, Beja, Nuer, local languages	Sunni Muslim, traditional beliefs, Christian	Sudanese dinar	www.sudan.gov.sd	120–121
Swaziland / Mbabane		17 364 / 6 704	1 032 000	Swazi, English	Christian, traditional beliefs	Emalangeni, South African rand	www.gov.sz	133
Tanzania / Dodoma		945 087 / 364 900	38 329 000	Swahili, English, Nyamwezi, local languages	Shi'a Muslim, Sunni Muslim, traditional beliefs, Christian	Tanzanian shilling	www.tanzania.go.tz	128–129
Togo / Lomé		56 785 / 21 925	6 145 000	French, Ewe, Kabre, local languages	Traditional beliefs, Christian, Sunni Muslim	CFA franc	www.republicoftogo.com	125
Tunisia / Tunis		164 150 / 63 379	10 102 000	Arabic, French	Sunni Muslim	Tunisian dinar	www.tunisiaonline.com	123
Uganda / Kampala		241 038 / 93 065	28 816 000	English, Swahili, Luganda, local languages	Roman Catholic, Protestant, Sunni Muslim, traditional beliefs	Ugandan shilling	www.government.go.ug	128
Zambia / Lusaka		752 614 / 290 586	11 668 000	English, Bemba, Nyanja, Tonga, local languages	Christian, traditional beliefs	Zambian kwacha	www.zambiatourism.com	127
Zimbabwe / Harare		390 759 / 150 873	13 010 000	English, Shona, Ndebele	Christian, traditional beliefs	Zimbabwean dollar	www.zim.gov.zw	131

Dependencies

Dependencies / capital		territorial status	sq km / sq miles	population	languages	religions	currency	official website	map
Canary Islands (Islas Canarias) / Santa Cruz de Tenerife/Las Palmas		Autonomous Community of Spain	7 447 / 2 875	1 944 700	Spanish	Roman Catholic	Euro	www.gobcan.es	122
Ceuta / Ceuta		Spanish Territory	19 / 7	74 931	Spanish, Arabic	Roman Catholic, Muslim	Euro	www.ciceuta.es	122
Madeira / Funchal		Autonomous Region of Portugal	779 / 301	245 012	Portuguese	Roman Catholic, Protestant	Euro	www.gov-madeira.pt/madeira	122
Mayotte / Dzaoudzi		French Departmental Collectivity	373 / 144	186 026	French, Mahorian	Sunni Muslim, Christian	Euro		129
Melilla / Melilla		Spanish Territory	13 / 5	68 463	Spanish, Arabic	Roman Catholic, Muslim	Euro	www.camelilla.es	123
Réunion / St-Denis		French Overseas Department	2 551 / 985	785 000	French, creole	Roman Catholic	Euro		218
St Helena and Dependencies / Jamestown		United Kingdom Overseas Territory	121 / 47	5 000	English	Protestant, Roman Catholic	St Helena pound	www.sainthelena.gov.sh	216–217
Western Sahara / Laâyoune		Disputed territory (Morocco)	266 000 / 102 703	341 000	Arabic	Sunni Muslim	Moroccan dirham		122

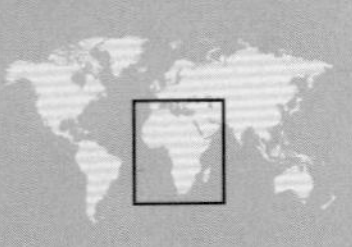

Africa has had a long history of conflict, disease, drought and troubled politics. The Second World War saw the end of European overseas empires as they found it impossible to defend their colonies against nationalist movements. The legacy was commonly political instability, religious and tribal conflict, impoverishment and oppression. While some countries are making progress towards development, internal conflict, frequent droughts and food shortages are normal in many regions. The level of debt is often crippling and there are many injustices and widespread corruption.

Endemic tropical diseases have long caused health problems in this continent. Underdeveloped health structures and lack of education have contributed and the current widespread problem of HIV/AIDS shows that the problems continue. Many countries have set up programmes to educate the population on health issues but lack of money means that there are limitations to their work and also, medicines are often not available even for easily treatable diseases.

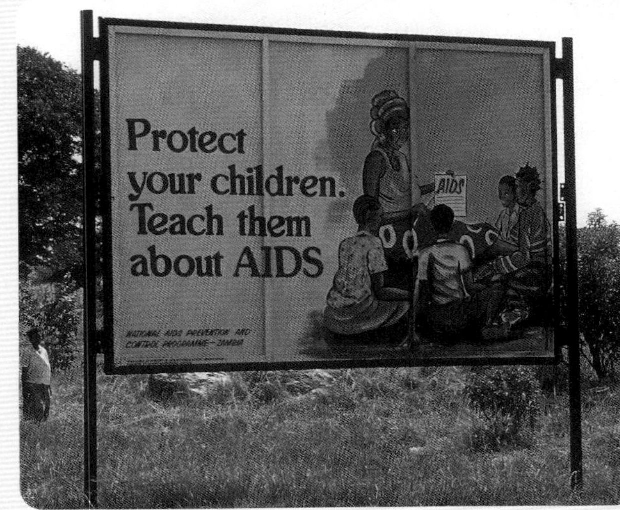

This AIDS poster is from **Zambia** which is one of the countries worst affected by the AIDS epidemic. Typically half of all people in sub-Saharan Africa who are infected with HIV contract it before they are twenty five.

Western Europe 580 000

Eastern Europe and Central Asia 1 300 000

North America 1 000 000

East Asia 900 000

South and South-East Asia 6 500 000

Caribbean 430 000

North Africa and Middle East 480 000

Oceania 32 000

Latin America 1 600 000

Sub-Saharan Africa 25 000 000

Global Total 37 800 000

Population living with HIV/AIDS
percentage of population

- over 15
- 8.1–15
- 5.1–8
- 2.1–5
- 0.4–2
- 0–0.3
- no data

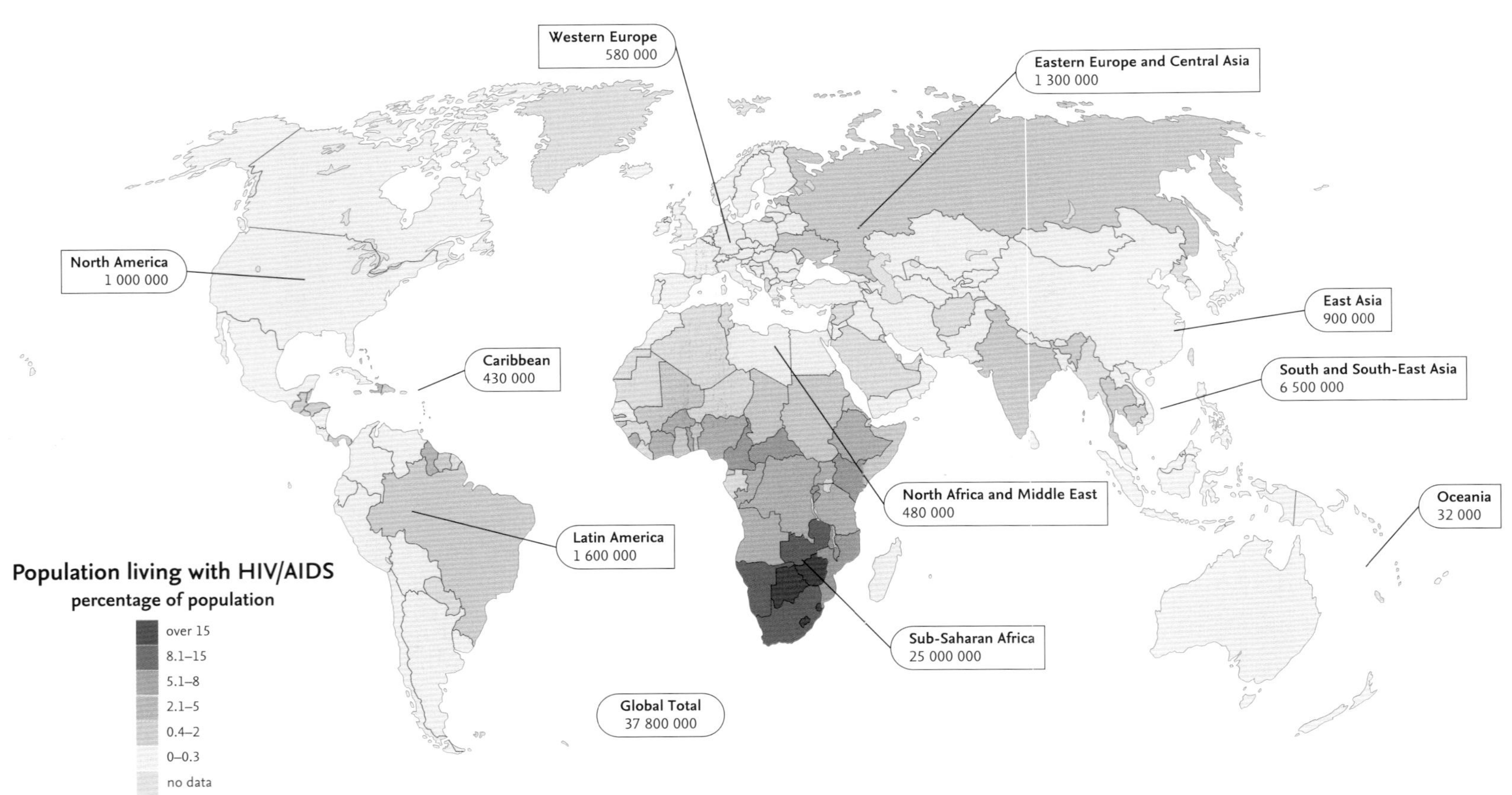

AIDS epidemic

At the end of 2003, there were around 25 million adults and children living with HIV in sub-Saharan Africa. In 2003 alone 2.2 million people died from AIDS there. The 12 million children orphaned by AIDS represent 80 per cent of the world's AIDS orphans.

The numbers of adults dying of AIDS is expected to increase. This means that more children will grow up without parental care and deprived of shelter, food, health and education. In many African countries the traditional family structures are no longer coping. Children are being raised by grandparents or are on their own. There is some help for these children and there are encouraging signs in several of the countries worst affected, which offer various types of support for orphans both in orphanages and in their own homes.

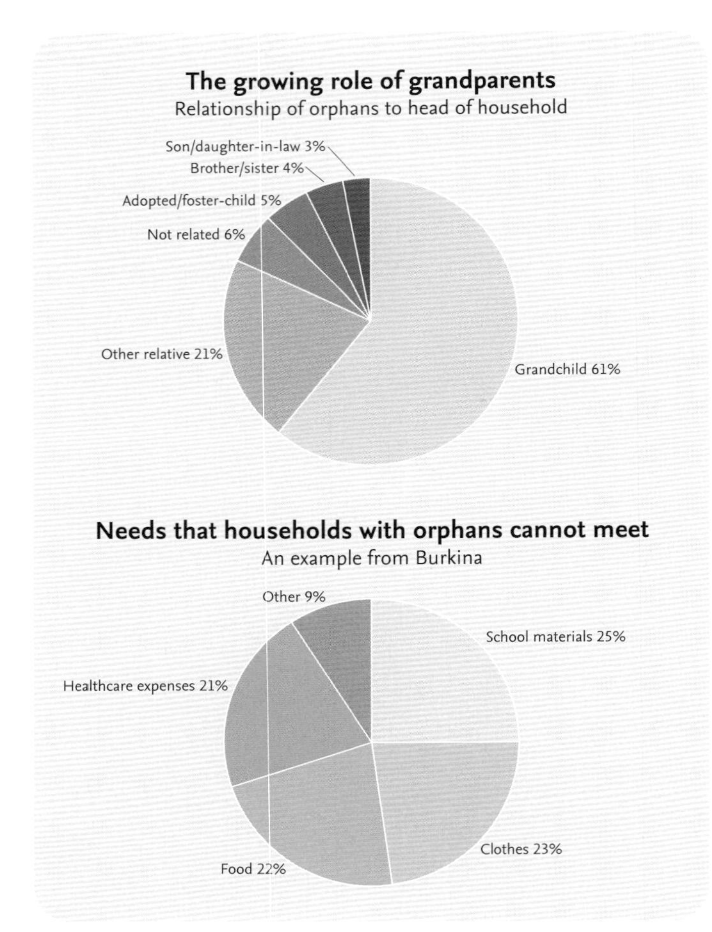

The growing role of grandparents
Relationship of orphans to head of household

- Son/daughter-in-law 3%
- Brother/sister 4%
- Adopted/foster-child 5%
- Not related 6%
- Other relative 21%
- Grandchild 61%

Needs that households with orphans cannot meet
An example from Burkina

- Other 9%
- School materials 25%
- Healthcare expenses 21%
- Clothes 23%
- Food 22%

Sub-Saharan Africa 2003

	orphans due to AIDS			adult AIDS deaths	
1	Nigeria	1 800 000	1	South Africa	5 100 000
2	South Africa	1 100 000	2	Nigeria	3 300 000
3	Tanzania	980 000	3	Zimbabwe	1 600 000
4	Zimbabwe	980 000	4	Tanzania	1 500 000
5	Uganda	940 000	5	Ethiopia	1 400 000
6	Congo, Dem. Rep.	770 000	6	Mozambique	1 200 000
7	Ethiopia	720 000	7	Kenya	1 100 000
8	Kenya	650 000	8	Congo, Dem. Rep.	1 000 000
9	Malawi	500 000	9	Zambia	830 000
10	Mozambique	470 000	10	Malawi	810 000

Conflicts

By 1975 most African states were independent of European colonial rule. However there were weak economies, fragile political systems and ecological problems, related to population increase and urbanisation. Serious droughts have led to famines and political instability, creating refugees and the AIDS epidemic adds to the existing problems of endemic tropical diseases. African states generally had poor welfare states and inadequate public utilities, and widespread corruption actively discouraged foreign investment.

The colonial country boundaries have led to problems of ethnic, religious and political rivalry, with several major civil wars and secessionist movements. There have also been many political problems with ruling politicians suppressing opposition parties. In some countries the military seized power but were ill-suited to civil government, however they were unwilling to surrender their power and in many cases this has led to a succession of coups.

Estimated deaths in recent conflicts	
Democratic Republic of the Congo	2 500 000
Sudan	2 000 000
Angola	500 000
Rwanda	500 000
Liberia	300 000
Algeria	80 000
Eritrea/Ethiopia	70 000

Want to know more?	
▶ World Countries	8–9
▶ Life expectancy in Africa	20–21
▶ World's poorest countries	22–23
▶ Statistical information for Africa	118–119
▶ Detailed reference maps of Africa	120–133

Internet links	
UNESCO	portal.unesco.org
United Nations Peace and Security	www.un.org/peace
World Health Organisation	www.who.int
UNAIDS	www.unaids.org

Facts

In sub-Saharan Africa there are seven countries where more than 20 per cent of adults now have HIV.

95 per cent of the world's AIDS orphans live in Africa.

Twenty eight African sub-Saharan states, have been at war since 1980.

Around 30 per cent of the population of the Darfur region of Sudan (2 million), have fled their homes in the recent conflict.

Independence and internal unrest

(1994) Recent internal conflict and date(s)

Recent territorial or border dispute

Country of origin and asylum for refugees

1960 Date of independence

Former colonial power/protectorate/trusteeship

Former Spanish colony, occupied by Morocco since 1975

An estimated 2 million people from the Darfur region of Sudan are currently displaced.

There have been almost constant conflicts in Sudan since 1956. The current conflict is in the Darfur region.

The Eritrea-Ethiopia border war started after Eritrea replaced the Ethiopian birr with it's own currency, the Nafka.

Liberia was founded by slaves freed from the USA in 1847

Liberia has suffered a chaotic and many sided conflict since 1990 due to offensives by rebel factions opposed to the government.

The Angolan civil war lasted from 1975 to 2002 creating an estimated 3 million refugees.

Since independence in 1975 the Comoros have had many coups, countercoups and repeated attempts at secession by smaller islands.

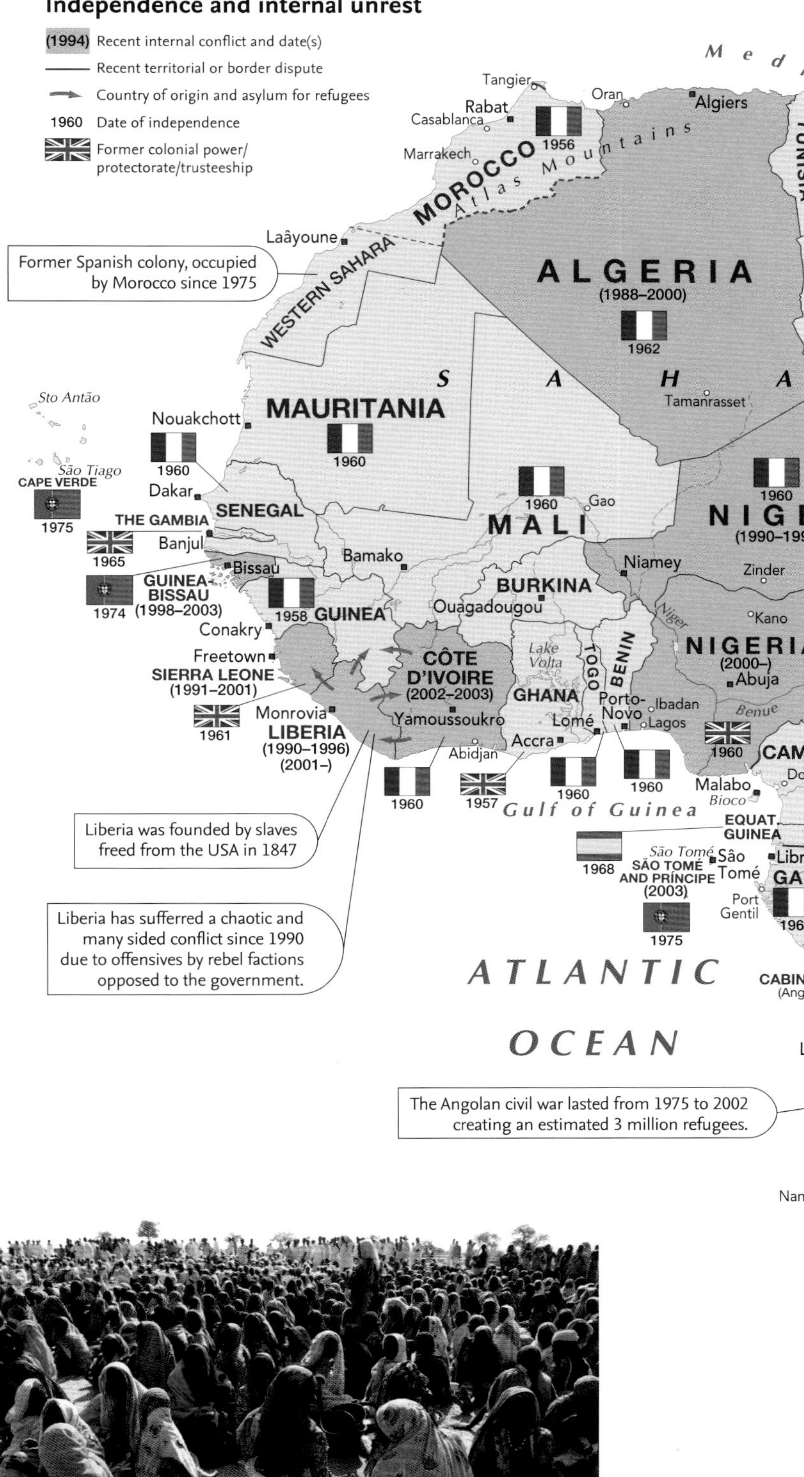

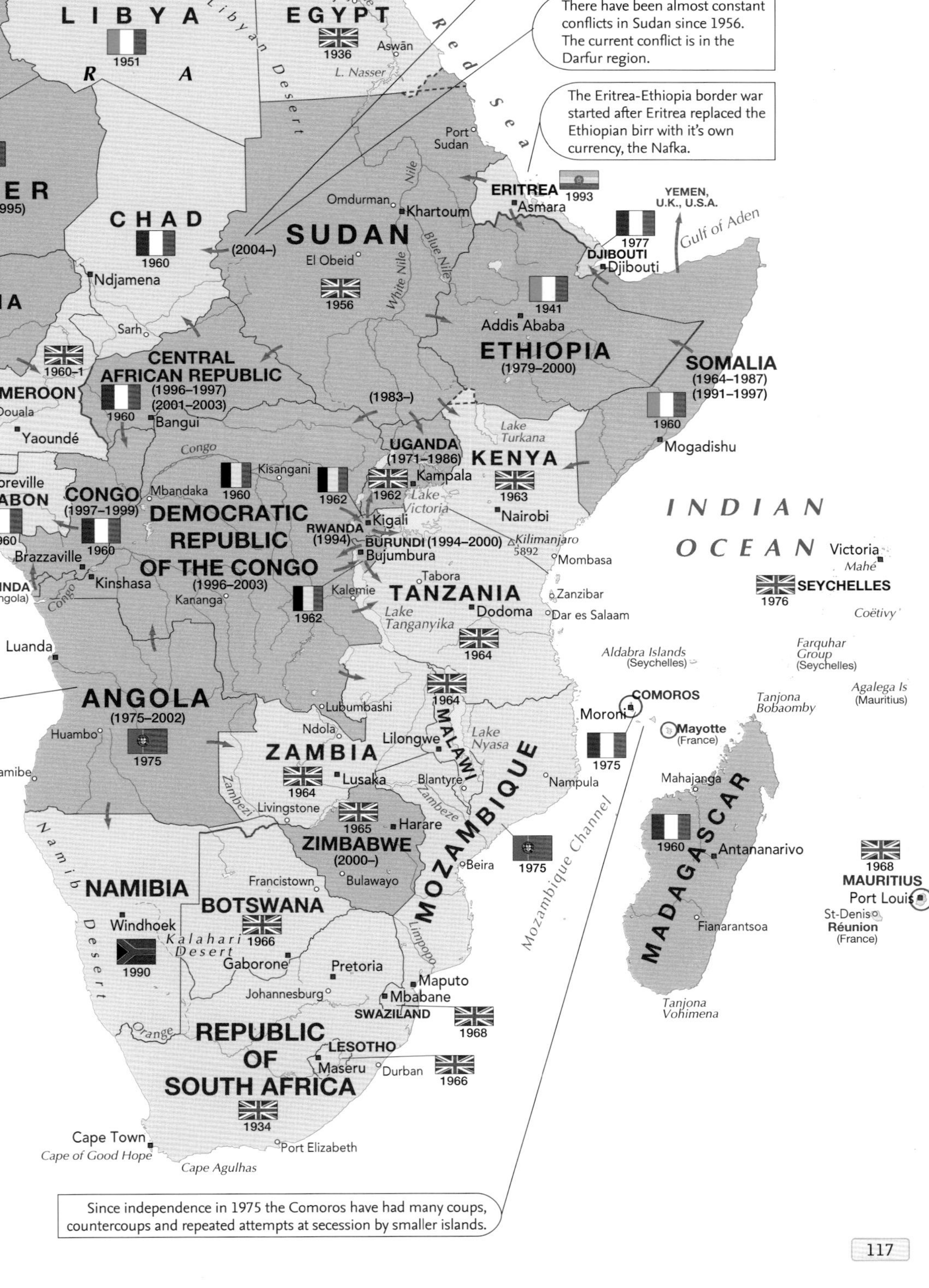

Refugees newly arrived at the **Brejin** camp in eastern **Chad** are waiting for aid distribution. These people have fled the Arab militias in the western Darfur region of Sudan with very few posessions.

Timeline:

- **4000–3000 BC** Desiccation of the Sahara begins
- **1540–1069 BC** The 'New Kingdom' in Egypt
- **149–146 BC** Third Punic War: Rome destroys Carthage
- **1450** Apogee of Songhay empire; university at Timbuktu
- **1415** Portuguese capture first territories in Africa
- **1300** Emergence of empire of Benin (Nigeria)
- **44** Mauretania (Morocco) annexed by Rome
- **1171** Saladin defeats Fatimids and conquers Egypt
- **1056** Almoravids conquer North Africa and southern Spain
- **1510** First African slaves to America
- **1652** Dutch found Cape Colony (South Africa)
- **1807** Abolition of the slave trade in the British Empire
- **1885** King of Belgium acquires the Congo
- **1869** Suez Canal opens
- **1852** South African republic (Transvaal) established
- **1836** The 'Great Trek' by Boer colonists in South Africa

Timescale: 4000, 3000, 2000, 1000, BC, AD, 100, 200, 300, 400, 500, 600, 700, 800, 900, 1000, 1100, 1200, 1300, 1400, 1500, 1600, 1700, 1800, 1810, 1820, 1830, 1840, 1850, 1860, 1870, 1880

- **641** Arabs conquer Egypt and begin conquest of North Africa
- **1200–1400** Buildings of Great Zimbabwe
- **1822** Liberia founded as colony for freed slaves
- **700** Rise of the empire of Ghana: decline of Aksum
- **1853** Livingstone's explorations begin
- **30 BC** Deaths of Antony and Cleopatra: Egypt a Roman province
- **1806** British capture Cape Colony
- **1152 BC** Death of Rameses III, last great pharaoh of Egypt
- **1700** Rise of Ashanti kingdom (Gold Coast)
- **1882** British occupy Egypt
- **2686–2181 BC** The 'Old Kingdom' (pyramid building) in Egypt
- **1487** Portuguese explorer Bartholomew Dias rounds Cape Horn
- **1571** Portuguese colony established in Angola

	Population							Economy					
	total population	population change (%)	urban population (%)	total fertility	population by age 0-14 (%)	population by age 60+ (%)	2050 projected population	total Gross National Income (GNI) (US$M)	Gross National Income (GNI) per capita (US$)	debt service ratio (% GNI)	total debt service (US$)	aid receipts (% GNI)	military spending (% GDP)
World	6 464 750 000	1.2	48.3	2.7	28.2	10.4	9 075 903 000	34 491 458	5 500	...	...	...	2.4
Algeria	32 854 000	1.5	58.8	2.5	29.6	6.5	49 500 000	60 221	1 890	7.8	4 166 400 000	0.6	3.7
Angola	15 941 000	2.8	35.7	6.8	46.5	3.9	43 501 000	10 004	740	9.3	862 800 000	4.5	3.7
Benin	8 439 000	3.2	44.6	5.9	44.2	4.3	22 123 000	2 990	440	2.4	63 200 000	8.1	...
Botswana	1 765 000	0.1	51.6	3.2	37.6	5.1	1 658 000	5 911	3 430	1.2	60 000 000	0.8	4.0
Burkina	13 228 000	3.2	17.8	6.7	47.2	4.2	39 093 000	3 587	300	1.7	52 800 000	14.8	1.7
Burundi	7 548 000	3.0	9.9	6.8	45.0	4.2	25 812 000	702	100	3.3	23 300 000	24.2	7.6
Cameroon	16 322 000	1.9	51.4	4.7	41.2	5.6	26 891 000	10 287	640	3.9	357 800 000	6.6	1.4
Cape Verde	507 000	2.4	55.9	3.8	39.5	5.5	1 002 000	701	1 490	3.4	21 700 000	14.6	0.7
Central African Republic	4 038 000	1.3	42.7	5.0	43.0	6.1	6 747 000	1 019	260	0.1	900 000	5.8	...
Chad	9 749 000	3.4	24.9	6.7	47.3	4.7	31 497 000	2 104	250	1.5	29 100 000	11.6	1.4
Comoros	798 000	2.7	35.0	4.9	42.0	4.3	1 781 000	269	450	1.9	4 800 000	13.1	...
Congo	3 999 000	3.0	53.5	6.3	47.1	4.5	13 721 000	2 407	640	1.1	24 000 000	2.6	...
Congo, Dem. Rep.	57 549 000	2.8	31.6	6.7	47.3	4.3	177 271 000	5 369	100	16.8	926 700 032	21.3	...
Côte d'Ivoire	18 154 000	1.6	44.9	5.1	41.9	5.3	33 959 000	11 159	660	7.5	831 500 032	9.6	...
Djibouti	793 000	2.1	83.7	5.1	41.5	4.7	1 547 000	643	910	2.0	12 100 000	12.9	...
Egypt	74 033 000	1.9	42.1	3.3	33.6	7.1	125 916 000	93 850	1 390	2.3	2 065 799 936	1.4	2.7
Equatorial Guinea	504 000	2.3	48.1	5.9	44.4	6.0	1 146 000	437	930	1.0	3 600 000	...	...
Eritrea	4 401 000	4.3	19.9	5.5	44.8	4.0	11 229 000	850	190	1.2	9 200 000	30.8	...
Ethiopia	77 431 000	2.4	15.6	5.9	44.5	4.7	170 190 000	6 325	90	1.8	108 100 000	21.7	5.2
Gabon	1 384 000	1.7	83.8	4.0	40.0	6.2	2 279 000	4 813	3 580	9.8	410 100 000	1.7	...
The Gambia	1 517 000	2.9	26.1	4.8	40.1	6.0	3 106 000	442	310	4.8	19 200 000	15.3	0.9
Ghana	22 113 000	2.1	45.4	4.4	39.0	5.7	40 573 000	6 563	320	3.5	211 000 000	10.8	0.6
Guinea	9 402 000	2.2	34.9	5.9	43.7	5.6	22 987 000	3 372	430	4.3	135 800 000	7.9	1.7
Guinea-Bissau	1 586 000	3.0	34.0	7.1	47.5	4.7	5 312 000	202	140	7.6	14 800 000	30.5	3.1
Kenya	34 256 000	2.2	39.4	5.0	42.8	4.1	83 073 000	12 604	390	3.7	452 400 000	3.2	1.6
Lesotho	1 795 000	0.1	17.9	3.7	38.6	7.5	1 601 000	1 049	590	7.7	67 200 000	8.7	3.1
Liberia	3 283 000	1.4	46.7	6.8	47.1	3.6	10 653 000	445	130	0.2	900 000	11.0	...
Libya	5 853 000	2.0	86.3	3.0	30.1	6.5	9 553 000	...	...	...	...	...	...
Madagascar	18 606 000	2.8	26.5	5.4	44.0	4.8	43 508 000	4 848	290	1.7	72 900 000	8.6	1.2
Malawi	12 884 000	2.3	16.3	6.1	47.3	4.7	29 452 000	1 832	170	1.9	36 200 000	20.2	0.8
Mali	13 518 000	3.0	32.3	6.9	48.2	4.2	41 976 000	3 428	290	2.9	89 700 000	15.0	2.0
Mauritania	3 069 000	3.0	61.8	5.8	43.0	5.3	7 497 000	1 163	430	5.7	64 300 000	30.6	1.9
Mauritius	1 245 000	1.0	43.3	2.0	24.6	9.6	1 465 000	5 012	4 090	5.5	250 600 000	0.5	0.2
Morocco	31 478 000	1.5	57.5	2.8	31.1	6.8	46 397 000	39 661	1 320	10.4	3 690 800 128	1.4	4.1
Mozambique	19 792 000	2.0	35.6	5.5	44.0	5.2	37 604 000	3 897	210	2.2	75 600 000	60.3	2.5
Namibia	2 031 000	1.4	32.4	4.0	41.5	5.3	3 060 000	3 771	1 870	...	...	4.5	2.9
Niger	13 957 000	3.4	22.2	7.9	49.0	3.3	50 156 000	2 361	200	1.3	27 900 000	13.8	1.1
Nigeria	131 530 000	2.2	46.7	5.9	44.3	4.8	258 108 000	42 984	320	4.0	1 489 900 032	0.9	1.1
Rwanda	9 038 000	2.4	18.3	5.7	43.5	3.9	18 153 000	1 826	220	1.3	22 000 000	20.5	3.1
São Tomé and Príncipe	157 000	2.3	37.8	4.1	39.5	5.7	295 000	50	320	13.1	6 100 000	56.0	...
Senegal	11 658 000	2.4	49.6	5.1	42.6	4.9	23 108 000	5 563	550	4.5	218 700 000	9.2	1.5
Seychelles	81 000	0.9	49.9	...	...	...	99 000	626	7 480	2.3	14 600 000	1.3	1.7
Sierra Leone	5 525 000	4.1	38.8	6.5	42.8	5.5	13 786 000	808	150	3.1	23 000 000	47.0	2.2
Somalia	8 228 000	3.2	34.8	6.4	44.1	4.2	21 329 000	...	...	...	200 000	...	...
South Africa, Republic of	47 432 000	0.8	56.9	2.8	32.6	6.8	48 660 000	125 971	2 780	4.5	4 691 500 032	0.5	1.6
Sudan	36 233 000	1.9	38.9	4.5	39.2	5.6	66 705 000	15 372	460	0.2	23 400 000	2.5	3.0
Swaziland	1 032 000	0.2	23.5	4.0	41.0	5.4	1 026 000	1 492	1 350	1.6	20 200 000	1.8	1.5
Tanzania	38 329 000	2.0	35.4	5.0	42.6	5.1	66 845 000	10 201	290	1.6	145 400 000	13.2	...
Togo	6 145 000	2.7	35.1	5.4	43.5	4.9	13 544 000	1 492	310	1.0	13 100 000	3.8	...
Tunisia	10 102 000	1.1	63.7	2.0	25.9	8.6	12 927 000	22 211	2 240	7.2	1 437 799 936	1.3	1.6
Uganda	28 816 000	3.4	12.2	7.1	50.5	3.8	126 950 000	6 173	240	1.4	79 200 000	11.2	2.4
Zambia	11 668 000	1.7	35.7	5.7	45.8	4.6	22 781 000	3 945	380	8.7	308 500 000	18.1	0.6
Zimbabwe	13 010 000	0.7	34.9	3.6	40.0	5.4	15 805 000	6 165	480	1.4	57 600 000	...	3.2

1922 Egypt independent

1919 Former German colonies redistributed

11 Italy conquers Libya

910 Formation of the Union of South Africa

99–1902 Boer War

2002 End of civil wars in Angola and Sierra Leone

1993 Independence of Eritrea from Ethiopia

1980 Black majority rule established in Zimbabwe (Rhodesia)

1975 Portugal grants independence to Angola, Mozambique and Cape Verde

1967–1970 Nigerian civil war and secession of Biafra

1961 South Africa becomes an independent republic

1957 Independence of Gold Coast (renamed Ghana)

1956 Suez crisis: Anglo-French invasion

1952 Mau Mau rebellion in Kenya begins

1890 | 1900 | 1910 | 1920 | 1930 | 1940 | 1950 | 1960 | 1970 | 1980 | 1990 | 2000

1935 Italy conquers Abyssinia (Ethiopia)

1940–1941 Italians expelled from Somalia, Eritrea and Ethiopia

1942 Apartheid inaugurated in South Africa

1954–1962 Algerian war of independence

1974 Emperor Haile Selassie of Ethiopia killed by Marxist junta

1979 Idi Amin of Uganda deposed by Tanzanian invasion

1984 Major famine in Ethiopia and the Sahel

1890 British colonization of Rhodesia

1994 South African election ends apartheid era: Mandela president

1994 Ethnic massacres in Rwanda and Burundi

Want to know more?

World's countries	8–9
Maps of mortality and life expectancy	20–21
Map of overseas aid	22–23
Guide to Africa's countries	114–115

Internet links

The African Union	www.africa-union.org
UN Economic Commission for Africa	www.uneca.org
Southern African Development Community	www.sadc.int

Facts

The ancient Egyptians worshipped about 2 000 gods and goddesses, some of whom were said to wield great power.

Recent studies of the outer buildings of the ruins of Great Zimbabwe have revised its estimated population from 1 000 to 18 000.

Before the Suez Canal was built, the Pharaohs, ancient Greeks and Romans linked the Mediterranean and Red Sea by a canal through the Nile delta.

See page 335 for explanatory table and sources

Social indicators						Environment				Communications					
child mortality rate	life expectancy male	life expectancy female	literacy rate (%)	access to safe water (%)	doctors per 100 000 people	forest area (%)	annual change in forest area (%)	protected land area (%)	CO_2 emissions (metric tons per capita)	main telephone lines per 100 people	cellular mobile subscribers per 100 people	internet users per 10 000 people	international dialling code	time zone	
80	**63.3**	**67.6**	**87.3**	**83**	**...**	**29.6**	**-0.2**	**11.4**	**3.8**	**18.8**	**21.9**	**1 125**	**...**	**...**	**World**
41	68.1	71.3	90.4	87	85	0.9	1.3	5.1	2.9	6.9	4.6	160	213	+1	Algeria
260	38.8	41.5	...	50	5	56.0	-0.2	10.0	0.5	0.7	0.9	29	244	+1	Angola
154	48.4	53.0	55.5	68	10	24.0	-2.3	22.6	0.3	1.0	3.4	100	229	+1	Benin
112	38.9	40.5	89.1	95	29	21.9	-0.9	30.2	2.3	8.3	25.3	349	267	+2	Botswana
207	45.2	46.2	36.9	51	4	25.9	-0.2	15.4	0.1	0.5	1.9	39	226	GMT	Burkina
190	40.4	41.4	66.1	79	1	3.7	-9.0	5.4	0.0	0.3	0.9	20	257	+2	Burundi
166	45.1	47.4	94.4	63	7	51.3	-0.9	8.0	0.4	0.7	6.6	38	237	+1	Cameroon
35	67.0	72.8	89.2	80	17	21.1	9.3	3.8	0.3	15.6	11.6	444	238	-1	Cape Verde
180	38.5	40.6	69.9	75	4	36.8	-0.1	16.6	0.1	0.2	0.3	14	236	+1	Central African Republic
200	43.7	45.7	69.9	34	3	10.1	-0.6	9.4	0.0	0.2	0.8	19	235	+1	Chad
73	59.4	62.2	59.0	94	7	4.3	-4.3	...	0.1	1.7	0.3	63	269	+3	Comoros
108	46.6	49.7	97.8	46	25	64.6	-0.1	17.7	0.5	0.2	9.4	43	242	+1	Congo
205	40.8	42.8	83.7	46	7	59.6	-0.4	8.3	0.1	0.02	1.9	10	243	+1 to +2	Congo, Dem. Rep.
192	40.8	41.2	67.6	84	9	22.4	-3.1	16.9	0.7	2.0	7.4	144	225	GMT	Côte d'Ivoire
138	44.7	46.8	85.7	80	13	0.3	...	0.5	0.6	1.4	3.4	97	253	+3	Djibouti
39	66.7	71.0	71.3	98	218	0.1	3.3	5.7	2.2	12.7	8.5	393	20	+2	Egypt
146	47.8	50.5	97.4	44	25	62.5	-0.6	16.8	0.4	1.8	7.6	36	240	+1	Equatorial Guinea
85	51.2	54.2	72.0	57	5	13.5	-0.3	4.1	0.1	0.9	...	23	291	+3	Eritrea
169	44.6	46.3	57.2	22	3	4.2	-0.8	16.4	0.1	0.6	0.1	11	251	+3	Ethiopia
91	55.8	57.5	...	87	...	84.7	...	3.4	2.8	2.9	22.4	262	241	+1	Gabon
123	52.7	55.5	60.0	82	4	48.1	1.0	3.2	0.2	2.9	7.5	188	220	GMT	The Gambia
95	56.5	59.3	92.1	79	9	27.8	-1.7	15.4	0.3	1.4	3.6	78	233	GMT	Ghana
160	48.8	49.5	...	51	13	28.2	-0.5	6.4	0.2	0.3	1.4	52	224	GMT	Guinea
204	43.8	46.9	60.9	59	17	60.5	-0.9	0.0	0.2	0.8	0.1	148	245	GMT	Guinea-Bissau
123	43.5	45.6	95.8	62	14	30.0	-0.5	12.3	0.3	1.0	5.0	127	254	+3	Kenya
84	32.3	37.7	91.1	76	7	0.5	...	0.2	...	1.3	4.5	97	266	+2	Lesotho
235	40.7	42.2	71.7	62	...	31.3	-2.0	15.8	0.1	0.2	0.1	0	231	GMT	Liberia
16	70.8	75.4	97.0	72	120	0.2	1.4	0.1	10.9	13.6	1.8	289	218	+2	Libya
126	52.5	54.8	81.5	45	9	20.2	-0.9	3.1	0.1	0.4	1.7	43	261	+3	Madagascar
178	37.3	37.7	72.5	67	...	27.2	-2.4	16.3	0.1	0.8	1.3	34	265	+2	Malawi
220	48.0	49.1	69.9	48	4	10.8	-0.7	3.7	0.1	0.5	2.3	24	223	GMT	Mali
183	50.9	54.1	49.6	56	14	43.9	...	0.2	1.2	1.2	10.9	37	222	GMT	Mauritania
18	68.4	75.8	94.3	100	85	7.9	-0.6	29.8	2.4	28.5	37.9	1 229	230	+4	Mauritius
39	66.8	70.5	69.6	80	49	6.8	...	1.2	1.3	4.1	24.3	266	212	GMT	Morocco
158	36.6	39.6	62.8	42	2	39.0	-0.2	5.7	0.1	0.5	2.3	28	258	+2	Mozambique
65	42.9	45.6	92.3	80	29	9.8	-0.9	5.6	1.0	6.6	11.6	338	264	+2	Namibia
262	45.9	46.5	24.4	46	3	1.0	-3.7	8.2	0.1	0.2	0.2	13	227	+1	Niger
198	51.1	51.8	88.5	60	27	14.8	-2.6	6.0	0.3	0.7	2.6	61	234	+1	Nigeria
203	38.8	39.7	84.9	73	2	12.4	-3.9	7.7	0.1	0.3	1.6	31	250	+2	Rwanda
118	67.0	72.8	...	79	47	28.3	...	...	0.6	4.6	3.2	987	239	GMT	São Tomé and Príncipe
137	50.8	55.1	52.9	72	10	32.2	-0.7	11.0	0.4	2.2	5.6	217	221	GMT	Senegal
15	...	...	...	87	132	66.7	...	12.3	2.8	26.9	68.2	1 452	248	+4	Seychelles
284	33.1	35.5	...	57	9	14.7	-2.9	4.5	0.1	0.5	1.4	16	232	GMT	Sierra Leone
225	46.4	49.5	...	29	...	12.0	-1.0	0.3	...	1.0	0.3	90	252	+3	Somalia
66	45.1	50.7	91.8	87	25	7.3	-0.1	6.1	7.4	10.7	36.4	682	27	+2	South Africa, Republic of
93	54.1	57.1	79.1	69	16	25.9	-1.4	4.9	0.2	2.7	2.0	90	249	+3	Sudan
153	33.3	35.4	91.2	52	15	30.3	1.2	3.5	0.4	4.4	8.4	259	268	+2	Swaziland
165	42.5	44.1	91.6	73	4	43.9	-0.2	39.6	0.1	0.4	2.5	71	255	+3	Tanzania
140	48.2	51.1	77.4	51	6	9.4	-3.4	11.3	0.4	1.2	4.4	420	228	GMT	Togo
24	70.8	74.9	94.3	82	70	3.1	0.2	1.5	1.9	11.8	19.2	637	216	+1	Tunisia
140	45.4	46.9	80.3	56	5	21.0	-2.0	26.4	0.1	0.2	3.0	49	256	+3	Uganda
182	32.7	32.1	89.1	55	7	42.0	-2.4	41.4	0.2	0.8	2.2	61	260	+2	Zambia
126	33.7	32.6	97.6	83	6	49.2	-1.5	14.7	1.2	2.6	3.2	430	263	+2	Zimbabwe

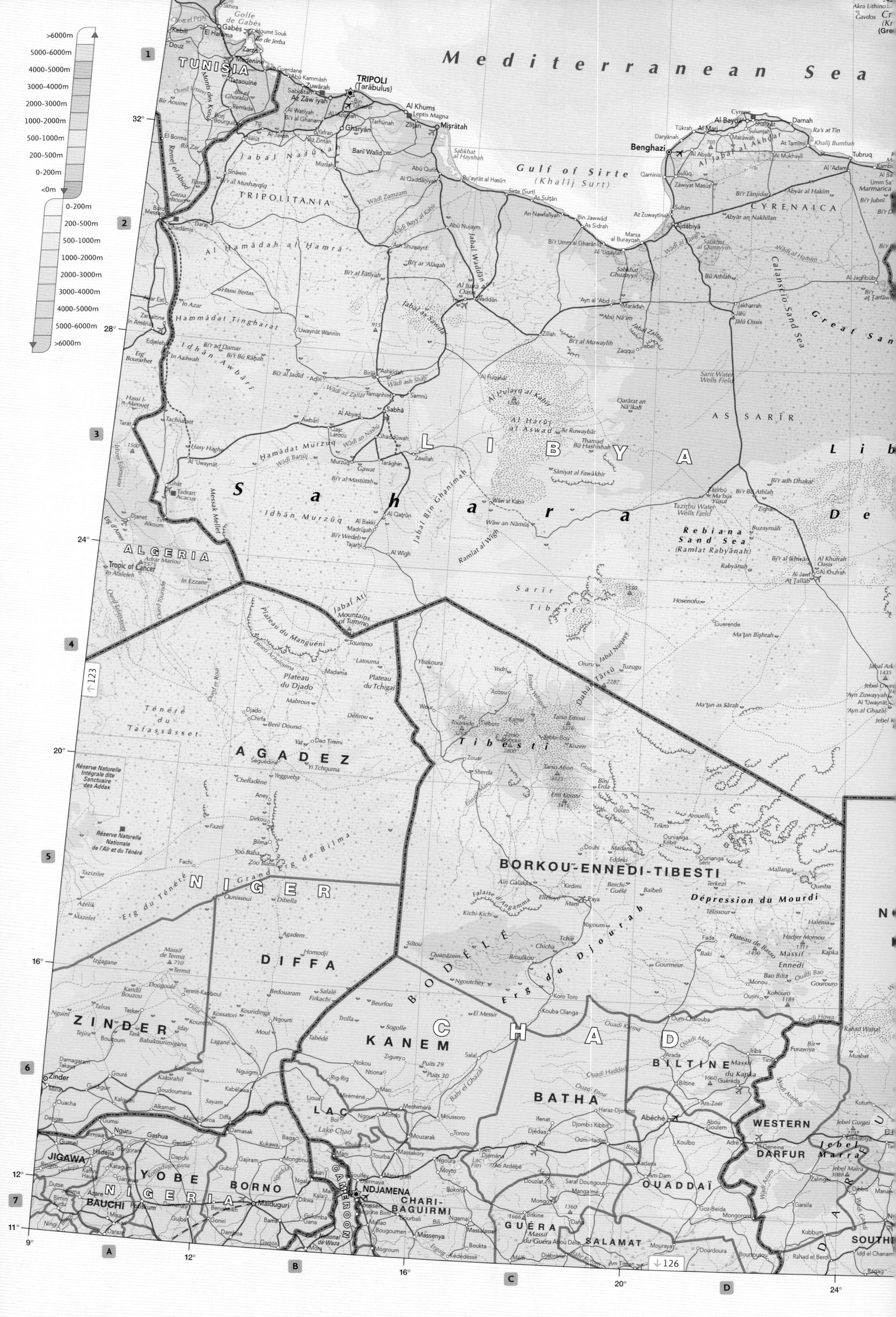
>6000m
5000-6000m
4000-5000m
3000-4000m
2000-3000m
1000-2000m
500-1000m
200-500m
0-200m
<0m
0-200m
200-500m
500-1000m
1000-2000m
2000-3000m
3000-4000m
4000-5000m
5000-6000m
>6000m
Mediterranean Sea
Gulf of Sirte
(Khalīj Surt)
TRIPOLI
(Ṭarābulus)
Benghazi
TUNISIA
TRIPOLITANIA
CYRENAICA
AS SARĪR
LIBYA
Sahara
ALGERIA
Tropic of Cancer
AGADEZ
NIGER
DIFFA
ZINDER
BORKOU-ENNEDI-TIBESTI
Tibesti
Dépression du Mourdi
KANEM
CHAD
BATHA
BILTINE
LAC
Lake Chad
NDJAMENA
CHARI-BAGUIRMI
GUÉRA
SALAMAT
OUADDAÏ
WESTERN DARFUR
JIGAWA
YOBE
BORNO
BAUCHI
NIGERIA
CAMEROON
Rebiana Sand Sea
(Ramlat Rabyānah)
Calanscio Sand Sea
Great Sand Sea
Ténéré du Tafassâsset
Erg du Djourab
Ḥamādat Murzuq
Idhān Murzūq
Idhān Awbārī
Al Ḥamādah al Ḥamrā'
↑123
↓126
32°
28°
24°
20°
16°
12°
11°
9°
12°
16°
20°
24°
1
2
3
4
5
6
7
A
B
C
D

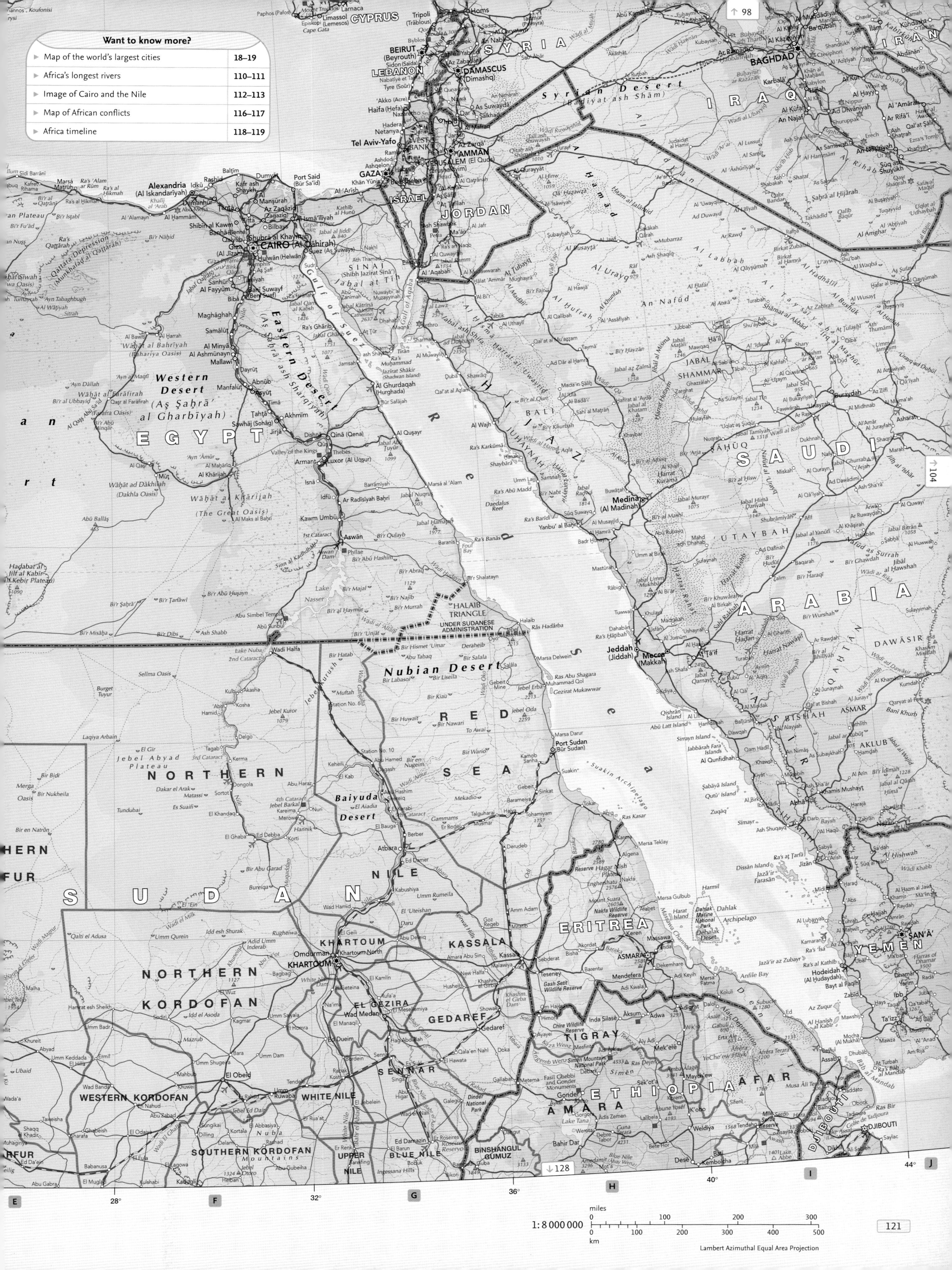

Want to know more?
Map of the world's largest cities 18–19
Africa's longest rivers 110–111
Image of Cairo and the Nile 112–113
Map of African conflicts 116–117
Africa timeline 118–119
98
104
128
CYPRUS
SYRIA
LEBANON
ISRAEL
JORDAN
IRAQ
IRAN
EGYPT
SAUDI ARABIA
SUDAN
ERITREA
ETHIOPIA
YEMEN
DJIBOUTI
BEIRUT
DAMASCUS
AMMAN
JERUSALEM
BAGHDAD
CAIRO (Al Qahirah)
KHARTOUM
ASMARA
SAN'A'
Syrian Desert
Western Desert
Eastern Desert
Nubian Desert
Red Sea
HALAIB TRIANGLE UNDER SUDANESE ADMINISTRATION
NORTHERN
NILE
KASSALA
NORTHERN KORDOFAN
WESTERN KORDOFAN
SOUTHERN KORDOFAN
WHITE NILE
SENNAR
GEDAREF
EL GEZIRA
BLUE NILE
UPPER NILE
TIGRAY
AMARA
AFAR
E F G H I J
28° 32° 36° 40° 44°
1:8 000 000
miles 0 100 200 300
km 0 100 200 300 400 500
Lambert Azimuthal Equal Area Projection

Africa Northwest Africa

Want to know more?

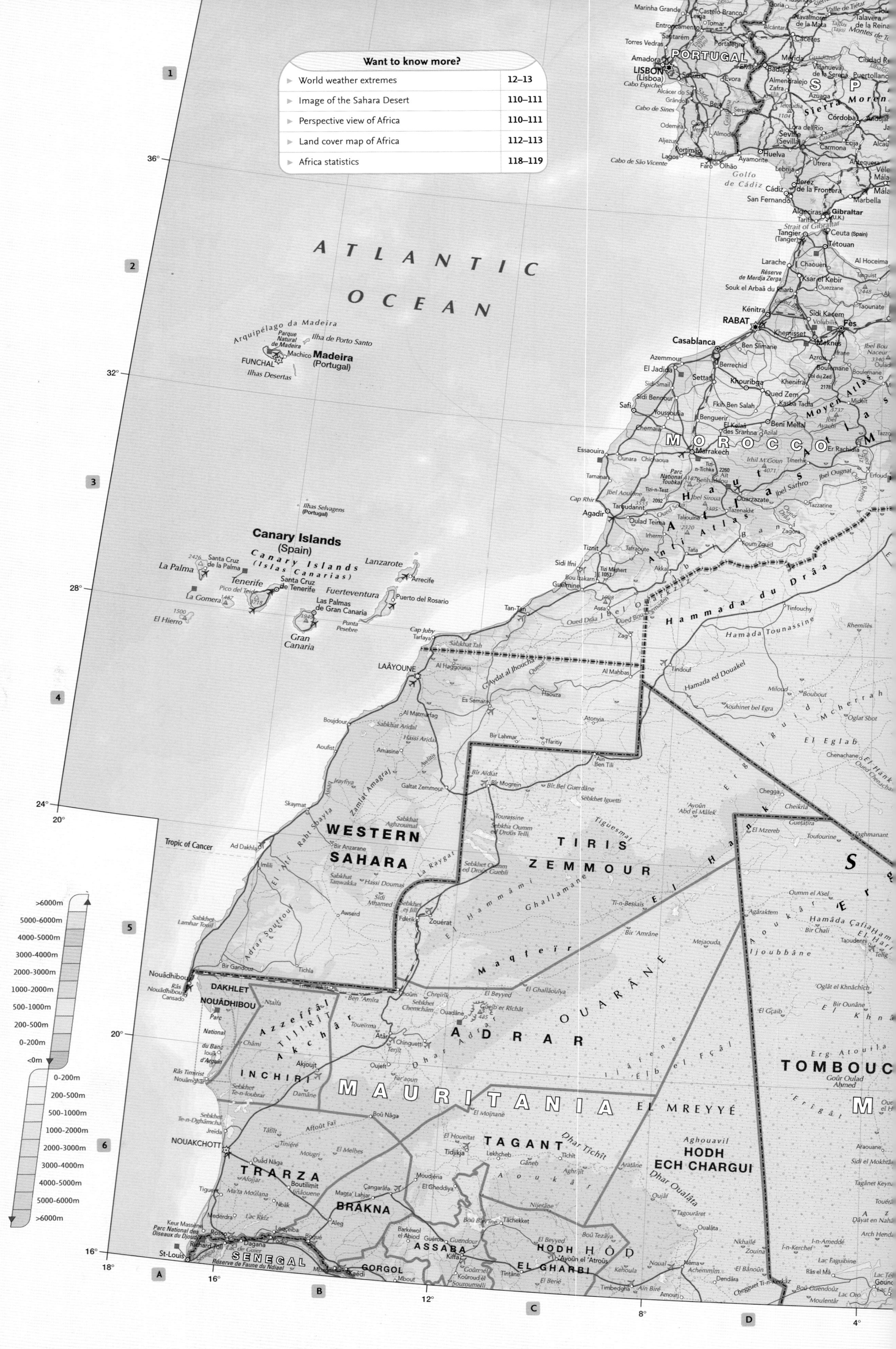

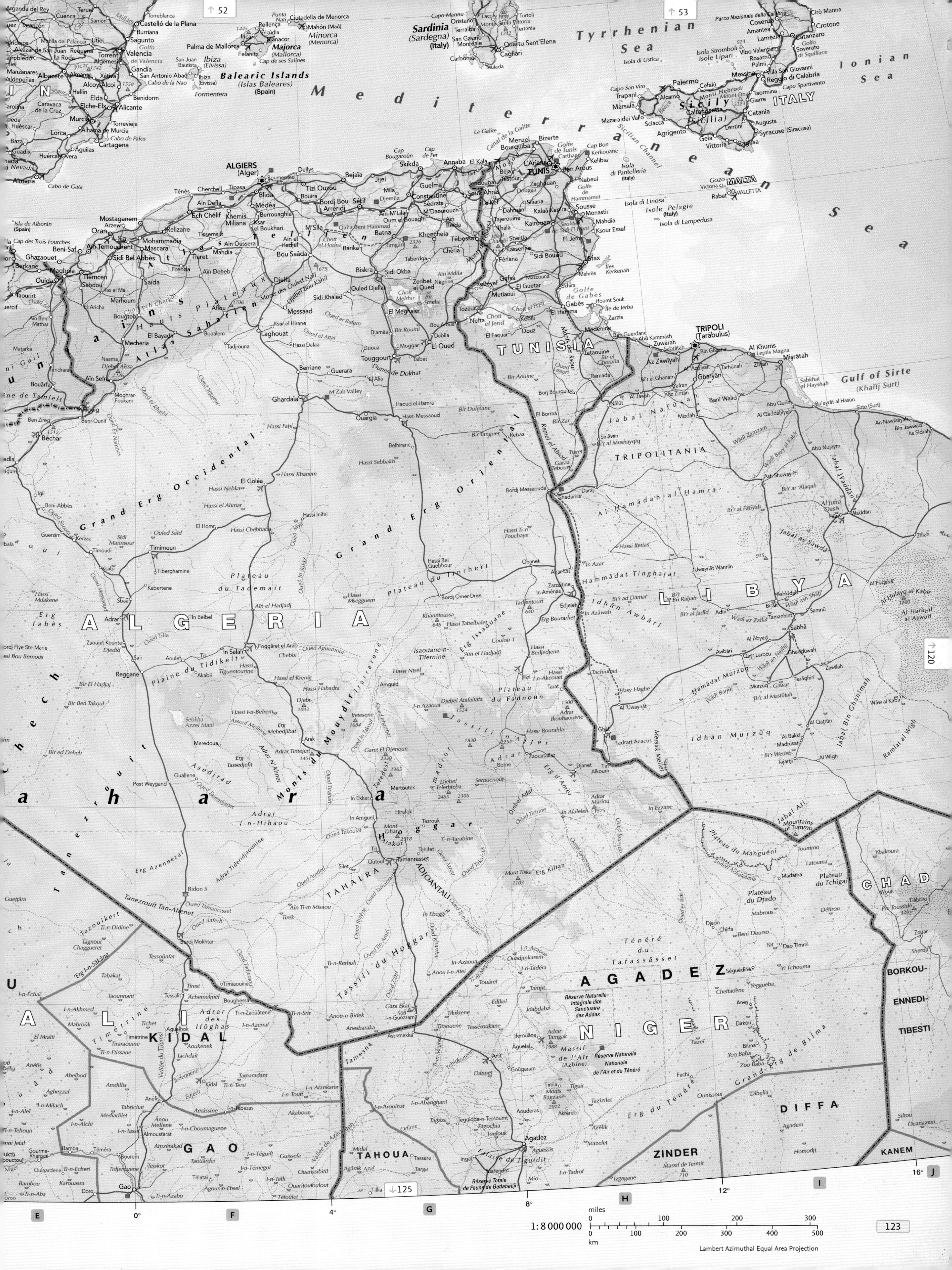

Mediterranean Sea
Tyrrhenian Sea
Ionian Sea
Sardinia (Sardegna) (Italy)
Balearic Islands (Islas Baleares) (Spain)
Majorca (Mallorca)
Minorca (Menorca)
Ibiza (Eivissa)
Formentera
Sicily (Sicilia)
ITALY
MALTA
VALLETTA
Gulf of Sirte (Khalīj Surt)
Golfe de Gabès
Golfe de Hammamet
Golfe de Tunis
Sicilian Channel
Canal de la Galite
Isole Pelagie (Italy)
Isola di Pantelleria (Italy)
ALGIERS (Alger)
TUNIS
TRIPOLI (Ṭarābulus)
ALGERIA
TUNISIA
LIBYA
NIGER
CHAD
MALI
AGADEZ
DIFFA
ZINDER
TAHOUA
GAO
KIDAL
KANEM
BORKOU-ENNEDI-TIBESTI
TRIPOLITANIA
Grand Erg Occidental
Grand Erg Oriental
Tell Atlas
Hauts Plateaux
Atlas Saharien
Plateau du Tademaït
Plateau du Tinrhert
Plaine du Tidikelt
Tanezrouft
Sahara
Hoggar
Tassili n'Ajjer
Tassili du Hoggar
Monts du Mouydir
Adrar des Ifôghas
Massif de l'Aïr (Azbine)
Ténéré du Tafassâsset
Erg du Ténéré
Grand Erg de Bilma
Plateau du Djado
Plateau du Manguéni
Plateau du Tchigaï
Al Ḥamādah al Ḥamrā'
Ḥammādat Tingharat
Idhān Awbārī
Idhān Murzūq
Ḥamādat Murzuq
Jabal Nafūsah
Jabal as Sawdā'
Oran
Constantine
Annaba
Sétif
Biskra
Ghardaïa
Ouargla
Touggourt
El Oued
Tamanrasset
Djanet
In Salah
Adrar
Reggane
Béchar
Sfax
Sousse
Gabès
Sabhā
Misrātah
Agadez
Arlit
Gao
Kidal
Bilma
1:8 000 000
miles 0 100 200 300
km 0 100 200 300 400 500
Lambert Azimuthal Equal Area Projection
E F G H I J
0° 4° 8° 12° 16°

↑ 52
↑ 53
↓ 125
↑ 120

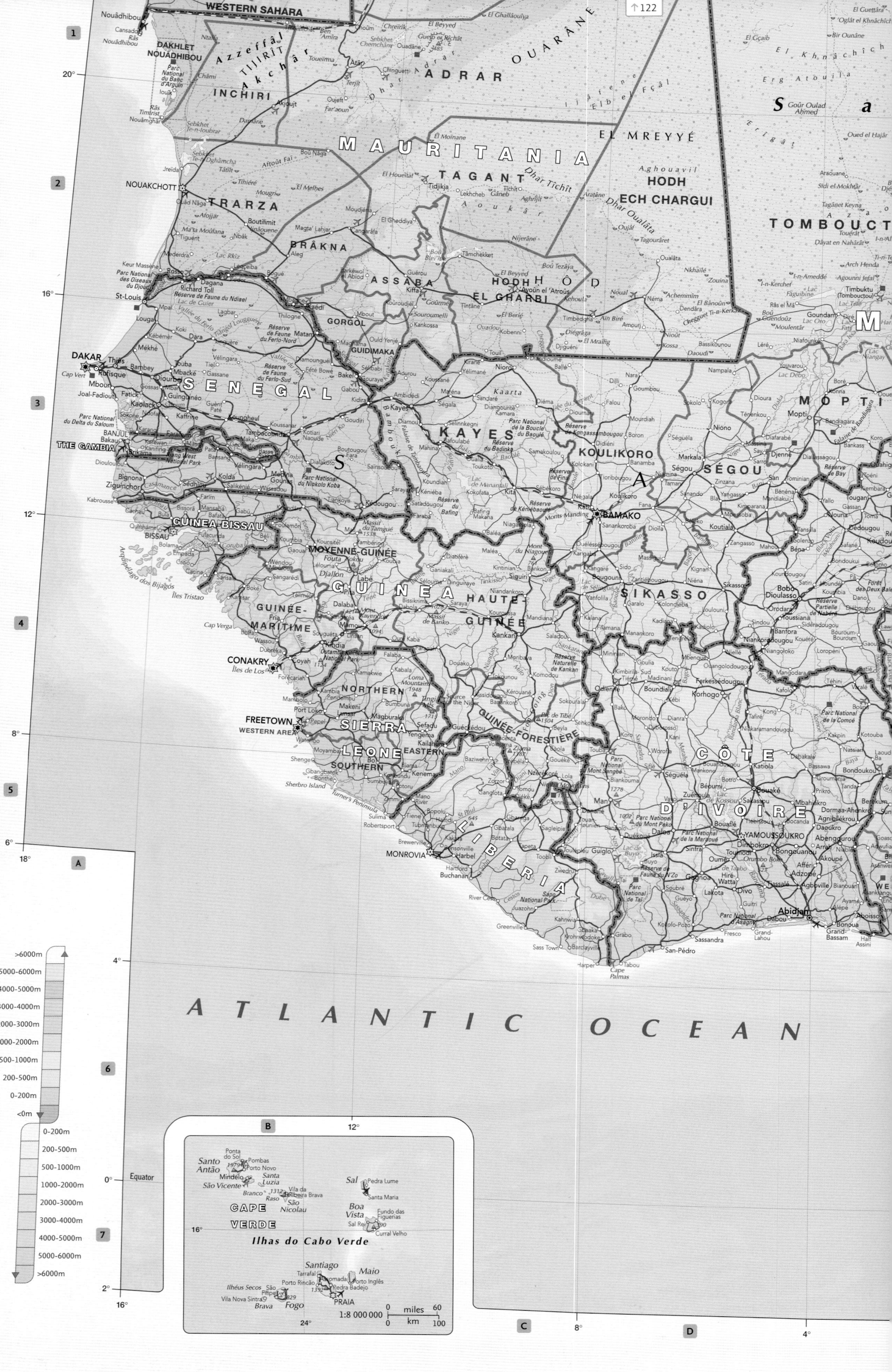

WESTERN SAHARA

MAURITANIA

MALI

SENEGAL

THE GAMBIA

GUINEA-BISSAU

GUINEA HAUTE

SIERRA LEONE

LIBERIA

CÔTE D'IVOIRE

ATLANTIC OCEAN

DAKAR

NOUAKCHOTT

NOUÂDHIBOU

BANJUL

BISSAU

CONAKRY

FREETOWN

MONROVIA

BAMAKO

YAMOUSSOUKRO

Abidjan

>6000m
5000-6000m
4000-5000m
3000-4000m
2000-3000m
1000-2000m
500-1000m
200-500m
0-200m
<0m

0-200m
200-500m
500-1000m
1000-2000m
2000-3000m
3000-4000m
4000-5000m
5000-6000m
>6000m

Equator

CAPE VERDE

Ilhas do Cabo Verde

Santo Antão
São Vicente
Mindelo
São Nicolau
Sal
Boa Vista
Maio
Santiago
Fogo
Brava
PRAIA

1:8 000 000

miles 60
km 100

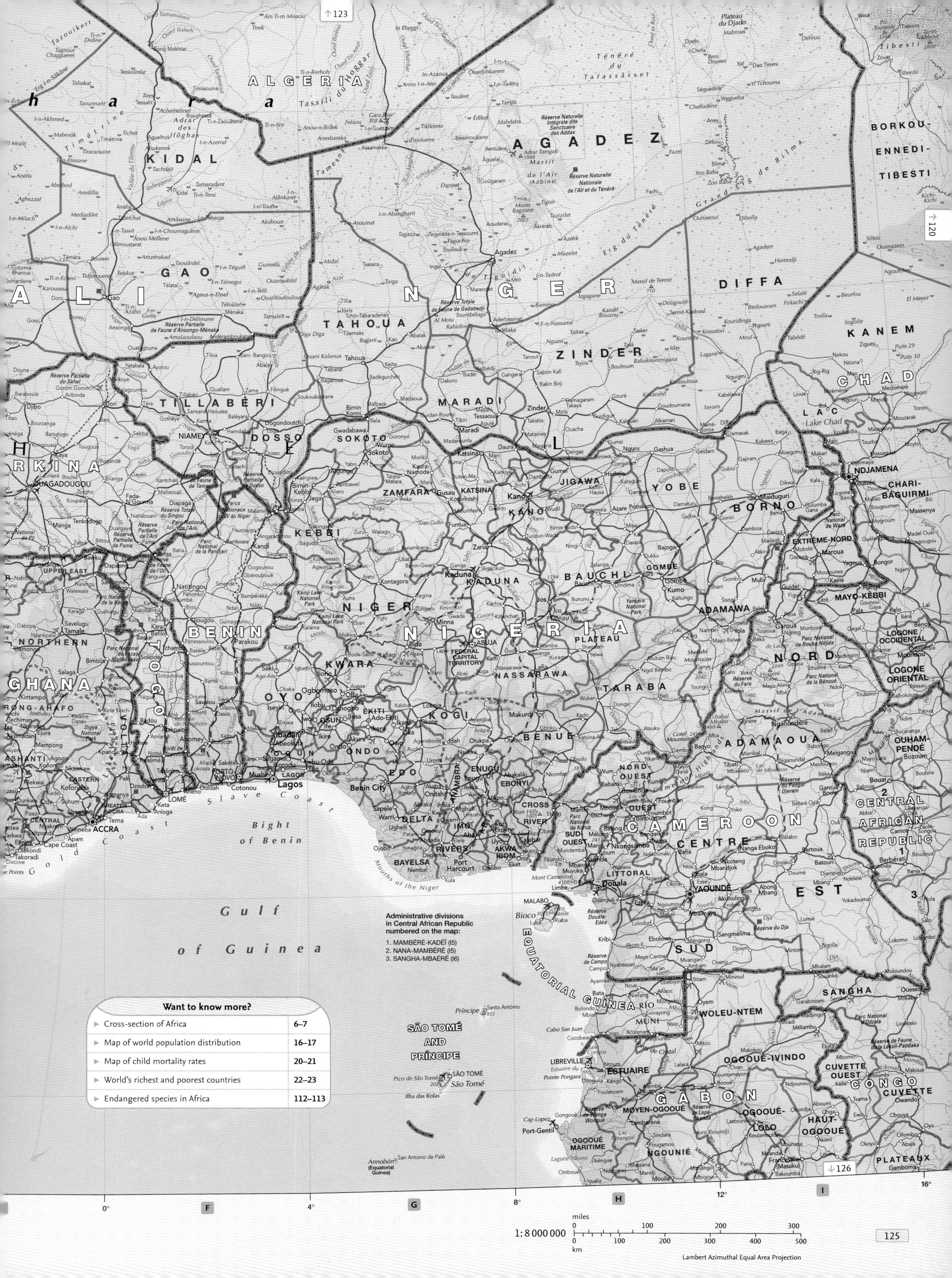

Want to know more?

Administrative divisions
in Central African Republic
numbered on the map:

1. MAMBÉRÉ-KADÉÏ (I5)
2. NANA-MAMBÉRÉ (I5)
3. SANGHA-MBAÉRÉ (I6)

miles
1 : 8 000 000

km

Lambert Azimuthal Equal Area Projection

↓ 126

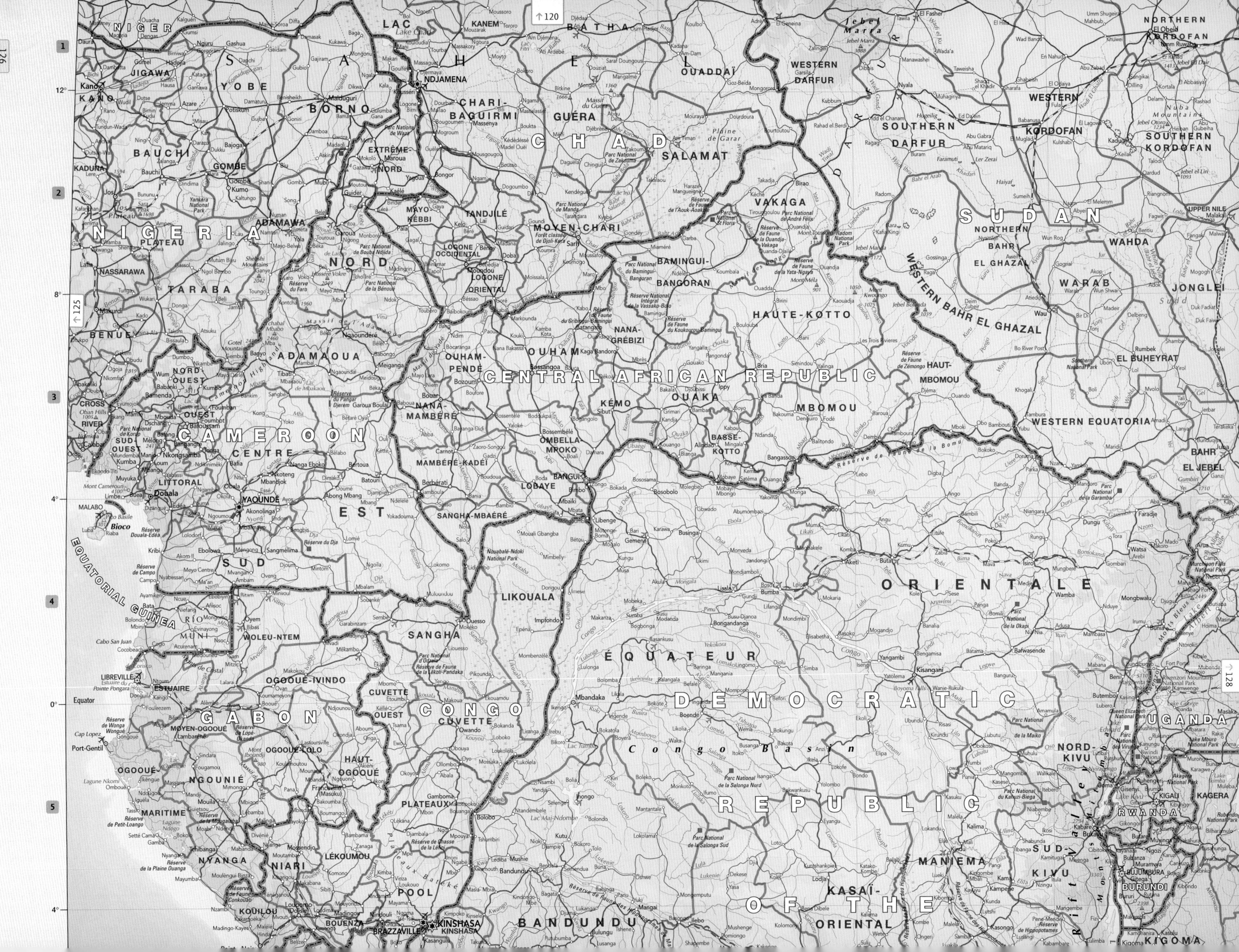
120
125
128
SUDAN
CHAD
CENTRAL AFRICAN REPUBLIC
CAMEROON
NIGERIA
GABON
CONGO
DEMOCRATIC REPUBLIC OF THE
EQUATORIAL GUINEA
UGANDA
RWANDA
BURUNDI
NORTHERN KORDOFAN
SOUTHERN KORDOFAN
WESTERN KORDOFAN
WESTERN DARFUR
SOUTHERN DARFUR
NORTHERN BAHR EL GHAZAL
WESTERN BAHR EL GHAZAL
WESTERN EQUATORIA
UPPER NILE
JONGLEI
WARAB
EL BUHEYRAT
BAHR EL JEBEL
WAHDA
OUADDAÏ
SALAMAT
GUÉRA
BATHA
KANEM
LAC
CHARI-BAGUIRMI
MOYEN-CHARI
TANDJILÉ
LOGONE OCCIDENTAL
LOGONE ORIENTAL
MAYO-KEBBI
VAKAGA
BAMINGUI-BANGORAN
HAUTE-KOTTO
HAUT-MBOMOU
MBOMOU
BASSE-KOTTO
OUAKA
KÉMO
NANA-GRÉBIZI
OUHAM
OUHAM-PENDÉ
NANA-MAMBÉRÉ
MAMBÉRÉ-KADEÏ
OMBELLA-MPOKO
LOBAYE
SANGHA-MBAÉRÉ
BANGUI
EXTRÊME-NORD
NORD
ADAMAOUA
EST
CENTRE
SUD
LITTORAL
OUEST
NORD-OUEST
SUD-OUEST
BORNO
YOBE
JIGAWA
KANO
KADUNA
BAUCHI
GOMBE
ADAMAWA
TARABA
PLATEAU
NASSARAWA
BENUE
CROSS RIVER
NIGER
LIKOUALA
SANGHA
CUVETTE
CUVETTE OUEST
PLATEAUX
POOL
LÉKOUMOU
BOUENZA
NIARI
KOUILOU
WOLEU-NTEM
ESTUAIRE
MOYEN-OGOOUÉ
OGOOUÉ-IVINDO
OGOOUÉ-LOLO
HAUT-OGOOUÉ
NGOUNIÉ
OGOOUÉ-MARITIME
NYANGA
ORIENTALE
ÉQUATEUR
BANDUNDU
KASAÏ-ORIENTAL
MANIEMA
SUD-KIVU
NORD-KIVU
KAGERA
RÍO MUNI
Congo Basin
Bioco
NDJAMENA
BANGUI
YAOUNDÉ
MALABO
LIBREVILLE
BRAZZAVILLE
KINSHASA
KIGALI
BUJUMBURA
Equator
12°
8°
4°
0°
4°
1
2
3
4
5

Want to know more?

▲ Life expectancy rates	20–21
▲ Image of the Congo river	110–111
▲ Land cover map of Africa	112–113
▲ Images of Lake Chad shrinking in size	112–113
▲ Map of African conflicts	116–117

1 : 8 000 000

Lambert Azimuthal Equal Area Projection

miles 0 100 200 300
km 0 100 200 300 400 500

>6000m
5000–6000m
4000–5000m
3000–4000m
2000–3000m
1000–2000m
500–1000m
200–500m
0–200m
<0m

0–200m
200–500m
500–1000m
1000–2000m
2000–3000m
3000–4000m
4000–5000m
5000–6000m
>6000m

ATLANTIC OCEAN

TANZANIA

RUKWA

NORTHERN

LUAPULA

CONGO

OCCIDENTAL

KATANGA

ZAMBIA

WESTERN

NORTH-WESTERN

COPPERBELT

CENTRAL

LUSAKA

SOUTHERN

EASTERN

MOZAMBIQUE

BAS-CONGO

ZAIRE

UIGE

LUNDA NORTE

MALANJE

LUNDA SUL

ANGOLA

MOXICO

CUANDO CUBANGO

CAPRIVI STRIP

OKAVANGO

NORTH-WEST

BOTSWANA

CENTRAL

MATABELELAND NORTH

ZIMBABWE

MASHONALAND WEST

MASHONALAND CENTRAL

MIDLANDS

HARARE

BENGO

LUANDA

CUANZA NORTE

CUANZA SUL

BENGUELA

HUAMBO

BIÉ

HUILA

NAMIBE

CUNENE

OVAMBOLAND

OMUSATI

OSHANA

OHANGWENA

OSHIKOTO

NAMIBIA

OTJOZONDJUPA

Lobito

Namibe

Luanda

Lubumbashi

Lusaka

Bulawayo

Cape Frio

127

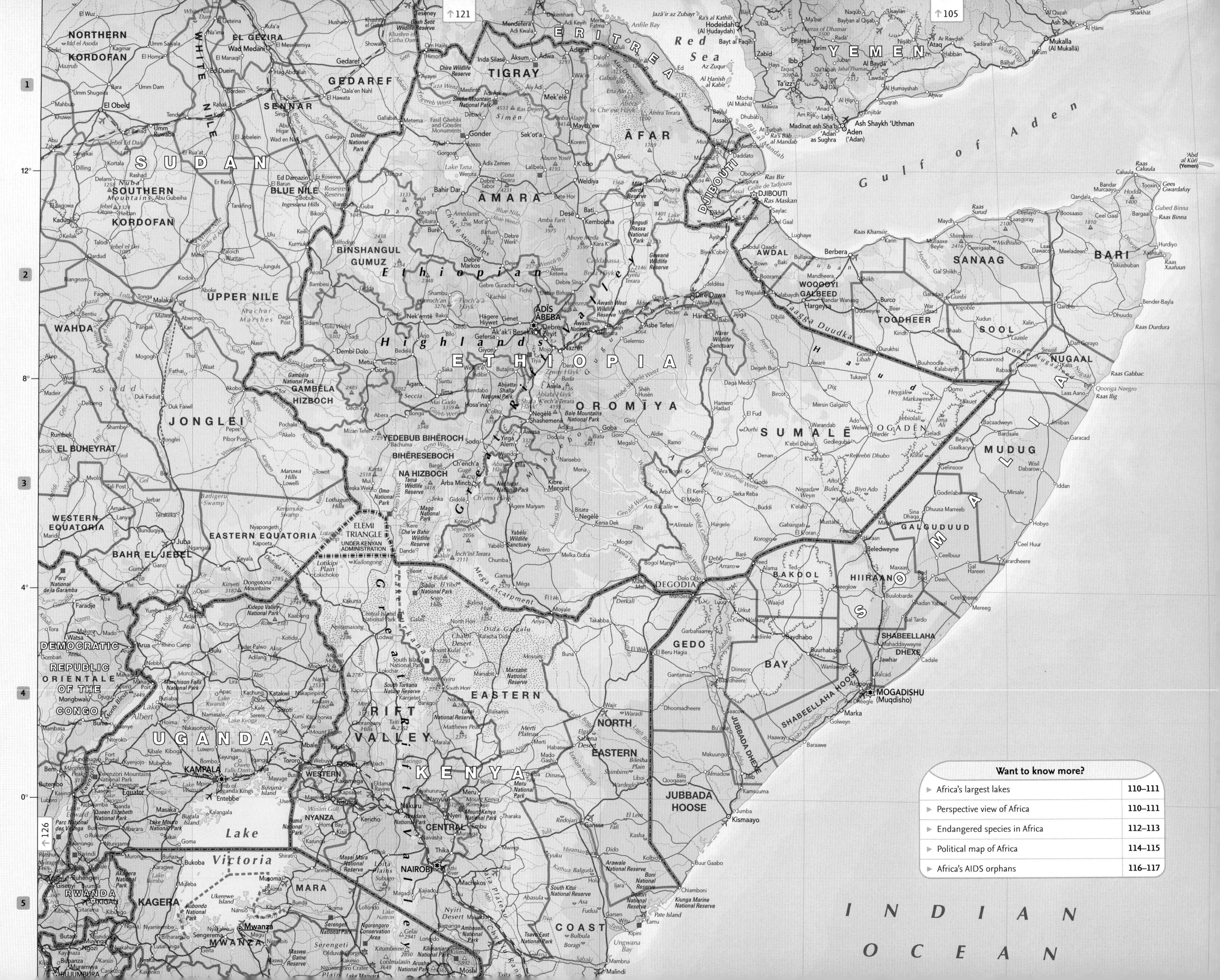

↑ 121

↓ 126

Want to know more?

▲ Africa's largest lakes	110–111
▲ Perspective view of Africa	110–111
▲ Endangered species in Africa	112–113
▲ Political map of Africa	114–115
▲ Africa's AIDS orphans	116–117

INDIAN OCEAN

Gulf of Aden

Red Sea

YEMEN

DJIBOUTI

ERITREA

ETHIOPIA

SOMALIA

Ethiopian Highlands

SUDAN

UGANDA

KENYA

Lake Victoria

Great Rift Valley

DEMOCRATIC REPUBLIC OF THE CONGO

RWANDA

BARI

NUGAAL

SOOL

SANAAG

AWDAL

WOQOOYI GALBEED

TOGDHEER

MUDUG

GALGUDUUD

OGĀDĒN

SUMALĒ

HIIRAAN

SHABEELLAHA DHEXE

SHABEELLAHA HOOSE

BAKOOL

BAY

GEDO

JUBBADA DHEXE

JUBBADA HOOSE

DECODIA

MOGADISHU (Muqdisho)

NORTH EASTERN

EASTERN

COAST

NAIROBI

CENTRAL

RIFT VALLEY

NYANZA

WESTERN

MARA

KAGERA

MWANZA

TIGRAY

AFAR

AMARA

OROMIYA

ADIS ABEBA

BINSHANGUL GUMUZ

GAMBĒLA HIZBOCH

YEDEBUB BIHĒROCH BIHĒRESEBOCH

NA HIZBOCH

GEDAREF

SENNAR

EL GEZIRA

WHITE NILE

BLUE NILE

NORTHERN KORDOFAN

SOUTHERN KORDOFAN

UPPER NILE

WAHDA

EL BUHEYRAT

JONGLEI

BAHR EL JEBEL

WESTERN EQUATORIA

EASTERN EQUATORIA

ELEMI TRIANGLE UNDER KENYAN ADMINISTRATION

ORIENTALE

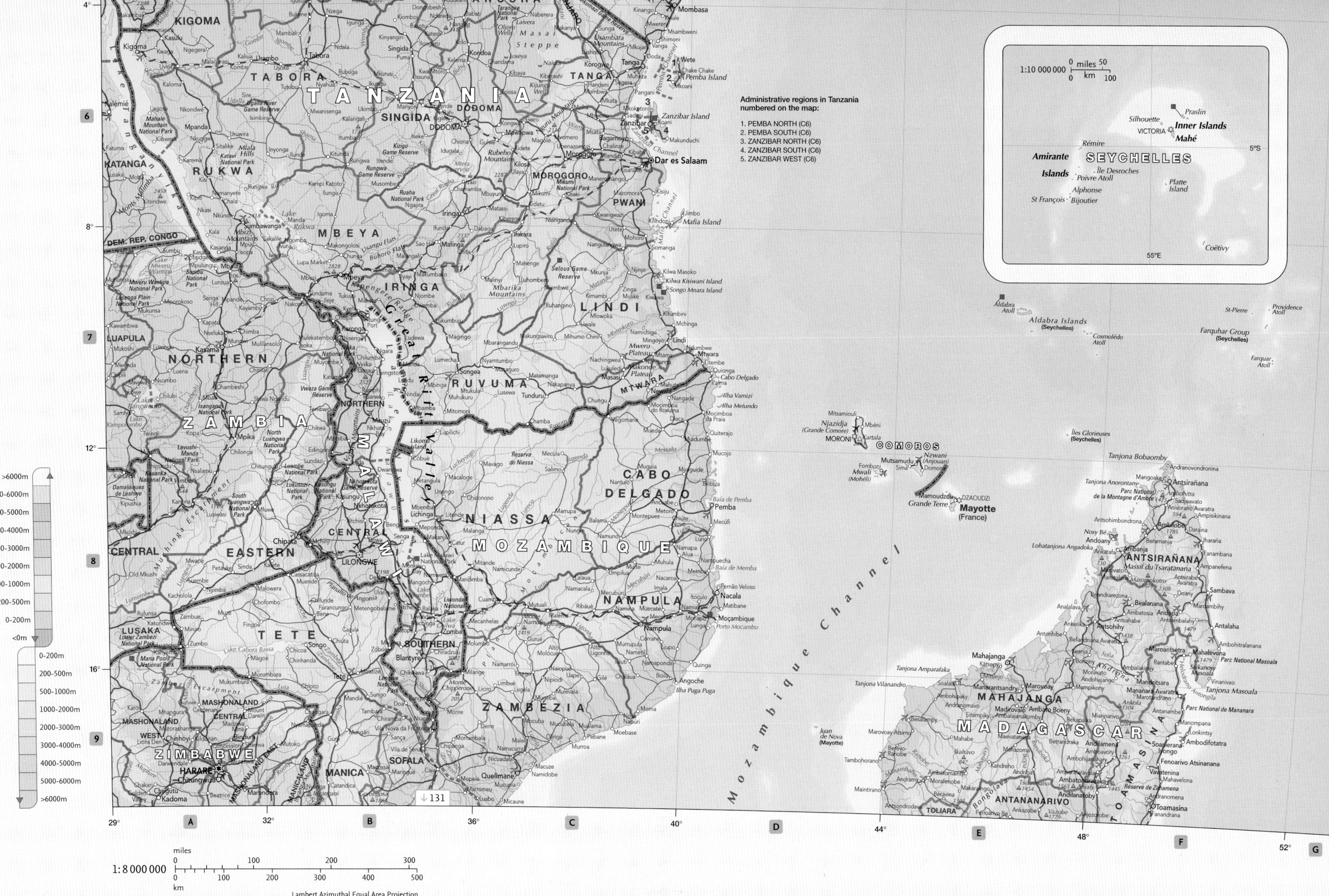

SEYCHELLES

Inner Islands
VICTORIA • Mahé
Silhouette
Praslin

Amirante Islands
Île Desroches
Poivre Atoll
Alphonse
St François • Bijoutier
Platte Island

Providence Atoll

St-Pierre

Farquhar Group (Seychelles)
Farquhar Atoll

Coëtivy

Aldabra Islands (Seychelles)
Aldabra Atoll

Cosmolédo Atoll

Îles Glorieuses (Seychelles)

1:10 000 000
0 miles 50
0 km 100

5°S
5°E
55°E

Administrative regions in Tanzania numbered on the map:
1. PEMBA NORTH (C6)
2. PEMBA SOUTH (C6)
3. ZANZIBAR NORTH (C6)
4. ZANZIBAR SOUTH (C6)
5. ZANZIBAR WEST (C6)

Mozambique Channel

COMOROS
MORONI
Njazidja (Grande Comore)
Mwali (Mohéli)
Nzwani (Anjouan)
Fomboni
Domoni
Mitsamiouli

Mayotte (France)
Mamoudzou • DZAOUDZI
Grande Terre

Juan de Nova (Mayotte)

MADAGASCAR

ANTSIRAÑANA

MAHAJANGA

ANTANANARIVO

TOLIARA

MANICA
MANICALAND

ZIMBABWE
HARARE
MASHONALAND
WEST
MASHONALAND
CENTRAL

TETE

TANZANIA
TABORA
KIGOMA
ARUSHA
SINGIDA
DODOMA
MBEYA
IRINGA
MOROGORO
TANGA
PWANI
LINDI
MTWARA
RUVUMA
Dar es Salaam
Zanzibar Island
Pemba Island
Mafia Island

Mombasa

DEM. REP. CONGO
KATANGA

ZAMBIA
NORTHERN
LUAPULA
RUKWA
CENTRAL
EASTERN
LUSAKA

MALAWI
LILONGWE
NORTHERN
CENTRAL
SOUTHERN
Blantyre
Lake Malawi

MOZAMBIQUE
NIASSA
CABO DELGADO
NAMPULA
ZAMBEZIA
SOFALA
Nampula
Pemba
Mozambique

Great Rift Valley
Lake Tanganyika

↓ 131

1:8 000 000
Lambert Azimuthal Equal Area Projection

miles
0 100 200 300
km
0 100 200 300 400 500

>6000m
5000–6000m
4000–5000m
3000–4000m
2000–3000m
1000–2000m
500–1000m
200–500m
0–200m
<0m

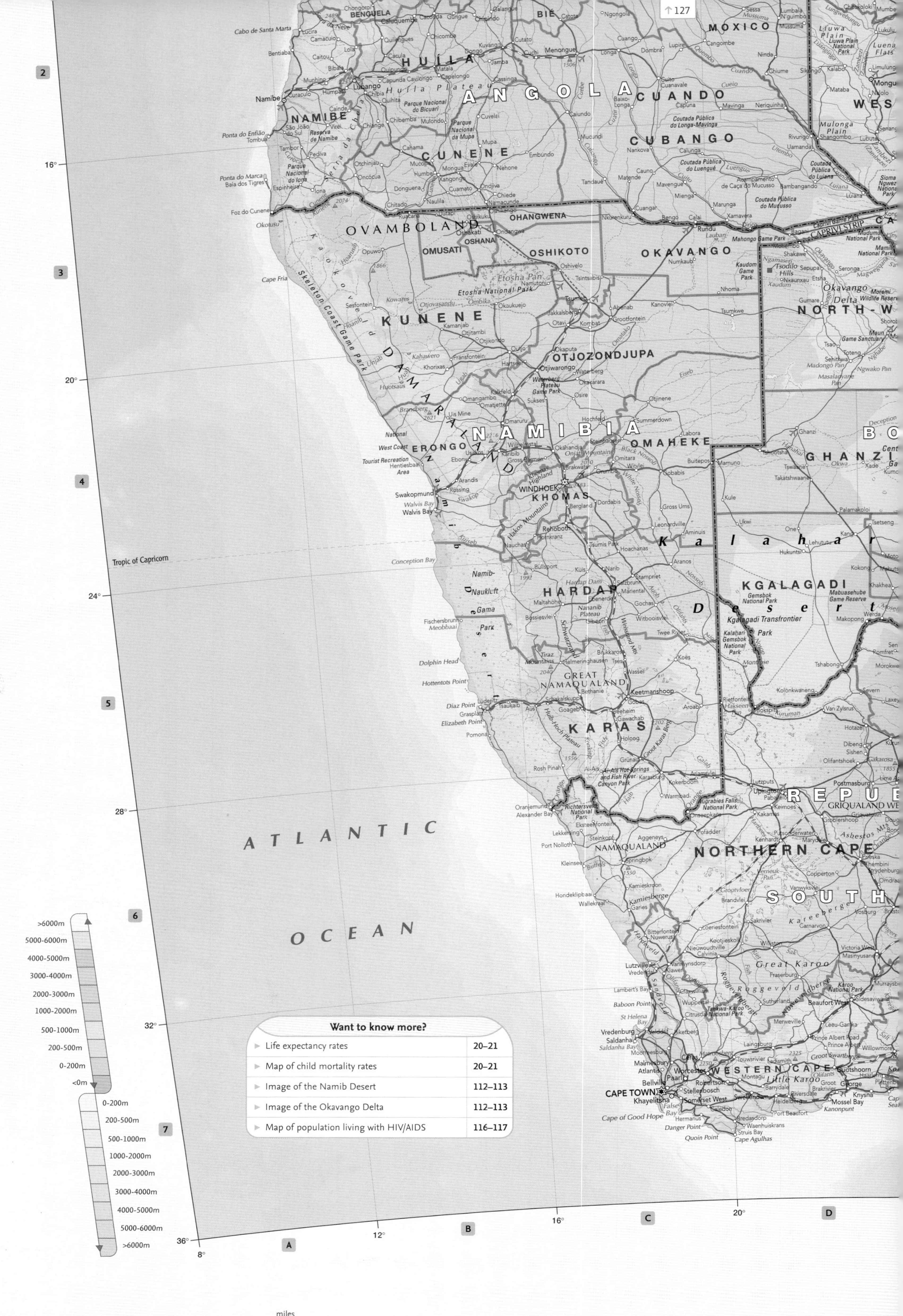

Africa Southern Africa

Want to know more?

▶ Life expectancy rates	20–21
▶ Map of child mortality rates	20–21
▶ Image of the Namib Desert	112–113
▶ Image of the Okavango Delta	112–113
▶ Map of population living with HIV/AIDS	116–117

>6000m
5000-6000m
4000-5000m
3000-4000m
2000-3000m
1000-2000m
500-1000m
200-500m
0-200m
<0m

0-200m
200-500m
500-1000m
1000-2000m
2000-3000m
3000-4000m
4000-5000m
5000-6000m
>6000m

1:8 000 000

miles
0   100   200   300

km
0   100   200   300   400   500

Lambert Azimuthal Equal Area Projection

↑129

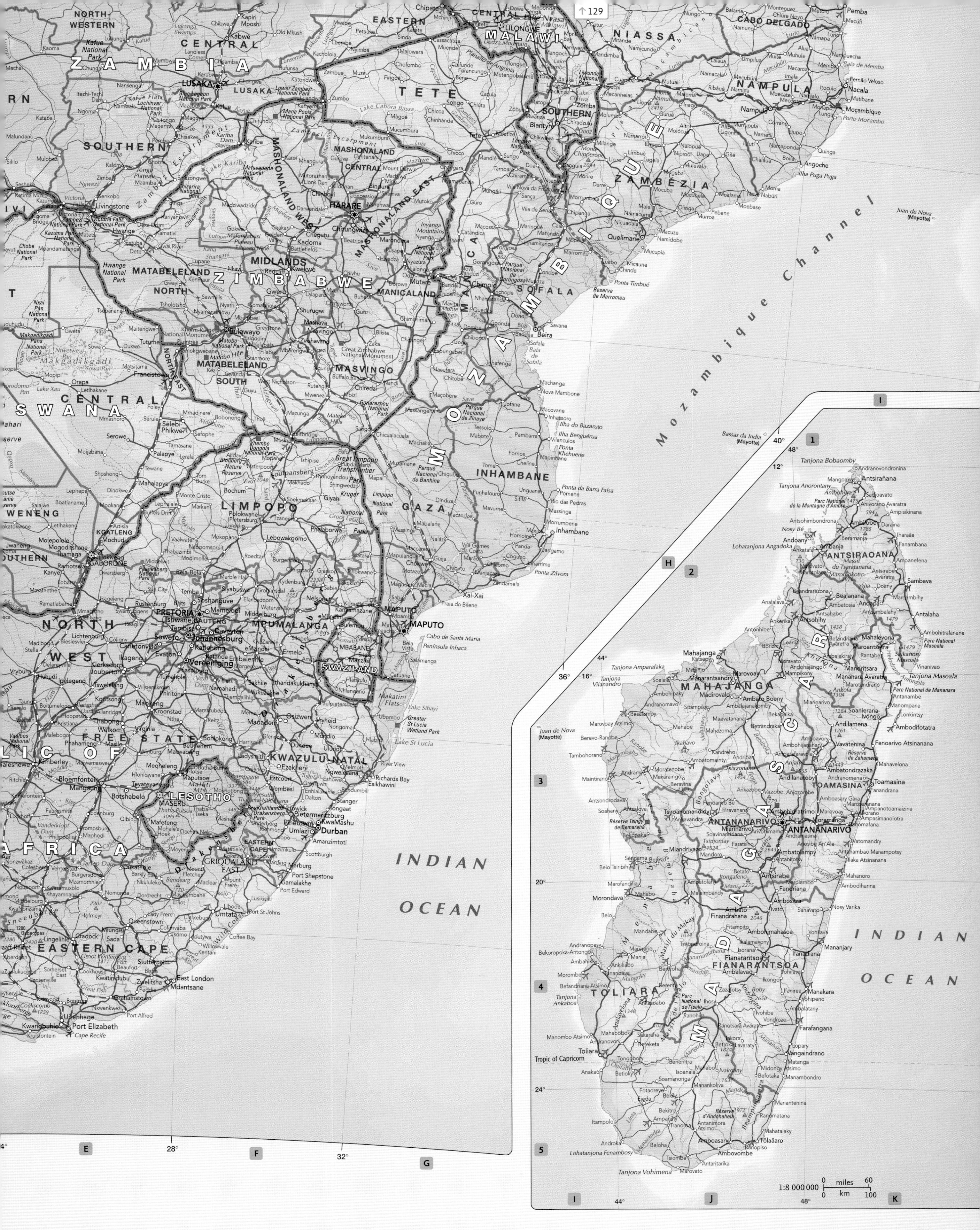
ZAMBIA
NORTH-WESTERN
CENTRAL
LUSAKA
SOUTHERN
EASTERN
MALAWI
CENTRAL
SOUTHERN
NIASSA
CABO DELGADO
NAMPULA
TETE
ZAMBÉZIA
MOZAMBIQUE
MANICA
SOFALA
INHAMBANE
GAZA
MAPUTO
ZIMBABWE
MASHONALAND CENTRAL
MASHONALAND WEST
MASHONALAND EAST
MIDLANDS
MATABELELAND NORTH
MATABELELAND SOUTH
MANICALAND
MASVINGO
BOTSWANA
CENTRAL
NORTH EAST
KWENENG
KGATLENG
SOUTHERN
LIMPOPO
MPUMALANGA
NORTH WEST
GAUTENG
FREE STATE
KWAZULU-NATAL
EASTERN CAPE
REPUBLIC OF SOUTH AFRICA
LESOTHO
SWAZILAND
Mozambique Channel
INDIAN OCEAN
LUSAKA
HARARE
Bulawayo
Livingstone
Blantyre
LILONGWE
Nampula
Quelimane
Beira
Inhambane
Xai-Xai
MAPUTO
MBABANE
GABORONE
PRETORIA
Johannesburg
Soweto
Vereeniging
Bloemfontein
Kimberley
MASERU
Pietermaritzburg
Durban
Richards Bay
East London
Port Elizabeth
Lake Kariba
Lake Cabora Bassa
Bassas da India (Mayotte)
Juan de Nova (Mayotte)
Tropic of Capricorn
MADAGASCAR
ANTSIRAOANA
MAHAJANGA
TOAMASINA
ANTANANARIVO
FIANARANTSOA
TOLIARA
Antsiranana
Mahajanga
Toamasina
Antsirabe
Fianarantsoa
Toliara
Morondava
Tôlañaro
INDIAN OCEAN
1:8 000 000
0 miles 60
0 km 100
E F G H I J K
1 2 3 4 5

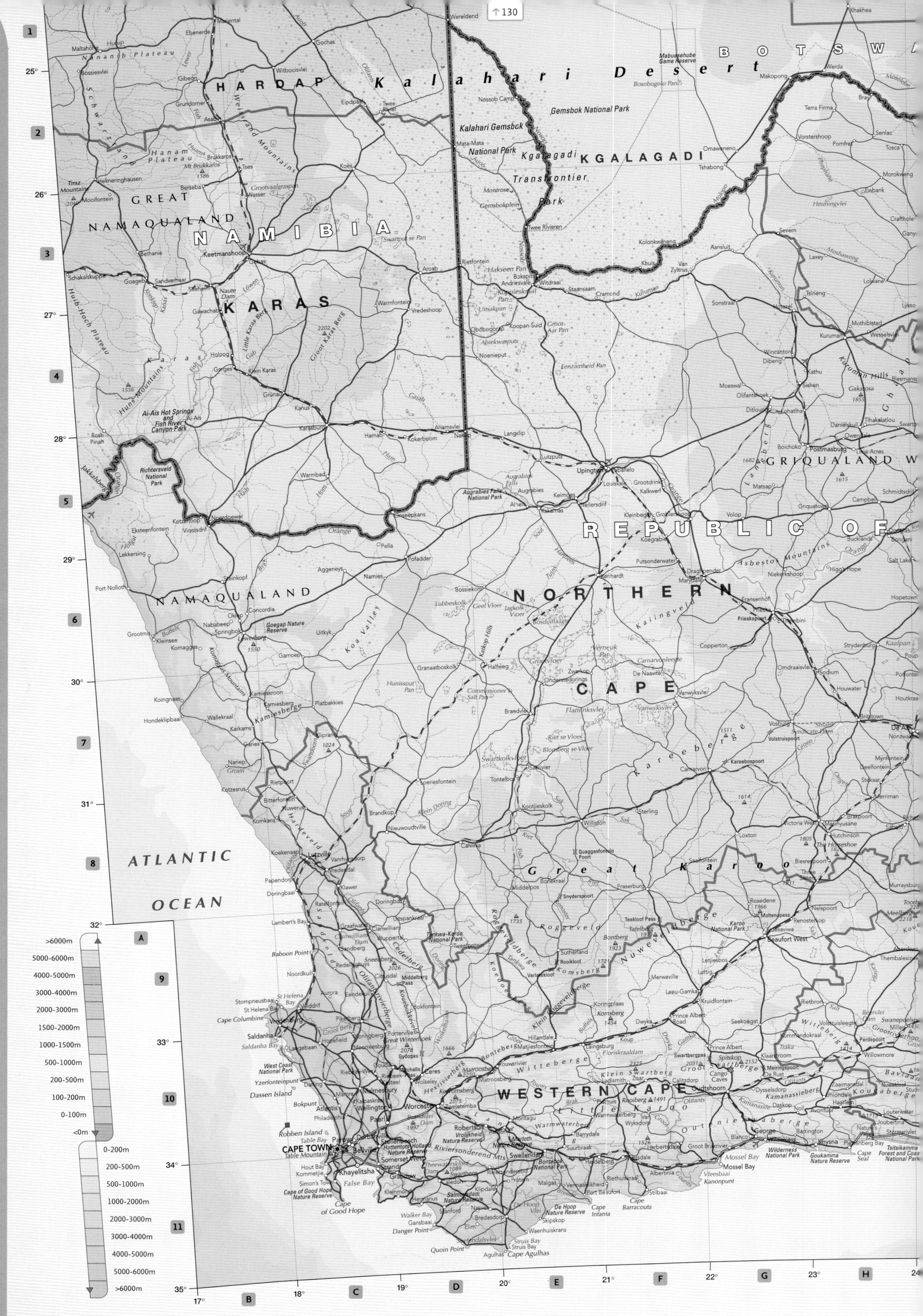

Africa Republic of South Africa

↑130
Kalahari Desert
BOTSWANA
HARDAP
KARAS
NAMIBIA
GREAT NAMAQUALAND
NAMAQUALAND
KGALAGADI
Kgalagadi Transfrontier Park
Kalahari Gemsbok National Park
Gemsbok National Park
Mabuasehube Game Reserve
Richtersveld National Park
Ai-Ais Hot Springs and Fish River Canyon Park
Augrabies Falls National Park
Goegap Nature Reserve
GRIQUALAND WEST
NORTHERN CAPE
WESTERN CAPE
Great Karoo
Little Karoo
Roggeveld
Kareeberge
Nuweveldberge
Komsberg
Swartberg
Langeberg
Cederberg
Koa Valley
Kamiesberge
Asbestos Mountains
Schwarzrand
Huns Mountains
Karas Mountains
Hanam Plateau
Nanib Plateau
Huib-Hoch Plateau
Weissrand Mountains
Orange
ATLANTIC OCEAN
Keetmanshoop
Upington
Springbok
Calvinia
Saldanha
Worcester
Paarl
Stellenbosch
CAPE TOWN
Table Mountain
Robben Island
Khayelitsha
Cape of Good Hope
Cape Agulhas
Mossel Bay
George
Knysna
Oudtshoorn
Beaufort West
Carnarvon
Prieska
Kuruman
Postmasburg
Sutherland
Port Nolloth
Alexander Bay
Lüderitz
Hermanus
Swellendam
Cape Columbine
Dassen Island
False Bay
Walker Bay
Danger Point
Quoin Point
West Coast National Park
Tankwa-Karoo National Park
Karoo National Park
Bontebok National Park
De Hoop Nature Reserve
Wilderness National Park
Goukamma Nature Reserve
Tsitsikamma Forest and Coastal National Park
>6000m
5000-6000m
4000-5000m
3000-4000m
2000-3000m
1500-2000m
1000-1500m
500-1000m
200-500m
100-200m
0-100m
<0m
0-200m
200-500m
500-1000m
1000-2000m
2000-3000m
3000-4000m
4000-5000m
5000-6000m
>6000m

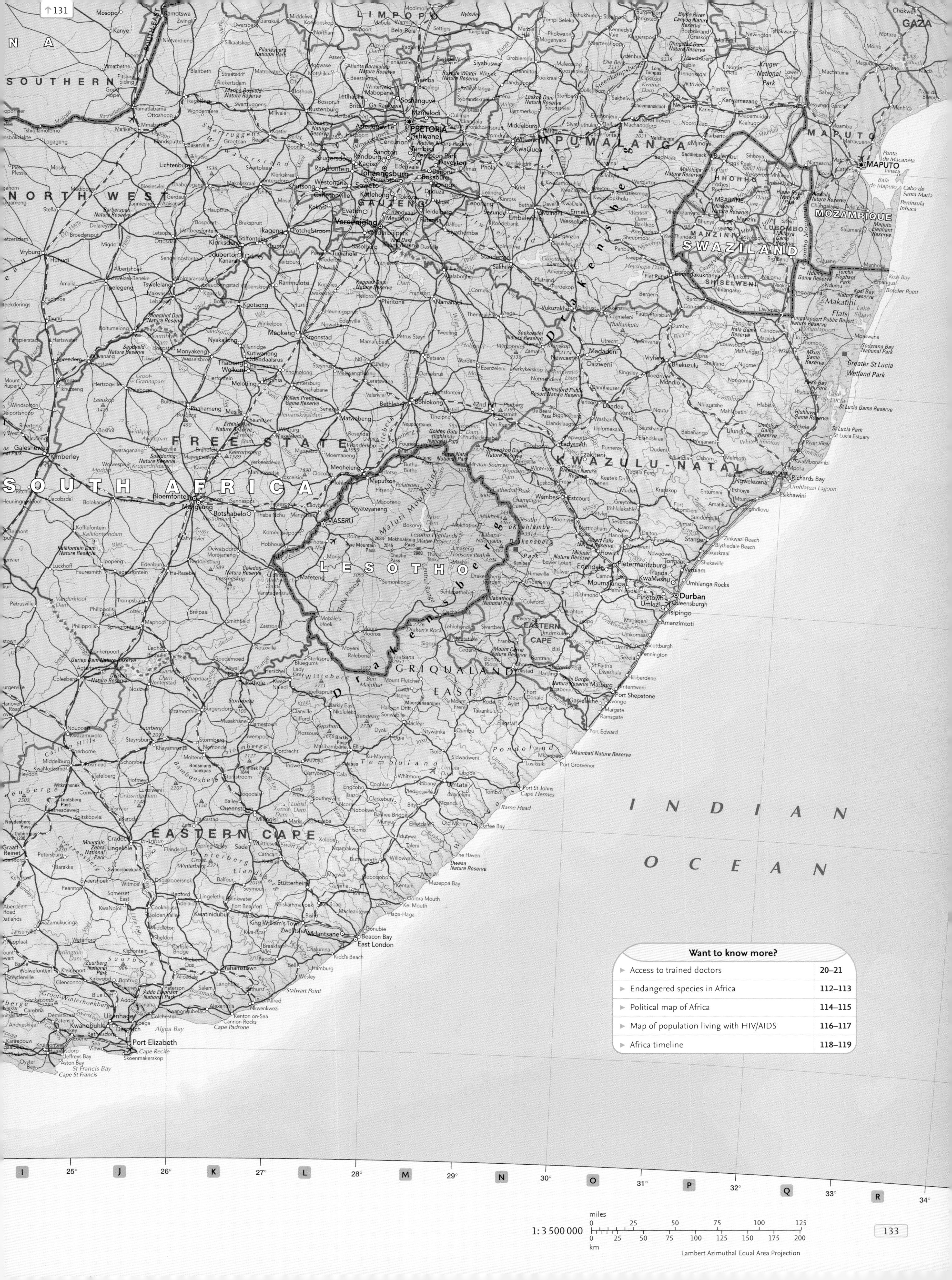

1 : 3 500 000

miles
0   25   50   75   100   125

km
0 25 50 75 100 125 150 175 200

Lambert Azimuthal Equal Area Projection

The continent of Oceania comprises Australia, the islands of New Zealand, New Guinea and numerous small islands and island groups in the Pacific Ocean, including Micronesia, Melanesia and Polynesia. The main landmass of Australia is largely desert, with many salt lakes and a low artesian basin in the east central area. The mountains of the Great Dividing Range run parallel to the east coast and are the source of the main river system, the Murray-Darling. The Great Barrier Reef, which stretches off the coast of Queensland, Australia, is the world's largest deposit of coral.

New Guinea is a mountainous island, most of which is covered with tropical forest. New Zealand has a great variety of landscape types, from tropical environments in the north of North Island to sub-Antarctic conditions in the south of South Island. North Island has extensive volcanic areas and South Island is mountainous, being dominated by the Southern Alps range.

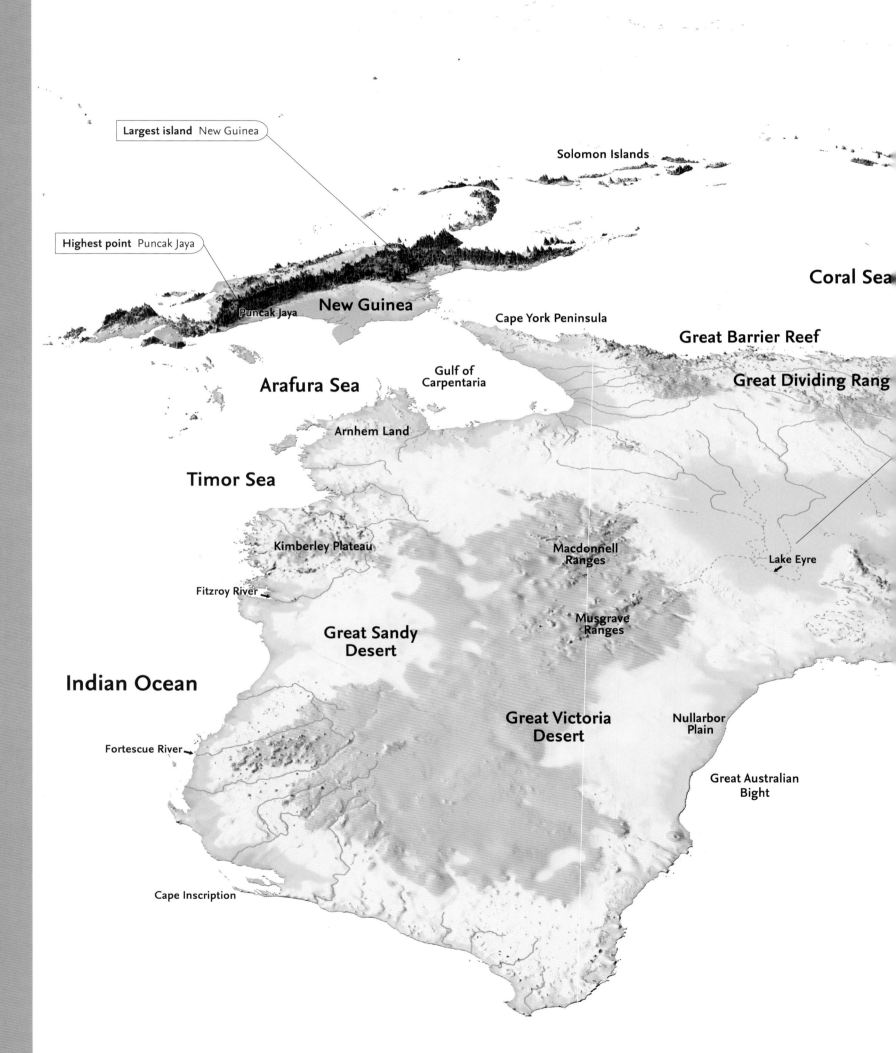

Largest island New Guinea

Highest point Puncak Jaya

Solomon Islands

Coral Sea

Puncak Jaya

New Guinea

Cape York Peninsula

Great Barrier Reef

Great Dividing Rang

Arafura Sea

Gulf of Carpentaria

Arnhem Land

Timor Sea

Kimberley Plateau

Macdonnell Ranges

Lake Eyre

Fitzroy River

Musgrave Ranges

Great Sandy Desert

Indian Ocean

Great Victoria Desert

Nullarbor Plain

Fortescue River

Great Australian Bight

Cape Inscription

Lake Eyre, situated in one of the driest regions in South Australia, is the largest salt lake in Australia. The lake actually comprises two lakes, Lake Eyre North and the much smaller Lake Eyre South. Salt has been washed into the lake from underlying marine sediments and when dry, which is its usual state, the lake bed is a glistening sheet of white salt. In this Space Shuttle photograph, the lake, viewed from the north, is in the process of drying out after being at a higher level.

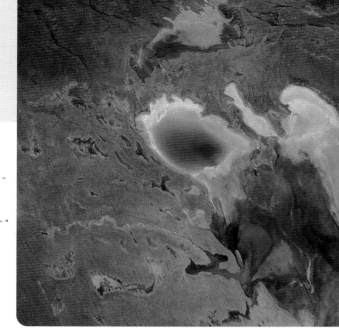

Fiji

New Caledonia

Pacific Ocean

North Island

Aoraki (Mount Cook)

South Island

Tasman Sea

Largest lake and lowest point Lake Eyre

Lachlan River
Murrumbidgee River
Darling River

Mount Kosciuszko

Murray River

Tasmania

Longest river and largest drainage basin Murray-Darling

Want to know more?

▶ Cross-section of Oceania		6–7
▶ Land cover map of Oceania		136–137
▶ Threats to coral reefs		140–141
▶ Maps of Oceania		144–153
▶ Map of Pacific Ocean		220–221

Internet links

Great Barrier Reef Marine Park Authority	www.gbrmpa.gov.au
Australian Government, Dept of the Environment	www.deh.gov.au
New Zealand Dept of Conservation	www.doc.govt.nz
The Maori people	www.maori.org.nz

Facts

The Great Barrier Reef is the world's largest coral reef which stretches for over 2 000 kilometres (1 249 miles).

New Zealand lies on the boundary of two tectonic plates, the Pacific and Indo-Australian plates. This forms part of the "ring of fire" around the Pacific Ocean, known for its active earthquakes and volcanoes.

Large areas of the interior (outback) of Australia are desert. Lakes are impermanent and salty and can vary in size and shape from year to year owing to the climate and can disappear in times of severe drought.

Many of the islands in Melanesia and Micronesia are coral atolls which are low lying, such as Tuvalu where the highest point is only 5 metres (16 feet) above sea level.

Highest mountains

Highest mountains	metres	feet	map
Puncak Jaya *Indonesia*	5 030	16 502	73 I7
Puncak Trikora *Indonesia*	4 730	15 518	73 I7
Puncak Mandala *Indonesia*	4 700	15 420	73 J7
Puncak Yamin *Indonesia*	4 595	15 075	73 I7
Mt Wilhelm *Papua New Guinea*	4 509	14 793	73 J8
Mt Kubor *Papua New Guinea*	4 359	14 301	73 J8

Longest rivers

Longest rivers	km	miles	map
Murray-Darling	3 750	2 330	146 C3
Darling	2 739	1 702	146 D3
Murray	2 589	1 608	146 C3
Murrumbidgee	1 690	1 050	147 E3
Lachlan	1 480	919	147 D3
Macquarie	950	590	147 E2

Largest islands

Largest islands	sq km	sq miles	map
New Guinea	808 510	312 167	73 J8
South Island, New Zealand	115 777	58 384	153 F11
North Island, New Zealand	227 414	44 702	152 J6
Tasmania	67 800	26 178	147 E5

Largest lakes

Largest lakes	sq km	sq miles	map
Lake Eyre	0-8 900	0-3 436	146 C2
Lake Torrens	0-5 780	0-2 232	146 C2

Land area

Total land area 8 844 516 sq km/3 414 887 sq miles (includes New Guinea and Pacific Island nations)		map
Most northerly point	**Eastern I.** *N. Pacific Ocean*	220 G4
Most southerly point	**Macquarie I.** *S.Pacific Ocean*	220 E9
Most westerly point	**Cape Inscription** *Australia*	151 A5
Most easterly point	**Île Clipperton** *N.Pacific Ocean*	221 K5
Lowest point	**Lake Eyre** *Australia*	146 C2

Aoraki (Mount Cook) on New Zealand's South Island, is the highest peak in the country at 3 754 metres (12 316 feet). The peak is part of the Southern Alps and the National Park surrounding it is designated a World Heritage area.

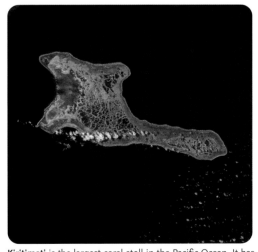

Kiritimati is the largest coral atoll in the Pacific Ocean. It has a shallow lagoon, which covers a large part of the island's 575 square kilometres (222 square miles). White sandy beaches surround the lagoon and line the island's coast.

Oceania is dominated by Australia which is largely desert with seasonal grass and scrubland. The main water area is Lake Eyre – a salt lake whose size fluctuates seasonally. New Guinea and its neighbouring islands are covered in tropical vegetation, while farther into the Pacific Ocean there are numerous scattered islands and island groups. Some are little more than coral reefs or atolls, only a few metres above sea level, but with a large variety of plant and animal species. The islands which make up New Zealand have a range of habitats from high alpine mountains to grassland, sub-tropical forests and cultivated areas. New Zealand sits on the edge of the Pacific tectonic plate and associated volcanic activity can be seen in the volcanoes, geysers and hot springs of North Island.

This view of **Bora Bora**, an island within the Society Islands of **French Polynesia** is typical of the South Pacific islands. Scattered groups of low-lying coral based islands host tropical or semi-tropical vegetation.

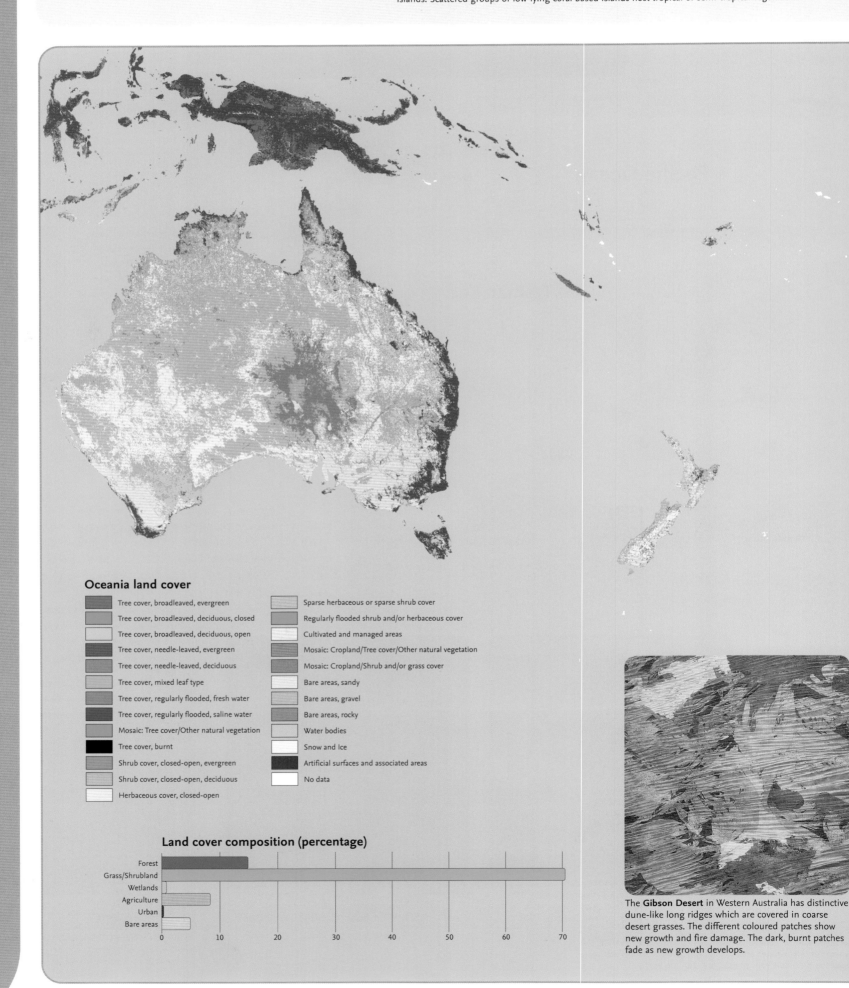

Oceania land cover

- Tree cover, broadleaved, evergreen
- Tree cover, broadleaved, deciduous, closed
- Tree cover, broadleaved, deciduous, open
- Tree cover, needle-leaved, evergreen
- Tree cover, needle-leaved, deciduous
- Tree cover, mixed leaf type
- Tree cover, regularly flooded, fresh water
- Tree cover, regularly flooded, saline water
- Mosaic: Tree cover/Other natural vegetation
- Tree cover, burnt
- Shrub cover, closed-open, evergreen
- Shrub cover, closed-open, deciduous
- Herbaceous cover, closed-open
- Sparse herbaceous or sparse shrub cover
- Regularly flooded shrub and/or herbaceous cover
- Cultivated and managed areas
- Mosaic: Cropland/Tree cover/Other natural vegetation
- Mosaic: Cropland/Shrub and/or grass cover
- Bare areas, sandy
- Bare areas, gravel
- Bare areas, rocky
- Water bodies
- Snow and Ice
- Artificial surfaces and associated areas
- No data

Land cover composition (percentage)

Forest, Grass/Shrubland, Wetlands, Agriculture, Urban, Bare areas (scale 0–70)

The **Gibson Desert** in Western Australia has distinctive dune-like long ridges which are covered in coarse desert grasses. The different coloured patches show new growth and fire damage. The dark, burnt patches fade as new growth develops.

Internet links

Red List of Threatened Species	www.redlist.org
UN Environment Programme	www.unep.org
IUCN the World Conservation Union	www.iucn.org
Images of Oceania	earthobservatory.nasa.gov

Facts

In 1859, twentyfour rabbits were released for hunting near Geelong. Now an estimated 200–300 million plague Australia.

It is common for a rabbit population to increase 8–10 fold in one breeding season.

In parts of the Northern Territory cane toads are spreading west at a rate of 50 kilometres (30 miles) a year.

On the tropical Solomon Islands 4 500 plant species have been identified which includes more than 230 varieties of orchid.

On New Zealand's South Island the **Banks Peninsula** is the only recognizable volcanic feature. It was formed by two overlapping volcanic centres, which are separated by Akaroa Harbour. Even after extensive erosion the radial drainage pattern typical of volcanoes is still evident. The **Canterbury Plain** behind the peninsula is a different habitat and is used for mixed cereal and livestock farming.

Endangered species

Even on the small, remote islands there are plants and animals under threat. There are species which have evolved to their unique habitat and so will be susceptible to any change in habitat or climate. Countries such as Papua New Guinea are under pressure to clear tropical forests for farmland while the Great Barrier Reef is dependent on clean, undisturbed water for the coral to flourish.

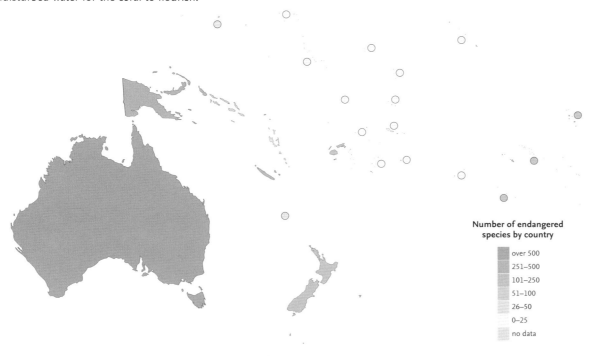

Number of endangered species by country

- over 500
- 251–500
- 101–250
- 51–100
- 26–50
- 0–25
- no data

The black-browed albatross is one of several **threatened species** of albatross. They roam the Southern Ocean for food but are vulnerable from predators when breeding on land. Sooty albatross numbers have dropped by 75 per cent in three generations.

Introduced species

In Australia, introduced species such as the European rabbit have proved to be major pests causing millions of dollars of damage each year. They cause land degradation and soil erosion as well as competing for food and shelter with the native species. In the 1950s the myxoma virus was introduced as was the calicivirus in 1995. Numbers declined for a while but soon recovered. When the rabbit numbers fell so did those for feral cats and foxes – predators of the rabbit. Native plants also reappeared, highlighting the damage the pests do.

Other species such as the cane toad were introduced in 1935 in northern Queensland to devour pests on sugar plantations. The toads are spreading westwards from the northeast coast. They are not officially registered as pests as their distribution is not nationwide, but they are being monitored for their environmental impact.

Coastal areas of **New Guinea** are home to mangrove forests which are considered the oldest unchanged ecosystem on the earth.

The greater bilby shown here, is one of several small **marsupials** which are vulnerable because they fall prey to feral cats and foxes. They also compete for food and burrows with rabbits.

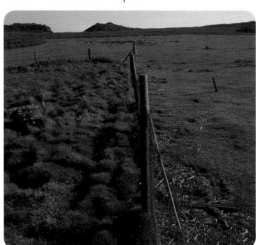

The difference a **rabbit fence** can make in protecting the vegetation can be clearly seen in this image – the longest fence built was 1 833 kilometres (1 139 miles) long – crossing the continent from north to south. Rabbits eat the tender young shoots of plants giving the vegetation no chance to recover.

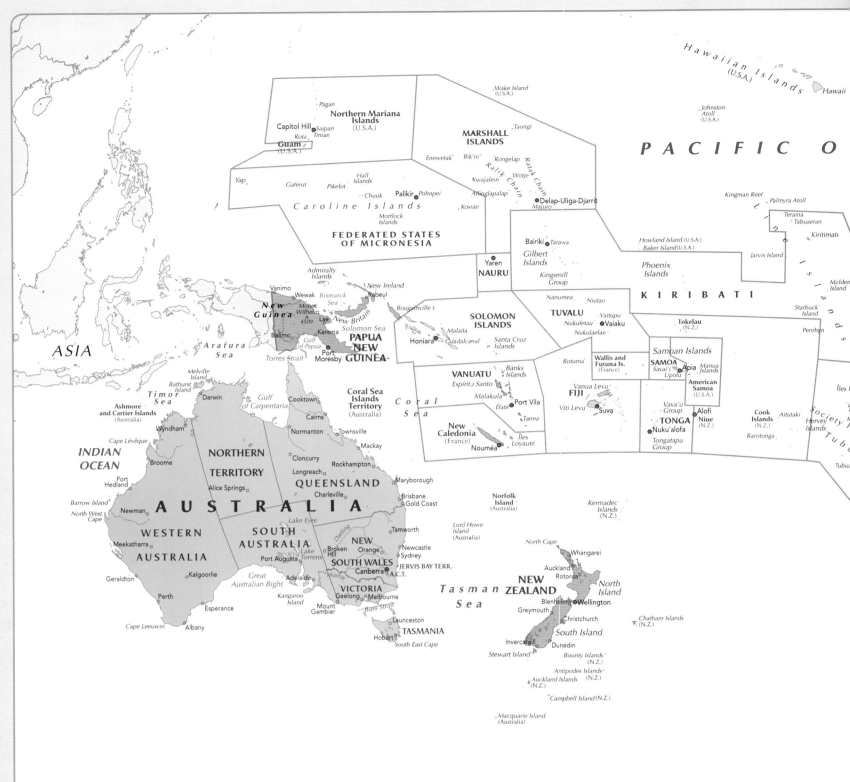

Countries capital		sq km sq miles	population	languages	religions	currency	official website	map
Australia Canberra		7 692 024 2 969 907	20 155 000	English, Italian, Greek	Protestant, Roman Catholic, Orthodox	Australian dollar	www.gov.au	144–145
Fiji Suva		18 330 7 077	848 000	English, Fijian, Hindi	Christian, Hindu, Sunni Muslim	Fiji dollar	www.fiji.gov.fj	145
Kiribati Bairiki		717 277	99 000	Gilbertese, English	Roman Catholic, Protestant	Australian dollar		145
Marshall Islands Dalap-Uliga-Djarrit		181 70	62 000	English, Marshallese	Protestant, Roman Catholic	US dollar	www.rmiembassyus.org	220
Micronesia, Federated States of Palikir		701 271	110 000	English, Chuukese, Pohnpeian, local languages	Roman Catholic, Protestant	US dollar	www.fsmgov.org	220
Nauru Yaren		21 8	14 000	Nauruan, English	Protestant, Roman Catholic	Australian dollar	www.un.int/nauru	145
New Zealand Wellington		270 534 104 454	4 028 000	English, Maori	Protestant, Roman Catholic	New Zealand dollar	www.govt.nz	152–153
Papua New Guinea Port Moresby		462 840 178 704	5 887 000	English, Tok Pisin (creole), local languages	Protestant, Roman Catholic, traditional beliefs	Kina	www.pngonline.gov.pg	144–145
Samoa Apia		2 831 1 093	185 000	Samoan, English	Protestant, Roman Catholic	Tala	www.govt.ws	145
Solomon Islands Honiara		28 370 10 954	478 000	English, creole, local languages	Protestant, Roman Catholic	Solomon Islands dollar	www.commerce.gov.sb	145
Tonga Nuku'alofa		748 289	102 000	Tongan, English	Protestant, Roman Catholic	Pa'anga	www.pmo.gov.to	145
Tuvalu Vaiaku		25 10	10 000	Tuvaluan, English	Protestant	Australian dollar		145
Vanuatu Port Vila		12 190 4 707	211 000	English, Bislama (creole), French	Protestant, Roman Catholic, traditional beliefs	Vatu	www.vanuatugovernment. gov.vu	145

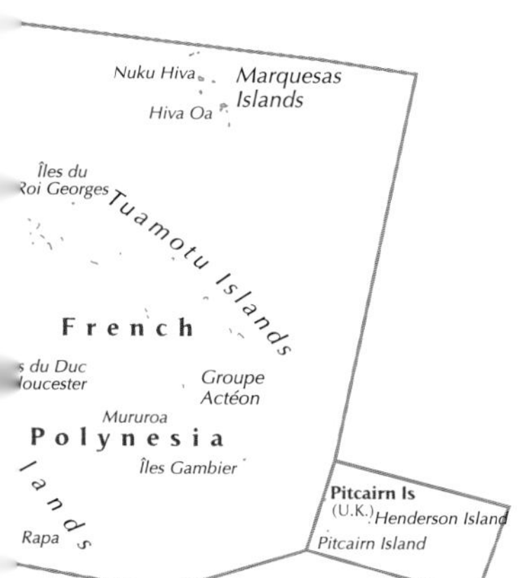

In 1908 this site in southeast New South Wales was chosen as the national capital of Australia, **Canberra**. The city now has a population of over 250 000. Parliament House is located on Capital Hill, to the south of Lake Burley Griffin in the centre of the circular roads.

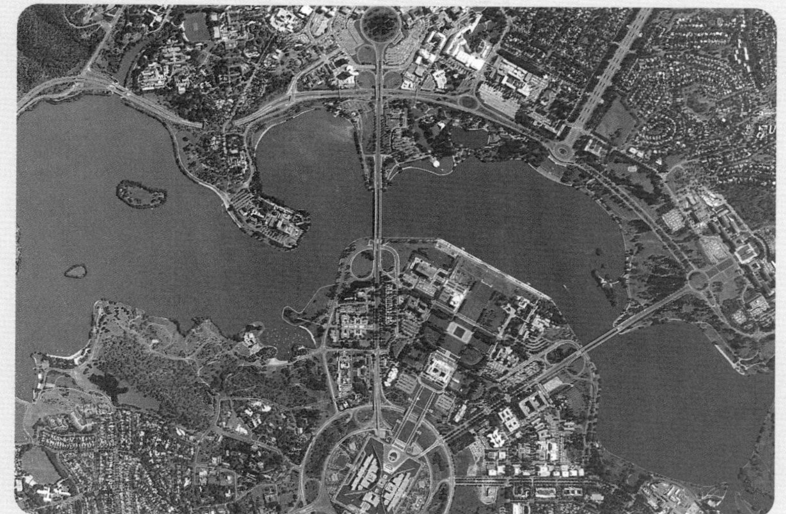

Want to know more?

▶	World landscapes	6–7
▶	Political map of the World	8–9
▶	Exploration of the Pacific	142–143
▶	Map of the Pacific Ocean	220–221
▶	Detailed maps of Oceania	144–153

Internet links

Asia-Pacific Economic Cooperation	www.apecsec.org.sg
Secretariat of the Pacific Community	www.spc.int
Australian Government	www.gov.au
Small Island Developing States Network	www.sidsnet.org
New Zealand Government	www.govt.nz

Facts

Over 90 per cent of Australia's population live in urban areas.

The longest straight railway line in the world crosses the Nullarbor Plain between South Australia and Western Australia running for 478 kilometres (297 miles).

New Caledonia has a population of over 200 000 but has twenty-nine vernacular Melanesian languages, six of which are taught in schools.

The Maori people who inhabited New Zealand before the Europeans, are getting more of their place names officially recognised, such as Aoraki for Mount Cook which means 'Cloud-piercer'.

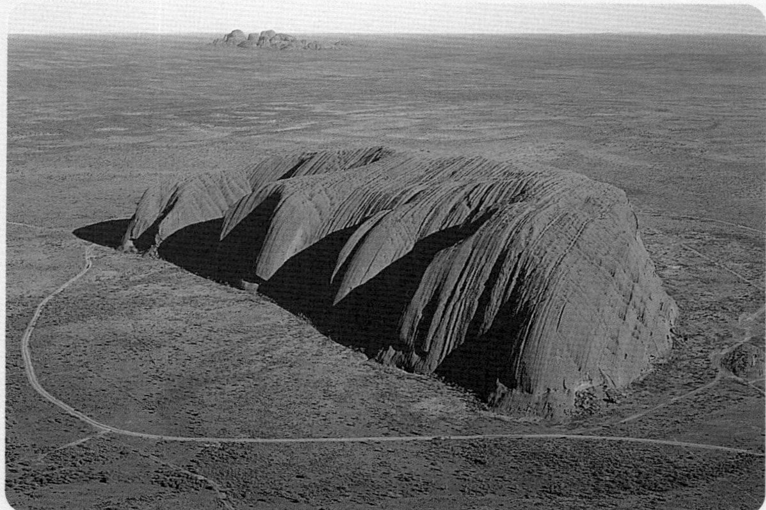

Uluṟu (Ayers Rock), is a large single rock outcrop which rises 350 metres (1 148 feet) above the vast plain of central Australia. The rock is composed of a collection of vertically bedded strata. In the far distance, a similar rock formation, the Olgas, can be seen.

Top 10 countries by area		sq km	sq miles	world rank
1	Australia	7 682 395	2 966 189	6
2	Papua New Guinea	462 840	178 704	54
3	New Zealand	270 534	104 454	75
4	Solomon Islands	28 370	10 954	142
5	Fiji	18 330	7 077	153
6	Vanuatu	12 190	4 707	157
7	Samoa	2 831	1 093	167
8	Tonga	748	289	173
9	Kiribati	717	277	174
10	Micronesia, Fed. States of	701	271	175

Top 10 countries by population		population	world rank
1	Australia	20 155 000	53
2	Papua New Guinea	5 887 000	103
3	New Zealand	4 028 000	123
4	Fiji	848 000	153
5	Solomon Islands	478 000	162
6	Vanuatu	211 000	172
7	Samoa	185 000	173
8	Micronesia, Federated States of	110 000	177
9	Tonga	102 000	179
10	Kiribati	99 000	180

Dependencies capital		territorial status	sq km sq miles	population	languages	religions	currency	official website	map
American Samoa Fagatogo		United States Unincorporated Territory	197 76	65 000	Samoan, English	Protestant, Roman Catholic	US dollar	www.government.as	145
Ashmore and Cartier Islands		Australian External Territory	5 2	uninhabited					150
Baker Island		United States Unincorporated Territory	1 0.4	uninhabited					145
Cook Islands Avarua		Self-governing New Zealand Territory	293 113	18 000	English, Maori	Protestant, Roman Catholic	New Zealand dollar	www.cook-islands.gov.ck	221
Coral Sea Islands Territory		Australian External Country	22 8	uninhabited					145
French Polynesia Papeete		French Overseas Territory	3 265 1 261	257 000	French, Tahitian, Polynesian languages	Protestant, Roman Catholic	CFP franc	www.presidence.pf	221
Guam Hagåtña		United States Unincorporated Territory	541 209	170 000	Chamorro, English, Tapalog	Roman Catholic	US dollar	ns.gov.gu	73
Howland Island		United States Unincorporated Territory	2 1	uninhabited					145
Jarvis Island		United States Unincorporated Territory	5 2	uninhabited					221
Johnston Atoll		United States Unincorporated Territory	3 1	uninhabited					221
Kingman Reef		United States Unincorporated Territory	1 0.4	uninhabited					221
Midway Islands		United States Unincorporated Territory	6 2	uninhabited					220
New Caledonia Nouméa		French Overseas Country	19 058 7 358	237 000	French, local languages	Roman Catholic, Protestant, Sunni Muslim	CFP franc	www.gouv.nc	145
Niue Alofi		Self-governing New Zealand Overseas Territory	258 100	1 000	English, Polynesian	Christian	New Zealand dollar	www.niuegov.com	145
Norfolk Island Kingston		Australian External Territory	35 14	2 601	English	Protestant, Roman Catholic	Australian dollar	www.norfolk.gov.nf	145
Northern Mariana Islands Capitol Hill		United States Commonwealth	477 184	81 000	English, Chamorro, local languages	Roman Catholic	US dollar	www.gov.mp	73
Palmyra Atoll		United States Unincorporated Territory	12 5	uninhabited					221
Pitcairn Islands Adamstown		United Kingdom Overseas Territory	45 17	47	English	Protestant	New Zealand dollar	www.government.pn	221
Tokelau		New Zealand Overseas Territory	10 4	1 000	English, Tokelauan	Christian	New Zealand dollar	www.tokelau.org.nz	145
Wake Island		United States Unincorporated Territory	7 3	uninhabited					220
Wallis and Futuna Islands Matā'utu		French Overseas Territory	274 106	15 000	French, Wallisian, Futunian	Roman Catholic	CFP franc	www.wallis.co.nc/assemblee.ter	145

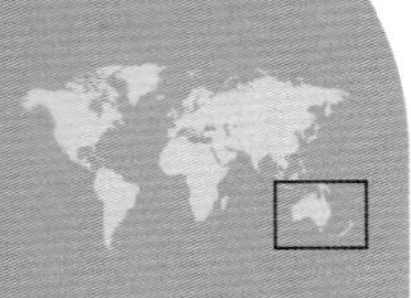
Oceania is a large and diverse region with several environmental issues affecting large proportions of its area. Dryland salinity is an increasing problem in Australia and one which has been around since, and was exacerbated by, European settlement of a naturally salty region. Of equal concern are the various threats to coral reefs and atolls. Groundwater resources on atolls are increasingly limited and living corals are subject to many destructive forces, both natural and man-made, which threaten the beauty and biodiversity of these delicate ecosystems. The region – which includes numerous low-lying island nations – is also particularly vulnerable to any rise in sea level caused by global warming.

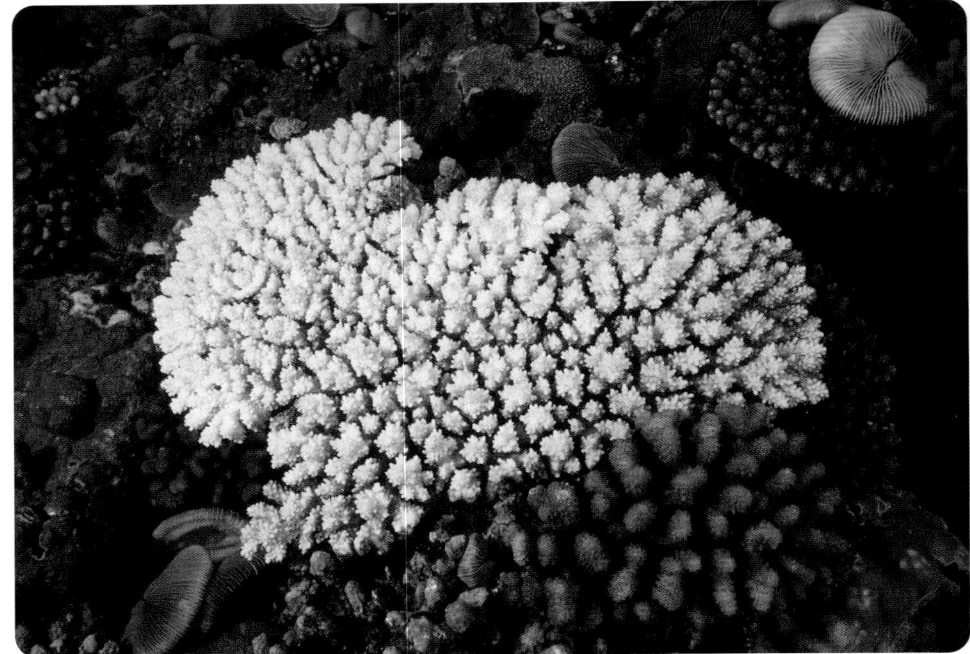

Bleached coral off Moorea, French Polynesia. Bleaching can be caused by an increase in water temperature, or by pollution such as that from leached fertilisers washed into the sea.

Reefs at risk in Oceania

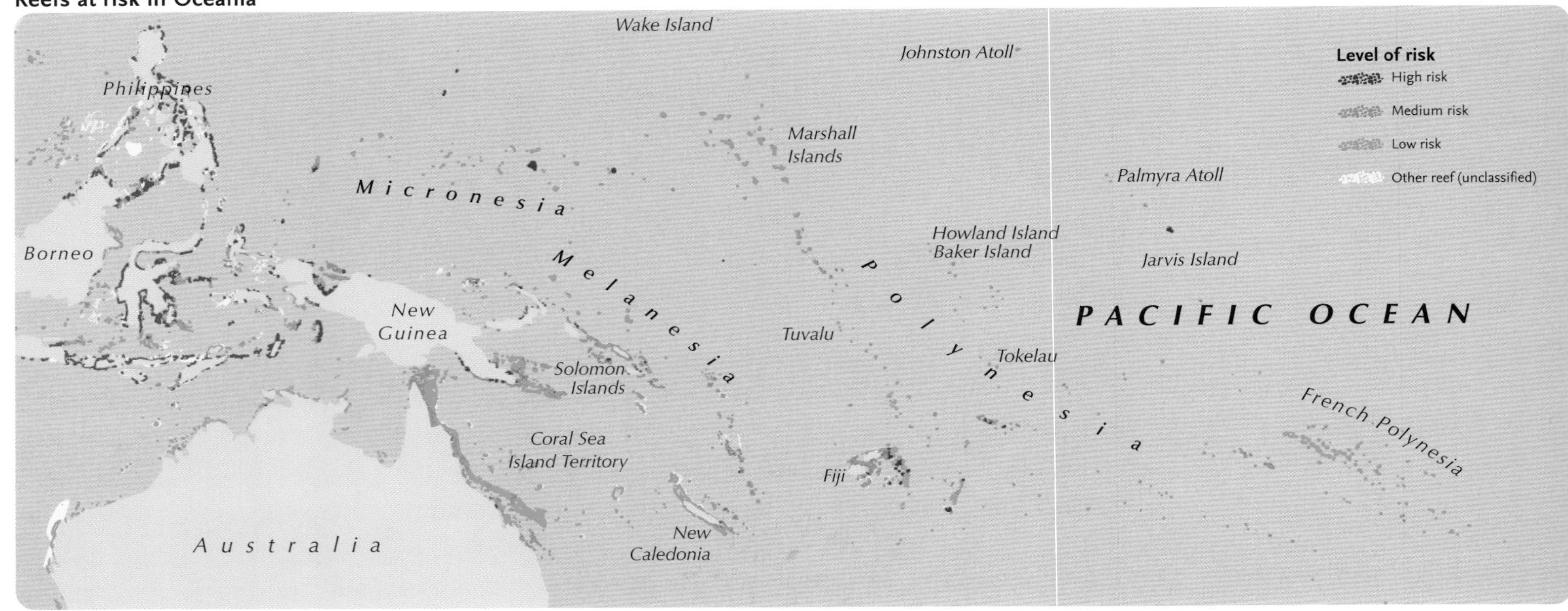

Level of risk

High risk
Medium risk
Low risk
Other reef (unclassified)

Oceania's coral reefs

Coral reefs are one of the world's most diverse marine habitats, supporting one-third of all fish species. Risks to reefs vary, but the main factors in their degradation are pollution (both marine and inland), over-exploitation, destructive fishing, erosion and proximity to coastal development. Global warming, rising sea level and natural disturbances also threaten coral. An increase in sea temperature causes coral to expel the algae *zoozanthella*, causing bleaching. Corals may adjust by swapping algae for more heat-tolerant species, but they are reaching their tolerance limits. In Fiji, corals suffered particularly widespread bleaching in 2000 and 2002. They are now recovering and there is much support for protecting areas around Fiji's reefs to ensure that any bleaching events are not made worse by overfishing, tourist damage and pollution.

Reefs at risk by region

region	percentage of reefs at each level of risk			Protected marine areas	
	low risk	medium risk	high risk	number	area (sq km/sq miles)
Pacific Ocean	59	31	10	92	372 809/143 904
Fiji	33	48	19	1	1/0.4
French Polynesia	82	18	0	1	124/48
Marshall islands	97	3	0	2	163/63
New Caledonia	83	13	4	5	530/205
Papua New Guinea	50	38	12	8	2 149/830
Solomon Islands	50	42	8	...	...

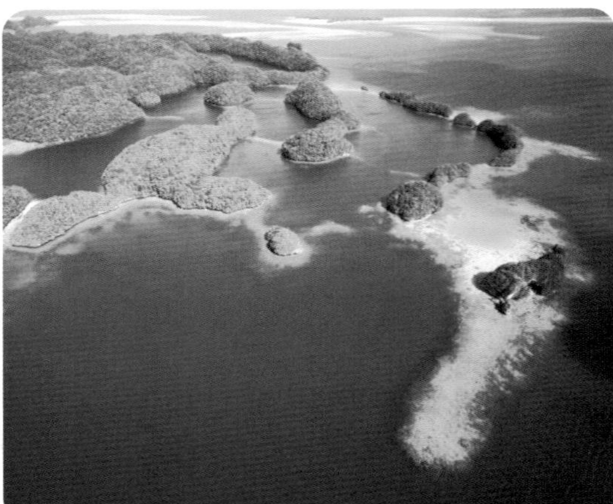

Fringing reefs are the most common type of coral reef. They form along the continental shelf or round tropical islands in shallow water. There is very little or no lagoon between the reef and the shore. This example is from Palau.

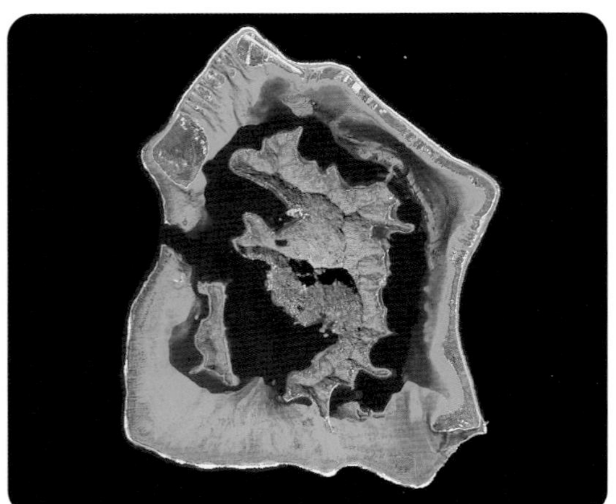

Barrier reefs grow parallel to shorelines and are usually separated from the land by a deep lagoon. They are so called because they form a barrier between the lagoon and the open sea, offering protection to the coastline. This image shows this effect on Bora-Bora in French Polynesia

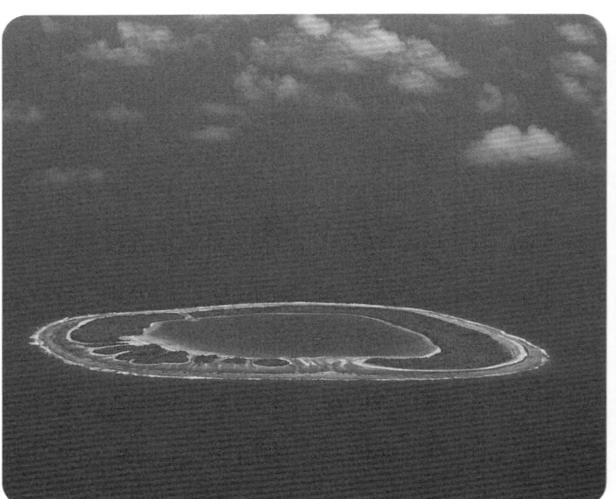

Coral atolls such as Mataiva in the Tuamotu Islands, French Polynesia, are rings of coral reef growing on top of old sunken volcanoes. They begin as fringing reefs surrounding a volcanic island, then, as the volcano sinks, the reef continues to grow, and eventually only the reef remains. There are over 300 atolls in the South Pacific.

Threat of rising sea level

St Petersburg
Hamburg
Venice
Tianjin
Tōkyō
Shanghai
Hong Kong
New York
Washington
Charlestown
Miami
West Indies
Dakar
Maldives
Palau
Marshall
Islands
Micronesia
Nauru
Kiribati
Seychelles
Tuvalu
American
Samoa
French
Comoros
Jakarta
Samoa
Samoa
Polynesia
Niue
Tonga
Cook Islands
Recife
Luanda
Beira
Durban
Adelaide
Montevideo
Buenos Aires
Wellington

**Areas at risk
of submersion**

- • Major cities
- ∾ Coastal areas at greatest risk
- •∾ Islands and archipelagos
- ∾ Low lying islands

Want to know more?

► Climate change	12–13
► Global coral reef risk	14–15
► Oceania statistics	142–143
► Map of the Pacific Ocean	220–221
► Detailed reference maps of Oceania	144–153

Internet links

The Global Coral Reef Monitoring Network	www.gcrmn.org
Wildlife Conservation Society: South Pacific	wcs.org/sw-around_the_globe/ Asia/southpacific
Dept of Agriculture, Forestry and Fisheries, Australia	www.affa.gov.au
Department of the Environment, Australia	www.deh.gov.au

Facts

By the end of 2000, 27 per cent of the world's coral reefs had been lost. Another 14 per cent are at risk of vanishing in the next twenty years.

If sea conditions are not ideal, coral becomes bleached, losing colour by expelling the pigmented algae. If conditions do not improve quickly the coral dies.

In some Pacific atoll communities groundwater has become polluted and there have been outbreaks of disease.

Dryland salinity destroys habitats around rivers and streams while the salt also destroys bitumen and concrete, affecting roads and railways.

Rising sea level

Although projections vary according to different models of climate change, it is predicted that at current rates of global warming, sea level will rise by approximately 40 centimetres (15 inches) by the 2080s. Such a rise places many regions at risk. When combined with predictions of population growth it is estimated that as many as 94 million people around the world will be at risk of flooding each year. Oceania's islands would be particularly threatened, and while many of the lowest-lying islands are unpopulated, they are valuable habitats which need protection.

Lowest Pacific islands	maximum height above sea level	land area sq km	sq miles	population
Kingman Reef	1m (3 ft)	1	0.4	0
Palmyra Atoll	2m (7 ft)	12	5	0
Ashmore and Cartier Islands	3m (10 ft)	5	2	0
Howland Island	3m (10 ft)	2	1	0
Johnston Atoll	5m (16 ft)	3	1	0
Tokelau	5m (16 ft)	10	4	1 000
Tuvalu	5m (16 ft)	25	10	10 000
Coral Sea Islands Territory	6m (20 ft)	22	8	0
Wake Island	6m (20 ft)	7	3	0
Jarvis Island	7m (23 ft)	5	2	0

Dryland salinity

Australia is a dry, and naturally salty continent. Its primary salinity comes from weathering rocks and the deposition of sea salt by rain and wind. Secondary salinity is the intensification of this natural salinity caused by land use changes since European settlement. The crops and plants which were introduced have shallower roots and use less water than the native vegetation they replaced. This has allowed more water to seep past the root zone and into the groundwater, causing the water table to rise, bringing salt to the surface. The salt then contaminates the land and the surface water, killing crops and pastureland. It also damages buildings, roads, bridges and pipelines. Excess salt reduces the diversity of native plants and animals, and impairs water quality for irrigation and human consumption – with potentially serious consequences for both urban and rural communities.

Australia's salinity hazard

Areas at risk
- Cropland or pasture
- Cropland

Irrigated areas
- >100 000ha
- 50 000–100 000ha
- 20 000–50 000ha
- 10 000–20 000ha

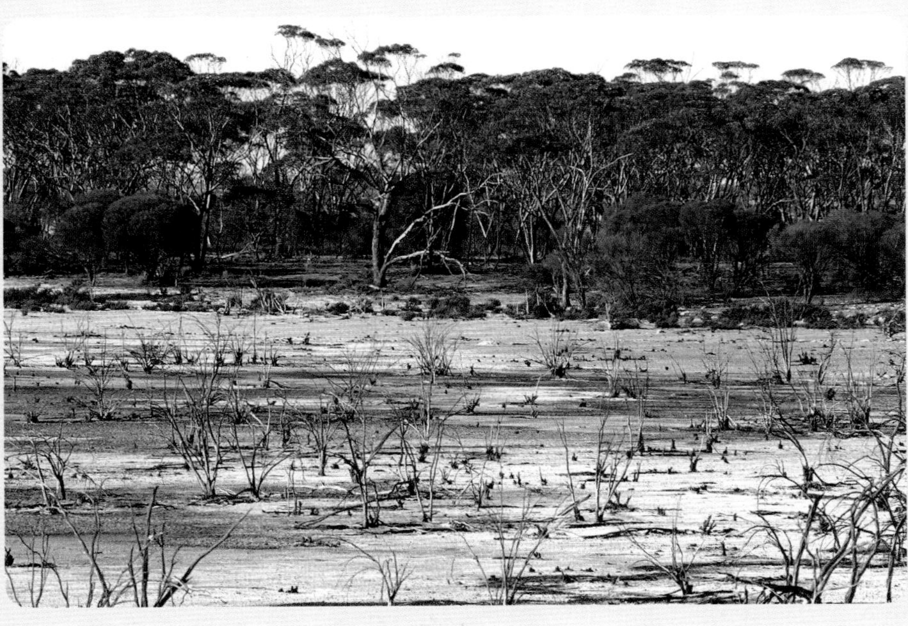

An area near **Kellerberrin**, Western Australia which is badly affected by salinity. Typical effects of salinity are soil erosion, loss of water quality in streams and rivers and destruction of vegetation.

Dryland salinity risk assessment

Plant species at risk	1500
Plant species in danger of extinction	450
2000 Area at risk or affected	57 000 sq km (22 000 sq m)
Roads at risk	20 000 km (12 427 miles)
Railways at risk	1 600 km (994 miles)
Vegetation ecosystems at risk	6 300 sq km (2 432 sq m)
2050 predictions Area at risk	170 000 sq km (65 637 sq m)
Roads at risk	52 000 km (32 311 miles)
Railways at risk	3 600 km (2237 miles)
Vegetation ecosystems at risk	20 000 sq km (7 722 sq m)

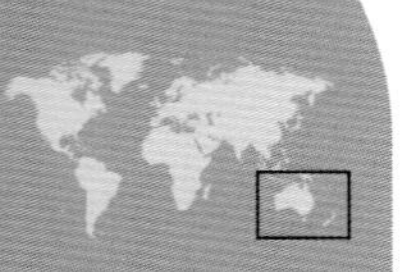

Oceania History and Statistics

50000–40000 BC First human migration to Australia from southeast Asia

4000 BC First migration to the Pacific islands from the west

800–950 Maori settlers populate New Zealand for the first time

1300–1000 BC Settlement of Fiji, Tonga and Samoa by Polynesians

400 Settlement of the Hawaiian islands

1768–1769 James Cook (British) begins exploration of the Pacific: first European landings in New Zealand

1520–1521 Ferdinand Magellan (Portuguese) crosses the Pacific

2000 BC Settlement of Melanesia and New Guinea from Asia

1500–1000 BC First settlement of the Mariana Islands and Micronesia

800 Polynesian settlers arrive in the Cook Islands

700–800 Easter Island first populated

300 Settlement of eastern Polynesia

1400–1600 Easter Island statues (moai)

300 BC Tuvalu (Ellice Islands) first settled by Polynesians

1642–1645 Abel Tasman (Dutch) discovers parts of Australia, New Zealand, Fiji, Tonga etc.

1893 New Zealand becomes the first country to give women the vote

1880 First frozen Australian beef sent to the UK

1874 Micronesia becomes a Spanish colony

1853 New Caledonia annexed by France

1845–1847 First Maori revolts against loss of lands

1788 First Fleet founds British colony in Australia (Sydney)

1789 Mutiny on *HMS Bounty*: European colonization of Pitcairn Island

1770 Cook claims New South Wales for Britain

1840 Treaty of Waitangi with the Maoris: Britain annexes New Zealand

1850 Australian colonies granted own government

1856 New Zealand granted own government

1874 Fiji becomes a British colony

1875–1876 One-third of Fijian population killed in measles epidemic

1888 Cook Islands become a British protectorate

1899 Micronesia sold by Spain to Germany

	Population							Economy					
	total population	population change (%)	urban population (%)	total fertility	population by age 0-14 (%)	population by age 60+ (%)	2050 projected population	total Gross National Income (GNI) (US$M)	Gross National Income (GNI) per capita (US$)	debt service ratio (% GNI)	total debt service (US$)	aid receipts (% GNI)	military spending (% GDP)
World	**6 464 750 000**	**1.2**	**48.3**	**2.7**	**28.2**	**10.4**	**9 075 903 000**	**34 491 458**	**5 500**	...	...	...	**2.4**
Australia	20 155 000	1.1	92.0	1.8	19.6	17.3	27 940 000	430 533	21 650	...	...	...	1.7
Fiji	848 000	0.9	51.7	2.9	31.7	6.4	934 000	1 969	2 360	1.6	27 800 000	1.9	2.2
Kiribati	99 000	2.1	47.3	...	...	...	177 000	84	880	...	...	22.9	...
Marshall Islands	62 000	3.5	66.3	...	...	...	150 000	143	2 710	...	...	48.4	...
Micronesia, Federated States of	110 000	0.6	29.3	4.4	39.0	4.9	99 000	261	2 090	...	...	45.6	...
Nauru	14 000	2.2	100.0	...	...	...	18 000	...	...	...	...	...	...
New Zealand	4 028 000	1.1	85.9	2.0	21.3	16.7	4 790 000	63 608	15 870	...	...	...	1.1
Papua New Guinea	5 887 000	2.1	13.2	4.1	40.3	3.9	10 619 000	2 823	510	10.4	277 500 000	7.6	0.8
Samoa	185 000	0.8	22.3	4.4	40.7	6.5	157 000	284	1 600	3.0	7 800 000	14.3	...
Solomon Islands	478 000	2.6	16.5	4.3	40.6	4.2	921 000	273	600	2.4	5 700 000	10.9	...
Tonga	102 000	0.4	33.4	3.5	35.9	8.8	75 000	152	1 490	2.0	2 700 000	16.5	...
Tuvalu	10 000	0.5	55.2	...	...	...	12 000	...	...	...	...	...	...
Vanuatu	211 000	2.0	22.8	4.2	39.9	5.1	375 000	248	1 180	1.0	2 200 000	11.9	...

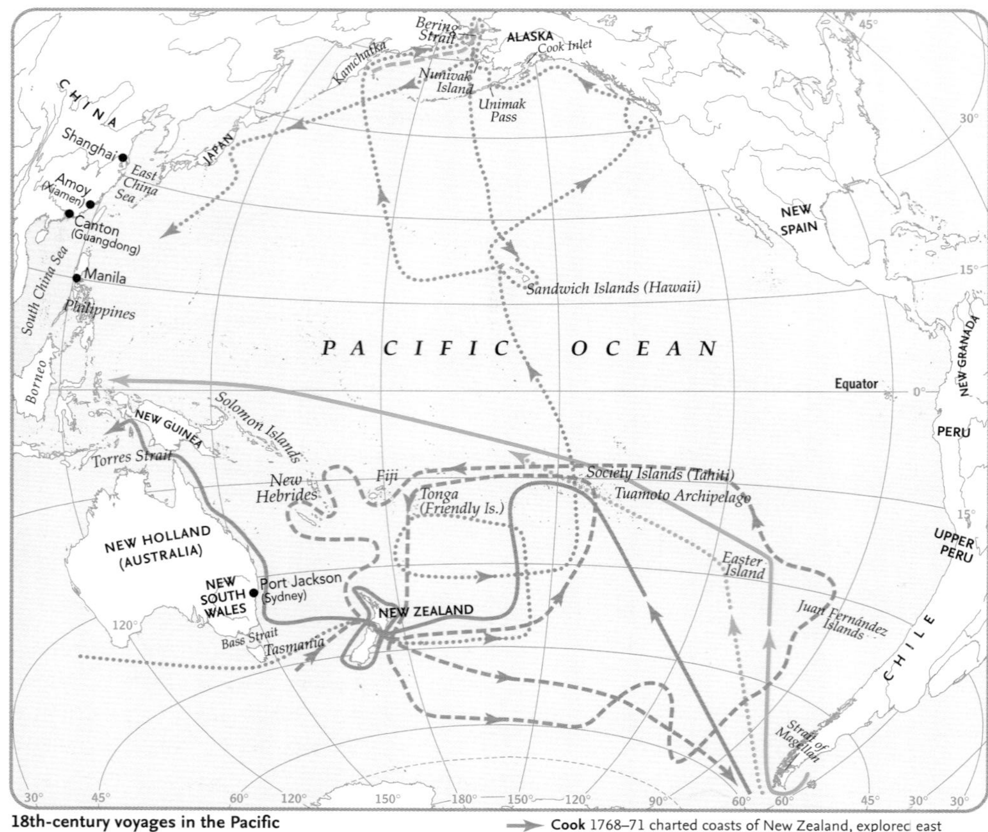

18th-century voyages in the Pacific

➤ **Roggeveen** 1722 discovered Easter Island and some of the Samoan group; circumnavigated globe.

➤ **Bering** 1728 sailed from Kamchatka, discovered strait seperating northeast Asia and northwest America.

⋯➤ **Wallis** 1766–8 discovered Society Islands (Tahiti), encouraged hope of habitable southern continent; circumnavigated globe.

➤ **Cook** 1768–71 charted coasts of New Zealand, explored east coast of Australia, confirmed existence of Torres Strait; circumnavigated globe.

➤ **Cook** 1772–5 made circuit of southern oceans in high latitude, charted New Hebrides, discovered many islands, ended hope of habitable southern continent; circumnavigated globe.

⋯➤ **Cook and Clerke** 1776–80 discovered Sandwich Islands (Hawaii), explored northwest coast of North America from Vancouver Island to Unimak Pass, sailed through Bering Strait to edge of pack ice, ended hope of navigable passage through the Arctic to the Atlantic.

European exploration in the Pacific 1720–1780

Most eighteenth-century voyages of discovery in the Pacific were searches for a habitable southern continent or for a usable northern strait between the Pacific and Atlantic oceans. Both proved imaginary. The expeditions instead confirmed the immensity of the Pacific and revealed the islands of New Zealand, a habitable eastern Australia, numerous island groups and a valuable whale fishery.

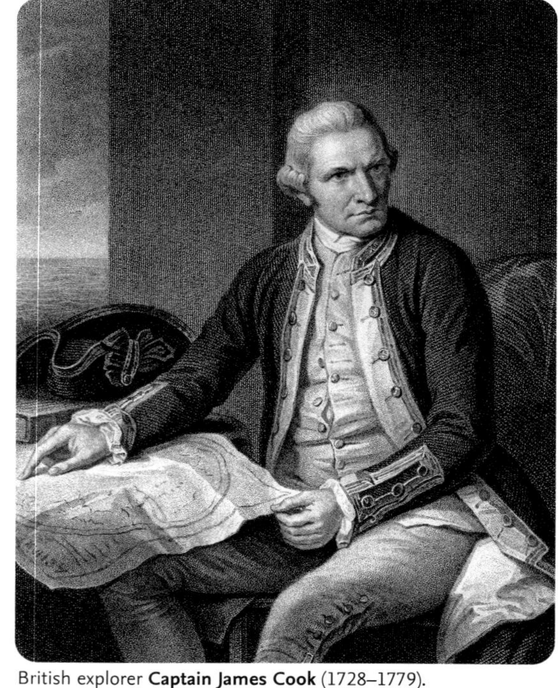

British explorer **Captain James Cook** (1728–1779).

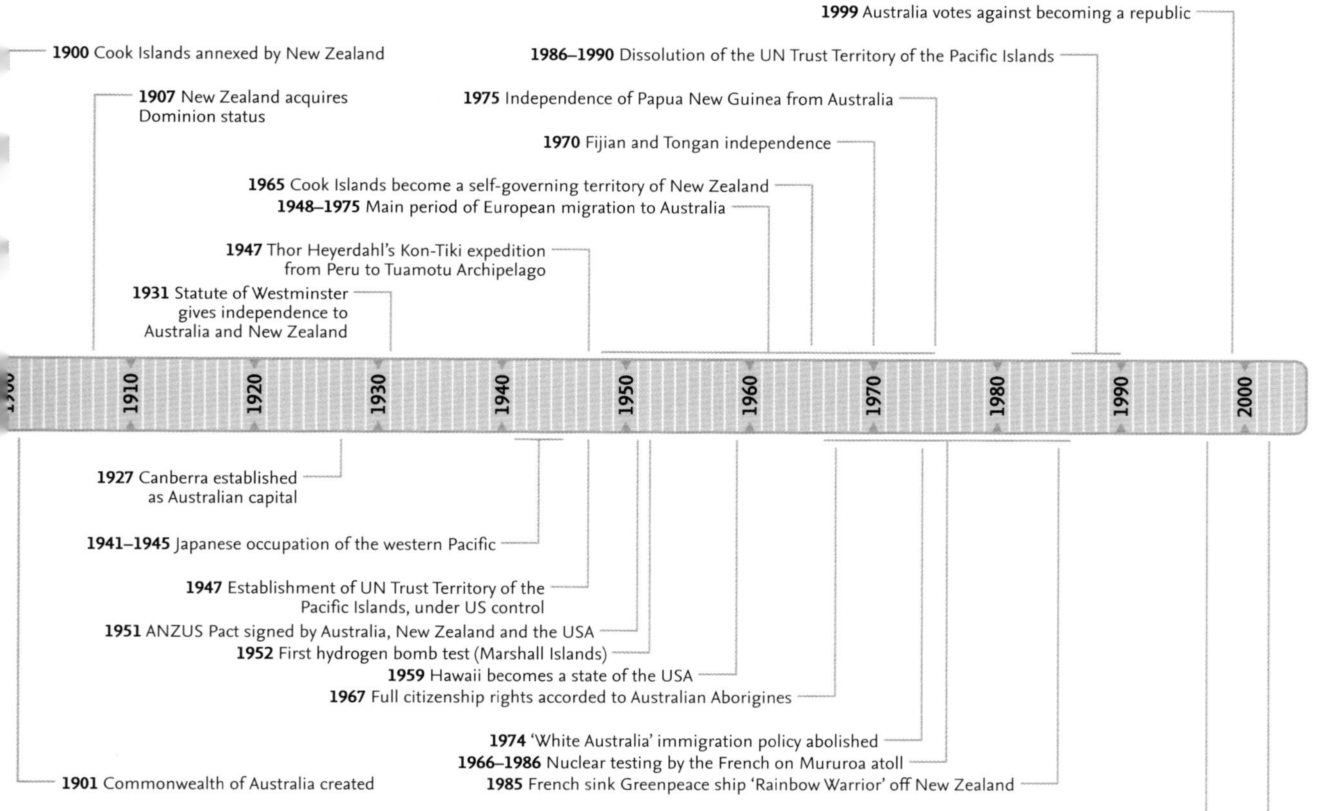

1999 Australia votes against becoming a republic

1900 Cook Islands annexed by New Zealand
1986–1990 Dissolution of the UN Trust Territory of the Pacific Islands

1907 New Zealand acquires Dominion status
1975 Independence of Papua New Guinea from Australia

1970 Fijian and Tongan independence

1965 Cook Islands become a self-governing territory of New Zealand
1948–1975 Main period of European migration to Australia

1947 Thor Heyerdahl's Kon-Tiki expedition from Peru to Tuamotu Archipelago

1931 Statute of Westminster gives independence to Australia and New Zealand

1910 1920 1930 1940 1950 1960 1970 1980 1990 2000

1927 Canberra established as Australian capital

1941–1945 Japanese occupation of the western Pacific

1947 Establishment of UN Trust Territory of the Pacific Islands, under US control
1951 ANZUS Pact signed by Australia, New Zealand and the USA
1952 First hydrogen bomb test (Marshall Islands)
1959 Hawaii becomes a state of the USA
1967 Full citizenship rights accorded to Australian Aborigines

1974 'White Australia' immigration policy abolished
1966–1986 Nuclear testing by the French on Mururoa atoll
1985 French sink Greenpeace ship 'Rainbow Warrior' off New Zealand
1901 Commonwealth of Australia created

1997 Western Samoa renamed Samoa
2002 Terrorist bombing in Bali (victims mainly Australian tourists)

Want to know more?

▶ World political map	8–9
▶ Guide to Oceania's countries	138–139
▶ Map of coral reefs at risk	140–141
▶ Pacific Ocean statistics	208–209
▶ Map of the Pacific Ocean	220–221

Internet links

Island countries	islands.unep.ch
The Pacific Community	www.spc.int
Maori culture	www.maori.org.nz
World Heritage Sites in Oceania	whc.unesco.org

Facts

Canberra became Australia's capital as a compromise, after a long dispute between Sydney and Melbourne.

Polynesia consists of over 1 000 islands.

Auckland, New Zealand, has the largest Polynesian population of any city in Oceania.

The Federated States of Micronesia consist of 607 islands, only 65 of which are inhabited.

Social indicators						Environment				Communications					See page 335 for explanatory table and sources
child mortality rate	life expectancy male	life expectancy female	literacy rate (%)	access to safe water (%)	doctors per 100 000 people	forest area (%)	annual change in forest area (%)	protected land area (%)	CO₂ emissions (metric tons per capita)	main telephone lines per 100 people	cellular mobile subscribers per 100 people	internet users per 10 000 people	international dialling code	time zone	
80	63.3	67.6	87.3	83	...	29.6	-0.2	11.4	3.8	18.8	21.9	1 125	...	...	World
6	76.4	82.0	...	100	247	20.1	-0.2	9.7	18.0	54.2	72.0	5 667	61	+8 to +11	Australia
20	68.1	71.5	99.2	93	34	44.6	-0.2	15.9	0.9	12.4	13.3	666	679	+12	Fiji
66	...	...	...	64	...	38.4	...	...	0.3	5.1	0.6	230	686	+12 to +14	Kiribati
61	...	...	...	85	...	...	...	...	...	8.3	1.1	259	692	+12	Marshall Islands
23	68.0	69.1	...	94	...	21.7	-4.5	6.7	...	8.7	1.5	510	691	+10 to +11	Micronesia, Federated States of
30	...	...	...	82	...	...	...	...	...	16.0	13.0	260	674	+12	Nauru
6	75.8	80.7	...	97	219	29.7	0.5	24.3	8.3	44.8	64.8	5 263	64	+13	New Zealand
93	56.8	58.7	76.9	39	6	67.6	-0.4	1.6	0.5	1.1	0.3	137	675	+10	Papua New Guinea
24	66.9	73.4	99.8	88	34	37.2	-2.1	...	0.8	6.5	1.5	222	685	-11	Samoa
22	67.9	70.7	...	70	13	88.8	-0.2	0.1	0.4	1.5	0.2	52	677	+11	Solomon Islands
19	68.0	69.1	...	100	35	5.5	...	23.7	1.2	11.3	3.4	292	676	+13	Tonga
51	...	...	...	93	...	...	...	...	...	6.5	...	1 250	688	+12	Tuvalu
38	67.5	70.5	...	60	12	36.7	0.1	1.4	0.4	3.2	3.8	361	678	+11	Vanuatu

Spread of railways 1870–2004

Lines opened since:
- 1870
- 1881
- 1895
- 1911
- 1925
- 1941
- 2004

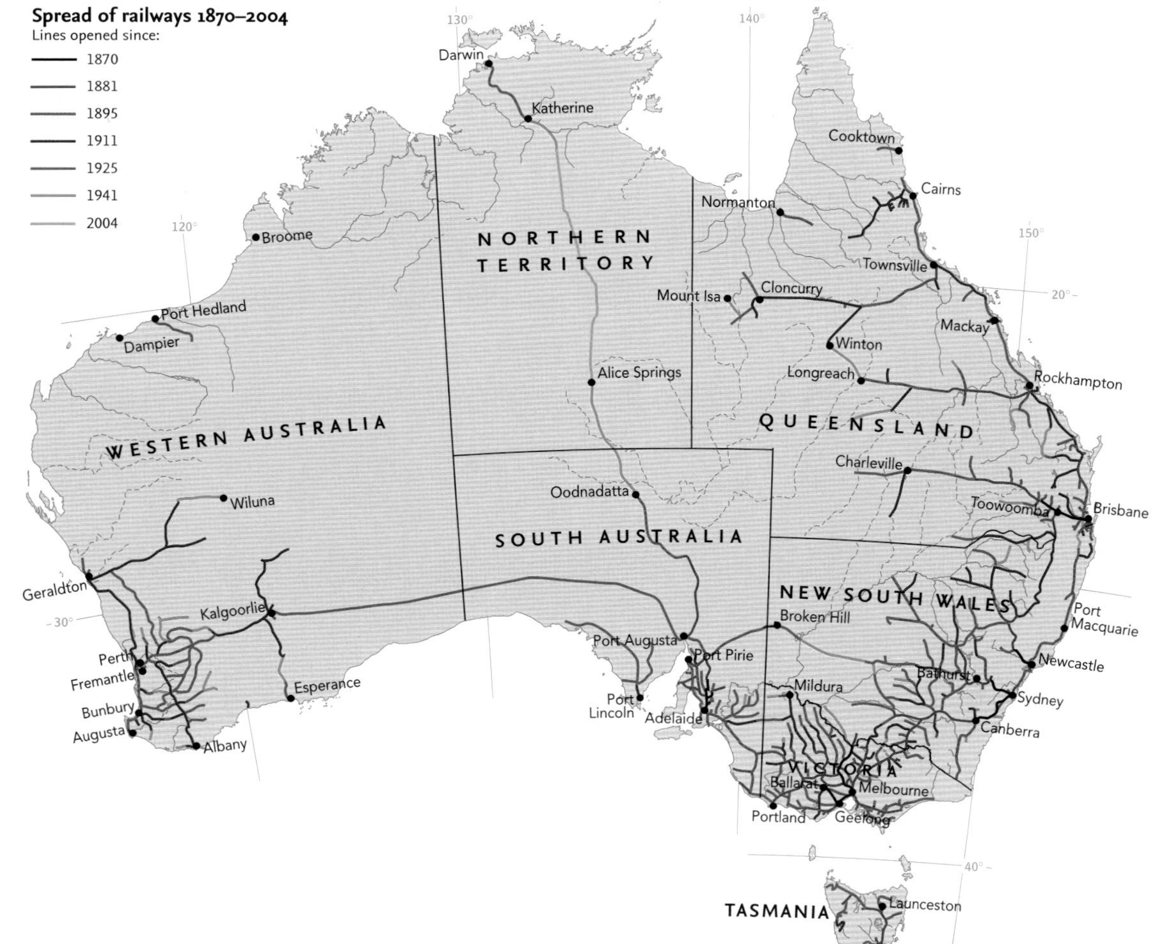

Darwin
Katherine
Cooktown
Normanton
Cairns
NORTHERN TERRITORY
Broome
Townsville
Mount Isa
Cloncurry
Port Hedland
Dampier
Winton
Mackay
Alice Springs
Longreach
Rockhampton
WESTERN AUSTRALIA
QUEENSLAND
Wiluna
Charleville
Oodnadatta
Toowoomba
Brisbane
SOUTH AUSTRALIA
NEW SOUTH WALES
Geraldton
Port Macquarie
Kalgoorlie
Broken Hill
Port Augusta
Newcastle
Perth
Port Pirie
Bathurst
Fremantle
Esperance
Sydney
Port Lincoln
Mildura
Canberra
Bunbury
Augusta
Adelaide
Albany
VICTORIA
Ballarat
Melbourne
Portland
Geelong
TASMANIA
Launceston
Hobart

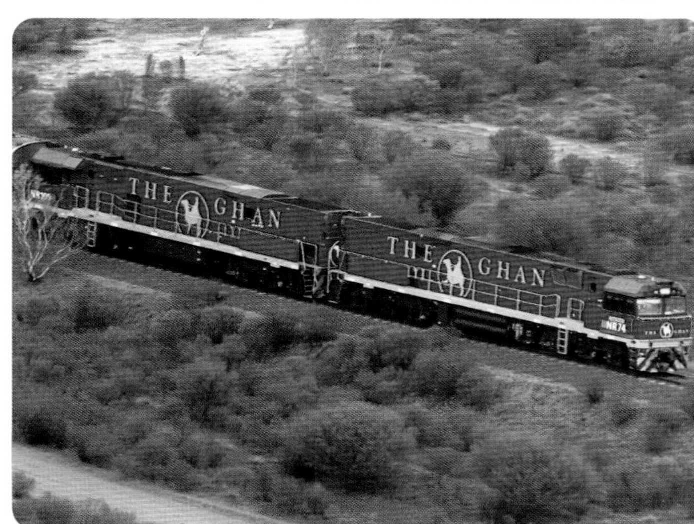

The Ghan train runs on the newly completed route between Adelaide and Darwin. It is named after Afghan camel drivers who used the same route over 150 years ago.

Railways in Australia

Australia's railways grew as a series of separate colonial systems, with incompatible gauges, each connecting a coastal metropolis to its vast hinterland. Only Queensland differed with its series of mini-systems. Standard gauge came late, connecting Sydney to Brisbane in 1930, to Melbourne in 1962 and to Perth in 1969. The most recent development was the completion of the north-south connection between Adelaide and Darwin – a journey of 2 897 kilometres (1 800 miles) – with the opening of the section north of Alice Springs in January 2004.

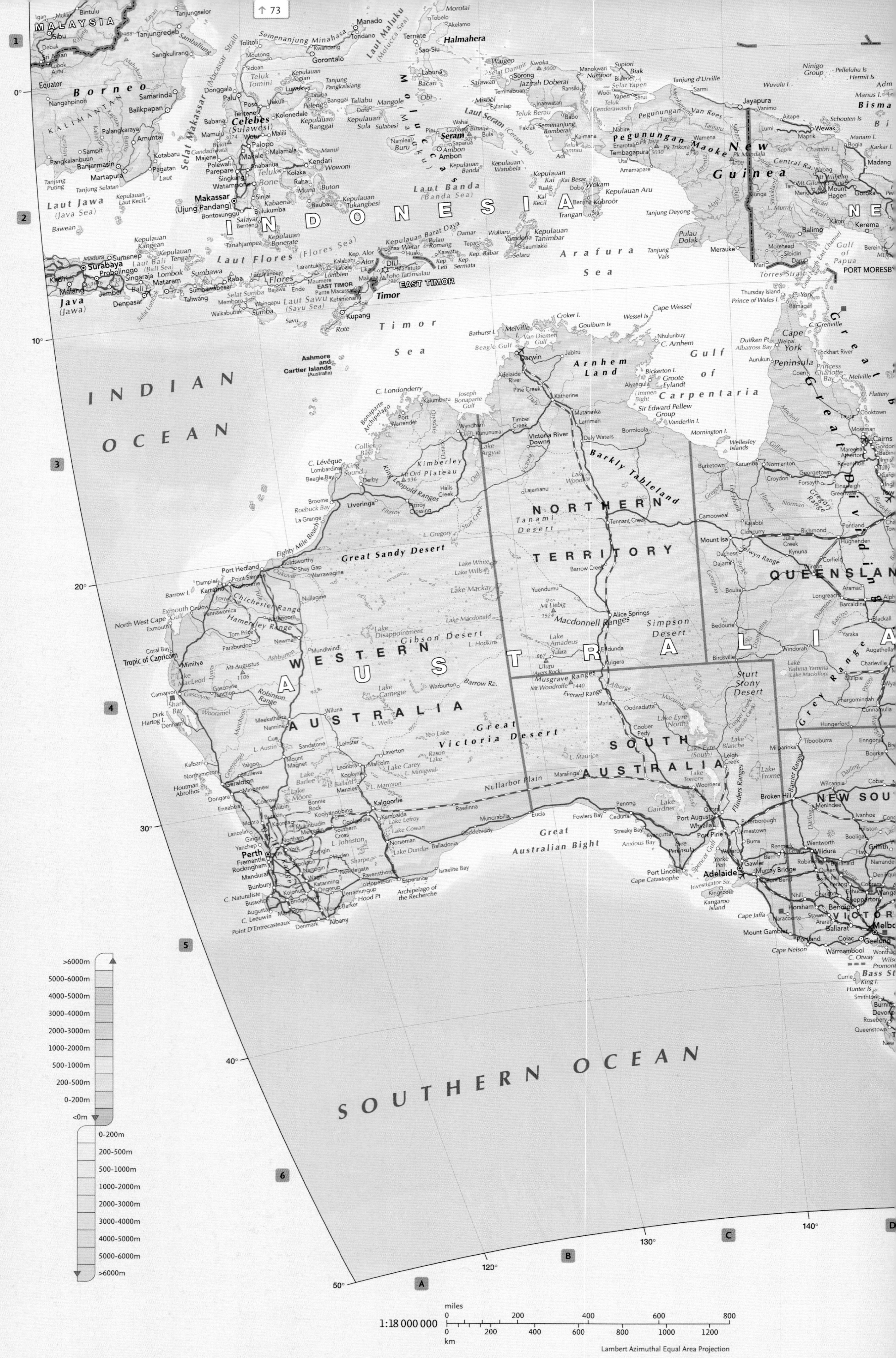

>6000m
5000-6000m
4000-5000m
3000-4000m
2000-3000m
1000-2000m
500-1000m
200-500m
0-200m
<0m

0-200m
200-500m
500-1000m
1000-2000m
2000-3000m
3000-4000m
4000-5000m
5000-6000m
>6000m

1:18 000 000

miles
0   200   400   600   800

0   200   400   600   800   1000   1200
km

Lambert Azimuthal Equal Area Projection

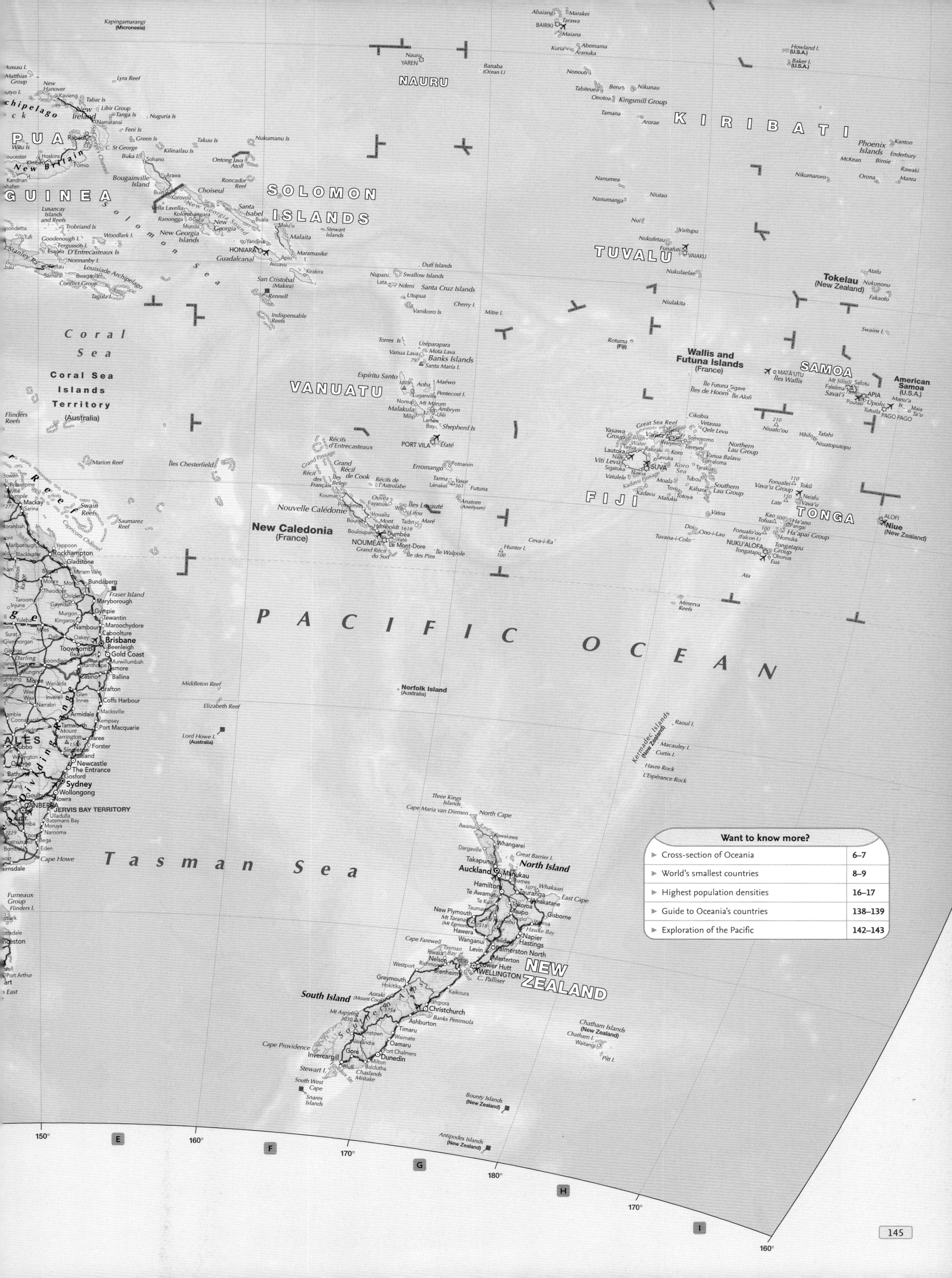

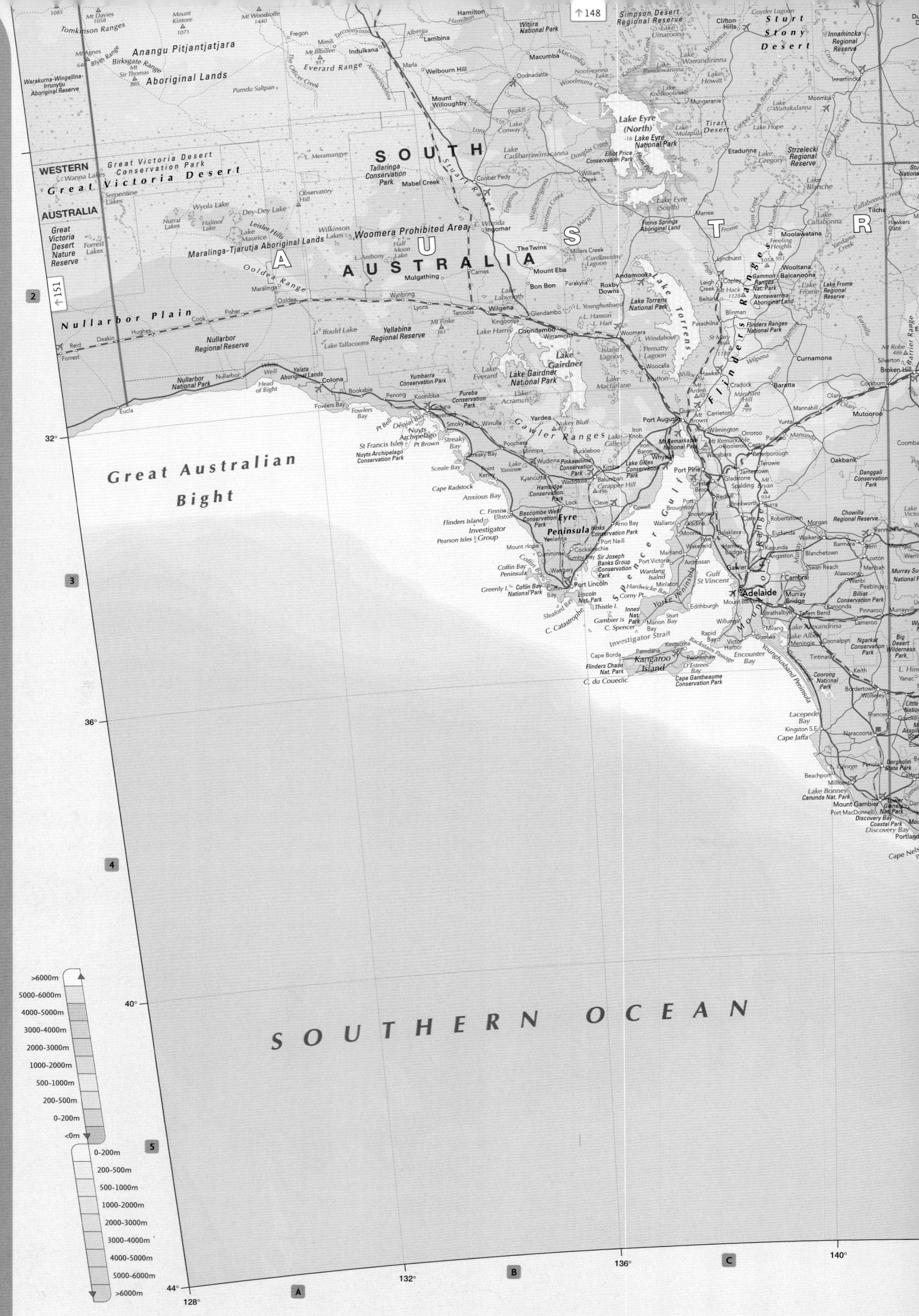

↑148
↑151
SOUTH AUSTRALIA
WESTERN AUSTRALIA
Great Victoria Desert
Great Victoria Desert Conservation Park
Great Victoria Desert Nature Reserve
Anangu Pitjantjatjara Aboriginal Lands
Maralinga-Tjarutja Aboriginal Lands
Woomera Prohibited Area
Nullarbor Plain
Nullarbor Regional Reserve
Nullarbor National Park
Yellabina Regional Reserve
Tallaringa Conservation Park
Simpson Desert Regional Reserve
Witjira National Park
Sturt Stony Desert
Innamincka Regional Reserve
Strzelecki Regional Reserve
Lake Eyre (North)
Lake Eyre (South)
Lake Eyre National Park
Lake Torrens
Lake Torrens National Park
Lake Gairdner
Lake Gairdner National Park
Lake Frome
Lake Frome Regional Reserve
Lake Callabonna
Lake Blanche
Flinders Ranges
Flinders Ranges National Park
Gawler Ranges
Stuart Range
Everard Range
Tomkinson Ranges
Ooldea Range
Eyre Peninsula
Yorke Peninsula
Spencer Gulf
Gulf St Vincent
Investigator Strait
Kangaroo Island
Encounter Bay
Lake Alexandrina
Great Australian Bight
SOUTHERN OCEAN
Adelaide
Port Augusta
Port Pirie
Port Lincoln
Whyalla
Ceduna
Coober Pedy
Roxby Downs
Andamooka
Woomera
Oodnadatta
Marla
Leigh Creek
Tarcoola
Maralinga
Ooldea
Eucla
Cook
Murray Bridge
Mount Gambier
Naracoorte
Kingston S.E.
Cape Jaffa
Port MacDonnell
Portland
Broken Hill
Mannahill
Yunta
Peterborough
Kadina
Wallaroo
Moonta
Victor Harbor
Kingscote
Penneshaw
Streaky Bay
Elliston
Tumby Bay
Cowell
Kimba
Wudinna
Minnipa
Iron Knob
Quorn
Hawker
Innamincka
Moomba
Marree
Lyndhurst
Copley
Coorong National Park
Younghusband Peninsula
Mount Lofty Ranges
Nuyts Archipelago
St Francis Isles
Pearson Isles
Investigator Group
Flinders Island
Cape Borda
Cape Catastrophe
Cape Spencer
32°
36°
40°
44°
128°
132°
136°
140°
A
B
C
2
3
4
5
>6000m
5000-6000m
4000-5000m
3000-4000m
2000-3000m
1000-2000m
500-1000m
200-500m
0-200m
<0m
0-200m
200-500m
500-1000m
1000-2000m
2000-3000m
3000-4000m
4000-5000m
5000-6000m
>6000m

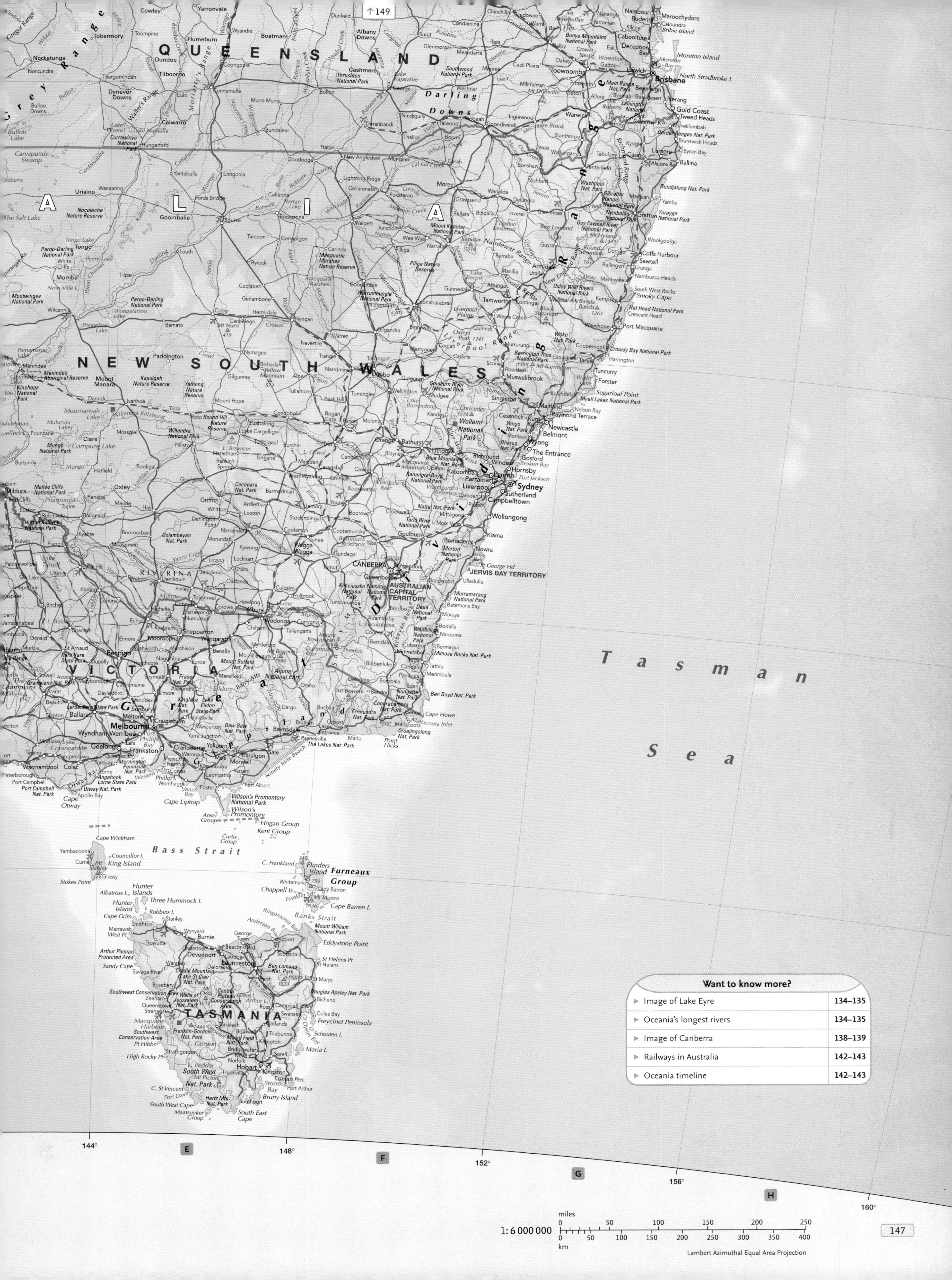

Want to know more?

1 : 6 000 000

Lambert Azimuthal Equal Area Projection

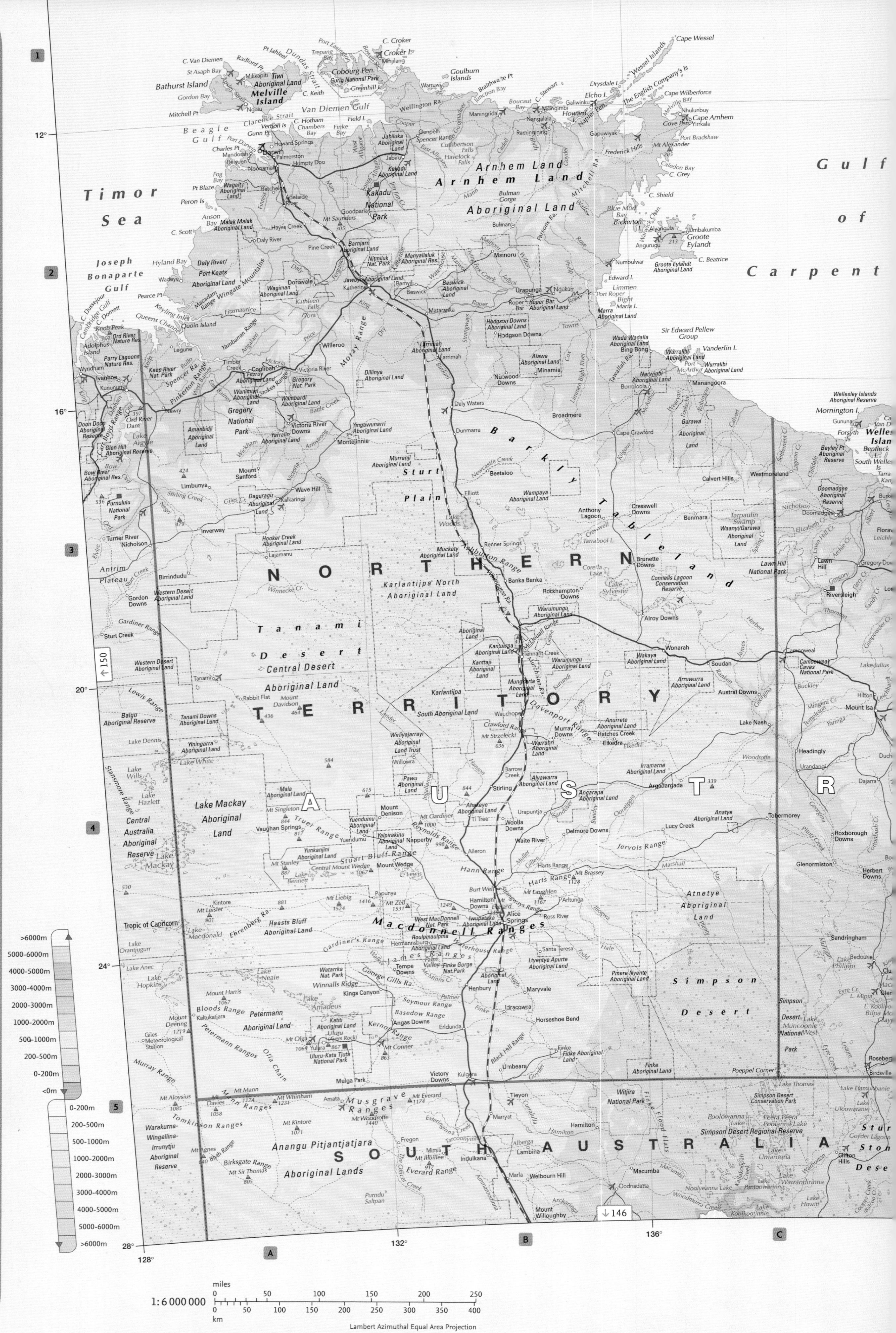

1:6 000 000

miles

km

Lambert Azimuthal Equal Area Projection

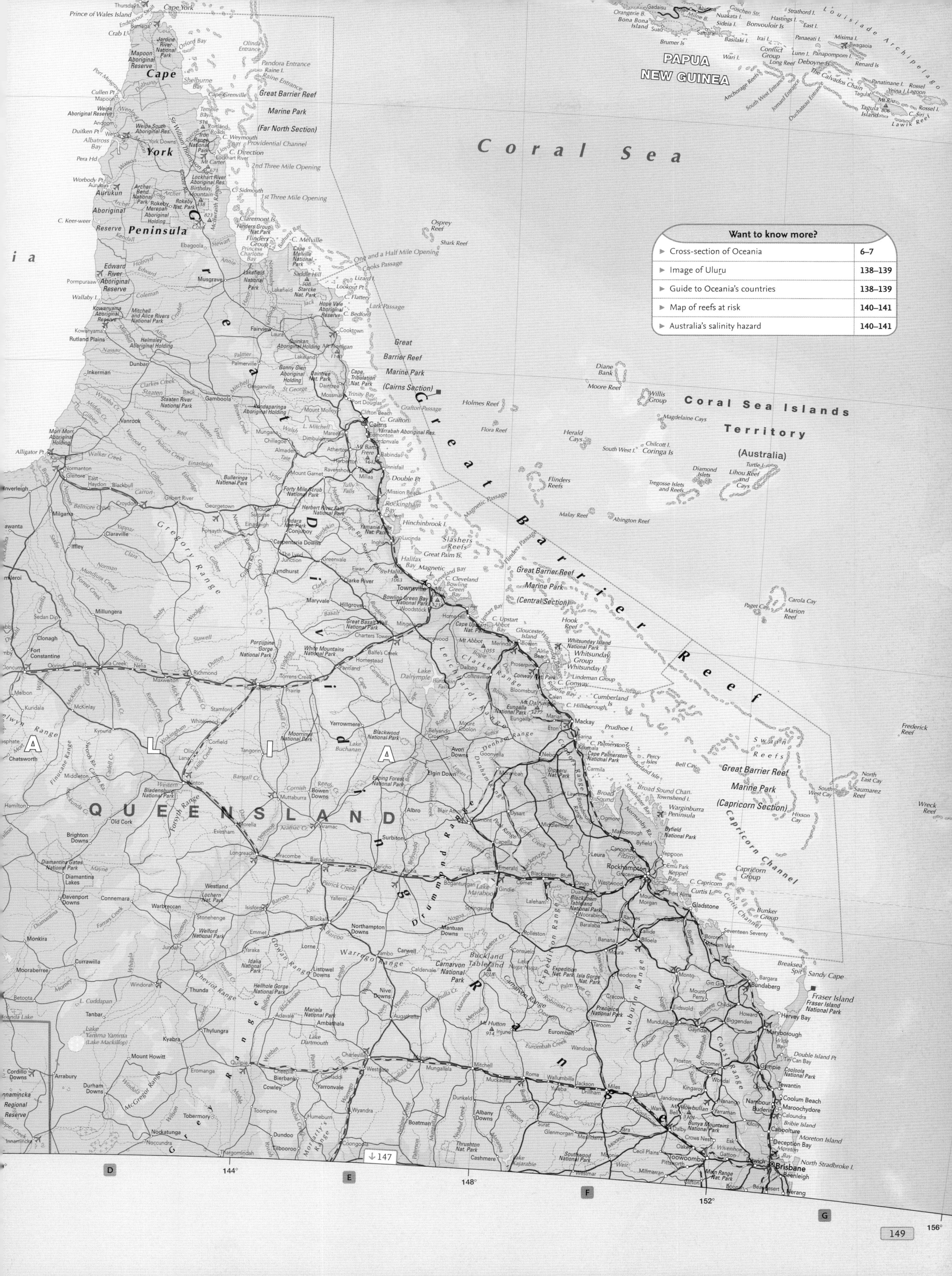

Thursday I.
Prince of Wales I.
Cape York
Endeavour Strait
Bamaga
Crab I.
Orford Bay
Cullen Pt
Mapoon
Olinda Entrance
Cape
Weipa
Aboriginal Reserve
York
Pandora Entrance
Raine Entrance
Raine I.
Great Barrier Reef
Marine Park
(Far North Section)

Coral Sea

PAPUA
NEW GUINEA
Louisiade Archipelago

Orangerie B.
Bona Bona Island
Milne B.
Goschen Str.
Strathord I.
Sideia I.
Bonvouloir Is
Suau
Brumer Is
Basilaki I.
Panaeati I.
Misima I.
Conflict Group
Long Reef
Deboyne Is
The Calvados Chain
Panatinane I.
Rossel I.
Tagula
Tagula Island
Panasesa I.

Coral Sea Islands
Territory
(Australia)

Want to know more?
► Cross-section of Oceania   6–7
► Image of Uluru   138–139
► Guide to Oceania's countries   138–139
► Map of reefs at risk   140–141
► Australia's salinity hazard   140–141

Diane Bank
Moore Reef
Holmes Reef
Osprey Reef
Shark Reef
Willis Group
Magdelaine Cays
Herald Cays
South West I.
Chilcott I.
Coringa Is
Flora Reef
Flinders Reefs
Tregosse Islets and Reefs
Diamond Islets
Lihou Reef and Cays
Turtle I.
Malay Reef
Abington Reef

QUEENSLAND

Cairns
Townsville
Mackay
Rockhampton
Gladstone
Bundaberg
Maryborough
Gympie
Brisbane

Great Barrier Reef
Marine Park
(Central Section)

Great Barrier Reef
Marine Park
(Capricorn Section)

Fraser Island
Fraser Island National Park

Swain Reefs

Frederick Reef

North East Cay
Saumarez Reef
Wreck Reef

Capricorn Channel

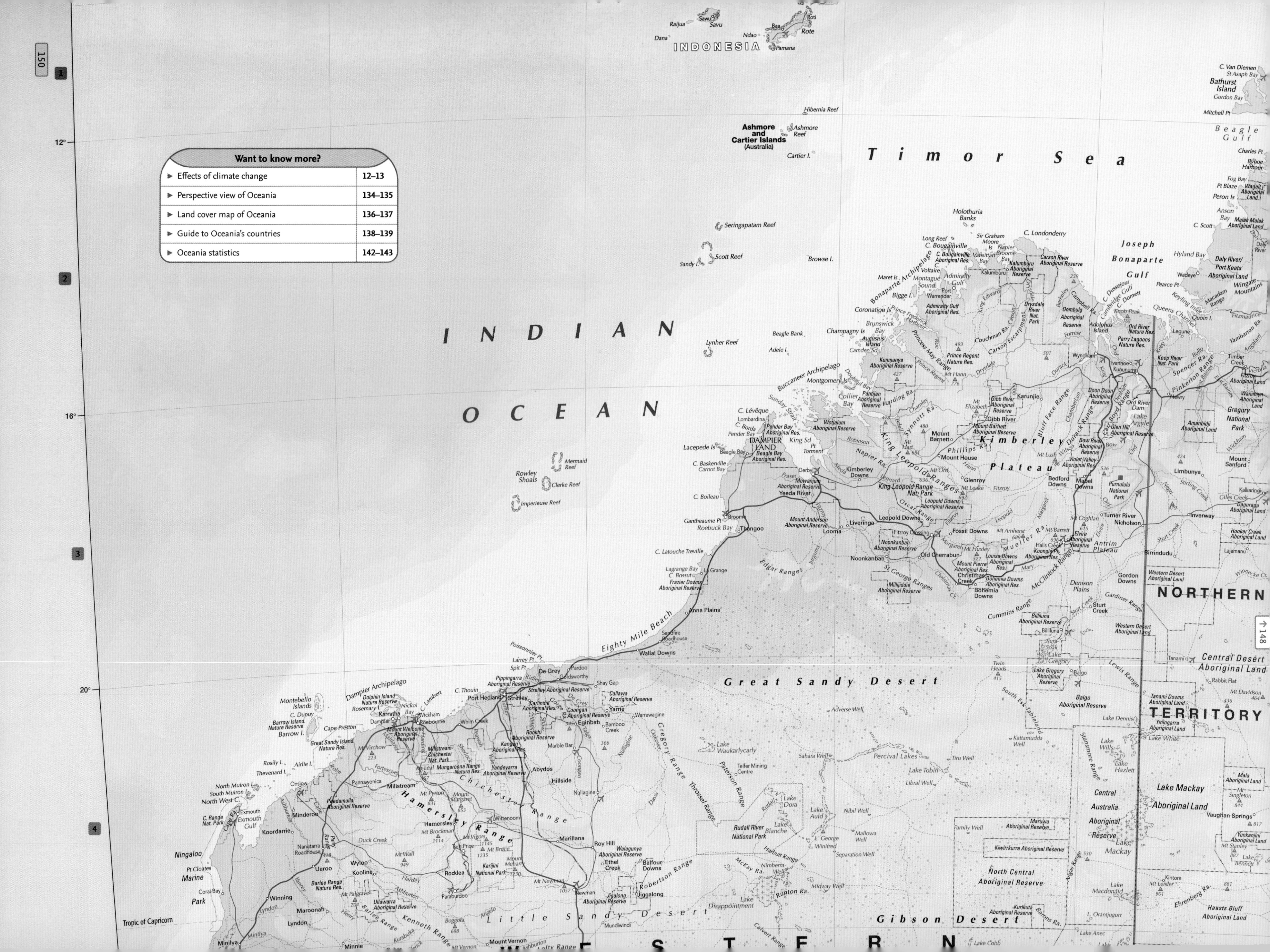

Oceania Western Australia

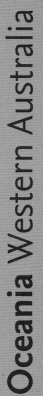

S O U T H   A U S T R A L I A

W E S T E R N   A U S T R A L I A

Great Victoria Desert

Nullarbor Plain

Great Australian Bight

1:6 000 000

Lambert Azimuthal Equal Area Projection

miles

km

>6000m
5000-6000m
4000-5000m
3000-4000m
2000-3000m
1000-2000m
500-1000m
200-500m
0-200m
<0m
0-200m
200-500m
500-1000m
1000-2000m
2000-3000m
3000-4000m
4000-5000m
5000-6000m
>6000m

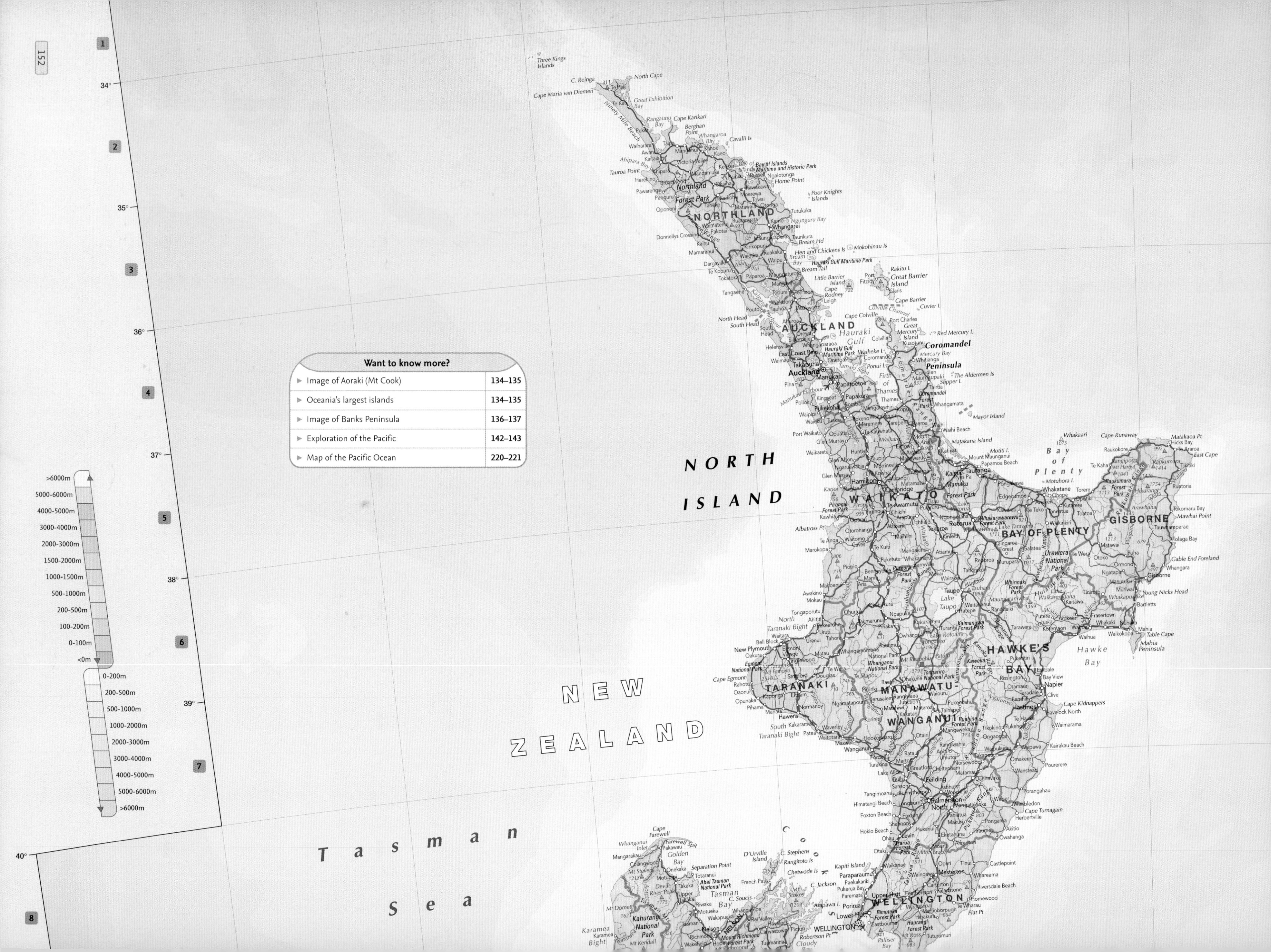

Want to know more?	
▸ Image of Aoraki (Mt Cook)	134–135
▸ Oceania's largest islands	134–135
▸ Image of Banks Peninsula	136–137
▸ Exploration of the Pacific	142–143
▸ Map of the Pacific Ocean	220–221

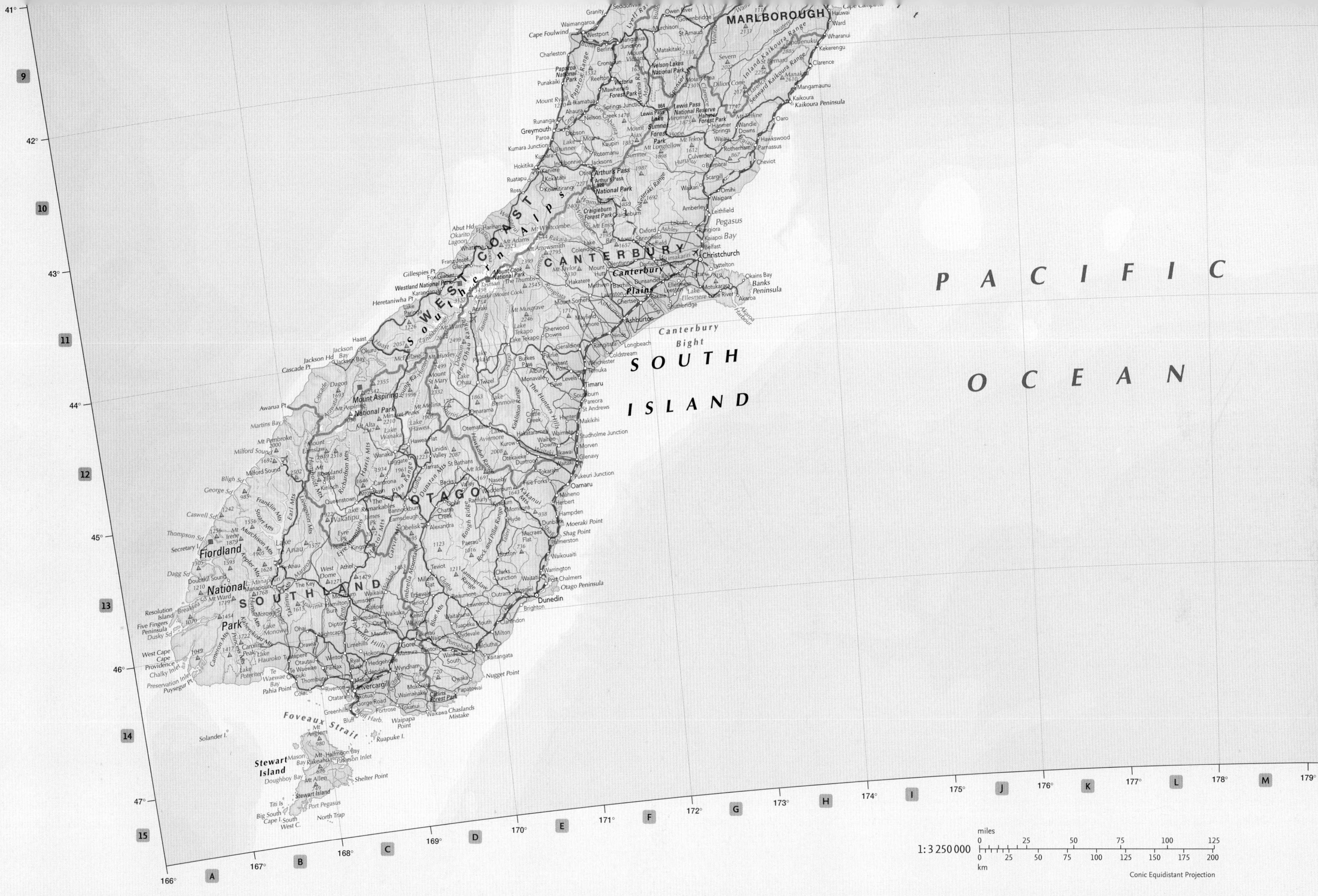

PACIFIC

OCEAN

MARLBOROUGH

SOUTH ISLAND

WEST COAST

CANTERBURY

Canterbury Plain

Canterbury Bight

OTAGO

SOUTHLAND

Fiordland National Park

Christchurch

Dunedin

Invercargill

Foveaux Strait

Stewart Island

Solander I.

1:3 250 000

Conic Equidistant Projection

North America Landscapes

North America is the largest continent in the western hemisphere. This view illustrates how the west coast is dominated by the Rocky Mountains which stretch from Alaska in the north through Canada, USA, Mexico and Central America. The Great Plains stretch gradually east of the Rockies, and extend from the Arctic Ocean to the Gulf of Mexico. The Appalachian Mountains dominate the east of the USA, with lowlands skirting the east coast of the continent and the Gulf of Mexico. Major water bodies are the Great Lakes, and Great Slave Lake and Great Bear Lake in the Arctic regions of Canada.

In the northeast, Hudson Bay is a huge inland sea connected to the Atlantic Ocean by the Hudson Strait. The large purple feature at the centre top of the image is the high, snow-covered plateau in Greenland. The Caribbean Sea contains numerous islands, stretching from the Bahamas to the north coast of South America. In the south the Isthmus of Panama forms the link between Central and South America.

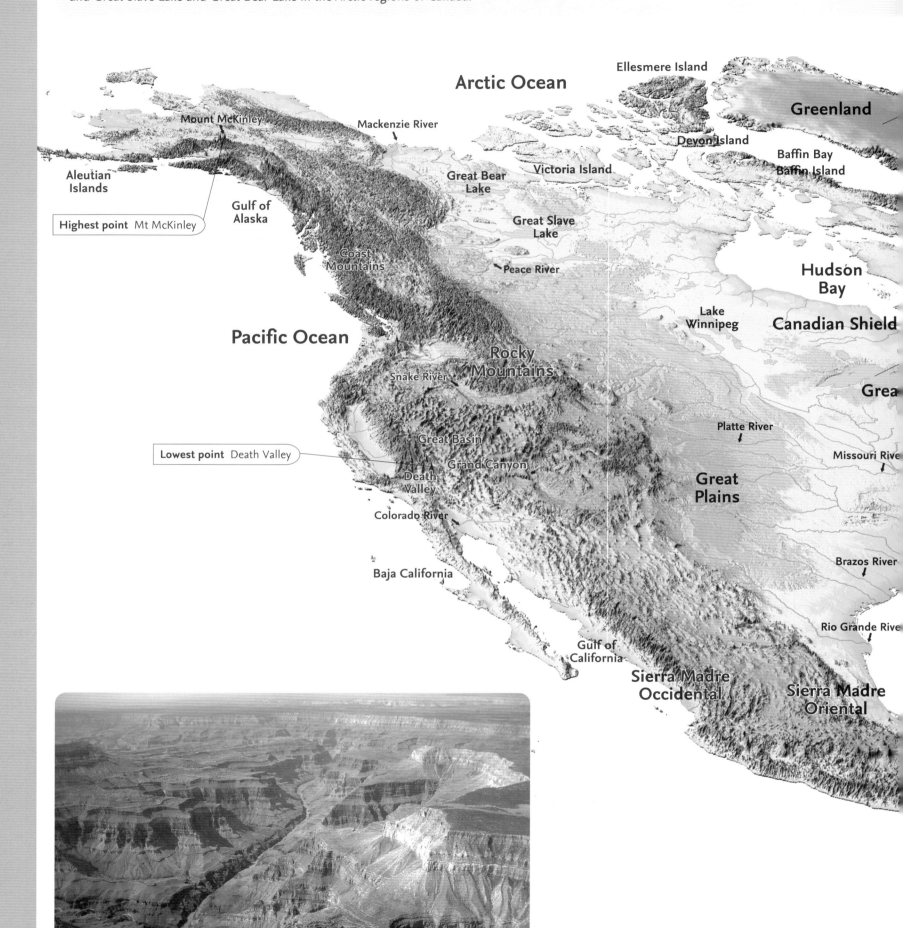

The **Grand Canyon** in northern Arizona, USA, is the largest canyon in the world and one of the most famous World Heritage Sites. It has been established as a National Park since 1919. This aerial view shows how the canyon has been carved out by the Colorado river, exposing many layers of sedimentary rock. The canyon reaches depths of over 1.5 kilometres (0.9 miles) and there are many peaks and smaller canyons within the main gorge.

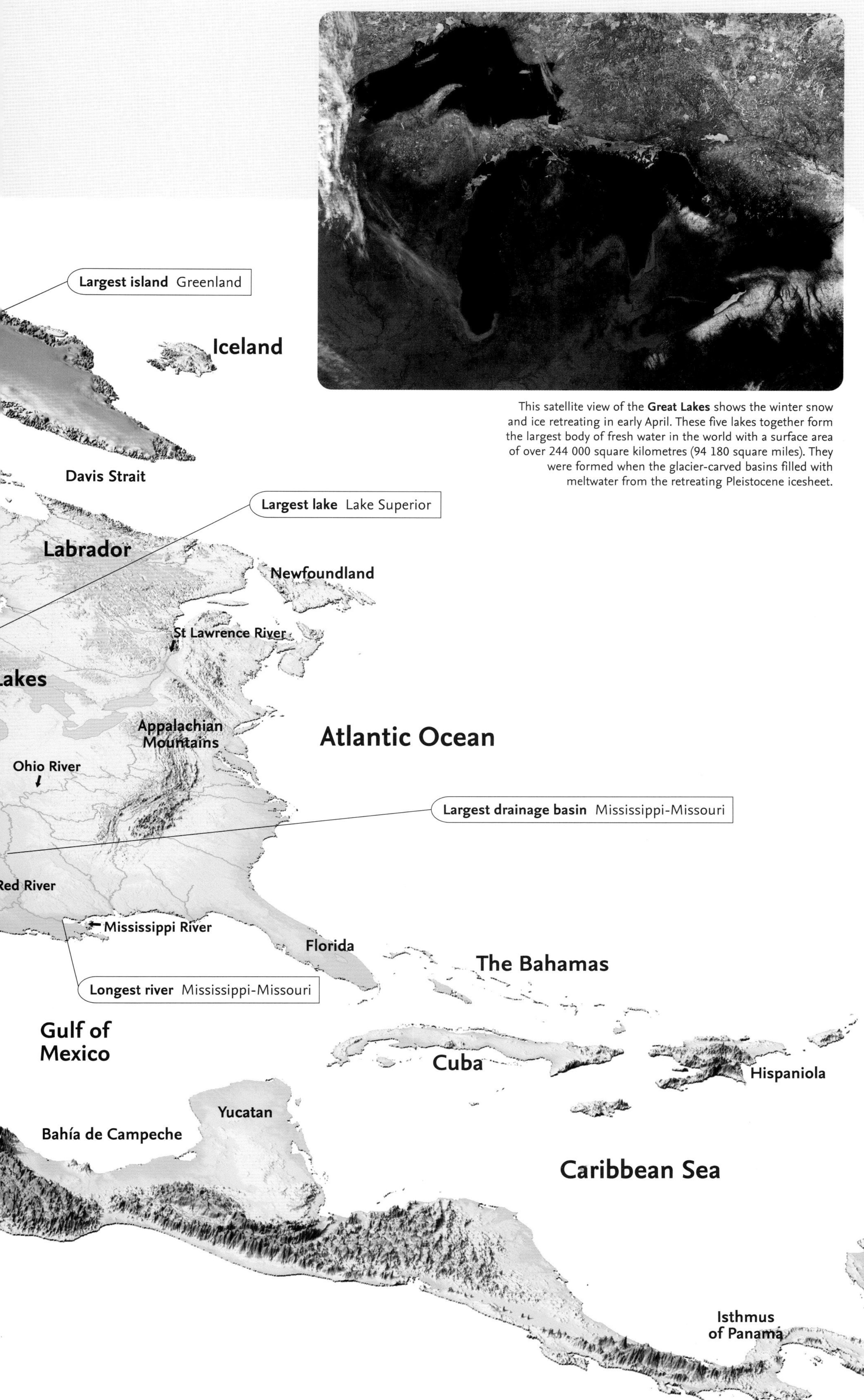

Want to know more?	
▶ Cross-section of North America	**6–7**
▶ World's largest lakes	**6–7**
▶ World weather extremes	**12–13**
▶ Land cover map of North America	**156–157**
▶ Atlantic hurricanes	**160–161**
▶ Maps of North America	**164–187**

Internet links	
Canadian natural resources	www.nrcan-rncan.gc.ca
Government of Canada	canada.gc.ca
The Great Lakes	www.great-lakes.net
US Geological Survey	www.usgs.gov
US weather and oceans information	www.noaa.gov

Facts

Canada has the longest coastline in the world.

The long chain of the Aleutian Islands which forms part of Alaska is the northern edge of the "ring of fire" where the edge of the Pacific tectonic plate causes volcanic and earthquake activity.

Devon Island in northern Canada is the world's largest uninhabited island.

When the volcano of Mt St Helens erupted in 1980, the first time since 1857, it lost 400 metres (1 312 feet) in height.

Largest island Greenland

Iceland

Davis Strait

Labrador

Newfoundland

St Lawrence River

Largest lake Lake Superior

Lakes

Appalachian Mountains

Ohio River

Atlantic Ocean

Largest drainage basin Mississippi-Missouri

Red River

Mississippi River

Longest river Mississippi-Missouri

Florida

The Bahamas

Gulf of Mexico

Cuba

Hispaniola

Yucatan

Bahía de Campeche

Caribbean Sea

Isthmus of Panama

This satellite view of the **Great Lakes** shows the winter snow and ice retreating in early April. These five lakes together form the largest body of fresh water in the world with a surface area of over 244 000 square kilometres (94 180 square miles). They were formed when the glacier-carved basins filled with meltwater from the retreating Pleistocene icesheet.

Highest mountains	metres	feet	map
Mt McKinley *USA*	6 194	20 321	164 D3
Mt Logan *Canada*	5 959	19 550	166 A2
Pico de Orizaba *Mexico*	5 610	18 855	185 F5
Mt St Elias *USA*	5 489	18 008	166 A2
Volcán Popocatépetl *Mexico*	5 452	17 887	185 F5
Mt Foraker *USA*	5 303	17 398	164 D3

Longest rivers	km	miles	map
Mississippi-Missouri	5 969	3 709	179 E6
Mackenzie-Peace-Finlay	4 241	2 635	164 F3
Missouri	4 086	2 539	178 E5
Mississippi	3 765	2 339	179 E6
Yukon	3 185	1 979	164 C3
Rio Grande	3 057	1 899	171 G8

Largest islands	sq km	sq miles	map
Greenland	2 175 600	840 004	165 O2
Baffin Island	507 451	195 927	165 L2
Victoria Island	217 291	83 897	165 H2
Ellesmere Island	196 236	75 767	165 K2
Cuba	110 860	42 803	186 D2
Newfoundland	108 860	42 031	169 J3
Hispaniola	76 192	29 418	187 F3

Largest lakes	sq km	sq miles	map
Lake Superior	82 100	31 698	172 D3
Lake Huron	59 600	23 011	173 K6
Lake Michigan	57 800	22 316	172 F7
Great Bear Lake	31 328	12 095	166 F1
Great Slave Lake	28 568	11 030	167 H2
Lake Erie	25 700	9 922	173 L9
Lake Winnipeg	24 387	9 415	167 L4
Lake Ontario	18 960	7 320	173 O7

Land area

Total land area 24 680 331 sq km/9 529 129 sq miles		map
Most northerly point	**Kap Morris Jesup** *Greenland*	165 P1
Most southerly point	**Punta Mariato** *Panama*	186 C6
Most westerly point	**Attu Island** *Aleutian Islands*	220 F2
Most easterly point	**Nordøstrundingen** *Greenland*	224 X1
Lowest point	**Death Valley** *USA*	183 H5

North America is a continent of environmental contrasts. From the northern archipelago of islands which are permanently frozen or semi-frozen with tundra and scrub vegetation, south to Central America and the Caribbean islands, which still have areas of tropical rain forest. The mountainous chain stretching down the continent's west coast starts in Alaska, becomes the Rocky Mountains and continues through Central America as the Sierra Madre. East of the mountains there are barren areas of desert and canyons with little vegetation but these give way to the grasslands of the Great Plains which are now heavily cultivated. Meanwhile, further east the Appalachian Mountains are much lower with a milder climate encouraging ecological diversity.

The Caribbean islands may well be known for their sunshine, coral reefs and sandy beaches but many are also home to lush forest-clad hills as seen here on **St Lucia**.

With the Richardson Mountains in the distance, the **Mackenzie** river flows north from the village of Alavik, seen on the river bend, to the Beaufort Sea, part of the Arctic Ocean. The river is only navigable between June and October.

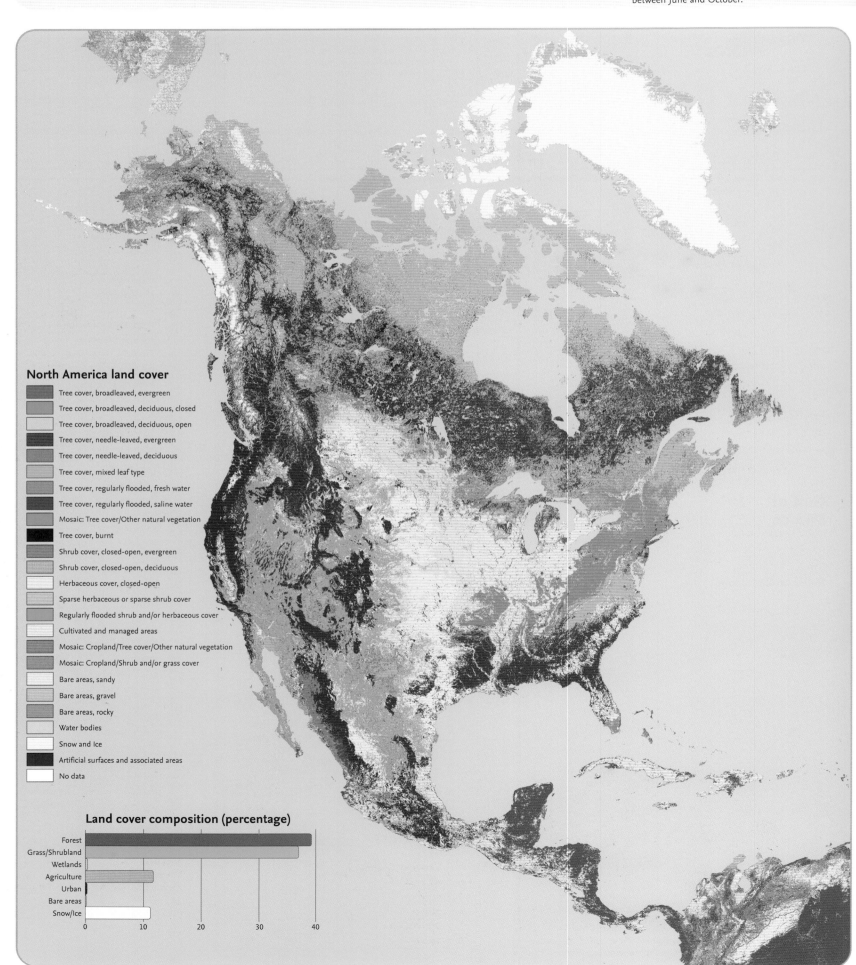

North America land cover

- Tree cover, broadleaved, evergreen
- Tree cover, broadleaved, deciduous, closed
- Tree cover, broadleaved, deciduous, open
- Tree cover, needle-leaved, evergreen
- Tree cover, needle-leaved, deciduous
- Tree cover, mixed leaf type
- Tree cover, regularly flooded, fresh water
- Tree cover, regularly flooded, saline water
- Mosaic: Tree cover/Other natural vegetation
- Tree cover, burnt
- Shrub cover, closed-open, evergreen
- Shrub cover, closed-open, deciduous
- Herbaceous cover, closed-open
- Sparse herbaceous or sparse shrub cover
- Regularly flooded shrub and/or herbaceous cover
- Cultivated and managed areas
- Mosaic: Cropland/Tree cover/Other natural vegetation
- Mosaic: Cropland/Shrub and/or grass cover
- Bare areas, sandy
- Bare areas, gravel
- Bare areas, rocky
- Water bodies
- Snow and Ice
- Artificial surfaces and associated areas
- No data

Land cover composition (percentage)

Forest
Grass/Shrubland
Wetlands
Agriculture
Urban
Bare areas
Snow/Ice

0   10   20   30   40

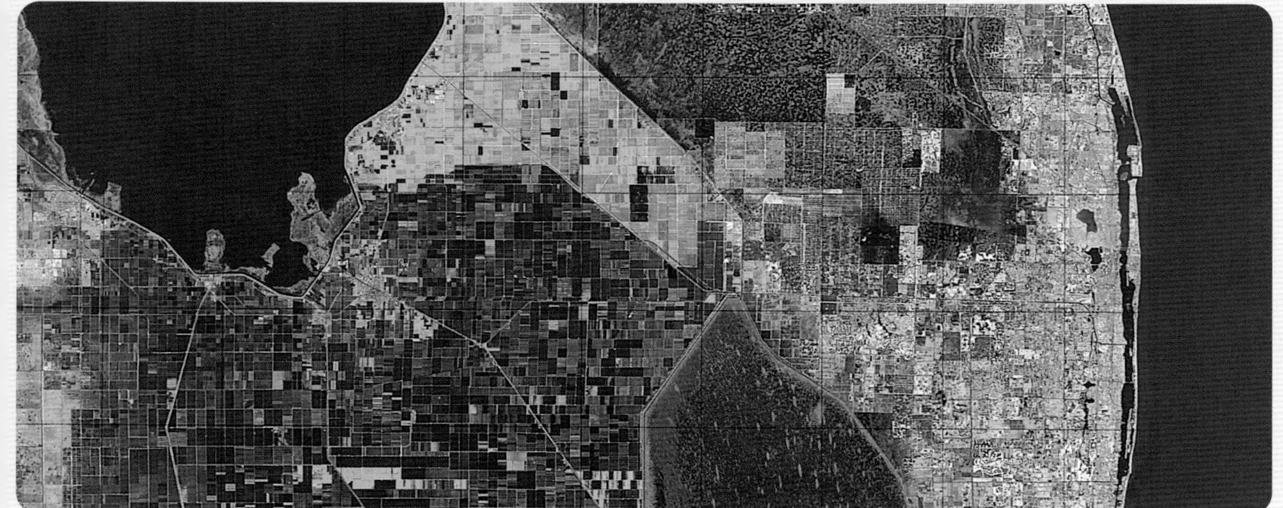

Regular field patterns of green (planted) and dark pink (unplanted) indicate mechanised cultivation. The fields extend to the edges of the **Everglades** and **Lake Okeechobee** in Florida. The urban area (blue/grey) clings to the Atlantic coast.

Internet links	
Red List of Threatened Species	www.redlist.org
UN Environment Programme	www.unep.org
IUCN the World Conservation Union	www.iucn.org
National Park Service	www.nps.gov
Images of North America	earthobservatory.nasa.gov

Facts

In the Canadian prairie states of Alberta, Saskatchewan and Manitoba there are over 5 000 lakes.

Three quarters of the top 150 prescription drugs in the U.S.A. are laboratory versions of chemicals found in plants, fungi, bacteria and vertebrates.

Yellowstone National Park is home to five threatened or endangered species and receives over three million visitors a year.

The Columbian icefield within Jasper National Park has rivers flowing into three different oceans.

Endangered species

The lure of oil and mineral resources has led man to encroach upon the harsh landscape of northern Canada, disrupting this fragile environment and the lifestyle of the native Inuit people. The vast cultivated plains of America leave little respite for wildlife. In Central America, as in other parts of the world at these latitudes, there is great pressure on the tropical rain forests to be felled for farmland.

Number of endangered species by country

- over 1000
- 501–1000
- 251–500
- 101–250
- 51–100
- 26–50
- 0–25
- no data

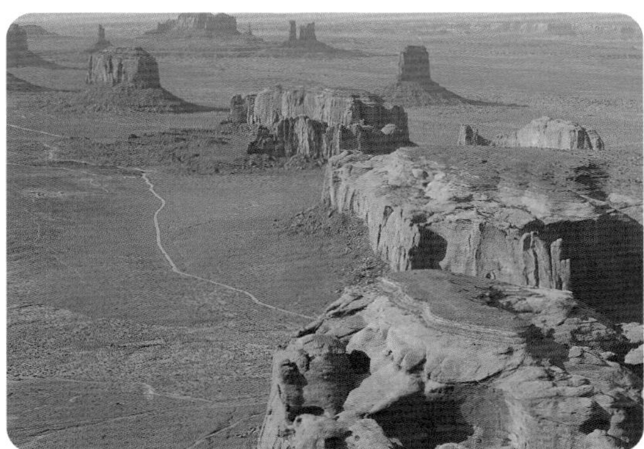

Monument Valley covers an area which is a Navajo Indian Reservation. The flat-topped, steep sided plateaus, or mesas, are made up from horizontal layers of weak rock with a more resistant cap. They are the product of hundreds of thousands of years of erosion. A small mesa is called a butte.

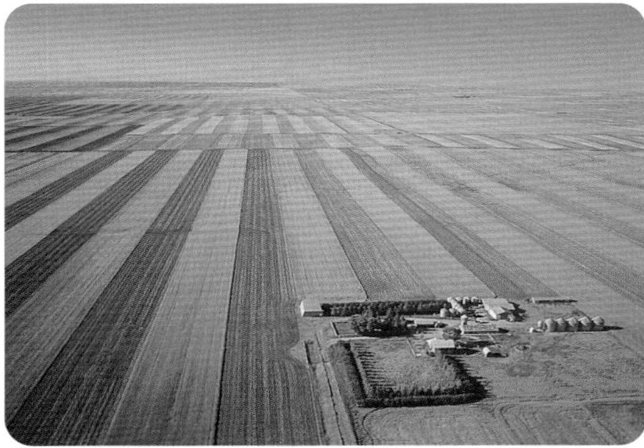

The natural habitat of the grasslands of **Montana** would have sustained herds of buffalo and also cattle or sheep ranching but today the emphasis is on extensive wheat farms using the most modern farming techniques.

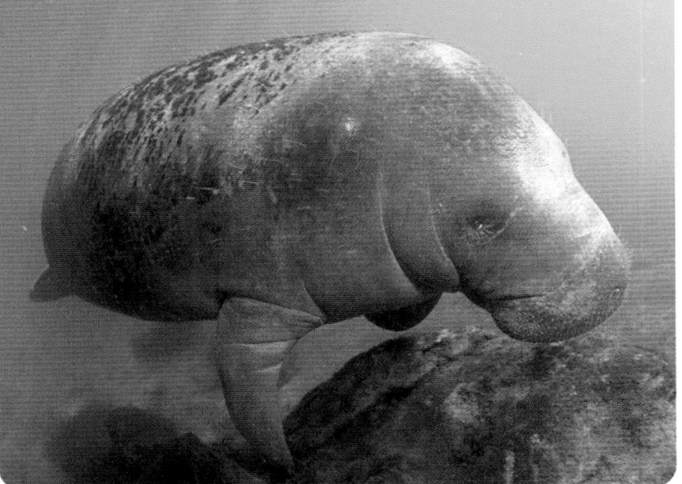

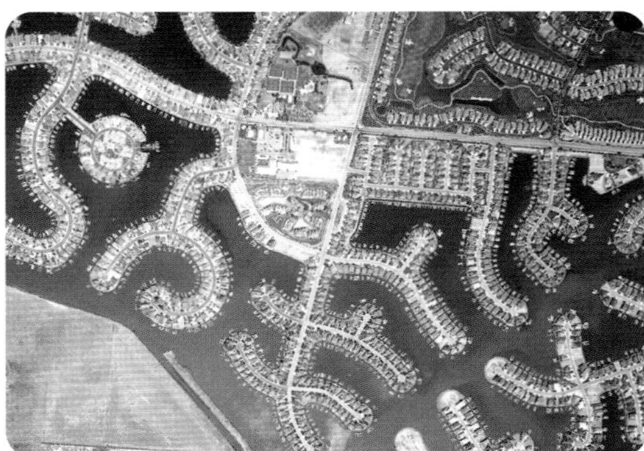

The demand for housing is constant and in **Stockton, California** the desire for a waterfront property has created this growing development of waterways and man-made promontories.

American **manatees** are at home in the warm waters of the **Gulf of Mexico** but numbers have suffered due to man's presence. They become caught in fishing nets and hit by boats' propellers. Also pollutants affect their food supplies.

Top 10 protected land by country

	country	percentage land protected
1	Belize	47.5
2	Guatemala	25.3
3	Dominican Republic	24.5
4	Costa Rica	23.4
5	Nicaragua	21.8
6	Honduras	20.8
7	Panama	19.5
8	Jamaica	15.9
9	United States	15.8
10	Canada	6.3

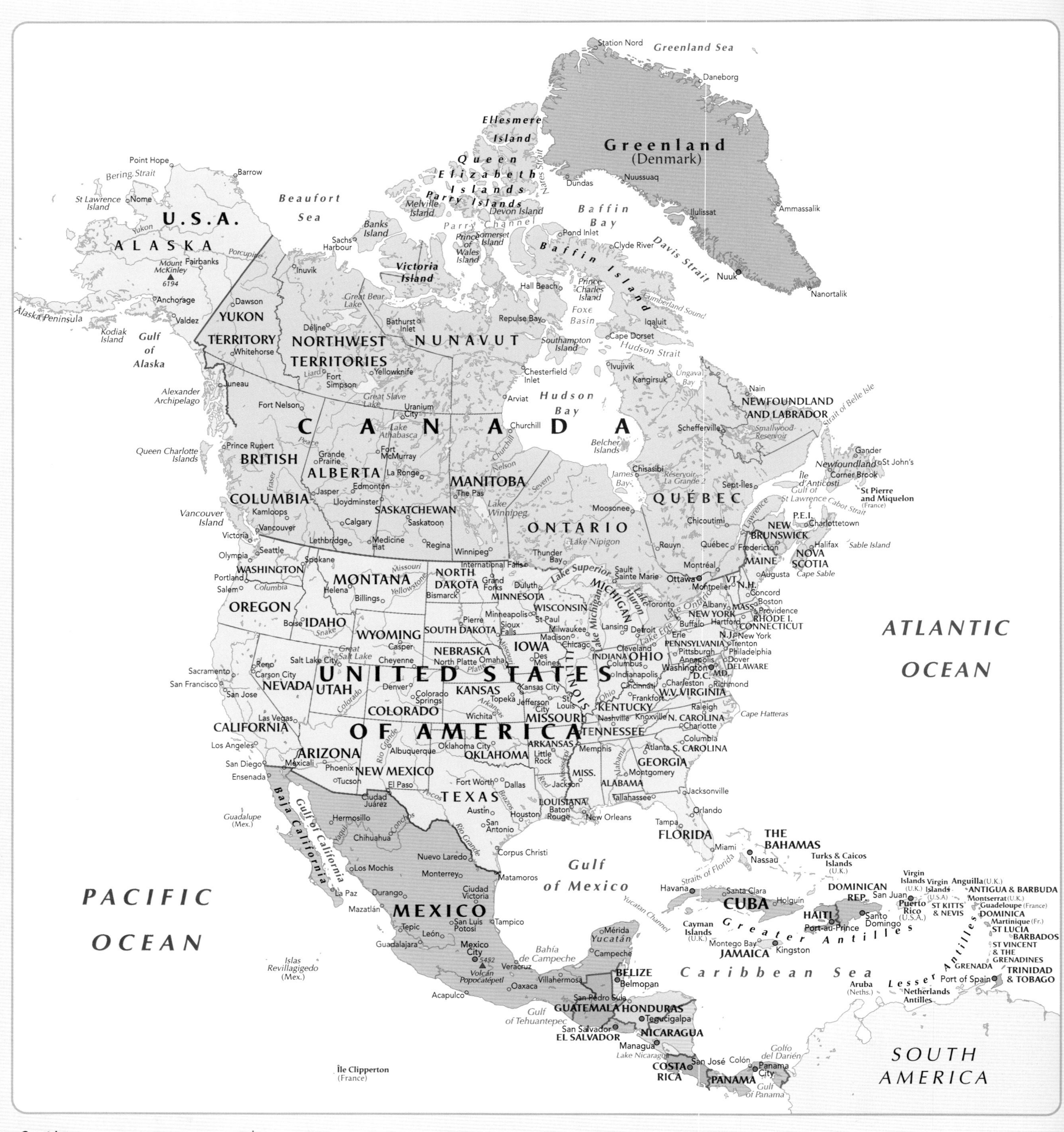

Countries capital		sq km sq miles	population	languages	religions	currency	official website	map
Antigua and Barbuda St John's		442 171	81 000	English, creole	Protestant, Roman Catholic	East Caribbean dollar	www.un.int/antigua	187
The Bahamas Nassau		13 939 5 382	323 000	English, creole	Protestant, Roman Catholic	Bahamian dollar	www.bahamas.gov.bs	186–187
Barbados Bridgetown		430 166	270 000	English, creole	Protestant, Roman Catholic	Barbados dollar	www.barbados.gov.bb	187
Belize Belmopan		22 965 8 867	270 000	English, Spanish, Mayan, creole	Roman Catholic, Protestant	Belize dollar	www.belize.gov.bz	185
Canada Ottawa		9 984 670 3 855 103	32 268 000	English, French	Roman Catholic, Protestant, Eastern Orthodox, Jewish	Canadian dollar	canada.gc.ca	164–165
Costa Rica San José		51 100 19 730	4 327 000	Spanish	Roman Catholic, Protestant	Costa Rican colón	www.casapres.go.cr	186
Cuba Havana (La Habana)		110 860 42 803	11 269 000	Spanish	Roman Catholic, Protestant	Cuban peso	www.cubagob.gov.cu	186–187
Dominica Roseau		750 290	79 000	English, creole	Roman Catholic, Protestant	East Caribbean dollar	www.dominica.co.uk	187
Dominican Republic Santo Domingo		48 442 18 704	8 895 000	Spanish, creole	Roman Catholic, Protestant	Dominican peso	www.presidencia.gov.do	187
El Salvador San Salvador		21 041 8 124	6 881 000	Spanish	Roman Catholic, Protestant	El Salvador colón, US dollar	www.casapres.gob.sv	185
Grenada St George's		378 146	103 000	English, creole	Roman Catholic, Protestant	East Caribbean dollar	www.grenadaconsulate.org	187
Guatemala Guatemala City		108 890 42 043	12 599 000	Spanish, Mayan languages	Roman Catholic, Protestant	Quetzal, US dollar	www.congreso.gob.gt	185
Haiti Port-au-Prince		27 750 10 714	8 528 000	French, creole	Roman Catholic, Protestant, Voodoo	Gourde	www.haiti.org	187
Honduras Tegucigalpa		112 088 43 277	7 205 000	Spanish, Amerindian languages	Roman Catholic, Protestant	Lempira	www.congreso.gob.hn	186
Jamaica Kingston		10 991 4 244	2 651 000	English, creole	Protestant, Roman Catholic	Jamaican dollar	www.jis.gov.jm	186
Mexico Mexico City		1 972 545 761 604	107 029 000	Spanish, Amerindian languages	Roman Catholic, Protestant	Mexican peso	www.presidencia.gob.mx	184–185
Nicaragua Managua		130 000 50 193	5 487 000	Spanish, Amerindian languages	Roman Catholic, Protestant	Córdoba	www.asamblea.gob.ni	186

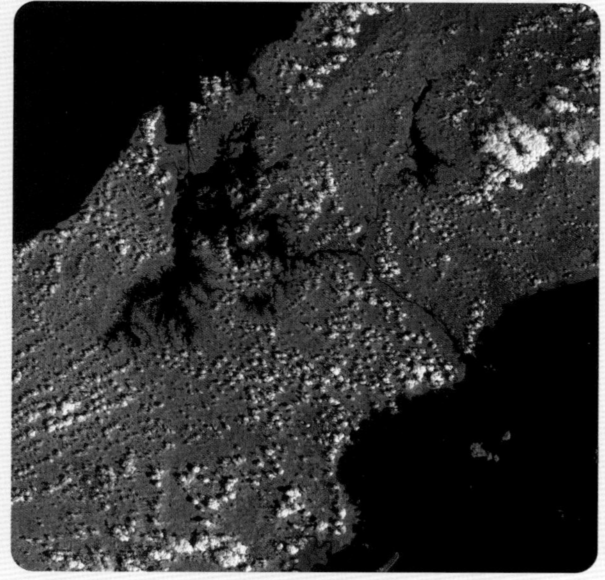

The **Panama Canal** is a vital shipping route between the Atlantic (seen top left of this image) and Pacific (bottom right) Oceans. Control of the Canal Zone rested with the USA until a 1977 treaty ceded the area to Panama, a transition which happened in 1979. Full control of the Canal passed to Panama on the last day of 1999.

Top 10 countries by area		sq km	sq miles	world rank
1	Canada	9 970 610	3 849 674	2
2	United States of America	9 809 378	3 787 422	3
3	Greenland	2 175 600	840 004	14
4	Mexico	1 972 545	761 604	15
5	Nicaragua	130 000	50 193	96
6	Honduras	112 088	43 277	101
7	Cuba	110 860	42 803	104
8	Guatemala	108 890	42 043	105
9	Panama	77 082	29 762	117
10	Costa Rica	51 100	19 730	127

Top 10 countries by population		population	world rank
1	United States of America	298 213 000	3
2	Mexico	107 029 000	11
3	Canada	32 268 000	36
4	Guatemala	12 599 000	70
5	Cuba	11 269 000	73
6	Dominican Republic	8 895 000	87
7	Haiti	8 528 000	88
8	Honduras	7 205 000	96
9	El Salvador	6 881 000	97
10	Nicaragua	5 487 000	107

Want to know more?

▸ World landscapes	6–7
▸ Political map of the world	8–9
▸ Colonization of North America	162–163
▸ Detailed maps of North America	164–187
▸ Peoples of the Arctic	214–215

Internet links

Organization of American States	www.oas.org
Caribbean Community CARICOM	www.caricom.org
US Census Bureau	www.census.gov
US Board on Geographic Names	geonames.usgs.gov

Facts

The Panama Canal, which opened in 1914, cut the journey between the Atlantic and Pacific Oceans by over 14 000 kilometres (8 700 miles).

The state of Alaska was bought by the USA from Russia for $7.2 million in 1867.

The Mississippi-Missouri is the longest river in North America at nearly 6 000 kilometres (3 728 miles).

Mexico City is the second largest city in the world with a population of over 19 million. It is also the highest city in North America at a height of 2 000 metres (6 562 feet). These conditions contribute to the air pollution which often hangs over the city.

Countries capital		sq km sq miles	population	languages	religions	currency	official website	map
Panama Panama City	★ ★	77 082 29 762	3 232 000	Spanish, English, Amerindian languages	Roman Catholic, Protestant, Sunni Muslim	Balboa	www.pa	186
St Kitts And Nevis Basseterre		261 101	43 000	English, creole	Protestant, Roman Catholic	East Caribbean dollar	www.stkittsnevis.net	187
St Lucia Castries		616 238	161 000	English, creole	Roman Catholic, Protestant	East Caribbean dollar	www.stlucia.gov.lc	187
St Vincent and the Grenadines Kingstown		389 150	119 000	English, creole	Protestant, Roman Catholic	East Caribbean dollar		187
Trinidad and Tobago Port of Spain		5 130 1 981	1 305 000	English, creole, Hindi	Roman Catholic, Hindu, Protestant, Sunni Muslim	Trinidad and Tobago dollar	www.gov.tt	187
United States of America Washington D.C.		9 826 635 3 794 085	298 213 000	English, Spanish	Protestant, Roman Catholic, Sunni Muslim, Jewish	US dollar	www.firstgov.gov	170–171

Dependencies capital		territorial status	sq km sq miles	population	languages	religions	currency	official website	map
Anguilla The Valley		United Kingdom Overseas Territory	155 60	12 000	English	Protestant, Roman Catholic	East Caribbean dollar	www.gov.ai	187
Aruba Oranjestad		Self-governing Netherlands Territory	193 75	99 000	Papiamento, Dutch, English	Roman Catholic, Protestant	Aruban florin	www.aruba.com	187
Bermuda Hamilton		United Kingdom Overseas Territory	54 21	64 000	English	Protestant, Roman Catholic	Bermuda dollar	www.gov.bm	171
Cayman Islands George Town		United Kingdom Overseas Territory	259 100	45 000	English	Protestant, Roman Catholic	Cayman Islands dollar	www.gov.ky	186
Clipperton, Île		French Overseas Territory	7 3	uninhabited					221
Greenland Nuuk (Godthåb)		Self-governing Danish Territory	2 175 600 840 004	57 000	Greenlandic, Danish	Protestant	Danish krone	www.nanoq.gl	165
Guadeloupe Basse-Terre		French Overseas Department	1 780 687	448 000	French, creole	Roman Catholic	Euro	www.cr-guadeloupe.fr	187
Martinique Fort-de-France		French Overseas Department	1 079 417	396 000	French, creole	Roman Catholic, traditional beliefs	Euro	www.cr-martinique.fr	187
Montserrat Plymouth		United Kingdom Overseas Territory	100 39	4 000	English	Protestant, Roman Catholic	East Caribbean dollar		187
Navassa Island		United States Unincorporated Territory	5 2	uninhabited					186
Netherlands Antilles Willemstad		Self-governing Netherlands Territory	800 309	183 000	Dutch, Papiamento, English	Roman Catholic, Protestant	Netherlands Antilles guilder	www.gov.an	187
Puerto Rico San Juan		United States Commonwealth	9 104 3 515	3 955 000	Spanish, English	Roman Catholic, Protestant	US dollar	www.gobierno.pr	187
St Pierre and Miquelon St-Pierre		French Territorial Collectivity	242 93	6 000	French	Roman Catholic	Euro		169
Turks and Caicos Islands Grand Turk		United Kingdom Overseas Territory	430 166	26 000	English	Protestant	US dollar		187
Virgin Islands (U.K.) Road Town		United Kingdom Overseas Territory	153 59	22 000	English	Protestant, Roman Catholic	US dollar		187
Virgin Islands (U.S.) Charlotte Amalie		United States Unincorporated Territory	352 136	112 000	English, Spanish	Protestant, Roman Catholic	US dollar	www.usvi.org	187

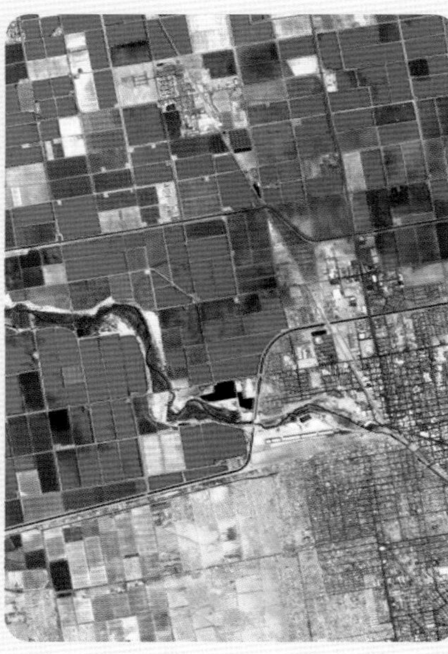

This satellite image combines visible and near-infrared wavelengths and clearly shows changes in land use across the **United States/Mexico border**. Areas of vegetation are displayed in red. The grid pattern of the lush agricultural fields of southern California is in stark contrast to the more barren area of northwest Mexico on the lower half of the image. The street pattern of the border town of Mexicali is also clearly seen.

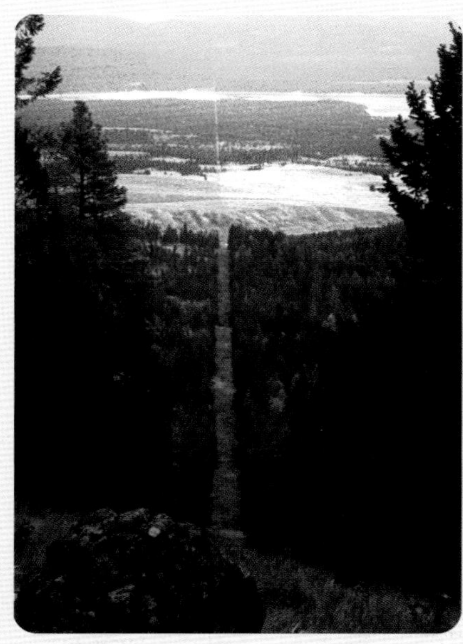

This photograph shows a section of the clearing which separates the **United States and Canada** along parts of their international boundary. The 8 891 kilometre (5 525 mile) border, which in this section follows the 49th parallel (49°N), is mapped and managed by the International Boundary Commission which was founded in 1908. The border here between Montana and British Columbia is typical of the six metre wide path of forest and brush which is kept clear.

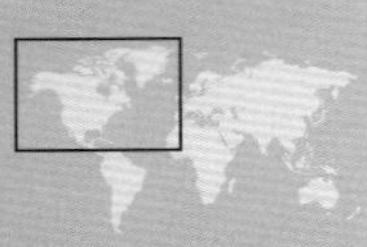
Tropical storms have different names around the world – typhoons, hurricanes, cyclones – but their features are the same. Strong winds and heavy rain can cause death and destruction to anything in their path. The hurricanes which originate in the Atlantic Ocean can cause major damage if they make landfall in the Caribbean and the USA. The effects of global warming may be a longer term problem and not immediately visible but the United Nation's Kyoto Protocol has helped focus world attention on the issue of climate change and the dangers of greenhouse gas emissions. Despite the USA being the world's greatest energy user, they chose to withdraw from the agreement.

The Saffir-Simpson hurricane scale

Tropical storms are reliant on warm water below them for energy and the slope of the continental shelf can affect the speed it hits landfall. Storms will abate when over land. The scale below ranks hurricanes from one to five in severity.

category	kilometres per hour	wind speed miles per hour	knots	storm surge above normal metres	feet
1	119–153	74–95	64–82	1.2–1.5	4–5
2	154–177	96–110	83–95	1.8–2.5	6–8
3	178–209	111–130	96–113	2.8–3.7	9–12
4	210–249	131–155	114–135	4–5.5	18
5	over 249	over 155	over 135	over 5.5	over 18

Tracks of tropical storms
Wind speeds often over 160 km per hour

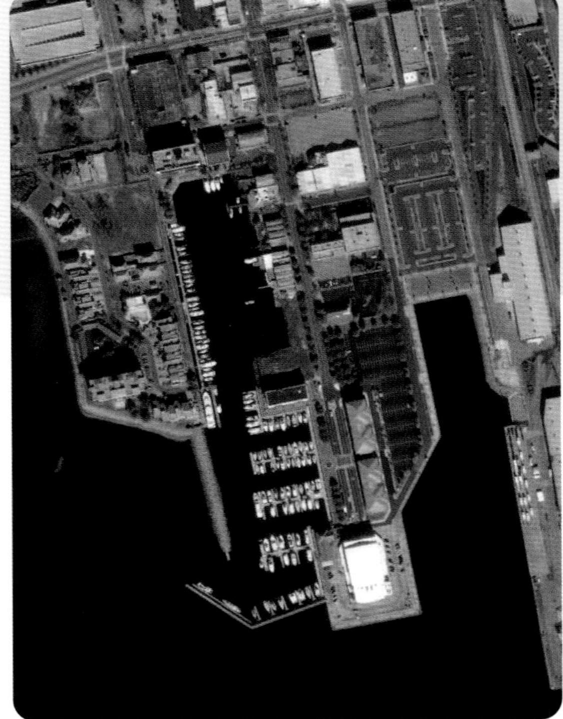

⇨ Cyclone track	⇨ Willy-willies	▨ Source area of tropical cyclones	◉ Major tropical storm (1994-2005)
⇨ Typhoon track	⇨ Hurricane track	▨ 'Tornado high risk areas'	

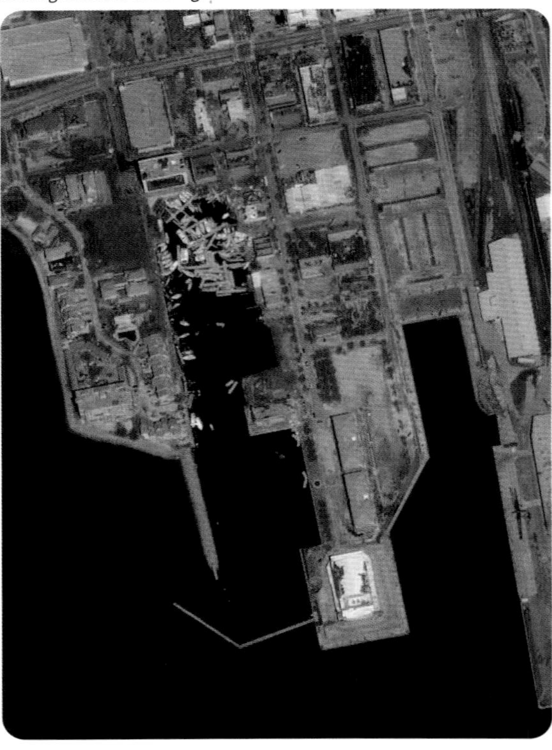

Pensacola, Florida before and two days after **Hurricane Ivan** struck, leaving roofless buildings and shattered boats.

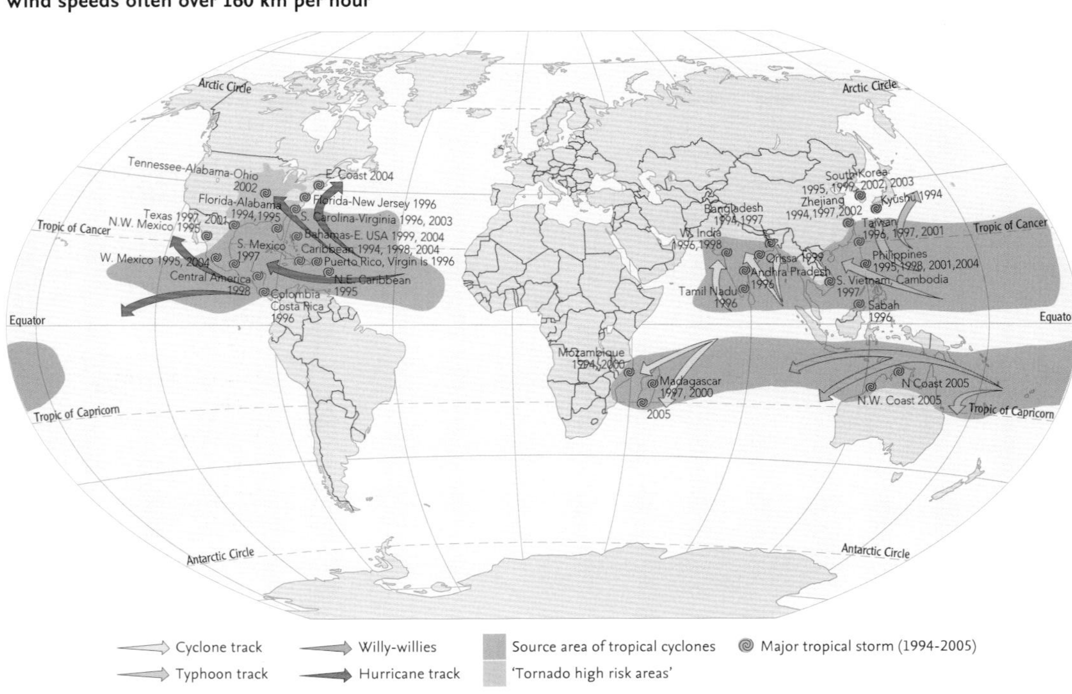

Major tropical storms, 2004

Hurricane strength
min ▬▬▬ max

NORTH AMERICA

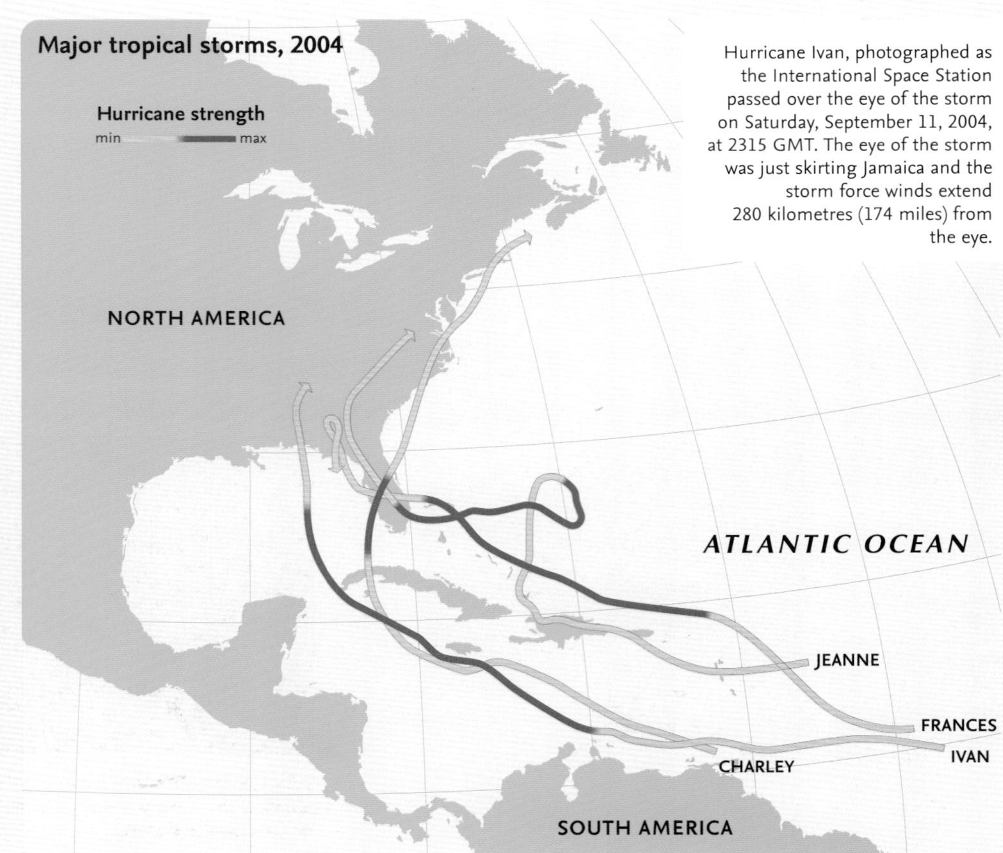

ATLANTIC OCEAN

JEANNE

FRANCES

CHARLEY

IVAN

SOUTH AMERICA

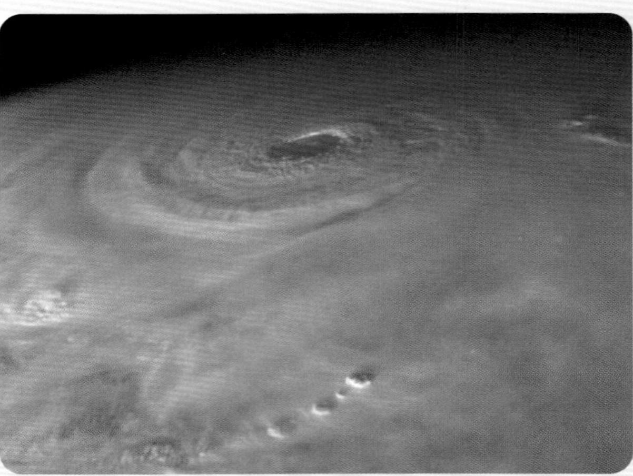

Hurricane Ivan, photographed as the International Space Station passed over the eye of the storm on Saturday, September 11, 2004, at 2315 GMT. The eye of the storm was just skirting Jamaica and the storm force winds extend 280 kilometres (174 miles) from the eye.

Six weeks of destruction

The Atlantic hurricane season generally lasts from June to December each year. In 2004 the season climaxed over six weeks starting in August when four major hurricanes hit the Caribbean and Florida one after another. Estimates of damage claims of around $23 billion, a final death toll of over 1 600 and approximately six million people without power were some of the after effects. Hurricanes Charley, Frances, Ivan and Jeanne all passed over Florida, at categories three or four (see table above), something which had not happened before in 130 years of record-keeping.

Energy consumption
Thousand tonnes of oil equivalent

- over 1 000 000
- 400 000–999 999
- 100 000–399 999
- 10 000–99 999
- 1 000–9 999
- 1–999
- no data

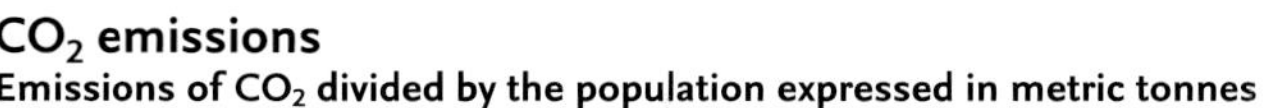

Want to know more?
▶ World climate and weather	12–13
▶ World health issues	20–21
▶ World's richest countries	22–23
▶ Endangered species in North America	156–157

Internet links
Carbon Dioxide Information Analysis Center	cdiac.esd.ornl.gov
UN Framework Convention on Climate Change	unfccc.int
Organization of Petroleum Exporting Countries	www.opec.org
Natural Resources Defense Council	www.nrdc.org
National Hurricane Center	www.nhc.noaa.gov

Facts

The average annual greenhouse gas emissions per person in the USA is 20 metric tonnes.

Energy sources are the largest single items in international trade.

The USA has 5 per cent of the global population but consumes over a quarter of the world's energy.

Atlantic and east Pacific based hurricanes are named alphabetically from A each year, with alternate male and female names.

Hurricanes get their name from Huracan, the Mayan god of wind and storms.

If Texas was a country it would be the world's 4th largest oil consumer.

CO$_2$ emissions
Emissions of CO$_2$ divided by the population expressed in metric tonnes

- 10 and over
- 5.0–9.9
- 2.5–4.9
- 1.0–2.4
- under 1.0
- no data

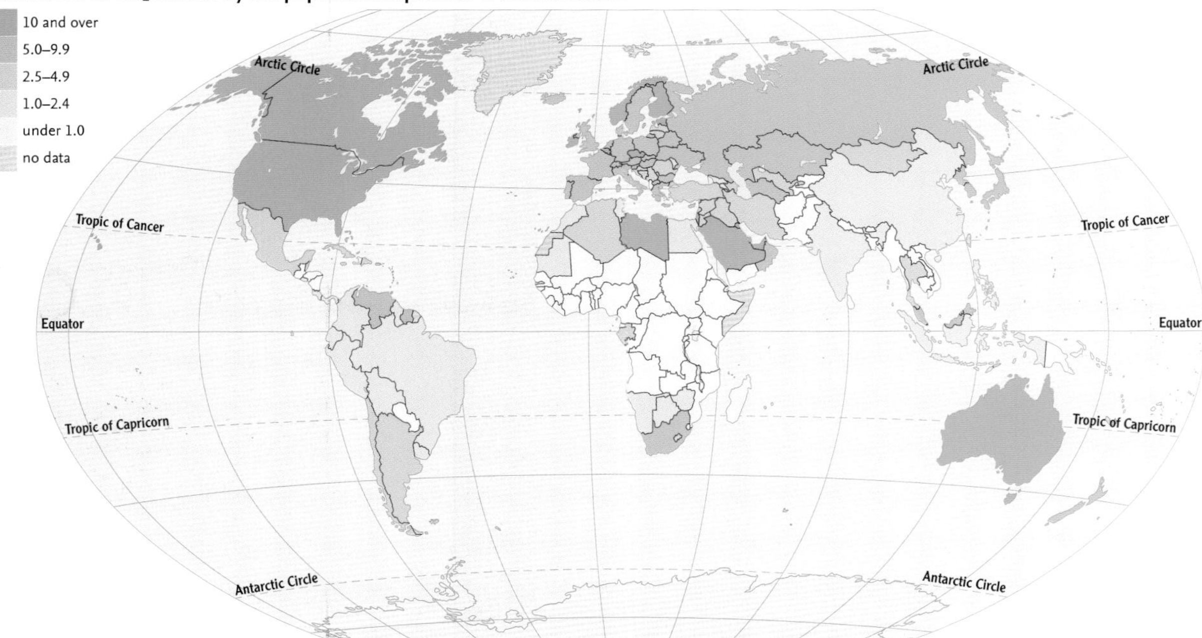

2003 World oil consumption
(thousand barrels daily)

	country	amount	world per cent share
1	USA	20 071	25.1
2	China	5 982	7.6
3	Japan	5 451	6.8
4	Germany	2 664	3.4
5	Russian Federation	2 503	3.4
6	India	2 426	3.1
7	South Korea	2 303	2.9
8	Canada	2 149	2.6
9	France	1 991	2.6
10	Italy	1 927	2.5

Energy consumption and its consequences

North America accounts for 30 per cent of the world's oil consumption with the USA alone using 25 per cent. Although the USA produces oil it is not self-sufficient. Texas produces over 1 100 000 barrels a day but uses more than twice that amount. With the Kyoto Protocol in 1997, the UN set out to take action on global warming. The USA initially signed up to a target of a 6 per cent reduction of greenhouse gas emissions.

As the treaty was ratified in 2004, the USA pulled out, worrying over the effect on the country's businesses, preferring to bring in their own measures. Since 1990 emissions have gone up 11 per cent and currently the USA is accountable for a quarter of the world's emissions which is 5 410 million metric tonnes a year.

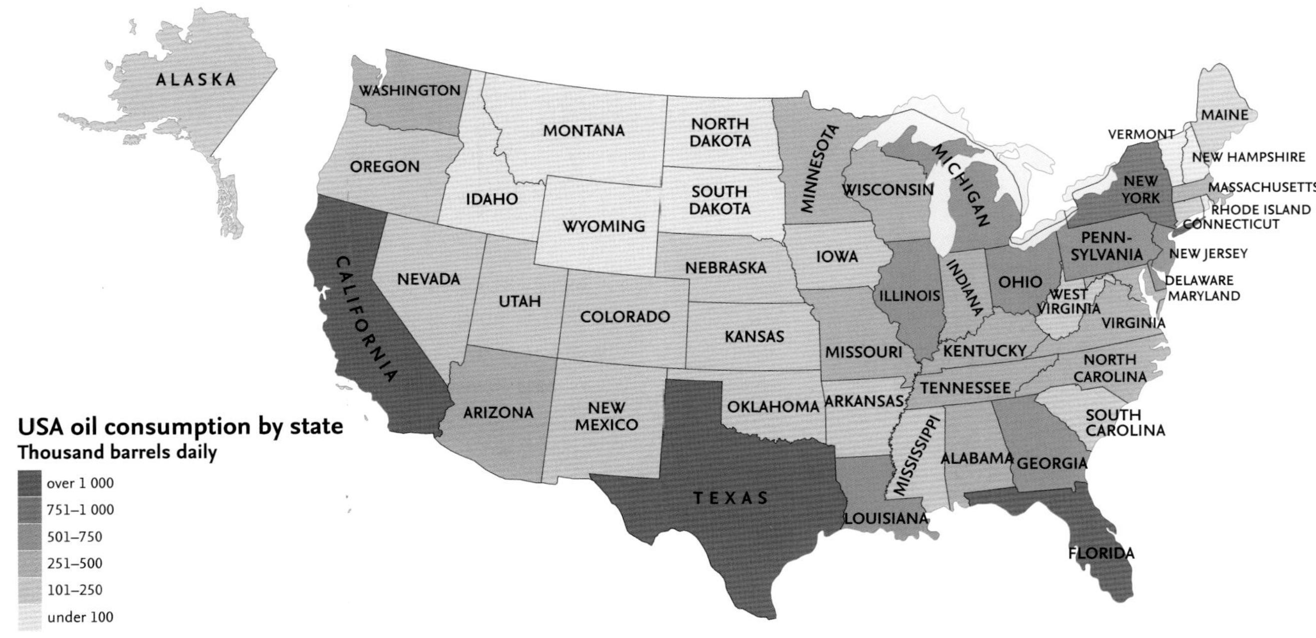

USA oil consumption by state
Thousand barrels daily

- over 1 000
- 751–1 000
- 501–750
- 251–500
- 101–250
- under 100

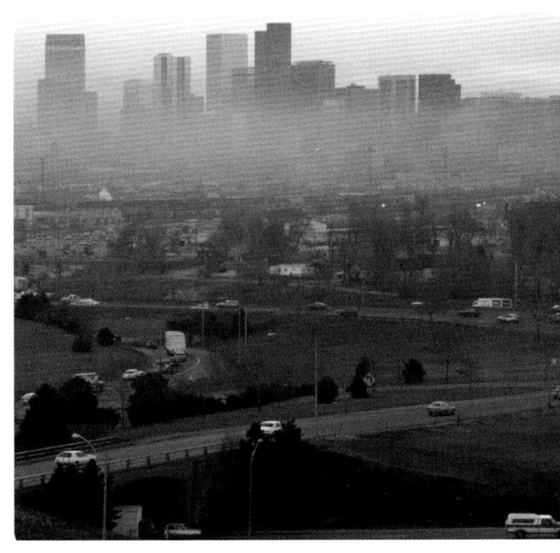

Individual states are introducing their own controls on **pollution** to try and prevent scenes such as this smog or 'brown cloud' in Denver.

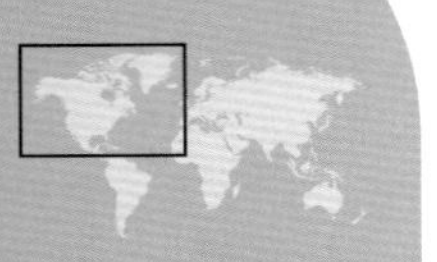

North America History and Statistics

8000 BC First people move into the Americas from Asia, across the Bering Strait

1750 BC Northernmost parts of Greenland settled

500 BC Foundation of Zapotec capital (Monte Albán), in Mexico

1608 French colonists found Quebec

1763 Treaty of Paris transfers most French North American possessions to Britain

100 Rise of Mayan capital Teotihuacán in Mexico

1776 American Declaration of Independence

300 Rise of Mayan civilization in Central America

1898 USA annexes Guam, Puerto Rico and the Philippines

1492 Columbus reaches America: discovery of the New World

1863 Slavery abolished in the USA

1803 Louisiana Purchase nearly doubles the size of the USA

1000 Vikings colonize Greenland and discover America (Vinland)

400 Settlement of the Hawaiian Islands

700 Mayan capital Teotihuacán destroyed

1100 Toltecs build capital at Tula (Mexico)
1100 Height of Pueblo culture (North America)

1325 Rise of Aztecs; Tenochtitlán founded
1493 First Spanish settlement in the New World (Hispaniola)

1519 Cortés begins conquest of Aztec empire
1607 First permanent English settlement in America (Jamestown, Virginia)

300 BC Rise of Hopewell chiefdoms in North America

1789 George Washington becomes first president of the United States

1845 Texas annexed by the USA

1846–1848 War between USA and Mexico: US conquers New Mexico and California

1861–1865 American Civil War

1150 BC Beginning of Olmec civilization in Mexico

1867 Russia sells Alaska to the USA
1867 Dominion of Canada established

3000 BC Maize first culivated in Central America

1620 Puritans land in New England (*Mayflower*)

1876 Telephone patented by Alexander Graham Bell (USA)

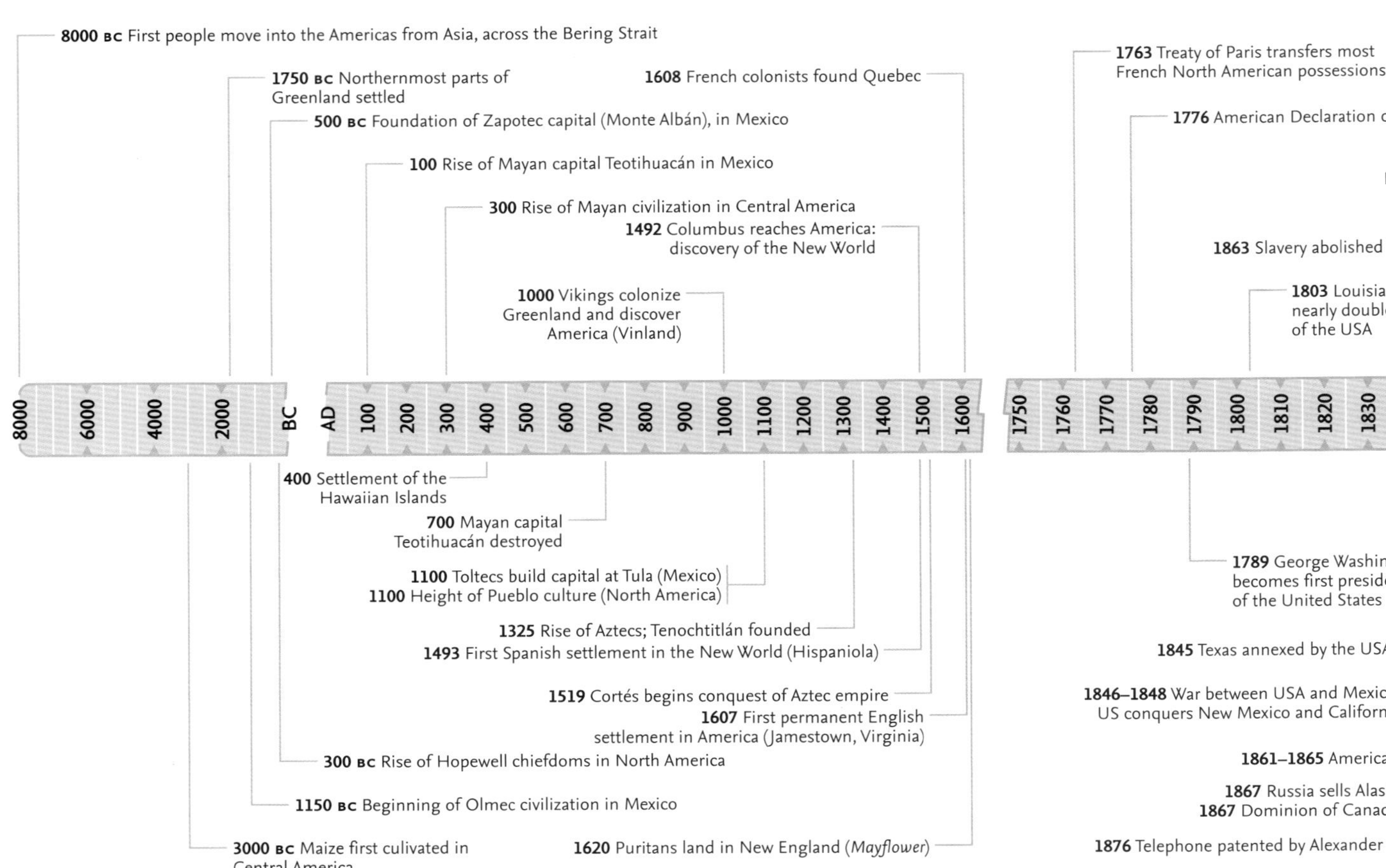

	Population							Economy					
	total population	population change (%)	urban population (%)	total fertility	population by age 0-14 (%)	60+ (%)	2050 projected population	total Gross National Income (GNI) (US$M)	Gross National Income (GNI) per capita (US$)	debt service ratio (% GNI)	total debt service (US$)	aid receipts (% GNI)	military spending (% GDP)
World	**6 464 750 000**	1.2	**48.3**	**2.7**	**28.2**	10.4	9 075 903 000	**34 491 458**	**5 500**	...		...	**2.4**
Antigua and Barbuda	81 000	1.3	37.7	...	...	...	112 000	719	9 160	...		2.0	...
The Bahamas	323 000	1.4	89.5	2.3	28.3	9.3	466 000	4 684	15 110	...		...	...
Barbados	270 000	0.3	51.7	1.5	18.9	13.2	255 000	2 512	9 270	...		0.1	...
Belize	270 000	2.2	48.3	3.2	36.8	5.9	442 000	807	3 190	22.7	188 000 000	2.7	...
Canada	32 268 000	1.0	80.4	1.5	17.6	17.9	42 844 000	756 770	23 930	...		...	1.1
Costa Rica	4 327 000	1.9	60.6	2.3	28.4	8.3	6 426 000	17 157	4 280	4.1	670 000 000	0.0	...
Cuba	11 269 000	0.3	75.6	1.6	19.1	15.3	9 749 000	...	...	...		...	...
Dominica	79 000	0.3	72.0	...	...	...	98 000	239	3 360	4.8	11 100 000	12.9	...
Dominican Republic	8 895 000	1.5	59.3	2.7	32.7	6.2	12 668 000	18 078	2 070	3.3	670 600 000	0.7	...
El Salvador	6 881 000	1.8	59.6	2.9	34.0	7.6	10 823 000	14 387	2 200	3.2	453 300 000	1.7	0.8
Grenada	103 000	0.3	40.7	...	...	...	157 000	396	3 790	6.8	25 600 000	2.6	...
Guatemala	12 599 000	2.4	46.3	4.6	43.2	6.1	25 612 000	23 486	1 910	1.8	412 000 000	1.1	0.6
Haiti	8 528 000	1.4	37.5	4.0	37.5	6.0	12 996 000	3 214	380	0.8	28 000 000	4.7	...
Honduras	7 205 000	2.3	45.6	3.7	39.2	5.6	12 776 000	6 760	970	6.2	396 800 000	6.8	...
Jamaica	2 651 000	0.5	52.1	2.4	31.2	10.2	2 586 000	7 285	2 760	11.6	842 099 968	0.3	...
Mexico	107 029 000	1.3	75.5	2.4	31.0	7.8	139 015 000	637 159	6 230	6.8	43 535 499 264	0.0	0.5
Nicaragua	5 487 000	2.0	57.3	3.3	38.9	4.9	9 371 000	3 989	730	4.0	151 400 000	13.6	1.4
Panama	3 232 000	1.8	57.1	2.7	30.4	8.8	5 093 000	12 681	4 250	13.9	1 677 200 000	0.2	...
St Kitts and Nevis	43 000	1.1	32.2	...	...	...	59 000	321	6 880	12.4	38 200 000	9.2	...
St Lucia	161 000	0.8	30.5	2.2	28.8	9.7	188 000	650	4 050	4.1	26 200 000	5.3	...
St Vincent and the Grenadines	119 000	0.5	58.3	2.3	29.2	8.9	105 000	361	3 300	3.8	13 200 000	1.4	...
Trinidad and Tobago	1 305 000	0.3	75.4	1.6	21.5	10.7	1 230 000	9 538	7 260	3.0	265 300 000	-0.1	...
United States of America	298 213 000	1.0	80.1	2.0	20.8	16.7	394 976 000	10 945 790	37 610	...		...	3.4

Colonial North America after 1713

Decimated by imported diseases, the aboriginal populations of North America lost control over their lands through a long process of displacement. France, Britain, Spain and Russia all claimed some degree of sovereignty over sections of the continent in the eighteenth century. Large European and enslaved African populations supplanted aboriginal peoples in eastern North America, but the European presence elsewhere remained limited at the end of the eighteenth century.

Land ownership
- British-claimed territory to 1763
- French-claimed territory to 1763
- Spanish territory, claimed 1650
- Ceded by France to Britain, 1763
- Ceded by France to Spain, 1763
- Additional Spanish territory by 1775
- Russian territory, claimed c. 1775
- USA from 1783

Colonization routes
- Spanish
- British
- Russian
- French

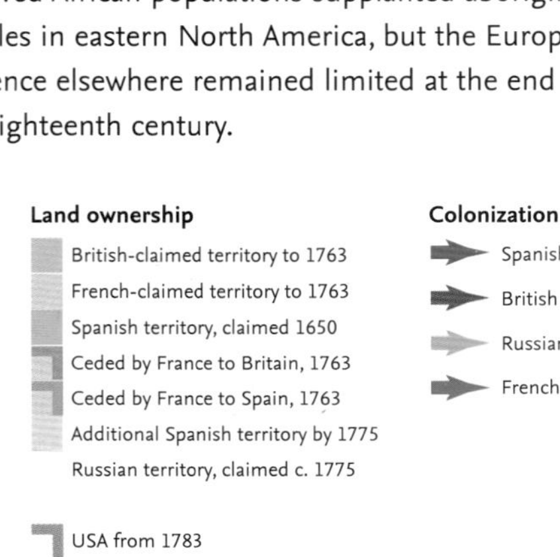

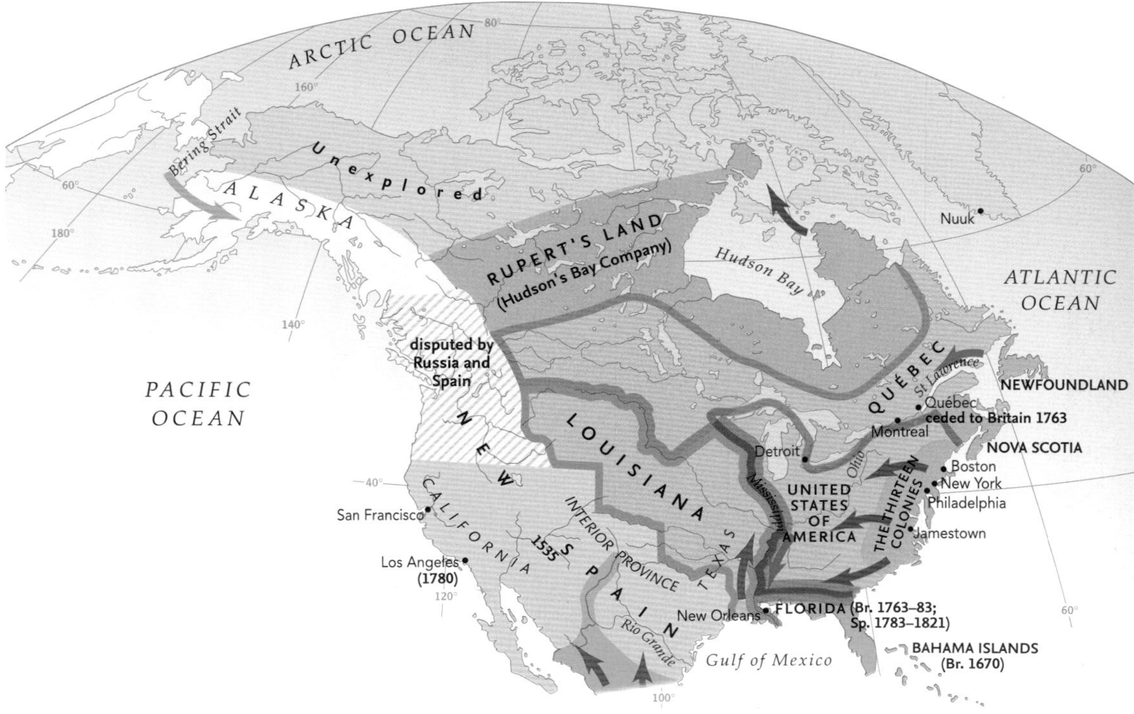

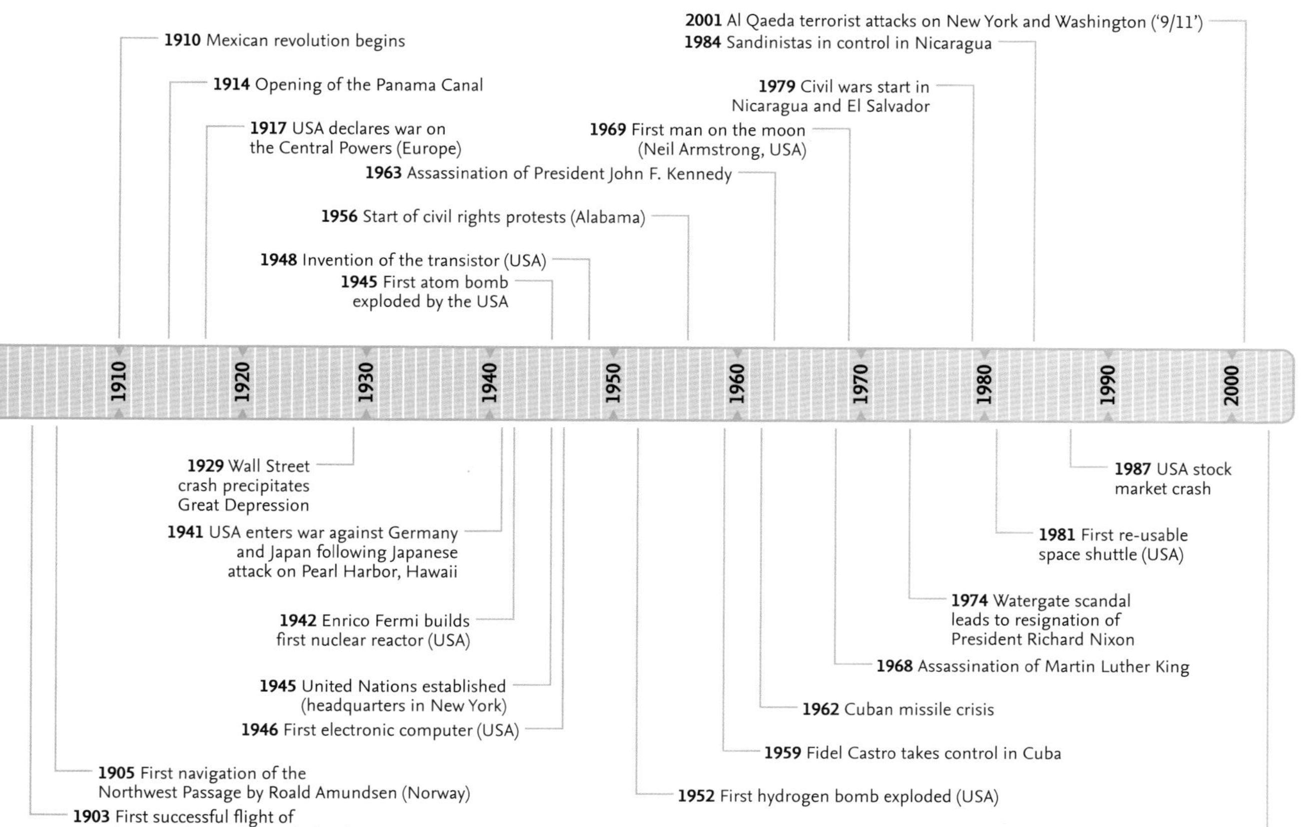

1910 Mexican revolution begins

2001 Al Qaeda terrorist attacks on New York and Washington ('9/11')
1984 Sandinistas in control in Nicaragua

1914 Opening of the Panama Canal

1979 Civil wars start in Nicaragua and El Salvador

1917 USA declares war on the Central Powers (Europe)

1969 First man on the moon (Neil Armstrong, USA)

1963 Assassination of President John F. Kennedy

1956 Start of civil rights protests (Alabama)

1948 Invention of the transistor (USA)

1945 First atom bomb exploded by the USA

1910 1920 1930 1940 1950 1960 1970 1980 1990 2000

1929 Wall Street crash precipitates Great Depression

1987 USA stock market crash

1941 USA enters war against Germany and Japan following Japanese attack on Pearl Harbor, Hawaii

1981 First re-usable space shuttle (USA)

1942 Enrico Fermi builds first nuclear reactor (USA)

1974 Watergate scandal leads to resignation of President Richard Nixon

1945 United Nations established (headquarters in New York)

1968 Assassination of Martin Luther King

1946 First electronic computer (USA)

1962 Cuban missile crisis

1905 First navigation of the Northwest Passage by Roald Amundsen (Norway)

1959 Fidel Castro takes control in Cuba

1903 First successful flight of petrol-powered aircraft (Wright brothers, USA)

1952 First hydrogen bomb exploded (USA)

2003 President George W. Bush declares war on terrorism

Internet links

Organization of American States	www.oas.org
Caribbean Community (CARICOM)	www.caricom.org
Aztec culture	www.aztecempire.com
The Panama Canal	www.pancanal.com
Island nations	islands.unep.ch

Facts

The Panama Canal is approximately 82 kilometres (51 miles) long with three sets of locks and can handle 12 000 ships a year.

The ship *Mayflower* left Plymouth on 6th September 1620 with 102 passengers and made landfall in New England on 11th November.

Guam became the only populated part of the USA to endure foreign occupation during World War II when Japan invaded in 1941.

Teotihuacán was the largest city in the New World with an estimated population of over 60 000.

Social indicators					Environment				Communications					See page 335 for explanatory table and sources
child mortality rate	life expectancy male	life expectancy female	literacy rate (%)	access to safe water (%)	doctors per 100 000 people	forest area (%)	annual change in forest area (%)	protected land area (%)	CO$_2$ emissions (metric tons per capita)	main telephone lines per 100 people	cellular mobile subscribers per 100 people	internet users per 10 000 people	international dialling code	time zone	
80	63.3	67.6	87.3	83	...	29.6	-0.2	11.4	3.8	18.8	21.9	1 125	...	...	World
12	...	...	...	91	105	20.5	...	0.0	4.9	48.8	49.0	1 282	1 268	-4	Antigua and Barbuda
14	63.9	70.3	97.4	97	163	84.1	...	1.7	5.9	41.5	39.0	2 649	1 242	-5	The Bahamas
13	74.5	79.5	...	100	137	4.7	...	0.0	4.4	49.7	51.9	3 708	1 246	-4	Barbados
39	69.9	73.0	98.2	91	102	59.1	-2.3	47.6	3.3	11.3	20.5	1 089	501	-6	Belize
6	76.7	81.9	...	100	187	26.5	...	6.3	14.2	62.9	41.7	5 128	1	-3.5 to -8	Canada
10	75.8	80.6	98.4	97	160	38.5	-0.8	23.5	1.4	25.1	11.1	1 931	506	-6	Costa Rica
8	74.8	78.7	99.8	91	596	21.4	1.3	1.3	2.8	5.1	0.2	107	53	-5	Cuba
14	...	...	...	97	49	61.3	-0.7	25.6	1.4	30.4	12.0	1 603	1 767	-4	Dominica
35	64.4	69.2	91.7	93	190	28.4	...	24.5	3.0	11.5	27.1	640	1 809	-4	Dominican Republic
36	67.7	73.7	89.0	82	126	5.8	-4.6	2.0	1.1	11.6	17.7	844	503	-6	El Salvador
23	...	...	...	95	81	14.7	0.9	0.0	2.1	31.7	7.1	1 690	1 473	-4	Grenada
47	63.0	68.9	80.3	95	109	26.3	-1.7	23.2	0.9	7.1	13.2	333	502	-6	Guatemala
118	49.0	50.0	66.2	71	25	3.2	-5.7	0.3	0.2	1.6	1.7	96	509	-5	Haiti
41	66.5	71.4	84.2	90	87	48.1	-1.0	20.8	0.7	4.8	4.9	252	504	-6	Honduras
20	73.7	77.8	94.5	93	85	30.0	-1.5	15.9	4.2	16.9	53.3	2 285	1 876	-5	Jamaica
28	70.4	76.4	97.2	91	156	28.9	-1.1	5.0	4.3	14.7	25.5	1 185	52	-6 to -8	Mexico
38	67.2	71.9	72.3	81	62	27.0	-3.0	21.9	0.7	3.2	3.8	168	505	-6	Nicaragua
24	72.3	77.4	97.0	91	121	38.6	-1.6	17.5	2.2	12.9	26.8	414	507	-5	Panama
22	...	...	...	99	117	11.1	-0.6	0.1	2.4	50.0	10.6	2 128	1 869	-4	St Kitts and Nevis
18	70.8	74.1	...	98	58	14.8	-4.9	13.8	2.1	32.0	9.0	824	1 758	-4	St Lucia
27	72.6	75.6	...	93	88	15.4	-1.4	11.1	1.4	23.4	8.5	598	1 784	-4	St Vincent and the Grenadines
20	68.4	74.4	99.8	91	75	50.5	-0.8	4.8	20.5	25.0	27.8	1 060	1 868	-4	Trinidad and Tobago
8	74.3	79.9	...	100	279	24.7	0.2	15.8	19.8	62.1	54.3	5 514	1	-5 to -10	United States of America

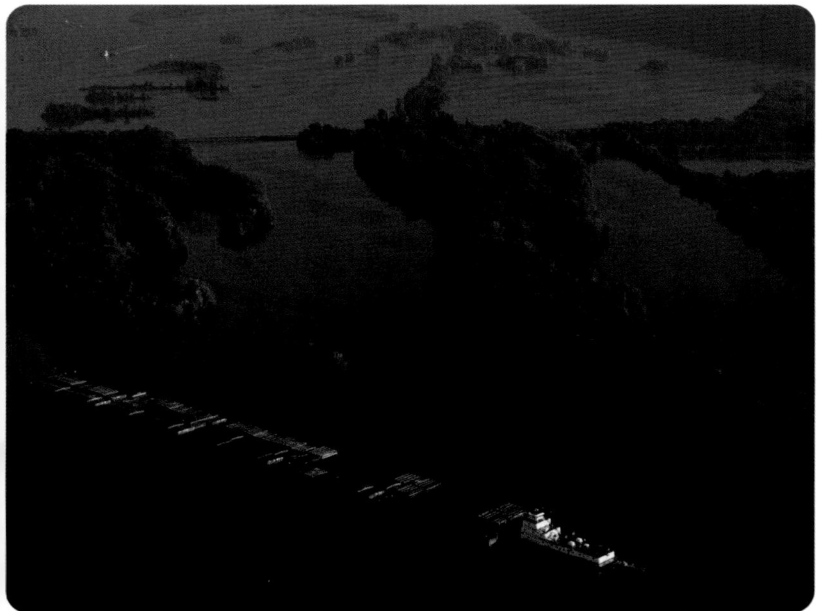

The **Mississippi**, part of the large Mississippi-Missouri river system, has featured heavily in the exploration, settlement and development of trade in the USA.

USA land transfers and expansion of settlement

In 1783 the fledgling nation of the United States of America extended from the Atlantic coast to the Mississippi river. Its territory was enlarged in just two great spates of expansion. During the first (1803–1819), three Virginian presidents acquired Louisiana and East and West Florida. During the second (1845–1853), Texas, Oregon, California and the remainder of the southwest were added, thereby completing the area occupied by the forty-eight contiguous states today.

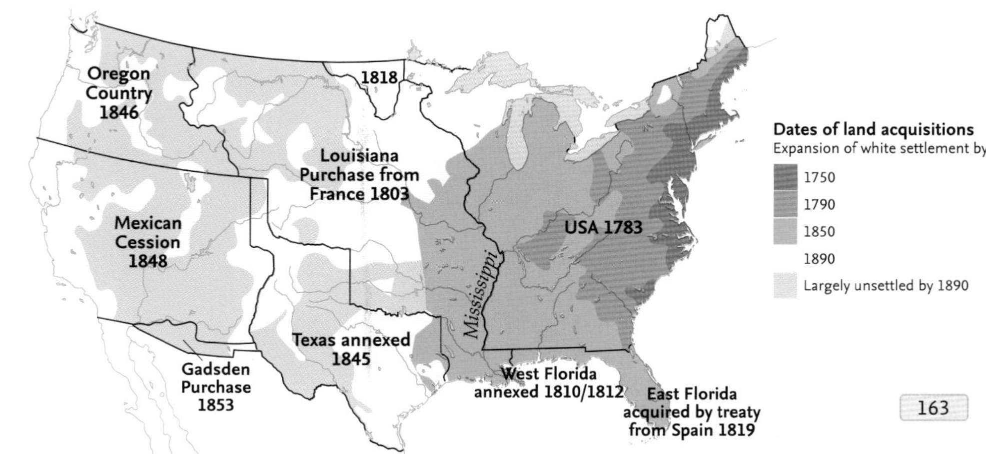

Oregon Country 1846

1818

Louisiana Purchase from France 1803

Mexican Cession 1848

USA 1783

Mississippi

Dates of land acquisitions
Expansion of white settlement by:
- 1750
- 1790
- 1850
- 1890
- Largely unsettled by 1890

Gadsden Purchase 1853

Texas annexed 1845

West Florida annexed 1810/1812

East Florida acquired by treaty from Spain 1819

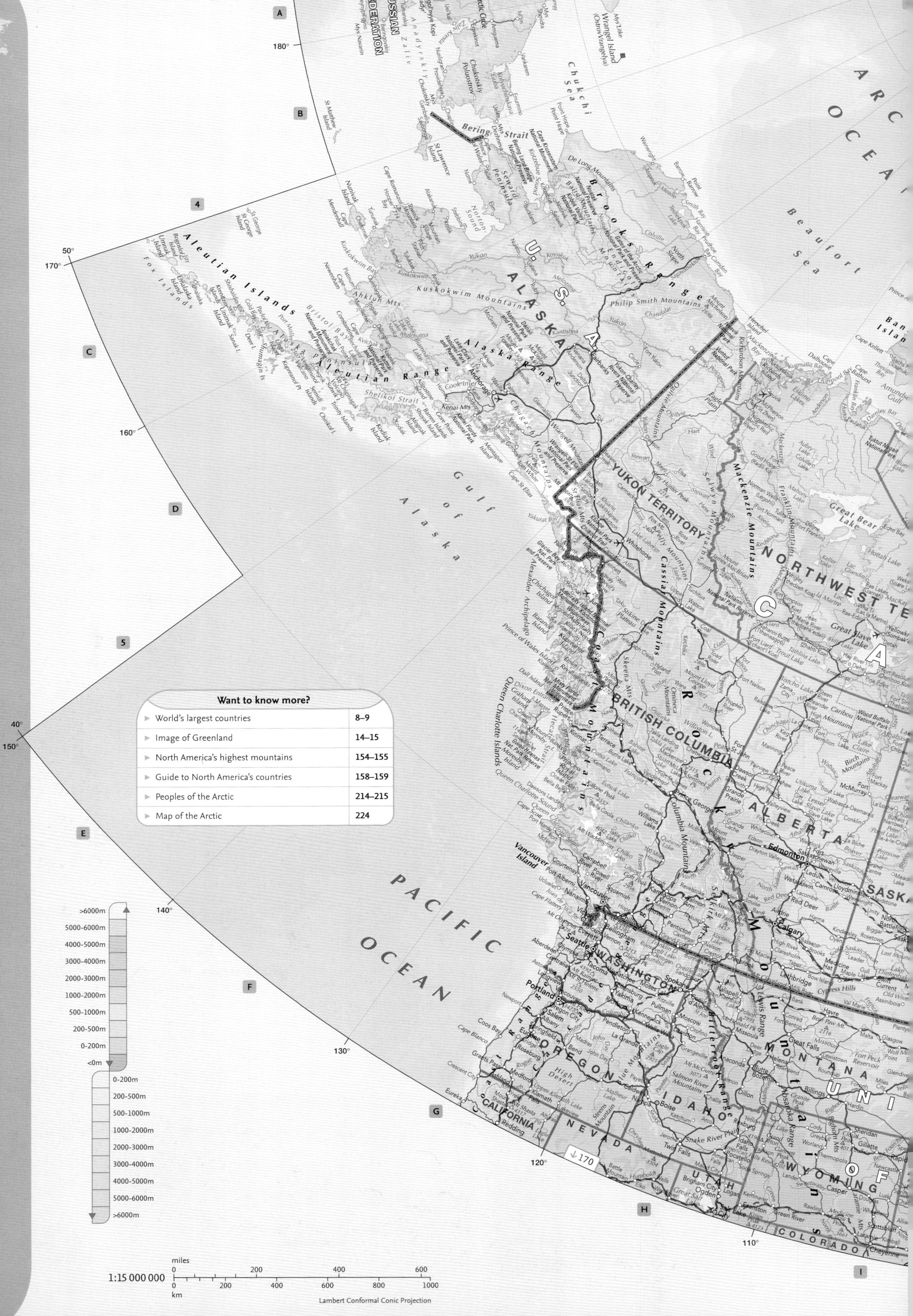

1:15 000 000

Lambert Conformal Conic Projection

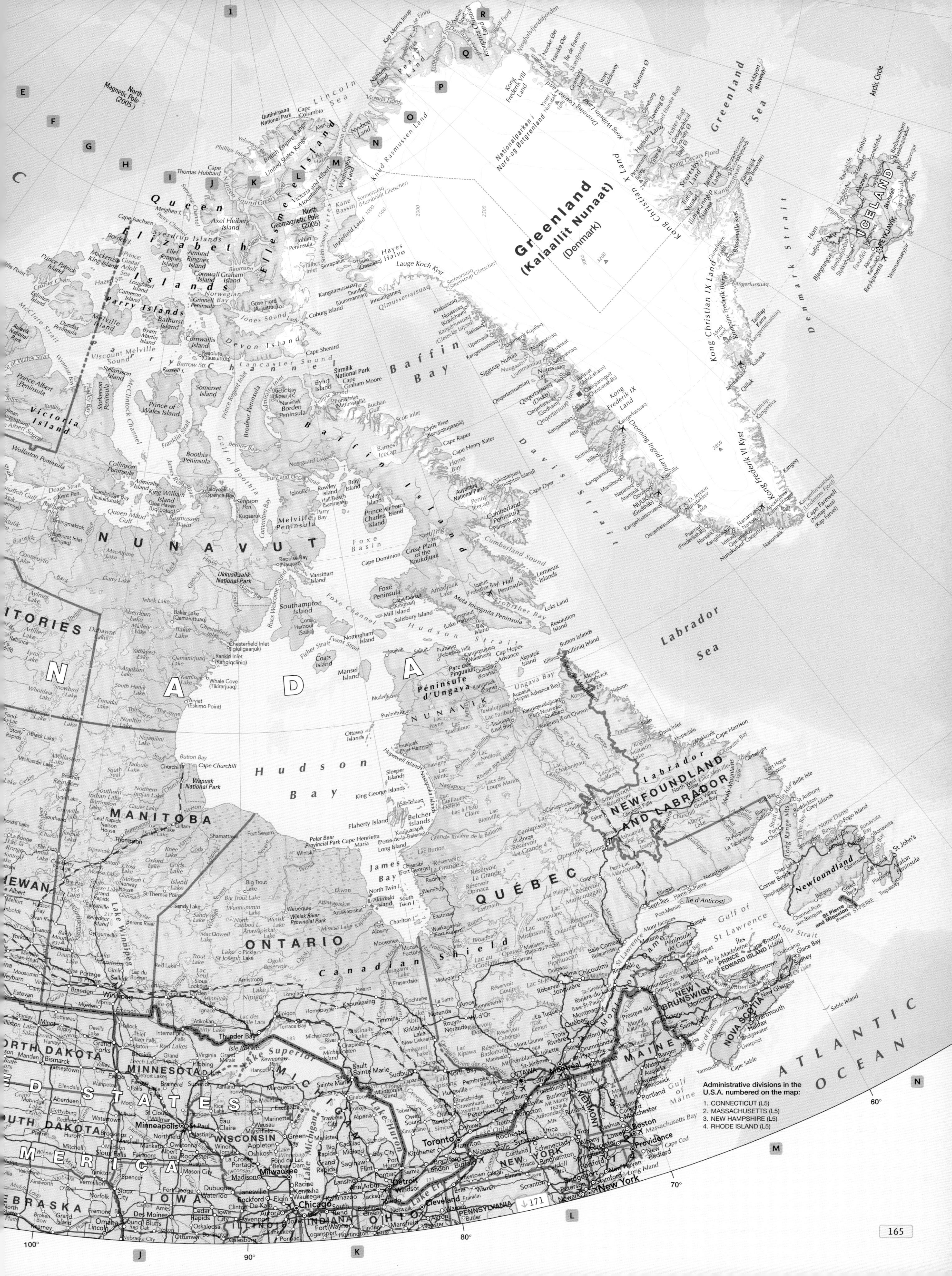
Greenland
(Kalaallit Nunaat)
(Denmark)
ICELAND
REYKJAVÍK
Greenland Sea
Denmark Strait
Labrador Sea
Baffin Bay
Davis Strait
Hudson Bay
Hudson Strait
Foxe Basin
James Bay
Lincoln Sea
ATLANTIC OCEAN
Queen Elizabeth Islands
Ellesmere Island
Baffin Island
Victoria Island
Devon Island
Axel Heiberg Island
Southampton Island
Arctic Circle
North Magnetic Pole (2005)
North Geomagnetic Pole (2005)
NUNAVUT
MANITOBA
ONTARIO
QUÉBEC
NEWFOUNDLAND AND LABRADOR
NEW BRUNSWICK
NOVA SCOTIA
PRINCE EDWARD ISLAND
Newfoundland
Gulf of St Lawrence
Canadian Shield
Péninsule d'Ungava
NUNAVIK
Lake Superior
Lake Michigan
Lake Huron
Lake Winnipeg
NORTH DAKOTA
SOUTH DAKOTA
MINNESOTA
WISCONSIN
MICHIGAN
IOWA
ILLINOIS
INDIANA
OHIO
PENNSYLVANIA
NEW YORK
VERMONT
MAINE
NEBRASKA
OTTAWA
Montréal
Québec
Toronto
Winnipeg
Chicago
Detroit
Boston
New York
Minneapolis
Milwaukee
Cleveland
Halifax
St John's
NUUK (Godthåb)
St Pierre and Miquelon (France)
Administrative divisions in the U.S.A. numbered on the map:
1. CONNECTICUT (L5)
2. MASSACHUSETTS (L5)
3. NEW HAMPSHIRE (L5)
4. RHODE ISLAND (L5)
↓171
60°
70°
80°
90°
100°

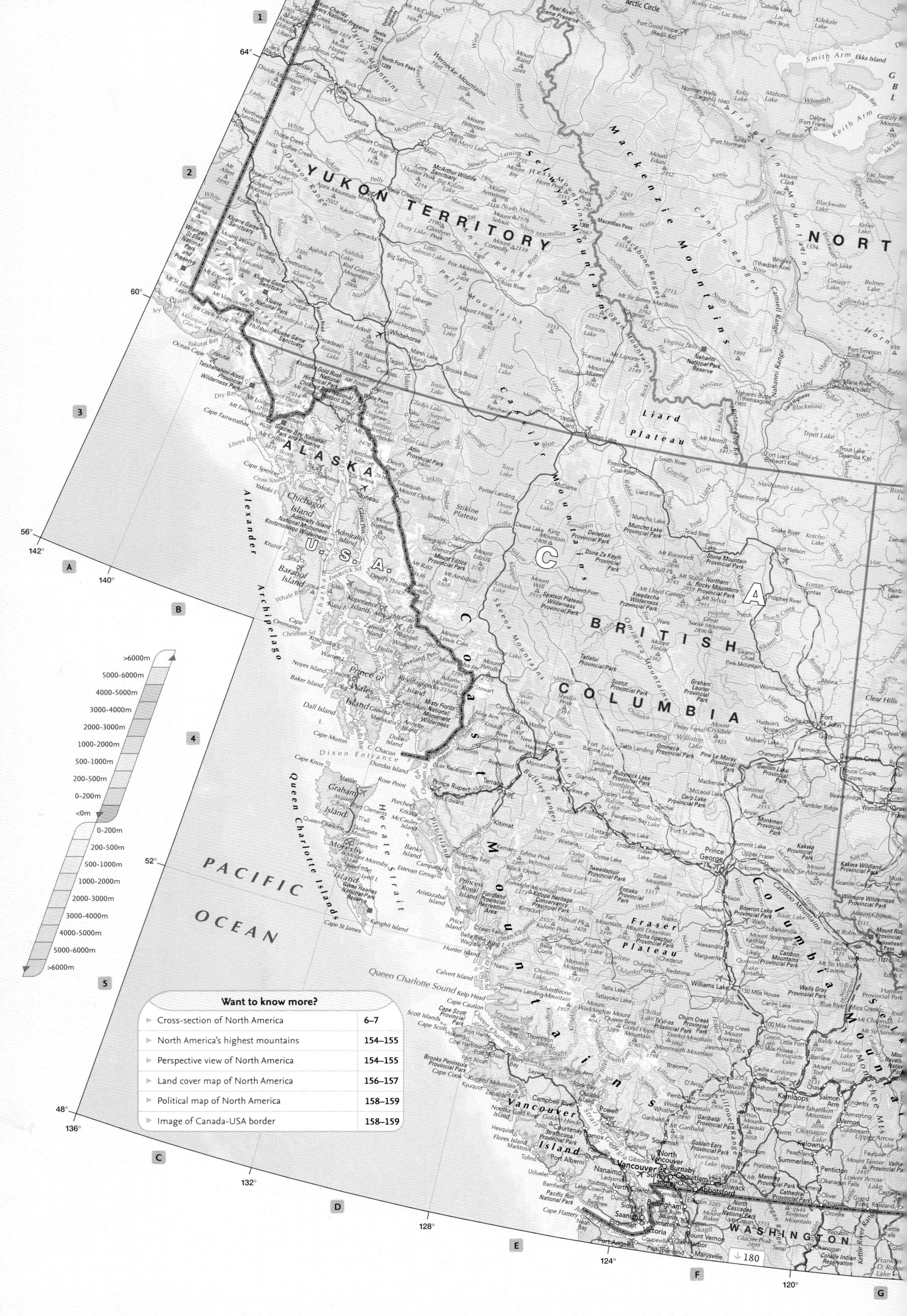

Want to know more?

>6000m
5000-6000m
4000-5000m
3000-4000m
2000-3000m
1000-2000m
500-1000m
200-500m
0-200m
<0m

0-200m
200-500m
500-1000m
1000-2000m
2000-3000m
3000-4000m
4000-5000m
5000-6000m
>6000m

↑164

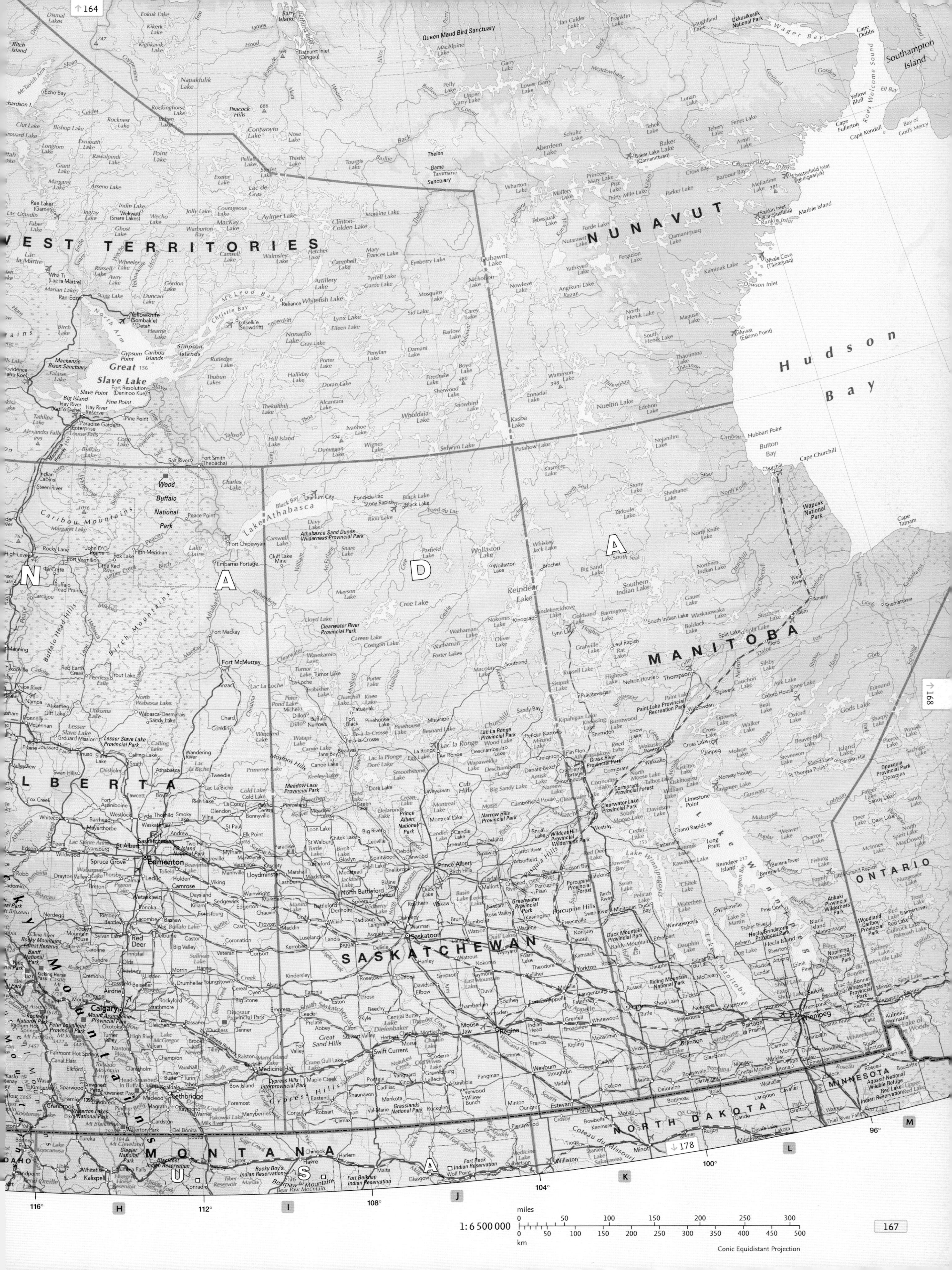
NUNAVUT
WEST TERRITORIES
Hudson Bay
Southampton Island
Wager Bay
Queen Maud Bird Sanctuary
Thelon Game Sanctuary
Great Slave Lake
Yellowknife
Wood Buffalo National Park
Lake Athabasca
Caribou Mountains
Birch Mountains
Reindeer Lake
Cree Lake
Wollaston Lake
Churchill
Wapusk National Park
MANITOBA
SASKATCHEWAN
ALBERTA
ONTARIO
Lake Winnipeg
Lake Winnipegosis
Lake Manitoba
Lake of the Woods
Edmonton
Calgary
Red Deer
Lethbridge
Medicine Hat
Saskatoon
Regina
Moose Jaw
Prince Albert
North Battleford
Swift Current
Brandon
Winnipeg
Thompson
Fort McMurray
Rocky Mountains
Banff National Park
MONTANA
NORTH DAKOTA
MINNESOTA
U.S.A.
CANADA
116°
112°
108°
104°
100°
96°
H
I
J
K
L
M
1:6 500 000
miles
0 50 100 150 200 250 300
km
0 50 100 150 200 250 300 350 400 450 500
Conic Equidistant Projection

→168
↓178

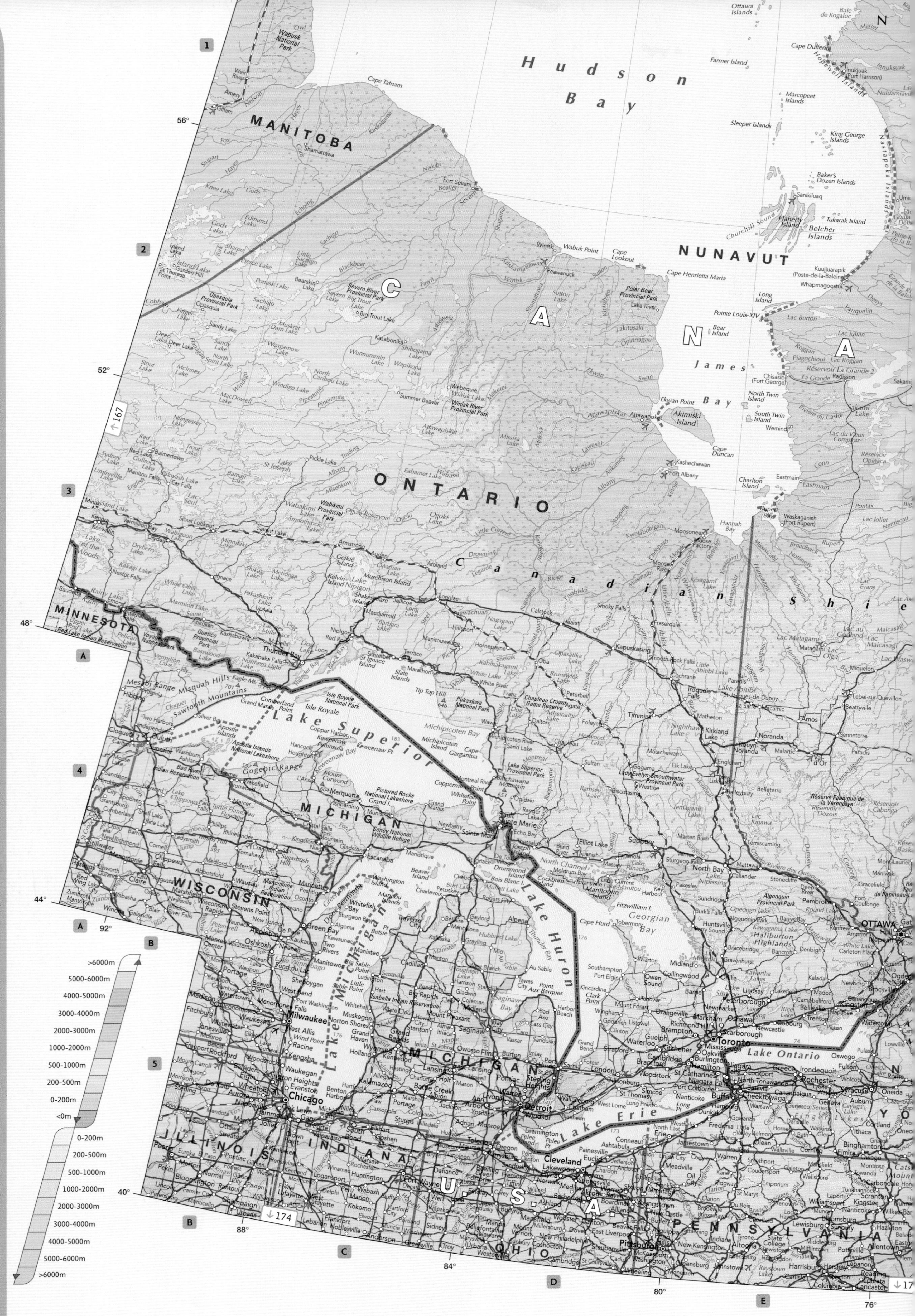

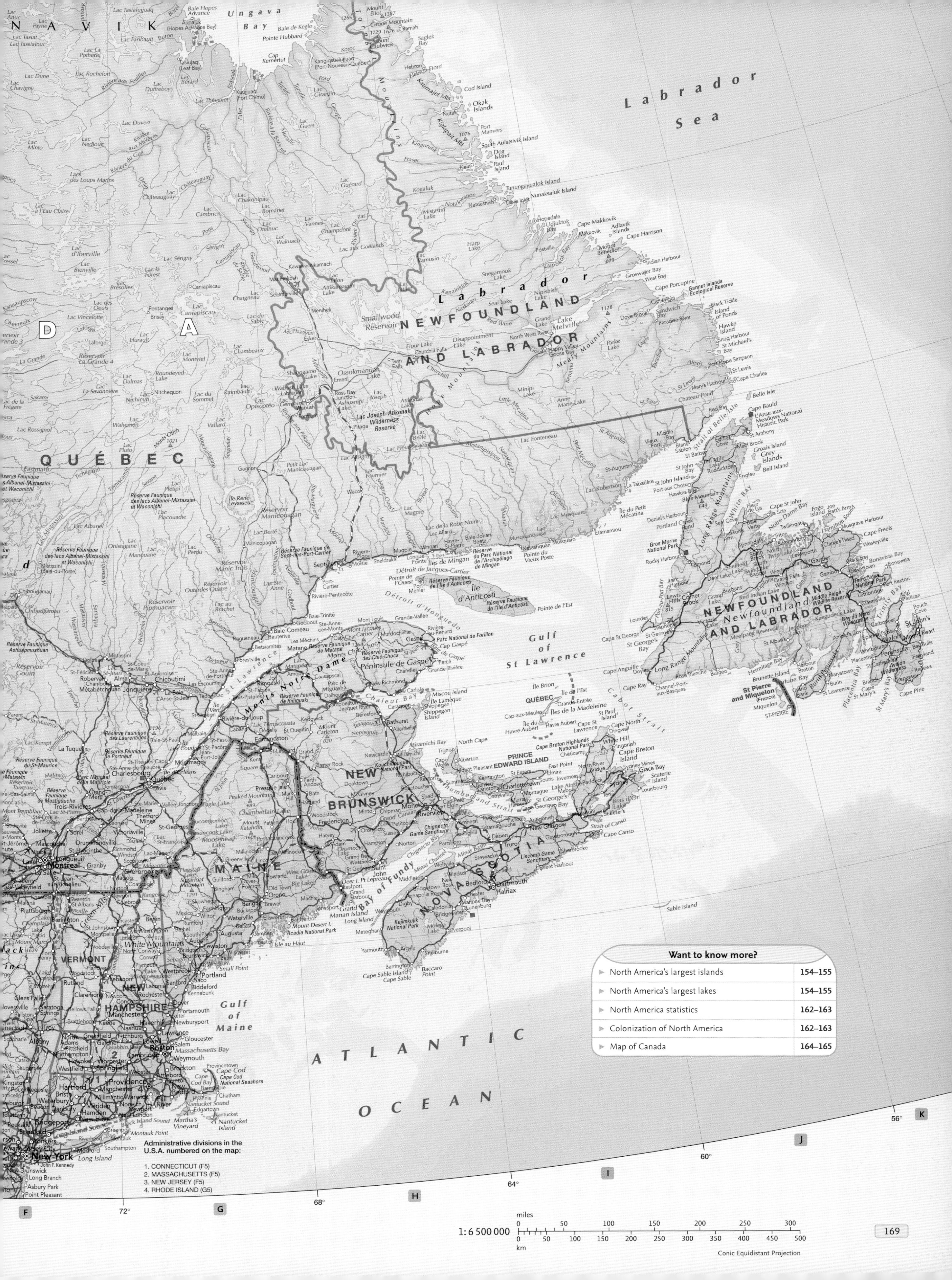

Want to know more?

Administrative divisions in the U.S.A. numbered on the map:
1. CONNECTICUT (F5)
2. MASSACHUSETTS (F5)
3. NEW JERSEY (F5)
4. RHODE ISLAND (G5)

miles
0   50   100   150   200   250   300

1 : 6 500 000
0   50 100 150 200 250 300 350 400 450 500
km

Conic Equidistant Projection

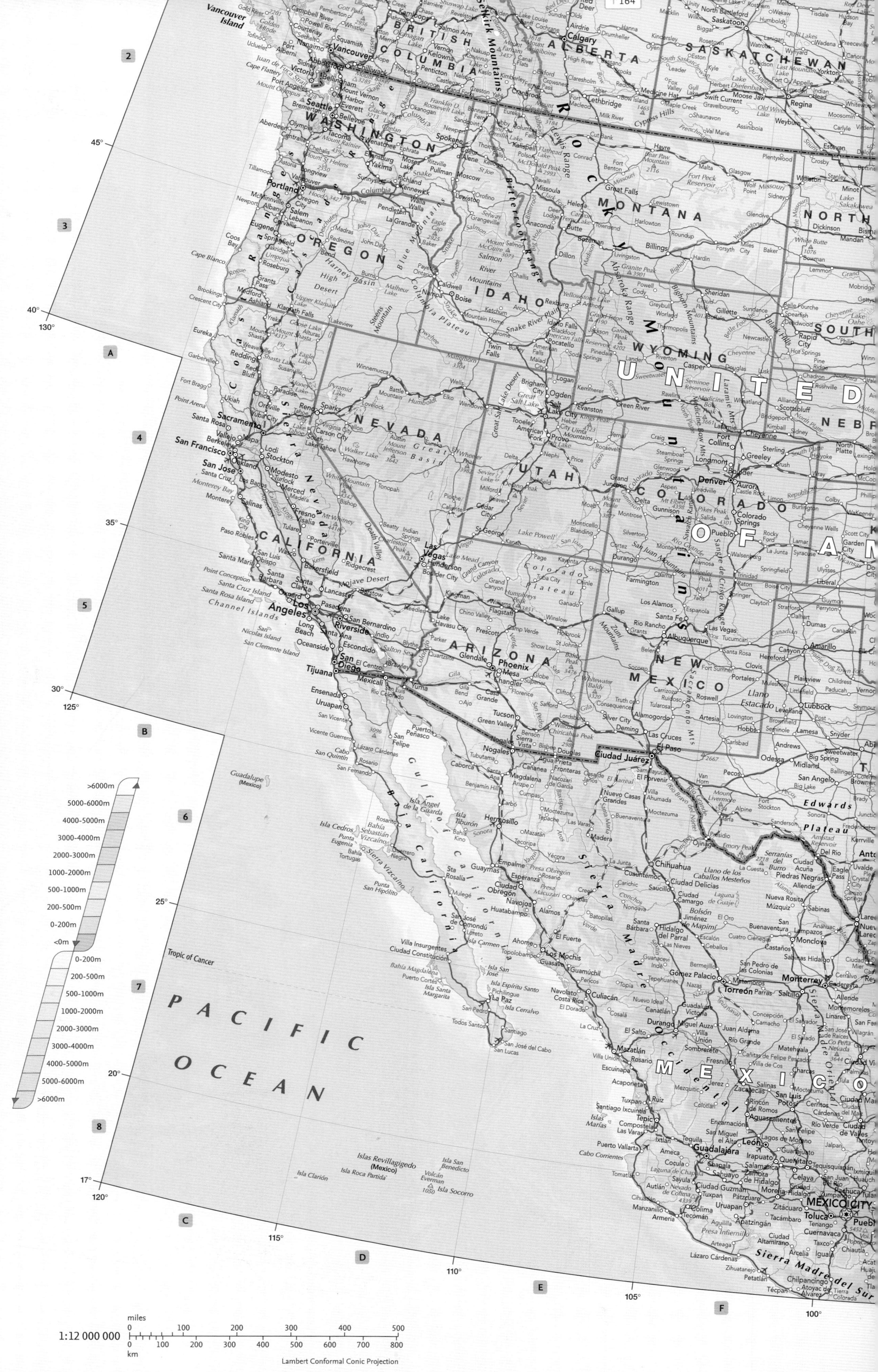

North America United States of America

miles
0 100 200 300 400 500

1:12 000 000

km
0 100 200 300 400 500 600 700 800

Lambert Conformal Conic Projection

Elevation scale:
>6000m
5000-6000m
4000-5000m
3000-4000m
2000-3000m
1000-2000m
500-1000m
200-500m
0-200m
<0m
0-200m
200-500m
500-1000m
1000-2000m
2000-3000m
3000-4000m
4000-5000m
5000-6000m
>6000m

PACIFIC OCEAN

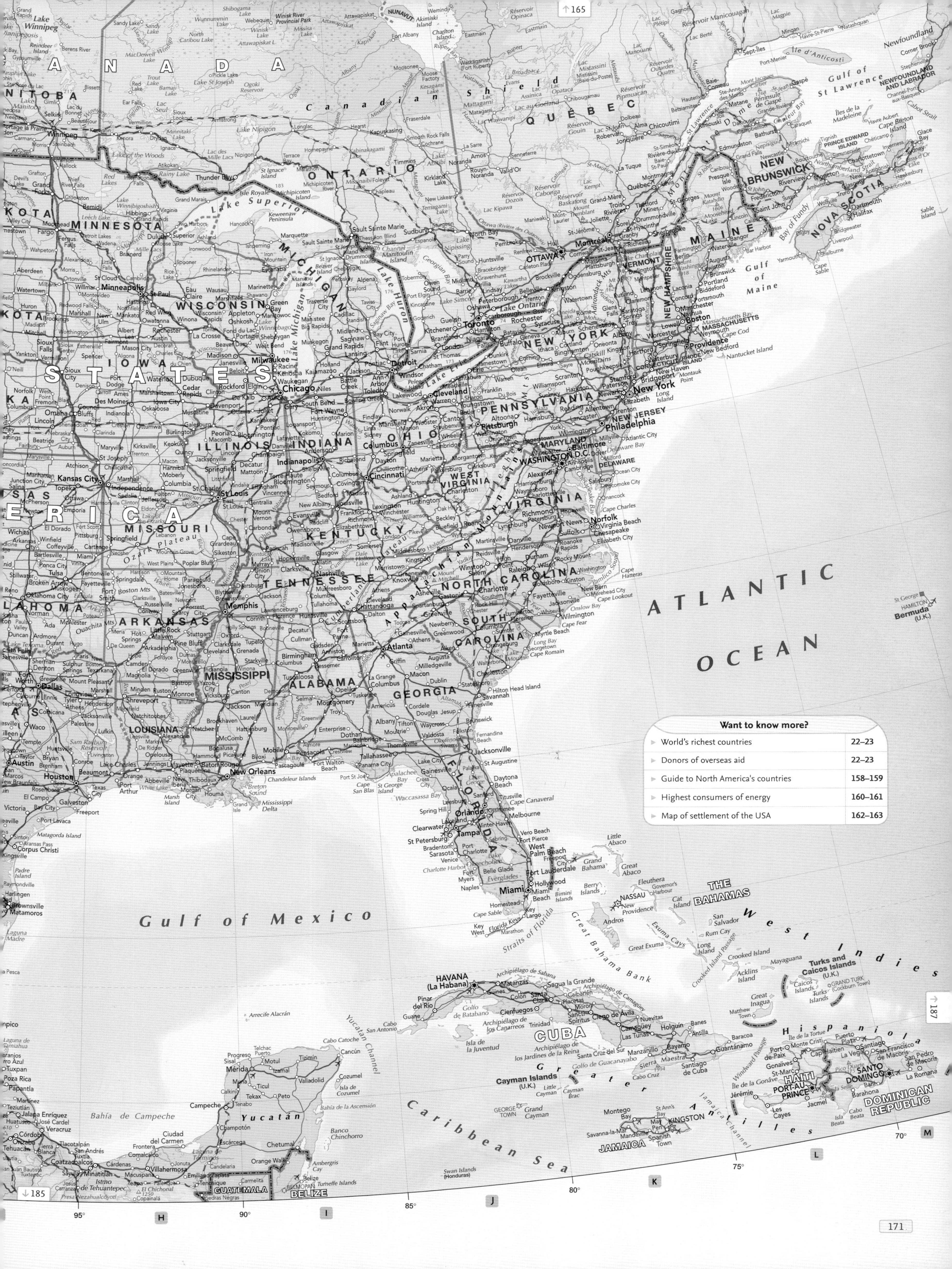

Want to know more?

▶ World's richest countries	22–23
▶ Donors of overseas aid	22–23
▶ Guide to North America's countries	158–159
▶ Highest consumers of energy	160–161
▶ Map of settlement of the USA	162–163

Want to know more?

>6000m
5000-6000m
4000-5000m
3000-4000m
2000-3000m
1500-2000m
1000-1500m
500-1000m
200-500m
100-200m
0-100m
<0m

0-50m
50-100m
100-200m
200-500m
500-1000m
1000-2000m
2000-3000m
3000-4000m
4000-5000m
5000-6000m
>6000m

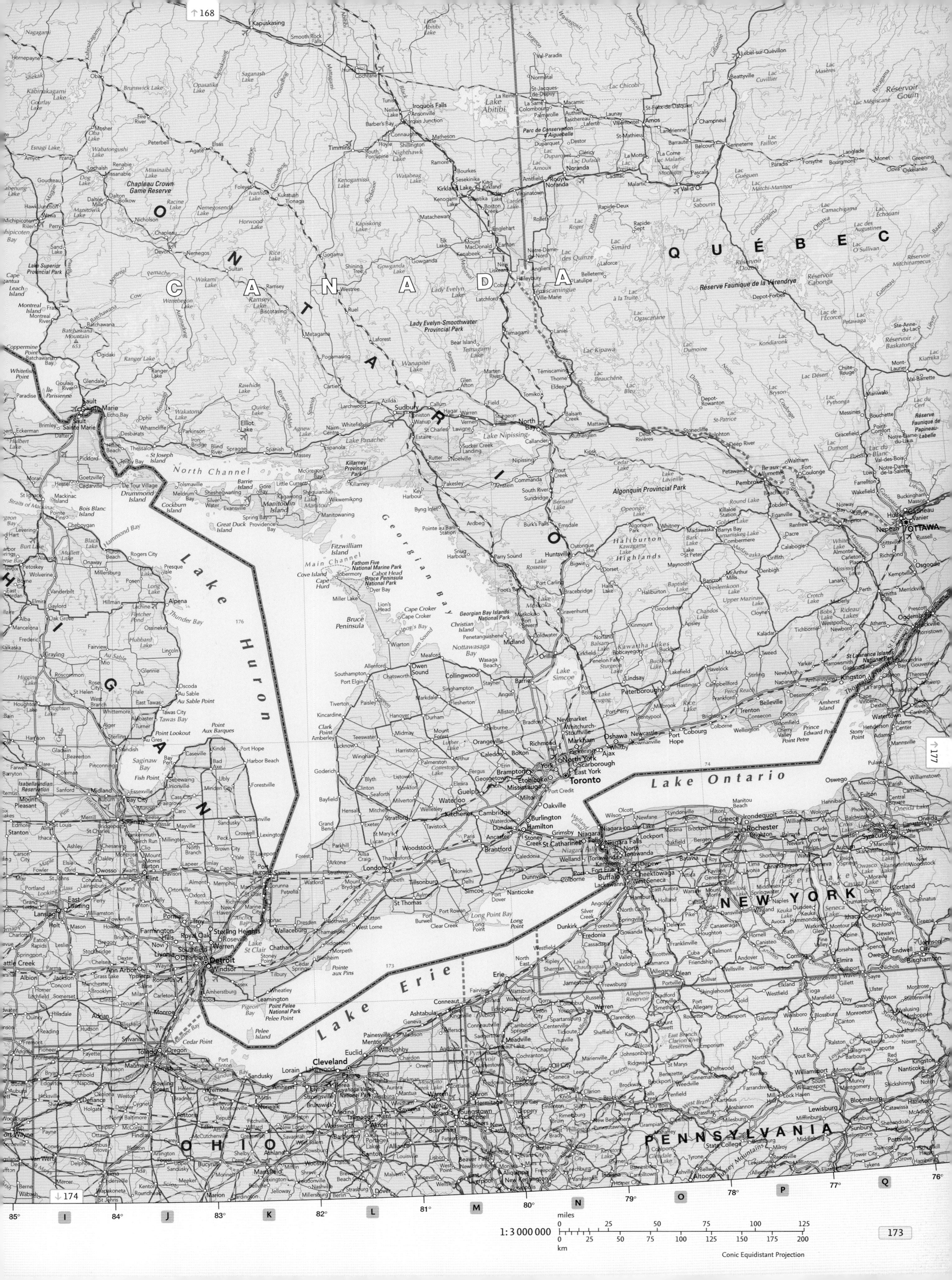

168
C A N A D A
O N T A R I O
Q U É B E C
M I C H I G A N
NEW YORK
PENNSYLVANIA
OHIO
Lake Huron
Lake Ontario
Lake Erie
Georgian Bay
North Channel
Lake St Clair
Lake Nipissing
Lake Simcoe
Lake Abitibi
Saginaw Bay
Thunder Bay
Long Point Bay
Algonquin Provincial Park
Chapleau Crown Game Reserve
Lady Evelyn-Smoothwater Provincial Park
Réserve Faunique de la Vérendrye
Haliburton Highlands
Georgian Bay Islands National Park
Fathom Five National Marine Park
Bruce Peninsula National Park
Point Pelee National Park
OTTAWA
Toronto
Detroit
Cleveland
Buffalo
Rochester
Hamilton
Sudbury
North Bay
Sault Sainte Marie
Windsor
London
Kingston
Syracuse
Erie
Toledo
Flint
Lansing
Saginaw
Timmins
Rouyn-Noranda
Val-d'Or
177
174
85° 84° 83° 82° 81° 80° 79° 78° 77° 76°
I J K L M N O P Q
1: 3 000 000
miles 0 25 50 75 100 125
km 0 25 50 75 100 125 150 175 200
Conic Equidistant Projection

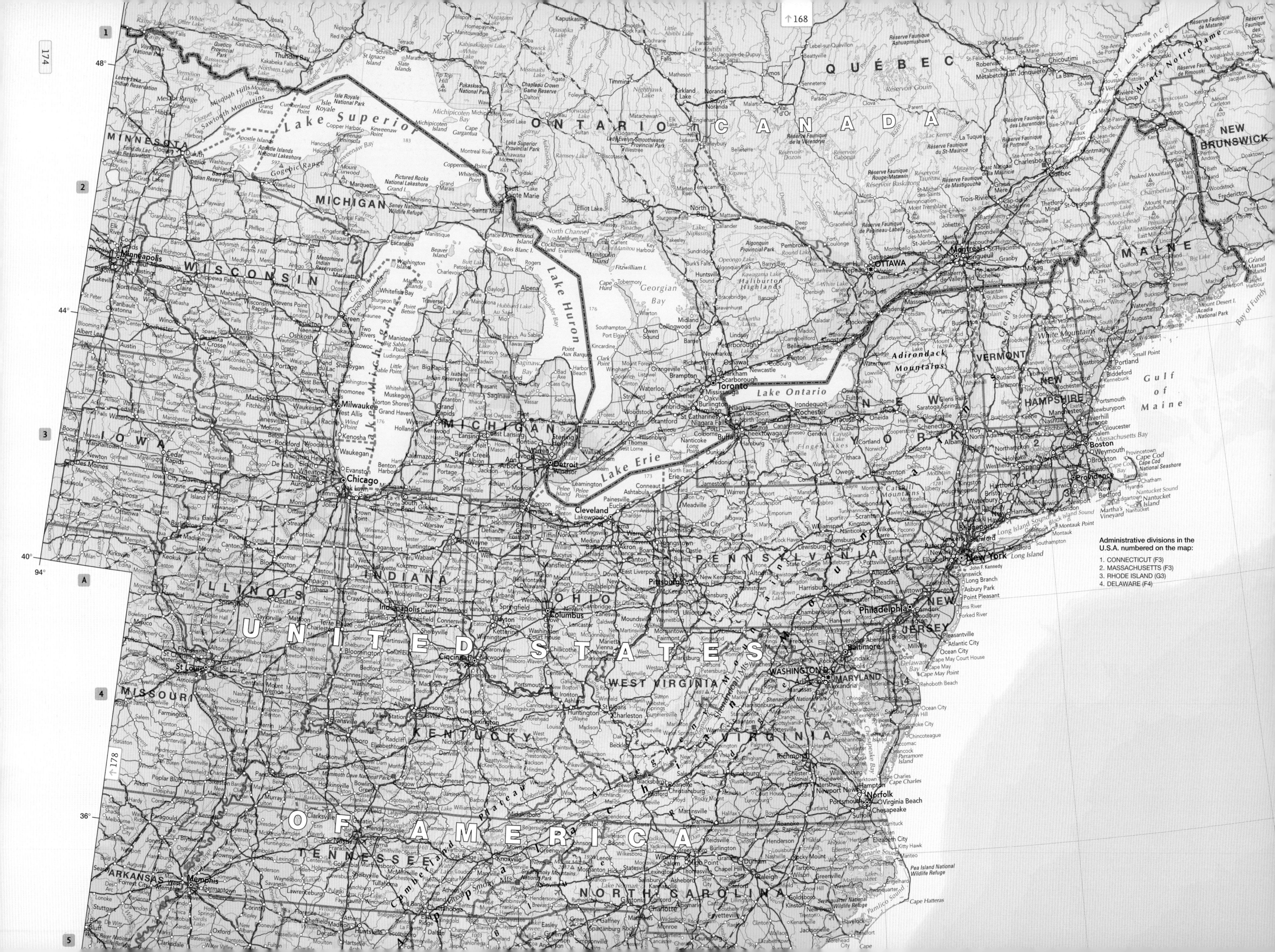

CANADA
ONTARIO
QUÉBEC
NEW BRUNSWICK
UNITED STATES OF AMERICA
MINNESOTA
WISCONSIN
MICHIGAN
IOWA
ILLINOIS
INDIANA
OHIO
MISSOURI
KENTUCKY
TENNESSEE
ARKANSAS
WEST VIRGINIA
VIRGINIA
NORTH CAROLINA
PENNSYLVANIA
NEW YORK
NEW JERSEY
MARYLAND
VERMONT
NEW HAMPSHIRE
MAINE
Lake Superior
Lake Michigan
Lake Huron
Lake Erie
Lake Ontario
Georgian Bay
Gulf of Maine
Bay of Fundy
OTTAWA
WASHINGTON D.C.
Administrative divisions in the U.S.A. numbered on the map:
1. CONNECTICUT (F3)
2. MASSACHUSETTS (F3)
3. RHODE ISLAND (G3)
4. DELAWARE (F4)

↑168
↑178

Want to know more?

1 : 6 500 000

Lambert Conformal Conic Projection

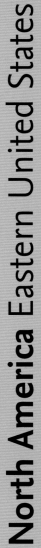

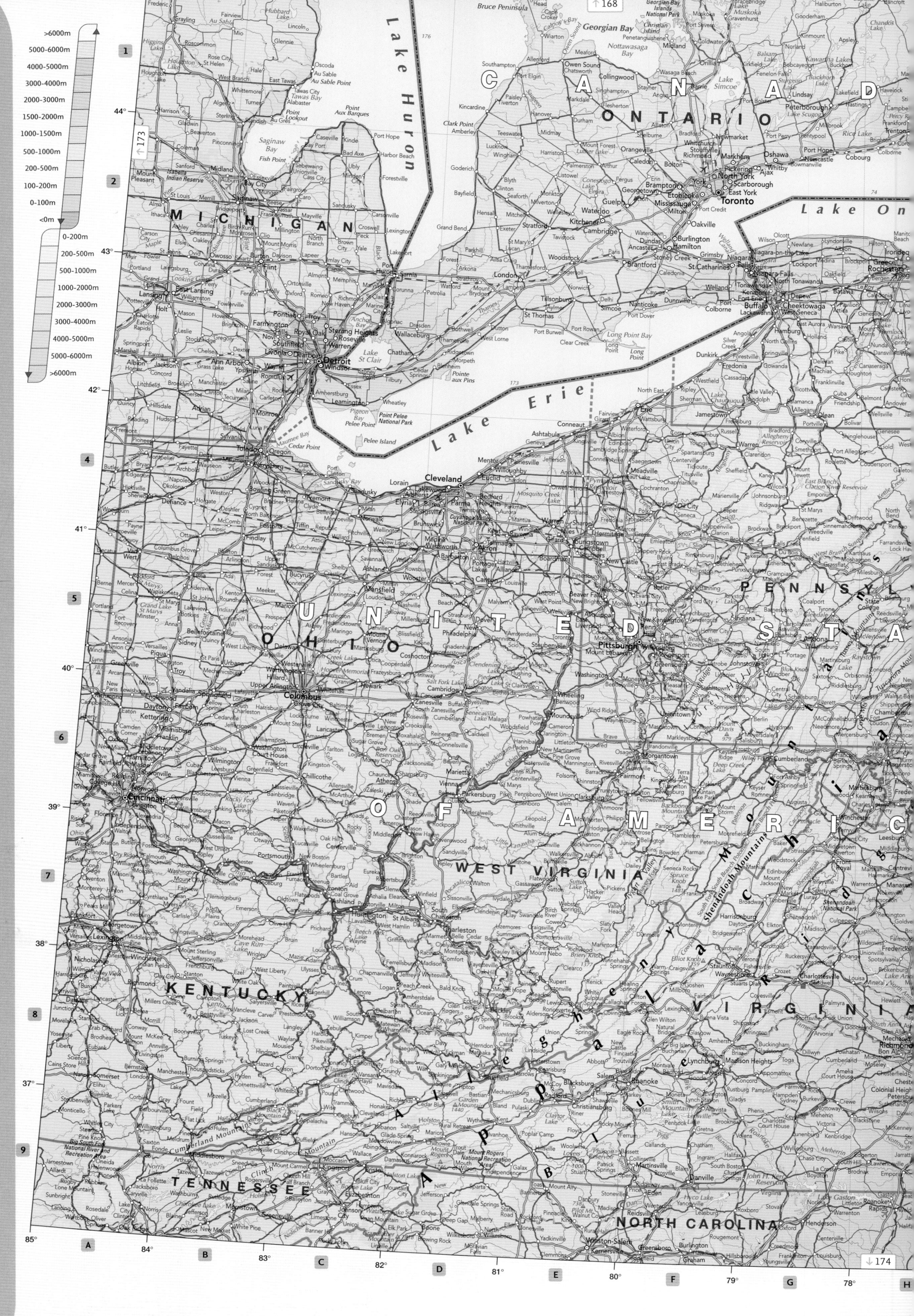
>6000m
5000-6000m
4000-5000m
3000-4000m
2000-3000m
1500-2000m
1000-1500m
500-1000m
200-500m
100-200m
0-100m
<0m
0-200m
200-500m
500-1000m
1000-2000m
2000-3000m
3000-4000m
4000-5000m
5000-6000m
>6000m
↑168
↑173
↓174
174
CANADA
ONTARIO
Lake Huron
Lake Ontario
Lake Erie
Georgian Bay
Toronto
Detroit
Cleveland
Pittsburgh
Columbus
Cincinnati
MICHIGAN
OHIO
UNITED STATES OF AMERICA
PENNSYLVANIA
WEST VIRGINIA
VIRGINIA
KENTUCKY
TENNESSEE
NORTH CAROLINA
Appalachian Mountains
Allegheny Mountains
Blue Ridge
44°
43°
42°
41°
40°
39°
38°
37°
85°
84°
83°
82°
81°
80°
79°
78°
A
B
C
D
E
F
G
H
1
2
4
5
6
7
8
9

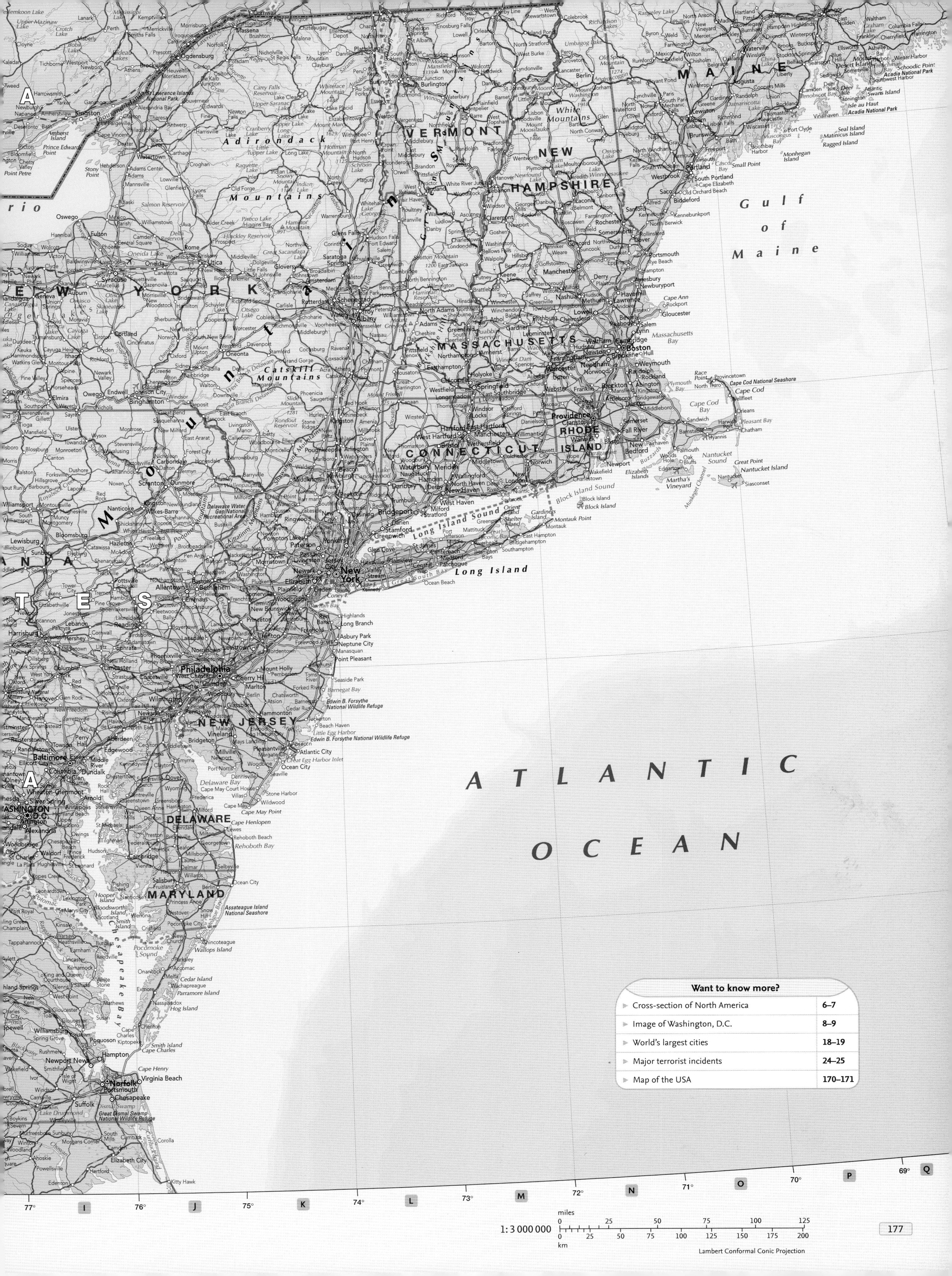

ATLANTIC

OCEAN

Gulf
of
Maine

MAINE

VERMONT

NEW
HAMPSHIRE

MASSACHUSETTS

RHODE
ISLAND

CONNECTICUT

NEW YORK

Long Island Sound

Long Island

NEW JERSEY

PENNSYLVANIA

DELAWARE

MARYLAND

Chesapeake Bay

miles

1:3 000 000

km

Lambert Conformal Conic Projection

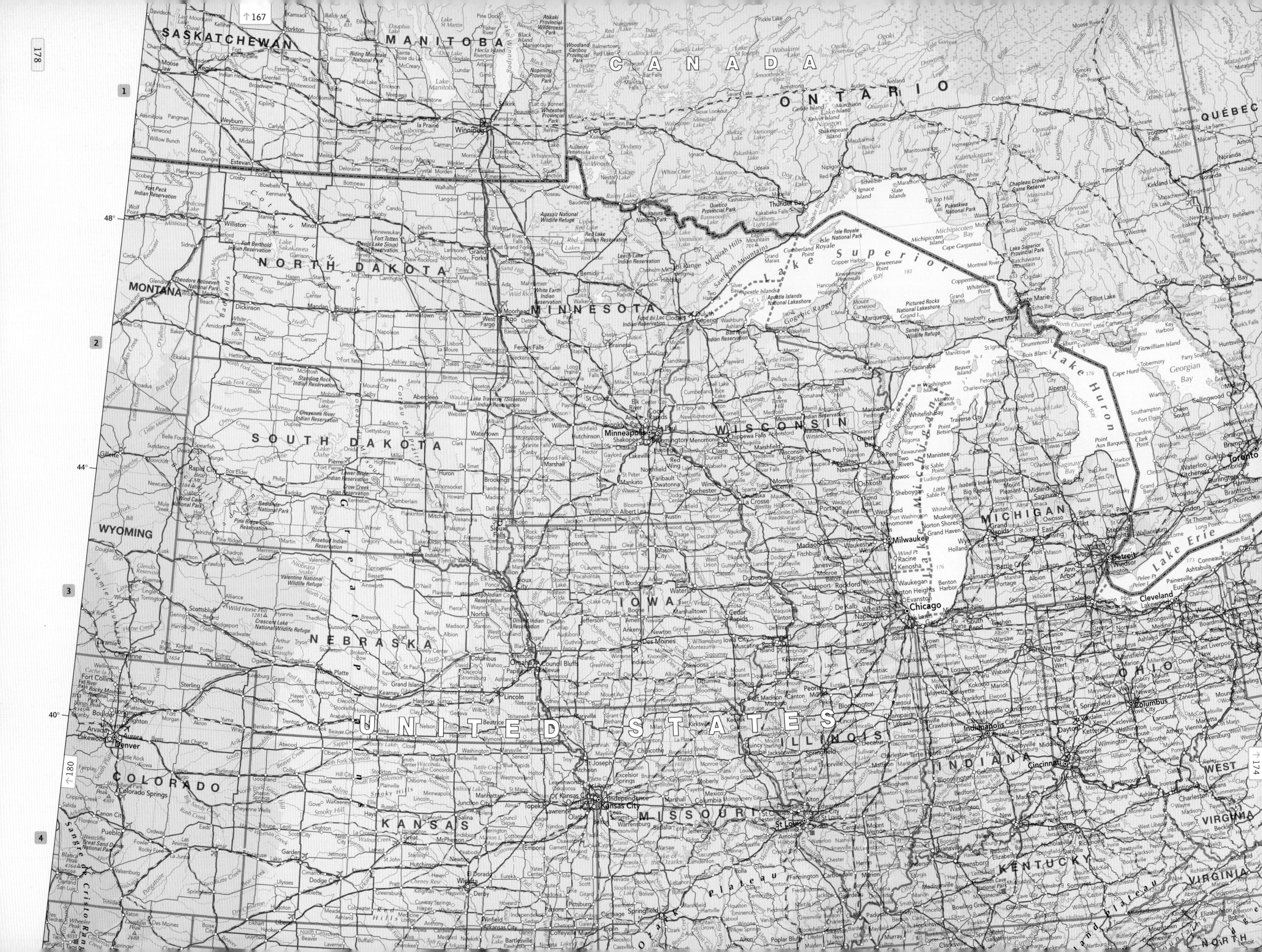

CANADA
ONTARIO
QUÉBEC
MANITOBA
SASKATCHEWAN
UNITED STATES
NORTH DAKOTA
SOUTH DAKOTA
MINNESOTA
WISCONSIN
MICHIGAN
IOWA
NEBRASKA
KANSAS
MISSOURI
ILLINOIS
INDIANA
OHIO
KENTUCKY
WEST VIRGINIA
VIRGINIA
COLORADO
WYOMING
MONTANA
Lake Superior
Lake Michigan
Lake Huron
Lake Erie
Great Plains
Chicago
Minneapolis
Detroit
Cleveland
Toronto
Winnipeg
Denver
Milwaukee
Indianapolis
Cincinnati
Kansas City
Omaha
Des Moines
St Louis
Columbus
↑167
↑174
↑180
1
2
3
4
48°
44°
40°

North America Central United States

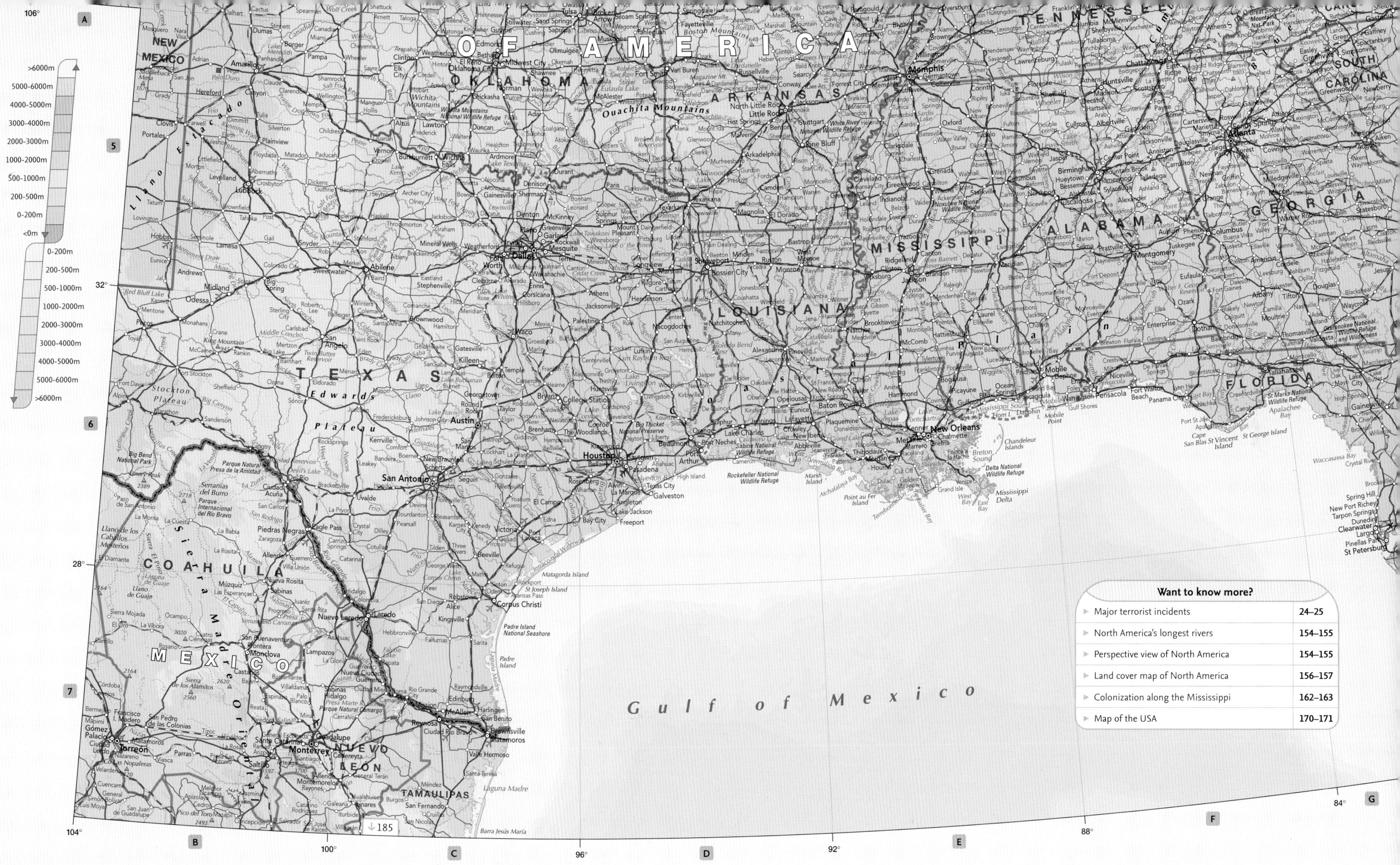
UNITED STATES OF AMERICA
NEW MEXICO
OKLAHOMA
ARKANSAS
TENNESSEE
SOUTH CAROLINA
GEORGIA
ALABAMA
MISSISSIPPI
LOUISIANA
TEXAS
FLORIDA
MEXICO
COAHUILA
NUEVO LEON
TAMAULIPAS
Gulf of Mexico
Ouachita Mountains
Edwards Plateau
Llano Estacado
Sierra Madre Oriental
Coastal Plain
Stockton Plateau
Dallas
Houston
San Antonio
Austin
New Orleans
Memphis
Atlanta
Oklahoma City
Little Rock
Jackson
Montgomery
Birmingham
Shreveport
Baton Rouge
Corpus Christi
Monterrey
Torreón
Laredo
Nuevo Laredo
Tallahassee
Mobile
Pensacola
Galveston
Beaumont
Lubbock
Amarillo
Abilene
Waco
Fort Worth
Chattanooga
Columbus
Brownsville
Matamoros
St Petersburg
Clearwater
Padre Island National Seashore
Matagorda Island
Big Bend National Park
Mississippi Delta
Chandeleur Islands
Laguna Madre
A
B
C
D
E
F
G
5
6
7
104°
100°
96°
92°
88°
84°
106°
32°
28°
>6000m
5000-6000m
4000-5000m
3000-4000m
2000-3000m
1000-2000m
500-1000m
200-500m
0-200m
<0m
0-200m
200-500m
500-1000m
1000-2000m
2000-3000m
3000-4000m
4000-5000m
5000-6000m
>6000m

↓185

1:6 500 000

miles 0 50 100 150 200 250 300

km 0 50 100 150 200 250 300 350 400 450 500

Lambert Conformal Conic Projection

Want to know more?

Major terrorist incidents	24–25
North America's longest rivers	154–155
Perspective view of North America	154–155
Land cover map of North America	156–157
Colonization along the Mississippi	162–163
Map of the USA	170–171

167

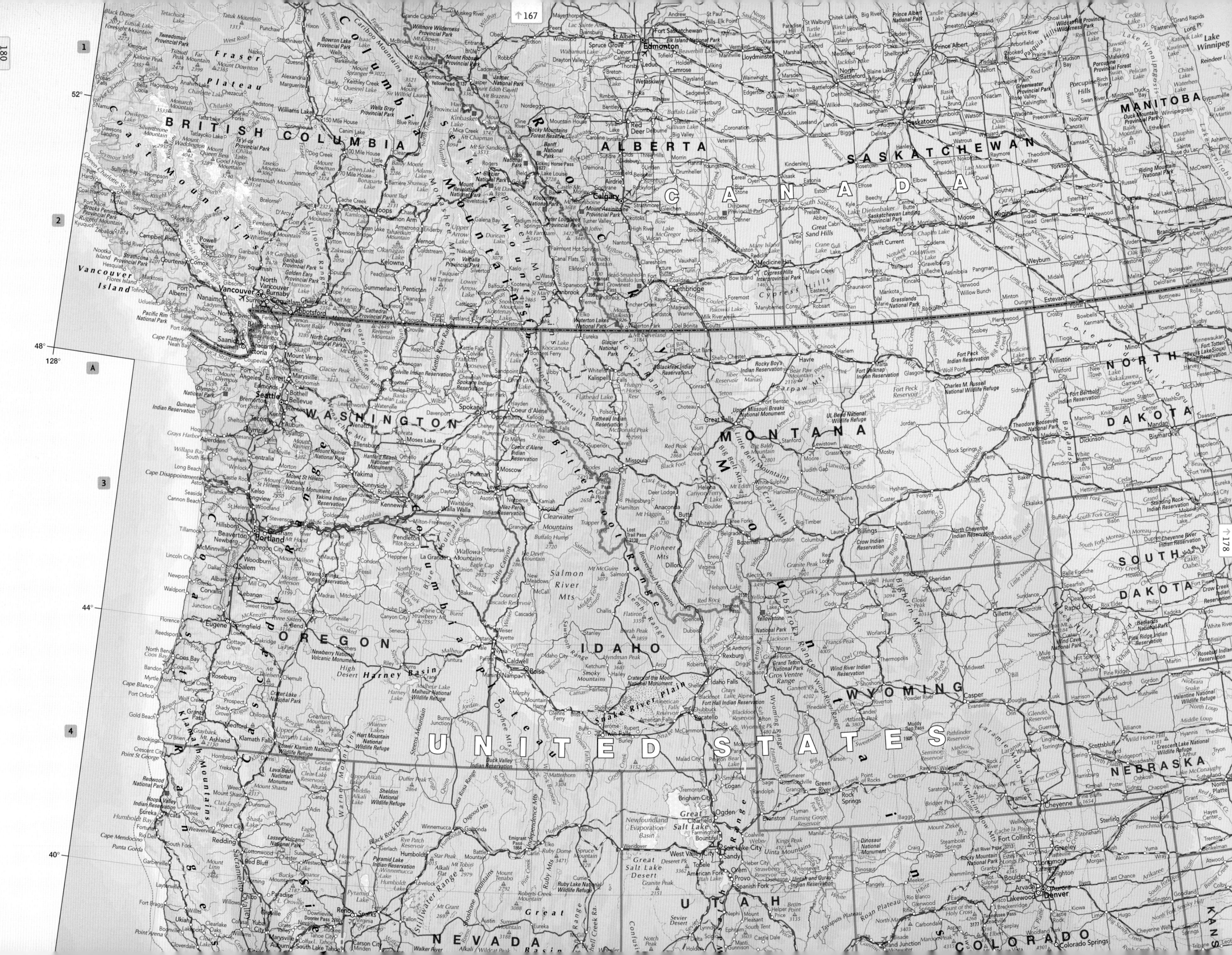

CANADA
UNITED STATES
BRITISH COLUMBIA
ALBERTA
SASKATCHEWAN
MANITOBA
WASHINGTON
OREGON
IDAHO
MONTANA
WYOMING
NORTH DAKOTA
SOUTH DAKOTA
NEBRASKA
COLORADO
UTAH
NEVADA
Rocky Mountains
Coast Mountains
Columbia Mountains
Selkirk Mountains
Cascade Range
Coast Ranges
Columbia Plateau
Fraser Plateau
Vancouver Island
Great Salt Lake
Seattle
Portland
Spokane
Vancouver
Victoria
Calgary
Edmonton
Saskatoon
Regina
Salt Lake City
Boise
Denver
Billings
Bismarck
Cheyenne

178

North America Western United States

↓184

1:6 500 000

Lambert Conformal Conic Projection

miles 0 50 100 150 200 250 300
km 0 50 100 150 200 250 300 350 400 450 500

Want to know more?

▲ Major volcanic eruptions	10–11
▲ Effects of climate change	12–13
▲ Image of Montana plains	156–157
▲ Image of pollution in Denver	160–161
▲ Map of the Pacific Ocean	220–221

HAWAII (U.S.A.)

1:6 500 000

miles 0 60 100
km 0 60 100

Elevation legend:
>6000m
5000–6000m
4000–5000m
3000–4000m
2000–3000m
1000–2000m
500–1000m
200–500m
0–200m
<0m
0–200m
200–500m
500–1000m
1000–2000m
2000–3000m
3000–4000m
4000–5000m
5000–6000m
>6000m

PACIFIC OCEAN

Gulf of California

MEXICO

CALIFORNIA · NEVADA · ARIZONA · NEW MEXICO · TEXAS · OKLAHOMA

UNITED STATES OF AMERICA

BAJA CALIFORNIA · BAJA CALIFORNIA SUR · SONORA · CHIHUAHUA · COAHUILA

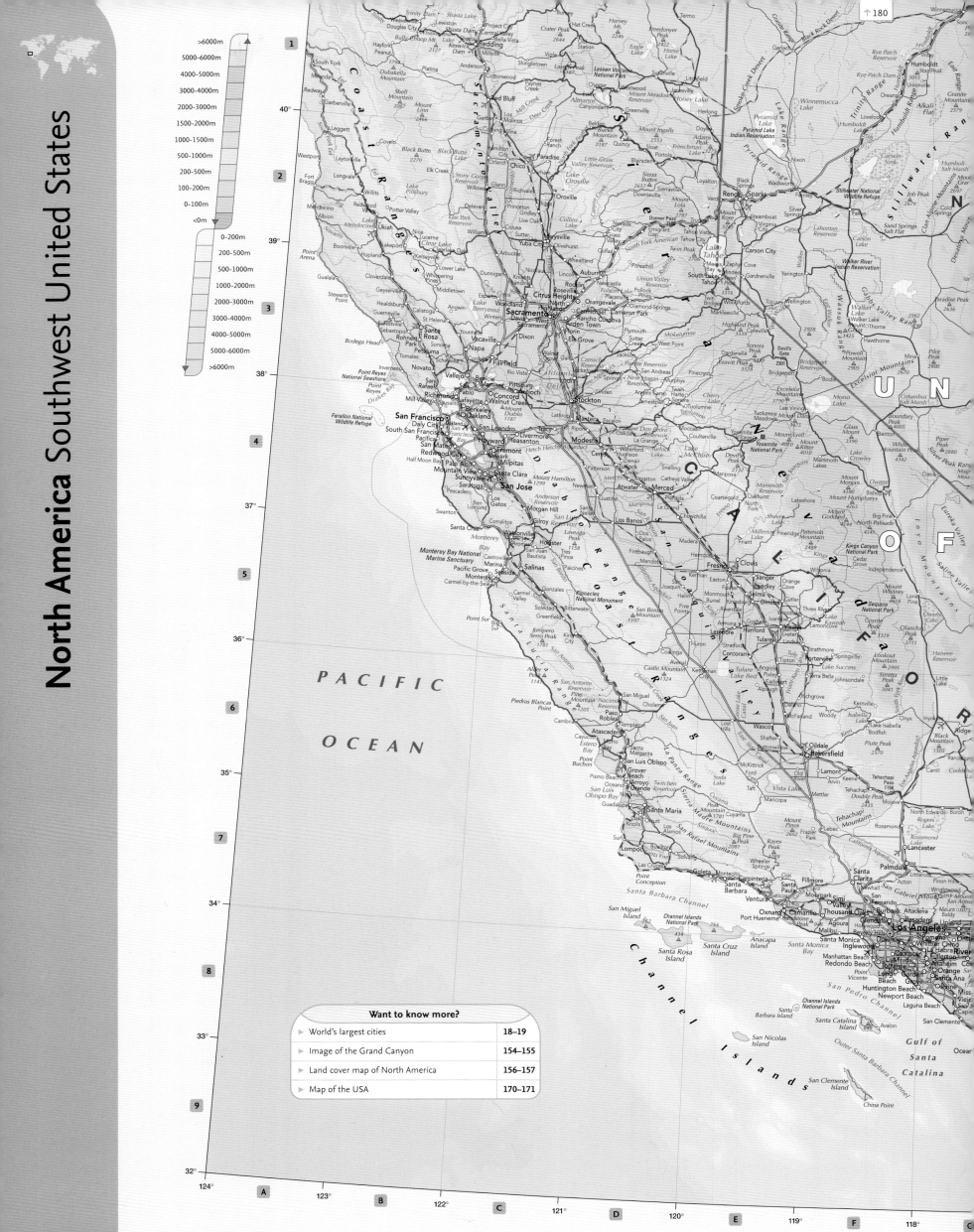

North America Southwest United States

PACIFIC

OCEAN

Want to know more?

>6000m
5000-6000m
4000-5000m
3000-4000m
2000-3000m
1500-2000m
1000-1500m
500-1000m
200-500m
100-200m
0-100m
<0m

0-200m
200-500m
500-1000m
1000-2000m
2000-3000m
3000-4000m
4000-5000m
5000-6000m
>6000m

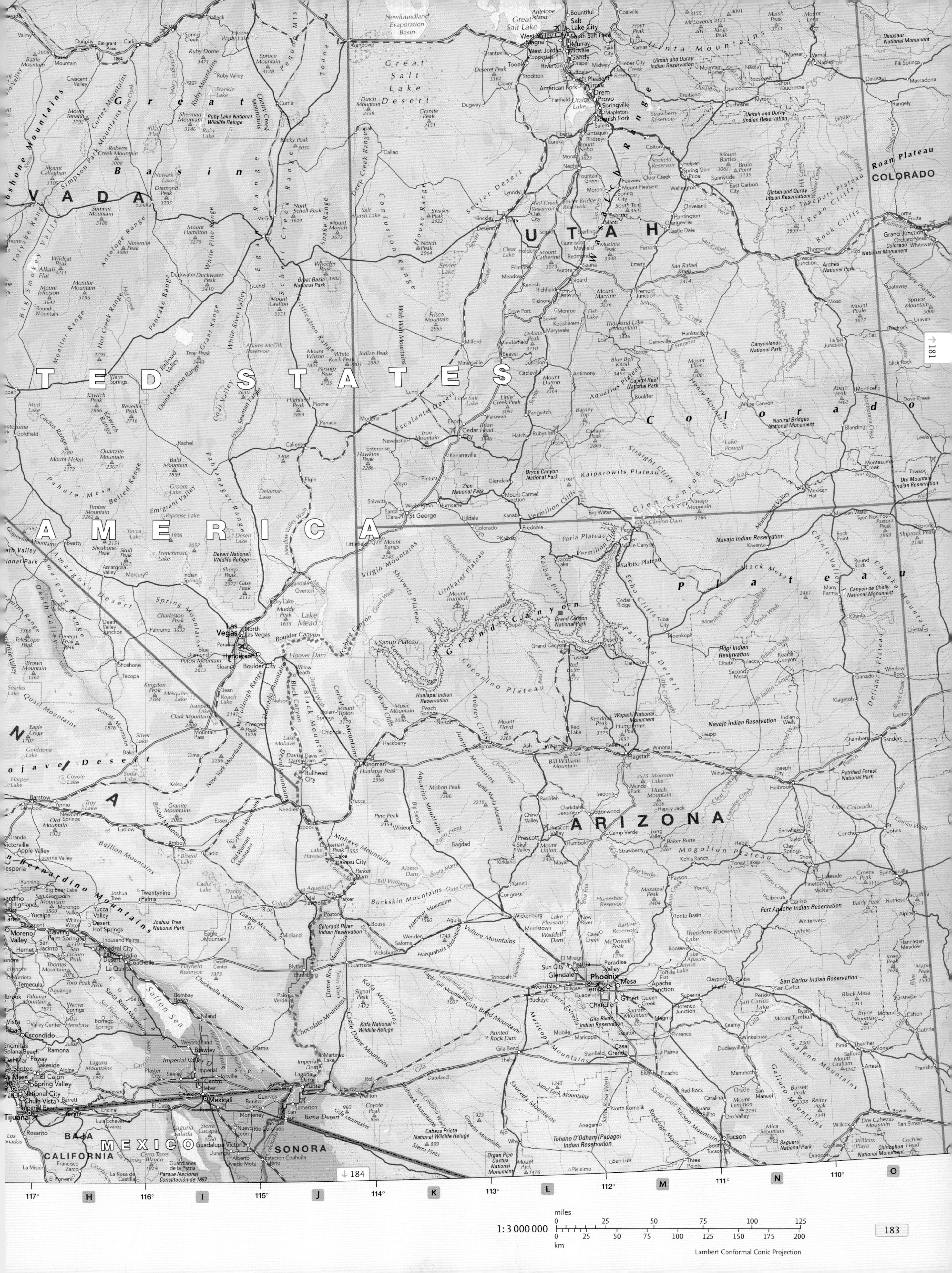
UTAH
ARIZONA
COLORADO
TED STATES
AMERICA
VADA
NIA
MEXICO
SONORA
BAJA CALIFORNIA
Great Basin
Great Salt Lake Desert
Newfoundland Evaporation Basin
Great Salt Lake
Salt Lake City
South Salt Lake
West Valley City
West Jordan
Murray
Midvale
Sandy
Magna
Riverton
Tooele
American Fork
Pleasant Grove
Orem
Provo
Springville
Spanish Fork
Park City
Heber City
Uinta Mountains
Uintah and Ouray Indian Reservation
Dinosaur National Monument
Vernal
Duchesne
Roosevelt
Price
Helper
Wellington
Green River
Moab
Arches National Park
Canyonlands National Park
Grand Junction
Roan Plateau
Book Cliffs
Roan Cliffs
East Tavaputs Plateau
San Rafael Knob
Sevier Desert
Sevier Lake
Delta
Fillmore
Nephi
Richfield
Salina
Manti
Castle Dale
Wasatch Plateau
Fish Lake
Capitol Reef National Park
Henry Mountains
Aquarius Plateau
Bryce Canyon National Park
Zion National Park
Cedar City
St George
Kanab
Escalante Desert
Kaiparowits Plateau
Straight Cliffs
Vermilion Cliffs
Glen Canyon
Glen Canyon Dam
Lake Powell
Natural Bridges National Monument
Blanding
Monticello
Mexican Hat
Navajo Mountain
Navajo Indian Reservation
Colorado Plateau
Black Mesa
Kayenta
Canyon de Chelly National Monument
Chuska Mountains
Chinle
Hopi Indian Reservation
Tuba City
Kaibab Plateau
Paria Plateau
Marble Canyon
Grand Canyon
Grand Canyon National Park
Coconino Plateau
Hualapai Indian Reservation
Uinkaret Plateau
Shivwits Plateau
Lake Mead
Boulder Canyon
Hoover Dam
Las Vegas
North Las Vegas
Henderson
Boulder City
Pahrump
Spring Mountains
Charleston Peak
Death Valley
Amargosa Desert
Amargosa Range
Desert National Wildlife Refuge
Pahute Mesa
Kawich Range
Great Basin National Park
Wheeler Peak
Ely
Eureka
Snake Range
Schell Creek Range
Egan Range
White Pine Range
Ruby Mountains
Ruby Lake National Wildlife Refuge
Elko
Wendover
Pioche
Caliente
Mojave Desert
Mohave Mountains
Barstow
Needles
Kingman
Bullhead City
Lake Havasu City
Parker
Colorado River Indian Reservation
Blythe
Joshua Tree National Park
Salton Sea
Palm Springs
Indio
Coachella
San Bernardino Mountains
Escondido
San Diego
Chula Vista
Tijuana
Mexicali
Calexico
El Centro
Imperial Valley
Yuma
San Luis
Kofa National Wildlife Refuge
Cabeza Prieta National Wildlife Refuge
Organ Pipe Cactus National Monument
Tohono O'Odham (Papago) Indian Reservation
Gila Bend
Gila River Indian Reservation
Phoenix
Glendale
Sun City
Peoria
Tempe
Mesa
Chandler
Apache Junction
Casa Grande
Tucson
Saguaro National Park
Sierra Vista
Wickenburg
Prescott
Chino Valley
Camp Verde
Sedona
Flagstaff
Humphreys Peak
Williams
Winslow
Holbrook
Petrified Forest National Park
Mogollon Plateau
Mogollon Rim
Payson
Show Low
Fort Apache Indian Reservation
San Carlos Indian Reservation
Theodore Roosevelt Lake
Globe
Safford
Pinaleno Mountains
Galiuro Mountains
Willcox
Chiricahua National Monument
1:3 000 000
miles
km
Lambert Conformal Conic Projection

↑181

↓184

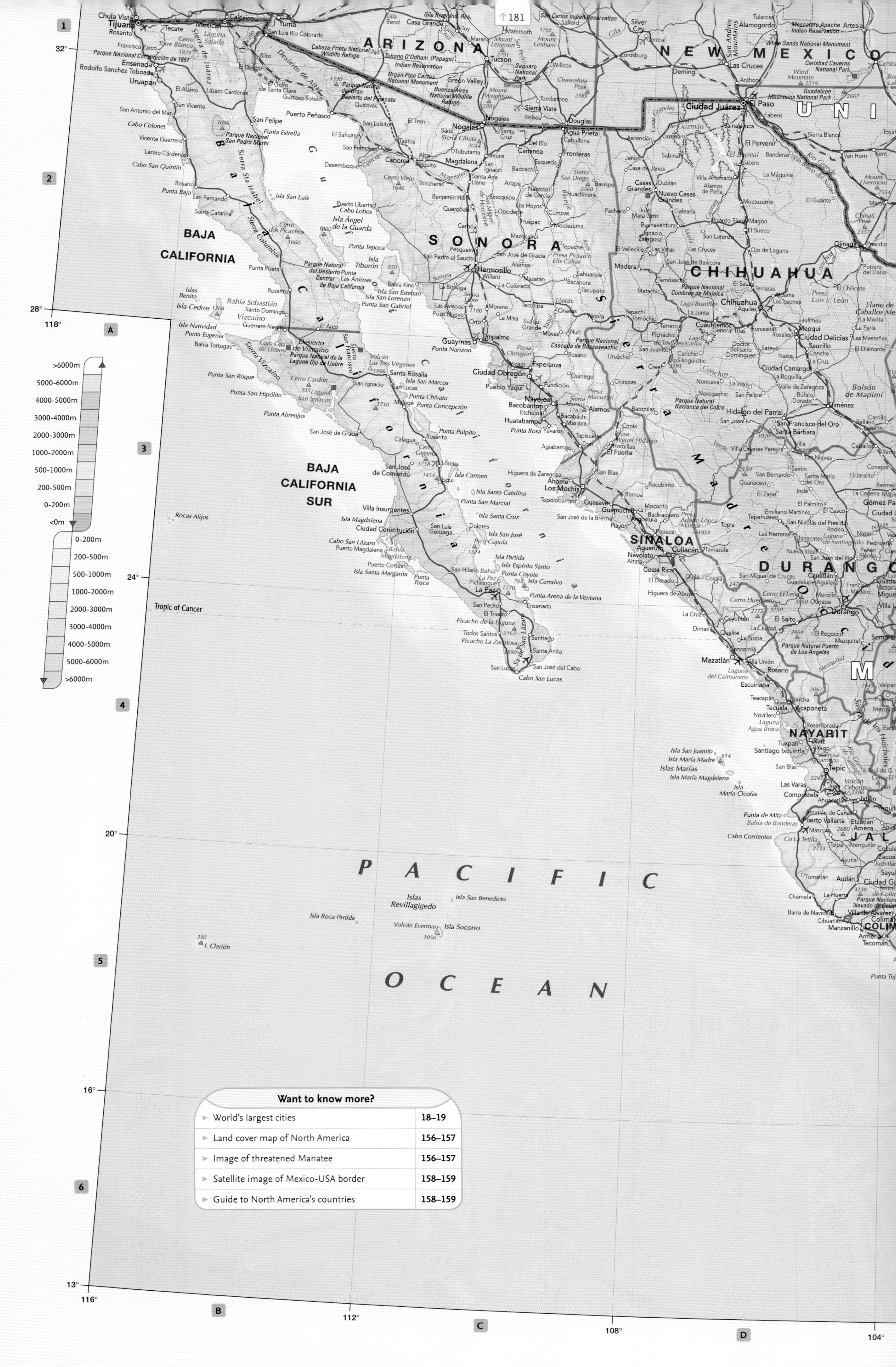

↑181

PACIFIC

OCEAN

Want to know more?

179

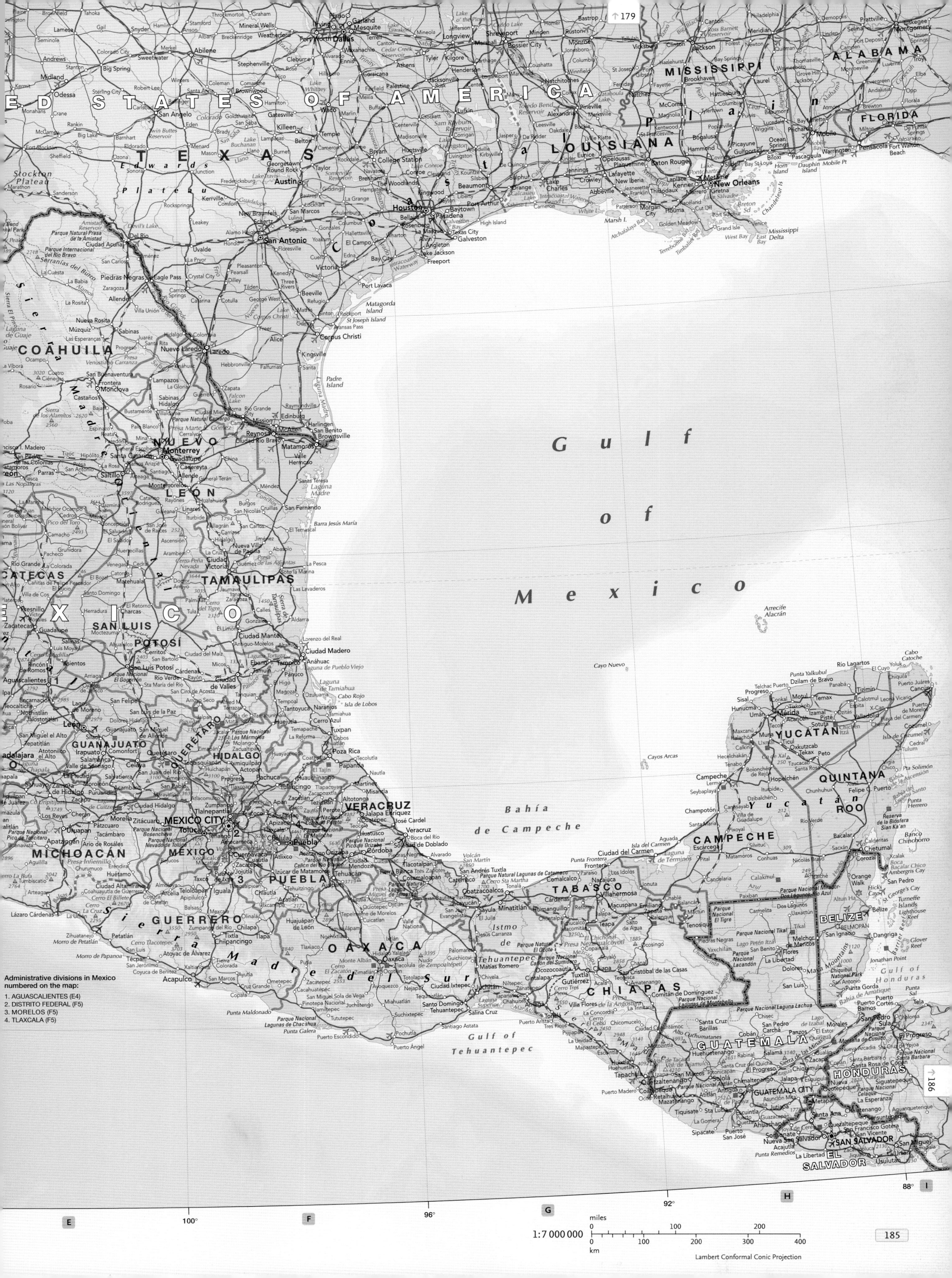
UNITED STATES OF AMERICA
TEXAS
LOUISIANA
MISSISSIPPI
ALABAMA
FLORIDA
Edwards Plateau
Stockton Plateau
Coastal Plain
Gulf of Mexico
Bahía de Campeche
Gulf of Tehuantepec
Gulf of Honduras
Mississippi Delta
Yucatán
Istmo de Tehuantepec
Sierra Madre Oriental
Sierra Madre del Sur
MEXICO
COAHUILA
NUEVO LEÓN
TAMAULIPAS
SAN LUIS POTOSÍ
ZACATECAS
GUANAJUATO
QUERÉTARO
HIDALGO
VERACRUZ
MICHOACÁN
MÉXICO
PUEBLA
GUERRERO
OAXACA
TABASCO
CHIAPAS
CAMPECHE
YUCATÁN
QUINTANA ROO
BELIZE
GUATEMALA
HONDURAS
EL SALVADOR
Dallas
Fort Worth
Shreveport
Jackson
Montgomery
Austin
San Antonio
Houston
Galveston
Corpus Christi
Baton Rouge
New Orleans
Mobile
Pensacola
Nuevo Laredo
Laredo
Monterrey
Saltillo
Matamoros
Brownsville
Ciudad Victoria
Tampico
San Luis Potosí
León
Guadalajara
Querétaro
MEXICO CITY
Toluca
Puebla
Veracruz
Cuernavaca
Acapulco
Oaxaca
Villahermosa
Campeche
Mérida
Cancún
Chetumal
BELMOPAN
Tuxtla Gutiérrez
GUATEMALA CITY
SAN SALVADOR
Tegucigalpa
Arrecife Alacrán
Cayo Nuevo
Cayos Arcas
Administrative divisions in Mexico numbered on the map:
1. AGUASCALIENTES (E4)
2. DISTRITO FEDERAL (F5)
3. MORELOS (F5)
4. TLAXCALA (F5)
100°
96°
92°
88°
E
F
G
H
I
1:7 000 000
miles
0
100
200
km
0
100
200
300
400
Lambert Conformal Conic Projection

186

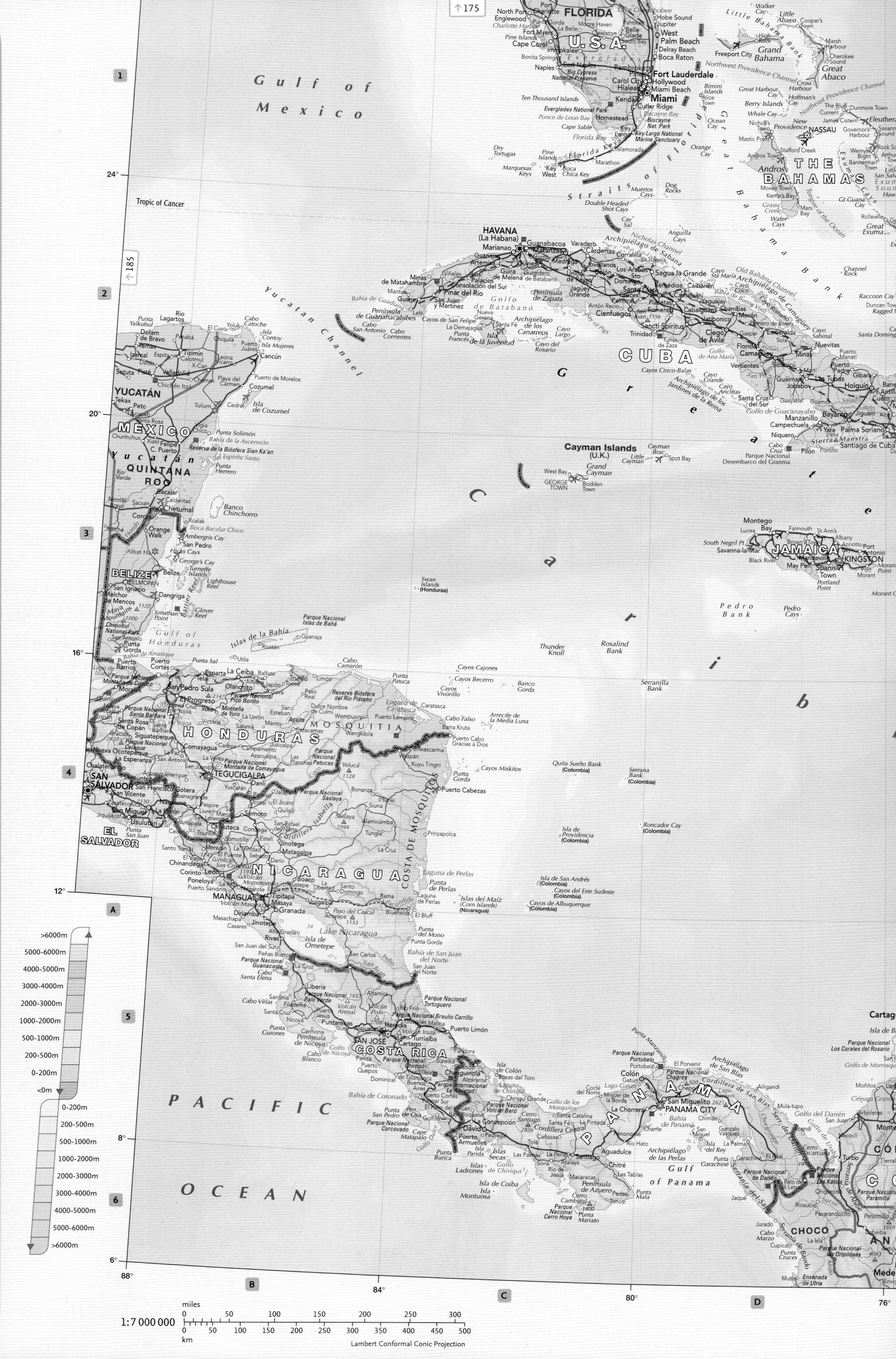

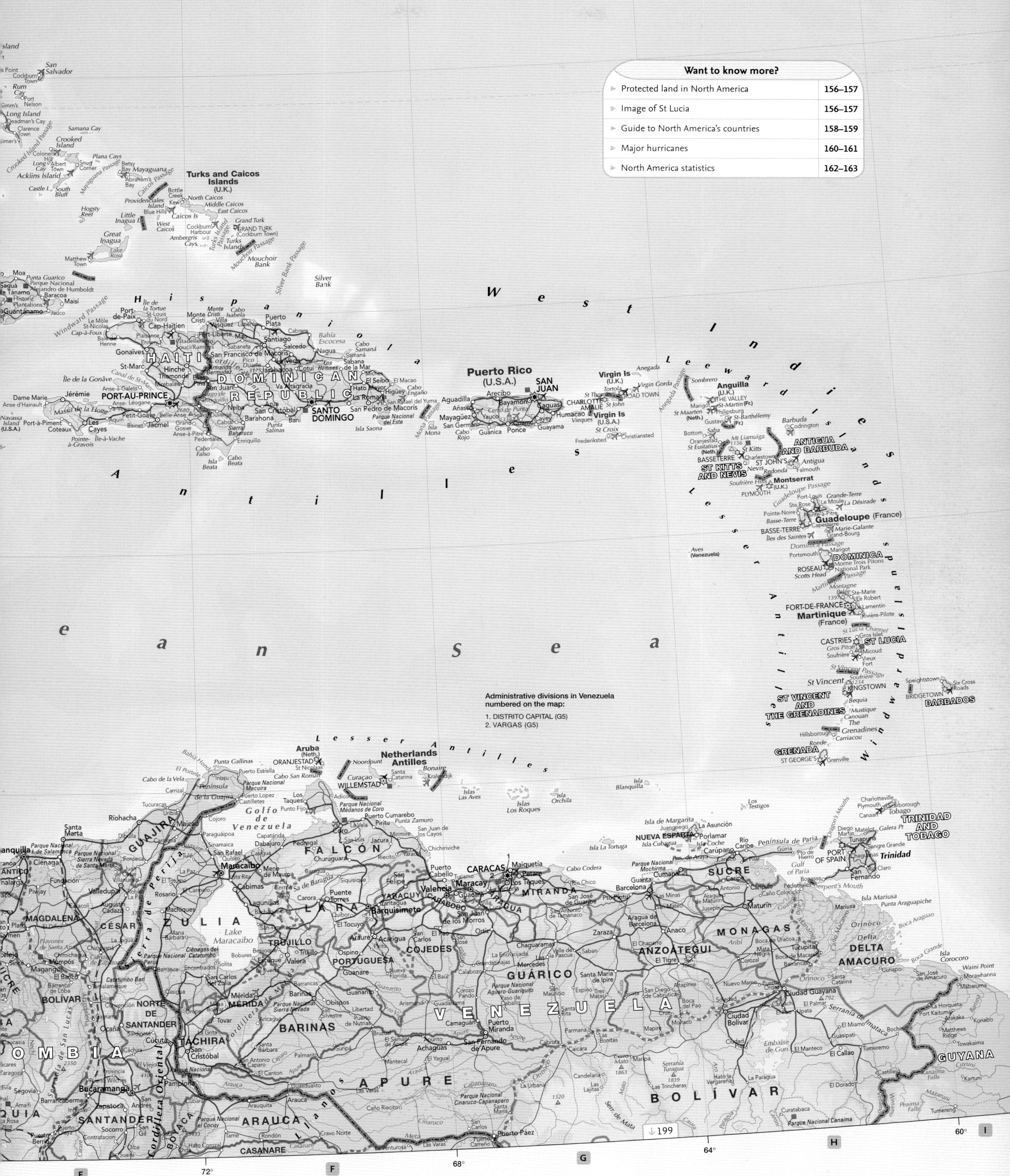

Administrative divisions in Venezuela
numbered on the map:

1. DISTRITO CAPITAL (G5)
2. VARGAS (G5)

South America Landscapes

The spectacular Andes mountains dominate the western side of South America, bordering the Pacific for the entire length of the landmass. They stretch from Tierra del Fuego in the south, to Panama in the north. This huge mountain system has many volcanoes, is the source of many of the continent's large rivers, including the Amazon and Orinoco, and surrounds the Atacama Desert, the driest place on earth. The Altiplano is a high plateau within the Andes between the main west and east mountain ranges. Other upland areas include the Brazilian Highlands in the northeast and Patagonia, where the land rises steadily from the Atlantic coast to the Andes. The Amazon Basin is a large lowland area, lying just south of the equator, through which the Amazon river and its many tributaries flow towards the huge delta on the Atlantic coast. The region contains vast areas of tropical rain forest. Huge, sparsely populated plains known as Llanos in the north and Pampas in the south provide further contrasts in the landscapes of the continent.

Gulf of Mexico

Caribbean Sea

Lake Maracaibo

Orinoco River Delta

Orinoco River

Angel Falls

Guiana Highlands

Llanos

Negro River

Japurá River

Amazon Basin

Galapagos Islands

Purus River

Selvas

Madeira River

Lake Titicaca

Largest lake Lake Titicaca

Altiplano

Atacama Desert

Pacific Ocean

Andes

Gran Chaco

Salado River

Paraná River

Highest point Cerro Aconcagua

Cerro Aconcagua

Uruguay River

Pampas

Río de la Plata

Colorado River

Negro River

Patagonia

Península Valdés

Lowest point Península Valdés

Largest island Isla Grande de Tierra del Fuego

Falkland Islands

Tierra del Fuego

Cape Horn

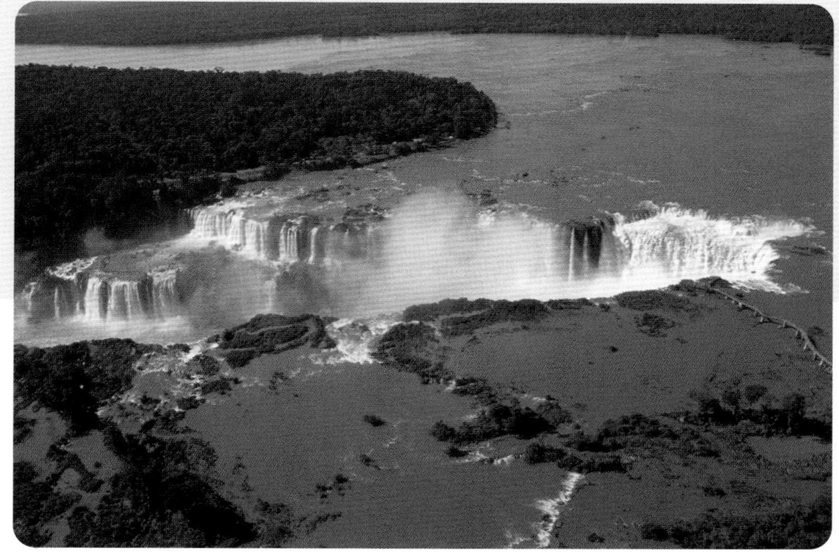

Iguaçu Falls are a spectacular sight from the air and on the ground. Here we can see a walkway extending out across the river to the edge of the falls. The countries of Argentina, Brazil and Paraguay all meet at the falls as the Iguaçu river flows into the Paraná on its way to the Atlantic Ocean.

Want to know more?

▶ Cross-section of South America — **6–7**
▶ World's longest rivers — **6–7**
▶ Endangered species in South America — **190–191**
▶ Images of deforestation — **194–195**
▶ Maps of South America — **198–207**

Internet links

Rainforest information	www.rainforestweb.org
Brazilian Institute of Geography and Statistics	www.ibge.gov.br
Latin American Network Information Center	lanic.utexas.edu
Mountain climbing in South America	www.peakbagger.com

Facts

The world's driest desert is the Atacama where only 1 mm of rain may fall as infrequently as once every 5–20 years.

Waterflow along the Amazon is over 1 500 times that of the river Thames.

Archipiélago Juan Fernández (Juan Fernandez Islands) off the coast of Chile are known to have been the origin of the famous castaway story, Robinson Crusoe.

Angel Falls, Venezuela is the highest waterfall in the world at 979 metres (3 212 feet). They were named in 1937 after Jimmie Angel whose plane crashed near them.

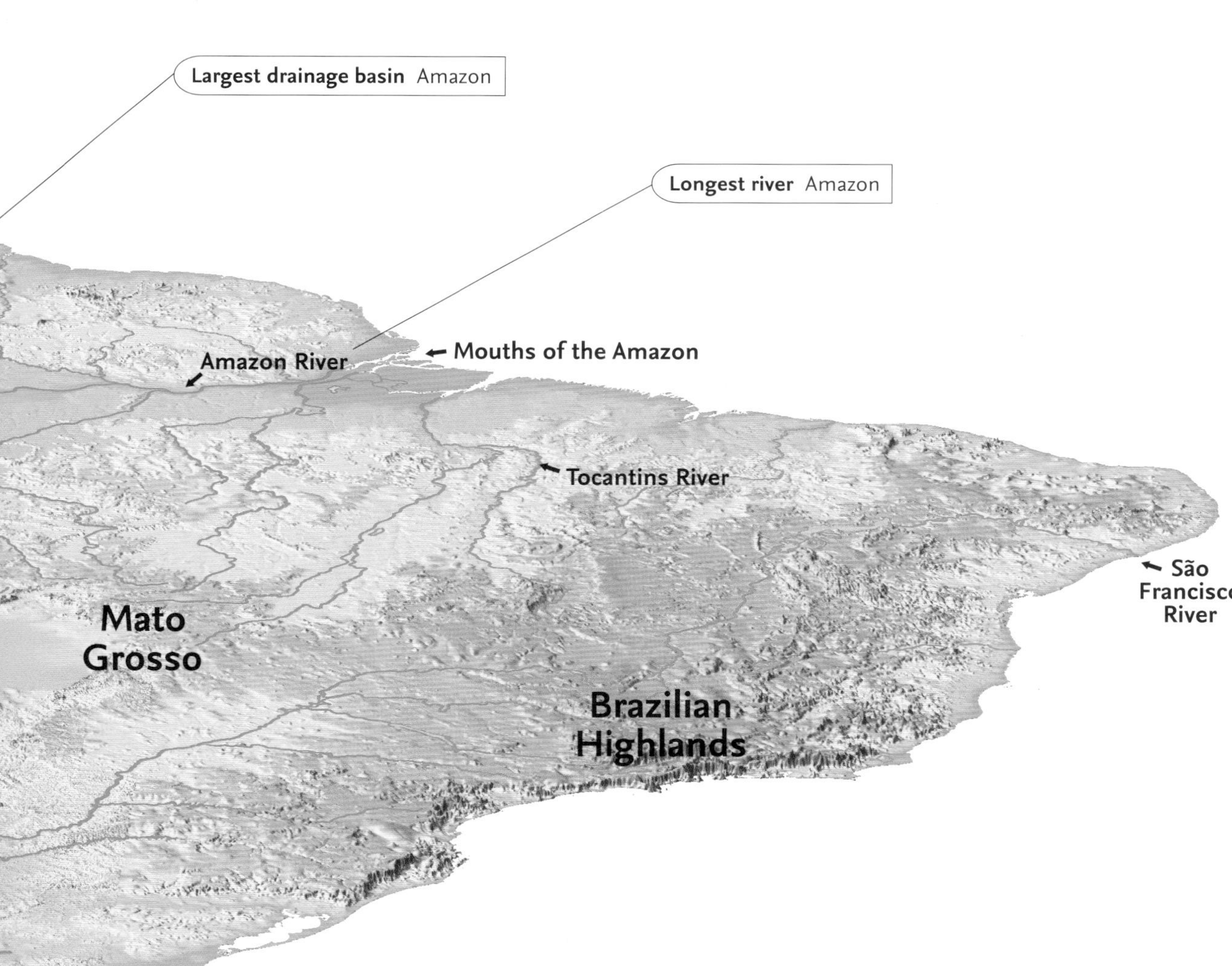

Largest drainage basin Amazon

Longest river Amazon

← Mouths of the Amazon

Amazon River →

← **Tocantins River**

← São Francisco River

Mato Grosso

Brazilian Highlands

Atlantic Ocean

Highest mountains

	metres	feet	map
Cerro Aconcagua *Argentina*	6 960	22 834	204 C4
Nevado Ojos del Salado *Argentina/Chile*	6 908	22 664	204 C2
Cerro Bonete *Argentina*	6 872	22 546	204 C2
Cerro Pissis *Argentina*	6 858	22 500	204 C2
Cerro Tupungato *Argentina/Chile*	6 800	22 309	204 C4
Cerro Mercedario *Argentina*	6 770	22 211	204 C3

Longest rivers

	km	miles	map
Amazon	6 516	3 964	202 B1
Rió de la Plata-Parana	4 500	2 796	204 F4
Purus	3 218	1 999	199 F5
Madeira	3 200	1 988	199 G5
São Francisco	2 900	1 802	202 E4
Tocantins	2 750	1 708	202 B2

Largest islands

	sq km	sq miles	map
Isla Grande de Tierra del Fuego	47 000	18 147	205 C9
Isla de Chiloé	8 394	3 240	205 B6
East Falkland	6 760	2 610	205 F8
West Falkland	5 413	2 090	205 F8

Largest lakes

	sq km	sq miles	map
Lake Titicaca	8 340	3 220	200 C3

Land area

Total land area 17 815 420 sq km/6 878 572 sq mls		map
Most northerly point	**Punta Gallinas** *Colombia*	198 D1
Most southerly point	**Cape Horn** *Chile*	205 D9
Most westerly point	**Galagapos Islands** *Ecuador*	216 H6
Most easterly point	**Ilhas Martin Vas** *Atlantic Oc.*	216 M7
Lowest point	**Península Valdés** *Argentina*	205 E6

The **Atacama Desert** is the driest place on earth and has practically no vegetation. The area has been exploited for mining, firstly of nitrates for fertiliser and more recently of copper and iron ore. This view from near San Pedro de Atacama, Chile shows the Patagonian Andes in the distance.

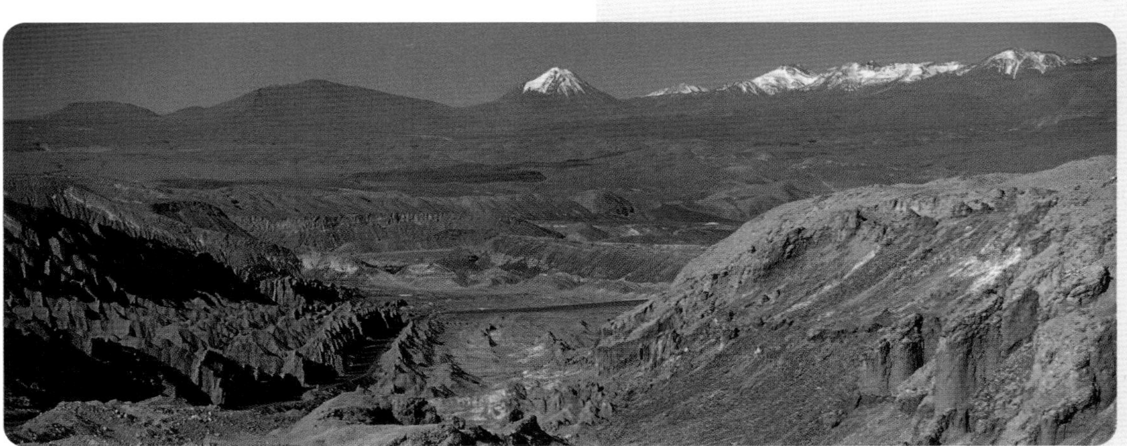

South America stretches from the cold lands of Tierra del Fuego in the south, close to Antarctica, north to the world's largest river basin straddling the equator. Covering 7 million square kilometres (2.7 million square miles), the Amazon basin is home to many rivers dissecting the tropical rain forest. Previously difficult to penetrate, the rain forest is rapidly being cleared by loggers, farmland is replacing a precious natural resource and many species of plants and animals are under threat. The Andes form a high, rugged barrier down the west coast of the continent with volcanoes and deserts, and the grasslands to the east of the Andes support cattle ranching. Much of the population lives in the eastern part of the continent. Dams provide much needed water for irrigation and cities, but often at the cost of rich natural habitats.

From the foothills of the Andes to the east coast of Argentina the **Pampas grasslands** support a major livestock industry and farming of flax and grain.

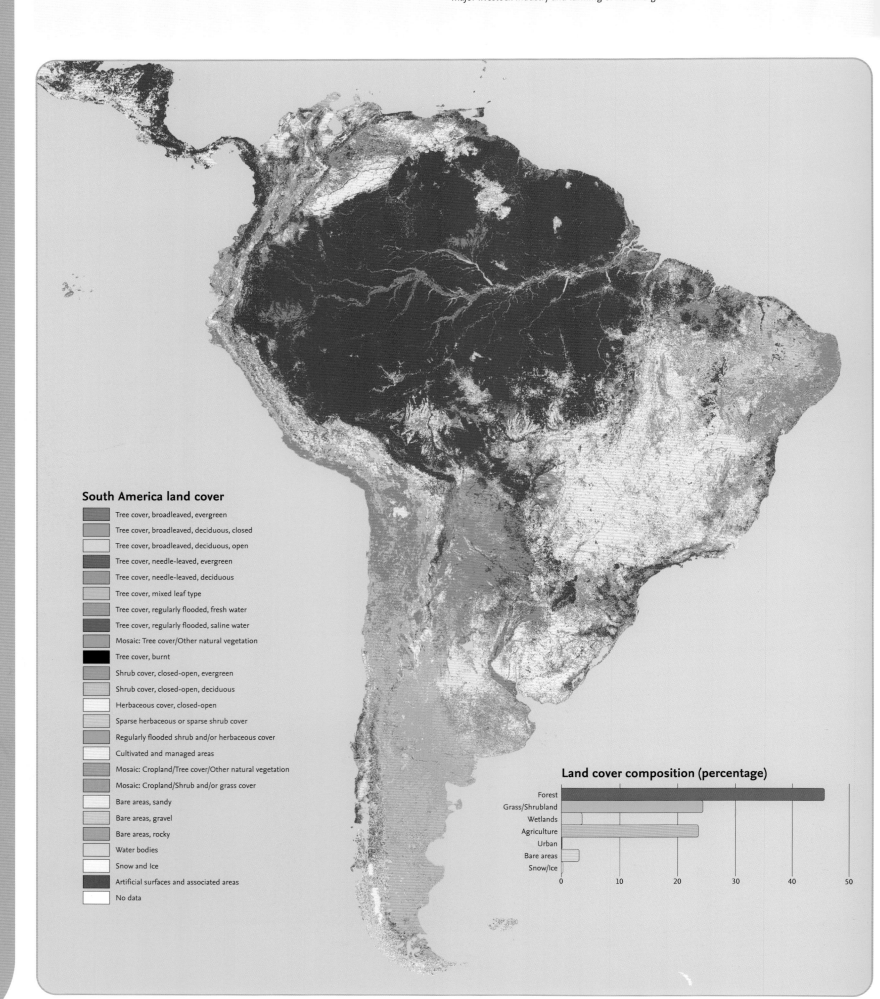

South America land cover

- Tree cover, broadleaved, evergreen
- Tree cover, broadleaved, deciduous, closed
- Tree cover, broadleaved, deciduous, open
- Tree cover, needle-leaved, evergreen
- Tree cover, needle-leaved, deciduous
- Tree cover, mixed leaf type
- Tree cover, regularly flooded, fresh water
- Tree cover, regularly flooded, saline water
- Mosaic: Tree cover/Other natural vegetation
- Tree cover, burnt
- Shrub cover, closed-open, evergreen
- Shrub cover, closed-open, deciduous
- Herbaceous cover, closed-open
- Sparse herbaceous or sparse shrub cover
- Regularly flooded shrub and/or herbaceous cover
- Cultivated and managed areas
- Mosaic: Cropland/Tree cover/Other natural vegetation
- Mosaic: Cropland/Shrub and/or grass cover
- Bare areas, sandy
- Bare areas, gravel
- Bare areas, rocky
- Water bodies
- Snow and Ice
- Artificial surfaces and associated areas
- No data

Land cover composition (percentage)

Forest	
Grass/Shrubland	
Wetlands	
Agriculture	
Urban	
Bare areas	
Snow/Ice	

0   10   20   30   40   50

The source of the river **Amazon** is in the Andes of southern Peru. It is fed by many tributaries on its journey across the continent. The humid tropical climate produces lush, dense forest vegetation, home to a great variety of animal life.

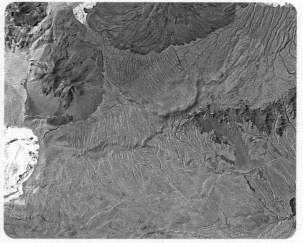

The **Atacama Desert** in northern Chile is the driest place on earth, but this barren area is rich in minerals and is a major source of the world's nitrates. Seasonal rains carve out the dry river valleys depositing minerals in the salt pans which appear white in this satellite image.

Internet links	
Red List of Threatened Species	www.redlist.org
UN Environment Programme	www.unep.org
IUCN the World Conservation Union	www.iucn.org
Images of South America	earthobservatory.nasa.gov

Facts

The Amazon can take ocean-going ships up as far as Manaus, about 1 200 kilometres (756 miles) from the delta.

Illegal trafficking of alpacas from Peru to Bolivia, Chile and beyond means the quality of the wool is declining as the finest animals fetch a high black market price.

The Parque Nacional Kaa-Iya del Gran Chacois the largest national park in Bolivia and was set up by three indigenous people who now help to administer it.

Lake Maracaibo has been suffering from an increasing growth of duckweed, covering up to 18 per cent of the lake. It needs to be constantly removed as it can double its size in two days.

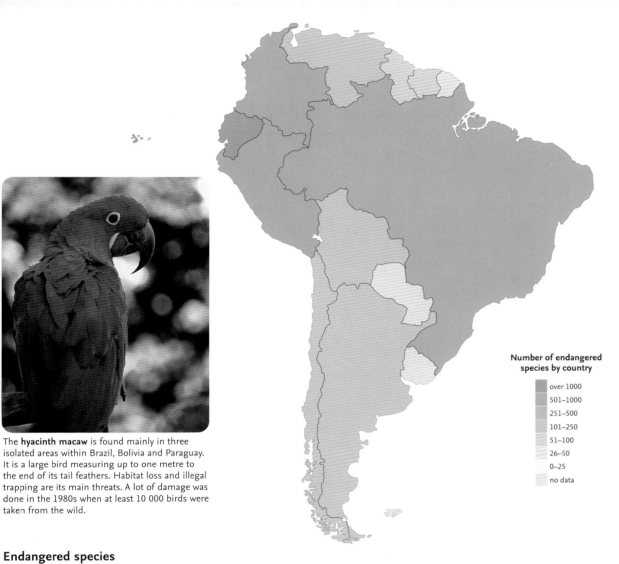

Number of endangered species by country

- over 1000
- 501–1000
- 251–500
- 101–250
- 51–100
- 26–50
- 0–25
- no data

The **hyacinth macaw** is found mainly in three isolated areas within Brazil, Bolivia and Paraguay. It is a large bird measuring up to one metre to the end of its tail feathers. Habitat loss and illegal trapping are its main threats. A lot of damage was done in the 1980s when at least 10 000 birds were taken from the wild.

Top 10 protected land by country

	country	percentage land protected
1	Colombia	72.3
2	Venezuela	70.3
3	Ecuador	26.0
4	Bolivia	19.4
5	Brazil	18.0
6	Peru	16.7
7	Suriname	12.7
8	Argentina	6.3
9	Paraguay	4.1
10	Chile	3.6

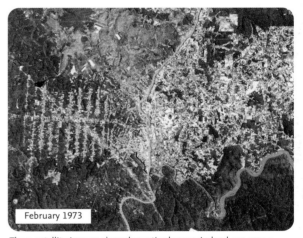

February 1973

These satellite images show dramatic changes in land use over a period of 30 years in eastern Paraguay and southwest Brazil. The building of the **Itaipu dam**, which was completed in the early 1980s and is seen at the top of the 2003 image, accelerated the clearing of forest for farmland and for workers' homes. The spectacular Iguaçu Falls and its surrounding forest, in the lower right of the images, are protected as a national park, mainly in Argentina – vital protection of a rapidly disappearing habitat.

Endangered species

Tropical rain forests are home to the majority of plant and animal species in the world and there are probably many yet to be officially recognized. Deforestation of the Amazon basin is a threat to the existence of many species. There is a less tangible threat to habitats in the southern part of the continent where global warming is affecting the extent of glaciers and ice in the mountains and consequently the amount of meltwater in the coastal regions.

May 2003

Mines in the Andes mainly produce copper, tin and lead. This mine in the **Rondônia** area of Brazil produces tin. In the northeast of the continent mining is for iron, aluminium and manganese.

The southern tip of South America is a dramatic mixture of high mountains, glaciers, lakes and a fragmented coastline. This view is of the **Torres del Paine National Park**.

Countries capital		sq km sq miles	population	languages	religions	currency	official website	map
Argentina Buenos Aires		2 766 889 1 068 302	38 747 000	Spanish, Italian, Amerindian languages	Roman Catholic, Protestant	Argentinian peso	www.info.gov.ar	204–205
Bolivia La Paz/Sucre		1 098 581 424 164	9 182 000	Spanish, Quechua, Aymara	Roman Catholic, Protestant, Baha'i	Boliviano	www.bolivia.gov.bo	200–201
Brazil Brasília		8 514 879 3 287 613	186 405 000	Portuguese	Roman Catholic, Protestant	Real	www.brazil.gov.br	202–203
Chile Santiago		756 945 292 258	16 295 000	Spanish, Amerindian languages	Roman Catholic, Protestant	Chilean peso	www.gobiernodechile.cl	204–205
Colombia Bogotá		1 141 748 440 831	45 600 000	Spanish, Amerindian languages	Roman Catholic, Protestant	Colombian peso	www.gobiernoenlinea.gov.co	198
Ecuador Quito		272 045 105 037	13 228 000	Spanish, Quechua, and other Amerindian languages	Roman Catholic	US dollar	www.ec-gov.net	198
Guyana Georgetown		214 969 83 000	751 000	English, creole, Amerindian languages	Protestant, Hindu, Roman Catholic, Sunni Muslim	Guyana dollar	www.gina.gov.gy	199
Paraguay Asunción		406 752 157 048	6 158 000	Spanish, Guaraní	Roman Catholic, Protestant	Guaraní	www.presidencia.gov.py	201
Peru Lima		1 285 216 496 225	27 968 000	Spanish, Quechua, Aymara	Roman Catholic, Protestant	Sol	www.peru.gob.pe	200
Suriname Paramaribo		163 820 63 251	449 000	Dutch, Surinamese, English, Hindi,	Hindu, Roman Catholic, Protestant, Sunni Muslim	Suriname guilder	www.kabinet.sr.org	199
Uruguay Montevideo		176 215 68 037	3 463 000	Spanish	Roman Catholic, Protestant, Jewish	Uruguayan peso	www.presidencia.gub.uy	204
Venezuela Caracas		912 050 352 144	26 749 000	Spanish, Amerindian languages	Roman Catholic, Protestant	Bolívar	www.gobiernoenlinea.ve	198–199

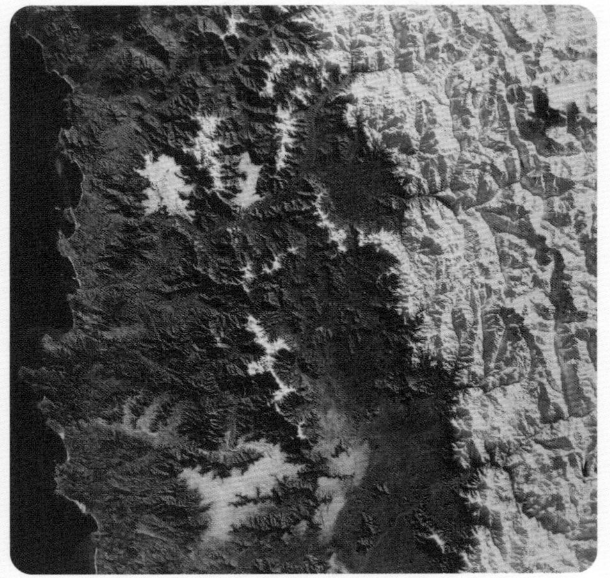

Top 10 countries by area		sq km	sq miles	world rank
1	Brazil	8 547 379	3 300 161	5
2	Argentina	2 766 889	1 068 302	8
3	Peru	1 285 216	496 225	20
4	Colombia	1 141 748	440 831	26
5	Bolivia	1 098 581	424 164	28
6	Venezuela	912 050	352 144	33
7	Chile	756 945	292 258	38
8	Paraguay	406 752	157 048	59
9	Ecuador	272 045	105 037	74
10	Guyana	214 969	83 000	83

Top 10 countries by population		population	world rank
1	Brazil	186 405 000	5
2	Colombia	45 600 000	28
3	Argentina	38 747 000	30
4	Peru	27 968 000	41
5	Venezuela	26 749 000	43
6	Chile	16 295 000	60
7	Ecuador	13 228 000	67
8	Bolivia	9 182 000	84
9	Paraguay	6 158 000	100
10	Uruguay	3 463 000	127

In this Landsat satellite image, **Santiago**, capital city and main industrial centre of Chile, can be seen to the left of the snow-capped Andes mountains which form a natural boundary between Chile and its easterly neighbour, Argentina. The city, which has suffered many earthquakes and floods, was established as Chile's capital when the country became independent in 1818.

Want to know more?

▶ World landscapes	**6–7**
▶ Political map of the World	**8–9**
▶ South America land cover map	**190–191**
▶ Images of deforestation	**194–195**
▶ Detailed maps of South America	**198–207**

Internet links

Organization of American States	www.oas.org
South America travel advice	www.fco.gov.uk
Visit Buenos Aires	www.bue.gov.ar
Visit Rio de Janeiro	www.therioguide.com

Facts

Brasília, the capital of Brazil, was planned and built from scratch in a then-remote part of the inland plateau. The capital was moved from Rio de Janeiro in 1960.

The São Paulo conurbation has a population of over 18 million. It was the first South American city to exceed the 10 million mark.

Machu Picchu in Peru is one of the world's most famous archaeological sites. It was discovered by Hiram Bingham in 1911.

Chile is over 4 000 kilometres (2 486 miles) long but its average width is only 177 kilometres (110 miles).

Dependencies capital		territorial status	sq km sq miles	population	languages	religions	currency	official website	map
Falkland Islands Stanley		United Kingdom Overseas Territory	12 170 4 699	3 000	English	Protestant, Roman Catholic	Falkland Islands pound	www.falklands.gov.fk	205
French Guiana Cayenne		French Overseas Department	90 000 34 749	187 000	French, creole	Roman Catholic	Euro	www.guyane.pref.gouv.fr	199
South Georgia and South Sandwich Islands		United Kingdom Overseas Territory	4 066 1 570	uninhabited					217

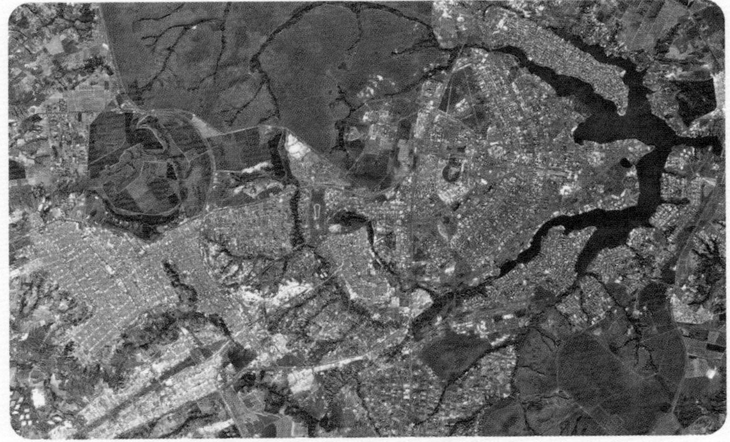

Construction of **Brasília** as the administrative and political centre of Brazil began in 1956 and four years later it replaced Rio de Janeiro as the capital city of Brazil. It is located on the Paraná, a headstream of the Tocantins river. In this infrared satellite image the city is in the centre, where buildings appear as light blue-grey. Vegetation along the small tributary rivers shows as red.

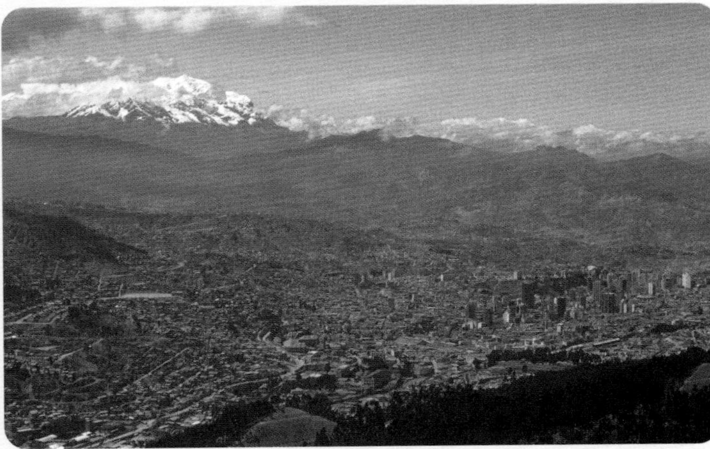

The Bolivian city of **La Paz** is the highest capital city in the world. It lies just southeast of Lake Titicaca, in a valley between the Cordillera Oriental and the Andes, sheltered from the severe winds and weather of the Altiplano. The city was established by the Spanish conquistadors in the mid-1500s.

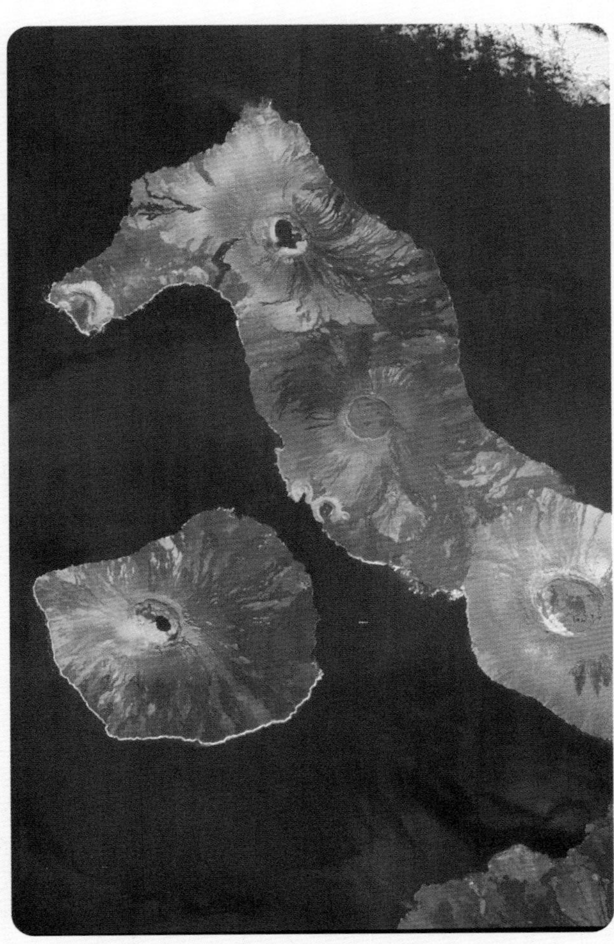

The **Galapagos Islands**, a group of islands created by volcanic activity, are renowned for their rich and unique wildlife. Vegetation, which appears red in this satellite image, is limited as the landscape is dominated by lava flows. The islands are part of Ecuador, lying over 1 000 kilometres (621 miles) off the country's west coast.

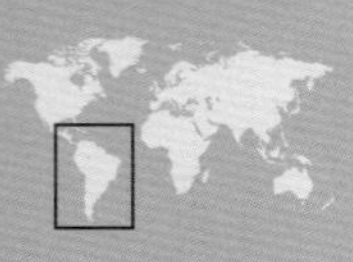

South America is home to vast areas of tropical rainforest, in particular the Amazon Basin. This huge and invaluable resource has been described as 'the lungs of the world' and yet the forests are under great threat as rates of deforestation increase. Deforestation increases carbon dioxide (CO_2) levels in the atmosphere, thereby impacting on global climate, and threatens the eradication of many species of flora and fauna. On the other side of the Andes, Colombia leads the way in the production and trafficking of illegal drugs. This trade, and the crimes commonly associated with it, can impact society and individuals in devastating ways, creating instability, fear and danger in many communities.

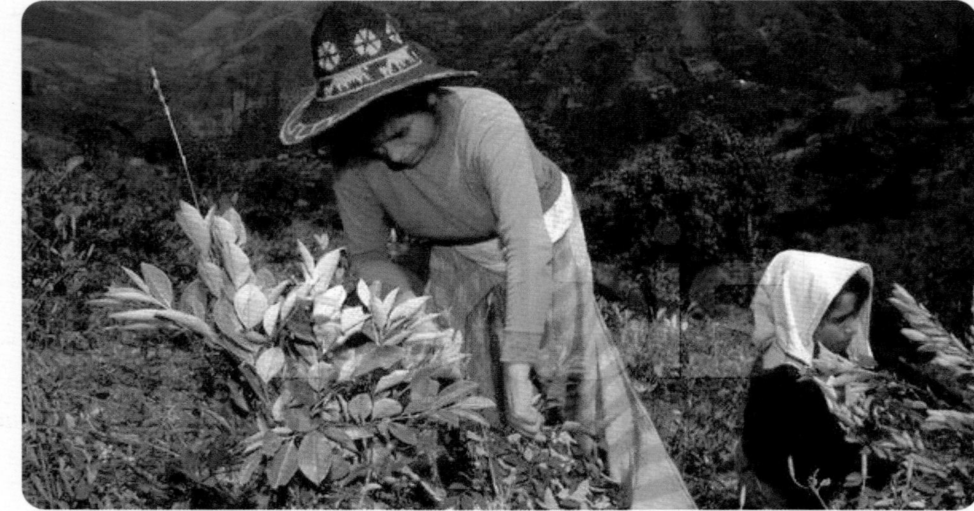

In some areas of South America **coca** is grown legally for traditional uses. Local people chew it or use it to make a tea to combat hunger and altitude sickness. Farmers of legal and illegal crops are being encouraged to substitute coca with other crops such as coffee.

The international drugs trade
Main producers and trafficking routes for opiates (opium, morphine, heroin) and cocaine

Cocaine producer
Opiate producer

Cocaine trafficking route
Opiate trafficking route

Afghanistan
Opiate production 2003: 3 600 metric tonnes

Mexico
Opiate production 2003: 84 metric tonnes

Colombia
Cocaine production 2003: 440 metric tonnes

Peru
Cocaine production 2003: 155 metric tonnes

Myanmar
Opiate production 2003: 810 metric tonnes

World
Opiate production 2003: 4 765 metric tonnes
Cocaine production 2003: 655 metric tonnes

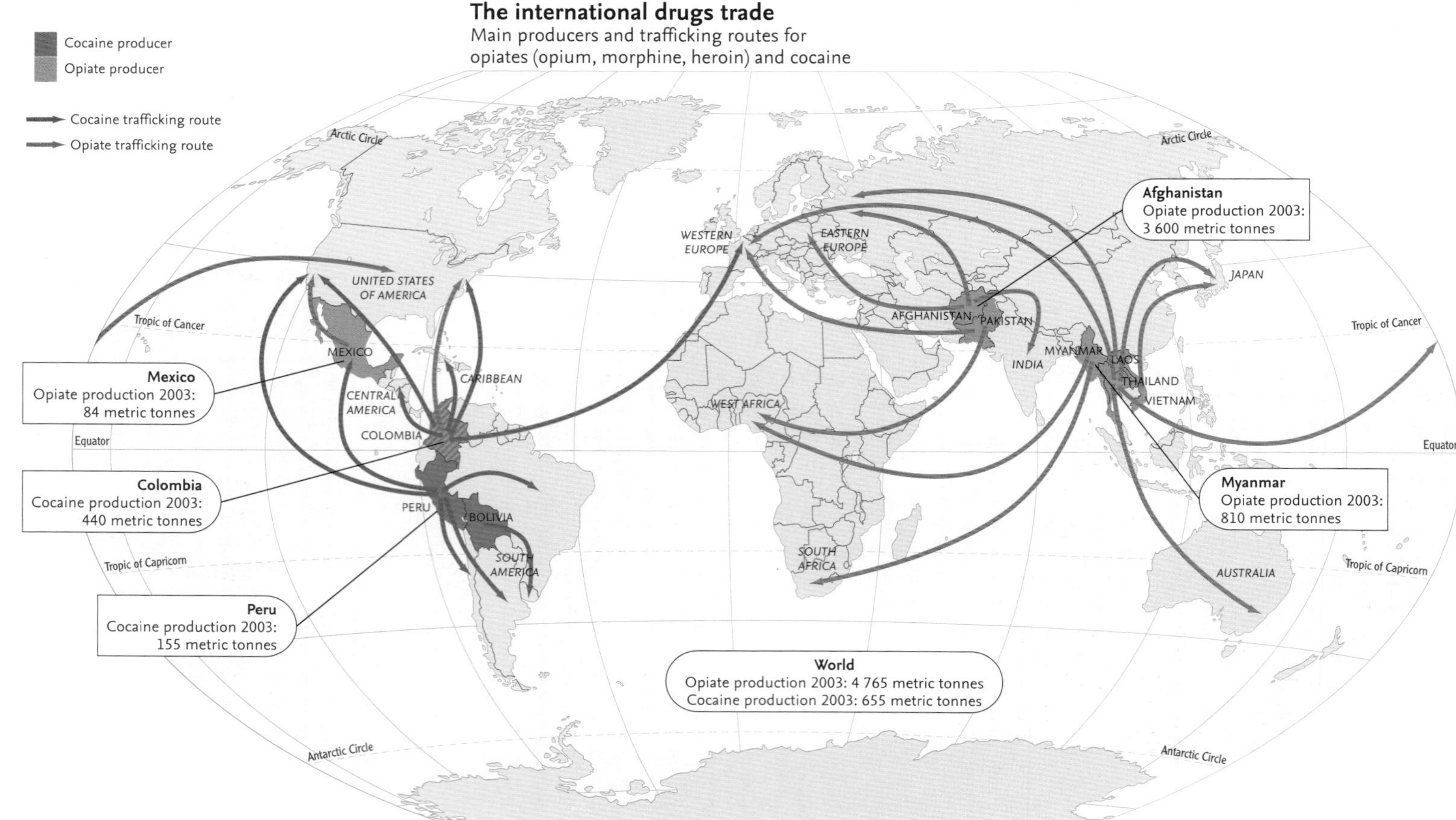

The drugs trade

For the third year in a row, Colombia has seen a decline in coca cultivation – 16 per cent from 2002–2003. Crop eradication, voluntary or forced and improved help for other forms of cultivation have aided this decline but the reduction from 1 020 to 860 square kilometres (102 000 to 86 000 hectares) does not take into account possible improved crop yield. It is thought that 3–8 per cent of Colombia's GDP comes from the illegal drugs trade and with the country producing 67 per cent of the world's cocaine it is a major concern. This equates to a potential value of US$350 million. This trade has fuelled a dangerous and volatile environment resulting in Colombia having the highest murder rate in the world.

Cocaine abuse
Percentage of population abusing cocaine

	country	per cent
1	Spain	2.6
2	USA	2.5
3	Ireland	2.4
4	UK	2.1
5	Argentina	1.9
6	Colombia	1.6
7	Chile	1.6
8	Australia	1.5
9	Panama	1.4
10	Canada	1.2

Trend in cocaine seizures, 2001–2002
Amounts in metric tonnes

Japan 0.02
Nigeria 0.04
Uruguay 0.04
Australia 0.1
Canada 0.2
Near and Middle East 0.2
Suriname 0.3
Argentina 1.1
Chile 2   Thailand 0.01
Bolivia 5.1   Zambia 0.02
Ecuador 5.1   East Africa 0.03
Brazil 9   Paraguay 0.2
Mexico 12   South Africa 0.4
Central America 12.9   Eastern Europe 0.6
Caribbean 13   Peru 14.6
Europe 45   Venezuela 17.8
USA 106   Colombia 119

decrease in metric tonnes   increase in metric tonnes

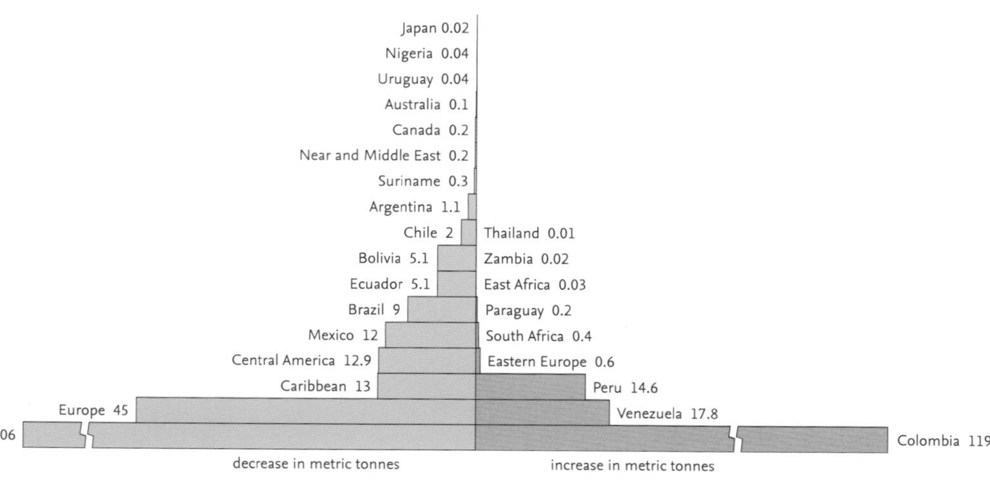

In **Colombia** soldiers are involved in destroying illegal drug processing laboratories as well as crop eradication by spraying.

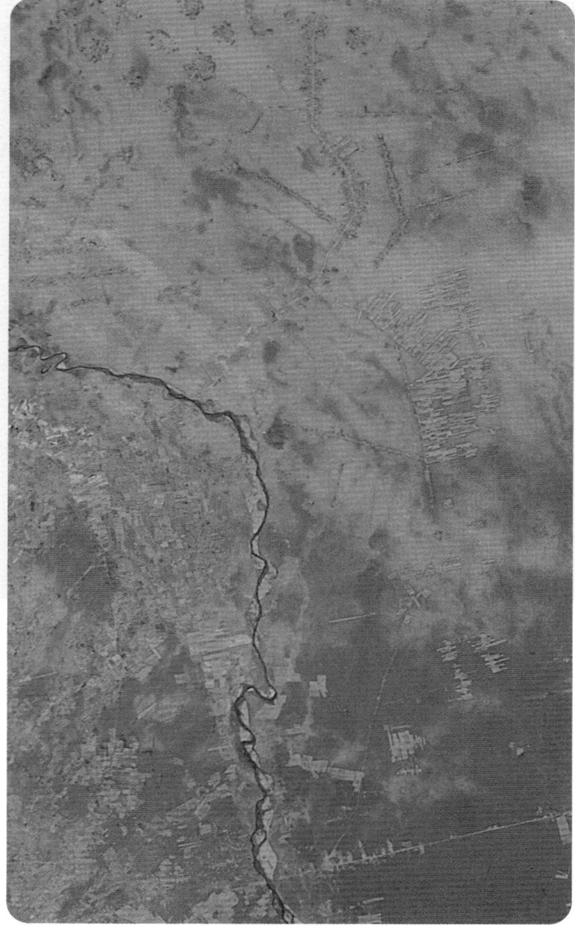

Forest clearing is worked in a pattern outwards from the roads that are initially laid for access of heavy machinery. Relatively few species of tree are used for timber products. Vegetation is burned for fuel and to supply nutrients to the soil as unlike temperate forests the trees and plants, not the soil hold the nutrients.

Deforestation in Brazil, 1990–2003

Area (thousand square kilometres)

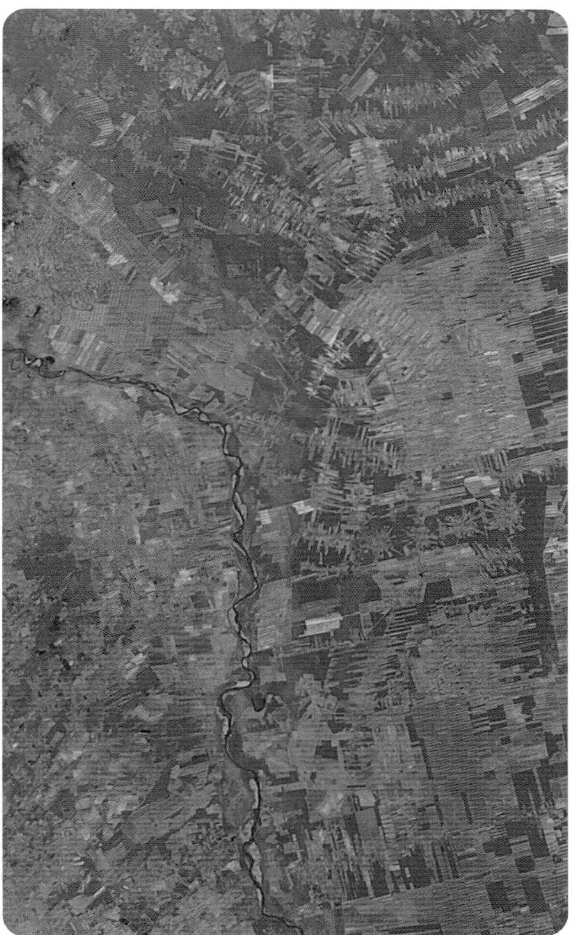

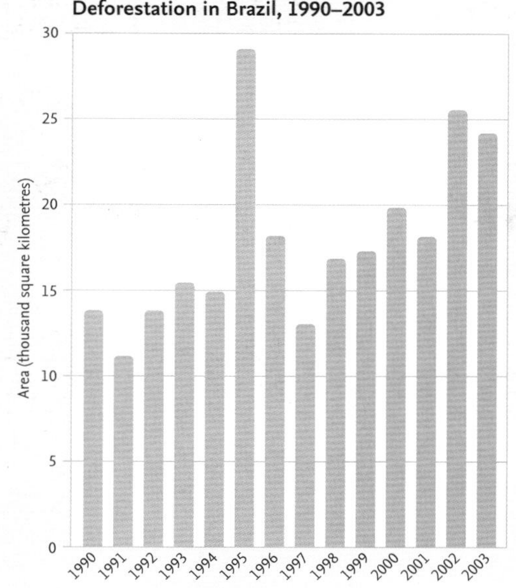

Deforestation

One per cent of tropical rainforest is lost in South America every year. The rainforest is cleared for a variety of reasons; cattle ranching, soya farming, mineral exploration and logging. For poor farmers the 'slash-and-burn' agricultural system is a short-term solution as the soil becomes infertile after about three years and a new area has to be cleared. Commercial agricultural methods work on a larger scale and have a greater affect. Where land is abandoned it takes fifty years or more for the forest to grow back. Illegal logging is a serious problem – in 2001 Ibama, the Brazilian environmental agency seized US$40 million worth of illegally felled mahogany.

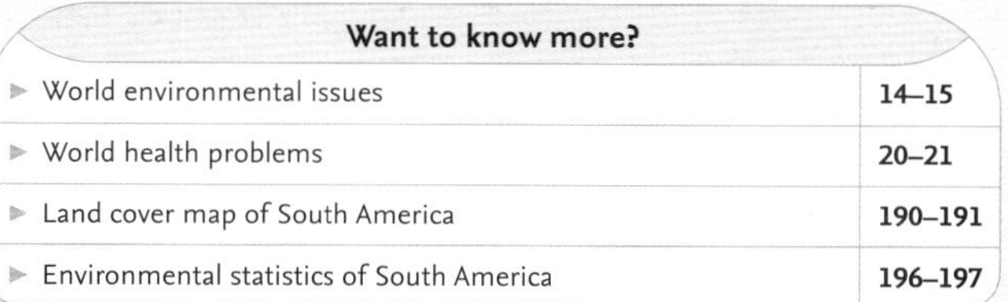

Want to know more?

▶ World environmental issues	14–15
▶ World health problems	20–21
▶ Land cover map of South America	190–191
▶ Environmental statistics of South America	196–197

Internet links

UN office on drugs and crime	**www.unodc.org**
International Tropical Timber Organization	**www.itto.org**
International Tropical Timber Information System	**www.ittis.org**
Global Forest Watch	**www.globalforestwatch.org**
World Resources Unit	**www.earthtrends.org**

Facts

If Amazonia were a country it would be the ninth largest in the world.

Amazonia produces approximately 20 per cent of the world's oxygen.

Colombia accounts for two-thirds of reported kidnappings in the world. Many are believed to be related to the drugs trade.

Approximately 3 per cent of the world's population use illicit drugs annually – approximately 190 million people.

A mahogany tree can take nearly 100 years to grow to a 'harvestable' size.

Causes of deforestation in the Amazon Basin within Brazil

Land use

- Cropland and woodland
- Grassland and grazing
- Grassland and woodland
- Tropical forest
- Temperate forest
- Scrubland or desert
- Swamp or marsh
- Deforestation

- ▬ Hydro-electric power dam
- ▬ Hydro-electric power dam (planned)
- ◆ Mining operations
- ── Extent of Amazonia in Brazil

Communications

- ── Railway
- ---- Railway (planned)
- ── Road
- ---- Road (planned)

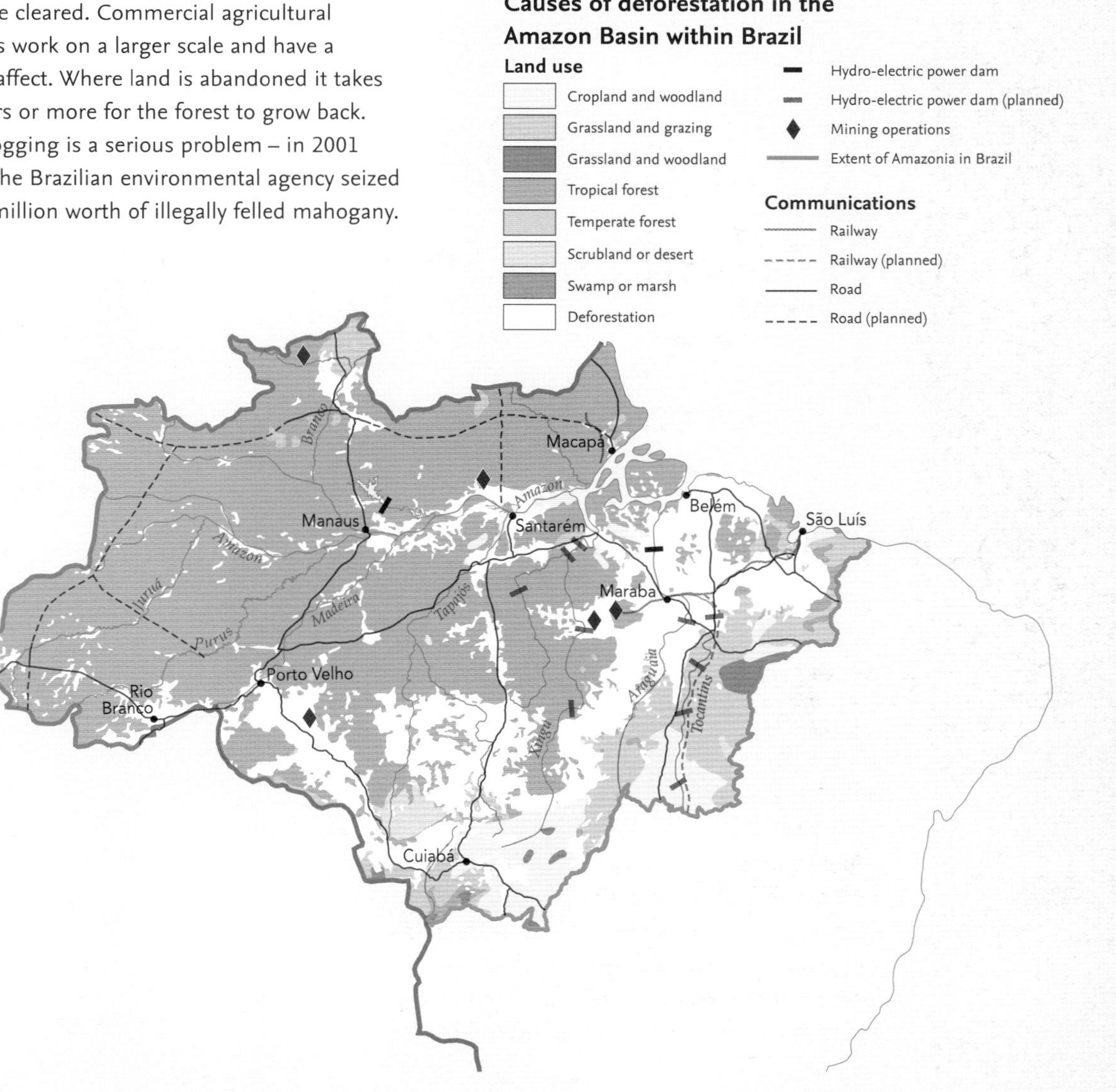

Timber products in Brazil, 2000
Products by type and use (1 000 cubic metres)
Values in brackets indicate volume in tropical species

Production

Veneer 200 (150)
Plywood 2 200 (1 100)
Sawn 18 500 (9 805)
Logs 46 000 (24 380)

Total: 66 900 (35 435)

Consumption

Veneer 117 (99)
Plywood 1 228 (528)
Sawn 17 038 (9 200)
Logs 45 613 (24 631)

Total: 63 996 (34 458)

Imports

Plywood 2 (2)
Logs 13 (10)
Veneer 27 (23)
Sawn 238 (174)

Total: 280 (209)

Exports

Logs 400 (0)
Plywood 974 (575)
Sawn 1 700 (901)
Veneer 110 (74)

Total: 3 184 (1 550)

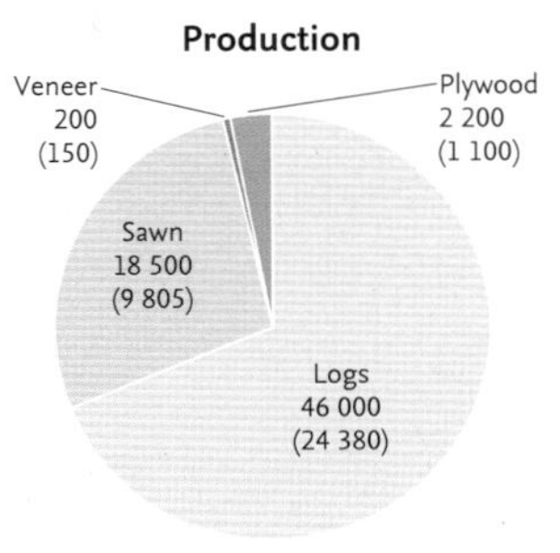

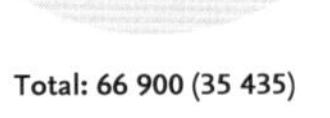

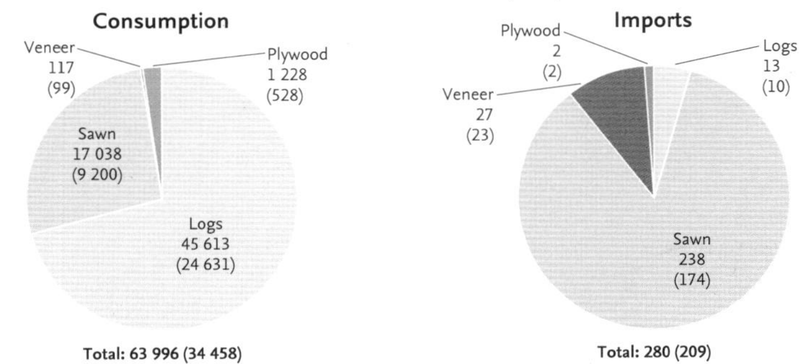

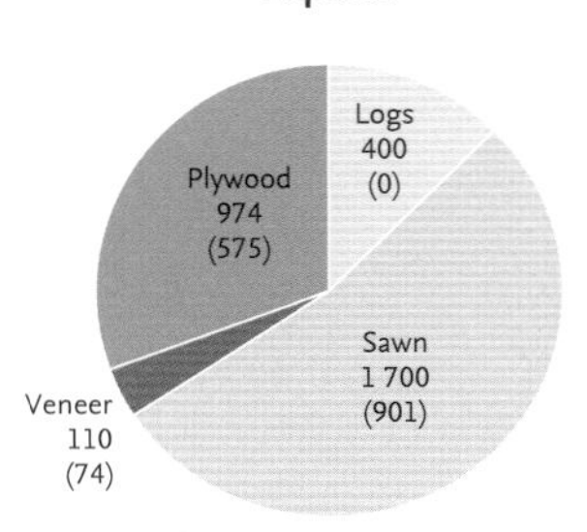

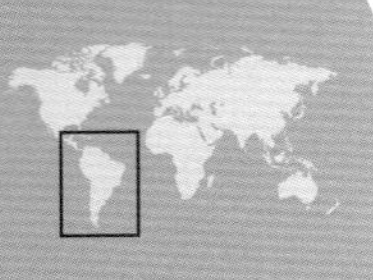

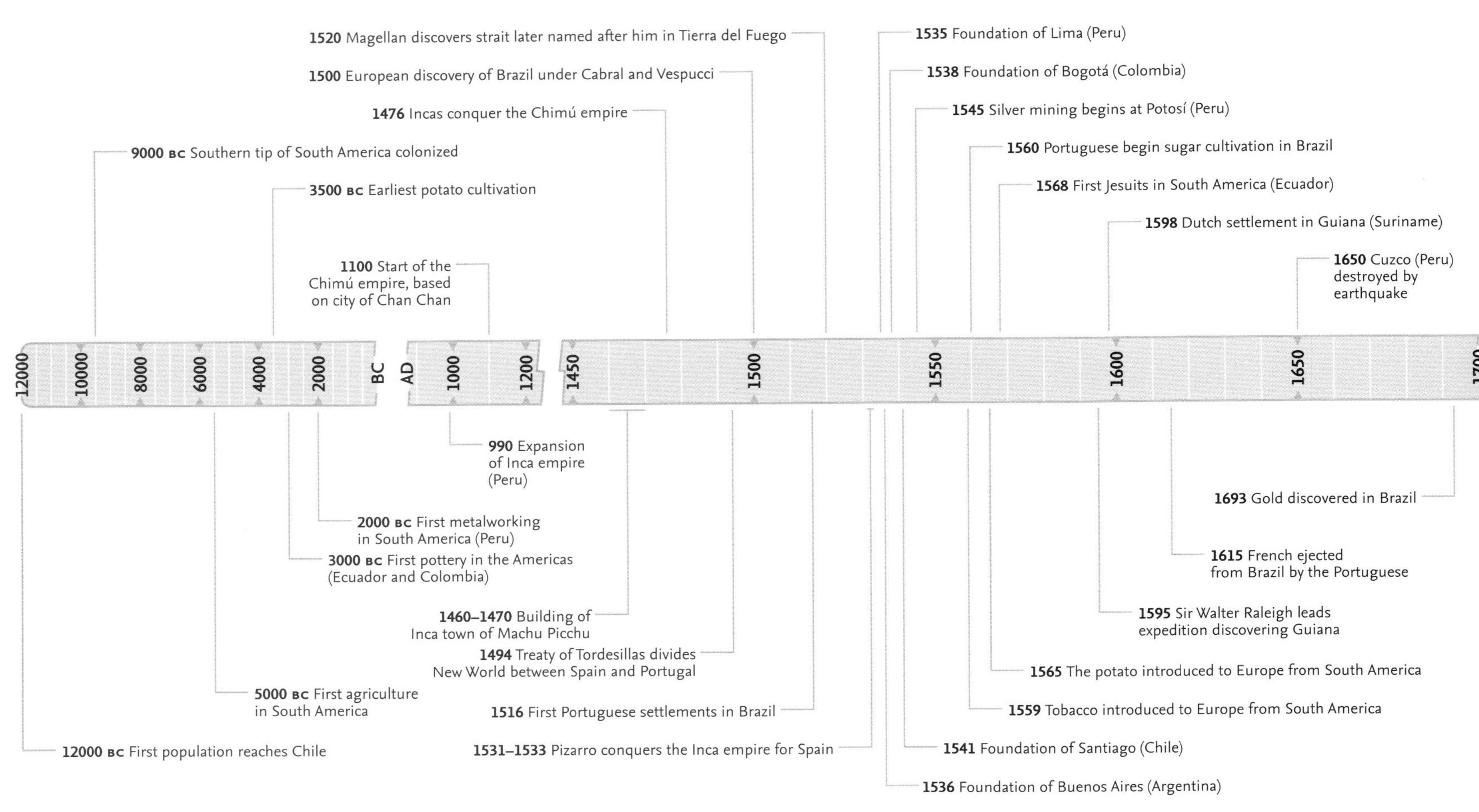

1520 Magellan discovers strait later named after him in Tierra del Fuego

1500 European discovery of Brazil under Cabral and Vespucci

1476 Incas conquer the Chimú empire

9000 BC Southern tip of South America colonized

3500 BC Earliest potato cultivation

1100 Start of the Chimú empire, based on city of Chan Chan

1535 Foundation of Lima (Peru)

1538 Foundation of Bogotá (Colombia)

1545 Silver mining begins at Potosí (Peru)

1560 Portuguese begin sugar cultivation in Brazil

1568 First Jesuits in South America (Ecuador)

1598 Dutch settlement in Guiana (Suriname)

1650 Cuzco (Peru) destroyed by earthquake

990 Expansion of Inca empire (Peru)

2000 BC First metalworking in South America (Peru)

3000 BC First pottery in the Americas (Ecuador and Colombia)

1460–1470 Building of Inca town of Machu Picchu

1494 Treaty of Tordesillas divides New World between Spain and Portugal

5000 BC First agriculture in South America

1516 First Portuguese settlements in Brazil

12000 BC First population reaches Chile

1531–1533 Pizarro conquers the Inca empire for Spain

1693 Gold discovered in Brazil

1615 French ejected from Brazil by the Portuguese

1595 Sir Walter Raleigh leads expedition discovering Guiana

1565 The potato introduced to Europe from South America

1559 Tobacco introduced to Europe from South America

1541 Foundation of Santiago (Chile)

1536 Foundation of Buenos Aires (Argentina)

	Population						Economy					
	total population	population change (%)	urban population (%)	total fertility	population by age 0-14 (%)	population by age 60+ (%)	2050 projected population	total Gross National Income (GNI) (US$M)	Gross National Income (GNI) per capita (US$)	debt service ratio (% GNI)	total debt service (US$)	aid receipts (% GNI)	military spending (% GDP)
World	**6 464 750 000**	**1.2**	**48.3**	**2.7**	**28.2**	**10.4**	**9 075 903 000**	**34 491 458**	**5 500**	**...**	**...**	**...**	**2.4**
Argentina	38 747 000	1.0	90.1	2.4	26.4	13.9	51 382 000	140 114	3 650	6.1	5 825 699 840	0.1	1.2
Bolivia	9 182 000	2.0	63.4	4.0	38.1	6.7	14 908 000	7 985	890	6.3	476 000 000	9.0	1.7
Brazil	186 405 000	1.4	83.1	2.4	27.9	8.8	253 105 000	478 922	2 710	11.7	51 631 599 616	0.1	1.6
Chile	16 295 000	1.1	87.0	2.0	24.9	11.6	20 657 000	69 193	4 390	11.9	7 728 999 936	0.0	2.9
Colombia	45 600 000	1.6	76.5	2.6	31.0	7.5	65 679 000	80 488	1 810	8.9	6 920 699 904	0.6	3.7
Ecuador	13 228 000	1.5	61.8	2.8	32.4	8.3	19 214 000	23 347	1 790	9.7	2 192 900 096	1.0	...
Guyana	751 000	0.2	37.6	2.3	29.3	7.4	488 000	689	900	11.6	77 500 000	9.7	...
Paraguay	6 158 000	2.4	57.2	3.9	37.6	5.6	12 095 000	6 213	1 100	5.8	327 000 000	1.0	0.9
Peru	27 968 000	1.5	73.9	2.9	32.2	7.8	42 552 000	58 458	2 150	6.1	3 356 499 968	0.9	1.3
Suriname	449 000	0.7	76.1	2.6	30.1	9.0	429 000	841	1 990	...	...	1.3	...
Uruguay	3 463 000	0.7	92.6	2.3	24.3	17.4	4 043 000	12 904	3 790	10.5	1 280 000 000	0.1	1.3
Venezuela	26 749 000	1.8	87.7	2.7	31.2	7.6	41 991 000	89 150	3 490	8.2	7 487 399 936	0.1	1.2

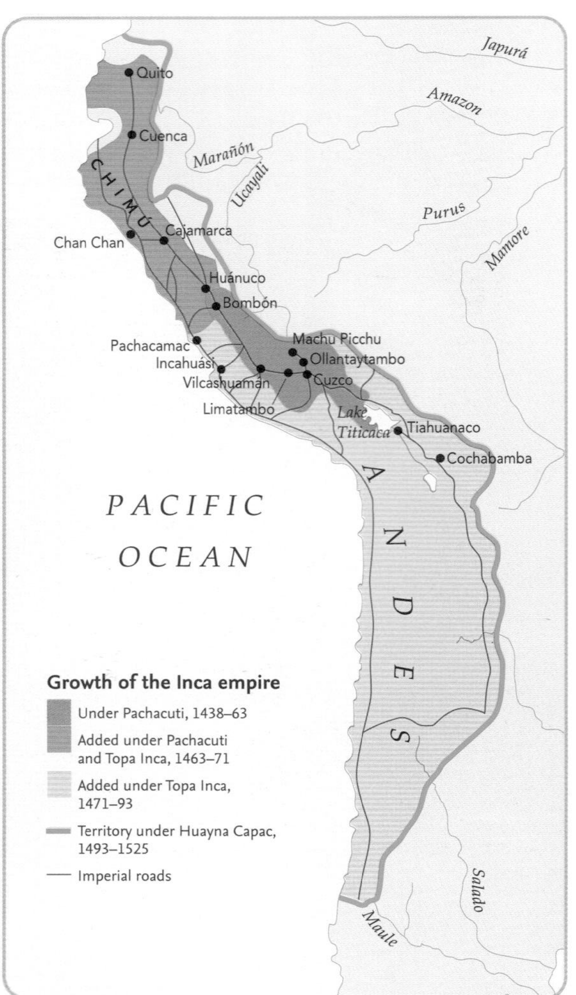

Growth of the Inca empire

Under Pachacuti, 1438–63

Added under Pachacuti and Topa Inca, 1463–71

Added under Topa Inca, 1471–93

Territory under Huayna Capac, 1493–1525

Imperial roads

The Inca empire, 1438–1525

The Inca empire expanded rapidly in the fifteenth century. From Cuzco, the Inca emperor exerted rigid control over this extensive territory by means of a highly trained bureaucracy, a state religion, a powerful army and an advanced communications network. The final expansion under Huayna Capac put the Inca world under great strain, however, and by the time of its conquest by the Spanish conquistador Pizarro in 1533, civil war had split the empire in two.

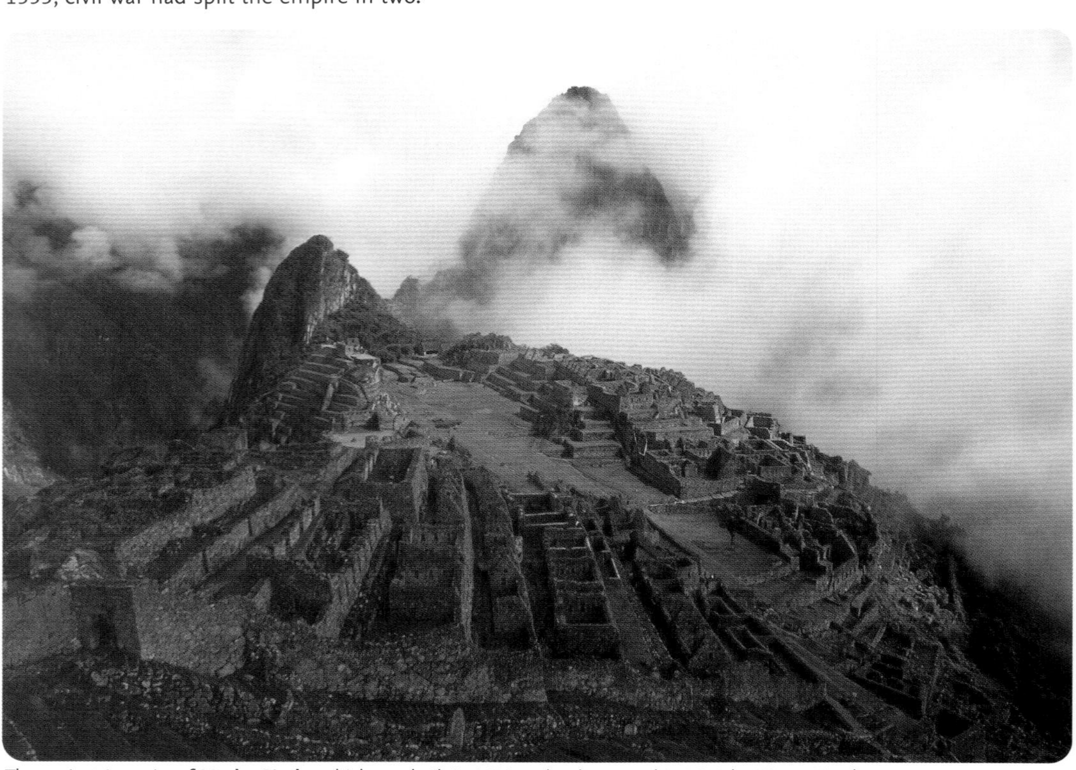

The ancient Inca city of **Machu Picchu** which was built in 1500 and rediscovered in 1911 by Hiram Bingham.

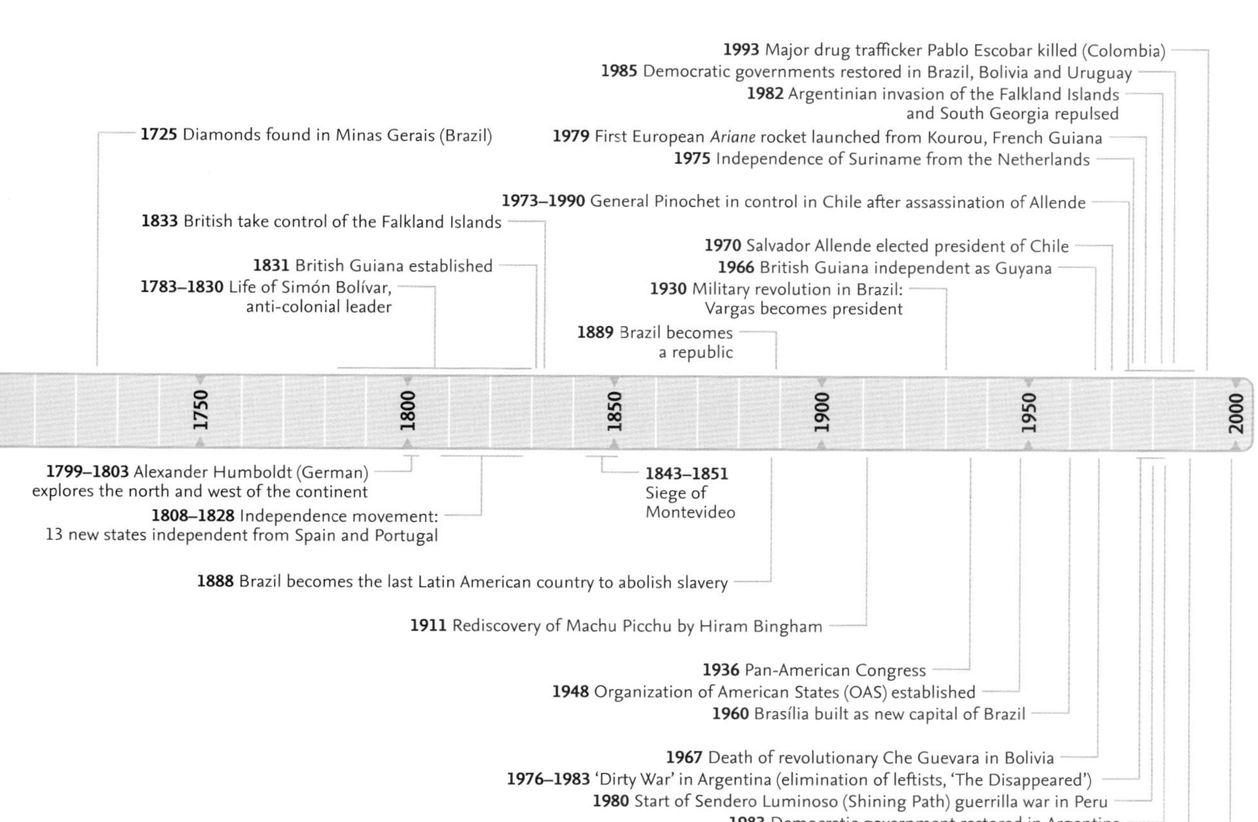

1993 Major drug trafficker Pablo Escobar killed (Colombia)
1985 Democratic governments restored in Brazil, Bolivia and Uruguay
1982 Argentinian invasion of the Falkland Islands and South Georgia repulsed
1979 First European *Ariane* rocket launched from Kourou, French Guiana
1975 Independence of Suriname from the Netherlands
1725 Diamonds found in Minas Gerais (Brazil)
1973–1990 General Pinochet in control in Chile after assassination of Allende
1833 British take control of the Falkland Islands
1970 Salvador Allende elected president of Chile
1966 British Guiana independent as Guyana
1831 British Guiana established
1783–1830 Life of Simón Bolívar, anti-colonial leader
1930 Military revolution in Brazil: Vargas becomes president
1889 Brazil becomes a republic

1750 · 1800 · 1850 · 1900 · 1950 · 2000

1799–1803 Alexander Humboldt (German) explores the north and west of the continent
1808–1828 Independence movement: 13 new states independent from Spain and Portugal
1843–1851 Siege of Montevideo
1888 Brazil becomes the last Latin American country to abolish slavery
1911 Rediscovery of Machu Picchu by Hiram Bingham
1936 Pan-American Congress
1948 Organization of American States (OAS) established
1960 Brasília built as new capital of Brazil
1967 Death of revolutionary Che Guevara in Bolivia
1976–1983 'Dirty War' in Argentina (elimination of leftists, 'The Disappeared')
1980 Start of Sendero Luminoso (Shining Path) guerrilla war in Peru
1983 Democratic government restored in Argentina
1989 Democratic government restored in Chile
1999 Panama assumes sole responsibility for operation of Panama Canal

Want to know more?

▶ Map of population distribution	16–17
▶ International debt	22–23
▶ North America timeline	162–163
▶ Guide to South America's countries	194–195
▶ International drugs trade	194–195

Internet links

Organization of American States	www.oas.org
South American conservation	www.unep-wcmc.org
Latin America	lanic.utexas.edu
Explore Patagonia	www.patagoniaaustral.net
Heritage sites in South America	whc.unesco.org

Facts

Ferdinand Magellan, the Portuguese explorer, set off sanctioned by Spain to sail westwards to the Spice Islands. He traversed the southern tip of the American continent but was killed in the Philippines.

The Galapagos Islands were a favourite hideout of sixteenth-century pirates and were also vital for re-provisioning ships with fresh water and meat.

The Falkland Islands have been claimed by England, France, Spain and Argentina but have been occupied by the British since 1833.

Simon Bolivar, a Venezuelan, was responsible for the independence of Bolivia, Colombia, Peru, Ecuador, Panama and Venezuela from Spain.

Social indicators					Environment				Communications					
child mortality rate	life expectancy male	female	literacy rate (%)	access to safe water (%)	doctors per 100 000 people	forest area (%)	annual change in forest area (%)	protected land area (%)	CO_2 emissions (metric tons per capita)	main telephone lines per 100 people	cellular mobile subscribers per 100 people	internet users per 10 000 people	international dialling code	time zone	See page 335 for explanatory table and sources
80	63.3	67.6	87.3	83	...	29.6	-0.2	11.4	3.8	18.8	21.9	1 125	...	...	World
20	70.6	77.7	98.6	94	304	12.7	-0.8	6.3	3.9	21.9	17.8	1 120	54	-3	Argentina
66	61.8	66.0	96.3	85	76	48.9	-0.3	19.4	1.3	7.1	16.7	324	591	-4	Bolivia
35	64.0	72.6	93.0	89	206	64.3	-0.4	18.0	1.8	22.3	26.4	822	55	-2 to -5	Brazil
9	73.0	79.0	99.0	95	115	20.7	-0.1	3.6	3.9	23.0	42.8	2 720	56	-3	Chile
21	69.2	75.3	97.2	92	94	47.8	-0.4	72.3	1.4	20.0	14.1	624	57	-5	Colombia
27	68.3	73.5	97.5	86	145	38.1	-1.2	27.0	2.0	11.9	18.4	438	593	-5	Ecuador
69	60.1	66.3	99.8	83	26	78.5	-0.3	2.3	2.1	9.2	9.9	1 422	592	-4	Guyana
29	68.6	73.1	97.3	83	49	58.8	-0.5	4.1	0.7	4.6	29.9	202	595	-3	Paraguay
34	67.3	72.4	97.1	81	103	50.9	-0.4	16.7	1.1	6.7	10.6	1 039	51	-5	Peru
39	68.5	73.7	...	92	50	90.5	...	12.7	5.0	15.2	32.0	416	597	-3	Suriname
14	71.6	78.9	99.3	98	387	7.4	5.0	0.4	1.6	28.0	19.3	1 190	598	-3	Uruguay
21	70.9	76.7	98.2	83	200	56.1	-0.4	70.4	6.5	11.3	25.6	506	58	-4	Venezuela

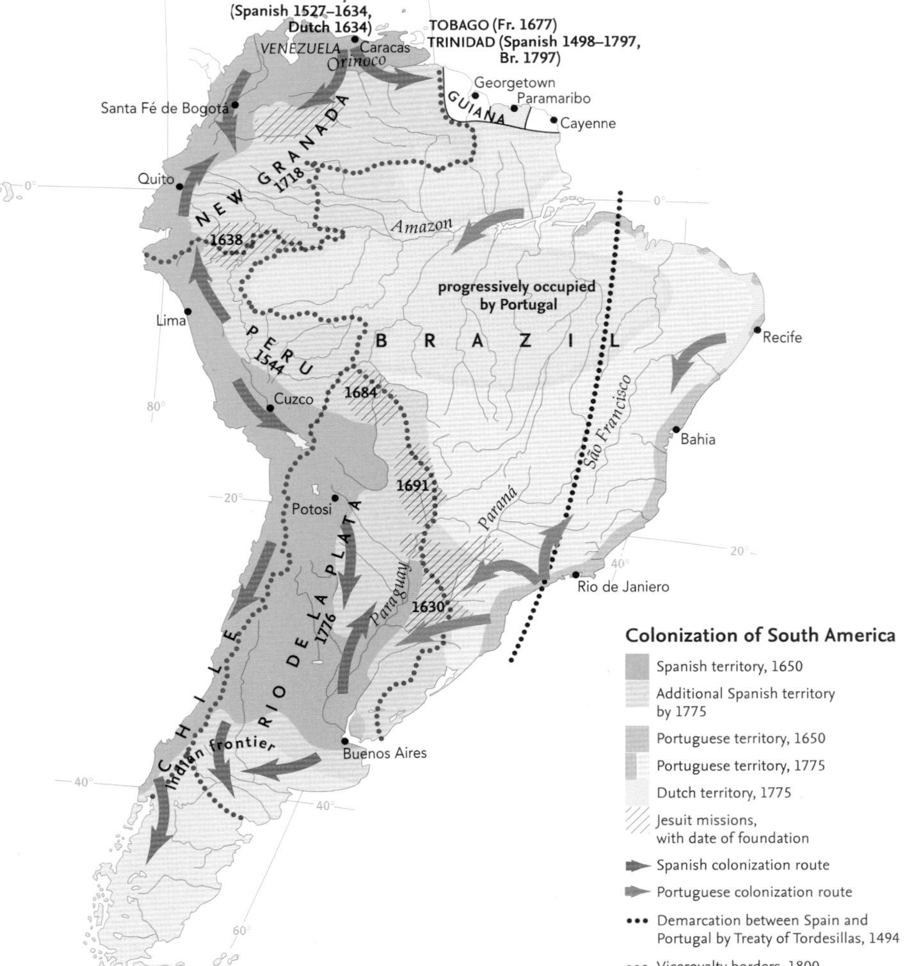

CURAÇAO (Spanish 1527–1634, Dutch 1634)
TOBAGO (Fr. 1677)
TRINIDAD (Spanish 1498–1797, Br. 1797)
VENEZUELA
Orinoco
Caracas
Santa Fé de Bogotá
GUIANA
Georgetown
Paramaribo
Cayenne
NEW GRANADA
1718
Quito
1638
Amazon
progressively occupied by Portugal
Lima
PERU
1544
B R A Z I L
São Francisco
Recife
Cuzco
1684
Potosí
1691
RIO DE LA PLATA
Paraguay
Paraná
1630
Bahia
Rio de Janiero
CHILE
Indian Frontier
1776
Buenos Aires

Colonization of South America

- Spanish territory, 1650
- Additional Spanish territory by 1775
- Portuguese territory, 1650
- Portuguese territory, 1775
- Dutch territory, 1775
- Jesuit missions, with date of foundation
- ➤ Spanish colonization route
- ➤ Portuguese colonization route
- ••• Demarcation between Spain and Portugal by Treaty of Tordesillas, 1494
- ••• Viceroyalty borders, 1800 (with date of foundation)

Colonial South America

In the sixteenth century, Spaniards colonized much of South and Central America. A great deal of their power and wealth arose from the conquest of the Aztec and Inca empires. In the seventeenth century, both Spain and Portugal were placed on the defensive by the colonial ambitions of France, Holland and Britain. From around 1808, the Spanish and Portuguese colonies began to gain their independence.

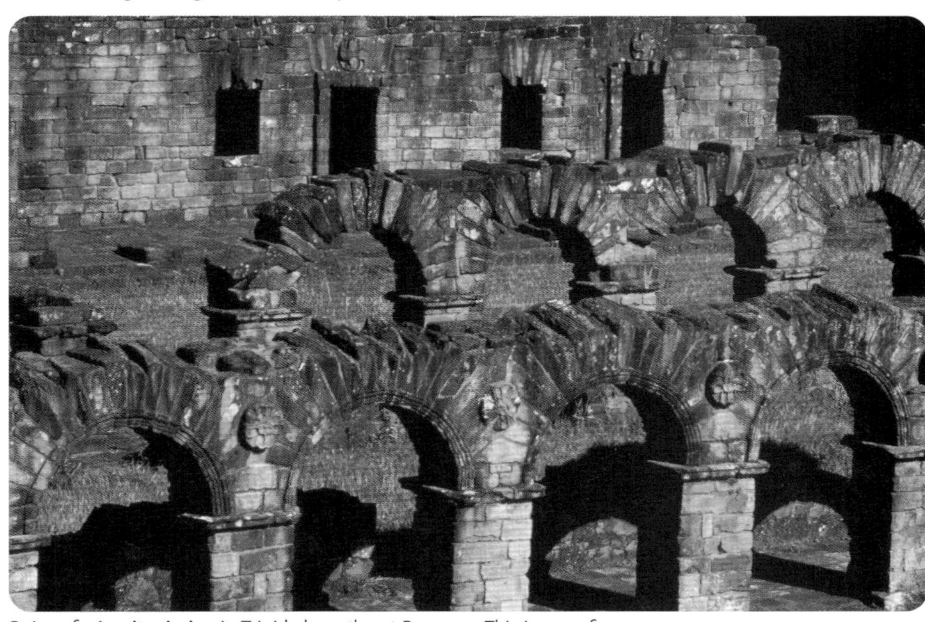

Ruins of a **Jesuit mission** in Trinidad, southeast Paraguay. This is one of many missions established during the seventeenth and eighteenth centuries throughout South America.

Administrative regions
numbered on the map:
COLOMBIA
1. QUINDIO (C3)
2. RISARALDA (C3)
3. BOGOTÁ (C3)
ECUADOR
4. BOLÍVAR (B5)
5. CHIMBORAZO (B5)
6. TUNGURAHUA (B5)
7. ZAMORA-CHINCHIPE (B5)
VENEZUELA
8. DISTRITO CAPITAL (E2)
9. VARGAS (E3)

Caribbean

PACIFIC

OCEAN

PANAMA

COLOMBIA

ECUADOR

PERU

>6000m
5000-6000m
4000-5000m
3000-4000m
2000-3000m
1000-2000m
500-1000m
200-500m
0-200m
<0m

0-200m
200-500m
500-1000m
1000-2000m
2000-3000m
3000-4000m
4000-5000m
5000-6000m
>6000m

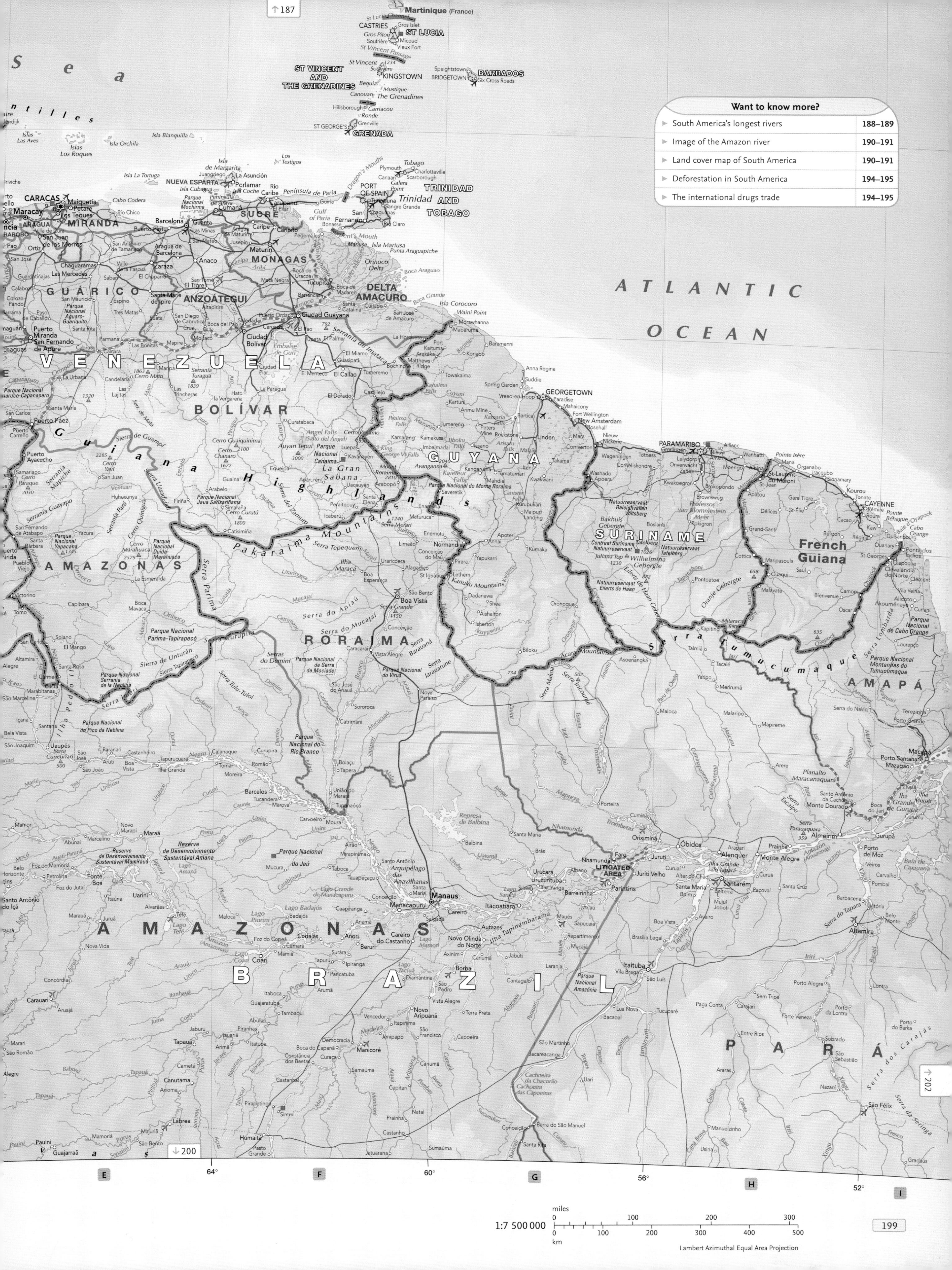

Want to know more?
South America's longest rivers 188–189
Image of the Amazon river 190–191
Land cover map of South America 190–191
Deforestation in South America 194–195
The international drugs trade 194–195
ATLANTIC
OCEAN
Sea
Antilles
Martinique (France)
ST LUCIA
CASTRIES
ST VINCENT AND THE GRENADINES
KINGSTOWN
BARBADOS
BRIDGETOWN
GRENADA
ST GEORGE'S
TRINIDAD AND TOBAGO
PORT OF SPAIN
Trinidad
Tobago
CARACAS
VENEZUELA
MIRANDA
SUCRE
MONAGAS
DELTA AMACURO
ANZOÁTEGUI
GUÁRICO
BOLÍVAR
AMAZONAS
Ciudad Guayana
Ciudad Bolívar
Barcelona
Cumaná
Maturín
Guiana Highlands
Pakaraima Mountains
GUYANA
GEORGETOWN
SURINAME
PARAMARIBO
French Guiana
CAYENNE
AMAPÁ
RORAIMA
Boa Vista
Serra Tumucumaque
AMAZONAS
BRAZIL
PARÁ
Manaus
Macapá
Santarém
Óbidos
Altamira
Itaituba
Parintins
Itacoatiara
Humaitá
Lambert Azimuthal Equal Area Projection
1:7 500 000
miles 0 100 200 300
km 0 100 200 300 400 500
64°
60°
56°
52°
E F G H I

↑187
↓200
→202

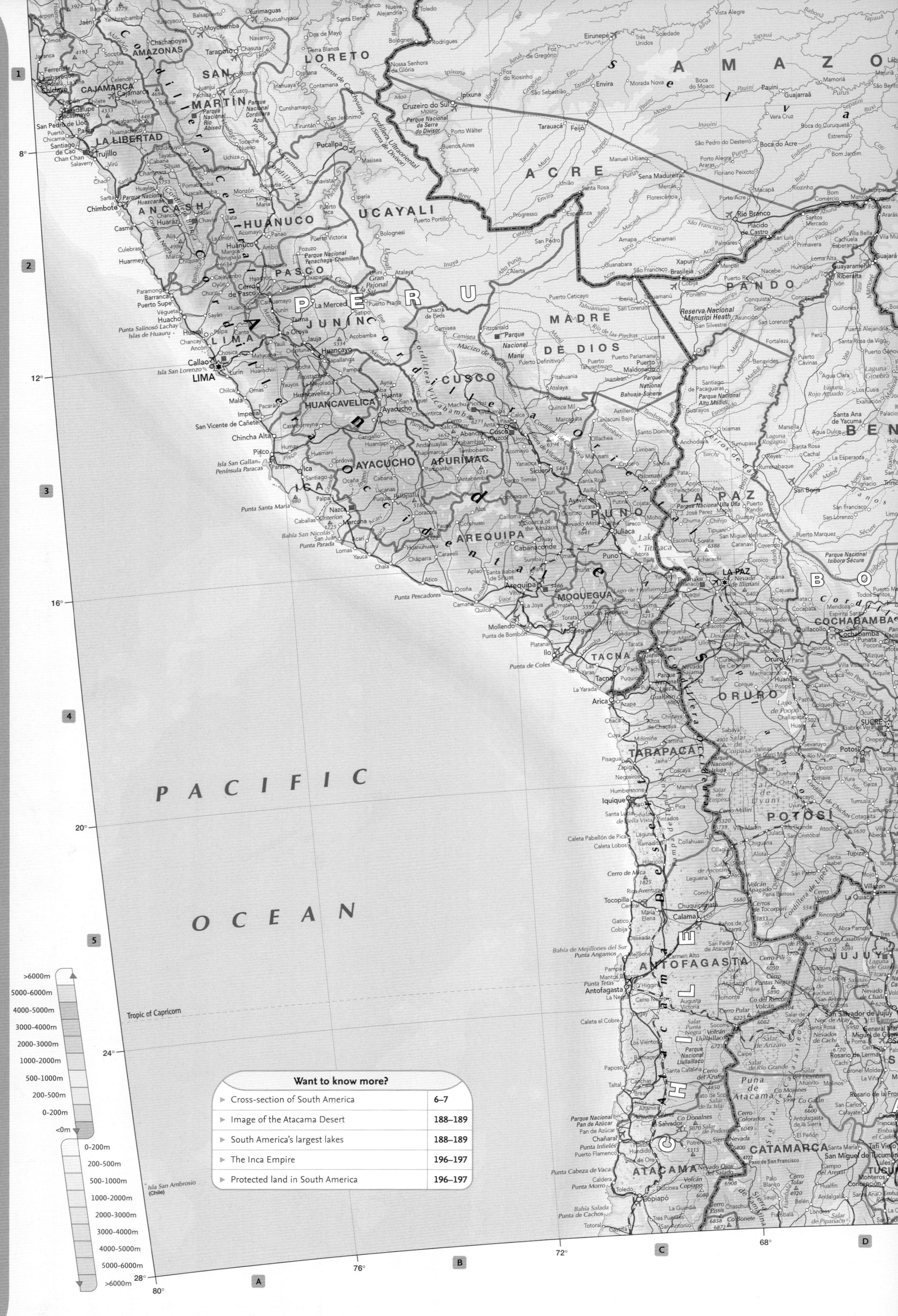

Want to know more?

>6000m
5000-6000m
4000-5000m
3000-4000m
2000-3000m
1000-2000m
500-1000m
200-500m
0-200m
<0m

0-200m
200-500m
500-1000m
1000-2000m
2000-3000m
3000-4000m
4000-5000m
5000-6000m
>6000m

↑199

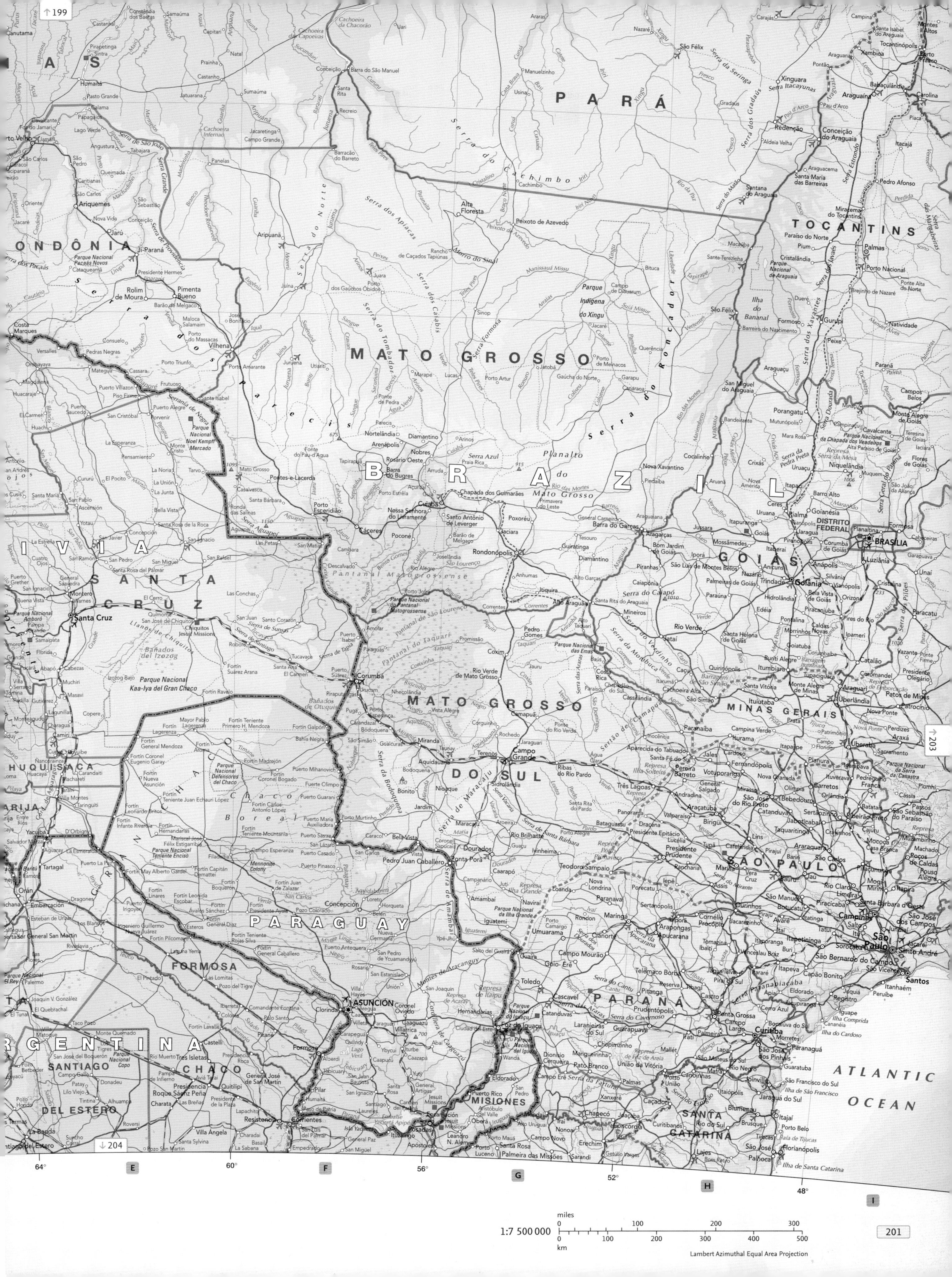

PARÁ
TOCANTINS
RONDÔNIA
MATO GROSSO
BRAZIL
Planalto do Mato Grosso
GOIÁS
DISTRITO FEDERAL
BRASÍLIA
MATO GROSSO DO SUL
MINAS GERAIS
SÃO PAULO
PARANÁ
SANTA CATARINA
BOLIVIA
SANTA CRUZ
CHUQUISACA
TARIJA
PARAGUAY
ASUNCIÓN
CHACO
ARGENTINA
FORMOSA
SANTIAGO DEL ESTERO
MISIONES
ATLANTIC OCEAN
Pantanal Matogrossense
Chaco Boreal
São Paulo
Rio Verde
Campo Grande
Cuiabá
Corumbá
Santa Cruz
Curitiba
Florianópolis
Santos
64°
60°
56°
52°
48°
E
F
G
H
I
1:7 500 000
miles
0
100
200
300
km
0
100
200
300
400
500
Lambert Azimuthal Equal Area Projection

→203

↓204

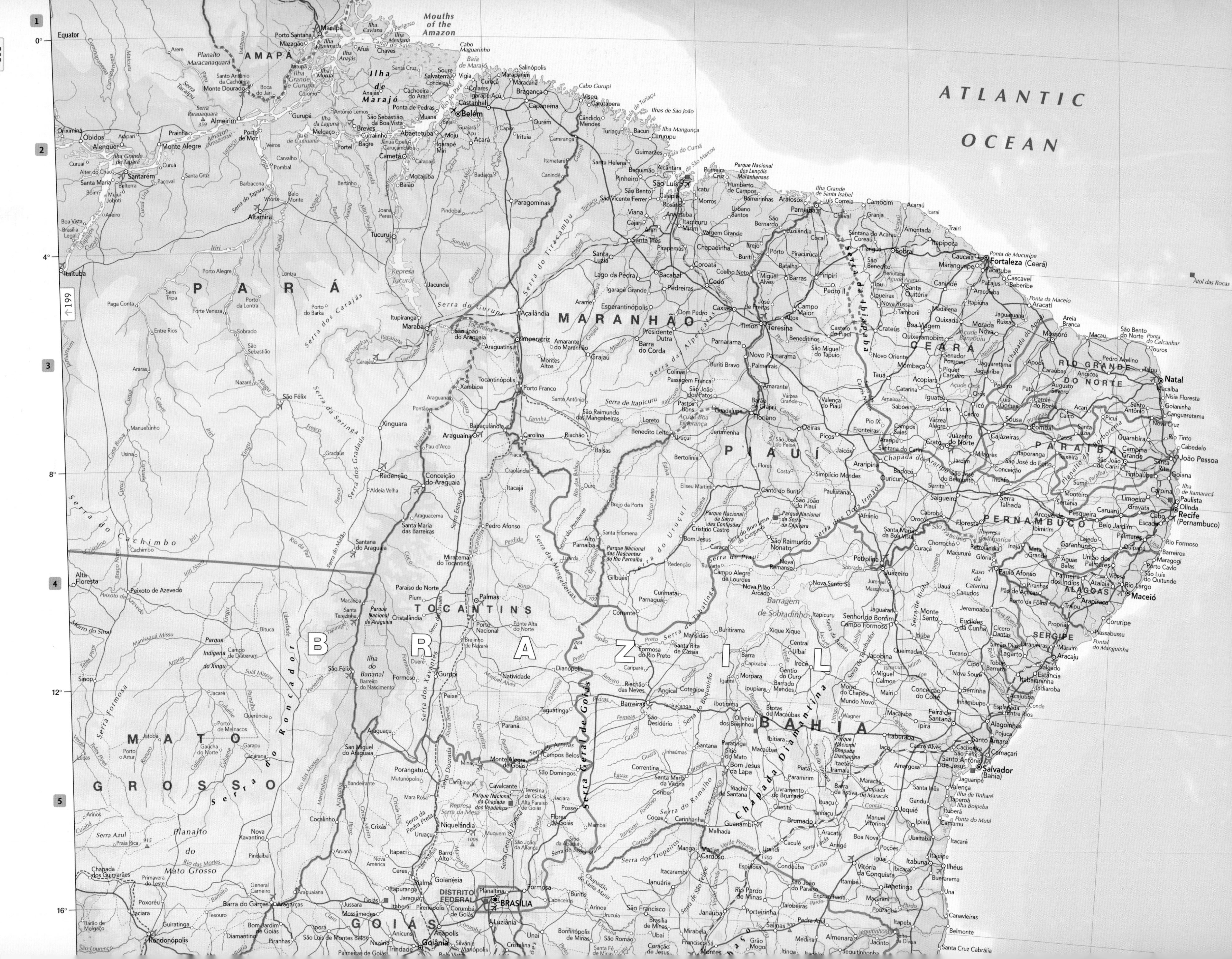
ATLANTIC
OCEAN
BRAZIL
PARÁ
MARANHÃO
PIAUÍ
CEARÁ
RIO GRANDE DO NORTE
PARAÍBA
PERNAMBUCO
ALAGOAS
SERGIPE
BAHIA
TOCANTINS
GOIÁS
MATO GROSSO
AMAPÁ
DISTRITO FEDERAL
BRASÍLIA
Belém
São Luís
Teresina
Fortaleza (Ceará)
Natal
João Pessoa
Recife (Pernambuco)
Maceió
Aracaju
Salvador (Bahia)
Palmas
Goiânia
Mouths of the Amazon
Ilha de Marajó
Chapada Diamantina
Serra Geral de Goiás
Serra do Roncador
Serra da Ibiapaba
Equator
0°
4°
8°
12°
16°
199
1
2
3
4
5

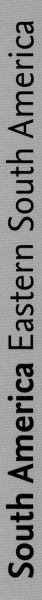

Want to know more?

▲ Cities of over 10 million people	18–19
▲ Image of Brasília	192–193
▲ South America's largest countries	192–193
▲ Colonial South America	196–197
▲ South America statistics	196–197

ATLANTIC

OCEAN

1:7 500 000

Lambert Azimuthal Equal Area Projection

miles

km

>6000m
5000–6000m
4000–5000m
3000–4000m
2000–3000m
1000–2000m
500–1000m
200–500m
0–200m
<0m

0–200m
200–500m
500–1000m
1000–2000m
2000–3000m
3000–4000m
4000–5000m
5000–6000m
>6000m

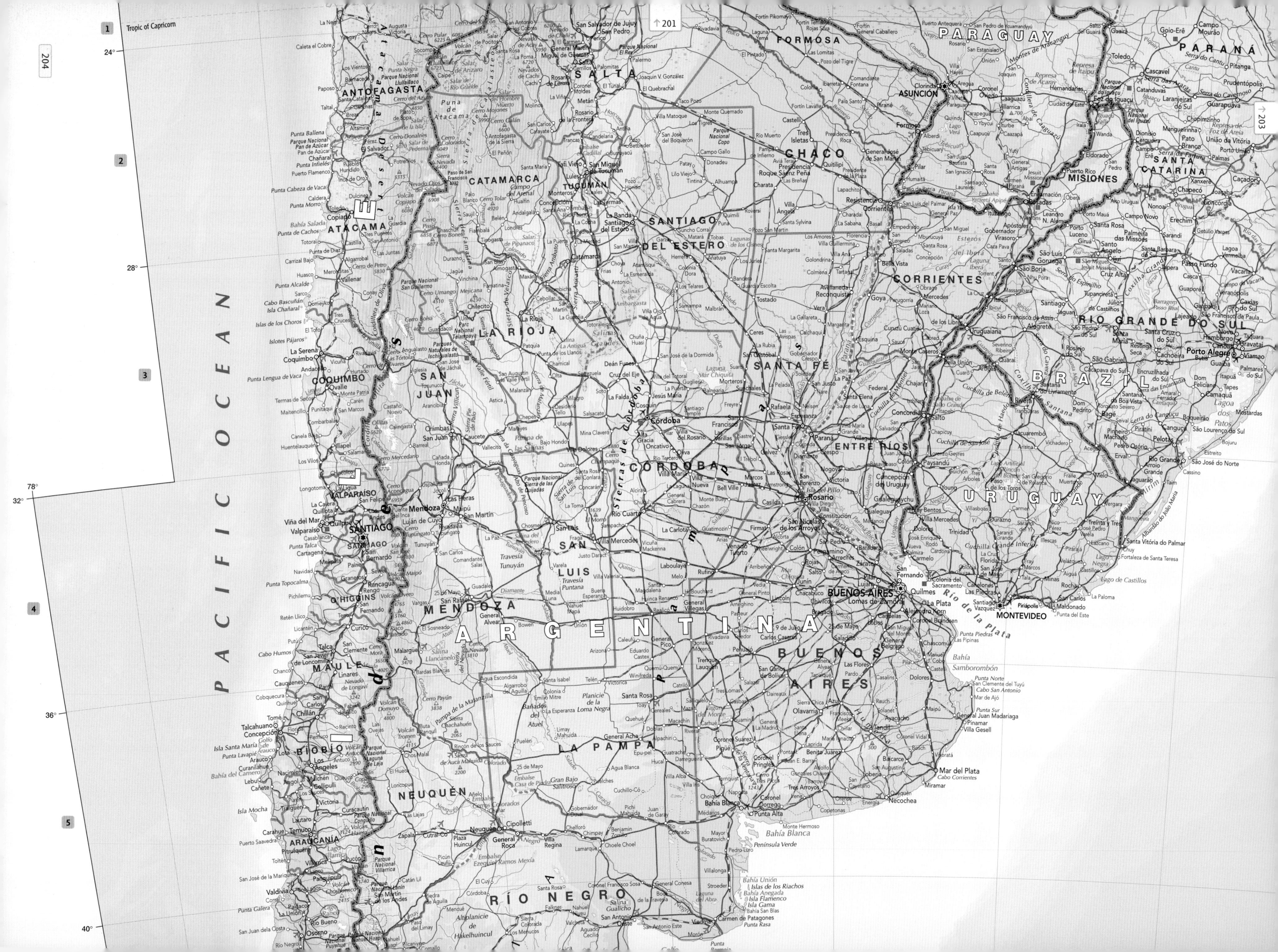

Tropic of Capricorn
PARAGUAY
ASUNCIÓN
PARANÁ
SANTA CATARINA
RIO GRANDE DO SUL
BRAZIL
URUGUAY
MONTEVIDEO
Río de la Plata
BUENOS AIRES
ARGENTINA
FORMOSA
SALTA
CHACO
MISIONES
CORRIENTES
TUCUMÁN
CATAMARCA
SANTIAGO DEL ESTERO
SANTA FE
ENTRE RÍOS
LA RIOJA
SAN JUAN
CÓRDOBA
SAN LUIS
MENDOZA
LA PAMPA
NEUQUÉN
RÍO NEGRO
ANTOFAGASTA
ATACAMA
COQUIMBO
VALPARAÍSO
SANTIAGO
O'HIGGINS
MAULE
BIOBÍO
ARAUCANÍA
PACIFIC OCEAN
Atacama Desert
Sierras de Córdoba
Bahía Blanca
Bahía Samborombón
↑201
↑203

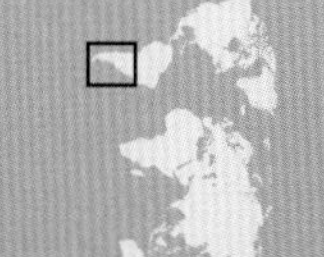

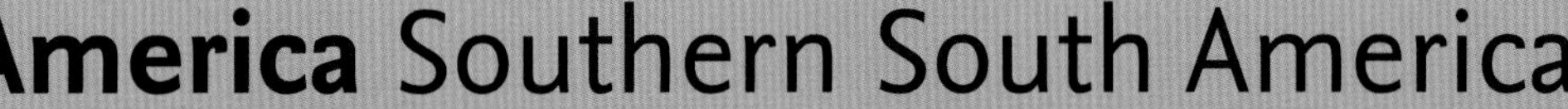

South Georgia (U.K.)

1:7 500 000

ATLANTIC OCEAN

Falkland Islands (U.K.)

West Falkland   East Falkland

1:7 500 000

Lambert Azimuthal Equal Area Projection

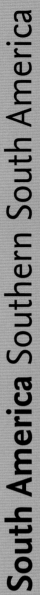

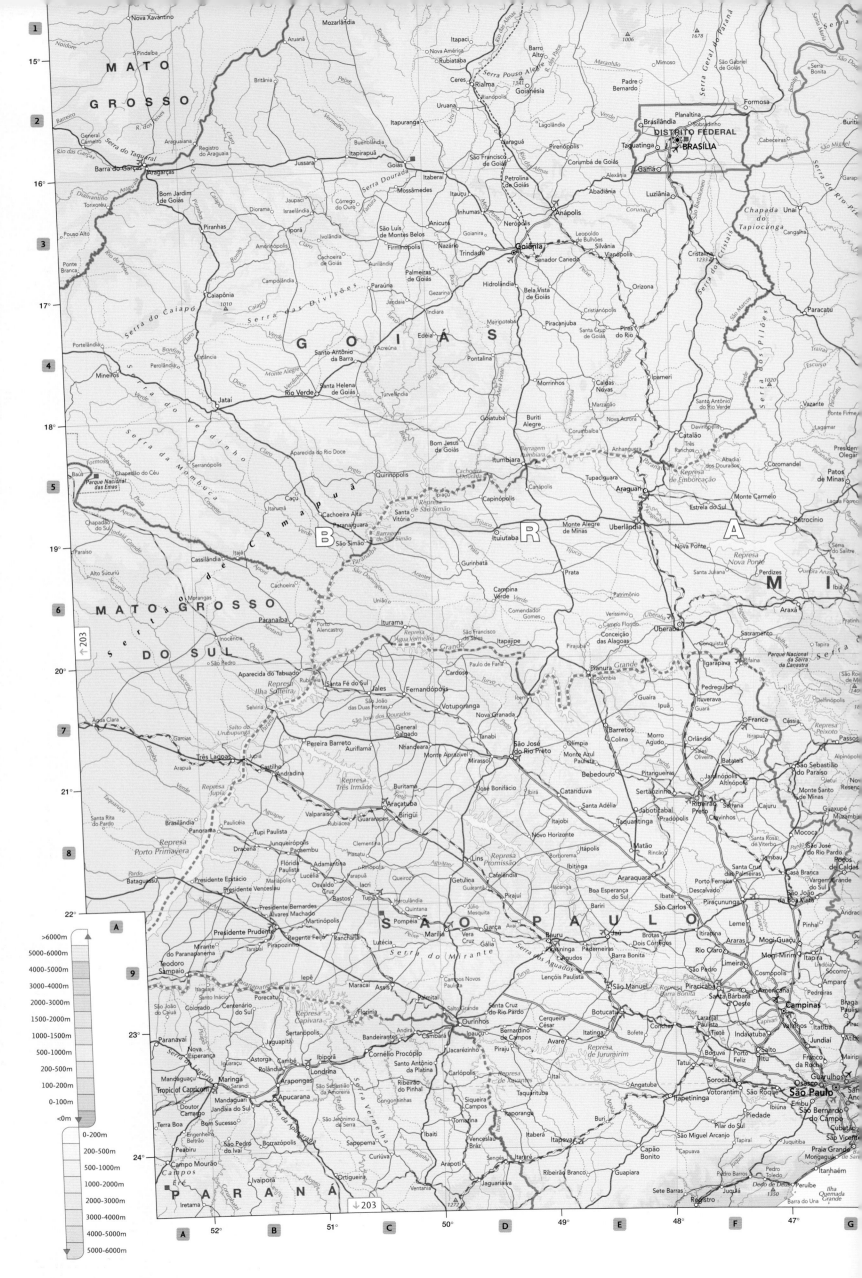

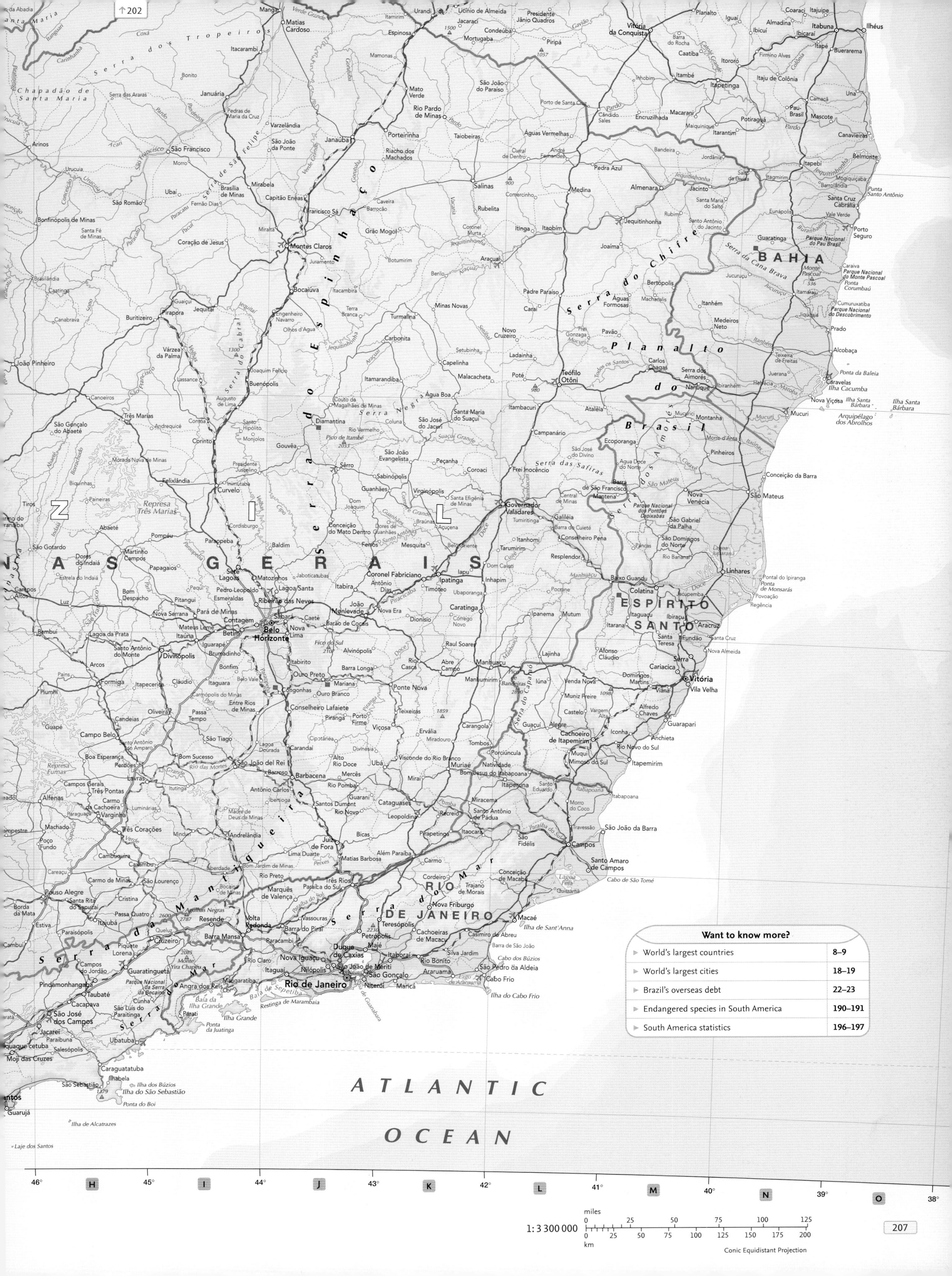
↑202
BAHIA
MINAS GERAIS
ESPÍRITO SANTO
RIO DE JANEIRO
ATLANTIC OCEAN
Serra do Espinhaço
Serra do Cabral
Serra dos Tropeiros
Chapadão de Santa Maria
Serra do Chifre
Planalto do Brasil
Serra dos Aimorés
Serra das Safiras
Serra da Mantiqueira
Serra do Mar
Serra do Caparaó
Serra Negra
Serra da Cana Brava
Represa Três Marias
Represa Furnas
Belo Horizonte
Rio de Janeiro
Vitória
Vila Velha
Montes Claros
Governador Valadares
Teófilo Otôni
Vitória da Conquista
Juiz de Fora
Ilhéus
Porto Seguro
Campos
Niterói
São Gonçalo
Petrópolis
Teresópolis
Nova Friburgo
Volta Redonda
Cabo Frio
Macaé
Linhares
São Mateus
Ipatinga
Coronel Fabriciano
Divinópolis
Sete Lagoas
Ouro Preto
Diamantina
Barbacena
São João del Rei
Conselheiro Lafaiete
Pouso Alegre
Taubaté
São José dos Campos
Guaratinguetá
Jacareí
Moji das Cruzes
Guarujá
Cachoeiro de Itapemirim
Colatina
Caratinga
Manhuaçu
Muriaé
Ubá
Cataguases
Poços
Varginha
Três Corações
Lavras
Formiga
Campo Belo
Itajubá
Resende
Barra Mansa
Angra dos Reis
Ubatuba
Caraguatatuba
Ilha Grande
Ilha do São Sebastião
Ilha dos Búzios
Ilha de Alcatrazes
Laje dos Santos
Ponta do Boi
Baía de Sepetiba
Baía de Guanabara
Restinga de Marambaia
Cabo de São Tomé
Ilha do Cabo Frio
Ilha de Sant'Anna
Arquipélago dos Abrolhos
Ilha Santa Bárbara
Parque Nacional do Monte Pascoal
Parque Nacional do Descobrimento
Parque Nacional do Pau Brasil
Parque Nacional dos Pontões Capixabas
Parque Nacional da Serra da Bocaina
Pico de Itambé 2033
Conic Equidistant Projection
1: 3 300 000
miles 0 25 50 75 100 125
km 0 25 50 75 100 125 150 175 200
46° 45° 44° 43° 42° 41° 40° 39° 38°
H I J K L M N O
Want to know more?
World's largest countries 8–9
World's largest cities 18–19
Brazil's overseas debt 22–23
Endangered species in South America 190–191
South America statistics 196–197

Between them, the world's oceans and polar regions cover approximately seventy per cent of the earth's surface. The oceans contain ninety-six per cent of the earth's water and a vast range of flora and fauna. They are a major influence on the world's climate, particularly through ocean currents. The Arctic and Antarctica are the coldest and most inhospitable places on the earth. They both have vast amounts of ice which, if global warming continues, could have a major influence on the sea level across the globe. Our understanding of the oceans and polar regions has increased enormously over the last twenty years through the development of new technologies, particularly that of satellite remote sensing, which can generate vast amounts of data relating to, for example, topography (both on land and the seafloor), land cover and sea surface temperature.

Pressure ridges form in Arctic sea ice when ice floes collide. As the floes are pushed together, a wall of broken ice is forced up. The height of such ridges is typically four to five metres, but they can reach as much as fifteen metres.

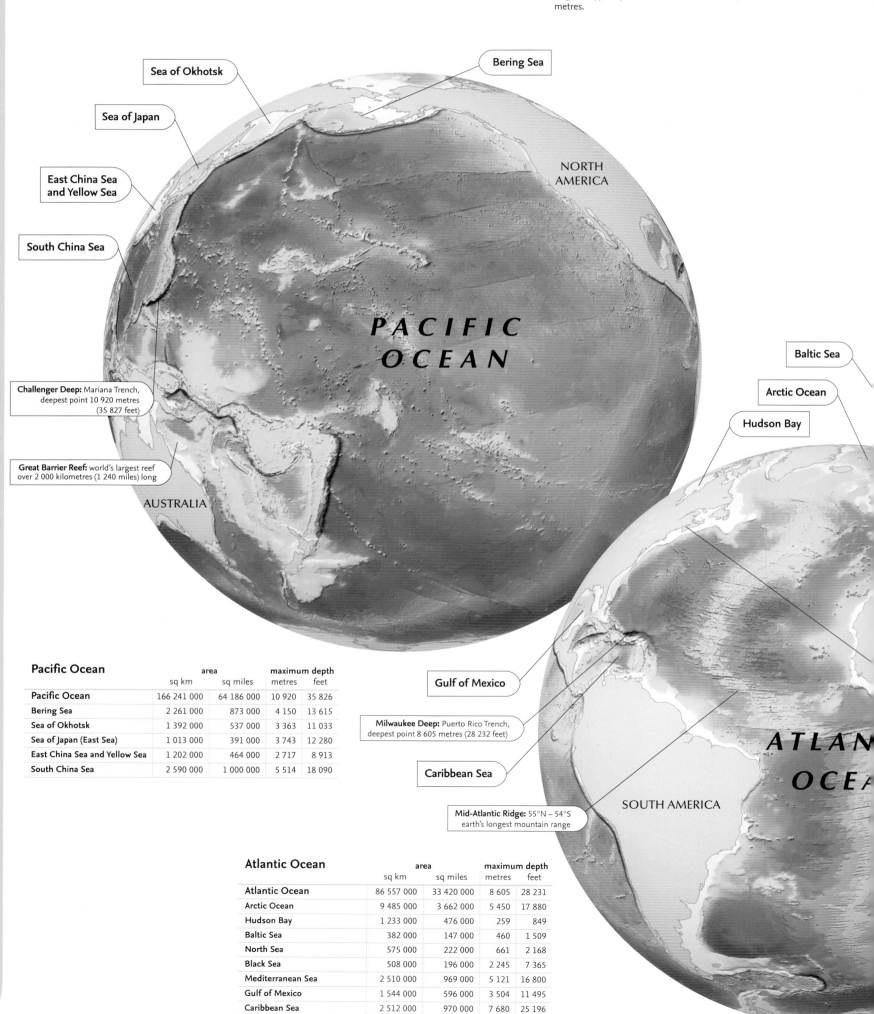

Sea of Okhotsk

Bering Sea

Sea of Japan

East China Sea and Yellow Sea

South China Sea

NORTH AMERICA

PACIFIC OCEAN

Challenger Deep: Mariana Trench, deepest point 10 920 metres (35 827 feet)

Great Barrier Reef: world's largest reef over 2 000 kilometres (1 240 miles) long

AUSTRALIA

Baltic Sea

Arctic Ocean

Hudson Bay

Gulf of Mexico

Milwaukee Deep: Puerto Rico Trench, deepest point 8 605 metres (28 232 feet)

Caribbean Sea

Mid-Atlantic Ridge: 55°N – 54°S earth's longest mountain range

SOUTH AMERICA

ATLAN OCEA

Pacific Ocean	area		maximum depth	
	sq km	sq miles	metres	feet
Pacific Ocean	166 241 000	64 186 000	10 920	35 826
Bering Sea	2 261 000	873 000	4 150	13 615
Sea of Okhotsk	1 392 000	537 000	3 363	11 033
Sea of Japan (East Sea)	1 013 000	391 000	3 743	12 280
East China Sea and Yellow Sea	1 202 000	464 000	2 717	8 913
South China Sea	2 590 000	1 000 000	5 514	18 090

Atlantic Ocean	area		maximum depth	
	sq km	sq miles	metres	feet
Atlantic Ocean	86 557 000	33 420 000	8 605	28 231
Arctic Ocean	9 485 000	3 662 000	5 450	17 880
Hudson Bay	1 233 000	476 000	259	849
Baltic Sea	382 000	147 000	460	1 509
North Sea	575 000	222 000	661	2 168
Black Sea	508 000	196 000	2 245	7 365
Mediterranean Sea	2 510 000	969 000	5 121	16 800
Gulf of Mexico	1 544 000	596 000	3 504	11 495
Caribbean Sea	2 512 000	970 000	7 680	25 196

The world's most southerly volcano, **Mount Erebus**, lies on Ross Island, in the Ross Sea. It is still active and monitored constantly. It was the scene of a tragic air crash in 1979 when 257 passengers on a sightseeing flight were killed.

Want to know more?	
▶ World landscapes	6–7
▶ World climate and weather	12–13
▶ Maps of Arctic sea ice extent	214–215
▶ Maps of the oceans	216–221
▶ Maps of the polar regions	222–224

Internet links	
Observe the oceans	www.noaa.gov
Ocean exploration	sio.ucsd.edu
Mapping the oceans	www.ngdc.noaa.gov/mgg/gebco
Polar research	www.spri.cam.ac.uk

Facts

If all of Antarctica's ice melted, world sea level would rise by more than 60 metres (197 feet).

The Arctic Ocean produces up to 50 000 icebergs per year.

The Mid-Atlantic Ridge in the Atlantic Ocean is the earth's longest mountain range.

The world's greatest tidal range – 21 metres (69 feet) – is in the Bay of Fundy, Nova Scotia, Canada.

The circumpolar current in the Southern Ocean carries 125 million cubic metres (30 million cubic miles) of water per second.

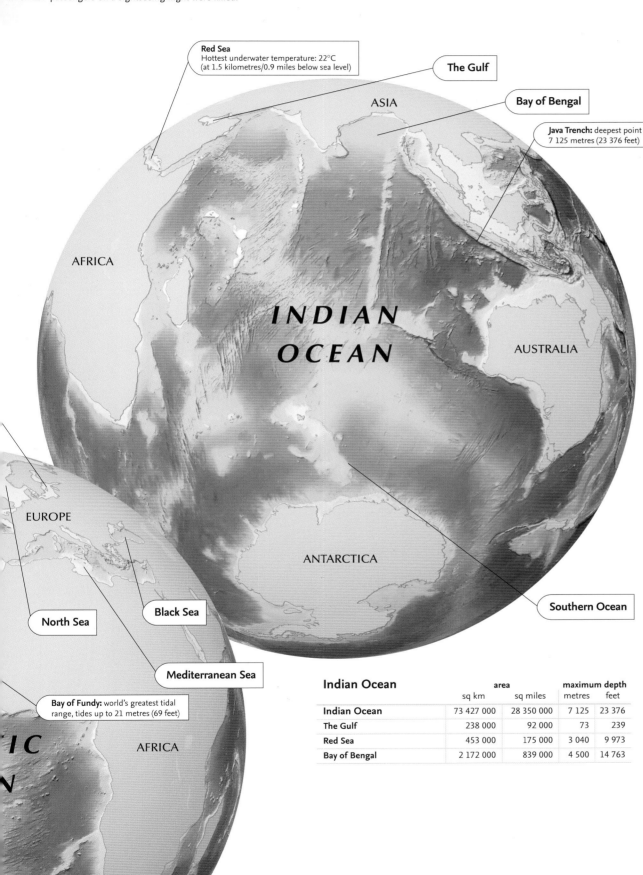

Red Sea
Hottest underwater temperature: 22°C
(at 1.5 kilometres/0.9 miles below sea level)

The Gulf

Bay of Bengal

Java Trench: deepest point
7 125 metres (23 376 feet)

ASIA

AFRICA

INDIAN OCEAN

AUSTRALIA

ANTARCTICA

EUROPE

North Sea

Black Sea

Mediterranean Sea

Bay of Fundy: world's greatest tidal range, tides up to 21 metres (69 feet)

AFRICA

Southern Ocean

Antarctica

highest mountains	metres	feet
Vinson Massif	4 897	16 066
Mt Tyree	4 852	15 918
Mt Kirkpatrick	4 528	14 856
Mt Markham	4 351	14 275
Mt Jackson	4 190	13 747
Mt Sidley	4 181	13 717

area	sq km	sq miles
Total land area (excluding ice shelves)	12 093 000	4 667 898
Ice shelves	1 559 000	601 774
Exposed rock	49 000	18 914

heights	metres	feet
Lowest bedrock elevation (Bentley Subglacial Trench)	- 2 496	- 8 189
Maximum ice thickness (Astrolabe Subglacial Basin)	4 776	15 669
Mean ice thickness (including ice shelves)	1 859	6 099

volume	cubic km	cubic miles
Ice sheet including ice shelves	25 400 000	6 094 000

climate	°C	°F
Lowest screen temperature (Vostok Station, 21st July 1983)	-89.2	-128.6
Coldest place – Annual mean (Plateau Station)	-56.6	-69.9

Indian Ocean	area		maximum depth	
	sq km	sq miles	metres	feet
Indian Ocean	73 427 000	28 350 000	7 125	23 376
The Gulf	238 000	92 000	73	239
Red Sea	453 000	175 000	3 040	9 973
Bay of Bengal	2 172 000	839 000	4 500	14 763

Arctic

temperature	°C	°F
Summer temperature at North Pole	near 0	32
Winter temperature at North Pole	-30	-22
Lowest temperature recorded in the Arctic (Verkhoyansk, northeastern Siberia, 1933)	-68	-90

sea ice extent	sq km	sq miles
Minimum sea ice extent in summer	5 000 000	1 930 000
Maximum sea ice extent in winter	16 000 000	6 180 000

ice thickness	metres	feet
Average sea ice thickness	2	6.6
Maximum ice thickness (Greenland ice sheet)	3 400	11 155

precipitation	mm	inches
Average precipitation (mainly snow) in the Arctic basin – rain equivalent	130	5.1
Average precipitation (mainly snow) in the Arctic coastal areas – rain equivalent	260	10.2

The world's major oceans are the Pacific, the Atlantic and the Indian Oceans. The Arctic Ocean is generally considered as part of the Atlantic, and the Southern Ocean, which stretches around the whole of Antarctica is usually treated as an extension of each of the three major oceans.

One of the most important factors affecting the earth's climate is the circulation of water within and between the oceans. Differences in temperature and surface winds create ocean currents which move enormous quantities of water around the globe (see world climate map page 12). These currents re-distribute heat which the oceans have absorbed from the sun, and so have a major effect on the world's climate system. El Niño is one climatic phenomenon directly influenced by these ocean processes.

This perspective view of the **ocean floor** shows trenches, ridges and basins of the western Pacific Ocean. The image extends from Australia and Melanesia at the bottom to the Philippines at the top. The Mariana Trench, the world's deepest, is in the upper centre.

This image of **global seafloor topography** has been produced from a combination of shipboard depth soundings and gravity data derived from satellite measurements. The range of colours represents different depths of the ocean – from orange and yellow on the shallow continental shelves to dark blues in the deepest ocean trenches. The heavily fractured mid-ocean ridges (ranging from green to yellow) are particularly prominent.

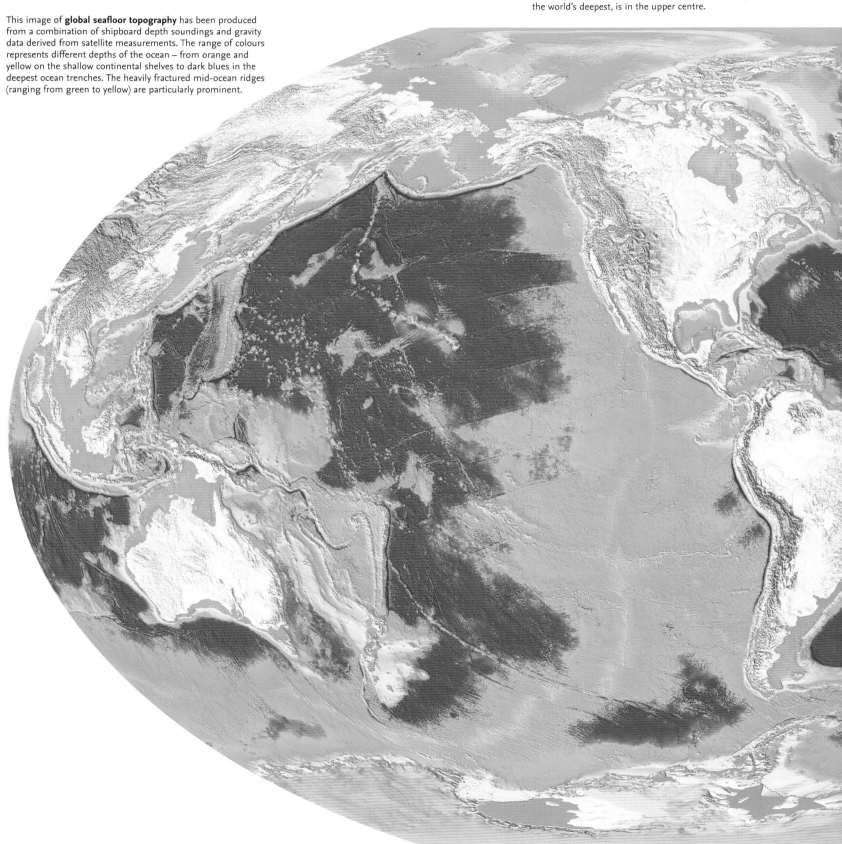

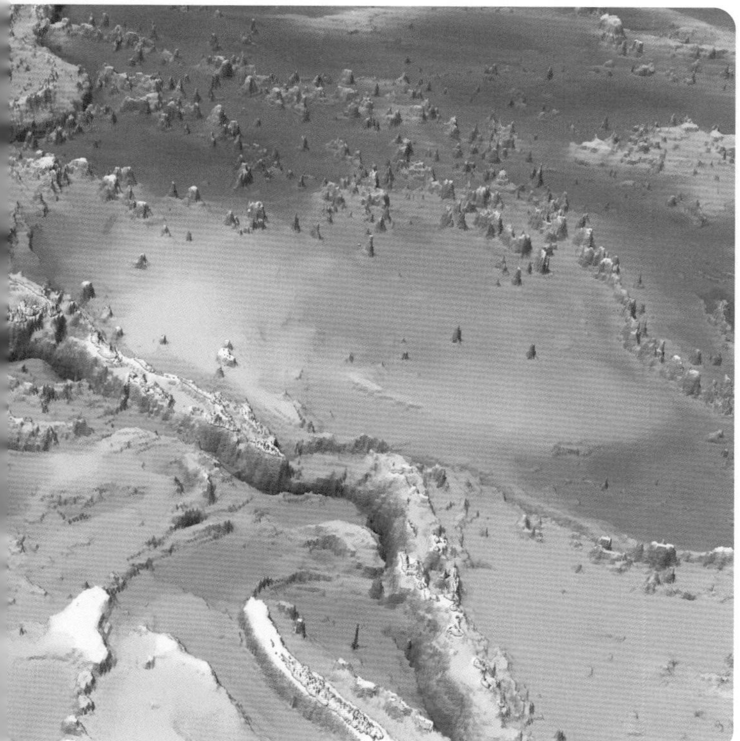

Observing the oceans

Methods of direct and indirect observation of the oceans have developed enormously over the last forty years. These techniques have provided the amount and quality of data required to greatly develop our understanding of the oceans. Earth observing satellites have become increasingly important. Radiometers on board satellites allow sea surface temperatures to be monitored and radar altimeters permit ocean surface currents to be inferred from measurements of sea surface height. Such developments meant that by the early 1990s routine monitoring of ocean surface currents was possible. The combination of satellite altimetry and other observation methods has also allowed a detailed picture of the ocean floor to be established.

Internet links	
Research the oceans	www.soc.soton.ac.uk
Shipping and the environment	www.imo.org
Ocean conservation	www.iucn.org/themes/marine
El Niño	www.elnino.noaa.gov
Shipping and the environment	www.imo.org

Facts

The Pacific was named by the 16th-century explorer Ferdinand Magellan after the calm waters he experienced there.

The Pacific is estimated to contain over 315 million cubic kilometres (76 million cubic miles) of water and has an average depth of over 4 000 metres (13 123 feet).

The Mid-Atlantic ridge runs down the centre of the Atlantic. It marks the boundary between two of the Earth's tectonic plates and is an active volcanic zone which is pulling Europe and America apart at a rate of over 2 centimetres (0.8 inches) per year.

The North Atlantic Drift is an ocean current originating in the Gulf of Mexico. It carries warm water towards the Arctic Ocean and modifies the climate of northwest Europe.

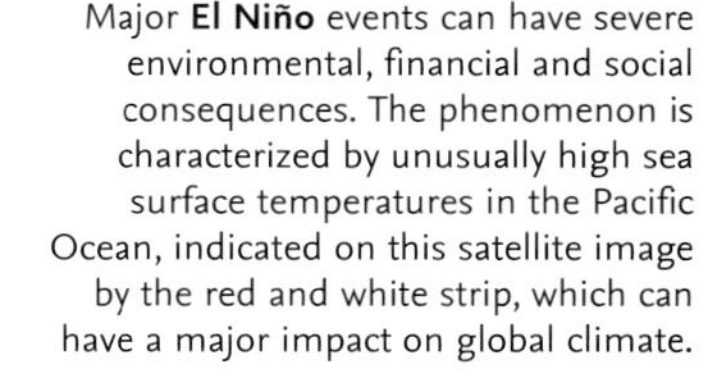

Major **El Niño** events can have severe environmental, financial and social consequences. The phenomenon is characterized by unusually high sea surface temperatures in the Pacific Ocean, indicated on this satellite image by the red and white strip, which can have a major impact on global climate.

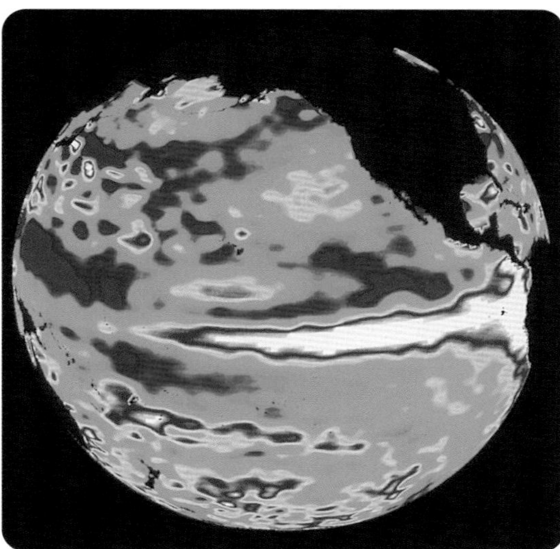

Oceans and climate

The oceans absorb solar radiation and by storing this heat, exert an extraordinary influence on the earth and its atmosphere. The circulation of water throughout the oceans, involving the redistribution of enormous amounts of heat energy, is critical to world climate and climate change. Any study of the relationships between such aspects of the Earth and its climate relies upon a clear understanding of the role of the oceans and of the complex processes within them. The precise nature and effect of the processes varies geographically, as demonstrated by the El Niño phenomenon which can influence weather patterns throughout the world.

Ocean transport of heat
Values in petawatts (PW). One Petawatt is approximately sixty times the global consumption of energy.

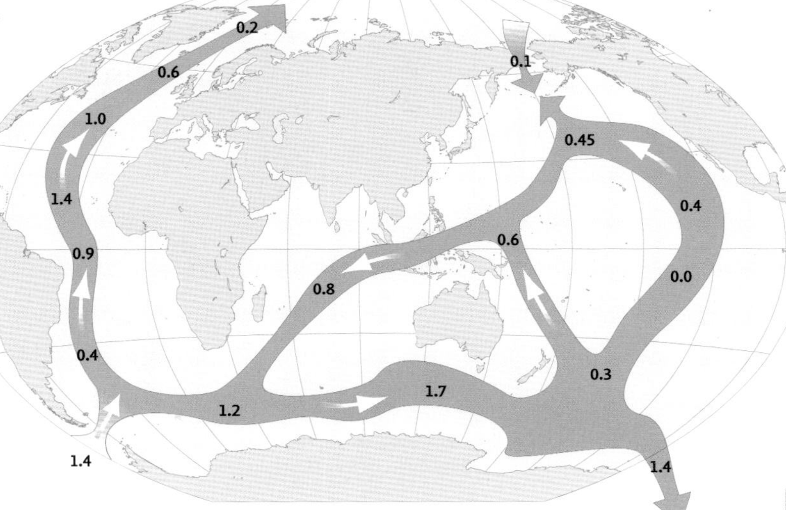

Antarctica Features

While the Arctic region consists mainly of the Arctic Ocean, Antarctica is a huge landmass, covered by a permanent ice cap which reaches a maximum thickness of over four kilometres. Antarctica has no permanent population, unlike the Arctic regions of Europe, Asia and North America. The only minor settlements are research stations which serve as bases for scientific research. Such research, and the continent as a whole, is subject to the Antarctic Treaty of 1959 which does not recognize individual land claims and protects the continent in the interests of international scientific cooperation. There has been a significant rise over the last thirty years in tourism in Antarctica – an activity which itself demands close control to ensure the unique environment of the continent is not threatened.

650 Possible first sighting of Antarctica by Polynesians

1892–1895 Norwegian whaling and sealing expeditions

1872–1876 HMS Challenger

1838–1942 Wilkes (USA) coastal mapping expedition

1820–1824 US and British sealing explorations under Palmer, Weddell and others

1774 Cook discovers and names South Georgia and the South Sandwich Islands

1739–1741 Bouvet's expedition (French) (Bouvet Island)

600	1000	1500	1600	1700	1720	1740	1760	1780	1800	1820	1840	1860	1880	1900

1771–1772 Kerguelen's expedition (French) (Kerguelen Islands)

1819–1821 Bellingshausen (Russian) first sighting of the mainland

1839–1843 Ross's naval expedition (Ross Ice Shelf etc.)

1578 Drake comes across sea ice south of Tierra del Fuego

1892–1893 British whaling expedition from Dundee

1889–1900 Borchgrevink (UK/Norway) mapping expedition

1502 Possible first sighting of Antarctica and/or South Georgia by Amerigo Vespucci

The unique beauty of **Antarctica** is evident in this image of the continent – a mosaic of twenty-five separate satellite images. The image is impressive in its depiction of the major physical features of the continent, including the Ronne Ice Shelf, including Berkner Island, and the Transantarctic Mountains.

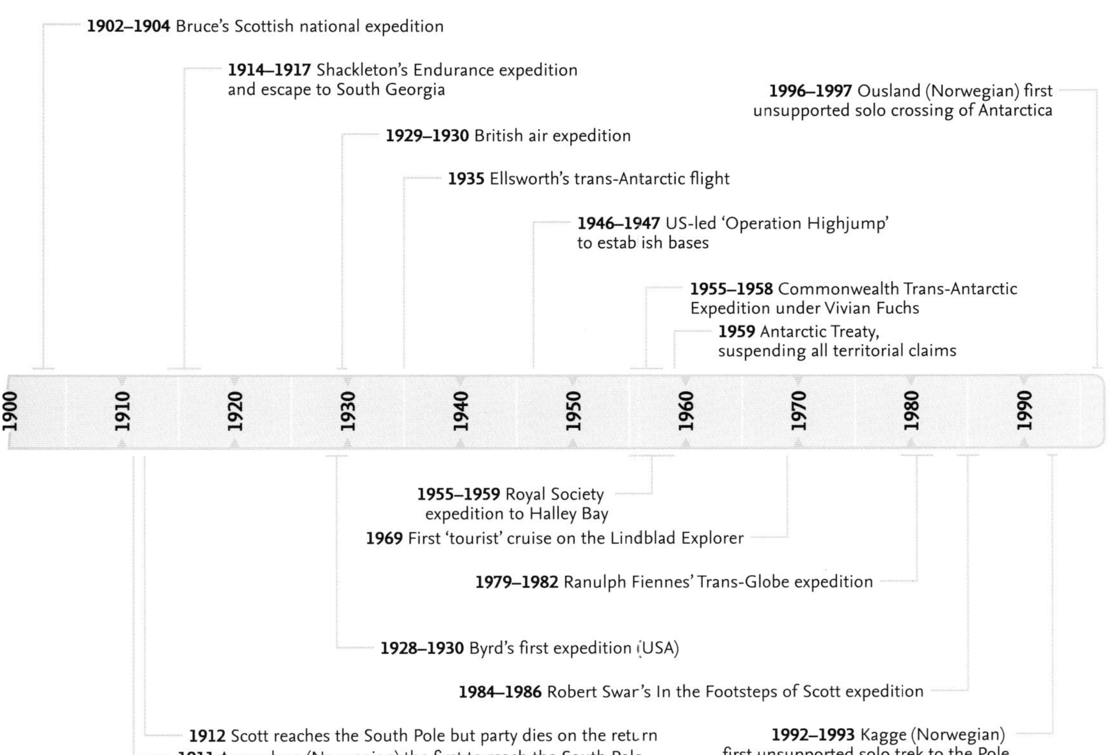

1902–1904 Bruce's Scottish national expedition

1914–1917 Shackleton's Endurance expedition
and escape to South Georgia

1996–1997 Ousland (Norwegian) first
unsupported solo crossing of Antarctica

1929–1930 British air expedition

1935 Ellsworth's trans-Antarctic flight

1946–1947 US-led 'Operation Highjump'
to establish bases

1955–1958 Commonwealth Trans-Antarctic
Expedition under Vivian Fuchs

1959 Antarctic Treaty,
suspending all territorial claims

1900 1910 1920 1930 1940 1950 1960 1970 1980 1990

1955–1959 Royal Society
expedition to Halley Bay

1969 First 'tourist' cruise on the Lindblad Explorer

1979–1982 Ranulph Fiennes' Trans-Globe expedition

1928–1930 Byrd's first expedition (USA)

1984–1986 Robert Swan's In the Footsteps of Scott expedition

1912 Scott reaches the South Pole but party dies on the return
1911 Amundsen (Norwegian) the first to reach the South Pole

1992–1993 Kagge (Norwegian)
first unsupported solo trek to the Pole

Want to know more?

▶ World landscapes — 6–7
▶ World climate and weather — 12–13
▶ Arctic features — 214–215
▶ Map of Antarctica — 222–223

Internet links

British Antarctic Survey	www.bas.ac.uk
Scott Polar Research Institute, Cambridge	www.spri.cam.ac.uk
Antarctic tourism	www.iaato.org
National Snow and Ice Data Center, University of Colorado	www.nsidc.org
Australian Antarctic Division	www.aad.gov.au

Facts

Some areas of Antarctica are never snow-covered and consist of bare rock.

There are some large lakes deep below the Antarctic ice which are believed to have no contact with the surface, yet may sustain their own ecosystems.

The South pole is at a height of 2 835 metres (9 301 feet) above sea level.

The largest iceberg recorded had an area of about 31 000 square kilometres (12 000 square miles), an area larger than Belgium.

Tourism in Antarctica

The Antarctic tourist 'industry' was born in 1969 when the Lindblad Explorer, the first purpose-built Antarctic tour ship began operating. Now, over 20 000 tourists visit the continent each year – a large increase from just over 8 000 ten years ago. The USA and Germany are the largest single contributors to the total number of visitors. The most popular destination is the Antarctic Peninsula (see table and map), although visits are also possible to the Weddell Sea, Ross Sea and East Antarctica regions. Tourist activities can present a threat to the wildlife and delicate environment of the continent. Strict controls over visits are imposed by the Antarctic Treaty and also by the International Association of Antarctica Tour Operators (IAATO) which represents travel companies operating in the region.

Top 10 tourist sites in Antarctica
Number of visitors per site, 2003–2004

		visitors
1	Antarctic Peninsula Region	24 535
2	Cuverville Island	13 980
3	Goudier Island	12 496
4	Almirante Brown Base	12 233
5	Whalers Bay, Deception Island	11 928
6	Half Moon Island	10 871
7	Neko Harbor	9 627
8	Waterboat Point	8 129
9	Jougla Point, Douomer Island	7 913
10	Petermann Island	7 543

Top 10 tourist sites in Antarctica

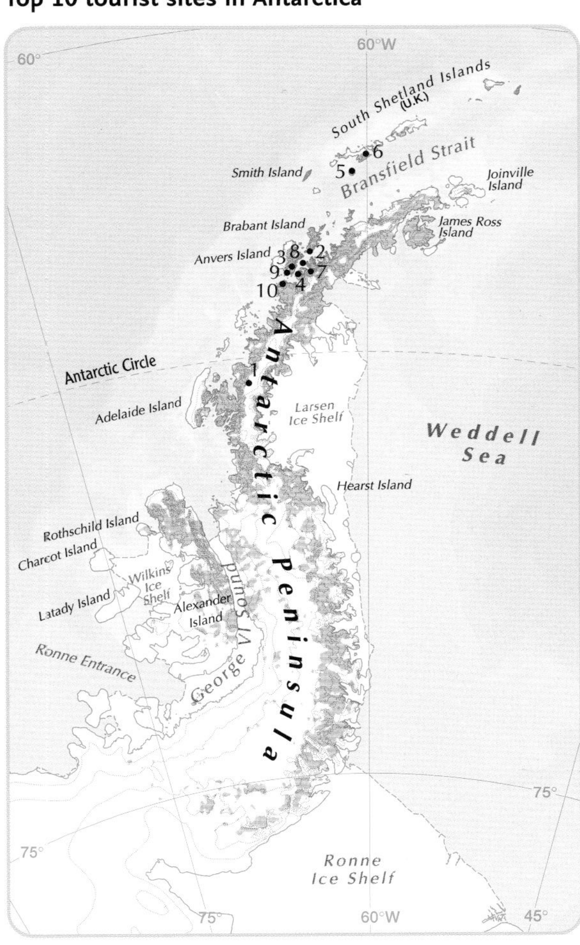

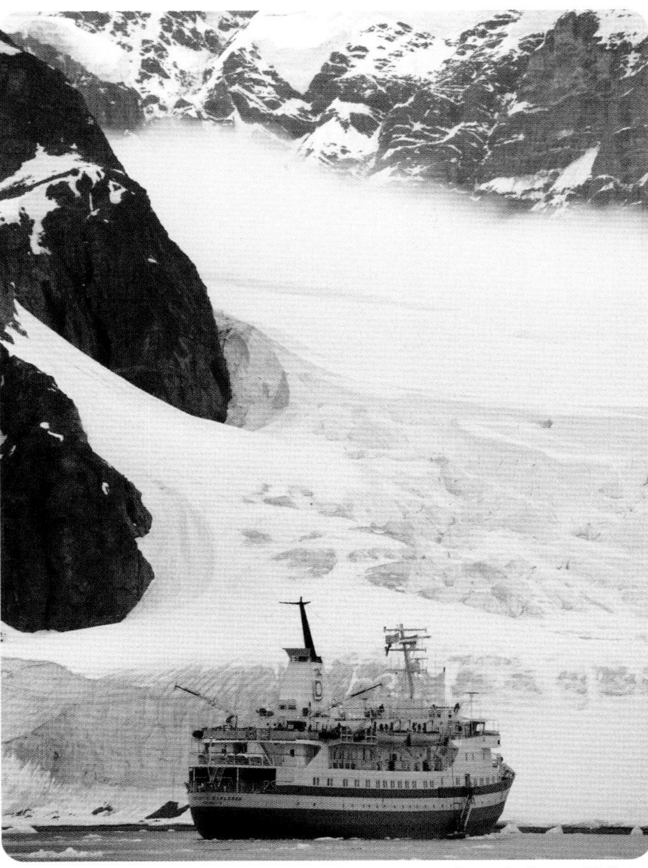

Tourists aboard the **cruise ship** *Polar Circle* as it passes through the Weddell Sea. Most Antarctic tourism is ship-borne with tourists transported ashore for periods of up to three hours at a time. Most cruises depart from Ushuaia, Argentina, or Port Stanley, Falkland Islands.

Ozone depletion and global warming

Since the 1970s, measurements have shown a thinning of the protective layer of ozone in the Earth's atmosphere and the appearance of an ozone 'hole' over Antarctica. This hole allows harmful ultraviolet-B radiation to penetrate to the continent. A major cause of this ozone depletion appears to be the emission, through human activity, of greenhouse gasses such as carbon dioxide, methane and chlorofluorocarbons (CFCs). These gasses also act to trap outgoing radiation, thereby keeping the earth's surface warmer than it would be otherwise – the phenomenon known as the greenhouse effect. Monitoring of such processes presents strong evidence for global warming and it is estimated that the world is now 0.6°C warmer than it was 100 years ago.

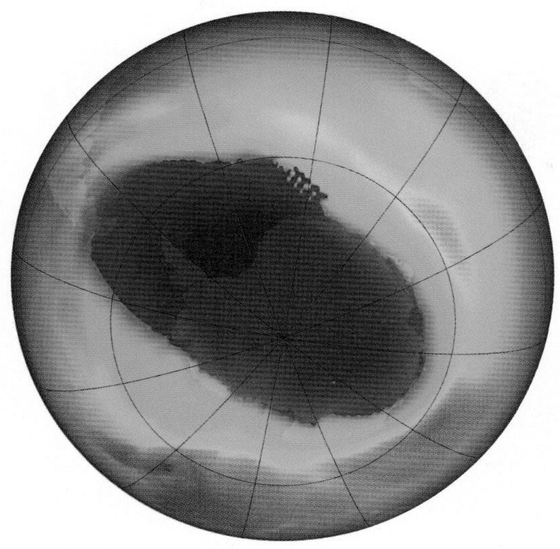

An image of the **ozone hole over Antarctica** captured by the Aura earth observing satellite, launched in July 2004. Yellow, orange and red areas represent relatively high levels of ozone, while dark blue-purple represents dramatically lower levels covering a huge area over the whole of the continent.

The Arctic region is generally defined as the area including the Arctic Ocean – which lies entirely within the Arctic Circle – and the immediate hinterlands of those land areas adjacent to it. A large proportion of the ocean itself is permanently covered in sea ice, which in some places reaches a thickness of over 4 metres (13 feet). The extent of this ice varies seasonally and the impact of global warming on its overall extent is being closely monitored. It generates up to 50 000 icebergs per year. The ocean is almost landlocked, and is connected to the Pacific Ocean only by the narrow Bering Strait – an important shipping route for Russian merchant ships. Sharing similarly extreme climatic conditions to Antarctica, the main difference between the two polar regions is the habitation of the Arctic by numerous ethnic groups.

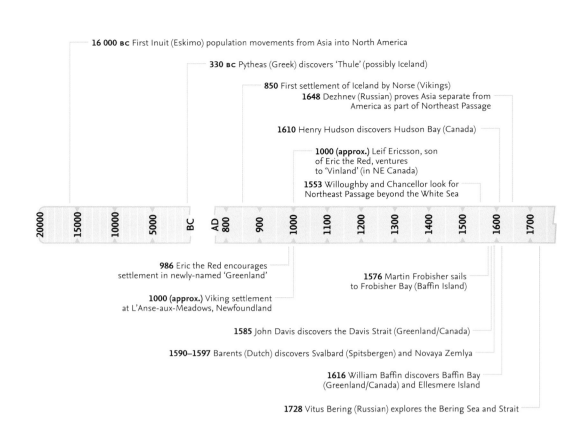

16 000 BC First Inuit (Eskimo) population movements from Asia into North America

330 BC Pytheas (Greek) discovers 'Thule' (possibly Iceland)

850 First settlement of Iceland by Norse (Vikings)
1648 Dezhnev (Russian) proves Asia separate from America as part of Northeast Passage

1610 Henry Hudson discovers Hudson Bay (Canada)

1000 (approx.) Leif Ericsson, son of Eric the Red, ventures to 'Vinland' (in NE Canada)

1553 Willoughby and Chancellor look for Northeast Passage beyond the White Sea

986 Eric the Red encourages settlement in newly-named 'Greenland'

1576 Martin Frobisher sails to Frobisher Bay (Baffin Island)

1000 (approx.) Viking settlement at L'Anse-aux-Meadows, Newfoundland

1585 John Davis discovers the Davis Strait (Greenland/Canada)

1590–1597 Barents (Dutch) discovers Svalbard (Spitsbergen) and Novaya Zemlya

1616 William Baffin discovers Baffin Bay (Greenland/Canada) and Ellesmere Island

1728 Vitus Bering (Russian) explores the Bering Sea and Strait

The nomadic lifestyle of the **Nenets people** is typical of many Arctic groups, but is becoming less common. The Nenets have long herded reindeer on both sides of the Ural Mountains and hunted seals and whales off the coasts of the Barents and Kara seas.

Peoples of the Arctic

The Arctic regions of Alaska, northern Canada, Greenland, and northern Scandinavia and Russian Federation contain the homelands of a diverse range of indigenous peoples. They are heavily dependent on the natural resources in the region, and recently, conflicts have arisen with governments eager to exploit these rich resources. There have also been moves towards greater autonomy for such groups. Most notably, in 1992 the Tungavik Federation of Nunavut and the government of Canada signed an agreement which addressed Inuit land claims and harvesting rights and established the new Canadian territory of Nunavut.

The main **indigenous groups** in the Arctic are shown on this map. These native peoples have subsisted for thousands of years on the resources of land and sea, as hunters, fishermen and reindeer herders.

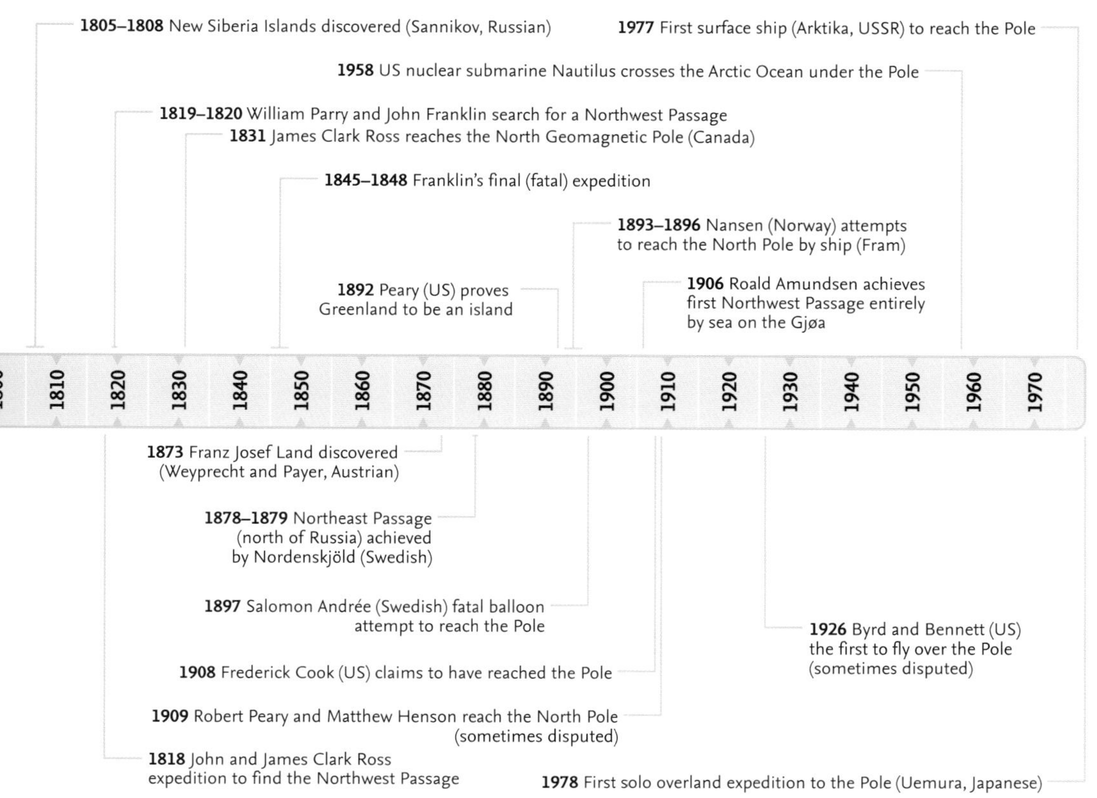

1805–1808 New Siberia Islands discovered (Sannikov, Russian)

1977 First surface ship (Arktika, USSR) to reach the Pole

1958 US nuclear submarine Nautilus crosses the Arctic Ocean under the Pole

1819–1820 William Parry and John Franklin search for a Northwest Passage

1831 James Clark Ross reaches the North Geomagnetic Pole (Canada)

1845–1848 Franklin's final (fatal) expedition

1893–1896 Nansen (Norway) attempts to reach the North Pole by ship (Fram)

1892 Peary (US) proves Greenland to be an island

1906 Roald Amundsen achieves first Northwest Passage entirely by sea on the Gjøa

1800 1810 1820 1830 1840 1850 1860 1870 1880 1890 1900 1910 1920 1930 1940 1950 1960 1970

1873 Franz Josef Land discovered (Weyprecht and Payer, Austrian)

1878–1879 Northeast Passage (north of Russia) achieved by Nordenskjöld (Swedish)

1897 Salomon Andrée (Swedish) fatal balloon attempt to reach the Pole

1908 Frederick Cook (US) claims to have reached the Pole

1926 Byrd and Bennett (US) the first to fly over the Pole (sometimes disputed)

1909 Robert Peary and Matthew Henson reach the North Pole (sometimes disputed)

1818 John and James Clark Ross expedition to find the Northwest Passage

1978 First solo overland expedition to the Pole (Uemura, Japanese)

Internet links

National Snow and Ice Data Center, University of Colorado	www.nsidc.org
Scott Polar Research Institute, Cambridge	www.spri.cam.ac.uk
Government of Nunavut, Canada	www.gov.nu.ca/Nunavut/
Arctic exploration	www.quarkexpeditions.com/arctic/exploration

Facts

Many features in the Arctic are named after the early explorers, including the Englishman John Davis, the Dutchman Willem Barents, Vitus Bering from Denmark and the Norwegian Fridtjof Nansen.

The term Inuit is now used to refer to the Arctic people formerly called Eskimos. An individual is called an Inuk, and the language of the Inuit, with its own special alphabet, is Inuktitut.

The Magnetic Pole – north on a compass – lies approximately 900 kilometres (560 miles) to the south of the North Pole, towards Canada.

Because of the number of major rivers flowing into it and its low evaporation rate, the Arctic is the least salty of all the oceans.

Arctic sea ice extents

Although much of the Arctic Ocean is constantly frozen, there are wide variations in the amount of sea ice throughout the year, as shown by these satellite-generated images. The lightest areas show almost completely frozen sea which extends as far south as Hudson Bay, Canada in February. By September, most of this ice has melted and that remaining is thinner and less concentrated, as indicated by the red-pink areas. Observation of changes in the extent of the sea ice are important in monitoring climate change, and it is now clear that the Arctic ice is getting thinner, and is less extensive than in the past. The images indicate this sort of change, particularly with the total extent of ice in September 2004 being significantly less than in September 1980.

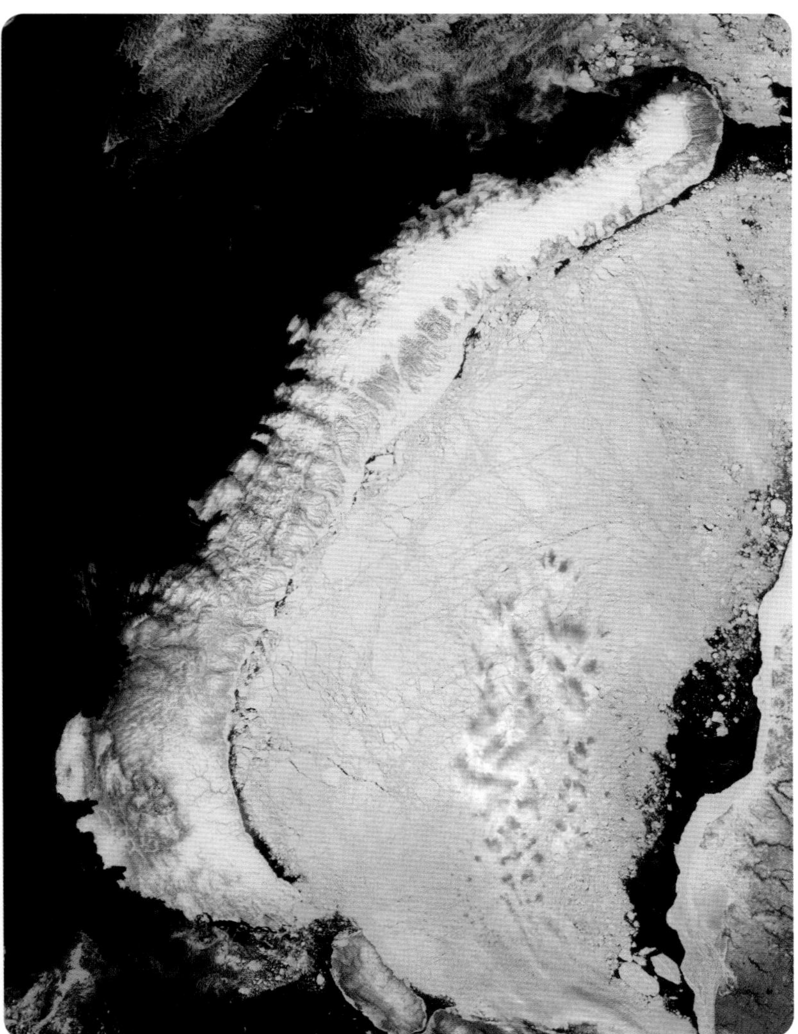

This satellite image shows the island of **Novaya Zemlya** and a section of the northern coast of the Russian Federation. The warming influence of sea currents is evident in this image with the North Atlantic Drift, or Gulf Stream, being a major factor in the clear water of the Barents Sea to the left of the island. This contrasts with the ice-filled waters of the colder Kara Sea to the right of the island.

Sea ice concentration

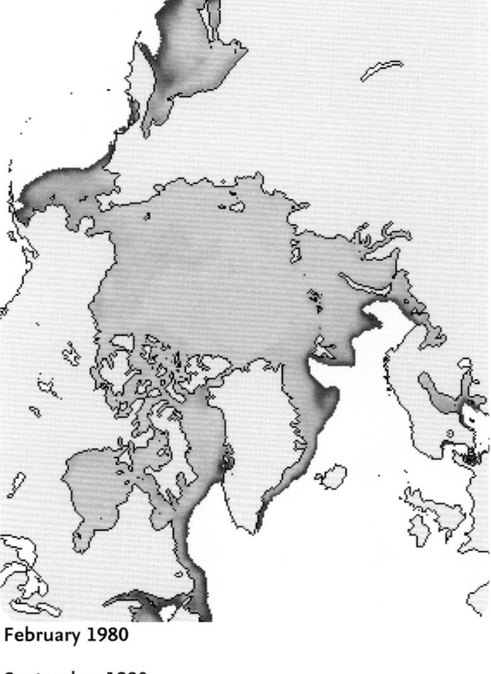

February 1980

February 2005

September 1980

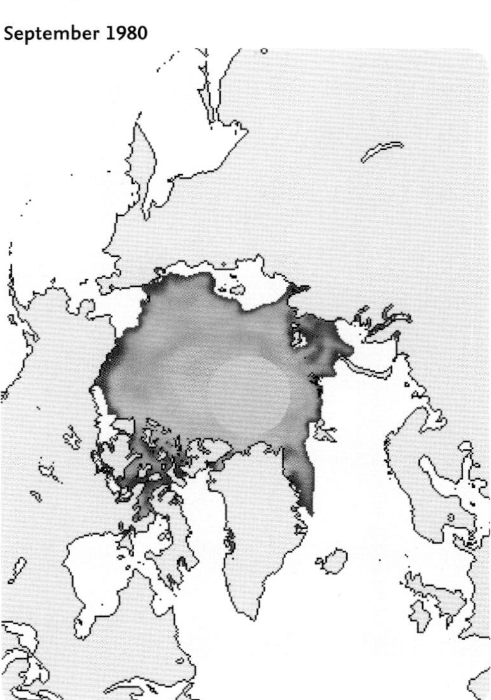

September 2004

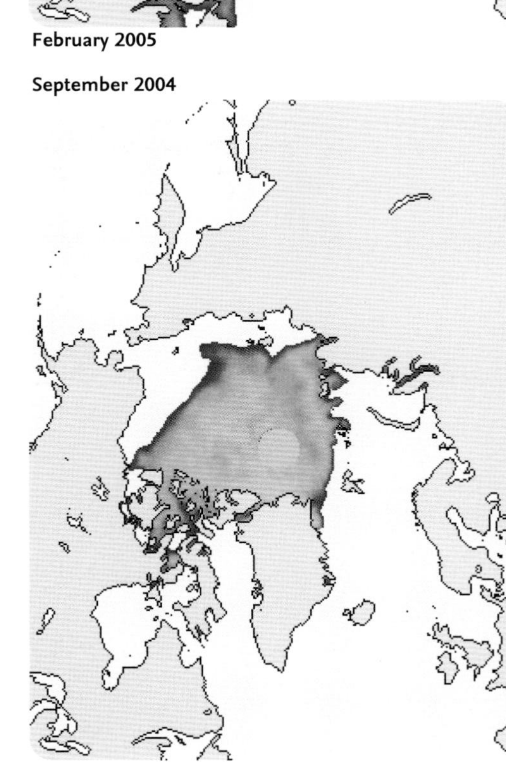

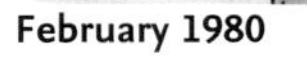

per cent

0 5 10 15 20 25 30 35 40 45 50 55 60 65 70 75 80 85 90 95 100

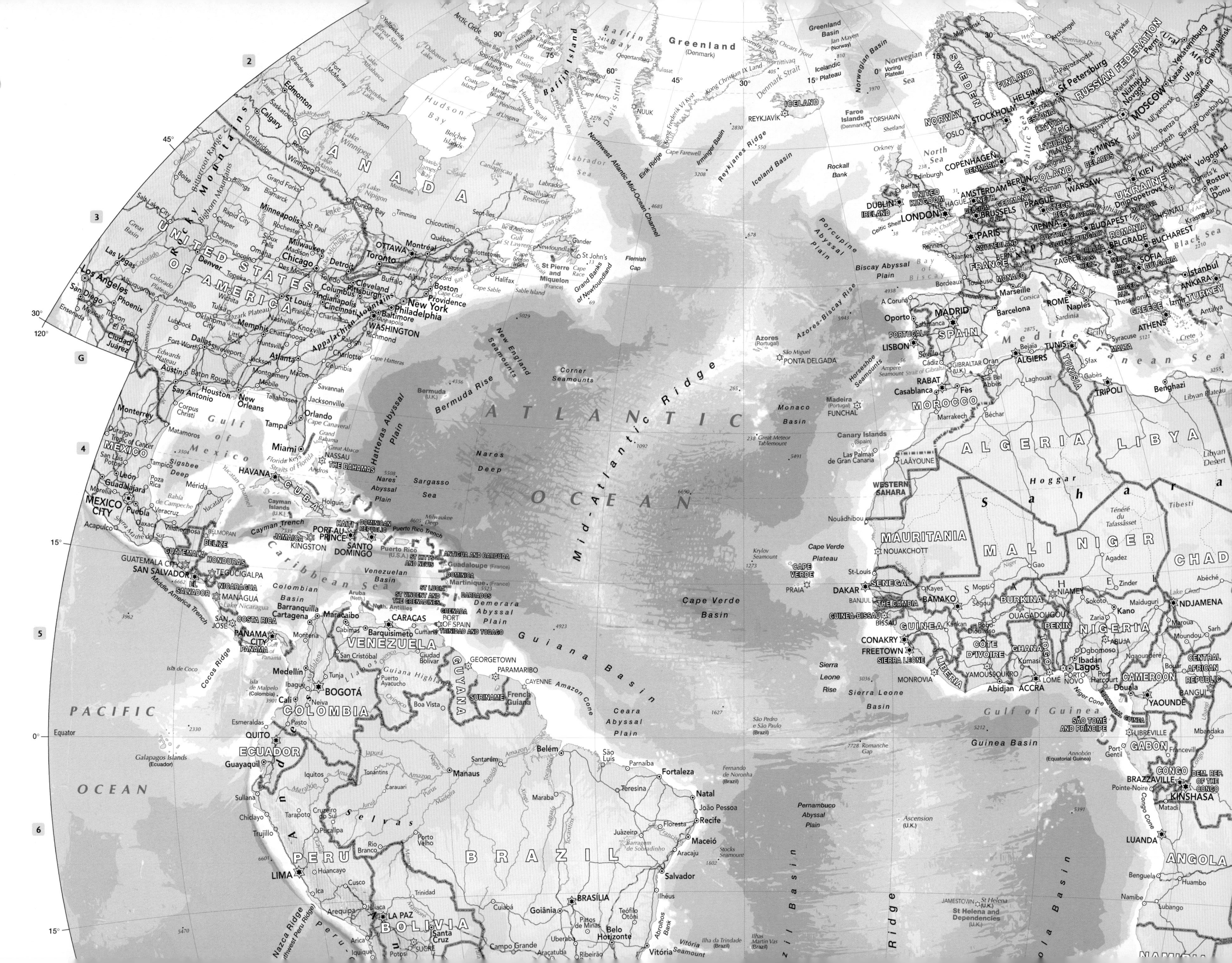
ATLANTIC OCEAN
PACIFIC OCEAN
Mid-Atlantic Ridge
CANADA
UNITED STATES OF AMERICA
MEXICO
BRAZIL
Greenland
(Denmark)
ICELAND
RUSSIAN FEDERATION
ALGERIA
LIBYA
MALI
NIGER
CHAD
MAURITANIA
NIGERIA
VENEZUELA
COLOMBIA
PERU
BOLIVIA
ECUADOR
GUYANA
CUBA
Caribbean Sea
Gulf of Mexico
Sargasso Sea
Hudson Bay
Labrador Sea
Mediterranean Sea
Gulf of Guinea
Guinea Basin
Cape Verde Basin
Canary Islands
Azores
Bermuda Rise
Northwest Atlantic Mid-Ocean Channel
Reykjanes Ridge
Rocky Mountains
Arctic Circle
Tropic of Cancer
Equator
WASHINGTON
OTTAWA
MEXICO CITY
LONDON
PARIS
MADRID
LISBON
ROME
MOSCOW
BRASÍLIA
BOGOTÁ
CARACAS
LIMA
QUITO
LA PAZ
DAKAR
ACCRA
KINSHASA
LUANDA
ALGIERS
TUNIS
TRIPOLI
NDJAMENA
REYKJAVÍK
NUUK
HAVANA
PANAMA CITY
New York
Chicago
Los Angeles
Montréal
Toronto
São Luís
Salvador
Recife
Fortaleza
Manaus
Belém
Lagos
Casablanca
Barcelona
Istanbul
2
3
4
5
6
G
30°
45°
60°
75°
90°
120°
15°
0°

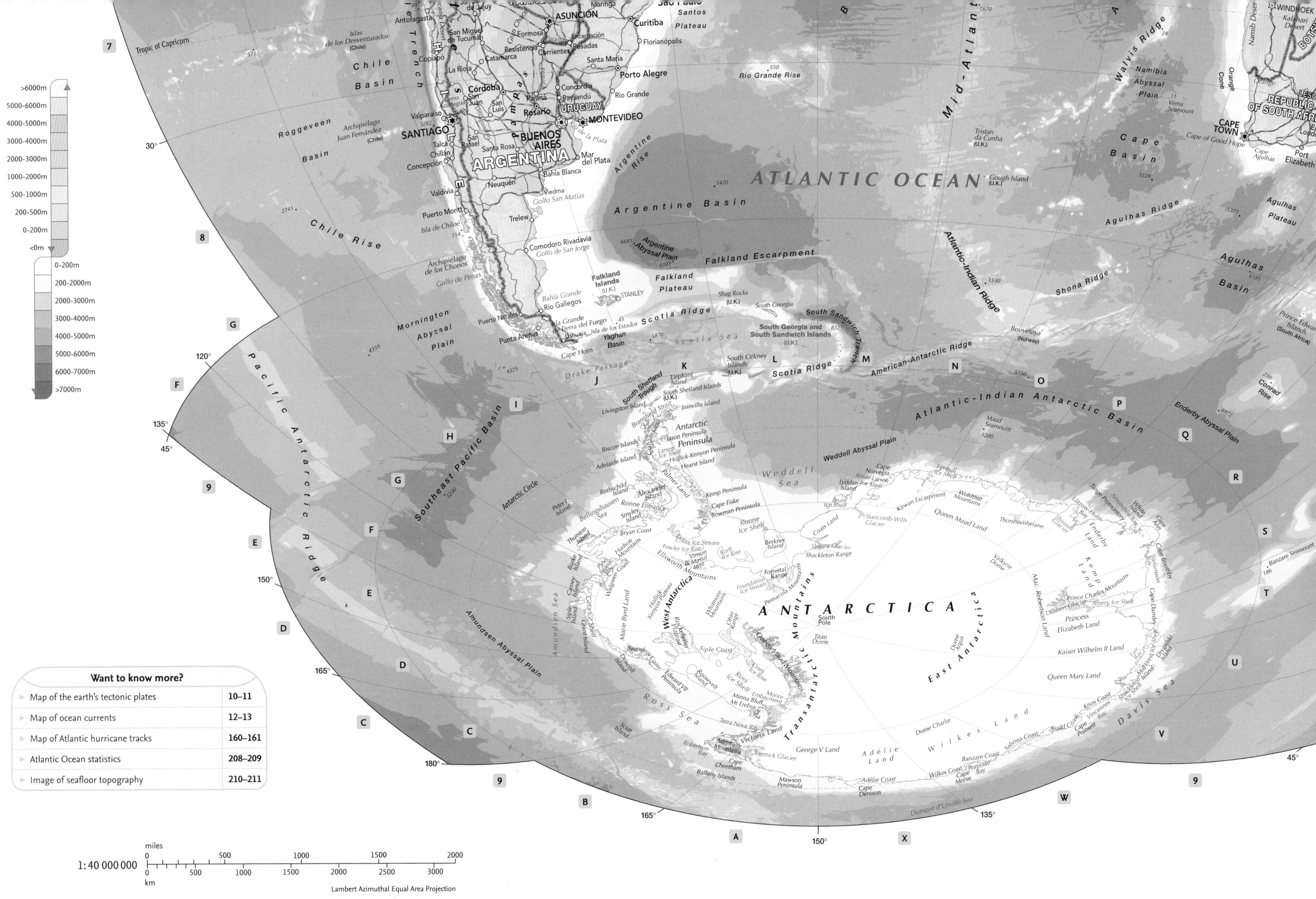

1 : 40 000 000

Lambert Azimuthal Equal Area Projection

miles

0   500   1000   1500   2000

km

0   500   1000   1500   2000   2500   3000

Want to know more?

▲ Map of the earth's tectonic plates	10–11
▲ Map of ocean currents	12–13
▲ Map of Atlantic hurricane tracks	160–161
▲ Atlantic Ocean statistics	208–209
▲ Image of seafloor topography	210–211

>6000m
5000–6000m
4000–5000m
3000–4000m
2000–3000m
1000–2000m
500–1000m
200–500m
0–200m

0–200m
200–2000m
2000–3000m
3000–4000m
4000–5000m
5000–6000m
6000–7000m
>7000m
<0m

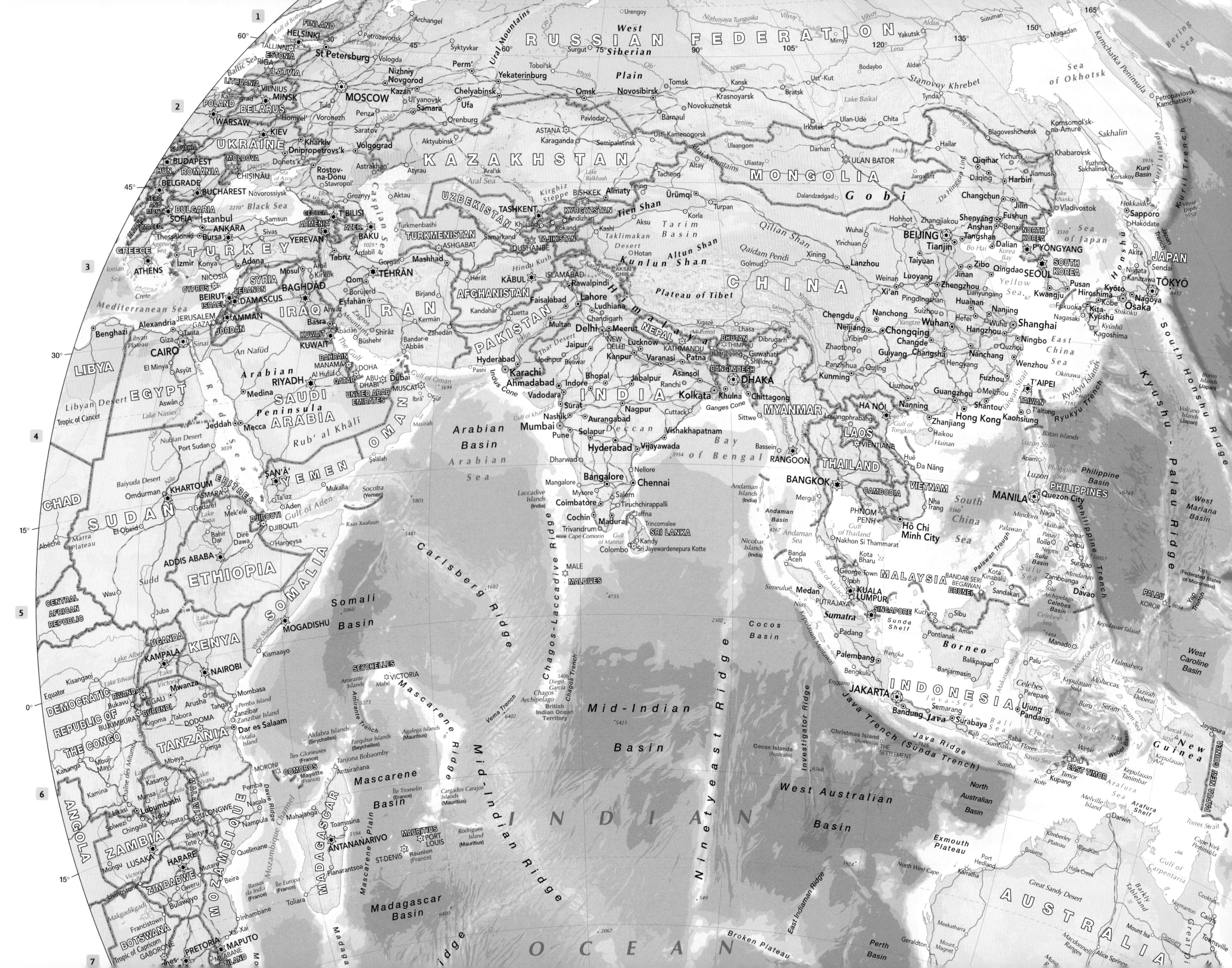
RUSSIAN FEDERATION
KAZAKHSTAN
MONGOLIA
CHINA
INDIA
PAKISTAN
AFGHANISTAN
IRAN
IRAQ
SAUDI ARABIA
YEMEN
OMAN
TURKEY
EGYPT
LIBYA
CHAD
SUDAN
ETHIOPIA
SOMALIA
KENYA
TANZANIA
ANGOLA
ZAMBIA
MOZAMBIQUE
MADAGASCAR
MYANMAR
THAILAND
MALAYSIA
INDONESIA
PHILIPPINES
JAPAN
AUSTRALIA
INDIAN OCEAN
Arabian Sea
Bay of Bengal
South China Sea
Sea of Okhotsk
Caspian Sea
Black Sea
Mediterranean Sea
Red Sea

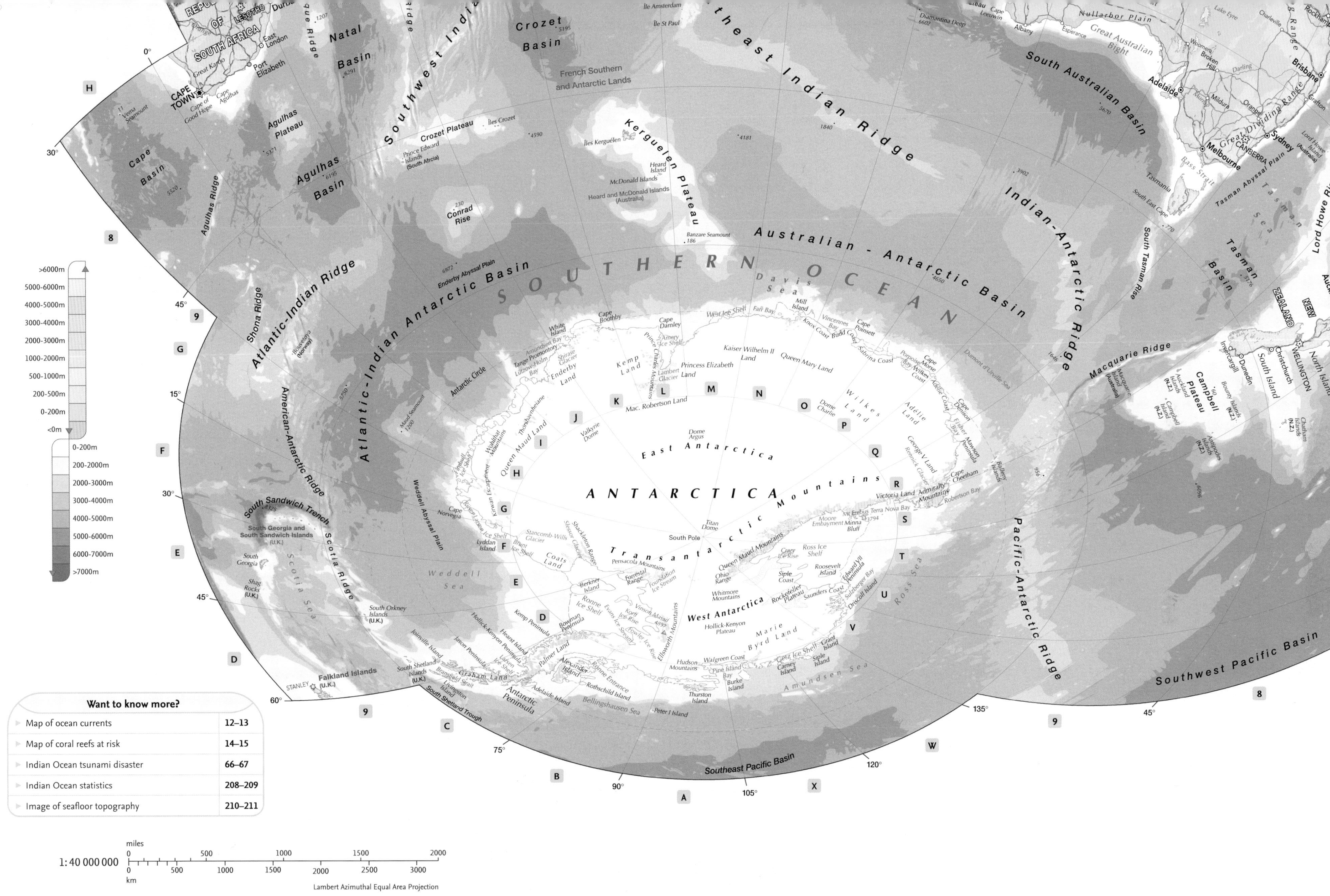

Want to know more?	
Map of ocean currents	12–13
Map of coral reefs at risk	14–15
Indian Ocean tsunami disaster	66–67
Indian Ocean statistics	208–209
Image of seafloor topography	210–211

1:40 000 000

Lambert Azimuthal Equal Area Projection

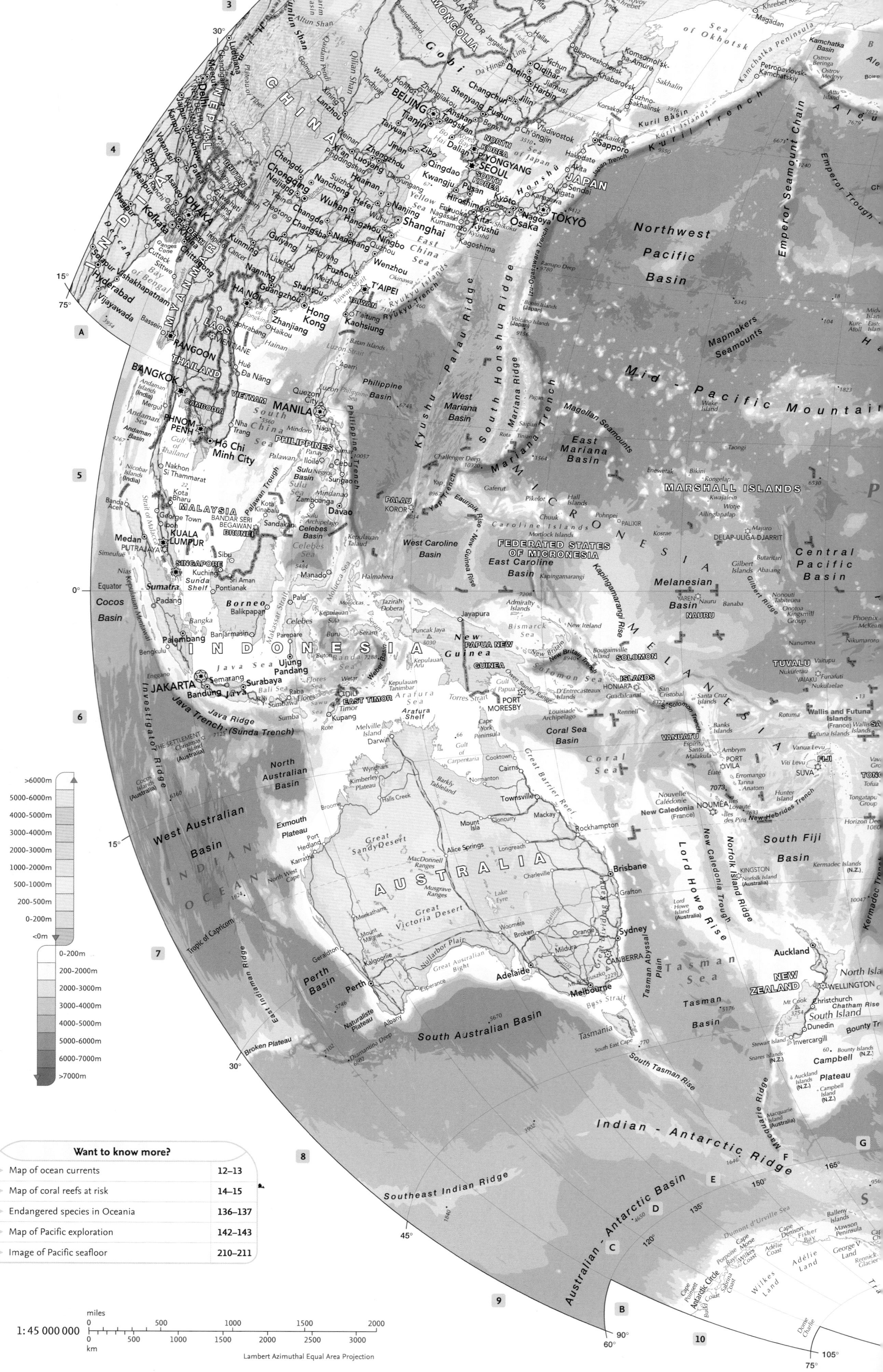

>6000m
5000-6000m
4000-5000m
3000-4000m
2000-3000m
1000-2000m
500-1000m
200-500m
0-200m
<0m

0-200m
200-2000m
2000-3000m
3000-4000m
4000-5000m
5000-6000m
6000-7000m
>7000m

1:45 000 000

miles
0   500   1000   1500   2000

km
0   500   1000   1500   2000   2500   3000

Lambert Azimuthal Equal Area Projection

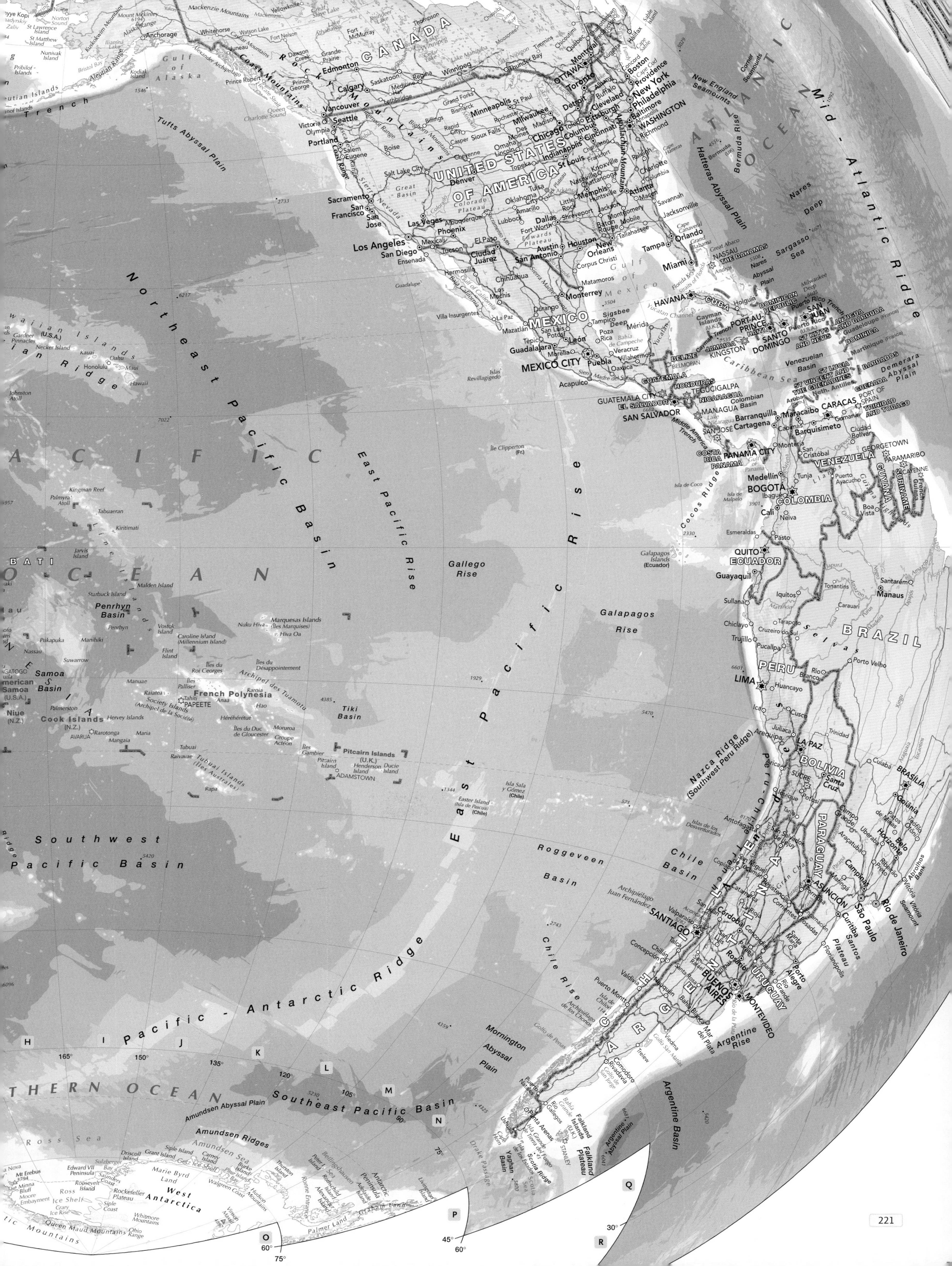

Antarctica

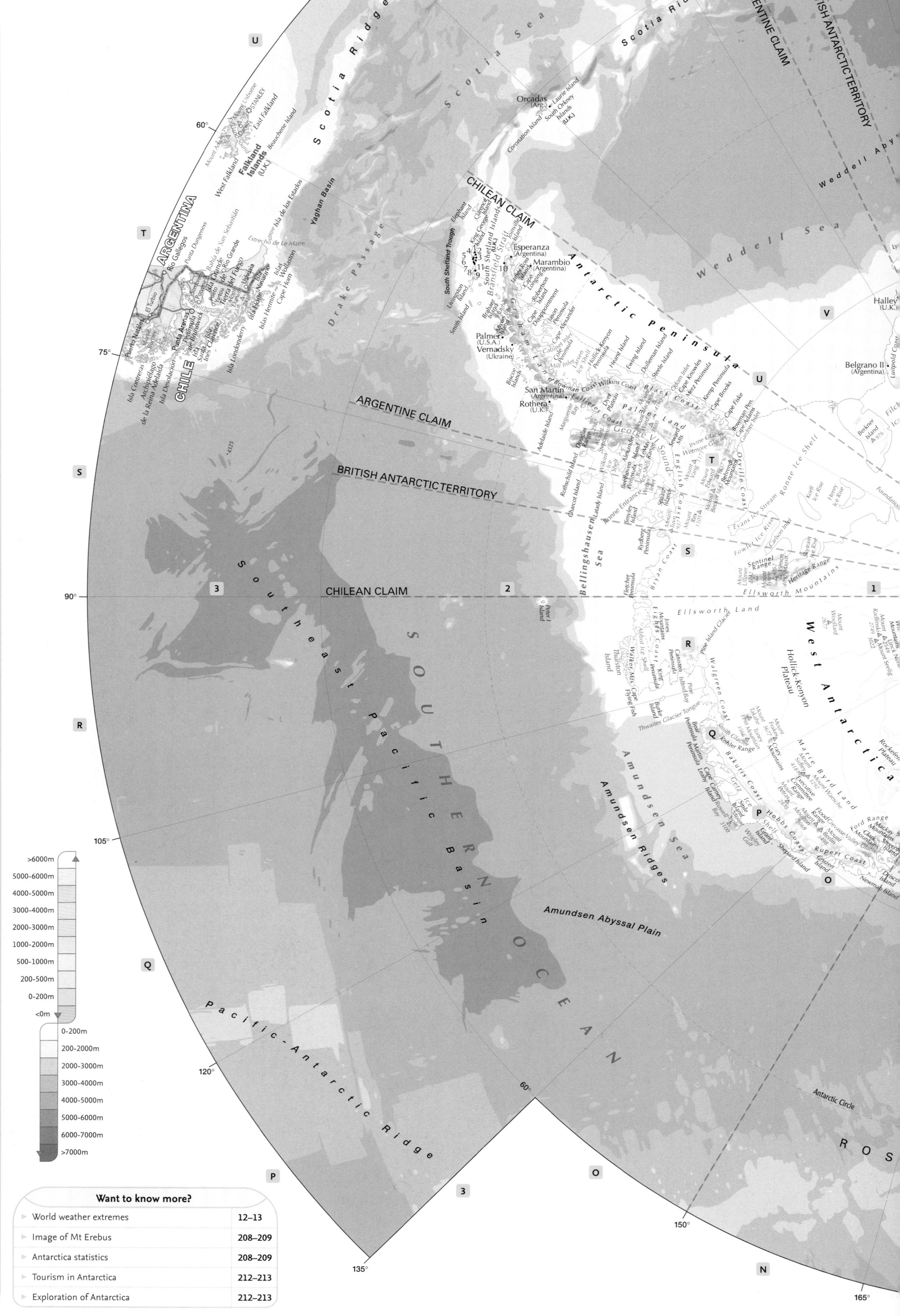

>6000m
5000-6000m
4000-5000m
3000-4000m
2000-3000m
1000-2000m
500-1000m
200-500m
0-200m
<0m

0-200m
200-2000m
2000-3000m
3000-4000m
4000-5000m
5000-6000m
6000-7000m
>7000m

Want to know more?

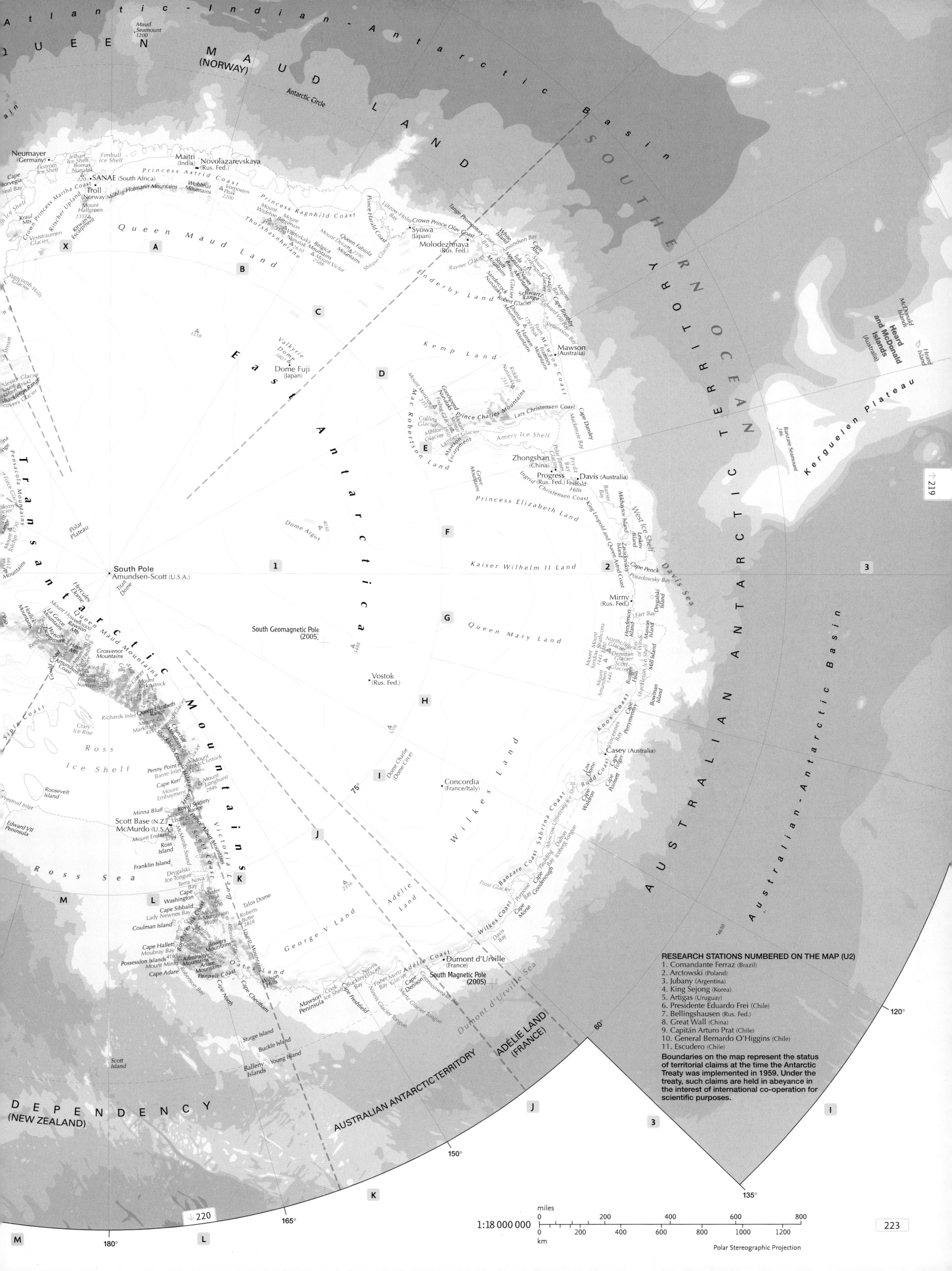

Atlantic-Indian-Antarctic Basin
Maud Seamount 1200
QUEEN MAUD LAND (NORWAY)
Antarctic Circle
SOUTHERN OCEAN
Neumayer (Germany)
Maitri (India)
Novolazarevskaya (Rus. Fed.)
SANAE (South Africa)
Troll (Norway)
Princess Astrid Coast
Princess Martha Coast
Mühlig-Hofmann Mountains
Wohlthat Mountains
Princess Ragnhild Coast
Queen Maud Land
Sør Rondane Mountains
Belgica Mountains
Queen Fabiola Mountains
Prince Harald Coast
Lützow-Holm Bay
Syowa (Japan)
Molodezhnaya (Rus. Fed.)
Crown Prince Olav Coast
Tange Promontory
Enderby Land
Amundsen Bay
Scott Mountains
Rayner Glacier
Kemp Land
Mawson (Australia)
Mawson Coast
Valkyrie Dome
Dome Fuji (Japan)
East Antarctica
Prince Charles Mountains
Lars Christensen Coast
Amery Ice Shelf
Cape Darnley
Mac Robertson Land
Zhongshan (China)
Progress (Rus. Fed.)
Davis (Australia)
Prydz Bay
Vestfold Hills
Ingrid Christensen Coast
Princess Elizabeth Land
King Leopold and Queen Astrid Coast
West Ice Shelf
Kerguelen Plateau
Heard and McDonald Islands (Australia)
McDonald Islands
Heard Island
Banzare Seamount
AUSTRALIAN ANTARCTIC TERRITORY
Polar Plateau
Dome Argus
South Pole
Amundsen-Scott (U.S.A.)
Titan Dome
Kaiser Wilhelm II Land
Cape Penck
Posadowsky Bay
Davis Sea
Mirny (Rus. Fed.)
Drygalski Island
Queen Mary Land
South Geomagnetic Pole (2005)
Vostok (Rus. Fed.)
Shackleton Ice Shelf
Bowman Island
Knox Coast
Casey (Australia)
Australian-Antarctic Basin
Transantarctic Mountains
Pensacola Mountains
Queen Maud Mountains
Grosvenor Mountains
Amundsen Coast
Gould Coast
Siple Coast
Richards Inlet
Queen Elizabeth Range
Mount Kirkpatrick
Mount Markham 4351
Ross Ice Shelf
Roosevelt Island
Edward VII Peninsula
Crary Ice Rise
Penny Point
Barne Inlet
Cape Kerr
Moore Embayment
Mount Longhurst 2846
Minna Bluff
Scott Base (N.Z.)
McMurdo (U.S.A.)
Mount Erebus 3794
Ross Island
Royal Society Range
Scott Coast
Victoria Land
Franklin Island
Drygalski Ice Tongue
Terra Nova Bay
Ross Sea
Cape Washington
Cape Sibbald
Lady Newnes Bay
Coulman Island
Cape Hallett
Moubray Bay
Possession Islands
Mount Minto
Cape Adare
Admiralty Mountains
Pennell Coast
Robertson Bay
Cape North
Oates Land
Talos Dome
Dome Charlie (Dome Circe)
Concordia (France/Italy)
Wilkes Land
Budd Coast
Sabrina Coast
Banzare Coast
Wilkes Coast
George V Land
Adélie Land
Dumont d'Urville (France)
South Magnetic Pole (2005)
Adélie Coast
Mawson Peninsula
Cook Ice Shelf
Ninnis Glacier Tongue
Mertz Glacier Tongue
Commonwealth Bay
Dumont d'Urville Sea
Sturge Island
Buckle Island
Young Island
Balleny Islands
Scott Island
ROSS DEPENDENCY (NEW ZEALAND)
AUSTRALIAN ANTARCTIC TERRITORY
ADÉLIE LAND (FRANCE)
60°
75°
120°
135°
150°
165°
180°
RESEARCH STATIONS NUMBERED ON THE MAP (U2)
1. Comandante Ferraz (Brazil)
2. Arctowski (Poland)
3. Jubany (Argentina)
4. King Sejong (Korea)
5. Artigas (Uruguay)
6. Presidente Eduardo Frei (Chile)
7. Bellingshausen (Rus. Fed.)
8. Great Wall (China)
9. Capitán Arturo Prat (Chile)
10. General Bernardo O'Higgins (Chile)
11. Escudero (Chile)
Boundaries on the map represent the status of territorial claims at the time the Antarctic Treaty was implemented in 1959. Under the treaty, such claims are held in abeyance in the interest of international co-operation for scientific purposes.
1:18 000 000
miles 0 200 400 600 800
km 0 200 400 600 800 1000 1200
Polar Stereographic Projection

↑219
↓220

↑ 220

Polar Stereographic Projection

1:24 000 000

Elevation legend (m):
- >6000m
- 5000–6000m
- 4000–5000m
- 3000–4000m
- 2000–3000m
- 1000–2000m
- 500–1000m
- 200–500m
- 0–200m
- <0m

- 0–200m
- 200–2000m
- 2000–3000m
- 3000–4000m
- 4000–5000m
- 5000–6000m
- 6000–7000m
- >7000m

Want to know more?	
▶ World's largest protected areas	14–15
▶ Image of Iceland	28–29
▶ Arctic statistics	208–209
▶ Exploration of the Arctic	214–215
▶ Peoples of the Arctic	214–215

miles
0 200 400 600 800 1000

km
0 200 400 600 800 1000 1200 1400 1600

Oceans and seas: PACIFIC OCEAN, Bering Sea, Aleutian Basin, Kamchatka Basin, Sea of Okhotsk, Chukchi Sea, East Siberian Sea, Laptev Sea, Kara Sea, ARCTIC OCEAN, Beaufort Sea, Barents Sea, Greenland Sea, Norwegian Sea, Baffin Bay, Davis Strait, Denmark Strait, North Sea, Lincoln Sea

Regions and features: U.S.A., CANADA, RUSSIAN FEDERATION, Greenland (Kalaallit Nunaat) (Denmark), ICELAND, NORWAY, SWEDEN, FINLAND, DENMARK, UNITED KINGDOM, ESTONIA, LATVIA, LITHUANIA, BELARUS

North Pole, North Magnetic Pole (2005), North Geomagnetic Pole (2005)

Arctic Circle

216

Introduction to the index

The index includes all names shown on the reference maps in the atlas. Each entry includes the country or geographical area in which the feature is located, a page number and an alphanumeric reference. Additional entry details and aspects of the index are explained below.

Referencing

Names are referenced by page number and by grid reference. The grid reference relates to the alphanumeric values which appear in the margin of each map. These reflect the graticule on the map – the letter relates to longitude divisions, the number to latitude divisions.

Names are generally referenced to the largest scale map page on which they appear. For large geographical features, including countries, the reference is to the largest scale map on which the feature appears in its entirety, or on which the majority of it appears.

Rivers are referenced to their lowest downstream point – either their mouth or their confluence with another river. The river name will generally be positioned as close to this point as possible.

Alternative names

Alternative names appear as cross-references and refer the user to the index entry for the form of the name used on the map. Details of alternative names and their types also appear within the main entry. The different types of name form included are: alternative forms or spellings currently in common use; English conventional name forms normally used in English-language contexts; historical and former names; and long and short name forms.

For rivers with multiple names – for example those which flow through several countries – all alternative name forms are included within the main index entries, with details of the countries in which each form applies.

Administrative qualifiers

Administrative divisions are included in an entry to differentiate duplicate names – entries of exactly the same name and feature type within the one country. In such cases, duplicate names are alphabetized in the order of the administrative division names.

Descriptors

Entries, other than those for towns and cities, include a descriptor indicating the type of geographical feature. Descriptors are not included where the type of feature is implicit in the name itself, unless there is a town or city of exactly the same name.

Name forms and alphabetical order

Name forms are as they appear on the maps, with additional alternative forms included as cross-references. Names appear in full in the index, although they may appear in abbreviated form on the maps.

The Icelandic characters Þ and þ are transliterated and alphabetized as 'Th' and 'th'. The German character ß is alphabetized as 'ss'. Names beginning with Mac or Mc are alphabetized exactly as they appear. The terms Saint, Sainte, etc, are abbreviated to St, Ste, etc, but alphabetized as if in the full form.

Name form policies are explained in the Introduction to the Atlas (pp 4–5).

Numerical entries

Entries beginning with numerals appear at the beginning of the index, in numerical order. Elsewhere, numerals are alphabetized before 'a'.

Permuted terms

Names beginning with generic geographical terms are permuted – the descriptive term is placed after, and the index alphabetized by, the main part of the name. For example, Mount Everest is indexed as Everest, Mount; Lake Superior as Superior, Lake. This policy is applied to all languages. Permuting has not been applied to names of towns, cities or administrative divisions beginning with such geographical terms. These remain in their full form, for example, Lake Isabella, USA.

Gazetteer entries and connections

Selected entries include gazetteer information. Important geographical facts which relate specifically to the entry are included within the entry.

Entries for features which also appear on, or which have a topical link to, the thematic pages of the atlas include a connection to those pages indicated by the symbol ▶▶.

UNESCO World Heritage Sites

Places or features which are designated as UNESCO World Heritage Sites, or which contain such sites, are identified within their index entries. Some locations identified in this way may contain more than one World Heritage Site.

Abbreviations

admin. dist.	administrative district	Indon.	Indonesia	pref.	prefecture
admin. div.	administrative division	is	islands	prov.	province
admin. reg.	administrative region	Kazakh.	Kazakhstan	pt	point
Afgh.	Afghanistan	KS	Kansas	Qld	Queensland
AK	Alaska	KY	Kentucky	Que.	Québec
AL	Alabama	Kyrg.	Kyrgyzstan	r.	river
Alg.	Algeria	l.	lake	r. mouth	river mouth
AR	Arkansas	LA	Louisiana	r. source	river source
Arg.	Argentina	lag.	lagoon	reg.	region
aut. comm.	autonomous community	Lith.	Lithuania	res.	reserve
aut. div.	autonomous division	Lux.	Luxembourg	resr	reservoir
aut. reg.	autonomous region	MA	Massachusetts	RI	Rhode Island
aut. rep.	autonomous republic	Madag.	Madagascar	Rus. Fed.	Russian Federation
AZ	Arizona	Man.	Manitoba	S.	South
Azer.	Azerbaijan	MD	Maryland	S.A.	South Australia
b.	bay	ME	Maine	salt l.	salt lake
Bangl.	Bangladesh	Mex.	Mexico	Sask.	Saskatchewan
B.C.	British Columbia	MI	Michigan	SC	South Carolina
Bol.	Bolivia	MN	Minnesota	SD	South Dakota
Bos.-Herz.	Bosnia-Herzegovina	MO	Missouri	sea chan.	sea channel
Bulg.	Bulgaria	Moz.	Mozambique	Serb. and Mont.	Serbia and Montenegro
c.	cape	MS	Mississippi	Sing.	Singapore
CA	California	MT	Montana	Switz.	Switzerland
Cent. Afr. Rep.	Central African Republic	mt.	mountain	Tajik.	Tajikistan
CO	Colorado	mts	mountains	Tanz.	Tanzania
Col.	Colombia	N.	North	Tas.	Tasmania
CT	Connecticut	nat. park	national park	terr.	territory
Czech Rep.	Czech Republic	nature res.	nature reserve	Thai.	Thailand
DC	District of Columbia	N.B.	New Brunswick	TN	Tennessee
DE	Delaware	NC	North Carolina	Trin. and Tob.	Trinidad and Tobago
Dem. Rep. Congo	Democratic Republic of the Congo	ND	North Dakota	Turkm.	Turkmenistan
depr.	depression	NE	Nebraska	TX	Texas
des.	desert	Neth.	Netherlands	U.A.E.	United Arab Emirates
Dom. Rep	Dominican Republic	NH	New Hampshire	U.K.	United Kingdom
E.	East, Eastern	NJ	New Jersey	Ukr.	Ukraine
Equat. Guinea	Equatorial Guinea	NM	New Mexico	union terr.	union territory
esc.	escarpment	N.S.	Nova Scotia	U.S.A.	United States of America
est.	estuary	N.S.W.	New South Wales	UT	Utah
Eth.	Ethiopia	N.T.	Northern Territory	Uzbek.	Uzbekistan
Fin.	Finland	NV	Nevada	VA	Virginia
FL	Florida	N.W.T.	Northwest Territories	Venez.	Venezuela
for.	forest	NY	New York	Vic.	Victoria
Fr. Guiana	French Guiana	N.Z.	New Zealand	vol.	volcano
g.	gulf	OH	Ohio	vol. crater	volcanic crater
GA	Georgia	OK	Oklahoma	VT	Vermont
Guat.	Guatemala	OR	Oregon	W.	West, Western
HI	Hawaii	PA	Pennsylvania	WA	Washington
Hond.	Honduras	Pak.	Pakistan	W.A.	Western Australia
i.	island	P.E.I.	Prince Edward Island	WI	Wisconsin
IA	Iowa	pen.	peninsula	WV	West Virginia
ID	Idaho	Phil.	Philippines	WY	Wyoming
IL	Illinois	plat.	plateau	Y.T.	Yukon Territory
imp. l.	impermanent lake	P.N.G.	Papua New Guinea		
IN	Indiana	Port.	Portugal		

1

1st Cataract *rapids* Egypt **121** G3
2nd Cataract *rapids* Sudan **121** F4
3rd Cataract *rapids* Sudan **121** F5
4th Cataract *rapids* Sudan **121** G5
5th Cataract *rapids* Sudan **121** G5
9 de Julio Arg. **204** E4
long form Nueve de Julio
15th of May City Egypt *see* **Medinet 15 Mayo**
25 de Mayo *Mendoza* Arg. **204** C4
long form Veinticinco de Mayo
25 de Mayo *Buenos Aires* Arg. **204** E4
long form Veinticinco de Mayo
25 de Mayo *La Pampa* Arg. **204** D5
long form Veinticinco de Mayo
26 Bakı Komissarı Azer. **107** G3
also known as imeni 26 Bakinskikh Komissarov; *formerly known as* Neftechala; *long form* İyirmi Altı Bakı Komissarı
42nd Hill S. Africa **133** N5
70 Mile House Canada **166** F5
100 Mile House Canada **166** F5
150 Mile House Canada **166** F4

A

Aabenraa Denmark **45** J5
also spelt Åbenrå
Aachen Germany **48** D5
formerly known as Aix-la-Chapelle; *historically known as* Aquae Grani *or* Aquisgranum
UNESCO World Heritage Site
Aadan Yabaal Somalia **128** E4
Aakirkeby Denmark **45** K5
Aalborg Denmark **45** J4
also spelt Ålborg
Aalborg Bugt *b.* Denmark **45** J4
Aalen Germany **48** H7
Aalesund Norway *see* **Ålesund**
Aaley Lebanon *see* **Aley**
Aalst Belgium **51** K2
also spelt Alost
Aanaar Fin. *see* **Inari**
Äänekoski Fin. **44** N3
Aansluit S. Africa **132** G3
Aarau Switz. **51** O5
Aarberg Switz. **51** N5
Aareavaara Sweden **44** M2
Aarhus Denmark *see* **Århus**
Aarlen Belgium *see* **Arlon**
Aars Denmark **45** J4
Aarschot Belgium **51** K2
Aasiaat Greenland **165** N3
also known as Egedesminde
Aath Belgium *see* **Ath**
Aavasaksa Fin. **44** M2
Aba China **86** B1
also known as Ngawa
Aba Dem. Rep. Congo **126** F4
Aba Nigeria **125** G5
Abā ad Dūd Saudi Arabia **104** D2
Abā al Afan *oasis* Saudi Arabia **105** E4
Abā al Qūr, Sha'īb *watercourse* Saudi Arabia **109** M6
Abā ar Ruwāth, Wādī *watercourse* Saudi Arabia **109** N7
Abacaxis *r.* Brazil **199** G6
Ābādān Iran **100** B4
English form Abadan
Abadan Iran *see* **Ābādān**
Ābādān, Jazīrah *i.* Iran/Iraq **105** E1
Ābādeh Iran **100** C4
Ābādeh Ţashk Iran **100** C4
Abadia dos Dourados Brazil **206** F5
Abadiânia Brazil **206** E3
Abadla Alg. **123** E3
Abádszalók Hungary **49** R8
Abaeté Brazil **207** H6
Abaeté *r.* Brazil **207** H5
Abaetetuba Brazil **202** B2
Abagnar Qi China *see* **Xilinhot**
Abag Qi China *see* **Xin Hot**
Abaí Para. **201** G6
Abaiang *atoll* Kiribati **145** G1
also spelt Apaiang; *formerly known as* Apia
A Baiuca Spain **54** C1
Abaji Nigeria **125** G4
Abajo Peak U.S.A. **183** O4
Abakaliki Nigeria **125** H5
Abakan Rus. Fed. **80** E2
formerly known as Ust'-Abakanskoye
Abala Congo **126** B5
Abala Niger **125** F3
Abalak Niger **125** G3
Abalyanka *r.* Belarus **43** L7
Abana Turkey **106** C2
Abancay Peru **200** B3
Abanga *r.* Gabon **126** A5
Abapó Bol. **201** E4
Abariringa *i.* Kiribati *see* **Kanton**
Abarkūh, Kavīr-e *des.* Iran **100** C4
Abarqū Iran **100** C4
A Barrela Spain **54** D2
Abarshahr Iran *see* **Neyshābūr**
Ābār 'Uwayrid Ţahtānī *well* Syria **109** K3
Abashiri Japan **90** I2
Abashiri-wan *b.* Japan **90** I2
Abasolo Mex. **185** F3
Abasula *waterhole* Kenya **128** C5
Abau P.N.G. **145** D3
Abava *r.* Latvia **42** C4
Abay *Karagandinskaya Oblast'* Kazakh. **103** H2
also known as Churubay Nura; *formerly known as* Abay Bazar
Abay *Vostochnyy Kazakhstan* Kazakh. *see* **Karaul**
Abaya, Lake Eth. **128** C3
also known as Ābaya Hāyk'; *formerly known as* Margherita, Lake
Ābaya Hāyk' *l.* Eth. *see* **Abaya, Lake**
Abay Bazar Kazakh. *see* **Abay**
Ābay Wenz *r.* Eth./Sudan **128** C2 *see* **Blue Nile**
Abaza Rus. Fed. **80** E2
Abba Cent. Afr. Rep. **126** B3
Abbadia San Salvatore Italy **56** D6
Abbāsābād Iran **100** D3
Abbasanta *Sardinia* Italy **57** A8
Abbatis Villa France *see* **Abbeville**
Abbaye, Point U.S.A. **172** E4
Abbe, Lake Djibouti/Eth. **128** D2
Abbeville France **51** H2
historically known as Abbatis Villa
Abbeville *GA* U.S.A. **175** D6
Abbeville *LA* U.S.A. **179** D6
Abbeville *SC* U.S.A. **175** D5
Abbey Canada **167** I5
Abbeyfeale Ireland **47** C11
Abbiategrasso Italy **56** A3
Abborrträsk Sweden **44** L2
Abbot, Mount Australia **149** E4
Abbot Bay Australia **149** E3
Abbot Ice Shelf Antarctica **222** R2
Abbotsford Canada **166** F5
Abbotsford U.S.A. **172** C6
Abbott *NM* U.S.A. **181** F5
Abbott *VA* U.S.A. **176** E8
Abbott *WV* U.S.A. **176** E7
Abbottabad Pak. **101** H3
Abchuha Belarus **43** K7
Abd, Oued el *watercourse* Alg. **55** L9
'Abd al 'Azīz, Jabal *hill* Syria **109** L1
'Abd al 'Azīz, Jabal *plat.* Syria **109** K1
'Abd al Kūrī *i.* Yemen **105** F5
'Abd Allah, Khawr *sea chan.* Iraq/Kuwait **107** G5
Abd al Ma'asīr *well* Saudi Arabia **109** J7
Ābdānān Iran **100** A3
Abdollāhābād Iran **100** D2
Abdulino Rus. Fed. **41** J5
Abéché Chad **120** D6
also known as Abeshr
Ab-e Garm, Chashmeh-ye *spring* Iran **100** D3
Abejukolo Nigeria **125** G5
Abelbod *well* Mali **125** E2
Abellinum Italy *see* **Avellino**
Abel Tasman National Park N.Z. **152** H8
Abemama *atoll* Kiribati **145** G1
also spelt Apamama
Abenab Namibia **130** C3
Abengourou Côte d'Ivoire **124** E5
Abenójar Spain **54** G6
Åbenrå Denmark *see* **Aabenraa**
Abensberg Germany **48** I7
Abeokuta Nigeria **125** F5
Abera Eth. **128** B3
Aberaeron U.K. **47** H11
Aberchirder U.K. **46** J6
Abercorn Zambia *see* **Mbala**
Abercrombie *r.* Australia **147** F3
Aberdare U.K. **47** I12
Aberdare National Park Kenya **128** C5
Aberdaron U.K. **47** H11
Aberdaugleddau U.K. *see* **Milford Haven**
Aberdeen Australia **147** F3
Aberdeen *Hong Kong* China **87** [inset]
also known as Heung Kong Tsai
Aberdeen S. Africa **132** I9
Aberdeen U.K. **46** J6
historically known as Devana
Aberdeen *MD* U.S.A. **177** I6
Aberdeen *MS* U.S.A. **175** B5
Aberdeen *OH* U.S.A. **176** B7
Aberdeen *SD* U.S.A. **178** C2
Aberdeen *WA* U.S.A. **180** B3
Aberdeen Island *Hong Kong* China **87** [inset]
also known as Ap Lei Chau
Aberdeen Lake Canada **167** L1
Aberdeen Road S. Africa **133** I9
Aberfeldy U.K. **46** I7
Aberfoyle U.K. **46** H7
Abergavenny U.K. **47** I12
also known as Y Fenni; *historically known as* Gobannium
Ābergelē Eth. **104** B5
Abergwaun U.K. *see* **Fishguard**
Aberhonddu U.K. *see* **Brecon**
Abermaw U.K. *see* **Barmouth**
Abernathy U.S.A. **179** B5
Abertawe U.K. *see* **Swansea**
Aberteifi U.K. *see* **Cardigan**
Aberystwyth U.K. **47** H11
Abeshr Chad *see* **Abéché**
Abez' Rus. Fed. **40** L2
Abhā Saudi Arabia **104** C4
Abhā, Jabal *hill* Saudi Arabia **104** C2
Abhanpur India **97** D5
Abhar Iran **100** B2
Abhar Rūd *r.* Iran **100** B3
Abia *state* Nigeria **125** G5
Abiad, Bahr el *r.* Sudan/Uganda **128** B2 *see* **White Nile**
Ābīata Hāyk' *l.* Eth. **128** C3
Abibe, Serranía de *mts* Col. **198** B2

►**Abidjan** Côte d'Ivoire **124** D5
Former capital of Côte d'Ivoire.

Abiekwasputs *salt pan* S. Africa **132** E4
Abijatta-Shalla National Park Eth. **128** C3
also known as Rift Valley Lakes National Park
Ab-i-Kavīr *salt flat* Iran **100** D3
Abiko Japan **91** G7
Abilene *KS* U.S.A. **178** C4
Abilene *TX* U.S.A. **179** C5
Abingdon U.K. **47** K12
Abingdon *IL* U.S.A. **172** C10
Abingdon *VA* U.S.A. **176** C9
Abington U.S.A. **177** O3
Abington Reef *reef* Australia **149** F3
Abinsk Rus. Fed. **41** F7
Ab-i-Panja *r.* Afgh./Tajik. *see* **Panj**
Abisko nationalpark *nat. park* Sweden **44** L1
Abitibi *r.* Canada **168** D3
Abitibi, Lake Canada **168** D3
Abnūb Egypt **121** F3
Åbo Fin. *see* **Turku**
Abohar India **96** B3
Aboisso Côte d'Ivoire **124** E5
Aboke Sudan **128** B2
Abomey Benin **125** F5
UNESCO World Heritage Site
Abongabong, Gunung *mt.* Indon. **76** B1
Abong Mbang Cameroon **125** I6
Aboot Oman **105** F4
Aborlan Phil. **74** A4
Abou Déia Chad **126** C2
Abou Goulem Chad **120** D6
Aboumi Gabon **126** B5
Abqaiq Saudi Arabia **105** E2
also known as Buqayq
Abra, Laguna del *l.* Arg. **204** E6
Abrād, Wādī *watercourse* Yemen **105** D5
Abraham's Bay Bahamas **187** E2
Abraka Nigeria **125** G5
Abrams U.S.A. **172** E6
Abra Pampa Arg. **200** D5
Abre Campo Brazil **207** K7
Abreojos, Punta *pt* Mex. **184** B3
'Abri Sudan **121** F4
Abrolhos, Arquipélago dos *is* Brazil **207** O5
Abrosovo Rus. Fed. **43** Q3
Abrud Romania **58** E2
Abruka *i.* Estonia **42** D3
Abruzzi *admin. reg.* Italy *see* **Abruzzo**
Abruzzo *admin. reg.* Italy **56** F6
also spelt Abruzzi
Abruzzo, Parco Nazionale d' *nat. park* Italy **56** F7
'Abs Yemen **104** C4
Absalom, Mount Antarctica **223** W1
Absaroka Range *mts* U.S.A. **180** E3
Absecon U.S.A. **177** K6
Abşeron Yarımadası *pen.* Azer. **107** G2
also known as Apsheronskiy Poluostrov
Absterna, Vozyera *l.* Belarus **42** I6
Abtar, Jabal al *hills* Syria **109** I3
Abū aḑ Ḑuhūr Syria **109** I2
Abū al Abyaḑ *i.* U.A.E. **105** F2
Abū al Ḩusayn, Qā' *imp. l.* Jordan **109** J5
Abū 'Alī *i.* Saudi Arabia **105** E2
Abū al Kūfah *waterhole* Iraq **109** N3
Abū al Maţāmīr Egypt **108** B7
Abū 'Āmūd, Wādī *watercourse* Jordan **108** H7
Abū 'Arīsh Saudi Arabia **104** C4
Abū Ballāş *hill* Egypt **121** E3
Abū Dā'ir *des.* Yemen **105** D4
Abu Deleiq Sudan **121** G6

►**Abu Dhabi** U.A.E. **105** F2
Capital of the United Arab Emirates. Also spelt Abū Ẓabī.

Abū Ḑībā' *waterhole* Saudi Arabia **104** B3
Abū Durbah Egypt **108** E9
Abufari Brazil **199** F6
Abū Farrūkh, Wādī *watercourse* Iraq **109** O4
Abu Gabra Sudan **126** E2
Abu Gamel Sudan **104** B5
Abū Ghar, Wādī *watercourse* Iraq **109** M5
Abū Ghizlān *waterhole* Iraq **109** O3
Abū Ghurayb Iraq **109** P4
Abu Gubeiha Sudan **128** A2
Abū Ḩād, Wādī *watercourse* Egypt **108** E9
Abū Ḩafnah, Wādī *watercourse* Jordan **109** J5
Abū Ḩallūfah, Jabal *hill* Jordan **109** H6
Abu Hamed Sudan **121** G5
Abū Ḩammād Egypt **108** C7
Abu Haraz Sudan **121** G5
Abu Hashim Sudan **121** G5
Abū Ḩaşwah, Jabal *hill* Egypt **108** E9
Abu Higar Sudan **121** G6
Abū Ḩummuş Egypt **108** B6

►**Abuja** Nigeria **125** G4
Capital of Nigeria.

Abū Jaḩaf, Wādī *watercourse* Iraq **109** O5
Abū Kabīr Egypt **108** C7
Abū Kamāl Syria **109** L3
Abū Kammāsh Libya **120** A1
Abū Khamsāt, Sha'īb *watercourse* Iraq **109** O6
Abukuma-kōchi *plat.* Japan **90** G6
Abu La'ot *watercourse* Sudan **121** F6
Abū Latt Island Saudi Arabia **104** C4
Abū Madd, Ra's *hd* Saudi Arabia **104** B2
Abu Matariq Sudan **126** E2
Abū Mīnā *tourist site* Egypt **108** A7
UNESCO World Heritage Site
Abumombazi Dem. Rep. Congo **126** D4
Abu Musa *i.* The Gulf **105** F2
also known as Abū Mūsá, Jazīreh-ye
Abū Mūsá, Jazīreh-ye *i.* The Gulf *see* **Abu Musa**
Abunã *r.* Bol. **200** D2
Abunã Brazil **200** D2
Abunai Brazil **199** E5
Abū Nā'im *well* Libya **120** C2
Ābune Yosēf *mt.* Eth. **128** C1
Abū Nujaym Libya **120** B2
Abū Qīr, Khalīj *b.* Egypt **108** B6
Abū Qurīn Libya **120** B2
Abū Rāqah *well* Saudi Arabia **104** B2
Abū Rawthah, Jabal *mt.* Egypt **108** F8
Aburo *mt.* Dem. Rep. Congo **126** F4
Abu Road India **96** B4
also known as Kharari
Abū Rubayq Saudi Arabia **104** B3
Abū Rujmayn, Jabal *mts* Syria **109** J3
Abū Salīm, Birkat *waterhole* Saudi Arabia **104** C2
Abū Sallah, Wādī *watercourse* Saudi Arabia **109** I9
Abū Sawādah *well* Saudi Arabia **105** E2
Abu Shagara, Ras *pt* Sudan **121** H4
Abu Simbel Egypt **121** F4
Abu Simbel Temple *tourist site* Egypt **121** F4
UNESCO World Heritage Site
Abū Şukhayr Iraq **107** F5
Abū Sulţān Egypt **108** D7
Abuta Japan **90** G3
Abu Tabaq *well* Sudan **121** G4
Abū Ţarfā', Wādī *watercourse* Egypt **108** E8
Abut Head N.Z. **153** E11
Abū Tīj Egypt **106** B6
Abū Ţuyūr, Jabal *mt.* Egypt **121** G3
Abū Ujayyijāt *well* Saudi Arabia **109** H9
Abū 'Uwayqilah *well* Egypt **108** F7
Abuye Meda *mt.* Eth. **128** C2
Abuyog Phil. **74** C4
Abu Zabad Sudan **121** F6
Abū Ẓabī U.A.E. *see* **Abu Dhabi**
Abū Zanīmah Egypt **121** G2
Abwong Sudan **128** B2
Åby Sweden **45** L4
Abyad Sudan **121** E6
Abyaḑ, Jabal al *hills* Saudi Arabia **108** G9
Abyaḑ, Jabal al *mts* Syria **109** I3
Abyān *governorate* Yemen **105** D5
Abyār al Hakīm *well* Libya **120** D2
Abyār an Nakhīlan *well* Libya **120** D2
Abyār Banī Murr *well* Saudi Arabia **108** G9
Abydos Australia **150** B4
Abyei Sudan **126** F2
Åbyn Sweden **44** M2
Abyssinia *country* Africa *see* **Ethiopia**
Abzakovo Rus. Fed. **102** D1
Abzanovo Rus. Fed. **102** D2
Acacias Col. **198** C4
Academician Vernadskiy *research station* Antarctica *see* **Vernadsky**
Academy Bay Rus. Fed. *see* **Akademii, Zaliv**
Academy Glacier Antarctica **223** T1
Acadia *prov.* Canada *see* **Nova Scotia**
Acadia National Park U.S.A. **177** Q1
Açailândia Brazil **202** C3
Acajutiba Brazil **202** E4
Acajutla El Salvador **185** H6
Acala Mex. **185** G5
Acamarachi *mt.* Chile *see* **Pili, Cerro**
Acambaro Mex. **185** E4
Acampamento de Caça do Mucusso Angola **127** D9
Acancéh Mex. **185** H4
Acandí Col. **198** B2
Acaponeta Mex. **184** D4
Acapulco Mex. **185** F5
long form Acapulco de Juárez
Acapulco de Juárez Mex. *see* **Acapulco**
Acará Brazil **202** B2
Acará *r.* Brazil **202** B2
Acarai Mountains *hills* Brazil/Guyana **199** G4
Acará Miri *r.* Brazil **202** B2
Acaraú Brazil **202** D2
Acaraú *r.* Brazil **202** D2
Acaray, Represa de *resr* Para. **201** G6
A Carballa Spain **54** C1
Acarí Brazil **202** E3
Acari *r.* Brazil **207** H2
Acarí Peru **200** B3
Acarí *r.* Peru **200** B3
Acarigua Venez. **198** D2
Acatlan Mex. **185** F5
Acatzingo Mex. **185** F5
Acay, Nevado de *mt.* Arg. **200** D6
Acayucán Mex. **185** G5
Accho Israel *see* **'Akko**
Accomac U.S.A. **177** J8
also spelt Accomack
Accomack U.S.A. *see* **Accomac**

►**Accra** Ghana **125** E5
Capital of Ghana.

Aceguá Brazil **204** G3
►**Aceh** *admin. dist.* Indon. **76** B1
formerly spelt Acheh *or* Atjeh; *historically known as* Achin
►►**66–67 Asia** Tsunami
Aceuchal Spain **54** E6
Achacachi Bol. **200** C4
Achaguas Venez. **199** D3
Achalpur India **96** C5
formerly known as Dadra *or* Elichpur
Achampet India **94** C2
Achan Rus. Fed. **82** E2
formerly known as Bolon'
Achanta India **94** D2
Achayvayam Rus. Fed. **39** R3
Acheh *admin. dist.* Indon. *see* **Aceh**
Achemelmel *well* Mali **123** F5
Achemmîm *well* Mauritania **124** D2
Acheng China **82** B3
Achern Germany **48** F7
Achhota India **94** D1
Achikulak Rus. Fed. **107** F1
Achill Island Ireland **47** B10
Achim Germany **48** G2
Achin *admin. dist.* Indon. *see* **Aceh**
Achinsk Rus. Fed. **80** E1
Achisay Kazakh. **103** G4
also spelt Ashchysay
Achit Rus. Fed. **40** K4
Achit Nuur *l.* Mongolia **84** A1
Achkhoy-Martan Rus. Fed. **107** F2
formerly known as Novoselskoye
Achlades, Akra *pt* Greece **59** G12
Achnasheen U.K. **46** G6
Achosa-Rudnya Belarus **43** M9
Aci Castello *Sicily* Italy **57** H11
Aci Catena *Sicily* Italy **57** H11
Acıgöl *l.* Turkey **106** B3
Acıpayam Turkey **106** B3
Acireale *Sicily* Italy **57** H11
Ackerman U.S.A. **175** B5
Ackley U.S.A. **174** A3
Acklins Island Bahamas **187** E2
Acobamba *Huancavelica* Peru **200** B3
Acobamba *Junín* Peru **200** B2
Acomayo *Cusco* Peru **200** C3
Acomayo *Huánuco* Peru **200** A2

►**Aconcagua, Cerro** *mt.* Arg. **204** C4
Highest mountain in South America.
►►**188–189 South America** Landscapes

Acopiara Brazil **202** E3
Acora Peru **200** C3
Açores, Arquipélago dos *is* Port **54** [inset]
A Coruña Spain **54** C1
English form Corunna; *also spelt* La Coruña
Acostambo Peru **200** B3
Acoyapa Nicaragua **186** B5
Acquapendente Italy **56** D6
Acqui Terme Italy **56** A4
historically known as Aquae Statiellae
Acra U.S.A. **177** K3
Acragas *Sicily* Italy *see* **Agrigento**
Acraman, Lake *salt flat* Australia **146** B3
Acre *r.* Brazil **200** D2
formerly known as Aquiry
Acre *state* Brazil **200** C2
Acre Israel *see* **'Akko**
Acreúna Brazil **206** C4
Acri Italy **57** I9
Ács Hungary **49** P8
Actaeon Group *is* Fr. Polynesia *see* **Actéon, Groupe**
Actéon, Groupe *is* Fr. Polynesia **221** J7
English form Actaeon Group
Acton Canada **173** M7
Acton U.S.A. **182** F7
Actopán Mex. **185** F4
Açuã *r.* Brazil **201** D1
Açuçena Brazil **207** K6
Acunum Acusio France *see* **Montélimar**
Acurenam Equat. Guinea **125** H6
Açurizal Brazil **201** F3
Ada Ghana **125** F5
Ada *Vojvodina, Srbija* Serb. and Mont. **58** B3
Ada *MN* U.S.A. **178** C2
Ada *OH* U.S.A. **176** B5
Ada *OK* U.S.A. **179** C5
Ādaba Eth. **128** C3
Adabazar Turkey *see* **Adapazarı**
Adaf, Djebel *mts* Alg. **123** H5
Adaja *r.* Spain **54** G3
Adak Sweden **44** L2
Adalia Turkey *see* **Antalya**
Adam Oman **105** G3
Adam, Mount *hill* Falkland Is **205** F8
Adamantina Brazil **206** B8
Adamaoua *prov.* Cameroon **125** I5
Adamaoua, Massif de l' *mts* Cameroon **125** I5
Adamas Greece **59** F12
also spelt Adhámas
Adamawa *state* Nigeria **125** H4
Adamclisi Romania **58** I4
Adamello *mt.* Italy **56** C2
Adamello-Brenta, Parco Naturale *nature res.* Italy **56** C2
Adaminaby Australia **147** F4
Adamovka Rus. Fed. **102** D2
Adams *KY* U.S.A. **176** C7
Adams *MA* U.S.A. **177** L3
Adams *NY* U.S.A. **177** I2
Adams *WI* U.S.A. **172** D7
Adams, Cape Antarctica **222** T2
Adams, Mount N.Z. **153** E11
Adam's Bridge *sea feature* India/Sri Lanka **94** C4
Adams Center U.S.A. **177** I2
Adams Lake Canada **166** G5
Adams McGill Reservoir U.S.A. **183** I3
Adams Mountain U.S.A. **166** D4
Adam's Peak Sri Lanka **94** D5
also known as Samanala *or* Sri Pada
Adams Peak U.S.A. **182** D2

►**Adamstown** Pitcairn Is **221** K7
Capital of the Pitcairn Islands.

Adamstown U.S.A. **177** I5
'Adan Yemen *see* **Aden**
Adana Turkey **106** C3
also known as Seyhan; *historically known as* Ataniya
Adana *prov.* Turkey **108** G1
Adana Yemen *see* **Aden**
'Adan as Sughra Yemen **104** D5
English form Little Aden
Adang, Teluk *b.* Indon. **77** G3
Adani Nigeria **125** G5
Adapazarı Turkey **106** B2
formerly known as Adabazar
Adaran, Jabal *mt.* Yemen **105** D5
Adare Ireland **47** D11
Adare, Cape Antarctica **223** L2
Adarmo, Khawr *watercourse* Sudan **104** A3
Adatara-san *vol.* Japan **90** G5
Adavale Australia **149** E5
Ādaži Latvia **42** F4
Adban Afgh. **101** G2
Adda *r.* Italy **56** B3
Aḑ Ḑab'ah Egypt **53** H5
Ad Dabbah Sudan *see* **Ed Debba**
Ad Dafīnah Saudi Arabia **104** C3
Ad Daghghārah Iraq **107** F4
Ad Dahnā' *des.* Saudi Arabia **105** D3
also spelt Dahana
Ad Dākhilīyah *admin. reg.* Oman **105** G3
Ad Dakhla W. Sahara **122** B5
also spelt Dakhla; *formerly known as* Villa Cisneros
Aḑ Ḑāli' Yemen **104** D5
Aḑ Ḑāli' *governorate* Yemen **105** D5
Ad Damir Sudan *see* **Ed Damer**
Ad Dammām Saudi Arabia *see* **Dammam**
Addanki India **94** C3
Ad Daqahlīyah *governorate* Egypt **108** C6
Ad Dār al Ḩamrā' Saudi Arabia **104** B2
Ad Darb Saudi Arabia **104** C4
Adda Sud, Parco dell' *park* Italy **56** B3
Addatigala India **94** D2
Ad Dawādimī Saudi Arabia **104** D2
Ad Dawḩah Qatar *see* **Doha**
Ad Daww *plain* Syria **109** I3
Addax, Réserve Naturelle Intégrale dite Sanctuaire des *nature res.* Niger **125** H2
Ad Dayr Egypt **108** C7
Ad Dibdibah *plain* Saudi Arabia **105** D2
Ad Dibīn Yemen **105** E4
Ad Dikākah *des.* Saudi Arabia **105** E4
Ad Dilam Saudi Arabia **105** D3
Ad Dir'īyah Saudi Arabia **105** D2

►**Addis Ababa** Eth. **128** C2
Capital of Ethiopia. Also spelt Ādīs Ābeba.

Addison U.S.A. **177** H3
Ad Dīwānīyah Iraq **107** F5
also spelt Diwaniyah
Ad Dīwānīyah *governorate* Iraq *see* **Al Qādisīyah**
Addo S. Africa **133** J10
Addo Elephant National Park S. Africa **133** J10
Addoo Atoll Maldives *see* **Addu Atoll**
Addu Atoll Maldives **93** D11
also known as Seenu Atoll; *also spelt* Addoo Atoll
Aḑ Ḑulū'īyah Iraq **109** P3
Ad Duwayd *well* Saudi Arabia **107** E5
Ad Duwayḩirah Saudi Arabia **104** D2
Ad Duwaym Sudan *see* **Ed Dueim**
Ad Duwayris *well* Saudi Arabia **105** E3
Adel *GA* U.S.A. **175** D6
Adel *IA* U.S.A. **178** D3

►**Adelaide** Australia **146** C3
State capital of South Australia.

Adelaide Bahamas **175** E7
Adelaide S. Africa **133** K9
Adelaide Island Antarctica **222** T2
Adelaide River Australia **148** A2
Adelebsen Germany **48** G4
Adele Island Australia **150** C2
Adelfoi *i.* Greece **59** H12
Adélie Coast Antarctica **223** J2
Adélie Coast *reg.* Antarctica *see* **Adélie Land**
Adélie Land *reg.* Antarctica **223** J2
also known as Adélie Coast *or* Terre Adélie
Adelong Aboriginal Reserve Australia **151** C6
Adelsheim Germany **48** G6
Adelunga Uzbek. **103** G4
Aden Yemen **104** D5
also spelt 'Adan; *historically known as* Adana
Aden, Gulf of Somalia/Yemen **128** E2
Adena U.S.A. **176** E5
Adenau Germany **48** D5
Adendorp S. Africa **133** I9
Aderbissinat Niger **125** G3
Aderno *Sicily* Italy *see* **Adrano**
Adesar India **96** A5
Adhaman az Zaur, Wādī *watercourse* Iraq **109** N5
Adhámas Greece *see* **Adamas**
Adhan, Jabal *mt.* U.A.E. **105** G2
Adhanah, Wādī *watercourse* Yemen **104** D5
Adh Dhayd U.A.E. **105** F2
Adh Dhāyūf *well* Saudi Arabia **104** D2
'Adhfā' *well* Saudi Arabia **107** E5
'Ādhirīyāt, Jibāl al *mts* Jordan **109** H7
Adhoi India **96** A5
Adi *i.* Indon. **73** H7
Ādī Ārk'ay Eth. **128** C1
Adícora Venez. **198** D2
Ādī Da'iro Eth. **104** B5
'Adid Umm Inderab *well* Sudan **121** F6
Adige *r.* Italy **56** E3
Adigey Autonomous Oblast *aut. rep.* Rus. Fed. *see* **Adygeya, Respublika**
Ādīgrat Eth. **128** C1
Adıgüzel Barajı *resr* Turkey **106** B3
Adi Keyih Eritrea **121** H6
Adi Kwala Eritrea **121** H6
Adilabad India **94** C2
Adilang Uganda **128** B4
Adilcevaz Turkey **107** E3
Adin U.S.A. **180** B4
Adīrī Libya **120** B3
Adirondack Mountains U.S.A. **177** K1
Ādīs Ābeba Eth. *see* **Addis Ababa**
Ādīs Zemen Eth. **128** C1
Adi Ugri Eritrea *see* **Mendefera**
Adıyaman Turkey **107** D3
Adjoantali *reg.* Alg. **123** G5
Adjud Romania **58** I2
Adjumani Uganda **128** A4
Adjuntas, Presa de las *resr* Mex. **185** F4
Adlavik Islands Canada **169** J2
Admiralty Gulf Australia **150** D2
Admiralty Gulf Aboriginal Reserve Australia **150** D2
Admiralty Inlet Canada **165** K2
Admiralty Island Canada **165** I3
Admiralty Island U.S.A. **164** F4
Admiralty Island National Monument-Kootznoowoo Wilderness *nat. park* U.S.A. **164** F4
Admiralty Islands P.N.G. **73** K7
Admiralty Mountains Antarctica **223** L2
Ādo Eth. **128** E3
Ado-Ekiti Nigeria **125** G5
Adok Sudan **128** A2
Adolfo Gonzáles Chaves Arg. **204** E5
Adolfsström Sweden **44** L2
Adolphus Island Australia **150** E2
Adonara *i.* Indon. **75** B5
also spelt Adunara
Adoni India **94** C3
Adour *r.* France **50** E9
Adra India **97** E5
Adra Spain **55** H8
Adra *r.* Spain **55** I8
Adramyttium Turkey *see* **Edremit**
Adramyttium, Gulf of Turkey *see* **Edremit Körfezi**
Adrano *Sicily* Italy **57** G11
also spelt Aderno; *historically known as* Hadranum
Adrar Alg. **123** E4
Adrar *mts* Alg. **123** G4
Adrar *hills* Mali *see* **Ifôghas, Adrar des**
Adrar *admin. reg.* Mauritania **122** C5
Adraskand *r.* Afgh. **101** E3
Adrasmon Tajik. **101** G1
Adré Chad **120** D6
Adrian *MI* U.S.A. **173** I9
Adrian *TX* U.S.A. **179** B5
Adrianople Turkey *see* **Edirne**
Adrianopolis Turkey *see* **Edirne**
Adriatic Sea Europe **56** F4
Adua Eth. *see* **Ādwa**
Adunara *i.* Indon. *see* **Adonara**
Adur India **94** C4
Adusa Dem. Rep. Congo **126** F4
Adusa, Qalti el *well* Sudan **121** E5
Adutiškis Lith. **42** H6
Aduwa Eth. *see* **Ādwa**
Adverse Well Australia **150** C4
Ādwa Eth. **128** C1
also spelt Aduwa; *formerly spelt* Adua
Adwufia Ghana **124** E5
Adyān, Fayḑat al *waterhole* Iraq **109** M6
Adycha *r.* Rus. Fed. **39** N3
Adygeya *aut. rep.* Rus. Fed. *see* **Adygeya, Respublika**
Adygeya, Respublika *aut. rep.* Rus. Fed. **41** F7
formerly known as Adigey Autonomous Oblast *or* Adygeyskaya Avtonomnaya Oblast'; *short form* Adygeya
Adygeysk Rus. Fed. **41** F7
formerly known as Teuchezhsk
Adygeyskaya Avtonomnaya Oblast' *aut. rep.* Rus. Fed. *see* **Adygeya, Respublika**
Adyk Rus. Fed. **41** H7
formerly known as Yuzhnyy
Adzopé Côte d'Ivoire **124** E5
Adz'va *r.* Rus. Fed. **40** L2
Adz'vavom Rus. Fed. **40** K2
Aegean Sea Greece/Turkey **59** F10
Aegina *i.* Greece *see* **Aigina**
Aegna *i.* Estonia **42** F2
Aegviidu Estonia **42** G2
Aegyptus *country* Africa *see* **Egypt**
Aela Jordan *see* **Al 'Aqabah**
Aelana Jordan *see* **Al 'Aqabah**
Aelia Capitolina Israel/West Bank *see* **Jerusalem**
Aelōnlaplap *atoll* Marshall Is *see* **Ailinglaplap**
Aenus Turkey *see* **Enez**
Ærø *i.* Denmark **48** H1
Aerzen Germany **48** G3
Aesernia Italy *see* **Isernia**
A Estrada Spain **54** C2
Äetsä Fin. **45** M3
Afabet Eritrea **121** H5
Afal *watercourse* Saudi Arabia *see* **'Ifāl, Wādī**
Afanas'yevo Rus. Fed. **40** J4
Afándou Greece *see* **Afantou**
Afantou Greece **59** J12
also spelt Afándou
Āfar *admin. reg.* Eth. **128** D1
Afar Oman **105** G3
Afar Depression Eritrea/Eth. **121** I6
Āfdem Eth. **128** D2
A Feira do Monte Spain **54** D1
Afféri Côte d'Ivoire **124** E5
Affreville Alg. *see* **Khemis Miliana**
Afghānestān *country* Asia *see* **Afghanistan**
►**Afghanistan** *country* Asia **101** E3
spelt Afghānestān in Dari and Pushtu
►►**64–65 Asia** Countries
Afgooye Somalia **128** E4
'Afīf Saudi Arabia **104** C3
Afikpo Nigeria **125** G5
Afim'ino Rus. Fed. **43** P4
Afiun Karahissar Turkey *see* **Afyon**
Åfjord Norway **44** J3
Aflou Alg. **123** F2
Afmadow Somalia **128** D4
Afognak Island U.S.A. **164** D4
Afojjar *well* Mauritania **124** B2
A Fonsagrada Spain **54** D1
also known as Fonsagrada
Afonso Cláudio Brazil **207** L7
Afragola Italy **56** G8
Afrânio Brazil **202** D4
Āfrēra Terara *vol.* Eth. **128** D1
Āfrēra YeChe'ew Hāyk' *l.* Eth. **128** D1
Africa Nova *country* Africa *see* **Tunisia**
'Afrīn Syria **109** H1
'Afrīn, Nahr *r.* Syria/Turkey **109** H1
Afşar Barajı *resr* Turkey **59** J10
Afşin Turkey **107** D3
also known as Efsus
Afsluitdijk *barrage* Neth. **48** C3
Aftol *well* Eth. **128** E3
Afton *NY* U.S.A. **177** J3
Afton *WY* U.S.A. **180** E4
Aftoût Faï *depr.* Mauritania **124** B2
Afuá Brazil **202** B2
'Afula Israel **108** G5
Afyon Turkey **106** B3
also known as Afyonkarahisar; *historically known as* Afiun Karahissar
Afyonkarahisar Turkey *see* **Afyon**
Aga *r.* Rus. Fed. **85** G1
Aga-Buryat Autonomous Okrug *admin. div.* Rus. Fed. *see* **Aginskiy Buryatskiy Avtonomnyy Okrug**
Agadem *well* Niger **125** I2
Agadès Niger *see* **Agadez**
Agadez Niger **125** G2
also spelt Agadès
Agadez *dept* Niger **125** H2
Agadir Morocco **122** C3
Agadyr' Kazakh. **103** H2
also spelt Aqadyr
Agaie Nigeria **125** G4
Agalega Islands Mauritius **218** K6
Agalta *nat. park* Hond. **186** B4
Agana Guam *see* **Hagåtña**
A Gándara de Altea Spain **54** C1
Agapovka Rus. Fed. **102** D1
Agar India **96** C5
Agârak *well* Niger **125** G2
Agâraktem *well* Mali **122** D5
Āgaro Eth. **128** C3
Agartala India **97** F5
Agashi India **94** B2
Agassiz National Wildlife Refuge *nature res.* U.S.A. **178** D1
Agate Canada **168** D3
Agathe France *see* **Agde**
Agathonisi *i.* Greece **59** H11
Agatti *i.* India **94** B4
Agawa *r.* Canada **173** I3
Agbor Bojiboji Nigeria **125** G5
Agboville Côte d'Ivoire **124** D5
Ağcabädi Azer. **107** F2
also spelt Agdzhabedi
Ağdam Azer. **107** F3
Ağdaş Azer. **107** F2
also spelt Agdash
Agdash Azer. *see* **Ağdaş**
Agde France **51** J9
historically known as Agathe
Agdzhabedi Azer. *see* **Ağcabädi**
Agedabia Libya *see* **Ajdābiyā**
Agen France **50** G8
historically known as Aginum
Agenebode Nigeria **125** G5
Āgere Maryam Eth. **128** C3
Ageyevo Rus. Fed. **43** R7
Aggeneys S. Africa **132** C6
Aggershus *county* Norway *see* **Akershus**
Aggteleki *nat. park* Hungary **49** R7
UNESCO World Heritage Site
Agharri, Sha'īb al *watercourse* Iraq **109** L4
Aghezzaf *well* Mali **125** E2
also spelt Arezzaf
Aghil Pass China/Jammu and Kashmir **89** B4
Aghireşu Romania **58** E2
Aghouavil *des.* Mauritania **124** D2
Aghrîjît *well* Mauritania **124** C2
Aghzoumal, Sabkhat *salt pan* W. Sahara **122** B4
Agia Greece **59** D9
also spelt Ayiá
Agiabampo Mex. **184** C3
Agia Eirinis, Akra *pt* Greece **59** G9
Agia Marina Greece **59** H11
Agiasos Greece **59** H9
also spelt Ayiásos
Agia Vervara Greece **59** G13
Agigea Romania **58** J4
Agighiol Romania **58** J3
Agiguan *i.* N. Mariana Is *see* **Aguijan**
Ağın Turkey **107** D3
Aginskiy Buryatskiy Avtonomnyy Okrug *admin. div.* Rus. Fed. **85** G1
English form Aga-Buryat Autonomous Okrug
Aginskoye Rus. Fed. **85** G1
Aginum France *see* **Agen**
Agioi Apostoloi Greece **59** E10
Agios Dimitrios Greece **59** E11
also spelt Áyios Dhimítrios
Agios Dimitrios, Akra *pt* Greece **59** F11
also spelt Áyios Dhimítris, Ákra
Agios Efstratios Greece **59** F9
Agios Efstratios *i.* Greece **59** G9
also spelt Áyios Evstrátios
Agios Fokas, Akra *pt* Greece **59** H9
Agios Georgios *i.* Greece **59** E11
also spelt Áyios Yeóryios
Agios Ioannis, Akra *pt* Greece **59** G13
Agios Kirykos Greece **59** H11
Agios Konstantinos Greece **59** D10
Agios Nikolaos Greece **59** G13
also spelt Áyios Nikólaos
Agios Paraskevi Greece **59** H9
Agios Petros Greece **59** D11

Agiou Orous, Kolpos b. Greece 59 E8
Agirwat Hills Sudan 121 G5
Agisanang S. Africa 133 J3
Agly r. France 51 J10
Agnantero Greece 59 C9
Agnes, Mount hill Australia 146 A1
Agnew Australia 151 C6
Agnew Lake Canada 173 L4
Agnibilékrou Côte d'Ivoire 124 E5
Agnita Romania 58 F3
Agniye-Afanas'yevsk Rus. Fed. 82 E2
Agno r. Italy 56 D3
Agnone Italy 56 G7
Ago-Are Nigeria 125 F4
Agogo Ghana 125 E5
Agona Junction Ghana 125 E5
Agong China 84 D4
Agounni Jefal well Mali 124 E2
Agoura U.S.A. 182 F7
Agous-n-Ehsel well Mali 125 F2
also known as Ehcel
Agout r. France 51 H9
Agra India 96 C4
UNESCO World Heritage Site
Agrakhanskiy Poluostrov pen. Rus. Fed. 102 A4
Agram Croatia see Zagreb
Agreda Spain 55 J3
Agri r. Italy 57 I8
Ağrı Turkey 107 E3
also known as Karaköse
Agria Gramvousa i. Greece 59 E13
Ağrı Dağı mt. Turkey see Ararat, Mount
Agrigan i. N. Mariana Is see Agrihan
Agrigento Sicily Italy 57 F11
formerly known as Girgenti; historically known as Acragas or Agrigentum
UNESCO World Heritage Site
Agrigentum Sicily Italy see Agrigento
Agrihan i. N. Mariana Is 73 K3
also spelt Agrigan; formerly spelt Grigan
Agrii r. Romania 58 E1
Agrinio Greece 59 C10
Agropoli Italy 57 G8
Agryz Rus. Fed. 40 J4
Ågskaret Norway 44 K2
Ağstafa Azer. 107 F2
Ağsu Azer. 107 G2
also spelt Akhsu
Agtertang S. Africa 133 J7
Agua Blanca Arg. 204 D5
Água Boa Brazil 207 K4
Agua Brava, Laguna lag. Mex. 184 D4
Agua Clara Bol. 200 D3
Água Clara Brazil 206 A7
Aguaclara Col. 198 C3
Aguada Mex. 185 H5
Aguadilla Puerto Rico 187 G3
Aguado Cecilio Arg. 204 D6
Agua Doce do Norte Brazil 207 L5
Aguados, Serra dos mts Brazil 206 D9
Agua Dulce Bol. 200 D3
Aguadulce Panama 186 C5
Agua Escondida Arg. 204 C5
Agua Fria r. U.S.A. 183 L8
Aguamilpa, Presa l. Mex. 184 D4
Aguanaval r. Mex. 185 E3
Aguanga U.S.A. 183 H8
Aguanqueterique Hond. 186 B4
Aguanus r. Canada 169 I3
Aguapeí Brazil 201 F4
Aguapeí r. Mato Grosso do Sul Brazil 206 B8
also known as Feio
Aguapeí r. Brazil 201 F3
Aguapeí, Serra hills Brazil 201 F4
Agua Prieta Mex. 184 C2
Aguarague, Cordillera de mts Bol. 201 E5
Aguaray Arg. 201 E5
A Guarda Spain 54 C3
also spelt La Guardia
Aguaro-Guariquito, Parque Nacional nat. park Venez. 199 E2
Aguaruto Mex. 184 D3
Aguas r. Spain 55 J7
Águas Belas Brazil 202 E4
Aguascalientes Mex. 185 E4
Aguascalientes state Mex. 185 E4
Águas Formosas Brazil 203 D6
Águas Vermelhas Brazil 207 L2
Aguasvivas r. Spain 55 K3
Água Verde r. Brazil 201 F3
Água Vermelha, Represa resr Brazil 206 C6
Aguaytia Peru 200 B2
Agudo Spain 54 G6
Agudos Brazil 206 E9
Águeda Port. 54 C4
Águeda r. Port./Spain 54 E3
Aguelal Niger 125 H2
Aguelhok Mali 125 F2
Aguemour, Oued watercourse Alg. 123 F4
Aguessis well Niger 123 H6
Aguié Niger 125 G3
Aguijan i. N. Mariana Is 73 K4
also spelt Aguigan
Águila mt. Spain 55 J4
Aguila U.S.A. 183 K8
Aguilar de Campóo Spain 54 G2
Águilas Spain 55 J7
Aguililla Mex. 185 E5
Aguisan Phil. 74 B4
Āgula'i Eth. 104 B5
Agulhas S. Africa 132 E11

▶Agulhas, Cape S. Africa 132 E11
Most southerly point of Africa.
▶▶110–111 Africa Landscapes

Agulhas Negras mt. Brazil 203 C7
Aguntum Italy see San Candido
Agusan r. Phil. 74 C4
Agutaya i. Phil. 74 B4
Ağva Turkey 106 B2
Agvali Rus. Fed. 102 A4
Agwarra Nigeria 125 G4
Agwei r. Sudan 128 B3
Ahaggar plat. Alg. see Hoggar
Ahakeye Aboriginal Land res. Australia 148 B4
Ahar Iran 100 A2
Ahaura N.Z. 153 F10
Ahaura r. N.Z. 153 F10
Ahaus Germany 48 E3
Ahigal Spain 54 E4
Ahillo mt. Spain 54 G7
Ahimanawa Range mts N.Z. 152 K6
Ahioma P.N.G. 149 F1
Ahipara N.Z. 152 H3
Ahipara Bay N.Z. 152 H3
Ahiri India 94 D2
Ahititi N.Z. 152 I6
Ahja r. Estonia 42 I3
Ahklun Mountains U.S.A. 164 C4
Ahlat Turkey 107 E3
Ahlen Germany 48 E4
Ahmadabad India 96 B5
formerly spelt Ahmedabad
Aḥmadābād Iran 101 E3
Aḥmad al Bāqir, Jabal mt. Jordan 108 G8
Ahmadnagar India 94 B2
formerly spelt Ahmednagar
Ahmadpur India 94 C2
also known as Rajura
Ahmadpur East Pak. 101 G4
Ahmadpur Sial Pak. 101 G4
Ahmar Mountains Eth. 128 D2
Ahmedabad India see Ahmadabad
Ahmednagar India see Ahmadnagar
Ahmetli Turkey 59 I10
Ahoada Nigeria 125 G5
Ahome Mex. 184 C3
Ahore India 96 B4
Ahoskie U.S.A. 177 I9
Ahram Iran 100 B4
Ahrâmât el Jîzah tourist site Egypt see Pyramids of Giza
Ahraura India 97 D4
Ahrensburg Germany 48 H2
Āhtäri Fin. 40 C3
Ahtme Estonia 42 I2
Āhū Iran 100 B4
Ahuacatlán Mex. 184 D4
Ahuachapán El Salvador 185 H6
Ahualulco Jalisco Mex. 184 E4
Ahualulco San Luis Potosí Mex. 185 E4
Ahun France 51 I6
Ahunapalu Estonia 42 I3
Ahuriri r. N.Z. 153 E12
Ahuroa N.Z. 152 I4
Ahvāz Iran 100 B4
also spelt Ahwāz
Ahvenanmaa is Fin. see Åland Islands
Ahwa India 94 B1
Aḥwar Yemen 105 D5
Ahwāz Iran see Ahvāz
Ahzar, Vallée de l' watercourse Niger 125 F3
Ai-Ais Namibia 130 C5
Ai-Ais Hot Springs and Fish River Canyon Park nature res. Namibia 130 C5
Aibag Gol r. China 85 F3
Aibetsu Japan 90 H3
Aichach Germany 48 I7
Aichi pref. Japan 91 E7
Aid U.S.A. 176 C7
Aida Japan 91 D7
Aigiali Greece 59 G12
also spelt Ayiáli
Aigialousa Cyprus 108 F2
also known as Yialousa
Aigina Greece 59 E11
Aigina i. Greece 59 E11
English form Aegina; also spelt Aíyina
Aiginio Greece 58 D8
also known as Aiyínion
Aigio Greece 59 D10
also known as Aíyion
Aigle Switz. 51 M6
Aigle de Chambeyron mt. France 51 M8
Aigoual, Mont mt. France 51 J8
Aiguá Uruguay 204 G4
Aiguebelle, Parc de Conservation d' nature res. Canada 173 O2
Aigües Tortes i Estany de Sant Maurici, Parc Nacional d' nat. park Spain 55 L2
Aiguille de Scolette mt. France/Italy 51 M7
Aiguilles d'Arves mts France 51 M7
Aiguille Verte mt. France 51 M7
Aigurande France 50 H6
Ai He r. China 83 B4
Aihua China see Yunxian
Aihui China see Heihe
Aija Peru 200 A2
Aijal India see Aizawl
Aiken U.S.A. 175 D5
Ailao Shan mts China 86 B3
Aileron Australia 148 B4
Aileu East Timor 75 C5
Ailigandi Panama 186 D5
Ailing China 87 D3
Ailinglabelab atoll Marshall Is see Ailinglaplap
Ailinglaplap atoll Marshall Is 220 G6
also spelt Aelōnlaplap or Ailinglabelab; formerly known as Lambert
Ailly-sur-Noye France 51 I3
Ailsa Craig Canada 173 L7
Ailsa Craig i. U.K. 47 G8
Aimogasta Arg. 204 D3
Aimorés, Serra dos hills Brazil 203 D6
Ain r. France 51 L7
Ainaži Latvia 42 F4
Aïn Beïda Alg. 123 G2
formerly known as Daoud
Aïn Beni Mathar Morocco 123 E2
'Aïn Ben Tili Mauritania 122 C4
Aïn Bessem Alg. 55 O8
Aïn Biré well Mauritania 124 C2
Aïn Boucif Alg. 55 O9
Aïn Defla Alg. 123 F1
formerly known as Duperré
Aïn Deheb Alg. 123 F2
Aïn Draham Tunisia 57 A12
Aïn el Hadjadj well Alg. 123 F3
Aïn el Hadjadj well Alg. 123 G4
Aïn el Hadjel Alg. 123 F2
Aïn Galakka spring Chad 120 C5
Aïn Mdila well Alg. 123 G2
Aïn-M'Lila Alg. 123 G1
Ainos nat. park Greece 59 B10
Aïn Oussera Alg. 123 F2
Aïn Salah Alg. see In Salah
Aïn Sefra Alg. 123 E2
Ainslie, Lake Canada 169 I4
Ainsworth IA U.S.A. 172 B9
Ainsworth NE U.S.A. 178 C3
Aintab Turkey see Gaziantep
Aïn Taya Alg. 55 O8
Aïn Tédélès Alg. 55 L9
Aïn Temouchent Alg. 123 E2
Aïn Ti-m Misaou well Alg. 123 F5
Aipe Col. 198 C4
Aiquile Bol. 200 D4
Air i. Indon. 77 D2
also known as Raibu
Aïr, Massif de l' mts Niger 125 H2
also known as Azbine
Airão Brazil 199 F5
Airbangis Indon. 76 B2
Airdrie Canada 167 H5
Aire r. France 51 K3
Aire-sur-l'Adour France 50 F9
Aïr et du Ténéré, Réserve Naturelle Nationale de l' nature res. Niger 125 H2
UNESCO World Heritage Site
Air Force Island Canada 165 L3
Airgin Sum China 85 F3
Airhitam r. Indon. 77 D2
Airhitam, Teluk b. Indon. 77 E3
Airlie Beach Australia 149 F4
Airlie Island Australia 150 A4
Airolo Switz. 51 O6
Airpanas Indon. 75 C4
Air Ronge Canada 167 J4
Airvault France 50 F6
Aisatung Mountain Myanmar 78 A3
Aisch r. Germany 48 I6
Aisén admin. reg. Chile 205 B7
Aishalton Guyana 199 G4
Ai Shan hill China 85 I4
Aishihik Canada 166 B2
Aishihik Lake Canada 166 B2
Aisimi Greece see Aisymi
Aisne r. France 51 I3
Aïssa, Djebel mt. Alg. 123 E2
Aisymi Greece 58 G7
also spelt Aisimi
Aitamännikkö Fin. 44 N2
Aitana mt. Spain 55 K6
Aitape P.N.G. 73 J7
also spelt Eitape
Aït Benhaddou tourist site Morocco 122 D3
UNESCO World Heritage Site
Aitkin U.S.A. 174 A2
Aitoliko Greece 59 C10
Aitova Rus. Fed. 41 J5
Aiud Romania 58 E2
also known as Nagyenyed
Aiviekste r. Latvia 42 G5
Aix France see Aix-en-Provence
Aix r. France 51 K7
Aix-en-Othe France 51 J4
Aix-en-Provence France 51 L9
historically known as Aquae Sextiae; short form Aix
Aixe-sur-Vienne France 50 H7
Aix-la-Chapelle Germany see Aachen
Aix-les-Bains France 51 L7
historically known as Aquae Gratianae
Āīy Ādī Eth. 128 C1
Aiyiáli Greece see Aigiali
Aíyina i. Greece see Aigina
Aiyínion Greece see Aiginio
Aíyion Greece see Aigio
Aizawl India 97 G5
formerly spelt Aijal
Aizenay France 50 E6
Aizkraukle Latvia 42 G5
formerly known as Stučka or Stuchka or imeni Petra Stuchki
Aizpute Latvia 42 C5
Aizu-wakamatsu Japan 90 F6
Ajā Egypt 108 C7
Ajā, Jibāl mts Saudi Arabia 104 C2
Ajaccio Corsica France 52 D3
Ajaccio, Golfe d' b. Corsica France 56 A7
Ajaigarh India 96 D4
Ajajú r. Col. 198 C4
Ajalpán Mex. 185 F5
Ajanta India 94 B1
UNESCO World Heritage Site
Ajanta Range hills India see Sahyadriparvat Range
Ajasse Nigeria 125 G4
Ajax Canada 173 N7
Ajax, Mount N.Z. 153 G10
Ajayameru India see Ajmer
Ajban U.A.E. 105 F2
Aj Bogd Uul mts Mongolia 84 B2
Ajdābiyā Libya 120 D2
formerly spelt Agedabia
Ajdovščina Slovenia 56 F3
a-Jiddét des. Oman see Ḥarāsīs, Jiddat al
Ajigasawa Japan 90 G4
'Ajīj, Wādī al watercourse Iraq 109 M2
Ajimganj India 97 F4
Ajka Hungary 49 O8
'Ajlūn Jordan 108 G5
'Ajmah, Jabal al mts Egypt 104 A1
'Ajmah, Jabal al plat. Egypt 108 E8
Ajman U.A.E. 105 F2
Ajmer India 96 B4
formerly known as Ajayameru or Ajmer-Merwara
Ajmer-Merwara India see Ajmer
Ajo U.S.A. 183 L9
Ajo, Mount U.S.A. 183 L9
Ajra India 94 B2
Ajuy Phil. 74 B4
Ajyyap Turkm. 102 C5
Akāashat Iraq 107 D4
Akabira Japan 90 H3
Akabli Alg. 123 F4
Akaboun well Mali 125 F2
Akademii, Zaliv b. Rus. Fed. 82 E1
English form Academy Bay
Akademik Nauk, Khrebet mt. Tajik. see Akademiyai Fanho, Qatorkŭhi
Akademiyai Fanho, Qatorkŭhi mt. Tajik. 101 G2
also known as Akademii Nauk, Khrebet
Akagera National Park Rwanda 126 F5
also known as Kagera, Parc National de la or L'Akagera, Parc National de
Akagi Japan 91 C7
Aka shi-dake mt. Japan 91 F7
Āk'ak'i Beseka Eth. 128 C2
Akalkot India 94 C2
Akama, Akra c. Cyprus see Arnauti, Cape
Akamagaseki Japan see Shimonoseki
Akamkpa Nigeria 125 H5
Akan Japan 90 I3
Akan-ko l. Japan 90 H3
Akan National Park Japan 90 I3
Akarkar well Niger 125 G3
Akarnanika mts Greece 59 B10
Akaroa N.Z. 153 G11
Akaroa Harbour N.Z. 153 G11
Akas reg. India 97 G4
'Akāsh, Wādī watercourse Iraq 109 L3
Akasha Sudan 121 F4
'Akāshāt Iraq 109 K4
Akashi Japan 91 D7
Äkäsjokisuu Fin. 44 M2
Akbakay Kazakh. 103 H3
Akbalyk Kazakh. 103 I3
also spelt Aqbalyq
Akbarābād Iran 100 C4
Akbarpur Uttar Pradesh India 96 D4
Akbarpur Uttar Pradesh India 97 D4
Akbasty Kazakh. 102 E3
Akbaytal Tajik. see Rabotoqbaytal
Akbaytal Pass Tajik. 101 H2
Akbeit Kazakh. 103 G2
also spelt Aqbeyit
Akbou Alg. 55 P8
Akbulak Rus. Fed. 102 C2
Akçadağ Turkey 107 D3
Akçakale Turkey 107 D3
Akcakertikbeli Geçidi pass Turkey 59 J9
Akçakoca Turkey 106 B2
Akçali Dağ mt. Turkey 106 C3
Akçalı Dağları mts Turkey 108 D1
Akçaova Turkey 59 I11
Akçay r. Turkey 59 J11
Akchâr reg. Mauritania 124 B2
Akchatau Kazakh. 103 H3
Akchi Kazakh. see Akshiy
Akdağ mt. Turkey 59 J9
Akdağlar mts Turkey 106 B3
Akdağmadeni Turkey 106 C3
Akdepe Turkm. 102 D4
formerly known as Leninsk
Akdere Turkey 108 E1
Ak Dovurak Rus. Fed. 84 A1
Akelamo Indon. 75 D2
Akelo Sudan 128 B3
Åkersberga Sweden 45 L4
Akershus county Norway 45 J3
formerly spelt Aggershus
Åkerstrømmen Norway 45 J3
Akespe Kazakh. 103 E3
Aketi Dem. Rep. Congo 126 D4
Akgyr Erezi hills Turkm. 102 C4
also known as Akkyr, Gory
Akhalgori Georgia 107 F2
formerly known as Leningori
Akhalk'alak'i Georgia 107 E2
Akhal Oblast admin. div. Turkm. see Akhal'skaya Oblast'
Akhal'skaya Oblast' admin. div. Turkm. 102 D5
English form Akhal Oblast; formerly known as Ashkhabadskaya Oblast'
Akhalts'ikhe Georgia 107 E2
Akhḍar, Al Jabal al mts Libya 120 D2
Akhḍar, Jabal mts Oman 105 G3
Akhḍar, Wādī al watercourse Saudi Arabia 109 H9
Akheloy Bulg. 58 I6
Akhisar Turkey 106 A3
historically known as Thyatira
Akhmīm Egypt 121 F3
also spelt Ekhmīm; historically known as Chemmis or Panoplis
Akhnoor Jammu and Kashmir 96 B2
Akhsu Azer. see Ağsu
Akhta Armenia see Hrazdan
Akhtarīn Syria 109 I1
Akhtubinsk Rus. Fed. 102 A2
Akhty Rus. Fed. 102 A4
Akhtyrka Ukr. see Okhtyrka
Aki Japan 91 C8
Akiéni Gabon 126 B5
Akimiski Island Canada 168 D2
Akıncılar İzmir Turkey see Selçuk
Akıncılar Sivas Turkey 107 D2
Akishma r. Rus. Fed. 82 D1
Akita Japan 90 G5
Akita pref. Japan 90 G5
Akitio N.Z. 152 K8
Akjoujt Mauritania 124 B2
Akka Morocco 122 C3
Akkajaure l. Sweden 44 L2
Akkem Rus. Fed. 88 D1
Akkerman Ukr. see Bilhorod-Dnistrovs'kyy
Akkermanovka Rus. Fed. 102 D2
Akkeshi Japan 90 I3
Akkeshi-wan b. Japan 90 I3
Akkistau Kazakh. 102 B3
also known as Aqqystaū
'Akko Israel 108 G5
historically known as Accho or Acre or St-Jean-d'Acre or Ptolemais
UNESCO World Heritage Site
Akkol' Akmolinskaya Oblast' Kazakh. 103 G1
also spelt Aqköl; formerly known as Alekseyevka
Akkol' Almatinskaya Oblast' Kazakh. 103 H3
Akkol' Atyrauskaya Oblast' Kazakh. 41 I7
also spelt Akkul' or Aqköl
Akkol' Zhambylskaya Oblast' Kazakh. 103 G4
Akköy Aydın Turkey 106 A3
Akköy Denizli Turkey 59 K11
Akku Kazakh. 103 I2
formerly known as Lebyazh'ye
Akkul' Kazakh. see Akkol'
Akkum Kazakh. 103 F3
Akkuş Turkey 107 D2
Akkyr, Gory hills Turkm. see Akgyr Erezi
Aklavik Canada 164 F3
Aklera India 96 C4
Aklub reg. Saudi Arabia 104 D4
Ak-Mechet Kazakh. see Kyzylorda
Akmena r. Lith. 42 D6
Akmenė Lith. 42 D5
Akmeņrags pt Latvia 42 C5
Akmeqit China 89 B4
Akmeshit Kazakh. 103 G2
Akmola Kazakh. see Astana
Akmola Oblast admin. div. Kazakh. see Akmolinskaya Oblast'
Akmolinsk Kazakh. see Astana
Akmolinskaya Oblast' admin. div. Kazakh. 103 G2
English form Aqmola Oblast; also known as Aqmola Oblysy; formerly known as Akmola Oblast or Tselinogradskaya Oblast'
Akniste Latvia 42 G5
Aknoul Morocco 122 E2
Akō Japan 91 D7
Akobo Sudan 128 B3
Akobo Wenz r. Eth./Sudan 128 B3
Akodia India 96 C5
Akola Maharashtra India 94 B2
Akola Maharashtra India 94 C1
Akom II Cameroon 125 H6
Akonolinga Cameroon 125 I6
Akop Sudan 126 F2
Akordat Eritrea 121 H6
Akören Turkey 106 C3
Akot India 96 C5
Akouménaye Fr. Guiana 199 H4
Akoupé Côte d'Ivoire 124 E5
Ak-Oyuk, Gora mt. Rus. Fed. 84 A1
Akpatok Island Canada 165 M3
Akqi China 88 B3
Akraifnio Greece 59 E10
Akranes Iceland 44 [inset] B2
Akrathos, Akra pt Greece 59 F8
Akre Iraq 109 O1
Akrérèb Niger 125 H2
Akritas, Akra pt Greece 59 C12
Akron CO U.S.A. 178 B3
Akron IN U.S.A. 172 G9
Akron OH U.S.A. 176 D4
Akrotiri Bay Cyprus 108 E3
also known as Akrotírion Bay or Akrotiriou, Kolpos
Akrotirion Bay Cyprus see Akrotiri Bay
Akrotiriou, Kolpos b. Cyprus see Akrotiri Bay
Akrotiri Sovereign Base Area military base Cyprus 108 D3

▶Aksai Chin terr. Asia 89 B5
Disputed territory (China/India). Also known as Aqsayqin Hit.

Aksakal Turkey 59 J8
Aksakovo Bulg. 58 I5
Aksakovo Rus. Fed. 40 J5
Aksaray Turkey 106 C3
Aksarka Rus. Fed. 38 G3
Aksay China 84 B4
also known as Hongliuwan
Aksay Kazakh. 102 C2
also spelt Aqsay; formerly known as Kazakhstan
Ak-Say r. Kyrg. 103 H4
Aksay Rus. Fed. 41 F7
Akşehir Turkey 106 B3
historically known as Philomelium
Akşehir Gölü l. Turkey 106 B3
Akseki Turkey 106 B3
Aksenovo Rus. Fed. 41 J5
Aks-e Rostam r. Iran 100 C4
Aksha Rus. Fed. 85 G1
Akshatau Kazakh. 102 C2
Akshiganak Kazakh. 103 E2
Akshiy Kazakh. 103 I4
also spelt Aqshī; formerly spelt Akchi
Akshukur Kazakh. 102 B4
also spelt Aqshuqyr
Aksu Xinjiang China 88 C3
Aksu Xinjiang China 88 C3
Aksu Almatinskaya Oblast' Kazakh. 103 I3
also spelt Aqsū
Aksu Pavlodarskaya Oblast' Kazakh. 103 I1
also spelt Aqsū; formerly known as Ermak or Yermak
Aksu Severnyy Kazakhstan Kazakh. 103 G1
also spelt Aqsū
Aksu Yuzhnyy Kazakhstan Kazakh. 103 G4
Aksu Zapadnyy Kazakhstan Kazakh. 102 C2
Aksu r. Kazakh. 103 I3
Aksu r. Tajik. see Oqsu
Aksu Turkey 108 B1
Aksu r. Turkey 107 B3
Aksuat Kustanayskaya Oblast' Kazakh. 103 F2
Aksuat Vostochnyy Kazakhstan Kazakh. 88 C2
also spelt Aqsūat
Aksuat, Ozero salt l. Kazakh. see Bol'shoy Aksuat, Ozero
Aksu-Ayuly Kazakh. 103 H2
also spelt Aqsū-Ayuly
Aksu He r. China 88 C3
Āksum Eth. 128 C1
historically known as Axum
UNESCO World Heritage Site
Aksüme China 88 C2
Aksuyek Kazakh. 103 H3
Aksu-Zhabaglinskiy Zapovednik nature res. Kazakh. 103 G4
Aktag mt. China 89 D4
Ak-Tal Rus. Fed. 88 F1
Aktash Uzbek. see Oqtosh
Aktau Karagandinskaya Oblast' Kazakh. 103 G3
Aktau Karagandinskaya Oblast' Kazakh. 103 H2
Aktau Mangistauskaya Oblast' Kazakh. 102 B4
also spelt Aqtaū; formerly known as Shevchenko
Aktepe Turkey 109 H1
Akto China 88 B4
Aktobe Kazakh. 102 D2
also known as Aqtöbe
Aktogay Karagandinskaya Oblast' Kazakh. 103 H2
also spelt Aqtoghay
Aktogay Pavlodarskaya Oblast' Kazakh. 103 H1
also spelt Aqtoghay; formerly known as Krasnokutsk or Krasnokutskoye
Aktogay Vostochnyy Kazakhstan Kazakh. 103 I3
Aktsyabrskaya Belarus 43 L6
also spelt Oktyabr'skaya
Aktsyabrski Belarus 43 J9
also spelt Oktyabr'skiy; formerly known as Karpilovka
Aktsyabrski Belarus 43 K7
also spelt Oktyabr'skiy
Aktumsyk Kazakh. 102 D3
Aktumsyk, Mys pt Uzbek. 102 D3
Ak-Tüz Kyrg. 103 H4
also spelt Aktyuz
Aktyubinskaya Oblast' admin. div. Kazakh. 102 D2
English form Aktyubinsk Oblast; also known as Aqtöbe Oblysy
Aktyubinsk Oblast admin. div. Kazakh. see Aktyubinskaya Oblast'
Aktyuz Kyrg. see Ak-Tüz
Akujärvi Fin. 44 N1
Akula Dem. Rep. Congo 126 D4
Akulichi Rus. Fed. 43 O8
Akulivik Canada 165 L3
Akumadan Ghana 125 E5
Akune Japan 91 B8
Akur mt. Uganda 128 B4
Akure Nigeria 125 G5
Akureyri Iceland 44 [inset] C2
Akwa Ibom state Nigeria 125 G5
Akwanga Nigeria 125 H4
Akyab Myanmar see Sittwe
Ak"yar Rus. Fed. 102 D2
Akyatan Gölü salt l. Turkey 108 G1
Akzhal Karagandinskaya Oblast' Kazakh. 103 H3
Akzhal Vostochnyy Kazakhstan Kazakh. 103 J2
also spelt Aqzhal
Akzhar Aktyubinskaya Oblast' Kazakh. 102 D2
formerly known as Novorossiyskiy
Akzhar Kzyl-Ordinskaya Oblast' Kazakh. 103 F3
Akzhar Vostochnyy Kazakhstan Kazakh. 88 C2
also spelt Aqzhar
Akzhar Zhambylskaya Oblast' Kazakh. 103 G4
Akzhaykyn, Ozero salt l. Kazakh. 103 F3
also known as Aqzhayqyn Köli
Ål Norway 45 J3
Ala r. Belarus 43 K9
Ala Italy 56 D3
'Alā, Jabal al hills Syria 109 H2
Alabama r. U.S.A. 175 C6
Alabama state U.S.A. 175 C5
Alabaster AL U.S.A. 175 C5
Alabaster MI U.S.A. 173 J6
Al 'Abṭīyah well Iraq 107 F5
Ala-Buka Kyrg. 103 G4
Al Abyaḍ Libya 120 B3
Al Abyār Libya 120 D1
Alaca Turkey 106 C2
also known as Huseyinabat
Alacahan Turkey 107 D3
Alaçam Turkey 106 C2
Alaçam Dağları mts Turkey 59 J9
Alacant Spain see Alicante
Alaçatı Turkey 59 H10
Alacrán, Arrecife reef Mex. 185 H4
Al Adabīyah Egypt 108 D8
Aladag mt. Bulg. 58 G7
Aladağ Turkey 106 C3
also known as Bademli
Ala Dag mt. Turkey 107 E3
Ala Dağlar mts Turkey 107 E3
Ala Dağları mts Turkey 106 C3
Al 'Adam Libya 120 D2
Alaejos Spain 54 F3
Al Aflāj reg. Saudi Arabia 105 D3
Alagadiço Brazil 199 F4
Alagapuram India 94 C4
Alag Hayrhan Uul mt. Mongolia 84 B2
Alagir Rus. Fed. 41 H8
Alagoas state Brazil 202 E4
Alagoinhas Brazil 202 E5
Alagón Spain 55 J3
Alagón r. Spain 54 E5
Alah r. Phil. 74 C5
Alahanpanjang Indon. 76 C3
Alahärmä Fin. 44 M3
Al Aḥmadī Kuwait 107 G5
Alaid, Ostrov i. Rus. Fed. see Atlasova, Ostrov
Alaior Spain 55 P5
Alai Range mts Asia 99 I2
also known as Alay Kyrka Toosu or Alayskiy Khrebet
Ālaivān Iran 100 C3
Al Ajā'is hills Saudi Arabia 109 K8
Al 'Ajā'iz well Oman 105 G4
Al Ajām Saudi Arabia 105 E2
Alajärvi Fin. 44 M3
Alajaure naturreservat nature res. Sweden 44 M1
Al Ajfar Saudi Arabia 104 C2
Alajõgi r. Estonia 42 I2
Al 'Ajrūd Egypt 108 D7
Al 'Ajrūd well Egypt 108 F7
Alajuela Costa Rica 186 B5
Alakanuk U.S.A. 164 C3
Al Akhḍar Saudi Arabia 104 B2
Alakol', Ozero salt l. Kazakh. 88 C2
also known as Ala Kul
Ala Kul salt l. Kazakh. see Alakol', Ozero
Alakurtti Rus. Fed. 44 O2
Al 'Alamayn Egypt 121 F2
also spelt El 'Alamein
Alalaú r. Brazil 199 F5
Al 'Alayyah Saudi Arabia 104 C4
Alama Somalia 128 D3
Al 'Amādīyah Iraq 107 E3
Alamagan i. N. Mariana Is 73 K3
also spelt Alamaguan
Alamaguan i. N. Mariana Is see Alamagan
Al'Amār Saudi Arabia 104 D2
Al 'Amārah Iraq 107 F5
also known as Amārah
'Alam ar Rūm, Ra's pt Egypt 121 E2
'Alāmarvdasht watercourse Iran 100 C4
Ālamat'ā Eth. 104 B5
Al Amghar waterhole Iraq 107 F5
Al Amghar waterhole Saudi Arabia 109 N7
Alamicamba Nicaragua 186 B4
Alaminos Phil. 74 A2
Al 'Āmirīyah Egypt 108 A6
Alamito Creek r. U.S.A. 181 F7
Alamitos, Sierra de los mt. Mex. 185 E3
Al Amlah Saudi Arabia 104 C3
Alamo U.S.A. 174 B5
Alamo Dam U.S.A. 183 K7
Alamogordo U.S.A. 181 F6
Alamo Heights U.S.A. 179 C6
Alamos Sonora Mex. 184 C2
Alamos Sonora Mex. 184 C3
Alamos r. Mex. 185 E3
Alamos, Sierra mts Mex. 184 C3
Alamosa U.S.A. 181 F5
Alamosa Creek r. U.S.A. 181 F6
Alamos de Peña Mex. 184 D2
Alampur India 94 C3
Al 'Anad Yemen 104 D5
Alanäs Sweden 44 K2
Al Anbār governorate Iraq 107 E4
Åland is Fin. see Åland Islands
Aland r. Germany 48 I2
Aland India 94 C2
Aland r. Iran 107 F3
Åland Islands Fin. 45 L3
also known as Ahvenanmaa; short form Åland
Ålands Hav sea chan. Fin./Sweden 45 L4
Alandur India 94 D3
Alangalang, Tanjung pt Indon. 77 G3
Alang Besar i. Indon. 76 C2
Alange, Embalse de resr Spain 54 E6
Alanggantang i. Indon. 76 D3
Alanson U.S.A. 173 I5
Alanya Turkey 106 C3
historically known as Coracesium
'Ālā' od Dīn Iran 100 C4
Alapaha r. U.S.A. 175 D6
Alapakam India 94 C4
Alaplı Turkey 41 D8
Alappuzha India see Alleppey
Alapur India 96 C4
Al 'Aqabah Jordan 108 G8
also spelt 'Aqaba; historically known as Aela or Aelana
Al 'Aqīq Saudi Arabia 104 C3
Al 'Āqūlah well Saudi Arabia 105 E3
Al 'Arabīyah i. Saudi Arabia 107 G6
Al 'Arabīyah as Sa'ūdīyah country Asia see Saudi Arabia
Alarcón, Embalse de resr Spain 55 I5
Al 'Āriḍah Saudi Arabia 104 C4
Al Arīn Saudi Arabia 104 C4
Al 'Arīsh Egypt 121 G2
Al Arṭāwīyah Saudi Arabia 105 D2
Alas Indon. 77 G5
Alas, Selat sea chan. Indon. 77 G5
Alaşehir Turkey 106 B3
historically known as Philadelphia
Alash r. Rus. Fed. 88 E1
Alash, Plato plat. Rus. Fed. 88 E1
Alashiya country Asia see Cyprus
Al Ashmūnayn Egypt 121 F3
historically known as Hermopolis Magna
Al 'Āshūrīyah well Iraq 107 E5
Alaska state U.S.A. 164 E3
Alaska, Gulf of U.S.A. 164 E4
Alaska Highway Canada/U.S.A. 166 A2
Alaska Peninsula U.S.A. 164 C4
Alaska Range mts U.S.A. 164 E3
Alas Purwo National Park Indon. 77 F5
Al 'Assāfīyah Saudi Arabia 104 B1
Alassio Italy 56 A4
Älät Azer. 107 G3
Alat Uzbek. see Olot
Alataw Shankou pass China/Kazakh. see Dzungarian Gate
Al 'Athāmīn hill Iraq 109 O7
Alatri Italy 56 F7
historically known as Aletrium
Al Atwā' well Saudi Arabia 104 C1
Alatyr' Rus. Fed. 40 H5
Alatyr' r. Rus. Fed. 40 H5
Alauksts l. Latvia 42 G4
Alausí Ecuador 198 B5
Alaverdi Armenia 107 F2
UNESCO World Heritage Site
Alavieska Fin. 44 N2
Ala-Vuokki Fin. 44 O2
Alavus Fin. 44 M3
Alawa Aboriginal Land res. Australia 148 B2
Al Awābī Oman 105 G3
Al 'Awdah Saudi Arabia 105 D2
Alawoona Australia 146 D3
Al Awshazīyah Saudi Arabia 104 C2
Alaykel' Kyrg. see Kök-Art
Alaykuu Kyrg. see Kök-Art
Alay Kyrka Toosu mts Asia see Alai Range
Al 'Ayn Oman 105 G3
Al 'Ayn Saudi Arabia 104 B2
Al 'Ayn U.A.E. 105 F2
Alayskiy Khrebet mts Asia see Alai Range
Al 'Ayyāṭ Egypt 108 C8
Al A'ẓamīyah Iraq 109 P4
Alazani r. Azer./Georgia 107 F2
Alazeya r. Rus. Fed. 39 P2
Al 'Azīzīyah Iraq 107 F4

▶Al 'Azīzīyah Libya 120 B1
Highest recorded shade temperature in the world.
▶▶12–13 World Climate and Weather

Alba Italy 51 O8
Alba U.S.A. 173 I6
Alba Adriatica Italy 56 F6
Al Ba'ā'ith Saudi Arabia 104 C2
Al Ba'āj Iraq 109 M1
Al Bāb Syria 109 I1
Albacete Spain 55 J5
Al Badā'i' Saudi Arabia 104 B2
Alba de Tormes Spain 54 F4
Al Badī' Saudi Arabia 105 D3
Al Bādiyah al Janūbīyah hill Iraq 107 F5
Ålbæk Denmark 45 J4
Ålbæk Bugt b. Denmark 45 J4
Al'bagan, Gora mt. Rus. Fed. 88 D1
Al Bāḥah prov. Saudi Arabia 104 C3
Al Baḥr al Aḥmar governorate Egypt 108 C9
Al Bahrayn country Asia see Bahrain
Alba Iulia Romania 58 E2
also known as Gyulafehérvár; formerly known as Karlsburg; historically known as Apulum
Al Bajā' well U.A.E. 105 E2
Al Ba'jah Saudi Arabia 104 C2
Al Bakhrā well Saudi Arabia 105 D2
Al Bakkī Libya 120 B3
Albalate de Arzobispo Spain 55 K3
Albanel, Lac l. Canada 169 F3
Albanel-Mistassini et Waconichi, Réserve Faunique des lacs nature res. Canada 169 F3
▶Albania country Europe 58 A7
known as Shqipërisë, Republika e in Albanian
▶▶32–33 Europe Countries
Albano Brazil 199 G5
Albany Australia 151 B7
Albany r. Canada 168 D2
Albany Jamaica 186 D3
Albany GA U.S.A. 175 C6
Albany MO U.S.A. 178 D3

▶Albany NY U.S.A. 177 L3
State capital of New York. Historically known as Fort Orange.

Albany OH U.S.A. 176 C6
Albany OR U.S.A. 180 B3
Albany TX U.S.A. 179 C5
Albany Downs Australia 147 F1
Albardão do João Maria coastal area Brazil 204 G4
Al Bardawīl depr. Saudi Arabia 109 K6
Al Bardī Libya 120 E2
Al Bārīdah hills Saudi Arabia 109 K8
Al Barīt waterhole Iraq 109 N6
Al Barrah Saudi Arabia 105 D2
Al Baṣrah Iraq see Basra
Al Baṣrah governorate Iraq 107 F5
Al Baṭḥa' marsh Iraq 107 F5
Al Bāṭinah admin. reg. Oman 105 G3
Al Bāṭinah reg. Oman 105 G2
Al Bāṭinah i. Saudi Arabia 105 E2
Albatross Bay Australia 149 D2
Albatross Island Australia 147 E5
Albatross Point N.Z. 152 I6

Al Bawītī Egypt **121** F2
Al Bayḍā' Libya **120** D1
also spelt Beida
Al Bayḍā' Yemen **105** D5
Al Bayḍā' governorate Yemen **105** D5
Albay Gulf Phil. **74** B3
Albemarle U.S.A. **174** D5
Albemarle Sound sea chan. U.S.A. **174** E5
Albenga Italy **56** A4
Alberche r. Spain **54** G5
Alberdi Para. **201** F6
Alberga watercourse Australia **146** B1
Albergaria-a-Velha Port. **54** C4
Albergian, Monte mt. Italy **51** M7
Alberobello Italy **57** J8
UNESCO World Heritage Site
Albert Australia **147** E3
Albert r. Australia **148** C3
Albert France **51** I3
Albert, Lake Australia **146** C3
►**Albert, Lake** Dem. Rep. Congo/Uganda **128** A4
formerly known as Mobutu, Lake or Mobutu Sese Seko, Lake
►►**110–111 Africa** Landscapes
Albert, Parc National nat. park Dem. Rep. Congo see **Virunga, Parc National des**
Alberta prov. Canada **167** H4
Albert Falls Nature Reserve S. Africa **133** O6
Albertinia S. Africa **132** F11
Albertirsa Hungary **49** Q8
Albert Kanaal canal Belgium **51** L2
Albert Lea U.S.A. **174** A3
Albert Nile r. Sudan/Uganda **126** G4
Alberto de Agostini, Parque Nacional nat. park Chile **205** C9
Alberton Canada **169** H4
Alberto Oviedo Mota Mex. **183** I9
Albertshoek S. Africa **133** J4
Albert Town Bahamas **187** E2
Albertville Dem. Rep. Congo see **Kalemie**
Albertville France **51** M7
Albertville U.S.A. **174** C5
Albeşti Romania **58** I2
Albi France **51** I9
Albia U.S.A. **174** A3
Al Bi'ār Saudi Arabia **104** B3
Al Bīḍah des. Saudi Arabia **105** E2
Albignasego Italy **56** D3
Albina Suriname **199** H3
Albino Italy **56** B3
Albion CA U.S.A. **182** A2
Albion IN U.S.A. **174** C3
Albion MI U.S.A. **173** I8
Albion NE U.S.A. **178** C3
Albion NY U.S.A. **176** G2
Albion PA U.S.A. **176** E4
Al Bi'r Saudi Arabia **104** B1
also known as Bi'r Ibn Hirmās
Al Birk Saudi Arabia **104** C4
Al Birkah Saudi Arabia **104** C3
Al Biyāḍh reg. Saudi Arabia **105** D3
Alborán, Isla de i. Spain **55** H9
Ålborg Denmark see **Aalborg**
Alborz, Reshteh-ye mts Iran see **Elburz Mountains**
Albota Romania **58** F4
Albox Spain **55** I7
Albro Australia **149** E4
Albstadt Germany **48** G7
Al Budayyi' Bahrain **105** E2
Albufeira Port. **54** C7
Ālbū Ghars, Sabkhat salt l. Iraq **109** M3
Al Buḥayrah governorate Egypt **108** B7
Al Bukayrīyah Saudi Arabia **104** C2
Albula Alpen mts Switz. **51** P6
Albuñol Spain **55** H8
Albuquerque U.S.A. **181** F6
Albuquerque, Cayos de is Caribbean Sea **186** C4
Al Buraymī Oman **105** F2
Alburg U.S.A. **177** L1
Al Burj Egypt **108** C6
Alburno, Monte mt. Italy **57** H8
Alburquerque Spain **54** E5
Al Burumbul Egypt **108** C8
Albury Australia **147** E4
Albury N.Z. **153** E12
Al Buşayrah Syria **109** L2
also spelt Buseire
Al Busayṭā' plain Saudi Arabia **107** D5
Al Buşayyah Iraq **107** F5
Al Bushūk well Saudi Arabia **104** D1
Al Buṭayn plain Saudi Arabia **105** D2
Al Buwī well Oman **105** G4
Alca Peru **200** B3
Alcácer do Sal Port. **54** C6
Alcáçovas r. Port. **54** C6
Alcalá de Guadaira Spain **54** F7
Alcalá de Henares Spain **55** H4
Alcalá de los Gazules Spain **54** F8
Alcalà de Xivert Spain **55** L4
Alcalá la Real Spain **54** H7
Alcalde, Punta pt Chile **204** C3
Alcamo Sicily Italy **57** E11
Alcanadre r. Spain **55** L3
Alcanar Spain **55** L4
Alcañiz Spain **55** K3
Alcântara Brazil **202** C2
Alcántara Spain **54** E5
Alcántara, Embalse de resr Spain **54** E5
Alcántara II, Embalse de resr Spain **54** E5
Alcantara Lake Canada **167** I2
Alcantarilla Spain **55** J7
Alcaraz Spain **55** I6
Alcaraz, Sierra de mts Spain **55** I6
Alcaria Ruiva hill Port. **54** D7
Alcarrache r. Port./Spain **54** D6
Alcatrazes, Ilha de i. Brazil **207** H11
Alcaudete Spain **54** G7
Alcázar de San Juan Spain **55** H5
Alcazarquivir Morocco see **Ksar el Kebir**
Alchevs'k Ukr. **41** F6
formerly known as Kommunarsk or Voroshilovsk
Alcira Arg. **204** D4
Alcira Spain see **Alzira**
Alcobaça Brazil **203** E6
Alcobaça Port. **54** B5
UNESCO World Heritage Site
Alconchel Spain **54** D6
Alcorneo r. Port./Spain **54** E5
Alcorta Arg. **204** E4
Alcoy-Alcoi Spain **55** K6
Alcubierre, Sierra de mts Spain **55** K3
Alcúdia Spain **55** O5
Aldabra Atoll Seychelles **129** E7
UNESCO World Heritage Site
Aldabra Islands Seychelles **129** E7
Al Daljamūn Egypt **108** B7
Aldama Chihuahua Mex. **184** D2
Aldama Tamaulipas Mex. **185** F4
Aldan Rus. Fed. **39** M4
Aldan r. Rus. Fed. **39** M3
Aldeburgh U.K. **47** N11
Aldeia Velha Brazil **202** B4
Aldeia Viçosa Angola **127** B7
Alder Creek U.S.A. **177** J2
Alderney i. Channel Is **50** D3
also known as Aurigny
Alder Peak U.S.A. **182** C6
Aldershot U.K. **47** L12
Alderson U.S.A. **176** E8
Al Dhafrah reg. U.A.E. **105** F3
Aldie Eth. **128** D3
Aledo U.S.A. **174** B3
Aleg Mauritania **124** B2
Alegre Brazil **203** D7
Alegrete Brazil **203** A9
Alegros Mountain U.S.A. **181** E6
Alejandro de Humboldt, Parque Nacional nat. park Mex. **187** E2
UNESCO World Heritage Site
Alejandro Korn Arg. **204** F4
Alekhovshchina Rus. Fed. **43** O1
Aleksandra, Mys hd Rus. Fed. **82** E1
Aleksandra Bekovicha-Cherkasskoga, Zaliv b. Kazakh. **102** B4
Aleksandriya Ukr. see **Oleksandriya**
Aleksandropol Armenia see **Gyumri**
Aleksandrov Rus. Fed. **43** T5
Aleksandrovac Srbija Serb. and Mont. **58** C5
Aleksandrov Gay Rus. Fed. **102** B2
Aleksandrovka Rus. Fed. **41** J5
Aleksandrovo Bulg. **58** G6
Aleksandrovo Bulg. **58** F5
Aleksandrovsk Rus. Fed. **40** K4
formerly known as Aleksandrovskiy
Aleksandrovsk Ukr. see **Zaporizhzhya**
Aleksandrovskaya Rus. Fed. **43** R2
Aleksandrovskiy Rus. Fed. see **Aleksandrovsk**
Aleksandrovskoye Stavropol'skiy Kray Rus. Fed. **41** G7
Aleksandrovskoye Stavropol'skiy Kray Rus. Fed. **41** H7
Aleksandrovskoye Tomskaya Oblast' Rus. Fed. **38** H3
Aleksandrovsk-Sakhalinskiy Rus. Fed. **82** F2
Aleksandrów Kujawski Poland **49** P3
Aleksandrów Łódzki Poland **49** Q4
Aleksandry, Zemlya i. Rus. Fed. **38** E1
English form Alexandra Land
Alekseyevka Akmolinskaya Oblast' Kazakh. see **Akkol'**
Alekseyevka Pavlodarskaya Oblast' Kazakh. **103** H2
Alekseyevka Vostochnyy Kazakhstan Kazakh. see **Terekty**
Alekseyevka Belgorodskaya Oblast' Rus. Fed. **41** F6
Alekseyevka Belgorodskaya Oblast' Rus. Fed. **41** F6
Alekseyevka Bryanskaya Oblast' Rus. Fed. **43** N8
Alekseyevskaya Rus. Fed. **41** G6
Aleksin Rus. Fed. **43** S7
Aleksinac Srbija Serb. and Mont. **58** C5
Aleksino-Shatur Rus. Fed. **43** U6
Alèmbé Gabon **126** A5
'Alem Ketema Eth. **128** C2
'Alem Maya Eth. **128** D2
Além Paraíba Brazil **203** D7
Ålen Norway **44** J3
Alençon France **50** G4
Alenquer Brazil **199** H5
Alentejo reg. Port. **54** C6
'Alenuihāhā Channel U.S.A. **181** [inset] Z1
Alep Syria see **Aleppo**
Alépé Côte d'Ivoire **124** E5
Aleppo Syria **109** I1
also known as Ḥalab or Yamkhad; also spelt Alep; historically known as Beroea
UNESCO World Heritage Site
Aler r. India **94** C2
Alert Canada **165** M1
Alerta Peru **200** C2
Alert Bay Canada **166** E5
Alès France **51** K8
Aleşd Romania **58** D1
Aleshki Ukr. see **Tsyurupyns'k**
Aleshnya Rus. Fed. **43** O8
Aleşkirt Turkey see **Eleşkirt**
Alessandria Italy **56** A4
UNESCO World Heritage Site
Alessio Albania see **Lezhë**
Ålesund Norway **44** I3
also spelt Aalesund
Aletrium Italy see **Alatri**
Aletschhorn mt. Switz. **51** N6
Aleutian Islands U.S.A. **220** H2
Aleutian Range mts U.S.A. **164** D4
Alevina, Mys c. Rus. Fed. **39** P4
Alevişik Turkey see **Samandağı**
Alexander, Cape Antarctica **222** T2
Alexander, Mount hill Australia **148** C2
Alexander Archipelago is U.S.A. **164** F4
Alexander Bay S. Africa **130** C6
Alexander City U.S.A. **175** C5
Alexander Island Antarctica **222** T2
Alexandra Australia **147** E4
Alexandra r. Australia **149** C3
Alexandra N.Z. **153** D13
Alexandra, Cape S. Georgia **205** [inset]
Alexandra Channel India **95** G3
Alexandra Falls Canada **167** G2
Alexandra Land i. Rus. Fed. see **Aleksandry, Zemlya**
Alexandreia Greece **58** D8
Alexandretta Turkey see **İskenderun**
Alexandria Afgh. see **Ghaznī**
Alexandria B.C. Canada **166** F4
Alexandria Ont. Canada **169** F4

►**Alexandria** Egypt **121** F2
5th most populous city in Africa. Also known as Al Iskandarīyah or El Iskandarîya.

Alexandria Romania **58** G5
Alexandria S. Africa **133** K10
Alexandria Turkm. see **Mary**
Alexandria U.K. **46** H8
Alexandria KY U.S.A. **176** A7
Alexandria LA U.S.A. **179** D6
Alexandria MN U.S.A. **178** D2
Alexandria SD U.S.A. **178** C3
Alexandria VA U.S.A. **177** H7
Alexandria Arachoton Afgh. see **Kandahār**
Alexandria Areion Afgh. see **Herāt**
Alexandria Bay U.S.A. **177** J1
Alexandria Prophthasia Afgh. see **Farāh**
Alexandrina, Lake Australia **146** C3
Alexandroupoli Greece **58** G8
Alexânia Brazil **206** E3
Alexis r. Canada **169** J2
Aley Lebanon **108** G4
also spelt Aaley
Aley r. Rus. Fed. **103** J1
Aleyak Iran **100** D2
Aleysk Rus. Fed. **103** J1
Al Fallūjah Iraq **109** O4
also known as Fallūjah
Alfambra r. Spain **55** J4
Al Fardah Yemen **105** E5
Alfaro Spain **55** J2
Alfarràs Spain **55** L3
Al Farūq reg. Saudi Arabia **105** E2
Al Farwānīyah Kuwait **107** F5
Al Fas Morocco see **Fès**
Al Fashn Egypt **106** B5
Alfatar Bulg. **58** I5
Al Fatḥah Iraq **107** E4
Al Fatk Yemen **105** F4
Al Fāw Iraq **107** G5
Al Fayyūm Egypt **121** F2
also spelt El Faiyûm
Al Fayyūm governorate Egypt **108** B8
Al Fāzih Yemen **104** C5
Alfeios r. Greece **59** C11
also spelt Alfíos
Alfeld (Leine) Germany **48** G4
Alfenas Brazil **203** C7
Alfíos r. Greece see **Alfeios**
Alföld plain Hungary **49** R9
Alford U.K. **46** J6
Alfred U.S.A. **177** O2
Alfred and Marie Range hills Australia **151** D5
Alfred M. Terrazas Mex. **185** F4
Alfredo Chaves Brazil **207** M7
Alfredton N.Z. **152** J8
Alfta Sweden **45** L3
Al Fujayrah U.A.E. see **Fujairah**
Al Fuqahā' Libya **120** C3
Al Furāt r. Iraq/Syria see **Euphrates**
Alga Kazakh. **102** D2
also spelt Algha
Algabas Kazakh. **102** C2
Algar Spain **54** F8
Ålgård Norway **45** I4
Algarinejo Spain **54** G7
Algarrobal Chile **204** C3
Algarrobo del Aguilla Arg. **204** D5
Algarve reg. Port. **54** C7
Algasovo Rus. Fed. **41** G5
Algeciras Spain **54** F8
Algemesí Spain **55** K5
Algena Eritrea **121** H5
Alger Alg. see **Algiers**
Alger U.S.A. **173** I6

►**Algeria** country Africa **123** E4
2nd largest country in Africa.
►►**114–115 Africa** Countries

Algha Kazakh. see **Alga**
Al Ghāfāt Oman **105** G3
Al Gharbīyah governorate Egypt **108** C7
Al Ghardaqah Egypt see **Al Ghurdaqah**
Al Gharīth Saudi Arabia **104** C3
Al Ghāṭ Saudi Arabia **105** D2
Al Ghawr plain Jordan/West Bank **108** G7
also spelt El Ghor
Al Ghayḍah Yemen **105** F4
Al Ghayl Saudi Arabia **105** D3
Alghero Sardinia Italy **57** A8
Al Ghubr reg. Oman **105** G4
Al Ghurdaqah Egypt **121** G3
also known as Al Ghardaqah
Al Ghuwayr well Qatar **105** E2
Al Ghwaybiyah Saudi Arabia **105** E2

►**Algiers** Alg. **123** F1
Capital of Algeria. Also known as Al Jaza'ir or Argel or El Djezair; also spelt Alger; historically known as Icosium.
UNESCO World Heritage Site

Alginet Spain **55** K5
Algoa Bay S. Africa **133** J10
Algodón r. Peru **198** D5
Algodor r. Spain **54** H5
Algoma U.S.A. **172** F6
Algona U.S.A. **178** D3
Algonac U.S.A. **173** K8
Algonquin Park Canada **168** E4
Algonquin Provincial Park Canada **173** O5
Algorta Spain **55** I1
Algōsh Iraq **109** O1
Älgsjö Sweden **44** L2
Algueirao Moz. see **Hacufera**
Algueirão-Mem Martins Port. **54** B6
Al Habakah well Saudi Arabia **107** E5
Al Ḥabbānīyah Iraq **107** E4
Al Ḥadaqah well Saudi Arabia **104** D1
Al Ḥadbah reg. Saudi Arabia **104** C3
Al Ḥadd Bahrain **105** E2
Al Ḥaddādī Egypt **108** B6
Al Haddār Saudi Arabia **105** D3
Al Hadhālīl plat. Saudi Arabia **107** E5
Al Ḥadīthah Iraq **107** E4
Al Ḥaḍr Iraq see **Hatra**
Al Ḥafár well Saudi Arabia **104** C1
Al Ḥaffah Syria **108** H2
Al Haggounia W. Sahara **122** B4
Al Ḥā'ir Saudi Arabia **105** D2
Al Hajar Oman **105** G3
Al Ḥajar al Gharbī mts Oman **105** G2
Al Ḥajar ash Sharqī mts Oman **105** G3
Al Ḥajr Yemen **105** D4
Al Ḥallānīyah i. Oman **105** G4
Alhama r. Spain **55** J2
Al Ḥamād plain Asia **98** B3
Alhama de Granada Spain **54** H7
Alhama de Murcia Spain **55** J7
Al Ḥamar Saudi Arabia **105** D3
Al Ḥāmi Yemen **105** E5
Alhamilla, Sierra hills Spain **55** I8
Al Ḥammām Egypt **121** F2
Al Hammām well Iraq **107** E5
Al Ḥamrā' Saudi Arabia **104** B3
Al Ḥāmūl Egypt **108** C6
Al Ḥanākīyah Saudi Arabia **104** C2
Al Ḥanīsh al Kabīr i. Yemen **104** C5
Al Haniyah esc. Iraq **107** F5
Al Ḥaqlānīyah Iraq **109** N3
Al Ḥaqū Saudi Arabia **104** C4
Al Hariq Saudi Arabia **105** D3
Al Ḥarrah Egypt **121** F2
Al Ḥarrah reg. Saudi Arabia **109** J7
Al Harūj al Aswad hills Libya **120** C3
Al Hasa reg. Saudi Arabia **105** E2
Al Ḥasakah Syria **109** L1
Al Ḥasakah governorate Syria **109** L1
Al Ḥasāni i. Saudi Arabia **104** B2
Al Hāshimīyah Iraq **107** F4
Al Ḥasī well Saudi Arabia **105** D3
Al Ḥāsikīyah i. Oman **105** F4
Al Ḥaşwah Iraq **109** P5
Al Ḥatīfah plain Saudi Arabia **105** D2
Al Ḥawāyā des. Saudi Arabia **105** E3
Al Hawi salt pan Saudi Arabia **109** J8
Al Ḥawījah Iraq **109** O2
Al Ḥawīyah Saudi Arabia **104** C3
Al Hawjā' Saudi Arabia **109** J9
Al Ḥawrā Yemen **105** D5
Al Ḥawṭah reg. Saudi Arabia **105** D3
Al Ḥayy Iraq **107** F4
Al Ḥayyānīyah waterhole Saudi Arabia **109** N9
Al Ḥayz Egypt **106** B5
Al Ḥazm Saudi Arabia **104** B1
Al Ḥazm al Jawf Yemen **104** D4
Alheit S. Africa **132** E5
Al Ḥibāk des. Saudi Arabia **105** F4
Al Ḥillah Iraq see **Hillah**
Al Ḥillah governorate Iraq see **Bābil**
Al Ḥillah Saudi Arabia **105** D3
Al Ḥilwah Saudi Arabia **105** D3
Al Ḥimārah well Saudi Arabia **105** E2
Al Hindīyah Iraq **107** F4
Al Ḥinnāh Saudi Arabia **105** E2
Al Ḥinw mt. Saudi Arabia **107** D5
Al Hirrah well Saudi Arabia **105** E3
Al Ḥishwah hills Yemen **104** D4
Al Ḥismā plain Saudi Arabia **104** A1
Al Ḥişn Jordan **108** G5
also spelt Husn
Al Ḥişn Yemen **105** D5
Al Hoceima Morocco **122** E2
formerly known as Villa Sanjurjo
Alhuampa Arg. **204** E2
Al Ḥudaydah Yemen see **Hodeidah**
Al Ḥudaydah governorate Yemen **104** C5
Al Ḥudūd ash Shamālīyah prov. Saudi Arabia **104** C1
Al Ḥufayrah well Saudi Arabia **105** E2
Al Ḥufrah reg. Saudi Arabia **104** B1
Al Hufūf Saudi Arabia **105** E2
also spelt Hofūf; also known as Hufūf
Al Hūj hills Saudi Arabia **104** B1
Al Ḥulayq al Kabīr hills Libya **120** C3
Al Ḥumayshah Yemen **105** D5
Al Ḥumrah reg. U.A.E. **105** F3
Al Ḥunayy Saudi Arabia **105** E2
Al Husayfīn Oman **105** G2
Al Ḥusaynīyah Egypt **108** C7
Al Ḥuthūl hill Saudi Arabia **109** K8
Al Huwatsah Oman **105** G3
Al Huwaylah Qatar **105** E2
Al Ḥuwaymi Yemen **105** D5
Al Ḥuwayyiṭ Saudi Arabia **104** C2
Al Ḥuwayz Syria **109** H2
Al Huwwah Saudi Arabia **105** D3
Ali China **89** B5
also known as Shiquanhe
'Alīābād Afgh. **101** G2
'Alīābād Golestān Iran **100** C2
'Alīābād Hormozgan Iran **100** C4
'Alīābād Khorāsan Iran **100** D3
'Alīābād Khorāsan Iran **101** E4
'Alīābād Kordestān Iran **100** A3
'Alīābād Qom Iran **100** B3
Alīābād, Kūh-e mt. Iran **100** B3
Aliağa Turkey **106** A3
Aliakmonas r. Greece **59** D8
Aliakmonas, Limni l. Greece **59** C8
Aliambata East Timor **75** C5
Aliartos Greece **59** E10
Alibag India **94** B2
Äli Bayramlı Azer. **107** G3
Alibey Adası i. Turkey **59** H9
Alibunar Vojvodina, Srbija Serb. and Mont. **58** B3
Alicante Spain **55** K6
also spelt Alacant
Alice Australia **149** E4
Alice r. Australia **149** D2
Alice watercourse Australia **149** E5
Alice S. Africa **133** K9
Alice U.S.A. **179** C7
Alice, Punta pt Italy **57** J9
Alice Arm Canada **166** D4
Alicedale S. Africa **133** K10
Alice Springs Australia **148** B4
Alice Town Bahamas **186** D1
Aliceville U.S.A. **175** B5
Alichur Tajik. **101** H2
Alichur r. Tajik. **101** H2
Alichuri Janubí, Qatorkŭhi mts Tajik. **101** H2
also known as Yuzhno-Alichurskiy, Khrebet
Alicia Phil. **74** B5
Alick Creek r. Australia **149** D4
Alicoto Fr. Guiana **199** H4
Alicudi, Isola i. Isole Lipari Italy **57** G10
Al 'Idd U.A.E. **105** F3
Al 'Idwah well Saudi Arabia **104** C2
Aliero Nigeria **125** G3
Alife Italy **56** G7
Aligarh India **96** C4
Alīgūdarz Iran **100** B3
Alihe China **85** I1
also known as Oroqen Zizhiqi
Alījūq, Kūh-e mt. Iran **100** B4
'Alī Kheyl Afgh. **101** G3
Al Ikhwān is Yemen **105** F5
English form The Brothers
Al 'Ilw al Aḥmar al Qiblī hill Egypt **108** B9
Alima r. Congo **126** C5
Al Imām Iraq **109** P5
Al Imārāt al 'Arabīyah at Muttaḥidah country Asia see **United Arab Emirates**
Alimia i. Greece **59** I12
Alindao Cent. Afr. Rep. **126** D3
Alinghar r. Afgh. **101** G3
Alingsås Sweden **45** K4
Alintale well Eth. **128** D3
Aliova r. Turkey **106** B3
Alipur India **94** C1
Alipur Pak. **101** G4
Alipur Duar India **97** F4
Aliquippa U.S.A. **176** E5
Alirajpur India **96** B5
Ali Sabieh Djibouti **128** D2
Al 'Īsāwīyah Saudi Arabia **107** D5
Al Iskandarīyah Egypt see **Alexandria**
Al Iskandarīyah governorate Egypt **108** A6
Al Iskandarīyah Iraq **107** F4
Aliskerovo Rus. Fed. **39** Q3
Al Ismā'īlīyah Egypt **121** G2
also spelt Ismâ'ilîya
Al Ismā'īlīyah governorate Egypt **108** D7
Aliste r. Spain **54** E3
Alitâive mt. Sweden **44** L2
Al Ittihab Yemen see **Madīnat ash Sha'b**
Aliveri Greece **59** F10
Aliwal North S. Africa **133** K7
Alix Canada **167** H4
Aliyaha r. Ukr. **58** K3
Al Jafr Jordan **109** H7
Al Jāfūrah des. Saudi Arabia **105** E2
Al Jaghbūb Libya **120** E2
Al Jahrah Kuwait **107** F5
Al Jamālīyah Egypt **108** C6
Al Jamalīyah Qatar **105** E2
Al Jarāwī well Saudi Arabia **109** J7
Al Jarf mts Saudi Arabia **104** B2
Al Jawārah well Oman **105** G4
Al Jawb reg. Saudi Arabia **105** E3
Al Jawf Libya **120** D3
Al Jawf Saudi Arabia **107** D5
also spelt Al Jauf
Al Jawf prov. Saudi Arabia **104** B1
Al Jawf governorate Yemen **105** D4
Al Jawlān hills Syria see **Golan**
Al Jawsh Libya **120** A1
Al Jaza'ir Alg. see **Algiers**
Al Jazā'ir reg. Iraq/Syria **109** K1
Alj Beyk Iran **100** C2
Aljezur Port. **54** C7
Al Jībān reg. Saudi Arabia **105** E2
Al Jid well Iraq **109** K5
Al Jilh esc. Saudi Arabia **104** D2
Al Jisr Iraq **109** P4
Al Jithāmīyah Saudi Arabia **104** C2
Al Jīzah Egypt see **Giza**
Al Jīzah governorate Egypt **108** A9
Al Ju'ayfirah Saudi Arabia **104** C4
Al Jubayl Saudi Arabia **105** E2
Al Jubayl hills Saudi Arabia **105** D2
Al Jubaylah Saudi Arabia **105** D2
Aljucén r. Spain **54** E6
Al Jufra Oasis Libya **120** B2
Al Julaydah well Saudi Arabia **105** D1
Al Jumūm Saudi Arabia **104** B3
Al Junaynah Saudi Arabia **104** C3
Al Jurayd i. Saudi Arabia **105** E2
Al Jurayfah Saudi Arabia **105** D2
Al Jurayr well Saudi Arabia **104** C3
Al Jurdhāwīyah Saudi Arabia **104** C2
Al Juwayf depr. Syria **109** I4
Al Juwayfah well Saudi Arabia **105** E3
Al Kahfah Saudi Arabia **104** C2
Al Kalbān Oman **105** G3
Alkaliya r. Ukr. **58** L3
Alkamari Niger **125** H3
Al Kāmil Oman **105** G3
Al Karābilah Iraq **109** M3
Al Karak Jordan **108** G6
also known as Karak
Al Karāmah Jordan **108** G6
Al Karmah Iraq **109** O4
Al Kāẓimīyah Iraq **107** F4
also known as Kādhimain or Kāẓimīyah
Al Khābūrah Oman **105** G3
Al Khaḍrā' well Saudi Arabia **104** C1
Al Khafaq well Saudi Arabia **105** D2
Al Khafqān salt pan Saudi Arabia **104** C3
Al Khalf Saudi Arabia **104** C2
Al Khalīf Oman **105** G3
Al Khalīl West Bank see **Hebron**
Al Khāliş Iraq **107** F4
Al Khamāsīn Saudi Arabia **104** D3
Al Kharfah Saudi Arabia **105** D3
Al Khārijah Egypt see **El Khârga**
Al Kharj reg. Saudi Arabia **105** D3
Al Kharkhayr oasis Saudi Arabia **105** E4
Al Kharrārah Qatar **105** E2
Al Khaşab Oman **105** G2
Al Khasfah well Oman **105** F4
Al Khāşirah Saudi Arabia **104** C3
Al Khatam reg. U.A.E. **105** F2
Al Khaṭāṭibah Egypt **108** B7
Al Khaṭīmī vol. Saudi Arabia **109** J6
Al Khawkhah Yemen **104** C5
Al Khawr Qatar **105** E2
Al Khawtamah i. Yemen **104** C5
Al Khīşah well Saudi Arabia **105** E2
Al Khizāmī well Saudi Arabia **105** E2
Al Khobar Saudi Arabia **105** E2
Al Khubrah Saudi Arabia **105** E2
Al Khuff reg. Saudi Arabia **104** D2
Al Khufrah Libya **120** D3
Al Khufrah Oasis Libya **120** D3
Al Khums Libya **120** B1
also spelt Homs
Al Khunfah sand area Saudi Arabia **104** B1
Al Khunn Saudi Arabia **105** E3
Al Khuwayr Qatar **105** E2
Al Kidan well Saudi Arabia **105** F3
Al Kifl Iraq **107** F4
Al Kir'ānah Qatar **105** E2
Alkmaar Neth. **48** B3
Al Kūfah Iraq **107** F4
also known as Kūfah
Al Kufla well Saudi Arabia **105** E3
Al Kumayt Iraq **107** F4
Al Kurá lava field Saudi Arabia **104** B2
Al Kusūr hills Saudi Arabia **109** J6
Al Kūt Iraq **107** F4
also known as Kut-al-Imara
Al Kuwayt country Asia see **Kuwait**
Al Kuwayt Kuwait see **Kuwait**
Al Labbah plain Saudi Arabia **107** E5
Allada Benin **125** F5
Al Lādhiqīyah Syria see **Latakia**
Al Lādhiqīyah governorate Syria **108** G2
Allagadda India **94** C3
Allahabad India **97** D4
Al Lajā lava field Syria **109** H5
Allakh-Yun' Rus. Fed. **39** N3
Allanridge S. Africa **133** K4
Allapalli India **94** D2
'Allāqī, Wādī al watercourse Egypt **121** G4
Allardt U.S.A. **176** A9
Allardville Canada **169** H4
Allariz Spain **54** D2
Al Latakhīyah well Yemen **105** E4
Alldays S. Africa **131** F4
Allegan U.S.A. **172** H8
Allegany U.S.A. **176** G3
Allegheny r. U.S.A. **176** F5
Allegheny Mountains U.S.A. **176** C9
Allegheny Reservoir U.S.A. **176** G4
Allemanskraaldam resr S. Africa **133** L5
Allen Phil. **74** C3
Allen, Lough l. Ireland **47** D9
Allen, Mount hill N.Z. **153** B15
Allen, Mount U.S.A. **166** A2
Allendale U.S.A. **175** D5
Allende Coahuila Mex. **185** E2
Allende Nuevo León Mex. **185** E3
Allendorf (Lumda) Germany **51** O2
Allenford Canada **173** L6
Allenstein Poland see **Olsztyn**
Allensville OH U.S.A. **176** C6
Allensville PA U.S.A. **176** H5
Allentown U.S.A. **177** J5
Alleppey India **94** C4
also known as Alappuzha
Aller r. Germany **48** G3
Allianc Suriname **199** H3
Alliance NE U.S.A. **178** B3
Alliance OH U.S.A. **176** D5
Al Lībīyah country Africa see **Libya**
Allier r. France **51** J6
Al Līfīyah well Iraq **107** E5
Alligator Point Australia **149** D3
Al Lihābah well Saudi Arabia **105** D2
Allikher India **94** C2
Allinge-Sandvig Denmark **45** K5
Al Lişāfah well Saudi Arabia **105** D2
Al Lisān pen. Jordan **108** G6
Allison U.S.A. **174** A3
Alliston Canada **173** N6
Al Līth Saudi Arabia **104** C3
Al Liwā' oasis U.A.E. **105** F3
Alloa U.K. **46** I7
Allonnes Pays de la Loire France **50** G5
Allora Australia **147** G2
Allouez U.S.A. **172** E6
Allschwil Switz. **51** N5
Allu Indon. **75** A4
Al Luḥayyah Yemen **104** C5
Allumettes, Île aux i. Canada **173** P5
Allur India **94** D3
Alluru Kottapatnam India **94** D3
Al Lussuf well Iraq **107** E5
Alma Canada **169** G3
formerly known as St-Joseph-d'Alma
Alma KS U.S.A. **178** C4
Alma MI U.S.A. **173** I7
Alma NE U.S.A. **178** C3
Al Ma'ānīyah Iraq **107** E5
Alma-Ata Kazakh. see **Almaty**
Alma-Ata Oblast admin. div. Kazakh. see **Almatinskaya Oblast'**
Almacelles Spain **55** L3
Al Machmin waterhole Iraq **109** N6
Almada Port. **54** B6
Al Madāfi' plat. Saudi Arabia **104** B1
Al Madā'in Iraq **109** P4
Al Ma'danīyāt well Iraq **107** F5
Al Maḍāyā Saudi Arabia **104** C4
Almaden Australia **149** E3
Almadén Spain **54** G6
Almadina Brazil **207** N1
Al Madīnah Iraq **100** A4
Al Madīnah Saudi Arabia see **Medina**
Al Madīnah prov. Saudi Arabia **104** B2
Al Mafraq Jordan **108** H5
also known as Mafraq
Al Maghrib reg. U.A.E. **105** F3
Almagro i. Phil. **74** C4
Al Mahākīk reg. Saudi Arabia **105** E3
Al Maḥallah al Kubrá Egypt **108** C7
Al Maḥārīq Egypt **121** F3
Al Maḥāwīl Iraq **109** P5
Al Mahbas W. Sahara **122** C4
Al Mahḍam Saudi Arabia **104** C3
Al Maḥiā depr. Saudi Arabia **104** B2
Al Maḥmūdīyah Iraq **107** F4
Al Mahrah governorate Yemen **105** E4
Al Mahrah reg. Yemen **105** E5
Al Maḥwīt Yemen **104** C5
Al Maḥwīt governorate Yemen **104** C5
Al Majma'ah Saudi Arabia **105** D2
Almăjului, Munții mts Romania **58** D4
Al Maks Egypt **108** A6
Al Maks al Baḥrī Egypt **121** F3
Al Mallāḥah marsh Egypt **108** E9
Al Malsūnīyah reg. Saudi Arabia **105** E2
Almalyk Uzbek. see **Olmaliq**
Al Ma'mūrah Egypt **108** B6
Al Manadir reg. Oman **105** F3
Al Manāmah Bahrain see **Manama**
Al Manjūr well Saudi Arabia **105** D3
Almanor, Lake U.S.A. **182** C1
Almansa Spain **55** J6
Al Manşūrah Egypt **121** F2
also spelt El Mansûra
Al Manşūrīyah Egypt **108** C7
Almanzor mt. Spain **54** F4
Almanzora r. Spain **55** J7
Al Ma'qil Iraq **107** F5
Almār Afgh. **101** F3
Almar r. Spain **54** F4
Al Mariyyah U.A.E. **105** F3
Al Marj Libya **120** D1
also known as Barce
Almas r. Brazil **201** H3
Almaş r. Romania **58** E1
Almas, Rio das r. Brazil **206** D1
Al Masana'a Oman **105** G3
Al Maṭarīyah Egypt **108** D6
Almatinskaya Oblast' admin. div. Kazakh. **103** I3
English form Almaty Oblast; also known as Almaty Oblysy; formerly known as Alma-Ata Oblast
Al Matmarfag W. Sahara **122** B4

►**Almaty** Kazakh. **103** I4
Former capital of Kazakhstan. English form Alma-Ata; formerly known as Vernyy.

Almaty Oblast admin. div. Kazakh. see **Almatinskaya Oblast'**
Almaty Oblysy admin. div. Kazakh. see **Almatinskaya Oblast'**
Al Mawşil Iraq see **Mosul**
Al Mayādīn Syria **109** L2
Almazán Spain **55** I3
Almeida Port. **54** E4
Almeirim Brazil **199** H5
Almeirim Port. **54** C5
Almelo Neth. **48** D3
Almenara Brazil **202** D6
Almenara Spain **55** K5
Almenara, Sierra de hills Spain **55** J7
Almendra, Embalse de resr Spain **54** E3
Almendralejo Spain **54** E6
Almere Neth. **48** C3
Almería Spain **55** I8
Almería, Golfo de b. Spain **55** I8
Almetievsk Rus. Fed. see **Al'met'yevsk**
Al'met'yevsk Rus. Fed. **40** J5
also spelt Almetievsk
Älmhult Sweden **45** K4
Al Midhnab Saudi Arabia **104** D2
Al Miḥrāḍ reg. Saudi Arabia **105** F3
Almina, Punta pt Spain **54** F9
Al Mindak Saudi Arabia **104** C3
Al Mintirib Oman **105** G3
Al Minyā Al Jīzah Egypt **108** C8
Al Minyā Al Minyā Egypt **121** F2
Al Minyā governorate Egypt **108** B9
Almirantazgo, Seno del sea chan. Chile **205** C9
Almirante Panama **186** C5
Al Mirfa U.A.E. **105** F2
Almirós Greece see **Almyros**
Al Mish'āb Saudi Arabia **105** E1
Al Mismīyah Syria **109** H4
Almodôvar Port. **54** C7
Almodóvar del Campo Spain **54** G6
Almoloya Mex. **185** E5
Almont U.S.A. **173** J8
Almonte Canada **173** Q5
Almonte Spain **54** E7
Almonte r. Spain **54** E5
Almora India **96** C3
Almoradí Spain **55** K6
Almorox Spain **54** G4
Al Mota well Niger **125** G3
Almoustarat Mali **125** F2
Al Mu'ayzīlah hill Saudi Arabia **109** J8
Al Mubarrez Saudi Arabia **105** E2
Al Muḍairib Oman **105** G3
Al Mudawwarah Jordan **108** H8
Al Muḥarraq Bahrain **105** E2
Al Muḥarraqah Egypt **108** C8
Al Muḥtaṭab depr. Saudi Arabia **109** H9
Al Mukallā Yemen see **Mukalla**
Al Mukhā Yemen see **Mocha**
Al Mukhaylī Libya **120** D1
Al Munbaṭiḥ des. Saudi Arabia **105** E3
Al Mundafan pass Saudi Arabia **105** D4
Almuñécar Spain **54** H8
historically known as Sexi
Al Muqdādīyah Iraq **107** F4
Al Murayr well Saudi Arabia **109** K7
Al Mūrītānīyah country Africa see **Mauritania**
Al Murūt well Saudi Arabia **107** D5
Almus Turkey **107** D2
also known as Tozanlı
Al Musannāh ridge Saudi Arabia **105** D1
Al Musayjīd Saudi Arabia **104** B2
Al Musayyib Iraq **109** P5
Al Muthanná governorate Iraq **107** F5
Al Muwayh Saudi Arabia **104** C3
Al Muwayliḥ Saudi Arabia **104** A2
Almyropotamos Greece **59** F10
Almyros Greece **59** D9
also spelt Almirós
Almyrou, Ormos b. Greece **59** F13
Alness U.K. **46** H6
Alnwick U.K. **46** K8

►**Alofi** Niue **145** I3
Capital of Niue.

Alofi, Île i. Wallis and Futuna Is **145** H3
Aloi Uganda **128** B4
Aloja Latvia **42** F4
Alol' Rus. Fed. **43** K5
Alolya r. Rus. Fed. **43** J5
Along India **97** G3
Alonnisos i. Greece **59** E9
Alonso r. Brazil **206** B11
Alor i. Indon. **75** C5
Alor, Kepulauan is Indon. **75** C5
Alor, Selat sea chan. Indon. **75** B5
Álora Spain **54** G8
Alor Setar Malaysia **76** C1
also spelt Alur Setar; formerly spelt Alor Star
Alor Star Malaysia see **Alor Setar**
Alosno Spain **54** D7
Alost Belgium see **Aalst**
Alot India **96** B5
Alota Bol. **200** D5
Alotau P.N.G. **149** F1
Aloysius, Mount Australia **151** E5
Alpachiri Arg. **204** E5
Alpagut Turkey **59** J9
Alpaugh U.S.A. **182** E6
Alpena U.S.A. **173** J5
Alpercatas, Serra das hills Brazil **202** C3
Alpha Australia **149** E4
Alpha S. Africa **133** P4
Alpha U.S.A. **172** C9
Alphonse Island i. Seychelles **129** [inset]
Alpi Apuane, Parco Naturale delle nature res. Italy **56** C4
Alpine AZ U.S.A. **183** O8
Alpine CA U.S.A. **183** H9
Alpine NY U.S.A. **177** I3
Alpine TX U.S.A. **179** B6
Alpine WY U.S.A. **180** E4
Alpine National Park Australia **147** E4
Alpinópolis Brazil **206** G7
►**Alps** mts Europe **51** M7
►►**28–29 Europe** Landscapes
Al Qā' valley Egypt **108** E9
Al Qā' Saudi Arabia **104** C3
Al Qa'āmīyāt reg. Saudi Arabia **105** D4
Al Qaddāḥīyah Libya **120** B2
Al Qādisīyah governorate Iraq **107** F5
formerly known as Ad Dīwānīyah

Al Qadmūs Syria 108 H2
Al Qaffāy i. U.A.E. 105 F2
Al Qafrah Yemen 105 D5
Al Qāhirah Egypt see **Cairo**
Al Qāhirah governorate Egypt 108 C8
Al Qaḩmah Saudi Arabia 104 C4
Al Qā'im Iraq 109 L3
Al Qā'īyah Saudi Arabia 104 C2
Al Qā'īyah well Saudi Arabia 105 D2
Al Qalībah Saudi Arabia 104 B1
Al Qāmishlī Syria 107 E3
Al Qanāţir al Qāhirīyah Egypt 108 C7
Al Qanţarah Egypt 106 C5
Al Qanţarah ash Sharqīyah Egypt 108 D7
Al Qar'ah well Saudi Arabia 105 D2
Al Qar'ah lava field Syria 109 H5
Al Qarn Yemen 105 D5
Al Qaryatayn Syria 109 I3
Al Qaşīm prov. Saudi Arabia 104 C2
Al Qaşr Egypt 121 F3
Al Qaşr Saudi Arabia 104 C2
Al Qaşş Abū Sa'īd plat. Egypt 121 E3
Al Qaţīf Saudi Arabia 105 E2
Al Qaţn Yemen 105 E5
Al Qaţrānah Jordan 108 H6
Al Qaţrūn Libya 120 B3
Al Qawnas reg. Saudi Arabia 105 D3
Al Qayşūmah Saudi Arabia 105 D1
Al Qāyşūmah well Saudi Arabia 107 E5
Al Qiblīyah i. Oman 105 G4
Al Qulayyibah waterhole Saudi Arabia 109 N9
Al Qumur country Africa see **Comoros**
Al Qunayţirah Syria 108 G4
Al Qunayţirah governorate Syria 108 G4
Al Qunfidhah Saudi Arabia 104 C4
Al Qurayn Saudi Arabia 104 C2
Al Qurayni oasis Saudi Arabia 105 F3
Al Qurayyah Saudi Arabia 104 C2
Al Qurayyah U.A.E. 105 G2
Al Qurayyāt Saudi Arabia 107 D5
Al Qurnah Iraq 107 F5
Al Quşayr Egypt 121 G3
Al Quwārah Saudi Arabia 104 C2
Al Quwayi' Saudi Arabia 105 D3
Al Quwayīyah Saudi Arabia 105 D2
Al Quwayrah Jordan 108 G8
Al Quzah Yemen 105 E5
Al Rabbād reg. U.A.E. 105 F3
Alrar Est Alg. 123 H3
Alroy Downs Australia 148 C3
Alsace admin. reg. France 51 N4
Alsace, Plaine d' valley France 51 N5
Al Samha U.A.E. 100 C5
Al Samīt well Iraq 107 E5
Alsask Canada 167 I5
Alsek r. U.S.A. 164 F4
Alsfeld Germany 48 G5
Al'skiy Khrebet mt. Rus. Fed. 82 E1
Alston U.K. 47 J9
Alstonville Australia 147 G2
Alsunga Latvia 42 C5
Alsviķi Latvia 42 H4
Alta Norway 44 M1
Alta, Mount N.Z. 153 C12
Altadena U.S.A. 182 F7
Altaelva r. Norway 44 M1
Altafjorden sea chan. Norway 44 M1
UNESCO World Heritage Site
Alta Floresta Brazil 201 F2
Alta Gracia Arg. 204 D3
Alta Gracia Nicaragua 186 B5
Altai Mountains Asia 88 D1
also known as Altayskiy Khrebet
UNESCO World Heritage Site
Altamaha r. U.S.A. 175 D6
Altamira Amazonas Brazil 199 E4
Altamira Pará Brazil 199 H5
Altamira Chile 204 C2
Altamira Col. 198 C4
Altamira Costa Rica 186 B5
Altamíra Mex. 185 F4
Altamira, Cuevas de tourist site Spain 54 G1
UNESCO World Heritage Site
Altamira, Sierra de mts Spain 54 F5
Altamonte Springs City U.S.A. 175 D6
Altamura Italy 57 I8
Altan Rus. Fed. 85 F1
Altanbulag Mongolia 85 E2
Altan Emel China 85 H1
also known as Xin Barag Youqi
Altan Ovoo mt. China/Mongolia 84 A2
Altan Shiret China 85 F4
also known as Ejin Horo Qi; also spelt Altan Xiret
Altan Xiret China see **Altan Shiret**
Alta Paraiso de Goiás Brazil 202 C5
Altapirire Venez. 199 E2
Altar Mex. 184 C2
Altar r. Mex. 181 E7
Altar, Desierto de des. Mex. 184 B1
Altata Mex. 184 D3
Altavista U.S.A. 176 F8
Altay China 84 A2
Altay Mongolia 84 C2
Altay, Respublika aut. rep. Rus. Fed. 84 A1
English form Altay Republic; formerly known as Gorno-Altayskaya Avtonomnaya Oblast' or Gornyy Altay
Altay Kray admin. div. Rus. Fed. see **Altayskiy Kray**
Altay Republic aut. rep. Rus. Fed. see **Altay, Respublika**
Altayskiy Khrebet mts Asia see **Altai Mountains**
Altayskiy Kray admin. div. Rus. Fed. 88 C1
English form Altay Kray
Altayskiy Zapovednik nature res. Rus. Fed. 84 A1
Altdorf Switz. 51 O6
Altea Spain 55 K6
Alteidet Norway 44 M1
Altenburg Germany 49 J5
Altenkirchen (Westerwald) Germany 48 E5
Altenqoke China 84 B4
Alter do Chão Brazil 199 H5
Alter do Chão Port. 54 D5
Altevatnet l. Norway 44 L1
Altin Köprü Iraq 107 F4
Altınoluk Turkey 59 H9
Altinópolis Brazil 206 F8
Altınova Turkey 59 H9
Altınözü Turkey 108 H1
Altıntaş Turkey 106 B3
Altınyaka Turkey 108 B1
Altiplano plain Bol. 200 C4
Altmühltal park Germany 48 I7
Altnaharra U.K. 46 H5
Alto U.S.A. 172 H8
Alto Araguaia Brazil 203 A6
Alto Cedro Cuba 186 E2
Alto Chicapa Angola 127 C7
Alto Cruz mt. Spain 55 I3
Alto Cuchumatanes mts Guat. 185 H6
Alto de Cabezas mt. Spain 55 H2
Alto de Covelo pass Spain 54 D2
Alto del Moncayo mt. Spain 55 J3
Alto de Pencoso hills Arg. 204 D4
Alto do Trevim mt. Port. 54 C4
Alto Douro Wine Region Port. 54 D3
UNESCO World Heritage Site
Alto Garças Brazil 202 A6
Alto Ligonha Moz. 131 H2
Alto Madidi, Parque Nacional nat. park Bol. 200 C3
Alto Molócuè Moz. 131 H2
Alton U.K. 47 L12
Alton IL U.S.A. 174 B4
Alton KY U.S.A. 176 A7
Alton MO U.S.A. 174 B4
Alton NH U.S.A. 177 N2
Altona B.C. Canada 166 F3
Altona Man. Canada 167 L5
Alto Nevado mt. Chile 205 B7
Altoona PA U.S.A. 176 G5
Altoona WI U.S.A. 172 B6
Alto Pacajá r. Brazil 202 B2
Alto Parnaíba Brazil 202 C4
Alto Purús r. Peru 200 C2
Alto Rio Doce Brazil 207 J8
Alto Río Senguerr Arg. 205 C7
Altos Brazil 202 D3
Altos de Chacaya Chile 200 C4
Altos de Chinchilla mts Spain 55 J6
Alto Sucuriú Brazil 206 A6
Alto Taquarí Brazil 203 A6
Altotero mt. Spain 55 H2
Altotonga Mex. 185 F5
Altötting Germany 49 J7
Alto Uruguai Brazil 203 A8
Altukhovo Rus. Fed. 43 P9
Altun Ha tourist site Belize 185 H5
Altun Shan mt. China 84 B4
Altun Shan mts China 84 B4
also known as Astin Tag
Alturas U.S.A. 180 B4
Altus U.S.A. 179 C5
Altyn-Topkan Tajik. see **Oltintopkan**
Alu Estonia 42 F2
Alua Moz. 131 H2
Al 'Ubaydī Iraq 109 M3
Al Ubaylah Saudi Arabia 105 E3
Alucra Turkey 107 D2
Al 'Uḑaylīyah Saudi Arabia 105 E2
Al Udayn Yemen 104 C5
Alūksne Latvia 42 I4
Alūksnes l. Latvia 42 I4
Al 'Ulā Saudi Arabia 104 B2
Al'ulah reg. Yemen 105 D5
Alūm Iran 100 B3
Alum Bridge U.S.A. 176 E6
Alum Creek Lake U.S.A. 176 C5
Alunda Sweden 45 L3
Aluniş Romania 58 F2
Alupka Ukr. 106 C1
Al 'Uqaylah Libya 120 C2
Al 'Uqaylah Saudi Arabia see **An Nabk**
Al 'Uqayr Saudi Arabia 105 E2
Al Uqşur Egypt see **Luxor**
Alur India 94 C3
Al Urayq des. Saudi Arabia 107 D5
Al 'Urdun country Asia see **Jordan**
Alur Setar Malaysia see **Alor Setar**
Alushta Ukr. 41 E7
Al Uthaylī Saudi Arabia 104 B1
Aluva India see **Alwaye**
Al 'Uwayjā' well Saudi Arabia 105 D3
Al 'Uwayjā' well Saudi Arabia 105 E3
Al 'Uwaynah well Saudi Arabia 105 E2
Al 'Uwaynāt Libya 120 E4
Al 'Uwaynāt Libya 120 A3
Al 'Uwaynidhiyah i. Saudi Arabia 104 B2
Al 'Uwayqīlah Saudi Arabia 107 E5
Al Uyainah Saudi Arabia 105 D2
Al 'Uyaynah well Saudi Arabia 108 H9
Al 'Uẓaym Saudi Arabia 104 C2
Al 'Uzayr Iraq 107 F5
Alva r. Port. 54 C4
Alva U.S.A. 178 C4
Alvand, Kūh-e mt. Iran 100 B3
Alvão, Parque Natural do nature res. Port. 54 D3
Alvarado Mex. 185 G5
Alvarado U.S.A. 179 C5
Alvarães Brazil 199 E5
Álvares Machado Brazil 206 B9
Älvdalen Sweden 45 K3
Alvdalen valley Sweden 45 K3
Alvedro airport Spain 54 C1
Alverca Port. 54 B6
Alvesta Sweden 45 K4
Alvin TX U.S.A. 179 D6
Alvin WI U.S.A. 172 E5
Alvinópolis Brazil 207 J7
Älvkarleby Sweden 45 L3
Älvsbyn Sweden 44 M2
Al Wādī at Jadīd governorate Egypt 106 A6
Al Wafrah Kuwait 107 F5
also spelt Wafra
Al Wajh Saudi Arabia 104 B2
Al Wakrah Qatar 105 E2
Al Wannān Saudi Arabia 105 E2
Al Waqbá well Saudi Arabia 105 D1
Alwar India 96 C4
Al Warī'ah Saudi Arabia 105 D2
Al Wāsiţah Egypt 108 C8
Al Wāţiyah well Egypt 121 E2
Al Watīyah Libya 120 A1
Alwaye India 94 C4
also known as Aluva
Al Widyān plat. Iraq/Saudi Arabia 107 E4
Al Wīgh Libya 120 B3
Al Wusayl Qatar 105 E2
Al Wusayţ well Saudi Arabia 104 D1
Al Wusţá admin. reg. Oman 105 G3
Alxa Youqi China see **Ehen Hudag**
Alxa Zuoqi China see **Bayan Hot**
Al Yamāmah Saudi Arabia 105 D2
Alyangula Australia 148 C2
Al Yāsāt i. U.A.E. 105 E2
Alyawarra Aboriginal Land res. Australia 148 B4
Alytus Lith. 42 F7
Al Yūsufīyah Iraq 109 P4
Alzada U.S.A. 178 A2
Alzey Germany 48 F6
Alzira Spain 55 K5
also spelt Alcira
Amacayacu, Parque Nacional nat. park Col. 198 D5
Ämådalen Sweden 45 K3
Amadeus, Lake salt flat Australia 148 A5
Amadi Sudan 128 A3
Amadjuak Lake Canada 165 L3
Amadora Port. 54 B6
Amadror plain Alg. 123 G4
Amaga Col. 198 C3
Amagi Japan 91 B8
Amahai Indon. 75 D3
Amakusa-Kami-shima i. Japan 91 B8
Amakusa-nada b. Japan 91 A8
Amakusa-Shimo-shima i. Japan 91 B8
Amal Oman 105 F4
Åmål Sweden 45 K4
Amalaoulaou well Mali 125 F3
Amalapuram India 94 D2
Amalat r. Rus. Fed. 81 J2
Amalfi Col. 198 C3
UNESCO World Heritage Site
Amalia S. Africa 133 J4
Amaliada Greece 59 C11
Amalner India 96 B5
Amamapare Indon. 73 I7
Amambaí Brazil 201 G5
Amambaí, Serra de hills Brazil/Para. 201 G5
Amami-Ō-shima i. Japan 81 L7
Amami-shotō is Japan 81 L7
Amamula Dem. Rep. Congo 126 E5
Amån r. Sweden 45 K3
Amanã, Lago l. Brazil 199 E5
Amanbidji Aboriginal Land res. Australia 148 A3
Amanda U.S.A. 176 C6
Amandola Italy 56 F6
Amangel'dy Aktyubinskaya Oblast' Kazakh. 102 D2
also spelt Amankeldi
Amangel'dy Kustanayskaya Oblast' Kazakh. 103 F2
also spelt Amankeldi
Amankaragay Kazakh. 103 F1
also spelt Amanqaraghay
Amankeldi Aktyubinskaya Oblast' Kazakh. see **Amangel'dy**
Amankeldi Kustanayskaya Oblast' Kazakh. see **Amangel'dy**
Amanotkel' Kazakh. 103 E3
Amanqaraghay Kazakh. see **Amankaragay**
Amantea Italy 57 I9
Amanzimtoti S. Africa 133 O7
Amapa Brazil 200 C2
Amapá state Brazil 199 I4
Amapala Hond. 186 B4
Amapari r. Brazil 199 I4
Āmara admin. reg. Eth. 128 C2
Amara Abu Sin Sudan 121 G6
Amaradia r. Romania 58 E4
Amārah Iraq see **Al 'Amārah**
Amaral Ferrador Brazil 203 A9
Amarante Brazil 202 D3
Amarante do Maranhão Brazil 202 C3
Amarapura Myanmar 78 B3
Amaravati r. India 94 C4
Amardalay Mongolia 85 E2
Amargosa Brazil 202 E5
Amargosa watercourse U.S.A. 181 C5
Amargosa Desert U.S.A. 183 H5
Amargosa Range mts U.S.A. 183 H5
Amargosa Valley U.S.A. 183 H5
Amargura Island Tonga see **Fonualei**
Amarillo U.S.A. 179 B5
Amarkantak India 97 D5
Amaro, Monte mt. Italy 56 G6
Amarpur India 97 F5
Amarwara India 96 C5
Amasa U.S.A. 172 E4
Amasia Turkey see **Amasya**
Amasine W. Sahara 122 B4
Amasra Turkey 106 C2
Amâssine well Mali 125 F2
Amasya Turkey 106 C2
historically known as Amasia
Amata Australia 151 E5
Amataurá Brazil 199 D5
Amatenango Mex. 185 G5
Amatikulu S. Africa 133 P6
Amatique, Bahía de b. Guat. 185 H6
Amatlán de Cañas Mex. 184 D4

►**Amazon** r. S. America 202 B1
Longest river in South America and 2nd in the world. Also spelt Amazonas.
►►**6–7 World** Landscapes
►►**188–189 South America** Landscapes

Amazon, Mouths of the Brazil 202 B1
Amazon, Source of the Peru 200 C3
Amazonas state Brazil 199 E6
Amazonas dept Col. 198 D5
Amazonas dept Peru 198 B6
Amazonas r. S. America see **Amazon**
Amazonas state Venez. 199 E4
Amazónia, Parque Nacional nat. park Brazil 199 G6
Āmba Ālagē mt. Eth. 128 C1
Ambad India 94 B2
Amba Farit mt. Eth. 128 C2
Ambahikily Madag. 131 [inset] I4
Ambajogai India 94 C2
also spelt Ambejogai
Ambala India 96 C3
Ambalajanakomby Madag. 131 [inset] J3
Ambalakirajy Madag. 131 [inset] K2
Ambalangoda Sri Lanka 94 D5
Ambalatany Madag. 131 [inset] J4
Ambalavao Madag. 131 [inset] J4
Ambam Cameroon 125 H6
Ambanja Madag. 131 [inset] K2
Ambar Iran 100 D4
Ambarchik Rus. Fed. 39 Q3
Ambarès-et-Lagrave France 50 F8
Ambargasta, Salinas de salt pan Arg. 204 D3
Ambarnyy Rus. Fed. 40 E2
Ambasamudram India 94 C4
Ambassa India 97 F5
Ambathala Australia 149 E5
Ambato Ecuador 198 B5
Ambato, Sierra mts Arg. 204 D3
Ambato Boeny Madag. 131 [inset] J3
Ambato Finandrahana Madag. 131 [inset] J4
Ambatolahy Madag. 131 [inset] J4
Ambatolampy Madag. 131 [inset] J3
Ambatomainty Madag. 131 [inset] J3
Ambatondrazaka Madag. 131 [inset] K3
Ambatosia Madag. 131 [inset] K2
Ambazac France 50 H7
Ambejogai India see **Ambajogai**
Ambelau i. Indon. 75 C3
Ambelón Greece see **Ampelonas**
Amberg Germany 48 I6
Amberg U.S.A. 172 F5
Ambergris Cay i. Belize 185 I5
Ambergris Cays is Turks and Caicos Is 187 F2
Ambérieu-en-Bugey France 51 L7
Amberley Canada 173 L6
Amberley N.Z. 153 G11
Ambert France 51 J7
Ambgaon India 94 D1
Ambianum France see **Amiens**
Ambidédi Mali 124 C3
Ambika r. India 94 B1
Ambikapur India 97 D5
Ambilobe Madag. 131 [inset] K2
Ambition, Mount Canada 166 D3
Amble U.K. 46 K8
Ambleside U.K. 47 J9
Amblève r. Belgium 51 L2
Ambo India 97 E5
Ambo Peru 200 A2
Amboasary Madag. 131 [inset] J5
Amboasary Gara Madag. 131 [inset] K3
Amboavory Madag. 131 [inset] K3
Ambodifotatra Madag. 131 [inset] K3
Ambodiharina Madag. 131 [inset] K4
Ambohidratrimo Madag. 131 [inset] J3
UNESCO World Heritage Site
Ambohijanahary Madag. 131 [inset] K3
Ambohimahasoa Madag. 131 [inset] J4
Ambohipaky Madag. 131 [inset] J3
Ambohitra mt. Madag. 131 [inset] K2
Ambohitralanana Madag. 131 [inset] K2
Amboina Indon. see **Ambon**
Amboise France 50 G5
Ambon Indon. 75 D3
formerly known as Amboina
Ambon i. Indon. 75 C3
Amboró, Parque Nacional nat. park Bol. 201 D4
Amboseli National Park Kenya 128 C5
Ambositra Madag. 131 [inset] J4
Ambovombe Madag. 131 [inset] J5
Amboy CA U.S.A. 183 I7
Amboy IL U.S.A. 172 D9
Ambre, Cap d' c. Madag. see **Bobaomby, Tanjona**
Ambrim i. Vanuatu see **Ambrym**
Ambriz Angola 127 B6
Ambriz, Coutada do nature res. Angola 127 B6
Ambrizete Angola see **N'zeto**
Ambrosio Brazil 198 D5
Ambrym i. Vanuatu 145 F3
also spelt Ambrim
Ambunten Indon. 77 F4
Ambur India 94 C3
Åmdals Verk Norway 45 J4
Am-Dam Chad 120 D6
Amded, Oued watercourse Alg. 123 F5
Amderma Rus. Fed. 40 L1
Amdillis well Mali 125 E2
Am Djéména Chad 120 C6
Amdo China see **Lharigarbo**
Amealco Mex. 185 E4
Ameca Mex. 184 D4
Amecameca Mex. 185 F5
Amedamit mt. Eth. 128 C2
Ameghino Arg. 204 E4
Ameland i. Neth. 48 C2
Amelia Italy 56 E6
Amelia Court House U.S.A. 176 H8
Amellu India 96 D4
Amendolara Italy 57 I9
Amenia U.S.A. 177 L4
Amer, Erg d' des. Alg. 123 H4
American, North Fork r. U.S.A. 182 C3
Americana Brazil 206 F9
American Falls U.S.A. 180 D4
American Falls Reservoir U.S.A. 180 D4
American Fork U.S.A. 183 M1

►**American Samoa** terr. S. Pacific Ocean 145 I3
United States Unincorporated Territory. Formerly known as Eastern Samoa.
►►**138–139 Oceania** Countries

Americus U.S.A. 175 C5
Ameringkogel mt. Austria 49 L8
Amersfoort Neth. 48 C3
Amersfoort S. Africa 133 N4
Amery Canada 167 M3
Amery Ice Shelf Antarctica 223 E2
Ames U.S.A. 174 A3
Amesbury U.S.A. 177 O3
Amet India 96 B4
Amethi India 97 D4
Amfilochia Greece 59 C10
Amfissa Greece 59 D10
Amga Rus. Fed. 39 N3
Amgalang China 85 H1
also known as Xin Barag Zuoqi
Amgu Rus. Fed. 82 E3
Amguema Rus. Fed. 39 S3
Amguid Alg. 123 G4
Amgun' r. Rus. Fed. 82 E1
Amherst Canada 169 H4
Amherst MA U.S.A. 177 M3
Amherst OH U.S.A. 176 C4
Amherst VA U.S.A. 176 F8
Amherst, Mount hill Australia 150 D3
Amherstburg Canada 173 J8
Amherstdale U.S.A. 176 D8
Amherst Island Canada 173 Q6
Amherstview Canada 173 Q6
Amida Turkey see **Diyarbakır**
Amidon U.S.A. 178 B2
Amiens France 51 I3
historically known as Ambianum or Samarobriva
UNESCO World Heritage Site
'Amīj, Wādī watercourse Iraq 107 E4
Amik Ovası marsh Turkey 107 D3
Amilḩayt, Ramlat des. Oman 105 F4
Amilḩayt, Wādī al r. Oman 105 F4
Amilly France 51 I5
'Amīnābād Iran 100 C4
Amíndhaion Greece see **Amyntaio**
Amindivi i. India see **Amini**
Amindivi Islands India 94 B4
Amini i. India 94 B4
also known as Amindivi
Amino Japan 91 D7
Aminuis Namibia 130 C4
Amioun Lebanon 108 G3
Amipshahr India 96 C3
Amīrābād Eşfahān Iran 100 B3
Amīrābād Īlām Iran 100 A3
Amirabad Iran see **Fūlād Maīalleh**
Amirante Islands Seychelles 129 [inset]
Āmirlī Iraq 109 P3
Amisk Lake Canada 167 K4
Amistad, Represa de resr Mex./U.S.A. see **Amistad Reservoir**
Amistad Reservoir Mex./U.S.A. 185 E2
also known as Amistad, Represa de
Amisus Turkey see **Samsun**
Amite U.S.A. 175 B6
Amite Creek r. U.S.A. 175 B6
Amla India 96 C5
also known as Sarni
Amlaḩ, Jabal al hill Saudi Arabia 104 C4
Amlamé Togo 125 F5
Amlash Iran 100 B2
Amlekhganj Nepal 97 E4
Åmli Norway 45 J4
Amlwch U.K. 47 H10
'Amm Adam Sudan 121 H5
Amman Jordan see **'Ammān**

►**'Ammān** Jordan 108 G6
Capital of Jordan. English form Amman; historically known as Philadelphia or Rabbath Ammon.

Ammanazar Turkm. 102 C5
Ämmänsaari Fin. 44 O2
'Ammār reg. Yemen 105 D5
'Ammār, Tall hill Syria 109 H5
Ammarnäs Sweden 44 L2
Ammaroodinna watercourse Australia 146 B1
Ammassalik Greenland 165 P3
also known as Tasiilaq; also spelt Angmagssalik
Ammer r. Germany 48 I8
Ammerån r. Sweden 44 L3
Ammersee l. Germany 48 I8
Ammochostos Cyprus see **Famagusta**
Ammochostos Bay Cyprus 108 F2
also known as Famagusta Bay
Am Nābiyah Yemen 104 C5
Amne Machin Range mts China see **A'nyêmaqên Shan**
Amnok-kang r. China/N. Korea see **Yalu Jiang**
Amod India 96 B5
Amo Jiang r. China 86 B4
Amol Iran 100 C2
Amolar Brazil 201 F4
Amoliani i. Greece 59 E8
Amontada Brazil 202 E2
Amor mt. Spain 54 G5
Amorebieta Spain 55 I1
Amores r. Arg. 204 F3
Amorgos i. Greece 59 G12
Amorinópolis Brazil 206 B3
Amory U.S.A. 175 B5
Amos Canada 168 E3
Åmot Buskerud Norway 45 J4
Åmot Telemark Norway 45 I4
also known as Ytre Vinje
Amotape, Cerros de mts Peru 198 A6
Åmotfors Sweden 45 K4
Amourj Mauritania 124 D2
Amoy China see **Xiamen**
Ampah Indon. 77 F3
Ampanefena Madag. 131 [inset] K2
Ampani India 95 D2
Ampanihy Madag. 131 [inset] J5
Ampanotoamaizina Madag. 131 [inset] K3
Amparafaka, Tanjona pt Madag. 131 [inset] J2
Amparafaravola Madag. 131 [inset] K3
Amparai Sri Lanka 94 D5
Amparo Brazil 206 G9
Ampasimanolotra Madag. 131 [inset] K3
formerly known as Vohibinany
Ampelonas Greece 59 D9
also known as Ambelón
Ampenan Indon. 77 G5
Amper r. Germany 48 I7
Amper Nigeria 125 H4
Amphitrite Group is Paracel Is 72 D3
Ampibaku Indon. 75 B3
Ampisikinana Madag. 131 [inset] K2
formerly spelt Ampitsikinana
Ampitsikinana Madag. see **Ampisikinana**
Ampoa Indon. 75 B3
Amposta Spain 55 L4
Amqui Canada 169 H3
Amrabad India 94 C2
'Amrah, Jabal hill Saudi Arabia 104 C2
Amrān Yemen 104 C5
Amrān governorate Yemen 105 C4
Amraoti India see **Amravati**
Amravati India 94 C1
formerly spelt Amraoti
Amreli India 96 A5
Am Rijā' Yemen 121 J6
Amritsar India 96 B3
Amroha India 96 C3
Amrum i. Germany 48 F1
Åmsele Sweden 44 L2
Amstelveen Neth. 48 B3

►**Amsterdam** Neth. 48 B3
Official capital of the Netherlands.
UNESCO World Heritage Site
►►**8–9 World** Countries

Amsterdam S. Africa 133 O3
Amsterdam NY U.S.A. 177 K3
Amsterdam OH U.S.A. 176 E5
Amsterdam, Île i. Indian Ocean 219 M8
English form Amsterdam Island
Amsterdam Island Indian Ocean see **Amsterdam, Île**
Amstetten Austria 49 L7
Am Timan Chad 126 D2
Amú r. Col. 198 C4
Amu Co l. China 89 E5
'Amūd, Jabal al mt. Saudi Arabia 109 K7
Amudar'ya r. Asia 99 F1
English form Amu Darya; also known as Dar"yoi Amu; also spelt Amudaryo, Amyderya; historically known as Oxus
Amu Darya r. Asia see **Amudar'ya**
Amudaryo r. Asia see **Amudar'ya**
Amund Ringnes Island Canada 165 J2
Amundsen, Mount Antarctica 223 G2
Amundsen Bay Antarctica 223 D2
Amundsen Coast Antarctica 223 O1
Amundsen Glacier Antarctica 223 N1
Amundsen Gulf Canada 164 G2
Amundsen-Scott research station Antarctica 223 A1
Amundsen Sea Antarctica 222 Q2
Amuntai Indon. 77 F3
Amur r. Rus. Fed. 82 F1
also known as Heilong Jiang
'Amur, Wadi watercourse Sudan 121 G5
Amurang Indon. 75 C2
Amur Oblast admin. div. Rus. Fed. see **Amurskaya Oblast'**
Amursk Rus. Fed. 82 E2
formerly known as Padali
Amurskaya Oblast' admin. div. Rus. Fed. 82 C1
English form Amur Oblast
Amurskiy Rus. Fed. 102 D1
Amurskiy Liman strait Rus. Fed. 82 F1
Amurzet Rus. Fed. 82 C3
Amvrakikos Kolpos b. Greece 59 B10
Amyderya r. Asia see **Amudar'ya**
Amyntaio Greece 58 C8
also known as Amíndhaion
Amyot Canada 173 I2
Amzacea Romania 58 J5
Amzérakad well Mali 125 F2
Am-Zoer Chad 120 D6
Ana r. Turkey 58 I7
Anaa atoll Fr. Polynesia 221 J7
Anabanua Indon. 75 B3
Anabar r. Rus. Fed. 39 L2
Ana Branch r. Australia 146 D3
Anabtā West Bank 108 G5
Anacapa Island U.S.A. 182 E7
Anaco Venez. 199 E2
Anaconda U.S.A. 180 D3
Anacortes U.S.A. 180 B2
Anadarko U.S.A. 179 C5
Anadolu Dağları mts Turkey 107 D2
Anadyr' Rus. Fed. 39 R3
Anadyr' r. Rus. Fed. 39 R3
Anadyr, Gulf of Rus. Fed. see **Anadyrskiy Zaliv**
Anadyrskiy Zaliv b. Rus. Fed. 39 S3
English form Anadyr, Gulf of
Anafi Greece 59 G12
Anafi i. Greece 59 G12
Anagé Brazil 202 D5
Anagni Italy 56 F7
historically known as Anagnia
Anagnia Italy see **Anagni**
'Ānah Iraq 107 E4
Anaheim U.S.A. 182 G8
Anahim Lake Canada 166 E4
Anáhuac Nuevo León Mex. 185 E3
Anáhuac Veracruz Mex. 185 F4
Anahuac U.S.A. 179 D6
Anaimalai Hills India 94 C4
Anai Mudi Peak India 94 C4
Anaiteum i. Vanuatu see **Anatom**
Anajás Brazil 202 B2
Anajás, Ilha i. Brazil 202 B2
Anajatuba Brazil 202 C2
Anakao Madag. 131 [inset] I4
Anakapalle India 95 D2
Anakie Australia 149 E4
Analalava Madag. 131 [inset] J2
Analavelona mts Madag. 131 [inset] I4
Anamã Brazil 199 F5
Ana María, Golfo de b. Cuba 186 D2
Anambas, Kepulauan is Indon. 77 D2
Anambra state Nigeria 125 G5
Anamosa U.S.A. 174 B3
Anamu r. Brazil 199 G4
Anamur Turkey 106 C3
Anan Japan 91 D8
Anand India 96 B5
Anandapur India 97 E5
Anandpur India 96 C3
Anandpur r. India 97 E5
Ananes i. Greece 59 F12
Anan'ev Kyrg. 103 I4
also known as Anan'yevo
Anangu Pitjantjatjara Aboriginal Lands res. Australia 146 A1
Anantapur India 94 C3
Anantnag Jammu and Kashmir 96 B2
also known as Islamabad
Anant Peth India 96 C4
Ananyev Ukr. see **Anan'yiv**
Anan'yevo Kyrg. see **Anan'ev**
Anan'yiv Ukr. 41 D7
also spelt Ananyev
Anapa Rus. Fed. 41 F7
Anápolis Brazil 206 E3
Anapú r. Brazil 199 I5
Anár Fin. see **Inari**
Anār Iran 100 C4
Anārak Iran 100 C3
Anarbar r. Iran 100 B3
Anardara Afgh. 101 E3
Anare Mountains Antarctica 223 L2
Añasco Puerto Rico 187 G3
Ånäset Sweden 44 M2
Anatahan i. N. Mariana Is 73 K3
formerly spelt Anatajan
Anatajan i. N. Mariana Is see **Anatahan**
Anatolia reg. Turkey 106 B3
Anatoliki Makedonia kai Thraki admin. reg. Greece 58 G7
Anatom i. Vanuatu 145 F4
also known as Anetchom, Île or Aneytioum, Île or Kéamu; also spelt Aneityum or Anaiteum
Añatuya Arg. 204 E3
Anatye Aboriginal Land res. Australia 148 C4
Anauá r. Brazil 199 F4
Anavilhanas, Arquipélago das is Brazil 199 F5
Anaypazari Turkey see **Gülnar**
Anaz mts Saudi Arabia 109 H9
Anbei China 84 C3
Anbyon N. Korea 83 B5
Ancares, Serra dos mts Spain 54 D2
Ancash dept Peru 200 A2
Ancaster Canada 173 N7
Ancasti, Sierra mts Arg. 204 D3
Ancenis France 50 E5
Anchán Arg. 205 D6
Anchang China 86 C2
also known as Anxian
Anchau Nigeria 125 H4
Anchieta Brazil 207 M7
Anchodaya Bol. 200 C3
Anchorage U.S.A. 164 E3
Anchorage Island atoll Cook Is see **Suwarrow**
Anchorage Reefs reef P.N.G. 149 F1
Anchor Bay U.S.A. 173 K8
Anchuthengu India see **Anjengo**
Anci China see **Langfang**
Ančia r. Lith. 42 D6
Anclitas, Cayo i. Cuba 186 D2
An Cóbh Ireland see **Cobh**
Ancón Peru 200 A2
Ancona Italy 56 F5
Ancuabe Moz. 129 C8
Ancud Chile 205 B6
Ancud, Golfo de g. Chile 205 B6
Ancyra Turkey see **Ankara**
Anda Heilong. China 82 B3
Anda Heilong. China see **Daqing**
Anda i. Indon. 75 C1
Andacollo Chile 204 C3
Andahuaylas Peru 200 B3
Andal India 97 E5
also spelt Ondal
Andalgalá Arg. 204 D2
Åndalsnes Norway 44 I3
Andalucía aut. comm. Spain 54 G7
English form Andalusia
Andalusia S. Africa see **Jan Kempdorp**
Andalusia aut. comm. Spain see **Andalucía**
Andalusia AL U.S.A. 175 C6
Andalusia IL U.S.A. 172 C9
Andām, Wādī r. Oman 105 G3
Andaman and Nicobar Islands union terr. Andaman & Nicobar Is India 95 G4
Andaman Islands India 95 G3
Andaman Sea Indian Ocean 79 A6
Andaman Strait India 95 G3
also known as Middle Strait
Andamooka Australia 146 C2
Andapa Madag. 131 [inset] K2
Andarāb Afgh. 101 G3
also known as Banow
Andarob Tajik. 101 G2
also spelt Anderob
Ande China 86 C4
Andeba Ye Midir Zerf Chaf pt Eritrea 104 C5
Andeg Rus. Fed. 40 J2
Andegavum France see **Angers**
Andelle r. France 50 H3
Andenes Norway 44 L1
Andenne Belgium 51 L2
Andéramboukane Mali 125 F3
Ånderdalen Nasjonalpark nat. park Norway 44 L1
Andermatt Switz. 51 O6
Andernos-les-Bains France 50 E8
Anderob Tajik. see **Andarob**
Anderson r. Canada 164 G3
Anderson AK U.S.A. 164 E3
Anderson CA U.S.A. 182 B1
Anderson IN U.S.A. 174 C3
Anderson MO U.S.A. 178 D4
Anderson SC U.S.A. 174 D5
Anderson Bay Australia 147 E5
Anderson Reservoir U.S.A. 182 C4
Andes Col. 198 C3
Andes mts S. America 200 A2
Andévalo, Sierra de hills Spain 54 D7
Andfjorden sea chan. Norway 44 L1
Andhíparos i. Greece see **Antiparos**
Andhra Pradesh state India 94 C2
Andía, Sierra de mts Spain 55 J2
Andijon Uzbek. 103 H4
also spelt Andizhan
Andijon admin. div. Uzbek. 103 H4
English form Andizhan Oblast; also known as Andijon Wiloyati
Andijon Wiloyati admin. div. Uzbek. see **Andijon**
Andikíra Greece see **Antikyra**
Andikithira i. Greece see **Antikythira**
Andilamena Madag. 131 [inset] K3
Andilanatoby Madag. 131 [inset] K3
Andīmeshk Iran 100 B3
Andímilos i. Greece see **Antimilos**
Andípaxoi i. Greece see **Antipaxoi**
Andípsara i. Greece see **Antipsara**
Andirá Brazil 206 C10
Andir He r. China 89 C4
Andırın Turkey 107 D3
Andirlangar China 89 C4
Andiyskoye Koysu r. Rus. Fed. 102 A4
Andiyur India 94 C4
Andizhan Uzbek. see **Andijon**
Andizhan Oblast admin. div. Uzbek. see **Andijon**
Andkhui r. Afgh. 101 F2
Andkhvoy Afgh. 101 F2
Andoany Madag. 131 [inset] K2
formerly known as Hell-Ville
Andoas Peru 198 B5
Andoas Nuevo Ecuador 198 B5
Andoga r. Rus. Fed. 43 S2
Andogskaya Gryada hills Rus. Fed. 43 S2
Andohahela, Réserve d' nature res. Madag. 131 [inset] J5
Andohajango Madag. 131 [inset] K2
Andol India 94 C2
Andola India 94 C2
Andong China see **Dandong**
Andong S. Korea 83 C5
Andongwei China 85 H5
Andoom Australia 149 D2
►**Andorra** country Europe 55 M2
►►**32–33 Europe** Countries
Andorra Spain 55 K4

►**Andorra la Vella** Andorra 55 M2
Capital of Andorra. Also spelt Andorra la Vieja.

Andorra la Vieja Andorra see **Andorra la Vella**
Andover U.K. 47 K12
Andover MA U.S.A. 177 N3
Andover NH U.S.A. 177 N2
Andover NY U.S.A. 176 H3
Andover OH U.S.A. 176 E4
Andøya i. Norway 44 K1
Andozero, Ozero l. Rus. Fed. 43 S2
Andradas Brazil 206 G9
Andrade U.S.A. 183 J9
Andradina Brazil 206 B7
Andramasina Madag. 131 [inset] J3
Andramy Madag. 131 [inset] J3
Andranomavo Madag. 131 [inset] J3
Andranomena Madag. 131 [inset] K3
Andranopasy Madag. 131 [inset] I4

Andranovondronina Madag. 131 [inset] K2
Andranovory Madag. 131 [inset] J4
Andreanof Islands U.S.A. 221 H2
Andreapol' Rus. Fed. 43 N5
André Félix, Parc National de nat. park Cent. Afr. Rep. 126 D2
André Fernandes Brazil 207 L2
Andrelândia Brazil 203 C7
Andrequicé Brazil 207 I5
Andrew Canada 167 H4
Andrew Bay Myanmar 78 A4
Andrews SC U.S.A. 175 E5
Andrews TX U.S.A. 179 B5
Andreyevka Kazakh. 103 J3
Andreyevka Rus. Fed. 102 B1
Andreyevskoye Rus. Fed. see Dneprovskoye
Andreykovichi Rus. Fed. 43 O9
Andreykovo Rus. Fed. 43 P6
Andria Italy 56 I7
Andriba Madag. 131 [inset] J3
Andrieskraal S. Africa 133 I10
Andriesvale S. Africa 132 E3
Andringitra mts Madag. 131 [inset] J4
Androka Madag. 131 [inset] J5
Androna reg. Madag. 131 [inset] K2
Androniki Rus. Fed. 43 U4
Andropov Rus. Fed. see Rybinsk
Andros i. Bahamas 186 D1
Andros Greece 59 F11
Andros i. Greece 59 F11
Androscoggin r. U.S.A. 177 P2
Androsovka Rus. Fed. 102 B1
Andros Town Bahamas 186 D1
Andrott i. India 94 B4
Andrushevka Ukr. see Andrushivka
Andrushivka Ukr. 41 D6
also spelt Andrushevka
Andrychów Poland 49 Q6
Andselv Norway 44 L1
Andsnes Norway 44 M1
Andújar Spain 54 G6
Andulo Angola 127 C7
Anec, Lake salt flat Australia 150 E4
Anecón Grande mt. Arg. 205 C6
Āneen-Kio terr. N. Pacific Ocean see Wake Island
Anéfis Mali 125 F2
Anéfis well Mali 125 E2
Anegada i. Virgin Is (U.K.) 187 G3
Anegada, Bahía b. Arg. 204 E6
Anegada Passage Virgin Is (U.K.) 187 H3
Anegam U.S.A. 183 L9
Aného Togo 125 F5
Aneityum i. Vanuatu see Anatom
'Aneiza, Jabal hill Iraq see 'Unayzah, Jabal
Anekal India 94 C3
Añelo Arg. 204 C5
Anemourion tourist site Turkey 108 D1
Anesbaraka well Alg. 123 G6
Anet France 50 H4
Anetchom, Île i. Vanuatu see Anatom
Aneto mt. Spain 55 L2
Aney Niger 125 I2
Aneytioum, Île i. Vanuatu see Anatom
Anfile Bay Eritrea 121 I6
Anfu China 87 E3
also known as Pingdu
Angadippuram India 94 C4
Angadoka, Lohatanjona hd Madag. 131 [inset] J2
Angahook Lorne State Park nature res. Australia 147 D4
Angalarri r. Australia 148 A2
Angamma, Falaise d' esc. Chad 120 C5
Angamos, Isla i. Chile 205 B8
Angamos, Punta pt Chile 200 C5
Ang'angxi China 85 I2

▶Angara r. Rus. Fed. 84 E1
Part of the Yenisey-Angara-Selenga, 3rd longest river in Asia. English form Upper Tunguska; also known as Verkhnyaya Tunguska.
▶▶60–61 Asia Landscapes

Angaradébou Benin 125 F4
Angarapa Aboriginal Land res. Australia 148 B4
Angarsk Rus. Fed. 80 G2
Angas Downs Australia 148 B5
Angas Range hills Australia 150 E4
Angaston Australia 146 C3
Angat Phil. 74 B3
Angatuba Brazil 206 E10
Angaur i. Palau 73 H5
also spelt Ngeaur or Niaur
Ånge Sweden 44 K3
Ángel, Salto waterfall Venez. see Angel Falls
Ángel de la Guarda, Isla i. Mex. 184 B2
Angeles Phil. 74 B3

▶Angel Falls Venez. 199 F3
Highest waterfall in the world. Also known as Ángel, Salto.

Ängelholm Sweden 45 K4
Angelina r. U.S.A. 179 D6
Angellala Creek r. Australia 149 E5
Angelo r. Australia 150 B4
Angels Camp U.S.A. 182 D3
Ångereb Eth. 104 B5
Angereb Wenz r. Eth. 128 C1
Ångermanälven r. Sweden 44 L3
Angermünde Germany 49 L2
Angers France 50 F5
historically known as Andegavum or Juliomagus
Anggana Indon. 77 G3
Angical Brazil 202 C4
Angicos Brazil 202 E3
Angikuni Lake Canada 167 L2
Angiola U.S.A. 182 E6
Angkor tourist site Cambodia 79 C5
UNESCO World Heritage Site
Anglem, Mount hill N.Z. 153 B14
also known as Hananui
Anglesey i. U.K. 47 H10
also known as Ynys Môn
Angleton U.S.A. 179 D6
Angliers Canada 173 N3
Anglin r. France 50 G6
Anglo-Egyptian Sudan country Africa see Sudan
Angmagssalik Greenland see Ammassalik
Ang Mo Kio Sing. 76 [inset]
Ango Dem. Rep. Congo 126 E3
Angoche Moz. 131 H3
formerly known as António Enes
Angohrān Iran 100 D5
Angol Chile 204 B5
▶Angola country Africa 127 C7
formerly known as Portuguese West Africa
▶▶114–115 Africa Countries
Angola IN U.S.A. 174 C3
Angola NY U.S.A. 176 F3
Angonia, Planalto de plat. Moz. 131 G2
Angoon U.S.A. 164 F4
Angora Turkey see Ankara
Angostura Mex. 184 C3
Angoulême France 50 G7
historically known as Iculisma
Angra do Heroísmo Arquipélago dos Açores 54 [inset]
UNESCO World Heritage Site
Angra dos Reis Brazil 207 I10
Angren Uzbek. 103 G4
Ångsö naturreservat nature res. Sweden 45 L4
Ang Thong Thai. 79 C5
Angu Dem. Rep. Congo 126 E4
Angualasto Arg. 204 C3
Anguang China 85 I2

▶Anguilla terr. West Indies 187 H3
United Kingdom Overseas Territory.
▶▶158–159 North America Countries

Anguilla Cays is Bahamas 186 D2
Anguille, Cape Canada 169 J4
Angul India 95 E1
Anguli Nur l. China 85 G3
Anguo China 85 G4
Angurugu Australia 148 C2
Angus Canada 173 N6
Angustura Brazil 201 E2
Angwin U.S.A. 182 B3
Anhanguera Brazil 206 E5
Anholt i. Denmark 45 J4
Anhua China 87 D2
also known as Dongping
Anhui prov. China 87 F1
English form Anhwei
Anhumas Brazil 202 A6
Anhwei prov. China see Anhui
Aniak U.S.A. 164 D3
Aniakchak National Monument and Preserve nat. park U.S.A. 164 D4
Anicuns Brazil 206 D3
Anidhros i. Greece see Anydro
Anié Togo 125 F5
Anie, Pic d' mt. France 50 F10
Aniene r. Italy 56 E7
Anikhovka Rus. Fed. 103 E2
Anikovo Rus. Fed. 40 G4
Animas r. U.S.A. 181 E5
Anina Romania 58 C3
Anishino Rus. Fed. 43 S7
Añisoc Equat. Guinea 125 H6
Anitaguipan Point Phil. 74 C4
Anıtlı Turkey 108 D1
Aniva Rus. Fed. 82 F3
Aniva, Mys c. Rus. Fed. 82 F3
Aniva, Zaliv b. Rus. Fed. 82 F3
Anivorano Madag. 131 [inset] K3
Anivorano Avaratra Madag. 131 [inset] K2
Aniwa U.S.A. 172 D5
Anjad India 96 B5
Anjafy mt. Madag. 131 [inset] J3
Anjalankoski Fin. 45 N3
Anjangaon India 96 C5
Anjar India 96 A5
Anjengo India 94 C4
also known as Anchuthengu
Anji China 87 F2
also known as Dipu
Anji India 94 C1
Anjiang China see Qianyang
Anjihai China 88 D2
Anjir Avand Iran 100 C3
Anjō Japan 91 E7
Anjoman Iran 100 D3
Anjou reg. France 50 F5
Anjou, Val d' valley France 50 F5
Anjouan i. Comoros see Nzwani
Anjozorobe Madag. 131 [inset] J3
Anjŭ N. Korea 83 B5
Anjuman reg. Afgh. 101 G3
Anka Nigeria 125 G3
Ankaboa, Tanjona pt Madag. 131 [inset] I4
formerly known as St-Vincent, Cap
Ankang China 87 D1

▶Ankara Turkey 106 C3
Capital of Turkey. Historically known as Ancyra or Angora.

Ankaratra mts Madag. 131 [inset] J3
Ankarsrum Sweden 45 L4
Ankatafa Madag. 131 [inset] K2
Ankavandra Madag. 131 [inset] J3
Ankazoabo Madag. 131 [inset] J4
Ankazobe Madag. 131 [inset] J3
Ankeny U.S.A. 174 A3
Ankerika Madag. 131 [inset] J2
An Khê Vietnam 79 E5
formerly known as An Tuc
Ankiliabo Madag. 131 [inset] I4
Anklam Germany 49 K2
Ankleshwar India 96 B5
formerly spelt Anklesvar
Anklesvar India see Ankleshwar
Ankofa mt. Madag. 131 [inset] K3
Ankogel mt. Austria 49 K8
Ankola India 94 B3
Ankouzhen China 85 E5
An'kovo Rus. Fed. 43 U5
Ankpa Nigeria 125 G5
Anling China see Yanling
An Lôc Vietnam 79 D6
Anloga Ghana 125 F5
Anlong China 86 C3
Ânlong Vêng Cambodia 79 D5
Anlu China 87 E2
Anmoore U.S.A. 176 E6
An Muileann gCearr Ireland see Mullingar
Anmyŏn-do i. S. Korea 83 B5
Ann, Cape Antarctica 223 D2
Ann, Cape U.S.A. 177 O3
Anna Rus. Fed. 41 G6
Anna U.S.A. 174 B4
Anna, Lake U.S.A. 176 H7
Annaba Alg. 123 G1
formerly known as Bône; historically known as Bona or Hippo Regius
Annaberg-Buchholtz Germany 49 K5
An Nabk Saudi Arabia 109 I6
also known as Al 'Uqaylah
An Nabk Syria 109 H3
An Nafūd des. Saudi Arabia 104 C1
Annai Guyana 199 G4
An Najaf Iraq 107 F5
also known as Najaf
An Najaf governorate Iraq 107 E5
Annalee r. Ireland 47 E9
Annam reg. Vietnam 78 D4
Annam Highlands mts Laos/Vietnam 78 D4
Annan U.K. 47 I9
Annan r. U.K. 47 I9
'Annān, Wādī al watercourse Syria 109 J3
Annandale U.S.A. 177 H7
Anna Plains Australia 150 C3

▶Annapolis U.S.A. 177 I7
State capital of Maryland. Historically known as Anne Arundel Town or Providence.

Annapolis Royal Canada 169 H4
Annapurna Conservation Area nature res. Nepal 97 E3

▶Annapurna I mt. Nepal 97 D3
10th highest mountain in the world and in Asia.
▶▶6–7 World Landscapes
▶▶60–61 Asia Landscapes

Annapurna II mt. Nepal 97 E3
Ann Arbor U.S.A. 173 J8
Anna Regina Guyana 199 G3
An Nás Ireland see Naas
An Nashū, Wādī watercourse Libya 120 B3
An Nāṣirīyah Iraq 107 F5
also known as Nāṣirīyah
Annaspan imp. l. S. Africa 133 J5
An Naṣrānī, Jabal mts Syria 109 I4
An Nawfalīyah Libya 120 C2
Annean, Lake salt flat Australia 151 B5
Anne Arundel Town U.S.A. see Annapolis
Annecy France 51 M7
Annecy, Lac d' l. France 51 M7
Annecy-le-Vieux France 51 M7
Anne Marie Lake Canada 169 I2
Annemasse France 51 M6
Annette Island U.S.A. 166 D4
Annie r. Australia 149 D2
Annikvere Estonia 42 H2
An Nimārah Syria 109 I5
An Nimāṣ Saudi Arabia 104 C4
Anning China 86 B3
formerly known as Lianran
Anning He r. China 86 B3
Annino Rus. Fed. 43 S2
An Nīr, Jabal hills Saudi Arabia 104 C2
Anniston U.S.A. 175 C5
Annobón i. Equat. Guinea 125 G7
formerly known as Pagalu
Annonay France 51 K7
Annotto Bay Jamaica 186 D3
An Nu'ayrīyah Saudi Arabia 105 E2
An Nukhaylah waterhole Iraq 109 P4
An Nu'mānīyah Iraq 107 F4
An Nuqay'ah Qatar 105 E2
An Nuṣayrīyah, Jabal mts Syria 108 H2
Annville U.S.A. 176 B8
Anogeia Greece 59 F13
also spelt Anóyia
Anoka U.S.A. 174 A2
Anori Brazil 199 F5
Anorontany, Tanjona hd Madag. 131 [inset] I2
Anosibe An'Ala Madag. 131 [inset] K3
Anou I-n-Atei well Alg. 123 G5
Ânou Mellene well Mali 125 F2
Anou-n-Bidek well Alg. 123 G6
Ano Viannos Greece 59 G13
Anóyia Greece see Anogeia
Anpu China 87 D4
Anpu Gang b. China 87 D4
Anqing China 87 F2
Anqiu China 85 H4
Anren China 87 E3
Ansai China 85 F4
also known as Zhenwudong
Anse-à-Galets Haiti 187 E3
Anse-à-Pitre Haiti 187 F3
Anse-à-Veau Haiti 187 E3
Anseba Shet watercourse Eritrea 104 B4
Anse d'Hainault Haiti 187 E3
Anser Group is Australia 147 E4
Anserma Col. 198 C3
Anshan China 85 I3
Anshun China 86 C3
Anshunchang China 86 B2
Ansina Uruguay 204 G3
An Sirhān, Wādī watercourse Saudi Arabia 107 D5
Ansjö Sweden 44 L3
Anson U.S.A. 179 C5
Anson Bay Australia 148 A2
Ansongo Mali 125 F3
Ansongo-Ménaka, Réserve Partielle de Faune d' nature res. Mali 125 F3
Ansonia U.S.A. 176 A5
Ansonville Canada 173 M2
Ansted U.S.A. 176 D7
Anstruther U.K. 46 J7
Ansu China see Xushui
Anta India 96 C4
Anta Peru 200 B3
Antabamba Peru 200 B3
Antakya Turkey 106 D3
also known as Hatay; historically known as Antioch or Antiochia
Antalaha Madag. 131 [inset] K2
Antalya Turkey 106 B3
also spelt Adalia; historically known as Attaleia or Attalia
Antalya prov. Turkey 108 B1
Antalya Körfezi g. Turkey 106 B3
Antanambao Manampotsy Madag. 131 [inset] K3
Antanambe Madag. 131 [inset] K3

▶Antananarivo Madag. 131 [inset] J3
Capital of Madagascar. Formerly spelt Tananarive; short form Tana.

Antananarivo prov. Madag. 131 [inset] J3
Antanifotsy Madag. 131 [inset] J3
Antanimora Atsimo Madag. 131 [inset] J5
An tAonach Ireland see Nenagh

▶Antarctica 222
Most southerly and coldest continent, and the continent with the highest average elevation.
▶▶212–213 Antarctica Features

▶Antarctic Peninsula Antarctica 222 T2
▶▶212–213 Antarctica Features
Antaritarika Madag. 131 [inset] J5
Antelope Island U.S.A. 183 L1
Antelope Range mts U.S.A. 183 H2
Antequera Spain 54 G7
Anthony KS U.S.A. 178 C4
Anthony NM U.S.A. 181 F6
Anthony, Lake salt flat Australia 146 B2
Anthony Lagoon Australia 148 B3
Anti Atlas mts Morocco 122 C3
also known as Petit Atlas
Antibes France 51 N9
Anticosti, Île d' i. Canada 169 I3
English form Anticosti Island
Anticosti Island Canada see Anticosti, Île d'
Antifer, Cap d' c. France 50 G3
Antigo U.S.A. 172 D5
Antigonish Canada 169 I4
Antigua i. Antigua and Barbuda 187 H3
Antigua Guat. see Antigua Guatemala
Antigua country West Indies see Antigua and Barbuda
▶Antigua and Barbuda country West Indies 187 H3
short form Antigua
▶▶158–159 North America Countries
Antigua Guatemala Guat. 185 H6
short form Antigua
UNESCO World Heritage Site
Antiguo-Morelos Mex. 185 F4
Antikyra Greece 59 D10
also spelt Andikira
Antikythira i. Greece 59 E13
also spelt Andikithira
Antikythiro, Steno sea chan. Greece 59 E13
Anti Lebanon mts Lebanon/Syria see Sharqī, Jabal ash
Antilla Arg. 204 D2
Antilla Cuba 186 E2
Antimilos i. Greece 59 F12
also spelt Andímilos
Antimony U.S.A. 183 M3
An tInbhear Mór Ireland see Arklow
Antioch Turkey see Antakya
Antioch CA U.S.A. 182 C3
Antioch IL U.S.A. 172 E8
Antiocheia ad Cragum tourist site Turkey 108 D1
Antiochia Turkey see Antakya
Antioquia Col. 198 C3
Antioquia dept Col. 198 C3
Antiparos i. Greece 59 G11
also spelt Andíparos
Antipaxoi i. Greece 59 B9
also spelt Andípaxoi
Antipino Rus. Fed. 43 O6
Antipodes Islands N.Z. 145 G6
UNESCO World Heritage Site
Antipsara i. Greece 59 G10
also spelt Andípsara
Antitilos i. Greece 59 I12
Antium Italy see Anzio
Antlers U.S.A. 179 D5
An t-Ob U.K. see Leverburgh
Antofagasta Chile 200 C5
Antofagasta admin. reg. Chile 200 C5
Antofagasta de la Sierra Arg. 204 D2
Antonhibe Madag. 131 [inset] J2
Antônio Carlos Brazil 207 J8
Antonio de Biedma Arg. 205 D7
Antônio Dias Brazil 207 K6
António Enes Moz. see Angoche
Antônio Lemos Brazil 202 B2
Antón Recio Cuba 186 C2
Antopal' Belarus 42 F9
Antrim U.K. 47 F9
Antrim Hills U.K. 47 F8
Antrim Plateau Australia 150 E3
Antrodoco Italy 56 F6
Antropovo Rus. Fed. 40 G4
Antsahabe Madag. 131 [inset] K2
Antsalova Madag. 131 [inset] J3
Antsambalahy Madag. 131 [inset] K2
Antseranana Madag. see Antsirañana
Antsiferovo Rus. Fed. 43 O3
Antsirabe Madag. 131 [inset] J3
Antsirabe Avaratra Madag. 131 [inset] K2
Antsirañana Madag. 131 [inset] K2
formerly known as Diégo Suarez; formerly spelt Antseranana
Antsirañana prov. Madag. 131 [inset] K2
Antsla Estonia 42 H4
Antsohihy Madag. 131 [inset] J2
Antsohimbondrona Madag. 131 [inset] K2
formerly known as Port St-Louis
Antsondrodava Madag. 131 [inset] J3
Anttis Sweden 44 M2
Anttola Fin. 45 N3
Antu China see Songjiang
An Tuc Vietnam see An Khê
Antuco Chile 204 C5
Antuco, Volcán vol. Chile 204 C5
Antufash, Jazīrat i. Yemen 104 C5
English form Antufush Island
Antufush Island Yemen see Antufash, Jazīrat
Antwerp Belgium 51 K1
also known as Anvers; Egypt also spelt Antwerpen
Antwerp U.S.A. 177 J1
Antwerpen Belgium see Antwerp
Antwerpen prov. Belgium 48 B4
UNESCO World Heritage Site
An Uaimh Ireland see Navan
Anuc, Lac l. Canada 169 F1
Anuchino Rus. Fed. 82 D4
Anueque, Sierra mts Arg. 205 C6
Anupgarh India 96 B3
Anuradhapura Sri Lanka 94 D4
UNESCO World Heritage Site
Anurrete Aboriginal Land res. Australia 148 B4
Anvers Belgium see Antwerp
Anvers Island Antarctica 222 T2
Anvil Range mts Canada 166 C2
Anxi Fujian China 87 F3
also known as Fengcheng
Anxi Gansu China 84 B3
also known as Yuanquan
Anxian China see Anchang
Anxiang China 87 E2
Anxin China 85 G4
also known as Xin'an
Anxious Bay Australia 146 B3
Anxur Italy see Terracina
Anyang Guangxi China see Du'an
Anyang Henan China 85 G4
also known as Zhangde
Anyang S. Korea 83 B5
Anyar Indon. 77 D4
Anydro i. Greece 59 G12
also known as Ánidhros
A'nyêmaqên Shan mts China 86 A1
English form Amne Machin Range
Anyi China 87 E2
also known as Longjin
Anykščiai Lith. 42 G6
Anyuan Jiangxi China 87 E3
also known as Xinshan
Anyuan Jiangxi China 87 E3
Anyue China 86 C2
also known as Yueyang
Anyuy r. Rus. Fed. 82 E2
Anyuysk Rus. Fed. 39 Q3
Anzac Alta Canada 167 I3
Anzac B.C. Canada 166 F4
Anze China 85 G4
Anzhero-Sudzhensk Rus. Fed. 80 D1
Anzi Dem. Rep. Congo 126 D5
Anzio Italy 56 E7
historically known as Antium
Anzoátegui state Venez. 199 E2
Aoba i. Vanuatu 145 F3
also known as Omba; also spelt Oba
Aoga-shima i. Japan 91 F8
Aohan Qi China see Xinhui
Aomen China see Macao
Aomori Japan 90 G4
Aomori pref. Japan 90 G4
Aoos r. Greece 59 B8
Ao Phang Nga National Park Thai. 79 B6
Aoraki N.Z. 153 E11

▶Aoraki mt. N.Z. 153 E11
Highest mountain in New Zealand. Also known as Aorangi or Cook, Mount

Aôral, Phnum mt. Cambodia 79 D5
Aorangi mt. N.Z. see Aoraki
Aorere r. N.Z. 152 G8
Aosta Italy 51 N7
Aotearoa country Oceania see New Zealand
Aouderas Niger 125 H2
Aoufist W. Sahara 122 B4
Aouhinet bel Egra well Alg. 122 D4
Aouk, Bahr r. Cent. Afr. Rep./Chad 126 C2
Aoukalé r. Cent. Afr. Rep./Chad 126 D2
Aouk-Aoakole, Réserve de Faune de l' nature res. Cent. Afr. Rep. 126 D2
Aoukâr reg. Mali/Mauritania 122 D5
Aoukenek well Mali 125 F2
Aoulef Alg. 123 F4
Aoulime, Jbel mt. Morocco 122 C3
Aourou Mali 124 C3
Aoxi China see Le'an
Aoya Japan 91 D7
Aoyang China see Shanggao
Aozou Chad 120 C4
Apa r. Brazil 201 F5
Apac Uganda 128 B4
Apache U.S.A. 179 C5
Apache, Lake U.S.A. 183 M8
Apache Junction U.S.A. 183 M8
Apagado, Volcán vol. Bol. 200 D5
Apahida Romania 58 E2
Apaiaí r. Brazil 206 E10
Apaiang atoll Kiribati see Abaiang
Apalachee Bay U.S.A. 175 C6
Apalachicola U.S.A. 175 C6
Apalachicola r. U.S.A. 175 C6
Apalachicola Bay U.S.A. 175 C6
Apam Ghana 125 E5
Apamama atoll Kiribati see Abemama
Apamea Turkey see Dinar
Apan Mex. 185 F5
Apaporis r. Col. 198 D5
Apar, Teluk b. Indon. 77 G3
Aparecida do Rio Doce Brazil 206 B5
Aparecida do Tabuado Brazil 206 B7
Aparima N.Z. see Riverton
Aparima r. N.Z. 153 C14
Aparri Phil. 74 B2
Aparurén Venez. 199 F3
Apas, Sierra hills Arg. 205 D6
Apaščia r. Lith. 42 F5
Apatin Vojvodina, Srbija Serb. and Mont. 56 K3
Apatity Rus. Fed. 44 P2
Apatou Fr. Guiana 199 H3
Apatzingán Mex. 185 E5
Ape Latvia 42 H4
Apediá r. Brazil 201 E2
Apeldoorn Neth. 48 C3
Apennines mts Italy 53 D3
also known as Appennino
Apere r. Bol. 200 D3
Apex Mountain Canada 166 B2
Aphrodite's Birthplace tourist site Cyprus 108 D3
also known as Petra tou Romiou
Api Dem. Rep. Congo 126 E4
Api mt. Nepal 96 D3
Api, Tanjung pt Indon. 75 B3
Apia Col. 198 C3
Apia atoll Kiribati see Abaiang

▶Apia Samoa 145 H3
Capital of Samoa.

Apiacas, Serra dos hills Brazil 201 F2
Apiaí Brazil 203 B8
Apiaú, Serra do mts Brazil 199 F4
Apio Solomon Is 145 F2
Apipilulco Mex. 185 F5
Apishapa r. U.S.A. 178 B4
Apiti N.Z. 152 J7
Apizaco Mex. 185 F5
Apizolaya Mex. 179 B7
Aplao Peru 200 B4
Ap Lei Chau i. Hong Kong China see Aberdeen Island
Apo, Mount vol. Phil. 74 C5
Apodi Brazil 202 E3
Apodi, Chapada do hills Brazil 202 E3
Apo East Passage Phil. 74 B3
Apoera Suriname 199 G3
Apolda Germany 48 I4
Apollinopolis Magna Egypt see Idfū
Apollo Bay Australia 147 D4
Apollonia Bulg. see Sozopol
Apollonia Greece 59 F12
Apolo Bol. 200 C3
Apopka U.S.A. 175 D6
Aporé r. Brazil 206 C6
Apostle Islands U.S.A. 172 C4
Apostle Islands National Lakeshore nature res. U.S.A. 172 C3
Apostolens Tommelfinger mt. Greenland 165 O3
Apóstoles Arg. 204 G2
Apostolos Andreas, Cape Cyprus 108 F2
also known as Zafer Burnu
Apoteri Guyana 199 G3
Apo West Passage Phil. 74 B3
Appalachia U.S.A. 176 C9
Appalachian Mountains U.S.A. 176 B9
Appalla i. Fiji see Kabara
Appennino mts Italy see Apennines
Appennino Abruzzese mts Italy 56 F6
Appennino Lucano mts Italy 57 H8
Appennino Napoletano mts Italy 56 H7
Appennino Tosco-Emiliano mts Italy 56 C5
Appiano sulla Strada del Vino Italy 56 D2
Applecross U.K. 46 G6
Appleton MN U.S.A. 178 C2
Appleton WI U.S.A. 172 E6
Apple Valley U.S.A. 183 G7
Appomattox U.S.A. 176 G8
Aprelevka Rus. Fed. 43 S6
Aprilia Italy 56 E7
Apsheronsk Rus. Fed. 41 F7
formerly known as Apsheronskaya
Apsheronskaya Rus. Fed. see Apsheronsk
Apsheronskiy Poluostrov pen. Azer. see Abşeron Yarımadası
Apsley Canada 173 O6
Apsley Strait Australia 148 A1
Apt France 51 L9
Apucarana Brazil 206 B10
Apucarana, Serra da hills Brazil 206 B10
Apulum Romania see Alba Iulia
Apurahuan Phil. 74 A4
Apure r. Venez. 198 E3
Apure state Venez. 198 D3
Apurímac dept Peru 200 B3
Apurimac r. Peru 200 B3
Apurito Venez. 198 D3
Aq"a Georgia see Sokhumi
'Aqaba Jordan see Al 'Aqabah
Aqaba, Gulf of Asia 104 A1
'Aqabah, Wādī al watercourse Egypt 108 E7
Aqadyr Kazakh. see Agadyr'
Aqal China 88 B3
Aqbalyq Kazakh. see Akbalyk
Aqbeyit Kazakh. see Akbeit
Āqchah Afgh. 101 F2
Aq Chai r. Iran 107 F3
'Aqdā Iran 100 C3
Aqdoghmish r. Iran 100 A2
Aqiq Sudan 121 H5
Aqiq, Khalīg b. Sudan 104 B4
'Aqīq, Wādī al watercourse Saudi Arabia 104 C2
Aqitag mt. China 88 E3
Aqköl Akmolinskaya Oblast' Kazakh. see Akkol'
Aqköl Atyrauskaya Oblast' Kazakh. see Akkol'
Aqla well Saudi Arabia 104 B2
Aqmola Kazakh. see Astana
Aqmola Oblast admin. div. Kazakh. see Akmolinskaya Oblast'
Aqmola Oblysy admin. div. Kazakh. see Akmolinskaya Oblast'
Āq Qal'eh Iran 100 C2
formerly known as Pahlavī Dezh
Aqqan China 89 D4
formerly known as Atqan
Aqqikkol Hu salt l. China 89 E4
Aqqystaū Kazakh. see Akkistau
Aqra', Wādī al watercourse Saudi Arabia 109 L7
'Aqraba West Bank 108 G5
'Aqrah Iraq 107 E3
'Aqran hill Saudi Arabia 109 J6
Aqsay Kazakh. see Aksay
Aqsayqin Hit terr. Asia see Aksai Chin
Aqshataū Kazakh. see Akchatau
Aqshī Kazakh. see Akshiy
Aqshuqyr Kazakh. see Akshukur
Aqsū Almatinskaya Oblast' Kazakh. see Aksu
Aqsū Pavlodarskaya Oblast' Kazakh. see Aksu
Aqsū Severnyy Kazakhstan Kazakh. see Aksu
Aqsūat Kazakh. see Aksuat
Aqsū-Ayuly Kazakh. see Aksu-Ayuly
Aqtaū Kazakh. see Aktau
Aqtöbe Kazakh. see Aktobe
Aqtöbe Oblysy admin. div. Kazakh. see Aktyubinskaya Oblast'
Aqtoghay Karagandinskaya Oblast' Kazakh. see Aktogay
Aqtoghay Pavlodarskaya Oblast' Kazakh. see Aktogay
Aquae Grani Germany see Aachen
Aquae Gratianae France see Aix-les-Bains
Aquae Sextiae France see Aix-en-Provence
Aquae Statiellae Italy see Acqui Terme
Aquarius Mountains U.S.A. 183 K7
Aquarius Plateau U.S.A. 183 M4
Aquaviva delle Fonti Italy 56 I8
Aquidabánmi r. Para. 201 F5
Aquidauana Brazil 201 G5
Aquidauana r. Brazil 201 F4
Aquila Mex. 184 E5
Aquilēia Italy 56 F3
UNESCO World Heritage Site
Aquiles Mex. 184 D2
Aquin Haiti 187 E3
Aquincum Hungary see Budapest
Aquiry r. Brazil see Acre
Aquisgranum Germany see Aachen
Aquitaine admin. reg. France 50 F8
Aqzhal Kazakh. see Akzhal
Aqzhar Kazakh. see Akzhar
Aqzhayqyn Köli salt l. Kazakh. see Akzhaykyn, Ozero
Ara India 97 E4
formerly spelt Arrah
Ara r. Spain 55 L2
Āra Ārba Eth. 128 D3
Arab U.S.A. 174 C5
Arab, Bahr el watercourse Sudan 126 F2
'Arab, Khalīj al b. Egypt 121 F2
'Arabābād Iran 100 D3
Ara Bacalle well Eth. 128 D3
'Arabah, Wādī watercourse Egypt 108 D8
'Arabah, Wādī r. Yemen 105 E4
'Arabah, Wādī al watercourse Israel/Jordan 108 G8
also known as Ha 'Arava
Arabelo Venez. 199 E3
Arabian Gulf Asia see The Gulf
Arabian Oryx Sanctuary Saudi Arabia 105 G4
UNESCO World Heritage Site
Arabian Sea Indian Ocean 99 H6
Ara Bonel Eth. 128 D3
Arabopó Venez. 199 F3
Araç Turkey 106 C2
Araça r. Brazil 199 F5
Aracaju Brazil 202 E4
Aracanguy, Montes de hills Para. 201 G6
Aracar, Volcán vol. Arg. 200 D6
Aracati Brazil 202 E3
Aracatu Brazil 202 D5
Araçatuba Brazil 206 C8
Aracena Spain 54 E7
Aracena, Isla i. Chile 205 C9
Aracena, Sierra de hills Spain 54 D7
Arachthos r. Greece 59 C9
also spelt Arakhthos
Aračinovo Macedonia 58 C6
Aracoiaba Brazil 202 E3
Aracruz Brazil 203 D6
Araçuaí Brazil 203 D6
Araçuaí r. Brazil 203 D6
'Arad Israel 108 G6
Arad Romania 58 C2
Arada Chad 120 D6
'Arādah U.A.E. 105 F3
Arādān Iran 100 C3
Aradeib, Wadi watercourse Sudan 120 D6
Arafura Sea Australia/Indon. 144 C2
Aragarças Brazil 206 A2
Aragón aut. comm. Spain 55 K3
UNESCO World Heritage Site
Aragón r. Spain 55 J2
Aragoncillo mt. Spain 55 I4
Aragua state Venez. 199 E2
Araguacema Brazil 202 B4
Araguaçu Brazil 202 B5
Aragua de Barcelona Venez. 199 E2
Aragua de Maturín Venez. 199 F2
Araguaia r. Brazil 206 A3
Araguaia, Parque Nacional de nat. park Brazil 202 B4
Araguaiana Brazil 206 B2
Araguaína Brazil 202 B3
Araguana Brazil 202 B3
Araguao, Boca r. mouth Venez. 199 F2
Araguapiche, Punta pt Venez. 199 F2
Araguari Brazil 206 E5
Araguari r. Amapá Brazil 199 I4
Araguari r. Minas Gerais Brazil 206 E5
Araguatins Brazil 202 B3
Aragvi r. Georgia 107 F2
'Arah, Ra's pt Yemen 104 C5
'Arah, Wādī r. Oman 105 F4
Arai Japan 90 F6
Araiosos Brazil 202 D2
Arak Alg. 123 F4
Arāk Iran 100 B3
formerly known as Sultanabad
Arak Syria 109 J3
Arakai-yama mt. Japan 90 F6
Arakaka Guyana 199 F3
Arakan state Myanmar 78 A3
also known as Rakhaing or Rakhine or Yagaing
Arakan Yoma mts Myanmar 78 A3
Arakhthos r. Greece see Arachthos
Arakkonam India 94 C3
formerly spelt Arkonam
Aral China 88 C3
Aral Kazakh. see Aral'sk
Aral Tajik. see Vose

▶Aral Sea salt l. Kazakh./Uzbek. 102 D3
4th largest lake in Asia. Also known as Aral Tengizi or Orol Dengizi.
▶▶6–7 World Landscapes
▶▶60–61 Asia Landscapes

Aral'sk Kazakh. 103 E3
also known as Aral
Aralsor, Ozero l. Kazakh. 102 B2
Aralsor, Ozero salt l. Kazakh. 102 C2
Aral Tengizi salt l. Kazakh./Uzbek. see Aral Sea
Aramac Australia 149 E4
Aramac Creek watercourse Australia 149 E4
Aramah plat. Saudi Arabia 105 D2
A Ramallosa Spain 54 C2
Aramberri Mex. 185 F3
Arame Brazil 202 C3
Aramia r. P.N.G. 73 J8
Aran r. India 94 C2
Arancibia Arg. 204 C3
Aranda de Duero Spain 55 H3
Arandelovac Srbija Serb. and Mont. 58 B4
Arandis Namibia 130 B4
Arang India 97 D5
Arani India 94 C3
Aran Island Ireland 47 D9
Aran Islands Ireland 47 C10
Aranjuez Spain 55 H4
UNESCO World Heritage Site
Aranos Namibia 130 C5
Aransas Pass U.S.A. 179 C7
Arantangi India 94 C4
Arantes r. Brazil 206 C6
Aranuka atoll Kiribati 145 G1
formerly known as Henderville
Aranyaprathet Thai. 79 C5
Arao Japan 91 B8
Araouane Mali 124 E2
Arapaho U.S.A. 179 C5
Arapahoe U.S.A. 178 C3
Arapari Brazil 199 H5
Arapawa Island N.Z. 152 I9
Arapgir Turkey 107 D3
Arapicos Ecuador 198 B5
Arapiraca Brazil 202 E4
Arapis, Akra pt Greece 59 F8
Arapongas Brazil 206 B10
Araputi Brazil 206 D11
Arapsun Turkey see Gülşehir
Arapuá Brazil 206 A7
Arapuni N.Z. 152 J5
'Ar'ar Saudi Arabia 107 E5
'Ar'ar, Wādī watercourse Iraq/Saudi Arabia 107 E5
Arara r. Brazil 199 F5
Araracuara Col. 198 C5
Araracuara, Cerros de hills Col. 198 C5

Araranguá Brazil 203 B9
Araraquara Brazil 206 E8
Araras Amazonas Brazil 200 C2
Araras Pará Brazil 199 H6
Ararás Brazil 200 D2
Araras São Paulo Brazil 206 F9
Araras, Açude resr Brazil 202 D3
Araras, Serra das hills Brazil 203 A6
Araras, Serra das mts Brazil 203 A8
Ararat Armenia 107 F3
Ararat Australia 147 D4
Ararat, Mount Turkey 107 F3
also known as Ağrı Dağı
Arari Brazil 202 C2
Araria India 97 E4
Araripe Brazil 202 D3
Araripe, Chapada do hills Brazil 202 D3
Araripina Brazil 202 D3
Araruama Brazil 207 K9
Araruama, Lago de lag. Brazil 207 K9
Aras Turkey 107 E3
also known as Velibaba
Aras r. Turkey see **Araz**
Ar-Asgat Mongolia 85 E1
Araṭâne well Mauritania 124 C2
Arataú r. Brazil 202 B2
Aratürük China see **Yiwu**
Arauá r. Brazil 199 F6
Arauá r. Brazil 199 F6
Arauã r. Brazil 200 D2
Arauca Col. 198 D3
Arauca dept Col. 198 D3
Arauca r. Venez. 198 E3
Araucanía admin. reg. Chile 204 B5
Arauco Chile 204 B5
Arauco, Golfo de b. Chile 204 B5
Arauquita Col. 198 D3
Araure Venez. 198 D2
Aravaipa Creek watercourse U.S.A. 183 N9
Aravalli Range mts India 96 B4
Aravete Estonia 42 G2
Araviana r. Spain 55 I3
Aravissos Greece 58 D8
Arawa P.N.G. 145 E2
Arawale National Reserve nature res. Kenya 128 D5
Arawata r. N.Z. see **Arawhata**
Arawhana mt. N.Z. 152 L6
Arawhata r. N.Z. 153 C12
formerly spelt Arawata
Araxá Brazil 206 G6
Araxos, Akra pt Greece 59 C10
Araya, Península de pen. Venez. 199 E2
Arayıt Dağı mt. Turkey 106 B3
Araz r. Azer. 107 G2
also spelt Aras
Arba r. Spain 55 J3
Arbailu Iraq see **Arbīl**
Ārba Minch Eth. 128 C3
Arbela Iraq see **Arbīl**
Arbīl Iraq 107 F3
also known as Hawlēr; also spelt Irbil; historically known as Arbailu or Arbela
Arbīl governorate Iraq 107 E4
Arboga Sweden 45 K4
Arbois France 51 L6
Arboletes Col. 198 B2
Arbon Switz. 51 P5
Arborfield Canada 167 K4
Arborg Canada 167 L5
Arbrå Sweden 45 L3
Arbroath U.K. 46 J7
Arbuckle U.S.A. 182 B2
Arbu Lut, Dasht-e des. Afgh. 101 E4
Arc r. France 51 M7
Arcachon France 50 E8
Arcachon, Bassin d' inlet France 50 E8
Arcadia FL U.S.A. 175 D7
Arcadia LA U.S.A. 179 D5
Arcadia MI U.S.A. 172 G6
Arcadia WI U.S.A. 172 B6
Arcalod, Pointe d' mt. France 51 M7
Arcanum U.S.A. 176 A6
Arcas, Cayos is Mex. 185 H4
Arcata U.S.A. 180 A4
Arc Dome mt. U.S.A. 183 G3
Arcelia Mex. 185 E5
Arc-et-Senans France 51 L6
UNESCO World Heritage Site
Archangel Rus. Fed. 40 G2
also known as Arkhangel'sk; historically known as Novyy Kholmogory
Archangel Oblast admin. div. Rus. Fed. see **Arkhangel'skaya Oblast'**
Archangelos Greece 59 J12
Archar r. Bulg. 58 D5
Archbold U.S.A. 176 A4
Archena Spain 55 J6
Archer r. Australia 149 D2
Archer Bend National Park Australia 149 D2
Archer City U.S.A. 179 C5
Arches National Park U.S.A. 183 O3
Arch Henda well Mali 124 E2
Archidona Spain 54 G7
Archie Creek r. Australia 148 C3
Archipélago de Mingan, Réserve du Parc National de l' nat. park Canada 169 I3
Arci, Monte hill Sardinia Italy 57 A9
Arcipelago de la Maddalena, Parco Nazionale dell' nat. park Sardinia Italy 56 B7
Ärçivan Azer. 107 G3
Arckaringa watercourse Australia 146 B2
Arçman Turkm. 102 D5
Arco Italy 56 C3
Arco U.S.A. 180 D4
Arcola U.S.A. 176 H7
Arconce r. France 51 J6
Arcos Brazil 207 H7
Arcos de Jalón Spain 55 I3
Arcos de la Frontera Spain 54 F8
Arcos de Valdevez Port. 54 C3
Arcot India 94 C3
Arcoverde Brazil 202 E4
Arctic Bay Canada 165 K2
also known as Ikpiarjuk
Arctic Institute Islands Rus. Fed. see **Arkticheskogo Instituta, Ostrova**
►**Arctic Ocean** 224 O1
►►**214–215 Arctic** Features
Arctic Red r. Canada 166 C1
Arctic Red River Canada see **Tsiigehtchic**
Arctowski research station Antarctica 222 U2
long form Henryk Arctowski
Arda r. Bulg. 58 H7
also known as Ardas
Ardabīl Iran 100 B2
Ardabīl prov. Iran 100 A2
Ardahan Turkey 107 E2
Ardāk Iran 101 D2
Ardakān Fārs Iran 100 C4
Ardakān Yazd Iran 100 C3
Ardal Iran 100 B4
Årdal Norway 45 I3
Årdalstangen Norway 45 I3
Ardas r. Greece 58 H7
Arḍ aş Şawwān plain Jordan 109 I7
Ardatov Nizhegorodskaya Oblast' Rus. Fed. 40 G5
Ardatov Respublika Mordoviya Rus. Fed. 40 H5
Ardbeg Canada 173 M5
Ardèche r. France 51 K8
Ardee Ireland 47 F10
Arden, Mount hill Australia 146 C3
Ardennes plat. Belgium 51 K3
also known as L'Ardenne, Plateau de
Ardentes France 50 H6
Arden Town U.S.A. 182 C3
Ardestān Iran 100 C3
Ardglass U.K. 47 G9
Ardila r. Port. 54 D6
Ardino Bulg. 58 G7
Ardkeen N.Z. 152 L6
Ardlethan Australia 147 E3
Ardmore U.S.A. 179 C5
Ardnamurchan, Point of U.K. 46 F7
Ardon Rus. Fed. 107 F2
Ardrossan Australia 146 C3
Ardrossan U.K. 46 H8
Ards Peninsula U.K. 47 G9
Ardvasar U.K. 46 G6
Åre Sweden 44 K3
Areado Brazil 207 G8
Arebi Dem. Rep. Congo 126 F4
Arecibo Puerto Rico 187 G3
Arefino Rus. Fed. 43 U3
Arefu Romania 58 F3
Areguá Para. 201 F6
Areia Branca Brazil 202 E3
Arekhawsk Belarus 43 L7
also spelt Orekhovsk; formerly known as Orekhi-Vydritsa
Arel Belgium see **Arlon**
Arelas France see **Arles**
Arelate France see **Arles**
Arena reef Phil. 74 B4
Arena, Point U.S.A. 182 A3
Arena de la Ventana, Punta pt Mex. 184 C3
Arenal, Campo del plain Arg. 204 D2
Arenal, Puerto del pass Spain 55 I6
Arenal, Volcán vol. Costa Rica 186 B5
Arena Point Phil. 74 B3
Arenápolis Brazil 201 F3
Arenas, Punta de pt Arg. 205 C9
Arenas de San Pedro Spain 54 F4
Arendal Norway 45 J4
Arendsee (Altmark) Germany 48 I3
Arenys de Mar Spain 55 N3
Arenzano Italy 56 A4
Areopoli Greece 59 D12
Areponapuchi Mex. 181 F8
Arequipa Peru 200 C4
UNESCO World Heritage Site
Arequipa dept Peru 200 B3
Arere Brazil 199 H5
Ārēro Eth. 128 C3
Ares mt. Spain 55 K4
Aresa r. Belarus 42 J9
Arévalo Spain 54 G3
Areza Eritrea 104 B5
Arezzaf well Mali see **Aghezzaf**
Arezzo Italy 56 D5
historically known as Arretium
'Arfajah well Saudi Arabia 107 D5
Arfara Greece 59 D11
Arga r. Spain 55 J2
Argadargada Australia 148 C4
Argalant Mongolia 85 F2
Argalasti Greece 59 E9
Argallanes, Sierra de los hills Spain 54 F6
Argan China 88 E3
Arganda del Rey Spain 55 H4
Arganil Port. 54 C4
Argao Phil. 74 B4
Argatay Mongolia 85 E2
Argel Alg. see **Algiers**
Argelès-Gazost France 50 F9
Argelès-sur-Mer France 51 J10
Argens r. France 51 M9
Argenta Italy 56 D4
Argentan France 50 F4
Argentario, Monte hill Italy 56 D6
Argentat France 51 H7
Argentera, Cima dell' mt. Italy 51 N8

►**Argentina** country S. America 204 C4
2nd largest country in South America and 8th in the world. 3rd most populous country in South America. Long form Argentine Republic.
►►**8–9 World** Countries
►►**192–193 South America** Countries

Argentina Range mts Antarctica 223 V1
Argentine Republic country S. America see **Argentina**
Argentino, Lago l. Arg. 205 B8
Argenton r. France 50 F5
Argentoratum France see **Strasbourg**
Argentre France 50 F4
Argeş r. Romania 58 H4
Argeşel r. Romania 58 F4
Arghandab r. Afgh. 101 F4
Arghastan r. Afgh. 101 F4
Argolikos Kolpos b. Greece 59 D11
Argonne U.S.A. 172 E5
Argos Greece 59 D11
Argos U.S.A. 172 G9
Argos Orestiko Greece 59 C8
Argostoli Greece 59 B10
Arguedas Spain 55 J2
►**Argun'** r. China/Rus. Fed. 85 H1
also known as Ergun He
►►**60–61 Asia** Landscapes
Argun r. Georgia/Rus. Fed. 107 F2
Argun Rus. Fed. 107 F2
Argungu Nigeria 125 G3
Argunskiy Khrebet mts Rus. Fed. 85 H1
Argus Range mts U.S.A. 182 G6
Arguut Mongolia 84 D2
Argyle Canada 169 H5
Argyle IA U.S.A. 172 B10
Argyle WI U.S.A. 172 D8
Argyle, Lake Australia 150 E3
Argyrokastron Albania see **Gjirokastër**
Arḩab reg. Yemen 104 D5
Arhangay prov. Mongolia 84 D2
Ar Horqin Qi China see **Tianshan**
Århus Denmark 45 J4
also spelt Aarhus
Aria N.Z. 152 I6
Ariaga i. Indon. 75 C1
Ariake-kai b. Japan 91 B8
Ariamsvlei Namibia 130 C6
Ariano Irpino Italy 56 H7
Arias Arg. 204 E4
Ari Atoll Maldives 93 D10
Ariaú Brazil 199 G5
Aribí r. Venez. 199 F2
Aribinda Burkina 125 E3
Arica Chile 200 C4
Arica Col. 198 D5
Aricagua Venez. 198 D2
Arid, Cape Australia 151 C7
Arida Japan 91 D7
Aridaia Greece 58 D8
Aridal, Sabkhat salt pan W. Sahara 122 B4
Arid Island N.Z. see **Rakitu Island**
Ariège r. France 50 H9
Arieş r. Romania 58 E2
Arieşul Mic r. Romania 58 E2
Arigiyn Gol r. Mongolia 84 D1
Arīḩā Syria 109 H2
Arihā West Bank see **Jericho**
Arikaree r. U.S.A. 178 B3
Arilje Srbija Serb. and Mont. 58 B5
Arimã Brazil 199 F6
Ariminum Italy see **Rimini**
Arimu Mine Guyana 199 G3
'Arīn, Wādī al watercourse Saudi Arabia 104 C4
Arinagour U.K. 46 F7
Arinos Mato Grosso Brazil 201 G3
Arinos Minas Gerais Brazil 202 C5
Arinos r. Brazil 201 F2
Ario de Rosáles Mex. 185 E5
Ariogala Lith. 42 E6
Ariporo r. Col. 198 D3
Aripuanã Brazil 201 F2
Aripuanã r. Brazil 199 F6
Ariquemes Brazil 201 E2
Ariranhá r. Brazil 203 A6
Arisaig U.K. 46 G7
Arisaig, Sound of sea chan. U.K. 46 G7
Arisaru Falls Guyana 199 G3
'Arīsh, Wādī al watercourse Egypt 108 E6
Arismendi Venez. 198 D2
Aristazabal Island Canada 166 D4
Aristizábal, Cabo c. Arg. 205 D7
Aristóbulo del Valle Arg. 201 G6
Aritwala Pak. 101 H4
Arivonimamo Madag. 131 [inset] J3
Arixang China see **Wenquan**
Ariya waterhole Kenya 128 C4
Ariyalur India 94 C4
Arizaro, Salar de salt flat Arg. 200 D6
Arizgoiti Spain 55 I1
Arizona Arg. 204 D4
Arizona state U.S.A. 183 M7
Arizpe Mex. 184 C2
'Arjah Saudi Arabia 104 D2
Årjäng Sweden 45 K4
Arjasa Indon. 77 F4
'Arjāwī, Wādī al watercourse Iraq 109 O5
Arjeplog Sweden 44 L2
Ārjo Eth. 128 C2
Arjona Col. 198 C2
Arjona Spain 54 G7
Arjuni India 96 D5
Arkadak Rus. Fed. 41 G6
Arkadelphia U.S.A. 179 D5
Arkagala Rus. Fed. 39 O3
Arkalgud India 94 C3
Arkalochori Greece 59 G13
Arkalyk Kazakh. 103 F2
also spelt Arqalyq
Arkansas r. U.S.A. 179 E5
Arkansas state U.S.A. 174 A5
Arkansas City AR U.S.A. 175 B5
Arkansas City KS U.S.A. 178 C4
Arkata r. Bulg. 58 D6
Arkatag Shan mts China 89 E4
Arkell, Mount Canada 166 C2
Arkenu, Jabal mt. Libya 120 E4
Arkhangel'sk Rus. Fed. see **Archangel**
Arkhangel'skaya Oblast' admin. div. Rus. Fed. 40 G3
English form Archangel Oblast
Arkhangel'skoye Respublika Bashkortostan Rus. Fed. 40 K5
Arkhangel'skoye Tul'skaya Oblast' Rus. Fed. 43 S8
Arkhara Rus. Fed. 82 C2
Arkhara r. Rus. Fed. 82 C2
Arkhipovka Primorskiy Kray Rus. Fed. 82 D4
Arkhipovka Smolenskaya Oblast' Rus. Fed. 43 M7
Árki i. Greece see **Arkoi**
Arklow Ireland 47 F11
also known as An tInbhear Mór
Arkoi i. Greece 59 H11
also known as Árki
Arkona Canada 173 L7
Arkona, Kap c. Germany 49 K1
Arkonam India see **Arakkonam**
Arkösund Sweden 45 L4
►**Arkticheskiy, Mys** c. Rus. Fed. 224 G1
►►**60–61 Asia** Landscapes

►**Arkticheskiy, Mys** is Rus. Fed. 39 J1
Most northerly point of Asia.

Arkticheskogo Instituta, Ostrova is Rus. Fed. 39 I2
English form Arctic Institute Islands
Arkul' Rus. Fed. 40 I4
Ärla Sweden 45 L4
Arlanc France 51 J7
Arlandag mt. Turkm. 102 C5
Arlanza r. Spain 55 G2
Arlanzón r. Spain 54 G2
Arles France 51 K9
historically known as Arelas or Arelate
UNESCO World Heritage Site
Arli Burkina 125 F4
Arli, Parc National de l' nat. park Burkina 125 F4
Arli, Réserve Partielle de l' nature res. Burkina 125 F4
Arlington IA U.S.A. 172 B8
Arlington IL U.S.A. 172 D9
Arlington NY U.S.A. 177 L4
Arlington OH U.S.A. 176 B5
Arlington OR U.S.A. 180 B3
Arlington VA U.S.A. 177 H7
Arlington WI U.S.A. 172 D7
Arlington Heights U.S.A. 174 B3
Arlit Niger 125 G2
Arlon Belgium 51 L3
also known as Arel; also spelt Aarlen
Arltunga Australia 148 B4
Arlyeya Belarus 43 K6
Arm r. Canada 167 J5
Armadale Australia 151 A7
Armadores i. Indon. 75 C1
Armageddon tourist site Israel see **Tel Megiddo**
Armagh U.K. 47 F9
Armah, Wādī r. Yemen 105 E4
Armançon r. France 51 J5
Armando Bermudez nat. park Dom. Rep. 187 F3
Armant Egypt 121 G3
historically known as Hermonthis
Armathia i. Greece 59 H13
Armavir Armenia 107 F2
formerly spelt Oktemberyan
Armavir Rus. Fed. 41 G7
►**Armenia** country Asia 107 F2
known as Haikakan in Armenian; formerly known as Armyanskaya S.S.R.; historically known as Urartu
►►**64–65 Asia** Countries
Armenia Col. 198 C3
Armenistis, Akra pt Greece 59 I12
Armenki Rus. Fed. 43 V4
Armenopolis Romania see **Gherla**
Armeria Mex. 184 E5
Armi, Capo dell' c. Italy 57 H11
Armidale Australia 147 F2
Armit Lake Canada 167 N1
Armona U.S.A. 182 E5
Armori India 94 D1
Armorique, Parc Régional d' park France 50 C4
Armour U.S.A. 178 C3
Armstrong Arg. 204 E4
Armstrong r. Australia 148 A3
Armstrong B.C. Canada 166 G5
Armstrong Ont. Canada 168 B3
Armstrong, Mount Canada 166 C2
Armstrong Island Cook Is see **Rarotonga**
Armu r. Rus. Fed. 82 E3
Armur India 94 C2
Armutçuk Dağı mts Turkey 106 A3
Armutlu Turkey 58 J8
Armutova Turkey see **Gömeç**
Armyans'k Ukr. 41 E7
Armyanskaya S.S.R. country Asia see **Armenia**
Arnå r. Denmark 48 F1
Arna Greece 59 D12
Árnafjall hill Faroe Is 46 E1
Arnage France 50 G5
Arnaia Greece 58 E8
Arnaoutis, Cape Cyprus see **Arnauti, Cape**
Arnarfjörður inlet Iceland 44 [inset] A2
Arnaud r. Canada 169 G1
Arnauti, Cape Cyprus 108 D2
also known as Akama, Akra; also spelt Arnaoutis, Cape
Arnavutköy Turkey 58 J7
Arnay-le-Duc France 51 K5
Arnedo Spain 55 I2
Arneiroz Brazil 202 D3
Arnemark Sweden 44 M2
Årnes Norway 45 J3
Arnett U.S.A. 179 C4
Arnhem Neth. 48 C4
Arnhem, Cape Australia 148 C2
Arnhem Land reg. Australia 148 B2
Arnhem Land Aboriginal Land res. Australia 148 B2
Arnionys 1 Lith. 42 G6
Arnisdale U.K. 46 G6
Arnissa Greece 58 C8
Arno r. Italy 56 C5
Arno Bay Australia 146 C3
Arnoia r. Spain 54 C2
also spelt Arnoya
Arnold MD U.S.A. 177 I6
Arnold MI U.S.A. 172 F4
Arnold MO U.S.A. 174 B4
Arnold's Cove Canada 169 K4
Arnoldstein Austria 49 K9
Arnon r. France 51 I5
Arnon r. Jordan see **Mawjib, Wādī al**
Arnoux, Lac l. Canada 173 N2
Arnøya i. Norway 44 M1
Arnoya r. Spain see **Arnoia**
Arnprior Canada 168 E4
Arnsberg Germany 48 F4
Arnstadt Germany 48 H5
Arnstein Canada 173 N5
Arnstorf Germany 49 J7
Arntfield Canada 173 N2
Aro r. Venez. 199 E3
Aroab Namibia 130 C5
Aroania mt. Greece 59 D11
Aroeira Brazil 203 A7
Aroland Canada 168 C3
Arolsen Germany 48 G4
Aroma Sudan 104 B5
Aromas U.S.A. 182 C5
Aron r. France 51 J6
Aron India 96 C4
Arona Italy 56 A3
Arorae i. Kiribati 145 G2
also spelt Arore; formerly known as Hurd Island
Arore i. Kiribati see **Arorae**
Aroroy Phil. 74 B3
Aros r. Mex. 184 C2
Arosa, Ría de est. Spain see **Arousa, Ría de**
Arossi i. Solomon Is see **San Cristobal**
Arouca Port. 54 C4
Arouelli well Chad 120 D5
Arousa, Ría de est. Spain 54 B2
also spelt Arosa, Ría de
Arpa r. Armenia/Turkey 107 E2
Arpaçay Turkey 107 E2
Arpaçsakarlar Turkey 108 F1
Arpajon-sur-Cère France 51 I8
Arqalyq Kazakh. see **Arkalyk**
Arquata del Tronto Italy 56 F6
Arquipélago dos Açores terr. N. Atlantic Ocean see **Arquipélago dos Açores**

►**Arquipélago dos Açores** aut. reg. Port. 54 [inset]
Autonomous Region of Portugal. English form Azores.
►►**32–33 Europe** Countries

Arra r. Pak. 101 F5
Arrábida, Parque Natural da nature res. Port. 54 C6
Arrabury Australia 149 D5
Ar Radīsīyah Baḩrī Egypt 121 G3
Arrah Côte d'Ivoire 124 E5
Arrah India see **Ara**
Ar Raḩá hill Saudi Arabia 109 K7
Ar Raḩḩālīyah Iraq 107 E4
Ar Rāhidah Yemen 104 D5
Arraias r. Brazil 202 A4
Arraias, Serra de hills Brazil 202 C5
Arraiolos Port. 54 D6
Ar Ramādī Iraq 107 E4
also known as Ramādī
Ar Ramthā Jordan 108 H5
Arran i. U.K. 46 G8
Ar Raqqah Syria 109 K2
also spelt Raqqa; historically known as Nicephorium
Ar Raqqah governorate Syria 109 J1
Arraro well Eth. 128 D3
Arras France 51 I2
historically known as Nemetocenna
Ar Ra's al Abyaḑ pt Saudi Arabia 104 B3
Arrasate Spain 55 I1
also known as Mondragón
Ar Rāshidīyah Iraq 109 P4
Ar Rass Saudi Arabia 104 C2
Arrats r. France 50 G8
Ar Rawḑ well Saudi Arabia 107 E5
Ar Rawḑah Egypt 108 B8
Ar Rawḑah Saudi Arabia 104 C3
Ar Rawḑah Yemen 105 D5
Ar Rāwuk Yemen 105 E5
Ar Rayḩānī Oman 105 F3
Ar Rayn Saudi Arabia 105 D3
Ar Rayyān Qatar 105 E2
Arrecifal Col. 198 D4
Arrecife Canary Is 122 B3
Arrecifes Arg. 204 E4
Arrée, Monts d' hills France 50 B4
Arretium Italy see **Arezzo**
Arriagá Mex. 185 G5
Arriaga Mex. 185 E4
Arribeños Arg. 204 E4
Ar Rifā'ī Iraq 107 F5
Ar Rihāb salt flat Iraq 107 F5
Ar Rimāl des. Saudi Arabia 105 F3
Arrington U.S.A. 176 G8
Ar Riyāḑ Saudi Arabia see **Riyadh**
Ar Riyāḑ prov. Saudi Arabia 104 D2
Arroio Grande Brazil 204 G4
Arronches Port. 54 D5
Arros r. France 50 F9
Arroux r. France 51 J6
Arrow r. Canada 172 D2
Arrow, Lough l. Ireland 47 D9
Arrow Creek r. U.S.A. 180 E3
Arrow Lake Canada 172 C2
Arrowsmith, Mount N.Z. 153 E11
Arrowtown N.Z. 153 C12
Arroyo de la Luz Spain 54 E5
Arroyo Grande U.S.A. 182 D6
Arroyo Seco Mex. 185 F4
UNESCO World Heritage Site
Ar Rubay'iyah Saudi Arabia 104 D2
Arruda Brazil 201 F3
Ar Rumādīyat Saudi Arabia 104 C2
Ar Rumaythah Bahrain 105 E2
Ar Rumaythah Iraq 107 F5
Ar Rummānah Iraq 109 M3
Ar Ruq'ī well Saudi Arabia 105 D1
Ar Ruşāfah Syria 109 J2
Ar Ruşayfah Jordan 108 H5
Ar Rustāq Oman 105 G3
Ar Ruţbah Iraq 107 E4
Ar Ruwaybāt well Libya 120 C3
Ar Ruwayḑah Saudi Arabia 104 D3
Arruwurra Aboriginal Land res. Australia 148 C4
Ars Iran 100 A2
Arsaköy Turkey 59 K12
Ärsarybaba Erezi hills Turkm. 102 C4
also known as Irsarybaba, Gory
Arsenajān Iran 100 C4
Arseno Lake Canada 167 H1
Arsen'yev Rus. Fed. 82 D3
Arsen'yevo Rus. Fed. 43 R8
Arshaly Kazakh. 103 H2
Arshanskaye Wzvyshsha hills Belarus 43 K7
Arsikere India 94 C3
Arsk Rus. Fed. 40 I4
Arslanköy Turkey 108 F1
Arta Greece 59 B9
Artashat Armenia 107 F3
formerly known as Kamarlu
Arteaga Coahuila Mex. 185 E3
Arteaga Michoacán Mex. 185 E5
Artem Rus. Fed. 82 D4
Artemisa Cuba 186 C2
Artemivs'k Ukr. 41 F6
also spelt Artemovsk; formerly known as Bakhmut
Artemovsk Ukr. see **Artemivs'k**
Artemovskiy Irkutskaya Oblast' Rus. Fed. 39 L4
Artemovskiy Primorskiy Kray Rus. Fed. 82 D4
Artenay France 51 H4
Artesa de Segre Spain 55 M3
Artesia AZ U.S.A. 183 O9
Artesia NM U.S.A. 181 F6
Arthur Canada 173 M7
Arthur NE U.S.A. 178 B3
Arthur TN U.S.A. 176 B9
Arthur, Lake S. Africa 133 J9
Arthur, Lake U.S.A. 176 E5
Arthur Lake Australia 147 E5
Arthur Pieman Protected Area nature res. Australia 147 E5
Arthur's Pass N.Z. 153 F10
Arthur's Pass National Park N.Z. 153 F10
Arthur's Town Bahamas 186 E1
Artigas research station Antarctica 222 U2
Artigas Uruguay 204 F3
Art'ik Armenia 107 E2
Artillery Lake Canada 167 I2
Artisia Botswana 131 E5
Artjärvi Fin. 42 H1
Artos Dağı mt. Turkey 107 E3
Artova Turkey 107 D2
Artrutx, Cap d' c. Spain 55 O5
Artsakh aut. reg. Azer. see **Dağlıq Qarabağ**
Arts Bogd Uul mts Mongolia 84 D2
Artsiz Ukr. see **Artsyz**
Artsyz Ukr. 41 D7
also spelt Artsiz
Artur de Paiva Angola see **Kuvango**
Artux China 88 B4
Artvin Turkey 107 E2
also known as Çoruh
Artyk Turkm. 102 D5
Aru Dem. Rep. Congo 126 F4
Aru, Kepulauan is Indon. 73 H8
Arua Uganda 128 A4
Aruajá Brazil 199 E6
Aruanã Brazil 206 B1

►**Aruba** terr. West Indies 198 D1
Self-governing Netherlands Territory.
►►**158–159 North America** Countries

Arudy France 50 F9
Arumã Brazil 199 F6
Arun r. Nepal 97 E4
Arunachal Pradesh state India 97 G4
formerly known as North-East Frontier Agency
Arun Gol r. China 85 J2
Arun Qi China see **Naji**
Aruppukkottai India 94 C4
Arus, Tanjung pt Indon. 75 B2
Arusha Tanz. 128 C5
Arusha admin. reg. Tanz. 129 C5
Arusha National Park Tanz. 128 C5
Arut r. Indon. 77 E3
Aruti Brazil 199 E5
Aruwimi r. Dem. Rep. Congo 126 D4
Arvada U.S.A. 180 F5
Arvayheer Mongolia 84 D2
Arvi India 94 C1
Arviat Canada 167 M2
formerly known as Eskimo Point
Arvidsjaur Sweden 44 L2
Arvika Sweden 45 K4
Årviksand Norway 44 M1
Arvin U.S.A. 182 F6
Arvonia U.S.A. 176 G8
Arwā' Saudi Arabia 104 D3
Arwād i. Syria 108 G3
Arwala Indon. 75 C4
Arxan China 85 H2
Aryanah Tunisia see **L'Ariana**
Arykbalyk Kazakh. 103 G1
also spelt Aryqbayq
Aryqbayq Kazakh. see **Arykbalyk**
Arys' Kazakh. 103 G4
Arys' r. Kazakh. 103 G4
Arys, Ozero salt l. Kazakh. 103 F3
Aryskannyg-Aryg Rus. Fed. 88 E1
Arzamas Rus. Fed. 40 G5
Arzanah i. U.A.E. 105 F2
Arzew Alg. 123 E2
Arzew, Golfe d' g. Alg. 55 K9
Arzgir Rus. Fed. 41 H7
Arzila Morocco see **Asilah**
Arzúa Spain 54 C2
Arzubikha Rus. Fed. 43 V1
Aš Czech Rep. 49 J5
Asa waterhole Kenya 128 C5
Åsa Sweden 45 K4
Asab Namibia 132 B2
Asaba Nigeria 125 G5
Asad, Buḩayrat al resr Syria 109 J1
Asadābād Afgh. 101 G3
Asadābād Hamadān Iran 100 B3
Asadābād Khorāsan Iran 101 D3
'Aşāfīr, Birkat al waterhole Saudi Arabia 109 O8
Asagny, Parc National d' nat. park Côte d'Ivoire 124 D5
Asahan r. Indon. 76 B2
Asahi Chiba Japan 91 G7
Asahi Toyama Japan 91 E6
Asahi-dake mt. Japan 90 F5
Asahi-dake vol. Japan 90 H3
Asahi-gawa r. Japan 91 C7
Asahikawa Japan 90 H3
Asaka Uzbek. 103 H4
also spelt Assake; formerly known as Leninsk
Āsalē l. Eth. 128 D1
Asālem Iran 100 B2
'Asalū, Chāh-e well Iran 100 C4
Asama-yama vol. Japan 91 F6
Asankranguaa Ghana 124 E5
Asan-man b. S. Korea 83 B5
Asansol India 97 E5
Asanwenso Ghana 124 E5
Āsayita Eth. 128 D2
Asbestos Hill Canada see **Purtuniq**
Asbestos Mountains S. Africa 132 G6
Āsbe Teferi Eth. 128 D2
Asbury Park U.S.A. 177 K5
Ascalon Israel see **Ashqelon**
Ascea Italy 57 H8
Ascensión Bol. 201 E3
Ascensión Chihuahua Mex. 184 D2
Ascensión Nuevo León Mex. 185 F3
Ascension atoll Micronesia see **Pohnpei**

►**Ascension** i. S. Atlantic Ocean 216 N6
Dependency of St Helena.

Ascensión, Bahía de la b. Mex. 185 I5
Aschaffenburg Germany 48 G6
Ascheberg Germany 48 E4
Aschersleben Germany 48 I4
Asciano Italy 56 D5
Ascoli Piceno Italy 56 F6
historically known as Asculum or Asculum Picenum
Ascoli Satriano Italy 56 H7
historically known as Ausculum or Ausculum Apulum
Ascotán Chile 200 C5
Ascotán, Salar de salt flat Chile 200 C5
Asculum Italy see **Ascoli Piceno**
Asculum Picenum Italy see **Ascoli Piceno**
Ascutney U.S.A. 177 M2
Åse Norway 44 K1
Āseb Eritrea see **Assab**
Asedjrad plat. Alg. 123 F4
Āsela Eth. 128 C3
Åsele Sweden 44 L2
Āsendabo Eth. 128 C3
Asenovgrad Bulg. 58 F6
Åseral Norway 45 I4
Aseri Estonia 42 H2
A Serra de Outes Spain 54 C2
Aşfāk Iran 100 D3
Aşfar, Jabal al mt. Jordan 109 H5
Aşfar, Tall al hill Saudi Arabia 109 M7
Aşfar, Tall al hill Syria 109 H4

►**Aşgabat** Turkm. 102 D5
Capital of Turkmenistan. Formerly spelt Ashkhabad; historically known as Poltoratsk.

Ásgarður Iceland 44 [inset] B2
Asha Rus. Fed. 40 K5
Ashanti admin. reg. Ghana 125 E5
Asharat Saudi Arabia 105 D2
Ashbourne U.K. 47 K10
Ashburn U.S.A. 175 D6
Ashburton watercourse Australia 150 A4
Ashburton N.Z. 153 F11
Ashburton r. N.Z. 153 F12
also known as Hakatere
Ashburton Bay Canada 172 G2
Ashburton Range hills Australia 148 B3
Ashchikol', Ozero salt l. Kazakh. 103 F3
Ashchikol', Ozero salt l. Kazakh. 103 G4
Ashchysay Kazakh. see **Achisay**
Ashcroft Canada 166 F5
Ashdod Israel 108 F6
historically known as Azotus
Ashdown U.S.A. 179 D5
Asheboro U.S.A. 174 E5
Ashern Canada 167 L5
Asheville U.S.A. 174 D5
Ashevo Rus. Fed. 43 K4
Asheweig r. Canada 168 C2
Ashford Australia 147 F2
Ashford U.K. 47 M12
Ash Fork U.S.A. 183 L6
Ashhurst N.Z. 152 J8
Ashibetsu Japan 90 H3
Ashikaga Japan 91 F6
Ashington U.K. 47 K8
Ashiro Japan 90 G4
Ashizuri-misaki pt Japan 91 C8
Ashizuri-Uwakai National Park Japan 83 D6
Ashkazar Iran 100 C4
Ashkelon Israel see **Ashqelon**
Ashkhabad Turkm. see **Aşgabat**
Ashkhabadskaya Oblast' admin. div. Turkm. see **Akhal'skaya Oblast'**
Ashkīdah Libya 120 B3
Ashkum U.S.A. 172 F10
Ashkun reg. Afgh. 101 G3
Ashland AL U.S.A. 175 C5
Ashland KS U.S.A. 178 C4
Ashland KY U.S.A. 176 C7
Ashland NE U.S.A. 178 C3
Ashland NH U.S.A. 177 N2
Ashland OH U.S.A. 176 C5
Ashland OR U.S.A. 180 B4
Ashland VA U.S.A. 176 H8
Ashland WI U.S.A. 172 C4
Ashland City U.S.A. 174 C4
Ashley r. N.Z. 153 G11
also known as Rakahuri
Ashley IN U.S.A. 173 H9
Ashley MI U.S.A. 173 I7
Ashley ND U.S.A. 178 C2
Ashley OH U.S.A. 176 C5

►**Ashmore and Cartier Islands** terr. Australia 144 B3
Australian External Territory.
►►**138–139 Oceania** Countries

Ashmore Reef reef Australia 150 C2
Ashmūn Egypt 108 B7
Ashmyanskaye Wzvyshsha hills Belarus 42 G7
Ashmyany Belarus 42 G7
also spelt Oshmyany
Ashmyany Belarus 42 H7
Ashoknagar India 96 C4
Ashoro Japan 90 H3
Ashqar, Barqā al reg. Yemen 105 D4
Ashqelon Israel 108 F6
also spelt Ashkelon; historically known as Ascalon
Ash Sha'ār Saudi Arabia 104 C4
Ash Shabakah Iraq 107 E5
Ash Shabb well Egypt 121 F4
Ash Shabrūm waterhole Saudi Arabia 109 O7
Ash Shaddādah Syria 109 L1
Ash Shafa Saudi Arabia 104 C3
Ash Shā'ib hill Egypt 108 B8
Ash Shakk Iraq 109 O2
Ash Sham Syria see **Damascus**
Ash Sha'm U.A.E. 105 G2
Ash Shanāfīyah Iraq 107 F5
also spelt Shināfīyah
Ash Shaqīq well Saudi Arabia 107 E5
Ash Sha'rā' Saudi Arabia 104 D2
Ash Sharāh mts Jordan 108 G7
Ash Sharawrah Saudi Arabia 105 D4
Ash Shāriqah U.A.E. see **Sharjah**
Ash Sharqāţ Iraq 107 E4
also spelt Sharqat; historically known as Ashur
UNESCO World Heritage Site
Ash Sharqīyah governorate Egypt 108 C7
Ash Sharqīyah admin. reg. Oman 105 G3
Ash Sharqīyah reg. Oman 105 G3
Ash Sharqīyah prov. Saudi Arabia 105 E3
Ash Shaţrah Iraq 107 F5
Ash Shawbak Jordan 108 G7
also spelt Shaubak
Ash Shawr hill Iraq 109 L4
Ash Shaykh 'Uthman Yemen 104 D5
English form Sheikh Othman
Ash Shiblīyāt hill Saudi Arabia 109 I8
Ash Shiḩr Yemen 105 E5
Ash Şhināş Oman 105 G2
Ash Shişar well Oman 105 F4
Ash Shu'āybah Saudi Arabia 104 C2
Ash Shu'bah Saudi Arabia 104 D1
Ash Shubaykīyah Saudi Arabia 104 C2
Ash Shuhadā' Egypt 108 B7
Ash Shumlūl Saudi Arabia 105 D2
Ash Shuqayq Saudi Arabia 104 C4
Ash Shurayf Saudi Arabia see **Khaybar**
Ash Shuwayḩiţīyah waterhole Saudi Arabia 109 L7
Ash Shuwayrif Libya 120 B2
Ashta Madhya Pradesh India 96 C5
Ashta Maharashtra India 94 B2
Ashtabula U.S.A. 176 E4

Ashtarak Armenia 107 F2
Ashti *Maharashtra* India 94 B2
Ashti *Maharashtra* India 94 C2
Ashti *Maharashtra* India 96 C5
Ashton S. Africa 132 E10
Ashton *ID* U.S.A. 180 E3
Ashton *IL* U.S.A. 172 D9
Ashuanipi *r.* Canada 169 H2
Ashuanipi Lake Canada 169 H2
Ashuapmushuan *r.* Canada 174 F1
formerly known as Chamouchouane
Ashuapmushuan, Réserve Faunique *nature res.* Canada 169 F3
Ashur Iraq *see* **Ash Sharqāţ**
Ashville *AL* U.S.A. 175 C5
Ashville *ME* U.S.A. 177 Q1
Ashville *PA* U.S.A. 176 G5
Ashwabay, Mount *hill* U.S.A. 172 C4
Ashwaubenon U.S.A. 172 E6
'Āşī *r.* Lebanon/Syria *see* **Orontes**
'Āşī, Nahr al *r.* Asia *see* **Orontes**
Asid Gulf Phil. 74 B3
Asientos Mex. 185 E4
Asifabad India 94 C2
Asika India 95 E2
Asikkala Fin. 45 N3
Asilah Morocco 54 E9
formerly spelt Arzila
Asillo Peru 200 C3
Asimi Greece 59 G13
Asinara, Golfo dell' *b. Sardinia* Italy 56 A8
Asinara, Isola *i. Sardinia* Italy 56 A7
Asind India 96 B4
Asino Rus. Fed. 39 I4
Asintorf Belarus 43 L7
Asipovichy Belarus 43 J8
also spelt Osipovichi
'Asīr *prov.* Saudi Arabia 104 C3
'Asīr *reg.* Saudi Arabia 104 C3
Asisium Italy *see* **Assisi**
Askainen Fin. 42 C1
Aşkale Turkey 107 E3
Askarovo Rus. Fed. 102 D1
Asker Norway 45 J4
Askersund Sweden 45 K4
Askim Norway 45 J4
Askino Rus. Fed. 40 K4
Askio *mt.* Greece 59 C8
Askira Nigeria 125 I4
Askival *hill* U.K. 46 F7
Askiz Rus. Fed. 80 E2
Askola Fin. 45 N3
Askol'd, Ostrov *i.* Rus. Fed. 90 C3
Askot India 96 D3
Askvoll Norway 45 I3
Aslam, Wādī *watercourse* Saudi Arabia 104 D3
Aşlāndūz Iran 100 A2
Aslanköy *r.* Turkey 108 F1
Aslik *r.* Belarus 43 K8
Aslóközpont Hungary *see* **Mórahalom**
Asmar Afgh. 96 A2
Asmar *reg.* Afgh. 101 G3
Asmar *reg.* Saudi Arabia 104 C4

►**Asmara** Eritrea 121 H6
Capital of Eritrea. Also spelt Āsmera.

Āsmera Eritrea *see* **Asmara**
Åsnen *l.* Sweden 45 K4
As Neves Spain 54 C2
also spelt Nieves
Asoenangka Brazil 199 G4
Aso-Kuju National Park Japan 91 B8
Asola Italy 56 C3
Asopos *r.* Greece 59 D11
Asopos *r.* Greece 59 E10
Āsosa Eth. 128 B2
Asoteriba, Jebel *mt.* Sudan 121 H4
Asotin U.S.A. 180 C3
Aspang-Markt Austria 49 N8
Aspara Kazakh. 103 H4
Asparukhovo Bulg. 58 I6
Aspås Sweden 44 K3
Aspe Spain 55 K6
Aspeå Sweden 44 L3
Aspen U.S.A. 180 F5
Aspermont U.S.A. 179 B5
Aspiring, Mount N.Z. 153 C12
also known as Tititea
As Pontes de García Rodríguez Spain 54 D1
also spelt Puentes de García Rodríguez
Aspro, Cape Cyprus 108 D3
also known as Aspron, Cape
Asprokavos, Akra *pt* Greece 59 B9
Aspromonte, Parco Nazionale dell' *nat. park* Italy 57 H10
Aspron, Cape Cyprus *see* **Aspro, Cape**
Asprovalta Greece 58 E8
Aspur India 96 B5
Asquith Canada 167 J4
Assa Morocco 122 C3
As Sa'an Syria 109 I2
Assab Eritrea 121 I6
also spelt Āseb
Assaba *admin. reg.* Mauritania 124 C2
Aš Sab'ān Saudi Arabia 104 C2
As Sabkhah Syria 109 K2
As Sabsab *well* Saudi Arabia 105 E2
Assabu Japan 90 G4
Aş Şafā *lava field* Syria 109 H4
Aş Şafāqīs Tunisia *see* **Sfax**
Aş Şaff Egypt 121 F2
Aş Şāfī Jordan 108 G6
also spelt Safi
As Safīrah Syria 109 I1
Aş Şahāf Saudi Arabia 105 E2
Aş Şahīf Yemen 104 C5
Aş Şahn *hills* Iraq/Saudi Arabia 109 N7
Aş Şaḩrā' al Gharbīyah *des.* Egypt *see* **Western Desert**
Aş Şaḩrā' ash Sharqīyah *des.* Egypt *see* **Eastern Desert**
Assake Uzbek. *see* **Asaka**
Assake-Audan, Vpadina *depr.* Uzbek. 102 D4
'Assal, Lac *l.* Djibouti *see* **Assal, Lake**

►**Assal, Lake** Djibouti 128 D2
Lowest point in Africa. Also known as 'Assal, Lac.
►►110–111 **Africa** Landscapes

As Salamiyah Saudi Arabia 105 D2
Aş Şāliḩīyah Egypt 108 D7
Aş Şāliḩīyah Syria 109 L3
also known as Dura Europos
As Sallūm Egypt 106 A5
As Salmān Iraq 107 F5
As Salţ Jordan 108 G5
also known as Salt
Assam *state* India 97 F4
Assamakka Niger 125 G2
As Samāwah Iraq 107 F5
Aş Şanām *reg.* Saudi Arabia 105 E3
Assaq *watercourse* W. Sahara 122 B4
As Sarīr *reg.* Libya 120 D3
Assateague Island National Seashore *nature res.* U.S.A. 177 J8
As Sawādah *reg.* Saudi Arabia 105 D3
As Sawdā *i.* Oman 105 F4
Aş Şawrah Saudi Arabia 104 A2
As Saybīyah *waterhole* Saudi Arabia 109 M9
Assegaaibos S. Africa 133 I10
Assemini *Sardinia* Italy 57 B9
Assen Neth. 48 D2
Assen S. Africa 133 L2
Assens Denmark 45 J5
Assesse Belgium 51 L2

As Sidrah Libya 120 C2
Assigny, Lac *l.* Canada 169 H2
As Sikak Saudi Arabia 105 E2
Assiniboia Canada 167 J5
Assiniboine *r.* Canada 167 L5
Assiniboine, Mount Canada 167 H5
Assinica, Lac *l.* Canada 168 F3
Assinica, Réserve Faunique *nature res.* Canada 169 F3
Assis Brazil 206 C9
Assisi Italy 56 E5
historically known as Asisium
UNESCO World Heritage Site
Assomada Cape Verde 124 [inset]
Assouf Mellene *watercourse* Alg. 123 F4
Aş Şubayḩīyah Kuwait 107 F5
As Subaykhah Saudi Arabia 104 C4
As Sufāl Yemen 105 E5
Aş Şufayrī *well* Saudi Arabia 105 D1
As Sukhnah Syria 109 J3
As Sulaymānīyah Iraq 107 F4
also known as Sulaymānīyah
As Sulaymānīyah *governorate* Iraq 107 F4
As Sulaymī Saudi Arabia 104 C2
As Sulayyil Saudi Arabia 105 D3
Aş Şulb *reg.* Saudi Arabia 105 E2
As Sulţān Libya 120 C2
Aş Şummān *plat.* Saudi Arabia 105 D2
Aş Şummān *plat.* Saudi Arabia 105 E3
As Sūq Saudi Arabia 104 C3
As Sūrīyah *country* Asia *see* **Syria**
Aş Şuwar Syria 109 L2
As Suwaydā' Syria 109 H5
As Suwaydā' *governorate* Syria 109 H5
As Suwayḩ Oman 105 G3
As Suwayq Oman 105 G3
Aş Şuwayrah Iraq 107 F4
As Suwayriqīyah Saudi Arabia 104 C3
As Suways Egypt *see* **Suez**
As Suways *governorate* Egypt 108 C8
As Suwwādīyah Yemen 105 D5
Asta *r.* Norway 45 J3
Asta, Cima d' *mt.* Italy 56 D2
Astacus Turkey *see* **İzmit**
Astaffort France 50 G8
Astakida *i.* Greece 59 H13
Astakos Greece 59 C10
Astalu Island Pak. *see* **Astola Island**

►**Astana** Kazakh. 103 G2
Capital of Kazakhstan. Formerly known as Akmola or Aqmola or Akmolinsk or Tselinograd.

Astaneh Iran 100 B2
Astara Azer. 107 G3
Åsteby Sweden 45 K3
Asterabad Iran *see* **Gorgān**
Asti Italy 56 A4
Astica Arg. 204 D3
Astillero Peru 200 C3
Astin Tag *mts* China *see* **Altun Shan**
Astipálaia *i.* Greece *see* **Astypalaia**
Astola Island Pak. 101 E5
also spelt Astalu Island
Aston Bay S. Africa 133 I11
Astor Jammu and Kashmir 96 B2
Astor *r.* Pak. 101 H3
Astorga Brazil 206 B10
Astorga Spain 54 E2
historically known as Asturica Augusta
Astoria U.S.A. 180 B3
Astra Arg. 205 D7
Astrabad Iran *see* **Gorgān**
Astrakhan' Kazakh. *see* **Astrakhanka**
Astrakhan' Rus. Fed. 102 B3
Astrakhan' Bazar Azer. *see* **Cälilabad**
Astrakhanka Kazakh. 103 G2
also known as Astrakhan'
Astrakhan Oblast *admin. div.* Rus. Fed. *see* **Astrakhanskaya Oblast'**
Astrakhanskaya Oblast' *admin. div.* Rus. Fed. 102 A3
English form Astrakhan Oblast
Astravyets Belarus 42 G7
Astrida Rwanda *see* **Butare**
Astrolabe, Récifs de l' *reef* New Caledonia 145 F3
Astros Greece 59 D11
Astryna Belarus 42 F8
Astsyer *r.* Belarus 43 M8
Asturias *aut. comm.* Spain 54 E1
Asturica Augusta Spain *see* **Astorga**
Astypalaia Greece 59 H12
Astypalaia *i.* Greece 59 H12
also known as Astipálaia; *formerly known as* Stampalia
Asubulak Kazakh. 88 C1
also spelt Asūbulaq
Asūbulaq Kazakh. *see* **Asubulak**
Asunción Bol. 200 D2
Asunción *r.* Mex. 181 D7
Asuncion *i.* N. Mariana Is 73 K3

►**Asunción** Para. 201 F6
Capital of Paraguay.

Asunción Mita Guat. 185 H6
Asvyeya Belarus 42 J5
Asvyeyskaye, Vozyera *l.* Belarus 42 J5
Aswa *r.* Uganda 128 A4
Aswad Oman 105 G2
Aswad, Ar Ra's al *pt* Saudi Arabia 104 B3
Aswad, Wādī *watercourse* Oman 105 F3
Aswān Egypt 121 G3
Aswān *governorate* Egypt 104 A2
Aswan Dam Egypt 121 G3
Asyūţ Egypt 121 F3
historically known as Lycopolis
Asyūţ *governorate* Egypt 106 B6
Ata *i.* Tonga 145 H4
formerly known as Sola
Atabapo *r.* Col./Venez. 199 E3
Atabay Kazakh. 103 G4
Atacama *admin. reg.* Chile 204 C2
Atacama, Desierto de *des.* Chile *see* **Atacama Desert**
Atacama, Puna de *plat.* Arg. 204 D2
Atacama, Salar de *salt flat* Chile 200 C5

►**Atacama Desert** Chile 204 C2
Driest place in the world. Also known as Atacama, Desierto de.
►►12–13 **World** Climate and Weather
►►188–189 **South America** Landscapes

Atacames Ecuador 198 B4
Ataco Col. 198 C4
Atafaitafa, Djebel *mt.* Alg. 123 G4
Atafu *atoll* Tokelau 145 H2
formerly known as Duke of York
Atakent Kazakh. 103 G4
Atakent Turkey 108 F1
Atakor *mts* Alg. 123 G5
Atakpamé Togo 125 F5
Atalaia Brazil 202 F4
Atalaia *hill* Port. 54 C6
Atalaia do Norte Brazil 198 D6
Atalaya Panama 186 C5
Atalaya *Madre de Dios* Peru 200 C3
Atalaya *Ucayali* Peru 200 B2
Ataléia Brazil 203 D6
Atamanovka Rus. Fed. 85 G1
Atami Japan 91 F7
Atamisqui Arg. 204 E3
Atammik Greenland 165 N3
Atamyrat Turkm. 103 F5
Ataniya Turkey *see* **Adana**

Atāntūr, Ra's *pt* Egypt 108 F9
Atapuerca *tourist site* Spain 55 H2
UNESCO World Heritage Site
Atapupu Indon. 75 C5
'Ataq Yemen 105 D5
'Atāqah, Jabal *hill* Egypt 108 D8
Atâr Mauritania 122 B5
Ataran *r.* Myanmar 78 B4
Atascadero U.S.A. 182 D6
Atascosa *watercourse* U.S.A. 179 C6
Atasu Kazakh. 103 G2
Atatan He *r.* China 88 E4
Atatürk Milli Parkı *nat. park* Turkey 59 J12
Ataúro, Ilha de *i.* East Timor 75 C5
formerly known as Kambing, Pulau
Atáviros *mt.* Greece *see* **Attavyros**
Atayurt Turkey 108 E1
Atbara Sudan 121 G5
Atbara *r.* Sudan 121 G5
Atbasar Kazakh. 103 G2
At-Bashy Kyrg. 103 H4
Atchafalaya Bay U.S.A. 175 B6
Atchison U.S.A. 178 D4
Atebubu Ghana 125 E5
Ateca Spain 55 J3
Aten Bol. 200 C3
Atenguillo Mex. 184 D4
Ateransk Kazakh. *see* **Atyrau**
Aterno *r.* Italy 56 F6
Āteshān Iran 100 C3
Āteshkhāneh, Kūh-e *hill* Afgh. 101 E3
Atessa Italy 56 G6
Aţfīḩ Egypt 108 C8
Ath Belgium 51 J2
also spelt Aath
Athabasca Canada 167 H4
Athabasca *r.* Canada 167 I3
Athabasca, Lake Canada 167 I3
Athabasca Sand Dunes Wilderness Provincial Park Canada 167 I3
Athagarh India 95 E1
Athalia U.S.A. 176 C7
Athapapuskow Lake Canada 167 K4
Athboy Ireland 47 F10
Athenae Greece *see* **Athens**
Athenry Ireland 47 D10
Athens Canada 173 R6

►**Athens** Greece 59 E11
Capital of Greece. Also known as Athínai; also spelt Athina; historically known as Athenae.
UNESCO World Heritage Site

Athens *AL* U.S.A. 174 C5
Athens *GA* U.S.A. 175 D5
Athens *NY* U.S.A. 177 L3
Athens *OH* U.S.A. 176 C6
Athens *TN* U.S.A. 174 C5
Athens *TX* U.S.A. 179 D5
Atherton Australia 149 E3
Athi *r.* Kenya 128 C5
Athina Greece *see* **Athens**
Athínai Greece *see* **Athens**
Athi River Kenya 128 C5
Athlone Ireland 47 E10
also known as Baile Átha Luain
Athnā', Wādī al *watercourse* Jordan 109 J5
Athni India 94 B2
Athol N.Z. 153 C13
Athol U.S.A. 177 M3
Athos *mt.* Greece 59 F8
UNESCO World Heritage Site
Ath Thamad Egypt 121 G2
Ath Tharthār, Wādī *r.* Iraq 107 E4
Ath Thāyāt *hills* Saudi Arabia 109 K7
Ath Thāyat *mt.* Saudi Arabia 109 H8
Ath Thumāmī *well* Saudi Arabia 105 D2
Athy Ireland 47 F11
Ati Chad 120 C6
Ati, Jabal *mts* Libya 120 B4
Aţīābād Iran 100 D3
Atiak Uganda 128 B4
Atiamuri N.Z. 152 K6
Ati Ardébé Chad 120 C6
Atibaia Brazil 206 G10
Atico Peru 200 B4
Atiedo Sudan 126 E3
Atikaki Provincial Wilderness Park Canada 167 M5
Atikameg Canada 167 H4
Atikameg *r.* Canada 168 D2
Atik Lake Canada 167 M4
Atikokan Canada 168 B3
Atikonak Lake Canada 169 H2
Atimonan Phil. 74 B3
Atina Italy 56 F7
Atirampattinam India 94 C4
Atitlán Guat. 185 H6
Atitlán, Parque Nacional *nat. park* Guat. 185 H6
Atjeh *admin. dist.* Indon. *see* **Aceh**
'Atk, Wādī al *watercourse* Saudi Arabia 105 D2
Atka Rus. Fed. 39 P3
Atkarsk Rus. Fed. 41 H6
Atkri Indon. 75 D3
Atlacomulco Mex. 185 F5
Atlanta S. Africa 133 L2

►**Atlanta** *GA* U.S.A. 175 C5
State capital of Georgia.

Atlanta *TX* U.S.A. 179 D5
Atlantı Turkey 106 C3
Atlantic *IA* U.S.A. 178 D3
Atlantic *ME* U.S.A. 177 Q1
Atlantic City U.S.A. 177 K6
Atlántico *dept* Col. 198 C2

►**Atlantic Ocean** 216 K3
2nd largest ocean in the world.
►►208–209 **Oceans and Poles**

Atlantic Peak U.S.A. 180 E4
Atlantis S. Africa 132 C10
Atlas Bogd *mt.* Mongolia 84 C3
Atlas Méditerranéen *mts* Alg. *see* **Atlas Tellien**
Atlas Mountains Africa 122 D3
Atlasova, Ostrov *i.* Rus. Fed. 39 P4
formerly known as Alaid, Ostrov
Atlas Saharien *mts* Alg. 123 F2
English form Saharan Atlas
Atlas Tellien *mts* Alg. 123 F2
also known as Atlas Méditerranéen *or* Tell Atlas
Atlin Canada 166 C3
Atlin Lake Canada 166 C3
Atlin Provincial Park Canada 166 C3
'Atlit Israel 108 F5
Atlixco Mex. 185 F5
Atmakur *Andhra Pradesh* India 94 C3
Atmore U.S.A. 175 C6
Atna Norway 45 J3
Atner India 96 C5
Atnetye Aboriginal Land *res.* Australia 148 C4
Atnur India 94 C2
Atō Japan 91 B7
Atocha Bol. 200 D5
Atoka U.S.A. 179 C5
Atome Angola 127 B7
Atonyia W. Sahara 122 C4
Atotonilco el Alto Mex. 185 E4
Atouat *mt.* Laos 78 D4
Atouila, Erg *des.* Mali 122 D5
Atoyac de Álvarez Mex. 185 E5
Atpadi India 94 B2
Atqan China *see* **Aqqan**
Atqasuk U.S.A. 164 D2
Atrai *r.* India 97 F4
Atrak, Rūd-e *r.* Iran/Turkm. *see* **Atrek**

Åtran *r.* Sweden 45 K4
Atranh India 96 C4
Atrato *r.* Col. 198 B2
Atrek *r.* Iran/Turkm. 100 C2
also known as Atrak, Rūd-e *or* Etrek
Atri Italy 56 F6
Atropatene *country* Asia *see* **Azerbaijan**
Atrūsh Iraq 109 O1
Atsiki Greece 59 G9
Atsion U.S.A. 177 K6
Atsugi Japan 91 F7
Atsuku Nigeria 125 H5
Atsumi *Aichi* Japan 91 E7
Atsumi *Yamagata* Japan 90 F5
Atsumi-hantō *pen.* Japan 91 E7
Atsuta Japan 90 G3
Aţ Ţaff *reg.* U.A.E. 105 F2
Aţ Ţafīlah Jordan 108 G7
also spelt Tafila
Aţ Ţā'if Saudi Arabia 104 C3
At Tājī Iraq 109 P4
Attalea Turkey *see* **Antalya**
Attalia Turkey *see* **Antalya**
Attalla U.S.A. 175 C5
Aţ Ţallāb *oasis* Libya 120 D3
At Ta'mīm *governorate* Iraq 107 E4
At Tamīmī Libya 120 D1
Attapu Laos 79 D5
also spelt Attopeu
Attar, Oued el *watercourse* Alg. 123 G2
At Tarābīl *hill* Egypt 108 D8
Aţ Ţarfāt *waterhole* Iraq 109 L4
Aţ Ţārmīyah Iraq 109 P4
Attavyros *mt.* Greece 59 I12
also spelt Atáviros
Attawapiskat Canada 168 D2
Attawapiskat *r.* Canada 168 D2
Attawapiskat Lake Canada 168 C2
Aţ Ţawīl *mts* Saudi Arabia 107 D5
At Taysīyah *plat.* Saudi Arabia 104 C1
Aţ Ţayyibah Jordan 108 G7
Attendorn Germany 48 E4
Atteridgeville S. Africa 133 M2
Attersee *l.* Austria 49 K8
At Tibnī Syria 109 K2
Attica *IN* U.S.A. 174 C3
Attica *NY* U.S.A. 176 G3
Attica *OH* U.S.A. 176 C4
Attikamagen Lake Canada 169 H2
Attiki *admin. reg.* Greece 59 E11
Attingal India 94 C4
Attleboro U.S.A. 177 N4
Attock City Pak. 101 H3
Attopeu Laos *see* **Attapu**
Attu Greenland 165 N3
Aţ Ţubayq *reg.* Saudi Arabia 107 D5

►**Attu Island** U.S.A. 220 G2
Most westerly point of North America.
►►154–155 **North America** Landscapes

Aţ Ţulayḩī *well* Saudi Arabia 104 D2
Attunga Australia 147 F2
At Tūnisīyah *country* Africa *see* **Tunisia**
Aţ Ţūr Egypt 121 G2
Attur *Tamil Nadu* India 94 C4
Attur *Tamil Nadu* India 94 C4
At Turbah Yemen 104 C5
At Turbah Yemen 104 D5
Aţ Ţuwayyah *well* Saudi Arabia 104 C2
Atūd Yemen 105 E5
Atuel *r.* Arg. 204 D5
Åtvidaberg Sweden 45 K4
Atwari Bangl. 97 F4
Atwater U.S.A. 182 D4
Atwood U.S.A. 178 B4
Atyrau Kazakh. 102 B3
formerly known as Ateransk *or* Gur'yev
Atyrau Oblast *admin. div.* Kazakh. *see* **Atyrauskaya Oblast'**
Atyraū Oblysy *admin. div.* Kazakh. *see* **Atyrauskaya Oblast'**
Atyrauskaya Oblast' *admin. div.* Kazakh. 102 B3
English form Atyrau Oblast; *also known as* Atyraū Oblysy; *formerly known as* Gur'yevskaya Oblast'
Auati-Paraná *r.* Brazil 199 E5
Aubagne France 51 L9
Aube *r.* France 51 J4
Aubenas France 51 K8
Aubergenville France 50 H4
Aubigny-sur-Nère France 51 I5
Aubin France 51 I8
Aubinadong *r.* Canada 168 D4
Aubonne Switz. 51 M6
Auboué France 51 L3
Aubrey Cliffs *mts* U.S.A. 183 L6
Aubry Lake Canada 164 G3
Auburn *r.* Australia 149 F5
Auburn *AL* U.S.A. 175 C5
Auburn *CA* U.S.A. 182 C3
Auburn *IL* U.S.A. 174 B4
Auburn *IN* U.S.A. 174 C3
Auburn *MA* U.S.A. 177 N3
Auburn *ME* U.S.A. 177 O1
Auburn *MI* U.S.A. 173 I7
Auburn *NE* U.S.A. 178 D3
Auburn *NY* U.S.A. 177 I3
Auburn *WA* U.S.A. 180 B3
Auburndale U.S.A. 172 C6
Auburn Range *hills* Australia 149 F5
Aubusson France 51 I7
Auca Mahuida, Sierra de *mt.* Arg. 204 C5
Auce Latvia 42 D5
Auch France 50 G9
historically known as Augusta Auscorum *or* Elimberrum
Auche Myanmar 78 B2
Auchi Nigeria 125 G5

►**Auckland** N.Z. 152 I4
5th most populous city in Oceania.

Auckland *admin. reg.* N.Z. 152 I4
Auckland Islands N.Z. 220 G9
UNESCO World Heritage Site
Aude *r.* France 51 J9
Auden Canada 168 C3
Audenarde Belgium *see* **Oudenaarde**
Audierne, Baie d' *b.* France 50 B5
Audincourt France 51 M5
Audo Range *mts* Eth. 128 D3
Audru Estonia 42 F3
Audruicq France 51 I2
Audubon U.S.A. 178 D3
Aue Germany 49 J5
Auerbach in der Oberpfalz Germany 48 I6
Auersberg *mt.* Germany 51 S2
Auezov Kazakh. 103 J2
Augathella Australia 149 E5
Augrabies S. Africa 132 E5
Augrabies Falls S. Africa 132 E5
Augrabies Falls National Park S. Africa 132 E5
Au Gres U.S.A. 173 J6
Augsburg Germany 48 H7
historically known as Augusta Vindelicorum
Augsburg-Westliche Wälder *park* Germany 48 H7
Augšlīgatne Latvia 42 G4
Augšzemes augstiene *hills* Latvia 42 H5
Augusta Australia 151 A7
►**Augusta** *Sicily* Italy 57 H11
►►34–35 **Europe** Mediterranean Basin
Augusta *AR* U.S.A. 174 B5
Augusta *GA* U.S.A. 175 D5
Augusta *KS* U.S.A. 178 C4
Augusta *KY* U.S.A. 176 A7

►**Augusta** *ME* U.S.A. 177 P1
State capital of Maine.

Augusta *WI* U.S.A. 172 B6
Augusta *WV* U.S.A. 176 G6
Augusta, Golfo di *b. Sicily* Italy 57 H11
Augusta Auscorum France *see* **Auch**
Augusta Taurinorum Italy *see* **Turin**
Augusta Treverorum Germany *see* **Trier**
Augusta Victoria Chile 200 C6
Augusta Vindelicorum Germany *see* **Augsburg**
Augustin Cadazzi Col. 198 C2
Augustine Island U.S.A. 164 D4
Augustines, Lac des *l.* Canada 173 R3
Augusto Cardosa Moz. *see* **Metangula**
Augusto de Lima Brazil 207 I5
Augustodunum France *see* **Autun**
Augusto Severo Brazil 202 E3
Augustów Poland 49 T2
Augustowska, Puszcza *for.* Poland 49 U2
Augustowski, Kanał *canal* Poland 49 U2
Augustus, Mount Australia 151 B5
Augustus Island Australia 150 D2
Aujuittuq Canada *see* **Grise Fiord**
Aukan Island Eritrea 104 C5
Aukštaitijos nacionalinis parkas *nat. park* Lith. 42 H6
Aukštelkai Lith. 42 E6
Aukštelkė Lith. 42 E6
Auktsjaur Sweden 44 L2
Aulavik National Park Canada 165 H2
Auld, Lake *salt flat* Australia 150 C4
Auliye Ata Kazakh. *see* **Taraz**
Auliyekol' Kazakh. 103 F1
Aulla Italy 56 B4
Aulneau Peninsula Canada 167 M5
Aulnoye-Aymeries France 51 J2
Aulon Albania *see* **Vlorë**
Ault France 50 H2
Aumale France 50 H3
Aumance *r.* France 51 I6
Auna Nigeria 125 G4
Aungban Myanmar 78 B3
Aunglan Myanmar 78 A4
Auning Denmark 45 J4
Auob *watercourse* Namibia/S. Africa 132 E3
Aupaluk Canada 169 G1
formerly known as Hopes Advance Bay
Aur *i.* Malaysia 76 D2
Aura Fin. 45 M3
Aurad India 94 C2
Auraiya India 96 C4
Aurajoki *r.* Fin. 42 D1
Aurangabad *Bihar* India 97 E4
Aurangabad *Maharashtra* India 94 B2
Auray France 50 D5
Aure Norway 44 J3
Aurich Germany 48 E2
Auriflama Brazil 206 C7
Aurigny *i.* Channel Is *see* **Alderney**
Aurilândia Brazil 206 C3
Aurillac France 51 I8
Aurino *r.* Italy 56 D2
Auron *r.* France 51 I5
Auronzo di Cadore Italy 56 E2
Aurora Phil. 74 B5
Aurora S. Africa 132 C9
Aurora *CO* U.S.A. 180 F5
Aurora *IL* U.S.A. 174 B3
Aurora *IN* U.S.A. 176 A6
Aurora *MN* U.S.A. 172 A3
Aurora *MO* U.S.A. 178 D4
Aurora *NE* U.S.A. 178 C3
Aurora *OH* U.S.A. 176 D4
Aurora *UT* U.S.A. 183 M3
Aurora Island Vanuatu *see* **Maéwo**
Aurukun Australia 149 D2
Aurukun Aboriginal Reserve Australia 149 D2
Aurunci, Monti *mts* Italy 56 F7
Aus Namibia 130 C5
Ausa India 94 C2
Au Sable U.S.A. 173 J6
Au Sable *r.* U.S.A. 173 J6
Ausable *r.* U.S.A. 177 L1
Au Sable Forks U.S.A. 177 L1
Au Sable Point *MI* U.S.A. 172 G4
Au Sable Point *MI* U.S.A. 173 J6
Auschwitz Poland *see* **Oświęcim**
Ausculum Italy *see* **Ascoli Satriano**
Ausculum Apulum Italy *see* **Ascoli Satriano**
Austafjord Norway 44 J2
Aust-Agder *county* Norway 45 J4
Austari-Jökulsá *r.* Iceland 44 [inset] C2
Austertana Norway 44 O1
Austin *MN* U.S.A. 174 A3
Austin *NV* U.S.A. 183 G2

►**Austin** *TX* U.S.A. 179 C6
State capital of Texas.

Austin, Lake *salt flat* Australia 151 B5
Austral Downs Australia 148 C4
Australes, Îles *is* Fr. Polynesia *see* **Tubuai Islands**

►**Australia** *country* Oceania 144 A4
Largest country in Oceania and 6th in the world. Most populous country in Oceania. Historically known as New Holland.
►►8–9 **World** Countries
►►138–139 **Oceania** Countries

Australian-Antarctic Basin *sea feature* Indian Ocean 219 N9
Australian Antarctic Territory Antarctica 223 J2
Australian Capital Territory *admin. div.* Australia 147 F3
Australind Australia 151 A7
►**Austria** *country* Europe 49 J8
known as Österreich *in German*
►►32–33 **Europe** Countries
Austrumkursas augstiene *hills* Latvia 42 D5
Austurland *constituency* Iceland 44 [inset] D2
Austvågøy *i.* Norway 44 K1
Autazes Brazil 199 G5
Auterive France 50 H9
Autesiodorum France *see* **Auxerre**
Authie *r.* France 51 H2
Authier Canada 173 O2
Autlán Mex. 184 D5
Autti Fin. 44 N2
Autun France 51 K6
historically known as Augustodunum
Auvergne *admin. reg.* France 51 J7
Auvergne, Monts d' *mts* France 51 I7
Auvézère *r.* France 50 G7
Auxerre France 51 J5
historically known as Autesiodorum
Auxonne France 51 L5
Auyan Tepuí *plat.* Venez. 199 F3
Auyuittuq National Park Canada 165 M3
Auzoue *r.* France 50 G8
Ava Myanmar 78 A3
Ava *MO* U.S.A. 178 D4
Ava *NY* U.S.A. 177 J2
Avaí Brazil 206 D9
Availles-Limouzine France 50 G6
Avallon France 51 J5
Avalon U.S.A. 182 F8
Avalon Peninsula Canada 169 K4
Avalon Wilderness *nature res.* Canada 169 K4
Avān Iran 100 A2
Avanashi India 94 C4
Avanganna *mt.* Guyana 199 G3
Avanigadda India 94 D2
Avanos Turkey 106 C3

Avarau *atoll* Cook Is *see* **Palmerston**
Avaré Brazil 206 E10
Avaricum France *see* **Bourges**
Avarskoye Koysu *r.* Rus. Fed. 102 A4

►**Avarua** Cook Is 221 I7
Capital of the Cook Islands, on Rarotonga island.

Avaträsk Sweden 44 L2
Ave *r.* Port. 54 C3
Aveiro Brazil 199 H5
Aveiro Port. 54 C4
Aveiro *admin. dist.* Port. 54 C4
Aveiro, Ria de *est.* Port. 54 C4
Āvej Iran 100 B3
Avellaneda Arg. 204 F3
Avellino Italy 56 G8
historically known as Abellinum
Avenal U.S.A. 182 D5
Avenio France *see* **Avignon**
Averøya *i.* Norway 44 I3
Aversa Italy 56 G8
Aves *i.* West Indies 187 H4
Aves *is* West Indies *see* **Las Aves, Islas**
Avesnes-sur-Helpe France 51 J2
Avesta Sweden 45 L3
Aveyron *r.* France 51 H8
Avezzano Italy 56 F6
Avgan Geçidi *pass* Turkey 108 E1
Avgo *i. Kythira* Greece 59 E12
Avgo *i.* Greece 59 G13
Aviá Terai Arg. 204 E2
Aviemore U.K. 46 I6
Aviemore, Lake N.Z. 153 E12
Avigliano Italy 57 H8
Avignon France 51 K9
historically known as Avenio
UNESCO World Heritage Site
Ávila Spain 54 G4
Ávila, Sierra de *mts* Spain 54 F4
Avilés Spain 54 F1
UNESCO World Heritage Site
Aviño Spain 54 C1
Avinurme Estonia 42 H3
Avión *mt.* Spain 54 C2
Avis Port. 54 D5
Avisio *r.* Italy 56 D2
Avize France 51 K4
Avlama Dağı *mt.* Turkey 108 E1
Avlemonas Greece 59 E12
Avlida Greece 59 E10
Avlona Albania *see* **Vlorë**
Avlum Denmark 45 J4
Avnyugskiy Rus. Fed. 40 H3
Avoca Australia 147 D4
Avoca *r.* Australia 147 D3
Avoca S. Africa 133 P2
Avoca *IA* U.S.A. 178 D3
Avoca *NY* U.S.A. 176 H3
Avola *Sicily* Italy 57 H12
Avon *r.* Australia 151 B6
Avon *r. England* U.K. 47 J11
Avon *r. England* U.K. 47 J12
Avon *r. England* U.K. 47 K13
Avon *IL* U.S.A. 172 C10
Avon *NY* U.S.A. 176 H3
Avondale U.S.A. 183 L8
Avon Downs Australia 149 E4
Avonmore *r.* Ireland 47 F11
Avon Park U.S.A. 175 D7
Avontuur S. Africa 132 H10
Avoti Latvia 42 F5
Avram Iancu Romania 58 C2
Avranches France 50 E4
Avre *r.* France 51 I3
Avrig Romania 58 F3
Avrillé France 50 F5
Avsuyu Turkey 109 H1
Avuavu Solomon Is 145 F2
Avveel Fin. *see* **Ivalo**
Avvil Fin. *see* **Ivalo**
A'waj *r.* Syria 108 G4
Awaji-shima *i.* Japan 91 D7
Awakeri N.Z. 152 K6
Awakino N.Z. 152 I6
'Awālī Bahrain 105 E2
Awang Indon. 77 G5
Awanui N.Z. 152 H3
Awarawar, Tanjung *pt* Indon. 77 F4
Āwarē Eth. 128 E2
'Awāriḍ, Wādī al *watercourse* Syria 109 K3
Awarua Point N.Z. 153 C12
Āwasa Eth. 128 C3
Āwash Eth. 128 D2
Āwash *r.* Eth. 128 D2
UNESCO World Heritage Site
Awa-shima *i.* Japan 90 F5
Āwash National Park Eth. 128 C2
Āwash West Wildlife Reserve *nature res.* Eth. 128 C2
Awat China 88 C3
Āwatā Shet' *r.* Eth. 128 C3
Awatere *r.* N.Z. 153 I9
Awbārī Libya 120 B3
Awbārī, Idhān *des.* Libya 120 A3
Awd *reg.* Yemen 104 D5
'Awdah *well* Saudi Arabia 105 E3
'Awdah, Hawr al *imp. l.* Iraq 107 F5
Awdal *admin. div.* Somalia 128 D2
Aw Dheegle Somalia 128 E4
Awdiinle Somalia 128 D4
Awe, Loch *l.* U.K. 46 G7
Aweil Sudan 126 E2
Awgu Nigeria 125 G5
Awka Nigeria 125 G5
Awlitis *watercourse* W. Sahara 122 B4
Awry Lake Canada 167 H2
Awserd W. Sahara 122 B5
Awu *vol.* Indon. 75 C2
Axe *r.* U.K. 47 I13
Axel Heiberg Glacier Antarctica 223 N1
Axel Heiberg Island Canada 165 J2
Axente Sever Romania 58 F2
Axim Ghana 125 E5
Axinim Brazil 199 G6
Axioma Brazil 199 E6
Axios *r.* Greece 58 D8
Axmars naturreservat *nature res.* Sweden 45 L3
Axum Eth. *see* **Āksum**
Ay Kazakh. 103 J3
Ayabe Japan 91 D7
Ayachi, Jbel *mt.* Morocco 122 D2
Ayacucho Arg. 204 F5
Ayacucho Peru 200 B3
Ayacucho *dept* Peru 200 B3
Ayadaw Myanmar 78 A3
Ayagoz Kazakh. 103 J3
also spelt Ayaköz; *formerly spelt* Ayaguz
Ayagoz *watercourse* Kazakh. 103 J3
Ayaguz Kazakh. *see* **Ayagoz**
Ayakagytma, Vpadina *depr.* Uzbek. 103 F4
Ayakkuduk Uzbek. *see* **Oyoqquduq**
Ayakkum Hu *salt l.* China 89 E4
Ayaköz Kazakh. *see* **Ayagoz**
Ayamé Côte d'Ivoire 124 E5
Ayamiken Equat. Guinea 125 H6
Ayamonte Spain 54 D7
Ayan Rus. Fed. 39 N4
Ayancık Turkey 106 C2
Ayang N. Korea 83 B5
Ayangba Nigeria 125 G5
Ayanka Rus. Fed. 39 Q3
Ayapel, Serranía de *mts* Col. 198 C3
Ayaş Turkey 106 C2
Ayaviri Peru 200 C3
Ayayei Eth. 128 C1
Āybak Afgh. 101 G2

233

Balanga Phil. 74 B3
Balangala Dem. Rep. Congo 126 C4
Balangoda Sri Lanka 94 D5
Balapur India 94 C1
Balarampur India 97 E5
Balase r. Indon. 75 B3
Bălăşeşti Romania 58 I2
Balashi Rus. Fed. 102 B2
Balashikha Rus. Fed. 43 S6
Balashov Rus. Fed. 41 G6
Balasinor India 96 B5
Balassagyarmat Hungary 49 Q7
Balaton l. Hungary see **Balaton, Lake**
Balaton, Lake Hungary 49 O9 also known as Balaton
Balatonboglár Hungary 49 O9
Balatonfüred Hungary 49 O9
Balatonlelle Hungary 49 O9
Balauring Indon. 75 B5
Balazote Spain 55 I6
Balbieriškis Lith. 42 E7
Balbina Brazil 199 G5
Balbina, Represa de resr Brazil 199 G5
Balbriggan Ireland 47 F10
Balcad Somalia 128 E4
Balcanoona Australia 146 C2
Balcarce Arg. 204 F5
Balchik Bulg. 58 J5
Balclutha N.Z. 153 D14
Baldim Brazil 207 J6
Bald Knob AR U.S.A. 174 B5
Bald Knob WV U.S.A. 176 D8
Bald Mountain U.S.A. 183 I4
Baldock Lake Canada 167 L3
Baldwin U.S.A. 175 D6
Baldwinsville U.S.A. 177 I2
Baldwinville U.S.A. 177 M3
Baldy Mount Canada 166 G5
Baldy Mountain hill Canada 167 K5
Baldy Peak U.S.A. 183 O8
Bal'dzhikan Rus. Fed. 85 F1
Bale Indon. 76 C3
Bâle Switz. see **Basel**
Baléa Mali 124 C3
Baleares, Islas is Spain see **Balearic Islands**
Baleares Insulae is Spain see **Balearic Islands**
Balearic Islands is Spain 55 M5 also known as Baleares, Islas or Balears, Illes; historically known as Baleares Insulae
Balears, Illes is Spain see **Balearic Islands**
Baleh r. Sarawak Malaysia 77 F2
Baleia, Ponta da pt Brazil 203 E6
Baleine, Grande Rivière de la r. Canada 168 E2
Baleine, Petite Rivière de la r. Canada 168 E2
Baleine, Rivière à la r. Canada 169 H1 also known as Whale
Baleines, Pointe des pt France 50 E6
Bale Mountains National Park Eth. 128 C3
Băleni Romania 58 G4
Baleno Phil. 74 B3
Baler Phil. 74 B3
Baler Bay Phil. 74 B3
Balesa well Kenya 128 C4
Baleshwar India 97 E5
Balestrand Norway 45 I3
Balestrieri, Punta mt. Sardinia Italy 57 B8
Baley Rus. Fed. 85 H1
Baléyara Niger 125 F3
Balezino Rus. Fed. 40 J4
Balfate Hond. 186 B4
Balfe's Creek Australia 149 E4
Balfour Canada 167 G5
Balfour N.Z. 153 C13
Balfour E. Cape S. Africa 133 K9
Balfour Mpumalanga S. Africa 133 M3
Balfour Downs Australia 150 C4
Balgatay Mongolia 84 C2 formerly known as Shilüüstey
Balgazyn Rus. Fed. 88 F1
Balgo Australia 150 D4
Balgo Aboriginal Reserve Australia 150 E4
Balguda well Kenya 128 C5
Balguntay China 88 D3
Bālḩaf Yemen 105 E5
Balho Djibouti 128 D1
Bali India 96 B4
Bali i. Indon. 77 F5
►**Bali** prov. Indon. 77 F5
►►**24–25 World** Terrorism
Bali reg. Saudi Arabia 104 B2
Bali, Selat sea chan. Indon. 77 F5
Baliangao Phil. 74 B4
Baliapal India 97 E5
Bali Barat National Park Indon. 77 F5
Balichak India 97 E5
Balige Indon. 76 B2
Baliguda India 95 D1
Balihan China 85 H3
Balıkesir Turkey 106 A3
Balıkesir prov. Turkey 59 J9
Balık Gölü l. Turkey 107 E3
Balīkh r. Syria/Turkey 109 K2
Balıklıçeşme Turkey 59 I8
Balikpapan Indon. 77 G3
Balikpapan, Teluk b. Indon. 77 G3
Bălileşti Romania 58 F3
Balimbing Phil. 74 A5
Balimila Reservoir India 94 D2
Balimo P.N.G. 73 J8
Balin China 85 I1
Balingen Germany 48 F7
Balingian Sarawak Malaysia 77 F2
Balingian r. Sarawak Malaysia 77 F2
Balinqiao China see **Bairin Qiao**
Balintang Channel Phil. 74 B2
Bali Sea Indon. 77 F4
Balitondo Cent. Afr. Rep. 126 D3
Baliungan i. Phil. 74 B5
Baljurshī Saudi Arabia 104 C4
Balkanabat Turkm. 102 C5
Balkan Mountains Bulg./Serb. and Mont. 58 D5 also known as Stara Planina
Balkan Oblast admin. div. Turkm. see **Balkanskaya Oblast'**
Balkanskaya Oblast' admin. div. Turkm. 102 C4 English form Balkan Oblast; formerly known as Krasnovodskaya Oblast'
Balkashino Kazakh. 103 G1
Balkh Afgh. 101 F2 historically known as Bactra or Zariaspa
Balkh prov. Afgh. 101 F2
Balkhab r. Afgh. 101 F2
Balkhash Kazakh. 103 H3 also spelt Balqash

►**Balkhash, Lake** Kazakh. 103 H3
3rd largest lake in Asia. Also known as Balkhash, Ozero or Balqash Köli.
►►**60–61 Asia** Landscapes

Balkhash, Ozero l. Kazakh. see **Balkhash, Lake**
Balkonda India 94 C2
Balkuduk Kazakh. 102 A3
Balla Bangl. 97 F4
Balla Balla Zimbabwe see **Mbalabala**
Ballachulish U.K. 46 G7
Balladonia Australia 151 C7
Ballaghaderreen Ireland 47 D10
Ballangen Norway 44 L1
Ballantrae U.K. 47 H8
Ballarat Australia 147 D4
Ballard, Lake salt flat Australia 151 C6
Ballarpur India 94 C2
Ballater U.K. 46 I6
Ballé Mali 124 C3
Ballena, Punta pt Chile 204 C2
Ballenero, Canal sea chan. Chile 205 C9
Balleny Islands Antarctica 223 K2
Ballia India 97 E4
Ballina Australia 147 G2
Ballina Ireland 47 C9 also spelt Béal an Átha
Ballinasloe Ireland 47 D10 also spelt Béal Átha na Sluaighe
Ballineen Ireland 47 D12
Ballinger U.S.A. 179 C6
Ballinrobe Ireland 47 C10
Ballons des Vosges, Parc Naturel Régional des nature res. France 51 M5
Ballsh Albania 58 A8
Ballston Spa U.S.A. 177 L2
Bally U.S.A. 177 J5
Ballybunnion Ireland 47 C11
Ballycastle Ireland 47 C9
Ballycastle U.K. 47 F8
Ballyhaunis Ireland 47 D10
Ballymena U.K. 47 F9
Ballymoney U.K. 47 F8
Ballyshannon Ireland 47 D9
Balmaceda Aisén Chile 205 C7
Balmaceda Antofagasta Chile 200 C6
Balmaseda Spain 55 H1 also spelt Valmaseda
Balmazújváros Hungary 49 S8
Balmer India see **Barmer**
Balmertown Canada 167 M5
Balmoral Australia 146 D4
Balmoral N.Z. 153 G10
Balnearia Arg. 204 E3
Baloa Indon. 75 B3
Balochistan prov. Pak. 101 F4
Balochistan reg. Pak. 92 B5 formerly spelt Baluchistan
Balod India 94 D1
Baloda India 97 D5
Baloda Bazar India 97 D5
Balok, Teluk b. Indon. 77 D3
Balombo Angola 127 B8 formerly known as Norton de Matos
Balonne r. Australia 147 F2
Balotra India 96 B4
Balpyk Bi Kazakh. 103 I3 formerly known as Kīrov or Kirovskiy
Balqash Kazakh. see **Balkhash**
Balqash Köli l. Kazakh. see **Balkhash, Lake**
Balrampur India 97 D4
Balranald Australia 147 D3
Balş Romania 58 F4
Balsam Creek Canada 173 N4
Balsam Lake l. Canada 173 O6
Balsam Lake U.S.A. 172 A5
Balsapuerto Peru 198 B6
Balsareny Spain 55 M3
Balsas Brazil 202 C3
Balsas Mex. 185 F5
Balsas r. Mex. 185 E5
Balsas, Rio das r. Brazil 202 C3
Bal'shavik Belarus 43 L9
Bålsta Sweden 45 L4
Balta Ukr. 41 D7
Baltasana, Tossal de la mt. Spain 55 M3
Baltasi Rus. Fed. 40 I4
Baltasound U.K. 46 L3
Baltay Rus. Fed. 102 A1
Bălţi Moldova 41 C7 formerly spelt Bel'ts' or Bel'tsy
Baltic Sea g. Europe 45 L5
Balţīm Egypt 121 F2
Baltimore Ireland 47 C12
Baltimore MD U.S.A. 177 I6
Baltimore OH U.S.A. 176 C6
Baltinava Latvia 42 I5
Baltinglass Ireland 47 F11
Baltistan reg. Jammu and Kashmir 96 B2
Baltiysk Rus. Fed. 42 A7 historically known as Pillau
Baltoji Vokė Lith. 42 G7
Baltoro Glacier Jammu and Kashmir 96 C2
Baluarte Brazil 202 D4
Baluch Ab well Iran 100 D4
Baluchistan reg. Pak. see **Balochistan**
Balui r. Sarawak Malaysia 77 F2
Balumath India 97 E5
Balumbah Australia 146 C3
Balumundam Indon. 76 B2
Balupe r. Latvia 42 H5
Baluran, Gunung mt. Indon. 77 F3
Baluran National Park Indon. 77 F4
Balurghat India 97 F4
Balut i. Phil. 74 C5
Balvatnet l. Norway 44 K2
Balvi Latvia 42 I4
Balya Turkey 106 A3
Balyaga Rus. Fed. 85 F1
Balykchy Kyrg. 103 I4 formerly known as Issyk-Kul' or Ysyk-Köl or Rybach'ye
Balykshi Kazakh. 102 B3 also spelt Balyqshy
Balyktyg-Khem r. Rus. Fed. 84 C1
Balyqshy Kazakh. see **Balykshi**
Balzar Ecuador 198 B5
►**Bam** Iran 100 D4 UNESCO World Heritage Site
►►**10–11 World** Earthquakes and Volcanoes
Bām Iran 100 D2
Bama China 87 C3
Bama Nigeria 125 I4
Bamaga Australia 149 D1
Bamaji Lake Canada 168 B3

►**Bamako** Mali 124 D3
Capital of Mali.

Bamba r. Cent. Afr. Rep. 126 C3
Bamba Dem. Rep. Congo 127 C6
Bamba Mali 125 E2
Bambama Congo 126 B5
Bambang Phil. 74 B2
Bambangando Angola 127 D9
Bambannan i. Phil. 74 B5
Bambari Cent. Afr. Rep. 126 D3
Bamberg Germany 48 H6 UNESCO World Heritage Site
Bamberg U.S.A. 175 D5
Bambesi Eth. 128 B2
Bambey Senegal 124 A3
Bambili Dem. Rep. Congo 126 E4
Bambio Cent. Afr. Rep. 126 C4
Bamboesberg mts S. Africa 133 K8
Bamboi Ghana 125 E4
Bamboo Creek Australia 150 C4
Bambou well Mali 125 E2
Bambouk reg. Mali 124 C3
Bambouti Cent. Afr. Rep. 126 E3
Bambudi Eth. 128 B2
Bambuí Brazil 203 C7
Bamda China 86 A2
Bāmdezh Iran 100 B4
Bamenda Cameroon 125 H5
Bamendjing, Lac de l. Cameroon 125 H5
Bamfield Canada 166 E5
Bami Turkm. see **Bamy**
Bāmīān Afgh. 101 F3
Bāmīān prov. Afgh. 101 F3
Bamiancheng China 85 J3
Bamiantong China see **Muling**
Bamingui Cent. Afr. Rep. 126 D3
Bamingui r. Cent. Afr. Rep. 126 C2
Bamingui-Bangoran pref. Cent. Afr. Rep. 126 D2
Bamingui-Bangoran, Parc National du nat. park Cent. Afr. Rep. 126 C2 UNESCO World Heritage Site
Bamiyan r. Afgh. 101 G3
Bamiyan Valley tourist site Afgh. 101 F3 UNESCO World Heritage Site
Bammo well Niger 125 H3
Bamoa Mex. 184 C3
Bamor India 96 C4
Bam Posht reg. Iran 101 E5
Bam Posht, Kūh-e mts Iran 101 E5
Bampūr Iran 101 E5
Bampūr watercourse Iran 101 D5
Bamrūd Iran 101 E3
Bamy Turkm. 102 D5 also spelt Bami
Bamyili Australia 148 B2 also known as Barunga
Ban Burkina 124 E3
Bana, Wādī watercourse Yemen 105 D5
Banaba i. Kiribati 145 F2 also known as Ocean Island; also spelt Paanopa
Banabuiu, Açude resr Brazil 202 E3
Bañados del Atuel marsh Arg. 204 D5
Bañados del Izozog swamp Bol. 201 E4
Bañados de Otuquis marsh Bol. 201 F4
Banahao, Mount vol. Phil. 74 B3
Banalia Dem. Rep. Congo 126 E4
Banamba Mali 124 D3
Banan China 86 C2 formerly known as Baxian
Banana Australia 149 F5
Bananal, Ilha do i. Brazil 202 B4
Bananga India 95 G5
Banankoro Guinea 124 C4
Banapur India 95 E2
Banarlı Turkey 58 I7
Banas r. India 96 C4
Banās, Ra's pt Egypt 121 G4
Banatski Karlovac Vojvodina, Srbija Serb. and Mont. 58 C3
Banawaya i. Indon. 75 A4
Banaz Turkey 106 B3
Banaz r. Turkey 59 K10
Ban Ban Laos 78 C4
Banbān, 'Irq des. Saudi Arabia 105 D2
Banbar China see **Domartang**
Banbridge U.K. 47 F9
Ban Bua Yai Thai. 79 C5
Banbury U.K. 47 K11
Banca Romania 58 I2
Banc d'Arguin, Parc National du nat. park Mauritania 122 A5 UNESCO World Heritage Site
Ban Chiang tourist site Thai. 78 C4 UNESCO World Heritage Site
Banchory U.K. 46 J6
Bancoran i. Phil. 74 A5
Bancroft Canada 168 E4
Bancroft Zambia see **Chililabombwe**
Band Iran 100 D3
Banda Dem. Rep. Congo 126 E3
Banda Madhya Pradesh India 96 C4
Banda Uttar Pradesh India 96 D4
Banda, Kepulauan is Indon. 75 D4
Banda Aceh Indon. 76 A1 formerly known as Kutaraja
Banda Banda, Mount Australia 147 G2
Bandahara, Gunung mt. Indon. 76 B2
Bandai-Asahi National Park Japan 90 F6
Bandama r. Côte d'Ivoire 124 D5
Bandama Blanc r. Côte d'Ivoire 124 D4
Bandān Iran 101 E4
Bandaneira Indon. 75 D4
Bandān Kūh mts Iran 101 E4
Bandar India see **Machilipatnam**
Bandar Abbas Iran see **Bandar-e 'Abbās**
Bandaragung Indon. 76 D4
Bandarban Bangl. 97 G5
Bandar-e 'Abbās Iran 100 D5 English form Bandar Abbas; historically known as Gombroon
Bandar-e Anzalī Iran 100 B2 formerly known as Bandar-e Pahlavī
Bandar-e Chārak Iran 100 C5
Bandar-e Deylam Iran 100 B4
Bandar-e Emām Khomeynī Iran 100 B4 formerly known as Bandar-e Shāhpūr
Bandar-e Lengeh Iran 100 C5
Bandar-e Maqām Iran 100 C5
Bandar-e Ma'shur Iran 100 B4
Bandar-e Moghūyeh Iran 100 C5
Bandar-e Pahlavī Iran see **Bandar-e Anzalī**
Bandar-e Rīg Iran 100 B4
Bandar-e Shāh Iran see **Bandar-e Torkeman**
Bandar-e Shāhpūr Iran see **Bandar-e Emām Khomeynī**
Bandar-e Torkeman Iran 100 C2 formerly known as Bandar-e Shāh
Bandar Lampung Indon. 76 D4 also known as Telukbetung; formerly known as Tanjungkarang-Telukbetung
Bandar Murcaayo Somalia 128 F2
Bandarpunch mt. India 96 C3

►**Bandar Seri Begawan** Brunei 77 F1
Capital of Brunei. Formerly known as Brunei.

Bandar Wanaag Somalia 128 E2
Banda Sea Indon. 75 D4
Band-e Amīr, Daryā-ye r. Afgh. 101 F2
Bandeira Brazil 207 M2
Bandeirante Brazil 202 B5
Bandeirantes Brazil 206 C10
Bandeiras, Pico de mt. Brazil 203 D7
Bandera Arg. 204 E3
Bandera U.S.A. 179 C6
Banderas Mex. 184 D2
Banderas, Bahía de b. Mex. 184 D4
Bandhi Pak. 101 G5
Bandhogarh India 96 D5
Bandi r. India 96 B4
Bandia r. India 94 D2
Bandiagara Mali 124 E3 UNESCO World Heritage Site
Bandiagara, Falaise de esc. Mali 124 E3
Bandikui India 96 C4
Bandīnī Iran 101 D5
Bandipur Jammu and Kashmir 96 B2
Bandipur Nepal 97 E4
Bandipur National Park India 94 C4
Bandırma Turkey 106 A2
Bandjarmasin Indon. see **Banjarmasin**
Bandjer pass Serb. and Mont. 58 A5
Bandon Ireland 47 D12
Bandon r. Ireland 47 D12
Ban Don Thai. see **Surat Thani**
Bandon U.S.A. 180 A4
Ban Don, Ao b. Thai. 79 B6
Band Qīr Iran 100 B4
Bandra India 94 B2
Bandua Moz. 131 G3
Bandula Moz. 131 G3
Bandundu Dem. Rep. Congo 126 C5 formerly known as Banningville
Bandundu prov. Dem. Rep. Congo 126 C6
Bandung Indon. 77 D4
Bandya Australia 151 C6
Băneasa Romania 58 I4
Băneasa Romania 58 H4
Bāneh Iran 100 A3
Banemo Indon. 75 D2
Banera India 96 B4
Banes Cuba 186 E2
Banff Canada 167 H5
Banff U.K. 46 J6
Banff National Park Canada 167 G5 UNESCO World Heritage Site
Banfora Burkina 124 D4
Bang Cent. Afr. Rep. 126 B3
Banga Angola 127 B7
Banga Dem. Rep. Congo 127 D6
Banga Phil. 74 C5
Banga r. Phil. 74 C5
Bangai Point Phil. 74 C5
Bangall Creek watercourse Australia 149 E4
Bangalore India 94 C3
Banganapalle India 94 C3
Banganga r. India 96 C4
Bangangté Cameroon 125 H5
Bangaon India 97 F5
Bangar Brunei 77 F1
Bangar Phil. 74 B2
Bangara r. Bangl. 97 F5
Bangarapet India 94 C3
Bangassou Cent. Afr. Rep. 126 D3
Bangdag Co salt l. China 89 C5
Bangfai, Xé r. Laos 78 D4
Banggai Indon. 75 B3
Banggai i. Indon. 75 B3
Banggai, Kepulauan is Indon. 75 B3
Banggi i. Sabah Malaysia 77 G1
Banghāzī Libya see **Benghazi**
Banghiang, Xé r. Laos 78 D4
Bangil Indon. 77 F4
Bangka i. Indon. 75 C2
Bangka i. Indon. 77 D3
Bangka, Selat sea chan. Indon. 77 D3
Bangka-Belitung prov. Indon. 77 D3
Bangkala, Teluk b. Indon. 75 A4
Bangkalan Indon. 77 F4
Bangkaru i. Indon. 76 B2
Bangkinang Indon. 76 C2
Bangkir Indon. 75 B2
Bangko Indon. 76 C3
Bangkog Co salt l. China 89 E6

►**Bangkok** Thai. 79 C5
Capital of Thailand. Also known as Krung Thep.
►►**18–19 World** Cities

Bangkok, Bight of b. Thai. 79 C5
Bangkor China 89 D6
Bangkulu i. Indon. 75 B3
Bangla state India see **West Bengal**

►**Bangladesh** country Asia 97 F4
8th most populous country in the world. Formerly known as East Bengal or East Pakistan.
►►**16–17 World** Population
►►**64–65 Asia** Countries

Bangma Shan mts China 86 A4
Bang Mun Nak Thai. 78 C4
Bångnäs Sweden 44 K2
Ba Ngoi Vietnam 79 E6
Bangolo Côte d'Ivoire 124 D5
Bangong Co salt l. China/Jammu and Kashmir 89 B5 also spelt Pangong Tso
Bangor Gwynedd, Wales U.K. 47 H10
Bangor Northern Ireland U.K. 47 G9
Bangor ME U.S.A. 177 Q1
Bangor MI U.S.A. 172 G8
Bangor PA U.S.A. 177 J5
Bangriposi India 97 E5
Bangs, Mount U.S.A. 183 K5
Bangsalsepulun Indon. 77 G3
Bang Saphan Yai Thai. 79 B6
Bangsund Norway 44 J2
Bangu Dem. Rep. Congo 127 D7
Bangued Phil. 74 B2

►**Bangui** Cent. Afr. Rep. 126 C3
Capital of Central African Republic.

Bangui Phil. 74 B2
Bangula Malawi 129 B9
Bangunpurba Indon. 76 B2
Banguru Dem. Rep. Congo 126 E4
Bangweulu, Lake Zambia 127 F7
Banhā Egypt 121 F2 also spelt Benha
Banhine, Parque Nacional de nat. park Moz. 131 G4
Ban Houei Sai Laos see **Huayxay**
Ban Huai Khon Thai. 78 C4
Bani Burkina 125 E3
Bani Cent. Afr. Rep. 126 D3
Baní Dom. Rep. 187 F3
Bani r. Mali 124 D3
Bani Phil. 74 A2
Bani, Jbel ridge Morocco 122 C3
Bania Cent. Afr. Rep. 126 C3
Bani Atiyah reg. Saudi Arabia 106 D5
Bani-Bangou Niger 125 F3
Banifing r. Mali 124 D3
Banifing r. Mali 124 D3
Banī Forūr, Jazīreh-ye i. Iran 100 C5
Banihal Pass and Tunnel Jammu and Kashmir 96 B2
Banikoara Benin 125 F4
Banī Mazār Egypt 106 B5
Banī Sa'd Iraq 109 P4
Banister r. U.S.A. 176 G9
Banī Suwayf Egypt 121 F2 also spelt Beni Suef
Banī Suwayf governorate Egypt 108 A9
Băniţa Romania 58 E3 UNESCO World Heritage Site
Banite Bulg. 58 G7
Banī Thawr Saudi Arabia 104 C4
Banitsa Bulg. 58 E5
Banī Walīd Libya 120 B2
Banī Wuţayfān well Saudi Arabia 105 E2
Bāniyās Syria 108 G2 historically known as Caesarea Philippi or Paneas
Bani Yas reg. U.A.E. 105 F3
Banja Srbija Serb. and Mont. 58 A5
Banja Luka Bos.-Herz. 56 J4
Banjar India 96 C3
Banjarbaru Indon. 77 F3
Banjarmasin Indon. 77 F3 formerly spelt Bandjarmasin
Banjes, Liqeni i resr Albania 58 B8

►**Banjul** Gambia 124 A3
Capital of The Gambia. Formerly known as Bathurst.

Bankä Azer. 100 B2
Banka India 97 E4
Banka Banka Australia 148 B3
Bankapur India 94 B3
Bankass Mali 124 E3
Ban Khai Thai. 79 C5
Ban Khao Yoi Thai. 79 B5
Banki India 95 E1
Bankim Cameroon 125 H5
Bankkop S. Africa 133 O3
Banko, Massif de mt. Guinea 124 C4
Bankobankoang i. Indon. 77 G4
Bankol India 94 B2
Bankon Guinea 124 C4
Banks Island B.C. Canada 166 D4
Banks Island N.W.T. Canada 164 G2
Banks Islands Vanuatu 145 F3
Banks Lake U.S.A. 180 C3
Banks Peninsula N.Z. 153 H11
Banks Strait Australia 147 F5
Bankura India 97 E5
Bankya Bulg. 58 E6
Bankya Bulg. 58 D6
Ban Lamduan Thai. 79 C5
Banlan China 87 D3
Banloc Romania 58 C3
Ban Mae Mo Thai. 78 B4
Banmauk Myanmar 78 A2
Bann r. U.K. 47 F8
Ban Napè Laos 78 D4
Ban Na San Thai. 79 B6
Banner Hill U.S.A. 176 C9
Bannerman Town Bahamas 186 D1
Bannertown U.S.A. 176 E9
Banning U.S.A. 183 H8
Banningville Dem. Rep. Congo see **Bandundu**
Bannivka Ukr. 58 J3
Bannockburn N.Z. 153 D13
Ban Noi Myanmar 78 B4
Bannu Pak. 101 G3 formerly known as Edwardesabad
Bañolas Spain see **Banyoles**
Baños de Agua Santa Ecuador 198 B5
Baños de Puritama Chile 200 C5
Bánovce nad Bebravou Slovakia 49 P7
Banovići Bos.-Herz. 56 K4
Banow Afgh. see **Andarāb**
Ban Phaeng Thai. 78 D4
Ban Phai Thai. 78 C4
Banphot Phisai Thai. 78 B5
Ban Pong Thai. 79 B5
Banqiao China 86 C3
Bansang Gambia 124 B3
Ban Sawi Thai. 79 B6
Bansgaon India 97 D4
Bansi Rajasthan India 96 B4
Bansi Uttar Pradesh India 96 C4
Bansi Uttar Pradesh India 97 D4
Banská Bystrica Slovakia 49 Q7
Banská Štiavnica Slovakia 49 P7 UNESCO World Heritage Site
Bansko Bulg. 58 E7
Bansloi r. India 97 E4
Ban Sut Ta Thai. 78 B4
Banswada India 94 C2
Banswara India 96 B5
Banta i. Indon. 77 G5
Bantaeng Indon. 75 A4
Bantayan i. Phil. 74 B4
Bantè Benin 125 F4
Banten prov. Indon. 77 D4
Ban Tha Chang Thai. 79 B6
Ban Tha Kham Thai. 79 B6
Ban Tha Song Yang Thai. 78 B4
Banthat mts Cambodia see **Cardamom Range**
Ban Tha Tako Thai. 79 C5
Ban Tha Tum Thai. 79 C5
Ban Thepha Thai. 79 C7
Ban Thung Luang Thai. 79 B5
Bantry Ireland 47 C12
Bantry Bay Ireland 47 C12
Bantul Indon. 77 E4
Bantva India 96 A5
Bantval India 94 B3
Banyak, Pulau-pulau is Indon. 76 B2
Banyeres de Mariola Spain 55 K6
Banyo Cameroon 125 H5
Banyoles Spain 55 N2 also spelt Bañolas
Banyuasin r. Indon. 76 D3
Banyumas Indon. 77 E4
Banyuwangi Indon. 77 F5
Banzare Coast Antarctica 223 I2
Banzart Tunisia see **Bizerte**
Banzyville Dem. Rep. Congo see **Mobayi-Mbongo**
Bao, Embalse del resr Spain see **Vao, Embalse de**
Bao, Ouadi watercourse Chad 120 D5
Bao'an Guangdong China see **Shenzhen**
Bao'an Qinghai China 84 D5
Bao'an Shaanxi China see **Zhidan**
Bao Bilia well Chad 120 D5
Baochang China 85 G3 also known as Taibus Qi
Baocheng China 86 C1
Baodi China 85 H4
Baoding China 85 G4 UNESCO World Heritage Site
Baofeng China 87 E1
Baoji Shaanxi China 86 C1
Baoji Shaanxi China 87 C1 also known as Guozhen
Baokang Hubei China 87 D2
Baokang Nei Mongol China 85 I2 also known as Horqin Zuoyi Zhongqi
Bao Lac Vietnam 78 D3
Bao Lôc Vietnam 79 D6
Baoqing China 82 D3
Baoro Cent. Afr. Rep. 126 B3
Baoshan Shanghai China 87 G2
Baoshan Yunnan China 86 A3
Baotou China 85 F3
Baotou Shan mt. China/N. Korea 82 C4
Baoulé r. Mali 124 C3
Baoulé r. Mali 124 D3
Baoxing China 86 B2
Baoxiu China 86 B4
Baoying China 87 F1
Baoyou China see **Ledong**
Bap India 96 B4
Bapatla India 94 D3
Bapaume France 51 I2
Baptiste Lake Canada 173 O5
Bapu China see **Meigu**
Baqar, Maşrif Baḩr al canal Egypt 108 D6
Baqarah Saudi Arabia 104 C3
Baqên Xizang China 89 F5 also known as Dartang
Baqên Xizang China 89 F6 also known as Yêtatang
Baqiu China 87 E3 also known as Xiajiang
Baqrān Saudi Arabia 104 C3
Baqty Kazakh. see **Bakhty**
Ba'qūbah Iraq 107 F4
Bar Crna Gora Serb. and Mont. 58 A6
Bara Nigeria 125 H4
Bara Sudan 121 F6
Bara well Sudan 126 E2
Baraawe Somalia 128 E4
Barabai Indon. 77 F3
Barabanki India 96 D4
Barabanovo Rus. Fed. 43 T7
Barabash Rus. Fed. 90 B3
Barabhum India 97 E5
Barabinsk Rus. Fed. 80 B1
Baraboo U.S.A. 172 D7
Baraboo r. U.S.A. 172 D7
Baraboulé Burkina 125 E3
Baraboy r. Ukr. 58 L2
Baracaldo Spain see **Barakaldo**
Baracoa Cuba 187 E2
Baradá, Nahr r. Syria 108 H4
Baradero Arg. 204 F4
Baradine r. Australia 147 F2
Baraga U.S.A. 172 E4
Bărăganului, Câmpia plain Romania 58 I4
Baragoi Kenya 128 C4
Baragua Venez. 198 D2
Baragua, Sierra de mts Venez. 198 D2
Barahona Dom. Rep. 187 F3
Barail Range mts India 97 G4
Bara Issa r. Mali 124 E2
Barajevo Srbija Serb. and Mont. 58 B4
Barak Afgh. 101 G2
Barak r. India 97 G4
Baraka watercourse Eritrea/Sudan 121 H5
Barakaldo Spain 55 I1 also spelt Baracaldo
Barakke S. Africa 133 I9
Barakot India 97 E5
Barakovo Rus. Fed. 43 U7
Barakpay Kazakh. 103 F1 also spelt Baraqbay
Baralaba Australia 149 F5
Bara Lacha Pass India 96 C2
Baram r. Sarawak Malaysia 77 F1
Baram, Tanjung pt Sarawak Malaysia 77 F1
Baramanni Guyana 199 G3
Baramati India 94 B2
Barambah r. Australia 149 F5
Barameiya Sudan 121 H5
Baramulla Jammu and Kashmir 96 B2
Baran' Belarus 43 L7
Baran India 96 C4
Baran r. Pak. 101 G5
Bārān, Kūh-e mts Iran 101 E3
Baranavichy Belarus 42 H8 also spelt Baranovichi; formerly spelt Baranowicze
Barang, Dasht-i des. Afgh. 101 E3
Baranikha Rus. Fed. 39 Q3
Baranīs Egypt 121 G4
Baranivka Ukr. 41 C6
Barankul Kazakh. 102 C3
Baranoa Col. 187 E5
Baranof Island U.S.A. 164 F4
Baranovichi Belarus see **Baranavichy**
Baranowicze Belarus see **Baranavichy**
Barão de Cocais Brazil 207 J6
Barão de Grajaú Brazil 202 D3
Barão de Melgaço Brazil 201 G4
Barão de Melgaco Brazil 201 E2
Baraolt Romania 58 G2
Baraqbay Kazakh. see **Barakpay**
Baraqueville France 51 I8
Bararati r. Brazil 201 F1
Bārat, Chīyā-e hill Iraq 109 P1
Barat Daya, Kepulauan is Indon. 75 C4
Baratta Australia 146 C3
Barauaná, Serra mts Brazil 199 F4
Baraut India 96 C3
Baraya Col. 198 C4
Barbacena Minas Gerais Brazil 203 D7
Barbacena Pará Brazil 199 H5
►**Barbados** country West Indies 187 I4
►►**16–17 World** Population
►►**158–159 North America** Countries
Barbar, Jabal mt. Egypt 108 E8
Barbara Lake Canada 168 C3
Barbaria, Cap de c. Spain 55 M6
Barbaros Turkey 58 I8
Barbastro Spain 55 L2
Barbate de Franco Spain 54 F8
Bārbele Latvia 42 F5
Barber's Bay Canada 173 M2
Barberspan Nature Reserve S. Africa 133 J3
Barberton S. Africa 133 P2
Barberton U.S.A. 176 D4
Barbezieux-St-Hilaire France 50 F7
Barbigha India 97 E4
Barbosa Col. 198 C3
Barbour Bay Canada 167 M2
Barbours U.S.A. 177 I4
Barbourville U.S.A. 176 B9
Barboza Phil. 74 B4
Barbuda i. Antigua and Barbuda 187 H3
Bârca Romania 58 E5
Barcaldine Australia 149 E4
Barcău r. Romania 58 C1
Barce Libya see **Al Marj**
Barcellona Pozzo di Gotto Sicily Italy 57 H10
Barcelona Spain 55 N3 historically known as Barcino UNESCO World Heritage Site
Barcelona Venez. 199 E2
Barcelonnette France 51 M8
Barcelos Brazil 199 F5
Barcin Poland 49 O3
Barcino Spain see **Barcelona**
Barclay de Tolly atoll Fr. Polynesia see **Raroia**
Barclayville Liberia 124 C5
Barcoo watercourse Australia 149 D5
Barcoo Creek watercourse Australia see **Cooper Creek**
Barcoo National Park Australia see **Welford National Park**
Barcs Hungary 56 J3
Barczewo Poland 49 R2
Bärdä Azer. 107 F2
Barda Rus. Fed. 40 J4
Bardaale Somalia 128 E3
Bárðarbunga mt. Iceland 44 [inset] C2
Bardas Blancas Arg. 204 C4
Bardaskan Iran 100 D3
Bardawil, Khabrat al salt pan Saudi Arabia 109 J6
Bardawīl, Sabkhat al lag. Egypt 108 E6
Barddhaman India 97 E5 formerly spelt Burdwan
Bardejov Slovakia 49 S6 UNESCO World Heritage Site
Bardera Somalia see **Baardheere**
Bardsey Island U.K. 47 H11
Bard Shah Iran 100 B3
Bardsīr Iran 100 D4
Barðsneshorn pt Iceland 165 R3
Bardstown U.S.A. 174 C4
Barduli Italy see **Barletta**
Bardwell U.S.A. 174 B4
Barē Eth. 128 D3
Bareilly India 96 C3
Bareli India 96 C5
Barengapara India 97 F4
Barentin France 50 G3
Barenton France 50 F4
Barentsburg Svalbard 38 B2
Barents Island Svalbard see **Barentsøya**
Barentsøya i. Svalbard 38 C2 English form Barents Island
Barents Sea Arctic Ocean 38 E2
Barentu Eritrea 121 H6
Bareo Sarawak Malaysia 77 F2
Barfleur, Pointe de pt France 50 E3
Barga China 89 C6
Barga Italy 56 C4
Bargaal Somalia 128 F2
Bārgāh Iran 100 D5
Bargara Australia 149 G5
Bargē Eth. 128 C3
Barge Italy 51 N8
Bargi India 96 C5
Bargırı Turkey see **Muradiye**
Bargteheide Germany 48 H2
Barguna Bangl. 97 F5
Bargur India 94 C4
Barh India 97 E4
Barhaj India 97 D4
Barhalganj India 97 D4
Bar Harbor U.S.A. 177 Q1
Barharwa India 97 E4
Bari Dem. Rep. Congo 126 C4
Bari India 96 C4
Bari Italy 56 I7 historically known as Barium
Bari admin. reg. Somalia 128 F2
Ba Ria Vietnam 79 D6
Barīdī, Ra's hd Saudi Arabia 104 B2
Bari Doab lowland Pak. 101 H4
Barik Oman 105 G3
Barika Alg. 123 G2
Barikot Afgh. 101 G3
Barikot Nepal 97 D3
Barīm i. Yemen 104 C5 English form Perim Island
Barima r. Guyana 199 G2
Barima r. Venez. 187 H5

Bébédjia Chad 126 C2
Bebedouro Brazil 206 E7
Beberibe Brazil 202 E3
Bebra Germany 48 G5
Bêca China 86 A2
Beccles U.K. 47 N11
Bečej Vojvodina, Srbija Serb. and Mont. 58 B3
also known as Óbecse
Becerreá Spain 54 D2
Becerrero hill Spain 54 G7
Becerro, Cayos is Hond. 186 C4
Béchar Alg. 123 E3
formerly known as Colomb-Béchar
Becharof Lake U.S.A. 164 D4
Bechevinka Rus. Fed. 43 S2
Bechuanaland country Africa see Botswana
Beçin Turkey 59 I11
Becker, Mount Antarctica 222 T1
Beckley U.S.A. 176 D8
Becks N.Z. 153 D12
Becky Peak U.S.A. 183 J2
Beclean Romania 58 F1
Bečva r. Czech Rep. 49 O6
Beda Hāyk' l. Eth. 128 D2
Bédarieux France 51 J9
Bedeau Alg. see Ras el Ma
Bedel', Pereval pass China/Kyrg. see Bedel Pass
Bedelē Eth. 128 C2
Bedel Pass China/Kyrg. 88 B3
also known as Bedel', Pereval
Bedford Canada 169 I4
Bedford S. Africa 133 K9
Bedford U.K. 47 L11
Bedford IA U.S.A. 178 D3
Bedford IN U.S.A. 174 C4
Bedford KY U.S.A. 174 C4
Bedford NY U.S.A. 177 L4
Bedford PA U.S.A. 176 G5
Bedford VA U.S.A. 176 F8
Bedford, Cape Australia 149 E2
Bedford Downs Australia 150 D3
Bedford Heights U.S.A. 176 D4
Bedi India 96 A5
Bedinggong Indon. 77 D3
Bednja r. Croatia 56 I2
Bednodem'yanovsk Rus. Fed. 41 G5
Bedok Sing. 76 [inset]
Bedok, Sungai r. Sing. 76 [inset]
Bedok Jetty Sing. 76 [inset]
Bedok Reservoir Sing. 76 [inset]
Bedouaram well Niger 125 I3
Bedourie Australia 148 C5
Bedrock U.S.A. 183 P3
Bedum Neth. 48 D2
Beechal Creek watercourse Australia 147 E1
Beecher U.S.A. 172 F9
Beech Fork Lake U.S.A. 176 C7
Beechy Canada 167 J5
Beekeepers Nature Reserve Australia 151 A6
Beelitz Germany 49 J3
Beenleigh Australia 147 G1
Beer Somalia 128 E2
Beersheba Israel 108 F6
also spelt Be'ér Sheva'
Be'ér Sheva' Israel see Beersheba
Be'ér Sheva' watercourse Israel 108 F6
Beervlei Dam S. Africa 132 H10
Beeskow Germany 49 L3
Beestekraal S. Africa 133 L2
Beetaloo Australia 148 B3
Beethoven Peninsula Antarctica 222 T2
Beeville U.S.A. 179 C6
Befale Dem. Rep. Congo 126 D4
Befandriana Atsimo Madag. 131 [inset] I4
Befandriana Avaratra Madag. 131 [inset] K2
Befori Dem. Rep. Congo 126 D4
Befotaka Madag. 131 [inset] J4
Bega Australia 147 F4
Bega r. Romania 58 C3
Begamganj Bangl. 97 F5
Bégard France 50 C4
Begari r. Pak. 101 G4
Begicheva, Ostrov i. Rus. Fed. see
Bol'shoy Begichev, Ostrov
Begovat Uzbek. see Bekobod
Begun India 96 B4
Begusarai India 97 E4
Behābād Iran 101 D3
Béhague, Pointe pt Fr. Guiana 199 I3
Behbehān Iran 100 B4
Behm Canal sea chan. U.S.A. 166 D4
Behrendt Mountains Antarctica 222 T2
Behshahr Iran 100 C2
Behsūd Afgh. 101 F3
Bei'an China 82 B2
Bei'ao China see Dongtou
Beiba China 86 C1
Beibei China 86 C2
Beichuan China 86 C2
also known as Qushan
Beida Libya see Al Bayḍā'
Beigang Taiwan see Peikang
Beihai China 87 D4
historically known as Pakhoi
Bei Hulsan Hu salt l. China 84 B4
Bei Jiang r. China 87 E4

►Beijing China 85 H4
Capital of China. Formerly known as Peking; historically known as Khanbalik.
UNESCO World Heritage Site
►►18–19 World Cities

Beijing municipality China 85 H3
Beilen Neth. 48 D3
Beiliu China 87 D4
Béinamar Chad 126 B2
Beining China 85 I3
also known as Guangning; formerly known as Beizhen
Beinn Bhreac hill U.K. 46 G7
Beinn Mhòr hill U.K. 46 E6
Beinn na Faoghlia i. U.K. see Benbecula
Beipan Jiang r. China 86 C3
Beipiao China 85 I3
Beira Moz. 131 G3
Beira prov. Moz. see Sofala
Beira Alta reg. Port. 54 D4
Beira Baixa reg. Port. 54 D5
Beira Litoral reg. Port. 54 C4
Beiru He r. China 87 E1

►Beirut Lebanon 108 G4
Capital of Lebanon. Also spelt Bayrūt or Beyrouth; historically known as Berytus.

Beiseker Canada 167 H5
Beishan China 84 C3
Bei Shan mts China 84 B3
formerly spelt Pei Shan
Beitai Ding mts China 85 G4
Beitbridge Zimbabwe 131 F4
Beit Jālā West Bank 108 G6
Beitun China 88 D2
Beiuș Romania 58 D2
Beizhen China see Beining
Beja Brazil 202 B2
Beja Port. 54 D6
Beja admin. dist. Port. 54 C7
Béja Tunisia 123 H1
Bejaïa Alg. 123 G1
formerly known as Bougie; historically known as Saldae
Béjar Spain 54 F4
Bejestān Iran 100 D3
Beji r. Pak. 101 G4
Bejucos Mex. 185 E5
Béka Adamaoua Cameroon 125 I5
Béka Est Cameroon 125 I5
Béka Nord Cameroon 125 I4
Bekabad Uzbek. see Bekobod
Bekapaika Madag. 131 [inset] J3
Bekasi Indon. 77 D4
Bekdaş Turkm. 102 C4
Beke Dem. Rep. Congo 127 E7
Békés Hungary 49 S9
Békéscsaba Hungary 49 S9
Beketovskaya Rus. Fed. 43 U1
Bekilli Turkey 59 K10
Bekily Madag. 131 [inset] J5
Bekitro Madag. 131 [inset] J5
Bekkai Japan 90 I3
Beklemishevo Rus. Fed. 85 G1
Bekobod Uzbek. 92 C2
also spelt Bekabad; formerly spelt Begovat
Bekopaka Madag. 131 [inset] J3
Bekoropoka-Antongo Madag. 131 [inset] I4
Bekovo Rus. Fed. 41 G5
Bekwai Ghana 125 E5
Bekyem Ghana 125 E5
Bela Bihar India 97 E4
Bela Uttar Pradesh India 97 D4
Bela Pak. 101 F5
Belab r. Pak. 101 G4
Bela-Bela S. Africa 133 M1
Bélabo Cameroon 125 I5
Bela Crkva Vojvodina, Srbija Serb. and Mont. 58 C4
Belaga Sarawak Malaysia 77 F2
Bel'agash Kazakh. 103 J2
Bel Air U.S.A. 177 I6
Belalcázar Spain 54 F6
Belang Indon. 75 C2
Bela Palanka Srbija Serb. and Mont. 58 D5
Bělá pod Bezdězem Czech Rep. 49 L5
Belapur India 94 B2
►Belarus country Europe 42 H8
formerly known as Belorussia or Belorusskaya S.S.R. or Byelorussia or White Russia
►►32–33 Europe Countries
Belasica mts Bulg./Macedonia see Belasitsa
Belasitsa mts Bulg./Macedonia 58 D7
also known as Kerkini Oros; also spelt Belasica
Belau country N. Pacific Ocean see Palau
Bela Vista Angola 127 B6
Bela Vista Amazonas Brazil 199 E4
Bela Vista Mato Grosso do Sul Brazil 201 F5
Bela Vista Moz. 131 G5
Bela Vista de Goiás Brazil 206 E3
Belawan Indon. 76 B2
Belaya r. Rus. Fed. 39 R3
Belaya Glina Rus. Fed. 41 G7
Belaya Kalitva Rus. Fed. 41 G6
Belaya Kholunitsa Rus. Fed. 40 I4
Belayan r. Indon. 77 G3
Belayan, Gunung mt. Indon. 77 F2
Belaya Rechka Rus. Fed. 43 U5
Belaya Tserkva Ukr. see Bila Tserkva
Belbédji Niger 125 G3
Belcești Romania 58 I1
Bełchatów Poland 49 Q4
Belcher U.S.A. 176 C8
Belcher Islands Canada 168 E1
Belchiragh Afgh. 101 F3
Belcourt Canada 173 P2
Beldanga India 97 F5
Belden U.S.A. 182 C1
Beldibi Turkey 59 J12
Belding U.S.A. 173 H7
Beleapani reef India see Cherbaniani Reef
Belebey Rus. Fed. 40 J5
Beled Hungary 49 O8
Beledweyne Somalia 128 E3
Belek Turkm. 102 C5
Béléko Mali 124 D3
Bélèl Cameroon 125 I5
Belel Nigeria 125 I4
Belém Brazil 202 B2
Belén Arg. 204 D2
Belén Para. 201 F5
Belen Antalya Turkey 108 D1
Belen Hatay Turkey 106 D3
Belen U.S.A. 181 F6
Belén, Cuchilla de hills Uruguay 204 F3
Belene Bulg. 58 G5
Belep, Îles is New Caledonia 145 F3
Belesar, Encoro de resr Spain 54 D2
Belev Rus. Fed. 43 R8
Belevi Turkey 59 I10
Belfast N.Z. 153 G11
Belfast S. Africa 133 O2

►Belfast U.K. 47 G9
Capital of Northern Ireland.

Belfast U.S.A. 177 P1
Bēlfodiyo Eth. 128 B2
Belford U.K. 46 K8
Belfort France 51 M5
Belgaum India 94 B3
Belgian Congo country Africa see
Congo, Democratic Republic of the
Belgicafjella mts Antarctica see
Belgica Mountains
Belgica Mountains Antarctica 223 C2
also known as Belgicafjella
België country Europe see Belgium
Belgique country Europe see Belgium
►Belgium country Europe 51 K2
known as België in Dutch (Flemish) or Belgique in French; historically known as Spanish Netherlands
►►32–33 Europe Countries
Belgorod Rus. Fed. 41 F6
Belgorod-Dnestrovskyy Ukr. see
Bilhorod-Dnistrovs'kyy
Belgorod Oblast admin. div. Rus. Fed. see
Belgorodskaya Oblast'
Belgorodskaya Oblast' admin. div. Rus. Fed. 41 F6
English form Belgorod Oblast

►Belgrade Srbija Serb. and Mont. 58 B4
Capital of Serbia and Montenegro. Also spelt Beograd; historically known as Singidunum.

Belgrade ME U.S.A. 177 P1
Belgrade MT U.S.A. 180 E3
Belgrano II research station Antarctica 222 V1
long form General Belgrano II
Belhirane Alg. 123 G3
Béli Guinea-Bissau 124 B4
Beli Nigeria 125 H5
Belice r. Sicily Italy 57 E11
Beli Drim r. Serb. and Mont. 58 B6
Beliliou i. Palau see Peleliu
Beli Lom r. Bulg. 58 H5
Beli Manastir Croatia 56 K3
Belin-Béliet France 50 F8
Belington U.S.A. 176 F6
Belingwe Zimbabwe see Mberengwa
Belinskiy Rus. Fed. 41 G5
Belinț Romania 58 C3
Belinyu Indon. 77 D3
Beli Timok r. Serb. and Mont. 58 D4
Belitsa Bulg. 58 E7
Belitung i. Indon. 77 E3
also spelt Billiton
Belize Angola 126 B6

►Belize Belize 185 H5
Former capital of Belize.

►Belize country Central America 185 H5
formerly known as British Honduras
►►158–159 North America Countries
Bélizon Fr. Guiana 199 H3
Beljak Austria see Villach
Beljanica mt. Serb. and Mont. 58 C4
Belkina, Mys pt Rus. Fed. 90 E2
Bel'kovskiy, Ostrov i. Rus. Fed. 39 N2
Bell Australia 149 F5
Bell r. Australia 147 F3
Bell r. Canada 168 E3
Bell S. Africa 133 L10
Bell, Point Australia 146 B3
Bella Bella Canada 166 D4
Bellac France 50 H6
Bella Coola Canada 166 E4
Bella Coola r. Canada 166 E4
Bellagio Italy 56 B3
Bellaire MI U.S.A. 173 H6
Bellaire TX U.S.A. 179 D6
Bellaria Italy 56 E4
Bellary India 94 C3
Bellata Australia 147 F2
Bella Unión Uruguay 204 F3
Bella Vista Corrientes Arg. 204 F3
Bella Vista Santa Cruz Arg. 205 C8
Bella Vista Bol. 201 E3
Bella Vista Para. 201 F5
Bellavista Peru 198 C5
Bella Vista U.S.A. 182 B1
Bella Vista, Salar de salt flat Chile 200 C5
Bell Block N.Z. 152 I7
Bell Cay reef Australia 149 F4
Belle U.S.A. 176 D7
Belle-Anse Haiti 187 E3
formerly known as Saltrou
Belledonne mts France 51 L7
Bellefontaine U.S.A. 176 B5
Belle Fourche U.S.A. 178 B2
Belle Fourche r. U.S.A. 178 B2
Bellegarde-sur-Valserine France 51 L6
Belle Glade U.S.A. 175 D7
Belle-Île i. France 50 C5
Belle Isle i. Canada 169 K3
Belle Isle, Strait of Canada 169 J3
Bellemont U.S.A. 183 M6
Belleterre Canada 168 E4
Belleville Canada 168 E4
Belleville France 51 K6
Belleville U.S.A. 178 C4
Bellevue IA U.S.A. 174 B3
Bellevue MI U.S.A. 173 H8
Bellevue NE U.S.A. 178 D3
Bellevue OH U.S.A. 176 C4
Bellevue WA U.S.A. 180 B3
Belley France 51 L7
Bellin Canada see Kangirsuk
Bellingen Australia 147 G2
Bellingham U.K. 47 J8
Bellingham U.S.A. 180 B2
Bellingshausen research station Antarctica 222 U2
Bellingshausen Sea Antarctica 222 S2
Bellinzona Switz. 51 P6
UNESCO World Heritage Site
Bell Island Canada 169 K3
Bello Col. 198 C3
Bellows Falls U.S.A. 177 M2
Bellpat Pak. 101 G4
Bell Rock i. U.K. 46 J7
Belluno Italy 56 E2
Belluru India 94 C3
Bell Ville Arg. 204 E4
Bellville S. Africa 132 C10
Bellville OH U.S.A. 176 C5
Bellville TX U.S.A. 179 C6
Bellwood U.S.A. 176 G5
Belly r. Canada 167 H5
Bélmez Spain 54 F6
Belmont Australia 147 F3
Belmont S. Africa 133 I6
Belmont NH U.S.A. 177 N2
Belmont NY U.S.A. 176 G3
Belmonte Brazil 202 E5
Belmonte Port. 54 D4
Belmont-sur-Rance France 51 I9

►Belmopan Belize 185 H5
Capital of Belize.

Belmore Creek r. Australia 149 D3
Belmullet Ireland 47 C9
Belo Madag. 131 [inset] J4
Beloe More Rus. Fed. see Beloye More
Beloe More sea Rus. Fed. see White Sea
Beloevo Rus. Fed. see Beloyevo
Belogorsk Rus. Fed. 82 C2
formerly known as Kuybyshevka-Vostochnaya
Belogorsk Ukr. see Bilohirs'k
Belogradchik Bulg. 58 D5
Beloha Madag. 131 [inset] J5
Belo Horizonte Amazonas Brazil 199 E5
Belo Horizonte Minas Gerais Brazil 203 D6
Beloit KS U.S.A. 178 C4
Beloit WI U.S.A. 172 D8
Belo Jardim Brazil 202 E4
Belo Monte Pará Brazil 199 I5
Belo Monte Piauí Brazil see Batalha
Belomorsk Rus. Fed. 40 E2
Belonia India 97 F5
Beloomut Rus. Fed. 43 U7
Belo Oriente Brazil 207 K6
Beloozersk Belarus see Byelaazyorsk
Beloozerskiy Rus. Fed. 43 T6
Belopa Indon. 75 B3
Belorado Spain 55 H2
Belorechensk Rus. Fed. 41 F7
formerly known as Belorechenskaya
Belorechenskaya Rus. Fed. see Belorechensk
Belören Adıyaman Turkey 107 D3
Belören Konya Turkey 106 C3
also known as Sarıoğlan
Beloretsk Rus. Fed. 38 F4
Belorussia country Europe see Belarus
Belorusskaya S.S.R. country Europe see Belarus
Beloslav Bulg. 58 I5
Belostok Poland see Białystok
Belot, Lac l. Canada 166 E1
Belotintsi Bulg. 58 D5
Belo Tsiribihina Madag. 131 [inset] J3
Belousovka Kazakh. 88 C1
Belousovo Rus. Fed. 43 R6
Belo Vale Brazil 207 I7
Belovo Bulg. 58 F6
Belovo Rus. Fed. 80 D2
Beloyarovo Rus. Fed. 82 C2
Beloye Rus. Fed. 43 U3
Beloye, Ozero l. Rus. Fed. 43 S1
Beloye More Rus. Fed. 44 P2
also spelt Beloe More
Beloye More sea Rus. Fed. see White Sea
Beloyevo Rus. Fed. 40 J4
also spelt Beloevo
Belozerka Rus. Fed. 102 C1
Belozersk Rus. Fed. 43 S1
Belpre U.S.A. 176 D6
Beltana Australia 146 C2
Belted Range mts U.S.A. 183 H4
Belterra Brazil 199 H5
Beltes Gol r. Mongolia 84 C1
Belton MO U.S.A. 178 D4
Belton TX U.S.A. 179 C6
Bel'ts' Moldova see Bălți
Bel'tsy Moldova see Bălți
Belukha, Gora mt. Kazakh./Rus. Fed. 88 D1
Belur India 94 B3
Belush'ya Guba Rus. Fed. 40 J1
Belush'ye Rus. Fed. 40 H2
Beluzhiy Nos, Mys c. Rus. Fed. 40 M1
Belva U.S.A. 176 D7
Belvès France 50 H8
Belvidere IL U.S.A. 174 B3
Belvidere NJ U.S.A. 177 J5
Belyando r. Australia 149 E4
Belyando Crossing Australia 149 E4
Belyayevka Rus. Fed. 102 D2
Belyayevka Ukr. see Bilyayivka
Belyayevo Rus. Fed. 43 M6
Belyuen Australia 148 A2
Belyy Rus. Fed. 43 N6
Belyy, Ostrov i. Rus. Fed. 38 H2
Belyye Berega Rus. Fed. 43 P8
Belyye Stolby Rus. Fed. 43 S6
Belyy Gorodok Rus. Fed. 43 S5
Belyy Yar Rus. Fed. 39 I4
Belzig Germany 49 J3
Belzoni U.S.A. 175 B5
Bełżyce Poland 49 T4
Bemaraha, Plateau du Madag. 131 [inset] J3
Bembe Angola 127 B6
Bembèrèkè Benin 125 F4
Bembibre Spain 54 E2
Bemidji U.S.A. 178 D2
Béna Burkina 124 D3
Bena Dibele Dem. Rep. Congo 126 D6
Benagin Indon. 77 F3
Ben Alder mt. U.K. 46 H7
Benalla Australia 147 E4
Benalmádena Spain 54 G8
Ben 'Amîra well Mauritania 122 B5
Benares India see Varanasi
Ben Arous Tunisia 123 H1
Bénat, Cap c. France 51 M9
Benavente Spain 54 F2
Benavides Bol. 200 D3
Benbecula i. U.K. 46 E6
also known as Beinn na Faoghlia
Ben Boyd National Park Australia 147 F4
Benbury hill Ireland 47 C10
Bencha China 87 G1
Bencheng China see Luannan
Bencubbin Australia 151 B6
Bend U.S.A. 180 B3
Bendearg mt. S. Africa 133 L8
Bendela Dem. Rep. Congo 126 C5
Bender Moldova see Tighina
Bender-Bayla Somalia 128 F2
Benderville U.S.A. 172 F6
Bendery Moldova see Tighina
Bendigo Australia 147 E4
Bendoc Australia 147 F4
Bēne Latvia 42 E5
Bene Moz. 131 G2
Benedict, Mount hill Canada 169 J2
Beneditinos Brazil 202 D3
Benedito Leite Brazil 202 C3
Bénéna Mali 124 D3
Benenitra Madag. 131 [inset] J4
Benešov Czech Rep. 49 L6
Benevento Italy 56 G7
historically known as Beneventum
Beneventum Italy see Benevento
Benezette U.S.A. 176 G4
Benfeld France 51 N4
Beng, Nam r. Laos 78 C4
Benga Malawi 129 B8
Bengal, Bay of sea Indian Ocean 95 F2
Bengamisa Dem. Rep. Congo 126 E4
Bengbis Cameroon 125 I6
Bengbu China 87 F1
Benghazi Libya 120 D1
also spelt Banghāzī; historically known as Berenice
Beng He r. China 85 H5
Benghisa Point Malta 57 G13
also known as Il-Ponta ta' Benghajsa
Bengkalis Indon. 76 C2
Bengkalis i. Indon. 76 C2
Bengkayang Indon. 77 E2
Bengkulu Indon. 76 C3
Bengkulu prov. Indon. 76 C3
Bengo Angola 127 C9
Bengo prov. Angola 127 B7
Bengtsfors Sweden 45 K4
Benguela Angola 127 B8
Benguela prov. Angola 127 B8
Ben Guerdane Tunisia 123 H2
Benguerir Morocco 122 D2
Benguérua, Ilha i. Moz. 131 G4
Benha Egypt see Banhā
Ben Hiant hill U.K. 46 F7
Ben Hope hill U.K. 46 H5
Beni dept Bol. 200 D3
Beni r. Bol. 200 D2
Beni Dem. Rep. Congo 126 F4
Beni Nepal 97 D3
Beni-Abbès Alg. 123 E3
Beni Boufrah Morocco 54 G9
Benicarló Spain 55 L4
Benicasim Spain 55 L4
Benicia U.S.A. 182 B3
Benidorm Spain 55 K6
Beni Dourso well Niger 125 I1
Benifaió Spain 55 K5
also spelt Benifayo
Benifayo Spain see Benifaió
Benigánim Spain 55 K6
Beni Guil reg. Morocco 123 E2
Beni Hadifa Morocco 54 G9
Beni Mellal Morocco 122 D2
►Benin country Africa 125 F4
formerly known as Dahomey
►►114–115 Africa Countries
Benin r. Nigeria 125 G5
Benin, Bight of g. Africa 125 F5
formerly known as Biafra, Bight of
Benin City Nigeria 125 G5
Beni-Ounif Alg. 123 E3
Beni-Saf Alg. 123 E2
Benisheikh Nigeria 125 I4
Benissa Spain 55 L6
Beni Suef Egypt see Banī Suwayf
Benithora r. India 94 C2
Benito r. Equat. Guinea see Mbini
Benito, Islas is Mex. 184 B2
Benito Juárez Arg. 204 F5
Benito Juárez Mex. 183 J9
Benito Soliven Phil. 74 B2
Benjamim Constant Brazil 198 D6
Benjamin U.S.A. 179 C5
Benjamin, Isla i. Chile 205 B7
Benjamín Hill Mex. 184 C2
Benjamin Zorrillo Arg. 204 D5
Benjina Indon. 73 H8
Benkei-misaki pt Japan 90 G3
Benkelman U.S.A. 178 B3
Benken Switz. 51 P5
Benkovac Croatia 56 H4
Benkovski Bulg. 58 I5
Ben Lawers mt. U.K. 46 H7
Ben Lomond mt. Australia 147 F2
Ben Lomond hill U.K. 46 H7
Ben Lomond U.S.A. 182 B4
Ben Lomond National Park Australia 147 E5
Ben Macdhui mt. Lesotho 133 L7
Ben Macdui mt. U.K. 46 I6
Ben Mahidi Alg. 57 A12
Benmara Australia 148 C3
Ben More mt. N.Z. 153 F11
Ben More hill U.K. 46 F7
Ben More mt. U.K. 46 H7
Benmore, Lake N.Z. 153 E12
Ben More Assynt hill U.K. 46 H5
Bennett Canada 166 C3
Bennett IA U.S.A. 172 C9
Bennett WI U.S.A. 172 B4
Bennett, Lake salt flat Australia 148 A4
Bennetta, Ostrov i. Rus. Fed. 39 O2
English form Bennett Island
Bennett Island Rus. Fed. see Bennetta, Ostrov
Bennett Lake Canada 166 C3
Bennettsville U.S.A. 174 E5
Ben Nevis mt. U.K. 46 G7
Benneydale N.Z. 152 J6
Bennington NH U.S.A. 177 N2
Bennington VT U.S.A. 177 L3
Ben Ohau Range mts N.Z. 153 D12
Benoi Basin dock Sing. 76 [inset]
Benoni S. Africa 133 M3
Bénoué r. Cameroon 125 I4
Bénoué, Parc National de la nat. park Cameroon 125 I4
Bénoy Chad 126 C2
Ben Rinnes hill U.K. 46 I6
Bensheim Germany 48 F6
Ben Slimane Morocco 122 D2
formerly known as Boulhaut
Benson AZ U.S.A. 181 E7
Benson MN U.S.A. 178 D2
Bensonville Liberia 124 C5
Bens Run U.S.A. 176 D6
Bent Iran 101 D5
Benta Seberang Malaysia 76 C1
Benteng Indon. 75 B4
Bentiaba Angola 127 B8
formerly known as São Nicolau
Ben Tieb Morocco 55 H9
Bentinck Island Australia 148 C3
Bentinck Island Myanmar 79 B6
Bentiu Sudan 126 F2
Bent Jbaïl Lebanon 108 G4
Bentley Canada 167 H4
Bentleyville U.S.A. 176 E5
Bento Gomes r. Brazil 201 F4
Benton AR U.S.A. 179 D5
Benton CA U.S.A. 182 F4
Benton IL U.S.A. 174 B4
Benton KY U.S.A. 174 B4
Benton LA U.S.A. 179 D5
Benton MO U.S.A. 174 B4
Benton TN U.S.A. 174 C5
Bentong Malaysia see Bentung
Benton Harbor U.S.A. 172 G8
Bentonville U.S.A. 179 D4
Bên Tre Vietnam 79 D6
formerly known as Truc Giang
Bentsy Rus. Fed. 43 M5
Bentuang Karimun National Park Indon. 77 F2
Bentung Malaysia 76 C2
formerly spelt Bentong
Benua Indon. 75 B4
Benua i. Indon. 77 D2
Benuamartinus Indon. 77 F2
Benue r. Nigeria 125 G5
Benue state Nigeria 125 H5
Benum, Gunung mt. Malaysia 76 C2
Ben Vorlich hill U.K. 46 H7
Benwa Zambia 127 E7
Benwee Head Ireland 47 C9
Benwood U.S.A. 176 E5
Ben Wyvis mt. U.K. 46 H6
Benxi China 82 A4
Ben Zireg Alg. 123 E3
Beograd Srbija Serb. and Mont. see Belgrade
Beohari India 97 D4
Béoumi Côte d'Ivoire 124 D5
Bepagut, Gunung mt. Indon. 76 C4
Beppu Japan 91 B8
Beppu-wan b. Japan 91 B8
Bequia i. St Vincent 187 H4
Bequimão Brazil 202 C2
Bera Bangl. 97 F4
Berach r. India 96 B4
Bera de Bidasoa Spain 55 J1
Beramanja Madag. 131 [inset] K2
Berane Crna Gora Serb. and Mont. 58 A6
formerly known as Ivangrad
Bérard, Lac l. Canada 169 G1
Berasia India 96 C5
Berastagi Indon. 76 B2
Berat Albania 58 A8
Beratus, Gunung mt. Indon. 77 G3
Berau r. Indon. 77 G2
Berau, Teluk b. Indon. 73 H7
Beravina Madag. 131 [inset] J3
also spelt Berovina
Berbak National Park Indon. 76 D3
Berber Sudan 121 G5
Berbera Somalia 128 E2
Berbérati Cent. Afr. Rep. 126 B3
Berbice S. Africa 133 P4
Bercel Hungary 49 Q8
Berceto Italy 56 B4
Berchi-Guélé well Chad 120 C5
Berchogur Kazakh. 102 D2
also spelt Birshoghyr
Berchtesgaden, Nationalpark nat. park Germany 49 J8
Berck France 50 H2
Berd Armenia 107 F2
Berdichev Ukr. see Berdychiv
Berdigestyakh Rus. Fed. 39 M3
Berdsk Rus. Fed. 80 C2
Berdyans'k Ukr. 41 F7
formerly known as Osipenko
Berdychiv Ukr. 41 D6
also spelt Berdichev
Béré Chad 126 C2
Berea KY U.S.A. 176 A8
Berea OH U.S.A. 176 D4
Berebere Indon. 75 D2
Bereg Rus. Fed. 43 S1
Beregdaróc Hungary 49 T7
Beregovo Ukr. see Berehove
Berehove Ukr. 49 T7
also spelt Beregovo
Bereina P.N.G. 73 K8
Bereket Turkm. 102 C5
formerly spelt Kazandzhik
Bereketa Madag. 131 [inset] J4
Berekum Ghana 124 E5
Berel' Kazakh. 88 D1
Beremend Hungary 56 K3
Berendeyevo Rus. Fed. 43 U5
Berenguela Bol. 200 C4
Berenice Libya see Benghazi
Berens r. Canada 167 L4
Berens Island Canada 167 L4
Berens River Canada 167 L4
Berenty Madag. 131 [inset] J4
Beresford Canada 169 H4
Beresford U.S.A. 178 C3
Berești Romania 58 I2
Berettyó r. Hungary 49 S8
Berettyóújfalu Hungary 49 S8
Berevo Madag. 131 [inset] J3
Berevo-Ranobe Madag. 131 [inset] J3
Bereza Belarus see Byaroza
Berezayka Rus. Fed. 43 O4
Berezeni Romania 58 J2
Berezino Belarus see Byerazino
Berezino Belarus see Byerazino
Berezivka Ukr. 41 D7
also spelt Berezovka
Berezne Ukr. 41 C6
Bereznik Rus. Fed. 40 G3
formerly known as Semyonovskoye
Berezniki Rus. Fed. 40 K4
Berezov Rus. Fed. see Berezovo
Berezovaya r. Rus. Fed. 40 K3
Berezovka Belarus see Byarozawka
Berezovka Amurskaya Oblast' Rus. Fed. 82 B2
Berezovka Orenburgskaya Oblast' Rus. Fed. 102 D1
Berezovka Permskaya Oblast' Rus. Fed. 40 K4
Berezovka Ukr. see Berezivka
Berezovo Rus. Fed. 38 G3
formerly known as Berezov
Berezovyy Rus. Fed. 82 D2
Berezyne Ukr. 58 K2
Berga Spain 55 M2
Bergama Turkey 106 A3
Bergamo Italy 56 B3
historically known as Bergomum
Bergantes, Riu r. Spain 55 K4
Bergby Sweden 45 L3
Bergen Mecklenburg-Vorpommern Germany 49 K1
Bergen Niedersachsen Germany 48 G3
Bergen Norway 45 I3
UNESCO World Heritage Site
Bergen S. Africa 133 O4
Bergen U.S.A. 176 H2
Bergen op Zoom Neth. 48 B4
Bergerac France 50 G8
Bergerson, Mount Antarctica 223 B2
Berghan Point N.Z. 152 H2
Bergheim (Erft) Germany 48 D5
Bergisch Gladbach Germany 48 E5
Bergland Namibia 130 C4
Bergnäs Sweden 44 L2
Bergnäsviken Sweden 44 L2
Bergomum Italy see Bergamo
Bergsjö Sweden 45 L3
Bergstraße-Odenwald park Germany 48 G6
Bergsviken Sweden 44 M2
Bergues France 51 I2
Bergville S. Africa 133 N5
Berh Mongolia 85 F2
Berhala, Selat sea chan. Indon. 76 C3
Berhampur India see Baharampur
Berheci r. Romania 58 I2
Berikat, Tanjung pt Indon. 77 D3
Berilo Brazil 207 K3
Beringa, Ostrov i. Rus. Fed. 220 G2
Beringarra Australia 151 B5
Beringen Belgium 51 L1
Bering Land Bridge National Preserve nature res. U.S.A. 164 C3
Beringovskiy Rus. Fed. 39 R3
formerly known as Ugolnyy
Bering Sea N. Pacific Ocean 39 R4
Bering Strait Rus. Fed./U.S.A. 164 C3
Berīs, Ra's pt Iran 101 E5
Berislav Ukr. see Beryslav
Berja Spain 55 I8
Berkåk Norway 44 J3
Berkane Morocco 123 E2
Berkel r. Neth. 48 D3
Berkeley r. Australia 150 D2
Berkeley U.S.A. 182 B4
Berkeley Springs U.S.A. 176 G6
Berkner Island Antarctica 222 U1
Berkovitsa Bulg. 58 E5
Berkshire Hills U.S.A. 177 L3
Berland r. Canada 166 G4
Berlevåg Norway 44 O1
also known as Bearalváhki
Berlin land Germany 49 K3
UNESCO World Heritage Site

►Berlin Germany 49 K3
Capital of Germany.

Berlin MD U.S.A. 177 J7
Berlin NH U.S.A. 177 N1
Berlin NJ U.S.A. 177 K6
Berlin OH U.S.A. 176 D5
Berlin PA U.S.A. 176 G6
Berlin WI U.S.A. 172 E7
Berlin, Mount Antarctica 222 O1
Berlins N.Z. 153 F9
Berliște Romania 58 C4
Bermagui Australia 147 F4
Berme Turkm. 102 D5
Bermeja, Punta pt Arg. 204 E6
Bermejíllo Mex. 184 E3
Bermejo r. Arg. 204 D4
Bermejo r. Arg./Bol. 201 F6
Bermejo Bol. 201 D5
Bermeo Spain 55 I1

►Bermuda terr. N. Atlantic Ocean 216 J3
United Kingdom Overseas Territory.
►►158–159 North America Countries

►Bern Switz. 51 N6
Capital of Switzerland. Also spelt Berne.
UNESCO World Heritage Site

Bernalda Italy 57 I8
Bernalillo U.S.A. 181 F6
Bernarde, Sommet de la mt. France 51 M9
Bernardino de Campos Brazil 206 D10
Bernard Lake Canada 173 N5
Bernardo O'Higgins, Parque Nacional nat. park Chile 205 B8
Bernau Germany 49 K3
Bernau am Chiemsee Germany 49 J8
Bernay France 50 G3
Bernburg (Saale) Germany 48 I4
Berndorf Austria 49 N8
Berne Switz. see Bern
Berne U.S.A. 176 A5
Berner Alpen mts Switz. 51 N6
English form Bernese Alps
Berneray i. Western Isles, Scotland U.K. 46 E6
also known as Bhearnaraigh, Eilean
Berneray i. Western Isles, Scotland U.K. 46 E7
also spelt Bearnaraigh
Bernese Alps mts Switz. see Berner Alpen
Bernesga r. Spain 54 F2
Bernier Bay Canada 165 K2
Bernier Island Australia 151 A5
Bernina Pass Switz. 51 Q6
Berninches mt. Spain 55 I4
Bernkastel-Kues Germany 48 E6
Bernstadt U.S.A. 176 A8
Beroea Greece see Veroia
Beroea Syria see Aleppo
Beroroha Madag. 131 [inset] J4
Beroun Czech Rep. 49 L6
Berounka r. Czech Rep. 49 L6
Berovina Madag. see Beravina
Berovo Macedonia 58 D7
Berre, Étang de lag. France 51 L9
Berrechid Morocco 122 D2
Berri Australia 146 D3
Berriane Alg. 123 F2
Berridale Australia 147 F4
Berrigan Australia 147 E3
Berrouaghia Alg. 123 F1
Berry reg. France 50 H6
Berry Creek r. Canada 167 I5
Berryessa, Lake U.S.A. 182 B3
Berry Head U.K. 47 I13
Berry Islands Bahamas 186 D1
Berryville AR U.S.A. 179 D4
Berryville VA U.S.A. 176 H6
Berseba Namibia 132 B3
Bersenbrück Germany 48 E3
Bersuat Rus. Fed. 103 E1
Berté, Lac l. Canada 169 G3
Bertinho Brazil 202 B2
Bertolinía Brazil 202 D3
Bertópolis Brazil 207 M4

Bertoua Cameroon 125 I5
Bertraghboy Bay Ireland 47 C10
Beru atoll Kiribati 145 G2
also spelt Peru; formerly known as Francis
Beruniy Uzbek. 102 E4
formerly known as Shabbaz; formerly spelt Biruni
Beruri Brazil 199 F5
Beruwala Sri Lanka 94 C5
Berveni Romania 49 T8
Berwick-upon-Tweed U.K. 46 J8
Beryslav Ukr. 41 E7
also spelt Berislav
Berytus Lebanon see Beirut
Berzasca Romania 58 C4
Bērzaune Latvia 42 H5
Bērzpils Latvia 42 I5
Bès r. France 51 J8
Besah Indon. 77 G2
Besalampy Madag. 131 [inset] J3
Besalú Spain 55 N2
Besançon France 51 M5
historically known as Vesontio
Besar i. Indon. 75 B5
Besar, Gunung mt. Indon. 77 F3
Besar, Gunung mt. Malaysia 76 C1
Besbay Kazakh. 102 C3
Besbre r. France 51 J6
Besed' r. Rus. Fed. 43 M9
Beshariq Uzbek. 103 G4
also spelt Besharyk; formerly known as Kirovo
Besharyk Uzbek. see Beshariq
Beshkent Uzbek. 103 F5
Beshneh Iran 100 C4
Besh-Ter, Gora mt. Kyrg./Uzbek. see Besh-Ter Toosu
Besh-Ter Toosu mt. Kyrg./Uzbek. 103 G4
also known as Beshtor Toghi or Besh-Ter, Gora
Beshtor Toghi mt. Kyrg./Uzbek. see Besh-Ter Toosu
Besikama Indon. 75 C5
Beşir Turkm. 103 F5
Beşiri Turkey 107 E3
Besitang Indon. 76 B1
Beskid Niski hills Poland 49 S6
Beskid Sądecki mts Poland 49 R6
Beskra Alg. see Biskra
Beslan Rus. Fed. 41 H8
Beslet mt. Bulg. 58 E7
Besna Kobila mt. Serb. and Mont. 58 D6
Besnard Lake Canada 167 J4
Besni Turkey 107 D3
Besor watercourse Israel 108 F6
Beşparmak Dağları mts Cyprus see Pentadaktylos Range
Béssao Chad 126 B3
Bessarabka Moldova see Basarabeasca
Bessaz, Gora mt. Kazakh. 103 G4
Bessemer AL U.S.A. 175 C5
Bessemer MI U.S.A. 172 C4
Besshoky, Gora hill Kazakh. 102 C3
Bessines-sur-Gartempe France 50 H6
Bessonovka Rus. Fed. 41 H5
Bessou, Mont de hill France 51 I7
Bestamak Aktyubinskaya Oblast' Kazakh. 102 C2
Bestamak Vostochnyy Kazakhstan Kazakh. 103 I2
Bestobe Kazakh. 103 H1
Beswick Australia 148 B2
Beswick Aboriginal Land res. Australia 148 B2
Betafo Madag. 131 [inset] J3
Betanzos Bol. 200 D4
Betanzos Spain 54 C1
Bétaré Oya Cameroon 125 I5
Bete Grise U.S.A. 172 F3
Bete Hor Eth. 128 C2
Bétérou Benin 125 F4
Betet i. Indon. 76 D3
Beth, Oued r. Morocco 122 D2
Bethal S. Africa 133 N3
Bethanie Namibia 130 C5
Bethany MO U.S.A. 178 D3
Bethany OK U.S.A. 179 C5
Bethari Nepal 97 D4
Bethel AK U.S.A. 164 C3
Bethel ME U.S.A. 177 O1
Bethel OH U.S.A. 176 A7
Bethelsdorp S. Africa 133 J10
Bethesda MD U.S.A. 177 H6
Bethesda OH U.S.A. 176 D5
Bethesdaweg S. Africa 133 I8
Bethlehem S. Africa 133 M5
Bethlehem U.S.A. 177 J5
Bethlehem West Bank 108 G6
also spelt Bayt Lahm or Bet Lehem
Bethulie S. Africa 133 J7
Béthune France 51 I2
Betijoque Venez. 198 D2
Betim Brazil 207 I6
Betioky Madag. 131 [inset] J4
Betiri, Gunung mt. Indon. 77 F5
Bet Lehem West Bank see Bethlehem
Betlitsa Rus. Fed. 43 O7
Betma India 96 B5
Betong Thai. 79 C7
Betoota Australia 149 D5
Bétou Congo 126 C4
Betpak-Dala plain Kazakh. 103 G3
Betrandraka Madag. 131 [inset] J3
Betroka Madag. 131 [inset] J4
Bet She'an Israel 108 G5
Betsiamites Canada 169 G3
Betsiamites r. Canada 169 G3
Betsiboka r. Madag. 131 [inset] J2
Betsie, Point U.S.A. 172 G6
Betsy Bay Bahamas 187 E2
Betsy Lake U.S.A. 173 H4
Bettendorf U.S.A. 172 C9
Bettiah India 97 E4
Betul India 96 C5
Betwa r. India 96 C4
Betws-y-coed U.K. 47 I10
Betygala Lith. 42 E6
Béu Angola 127 B6
Beulah U.S.A. 178 B2
Beurfou well Chad 120 B6
Beuthen Poland see Bytom
Beuvron r. France 50 H5
Beverley U.K. 47 L10
Beverly MA U.S.A. 177 O3
Beverly OH U.S.A. 176 D6
Beverly Hills U.S.A. 182 F7
Beverungen Germany 48 G4
Beverwijk Neth. 48 B3
Bex Switz. 51 N6
Bextograk China 88 D4
Beyağaç Turkey 59 J11
Beyazköy Turkey 58 I7
Beyce Turkey see Orhaneli
Beydağ Turkey 59 J10
Bey Dağları mts Turkey 106 B3
Beykonak Turkey 108 B1
Beykoz Turkey 106 B2
Beyla Guinea 124 C4
Beylagan Azer. see Beyläqan
Beyläqan Azer. 107 F3
also spelt Beylagan; formerly known as Zhdanovsk
Beylul Eritrea 121 I6
Beyneu Kazakh. 102 C3
Beyoneisu Retugan i. Japan 91 F9
Beypazarı Turkey 106 B2
Beypınarı Turkey 107 D3
Beypore India 94 B4
Beyra Somalia 128 E3
Beyram Iran 100 C5
Beyrouth Lebanon see Beirut
Beyşehir Turkey 106 B3
Beyşehir Gölü l. Turkey 106 B3
Beytüşşebap Turkey 107 E3
also known as Elki
Bezameh Iran 100 D3
Bezbozhnik Rus. Fed. 40 I4
Bezdan Vojvodina, Srbija Serb. and Mont. 56 K3
Bezenjān Iran 100 D4
Bezhanitskaya Vozvyshennost' hills Rus. Fed. 43 K5
Bezhanitsy Rus. Fed. 43 K5
Bezhanovo Bulg. 58 F5
Bezhetsk Rus. Fed. 43 R4
Bezhetskiy Verkh reg. Rus. Fed. 43 R4
Béziers France 51 J9
Bezmein Turkm. see Büzmeýin
Bezwada India see Vijayawada
Bhabhar India 96 A4
Bhabhua India 97 D4
Bhabra India 96 B5
Bhachau India 96 A5
Bhadar r. India 96 A5
Bhadarwah Jammu and Kashmir 96 B2
Bhadaur India 101 H4
Bhadgaon Nepal see Bhaktapur
Bhadohi India 97 D4
Bhadra India 96 B3
Bhadrachalam India 94 D2
Bhadrachalam Road Station India see Kottagudem
Bhadrak India 97 E5
Bhadra Reservoir India 94 B3
Bhadravati India 94 B3
Bhag Pak. 101 F4
Bhagalpur India 97 E4
Bhagirathi r. India 97 F5
Bhainsa India 94 C2
Bhainsdehi India 96 C5
Bhairab Bazar Bangl. 97 F4
Bhairawa Nepal 97 D4
also known as Siddharthanagar; also spelt Bhairahawa
Bhairawaha Nepal see Bhairawa
Bhairi Hol mt. Pak. 101 F5
Bhakkar Pak. 101 G4
Bhaktapur Nepal 97 E4
also known as Bhadgaon
UNESCO World Heritage Site
Bhalki India 94 C2
Bhalwal Pak. 101 H3
Bhamgarh India 96 C5
Bhamo Myanmar 78 B2
Bhandara India 96 C5
Bhander India 96 C4
Bhanjanagar India 95 E2
Bhanpura India 96 B4
Bhanrer Range hills India 96 C5
Bharat country Asia see India
Bharatpur India 96 C4
Bharatpur Nepal 97 E4
Bhareli r. India 97 G4
Bhari r. Pak. 101 E5
Bharthana India 96 C4
Bharuch India 96 B5
formerly known as Broach; historically known as Barygaza or Bhrigukaccha
Bhatapara India 97 D5
Bhatghar Lake India 94 B2
Bhatiapara Ghat Bangl. 97 F5
Bhatinda India see Bathinda
Bhatkal India 94 B3
Bhatnair India see Hanumangarh
Bhatpara India 97 F5
Bhaun Gharibwal Pak. 101 H3
Bhavani India 94 C4
Bhavani r. India 94 C4
Bhavani Sagar l. India 94 C4
Bhavnagar India 96 B5
Bhawana Pak. 101 H4
Bhawanipatna India 95 D2
Bhearnaraigh, Eilean i. U.K. see Berneray
Bheemavaram India see Bhimavaram
Bhekuzulu S. Africa 133 O4
Bhera Pak. 101 H3
Bheri r. Nepal 97 D3
Bhigvan India 94 B2
Bhilai India 96 D5
Bhildi India 96 B4
Bhilwara India 96 B4
Bhima r. India 94 C2
Bhimavaram India 94 D2
formerly spelt Bheemavaram
Bhimbar Pak. 101 H3
Bhimnagar India 97 E4
Bhimphedi Nepal 97 E4
Bhind India 96 C4
Bhindar India 96 B4
Bhinga India 97 D4
Bhingar India 94 B2
Bhinmal India 96 B4
Bhiwandi India 94 B2
Bhiwani India 96 C3
Bhogat India 96 A5
Bhojpur Nepal 97 E4
Bhokardan India 94 B1
Bhola Bangl. 97 F5
Bhongaon India 96 C4
Bhongir India 94 C2
Bhongweni S. Africa 133 N7
Bhopal India 96 C5
Bhopalpatnam India 94 D2
Bhor India 94 B2
Bhrigukaccha India see Bharuch
Bhuban India 95 E1
Bhubaneshwar India 95 E1
formerly spelt Bhubaneswar
Bhubaneswar India see Bhubaneshwar
Bhuban Hills India 97 G4
Bhuj India 96 A5
Bhumiphol Dam Thai. 78 B4
Bhunya Swaziland 133 P3
Bhusawal India 96 B5
►Bhutan country Asia 97 F4
known as Druk-Yul in Dzongkha
►►64–65 Asia Countries
Bhuttewala India 96 A4
Bhuvanagiri India 94 C4
Biá r. Brazil 199 E5
Bia, Monts mts Dem. Rep. Congo 127 E7
Bia, Phou mt. Laos 78 C4
Biābān mts Iran 100 D5
Biafra, Bight of g. Africa see Benin, Bight of
Biak Irian Jaya Indon. 73 I7
Biak Sulawesi Tengah Indon. 75 B3
Biak i. Indon. 73 I7
Biała r. Poland 49 R5
Biała Piska Poland 49 T2
Biała Podlaska Poland 49 U3
Białobrzegi Poland 49 R4
Białogard Poland 49 M2
Białowieski Park Narodowy nat. park Poland 42 E9
UNESCO World Heritage Site
Biały Bór Poland 49 N2
Białystok Poland 49 U2
formerly spelt Belostok
Biancavilla Sicily Italy 57 G11
Bianco Italy 57 I10
Bianco, Monte mt. France/Italy see Blanc, Mont
Bianga Cent. Afr. Rep. 126 D3
Biankouma Côte d'Ivoire 124 D5
Bianouan Côte d'Ivoire 124 E5
Bianzhuang China see Cangshan
Biaora India 96 C5
Bi'ār Ghabāghib well Syria 109 K2
Biārjmand Iran 100 C2
Biaro i. Indon. 75 C2
Biarritz France 50 E9
Bi'ār Tabrāk well Saudi Arabia 105 D2
Biasca Switz. 51 O6
Bibā Egypt 121 F2
Bibai Japan 90 G3
Bibala Angola 127 B8
formerly known as Vila Arriaga
Bibas Gabon 126 A4
Bibbenluke Australia 147 F4
Bibbiena Italy 56 D5
Biberach an der Riß Germany 48 G7
Bibiani Ghana 124 E5
Bibirevo Rus. Fed. 43 N5
Bibiyana r. Bangl. 97 F4
Biblos Lebanon see Jbail
Bicas Brazil 207 J8
Bicaz Romania 58 H2
Bicheng China see Bishan
Bicheno Australia 147 F5
Bichevaya Rus. Fed. 82 D3
Bichi Nigeria 125 H3
Bichi r. Rus. Fed. 82 E1
Bicholim India 94 B3
Bichraltar Nepal 97 E4
Bichura Rus. Fed. 85 E1
Bichvint'a Georgia 107 E2
also known as Pitsunda
Bickerton Island Australia 148 C2
Bicuari, Parque Nacional do nat. park Angola 127 B8
Bid India 94 B2
also spelt Bir
Bida Nigeria 125 G4
Bidache France 50 E9
Bidadari, Tanjung pt Sabah Malaysia 77 G1
Bidar India 94 C2
Bidasar India 96 B4
Bidbid Oman 105 G3
Biddeford U.S.A. 177 O2
Bideford U.K. 47 H12
Bideford Bay U.K. see Barnstaple Bay
Bidente r. Italy 56 E4
Bidjovagge Norway 44 M1
Bīdkhan, Kūh-e mt. Iran 100 D4
Bidokht Iran 100 D3
Bidon 5 tourist site Alg. 123 F5
Bidzhan Rus. Fed. 82 C3
Bidzhar r. Rus. Fed. 82 D3
Bié Angola see Kuito
Bié prov. Angola 127 C8
Biebrza r. Poland 49 T2
Biebrzański Park Narodowy nat. park Poland 49 T2
Biedenkopf Germany 48 F5
Biel Switz. 51 N5
also known as Bienne
Bielawa Poland 49 N5
Bielefeld Germany 48 F3
Bielitz Poland see Bielsko-Biała
Biella Italy 56 A3
UNESCO World Heritage Site
Bielsko-Biała Poland 49 Q6
historically known as Bielitz
UNESCO World Heritage Site
Bielsk Podlaski Poland 49 U3
Bielstein hill Germany 51 P1
Bienenbüttel Germany 48 H2
Biên Hoa Vietnam 79 D6
Bienne r. France 51 L6
Bienne Switz. see Biel
Bienvenida hill Spain 54 E6
Bienvenue Fr. Guiana 199 H4
Bienville, Lac l. Canada 169 F2
Bierbank Australia 149 E5
Biertan Romania 58 F2
UNESCO World Heritage Site
Bierutów Poland 49 O4
Biesiesvlei S. Africa 133 J3
Biesiespoort S. Africa 132 H8
Bieszczady mts Poland 49 T6
Bieszczadzki Park Narodowy nat. park Poland 49 T6
Bièvre Belgium 51 L3
Biferno r. Italy 56 H7
Bifoun Gabon 126 A5
Bifröst Iceland 44 [inset] B2
Bifuka Japan 90 H2
Big r. U.S.A. 182 A2
Biga Turkey 106 A2
Biga r. Turkey 59 I8
Bigadiç Turkey 106 B3
Biganos France 50 F8
Biga Yarımadası pen. Turkey 59 H9
Big Baldy Mountain U.S.A. 180 E3
Big Bay U.S.A. 172 F4
Big Bay de Noc U.S.A. 172 F5
Big Bear Lake U.S.A. 183 H7
Big Belt Mountains U.S.A. 180 E3
Big Bend Swaziland 133 P3
Big Bend National Park U.S.A. 179 B6
Big Black r. U.S.A. 175 B5
Big Blue r. U.S.A. 178 C4
Big Canyon watercourse U.S.A. 179 B6
Big Cypress National Preserve nature res. U.S.A. 175 D7
Big Desert Wilderness Park nature res. Australia 146 D3
Big Eau Pleine Reservoir U.S.A. 172 D6
Biger Nuur salt l. Mongolia 84 C2
Big Fork r. U.S.A. 174 A1
Biggar Canada 167 J4
Biggar U.K. 46 I8
Biggar, Lac l. Canada 168 F3
Biggarsberg S. Africa 133 N5
Biggar Island Australia 150 D2
Biggenden Australia 149 G5
Bigger, Mount Canada 166 B3
Biggleswade U.K. 47 L11
Biggs U.S.A. 182 C2
Big Hole r. U.S.A. 180 D3
Bighorn r. U.S.A. 180 F3
Bighorn Mountains U.S.A. 180 F3
Bigil'dino Rus. Fed. 43 U8
Big Island i. Nunavut Canada 165 L3
Big Island i. N.W.T. Canada 167 G2
Big Island U.S.A. 176 F8
Big Kalzas Lake Canada 166 C2
Big Lake U.S.A. 179 B6
Big Lake l. U.S.A. 174 G2
Big Muddy Creek r. U.S.A. 180 F2
Bignona Senegal 124 A3
Bigobo Dem. Rep. Congo 127 E6
Big Otter r. U.S.A. 176 F8
Big Pine U.S.A. 182 F4
Big Pine Peak U.S.A. 182 F7
Big Rapids U.S.A. 172 H7
Big Rib r. U.S.A. 172 D6
Big River Canada 167 J4
Big Sable Point U.S.A. 172 G6
Big Salmon Canada 166 C2
Big Salmon r. Canada 166 C2
Big Sand Lake Canada 167 L3
Big Sandy r. U.S.A. 180 E4
Big Sandy watercourse U.S.A. 183 K7
Big Sandy Creek r. U.S.A. 178 B4
Big Sandy Lake Canada 167 J4
Big Sioux r. U.S.A. 178 C3
Big Smokey Valley valley U.S.A. 183 G3
Big South Cape Island N.Z. 153 B15
Big South Fork National River and Recreation Area park U.S.A. 176 A9
Big Spring U.S.A. 179 B5
Big Stone Canada 167 I5
Big Sur U.S.A. 182 C5
Big Thicket National Preserve nature res. U.S.A. 179 D6
Big Timber U.S.A. 180 E3
Big Trout Lake Canada 168 B2
Big Trout Lake l. Canada 168 B2
Big Valley Canada 167 H4
Big Water U.S.A. 183 M4
Bigwin Canada 173 N5
Bihać Bos.-Herz. 56 H4
Bihar state India 97 E4
Bihariganj India 97 E4
Bihar Sharif India 97 E4
Bihor, Vârful mt. Romania 58 D2
Bihoro Japan 90 I3
Bihpuriagaon India 97 G4
Bijagós, Arquipélago dos is Guinea-Bissau 124 A4
Bijainagar India 96 B4
Bijaipur India 96 C4
Bijapur India 94 B2
Bijār Iran 100 A3
Bijarpur India 94 D2
Bijawar India 96 C4
Bijbehara Jammu and Kashmir 96 B2
Bijeljina Bos.-Herz. 56 L4
Bijelolasica mt. Croatia 56 H3
Bijelo Polje Crna Gora Serb. and Mont. 58 A5
Bijie China 86 C3
Bijni India 97 F4
Bijnor India 96 C3
Bijolia India 96 B4
Bijoutier i. Seychelles 129 [inset]
Bijrān well Saudi Arabia 105 E2
Bijrān, Khashm hill Saudi Arabia 105 E2
Bikampur India 96 B4
Bikaner India 96 B3
Bikbauli Kazakh. 103 E3
Bikfaiya Lebanon 108 G4
Bikin Rus. Fed. 82 D3
Bikin r. Rus. Fed. 82 D3
Bikini atoll Marshall Is 220 G5
Bikita Zimbabwe 131 F4
Bikori Sudan 128 B2
Bikoro Dem. Rep. Congo 126 C5
Bikou China 86 C1
Bikramganj India 97 E4
Bilaa Point Phil. 74 C4
Bilād Banī Bū 'Alī Oman 105 G3
Bilād Banī Bū Ḩasan Oman 105 G3
Bilād Ghāmid reg. Saudi Arabia 104 C3
Bilād Zahrān reg. Saudi Arabia 104 C3
Bilanga Burkina 125 E3
Bilangbilangan i. Indon. 77 G2
Bilara India 96 B4
Bilari India 96 C3
Bilaspur Chhattisgarh India 97 D5
Bilaspur Himachal Pradesh India 96 C3
Biläsuvar Azer. 107 G3
formerly known as Pushkino
Bilatan i. Phil. 74 B5
Bila Tserkva Ukr. 41 D6
also spelt Belaya Tserkva
Bilauktaung Range mts Myanmar/Thai. 79 B5
Bilbao Spain 55 I1
also spelt Bilbo
Bilbays Egypt 121 F2
Bilbo Spain see Bilbao
Bilbor Romania 58 G1
Bildudalur Iceland 44 [inset] B2
Bileća Bos.-Herz. 56 K6
Bilecik Turkey 106 B2
Biled Romania 58 B3
Bilesha Plain Kenya 128 D4
Biłgoraj Poland 49 T5
Bilharamulo Tanz. 128 A5
Bilhaur India 96 D4
Bilhorod-Dnistrovs'kyy Ukr. 41 D7
also spelt Belgorod-Dnestrovskyy; formerly known as Akkerman; historically known as Cetatea Albă or Tyras
Bili Chad 126 C2
Bili r. Dem. Rep. Congo 126 D3
Bilibino Rus. Fed. 39 Q3
Bilibiza Moz. 129 D8
Bilikōl l. Kazakh. see Biylikol', Ozero
Bilin Myanmar 78 B4
Biliran i. Phil. 74 C4
Bilisht Albania 58 B8
Bilis Qooqaani Somalia 128 D4
Biliu He r. China 85 I4
Bill U.S.A. 180 F4
Billabalong Australia 151 A5
Billabong Creek r. Australia see Moulamein Creek
Billdal Sweden 45 J4
Billère France 50 F9
Billiat Conservation Park nature res. Australia 146 D3
Billiluna Australia 150 D3
Billiluna Aboriginal Reserve Australia 150 D3
Billings U.S.A. 180 E3
Billiton i. Indon. see Belitung
Bill of Portland hd U.K. 47 J13
also known as Portland Bill
Billund airport Denmark 45 J5
Bill Williams r. U.S.A. 183 J7
Bill Williams Mountain U.S.A. 183 L6
Bilma Niger 125 I2
Bilo Eth. 128 C2
Biloela Australia 149 F5
Bilohirs'k Ukr. 41 E7
also spelt Belogorsk; formerly known as Karasubazar
Bilohir"ya Ukr. 41 C6
Biloku Guyana 199 G4
Biloli India 94 C2
Biloluts'k Ukr. 41 F6
Bilovods'k Ukr. 41 F6
Biloxi U.S.A. 175 B6
Bilpa Morea Claypan salt flat Australia 148 C5
Bilqās Qism Awwal Egypt 108 C6
Bilshausen Germany 48 H4
Bilsi India 96 C3
Biltine Chad 120 D6
Biltine pref. Chad 120 D6
Bilugyun Island Myanmar 78 B4
Bilungala Indon. 75 B2
Bilwascarma Nicaragua 186 C4
Bilyayivka Ukr. 41 D7
also spelt Belyayevka
Bima r. Dem. Rep. Congo 126 E4
Bima Indon. 77 G5
Bima, Teluk b. Indon. 77 G5
Bimbe Angola 127 B7
Bimbila Ghana 125 F4
Bimbo Centr. Afr. Rep. 126 C3
Bimini Islands Bahamas 186 D1
Bimlipatam India 95 D2
Bina-Etawa India 96 C4
Binaija, Gunung mt. Indon. 75 D3
Binalbagan Phil. 74 B4
Bīnālūd, Kūh-e mts Iran 100 D2
Binarowa tourist site Poland 49 S6
UNESCO World Heritage Site
Binatang Sarawak Malaysia 77 E2
Binboğa Daği mt. Turkey 107 D3
Bincheng China 85 H4
formerly known as Binxian
Binchuan China 86 B3
also known as Niujing
Binder Chad 126 B2
Bindki India 96 D4
Bindu Dem. Rep. Congo 127 C6
Bindura Zimbabwe 131 F3
Binefar Spain 55 L3
Binga Zimbabwe 131 E3
Binga, Monte mt. Moz. 131 G3
Bingara Australia 147 F2
Bingaram i. India 94 B4
Bing Bong Australia 148 C2
Bingcaowan China 84 D4
Bingen am Rhein Germany 48 E6
Bingham U.S.A. 174 G2
Binghamton U.S.A. 177 J3
Bin Ghanīmah, Jabal hills Libya 120 B3
Bin Ghashir Libya 120 B1
Bingmei China see Congjiang
Bingöl Turkey 107 E3
also known as Çapakçur
Bingol Dağı mt. Turkey 107 E3
Bingxi China see Yushan
Bingzhongluo China 86 A2
Binicuil Phil. 74 B4
Bini Erda well Chad 120 C4
Binika India 97 D5
Binjai Indon. 76 B2
Bin Jawwād Libya 120 C2
Binna, Raas pt Somalia 128 F2
Binnaway Australia 147 F2
Binongko i. Indon. 75 C4
Binpur India 97 E5
Bīnshangul Gumuz admin. reg. Eth. 128 B2
Bintan i. Indon. 76 D2
Bintang, Bukit mts Malaysia 76 C1
Bintuan Phil. 74 B3
Bintuhan Indon. 76 C4
Bintulu Sarawak Malaysia 77 F2
Binubusan Phil. 74 B3
Binxian Heilong. China 82 B3
also known as Binzhou
Binxian Shaanxi China 87 D1
Binxian Shandong China see Bincheng
Binyang China 87 D4
also known as Binzhou
Bin-Yauri Nigeria 125 G4
Binz, Ostseebad Germany 49 K1
Binzhou Guangxi China see Binyang
Binzhou Heilong. China see Binxian
Binzhou Shandong China 85 H4
Biobío admin. reg. Chile 204 B5
Biobío r. Chile 204 B5
Bioco i. Equat. Guinea 125 H6
also spelt Bioko; formerly known as Fernando Poó or Macias Nguema
Biograd na Moru Croatia 56 H5
Biogradska Gora nat. park Serb. and Mont. 58 A6
Bioko i. Equat. Guinea see Bioco
Biokovo park Croatia 56 J5
Biquinhas Brazil 207 H5
Bir India see Bid
Bir, Ras pt Djibouti 128 D2
Bira Rus. Fed. 82 D2
Bira r. Rus. Fed. 82 D2
Bi'r Abā al 'Ajjāj well Saudi Arabia 104 B2
Bi'r Abraq well Egypt 121 G4
Bi'r Abū Daraj well Egypt 108 D8
Bir Abu Garad well Sudan 121 F5
Bi'r Abū Hashīm well Egypt 121 G4
Bi'r Abū Ḩuşayn well Egypt 121 F4
Bi'r Abū Jady oasis Syria 109 J1
Bi'r Abū Minqār well Egypt 121 E3
Bi'r ad Damar well Libya 120 A3
Bi'r ad Duwaydār well Egypt 108 D7
Bi'r adh Dhakar well Libya 120 D3
Bir Adiat well Mauritania 122 C4
Birāk Libya 120 B3
Birakan Rus. Fed. 82 C2
Bi'r al 'Ajramīyah well Egypt 108 C8
Bi'r al Amīr well Saudi Arabia 104 B2
Bi'r al Aţbaq well Saudi Arabia 104 B2
Bi'r al 'Awādī well Saudi Arabia 104 B3
Bi'r al Fātīyah well Libya 120 B2
Bi'r al Ghanam Libya 120 B1
Bi'r al Ḩalbā well Syria 109 J3
Bi'r al Ḩaymūr well Egypt 121 G4
Bi'r al Ḩisw well Saudi Arabia 104 C2
Bi'r al Ikhwān well Libya 120 D3
Bi'r al Jadīd well Libya 120 B3
Bi'r al Jāhilīyah well Saudi Arabia 104 C3
Bi'r al Jifjāfah well Egypt 108 E7
Bi'r al Khamsah well Egypt 106 A5
Bi'r al Māliḩah well Egypt 108 E8
Bi'r al Marba'ah well Syria 109 K3
Bi'r al Mashī well Saudi Arabia 104 B2
Bi'r al Mastūtah well Libya 120 B3
Bi'r al Mulūsi Iraq 107 E4
Bi'r al Mulūşī waterhole Iraq 109 L4
Bi'r al Munbaţiḩ well Syria 109 J3
Bi'r al Mushayqīq well Libya 120 B2
Bi'r al Muwayliḩ well Libya 120 C2
Bi'r al Qaţrānī well Egypt 121 E2
Bi'r al Qurr well Saudi Arabia 104 B2
Bi'r al Ubbayiḑ well Egypt 121 E3
Bi'r al 'Udayd well Egypt 108 F9
Bir 'Amrâne well Mauritania 122 C5
Birandozero Rus. Fed. 40 F3
Bi'r an Nakhīlī waterhole Iraq 109 N3
Bi'r an Nuşş well Egypt 121 E2
Bir Anzarane W. Sahara 122 B5
Birao Cent. Afr. Rep. 126 D2
Bir Aouine well Tunisia 123 H2
Bi'r ar 'Alaqah well Libya 120 B2
Bi'r 'Arja well Saudi Arabia 104 C2
Bi'r ar Rābiyah well Egypt 106 A5
Bi'r ar Rummānah Egypt 108 D6
Bi'r as Sakhā well Saudi Arabia 104 C3
Biratar Bulak spring China 88 E3
Biratnagar Nepal 97 E4
also known as Morang
Biratori Japan 90 H3
Bi'r aţ Ţarfāwī well Libya 120 E2
Bi'r aţ Tayyārīyah well Syria 109 K3
Bi'r aţ Ţuwayyah waterhole Iraq 109 L4
Bi'r 'Azīz well Saudi Arabia 105 E3
Bi'raz Zurq well Saudi Arabia 104 C4
Bi'r Başīrī well Syria 109 I3
Bi'r Baydā' well Egypt 108 F7
Bi'r Baydā well Saudi Arabia 104 B2
Bi'r Baylī well Egypt 120 E2
Bîr Bel Guerdâne well Mauritania 122 C4
Bir Ben Takoul well Alg. 123 E4
Bir Bidi well Sudan 121 E5
Bi'r Bū Athlah well Libya 120 D3
Bi'r Bu'ayrāt well Egypt 108 D8
Bi'r Budayy well Saudi Arabia 104 B2
Bi'r Bū Rāḩah well Libya 120 B3
Bi'r Buraym well Saudi Arabia 104 C3
Birch r. Canada 167 H3
Bir Chali well Mali 122 D5
Birch Hills Canada 167 J4
Birchip Australia 147 D3
Birch Lake N.W.T. Canada 167 G2
Birch Lake Sask. Canada 167 I4
Birch Lake U.S.A. 172 B3
Birch Mountains Canada 167 H3
Birch River Canada 167 K4
Birch River U.S.A. 176 E7
Birch Run U.S.A. 173 J7
Birchwood U.S.A. 172 B5
Bircot Eth. 128 D3
Bir Di Sudan 126 F3
Bi'r Dibs well Egypt 121 F4
Bi'r Diqnāsh well Egypt 120 E2
Bird Island N. Mariana Is see Farallon de Medinilla
Bir Dolmane well Alg. 123 H3
Birdsboro U.S.A. 177 J5
Birdseye U.S.A. 183 M2
Birdsville Australia 148 C5
Birdum r. Australia 148 B2
Birecik Turkey 107 D3
Bir ed Deheb well Alg. 123 E4
Bir el Fakama well Sudan 104 A4
Bir el Ghoralia well Tunisia 123 H2
Bir El Hadjaj well Alg. 123 E4
Birendranagar Nepal see Surkhet
Bir en Natrûn well Sudan 121 E5
Bir en Nugeim well Sudan 121 G5
Bir es Smeha well Alg. 123 G2
Bireun Indon. 76 B1
Bi'r Fāḑil well Saudi Arabia 105 E3
Bi'r Fajr well Saudi Arabia 104 B1
Bir Fanoidig well Sudan 104 A4
Bi'r Fardān well Saudi Arabia 105 E3
Bi'r Fu'ād well Egypt 121 E2
Bir Furawiya well Sudan 120 D6
Bir Gandouz W. Sahara 122 A5
Bi'r Ghawdah well Saudi Arabia 104 D3
Bir Hādī oasis Saudi Arabia 105 E4
Bi'r Ḩajal well Syria 109 K3
Birhan mt. Eth. 128 C2
Bi'r Haraqī well Saudi Arabia 104 C3
Bi'r Ḩasanah well Egypt 108 E7
Bir Hatab well Sudan 121 G4
Bi'r Ḩaymir well Saudi Arabia 104 B2
Bi'r Ḩayzān well Saudi Arabia 104 B2
Bir Hismet 'Umar well Sudan 121 G4
Bi'r Ḩudūf well Saudi Arabia 104 C3
Bi'r Ḩumaymah well Syria 109 K3
Bir Huwait well Sudan 121 G4
Bi'r Ḩuwaymidah well Saudi Arabia 104 C2
Bi'r Ibn Ghunayn well Saudi Arabia 104 B2
Bi'r Ibn Hirmās Saudi Arabia see Al Bi'r
Bi'r Ibn Sarrār well Saudi Arabia 104 C4
Bi'r Īdīmah well Saudi Arabia 104 D4
Birigüi Brazil 206 C8
Birin, Col de pass Alg. 55 N9
Birini Cent. Afr. Rep. 126 D3
Bi'r Iştabl well Egypt 121 E2
Bīrjand Iran 101 D3
Bi'r Jaydah well Saudi Arabia 104 B2
Bi'r Jifah well Yemen 105 D5
Bi'r Jindālī well Egypt 108 C8
Bi'r Jubnī well Libya 120 E2
Bi'r Jugjug well Saudi Arabia 104 C3
Birka tourist site Sweden 45 L4
UNESCO World Heritage Site
Birkeland Norway 45 J4
Birkenhead U.K. 47 I10
Bi'r Khamrān waterhole Iraq 109 O3
Bi'r Khurbah well Saudi Arabia 104 B2
Bi'r Khuwārah well Saudi Arabia 104 C3
Bir Kiau well Sudan 121 G4
Bīrkim Iraq 107 F3
Birkirkara Malta 57 G13
Birksgate Range hills Australia 146 A1
Bir Labasoi well Sudan 121 G4
Bîrlad Romania see Bârlad
Bi'r Lahfān well Egypt 108 E6
Bir Lahmar W. Sahara 122 C4
Birlik Zhambylskaya Oblast' Kazakh. 103 H3
formerly spelt Brlik
Birlik Zhambylskaya Oblast' Kazakh. 103 H4
also spelt Brlik
Bir Likeit el Fauqani well Sudan 104 A3
Bir Liseila well Sudan 121 G4
Bi'r Majal well Egypt 121 G4
Birmal reg. Afgh. 101 G3
Bi'r Malīyah well Saudi Arabia 104 C3
Birmingham U.K. 47 K11
Birmingham U.S.A. 175 C5
Bi'r Misāḩa well Egypt 121 E4
Birmitrapur India 97 E5
Bîr Mogreïn Mauritania 122 C4
formerly known as Fort Trinquet
Bi'r Muḩaymid al Wazwaz well Syria 109 J3
Bi'r Mujayfil well Saudi Arabia 108 G8
Bi'r Murrah well Egypt 121 G4
Bi'r Muwayliḩ well Syria 109 K3
Bi'r Nabt well Saudi Arabia 104 B2
Bi'r Nāḩid oasis Egypt 121 F2
Bi'r Najīb well Egypt 121 G4
Bi'r Najib well Syria 109 K3
Bi'r Nasīf Saudi Arabia 104 B2
Bir Nawari well Sudan 121 G4
Birni Benin 125 F4
Birnie i. Kiribati 145 H2
Birnin-Gaouré Niger 125 F3
Birnin-Gwari Nigeria 125 G4
Birnin-Kebbi Nigeria 125 G3
Birnin Konni Niger 125 G3
Birnin Kudu Nigeria 125 H4
Birniwa Nigeria 125 H3
Bir Nukheila well Sudan 121 E5
Birobidzhan Rus. Fed. 82 D2
Birofel'd Rus. Fed. 82 D2
Bir Ounâne well Mali 122 E5
Birpur India 97 E4
Bi'r Qaşīr as Sirr well Egypt 106 A5
Bi'r Qulayb well Egypt 121 G3
Birr Ireland 47 E10
Bi'r Rawḑ Sālim well Egypt 108 E7
Birrie r. Australia 147 E2
Birrindudu Australia 148 A3
Bir Roumi well Alg. 123 G2
Bi'r Şābil Iraq 107 E4
Bi'r Şahrā' well Egypt 121 F4
Bir Salala well Sudan 121 G4
Birsay U.K. 46 I4
Bi'r Shalatayn Egypt 121 G4
Bi'r Shamandūr well Syria 109 K1
Birshoghyr Kazakh. see Berchogur
Bi'r Simād waterhole Iraq 109 O3
Birsk Rus. Fed. 40 J5
Bir Sohanit well Sudan 104 A3
Birštonas Lith. 42 F7
Bi'r Ţābah Egypt 108 F8
Bi'r Ţalḩah well Saudi Arabia 105 D3
Bir Tanguer well Alg. 123 H3
Bi'r Tānjidar well Libya 120 D2
Bi'r Ţarfāwī well Egypt 121 F4
Bi'r Ţarūfāwī waterhole Iraq 109 O4
Birtavarre Norway 44 M1
Bi'r Thāl well Egypt 108 E8
Birthday Mountain hill Australia 149 D2
Birtle Canada 167 K5
Biru China 89 F6
also known as Biruxiong
Bi'r Udayb well Egypt 108 D8
Biruintsa Moldova see Ştefan Vodă
Bi'r Umm al Gharānīq Libya 120 C2
Bi'r Umm Fawākhīr well Egypt 104 A2
Bi'r Umm Missā well Saudi Arabia 104 B2
Biruni Uzbek. see Beruniy
Bi'r 'Unjāt well Egypt 121 G4
Birur India 94 B3
Bi'r Usaylīlah well Saudi Arabia 105 D3
Biruxiong China see Biru
Bir Wario well Sudan 121 G5
Bi'r Wedeb well Libya 120 B3
Bir Wurshah well Saudi Arabia 104 C3
Biryakovo Rus. Fed. 43 V2
Biržai Lith. 42 F5
Bir Zar well Tunisia 123 H3
Bisa i. Indon. 75 C3
Bisalpur India 96 C3
Bisau India 96 B3
Bisbee U.S.A. 181 E7
Biscarrosse France 50 E8
Biscarrosse et de Parentis, Étang de l. France 50 E8
Biscay, Bay of sea France/Spain 50 A7
Biscayne Bay U.S.A. 175 D7
Biscayne National Park U.S.A. 175 D7
Bischofshofen Austria 49 K8
Bischofswerda Germany 49 L4
Biscoe Islands Antarctica 222 T2
Biscotasing Canada 168 D4
Bisert' r. Rus. Fed. 40 K4
Bisertsi Bulg. 58 H5
Biševo i. Croatia 56 H6
Bisezhai China 86 B4
Bisha Eritrea 121 H6
Bīshah reg. Saudi Arabia 104 C4

Bom Jesus do Itabapoana Brazil 203 D7
Bømlo i. Norway 45 I4
Bomokandi r. Dem. Rep. Congo 126 E4
Bompas France 51 I10
Bom Retiro Brazil 203 B8
Bom Sucesso Minas Gerais Brazil 207 I8
Bom Sucesso Paraná Brazil 206 B10
Bomu, Réserve de Faune de la nature res. Dem. Rep. Congo 126 D3
Bon, Cap c. Tunisia 123 H1
Bona Alg. see Annaba
Bona, Mount U.S.A. 166 A2
Bonāb Iran 100 A2
Bona Bona Island P.N.G. 149 F1
Bon Air U.S.A. 176 H8
Bonaire i. Neth. Antilles 187 F4
Bonandolok Indon. 76 B2
Bonanza Nicaragua 186 B4
Bonaparte Archipelago is Australia 150 D2
Bonaparte Lake Canada 166 F5
Bonasse Trin. and Tob. 187 H5
Bonavista Canada 169 K3
Bonavista Bay Canada 169 K3
Bon Bon Australia 146 B2
Bondo Équateur Dem. Rep. Congo 126 D5
Bondo Orientale Dem. Rep. Congo 126 D4
Bondoc Peninsula Phil. 74 B3
Bondokodi Indon. 75 A5
Bondoukou Côte d'Ivoire 124 E4
Bondoukui Burkina 124 E4
Bondowoso Indon. 77 F4
Bonduel U.S.A. 172 E6
Bondyuzhskiy Rus. Fed. see Mendeleyevsk
Bône Alg. see Annaba
Bone Indon. 75 B4
Bone, Teluk b. Indon. 75 B4
Bonekraal S. Africa 132 E8
Bone Lake U.S.A. 172 A5
Bonelipu Indon. 75 B4
Bonerate Indon. 75 B4
Bonerate i. Indon. 75 B4
Bonerate, Kepulauan is Indon. 75 B4

▸Bonete, Cerro mt. Arg. 204 C2
3rd highest mountain in South America.
▸▸188–189 South America Landscapes

Bonfim Brazil 207 I7
Bonfim r. Brazil 206 A4
Bonfinópolis de Minas Brazil 202 C6
Bonga Eth. 128 C3
Bongabong Phil. 74 B3
Bongaigaon India 97 F4
Bongandanga Dem. Rep. Congo 126 D4
Bongani S. Africa 132 H6
Bongao Phil. 74 A5
Bongba China 89 C5
Bong Co l. China 89 E6
Bongka r. Indon. 75 B3
Bongo i. Phil. 74 C5
Bongo, Massif des mts Cent. Afr. Rep. 126 D2
Bongo, Serra do mts Angola 127 B7
Bongolava mts Madag. 131 [inset] J3
Bongor Chad 126 B2
Bongouanou Côte d'Ivoire 124 D5
Bông Sơn Vietnam 79 E5
Bonham U.S.A. 179 C5
Bönhamn Sweden 44 L3
Boni Mali 125 E3
Bonifacio Corsica France 52 D3
Bonifacio, Bocche di strait France/Italy see Bonifacio, Strait of
Bonifacio, Bouches de strait France/Italy see Bonifacio, Strait of
Bonifacio, Strait of strait France/Italy 56 A7
also known as Bonifacio, Bocche di or Bonifacio, Bouches de
Boni National Reserve nature res. Kenya 128 D5

▸Bonin Islands N. Pacific Ocean 220 E4
Part of Japan. Also known as Ogasawara-shotō.

Bonita Springs U.S.A. 175 D7
Bonito Mato Grosso do Sul Brazil 201 F5
Bonito Minas Gerais Brazil 207 I2
Bonito r. Brazil 206 B3
Bonito r. Brazil 206 G2

▸Bonn Germany 48 E5
Former capital of Germany. Historically known as Bonna.

Bonna Germany see Bonn
Bonnat France 51 H6
Bonners Ferry U.S.A. 180 C2
Bonnet, Lac du resr Canada 167 M5
Bonnet Plume r. Canada 166 C1
Bonneval France 50 H4
Bonneville France 51 M6
Bonney, Lake Australia 146 D4
Bonnie Rock Australia 151 B6
Bonny Glen Aboriginal Holding res. Australia 149 E3
Bonny Ridge S. Africa 133 N7
Bonnyville Canada 167 I4
Bono Sardinia Italy 57 B8
Bōno-misaki pt Japan 91 B9
Bononia Italy see Bologna
Bonorva Sardinia Italy 57 A8
Bonoua Côte d'Ivoire 124 E5
Bonpland, Mount N.Z. 153 C12
Bonsall U.S.A. 183 G8
Bonshaw Australia 147 F2
Bontberg mt. S. Africa 132 F9
Bonteberg mts S. Africa 132 D10
Bontebok National Park S. Africa 132 E11
Bonthe Sierra Leone 124 B5
Bontoc Phil. 74 B2
Bontomatane Indon. 75 B4
Bontosunggu Indon. 75 A4
Bontrand S. Africa 133 N7
Bontrug S. Africa 133 J10
Bonvouloir Islands P.N.G. 149 F1
Bonyhád Hungary 49 P9
Boo Sweden 45 L4
Boo, Kepulauan is Indon. 75 D3
Boodie Boodie Range hills Australia 151 C5
Bookabie Australia 146 B2
Book Cliffs ridge U.S.A. 183 O2
Booker U.S.A. 178 B4
Boola Guinea 124 C4
Booleroo Centre Australia 146 C3
Booligal Australia 147 E3
Boologooro Australia 151 A5
Boomi Australia 147 F2
Boon U.S.A. 172 H6
Boonah Australia 147 G1
Boone IA U.S.A. 174 A3
Boone NC U.S.A. 176 D9
Boone Lake U.S.A. 176 C9
Boones Mill U.S.A. 176 F8
Booneville AR U.S.A. 179 D5
Booneville KY U.S.A. 176 B8
Booneville MS U.S.A. 174 B5
Boons S. Africa 133 L2
Boonsboro U.S.A. 176 H6
Bööntsagaan Nuur salt l. Mongolia 84 C2
Boonville CA U.S.A. 182 A3
Boonville IN U.S.A. 174 C4
Boonville MO U.S.A. 178 D4
Boopi r. Bol. 200 D3
Boorabin National Park Australia 151 C6
Boorama Somalia 128 D2
Booroorban Australia 147 E3
Boorowa Australia 147 F3
Boosaaso Somalia 128 F2
Boothbay Harbor U.S.A. 177 P2
Boothby, Cape Antarctica 223 D2
Boothia, Gulf of Canada 165 K3
Boothia Peninsula Canada 165 J2
Booué Gabon 126 A5
Bopolu Liberia 124 C5
Boppard Germany 48 E5
Boqê China 89 E6
Boqueirão Brazil 204 G3
Boqueirão, Serra do hills Brazil 202 C5
Bor Rus. Fed. 40 H4
Bor Srbija Serb. and Mont. 58 D4
Bor Sudan 128 A3
Bor Turkey 106 C3
Boragi waterhole Kenya 128 C5
Borah Peak U.S.A. 180 D3
Borakalalo Nature Reserve S. Africa 133 L2
Boran Kazakh. see Buran
Boraphet, Bung l. Thai. 79 C5
Boraraigh i. U.K. see Boreray
Borås Sweden 45 K4
Borasambar India 95 D1
Borāzjān Iran 100 B4
Borba Brazil 199 G6
Borba Port. 54 D6
Borbollón, Embalse del resr Spain 54 E4
Borbon Phil. 74 C4
Borborema Brazil 206 D8
Borborema, Planalto da plat. Brazil 202 E3
Borca Romania 58 G1
Borcea, Braţul watercourse Romania 58 I4
Borchalo Georgia see Marneuli
Borchgrevink Coast Antarctica 223 K2
Borçka Turkey 107 E2
also known as Yeniyol
Borda, Cape Australia 150 C3
Borda da Mata Brazil 207 G9
Bor Dağı mt. Turkey 59 K11
Bordeaux France 50 F8
historically known as Burdigala
Bordehi India 96 C5
Bordein Sudan 121 G6
Borden-Carleton Canada 169 I4
Borden Island Canada 165 H2
Borden Peninsula Canada 165 K2
Bordentown U.S.A. 177 K5
Border Ranges National Park Australia 147 G2
Bordertown Australia 146 D4
Borðeyri Iceland 44 [inset] B2
Bordj Bou Arréridj Alg. 123 G1
Bordj Bounaama Alg. 55 M9
Bordj Flye Ste-Marie Alg. 123 E4
Bordj Messaouda Alg. 123 H3
Bordj Mokhtar Alg. 123 F5
Bordj Omar Driss Alg. see Bordj Omer Driss
Bordj Omer Driss Alg. 123 G3
formerly known as Fort Flatters or Zaouet el Kahla; formerly spelt Bordj Omar Driss
Bordj Zemoura Alg. 55 P8
Borðoy i. Faroe Is 46 F1
Bordu Kyrg. 103 H4
also known as Bordunskiy
Bordunskiy Kyrg. see Bordu
Boreas Nunatak Antarctica 223 X2
Borel r. Canada 169 G1
Borensberg Sweden 45 K4
Boreray i. U.K. 46 D6
also spelt Boraraigh
Borgå Fin. see Porvoo
Borgafjäll Sweden 44 K2
Borgarfjörður Iceland 44 [inset] D2
Borgarnes Iceland 44 [inset] B2
Børgefjell Nasjonalpark nat. park Norway 44 K2
Borger U.S.A. 179 B5
Borgholm Sweden 45 L4
Borgo Corsica France 51 P10
Borgo a Mozzano Italy 56 C5
Borgomanero Italy 56 A3
Borgo San Dalmazzo Italy 51 N8
Borgo San Lorenzo Italy 56 D5
Borgosesia Italy 56 A3
Borgo Val di Taro Italy 56 B4
Borgo Valsugana Italy 56 D2
Borgsjåbrotet mt. Norway 45 J3
Bori India 94 C1
Bori r. India 96 B5
Börili Kazakh. see Burli
Borilovo Rus. Fed. 43 Q8
Borino Bulg. 58 F7
Borinskoye Rus. Fed. 43 U9
Borisoglebsk Rus. Fed. 41 G6
Borisoglebskiy Rus. Fed. 43 U4
Borisov Belarus see Barysaw
Borisovka Rus. Fed. 41 F6
Borisovo-Sudskoye Rus. Fed. 43 R2
Borispol' Ukr. see Boryspil'
Bo River Post Sudan 126 E3
Borizny Madag. 131 [inset] J2
Borja mts Bos.-Herz. 56 J4
Borja Peru 198 B6
Borjas Blancas Spain see Les Borges Blanques
Borj Bourguiba Tunisia 123 H2
Borjomis Nakrdzali nature res. Georgia 107 E2
Borkavichy Belarus 43 J6
Borken Germany 48 D4
Borkenes Norway 44 L1
Borki Rus. Fed. 43 T9
Borkou-Ennedi-Tibesti pref. Chad 120 C5
Borkovskaya Rus. Fed. 40 I2
Borkum Germany 48 D2
Borkum i. Germany 48 D2
Borlänge Sweden 45 K3
Borlaug Norway 45 I3
Borlu Turkey 106 B3
Borna Germany 49 J4
Born-Berge hill Germany 48 H4
Borne Alg. 123 G4

▸Borneo i. Asia 77 F2
Largest island in Asia and 3rd in the world.
▸▸6–7 World Landscapes
▸▸60–61 Asia Landscapes

Bornes mts France 51 M7
Bornholm i. Denmark 45 K5
Bornholmsgattet strait Denmark/Sweden 45 K5
Borno state Nigeria 125 I4
Bornova Turkey 106 A3
Borobudur tourist site Indon. 77 E4
UNESCO World Heritage Site
Borodino Krasnoyarskiy Kray Rus. Fed. 39 I3
Borodino Moskovskaya Oblast' Rus. Fed. 43 Q6
Borodino Ukr. 58 K2
Borodinskoye Rus. Fed. 43 K1
Borodyanka Ukr. 41 D6
Borogontsy Rus. Fed. 39 N3
Borohoro Shan mts China 88 C2
Borok Rus. Fed. 43 T3
Boroko Indon. 75 B2
Borok-Sulezhskiy Rus. Fed. 43 R4
Boromo Burkina 124 E4
Boron Mali 124 D3
Boron U.S.A. 182 G7
Borongan Phil. 74 C4
Bororen Australia 149 F5
Borovan Bulg. 58 E5
Borovenka Rus. Fed. 43 O3
Borovichi Rus. Fed. 43 O3
Borovo Selo Croatia 56 K3
Borovoy Kirovskaya Oblast' Rus. Fed. 40 I4
Borovoy Respublika Kareliya Rus. Fed. 40 E2
Borovoy Respublika Komi Rus. Fed. 40 J3
Borovoye Kazakh. 103 G1
Borovsk Rus. Fed. 43 R6
Borovskoy Kazakh. 103 F1
Borrachudo r. Brazil 207 H5
Borrazópolis Brazil 206 B10
Borrego Springs U.S.A. 183 H8
Borroloola Australia 148 C3
Børsa Norway 44 J3
Borşa Romania 58 E2
Borşa Romania 53 G2
Borsad India 96 B5
Borsakelmas sho'rxogi salt marsh Uzbek. 102 D4
Borsec Romania 58 G2
Børselv Norway 44 N1
Borshchiv Ukr. 41 C6
Borshchovochnyy Khrebet mts Rus. Fed. 85 F1
Borsippa tourist site Iraq 107 F4
Borskoye Rus. Fed. 102 B1
Borsod-Abaúj-Zemplén county Hungary 49 R7
UNESCO World Heritage Site
Börßum Germany 48 H3
Bortala China see Bole
Bortala He r. China 88 C2
Bort-les-Orgues France 51 I7
Bor-Üdzüür Mongolia 84 B2
Borūjen Iran 100 B4
Borūjerd Iran 100 B3
Bor Ul Shan mts China 84 C3
Borun Iran 100 D3
Borushtitsa Bulg. 58 G6
Boryspil' Ukr. 40 D6
also spelt Borispol'
Borzna Ukr. 41 E6
Börzsönyi park Hungary 49 P8
Borzya Rus. Fed. 85 H1
Borzya r. Rus. Fed. 85 G1
Bosa Sardinia Italy 57 A8
Bosaga Kazakh. 103 H3
also spelt Bosagha; formerly known as Bosaginskiy
Bosagha Kazakh. see Bosaga
Bosaginskiy Kazakh. see Bosaga
Bosanska Dubica Bos.-Herz. 56 I3
also known as Kozarska Dubica
Bosanska Gradiška Bos.-Herz. 56 J3
also known as Gradiška
Bosanska Kostajnica Bos.-Herz. 56 I3
also known as Srpska Kostajnica
Bosanska Krupa Bos.-Herz. 56 I4
also known as Krupa or Krupa na Uni
Bosanski Brod Bos.-Herz. 56 K3
also known as Srpski Brod
Bosanski Novi Bos.-Herz. 56 I3
also known as Novi Grad
Bosanski Petrovac Bos.-Herz. 56 I4
also known as Petrovac
Bosanski Šamac Bos.-Herz. 56 K3
also known as Šamac
Bosberg mt. S. Africa 133 I9
Bosbokrand S. Africa 133 P1
Boscawen U.S.A. 177 N2
Boscawen Island Tonga see Niuatoputopu
Bosch Arg. 204 F5
Boscobel U.S.A. 172 C7
Bosduiflaagte salt pan S. Africa 132 E6
Bose China 86 C4
Bosencheve, Parque Nacional nat. park Mex. 185 E5
Boshchakul' Kazakh. see Bozshakol'
Boshnyakovo Rus. Fed. 82 F2
Boshoek S. Africa 133 L2
Boshof S. Africa 133 J5
Boshruyeh Iran 100 D3
Bosilegrad Srbija Serb. and Mont. 58 D6
formerly spelt Bosiljgrad
Bosiljgrad Srbija Serb. and Mont. see Bosilegrad
Boskol' Kazakh. 103 E1
also spelt Bozkōl; formerly spelt Buskul'
Boskovice Czech Rep. 49 N6
Boslanti Suriname 199 H3
Bosna r. Bos.-Herz. 56 K3
Bosna hills Bulg. 58 I6
Bosna i Hercegovina country Europe see Bosnia-Herzegovina
Bosna Saray Bos.-Herz. see Sarajevo
▸Bosnia-Herzegovina country Europe 56 J4
known as Bosna i Hercegovina in Bosnian
▸▸32–33 Europe Countries
Boso Dem. Rep. Congo 126 D4
Bosobogolo Pan salt pan Botswana 132 G2
Bosobolo Dem. Rep. Congo 126 C3
Bōsō-hantō pen. Japan 91 G7
Bososama Dem. Rep. Congo 126 D3
Bosoport S. Africa 133 K3
▸Bosporus strait Turkey 106 B2
also known as İstanbul Boğazı
▸▸32–33 Europe Countries
Bossaga Turkm. see Basaga
Bossangoa Cent. Afr. Rep. 126 C3
Bossembélé Cent. Afr. Rep. 126 C3
Bossemptélé Cent. Afr. Rep. see Bossentélé
Bossentélé Cent. Afr. Rep. 126 C3
formerly spelt Bossemptélé
Bossiekom S. Africa 132 E6
Bossier City U.S.A. 179 D5
Bossiesvlei Namibia 130 C5
Bosspruit S. Africa 133 L3
Bossut, Cape Australia 150 C3
Bostan China 89 D4
Bostān Iran 100 A4
Bosten Hu l. China 88 D3
also known as Bagrax Hu
Boston U.K. 47 L11

▸Boston U.S.A. 177 N3
State capital of Massachusetts.

Boston Creek Canada 173 N2
Boston Mountains U.S.A. 179 D5
Bosut r. Croatia 56 L3
Boswell IN U.S.A. 172 F10
Boswell PA U.S.A. 176 F5
Botad India 96 A5
Botata Liberia 124 C5
Boteå Sweden 44 L3
Boteler Point S. Africa 133 Q3
Boteni Romania 58 G3
Boteti r. Botswana 131 E4
Botev mt. Bulg. 58 F6
Botevgrad Bulg. 58 E6
Bothaville S. Africa 133 K4
Bothell U.S.A. 180 B3
Bothnia, Gulf of Fin./Sweden 44 L3
Bothwell Australia 147 E5
Bothwell Canada 173 L8
Boticas Port. 54 D3
Botin mt. Bos.-Herz. 56 K5
Botkins U.S.A. 176 A5
Botlikh Rus. Fed. 102 A4
Botna r. Moldova 58 K2
Botoşani Romania 53 H2
Botou China 85 H4
Botro Côte d'Ivoire 124 D5
Botshabelo S. Africa 133 K6
Botsmark Sweden 44 M2
▸Botswana country Africa 130 D4
formerly known as Bechuanaland
▸▸114–115 Africa Countries
Bottenviken g. Fin./Sweden 44 M2
Bottineau U.S.A. 178 B1
Bottle Creek Turks and Caicos Is 187 E2
Bottom Neth. Antilles 187 H3
Bottrop Germany 48 D4
Botucatu Brazil 206 E9
Botumirim Brazil 207 J3
Bouaflé Côte d'Ivoire 124 D5
Bou Ahmed Morocco 54 G9
Bouaké Côte d'Ivoire 124 D5
Boualem Alg. 123 F2
Bouandougou Côte d'Ivoire 124 D4
formerly spelt Buandougou
Bouanga Congo 126 C5
Bouar Cent. Afr. Rep. 126 B3
Bou Arada Tunisia 57 B12
Bouârfa Morocco 123 E2
Bou Aroua Alg. 123 G2
Bouba Ndjida, Parc National de nat. park Cameroon 125 I4
Boubin mt. Czech Rep. 49 K6
Boû Bleï'ine well Mauritania 124 C2
Boubout well Alg. 122 D4
Bouca Cent. Afr. Rep. 126 C3
Boucau France 50 E9
Boucaut Bay Australia 148 B2
Bouchette Canada 173 R4
Boucle du Baoulé, Parc National de la nat. park Mali 124 C3
Bouctouche Canada 169 H4
Boudh India 95 E1
Boudinar Morocco 54 H9
Boû Djébéha well Mali 124 E2
Boudoua Cent. Afr. Rep. 126 C3
Boudry Switz. 51 M6
Bouenza admin. reg. Congo 126 B6
Bouenza r. Congo 126 B6
Boufore Cent. Afr. Rep. 126 C3
Bougainville, Cape Australia 150 D2
Bougainville Island P.N.G. 145 E2
Bougaroûn, Cap c. Alg. 123 G1
Boughessa Mali 125 F2
formerly spelt Bouressa
Bougie Alg. see Bejaïa
Bougouemen Chad 126 B2
Bougouni Mali 124 D4
Bougtob Alg. 123 F2
Boû Guendoûz well Mali 124 D2
Bouguirat Alg. 55 L9
Bougzoul Alg. 55 N9
Bouillon Belgium 51 L3
Bouira Alg. 123 F1
Bou Izakarn Morocco 122 C3
Boujdour W. Sahara 122 B4
Bou Kahil, Djebel mts Alg. 123 F2
Boukoumbé Benin 125 F4
Boukta Chad 126 C2
Boulder Australia 151 C6
Boulder CO U.S.A. 180 F4
Boulder MT U.S.A. 180 D3
Boulder UT U.S.A. 183 M4
Boulder Canyon gorge U.S.A. 183 J5
Boulder City U.S.A. 183 J6
Bou Legmaden, Oued watercourse Alg./Morocco 122 C3
Boulemane Morocco 122 D2
Boulemane Morocco 122 D2
Boulevard U.S.A. 183 H9
Boulhaut Morocco see Ben Slimane
Boulia Australia 148 C4
Boulogne France see Boulogne-sur-Mer
Boulogne r. France 50 E5
Boulogne-Billancourt France 51 I4
Boulogne-sur-Mer France 50 H2
historically known as Gesoriacum; short form Boulogne
Boulou r. Cent. Afr. Rep. 126 E3
Boulouba Cent. Afr. Rep. 126 D3
Bouloupari New Caledonia 145 F4
Boulsa Burkina 125 E3
Boultoum Niger 125 H3
Boumango Gabon 126 B5
Boumba r. Cameroon 125 I6
Boumbé I r. Cent. Afr. Rep. 126 B3
Boumerdes Alg. 123 F1
Bouna Côte d'Ivoire 124 E4
Bou Naceur, Jbel mt. Morocco 122 E2
Boû Nâga Mauritania 124 B2
Boundary U.S.A. 166 A1
Boundary Peak U.S.A. 182 F4
Boundiali Côte d'Ivoire 124 D4
Boungou r. Cent. Afr. Rep. 126 D3
Bountiful U.S.A. 183 M1
Bounty Islands N.Z. 145 G6
UNESCO World Heritage Site
Bourail New Caledonia 145 F4
Bourarhet, Erg des des. Alg. 123 H4
Bourbince r. France 51 K6
Bourbon terr. Indian Ocean see Réunion
Bourbon-Lancy France 51 J6
Bourbonne-les-Bains France 51 L5
Bourbriac France 50 C4
Bourem Mali 125 E2
Bouressa Mali see Boughessa
Bourg France 50 F7
Bourganeuf France 50 H7
Bourg-en-Bresse France 51 L6
Bourges France 51 I5
historically known as Avaricum
UNESCO World Heritage Site
Bourgmont Canada 173 R2
Bourgneuf, Baie de b. France 50 D5
Bourgogne admin. reg. France 51 K5
Bourgoin-Jallieu France 51 L7
Bourg-St-Andéol France 51 K8
Bourg-St-Maurice France 51 M7
Bourke Australia 147 E2
Bourkes Canada 173 M2
Bournemouth U.K. 47 K13
Bouroum-Bouroum Burkina 124 E4
Bourtoutou Chad 126 D2
Bourzanga Burkina 125 E3
Bou Saâda Alg. 123 G2
Bou Salem Tunisia 57 A12
Bouse U.S.A. 183 J8
Bouse Wash watercourse U.S.A. 183 J7
Boussé Burkina 125 E3
Bousso Chad 126 C2
Boû Tezâya well Mauritania 124 C2
Boutilimit Mauritania 124 B2
Boutougou Fara Senegal 124 B3
Bouvet Island terr. S. Atlantic Ocean see Bouvetøya

▸Bouvetøya terr. S. Atlantic Ocean 217 O9
Dependency of Norway. English form Bouvet Island.

Boven Kapuas Mountains Indon./Malaysia see Kapuas Hulu, Pegunungan
Bow r. Australia 150 E3
Bow r. Canada 167 I5
Bowa China see Muli
Bowbells U.S.A. 178 B1
Bowden U.S.A. 176 F7
Bowditch atoll Tokelau see Fakaofo
Bowen Arg. 204 D4
Bowen Australia 149 F4
Bowen r. Australia 149 E4
Bowen, Mount Australia 147 F4
Bowen Downs Australia 149 E4
Bowen Strait Australia 148 B1
Bowers Mountains Antarctica 223 K2
Bowie AZ U.S.A. 183 O9
Bowie TX U.S.A. 179 C5
Bow Island Canada 167 I5
Bowkan Iran 100 A2
Bowling Green KY U.S.A. 174 C4
Bowling Green MO U.S.A. 174 B4
Bowling Green OH U.S.A. 176 B4
Bowling Green VA U.S.A. 177 H7
Bowling Green Bay Australia 149 E3
Bowling Green Bay National Park Australia 149 E3
Bowman U.S.A. 178 B2
Bowman, Mount Canada 166 F5
Bowman Coast Antarctica 222 T2
Bowman Island Antarctica 223 G2
Bowman Peninsula Antarctica 222 T2
Bowmanville Canada 173 O7
Bown Somalia 128 D2
Bowo Sichuan China see Bomai
Bowo Xizang China see Bomi
Bow River Aboriginal Reserve Australia 150 D3
Bowron r. Canada 166 F4
Bowron Lake Provincial Park Canada 166 F4
Bowser Lake Canada 166 D3
Boxberg Germany 48 G6
Box Elder U.S.A. 178 B2
Box Elder r. U.S.A. 178 B2
Boxholm Sweden 45 K4
Boxing China 85 H4
Boxtel Neth. 48 C4
Boyabat Turkey 106 C2
Boyacá dept Col. 198 C3
Boyadzhik Bulg. 58 H6
Boyalıca Turkey 58 K8
Boyalık Turkey see Çiçekdağı
Boyana tourist site Bulg. 58 E6
UNESCO World Heritage Site
Boyang China 87 F2
formerly known as Poyang
Boyanovichi Rus. Fed. 43 P8
Boyanovo Bulg. 58 H6
Boyd r. Australia 147 G2
Boyd Lagoon salt flat Australia 151 D5
Boyd Lake Canada 167 K2
Boydton U.S.A. 176 G9
Boyer r. U.S.A. 178 D3
Boyera Dem. Rep. Congo 126 C5
Boyertown U.S.A. 177 J5
Boykins U.S.A. 177 H9
Boyle Canada 167 H4
Boyle Ireland 47 D10
Boyne r. Qld Australia 149 F4
Boyne r. Qld Australia 149 F5
Boyne r. Ireland 47 F10
Boyne City U.S.A. 173 H5
Boyni Qara Afgh. 101 F2
Boyo Cent. Afr. Rep. 126 D3
Boyoma, Chutes waterfall Dem. Rep. Congo see Boyoma Falls
Boyoma Falls Dem. Rep. Congo 126 E4
also known as Boyoma, Chutes; formerly known as Stanley, Chutes
Boysun Uzbek. 103 F5
also spelt Baysun
Boyuibe Bol. 201 E5
Böyük Hinaldağ mt. Azer. 100 A1
Boyup Brook Australia 151 B7
Bozanbay Kazakh. 88 C1
Bozashy Tübegi pen. Kazakh. see Buzachi, Poluostrov
Bozburun Turkey 106 B3

▸Bozcaada i. Turkey 106 A3
Most westerly point of Asia. Also known as Tenedos.
▸▸60–61 Asia Landscapes

Bozdağ mt. Turkey 59 H10
Bozdağ mt. Turkey 109 H1
Boz Dağları mts Turkey 106 A3
Bozdoğan Turkey 106 B3
Bozeman U.S.A. 180 E3
Bozen Italy see Bolzano
Bozhou China 87 E1
Bozkır Turkey 106 C3
also known as Silistat
Bozköl Kazakh. see Boskol'
Bozkurt Turkey 59 K11
Bozouls France 51 I8
Bozoum Cent. Afr. Rep. 126 C3
Bozova Turkey 107 D3
also known as Hüvek
Bozovici Romania 58 D4
Bozqūsh, Kūh-e mts Iran 100 A2
Bozshakol' Kazakh. 103 H2
formerly spelt Boshchakul'
Boztumsyk Kazakh. 103 F2
Bozüyük Turkey 106 B3
Bozyazı Turkey 108 D1
Bra Italy 51 N8
Brabant Island Antarctica 222 T2
Brač i. Croatia 56 I5
Bracara Port. see Braga
Bracciano Italy 56 E6
Bracciano, Lago di l. Italy 56 E6
Bracebridge Canada 168 E4
Brachet, Lac au l. Canada 169 G3
Bräcke Sweden 44 K3
Brackettville U.S.A. 179 B6
Bracki Kanal sea chan. Croatia 56 I5
Bracknell U.K. 47 L12
Braço Norte r. Brazil 201 G2
Brad Romania 58 D2
Bradano r. Italy 57 I8
Bradenton U.S.A. 175 D7
Bradford Canada 173 N6
Bradford U.K. 47 K10
Bradford PA U.S.A. 176 G4
Bradford VT U.S.A. 177 M2
Bradley U.S.A. 172 F9
Bradner U.S.A. 176 B4
Bradshaw U.S.A. 176 D8
Brady U.S.A. 179 C6
Brady Creek r. U.S.A. 179 C6
Brady Glacier U.S.A. 166 B3
Braemar U.K. 46 I6
Braga Port. 54 C3
historically known as Bracara
Braga admin. dist. Port. 54 C3
Bragado Arg. 204 E4
Bragança Brazil 202 C2
Bragança Port. 54 E3
Bragança admin. dist. Port. 54 E3
Bragança Paulista Brazil 206 G9
Brahin Belarus 41 D6
Brahmakund India 97 H4
Brahmanbaria Bangl. 97 F5
Brahmani r. India 95 E1
Brahmapur India 95 E2
Brahmaputra r. China/India 89 D6
also known as Dihang (India) or Yarlung Zangbo (China)
Braidwood Australia 147 F3
Braidwood U.S.A. 172 E9
Brăila Romania 58 I3
Brăilei, Insula Mare a i. Romania 58 I4
Braine France 51 J3
Brainerd U.S.A. 178 D2
Braintree U.K. 47 M12
Braithwaite Point Australia 148 B1
Braives Belgium 51 L2
Brak r. S. Africa 132 E10
Brak watercourse S. Africa 132 C5
Brake (Unterweser) Germany 48 F2
Brâkna admin. reg. Mauritania 124 B2
Brakpoort S. Africa 132 E11
Brakspruit S. Africa 133 K3
Brakwater Namibia 130 C4
Bralorne Canada 166 F5
Bramhapuri India 94 C1
Bramming Denmark 45 J5
Brampton Canada 168 E5
Brampton U.K. 47 J9
Bramsche Germany 48 F3
Bramsöfjärden l. Sweden 45 L3
Brancaleone Italy 57 I11
Branch Canada 169 K4
Branco r. Mato Grosso Brazil 201 E2
Branco r. Roraima Brazil 199 F5
Branco i. Cape Verde 124 [inset]
Brandberg mt. Namibia 130 B4
Brändbo Sweden 45 L3
Brandbu Norway 45 J3
Brande Denmark 45 J5
Brandenburg Germany 49 J3
Brandenburg land Germany 49 K3
Brandenburg U.S.A. 174 C4
Brandenburger Wald- und Seengebiet park Germany 49 J3
Brandfort S. Africa 133 K5
Brandkop S. Africa 132 D8
Brändö Fin. 45 M3
Brandon Canada 167 L5
Brandon MS U.S.A. 175 B5
Brandon SD U.S.A. 178 C3
Brandon VT U.S.A. 177 L2
Brandon Head Ireland 47 B11
Brandon Mountain hill Ireland 47 B11
Brandonville U.S.A. 176 F6
Brandvlei S. Africa 132 E7
Brandvlei Dam resr S. Africa 132 D10
Brandvoll Norway 44 L1
Brani, Pulau i. Sing. 76 [inset]
Braniewo Poland 49 Q1
Brännberg Sweden 44 M2
Brannenburg Germany 48 J8
Bransfield Strait Antarctica 222 T2
Brańsk Poland 49 T3
Brantas r. Indon. 77 F4
Brantford Canada 168 D5
Brantôme France 50 G7
Brantwood U.S.A. 172 C5
Brás Brazil 199 G5
Brasaljce Kosovo, Srbija Serb. and Mont. 58 C6
Bras d'Or Lake Canada 169 I4
Brasil Brazil 198 D6
Brasil country S. America see Brazil
Brasil, Planalto do plat. Brazil 203 D6
Brasilândia Mato Grosso do Sul Brazil 206 A8
Brasilândia Minas Gerais Brazil 206 E2
Brasilândia Minas Gerais Brazil 207 G4
Brasileia Brazil 200 C2

▸Brasília Brazil 206 F2
Capital of Brazil.
UNESCO World Heritage Site
▸▸192–193 South America Countries

Brasília de Minas Brazil 202 C6
Brasília Legal Brazil 199 H5
Brasla r. Latvia 42 F4
Braslav Belarus see Braslaw
Braslaw Belarus 42 I6
also spelt Braslav
Braşov Romania 58 G3
formerly known as Oraşul Stalin; historically known as Kronstadt
Brasovo Rus. Fed. 43 P9
Brassey, Banjaran mts Sabah Malaysia 77 G1
Brassey, Mount Australia 148 B4
Brassey Range hills Australia 151 C5
Bratan mt. Bulg. 58 G6
Bratca Romania 58 D2

▸Bratislava Slovakia 49 O7
Capital of Slovakia. Also known as Pozsony; formerly known as Pressburg.

Bratsk Rus. Fed. 80 G1
Bratskoye Vodokhranilishche resr Rus. Fed. 80 G1
Brattleboro U.S.A. 177 M3
Brattmon Sweden 45 K3
Brattvåg Norway 44 I3
Bratunac Bos.-Herz. 56 L4
Braulio Carrillo, Parque Nacional nat. park Costa Rica 186 C5
Braúnas Brazil 207 K6
Braunau am Inn Austria 49 K7
Braunsbedra Germany 48 I4
Braunschweig Germany 48 H3
historically known as Brunswick
Brava i. Cape Verde 124 [inset]
Brave U.S.A. 176 E6
Bråviken inlet Sweden 45 L4
Bravo, Cerro mt. Bol. 201 D4
Bravo del Norte, Río r. Mex./U.S.A. 185 F3
also known as Rio Grande
Brawley U.S.A. 183 I9
Bray Ireland 47 F10
also spelt Bré
Bray S. Africa 132 H2
Braye r. France 50 G5
Bray Island Canada 165 L3
Bray-sur-Seine France 51 J4
Brazeau r. Canada 167 H4
Brazeau, Mount Canada 167 G4

▸Brazil country S. America 202 B4
Largest country in South America and 5th in the world. Most populous country in South America and 5th in the world. Spelt Brasil in Portuguese.
▸▸8–9 World Countries
▸▸16–17 World Population
▸▸192–193 South America Countries

Brazil U.S.A. 174 C4
Brazos r. U.S.A. 179 D6

▸Brazzaville Congo 126 B6
Capital of Congo.

Brčko Bos.-Herz. 56 K4
Brčko admin. div. Bos.-Herz. 56 K4
Brda r. Poland 49 P2
Brdy hills Czech Rep. 49 K6
Bré Ireland see Bray
Breakfast Vlei S. Africa 133 K10
Breaksea Sound inlet N.Z. 153 A13
Breaksea Spit Australia 149 G5
Bream Bay N.Z. 152 I3
Bream Head N.Z. 152 I3
Bream Tail c. N.Z. 152 I4
Breas Chile 204 C2
Breaza Romania 58 G3
Brebes Indon. 77 E4
Brechin U.K. 46 J7
Brecht Belgium 51 K1
Breckenridge CO U.S.A. 180 F5
Breckenridge MN U.S.A. 178 C2
Breckenridge TX U.S.A. 179 C5
Brecknock, Península pen. Chile 205 B9
Břeclav Czech Rep. 49 N7
Brecon U.K. 47 I12
also known as Aberhonddu
Brecon Beacons reg. U.K. 47 I12
Brecon Beacons National Park U.K. 47 I12
Breda Neth. 48 B4
Bredasdorp S. Africa 132 E11
Bredbo Australia 147 F3
Bredviken Sweden 44 K2
Bredy Rus. Fed. 103 E1
Breede r. S. Africa 132 E11
Bregalnica r. Macedonia 58 C7
Bregenz Austria 48 G8
Bregovo Bulg. 58 D4
Bréhal France 50 E4
Breiðafjörður b. Iceland 44 [inset] A2
Breiðdalsvík Iceland 44 [inset] D2
Breil-sur-Roya France 51 N9
Breipaal S. Africa 133 K7
Breisach am Rhein Germany 48 E7
Breivikbotn Norway 44 M1
Breivikeidet Norway 44 L1
Brejinho de Nazaré Brazil 202 B4
Brejo Brazil 202 D2
Brejo r. Brazil 202 D4
Brejo da Porta Brazil 202 C4
Brekstad Norway 44 J3
Bremen Germany 48 F2
UNESCO World Heritage Site

Bremen GA U.S.A. 175 C5
Bremen OH U.S.A. 176 C6
Bremer Bay Australia 151 B7
Bremerhaven Germany 48 F2
Bremer Range hills Australia 151 C7
Bremersdorp Swaziland see Manzini
Bremerton U.S.A. 180 B3
Bremervörde Germany 48 G2
Breń r. Poland 49 S5
Brenham U.S.A. 179 C6
Brenna Norway 44 K2
Brenne, Parc Naturel Régional de la nature res. France 50 H6
Brennero Italy 56 D2
Brennero, Passo di pass Austria/Italy see Brenner Pass
Brennerpaß pass Austria/Italy see Brenner Pass
Brenner Pass pass Austria/Italy 48 I9
also known as Brennero, Passo di or Brennerpaß
Breno Italy 56 C3
Brenta r. Italy 56 E3
Brenta, Gruppo di mts Italy 56 C2
Brentwood U.K. 47 M12
Brenzone Italy 56 C3
Brescia Italy 56 C3
historically known as Brixia
Breslau Poland see Wrocław
Bresle r. France 50 H2
Brésolles, Lac l. Canada 169 G2
Bressanone Italy 56 D2
Bressay i. U.K. 46 K3
Bressuire France 50 F6
Brest Belarus 42 E9
formerly known as Brest-Litovsk or Brześć nad Bugiem
Brest France 50 B4
Brest-Litovsk Belarus see Brest
Brest Oblast admin. div. Belarus see Brestskaya Voblasts'
Brestovac Srbija Serb. and Mont. 58 C5
Brestskaya Oblast' admin. div. Belarus see Brestskaya Voblasts'
Brestskaya Voblasts' admin. div. Belarus 42 G9
English form Brest Oblast; also known as Brestskaya Oblast'
Bretagne admin. reg. France 50 D4
English form Brittany
Bretagne reg. France see Brittany
Bretana Peru 198 C6
Brețcu Romania 58 H2
Breteuil Haute-Normandie France 50 G4
Breteuil Picardie France 51 I3
Brétigny-sur-Orge France 51 I4
Breton Canada 167 H4
Breton Sound b. U.S.A. 175 B6
Bretten Germany 48 F6
Breu r. Brazil/Peru 200 B2
Breueh, Pulau i. Indon. 76 A1
Brevard U.S.A. 174 D5
Breves Brazil 202 B2
Brewarrina Australia 147 E2
Brewer U.S.A. 177 Q1
Brewerville Liberia 124 C5
Brewster NE U.S.A. 178 C3
Brewster OH U.S.A. 176 D5
Brewster WA U.S.A. 180 C2
Brewster, Kap c. Greenland see Kangikajik
Brewster, Lake imp. l. Australia 147 E3
Brewton U.S.A. 175 C6
Breyten S. Africa 133 N3
Breytovo Rus. Fed. 43 S3
Brezhnev Rus. Fed. see Naberezhnyye Chelny
Brežice Slovenia 56 H3
Breznik Bulg. 58 D6
Breznița-Motru Romania 58 E4
Breznitsa Bulg. 58 E7
Brezno Slovakia 49 Q7
Brezovo Bulg. 58 G6
Brezovo Polje hill Croatia 56 J3
Bria Cent. Afr. Rep. 126 D3
Briakan Rus. Fed. 82 D1
Briançon France 51 M8
Brian Head mt. U.S.A. 183 L4
Briare France 51 I5
Bribie Island Australia 149 G5
Briceni Moldova 41 C6
formerly spelt Brichany
Brichany Moldova see Briceni
Bricquebec France 50 E3
Bridgehampton U.S.A. 177 M5
Bridgeman U.S.A. 172 G9
Bridgend U.K. 47 I12
also known as Pen-y-Bont ar Ogwr
Bridgeport AL U.S.A. 174 C5
Bridgeport CA U.S.A. 182 E3
Bridgeport CT U.S.A. 177 L4
Bridgeport MI U.S.A. 173 J7
Bridgeport NE U.S.A. 178 B3
Bridgeport TX U.S.A. 179 C5
Bridgeport Reservoir U.S.A. 182 E3
Bridger Peak U.S.A. 180 F4
Bridgeton U.S.A. 177 J6
Bridgetown Australia 151 B7
►Bridgetown Barbados 187 I4
Capital of Barbados.
Bridgetown Canada 169 H4
Bridgeville U.S.A. 177 J7
Bridgewater Australia 147 E5
Bridgewater Canada 169 H4
Bridgewater MA U.S.A. 177 O4
Bridgewater NY U.S.A. 177 J3
Bridgewater VA U.S.A. 176 G7
Bridgton U.S.A. 177 O1
Bridgwater U.K. 47 I12
Bridgwater Bay U.K. 47 I12
Bridlington U.K. 47 L9
Bridport Australia 147 E5
Bridport U.K. 47 J13
Brie reg. France 51 I4
Briec France 50 C4
Brie-Comte-Robert France 51 I4
Brieg Poland see Brzeg
Brienne-le-Château France 51 K4
Brienzer See l. Switz. 51 N6
Briery Knob mt. U.S.A. 176 E7
Brig Switz. 51 N6
Briggsville U.S.A. 172 D7
Brigham City U.S.A. 180 D4
Brighton Canada 173 P6
Brighton N.Z. 153 E13
Brighton U.K. 47 L13
Brighton CO U.S.A. 180 F5
Brighton IA U.S.A. 172 B9
Brighton MI U.S.A. 173 J8
Brighton NY U.S.A. 176 H2
Brighton WV U.S.A. 176 C7
Brighton Downs Australia 149 D4
Brignoles France 51 M9
Brihuega Spain 55 I4
Brikama Gambia 124 A3
Brillion U.S.A. 172 E6
Brilon Germany 48 F4
Brimley U.S.A. 173 I4
Brimnes Iceland 44 [inset] D2
Brimson U.S.A. 172 B3
Brindisi Italy 57 J8
historically known as Brundisium
Brinje Croatia 56 H3
Brinkley U.S.A. 174 B5
Brinkworth Australia 146 C3
Brion, Île i. Canada 169 I4
Brionne France 50 G3
Brioude France 51 J7
Brisay Canada 169 G2
►Brisbane Australia 147 G1
State capital of Queensland and 3rd most populous city in Oceania.
Brisighella Italy 56 D4
Bristol U.K. 47 J12
Bristol CT U.S.A. 177 M4
Bristol FL U.S.A. 175 C6
Bristol NH U.S.A. 177 N2
Bristol RI U.S.A. 177 N4
Bristol TN U.S.A. 176 C9
Bristol VT U.S.A. 177 L1
Bristol Bay U.S.A. 164 C4
Bristol Channel est. U.K. 47 H12
Bristol Lake U.S.A. 183 I7
Bristol Mountains U.S.A. 183 H7
Britânia Brazil 206 B2
Britannia Island New Caledonia see Maré
British Antarctic Territory Antarctica 222 S2
British Columbia prov. Canada 166 F5
British Empire Range mts Canada 165 K1
British Guiana country S. America see Guyana
British Honduras country Central America see Belize
►British Indian Ocean Territory terr. Indian Ocean 218 L6
United Kingdom Overseas Territory.
►►64–65 Asia Countries
British Solomon Islands country S. Pacific Ocean see Solomon Islands
Brito Godins Angola see Kiwaba N'zogi
Brits S. Africa 133 L2
Britstown S. Africa 132 H7
Brittany admin. reg. France see Bretagne
Brittany reg. France 50 C4
also known as Bretagne
Britton U.S.A. 178 C2
Brive-la-Gaillarde France 50 H7
Briviesca Spain 55 H2
Brixham U.K. 47 I13
Brixia Italy see Brescia
Brlik Zhambylskaya Oblast' Kazakh. see Birlik
Brlik Zhambylskaya Oblast' Kazakh. see Birlik
Brno Czech Rep. 49 N6
formerly spelt Brünn
UNESCO World Heritage Site
Broach India see Bharuch
Broad r. U.S.A. 174 D5
Broadalbin U.S.A. 177 K2
Broad Arrow Australia 151 C6
Broadback r. Canada 168 E3
Broad Bay U.K. see Tuath, Loch a'
Broadford U.K. 46 G6
Broad Law hill U.K. 46 I8
Broadmere Australia 148 B3
Broad Sound sea chan. Australia 149 F4
Broad Sound Channel Australia 149 F4
Broadsound Range hills Australia 149 F4
Broadus U.S.A. 180 F3
Broadview Canada 167 K5
Broadwater U.S.A. 178 B3
Broadway U.S.A. 176 G7
Broadwood N.Z. 152 H3
Broby Sweden 45 K4
Broceni Latvia 42 D5
Brochet Canada 167 K3
Brocken mt. Germany 48 H4
Brockman, Mount Australia 150 B4
Brockport NY U.S.A. 176 H2
Brockport PA U.S.A. 176 G4
Brockton U.S.A. 177 N3
Brockville Canada 168 F4
Brockway U.S.A. 176 G4
Brod Macedonia 58 C7
Broderick Heads Kenya see Webuye
Brodeur Peninsula Canada 165 K2
Brodhead KY U.S.A. 176 A8
Brodhead WI U.S.A. 172 D8
Brodheadsville U.S.A. 177 J5
Brodick U.K. 46 G8
Brodnax U.S.A. 176 G9
Brodnica Poland 49 Q2
Brody Ukr. 41 C6
Broedersput S. Africa 133 J3
Brok r. Poland 49 S3
Broke Inlet Australia 151 B7
Broken Arrow U.S.A. 179 D4
Broken Bay Australia 147 F3
Broken Bow NE U.S.A. 178 C3
Broken Bow OK U.S.A. 179 D5
Broken Bow Reservoir U.S.A. 179 D5
Brokenburg U.S.A. 176 H7
Brokenhead r. Canada 167 L5
Broken Hill Australia 146 D2
Broken Hill Zambia see Kabwe
Brokopondo Suriname 199 H3
Brokopondo Stuwmeer resr Suriname see Professor van Blommestein Meer
Bromberg Poland see Bydgoszcz
Bromnes Norway 44 L1
Bromo-Tengger-Semeru National Park Indon. 77 F4
Bromsgrove U.K. 47 J11
Brønderslev Denmark 45 J4
Brong-Ahafo admin. reg. Ghana 125 E5
Bronkhorstspruit S. Africa 133 M2
Bronnitsy Rus. Fed. 43 T6
Brønnøysund Norway 44 K2
Bronson FL U.S.A. 175 D6
Bronson MI U.S.A. 173 H9
Bronte Sicily Italy 57 G11
Brooke U.S.A. 176 H7
Brooke's Point Phil. 74 A4
Brookfield MO U.S.A. 178 D4
Brookfield WI U.S.A. 172 E7
Brookhaven U.S.A. 175 B6
Brookings OR U.S.A. 180 A4
Brookings SD U.S.A. 178 C2
Brookline U.S.A. 177 N3
Brooklyn U.S.A. 173 I8
Brooklyn Park U.S.A. 174 A2
Brookneal U.S.A. 176 G8
Brooks Canada 167 I5
Brooks ME U.S.A. 177 P1
Brooks WV U.S.A. 176 E8
Brooks, Cape Antarctica 222 T2
Brooks Brook Canada 166 C2
Brooks Peninsula Provincial Park Canada 166 E5
Brooks Range mts U.S.A. 164 E3
Brookston IN U.S.A. 172 G10
Brookston MN U.S.A. 172 A4
Brooksville FL U.S.A. 175 D6
Brooksville KY U.S.A. 176 A7
Brookton Australia 151 B7
Brookville U.S.A. 176 F4
Broom, Loch inlet U.K. 46 G6
Broome Australia 150 C3
Broomehill Australia 151 B7
Broons France 50 D4
Brora U.K. 46 I5
Brora r. U.K. 46 I5
Brøstadbotn Norway 44 L1
Broșteni Romania 58 G1
Brosville U.S.A. 176 F9
Brotas Brazil 206 E9
Brotas de Macaúbas Brazil 202 D5
Brothers U.S.A. 180 B4
Brou France 50 H4
Broughton Island Canada see Qikiqtarjuaq
Broulkou well Chad 120 C5
Brovary Ukr. 41 D6
Brown, Lake salt flat Australia 151 B6
Brown, Mount hill Australia 146 C3
Brown, Point Australia 146 B3
Brown City U.S.A. 173 K7
Brown Creek r. Australia 149 D3
Brown Deer U.S.A. 172 F7
Browne Range hills Australia 151 D5
Brownfield U.S.A. 179 B5
Brown Mountain U.S.A. 183 G6
Brown's Town Jamaica 186 D3
Brownstown U.S.A. 174 C4
Brownsville PA U.S.A. 176 F5
Brownsville TN U.S.A. 174 B5
Brownsville TX U.S.A. 179 C7
Brownsweg Suriname 199 H3
Brownwood U.S.A. 179 C6
Browse Island Australia 150 C2
Brozas Spain 54 E5
Brozha Belarus 43 K9
Bruay-la-Bussière France 51 I2
Bruce MS U.S.A. 174 B5
Bruce WI U.S.A. 172 B5
Bruce, Mount Australia 150 B4
Bruce Peninsula Canada 173 L6
Bruce Peninsula National Park Canada 173 L5
Bruce Rock Australia 151 B6
Bruchsal Germany 48 F6
Bruck an der Leitha Austria 49 N7
Bruck an der Mur Austria 49 M8
Bruges Belgium see Brugge
Brugge Belgium 51 J1
also spelt Bruges
UNESCO World Heritage Site
Bruhagen Norway 44 I3
Brühl Germany 48 D5
UNESCO World Heritage Site
Bruin KY U.S.A. 176 B7
Bruin PA U.S.A. 176 F4
Bruin Point mt. U.S.A. 183 N2
Bruint India 97 H3
Brukkaros Namibia 130 C5
Brukkaros, Mount Namibia 132 B2
Brûlé Canada 166 G4
Brule U.S.A. 172 B4
Brûlé, Lac l. Canada 169 I2
also known as Burnt Lake
Brumadinho Brazil 207 I7
Brumado Brazil 202 D5
Brumath France 51 N4
Brumer Islands P.N.G. 149 F1
Brumunddal Norway 45 J3
Brú Na Bóinne tourist site Ireland 47 F10
UNESCO World Heritage Site
Brundisium Italy see Brindisi
Bruneau U.S.A. 180 D4
Bruneau r. U.S.A. 180 D4
Bruneau, West Fork r. U.S.A. 180 D4
►Brunei country Asia 77 F1
►►64–65 Asia Countries
Brunei Brunei see Bandar Seri Begawan
Brunei Bay Malaysia 77 F1
Brunette Downs Australia 148 B3
Brunette Island Canada 169 K4
Brunflo Sweden 44 K3
Brunico Italy 56 D2
Brünn Czech Rep. see Brno
Brunna Sweden 45 L4
Brunner, Lake N.Z. 153 F10
Bruno Canada 167 J4
Bruno U.S.A. 172 A4
Brunsbüttel Germany 48 G2
Brunswick Germany see Braunschweig
Brunswick GA U.S.A. 175 D6
Brunswick MD U.S.A. 176 H6
Brunswick ME U.S.A. 177 P2
Brunswick MO U.S.A. 178 D4
Brunswick OH U.S.A. 176 D4
Brunswick, Península de pen. Chile 205 C9
Brunswick Bay Australia 150 D2
Brunswick Heads Australia 147 G2
Brunswick Junction Australia 151 A7
Brunswick Lake Canada 168 D3
Bruntál Czech Rep. 49 O6
Brunt Ice Shelf Antarctica 222 W2
Bruny Island Australia 147 E5
Brus Srbija Serb. and Mont. 58 C5
Brusa Turkey see Bursa
Brush U.S.A. 178 B3
Brushton U.S.A. 177 K1
Brusovo Rus. Fed. 43 Q4
Brusque Brazil 203 B8
Brussel Belgium see Brussels
►Brussels Belgium 51 K2
Capital of Belgium. Also spelt Brussel or Bruxelles.
UNESCO World Heritage Site
Brusturi-Drăgănești Romania 58 H1
Brusy Poland 49 O2
Bruthen Australia 147 E4
Bruxelles Belgium see Brussels
Bruyères France 51 M4
Bruzual Venez. 198 D2
Bryan OH U.S.A. 176 A4
Bryan TX U.S.A. 179 C6
Bryan, Mount hill Australia 146 C3
Bryan Coast Antarctica 222 S2
Bryansk Rus. Fed. 43 P8
Bryanskaya Oblast' admin. div. Rus. Fed. 43 O8
English form Bryansk Oblast
Bryansk Oblast admin. div. Rus. Fed. see Bryanskaya Oblast'
Bryanskoye Rus. Fed. 102 A3
Bryant AR U.S.A. 179 D5
Bryant WI U.S.A. 172 D5
Bryant Creek r. U.S.A. 178 D4
Bryant Pond U.S.A. 177 O1
Bryce Canyon National Park U.S.A. 183 L4
Bryce Mountain U.S.A. 183 O8
Bryn' Rus. Fed. 43 Q8
Bryne Norway 45 I4
Bryson, Lac l. Canada 173 P4
Bryukhovetskaya Rus. Fed. 41 F7
Brzava r. Serb. and Mont. 58 B3
Brzeg Poland 49 O5
historically known as Brieg
Brzeg Dolny Poland 49 N4
Brześć nad Bugiem Belarus see Brest
Brzozów Poland 49 T6
Bū well Yemen 105 D5
Bua Angola 127 B6
Bua Sweden 45 K4
Bu'aale Somalia 128 D4
Buad i. Phil. 74 C4
Buala Solomon Is 145 E2
Buandougou Côte d'Ivoire see Bouandougou
Buang i. Indon. 75 C2
Buatan Indon. 76 C2
Bū Athlah well Libya 120 D2
Bu'ayj well Saudi Arabia 105 E2
Bu'ayrāt al Hasūn Libya 120 B2
Bubanza Burundi 126 F5
Bubi r. Zimbabwe 131 F4
Būbīyān Island Kuwait 107 G5
Bubuan i. Phil. 74 B5
Bubuan i. Phil. 74 B5
Buca Turkey 59 I10
Bucak Turkey 106 B3
Bucaramanga Col. 198 C3
Bucas Grande i. Phil. 74 C4
Buccaneer Archipelago is Australia 150 C3
Bucegi, Munții mts Romania 58 G3
Buchan Australia 147 F4
Buchanan Liberia 124 C5
Buchanan MI U.S.A. 172 G9
Buchanan VA U.S.A. 176 F8
Buchanan, Lake salt flat Australia 149 E4
Buchanan, Lake U.S.A. 179 C6
Buchan Gulf Canada 165 L2
Buchans Canada 169 J3
►Bucharest Romania 58 H4
Capital of Romania. Also spelt București or Bükreș.
Buchen (Odenwald) Germany 48 G6
Bucholz in der Nordheide Germany 48 G2
Buchon, Point U.S.A. 182 D6
Buchy France 50 H3
Bucin, Pasul pass Romania 58 G2
Buckburn Draw watercourse U.S.A. 179 B6
Bückeburg Germany 48 G3
Buckeye U.S.A. 183 L8
Buckhannon U.S.A. 176 E7
Buckhannon r. U.S.A. 176 F6
Buckhaven U.K. 46 I7
Buckhorn Canada 173 O6
Buckhorn Lake Canada 173 O6
Buckie U.K. 46 J6
Buckingham Canada 173 R5
Buckingham U.K. 47 L11
Buckingham PA U.S.A. 177 J5
Buckingham VA U.S.A. 176 G8
Buckland U.S.A. 164 C3
Bucklands S. Africa 132 H6
Buckland Tableland reg. Australia 149 F5
Buckleboo Australia 146 C3
Buckle Island Antarctica 223 K2
Buckley watercourse Australia 148 C4
Buckley U.S.A. 172 E10
Buckley Bay Antarctica 223 J2
Buckskin Mountains U.S.A. 183 K7
Bucks Mountain U.S.A. 182 C2
Bucksport U.S.A. 177 Q1
Bučovice Czech Rep. 49 O6
Bucșani Romania 58 G4
București Romania see Bucharest
Bucyrus U.S.A. 176 C5
Bud Norway 44 I3
Buda Rus. Fed. 43 P8
Buda, Illa de i. Spain 55 L4
Budai park Hungary 49 P8
Buda-Kashalyova Belarus 43 L9
Budalin Myanmar 78 A3
►Budapest Hungary 49 Q8
Capital of Hungary. Historically known as Aquincum.
UNESCO World Heritage Site
Budaun India 96 C3
Budayyi'ah well Saudi Arabia 104 C3
Bud Bud Somalia 128 E3
Budd Coast Antarctica 223 H2
Buddi Eth. 128 D3
Buddusò Sardinia Italy 57 B8
Bude U.K. 47 H13
Budennovsk Rus. Fed. 41 H7
Buderim Australia 149 G5
Budești Romania 58 H4
Budīya, Jabal hills Egypt 108 E8
Budogoshch' Rus. Fed. 43 N2
Budongquan China 84 B5
Budoni Sardinia Italy 57 B8
Budszentmihály Hungary see Tiszavasvári
Budū, Ḩadabat al plain Saudi Arabia 105 E3
Budū', Sabkhat al salt pan Saudi Arabia 105 E3
Budureasa Romania 58 D2
Budva Crna Gora Serb. and Mont. 56 K6
Budweis Czech Rep. see České Budějovice
Budzilava Belarus 43 K6
Buea Cameroon 125 H5
Buëch r. France 51 L8
Buellton U.S.A. 182 D7
Buena Esperanza Arg. 204 D4
Buenaventura Col. 198 B4
Buenaventura Mex. 184 D2
Buena Vista Bol. 201 E4
Buenavista Mex. 185 E5
Buena Vista i. N. Mariana Is see Tinian
Buenavista Phil. 74 B3
Buena Vista CO U.S.A. 180 F5
Buena Vista GA U.S.A. 175 C5
Buena Vista VA U.S.A. 176 F8
Buena Vista, Bahía de b. Cuba 186 D2
Buendia, Embalse de resr Spain 55 I4
Buenga r. Angola 127 B6
Buengas Angola 127 B6
formerly known as Nova Esperança
Buenolândia Brazil 206 C2
Buenópolis Brazil 203 C6
►Buenos Aires Arg. 204 F4
Capital of Argentina. 2nd most populous city in South America, and 8th in the world.
►►18–19 World Cities
Buenos Aires prov. Arg. 204 E5
Buenos Aires Brazil 200 B2
Buenos Aires Amazonas Col. 198 D5
Buenos Aires Guaviare Col. 198 C4
Buenos Aires Costa Rica 186 C5
Buenos Aires, Lago l. Arg./Chile 205 B7
Buenos Aires National Wildlife Refuge nature res. U.S.A. 181 E7
Buen Pasto Arg. 205 C7
Buen Tiempo, Cabo c. Arg. 205 C8
Buerarema Brazil 202 E5
Buesaco Col. 198 B4
Bueu Spain 54 C2
Buey, Cabeza de mt. Spain 55 H6
Bufa Mex. 184 D3
Buffalo r. Canada 167 H2
Buffalo MO U.S.A. 178 D4
Buffalo NY U.S.A. 176 G3
Buffalo OH U.S.A. 176 D6
Buffalo OK U.S.A. 178 C4
Buffalo SD U.S.A. 180 G3
Buffalo TX U.S.A. 179 C6
Buffalo WI U.S.A. 172 B6
Buffalo WY U.S.A. 180 F3
Buffalo r. AR U.S.A. 179 D4
Buffalo r. TN U.S.A. 174 C5
Buffalo r. WI U.S.A. 172 B6
Buffalo Head Hills Canada 167 G3
Buffalo Head Prairie Canada 167 G3
Buffalo Hump mt. U.S.A. 180 D3
Buffalo Lake Alta Canada 167 H4
Buffalo Lake N.W.T. Canada 167 H2
Buffalo Narrows Canada 167 I4
Buffalo Range Zimbabwe 131 F4
Buffalo Valley valley U.S.A. 183 G1
Buffels r. Kwazulu-Natal S. Africa 133 O5
Buffels r. W. Cape S. Africa 132 E10
Buffels watercourse S. Africa 132 B6
Buffels Drift S. Africa 131 E4
Buford U.S.A. 175 C5
Buftea Romania 58 G4
Bug r. Poland 49 U4
Buga Col. 198 B4
Buga Mongolia 84 B2
Buga Nigeria 125 G4
Bugala Island Uganda 128 B5
Bugana Nigeria 125 G5
Bugant Mongolia 85 E1
Bugarach, Pic de mt. France 51 I10
Bugaz Ukr. see Zatoka
Bugdayly Turkm. 102 C5
Bugeat France 51 H7
Bugel, Tanjung pt Indon. 77 E4
Bugojno Bos.-Herz. 56 J4
Bugøyfjord Norway 44 O1
Bugrino Rus. Fed. 40 I1
Bugsuk i. Phil. 74 A4
Bugt China 85 I1
Buguey Phil. 74 B2
Bugui Point Phil. 74 B3
Bugul'ma Rus. Fed. 40 J5
Bugun' Kazakh. 103 E3
Bügür China see Luntai
Buguruslan Rus. Fed. 41 J5
Būhābād Iran 100 C4
Buharkent Turkey 59 J11
Buḩayrat Dahūk l. Iraq 98 C2
Buhera Zimbabwe 131 F3
Buh He r. China 84 C4
Buhi Phil. 74 B3
Bühl Germany 48 F7
Buhl ID U.S.A. 180 D4
Buhl MN U.S.A. 172 A3
Buhoro Flats plain Tanz. 129 B7
Buhriz Iraq 109 P4
Buhu r. Tanz. 129 B6
Buhuși Romania 58 H2
Buia Italy 56 F2
Buick Canada 166 F3
Builth Wells U.K. 47 I11
Buin P.N.G. 145 E2
Bui National Park Ghana 124 E4
Buinsk Rus. Fed. 40 I5
Bu'īn Zahrā Iran 100 B3
Buir Nur l. Mongolia 85 H2
Buitepos Namibia 130 C4
Būivydžiai Lith. 42 G7
Bujalance Spain 54 G7
Bujanovac Srbija Serb. and Mont. 58 C6
Bujoru Romania 58 G5
►Bujumbura Burundi 126 F5
Capital of Burundi. Formerly known as Usumbura.
Buk Poland 49 N3
Bukachacha Rus. Fed. 81 J2
Buka Daban mt. China 89 E4
Buka Island P.N.G. 145 E2
Bukama Dem. Rep. Congo 127 E7
Bukan' Rus. Fed. 43 P8
Būkand Iran 100 C4
Bukanskoye Rus. Fed. 103 J1
Bukavu Dem. Rep. Congo 126 F5
formerly known as Costermansville
Bukedi Dem. Rep. Congo 127 C6
Bukene Tanz. 129 B6
Bukeya Dem. Rep. Congo 127 E7
Bukhara Oblast admin. div. Uzbek. see Buxoro
Bukhava Belarus 43 K6
Bukhoro Uzbek. see Buxoro
Bukhoro Wiloyati admin. div. Uzbek. see Buxoro
Bukhtarminskoye Vodokhranilishche resr Kazakh. 88 D1
also known as Buqtyrma Bögeni
Bukide i. Indon. 75 C2
Bukima Tanz. 128 B5
Bukit Baka-Bukit Raya National Park Indon. 77 F3
Bukit Barisan Selatan National Park Indon. 76 D4
UNESCO World Heritage Site
Bukit Timah Sing. 76 [inset]
Bukittinggi Indon. 76 C3
also known as Fort de Kock
Bükk mts Hungary 49 R7
Bukkapatnam India 94 C3
Bükki nat. park Hungary 49 R7
Bükkzsérc Hungary 49 R8
Bukoba Tanz. 128 A5
Bukonys Lith. 42 F6
Bukowa r. Poland 49 T5
Bukowo, Jezioro lag. Poland 49 N1
Bükreș Romania see Bucharest
Buku, Tanjung pt Indon. 76 D3
Bukum, Pulau i. Sing. 76 [inset]
Būl, Kūh-e mt. Iran 100 C4
Bula Guinea-Bissau 124 B3
Bula Indon. 73 H7
Bülach Switz. 51 O5
Bulag Mongolia 85 F1
Bulagtay Mongolia 85 E1
Bulahdelah Australia 147 G3
Bulalacao i. Phil. 74 B4
Bulan Phil. 74 B3
Bulan i. Phil. 74 B5
Bulancak Turkey 107 D2
Bulandshahr India 96 C3
Bulanık Turkey 107 E3
Bulanovo Rus. Fed. 102 C1
Bulava Rus. Fed. 82 F2
Bulawa, Gunung mt. Indon. 75 B2
Bulawayo Zimbabwe 131 F4
Bulbula waterhole Kenya 128 C5
Buldan Turkey 106 B3
Buldhana India 94 C1
Buldibuyo Peru 200 A2
Buleda reg. Pak. 101 E5
Bulei well Eth. 128 E3
Bulembu Swaziland 133 P2
formerly known as Havelock
Bulgan Bulgan Mongolia 84 D1
Bulgan Hovd Mongolia see Bürenhayrhan
Bulgan Hovd Mongolia 84 B2
formerly known as Darvi
Bulgan Hövsgöl Mongolia 84 D1
Bulgan Ömnögovĭ Mongolia 84 D2
Bulgan prov. Mongolia 84 D1
Bulgan Gol r. Mongolia 84 A2
Bulgar Rus. Fed. see Bolgar
Bŭlgarevo Bulg. 58 J5
►Bulgaria country Europe 58 F6
spelt Bŭlgariya in Bulgarian
►►32–33 Europe Countries
Bŭlgariya country Europe see Bulgaria
Bulghah Saudi Arabia 104 C2
Buli Indon. 75 D2
Buli, Teluk b. Indon. 75 D2
Buliluyan, Cape Phil. 74 A4
Bulkley Ranges mts Canada 166 D4
Bullaque r. Spain 54 G6
Bullas Spain 55 J6
Bullaxaar Somalia 128 E2
Bulle Switz. 51 N6
Bullea, Lake salt flat Australia 146 D2
Bullen r. Canada 167 K1
Buller r. N.Z. 153 F9
Bullering National Park Australia 149 D3
Bullfinch Australia 151 B6
Bullhead City U.S.A. 183 J6
Bullion Mountains U.S.A. 183 H7
Bullmark Sweden 44 M2
Bullo r. Australia 148 A2
Bulloo watercourse Australia 147 D2
Bulloo Downs Australia 147 D2
Bulloo Lake salt flat Australia 147 D2
Bulls N.Z. 152 J8
Bull Shoals Lake U.S.A. 179 D4
Büllsport Namibia 130 C5
Bully Choop Mountain U.S.A. 182 B1
Bulman Australia 148 B2
Bulman Gorge Australia 148 B2
Bulmer Lake Canada 166 F2
Buloh, Pulau i. Sing. 76 [inset]
Buloke, Lake dry lake Australia 147 D4
Bulolo P.N.G. 73 K8
Bulqizë Albania 58 B7
Bultfontein S. Africa 133 K5
Bulu, Gunung mt. Indon. 77 G2
Buluan Phil. 74 C5
Bulubulu Indon. 75 B4
Buluk well Kenya 128 C3
Bulukumba Indon. 75 B4
Bulun Rus. Fed. 39 M2
Bulungu Bandundu Dem. Rep. Congo 126 C6
Bulungu Kasai Occidental Dem. Rep. Congo 127 D6
Bulung'ur Uzbek. 103 F5
formerly known as Krasnogvardeysk
Bulusan Phil. 74 C3
Bulwer S. Africa 133 N6
Bumba Bandundu Dem. Rep. Congo 127 C6
Bumba Équateur Dem. Rep. Congo 126 D4
Bumbah, Khalīj b. Libya 120 D1
Bumbat Mongolia 84 E2
Bumbești-Jiu Romania 58 E3
Bumbuna Sierra Leone 124 C4
Bumhkang Myanmar 78 B2
Bumpha Bum mt. Myanmar 78 B2
Buna Dem. Rep. Congo 126 C5
Buna Kenya 128 C4
Bunayyān well Saudi Arabia 105 E3
Bunazi Tanz. 128 A5
Bunbury Australia 151 A7
Bunclody Ireland 47 F11
formerly known as Newtownbarry
Buncrana Ireland 47 E8
Bunda Tanz. 128 B5
Bundaberg Australia 149 G5
Bundaleer Australia 147 E2
Bundey watercourse Australia 148 B4
Bundi India 96 B4
Bundibugyo Uganda 128 A4
Bundjalung National Park Australia 147 G2
Bundoran Ireland 47 D9
Bundu India 97 E5
Bunduqiya Sudan 128 A3
Bunë r. Albania/Serb. and Mont. 58 A7
Buner reg. Pak. 101 H3
Bunga r. Nigeria 125 H3
Bungalaut, Selat sea chan. Indon. 76 B3
Bungendore Australia 147 F3
Bunger Hills Antarctica 223 G2
Bungi Indon. 75 B4
Bungil Creek r. Australia 149 F5
Bungle Bungle National Park Australia see Purnululu National Park
Bungo Angola 127 B6
Bungoma Kenya 128 B4
Bungo-suidō sea chan. Japan 91 C8
Bungo-takada Japan 91 B8
Bunguran, Kepulauan is Indon. see Natuna, Kepulauan
Bunguran, Pulau i. Indon. see Natuna Besar
Buni, Ci r. Indon. 77 D4
Bunia Dem. Rep. Congo 126 F4
Buningonia well Australia 151 C6
Bunji Jammu and Kashmir 96 B2
Bunker Group atolls Australia 149 G4
Bunkeya Dem. Rep. Congo 127 E7
Bunkie U.S.A. 179 D6
Bunkris Sweden 45 K3
Bunnell U.S.A. 175 D6
Bunnythorpe N.Z. 152 J8
Buñol Spain 55 K5
Bünsum China 89 C6
Bunsuru watercourse Nigeria 125 G3
Buntok Indon. 77 F3
Buntokecil Indon. 77 F3
Bununu Nigeria 125 H4
Bunya Mountains National Park Australia 149 F5
Bünyan Turkey 106 C3
Bunyu i. Indon. 77 G2
Bunza Nigeria 125 G3
Buoač Bos.-Herz. 56 J4
Buoddobohki Fin. see Patoniva
Buonconvento Italy 56 D5
Buôn Ma Thuôt Vietnam 79 E5
Buorkhaya, Guba b. Rus. Fed. 39 N2
Bup r. China 89 D6
Buqayq Saudi Arabia see Abqaiq
Buqbuq Egypt 121 E2
Buqtyrma Bögeni resr Kazakh. see Bukhtarminskoye Vodokhranilishche
Bura Kenya 128 C5
Buraan Somalia 128 F2
Burakin Australia 151 B6
Buram Sudan 126 E2
Buran Kazakh. 88 D1
also spelt Boran
Buran Darat reef Sing. 76 [inset]
Buranhaém r. Brazil 207 N3
Burannoye Rus. Fed. 102 C2
Burano r. Italy 56 E5
Burauen Phil. 74 C4
Buraydah Saudi Arabia 104 C2
Burayevo Rus. Fed. 40 J5
Burbach Germany 48 F5
Burbank U.S.A. 182 F7
Burchell Lake Canada 172 C2
Burcher Australia 147 E3
Burco Somalia 128 E2
Burdalyk Turkm. 103 F5
Burdekin r. Australia 149 E3
Burdekin Falls Australia 149 E4
Burdigala France see Bordeaux
Burdur Turkey 106 B3
Burdur Gölü l. Turkey 106 B3
Burdwan India see Barddhaman
Burē Eth. 128 C2
Bure r. U.K. 47 N11
Bureå Sweden 44 M2
Bureinskiy Khrebet mts Rus. Fed. 82 D2
English form Bureya Range
Bureiqa well Sudan 121 F5
Bürenhayrhan Mongolia 84 A2
formerly known as Bulgan
Bürentsogt Mongolia 85 F2
Bureya r. Rus. Fed. 82 C2
Bureya-Pristan' Rus. Fed. see Novobureyskiy
Bureya Range mts Rus. Fed. see Bureinskiy Khrebet
Bureyinski Zapovednik nature res. Rus. Fed. 82 D2
Burgaltay Mongolia 84 E1
Burgas Bulg. 58 I6
Burgaw U.S.A. 174 E5
Burg bei Magdeburg Germany 48 I3
Burgdorf Niedersachsen Germany 48 H3
Burgdorf Niedersachsen Germany 48 H3
Burgdorf Switz. 51 N5
Burgeo Canada 169 J4
Burgersdorp S. Africa 133 K7
Burgersfort S. Africa 133 O1
Burgerville S. Africa 133 I7
Burges, Mount hill Australia 151 C6
Burgess U.S.A. 177 I8
Burget Tuyur waterhole Sudan 121 E4
Burghausen Germany 49 J7
Burghūth, Sabkhat al salt l. Syria 109 M3
Burgin U.S.A. 176 A8
Burglengenfeld Germany 48 J6
Burgos Mex. 185 F3
Burgos Spain 55 H2
UNESCO World Heritage Site
Burgsvik Sweden 45 L4
Burhabalanga r. India 97 E5
Burhan Budai Shan mts China 84 B5
Burhaniye Turkey 106 A3
Burhanpur India 96 C5
Burhanuddin Bangl. 97 F5
Burhar-Dhanpuri India 97 D5
Burhave (Butjadingen) Germany 48 F2
Burhi Gandak r. India 97 E4
Buri Brazil 206 E10
Burias i. Phil. 74 B3
Buriat-Mongol Republic aut. rep. Rus. Fed. see Buryatiya, Respublika
Buribay Rus. Fed. 102 D2
Burica, Punta pt Costa Rica 186 C5
Burin Canada 169 K4
Burin Peninsula Canada 169 K4
Buriram Thai. 79 C5
Buritama Brazil 206 C8

Buriti Brazil **202** D2
Buriti *r.* Brazil **201** F3
Buriti Alegre Brazil **206** D5
Buriti Bravo Brazil **202** D3
Buritirama Brazil **202** D4
Buritis Brazil **206** G2
Buritizeiro Brazil **207** I4
Burj al 'Arab Egypt **108** A7
Burjassot Spain **55** K5
Burj Mughayzil Egypt **108** B6
Burkan-Suu *r.* Kyrg. **103** I4
also known as Buurakan
Burkburnett U.S.A. **179** C5
Burke *watercourse* Australia **149** C4
Burke U.S.A. **178** C3
Burke Channel Canada **166** E5
Burke Island Antarctica **222** Q2
Burkes Pass N.Z. **153** E12
Burkesville U.S.A. **174** C4
Burketown Australia **148** C3
Burkeville U.S.A. **176** G8
Burkhala Rus. Fed. **39** O3
►**Burkina** *country* Africa **125** E3
formerly known as Upper Volta *or* Haute-Volta; *long form* Burkina Faso
►►**114–115 Africa** Countries
Burkina Faso *country* Africa *see* **Burkina**
Burk's Falls Canada **168** E4
Burkutty Kazakh. **103** I2
Burla Rus. Fed. **103** I1
Burley U.S.A. **180** D4
Burli Kazakh. **103** E1
also spelt Börili
Burlin Kazakh. **102** C2
Burlington Canada **168** E5
Burlington *CO* U.S.A. **178** B4
Burlington *IA* U.S.A. **174** B3
Burlington *KS* U.S.A. **178** D4
Burlington *NC* U.S.A. **176** F9
Burlington *VT* U.S.A. **177** L1
Burlington *WA* U.S.A. **180** B2
Burlington *WI* U.S.A. **172** E8
Burly Rus. Fed. **40** K5
Burma *country* Asia *see* **Myanmar**
Burmakino Rus. Fed. **43** V4
Burnaby Canada **166** F5
Burnet U.S.A. **179** C6
Burnett *r.* Australia **149** G5
Burney U.S.A. **182** C1
Burney, Monte *vol.* Chile **205** B9
Burnham U.S.A. **177** P1
Burnie Australia **147** E5
Burning Springs U.S.A. **176** B8
Burnley U.K. **47** J10
Burnoye Kazakh. *see* **Bauyrzhan Momyshuly**
Burns U.S.A. **180** C4
Burnside *r.* Canada **167** I1
Burnside U.S.A. **176** A9
Burnside, Lake *salt flat* Australia **151** C5
Burns Junction U.S.A. **180** C4
Burns Lake Canada **166** E4
Burnsville U.S.A. **176** E7
Burnt *r.* U.S.A. **180** C3
Burnt Lake Canada *see* **Brûlé, Lac**
Burntwood *r.* Canada **167** L4
Burntwood Lake Canada **167** K4
Burog Co *l.* China **89** D5
Buron *r.* Canada **169** G1
Burovoy Uzbek. **103** E4
Burqin China **88** D2
Burqin He *r.* China **88** D2
Burqu' Jordan **109** J5
Burra Australia **146** C3
Burra *i.* U.K. **46** K3
Burrel Albania **58** B7
Burrel U.S.A. **182** E5
Burren *reg.* Ireland **47** C10
Burrendong, Lake *resr* Australia **147** F3
Burren Junction Australia **147** F2
Burriana Spain **55** K5
Burrinjuck Reservoir Australia **147** F3
Burro, Serranías del *mts* Mex. **185** E2
Burr Oak U.S.A. **172** B7
Burr Oak Reservoir U.S.A. **176** C6
Burro Creek *watercourse* U.S.A. **183** K7
Burrow Head U.K. **47** H9
Burruyacú Arg. **204** D2
Bursa Turkey **106** B2
historically known as Brusa *or* Prusa
Bursa *prov.* Turkey **59** J8
Būr Safāga Egypt **121** G3
Būr Sa'īd Egypt *see* **Port Said**
Būr Sa'īd *governorate* Egypt **108** D6
Bursinskoye Vodokhranilishche *resr* Rus. Fed. **82** C2
Būr Sudan Sudan *see* **Port Sudan**
Burt Lake U.S.A. **173** I5
Burtnieku ezers *l.* Latvia **42** G4
Burton U.S.A. **173** J8
Burton, Lac *l.* Canada **168** E2
Burton upon Trent U.K. **47** K11
Burträsk Sweden **44** M2
Burtundy Australia **147** D3
Burt Well Australia **148** B4
Buru *i.* Indon. **75** C3
Burubaytal Kazakh. **88** A2
also spelt Būrylbaytal
Burūk, Wādī al *watercourse* Egypt **108** E7
Burullus, Bahra el *lag.* Egypt *see* **Burullus, Lake**
Burullus, Lake *lag.* Egypt **108** B6
also known as Burullus, Bahra el
Burultokay China *see* **Fuhai**
Burūn, Ra's *pt* Egypt **108** E6
►**Burundi** *country* Africa **126** F5
formerly known as Urundi
►►**114–115 Africa** Countries
Burunniy Rus. Fed. *see* **Tsagan Aman**
Bururi Burundi **126** F5
Burwash Landing Canada **166** B2
Burwell U.S.A. **178** C3
Burwick U.K. **46** J5
Buryatia *aut. rep.* Rus. Fed. *see* **Buryatiya, Respublika**
Buryatiya, Respublika *aut. rep.* Rus. Fed. **84** D1
English form Buryatia; *formerly known as* Buriat-Mongol Republic *or* Buryatskaya Mongolskaya A.S.S.R.
Buryatskaya Mongolskaya A.S.S.R. *aut. rep.* Rus. Fed. *see* **Buryatiya, Respublika**
Būrylbaytal Kazakh. *see* **Burubaytal**
Buryn' Ukr. **41** E6
Burynshyk Kazakh. **102** B3
Bury St Edmunds U.K. **47** M11
Burzil Pass Jammu and Kashmir **96** B2
Busalla Italy **56** A4
Busan S. Korea *see* **Pusan**
Būs'ān Yemen **104** C5
Busan Bay Phil. **74** B5
Busanga Dem. Rep. Congo **126** D5
Busca Italy **51** N8
Buseire Syria *see* **Al Buşayrah**
Būshehr Iran **100** B4
formerly spelt Bushire
Būshehr *prov.* Iran **100** B4
Bushenyi Uganda **128** A5
Bushire Iran *see* **Būshehr**
Bushkill U.S.A. **177** J4
Bushnell *FL* U.S.A. **175** D6
Bushnell *IL* U.S.A. **172** C10
Bushuikha Rus. Fed. **43** V2
Busia Kenya **128** B4
Busing, Pulau *i.* Sing. **76** [inset]
Businga Dem. Rep. Congo **126** D4
Busira *r.* Dem. Rep. Congo **126** C5
Buskerud *county* Norway **45** J3
Busko-Zdrój Poland **49** R5
Buskul' Kazakh. *see* **Boskol'**
Busobuso Indon. **75** D2
Buşrá ash Shām Syria **109** H5
UNESCO World Heritage Site
Busselton Australia **151** A7
Bussol', Proliv *strait* Rus. Fed. **81** Q3
Bustamante Mex. **185** E3
Buşteni Romania **58** G3
Bustillos, Lago *l.* Mex. **184** D2
Busto Arsizio Italy **56** A3
Busuanga Phil. **74** A3
Busuanga *i.* Phil. **74** A3
Busu-Djanoa Dem. Rep. Congo **126** D4
Büsum Germany **48** F1
Busu Modanda Dem. Rep. Congo **126** C4
Buta Dem. Rep. Congo **126** E4
Butajīra Eth. **128** C2
Butan Bulg. **58** E5
Buta Ranquil Arg. **204** C5
Butare Rwanda **126** F5
formerly known as Astrida
Butaritari *atoll* Kiribati **220** G6
also known as Makin
Butauanan *pt* Phil. **74** B3
Bute *i.* U.K. **46** G8
Butea Romania **58** H1
Butedale Canada **166** D4
Bute Inlet Canada **166** E5
Butembo Dem. Rep. Congo **126** F4
Butha-Buthe Lesotho **133** M5
Butha Qi China *see* **Zalantun**
Buthidaung Myanmar **78** A3
Butiá Brazil **203** B9
Butiaba Uganda **128** A4
Butler *AL* U.S.A. **175** B5
Butler *GA* U.S.A. **175** C5
Butler *IN* U.S.A. **176** A4
Butler *KY* U.S.A. **176** A7
Butler *MO* U.S.A. **178** D4
Butler *PA* U.S.A. **176** F5
Buton *i.* Indon. **75** B4
Buton, Selat *sea chan.* Indon. **75** B4
Butrimonys Lith. **42** G7
Butrint *tourist site* Albania **58** B9
UNESCO World Heritage Site
Butrintit, Liqeni i *l.* Albania **59** B9
Buttahatchee *r.* U.S.A. **175** B5
Butte *MT* U.S.A. **180** D3
Butte *NE* U.S.A. **178** C3
Butternut U.S.A. **172** C4
Butterworth Malaysia **76** C1
Butterworth S. Africa **133** M9
Buttes, Sierra *mt.* U.S.A. **182** D2
Butt of Lewis *hd* U.K. **46** F5
also known as Robhanais, Rubha
Button Bay Canada **167** M3
Button Islands Canada **165** M3
Buttonwillow U.S.A. **182** E6
Butuan Phil. **74** C4
Butuan Bay Phil. **74** C4
Butuo China **86** B3
also known as Temuli
Buturlinovka Rus. Fed. **41** G6
Butwal Nepal **97** D4
Butzbach Germany **48** F5
Bützow Germany **48** I2
Buuhoodle Somalia **128** E2
Buulobarde Somalia **128** E4
Buurakan *r.* Kyrg. *see* **Burkan-Suu**
Buur Gaabo Somalia **128** D5
Buurhabaka Somalia **128** E4
Buvåg Norway **44** K1
Buvuma Island Uganda **128** B4
Buwārah, Jabal *mt.* Saudi Arabia **108** F9
Buwāţah Saudi Arabia **104** B2
Buxar India **97** E4
Buxoro Uzbek. **103** F5
also spelt Bukhoro
UNESCO World Heritage Site
Buxoro *admin. div.* Uzbek. **103** E4
English form Bukhara Oblast; *also known as* Bukhoro Wiloyati
Buxtehude Germany **48** G2
Buxton U.K. **47** K10
Buy Rus. Fed. **40** G4
Buy *r.* Rus. Fed. **40** J4
Buyant *Bayanhongor* Mongolia **84** C2
Buyant *Bayan-Ölgiy* Mongolia **84** A1
Buyant *Hentiy* Mongolia **85** F2
Buyant Gol *r.* Mongolia **84** A1
Buyant Gol *r.* Mongolia **84** C2
Buyant-Ovoo Mongolia **85** E2
Buyant-Uhaa Mongolia **85** F2
Buyck U.S.A. **172** A2
Buynaksk Rus. Fed. **102** A4
Buyo Côte d'Ivoire **124** D5
Buyo, Lac de *l.* Côte d'Ivoire **124** D5
Buyuan Jiang *r.* China **86** B4
Büyükada *i.* Turkey **58** K8
Büyük Egri Dağ *mt.* Turkey **108** E1
Büyükkarıştıran Turkey **58** I7
Büyükkonuk Turkey **59** K11
Büyükmenderes *r.* Turkey **106** A3
Büyükorhan Turkey **59** J9
Büyükşahinbey Turkey **109** I1
Buyun Shan *mt.* China **85** I3
Buzachi, Poluostrov *pen.* Kazakh. **102** B3
also known as Bozashy Tübegi
Buzançais France **50** H6
Buzău Romania **58** H3
Buzău *r.* Romania **58** H3
Buzaymah *oasis* Libya **120** D3
Buzdyak Rus. Fed. **40** J5
Buzha *r.* Rus. Fed. **43** V6
Búzi Moz. **131** G3
Búzi *r.* Moz. **131** G3
Buziaş Romania **58** C3
Búzios, Cabo dos *c.* Brazil **207** L9
Búzios, Ilha dos *i.* Brazil **207** H10
Büzmeyin Turkm. *see* **Büzmeýin**
Büzmeýin Turkm. **102** D5
also spelt Büzmeyin; *formerly spelt* Bezmein
Buzuluk Rus. Fed. **102** C1
Buzuluk *r.* Rus. Fed. **41** G6
Buzzards Bay U.S.A. **177** O4
Bwagaoia P.N.G. **149** G1
Bwindi National Park Uganda **126** F5
UNESCO World Heritage Site
Byadgi India **94** B3
Byahoml' Belarus **42** J7
Byakar Bhutan *see* **Jakar**
Byala Bulg. **58** G5
Byala Bulg. **58** I6
Byala Slatina Bulg. **58** E5
Byalynichy Belarus **43** K8
Byalynkavichy Belarus **43** N8
Byam Martin Island Canada **165** I2
Byarezina *r.* Belarus **42** G8
Byarezina *r.* Belarus **43** L9
Byarezinski Biyasfyerny Zapavyednik *nature res.* Belarus **43** J7
Byaroza Belarus **42** F9
also spelt Bereza
Byarozawka Belarus **42** G8
also spelt Berezovka
Byblos *tourist site* Lebanon **108** G3
UNESCO World Heritage Site
Bychawa Poland **49** T4
Byczyna Poland **49** P4
Bydgoszcz Poland **49** P2
historically known as Bromberg
Byelaazyorsk Belarus **42** G9
also spelt Beloozersk
Byelitsk Belarus **43** L9
Byel'ki Belarus **42** I6
Byelorussia *country* Europe *see* **Belarus**
Byerastavitsa Belarus *see* **Pahranichny**
Byerazino Belarus **43** J8
also spelt Berezino
Byerazino Belarus **43** J7
also spelt Berezino
Byeraznyaki Belarus **42** I9
Byers U.S.A. **180** F5
Byershty Belarus **42** F8
Byeshankovichy Belarus **43** K6
Byesville U.S.A. **176** D6
Byesyedz' *r.* Belarus **43** M9
Byfield Australia **149** F4
Byfield National Park Australia **149** F4
Bygdeå Sweden **44** M2
Byglandsfjord Norway **45** I4
Bykhaw Belarus **43** L8
also spelt Bykhov
Bykhov Belarus *see* **Bykhaw**
Bykle Norway **45** I4
Bykovo Rus. Fed. **41** H6
Bykovskiy Rus. Fed. **39** M2
Bylas U.S.A. **183** N8
Bylot Island Canada **165** L2
Byng Inlet Canada **173** M5
Bynoe *r.* Australia **149** D3
Bynoe Harbour Australia **150** E2
Byramgore Reef *reef* India **94** A4
also known as Chereapani
Byrd Glacier Antarctica **223** K1
Byrka Rus. Fed. **85** H1
Byrkjelo Norway **45** I3
Byrock Australia **147** E2
Byron *IL* U.S.A. **172** D8
Byron *ME* U.S.A. **177** O1
Byron Bay Australia **147** G2
Byron Island Kiribati *see* **Nikunau**
Byrranga, Gory *mts* Rus. Fed. **39** J2
Byryne Ukr. **43** O9
Byske Sweden **44** M2
Byskeälven *r.* Sweden **44** M2
Byssa *r.* Rus. Fed. **82** C1
Bystrá *mt.* Slovakia **49** Q6
Bystretsovo Rus. Fed. **43** J4
Bystřice nad Pernštejnem Czech Rep. **49** N6
Bystrinskiy Golets, Gora *mt.* Rus. Fed. **85** F1
Bystrovka Kyrg. *see* **Kemin**
Bystryy Tanyp *r.* Rus. Fed. **40** J5
Bystrzyca *r.* Poland **49** N4
Bystrzyca *r.* Poland **49** T4
Bytantay *r.* Rus. Fed. **39** N3
Bytča Slovakia **49** P6
Bytom Poland **49** P5
historically known as Beuthen
Bytosh' Rus. Fed. **43** P8
Bytów Poland **49** O1
Byumba Rwanda **126** F5
Byurgyutli Turkm. **102** C5
Byxelkrok Sweden **45** L4
Byzantium Turkey *see* **İstanbul**
Bzura *r.* Poland **49** R3

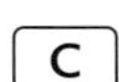

Ca, Sông *r.* Vietnam **78** D4
Caacupé Para. **201** F6
Caaguazú Para. **201** F6
Caaguazú, Cordillera de *hills* Para. **201** G6
Caála Angola **127** B8
formerly known as Robert Williams
Caapiranga Brazil **199** F5
Caapucú Para. **201** F6
Caarapó Brazil **203** A7
Caatiba Brazil **207** M2
Caatinga Brazil **207** H4
Caazapá Para. **201** F6
Cabaçal *r.* Brazil **201** F3
Cabaiguán Cuba **186** D2
Caballas Peru **200** B3
Caballo *mt.* Spain **55** H7
Caballococha Peru **198** D5
Caballos Mesteños, Llano de los *plain* Mex. **184** D2
Cabana *Ancash* Peru **200** A2
Cabana *Ayacucho* Peru **200** B3
Cabanaconde Peru **200** C3
Cabañaquinta Spain **54** F1
Cabanatuan Phil. **74** B3
Cabanères *hill* France **50** H9
Cabano Canada **169** G4
Čabar Croatia **56** G3
Cabdul Qaadir Somalia **128** D2
Cabeceiras Brazil **206** G2
Cabeço Rainha *mt.* Port. **54** D5
Cabedelo Brazil **202** F3
Cabeza del Buey Arg. **205** C6
Cabeza del Buey Spain **54** F6
Cabeza de Vaca, Punta *pt* Chile **204** C2
Cabeza Prieta National Wildlife Refuge *nature res.* U.S.A. **183** K9
Cabezas Bol. **201** E4
Cabezo Gordo *hill* Spain **54** D7
Cabimas Venez. **198** D2
Cabinda Angola **127** B6
Cabinda *prov.* Angola **127** B6
Cabinet Inlet Antarctica **222** T2
Cabinet Mountains U.S.A. **180** D2
Cabingan *i.* Phil. **74** B5
Cabistra Turkey *see* **Ereğli**
Cable U.S.A. **172** B4
Cabo Brazil **202** F4
Cabo Blanco Arg. **205** D7
Cabo Delgado *prov.* Moz. **131** H2
Cabo Frio Brazil **203** D7
Cabo Frio, Ilha do *i.* Brazil **207** L10
Cabollera, Peña *mt.* Spain **55** H3
Cabonga, Réservoir *resr* Canada **168** E4
Cabool U.S.A. **178** D4
Caboolture Australia **147** G1
Cabo Orange, Parque Nacional de *nat. park* Brazil **199** I4
Cabo Pantoja Peru **198** C5
Cabora Bassa, Lake *resr* Moz. **131** F2
also known as Cahora Bassa, Lago de
Cabo Raso Arg. **205** D7
Caborca Mex. **184** B2
Cabot Head Canada **173** L5
Cabot Strait Canada **169** I4
Cabo Verde *country* N. Atlantic Ocean *see* **Cape Verde**
Cabo Verde, Ilhas do *is* N. Atlantic Ocean **124** [inset]
Cabo Yubi Morocco *see* **Tarfaya**
Cabra *i.* Phil. **74** B3
Cabra Spain **54** G7
Cabra *r.* Spain **54** G7
Cabral Dom. Rep. **187** F3
Cabral, Serra do *mts* Brazil **203** C6
Cabras *Sardinia* Italy **57** A9
Cäbrayıl Azer. **107** F3
Cabred Arg. **204** F3
Cabrela *r.* Port. **54** C6
Cabrera Dom. Rep. **187** F3
Cabrera *i.* Spain **55** N5
Cabrera, Sierra de la *mts* Spain **54** E2
Cabri Canada **167** I5
Cabriel *r.* Spain **55** J5
Cabrobó Brazil **202** E4
Cabruta Venez. **199** E3
Cabugao Phil. **74** B2
Čabulja *mt.* Bos.-Herz. **56** J5
Cabullona Mex. **184** C2
Caçador Brazil **203** B8
Cacagoin China *see* **Qagca**
Cacahuatepec Mex. **185** F5
Čačak *Srbija* Serb. and Mont. **58** B5
Cacao Fr. Guiana **199** H3
Caçapava Brazil **207** H10
Caçapava do Sul Brazil **203** A9
Cacapon *r.* U.S.A. **176** G6
Cácares Col. **198** C3
Caccia, Capo *c. Sardinia* Italy **57** A8
Çäçe Turkm. **102** E5
also spelt Chäche
Cacém Port. **54** B6
Cáceres Brazil **201** F4
Cáceres Spain **54** E5
UNESCO World Heritage Site
Cachal Bol. **200** D3
Cache *r.* U.S.A. **174** B4
Cacheau *r.* Guinea-Bissau **124** A3
Cache Creek Canada **166** F5
Cache Creek *r.* U.S.A. **182** C3
Cache la Poudre *r.* U.S.A. **180** F4
Cacheu Guinea-Bissau **124** A3
Cachi Arg. **204** D2
Cachi, Nevados de *mts* Arg. **200** D6
Cachimbo Brazil **202** A4
Cachimbo, Serra do *hills* Brazil **202** A4
Cachimo Angola **127** D7
Cachina *r.* Chile **204** C2
Cachingues Angola **127** C8
Cáchira Col. **198** C3
Cachoeira *Bahia* Brazil **202** E5
Cachoeira *Mato Grosso do Sul* Brazil **206** B6
Cachoeira Alta Brazil **206** C5
Cachoeira de Goiás Brazil **206** C3
Cachoeira do Arari Brazil **202** B2
Cachoeira do Sul Brazil **203** A9
Cachoeiras de Macacu Brazil **207** K9
Cachoeiro de Itapemirim Brazil **203** D7
Cachos, Punta de *pt* Chile **204** C2
Cachuela Esperanza Bol. **200** D2
Cacine Guinea-Bissau **124** B4
Cacolo Angola **127** C7
Caconda Angola **127** B8
Cacongo Angola **127** B6
formerly known as Guilherme Capelo *or* Landana
Cactus U.S.A. **179** B4
Cactus Range *mts* U.S.A. **183** G4
Caçu Brazil **206** B5
Cacuaco Angola **127** B7
Cacula Angola **127** B8
Caculama Angola **127** C7
Caculé Brazil **202** D5
Cacumba, Ilha *i.* Brazil **207** N4
Cacuso Angola **127** B7
Cadale Somalia **128** E4
Čadca Slovakia **49** P6
Caddabassa *i.* Eth. **128** D2
Caddo Lake U.S.A. **179** D5
Cadell *r.* Australia **148** B2
Cadell Creek *watercourse* Australia **149** D4
Cadenberge Germany **48** G2
Cadereyta Mex. **185** E3
Cadí, Serra del *mts* Spain **55** M2
Cadibarrawirracanna, Lake *salt flat* Australia **146** B2
Cadig Mountains Phil. **74** B3
Cadillac *Que.* Canada **173** O2
Cadillac *Sask.* Canada **167** J5
Cadillac U.S.A. **172** H6
Cadiz Phil. **74** B4
Cádiz Spain **54** E8
historically known as Gades
Cadiz *CA* U.S.A. **183** I7
Cadiz *KY* U.S.A. **174** C4
Cadiz *OH* U.S.A. **176** E5
Cádiz, Bahía de *b.* Spain **54** E8
Cádiz, Golfo de *g.* Spain **54** D8
Cadiz Lake U.S.A. **183** I7
Cadomin Canada **167** G4
Cadott U.S.A. **172** B6
Cadotte *r.* Canada **167** G3
Cadoux Australia **151** B6
Caen France **50** F3
Caerdydd U.K. *see* **Cardiff**
Caere Italy *see* **Cerveteri**
Caerfyrddin U.K. *see* **Carmarthen**
Caergybi U.K. *see* **Holyhead**
Caernarfon U.K. **47** H10
formerly spelt Caernarvon; *historically known as* Segontia *or* Segontium
Caernarfon Bay U.K. **47** H10
Caernarfon Castle *tourist site* U.K. **47** H10
Caernarvon U.K. *see* **Caernarfon**
Caesaraugusta Spain *see* **Zaragoza**
Caesarea Alg. *see* **Cherchell**
Caesarea *tourist site* Israel **108** F5
Caesarea Cappadociae Turkey *see* **Kayseri**
Caesarea Philippi Syria *see* **Bāniyās**
Caesarodunum France *see* **Tours**
Caesaromagus U.K. *see* **Chelmsford**
Caeté Brazil **207** J6
Caeté *r.* Brazil **200** C2
Caetité Brazil **202** D5
Cafayate Arg. **204** D2
Cafelândia Brazil **206** D8
Caffa Ukr. *see* **Feodosiya**
Çafia, Hamâda *des.* Mali **122** D5
Cafuini *r.* Brazil **199** G4
Cagayan *i.* Phil. **74** B4
Cagayan *r.* Phil. **74** B2
Cagayan de Oro Phil. **74** C4
Cagayan de Tawi-Tawi *i.* Phil. **74** A5
Cagayan Islands Phil. **74** B4
Cagli Italy **56** E5
Cagliari *Sardinia* Italy **57** B9
historically known as Carales *or* Caralis
Cagliari, Golfo di *b. Sardinia* Italy **57** B9
Cagnano Varano Italy **56** H7
Cagnes-sur-Mer France **51** N9
Caguán *r.* Col. **198** C5
Caguas Puerto Rico **187** G3
Çagyl Turkm. **102** C4
Çagyllyşor Çöketligi *depr.* Turkm. **102** D4
Cahaba *r.* U.S.A. **175** C5
Cahama Angola **127** B9
Caha Mountains *hills* Ireland **47** C12
Cahersiveen Ireland *see* **Cahirciveen**
Cahir Ireland **47** E11
Cahirciveen Ireland **47** B12
also spelt Cahersiveen
Cahokia U.S.A. **178** E4
UNESCO World Heritage Site
Cahora Bassa, Lago de *resr* Moz. *see* **Cabora Bassa, Lake**
Cahore Point Ireland **47** F11
Cahors France **50** H8
Cahuapanas Peru **198** B6
Cahul Moldova **58** J3
formerly spelt Kagul *or* Kakhul
Caia Moz. **131** G3
formerly known as Vila Fontes
Caia *r.* Port. **54** D6
Caia, Barragem do *resr* Port. **54** D5
Caiabis, Serra dos *hills* Brazil **201** F3
Caianda Angola **127** D7
Caiapó *r.* Brazil **206** B2
Caiapó, Serra do *mts* Brazil **206** A4
Caiapônia Brazil **206** B3
Caiaza Angola **127** D7
Caibarién Cuba **186** D2
Cai Bâu, Đao *i.* Vietnam **78** D3
Cai Be Vietnam **79** D6
Caicara Venez. **199** E3
Caicó Brazil **202** E3
Caicos Islands Turks and Caicos Is **187** F2
Caicos Passage Bahamas/Turks and Caicos Is **187** E2
Caidian China **87** E2
formerly known as Hanyang
Caidu China *see* **Shangcai**
Caifuche Angola **127** D7
Caiguna Australia **151** D7
Caihua China **87** D2
Cailloma Peru **200** C3
Caimanero, Laguna del *lag.* Mex. **184** D4
Caiman Point Phil. **74** A3
Caimbambo Angola **127** B8
Caimodorro *mt.* Spain **55** J4
Cainde Angola **127** B8
Căineni Romania **58** F3
Caineville U.S.A. **183** M3
Cainnyigoin China **86** B1
Cains Store U.S.A. **176** A8
Caipe Arg. **200** C6
Caird Coast Antarctica **222** W1
Cairngorm Mountains U.K. **46** I6
Cairngorms National Park U.K. **46** I6
Cairns Australia **149** E3
Cairnsmore of Carsphairn *hill* U.K. **47** H8

►**Cairo** Egypt **121** F2
Capital of Egypt, and most populous city in Africa. Also known as El Qâhira or Al Qāhirah or Le Caire. UNESCO World Heritage Site
►►**18–19 World** Cities

Cairo *GA* U.S.A. **175** C6
Cairo *IL* U.S.A. **174** B4
Cairo, Monte *mt.* Italy **56** F7
Cairo Montenotte Italy **56** A4
Caisleán an Bharraigh Ireland *see* **Castlebar**
Caistor U.K. **47** L10
Caitou Angola **127** B8
Caiundo Angola **127** C8
Caiwarro Australia **147** E2
Caixi China **87** F3
Caiyuanzhen China *see* **Shengsi**
Caiza Bol. **200** D5
Caizi Hu *l.* China **87** F2
Cajabamba Peru **200** A1
Cajamarca Peru **200** A1
Cajamarca *dept* Peru **198** B6
Cajapió Brazil **202** C2
Cajarc France **50** H8
Cajari Brazil **202** C2
Cajatambo Peru **200** A2
Cajàzeiras Brazil **202** E3
Čajetina *Srbija* Serb. and Mont. **58** A5
Çajidiocan Phil. **74** B3
Čajniče Bos.-Herz. **56** L5
Cajones, Cayos *is* Hond. **186** C3
Cajuata Bol. **200** D4
Cajuru Brazil **206** F8
Caka China **84** C4
Caka'lho China *see* **Yanjing**
Caka Yanhu *l.* China **84** C4
Čakovec Croatia **56** I2
Çal Turkey **106** B3
Çal Turkey *see* **Çukurca**
Cala S. Africa **133** L8
Cala *r.* Spain **54** E7
Calabar Nigeria **125** H5
Calabogie Canada **173** Q5
Calabozo Venez. **199** E2
Calabria *admin. reg.* Italy **57** I10
Calabria, Parco Nazionale della *nat. park* Italy **57** I9
Calaburra, Punta de *pt* Spain **54** G8
Calacoto Bol. **200** C4
Calaf Spain **55** M3
Calafat Romania **58** D5
Calafate Arg. **205** B8
Cala Figuera, Cap de *c.* Spain **55** N5
Calagnaan *i.* Phil. **74** B4
Calagua Mex. **184** C3
Calagua Islands Phil. **74** B3
Calagurris Spain *see* **Calahorra**
Calahorra Spain **55** J2
historically known as Calagurris
Calai Angola **127** C9
Calais France **51** H2
Calais U.S.A. **174** H2
Calakmul *tourist site* Mex. **185** H5
UNESCO World Heritage Site
Calalasteo, Sierra de *mts* Arg. **204** D2
Calama Brazil **201** E2
Calama Chile **200** C5
Calamajué Mex. **181** D7
Calamar Col. **198** C4
Calamarca Bol. **200** C4
Calamian Group *is* Phil. **74** A4
Calamocha Spain **55** J4
Călan Romania **58** E3
Calanaque Brazil **199** E5
Calañas Spain **54** E7
Calanda Spain **55** K4
Calandagan *i.* Phil. **74** B4
Calandula Angola **127** C7
also spelt Kalandula; *formerly known as* Duque de Bragança
Calang Indon. **76** A1
Calanscio Sand Sea *des.* Libya **120** D2
Calapan Phil. **74** B3
Calapas *pass* S. Africa **133** L8
Calar Alta *mt.* Spain **55** I7
Călăraşi Moldova **58** J1
formerly spelt Kalarash
Călăraşi Romania **58** I4
Cala Santa Galdana Spain **55** O5
Calatafimi *Sicily* Italy **57** E11
Calatayud Spain **55** J3
Calau Germany **49** K4
Calauag Phil. **74** B3
Calavà, Capo *c. Sicily* Italy **57** G10
Calavite Passage Phil. **74** B3
Calawit *i.* Phil. **74** A3
Calayan *i.* Phil. **74** B2
Calbayog Phil. **74** C3
Calbiga Phil. **74** C4
Calca Peru **200** C3
Calcanhar, Ponta do *pt* Brazil **202** F3
Calcasieu *r.* U.S.A. **179** D6
Calcasieu Lake U.S.A. **179** D6
Calceta Ecuador **198** A5
Calchaqui Arg. **204** E3
Calcutta India *see* **Kolkata**
Căldăraru Romania **58** F4
Caldas *dept* Col. **198** C3
Caldas da Rainha Port. **54** B5
Caldas de Mombuy Spain *see* **Caldes de Montbui**
Caldas Novas Brazil **206** E4
Caldeirão Brazil **201** D2
Calder *r.* Canada **167** G1
Caldera Chile **204** C2
Calderitas Mex. **185** H5
Caldervale Australia **149** E5
Caldes de Montbui Spain **55** N3
also spelt Caldas de Mombuy
Çaldıran Turkey **107** E3
Caldwell *ID* U.S.A. **180** C4
Caldwell *KS* U.S.A. **178** C4
Caldwell *OH* U.S.A. **176** D6
Caldwell *TX* U.S.A. **179** C6
Caledon Canada **173** N7
Caledon *r.* Lesotho/S. Africa **133** K7
Caledon S. Africa **132** D11
Caledon Bay Australia **148** C2
Caledonia *N.S.* Canada **169** H4
Caledonia *Ont.* Canada **173** N7
Caledonia *admin. div.* U.K. *see* **Scotland**
Caledonia *MI* U.S.A. **172** H8
Caledonia *MN* U.S.A. **174** B3
Caledonia *NY* U.S.A. **176** H3
Caledon Nature Reserve S. Africa **133** K6
Calella Spain **55** N3
Calen Australia **149** F4
Calenzana *Corsica* France **51** O10
Calera U.S.A. **175** C5
Calera y Chozas Spain **54** F5
Caleta el Cobre Chile **200** C6
Caleta Josefina Chile **205** C9
Caleta Lobos Chile **200** C5
Caleta Pabellón de Pica Chile **200** C5
Caleufú Arg. **204** D4
Calexico U.S.A. **183** I9
Calf of Man *i.* Isle of Man **47** H9
Calgary Canada **167** H5
Calhoun U.S.A. **174** C5
Cali Col. **198** B4
Çalı Turkey **59** J8
Calicoan *i.* Phil. **74** C4
Calicut India **94** B4
also known as Kozhikode
Caliente U.S.A. **183** J4
California U.S.A. **178** D4
California *state* U.S.A. **182** D4
California, Golfo de *g.* Mex. *see* **California, Gulf of**
California, Gulf of Mex. **184** B2
also known as California, Golfo de; *historically known as* Cortes, Sea of
California Aqueduct U.S.A. **182** D5
California Aqueduct *canal* U.S.A. **182** C4
California Coastal National Monument U.S.A. **181** B6
California Delta U.S.A. **182** C3
Cälilabad Azer. **107** G3
also spelt Dzhalalabad; *formerly known as* Astrakhan' Bazar
Calilegua Arg. **201** D5
Calilegua, Parque Nacional *nat. park* Arg. **200** D5
Călimăneşti Romania **58** F3
Călimani, Munţii *mts* Romania **58** F1
Calingasta Arg. **204** C3
Calistoga U.S.A. **182** B3
Calitri Italy **56** H8
Calitzdorp S. Africa **132** F10
Çalkaya Turkey **108** B1
Calkiní Mex. **185** H4
Callabonna, Lake *salt flat* Australia **146** D2
Callabonna Creek *watercourse* Australia **146** D2
Callac France **50** C4
Callaghan U.S.A. **176** E8
Callaghan, Mount U.S.A. **183** H2
Callan Ireland **47** E11
Callander Canada **168** E4
Callander U.K. **46** H7
Callands U.S.A. **176** F9
Callang Phil. **74** B2
Callao Peru **200** A3
Callao U.S.A. **183** K2
Callawa Aboriginal Reserve Australia **150** C4
Calles Mex. **185** F4
Callicoon U.S.A. **177** J4
Callide Australia **149** F5
Calling Lake Canada **167** H4
Calling Lake *l.* Canada **167** H4
Calliope Australia **149** F5
Callipolis Turkey *see* **Gallipoli**
Callosa d'En Sarrià Spain **55** K6
Callosa de Segura Spain **55** K6
Callum Canada **173** M4
Callyharra Springs Australia **151** A5
Calmar Canada **167** H4
Calmar U.S.A. **174** B3
Călmăţui *r.* Romania **58** G5
Călnic Romania **58** E3
UNESCO World Heritage Site
Călniştea *r.* Romania **58** G4
Calolziocorte Italy **56** B3
Caloosahatchee *r.* U.S.A. **175** D7
Calore *r.* Italy **56** G7
Calotmul Mex. **185** H4
Caloundra Australia **149** G5
Čalovo Slovakia *see* **Veľký Meder**
Calpe Spain **55** L6
Calpoy's Bay Canada **173** L6
Calpulálpan Mex. **185** F5
Calstock Canada **168** C3
Caltagirone *Sicily* Italy **57** G11
UNESCO World Heritage Site
Caltanissetta *Sicily* Italy **57** G11
Çaltıbozkır Turkey **108** E1
Calucinga Angola **127** C7
Caluire-et-Cuire France **51** K7
Calulo Angola **127** B7
Calumet U.S.A. **172** E3
Calunda Angola **127** D8
Calunga Angola **127** C9
Caluquembe Angola **127** B8
Calusa *i.* Phil. **74** B4
Caluula Somalia **128** F2
Caluula, Raas *pt* Somalia **128** F2
Calvert *r.* Australia **148** C3
Calvert Hills Australia **148** C3
Calvert Island Canada **166** D5
Calvert Range *hills* Australia **150** C4
Calvi *Corsica* France **51** O10
Calvià Spain **55** N5
Calvinia S. Africa **132** D8
Calvitero *mt.* Spain **54** F4
Calzada de Calatrava Spain **54** H6
Cam *r.* U.K. **47** M11
Camabatela Angola **127** B7
Camacã Brazil **207** N2
Camaçari Brazil **202** E5
Camache Reservoir U.S.A. **182** D3
Camachigama *r.* Canada **168** E4
Camachigama, Lac *l.* Canada **173** Q3
Camacho Mex. **185** E3
Camacuio Angola **127** B8
Camacupa Angola **127** C8
formerly known as General Machado
Camaguán Venez. **199** E2
Camagüey Cuba **186** D2
Camagüey, Archipiélago de *is* Cuba **186** D2
Camah, Gunung *mt.* Malaysia **76** C1
Camaiú *r.* Brazil **199** G6
Camajuaní Cuba **186** D2
Çamalan Turkey *see* **Gülek**
Camamu Brazil **202** E5
Camana Peru **200** B4
Camanã *r.* Peru **200** B4
Camanongue Angola **127** D7
formerly known as Vila Bugaço; *formerly spelt* Kamenongue
Camapuã Brazil **203** A6
Camaquã Brazil **203** B9
Camaquã *r.* Brazil **204** H3
Camăr Romania **58** D1
Camará Brazil **199** F5
Camarão Brazil **199** F4
Camararé *r.* Brazil **201** F3
Camargo Bol. **200** D5
Camargo Mex. **185** F3
Camargo, Parque Natural *nature res.* Mex. **185** F3
Camargue, Parc Naturel Régional de *nature res.* France **51** K9
Camarillo U.S.A. **182** E7
Camariñas Spain **54** B1
Camarón, Cabo *c.* Hond. **186** B4
Camarones Arg. **205** D7
Camarones, Bahía *b.* Arg. **205** D7
Camas U.S.A. **180** B3
Camas *r.* U.S.A. **180** D4
Camas Creek *r.* U.S.A. **180** D4

Carrillo Mex. 184 E3
Carrington U.S.A. 178 C2
Carrion r. Spain 54 G2
Carrión de los Condes Spain 54 G2
Carrizal Col. 198 C2
Carrizal Bajo Chile 204 C3
Carrizo U.S.A. 183 N7
Carrizo Creek r. U.S.A. 179 B4
Carrizo Creek watercourse AZ U.S.A. 183 N8
Carrizo Creek watercourse CA U.S.A. 183 I8
Carrizos Mex. 185 F3
Carrizo Springs U.S.A. 179 C6
Carrizo Wash watercourse U.S.A. 183 O7
Carrizozo U.S.A. 181 F6
Carroll U.S.A. 178 D3
Carrollton AL U.S.A. 175 B5
Carrollton GA U.S.A. 175 C5
Carrollton IL U.S.A. 174 B4
Carrollton KY U.S.A. 174 C4
Carrollton MO U.S.A. 178 D4
Carrollton MS U.S.A. 175 B5
Carrolltown U.S.A. 176 G5
Carron r. Australia 149 D3
Carron r. U.K. 46 H6
Carrot r. Canada 167 K4
Carrot River Canada 167 K4
Carrsville U.S.A. 177 I9
Carruthersville U.S.A. 174 B4
Carry Falls Reservoir U.S.A. 177 K1
Çarşamba Turkey 107 D2
Carson r. Australia 150 D2
Carson U.S.A. 178 B2
Carson r. U.S.A. 182 E2
Carson City MI U.S.A. 173 I7

►Carson City NV U.S.A. 182 E2
State capital of Nevada.

Carson Escarpment Australia 150 D2
Carson Lake U.S.A. 182 F2
Carson River Aboriginal Reserve Australia 150 D2
Carson Sink l. U.S.A. 182 F2
Carsonville U.S.A. 173 K7
Carstensz-top mt. Indon. see Jaya, Puncak
Carswell Lake Canada 167 I3
Cartagena Chile 204 C4
Cartagena Col. 198 C2
UNESCO World Heritage Site
Cartagena Spain 55 K7
historically known as Carthago Nova
Cartago Col. 198 C3
Cartago Costa Rica 186 C5
Cártama Spain 54 G8
Cartaxo Port. 54 C5
Cartaya, Cap c. France 51 M9
Carter, Mount hill Australia 149 D2
Carteret Group is P.N.G. see Kilinailau Islands
Carteret Island Solomon Is see Malaita
Carters Range hills Australia 149 D4
Cartersville U.S.A. 175 C5
Carterton N.Z. 152 J9
Carthage tourist site Tunisia 123 H1
historically known as Carthago
UNESCO World Heritage Site
Carthage IL U.S.A. 174 B3
Carthage MO U.S.A. 178 D4
Carthage NC U.S.A. 174 E5
Carthage NY U.S.A. 177 J2
Carthage TN U.S.A. 174 C4
Carthage TX U.S.A. 179 D5
Carthago tourist site Tunisia see Carthage
Carthago Nova Spain see Cartagena
Cartier Canada 173 L4
Cartier Island Australia 150 C2
Cartwright Man. Canada 167 L5
Cartwright Nfld. and Lab. Canada 169 J2
Caruachi Venez. 199 F2
Caruarú Brazil 202 F4
Caruçambaba Brazil 202 B2
Cărunta, Vârful mt. Romania 58 H2
Carúpano Venez. 199 F2
Carutapera Brazil 202 C2
Carvalho Brazil 199 I5
Carver U.S.A. 176 B8
Carvin France 51 I2
Carvoeiro Brazil 199 F5
Carvoeiro, Cabo c. Port. 54 B5
Carwell Australia 149 E5
Cary U.S.A. 174 E5
Caryapundy Swamp Australia 147 D2
Caryville TN U.S.A. 176 A9
Caryville WI U.S.A. 172 B6
Casabindo, Cerro de mt. Arg. 200 D5
Casablanca Chile 204 C4
Casablanca Morocco 122 D2
also known as Dar el Beida.
Casa Branca Brazil 206 F8
Casa de Janos Mex. 184 C2
Casa de Piedra, Embalse resr Arg. 204 D5
Casa Grande U.S.A. 183 M9
Casale Monferrato Italy 56 A3
Casalins Arg. 204 F5
Casalmaggiore Italy 56 C4
Casalpusterlengo Italy 56 B3
Casalvasco Brazil 201 E3
Casamance r. Senegal 124 A3
Casanare dept Col. 198 D3
Casanare r. Col. 198 D3
Casares Nicaragua 186 B5
Casas Grandes Mex. 184 D2
UNESCO World Heritage Site
Casas Grandes r. Mex. 184 D2
Casas-Ibáñez Spain 55 J5
Casbas Arg. 204 E5
Casca Brazil 203 A9
Cascada de Bassaseachic, Parque Nacional nat. park Mex. 184 C2
Cascade Australia 151 C7
Cascade r. N.Z. 153 C12
Cascade IA U.S.A. 174 B3
Cascade ID U.S.A. 180 C3
Cascade Point N.Z. 153 C12
Cascade Range mts Canada/U.S.A. 164 G5
Cascade Reservoir U.S.A. 180 C3
Cascais Port. 54 B6
Cascal, Paso del pass Nicaragua 186 B5
Cascapédia r. Canada 169 H3
Cascavel Ceará Brazil 202 E3
Cascavel Paraná Brazil 203 A8
Căscioarele Romania 58 H4
Casco U.S.A. 172 F6
Casco Bay U.S.A. 177 P2
Caserta Italy 56 G7
UNESCO World Heritage Site
Caseville U.S.A. 173 J7
Casey research station Antarctica 223 H2
Casey Bay Antarctica 223 D2
Caseyr, Raas c. Somalia 128 F2
English form Guardafui, Cape
Cashel Ireland 47 E11
Cashmere Australia 147 F1
Cashton U.S.A. 172 C7
Casigua Falcón Venez. 198 D2
Casigua Zulia Venez. 198 C2
Casiguran Phil. 74 B2
Casiguran Sound sea chan. Phil. 74 B2
Casilda Arg. 204 E4
Casimcea Romania 58 J4
Casimcea r. Romania 58 J4
Casimiro de Abreu Brazil 207 K9
Casino Australia 147 G2
Casinos Spain 55 K5
Casita Mex. 181 E7
Čáslav Czech Rep. 49 M6
Casma Peru 200 A2
Casnewydd U.K. see Newport
Casnovia U.S.A. 172 H7
Casogoran Bay Phil. 74 C4
Casoli Italy 56 G6
Caspe Spain 55 K3
Casper U.S.A. 180 F4
Caspian U.S.A. 172 E4
Caspian Lowland Kazakh./Rus. Fed. 102 A3
also known as Kaspīy Mangy Oypaty or Prikaspiyskaya Nizmennost'

►Caspian Sea Asia/Europe 102 B4
Largest lake in the world and in Asia/Europe. Lowest point in Europe. Also known as Kaspiyskoye More.
►►6–7 World Landscapes
►►28–29 Europe Landscapes
►►60–61 Asia Landscapes

Cass r. U.S.A. 173 J7
Cassacatiza Moz. 131 G2
Cassadaga U.S.A. 176 F3
Cassai Angola 127 D7
Cassamba Angola 127 D8
Cassano allo Ionio Italy 57 I9
Cassara Brazil 201 E3
Cass City U.S.A. 173 J7
Casselman Canada 168 F4
Casselton U.S.A. 178 C2
Cássia Brazil 206 G7
Cassiar Mountains Canada 166 D3
Cassilândia Brazil 206 B6
Cassilis Australia 147 F3
Cassinga Angola 127 C8
also spelt Kassinga
Cassino Brazil 204 G4
Cassino Italy 56 F7
Cassis France 51 L9
Cassley r. U.K. 46 H6
Cassongue Angola 127 B7
Cassopolis U.S.A. 172 G9
Cassville MO U.S.A. 178 D4
Cassville WI U.S.A. 172 C8
Castalla Spain 55 K6
Castanhal Amazonas Brazil 199 F6
Castanhal Pará Brazil 202 C2
Castanheira de Pêra Port. 54 C4
Castanheiro Brazil 199 E5
Castanho Brazil 201 E1
Castaño Nuevo Arg. 204 C3
Castaños Mex. 185 E3
Castejón, Montes de mts Spain 55 J3
Castèl del Monte tourist site Italy 56 I7
UNESCO World Heritage Site
Castèl di Sangro Italy 56 G7
Castelfiorentino Italy 56 C5
Castelfranco Emilia Italy 56 D4
Castelfranco Veneto Italy 56 D3
Casteljaloux France 50 G8
Castellammare, Golfo di b. Sicily Italy 57 E10
Castellammare di Stabia Italy 57 G8
Castellane France 51 M9
Castellaneta Italy 57 I8
Castellanos mt. Spain 55 I6
Castellar de la Frontera Spain 54 F8
Castelldefels Spain 55 M3
Castell de Ferro Spain 55 H8
Castelli Buenos Aires Arg. 204 F5
Castelli Chaco Arg. 204 E2
Castell-nedd U.K. see Neath
Castell Newydd Emlyn U.K. see Newcastle Emlyn
Castello de Ampurias Spain see Castelló d'Empúries
Castelló de la Plana Spain see Castellón de la Plana
Castelló d'Empúries Spain 55 O2
also spelt Castello de Ampurias
Castellón de la Plana Spain 55 K5
also spelt Castelló de la Plana
Castelnaudary France 51 H9
Castelnau-de-Médoc France 50 F7
Castelnovo ne'Monti Italy 56 C4
Castelo Brazil 207 L7
Castelo Branco Port. 54 D5
Castelo Branco admin. dist. Port. 54 D4
Castelo de Vide Port. 54 D5
Castelo do Piaui Brazil 202 D3
Castèl San Pietro Terme Italy 56 D4
Castelsardo Sardinia Italy 56 A8
Castelsarrasin France 50 H8
Casteltermini Sicily Italy 57 F11
Castelvetrano Sicily Italy 57 E11
Castèl Volturno Italy 56 F7
Casterton Australia 146 D4
Castets France 50 E9
Castiglione dei Pepoli Italy 56 D4
Castiglione del Lago Italy 56 E5
Castiglione della Pescaia Italy 56 C6
Castiglione della Stiviere Italy 56 C3
Castiglion Fiorentino Italy 56 D5
Castile U.S.A. 176 G3
Castilho Brazil 206 B7
Castilla Chile 204 C2
Castilla Peru 198 A6
Castilla-La Mancha aut. comm. Spain 55 H5
Castilla y León aut. comm. Spain 55 G3
Castillejo Venez. 199 F3
Castilletes Col. 198 D2
Castillo, Canal del sea chan. Chile 205 B8
Castillo, Pampa del hills Arg. 205 C7
Castillos Uruguay 204 G4
Castillos, Lago de l. Uruguay 204 G4
Castlebar Ireland 47 C10
also known as Caisleán an Bharraigh
Castleblayney Ireland 47 F9
Castle Dale U.S.A. 183 M2
Castle Danger U.S.A. 172 B3
Castle Dome Mountains U.S.A. 183 J8
Castle Douglas U.K. 47 I9
Castlegar Canada 166 G5
Castle Island Bahamas 187 E2
Castleisland Ireland 47 C11
Castlemaine Australia 147 E4
Castle Mountain Canada 166 H5
formerly known as Eisenhower, Mount
Castle Mountain U.S.A. 182 D6
Castle Peak hill Hong Kong China 87 [inset]
also known as Tsing Shan
Castle Peak Bay Hong Kong China 87 [inset]
also known as Tsing Shan Wan
Castlepoint N.Z. 152 K8
Castlepollard Ireland 47 E10
Castlerea Ireland 47 D10
Castlereagh r. Australia 147 E2
Castle Rock CO U.S.A. 180 F5
Castle Rock WA U.S.A. 180 B3
Castle Rock Lake U.S.A. 172 C7
Castor Canada 167 I4
Castor, Rivière du r. Canada 168 E2
Castor Creek r. U.S.A. 179 D6
Castra Regina Germany see Regensburg
Castres France 51 I9
Castricum Neth. 48 B3

►Castries St Lucia 187 H4
Capital of St Lucia.

Castro Brazil 203 B8
Castro Chile 205 B6
Castro Alves Brazil 202 E5
Castrocaro Terme Italy 56 D4
Castro del Río Spain 54 G7
Castro de Rei Spain 54 D1
Castro Marim Port. 54 D7
Castro-Urdiales Spain 55 H1
Castro Verde Port. 54 C7
Castrovillari Italy 57 I9
Castroville U.S.A. 182 C5
Castrovirreyna Peru 200 B3
Castuera Spain 54 F6
Cast Uul mt. Mongolia 84 A1
Caswell Sound inlet N.Z. 153 B12
Çat Turkey 107 E3
Catabola Angola 127 C8
formerly known as Nova Sintra
Catacamas Hond. 186 B4
Catacaos Peru 198 A6
Catacocha Ecuador 198 B6
Cataguases Brazil 207 K8
Catahoula Lake U.S.A. 179 D6
Cataiñgan Phil. 74 B3
Çatak Turkey 107 E3
Catalão Brazil 206 F5
Çatalca Turkey 58 J7
Çatalca Yarımadası pen. Turkey 58 J7
Catalina U.S.A. 183 N9
Catalonia aut. comm. Spain see Cataluña
Cataluña aut. comm. Spain 55 M3
English form Catalonia; also spelt Catalunya
Catalunya aut. comm. Spain see Cataluña
Çatalzeytin Turkey 106 C2
Catamarca Arg. 204 D3
Catamarca prov. Arg. 204 D2
Catambia Moz. see Catandica
Catana Sicily Italy see Catania
Catanauan Phil. 74 B3
Catandica Moz. 131 G3
formerly known as Catambia or Vila Gouveia
Catanduanes i. Phil. 74 C3
Catanduva Brazil 206 D8
Catanduvas Brazil 203 A8
Catania Sicily Italy 57 H11
historically known as Catana
UNESCO World Heritage Site
Catania, Golfo di g. Sicily Italy 57 H11
Catán Lil Arg. 204 C5
Catanzaro Italy 57 I10
Cataqueamã Brazil 201 E2
Cataract U.S.A. 172 C6
Cataract Creek watercourse U.S.A. 183 L5
Catarina Brazil 202 E3
Catarina U.S.A. 179 C6
Catarino Rodriguez Mex. 185 E3
Catarman Phil. 74 C3
Catarroja Spain 55 K5
Catastrophe, Cape Australia 146 B3
Catata Nova Angola 127 B8
Catatumbo Bari nat. park Col. 198 C2
Catavi Bol. 200 D4
Catawba U.S.A. 172 C5
Catawba r. U.S.A. 174 D5
Catawissa U.S.A. 177 I5
Cat Ba, Đao i. Vietnam 78 D3
Catbalogan Phil. 74 C4
Cateel Phil. 74 C5
Cateel Bay Phil. 74 C5
Catemaco Mex. 185 G5
Catembe Moz. 133 Q3
Catengue Angola 127 B8
Catete Angola 127 B7
Catete r. Brazil 199 H6
Cathcart S. Africa 133 L9
Cathedral City U.S.A. 183 H8
Cathedral Peak Lesotho 133 N5
Cathedral Provincial Park Canada 166 F5
Catherine, Mount U.S.A. 183 L3
Catheys Valley U.S.A. 182 D4
Cathlamet U.S.A. 180 B3
Catió Guinea-Bissau 124 B4
Catisimiña Venez. 199 F3
Cat Island Bahamas 187 E1
Catlins Forest Park nature res. N.Z. 153 D14
Catoche, Cabo c. Mex. 185 I4
Catolé do Rocha Brazil 202 E3
Catolé Grande r. Brazil 207 M2
Catolo Angola 127 C7
Catorce Mex. 185 E4
Catota Angola 127 C8
Catoute mt. Spain 54 E2
Catria, Monte mt. Italy 56 E5
Catriló Arg. 204 E5
Catrimani Brazil 199 F4
Catrimani r. Brazil 199 F4
Catskill U.S.A. 177 L3
Catskill Mountains U.S.A. 177 K3
Cattenom France 51 M3
Cattle Creek N.Z. 153 E12
Cattolica Italy 56 E5
Catúa Arg. 200 D5
Catuane Moz. 131 G5
Catur Moz. 129 B8
Cauaxi r. Brazil 202 B2
Cauayan Phil. 74 B4
Caubvick, Mount Canada 169 I1
Cauca dept Col. 198 B4
Cauca r. Col. 198 C2
Caucaia Brazil 202 E2
Caucasia Col. 198 C3
Caucasus mts Asia/Europe 107 E2
also known as Bol'shoy Kavkaz
UNESCO World Heritage Site
Caucete Arg. 204 C3
Cauchari, Salar de salt flat Arg. 200 D5
Cauchon Lake Canada 167 L4
Caucomgomoc Lake U.S.A. 174 G2
Caudete Spain 55 K6
Caudry France 51 J2
Cauit Point Phil. 74 C4
Caulnes France 50 D4
Caulonia Italy 57 I10
Caunao r. Cuba 186 D2
Caungula Angola 127 C7
Cauno Angola 127 C9
Cauquenes Chile 204 B4
Caura r. Venez. 199 E3
Caurés r. Brazil 199 F5
Causapscal Canada 169 H3
Căușeni Moldova 58 K2
formerly spelt Kaushany
Caussade France 50 H8
Cautário r. Brazil 201 D3
Caution, Cape Canada 166 E5
Cauto r. Cuba 186 D2
Cava de'Tirreni Italy 57 G8
Cávado r. Port. 54 C3
Cavaglià Italy 56 A3
Cavaillon France 51 L9
Cavalcante Goiás Brazil 202 C5
Cavalcante Rondônia Brazil 201 E2
Cavalier U.S.A. 178 C1
Cavalleria, Cap de c. Spain 55 P4
Cavalli Islands N.Z. 152 H2
Cavally r. Côte d'Ivoire 124 D5
Cavan Ireland 47 E10
Çavdarhisar Turkey 59 K9
Çavdır Turkey 106 B3
Cave N.Z. 153 E12
Cave City AR U.S.A. 174 B4
Cave City KY U.S.A. 174 C4
Cave Creek U.S.A. 183 M8
Caveira Brazil 207 J3
Cavenagh Range hills Australia 151 E5
Cavera, Serra do hills Brazil 203 A9
Cavernoso, Serra do mts Brazil 203 A8
Cave Run Lake U.S.A. 176 B7
Caviana, Ilha i. Brazil 202 B1
Cavili reef Phil. 74 B4
Cavite Phil. 74 B3
Cavo, Monte hill Italy 56 E7
Cavone r. Italy 57 I8
Cavongo Angola 127 C8
Çavuşçu Turkey 106 B3
Çavuşköy Turkey 108 B1
Cawndilla Lake imp. l. Australia 147 D3
Cawnpore India see Kanpur
Cawood U.S.A. 176 B9
Caxambu Brazil 207 I8
Caxias Amazonas Brazil 198 D6
Caxias Maranhão Brazil 202 D3
Caxias do Sul Brazil 203 B9
Caxito Angola 127 B7
Caxiuana, Baía de l. Brazil 199 I5
Çay Turkey 106 B3
Cayambe-Coca, Reserva Ecológica nat. park Ecuador 198 B5
Çaybaşı Turkey see Çayeli
Cayce U.S.A. 175 D5
Çaycuma Turkey 106 C2
Çayeli Turkey 107 E2
also known as Çaybaşı

►Cayenne Fr. Guiana 199 H3
Capital of French Guiana.

Cayey Puerto Rico 187 G3
Çaygören Barajı resr Turkey 59 J9
Çayhan Turkey 106 C3
Çayhisar Turkey 59 J12
Çayırhan Turkey 106 B2
Caylus France 50 H8
Cayman Brac i. Cayman Is 186 D3

►Cayman Islands terr. West Indies 186 C3
United Kingdom Overseas Territory.
►►158–159 North America Countries

Cay Sal i. Bahamas 186 C2
Cay Santa Domingo i. Bahamas 186 E2
Cayucos U.S.A. 182 D6
Cayuga Canada 173 N8
Cayuga Heights U.S.A. 177 I3
Cayuga Lake U.S.A. 177 I3
Cazage Angola 127 D7
also spelt Cazaje
Cazaje Angola see Cazage
Cazalla de la Sierra Spain 54 F7
Căzănești Romania 58 I4
Caza Pava Arg. 204 F3
Cazaux et de Sanguinet, Étang de l. France 50 E8
Cazê China 89 D6
Cazenovia U.S.A. 177 J3
Cazères France 50 H9
Cažma Croatia 56 I3
Cazombo Angola 127 D7
Cazorla Spain 55 I7
Cazula Moz. 131 G2
Cea r. Spain 54 F2
Ceadâr-Lunga Moldova see Ciadîr-Lunga
Ceanannus Mór Ireland see Kells
Ceará Brazil see Fortaleza
Ceará state Brazil 202 E3
Ceatalchioi Romania 58 J3
Ceatharlach Ireland see Carlow
Ceballos Mex. 184 D3
Cebireis Dağı mt. Turkey 108 D1
Cebollar Arg. 204 D3
Ceboruco, Volcán vol. Mex. 184 D4
Cebreros Spain 54 G4
Cebu Phil. 74 B4
Cebu i. Phil. 74 B4
Ceccano Italy 56 F7
Cecil U.S.A. 172 E6
Cecil Plains Australia 147 F1
Cecil Rhodes, Mount hill Australia 151 C5
Cecilton U.S.A. 177 J6
Cecina Italy 56 C5
Cecina r. Italy 56 C5
Ceclavín Spain 54 E5
Cedar r. MI U.S.A. 173 I7
Cedar r. ND U.S.A. 178 B2
Cedar r. NE U.S.A. 178 C3
Cedar Bluff U.S.A. 176 D8
Cedar City U.S.A. 183 K4
Cedar Creek Reservoir U.S.A. 179 C5
Cedaredge U.S.A. 180 F5
Cedar Falls U.S.A. 174 A3
Cedar Grove CA U.S.A. 182 F5
Cedar Grove IN U.S.A. 176 A6
Cedar Grove WI U.S.A. 172 F7
Cedar Grove WV U.S.A. 176 D7
Cedar Island U.S.A. 177 J8
Cedar Lake Man. Canada 167 K4
Cedar Lake Ont. Canada 173 O4
Cedar Point U.S.A. 176 B4
Cedar Rapids U.S.A. 174 B3
Cedar Ridge U.S.A. 183 M5
Cedar River U.S.A. 172 F5
Cedar Run U.S.A. 177 K6
Cedar Springs Canada 173 K8
Cedar Springs U.S.A. 172 H7
Cedarville S. Africa 133 N7
Cedarville IL U.S.A. 172 D8
Cedarville MI U.S.A. 173 I5
Cedarville OH U.S.A. 176 B6
Cedegolo Italy 56 C2
Cedeira Spain 54 C1
Cedeño Hond. 186 B4
Cederberg mts S. Africa 132 C9
Cedral Quintana Roo Mex. 185 I4
Cedral San Luis Potosí Mex. 185 E4
Cedro Brazil 202 E3
Cedros Hond. 186 B4
Cedros Mex. 185 E3
Cedros, Cerro mt. Mex. 181 D7
Cedros, Isla i. Mex. 184 B2
Ceduna Australia 146 B3
Cee Spain 54 B2
Ceelayo Somalia 128 F2
Ceelbuur Somalia 128 E3
Ceel Dhaab Somalia 128 E2
Ceeldheere Somalia 128 E4
Ceel Gaal Bari Somalia 128 F2
Ceel Gaal Woqooyi Galbeed Somalia 128 D2
Ceel Huur Somalia 128 F3
Ceel Walaaq well Somalia 128 D4
Ceerigaabo Somalia 128 E2
Cefalù Sicily Italy 57 G10
historically known as Cephaloedium
Cega r. Spain 54 G3
Cegléd Hungary 49 Q8
Čegrane Macedonia 58 B7
Ceheng China 86 C3
also known as Zhelou
Cehu Silvaniei Romania 58 E1
Ceira r. Port. 54 C4
Çekerek Turkey 106 C2
also known as Hacıköy
Celano Italy 56 F6
Celaque, Parque Nacional nat. park Hond. 186 A4
Celaya Mex. 185 E4
Celbridge Ireland 47 F10
Célé r. France 50 H8

►Celebes i. Indon. 75 B3
4th largest island in Asia. Also known as Sulawesi.
►►60–61 Asia Landscapes

Celebes Sea Indon./Phil. 75 B2
Celendín Peru 198 B6
Celina OH U.S.A. 176 A5
Celina TN U.S.A. 174 C4
Celje Slovenia 56 H2
Cella Spain 55 J4
Celldömölk Hungary 49 O8
Celle Germany 48 H3
Celles-sur-Belle France 50 F6
Cellina r. Italy 56 E2
Celone r. Italy 56 H7
Celovec Austria see Klagenfurt
Celtic Sea Ireland/U.K. 47 F13
Cemaru, Gunung mt. Indon. 77 F2
Çemenibit Turkm. 101 E3
Cemilbey Turkey 106 C2
Çemişgezek Turkey 107 D3
Cempi, Teluk b. Indon. 77 G5
Cenad Romania 58 B2
Cenajo, Embalse del resr Spain 55 J6
Cencenighe Agordino Italy 56 D2
Cenderawasih, Teluk b. Indon. 73 I7
also known as Irian, Teluk
Çendir r. Turkm. 102 C5
also spelt Chendir
Cenei Romania 58 B3
Cenis, Col du Mont pass France 51 M7
Ceno r. Italy 56 C4
Cenon France 50 F8
Čenta Vojvodina, Srbija Serb. and Mont. 58 B3
Centane S. Africa see Kentani
Centenário do Sul Brazil 206 B9
Centenary Zimbabwe 131 F3
Centennial Wash watercourse U.S.A. 183 L8
Center ND U.S.A. 178 B2
Center NE U.S.A. 178 C3
Center TX U.S.A. 179 D6
Centerburg U.S.A. 176 C5
Center City U.S.A. 178 D2
Centereach U.S.A. 177 L5
Center Hill Lake resr U.S.A. 174 C5
Center Point U.S.A. 175 C5
Centerville IA U.S.A. 174 A3
Centerville MO U.S.A. 174 B4
Centerville NC U.S.A. 176 G9
Centerville OH U.S.A. 176 C7
Centerville PA U.S.A. 176 F4
Centerville TN U.S.A. 174 C5
Centerville TX U.S.A. 179 D6
Centerville WV U.S.A. 176 E6
Cento Italy 56 D4
Centraal Suriname Natuurreservaat nature res. Suriname 199 G4
UNESCO World Heritage Site
Centrafricaine, République country Africa see Central African Republic
Central admin. dist. Botswana 131 E4
Central Brazil 202 D4
Central Chile 200 C5
Central admin. reg. Ghana 125 E5
UNESCO World Heritage Site
Central prov. Kenya 128 C5
Central admin. reg. Malawi 129 B8
Central U.S.A. 181 E6
Central prov. Zambia 127 F8
Central, Cordillera mts Bol. 200 D4
Central, Cordillera mts Col. 198 B4
Central, Cordillera mts Dom. Rep. 187 F3
Central, Cordillera mts Panama 186 C5
Central, Cordillera mts Peru 200 A2
Central, Cordillera mts Phil. 74 B2
UNESCO World Heritage Site
Central African Empire country Africa see Central African Republic
►Central African Republic country Africa 126 C3
known as Centrafricaine, République in French; formerly known as Central African Empire or Ubangi-Shari
►►114–115 Africa Countries
Central Australia Aboriginal Reserve Australia 150 E4
Central Brahui Range mts Pak. 101 F4
Central Butte Canada 167 J5
Central City IA U.S.A. 174 B3
Central City NE U.S.A. 178 C3
Central City PA U.S.A. 176 G5
Central de Minas Brazil 207 L5
Central Desert Aboriginal Land res. Australia 148 A4
Central Falls U.S.A. 177 N4
Centralia IL U.S.A. 174 B4
Centralia WA U.S.A. 180 B3
Central Island National Park Kenya 128 C4
UNESCO World Heritage Site
Central Islip U.S.A. 177 L5
Central Kalahari Game Reserve nature res. Botswana 131 D4
Central Makran Range mts Pak. 101 F5
Central Mount Wedge Australia 148 A4
Central'noolesnoy Zapovednik nature res. Rus. Fed. 43 N5
Central Plateau Conservation Area nature res. Australia 147 E5
Central Provinces state India see Madhya Pradesh
Central Range mts Lesotho 133 M6
Central Range mts P.N.G. 73 J7
Central Russian Upland hills Rus. Fed. 43 R7
also known as Sredne-Russkaya Vozvyshennost'
Central Siberian Plateau Rus. Fed. 39 L3
also known as Siberia or Sredne-Sibirskoye Ploskogor'ye
Central Square U.S.A. 177 I2
Central Valley U.S.A. 182 B1
Centre prov. Cameroon 125 H5
Centre admin. reg. France 50 H5
Centre U.S.A. 175 C5
Centre, Canal du Belgium 51 J2
UNESCO World Heritage Site
Centreville AL U.S.A. 175 C5
Centreville MD U.S.A. 177 I6
Centreville VA U.S.A. 176 H7
Centurion S. Africa 133 M2
formerly known as Verwoerdburg
Cenxi China 87 D4
Ceos i. Greece see Kea
Céou r. France 50 H8
Cephaloedium Sicily Italy see Cefalù
Cephalonia i. Greece 59 B10
also known as Kefallinía; also spelt Kefallonia
Čepin Croatia 56 K3
Čepkelių nature res. Lith. 42 F8
Ceprano Italy 56 F7
Cepu Indon. 77 E4
Cer hills Serb. and Mont. 58 A4
Ceram i. Indon. see Seram
Ceram Sea Indon. see Seram Sea
Cerbat Mountains U.S.A. 183 J6
Cerbol r. Spain see Cérvol, Riu
Cercal hill Port. 54 C7
Čerchov mt. Czech Rep. 49 J6
Cère r. France 51 H8
Cerea Italy 56 D3
Cereal Canada 167 I5
Cereales Arg. 204 E5
Ceres Arg. 204 E3
Ceres Brazil 206 D2
Ceres S. Africa 132 D10
Ceres U.S.A. 182 D4
Céret France 51 I10
Cereté Col. 198 C2
Cerf, Lac du l. Canada 173 R4
Cerignola Italy 56 H7
Cerigo i. Greece see Kythira
Çerikli Turkey 106 C3
Cêringgolêb China see Dongco
Çerkeş Turkey 106 C2
Çerkezköy Turkey 58 J7
Cerknica Slovenia 56 G3
Cermei Romania 58 C2
Çermik Turkey 107 D3
Cerna Romania 58 J3
Cerna r. Romania 58 D3
Cerna r. Romania 58 D4
Cerna r. Romania 58 F4
Cernat Romania 58 H3
Cernăuți Ukr. see Chernivtsi
Cernavodă Romania 58 J4
Cernay France 51 N5
Cerqueira César Brazil 206 D10
Cerralvo Mex. 185 F3
Cerralvo, Isla i. Mex. 184 C3
Cërrik Albania 58 A7
Cerrillos Arg. 200 D6
Cerritos Mex. 185 E4
Cerro Azul Brazil 203 B8
Cerro Azul Mex. 185 F4
Cerro de Pasco Peru 200 A2
Cerro Hoya, Parque Nacional nat. park Panama 186 C6
Cerro Manantiales Chile 205 C9
Cerrón mt. Spain 55 H8
Cerrón, Cerro mt. Venez. 198 D2
Cerro Negro Chile 200 C5
Cerros Colorados, Embalse resr Arg. 204 C5
Cerros de Amotape, Parque Nacional nat. park Peru 198 A5
Certaldo Italy 56 D5
Certeju de Sus Romania 58 D3
Cervantes Australia 151 A6
Cervantes, Cerro mt. Arg. 205 B8
Cervaro r. Italy 56 H7
Cervati, Monte mt. Italy 57 H8
Cervenia Romania 58 G5
Cervera Spain 55 M3
Cervera de Pisuerga Spain 54 G2
Cerveteri Italy 56 E7
historically known as Caere
UNESCO World Heritage Site
Cervia Italy 56 E4
Cervialto, Monte mt. Italy 57 H8
Cervignano del Friuli Italy 56 F3
Cervina, Punta mt. Italy 56 D2
Cervione Corsica France 51 P10
Cervo Spain 54 D1
Cérvol, Riu r. Spain 55 L4
also spelt Cerbol
Cesar dept Col. 198 C2
Cesar r. Col. 198 C2
Cesarò Sicily Italy 57 G11
Cesena Italy 56 E4
Cesenatico Italy 56 E4
Cēsis Latvia 42 G4
historically known as Wenden
Česká Lípa Czech Rep. 49 L5
Česká Republika country Europe see Czech Republic
České Budějovice Czech Rep. 49 L7
formerly known as Budweis
České Středohoří hills Czech Rep. 49 K5
Českomoravská vysočina hills Czech Rep. 49 L6
Český Krumlov Czech Rep. 49 L7
UNESCO World Heritage Site
Český les mts Czech Rep./Germany 49 J6
Český Těšín Czech Rep. 49 P6
Česma r. Croatia 56 I3
Çeşme Turkey 106 A3
Cessnock Australia 147 F3
Cesson-Sévigné France 50 E4
Cestas France 50 F8
Cestos r. Liberia 124 C5
Cesuras Spain 54 C1
Cesvaine Latvia 42 H5
Cêtar China 84 D4
formerly known as Qaidar
Cetate Romania 58 E4
Cetatea Albă Ukr. see Bilhorod-Dnistrovs'kyy
Cetina r. Croatia 56 I5
Cetinje Crna Gora Serb. and Mont. 56 K6
Cetraro Italy 57 H9

►Ceuta N. Africa 54 F9
Spanish Territory.
►►114–115 Africa Countries

Ceva-i-Ra reef Fiji 145 G4
also spelt Theva-i-Ra
Cévennes mts France 51 J9
Cévennes, Parc National des nat. park France 51 J8
Čevetjävri Fin. see Sevettijärvi
Cevizli Turkey 109 I1
Cevizlik Turkey see Maçka
Ceyhan Turkey 106 C3
Ceyhan r. Turkey 107 C3
Ceyhan Boğazı r. mouth Turkey 108 G1
Ceylanpınar Turkey 107 E3
also known as Resülayn
Ceylon country Asia see Sri Lanka
Cèze r. France 51 K8
Chābahār Iran 101 E5
Chablais mts France 51 M6
Chablé Mex. 185 H5
Chablis France 51 J5
Chabre ridge France 51 L8
Chabrol i. New Caledonia see Lifou
Chabyêr Caka salt l. China 89 D6
Chaca Chile 200 C4
Chacabuco Arg. 204 E4
Chacarilla Bol. 200 C4
Chachahuén, Sierra mt. Arg. 204 C5
Chachapoyas Peru 198 B6
Chachaura-Binaganj India 96 C4
Chäche Turkm. see Çäçe
Chachersk Belarus 43 L9
Chachevichy Belarus 43 K8
Chachoengsao Thai. 79 C5
Chaco prov. Arg. 204 E2
formerly known as Presidente Juan Perón
Chaco Boreal reg. Para. 201 F5
Chaco Culture National Historical Park nat. park U.S.A. 181 F5
UNESCO World Heritage Site
Chacon, Cape U.S.A. 166 C4
Chacorão, Cachoeira da waterfall Brazil 199 G6
Chacra de Piros Peru 200 B2

►Chad country Africa 120 C6
5th largest country in Africa. Also spelt Tchad or Tshad.
►►114–115 Africa Countries

Chad, Lake Africa 120 B6
Chadaasan Mongolia 84 D2
Chadan Rus. Fed. 84 A1
Chadron U.S.A. 178 B3
Chadyr-Lunga Moldova see Ciadîr-Lunga
Chae Hom Thai. 78 B4
Chaek Kyrg. 103 H4
also spelt Chayek
Chaeryŏng N. Korea 83 B5
Chae Son National Park Thai. 78 B4
Chaffee U.S.A. 174 B4
Chaffers, Isla i. Chile 205 B7
Chaffey U.S.A. 172 A4
Chafurray Col. 198 C4
Chagai Pak. 101 F4
Chagai Hills Afgh./Pak. 101 E4
Chagalamarri India 94 C3
Chagan Kzyl-Ordinskaya Oblast' Kazakh. 103 F3
Chagan Vostochnyy Kazakhstan Kazakh. 103 I2
also spelt Shaghan
Chaganuzun Rus. Fed. 84 A1
Chagdo Kangri reg. China 89 D5
Chaghā Khūr mt. Iran 100 B4
Chaghcharān Afgh. 101 F3
Chaglinka r. Kazakh. 103 G1
Chagny France 51 K6
Chagoda Rus. Fed. 43 Q2
Chagoda r. Rus. Fed. 43 Q2
Chagodoshcha r. Rus. Fed. 43 R3
Chagos Archipelago is Indian Ocean 218 L6
Chagoyan Rus. Fed. 82 C1
Chagra r. Rus. Fed. 102 B1
Chagrayskoye Plato plat. Kazakh. see Shagyray, Plato

Chagres, Parque Nacional nat. park Panama 186 D5
Chaguanas Trin. and Tob. 187 H5
Chaguaramas Venez. 199 E2
Chagyllyshor, Vpadina depr. Turkm. 102 C4
Chaha r. Ukr. 58 K3
Chahah Burjal Afgh. 101 E4
Chāh Ākhvor Iran 101 D3
Chaharbagh Afgh. 101 G3
Chahār Maḩāll va Bakhtīārī prov. Iran 100 B3
Chah Baba well Iran 100 C3
Chāh Bahār, Khalīj-e b. Iran 101 E5
Chahbounia Alg. 55 N9
Chāh-e Āb Afgh. 101 G2
Chāh-e Nūklok Iran 100 C3
Chah Gheybī, Hāmūn-e salt pan Iran 101 E4
Chāh Ḩaqq Iran 100 C4
Chah Sandan Pak. 101 E4
Chahuites Mex. 185 G5
Chaibasa India 97 E5
Chaigneau, Lac l. Canada 169 H2
Chaigoubu China see Huai'an
Chai He r. China 82 A4
Chaillu, Massif du mts Gabon 126 A5
Chainat Thai. 79 C5
Chainjoin Co l. China 89 D5
Chai Si r. Thai. 79 C5
Chaitén Chile 205 B6
Chai Wan Hong Kong China 87 [inset]
Chaiwopu China 88 D3
Chaiya Thai. 79 B6
Chaiyaphum Thai. 79 C5
Chajarí Arg. 204 F3
Chakai India 97 E4
Chakar r. Pak. 101 G4
Chakari Zimbabwe 131 F3
Chake Chake Tanz. 129 C6
Chakhānsūr Afgh. 101 E4
Chakia India 97 D4
Chak Jhumra Pak. 101 H4
Chakonipau, Lac l. Canada 169 G1
Chakradharpur India 97 E5
Chakulia India 97 E5
Chakwal Pak. 101 H3
Chala Peru 200 B3
Chala Tanz. 129 A6
Chalais France 50 G7
Chalap Dalan mts Afgh. 101 F3
Chalatenango El Salvador 185 H6
Chaláua Moz. 131 H3
Chalaxung China 86 A1
Chalbi Desert Kenya 128 C4
Chalcedon Turkey see Kadıköy
Chalengkou China 84 B4
Chaleur Bay inlet Canada 169 H3
also known as Chaleurs, Baie de
Chaleurs, Baie de inlet Canada see Chaleur Bay
Chalía r. Arg. 205 C8
Chalīb Abū Munţār watercourse Iraq 109 L5
Chaling China 87 E3
Chalinze Tanz. 129 C6
Chalisgaon India 94 B1
Chalisseri India 94 C4
Chalkar, Ozero salt l. Kazakh. see Shalkar, Ozero
Chalki Greece 59 I12
Chalki i. Greece 59 I12
also spelt Khálki
Chalkida Greece 59 E10
also known as Khalkís
Chalkudysu Kazakh. 103 I4
Chalky Inlet N.Z. 153 A14
Challakere India 94 C3
Challans France 50 E6
Challapata Bol. 200 D4

►Challenger Deep sea feature N. Pacific Ocean 220 E5
Deepest point in the world (Mariana Trench).
►►208–209 Oceans and Poles

Challis U.S.A. 180 D3
Chalmette U.S.A. 175 B6
Chal'mny-Varre Rus. Fed. 40 F2
Chalonnes-sur-Loire France 50 F5
Châlons-en-Champagne France 51 K4
formerly known as Châlons-sur-Marne
Châlons-sur-Marne France see Châlons-en-Champagne
Chalon-sur-Saône France 51 K6
Chalt Jammu and Kashmir 96 B1
Chalumna S. Africa 133 L10
Châlus France 50 G7
Chālūs Iran 100 B2
Cham Germany 49 J6
Cham, Cu Lao i. Vietnam 78 E5
Chama U.S.A. 181 F5
Chama r. U.S.A. 181 F5
Chamamba Tanz. 129 B6
Chaman Pak. 101 F4
Chaman Bid Iran 100 D2
Chamao, Khao mt. Thai. 79 C5
Chamba India 96 C2
Chamba Tanz. 129 C7
Chambal r. India 96 C4
Chambas Cuba 186 D2
Chambeaux, Lac l. Canada 169 G2
Chamberlain r. Australia 150 D3
Chamberlain Canada 167 J5
Chamberlain U.S.A. 178 C3
Chamberlain Lake U.S.A. 174 G2
Chambers U.S.A. 183 O6
Chambers Bay Australia 148 A2
Chambersburg U.S.A. 176 H6
Chambers Island U.S.A. 172 F5
Chambéry France 51 L7
Chambeshi Zambia 127 F7
Chambeshi r. Zambia 127 F8
Chambi, Jebel mt. Tunisia 123 H2
Chambira r. Peru 198 C6
Chambord Canada 169 F3
Chambri Lake P.N.G. 73 J7
Chamdo China see Qamdo
Chame Panama 186 D5
Chamechaude mt. France 51 L7
Chamela Mex. 184 D5
Châmi well Mauritania 122 B5
Chamical Arg. 204 D3
Chamili i. Greece 59 H13
Ch'amo Hāyk' l. Eth. 128 C3
Chamoli India see Gopeshwar
Chamonix-Mont-Blanc France 51 M7
Chamouchouane r. Canada see Ashuapmushuan
Chamouse, Montagne de mt. France 51 L8
Champa India 97 D5
Champagne-Ardenne admin. reg. France 51 K4
Champagne Castle mt. S. Africa 133 N6
Champagnole France 51 L6
Champagny Islands Australia 150 D2
Champaign U.S.A. 174 B3
Champaqui, Cerro mt. Arg. 204 D3
Champara mt. Peru 200 A2
Champasak Laos 79 D5
UNESCO World Heritage Site
Champdoré, Lac l. Canada 169 H2
Champhai India 97 G5
Champion Canada 167 H5
Champion U.S.A. 172 F4
Champlain NY U.S.A. 177 L1
Champlain VA U.S.A. 177 I7
Champlain, Lake Canada/U.S.A. 174 F2
Champlain Canal U.S.A. 177 L2
Champlitte France 51 L5
Champneuf Canada 173 P2
Champotón Mex. 185 H5
Chamrajnagar India 94 C4
Cham Siyāh Iran 100 B4
Chamusca Port. 54 C5
Chamzinka Rus. Fed. 41 H5
Chana Thai. 79 C7
Chanak Turkey see Çanakkale
Chanal Mex. 185 G5
Chañar Arg. 204 C5
Chañaral Chile 204 C2
Chañaral, Isla i. Chile 204 C3
Chanārān Iran 101 D2
Chanaro, Cerro mt. Venez. 199 F3
Chança r. Port./Spain see Chanza
Chancay Peru 200 A2
Chan Chan tourist site Peru 200 A2
UNESCO World Heritage Site
Chanco Chile 204 B4
Chancos Peru 200 A2
Chanda India see Chandrapur
Chandalar r. U.S.A. 164 E3
Chandama Tanz. 129 C6
Chandausi India 96 C3
Chandbali India 95 E1
Chandeleur Islands U.S.A. 175 B6
Chanderi India 96 C4
Chandia India 96 D5
Chandigarh India 96 C3
Chandil India 97 E5
Chandler Canada 169 H3
Chandler AZ U.S.A. 183 M8
Chandler OK U.S.A. 179 C5
Chandless r. Brazil 200 C2
Chandmany Mongolia 84 C1
Chandos Lake Canada 173 P6
Chandpur Bangl. 97 F5
Chandpur India 96 C3
Chandragiri India 94 C3
Chandrapur India 94 C2
formerly known as Chanda
Chandur India 94 C1
Chandvad India 94 B1
Chang, Ko i. Thai. 79 C5
Changalane Moz. 133 Q3
Chang'an Guangxi China see Rong'an
Chang'an Shaanxi China 87 D1
also known as Weiqu
Chang-an S. Korea 91 A7
Changane r. Moz. 131 G5
Changara Moz. 131 G3
Changbai China 82 C4
Changbai Shan mts China/N. Korea 82 B4
formerly known as Ch'ang-pai Shan
Chang Cheng research station Antarctica see Great Wall
Changchow Fujian China see Zhangzhou
Changchow Jiangsu China see Changzhou
Changchun China 82 B4
historically known as Hsinking
Changdao China 85 I4
also known as Nanchangshan; formerly known as Sihou
Changde China 87 D2
formerly spelt Changteh
Changfeng China 87 F1
also known as Shuihu
Changge China 87 E1
Changgi-ap pt S. Korea 83 C5
Changgo China 89 D6
Changhai China see Sikuaishi
Chang Hu l. China 87 E2
Changhua Taiwan 87 G3
also spelt Zhanghua
Changhua Jiang r. China 87 D5
Changhŭng S. Korea 83 B6
Changi Sing. 76 [inset]
Changji China 88 D3
Changjiang China 87 D5
also known as Shiliu
Chang Jiang r. China see Yangtze Kiang
Chang Jiang r. China see Yangtze
Changjiang Kou r. mouth China see Yangtze, Mouth of the
Changjin N. Korea 83 B4
Changjin-gang r. N. Korea 83 B4
Changkiang China see Zhanjiang
Changle China 87 F3
Changleng China see Xinjian
Changli China 85 H4
Changling China 85 I2
Changliushui China 85 E4
Changlung Jammu and Kashmir 96 C2
Changning Hunan China 87 E3
Changning Jiangxi China see Xunwu
Changning Sichuan China 86 C2
Changnyŏn N. Korea 83 B5
Ch'ang-pai Shan mts China/N. Korea see Changbai Shan
Changping China 85 H3
UNESCO World Heritage Site
Changpu China see Suining
Changsan-got pt N. Korea 83 B5
Changsha China 87 E2
Changshan Qundao is China 85 I4
Changshi China 86 C3
Changshou China 86 C2
Changshoujie China 87 E2
Changshu China 87 G2
Changsŏng S. Korea 83 B6
Changtai China 87 F3
also known as Wu'an
Changteh China see Changde
Changting Fujian China 87 F3
also known as Tingzhou
Changting Heilong. China 82 C3
Changtu China 82 B4
Changuinola Panama 186 C5
Ch'angwŏn S. Korea 83 C6
Changwu China 85 E5
also known as Zhaoren
Changxing China 87 F2
also known as Zhicheng
Changxing Dao i. China 85 I4
Changyang China 87 D2
also known as Longzhouping
Changyi China 85 H4
Changyŏn N. Korea 83 B5
Changyuan Chongqing China see Rongchang
Changyuan Henan China 85 G5
Changzhi Shanxi China 85 G4
Changzhi Shanxi China 85 G5
also known as Handian
Changzhou China 87 F2
also known as Wujin; formerly spelt Changchow
Chañi, Nevado de mt. Arg. 200 D6
Chania Greece 59 F13
also spelt Khaniá; historically known as Canea or Cydonia
Chanion, Kolpos b. Greece 59 E13
Chankou China 84 E5
Channagiri India 94 B3
Channapatna India 94 C3
Channel Islands English Chan. 50 D3
also known as Normandes, Îles
Channel Islands U.S.A. 182 E8
Channel Islands National Park U.S.A. 182 E7
Channel-Port-aux-Basques Canada 169 J4
Channel Rock i. Bahamas 186 D2
Channel Tunnel tunnel France/U.K. 50 H1
Channing U.S.A. 172 E4
Chantada Spain 54 D2
Chantal'skiy mt. Rus. Fed. 39 R3
Chanthaburi Thai. 79 C5
Chantilly France 51 I3
Chantonnay France 50 E6
Chanumla India 95 G4
Chanute U.S.A. 178 D4
Chany, Ozero salt l. Rus. Fed. 80 B2
Chanza r. Port./Spain 54 D7
also spelt Chança
Chao Peru 200 A2
Chaobai Xinhe r. China 85 H4
Chaohu China 87 F2
Chao Hu l. China 87 F2
Chao Phraya r. Thai. 79 C5
Chaor China 85 I1
Chaouèn Morocco 122 D2
Chaoyang Guangdong China 87 F4
Chaoyang Heilong. China see Jiayin
Chaoyang Jilin China see Huinan
Chaoyang Liaoning China 85 I3
Chaoyang Hu l. China 89 D5
Chaozhong China 85 I1
Chaozhou China 87 F4
Chapada Diamantina, Parque Nacional nat. park Brazil 202 D5
Chapada dos Guimarães Brazil 201 G3
Chapada dos Veadeiros, Parque Nacional da nat. park Brazil 202 C5
UNESCO World Heritage Site
Chapadão do Céu Brazil 206 A5
Chapadão do Sul Brazil 206 A5
Chapadinha Brazil 202 D2
Chapais Canada 169 F3
Chapak Guzar Afgh. 101 F2
Chapala Mex. 185 E4
Chapala, Laguna de l. Mex. 185 E4
Chapare r. Bol. 200 D3
Cháparra Peru 200 B3
Chaparral Col. 198 C4
Chapayev Kazakh. 102 B2
Chapayevsk Rus. Fed. 102 B1
Chapayevskoye Kazakh. 103 H1
Chapecó Brazil 203 A8
Chapecó r. Brazil 203 A8
Chapel Hill U.S.A. 174 E5
Chapicuy Uruguay 204 F3
Chapimarca Peru 200 B3
Chapleau Canada 168 D4
Chapleau Crown Game Reserve nature res. Canada 168 D3
Chaplin Canada 167 J5
Chaplin Lake dry lake Canada 167 J5
Chaplino Rus. Fed. 39 S3
Chaplygin Rus. Fed. 41 F5
Chapman, Mount Canada 166 G5
Chapmanville PA U.S.A. 176 F4
Chapmanville WV U.S.A. 176 C8
Chappell U.S.A. 178 B3
Chappell Islands Australia 147 E5
Chapra India see Chhapra
Chapri Pass Afgh. 101 F3
Charadai Arg. 204 F2
Charagua Bol. 201 E4
Charana Bol. 200 C4
Charapita Col. 198 C5
Charata Arg. 204 E2
Charbonnel, Pointe de mt. France 51 N7
Charcas Mex. 185 E4
Char Chu r. China 89 F6
Charcot Island Antarctica 222 S2
Chard Canada 167 I4
Chard U.K. 47 J13
Chardara Kazakh. see Shardara
Chardara, Step' plain Kazakh. 103 F4
Chardarinskoye Vodokhranilishche resr Kazakh./Uzbek. 103 G4
also known as Shardara Bögeni
Chardon U.S.A. 176 D4
Chardzhou Turkm. see Türkmenabat
Chardzhouskaya Oblast' admin. div. Turkm. see Lebapskaya Oblast'
Charente r. France 50 F7
Charg Iran 100 C4
Chari r. Cameroon/Chad 125 I3
also spelt Shari
Chari-Baguirmi pref. Chad 126 C2
Chārīkār Afgh. 101 G3
Charikot Nepal 97 E4
Chariton U.S.A. 174 A3
Chariton r. U.S.A. 174 A4
Chärjew Turkm. see Türkmenabat
Charkayuvom Rus. Fed. 40 J2
Charkhari India 96 C4
Charkhi Dadri India 96 C3
Charkhlik China see Ruoqiang
Charleroi Belgium 51 K2
Charles, Cape U.S.A. 177 J8
Charlesbourg Canada 169 G4
Charles City IA U.S.A. 174 A3
Charles City VA U.S.A. 177 H8
Charles Lake Canada 167 I3
Charles M. Russell National Wildlife Refuge nature res. U.S.A. 180 F3
Charles Point Australia 148 A2
Charleston N.Z. 153 F9
Charleston IL U.S.A. 174 B4
Charleston MO U.S.A. 174 B4
Charleston MS U.S.A. 174 B5
Charleston SC U.S.A. 175 E5

►Charleston WV U.S.A. 176 D7
State capital of West Virginia.

Charleston Peak U.S.A. 183 I5
Charlestown St Kitts and Nevis 187 H3
Charlestown NH U.S.A. 177 M2
Charlestown RI U.S.A. 177 N4
Charles Town U.S.A. 176 H6
Charleville Australia 149 E5
Charleville Ireland see Rathluirc
Charleville-Mézières France 51 K3
Charlevoix U.S.A. 172 H5
Charlie Lake Canada 166 F3
Charlotte MI U.S.A. 173 I8
Charlotte NC U.S.A. 174 D5

►Charlotte Amalie Virgin Is (U.S.A.) 187 G3
Capital of the U.S. Virgin Islands.

Charlotte Bank sea feature S. China Sea 77 D1
Charlotte Court House U.S.A. 176 G8
Charlotte Harbor b. U.S.A. 175 D7
Charlotte Lake Canada 166 E4
Charlottenberg Sweden 45 K4
Charlottesville U.S.A. 176 G7
UNESCO World Heritage Site

►Charlottetown Canada 169 I4
Provincial capital of Prince Edward Island.

Charlotteville Trin. and Tob. 187 H5
Charlton Australia 147 D4
Charlton Island Canada 168 E2
Charmes France 51 M4
Charnitsa r. Belarus 43 L7
Charnley r. Australia 150 D3
Charomkhava Belarus 42 I6
Charomskoye Rus. Fed. 43 T2
Charozero Rus. Fed. 43 T1
Charron Lake Canada 167 M4
Charsadda Pak. 101 G3
Charsk Kazakh. see Shar
Charters U.S.A. 176 B7
Charters Towers Australia 149 E4
Chartres France 50 H4
UNESCO World Heritage Site
Chartreuse, Massif de la mts France 51 L7
Charyn Kazakh. 103 I4
also spelt Sharyn
Charyn r. Kazakh. 103 I4
Charysh r. Rus. Fed. 103 J1
Charyshskoye Rus. Fed. 88 C1
Chas India 97 E5
Chās mt. Port. 54 C4
Chaschuil Arg. 204 C2
Chascomús Arg. 204 F4
Chase Canada 166 G5
Chase U.S.A. 172 H7
Chase City U.S.A. 176 G9
Chashkent Turkm. 103 E5
Chashniki Belarus 43 K7
Chasia reg. Greece 59 C9
Chasico Arg. 205 D6
Chaska U.S.A. 178 D2
Chaslands Mistake c. N.Z. 153 D14
Chasŏng N. Korea 82 B4
Chasovenskaya Rus. Fed. 43 O1
Chassezac r. France 51 K8
Chassiron, Pointe de pt France 50 E6
Chastab, Kūh-e mts Iran 100 C3
Chastyye Rus. Fed. 40 J4
Chasuta Peru 198 B6
Chāt Iran 100 C2
Chatang China see Zhanang
Château-Arnoux France 51 L8
Châteaubriant France 50 E5
Château-Chinon France 51 J5
Château-du-Loir France 50 G5
Châteaudun France 50 H4
Chateaugay U.S.A. 177 K1
Châteaugiron France 50 E4
Château-Gontier France 50 F5
Châteauguay r. Canada 169 G1
Châteauguay, Lac l. Canada 169 G1
Châteaulin France 50 B4
Châteauneuf-en-Thymerais France 50 H4
Châteauneuf-sur-Loire France 51 I5
Chateau Pond l. Canada 169 J2
Châteauponsac France 50 H6
Châteaurenard France 51 K9
Château-Renault France 50 G5
Châteauroux France 50 H6
Château-Salins France 51 M4
Château-Thierry France 51 J3
Châtelaillon-Plage France 50 E6
Châtelet Belgium 51 K2
Châtellerault France 50 G6
Châtenois France 51 L4
Chatfield U.S.A. 178 D3
Chatham Canada 168 D5
Chatham U.K. 47 M12
Chatham MA U.S.A. 177 P4
Chatham MI U.S.A. 172 G4
Chatham NY U.S.A. 177 L3
Chatham VA U.S.A. 176 F9
Chatham, Isla i. Chile 205 B8
Chatham Island Samoa see Savai'i
Chatham Island S. Pacific Ocean 145 H6
also known as Rekohua
Chatham Islands S. Pacific Ocean 145 H6
Chatham Sound sea chan. Canada 166 D4
Chatham Strait U.S.A. 166 C3
Châtillon-sur-Indre France 50 H6
Châtillon-sur-Loire France 51 I5
Châtillon-sur-Seine France 51 K5
Chatkal r. Kyrg. 103 G4
Chatkal Range mts Kyrg. 103 G4
Chatom U.S.A. 175 B6
Chatra India 97 E4
Chatra Nepal 97 E4
Chatsu India 96 B4
Chatsworth Australia 149 D4
Chatsworth Canada 173 M6
Chatsworth GA U.S.A. 174 C5
Chatsworth IL U.S.A. 172 E10
Chatsworth NJ U.S.A. 177 K6
Chatsworth Zimbabwe 131 F3
Chattagam Bangl. see Chittagong
Chattahoochee U.S.A. 175 C6
Chattahoochee r. U.S.A. 179 F6
Chattanooga U.S.A. 174 C5
Chatto Creek N.Z. 153 D13
Chatturat Thai. 79 C5
Chatyrkël', Ozero l. Kyrg. see Chatyr-Köl
Chatyr-Köl l. Kyrg. 88 A3
also known as Chatyrkël', Ozero
Chatyr-Tash Kyrg. 103 I4
Châu Đôc Vietnam 79 D6
formerly known as Chau Phu
Chauffailles France 51 K6
Chauhtan India 96 A4
Chauk Myanmar 78 A3
Chauka r. India 96 D4
Chaukhamba mts India 96 C3
also known as Badarinath; also known as Badrinath Peaks
Chau Kung To i. Hong Kong China see Sunshine Island
Chaumont France 51 L4
Chauncey U.S.A. 176 C6
Chaungwabyin Myanmar 79 B5
Chaunskaya Guba b. Rus. Fed. 39 Q3
Chauny France 51 J3
Châu Ô Vietnam 79 E5
Chau Phu Vietnam see Châu Đôc
Chaurai India 96 C5
Chausey, Îles is France 50 E4
Chausy Belarus see Chavusy
Chautauqua, Lake U.S.A. 176 F3
Chauvay Kyrg. 103 H4
Chauvigny France 50 G6
Chauvin Canada 167 I4
Chavakachcheri Sri Lanka 94 D4
Chaval Brazil 202 D2
Chavan'ga Rus. Fed. 40 F2
Chavār Iran 100 A3
Chaves Brazil 202 B2
Chaves Port. 54 D3
Chaves Valdivia Peru 198 B6
Chavigny, Lac l. Canada 169 F1
Chavin tourist site Peru 200 A2
UNESCO World Heritage Site
Chaviva Col. 198 C3
Chavusy Belarus 43 L8
also spelt Chausy
Chawal r. Pak. 101 F4
Chay, Sông r. Vietnam 78 D3
Chayan Kazakh. see Shayan
Chayanta r. Bol. 200 D4
Chayatyn, Khrebet ridge Rus. Fed. 82 E1
Chayek Kyrg. see Chaek
Chayevo Rus. Fed. 43 S3
Chaykovskiy Rus. Fed. 40 J4
Chazhegovo Rus. Fed. 40 J3
Chazón Arg. 204 E4
Chazy U.S.A. 177 L1
Cheat r. U.S.A. 176 F6
Cheb Czech Rep. 49 J5
Chebanse U.S.A. 172 F9
Chebbi salt l. Alg. 123 F4
Cheboksary Rus. Fed. 40 H4
Cheboygan U.S.A. 173 I5
Chebsara Rus. Fed. 43 T2
Chechen', Ostrov i. Rus. Fed. 102 A4
Ch'ech'eng Taiwan 87 G4
Chechenia aut. rep. Rus. Fed. see Chechenskaya Respublika
Chechenskaya Respublika aut. rep. Rus. Fed. 41 H8
short form Chechnya; English form Chechenia or Chechnia; also known as Ichkeria
Cheche Pass Lesotho 133 M6
Chechnia aut. rep. Rus. Fed. see Chechenskaya Respublika
Chechnya aut. rep. Rus. Fed. see Chechenskaya Respublika
Chech'ŏn S. Korea 83 C5
Chęciny Poland 49 R5
Checotah U.S.A. 179 D5
Cheder Rus. Fed. 84 B1
Cheduba Island Myanmar see Man-aung Kyun
Cheduba Strait Myanmar 78 A4
Chée r. France 51 K4
Cheektowaga U.S.A. 176 G3
Cheepash r. Canada 168 D3
Cheepie Australia 149 E5
Cheetham, Cape Antarctica 223 K2
Chef-Boutonne France 50 F6
Cheffadène well Niger 125 I2
Chefoo China see Yantai
Chefornak U.S.A. 164 C3
Chegdomyn Rus. Fed. 82 D2
Chegga Mauritania 122 D4
Cheggué watercourse Mauritania 124 C2
Chegguet Ti-n-Kerkâz des. Mauritania 124 D2
Chegutu Zimbabwe 131 F3
formerly known as Hartley
Chehalis U.S.A. 180 B3
Chehalis r. U.S.A. 180 B3
Chehardeh Iran 100 D3
Cheharīz tourist site Iraq 107 F4
Chehel Chashmeh, Kūh-e hill Iran 100 A3
Chehel Dokhtarān, Kūh-e mt. Iran 101 E4
Chehell'āyeh Iran 100 D4
Cheikria well Alg. 122 D4
Cheil Nerei-Beuşniţa nat. park Romania 58 C3
Cheiron, Cime du mt. France 51 M9
Cheju S. Korea 83 B6
Cheju-do i. S. Korea 83 B6
English form Quelpart Island
Cheju-haehyŏp sea chan. S. Korea 83 B6
Chekalin Rus. Fed. 43 R7
Chek Chau i. Hong Kong China see Port Island
Chek Chue Hong Kong China see Stanley
Chekhov Moskovskaya Oblast' Rus. Fed. 43 S6
formerly known as Lopasnya
Chekhov Sakhalin Rus. Fed. 82 F3
Chekiang prov. China see Zhejiang
Chek Jawa, Tanjong pt Sing. 76 [inset]
Chek Lap Kok i. Hong Kong China 87 [inset]
Chek Mun Hoi Hap sea chan. Hong Kong China see Tolo Channel
Chekshino Rus. Fed. 43 V2
Chela, Serra da mts Angola 127 B9
Chelan U.S.A. 180 B3
Chelan, Lake U.S.A. 180 B2
Chelforó Arg. 204 D5
Chélif, Oued r. Alg. 55 L8
Cheline Moz. 131 G4
Chellal Alg. 55 P9
Chełm Poland 53 G1
historically known as Kholm
Chelmer r. U.K. 47 M12
Chełmno Poland 49 P2
Chelmsford U.K. 47 M12
historically known as Caesaromagus
Chelmsford U.S.A. 177 N3
Chelmsford Public Resort Nature Reserve S. Africa 133 N4
Chełmża Poland 49 P2
Chelsea U.S.A. 173 I8
Cheltenham N.Z. 152 J8
Cheltenham U.K. 47 J12
Chelva Spain 55 K5
Chelyabinsk Rus. Fed. 38 G4
Chelyabinskaya Oblast' admin. div. Rus. Fed. 103 E1
English form Chelyabinsk Oblast
Chelyabinsk Oblast admin. div. Rus. Fed. see Chelyabinskaya Oblast'
Chelyan U.S.A. 176 D7
Chelyuskin Rus. Fed. 39 K2
Chelyuskin, Mys c. Rus. Fed. 39 K2
Chemaïa Morocco 122 C2
Chemax Mex. 185 I4
Chembe Zambia 127 F7
Chemchâm, Sebkhet salt flat Mauritania 122 B5
Chêm Co l. China 89 B5
Chemillé France 50 F5
Chemmis Egypt see Akhmīm
Chemnitz Germany 49 J5
formerly known as Karl-Marx-Stadt
Chemulpo S. Korea see Inch'ŏn
Chemult U.S.A. 180 B4
Chemung r. U.S.A. 177 I4
Chenab r. India/Pak. 96 A3
Chenachane Alg. 122 D4
Chenachane, Oued watercourse Alg. 122 E4
Chenango r. U.S.A. 177 J3
Chenango Bridge U.S.A. 177 J3
Ch'ench'a Eth. 128 C3
Chendir r. Turkm. see Çendir
Cheney U.S.A. 180 C3
Cheney Reservoir U.S.A. 178 C4
Chengalpattu India 94 D3
formerly known as Chingleput
Chengam India 94 C3
Cheng'an China 85 G4
Chengbihe Shuiku resr China 86 C3
Chengbu China 87 D3
also known as Rulin
Chengcheng China 85 F5
Chengchow China see Zhengzhou
Chengde Hebei China 85 H3
UNESCO World Heritage Site
Chengde Hebei China 85 H3
►Chengdu China 86 C2
formerly spelt Chengtu
►►18–19 World Cities
Chengel'dy Kzyl-Ordinskaya Oblast' Kazakh. see Shengel'dy
Chengel'dy Yuzhnyy Kazakhstan Kazakh. 103 G4
Chenggong China 86 B3
also known as Longcheng
Chenghai China 87 F4
Cheng Hai l. China 86 B3
Chengjiang Jiangxi China see Taihe
Chengjiang Yunnan China 86 B3
Chengkou China 87 D2
also known as Gecheng
Chengmai China 87 D5
also known as Jinjiang
Chengqian China 85 H5
Chengqiao China see Chongming
Chengshou China see Yingshan
Chengtu China see Chengdu
Chengwu China 87 E1
Chengxian Gansu China 86 C1
Chengxian Guizhou China see Fuquan
Chengxiang Chongqing China see Wuxi
Chengxiang Jiangxi China see Quannan
Chengxiang Sichuan China see Tianquan
Chengxiang Sichuan China see Mianning
Chengyang China see Juxian
Chengzhong China see Ningming
Cheniu Shan i. China 85 H5
Chennai India 94 D3
formerly known as Madras
Chenoa U.S.A. 172 E10
Chenstokhov Poland see Częstochowa
Chentejn Nuruu mts Mongolia 85 E1
Chenting, Tanjong pt Sing. 76 [inset]
Chenxi China 87 D3
also known as Chenyang
Chenyang China see Chenxi
Chenying China see Wannian
Chenzhou China 87 E3
Cheom Ksan Cambodia see Chŏâm Khsant
Chepelare Bulg. 58 F7
Chepén Peru 200 A1
Chepes Arg. 204 D3
Chepo Panama 186 D5
Chepstow U.K. 47 J12
Cheptsa r. Rus. Fed. 40 I4
Chequamegon Bay U.S.A. 172 C4
Cher r. France 51 G5
Chera state India see Kerala
Cherán Mex. 185 E5
Cherangany Hills Kenya 128 B4
Cheraw U.S.A. 174 E5
Cherbaniani Reef reef India 94 A3
also known as Beleapani
Cherbourg France 50 E3
Cherchell Alg. 123 F1
historically known as Caesarea
Cherchen China see Qiemo
Cherdakly Rus. Fed. 41 I5
Cherdoyak Kazakh. 88 C1
Cherdyn' Rus. Fed. 40 K3
Chère r. France 50 E5
Chereapani reef India see Byramgore Reef
Cherekha r. Rus. Fed. 43 J4
Cheremisinovo Rus. Fed. 41 F6
Cheremkhovo Rus. Fed. 80 G2
Cheremshany Rus. Fed. 82 D3
formerly known as Sinancha
Cheremukhovka Rus. Fed. 40 I4
Cherepanovo Rus. Fed. 80 C2
Cherepovets Rus. Fed. 43 S2
Cherevkovo Rus. Fed. 40 H3
Chergui, Chott ech imp. l. Alg. 123 E2
Chéria Alg. 123 G2
Cherial India 94 C2
Cheriton U.S.A. 177 J8
Cheriyam i. India 94 B4
Cherkassy Ukr. see Cherkasy
Cherkasy Ukr. 41 E6
also spelt Cherkassy
Cherkessk Rus. Fed. 41 G7
Cherkutino Rus. Fed. 43 U5
Cherla India 94 D2
Chermenze Angola 127 D8
Chermoz Rus. Fed. 40 K4
Chern' Rus. Fed. 43 R8
Chern' r. Rus. Fed. 43 R8
Chernak Kazakh. 103 G4
also spelt Shornaq
Chernava Lipetskaya Oblast' Rus. Fed. 43 T9
Chernava Ryazanskaya Oblast' Rus. Fed. 43 U8
Chernaya Rus. Fed. 40 K1
Chernaya r. Rus. Fed. 40 K1
Chernaya r. Rus. Fed. 42 I3
Chernaya Kholunitsa Rus. Fed. 40 I4
Chernevo Moskovskaya Oblast' Rus. Fed. 43 T7
Chernevo Pskovskaya Oblast' Rus. Fed. 43 J3
Chernigov Ukr. see Chernihiv
Chernigovka Rus. Fed. 82 D3
Chernihiv Ukr. 41 D6
also spelt Chernigov
Cherni Lom r. Bulg. 58 G5
Cherninivka Ukr. 41 F7
Cherni Vrŭkh mt. Bulg. 58 E6
Chernivtsi Ukr. 41 C6
also known as Czernowitz; also spelt Chernovtsy; historically known as Cernăuţi
Chernobyl' Ukr. see Chornobyl'
Chernogorsk Rus. Fed. 80 E2
Chernoostrovskoye Rus. Fed. 39 I3
Chernorechenskiy Rus. Fed. 40 J3
Chernoretskoye Kazakh. 103 I1
Chernoushevo Rus. Fed. 43 N1
Chernovskoye Rus. Fed. 40 H4
Chernovtsy Ukr. see Chernivtsi
Chernoye More sea Asia/Europe see Black Sea
Chernushka Rus. Fed. 40 K4
Chernyakhiv Ukr. 41 D6
Chernyakhovsk Rus. Fed. 42 C7
historically known as Insterburg
Chernyanka Rus. Fed. 41 F6
Chernyayeve Rus. Fed. 82 B1
Chernysheva, Zaliv b. Kazakh. 102 D3
Chernyshevsk Rus. Fed. 81 J2
Chernyshevskiy Rus. Fed. 39 L3
Chernyshkovskiy Rus. Fed. 41 G6
Chernyy, Mys c. Rus. Fed. 40 J1
Chernyye Zemli reg. Rus. Fed. 41 H7
Chernyy Irtysh r. China/Kazakh. see Ertix He
Chernyy Otrog Rus. Fed. 102 C2
Chernyy Porog Rus. Fed. 40 E3
Chernyy Rynok Rus. Fed. see Kochubey
Chernyy Yar Rus. Fed. 102 A2
Cherokee IA U.S.A. 178 D3
Cherokee OK U.S.A. 178 C4
Cherokee Lake U.S.A. 176 B9
Cherokees, Lake o' the U.S.A. 178 D4
Cherokee Sound Bahamas 186 D1
Cherpessa Rus. Fed. 43 L5

►Cherrapunji India 97 F4
Highest recorded annual rainfall in the world.
►►12–13 World Climate and Weather

Cherry Creek r. U.S.A. 178 B2
Cherry Creek Mountains U.S.A. 183 J1
Cherryfield U.S.A. 177 R1
Cherry Hill U.S.A. 177 J6
Cherry Island Solomon Is 145 F3
Cherry Lake U.S.A. 182 E3
Cherry Valley Canada 173 P7
Cherskaya Rus. Fed. 43 J4
Cherskiy Rus. Fed. 39 Q3
formerly known as Nizhniye Kresty
Cherskiy Range mts Rus. Fed. see Cherskogo, Khrebet
Cherskogo, Khrebet mts Chitinskaya Oblast' Rus. Fed. 85 F1
English form Cherskiy Range
Cherskogo, Khrebet mts Respublika Sakha (Yakutiya) Rus. Fed. 39 O3
Chersonisos Methano pen. Greece 59 E11
Cherthala India see Shertally
Chertkov Ukr. see Chortkiv
Chertkovo Rus. Fed. 41 G6
Chertolino Rus. Fed. 43 O5
Chertsey N.Z. 153 F11
Cherusti Rus. Fed. 43 V6
Cherven Bryag Bulg. 58 F5
Chervonoarmeyskoye Ukr. see Vil'nyans'k
Chervonoarmiys'k Ukr. see Krasnoarmiys'k
Chervonograd Ukr. see Chervonohrad
Chervonohrad Ukr. 41 C6
also spelt Chervonograd; formerly known as Kristinopol' or Krystynopol
Chervonozavods'ke Ukr. 41 E6
Chervonoznam"yanka Ukr. 58 L1
Chervyen' Belarus 43 J8
Cherykaw Belarus 43 M8
Chesaning U.S.A. 173 I7
Chesapeake U.S.A. 177 I9
Chesapeake Bay U.S.A. 177 I7
Chesapeake Beach U.S.A. 177 I7
Cheshire U.S.A. 177 L3
Cheshme Vtoroy Turkm. 102 E5
Cheshskaya Guba b. Rus. Fed. 40 H2
Chesht-e Sharīf Afgh. 101 E3
Chesma Rus. Fed. 103 E1
Chesnokovka Rus. Fed. see Novoaltaysk
Chester Canada 169 H4
Chester U.K. 47 J10
historically known as Deva
Chester CA U.S.A. 182 C1
Chester IL U.S.A. 174 B4
Chester MT U.S.A. 180 E2
Chester NJ U.S.A. 177 K5
Chester OH U.S.A. 176 D6
Chester PA U.S.A. 177 J6
Chester SC U.S.A. 174 D5
Chester VA U.S.A. 176 H8
Chester r. U.S.A. 177 I7
Chesterfield U.K. 47 K10
Chesterfield MO U.S.A. 174 B4
Chesterfield SC U.S.A. 174 D5

Chesterfield VA U.S.A. 176 H8
Chesterfield, Îles is New Caledonia 145 E3
Chesterfield Inlet Canada 167 N2 also known as Igluligaarjuk
Chesterfield Inlet inlet Canada 167 M2
Chestertown U.S.A. 177 I6
Chestnut Ridge U.S.A. 176 F5
Chesuncook Lake U.S.A. 174 G2
Chetek U.S.A. 172 B5
Chéticamp Canada 169 I4
Chetlat i. India 94 B4
Chetopa U.S.A. 178 D4
Chetumal Mex. 185 H5
Chetwode Islands N.Z. 152 I8
Chetwynd Canada 166 F4
Cheung Chau Hong Kong China 87 [inset]
Chevelon Creek r. U.S.A. 183 N7
Cheviot N.Z. 153 H10
Cheviot U.S.A. 176 A6
Cheviot Hills U.K. 47 J8
Cheviot Range hills Australia 149 D5
Chevreulx r. Canada 169 F2
Che'w Bahir salt l. Eth. 128 C3
Che'w Bahir Wildlife Reserve nature res. Eth. 128 C3
Chewelah U.S.A. 180 C2
Cheyenne OK U.S.A. 179 C5

►**Cheyenne** WY U.S.A. 180 F4
State capital of Wyoming.

Cheyenne r. U.S.A. 178 B2
Cheyenne River Indian Reservation res. U.S.A. 178 B2
Cheyenne Wells U.S.A. 178 B4
Cheyne Bay Australia 151 B7
Cheyur India 94 D3
Cheyyar r. India 94 C3
Chezacut Canada 166 E4
Chhabra India 96 C4
Chhapar India 96 B4
Chhapra India 97 E4 formerly spelt Chapra
Chhata India 96 C4
Chhatak Bangl. 97 F4
Chhatarpur Jharkhand India 97 E4
Chhatarpur Madhya Pradesh India 96 C4
Chhatrapur India 95 E2
Chhattisgarh state India 97 D5
Chhay Arêng, Stœng r. Cambodia 79 C6
Chhibramau India 96 C4
Chhindwara India 96 C5
Chhipa Barod India 96 C4
Chhlong, Prêk r. Cambodia 79 D5
Chhota Chhindwara India 96 C5
Chhota Udepur India 96 B5
Chhuikhadan India 96 D5
Chhuk Cambodia see Phumĭ Chhuk
Chhukha Bhutan 97 F4
Chi, Lam r. Thai. 79 C5
Chi, Mae Nam r. Thai. 78 D5
Chiai Taiwan 87 G4 also spelt Jiayi
Ch'iak-san National Park S. Korea 83 C5
Chiamboni Kenya 128 D5
Chiang Dao Thai. 78 B4
Chiange Angola 127 B8 formerly known as Vila de Almoster
Chiang Kham Thai. 78 C4
Chiang Khan Thai. 78 C4
Chiang Mai Thai. 78 B4 also spelt Chiengmai
Chiang Rai Thai. 78 B4
Chiani r. Italy 56 E6
Chiapa Mex. 185 G5
Chiapas state Mex. 185 G5
Chiat'ura Georgia 107 E2
Chiautla Mex. 185 F5
Chiavari Italy 56 B4
Chiavenno Italy 56 B2
Chiba Japan 91 G7
Chiba pref. Japan 90 G7
Chibemba Angola 127 B8
Chibi China 87 E2
Chibia Angola 127 B8 formerly known as João de Almeida
Chibit Rus. Fed. 88 D1
Chibizovka Rus. Fed. see Zherdevka
Chiboma Moz. 131 G4
Chibougamau Canada 169 F3
Chibougamau, Lac l. Canada 169 F3
Chibu-Sangaku National Park Japan 91 E6 English form Japan Alps National Park
Chibuto Moz. 131 G5
Chibwe Zambia 127 F8
Chicacole India see Srikakulam

►**Chicago** U.S.A. 174 C3
4th most populous city in North America.
►►18–19 World Cities

Chicago Heights U.S.A. 172 F9
Chicago O'Hare airport U.S.A. 172 F9
Chicala Angola 127 C7
Chicamba Moz. 131 G3
Chicapa r. Angola 127 D6
Chic-Chocs, Monts mts Canada 169 H3
Chic-Chocs, Réserve Faunique des nature res. Canada 169 H3
Chicera Hamba hill Romania 58 F3
Chicha well Chad 120 C5
Chichagof Island U.S.A. 164 F4
Chichak r. Pak. 101 F5
Chichaoua Morocco 122 C3
Chichas, Cordillera de mts Bol. 200 D5
Chicheng Hebei China 85 G3
Chicheng Sichuan China see Pengxi
Chichén Itzá tourist site Mex. 185 H4 UNESCO World Heritage Site
Chichester U.K. 47 L13
Chichester Range mts Australia 150 B4
Chichgarh India 94 D1
Chichibu Japan 83 E6
Chichibu-Tama National Park Japan 91 F7
Chichijima-rettō is Japan 73 J1
Chichiriviche Venez. 199 D2
Chicholi India 96 C5
Chickahominy r. U.S.A. 177 I8
Chickasawhay r. U.S.A. 175 B6
Chickasha U.S.A. 179 C5
Chiclana de la Frontera Spain 54 E8
Chiclayo Peru 198 B6
Chico r. Chubut Arg. 205 C6
Chico r. Chubut Arg. 205 D7
Chico r. Santa Cruz Arg. 205 C8
Chico U.S.A. 182 C2
Chicoa Moz. 131 G2
Chicobea i. Fiji see Cikobia
Chicobi, Lac l. Canada 173 O2
Chicomba Angola 127 B8
Chicomo Moz. 131 G5
Chicomucelo Mex. 185 G6
Chiconono Moz. 129 B8
Chicopee U.S.A. 177 M3
Chico Sapocoy, Mount Phil. 74 B2
Chicoutimi Canada 169 G3
Chicoutimi r. Canada 169 G3
Chicualacuala Moz. 131 F4 formerly known as Malvérnia
Chicuma Angola 127 B8
Chidambaram India 94 C4
Chido S. Korea 83 B6
Chiede Angola 127 C9
Chiefland U.S.A. 175 D6
Chiemsee l. Germany 49 J8
Chiengi Zambia 127 F7
Chiengmai Thai. see Chiang Mai
Chienti r. Italy 56 F5
Chieo Lan Reservoir Thai. 79 B6
Chieri Italy 51 N7
Chiers r. France 51 L3
Chiese r. Italy 56 C3
Chieti Italy 56 G6 historically known as Teate
Chifeng China 85 H3 also known as Ulanhad
Chifre, Serra do mts Brazil 203 D6
Chifunde Moz. 131 G2 formerly known as Tembué
Chiganak Kazakh. 103 H3 also spelt Shyghanaq
Chiginagak Volcano, Mount U.S.A. 164 D4
Chignecto Bay Canada 169 H4
Chignecto Game Sanctuary nature res. Canada 169 H4
Chignik U.S.A. 164 D4
Chigorodó Col. 198 B3
Chigu China 89 E6
Chiguana Bol. 200 D5
Chigubo Moz. 131 G4
Chigu Co l. China 89 E6
Chihli, Gulf of China see Bo Hai
Chihuahua Mex. 184 D2
Chihuahua state Mex. 184 D2
Chiili Kazakh. 103 F3 also spelt Shīeli
Chijinpu China 84 C3
Chikalda India 96 C5
Chikan China 87 D4
Chikaskia r. U.S.A. 178 C4
Chik Ballapur India 94 C3
Chikhachevo Rus. Fed. 43 K4
Chikhali Kalan Parasia India 96 C5
Chikhli India 94 C1
Chikmagalur India 94 B3
Chikodi India 94 B2
Chikodi Road India 94 B2
Chikoy Rus. Fed. 85 E1
Chikoy r. Rus. Fed. 85 E1
Chikugo Japan 91 B8
Chikuma-gawa r. Japan 90 F6
Chikushino Japan 91 B8
Chikwa Zambia 129 B7
Chikwawa Malawi 129 B9
Chikyū-misaki pt Japan 90 G3
Chila Angola 127 B8
Chilanko r. Canada 166 F4
Chilanko Forks Canada 166 E4
Chilapa Mex. 185 F5
Chilas Jammu and Kashmir 96 B2
Chilaw Sri Lanka 94 C5
Chilca Peru 200 A3
Chilcaya Chile 200 C4
Chilcotin r. Canada 166 F5
Chilcott Island Australia 149 F3
Childers Australia 149 G5
Childress U.S.A. 179 B5
►**Chile** country S. America 205 B7
►►192–193 South America Countries
Chile Chico Chile 205 C7
Chilecito Arg. 204 D3
Chilengue, Serra do mts Angola 127 B8
Chilete Peru 200 A1
Chilhowie U.S.A. 176 D9
Chilia-Nouă Ukr. see Kiliya
Chilia Veche Romania 58 K3
Chilik Kazakh. 103 I4 also spelt Shelek
Chilik r. Kazakh. 103 I4
Chilika Lake India 95 E2
Chililabombwe Zambia 127 E8 formerly known as Bancroft
Chiliomodi Greece 59 D11 also known as Khiliomódhion
Chilko r. Canada 166 F4
Chilko Lake Canada 166 E5
Chilkoot Trail National Historic Site nat. park U.S.A. 164 F4
Chillagoe Australia 149 E3
Chillán Chile 204 B5
Chillar Arg. 204 F5
Chillicothe IL U.S.A. 172 D10
Chillicothe MO U.S.A. 178 D4
Chillicothe OH U.S.A. 176 C6
Chilliculco Peru 200 C4
Chillinji Jammu and Kashmir 96 B1
Chilliwack Canada 166 F5
Chilmari Bangl. 97 F4
►**Chiloé, Isla de** i. Chile 205 B6 long form Chiloé, Isla Grande de UNESCO World Heritage Site
►►188–189 South America Landscapes
Chiloé, Isla Grande de i. Chile see Chiloé, Isla de
Chilombo Angola 127 D8
Chilonga Zambia 127 F8
Chiloquin U.S.A. 180 B4
Chilpancingo Mex. 185 F5
Chiltern Australia 147 E4
Chiltern Hills U.K. 47 L12
Chilton U.S.A. 172 E6
Chiluage Angola 127 D7
Chilubi Zambia 127 F7
Chilumba Malawi 129 B7
Chilung Taiwan 87 G3 English form Keelung; also spelt Jilong
Chilwa, Lake Malawi 129 B8
Chimala Tanz. 129 B7
Chimaltenango Guat. 185 H6
Chimán Panama 186 D5
Chimanimani Zimbabwe 131 G3 formerly known as Mandidzuzure or Melsetter
Chi Ma Wan Hong Kong China 87 [inset]
Chimba Zambia 127 F7
Chimbas Arg. 204 C3
Chimbay Uzbek. see Chimboy
Chimborazo mt. Ecuador 198 B5
Chimborazo prov. Ecuador 198 B5
Chimbote Peru 200 A2
Chimboy Uzbek. 102 D4 also spelt Chimbay
Chimian Pak. 101 H4
Chimichaguá Col. 187 E5
Chimishliya Moldova see Cimişlia
Chimkent Kazakh. see Shymkent
Chimkentskaya Oblast' admin. div. Kazakh. see Yuzhnyy Kazakhstan
Chimoio Moz. 131 G3 formerly known as Vila Pery
Chimorra hill Spain 54 G6
Chimpay Arg. 204 D5
Chimtargha, Qullai mt. Tajik. 101 G2 also known as Chimtorga, Gora
Chimtorga, Gora mt. Tajik. see Chimtargha, Qullai
Chimyon Uzbek. 103 G4
Chin state Myanmar 78 A3

►**China** country Asia 80 D5
Most populous country in the world and in Asia. 2nd largest country in Asia and 4th largest in the world. Known in Chinese as Zhongguo; long form Zhongguo Renmin Gongheguo or Chung-hua Jen-min Kung-ho-kuo.
►►8–9 World Countries
►►16–17 World Population
►►64–65 Asia Countries

China Mex. 185 F3
China, Republic of country Asia see Taiwan
China Bakir r. Myanmar see To
Chinacates Mex. 184 D3
China Lake U.S.A. 177 P1
Chinandega Nicaragua 186 B4
China Point U.S.A. 182 F9
Chinati Peak U.S.A. 181 F7
Chinaz Uzbek. see Chinoz
Chincha Alta Peru 200 A3
Chinchaga r. Canada 166 G3
Chinchāl, Nahr r. Iraq 109 P3
Chinchilla Australia 149 F5
Chincholi India 94 C2
Chinchorro, Banco sea feature Mex. 185 I5
Chincolco Chile 204 C4
Chincoteague U.S.A. 177 J8
Chincoteague Bay U.S.A. 177 J8
Chinde Moz. 131 H3
Chin-do i. S. Korea 83 B6
Chindu China 86 A1 also known as Chuqung
Chindwin r. Myanmar 78 A3
Chineni Jammu and Kashmir 96 B2
Chinese Turkestan aut. reg. China see Xinjiang Uygur Zizhiqu
Chingaza, Parque Nacional nat. park Col. 198 C3
Chinghai prov. China see Qinghai
Chinghwa N. Korea 83 B5
Chingirlau Kazakh. 102 C2 also spelt Shynggyrlaū
Chingiz-Tau, Khrebet mts Kazakh. 103 I2
Chingleput India see Chengalpattu
Chingola Zambia 127 E8
Chinguar Angola 127 C8
Chinguețți Mauritania 122 B5
Chinguil Chad 126 C2
Chinhae S. Korea 83 C6
Chinhanda Moz. 131 G2
Chinhoyi Zimbabwe 131 F3 formerly spelt Sinoia
Chini India see Kalpa
Chiñijo Bol. 200 C3
Chining China see Jining
Chiniot Pak. 101 H4
Chinipas Mex. 184 C3
Chinit, Stœng r. Cambodia 79 D5
Chinju S. Korea 83 C6
Chinko r. Cent. Afr. Rep. 126 D3
Chinle U.S.A. 183 O5
Chinle Valley valley U.S.A. 183 O5
Chinle Wash watercourse U.S.A. 183 O5
Chinmen Taiwan 87 F3 also spelt Jinmen or Kinmen
Chinmen Tao i. Taiwan 87 F3 English form Quemoy
Chinna Ganjam India 94 D3
Chinnamanur India 94 C4
Chinnamp'o N. Korea see Namp'o
Chinna Salem India 94 C4
Chinnur India 94 C2
Chino Japan 91 F7
Chino U.S.A. 182 G7
Chino Creek watercourse U.S.A. 183 L7
Chinocup, Lake salt flat Australia 151 B7
Chinocup Nature Reserve Australia 151 B7
Chinon France 50 G5
Chinook U.S.A. 180 E2
Chino Valley U.S.A. 183 L7
Chinoz Uzbek. 103 G4 also spelt Chinaz
Chinsali Zambia 129 B7
Chintalnar India 94 D2
Chintamani India 94 C3
Chinteni Romania 58 E2
Chinú Col. 198 C2
Chinyama Litapi Zambia 127 D8
Chin'yavoryk Rus. Fed. 40 J3
Chioco Moz. 131 G3
Chioggia Italy 56 E3
Chiona Tanz. 129 B6
Chios Greece 59 H10
Chios i. Greece 59 G10 also spelt Khíos
Chios Strait Greece 59 H10 English form Khios Strait
Chipanga Moz. 131 G3
Chipata Zambia 129 B8 formerly known as Fort Jameson
Chipchihua, Sierra de mts Arg. 205 C6
Chipili Zambia 127 F7
Chipindo Angola 127 B8
Chiping China 85 H4
Chipinga Zimbabwe see Chipinge
Chipinge Zimbabwe 131 G4 formerly spelt Chipinga
Chipiona Spain 54 E8
Chipley U.S.A. 175 C6
Chiplun India 94 B2
Chipman Canada 169 H4
Chipoia Angola 127 C8
Chippenham U.K. 47 J12
Chipperone, Monte mt. Moz. 131 G3
Chippewa r. MN U.S.A. 178 D2
Chippewa r. WI U.S.A. 172 A6
Chippewa, Lake U.S.A. 172 B5
Chippewa Falls U.S.A. 172 B6
Chipping Norton U.K. 47 K12
Chiprovtsi Bulg. 58 D5
Chipundu Zambia 127 F8
Chipuriro Zimbabwe see Guruve
Chipurupalle Andhra Pradesh India 95 D2
Chipurupalle Andhra Pradesh India 95 D2
Chiquian Peru 200 A2
Chiquibul National Park Belize 185 H5
Chiquilá Mex. 185 I4
Chiquimula Guat. 185 H6
Chiquinquira Col. 198 C3
Chiquintirca Peru 200 B3
Chiquita, Mar l. Arg. 204 E4
Chiquitos, Llanos de plain Bol. 201 E4
Chiquitos Jesuit Missions tourist site Brazil 201 E4 UNESCO World Heritage Site
Chir r. Rus. Fed. 41 G6
Chirada India 94 D3
Chiradzulu Malawi 129 B8
Chirala India 94 D3
Chiramba Moz. 131 G3
Chirambirá, Punta pt Col. 198 B3
Chiras Afgh. 101 F3
Chirawa India 89 A6
Chirchiq Uzbek. 103 G4
Chirchiq r. Uzbek. 103 G4
Chiredzi Zimbabwe 131 F4
Chire Wildlife Reserve nature res. Eth. 128 C1
Chirfa Niger 125 I1
Chirgua r. Venez. 199 E2
Chiricahua National Monument nat. park U.S.A. 183 O9
Chiricahua Peak U.S.A. 181 E7
Chiriguaná Col. 198 C2
Chirikof Island U.S.A. 164 D4
Chiriquí, Golfo de b. Panama 186 C5
Chiriquí, Laguna de b. Panama 186 C5
Chiriquí Grande Panama 186 C5
Chiri-san mt. S. Korea 83 B6
Chiri-san National Park S. Korea 83 B6
Chirka-Kem' r. Rus. Fed. 44 P2
Chirnside U.K. 46 J8
Chirpan Bulg. 58 G6
Chirripó, Parque Nacional nat. park Costa Rica 186 C5
Chirundu Zimbabwe 131 F3
Chīrūyeh Iran 100 C5
Chisamba Zambia 127 F8
Chisana r. U.S.A. 166 A2
Chisasa Zambia 127 E8
Chisasibi Canada 168 E2
Chisec Guat. 185 H6
Chisekesi Zambia 127 E9
Chiselet Romania 58 H4
Chisenga Malawi 129 B7
Chishima-retto is Rus. Fed. see Kuril Islands
Chishmy Rus. Fed. 40 J5
Chisholm Canada 167 H4
Chisholm ME U.S.A. 177 O1
Chisholm MN U.S.A. 178 D2
Chishtian Mandi Pak. 101 H4
Chishui China 86 C2
Chishuihe China 86 C3
Chishui He r. China 86 C2
Chisimaio Somalia see Kismaayo

►**Chişinău** Moldova 58 J1
Capital of Moldova. Formerly spelt Kishinev.

Chişineu-Criş Romania 58 C2
Chisone r. Italy 51 N8
Chistopol' Rus. Fed. 40 I5
Chistopol'ye Kazakh. 103 F1
Chistyakovskoye Kazakh. 103 G1
Chita Bol. 200 D5
Chita Col. 198 C3
Chita Rus. Fed. 85 G1
Chita Tanz. 129 B7
Chitado Angola 127 B9
Chitaldrug India see Chitradurga
Chitalwana India 96 A4
Chita Oblast admin. div. Rus. Fed. see Chitinskaya Oblast'
Chitato Angola 127 D6 formerly known as Portugália
Chitayevo Rus. Fed. 40 I3
Chitek Lake Canada 167 J4
Chitek Lake l. Canada 167 L4
Chitembo Angola 127 C8
Chitinskaya Oblast' admin. div. Rus. Fed. 85 H1 English form Chita Oblast
Chitipa Malawi 129 B7
Chitobe Moz. 131 G4 formerly known as Machaze
Chitokoloki Zambia 127 D8
Chitongo Zambia 127 E9
Chitor India see Chittaurgarh
Chitose Japan 90 G3
Chitradurga India 94 C3 formerly known as Chitaldrug
Chitrakoot India 96 D4
Chitral Pak. 101 G3
Chitral r. Pak. 101 G3
Chitravati r. India 94 C3
Chitré Panama 186 C6
Chitrod India 96 A5
Chittagong Bangl. 97 F5 also spelt Chattagam
Chittagong admin. div. Bangl. 97 F5
Chittaranjan India 97 E5 formerly known as Mihidjan
Chittaurgarh India 96 B4 formerly known as Chitor; formerly spelt Chittorgarh
Chittoor India 94 C3
Chittorgarh India see Chittaurgarh
Chittur India 94 C4
Chitungulu Zambia 129 B8
Chitungwiza Zimbabwe 131 F3
Chiu Lung Hong Kong China see Kowloon
Chiume Angola 127 D8
Chiúre Novo Moz. 131 H2
Chiusa Sclafani Sicily Italy 57 F11
Chiúta Moz. 131 G2
Chiva Spain 55 K5
Chivasso Italy 56 A3
Chívato, Punta pt Mex. 184 C3
Chivay Peru 200 C3
Chive Bol. 200 C3
Chivela Mex. 185 G5
Chivhu Zimbabwe 131 F3 formerly known as Enkeldoorn
Chivilcoy Arg. 204 E4
Chiyirchik, Pereval pass Kyrg. see Chyyyrchyk Ashuusu
Chizarira Hills Zimbabwe 131 E3
Chizarira National Park Zimbabwe 131 E3
Chizha Vtoraya Kazakh. 102 B2
Chizhou China 87 F2
Chizu Japan 91 D7
Chkalov Rus. Fed. see Orenburg
Chkalovo Kazakh. 103 G1
Chkalovsk Rus. Fed. 40 G4
Chkalovskaya Oblast' admin. div. Rus. Fed. see Orenburgskaya Oblast'
Chkalovskiy Rus. Fed. 44 P2
Chkalovskoye Rus. Fed. 82 D3
Chlef Alg. 123 F1 also spelt Ech Chélif; formerly known as El Asnam or Orléansville
Chloride U.S.A. 183 J6
Chlumec nad Cidlinou Czech Rep. 49 M5
Chlya, Ozero l. Rus. Fed. 82 F1
Chmielnik Poland 49 R5
Choa Chu Kang Sing. 76 [inset]
Choa Chu Kang hill Sing. 76 [inset]
Chŏâm Khsant Cambodia 79 D5 also spelt Cheom Ksan
Choapa r. Chile 204 C3
Chobe National Park Botswana 131 E3
Choch'iwŏn S. Korea 83 B5
Chocianów Poland 49 M4
Chociwel Poland 49 M2
Chocó dept Col. 198 B3
Chocolate Mountains U.S.A. 183 I8
Chocontá Col. 198 C3
Choctawhatchee r. U.S.A. 175 C6
Chodavaram India 94 D2
Chodecz Poland 49 Q3
Chodelka r. Poland 49 S4
Cho-do i. N. Korea 83 B5
Chodro Rus. Fed. 84 A1
Choduralyg Rus. Fed. 84 C1
Chodzież Poland 49 N3
Choele Choel Arg. 204 D5
Chofombo Moz. 131 F2
Choghādak Iran 100 B4
Chogo Lungma Glacier Jammu and Kashmir 96 B2
Chograyskoye Vodokhranilishche resr Rus. Fed. 41 H7
Choiceland Canada 167 J4
Choique Arg. 204 E5
Choirokoitia Cyprus 108 E3 UNESCO World Heritage Site
Choiseul i. Solomon Is 145 E2 formerly known as Lauru
Choiseul Sound sea chan. Falkland Is 205 F8
Choix Mex. 184 C3
Chojna Poland 49 L3
Chojnice Poland 49 O2
Chojnów Poland 49 M4
Chōkai-san vol. Japan 90 G5
Ch'ok'ē Mountains Eth. 128 C2
Chokpar Kazakh. 103 H4 also spelt Shokpar or Shoqpar
Choksum China 89 D6
Chokue Moz. see Chókwé
Chokurdakh Rus. Fed. 39 O2
Chókwé Moz. 131 G5 formerly known as Vila de Trego Morais; formerly spelt Chokue
Cho La pass China 86 A2
Cholame U.S.A. 182 D6
Cholame Creek r. U.S.A. 182 D6
Chola Shan mts China 86 A1
Cholet France 50 F5
Choloma Hond. 186 B4
Cholpon-Ata Kyrg. 103 I4
Cholula Mex. 185 F5
Choluteca Hond. 186 B4
Choma Zambia 127 E9
Chŏmch'ŏn S. Korea 83 C5
Chomo China see Yadong
Chomo Ganggar mt. China 89 E6
Chomo Lhari mt. Bhutan 97 F4
Chomo Yummo mt. China/India 97 F3
Chomun India 96 B4
Chomutov Czech Rep. 49 K5
Chona r. Rus. Fed. 39 K3
Ch'ŏnan S. Korea 83 B5
Chon Buri Thai. 79 C5 also known as Bar Pla Soi
Chonchi Chile 205 B6
Chone Ecuador 198 A5
Chong'an China see Wuyishan
Ch'ŏngch'ŏn-gang r. N. Korea 83 B5
Ch'ongdo S. Korea 83 C6
Chonggye China see Qonggyai
Chŏngja S. Korea 91 A7
Ch'ŏngjin N. Korea 82 C4
Chŏngju N. Korea 83 B5
Ch'ŏngju S. Korea 83 B5
Chongkü China 86 A2
Chongli China 85 G3 also known as Xiwanzi
Chonglong China see Zizhong
Chongming China 87 G2 also known as Chengqiao
Chongming Dao i. China 87 G2
Chongoroi Angola 127 B8
Chŏngp'yŏng N. Korea 83 B5
Chongqing Chongqing China 86 C2 formerly spelt Chungking
Chongqing Sichuan China see Chongzhou
Chongqing municipality China 87 C2
Chongren China 87 E3 also known as Bashan
Chŏngŭp S. Korea 83 B6
Chongwe Zambia 127 F8
Chongyang China 87 E2 also known as Tiancheng
Chongyang Xi r. China 87 F3
Chongyi China 87 E3 also known as Hengshui
Chongyz-Tayga, Gora mt. Rus. Fed. 84 B1
Chongzhou China 86 B2 formerly known as Chongqing
Chongzuo China 87 C4 also known as Taiping
Chŏnju S. Korea 83 B6
Chonogol Mongolia 85 G2
Chonos, Archipiélago de los is Chile 205 B7
Chontalpa Mex. 185 G5
Chơn Thanh Vietnam 79 D6
►**Cho Oyu** mt. China/Nepal 97 E3
►►6–7 World Landscapes
►►60–61 Asia Landscapes
Chop Ukr. 49 T7
Chopan India 97 D4
Chopda India 96 B5
Chopimzinho Brazil 203 A8
Choptank r. U.S.A. 177 I7
Choqāy Zanbil tourist site Iran 107 G5 UNESCO World Heritage Site
Choquecamata Bol. 200 D4
Chor Pak. 101 G5
Chora Greece 59 C11 also spelt Khóra
Chorley U.K. 47 J10
Chornobyl' Ukr. 41 D6 also spelt Chernobyl'
Chornomors'ke Ukr. 41 E7
Chornomors'kyy Zapovidnyk nature res. Ukr. 41 D7
Choros, Islas de los is Chile 204 C3
Choroszcz Poland 49 T2
Chorrochó Brazil 202 E4
Chortkiv Ukr. 41 C6 also spelt Chertkov
Chorvoq suv ombori resr Kazakh./Uzbek. 103 G4
Chorwad India 94 A1
Ch'ŏrwŏn S. Korea 83 B5
Chorzele Poland 49 R2
Ch'osan N. Korea 83 B4
Chōsen-kaikyō sea chan. Japan/S. Korea see Nishi-suidō
Chōshi Japan 91 G7
Choshuenco, Volcán vol. Chile 204 B5
Chosica Peru 200 A2
Chos Malal Arg. 204 C5
Chosmes Arg. 204 D4
Choszczno Poland 49 M2
Chota Peru 198 B6
Chota Nagpur reg. India 97 D5
Choteau U.S.A. 180 D3
Chotila India 96 A5
Choûm Mauritania 122 B5
Chowan r. U.S.A. 177 I9
Chowchilla U.S.A. 182 D4
Chowghat India 94 B4
Chowilla Regional Reserve nature res. Australia 146 D3
Chown, Mount Canada 166 G4
Choya Arg. 204 D3
Choybalsan Mongolia 85 G2
Choyr Mongolia 85 F2
Chozi Zambia 129 B7
Chreïrîk well Mauritania 122 B5
Chřiby hills Czech Rep. 49 O6
Chrisman U.S.A. 174 C4
Chrissiesmeer S. Africa 133 O3
Christchurch N.Z. 153 G11
Christiana S. Africa 133 J4
Christiania Norway see Oslo
Christian Island Canada 173 M6
Christiansburg U.S.A. 176 E8
Christianshåb Greenland see Qasigiannguit
Christian Sound sea chan. U.S.A. 166 C4
Christiansted Virgin Is (U.S.A.) 187 G3
Christie U.S.A. 172 C6
Christie Bay Canada 167 I2
Christina r. Canada 167 I3
Christmas Creek Australia 150 D3
Christmas Creek r. Australia 150 D3

►**Christmas Island** terr. Indian Ocean 218 O6
Australian External Territory.
►►64–65 Asia Countries

Christopher, Lake salt flat Australia 151 D5
Christos Greece 59 H11 also spelt Hristós
Chrudim Czech Rep. 49 M6
Chrysi i. Greece 59 G14
Chrysochou Bay Cyprus 108 D2 also known as Chrysochous, Kolpos; also spelt Khrysokhou Bay
Chrysochous, Kolpos b. Cyprus see Chrysochou Bay
Chrysoupoli Greece 58 F8 also known as Khrisoúpolis
Chu Kazakh. see Shu
Chu r. Kazakh. 103 F3
Chuadanga Bangl. 97 F5
Chuali, Lago l. Moz. 133 Q1
Chuansha China 87 G2
Chubalung China 86 A2
Chubarovka Ukr. see Polohy
Chubarovo Rus. Fed. 43 R6
Chubartau Kazakh. see Barshatas
Chubbuck U.S.A. 180 D4
Chubut prov. Arg. 205 C6
Chubut r. Arg. 205 D6
Chuchkovo Rus. Fed. 41 G5
Chuckwalla Mountains U.S.A. 183 I8
Chucul Arg. 204 D4
Chucunaque r. Panama 186 D5
Chudniv Ukr. 41 D6
Chudovo Rus. Fed. 43 M2
Chudskoye, Ozero l. Estonia/Rus. Fed. see Peipus, Lake
Chudzin Belarus 42 H9
Chudz"yavr, Ozero l. Rus. Fed. 44 P1
Chugach Mountains U.S.A. 164 E3
Chūgoku-sanchi mts Japan 91 C7
Chugqênsumdo China see Jigzhi
Chuguchak China see Tacheng
Chuguyev Ukr. see Chuhuyiv
Chuguyevka Rus. Fed. 82 D3
Chuhai China see Zhuhai
Chuhuyiv Ukr. 41 F6 also spelt Chuguyev
Chu-Iliyskiye Gory mts Kazakh. 103 H3 UNESCO World Heritage Site
Chuka China 86 A2
Chukai Malaysia see Cukai
Chukchagirskoye, Ozero l. Rus. Fed. 82 E1
Chukchi Peninsula Rus. Fed. see Chukotskiy Poluostrov
Chukchi Sea Rus. Fed./U.S.A. 164 B3
Chukhloma Rus. Fed. 40 G4
Chukotskiy, Mys c. Rus. Fed. 39 S3
Chukotskiy Poluostrov pen. Rus. Fed. 39 S3 English form Chukchi Peninsula
Chulakkurgan Kazakh. see Sholakkorgan
Chulaktau Kazakh. see Karatau
Chulasa Rus. Fed. 40 H2
Chula Vista U.S.A. 183 G9
Chulkovo Rus. Fed. 43 R8
Chulucanas Peru 198 A6
Chulung Pass Pak. 96 C2
Chuluut Gol r. Mongolia 84 D1
Chulym Rus. Fed. 80 C1
Chulyshman r. Rus. Fed. 84 A1
Chulyshmanskoye Ploskogor'ye plat. Rus. Fed. 84 A1
Chum Rus. Fed. 40 L2
Chuma Bol. 200 C3
Chumba Eth. 128 C3
Chumbicha Arg. 204 D3
Chumda China 86 A1
Chumerna mt. Bulg. 58 G6
Chumikan Rus. Fed. 82 D1
Chum Phae Thai. 78 C4
Chumphon Thai. 79 B6
Chum Saeng Thai. 78 C5
Chuna r. Rus. Fed. 39 J4
Chuña Huasi Arg. 204 D3
Chun'an China 87 F2 also known as Pailing
Chuna-Tundra plain Rus. Fed. 44 P2
Ch'unch'ŏn S. Korea 83 B5
Chunchura India 97 F5
Chundzha Kazakh. 103 I4 also spelt Shonzha
Chunga Zambia 127 E8
Chung-hua Jen-min Kung-ho-kuo country Asia see China
Chung-hua Min-kuo country Asia see Taiwan
Ch'ungju S. Korea 83 B5
Chungking China see Chongqing
Ch'ungmu S. Korea see T'ongyŏng
Chŭngsan N. Korea 83 B5
Chungu Tanz. 129 C7
Chungyang Shanmo mts Taiwan 87 G4 also known as Taiwan Shan
Chunhua China 82 C4
Chunhuhux Mex. 185 H5
Chunxi China see Gaochun
Chunya r. Rus. Fed. 39 J3
Chunya Tanz. 129 B7
Chu Oblast admin. div. Kyrg. see Chüy
Chuôi, Hon i. Vietnam 79 D6
Chuosijia China see Guanyinqiao
Chupa Rus. Fed. 44 P2
Chūplū Iran 100 A2
Chuquicamata Chile 200 C5
Chuquisaca dept Bol. 201 D5
Chuqung China see Chindu
Chur Rus. Fed. 40 J4
Chur Switz. 51 P6 also spelt Coire; historically known as Curia
Churachandpur India 97 G4
Chūrān Iran 100 C4
Churapcha Rus. Fed. 39 N3
Churayevo Rus. Fed. 40 J5
Church Hill MD U.S.A. 177 J6
Church Hill TN U.S.A. 176 C9
Churchill Canada 167 M3
Churchill r. Man. Canada 167 M3
Churchill r. Nfld. and Lab. Canada 169 I2 formerly known as Hamilton
►**Churchill, Cape** Canada 167 M3
►►14–15 World Environmental Impacts
Churchill Falls Canada 169 I2
Churchill Lake Canada 167 I4
Churchill Mountains Antarctica 223 K1
Churchill Peak Canada 166 E3
Churchill Sound sea chan. Canada 168 E1
Churchville U.S.A. 176 F7
Chureg-Tag, Gora mt. Rus. Fed. 84 A1
Churia Ghati Hills Nepal 97 E4
Churilovo Rus. Fed. 43 L6
Churin Peru 200 A2
Churn Creek Provincial Park Canada 166 F5
Churov Rus. Fed. 40 H4
Churovichi Rus. Fed. 43 N9
Churu India 96 B3
Churubay Nura Kazakh. see Abay
Churuguara Venez. 198 D2
Chūrui Japan 90 H3
Churumuco Mex. 185 E5
Chushul Jammu and Kashmir 96 C2
Chuska Mountains U.S.A. 183 O5
Chusovaya r. Rus. Fed. 40 K4
Chusovoy Rus. Fed. 40 K4
Chust Ukr. see Khust
Chust Uzbek. 103 G4
Chute-Rouge Canada 173 Q4
Chutung Taiwan 87 G3 also known as Zhudong
Chuuk i. Micronesia 220 F5
Chuvashia aut. rep. Rus. Fed. see Chuvashskaya Respublika
Chuvashskaya A.S.S.R. aut. rep. Rus. Fed. see Chuvashskaya Respublika
Chuvashskaya Respublika aut. rep. Rus. Fed. 40 H5 English form Chuvashia; formerly known as Chuvashskaya A.S.S.R.
Chuwang-san National Park S. Korea 83 C5
Chuxiong China 86 B3
Chüy admin. div. Kyrg. 103 H4 English form Chu Oblast; also known as Chuyskaya Oblast'
Chuy Uruguay 204 G4
Chuyskaya Oblast' admin. div. Kyrg. see Chüy
Chuzhou Anhui China 87 F1
Chuzhou Jiangsu China 87 F1
Chyhirynskaye Vodaskhovishcha resr Belarus 43 K8
Chymyshliya Moldova see Cimişlia
Chyrvonaya Slabada Belarus 43 J9
Chyrvonaye, Vozyera l. Belarus 42 I9
Chyulu Range mts Kenya 128 C5
Chyyyrchyk Ashuusu pass Kyrg. 103 H4 also known as Chiyirchik, Pereval
Ciacova Romania 58 C3
Ciadâr-Lunga Moldova see Ciadîr-Lunga
Ciadîr-Lunga Moldova 58 J2 formerly spelt Ceadâr-Lunga or Ciadâr-Lunga or Chadyr-Lunga

Ciamis Indon. 77 E4
Ciampino *airport* Italy 56 E7
Cianjur Indon. 77 D4
Cianorte Brazil 201 G5
Cibadak Indon. 77 D4
Cibatu Indon. 77 E4
Cibecue U.S.A. 183 N7
Cibinong Indon. 77 D4
Cibitoke Burundi 126 F5
Cibolo Creek *r.* U.S.A. 179 C6
Cibuta, Sierra *mt.* Mex. 184 C2
Čićarija *mts* Croatia 56 F3
Çiçekdağı Turkey 106 C3
also known as Boyalık
Çiçekli *İzel* Turkey 108 G1
Çiçekli *Manisa* Turkey 59 J9
Cicero U.S.A. 172 F9
Cícero Dantas Brazil 202 E4
Čičevac *Srbija* Serb. and Mont. 58 C5
Cidacos *r.* Spain 55 J2
Cide Turkey 106 C2
Cidlina *r.* Czech Rep. 49 M5
Ciechanów Poland 49 R3
Ciechanowiec Poland 49 T3
Ciechocinek Poland 49 P3
Ciego de Ávila Cuba 186 D2
Ciénaga Col. 198 C2
Ciénagas del Catatumbo *nat. park* Venez. 198 D2
Cienfuegos Cuba 186 C2
Cíes, Illas *is* Spain 54 C2
Cieszanów Poland 49 U5
Cieszyn Poland 49 P6
Cieza Spain 55 J6
Çiftlikköy Turkey 109 I1
Çiftlik Turkey *see* Kelkit
Çiftlikköy Turkey 58 J7
Cifuentes Spain 55 I4
Cigeulis Indon. 77 D4
Cigüela *r.* Spain 55 H5
Cihanbeyli Turkey 106 C3
also known as Inevi
Cihangazi Turkey 59 K9
Cihuatlán Mex. 184 D5
Cijara, Embalse de *resr* Spain 54 G5
Cikai China *see* Gongshan
Çikes, Maja e *mt.* Albania 59 A8
Cikobia *i.* Fiji 145 H3
also spelt Thikombia; *formerly spelt* Chicobea *or* Ticumbia *or* Tikumbia
Čikola *r.* Croatia 56 I5
Cilacap Indon. 77 E4
Cilangkahan Indon. 77 D4
Çıldır Turkey 107 E2
also known as Zurzuna
Çıldır Gölü *l.* Turkey 107 E2
Çıldıroba Turkey 109 I1
Ciledug Indon. 77 E4
Cilento e del Vallo di Diano, Parco Nazionale del *nat. park* Italy 57 H8
UNESCO World Heritage Site
Cili China 87 D2
Cilician Gates *pass* Turkey *see* Gülek Boğazı
Cilieni Romania 58 F5
Cill Airne Ireland *see* Killarney
Cill Chainnigh Ireland *see* Kilkenny
Cill Mhantáin Ireland *see* Wicklow
Çilmämmetgum *des.* Turkm. 102 C4
Cilo Dağı *mt.* Turkey 107 F3
Çiloy Adası *i.* Azer. 107 G2
Cima U.S.A. 183 I6
Cimahi Indon. 77 D4
Cimarron *KS* U.S.A. 178 B4
Cimarron *NM* U.S.A. 181 F5
Cimarron *r.* U.S.A. 179 C4
Cimarron Creek *r.* U.S.A. 181 F5
Cimino, Monte *mt.* Italy 56 E6
Cimişlia Moldova 58 J2
formerly spelt Chimishliya *or* Chymyshliya
Cimone, Monte *mt.* Italy 56 C4
Cîmpeni Romania *see* Câmpeni
Cîmpia Turzii Romania *see* Câmpia Turzii
Cîmpina Romania *see* Câmpina
Cîmpulung Romania *see* Câmpulung
Cîmpulung Moldovenesc Romania *see* Câmpulung Moldovenesc
Cina, Tanjung *c.* Indon. 76 D4
Çınar Turkey 107 E3
also known as Hanakpınar
Çınarcık Turkey 58 K8
Cinaruco *r.* Venez. 198 E3
Cinaruco-Capanaparo, Parque Nacional *nat. park* Venez. 199 E3
Cinca *r.* Spain 55 L3
Cincar *mt.* Bos.-Herz. 56 J5
Cincinnati U.S.A. 176 A6
Cincinnatus U.S.A. 177 J3
Cinco-Balas, Cayos *is* Cuba 186 D2
Cinco de Outubro Angola *see* Xá-Muteba
Cincu Romania 58 F3
Çine Turkey 106 B3
Çine *r.* Turkey 59 I11
Ciney Belgium 51 L2
Cinfães Port. 54 C3
Cingoli Italy 56 F5
Cinque Island India 95 G4
Cinque Terre *reg.* Italy 56 B4
UNESCO World Heritage Site
Cintalapa Mex. 185 G5
Cinto, Monte *mt.* France 51 O10
Cintruénigo Spain 55 J2
Cinzas *r.* Brazil 206 C10
Ciolpani Romania 58 H4
Čiovo *i.* Croatia 56 I5
Cipatuja Indon. 77 E4
Ciping China *see* Jinggangshan
Cipó Brazil 202 E4
Cipo *r.* Brazil 207 I5
Cipolletti Arg. 204 D5
Cipotânea Brazil 207 J7
Circeo, Monte *hill* Italy 56 F7
Circeo, Parco Nazionale del *nat. park* Italy 56 E7
Circle *AK* U.S.A. 164 E3
Circle *MT* U.S.A. 180 F3
Circleville *OH* U.S.A. 176 C6
Circleville *UT* U.S.A. 183 L3
Cirebon Indon. 77 E4
formerly spelt Tjirebon
Cirencester U.K. 47 K12
historically known as Corinium
Cirene *tourist site* Libya *see* Cyrene
Ciriè Italy 51 N7
Ciriš *l.* Latvia 42 H5
Cirò Marina Italy 57 J9
Ciron *r.* France 50 F8
Cirque Mountain Canada 169 I1
Cirta Alg. *see* Constantine
Cisco U.S.A. 183 O3
Cisnădie Romania 58 F3
Cisnes, Lagunas de los *lakes* Arg. 204 E3
Cisterna di Latina Italy 56 E7
Cistierna Spain 54 F2
Citadelle/Sans Souci/Ramiers *tourist site* Haiti 187 E3
UNESCO World Heritage Site
Citlaltépetl *vol.* Mex. *see* Orizaba, Pico de
Čitluk Bos.-Herz. 56 J5
Citronelle U.S.A. 175 B6
Citrusdal S. Africa 132 D9
Citrus Heights U.S.A. 182 C3
Cittadella Italy 56 D3
Città di Castello Italy 56 E5
Cittanova Italy 57 I10
City of Derry *airport* U.K. 47 E8
Ciucaş, Vârful *mt.* Romania 58 G3
Ciucea Romania 58 D2
Ciudad Acuña Mex. 185 E2
Ciudad Altamirano Mex. 185 E5
Ciudad Bolívar Venez. 199 F2
Ciudad Camargo Mex. 184 D3
Ciudad Constitución Mex. 184 C3
also known as Villa Constitución
Ciudad Cuauhtémoc Mex. 185 H6
Ciudad del Carmen Mex. 185 H5
Ciudad del Este Para. 201 G6
formerly known as Puerto Presidente Stroessner
Ciudad Delicias Mex. 184 D2
Ciudad del Maíz Mex. 185 F4
Ciudad de Valles Mex. 185 F4
Ciudad Guayana Venez. 199 F2
Ciudad Guzmán Mex. 184 E5
Ciudad Hidalgo Mex. 185 E5
Ciudad Ixtepec Mex. 185 G5
Ciudad Juárez Mex. 184 D2
Ciudad Lerdo Mex. 184 E3
Ciudad Madero Mex. 185 F4
Ciudad Mante Mex. 185 F4
Ciudad Mendoza Mex. 185 F5
Ciudad Mier Mex. 185 F3
Ciudad Obregón Mex. 184 C3
Ciudad Piar Venez. 199 F3
Ciudad Real Spain 54 H6
Ciudad Río Bravo Mex. 185 F3
Ciudad Rodrigo Spain 54 E4
Ciudad Trujillo Dom. Rep. *see* Santo Domingo
Ciudad Victoria Mex. 185 F4
Ciudanoviţa Romania 58 C3
Ciumani Romania 58 G2
Ciutadella de Menorca Spain 55 O4
Civa Burnu *pt* Turkey 107 D2
Civetta, Monte *mt.* Italy 56 E2
Cividale del Friuli Italy 56 F2
Civita Castellana Italy 56 E6
historically known as Falerii
Civitanova Marche Italy 56 F5
Civitavecchia Italy 56 D6
Civitella Roveto Italy 56 F7
Civray France 50 G6
Çivril Turkey 106 B3
Cixi China 87 G2
also known as Hushan
Cixian China 85 G4
also known as Cizhou
Ciyao China 85 H5
Cizhou China *see* Cixian
Cizre Turkey 107 E3
Clackamas *r.* U.S.A. 180 B3
Clacton-on-Sea U.K. 47 N12
Clain *r.* France 50 G6
Claire, Lake Canada 167 H3
Clair Engle Lake *resr* U.S.A. 180 B4
Clairmont Canada 166 G4
Claise *r.* France 50 G6
Clam Lake U.S.A. 172 C4
Clan Alpine Mountains U.S.A. 182 G2
Clanton U.S.A. 175 C5
Clanville S. Africa 133 L8
Clanwilliam S. Africa 132 C9
Clanwilliam Dam S. Africa 132 C9
Clara *r.* Australia 149 D3
Clara Ireland 47 E10
Clara Island Myanmar 79 B6
Claraville Australia 149 D3
Clare *N.S.W.* Australia 147 D3
Clare *S.A.* Australia 146 C3
Clare *r.* Ireland 47 C10
Clare U.S.A. 173 I7
Clare Island Ireland 47 B10
Claremont U.S.A. 177 M2
Claremont Isles Australia 149 D2
Claremore U.S.A. 179 D4
Claremorris Ireland 47 D10
Clarence *r.* Australia 147 G2
Clarence N.Z. 153 H10
Clarence *r.* N.Z. 153 H10
Clarence U.S.A. 172 B9
Clarence, Isla *i.* Chile 205 C9
Clarence Island Antarctica 222 U2
Clarence Strait Australia 148 A1
Clarence Strait U.S.A. 166 C3
Clarence Town Bahamas 187 E2
Clarendon N.Z. 153 E14
Clarendon *AR* U.S.A. 174 B5
Clarendon *PA* U.S.A. 176 F4
Clarendon *TX* U.S.A. 179 B5
Clarenville Canada 169 K3
Claresholm Canada 167 H5
Clarinda U.S.A. 178 D3
Clarington U.S.A. 176 E6
Clarion *IA* U.S.A. 174 A3
Clarion *PA* U.S.A. 176 F4
Clarion *r.* U.S.A. 176 F4
Clarión, Isla *i.* Mex. 184 B5
Clarks N.Z. 152 J4
Clark U.S.A. 178 C2
Clark, Mount Canada 166 F1
Clarkdale U.S.A. 183 L7
Clarke *r.* Australia 149 E3
Clarkebury S. Africa 133 M8
Clarke Range *mts* Australia 149 E4
Clarke River Australia 149 E3
Clarkes Creek *r.* Australia 149 D3
Clarke's Head Canada 169 K3
Clark Fork *r. ID* U.S.A. 180 C2
Clark Fork *r. MT* U.S.A. 180 C2
Clark Hill Reservoir U.S.A. 175 D5
Clark Mountain U.S.A. 183 I6
Clark Mountains Antarctica 222 O1
Clark Point Canada 168 D4
Clarksburg U.S.A. 176 E6
Clarksdale U.S.A. 174 B5
Clark's Fork Yellowstone *r.* U.S.A. 180 E3
Clarks Junction N.Z. 153 E13
Clarkson S. Africa 133 I11
Clarkston U.S.A. 180 C3
Clarksville *AR* U.S.A. 179 D5
Clarksville *TN* U.S.A. 174 C4
Clarksville *TX* U.S.A. 179 D5
Claro *r. Goiás* Brazil 206 C6
Claro *r. Mato Grosso* Brazil 206 B2
Clatskanie U.S.A. 180 B3
Claude U.S.A. 179 B5
Cláudio Brazil 203 C7
Claveria Phil. 74 B2
Clavering Ø *i.* Greenland 165 Q2
Claxton U.S.A. 175 D5
Clay U.S.A. 176 D7
Clayburg U.S.A. 177 L1
Clay Center *KS* U.S.A. 178 C4
Clay Center *NE* U.S.A. 178 C3
Clay City U.S.A. 176 B8
Clayhole Wash *watercourse* U.S.A. 183 K4
Claymont U.S.A. 177 J6
Claypool U.S.A. 183 N8
Clay Springs U.S.A. 183 N7
Clayton *DE* U.S.A. 177 J6
Clayton *GA* U.S.A. 174 D5
Clayton *NM* U.S.A. 178 B4
Clayton *NY* U.S.A. 177 I1
Claytor Lake U.S.A. 176 E8
Clearco U.S.A. 176 F7
Clear Creek Canada 173 M8
Clear Creek U.S.A. 183 M2
Clear Creek *r. AZ* U.S.A. 183 N7
Clear Creek *r. WY* U.S.A. 180 F3
Clearfield *PA* U.S.A. 176 G4
Clearfield *UT* U.S.A. 180 D4
Clear Fork Brazos *r.* U.S.A. 179 C5
Clear Hills Canada 166 G3
Clear Island Ireland 47 C12
Clear Lake *IA* U.S.A. 174 A3
Clear Lake *SD* U.S.A. 178 C2
Clear Lake *WI* U.S.A. 172 A5
Clear Lake *l. CA* U.S.A. 182 B2
Clear Lake *l. UT* U.S.A. 183 L2
Clearlake Oaks U.S.A. 182 B2
Clear Lake Reservoir U.S.A. 180 B4
Clearmont U.S.A. 180 F3
Clear Spring U.S.A. 176 H6
Clearwater Canada 166 G5
Clearwater *r. Alta* Canada 167 H4
Clearwater *r. Alta/Sask.* Canada 167 I3
Clearwater U.S.A. 175 D7
Clearwater *r. ID* U.S.A. 180 C3
Clearwater *r. MN* U.S.A. 178 C2
Clear Water Bay Hong Kong China 87 [inset]
also known as Tsing Shui Wan
Clearwater Lake *l.* Canada 167 K4
Clearwater Lake U.S.A. 172 D5
Clearwater Lake Provincial Park Canada 167 K4
Clearwater Mountains U.S.A. 180 D3
Clearwater River Provincial Park Canada 167 I3
Cleburne U.S.A. 179 C5
Cle Elum U.S.A. 180 B3
Cléguérec France 50 C4
Clejani Romania 58 G4
Clément Fr. Guiana 199 H4
Clementi Sing. 76 [inset]
Clementina Brazil 206 C8
Clemmons U.S.A. 176 E9
Clemson U.S.A. 174 D5
Clendenin U.S.A. 176 D7
Clendening Lake U.S.A. 176 D5
Cleopatra Needle *mt.* Phil. 74 A4
Clères France 50 H3
Clerf Lux. *see* Clervaux
Clérey Canada 173 O2
Clerke Reef *reef* Australia 150 B3
Clermont Australia 149 E4
Clermont France 51 I3
Clermont U.S.A. 175 D6
Clermont-en-Argonne France 51 L3
Clermont-Ferrand France 51 J7
Clermont-l'Hérault France 51 J9
Clervaux Lux. 51 M2
also known as Clerf
Cles Italy 56 D2
Cleve Australia 146 C3
Cleveland *r.* Canada 167 O1
Cleveland *GA* U.S.A. 174 D5
Cleveland *MS* U.S.A. 175 B5
Cleveland *OH* U.S.A. 176 D4
Cleveland *TN* U.S.A. 174 C5
Cleveland *TX* U.S.A. 179 D6
Cleveland *UT* U.S.A. 183 N2
Cleveland *VA* U.S.A. 176 C9
Cleveland *WI* U.S.A. 172 F7
Cleveland, Cape Australia 149 E3
Cleveland, Mount U.S.A. 180 D2
Cleveland Bay Australia 149 E3
Cleveland Hills U.K. 47 K9
Clevelândia do Norte Brazil 199 I4
Cleveland Peninsula U.S.A. 166 C4
Cleves Germany *see* Kleve
Clew Bay Ireland 47 C10
Clewiston U.S.A. 175 D7
Clifden Ireland 47 B10
Cliffdale *r.* Australia 148 C3
Clifford S. Africa 133 L8
Clifftop U.S.A. 176 E7
Clifton Australia 147 F1
Clifton *AZ* U.S.A. 183 O8
Clifton *IL* U.S.A. 172 F10
Clifton Beach Australia 149 E3
Clifton Forge U.S.A. 176 F8
Clifton Hills Australia 146 C1
Clifton Park U.S.A. 177 L3
Climax Canada 167 I5
Climax U.S.A. 172 H8
Clinch *r.* U.S.A. 176 B9
Clinchco U.S.A. 176 C8
Clinch Mountain *mts* U.S.A. 176 C9
Clinchport U.S.A. 176 C9
Cline River Canada 167 G4
Clinton Canada 168 D5
Clinton N.Z. 153 D14
Clinton *AR* U.S.A. 179 D5
Clinton *IA* U.S.A. 174 B3
Clinton *KY* U.S.A. 174 B4
Clinton *LA* U.S.A. 175 B6
Clinton *ME* U.S.A. 177 P1
Clinton *MI* U.S.A. 173 J8
Clinton *MO* U.S.A. 178 D4
Clinton *MS* U.S.A. 175 B5
Clinton *NC* U.S.A. 174 E5
Clinton *NY* U.S.A. 177 J2
Clinton *OK* U.S.A. 179 C5
Clinton *TN* U.S.A. 176 A9
Clinton-Colden Lake Canada 167 J1
Clinton Creek Canada 166 A1
Clintonville *WI* U.S.A. 172 E6
Clintonville *WV* U.S.A. 176 E8
Clintwood U.S.A. 176 C8
Clio U.S.A. 173 J7
►Clipperton, Île *terr.* N. Pacific Ocean 221 L5
French Overseas Territory. Most easterly point of Oceania. English form Clipperton Island.
►►134–135 Oceania Landscapes
►►158–159 North America Countries
Clipperton Island *terr.* N. Pacific Ocean *see* Clipperton, Île
Clisham *hill* U.K. 46 F6
Clisson France 50 E5
Clitheroe U.K. 47 J10
Clive N.Z. 152 K7
Clive Lake Canada 167 G2
Cliza Bol. 200 D4
Cloates, Point Australia 150 A4
Clocolan S. Africa 133 L5
Clonagh Australia 149 D4
Clonakilty Ireland 47 D12
Cloncurry Australia 149 D4
Cloncurry *r.* Australia 149 D3
Clones Ireland 47 E9
Clonmel Ireland 47 E11
also spelt Cluain Meala
Cloppenburg Germany 48 F3
Cloquet U.S.A. 174 A2
Cloquet *r.* U.S.A. 174 A2
Clorinda Arg. 204 F2
Cloud Bay Canada 172 D2
Cloud Peak U.S.A. 180 F3
Cloudy Bay N.Z. 152 I9
Clova Canada 168 F3
Clover U.S.A. 183 L1
Cloverdale U.S.A. 182 A3
Clovis *CA* U.S.A. 182 E5
Clovis *NM* U.S.A. 179 B5
Cloyes-sur-le-Loir France 50 H5
Cloyne Canada 173 P6
Cluain Meala Ireland *see* Clonmel
Cluanie, Loch *l.* U.K. 46 G6
Cluff Lake Mine Canada 167 I3
Cluj-Napoca Romania 58 E2
also known as Kolozsvár
Cluny Australia 148 C5
Cluny France 51 K6
Cluses France 51 M6
Cluster Springs U.S.A. 176 G9
Clutha *r.* N.Z. 153 D14
Clut Lake Canada 167 G1
Clutterbuck Hills Australia 151 D5
Clwydian Range *hills* U.K. 47 I10
Clyde Canada 167 H4
Clyde *r.* U.K. 46 H8
Clyde *NY* U.S.A. 177 I2
Clyde *OH* U.S.A. 176 C4
Clyde, Firth of *est.* U.K. 46 H8
Clydebank U.K. 46 H8
Clyde River Canada 165 M2
also known as Kangiqtugaapik
Clydevale N.Z. 153 D14
Clyman U.S.A. 172 E7
Clymer U.S.A. 176 F5
Cnossus *tourist site* Greece *see* Knossos
Côa *r.* Port. 54 D3
UNESCO World Heritage Site
Coachella U.S.A. 183 H8
Coachella Canal U.S.A. 183 I9
Coahuayutla de Guerrero Mex. 185 E5
Coahuila *state* Mex. 185 E3
Coal *r.* Canada 166 E3
Coal City U.S.A. 172 E9
Coaldale Canada 167 H5
Coalgate U.S.A. 179 C5
Coal Grove U.S.A. 176 C7
Coal Harbour Canada 166 E5
Coalinga U.S.A. 182 D5
Coalport U.S.A. 176 G5
Coal River Canada 166 E3
Coal Valley *valley* U.S.A. 183 I4
Coalville U.S.A. 183 M1
Coamo Puerto Rico 187 G3
Coaraci Brazil 207 N1
Coari Brazil 199 F6
Coari *r.* Brazil 199 F6
Coari, Lago *l.* Brazil 199 F6
Coarsegold U.S.A. 182 E4
Coast *prov.* Kenya 128 D5
Coast *admin. reg.* Tanz. *see* Pwani
Coastal Plain U.S.A. 175 A6
Coast Mountains Canada 166 E4
Coast Range *hills* Australia 149 F5
Coast Ranges *mts* U.S.A. 182 A1
Coatepec Mex. 185 F5
Coatepeque Guat. 185 H6
Coatesville U.S.A. 177 J6
Coaticook Canada 169 G4
Coats Island Canada 165 K3
Coats Land *reg.* Antarctica 222 V1
Coatzacoalcos Mex. 185 G5
formerly known as Puerto México
Coatzintla Mex. 185 F4
Cobadin Romania 58 J4
Cobalt Canada 173 N3
Cobán Guat. 185 H6
Cobar Australia 147 E2
Cobargo Australia 147 F4
Cobb, Lake *salt flat* Australia 150 D5
Cobden Canada 173 Q5
Cobh Ireland 47 D12
also spelt An Cóbh; *formerly known as* Queenstown
Cobham *r.* Canada 167 M4
Cobija Bol. 200 C2
Cobija Chile 200 C5
Coblenz Germany *see* Koblenz
Cobleskill U.S.A. 177 K3
Cobos Mex. 185 F4
Cobourg Canada 168 E5
Cobourg Peninsula Australia 148 B1
Cobquecura Chile 204 B5
Cobra Australia 150 B5
Cobram Australia 147 E3
Cobres Arg. 200 D5
Cóbuè Moz. 129 B8
Coburg Germany 48 H5
Coburg Island Canada 165 L2
Coca Ecuador 198 B5
also known as El Coca; *short form* Francisco de Orellana
Coca Spain 54 G3
Cocachacra Peru 200 C4
Cocal Brazil 202 D2
Cocalinho Brazil 202 B5
Cocanada India *see* Kakinada
Cocapata Bol. 200 D4
Cocentaina Spain 55 K6
Cochabamba Bol. 200 D4
Cochabamba *dept* Bol. 200 D4
Cochamó Chile 205 B6
Coche, Isla *i.* Venez. 199 F2
Cochem Germany 48 E5
Co Chiên, Sông *r. mouth* Vietnam 79 D6
Cochin India 94 C4
also known as Kochi
Cochin *reg.* Vietnam 79 D6
Cochinos, Bahía de *b.* Cuba *see* Pigs, Bay of
Cochise U.S.A. 183 O9
Cochise Head *mt.* U.S.A. 183 O9
Cochran U.S.A. 175 D5
Cochrane *Alta* Canada 167 H5
Cochrane *Ont.* Canada 168 D3
Cochrane *r.* Canada 167 K3
Cochrane Chile 205 B7
Cochrane, Lago *l.* Arg./Chile 205 B7
Cochranton U.S.A. 176 E4
Cochranville U.S.A. 177 J6
Cockaleechie Australia 146 B3
Cockburn Australia 146 D3
Cockburn Harbour Turks and Caicos Is 187 F2
Cockburn Island Canada 168 D4
Cockburn Town Bahamas 187 E1
Cockburn Town Turks and Caicos Is *see* Grand Turk
Cockermouth U.K. 47 I9
Cocklebiddy Australia 151 D7
Cockscomb *mt.* S. Africa 133 I10
Coclé del Norte Panama 186 C5
Coco *r.* Brazil 202 B4
Coco *r.* Hond./Nicaragua 186 C4
also known as Segovia
Coco, Cayo *i.* Cuba 186 D2
Coco, Isla de *i.* N. Pacific Ocean 221 N5
UNESCO World Heritage Site
Cocobeach Gabon 126 A4
Coco Channel India 95 G3
Coconino Plateau U.S.A. 183 K6
Cocopara National Park Australia 147 E3
Cocorná Col. 198 C3
Cocos Brazil 202 C5
►Cocos Islands *terr.* Indian Ocean 218 N6
Australian External Territory. Also known as Keeling Islands.
►►64–65 Asia Countries
Cocula Mex. 184 E4
Cod, Cape U.S.A. 177 O4
Codăeşti Romania 58 I2
Codajás Brazil 199 F5
Codera, Cabo *c.* Venez. 199 E2
Coderre Canada 167 J5
Codigoro Italy 56 E4
Cod Island Canada 169 I1
Codlea Romania 58 G3
Codó Brazil 202 D3
Codogno Italy 56 B3
Codrington Antigua and Barbuda 187 H3
Codrington, Mount Antarctica 223 D2
Codroipo Italy 56 E3
Codru Moldova 58 J2
Cody U.S.A. 180 E3
Coeburn U.S.A. 176 C9
Coega S. Africa 133 J10
Coelho Neto Brazil 202 D3
Coen Australia 149 D2
Coen *r.* Australia 149 D2
Coerney S. Africa 133 J10
Coeroeni *r.* Suriname 199 G4
Coesfeld Germany 48 E4
Coëtivy *i.* Seychelles 129 [inset]
Coetzeesberg *mts* S. Africa 133 I9
Coetzersdam S. Africa 133 I3
Coeur d'Alene U.S.A. 180 C3
Coeur d'Alene *r.* U.S.A. 180 C3
Coeur d'Alene Indian Reservation *res.* U.S.A. 180 C3
Coeur d'Alene Lake U.S.A. 180 C3
Coffee Bay S. Africa 133 N8
Coffee Creek Canada 166 B2
Coffeyville U.S.A. 178 D4
Coffin Bay Australia 146 B3
Coffin Bay *b.* Australia 146 B3
Coffin Bay National Park Australia 146 B3
Coffin Bay Peninsula Australia 146 B3
Coffs Harbour Australia 147 G2
Cofimvaba S. Africa 133 L9
formerly known as St Mark's
Cofre de Perote, Parque Nacional *nat. park* Mex. 185 F5
Cogâlniceanu *airport* Romania *see* Kogălniceanu
Cogealac Romania 58 J4
Coggon U.S.A. 172 B8
Coghinas *r. Sardinia* Italy 57 A8
Coghlan S. Africa 133 M8
Coghlan, Mount *hill* Australia 150 D3
Cognac France 50 F7
Cogo Equat. Guinea 125 H6
Cogolin France 51 M9
Coguno Moz. 131 G5
Čohkarášša *mt.* Norway 44 N1
Čohkkiras Sweden *see* Jukkasjärvi
Cohocton U.S.A. 177 H3
Cohoes U.S.A. 177 L3
Cohuna Australia 147 E3
Coiba, Isla de *i.* Panama 186 C6
Coihaique Chile 205 B7
Coihaique Alto Chile 205 C7
Coimbatore India 94 C4
Coimbra Port. 54 C4
Coimbra *admin. dist.* Port. 54 C4
Coín Spain 54 G8
Coipasa, Salar de *salt flat* Bol. 200 C4
Coire Switz. *see* Chur
Cojasca Romania 58 G4
Cojata Peru 200 C3
Cojedes *state* Venez. 198 D2
Cojoro Venez. 187 F5
Cojudo Blanco, Cerro *mt.* Arg. 205 C7
Colac Australia 147 D4
Colac N.Z. 153 B14
Colair Lake India *see* Kolleru Lake
Çolaklı Turkey 108 C1
Colares Brazil 202 B2
Colatina Brazil 203 D6
Colborne Canada 173 P7
Colby *KS* U.S.A. 178 B4
Colby *WI* U.S.A. 172 C6
Colca *r.* Peru 200 B3
Colceag Romania 58 H4
Colchester S. Africa 133 J10
Colchester U.K. 47 M12
historically known as Camulodunum
Colchester U.S.A. 177 M4
Cold Bay U.S.A. 164 C4
also known as Fort Randall
Cold Lake Canada 167 I4
Cold Lake *l.* Canada 167 I4
Coldspring U.S.A. 179 D6
Cold Springs U.S.A. 182 G2
Coldstream Canada 166 G5
Coldstream N.Z. 153 F12
Coldstream U.K. 46 J8
Coldwater Canada 173 N6
Coldwater *KS* U.S.A. 178 C4
Coldwater *MI* U.S.A. 173 I9
Coldwater Creek *r.* U.S.A. 179 B4
Coldwell Canada 172 G2
Colebrook U.S.A. 177 N1
Coleford S. Africa 133 N6
Coleman *r.* Australia 149 D2
Coleman *MI* U.S.A. 173 I7
Coleman *TX* U.S.A. 179 C6
Coleman *WI* U.S.A. 172 E5
Çölemerik Turkey *see* Hakkâri
Colenso S. Africa 133 N5
Colentina *r.* Romania 58 G4
Cole Peninsula Antarctica 222 T2
Coleraine Australia 146 D4
Coleraine U.K. 47 F8
Coleroon *r.* India 94 C4
Coles, Punta de *pt* Peru 200 C4
Coles Bay Australia 147 F5
Colesberg S. Africa 133 J7
Colesburg U.S.A. 172 B8
Coleville U.S.A. 182 E3
Colfax *CA* U.S.A. 182 D2
Colfax *LA* U.S.A. 179 D6
Colfax *WA* U.S.A. 180 C3
Colfax *WI* U.S.A. 172 B6
Colhué Huapí, Lago *l.* Arg. 205 C7
Colibaşi Romania 58 F4
Colico Italy 56 B2
Coligny S. Africa 133 K3
Colima Mex. 184 E5
Colima *state* Mex. 184 E5
Colima, Nevado de *vol.* Mex. 184 E4
Colina Brazil 206 E7
Colinas Brazil 202 C3
Colíseu *r.* Brazil 202 A5
Coll *i.* U.K. 46 F7
Collado Bajo *mt.* Spain 55 J4
Collado Villalba Spain 54 H4
Collahuasi Chile 200 C5
Collalto *mt.* Austria/Italy 48 J9
also known as Hochgall
Collarenebri Australia 147 F2
Collecchio Italy 56 C4
Colle di Val d'Elsa Italy 56 D5
College Corner U.S.A. 176 A6
College Hill U.S.A. 176 A6
College Park U.S.A. 175 C5
College Station U.S.A. 179 C6
Collerina Australia 147 E2
Collesalvetti Italy 56 C5
Collie Australia 151 B7
Collier Bay Australia 150 D3
Collier Range *hills* Australia 151 B5
Collier Range National Park Australia 151 B5
Collierville U.S.A. 174 B5
Collingwood Canada 168 D4
Collingwood N.Z. 152 G8
Collins U.S.A. 175 B6
Collins Glacier Antarctica 223 E2
Collins Lake U.S.A. 182 C2
Collinson Peninsula Canada 165 I2
Collinsville Australia 149 E4
Collinsville *OK* U.S.A. 179 D4
Collinsville *VA* U.S.A. 176 F9
Collipulli Chile 204 B5
Collmberg *hill* Germany 49 K4
Collooney Ireland 47 D9
Colmar France 51 N4
Colmena Arg. 204 E3
Colmenar de Oreja Spain 55 H4
Colmenar Viejo Spain 54 H4
Colne U.K. 47 J10
Colo *r.* Australia 147 F3
Cologne Germany 48 D5
also spelt Köln; *historically known as* Colonia Agrippina
UNESCO World Heritage Site
Coloma *MI* U.S.A. 172 G8
Coloma *WI* U.S.A. 172 D6
Colomb-Béchar Alg. *see* Béchar
Colômbia Brazil 206 E7
Colombia Col. 198 C4
Colombia Mex. 185 F3
►Colombia *country* S. America 198 C4
2nd most populous and 4th largest country in South America.
►►192–193 South America Countries
►Colombo Sri Lanka 94 C5
Former capital of Sri Lanka.
Colombourg Canada 173 N2
Colomiers France 50 H9
Colón *Buenos Aires* Arg. 204 E4
Colón *Entre Ríos* Arg. 204 F4
Colón Cuba 186 C2
Colón Panama 186 D5
Colon U.S.A. 172 H9
Colón, Archipiélago de *is* Pacific Ocean *see* Galapagos Islands
Colón, Isla de *i.* Panama 186 C5
Colona Australia 146 B2
Colonelganj India 97 D4
Colonel Hill Bahamas 187 E2
Colonet, Cabo *c.* Mex. 184 A2
Colonia Arg. 204 E2
Colônia *r.* Brazil 207 N1
Colonia Micronesia 73 I5
Colonia Agrippina Germany *see* Cologne
Colonia del Sacramento Uruguay 204 F4
UNESCO World Heritage Site
Colonia Dora Arg. 204 E3
Colonia Emilio Mitre Arg. 204 D5
Colonia Julia Fenestris Italy *see* Fano
Colonia Las Heras Arg. 205 C7
Colonial Heights U.S.A. 176 H8
Colonia Suiza Uruguay 204 F4
Colonna, Capo *c.* Italy 57 J9
Colonsay *i.* U.K. 46 F7
Colorado *r. La Rioja* Arg. 204 D3
Colorado *r. San Juan* Arg. 204 C3
Colorado *r.* Arg. 204 E5
Colorado Brazil 206 B9
Colorado *r.* Mex./U.S.A. 184 B2
Colorado *r.* U.S.A. 179 C6
Colorado *state* U.S.A. 183 P2
Colorado City *AZ* U.S.A. 183 K5
Colorado City *TX* U.S.A. 179 B5
Colorado Desert U.S.A. 183 H8
Colorado National Monument *nat. park* U.S.A. 183 P2
Colorado Plateau U.S.A. 183 O4
Colorado River Aqueduct *canal* U.S.A. 183 J7
Colorado River Indian Reservation *res.* U.S.A. 183 J8
Colorados, Cerro *mt.* Arg. 204 C2
Colorado Springs U.S.A. 180 F5
Colorno Italy 56 C4
Colossae Turkey *see* Honaz
Colotlán Mex. 185 E4
Colquechaca Bol. 200 D4
Colquiri Bol. 200 D4
Colquitt U.S.A. 175 C6
Colson U.S.A. 176 C8
Colstrip U.S.A. 180 F3
Colton *CA* U.S.A. 183 G7
Colton *NY* U.S.A. 177 K1
Colton *UT* U.S.A. 183 M2
Columbia *KY* U.S.A. 174 C4
Columbia *LA* U.S.A. 179 D5
Columbia *MD* U.S.A. 177 I6
Columbia *MO* U.S.A. 178 D4
Columbia *MS* U.S.A. 175 B6
Columbia *NC* U.S.A. 174 E5
Columbia *NJ* U.S.A. 177 J5
Columbia *PA* U.S.A. 177 I5
►Columbia *SC* U.S.A. 175 D5
State capital of South Carolina.
Columbia *TN* U.S.A. 174 C5
Columbia *r.* U.S.A. 180 B3
Columbia, Cape Canada 165 L1
Columbia, Mount Canada 167 G4
Columbia, Sierra *mts* Mex. 184 B2
Columbia City U.S.A. 174 C3
Columbia Falls *ME* U.S.A. 177 R1
Columbia Falls *MT* U.S.A. 180 D2
Columbia Mountains Canada 166 F4
Columbia Plateau U.S.A. 180 C3
Columbine, Cape S. Africa 132 B9
Columbretes, Islas *is* Spain 55 L5
Columbus *GA* U.S.A. 175 C5
Columbus *IN* U.S.A. 174 C4
Columbus *KS* U.S.A. 178 D4
Columbus *MS* U.S.A. 175 B5
Columbus *MT* U.S.A. 180 E3
Columbus *NC* U.S.A. 174 D5
Columbus *NE* U.S.A. 178 C3
►Columbus *OH* U.S.A. 176 B6
State capital of Ohio.
Columbus *PA* U.S.A. 176 F4
Columbus *TX* U.S.A. 179 C6
Columbus *WI* U.S.A. 172 D7
Columbus Grove U.S.A. 176 A5
Columbus Junction U.S.A. 172 B9
Columbus Salt Marsh U.S.A. 182 F3
Coluna Brazil 207 K5
Colunga Spain 54 F1
Colusa U.S.A. 182 B2
Colville N.Z. 152 J4
Colville U.S.A. 180 C2
Colville *r.* U.S.A. 164 D2
Colville, Cape N.Z. 152 J4
Colville Channel N.Z. 152 J4
Colville Indian Reservation *res.* U.S.A. 180 C2
Colville Lake Canada 166 E1
Colwyn Bay U.K. 47 I10
also known as Bae Colwyn
Comacchio Italy 56 E4
Comacchio, Valli di *lag.* Italy 56 E4
Comai China 89 E6
also known as Damxoi
Comalcalco Mex. 185 G5
Comallo Arg. 204 C6
Comana Romania 58 H4
Comanche U.S.A. 179 C6
Comandante Ferraz *research station* Antarctica 222 U2
Comandante Fontana Arg. 204 F2
Comandante Luis Piedra Buena Arg. 205 C8
Comandante Salas Arg. 204 C4
Comanegra, Puig de *mt.* Spain 55 N2
Comăneşti Romania 58 H2
Comarnic Romania 58 G3
Comayagua Hond. 186 B4
Combahee *r.* U.S.A. 175 D5
Combarbalá Chile 204 C3
Comber U.K. 47 G9
Combermere Canada 173 P5
Combermere Bay Myanmar 78 A4
Combol *i.* Indon. 76 C2
Combourg France 50 E4
Comendador Gomes Brazil 206 D6
Comercinho Brazil 207 L3
Comet Australia 149 F4
Comet *r.* Australia 149 F4
Comfort *TX* U.S.A. 179 C6
Comfort *WV* U.S.A. 176 D7
Comilla Bangl. 97 F5
Comino *i.* Malta *see* Kemmuna
Comino, Capo *c. Sardinia* Italy 57 B8

Dame Marie Haiti 187 E3
Damghan Iran 100 C2
Damietta Egypt see Dumyât
Daming China 85 G4
Daming Shan mt. China 87 D4
Damjong China 97 G2
Damlasu Turkey 109 K1
Dammai i. Phil. 74 B5
Dammam Saudi Arabia 105 E2
also spelt Ad Dammām
Dammastock mt. Switz. 51 O6
Damme Germany 48 F3
Damoh India 96 C5
Damongo Ghana 125 E4
Damour Lebanon 108 G4
Dampelas, Tanjung pt Indon. 75 A2
Dampier Australia 150 B4
Dampier Archipelago is Australia 150 B4
Dampier Island P.N.G. see Karkar Island
Dampier Land reg. Australia 150 C3
Dampierre-sur-Salon France 51 L5
Dampier Strait P.N.G. 145 D2
Dampir, Selat sea chan. Indon. 73 H7
Dampit Indon. 77 F5
Damqoq Zangbo r. China see Maquan He
Dam Qu r. China 97 G2
Dâmrei, Chuŏr Phnum mts Cambodia 79 D6
Damroh India 97 G3
Damxoi China see Comai
Damxung China 89 E6
also known as Gongtang
Dan r. U.S.A. 176 G9
Dana i. Indon. 75 B5
Dana Nepal 97 D3
Dana, Mount U.S.A. 182 E4
Danakil reg. Eritrea/Eth. see Denakil
Danané Côte d'Ivoire 124 C5
Đa Nẵng Vietnam 78 E4
formerly known as Tourane
Đa Nẵng, Vung b. Vietnam 78 E4
Dananhu China 84 B3
Danao Phil. 74 C4
Danata Turkm. 102 C5
Danba China 86 B2
also known as Rongzhag or Zhanggu
Danbury CT U.S.A. 177 L4
Danbury NC U.S.A. 176 E9
Danbury NH U.S.A. 177 N2
Danbury WI U.S.A. 172 A4
Danby U.S.A. 177 M2
Danby Lake U.S.A. 183 I7
Dancheng Henan China 87 E1
Dancheng Zhejiang China see Xiangshan
Dande r. Angola 127 B7
Dande Eth. 128 C3
Dandeldhura Nepal 96 D3
Dandeli India 94 B3
Dando Angola 127 C7
Dandong China 83 B4
formerly known as Andong
Dandridge U.S.A. 174 D4
Danė r. Lith. 42 C6
Daneborg Greenland 165 Q2
Daneți Romania 58 F5
Dänew Turkm. see Galkynyş
Danfeng Shaanxi China 87 D1
also known as Longjuzhai
Danfeng Yunnan China see Shizong
Dâng, Đa r. Vietnam 79 D6
Dangan Liedao i. China 87 E4
Dangara Tajik. see Danghara
Dangbizhen Rus. Fed. 82 C3
Dangchang China 86 C1
Dangchengwan China see Subei
Dange Angola 127 B6
formerly known as Quitexe
Danger Islands atoll Cook Is see Pukapuka
Danger Point S. Africa 132 D11
Dangé-St-Romain France 50 G6
Danggali Conservation Park nature res. Australia 146 D3
Danghara Tajik. 101 G2
also spelt Dangara
Danghe Nanshan mts China 84 B4
Dangila Eth. 128 C2
Dangjin Shankou pass China 84 B4
Dangla Shan mts China see Tanggula Shan
Dan Gorayo Somalia 128 F2
Dangori India 97 G4
Dangqên China 89 E6
Dangriga Belize 185 H5
formerly known as Stann Creek
Dangshan China 87 F1
Dangtu China 87 F2
Dan-Gulbi Nigeria 125 G4
Dangur Eth. 128 B2
Dangur mts Eth. 128 B2
Dangyang China 87 D2
Daniel's Harbour Canada 169 J3
Daniëlskuil S. Africa 132 H5
Danielson U.S.A. 177 N4
Danielsrus S. Africa 133 M4
Danielsville U.S.A. 175 D5
Danilkovo Rus. Fed. 43 S2
Danilov Rus. Fed. 43 V3
Danilovgrad Crna Gora Serb. and Mont. 58 A6
Danilovka Kazakh. 103 G1
Danilovka Rus. Fed. 41 H6
Danilovskaya Vozvyshennost' hills Rus. Fed. 40 F4
Daning China 85 F4
Dänizkänarı Azer. 107 G2
Danjiang China see Leishan
Danjiangkou China 87 D1
formerly known as Junxian
Danjiangkou Shuiku resr China 87 D1
Danjo-guntō is Japan 91 A8
Ḑank Oman 105 G3
Dankov Rus. Fed. 43 U8
Dankova, Pik mt. Kyrg. 103 I4
Danlí Hond. 186 B4
Danling China 86 B2
Danmark Fjord inlet Greenland 165 Q1
English form Denmark Fjord
Dannebrog Ø i. Greenland see Qillak
Dannemora U.S.A. 177 L1
Dannenberg (Elbe) Germany 48 I2
Dannet well Niger 125 G2
Dannevirke N.Z. 152 K8
Dannhauser S. Africa 133 O5
Dano Burkina 124 E4
Dan Sai Thai. 78 C4
Danshui Taiwan see Tanshui
Dansville U.S.A. 176 H3
Danta Gujarat India 96 B4
Danta Rajasthan India 89 A7
Dantewara India 94 D2
Dantu China 87 F1
also known as Zhenjiang

►Danube r. Europe 58 J3
2nd longest river in Europe. Also spelt Donau (Austria/Germany) or Duna (Hungary) or Dunaj (Slovakia) or Dunărea (Romania) or Dunav (Bulgaria/Croatia/Serbia and Montenegro) or Dunay (Ukraine).
►►28–29 Europe Landscapes

Danube Delta Romania 58 K3
also known as Dunării, Delta
UNESCO World Heritage Site
Danubyu Myanmar 78 A4
Danumparai Indon. 77 F2
Danum Valley Conservation Area nature res. Sabah Malaysia 77 G1
Danville AR U.S.A. 179 D5
Danville IL U.S.A. 174 C3
Danville IN U.S.A. 174 C4
Danville KY U.S.A. 176 A8
Danville OH U.S.A. 176 C5
Danville VA U.S.A. 176 F9
Danville VT U.S.A. 177 M1
Danxian China see Danzhou
Danyang China 87 F2
Danzhai China 87 C3
also known as Longquan
Danzhou Guangxi China 87 D3
Danzhou Hainan China 87 D5
also known as Nada; formerly known as Danxian
Danzhou Shaanxi China see Yichuan
Danzig Poland see Gdańsk
Danzig, Gulf of Poland/Rus. Fed. see Gdańsk, Gulf of
Dao Phil. 74 B4
Dão r. Port. 54 C4
Daocheng China 86 B2
also known as Dabba or Jinzhu
Daojiang China see Daoxian
Daokou China see Huaxian
Daoshiping China 87 D2
Daotanghe China 84 D4
Dao Tay Sa is S. China Sea see Paracel Islands
Dao Timmi Niger 125 I1
Daoud Alg. see Aïn Beïda
Daoudi well Mauritania 124 D3
Daoukro Côte d'Ivoire 124 E5
Daoxian China 87 D3
also known as Daojiang
Daozhen China 87 C2
also known as Yuxi
Dapa Phil. 74 C4
Dapaong Togo 125 F4
Dapchi Nigeria 125 H3
Dapeng Wan b. Hong Kong China see Mirs Bay
Daphabum mt. India 97 H4
Daphnae tourist site Egypt 108 D7
also known as Kawm Dafanah
Daphne U.S.A. 175 C6
Daphni tourist site Greece 59 E11
UNESCO World Heritage Site
Dapiak, Mount Phil. 74 B4
Dapingdi China see Jiankang
Dapitan Phil. 74 B4
Da Qaidam Zhen China 84 B4
Daqiao China 86 B3
Daqing China 82 B3
also known as Anda; formerly known as Sartu
Daqing Shan mts China 85 F3
Daqin Tal China 85 I3
also known as Naiman Qi
Daqiu China 87 F3
Daqq-e Patargān salt flat Iran 101 E3
Daqq-e Tundi, Dasht-e imp. l. Afgh. 101 E3
Daquan China 84 B3
Daquanwan China 84 B3
Dāqūq Iraq 107 F4
Daqu Shan i. China 87 G2
Dara Senegal 124 B3
formerly spelt Dahra
Dar'ā Syria 108 H5
Dar'ā governorate Syria 108 H5
Daraá r. Brazil 199 E5
Dārāb Iran 100 C4
Daraga Phil. 74 B3
Dārah, Jabal mt. Egypt 106 C6
Darahanava Belarus 43 J8
Daraim Afgh. 96 A1
Daraina Madag. 131 [inset] K2
Daraj Libya 120 A2
Daram i. Phil. 74 C4
Dārān Iran 100 B3
Darasun Rus. Fed. 85 G1
Darasuram India 94 C4
UNESCO World Heritage Site
Daraut-Korgon Kyrg. 103 H5
also spelt Daraut-Kurgan
Daraut-Kurgan Kyrg. see Daraut-Korgon
Đaravica mt. Serb. and Mont. 58 B6
Darazo Nigeria 125 H4
Darb Saudi Arabia 104 C4
Darband Iran 100 D4
Darband Uzbek. 103 F5
formerly spelt Derbent
Darband, Kūh-e mt. Iran 100 D4
Darb-e Behesht Iran 100 D4
Darbėnai Lith. 42 C5
Dar Ben Karricha el Behri Morocco 54 F9
Darbhanga India 97 E4
Darcang China 86 A1
Dar Chabanne Tunisia 57 C12
Dar Chaoui Morocco 54 F9
D'Arcy Canada 166 F5
Darda Croatia 56 K3
Dardanelle AR U.S.A. 179 D5
Dardanelle CA U.S.A. 182 E3
Dardanelle, Lake U.S.A. 179 D5
Dardanelles strait Turkey 106 A2
also known as Çanakkale Boğazı; historically known as Hellespont
Dardo China see Kangding
Dar el Beida Morocco see Casablanca
Darende Turkey 107 D3

►Dar es Salaam Tanz. 129 C6
Former capital of Tanzania.

Dārestān Iran 100 C4
Darfield N.Z. 153 G11
Darfo Boario Terme Italy 56 C3
►Darfur reg. Sudan 120 E6
►►116–117 Africa Conflicts
Dargai Pak. 101 G3
Darganata Turkm. 103 E4
Dargaville N.Z. 152 H3
Dargin, Jezioro l. Poland 49 S1
Dargo Australia 147 E4
Darhan Mongolia 85 E1
Darhan Muminggan Lianheqi China see Bailingmiao
Darıca Turkey 58 K8
Darıcı Turkey 59 J9
Darien CT U.S.A. 177 L4
Darien GA U.S.A. 175 D6
Darién, Golfo del g. Col. 198 B2
Darién, Parque Nacional de nat. park Panama 186 D6
UNESCO World Heritage Site
Darién, Serranía del mts Panama 186 D5
Dar'inskiy Kazakh. 103 H2
also known as Darīya
Dar'inskoye Kazakh. 102 B2
Darío Nicaragua 186 B4
Darīya Kazakh. see Dar'inskiy
Darīz Oman 105 G3
Darjeeling India 97 F4
also spelt Darjiling
UNESCO World Heritage Site
Darjiling India see Darjeeling
Dârjiu Romania 58 G2
UNESCO World Heritage Site
Dārkhovīn Iran 100 B4
Darlag China 86 A1
also known as Gyümai

►Darling r. Australia 147 D3
2nd longest river in Oceania. Part of the longest (Murray-Darling).
►►134–135 Oceania Landscapes

Darling S. Africa 132 C10
Darling Downs hills Australia 147 F1
Darling Range hills Australia 151 A7
Darlington U.K. 47 K9
Darlington SC U.S.A. 175 E5
Darlington WI U.S.A. 172 C8
Darlington Dam resr S. Africa 133 J10
Darlington Point Australia 147 E3
Darlot, Lake salt flat Australia 151 C5
Darłowo Poland 49 N1
Dărmănești Romania 58 H2
Darma Pass China/India 89 C6
Darmaraopet India 94 C2
Darmstadt Germany 48 F6
Darna r. India 94 B1
Darnah Libya 120 D1
also spelt Derna
Darnall S. Africa 133 P6
Darnick Australia 147 D3
Darnley, Cape Antarctica 223 E2
Darnley Bay Canada 164 G3
Daroca Spain 55 J3
Darovskoy Rus. Fed. 40 H4
Dar Pahn Iran 100 D5
Darr watercourse Australia 149 D4
Darregueira Arg. 204 E5
Darreh Bīd Iran 100 D3
Darreh Gaz Iran 101 D2
also known as Moḩammadābād
Darreh Gozaru r. Iran see Gīzeh Rūd
Darreh-ye Bāhābād Iran 100 C4
Darreh-ye Shahr Iran 100 A3
Darreh-ye Shekārī r. Afgh. 101 G3
Darreh-ye Shekārī r. Afgh. 101 G3
Darro watercourse Eth. 128 D3
Darsa i. Yemen 105 F5
Darsi India 94 C3
Darß pen. Germany 49 J1
Darßer Ort c. Germany 49 J1
Darta Turkm. see Tarta
Dār Ta'izzah Syria 109 H1
Dartang China see Baqên
Dartford U.K. 47 M12
Dartmoor Australia 146 D4
Dartmoor hills U.K. 47 H13
Dartmoor National Park U.K. 47 I13
Dartmouth Canada 169 I4
Dartmouth U.K. 47 I13
Dartmouth, Lake salt flat Australia 149 E5
Dartmouth Reservoir Australia 147 E4
Daru P.N.G. 73 J8
Daru waterhole Sudan 121 G5
Daruba Indon. 75 D2
Daruvar Croatia 56 J3
Darvaza Turkm. see Derweze
Darvi Govĭ-Altay Mongolia 84 B2
Darvi Hovd Mongolia see Bulgan
Darvinskiy Gosudarstvennyy Zapovednik nature res. Rus. Fed. 43 S3
Darvoz, Qatorkŭhi mts Tajik. 101 G2
Darwendale Zimbabwe 131 F3
Darwha India 94 C1

►Darwin Australia 148 A2
Capital of Northern Territory. Historically known as Palmerston.

Darwin Falkland Is 205 F8
Darwin, Canal sea chan. Chile 205 B7
Darwin, Monte mt. Chile 205 C9
Darya Khan Pak. 101 G4
Dar'yalyktakyr, Ravnina plain Kazakh. 103 F3
Daryānah Libya 120 D1
Dar"yoi Amu r. Asia see Amudar'ya
Dar"yoi Sir r. Asia see Syrdar'ya
Dārzīn Iran 100 D4
Dās i. U.A.E. 105 F2
Dasada India 96 A5
Dasha He r. China 85 G4
Dashbalbar Mongolia 85 G1
Dashhowuz Turkm. see Daşoguz
Dashiqiao China 85 I3
formerly known as Yingkou
Dashitou China 88 E3
Dashizhai China 85 I2
Dashkawka Belarus 43 L8
Dashkesan Azer. see Daşkäsän
Dashkhovuz Oblast admin. div. Turkm. see Dashkhovuzskaya Oblast'
Dashkhovuzskaya Oblast' admin. div. Turkm. 102 D4
English form Dashkhovuz Oblast; formerly known as Tashauzskaya Oblast'
Dashköpri Turkm. see Daşköpri
Dashoguz Turkm. see Daşoguz
Dasht Iran 100 D2
Dasht r. Pak. 101 E5
Dashtak Iran 100 D2
formerly spelt Dashtak Qal'ehsi
Dashtak Qal'ehsi Iran see Dashtak
Dasht-e Bar Iran 100 D4
Dasht-e Palang r. Iran 100 C4
Dashtiari Iran 101 E5
Dashtobod Uzbek. 103 G4
Dashuikeng China 85 E4
Dashuiqiao China 84 C4
Dashuitou China 84 E4
Daska Pak. 101 H3
Daşkäsän Azer. 107 F2
also spelt Dashkesan
Daskop S. Africa 132 G10
Daşköpri Turkm. 103 E5
also spelt Dashköpri
Daşoguz Turkm. 102 D4
also known as Dashoguz; also spelt Dashhowuz; formerly known as Tashauz
Dasongshu China 86 C3
Daspar mt. Pak. 101 H2
Dassa Benin 125 F5
Dassalan i. Phil. 74 B5
Dassen Island S. Africa 132 C10
Dastakān, Ra's-e pt Iran 100 C5
Da Suifen He r. China 82 C4
Dasuya India 96 B3
Dasville S. Africa 133 M3
Datadian Indon. 77 F2
Datça Turkey 106 A3
Date Japan 90 G3
Date Creek watercourse U.S.A. 183 K7
Dateland U.S.A. 183 K9
Datha India 96 B5
Datia India 96 C4
Datian China 87 F3
also known as Junxi
Datian Ding mt. China 87 D4
Datong Fujian China see Tong'an
Datong Heilong. China 82 B3
Datong Qinghai China 84 D4
also known as Qiaotou
Datong Shanxi China 85 G3
UNESCO World Heritage Site
Datong He r. China 84 D4
Datong Shan mts China 84 C4
Datta Rus. Fed. 82 F2
Datu i. Indon. 77 E2
Datu, Tanjung c. Indon./Malaysia 77 E2
Datuk, Tanjung pt Indon. 76 C3
Datu Piang Phil. 74 C5
also known as Dulawan
Daudkandi Bangl. 97 F5
Daud Khel Pak. 101 G3
Daudnagar India 97 E4
Daudzeva Latvia 42 G5
Daugai Lith. 42 F7
Daugailiai Lith. 42 G6
Daugava r. Latvia 42 F4
Daugavpils Latvia 42 H6
also known as Dvinsk; formerly known as Dünaburg
Daugyvenė r. Lith. 42 E5
Daulatabad Afgh. 101 F2
Daulatabad Iran see Malāyer
Daulatpur Bangl. 97 F5
Daule Ecuador 198 B5
Daun Germany 48 D5
Daund India 94 B2
Daung Kyun i. Myanmar 79 B5
also known as Ross Island
Daungyu r. Myanmar 78 A3
Dauphin Canada 167 K5
Dauphiné reg. France 51 L7
Dauphiné, Alpes du mts France 51 L8
Dauphin Island U.S.A. 175 B6
Dauphin Lake Canada 167 L5
Daura Nigeria 125 H3
Daurie Creek r. Australia 151 A5
Dauriya Rus. Fed. 85 H1
Daurskiy Khrebet mts Rus. Fed. 85 F1
Dausa India 96 C4
Dâu Tiêng, Hô resr Vietnam 79 D6
Däväçi Azer. 107 G2
also spelt Divichi
Davangere India 94 B3
Davao Phil. 74 C5
Davao Gulf Phil. 74 C5
Dāvarān Iran 100 D4
Dāvar Panāh Iran 101 E5
also known as Dizak
Davel S. Africa 133 N3
Davenport IA U.S.A. 174 B3
Davenport NY U.S.A. 177 K3
Davenport WA U.S.A. 180 C3
Davenport Downs Australia 149 D5
Davenport Range hills Australia 148 B4
Daveyton S. Africa 133 M3
David Panama 186 C5
David City U.S.A. 178 C3
Davidson Canada 167 J5
Davidson, Mount hill Australia 148 A4
Davidson Lake Canada 167 L4
Davies, Mount Australia 146 A1
Davinópolis Brazil 206 F5
Davis research station Antarctica 223 F2
Davis r. Australia 150 C4
Davis i. Myanmar see Than Kyun
Davis CA U.S.A. 182 C3
Davis WV U.S.A. 176 F6
Davis, Mount hill U.S.A. 176 F6
Davis Bay Antarctica 223 I2
Davis Dam U.S.A. 183 J6
Davis Dam dam U.S.A. 183 J6
Davis Inlet Canada 169 I2
Davison U.S.A. 173 J7
Davis Sea Antarctica 223 G2
Davis Strait Canada/Greenland 165 N3
Davlekanovo Rus. Fed. 40 J5
Davlia Greece 59 D10
also spelt Dhávlia
Davos Switz. 51 P6
Davutlar Turkey 59 I11
Davy U.S.A. 176 D8
Davyd-Haradok Belarus 42 I9
Davydkovo Rus. Fed. see Tolbukhino
Davydovo Rus. Fed. 43 T4
Davy Lake Canada 167 I3
Dawa China 85 I3
Dawa Co l. China 89 D6
Dawāsir reg. Saudi Arabia 104 D3
Dawāsir, Wādī ad watercourse Saudi Arabia 104 D3
Dawa Wenz r. Eth. 128 D3
Dawaxung China 89 D6
Dawê China 86 B2
Dawei Myanmar see Tavoy
Dawei b. Myanmar see Tavoy
Dawen He r. China 85 H5
Dawera i. Indon. 75 D4
Dawhat Bilbul b. Saudi Arabia 105 E2
Dawhinava Belarus 42 I7
Dawna Range mts Myanmar/Thai. 78 B4
Dawqah Oman 105 F4
Dawqah Saudi Arabia 104 C4
Ḑawrān Yemen 104 D5
Dawson r. Australia 149 F4
Dawson Canada 166 B1
Dawson GA U.S.A. 175 C6
Dawson ND U.S.A. 180 H3
Dawson, Isla i. Chile 205 C9
Dawson, Mount Canada 167 G5
Dawson Bay Canada 167 K4
Dawson Creek Canada 166 F4
Dawson Inlet Canada 167 M2
Dawson Range mts Canada 166 A2
Dawsons Landing Canada 166 E5
Dawu Hubei China 87 E2
Dawu Qinghai China see Maqên
Dawu Sichuan China 86 B2
also known as Xianshui
Dawu Taiwan see Tawu
Dawukou China see Shizuishan
Dawu Shan hill China 87 E2
Dawwah Oman 105 G3
Dax France 50 E9
Daxian China see Dazhou
Daxiang Ling mts China 86 B2
Daxihaizi Shuiku l. China 88 D3
Daxin China 87 C4
also known as Taocheng
Daxing Yunnan China see Ninglang
Daxing Yunnan China see Lüchun
Daxue China see Wencheng
Da Xueshan mts China 86 B2
Dayan China see Lijiang
Dayang He r. China 85 I4
Dayangshu China 85 J1
Dayan Nuur l. Mongolia 84 A1
Dayao China 86 B3
also known as Jinbi
Dayao Shan mts China 87 D4
Ḑâyat en Nahârât well Mali 124 E2
Daye China 87 E2
Dayi China 86 B2
also known as Jinyuan
Daying Jiang r. China 86 A3
Dayishan China see Guanyun
Dāykundi Afgh. 101 F3
Dāykundi prov. Afgh. 101 F3
Dayl Oman 105 G2
Daylesford Australia 147 E4
Dayong China see Zhangjiajie
Dayr Abū Sa'īd Jordan 108 G5
Dayr az Zawr Syria 109 L2
also spelt Deir-ez-Zor
Dayr az Zawr governorate Syria 109 L2
Dayr Ḩāfīr Syria 109 I1
Dayrūţ Egypt 121 F3
Daysland Canada 167 H4
Dayton OH U.S.A. 176 A6
Dayton TN U.S.A. 174 C5
Dayton TX U.S.A. 179 D6
Dayton VA U.S.A. 176 G7
Dayton WA U.S.A. 180 C3
Daytona Beach U.S.A. 175 D6
Dayu China 87 E3
also known as Nan'ao
Dayu Indon. 77 F3
Dayu Ling mts China 87 E3
Da Yunhe canal China 87 F1
English form Grand Canal
Dayyīna i. U.A.E. 105 F2
Dazaifu Japan 91 B8
Dazhe China see Pingyuan
Dazhongji China see Dafeng
Dazhou China 87 C2
formerly known as Daxian
Dazhou Dao i. China 87 D5
Dazhu China 87 C2
also known as Zhuyang
Dazu China 86 C2
also known as Longgang
UNESCO World Heritage Site
De Aar S. Africa 132 I7
Dead r. U.S.A. 172 F4
Deadman's Cay Bahamas 187 E2
Dead Mountains U.S.A. 183 J7

►Dead Sea salt l. Asia 108 G6
Lowest point in the world and in Asia. Also known as Lut, Bahrat or HaMelaḥ, Yam.
►►60–61 Asia Landscapes

Deadwood U.S.A. 178 B2
Deakin Australia 151 E6
Deal U.K. 47 N12
Dealesville S. Africa 133 J5
Dean r. Canada 166 E4
De'an China 87 E2
also known as Puting
Dean Channel Canada 166 E4
Deán Funes Arg. 204 D3
Deanuvuotna inlet Norway see Tanafjorden
Dearborn U.S.A. 173 J8
Dease r. B.C. Canada 166 D3
Dease r. N.W.T. Canada 167 G1
Dease Arm b. Canada 166 F1
Dease Lake Canada 166 D3
Dease Lake l. Canada 166 D3
Dease Strait Canada 165 I3
Death Valley U.S.A. 183 H5

►Death Valley depr. U.S.A. 183 G5
Lowest point in the Americas.
►►154–155 North America Landscapes

Death Valley Junction U.S.A. 183 H5
Death Valley National Park U.S.A. 183 G5
Deaver U.S.A. 180 E3
Debagram India 97 F5
Debak Sarawak Malaysia 77 E2
Debao China 86 C4
Debar Macedonia 58 B7
Debark Eth. 128 C1
Debay well Yemen 105 E4
Debden Canada 167 J4
De Beers Pass S. Africa 133 N5
Debert Canada 169 I4
Debesy Rus. Fed. 40 J4
Dębica Poland 49 S5
De Biesbosch, Nationaal Park nat. park Neth. 48 B4
Debila Alg. 123 G2
Debin Rus. Fed. 39 P3
Dęblin Poland 49 S4
Dębno Poland 49 R6
UNESCO World Heritage Site
Dębno Poland 49 L3
Débo, Lac l. Mali 124 D3
Deborah East, Lake salt flat Australia 151 B6
Deborah West, Lake salt flat Australia 151 B6
Deboyne Islands P.N.G. 149 G1
Debre Birhan Eth. 128 C2
Debrecen Hungary 49 S8
Debre Markos Eth. 128 C2
Debre Sīna Eth. 128 C2
Debre Tabor Eth. 128 C2
Debre Werk' Eth. 128 C2
Debre Zeyit Eth. 128 C2
Debrzno Poland 49 O2
Deçan Kosovo, Srbija Serb. and Mont. see Dečani
Dečani Kosovo, Srbija Serb. and Mont. 58 B6
also spelt Deçan
UNESCO World Heritage Site
Decatur AL U.S.A. 174 C5
Decatur GA U.S.A. 175 C5
Decatur IL U.S.A. 174 B4
Decatur IN U.S.A. 176 A5
Decatur MI U.S.A. 172 H8
Decatur MS U.S.A. 175 B5
Decatur TN U.S.A. 174 C5
Decatur TX U.S.A. 179 C5
Decazeville France 51 I8

►Deccan plat. India 94 C2
Plateau making up most of southern and central India.

Deception watercourse Botswana 130 E4
Deception Bay Australia 147 G1
Dechang China 86 B3
also known as Dezhou
Decheng China see Deqing
Děčín Czech Rep. 49 L5
Decize France 51 J6
Decorah U.S.A. 174 B3
Dedap i. Indon. see Penasi, Pulau
Dedaye Myanmar 78 A4
Dedebağı Turkey 59 K11
Dedegöl Dağları mts Turkey 106 B3
Deder Eth. 128 D2
Dedinovo Rus. Fed. 43 U6
Dedo de Deus mt. Brazil 206 F11
Dedop'listsqaro Georgia 107 F2
formerly known as Tsiteli Tskaro
Dédougou Burkina 124 E3
Dedovichi Rus. Fed. 43 K4
Dedurovka Rus. Fed. 102 C2
Dedza Malawi 129 B8
Dedza Mountain Malawi 131 G2
Dee r. England/Wales U.K. 47 I10
Dee r. Scotland U.K. 46 J6
Deeg India 96 C4
Deelfontein S. Africa 132 H7
Deep Bay Hong Kong China 87 [inset]
also known as Shenzhen Wan
Deep Bight inlet Australia 150 D2
Deep Creek Lake U.S.A. 176 F6
Deep Creek Range mts U.S.A. 183 K2
Deep Gap U.S.A. 176 D9
Deep River Canada 168 E4
Deep River U.S.A. 177 M4
Deer Creek r. U.S.A. 182 B2
Deer Creek Reservoir U.S.A. 183 M1
Deeri Somalia 128 E3
Deering, Mount Australia 151 E5
Deer Island Canada 169 H4
Deer Island AK U.S.A. 164 C4
Deer Island ME U.S.A. 177 Q1
Deer Isle U.S.A. 177 Q1
Deer Lake Nfld. and Lab. Canada 169 J3
Deer Lake Ont. Canada 167 M4
Deer Lake l. Canada 167 M4
Deer Lodge U.S.A. 180 D3
Deer Park U.S.A. 180 C3
Deerpass Bay Canada 166 F1
Deesa India see Disa
Defeng China see Liping
Defensores del Chaco, Parque Nacional nat. park Para. 201 E5
Defiance U.S.A. 176 A4
Defiance Plateau U.S.A. 183 O6
Défirou well Niger 125 I1
De Funiak Springs U.S.A. 175 C6
Degana India 96 B4
Degano r. Italy 56 E2
Dêgê China 86 A2
also known as Gengqing
Degebe r. Port. 54 D6
Degeberga Sweden 45 K5
Degeh Bur Eth. 128 D2
Dégelis Canada 169 G4
formerly known as Ste-Rose-du-Dégelé
Degema Nigeria 125 G5
Degerfors Sweden 45 K4
Deggendorf Germany 49 J7
Degh r. Pak. 101 H4
Değirmencik r. Turkey 59 J9
Değirmenlik Cyprus see Kythrea
Degodia reg. Eth. 128 D3
De Grey Australia 150 B4
De Grey r. Australia 150 B4
Degtevo Rus. Fed. 41 G6
Degtyarevka Rus. Fed. 43 N8
Dehaj Iran 100 C4
Dehak Iran 101 E5
Dehalak Deset i. Eritrea 121 I6
Deh Bakrī Iran 100 D4
Deh Barez Iran see Fāryāb
Deh-Dasht Iran 100 B4
Dehdez Iran 100 B4
Dehej India 96 B5
Deh-e Khalīfeh Iran 100 B4
Deh-e Kohneh Iran 100 B4
Dehel Island Eritrea 104 B5
Dehgāh Iran 100 B2
Deh Golān Iran 100 A3
Dehi Afgh. 101 F3
Deh Khvājeh Iran 100 C4
Dehkūyeh Iran 100 C5
Dehlorān Iran 100 A3
Deh Mollā Iran 100 B4
De Hoge Veluwe, Nationaal Park nat. park Neth. 48 C3
De Hoop Nature Reserve S. Africa 132 E11
De Hoop Vlei l. S. Africa 132 E11
Dehqonobod Uzbek. 103 F5
also spelt Dekhkanabad
Dehra Dun India 96 C3
Dehri India 97 E4
Deh Shū Afgh. 101 E4
Dehua China 87 F3
also known as Longxun
Dehui China 82 B3
Deim Zubeir Sudan 126 E3
Deinze Belgium 51 J2
Deïr el Qamar Lebanon 108 G4
Deir-ez-Zor Syria see Dayr az Zawr
Dej Romania 58 E1
Dejë, Mal mt. Albania 58 B7
Dejen Eth. 128 C2
Deji China see Rinbung
Dejiang China 87 D2
also known as Jiangsi
Deka Drum Zimbabwe 131 E3
De Kalb IL U.S.A. 174 B3
De Kalb MS U.S.A. 175 B5
De Kalb TX U.S.A. 179 D5
De Kalb Junction U.S.A. 177 J1
De-Kastri Rus. Fed. 81 O2
Dekemhare Eritrea 121 H6
Dekese Dem. Rep. Congo 126 D5
Dekhkanabad Uzbek. see Dehqonobod
Dékoa Cent. Afr. Rep. 126 C3
Delaki Indon. 75 C5
Delamar Lake U.S.A. 183 J4
Delami Sudan 128 A2
De Land U.S.A. 175 D6
Delano U.S.A. 182 E6
Delano Peak U.S.A. 183 L3

►Delap-Uliga-Djarrit Marshall Is 220 G5
Capital of the Marshall Islands, on Majuro atoll. Also spelt Dalap-Uliga-Darrit or Djarrit-Uliga-Dalap.

Delārām Afgh. 101 E3
Delareyville S. Africa 133 J3
Delaronde Lake Canada 167 J4
Delavan U.S.A. 172 E8
Delaware U.S.A. 176 B5
Delaware r. KS U.S.A. 178 D4
Delaware r. NJ/PA U.S.A. 177 J6
Delaware state U.S.A. 177 J7
Delaware, East Branch r. U.S.A. 177 J4
Delaware, West Branch r. U.S.A. 177 J4
Delaware Bay U.S.A. 177 J6
Delaware City U.S.A. 177 J6
Delaware Water Gap National Recreational Area park U.S.A. 177 K4
Delay r. Canada 169 G1
Delbarton U.S.A. 176 C8
Delbeng Sudan 126 F3
Del Bonita Canada 167 H5
Delburne Canada 167 H4
Delčevo Macedonia 58 D7
Dêlêg China 89 D6
Delegate Australia 147 F4
Delémont Switz. 51 N5
Delevan CA U.S.A. 182 B2
Delevan NY U.S.A. 176 G3
Delfinópolis Brazil 206 G7
Delft Neth. 48 B3
Delft Island Sri Lanka 94 C4
Delfzijl Neth. 48 D2
Delgado, Cabo c. Moz. 129 D7
Delgermörön Mongolia 84 C2
Delger Mörön r. Mongolia 84 D1
Delgo Sudan 121 F4
Delhi Canada 173 M8
Delhi China 84 C4
formerly known as Delingha

►Delhi India 96 C3
3rd most populous city in Asia and 6th in the world.
UNESCO World Heritage Site
►►18–19 World Cities

Delhi admin. div. India 89 B6
Delhi CA U.S.A. 182 D4
Delhi LA U.S.A. 175 B5
Delhi NY U.S.A. 177 K3
Deli i. Indon. 77 D4
Deli r. Turkey 107 E3
Delice Turkey 106 C3
Delice r. Turkey 106 C2
Délices Fr. Guiana 199 H3
Delījān Iran 100 B3
Deliktaş Turkey 59 H10
Déljne Canada 166 F1
formerly known as Fort Franklin
Delingha China see Delhi
Delisle Canada 167 J5
Delitua Indon. 76 B2
Delitzsch Germany 49 J4
Dell Rapids U.S.A. 178 C3
Dellys Alg. 123 F1
Del Mar U.S.A. 183 G9
Delmar DE U.S.A. 177 J7
Delmar IA U.S.A. 172 C8
Delmas S. Africa 133 M3
Delmenhorst Germany 48 F2
Delmont U.S.A. 176 F5
Delmore Downs Australia 148 B4
Delnice Croatia 56 G3
Del Norte U.S.A. 181 F5
De-Longa, Ostrova is Rus. Fed. 39 P2
English form De Long Islands
De Long Islands Rus. Fed. see De-Longa, Ostrova
De Long Mountains U.S.A. 164 C3
De Long Strait Rus. Fed. see Longa, Proliv
Deloraine Australia 147 E5
Deloraine Canada 167 K5
Delphi tourist site Greece 59 D10
UNESCO World Heritage Site
Delphi U.S.A. 174 C3
Delphos U.S.A. 176 A5
Delportshoop S. Africa 133 I5

Delray Beach U.S.A. 175 D7
Del Río Mex. 184 C2
Del Rio U.S.A. 179 B6
Delsbo Sweden 45 L3
Delta state Nigeria 125 G5
Delta CO U.S.A. 181 E5
Delta OH U.S.A. 176 A4
Delta UT U.S.A. 183 L2
Delta Amacuro state Venez. 199 F2
Delta du Saloum, Parc National du nat. park Senegal 124 A3
Delta Junction U.S.A. 164 E3
Delta National Wildlife Refuge nature res. U.S.A. 175 B6
Delta Reservoir U.S.A. 177 J2
Deltona U.S.A. 175 D6
Delungra Australia 147 F2
Delvada India 94 A1
Delvinë Albania 59 B9
Dema r. Rus. Fed. 102 C1
Demak Indon. 77 E4
Demanda, Sierra de la mts Spain 55 H2
Demavend mt. Iran see **Damāvand, Qolleh-ye**
Demba Dem. Rep. Congo 127 D6
Dembava Lith. 42 F6
Dembia Cent. Afr. Rep. 126 E3
Dembī Dolo Eth. 128 B2
Demerara Guyana see **Georgetown**
Demidov Rus. Fed. 43 M6
Deming U.S.A. 181 F6
Demini r. Brazil 199 F5
Demini, Serras do mts Brazil 199 F4
Demirci Turkey 106 B3
Demir Hisar Macedonia 58 C7
Demirköprü Barajı resr Turkey 106 B3
Demirköy Turkey 58 I7
Demirler r. Turkey 59 K10
Demistkraal S. Africa 133 I10
Demmin Germany 49 K2
Democracia Brazil 199 F6
Demopolis U.S.A. 175 C5
Dempo, Gunung vol. Indon. 76 C4
Dempster Highway Canada 166 B1
Dêmqog Jammu and Kashmir 96 C2
Demyakhi Rus. Fed. 43 N6
Dem'yanovo Rus. Fed. 40 H3
Demyansk Rus. Fed. 43 N4
De Naawte S. Africa 132 F7
Denair U.S.A. 182 D4
Denakil reg. Eritrea/Eth. 121 I6
also spelt Danakil
Denali National Park and Preserve U.S.A. 164 D3
formerly known as Mount McKinley National Park
Denan Eth. 128 D3
Denare Beach Canada 167 K4
Denbigh Canada 168 E4
Denbigh U.K. 47 I10
also spelt Dinbych
Den Bosch Neth. see **'s-Hertogenbosch**
Den Burg Neth. 48 B2
Den Chai Thai. 78 C4
Dendang Indon. 77 D3
Dendâra Mauritania 124 D2
Dendermonde Belgium 51 K1
also known as Termonde
Đeneral Janković Kosovo, Srbija Serb. and Mont. 58 C6
also spelt Djeneral Janković
Denetiah Provincial Park Canada 166 E3
Denezhkin Kamen', Gora mt. Rus. Fed. 40 K3
Dengas Niger 125 H3
Denge Nigeria 125 G3
Dengfeng China 87 E1
Dênggar China 89 D6
Dengjiabu China see **Yujiang**
Dêngka China see **Têwo**
Dêngkagoin China see **Têwo**
Dengkou China 85 E3
also known as Bayan Gol
Dêngqên China 97 G3
also known as Gyamotang
Dengta China 87 E4
Denguiro Cent. Afr. Rep. 126 D3
Dengxian China see **Dengzhou**
Dengzhou Henan China 87 E1
formerly known as Dengxian
Dengzhou Shandong China see **Penglai**
Den Haag Neth. see **The Hague**
Denham Australia 151 A5
Denham r. Australia 150 E2
Denham Range mts Australia 149 F4
Denham Sound sea chan. Australia 151 A5
Den Helder Neth. 48 B3
Denholm Canada 167 I4
Denia Spain 55 L6
Denial Bay Australia 146 B3
Deniliquin Australia 147 E3
Deninoo Kue Canada see **Fort Resolution**
Deniskovichi Rus. Fed. 43 M9
Denison IA U.S.A. 178 D3
Denison TX U.S.A. 179 C5
Denison, Cape Antarctica 223 J2
Denison Plains Australia 150 E3
Denisovka Kazakh. 103 E1
formerly known as Ordzhonikidze
Denizli Turkey 106 B3
historically known as Laodicea or Laodicea ad Lycum
Denizli prov. Turkey 59 K11
Denman Australia 147 F3
Denman Glacier Antarctica 223 G2
Denmark Australia 151 B7
►**Denmark** country Europe 45 J5
►►**32–33 Europe** Countries
Denmark U.S.A. 172 F6
Denmark Fjord inlet Greenland see **Danmark Fjord**
Denmark Strait Greenland/Iceland 165 Q3
Dennilton S. Africa 133 N2
Dennis, Lake salt flat Australia 150 E4
Dennison U.S.A. 176 D5
Dennisville U.S.A. 177 K6
Denov Uzbek. 103 F5
also spelt Denow
Denow Uzbek. see **Denov**
Denpasar Indon. 77 F5
Densongi Indon. 75 B3
Denton MD U.S.A. 177 J7
Denton TX U.S.A. 179 C5
D'Entrecasteaux, Point Australia 151 A7
D'Entrecasteaux, Récifs reef New Caledonia 145 F3
D'Entrecasteaux Islands P.N.G. 145 E2
D'Entrecasteaux National Park Australia 151 A7
Dents du Midi mt. Switz. 51 M6

►**Denver** U.S.A. 180 F5
State capital of Colorado.

Denys r. Canada 168 E2
Deo India 97 E4
Deoband India 96 C3
Deobhog India 95 D2
Deogarh Orissa India 97 E5
Deogarh Rajasthan India 96 B4
Deogarh mt. India 97 D5
Deoghar India 97 E4
also spelt Devghar
Deoli India 94 C1
Déols France 50 H6
Deori India 96 C5
Deoria India 97 D4
Deosai, Plains of Jammu and Kashmir 96 B2
Deothang Bhutan 97 F4
Dep r. Rus. Fed. 82 B1
Depalpur India 96 B5
De Pas, Rivière r. Canada 169 H2
De Pere U.S.A. 172 E6
Depew U.S.A. 176 G3
Deposit U.S.A. 177 J3
Depot-Forbes Canada 173 Q3
Depot-Rowanton Canada 173 P4
Depsang Point hill Aksai Chin 89 B5
Depue U.S.A. 172 D9
Deputatskiy Rus. Fed. 39 N3
Dêqên Xizang China 89 E6
Dêqên Xizang China 89 E6
Dêqên Xizang China see **Dagzê**
Dêqên Yunnan China 86 A2
also known as Kaiping
Deqing Guangdong China 87 D4
also known as Decheng
Deqing Zhejiang China 87 G2
De Queen U.S.A. 179 D5
De Quincy U.S.A. 179 D6
Der, Lac du l. France 51 K4
Dera Eth. 128 C2
Dera Bugti Pak. 101 G4
Dera Ghazi Khan Pak. 101 G4
Deraheib reg. Sudan 121 G4
Dera Ismail Khan Pak. 101 G4
Derajat reg. Pak. 101 G4
Deram, Mount Antarctica 223 C2
Derbent Rus. Fed. 102 B4
UNESCO World Heritage Site
Derbent Turkey 59 J10
Derbent Uzbek. see **Darband**
Derbesiye Turkey see **Şenyurt**
Derby Australia 150 C3
Derby S. Africa 133 L2
Derby U.K. 47 K11
Derby CT U.S.A. 177 L4
Derby KS U.S.A. 178 C4
formerly known as El Paso
Derby Line U.S.A. 177 M1
Derecske Hungary 49 S8
Dereham U.K. 47 M11
Dereköy Antalya Turkey 108 D1
Dereköy Denizli Turkey 59 K11
Dereva Rus. Fed. 43 N2
Derg, Lough l. Ireland 47 D11
Dergachi Rus. Fed. 102 B2
Dergachi Ukr. see **Derhachi**
Dergholm State Park nature res. Australia 146 D4
Derhachi Ukr. 41 F6
also spelt Dergachi
De Ridder U.S.A. 179 D6
Derik Turkey 107 E3
Derinkuyu Turkey 106 C3
Derkali well Kenya 128 D4
Derna Libya see **Darnah**
Dêrong China 86 A2
also known as Songmai
Déroute, Passage de la strait Channel Is/France 50 D3
Derow Iran 102 B5
Derre Moz. 131 H3
Derry U.K. see **Londonderry**
Derry U.S.A. 177 N3
Derryveagh Mountains hills Ireland 47 D9
Derstei China 84 D3
Dêrub China 89 B5
also known as Rutog
Derudeb Sudan 121 H5
De Rust S. Africa 132 G10
Deruta Italy 56 E6
Derventa Bos.-Herz. 56 J4
Derwent r. Australia 147 E5
Derwent r. Derbyshire, England U.K. 47 K11
UNESCO World Heritage Site
Derwent r. England U.K. 47 L10
Derweze Turkm. 102 D4
also spelt Darvaza
Deryugino Rus. Fed. 43 Q9
Derza r. Rus. Fed. 43 P5
Derzhavino Rus. Fed. 102 C1
Derzhavinsk Kazakh. 103 F2
formerly known as Derzhavinskiy
Derzhavinskiy Kazakh. see **Derzhavinsk**
Desa Romania 58 E5
Desaguadero r. Arg. 204 D4
Desaguadero r. Bol. 200 C4
Désappointement, Îles du is Fr. Polynesia 221 J6
English form Disappointment Islands
Des Arc U.S.A. 174 B5
Desatoya Mountains U.S.A. 182 G2
Desbarats Canada 173 J4
Descalvado Mato Grosso Brazil 201 F4
Descalvado São Paulo Brazil 206 F8
Descartes France 50 G6
Deschambault Lake Canada 167 K4
Deschambault Lake l. Canada 167 K4
Deschutes r. U.S.A. 170 B2
Descombrimento, Parque Nacional do nat. park Brazil 207 N4
Desē Eth. 128 C2
formerly spelt Dessye
Deseada Chile 200 C5
Deseado Arg. 205 D7
Deseado r. Arg. 205 D7
Desembarco del Granma, Parque Nacional nat. park Cuba 186 D3
UNESCO World Heritage Site
Desembarco Del Granma National Park tourist site Cuba 186 D3
Desemboque Mex. 184 B2
Desengaño, Punta pt Arg. 205 D8
Deseret U.S.A. 183 L2
Deseret Peak U.S.A. 183 L1
Deseronto Canada 173 P6
Désert, Lac l. Canada 173 Q4
Desertas, Ilhas is Madeira 122 A2
Desert Canal Pak. 101 G4
Desert Center U.S.A. 183 I8
Desert Hot Springs U.S.A. 183 H8
Désertines France 51 I6
Desert Lake U.S.A. 183 I5
Desert National Wildlife Refuge nature res. U.S.A. 183 I5
Desert View U.S.A. 183 M5
Deshler U.S.A. 176 B4
Deshnok India 96 B4
Desiderio Tello Arg. 204 D3
Desierto Central de Baja California, Parque Natural del nature res. Mex. 184 B2
Desíerto de Sechura des. Peru 198 A6
Deskati Greece 59 C9
also spelt Dheskáti
De Smet U.S.A. 178 C2

►**Des Moines** IA U.S.A. 174 A3
State capital of Iowa.

Des Moines NM U.S.A. 178 B4
Des Moines r. U.S.A. 178 D2
Desna r. Rus. Fed./Ukr. 41 D6
Desnăţui r. Romania 58 E5
Desnogorsk Rus. Fed. 43 O7
Desnogorskoye Vodokhranilishche resr Rus. Fed. 43 O7
Desnudo, Cerro mt. Arg. 205 C7
Desolación, Isla i. Chile 205 B9
Desolation Point Phil. 74 C4
DeSoto U.S.A. 172 B7
Despatch S. Africa 133 J10
Despen Rus. Fed. 84 B1
Des Plaines U.S.A. 172 F8
Despotovac Srbija Serb. and Mont. 58 C4
Desroches, Île i. Seychelles 129 [inset]
Dessau Germany 49 J4
UNESCO World Heritage Site
Dessye Eth. see **Desē**
Destor Canada 173 O2
D'Estrees Bay Australia 146 C3
Destruction Bay Canada 166 B2
Desvres France 51 H2
Deta Romania 58 C3
Detah Canada 167 H2
Detchino Rus. Fed. 43 R7
Dete Zimbabwe 131 E3
formerly spelt Dett
De Teut Natuurreservaat nature res. Belgium 51 L2
Deti Jon b. Albania/Greece 59 A8
Đetinja r. Serb. and Mont. 58 B5
Detmold Germany 48 F4
Detour, Point U.S.A. 172 G5
De Tour Village U.S.A. 173 J5
Detrital Wash watercourse U.S.A. 183 J5
Detroit U.S.A. 173 J8
Detroit Lakes U.S.A. 178 D2
Dett Zimbabwe see **Dete**
Det Udom Thai. 79 D5
Detva Slovakia 49 Q7
Deua National Park Australia 147 F3
Deurne Neth. 48 C4
Deutschland country Europe see **Germany**
Deutschlandsberg Austria 49 M9
Deutsch-Luxemburgischer Naturpark nature res. Germany 48 D6
Deux-Rivières Canada 173 O4
Deva Romania 58 D3
Deva U.K. see **Chester**
Devadurga India 94 C2
Devakottai India 94 C4
Devana U.K. see **Aberdeen**
Devanhalli India 94 C3
Devarkonda India 94 C2
Deve Bair pass Macedonia see **Velbŭzhdki Prokhod**
Devecser Hungary 49 O8
Develi Turkey 106 C3
also known as Everek
Deveron r. U.K. 46 J6
Devesel Romania 58 D4
Devét Skal hill Czech Rep. 49 N6
Devgadh Bariya India 96 B5
Devghar India see **Deoghar**
Devikot India 96 A4
Devil River Peak N.Z. 152 G8
Devils r. U.S.A. 179 B6
Devil's Gate pass U.S.A. 182 E3
Devil's Island U.S.A. 172 C3
Devil's Lake U.S.A. 178 C1
Devil's Lake l. U.S.A. 179 B6
Devil's Paw mt. U.S.A. 164 F4
Devil's Peak U.S.A. 182 E4
Devil's Point Bahamas 187 E1
Devil's Thumb mt. Canada/U.S.A. 166 C3
Devin Bulg. 58 F7
Devine U.S.A. 179 C6
Devizes U.K. 47 K12
Devli India 96 B4
Devnya Bulg. 58 I5
Devoll r. Albania 58 A8
Dévoluy mts France 51 L8
Devon Alta Canada 180 D1
Devon Ont. Canada 173 J3
Devon S. Africa 133 M3
Devon Island Canada 165 J2
Devonport Australia 147 E5
Devore U.S.A. 182 G7
Devrek Turkey 106 B2
Devrez r. Turkey 106 C2
Devrukh India 94 B2
Dewa, Tanjung pt Indon. 76 A2
Dewakang Besar i. Indon. 77 G4
Dewanganj Bangl. 97 F4
Dewas India 96 C5
De Weerribben, Nationaal Park nat. park Neth. 48 D3
Dewelē Eth. 128 D2
Dewetsdorp S. Africa 133 K6
De Witt AR U.S.A. 174 B5
De Witt IA U.S.A. 174 B3
Dexing China 87 F2
formerly known as Yincheng
Dexter MI U.S.A. 173 J8
Dexter MO U.S.A. 174 B4
Dexter NM U.S.A. 181 F6
Dexter NY U.S.A. 177 I1
Deyang China 86 C2
Dey-Dey Lake salt flat Australia 146 A2
Deyhuk Iran 100 D3
Deynau Turkm. see **Galkynyş**
Deyong, Tanjung pt Indon. 73 I8
Deyyer Iran 100 B5
Dez r. Iran 100 B4
Dez, Sadd-e resr Iran 107 G4
formerly known as Mohammad Reza Shah Pahlavi Dam
Dezadeash Canada 166 B2
Dezadeash Lake Canada 166 B2
Dezfūl Iran 100 B3

►**Dezhneva, Mys** c. Rus. Fed. 39 T3
Most easterly point of Asia. English form East Cape.
►►**60–61 Asia** Landscapes

Dezhou Shandong China 85 H4
Dezhou Sichuan China see **Dechang**
Dezh Shāhpūr Iran see **Marīvān**
Dhading Nepal 97 E4
Dhahab Egypt 121 G2
Dhahab, Marsá b. Egypt 108 F9
Dhahab, Wādī adh r. Syria 108 G5
Dhāhiriya West Bank 108 F6
Dhahlān, Jabal hill Saudi Arabia 104 D2
Dhahran Saudi Arabia 105 E2
also spelt Aẓ Ẓahrān

►**Dhaka** Bangl. 97 F5
Capital of Bangladesh. Formerly spelt Dacca.
►►**18–19 World** Cities

Dhaka admin. div. Bangl. 97 F5
Dhalbhum reg. India 97 E5
Dhaleswari r. Bangl. 97 F5
Dhaleswari r. India 97 G4
Dhalgaon India 94 B2
Dhamār Yemen 104 D5
Dhamār governorate Yemen 104 D5
Dhamnod India 96 B5
Dhampur India 96 C3
Dhamtari India 94 D1
Dhanbad India 97 E5
Dhandhuka India 96 B5
Dhanera India 96 B4
Dhangarhi Nepal 96 D3
Dhang Range mts Nepal 97 D3
Dhankuta Nepal 97 E4
Dhar India 96 B5
Ḍhar Adrar hills Mauritania 124 B2
Dharampur India 94 B1
Dharan Bazar Nepal 97 E4
Dharapuram India 94 C4
Dhari India 96 A5
Dharmanagar India 97 G4
Dharmapuri India 94 C3
Dharmavaram India 94 C3
Dharmjaygarh India 97 D5
also known as Rabkob
Dharmkot India 96 B3
Dharoor watercourse Somalia 128 F2
Ḍhar Oualâta hills Mauritania 124 D2
Ḍhar Tîchît hills Mauritania 124 C2
Dharug National Park Australia 147 F3
Dharur India 94 C2
Dharwad India 94 B3
formerly known as Dharwar
Dharwar India see **Dharwad**
Dhasa India 96 A5
Dhasan r. India 96 C4

►**Dhaulagiri** mt. Nepal 97 D3
7th highest mountain in the world and in Asia. Also spelt Dhawlagiri.
►►**6–7 World** Landscapes
►►**60–61 Asia** Landscapes

Dhaurahra India 96 D4
Dhávlia Greece see **Davlia**
Dhawlagiri mt. Nepal see **Dhaulagiri**
Dhekelia Sovereign Base Area military base Cyprus 108 E2
Dhekiajuli India 97 G4
Dhenkanal India 95 E1
Dheskáti Greece see **Deskati**
Dhiafánion Greece see **Diafani**
Dhi'b, Ra's pt Egypt 108 E9
Dhībān Jordan 108 G6
Dhidhimótikhon Greece see **Didymoteicho**
Dhing India 97 G4
Dhī Qār governorate Iraq 107 F5
Dhirwah, Wādī adh watercourse Jordan 109 H6
Dhodhekánisos is Greece see **Dodecanese**
Dhofar admin. reg. Oman see **Ẓufār**
Dhokós i. Greece see **Dokos**
Dhola India 96 A5
Dholka India 96 B5
Dholpur India 96 C4
Dhomokós Greece see **Domokos**
Dhone India 94 C3
Dhoomadheere Somalia 128 D4
Dhoraji India 96 A5
Dhori India 96 A5
Dhragonádha i. Greece see **Dragonada**
Dhragónisos i. Greece see **Dragonisi**
Dhrangadhra India 96 A5
Dhrol India 96 A5
Dhrosiá Greece see **Drosia**
Dhubāb Yemen 104 C5
Dhubri India 97 F4
also spelt Dhuburi
Dhuburi India see **Dhubri**
Dhule India 94 B1
formerly known as Dhulia
Dhulia India see **Dhule**
Dhulian India 97 E4
Dhuma India 96 C5
Dhunche Nepal 97 E4
Dhuudo Somalia 128 F2
Dhuusa Marreeb Somalia 128 E3
Dhuwaybān basin Saudi Arabia 104 B2
Dhytikí Ellás admin. reg. Greece see **Dytiki Ellas**
Dhytikí Makedhonía admin. reg. Greece see **Dytiki Makedonia**
Dia i. Greece 59 G13
Diablo, Mount U.S.A. 182 C4
Diablo Range mts U.S.A. 182 C4
Diaca Moz. 129 C7
Diafani Greece 59 I13
also known as Dhiafánion
Diafarabé Mali 124 D3
Diaka r. Mali 124 D3
Dialakoto Senegal 124 B3
Diallassagou Mali 124 E3
Diamante Arg. 204 E4
Diamante r. Arg. 204 D4
Diamante Italy 57 H9
Diamantina watercourse Australia 149 C5
Diamantina Amazonas Brazil 199 F6
Diamantina Minas Gerais Brazil 203 D6
UNESCO World Heritage Site
Diamantina, Chapada plat. Brazil 202 D5
Diamantina Gates National Park Australia 149 D4
Diamantina Lakes Australia 149 D4
Diamantino Mato Grosso Brazil 201 F3
Diamantino Mato Grosso Brazil 202 A6
Diamantino r. Brazil 206 A3
Diamond Harbour India 97 F5
Diamond Islets Australia 149 F3
Diamond Peak U.S.A. 183 I2
Diamond Springs U.S.A. 182 D3
Diamondville U.S.A. 180 E4
Diamou Mali 124 C3
Diamounguél Senegal 124 B3
Dianbai China 87 D4
also known as Shuidong
Dianbu China see **Feidong**
Diancang Shan mt. China 86 B3
Dian Chi l. China 86 B3
Diandioumé Mali 124 C3
Diane Bank sea feature Australia 149 F2
Diangounté Kamara Mali 124 C3
Diani r. Guinea 124 C5
Dianjiang China 87 C2
also known as Guixi
Diano Marina Italy 56 A5
Dianópolis Brazil 202 C4
Dianra Côte d'Ivoire 124 D4
Diaobingshan China see **Tiefa**
Diaokou China 85 H4
Diaoling China 82 C3
Diapaga Burkina 125 F3
Diaporioi i. Greece 59 E11
Diarizos r. Cyprus 108 D3
Diatifèrè Guinea 124 C4
Diavolo, Mount hill India 95 G3
Diaz Point Namibia 130 B5
Dibā al Ḥiṣn U.A.E. 105 G2
Ḍibab Oman 105 G3
Dibang r. India see **Dingba Qu**
Dibaya Dem. Rep. Congo 127 D6
Dibbis Sudan 120 E6
Dibek Dağı mt. Turkey 59 J10
Dibella well Niger 125 I2
Dibeng S. Africa 132 G4
Dībīlē Eth. 128 D2
Dibis Iraq 109 P2
Ḍibīy, Jabal hills Saudi Arabia 104 C2
Dibrugarh India 97 G4
Dibulla Col. 198 C2
Dickens U.S.A. 179 B5
Dickeyville U.S.A. 172 C8
Dickinson U.S.A. 178 B2
Dickson U.S.A. 174 C4
Dicle r. Turkey 107 E3 see **Tigris**
Dida Galgalu reg. Kenya 128 C4
Dīdah well Saudi Arabia 104 D2
Dīdī, Jabal ad hill Syria 109 K2
Didicas i. Phil. 74 B2
Didiéni Mali 124 C3
Didinga Hills Sudan 128 B3
Dido waterhole Kenya 128 D5
Didsbury Canada 167 H5
Didwana India 96 B4
Didymoteicho Greece 58 H7
also known as Dhidhimótikhon
Didžiasalis Lith. 42 H6
Didžiulis l. Lith. 42 F7
Die France 51 L8
Die Berg mt. S. Africa 133 O2
Diébougou Burkina 124 E4
Dieburg Germany 48 F6
Diedenhofen France see **Thionville**
Diefenbaker, Lake Canada 167 I5
Diège r. France 51 I7
Diego de Almagro, Isla i. Chile 205 B8
Diego Garcia i. British Indian Ocean Terr. 218 L6
Diego Martin Trin. and Tob. 187 H5
Diégo Suarez Madag. see **Antsirañana**
Diégrâga well Mauritania 124 C3
Diéké Guinea 124 C5
Diekirch Lux. 51 M3
Diéma Mali 124 C3
Diemelsee park Germany 48 F4
Điên Biên Phu Điên Biên Phu Vietnam 78 C3
Diên Châu Vietnam 78 D4
Dienvidsusēja r. Latvia 42 F5
Diepholz Germany 48 F3
Dieppe France 50 H3
Dierks U.S.A. 179 D5
Di'er Nonchang Qu r. China 85 E4
Di'er Songhua Jiang r. China 82 B3
Diest Belgium 51 L2
Dietikon Switz. 51 O5
Dieveniškės Lith. 42 G7
Diffa Niger 125 I3
Diffa dept Niger 125 I2
Difnein Island Eritrea 104 B4
Dig well Eth. 128 E3
Diga Diga well Niger 125 F3
Digapahandi India 95 E2
Digba Dem. Rep. Congo 126 E3
Digboi India 97 G4
Digby Canada 169 H4
Digerbergen hill Sweden 45 K3
Digerberget hill Sweden 45 K3
Diggi India 96 B4
Dighton U.S.A. 178 B4
Diglur India 94 C2
Digne-les-Bains France 51 M8
Digoin France 51 J6
Digos Phil. 74 C5
Digras India 94 C1
Digri Pak. 101 G5
Digul r. Indon. 73 I8
Digya National Park Ghana 125 E5
Dihang r. India 97 G3 see **Brahmaputra**
Diib, Wadi watercourse Sudan 104 B3
Diinsoor Somalia 128 D4
Dijlah, Nahr r. Iraq/Syria 107 F4 see **Tigris**
Dijlah - Ath Tharthār, Qanāt canal Iraq 109 O4
English form Tharthār Canal
Dijon France 51 L5
Dik Chad 126 C2
Dikanäs Sweden 44 L2
Diken India 96 B4
Dikhil Djibouti 128 D2
Dikho r. India 97 G4
Dikili Turkey 106 A3
Diksmuide Belgium 51 I1
Dikson Rus. Fed. 39 I2
Dikwa Nigeria 125 I3
Dīla Eth. 128 C3
Dilaram Iran 100 D4
Dilek Yarımadası Milli Parkı nat. park Turkey 59 I11
Dili Dem. Rep. Congo 126 E4

►**Dili** East Timor 75 C5
Capital of East Timor.

Dilia watercourse Niger 125 I3
Dilijan Armenia 107 F2
also spelt Dilizhan
Dilijan Argelanots' nature res. Armenia 107 F2
Di Linh Vietnam 79 E6
Dilion Cone mt. N.Z. 153 H10
Dilizhan Armenia see **Dilijan**
Dillenburg Germany 48 F5
Dilley U.S.A. 179 C6
Dilli Mali 124 D3
Dilling Sudan 121 F6
Dillingen an der Donau Germany 48 H7
Dillingham U.S.A. 164 D4
Dillinya Aboriginal Land res. Australia 148 B2
Dillon Canada 167 I4
Dillon r. Canada 167 I4
Dillon MT U.S.A. 180 D3
Dillon SC U.S.A. 174 E5
Dillsburg U.S.A. 177 H5
Dillwyn U.S.A. 176 G8
Dilolo Dem. Rep. Congo 127 D7
Dilos i. Greece 59 G11
UNESCO World Heritage Site
Diltāwa Iraq 107 F4
Dimako Cameroon 125 I5
Dimapur India 97 G4
Dimas Mex. 184 D4
Dimashq Syria see **Damascus**
Dimashq governorate Syria 109 I4
Dimbelenge Dem. Rep. Congo 127 D6
Dimbokro Côte d'Ivoire 124 D5
Dimboola Australia 147 D4
Dimbulah Australia 149 E3
Dimitrovgrad Bulg. 58 G6
Dimitrovgrad Rus. Fed. 41 I5
formerly known as Melekess
Dimitrovgrad Srbija Serb. and Mont. 58 D5
formerly known as Tsaribrod
Dimitrovo Bulg. see **Pernik**
Dimmitt U.S.A. 179 B5
Dīmona Israel 108 G6
Dinagat i. Phil. 74 C4
Dinagat Sound sea chan. Phil. 74 C4
Dinajpur Bangl. 97 F4
Dinan France 50 D4
Dinanagar India 96 B2
Dinangourou Mali 125 E3
Dinant Belgium 51 K2
Dinapur India 97 E4
Dinar Turkey 106 B3
historically known as Apamea
Dīnār, Kūh-e mt. Iran 100 B4
Dinara mt. Bos.-Herz. 56 I4
Dinara Planina mts Bos.-Herz./Croatia see **Dinaric Alps**
Dinard France 50 D4
Dinaric Alps mts Bos.-Herz./Croatia 56 I4
also known as Dinara Planina
Dinas well Kenya 128 C4
Dinbych U.K. see **Denbigh**
Dinbych-y-Pysgod U.K. see **Tenby**
Dinder r. Sudan 121 G6
Dinder el Agaliyin r. Sudan 104 A5
Dinder National Park Sudan 121 G6
Dindi r. India 94 C2
Dindigul India 94 C4
Dindima Nigeria 125 H4
Dindiza Moz. 131 G4
Dindori Madhya Pradesh India 96 D5
Dindori Maharashtra India 94 B1
Dinek Turkey 106 C3
Dinga Dem. Rep. Congo 127 C6
Dinga Pak. 101 H3
Dingalan Bay Phil. 74 B3
Dingba Qu r. India 97 G4
also known as Dibang
Dingbian China 85 E4
Dingbujie China 87 E2
Dingelstädt Germany 48 H4
Dingin, Bukit mt. Indon. 76 C3
Dingla Nepal 97 E4
Dingle Ireland 47 B11
Dingle Bay Ireland 47 B11
Dingnan China 87 E3
also known as Lishi
Dingo Australia 149 F4
Dingolfing Germany 49 J7
Dingping China see **Linshui**
Dingras Phil. 74 B2
Dingtao China 85 G5
Dinguiraye Guinea 124 C4
Dingwall Canada 169 I4
Dingwall U.K. 46 H6
Dingxi China 84 E5
Dingxian China see **Dingzhou**
Dingxiang China 85 G4
Dingxin China 84 C3
Dingxing China 85 G4
Dingyuan China 87 F1
Dingzhou China 85 G4
formerly known as Dingxian
Dingzi Gang b. China 85 I4
Dingzikou China 84 B4
Đinh An, Cửa r. mouth Vietnam 79 D6
Dinhata India 97 F4
Dinh Lâp Vietnam 78 D3
Dini, Mount P.N.G. 73 J8
Dinkel r. Neth. 48 D3
Dinkelsbühl Germany 48 H6
Dinnebito Wash watercourse U.S.A. 183 M6
Dinngyê China 89 D6
also known as Gyangkar
Dinokwe Botswana 131 E4
Dinosaur U.S.A. 183 O1
Dinosaur National Monument nat. park U.S.A. 183 O1
Dinosaur Provincial Park Canada 167 I5
UNESCO World Heritage Site
Dintiteladas Indon. 77 D4
Dinuba U.S.A. 182 E5
Dinwiddie U.S.A. 176 H8
Dioïla Mali 124 D3
Diois, Massif du mts France 51 L8
Dion r. Guinea 124 C4
Dionísio Brazil 207 K6
Dionísio Cerqueira Brazil 203 A8
Diorama Brazil 206 B3
Dioscurias Georgia see **Sokhumi**
Diosig Romania 58 D1
Diospolis Magna tourist site Egypt see **Thebes**
Diouloulou Senegal 124 A3
Dioumara Mali 124 C3
Dioundiou Niger 125 F3
Dioura Mali 124 D3
Diourbel Senegal 124 A3
Dipalpur Pak. 101 H4
Dipayal Nepal 96 D3
Diphu India 97 G4
Dipkarpaz Cyprus see **Rizokarpason**
Diplo Pak. 101 G5
Dipolog Phil. 74 B4
Dipperu National Park Australia 149 F4
Dipton N.Z. 153 C13
Dipu China see **Anji**
Dir Pak. 92 D3
Dir reg. Pak. 101 G3
Dīrah U.A.E. 105 F2
Dirang India 97 G4
Diré Mali 124 E2
Direction, Cape Australia 149 D2
Dirē Dawa Eth. 128 D2
Dirfys mts Greece 59 E10
Dirhami Estonia 42 E2
Diriamba Nicaragua 186 B5
Dirico Angola 127 D9
Dirillo r. Sicily Italy 57 G11
Dirimii Geçidi pass Turkey 108 A1
Dirk Hartog Island Australia 151 A5
Dirkou Niger 125 I2
Dirranbandi Australia 147 F2
Ḍirs Saudi Arabia 104 C4
Dirschau Poland see **Tczew**
Dirty Devil r. U.S.A. 183 N4
Disa India 96 B4
formerly spelt Deesa
Disang r. India 97 G4
Disappointment, Cape Antarctica 222 T2
Disappointment, Cape S. Georgia 205 [inset]
Disappointment, Cape U.S.A. 180 A3
Disappointment, Lake salt flat Australia 150 C4
Disappointment Islands Fr. Polynesia see **Désappointement, Îles du**
Disappointment Lake Canada 169 I2
Discovery Bay Australia 146 D4
Discovery Bay Hong Kong China 87 [inset]
also known as Tai Pak Wan
Discovery Bay Coastal Park nature res. Australia 146 D4
Disentis Muster Switz. 51 O6
Disgrazia, Monte mt. Italy 56 B2
Dishnā Egypt 121 G3
Disko i. Greenland see **Qeqertarsuaq**
Disko Bugt b. Greenland see **Qeqertarsuup Tunua**
Dismal Lakes Canada 167 G1
Dismal Mountains Antarctica 223 D2
Dismal Swamp U.S.A. 177 I9
Disneyland Resort Paris tourist site France 51 I4
Dispur India 97 F4
Disputanta U.S.A. 177 H8
Disraëli Canada 169 G4
Diss U.K. 47 N11
Dissān Island Saudi Arabia 104 C4
Distrito Federal admin. dist. Brazil 206 F2
English form Federal District
Distrito Federal admin. dist. Mex. 185 F5
Distrito Federal admin. dist. Venez. 199 E2
English form Federal District
Disūq Egypt 108 B6
Ditloung S. Africa 132 G5
Dittaino r. Sicily Italy 57 H11
Diu India 94 A1
Diuata Mountains Phil. 74 C4
Diuata Point Phil. 74 C4
Dīvān Darreh Iran 100 A3
Divehi country Indian Ocean see **Maldives**
Divénié Congo 126 B5
Dives r. France 50 F3
Divichi Azer. see **Däväçi**
Divide Mountain U.S.A. 166 A2
Divilacan Bay Phil. 74 B2
Divinésia Brazil 207 J7
Divinópolis Brazil 203 C7
Divisões, Serra das mts Brazil 206 B4
also known as Santa Marta, Serra de
Divisor, Sierra de mts Peru see **Ultraoriental, Cordillera**
Divjaka nat. park Albania 58 A8
Divnoye Rus. Fed. 41 G7
Divo Côte d'Ivoire 124 D5
Divo Rus. Fed. 43 M6
Divor r. Port. 54 C6
Divounia i. Greece 59 H13
Divriği Turkey 107 D3
UNESCO World Heritage Site
Divuma Dem. Rep. Congo 127 D7
Div'ya Rus. Fed. 40 K4
Diwaniyah Iraq see **Ad Dīwānīyah**
Dixcove Ghana 125 E5
Dixfield U.S.A. 177 O1
Dix Milles, Lac des l. Canada 173 S3
Dixmont U.S.A. 177 P1
Dixon CA U.S.A. 182 C3
Dixon IL U.S.A. 174 B3
Dixon Entrance sea chan. Canada/U.S.A. 164 F4
Dixon's Bahamas 175 F7
Dixonville Canada 167 G3
Diyadin Turkey 107 E3
Diyālá governorate Iraq 107 F4
Diyarbakır Turkey 107 E3
historically known as Amida
Diyodar India 96 A4
Diz Pak. 101 E5
Dizak Iran see **Dāvar Panāh**
Dizangué Cameroon 125 H6
Diz Chah Iran 100 C3
Dize Turkey see **Yüksekova**
Dizney U.S.A. 176 B9
Dja r. Cameroon 125 I6
Dja, Réserve du nature res. Cameroon 125 I6
UNESCO World Heritage Site
Djado Niger 125 I1
Djado, Plateau du Niger 125 I1

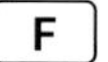

Fabens U.S.A. 181 F7
Faber, Mount hill Sing. 76 [inset]
Faber Lake Canada 167 G2
Fabero Spain 54 E2
Fabriano Italy 56 E5
Facatativá Col. 198 C3
Fachi Niger 125 H2
Factoryville U.S.A. 177 J4
Facundo Arg. 205 C7
Fada Chad 120 D5
Fada-N'Gourma Burkina 125 F3
Faḍīlah well Saudi Arabia 105 E3
Faḍli reg. Yemen 105 D5
Fadnoun, Plateau du Alg. 123 H4
Faenza Italy 56 D4
Færingehavn Greenland see Kangerluarsoruseq
Færoerne terr. N. Atlantic Ocean see Faroe Islands
Faeroes terr. N. Atlantic Ocean see Faroe Islands
Fafa r. Cent. Afr. Rep. 126 C3
Fafanlap Indon. 73 H7
Fafe Port. 54 C3
Fafen Shet' watercourse Eth. 128 E3
Fafi waterhole Kenya 128 D5
Faga watercourse Burkina 125 F3
Făgăraş Romania 58 F3
Fagersta Sweden 45 K4
UNESCO World Heritage Site
Făget Romania 58 D3
Fagnano, Lago l. Arg./Chile 205 C9
Fagne reg. Belgium 51 K2
Fagochia well Niger 125 G2
Faguibine, Lac l. Mali 124 D2
Fagurhólsmýri Iceland 44 [inset] C3
Fagwir Sudan 128 A2
Fahlīān, Rūdkhāneh-ye watercourse Iran 100 B4
Fahraj Iran 100 C4
Fahūd, Jabal hill Oman 105 G3
Faial i. Arquipélago dos Açores 54 [inset]
Fā'id Egypt 108 D7
Faillon, Lac l. Canada 173 Q2
Fairbanks U.S.A. 164 E3
Fairborn U.S.A. 176 A6
Fairbury U.S.A. 178 C3
Fairchild U.S.A. 172 C6
Fairfax N.Z. 153 C14
Fairfax LA U.S.A. 172 B9
Fairfax VA U.S.A. 177 H7
Fairfax VT U.S.A. 177 L1
Fairfield CA U.S.A. 182 B3
Fairfield IA U.S.A. 174 B3
Fairfield ID U.S.A. 180 D4
Fairfield IL U.S.A. 174 B4
Fairfield OH U.S.A. 176 A6
Fairfield TX U.S.A. 179 C6
Fairfield UT U.S.A. 183 L1
Fairfield VA U.S.A. 176 F8
Fairgrove U.S.A. 173 J7
Fairhaven U.S.A. 177 O4
Fair Haven U.S.A. 177 L2
Fair Head U.K. 47 F8
Fair Hill U.S.A. 177 J6
Fair Isle i. U.K. 46 K4
Fairlee U.S.A. 177 M2
Fairlie N.Z. 153 E12
Fairmont MN U.S.A. 178 D3
Fairmont WV U.S.A. 176 E6
Fairmont Hot Springs Canada 167 H5
Fairplay U.S.A. 180 F5
Fairview Australia 149 E2
Fairview Canada 166 G3
Fairview IL U.S.A. 172 C10
Fairview KY U.S.A. 176 B7
Fairview MI U.S.A. 173 I6
Fairview OK U.S.A. 179 C4
Fairview PA U.S.A. 176 E3
Fairview UT U.S.A. 183 M2
Fairview WI U.S.A. 172 C7
Fairview Park Hong Kong China 87 [inset]
Fairweather, Cape U.S.A. 166 B3
Fairweather, Mount Canada/U.S.A. 164 F4
Fais i. Micronesia 73 J5
formerly known as Tromelin Island
Faisalabad Pak. 101 H4
formerly known as Lyallpur
Faizabad Badakhshān Afgh. see Feyzābād
Faizabad Fāryāb Afgh. 101 F2
Faizabad India 97 D4
Fāj aş Şulubī watercourse Saudi Arabia 109 M7
Fajj, Wādī al watercourse Iraq 109 O5
Fajr, Wādī watercourse Saudi Arabia 107 D5
Fakaofo atoll Tokelau 145 H2
also spelt Fakaofu; formerly known as Bowditch
Fakaofu atoll Tokelau see Fakaofo
Fakel Rus. Fed. 40 J4
formerly known as Sergiyevskiy
Fakenham U.K. 47 M11
Fåker Sweden 44 K3
Fakfak Indon. 73 H7
Fakhrabad Iran 100 C4
Fakiragram India 97 F4
Fakiyska Reka r. Bulg. 58 I6
Fakse Denmark 45 K5
Fakse Bugt b. Denmark 45 K5
Faku China 85 I3
Falaba Sierra Leone 124 C4
Falagountou Burkina 125 F3
Falaise France 50 F4
Falaise Lake Canada 167 G2
Falakata India 97 F4
Falam Myanmar 78 A3
Falavarjan Iran 100 B3
Falcarragh Ireland 47 D8
Falces Spain 55 J2
Fălciu Romania 58 J2
Falcón state Venez. 198 D2
Falcon, Cap c. Alg. 55 K9
Falconara Marittima Italy 56 F5
Falcone, Capo del c. Sardinia Italy 56 A8
Falcon Island Tonga see Fonuafu'u
Falcon Lake Canada 167 M5
Falcon Lake l. Mex./U.S.A. 185 F3
Falelima Samoa 145 H3
Falémé r. Mali/Senegal 124 B3
Falerii Italy see Civita Castellana
Falfurrias U.S.A. 179 C7
Falher Canada 167 G4
Falkat watercourse Eritrea 104 B4
Falkenberg Germany 49 K4
Falkenberg Sweden 45 K4
Falkensee Germany 49 K3
Falkirk U.K. 46 I8

►Falkland Islands terr. S. Atlantic Ocean 205 F8
United Kingdom Overseas Territory. Also known as Malvinas, Islas.
►►192–193 South America Countries

Falkland Sound sea chan. Falkland Is 205 E9
Falkner Arg. 204 D6
Falkonera i. Greece 59 E12
Falköping Sweden 45 K4
Fall r. U.S.A. 178 D4
Fall Branch U.S.A. 176 C9
Fallbrook U.S.A. 183 G8
Fall Creek U.S.A. 172 B6
Fallieres Coast Antarctica 222 T2
Fallon U.S.A. 182 F2
Fall River U.S.A. 177 N4
Fall River Pass U.S.A. 180 F4
Falls City U.S.A. 178 D3
Falls Creek U.S.A. 176 G4
Fallūjah Iraq see Al Fallūjah
Falmouth Antigua and Barbuda 187 H3
Falmouth Jamaica 186 D3
Falmouth U.K. 47 G13
Falmouth KY U.S.A. 176 A7
Falmouth MA U.S.A. 177 O4
Falmouth ME U.S.A. 177 O2
Falmouth VA U.S.A. 176 H7
Falou Mali 124 D3
False r. Canada 169 G1
False Bay S. Africa 132 C11
False Bay Park S. Africa 133 Q4
False Point India 95 E1
Falso, Cabo c. Dom. Rep. 187 F3
Falso, Cabo c. Hond. 186 C4
Falso Cabo de Hornos c. Chile 205 C9
Falster i. Denmark 45 J5
Fălticeni Romania 58 H1
Falun Sweden 45 K3
UNESCO World Heritage Site
Falzarego, Passo di pass Italy 56 E2
Famagusta Cyprus 108 E2
also known as Ammochostos or Gazimağusa or Magosa
Famagusta Bay Cyprus see Ammochostos Bay
Famatina Arg. 204 D3
Famatina, Sierra de mts Arg. 204 C3
Famenin Iran 100 B3
Fame Range hills Australia 151 C5
Family Lake Canada 167 M5
Family Well Australia 150 D4
Fana Mali 124 D3
Fanad Head Ireland 47 E8
Fanambana Madag. 131 [inset] K2
Fanandrana Madag. 131 [inset] K3
Fanari, Akra pt Greece 59 H11
Fanchang China 87 F2
Fandriana Madag. 131 [inset] J4
Fang Thai. 78 B4
Fangak Sudan 128 A2
Fangcheng Guangxi China see Fangchenggang
Fangcheng Henan China 87 E1
Fangchenggang China 87 D4
formerly known as Fangcheng
Fangdou Shan mts China 87 D2
Fangliao Taiwan 87 G4
Fangshan Taiwan 87 G4
Fangxian China 87 D1
Fangzheng China 82 C3
Fani i Vogël r. Albania 58 A7
Fanipal' Belarus 42 I8
Fankuai China 87 D2
formerly known as Fankuaidian
Fankuaidian China see Fankuai
Fanling Hong Kong China 87 [inset]
Fannrem Norway 44 J3
Fannūj Iran 101 D5
Fanø i. Denmark 45 J5
Fano Italy 56 F5
historically known as Colonia Julia Fenestris or Fanum Fortunae
Fanoualie i. Tonga see Fonualei
Fanshan Anhui China 87 F2
Fanshan Zhejiang China 87 G3
Fanshi China 85 G4
Fanum Fortunae Italy see Fano
Fanxian China 85 G5
also known as Yingtaoyuan
Farab Turkm. see Farap
Faraba Mali 124 C3
Farab-Pristan' Turkm. see Jeýhun
Faradje Dem. Rep. Congo 126 F4
Faradofay Madag. see Tôlañaro
Farafangana Madag. 131 [inset] J4
Farafenni Gambia 124 B3
Farafra Oasis Egypt 121 F3
Farāgheh Iran 100 C4
Farāh Afgh. 101 E3
historically known as Alexandria Prophthasia
Farāh prov. Afgh. 101 E3
Faraḥābād Iran see Khezerābād
Farah Rūd watercourse Afgh. 101 E4
Farakhulm Afgh. 101 G3
Farallon de Medinilla i. N. Mariana Is 73 K3
also known as Bird Island
Farallon de Pajaros vol. N. Mariana Is 73 J2
Farallones de Cali, Parque Nacional nat. park Col. 198 B4
Farallon National Wildlife Refuge nature res. U.S.A. 182 A4
Faramuti l. Sudan 126 E2
Faranah Guinea 124 C4
Faraoani Romania 58 H2
Far'aoun well Mauritania 124 B2
Farap Turkm. 103 E5
formerly spelt Farab
Fararah Oman 105 F4
Farasān Saudi Arabia 104 C4
Farasān, Jazā'ir is Saudi Arabia 104 C4
Faratsiho Madag. 131 [inset] J3
Faraulep atoll Micronesia 73 J5
also known as Fattoilep; also spelt Foraulep; formerly known as Gardner
Fardes r. Spain 55 I7
Farewell, Cape Greenland 165 O3
also known as Farvel, Kap or Nunap Isua or Uummannarsuaq
Farewell, Cape N.Z. 152 G8
Farewell Spit N.Z. 152 G8
Färgelanda Sweden 45 K4
Farghona Uzbek. see Farg'ona
Farghona Wiloyati admin. div. Uzbek. see Farg'ona
Fargo U.S.A. 178 C2
Farg'ona Uzbek. 103 G4
also spelt Farghona; formerly known as Novyy Margelan or Skobelev
Farg'ona admin. div. Uzbek. 103 G4
English form Fergana Oblast; also known as Farghona Wiloyati
Faribault U.S.A. 174 A2
Faribault, Lac l. Canada 169 G1
Faridabad India 96 C3
Faridkot India 96 B3
Faridpur Bangl. 97 F5
Faridpur India 96 C3
Fārigh, Wādī al watercourse Libya 120 C2
Färila Sweden 45 K3
Farim Guinea-Bissau 124 B3
Farīmān Iran 101 D3
Farinha r. Brazil 202 C3
Fāris, Qalamat oasis Saudi Arabia 105 E4
Farish Uzbek. 103 F4
also spelt Forish
Fāriskūr Egypt 108 C6
Färjestaden Sweden 45 L4
Farkadhon Greece 59 D9
Farkhar Afgh. see Farkhato
Farkhato Afgh. 101 G2
also known as Farkhar
Farkhor Tajik. 101 G2
also spelt Parkhar
Farley U.S.A. 172 B8
Farmahin Iran 100 B3
Farmakonisi i. Greece 59 I11
Farmer City U.S.A. 174 B3
Farmer Island Canada 168 D1
Farmerville U.S.A. 179 D5
Farmington Canada 166 F4
Farmington IA U.S.A. 172 B10
Farmington IL U.S.A. 172 C10
Farmington ME U.S.A. 177 O1
Farmington MO U.S.A. 174 B4
Farmington NH U.S.A. 177 N2
Farmington NM U.S.A. 181 E5
Farmington UT U.S.A. 180 E4
Farmington Hills U.S.A. 173 J8
Far Mountain Canada 166 E4
Farmville U.S.A. 176 G8
Farne Islands U.K. 46 K8
Farnham U.S.A. 177 I8
Farnham, Lake salt flat Australia 151 D5
Farnham, Mount Canada 167 G5
Faro Brazil 199 G5
Faro r. Cameroon 125 I4
Faro Canada 166 C2
Faro Port. 54 D7
Faro admin. dist. Port. 54 C7
Fårö i. Sweden 45 L4
Faro, Réserve du nature res. Cameroon 125 I4
Faro, Serra do mts Spain 54 D2

►Faroe Islands terr. N. Atlantic Ocean 46 E2
Self-governing Danish Territory. Also spelt Faeroes; also known as Færoerne or Føroyar.
►►32–33 Europe Countries

Fårösund Sweden 45 L4
Farquhar Atoll Seychelles 129 F7
Farquhar Group is Seychelles 129 F7
Farquharson Tableland hills Australia 151 C5
Farrandsville U.S.A. 176 H4
Farrars Creek watercourse Australia 149 D5
Farrāsh, Jabal al hill Saudi Arabia 104 C4
Farrāshband Iran 100 C4
Farr Bay Antarctica 223 G2
Farrellton Canada 173 R5
Farrokhī Iran 101 D3
Farrukhabad India see Fatehgarh
Fārs prov. Iran 100 C4
historically known as Pars or Parsa or Persis
Farsakh Iran 100 C3
Farsala Greece 59 D9
Farsaliotis r. Greece 59 D9
Fārsī, Jazīreh-ye i. Iran 107 G6
Farson U.S.A. 180 E4
Farsund Norway 45 I4
Fartak, Jabal mts Yemen 105 E5
Fartak, Ra's c. Yemen 105 F5
Fărţăneşti Romania 58 I3
Fartura r. Brazil 206 C3
Fartura, Serra da mts Brazil 203 A8
Fārūj Iran 100 D2
Farvel, Kap c. Greenland see Farewell, Cape
Farwell MI U.S.A. 173 I7
Farwell TX U.S.A. 179 B5
Fāryāb prov. Afgh. 101 F2
Fāryāb Hormozgan Iran 100 D5
also known as Deh Barez
Fāryāb Kermān Iran 100 D4
Farynava Belarus 43 J6
Fasā Iran 100 C4
Fasano Italy 56 J8
Fåset Norway 45 J3
Faşikan Geçidi pass Turkey 108 D1
Fasil Ghebbi and Gonder Monuments tourist site Eth. 128 C1
UNESCO World Heritage Site
Fāsteh, Ra's-e pt Iran 101 E5
Fastiv Ukr. 41 D6
also spelt Fastov
Fastov Ukr. see Fastiv
Fatehabad India 96 B3
Fatehgarh Madhya Pradesh India 96 C4
Fatehgarh Uttar Pradesh India 96 C4
formerly known as Farrukhabad
Fatehnagar India 96 B4
Fatehpur Rajasthan India 96 B4
Fatehpur Uttar Pradesh India 96 D4
Fatehpur Sikri India 96 C4
UNESCO World Heritage Site
Fateyevka Rus. Fed. 43 P9
Fatezh Rus. Fed. 43 Q9
Fatḥābād Iran 100 C4
Fathai Sudan 128 A2
Fathom Five National Marine Park Canada 173 L5
Fati, Lac l. Mali 124 E2
Fatick Senegal 124 A3
Fattoilep atoll Micronesia see Faraulep
Fatuma Dem. Rep. Congo 127 F6
Faulkton U.S.A. 178 C2
Faulquemont France 51 M3
Fauquier Canada 166 G5
Fauresmith S. Africa 133 J6
Fauske Norway 44 K2
Faust Canada 167 H4
Favalto, Monte mt. Italy 56 E5
Favignana Sicily Italy 57 E11
Favignana, Isola i. Sicily Italy 57 E11
Fawcett Canada 167 H4
Fawn r. Canada 168 B2
Fawnleas S. Africa 133 O6
Fawwārah Saudi Arabia 104 C2
Faxaflói b. Iceland 44 [inset] B2
Faxälven r. Sweden 44 L3
Faya Chad 120 C5
also known as Largeau
Fayaoué New Caledonia 145 F4
Fayette AL U.S.A. 175 C5
Fayette IA U.S.A. 172 B8
Fayette MI U.S.A. 172 G5
Fayette MO U.S.A. 178 D4
Fayette MS U.S.A. 175 B6
Fayette OH U.S.A. 176 A4
Fayetteville AR U.S.A. 179 D4
Fayetteville GA U.S.A. 175 C5
Fayetteville NC U.S.A. 174 E5
Fayetteville NY U.S.A. 177 I2
Fayetteville PA U.S.A. 176 H6
Fayetteville TN U.S.A. 174 C5
Fayetteville WV U.S.A. 176 D7
Fayfā Saudi Arabia 104 C4
Fayḥālah, Wādī watercourse Saudi Arabia 109 O8
Faylakah i. Kuwait 107 G5
Fayl-la-Forêt France 51 L5
Fayrān well Egypt 108 E9
Fayrān, Wādī watercourse Egypt 108 E9
Fayranī, Jabal mt. Egypt 108 F9
Fazair al Ghrazi watercourse Saudi Arabia 109 H8
Fazao Malfakassa, Parc National de nat. park Togo 125 F4
Fazeï well Niger 125 H2
Fazilka India 96 B3
Fazrān, Jabal hill Saudi Arabia 105 E2
Fdérik Mauritania 122 B5
formerly known as Fort Gouraud
Fead Group is P.N.G. see Nuguria Islands
Feale r. Ireland 47 C11
Fear, Cape U.S.A. 175 E5
Feather r. U.S.A. 182 C3
Feather, North Fork r. U.S.A. 182 C2
Featherston N.Z. 152 J9
Fécamp France 50 G3
Federacija Bosna i Hercegovina aut. div. Bos.-Herz. 56 K4
English form Federation of Bosnia and Herzegovina; also known as Muslim-Croat Federation
Federal Arg. 204 F3
Federal Capital Territory admin. div. Nigeria 125 G4
Federal District admin. dist. Brazil see Distrito Federal
Federal District admin. dist. Venez. see Distrito Federal
Federalsburg U.S.A. 177 J7
Federated Malay States country Asia see Malaysia
Federation of Bosnia and Herzegovina aut. div. Bos.-Herz. see Federacija Bosna i Hercegovina
Fedorov Kazakh. see Fedorovka
Fedorovka Kustanayskaya Oblast' Kazakh. 103 E1
Fedorovka Pavlodarskaya Oblast' Kazakh. 103 I1
Fedorovka Zapadnyy Kazakhstan Kazakh. 102 B2
also known as Fedorov
Fedorovka Rus. Fed. 102 C1
Fedorovskoye Rus. Fed. 43 U5
Feerfeer Somalia 128 E3
Fehérgyarmat Hungary 49 T8
Fehet Lake Canada 167 M1
Fehmarn i. Germany 48 I1
Fehmarn Belt strait Denmark/Germany 45 J5
also known as Femer Bælt
Fehrbellin Germany 49 J3
Feia, Lagoa lag. Brazil 203 D7
Feicheng China see Feixian
Feidong China 87 F2
also known as Dianbu
Feijó Brazil 200 C2
Feilding N.Z. 152 J8
Fei Ngo Shan hill Hong Kong China see Kowloon Peak
Feio r. Brazil see Aguapeí
Feira Zambia see Luangwa
Feira de Santana Brazil 202 E5
Feixi China 87 F2
also known as Shangpai; formerly known as Shangpaihe
Feixian China 85 H5
also known as Feicheng
Feixiang China 85 G4
Fejaj, Chott el salt l. Tunisia 123 H2
Fejø i. Denmark 48 I1
Feke Turkey 106 C3
Felanitx Spain 55 O5
Felaou well Alg. 125 G2
Feldberg mt. Germany 51 N5
Feldkirch Austria 48 G8
Feldkirchen in Kärnten Austria 49 L9
Feldru Romania 58 F1
Feliciano r. Arg. 204 F3
Felicity U.S.A. 176 A7
Felidhu Atoll Maldives 93 D10
Felipe C. Puerto Mex. 185 H5
Felixlândia Brazil 203 C6
Felixstowe U.K. 47 N12
Felletin France 51 I7
Fellowsville U.S.A. 176 F6
Felsberg Germany 48 G4
Felsina Italy see Bologna
Feltre Italy 56 D2
Femeas r. Brazil 202 C5
Femer Bælt strait Denmark/Germany see Fehmarn Belt
Femminamorta, Monte mt. Italy 57 I9
Femø i. Denmark 48 I1
Femundsmarka Nasjonalpark nat. park Norway 44 K3
Fenambosy, Lohatanjona pt Madag. 131 [inset] J5
Fene Spain 54 C1
Fenelon Falls Canada 173 O6
Fener Burnu hd Turkey 108 G1
also known as Karataş Burnu
Fénérive Madag. see Fenoarivo Atsinanana
Fengari mt. Greece 59 G8
Fengcheng Fujian China see Lianjiang
Fengcheng Fujian China see Anxi
Fengcheng Fujian China see Yongding
Fengcheng Guangdong China see Xinfeng
Fengcheng Guangxi China see Fengshan
Fengcheng Jiangxi China 87 E2
Fengcheng Liaoning China 83 B4
Fengchuan China see Fengxin
Fengdu China 87 C2
also known as Xiucaiwan; formerly known as Mingshan
Fenggang Fujian China see Shaxian
Fenggang Guizhou China 87 C3
also known as Longquan
Fenggang Jiangxi China see Yihuang
Fenggeling China 86 C1
Fenghua China 87 G2
Fenghuang China 87 D3
also known as Tuojiang
Fengjiaba China see Wangcang
Fengjie China 87 D2
also known as Yong'an
Fengkai China 87 D4
also known as Jiangkou
Fenglin Taiwan 87 G4
Fengming China see Qishan
Fengnan China 85 H4
Fengning China 85 H3
also known as Dage or Dagezhen
Fengqi China see Luochuan
Fengqing China 86 A3
also known as Fengshan
Fengqiu China 87 E1
Fengrun China 85 H4
Fengshan Fujian China see Luoyuan
Fengshan Guangxi China 86 C3
also known as Fengcheng
Fengshan Hubei China see Luotian
Fengshan Yunnan China see Fengqing
Fengshuba Shuiku resr China 87 E3
Fengshui Shan mt. China 82 A1
Fengtai China 87 F1
Fengtongzai Giant Panda Reserve nature res. China 86 B2
Fengxian Jiangsu China 87 F1
Fengxian Shaanxi China 86 C1
also known as Shuangshipu
Fengxian Shanghai China 87 G2
also known as Nanqiao
Fengxiang Heilong. China see Luobei
Fengxiang Yunnan China see Lincang
Fengxin China 87 E2
also known as Fengchuan
Fengyang China 87 F1
also known as Fucheng
Fengyi Guizhou China see Zheng'an
Fengyi Sichuan China see Maoxian
Fengyüan Taiwan 87 G3
Fengzhen China 85 G3
Fen He r. China 85 F5
Fenhe Shuiku resr China 85 F4
Feni Bangl. 97 F5
Feni Islands P.N.G. 145 E2
Fenny r. Bangl./India 97 F5
Feno, Capo di c. Corsica France 56 A7
Fenoarivo Atsinanana Madag. 131 [inset] K3
formerly known as Fénérive
Fenoarivo Be Madag. 131 [inset] J3
Fenshui China 87 F2
Fenton U.S.A. 173 J8
Fenua Ura atoll Fr. Polynesia see Manuae
Fenwick U.S.A. 176 E7
Fenyang China 85 F4
Fenyi China 87 E3
Feodosiya Ukr. 41 E7
also known as Caffa or Kafa or Kefe; historically known as Theodosia
Fer, Cap de c. Alg. 123 G1
Férai Greece see Feres
Ferapontovo Rus. Fed. 43 T2
Ferdinandshof Germany 49 K2
Ferdows Iran 100 D3
Fère-Champenoise France 51 J4
Feres Greece 58 H8
also known as Férai
Fergana Oblast admin. div. Uzbek. see Farg'ona
Fergana Range mts Kyrg. see Fergana Too Tizmegi
Fergana Too Tizmegi mts Kyrg. 103 H4
English form Fergana Range; also known as Ferganskiy Khrebet
Ferganskiy Khrebet mts Kyrg. see Fergana Too Tizmegi
Fergus Canada 173 M7
Fergus Falls U.S.A. 178 C2
Ferguson Lake Canada 167 L2
Fergusson r. Australia 148 A2
Fergusson Island P.N.G. 145 E2
Fériana Tunisia 123 H2
Ferjukot Iceland 44 [inset] B2
Ferkessédougou Côte d'Ivoire 124 D4
Ferlach Austria 49 L9
Ferlo, Vallée du watercourse Senegal 124 B3
Ferlo-Nord, Réserve de Faune du nature res. Senegal 124 B3
Ferlo-Sud, Réserve de Faune du nature res. Senegal 124 B3
Fermo Italy 56 F5
historically known as Firmum or Firmum Picenum
Fermont Canada 169 H2
Fermoselle Spain 54 E3
Fermoy Ireland 47 D11
Fernandina Beach U.S.A. 175 D6
Fernando de Magallanes, Parque Nacional nat. park Chile 205 B9
Fernando de Noronha i. Brazil 216 L6
UNESCO World Heritage Site
Fernandópolis Brazil 206 C7
Fernando Poó i. Equat. Guinea see Bioco
Fernán Núñez Spain 54 G7
Fernão Dias Brazil 207 I3
Fernão Veloso Moz. 131 I2
Ferndale U.S.A. 180 B2
Ferndown U.K. 47 K13
Fernhill N.Z. 152 K7
Fernie Canada 167 H5
Fernley U.S.A. 182 E2
Ferns Ireland 47 F11
Ferozepore India see Firozpur
Ferrara Italy 56 D4
UNESCO World Heritage Site
Ferrato, Capo c. Sardinia Italy 57 B9
Ferreira Spain 54 D1
Ferreira do Alentejo Port. 54 C6
Ferrellsburg U.S.A. 176 C7
Ferreñafe Peru 198 B6
Ferriday U.S.A. 175 B6
Ferro, Capo c. Sardinia Italy 56 B7
Ferrol Spain 54 C1
also known as El Ferrol; long form El Ferrol del Caudillo
Ferron U.S.A. 183 M2
Ferros Brazil 203 D6
Ferrum U.S.A. 176 E9
Ferryland Canada 169 K4
Ferryville Tunisia see Menzel Bourguiba
Fertő l. Austria/Hungary 49 N8
UNESCO World Heritage Site
Fertő-tavi nat. park Hungary 49 N8
Ferzikovo Rus. Fed. 43 R7
Fès Morocco 122 D2
also spelt Al Fas or Fez
UNESCO World Heritage Site
Feshi Dem. Rep. Congo 127 C6
Fessenden U.S.A. 178 C2
Fet Dom, Tanjung pt Indon. 75 D3
Fété Bowé Senegal 124 B3
Feteşti Romania 58 I4
Feteşti-Gară Romania 58 I4
Fethard Ireland 47 E11
Fethiye Malatya Turkey see Yazıhan
Fethiye Muğla Turkey 106 B3
Fetisovo Kazakh. 102 C4
Fetlar i. U.K. 46 L3
Feuilles, Rivière aux r. Canada 169 G1
Feurs France 51 K7
Fevral'sk Rus. Fed. 82 C1
Fevzipaşa Turkey 107 D3
Feyzābād Afgh. 101 G2
also spelt Faizabad
Feyẕābād Iran 100 C4
Fez Morocco see Fès
Fiambalá Arg. 204 D2
Fiambala r. Arg. 204 D2
Fian Ghana 124 E4
Fianarantsoa Madag. 131 [inset] J4
Fianarantsoa prov. Madag. 131 [inset] J4
Fianga Chad 126 B2
Fiano Romano Italy 56 E6
Ficalho hill Port. 54 D7
Fichē Eth. 128 C2
Fichtelgebirge hills Germany 51 S2
Fichtelgebirge park Germany 48 J5
Ficksburg S. Africa 133 L5
Fidā oasis Saudi Arabia 105 F4
Fidenza Italy 56 C4
Fidīmīn Egypt 108 B8
Fidjeland Norway 45 I4
Fidlův Kopec hill Czech Rep. 49 O6
Field B.C. Canada 167 G5
Field Ont. Canada 173 M4
Field U.S.A. 176 B9
Field Island Australia 148 B2
Fiemanka r. Latvia 42 H5
Fieni Romania 58 G3
Fier Albania 58 A8
Fiery Creek r. Australia 148 C3
Fierzes, Liqeni i resr Albania 58 B6
Fife Lake U.S.A. 172 H6
Fife Ness pt U.K. 46 J7
Fifield U.S.A. 172 C5
Fifteenth of May City Egypt see Medinet 15 Mayo
Fifth Cataract rapids Sudan see 5th Cataract
Fifth Meridian Canada 167 H3
Figalo, Cap c. Alg. 55 J9
Figari, Capo c. Sardinia Italy 56 B8
Figeac France 51 I8
Figueira r. Port. 54 C6
Figueira da Foz Port. 54 C4
Figueiró dos Vinhos Port. 54 C5
Figueras Spain see Figueres
Figueres Spain 55 N2
also spelt Figueras
Figuig Morocco 123 E2
Figuil Cameroon 125 I4

►Fiji country S. Pacific Ocean 145 G3
4th most populous and 5th largest country in Oceania.
►►138–139 Oceania Countries

Fīk' Eth. 128 D2
Filabusi Zimbabwe 131 F4
Filadelfia Costa Rica 186 B5
Filadelfia Italy 57 I10
Filadelfia Para. 201 E5
Fil'akovo Slovakia 49 Q7
Filamana Mali 124 D4
Filchner Ice Shelf Antarctica 222 V1
Filey U.K. 47 L9
Filiaşi Romania 58 E4
Filiates Greece 59 B9
Filiatra Greece 59 C11
Filibe Bulg. see Plovdiv
Filicudi, Isola i. Isole Lipari Italy 57 G10
Filingué Niger 125 F3
Filiouri r. Greece 58 G8
Filipinas country Asia see Philippines
Filippa, Mys hd Rus. Fed. 82 E1
Filippiada Greece 59 B9
Filippoi tourist site Greece 58 F7
Filipstad Sweden 45 K4
Fillan Norway 44 J3
Fillíra Greece see Fillyra
Fillmore CA U.S.A. 182 F7
Fillmore UT U.S.A. 183 L3
Fillyra Greece 58 G7
also spelt Fillíra
Filtu Eth. 128 D3
Fimbull Ice Shelf Antarctica 223 A2
Fina, Réserve de nature res. Mali 124 C3
Finale Ligure Italy 56 A4
Fincastle U.S.A. 176 F8
Finch'a'ā Hāyk' l. Eth. 128 C2
Findhorn r. U.K. 46 I6
Fındık Turkey 107 E3
also known as Parona
Findlay U.S.A. 176 B4
Fine U.S.A. 177 J1
Finger Lake Canada 167 M4
Finger Lakes U.S.A. 177 I3
Fingeshwar India 94 D1
Fingoè Moz. 131 F2
Finiels, Sommet de mt. France 51 J8
Finike Turkey 106 B3
Finike Körfezi b. Turkey 106 B3
Finisterre Spain see Fisterra
Finisterre, Cabo c. Spain see Finisterre, Cape
Finisterre, Cape Spain 54 B2
also known as Finisterre, Cabo or Fisterra, Cabo
Finke Australia 148 B5
Finke watercourse Australia 148 B5
Finke, Mount hill Australia 146 B2
Finke Aboriginal Land res. Australia 148 C5
Finke Bay Australia 148 A2
Finke Flood Flats lowland Australia 148 B5
Finke Gorge National Park Australia 148 B5
►Finland country Europe 44 M3
known as Suomi in Finnish
►►32–33 Europe Countries
Finland U.S.A. 172 B3
Finland, Gulf of Europe 42 D2
Finlay r. Canada 166 E3
Finlay, Mount Canada 166 E3
Finlay Forks Canada 166 F4
Finlayson U.S.A. 172 A4
Finley Australia 147 E3
Finley U.S.A. 178 C2
Finmark Canada 172 D2
Finn r. Ireland 47 E9
Finne ridge Germany 48 I4
Finnigan, Mount Australia 149 E2
Finniss r. Australia 148 A2
Finniss, Cape Australia 146 B3
Finnis Springs Aboriginal Land res. Australia 146 C2
Finnmark county Norway 44 N1
Finnmarksvidda reg. Norway 44 M1
Finnskog Norway 45 K3
Finnsnes Norway 44 L1
Finschhafen P.N.G. 73 K8
Finspång Sweden 45 K4
Finsteraarhorn mt. Switz. 51 O6
Finsterwalde Germany 49 K4
Finström Fin. 42 A1
Fintona U.K. 47 E9
Finucane Range hills Australia 149 D4
Fiora r. Italy 56 D6
Fiordland National Park N.Z. 153 B13
UNESCO World Heritage Site
Fiordland Provincial Recreation Area Canada 166 D4
Fiorenzuola d'Arda Italy 56 B4
Fir reg. Saudi Arabia 105 D1
Fırat r. Turkey 107 D3 see Euphrates
Firavahana Madag. 131 [inset] J3
Firebaugh U.S.A. 182 D5
Firedrake Lake Canada 167 J2
Firenze Italy see Florence
Fire River Canada 173 J2
Fireside Canada 166 E3
Firesteel Creek r. U.S.A. 178 C3
Firiña Venez. 199 E3
Firk, Sha'īb watercourse Iraq 107 F5
Firkachi well Niger 125 I3
Firmat Arg. 204 E4
Firmino Alves Brazil 207 N1
Firminópolis Brazil 206 C3
Firminy France 51 K7
Firmum Italy see Fermo
Firmum Picenum Italy see Fermo
Firovo Rus. Fed. 43 O4
Firozabad India 96 C4
Firozkoh reg. Afgh. 101 F3
Firozpur Haryana India 96 C4
Firozpur Punjab India 96 B3
formerly spelt Ferozepore
First Cataract rapids Egypt see 1st Cataract
Firuzabad Iran see Rāsk
Fīrūzābād Iran 100 C4
Fīrūzeh Iran 100 D2
Fīrūzkūh Iran 100 C3
Fischersbrunn Namibia 130 B5
Fish watercourse Namibia 130 C6
Fish r. S. Africa 132 E7
Fisher Australia 146 A2
Fisher Bay Antarctica 223 J2
Fisher Glacier Antarctica 223 E2
Fisher River Canada 167 L5
Fisher Strait Canada 165 K3
Fishersville U.S.A. 176 G7
Fishguard U.K. 47 H12
also known as Abergwaun
Fishing Creek U.S.A. 177 I7
Fishing Lake Canada 167 M4
Fish Lake Canada 166 F2
Fish Lake MN U.S.A. 172 A4
Fish Lake UT U.S.A. 183 M3
Fish Point U.S.A. 173 J7
Fiskå Norway 44 I3
Fiske, Cape Antarctica 222 T2
Fiskebøl Norway 44 K1
Fiskenæsset Greenland see Qeqertarsuatsiaat
Fismes France 51 J3
Fisterra Spain 54 B2
also spelt Finisterre
Fisterra, Cabo c. Spain see Finisterre, Cape
Fitampito Madag. 131 [inset] J4
Fitchburg MA U.S.A. 177 N3
Fitchburg WI U.S.A. 172 D8
Fitchville U.S.A. 176 C4
Fitíai Greece see Fyteies
Fitjar Norway 45 I4
Fitri, Lac l. Chad 120 C6
Fitzcarrald Peru 200 B2
Fitzgerald U.S.A. 175 D6
Fitzgerald River National Park Australia 151 B7
Fitz Hugh Sound sea chan. Canada 166 D5
Fitzmaurice r. Australia 148 A2
Fitz Roy Arg. 205 D7
Fitzroy r. Qld Australia 149 F4
Fitzroy r. W.A. Australia 150 C3
Fitz Roy, Cerro mt. Arg. 205 B8
Fitzroy Aboriginal Land res. Australia 148 A2
Fitzroy Crossing Australia 150 D3
Fitzwilliam Island Canada 168 D4
Fiume Croatia see Rijeka
Fiumefreddo di Sicilia Sicily Italy 57 H11
Five Fingers Peninsula N.Z. 153 A13
Five Forks N.Z. 153 E13
Five Points U.S.A. 182 D5
Fivizzano Italy 56 C4
Fizi Dem. Rep. Congo 126 F6
Fizuli Azer. see Füzuli
Fjällsjönäs Sweden 44 L2
Fjellbu Norway 44 L1
Fjerritslev Denmark 45 J4
Fkih Ben Salah Morocco 122 D2
Flå Norway 45 J3
Flaga Iceland 44 [inset] C3
Flagstaff S. Africa 133 N8
also known as Siphaqeni
Flagstaff U.S.A. 183 M6
Flagstaff Lake U.S.A. 174 G2
Flaherty Island Canada 168 E1
Flakaberg Sweden 44 M2
Flåm Norway 45 I3
Flambeau r. U.S.A. 172 B5
Flamborough Head U.K. 47 L9
Flamenco, Isla i. Arg. 204 E6

Frosinone Italy 56 F7
historically known as Frusino
Frosta Norway 44 J3
Frostburg U.S.A. 176 G6
Frost Glacier Antarctica 223 I2
Frøya i. Norway 44 J3
Fruges France 51 I2
Fruita U.S.A. 183 P2
Fruitland IA U.S.A. 172 B9
Fruitland MD U.S.A. 177 J7
Fruitland UT U.S.A. 183 N1
Fruitport U.S.A. 172 G7
Fruitvale U.S.A. 183 P2
Fruktovaya Rus. Fed. 43 U7
Frunze Batken Kyrg. 103 G4
also known as Frunzenskoye
Frunze Bishkek Kyrg. see Bishkek
Frunzenskoye Kyrg. see Frunze
Frunzivka Ukr. 58 K1
Frusino Italy see Frosinone
Fruska Gora nat. park Serb. and Mont. 58 A3
Frutigen Switz. 51 N6
Frutillar Chile 205 B6
Frutuoso Brazil 201 E3
Fryanovo Rus. Fed. 43 T5
Fryazino Rus. Fed. 43 T6
Frýdek-Místek Czech Rep. 49 P6
Fryeburg U.S.A. 177 O1
Fu'an China 87 F3
Fucheng Anhui China see Fengyang
Fucheng Shaanxi China see Fuxian
Fuchū Japan 91 C7
Fuchuan China 87 D3
also known as Fuyang
Fuchun Jiang r. China 87 G2
Fudai Japan 90 G4
Fude China 87 F3
Fuding China 87 G3
Fudua waterhole Kenya 128 C5
Fudul reg. Saudi Arabia 105 D3
Fuengirola Spain 54 G8
Fuenlabrada Spain 54 H4
Fuente-Álamo Spain 55 J6
Fuente Álamo Spain 55 J7
Fuente Albilla, Cerro de mt. Spain 55 J6
Fuente de Cantos Spain 54 E6
Fuente Obejuna Spain 54 F6
Fuentesaúco Spain 54 F3
Fuentes de Ebro Spain 55 K3
Fuerte Olimpo Para. 201 F5
Fuerteventura i. Canary Is 122 B3
Fuga i. Phil. 74 B2
Fugloy i. Faroe Is 46 F1
Fuglstad Norway 44 K2
Fugou China 87 E1
Fugu China 85 F4
Fuguo China see Zhanhua
Fuhai China 88 D2
also known as Burultokay
Fuḩaymī Iraq 109 N3
Fujairah U.A.E. 105 G2
also spelt Al Fujayrah or Fujeira
Fujeira U.A.E. see Fujairah
Fuji China see Xiaoshi
Fuji Japan 91 F7
Fujian prov. China 87 F3
English form Fukien
Fu Jiang r. China 86 C2
Fujieda Japan 91 F7
Fuji-Hakone-Izu National Park Japan 91 F7
Fujiidera Japan 91 D7
Fujin China 82 C3
Fujinomiya Japan 91 F7
Fujioka Japan 91 F6
Fuji-san vol. Japan 91 F7
Fujiyoshida Japan 91 F7
Fukagawa Japan 90 H3
Fūkah Egypt 106 A5
Fukang China 88 D2
Fukaura Japan 90 F4
Fukaya Japan 91 F6
Fukien prov. China see Fujian
Fukuchiyama Japan 91 D7
Fukue Japan 91 A8
Fukue-jima i. Japan 91 A8
Fukui Japan 91 E6
Fukui pref. Japan 91 E7
Fukuno Japan 91 E6
Fukuoka Japan 91 B8
Fukuoka pref. Japan 91 B8
Fukushima Fukushima Japan 90 G6
Fukushima Hokkaidō Japan 90 G4
Fukushima pref. Japan 90 G6
Fukuyama Japan 91 B9
Fūl, Jabal hill Egypt 108 D8
Fulacunda Guinea-Bissau 124 B4
Fūlād Maïalleh Iran 100 C2
also known as Amirabad
Fulayj Oman 105 G3
Fulchhari Bangl. 97 F4
Fulda Germany 48 G5
Fulda r. Germany 48 G4
Fule China 86 C3
Fuli China see Jixian
Fuliji China 87 F1
Fulin China see Hanyuan
Fuling China 87 C2
Fulitun China see Jixian
Fullerton CA U.S.A. 182 G8
Fullerton NE U.S.A. 178 C3
Fullerton, Cape Canada 167 N2
Fulnek Czech Rep. 49 O6
Fulton KY U.S.A. 174 B4
Fulton MO U.S.A. 174 B4
Fulton MS U.S.A. 174 B5
Fulton NY U.S.A. 177 I2
Fulufjällets national park nature res. Sweden 45 K3
Fulunäs Sweden 45 K3
Fumay France 51 K3
Fumel France 50 G8
Fumin China 86 B3
also known as Yongding
Funabashi Japan 91 F7
Funafuti atoll Tuvalu 145 G2
formerly known as Ellice Island
Funan Anhui China 87 E1
Funan Guangxi China see Fusui
Funäsdalen Sweden 44 K3

►Funchal Madeira 122 A2
Capital of Madeira.

Fundación Col. 198 C2
Fundão Brazil 203 D6
Fundão Port. 54 D4
Fundi Italy see Fondi
Fundición Mex. 184 C3
Fundo das Figuerias Cape Verde 124 [inset]
Fundulea Romania 58 H4
Fundy, Bay of g. Canada 169 H4
Fünen i. Denmark see Fyn
Funeral Peak U.S.A. 183 H5
Fünfkirchen Hungary see Pécs
Fung Wong Shan hill Hong Kong China see Lantau Peak
Funhalouro Moz. 131 G4
Funing Jiangsu China 87 F1
Funing Yunnan China 86 C4
also known as Xinhua
Funiu Shan mts China 87 D1
Funnel Creek r. Australia 149 F4
Funsi Ghana 125 E4
Funtua Nigeria 125 G4
Funzie U.K. 46 L3
Fuping China 85 G4
Fuqing China 87 F3
Fuquan China 87 C3
also known as Chengxian
Furancungo Moz. 131 G2
Furano Japan 90 H3
Fürgun, Kūh-e mt. Iran 100 D5
Furmanov Rus. Fed. 40 G4
Furmanovka Kazakh. see Moyynkum
Furmanovo Kazakh. see Zhalpaktal
Furmanovo Rus. Fed. 90 D3
Furnas, Represa resr Brazil 207 G8
Furneaux Group is Australia 147 F5
Furnes Belgium see Veurne
Furong China see Wan'an
Fürstenau Germany 48 E3
Fürstenberg Germany 49 K2
Fürstenfeld Austria 49 N8
Fürstenfeldbruck Germany 48 I7
Fürstenwalde Germany 49 L3
Fürth Germany 48 H6
Furth im Wald Germany 49 J6
Furubira Japan 90 G3
Furudal Sweden 45 K3
Furukawa Japan 90 G5
Fury and Hecla Strait Canada 165 K3
Fusagasugá Col. 198 C3
Fusan S. Korea see Pusan
Fushan Shandong China 85 I4
Fushan Shanxi China 85 F5
Fushë-Krujë Albania 58 A7
Fushun Liaoning China 82 A4
Fushun Sichuan China 86 C2
Fusong China 82 B4
Fusui China 87 C4
also known as Xinning; formerly known as Funan
Futago-san vol. Japan 91 B8
Futaleufú Chile 205 C6
Fu Tau Pun Chau i. Hong Kong China 87 [inset]
Futog Vojvodina, Srbija Serb. and Mont. 58 A3
Futtsu Japan 91 F7
Futuna i. Vanuatu 145 G3
also spelt Fotuna; formerly known as Erronan
Futuna, Île i. Wallis and Futuna Is 145 H3
Futuna Islands Wallis and Futuna Is 145 H3
English form Hoorn Islands; also known as Hoorn, Îles de or Horne, Îles de.
Futun Xi r. China 87 F3
Fuwah Egypt 108 B6
Fuwayriṭ Qatar 105 E2
Fuxian Liaoning China see Wafangdian
Fuxian Shaanxi China 85 F5
also known as Fucheng
Fuxian Hu l. China 86 B3
Fuxin Liaoning China 85 I3
also known as Fuxinzhen
Fuxin Liaoning China 85 I3
Fuxing China see Wangmo
Fuxinzhen China see Fuxin
Fuya Japan 90 F5
Fuyang Anhui China 87 E1
Fuyang Guangxi China see Fuchuan
Fuyang Zhejiang China 87 F2
Fuyang He r. China 85 H4
Fuying Dao i. China 87 G3
Fuyu Heilong. China 85 J2
Fuyu Jilin China see Songyuan
Fuyu Jilin China 82 B3
formerly known as Sanchahe
Fuyuan Heilong. China 82 D2
Fuyuan Yunnan China 86 C3
also known as Zhong'an
Fuyun China 84 A2
also known as Koktokay
Füzesabony Hungary 49 R8
Füzesgyarmat Hungary 49 S8
Fuzhou Fujian China 87 F3
formerly spelt Foochow
Fuzhou Jiangxi China 87 F3
formerly known as Linchuan
Füzuli Azer. 107 F3
also spelt Fizuli; formerly known as Karyagino
Fwamba Dem. Rep. Congo 127 D6
Fyn county Denmark 45 J5
Fyn i. Denmark 38 B4
also known as Fünen
Fyne, Loch inlet U.K. 46 G8
Fyresvatn l. Norway 45 J4
F.Y.R.O.M. country Europe see Macedonia
Fyteies Greece 59 C10
also known as Fitíai

G

Gaâfour Tunisia 57 B12
Gaalkacyo Somalia 128 E3
Gaat r. Sarawak Malaysia 77 F2
Gab watercourse Namibia 132 B4
Gabakly Turkm. 103 E5
also spelt Kabakly
Gabangab well Eth. 128 E3
Gabas r. France 50 F9
Gabasumdo China see Tongde
Gabbac, Raas pt Somalia 128 F2
Gabbs Valley Range mts U.S.A. 182 F3
Gabd Pak. 101 E5
Gabela Angola 127 B7
Gaberones Botswana see Gaborone
Gabès Tunisia 123 H2
Gabès, Golfe de g. Tunisia 123 H2
English form Gabès, Gulf of
Gabès, Gulf of Tunisia see Gabès, Golfe de
Gabgaba, Wadi watercourse Sudan 121 G4
Gable End Foreland hd N.Z. 152 M6
►Gabon country Africa 126 A5
►►114–115 Africa Countries
Gabon, Estuaire du est. Gabon 126 A4

►Gaborone Botswana 131 E5
Capital of Botswana. Formerly spelt Gaberones.

Gabou Senegal 124 B3
Gabriel Vera Bol. 200 D4
Gabriel y Galán, Embalse de resr Spain 54 E4
Gābrīk Iran 100 D5
Gābrīk watercourse Iran 100 D5
Gabrovnitsa Bulg. 58 E5
Gabrovo Bulg. 58 G6
Gabú Guinea-Bissau 124 B3
Gabuli vol. Eth. 128 D1
Gacé France 50 G4
Gacko Bos.-Herz. 56 K5
Gädäbäy Azer. 107 F2
Gadabedji, Réserve Totale de Faune de nature res. Niger 125 G3
Gadag India 94 B3
Gadaisu P.N.G. 149 F1
Gadchiroli India 94 D1
Gäddede Sweden 44 K2
Gadê China 86 A1
also known as Pagqên
Gadebusch Germany 48 I2
Gades Spain see Cádiz
Gadhada India 96 A5
Gadhra India 94 A1
Gadsden U.S.A. 175 C5
Gadwal India 94 C2
Gadyach Ukr. see Hadyach
Gadyn Turkm. 103 E5
Gadzi Cent. Afr. Rep. 126 C3
Gadžin Han Srbija Serb. and Mont. 58 D5
Gael Hamke Bugt b. Greenland 165 Q2
Găeşti Romania 58 G4
Gaeta Italy 56 F7
Gaeta, Golfo di g. Italy 56 F7
Gafanha da Nazaré Port. 54 C4
Gaferut i. Micronesia 73 K5
Gaffney U.S.A. 174 D5
Gafsa Tunisia 123 H2
historically known as Capsa
Gag i. Indon. 75 D3
Gagal Chad 126 B2
Gagaon India 96 B5
Gagarin Rus. Fed. 43 Q6
formerly known as Gzhatsk
Gagarin Uzbek. 103 G4
formerly known as Yerzhar
Gagere watercourse Nigeria 125 G3
Gagliano del Capo Italy 57 K9
Gagnoa Côte d'Ivoire 124 D5
Gagnon Canada 169 G3
Gago Coutinho Angola see Lumbala N'guimbo
Gagra Georgia 107 E2
Gaiab watercourse Namibia 130 C6
Gaibandha Bangl. 97 F4
Găiceana Romania 58 I2
Gail r. Austria 49 K9
Gail U.S.A. 179 B5
Gaillac France 50 H9
Gaillimh Ireland see Galway
Gaillon France 50 H3
Gaindainqoinkor China see Gaindainqoinkor
Gaindainqoinkor China 89 E6
also known as Gaindaingoinkor
Gainesboro U.S.A. 178 F4
Gainesville FL U.S.A. 175 D6
Gainesville GA U.S.A. 174 D5
Gainesville MO U.S.A. 178 D4
Gainesville TX U.S.A. 179 C5
Gainsborough U.K. 47 L10
Gairdner r. Australia 151 B7
Gairdner, Lake imp. l. Australia 146 B2
Gairloch U.K. 46 G6
Gairo Tanz. 129 C6
Gaixian China see Gaizhou
Gaizhou China 85 I3
formerly known as Gaixian
Gaiziņkalns hill Latvia 42 G5
Gaja r. Hungary 49 P8
Gajah Hutan, Bukit hill Malaysia 76 C1
Gajapatinagaram India 95 D2
Gaji r. Nigeria 125 H4
Gajiram Nigeria 125 I3
Gajol India 97 F4
Gakarosa mt. S. Africa 132 H4
Gakem Nigeria 125 H5
Gakuch Jammu and Kashmir 96 B1
Gala China 89 E6
Galaasiya Uzbek. see Galaosiyo
Galán, Cerro mt. Arg. 204 D2
Galana r. Kenya 128 D5
Galand Iran 100 C2
Galang Besar i. Indon. 76 D2
Galangue Angola 127 C8
Galanta Slovakia 49 O7
Galaosiyo Uzbek. 103 F5
also spelt Galaasiya
Galápagos, Islas is Pacific Ocean see Galapagos Islands

►Galapagos Islands is Pacific Ocean 221 M6
Part of Ecuador. Most westerly point of South America. Also known as Galápagos, Islas or Colón, Archipiélago de.
UNESCO World Heritage Site
►►14–15 World Environmental Impacts
►►188–189 South America Landscapes
►►192–193 South America Countries

Galas well Kenya 128 C4
Galashiels U.K. 46 J8
Galata Bulg. 58 I5
Galatea N.Z. 152 K6
Galaţi Romania 58 J3
Galatina Italy 57 K8
Galatini Greece 59 C8
Galatista Greece 59 E8
Galatone Italy 57 K8
Galatzó, Puig des mt. Spain 55 N5
Galax U.S.A. 176 E9
Galaýmor Turkm. 101 E3
also spelt Galaymor
Galaymor Turkm. see Galaýmor
Galdhøpiggen mt. Norway 45 J3
Galeana Chihuahua Mex. 184 D2
Galeana Nuevo León Mex. 185 E3
Galegu Sudan 121 G6
Galela Indon. 75 C2
Galena AK U.S.A. 164 D3
Galena IL U.S.A. 174 B3
Galena KS U.S.A. 178 D4
Galena MD U.S.A. 177 J6
Galena MO U.S.A. 178 D4
Galena Bay Canada 166 G5
Galera, Punta pt Chile 204 B6
Galera, Punta pt Ecuador 198 A4
Galera, Punta pt Mex. 185 F6
Galera Point Trin. and Tob. 187 H5
Galeras vol. Col. 198 B4
Galesburg IL U.S.A. 174 B3
Galesburg MI U.S.A. 172 H8
Galeshewe S. Africa 133 I5
Galesville U.S.A. 172 B6
Galeton U.S.A. 176 H4
Galga r. Hungary 49 Q8
Galguduud admin. reg. Somalia 128 E3
Gal Hareeri Somalia 128 E3
Gália Brazil 206 D9
Galicea Mare Romania 58 E4
Galich Rus. Fed. 40 G4
Galichskaya Vozvyshennost' hills Rus. Fed. 40 G4
Galicia aut. comm. Spain 54 D2
Galičica nat. park Macedonia 58 B7
Galilee, Sea of l. Israel 108 G5
also known as Tiberias, Lake or Kinneret, Yam
Galiléia Brazil 207 L6
Galissas Greece 59 F11
Galite, Canal de la sea chan. Tunisia 123 H1
Galitsa Rus. Fed. 43 S8
Galiuro Mountains U.S.A. 183 N9
Galiwinku Australia 148 B2
Galkynyş Turkm. 103 E5
also spelt Dänew; formerly spelt Deynau
Gallabat Sudan 121 H6
G'allaorol Uzbek. 103 F4
also spelt Ghallaorol
Gallarate Italy 56 A3
Gallatin MO U.S.A. 178 D4
Gallatin TN U.S.A. 174 C4
Gallatin r. U.S.A. 180 E3
Galle Sri Lanka 94 D5
UNESCO World Heritage Site
Gállego r. Spain 55 K3
Gallegos r. Arg. 205 C8
Gallegos, Cabo c. Chile 205 B7
Gallia country Europe see France

►Gallinas, Punta pt Col. 198 D1
Most northerly point of South America.
►►188–189 South America Landscapes

Gallipoli Italy 57 K8
Gallipoli Turkey 106 A2
also spelt Gelibolu; historically known as Callipolis
Gallipolis U.S.A. 176 C7
Gällivare Sweden 44 M2
Gallneukirchen Austria 49 L7
Gallo r. Spain 55 I4
Gällö Sweden 44 K3
Gallo, Capo c. Sicily Italy 57 F10
Gallup KY U.S.A. 176 C7
Gallup NM U.S.A. 181 E6
Gallur Spain 55 J3
Gallura reg. Sardinia Italy 56 A8
Galma watercourse Nigeria 125 G4
Galoya Sri Lanka 94 D4
Gal Oya National Park Sri Lanka 94 D5
Gal Shiikh Somalia 128 E2
Galt U.S.A. 182 C3
Gal Tardo Somalia 128 E4
Galtat Zemmour W. Sahara 122 B4
Galtee Mountains hills Ireland 47 D11
Galtymore hill Ireland 47 D11
Galūgāh, Kūh-e mts Iran 100 C4
Galūgāh-e Āsīyeh Iran 101 D3
Galunggung, Gunung vol. Indon. 77 E4
Galva U.S.A. 172 C9
Galveias Port. 54 D5
Galveston IN U.S.A. 172 G10
Galveston TX U.S.A. 179 D6
Galveston Bay U.S.A. 179 D6
Galvez Arg. 204 E4
Galwa Nepal 97 D3
Galway Ireland 47 C10
also spelt Gaillimh
Galway Bay Ireland 47 C10
Gâm, Sông r. Vietnam 78 D3
Gamá Brazil 206 E3
Gama, Isla i. Arg. 204 E6
Gamaches France 50 H3
Gamagōri Japan 91 E7
Gamalakhe S. Africa 133 O7
Gamalama vol. Indon. 75 C2
Gamarra Col. 198 C2
Gámas Fin. see Kaamanen
Gamawa Nigeria 125 H3
Gamay Bay Phil. 74 C3
Gamba China see Gongbalou
Gamba Gabon 126 A5
Gambēla Eth. 128 B2
Gambēla Hizboch admin. reg. Eth. 128 B3
Gambēla National Park Eth. 128 B3
Gambell U.S.A. 164 B3
Gambia r. Gambia 124 A3
UNESCO World Heritage Site
Gambie r. Senegal 124 B3
Gambier, Îles is Fr. Polynesia 221 K7
English form Gambier Islands; also known as Mangareva Islands
Gambier Islands Australia 146 C3
Gambier Islands Fr. Polynesia see Gambier, Îles
Gambo Canada 169 K3
Gamboma Congo 126 B5
Gamboola Australia 149 D3
Gamboula Cent. Afr. Rep. 126 B3
Gamda China see Zamtang
Gamka r. S. Africa 132 F10
Gamkunoro, Gunung vol. Indon. 75 C2
Gamlakarleby Fin. see Kokkola
Gamleby Sweden 45 L4
Gammams well Sudan 121 G5
Gammelstaden Sweden 44 M2
Gammon Ranges National Park Australia 146 C2
Gamoep S. Africa 132 C6
Gamova, Mys pt Rus. Fed. 82 C4
Gampaha Sri Lanka 94 D5
Gampola Sri Lanka 94 D5
Gams Switz. 51 P5
Gamshadzai Kūh mts Iran 101 E4
Gamtog China 86 A2
Gamtoos r. S. Africa 133 J10
Gamud mt. Eth. 128 C3
Gamvik Norway 44 O1
Gana China 86 B1
formerly known as Gengda
Ganado U.S.A. 183 O6
Gananoque Canada 168 E4
Ganāveh Iran 100 B4
Gäncä Azer. 107 F2
also spelt Gandzha; formerly known as Kirovabad; formerly spelt Gyandzha
Gand Belgium see Ghent
Ganda Angola 127 B8
formerly known as Mariano Machado
Gandadiwata, Bukit mt. Indon. 75 A3
Gandai India 96 D5
Gandajika Dem. Rep. Congo 127 D6
Gandarbal Jammu and Kashmir 96 B2
Gandari Mountain Pak. 101 G4
Gandava Pak. 101 F4
Gander Canada 169 K3
Gander r. Canada 169 K3
Ganderkesee Germany 48 F2
Gander Lake Canada 169 K3
Gandesa Spain 55 L3
Gandevi India 94 B1
Gandhidham India 96 A5
Gandhinagar India 96 B5
Gandhi Sagar resr India 96 B4
Gandi, Wadi watercourse Sudan 126 E2
Gandía Spain 55 K6
Gandomān Iran 100 B4
Gandu Brazil 202 E5
Gandvik Norway 44 O1
Gandzha Azer. see Gäncä
Gâneb well Mauritania 124 C2
Ganga r. Bangl./India see Ganges
Ganga Nigeria 125 G4
Ganga r. Sri Lanka 94 D5
Gangaikondacholapuram India 94 C4
UNESCO World Heritage Site
Gangakher India 94 C2
Gangán Arg. 205 C6
Gangán, Pampa de plain Arg. 205 C6
Ganganagar India 96 B3
Gangapur Maharashtra India 94 B2
Gangapur Rajasthan India 96 B4
Gangapur Rajasthan India 96 C4
Gangara Niger 125 H3
Gangavali r. India 94 B3
Gangaw Myanmar 78 A3
Gangawati India 94 C3
Gangaw Range mts Myanmar 78 B3
Gangca China 84 D4
also known as Shaliuhe
Gangdhar India 96 B5
Gangdisê Shan mts China 89 C6
English form Kailas Range
Ganges r. Bangl./India 96 F5
also known as Ganga or Padma (Bangl.)
Ganges France 51 J9
Ganges, Mouths of the Bangl./India 97 F5
Gangi Sicily Italy 57 G11
Ganglota Liberia 124 C5
Gangouyi China 84 E5
Gangra Turkey see Çankırı
Gangrar India 96 B4
Gangtok India 97 F4
Gangu China 86 C1
Gangziyao China 85 G4
Gan He r. China 85 J1
Ganhezi China 88 E2
Gani Indon. 75 D3
Ganiakali Guinea 124 C4
Ganjam India 95 E2
Gan Jiang r. China 87 F2
Ganjig China 85 I3
also known as Horqin Zuoyi Houqi
Gankovo Rus. Fed. 43 O2
Ganluo China 86 B2
also known as Xinshiba
Gannan China 85 I2
Gannat France 51 J6
Gannet Islands Ecological Reserve Canada 169 J2
Gannett Peak U.S.A. 180 E4
Ganq China 84 B4
Ganquan China 85 F4
Gansbaai S. Africa 132 D11
Gänserndorf Austria 49 N7
Ganshui China 86 C2
Ganskuil S. Africa 133 K1
Gansu prov. China 84 C3
English form Kansu
Gantamaa Somalia 128 D4
Gantapara India 95 D1
Gantheaume Point Australia 150 C3
Gant'iadi Georgia 107 E2
formerly known as Pilenkovo
Ganting China see Huxian
Gantsevichi Belarus see Hantsavichy
Ganxian China 87 E3
also known as Meilin
Ganyal r. India 94 C1
Ganye Nigeria 125 I4
Ganyesa S. Africa 132 I3
Ganyu China 87 F1
also known as Qingkou
Ganyushkino Kazakh. 102 B3
Ganzhe China see Minhou
Ganzhou China 87 E3
Ganzi Sudan 128 A3
Ganzurino Rus. Fed. 85 E1
Gao Mali 125 E2
UNESCO World Heritage Site
Gao admin. reg. Mali 125 F2
Gao'an China 87 E2
Gaocheng Hebei China 85 G4
Gaocheng Sichuan China see Litang
Gaochun China 87 F2
also known as Chunxi
Gaocun China see Mayang
Gaojian China 87 G2
Gaolan China 84 D4
formerly known as Shidongsi
Gaoleshan China see Xianfeng
Gaoliangjian China see Hongze
Gaoligong Shan mts China 86 A3
Gaoling China 87 D1
also known as Luyuan
Gaomi China 85 H4
Gaomutang China 87 D3
Gaoping China 85 G5
Gaoqing China 85 H4
also known as Tianzhen
Gaotai China 84 C4
Gaotang China 85 H4
Gaotangling China see Wangcheng
Gaotingzhen China see Daishan
Gaotouyao China 85 F4
Gaoua Burkina 124 E4
Gaoual Guinea 124 B4
Gaoxian China see Wenjiang
Gaoxiong Taiwan see Kaohsiung
Gaoyang China 85 G4
Gaoyi China 85 G4
Gaoyou China 87 F1
Gaoyou Hu l. China 87 F1
Gaozhou China 87 D4
Gap France 51 M8
Gapan Phil. 74 B3
Gap Carbon c. Alg. 55 K9
Gapuwiyak Australia 148 B2
Gaqoi China 89 C6
Gar China 99 K3
also known as Gargunsa or Shiquanhe
Gar Pak. 101 E5
Gar' r. Rus. Fed. 82 C1
Garaa Tebourt well Tunisia 123 H3
Garabekewül Turkm. 103 F5
formerly spelt Karabekaul
Garabil Belentligi hills Turkm. 103 E5
also known as Karabil', Vozvyshennost'
Garabinzam Congo 126 B4
Garabogazköl Turkm. 102 C4
formerly spelt Kara-Bogaz-Gol
Garabogazköl Aýlagy b. Turkm. see Garabogazköl Aýlagy
Garabogazköl Aýlagy b. Turkm. 102 C4
also known as Garabogazköl Aylagy
Garabogazköl Bogazy sea chan. Turkm. 102 C4
also known as Kara-Bogaz-Gol, Proliv
Garacad Somalia 128 F3
Garachiné Panama 186 D5
Garachiné, Punta pt Panama 186 D5
Garadag Somalia 128 E2
Gara Ekar hill Alg. 123 G6
Garagoa Col. 198 C3
Garagum des. Kazakh. see Karakum Desert
Garagum des. Turkm. see Karakum Desert
Garagum Kanaly canal Turkm. 103 E5
Garah Australia 147 F2
Garalo Mali 124 D4
Garamätnyýaz Turkm. 103 F5
also spelt Garamätnyyaz
Garamätnyyaz Turkm. see Garamätnyýaz
Garamba r. Dem. Rep. Congo 126 F4
Garamba, Parc National de la nat. park Dem. Rep. Congo 126 F3
UNESCO World Heritage Site
Garanhuns Brazil 202 E4
Ga-Rankuwa S. Africa 133 L2
Garapu Brazil 202 A5
Garapuava Brazil 206 G3
Garar, Plaine de plain Chad 126 D2
Garawa Aboriginal Land res. Australia 148 C3
Garba Cent. Afr. Rep. 126 D2
Garbahaarrey Somalia 128 D4
Garba Tula Kenya 128 C4
Garberville U.S.A. 182 A1
Garbo China see Lhozhag
Garbosh, Kūh-e mt. Iran 100 B3
Gârbova, Vârful hill Romania 58 H3
Garbsen Germany 48 G3
Garça Brazil 206 D9
Garças, Rio das r. Brazil 206 A2
Gârceni Romania 58 I2
Garcias Brazil 206 A7
Garcia Sola, Embalse de resr Spain 54 F5
Gârcina Romania 58 H2
Gard r. France 51 K9
Garda Italy 56 C3
Garda, Lago di l. Italy see Garda, Lake
Garda, Lake Italy 56 C3
also known as Garda, Lago di
Gardabani Georgia 107 F2
Gârda de Sus Romania 58 D2
Garde Lake Canada 167 J2
Gardelegen Germany 48 I3
Garden City U.S.A. 178 B4
Garden Corners U.S.A. 172 G5
Garden Grove U.S.A. 182 G8
Garden Hill Canada 167 M4
Garden Island U.S.A. 172 H5
Garden Mountain U.S.A. 176 D8
Gardermoen airport Norway 45 J3
also known as Oslo
Gardēz Afgh. 101 G3
Gardinas Belarus see Hrodna
Gardiner U.S.A. 177 P1
Gardiner, Mount Australia 148 B4
Gardiner Range hills Australia 148 A3
Gardiners Island U.S.A. 177 M4
Gardiner's Range mts Australia 148 B4
Gardner atoll Micronesia see Faraulep
Gardner IL U.S.A. 172 E9
Gardner MA U.S.A. 177 N3
Gardner Inlet Antarctica 222 T1
Gardner Island Kiribati see Nikumaroro
Gardner Pinnacles is U.S.A. 221 H4
formerly known as Man-of-War Rocks or Pollard Islands
Gardnerville U.S.A. 182 E3
Gardno, Jezioro lag. Poland 49 O1
Gárdony Hungary 49 P8
Gardsjönås Sweden 44 L2
Gärdslösa Sweden 45 L4
Gáregasnjárga Fin. see Karigasniemi
Gares Spain see Puente la Reina
Garešnica Croatia 56 I3
Garet El Djenoun mt. Alg. 123 G4
Gare Tigre Fr. Guiana 199 H3
Garfield U.S.A. 181 F5
Garforth U.K. 47 K10
Gargalianoi Greece 59 C11
Gargáligas r. Spain 54 F5
Gargano, Parco Nazionale del nat. park Italy 56 H7
Gargantua, Cape Canada 168 C4
Gargunsa China see Gar
Gargždai Lith. 42 C6
Garhakota India 96 C5
Garhbeta India 97 E5
Garhi India 96 B5
Garhi Khairo Pak. 101 F4
Garhi Malehra India 96 C4
Garhmuktesar India 96 C3
Garhshankar India 96 C3
Garhwa India 97 D4
Garibaldi Brazil 203 B9
Garibaldi Canada 166 F5
Garibaldi, Mount Canada 166 F5
Garibaldi Provincial Park Canada 166 F5
Gariep Dam resr S. Africa 133 J7
Gariep Dam Nature Reserve S. Africa 133 J7
Garies S. Africa 132 B7
Garissa Kenya 128 C5
Garkalne Latvia 42 F4
Garkung Caka l. China 89 D5
Garland U.S.A. 179 C5
Garliava Lith. 42 E7
Gârliciu Romania 58 J4
Garlin France 50 F9
Garm Tajik. see Gharm
Garmab Afgh. 101 F3
Garm Ab, Chashmeh-ye spring Iran 100 D3
Garmdasht Iran 100 B4
Garmeh Iran 100 D2
Garmī Iran 100 B2
Garmisch-Partenkirchen Germany 48 I8
Garmsar Iran 100 C3
Garmsel reg. Afgh. 101 E4
Garner IA U.S.A. 174 A3
Garner KY U.S.A. 176 C8
Garneti Canada see Rae Lakes
Garnett U.S.A. 178 D4
Garnpung Lake imp. l. Australia 147 D3
Garo Hills India 97 F4
Garonne r. France 50 F8
Garoowe Somalia 128 F2
Garoth India 96 B4
Garou, Lac l. Mali 124 E2
Garoua Cameroon 125 I4
Garoua Boulai Cameroon 125 I5
Garqêntang China see Sog
Garrett U.S.A. 173 H9
Garrison KY U.S.A. 176 B7
Garrison ND U.S.A. 178 B2
Garrucha Spain 55 J7
Garryçyrla Turkm. 102 E5
formerly known as Karrychirla
Garrygala Turkm. 102 D5
formerly spelt Kara-Kala
Garry Lake Canada 167 K1
Garryowen S. Africa 133 L8
Garsen Kenya 128 D5
Garshy Turkm. see Garşy
Garsila Sudan 120 D6
Garşy Turkm. 102 C4
also spelt Garshy
Gartar China see Qianning
Gartempe r. France 50 G6
UNESCO World Heritage Site
Gartog China see Markam
Gartok China see Garyarsa
Garut Indon. 77 D4
Garvie Mountains N.Z. 153 C13
Garwolin Poland 49 S4
Gar Xincun China 89 C5
Gary IN U.S.A. 174 C3
Gary WV U.S.A. 176 D8
Garyarsa China 89 C6
also known as Gartok
Garyi China 86 A2
Garyū-zan mt. Japan 91 C7
Garza Arg. 204 E3
Gar Zangbo r. China 89 B5
Garzê China 86 A2
Garzón Col. 198 C4
Gasan-Kuli Turkm. see Esenguly
Gascogne reg. France see Gascony
Gascogne, Golfe de g. France/Spain see Gascony, Gulf of
Gasconade r. U.S.A. 174 B4
Gascony reg. France 50 F9
also spelt Gascogne
Gascony, Gulf of France/Spain 50 E8
also known as Gascogne, Golfe de or Gascuña, Golfo de
Gascoyne r. Australia 151 A5
Gascoyne, Mount hill Australia 151 B5
Gascoyne Junction Australia 151 A5
Gascuña, Golfo de g. France/Spain see Gascony, Gulf of
Gasherbrum I mt. Jammu and Kashmir 96 C2
Gash Setit Wildlife Reserve nature res. Eritrea 121 H6
Gasht Iran 101 E5
Gas Hu salt l. China 88 E4
Gashua Nigeria 125 H3
Gaspar Cuba 186 D2
Gaspar, Selat sea chan. Indon. 77 D3
Gaspé Canada 169 H3
Gaspé, Baie de b. Canada 169 H3
Gaspé, Cap c. Canada 169 H3
Gaspé, Péninsule de pen. Canada 169 H3
Gassan Burkina 124 E3
Gassan vol. Japan 90 G5
Gassane Senegal 124 B3
Gassaway U.S.A. 176 E7
Gassol Nigeria 125 H4
Gass Peak U.S.A. 183 I5
Gasteiz Spain see Vitoria-Gasteiz
Gastello Rus. Fed. 82 F2
Gaston U.S.A. 176 H9
Gaston, Lake U.S.A. 176 H9
Gastonia U.S.A. 174 D5
Gastouni Greece 59 C11
Gastre Arg. 205 C6
Gata, Cabo de c. Spain 55 I8
Gata, Cape Cyprus 108 E3
also known as Gatas, Akra
Gata, Sierra de mts Spain 54 E4
Gataga r. Canada 166 E3
Gătaia Romania 58 C3
Gatas, Akra c. Cyprus see Gata, Cape
Gatchina Rus. Fed. 43 L2
Gateshead U.K. 47 K9
Gates of the Arctic National Park and Preserve U.S.A. 164 D3
Gatesville U.S.A. 179 C6
Gateway U.S.A. 183 P3
Gatico Chile 200 C5
Gatineau Canada 168 F4
Gatineau r. Canada 168 F4
Gatlinburg U.S.A. 179 G5
Gatong China see Jomda
Gatooma Zimbabwe see Kadoma
Gatton Australia 147 G1

Głogów Poland **49** N4
historically known as Glogau
Głogówek Poland **49** O5
Głogów Małopolski Poland **49** S5
Glomfjord Norway **44** K2
Glomma *r.* Norway **45** J4
Glommersträsk Sweden **44** L2
Glória Brazil **202** E4
Glorieuses, Îles *is* Indian Ocean **129** E7
English form Glorioso Islands
Glorioso Islands Indian Ocean *see* **Glorieuses, Îles**
Gloucester Australia **147** F2
Gloucester P.N.G. **145** D2
Gloucester U.K. **47** J12
historically known as Glevum
Gloucester *MA* U.S.A. **177** O3
Gloucester *VA* U.S.A. **177** I8
Gloucester Island Australia **149** F4
Gloucester Point U.S.A. **177** I8
Glover Reef *reef* Belize **185** I5
Gloversville U.S.A. **177** K2
Glovertown Canada **169** K3
Glöwen Germany **48** J3
Głowno Poland **49** Q4
Głubczyce Poland **49** O5
Glubinnoye Rus. Fed. **82** D3
Glubokiy Rus. Fed. **41** G6
Glubokoye Belarus *see* **Hlybokaye**
Glubokoye Kazakh. **88** C1
Glubokoye, Ozero *l.* Rus. Fed. **43** K1
Glücksburg (Ostsee) Germany **48** G1
Glückstadt Germany **48** G2
Gluggarnir *hill* Faroe Is **46** F2
Glukhov Ukr. *see* **Hlukhiv**
Gmelinka Rus. Fed. **102** A2
Gmünd Austria **49** L7
Gmunden Austria **49** K8
Gnadenhutten U.S.A. **176** D5
Gnarp Sweden **45** L3
Gnarrenburg Germany **48** G2
Gnesen Poland *see* **Gniezno**
Gniew Poland **49** P2
Gniewkowo Poland **49** P3
Gniezno Poland **49** O3
historically known as Gnesen
Gnisvärd Sweden **45** L4
Gnjilane *Kosovo, Srbija* Serb. and Mont. **58** C6
Gnoien Germany **49** J2
Gnowangerup Australia **151** B7
Gnows Nest Range *hills* Australia **151** B6
Goa *state* India **94** B3
UNESCO World Heritage Site
Goageb Namibia **130** C5
Goalpara India **97** F4
Goang Indon. **75** A5
Goaso Ghana **124** E5
Goat Fell *hill* U.K. **46** G8
Goba Eth. **128** D3
Gobabis Namibia **130** C4
Gobannium U.K. *see* **Abergavenny**
Gobas Namibia **130** C5
Gobernador Crespo Arg. **204** E3
Gobernador Duval Arg. **204** D5
Gobernador Gregores Arg. **205** C8
Gobernador Mayer Arg. **205** C8
Gobernador Virasoro Arg. **204** F3
Gobi *des.* China/Mongolia **85** E2
English form Gobi Desert
Gobi Desert China/Mongolia *see* **Gobi**
Gobiki Rus. Fed. **43** O8
Göblberg *hill* Austria **49** K7
Gobō Japan **91** D8
Goch Germany **48** D4
Gochas Namibia **130** C5
Go Công Vietnam **79** D6
Godagari Bangl. **97** F4
Godavari *r.* India **94** D2
Godbout Canada **169** H3
Godbout *r.* Canada **169** H3
Godda India **97** E4
Goddard, Mount U.S.A. **182** F4
Godē Eth. **128** D3
Godeal *hill* Port. **54** C6
Godech Bulg. **58** E5
Goderich Canada **168** D5
Goderville France **50** G3
Godhavn Greenland *see* **Qeqertarsuaq**
Godhra India **96** B5
Godinlabe Somalia **128** E3
Godo, Gunung *mt.* Indon. **75** C3
Gödöllő Hungary **49** Q8
Gods *r.* Canada **167** M3
Gods Lake Canada **167** M4
God's Mercy, Bay of Canada **167** O2
Godthåb Greenland *see* **Nuuk**
Godučohkka *mt.* Sweden **44** L1
also spelt Kåtotjåkka
Godwin-Austen, Mount China/Jammu and Kashmir *see* **K2**
Goedemoed S. Africa **133** K7
Goedgegun Swaziland *see* **Nhlangano**
Goegap Nature Reserve S. Africa **132** C6
Goéland, Lac au *l.* Canada **168** E3
Goélands, Lac aux *l.* Canada **169** I2
Goes Neth. **48** A4
Goetzville U.S.A. **173** I4
Goffstown U.S.A. **177** N2
Gogama Canada **168** D4
Gogebic, Lake U.S.A. **172** D4
Gogebic Range *hills* U.S.A. **172** D4
Göğeç Turkey **109** K1
Gogland, Ostrov *i.* Rus. Fed. **42** H1
Gogoi Moz. **131** G4
Gogolevka Rus. Fed. **43** M7
Gogoșu Romania **58** D4
Gogounou Benin **125** F4
Gogra India *see* **Ghaghra**
Gogra *r.* India *see* **Ghaghara**
Gogrial Sudan **126** F2
Gogunda India **96** B4
Gohad India **96** C4
Gohana India **96** C3
Goharganj India **96** C5
Goiana Brazil **202** F3
Goianésia Brazil **206** D2
Goiânia Brazil **206** D3
Goianinha Brazil **202** F3
Goianira Brazil **206** D3
Goiás Brazil **206** C2
UNESCO World Heritage Site
Goiás *state* Brazil **206** C3
Goiatuba Brazil **206** D5
Goincang China **86** B1
Goio-Erê Brazil **203** A8
Goi-Pula Dem. Rep. Congo **127** E6
Goito Italy **56** C3
Gojeb Wenz *r.* Eth. **128** C3
Gojra Pak. **101** H4
Gokak India **94** B2
Gokarn India **94** B3
Gök Çay *r.* Turkey **108** D1
Gökçeada *i.* Turkey **106** A2
also known as İmroz
Gökçedağ Turkey **106** B3
Gökçen Turkey **59** I10
Gökçeören Turkey **59** J10
Gökdepe Turkm. *see* **Gëkdepe**
Gökdere *r.* Turkey **108** D1
Gökirmak *r.* Turkey **106** C2
Goklenkuy, Solonchak *salt l.* Turkm. **102** D4
Gökova Turkey *see* **Ula**
Gökova Körfezi *b.* Turkey **106** A3
Gokprosh Hills Pak. **101** E5
Göksun Turkey **107** D3
Göksu Nehri *r.* Turkey **106** C3
Goksu Parkı Turkey **108** E1
Gokteik Myanmar **78** B3
Göktepe Turkey **108** D1
Gokwe Zimbabwe **131** F3
Gol Norway **45** J3
Gola India **96** D3
Golaghat India **97** G4
Golakganj India **97** F4
Golan *hills* Syria **108** G4
also spelt Al Jawlān *or* HaGolan
Gołańcz Poland **49** O3
Golbāf Iran **100** D4
Golbahār Afgh. **101** G3
Gölbaşı Turkey **107** D3
Golconda India **94** C2
Golconda *IL* U.S.A. **174** B4
Golconda *NV* U.S.A. **183** G1
Gölcük *Balıkesir* Turkey **59** I9
Gölçük Turkey *see* **Etili**
Gölcük *Kocaeli* Turkey **106** B2
Gölcük *r.* Turkey **59** J9
Golczewo Poland **49** L2
Gold U.S.A. **176** H4
Gołdap Poland **49** T1
Gołdapa *r.* Poland **49** S1
Gold Beach U.S.A. **180** A4
Goldberg Germany **49** J2
Gold Coast *country* Africa *see* **Ghana**
Gold Coast Australia **147** G2
formerly known as South Coast Town
Gold Coast *coastal area* Ghana **125** E5
Golden Canada **167** G5
Golden Bay N.Z. **152** G8
Goldendale U.S.A. **180** B3
Golden Downs N.Z. **153** G9
Golden Ears Provincial Park Canada **166** F5
Golden Gate Highlands National Park S. Africa **133** M5
Golden Hinde *mt.* Canada **166** E5
Golden Lake Canada **168** E4
Golden Meadow U.S.A. **175** B6
Golden Valley S. Africa **133** J9
Golden Valley Zimbabwe **131** F3
Goldfield U.S.A. **183** G4
Gold River Canada **166** E5
Goldsand Lake Canada **167** K3
Goldsboro U.S.A. **174** E5
Goldstone Lake U.S.A. **183** H6
Goldsworthy Australia **150** B4
Goldthwaite U.S.A. **179** C6
Goldvein U.S.A. **176** H7
Göle Turkey **107** E2
also known as Merdenik
Goleniów Poland **49** L2
Golestān Afgh. **101** E3
Golestān *prov.* Iran **100** C2
Goleta U.S.A. **182** E7
Golfito Costa Rica **186** C5
Golfo di Orosei Gennargentu e Asinara, Parco Nazionale del *nat. park Sardinia* Italy **57** B8
Gölgeli Dağları *mts* Turkey **106** B3
Gölhisar Turkey **59** K11
Goliad U.S.A. **179** C6
Golija *nat. park* Serb. and Mont. **58** B5
Golija Planina *mts* Serb. and Mont. **58** B5
Golingka China *see* **Gongbo'gyamda**
Golitsyno Rus. Fed. **43** S6
Gölköy Turkey **107** D2
also known as Kuşluyan
Gollel Swaziland *see* **Lavumisa**
Gölmarmara Turkey **59** I10
Golmberg *hill* Germany **49** K3
Golmud China **84** B4
Golmud He *r.* China **84** B4
Golo *i.* Phil. **74** B3
Golobino Rus. Fed. **43** V6
Golodnaya Step' *plain* Uzbek. **103** F4
Golondrina Arg. **204** E3
Gölovası Turkey **108** G1
Golovnino Rus. Fed. **90** I3
Golpāyegān Iran **100** B3
Gölpazarı Turkey **106** B2
Golspie U.K. **46** I6
Golub-Dobrzyń Poland **49** Q2
Golubovka Kazakh. **103** H1
Golungo Alto Angola **127** B7
Goluzino Rus. Fed. **43** V2
Gol Vardeh Iran **101** E3
Golweyn Somalia **128** E4
Golyama Syutkya *mt.* Bulg. **58** F7
Golyama Zhelyazna Bulg. **58** F6
Golyam Perelik *mt.* Bulg. **58** F7
Golyam Persenk *mt.* Bulg. **58** F7
Golyashi Belarus *see* **Sasnovy Bor**
Gölyazı Turkey **59** J8
Golynki Rus. Fed. **43** M7
Golyshi Rus. Fed. *see* **Vetluzhskiy**
Goma Dem. Rep. Congo **126** F5
Goma Uganda **128** A5
Gomang Co *salt l.* China **89** E6
Gomati *r.* India **96** D4
Gombak, Bukit *hill* Sing. **76** [inset]
Gombari Dem. Rep. Congo **126** F4
Gombe Nigeria **125** H4
Gombe *state* Nigeria **125** H4
Gombe *r.* Tanz. **129** A6
Gombi Nigeria **125** I4
Gombroon Iran *see* **Bandar-e 'Abbās**
Gömeç Turkey **59** H9
also known as Armutova
Gomel' Belarus *see* **Homyel'**
Gomel Oblast *admin. div.* Belarus *see* **Homyel'skaya Voblasts'**
Gomel'skaya Oblast' *admin. div.* Belarus *see* **Homyel'skaya Voblasts'**
Gómez Palacio Mex. **184** E3
Gómez Rendón Ecuador **198** A5
Gōmil, Rūbār-e *r.* Iraq **109** O1
Gomīshān Iran **100** C2
Gomo China **89** D5
Gomo Co *salt l.* China **89** D5
Gomorovichi Rus. Fed. **43** P1
Gomumu *i.* Indon. **75** C3
Gonabad Iran *see* **Jūymand**
Gonaïves Haiti **187** E3
Gonarezhou National Park Zimbabwe **131** F4
Gonâve, Île de la *i.* Haiti **187** E3
Gonbad, Chāh-e *well* Iran **100** C3
Gonbad-e Kavus Iran **100** C2
Gonda India **97** D4
Gondal India **96** A5
Gonda Libah *well* Eth. **128** E2
Gondar Col. **198** C5
Gondar Eth. *see* **Gonder**
Gonder Eth. **128** C1
formerly spelt Gondar
Gondey Chad **126** C2
Gondia India **96** D5
Gondomar Spain **54** C2
Gönen Turkey **106** A2
Gönen *r.* Turkey **59** I8
Gonfreville-l'Orcher France **50** G3
Gong'an China **87** E2
also known as Douhudi; *formerly known as* Doushi
Gongbalou China **89** E6
also known as Gamba
Gongbo'gyamda China **89** F6
also known as Golingka
Gongcheng China **87** D3
Gonggar China **89** E6
also known as Gyixong
Gongga Shan *mt.* China **86** B2
also known as Minya Konka
Gonghe *Qinghai* China **84** D4
also known as Qabqa
Gonghe *Yunnan* China *see* **Mouding**
Gonghui China **85** G3
Gongjiang China *see* **Yudu**
Gongliu China **88** C3
also known as Tokkuztara
Gongola *r.* Nigeria **125** I4
Gongolgon Australia **147** E2
Gongoué Gabon **126** A5
Gongpoquan China **84** C3
Gongquan China **86** C2
also known as Gongxian
Gongshan China **86** A3
also known as Cikai
Gongtang China *see* **Damxung**
Gongwang Shan *mts* China **86** B3
Gongxian *Henan* China *see* **Gongyi**
Gongxian *Sichuan* China *see* **Gongquan**
Gongyi China **87** E1
formerly known as Gongxian *or* Xiaoyi
Gongzhuling China **82** B4
formerly known as Huaide
Goniądz Poland **49** T2
Goniri Nigeria **125** I4
Gonjo China *see* **Kasha**
Gonnesa *Sardinia* Italy **57** A9
Gonnoi Greece **59** D9
Gonnosfanadiga *Sardinia* Italy **57** A9
Gōnoura Japan **91** A8
Gonubie S. Africa **133** M9
Gonzáles Mex. **185** F4
Gonzales *CA* U.S.A. **182** C5
Gonzales *TX* U.S.A. **179** C6
González Moreno Arg. **204** E4
Gonzalo Vásquez Panama **186** D5
Goochland U.S.A. **176** H8
Goode U.S.A. **176** F8
Goodenough, Cape Antarctica **223** I2
Goodenough Island P.N.G. **145** E2
Gooderham Canada **173** O6
Good Harbor Bay U.S.A. **172** H5
Good Hart U.S.A. **173** H5
Good Hope Botswana **133** J2
Good Hope U.S.A. **172** C10
Good Hope, Cape of S. Africa **132** C11
Good Hope Mountain Canada **166** E5
Goodland U.S.A. **178** B4
Goodman U.S.A. **172** E5
Goodooga Australia **147** E2
Goodparla Australia **148** B2
Goodrich U.S.A. **172** C5
Goodspeed Nunataks *nunataks* Antarctica **223** E2
Goodwood *r.* Canada **169** G2
Goole U.K. **47** L10
Goolgowi Australia **147** E3
Goolwa Australia **146** C3
Goomadeer *r.* Australia **148** B1
Goomalling Australia **151** B6
Goombalie Australia **147** E2
Goomeri Australia **149** G5
Goonda Moz. **131** G3
Goondiwindi Australia **147** F2
Goongarrie, Lake *salt flat* Australia **151** C6
Goongarrie National Park Australia **151** C6
Goonyella Australia **149** E4
Goorly, Lake *salt flat* Australia **151** B6
Goose *r.* Canada **169** I2
Goose *r.* U.S.A. **178** C2
Goose Bay Canada *see* **Happy Valley-Goose Bay**
Goose Creek U.S.A. **175** D5
Goose Creek *r.* U.S.A. **180** D4
Goose Green Falkland Is **205** F8
Goose Lake U.S.A. **180** B4
Goose Lake Canal *r.* U.S.A. **182** E6
Gooty India **94** C3
Gop India **95** E2
Gopalganj Bangl. **97** F5
Gopalganj India **97** E4
Gopeshwar India **96** C3
formerly known as Chamoli
Gopichettipalayam India **94** C4
Gopiganj India **97** D4
Göppingen Germany **48** G7
Góra Poland **49** N4
Goradiz Azer. *see* **Horadiz**
Goragorskiy Rus. Fed. **41** H8
Góra Kalwaria Poland **49** S4
Gorakhpur India **97** D4
Goražde Bos.-Herz. **56** K5
Gorbachevo Rus. Fed. **43** S8
Gorchukha Rus. Fed. **40** G4
Gorczański Park Narodowy *nat. park* Poland **49** R6
Gorda, Banco *sea feature* Hond. **186** C4
Gorda, Punta *pt* Nicaragua **186** C4
Gorda, Punta *pt* U.S.A. **180** A4
Gorda, Sierra *mts* Spain **54** G7
Gördalen Sweden **45** K3
Gördes Turkey **106** B3
Gordeyevka Rus. Fed. **43** M9
Gordon *r.* Canada **167** O1
Gordon *NE* U.S.A. **178** B3
Gordon *WI* U.S.A. **172** B4
Gordon, Isla *i.* Chile **205** C9
Gordon, Lake Australia **147** E5
Gordon Bay Australia **148** A1
Gordon Downs Australia **150** E3
Gordon Lake Canada **167** H2
Gordonsville U.S.A. **176** G7
Gordonvale Australia **149** E3
Goré Chad **126** C3
Gorē Eth. **128** B2
Gore N.Z. **153** C14
Gore U.S.A. **176** G6
Gore Bay Canada **173** K5
Gorelki Rus. Fed. **43** S7
Goreloye Rus. Fed. **41** G5
Göreme Milli Parkı *nat. park* Turkey **106** C3
UNESCO World Heritage Site
Gore Point U.S.A. **164** D4
Goretovo Rus. Fed. **43** Q6
Gorey Ireland **47** F11
Gorg Iran **101** D4
Gorgān Iran **100** C2
also spelt Gurgan; *formerly known as* Asterabad *or* Astrabad; *historically known as* Hyrcania *or* Varkana
Gorgān, Khalīj-e *b.* Iran **100** C2
Gorge Range *hills* Australia **150** B4
Gorge Range *mts* Australia **149** E3
Gorge Road N.Z. **153** C14
Gorges Namibia **132** B4
Gorgol *admin. reg.* Mauritania **124** B2
Gorgona, Isola di *i.* Italy **56** B5
Gorgora Eth. **128** C1
Gorgoram Nigeria **125** H3
Gorgova, Lacul *l.* Romania **58** K3
Gorham U.S.A. **177** N1
Gori Georgia **107** F2
Gorinchem Neth. **48** B4
Goris Armenia **107** F3
Goritsa Bulg. **58** I6
Goritsy Rus. Fed. **43** R4
Gorizia Italy **56** F3
Gorka Rus. Fed. **43** T5
Gorkhā Nepal **97** E4
Gorki Belarus *see* **Horki**
Gor'kiy Rus. Fed. *see* **Nizhniy Novgorod**
Gor'kovskaya Oblast' *admin. div.* Rus. Fed. *see* **Nizhegorodskaya Oblast'**
Gor'kovskoye Vodokhranilishche *resr* Rus. Fed. **43** V4
Gor'koye, Ozero *salt l.* Rus. Fed. **103** J1
Gor'koye, Ozero *salt l.* Rus. Fed. **103** J1
Gorlice Poland **49** S6
Görlitz Germany **49** L4
Gorlovka Ukr. *see* **Horlivka**
Gorlovo Rus. Fed. **43** U8
Gormi India **96** C4
Gorna Dzhumaya Bulg. *see* **Blagoevgrad**
Gorna Oryakhovitsa Bulg. **58** G5
Gorni Dŭbnik Bulg. **58** F5
Gornja Radgona Slovenia **56** H2
Gornja Toponica *Srbija* Serb. and Mont. **58** C5
Gornji Matejevac *Srbija* Serb. and Mont. **58** C5
Gornji Milanovac *Srbija* Serb. and Mont. **58** B4
Gornji Vakuf Bos.-Herz. **56** J5
also known as Uskoplje
Gorno Ablanovo Bulg. **58** G5
Gorno-Altaysk Rus. Fed. **80** D2
Gorno-Altayskaya Avtonomnaya Oblast' *aut. rep.* Rus. Fed. *see* **Altay, Respublika**
Gorno-Badakhshan *aut. rep.* Tajik. *see* **Kŭhistoni Badakhshon**
Gornopravdinsk Rus. Fed. **38** G3
Gornotrakiyska Nizina *lowland* Bulg. **58** G6
Gornozavodsk *Permskaya Oblast'* Rus. Fed. **40** K4
formerly known as Novopashiyskiy
Gornozavodsk *Sakhalin* Rus. Fed. **82** F3
Gornyak *Altayskiy Kray* Rus. Fed. **88** C1
Gornyak *Ryazanskaya Oblast'* Rus. Fed. **43** U8
Gornye Klyuchi Rus. Fed. **82** D3
Gornyy *Khabarovskiy Kray* Rus. Fed. **82** E2
formerly known as Solnechnyy
Gornyy *Primorskiy Kray* Rus. Fed. **90** C2
Gornyy *Saratovskaya Oblast'* Rus. Fed. **102** B2
Gornyy Altay *aut. rep.* Rus. Fed. *see* **Altay, Respublika**
Gornyy Badakhshan *aut. rep.* Tajik. *see* **Kŭhistoni Badakhshon**
Gornyy Balykley Rus. Fed. **41** H6
Goro Eth. **128** D3
Goro *i.* Fiji *see* **Koro**
Goroch'an *mt.* Eth. **128** C2
Gorodenka Ukr. *see* **Horodenka**
Gorodets Rus. Fed. **40** G4
Gorodishche *Penzenskaya Oblast'* Rus. Fed. **41** H5
Gorodishche *Volgogradskaya Oblast'* Rus. Fed. **41** H6
Gorodok Belarus *see* **Haradok**
Gorodok Belarus *see* **Haradok**
Gorodok Rus. Fed. *see* **Zakamensk**
Gorodok Ukr. *see* **Horodok**
Gorodovikovsk Rus. Fed. **41** G7
formerly known as Bashanta
Goroka P.N.G. **73** K8
Goroke Australia **146** D4
Gorokhovets Rus. Fed. **40** G4
Gorom Gorom Burkina **125** E3
Gorong, Kepulauan *is* Indon. **73** H7
Gorongosa Moz. **131** G3
formerly known as Vila Paiva de Andrada
Gorongosa *mt.* Moz. **131** G3
Gorongosa, Parque Nacional de *nat. park* Moz. **131** G3
Gorontalo Indon. **75** B2
Gorontalo *prov.* Indon. **75** B2
Gorontalo *prov.* Indon. **75** D2
Goronyo Nigeria **125** G3
Goroubi *watercourse* Niger **125** F3
Gorouol *r.* Burkina/Niger **125** F3
Górowo Iławeckie Poland **49** R1
Gorshechnoye Rus. Fed. **41** F6
Gór Stołowych, Park Narodowy *nat. park* Poland **49** N5
Goru, Vârful *mt.* Romania **58** H3
Görükle Turkey **59** J8
Gorumna Island Ireland **47** C10
Gorutuba *r.* Brazil **207** J2
Goryachiy Klyuch Rus. Fed. **41** F7
Górzno Poland **49** Q2
Gorzów Wielkopolski Poland **49** M3
historically known as Landsberg
Gosainthan *mt.* China *see* **Xixabangma Feng**
Goschen Strait P.N.G. **149** F1
Gosford Australia **147** F3
Goshen *CA* U.S.A. **182** E5
Goshen *IN* U.S.A. **174** C3
Goshen *NH* U.S.A. **177** M2
Goshen *VA* U.S.A. **176** F8
Goshoba Turkm. *see* **Goșoba**
Goshogawara Japan **90** G4
Goslar Germany **48** H4
UNESCO World Heritage Site
Goșoba Turkm. **102** C4
also spelt Goshoba
Gospić Croatia **56** H4
Gossas Senegal **124** A3
Gosse *watercourse* Australia **148** B3
Gossi Mali **125** E3
Gossinga Sudan **126** E2
Gostivar Macedonia **58** B7
Gostyń Poland **49** O4
Gostynin Poland **49** Q3
Gosu China **86** A1
Gota Eth. **128** D2
Götaälven *r.* Sweden **45** J4
Göteborg Sweden *see* **Gothenburg**
Gotel Mountains Cameroon/Nigeria **125** H5
Gotemba Japan *see* **Gotenba**
Gotenba Japan **91** F7
also spelt Gotemba
Götene Sweden **45** K4
Gotenhafen Poland *see* **Gdynia**
Gotha Germany **48** H5
Gothem Sweden **45** L4
Gothenburg Sweden **45** J4
also spelt Göteborg
Gothenburg U.S.A. **178** B3
Gothèye Niger **125** F3
Gotland *i.* Sweden **45** L4
Gotō-rettō *is* Japan **91** A8
Gotse Delchev Bulg. **58** E7
Gotska Sandön Sweden **45** L4
Gotska Sandön *i.* Sweden **45** L4
Gōtsu Japan **91** C7
Gottero, Monte *mt.* Italy **56** B4
Göttingen Germany **48** G4
Gottne Sweden **44** L3
Gott Peak Canada **166** F5
Gottwaldow Czech Rep. *see* **Zlín**
Gotval'd Ukr. *see* **Zmiyiv**
Gouako Cent. Afr. Rep. **126** D3
Gouda Neth. **48** B3
Gouda S. Africa **132** D10
Goudiri Senegal **124** B3
Goudoumaria Niger **125** H3
Goudreau Canada **173** I2
Gouéké Guinea **124** C4
Goûgaram Niger **125** G2

►**Gough Island** S. Atlantic Ocean **217** N8
Dependency of St Helena.
UNESCO World Heritage Site

Gouin, Réservoir *resr* Canada **169** F3
Goukamma Nature Reserve S. Africa **132** G11
Goulais River Canada **173** I4
Goulburn Australia **147** F3
Goulburn *r.* Australia **147** E4
Goulburn Islands Australia **148** B1
Goulburn River National Park Australia **147** F3
Gould, Mount *hill* Australia **151** B5
Gould City U.S.A. **172** H4
Gould Coast Antarctica **223** O1
Goulféy Cameroon **125** I3
Goulia Côte d'Ivoire **124** D4
Goulou *atoll* Micronesia *see* **Ngulu**
Goumbou Mali **124** D3
Goumenissa Greece **58** D8
Gouna Cameroon **125** I4
Goundam Mali **124** E2
Goundi Chad **126** C2
Gounou-Gaya Chad **126** B2
Gouraya Alg. **55** M8
Gouraye Mauritania **124** B3
Gourcy Burkina **124** E3
Gourdon France **50** H8
Gouré Niger **125** H3
Gourin France **50** C4
Gouripur Bangl. **97** F4
Gourits *r.* S. Africa **132** F11
Gourlay Lake Canada **173** I2
Gourma-Rharous Mali **125** E2
Goûrmél *well* Mauritania **124** C2
Gourmeur *well* Chad **120** D5
Gournay-en-Bray France **50** H3
Gouro Chad **120** C5
Goûr Oulad Aḥmed *reg.* Mali **122** D5
Gourouro *well* Chad **120** D5
Goussainville France **51** I3
Gouvêa Brazil **207** J5
Gouveia Port. **54** D4
Gouverneur U.S.A. **177** J1
Gove U.S.A. **178** B4
Gove, Barragem do *resr* Angola **127** B8
Govedartsi Bulg. **58** E6
Govena, Mys *hd* Rus. Fed. **39** Q4
Gove Peninsula Australia **148** C2
Governador Valadares Brazil **203** D6
Governor Generoso Phil. **74** C5
Governor's Harbour Bahamas **186** D1
Govĭ-Altay *prov.* Mongolia **84** B2
Govĭ Altayn Nuruu *mts* Mongolia **84** C2
Govind Ballash Pant Sagar *resr* India **97** D4
Govindgarh India **97** D4
Govind Sagar *resr* India **96** C3
Govurdak Turkm. *see* **Gowurdak**
Gowanda U.S.A. **176** G3
Gowan Range *hills* Australia **149** E5
Gowd-e Aḥmar Iran **100** C4
Gowdeh, Rūd-e *watercourse* Iran **100** C5
Gowenbridge N.Z. **153** G9
Gowganda Canada **173** M3
Gowganda Lake Canada **173** M3
Gowmal Kalay Afgh. **101** G3
Gowurdak Turkm. **103** F5
also spelt Govurdak; *formerly spelt* Gaurdak
Goya Arg. **204** F3
Göyçay Azer. **107** F2
Goyder *r.* Australia **148** B2
Goyder *watercourse* Australia **148** B5
Goyder Lagoon *salt flat* Australia **146** C1
Goýmatdag *hills* Turkm. **102** C4
also known as Goymatdag
Goymatdag *hills* Turkm. *see* **Goýmatdag**
Göynük *Antalya* Turkey **108** B1
Göynük *Bingöl* Turkey **107** E3
also known as Oğnut
Göynük *Bolu* Turkey **106** B2
Göynükbelen Turkey **59** K9
Goyō-zan *mt.* Japan **90** G5
Göytäpä Azer. **107** G3
Gozareh Afgh. **101** E3
Goz-Beïda Chad **120** D6
Gözcüler Turkey **108** G1
Gözene Turkey **107** D3
Gozha Co *salt l.* China **89** C5
Gözne Turkey **108** F1
Gozo *i.* Malta **57** G12
also known as Għawdex
Goz Regeb Sudan **121** G5
Graaff-Reinet S. Africa **133** I9
Graafwater S. Africa **132** C9
Grabia *r.* Poland **49** P4
Grabo Côte d'Ivoire **124** D5
Grabouw S. Africa **132** D11
Grabovica *Srbija* Serb. and Mont. **58** D4
Grabow Germany **48** I2
Grabowa *r.* Poland **49** N1
Grabów nad Prosną Poland **49** P4
Gračac Croatia **56** H4
Gračanica Bos.-Herz. **56** K4
Gračanica Jezero *l.* Serb. and Mont. **58** A6
Graçay France **50** H5
Grace, Lake *salt flat* Australia **151** B7
Gracefield Canada **168** E4
Gracemere Australia **149** F4
Grachevka Rus. Fed. **102** C1
Grachi Kazakh. **103** I2
Gracias Hond. **186** A4
Graciosa *i.* Arquipélago dos Açores **54** [inset]
Gradačac Bos.-Herz. **56** K4
Gradaús Brazil **202** B3
Gradaús, Serra dos *hills* Brazil **202** B4
Gradets Bulg. **58** H6
Gradignan France **50** F8
Gradishte *hill* Bulg. **58** H6
Gradiška Bos.-Herz. *see* **Bosanska Gradiška**
Gradište Croatia **56** K3
Grădiștea Romania **58** H4
Grado Italy **56** F3
Grado Spain **54** E1
Grady U.S.A. **179** B5
Gräfenhainichen Germany **49** J4
Gräftåvallen Sweden **44** K3
Grafton Australia **147** G2
Grafton *ND* U.S.A. **178** C1
Grafton *WI* U.S.A. **172** F7
Grafton *WV* U.S.A. **176** E6
Grafton, Cape Australia **149** E3
Grafton, Mount U.S.A. **183** J3
Grafton Passage Australia **149** E3
Graham *NC* U.S.A. **176** F9
Graham *TX* U.S.A. **179** C5
Graham, Mount U.S.A. **183** O9
Graham Bell Island Rus. Fed. *see* **Greem-Bell, Ostrov**
Graham Island *B.C.* Canada **166** C4
Graham Island *Nunavut* Canada **165** J2
Graham Lake U.S.A. **177** Q1
Graham Land *reg.* Antarctica **222** T2
Graham Laurier Provincial Park Canada **166** F3
Graham Moore, Cape Canada **165** L2
Grahamstown S. Africa **133** K10
Graiguenamanagh Ireland **47** F11
Grajagan Indon. **77** F5
Grajaú Brazil **202** C3
Grajaú *r.* Brazil **202** C2
Grajewo Poland **49** T2
Gram Denmark **45** J5
Gramada *mt.* Serb. and Mont. **58** D6
Gramat France **50** H8
Gramatikovo Bulg. **58** I6
Grammichele *Sicily* Italy **57** G11
Grammos *mt.* Greece **59** B8
Gramoz, Mal *mt.* Albania/Greece **59** B8
Grampian U.S.A. **176** G5
Grampian Mountains U.K. **46** H7
Grampians National Park Australia **147** D4
Gramsh Albania **58** B8
Gran Hungary *see* **Esztergom**
Granaatboskolk S. Africa **132** D7
Granada Col. **198** C4
Granada Nicaragua **186** B5
Granada Spain **55** H7
UNESCO World Heritage Site
Granado *hill* Spain **54** D7
Gran Altiplanicie Central *plain* Arg. **205** C8
Granard Ireland **47** E10
Gran Bajo *depr.* Arg. **205** D7
Gran Bajo Salitroso *salt flat* Arg. **204** D5
Gran Bajo San Julián *valley* Arg. **205** C8
Granbury U.S.A. **179** C5
Granby Canada **169** F4
Granby U.S.A. **180** F4
Gran Canaria *i.* Canary Is **122** B4
English form Grand Canary
Gran Chaco *reg.* Arg./Para. **201** E6
Grand *r. MO* U.S.A. **174** C3
Grand *r. SD* U.S.A. **178** B2
Grand, North Fork *r.* U.S.A. **178** B2
Grand, South Fork *r.* U.S.A. **178** B2
Grandas Spain **54** E1
Grand Atlas *mts* Morocco *see* **Haut Atlas**
Grand Bahama *i.* Bahamas **186** D1
Grand Bank Canada **169** K4
Grand-Bassam Côte d'Ivoire **124** E5
Grand Bay U.S.A. **175** B6
Grand Bay-Westfield Canada **169** H4
Grand Bend Canada **168** D5
Grand Bérard *mt.* France **51** M8
Grand-Bourg Guadeloupe **187** H4
Grand Canal China *see* **Da Yunhe**
Grand Canal Ireland **47** E10
Grand Canary *i.* Canary Is *see* **Gran Canaria**
Grand Canyon U.S.A. **183** L5
►**Grand Canyon** *gorge* U.S.A. **183** L5
►►**154–155 North America** Landscapes
Grand Canyon National Park U.S.A. **183** L5
UNESCO World Heritage Site
Grand Canyon-Parashant National Monument *nat. park* U.S.A. **181** D5
Grand Cayman *i.* Cayman Is **186** C3
Grand Centre Canada **167** I4
Grand Combin *mt.* Switz. **51** N7
Grand Detour U.S.A. **172** D9
Grande *r.* Arg. **204** C5
Grande *r. Santa Cruz* Bol. **201** E4
Grande *r. Santa Cruz* Bol. **201** E4
also known as Guapay
Grande *r. Bahia* Brazil **202** D4
Grande *r. São Paulo* Brazil **206** C7
Grande *r.* Peru **200** B3
Grande, Bahía *b.* Arg. **205** C8
Grande, Cayo *i.* Cuba **186** D2
Grande, Cerro *mt.* Mex. **185** F5
Grande, Ciénaga *lag.* Col. **198** C2
Grande, Ilha *i.* Brazil **203** C7
Grande, Serra *hills* Brazil **201** E2
Grande, Serra *mt.* Brazil **199** F4
also known as Carauná
Grande Cache Canada **166** G4
Grande Casse, Pointe de la *mt.* France **51** M7
Grande Comore *i.* Comoros *see* **Njazidja**
Grande de Manacapuru, Lago *l.* Brazil **199** F5
Grande-Entrée Canada **169** I4
Grande Leyre *r.* France **50** F8
Grande Prairie Canada **166** G4
Grand Erg de Bilma *des.* Niger **125** I2
Grand Erg Occidental *des.* Alg. **123** E3
English form Great Western Erg
Grand Erg Oriental *des.* Alg. **123** G3
English form Great Eastern Erg
Grande-Rivière Canada **169** H3
Grande Ronde *r.* U.S.A. **180** C3
Grandes, Salinas *salt marsh* Arg. **200** D5
Grandes, Salinas *salt marsh* Arg. **204** D3
Gran Desierto del Pinacate, Parque Natural del *nature res.* Mex. **184** B2
Grande-Terre *i.* Guadeloupe **187** H3
Grande Terre *i.* Mayotte **129** E8
Grande Tête de l'Obiou *mt.* France **51** L8
Grande-Vallée Canada **169** H3
Grand Falls Canada **169** H4
Grand Falls-Windsor Canada **169** K3
Grandfather Mountain U.S.A. **176** D9
Grand Forks Canada **166** G5
Grand Forks U.S.A. **178** C2
Grand-Fougeray France **50** E5
Grand Gorge U.S.A. **177** K3
Grand Gosier Haiti **187** F3
Grand Harbour Canada **169** H4
Grand Haven U.S.A. **172** G7
Grandin, Lac *l.* Canada **167** G1
Grand Island U.S.A. **178** C3
Grand Island *i.* U.S.A. **172** G4
Grand Isle U.S.A. **175** B6
Grand Junction *CO* U.S.A. **183** P2
Grand Junction *MI* U.S.A. **172** G8
Grand-Lahou Côte d'Ivoire **124** D5
Grand Lake *N.B.* Canada **169** H4
Grand Lake *Nfld. and Lab.* Canada **169** I2
Grand Lake *Nfld. and Lab.* Canada **169** J3
Grand Lake *LA* U.S.A. **179** D6
Grand Lake *LA* U.S.A. **179** E6
Grand Lake *MI* U.S.A. **173** J5
Grand Lake St Marys U.S.A. **176** A5
Grand Ledge U.S.A. **173** I8
Grand Manan Island Canada **169** H4
Grand Marais *MI* U.S.A. **172** H4
Grand Marais *MN* U.S.A. **174** B2
Grand Marsh U.S.A. **172** D7
Grand-Mère Canada **169** F4
Grândola Port. **54** C6
Grândola, Serra de *mts* Port. **54** C6
Grand Pacific Glacier Canada **166** B3
Grand Passage New Caledonia **145** F3
Grand Rapids Canada **167** L4
Grand Rapids *MI* U.S.A. **172** H8
Grand Rapids *MN* U.S.A. **174** A2
Grand St Bernard, Col du *pass* Italy/Switz. *see* **Great St Bernard Pass**
Grand-Santi Fr. Guiana **199** H3
Grand Teton *mt.* U.S.A. **180** E4
Grand Teton National Park U.S.A. **180** E4
Grand Traverse Bay U.S.A. **172** H6

►**Grand Turk** Turks and Caicos Is **187** F2
Capital of the Turks and Caicos Islands. Also known as Cockburn Town.

Grand Turk *i.* Turks and Caicos Is **187** F2
Grand Valley *valley* Swaziland **133** P3
Grand View U.S.A. **172** B4
Grandville U.S.A. **172** H8
Grandvilliers France **51** H3
Grand Wash *watercourse* U.S.A. **183** J5
Grand Wash Cliffs *mts* U.S.A. **183** J6
Grañén Spain **55** K3
Graneros Chile **204** C4
Granger U.S.A. **180** E4
Grängesberg Sweden **45** K3
Grangeville U.S.A. **180** C3
Granhult Sweden **44** M2
Granisle Canada **166** E4
Granite City U.S.A. **174** B4
Granite Falls U.S.A. **178** D2
Granite Mountain U.S.A. **182** G1
Granite Mountains *CA* U.S.A. **183** I7
Granite Mountains *CA* U.S.A. **183** I8
Granite Peak *MT* U.S.A. **180** E3
Granite Peak *UT* U.S.A. **183** K1
Granite Range *mts* U.S.A. **182** E1
Granitogorsk Kazakh. **103** H4
Granitola, Capo *c. Sicily* Italy **57** E11
Granity N.Z. **153** F9
Granja Brazil **202** D2
Gran Laguna Salada *l.* Arg. **205** D7
Gran Morelos Mex. **181** F7
Granollers Spain **55** N3
Gran Pajonal *plain* Peru **200** B2
Gran Paradiso *mt.* Italy **51** N7
Gran Paradiso, Parco Nazionale del *nat. park* Italy **51** N7
Gran Pilastro *mt.* Austria/Italy **48** I9
also known as Hochfeiler
Gran San Bernardo, Colle del *pass* Italy/Switz. *see* **Great St Bernard Pass**
Gran Sasso d'Italia *mts* Italy **56** F6
Gran Sasso e Monti della Laga, Parco Nazionale del *nat. park* Italy **56** F6
Gransee Germany **49** K2
Grant U.S.A. **178** B3
Grant, Mount *NV* U.S.A. **182** F3
Grant, Mount *NV* U.S.A. **182** G2

Grant City U.S.A. 178 D3
Grantham U.K. 47 L11
Grant Island Antarctica 222 P2
Grant Lake Canada 167 G1
Granton U.S.A. 172 C6
Grantown-on-Spey U.K. 46 I6
Grant Park U.S.A. 172 F9
Grant Range *mts* U.S.A. 183 I3
Grants U.S.A. 181 F6
Grantsburg U.S.A. 172 A5
Grants Pass U.S.A. 180 B4
Grantsville U.S.A. 183 L1
Granville Canada 166 B2
Granville France 50 E4
Granville *AZ* U.S.A. 183 O8
Granville *IL* U.S.A. 172 D9
Granville *NY* U.S.A. 177 L2
Granville *OH* U.S.A. 176 C5
Granville Lake Canada 167 K3
Granvin Norway 45 I3
Grão Mogol Brazil 202 D6
Grapevine Mountains U.S.A. 183 G5
Gras, Lac de *l.* Canada 167 I1
Graskop S. Africa 133 O1
Gräsö *i.* Sweden 45 L3
Grasplatz Namibia 130 B5
Grass *r.* Canada 167 L3
Grass *r.* U.S.A. 177 K1
Grasse France 51 M9
Grassflat U.S.A. 176 G4
Grass Lake U.S.A. 173 I8
Grasslands National Park Canada 167 J5
Grass Patch Australia 151 C7
Grassrange U.S.A. 180 E3
Grassridgedam *l.* S. Africa 133 J8
Grass River Provincial Park Canada 167 K4
Grass Valley U.S.A. 182 C2
Grassy Australia 147 E5
Grassy Creek *r.* Bahamas 186 D2
Grästorp Sweden 45 K4
Gratiot U.S.A. 172 C8
Gratkorn Austria 49 M8
Graudenz Poland *see* Grudziądz
Graulhet France 51 H9
Graus Spain 55 L2
Gravata Brazil 202 F4
Gravatai Brazil 203 B9
Gravdal Norway 44 K1
Grave, Pointe de *pt* France 50 E7
Gravelbourg Canada 167 J5
Gravenhurst Canada 168 E4
Grave Peak U.S.A. 180 D3
Grāveri Latvia 42 I5
Gravesend Australia 147 F2
Gravette U.S.A. 179 D4
Gravina in Puglia Italy 57 I8
Gravina Island U.S.A. 166 D4
Gravois, Pointe-à- *pt* Haiti 187 E3
Grawn U.S.A. 172 H6
Gray France 51 L5
Gray *GA* U.S.A. 175 D5
Gray *KY* U.S.A. 176 A9
Gray *ME* U.S.A. 177 O2
Gray *TN* U.S.A. 176 C9
Grayback Mountain U.S.A. 180 B4
Gray Lake Canada 167 I2
Grayling *r.* Canada 166 E3
Grayling U.S.A. 173 I6
Grays Harbor *inlet* U.S.A. 180 A3
Grays Lake U.S.A. 180 E4
Grayville U.S.A. 174 C4
Graz Austria 49 M8
UNESCO World Heritage Site
Grdelica *Srbija* Serb. and Mont. 58 D6
Greasy Lake Canada 166 F2
Great Abaco *i.* Bahamas 186 D1
Great Australian Bight *g.* Australia 146 A3
Great Bahama Bank *sea feature* Bahamas 186 D1
Great Barrier Island N.Z. 152 J4
Great Barrier Reef *reef* Australia 149 E1
UNESCO World Heritage Site
Great Barrier Reef Marine Park (Cairns Section) Australia 149 E3
►Great Barrier Reef Marine Park (Capricorn Section) Australia 149 F4
►►14–15 World Environmental Impacts
Great Barrier Reef Marine Park (Central Section) Australia 149 F3
Great Barrier Reef Marine Park (Far North Section) Australia 149 E2
Great Barrington U.S.A. 177 L3
Great Basalt Wall National Park Australia 149 E3
Great Basin U.S.A. 183 H2
Great Basin National Park U.S.A. 183 J3
Great Bear *r.* Canada 166 E1

►Great Bear Lake Canada 166 F1
4th largest lake in North America and 7th in the world.
►►6–7 World Landscapes
►►154–155 North America Landscapes

Great Belt *sea chan.* Denmark 45 J5
also known as Store Bælt
Great Bend *KS* U.S.A. 178 C4
Great Bend *PA* U.S.A. 177 J4
Great Bitter Lake Egypt 108 D7
also known as Murrat el Kubra, Buheirat
Great Blasket Island Ireland 47 B11

►Great Britain *i.* U.K. 47 J9
Largest island in Europe and 8th in the world.
►►6–7 World Landscapes
►►28–29 Europe Landscapes

Great Coco Island Cocos Is 79 A5
Great Dismal Swamp National Wildlife Refuge *nature res.* U.S.A. 177 I9
Great Dividing Range *mts* Australia 145 D5
Great Duck Island Canada 173 K5
Great Eastern Erg *des.* Alg. *see* Grand Erg Oriental
Great Egg Harbor Inlet U.S.A. 177 K6
Greater Accra *admin. reg.* Ghana 125 F5
UNESCO World Heritage Site
Greater Antilles *is* Caribbean Sea 171 J7
Greater Khingan Mountains China *see* Da Hinggan Ling
Greater St Lucia Wetland Park *nature res.* S. Africa 132 Q4
UNESCO World Heritage Site
Greater Tunb *i.* The Gulf 105 F2
also known as Tonb-e Bozorg, Jazīreh-ye *or* Ţunb al Kubrá
Great Exhibition Bay N.Z. 152 H2
Great Exuma *i.* Bahamas 186 E2
Great Falls U.S.A. 180 E3
Great Fish *r.* S. Africa 133 L10
Greatford N.Z. 152 J8
Great Gandak *r.* India 97 E4
Great Ganges *atoll* Cook Is *see* Manihiki
Great Guana Cay *i.* Bahamas 186 D1
Great Harbour Cay *i.* Bahamas 186 D1
Great Inagua *i.* Bahamas 187 E2
Great Karoo *plat.* S. Africa 132 H9
also known as Karroo
Great Kei *r.* S. Africa 133 M9
Great Lake Australia 147 E5

►Great Lakes Canada/U.S.A. 172
Consist of Lakes Erie, Huron, Michigan, Ontario and Superior.
►►154–155 North America Landscapes

Great Limpopo Transfrontier Park *nat. park* Africa 131 F4
Great Mercury Island N.Z. 152 J4
Great Miami *r.* U.S.A. 176 A6
Great Namaqualand *reg.* Namibia 130 C5
Great Nicobar *i.* India 95 G5
Great North East Channel Australia/P.N.G. 144 D2
Great Ouse *r.* U.K. 47 M11
Great Oyster Bay Australia 147 F5
Great Palm Islands Australia 149 E3
Great Peconic Bay U.S.A. 177 M5
Great Plains U.S.A. 178 B3
Great Point U.S.A. 177 O4
Great Rift Valley *valley* Africa 128 C5
Great Ruaha *r.* Tanz. 129 C6
Great Sacandaga Lake U.S.A. 177 K2
Great St Bernard Pass Italy/Switz. 51 N7
also known as Grand St Bernard, Col du *or* Gran San Bernardo, Colle del
Great Salt Lake U.S.A. 183 L1
Great Salt Lake Desert U.S.A. 183 K1
Great Sand Dunes National Park U.S.A. 181 F5
Great Sand Hills Canada 167 I5
Great Sand Sea *des.* Egypt/Libya 120 E2
Great Sandy Desert Australia 150 C4
Great Sandy Island Australia *see* Fraser Island
Great Sandy Island Nature Reserve Australia 150 A4
Great Sea Reef *reef* Fiji 145 G3

►Great Slave Lake Canada 167 H2
Deepest and 5th largest lake in North America, and 10th in the world.
►►154–155 North America Landscapes

Great Smoky Mountains U.S.A. 174 C5
Great Smoky Mountains National Park U.S.A. 174 D5
UNESCO World Heritage Site
Great Snow Mountain Canada 166 E3
Great South Bay U.S.A. 177 L5
Great Usutu *r.* Africa *see* Usutu
Great Victoria Desert Australia 151 E6
Great Victoria Desert Conservation Park *nature res.* Australia 146 A2
Great Victoria Desert Nature Reserve Australia 151 E6
Great Wall *research station* Antarctica 222 U2
also known as Chang Cheng
►Great Wall *tourist site* China 85 H3
UNESCO World Heritage Site
►►64–65 Asia Countries
Great Western Erg *des.* Alg. *see* Grand Erg Occidental
Great West Torres Islands Myanmar 79 B6
Great Winterhoek *mt.* S. Africa 132 D10
Great Yarmouth U.K. 47 N11
short form Yarmouth
Great Zab *r.* Iraq *see* Zāb al Kabīr, Nahr az
Great Zimbabwe National Monument *tourist site* Zimbabwe 131 F4
short form Zimbabwe
UNESCO World Heritage Site
Grebbestad Sweden 45 J4
Grebenkovskiy Ukr. *see* Hrebinka
Grebnevo Rus. Fed. 43 U7
Grebyonka Ukr. *see* Hrebinka
Greci, Vârful *hill* Romania 58 J3
Greco, Cape Cyprus *see* Greko, Cape
Greco, Monte *mt.* Italy 56 F7
Gredos, Sierra de *mts* Spain 54 F4
Greec Chile 205 C9
►Greece *country* Europe 59 C10
known as Ellas in Greek; *historically known as* Hellas
►►32–33 Europe Countries
Greece U.S.A. 176 H2
Greeley U.S.A. 180 F4
Greely Center U.S.A. 178 C3
Greely Fiord *inlet* Canada 165 K1
Greem-Bell, Ostrov *i.* Rus. Fed. 39 G1
English form Graham Bell Island
Green *r.* Canada 171 M2
Green *r. KY* U.S.A. 174 C4
Green *r. ND* U.S.A. 178 B2
Green *r. WY* U.S.A. 183 O3
Green Bay U.S.A. 172 E6
Green Bay *b.* U.S.A. 172 F5
Greenbrier *r.* U.S.A. 176 E8
Greenbushes Australia 151 B7
Greencastle Bahamas 175 E7
Greencastle *IN* U.S.A. 174 C4
Greencastle *PA* U.S.A. 176 H6
Green Cove Springs U.S.A. 175 D6
Greendale *IN* U.S.A. 176 A6
Greendale *KY* U.S.A. 176 A7
Greene *ME* U.S.A. 177 O1
Greene *NY* U.S.A. 177 J3
Greeneville U.S.A. 176 C9
Greenfield *CA* U.S.A. 182 C5
Greenfield *IA* U.S.A. 178 D3
Greenfield *IN* U.S.A. 174 C4
Greenfield *MA* U.S.A. 177 M3
Greenfield *MO* U.S.A. 178 D4
Greenfield *OH* U.S.A. 176 B6
Greenfield *WI* U.S.A. 172 E8
Green Head Australia 151 A6
Greenhill Island Australia 148 B1
Greenhills N.Z. 153 C14
Greening Canada 173 S2
Green Island *i.* Taiwan *see* Lü Tao
Green Island U.S.A. 172 C8
Green Island Bay Phil. 74 A4
Green Islands P.N.G. 145 E2
Green Lake Canada 167 J4
Green Lake *l.* Canada 166 F5
Green Lake U.S.A. 172 E7

►Greenland *terr.* N. America 165 O2
Self-governing Danish Territory. Largest island in the world and in North America. 3rd largest political entity in North America. Known as Grønland in Danish or Kalaallit Nunaat in Greenlandic.
►►6–7 World Landscapes
►►154–155 North America Landscapes
►►158–159 North America Countries

Greenland U.S.A. 172 D4
Greenly Island Australia 146 B3
Green Mountains U.S.A. 177 M1
Greenock U.K. 46 H8
Greenough Australia 151 A6
Greenough *r.* Australia 151 A6
Greenport U.S.A. 177 M4
Green River U.S.A. 180 E4
Greensboro *AL* U.S.A. 175 C5
Greensboro *GA* U.S.A. 175 D5
Greensboro *MD* U.S.A. 177 J7
Greensboro *NC* U.S.A. 176 F9
Greensburg *IN* U.S.A. 174 C4
Greensburg *KS* U.S.A. 178 C4
Greensburg *KY* U.S.A. 174 C4
Greensburg *LA* U.S.A. 175 B6
Greensburg *PA* U.S.A. 176 F5
Greens Peak U.S.A. 183 O7
Green Swamp U.S.A. 175 E5
Greenup *IL* U.S.A. 174 B4
Greenup *KY* U.S.A. 176 C7
Greenvale Australia 149 E3
Green Valley U.S.A. 181 E7
Greenville Canada 166 D4
Greenville Liberia 124 C5
Greenville *AL* U.S.A. 175 C6
Greenville *CA* U.S.A. 182 D1
Greenville *IL* U.S.A. 174 B4
Greenville *KY* U.S.A. 174 C4
Greenville *ME* U.S.A. 174 G2
Greenville *MI* U.S.A. 172 H7
Greenville *MO* U.S.A. 174 B4
Greenville *MS* U.S.A. 175 B5
Greenville *NC* U.S.A. 174 E5
Greenville *NH* U.S.A. 177 N3
Greenville *OH* U.S.A. 176 A5
Greenville *PA* U.S.A. 176 E4
Greenville *SC* U.S.A. 174 D5
Greenville *TX* U.S.A. 179 C5
Greenwater Lake Canada 172 C2
Greenwater Provincial Park Canada 167 K4
Greenwich *atoll* Micronesia *see* Kapingamarangi
Greenwich U.K. 47 M12
UNESCO World Heritage Site
Greenwich *CT* U.S.A. 177 L4
Greenwich *NY* U.S.A. 177 L2
Greenwich *OH* U.S.A. 176 C4
Greenwood *AR* U.S.A. 179 D5
Greenwood *IN* U.S.A. 174 C4
Greenwood *MS* U.S.A. 175 B5
Greenwood *SC* U.S.A. 175 D5
Greenwood *WI* U.S.A. 172 C6
Greer U.S.A. 174 D5
Greers Ferry Lake U.S.A. 179 D5
Gregório *r.* Brazil 198 D6
Gregory *r.* Australia 148 C3
Gregory *MI* U.S.A. 173 I8
Gregory *SD* U.S.A. 178 C3
Gregory, Lake *salt flat S.A.* Australia 146 C2
Gregory, Lake *salt flat W.A.* Australia 150 D4
Gregory, Lake *salt flat W.A.* Australia 151 B5
Gregory Downs Australia 148 C3
Gregory National Park Australia 148 A3
Gregory Range *hills Qld* Australia 149 D3
Gregory Range *hills W.A.* Australia 150 C4
Greifswald Germany 49 K1
Greifswalder Bodden *b.* Germany 49 K1
Greifswalder Oie *i.* Germany 49 K1
Greiz Germany 49 J5
Greko, Cape Cyprus 108 F3
also spelt Greco, Cape
Gremikha Rus. Fed. 40 F1
Gremyachev Rus. Fed. 43 T7
Gremyachinsk *Permskaya Oblast'* Rus. Fed. 40 K4
Gremyachinsk *Respublika Buryatiya* Rus. Fed. 81 H2
Grenå Denmark 45 J4
Grenada U.S.A. 175 B5
►Grenada *country* West Indies 187 H4
►►158–159 North America Countries
Grenade France 50 H9
Grenade-sur-l'Adour France 50 F9
Grenchen Switz. 51 N5
Grenen *spit* Denmark 45 J4
English form The Skaw
Grenfell Australia 147 F3
Grenfell Canada 167 K5
Grenoble France 51 L7
Grense-Jakobselv Norway 44 O1
Grenville Grenada 187 H4
Grenville, Cape Australia 149 D1
Grenville Island Fiji *see* Rotuma
Greshak Pak. 101 F5
Gresham U.S.A. 180 B3
Gresik Indon. 77 F4
Gressåmoen Nasjonalpark *nat. park* Norway 44 K2
Gretna *LA* U.S.A. 175 B6
Gretna *VA* U.S.A. 176 F9
Grevelingen *sea chan.* Neth. 48 A4
Greven Germany 48 E3
Grevena Greece 59 C8
Grevenbroich Germany 48 D4
Grevenmacher Lux. 51 M3
Grevesmühlen Germany 48 I2
Grey *r.* Canada 169 J4
Grey *r.* N.Z. 153 F10
also known as Māwheranui
Grey, Cape Australia 148 C2
Greybull U.S.A. 180 E3
Greybull *r.* U.S.A. 180 E3
Grey Hunter Peak Canada 166 C2
Grey Islands Canada 169 K3
Greylock, Mount U.S.A. 177 L3
Greymouth N.Z. 153 F10
Grey Range *hills* Australia 147 D2
Grey's Plains Australia 151 A5
Greystone Zimbabwe 131 F4
Greytown S. Africa 133 O6
Grez-Doiceau Belgium 51 K2
Gria, Akra *pt* Greece 59 F11
Gribanovskiy Rus. Fed. 41 G6
Gribingui *r.* Cent. Afr. Rep. 126 C2
Gribingui-Bamingui, Réserve de Faune du *nature res.* Cent. Afr. Rep. 126 C3
Gridley *CA* U.S.A. 182 C2
Gridley *IL* U.S.A. 172 E10
Grieskirchen Austria 49 K7
Griffin U.S.A. 175 C5
Griffith Australia 147 E3
Griffith Canada 173 P5
Griffiths Point Canada 165 G2
Griffithsville U.S.A. 176 D7
Grigan *i.* N. Mariana Is *see* Agrihan
Grigiškės Lith. 42 G7
Grignols France 50 F8
Grigoriopol Moldova 58 K1
Grik Malaysia *see* Gerik
Grim, Cape Australia 147 E5
Grimari Cent. Afr. Rep. 126 D3
Grimeton *tourist site* Sweden 45 K4
UNESCO World Heritage Site
Grimma Germany 49 J4
Grimmen Germany 49 K1
Grimsby Canada 173 N7
Grimsby U.K. 47 L10
Grímsey *i.* Iceland 44 [inset] C2
Grimshaw Canada 167 G3
Grímsstaðir Iceland 44 [inset] C2
Grimstad Norway 45 J4
Grindaheim Norway 45 J3
Grindavík Iceland 44 [inset] B3
Grindsted Denmark 45 J5
Grindu Romania 58 H4
Grindu Romania 58 J3
Grindul Chituc *spit* Romania 58 J4
Grinduşu, Vârful *mt.* Romania 58 H2
Grinevo Rus. Fed. 43 O9
Grinnell U.S.A. 174 A3
Grinnell Peninsula Canada 165 J2
Grinţieş Romania 58 G1
Grintovec *mt.* Slovenia 56 G2
Griqualand East *reg.* S. Africa 133 N7
Griqualand West *reg.* S. Africa 132 H5
Griquatown S. Africa 132 H5
Grise Fiord Canada 165 K2
also known as Aujuittuq
Grishino Ukr. *see* Krasnoarmiys'k
Grisik Indon. 76 C3
Gris Nez, Cap *c.* France 50 H2
Grisolles France 50 H9
Grisslehamn Sweden 45 L3
Gritley U.K. 46 J5
Grizim *well* Alg. 123 E4
Grizzly Bear Mountain *hill* Canada 166 F1
Grmeč *mts* Bos.-Herz. 56 I4
Groais Island Canada 169 K3
Grobbendonk Belgium 51 K1
Grobiņa Latvia 42 C5
Groblersdal S. Africa 133 N2
Groblershoop S. Africa 132 G5
Gröbming Austria 49 K8
Grocka *Srbija* Serb. and Mont. 58 B4
Grodków Poland 49 O5
Grodnenskaya Oblast' *admin. div* Belarus *see* Hrodzyenskaya Voblasts'
Grodno Belarus *see* Hrodna
Grodno Oblast *admin. div.* Belarus *see* Hrodzyenskaya Voblasts'
Grodzisk Mazowiecki Poland 49 R3
Grodzisk Wielkopolski Poland 49 N3
Groen *watercourse N. Cape* S. Africa 132 H7
Groen *watercourse N. Cape/W. Cape* S. Africa 132 B7
Groesbeck U.S.A. 179 C6
Gröf Iceland 44 [inset] B2
Groganville Australia 149 E3
Groix, Île de *i.* France 50 C5
Grójec Poland 49 R4
Grombalia Tunisia 57 C12
Grömitz Germany 48 H1
Gronau (Westfalen) Germany 48 E3
Grong Norway 44 K2
Groningen Neth. 48 D2
Groningen Suriname 199 H3
Grønland *terr.* N. America *see* Greenland
Grønnedal Greenland *see* Kangilinnguit
Groom Lake U.S.A. 183 I4
Groot *r. E. Cape* S. Africa 132 I10
Groot *r. W. Cape* S. Africa 132 D9
Groot *r. W. Cape* S. Africa 132 F10
Groot-Aar Pan *salt pan* S. Africa 132 E4
Groot Berg *r.* S. Africa 132 C9
Groot Brak *r.* S. Africa 133 J8
Groot Brakrivier S. Africa 132 G11
Grootdraaidam *dam* S. Africa 133 N3
Grootdrink S. Africa 132 F5
Groote Eylandt *i.* Australia 148 C2
Groote Eylandt Aboriginal Land *res.* Australia 148 C2
Grootfontein Namibia 130 C3
Groot-Grannapan *salt pan* S. Africa 133 J5
Groot Karas Berg *plat.* Namibia 130 C5
Groot Letaba *r.* S. Africa 131 F4
Grootmis S. Africa 132 B6
Grootpan S. Africa 133 K2
Grootrivierhoogte *mts* S. Africa 132 H10
Groot Swartberge *mts* S. Africa 132 F10
Grootvaalgraspan *salt pan* Namibia 132 C3
Grootvloer *salt pan* S. Africa 132 E6
Groot Winterberg *mt.* S. Africa 133 K9
Groot-Winterhoekberge *mts* S. Africa 133 I10
Gropeni Romania 58 I3
Grosa, Isla *i.* Spain 55 K7
Gros Islet St Lucia 187 H4
Gros Morne National Park Canada 169 J3
UNESCO World Heritage Site
Grosne *r.* France 51 K6
Gros Piton *mt.* St Lucia 187 H4
UNESCO World Heritage Site
Gross Barmen Namibia 130 C4
Große Aue *r.* Germany 48 G3
Großenhain Germany 49 K4
Großenkneten Germany 48 F3
Großenlüder Germany 48 G5
Großer Arber *mt.* Germany 49 K6
Großer Beerberg *hill* Germany 48 H5
Grosser Bösenstein *mt.* Austria 49 L8
Grosser Priel *mt.* Austria 49 L8
Großer Rachel *mt.* Germany 49 K7
Grosser Speikkofel *mt.* Austria 49 K9
Grosser Speikkogel *mt.* Austria 49 L9
Grosseto Italy 56 D6
Groß-Gerau Germany 48 F6
Großglockner *mt.* Austria 49 J8
Groß-Hesepe Germany 48 E3
Großräschen Germany 49 L4
Groß Schönebeck Germany 49 K3
Gross Ums Namibia 130 C4
Großvenediger *mt.* Austria 49 J8
Grosuplje Slovenia 56 G3
Grosvenor Mountains Antarctica 223 L1
Gros Ventre Range *mts* U.S.A. 180 E4
Groswater Bay Canada 169 J2
Groton *CT* U.S.A. 177 M4
Groton *NY* U.S.A. 177 I3
Groton *SD* U.S.A. 178 C2
Grottoes U.S.A. 176 G7
Grouard Lake Canada 167 G1
Grouard Mission Canada 167 G4
Grouin, Pointe du *pt* France 50 E4
Groumania Côte d'Ivoire 124 E5
Groundhog *r.* Canada 168 D3
Grove U.S.A. 178 D4
Grove City *OH* U.S.A. 176 B6
Grove City *PA* U.S.A. 176 E4
Grove Hill U.S.A. 175 C6
Grövelsjön Sweden 45 K3
Grove Mountains Antarctica 223 F2
Grover Beach U.S.A. 182 D6
Groveton *NH* U.S.A. 177 N1
Groveton *TX* U.S.A. 179 D6
Grovfjord Norway 44 L1
Growler Mountains U.S.A. 183 K9
Grozd'ovo Bulg. 58 I5
Groznyy Rus. Fed. 41 H8
also known as Dzhokhar Ghala
Grubišno Polje Croatia 56 J3
Grudovo Bulg. *see* Sredets
Grudziądz Poland 49 P2
historically known as Graudenz
Grumăzeşti Romania 58 H1
Grums Sweden 45 K4
Grünau Namibia 130 C5
Grünau-Grünheider Wald und Seengebiet *park* Germany 49 K3
Grünberg Poland *see* Zielona Góra
Grundagssätern Sweden 45 K3
Grundarfjörður Iceland 44 [inset] B2
Grundforsen Sweden 45 K3
Grundlsee *nature res.* Austria 49 K8
Grundorner Namibia 132 B2
Grundsuna Sweden 44 L3
Grundy U.S.A. 176 C8
Gruñidora Mex. 185 E3
Gruver U.S.A. 179 B4
Gruzdžiai Lith. 42 E5
Gruzinskaya S.S.R. *country* Asia *see* Georgia
Gryazi Rus. Fed. 41 F5
Gryaznoye Rus. Fed. 43 U7
Gryazovets Rus. Fed. 43 V3
Grybów Poland 49 R6
Gryfice Poland 49 M2
Gryfino Poland 49 L2
Gryfów Śląski Poland 49 M4
Gryllefjord Norway 44 L1
Grytviken S. Georgia 205 [inset]
Gua India 97 E5
Guà *r.* Italy 56 D3
Guabito Panama 186 C5
Guacanayabo, Golfo de *b.* Cuba 186 D2
Guacara Venez. 187 G5
Guacharía *r.* Col. 198 D3
Guaçu Brazil 203 A7
Guaçuí Brazil 207 L7
Guadaira *r.* Spain 54 E7
Guadajira *r.* Spain 54 E6
Guadajoz *r.* Spain 54 G7
Guadalajara Mex. 185 E4
UNESCO World Heritage Site
Guadalajara Spain 55 H4
Guadalaviar *r.* Spain 55 J4
Guadalcacín, Embalse de *resr* Spain 54 F8
Guadalcanal *i.* Solomon Is 145 F2
Guadalcanal Spain 54 F6
Guadalén *r.* Spain 55 H6
Guadales Arg. 204 D4
Guadalhorce *r.* Spain 54 G8
Guadalhorce, Embalse de *resr* Spain 54 G8
Guadalimar *r.* Spain 55 H7
Guadalmez *r.* Spain 54 G6
Guadalope *r.* Spain 55 K3
Guadalquivir *r.* Spain 55 E8
Guadalupe Brazil 202 D3
Guadalupe *Nuevo León* Mex. 185 E3
Guadalupe *Zacatecas* Mex. 185 E4
Guadalupe *i.* Mex. 170 C6
Guadalupe *watercourse* Mex. 183 H9
Guadalupe Peru 200 A1
Guadalupe Spain 54 F5
UNESCO World Heritage Site
Guadalupe *AZ* U.S.A. 183 M8
Guadalupe *CA* U.S.A. 182 D7
Guadalupe *r.* U.S.A. 179 C6
Guadalupe, Sierra de *mts* Spain 54 F5
Guadalupe Aguilera Mex. 184 D3
Guadalupe Mountains National Park U.S.A. 181 F7
Guadalupe Victoria *Baja California Norte* Mex. 183 I9
Guadalupe Victoria *Durango* Mex. 184 D3
Guadamez *r.* Spain 54 F6
Guadarrama *r.* Spain 54 G5
Guadarrama Venez. 199 D2
Guadarrama, Puerto de *pass* Spain 54 G4
Guadarrama, Sierra de *mts* Spain 54 G4
Guadazaón *r.* Spain 55 J5

►Guadeloupe *terr.* West Indies 187 H3
French Overseas Department.
►►158–159 North America Countries

Guadeloupe Passage Caribbean Sea 187 H3
Guadiamar *r.* Spain 54 E8
Guadiana *r.* Port./Spain 54 D7
Guadiana, Bahía de *b.* Cuba 186 B2
Guadiana Menor *r.* Spain 55 H7
Guadiaro *r.* Spain 54 F8
Guadiato *r.* Spain 54 F7
Guadiela *r.* Spain 55 I4
Guadiervas *r.* Spain 54 F4
Guadix Spain 55 H7
Guafo, Isla *i.* Chile 205 B6
Guagua Phil. 74 B3
Guaíba Brazil 203 B9
Guaiçuí Brazil 203 C6
Guaicuras Brazil 201 F5
Guaillabamba *r.* Ecuador 198 B4
Guáimaro Cuba 186 D2
Guaina Venez. 199 F3
Guainía *dept* Col. 198 D4
Guainía *r.* Col./Venez. 198 E4
Guaiquinima, Cerro *mt.* Venez. 199 F3
Guaíra *Paraná* Brazil 203 A8
Guaíra *São Paulo* Brazil 206 E7
Guaitecas, Islas *is* Chile 205 B6
Guaizihu China 84 D3
Guajará Açu Brazil 202 B2
Guajará Mirim Brazil 200 D2
Guajaratuba Brazil 199 F6
Guajarraã Brazil 200 D1
Guaje, Laguna de *l.* Mex. 185 E2
Guaje, Llano de *plain* Mex. 185 E3
Guajira, Península de la *pen.* Col. 198 D2
Gualaceo Ecuador 198 B5
Gualala U.S.A. 182 A3
Gualán Guat. 185 H6
Gualaquiza Ecuador 198 B5
Gualdo Tadino Italy 56 E5
Gualeguay Arg. 204 F4
Gualeguay *r.* Arg. 204 F4
Gualeguaychu Arg. 204 F4
Gualicho, Salina *salt flat* Arg. 204 D6
Gualjaina Arg. 205 C6
Guallatiri *vol.* Chile 200 C4

►Guam *terr.* N. Pacific Ocean 73 J4
United States Unincorporated Territory.
►►138–139 Oceania Countries

Guamblin, Isla *i.* Chile 205 B7
Guamini Arg. 204 E5
Guamo Cuba 186 D2
Guampí, Sierra de *mts* Venez. 199 E3
Guamúchil Mex. 184 C3
Gu'an China 85 H4
Guanabacoa Cuba 186 C2
Guanabara Brazil 200 C2
Guanabara, Baía de *b.* Brazil 207 J9
Guanacaste, Parque Nacional *nat. park* Costa Rica 186 B5
UNESCO World Heritage Site
Guanacevi Mex. 184 D3
Guanahacabibes, Península de *pen.* Cuba 186 B2
Guanaja Hond. 186 B3
Guanajay Cuba 186 C2
Guanajuato Mex. 185 E4
UNESCO World Heritage Site
Guanajuato *state* Mex. 185 E4
Guanambi Brazil 202 D5
Guanare Venez. 198 D2
Guanare Viejo *r.* Venez. 198 E2
Guanarito Venez. 198 D2
Guanarito *r.* Venez. 198 D2
Guanay Bol. 200 D3
Guandacol Arg. 204 C3
Guandaokou China 87 D1
Guandi Shan *mt.* China 85 F4
Guandu *r.* Brazil 207 L6
Guandu China 87 E3
Guane Cuba 186 B2
Guang'an China 86 C2
also known as Nonghui
Guangchang China 87 F3
also known as Xujiang
Guangde China 87 F2
also known as Taozhou
Guangdong *prov.* China 87 E4
English form Kwangtung
Guangfeng China 87 F2
also known as Yongfeng
Guanghai China 87 E4
Guanghan China 86 C2
Guanghua China *see* Laohekou
Guangling China 85 G4
Guangmao Shan *mt.* China 86 B3
Guangming China *see* Xide
Guangming Ding *mt.* China 87 F2
Guangnan China 86 C3
also known as Liancheng
Guangning *Guangdong* China 87 E4
also known as Nanjie
Guangning *Liaoning* China *see* Beining
Guangrao China 85 H4
Guangshan China 87 E2
Guangshui China 87 E2
Guangxi *aut. reg.* China *see* Guangxi Zhuangzu Zizhiqu
Guangxi Zhuangzu Zizhiqu *aut. reg.* China 87 D4
short form Guangxi; *English form* Kwangsi *or* Kwangsi Chuang Autonomous Region
Guangyuan China 86 C1
Guangze China 87 F3
also known as Hangchuan
Guangzhou China 87 E4
English form Canton; *formerly spelt* Kwangchow
Guanhães Brazil 203 D6
Guanhães *r.* Brazil 207 K6
Guan He *r.* China 87 F1
Guanhe Kou *r. mouth* China 87 F1
Guánica Puerto Rico 187 G3
Guanipa *r.* Venez. 199 F2
Guanling China 86 C3
also known as Guansuo
Guanmian Shan *mts* China 87 D2
Guanpo China 87 D1
Guansuo China *see* Guanling
Guanta Venez. 199 E2
Guantánamo Cuba 187 E2
Guantao China 85 G4
Guanxian China *see* Dujiangyan
Guanyang China 87 D3
Guanyinqiao China 86 B2
formerly known as Chuosijia
Guanyun China 87 F1
also known as Yishan; *formerly known as* Dayishan
Guapay *r.* Bol. *see* Grande
Guapé Brazil 203 C7
Guapí Col. 198 B4
Guapiara Brazil 206 E11
Guápiles Costa Rica 186 C5
Guaporé *r.* Bol./Brazil 200 D2
Guaporé Brazil 203 B9
Guaporé *state* Brazil *see* Rondônia
Guaqui Bol. 200 C4
Guará Brazil 206 F7
Guará *r.* Brazil 202 C5
Guara, Sierra de *mts* Spain 55 K2
Guarabira Brazil 202 F3
Guaranda Ecuador 198 B5
Guarani Brazil 207 J8
Guarantã Brazil 206 D8
Guarapari Brazil 203 D7
Guarapuava Brazil 203 B8
Guararapes Brazil 206 C8
Guaratinga Brazil 202 E6
Guaratinguetá Brazil 207 H9
Guaratuba Brazil 203 B8
Guarayos Bol. 200 C3
Guarda Port. 54 D4
Guarda *admin. dist.* Port. 54 D4
Guardafui, Cape Somalia *see* Caseyr, Raas
Guardal *r.* Spain 55 I7
Guardamar del Segura Spain 55 K6
Guardatinajas Venez. 199 E2
Guardia Escolta Arg. 204 E3
Guardiagrele Italy 56 G6
Guardianes de la Patria Mex. 183 I9
Guardo Spain 54 G2
Guardunha, Serra de *mts* Port. 54 D5
Guareña Spain 54 E6
Guariba *r.* Brazil 201 E1
Guárico *state* Venez. 199 E2
Guarico, Punta *pt* Cuba 187 E2
Guarrojo *r.* Col. 198 D3
Guarujá Brazil 207 G10
Guarulhos Brazil 206 G10
Guasare *r.* Venez. 187 F5
Guasave Mex. 184 C3
Guasdualito Venez. 198 D3
Guasipati Venez. 199 F3
Guastatoya Guat. 185 H6
also known as El Progreso
Guasuba *r.* India 97 F5

►Guatemala *country* Central America 185 H6
4th most populous country in North America.

Guatemala Guat. *see* Guatemala City

►Guatemala City Guat. 185 H6
Capital of Guatemala. Also known as Guatemala.
►►158–159 North America Countries

Guatimozin Arg. 204 E4
Guatrache Arg. 204 E5
Guatrochi Arg. 205 D6
Guaviare *dept* Col. 198 D4
Guaviare *r.* Col. 198 E3
Guaxupé Brazil 206 G8
Guayabal Col. 198 D3
Guayabal Cuba 186 D2
Guayaguas, Sierra da *mts* Arg. 204 D3
Guayama Puerto Rico 187 G3
Guayapo, Serranía *mts* Venez. 199 E3
Guayaquil Ecuador 198 B5
Guayaquil, Golfo de *g.* Ecuador 198 A5
Guayaramerín Bol. 200 D2
Guayas *prov.* Ecuador 198 A5
Guayatayoc, Laguna de *imp. l.* Arg. 200 D5
Guaymas Mex. 184 C3
Guayquiraró *r.* Arg. 204 F3
Guazacapán Guat. 185 H6
Guba Eth. 128 B2
Gubadag Turkm. 102 D4
formerly known as Tel'mansk
Guba Dolgaya Rus. Fed. 40 K1
Gubakha Rus. Fed. 40 K4
Gûbâl, Gezîret *i.* Egypt 104 A2
English form Gûbâl Island
Gûbâl Island Egypt *see* Gûbâl, Gezîret
Guban *plain* Somalia 128 E2
Gubat Phil. 74 C3
Gubbi India 94 C3
Gubbio Italy 56 E5
historically known as Iguvium
Gubdor Rus. Fed. 40 K3
Gubed Binna *b.* Somalia 128 F2
Guben Germany 49 L4
formerly known as Wilhelm-Pieck-Stadt
Gŭbene Bulg. 58 G6
Gubin Poland 49 L4
Gubino Rus. Fed. 43 Q6
Gubio Nigeria 125 I3
Gubkin Rus. Fed. 41 F6
Gucheng *Hebei* China 85 G4
also known as Zhengkou; *formerly known as* Zhengjiakou
Gucheng *Hubei* China 87 D1
Gudalur India 94 C4
Gudar, Sierra de *mts* Spain 55 K4
Gudari India 95 D2
Gudaut'a Georgia 107 E2
Gudbrandsdalen *valley* Norway 45 J3
Guddu Barrage Pak. 101 G4
Gudermes Rus. Fed. 102 A4
Gudi Nigeria 125 H4
Gudivada India 94 D2
Gudiyattam India 94 C3
Gudong He *r.* China 82 C4
Gudri *r.* Pak. 101 E5
Güdül Turkey 106 C2
Gudur *Andhra Pradesh* India 94 C3
Gudur *Andhra Pradesh* India 94 C3
Gudvangen Norway 45 I3
Gudzhal *r.* Rus. Fed. 82 D2
Gudžiūnai Lith. 42 E6
Gué, Rivière du *r.* Canada 169 G1
Guebwiller France 51 N5
Guéckédou Guinea 124 C4
Guéguen, Lac *l.* Canada 173 P2
Guelb er Rîchât *hill* Mauritania 122 C5
Guélengdeng Chad 126 B2
Guelma Alg. 123 G1
Guelmine Morocco 122 C3
Guelph Canada 168 D5
Guémez Mex. 185 F4
Guendour *well* Mauritania 122 C6
Guéné Benin 125 F4
Guènt Paté Senegal 124 B3
Guer France 50 D5
Guéra *pref.* Chad 126 C2
Guéra, Massif du *mts* Chad 126 C2
Guérande France 50 D5
Guerara Alg. 123 G2
Guérard, Lac *l.* Canada 169 H1
Guercif Morocco 123 E2
Guéré *watercourse* Chad 120 C5
Guéréda Chad 120 D6
Guerende Libya 120 D4

H

Iton r. France 50 H3
Itongafeno mt. Madag. 131 [inset] J4
Itororó Brazil 207 M2
Itsuki Japan 91 B8
Itsukushima i. Japan 83 D6
UNESCO World Heritage Site
Itsukushima Shrine tourist site Japan 91 C7
Ittiri Sardinia Italy 57 A8
Ittoqqortoormiit Greenland 165 Q2
also known as Scoresbysund
Itu Brazil 206 F10
Itu Nigeria 125 G5
Itu Abu Island S. China Sea 72 D4
Ituaçu Brazil 202 D5
Ituberá Brazil 202 E5
Ituí r. Brazil 198 D6
Ituiutaba Brazil 206 D5
Itula Dem. Rep. Congo 126 E5
Itumba Tanz. 129 B6
Itumbiara Brazil 206 D5
Itumbiara, Barragem resr Brazil 206 D5
Itungi Port Malawi 129 B7
Ituni Guyana 199 G3
Itupiranga Brazil 202 B3
Iturama Brazil 206 C6
Iturbe Para. 201 F6
Iturbide Campeche Mex. 185 H5
Iturbide Nuevo León Mex. 185 F3
Ituri r. Dem. Rep. Congo 126 E4
Iturup, Ostrov i. Rus. Fed. 82 G3
also known as Etorofu-tō
Itutinga Brazil 207 I8
Ituverava Brazil 206 F7
Ituxi r. Brazil 200 D1
also known as Iquiri
Ituzaingo Arg. 204 F2
Ityopia country Africa see **Ethiopia**
Itzehoe Germany 48 G2
Iuaretê Brazil 198 D4
Iuka U.S.A. 174 B5
Iul'tin Rus. Fed. 39 S3
Iuluti Moz. 131 H2
Iúna Brazil 207 L7
Iutica Brazil 198 D4
Ivaí r. Brazil 206 A10
Ivaiporã Brazil 206 B11
Ivakoany mt. Madag. 131 [inset] J4
Ivalo Fin. 44 N1
also known as Avveel or Avvil
Ivalojoki r. Fin. 44 N1
Ivanava Belarus 42 G9
also spelt Ivanovo
Ivanec Croatia 56 I2
Ivangorod Rus. Fed. 43 J2
Ivangrad Crna Gora Serb. and Mont. see **Berane**
Ivanhoe N.S.W. Australia 147 E3
Ivanhoe W.A. Australia 150 E2
Ivanhoe r. Canada 168 D3
Ivanhoe CA U.S.A. 182 E5
Ivanhoe MN U.S.A. 178 C2
Ivanhoe VA U.S.A. 176 E9
Ivanhoe Lake N.W.T. Canada 167 J2
Ivanhoe Lake Ont. Canada 173 K2
Ivanić-Grad Croatia 56 I3
Ivanishchi Rus. Fed. 43 V6
Ivanivka Ukr. 58 L2
Ivanjica Srbija Serb. and Mont. 58 B5
Ivankiv Ukr. 41 D6
Ivankovo Croatia 56 K3
Ivan'kovo Rus. Fed. 43 S7
Ivan'kovskiy Rus. Fed. 43 V5
Ivan'kovskoye Vodokhranilishche resr Rus. Fed. 43 R5
Ivankovtsy Rus. Fed. 82 D2
Ivano-Frankivs'k Ukr. 41 C6
also spelt Ivano-Frankovsk; formerly known as Stanislav
Ivano-Frankovsk Ukr. see **Ivano-Frankivs'k**
Ivanovka Kazakh. see **Kokzhayyk**
Ivanovka Amurskaya Oblast' Rus. Fed. 82 B2
Ivanovka Orenburgskaya Oblast' Rus. Fed. 102 C1
Ivanovo Belarus see **Ivanava**
Ivanovo tourist site Bulg. 58 G5
UNESCO World Heritage Site
Ivanovo Ivanovskaya Oblast' Rus. Fed. 40 G4
Ivanovo Pskovskaya Oblast' Rus. Fed. 43 L5
Ivanovo Tverskaya Oblast' Rus. Fed. 43 S3
Ivanovo Oblast admin. div. Rus. Fed. see **Ivanovskaya Oblast'**
Ivanovskaya Oblast' admin. div. Rus. Fed. 43 U4
English form Ivanovo Oblast
Ivanovskiy Khrebet mts Kazakh. 88 C1
Ivanovskoye Orlovskaya Oblast' Rus. Fed. 43 R8
Ivanovskoye Yaroslavskaya Oblast' Rus. Fed. 43 U5
Ivanpah Lake U.S.A. 183 I6
Ivanšćica mts Croatia 56 H2
Ivanski Bulg. 58 I5
Ivanteyevka Rus. Fed. 102 B1
Ivantsevichi Belarus see **Ivatsevichy**
Ivato Madag. 131 [inset] J4
Ivatsevichy Belarus 42 G9
also spelt Ivantsevichi
Ivaylovgrad Bulg. 58 H7
Ivaylovgrad, Yazovir resr Bulg. 58 G7
Ivdel' Rus. Fed. 38 G3
Iveşti Romania 58 I3
Iveşti Romania 58 I2
Ivi, Cap c. Alg. 55 L8
Ivindo r. Gabon 126 B5
Ivinheima Brazil 203 A7
Ivittuut Greenland 165 O3
Iviza i. Spain see **Ibiza**
Ivohibe Madag. 131 [inset] J4
Ivolândia Brazil 206 C3
Ivolginsk Rus. Fed. 85 E1
Ivón Bol. 200 D2
Ivor U.S.A. 177 I9
Ivory Coast country Africa see **Côte d'Ivoire**
Ivösjön l. Sweden 45 K4
Ivot Rus. Fed. 43 P8
Ivrea Italy 51 N7
İvrindi Turkey 59 I9
Ivris Ugheltekhili pass Georgia 107 F2
Ivugivik Canada see **Ivujivik**
Ivujivik Canada 165 L3
formerly spelt Ivugivik
Ivuna Tanz. 129 B7
Ivvavik National Park Canada 164 F3
Ivyanyets Belarus 42 H8
Ivydale U.S.A. 176 D7
Iwaizumi Japan 90 G5
Iwaki Japan 90 G6
Iwaki-san vol. Japan 90 G4
Iwakuni Japan 91 C7
Iwamatsu Japan 91 C8
Iwamizawa Japan 90 G3
Iwan r. Indon. 77 F2
Iwanai Japan 90 G3
Iwanda Tanz. 129 B7
Iwanuma Japan 90 G5
Iwata Japan 91 E7
Iwate Japan 90 G5
Iwate pref. Japan 90 G5
Iwate-san vol. Japan 90 G5
Iwo Nigeria 125 G5
Iwo Jima i. Japan see **Iō-jima**
Iwupataka Aboriginal Land res. Australia 148 B4
Iwye Belarus 42 G8
Ixcamilpa Mex. 185 F5
Ixiamas Bol. 200 C3
Ixmiquilpán Mex. 185 F4
Ixopo S. Africa 133 O7
Ixtacomitán Mex. 185 G5
Ixtlán Nayarit Mex. 184 D4
Ixtlán Oaxaca Mex. 185 F5
Iya i. Indon. 75 B5
Iya r. Rus. Fed. 80 G1
Iyayi Tanz. 129 B7
İyirmi Altı Bakı Komissarı Azer. see **26 Bakı Komissarı**
Iyo Japan 91 C8
Iyomishima Japan 91 C8
Iyo-nada b. Japan 91 C8
Izabal, Lago de l. Guat. 185 H6
Izaga, Peña de mt. Spain 55 J2
Izamal Mex. 185 H4
Izapa tourist site Mex. 185 G6
Izari-dake mt. Japan 90 G3
Izazi Tanz. 129 B6
Izbăşeşti hill Romania 58 F3
'Izbat al Burj Egypt 108 C6
'Izbat al Jazīrah Egypt 108 C6
'Izbat Jamaşah al Gharbīyah Egypt 108 C6
Izberbash Rus. Fed. 102 A4
Izdeshkovo Rus. Fed. 43 O6
Īzeh Iran 100 B4
Izgagane well Niger 125 H2
Izhevsk Rus. Fed. 40 J4
formerly known as Ustinov
Izhma Respublika Komi Rus. Fed. 40 J2
Izhma Respublika Komi Rus. Fed. see **Sosnogorsk**
Izhma r. Rus. Fed. 40 J2
Izkī Oman 105 G3
Izmail Ukr. see **Izmayil**
Izmalkovo Rus. Fed. 43 S9
Izmayil Ukr. 41 D7
also spelt Izmail; formerly spelt Ismail
Izmeny, Proliv sea chan. Japan/Rus. Fed. see **Notsuke-suidō**
İzmir Turkey 106 A3
historically known as Smyrna
İzmir prov. Turkey 59 I10
İzmir Körfezi g. Turkey 106 A3
İzmit Turkey 106 B2
also known as Kocaeli; historically known as Astacus or Nicomedia
İzmit Körfezi b. Turkey 106 B2
Izmorene Morocco 54 H9
Iznajar, Embalse de resr Spain 54 G7
Iznalloz Spain 55 H7
İznik Turkey 58 K8
historically known as Nicaea
İznik Gölü l. Turkey 106 B2
Iznoski Rus. Fed. 43 Q7
Izoard, Col d' pass France 51 M8
Izobil'noye Rus. Fed. see **Izobil'nyy**
Izobil'nyy Rus. Fed. 41 G7
formerly known as Izobil'noye
Izola Slovenia 56 F3
Izoplit Rus. Fed. 43 R5
Izozog Bajo Bol. 201 E4
Izra' Syria 108 H5
Iztochni Rodopi mts Bulg. 58 G7
Izúcar de Matamoros Mex. 185 F5
Izu-hantō pen. Japan 91 F7
Izuhara Japan 91 A7
Izumi Japan 91 B8
Izumisano Japan 91 D7
Izumo Japan 91 C7

►**Izu-Ogasawara Trench** sea feature N. Pacific Ocean 220 E3
5th deepest trench in the world.

Izu-shotō is Japan 91 F7
Izu-tobu vol. Japan 91 F7
Izvestiy Tsentral'nogo Ispolnitel'nogo Komiteta, Ostrova Rus. Fed. 39 I2
Izvestkovyy Rus. Fed. 82 C2
Izvoarele Romania 58 G4
Izvoarele Romania 58 F4
Izvoarele Romania 58 H3
Izvoru Romania 58 G4
Izyaslav Ukr. 41 C6
Iz"yayu Rus. Fed. 40 K2
Izyndy Kazakh. 102 D3
Izyum Ukr. 41 F6

J

Jaama Estonia 42 I2
Ja'ar Yemen 105 D5
Ja'ār, Birkat al salt l. Egypt 108 B7
Jaba watercourse Iran 100 D3
Jabal as Sirāj Afgh. 101 G3
Jabal Dab Saudi Arabia 105 E3
Jabalón r. Spain 54 G6
Jabalpur India 96 C5
formerly spelt Jubbulpore
Jabal 'Uwaybid Egypt 108 D7
Jabbārah Fara Islands Saudi Arabia 104 C4
Jabbūl, Sabkhat al salt flat Syria 109 I2
Jabiluka Aboriginal Land res. Australia 148 B2
Jabir reg. Oman 105 G3
Jabiru Australia 148 B2
Jablah Syria 108 G2
Jablanica Bos.-Herz. 56 J5
Jablanica r. Serb. and Mont. 58 C5
Jablonec nad Nisou Czech Rep. 49 M5
Jabłonowo Pomorskie Poland 49 Q2
Jablunkov Czech Rep. 49 P6
Jaboticabal Brazil 206 E8
Jaboticatubas Brazil 207 J6
Jabuka i. Croatia 56 H5
Jabuka Vojvodina, Srbija Serb. and Mont. 58 B4
Jabung, Tanjung pt Indon. 76 D3
Jaburu Brazil 199 E6
Jabuti Brazil 199 G6
Jaca Spain 55 K2
Jacala Mex. 185 F4
Jacaraci Brazil 207 K1
Jacaré Mato Grosso Brazil 202 A5
Jacaré Rondônia Brazil 201 D2
Jacaré r. Brazil 199 F6
Jacaré r. Brazil 202 D4
Jacareacanga Brazil 199 G6
Jacareí Brazil 207 G10
Jacaretinga Brazil 201 F2
Jacarézinho Brazil 206 D10
Jáchal r. Arg. 204 D3
Jaciara Brazil 202 A5
Jacinto Brazil 202 D6
Jaciparaná Brazil 201 D2
Jaciparaná r. Brazil 201 D2
Jack r. Australia 149 E2
Jackfish Canada 172 G2
Jackfish Lake Canada 167 I4
Jack Lee, Lake resr U.S.A. 179 D5
Jacksboro TN U.S.A. 176 A9
Jacksboro TX U.S.A. 179 C5
Jackson Australia 149 F5
Jackson AL U.S.A. 175 C6
Jackson CA U.S.A. 182 D3
Jackson GA U.S.A. 175 D5
Jackson KY U.S.A. 176 B8
Jackson MI U.S.A. 173 I8
Jackson MN U.S.A. 178 D3
Jackson MO U.S.A. 174 B4

►**Jackson** MS U.S.A. 175 B5
State capital of Mississippi.

Jackson NC U.S.A. 176 H9
Jackson OH U.S.A. 176 C6
Jackson TN U.S.A. 174 B5
Jackson WI U.S.A. 172 E7
Jackson WY U.S.A. 180 E4
Jackson, Cape N.Z. 152 I8
Jackson, Mount Antarctica 222 T2
Jackson Bay N.Z. 153 C11
Jackson Bay b. N.Z. 153 C11
also known as Okahu
Jackson Head N.Z. 153 C11
Jackson Island Rus. Fed. see **Dzheksona, Ostrov**
Jackson Lake U.S.A. 180 E4
Jacksonport U.S.A. 172 F6
Jacksons N.Z. 153 F10
Jackson's Arm Canada 169 J3
Jacksonville AL U.S.A. 175 C5
Jacksonville AR U.S.A. 179 D5
Jacksonville FL U.S.A. 175 D6
Jacksonville IL U.S.A. 174 B4
Jacksonville NC U.S.A. 174 E5
Jacksonville OH U.S.A. 176 C6
Jacksonville TX U.S.A. 179 D6
Jacksonville Beach U.S.A. 175 D6
Jack Wade U.S.A. 166 A1
Jacmel Haiti 187 E3
Jaco i. East Timor 75 C5
also known as Jako
Jacobabad Pak. 101 G4
Jacobina Brazil 202 D4
Jacob Lake U.S.A. 183 L5
Jacobsdal S. Africa 133 I6
Jacques-Cartier, Détroit de sea chan. Canada 169 H3
also known as Jacques Cartier Passage
Jacques Cartier, Mont mt. Canada 169 H3
Jacques Cartier Passage Canada see **Jacques-Cartier, Détroit de**
Jacquet River Canada 169 H4
Jacuba r. Brazil 206 A5
Jacuí Brazil 206 G8
Jacuí r. Brazil 203 B9
Jacuípe r. Brazil 202 E5
Jacunda Brazil 202 B3
Jacundá r. Brazil 202 B2
Jacupemba Brazil 207 M6
Jacupiranga Brazil 203 C8
Jacura Venez. 198 D2
Jadar r. Bos.-Herz. 56 L4
Jadar r. Serb. and Mont. 58 A4
Jadcherla India 94 C2
Jaddangi India 95 D2
Jaddi, Ras pt Pak. 101 E5
Jadebusen b. Germany 48 F2
Jadhdhānah Saudi Arabia 104 C4
Jādib Yemen 105 F4
J. A. D. Jensen Nunatakker nunataks Greenland 165 O3
Jadotville Dem. Rep. Congo see **Likasi**
Jadova r. Croatia 56 H4
Jadovnik mt. Bos.-Herz. 56 I4
Jaén Peru 198 B6
Jaen Phil. 74 B3
Jaén Spain 54 H7
Jæren reg. Norway 45 I4
Ja'farābād Ardabīl Iran 100 B2
Ja'farābād Khorāsan Iran 100 D2
Jaffa Israel see **Tel Aviv-Yafo**
Jaffa, Cape Australia 146 C4
Jaffna Sri Lanka 94 C4
Jaffrey U.S.A. 177 M3
Jafr, Qa' al imp. l. Jordan 109 H7
Jagadhri India 96 C3
Jägala r. Estonia 42 G2
Jagalur India 94 C3
Jagdalak Afgh. 101 G3
Jagdalpur India 94 D2
Jagdaqi China 85 J1
Jagdishpur India 89 C7
Jagdispur India 97 E4
Jagersfontein S. Africa 133 J6
Jaggang China 89 B5
Jaggayyapeta India 94 D2
Jaghīn Iran 100 D5
Jaghjaghah, Nahr r. Syria/Turkey 109 M1
Jagīn watercourse Iran 100 D5
Jagkolk Vloer salt pan S. Africa 132 E6
Jagodina Srbija Serb. and Mont. 58 C5
formerly known as Svetozarevo
Jagok Tso salt l. China see **Urru Co**
Jagsamka China see **Luding**
Jagst r. Germany 48 G6
Jagtial India 94 C2
Jaguapitã Brazil 206 B10
Jaguarão r. Brazil/Uruguay 204 G4
also known as Yaguarón
Jaguarão Uruguay 204 G4
Jaguarari Brazil 202 D4
Jaguaretama Brazil 202 E3
Jaguari Brazil 203 A9
Jaguariaíva Brazil 206 D11
Jaguaribe Brazil 202 E3
Jaguaribe r. Brazil 202 E3
Jaguaripe Brazil 202 E5
Jaguaruana Brazil 202 E3
Jagüe Arg. 204 C3
Jagüey Grande Cuba 186 C2
Jahām, 'Irq des. Saudi Arabia 105 D2
Jahanabad India see **Jehanabad**
Jahān Dāgh mt. Iran 100 B2
Jahannam, Qārat hill Egypt 108 B8
Jahleel, Point Australia 148 A1
Jahmah well Iraq 107 F5
Jahrom Iran 100 C4
Jāhyad Iran 100 D5
Jaicós Brazil 202 D3
Jaigarh India 94 B2
Jailolo Indon. 75 C2
Jailolo, Selat sea chan. Indon. 75 D3
Jailolo Gilolo i. Indon. see **Halmahera**
Jaiña Chile 200 C4
Jainca China 84 D5
also known as Magitang
Jaintiapur Bangl. 97 G4
Jaipur India 96 B4
Jais India 97 D4
Jaisalmer India 96 A4
Jaisamand Lake India 96 B4
Jaisinghnagar India 97 D5
Jaitaran India 96 B4
Jaitgarh hill India 94 C1
Jaitpur India 96 C4
Jajarkot Nepal 97 D3
Jajce Bos.-Herz. 56 J4
Jajnagar state India see **Orissa**
Jakar Bhutan 97 F4
also known as Byakar

►**Jakarta** Indon. 77 D4
Capital of Indonesia. 5th most populous city in Asia and 9th in the world. Formerly spelt Djakarta; historically known as Batavia or Sunda Kalapa.
►►18–19 **World** Cities

Jakhan India 101 G6
Jakharrah Libya 120 D2
Jakin mt. Afgh. 101 F4
Jakkalsberg Namibia 130 C3
Jakkalsberg hills Namibia 132 A5
Jakkī Kowr Iran 101 E5
Jäkkvik Sweden 44 L2
Jakliat India 96 B3
Jako i. East Timor see **Jaco**
Jakobshavn Greenland see **Ilulissat**
Jakobstad Fin. 44 M3
also known as Pietersaari
Jakupica mts Macedonia 58 C7
Jal U.S.A. 179 B5
Jalaid China see **Inder**
Jalājil Saudi Arabia 105 D2
Jalālābād Afgh. 101 G3
Jalalabad Punjab India 96 B3
Jalalabad Uttar Pradesh India 96 C3
Jalalabad Uttar Pradesh India 96 C4
Jalal-Abad Kyrg. 103 H4
also spelt Dzhalal-Abad
Jalal-Abad admin. div. Kyrg. 103 H4
English form Jalal-Abad Oblast; also known as Dzhalal-Abadskaya Oblast'
Jalal-Abad Oblast admin. div. Kyrg. see **Jalal-Abad**
Jalālah al Baḩrīyah, Jabal plat. Egypt 108 C8
Jalalpur Gujarat India 94 B1
Jalalpur Uttar Pradesh India 97 D4
Jalāmid, Ḩazm al ridge Saudi Arabia 107 D5
Ja'lān, Jabal mts Oman 105 G3
Jalandhar India 96 B3
formerly spelt Jullundur
Jalan Kayu Sing. 76 [inset]
Jalapa Guat. 185 H6
Jalapa Tabasco Mex. 185 G5
Jalapa Veracruz Mex. 185 F5
also known as Xalapa
Jalapa Nicaragua 186 B4
Jalapur Pak. 101 H3
Jalapur Pirwala Pak. 101 G4
Jalasjärvi Fin. 44 M3
Jalaun India 96 C4
Jalawlā' Iraq 107 F4
also spelt Jalūlā
Jalboi r. Australia 148 B2
Jaldak Afgh. 101 F4
Jaldhaka r. Bangl. 97 F4
Jaldrug India 94 C2
Jales Brazil 206 C7
Jalesar India 96 C4
Jaleshwar India 97 E5
Jaleshwar Nepal see **Jaleswar**
Jaleswar Nepal 97 E4
also spelt Jaleshwar
Jalgaon India 96 B5
Jalībah Iraq 107 F5
Jalingo Nigeria 125 H4
Jalisco state Mex. 184 D5
Jallābī Iran 100 D5
Jalna India 94 B2
Jālo Iran 101 E5
Jalón r. Spain 55 J3
Jalore India 96 B4
Jalostotitlán Mex. 185 E4
Jalovik Srbija Serb. and Mont. 58 A4
Jalpa Mex. 185 E4
Jalpaiguri India 97 F4
Jalpan Mex. 185 F4
UNESCO World Heritage Site
Jalrez Afgh. 101 G3
Jālū Libya 120 D2
Jalūlā Iraq see **Jalawlā'**
Jālū Oasis Libya 120 D2
Jām r. Iran 101 E3
Jām reg. Iran 101 E3
Jam, Minaret of tourist site Afgh. 101 F3
UNESCO World Heritage Site
Jamaica Cuba 187 E2
►**Jamaica** country West Indies 186 D3
►►158–159 **North America** Countries
Jamaica Channel Haiti/Jamaica 187 E3
Jämaja Estonia 42 D3
Jamalpur Bangl. 97 F4
Jamalpur India 97 E4
Jamanxim r. Brazil 199 G6
Jamari Brazil 201 E2
Jamba Angola 127 C8
Jambi Indon. 76 C3
also known as Telanaipura
Jambi prov. Indon. 76 C3
Jambin Australia 149 F5
Jambo India 96 B4
Jamboaye r. Indon. 76 B1
Jambongan i. Sabah Malaysia 77 G1
Jambuair, Tanjung pt Indon. 76 B1
Jambūr Iraq 109 P2
Jambusar India 96 B5
Jamekunte India 94 C2
James watercourse Australia 148 C4
James r. Canada 167 I1
James r. MO U.S.A. 178 D4
James r. ND/SD U.S.A. 178 C3
James r. VA U.S.A. 177 I8
James, Isla i. Chile 205 B7
Jamesabad Pak. 101 G5
James Bay Canada 168 D2
Jamesburg U.S.A. 177 K5
James Cistern Bahamas 186 D1
Jameson Land reg. Greenland 165 Q2
Jameson Range hills Australia 151 D5
James Peak N.Z. 153 C13
James Ranges mts Australia 148 B5
James Ross Island Antarctica 222 U2
James Ross Strait Canada 165 J3
Jamestown Australia 146 C3
Jamestown Canada see **Wawa**
Jamestown S. Africa 133 K8

►**Jamestown** St Helena 216 N7
Capital of St Helena and Dependencies.

Jamestown CA U.S.A. 182 D4
Jamestown KY U.S.A. 174 C4
Jamestown ND U.S.A. 178 C2
Jamestown NY U.S.A. 176 F3
Jamestown PA U.S.A. 176 E4
Jamestown TN U.S.A. 176 A9
Jämijärvi Fin. 45 M3
Jamiltepec Mex. 185 F5
Jamkhandi India 94 B2
Jamkhed India 94 B2
Jammalamadugu India 94 C3
Jammerbugten b. Denmark 45 J4
Jammu Jammu and Kashmir 96 B2

►**Jammu and Kashmir** terr. Asia 96 C2
Disputed territory (India/Pakistan). Short form Kashmir.
►►64–65 **Asia** Countries

Jamnagar India 96 A5
formerly known as Navangar
Jamner India 94 B1
Jamni r. India 96 C4
Jamno, Jezioro lag. Poland 49 N1
Jampang Kulon Indon. 77 D4
Jampur Pak. 101 G4
Jämsä Fin. 45 N3
Jamsah Egypt 121 G3
Jämsänkoski Fin. 45 N3
Jamshedpur India 97 E5
Jamtara India 97 E5
Jamtari Nigeria 125 H5
Jämtland county Sweden 44 K3
Jamui India 97 E4
Jamuk, Gunung mt. Indon. 77 G2
Jamu Mare Romania 58 C3
Jamuna r. Bangl. 97 F5
Jamuna r. India 97 G4
Janā i. Saudi Arabia 105 E2
Janāb, Wādī al watercourse Jordan 109 H6
Janāj Egypt 108 B7
Janakpur India 97 D5
Janakpur Nepal 97 E4
Janaúba Brazil 202 D5
Jandaia Brazil 206 C4
Jandaia do Sul Brazil 206 B10
Jandaq Iran 100 C3
Jandiala India 96 B3
Jandiatuba r. Brazil 198 D5
Jandongi Dem. Rep. Congo 126 D4
Jandowae Australia 149 F5
Jándula r. Spain 54 G6
Jandulilla r. Spain 55 H7
Janeiro r. Brazil 202 C5
Janesville CA U.S.A. 182 D1
Janesville WI U.S.A. 172 D8
Jang, Tanjung pt Indon. 76 D3
Jangal Iran 101 D3
Jangamo Moz. 131 G5
Jangaon India 94 C2
Jangeldi Uzbek. see **Jongeldi**
Jangipur India 97 F4
Jangnga Turkm. see **Jaňňa**
Jangngai Ri mts China 89 D5
Jangngai Zangbo r. China 89 D5
Jānī Beyglū Iran 100 A2
Janikowo Poland 49 P3
Janja Bos.-Herz. 56 L4
Janja r. Bos.-Herz. 56 L4
Janjevo Kosovo, Srbija Serb. and Mont. 58 C6
Jan Kempdorp S. Africa 133 I4
formerly known as Andalusia
Jankov Kamen mt. Serb. and Mont. 58 B5

►**Jan Mayen** i. Arctic Ocean 224 X2
Part of Norway.

Jāņmuiža Latvia 42 G4
Jaňňa Turkm. 102 C4
also spelt Jangnga
Jannatābād Iran 100 B3
Jañona mt. Spain 54 E4
Janos Mex. 184 C2
Jánoshalma Hungary 49 Q9
Jánossomorja Hungary 49 O8
Janów Lubelski Poland 49 T5
Jans Bay Canada 167 I4
Jansenville S. Africa 133 I9
Jânua Coeli Brazil 202 B2
Januária Brazil 202 C5
Janūbī, Al Fulayj al watercourse Saudi Arabia 105 D1
Janûb Sînâ' governorate Egypt 108 E8
English form South Sinai; also known as Sinai al Janûbîya
Janwada India 94 C2
Janzar mt. Pak. 101 E5
Janzé France 50 E5
Jaora India 96 B5

►**Japan** country Asia 90 E5
10th most populous country in the world. Known as Nihon or Nippon in Japanese.
►►16–17 **World** Population
►►64–65 **Asia** Countries

Japan, Sea of N. Pacific Ocean 83 D5
also known as East Sea or Nippon Hai
Japan Alps National Park Japan see **Chibu-Sangaku National Park**
Japón Hond. 186 B4
Japurá r. Brazil 198 E5
Japvo Mount India 97 G4
Jaqué Panama 186 D6
Jarabacoa Dom. Rep. 187 F3
Jarābulus Syria 109 J1
Jarad Saudi Arabia 104 C4
Jaraguá Brazil 206 D2
Jaraguá do Sul Brazil 203 B8
Jaraguari Brazil 203 A7
Jaraiz de la Vera Spain 54 F4
Jarama r. Spain 55 H4
Jarash Jordan 108 G5
Jarauçu r. Brazil 199 H5
Järbo Sweden 45 L3
Jarboesville U.S.A. see **Lexington Park**
Jar-bulak Kazakh. see **Kabanbay**
Jardim Ceará Brazil 202 E3
Jardim Mato Grosso do Sul Brazil 201 F5
Jardín r. Spain 55 I6
Jardine River National Park Australia 149 D1
Jardines de la Reina, Archipiélago de los is Cuba 186 D2
Jardinópolis Brazil 206 F8
Jargalant Arhangay Mongolia 84 D2
Jargalant Bayanhongor Mongolia 84 C2
Jargalant Bayan-Ölgiy Mongolia 84 A2
Jargalant Dornod Mongolia 85 G2
Jargalant Govĭ-Altay Mongolia 84 C2
Jargalant Hovd Mongolia see **Hovd**
Jargalant Töv Mongolia 85 E1
Jargalant Hayrhan mt. Mongolia 84 B2
Jargalthaan Mongolia 85 F2
Jari r. Brazil 199 I5
Jaria Jhanjail Bangl. 97 F4
Jarmen Germany 49 K2
Järna Dalarna Sweden 45 K3
Järna Stockholm Sweden 45 L4
Jarnac France 50 F7
Jarocin Poland 49 O4
Jaroměř Czech Rep. 49 M5
Jarosław Poland 49 T5
Järpen Sweden 44 K3
Jarqo'rgo'n Uzbek. 103 F5
also spelt Jarqŭrghon
Jarqŭrghon Uzbek. see **Jarqo'rgo'n**
Jarrāḩ, Wādī watercourse Syria 109 M1
Jarrāhi watercourse Iran 100 B4
Jarratt U.S.A. 176 H9
Jarrettsville U.S.A. 177 I6
Jartai China 85 E4
Jartai Yanchi salt l. China 84 E4
Jarú Brazil 201 E2
Jarūb Yemen 105 F4
Jarud China see **Lubei**
Jarut mt. Serb. and Mont. 58 B5
Järvakandi Estonia 42 F3
Järvenpää Fin. 45 N3

►**Jarvis Island** terr. N. Pacific Ocean 221 I6
United States Unincorporated Territory.
►►138–139 **Oceania** Countries

Järvsand Sweden 44 K2
Järvsö Sweden 45 L3
Jarwa India 97 D4
Jasdan India 96 A5
Jashpurnagar India 97 E5
Jasień Poland 49 M4
Jasiołka r. Poland 49 S6
Jāsk Iran 100 D5
Jāsk-e Kohneh Iran 100 D5
Jasliq Uzbek. 102 D4
also spelt Zhaslyk
Jasło Poland 49 S6
Jašlūnai Lith. 42 G7
Jasmund pen. Germany 49 K1
Jasmund, Nationalpark nature res. Germany 49 K1
Jaso India 96 D4
UNESCO World Heritage Site
Jason Peninsula Antarctica 222 T2
Jasper Canada 166 G4
Jasper AL U.S.A. 175 C5
Jasper AR U.S.A. 179 D4
Jasper FL U.S.A. 175 D6
Jasper GA U.S.A. 174 C5
Jasper IN U.S.A. 174 C4
Jasper NY U.S.A. 176 H3
Jasper OH U.S.A. 176 B6
Jasper TN U.S.A. 174 C5
Jasper TX U.S.A. 179 D6
Jasper National Park Canada 167 G4
UNESCO World Heritage Site
Jaşşān Iraq 107 F4
Jassy Romania see **Iaşi**
Jastarnia Poland 49 P1
Jastrebarsko Croatia 56 H3
Jastrowie Poland 49 N2
Jastrzębie-Zdrój Poland 49 P6
historically known as Bad Königsdorff
Jászárokszállás Hungary 49 Q8
Jászberény Hungary 49 Q8
Jataí Brazil 206 B4
Jatapu r. Brazil 199 G5
Jatara India 96 C4
Jati Pak. 101 G5
also known as Mughalbhin
Jatibarang Indon. 77 E4
Jatibonico Cuba 186 D2
Játiva Spain see **Xátiva**
Jatiwangi Indon. 77 E4
Jatobá Brazil 202 A5
Jatoi Pak. 101 G4
Jättendal Sweden 45 L3
Jatuarana Brazil 201 E1
Jaú Brazil 206 E9
Jaú r. Brazil 199 F5
Jaú, Parque Nacional do nat. park Brazil 199 F5
UNESCO World Heritage Site
Jauaperi r. Brazil 199 F5
Jaua Sarisariñama, Parque Nacional nat. park Venez. 199 E3
Jauco Cuba 187 E2
Jauja Peru 200 B2
Jaumave Mex. 185 F4
Jauna r. Brazil 199 F6
Jaunanna Latvia 42 I4
Jaunay-Clan France 50 G6
Jaunjelgava Latvia 42 G5
Jaunkalsnava Latvia 42 G5
Jaunlutriņi Latvia 42 D5
Jaunmārupe Latvia 42 E5
Jaunpiebalga Latvia 42 H4
Jaunpils Latvia 42 E5
Jaunpur India 97 D4
Jaupaci Brazil 206 C3
Jauru Brazil 203 A6
Jauru r. Brazil 201 F4

►**Java** i. Indon. 77 D5
5th largest island in Asia. Also spelt Jawa.
►►60–61 **Asia** Landscapes

Javadi Hills India 94 C3
Javaés r. Brazil see **Formoso**
Javaés, Serra dos hills Brazil 202 B4
Javalambre mt. Spain 55 K4
Javalambre, Sierra de mts Spain 55 J4
Javand Afgh. 101 F3
Javari r. Brazil 198 D6
also spelt Yavari
Javarthushuu Mongolia 85 G1
Java Sea Indon. 77 E4

►**Java Trench** sea feature Indian Ocean 218 N6
Deepest point in the Indian Ocean.
►►208–209 **Oceans and Poles**

Jávea-Xábia Spain 55 L6
Javier, Isla i. Chile 205 B7
Javor mts Serb. and Mont. 58 B5
Javořice hill Czech Rep. 49 M6
Javorie mt. Slovakia 49 Q7
Javornik mt. Slovenia 56 H2
Javorníky mts Slovakia 49 P6
Jävre Sweden 44 M2
Jawa i. Indon. see **Java**
Jawa Barat prov. Indon. 77 D4
Jawad India 96 B4
Jawai r. India 96 A4
Jawala Mukhi India 96 C3
Jawar India 96 C5
Jawa Tengah prov. Indon. 77 E4
Jawa Timur prov. Indon. 77 F4
Jawbān Bayk Syria 109 I1
Jawf, Wādī al watercourse Yemen 104 D5
Jawhar India 94 B2
Jawhar Somalia 128 E4
Jawor Poland 49 N4
UNESCO World Heritage Site
Jaworzno Poland 49 Q5
Jawoyn Aboriginal Land res. Australia 148 B2
Jay U.S.A. 179 D4

►**Jaya, Puncak** mt. Indon. 73 I7
Highest mountain in Oceania. Formerly known as Carstensz-top or Sukarno, Puntjak.
►►134–135 **Oceania** Landscapes

Jayanca Peru 198 B6
Jayanti India 97 F4
Jayapura Indon. 73 J7
formerly known as Hollandia or Sukarnapura
Jayb, Wādī al watercourse Israel/Jordan 108 G6
Jayfī, Wādī al watercourse Egypt 108 F7
Jaynagar Bihar India 97 E4
Jaynagar W. Bengal India 97 F5
Jaypur India 95 D2
Jayrūd Syria 109 H4
Jayton U.S.A. 179 B5
Jazīrat al Hamrā U.A.E. 105 F2
Jazminal Mex. 185 E3
Jaz Mūrīān, Hāmūn-e salt marsh Iran 100 D5
Jbail Lebanon 108 G3
historically known as Biblos
J. C. Murphey Lake U.S.A. 172 F9
Jean U.S.A. 183 I6
Jeanerette U.S.A. 175 B6
Jean Marie River Canada 166 F2
also known as Tthedzehk'edeli
Jebāl Bārez, Kūh-e mts Iran 100 D4
Jebel Libya 120 C2
Jebel Romania 58 C3
Jebel Turkm. 102 C5
also spelt Dzhebel
Jebel, Bahr el r. Sudan/Uganda see **White Nile**
Jebel Abyad Plateau Sudan 121 F5
Jebel Ali U.A.E. see **Mina Jebel Ali**
Jeberos Peru 198 B6
Jebha Morocco 54 G9
Jebus Indon. 77 D3
Jedburgh U.K. 46 J8
Jeddah Saudi Arabia 104 B3
also spelt Jiddah
Jeddore Lake Canada 169 K3
Jedeida Tunisia 57 B12
Jędrzejów Poland 49 R5
Jedwabne Poland 49 T2
Jeetze r. Germany 48 I2
Jefferson IA U.S.A. 178 D3
Jefferson NC U.S.A. 176 D9
Jefferson OH U.S.A. 176 E4
Jefferson TX U.S.A. 179 D5
Jefferson WI U.S.A. 172 E7
Jefferson r. U.S.A. 180 E3
Jefferson, Mount U.S.A. 183 H3
Jefferson, Mount vol. U.S.A. 180 B3

►**Jefferson City** MO U.S.A. 178 D4
State capital of Missouri.

Jefferson City TN U.S.A. 176 B9
Jeffersonton U.S.A. 176 H7
Jeffersonville IN U.S.A. 174 C4
Jeffersonville KY U.S.A. 176 B8
Jeffersonville OH U.S.A. 176 B6
Jeffrey U.S.A. 176 D8
Jeffreys Bay S. Africa 133 I11
Jega Nigeria 125 G3
Jehanabad India 97 E4
formerly spelt Jahanabad
Jēkabpils Latvia 42 G5
Jelbart Ice Shelf Antarctica 223 X2

Jelcz-Laskowice Poland 49 O4
Jeldēsa Eth. 128 D2
Jelenia Góra Poland 49 M5
historically known as Hirschberg
Jelep La pass China/India 89 E7
Jelgava Latvia 42 E5
Jellico U.S.A. 176 A9
Jellicoe Canada 168 C3
Jelling Denmark 45 J5
UNESCO World Heritage Site
Jelloway U.S.A. 176 C5
Jelondí Tajik. 101 H2
also spelt Dzhelondi; also spelt Dzhilandy
Jelow Gīr Iran 100 A3
Jemaja i. Indon. 77 D2
Jember Indon. 77 F5
Jemez Pueblo U.S.A. 181 F6
Jeminay China 88 D2
also known as Topterek
Jeminay Kazakh. 88 D2
Jemma Bauchi Nigeria 125 H4
Jemma Kaduna Nigeria 125 H4
Jemmel Tunisia 57 C13
Jemnice Czech Rep. 49 M6
Jempang, Danau l. Indon. 77 G3
Jena Germany 48 I5
Jena U.S.A. 179 D6
Jenda Malawi 129 B8
Jendouba Tunisia 123 H1
Jengish Chokusu mt. China/Kyrg. see Pobeda Peak
Jenīn West Bank 108 G5
Jenipapo Brazil 199 F6
Jenkinjones U.S.A. 176 D8
Jenkins U.S.A. 176 C8
Jenkintown U.S.A. 177 J5
Jenne Mali see Djenné
Jenner Canada 167 I5
Jennersdorf Austria 49 N9
Jennings r. Canada 166 C3
Jennings U.S.A. 179 D6
Jenpeg Canada 167 L4
Jepara Indon. 77 E4
Jeparit Australia 147 D4
Jeppo Fin. 44 M3
Jequié Brazil 202 D5
Jequitaí Brazil 203 C6
Jequitaí r. Brazil 207 I4
Jequitinhonha Brazil 202 D6
Jequitinhonha r. Brazil 207 O2
Jerba, Île de i. Tunisia 123 H2
Jerbar Sudan 128 A3
Jereh Iran 107 G5
Jérémie Haiti 187 E3
Jeremoabo Brazil 202 E4
Jerer Shet' watercourse Eth. 128 D3
Jereweh Indon. 77 G5
Jerez Mex. 185 E4
Jerez de la Frontera Spain 54 E8
Jerez de los Caballeros Spain 54 E6
Jerfojaur Sweden 44 L2
Jergol Norway 44 N1
Jergucat Albania 59 B9
Jericho Australia 149 E4
Jericho West Bank 108 G6
also known as Arīḥā; also spelt Yeriḥo; historically known as Tell es-Sultan
Jerid, Chott el salt l. Tunisia 123 H2
Jerijeh, Tanjung pt Sarawak Malaysia 77 E2
Jerilderie Australia 147 E3
Jermyn U.S.A. 177 J4
Jerome AZ U.S.A. 183 L7
Jerome ID U.S.A. 180 D4
Jerramungup Australia 151 B7

▶Jersey terr. Channel Is 50 D3
United Kingdom Crown Dependency.
▶▶32–33 Europe Countries

Jersey City U.S.A. 177 K5
Jerseyville U.S.A. 174 B4
Jerte r. Spain 54 E5
Jerumenha Brazil 202 D3

▶Jerusalem Israel/West Bank 108 G6
De facto capital of Israel. Also known as El Quds; also spelt Yerushalayim; historically known as Aelia Capitolina or Hierosolyma.
UNESCO World Heritage Site

Jerusalem N.Z. 152 J7
Jervis Bay Australia 147 F3
Jervis Bay Territory admin. div. Australia 147 F3
also known as Commonwealth Territory
Jervois Range hills Australia 148 B4
Jesenice Slovenia 56 G2
Jeseník Czech Rep. 49 O5
Jesi Italy 56 F5
Jesmond Canada 166 F5
Jesolo Italy 56 E3
Jesselton Sabah Malaysia see Kota Kinabalu
Jessen Germany 49 J4
Jessheim Norway 45 J3
Jessore Bangl. 97 F5
Jesuit Missions tourist site Arg. 204 G2
UNESCO World Heritage Site
Jesuit Missions tourist site Para. 204 G2
UNESCO World Heritage Site
Jesu Maria Island P.N.G. see Rambutyo Island
Jesup U.S.A. 175 D6
Jesús Carranza Mex. 185 G5
Jesús María Arg. 204 D3
Jesús María, Barra spit Mex. 185 F3
Jetalsar India 96 A5
Jethro tourist site Saudi Arabia 104 A1
also known as Maghā'ir Shu'ayb
Jetmore U.S.A. 178 C4
Jevnaker Norway 45 J3
Jewett City U.S.A. 177 N4
Jewish Autonomous Oblast admin. div. Rus. Fed. see Yevreyskaya Avtonomnaya Oblast'
Jeýhun Turkm. 103 E5
also spelt Jeyhun; formerly known as Farab-Pristan'
Jeyhun Turkm. see Jeýhun
Jeziorak, Jezioro l. Poland 49 Q2
Jeziorany Poland 49 R2
Jeziorka r. Poland 49 S3
Jeziorsko, Jezioro l. Poland 49 P4
Jezzine Lebanon 108 G4
Jhabua India 96 B5
Jha Jha India 97 E4
Jhajjar India 96 C3
Jhajju India 96 B4
Jhalakati Bangl. 97 F5
Jhalawar India 96 C4
Jhalida India 97 E5
Jhal Magsi Pak. 101 F4
Jhalrapatan India 96 C4
Jhang Pak. 101 H4
Jhanjharpur India 97 E4
Jhansi India 96 C4
Jhanzi r. India 97 G4
Jhapa Nepal 97 E4
Jhargram India 97 E5
Jharia India 97 E5
Jharkhand state India 97 E5
Jharsuguda India 97 E5
Jhatpat Pak. 101 G4
Jhawani Nepal 97 E4
Jhelum r. India/Pak. 96 B3
Jhelum Pak. 101 H3
UNESCO World Heritage Site
Jhenaidah Bangl. 97 F5
also known as Jhenaidaha
Jhenaidaha Bangl. see Jhenaidah
Jhinjhuvada India 96 A5
Jhinkpani India 97 E5
Jhudo Pak. 101 G5
Jhumritilaiya India 97 E4
Jhunjhunun India 96 B3
Jhusi India 97 D4
Jiachuan China 86 C1
formerly known as Jiachuanzhen
Jiachuanzhen China see Jiachuan
Jiading Jiangxi China see Xinfeng
Jiading Shanghai China 87 G2
Jiahe China 87 E3
Jiajiang China 86 B2
Jialing Jiang r. China 86 C2
Jialu China see Jiaxian
Jialu He r. China 87 E1
Jiamusi China 82 C3
Ji'an Jiangxi China 87 E3
also known as Dunhou
Ji'an Jiangxi China 87 E3
Ji'an Jilin China 83 B4
UNESCO World Heritage Site
Jianchang Jiangxi China see Nancheng
Jianchang Liaoning China 85 H3
Jianchuan China 86 A3
also known as Jinhua
Jiandaoyu China see Guojiaba
Jiande China 87 F2
Jiang'an China 86 C2
Jiangbei China see Yubei
Jiangcheng China 86 B4
also known as Menglie
Jiangchuan China 86 B3
also known as Dajie
Jiangcun China 87 D3
Jiangdu China 87 F1
formerly known as Xiannümiao
Jiange China see Pu'an
Jiangjiehe China 87 C3
Jiangjin China 86 C2
Jiangjunmiao China 88 E2
Jiangjunmu China 85 G4
Jiangjuntai China 84 C3
Jiangkou Guangdong China see Fengkai
Jiangkou Guizhou China 87 D3
also known as Shuangjiang
Jiangkou Shaanxi China 86 C1
Jiangkou Sichuan China see Pingchang
Jiangle China 87 F3
also known as Guyong
Jiangling China see Jingzhou
Jiangluozhen China 86 C1
Jiangmen China 87 E4
Jiangna China see Yanshan
Jiangning China see Dongshan
Jiangshan China 87 F2
Jiangsi China see Dejiang
Jiangsu prov. China 87 F1
English form Kiangsu
Jiangtaibu China 85 E5
Jiangxi prov. China 87 E3
English form Kiangsi
Jiangxia China 87 E2
formerly known as Wuchang
Jiangxian China 85 F5
Jiangxigou China 84 D4
Jiangyan China 87 G1
formerly known as Taixian
Jiangyin China 87 G2
Jiangyong China 87 D3
Jiangyou China 86 C2
formerly known as Zhongba
Jiangyu China 85 H4
Jiangzhesongrong China 89 D6
Jianhu China 87 F1
Jian Jiang r. China 87 D4
Jianjun China see Yongshou
Jiankang China 85 F4
also known as Dapingdi
Jianli China 87 E2
also known as Rongcheng
Jianning China 87 F3
also known as Suicheng
Jian'ou China 87 F3
Jianping Liaoning China 85 H3
also known as Yebaishou
Jianping Liaoning China 85 H3
Jianqiao China 85 H4
Jianshe Qinghai China 86 A1
Jianshe Sichuan China see Baiyü
Jianshi China 87 D2
also known as Yezhou
Jianshui China 86 B4
also known as Lin'an
Jianxing China 86 C2
Jianyang Fujian China 87 F3
Jianyang Sichuan China 86 C2
Jiaochang China 86 B1
formerly known as Jiaochangba
Jiaochangba China see Jiaochang
Jiaocheng Guangdong China see Jiaoling
Jiaocheng Shanxi China 85 G4
Jiaohe China 82 B4
Jiaojiang China see Taizhou
Jiaokou China 85 F4
Jiaokui China see Yiliang
Jiaolai He r. China 85 H4
Jiaolai He r. China 85 I3
Jiaoling China 87 F3
also known as Jiaocheng
Jiaonan China 85 H5
formerly known as Wanggezhuang
Jiaowei China 87 F3
Jiaozhou China 85 I4
Jiaozhou Wan b. China 85 I4
Jiaozuo China 85 G5
Jiapigou China 82 B4
Jiasa China 86 B3
Jiashan China see Mingguang
Jiashi China 88 B4
also known as Payzawat
Jia Tsuo La pass China 89 D6
Jiaxian Henan China 87 E1
Jiaxian Shaanxi China 85 F4
also known as Jialu
Jiaxiang China 85 H5
Jiaxing China 87 G2
Jiayi Taiwan see Chiai
Jiayin China 82 C2
also known as Chaoyang
Jiayu China 87 E2
also known as Yuyue
Jiayuguan China 84 C4
Jiazi China 87 F4
Jibou Romania 58 E1
Jibsh, Ra's c. Oman 105 G3
Jibūtī country Africa see Djibouti
Jibuti Djibouti see Djibouti
Jicarilla Apache Indian Reservation res. U.S.A. 181 F5
Jičín Czech Rep. 49 M5
Jiddah Saudi Arabia see Jeddah
Jiddī, Jabal al hill Egypt 121 G2
English form Giddi Pass
Jidong China 82 C3
Jiehkkevárri mt. Norway 44 L1
Jiehu China see Yinan
Jieshi China 87 E4
Jieshi Wan b. China 87 E4
Jieshou China 87 E1
Jiesia r. Lith. 42 E7
Jiexi China 87 E4
also known as Hepo
Jiexiu China 85 F4
Jieyang China 87 F4
Jieznas Lith. 42 F7
Jigalong Aboriginal Reserve Australia 150 C4
Jigawa state Nigeria 125 H3
Jigerbent Turkm. 103 E4
also spelt Dzhigirbent
Jiggalong Australia 150 C4
Jiggs U.S.A. 183 I1
Jiguaní Cuba 186 D2
Jigzhi China 86 B1
also known as Chugqênsumdo
Jihār, Wādī al watercourse Syria 109 I3
Jihlava Czech Rep. 49 M6
Jihlava r. Czech Rep. 49 N7
Jijel Alg. 123 G1
formerly spelt Djidjelli
Jijia r. Romania 58 J2
Jijiga Eth. 128 D2
Jijona-Xixona Spain 55 K6
Jijü China 86 B2
Jil'ād reg. Jordan 108 G5
English form Gilead
Jīlān ash Shuwayḥiṭīyah esc. Saudi Arabia 109 K7
Jilava Romania 58 H4
Jilbadji Nature Reserve Australia 151 B6
Jilf al Kabīr, Haḍabat al plat. Egypt see Gilf Kebir Plateau
Jilga r. Afgh. 101 G3
Jilh al 'Ishār plain Saudi Arabia 105 D2
Jilib Somalia 128 D4
Jili Hu l. China 88 D2
Jilin China 82 B4
also known as Kirin
Jilin prov. China 85 J3
English form Kirin
Jiling China 84 D4
Jilin Hada Ling mts China 82 B4
Jiloca r. Spain 55 J3
Jilong Taiwan see Chilung
Jīma Eth. 128 C3
Jima Ali well Eth. 128 E3
Jimaní Haiti 187 F3
Jimbo Tanz. 129 C6
Jimbolia Romania 58 B3
Jimda China see Zindo
Jimena de la Frontera Spain 54 F8
Jiménez Chihuahua Mex. 184 D3
Jiménez Coahuila Mex. 185 E2
Jiménez Tamaulipas Mex. 185 F3
Jimeta Nigeria 125 I4
Jimi r. P.N.G. 73 J7
Jim Jim Creek r. Australia 148 B2
Jimo China 85 I4
Jimsar China 88 E3
Jina Romania 58 E3
Jinan China 85 H4
formerly spelt Tsinan
Jin'an China see Songpan
Jinbi China see Dayao
Jinchang China 84 D4
formerly known as Jinchuan
Jincheng Shanxi China 85 G5
Jincheng Sichuan China see Leibo
Jincheng Sichuan China see Yilong
Jincheng Yunnan China see Wuding
Jinchengjiang China see Hechi
Jinchuan Gansu China see Jinchang
Jinchuan Jiangxi China see Xingan
Jinchuan Sichuan China 86 B2
also known as Quqên
Jind India 96 C3
Jindřichův Hradec Czech Rep. 49 M6
Jin'e China see Longchang
Jinfosi China 84 C4
Jing China see Jinghe
Jing'an China see Doumen
Jingbian China 85 F4
also known as Zhangjiapan
Jingchuan China 85 E5
Jingde China 87 F2
also known as Jingyang
Jingdezhen China 87 F2
Jingdong China 86 B3
also known as Jinping
Jinggangshan China 87 E3
formerly known as Ciping
Jinggang Shan hill China 87 E3
Jinggongqiao China 87 F2
Jinggu China 86 B4
also known as Weiyuan
Jinghai China 85 H4
Jinghe China 88 C2
also known as Jing
Jing He r. China 87 D1
Jinghong China 86 B4
formerly known as Yunjinghong
Jingjiang China 87 G1
Jingle China 85 G4
Jingmen China 87 E2
Jingning China 85 E5
Jingpeng China 85 H3
also known as Hexigten Qi
Jingpo Hu resr China 82 C4
Jingshan China 87 E2
also known as Xinshi
Jingtai China 84 D4
also known as Yitiaoshan
Jingtieshan China 84 C4
formerly known as Huashugou
Jingxi China 86 C4
also known as Xinjing
Jingxian Anhui China 87 F2
Jingxian Hunan China see Jingzhou
Jingxin China see Yongshan
Jingyan China 86 C2
also known as Yancheng
Jingyang China see Jingde
Jingyu China 82 B4
Jingyuan China 84 E4
Jingzhou Hubei China 87 E2
formerly known as Jiangling
Jingzhou Hubei China 87 E2
formerly known as Shashi
Jingzhou Hunan China 87 D3
also known as Quyang; formerly known as Jingxian
Jinhe China see Jinping
Jinhua Yunnan China see Jianchuan
Jinhua Zhejiang China 87 F2
Jining Nei Mongol China 85 G3
also spelt Tsining
Jining Shandong China 85 H5
formerly known as Chining
Jinja Uganda 128 B4
Jinjiang Fujian China 87 F3
Jinjiang Hainan China see Chengmai
Jinjiang Yunnan China 86 B3
Jin Jiang r. China 87 D3
Jin Jiang r. China 87 E2
Jinka Eth. 128 C3
Jinkouhe China 86 B2
Jinmen Taiwan see Chinmen
Jinmu Jiao pt China 87 D5
Jinning China 86 B3
also known as Kunyang
Jinotega Nicaragua 186 B4
Jinotepe Nicaragua 186 B5
Jinping Guizhou China 87 D3
also known as Sanjiang
Jinping Yunnan China see Jingdong
Jinping Yunnan China 86 B4
also known as Jinhe
Jinping Yunnan China see Qiubei
Jinping Shan mts China 86 B3
Jinsen S. Korea see Inch'ŏn
Jinsha China 86 C3
Jinsha Jiang r. China 78 B1
Jinsha Jiang r. China see Yangtze Kiang
Jinsha Jiang r. China see Yangtze
Jinshan Nei Mongol China 85 H3
also known as Harqin Qi
Jinshan Shanghai China see Zhujing
Jinshan Yunnan China see Lufeng
Jinshi Hunan China 87 D2
Jinshi Hunan China see Xinning
Jinta China 84 C4
Jintan China 87 F2
Jintang China 86 C2
also known as Zhaozhen
Jintotolo Channel Phil. 74 B4
Jintur India 94 C2
Jinxi Jiangxi China 87 F3
also known as Xiugu
Jinxi Liaoning China see Lianshan
Jin Xi r. China 87 F3
Jinxian Jiangxi China 87 F2
also known as Minhe
Jinxian Liaoning China see Linghai
Jinxiang Shandong China 85 H5
Jinxiang Zhejiang China 87 G3
Jinxiu China 87 D3
Jinyang China 86 B3
also known as Tiandiba
Jinyuan China see Dayi
Jinyun China 87 G2
also known as Wuyun
Jinz, Qā' al salt flat Jordan 108 H7
Jinzhai China 87 E2
also known as Meishan
Jinzhong China 85 G4
Jinzhou Liaoning China 85 I3
Jinzhou Liaoning China 85 I4
Jinzhou Wan b. China 85 I4
Jinzhu China see Daocheng
Ji-Paraná Brazil 201 E2
Jiparaná r. Brazil 201 E2
Jipijapa Ecuador 198 A5
Ji Qu r. China 80 F6
Jiquilisco El Salvador 185 H6
Jiquilpan de Juárez Mex. 185 E5
Jiquitaia Brazil 207 N4
Jirā', Wādī watercourse Egypt 108 E8
Jirānīyāt, Shi'bān al watercourse Saudi Arabia 109 J6
Jirau Brazil 200 D2
Jirgatol Tajik. 101 G2
also spelt Dzhirgatal'
Jiri r. India 97 G4
Jirin Gol China 85 H2
Jirjā Egypt 121 F3
Jirkov Czech Rep. 49 K5
Jīroft Iran 100 D4
also known as Sabzvārān
Jirriiban Somalia 128 F3
Jirwān Saudi Arabia 105 E3
Jirzah Egypt 108 C8
Jishan China 85 F5
Jishi China see Xunhua
Jishou China 87 D2
Jishui China see Yongfeng
Jisr ash Shughūr Syria 108 H2
Jitian China see Lianshan
Jitra Malaysia 76 C1
Jiu r. Romania 58 E5
Jiudengkou China 85 E4
Jiuding Shan mt. China 86 B2
Jiugong Shan mt. China 87 E2
Jiujiang Jiangxi China 87 E2
also known as Shahejie; formerly known as Shahezhen
Jiujiang Jiangxi China 87 F2
Jiulian China see Mojiang
Jiuling Shan mts China 87 E2
Jiulong Hong Kong China see Kowloon
Jiulong Sichuan China 86 B2
also known as Gyaisi
Jiulong Sichuan China see Yuechi
Jiuquan China 84 C4
formerly known as Suzhou
Jiutai China 82 B3
Jiuxian China 85 F4
Jiuxu China 78 D2
Jiuzhaigou China 86 C1
also known as Yongle
UNESCO World Heritage Site
Jiuzhen China 87 F3
Jiwani Pak. 101 E5
Jiwen China 85 I1
Jixi Anhui China 87 F2
also known as Huayang
Jixi Heilong. China 82 C3
Jixian Hebei China see Jizhou
Jixian Heilong. China 82 C3
also known as Fuli; formerly known as Fulitun
Jixian Henan China see Weihui
Jixian Shanxi China 85 F4
Jiyuan China 85 G5
Jiz, Wādī al r. Yemen 105 F4
Jīzān Saudi Arabia 104 C4
Jīzān prov. Saudi Arabia 104 C4
Jizera r. Czech Rep. 49 L5
Jizerské hory mts Czech Rep. 49 M5
Jizhou China 85 G4
formerly known as Jixian
Jizl watercourse Saudi Arabia 104 B2
Jizō-zaki pt Japan 91 C7
Jizzakh Uzbek. see Jizzax
Jizzakh Wiloyati admin. div. Uzbek. see Jizzax
Jizzax Uzbek. 103 F4
also spelt Jizzakh
Jizzax admin. div. Uzbek. 103 F5
English form Dzhizak Oblast; also known as Jizzakh Wiloyati
Joaçaba Brazil 203 B8
Joachimsthal Germany 49 K3
Joaíma Brazil 202 D6
Joal-Fadiout Senegal 124 A3
Joana Peres Brazil 202 B2
João Belo Moz. see Xai-Xai
João de Almeida Angola see Chibia
João Monlevade Brazil 207 J6
João Pessoa Brazil 202 F3
João Pinheiro Brazil 203 C6
Joaquim Felício Brazil 207 I4
Joaquín V. González Arg. 204 D2
Jobabo Cuba 186 D2
Jobat India 96 B5
Job Peak U.S.A. 182 F2
Jockfall Sweden 44 M2
Jocoli Arg. 204 C4
Joda India 97 E5
Jódar Spain 55 H7
Jodhpur India 96 B4
Jodiya India 96 A5
Joe Batt's Arm Canada 169 K3
Joensuu Fin. 44 O3
Joesjö Sweden 44 K2
Jōetsu Japan 90 F6
Jofane Moz. 131 G4
Joffre, Mount Canada 167 H5
Jogbani India 97 E4
Jogbura Nepal 96 D3
Jõgeva Estonia 42 H3
Jogighopa India 97 F4
Jogindarnagar India 96 C3
Jogjakarta Indon. see Yogyakarta
Jõgua Estonia 42 I2
Johannesburg S. Africa 133 L3
Johan Peninsula Canada 165 L2
Jōhen Japan 91 C8
Johilla r. India 96 D5
John Day U.S.A. 180 C3
John Day r. U.S.A. 180 B3
John Day, Middle Fork r. U.S.A. 180 C3
John Day, North Fork r. U.S.A. 180 C3
John D'Or Prairie Canada 167 H3
John F. Kennedy airport U.S.A. 177 L5
John H. Kerr Reservoir U.S.A. 176 G9
John Jay, Mount Canada/U.S.A. 166 D3
Johnny Hoe r. Canada 166 F1
John o'Groats U.K. 46 I5
Johnson U.S.A. 177 M1
Johnsonburg U.S.A. 176 G4
Johnson City NY U.S.A. 177 J3
Johnson City TN U.S.A. 176 C9
Johnson City TX U.S.A. 179 C6
Johnsondale U.S.A. 182 F6
Johnston U.S.A. 175 D5
Johnston, Lake salt flat Australia 151 C7
Johnston and Sand Islands atoll N. Pacific Ocean see Johnston Atoll

▶Johnston Atoll N. Pacific Ocean 220 H4
United States Unincorporated Territory. Also known as Johnston and Sand Islands.
▶▶138–139 Oceania Countries

Johnstone Lake Canada see Old Wives Lake
Johnstone Strait Canada 166 E5
Johnston Range hills Australia 151 B6
Johnstown NY U.S.A. 177 K2
Johnstown OH U.S.A. 176 C5
Johnstown PA U.S.A. 176 G5
Johor state Malaysia 76 C2
Johor, Selat strait Malaysia/Sing. 76 [inset]
Johor, Sungai Malaysia 76 [inset]
Johor Bahru Malaysia 76 C2
Jõhvi Estonia 42 I2
Joigny France 51 J5
Joinville Brazil 203 B8
Joinville France 51 L4
Joinville Island Antarctica 222 U2
Jojutla Mex. 185 F5
Jokela Fin. 42 F1
Jøkelbugten b. Greenland 165 Q2
Jokioinen Fin. 45 M3
Jokiperä Fin. 44 M3
Jokkmokk Sweden 44 L2
Jökulbunga hill Iceland 44 [inset] B2
Jökulfirðir inlet Iceland 44 [inset] B2
Jökulsá á Dál r. Iceland 44 [inset] D2
Jökulsá á Fjöllum r. Iceland 44 [inset] C2
Jolarpettai India 94 C3
Jolfā Iran 107 G4
Joliet U.S.A. 174 B3
Joliet, Lac l. Canada 168 E3
Joliette Canada 169 F4
Jolly Lake Canada 167 H1
Jolo Phil. 74 B5
Jolo i. Phil. 74 B5
Jomala Fin. 42 A1
Jomalig i. Phil. 74 B3
Jomard Entrance sea chan. P.N.G. 149 F1
Jombang Indon. 77 F4
Jomda China 86 A2
also known as Gatong
Jømna Norway 45 J3
Jomsom Nepal 97 D3
Jonāḩ Iran 100 C5
Jonancy U.S.A. 176 C8
Jonathan Point Belize 185 H5
Jonava Lith. 42 F6
Jondal Norway 45 I3
Jondor Uzbek. 103 F5
Jonê China 86 B1
also known as Liulin
Jonesboro AR U.S.A. 174 B5
Jonesboro IL U.S.A. 174 B4
Jonesboro LA U.S.A. 179 D5
Jonesboro TN U.S.A. 176 C9
Jones Mills U.S.A. 176 F5
Jones Mountains Antarctica 222 R2
Jonesport U.S.A. 174 H2
Jones Sound sea chan. Canada 165 K2
Jonestown KY U.S.A. 176 A8
Jonestown PA U.S.A. 177 I5
Jonesville LA U.S.A. 175 B6
Jonesville NC U.S.A. 176 E9
Jonesville VA U.S.A. 176 B9
Jongeldi Uzbek. 103 E4
also spelt Jangeldi; formerly spelt Dzhankel'dy or Dzhingil'dy
Jonglei Sudan 128 A3
Jonglei state Sudan 128 B3
Jonglei Canal Sudan 128 A3
Joniškėlis Lith. 42 F5
Joniškis Lith. 42 E5
Jonk r. India 97 D5
Jönköping Sweden 45 K4
Jönköping county Sweden 45 K4
Jonquière Canada 169 G3
Jonuta Mex. 185 G5
Jonzac France 50 F7
Joplin U.S.A. 178 D4
Joppa Israel see Tel Aviv-Yafo
Jora India 96 C4
▶Jordan country Asia 108 G7
known as Al 'Urdun in Arabic
▶▶64–65 Asia Countries
Jordan r. Asia 108 G6
Jordan MT U.S.A. 180 F3
Jordan NY U.S.A. 177 I2
Jordan r. OR U.S.A. 180 C4
Jordan r. UT U.S.A. 183 L1
Jordânia Brazil 207 M2
Jordet Norway 45 K3
Jorge Montt, Isla i. Chile 205 B8
Jorhat India 97 G4
Jorm Afgh. 101 G2
Jormvattnet Sweden 44 K2
Jörn Sweden 44 M2
Joroinen Fin. 44 N3
Jørpeland Norway 45 I4
Jos Nigeria 125 H4
Jose Abad Santos Phil. 74 C5
José Bonifácio Rondônia Brazil 201 E3
José Bonifácio São Paulo Brazil 206 D8
José Cardel Mex. 185 F5
José de Freitas Brazil 202 D3
José de San Martín Arg. 205 C7
José Enrique Rodó Uruguay 204 F4
Joselândia Brazil 201 F4
José Pañganiban Phil. 74 B3
José Pedro Varela Uruguay 204 G4
Joseph, Lac l. Canada 169 H2
Joseph Bonaparte Gulf Australia 150 E2
Joseph City U.S.A. 183 N7
Joshimath India 96 C3
Jōshinetsu-kōgen National Park Japan 91 F6
Joshipur India 97 E5
Joshua Tree U.S.A. 183 H7
Joshua Tree National Park U.S.A. 183 I8
Jos Plateau Nigeria 125 H4
Josselin France 50 D5
Jossund Norway 44 J2
Jostedalsbreen glacier Norway 45 I3
Jostedalsbreen Nasjonalpark nat. park Norway 45 I3
Josvainiai Lith. 42 E6
Jotunheimen mts Norway 45 J3
Jotunheimen Nasjonalpark nat. park Norway 45 J3
Joubertina S. Africa 132 H10
Jouberton S. Africa 133 K3
Joué-lès-Tours France 50 G5
Joukokylä Fin. 44 N2
Joûnié Lebanon 108 G4
Jourdanton U.S.A. 179 C6
Joussard Canada 167 H4
Joutsa Fin. 45 N3
Joutseno Fin. 45 O3
Joutsijärvi Fin. 44 N2
Jovellanos Cuba 186 C2
Jowai India 97 G4
Jowzjān prov. Afgh. 101 F2
Joy, Mount Canada 166 C2
Joya de Cerén tourist site El Salvador 185 H6
UNESCO World Heritage Site
Joypurhat Bangl. 97 F4
Jozini S. Africa 133 Q4
Jrayfiya well W. Sahara 122 B4
Jreïda Mauritania 124 A2
Juan Aldama Mex. 185 E3
Juancheng China 85 G5
Juan de Fuca Strait Canada/U.S.A. 164 G5
Juan de Garay Arg. 204 D5
Juan de Nova i. Indian Ocean 129 D9
Juan E. Barra Arg. 204 E5
Juan Escutia Mex. 184 D4
Juan Fernández, Archipiélago is S. Pacific Ocean see Juan Fernández Islands
Juan Fernández Islands S. Pacific Ocean 221 N8
also known as Juan Fernández, Archipiélago
Juangriego Venez. 199 F2
Juan Jorge Arg. 204 F3
Juanjuí Peru 200 A1
Juankoski Fin. 44 O3
Juan Mata Ortíz Mex. 184 C2
Juanshui China see Tongcheng
Juan Stuven, Isla i. Chile 205 B7
Juara Brazil 201 F2
Juaréz Mex. 185 E3
Juárez, Sierra de mts Mex. 184 A1
Juatinga, Ponta da pt Brazil 207 I10
Juàzeiro Brazil 202 D4
Juàzeiro do Norte Brazil 202 E3
Juazohn Liberia 124 C5
Juba r. Somalia see Jubba
Juba Sudan 128 A3
Juban Yemen 104 D5
Jubany research station Antarctica 222 U2
long form Teniente Jubany
Jubba r. Somalia 128 D5
also spelt Juba; formerly spelt Giuba
Jubbada Dhexe admin. reg. Somalia 128 D4
Jubbada Hoose admin. reg. Somalia 128 D4
Jubbah Saudi Arabia 104 C1
Jubbulpore India see Jabalpur
Jubilee Lake salt flat Australia 151 D6
Jubing Nepal 97 E4
Juby, Cap c. Morocco 122 B4
Júcar r. Spain 55 K5
Jucas Brazil 202 E3
Juchatengo Mex. 185 F5
Juchitán Mex. 185 G5
Juchitlán Mex. 184 D4
Jucuruçu Brazil 203 E6
Jucuruçu r. Brazil 207 N4
Judaberg Norway 45 I4
Judaidat al Hamir Iraq 107 E5
Judaydah waterhole Iraq 109 M5
Judaydah Syria 109 K2
Judayyidat 'Ar'ar well Iraq 107 E5
Judenburg Austria 49 L8
Judian China 86 A3
Judith r. U.S.A. 180 E3
Judith Gap U.S.A. 180 E3
Juegang China see Rudong
Juego de Bolos mt. Spain 55 H6
Juelsminde Denmark 45 J5
Juerana Brazil 207 N4
Jufari r. Brazil 199 F5
Jufrah, Wādī al watercourse Egypt 108 C7
Jugon-les-Lacs France 50 D4
Juh China 85 F4
Juhaynah reg. Saudi Arabia 104 B2
Juḩaysh, Qalamat al oasis Saudi Arabia 105 E3
Juigalpa Nicaragua 186 B4
Juillac France 50 H7
Juillet, Lac l. Canada 169 I2
Juína Brazil 201 F2
Juina r. Brazil 201 F3
Juist i. Germany 48 E2
Juiz de Fora Brazil 203 D7
Jujuhan r. Indon. 76 C3
Ju Ju Klu Turkm. 102 E5
Jujuy prov. Arg. 200 D5
Jukkasjärvi Sweden 44 M2
also known as Čohkkiras
Julaca Bol. 200 D5
Julesburg U.S.A. 178 B3
Juli Peru 200 C4
Julia Brazil 199 E5
Juliaca Peru 200 C3
Julia Creek Australia 149 D4
Julian U.S.A. 183 H8
Julian, Lac l. Canada 168 E2
Julian Alps mts Slovenia see Julijske Alpe
Julianatop mt. Indon. see Mandala, Puncak
Juliana Top mt. Suriname 199 G4
Julianehåb Greenland see Qaqortoq
Julijske Alpe mts Slovenia 56 F2
English form Julian Alps
Julimes Mex. 184 D2
Júlio de Castilhos Brazil 203 A9
Juliomagus France see Angers
Júlio Mesquita Brazil 206 D9
Julius, Lake Australia 148 C4
Jullundur India see Jalandhar
Juma r. Brazil 199 E6
Juma Uzbek. 103 F5
also spelt Dzhuma
Juma He r. China 85 G4
Jumangguin China 86 A1
Jumba Somalia 128 D5
Jumilla Spain 55 J6
Jumla Nepal 97 D3
Jumna r. India see Yamuna
Jump r. U.S.A. 172 B5
Jumprava Latvia 42 F5
Junagadh India 96 A5
Junagarh India 95 D2
Junan China 85 H5
also known as Shizilu
Junaynah, Ra's al mt. Egypt 108 E8
Jun Bulen China 85 H2
Junction TX U.S.A. 179 C6
Junction UT U.S.A. 183 L3
Junction Bay Australia 148 B1
Junction City KS U.S.A. 178 C4
Junction City KY U.S.A. 176 A8
Junction City OR U.S.A. 180 B3
Jundah Australia 149 D5
Jundiaí Brazil 206 G10

▶Juneau U.S.A. 164 F4
State capital of Alaska.

Juneau Icefield Canada 166 C3
Junee Australia 147 E3
Jūn el Khudr b. Lebanon 108 G4
Jungar Qi China see Shagedu
Jungfrau mt. Switz. 51 O6
UNESCO World Heritage Site
Junggar Pendi basin China 88 D2
English form Dzungarian Basin
Jungshahi Pak. 101 F5
Junguls Sudan 128 B2
Juniata r. U.S.A. 177 H5
Junik Kosovo, Srbija Serb. and Mont. 58 B6
Junín Arg. 204 E4
Junín Peru 200 A2
Junín dept Peru 200 B2
Junior U.S.A. 176 F7
Juniper Mountains U.S.A. 183 K6
Junipero Serro Peak U.S.A. 182 C5
Junkerdalen Balvatnet nature res. Norway 44 K2
Junlian China 86 C2

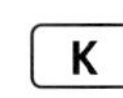

Karpathos Greece 59 I13
Karpathos *i.* Greece 59 I13
formerly known as Scarpanto
Karpathou, Steno *sea chan.* Greece 59 I12
Karpaty *mts* Europe *see* **Carpathian Mountains**
Karpenisi Greece 59 C10
Karpilovka Belarus *see* **Aktsyabrski**
Karpinsk Rus. Fed. 38 G4
Karpogory Rus. Fed. 40 H2
Karpovychi Ukr. 43 N9
Karpuz *r.* Turkey 108 C1
Karpuzlu *Aydın* Turkey 59 I11
Karpuzlu *Edirne* Turkey 58 H8
Karratha Australia 150 B4
Karrats Fjord *inlet* Greenland *see* **Nuugaatsiaap Imaa**
Karrī Iran 100 B4
Karringmelkspruit S. Africa 133 L7
Karroo *plat.* S. Africa *see* **Great Karoo**
Karroun Hill Nature Reserve Australia 151 B6
Karrukh Afgh. 101 E3
Karrychirla Turkm. *see* **Garryçyrla**
Kars Turkey 107 E2
Karsakpay Kazakh. 103 F3
also spelt Qarsaqbay
Kärsämäki Fin. 44 N3
Kārsava Latvia 42 I5
Karshi Uzbek. *see* **Qarshi**
Karşıyaka *Balıkesir* Turkey 58 J8
Karşıyaka *İzmir* Turkey 59 I10
Karsiyang India 97 F4
Karskiye Vorota, Proliv *strait* Rus. Fed. 40 K1
English form Kara Strait
Karskoye More *sea* Rus. Fed. *see* **Kara Sea**
Karstädt Germany 48 I2
Karsu Turkey 109 H1
Karsun Rus. Fed. 41 H5
Kartal Turkey 106 B2
Kartala *vol.* Comoros 129 D7
Kartaly Rus. Fed. 103 E1
Kartarpur India 96 B3
Kartena Lith. 42 C6
Karthaus U.S.A. 176 G4
Kartsevo Rus. Fed. 43 L5
Kartsino, Akra *pt* Greece 59 F10
Karttula Fin. 44 N3
Kartuni Guyana 199 G3
Kartuzy Poland 49 P1
Karubwe Zambia 127 F8
Kārūkh, Jabal *mt.* Iraq 109 P1
Karumai Japan 90 G4
Karumba Australia 149 D3
Karun, Kūh-e *hill* Iran 100 B4
Kārūn, Rūd-e *r.* Iran 100 B4
Karunagapalli India 94 C4
Karungi Sweden 44 M2
Karungu Kenya 128 B5
Karuni Indon. 75 A5
Karunjie Australia 150 D3
Karup Denmark 45 J4
Karur India 94 C4
Karuzi Burundi 126 F5
Karvetnagar India 94 C3
Karvia Fin. 45 M3
Karviná Czech Rep. 49 P6
Karwar India 94 B3
Karwendelgebirge *nature res.* Austria 48 I8
Karwi India 96 D4
Karya Greece 59 B10
Karyagino Azer. *see* **Füzuli**
Karyes Greece 59 F8
Karymskoye Rus. Fed. 85 G1
Karynzharyk, Peski *des.* Kazakh. 102 C4
Karystos Greece 59 F10
also spelt Káristos
Kaş Turkey 106 B3
Kasa India 94 B2
Kasaba Turkey *see* **Turgutlu**
Kasaba Lodge Zambia 127 F7
Kasabonika Canada 168 B2
Kasaï *r.* Dem. Rep. Congo 127 C5
Kasai Japan 91 D7
Kasaï, Plateau du Dem. Rep. Congo 127 D6
Kasaï-Occidental *prov.* Dem. Rep. Congo 127 D6
Kasaï-Oriental *prov.* Dem. Rep. Congo 126 E6
Kasaji Dem. Rep. Congo 127 D7
Kasama Japan 91 G6
Kasama Zambia 127 F7
Kasan Uzbek. *see* **Koson**
Kasane Botswana 131 E3
Kasanga Tanz. 129 A7
Kasangulu Dem. Rep. Congo 126 B6
Kasanka National Park Zambia 127 F8
Kasansay Uzbek. *see* **Kosonsoy**
Kasanza Dem. Rep. Congo 127 C6
Kasar, Ras *pt* Sudan 121 H5
Kasaragod India 94 B3
Kasari *r.* Estonia 42 E3
Kasatkino Rus. Fed. 82 C2
Kasba Lake Canada 167 K2
Kasba Tadla Morocco 122 D2
Kasbi Uzbek. 103 F5
Kaseda Japan 91 B9
Kasempa Zambia 127 E8
Kasenga *Katanga* Dem. Rep. Congo 127 D7
Kasenga *Katanga* Dem. Rep. Congo 127 F7
Kasenye Dem. Rep. Congo 126 F4
Kasese Dem. Rep. Congo 126 E5
Kasese Uganda 128 A4
Kasevo Rus. Fed. *see* **Neftekamsk**
Kasganj India 96 C4
Kasha China 86 A2
also known as Gonjo
Kasha *waterhole* Kenya 128 D5
Kashabowie Canada 168 B3
Kāshān Iran 100 B3
Kashary Rus. Fed. 41 G6
Kashechewan Canada 168 D2
Kashgar China *see* **Kashi**
Kashi China 88 B4
formerly known as Kashgar *or* Kaxgar
Kashihara Japan 91 D7
Kashima Japan 91 B8
Kashima-nada *b.* Japan 91 G6
Kashin Rus. Fed. 43 S4
Kashinka *r.* Rus. Fed. 43 S4
Kashiobwe Dem. Rep. Congo 127 F7
Kashipur India 96 C3
Kashira Rus. Fed. 43 T7
Kashirka *r.* Rus. Fed. 43 T7
Kashiwazaki Japan 90 F6
Kashkadar'ya *r.* Uzbek. *see* **Qashqadaryo**
Kashkadarya Oblast *admin. div.* Uzbek. *see* **Qashqadaryo**
Kashkanteniz Kazakh. 103 H3
also spelt Kashken-Teniz *or* Qashqantengiz
Kashken-Teniz Kazakh. *see* **Kashkanteniz**
Kashkurino Rus. Fed. 43 M6
Kāshmar Iran 100 D3
Kashmir *terr.* Asia *see* **Jammu and Kashmir**
Kashmir, Vale of *valley* India 96 B2
Kashmor Pak. 101 G4
Kashmund *reg.* Afgh. 101 G3
Kashyukulu Dem. Rep. Congo 127 E6
Kasi India *see* **Varanasi**
Kasia India 97 D4
Kasilovo Rus. Fed. 43 O8
Kasimbar Indon. 75 A3
Kasimov Rus. Fed. 40 G5
Kasingi Dem. Rep. Congo 126 F4
Kasiruta *i.* Indon. 75 C3
Kaskaskia *r.* U.S.A. 174 B4
Kaskattama *r.* Canada 167 N3
Kaskelen Kazakh. 103 I4
also spelt Qaskelen
Kaskinen Fin. 44 M3
also known as Kaskö
Kas Klong *i.* Cambodia *see* **Kŏng, Kaôh**
Kaskö Fin. *see* **Kaskinen**
Kaskyrbulak Yuzhnyy, Gora *hill* Turkm. 102 C4
Kaslo Canada 167 G5
Kasmere Lake Canada 167 K3
Kasnya *r.* Rus. Fed. 43 P6
Kasomeno Dem. Rep. Congo 127 F7
Kasongan Indon. 77 F3
Kasongo Dem. Rep. Congo 126 E6
Kasongo-Lunda Dem. Rep. Congo 127 C6
Kasonguele Dem. Rep. Congo 127 E6
Kasos *i.* Greece 59 H13
Kasou, Steno *sea chan.* Greece 59 I13
Kaspi Georgia 107 F2
Kaspiy Mangy Oypaty *lowland* Kazakh./Rus. Fed. *see* **Caspian Lowland**
Kaspiysk Rus. Fed. 102 A4
Kaspiyskiy Rus. Fed. *see* **Lagan'**
Kaspiyskoye More *sea* Asia/Europe *see* **Caspian Sea**
Kasplya Rus. Fed. 43 M7
Kasplya *r.* Rus. Fed. 43 L6
Kasrawad India 96 B5
Kasrik Turkey *see* **Gürpınar**
Kassa Slovakia *see* **Košice**
Kassaare laht *b.* Estonia 42 D3
Kassala Sudan 121 H6
Kassala *state* Sudan 121 G6
Kassandra *pen.* Greece 59 E8
Kassandras, Akra *pt* Greece 59 E9
Kassandras, Kolpos *b.* Greece 59 E8
Kassandreia Greece 59 E8
Kassel Germany 48 G4
Kasserine Tunisia 123 H2
Kassinga Angola *see* **Cassinga**
Kassouloua *well* Niger 125 H3
Kastamonu Turkey 106 C2
also known as Çandar
Kastelli *Kriti* Greece 59 E13
also known as Kastéllion
Kastelli *Kriti* Greece 59 G13
Kastéllion Greece *see* **Kastelli**
Kastellorizon *i.* Greece *see* **Megisti**
Kastellou, Akra *pt* Greece 59 I13
Kastoria Greece 58 C8
Kastorias, Limni *l.* Greece 58 C8
Kastornoye Rus. Fed. 41 F6
Kastos *i.* Greece 59 B10
Kastrakiou, Techniti Limni *resr* Greece 59 C10
Kastre Estonia 42 I3
Kastrova Belarus 43 J5
Kastsyukovichi Belarus 43 N8
also spelt Kostyukovichi
Kastsyukowka Belarus 43 L9
Kasugai Japan 91 E7
Kasuku Dem. Rep. Congo 126 E5
Kasulu Tanz. 129 A6
Kasumiga-ura *l.* Japan 91 G6
Kasumkent Rus. Fed. 102 B4
Kasungu Malawi 129 B8
Kasungu National Park Malawi 129 B8
Kasur Pak. 101 H4
Kataba Zambia 127 E9
Katagum Nigeria 125 H3
Katahdin, Mount U.S.A. 174 G2
Kataklik Jammu and Kashmir 96 C2
Katako-Kombe Dem. Rep. Congo 126 E5
Katakolo, Akra *pt* Greece 59 C11
Katakwi Uganda 128 B4
Katanda Dem. Rep. Congo 126 D6
Katanga *prov.* Dem. Rep. Congo 127 E7
formerly known as Shaba
Katangi *Madhya Pradesh* India 96 C5
Katangi *Madhya Pradesh* India 96 C5
Katangli Rus. Fed. 82 F2
Katanning Australia 151 B7
Kata Pusht Iran 100 B2
Katashin Rus. Fed. 43 N9
Katastari Greece 59 B11
Katavi National Park Tanz. 129 A6
Katawaz Afgh. 101 G3
Katawaz *reg.* Afgh. 101 F3
Katchall *i.* India 95 G5
Katchamba Togo 125 F4
Katea Dem. Rep. Congo 127 E6
Katerini Greece 59 D8
Katesh Tanz. 129 B6
Kate's Needle *mt.* Canada/U.S.A. 164 F4
Katete Zambia 129 B8
Katghora India 97 D5
Katha Myanmar 78 B2
Katherîna, Gebel *mt.* Egypt 121 G2
Katherine Australia 148 B2
Katherine *r.* Australia 148 A2
Katherine Gorge National Park Australia *see* **Nitmiluk National Park**
Kathi India 96 B5
Kathiawar *pen.* India 96 A5
Kathīb, Ra's al *pt* Yemen 104 C5
Kathleen Falls Australia 148 A2

▸**Kathmandu** Nepal 97 E4
Capital of Nepal. English form Katmandu.
UNESCO World Heritage Site

Kathu S. Africa 132 H4
Kathua Jammu and Kashmir 96 B2
Kathua *watercourse* Kenya 128 C5
Kati Mali 124 C3
Katibas *r. Sarawak* Malaysia 77 F2
Kati-ér *r.* Hungary 49 S8
Katihar India 97 E4
Katikati N.Z. 152 J5
Katikati S. Africa 133 L9
Katima Mulilo Namibia 131 E3
Katimik Lake Canada 167 L4
Katino Rus. Fed. 43 U8
Katiola Côte d'Ivoire 124 D4
Kā Tiritiri o te Moana *mts* N.Z. *see* **Southern Alps**
Katiti Aboriginal Land *res.* Australia 148 A5
Katkop Hills S. Africa 132 E7
Katlabukh, Ozero *l.* Ukr. 58 J3
Katlehong S. Africa 133 M3
Katma China 88 D4
Katmai National Park and Preserve U.S.A. 164 D4
Katmandu Nepal *see* **Kathmandu**
Kato Achaïa Greece 59 C10
Kat O Chau *i. Hong Kong* China *see* **Crooked Island**
Katochi Greece 59 C10
Kato Figaleia Greece 59 C11
Kat O Hoi *b. Hong Kong* China *see* **Crooked Harbour**
Katol India 96 C5
Kätölandet *i.* Fin. 44 M3
Katombe Dem. Rep. Congo 127 D6
Katompi Dem. Rep. Congo 127 E6
Katondwe Zambia 127 F8
Kato Nevrokopi Greece 58 E7
Katong Sing. 76 [inset]
Katonga *r.* Uganda 128 A4
Katon-Karagay Kazakh. 88 D1
also spelt Katonqaraghay
Katonqaraghay Kazakh. *see* **Katon-Karagay**
Katoomba Australia 147 F3
Katoposa, Gunung *mt.* Indon. 75 B3
Katosan India 96 B5
Kato Tithorea Greece 59 D10
Kåtotjåkka *mt.* Sweden *see* **Godučohkka**
Katowice Poland 49 Q5
formerly known as Stalinogród; *historically known as* Kattowitz
Katoya India 97 F5
formerly spelt Katwa
Katpur India 96 B5
Katrineholm Sweden 45 L4
Katse Dam Lesotho 133 M6
Katsepy Madag. 131 [inset] J2
Katsikas Greece 59 B9
Katsina Nigeria 125 G3
Katsina *state* Nigeria 125 G4
Katsina-Ala Nigeria 125 H5
Katsumoto Japan 91 A8
Katsuura Japan 91 G7
Katsuyama Japan 91 E6
Kattamudda Well Australia 150 D4
Kattaqo'rg'on Uzbek. 103 F5
also spelt Kattaqŭrghon
Kattaqŭrghon Uzbek. *see* **Kattaqo'rg'on**
Kattasang Hills Afgh. 101 F3
Kattavia Greece 59 I13
Kattegat *strait* Denmark/Sweden 45 J4
Kattisavan Sweden 44 L2
Kattowitz Poland *see* **Katowice**
Kattuputtur India 94 C4
Katumba Dem. Rep. Congo 127 E6
Katumbi Malawi 129 B7
Katun' *r.* Rus. Fed. 88 D1
Katunino Rus. Fed. 40 H4
Katunskiy Khrebet *mts* Rus. Fed. 88 D1
Katwa India *see* **Katoya**
Katwijk aan Zee Neth. 48 B3
Katyk Ukr. *see* **Shakhtars'k**
Katyn' Rus. Fed. 43 M7
Kąty Wrocławskie Poland 49 N4
Kaua'i *i.* U.S.A. 181 [inset] Y1
Kaua'i Channel U.S.A. 181 [inset] Y1
Kaudom Game Park *nature res.* Namibia 130 D3
Kaufbeuren Germany 48 H8
Kaufman U.S.A. 179 C5
Kauhajoki Fin. 44 M3
Kauhanevan-Pohjankankaan kansallispuisto *nat. park* Fin. 45 M3
Kauhava Fin. 44 M3
Kaukauna U.S.A. 172 E6
Kaukkwè Hills Myanmar 78 B2
Kaukonen Fin. 44 N2
Kauksi Estonia 42 I2
Kaulinranta Fin. 44 M2
Kaumajet Mountains Canada 169 I1
Kaunakakai U.S.A. 181 [inset] Z1
Kaunas Lith. 42 E7
formerly known as Kovno
Kaunata Latvia 42 I5
Kaundy, Vpadina *depr.* Kazakh. 102 C4
Kaunia Bangl. 97 F4
Kauno marios *l.* Lith. 42 F7
Kaupiri N.Z. 153 F10
Kaura-Namoda Nigeria 125 G3
Kau Sai Chau *i. Hong Kong* China 87 [inset]
Kaushany Moldova *see* **Căuşeni**
Kaustinen Fin. 44 M3
Kautokeino Norway 44 M1
Kau-ye Kyun *i.* Myanmar 79 B6
Kavacha Rus. Fed. 39 Q3
Kavadarci Macedonia 58 D7
Kavajë Albania 58 A7
Kavak *Çanakkale* Turkey 58 H8
Kavak *Samsun* Turkey 106 D2
Kavak Dağı *hill* Turkey 59 H9
Kavaklıdere *Manisa* Turkey 59 J10
Kavaklıdere *Muğla* Turkey 59 J11
Kavala Greece 58 F8
Kavalas, Kolpos *b.* Greece 58 F8
Kavalerovo Rus. Fed. 82 D3
Kavali India 94 D3
Kavalpatnam India 94 C4
Kavalyova Belarus 43 L6
Kavanayen Venez. 199 F3
Kavār Iran 100 C4
Kavaratti India 94 B4
Kavaratti *i.* India 94 B4
Kavarna Bulg. 58 J5
Kavarskas Lith. 42 F6
Kavendou, Mont *mt.* Guinea 124 B4
Kaveri *r.* India 94 C4
Kaveripatnam India 94 C3
Kavi India 96 B5
Kavieng P.N.G. 145 E2
Kavīr Iran 100 B3
Kavīr, Chāh-e *well* Iran 100 D3
Kavīr, Dasht-e *des.* Iran 100 C3
Kavīr Kūshk *well* Iran 100 D3
Kavirondo Gulf Kenya *see* **Winam Gulf**
Kavkazskiy Zapovednik *nature res.* Rus. Fed. 41 G8
Kaw Fr. Guiana 199 H3
Kawabe Japan 90 G5
Kawachi-nagano Japan 91 D7
Kawagama Lake Canada 168 E4
Kawagoe Japan 91 F7
Kawaguchi Japan 91 F7
Kawahara Japan 91 D7
Kawai Japan 90 G5
Kawaihae U.S.A. 181 [inset] Z1
Kawaihoa Point U.S.A. 181 [inset] Y1
Kawakawa N.Z. 152 I3
Kawamata Japan 90 G6
Kawambwa Zambia 127 F7
Kawaminami Japan 91 B8
Kawana Zambia 127 E8
Kawangkoan Indon. 75 C2
Kawanishi Japan 91 D7
Kawardha India 96 D5
Kawartha Lakes Canada 168 E4
Kawasa Dem. Rep. Congo 127 F7
Kawasaki Japan 91 F7
Kawashiri-misaki *pt* Japan 91 B7
Kawato Indon. 75 B3
Kawaura Japan 91 B8
Kawawachikamach Canada 169 H2
Kawe *i.* Indon. 75 D2
Kaweah, Lake U.S.A. 182 F5
Kaweka Forest Park *nature res.* N.Z. 152 K7
Kaweka Range *mts* N.Z. 152 K7
Kawene Canada 172 B2
Kawerau N.Z. 152 K6
Kawhia N.Z. 152 I6
Kawich Peak U.S.A. 183 H4
Kawich Range *mts* U.S.A. 183 H4
Kawinaw Lake Canada 167 L4
Kawio *i.* Indon. 75 C1
Kawkabān Yemen 104 C5
Kawkareik Myanmar 78 B4
Kaw Lake U.S.A. 178 C4
Kawlin Myanmar 78 A3
Kawludo Myanmar 78 B4
Kawmapyin Myanmar 79 B5
Kawm Dafanah *tourist site* Egypt *see* **Daphnae**
Kawm Hamādah Egypt 108 B7
Kawm Umbū Egypt 121 G3
Kawngmeum Myanmar 78 B3
Kawthaung Myanmar 79 B6
Kawthoolei *state* Myanmar *see* **Kayin**
Kawthule *state* Myanmar *see* **Kayin**
Kaxgar China *see* **Kashi**
Kaxgar He *r.* China 88 B4
Kax He *r.* China 88 C3
Kaxtax Shan *mts* China 89 C4
Kaya Burkina 125 E3
Kaya S. Korea 91 A7
Kayacı Dağı *hill* Turkey 59 H9
Kayadibi Turkey 107 D3
Kayah *state* Myanmar 78 B4
Kayambi Zambia 129 A7
Kayan *r.* Indon. 77 E3
Kayan *r.* Indon. 77 G2
Kayan Myanmar 78 B4
Kayanaza Burundi 126 F5
Kayangel Atoll Palau 73 H5
also known as Ngcheangel
Kayankulam India 94 C4
Kayar India 94 C2
Kayasa Indon. 75 C2
Kaya-san National Park S. Korea 91 A7
UNESCO World Heritage Site
Kaybagar, Ozero *l.* Kazakh. *see* **Koybagar, Ozero**
Kayd, Wādī *watercourse* Egypt 108 F9
Kaydak, Sor *dry lake* Kazakh. 102 C3
Kaydanovo Belarus *see* **Dzyarzhynsk**
Kayenta U.S.A. 183 N5
Kayes Mali 124 C3
Kayes *admin. reg.* Mali 124 C3
Kayga Kazakh. 103 F2
also known as Qayghy; *formerly known as* Kaygy
Kaygy Kazakh. *see* **Kayga**
Kayin *state* Myanmar 78 B4
also known as Karan; *formerly known as* Karen *or* Kawthoolei *or* Kawthule
Kaymanachikha Kazakh. 103 H1
Kaymaz Turkey 106 B3
Kaynar *Vostochnyy Kazakhstan* Kazakh. 103 I2
also spelt Qaynar
Kaynar *Zhambylskaya Oblast'* Kazakh. 103 H4
Kaynar Turkey 107 D3
Kaynarlı *r.* Turkey 58 I7
Kayoa *i.* Indon. 75 C2
Kayrakkum Tajik. *see* **Qayroqqum**
Kayrakkumskoye Vodokhranilishche *resr* Tajik. *see* **Qayroqqum, Obanbori**
Kayseri Turkey 106 C3
historically known as Caesarea Cappadociae *or* Mazaca
Kaysersberg France 51 N4
Kayuadi *i.* Indon. 75 B4
Kayuagung Indon. 76 D3
Kayunga Uganda 128 B4
Kayuyu Dem. Rep. Congo 126 E5
Kayyerkan Rus. Fed. 39 I3
Kayyngdy Kyrg. 103 H4
formerly spelt Kainda *or* Kaindy; *formerly known as* Molotovsk
Kazachka Rus. Fed. 43 T8
Kazach'ye Rus. Fed. 39 N2
Kazakh Azer. *see* **Qazax**
Kazakhdar'ya Uzbek. *see* **Qozoqdaryo**
Kazakhskaya S.S.R. *country* Asia *see* **Kazakhstan**
Kazakhskiy Melkosopochnik *plain* Kazakh. 103 G2
Kazakhskiy Zaliv *b.* Kazakh. 102 C4
also known as Qazaq Shyghanaghy

▸**Kazakhstan** *country* Asia 102 C2
4th largest country in Asia and 9th in the world. Also spelt Kazakstan or Qazaqstan in Kazakh; formerly known as Kazakhskaya S.S.R.
▸▸8–9 **World** Countries
▸▸64–65 **Asia** Countries

Kazakhstan Kazakh. *see* **Aksay**
Kazaki Rus. Fed. 43 T9
Kazakstan *country* Asia *see* **Kazakhstan**
Kazalinsk Kazakh. 103 E3
also known as Qazaly
Kazan *r.* Canada 167 M2
Kazan' Rus. Fed. 40 I5
UNESCO World Heritage Site
Kazanchunkur Kazakh. 103 J2
Kazancı Turkey 106 C3
Kazandzhik Turkm. *see* **Bereket**
Kazanje, Mal *mt.* Albania 59 B9
Kazanka *r.* Rus. Fed. 40 I5
Kazanketken Uzbek. *see* **Qozonketkan**
Kazanlı Turkey 108 F1
Kazanlŭk Bulg. 58 G6
UNESCO World Heritage Site
Kazanovka Rus. Fed. 43 T8
Kazanovo Rus. Fed. 85 G1
Kazan-rettō *is* N. Pacific Ocean *see* **Volcano Islands**
Kazatin Ukr. *see* **Kozyatyn**
Kazatskiy Kazakh. 102 D2
Kaza Wenz *r.* Eth. 128 C1

▸**Kazbek** *mt.* Georgia/Rus. Fed. 107 F2
4th highest mountain in Europe. Also known as Mqinvartsveri.
▸▸28–29 **Europe** Landscapes

Kaz Dağı *mts* Turkey 106 A3
Kāzerūn Iran 100 B4
Kazgorodok Kazakh. 103 G1
Kazhim Rus. Fed. 40 I3
Kazhmak *r.* Pak. 101 E5
Kazıkbeli Geçidi *pass* Turkey 59 K11
Kazi Magomed Azer. *see* **Qazimämmäd**
Kazimierza Wielka Poland 49 R5
Kazimierz Dolne Poland 49 S4
Kāẓimīyah Iraq *see* **Al Kāẓimīyah**
Kazincbarcika Hungary 49 R7
Kazinka *Lipetskaya Oblast'* Rus. Fed. 43 U9
formerly known as Novaya Zhizn
Kazinka *Ryazanskaya Oblast'* Rus. Fed. 43 U8
Kaziranga National Park India 97 G4
UNESCO World Heritage Site
Kazlowshchyna Belarus 42 G8
Kazlowshchyna Belarus 42 J6
Kazlų Rūda Lith. 42 E7
Kazo Japan 91 F6
Kaztalovka Kazakh. 102 B2
Kazuma Pan National Park Zimbabwe 131 E3
Kazumba Dem. Rep. Congo 127 D6
Kazungula Zambia 127 E9
Kazuno Japan 90 G4
Kazy Turkm. 102 D5
Kazyany Belarus 43 K6
Kazygurt Kazakh. 103 G4
also spelt Qazyqurt; *formerly known as* Lenin *or* Leninskoye
Kazym *r.* Rus. Fed. 38 G3
Kazymskiy Mys Rus. Fed. 38 G3
Kçirë Albania 58 A6
Kea Greece 59 F11
Kea *i.* Greece 59 F11
English form Ceos
Kea'au U.S.A. 181 [inset] Z2
Keahole Point U.S.A. 181 [inset] Z2
Kealakekua Bay U.S.A. 181 [inset] Z2
Keālia U.S.A. 181 [inset] Z2
Keams Canyon U.S.A. 183 N6
Kéamu *i.* Vanuatu *see* **Anatom**
Kearney U.S.A. 178 C3
Kearneysville U.S.A. 176 H6
Kearny U.S.A. 183 N8
Keas, Steno *sea chan.* Greece 59 F11
Keate's Drift S. Africa 133 O5
Keban Turkey 107 D3
Keban Barajı *resr* Turkey 107 D3
Kebatu *i.* Indon. 77 E3
Kebbi *state* Nigeria 125 F3
Kébémèr Senegal 124 A3
Kébi *r.* Cameroon 125 I4
Kébi Côte d'Ivoire 124 D4
Kebili Tunisia 123 H2
Kebīr, Nahr al *r.* Lebanon/Syria 108 G3
Kebkabiya Sudan 120 E6
Kebnekaise *mt.* Sweden 44 L2
K'ebrī Dehar Eth. 128 E3
Kebumen Indon. 77 E4
Kecel Hungary 49 Q9
Kech *reg.* Pak. 101 E5
K'ech'a Terara *mt.* Eth. 128 C3
Kéché Cent. Afr. Rep. 126 D2
Kechika *r.* Canada 166 E3
Keçiborlu Turkey 106 B3
Kecskemét Hungary 49 Q9
Kedah *state* Malaysia 76 C1
Kėdainiai Lith. 42 E6
Kedairu Passage Fiji *see* **Kadavu Passage**
Kédédéssé Chad 126 C2
Kedgwick Canada 169 H4
Kedian China 87 E2
Kediri Indon. 77 F4
Kedong China 82 B3
Kédougou Senegal 124 B3
Kedva *r.* Rus. Fed. 40 J2
Kędzierzyn-Koźle Poland 49 P5
historically known as Heydebreck
Keele *r.* Canada 166 E1
Keele Peak Canada 166 D2
Keeley Lake Canada 167 I4
Keeling Islands *terr.* Indian Ocean *see* **Cocos Islands**
Keelung Taiwan *see* **Chilung**
Keenapusan *i.* Phil. 74 A5
Keene *CA* U.S.A. 182 F6
Keene *NH* U.S.A. 177 M3
Keene *OH* U.S.A. 176 D5
Keep *r.* Australia 148 A2
Keepit, Lake *resr* Australia 147 F2
Keep River National Park Australia 148 A2
Keeromsberg *mt. Free State* S. Africa 133 K5
Keeromsberg *mt. W. Cape* S. Africa 132 D10
Keer-weer, Cape Australia 149 D2
Keetmanshoop Namibia 130 C5
Keewatin Canada 167 M5
Keewatin U.S.A. 174 A2
Kefallinia *i.* Greece *see* **Cephalonia**
Kefallonia *i.* Greece *see* **Cephalonia**
Kefalos Greece 59 H12
Kefalos, Akra *pt* Greece 59 F11
Kefamenanu Indon. 75 C5
Kefe Ukr. *see* **Feodosiya**
Keffi Nigeria 125 G4
Keflavík Iceland 44 [inset] B2
Kê Ga, Mui *pt* Vietnam 79 E6
Kegalla Sri Lanka 94 D5
Kegayli Uzbek. *see* **Kegeyli**
Kegen Kazakh. 103 I4
Kegeyli Uzbek. 102 D4
also spelt Kegayli
Keglo, Baie de *b.* Canada 169 H1
Keg River Canada 167 G3
Kegul'ta Rus. Fed. 41 H7
Ķegums Latvia 42 F5
Keheili Sudan 121 G5
Kehl Germany 48 E7
Kehoula *well* Mauritania 124 C2
Kehra Estonia 42 G2
Kehsi Mansam Myanmar 78 B3
Kehtna Estonia 42 F3
Keighley U.K. 47 K10
Keihoku Japan 91 D7
Keila Estonia 42 F2
Keila *r.* Estonia 42 F2
Keilak Sudan 126 F2
Keili Sudan 128 B2
Kei Ling Ha Hoi *b. Hong Kong* China *see* **Three Fathoms Cove**
Keimoes S. Africa 132 E5
Kei Mouth S. Africa 133 M9
Kei Road S. Africa 133 L9
Keiskama *r.* S. Africa 133 L10
Keiskammahoek S. Africa 133 L9
Keïta Niger 125 G3
Kéïta, Bahr *r.* Chad 126 C2
Keitele Fin. 44 N3
Keitele *l.* Fin. 44 N3
Keith Australia 146 D4
Keith U.K. 46 J6
Keith, Cape Australia 148 A1
Keith Arm *b.* Canada 166 F1
Keithley Creek Canada 166 F4
Keithsburg U.S.A. 172 C9
Kejimkujik National Park Canada 169 H4
Kekaha U.S.A. 181 [inset] Y1
Kök-Art Kyrg. *see* **Kök-Art**
Ķekava Latvia 42 F5
Këkaygyr Kyrg. *see* **Kök-Aygyr**
Kekerengu N.Z. 153 H10
Kékes *mt.* Hungary 49 R8
Kekova Adası *i.* Turkey 108 A1
Kekra Rus. Fed. 39 O4
Kekri India 96 B4
Kök-Tash Kyrg. *see* **Kök-Tash**
K'elafo Eth. 128 E3
Kelai *atoll* Maldives 94 B5
Kelan China 85 F4
Kelang *i.* Indon. 75 C3
Kelang Malaysia *see* **Klang**
Kelantan *r.* Malaysia 76 C1
Kelantan *state* Malaysia 76 C1
Kelārdasht Iran 100 B2
Kelawar *i.* Indon. 77 E3
Kelbia, Sebkhet *salt pan* Tunisia 57 C13
Kele Uganda 128 B4
Kelekçi Turkey 59 K11
Kelema Tanz. 129 B6
Keles Turkey 59 K9
Keles Uzbek. 103 G4
Kelheim Germany 48 I7
Kelibia Tunisia 123 H1
Kelif Turkm. 103 F5
Kelif Uzboýy *marsh* Turkm. 103 E5
Kelkit Turkey 107 D2
also known as Çiftlik
Kelkit *r.* Turkey 107 D2
Kellavere *hill* Estonia 42 H2
Kéllé Congo 126 B5
Kellerberrin Australia 151 B6
Keller Lake Canada 166 F2
Kellerovka Kazakh. 103 G1
Kellett, Cape Canada 164 G2
Kelliher Canada 167 K5
Kellogg U.S.A. 180 C3
Kelloselkä Fin. 44 O2
Kells Ireland 47 F10
also known as Ceanannus Mór
Kelly Lake Canada 166 E1
Kelly Range *hills* Australia 151 C5
Kelmė Lith. 42 D6
Kelo Chad 126 B2
Kelowna Canada 166 G5
Kelp Head Canada 166 E5
Kelsey U.S.A. 172 A3
Kelseyville U.S.A. 182 B3
Kelso N.Z. 153 D13
Kelso U.K. 46 J8
Kelso *CA* U.S.A. 183 I6
Kelso *WA* U.S.A. 180 B3
Keltie, Jebel *mt.* Morocco 54 F9
Keluang Malaysia 76 C2
formerly spelt Kluang
Keluĵärvi Fin. 44 N2
Kelvington Canada 167 K4
Kelvin Island Canada 168 B3
Kelwara India 101 H5
Kem' Rus. Fed. 40 E2
Kem' *r.* Rus. Fed. 40 E2
Kema *r.* Rus. Fed. 43 S1
Ke Macina Mali *see* **Massina**
Kemah Turkey 107 D3
Kemal Turkey 58 H7
Kemaliye Turkey 107 D3
also known as Eğin
Kemalpaşa Turkey 59 I10
Kemano Canada 166 E4
Kembé Cent. Afr. Rep. 126 D3
Kembolcha Eth. 128 C2
Kemeneshát *hills* Hungary 49 O8
Kemer *Antalya* Turkey 106 B3
Kemer *Antalya* Turkey 108 A1
Kemer *Muğla* Turkey 106 B3
Kemer Barajı *resr* Turkey 106 B3
Kemerovo Rus. Fed. 80 D1
Kemerovo Oblast *admin. div.* Rus. Fed. *see* **Kemerovskaya Oblast'**
Kemerovskaya Oblast' *admin. div.* Rus. Fed. 80 D2
English form Kemerovo Oblast
Kemi Fin. 44 N2
Kemihaara Fin. 44 O2
Kemijärvi Fin. 44 N2
Kemijärvi *l.* Fin. 44 N2
Kemijoki *r.* Fin. 44 N2
Kemin Kyrg. 103 H4
formerly known as Bystrovka
Keminmaa Fin. 44 N2
Kemiö Fin. *see* **Kimito**
Kemir Turkm. *see* **Keymir**
Kemlya Rus. Fed. 40 H5
Kemmerer U.S.A. 180 E4
Kemmuna *i.* Malta 57 G12
also known as Comino
Kémo *pref.* Cent. Afr. Rep. 126 C3
Kemp, Lake U.S.A. 179 C5
Kempazh *r.* Rus. Fed. 40 L2
Kempele Fin. 44 N2
Kempen *reg.* Belgium 51 K1
Kempendyay Rus. Fed. 39 L3
Kempisch Kanaal *canal* Belgium 51 L1
Kemp Land *reg.* Antarctica 223 D2
Kemp Peninsula Antarctica 222 U2
Kemp's Bay Bahamas 186 D1
Kempsey Australia 147 G2
Kempt, Lac *l.* Canada 169 F4
Kempten (Allgäu) Germany 48 H8
Kempton Australia 147 E5
Kempton Park S. Africa 133 M3
Kemptville Canada 173 R5
Kemujan *i.* Indon. 77 E4
Ken *r.* India 96 D4
Kenabeek Canada 173 N3
Kenai U.S.A. 164 D3
Kenai Fiords National Park U.S.A. 164 D4
Kenai Mountains U.S.A. 164 D4
Kenamu *r.* Canada 169 J2
Kenamuke Swamp Sudan 128 B3
Kenansville U.S.A. 174 E5
Kenbridge U.S.A. 176 G9
Kendal Indon. 77 E4
Kendal U.K. 47 J9
Kendall *r.* Australia 149 D2
Kendall U.S.A. 175 D7
Kendall, Cape Canada 167 O2
Kendall, Mount N.Z. 152 G9
Kendallville U.S.A. 172 H9
Kendari Indon. 75 B3
Kendawangan Indon. 77 E3
Kendawangan *r.* Indon. 77 E3
Kendégué Chad 126 C2
Kendrikí Makedhonía *admin. reg.* Greece *see* **Kentriki Makedonia**
Kendrapara India 95 E1
Kendrew S. Africa 133 I9
Kendrick Peak U.S.A. 183 M6
Kendua Bangl. 97 F4
Kendyktas *mts* Kazakh. 103 H4
Kendyrli-Kayasanskoye, Plato *plat.* Kazakh. 102 C4
Kendyrlisor, Solonchak *salt l.* Kazakh. 102 C4
Kenedy U.S.A. 179 C6
Keneka *r.* S. Africa 133 N7
Kenema Sierra Leone 124 C5
Kenepai, Gunung *mt.* Indon. 77 E2
Kenge Dem. Rep. Congo 126 C6
Kengere Dem. Rep. Congo 127 E7
Keng Hkam Myanmar 78 B3
Kengis Sweden 44 M2
Kengkhar Bhutan 97 F4
Keng Lap Myanmar 78 C3
Keng Lon Myanmar 78 B3
Keng-Peli Uzbek. 102 D4
Keng Tawng Myanmar 78 B3
Kengtung Myanmar 78 B3
Kenhardt S. Africa 132 F6
Kéniéba Mali 124 C3
Kéniébaoulé, Réserve de *nature res.* Mali 124 C3
Kénitra Morocco 122 D2
formerly known as Port-Lyautey
Kenli China 85 H4
Kenmare Ireland 47 C12
Kenmare U.S.A. 178 B1
Kenmare River *inlet* Ireland 47 B12
Kenmaur Zimbabwe 131 F3
Kenmore U.S.A. 176 G3
Kenn Germany 48 D6
Kennebec U.S.A. 178 C3
Kennebec *r.* U.S.A. 174 G2
Kennebunk U.S.A. 177 O2
Kennebunkport U.S.A. 177 O2
Kennedy Australia 149 E3
Kennedy *r.* Australia 149 E2
Kennedy, Cape U.S.A. *see* **Canaveral, Cape**
Kennedy Range *hills* Australia 151 A5
Kennedy Range National Park Australia 151 A5
Kennedy's Vale S. Africa 133 O1
Kennedy Town *Hong Kong* China 87 [inset]
Kennedyville U.S.A. 177 J6
Kenner U.S.A. 175 B6
Kennet *r.* U.K. 47 L12
Kenneth Range *hills* Australia 150 B4
Kennett U.S.A. 174 B4
Kennewick U.S.A. 180 C3
Kenogami *r.* Canada 168 C3
Kenogami Lake Canada 173 M2
Kenogamissi Lake Canada 173 L2
Keno Hill Canada 166 C2
Kenora Canada 167 M5
Kenosha U.S.A. 172 F8
Kenova U.S.A. 176 C7
Kenozero, Ozero *l.* Rus. Fed. 40 F3
Kensington Canada 169 I4
Kent *OH* U.S.A. 176 D4
Kent *TX* U.S.A. 181 F7
Kent *VA* U.S.A. 176 D9
Kent *WA* U.S.A. 180 B3
Kentani S. Africa 133 M9
also spelt Centane
Kentau Kazakh. 103 G4
Kent Group *is* Australia 147 E4
Kentland U.S.A. 174 C3
Kenton *MI* U.S.A. 172 E4
Kenton *OH* U.S.A. 176 B5
Kenton-on-Sea S. Africa 133 K10
Kent Peninsula Canada 165 I3
Kentriki Makedonia *admin. reg.* Greece 58 E8
also spelt Kendrikí Makedhonía
Kentucky *r.* U.S.A. 176 B8
Kentucky *state* U.S.A. 176 A8
Kentucky Lake U.S.A. 174 B4
Kentwood *LA* U.S.A. 175 B6
Kentwood *MI* U.S.A. 172 H8
▸**Kenya** *country* Africa 128 C4
▸▸114–115 **Africa** Countries

▸**Kenya, Mount** Kenya 128 C5
2nd highest mountain in Africa. Also known as Kirinyaga.
▸▸110–111 **Africa** Landscapes

Kenyir, Tasik *resr* Malaysia 76 C1
Kenzingen Germany 48 E7
Keokuk U.S.A. 174 B3
Keoladeo National Park India 96 C4
UNESCO World Heritage Site
Keonjhar India 97 E5
Keosauqua U.S.A. 174 B3
Keowee, Lake *resr* U.S.A. 174 D5
Kepa Rus. Fed. 44 P2
Kepa *r.* Rus. Fed. 44 P2
Kepahiang Indon. 76 C3

Kokterek Kazakh. 103 I3
Koktobe Kazakh. 103 I1
Koktokay *Xinjiang* China see **Fuyun**
Koktokay *Xinjiang* China 84 A2
Koktuma Kazakh. 88 C2
Koku, Tanjung *pt* Indon. 75 B4
Kokubu Japan 91 B9
Kok-Yangak Kyrg. see **Kök-Janggak**
Kokyar China 88 B4
Kokzhayyk Kazakh. 88 C1
  formerly known as Ivanovka
Kola Rus. Fed. 44 P1
Kola *r.* Rus. Fed. 44 P1
Kolab *r.* India see **Sabari**
Kolabira India 97 E5
Kolachi *r.* Pak. 101 F5
Kola Diba Eth. 104 B5
Kolaghat India 97 E5
Kolahoi *mt.* Jammu and Kashmir 96 B2
Kolaka Indon. 75 B4
Kolana Indon. 75 C5
Ko Lanta Thai. 79 B7
Kola Peninsula Rus. Fed. 40 F2
  also known as Kol'skiy Poluostrov
Kolar *Chhattisgarh* India 94 D2
Kolar *Karnataka* India 94 C3
Kolaras India 96 C4
Kolar Gold Fields India 94 C3
Kolari India 44 M2
Kolarovgrad Bulg. see **Shumen**
Kolašin *Crna Gora* Serb. and Mont. 58 A6
Kolayat India 96 B4
Kolbano Indon. 75 C5
Kolberg Poland see **Kołobrzeg**
Kolbio Kenya 128 D5
Kolchanovo Rus. Fed. 43 N1
Kol'chugino Rus. Fed. 43 U5
Kolda Senegal 124 B3
Kolding Denmark 45 J5
Kole *Kasai Oriental* Dem. Rep. Congo 126 D5
Kole *Orientale* Dem. Rep. Congo 126 E4
Koléa Alg. 55 N8
Kolendo Rus. Fed. 82 F1
Koler Sweden 44 M2
Kolga-Jaani Estonia 42 G3
Kolguyev, Ostrov *i.* Rus. Fed. 40 I1
Kolhan *reg.* India 97 E5
Kolhapur India 94 B2
Kolho Fin. 45 N3
Kolhumadulu Atoll Maldives 93 D10
Koliba *r.* Guinea/Guinea-Bissau 124 B3
Kolikata India see **Kolkata**
Kolima *l.* Fin. 44 N3
Kolín Czech Rep. 49 M5
Kolin *kansallispuisto nat. park* Fin. 44 O3
K'olíto Eth. 128 C3
Kõljala Estonia 42 D3
Kolkasrags *pt* Latvia 42 D4

▶Kolkata India 97 F5
  4th most populous city in Asia, and 7th in the world. Also spelt Calcutta *or* Kolikata.
  ▶▶18–19 World Cities

Kolkhozabad Tajik. see **Kolkhozobod**
Kolkhozobod Tajik. 101 G2
  also spelt Kolkhozabad; *formerly known as* Kaganovichabad
Kollam India see **Quilon**
Kollegal India 94 C3
Kolleru Lake India 94 D2
  also known as Colair Lake
Kollo Niger 125 F3
Köln Germany see **Cologne**
Kolno Poland 49 S2
Kofo Poland 49 N5
Kolo Tanz. 129 B6
Kołobrzeg Poland 49 M1
  historically known as Kolberg
Kolodenskoye, Ozero *l.* Rus. Fed. 43 S2
Kologriv Rus. Fed. 40 H4
Kolokani Mali 124 C3
Kolokolkova, Guba *b.* Rus. Fed. 40 J1
Koloksha *r.* Rus. Fed. 43 V5
Kolombangara *i.* Solomon Is 145 E2
  also known as Nduke
Kolomea Ukr. see **Kolomyya**
Kolomna Rus. Fed. 43 T6
Kolomonyi Dem. Rep. Congo 126 D6
Kolomyja Ukr. see **Kolomyya**
Kolomyya Ukr. 41 C6
  also spelt Kolomea *or* Kołomyja
Kolondiéba Mali 124 D4
Kolonedale Indon. 75 B3
Kolonjë Albania 58 A8
Kolonkwaneng Botswana 130 D5
Kolono Indon. 75 B4
Koloshma *r.* Rus. Fed. 43 Q1
Kolowana Watobo, Teluk *b.* Indon. 75 B4
Kolozero, Ozero *l.* Rus. Fed. 44 P1
Kolozsvár Romania see **Cluj-Napoca**
Kolp' *r.* Rus. Fed. 43 R2
Kolpashevo Rus. Fed. 39 I4
Kolpino Rus. Fed. 43 Q2
Kolpny Rus. Fed. 43 R9
Kol'qduduq Uzbek. 103 E4
  also spelt Kalqudauq
Kol'skiy Poluostrov *pen.* Rus. Fed. see **Kola Peninsula**
Kölsvallen Sweden 45 K3
Koltubanovskiy Rus. Fed. 102 B1
Kolubara *r.* Serb. and Mont. 58 B4
Kölük Turkey see **Kâhta**
Koluli Eritrea 121 I6
Koluton Kazakh. 103 G2
Kolva *r.* Rus. Fed. 40 K2
Kolva *r.* Rus. Fed. 40 K3
Kolvereid Norway 44 J2
Kolvik Norway 44 N1
Kolvitsa Rus. Fed. 44 P2
Kolvitskoye, Ozero *l.* Rus. Fed. 44 P2
Kolwa *reg.* Pak. 101 F5
Kolwezi Dem. Rep. Congo 127 E7
Kolya *r.* Rus. Fed. 39 Q3
Kolyma *r.* Rus. Fed. 39 Q3
Kolyma Lowland Rus. Fed. see **Kolymskaya Nizmennost'**
Kolyma Range Rus. Fed. see **Kolymskiy, Khrebet**
Kolymskaya Nizmennost' *lowland* Rus. Fed. 39 P3
  English form Kolyma Lowland
Kolymskiy, Khrebet *mts* Rus. Fed. 39 Q3
  English form Kolyma Range; *also known as* Gydan, Khrebet
Kolymskoye Vodokhranilishche *resr* Rus. Fed. 39 O3
Kolyshley Rus. Fed. 41 I6
Kolyuchinskaya Guba *b.* Rus. Fed. 39 S3
Kolyvan' Rus. Fed. 80 D1
Kol'zhat Kazakh. 88 C3
Kom China 88 D1
Kom *mt.* Bulg. 58 E5
Komadugu-gana *watercourse* Nigeria 125 I3
Komaga-take *mt.* Japan 90 F6
Komaga-take *vol.* Japan 90 G3
Komaggas S. Africa 132 B6
Komaggas Mountains S. Africa 132 B6
Komaki Japan 91 E7
Komandnaya, Gora *mt.* Rus. Fed. 82 C2
Komandorskiye Ostrova *is* Rus. Fed. 39 Q4
Komarichi Rus. Fed. 43 P9
Komárno Slovakia 49 P8

Koza Rus. Fed. 43 U3
Kozağacı Turkey see Günyüzü
Kō-zaki pt Japan 91 A7
Kozan Turkey 106 C3
also known as Sis
Kozani Greece 59 C8
Kozar, Ras pt Eritrea 104 C5
Kozara mts Bos.-Herz. 56 I3
Kozara nat. park Bos.-Herz. 56 J3
Kozarska Dubica Bos.-Herz. see Bosanska Dubica
Kozel'sk Rus. Fed. 43 Q7
Kozen well Chad 120 C4
Kozhabakhy Kazakh. 103 E3
Kozhakol', Ozero l. Kazakh. 103 G2
also known as Qozhaköl
Kozhevnikovo Rus. Fed. 39 L2
Kozhikode India see Calicut
Kozhim-Iz, Gora mt. Rus. Fed. 40 K3
Kozhva Rus. Fed. 40 K2
Kozhva r. Rus. Fed. 40 K2
Kozhym r. Rus. Fed. 40 K2
Kozienice Poland 49 S4
Kozlikha Rus. Fed. 43 V1
Kozloduy Bulg. 58 E5
Kozlovka Chuvashskaya Respublika Rus. Fed. 40 I5
Kozlovka Voronezhskaya Oblast' Rus. Fed. 41 G6
Kozlovo Rus. Fed. 43 R5
Kozlu Turkey 106 B2
Kozluk Bos.-Herz. 56 L4
Koźmin Wielkopowski Poland 49 O4
Koz'modem'yansk Rus. Fed. 40 H4
Kozmoldak Kazakh. 103 G4
Koznitsa mt. Bulg. 58 E6
Kożuchów Poland 49 M4
Kožuf mts Greece/Macedonia 58 D7
Kōzu-shima i. Japan 91 F7
Kozyatyn Ukr. 41 D6
also spelt Kazatin
Kozyörük Turkey 58 H7
Kpalimé Togo 125 F5
Kpandae Ghana 125 E4
Kpandu Ghana 125 F5
Kpungan Pass India/Myanmar 97 H4
Kra, Isthmus of isthmus Thai. 79 B6
Kraai r. S. Africa 133 K7
Kraankuil S. Africa 132 I6
Krabi Estonia 42 H4
Krabi Thai. 79 B6
Kra Buri Thai. 79 B6
Krâchéh Cambodia 79 D5
also spelt Kratie
Kräckelbäcken Sweden 45 K3
Kraftino, Ozero l. Rus. Fed. 43 P4
Kragan Indon. 77 E4
Kragerø Norway 45 J4
Kragujevac Srbija Serb. and Mont. 58 B4
Krajenka Poland 49 O2
Krakatau i. Indon. 77 D4
Krakatau Volcano National Park Indon. 76 D4
Krakau Poland see Kraków
Kråklivollen Norway 44 J3
Kraków Poland 49 Q5
historically known as Cracovia or Cracow or Krakau
UNESCO World Heritage Site
Krakow U.S.A. 172 E6
Kralendijk Neth. Antilles 187 F4
Kraljevića Croatia 56 G3
Kraljevo Srbija Serb. and Mont. 58 B5
formerly known as Rankovićevo
Kráľova hoľa mt. Slovakia 49 R7
Kráľovský Chlmec Slovakia 49 S7
Kralupy nad Vltavou Czech Rep. 49 L5
Kramators'k Ukr. 41 F6
Kramfors Sweden 44 L3
Krammer est. Neth. 48 B4
Kranidi Greece 59 E11
Kranj Slovenia 56 G2
Kranji Reservoir Sing. 76 [inset]
Kransfontein S. Africa 133 M5
Kranskop S. Africa 133 O5
Kranskop mt. S. Africa 133 N4
Krapanj Croatia 56 H5
Krapina Croatia 56 H2
Krapinske Toplice Croatia 56 H2
Krapivna Kaluzhskaya Oblast' Rus. Fed. 43 Q8
Krapivna Smolenskaya Oblast' Rus. Fed. 43 O7
Krapkowice Poland 49 O5
Krasavino Rus. Fed. 40 H3
Krasilov Ukr. see Krasyliv
Krasino Rus. Fed. 40 J1
Kraskino Rus. Fed. 82 C4
Krāslava Latvia 42 I6
Kraslice Czech Rep. 49 J5
Krasnapollye Belarus 43 M8
Krasnasyel'ski Belarus 42 F8
Krasnaya Gora Rus. Fed. 43 M8
Krasnaya Gorbatka Rus. Fed. 40 G5
Krasnaya Polyana Kazakh. 103 H2
Krasnaya Polyana Rus. Fed. 41 G8
Krasnaya Slabada Belarus 42 I9
Krasnaya Zarya Rus. Fed. 43 S9
Kraśnik Poland 49 T5
Krasnoarmeysk Kazakh. see Tayynsha
Krasnoarmeysk Moskovskaya Oblast' Rus. Fed. 43 T5
Krasnoarmeysk Saratovskaya Oblast' Rus. Fed. 41 H6
Krasnoarmeysk Ukr. see Krasnoarmiys'k
Krasnoarmeyskaya Rus. Fed. see Poltavskaya
Krasnoarmeyskiy Chukotskiy Avtonomnyy Okrug Rus. Fed. 39 R3
Krasnoarmeyskiy Rostovskaya Oblast' Rus. Fed. 41 G7
formerly known as Kuberle
Krasnoarmiys'k Ukr. 41 F6
also spelt Krasnoarmeysk; formerly known as Chervonoarmiys'k or Grishino or Postysheve
Krasnoborskiy Rus. Fed. 43 Q2
Krasnoborsk Rus. Fed. 40 H3
Krasnodar Rus. Fed. 41 F7
formerly known as Yekaterinodar
Krasnodar Kray admin. div. Rus. Fed. see Krasnodarskiy Kray
Krasnodarskiy Kray admin. div. Rus. Fed. 41 F7
English form Krasnodar Kray
Krasnodon Ukr. 41 F6
Krasnofarfornyy Rus. Fed. 43 M2
Krasnogorka Kazakh. see Ul'ken Sulutor
Krasnogorodskoye Rus. Fed. 43 J5
Krasnogorsk Moskovskaya Oblast' Rus. Fed. 43 S6
Krasnogorsk Sakhalin Rus. Fed. 82 F2
Krasnogorskoye Rus. Fed. 40 J4
Krasnograd Ukr. see Krasnohrad
Krasnogvardeysk Uzbek. see Bulung'ur
Krasnogvardeyskiy Rus. Fed. 43 S6
Krasnogvardeyskoye Rus. Fed. 41 G7
formerly known as Yevdokimovskoye
Krasnohrad Ukr. 41 E6
also spelt Krasnograd; formerly known as Konstantinograd
Krasnohvardiys'ke Ukr. 41 E7
Krasnokamensk Rus. Fed. 85 H1
Krasnokamsk Rus. Fed. 40 J4
Krasnokholm Rus. Fed. 102 C2
Krasnokutsk Kazakh. see Aktogay
Krasnokutskoye Kazakh. see Aktogay
Krasnolesnyy Rus. Fed. 41 F6
Krasnoles'ye Rus. Fed. 42 D7
Krasnomayskiy Rus. Fed. 43 P4
Krasnoostrovskiy Rus. Fed. 43 J1
Krasnoperekops'k Ukr. 41 E7
Krasnopol'ye Rus. Fed. 82 F2
Krasnorechenskiy Rus. Fed. 82 D3
Krasnosel'kup Rus. Fed. 39 I3
Krasnosel'skoye Rus. Fed. 43 K1
Krasnoslobodsk Rus. Fed. 41 G5
Krasnotur'insk Rus. Fed. 38 G4
Krasnoufimsk Rus. Fed. 40 K4
Krasnousol'skiy Rus. Fed. 40 K5
Krasnovishersk Rus. Fed. 40 K3
Krasnovodsk Turkm. see Türkmenbaşy
Krasnovodskaya Oblast' admin. div. Turkm. see Balkanskaya Oblast'
Krasnovodskoye Plato plat. Turkm. 102 C4
Krasnoyarovo Rus. Fed. 82 C2
Krasnoyarsk Rus. Fed. 80 E1
Krasnoyarskiy Rus. Fed. 102 D2
Krasnoyarskiy Kray admin. div. Rus. Fed. 80 E1
English form Krasnoyarsk Kray
Krasnoyarsk Kray admin. div. Rus. Fed. see Krasnoyarskiy Kray
Krasnoye Belgorodskaya Oblast' Rus. Fed. 41 F6
Krasnoye Bryanskaya Oblast' Rus. Fed. 43 O8
Krasnoye Lipetskaya Oblast' Rus. Fed. 43 T9
Krasnoye Pskovskaya Oblast' Rus. Fed. 43 K5
Krasnoye Respublika Kalmykiya - Khalm'g-Tangch Rus. Fed. see Ulan Erge
Krasnoye Smolenskaya Oblast' Rus. Fed. 43 M7
Krasnoye, Ozero l. Rus. Fed. 39 R3
Krasnoye Plamya Rus. Fed. 43 T5
Krasnoye Znamya Rus. Fed. 43 Q4
Krasnozatonskiy Rus. Fed. 40 I3
Krasnozavodsk Rus. Fed. 43 T5
Krasnoznamensk Rus. Fed. 42 D7
Krasnoznamenskiy Kazakh. see Yegindykol'
Krasnystaw Poland 49 U5
Krasnyy Rus. Fed. 43 M7
Krasnyy Chikoy Rus. Fed. 85 F1
Krasnyye Baki Rus. Fed. 40 H4
Krasnyye Barrikady Rus. Fed. 102 A3
Krasnyye Tkachi Rus. Fed. 43 U4
Krasnyy Kamyshanik Rus. Fed. see Komsomol'skiy
Krasnyy Kholm Rus. Fed. 43 S3
Krasnyy Kut Rus. Fed. 102 A2
Krasnyy Luch Rus. Fed. 43 L4
Krasnyy Luch Ukr. 41 F6
Krasnyy Lyman Ukr. 41 F6
Krasnyy Oktyabr' Rus. Fed. 43 T5
Krasnyy Profintern Rus. Fed. 43 V4
Krasnyy Rog Bryanskaya Oblast' Rus. Fed. 43 O8
Krasnyy Rog Bryanskaya Oblast' Rus. Fed. 43 O9
Krasnyy Tekstil'shchik Rus. Fed. 41 H6
Krasnyy Yar Kazakh. 103 G1
Krasnyy Yar Rus. Fed. 102 B3
Krasyliv Ukr. 41 C6
also spelt Krasilov
Kratie Cambodia see Krâchéh
Kratovo Macedonia 58 D6
Krauja Latvia 42 H6
Kraul Mountains Antarctica 223 X2
Kraulshavn Greenland see Nuussuaq
Krâvanh, Chuŏr Phnum mts Cambodia see Cardamom Range
Kraynovka Rus. Fed. 102 A4
Krechevitsy Rus. Fed. 43 M3
Krefeld Germany 48 D4
Krekenava Lith. 42 F6
Kremaston, Techniti Limni resr Greece 59 C10
Kremen mt. Croatia 56 H4
Kremenchug Ukr. see Kremenchuk
Kremenchuk Ukr. 41 E6
also spelt Kremenchug
Kremenchuts'ka Vodoskhovyshche resr Ukr. 41 E6
Kremenki Rus. Fed. 43 S7
Kremenskoye Rus. Fed. 43 Q6
Kremges Ukr. see Svitlovods'k
Kreml' Rus. Fed. see Solovetskiy
Kremmidi, Akra pt Greece 59 E12
Kremmling U.S.A. 180 F4
Krems an der Donau Austria 49 M7
Kremsmünster Austria 49 L7
Krenitzin Islands U.S.A. 164 C4
Krepoljin Srbija Serb. and Mont. 58 C4
Kresna Bulg. 58 E7
Kresta, Zaliv g. Rus. Fed. 39 S3
Krestena Greece 59 C11
Krest-Khal'dzhayy Rus. Fed. 39 N3
Krestovka Rus. Fed. 40 J2
Kresttsy Rus. Fed. 43 N3
Kresty Moskovskaya Oblast' Rus. Fed. 43 S6
Kresty Pskovskaya Oblast' Rus. Fed. 43 M6
Kresty Tul'skaya Oblast' Rus. Fed. 43 T8
Krestyakh Rus. Fed. 39 L3
Kretinga Lith. 42 C6
Kreuth Germany 48 I8
Kreuzau Germany 48 D5
Kreuzeck Gruppe mts Austria 49 K9
Kreuzlingen Switz. 51 P5
Kreuztal Germany 48 E5
Kreva Belarus 42 H7
Kribi Cameroon 125 H6
Krichev Belarus see Krychaw
Krichim Bulg. 58 F6
Krieglach Austria 49 M8
Kriel S. Africa 133 N3
Krievukalns hill Latvia 42 C5
Krieza Greece 59 F10
Krikellos Greece 59 C10
Krikelos, Akra pt Greece 59 H12
Krikovo Moldova see Cricova
Kril'on, Mys c. Rus. Fed. 82 F3
Krios, Akra pt Greece 59 E13
Krishna r. India 94 D2
formerly known as Kistna
Krishnagiri India 94 C3
Krishnai r. India 97 F4
Krishnanagar India 97 F5
Krishnaraja Sagara l. India 94 C3
Krishnarajpet India 94 C3
Kristdala Sweden 45 L4
Kristiania Norway see Oslo
Kristiansand Norway 45 I4
Kristianstad Sweden 45 K4
Kristiansund Norway 44 I3
Kristiinankaupunki Fin. see Kristinestad
Kristinehamn Sweden 45 K4
Kristinestad Fin. 45 M3
also known as Kristiinankaupunki
Kristinopol' Ukr. see Chervonohrad
Kriti admin. reg. Greece 59 F14
Kriti i. Greece see Crete
Kriūkai Lith. 42 E6
Kriulyany Moldova see Criuleni
Kriusha Rus. Fed. 43 U7
Krivača mt. Serb. and Mont. 58 B5
Krivaja r. Bos.-Herz. 56 K4
Krivandino Rus. Fed. 43 U6
Kriva Palanka Macedonia 58 D6
Kriva Reka r. Macedonia 58 C6
Křivoklátská vrchovina hills Czech Rep. 49 K6
Krivoles Rus. Fed. 43 N8
Krivoy Porog Rus. Fed. 40 E2
Krivoy Rog Ukr. see Kryvyy Rih
Križevci Croatia 56 I2
Krk mt. Bos.-Herz. 56 L4
Krk Croatia 56 G3
Krk i. Croatia 56 G3
Krka r. Croatia 56 H5
Krka r. Slovenia 56 H3
Krkonošský národní park nat. park Czech Rep./Poland 49 M5
also known as Karkonoski Park Narodowy
Krnjača Srbija Serb. and Mont. 58 B4
Krnov Czech Rep. 49 O5
Krobia Poland 49 N4
Krohnwodoke Liberia 124 D5
Kroknes Norway 44 O1
Krokom Sweden 44 K3
Króksfjarðarnes Iceland 44 [inset] B2
Krokstadøra Norway 44 J3
Krolevets' Ukr. 41 E6
Kroma r. Rus. Fed. 43 Q9
Kromdraai S. Africa 133 N2
Kroměříž Czech Rep. 49 O6
UNESCO World Heritage Site
Kromy Rus. Fed. 43 Q9
Kronach Germany 48 I5
Kronfjell hill Norway 45 J4
Kröng Kaôh Kŏng Cambodia 79 C6
Kronli India 97 G3
Kronoberg county Sweden 45 K4
Kronoby Fin. 44 M3
Kronotskiy Poluostrov pen. Rus. Fed. 39 Q4
Kronotskiy Zaliv b. Rus. Fed. 39 Q4
Kronotskoye Ozero l. Rus. Fed. 39 Q4
Kronprins Christian Land reg. Greenland 165 Q1
Kronprins Frederik Bjerge nunataks Greenland 165 P3
Kronshagen Germany 48 H1
Kronshtadt Rus. Fed. 43 K2
English form Kronstadt
Kronstadt Romania see Brașov
Kronstadt Rus. Fed. see Kronshtadt
Kroonstad S. Africa 133 L4
Kropotkin Rus. Fed. 41 G7
Kropp Germany 48 G1
Krosno Poland 49 S6
Krosno Odrzańskie Poland 49 M3
Krossen Norway 45 J4
Krotoszyn Poland 49 O4
Krotz Springs U.S.A. 175 B6
Krousonas Greece 59 F13
Kroya Indon. 77 E4
Krško Slovenia 56 H3
Krstača mt. Serb. and Mont. 58 B6
Krugersdorp S. Africa 133 K5
Kruger National Park S. Africa 133 P2
Krugersdorp S. Africa 133 L3
Krugerspos S. Africa 133 O1
Kruglyakov Rus. Fed. see Oktyabr'skiy
Kruhlaye Belarus 43 K7
Krui Indon. 76 C4
Kruidfontein S. Africa 132 F9
Kruisfontein S. Africa 133 I11
Krujë Albania 58 A7
Krumë Albania 58 B6
Krumovgrad Bulg. 58 G7
Krungkao Thai. see Ayutthaya
Krung Thep Thai. see Bangkok
Kruoja r. Lith. 42 E5
Krupa Bos.-Herz. see Bosanska Krupa
Krupa na Uni Bos.-Herz. see Bosanska Krupa
Krupanj Srbija Serb. and Mont. 58 A4
Krupina Slovakia 49 Q7
Krupki Belarus 43 K7
Kruševac Srbija Serb. and Mont. 58 C5
Kruševo Macedonia 58 C7
Krušné hory mts Czech Rep. 49 J5
Krustkalnu rezervāts nature res. Latvia 42 H5
Kruszwica Poland 49 P3
Krutoye Orlovskaya Oblast' Rus. Fed. 43 S9
Krutoye Smolenskaya Oblast' Rus. Fed. 43 M6
Kruzof Island U.S.A. 166 C3
Krybinka r. Belarus 43 K6
Krychaw Belarus 43 M8
also spelt Krichev
Kryezi Albania 58 B6
Krym' pen. Ukr. see Crimea
Krymsk Rus. Fed. 41 F7
formerly known as Krymskaya
Krymskaya Rus. Fed. see Krymsk
Kryms'kyy Pivostriv pen. Ukr. see Crimea
Kryms'kyy Zapovidnyk nature res. Ukr. 106 C1
Krynica Poland 49 R6
Krynica Morska Poland 49 Q1
Krynki Belarus 43 L6
Krystynopol Ukr. see Chervonohrad
Krytiko Pelagos sea Greece 59 G12
Kryvichy Belarus 42 I7
Kryvyy Rih Ukr. 41 E7
also spelt Krivoy Rog
Krzepice Poland 49 P5
Krzna r. Poland 49 U3
Krzna Południowa r. Poland 49 T4
Krzyż Wielkopolski Poland 49 N3
Ksabi Alg. 123 E3
Ksar Chellala Alg. 55 N9
formerly known as Reïbell
Ksar el Boukhari Alg. 123 F2
formerly known as Boghari
Ksar el Hirane Alg. 123 F2
Ksar el Kebir Morocco 122 D2
formerly spelt Alcazarquivir
Ksar-es-Souk Morocco see Er Rachidia
Ksenofontova Rus. Fed. 40 J3
Kshen' r. Rus. Fed. 43 S9
Ksour, Monts des mts Alg. 120 A1
Ksour, Monts des mts Tunisia 123 H2
Ksour Essaf Tunisia 123 H2
Kstovo Rus. Fed. 40 H4
Ktsyn' Rus. Fed. 43 Q8
Kū', Jabal al hill Saudi Arabia 105 D2
Ku, Wadi el watercourse Sudan 121 E6
Kuaidamao China see Tonghua
Kuala Belait Brunei 77 F1
Kuala Dungun Malaysia see Dungun
Kualajelai Indon. 77 E3
Kuala Kangsar Malaysia 76 C1
Kualakapuas Indon. 77 F3
Kuala Kerai Malaysia 76 C1
Kualakuayan Indon. 77 F3
Kuala Kubu Baharu Malaysia 76 C2
Kualakurun Indon. 77 F3
Kuala Lipis Malaysia 76 C1

►Kuala Lumpur Malaysia 76 C2
Joint capital of Malaysia.
►►8–9 World Countries

Kualapembuang Indon. 77 F3
Kuala Penyu Sabah Malaysia 77 F1
Kuala Pilah Malaysia 76 C2
Kualapu'u U.S.A. 181 [inset] Z1
Kualasampit Indon. 77 F3
Kualasimpang Indon. 76 B1
Kuala Terengganu Malaysia 76 C1
Kualatungal Indon. 76 C3
Kuamut Sabah Malaysia 77 G1
Kuamut r. Sabah Malaysia 77 G1
Kuancheng China 85 H3
Kuandian China 83 B4
Kuangyuan China see Yiliang
Kuanshan Taiwan 87 G4
Kuantan Malaysia 76 C2
Kuaotunu N.Z. 152 J4
Kuba Azer. see Quba
Kuban' r. Rus. Fed. 41 F7
Kubār Syria 109 K2
Kubārah Oman 105 G3
Kübassaare poolsaar pen. Estonia 42 E3
Kubaysah Iraq 107 E4
Kubbum Sudan 126 D2
Kubena r. Rus. Fed. 43 U2
Kubenskoye Rus. Fed. 43 U2
Kubenskoye, Ozero l. Rus. Fed. 43 U2
Kuberle Rus. Fed. see Krasnoarmeyskiy
Kubinka Rus. Fed. 43 R6
Kubitzer Bodden b. Germany 49 K1
Kubnya r. Rus. Fed. 40 I5
Kubokawa Japan 91 C8
►Kubor, Mount P.N.G. 73 J8
►►134–135 Oceania Landscapes
Kubrat Bulg. 58 H5
Kubrinsk Rus. Fed. 43 T5
Kubumesaäi Indon. 77 F2
Kučevo Srbija Serb. and Mont. 58 C4
Kuchaman India 96 B4
Kuchema Rus. Fed. 40 G2
Kuchera India 96 B4
Kuching Sarawak Malaysia 77 E2
also spelt Kucing
Kuchinotsu Japan 91 B8
Kuchurhan r. Ukr. 58 K2
Kucing Sarawak Malaysia see Kuching
Kuçovë Albania 58 A8
formerly known as Qyteti Stalin
Küçükköy Turkey 59 H9
Küçükmenderes r. Turkey 59 H8
Küçükmenderes r. Turkey 59 I11
Kuda India 96 A5
Kudachi India 94 B2
Kudal India 94 B3
Kudamatsu Japan 91 B8
Kudap Indon. 76 C2
Kudara-Somon Rus. Fed. 85 E1
Kudat Sabah Malaysia 77 G1
Kudev r. Rus. Fed. 42 J4
Kudever' Rus. Fed. 43 K5
Kudirkos Naumiestis Lith. 42 D7
Kudligi India 94 C3
Kudremukh mt. India 94 B3
Kudrinskaya Rus. Fed. 43 Q7
Kudu Nigeria 125 G4
Kudus Indon. 77 E4
Kudymkar Rus. Fed. 40 J4
Kueishan Tao i. Taiwan 87 G3
Kūfah Iraq see Al Kūfah
Kufstein Austria 48 J8
Kugaaruk Canada 165 K3
Kugaly Kazakh. 103 I3
also spelt Qoghaly
Kugesi Rus. Fed. 40 H4
Kugka Lhai China 89 E6
Kugluktuk Canada 165 H3
formerly known as Coppermine
Kugmallit Bay Canada 164 F3
Kūh, Ra's-al- pt Iran 100 D5
Kūhak Iran 101 E5
Kūhbonān Iran 100 D4
Kūhdasht Iran 100 A3
Kūhestak Iran 100 D5
Kūhīn Iran 100 B2
Kūhīrī Iran 101 E5
Kŭhistoni Badakhshon aut. rep. Tajik. 101 H2
also known as Gorno-Badakhshan or Gornyy Badakhshan; formerly known as Badakhshoni Kŭhī; short form Badakhshan
Kühlung park Germany 48 I1
Kühlungsborn, Ostseebad Germany 48 I1
Kuhmo Fin. 44 O2
Kuhmoinen Fin. 45 N3
Kūhpāyeh Iran 100 C3
Kūhpāyeh mt. Iran 100 D4
Kūhrān, Kūh-e mt. Iran 100 D5
Kühtang r. Iran 100 B4
Kui Buri Thai. 79 B5
Kuimetsa Estonia 42 G2
Kuis Namibia 130 C5
Kuiseb watercourse Namibia 130 B4
Kuitan China 87 E4
Kuitin China see Kuytun
Kuito Angola 127 C8
formerly known as Bié
Kuiu Island U.S.A. 166 C3
Kuivaniemi Fin. 44 N2
Kuivastu Estonia 42 E3
Kuja r. Latvia 42 H5
Kujang India 95 E1
Kujang N. Korea 83 B5
Kuji Japan 90 G4
Kuji-wan b. Japan 90 G4
Kujū-san vol. Japan 91 B8
Kukālār, Kūh-e hill Iran 100 B4
Kukan Rus. Fed. 82 D2
Kukatush Canada 173 K2
Kukawa Nigeria 125 I3
Kukerin Australia 151 B7
Kukës Albania 58 B6
Kuki Japan 91 F6
Kukkola Fin. 44 N2
Kukmor Rus. Fed. 40 I4
Kukoboy Rus. Fed. 43 U3
Kukruse Estonia 42 I2
Kukshi India 96 B5
Kukunuru India 94 D2
Kukup Malaysia 76 C2
Kükürtli Turkm. 102 D5
formerly known as Sernyy Zavod
Kukusan, Gunung hill Indon. 77 F3
Kukushtan Rus. Fed. 40 K4
Kül r. Iran 100 C5
Kula Bulg. 58 D5
Kula r. Moldova see Cula
Kula Nigeria 125 G5
Kula Vojvodina, Srbija Serb. and Mont. 58 A3
Kula mt. Serb. and Mont. 58 A6
Kula Turkey 106 B3
Kulabu, Gunung mt. Indon. 76 B2
Kulachi Pak. 101 G4
Kulagi Rus. Fed. 43 N9
Kulagino Kazakh. 102 B2
Kula Kangri mt. Bhutan 97 F3
Kulal, Mount Kenya 128 C4
Kulaly, Ostrov i. Kazakh. 102 B3
also known as Qulaly Araly
Kulan Kazakh. 103 H4
Kulandy Kazakh. 102 D3
also spelt Qulandy
Kulaneh reg. Pak. 101 E5
Kulanotpes watercourse Kazakh. 103 G2
also spelt Qulanötpes
Kulao r. Pak. 101 F4
Kular Rus. Fed. 39 N2
Kulassein i. Phil. 74 B5
Kulat, Gunung mt. Indon. 77 G2
Kulautuva Lith. 42 E7
Kulawi Indon. 75 A3
Kulb Sudan 121 F4
Kuldīga Latvia 42 C5
Kuldja China see Yining
Kul'dur Rus. Fed. 82 C2
Kule Botswana 130 D4
Kulebaki Rus. Fed. 40 G5
Kuleshi Rus. Fed. 43 S9
Kulgera Australia 148 B5
Kulgunino Rus. Fed. 102 D1
Kuliai Lith. 42 C6
Kuligi Rus. Fed. 40 J4
Kulikovo Arkhangel'skaya Oblast' Rus. Fed. 40 H3
Kulikovo Lipetskaya Oblast' Rus. Fed. 43 U9
Kulim Malaysia 76 C1
Kulittalai India 94 C4
Kulkyne watercourse Australia 147 E2
Kullamaa Estonia 42 F3
Kullu India 96 C3
Kulmbach Germany 48 I5
Kŭlob Tajik. 101 G2
also spelt Kulyab
Kulotino Rus. Fed. 43 O3
Kuloy Rus. Fed. 40 G3
Kuloy r. Rus. Fed. 40 G2
Kulp Turkey 107 E3
also known as Pasur
Kul'sary Kazakh. 102 C3
also spelt Qulsary
Kulshabi Sudan 126 F2
Kultuk Rus. Fed. 84 D1
Kulu Turkey 106 C3
Kulübe Tepe mt. Turkey 106 B3
Kulunda Rus. Fed. 103 I1
Kulunda r. Rus. Fed. 103 I1
Kulundinskaya Step' plain Kazakh./Rus. Fed. 103 H1
Kulundinskoye, Ozero salt l. Rus. Fed. 103 I1
Kulusuk Greenland 165 P3
also known as Kap Dan
Külvand Iran 100 C4
Kulwin Australia 147 D3
Kulyab Tajik. see Kŭlob
Kuma r. Rus. Fed. 44 O2
Kuma r. Rus. Fed. 102 A3
Kumagaya Japan 91 F6
Kumai, Teluk b. Indon. 77 E3
Kumaishi Japan 90 F3
Kumak r. Rus. Fed. 102 D2
Kumalar Dağı mts Turkey 106 B3
Kumamoto Japan 91 B8
Kumamoto pref. Japan 91 B8
Kumano Japan 91 E8
Kumanovo Macedonia 58 C6
Kumara N.Z. 153 F10
Kumara Junction N.Z. 153 F10
Kumarkhali Bangl. 97 F5
Kumasi Ghana 125 E5
UNESCO World Heritage Site
Ku-Mayima S. Africa 133 M8
Kumayri Armenia see Gyumri
Kumba Cameroon 125 H5
Kumbağ Turkey 58 I8
Kumbakonam India 94 C4
Kümbet Turkey 106 B3
Kumbharli Ghat mt. India 94 B2
Kumbher Nepal 97 D3
Kumbla India 94 B3
Kumbo Cameroon 125 H5
Kumbri Latvia 42 D5
Kumchuru Botswana 130 D4
Kum-Dag Turkm. see Gumdag
Kumdah Saudi Arabia 105 D3
Kumel well Iran 100 C3
Kumertau Rus. Fed. 102 C1
Kŭm-gang r. S. Korea 83 B6
Kumgang-san mt. N. Korea 83 C5
English form Keumgang, Mount; formerly known as Kongang, Mount
Kumguri India 97 F4
Kumharsain India 89 B6
Kumher India 96 C4
Kŭmho-gang r. S. Korea 83 C6
Kumi S. Korea 83 C5
Kumi Uganda 128 B4
Kumkale Turkey 59 H9
Kum Kuduk well China 88 E3
Kumla Sweden 45 K4
Kumlinge Fin. 45 M3
Kumlu Turkey 109 H1
Kumluca Turkey 108 B1
Kummerower See l. Germany 49 J2
Kumo Nigeria 125 H4
Kŭmŏ-do i. S. Korea 83 B6
Kumola watercourse Kazakh. 103 F3
also spelt Qumola
Kumon Range mts Myanmar 78 B2
Kumphawapi Thai. 78 C4
Kumputunturi hill Fin. 44 N2
Kumta India 94 B3
Kumu Dem. Rep. Congo 126 E4
Kumukahi, Cape U.S.A. 181 [inset] Z2
Kumul China see Hami
Kumund India 95 D1
Kümüx China 88 E3
Kumylzhenskaya Rus. Fed. see Kumylzhenskiy
Kumylzhenskiy Rus. Fed. 41 G6
formerly known as Kumylzhenskaya
Kumyshtag, Pik mt. Kyrg. 103 G4
also spelt Kyumyush-Tak, Pik
Kun r. Myanmar 78 B4
Kunar prov. Afgh. 101 G3
Kunar r. Afgh. 101 G3
Kunashir, Ostrov i. Rus. Fed. 82 G3
Kunashirskiy Proliv sea chan. Japan/Rus. Fed. see Nemuro-kaikyō
Kunchaung Myanmar 78 B3
Kunda Dem. Rep. Congo 126 E5
Kunda Estonia 42 H2
Kunda r. Estonia 42 H2
Kunda India 97 D4
Kunda-dia-Baze Angola 127 C7
Kunda laht b. Estonia 42 H2
Kundapura India 94 B3
formerly spelt Coondapoor
Kundar r. Afgh./Pak. 101 G3
Kundelungu, Parc National de nat. park Dem. Rep. Congo 127 E7
Kundelungu Ouest, Parc National de nat. park Dem. Rep. Congo 127 E7
Kundgol India 94 B3
Kundian Pak. 101 G3
Kundur i. Indon. 76 C2
Kunduz Afgh. 101 G2
also spelt Kondūz; historically known as Drapsaca
Kunduz prov. Afgh. 101 G2
Kunene admin. reg. Namibia 130 B3
Kunene r. Namibia 127 A9
also spelt Cunene
Künes China see Xinyuan
Künes Chang China 88 C3
Künes He r. China 88 C3
Künes Linchang China 88 D3
Kungälv Sweden 45 J4
Kungei Alatau mts Kazakh./Kyrg. 103 I4
also spelt Küngöy Ala-Too
Kunggar China see Maizhokunggar
Kunghit Island Canada 166 D4
Küngöy Ala-Too mts Kazakh./Kyrg. see Kungei Alatau
Kungradkol' Uzbek. 102 E4
Kungsbacka Sweden 45 K4
Kungshamn Sweden 45 J4
Kungsör Sweden 45 L4
Kungu Dem. Rep. Congo 126 C4
Kungur mt. China see Kongur Shan
Kungur Rus. Fed. 40 K4
Kungyangon Myanmar 78 A4
Kunhegyes Hungary 49 R8
Kuni r. India 94 C2
Kunié i. New Caledonia see Pins, Île des
Kunigai India 94 C3
Kunimi-dake mt. Japan 91 B8
Kuningaküla Estonia 42 I2
Kuningan Indon. 77 E4
Kunisaki Japan 91 B8
Kunjabar India 95 E1
Kunlavav India 96 A5
Kunlong Myanmar 78 B3
Kunlui r. India/Nepal 97 F4
Kunlun Shan mts China 84 B5
Kunlun Shankou pass China 84 B5
Kunmadaras Hungary 49 R8
Kunming China 86 B3
Kunmunya Aboriginal Reserve Australia 150 D2
Kuno r. India 96 C4
Kunoy i. Faroe Is 46 F1
Kunsan S. Korea 83 B6
Kunshan China 87 G2
Kunszentmárton Hungary 49 R9
Kunszentmiklós Hungary 49 Q8
Kuntshankoie Dem. Rep. Congo 126 D5
Kununurra Australia 150 E2
Kunwak r. Canada 167 L2
Kunwari r. India 96 C4
Kun'ya Rus. Fed. 43 L5
Kun'ya r. Rus. Fed. 43 M4
Kunyang Henan China see Yexian
Kunyang Yunnan China see Jinning
Kunyang Zhejiang China see Pingyang
Kunya-Urgench Turkm. see Köneürgenç
Kunyu Shan mts China 85 I4
Künzelsau Germany 48 G6
Kuocang Shan mts China 87 G2
Kuolayarvi Rus. Fed. 44 O2
Kuopio Fin. 44 N3
Kuosku Fin. 44 O2
Kupa r. Croatia/Slovenia 56 I3
Kupang Indon. 75 B5
Kupang, Teluk b. Indon. 75 B5
Kupanskoye Rus. Fed. 43 T5
Kupari India 97 E5
Kupiškis Lith. 42 F6
Kuprava Latvia 42 I4
Kupreanof Island U.S.A. 164 F4
Kupreanof Point U.S.A. 164 D4
Kupuy Rus. Fed. 43 L5
Kupwara Jammu and Kashmir 96 B2
Kup"yans'k Ukr. 41 F6
Kuqa China 88 C3
Kür r. Azer. 107 G3
Kur r. Rus. Fed. 82 D2
Kura r. Azer./Georgia 107 F2
Kura r. Georgia 107 F2
Kura r. Rus. Fed. 41 G8
Kurabuka r. Australia 150 B5
Kuragaty Kazakh. 103 H4
also spelt Qoraghaty
Kuragwi Nigeria 125 H4
Kurakh Rus. Fed. 102 A4
Kura kurk sea chan. Estonia/Latvia see Irbe Strait
Kuramā, Ḩarrat lava field Saudi Arabia 104 C2
Kurashasayskiy Kazakh. 102 D2
Kurashiki Japan 91 C7
Kurasia India 97 D5
Kura Soak well Australia 150 D3
Kurayn i. Saudi Arabia 105 E2
Kurayoshi Japan 91 C7
Kurayskiy Khrebet mts Rus. Fed. 84 A1
Kurba Rus. Fed. 43 U4
Kurban Dağı mt. Turkey 58 K8
Kurbin He r. China 82 C2
Kurca r. Romania 58 B2
Kurchatov Rus. Fed. 41 E6
Kurchum Kazakh. 88 C1
also spelt Kürshim; formerly known as Kurmashkino
Kurchum r. Kazakh. 88 C1
Kürdämir Azer. 107 G2
also spelt Kyurdamir
Kurday Kazakh. 103 H4
also spelt Qorday
Kür Dili pt Azer. 107 G3
Kurduvadi India 94 B2
Kŭrdzhali Bulg. 58 G7
Kure Japan 91 C7
Küre Turkey 106 C2
Kure Atoll U.S.A. 220 H4
also known as Ocean Island
Kuressaare Estonia 42 D3
formerly known as Kingissepa
Kureya r. Rus. Fed. 43 K3
Kureyskoye Vodokhranilishche resr Rus. Fed. 39 I3
Kurgal'dzhino Kazakh. see Korgalzhyn
Kurgan Rus. Fed. 38 G4
Kurganinsk Rus. Fed. 41 G7
formerly known as Kurgannaya
Kurgannaya Rus. Fed. see Kurganinsk
Kurgantyube Tajik. see Qŭrghonteppa
Kuri India 96 A4
Kuria is Kiribati 145 G1
Kuria Muria Bay Oman see Ḩalāniyāt, Khalīj al
Kuria Muria Islands Oman see Ḩalāniyāt, Juzur al
Kuridala Australia 149 D4
Kurigram Bangl. 97 F4
Kurikka Fin. 44 M3
Kurikoma-yama vol. Japan 90 G5
Kurile, Mal mt. Albania 58 A6
Kuril Islands Rus. Fed. 82 G3
also known as Kuril'skiye Ostrova or Chishima-retto
Kurilovka Rus. Fed. 102 B2
Kuril'sk Rus. Fed. 81 P3
Kuril'skiye Ostrova is Rus. Fed. see Kuril Islands
Kuriyama Japan 90 G3
Kurkino Rus. Fed. 43 T8
Kurkurabazhi, Gora mt. Rus. Fed. 84 A1
Kurlkuta Aboriginal Reserve Australia 150 D4
Kurlovskiy Rus. Fed. 40 G5
Kurmanayevka Rus. Fed. 102 B1
Kurmashkino Kazakh. see Kurchum
Kurmene Latvia 42 F5
Kurmuk Sudan 128 B2
Kurnool India 94 C3
Kurobe Japan 91 E6
Kuroishi Japan 90 G4
Kuroiso Japan 90 G6
Kuromatsunai Japan 90 G3
Kuror, Jebel mt. Sudan 121 F4
Kuro-shima i. Japan 91 A9
Kurovskiy Rus. Fed. 82 B1
Kurovskoy Rus. Fed. 43 R7
Kurovskoye Rus. Fed. 43 T6
Kurow N.Z. 153 E12
Kurram r. Afgh./Pak. 101 G3
Kurri Kurri Australia 147 F3
Kuršėnai Lith. 42 D5
Kursh, Jabal hill Saudi Arabia 104 C3
Kürshim Kazakh. see Kurchum
Kurshskiy Zaliv b. Lith./Rus. Fed. see Courland Lagoon
Kurshynavichy Belarus 42 H9
Kursīši Latvia 42 D5
Kuršių marios b. Lith./Rus. Fed. see Courland Lagoon
Kuršių neringos nacionalinis parkas nat. park Lith. 42 B6
UNESCO World Heritage Site
Kursk Rus. Fed. 41 F6
Kurskaya Rus. Fed. 41 H7
Kurskaya Oblast' admin. div. Rus. Fed. 41 F6
English form Kursk Oblast
Kurskiy Zaliv b. Lith./Rus. Fed. see Courland Lagoon
Kursk Oblast admin. div. Rus. Fed. see Kurskaya Oblast'
Kuršumlija Srbija Serb. and Mont. 58 C5
Kurşunlu Turkey 106 C2
Kurtalan Turkey 107 E3
also known as Misraç
Kurti r. Kazakh. see Kurtty
Kurtoğlu Burnu pt Turkey 106 B3
Kurtpınar Turkey 108 G1
Kurttepe Turkey 108 G1
Kurtty r. Kazakh. 103 I3
also spelt Kürti or Kurty
Kurty r. Kazakh. see Kurtty
Kuru Fin. 45 M3
Kuru r. Greece see Kourou
Kuru India 97 E5
Kuru watercourse Sudan 126 E2
Kurucaşile Turkey 106 C2
Kurud India 94 D1
Kurukshetra India 96 C3
Kuruktag mts China 88 D3
Kuruman S. Africa 132 H4
Kuruman watercourse S. Africa 132 E3
Kuruman Hills S. Africa 132 H4
Kurume Japan 91 B8
Kurumkan Rus. Fed. 81 I2
Kurun r. Sudan 128 B3
Kurundi watercourse Australia 148 B4
Kurundvad India 94 B2
Kurunegala Sri Lanka 94 D5
Kurunzulay Rus. Fed. 85 H1
Kurupam India 95 D2

Lakefield Canada 168 E4
Lakefield National Park Australia 149 E2
Lake Fork r. U.S.A. 183 O1
Lake Frome Regional Reserve nature res. Australia 146 C2
Lake Gairdner National Park Australia 146 B2
Lake Geneva U.S.A. 172 E8
Lake Gilles Conservation Park nature res. Australia 146 C3
Lake Grace Australia 151 B7
Lake Gregory Aboriginal Reserve Australia 150 D4
Lake Harbour Canada see **Kimmirut**
Lake Havasu City U.S.A. 183 J7
Lakehurst U.S.A. 177 K5
Lake Isabella U.S.A. 182 F6
Lake Jackson U.S.A. 179 D6
Lake King Australia 151 B7
Lake King Nature Reserve Australia 151 B7
Lakeland Australia 149 E2
Lakeland FL U.S.A. 175 D7
Lakeland GA U.S.A. 175 D6
Lake Linden U.S.A. 172 E3
Lake Louise Canada 167 G5
Lake Mackay Aboriginal Land res. Australia 148 A4
Lake Magenta Nature Reserve Australia 151 B7
Lake Malawi National Park Malawi 129 B8
UNESCO World Heritage Site
Lake Manyara National Park Tanz. 128 B5
Lake Mburo National Park Uganda 128 A5
Lake Mills U.S.A. 174 A3
Lake Nash Australia 148 C4
Lake Paringa N.Z. 153 D11
Lake Placid U.S.A. 177 L1
Lakeport CA U.S.A. 182 B2
Lakeport MI U.S.A. 173 K7
Lake Providence U.S.A. 175 B5
Lake Pukaki N.Z. 153 E12
Lake Range mts U.S.A. 182 E1
Lake River Canada 168 D2
Lake St Peter Canada 173 O5
Lakes Entrance Australia 147 F4
Lakeshore U.S.A. 182 E4
Lakeside AZ U.S.A. 183 O7
Lakeside CA U.S.A. 183 H9
Lakeside NJ U.S.A. 177 K4
Lake Sumner Forest Park nature res. N.Z. 153 G10
Lake Superior Provincial Park Canada 173 I3
Lake Tekapo N.Z. 153 E12
Lake Torrens National Park Australia 146 C2
Lake Traverse (Sisseton) Indian Reservation res. U.S.A. 178 C2
Lakeview OH U.S.A. 176 B5
Lakeview OR U.S.A. 180 B4
Lake Village U.S.A. 175 B5
Lakeville U.S.A. 174 A2
Lake Wales U.S.A. 175 D7
Lakewood CO U.S.A. 180 F5
Lakewood OH U.S.A. 176 D4
Lakewood WI U.S.A. 172 E5
Lakhdaria Alg. 55 O8
Lakhdenpokh'ya Rus. Fed. 45 O3
Lakheri India 96 C4
Lakhimpur India 96 D4
Lakhipur India 97 G4
Lakhisarai India 97 E4
also spelt Luckeesarai
Lakhish r. Israel 108 F6
Lakhnadon India 96 C5
Lakhpat India 96 A5
Lakhtar India 96 A5
Lakhva r. Belarus 43 L8
Lakin U.S.A. 178 B4
Lakinsk Rus. Fed. 43 U5
formerly known as Lakinskiy
Lakinskiy Rus. Fed. see **Lakinsk**
Lakitusaki r. Canada 168 D2
Lakki Pak. 101 G3
Lakkoma Greece 59 G8
Lakonikos Kolpos b. Greece 59 D12
Lakor i. Indon. 75 D5
Lakota Côte d'Ivoire 124 D5
Lakota U.S.A. 178 C1
Laksefjorden sea chan. Norway 44 N1
Lakselv Norway 44 N1
Laksfors Norway 44 K2
Lakshadweep is India see **Laccadive Islands**
Lakshadweep union terr. India 94 B4
formerly known as Laccadive, Minicoy and Amindivi Islands
Laksham Bangl. 97 F5
Lakshettipet India 94 C2
Lakshmeshwar India 94 B3
Lakshmikantapur India 97 F5
Laktyshy Vodaskhovishcha resr Belarus 42 H9
Lala Phil. 74 B5
Lalago Tanz. 128 B5
La Laguna Arg. 204 E4
Lala Musa Pak. 101 H3
Lalapanzi Zimbabwe 131 F3
Lalapaşa Turkey 58 H7
Lalara Gabon 126 A4
Lalaua Moz. 131 H2
L'Albufera l. Spain 55 K5
L'Alcora Spain 55 K4
Laleham Australia 149 F4
Läleh Zār, Kūh-e mt. Iran 100 D4
Lalganj India 97 E4
Lalgudi India 94 C4
Lālī Iran 100 B3
Lalibela Eth. 128 C1
UNESCO World Heritage Site
La Libertad Ecuador 198 A5
La Libertad El Salvador 185 H6
La Libertad Guat. 185 H5
La Libertad Nicaragua 186 B4
La Libertad dept Peru 200 A2
La Ligua Chile 204 C4
Laliki Indon. 75 C4
Lalimboee Indon. 75 B3
Lalin China 82 B3
Lalín Spain 54 C2
Lalinde France 50 G8
La Línea de la Concepción Spain 54 F8
Lalin He r. China 82 B3
Lalitpur India 96 C4
Lalitpur Nepal see **Patan**
Lal-Lo Phil. 74 B2
Lalmikor Uzbek. 103 F5
also spelt Lyal'mikar
Lalmonirhat Bangl. 97 F4
La Loche Canada 167 I3
La Loche, Lac l. Canada 167 I3
La Loma Bol. 201 D5
La Loupe France 50 H4
La Louvière Belgium 51 K2
UNESCO World Heritage Site
Lalpur India 96 A5
Lal'sk Rus. Fed. 40 H3
Lalsot India 96 C4
Laluin i. Indon. 75 C3
Lalung La pass China 89 D6
Lama Bangl. 97 G5
La Macarena, Parque Nacional nat. park Col. 198 C4
La Maddalena Sardinia Italy 56 B7
Lamag Sabah Malaysia 77 G1
Lamaing Myanmar 79 B5
La Malbaie Canada 169 G4
La Malinche, Parque Nacional nat. park Mex. 185 F5
Lamam Laos 79 D5
La Mancha Mex. 185 E3
La Manche strait France/U.K. see **English Channel**
La Manga del Mar Menor Spain 55 K7
La Máquina Mex. 184 D2
Lamar CO U.S.A. 178 B4
Lamar MO U.S.A. 178 D4
Lamard Iran 100 C5
Lamarque Arg. 204 D5
La Marque U.S.A. 179 D6
La Martre, Lac l. Canada 167 G2
Lamas r. Turkey 108 F1
La Mauricie, Parc National de nat. park Canada 169 F4
La Maya Cuba 186 E2
Lamballe France 50 D4
Lambaréné Gabon 126 A5
Lambayeque Peru 198 B6
Lambayeque dept Peru 198 B6
Lambay Island Ireland 47 G10
Lambeng Indon. 77 F3
Lambert atoll Marshall Is see **Ailinglaplap**
Lambert, Cape Australia 150 B4

►**Lambert Glacier** Antarctica 223 E2
Largest series of glaciers in the world.

Lambert's Bay S. Africa 132 C9
Lambertville U.S.A. 177 K5
Lambeth Canada 173 L8
Lambi India 96 B3
Lambina Australia 146 B1
Lambro r. Italy 56 B3
Lamego Port. 54 D3
La Mejorada Peru 200 B3
Lamen Bay Vanuatu 145 F3
Lamèque, Île i. Canada 169 H4
La Merced Arg. 204 D3
La Merced Peru 200 B2
Lameroo Australia 146 D3
La Mesa U.S.A. 183 G9
Lamesa U.S.A. 179 B5
L'Ametlla de Mar Spain 55 L4
Lamezia Italy 57 I10
Lamhar Touil, Sabkhet imp. l. W. Sahara 122 A5
Lamia Greece 59 D10
Lamigan Point Phil. 74 C5
Lamington National Park Australia 147 G2
Lamir Iran 100 B2
La Mirada U.S.A. 182 F8
formerly known as Mirada Hills
La Misa Mex. 184 C2
La Misión Mex. 183 H9
Lamitan Phil. 74 B5
Lamma Island Hong Kong China 87 [inset]
also known as Pok Liu Chau
Lammerkop S. Africa 133 N2
Lammerlaw Range mts N.Z. 153 D13
Lammermuir Hills U.K. 46 J8
Lammhult Sweden 45 K4
Lammi Fin. 45 N3
Lammijärv lake channel Estonia/Rus. Fed. 42 I3
La Moille U.S.A. 172 D9
Lamoille r. U.S.A. 177 L1
La Moine r. U.S.A. 174 B4
La Mojonera Spain 55 I8
Lamon Bay Phil. 74 B3
Lamone r. Italy 56 E4
Lamongan Indon. 77 F4
Lamoni U.S.A. 174 A3
Lamont U.S.A. 182 F6
La Morita Chihuahua Mex. 184 D2
La Morita Coahuila Mex. 179 B6
Lamotrek atoll Micronesia 73 K5
La Motte Canada 173 O2
Lamotte-Beuvron France 51 I5
La Motte-Servolex France 51 L7
La Moure U.S.A. 178 C2
Lampa Peru 200 C3
Lampang Thai. 78 B4
Lam Pao Reservoir Thai. 78 C4
Lampasas U.S.A. 179 C6
Lampasas r. U.S.A. 179 C6
Lampazos Mex. 185 E3
Lampedusa, Isola di i. Sicily Italy 57 E13
Lampeland Norway 45 J4
Lampeter U.K. 47 H11
also known as Llanbedr
Lamphun Thai. 78 B4
Lampozhnya Rus. Fed. 40 H2
Lampsacus Turkey see **Lâpseki**
Lampung prov. Indon. 76 D4
Lampung, Teluk b. Indon. 76 D4
Lamta India 96 D5
Lam Tin Hong Kong China 87 [inset]
Lamu Kenya 128 D5
UNESCO World Heritage Site
Lamu Myanmar 78 A4
La Muela mt. Spain 55 J5
La Mure France 51 L8
Lana Australia 149 D4
Lana Italy 56 D2
Lāna'i i. U.S.A. 181 [inset] Z1
also known as Ranai
Lāna'i City U.S.A. 181 [inset] Z1
Lanao, Lake Phil. 74 C5
Lanark Canada 173 Q5
Lanark U.K. 46 I8
Lanark U.S.A. 172 D8
Lanas Sabah Malaysia 77 G1
Lanbi Kyun i. Myanmar 79 B6
also known as Sullivan Island
Lanboyan Point Phil. 74 B4
Lancang China 86 A4
also known as Menglang
Lancang Jiang r. China see **Mekong**
Lancaster U.K. 47 J9
Lancaster CA U.S.A. 182 F7
Lancaster KY U.S.A. 176 A8
Lancaster MO U.S.A. 174 A3
Lancaster NH U.S.A. 177 N1
Lancaster OH U.S.A. 176 C6
Lancaster PA U.S.A. 177 I5
Lancaster SC U.S.A. 174 D5
Lancaster VA U.S.A. 177 I8
Lancaster WI U.S.A. 172 C8
Lancaster Sound strait Canada 165 K2
Lancelin Australia 151 A6
Lanch'khut'i Georgia 107 E2
Lanchow China see **Lanzhou**
Lanciano Italy 56 G6
Lancing U.S.A. 176 A9
Lanco Chile 204 B5
Lancun China 85 I4
Łańcut Poland 49 T5
Lancy Switz. 51 M6
Landa de Matamoros Mex. 185 F4
UNESCO World Heritage Site
Landak r. Indon. 77 E3
Landana Angola see **Cacongo**
Landau an der Isar Germany 49 J7
Landau in der Pfalz Germany 48 F6
Landeck Austria 48 H8
Lander watercourse Australia 148 A4
Lander U.S.A. 180 E4
Landerneau France 50 B4
Landes reg. France 50 F8
Landes de Gascogne, Parc Naturel Régional des nature res. France 50 F8
Landes de Lanvaux reg. France 50 D5
Landes du Mené reg. France 50 D4
Landfall Island India 95 G3
Landik, Gunung mt. Indon. 76 C3
Landis Canada 167 I4
Landivisiau France 50 B4
Landless Corner Zambia 127 F8
Land O' Lakes U.S.A. 172 D4
Landön Sweden 44 K3
Landor Australia 151 B5
Landquart Switz. 51 P5
Landrienne Canada 173 P2
Landrum U.S.A. 174 D5
Landsberg Poland see **Gorzów Wielkopolski**
Landsberg am Lech Germany 48 H7
Landsborough r. N.Z. 153 D11
Land's End pt U.K. 47 G13
Landshut Germany 48 J7
Landskrona Sweden 45 K5
La Nedei mt. Romania 58 E3
La Negra Chile 200 C5
Lane Pool Reserve nature res. Australia 151 B7
La Neuveville Switz. 51 N5
Lanfeng China see **Lankao**
Lang, Nam r. Myanmar 78 B2
La Nga, Sông r. Vietnam 79 D6
La'nga Co l. China 89 C6
Langadhás Greece see **Lagkadas**
Langai r. India 97 G4
Langan r. Sweden 44 K3
Langao China 87 D1
Langar Badakhshān Afgh. 101 H2
Langar Parvān Afgh. 101 G3
Langar Iran 101 E3
Langar Navoiy Uzbek. 103 F4
also spelt Lyangar
Langar Qashqadaryo Uzbek. 103 F5
formerly spelt Lyangar
Langara Indon. 75 B4
Langberg mts S. Africa 132 G5
Langdon U.S.A. 178 C1
Langeac France 51 J7
Langeais France 50 G5
Langebaan S. Africa 132 C10
Langeberg mts S. Africa 132 D10
Langehorn S. Africa 133 I3
Langeland i. Denmark 45 J5
Langelands Bælt strait Denmark 45 J5
Längelmäki Fin. 45 N3
Längelmävesi l. Fin. 40 C3
Langen Germany 48 F2
Langenburg Canada 167 K5
Langenlois Austria 49 M7
Langenthal Switz. 51 N5
Langeoog Germany 48 E2
Langeoog i. Germany 48 E2
Langepas Rus. Fed. 38 H3
Langesund Norway 45 J4
Langfang China 85 H4
also known as Anci
Långfjallets naturreservat nature res. Sweden 45 K3
Langgapayung Indon. 76 C2
Langgar China 89 F6
Langgöns Germany 48 F5
Langham Canada 167 J4
Langholm U.K. 46 J8
Langholm S. Africa 133 K10
Langholm U.K. 47 J8
Langjökull ice cap Iceland 44 [inset] B2
Langka Indon. 76 B1
Langkawi i. Malaysia 76 B1
Langkesi, Kepulauan is Indon. 75 C4
Lang Kha Toek, Khao mt. Thai. 79 B6
Langkho Myanmar 78 B3
Langklip S. Africa 132 E5
Langkon Sabah Malaysia 77 G1
Langlade Canada 173 R2
Langley Canada 166 F5
Langley U.S.A. 176 C8
Langlo watercourse Australia 149 E5
Langmusi China see **Dagcanglhamo**
Langogne France 51 J8
Langon France 50 F8
Langong, Xé r. Laos 78 D4
Langøya i. Norway 44 K1
Langqên Zangbo r. China 89 B6
Langqi China 87 F3
Langreo Spain 54 F1
Langres France 51 L5
Langres, Plateau de France 51 K5
Langsa Indon. 76 B1
Langsa, Teluk b. Indon. 76 B1
Långsele Sweden 44 L3
Langshan China 85 E3
Lang Shan mts China 85 E3
Langslett Norway 44 M1
Lang Sơn Vietnam 78 D3
Langtang National Park Nepal 97 E3
Langtao Myanmar 78 B2
Långträsk Sweden 44 M2
Langtry U.S.A. 179 B6
Languan China see **Lantian**
Languedoc-Roussillon admin. reg. France 51 I10
Languiaru r. Brazil see **Iquê**
Languiñeo Arg. 205 C6
Langundu, Tanjung pt Indon. 77 G5
Långvinds bruk Sweden 45 L3
Langwedel Germany 48 G3
Langya Shan mt. China 85 G4
Langzhong China 86 C2
Laniel Canada 173 N3
Lanigan Canada 167 J5
Lanín, Parque Nacional nat. park Arg. 204 C5
Lanín, Volcán vol. Arg./Chile 204 C5
Lanjak, Bukit mt. Sarawak Malaysia 77 E2
Lanji India 96 D5
Lanka country Asia see **Sri Lanka**
Lankao China 87 E1
formerly known as Lanfeng
Länkäran Azer. 107 G3
also spelt Lenkoran'
Lan Kok Tsui pt Hong Kong China see **Black Point**
Lanlacuni Bajo Peru 200 C3
Lannemezan France 50 G9
Lannion France 50 C4
L'Annonciation Canada 169 F4
La Noria Bol. 201 E3
La Noria Mex. 184 D4
Lansdale U.S.A. 177 J5
L'Anse U.S.A. 172 E4
L'Anse-aux-Meadows National Historic Park Canada 169 K3
UNESCO World Heritage Site
L'Anse-St-Jean Canada 169 G3
Lansford U.S.A. 177 J5
Lansing r. Canada 166 C2
Lansing IA U.S.A. 172 B7

►**Lansing** MI U.S.A. 173 I8
State capital of Michigan.

Länsi-Suomi prov. Fin. 44 M3
Lansjärv Sweden 44 M2
Lanta, Ko i. Thai. 79 B7
Lantau Island Hong Kong China 87 [inset]
also known as Tai Yue Shan
Lantau Peak hill Hong Kong China 87 [inset]
also known as Fung Wong Shan
Lanterne r. France 51 M5
Lantian Hunan China see **Lianyuan**
Lantian Shaanxi China 87 D1
also known as Languan
Lanusei Sardinia Italy 57 B9
Lanuza Phil. 74 C4
Lanuza Bay Phil. 74 C4
Lanxi Heilong. China 82 B3
Lanxi Zhejiang China 87 F2
Lanxian China 85 F4
also known as Dongcun
Lanya Sudan 128 A3
Lanyi He r. China 85 F4
Lan Yü i. Taiwan 87 G4
Lanzarote i. Canary Is 122 B3
Lanzhou China 84 D4
also spelt Lanchow
Lanzijing China 85 I2
Lanzo Torinese Italy 51 N7
Lao r. Italy 57 H9
Lao, Nam Mae r. Thai. 78 B4
Laoag Phil. 74 B2
Laoang Phil. 74 C3
Laobie Shan mts China 86 A4
Laobukou China 87 D3
Lao Cai Vietnam 78 C3
Laodicea Syria see **Latakia**
Laodicea Turkey see **Denizli**
Laodicea ad Lycum Turkey see **Denizli**
Laodicea ad Mare Syria see **Latakia**
Laofengkou China 88 C2
Laoha He r. China 85 I3
Laoheishan China 82 C4
Laohekou China 87 D1
formerly known as Guanghua
Laohutun China 85 I4
Laojunmiao China see **Yumen**
Lao Ling mts China 82 B4
Laolong China see **Longchuan**
Laon France 51 J3
Laona U.S.A. 172 E5
La Oroya Peru 200 B2
►**Laos** country Asia 78 C4
►►64–65 **Asia** Countries
Laoshan China 85 I4
also known as Licun
Laotieshan Shuidao sea chan. China see **Bohai Haixia**
Laotougou China 82 C4
Laotuding Shan hill China 82 B4
Laou, Oued r. Morocco 54 F9
Laoudi-Ba Côte d'Ivoire 124 E4
Laowohi pass Jammu and Kashmir see **Khardung La**
Laoximiao China 84 D3
Laoye Ling mts China 82 C4
Lapa Brazil 203 B8
Lapac i. Phil. 74 B5
Lapachito Arg. 204 F2
Lapai Nigeria 125 G4
Lapalisse France 51 J6
La Palma i. Canary Is 122 A3
La Palma Panama 186 D5
La Palma U.S.A. 183 M9
La Palma del Condado Spain 54 E7
La Paloma Uruguay 204 G4
La Pampa prov. Arg. 204 D5
formerly known as Eva Perón
La Panza Range mts U.S.A. 182 D6
La Paragua Venez. 199 F3
Laparan i. Phil. 74 A5
La Paya, Parque Nacional nat. park Col. 198 C4
La Paz Entre Ríos Arg. 204 F3
La Paz Mendoza Arg. 204 D4

►**La Paz** Bol. 200 C4
Official capital of Bolivia.
►►8–9 **World** Countries
►►192–193 **South America** Countries

La Paz dept Bol. 200 C3
La Paz Hond. 186 B4
La Paz Mex. 184 C3
La Paz Nicaragua 186 B4
UNESCO World Heritage Site
Lapaz U.S.A. 172 G9
La Paz Venez. 198 C2
La Paz, Bahía b. Mex. 184 C3
La Pedrera Col. 198 D5
Lapeer U.S.A. 173 J7
La Pelada Arg. 204 E3
La Peña Panama 186 C5
La Perla Mex. 184 D2
La Pérouse Strait Japan/Rus. Fed. 90 G2
also known as Sōya-kaikyō
La Pesca Mex. 185 F4
La Piedad Mex. 185 E4
La Pine U.S.A. 180 B4
Lapinig Phil. 74 C3
Lapinlahti Fin. 44 N3
La Pintada Panama 186 C5
Laplace U.S.A. 175 B6
Lap Lae Thai. 78 C4
Laplandskiy Zapovednik nature res. Rus. Fed. 44 P2
La Plata Arg. 204 F4
formerly known as Eva Perón
La Plata MD U.S.A. 177 I7
La Plata MO U.S.A. 178 D3
La Plata, Río de sea chan. Arg./Uruguay 204 F4
La Plaza Spain 54 E1
La Plonge, Lac l. Canada 167 J4
Lapmežciems Latvia 42 E4
La Pobla de Segur Spain 55 L2
La Pola de Gordón Spain 54 F2
La Poma Arg. 200 D6
Lapominka Rus. Fed. 40 G2
La Porte U.S.A. 174 C3
Laporte U.S.A. 177 I4
Laporte, Mount Canada 166 E2
Laposo, Bukit mt. Indon. 75 A4
La Potherie, Lac l. Canada 169 F1
Lapovo Srbija Serb. and Mont. 58 C4
La Poyata Col. 198 C3
Lappajärvi l. Fin. 44 M3
Lappeenranta Fin. 45 O3
Lappi Fin. 45 M3
UNESCO World Heritage Site
Lappi prov. Fin. 44 N2
Lappland reg. Europe 44 L2
UNESCO World Heritage Site
Lappohja Fin. 42 E2
Lappträsk Sweden 44 M2
Laprida Arg. 204 E5
La Pryor U.S.A. 179 C6
Lâpseki Turkey 106 A2
historically known as Lampsacus
Laptevo Rus. Fed. see **Yasnogorsk**
Laptev Sea Rus. Fed. 39 M2
also known as Laptevykh, More
Laptevykh, More sea Rus. Fed. see **Laptev Sea**
Lapua Fin. 44 M3
Lapuanjoki r. Fin. 44 M3
La Puebla Spain see **Sa Pobla**
La Puebla del Río Spain 54 E7
La Puebla de Montalbán Spain 54 G5
La Puerta Catamarca Arg. 204 D3
La Puerta Córdoba Arg. 204 E3
La Puerta Venez. 198 D2
Lapu-Lapu Phil. 74 B4
Lapurdum France see **Bayonne**
Lăpuşnicu Mare Romania 58 C4
Lapušnik Kosovo, Srbija Serb. and Mont. 58 B6
Łapy Poland 49 T3
Laqiya Arbain well Sudan 121 F4
La Quiaca Arg. 200 D5
L'Aquila Italy 56 F6
La Quinta U.S.A. 183 H8
Lār Iran 100 C5
Lara Australia 147 E4
Lara state Venez. 198 D2
Laracha Spain 54 C1
Larache Morocco 122 D2
formerly spelt El Araïche; *historically known as* Lixus
Laragne-Montéglin France 51 L8
Lārak i. Iran 100 D5
Laramie U.S.A. 180 F4
Laramie r. U.S.A. 180 F4
Laramie Mountains U.S.A. 180 F4
Laranda Turkey see **Karaman**
Laranjal Brazil 199 G6
Laranjal Paulista Brazil 206 F10
Laranjeiras Brazil 202 E4
Laranjeiras do Sul Brazil 203 A8
Laranjinha r. Brazil 206 C9
Larantuka Indon. 75 B5
Larat i. Indon. 73 H8
La Raygat reg. W. Sahara 122 B5
Larba Alg. 55 O8
L'Arbresle France 51 K7
Lärbro Sweden 45 L4
Larchwood Canada 173 L4
L'Ardenne, Plateau de Belgium see **Ardennes**
Larder Lake Canada 173 N2
Larder Lake l. Canada 173 N2
Laredo Spain 55 H1
Laredo U.S.A. 179 C7
La Reforma Sonora Mex. 181 E7
La Reforma Veracruz Mex. 185 F4
La Reina Adelaida, Archipiélago de is Chile 205 B9
English form Queen Adelaide Islands
La Reine Canada 173 N2
La Réole France 50 F8
Largeau Chad see **Faya**
L'Argentière-la-Bessée France 51 M8
Largo U.S.A. 175 D7
Largo, Cayo i. Cuba 186 C2
Largs U.K. 46 H8
Lārī Iran 100 A2
L'Ariana Tunisia 123 H1
also spelt Aryanah
Lariang Indon. 75 A3
Lariang r. Indon. 75 A3
Larimore U.S.A. 178 C1
La Rinconada Spain 54 F7
Larino Italy 56 G7
La Rioja Arg. 204 D3
La Rioja prov. Arg. 204 D3
La Rioja aut. comm. Spain 55 I2
Larionovo Rus. Fed. 43 L1
Larisa Greece 59 D9
also known as Yenişehir; *also spelt* Larissa
Larissa Greece see **Larisa**
Laristan reg. Iran 100 D5
Larkana Pak. 101 G5
Lark Harbour Canada 169 J3
Lar Koh mt. Afgh. 101 E3
Lark Passage Australia 149 E2
Larnaca Cyprus 108 E3
also spelt Larnaka
Larnaka Cyprus see **Larnaca**
Larne U.K. 47 G9
Larned U.S.A. 178 C4
Laro Cameroon 125 I4
La Robla Spain 54 F2
La Roche-en-Ardenne Belgium 51 L2
La Rochefoucauld France 50 G7
La Rochelle France 50 E6
La Roche-sur-Yon France 50 E6
La Roda Spain 55 I5
La Romana Dom. Rep. 187 F3
La Ronge Canada 167 J4
La Ronge, Lac l. Canada 167 J4
La Rosa Mex. 185 E3
La Rosa de Castilla Mex. 183 H9
La Rosita Mex. 185 E2
Larouco, Serra do mts Spain 54 D3
Larrey Point Australia 150 B3
Larrimah Australia 148 B2
Larrimah Aboriginal Land res. Australia 148 B2
also known as Wubalawun
Lars Christensen Coast Antarctica 223 E2
Larsen Ice Shelf Antarctica 222 T2
Larsnes Norway 44 I3
La Rubia Arg. 204 E3
Larvik Norway 45 J4
Lar'yak Rus. Fed. 39 I3
Larzac, Causse du plat. France 51 J8
La Sabana Arg. 204 F2
La Sabana Col. 198 D4
La Sal U.S.A. 183 O3
La Sal Junction U.S.A. 183 O3
La Salle Canada 169 F4
La Salle U.S.A. 174 B3
Las Animas U.S.A. 178 B4
Las Ánimas, Punta pt Mex. 184 B2
Las Anod Somalia see **Laascaanood**
La Sarre Canada 168 E3
La Sauvette hill France 51 M9
Las Aves, Islas is West Indies 187 G5
short form Aves
Las Avispas Arg. 204 E3
Las Avispas Mex. 184 C2
La Savonnière, Lac l. Canada 169 F2
Las Bonitas Venez. 199 E3
Las Breñas Arg. 204 E2
Las Chapas Arg. 205 D6
La Scie Canada 169 K3
Las Conchas Bol. 201 F4
Las Cruces Mex. 184 D2
Las Cruces CA U.S.A. 182 D7
Las Cruces NM U.S.A. 181 F6
La Selle, Pic mt. Haiti 187 F3
La Serena Chile 204 C3
Las Esperanças Mex. 185 E3
Las Flores Buenos Aires Arg. 204 F5
Las Flores Salta Arg. 201 E6
Lashburn Canada 167 I4
Las Heras Arg. 204 C4
Las Hermosas, Parque Nacional nat. park Col. 198 C4
Las Herreras Mex. 184 D3
Lashio Myanmar 78 B3
Lashkar Gāh Afgh. 101 F4
Las Horquetas Arg. 205 C8
La Sila reg. Italy 57 I9
Łasin Poland 49 Q2
Las Juntas Chile 204 C3
Las Lajas Arg. 204 C5
Las Lajitas Venez. 199 E3
Las Lavaderos Mex. 185 F4
Las Lomas Peru 198 A6
Las Lomitas Arg. 201 E6
Las Marismas marsh Spain 54 E7
Las Martinetas Arg. 205 D7
Las Médulas tourist site Spain 54 E2
UNESCO World Heritage Site
Las Mercedes Venez. 199 E2
Las Mesteñas Mex. 184 D2
Las Minas Venez. 199 E2
Las Mulatas is Panama see **San Blas, Archipiélago de**
Las Nieves Mex. 184 D3
Las Nopaleras, Cerro mt. Mex. 185 E3
La Solana Spain 55 H6
Lasolo, Teluk b. Indon. 75 B3
Las Orquideas, Parque Nacional nat. park Col. 198 B3
La Souterraine France 50 H6
Las Ovejas Arg. 204 C5
Las Palmas watercourse Mex. 183 G9
Las Palmas Panama 186 C5

►**Las Palmas de Gran Canaria** Canary Is 122 B3
Joint capital of the Canary Islands.

Las Petas Bol. 201 F4
La Spezia Italy 56 B4
Las Piedras Uruguay 204 F4
Las Pipinas Arg. 204 F4
Las Planchas Hond. 186 B4
Las Plumas Arg. 205 D6
Laspur Pak. 101 H2
Las Rosas Arg. 204 E4
Las Rozas de Madrid Spain 54 H4
Lassance Brazil 207 I4
Lassay-les-Châteaux France 50 F4
Lassen Peak vol. U.S.A. 182 C1
Lassen Volcanic National Park U.S.A. 182 C1
Las Tablas Panama 186 C6
Lastarria, Parque Nacional de nat. park Chile 205 B7
Last Chance U.S.A. 178 B4
Las Termas Arg. 204 D2
Last Mountain Lake Canada 167 J5
Las Torres de Cotillas Spain 55 J6
Las Tórtolas, Cerro mt. Chile 204 C3
Lastoursville Gabon 126 B5
Lastovo i. Croatia 56 I6
Lastovski Kanal sea chan. Croatia 56 I6
Las Tres Vírgenes, Volcán vol. Mex. 184 B3
Las Trincheras Venez. 199 E3
Las Tunas Cuba 186 D2
Lasva Estonia 42 I4
Las Varas Col. 199 D3
Las Varas Chihuahua Mex. 184 D2
Las Varas Nayarit Mex. 184 D4
Las Varas Venez. 198 D3
Las Varillas Arg. 204 E3
Las Vegas NM U.S.A. 181 F6
Las Vegas NV U.S.A. 183 I5
Las Villuercas mt. Spain 54 F5
Las Yaras Peru 200 C4
Lata Solomon Is 145 F3
La Tabatière Canada 169 J3
Latacunga Ecuador 198 B5
Latady Island Antarctica 222 S2
La Tagua Col. 198 C5
Latakia Syria 108 G2
also known as Lattaquié; *also spelt* Al Lādhiqīyah; *historically known as* Laodicea or Laodicea ad Mare
Latalata i. Indon. 75 C3
Latchford Canada 173 N3
Late i. Tonga 145 H3
also known as Latte Island or Lette Island
Latehar India 97 E5
Latemar mt. Italy 56 D2
La Teste-de-Buch France 50 E8
La Tetilla, Cerro mt. Mex. 184 D4
Latgales augstiene reg. Latvia 42 I5
Latham Australia 151 B6
Lathi India 96 A5
Lathrop U.S.A. 182 C4
Lātīdān Iran 100 C5
Latimojong Mountains Reserve nature res. Indon. 75 B3
Latina Italy 56 E7
Latisana Italy 56 F3
La Toma Arg. 204 D4
La Tortuga, Isla i. Venez. 199 E2
Latorytsya r. Ukr. 49 T7
Latouche Treville, Cape Australia 150 C3
Latouma well Niger 123 I5
La Tour-du-Pin France 51 L7
La Tremblade France 50 E7
La Trinidad Nicaragua 186 B4
La Trinidad Phil. 74 B2
La Trinitaria Mex. 185 G5
La Trinité France 51 N9
Latrobe Australia 147 E5
Latrobe U.S.A. 176 F5
Latronico Italy 57 I8
La Troya r. Arg. 204 C3
Latskoye Rus. Fed. 43 T3
Lattaquié Syria see **Latakia**
Latte Island Tonga see **Late**
Lattes France 51 J9
Latulipe Canada 173 N3
La Tuque Canada 169 F4
Latur India 94 C2
►**Latvia** country Europe 42 E5
spelt Latvija *in Latvian; formerly known as* Latviyskaya S.S.R.
►►32–33 **Europe** Countries
Latvija country Europe see **Latvia**
Latviyskaya S.S.R. country Europe see **Latvia**
Lau Nigeria 125 H4
Lau r. Sudan 128 A3
Laua r. India 97 E5
Lauban watercourse Namibia 130 D3
Lauca, Parque Nacional nat. park Chile 200 C4
Lauenburg (Elbe) Germany 48 H2
Lauf an der Pegnitz Germany 48 I6
Laufen Germany 49 J8
Laufen Switz. 51 N5
Laugarbakki Iceland 44 [inset] B2
Lauge Koch Kyst reg. Greenland 165 M2
Laughland Lake Canada 167 M1
Laughlen, Mount Australia 148 B4
Laughlin Peak U.S.A. 181 F5
Lauhanvuoren kansallispuisto nat. park Fin. 45 M3
Lauka Estonia 42 D3
Laukaa Fin. 44 N3
Laukuva Lith. 42 D6
Laun Thai. 79 B6
Launay Canada 173 O2
Launceston Australia 147 E5
Launceston U.K. 47 H13
Launglon Myanmar 79 B5
Launglon Bok Islands Myanmar 79 B5
La Unidad Mex. 185 G6
La Unión Bol. 201 E3
La Unión Chile 204 B6
La Unión Col. 198 B4
La Unión El Salvador 185 I6
La Unión Hond. 186 B4
La Unión Mex. 185 E5
La Unión Huánuco Peru 200 A2
La Unión Piura Peru 198 A6
La Unión Spain 55 K7
Laur Phil. 74 B3
Laura Australia 149 E2
La Urbana Venez. 199 E3
Laurel DE U.S.A. 177 J7
Laurel MS U.S.A. 175 B6
Laurel MT U.S.A. 180 E3
Laureldale U.S.A. 177 J5
Laureles Para. 201 F6
Laurel Hill hills U.S.A. 176 F6
Laurencekirk U.K. 46 J7
Laurens IA U.S.A. 178 D3
Laurens SC U.S.A. 174 D5
Laurentides, Réserve Faunique des nature res. Canada 169 G4
Lauri India 96 D4
Lauria Italy 57 H8
Laurie Island S. Atlantic Ocean 222 V2
Laurinburg U.S.A. 174 E5
Lauriston N.Z. 153 F11
Laurium U.S.A. 172 E3
Lauru i. Solomon Is see **Choiseul**
Lausanne Switz. 51 M6
Lausitzer Grenzwall park Germany 49 K4
Laut i. Indon. 77 E1
Laut i. Indon. 77 E3
Laut i. Indon. 77 G3
Laut, Selat sea chan. Indon. 77 F3
Lauta Germany 49 L4
Lautaro Chile 204 B5
Lautaro, Volcán vol. Chile 205 B8
Lautem East Timor 75 C5
Lauterbrunnen Switz. 51 N6
Lautersbach (Hessen) Germany 48 G5
Laut Kecil, Kepulauan is Indon. 77 F4
Lautoka Fiji 145 G3
Laut Taka Bonerate National Park Indon. 75 B4
Lauttawar, Danau l. Indon. 76 B1
Lauvsnes Norway 44 J2
Lauvuskylä Fin. 44 O3
Lauwersmeer l. Neth. 48 D2
Lava r. Rus. Fed. 49 S1
Lava Beds National Monument nat. park U.S.A. 180 B4
Lavaca r. U.S.A. 179 C6
Laval Canada 169 F4
Laval France 50 F4
Lavalette U.S.A. 176 C7
La Vall d'Uixó Spain 55 K5
Lāvān Iran 100 C5

278

Liannan China 87 E3
also known as Sanjiang
Lianping China 87 E3
also known as Yuanshan
Lianran China see Anning
Lianshan Guangdong China 87 E3
also known as Jitian
Lianshan Liaoning China 85 I3
formerly known as Jinxi
Liant, Cape pt Thai. see Samae San, Laem
Liantang China see Nanchang
Liantuo China 87 D2
Lianxian China see Lianzhou
Lianyin China 82 A1
Lianyuan China 87 D3
formerly known as Lantian
Lianyungang China 87 F1
Lianzhou Guangdong China 87 E3
formerly known as Lianxian
Lianzhou Guangxi China see Hepu
Lianzhushan China 82 C3
Liaocheng China 85 G4
Liaodong Bandao pen. China 85 I3
Liaodong Wan b. China 85 I3
Liaodun China 84 B3
Liaodunzhan China 84 B3
Liao He r. China 85 I3
Liaoning prov. China 85 I3
Liaoyang China 85 I3
Liaoyuan China 82 B4
Liaozhong China 85 I3
Liapades Greece 59 A9
Liaqatabad Pak. 101 G3
Liard r. Canada 166 F2
Liard Highway Canada 166 F2
Liard Plateau Canada 166 E2
Liard River Canada 166 E3
Liari Pak. 101 F5
Liat i. Indon. 77 D3
Liathach mt. U.K. 46 G6
Liban country Asia see Lebanon
Liban, Jebel mts Lebanon 108 H3
Libano Col. 198 C3
Libau Latvia see Liepāja
Libby U.S.A. 180 D2
Libenge Dem. Rep. Congo 126 C4
Liberal U.S.A. 178 B4
Liberdade Brazil 207 I9
Liberdade r. Amazonas Brazil 200 C1
Liberdade r. Mato Grosso Brazil 202 A4
Liberec Czech Rep. 49 M5
►Liberia country Africa 124 C5
►►114–115 Africa Countries
Liberia Costa Rica 186 B5
Libertad Venez. 198 D2
Libertador General San Martín Arg. 201 D5
Liberty AK U.S.A. 166 A1
Liberty IN U.S.A. 176 A6
Liberty KY U.S.A. 176 A8
Liberty ME U.S.A. 177 P1
Liberty MO U.S.A. 178 D4
Liberty NY U.S.A. 177 K4
Liberty TX U.S.A. 179 D6
Libertyville U.S.A. 172 F8
Libmanan Phil. 74 B3
Libnī, Jabal hill Egypt 108 E7
Libo China 87 C3
also known as Yuping
Libobo, Tanjung pt Indon. 75 D3
Libode S. Africa 133 N8
Libohovë Albania 59 B8
Liboi Kenya 128 D4
Libong, Ko i. Thai. 79 B7
Libourne France 50 F8
Libral Well Australia 150 D4
Librazhd Albania 58 B7
Libre, Sierra mts Mex. 184 C2
►Libreville Gabon 126 A4
Capital of Gabon.
Libuganon r. Phil. 74 C5
►Libya country Africa 120 B3
4th largest country in Africa. Spelt Al Lībīyah in Arabic.
►►114–115 Africa Countries
Libyan Desert Egypt/Libya 120 E3
Libyan Plateau Egypt 121 E2
Licantén Chile 204 B4
Licata Sicily Italy 57 F11
Lice Turkey 107 E3
Lichas pen. Greece 59 D10
also spelt Likhás
Licheng Fujian China see Xianyou
Licheng Guangxi China see Lipu
Licheng Shandong China 85 H4
also known as Hongjialou
Licheng Shanxi China 85 G4
Lichfield N.Z. 152 J6
Lichfield U.K. 47 K11
Lichinga Moz. 129 B8
formerly known as Vila Cabral
Lichte Germany 48 I5
Lichtenburg S. Africa 133 K3
Lichtenfels Germany 48 I5
Lichuan Hubei China 87 D2
Lichuan Jiangxi China 87 F3
also known as Rifeng
Licínio de Almeida Brazil 207 K1
Liciro Moz. 131 H3
Licking r. U.S.A. 176 A6
Lički Osik Croatia 56 H4
Licun China see Laoshan
Lid' r. Rus. Fed. 43 Q2
Lida Belarus 42 G8
Lidjombo Cent. Afr. Rep. 126 C4
Lidköping Sweden 45 K4
Lidsjöberg Sweden 44 K2
Lidumnieki Latvia 42 I5
Lidzbark Poland 49 Q2
Lidzbark Warmiński Poland 49 R1
Liebenbergs Vlei r. S. Africa 133 M4
Liebenwalde Germany 49 K3
Liebig, Mount Australia 148 A4
Liebling Romania 58 C3
►Liechtenstein country Europe 51 P5
►►32–33 Europe Countries
Liège Belgium 51 L2
also known as Luik
Liegnitz Poland see Legnica
Lieksa Fin. 44 O3
Lielais Ludzas l. Latvia 42 I5
Lielupe r. Latvia 42 F4
Lielvārde Latvia 42 F5
Lien Sweden 44 L3
Liên Nghia Vietnam 79 E6
Liên Sơn Vietnam 79 E5
Lienz Austria 49 J9
Liepāja Latvia 42 C5
also spelt Liepaya; formerly spelt Libau
Liepaya Latvia see Liepāja
Liepna Latvia 42 I4
Liesjärven kansallispuisto nat. park Fin. 42 E1
Liestal Switz. 51 N5
Lieto Fin. 42 D1
Liétor Spain 55 J6
Lietuva country Europe see Lithuania
Liévin France 51 I2
Lièvre r. Canada 168 F4
Liezen Austria 49 L8
Lifamatola i. Indon. 75 C3
Lifanga Dem. Rep. Congo 126 D4
Liffey r. Ireland 47 F10
Lifford Ireland 47 E9
Liffré France 50 E4
Lifi Mahuida mt. Arg. 205 C6
Lifou i. New Caledonia 145 F4
also spelt Lifu; formerly known as Chabrol
Lifu i. New Caledonia see Lifou
Lifudzin Rus. Fed. see Rudnyy
Ligao Phil. 74 B3
Līgatne Latvia 42 G4
Lighthouse Reef reef Belize 185 I5
Lightning Ridge Australia 147 E2
Ligny-en-Barrois France 51 L4
Ligonha r. Moz. 131 H3
Ligonier IN U.S.A. 172 H9
Ligonier PA U.S.A. 176 F5
Ligoúrion Greece see Lygourio
Ligui Mex. 184 C3
Ligure, Mar sea France/Italy see Ligurian Sea
Liguria admin. reg. Italy 56 A4
Ligurian Sea France/Italy 51 O9
also known as Ligure, Mar or Ligurienne, Mer
Ligurienne, Mer sea France/Italy see Ligurian Sea
Ligurta U.S.A. 183 J9
Lihir Group is P.N.G. 145 E2
formerly known as Gerrit Denys
Lihou Reef and Cays reef Australia 149 F3
Līhu'e U.S.A. 181 [inset] Y1
Lihula Estonia 42 E3
Liidli Kue Canada see Fort Simpson
Liivi laht b. Estonia/Latvia see Riga, Gulf of
Lijiang Yunnan China 86 B3
also known as Dayan
UNESCO World Heritage Site
Lijiang Yunnan China see Yuanjiang
Lijiazhai China 87 E2
Lik, Nam r. Laos 78 C4
Lika reg. Croatia 56 H4
Likak Iran 100 B4
Likala Dem. Rep. Congo 126 C4
Likasi Dem. Rep. Congo 127 E7
formerly known as Jadotville
Likati Dem. Rep. Congo 126 D4
Likati r. Dem. Rep. Congo 126 E4
Likely Canada 166 F4
Likhachevo Ukr. see Pervomays'kyy
Likhachyovo Ukr. see Pervomays'kyy
Likhás pen. Greece see Lichas
Likhoslavl' Rus. Fed. 43 Q4
Likimi Dem. Rep. Congo 126 D4
Likino-Dulevo Rus. Fed. 43 T6
Likisia East Timor see Liquiçá
Likma India 94 D1
Likolia Dem. Rep. Congo 126 D5
Likoma Island i. Malawi 129 B8
Likouala admin. reg. Congo 126 C4
Likouala r. Congo 126 C5
Likouala aux Herbes r. Congo 126 C5
Liku Indon. 77 E2
Liku Sarawak Malaysia 77 F1
Likupang Indon. 75 C2
L'Île-Rousse Corsica France 51 O10
Lilienfeld Austria 49 M7
Lilienthal Germany 48 F2
Liling China 87 E3
Liljendal Fin. 42 H1
Lilla Pak. 101 H3
Lilla Edet Sweden 45 K4
Lilla Luleälven r. Sweden 44 M2
Lillbläiken hill Sweden 44 L2
Lille Belgium 51 K1
Lille France 51 J2
Lille Bælt sea chan. Denmark see Little Belt
Lillebonne France 50 G3
Lillehammer Norway 45 J3
Lillesand Norway 45 J4
Lillestrøm Norway 45 J4
Lilley U.S.A. 172 H7
Lillian, Point hill Australia 151 D5
Lillie Glacier Antarctica 223 L2
Lillington U.S.A. 174 E5
Lillooet Canada 166 F5
Lillooet r. Canada 166 F5
Lillooet Range mts Canada 166 F5
Lilo r. Dem. Rep. Congo 126 E5
Lilong India 97 G4
►Lilongwe Malawi 129 B8
Capital of Malawi.
Lilo Viejo Arg. 204 E2
Liloy Phil. 74 B4
Lily U.S.A. 172 E5
Lim r. Serb. and Mont. 58 A5
►Lima Peru 200 A3
Capital of Peru and 4th most populous city in South America.
UNESCO World Heritage Site
Lima dept Peru 200 A2
Lima MT U.S.A. 180 D3
Lima NY U.S.A. 176 H3
Lima OH U.S.A. 176 A5
Limaão Brazil 199 F4
Lima Duarte Brazil 207 J8
Līmah Oman 105 G2
Lima Islands China see Wanshan Qundao
Liman Rus. Fed. 102 A3
Limanowa Poland 49 R6
Limar Indon. 75 C4
Limarí r. Chile 204 C3
Limas Indon. 76 D2
Limassol Cyprus 108 E3
also known as Lemesos
Limavady U.K. 47 F8
Limay r. Arg. 204 D5
Limay Mahuida Arg. 204 D5
Limbach-Oberfrohna Germany 49 J5
Limbang r. Sarawak Malaysia 77 F1
Limbani Peru 200 C3
Limbaži Latvia 42 F4
Limbdi India 96 A5
Limbe Cameroon 125 H5
formerly known as Victoria
Limboto Indon. 75 B2
Limboto, Danau l. Indon. 75 B2
Limbuè Moz. 131 H3
Limbungan Indon. 77 F3
Limbunya Australia 148 A3
Limburg prov. Belgium 48 C4
UNESCO World Heritage Site
Limburg an der Lahn Germany 48 F5
Lim Chu Kang Sing. 76 [inset]
Lim Chu Kang hill Sing. 76 [inset]
Lime Acres S. Africa 132 H5
Limehills N.Z. 153 C14
Limeira Brazil 206 F9
Limenaria Greece 58 F8
Limerick Ireland 47 D11
also spelt Luimneach
Limestone U.S.A. 176 C9
Limestone Point Canada 167 L4
Limfjorden sea chan. Denmark 45 J4
Limia r. Spain 54 C3
Limin Chersonisou Greece 59 G13
Limingen Norway 44 K2
Limingen l. Norway 44 K2
Liminka Fin. 44 N2
Limmen Bight b. Australia 148 C2
Limmen Bight River r. Australia 148 B2
Limni Greece 59 E10
Limnos i. Greece 59 G9
also spelt Lemnos
Limoeiro Brazil 202 F3
Limoges France 50 H7
Limón Hond. 186 B4
Limon U.S.A. 178 B4
Limonum France see Poitiers
Limoquije Bol. 200 D3
Limousin admin. reg. France 50 H7
Limousin, Plateaux du France 50 H7
Limoux France 51 I9
Limpopo prov. S. Africa 133 M1
formerly known as Northern Transvaal
Limpopo r. S. Africa/Zimbabwe 131 G5
Limpopo National Park nat. park S. Africa 131 F4
Limu China 87 D3
Limulunga Zambia 127 D8
Linaälven r. Sweden 44 M2
Līnah Saudi Arabia 104 C1
Linakeng Lesotho 133 M6
Linakhamari Rus. Fed. 44 O1
Lin'an Yunnan China see Jianshui
Lin'an Zhejiang China 87 F2
Linao Bay Phil. 74 C5
Linapacan i. Phil. 74 A4
Linapacan Strait Phil. 74 A4
Linares Chile 204 C4
Linares Mex. 185 F3
Linares Spain 55 H6
Linas, Monte mt. Sardinia Italy 57 A9
Linau Balui plat. Sarawak Malaysia 77 F2
Lincang China 86 B4
also known as Fengxiang
Lincheng Hainan China see Lingao
Lincheng Hunan China see Huitong
Linchuan China see Fuzhou
Linck Nunataks nunataks Antarctica 222 R1
Lincoln Arg. 204 E4
Lincoln U.K. 47 L10
historically known as Lindum
Lincoln CA U.S.A. 182 C3
Lincoln IL U.S.A. 174 B3
Lincoln KS U.S.A. 178 C4
Lincoln ME U.S.A. 174 G2
Lincoln MI U.S.A. 173 J6
►Lincoln NE U.S.A. 178 C3
State capital of Nebraska.
Lincoln City U.S.A. 180 A3
Lincoln Island Paracel Is 72 D3
Lincoln National Park Australia 146 B3
Lincoln Sea Canada/Greenland 165 O1
Lincolnshire Wolds hills U.K. 47 L10
Linda, Serra hills Brazil 202 D5
Lindas Norway 46 R3
Lindau (Bodensee) Germany 48 G8
Lindeman Group is Australia 149 F4
Linden Canada 167 H5
Linden Guyana 199 G3
formerly known as Mackenzie
Linden AL U.S.A. 175 C5
Linden CA U.S.A. 182 C3
Linden NJ U.S.A. 177 K5
Linden TN U.S.A. 174 C5
Linden TX U.S.A. 179 D5
Lindenow Fjord inlet Greenland see Kangerlussuatsiaq
Lindesberg Sweden 45 K4
Líndhos Greece see Lindos
Lindi r. Dem. Rep. Congo 126 E4
Lindi Tanz. 129 C7
Lindi admin. reg. Tanz. 129 C7
Lindian China 85 J2
Lindisfarne i. U.K. see Holy Island
Lindley S. Africa 133 L4
Lindóia Brazil 206 G9
Lindome Sweden 45 K4
Lindong China 85 H3
also known as Bairin Zuoqi
Lindos Greece 59 J12
also spelt Líndhos
Lindos, Akra pt Greece 59 J12
Lindsay Canada 168 E4
Lindsay U.S.A. 182 E5
Lindsborg U.S.A. 178 C4
Lindsdal Sweden 45 L4
Lindside U.S.A. 176 E8
Lindum U.K. see Lincoln
Line Islands S. Pacific Ocean 221 I5
Linets Rus. Fed. 43 Q9
Linfen China 85 F4
Lingamparti India 94 D2
Linganamakki Reservoir India 94 B3
Lingao China 87 D5
also known as Lincheng
Lingayen Phil. 74 B2
Lingayen Gulf Phil. 74 B2
Lingbao China 87 D1
formerly known as Guoluezhen
Lingbi China 87 F1
Lingcheng Guangxi China see Lingshan
Lingcheng Hainan China see Lingshui
Lingcheng Shandong China see Lingxian
Lingchuan Guangxi China 87 D3
Lingchuan Shanxi China 85 G5
Lingelethu S. Africa 133 K9
Lingelihle S. Africa 133 J9
Lingen (Ems) Germany 48 E3
Lingga i. Indon. 76 D3
Lingga, Kepulauan is Indon. 76 D3
Linggo Co l. China 89 E5
Linghai China 85 I3
also known as Dalinghe; formerly known as Jinxian
Lingig Phil. 74 C5
Lingle U.S.A. 180 F4
Lingomo Dem. Rep. Congo 126 D4
Lingqiu China 85 G4
Lingshan China 87 D4
also known as Lingcheng
Lingshan Wan b. China 85 I5
Lingshi Bhutan 97 F4
also spelt Lingzhi
Lingshi China 85 F4
Lingshui China 87 D5
also known as Lingcheng
Lingshui Wan b. China 87 D5
Lingsugur India 94 C2
Lingtai China 85 E5
also known as Zhongtai
Linguère Senegal 124 B3
Lingui China 87 D3
Lingxi China see Yongshun
Lingxian Hunan China see Yanling
Lingxian Shandong China 85 H4
also known as Lingcheng
Lingxiang China 87 E2
Lingyuan China 85 H3
Lingyun China 86 C3
also known as Sicheng
Lingzhi Bhutan see Lingshi
Lingzi Thang Plains l. Aksai Chin 89 B5
Linhai China 87 G2
Linhares Brazil 203 D6
Linhe China 85 E3
Linhpa Myanmar 78 A2
Linidis Valley N.Z. 153 D12
Linjiang Fujian China see Shanghang
Linjiang Jilin China 82 B4
Linköping Sweden 45 K4
Linkou China 82 C3
Linksness U.K. 46 I5
Linkuva Lith. 42 E5
Linli China 87 D2
Linlü Shan mt. China 85 G4
Linmingguan China see Yongnian
Linn U.S.A. 174 B4
Linn, Mount U.S.A. 182 B1
Linnansaaren kansallispuisto nat. park Fin. 44 O3
Linnhe, Loch inlet U.K. 46 G7
Linosa, Isola di i. Sicily Italy 57 E13
Linova Belarus 42 F9
Linqing China 85 G4
Linru China see Ruzhou
Lins Brazil 206 D8
Linsan Guinea 124 B4
Linshui China 86 C2
also known as Dingping
Linta r. Madag. 131 [inset] J5
Lintah, Selat sea chan. Indon. 75 A5
Lintan China 86 B1
Lintao China 84 D5
also known as Taoyang
Linth r. Switz. 51 P5
Linthal Switz. 51 P6
Linton U.S.A. 178 B2
Lintong China 87 D1
also known as Lishan
Linville U.S.A. 176 D9
Linxi China 85 H3
Linxia China 84 D5
Linxian Henan China see Linzhou
Linxian Shanxi China 85 F4
Linxiang China 87 E2
Linyanti r. Botswana/Namibia 131 E3
Linyanti Swamp Namibia 130 D3
Linyi Shandong China 85 H4
Linyi Shandong China 85 H5
Linyi Shanxi China 85 F5
Linying China 87 E1
Linz Austria 49 L7
Linze China 84 D4
formerly known as Shahepu or Shahezhen
Linzhou China 85 G4
formerly known as Linxian
Lioma Moz. 131 H2
Lion, Golfe du g. France 51 J10
English form Lions, Gulf of
Lions, Gulf of France see Lion, Golfe du
Lions Den Zimbabwe 131 F3
Lion's Head Canada 173 L6
Lioua Chad 120 B6
Liouesso Congo 126 B4
Lipa Phil. 74 B3
Lipari Isole Lipari Italy 57 G10
Lipari, Isola i. Isole Lipari Italy 57 G10
Lipari, Isole is Italy 57 G10
UNESCO World Heritage Site
Lipatkain Indon. 76 C2
Lipawki Belarus 42 I6
Liperi Fin. 44 O3
Lipetsk Rus. Fed. 43 U9
Lipetskaya Oblast' admin. div. Rus. Fed. 43 T9
English form Lipetsk Oblast
Lipetsk Oblast admin. div. Rus. Fed. see Lipetskaya Oblast'
Lipez, Cordillera de mts Bol. 200 D5
Lipiany Poland 49 L2
Lipin Bor Rus. Fed. 43 S1
Liping China 87 D3
also known as Defeng
Lipitsy Rus. Fed. 43 S8
Lipki Rus. Fed. 43 S8
Lipljan Kosovo, Srbija Serb. and Mont. 58 C6
Lipnaya Gorka Rus. Fed. 43 O2
Lipnica Murowana Poland 49 R6
UNESCO World Heritage Site
Lipník nad Bečvou Czech Rep. 49 O6
Lipno Poland 49 Q3
Lipno, Vodní nádrž resr Czech Rep. 49 L7
Lipova Romania 58 C2
Lipovtsy Rus. Fed. 90 B2
Lipovu Romania 58 E4
Lippe r. Germany 48 D4
Lippstadt Germany 48 F4
Lipscomb U.S.A. 179 B4
Lipsk Poland 49 U2
Lipsko Poland 49 S4
Lipsoí i. Greece see Leipsoi
Lipti Lekh pass Nepal 96 D3
Liptovská Mara, Vodná nádrž resr Slovakia 49 Q6
Liptovský Hrádok Slovakia 49 Q6
Liptovský Mikuláš Slovakia 49 Q6
Liptrap, Cape Australia 147 E4
Liptsy Rus. Fed. 43 P6
Lipu China 87 D3
also known as Licheng
Lipusz Poland 49 O1
Liquiçá East Timor 75 C5
also spelt Likisia or Liquissa
Liquissa East Timor see Liquiçá
Lira Uganda 128 B4
Liran i. Indon. 75 C4
Liranga Congo 126 C5
Liri r. Italy 56 F7
Liri, Jebel el mt. Sudan 128 A2
Lirung Indon. 75 C2
Lis Albania 58 B7
Lisa Romania 58 F3
Lisakovsk Kazakh. 103 E1
Lisala Dem. Rep. Congo 126 D4
Lisboa Port. see Lisbon
Lisboa admin. dist. Port. 54 B5
►Lisbon Port. 54 B6
Capital of Portugal. Also spelt Lisboa; historically known as Olisipo.
UNESCO World Heritage Site
Lisbon IL U.S.A. 172 E9
Lisbon ME U.S.A. 177 O1
Lisbon ND U.S.A. 178 C2
Lisbon NH U.S.A. 177 N1
Lisbon OH U.S.A. 176 E5
Lisbon Falls U.S.A. 177 O2
Lisburn U.K. 47 F9
Liscannor Bay Ireland 47 C11
Liscomb Game Sanctuary nature res. Canada 169 I4
Lisdoonvarna Ireland 47 C10
Lisec mt. Macedonia 58 D7
Lishan China see Lintong
Lishan Taiwan 87 G3
Lishe Jiang r. China 86 B3
Lishi Jiangxi China see Dingnan
Lishi Shanxi China 85 F4
Līshtar-e Bālā Iran 100 B4
Lishu China 82 B4
Lishui Jiangsu China 87 F2
Lishui Zhejiang China 87 F2
Li Shui r. China 87 D2
Lisichansk Ukr. see Lysychans'k
Lisieux France 50 G3
Lisiy Nos Rus. Fed. 43 L1
Liskeard U.K. 47 H13
Liski Rus. Fed. 41 F6
formerly known as Georgiu-Dezh
L'Isle-en-Dodon France 50 G9
L'Isle-Jourdain France 50 H9
L'Isle-sur-la-Sorgue France 51 L9
L'Isle-sur-le-Doubs France 51 M5
Lismore Australia 147 G2
Lismore Ireland 47 E11
Lismore N.Z. 153 F11
Lisne Ukr. 58 K2
Liss mt. Saudi Arabia 109 J6
Lissa Croatia see Vis
Lissa Poland see Leszno
Lisseri, Oued watercourse Tunisia 123 H2
Listafjorden b. Norway 45 I4
Lister, Mount Antarctica 223 K1
Listore watercourse Australia 148 C5
Listowel Canada 168 D5
Listowel Ireland 47 C11
Listowel Downs Australia 149 E5
Listvyaga, Khrebet mts Kazakh./Rus. Fed. 88 D1
Listvyanka Rus. Fed. 84 E1
Liswarta r. Poland 49 P4
Lit Sweden 44 K3
Litang Guangxi China 87 D4
Litang Sichuan China 86 B2
also known as Gaocheng
Litang Qu r. China 86 B2
Litani r. Fr. Guiana/Suriname 199 H4
Līṭānī, Nahr el r. Lebanon 108 G4
Litchfield CA U.S.A. 182 D1
Litchfield IL U.S.A. 174 B4
Litchfield MI U.S.A. 173 I8
Litchfield MN U.S.A. 178 D2
Litembe Tanz. 129 D7
Litene Latvia 42 I4
Līth, Wādī al watercourse Saudi Arabia 104 C3
Lithgow Australia 147 F3
Lithino, Akra pt Greece 59 F14
►Lithuania country Europe 42 E6
known as Lietuva in Lithuanian; formerly known as Litovskaya S.S.R.
►►32–33 Europe Countries
Litija Slovenia 56 G2
Lititz U.S.A. 177 I5
Litke, Mys c. Rus. Fed. 39 S2
Litochoro Greece 59 D8
Litoměřice Czech Rep. 49 L5
Litomyšl Czech Rep. 49 N6
UNESCO World Heritage Site
Litovel Czech Rep. 49 O6
Litovko Rus. Fed. 82 D2
Litovskaya S.S.R. country Europe see Lithuania
Little r. LA U.S.A. 179 D6
Little r. OK U.S.A. 179 D5
Little r. TX U.S.A. 179 C6
Little Abaco i. Bahamas 186 D1
Little Abitibi r. Canada 168 D3
Little Abitibi Lake Canada 168 D3
Little Aden Yemen see 'Adan as Sughra
Little Andaman i. India 95 G4
Little Bahama Bank sea feature Bahamas 186 D1
Little Barrier i. N.Z. 152 J4
Little Bay de Noc U.S.A. 172 F5
Little Belt sea chan. Denmark 45 J5
also known as Lille Bælt
Little Belt Mountains U.S.A. 180 E3
Little Bighorn r. U.S.A. 180 F3
Little Bitter Lake Egypt 108 D7
also known as Murrat el Sughra, Buheirat
Little Blue r. U.S.A. 178 C4
Little Bow r. Canada 167 H5
Little Buffalo r. Canada 167 H2
Little Cayman i. Cayman Is 186 C3
Little Churchill r. Canada 167 M3
Little Coco Island Cocos Is 79 A5
Little Colorado r. U.S.A. 183 M5
Little Creek Peak U.S.A. 183 L4
Little Current Canada 168 D4
Little Current r. Canada 168 C3
Little Desert National Park Australia 146 D4
Little Egg Harbor inlet U.S.A. 177 K6
Little Exuma i. Bahamas 186 E2
Little Falls MN U.S.A. 178 D2
Little Falls NY U.S.A. 177 K2
Littlefield AZ U.S.A. 183 K5
Littlefield TX U.S.A. 179 B5
Little Fish r. S. Africa 133 K10
Little Fork r. U.S.A. 174 A1
Little Fort Canada 166 F5
Little Grand Rapids Canada 167 M4
Little Grass Valley Reservoir U.S.A. 182 C2
Little Inagua Island Bahamas 187 E2
Little Kanawha r. U.S.A. 176 D6
Little Karas Berg plat. Namibia 132 C4
Little Karoo plat. S. Africa 132 E10
Little Lake U.S.A. 182 G6
Little Mecatina r. Canada see Petit Mécatina
Little Mecatina Island Canada see Petit Mécatina, Île du
Little Miami r. U.S.A. 176 A6
Little Minch sea chan. U.K. 46 E6
Little Missouri r. U.S.A. 178 B2
Little Muskingum r. U.S.A. 176 D6
Little Nicobar i. India 95 G5
Little Olifants r. S. Africa 133 N2
Little Pamir mts Afgh. 101 H2
Little Pic r. Canada 172 G2
Little Powder r. U.S.A. 180 F3
Little Rann marsh India 96 A5
Little Red r. U.S.A. 179 E5
Little Red River Canada 167 H3
Little River N.Z. 153 G11
Little River U.S.A. 175 E5
►Little Rock U.S.A. 179 D5
State capital of Arkansas.
Littlerock U.S.A. 182 G7
Little Sable Point U.S.A. 172 G7
Little Sachigo Lake Canada 168 A2
Little Salmon Lake Canada 166 C2
Little Salt Lake U.S.A. 183 L4
Little Sandy Desert Australia 150 B4
Little San Salvador i. Bahamas 186 E1
Little Sioux r. U.S.A. 178 C3
Little Smoky Canada 167 G4
Little Smoky r. Canada 167 G4
Little Snake r. U.S.A. 180 E4
Littlestown U.S.A. 177 H6
Little Tibet reg. Jammu and Kashmir see Ladakh
Littleton NC U.S.A. 176 H9
Littleton NH U.S.A. 177 N1
Littleton WV U.S.A. 176 E6
Little Traverse Bay U.S.A. 173 H5
Little Tupper Lake U.S.A. 177 K1
Little Turtle Lake Canada 172 A2
Little Valley U.S.A. 176 G3
Little Wabash r. U.S.A. 174 B4
Little Wanganui N.Z. 152 G9
Little White r. U.S.A. 178 B3
Little Wichita r. U.S.A. 179 C5
Little Wind r. U.S.A. 180 E4
Little Wood r. U.S.A. 180 D4
Little Zab r. Iraq see Zāb aş Şaghīr, Nahr az
Littoral prov. Cameroon 125 H5
Litunde Moz. 129 B8
Lituya Bay U.S.A. 166 B3
Litvínov Czech Rep. 49 K5
Liu Estonia 42 F3
Liuba China 86 C1
Liuchiu Yü i. Taiwan 87 G4
Liuchong He r. China 86 C3
Liuchow China see Liuzhou
Liugong Dao i. China 85 I4
Liugu He r. China 85 I3
Liuhe China 82 B4
Liu He r. China 85 H3
Liu He r. China 85 I3
Liuheng Dao i. China 87 G2
Liujiachang China 87 D2
Liujiang China 87 D3
also known as Labao
Liujiaxia China see Yongjing
Liujiaxia Shuiku resr China 84 D5
Liulin Gansu China see Jonê
Liulin Shanxi China 85 F4
Liupai China see Tian'e
Liupan Shan mts China 85 E5
Liupanshui China see Lupanshui
Liupo Moz. 131 H2
Liure Hond. 186 B4
Liushuquan China 84 B3
Liuwa Plain Zambia 127 D8
Liuwa Plain National Park Zambia 127 D8
Liuyang China 87 E2
Liuyang He r. China 87 E2
Liuzhangzhen China see Yuanqu
Liuzhou China 87 D3
formerly known as Liuchow
Livada, Akra pt Greece 59 G11
Livadi i. Greece 59 H12
Livadiya Rus. Fed. 82 D4
Līvāni Latvia 42 H5
Livanjsko Polje plain Bos.-Herz. 56 I4
Livarot France 50 G3
Līvbērze Latvia 42 E5
Live Oak CA U.S.A. 182 C2
Live Oak FL U.S.A. 175 D6
Liveringa Australia 150 D3
Livermore U.S.A. 182 C4
Livermore, Mount U.S.A. 181 F7
Liverpool Australia 147 F3
Liverpool Canada 169 H4
Liverpool U.K. 47 J10
UNESCO World Heritage Site
Liverpool U.S.A. 177 I2
Liverpool Bay Canada 164 F3
Liverpool Plains Australia 147 F2
Liverpool Range mts Australia 147 F2
Livingston U.K. 46 I8
Livingston AL U.S.A. 175 B5
Livingston CA U.S.A. 182 D4
Livingston KY U.S.A. 176 A8
Livingston LA U.S.A. 175 B6
Livingston MT U.S.A. 180 E3
Livingston NJ U.S.A. 177 K5
Livingston TX U.S.A. 179 D6
Livingston WI U.S.A. 172 C8
Livingston, Lake U.S.A. 179 D6
Livingstone Zambia 127 E9
also known as Maramba
Livingstonia Malawi 129 B7
Livingston Island Antarctica 222 T2
Livingston Manor U.S.A. 177 K4
Livingston Mountains N.Z. 153 C12
Livno Bos.-Herz. 56 J5
Livny Rus. Fed. 43 S9
Livo r. Rus. Fed. 44 O2
Livonia MI U.S.A. 173 J8
Livonia NY U.S.A. 176 H3
Livorno Italy 56 C5
historically known as Leghorn
Livradois, Monts du mts France 51 J7
Livradois Forez, Parc Naturel Régional du nature res. France 51 J7
Livramento do Brumado Brazil 202 D5
Livron-sur-Drôme France 51 K8
Liwā Oman 105 G2
Liwā', Wādī al watercourse Syria 109 H5
Liwale Tanz. 129 C7
Liwiec r. Poland 49 S3
Liwonde Malawi 129 B8
Liwonde National Park Malawi 129 B8
Liwu China see Lixian
Lixian Gansu China 86 C1
Lixian Hebei China 85 G4
also known as Liwu
Lixian Hunan China 87 D2
Lixian Sichuan China 86 B2
also known as Zagunao
Lixin China 87 F1
Lixouri Greece 59 B10
Lixus Morocco see Larache
Liyang China 87 F2
Liyuan China see Sangzhi
Liz r. Port. 54 C5
Lizarda Brazil 202 C4
Lizard Island Australia 149 E2
Lizard Point U.K. 47 G14
Lizarra Spain see Estella
Lizemores U.S.A. 176 D7
Liziping China 86 B2
Lizonne r. France 50 G7
Ljig Srbija Serb. and Mont. 58 B4
Ljubija Bos.-Herz. 56 I4
►Ljubljana Slovenia 56 G2
Capital of Slovenia. Historically known as Emona or Laibach.
Ljubuški Bos.-Herz. 56 J5
Ljugarn Sweden 45 L4
Ljungå Sweden 44 L3
Ljungan r. Sweden 45 L3
Ljungaverk Sweden 44 L3
Ljungby Sweden 45 K4
Ljungskile Sweden 45 J4
Ljusdal Sweden 45 L3
Ljusnan r. Sweden 45 L3
Ljusne Sweden 45 L3
Ljutomer Slovenia 56 I2
Llagostera Spain 55 N3
Llaima, Volcán vol. Chile 204 C5
Llanbedr U.K. see Lampeter
Llançà Spain 55 O2
also spelt Llansá
Llancanelo, Salina salt flat Arg. 204 C4
Llandeilo U.K. 47 I12
Llandovery U.K. 47 I12
also known as Llanymddyfri
Llandrindod Wells U.K. 47 I11
Llandudno U.K. 47 I10
Llanelli U.K. 47 H12
Llanes Spain 54 G1
Llangollen U.K. 47 I11
Llangurig U.K. 47 I11
Llano Mex. 184 C2
Llano U.S.A. 179 C6
Llano r. U.S.A. 179 C6
Llano Estacado plain U.S.A. 179 B5
Llanos plain Col./Venez. 198 D3
Llanquihue, Lago l. Chile 205 B6
Llansá Spain see Llançà
Llanymddyfri U.K. see Llandovery
Llata Peru 200 A2
Lleida Spain 55 L3
also spelt Lérida
Llentrisca, Cap c. Spain 55 M6
Llerena Spain 54 E6
Llica Bol. 200 C4
Llíria Spain 55 K5
Llodio Spain 55 I1
Lloret de Mar Spain 55 N3
Llorgara nat. park Albania 59 A8
Lloyd Bay Australia 149 D2
Lloyd George, Mount Canada 166 E3
Lloyd Lake Canada 167 I3
Lloydminster Canada 167 I4
Llucmayor Spain see Llucmajor
Llucmajor Spain 55 N5
also spelt Llucmayor
Llullaillaco, Parque Nacional nat. park Chile 200 C6
Llullaillaco, Volcán vol. Chile 200 C6
Lô, Sông r. China/Vietnam 86 C4
Loa r. Chile 200 C5
Loa U.S.A. 183 M3
Loagan Bunut National Park Sarawak Malaysia 77 F2
Loakulu Indon. 77 G3
Loanda Brazil 203 A7
Loano Italy 56 A4
Loay Phil. 74 C4
Lob' r. Rus. Fed. 43 Q5
Loban' r. Rus. Fed. 40 I4
Lobanovo Rus. Fed. 43 T8
Lobata Indon. 75 B3
Lobatse Botswana 131 E5
Löbau Germany 49 L4
Lobaye pref. Cent. Afr. Rep. 126 C3
Lobaye r. Cent. Afr. Rep. 126 C4
Löbenberg hill Germany 49 J4

Loberia Arg. 204 F5
Łobez Poland 49 M2
Lobito Angola 127 B8
Lobitos Peru 198 A6
Lobnya Rus. Fed. 43 S5
Loboko Congo 126 C5
Lobón Spain 54 E6
Lobos Arg. 204 F4
Lobos, Cabo c. Mex. 184 B2
Lobos, Isla de i. Mex. 185 F4
Lobos de Afuera, Islas is Peru 198 A6
Lobos de Tierra, Isla i. Peru 198 A6
Loburg Germany 48 J3
Loburn N.Z. 153 G11
Łobżenica Poland 49 O2
Locarno Switz. 51 O6
Lochaline U.K. 46 G7
Lochalsh Canada 173 I2
Lo Chau i. Hong Kong China see Beaufort Island
Loch Baghasdail U.K. see Lochboisdale
Lochboisdale U.K. 46 E6
also spelt Loch Baghasdail
Lochern National Park Australia 149 D5
Loches France 50 G5
Loch Garman Ireland see Wexford
Lochgilphead U.K. 46 G7
Lochiel S. Africa 133 O3
Lochinvar National Park Zambia 127 E8
Lochinver U.K. 46 G5
Loch Lomond & the Trossachs National Park nat. park U.K. 46 H7
Lochmaddy U.K. 46 E6
also known as Loch nam Madadh
Lochnagar mt. U.K. 46 I7
Loch nam Madadh U.K. see Lochmaddy
Łochów Poland 49 S3
Lochranza U.K. 46 G8
Lochsa r. U.S.A. 180 D3
Lochy, Loch l. U.K. 46 H7
Lock Australia 146 B3
Lockbourne U.S.A. 176 C6
Lockeford U.S.A. 182 C3
Lockerbie U.K. 47 I8
Lockhart Australia 147 E3
Lockhart U.S.A. 179 C6
Lockhart River Australia 149 D2
Lockhart River Aboriginal Reserve Australia 149 D2
Lock Haven U.S.A. 176 H4
Löcknitz r. Germany 48 I2
Lockport U.S.A. 176 G2
Locminé France 50 D5
Lôc Ninh Vietnam 79 D6
Locorotondo Italy 57 J8
Locri Italy 57 I10
Locumba r. Peru 200 C4
Lod Israel 108 F6
also known as Lydda
Loddon r. Australia 147 D3
Lode Latvia 42 G4
Lodève France 51 J9
Lodeynoye Pole Rus. Fed. 43 O1
Lodge, Mount Canada/U.S.A. 166 B3
Lodge Creek r. Canada/U.S.A. 167 I5
Lodhikheda India 96 C5
Lodhran Pak. 101 G4
Lodi Italy 56 B3
Lodi CA U.S.A. 182 C3
Lodi OH U.S.A. 176 C4
Lodi WI U.S.A. 172 D7
Løding Norway 44 K2
Lødingen Norway 44 K1
Lodja Dem. Rep. Congo 126 D5
Lodomeria Rus. Fed. see Vladimir
Lodosa Spain 55 I2
Lodrani India 96 A5
Lodwar Kenya 128 B4
Łódź Poland 49 Q4
English form Lodz
Lodz Poland see Łódź
Loei Thai. 78 C4
Loerie S. Africa 133 J10
Loeriesfontein S. Africa 132 D7
Lofoten is Norway 44 K1
Lofsdalen Sweden 45 K3
Lofter S. Africa 133 J7
Lofty Range hills Australia 150 B5
Log Rus. Fed. 41 G6
Loga Niger 125 F3
Logageng S. Africa 133 I2
Logan IA U.S.A. 178 D3
Logan NM U.S.A. 181 G6
Logan OH U.S.A. 176 C6
Logan UT U.S.A. 180 E4
Logan WV U.S.A. 176 D8

►Logan, Mount Canada 166 A2
2nd highest mountain in North America.
►►154–155 North America Landscapes

Logan, Mount U.S.A. 180 B2
Logan Creek r. Australia 149 E4
Logan Creek r. U.S.A. 178 C3
Logandale U.S.A. 183 J5
Logan Lake Canada 166 F5
Logan Mountains Canada 166 D2
Logansport IN U.S.A. 174 C3
Logansport LA U.S.A. 179 D6
Logatec Slovenia 56 G3
Lögdeälven r. Sweden 44 L3
Loge r. Angola 127 B6
Logone r. Africa 126 B1
Logone Birni Cameroon 125 I4
Logone Occidental pref. Chad 126 B2
Logone Oriental pref. Chad 126 C2
Logreşti Romania 58 E4
Logroño Spain 55 I2
Løgstør Denmark 45 J4
Logtak Lake India 97 G4
Logudoro reg. Sardinia Italy 57 A8
Lohardaga India 97 E5
Loharu India 96 B3
Lohatlha S. Africa 132 H5
Lohawat India 96 B4
Lohil r. China/India see Zayü Qu
Lohilahti Fin. 45 O3
Lohiniva Fin. 44 N2
Lohja Fin. 45 N3
Lohjanjärvi l. Fin. 42 E1
Löhne Germany 48 F3
Lohne (Oldenburg) Germany 48 F3
Lohtaja Fin. 44 M2
Lohusuu Estonia 42 I3
Loi, Nam r. Myanmar 78 C3
Loikaw Myanmar 78 B4
Loi Lan mt. Myanmar/Thai. 78 B4
Loi-lem Myanmar 78 B3
Loimaa Fin. 45 M3
Loimaan kunta Fin. 42 D1
Loipyet Hills Myanmar 78 B2
Loir r. France 50 F5
Loir, Les Vaux du valley France 50 G5
Loire r. France 51 D5
UNESCO World Heritage Site
Loire et de l'Allier, Plaines de la plain France 51 J6
Loisach r. Germany 48 I8
Loi Sang mt. Myanmar 78 B3
Loi Song mt. Myanmar 78 B3
Loita Plains Kenya 128 B5
Loja Ecuador 198 B6
Loja prov. Ecuador 198 B6
Loja Spain 54 G7
Lokan r. Sabah Malaysia 77 G1
Lokandu Dem. Rep. Congo 126 E5
Lokan tekojärvi l. Fin. 44 N2
Lokchim r. Rus. Fed. 40 I3
Lokeren Belgium 51 K1
Loki vol. Iceland 44 [inset] C2
Lokichar Kenya 128 B4
Lokichokio Kenya 128 B3
Lokilalaki, Gunung mt. Indon. 75 B3
Lokka Fin. 44 N2
Løkken Denmark 45 J4
Løkken Norway 44 J3
Loknya Rus. Fed. 43 L5
Lokofe Dem. Rep. Congo 126 D5
Lokoja Nigeria 125 G5
Lokolama Dem. Rep. Congo 126 C5
Lokolo r. Dem. Rep. Congo 126 C5
Lokomo Cameroon 125 I6
Lokoro r. Dem. Rep. Congo 126 C5
Lokosafa Cent. Afr. Rep. 126 C4
Lokossa Benin 125 F5
Lokot' Rus. Fed. 43 P9
Loksa Estonia 42 G2
Løksebotn Norway 44 L1
Loks Land i. Canada 165 M3
Lokutu Dem. Rep. Congo see Elisabetha
Lol Sudan 126 F3
Lol watercourse Sudan 126 F2
Lola Angola 127 B8
Lola Guinea 124 C5
Lola, Mount U.S.A. 182 D2
Lolland i. Denmark 45 J5
Lolle watercourse Sudan 128 A2
Lollondo Tanz. 128 B5
Lolo Dem. Rep. Congo 126 D4
Lolo U.S.A. 180 D3
Loloda Indon. 75 C2
Loloda Utara, Kepulauan is Indon. 75 C2
Lolodorf Cameroon 125 H6
Lolo Pass U.S.A. 180 D3
Lolowau Indon. 76 B2
Lolwane S. Africa 132 H3
Lom Bulg. 58 E5
Lom r. Bulg. 58 E5
Lom Norway 45 J3
Lom Rus. Fed. 43 U4
Loma U.S.A. 183 P2
Loma Alta Bol. 200 D2
Lomako r. Dem. Rep. Congo 126 D4
Lomaloma Fiji 145 H3
Lomami r. Dem. Rep. Congo 126 D4
Loma Mountains Sierra Leone 124 C4
Loma Negra, Planicie de la plain Arg. 204 D5
Lomar Pass Afgh. 101 F3
Lomas Peru 200 B3
Lomas Coloradas hills Arg. 205 D6
Lomas de Zamora Arg. 204 F4
Lomati r. S. Africa see Mlumati
Lombarda, Serra hills Brazil 199 H4
Lombardia admin. reg. Italy 56 B3
Lombardina Australia 150 C3
Lomblen i. Indon. 75 B5
Lombok Indon. 77 G5
Lombok i. Indon. 77 G5
Lombok, Selat sea chan. Indon. 77 F5

►Lomé Togo 125 F5
Capital of Togo.

Lomela r. Dem. Rep. Congo 126 D5
Lomié Cameroon 125 I6
Lomira U.S.A. 172 E7
Lommel Belgium 51 L1
Lomond Canada 169 J3
Lomond, Loch l. U.K. 46 H7
Lomonosov Rus. Fed. 43 K2
Lomont hills France 51 M5
Lomovoye Rus. Fed. 40 G2
Lomphat Cambodia see Lumphăt
Lompobattang, Gunung mt. Indon. 75 A4
Lompoc U.S.A. 182 D7
Lom Sak Thai. 78 C4
Lomsjö Sweden 44 L2
Łomża Poland 49 T2
Lonar India 94 C2
Lonato Italy 56 C3
Lonavale India 94 B2
Loncopue Arg. 204 C5
Londa Bangl. 97 F5
Londa India 94 B3
Londinium U.K. see London
Londoko Rus. Fed. 82 D2
London Canada 168 D5

►London U.K. 47 L12
Capital of the United Kingdom and of England. 4th most populous city in Europe. Historically known as Londinium.
UNESCO World Heritage Site
►►18–19 World Cities

London KY U.S.A. 176 A8
London OH U.S.A. 176 B6
London City airport U.K. 47 M12
Londonderry U.K. 47 E9
also known as Derry or Doire
Londonderry U.S.A. 177 M2
Londonderry, Cape Australia 150 D2
Londonderry, Isla i. Chile 205 C9
London Gatwick airport U.K. 47 L12
London Heathrow airport U.K. 47 L12
London Stansted airport U.K. 47 M12
Londres Arg. 204 D2
Londrina Brazil 206 B10
Lone Mountain U.S.A. 176 A9
Lone Pine U.S.A. 182 F5
Long Thai. 78 B4
Longa Angola 127 C8
Longa r. Bengo/Cuanza Sul Angola 127 B7
Longa r. Cuando Cubango Angola 127 C9
Longa Greece 59 C12
Longa, Proliv sea chan. Rus. Fed. 39 R2
English form De Long Strait
Longagung Indon. 77 F2
Long Akah Sarawak Malaysia 77 F2
Longa-Mavinga, Coutada Pública do nature res. Angola 127 D9
Long'an Guangxi China 87 C4
Long'an Sichuan China see Pingwu
Longarone Italy 56 E2
Longaví, Nevado de mt. Chile 204 C5
Long Bay U.S.A. 175 E5
Longbeach N.Z. 153 F12
Long Beach CA U.S.A. 182 F8
Long Beach WA U.S.A. 180 A3
Longbia Indon. 77 G2
Longboh Indon. 77 F2
Long Branch U.S.A. 177 L5
Longburn N.Z. 152 J8
Long Cay i. Bahamas 187 E2
Longchang China 86 C2
also known as Jin'e
Longcheng Anhui China see Xiaoxian
Longcheng Guangdong China see Longmen
Longcheng Jiangxi China see Pengze
Longcheng Yunnan China see Chenggong
Longchuan Guangdong China 87 E3
also known as Laolong
Longchuan Yunnan China see Nanhua
Longchuan Jiang r. China 86 A4
Long Creek r. Canada 167 K5
Long Eaton U.K. 47 K11
Longfellow, Mount N.Z. 153 G10
Longford Ireland 47 E10
Longgang Chongqing China see Dazu
Longgang Guangdong China 87 E4
Longgi r. Indon. 77 G2
Long Harbour Hong Kong China 87 [inset]
also known as Tai Tan Hoi Hap
Longhope U.K. 46 I5
Longhua China 85 H3
Longhui China 87 D3
also known as Taohong; formerly known as Taohuaping
Longhurst, Mount Antarctica 223 K1
Longibau Indon. 77 G2
Longido Tanz. 128 C5
Longikis Indon. 77 G3
Longing, Cape Antarctica 222 U2
Longiram Indon. 77 F3
Long Island Bahamas 187 E2
Long Island N.S. Canada 169 H4
Long Island Nunavut Canada 168 E2
Long Island India 95 G3
Long Island P.N.G. 73 K8
Long Island U.S.A. 177 M5
Long Island Sound sea chan. U.S.A. 177 L4
Longjiang China 85 I2
Long Jiang r. China 87 D3
Longjin Fujian China see Qingliu
Longjin Jiangxi China see Anyi
Longjuzhai China see Danfeng
Longkou China 85 I4
Longkou Gang b. China 85 I4
Longlac Canada 168 C3
Long Lake l. Canada 168 C3
Long Lake U.S.A. 177 K2
Long Lake l. MI U.S.A. 172 H6
Long Lake l. MI U.S.A. 173 J5
Long Lake l. NY U.S.A. 177 K1
Longli China 86 C3
also known as Longshan
Longlin China 86 C3
also known as Xinzhou
Longmeadow U.S.A. 177 M3
Longmen China 87 E4
also known as Longcheng
Longmen Shan mts China 86 C1
Longming China 86 C4
Longmont U.S.A. 180 F4
Longnan China 87 E3
Longnawan Indon. 77 F2
Longobucco Italy 57 I9
Longonjo Angola 127 B8
Longotoma Chile 204 C4
Longpahangai Indon. 77 F2
Long Phu Vietnam 79 D6
Longping China see Luodian
Long Point Canada 168 D5
Long Point Man. Canada 167 L4
Long Point Ont. Canada 168 D5
Long Point Bay Canada 173 M8
Long Prairie U.S.A. 178 D2
Longpujungan Indon. 77 F2
Longquan Guizhou China see Danzhai
Longquan Guizhou China see Fenggang
Longquan Zhejiang China 87 F2
Longquan Xi r. China 87 G2
Long Range Mountains Canada 169 J3
Longreach Australia 149 E4
Long Reef reef Australia 150 D2
Long Reef reef P.N.G. 149 F1
Longriba China 86 B1
Long Ridge U.S.A. 176 A7
Longshan Guizhou China see Longli
Longshan Hunan China 87 D2
also known as Min'an
Longsheng China 87 D3
Longshou Shan mts China 84 D4
Longs Peak U.S.A. 180 F4
Long Teru Sarawak Malaysia 77 F2
Longtian China 87 D2
Longtom Lake Canada 167 G1
Long Tompas pass S. Africa 133 O2
Longtown U.K. 47 J8
Longué-Jumelles France 50 F5
Longue-Pointe Canada 169 H3
Longueuil Canada 69 F4
Longuyon France 51 L3
Longvale U.S.A. 182 A2
Long Valley U.S.A. 183 M7
Longview TX U.S.A. 179 D5
Longview WA U.S.A. 180 B3
Longwangmiao China 90 C2
Longwei Co l. China 89 E5
Longxi China 86 C1
Longxian Guangdong China see Wengyuan
Longxian Shaanxi China 86 C1
Longxi Shan mt. China 87 F3
Longxun China see Dehua
Long Xuyên Vietnam 79 D6
Longyan China 87 F3
Longyao China 85 G4

►Longyearbyen Svalbard 38 B2
Capital of Svalbard.

Longzhen China 82 B2
Longzhou China 86 C4
Longzhouping China see Changyang
Lonigo Italy 56 D3
Lonja r. Croatia 56 I3
Lonjsko Polje plain Croatia 56 I3
Lonkintsy Madag. 131 [inset] K3
Lonoke U.S.A. 174 B5
Lönsboda Sweden 45 K4
Lønsdalen valley Norway 44 K2
Lons-le-Saunier France 51 L6
Lontar i. Indon. 75 D4
Lonton Myanmar 78 B2
Lontra Brazil 199 I6
Lontra r. Mato Grosso do Sul Brazil 203 A7
Lontra r. Tocantins Brazil 202 B3
Loo Estonia 42 F2
Looc Phil. 74 B3
Loochoo Islands Japan see Ryukyu Islands
Looking Glass r. U.S.A. 173 I8
Lookout, Cape Canada 168 D2
Lookout, Cape U.S.A. 174 E5
Lookout, Point U.S.A. 173 J6
Lookout Mountain U.S.A. 182 F5
Lookout Point Qld Australia 149 E2
Lookout Point W.A. Australia 151 B7
Loolmalasin vol. crater Tanz. 128 B5
Looma Australia 150 D3
Loon Canada 168 B3
Loon r. Canada 167 H3
Loongana Australia 151 D6
Loon Lake Canada 167 I4
Loop Head Ireland 47 C11
Lootsberg Pass S. Africa 133 I8
Lop China 89 C4
Lopandino Rus. Fed. 43 P9
Lopary Madag. 131 [inset] J4
Lopasnya Rus. Fed. see Chekhov
Lopasnya r. Rus. Fed. 43 S7
Lopatina, Gora mt. Rus. Fed. 82 F2
Lopatino Rus. Fed. 41 H5
Lopatinskiy Rus. Fed. 43 T6
Lopatka, Cape Rus. Fed. see Lopatka, Mys
Lopatka, Mys c. Kamchatskaya Oblast' Rus. Fed. 39 P4
Lopatka, Mys c. Respublika Sakha (Yakutiya) Rus. Fed. 39 P2
English form Lopatka, Cape
Lopatovo Rus. Fed. 43 J4
Lopazna Rus. Fed. 43 N8
Lop Buri Thai. 79 C5
also known as Tha Hin
Lopé-Okanda, Réserve de nature res. Gabon 126 A5
Lopez Phil. 74 B3
Lopez, Cap c. Gabon 126 A5
Lopnur China see Yuli
Lop Nur salt l. China 88 E3
Lopori r. Dem. Rep. Congo 126 C4
Lopphavet b. Norway 44 M1
Loppi Fin. 45 N3
Lora r. Afgh. 101 F4
Lora watercourse Australia 146 B2
Lora Norway 45 J3
Lora, Hamun-i- dry lake Pak. 101 F4
Lora del Río Spain 54 F7
Lorain U.S.A. 176 C4
Loralai Pak. 101 G4
Loralai r. Pak. 101 G4
Lorca Spain 55 J7
Lord Howe Atoll Solomon Is see Ontong Java Atoll
Lord Howe Island Australia 145 E5
UNESCO World Heritage Site
Lord Loughborough Island Myanmar 79 B6
Lordsburg U.S.A. 181 E6
Lore Lindu National Park Indon. 75 B3
Lorena Brazil 203 C7
Lorengau P.N.G. 73 K7
Lorentz r. Indon. 73 I8
Lorenzo del Real Mex. 185 F4
Lorenzo Geyres Uruguay 204 F4
Lorestān prov. Iran 100 B3
Loreto Brazil 202 C3
Loreto Italy 56 F5
Loreto Mex. 184 C3
Loreto Para. 201 F5
Loreto dept Peru 198 C5
Loreto Phil. 74 C4
Loretta U.S.A. 172 C5
Lorian Swamp Kenya 128 C4
Lorica Col. 198 C2
Lorient France 50 C5
Lorillard r. Canada 167 N1
Lormi India 97 D5
Lorn, Firth of est. U.K. 46 G7
Lorne Qld Australia 149 E5
Lorne Vic. Australia 147 D4
Loro r. China 89 F6
Loropéni Burkina 124 E4
Lörrach Germany 48 E8
Lorrain, Plateau France 51 M4
Lorraine Australia 148 C3
Lorraine admin. reg. France 51 M4
Lorraine, Parc Naturel Régional de park France 51 L4
Lorsch Germany 48 F6
UNESCO World Heritage Site
Lort r. Australia 151 C7
Lörudden Sweden 45 L3
Los, Îles de is Guinea 124 B4
Losai National Reserve nature res. Kenya 128 C4
Losal India 96 B4
Los Alamos CA U.S.A. 182 D7
Los Alamos NM U.S.A. 181 F6
Los Alerces, Parque Nacional nat. park Arg. 205 C6
Los Amores Arg. 204 F3
Los Andes Chile 204 C4
Los Ángeles Chile 204 B5

►Los Angeles U.S.A. 182 F7
3rd most populous city in North America.
►►18–19 World Cities

Los Angeles Aqueduct canal U.S.A. 182 F6
Los Antiguos Arg. 205 C7
Los Arabos Cuba 186 C2
Los Banos U.S.A. 182 D4
Los Barreros mt. Spain 55 I6
Los Barrios Spain 54 F8
Los Blancos Arg. 201 E5
Los Chiles Costa Rica 186 B5
Los Corales del Rosario, Parque Nacional nat. park Col. 198 C2
Los Coronados, Islas is Mex. 183 G9
Los Corrales de Buelna Spain 54 G1
Los Cusis Beni Bol. 200 D3
Los Cusis Beni Bol. 201 D3
Los Desventurados, Islas de is S. Pacific Ocean 221 N7
Los Difuntos, Lago de l. Uruguay see Negra, Lago
Losevo Rus. Fed. 41 G6
Loseya well Tanz. 129 C6
Los Gatos U.S.A. 182 C4
Los Glaciares, Parque Nacional nat. park Arg. 205 B8
UNESCO World Heritage Site
Los Haitises nat. park Dom. Rep. 187 F3
Los Hoyos Mex. 184 C2
Los Huemules, Parque Nacional nat. park Chile 205 B7
Łosice Poland 49 T3
Los Idolos Mex. 185 G5
Lošinj i. Croatia 56 G4
Los Juries Arg. 204 E3
Los Katios, Parque Nacional nat. park Col. 198 B3
UNESCO World Heritage Site
Loskop S. Africa 133 N5
Loskop Dam Nature Reserve S. Africa 133 N2
Los Lagos Chile 204 B5
Los Lagos admin. reg. Chile 204 E6
Loslau Poland see Wodzisław Śląski
Los Leones Mex. 184 D2
Los Lunas U.S.A. 181 F6
Los Mármoles, Parque Nacional nat. park Mex. 185 F4
Los Menucos Arg. 204 C6
Los'mino Rus. Fed. 43 P6
Los Mochis Mex. 184 C3
Los Molinos U.S.A. 182 B1
Los Navalmorales Spain 54 G5
Los Nevados, Parque Nacional nat. park Col. 198 C3
Los Palacios Cuba 186 C2
Los Palacios y Villafranca Spain 54 F7
Lospatos East Timor 75 C5
Los Pedroches plat. Spain 54 F6
Los Reyes Mex. 185 E5
Los Ríos prov. Ecuador 198 B5
Los Roques, Islas is Venez. 199 E2
Los Sauces Chile 204 B5
Lossiemouth U.K. 46 I6
Los Taques Venez. 198 D2
Lost Creek U.S.A. 176 E8
Los Telares Arg. 204 E3
Los Teques Venez. 199 E2
Los Testigos is Venez. 199 F2
Lost Hills U.S.A. 182 E6
Los Tigres Arg. 204 E2
Lost Trail Pass U.S.A. 180 D3
Losvida, Vozyera l. Belarus 43 L6
Los Vientos Chile 200 C6
Los Vilos Chile 204 C3
Los Yébenes Spain 54 H5
Lot r. France 51 G8
Lota Chile 204 B5
Lotagipi Swamp Kenya 128 B3
Lote Norway 45 I3
Løten Norway 45 J3
Lotfābād Turkm. 102 D5
Loth U.K. 46 J4
Lothagum Hills Sudan 128 B3
Lothair S. Africa 133 O3
Lotikipi Plain Kenya 128 B3
Loto Dem. Rep. Congo 126 D5
Lotoi r. Dem. Rep. Congo 126 C5
Lotoshino Rus. Fed. 43 Q5
Lot's Wife i. Japan see Sōfu-gan
Lotta r. Fin./Rus. Fed. 44 O1
also spelt Lutto
Louangnamtha Laos 78 C3
also spelt Luang Nam Tha
Louangphabang Laos 78 C4
also spelt Luang Prabang
UNESCO World Heritage Site
Louang Phrabang Range mts Laos/Thai. 78 C4
L'Ouanne r. France 51 I5
Loubomo Congo 126 B6
also known as Dolisie
Loučná hill Czech Rep. 49 K5
Loudéac France 50 D4
Loudi China 87 D3
Loudima Congo 126 B6
Loudon U.S.A. 174 C5
Loudonville U.S.A. 176 C5
Loudun France 50 G5
Louéssé r. Congo 126 B5
Louga Senegal 124 A3
Loughborough U.K. 47 K11
Lougheed Island Canada 165 I2
Loughrea Ireland 47 D10
Louhans France 51 L6
Louisa KY U.S.A. 176 C7
Louisa VA U.S.A. 176 H7
Louisa Downs Aboriginal Reserve Australia 150 D3
Louisbourg Canada 169 J4
formerly spelt Louisburg
Louisburg Canada see Louisbourg
Louisburg U.S.A. 176 G9
Louise Falls Canada 167 G2
Louis-Gentil Morocco see Youssoufia
Louisiade Archipelago is P.N.G. 149 G1
Louisiana U.S.A. 174 B4
Louisiana state U.S.A. 175 B6
Louisvale S. Africa 132 F5
Louisville GA U.S.A. 175 D5
Louisville IL U.S.A. 174 B4
Louisville KY U.S.A. 174 C4
Louisville MS U.S.A. 175 B5
Louisville OH U.S.A. 176 D5
Louis-XIV, Pointe pt Canada 168 E2
Loukhi Rus. Fed. 44 P2
Loukoléla Congo 126 C5
Loukouo Congo 126 B5
Loulé Port. 54 C7
Louloumi Mali 124 D4
Loum Cameroon 125 H5
Louny Czech Rep. 49 K5
Loup r. U.S.A. 178 C3
Loup City U.S.A. 178 C3
Loups Marins, Lacs des lakes Canada 169 F1
Lourdes Canada 169 J3
Lourdes France 50 F9
Lourenço Brazil 199 I4
Lourenço Marques Moz. see Maputo
Lourinhã Port. 54 B5
Lousã Port. 54 C4
Louterwater S. Africa 132 H10
Louth Australia 147 E2
Louth U.K. 47 L10
Loutra Greece 59 F11
Loutra Aidipsou Greece 59 E10
Loutraki Greece 59 D11
Louvain Belgium see Leuven
Louviers France 50 H3
Louwsburg S. Africa 133 P4
Lövånger Sweden 44 M2
Lovasberény Hungary 49 P8
Lovat' r. Rus. Fed. 43 M3
Lövberga Sweden 44 K3
Lovćen mts Serb. and Mont. 56 K6
Lovech Bulg. 58 F5
Loveland U.S.A. 180 F4
Lovell ME U.S.A. 177 O1
Lovell WY U.S.A. 180 E3
Lovelock U.S.A. 182 F1
Lovenia, Mount U.S.A. 183 N1
Lovere Italy 56 C3
Lovers' Leap mt. U.S.A. 176 E9
Loves Park U.S.A. 172 D8
Loviisa Fin. 45 N3
Lovington U.S.A. 179 B5
Lovozero Rus. Fed. 40 E1
Lovran Croatia 56 G3
Lovrin Romania 58 B3
Lövstabukten b. Sweden 45 L3
Lovtsy Rus. Fed. 43 U6
Lóvua Angola 127 D6
Lóvua Angola 127 D7
Low Canada 173 R5
Lowa Dem. Rep. Congo 126 E5
Lowa r. Dem. Rep. Congo 126 E5
Lowarai Pass Pak. 101 G3
Lowell IN U.S.A. 172 F9
Lowell MA U.S.A. 177 N3
Lowell MI U.S.A. 172 H8
Lowell OR U.S.A. 180 B4
Lowell VT U.S.A. 177 M1
Lowelli Sudan 128 B3
Löwen watercourse Namibia 132 B4
Lower Arrow Lake Canada 166 G5
Lower Brule Indian Reservation res. U.S.A. 178 C2
Lower California pen. Mex. see Baja California
Lower Garry Lake Canada 167 L1
Lower Glenelg National Park Australia 146 D4
Lower Granite Gorge U.S.A. 183 K6
Lower Hutt N.Z. 152 I9
Lower Klamath National Wildlife Refuge nature res. U.S.A. 180 B4
Lower Laberge Canada 166 C2
Lower Lake U.S.A. 182 B3
Lower Loteni S. Africa 133 N6
Lower Lough Erne l. U.K. 47 E9
Lower Peirce Reservoir Sing. 76 [inset]
Lower Pitseng S. Africa 133 M7
Lower Red Lake U.S.A. 178 D2
Lower Sabie S. Africa 133 P2
Lower Saxony land Germany see Niedersachsen
Lower Tunguska r. Rus. Fed. see Nizhnyaya Tunguska
Lower Zambezi National Park Zambia 127 F8
Lowestoft U.K. 47 N11
Lowgar prov. Afgh. 101 G3
Łowicz Poland 49 Q3
Low Island Kiribati see Starbuck Island
Lowmoor U.S.A. 176 F8
Lowsville U.S.A. 176 E6
Lowville U.S.A. 177 J2
Loxton Australia 146 D3
Loxton S. Africa 132 G8
Loyalsock Creek r. U.S.A. 177 I4
Loyalton U.S.A. 182 D2
Loyalty Islands New Caledonia see Loyauté, Îles
Loyang China see Luoyang
Loyauté, Îles is New Caledonia 145 F4
English form Loyalty Islands
Loyd U.S.A. 172 C7
Loyengo Swaziland 133 P3
Loyev Belarus see Loyew
Loyew Belarus 41 D6
also spelt Loyev
Loyno Rus. Fed. 40 J4
Loyola, Punta pt Arg. 205 C8
Løypskardtinden mt. Norway 44 K2
Lozère, Mont mt. France 51 J8
Loznica Srbija Serb. and Mont. 58 A4
Loznitsa Bulg. 58 H5
Lozova Ukr. 41 F6
also spelt Lozovaya
Lozovaya Kazakh. see Lozovoye
Lozovaya Ukr. see Lozova
Lozovik Srbija Serb. and Mont. 58 C4
Lozovoye Kazakh. 103 I1
formerly known as Lozovaya
Loz'va r. Rus. Fed. 40 L3
Ltyentye Apurte Aboriginal Land res. Australia 148 B5
also known as Santa Teresa Aboriginal Land
Luabo Moz. 131 H3
Luacano Angola 127 D7
Luachimo r. Angola/Dem. Rep. Congo 127 D6
Lua Dekere r. Dem. Rep. Congo 126 C4
Luakila Dem. Rep. Congo 126 E6
Luala r. Moz. 131 H3
Luambe National Park Zambia 129 B8
Luampa r. Zambia 127 E8
Lu'an China 87 F2
Luanchuan China 87 D1
Luanco Spain 54 F1

►Luanda Angola 127 B7
Capital of Angola.

Luanda prov. Angola 127 B7
Luando Angola 127 C7
Luando r. Angola 127 C7
Luando, Reserva Natural Integral do nature res. Angola 127 C7
Luang, Huai r. Thai. 78 C4
Luang, Khao mt. Thai. 79 B6
Luang, Thale lag. Thai. 79 C7
Luanginga r. Zambia 127 D8
Luang Nam Tha Laos see Louangnamtha
Luang Prabang Laos see Louangphabang
Luanguinga r. Angola 127 D8
Luangwa Zambia 127 F8
formerly known as Feira
Luangwa r. Zambia 127 F8
Luanhaizi China 84 B5
Luan He r. China 85 H4
Luannan China 85 H4
also known as Bencheng
Lua Nova Brazil 199 G6
Luanping China 85 H3
Luanshya Zambia 127 F8
Luanxian China 85 H4
also known as Luanzhou
Luanza Dem. Rep. Congo 127 F7
Luanzhou China see Luanxian
Luao Angola see Luau
Luapula prov. Zambia 127 F7
Luar, Danau l. Indon. 77 F2
Luarca Spain 54 E1
Luashi Dem. Rep. Congo 127 D7
Luatamba Angola 127 D8
Luau Angola 127 D7
formerly known as Teixeira de Sousa or Vila Teixeira de Sousa; formerly spelt Luao
Luba Equat. Guinea 125 H6
formerly known as San Carlos
Lubaczów Poland 49 U5
Lubalo Angola 127 C7
Lubań Poland 49 M4
Lubāna Latvia 42 H5
Lubānas ezers l. Latvia 42 H5
Lubang Phil. 74 B3
Lubang i. Phil. 74 B3
Lubang Islands Phil. 74 A3
Lubango Angola 127 B8
formerly known as Sá da Bandeira
Lubao Dem. Rep. Congo 127 E6
Lubartów Poland 49 T4
Lubawa Poland 49 Q2
Lübbecke Germany 48 F3
Lübben Germany 49 K4
Lübbenau Germany 49 K4
Lubbeskolk salt pan S. Africa 132 D6
Lubbock U.S.A. 179 B5
Lübeck Germany 48 H2
UNESCO World Heritage Site
Lubeck U.S.A. 176 D6
Lübecker Bucht b. Germany 48 H1
Lubefu Dem. Rep. Congo 126 E6
Lubei China 85 I2
also known as Jarud
Lubelska, Wyżyna hills Poland 49 T4
Lüben Poland see Lubin
Lubenka Kazakh. 102 C2
Lubero Dem. Rep. Congo 126 F5
Lubéron, Montagne du ridge France 51 L9
Lubéron, Parc Naturel Régional du nature res. France 51 L9
Lubersac France 50 H7
Lubie, Jezioro l. Poland 49 M2
Lubienka r. Poland 49 P3
Lubień Kujawski Poland 49 Q3
Lubin Poland 49 N4
historically known as Lüben
Lubisi Dam resr S. Africa 133 L8
Lublin Poland 49 T4
Lubliniec Poland 49 P5
Lubnān country Asia see Lebanon
Lubny Ukr. 41 E6
Lubok Antu Sarawak Malaysia 77 E2
Lubombo admin. dist. Swaziland 133 P3
Luboń Poland 49 N3
Lubosalma Rus. Fed. 44 O3
Lubraniec Poland 49 P3
Lubrín Spain 55 I7
Lübtheen Germany 48 I2
Lubuagan Phil. 74 B2
Lubudi Dem. Rep. Congo 127 E7
Lubudi r. Dem. Rep. Congo 127 E7
Lubuklinggau Indon. 76 C3
Lubukpakam Indon. 76 B2
Lubuksikaping Indon. 76 C2
Lubumbashi Dem. Rep. Congo 127 E7
formerly known as Élisabethville
Lubunda Dem. Rep. Congo 127 E6
Lubungu Zambia 127 E8
Lubuta Zambia 127 D9
Lubutu Dem. Rep. Congo 126 E5
Lubutu r. Dem. Rep. Congo 126 E5
Lubwe Zambia 127 F7
Lubyanki Rus. Fed. 43 Q9
Lucala Angola 127 B7
Lucan Canada 173 L7
Lucanas Peru 200 B3
Lučani Srbija Serb. and Mont. 58 B5
Lucania, Mount Canada 166 A2
Lucaoshan China 84 B4
Lucapa Angola 127 D7
formerly known as Lukapa
Lucas Brazil 201 G3
Lucasville U.S.A. 176 C7
Lucca Italy 56 C5
Lucé France 50 H4
Lucea Jamaica 186 D3
Luce Bay U.K. 47 H9
Lucedale U.S.A. 175 B6
Lucélia Brazil 206 B8
Lucena Phil. 74 B3
Lucena Spain 54 G7
Lučenec Slovakia 49 Q7
Lucera Italy 56 H7
Lucerna Peru 200 C3
Lucerne Switz. 51 O5
also spelt Luzern
Lucerne U.S.A. 182 B2
Lucerne Valley U.S.A. 183 H7
Lucero Mex. 184 D2
Lucha r. Rus. Fed. 82 C1
Luchay Belarus 42 I6
Luchegorsk Rus. Fed. 82 D3
Lucheng Guangxi China see Luchuan
Lucheng Shanxi China 85 G4
Lucheng Sichuan China see Kangding
Lucheringo r. Moz. 129 C7
Luchki Rus. Fed. 43 U5
Luchosa r. Belarus 43 L6
Lüchow Germany 48 I3
Luchuan China 87 D4
also known as Lucheng
Lüchun China 86 B4
also known as Daxing
Lucinda Australia 149 E3
Lucipara, Kepulauan is Indon. 75 C4
Lucira Angola 127 B8
Luciu Romania 58 I4

Łuck Ukr. *see* **Luts'k**
Luck U.S.A. **172** A5
Luckau Germany **49** K4
Luckeesarai India *see* **Lakhisarai**
Luckenwalde Germany **49** K3
Luckhoff S. Africa **133** I6
Lucknow Canada **173** L7
Lucknow India **96** D4
Luçon France **50** E6
Lücongpo China **87** D2
Lucunga Angola **127** B6
Lucusse Angola **127** D8
Lucy Creek Australia **148** C4
Lüda China *see* **Dalian**
Luda Kamchiya *r.* Bulg. **58** I5
Ludbreg Croatia **56** I2
Lüdenscheid Germany **48** E4
Lüderitz Namibia **130** B5
Ludewa Tanz. **129** B7
Ludhiana India **96** B3
Ludian China **86** B3
also known as Wenping
Luding China **86** B2
also known as Jagsamka *or* Luqiao
Ludington U.S.A. **172** G7
Ludlow U.K. **47** J11
Ludlow *CA* U.S.A. **183** H7
Ludlow *VT* U.S.A. **177** M2
Ludogorie *reg.* Bulg. **58** H5
Ludogorsko Plato *plat.* Bulg. **58** H5
Ludoni Rus. Fed. **43** K3
Ludowici U.S.A. **175** D6
Luduş Romania **58** F2
Ludvika Sweden **45** K3
Ludwigsburg Germany **48** G7
Ludwigsfelde Germany **49** K3
Ludwigshafen am Rhein Germany **48** F6
Ludwigslust Germany **48** I2
Ludwigsort Rus. Fed. *see* **Ladushkin**
Ludza Latvia **42** I5
Ludza *r.* Latvia **42** J4
Luebo Dem. Rep. Congo **127** D6
Lueki Dem. Rep. Congo **126** E5
Lueki *r.* Dem. Rep. Congo **126** E5
Luembe Zambia **127** F8
Luena Angola **127** C7
formerly known as Luso
Luena Dem. Rep. Congo **127** E7
Luena Zambia **127** F7
Luena *r.* Zambia **127** D8
Luena Flats *plain* Zambia **127** D8
Luengé, Coutada Pública do *nature res.* Angola **127** D9
Luengue *r.* Angola **127** D9
Luenha *r.* Moz./Zimbabwe **131** G3
Luepa Venez. **199** F3
Lüeyang China **86** C1
Lufeng *Guangdong* China **87** E4
Lufeng *Hunan* China *see* **Xupu**
Lufeng *Yunnan* China **86** B3
also known as Jinshan
Lufira *r.* Dem. Rep. Congo **127** E7
Lufira, Lac de retenue de la *resr* Dem. Rep. Congo **127** E7
Lufkin U.S.A. **179** D6
Lufu China *see* **Shilin**
Lug *r.* Serb. and Mont. **58** C4
Luga Rus. Fed. **43** K3
Luga *r.* Rus. Fed. **43** J2
Lugano Switz. **51** O6
Lugano, Lago di *l.* Italy/Switz. **56** B2
UNESCO World Heritage Site
Lugansk Ukr. *see* **Luhans'k**
Luganville Vanuatu **145** F3
Lugdunum France *see* **Lyon**
Lugela Moz. **131** H3
Lugela *r.* Moz. **131** H3
Lugenda *r.* Moz. **131** H1
Lugg *r.* U.K. **47** J11
Luggate N.Z. **153** D12
Luggudontsen *mt.* China **89** E6
Lughaye Somalia **128** D2
Lugnaquilla *hill* Ireland **47** F11
Lugo Italy **56** D4
Lugo Spain **54** D1
UNESCO World Heritage Site
Lugoj Romania **58** C3
Lugovaya Rus. Fed. **43** S5
Lugovaya Proleyka Rus. Fed. *see* **Primorsk**
Lugovoy Kazakh. **103** H4
Lugus *i.* Phil. **74** B5
Luhanka Fin. **45** N3
Luhans'k Ukr. **41** F6
also spelt Lugansk; *formerly known as* Voroshilovgrad
Luhawskiya Belarus **43** L6
Luhe China **87** F1
Lu He *r.* China **85** F4
Luḩfī, Wādī *watercourse* Jordan **109** H5
Luhin Sum China **85** H2
Luhit *r.* China/India *see* **Zayü Qu**
Luhit *r.* India **97** G3
Luhombero Tanz. **129** C7
Luhua China *see* **Heishui**
Luhuo China **86** B2
also known as Xindu *or* Zhaggo
Luhyny Ukr. **41** D6
Luia Angola **127** D7
Luia *r.* Angola **127** D6
Luia *r.* Moz. **131** G3
Luiana Angola **127** D9
Luiana *r.* Angola **127** D9
Luiana, Coutada Pública do *nature res.* Angola **127** D9
Luica Romania **58** H4
Luichow Peninsula China *see* **Leizhou Bandao**
Luik Belgium *see* **Liège**
Luilaka *r.* Dem. Rep. Congo **126** D5
Luimneach Ireland *see* **Limerick**
Luing *i.* U.K. **46** G7
Luino Italy **56** A3
Luio *r.* Angola **127** D8
Luiro *r.* Fin. **44** N2
Luís Correia Brazil **202** D2
Luis Echeverría Álvarez Mex. **183** H9
Luís Gomes Brazil **202** E3
Luishia Dem. Rep. Congo **127** E7
Luis L. León, Presa *resr* Mex. **184** D2
Luis Moya *Durango* Mex. **184** E3
Luis Moya *Zacatecas* Mex. **185** E4
Luitpold Coast Antarctica **222** V1
Luiza Dem. Rep. Congo **127** D6
Luizi Dem. Rep. Congo **127** E6
Luján Arg. **204** F4
Luján de Cuyo Arg. **204** C4
Lujiang China **87** F2
Lukachek Rus. Fed. **82** D1
Lukala Dem. Rep. Congo **127** B6
Lukanga Dem. Rep. Congo **126** C6
Lukanga Swamps Zambia **127** E8
Lukapa Angola *see* **Lucapa**
Lukavac Bos.-Herz. **56** K4
Luke, Mount *hill* Australia **151** B5
Lukenga, Lac *l.* Dem. Rep. Congo **127** E7
Lukenie *r.* Dem. Rep. Congo **126** C5
Lukh *r.* Rus. Fed. **40** G4
Lukhovitsy Rus. Fed. **43** U7
Lŭki Bulg. **58** F7
Lukinskaya Rus. Fed. **43** P1
Luk Keng *Hong Kong* China **87** [inset]
Lukolela *Équateur* Dem. Rep. Congo **126** C5
Lukolela *Kasai Oriental* Dem. Rep. Congo **127** E6
Lukomskaye, Vozyera *l.* Belarus **43** K7
Lukou China *see* **Zhuzhou**
Lukovac *r.* Bos.-Herz. **56** L4
Lukovë Albania **59** A9
Lukovit Bulg. **58** F5
Lukovnikovo Rus. Fed. **43** P5
Łuków Poland **49** T4
Lukoyanov Rus. Fed. **40** H5
Luksagu Indon. **75** B3
Lukšiai Lith. **42** E7
Lukuga *r.* Dem. Rep. Congo **127** E6
Lukula Dem. Rep. Congo **127** B6
Lukuledi Tanz. **129** C7
Lukulu Zambia **127** D8
Lukumburu Tanz. **129** B7
Lukuni Dem. Rep. Congo **127** C6
Lukusashi *r.* Zambia **127** F8
Lukusuzi National Park Zambia **129** B8
Lula *r.* Dem. Rep. Congo **126** D5
Luleå Sweden **44** M2
UNESCO World Heritage Site
Luleälven *r.* Sweden **44** M2
Lüleburgaz Turkey **106** A2
Lules Arg. **204** D2
Luliang China **86** B3
also known as Zhongshu
Lüliang Shan *mts* China **85** F4
Lulimba Dem. Rep. Congo **126** F6
Luling U.S.A. **179** C6
Lulong China **85** H4
Lulonga Dem. Rep. Congo **126** C4
Lulonga *r.* Dem. Rep. Congo **126** C4
Lulu *r.* Dem. Rep. Congo **126** D4
Luluabourg Dem. Rep. Congo *see* **Kananga**
Lülung China **89** D6
Lulworth, Mount *hill* Australia **151** B5
Lumachomo China **89** D6
Lumai Angola **127** D8
Lumajang Indon. **77** F5
Lumajangdong Co *salt l.* China **89** C5
Lümanda Estonia **42** D3
Lūmār Iran **107** F4
Lumbala *Moxico* Angola *see* **Lumbala N'guimbo**
Lumbala *Moxico* Angola *see* **Lumbala Kaquengue**
Lumbala Kaquengue Angola **127** D8
formerly known as Lumbala
Lumbala N'guimbo Angola **127** D8
formerly known as Gago Coutinho *or* Lumbala
Lumber *r.* U.S.A. **174** E5
Lumberton U.S.A. **174** E5
Lumbini Nepal **97** D4
UNESCO World Heritage Site
Lumbis Indon. **77** G1
Lumbrales Spain **54** E4
Lumding India **97** G4
Lumecha Tanz. **129** B7
Lumezzane Italy **56** C3
Lumi P.N.G. **73** J7
Lumijoki Fin. **44** N2
Lumina Romania **58** J4
Luminárias Brazil **207** I8
Lum-nan-pai Wildlife Reserve Thai. **78** B4
Lumparland Fin. **45** M3
Lumphăt Cambodia **79** D5
also spelt Lomphat
Lumpkin U.S.A. **175** C5
Lumsden Canada **167** J5
Lumsden N.Z. **153** C13
Lumut, Gunung *mt.* Indon. **77** F3
Lumut, Tanjung *pt* Indon. **77** D3
Lumwana Zambia **127** E7
Lün Mongolia **85** E2
Luna Phil. **74** B2
Luna *hill* Spain **54** F8
Luna *r.* Spain **54** F2
Lunan Lake Canada **167** M1
Lunan Shan *mts* China **86** B3
Luna Pier U.S.A. **173** J9
Lunavada India **96** B5
Lunayyir, Ḩarrat *lava field* Saudi Arabia **104** B2
Lunca Romania **58** F5
Lunca Bradului Romania **58** G2
Lunca Ilvei Romania **58** F1
Luncani Romania **58** E3
UNESCO World Heritage Site
Luncavăţ *r.* Romania **58** F4
Lund Sweden **45** K5
Lund *NV* U.S.A. **183** I3
Lund *UT* U.S.A. **183** K3
Lunda Norte *prov.* Angola **127** C7
Lundar Canada **167** L5
Lunda Sul *prov.* Angola **127** D7
Lundazi Zambia **129** B8
Lundbreck Canada **167** H5
Lundi *r.* Zimbabwe *see* **Runde**
Lunds U.S.A. **172** E6
Lundu Tanz. **129** B7
Lundy *i.* U.K. **47** H12
Lune *r.* U.K. **47** J9
Lüneburg Germany **48** H2
Lüneburger Heide *reg.* Germany **48** H2
Lüneburger Heide, Naturpark *nature res.* Germany **48** G2
Lunel France **51** K9
Lünen Germany **48** E4
Lunenburg Canada **169** H4
UNESCO World Heritage Site
Lunenburg U.S.A. **176** G9
Lunestedt Germany **48** F2
Lunéville France **51** M4
Lunga Moz. **131** I2
Lunga *r.* Zambia **127** E8
Lunggar China **89** C6
Lunggar Shan *mts* China **89** C6
Lung Kwu Chau *i. Hong Kong* China **87** [inset]
Lungleh India *see* **Lunglei**
Lunglei India **97** G5
formerly spelt Lungleh
Lungmari *mt.* China **89** D6
Lungmu Co *salt l.* China **89** C5
Lungro Italy **57** I9
Lungué-Bungo *r.* Angola **127** D8
Lungwebungu *r.* Zambia **127** D8
Lunh Nepal **97** D3
Luni *r.* India **96** A4
Luni *r.* Pak. **101** G4
Luninets Belarus *see* **Luninyets**
Lunino Rus. Fed. **41** H5
Luninyets Belarus **42** H9
also spelt Luninets
L'Union France **50** H9
Lunkaransar India **96** B3
Lunkha India **96** B3
Lunkho *mt.* Afgh./Pak. **101** H2
Lunkkaus Fin. **44** N2
Lunna Belarus **42** F8
Lunn Island P.N.G. **149** F1
Lunsar Sierra Leone **124** B4
Lunsemfwa *r.* Zambia **127** F8
Lunsklip S. Africa **131** F5
Luntai China **88** D3
also known as Bügür
Lunxhërisë, Mali i *ridge* Albania **59** B8
Lunyuk Indon. **77** G5
Lunzua Zambia **127** F7
Luobei China **82** C3
also known as Fengxiang
Luobuzhuang China **88** E4
Luocheng *Fujian* China *see* **Hui'an**
Luocheng *Gansu* China **84** C4
Luocheng *Guangxi* China **87** D3
also known as Dongmen
Luochuan China **85** F5
also known as Fengqi
Luodian China **86** C3
also known as Longping
Luoding China **87** D4
Luodonselkä *sea chan.* Fin. **44** N2
Luodou Sha *i.* China **87** D4
Luohe China **87** E1
Luo He *r. Henan* China **87** E1
Luo He *r. Shaanxi* China **87** D1
Luoma Hu *l.* China **87** F1
Luonan China **87** D1
Luoning China **87** D1
Luonteri *l.* Fin. **45** N3
Luoping China **86** C3
also known as Luoxiong
Luopioinen Fin. **45** N3
Luoshan China **87** E1
Luotian China **87** E2
also known as Fengshan
Luovttejohka Norway **44** O1
Luoxiao Shan *mts* China **87** E3
Luoxiong China *see* **Luoping**
Luoyang *Guangdong* China *see* **Boluo**
Luoyang *Henan* China **87** E1
formerly known as Loyang
UNESCO World Heritage Site
Luoyang *Zhejiang* China *see* **Taishun**
Luoyuan China **87** F3
also known as Fengshan
Luozi Dem. Rep. Congo **126** B6
Luozigou China **82** C4
Lupa Market Tanz. **129** B7
Lupane Zimbabwe **131** E3
Lupanshui China **86** C3
also known as Shuicheng *or* Xiayingpan *or* Zhongshan; *formerly spelt* Liupanshui
Lupar *r. Sarawak* Malaysia **77** E2
Łupawa *r.* Poland **49** O1
Lupeni Romania **58** G2
Lupeni Romania **58** E3
Luperón Dom. Rep. **187** F3
Lupilichi Moz. **129** B7
formerly known as Olivença
Lupire Angola **127** C8
Lupiro Tanz. **129** C7
Lupon Phil. **74** C5
Luppa Germany **49** J4
Lupton U.S.A. **183** O6
Lup'ya *r.* Rus. Fed. **40** J3
Luqiao China *see* **Luding**
Luqu China **86** B1
also known as Ma'ngê
Lu Qu *r.* China *see* **Tao He**
Luquan *Hebei* China **85** G4
formerly known as Huolu
Luquan *Yunnan* China **86** B3
also known as Pingshan
Luquembo Angola **127** C7
Lūrā Shīrīn Iran **107** F3
Luray U.S.A. **176** G7
Lure France **51** M5
Lure, Sommet de *mt.* France **51** L8
Lureco *r.* Moz. **129** C8
Luremo Angola **127** C7
Lurgan U.K. **47** F9
Lūrg-e Shotorān *salt pan* Iran **101** D3
Luribay Bol. **200** D4
Lurín Peru **200** A3
Luring China *see* **Gêrzê**
Lúrio Moz. **131** I2
Lurio *r.* Moz. **131** I2
Lusaheia *park* Norway **45** I4
Lusahunga Tanz. **128** A5
Lusaka Dem. Rep. Congo **127** F6

►**Lusaka** Zambia **127** F8
Capital of Zambia.

Lusaka *prov.* Zambia **127** F8
Lusambo Dem. Rep. Congo **126** D6
Lusancay Islands and Reefs P.N.G. **145** E2
Lusanga Dem. Rep. Congo **126** C6
formerly known as Leverville
Lusangi Dem. Rep. Congo **126** E6
Luseland Canada **167** I4
Lusenga Plain National Park Zambia **127** F7
Lusewa Tanz. **129** C7
Lush, Mount *hill* Australia **150** D3
Lushan China **86** B2
also known as Luyang
Lushan National Park China **87** E2
UNESCO World Heritage Site
Lushar China *see* **Huangzhong**
Lushi China **87** D1
Lushnjë Albania **58** A8
Lushoto Tanz. **129** C6
Lüshun China **85** I4
formerly known as Port Arthur *or* Ryojun
Lüsi China **87** G1
Lusi *r.* Indon. **77** E4
Lusignan France **50** G6
Lusikisiki S. Africa **133** N8
Lusiwasi Zambia **127** F8
Lusk U.S.A. **180** F4
Luso Angola *see* **Luena**
Lussac-les-Châteaux France **50** G6
Lussusso Angola **127** B7
Luster Norway **45** I3
UNESCO World Heritage Site
Lusushwana *r.* Swaziland **133** P3
Lusutufu *r.* Africa *see* **Usutu**
Lut, Bahrat *salt l.* Asia *see* **Dead Sea**
Lut, Dasht-e *des.* Iran **100** D4
Lutai China *see* **Ninghe**
Lü Tao *i.* Taiwan **87** G4
English form Green Island; *also known as* Huoshao Tao
Lutécia Brazil **206** C9
Luterskie, Jezioro *l.* Poland **49** R2
Lutetia France *see* **Paris**
Lūt-e Zangī Aḩmad *des.* Iran **100** D4
Luther Lake Canada **173** M7
Luthersburg U.S.A. **176** G4
Lutherstadt Wittenberg Germany **49** J4
also known as Wittenberg
Lutiba Dem. Rep. Congo **126** F5
Lütjenburg Germany **48** H1
Luton U.K. **47** L12
Lutong *Sarawak* Malaysia **77** F1
Lutope *r.* Zimbabwe **131** F3
Łutselk'e Canada **167** I2
formerly known as Snowdrift
Lutshi Dem. Rep. Congo **126** E6
Luts'k Ukr. **41** C6
formerly spelt Łuck
Luttig S. Africa **132** G9
Lutto *r.* Fin./Rus. Fed. *see* **Lotta**
Lutuai Angola **127** D8
Lutynia *r.* Poland **49** O3
Lutz U.S.A. **175** D6
Lützow-Holm Bay Antarctica **223** C2
Lutzputs S. Africa **132** E5
Lutzville S. Africa **132** C8
Luumäki Fin. **45** N3
Luuq Somalia **128** D4
Luve Swaziland **133** P3
Luverne *AL* U.S.A. **175** C6
Luverne *MN* U.S.A. **178** C3
Luvia Fin. **45** M3
Luvo Angola **127** B6
Luvozero Rus. Fed. **44** O2
Luvua *r.* Dem. Rep. Congo **127** E6
Luvuei Angola **127** D8
Luvuvhu *r.* S. Africa **131** F4
Luwegu *r.* Tanz. **129** C7
Luwero Uganda **128** B4
Luwingu Zambia **127** F7
Luwo *i.* Indon. **75** D2
Luwuk Indon. **75** B3
►**Luxembourg** *country* Europe **51** L3
Letzeburgish form Lëtzebuerg; *also spelt* Luxemburg
►►**32–33 Europe** Countries

►**Luxembourg** Lux. **51** M3
Capital of Luxembourg.
UNESCO World Heritage Site

Luxemburg *country* Europe *see* **Luxembourg**
Luxemburg *IA* U.S.A. **172** B8
Luxemburg *WI* U.S.A. **172** F6
Luxeuil-les-Bains France **51** M5
Luxi *Hunan* China *see* **Wuxi**
Luxi *Yunnan* China **86** A3
also known as Mangshi
Luxi *Yunnan* China **86** B3
also known as Zhongshu
Luxolweni S. Africa **133** J8
Luxor Egypt **121** G3
also spelt El Uqşur *or* Al Uqşur
Luyang China *see* **Lushan**
Luya Shan *mts* China **85** F4
Luy de France *r.* France **50** F9
Luyi China **87** E1
Luyuan China *see* **Gaoling**
Luz Brazil **207** H6
Luza Rus. Fed. **40** H3
Luza *r.* Rus. Fed. **40** H3
Luza *r.* Rus. Fed. **40** K2
Luzech France **50** H8
Luzern Switz. *see* **Lucerne**
Luzha *r.* Rus. Fed. **43** R7
Luzhai China **87** D3
Luzhi China **86** C3
also known as Xiayingpan
Luzhou China **86** C2
Luziânia Brazil **206** F3
Lužické hory *mts* Czech Rep. **49** L5
Luzilândia Brazil **202** D2
Lūžņas Latvia **42** C4
Lužnice *r.* Czech Rep. **49** L6
►**Luzon** *i.* Phil. **74** B3
►►**60–61 Asia** Landscapes
Luzon Strait Phil. **74** B1
Luzy France **51** J6
Luzzi Italy **57** I9
L'viv Ukr. **41** C6
English form Lvov; *also spelt* L'vov; *formerly spelt* Lwów; *historically known as* Lemberg
UNESCO World Heritage Site
Lvov Ukr. *see* **L'viv**
L'vov Ukr. *see* **L'viv**
L'vovskiy Rus. Fed. **43** S6
Lwów Ukr. *see* **L'viv**
Lwówek Poland **49** N3
Lyady Belarus **43** M7
Lyady Rus. Fed. **43** J3
Lyakhavichy Belarus **42** H8
also spelt Lyakhovichi
Lyakhovichi Belarus *see* **Lyakhavichy**
Lyakhovskiye Ostrova *is* Rus. Fed. **39** O2
Lyallpur Pak. *see* **Faisalabad**
Lyal'mikar Uzbek. *see* **Lalmikor**
Lyamtsa Rus. Fed. **40** F2
Lyangar *Navoiy* Uzbek. *see* **Langar**
Lyangar *Qashqadaryo* Uzbek. *see* **Langar**
Lyapin *r.* Rus. Fed. **40** L3
Lyaskelya Rus. Fed. **44** O3
Lyaskovets Bulg. **58** G5
Lyasnaya Belarus **42** G9
Lyasnaya *r.* Belarus **42** E9
Lybster U.K. **46** I5
Lychkovo Rus. Fed. **43** N4
Lyck Poland *see* **Ełk**
Lycksele Sweden **44** L2
Lycopolis Egypt *see* **Asyūţ**
Lydda Israel *see* **Lod**
Lyddan Island Antarctica **222** W2
Lydenburg S. Africa **133** O2
Lydia *reg.* Turkey **59** I10
Łydynia *r.* Poland **49** R3
Lyebyada *r.* Belarus **42** G8
Lyel'chytsy Belarus **41** D6
Lyell, Mount U.S.A. **182** E4
Lyell Island Canada **166** D4
Lyell Range *mts* N.Z. **153** G9
Lyenina Belarus **43** M9
Lyepyel' Belarus **43** J7
also spelt Lepel'
Lygourio Greece **59** E11
also known as Ligoúrion
Lygumai Lith. **42** E5
Lykens U.S.A. **177** I5
Lykoshino Rus. Fed. **43** O3
Lykso S. Africa **132** I4
Lyman Ukr. **58** K3
Lyman U.S.A. **180** E4
Lymans'ke Ukr. **58** K2
Lyme Bay U.K. **47** J13
Lymington U.K. **47** K13
Łyna *r.* Poland **49** S1
Lynch U.S.A. **176** C9
Lynchburg *TN* U.S.A. **174** C5
Lynchburg *VA* U.S.A. **176** F8
Lynches *r.* U.S.A. **175** E5
Lynch Station U.S.A. **176** F8
Lynchville U.S.A. **177** O1
Lynd *r.* Australia **149** D3
Lyndhurst *Qld* Australia **149** E3
Lyndhurst *S.A.* Australia **146** C2
Lyndon Australia **150** A4
Lyndon *r.* Australia **150** A4
Lyndon U.S.A. **178** D4
Lyndonville *NY* U.S.A. **176** G2
Lyndonville *VT* U.S.A. **177** M1
Lyngdal Norway **45** I4
Lyngen *sea chan.* Norway **44** M1
Lyngseidet Norway **44** M1
Lynher Reef *reef* Australia **150** C2
Lynn U.K. *see* **King's Lynn**
Lynn *IN* U.S.A. **176** A5
Lynn *MA* U.S.A. **177** O3
Lynn Canal *sea chan.* U.S.A. **166** C3
Lynndyl U.S.A. **183** L2
Lynn Haven U.S.A. **175** C6
Lynn Lake Canada **167** K3
Lynton U.K. **47** I12
Lyntupy Belarus **42** H6
Lynx Lake Canada **167** J2
Lynxville U.S.A. **172** B7
Lyon France **51** K7
English form Lyons; *historically known as* Lugdunum
UNESCO World Heritage Site
Lyon Mountain U.S.A. **177** L1
Lyonnais, Monts du *hills* France **51** K7
Lyons Australia **146** B2
Lyons *r.* Australia **151** A5
Lyons France *see* **Lyon**
Lyons *GA* U.S.A. **175** D5
Lyons *KS* U.S.A. **178** C4
Lyons *NY* U.S.A. **177** I2
Lyons Falls U.S.A. **177** J2
Lyozna Belarus **43** L6
Lyra Reef *reef* P.N.G. **145** E2
Lysá hora *mt.* Czech Rep. **49** P6
Lysekil Sweden **45** J4
Lyshchichi Rus. Fed. **43** N9
Łysica *hill* Poland **49** R5
Lyskovo Rus. Fed. **40** H4
Ly Sơn, Đao *i.* Vietnam **79** E5
Lys'va Rus. Fed. **40** K4
Lysychans'k Ukr. **41** F6
also spelt Lisichansk
Lysyye Gory Rus. Fed. **41** H6
Lytham St Anne's U.K. **47** I10
Lytkarino Rus. Fed. **43** S6
Lyttelton N.Z. **153** G11
Lytton Canada **166** F5
Lyuban' Belarus **42** J9
Lyuban' Rus. Fed. **43** M2
Lyubanskaye Vodaskhovishcha *resr* Belarus **42** J9
Lyubavichi Rus. Fed. **43** L7
Lyubazh Rus. Fed. **43** Q9
Lyubcha Belarus **42** H8
Lyubertsy Rus. Fed. **43** S6
Lyubeshiv Ukr. **41** C6
Lyubim Rus. Fed. **43** V3
Lyubimets Bulg. **58** H7
Lyubimovka Rus. Fed. **43** T8
Lyubishchytsy Belarus **42** G9
Lyubitovo Rus. Fed. **43** P3
Lyubokhna Rus. Fed. **43** P8
Lyubomirovo Rus. Fed. **43** T2
Lyubotin Ukr. *see* **Lyubotyn**
Lyubotyn Ukr. **53** J2
also spelt Lyubotin
Lyubyacha Belarus **42** I8
Lyubytino Rus. Fed. **43** O3
Lyudinovo Rus. Fed. **43** P8
Lyugovichi Rus. Fed. **43** O1
Lyulyakovo Bulg. **58** I6
Lyunda *r.* Rus. Fed. **40** H4
Lyusina Belarus **42** H9
Lyzha *r.* Rus. Fed. **40** K2
Lzha *r.* Rus. Fed. **43** J4

M

Ma *r.* Myanmar **78** B3
Ma, Nam *r.* Laos **78** C3
Ma, Sông *r.* Vietnam **78** D4
Maalhosmadulu Atoll Maldives **94** B5
Maamakundhoo *i.* Maldives *see* **Makunudhoo**
Maamba Zambia **127** E9
Ma'an Cameroon **125** H6
Ma'ān Jordan **108** G7
Maaninka Fin. **44** N3
Maaninkavaara Fin. **44** O2
Maanselkä Fin. **44** O3
Ma'anshan China **87** F2
Maanyt *Bulgan* Mongolia **84** D1
Maanyt *Töv* Mongolia **85** E2
Maardu Estonia **42** G2
Maarianhamina Fin. *see* **Mariehamn**
Ma'āriḍ, Banī *des.* Saudi Arabia **105** D4
Ma'arrat an Nu'mān Syria **109** H2
Maartenshoop S. Africa **133** O1
Maas *r.* Neth. **48** B4
also spelt Meuse (Belgium/France)
Maaseik Belgium **51** L1
Maasin Phil. **74** C4
Maas-Schwalm-Nette *nat. park* Germany/Neth. **48** C4
Maastricht Neth. **48** C5
Maatsuyker Group *is* Australia **147** E5
Maba China **87** F1
Maba Indon. **75** D2
Maba, Ouadi *watercourse* Chad **120** D6
Mabalacat Phil. **74** B3
Mabalane Moz. **131** G4
Mabana Dem. Rep. Congo **126** F4
Mabanda Gabon **126** A5
Ma'bar Yemen **104** D5
Mabaruma Guyana **199** G2
Mabating China *see* **Hongshan**
Mabein Myanmar **78** B3
Mabel Creek Australia **146** B2
Mabel Downs Australia **150** D3
Mabella Canada **168** B3
Maberly Canada **173** Q6
Mabian China **86** B2
also known as Minjian
Mablethorpe U.K. **47** M10
Mably France **51** K6
Mabopane S. Africa **133** M2
Mabote Moz. **131** G4
Mabou Canada **169** I4
Mabrak, Jabal *mt.* Jordan **108** G7
Mabroûk *well* Mali **125** E2
Mabrous *well* Niger **125** I1
Mabuasehube Game Reserve *nature res.* Botswana **130** D5
Mabudis *i.* Phil. **74** B1
Mabula S. Africa **133** L1
Ma'būs Yūsuf *oasis* Libya **120** D3
Mabutsane Botswana **130** D5
Macá, Monte *mt.* Chile **205** B7
Macachín Arg. **204** E5
Macadam Plains Australia **151** B5
Macadam Range *hills* Australia **148** A2
Macaé Brazil **203** D7
Macael Spain **55** I7
Macaíba Brazil **202** F3
Macajalar Bay Phil. **74** C4
Macajuba Brazil **202** D5
Macaloge Moz. **129** B8
formerly known as Miranda *or* Vila Miranda
MacAlpine Lake Canada **167** K1
Macamic Canada **168** E3
Macan, Kepulauan *atolls* Indon. *see* **Taka'Bonerate, Kepulauan**
Macandze Moz. **131** G4
Macaneta, Ponta de *pt* Moz. **133** Q2
Macao China **87** E4
also known as Aomen; *also spelt* Macau
Macapá *Amapá* Brazil **199** I4
Macapá *Amazonas* Brazil **200** D2
Macará Ecuador **198** B6
Macaracas Panama **186** C6
Macarani Brazil **202** D5
Macarena, Cordillera *mts* Col. **198** C4
Macareo, Caño *r.* Venez. **199** F2
Macas Ecuador **198** B5
Maçãs *r.* Port./Spain **54** E3
Macassar Indon. *see* **Makassar**
Macassar Strait Indon. *see* **Selat Makassar**
Macau Brazil **202** E3
Macau China *see* **Macao**
Macauã *r.* Brazil **200** C2
Macaúba Brazil **202** B4
Macaúbas Brazil **202** D5
Macauley Island N.Z. **145** H5
Macayari Col. **198** C4
Macbride Head Falkland Is **205** F8
Maccaretane Moz. **131** G5
Macclenny U.S.A. **175** D6
Macclesfield U.K. **47** J10
Macclesfield Bank *sea feature* S. China Sea **72** D3
also known as Zhongsha Qundao
Macdiarmid Canada **168** B3
Macdonald, Lake *salt flat* Australia **150** E4
Macdonnell Ranges *mts* Australia **148** A4
MacDowell Lake Canada **167** M4
Macedo de Cavaleiros Port. **54** E3
Macedon *country* Europe *see* **Macedonia**
►**Macedonia** *country* Europe **58** C7
spelt Makedonija in Macedonian; *historically known as* Macedon; *long form* Former Yugoslav Republic of Macedonia; *short form* F.Y.R.O.M.
►►**32–33 Europe** Countries
Maceió Brazil **202** F4
Maceio, Ponta da *pt* Brazil **202** E3
Macenta Guinea **124** C4
Macerata Italy **56** F5
Macfarlane, Lake *salt flat* Australia **146** C3
Macgillycuddy's Reeks *mts* Ireland **47** C12
Mach Pak. **101** F4
Macha Rus. Fed. **39** L3
Machacalis Brazil **207** M4
Machacamarca Bol. **200** D4
Machachi Ecuador **198** B5
Machadinho *r.* Brazil **201** E2
Machado Brazil **207** H8
Machadodorp S. Africa **133** O2
Machai Zambia **127** E8
Machaila Moz. **131** G4
Machakos Kenya **128** C5
Machala Ecuador **198** B5
Machali China *see* **Madoi**
Machanga Moz. **131** G4
Machareti Bol. **201** E5
Machar Marshes Sudan **128** B2
Machattie, Lake *salt flat* Australia **148** C5
Machatuine Moz. **133** Q2
Machaze Moz. *see* **Chitobe**
Machecoul France **50** E6
Macheng China **87** E2
Macherla India **94** C2
Machesney Park U.S.A. **172** D8
Machhiwara India **96** C3
formerly spelt Machiwara
Machhlishahr India **97** D4
Machias *ME* U.S.A. **174** H2
Machias *NY* U.S.A. **176** G3
Machico Madeira **122** A2
Machilipatnam India **94** D2
also known as Masulipatam; *formerly known as* Bandar
Machinga Malawi **129** B8
Machiques Venez. **198** C2
Machiwara India *see* **Machhiwara**
Māch Kowr Iran **101** E5
Macho, Arroyo del *watercourse* U.S.A. **181** F6
Machu Picchu *tourist site* Peru **200** B3
UNESCO World Heritage Site
Machupo *r.* Bol. **201** D3
Machynlleth U.K. **47** I11
Macia Moz. **131** G5
Macias Nguema *i.* Equat. Guinea *see* **Bioco**
Măcin Romania **58** J3
Macintyre *r.* Australia **147** F2
Macintyre Brook *r.* Australia **147** F2
Macizo de Tocate *mts* Peru **200** B3
Maçka Turkey **107** D2
also known as Cevizlik
Mackay Australia **149** F4
MacKay *r.* Canada **167** I3
Mackay, Lake *salt flat* Australia **150** E4
MacKay Lake Canada **167** I2
Mackay Mountains Antarctica **222** O1
Mackenzie *r.* Australia **149** F4
Mackenzie *B.C.* Canada **166** F4
Mackenzie *Ont.* Canada **172** E2
Mackenzie *r.* Canada **166** E2
Mackenzie Guyana *see* **Linden**
Mackenzie *atoll* Micronesia *see* **Ulithi**
Mackenzie Bay Antarctica **223** E2
Mackenzie Bay Canada **164** F3
Mackenzie Bison Sanctuary *nature res.* Canada **167** G2
Mackenzie Highway Canada **167** G2
Mackenzie King Island Canada **165** H2
Mackenzie Mountains Canada **166** C1

►**Mackenzie-Peace-Finlay** *r.* Canada **166**
2nd longest river in North America.
►►**154–155 North America** Landscapes

Mackillop, Lake *salt flat* Australia *see* **Yamma Yamma, Lake**
Mackinac, Straits of *lake channel* U.S.A. **173** H5
Mackinac Island U.S.A. **173** I5
Mackinaw *r.* U.S.A. **174** B3
Macklin Canada **167** I4
Macksville Australia **147** G2
Mackunda Creek *watercourse* Australia **149** D4
Maclean Australia **147** G2
Macleantown S. Africa **133** L9
Maclear S. Africa **133** M8
Macleay *r.* Australia **147** G2
MacLeod Canada *see* **Fort Macleod**
MacLeod, Lake *imp. l.* Australia **150** A5
Macmillan *r.* Canada **166** C2
Macmillan Pass Canada **166** D2
Maçobere Moz. **131** G4
Macocola Angola **127** C6
Macomb U.S.A. **174** B3
Macomer *Sardinia* Italy **57** A8
Mâcon France **51** K6
Macon *GA* U.S.A. **175** D5
Macon *MO* U.S.A. **178** D4
Macon *MS* U.S.A. **175** B5
Macon *OH* U.S.A. **176** B7
Macon, Bayou *r.* U.S.A. **175** B6
Macondo Angola **127** D8
Macossa Moz. **131** G3
Macotera Spain **54** F4
Macoun Lake Canada **167** K3
Macovane Moz. **131** G4
Macpherson Robertson Land *reg.* Antarctica *see* **Mac. Robertson Land**
►**Macquarie** *r. N.S.W.* Australia **147** E2
►►**134–135 Oceania** Landscapes
Macquarie *r. Tas.* Australia **147** E5
Macquarie Harbour Australia **147** E5

►**Macquarie Island** S. Pacific Ocean **220** F9
Part of Australia. Most southerly point of Oceania.
UNESCO World Heritage Site
►►**134–135 Oceania** Landscapes

Macquarie Marshes Australia **147** E2
Macquarie Marshes Nature Reserve Australia **147** E2
Macquarie Mountain Australia **147** F3
Macraes Flat N.Z. **153** E13
MacRitchie Reservoir Sing. **76** [inset]
Mac. Robertson Land *reg.* Antarctica **223** E2
long form Macpherson Robertson Land
Macroom Ireland **47** D12
Mactún Mex. **185** H5
Macú Brazil **198** D4
Macuira, Parque Nacional *nat. park* Col. **198** D1
Macuje Col. **198** C4
Macukull Albania **58** B7
Macumba Australia **146** B1
Macumba *watercourse* Australia **146** C1
Macururé Brazil **202** E4
Macusani Peru **200** C3
Macuspana Mex. **185** G5
Macuzari, Presa *resr* Mex. **184** C3
Macuze Moz. **131** H3
Mādabā Jordan **108** G6
Madadeni S. Africa **133** O4

►**Madagascar** *country* Africa **131** [inset] J4
Largest island in Africa and 4th in the world.
►►**6–7 World** Landscapes
►►**14–15 World** Environmental Impacts
►►**110–111 Africa** Landscapes
►►**114–115 Africa** Countries

Madagli Nigeria **125** I4
UNESCO World Heritage Site
Madā'in Şāliḩ Saudi Arabia **104** B2
Madalena Brazil **202** E3
Madama Niger **123** I5
Madan Bulg. **58** F7
Madana Chad **126** C2
Madana *well* Chad **120** C5
Madanapalle India **94** C3
Madang P.N.G. **73** K8
Madaora India **96** C4
Madaoua Niger **125** G3
Madara Bulg. **58** I5
UNESCO World Heritage Site
Mădăraş Romania **58** C2

Malone U.S.A. 177 K1
Malong China 86 B3
also known as Tongquan
Malonga Dem. Rep. Congo 127 D7
Małopolska, Wyżyna hills Poland 49 R5
Maloshuyka Rus. Fed. 40 F3
Malovan pass Bos.-Herz. 56 J5
Malovăț Romania 58 D4
Malowera Moz. 131 F2
formerly spelt Maluera
Måløy Norway 44 I3
Maloyaroslavets Rus. Fed. 43 R6
Maloye Borisovo Rus. Fed. 43 R2
Malozemel'skaya Tundra lowland Rus. Fed. 40 I2
Malpelo, Isla de i. N. Pacific Ocean 198 A4
Malpica Spain 54 C1
Mālpils Latvia 42 F4
Malprabha r. India 94 C2
Malpura India 96 B4
Malše r. Czech Rep. 49 L7
Malsiras India 94 B2
►Malta country Europe 57 G13
►►16–17 World Population
►►32–33 Europe Countries
Malta Latvia 42 I5
Malta r. Latvia 42 I5
Malta i. Malta 57 G13
Malta U.S.A. 180 F2
Maltahöhe Namibia 130 C5
Maltam Cameroon 125 I3
Maltion luonnonpuisto nature res. Fin. 44 O2
Malton U.K. 47 L9
Maluera Moz. see Malowera
Malukken is Indon. see Moluccas
Maluku is Indon. see Moluccas
Maluku prov. Indon. 75 D3
Ma'lūlā, Jabal mts Syria 109 H4
Malului, Vârful hill Romania 58 D2
Malumfashi Nigeria 125 G4
Malundano Zambia 127 E9
Malung Sweden 45 K3
Maluti Mountains Lesotho 133 M6
Malu'u Solomon Is 145 F2
Malvan India 94 B2
Malvasia Greece see Monemvasia
Malvern AR U.S.A. 179 D5
Malvern OH U.S.A. 176 D5
Malvérnia Moz. see Chicualacuala
Malvinas, Islas terr. S. Atlantic Ocean see Falkland Islands
Malwa reg. India 96 C5
Malwal Sudan 128 A2
Malxe r. Germany 49 L4
Malý Dunaj r. Slovakia 49 P8
Malykay Rus. Fed. 39 L3
Malyn Ukr. 41 D6
also spelt Malin
Malyy, Ostrov i. Rus. Fed. 43 J1
Malyy Anyuy r. Rus. Fed. 39 Q3
Malyye Soli Rus. Fed. 43 V4
Malyy Irgiz r. Rus. Fed. 41 I5
Malyy Kavkaz mts Asia see Lesser Caucasus
Malyy Kunaley Rus. Fed. 85 E1
Malyy Lyakhovskiy, Ostrov i. Rus. Fed. 39 O2
Malyy Taymyr, Ostrov i. Rus. Fed. 39 K2
Malyy Uzen' r. Kazakh./Rus. Fed. 102 B2
also known as Kishiözen
Malyy Yenisey r. Rus. Fed. 84 B1
Malyy Zelenchuk r. Rus. Fed. 107 E1
Mama r. Rus. Fed. 39 O3
Mamadysh Rus. Fed. 40 I5
Mamafubedu S. Africa 133 M4
Mamahabane S. Africa 133 L5
Mamallapuram India 94 D3
UNESCO World Heritage Site
Mamaranui N.Z. 152 H3
Mamasa Indon. 75 A3
Mambahenauhan i. Phil. 74 A5
Mambai Brazil 202 C5
Mambajao Phil. 74 C4
Mambal Cameroon 125 I5
Mambali Tanz. 129 B6
Mambasa Dem. Rep. Congo 126 F4
Mambéré r. Cent. Afr. Rep. 126 C4
Mambéré-Kadéï pref. Cent. Afr. Rep. 126 B3
Mambi Indon. 75 A3
Mambili r. Congo 126 C4
Mambolo Sierra Leone 124 B4
Mambrui Kenya 128 D5
Mamburao Phil. 74 B3
Mamelodi S. Africa 133 M2
Mamers France 50 G4
Mamfe Cameroon 125 H5
Mamiá Brazil 199 F6
Mamili National Park Namibia 130 D3
Mamiña Chile 200 C5
Mamison Pass Georgia/Rus. Fed. 107 E2
Mammoth U.S.A. 183 N9
Mammoth Cave National Park U.S.A. 174 C4
UNESCO World Heritage Site
Mammoth Lakes U.S.A. 182 F4
Mammoth Reservoir U.S.A. 182 E4
Mamonas Brazil 207 K2
Mamonovo Kaliningradskaya Oblast' Rus. Fed. 42 A7
historically known as Heiligenbeil
Mamonovo Ryazanskaya Oblast' Rus. Fed. 43 U8
Mamontovo Rus. Fed. 103 J1
Mamoré r. Bol./Brazil 200 D2
Mamori Brazil 199 E5
Mamori, Lago l. Brazil 199 F5
Mamoriá Brazil 200 D1
Mamou Guinea 124 B4
Mamoudzou Mayotte 129 E8
also spelt Mamoutsou or Mamutzu
Mamoutsou Mayotte see Mamoudzou
Mampikony Madag. 131 [inset] J3
Mampong Ghana 125 E5
Mamre S. Africa 132 C10
Mamry, Jezioro l. Poland 49 S1
Mamuju Indon. 75 A3
Ma'mūl Oman 105 F4
Mamuno Botswana 130 D4
Mamuras Albania 58 A7
Mamurogawa Japan 90 G5
Mamutzu Mayotte see Mamoudzou
Man Côte d'Ivoire 124 D5
Man r. India 94 B2
Man U.S.A. 176 D8
►Man, Isle of i. Irish Sea 47 H9
United Kingdom Crown Dependency.
►►32–33 Europe Countries
Mana Fr. Guiana 199 H3
Mānā U.S.A. 181 [inset] Y1
Mana Bárbara Venez. 198 C2
Manabí prov. Ecuador 198 B5
Manacacias r. Col. 198 C3
Manacapuru Brazil 199 F5
Manacor Spain 55 O5
Manado Indon. 75 C2
►Managua Nicaragua 186 B4
Capital of Nicaragua.
Managua, Lago de l. Nicaragua 186 B4
Manaḩ Oman 105 G3
Manaia N.Z. 152 I7
Manakara Madag. 131 [inset] J4
Manakau mt. N.Z. 153 H10
Manākhah Yemen 104 C5
Manali India 96 C2
►Manama Bahrain 105 E2
Capital of Bahrain. Also spelt Al Manāmah.
►►8–9 World Countries
Manamadurai India 94 C4
Manambaho r. Madag. 131 [inset] J3
Manambondro Madag. 131 [inset] J4
Manamelkudi India 94 C4
Manam Island P.N.G. 73 K7
also known as Vulcan Island
Manamo, Caño r. Venez. 199 F2
Manamoc i. Phil. 74 B4
Mananantañana r. Madag. 131 [inset] J4
Mananara r. Madag. 131 [inset] J4
Mananara, Parc National de nat. park Madag. 131 [inset] K3
Mananara Avaratra Madag. 131 [inset] K3
Manangoora Australia 148 C3
Mananjary Madag. 131 [inset] K4
Manankoliva Madag. 131 [inset] J5
Manankoro Mali 124 D4
Manantali, Lac de l. Mali 124 C3
Manantavadi India 94 C4
Manantenina Madag. 131 [inset] J5
Mana Pass China/India 89 B6
Mana Pools National Park Zimbabwe 131 F3
UNESCO World Heritage Site
Manapouri N.Z. 153 B13
►Manapouri, Lake N.Z. 153 B13
Deepest lake in Oceania.
Manapparai India 94 C4
Manarantsandry Madag. 131 [inset] J3
Manas China 88 D2
Manas r. India 97 F4
Manas, Gora mt. Uzbek. 103 G4
Manasa India 96 B4
Manas He r. China 88 D2
Manas Hu l. China 88 D2
Manāşīr reg. U.A.E. 105 F3
►Manaslu mt. Nepal 97 E3
8th highest mountain in the world and in Asia.
►►6–7 World Landscapes
►►60–61 Asia Landscapes
Manasquan U.S.A. 177 K5
Manassas U.S.A. 176 H7
Manastir Macedonia see Bitola
Manas Wildlife Sanctuary nature res. Bhutan 97 F4
UNESCO World Heritage Site
Manatang Indon. 75 C5
Manatuto East Timor 75 C5
Man-aung Myanmar 78 A4
Man-aung Kyun i. Myanmar 78 A4
also known as Cheduba Island
Manaus Brazil 199 F5
Manavgat Turkey 106 B3
Manavgat r. Turkey 108 C1
Manawa U.S.A. 172 E6
Manawar India 96 B5
Manawaru N.Z. 152 J5
Manawashei Sudan 120 E6
Manawatu r. N.Z. 152 J8
Manawatu-Wanganui admin. reg. N.Z. 152 J7
Manay Phil. 74 C5
Manayenki Rus. Fed. 43 R8
Manbazar India 97 E5
Manbij Syria 109 I1
Mancelona U.S.A. 173 H6
Manchar India 94 B2
Manchester U.K. 47 J10
Manchester CT U.S.A. 177 M4
Manchester IA U.S.A. 174 B3
Manchester KY U.S.A. 176 B8
Manchester MD U.S.A. 177 I6
Manchester MI U.S.A. 173 I8
Manchester NH U.S.A. 177 N3
Manchester OH U.S.A. 176 B7
Manchester TN U.S.A. 174 C5
Manchhar Lake Pak. 101 F5
Manciano Italy 56 D6
Mancılık Turkey 107 D3
Mancınık Dağı mts Turkey 59 I9
Mancos r. U.S.A. 183 P5
Mand Pak. 101 E5
Mand, Rūd-e r. Iran 100 B4
also known as Qara Āghach
Manda Bangl. 97 F4
Manda Malawi 129 B7
Manda Tanz. 129 B6
Manda, Jebel mt. Sudan 126 E2
Manda, Parc National de nat. park Chad 126 C2
Mandabe Madag. 131 [inset] J4
Mandaguaçu Brazil 206 A10
Mandaguari Brazil 206 B10
Mandai Sing. 76 [inset]
Mandal Afgh. 101 E3
Mandal Gujarat India 96 A5
Mandal Rajasthan India 96 B4
Mandal Bulgan Mongolia 84 D1
Mandal Töv Mongolia 85 E1
Mandal Norway 45 I4
►Mandala, Puncak mt. Indon. 73 J7
3rd highest mountain in Oceania. Formerly known as Julianatop.
►►134–135 Oceania Landscapes
Mandalay Myanmar 78 B3
also spelt Mandale
Mandalay admin. div. Myanmar 78 A3
also spelt Mandale
Mandale Myanmar see Mandalay
Mandale admin. div. Myanmar see Mandalay
Mandalgarh India 96 B4
Mandalgovĭ Mongolia 85 E2
Mandalī Iraq 107 F4
Mandalt China 85 G3
also known as Sonid Zuoqi
Mandan U.S.A. 178 B2
Mandaon Phil. 74 B3
Mandapam India 94 C4
Mandar, Teluk b. Indon. 75 A3
Mandas Sardinia Italy 57 B9
Mandav Hills India 96 A5
Mandé, Mont de hill France 51 K6
Mandelieu-la-Napoule France 51 M9
Mandello del Lario Italy 56 B3
Mandera Kenya 128 D4
Manderfield U.S.A. 183 L3
Mandeville Jamaica 186 D3
Mandeville N.Z. 153 C13
Mandha India 96 A4
Mandheera Somalia 128 E2
Mandhoúdhíon Greece see Mantoudi
Mandi India 96 C3
Mandiakui Mali 124 D3
Mandiana Guinea 124 C4
Mandi Angin, Gunung mt. Malaysia 76 C1
Mandi Burewala Pak. 101 H4
Mandidzuzure Zimbabwe see Chimanimani
Mandié Moz. 131 G3
Mandimba Moz. 131 G2
Manding, Monts mts Mali 124 C3
Mandioli i. Indon. 75 C3
Mandji Gabon 126 A5
Mandla India 96 D5
Mandor India 96 B4
Mandorah Australia 148 A2
Mandoro Dem. Rep. Congo 126 F3
Mandoro Madag. 131 [inset] J3
Mandor Reserve nature res. Indon. 77 E2
Mandouri Togo 125 F4
Mandra Greece 59 E10
Mandraki Greece 59 I12
Mandrare r. Madag. 131 [inset] J5
Mandrenska r. Bulg. see Sredetska Reka
Mandritsara Madag. 131 [inset] K2
Mandsaur India 96 B4
Mandul i. Indon. 77 G2
Mandurah Australia 151 A7
Manduria Italy 57 J8
Mandvi Gujarat India 96 A5
Mandvi Gujarat India 96 B5
Mandya India 94 C3
Manekwara India 96 A5
Manendragarh India 97 D5
Maner India 97 E4
Maner r. India 94 C2
Manerbio Italy 56 C3
Maneromango Tanz. 129 C6
Manesht Kūh mt. Iran 100 A3
Mănești Romania 58 G4
Maneva Madag. see Mahaboboka
Manevychi Ukr. 41 C6
Manfalūţ Egypt 121 F3
Manfredonia Italy 56 H7
Manfredonia, Golfo di g. Italy 56 I7
Manga Brazil 202 D5
Manga Burkina 125 E4
Mangabeiras, Serra das hills Brazil 202 C4
Manga Grande Angola 127 B6
Mangai Dem. Rep. Congo 126 C6
Mangai, Réserve de Faune des Hippopotames de nature res. Dem. Rep. Congo 126 C5
Mangaia i. Cook Is 221 I7
also spelt Mangea
Mangakino N.Z. 152 J6
Mangalagiri India 94 D2
Mangaldai India 97 G4
Mangalia Romania 58 J5
Mangalmé Chad 120 C6
Mangalore India 94 B3
Mangalvedha India 94 B2
Mangamaunu N.Z. 153 H10
Mangamuka N.Z. 152 H3
Mangania Dem. Rep. Congo 126 D4
Manganui r. N.Z. 152 H3
Mangaon India 94 B2
Mangapet India 94 D2
Mangarakau N.Z. 152 G8
Mangaratiba Brazil 207 I9
Mangareva Islands Fr. Polynesia see Gambier, Îles
Mangatainoka N.Z. 152 J8
Mangatawhiri N.Z. 152 J5
Mangaung S. Africa 133 K6
Mangawan India 97 D4
Mangaweka N.Z. 152 J7
Mangawhai N.Z. 152 I4
Mangde Chhu r. Bhutan see Trongsa Chhu
Ma'ngê China see Luqu
Mangea i. Cook Is see Mangaia
Mangembe Dem. Rep. Congo 126 E6
Manger Norway 45 I3
Manggar Indon. 77 E3
Mangghyshlaq Kazakh. see Mangystau
Mangghystaū Kazakh. see Mangystau
Mangghystaū Oblysy admin. div. Kazakh. see Mangistauskaya Oblast'
Mangghyt Uzbek. see Mang'it
Manghit Uzbek. see Mang'it
Mangistau, Gory hills Kazakh. 102 B3
Mangistauskaya Oblast' admin. div. Kazakh. 102 C4
also known as Mangghystaū Oblysy; formerly known as Mangyshlak Oblast or Mangyshlakskaya Oblast'
Mang'it Uzbek. 102 E4
also spelt Mangghyt or Manghit
Mangkalihat, Tanjung pt Indon. 77 G2
Mangkutup r. Indon. 77 F3
Manglares, Punta pt Col. 198 B4
Mangnai China 88 E4
Mangnai Zhen China 88 E4
Mangoaka Madag. 131 [inset] K2
Mangochi Malawi 129 B8
formerly known as Fort Johnston
Mangodara Burkina 124 D4
Mangoky r. Toliara Madag. 131 [inset] I4
Mangoky r. Toliara Madag. 131 [inset] J4
Mangole i. Indon. 75 C3
Mangole, Selat sea chan. Indon. 75 C3
Mangoli India 94 B2
Mangombe Dem. Rep. Congo 126 E5
Mangonui N.Z. 152 H3
Mangoro r. Madag. 131 [inset] K3
Mangqystaū Shyghanaghy b. Kazakh. see Mangyshlakskiy Zaliv
Mangra China see Guinan
Mangral India 96 A5
Mangrol India 96 C4
Mangrul India 94 C1
Mangshi China see Luxi
Mangualde Port. 54 D4
Manguari Brazil 198 D5
Manguchar Pak. 101 F4
Mangueira, Lago l. Brazil 204 G4
Mangueirinha Brazil 203 A8
Manguéni, Plateau du Niger 123 H5
Mangui China 82 A2
Manguinha, Pontal do pt Brazil 202 E4
Mangula Zimbabwe see Mhangura
Mangum U.S.A. 179 C5
Mangunça, Ilha i. Brazil 202 C2
Mangut Rus. Fed. 85 G1
Mangyshlak Kazakh. see Mangystau
Mangyshlak, Poluostrov pen. Kazakh. 102 B3
also known as Tüpqaraghan Tübegi
Mangyshlak Oblast admin. div. Kazakh. see Mangistauskaya Oblast'
Mangyshlakskaya Oblast' admin. div. Kazakh. see Mangistauskaya Oblast'
Mangyshlakskiy Zaliv b. Kazakh. 102 B3
also known as Mangqystaū Shyghanaghy
Mangystau Kazakh. 102 B4
also spelt Mangghystaū; formerly known as Mangghyshlaq or Mangyshlak
Manhan Hovd Mongolia see Tögrög
Manhan Hövsgöl Mongolia 84 C1
Manhattan U.S.A. 178 C4
Manhattan Beach U.S.A. 182 F8
Manhica Moz. 133 Q2
Manhoca Moz. 133 Q3
Manhuaçu Brazil 203 D7
Manhuaçu r. Brazil 207 L6
Manhumirim Brazil 207 L7
Mani Chad 120 B6
Mani well Chad 120 C5
Mani China 89 D5
Mani Col. 198 C3
Mani Nigeria 125 G3
Mānī', Wādī al watercourse Iraq 109 M3
Mania r. Madag. 131 [inset] J3
Maniago Italy 56 E2
Maniakoi Greece 58 C8
Maniari Tank resr India 97 D5
also known as Khuria Tank
Manica Moz. 131 G3
Manica prov. Moz. 131 G3
Manicaland prov. Zimbabwe 131 G3
Manicoré Brazil 199 F6
Manicoré r. Brazil 199 F6
Manicouagan Canada 169 G3
Manicouagan r. Canada 169 G3
Manicouagan, Petit Lac l. Canada 169 H2
Manicouagan, Réservoir resr Canada 169 G3
Manic Trois, Réservoir resr Canada 169 G3
Maniema prov. Dem. Rep. Congo 126 E5
Manīfah Saudi Arabia 105 E2
Maniganggo China 86 A2
Manigotagan Canada 167 L5
Manihari India 97 E4
Manihiki atoll Cook Is 221 I6
formerly known as Great Ganges or Humphrey Island
Maniitsoq Greenland 165 N3
also known as Sukkertoppen
Maniji r. Pak. 101 F5
Manika, Plateau de la Dem. Rep. Congo 127 E7
Manikchhari Bangl. 97 G5
Manikganj Bangl. 97 F5
Manikgarh India see Rajura
Manikpur India 96 D4
►Manila Phil. 74 B3
Capital of the Philippines.
UNESCO World Heritage Site
►►18–19 World Cities
Manila U.S.A. 180 E4
Manila Bay Phil. 74 B3
Manilaid i. Estonia 42 F3
Manilla Australia 147 F2
Manily Rus. Fed. 39 Q3
Manimbaya, Tanjung pt Indon. 75 A3
Maningrida Australia 148 B2
Maninjau, Danau l. Indon. 76 C3
Manipa i. Indon. 75 C3
Manipa, Selat sea chan. Indon. 75 C3
Manipur India see Imphal
Manipur state India 97 G4
Manipur r. India/Myanmar 97 G5
Manisa Turkey 106 A3
Manisa prov. Turkey 59 J10
Manises Spain 55 K5
Manissauá Missu r. Brazil 202 A4
Manistee U.S.A. 172 G6
Manistee r. U.S.A. 172 G6
Manistique U.S.A. 172 G5
Manistique Lake U.S.A. 172 H4
Manitoba prov. Canada 167 L4
Manitoba, Lake Canada 167 L5
Manito Lake Canada 167 I4
Manitou Canada 167 L5
Manitou r. Canada 169 H3
Manitou, Lake Canada 168 D4
Manitou Beach U.S.A. 176 H2
Manitou Falls Canada 168 A3
Manitou Island U.S.A. 172 F3
Manitou Islands U.S.A. 172 G5
Manitoulin Island Canada 168 D4
Manitouwadge Canada 168 C3
Manitowaning Canada 173 L5
Manitowik Lake Canada 173 I2
Manitowish Waters U.S.A. 172 D4
Manitowoc U.S.A. 172 F6
Maniwaki Canada 168 F4
Manizales Col. 198 C3
Manja Madag. 131 [inset] J4
Manjacaze Moz. 131 G5
Manjak Madag. 131 [inset] J3
Manjam Umm Qurayyāt waterhole Egypt 104 A3
Manjarabad India 94 B3
Manjeri India 94 C4
Manjhand Pak. 101 G5
Man Jiang r. China 82 B4
Manjil Iran 100 B2
Manjimup Australia 151 B7
Manjo Cameroon 125 H5
Manjra r. India 94 C2
Man Kabat Myanmar 78 B2
Mankachar India 97 F4
Mankanza Dem. Rep. Congo see Makanza
Mankato KS U.S.A. 178 C4
Mankato MN U.S.A. 178 D2
Mankono Côte d'Ivoire 124 D4
Mankota Canada 167 J5
Manlleu Spain 55 N3
Manly U.S.A. 174 A3
Manmad India 94 B1
Mann r. Australia 148 B2
Mann, Mount Australia 148 A5
Manna Indon. 76 C4
Mannahill Australia 146 C3
Mannar Sri Lanka 94 C4
Mannar, Gulf of India/Sri Lanka 94 C4
Mannargudi India 94 C4
Manneru r. India 94 D3
Mannheim Germany 48 F6
Mannicolo Islands Solomon Is see Vanikoro Islands
Männikuste Estonia 42 F3
Manning Canada 167 G3
Manning ND U.S.A. 178 B2
Manning SC U.S.A. 175 D5
Manning Provincial Park Canada 166 F5
Mannington U.S.A. 176 E6
Männlifluh mt. Switz. 51 N6
Mann Ranges mts Australia 148 A5
Mannsville U.S.A. 177 I2
Mannu r. Sardinia Italy 57 A8
Mannu r. Sardinia Italy 57 A9
Mannu r. Sardinia Italy 57 B9
Mannu, Capo c. Sardinia Italy 57 A8
Mannville Canada 167 I4
Mano r. Liberia/Sierra Leone 124 C5
Manoa Bol. 200 D2
Man-of-War Rocks is U.S.A. see Gardner Pinnacles
Manoharpur India 89 B7
Manohar Thana India 96 C4
Manokotak U.S.A. 164 D4
Manokwari Indon. 73 H7
Manombo Atsimo Madag. 131 [inset] I4
Manompana Madag. 131 [inset] K3
Manono Dem. Rep. Congo 127 E6
Manora Head Pak. 101 F5
Mano River Liberia 124 C5
Manos, Cueva de las cave Arg. 205 C7
UNESCO World Heritage Site
Manosque France 51 L9
Manouane, Lac l. Canada 169 G3
Mano-wan b. Japan 90 F6
Man Pan Myanmar 78 B3
Manp'o N. Korea 83 B4
Manpur India 96 B5
Manra i. Kiribati 145 H2
formerly known as Sydney Island
Manresa Spain 55 M3
Mansa Gujarat India 96 B5
Mansa Punjab India 96 B3
Mansa Zambia 127 F7
formerly known as Fort Rosebery
Mansabá Guinea-Bissau 124 B3
Mansa Konko Gambia 124 B3
Man Sam Myanmar 78 B3
Mansehra Pak. 101 H3
Mansel Island Canada 165 L3
Mansel'kya ridge Fin./Rus. Fed. 44 O2
Mansfield Australia 147 E4
Mansfield U.K. 47 K10
Mansfield AR U.S.A. 179 D5
Mansfield LA U.S.A. 179 D5
Mansfield MA U.S.A. 177 N3
Mansfield OH U.S.A. 176 C5
Mansfield PA U.S.A. 177 H4
Mansfield, Mount U.S.A. 177 M1
Man Si Myanmar 78 B2
Mansi Myanmar 78 A2
Mansidão Brazil 202 D4
Manso r. Brazil see Mortes, Rio das
Manso-Nkwanta Ghana 125 E5
Mansuela Indon. 75 D3
Mansurlu Turkey 106 C3
also known as Tapan
Manta Ecuador 198 A5
long form San Pablo de Manta
Mantalingajan, Mount Phil. 74 A4
Mantantale Dem. Rep. Congo 126 D5
Mantaro r. Peru 200 B3
Manteca U.S.A. 182 C4
Mantecal Venez. 198 D3
Mantehage i. Indon. 75 C2
Manteigas Port. 54 D4
Mantena Brazil 203 D6
Manteno U.S.A. 172 F9
Manteo U.S.A. 174 F5
Mantes-la-Jolie France 50 H4
Manthani India 94 C2
Manti U.S.A. 183 M2
Mantiqueira, Serra da mts Brazil 203 C7
Manto Hond. 186 B4
Manton U.S.A. 172 H6
Mantorville U.S.A. 168 A4
Mantos Blancos Chile 200 C5
Mantoudi Greece 59 E10
also known as Mandhoúdhíon
Mantova Italy see Mantua
Mäntsälä Fin. 45 N3
Mänttä Fin. 45 N3
Mantua Cuba 186 B2
Mantua Italy 56 C3
also spelt Mantova
Mantua U.S.A. 176 D4
Mantuan Downs Australia 149 E5
Manturovo Rus. Fed. 40 H4
Mäntyharju Fin. 45 N3
Mäntyjärvi Fin. 44 N2
Manu r. Bol. see Mapiri
Manú r. Peru 200 C3
Manu, Parque Nacional nat. park Peru 200 B3
UNESCO World Heritage Site
Manuae atoll Fr. Polynesia 221 I7
also known as Fenua Ura; formerly known as Scilly, Île
Manu'a Islands American Samoa 145 I3
Manubi S. Africa 133 M9
Manuel Alves r. Brazil 202 B4
Manuel J. Cobo Arg. 204 F4
Manuel Rodriguez, Isla i. Chile 205 B9
Manuel Urbano Brazil 200 C2
Manuel Vitorino Brazil 202 D5
Manuelzinho Brazil 202 A3
Manui i. Indon. 75 B3
Manūjān Iran 100 D5
Manukan Phil. 74 B4
Manukau N.Z. 152 I4
Manukau Harbour N.Z. 152 I5
Manuk Manka i. Phil. 74 A5
Manunda watercourse Australia 146 C3
Manupari r. Bol. 200 D2
Manurimi r. Bol. 200 D2
Manuripi r. Bol. 200 D2
Manuripi Heath, Reserva Nacional nature res. Bol. 200 C2
Manusela National Park Indon. 75 D3
Manus Island P.N.G. 73 K7
Manutuke N.Z. 152 L6
Manvi India 94 C3
Manwat India 94 C2
Many U.S.A. 179 D6
Manyallaluk Aboriginal Reserve Australia 148 B2
Manyame r. Moz./Zimbabwe 131 F2
formerly known as Hunyani
Manyara, Lake salt l. Tanz. 129 B5
Manyas Turkey 59 I8
Manyas Gölü l. Turkey see Kuş Gölü
Manyatseng S. Africa 133 L6
Manyberries Canada 167 I5
Manych-Gudilo, Ozero l. Rus. Fed. 41 G7
Many Farms U.S.A. 183 O5
Manyinga Zambia 127 E8
Many Island Lake Canada 167 I5
Manyoni Tanz. 129 B6
Many Peaks, Mount hill Australia 151 B7
Manzala, Bahra el lag. Egypt see Manzala, Lake
Manzala, Lake lag. Egypt 108 D6
also known as Manzala, Bahra el
Manzanal, Puerto del pass Spain 54 E2
Manzanares Spain 55 H5
Manzaneda, Cabeza de mt. Spain 54 D2
Manzanillo Cuba 186 D2
Manzanillo Mex. 184 D5
Manzanillo, Punta pt Panama 186 D5
Manzanza Dem. Rep. Congo 126 F6
Manzariyeh Iran 100 B3
Manzengele Dem. Rep. Congo 127 C6
Manzhouli China 85 H1
Manzini Swaziland 133 P3
formerly known as Bremersdorp
Manzini admin. dist. Swaziland 133 P3
Manzovka Rus. Fed. see Sibirtsevo
Mao Chad 120 B6
Mao Dom. Rep. 187 F3
formerly known as Valverde
Maó Spain see Mahón
Mao, Nam r. Myanmar see Shweli
Maoba Guizhou China 86 C3
Maoba Hubei China 87 D2
Maocifan China 87 E2
Mao'ergai China 86 B1
Maoke, Pegunungan mts Indon. 73 I7
Maokeng S. Africa 133 L4
Maokui Shan mt. China 83 A4
Maomao Shan mt. China 84 D4
Maoming China 87 D4
Ma On Shan hill Hong Kong China 87 [inset]
Maopi Cape Taiwan see Maopi T'ou
Maopi T'ou c. Taiwan 87 G4
English form Maopi Cape
Maopora i. Indon. 75 C4
Maotou Shan mt. China 86 B3
Maowen China see Maoxian
Maoxian China 86 B2
also known as Fengyi; formerly known as Maowen
Mapai Moz. 131 F4
Mapam Yumco l. China 89 C6
Mapane Indon. 75 B3
Mapanza Zambia 127 E9
Mapastepec Mex. 185 G6
Maphodi S. Africa 133 J7
Mapi r. Indon. 73 I8
Mapiche, Serranía mts Venez. 199 E3
Mapimí Mex. 184 E3
Mapinhane Moz. 131 G4
Mapire Venez. 199 E3
Mapireme Brazil 199 H4
Mapiri Bol. 200 C3
Mapiri r. Bol. 200 D2
also known as Manu
Mapirpán Col. 198 C4
Mapiu N.Z. 152 J6
Maple r. IA U.S.A. 178 D3
Maple r. MI U.S.A. 173 I8
Maple r. ND U.S.A. 178 C2
Maple r. ND U.S.A. 178 C2
Maple Creek Canada 167 I5
Maple Peak U.S.A. 183 O8
Mapleton IA U.S.A. 178 D3
Mapleton UT U.S.A. 183 M1
Maplewood U.S.A. 172 F6
Mapoon Australia 149 D1
Mapoon Aboriginal Reserve Australia 149 D2
Mapor i. Indon. 76 D2
Mapoteng Lesotho 133 L6
Maprik P.N.G. 73 J7
Mapuca India 94 B3
Mapuera r. Brazil 199 G5
Mapulanguene Moz. 131 G5
Mapunda Dem. Rep. Congo 127 E7
►Maputo Moz. 131 G5
Capital of Mozambique. Formerly known as Lourenço Marques.
Maputo prov. Moz. 131 G5
Maputo r. Moz./S. Africa 133 Q3
Maputo, Baía de b. Moz. 133 Q3
Maputo Elephant Reserve nature res. Moz. 133 Q3
Maputsoe Lesotho 133 L5
Maqanshy Kazakh. see Makanchi
Maqar an Na'am well Iraq 107 E5
Maqat Kazakh. see Makat
Maqên China 86 B1
also known as Dawu
Maqên Kangri mt. China 86 A1
Maqla, Jabal al mt. Saudi Arabia 108 G9
Maqnā Saudi Arabia 108 F9
Maqrat Yemen 105 E5
Maqţeïr reg. Mauritania 122 C5
Maqu China 86 B1
also known as Nyinma
Ma Qu r. China see Yellow
Maquan He r. China 89 D6
also known as Damqoq Zangbo
Maqueda Channel Phil. 74 B3
Maquela do Zombo Angola 127 B6
Maquinchao Arg. 204 C6
Maquoketa U.S.A. 174 B3
Maquoketa r. U.S.A. 174 B3
Maquon U.S.A. 172 C10
Mar r. Pak. 101 F5
Mar, Serra do mts Rio de Janeiro/São Paulo Brazil 203 C7
Mar, Serra do mts Rio Grande do Sul/Santa Catarina Brazil 203 B9
Mar, Serra do mts Brazil 207 J9
Mara r. Canada 167 I1
Mara Guyana 199 G3
Mara India 97 D5
Mara admin. reg. Tanz. 128 B5
Maraã Brazil 199 E5
Maraba Brazil 202 B3
Marabahan Indon. 77 F3
Marabatua i. Indon. 77 F4
Marabitanas Brazil 199 E4
Maraboon, Lake resr Australia 149 F4
Maracá r. Brazil 199 I5
Maracá, Ilha i. Brazil 199 F4
Maracaí Brazil 206 C9
Maracaibo Venez. 198 D2
Maracaibo, Lago de l. Venez. see Maracaibo, Lake
Maracaibo, Lake Venez. 198 D2
also known as Maracaibo, Lago de
Maracaju Brazil 201 G5
Maracaju, Serra de hills Brazil 201 G5
Maracanã Brazil 202 C2
Maracanaquará, Planalto plat. Brazil 199 H5
Maracanda Uzbek. see Samarqand
Maracás Brazil 202 D5
Maracás, Chapada de hills Brazil 202 D5
Maracay Venez. 199 E2
Marachkova Belarus 43 J6
Marādah Libya 120 C2
Maradi Niger 125 G3
Maradi dept Niger 125 G3
Marāgheh Iran 100 A2
Maragogi Brazil 202 F4
Maragondon Phil. 74 B3
Marah Saudi Arabia 105 D2
Marahoué r. Côte d'Ivoire 124 D5
Marahuaca, Cerro mt. Venez. 199 E4
Marais des Cygnes r. U.S.A. 178 D4
Marais du Cotentin et du Bessin, Parc Naturel Régional des nature res. France 50 E3
Marais Poitevin, Val de Sèvre et Vendée, Parc Naturel Régional nature res. France 50 F6
Marajó, Baía de est. Brazil 202 B2
Marajó, Ilha de i. Brazil 202 B2
Marakei atoll Kiribati 145 G1
also spelt Maraki; formerly known as Matthew
Maraki atoll Kiribati see Marakei
Marakkanam India 94 C3
Maralal Kenya 128 C4
Maralbashi China see Bachu
Maraldy Kazakh. 103 I1
Maraldy, Ozero salt l. Kazakh. 103 I1
Maralinga Australia 146 A2
Maralinga-Tjarutja Aboriginal Lands res. Australia 146 A2
Maralwexi China see Bachu
Maramasike i. Solomon Is 145 F2
Maramba Zambia see Livingstone
Marambio research station Antarctica 222 U2
long form Vicecomodoro Marambio
Marampit i. Indon. 75 C1
Maran mt. Pak. 101 F4
Marana U.S.A. 183 M9
Marand Iran 100 A2
Marandellas Zimbabwe see Marondera
Marang Myanmar 79 B6
Maranguape Brazil 202 E2
Maranhão r. Brazil 206 E1
Maranhão state Brazil 202 C3
Maranoa r. Australia 147 F1
Marañón r. Peru 198 C6
Marans France 50 F6
Marão Moz. 131 G5
formerly known as Mau-é-ele
Marão mt. Port. 54 D3
Maraoué, Parc National de la nat. park Côte d'Ivoire 124 D5
Marapanim Brazil 202 C2
Marape Brazil 201 F3
Marapi, Gunung vol. Indon. 76 C3
Marari Brazil 199 E6
Mararoa r. N.Z. 153 B13
Mara Rosa Brazil 202 B5
Maraş Cyprus see Varosia
Maraş Turkey see Kahramanmaraş
Marasende i. Indon. 77 G4
Mărășești Romania 58 I3
Mărașu Romania 58 I4
Maratea Italy 57 H9
Marathia, Akra pt Greece 59 B11
Marathokampos Greece 59 H11
Marathon Canada 168 C3
Marathón Greece see Marathonas
Marathon FL U.S.A. 175 D7
Marathon TX U.S.A. 179 B6
Marathon WI U.S.A. 172 D6
Marathonas Greece 59 E10
also known as Marathón
Maratua i. Indon. 77 G2
Marauá Brazil 199 E5
Marauiá r. Brazil 199 E5
Maravatío Mex. 185 E5
Maravillas Creek watercourse U.S.A. 179 B6
Marāwah Libya 120 D1
Marawi Phil. 74 C4
Marawwaḩ, Jazīrat i. U.A.E. 105 F2
Marayes Arg. 204 D3
Maray Lake Pak. 101 G4
Mar'ayt Yemen 105 E4
Märäzä Azer. 107 G2
Marbella Spain 54 G8
Marble Bar Australia 150 B4
Marble Canyon U.S.A. 183 M5
Marble Canyon gorge U.S.A. 183 M5
Marble Hall S. Africa 133 N1
Marble Hill U.S.A. 174 B4
Marble Island Canada 167 N2
Marbul Pass Jammu and Kashmir 96 B2
Marburg S. Africa 133 O7
Marburg Slovenia see Maribor
Marburg an der Lahn Germany 48 F5

Marca Peru **200** A2
Marca, Ponta do *pt* Angola **127** A9
Marcal *r.* Hungary **49** O8
Marcali Hungary **49** O9
Marcapata Peru **200** C3
Marcelino Brazil **199** E5
Marcellus *MI* U.S.A. **172** H8
Marcellus *NY* U.S.A. **177** I3
March *r.* Austria/Slovakia *see* **Morava**
March U.K. **47** M11
Marchant Hill Australia **146** C3
Marche *reg.* France **50** H6
Marche *admin. reg.* Italy **56** E5
Marche, Plateaux de la France **50** H6
Marche-en-Famenne Belgium **51** L2
Marchena Spain **54** F7
Mar Chiquita, Laguna *l.* Arg. **204** E3
Marchtrenk Austria **49** L7
Mārciena Latvia **42** H5
Marcona Peru **200** B3
Marcopeet Islands Canada **168** E1
Marcos Juárez Arg. **204** E4
Marcy, Mount U.S.A. **177** L1
Mardan Pak. **101** H3
Mar de Ajó Arg. **204** F5
Mar del Plata Arg. **204** F5
Mardīan Afgh. **101** F2
Mardın Turkey **107** E3
Mårdudden Sweden **44** M2
Mardzad Mongolia **84** D2
Maré *i.* New Caledonia **145** F4
formerly known as Britannia Island
Mare de Déu del Toro *hill* Spain **55** P5
Maree, Loch *l.* U.K. **46** G6
Mareeba Australia **149** E3
Mareh Iran **101** D5
Maréna Mali **124** C3
Marendet Niger **125** G2
Marengo *IA* U.S.A. **174** A3
Marengo *IL* U.S.A. **172** E8
Marengo *WI* U.S.A. **172** C4
Marenisco U.S.A. **172** D4
Marennes France **50** E7
Marerano Madag. **131** [inset] J4
Maret Islands Australia **150** D2
Marettimo, Isola *i. Sicily* Italy **57** E11
Mareuil France **50** G7
Mareuil-sur-Lay-Dissais France **50** E6
Marevo Rus. Fed. **43** N4
Marfa U.S.A. **181** F7
Margam Ri *mts* China **89** D5
Marganets Kazakh. *see* **Zhezdy**
Marganets Ukr. *see* **Marhanets'**
Margao India *see* **Madgaon**
Margaret *r.* Australia **150** D3
Margaret *watercourse* Australia **146** C2
Margaret, Mount *hill* Australia **150** B4
Margaret Lake *Alta* Canada **167** H3
Margaret Lake *N.W.T.* Canada **167** G1
Margaret River Australia **151** A7
Margaretville U.S.A. **177** K3
Margarita Arg. **204** E3
Margarita, Isla de *i.* Venez. **199** F2
Margaritovo Rus. Fed. **90** D3
Margate S. Africa **133** O7
Margate U.K. **47** N12
Margate City U.S.A. **177** K6
Mărgău Romania **58** D2
Margeride, Monts de la *mts* France **51** J7
Margherita India **97** G4
Margherita, Lake Eth. *see* **Abaya, Lake**
Margherita di Savoia Italy **56** I7

▸**Margherita Peak** Dem. Rep. Congo/Uganda **126** F4
3rd highest mountain in Africa. Also known as Stanley, Mount or Marguerite, Pic.
▸▸**110–111 Africa** Landscapes

Marghilon Uzbek. *see* **Marg'ilon**
Marghita Romania **58** D1
Marg'ilon Uzbek. **103** G4
also spelt Marghilon
Margionys Lith. **42** F8
Margog Caka *l.* China **89** D5
Margos Peru **200** A2
Margosatubig Phil. **74** B5
Māgow, Dasht-e *des.* Afgh. **101** E4
Marguerite Canada **166** F4
Marguerite, Pic *mt.* Dem. Rep. Congo/Uganda *see* **Margherita Peak**
Marguerite Bay Antarctica **222** T2
Margyang China **89** E6
Marhaj Khalīl Iraq **107** F4
Marhamat Uzbek. **103** H4
Marhan Dāgh *hill* Iraq **107** E3
Marhanets' Ukr. **41** E7
also spelt Marganets; *formerly known as* Komintern
Marhoum Alg. **123** E2
Mari *r.* Brazil **201** D1
Mari Myanmar **78** B2
Mari P.N.G. **73** J8
Maria *r.* Brazil **203** A7
Maria *atoll* Fr. Polynesia **221** I7
María Cleofas, Isla *i.* Mex. **184** D4
María Elena Chile **200** C5
Mariager Denmark **45** J4
María Ignacia Arg. **204** F5
Maria Island *N.T.* Australia **148** B2
Maria Island *Tas.* Australia **147** F5
Mariala National Park Australia **149** E5
María Madre, Isla *i.* Mex. **184** D4
María Magdelena, Isla *i.* Mex. **184** D4
Marian Australia **149** F4
Mariana Brazil **207** J7
Marianao Cuba **186** C2

▸**Mariana Trench** *sea feature* N. Pacific Ocean **220** E5
Deepest trench in the world.

Mariani India **97** G4
Mariánica, Cordillera *mts* Spain *see* **Morena, Sierra**
Marian Lake Canada **167** G2
Marianna *AR* U.S.A. **174** B5
Marianna *FL* U.S.A. **175** C6
Mariannelund Sweden **45** K4
Mariano Loza Arg. **204** F3
Mariano Machado Angola *see* **Ganda**
Mariánské Lázně Czech Rep. **49** J6
historically known as Marienbad
Mariapiri, Mesa de *hills* Col. **198** D4
Mariápolis Brazil **206** B8
Marias *r.* U.S.A. **180** E3
Marías, Islas *is* Mex. **184** D4

▸**Mariato, Punta** *pt* Panama **186** C6
Most southerly point of North America.
▸▸**154–155 North America** Landscapes

Maria van Diemen, Cape N.Z. **152** G2
Mariazell Austria **49** M8
Ma'rib Yemen **105** D5
Ma'rib *governorate* Yemen **105** D5
Maribel U.S.A. **172** F6
Maribo Denmark **48** I1
Maribor Slovenia **56** H2
historically known as Marburg
Maricá Brazil **207** K9
Marica *r.* Bulg. *see* **Maritsa**
Marico *r.* S. Africa **133** K1
Marico Bosveld Nature Reserve S. Africa **133** K2
Maricopa *AZ* U.S.A. **183** L8
Maricopa *CA* U.S.A. **182** E6
Maricopa Mountains U.S.A. **183** L8
Maricourt Canada *see* **Kangiqsujuaq**
Maridi Sudan **126** F3
Maridi *watercourse* Sudan **126** F3
Marié *r.* Brazil **199** E6
Marie Byrd Land *reg.* Antarctica **222** P1
Marie-Galante *i.* Guadeloupe **187** H4
Mariehamn Fin. **45** L3
also spelt Maarianhamina
Mari El *aut. rep.* Rus. Fed. *see* **Mariy El, Respublika**
Mariembero *r.* Brazil **202** B5
also known as Cristalino
Marienbad Czech Rep. *see* **Mariánské Lázně**
Marienburg Poland *see* **Malbork**
Mariental Namibia **130** C5
Marienville U.S.A. **176** F4
Marienwerder Poland *see* **Kwidzyn**
Mariestad Sweden **45** K4
Mariet *r.* Canada **168** E1
Marietta *GA* U.S.A. **175** C5
Marietta *OH* U.S.A. **176** D6
Marietta *OK* U.S.A. **179** C5
Mariga *r.* Nigeria **125** G4
Marigliano Italy **56** G8
Marignane France **51** L9
Marigot Dominica **187** H4
Marigot West Indies **187** H3
Marii, Mys *pt* Rus. Fed. **82** F1
Mariinsk Rus. Fed. **80** D1
Mariinskoye Rus. Fed. **103** E1
Marijampolė Lith. **42** E7
formerly known as Kapsukas
Marikostinovo Bulg. **58** E7
Marília Brazil **206** D9
Marillana Australia **150** B4
Marimba Angola **127** C7
Marín Spain **54** C2
Marina U.S.A. **182** C5
Marina di Gioiosa Ionica Italy **57** I10
Mar'ina Gorka Belarus *see* **Mar"ina Horka**
Mar"ina Horka Belarus **42** J8
also spelt Mar'ina Gorka
Marinduque *i.* Phil. **74** B3
Marine City U.S.A. **173** K8
Marinella, Golfo di *b. Sardinia* Italy **56** B7
Mariner Glacier Antarctica **223** L2
Marinette U.S.A. **172** F5
Maringá Brazil **206** B10
Maringa *r.* Dem. Rep. Congo **126** C4
Maringo U.S.A. **176** C5
Maringué Moz. **131** G3
Marinha Grande Port. **54** C5
Marinjab Iran **100** B3
Mar'insko Rus. Fed. **43** J3
Marion *AL* U.S.A. **175** C5
Marion *AR* U.S.A. **174** B5
Marion *IA* U.S.A. **172** B8
Marion *IL* U.S.A. **174** B4
Marion *IN* U.S.A. **174** C3
Marion *KS* U.S.A. **178** C4
Marion *KY* U.S.A. **174** B4
Marion *NC* U.S.A. **174** D5
Marion *OH* U.S.A. **176** B5
Marion *SC* U.S.A. **175** E5
Marion *VA* U.S.A. **176** D9
Marion *WI* U.S.A. **172** E6
Marion, Lake U.S.A. **175** D5
Marion Bay Australia **146** C3
Marion Lake U.S.A. **178** C4
Marion Reef *reef* Australia **149** G3
Mariou, Adrar *mt.* Alg. **123** H5
Maripa Venez. **199** E3
Maripasoula Fr. Guiana **199** H4
Maripipi *i.* Phil. **74** C4
Mariposa U.S.A. **182** E4
Mariposa *r.* U.S.A. **182** D4
Mariquita Col. **198** C3
Marir, Gezîret *i.* Egypt **104** A3
English form Mirear Island
Marisa Indon. **75** B2
Mariscal José Félix Estigarribia Para. **201** E5
Mărişel Romania **58** E2
Mărişelu Romania **58** F1
Marite S. Africa **133** P1
Maritime Alps *mts* France/Italy **51** M8
also known as Maritimes, Alpes or Marittime, Alpi
Maritime Kray *admin. div.* Rus. Fed. *see* **Primorskiy Kray**
Maritimes, Alpes *mts* France/Italy *see* **Maritime Alps**
Maritsa Bulg. *see* **Simeonovgrad**
Maritsa *r.* Bulg. **58** H7
also spelt Marica
Marittime, Alpi *mts* France/Italy *see* **Maritime Alps**
Mari-Turek Rus. Fed. **40** I4
Mariupol' Ukr. **41** F7
formerly known as Zhdanov
Mariusa *nat. park* Venez. **199** F2
Mariusa, Isla *i.* Venez. **199** F2
Marīvān Iran **107** F4
formerly known as Dezh Shāhpūr
Mariy El, Respublika *aut. rep.* Rus. Fed. **40** I4
English form Mari El; *formerly known as* Mariyskaya A.S.S.R. *or* Mary A.S.S.R.
Mariyskaya A.S.S.R. *aut. rep.* Rus. Fed. *see* **Mariy El, Respublika**
Mārjamaa Estonia **42** F3
Marjan Afgh. *see* **Wazi Khwa**
Marjayoûn Lebanon **108** G4
Markā *i.* Saudi Arabia **104** C4
Marka Somalia **128** E4
formerly spelt Merca
Markakol', Ozero *l.* Kazakh. **88** D1
also known as Marqakōl
Markala Mali **124** D3
Markam China **86** A2
also known as Gartog
Markapur India **94** C3
Markaryd Sweden **45** K4
Markawene *well* Eth. **128** E3
Markaz, Ra's *c.* Oman **105** G4
Markazī *prov.* Iran **100** B3
Markdale Canada **173** M6
Marken S. Africa **131** F4
Markermeer *l.* Neth. **48** C3
Market Harborough U.K. **47** L11
Market Rasen U.K. **47** L10
Market Weighton U.K. **47** L10
Markha *r.* Rus. Fed. **39** L3
Markham Canada **168** E5
Markham, Mount Antarctica **223** K1
Markit China **88** B4
Markitta Sweden **44** M2
Markleeville U.S.A. **182** E3
Markleysburg U.S.A. **176** F6
Markog Qu *r.* China **86** B1
Markounda Cent. Afr. Rep. **126** C3
Markovo *Chukotskiy Autonomnyy Okrug* Rus. Fed. **39** R3
Markovo *Ivanovskaya Oblast'* Rus. Fed. **43** V4
Markoye Burkina **125** F3
Marks Rus. Fed. **102** A2
Marks U.S.A. **174** B5
Marksville U.S.A. **175** A6
Marktheidenfeld Germany **48** G6
Marktoberdorf Germany **48** H8
Marktosis Canada **166** E5
Marktredwitz Germany **48** J5
Marl Germany **48** E4
Marla Australia **146** B1
Marlboro U.S.A. **177** L4
Marlborough Australia **149** F4
Marlborough *admin. reg.* N.Z. **153** H9
Marlborough *MA* U.S.A. **177** N3
Marlborough *NH* U.S.A. **177** M3
Marle France **51** J3
Marlin U.S.A. **179** C6
Marlinton U.S.A. **176** E7
Marlo Australia **147** F4
Marloth Nature Reserve S. Africa **132** E11
Marlton U.S.A. **177** K6
Marmagao India **94** B3
formerly spelt Mormugao
Marmande France **50** G8
Marmara Turkey **58** I8
Marmara, Sea of *g.* Turkey **106** B2
also known as Marmara Denizi
Marmara Adası *i.* Turkey **58** I8
Marmara Denizi *g.* Turkey *see* **Marmara, Sea of**
Marmaraereğlisi Turkey **58** I8
Marmara Gölü *l.* Turkey **59** J10
Marmarica *reg.* Libya **120** E2
Marmaris Turkey **106** B3
Marmaro Greece **59** H10
Marmelos *r.* Brazil **201** E1
Marmet U.S.A. **176** D7
Marmion, Lake *salt l.* Australia **151** C6
Marmion Lake Canada **168** B3
Marmolada *mt.* Italy **56** D2
Marmolejo Spain **54** G6
Marne *r.* France **51** I4
Marne Germany **48** G2
Marne, Source de la *tourist site* France **48** C8
Marne-la-Vallée France **51** I4
Marneuli Georgia **107** F2
formerly known as Borchalo *or* Sarvani
Maro Chad **126** C2
Maroambihy Madag. **131** [inset] K2
Maroantsetra Madag. **131** [inset] K2
Maroba *r.* Brazil **207** N4
Marofandilia Madag. **131** [inset] J4
Marokopa N.Z. **152** I6
Marol Jammu and Kashmir **96** C2
Marolambo Madag. **131** [inset] K4
Maroldsweisach Germany **48** H5
Marolles-les-Braults France **50** G4
Maromokotro *mt.* Madag. **131** [inset] K2
Marondera Zimbabwe **131** F3
formerly spelt Marandellas
Maroni *r.* Fr. Guiana **199** H3
Maronne *r.* France **51** H7
Maroochydore Australia **149** G5
Maroonah Australia **150** A4
Maroon Peak U.S.A. **180** F5
Maros Indon. **75** A4
Maros *r.* Romania **58** B2
Maroseranana Madag. **131** [inset] K3
Maros-Körös Köze *plain* Hungary **49** R9
Maroslele Hungary **49** R9
Marosvásárhely Romania *see* **Târgu Mureş**
Marotandrano Madag. **131** [inset] K3
Marotolana Madag. **131** [inset] K2
Maroua Cameroon **125** I4
Marova Brazil **199** F5
Marovato *Antsirañana* Madag. **131** [inset] K2
Marovato *Toliara* Madag. **131** [inset] J5
Marovoay *Mahajanga* Madag. **131** [inset] J3
Marovoay *Toamasina* Madag. **131** [inset] K3
Marovoay Atsimo Madag. **131** [inset] J3
Marowali Indon. **75** B3
Marowijne *r.* Suriname **199** H3
Marqab al Khubbāz *hill* Iraq **109** N4
Marqādah Syria **109** L2
Marqakōl *l.* Kazakh. *see* **Markakol', Ozero**
Marquard S. Africa **133** L5
▸**Marquesas Islands** Fr. Polynesia **221** J6
also known as Marquises, Îles
▸▸**14–15 World** Environmental Impacts
Marquesas Keys *is* U.S.A. **175** D7
Marquês de Valença Brazil **207** J9
Marquette U.S.A. **172** F4
Marquise France **50** H2
Marquises, Îles *is* Fr. Polynesia *see* **Marquesas Islands**
Marra *r.* Australia **147** E2
Marra, Jebel *mt.* Sudan **120** E6
Marra Aboriginal Land *res.* Australia **148** B2
Marracuene Moz. **133** Q2
formerly known as Vila Luísa
Marradi Italy **56** D4
Marra, Jebel *plat.* Sudan **120** E6
Marrāk *i.* Saudi Arabia **104** C4
Marrakech Morocco **122** D3
English form Marrakesh
UNESCO World Heritage Site
Marrakesh Morocco *see* **Marrakech**
Marrawah Australia **147** E5
Marree Australia **146** C2
Marrero U.S.A. **175** B6
Marresale Rus. Fed. **40** M1
Marromeu Moz. **131** G3
Marromeu, Reserva de *nature res.* Moz. **131** G3
Marrupa Moz. **129** C8
Marryat Australia **148** B5
Mars *r.* France **51** I7
Mars U.S.A. **176** E5
Marsá al 'Alam Egypt **121** G3
Marsa al Burayqah Libya **120** C2
Marsabit Kenya **128** C4
Marsabit National Reserve *nature res.* Kenya **128** C4
Marsa Darur Sudan **121** H5
Marsa Delwein Sudan **121** H4
Marsá Iljī Egypt **104** A2
Marsala *Sicily* Italy **57** E11
Marsa Mar'ob Sudan **104** B3
Marsá Maţrūḩ Egypt **121** E2
historically known as Paraetonium
Marsa Oseif Sudan **104** B3
Marsa Salak Sudan **104** B3
Marsa Shin'ab Sudan **104** B3
Marsá Ţunḑubah Egypt **104** A2
Mars Bay Bahamas **186** D2
Marsberg Germany **48** F4
Marsciano Italy **56** E6
Marsden Australia **147** E3
Marsden Canada **167** I4
Marseille France **51** L9
English form Marseilles; *historically known as* Massilia
Marseilles France *see* **Marseille**
Marseilles U.S.A. **172** E9
Marsella Bol. **200** D3
Marsfjället *mt.* Sweden **44** K2
Marshah, Jabal *mt.* Saudi Arabia **108** F9
Marshall *watercourse* Australia **148** C4
Marshall Canada **167** I4
Marshall *AR* U.S.A. **179** D5
Marshall *IL* U.S.A. **174** C4
Marshall *MI* U.S.A. **173** I8
Marshall *MN* U.S.A. **178** D2
Marshall *MO* U.S.A. **178** D4
Marshall *TX* U.S.A. **179** D5
Marshall *VA* U.S.A. **176** H7
▸**Marshall Islands** *country* N. Pacific Ocean **220** H5
also known as Majōl
▸▸**16–17 World** Population
▸▸**138–139 Oceania** Countries
Marshalltown U.S.A. **174** A3
Marshfield *MO* U.S.A. **178** D4
Marshfield *WI* U.S.A. **172** C6
Marsh Harbour Bahamas **186** D1
Mars Hill U.S.A. **174** H2
Marsh Island U.S.A. **175** B6
Marsh Lake Canada **166** C2
Marsh Lake *l.* Canada **166** C2
Marsh Peak U.S.A. **183** O1
Marshūn Iran **100** B2
Marsing U.S.A. **180** C4
Märsta Sweden **45** L4
Marsyangdi *r.* Nepal **97** E4
Marta Italy **56** D6
Marta *r.* Italy **56** D6
Martanai Besar *i. Sabah* Malaysia **77** G1
Martapura *Kalimantan Selatan* Indon. **77** F3
Martapura *Sumatra* Indon. **76** D4
Martel France **50** H8
Marten River Canada **168** E4
Marte R. Gómez, Presa *resr* Mex. **185** F3
Martés *mt.* Spain **55** K5
Martés, Serra *mts* Spain **55** J5
Martha's Vineyard *i.* U.S.A. **177** O4
Martí Cuba **186** D2
Martigny Switz. **51** N6
Martim Vaz, Ilhas *is* S. Atlantic Ocean *see* **Martin Vas, Ilhas**
Martin *r.* Canada **166** F2
Martin Slovakia **49** P6
Martín *r.* Spain **55** K3
Martin U.S.A. **178** B3
Martin, Lake U.S.A. **175** C5
Martina Franca Italy **57** J8
Martinborough N.Z. **152** J9
Martinet Spain **55** M2
Martínez Mex. **185** F4
Martinez *CA* U.S.A. **182** B3
Martinez *GA* U.S.A. **175** D5
Martinez Lake U.S.A. **183** J9
Martinho Campos Brazil **203** C6

▸**Martinique** *terr.* West Indies **187** H4
French Overseas Department.
▸▸**158–159 North America** Countries

Martinique Passage Dominica/Martinique **187** H4
Martino Greece **59** E10
Martinópolis Brazil **206** B9
Martin Peninsula Antarctica **222** Q2
Martins Bay N.Z. **153** B12
Martinsburg *OH* U.S.A. **176** C5
Martinsburg *PA* U.S.A. **176** G5
Martinsburg *WV* U.S.A. **176** H6
Martinsville *IN* U.S.A. **174** C4
Martinsville *VA* U.S.A. **176** F9

▸**Martin Vas, Ilhas** *is* S. Atlantic Ocean **217** M7
Most easterly point of South America. English form Martin Vaz Islands; also spelt Martim Vaz, Ilhas.
▸▸**188–189 South America** Landscapes

Martin Vaz Islands S. Atlantic Ocean *see* **Martin Vas, Ilhas**
Martök Kazakh. *see* **Martuk**
Marton N.Z. **152** J8
Martorell Spain **55** M3
Martos Spain **54** H7
Martuk Kazakh. **102** D2
also spelt Martök
Martuni Armenia **107** F2
Maru Nigeria **125** G3
Maruchak Afgh. **101** E3
Marudi *Sarawak* Malaysia **77** F1
Marudu, Teluk *b. Sabah* Malaysia **77** G1
Marugame Japan **91** C7
Maruia *r.* N.Z. **153** G9
Maruim Brazil **202** E4
Marukhis Ugheltekhili *pass* Georgia/Rus. Fed. **107** E2
Marum, Mount *vol.* Vanuatu **145** F3
Mārūn *r.* Iran **100** B4
Marunga Angola **127** D9
Marusthali *reg.* India **96** A4
Maruwa Aboriginal Reserve Australia **150** D4
Maruwa Hills Sudan **128** B3
Marvast Iran **100** C4
Marv Dasht Iran **100** C4
Marvejols France **51** J8
Marvine, Mount U.S.A. **183** M3
Marwar Junction India **96** B4
Marwayne Canada **167** I4
Mary *r. N.T.* Australia **148** A2
Mary *r. Qld* Australia **149** G5
Mary *r. W.A.* Australia **150** D3
Mary Turkm. **103** E5
historically known as Alexandria *or* Merv
UNESCO World Heritage Site
Mary A.S.S.R. *aut. rep.* Rus. Fed. *see* **Mariy El, Respublika**
Maryborough *Qld* Australia **149** G5
Maryborough *Vic.* Australia **147** D4
Marydale S. Africa **132** G6
Mar'yevka Rus. Fed. **102** B1
Mary Frances Lake Canada **167** J2
Maryland *state* U.S.A. **177** I7
Mary Oblast *admin. div.* Turkm. *see* **Maryyskaya Oblast'**
Mary's Harbour Canada **169** K2
Marystown Canada **169** K4
Marysvale U.S.A. **183** L3
Marysville *CA* U.S.A. **182** C2
Marysville *KS* U.S.A. **178** C4
Marysville *MI* U.S.A. **173** K8
Marysville *OH* U.S.A. **176** B5
Marysville *WA* U.S.A. **180** B2
Maryvale *N.T.* Australia **148** B5
Maryvale *Qld* Australia **149** E3
Maryville *MO* U.S.A. **178** D3
Maryville *TN* U.S.A. **174** D5
Maryyskaya Oblast' *admin. div.* Turkm. **103** E5
English form Mary Oblast
Marzagão Brazil **206** E4
Marzo, Cabo *c.* Col. **198** B3
Masachapa Nicaragua **186** B5
Masada *tourist site* Israel **108** G6
also spelt Metsada *or* Mezada
UNESCO World Heritage Site
Maşaff, Wādī *watercourse* Syria/Turkey **109** L1
Masaguro Tanz. **129** C7
Masāhūn, Kūh-e *mt.* Iran **100** C4
Masai Mara National Reserve *nature res.* Kenya **128** B5
Masai Steppe *plain* Tanz. **129** C6
Masaka Uganda **128** A5
Masakhane S. Africa **133** K8
Masalanyane Pan *salt pan* Botswana **130** D4
Masalembu Besar *i.* Indon. **77** F4
Masalembu Kecil *i.* Indon. **77** F4
Masallı Azer. **107** G3
Masamba Indon. **75** B3
Masamba *mt.* Indon. **75** B3
Masan S. Korea **83** C6
Masāqif *i.* Saudi Arabia **104** C4
Masasi Tanz. **129** C7
Masavi Bol. **201** E4
Masaya Nicaragua **186** B5
Masaya, Volcán *vol.* Nicaragua **186** B5
Masbate Phil. **74** B3
Masbate *i.* Phil. **74** B3
Mascara Alg. **123** F2
also spelt Mouaskar
Mascot U.S.A. **176** B9
Mascota Mex. **184** D4
Mascote Brazil **207** N2
Mascouche Canada **169** F4
Masein Myanmar **78** A3
Ma Sekatok *b.* Indon. **77** G2
Masela Indon. **75** D5
Masela *i.* Indon. **75** D5
Maseno Kenya **128** B4
Masères, Lac *l.* Canada **173** Q2

▸**Maseru** Lesotho **133** L6
Capital of Lesotho.

Masfjorden Norway **45** I3
Mashaba Zimbabwe *see* **Mashava**
Mashābih *i.* Saudi Arabia **104** B2
Mashai Lesotho **133** M6
Mashala Dem. Rep. Congo **126** D6
Mashan China **87** D4
also known as Baishan
Mashava Zimbabwe **131** F4
formerly spelt Mashaba
Masherbrum *mt.* Jammu and Kashmir **96** C2
Masheve Ukr. **43** N9
Mashhad Iran **101** D2
English form Meshed
Mashi *r.* India **96** B4
Mashike Japan **90** G3
Mashkel, Hamun-i- *salt flat* Pak. **101** E4
Mashket *r.* Pak. **101** E5
Mashki Chah Pak. **101** E4
Māshkīd *r.* Iran **101** E5
Mashonaland Central *prov.* Zimbabwe **131** F3
Mashonaland East *prov.* Zimbabwe **131** F3
Mashonaland West *prov.* Zimbabwe **131** F3
Mashtagi Azer. *see* **Maştağa**
Masiáca Mex. **184** C3
Masia-Mbia Dem. Rep. Congo **126** C5
Masibambane S. Africa **133** L8
Masīf Balţīm Egypt **108** C6
Masīlah, Wādī al *watercourse* Yemen **105** E5
Masilo S. Africa **133** K5
Masi-Manimba Dem. Rep. Congo **126** C6
Masindi Uganda **128** A4
Masinloc Phil. **74** A3
Masinyusane S. Africa **132** H8
Masira, Gulf of Oman *see* **Maşīrah, Khalīj**
Masira Channel Oman *see* **Maşīrah, Tur'at**
Maşīrah, Jazīrat *i.* Oman **105** G3
English form Masira Island
Maşīrah, Khalīj *b.* Oman **105** G4
English form Masira, Gulf of
Maşīrah, Tur'at *sea chan.* Oman **105** G3
English form Masira Channel
Masira Island Oman *see* **Maşīrah, Jazīrat**
Masis Armenia **107** F2
Masisea Peru **200** B2
Masjaing S. Africa **133** M5
Masjed Soleymān Iran **100** B4
Mask, Lough *l.* Ireland **47** C10
Maskanah Syria **109** J1
Maskūtān Iran **101** D5
Maslti Pak. **101** F4
Masna'ah Yemen **105** E5
Masoala, Parc National *nat. park* Madag. **131** [inset] K2
Masoala, Parc National de *nat. park* Madag. **129** F8
Masoala, Saikanosy *pen.* Madag. **131** [inset] K2
Masoala, Tanjona *c.* Madag. **131** [inset] K2
Masohi Indon. **75** D3
Mason *KY* U.S.A. **176** A7
Mason *MI* U.S.A. **173** I8
Mason *OH* U.S.A. **176** A6
Mason *TX* U.S.A. **179** C6
Mason *WI* U.S.A. **172** B4
Mason *WV* U.S.A. **176** C6
Mason, Lake *salt flat* Australia **151** B5
Mason Bay N.Z. **153** B14
Mason City U.S.A. **174** A3
Masoni *i.* Indon. **75** C3
Masontown *PA* U.S.A. **176** F6
Masontown *WV* U.S.A. **176** F6
Masqaţ Oman *see* **Muscat**
Masqaţ *governorate* Oman **105** G3
Masqaţ *reg.* Oman **105** G2
also spelt Muscat
Massa Italy **56** C4
Massachusetts *state* U.S.A. **177** M3
Massachusetts Bay U.S.A. **177** O3
Massadona U.S.A. **183** P1
Massafra Italy **57** J8
Massaguet Chad **120** B6
Massakory Chad **120** B6
Massalassef Chad **126** C2
Massa Marittimo Italy **56** C5
Massambará Brazil **204** G3
Massana Gabon **126** A5
Massangena Moz. **131** G4
Massango Angola **127** C7
Massaroca Brazil **202** D4
Massarosa Italy **56** C5
Massau Angola **127** C6
Massawa Eritrea **121** H6
also spelt Mits'iwa
Massawa Channel Eritrea **121** H5
Massena U.S.A. **177** K1
Massenya Chad **126** C2
Masset Canada **166** C4
Masset Inlet Canada **166** C4
Masseube France **50** G9
Massey Canada **168** D4
Massiac France **51** J7
Massieville U.S.A. **176** C6
Massif Central *mts* France **51** J7
Massigui Mali **124** D4
Massilia France *see* **Marseille**
Massina Mali **124** D3
formerly spelt Ke Macina
Massinga Moz. **131** G4
Massingir Moz. **131** G4
Massintonto *r.* Moz./S. Africa **133** Q2
Masson Canada **173** R5
Masson Island Antarctica **223** G2
Maştağa Azer. **107** G2
also spelt Mashtagi
Mastchoh Tajik. **101** G2
also known as Matcha
Masterton N.Z. **152** J8
Masticho, Akra *pt* Greece **59** H10
Mastic Point Bahamas **186** D1
Mastigouche, Réserve Faunique de *nature res.* Canada **169** F4
Mastrevik Norway **46** Q3
Mastuj Pak. **101** H2
Mastung Pak. **101** F4
Mastūrah Saudi Arabia **104** B3
Masty Belarus **42** F8
also spelt Mosty
Masuda Japan **91** B7
Masuika Dem. Rep. Congo **127** D6
Masuku Gabon *see* **Franceville**
Masuleh Iran **100** B2
Masulipatam India *see* **Machilipatnam**
Masuna *i.* American Samoa *see* **Tutuila**
Masurai, Bukit *mt.* Indon. **76** C3
Masvingo Zimbabwe **131** F4
formerly known as Fort Victoria *or* Nyanda
Masvingo *prov.* Zimbabwe **131** F4
Maswa Tanz. **128** B5
Maswe Game Reserve *nature res.* Tanz. **128** B5
Maşyāf Syria **109** H2
Mat *r.* Albania **58** A7
Mata *r.* N.Z. **152** M5
Mata, Serranía de *mts* Venez. **199** E3
Mata Amarilla Arg. **205** C8
Mataba Zambia **127** D8
Matabaan Somalia **128** E3
Matabeleland North *prov.* Zimbabwe **131** E3
Matabeleland South *prov.* Zimbabwe **131** F4
Matabhanga India **97** F4
Matachewan Canada **168** D4
Matachic Mex. **184** D2
Matadi Dem. Rep. Congo **127** B6
Matador U.S.A. **179** B5
Matagalpa Nicaragua **186** B4
Matagami Canada **168** E3
Matagami, Lac *l.* Canada **168** E3
Matagorda Island U.S.A. **179** C6
Mata Grande Brazil **202** E4
Matahiwi N.Z. **152** J7
Mataigou China *see* **Taole**
Matak *i.* Indon. **77** D2
Matak Kazakh. **103** H2
Matakana Island N.Z. **152** K5
Matakaoa Point N.Z. **152** M5
Matakitaki N.Z. **153** G9
Matala Angola **127** B8
Matale Sri Lanka **94** D5
Mataleng S. Africa **133** I5
Maţālī', Jabal *hill* Saudi Arabia **104** C2
Matam Senegal **124** B3
Matamata N.Z. **152** J5
Mata-Mata S. Africa **132** E2
Matamau N.Z. **152** K8
Matamey Niger **125** H3
Matamoras U.S.A. **177** K4
Matamoros *Campeche* Mex. **185** H5
Matamoros *Coahuila* Mex. **185** E3
Matamoros *Tamaulipas* Mex. **185** F3
Ma'ta Moûlana *well* Mauritania **124** B2
Matana, Danau *l.* Indon. **75** B3
Matanal Point Phil. **74** B5
Ma'ţan as Sārah *well* Libya **120** D4
Ma'ţan Bishrah *well* Libya **120** D4
Matandu *r.* Tanz. **129** C7
Matane Canada **169** H3
Matane, Réserve Faunique de *nature res.* Canada **169** H3
Mata Negra Venez. **199** F2
Matanga Madag. **131** [inset] J4
Matangi N.Z. **152** J5
Matanzas Cuba **186** C2
Matanzilla, Pampa de la *plain* Arg. **204** C5
Matão Brazil **206** E8
Matão, Serra do *hills* Brazil **202** B4
Matapalo, Cabo *c.* Costa Rica **186** C5
Matapan, Cape *pt* Greece *see* **Tainaro, Akra**
Mata Panew *r.* Poland **49** P5
Matapédia, Lac *l.* Canada **169** H3
Mataporquera Spain **54** G2
Maţār *well* Saudi Arabia **105** D2
Matará Arg. **204** E3
Matara Sri Lanka **94** D5
also known as Matturai
Mataragka Greece **59** C10
also spelt Matarânga
Mataram Indon. **77** G5
Matarânga Greece *see* **Mataragka**
Mataranka Australia **148** B2
Matārimah, Ra's *pt* Egypt **108** D8
Matarinao Bay Phil. **74** C4
Matarka Morocco **123** E2
Mataró Spain **55** N3
Mataroa N.Z. **152** J7
Matarombea *r.* Indon. **75** B3
Mataruška Banja *Srbija* Serb. and Mont. **58** B5
Matasiri *i.* Indon. **77** F4
Matassi *well* Sudan **121** F5
Matassi Tanz. **129** C6
Matatiele S. Africa **133** M7
Matatila Dam India **96** C4
Matau N.Z. **152** I7
Mataura N.Z. **153** C14
Mataura *r.* N.Z. **153** C14

▸**Matā'utu** Wallis and Futuna Is **145** H3
Capital of Wallis and Futuna Islands.

Matawai N.Z. **152** L6
Matawaia N.Z. **152** H3
Matawin *r.* Canada **169** F4
Matay Kazakh. **103** I3
Maţbakh, Ra's al *pt* Qatar **105** E2
Matcha Tajik. *see* **Mastchoh**
Matchi-Manitou, Lac *l.* Canada **173** P2
Mategua Bol. **201** E3
Matehuala Mex. **185** E4
Matei Romania **58** F2
Mateke Hills Zimbabwe **131** F4
Matelica Italy **56** F5
Matelot Trin. and Tob. **187** H5
Matemanga Tanz. **129** C7
Matende Angola **127** C9
Matera Italy **57** I8
UNESCO World Heritage Site
Matese, Monti del *mts* Italy **56** G7
Mátészalka Hungary **49** T8
Matetsi Zimbabwe **131** E3
Mateur Tunisia **57** B11
Matheus Leme Brazil **207** I6
Matewan U.S.A. **176** C8
Matha France **50** F7
Matheson Canada **168** D3
Mathews U.S.A. **177** I8
Mathias U.S.A. **176** G7
Mathis U.S.A. **179** C6
Mathraki *i.* Greece **59** A9
Mathura India **96** C4
Mati Phil. **74** C5
Matiacoali Burkina **125** F3
Matianxu China **87** E3
Matiari Pak. **101** G5
Matias Barbosa Brazil **207** J8
Matias Cardoso Brazil **202** D5
Matías Romero Mex. **185** G5
Matibane Moz. **131** I2
Matimekosh Canada **169** H2
Matina Costa Rica **186** C5
Matinicus Island U.S.A. **177** Q2
Matizi China **86** B1
Matjiesfontein S. Africa **132** E10
Matla *r.* India **97** F5
Matli Pak. **101** G5
Matlock U.K. **47** K10
Matlwangtlwang S. Africa **133** L4
Matna Sudan **104** A5
Mato *r.* Venez. **199** E3
Mato, Cerro *mt.* Venez. **199** E3
Matoaka U.S.A. **176** D8
Matobo Hills Zimbabwe **131** F4
also spelt Matopo Hills
UNESCO World Heritage Site
Matobo National Park Zimbabwe **131** F4
formerly known as Rhodes Matopos National Park
Matogrossense, Pantanal *marsh* Brazil **201** G4
Mato Grosso Brazil **201** F3
Mato Grosso *state* Brazil **206** A2
Mato Grosso, Planalto do *plat.* Brazil **202** A5
Mato Grosso do Sul *state* Brazil **206** A6
Matola Moz. **131** G5
Matondo Moz. **131** G3
Matope Malawi **129** B8
Matopo Hills Zimbabwe *see* **Matobo Hills**
Matos *r.* Bol. **200** D3
Matosinhos Port. **54** C3
Matou China *see* **Pingguo**
Mato Verde Brazil **207** K2
Matozinhos Brazil **207** I6
Mátra *mts* Hungary **49** Q8
Maţraḩ Oman **105** G3
Mátrai *park* Hungary **49** R8
Matrei in Osttirol Austria **49** J9
Matroosberg S. Africa **132** D10
Matroosberg *mt.* S. Africa **132** D10
Matrooster S. Africa **133** K2
Maţrūḩ *governorate* Egypt **108** A8
Matsalu riiklik looduskaitseala *nature res.* Estonia **42** E3
Matsap S. Africa **132** G5
Matsesta Rus. Fed. **107** D2
Matsitama Botswana **131** E4
Matsudo Japan **91** F7
Matsue Japan **91** C7
Matsumae Japan **90** G4
Matsumoto Japan **91** E6
Matsusaka Japan **91** E7
Matsu Tao *i.* Taiwan **87** G3
Matsuura Japan **91** A8
Matsuyama Japan **91** C8
Matsuzaki Japan **91** F7

Mattagami r. Canada 168 D3
Mattamuskeet, Lake U.S.A. 174 E5
Mattawa Canada 168 E4
Matterhorn mt. Italy/Switz. 51 N7
Matterhorn mt. U.S.A. 180 D4
Mattersburg Austria 49 N8
Matthew atoll Kiribati see **Marakei**
Matthews U.S.A. 174 D5
Matthews Peak Kenya 128 C4
Matthews Ridge Guyana 199 F3
Matthew Town Bahamas 187 E2
Maṭṭī, Sabkhat salt pan Saudi Arabia 105 F3
Mattituck U.S.A. 177 M5
Mattmar Sweden 44 K3
Mattō Japan 91 E6
Mattoon U.S.A. 174 B4
Måttsund Sweden 44 M2
Matturai Sri Lanka see **Matara**
Matu Sarawak Malaysia 77 E2
Matua, Ostrov i. Rus. Fed. 81 Q3
Matucana Peru 200 A2
Matugama Sri Lanka 94 D5
Matuku i. Fiji 145 G3
Matumbo Angola 127 C8
Matun Afgh. see **Khowst**
Maturín Venez. 199 F2
Maturuca Brazil 199 F3
Matusadona National Park Zimbabwe 131 F3
Matutuang i. Indon. 75 C1
Matveyev, Ostrov i. Rus. Fed. 40 K1
Matveyevka Rus. Fed. 102 C1
Matwabeng S. Africa 133 L5
Matxitxako, Cabo c. Spain 55 I1
Maty Island P.N.G. see **Wuvulu Island**
Matyrskiy Rus. Fed. 43 U9
Mau Madhya Pradesh India 96 C4
Mau Uttar Pradesh India 97 D4
Mau Aimma India 97 D4
Maubermé, Pic de mt. France/Spain 55 L2
Maubeuge France 51 J2
Maubin Myanmar 78 A4
Ma-ubin Myanmar 78 B2
Maubourguet France 50 G9
Mauchsberg S. Africa 133 O2
Maudaha India 96 D4
Maude Australia 147 E3
Mau-é-ele Moz. see **Marão**
Maués Brazil 199 G5
Maués r. Brazil 199 G5
Mauganj India 97 D4
Maug Islands N. Mariana Is 73 K2
Mauguio France 51 K9
Maui i. U.S.A. 181 [inset] Z1
Maukkadaw Myanmar 78 A3
Maulbronn Germany 48 F7
UNESCO World Heritage Site
Maule admin. reg. Chile 204 B4
Maule r. Chile 204 B4
Mauléon France 50 F6
Mauléon-Licharre France 50 F9
Maullín Chile 205 B6
Maumaupaki hill N.Z. 152 J5
Maumee U.S.A. 176 B4
Maumee r. U.S.A. 176 B4
Maumee Bay U.S.A. 176 B4
Maumere Indon. 75 B5
Maun Botswana 130 D3
Mauna Kea vol. U.S.A. 181 [inset] Z2
Mauna Loa vol. U.S.A. 181 [inset] Z2
Maunath Bhanjan India 97 D4
Maun Game Sanctuary nature res. Botswana 130 D3
Maungataniwha mt. N.Z. 152 K6
Maungatapere N.Z. 152 I3
Maungaturoto N.Z. 152 I4
Maungdaw Myanmar 78 A3
Maungmagan Islands Myanmar 79 B5
Maungmagon Myanmar 79 B5
Maupin U.S.A. 180 B3
Mau Ranipur India 96 C4
Maurawan India 96 D4
Maurepas, Lake U.S.A. 175 B6
Maures, Massif des hills France 51 M9
Mauri r. Bol. 200 C4
Mauriac France 51 I7
Maurice country Indian Ocean see **Mauritius**
Maurice, Lake salt flat Australia 146 A2
▸**Mauritania** country Africa 122 B6
spelt Al Mūrītānīyah in Arabic or Mauritanie in French
▸▸8–9 **World** Countries
▸▸114–115 **Africa** Countries
Mauritanie country Africa see **Mauritania**
▸**Mauritius** country Indian Ocean 218 K7
also known as Maurice
▸▸16–17 **World** Population
▸▸114–115 **Africa** Countries
Mauro, Monte mt. Italy 56 G7
Mauron France 50 D4
Maurs France 51 I8
Mauston U.S.A. 172 C7
Mauvezin France 50 G9
Mauzé-sur-le-Mignon France 50 F6
Mava Dem. Rep. Congo 126 E4
Mavaca r. Venez. 199 E4
Mavago Moz. 129 C8
Mavasjaure l. Sweden 44 L2
Mavengue Angola 127 C9
Mavinga Angola 127 D8
Mavisdale U.S.A. 176 C8
Mavita Moz. 131 G3
Mavra i. Greece 59 H12
Mavrothalassa Greece 58 E8
Mavrovo nat. park Macedonia 58 B7
Mavume Moz. 131 G4
Mavuya S. Africa 133 L8
Mawa, Bukit mt. Indon. 77 F2
Ma Wan i. Hong Kong China 87 [inset]
Māwān, Khashm hill Saudi Arabia 105 D3
Mawana India 96 C3
Mawanga Dem. Rep. Congo 127 C6
Mawasangka Indon. 75 B4
Mawdaung Pass Myanmar/Thai. 79 B6
Mawei China 87 F3
Mawhai Point N.Z. 152 M6
Mawheraiti N.Z. 153 F10
Māwheranui r. N.Z. see **Grey**
Māwiyah Yemen 104 D5
Mawjib, Wādī al r. Jordan 108 G6
also known as Arnon
Mawkhi Myanmar 78 B4
Mawkmai Myanmar 78 B3
Mawlaik Myanmar 78 A3
also known as Upper Chindwin
Mawlamyaing Myanmar 78 B4
also known as Mawlamyine or Moulmein
Mawlamyainggyun Myanmar 78 A4
Mawlamyine Myanmar see **Mawlamyaing**
Mawphlang India 97 F4
Mawqaq Saudi Arabia 104 C2
Mawshij Yemen 104 C5
Mawson research station Antarctica 223 E2
Mawson Coast Antarctica 223 E2
Mawson Escarpment Antarctica 223 E2
Mawson Peninsula Antarctica 223 K2
Maw Taung mt. Myanmar 79 B6
Mawza Yemen 104 C5
Maxaas Somalia 128 E3
Maxán Arg. 204 D3
Maxcanú Mex. 185 H4
Maxhamish Lake Canada 166 F3
Maxia, Punta mt. Sardinia Italy 57 A9
Măxineni Romania 58 I3
Maxixe Moz. 131 G4
Maxmo Fin. 44 M3
Maxwell N.Z. 152 I7
Maxwelton Australia 149 D4
Maya Chad 126 C3
Maya i. Indon. 77 E3
Maya r. Rus. Fed. 39 N3
Mayaguana i. Bahamas 187 E2
Mayaguana Passage Bahamas 187 E2
Mayagüez Puerto Rico 187 G3
Mayahi Niger 125 G3
Mayak Rus. Fed. 102 C2
Mayakovskiy, Qullai mt. Tajik. 101 G2
also known as Mayakovskogo, Pik
Mayakovskogo, Pik mt. Tajik. see **Mayakovskiy, Qullai**
Mayakum Kazakh. 103 G4
also spelt Mayaqum
Mayala Dem. Rep. Congo 127 C6
Mayama Congo 126 B5
Mayamba Dem. Rep. Congo 126 C6
Mayamey Iran 100 C2
Maya Mountains Belize/Guat. 185 H5
Mayan China see **Mayanhe**
Mayang China 87 D3
also known as Gaocun
Mayanhe China 86 C1
formerly known as Mayan
Mayaqum Kazakh. see **Mayakum**
Mayarí Cuba 186 E2
Maya-san mt. Japan 90 F5
Maybeury U.S.A. 176 D8
Maybole U.K. 46 H8
Maych'ew Eth. 128 C1
Maydh Somalia 128 E2
Maydos Turkey see **Eceabat**
Mayen Germany 48 E5
Mayenne France 50 F4
Mayenne r. France 50 F5
Mayer U.S.A. 183 L7
Mayêr Kangri mt. China 89 D5
Mayersville U.S.A. 175 B5
Mayerthorpe Canada 167 H4
Mayet France 50 G5
Mayfa'ah Yemen 105 D5
Mayfield N.Z. 153 F11
Mayfield KY U.S.A. 174 B4
Mayfield UT U.S.A. 183 M2
Mayhan Mongolia 84 D2
Mayi He r. China 82 C3
Maykain Kazakh. 103 H2
also spelt Mayqayyng
Maykamys Kazakh. 103 I3
Maykhura Tajik. 101 G2
Maykop Rus. Fed. 41 G7
Mayluu-Suu Kyrg. 103 H4
formerly known as Mayly-Say
Mayly-Say Kyrg. see **Mayluu-Suu**
Maymak Kazakh. 103 G4
Mayna Respublika Khakasiya Rus. Fed. 80 E2
Mayna Ul'yanovskaya Oblast' Rus. Fed. 41 H5
Maynardville U.S.A. 174 D4
Mayne watercourse Australia 149 D4
Maynooth Canada 173 P5
Mayo Canada 166 C2
formerly known as Mayo Landing
Mayo r. Mex. 181 E8
Mayo r. Peru 198 B6
Mayo U.S.A. 175 D6
Mayo Alim Cameroon 125 I4
Mayo-Belwa Nigeria 125 I4
Mayo Darlé Cameroon 125 H5
Mayo-Kébbi pref. Chad 126 B2
Mayoko Congo 126 B5
Mayo Lake Canada 166 C2
Mayo Landing Canada see **Mayo**
Mayo Lara Cent. Afr. Rep. 126 B3
Mayon vol. Phil. 74 B3
Mayor, Puig mt. Spain see **Major, Puig**
Mayor Buratovich Arg. 204 E5
Mayor Island N.Z. 152 K5
Mayor Pablo Lagerenza Para. 201 E4

▸**Mayotte** terr. Africa 129 E8
French Departmental Collectivity.
▸▸114–115 **Africa** Countries

May Pen Jamaica 186 D3
Mayqayyng Kazakh. see **Maykain**
Mayraira Point Phil. 74 B2
Maysah, Tall al mt. Jordan 108 G6
Maysān governorate Iraq 107 F5
Mayskiy Amurskaya Oblast' Rus. Fed. 82 C1
Mayskiy Kabardino-Balkarskaya Respublika Rus. Fed. 41 H8
Mayskiy Permskaya Oblast' Rus. Fed. 40 J4
Mayskiy, Khrebet mts Rus. Fed. 82 D1
Mayskoye Kazakh. 103 I2
Mays Landing U.S.A. 177 K6
Mayson Lake Canada 167 J3
Maysville KY U.S.A. 176 B7
Maysville MO U.S.A. 178 D4
Maytag China see **Dushanzi**
Mayu i. Indon. 75 C2
Mayu r. Myanmar 78 A3
Mayuge Uganda 128 B4
Mayumba Gabon 126 A5
Mayum La pass China 89 C6
Mayuram India 94 C4
Mayville MI U.S.A. 173 J7
Mayville ND U.S.A. 178 C2
Mayville NY U.S.A. 176 F3
Mayville WI U.S.A. 172 E7
Mayya Rus. Fed. 39 N3
Maza Arg. 204 E5
Maza Rus. Fed. 43 R2
Mazabuka Zambia 127 E8
Mazaca Turkey see **Kayseri**
Mazagan Morocco see **El Jadida**
Mazagão Brazil 199 I5
Ma'zah, Jabal hill Syria 109 L2
Maza Jugla r. Latvia 42 F5
Mazamet France 51 I9
Mazán Peru 198 C5
Māzandarān prov. Iran 100 B2
Mazao Dem. Rep. Congo 127 D7
Mazapil Mex. 185 E3
Mazar China 89 B4
Mazar, Koh-i- mt. Afgh. 101 F3
Mazāra Oman 105 G3
Mazara, Val di valley Sicily Italy 57 E11
Mazara del Vallo Sicily Italy 57 E11
Mazār-e Sharīf Afgh. 101 F2
Mazarrón Spain 55 J7
Mazartag mt. China 88 B4
Mazaruni r. Guyana 199 G3
Mazatán Mex. 184 C2
Mazatenango Guat. 185 H6
Mazatlán Mex. 184 D4
Mazatzal Peak U.S.A. 183 M7
Mazāvī watercourse Iran 100 D5
Mažeikiai Lith. 42 D5
Mazelet well Niger 125 H2
Mazeppa Bay S. Africa 133 M9
Maẓhūr, 'Irq al des. Saudi Arabia 104 C2
Mazı Turkey 59 I11
Mazie U.S.A. 176 C7
Mazirbe Latvia 42 D4
Mazocahui Mex. 184 C2
Mazocruz Peru 200 C4
Mazomanie U.S.A. 172 D7
Mazomeno Dem. Rep. Congo 126 E6
Mazomora Tanz. 129 C6
Mazong Shan mt. China 84 C3
Mazong Shan mts China 84 B3
Mazowe r. Zimbabwe 131 G3
Mazowiecka, Nizina reg. Poland 49 R3
Mazrub well Sudan 121 F6
Mazsalaca Latvia 42 G4
Māzū Iran 100 B3
Mazunga Zimbabwe 131 F4
Mazurskie, Pojezierze reg. Poland 49 R2
Mazyr Belarus 43 K9
also spelt Mozyr'
Mazzouna Tunisia 123 H2
Mba Cameroon 125 H5

▸**Mbabane** Swaziland 133 P3
Capital of Swaziland.

Mbacké Senegal 124 B3
Mbaéré r. Cent. Afr. Rep. 126 C4
Mbagne Mauritania 124 B2
Mbahiakro Côte d'Ivoire 124 D5
Mbaïki Cent. Afr. Rep. 126 C4
Mbakaou Cameroon 125 I5
Mbakaou, Lac de l. Cameroon 125 I5
Mbala Zambia 127 F7
formerly known as Abercorn
Mbalabala Zimbabwe 131 F4
formerly spelt Balla Balla
Mbalam Cameroon 125 I6
Mbale Uganda 128 B4
Mbalmayo Cameroon 125 H6
Mbam r. Cameroon 125 H5
Mbamba Bay Tanz. 129 B7
Mbandaka Dem. Rep. Congo 126 C5
formerly known as Coquilhatville
Mbandjok Cameroon 125 H5
Mbang Cameroon 125 I6
Mbanga Cameroon 125 H5
M'banza Congo Angola 127 B6
formerly known as São Salvador or São Salvador do Congo
Mbanza-Ngungu Dem. Rep. Congo 127 B6
formerly known as Songololo or Thysville
Mbar Senegal 124 B3
Mbarangandu Tanz. 129 C7
Mbarara Uganda 128 A5
Mbari r. Cent. Afr. Rep. 126 D3
Mbarika Mountains Tanz. 129 C7
Mbaswana S. Africa 133 Q4
Mbata Cent. Afr. Rep. 126 C4
Mbati Zambia 127 F7
Mbé Cameroon 125 I5
Mbé Congo 126 B5
Mbemba Moz. 129 B8
Mbembesi Zimbabwe 131 F3
Mbemkuru r. Tanz. 129 C7
Mbéni Comoros 129 D7
Mbenqué Côte d'Ivoire 124 D4
Mberengwa Zimbabwe 131 F4
formerly known as Belingwe
Mbereshi Zambia 127 F7
Mbeya Tanz. 129 B7
Mbeya admin. reg. Tanz. 129 B7
Mbi r. Cameroon 125 I5
Mbi r. Cent. Afr. Rep. 126 C3
Mbigou Gabon 126 A5
Mbinda Congo 126 B5
Mbinga Tanz. 129 B7
Mbini Equat. Guinea 125 H6
Mbini r. Equat. Guinea 125 H6
formerly known as Benito
Mbizi Zimbabwe 131 F4
Mbizi Mountains Tanz. 129 A7
Mbo Cent. Afr. Rep. 126 C2
Mboki Cent. Afr. Rep. 126 E3
Mbomo Congo 126 B4
Mbomou pref. Cent. Afr. Rep. 126 D3
Mbomou r. Cent. Afr. Rep./Dem. Rep. Congo 126 D3
Mbon Congo 126 B5
Mbouda Cameroon 125 H5
Mbour Senegal 124 A3
Mbout Mauritania 124 B2
Mbowela Zambia 127 E8
Mbozi Tanz. 129 B7
Mbrès Cent. Afr. Rep. 126 C3
Mbrostar Albania 58 A8
Mbuji-Mayi Dem. Rep. Congo 127 D6
Mbulu Tanz. 129 B5
Mbuluzi r. Swaziland 133 Q3
Mburucuyá Arg. 204 F3
Mbutini Hills Swaziland 133 P3
Mbuyuni Tanz. 129 C6
Mbwewe Tanz. 129 C6
McAdam Canada 169 H4
McAdoo U.S.A. 177 J5
McAlester U.S.A. 179 D5
McAllen U.S.A. 179 C7
McAllister U.S.A. 172 F5
McArthur r. Australia 148 C2
McArthur U.S.A. 176 C6
McArthur Mills Canada 173 P5
McArthur Wildlife Sanctuary nature res. Canada 166 C2
McBain U.S.A. 173 H6
McBride Canada 166 F4
McCall U.S.A. 180 C3
McCamey U.S.A. 179 B6
McCammon U.S.A. 180 D4
McCaslin Mountain hill U.S.A. 172 E5
McCauley Island Canada 166 D4
McClintock, Mount Antarctica 223 K1
McClintock Channel Canada 165 I2
McClintock Range hills Australia 150 D3
McClure, Lake U.S.A. 182 D4
McClure Strait Canada 165 H2
McClusky U.S.A. 178 B2
McComb MS U.S.A. 175 B6
McComb OH U.S.A. 176 B4
McConaughy, Lake U.S.A. 178 B3
McConnellsburg U.S.A. 176 H6
McConnelsville U.S.A. 176 D6
McCook U.S.A. 178 B3
McCormick U.S.A. 175 D5
McCoy U.S.A. 176 E8
McCrea r. Canada 167 H2
McCreary Canada 167 L5
McCullough Range mts U.S.A. 183 I6
McCullum, Mount Canada 166 B1
McCutchenville U.S.A. 176 B5
McDame Canada 166 D3
McDonald Islands Indian Ocean 219 L9
McDonald Peak U.S.A. 180 D3
McDonnell Creek watercourse Australia 146 C2
McDouall Range hills Australia 148 B3
McDowell Peak U.S.A. 183 M8
McFarland CA U.S.A. 182 E6
McFarland WI U.S.A. 172 D7
McFarlane r. Canada 167 J3
McFarlane, Mount N.Z. 153 D11
McGill U.S.A. 183 J2
McGivney Canada 169 H4
McGrath AK U.S.A. 164 D3
McGrath MN U.S.A. 174 A2
McGregor r. Canada 166 F4
McGregor, Lake Canada 167 H5
McGregor Bay Canada 173 L4
McGregor Range hills Australia 147 D1
McGuire, Mount U.S.A. 180 D3
Mcherrah reg. Alg. 122 D4
Mchinga Tanz. 129 C7
Mchinji Malawi 129 B8
formerly known as Fort Manning
McIlwraith Range hills Australia 149 D2
McInnes Lake Canada 167 M4
McIntosh U.S.A. 178 B2
McKay Range hills Australia 150 C4
McKean i. Kiribati 145 H2
formerly known as Drummond Island
McKee U.S.A. 176 A8
McKeesport U.S.A. 176 F5
McKees Rocks U.S.A. 176 E5
McKenney U.S.A. 176 H9
McKenzie U.S.A. 174 B4
McKenzie r. U.S.A. 180 B3
McKinlay Australia 149 D4
McKinlay r. Australia 149 D4

▸**McKinley, Mount** U.S.A. 164 D3
Highest mountain in North America.
▸▸154–155 **North America** Landscapes

McKinney U.S.A. 179 C5
McKittrick U.S.A. 182 E6
McLeansboro U.S.A. 174 B4
McLennan Canada 167 G4
McLeod r. Canada 167 H4
McLeod Bay Canada 167 I2
McLeod Lake Canada 166 F4
McLeod's Island Myanmar 79 B6
McMinns Creek watercourse Australia 148 B5
McMinnville OR U.S.A. 180 B3
McMinnville TN U.S.A. 174 C5
McMurdo research station Antarctica 223 L1
McMurdo Sound b. Antarctica 223 L1
McNary U.S.A. 183 O7
McNaughton U.S.A. 172 D5
McNaughton Lake Canada see **Kinbasket Lake**
McPhadyen r. Canada 169 H2
McPherson U.S.A. 178 C4
McPherson Range mts Australia 147 G2
McQuesten r. Canada 166 B2
McRae U.S.A. 175 D5
McTavish Arm b. Canada 167 G1
McVeytown U.S.A. 176 H5
McVicar Arm b. Canada 166 F1
McWhorter U.S.A. 176 E6
Mda r. Rus. Fed. 43 N3
Mdantsane S. Africa 133 L9
M'Daourouch Alg. 123 G1
Mdiq Morocco 54 F9
formerly known as Rincon
M'Đrak Vietnam 79 E5
Mê, Hon i. Vietnam 78 D4
Mead, Lake resr U.S.A. 183 J5
Meade U.S.A. 178 B4
Meade r. U.S.A. 164 D2
Meadow Australia 151 A5
Meadow U.S.A. 183 L3
Meadowbank r. Canada 167 L1
Meadow Bridge U.S.A. 176 E8
Meadow Lake Canada 167 I4
Meadow Lake Provincial Park Canada 167 I4
Meadow Valley Wash r. U.S.A. 183 J5
Meadowview U.S.A. 176 D9
Meadville MS U.S.A. 175 B6
Meadville PA U.S.A. 176 E4
Meaford Canada 173 M6
Meaken-dake vol. Japan 90 I3
Mealhada Port. 54 C4
Mealy Mountains Canada 169 J2
Meandarra Australia 147 F1
Meander River Canada 167 G3
Meares i. Indon. 75 C1
Mearim r. Brazil 202 C2
Meaux France 51 I4
Mebridege r. Angola 127 B6
Mebtoun, Oued el watercourse Alg. 55 K9
Mebu India 97 G3
Mebulu, Tanjung pt Indon. 77 F5
Mecanhelas Moz. 131 G2
Mecca Saudi Arabia 104 B3
also spelt Makkah
Mecca U.S.A. 181 C6
Mechanic Falls U.S.A. 177 O1
Mechanicsburg OH U.S.A. 176 B5
Mechanicsburg VA U.S.A. 176 E8
Mechanicsville U.S.A. 176 H8
Mechanicville U.S.A. 177 L3
Mechelen Belgium 51 K1
also known as Malines
Mecherchar i. Palau see **Eil Malk**
Mecheria Alg. 123 E2
Mechernich Germany 48 D5
Mechiméré Chad 120 B6
Mechka r. Bulg. 58 G6
Mecidiye Edirne Turkey 58 H8
Mecidiye Manisa Turkey 59 I10
Mecitözü Turkey 106 C2
Meckenheim Germany 48 E5
Mecklenburger Bucht b. Germany 48 I1
Mecklenburg-Vorpommern land Germany 49 J2
English form Mecklenburg - West Pomerania
Mecklenburg - West Pomerania land Germany see **Mecklenburg-Vorpommern**
Meconta Moz. 131 H2
Mecubúri Moz. 131 H2
Mecubúri r. Moz. 131 I2
Mecúfi Moz. 131 I2
Mecula Moz. 129 C8
Meda r. Australia 150 C3
Meda Port. 54 D4
Meda mt. Spain 54 D2
Medak India 94 C2
Medan Indon. 76 B2
Medang i. Indon. 77 G5
Médanos Buenos Aires Arg. 204 E5
Médanos Entre Ríos Arg. 204 F4
Medanosa, Punta pt Arg. 205 D8
Médanos de Coro, Parque Nacional nat. park Venez. 198 D2
Medaryville U.S.A. 172 G9
Medchal India 94 C2
Médéa Alg. 123 F1
also known as Lemdiyya
Medeiros Neto Brazil 207 M4
Medellín Col. 198 C3
Medenine Tunisia 123 H2
Meder Eritrea 104 C5
Mederdra Mauritania 124 B2
Medford NY U.S.A. 177 M5
Medford OK U.S.A. 178 C4
Medford OR U.S.A. 180 B4
Medford WI U.S.A. 172 C5
Medgidia Romania 58 J4
Mediadilet well Mali 125 E2
Media Luna Arg. 204 D4
Media Luna, Arrecife de la reef Hond. 186 C4
Mediapolis U.S.A. 172 B9
Mediaş Romania 58 F2
Medicine Bow r. U.S.A. 180 F4
Medicine Bow Mountains U.S.A. 180 F4
Medicine Bow Peak U.S.A. 180 F4
Medicine Hat Canada 167 I5
Medicine Lake U.S.A. 180 F2
Medicine Lodge U.S.A. 178 C4
Medina Brazil 202 D6
Medina Col. 198 C3
Medina Saudi Arabia 104 B2
also spelt Al Madīnah
Medina NY U.S.A. 176 G2
Medina OH U.S.A. 176 D4
Medina r. U.S.A. 179 C6
Medinaceli Spain 55 I3
Medina del Campo Spain 54 G3
Medina de Pomar Spain 55 H2
Medina de Rioseco Spain 54 F3
Medina Gounas Senegal 124 B3
Medina-Sidonia Spain 54 F8
Medinet 15 Mayo Egypt 108 C8
English form 15th of May City or Fifteenth of May City
Medinet el Amal Egypt 108 C8
Medinet el Sadat Egypt 108 B7
Medinipur India 97 E5
formerly spelt Midnapore
Mediolanum Italy see **Milan**
Mediterranean Sea 53 C4
Medje Dem. Rep. Congo 126 E4
Medjedel Alg. 55 O9
Medjerda, Monts de la mts Alg. 57 A12
Mednogorsk Rus. Fed. 102 D2
Mednoye Rus. Fed. 43 Q5
Mednyy, Ostrov i. Rus. Fed. 220 G2
Médoc reg. France 50 E7
Mêdog China 97 G3
also known as Dongbo
Medora U.S.A. 178 B2
Médouneu Gabon 126 A4
Medstead Canada 167 I4
Medu Kongkar China see **Maizhokunggar**
Meduro atoll Marshall Is see **Majuro**
Medveđa Srbija Serb. and Mont. 58 C6
Medvedevo Rus. Fed. 40 H4
Medveditsa r. Rus. Fed. 41 G6
Medvednica mts Croatia 56 H3
Medvedok Rus. Fed. 40 I4
Medvėgalio kalnis hill Lith. 42 D6
Medvezh'i, Ostrova is Rus. Fed. 39 Q2
Medvezh'yegorsk Rus. Fed. 40 E3
Medyn' Rus. Fed. 43 Q7
Medzilaborce Slovakia 49 S6
Meeberrie Australia 151 A5
Meekatharra Australia 151 B5
Meeker CO U.S.A. 180 F4
Meeker OH U.S.A. 176 B5
Meeks Bay U.S.A. 182 D2
Meeladeen Somalia 128 F2
Meelberg mt. S. Africa 132 I9
Meelpaeg Reservoir Canada 169 J3
Meerane Germany 49 J5
Meerapalu Estonia 42 I3
Meerut India 96 C3
Mefta Sidi Boubekeur Alg. 55 K9
Mēga Eth. 128 C3
Mega i. Indon. 76 C3
Mega Escarpment Eth./Kenya 128 C3
Megali Panagia Greece 59 E8
Megalo Eth. 128 D3
Megalo Chorio Greece 59 I12
Megalopoli Greece 59 D11
Megalos Anthropofas i. Greece 59 H11
Meganisi i. Greece 59 B10
Mégantic, Lac l. Canada 169 G4
Megara Greece 59 E10
Megezez mt. Eth. 128 C2

▸**Meghalaya** state India 97 F4
Highest mean annual rainfall in the world.
▸▸12–13 **World** Climate and Weather

Meghasani mt. India 97 E5
Meghna r. Bangl. 97 F5
Meghri Armenia 107 F3
also spelt Megri
Megion Rus. Fed. 38 H3
Mégiscane, Lac l. Canada 173 R2
Megisti i. Greece 59 K12
formerly known as Kastellorizon
Megletsy Rus. Fed. 43 P3
Meglino, Ozero l. Rus. Fed. 43 Q3
Megra r. Rus. Fed. 43 Q1
Megrega Rus. Fed. 43 O1
Megri Armenia see **Meghri**
Megrozero Rus. Fed. 43 O1
Mehadica Romania 58 D3
Mehamn Norway 44 N1
Mehar Pak. 101 F5
Meharry, Mount Australia 150 B4
Mehdia Tunisia see **Mahdia**
Mehedeby Sweden 45 L3
Mehedjibat, Erg des. Alg. 123 F4
Mehekar India 94 C1
Meherpur Bangl. 97 F5
Meherrin U.S.A. 176 G8
Meherrin r. U.S.A. 176 I9
Mehidpur India 96 B5
Mehlville U.S.A. 174 B4
Mehmadabad India 96 B5
Mehndawal India 97 D4
Mehrābān Iran 100 A2
Mehrān Iran 100 A3
Mehrān watercourse Iran 100 C5
Mehrān Iraq 107 F4
Mehtar Lām Afgh. 101 G3
Mehun-sur-Yèvre France 51 I5
Meia Ponte r. Brazil 206 D5
Meicheng Anhui China see **Qianshan**
Meicheng Fujian China see **Minqing**
Meichengzhen China 87 D2
Meidougou Cameroon 125 I5
Meiganga Cameroon 125 I5
Meighen Island Canada 165 J2
Meigu China 86 B2
also known as Bapu
Meihekou China 82 B4
formerly known as Hailong
Meijiang China see **Ningdu**
Mei Jiang r. China 87 E3
Meikeng China 87 E3
Meikle r. Canada 166 G3
Meiktila Myanmar 78 A3
Meilen Switz. 51 O5
Meilin China see **Ganxian**
Meilleur r. Canada 166 E2
Meilü China see **Meilu**
Meilu China 87 D4
also known as Meilü
Meiningen Germany 48 H5
Meira Spain 54 D1
Meiringen Switz. 51 O6
Meiringspoort pass S. Africa 132 G10
Meishan Anhui China see **Jinzhai**
Meishan Sichuan China 86 B2
also known as Dongpo
Meißen Germany 49 K4
Meißner-Kaufunger Wald, Naturpark nature res. Germany 48 G4
Meister r. Canada 166 D2
Meitan China 87 C3
also known as Yiquan
Meitingen Germany 48 H7
Meixi China 82 C3
Meixian Guangdong China see **Meizhou**
Meixian Shaanxi China 87 C1
Meixing China see **Xiaojin**
Meizhou China 87 F3
formerly known as Meixian
Mej r. India 96 C4
Méjan, Sommet de mt. France 51 K8
Mejaouda well Mauritania 122 D5
Mejez el Bab Tunisia 57 B12
Mejicana mt. Arg. 204 D3
Mejillones Chile 200 C5
Mejillones del Sur, Bahía de b. Chile 200 C5
Mekadio well Sudan 121 G5
Mékambo Gabon 126 B4
Mek'elē Eth. 128 C1
Mekhbaza Rus. Fed. 43 O1
Mékhé Senegal 124 A3
Mekhtar Pak. 101 G4
Mekkaw Nigeria 125 F5
Meknès Morocco 122 D2
UNESCO World Heritage Site
▸**Mekong** r. Asia 78 D4
also known as Lancang Jiang (China) or Mènam Khong (Laos/Thailand)
▸▸60–61 **Asia** Landscapes
Mekong, Mouths of the Vietnam 79 D6
Méla, Mont hill Cent. Afr. Rep. 126 D2
Melaka Malaysia 76 C2
formerly spelt Malacca
Melaka state Malaysia 76 C2
formerly spelt Malacca
Melalo, Tanjung pt Indon. 77 D3
Melanesia is Oceania 220 F6
Melar Iceland 44 [inset] B2
Melawi r. Indon. 77 E2

▸**Melbourne** Australia 147 E4
State capital of Victoria. 2nd most populous city in Oceania.
UNESCO World Heritage Site

Melbourne AR U.S.A. 174 B4
Melbourne FL U.S.A. 175 D6
Melbu Norway 44 K1
Melchor, Isla i. Chile 205 B7
Melchor de Mencos Guat. 185 H5
Melchor Ocampo Mex. 185 E3
Meldal Norway 44 J3
Meldola Italy 56 E4
Meldorf Germany 48 G1
Meldrum U.S.A. 176 B9
Meldrum Bay Canada 168 D4
Mele, Capo c. Italy 56 A5
Melech r. Rus. Fed. 43 R4
Melekess Rus. Fed. see **Dimitrovgrad**
Melenci Vojvodina, Srbija Serb. and Mont. 58 B3
Melendiz Dağı mt. Turkey 106 C3
Melenki Rus. Fed. 40 G5
Melet Turkey see **Mesudiye**
Meleuz Rus. Fed. 102 C1
Mélèzes, Rivière aux r. Canada 169 G1
Melfa U.S.A. 177 J8
Mélfi Chad 126 C2
Melfi Italy 56 H8
Melfort Canada 167 J4
Melgaço Brazil 202 B2
Melgar de Fernamental Spain 54 G2
Melhus Norway 44 J3
Meliadine Lake Canada 167 M2
Melide Spain 54 D2
also spelt Mellid
Meligalas Greece 59 C11

▸**Melilla** N. Africa 55 I9
Spanish Territory. Formerly known as Rusaddir.
▸▸114–115 **Africa** Countries

Melilli Sicily Italy 57 H11
Melimoyu, Monte mt. Chile 205 B7
Melina, Mount N.Z. 153 D12
Melintang, Danau l. Indon. 77 G3
Melipilla Chile 204 C4
Melita Canada 167 K5
Melitene Turkey see **Malatya**
Melito di Porto Salvo Italy 57 H11
Melitopol' Ukr. 41 E7
Melk Austria 49 M7
Melka Guba Eth. 128 C3
Mellakoski Fin. 44 N2
Mellansel Sweden 44 L3
Mellansjö Sweden 45 K3
Mellanström Sweden 44 L2
Melle Germany 48 F3
Mellègue, Barrage dam Tunisia 57 A12
Mellerud Sweden 45 K4
Mellid Spain see **Melide**
Mellit Sudan 121 E6
Mellizo Sur, Cerro mt. Chile 205 B8
Mellor Glacier Antarctica 223 E2
Mellrichstadt Germany 48 H5
Mellum i. Germany 48 F2
Melmele watercourse Chad 120 C6
Melmoth S. Africa 133 P5
Mel'nichoye Rus. Fed. 82 D3
Mělník Czech Rep. 49 L5
Mel'nikovo Rus. Fed. 43 K1
Melo Arg. 204 E4
Melo Uruguay 204 G4
Meloding S. Africa 133 K5
Melolo Indon. 75 B5
Mélong Cameroon 125 H5
Melovoye Ukr. see **Milove**
Melozitna r. U.S.A. 164 D3
Melrhir, Chott salt l. Alg. 123 G2
Melrose Australia 151 C5
Melrose U.K. 46 J8
Melrose U.S.A. 178 D2
Melsetter Zimbabwe see **Chimanimani**
Melsungen Germany 48 G4
Melta, Mount Sabah Malaysia see **Tawai, Bukit**
Meltaus Fin. 44 N2
Melton Australia 147 E4
Melton Mowbray U.K. 47 L11
Meluan Sarawak Malaysia 77 E2
Melun France 51 I4
Melur India 94 C4
Melut Sudan 128 B2
Melville Canada 167 K5
Melville, Cape Australia 149 E2
Melville, Cape Phil. 74 A5
Melville, Lake Canada 169 J2
Melville Bay Australia 148 C2
Melville Bugt b. Greenland see **Qimusseriarsuaq**
Melville Island Australia 148 A1
Melville Island Canada 165 I2
Melville Peninsula Canada 165 K3
Melvin, Lough l. Ireland/U.K. 47 D9
Mélykút Hungary 49 Q9
Memaliaj Albania 59 A8
Mêmar Co salt l. China 89 C5
Memba Moz. 131 I2
Memba, Baía de b. Moz. 131 I2
Memberamo r. Indon. 73 I7
Memboro Indon. 75 A5
Memel Lith. see **Klaipėda**
Memel S. Africa 133 N4
Mēmele r. Latvia 42 F5
Memiakalnis hill Lith. 42 H6
Memmingen Germany 48 H8
Memphis tourist site Egypt 121 F2
UNESCO World Heritage Site
Memphis MI U.S.A. 173 K8
Memphis MO U.S.A. 174 A3
Memphis TN U.S.A. 174 B5
Memphis TX U.S.A. 179 B5
Memuro-dake mt. Japan 90 H3
Mena Eth. 128 C3
Mena Indon. 75 C5
Mena Ukr. 41 E6
Mena U.S.A. 179 D5
Menabe mts Madag. 131 [inset] J4
Ménaka Mali 125 F3
Mènam Khong r. Asia 78 D4 see **Mekong**
Menanga Indon. 75 C3
Menarandra r. Madag. 131 [inset] J5
Menard U.S.A. 179 C6
Menasha U.S.A. 172 E6
Mencal mt. Spain 55 H7
Mencué Arg. 204 C6
Mendanau i. Indon. 77 D3
Mendarda India 96 A5
Mendarik i. Indon. 77 D2
Mendawai Indon. 77 F3
Mendawai r. Indon. 77 F3
Mende France 51 J8
Mendebo Mountains Eth. 128 C3
Mendefera Eritrea 121 H6
also known as Adi Ugri
Mendeleyevsk Rus. Fed. 40 J5
formerly known as Bondyuzhskiy
Menden (Sauerland) Germany 48 E4
Mendenhall U.S.A. 175 B6
Mendenhall, Cape U.S.A. 164 C4
Mendenhall Glacier U.S.A. 166 C3
Menderes Turkey 59 I10
Méndez Mex. 185 F3
Mendez-Nuñez Phil. 74 B3

Mendi P.N.G. 73 J8
Mendip Hills U.K. 47 J12
Mendocino U.S.A. 182 A2
Mendocino, Cape U.S.A. 180 A4
Mendocino, Lake U.S.A. 182 A2
Mendota *CA* U.S.A. 182 D5
Mendota *IL* U.S.A. 174 B3
Mendota, Lake U.S.A. 172 D7
Mendoza Arg. 204 C4
Mendoza *prov.* Arg. 204 C4
Mendoza Bol. 200 D4
Mene de Mauroa Venez. 198 D2
Menemen Turkey 59 I10
Menez Bré *hill* France 50 C4
Menfi *Sicily* Italy 57 E11
Menga, Puerto de *pass* Spain 54 F4
Mengalum *i.* Malaysia 77 F1
Mengban China 86 B4
Mengcheng China 87 F1
Mengen Turkey 106 C2
Menggala Indon. 76 D4
Menghai China 86 B4
also known as Xiangshan
Mengíbar Spain 54 H7
Mengkiang *r.* Indon. 77 E2
Mengkoka, Gunung *mt.* Indon. 75 B3
Menglang China *see* **Lancang**
Menglie China *see* **Jiangcheng**
Mengmeng China *see* **Shuangjiang**
Mengong Cameroon 125 H6
Mengshan China 87 D3
Mengxian China *see* **Mengzhou**
Mengyang China *see* **Mingshan**
Mengyin China 85 H5
Mengzhou China 87 E1
formerly known as Mengxian
Mengzi China 86 B4
also known as Wenlan
Menihek Canada 169 H2
Menindee Australia 147 D3
Menindee, Lake Australia 147 D3
Menindee Aboriginal Reserve Australia 147 D3
Meningie Australia 146 C3
Menkere Rus. Fed. 39 M3
Menna *r.* Eth. 104 B5
Mennecy France 51 I4
Mennonite Colony *res.* Para. 201 F5
Menominee U.S.A. 172 F5
Menominee *r.* U.S.A. 172 F5
Menominee Indian Reservation *res.* U.S.A. 172 E5
Menomonee Falls U.S.A. 172 E7
Menomonie U.S.A. 172 B6
Menongue Angola 127 C8
formerly known as Serpa Pinto
Menor, Mar *lag.* Spain 55 K7
Menorca *i.* Spain *see* **Minorca**
Mensalong Indon. 77 G2
Men'shikova, Mys *c.* Rus. Fed. 40 K1
Mentakab Malaysia *see* **Mentekab**
Mentarang *r.* Indon. 77 G2
Mentawai, Kepulauan *is* Indon. 76 B3
Mentawai, Selat *sea chan.* Indon. 76 C3
Mentaya *r.* Indon. 77 F3
Mentekab Malaysia 76 C2
formerly spelt Mentakab
Mentiras *hill* Port. 54 D6
Mentiras *mt.* Spain 55 I6
Mentok Indon. 76 D3
Menton France 51 N9
Mentone U.S.A. 179 B6
Mentor U.S.A. 176 D4
Mentuba *r.* Indon. 77 F3
Menufia *governorate* Egypt *see* **Minûfîya**
Menukung Indon. 77 F3
Menumbok *Sabah* Malaysia 77 F1
Menunu Indon. 75 B2
Menyapa, Gunung *mt.* Indon. 77 G2
Menyuan China 84 D4
also known as Haomen
Menza *r.* Rus. Fed. 85 F1
Menzel Bourguiba Tunisia 123 H1
formerly known as Ferryville
Menzelet Barajı *resr* Turkey 107 D3
Menzelinsk Rus. Fed. 40 J5
Menzel Temime Tunisia 57 D12
Menzies Australia 151 C6
Menzies, Mount Antarctica 223 E2
Meobbaai *b.* Namibia 130 B5
Meoqui Mex. 184 D2
Mepala Angola 127 B6
Meponda Moz. 131 G1
Meppel Neth. 48 D3
Meppen Germany 48 E3
Meqheleng S. Africa 133 L5
Mequéns *r.* Brazil 201 E3
Mequinenza, Embalse de *resr* Spain 55 L3
Mequon U.S.A. 172 F7
Mer France 50 H5
Merah Indon. 77 G2
Merak Indon. 77 D4
Meråker Norway 44 J3
Meramangye, Lake *salt flat* Australia 146 B2
Meramec *r.* U.S.A. 178 E4
Merano Italy 56 D2
Merapi, Gunung *vol. Java* Indon. 77 E4
Merapi, Gunung *vol. Java* Indon. 77 F5
Merari, Serra *mt.* Brazil 199 F3
Meratswe *r.* Botswana 131 E4
Meratus, Pegunungan *mts* Indon. 77 F3
Merauke Indon. 73 J8
Merbau Indon. 76 C2
Merbein Australia 147 D3
Merca Somalia *see* **Marka**
Mercadal Spain 55 P5
Mercantour, Parc National du *nat. park* France 51 M8
Merced U.S.A. 182 D4
Merced *r.* U.S.A. 182 D4
▶**Mercedario, Cerro** *mt.* Arg. 204 C3
▶▶**188–189 South America** Landscapes
Mercedes Arg. 204 F3
Mercedes Uruguay 204 F4
Merceditas Chile 204 C3
Mercer *ME* U.S.A. 177 P1
Mercer *OH* U.S.A. 176 A5
Mercer *PA* U.S.A. 176 E4
Mercer *WI* U.S.A. 172 C4
Mercersburg U.S.A. 176 H6
Mercês *Acre* Brazil 200 C2
Mercês *Minas Gerais* Brazil 203 D7
Mercier Bol. 200 C2
Mercury U.S.A. 183 I5
Mercury Bay N.Z. 152 J4
Merdenik Turkey *see* **Göle**
Merdja Zerga, Réserve de *nature res.* Morocco 122 D2
Meredith U.S.A. 177 N2
Meredith, Cape Falkland Is 205 E9
Meredith, Lake U.S.A. 179 B5
Meredoua Alg. 123 F4
Mereeg Somalia 128 E4
Merefa Ukr. 41 F6
Meremäe Estonia 42 I4
Meremere N.Z. 152 J5
Merenkurkku *strait* Fin./Sweden 44 M3
Merepah Aboriginal Holding *res.* Australia 149 D2
Merezha Rus. Fed. 43 R2
Merga Oasis Sudan 121 E5
Mergenevo Kazakh. 102 B2
Mergui Myanmar *see* **Myeik**
Mergui Archipelago *is* Myanmar 79 B6
Merhei, Lacul *l.* Romania 58 K3
Meribah Australia 146 D3
Meriç *r.* Greece/Turkey 58 H8
Meriç *r.* Greece/Turkey *see* **Evros**
Meriç Turkey 58 H7
Merichas Greece 59 F11
Mérida Mex. 185 H4
Mérida Spain 54 E6
historically known as Emerita Augusta
UNESCO World Heritage Site
Mérida Venez. 198 D2
Mérida *state* Venez. 198 D2
Mérida, Cordillera de *mts* Venez. 198 D3
Meriden U.S.A. 177 M4
Meridian *MS* U.S.A. 175 B5
Meridian *TX* U.S.A. 179 C6
Mérignac France 50 F8
Merijärvi Fin. 44 N2
Merikarvia Fin. 45 M3
Merimbula Australia 147 F4
Merín, Laguna *l.* Brazil/Uruguay *see* **Mirim, Lagoa**
Merinda Australia 149 F4
Meringur Australia 146 D3
Merir *i.* Palau 73 H6
historically known as Warren Hastings Island
Merirumã Brazil 199 H4
Merivale *r.* Australia 149 E5
Merke Kazakh. 103 H4
Merkel U.S.A. 179 B5
Merkinė Lith. 42 F7
Merlimau, Pulau *reg.* Sing. 76 [inset]
Mermaid Reef *reef* Australia 150 B3
Merolia Australia 151 C6
Meron, Har *mt.* Israel 108 G5
Merošina *Srbija* Serb. and Mont. 58 C5
Merowe Sudan 121 F5
Merredin Australia 151 B6
Merrick *hill* U.K. 47 H8
Merrickville Canada 173 R6
Merrill *MI* U.S.A. 173 I7
Merrill *WI* U.S.A. 172 D5
Merrill, Mount Canada 166 E2
Merrillan U.S.A. 172 C6
Merrillville U.S.A. 172 F9
Merriman S. Africa 132 H8
Merriman U.S.A. 178 B3
Merritt Canada 166 F5
Merritt Island U.S.A. 175 D6
Merritt Island National Wildlife Refuge *nature res.* U.S.A. 175 D6
Merrygoen Australia 147 F2
Mersa Fatma Eritrea 121 I6
Mersa Gulbub Eritrea 121 H5
Mersa Teklay Eritrea 121 H5
Mersch Lux. 51 M3
Merse *r.* Italy 56 D5
Merseburg (Saale) Germany 48 I4
Mersin Turkey 106 C3
formerly known as İçel
Mersin *prov.* Turkey 108 E1
Mersing Malaysia 76 C2
Mersing, Bukit *mt. Sarawak* Malaysia 77 F2
Mersin Galgalo Eth. 128 E3
Mērsrags Latvia 42 E4
Mērsrags *pt* Latvia 42 E4
Merta India 96 B4
Merta Road India 96 B4
Merthyr Tydfil U.K. 47 I12
Merti Kenya 128 C4
Merti Plateau Kenya 128 C4
Mértola Port. 54 D7
Mertoutek Alg. 123 G4
Mertvyy Kultuk, Sor *dry lake* Kazakh. 102 C3
also known as Öli Qoltyq Sory
Mertz Glacier Antarctica 223 J2
Mertz Glacier Tongue Antarctica 223 J2
Mertzon U.S.A. 179 B6
Méru France 51 I3
Meru Kenya 128 C4

▶**Meru** *vol.* Tanz. 128 C5
4th highest mountain in Africa.
▶▶**110–111 Africa** Landscapes

Meru Betiri National Park Indon. 77 F5
Merui Pak. 101 E4
Meru National Park Kenya 128 C4
Merv Turkm. *see* **Mary**
Merweville S. Africa 132 F9
Merzifon Turkey 106 C2
Merzig Germany 48 D6
Merz Peninsula Antarctica 222 T2
Mesa S. Africa 133 K3
Mesa *r.* Spain 55 J3
Mesa U.S.A. 183 M8
Mesabi Range *hills* U.S.A. 174 A2
Mesa Bolívar Venez. 198 D2
Mesagne Italy 57 J8
Mesara, Ormos *b.* Greece 59 F13
Mesa Verde National Park U.S.A. 181 E5
UNESCO World Heritage Site
Mescalero Apache Indian Reservation *res.* U.S.A. 181 F6
Meschede Germany 48 F4
Meselefors Sweden 44 L2
Mesfinto Eth. 128 C1
Mesgouez, Lac *l.* Canada 169 F3
Mesha *r.* Rus. Fed. 40 I5
Meshchovsk Rus. Fed. 43 Q7
Meshed Iran *see* **Mashhad**
Meshekli Uzbek. 103 E4
Meshkān Iran 100 D2
Meshoppen U.S.A. 173 Q9
Mesimeri Greece 59 E8
Meslay-du-Maine France 50 F5
Mesola Italy 56 E4
Mesolongi Greece 59 C10
English form Missolonghi; *also known as* Mesolóngion
Mesolóngion Greece *see* **Mesolongi**
Mesquita Brazil 203 D6
Mesquite U.S.A. 179 C5
Mesquite Lake U.S.A. 183 I6
Messaad Alg. 123 F2
Messak Mellet *hills* Libya 120 A3
Messalo *r.* Moz. 129 D7
Messana *Sicily* Italy *see* **Messina**
Messaoud, Oued *watercourse* Alg. 123 E4
Messel Germany 48 F6
UNESCO World Heritage Site
Messier, Canal *sea chan.* Chile 205 B8
Messina *Sicily* Italy 57 H10
historically known as Messana *or* Zancle
Messina, Strait of *strait* Italy 57 H10
also known as Stretta di Messina
Messines Canada 173 Q4
Messini Greece 59 D11
Messiniakos Kolpos *b.* Greece 59 D12
Meßkirch Germany 48 G8
Messlingen Sweden 44 K3
Mesta *r.* Greece *see* **Nestos**
Mestghanem Alg. *see* **Mostaganem**
Meston, Akra *pt* Greece 59 G10
Mesudiye Turkey 107 D2
also known as Melet
Mesuji *r.* Indon. 77 D4
Meta *dept* Col. 198 C4
Meta *r.* Col./Venez. 198 E3
Métabetchouan Canada 169 G3
Metagama Canada 173 L3
Meta Incognita Peninsula Canada 165 M3
Metairie U.S.A. 179 E6
Metaliferi, Munții *mts* Romania 58 D2
Metallifere, Colline *mts* Italy 56 C5
Metallostroy Rus. Fed. 43 L2
Metamora U.S.A. 172 D10
Metán Arg. 204 D2
Metanara Eth. 128 C2
Metangula Moz. 129 B8
formerly known as Augusto Cardosa
Metapán El Salvador 185 H6
Metauro *r.* Italy 56 F5
Meteghan Canada 169 H4
Metelys *l.* Lith. 42 E7
Metema Eth. 128 C1
Metengobalame Moz. 131 G2
Meteora *tourist site* Greece 59 C9
UNESCO World Heritage Site
Meteor Creek *r.* Australia 149 F5
Methoni Greece 59 C12
Methuen U.S.A. 177 N3
Methven N.Z. 153 F11
Metionga Lake Canada 168 B3
Metković Croatia 56 J5
Metlakatla U.S.A. 166 D4
Metlaoui Tunisia 123 H2
Metlika Slovenia 56 H3
Metoro Moz. 131 H2
Metro Indon. 76 D4
Metropolis U.S.A. 174 B4
Metsada *tourist site* Israel *see* **Masada**
Metsäkylä Fin. 44 O2
Metsovo Greece 59 C9
Metter U.S.A. 175 D5
Mettler U.S.A. 182 F6
Mettuppalaiyam India 94 C4
Mettur India 94 C4
Metu Eth. 128 B2
Metundo, Ilha *i.* Moz. 129 D7
Metz France 51 M3
Metzingen Germany 48 G7
Meu *r.* France 50 E4
Meulaboh Indon. 76 B1
Meung-sur-Loire France 50 H5
Meurthe *r.* France 51 M4
Meuse *r.* Belgium/France 51 L1
also spelt Maas (Netherlands)
Mêwa China 86 B1
Mexcala Mex. 185 F5
Mexia U.S.A. 179 C6
Mexiana, Ilha *i.* Brazil 202 B1
Mexicali Mex. 184 B1
Mexican Hat U.S.A. 183 O4
Mexicanos, Lago de los *l.* Mex. 184 D2
Mexican Water U.S.A. 183 O5

▶**Mexico** *country* Central America 184 D4
2nd most populous and 4th largest country in North America.
▶▶**16–17 World** Population
▶▶**158–159 North America** Countries

México Mex. *see* **Mexico City**
México *state* Mex. 185 F5
Mexico *ME* U.S.A. 177 O1
Mexico *MO* U.S.A. 174 B4
Mexico *NY* U.S.A. 177 I2
Mexico, Gulf of Mex./U.S.A. 171 G7

▶**Mexico City** Mex. 185 F5
Capital of Mexico. Most populous city in North America and 2nd in the world. Also known as México.
UNESCO World Heritage Site
▶▶**18–19 World** Cities

Meybod Iran 100 C3
Meydanī, Ra's-e *pt* Iran 100 D5
Meydān Shahr Afgh. 101 G3
Meyenburg Germany 49 J2
Meyersdale U.S.A. 176 F6
Meyerton S. Africa 133 M3
Meylan France 51 L7
Meymac France 51 I7
Meymaneh Afgh. 101 F3
Meymeh Iran 100 B3
Meynypil'gyno Rus. Fed. 39 R3
Meyo Centre Cameroon 125 H6
Meyssac France 50 H7
Meza Myanmar 78 B2
Meza *r.* Rus. Fed. 43 V3
Mezada *tourist site* Israel *see* **Masada**
Mezas *mt.* Spain 54 E4
Mezcalapa *r.* Mex. 185 G5
Mezdra Bulg. 58 E5
Mèze France 51 J9
Mezen' Rus. Fed. 40 H2
Mezen' *r.* Rus. Fed. 40 H2
Mézenc, Mont *mt.* France 51 K8
Mezenskaya Guba *b.* Rus. Fed. 40 G2
Mezha *r.* Rus. Fed. 43 M6
Mezhdurechensk *Kemerovskaya Oblast'* Rus. Fed. 80 D2
formerly known as Olzheras
Mezhdurechensk *Respublika Komi* Rus. Fed. 40 I3
Mezhdurechenskiy Rus. Fed. 38 G4
Mezhdurechnye Rus. Fed. *see* **Shali**
Mezhdusharskiy, Ostrov *i.* Rus. Fed. 40 J1
Mézidon-Canon France 50 F3
Mézin France 50 G8
Mezinovskiy Rus. Fed. 43 V6
Mezitli Turkey 108 F1
Mezőberény Hungary 49 S9
Mezőhegyes Hungary 49 R9
Mezőkovácsháza Hungary 49 R9
Mezőkövesd Hungary 49 R8
Mezőtúr Hungary 49 R9
Mezquital Mex. 184 D4
Mezquital *r.* Mex. 184 D4
Mezquitic Mex. 184 E4
Mežvidi Latvia 42 I5
Mezzolombardo Italy 56 D2
Mfouati Congo 126 B6
Mfuwe Zambia 127 F8
Mgachi Rus. Fed. 82 F2
Mgbidi Nigeria 125 G5
Mglin Rus. Fed. 43 N8
Mgwali *r.* S. Africa 133 M8
Mhàil, Rubh' a' *pt* U.K. 46 F8
Mhangura Zimbabwe 131 F3
formerly spelt Mangula
Mhasvad India 94 B2
Mhlambanyatsi Swaziland 133 P3
Mhlume Swaziland 133 P3
Mhluzi S. Africa 133 N2
Mhow India 96 B5
Mi *r.* Myanmar 78 A3
Miacatlan Mex. 185 F5
UNESCO World Heritage Site
Miagao Phil. 74 B4
UNESCO World Heritage Site
Miahuatlán Mex. 185 F5
Miajadas Spain 54 F5
Miaméré Cent. Afr. Rep. 126 C2
Miami *AZ* U.S.A. 183 N8

▶**Miami** *FL* U.S.A. 175 D7
5th most populous city in North America.

Miami *OK* U.S.A. 178 D4
Miami *TX* U.S.A. 179 B5
Miami Beach U.S.A. 175 D7
Miamisburg U.S.A. 176 A6
Miamitown U.S.A. 176 A6
Miānābād Iran 100 D2
Mianaz Pak. 101 E5
Miancaowan China 84 C5
Mian Chanmun Pak. 101 H4
Mianchi China 87 D1
Mīāndasht Iran 100 D2
Miandowāb Iran 100 A2
Miandrivazo Madag. 131 [inset] J3
Mianduhe China 85 I1
Mīāneh Iran 100 A2
Miangas *i.* Phil. 74 C5
Miani Hor *b.* Pak. 101 F5
Mianmian Shan *mts* China 86 B3
Mianning China 86 B2
also known as Chengxiang
Mianwali Pak. 101 G3
Mianxian China 86 C1
Mianyang *Hubei* China *see* **Xiantao**
Mianyang *Sichuan* China 86 C2
Mianzhu China 86 C2
Miaodao Liedao *is* China 85 I4
Miao'ergou China 88 C2
also known as Utu
Miaogao China *see* **Suichang**
Miaoli Taiwan 87 G3
Miarinarivo *Antananarivo* Madag. 131 [inset] J3
Miarinarivo *Toamasina* Madag. 131 [inset] J3
Miass Rus. Fed. 38 G4
Miastko Poland 49 N1
Mica, Cerro de *mt.* Chile 200 C5
Mica Creek Canada 166 G4
Mica Mountain U.S.A. 183 N9
Micang Shan *mts* China 86 C1
Micaune Moz. 131 H3
Michalovce Slovakia 49 S7
Michel Canada 167 I4
Michelson, Mount U.S.A. 164 E3
Micheng China *see* **Midu**
Miches Dom. Rep. 187 F3
Michigamme Lake U.S.A. 172 E4
Michigamme Reservoir U.S.A. 172 E4
Michigan *state* U.S.A. 173 E4

▶**Michigan, Lake** U.S.A. 172 F7
3rd largest lake in North America and 5th in the world.
▶▶**6–7 World** Landscapes
▶▶**154–155 North America** Landscapes

Michigan City U.S.A. 174 C3
Michipicoten Bay Canada 168 C4
Michipicoten Island Canada 168 C4
Michipicoten River Canada 168 C4
Michoacán *state* Mex. 185 E5
Michurin Bulg. *see* **Tsarevo**
Michurinsk Rus. Fed. 41 G5
Micos Mex. 185 F4
Micoud St Lucia 187 H4
Micronesia *is* Pacific Ocean 220 E5
▶**Micronesia, Federated States of** *country* N. Pacific Ocean 220 G5
▶▶**138–139 Oceania** Countries
Midai *i.* Indon. 77 D2
Midal *well* Niger 125 G2
Midale Canada 167 K5
Middelberg Pass S. Africa 132 D9
Middelburg Neth. 48 A4
Middelburg *E. Cape* S. Africa 133 J8
Middelburg *Mpumalanga* S. Africa 133 N2
Middelfart Denmark 45 J5
Middelharnis Neth. 48 B4
Middelpos S. Africa 132 E8
Middelwit S. Africa 133 L1
Middenbeemster Neth. 48 B3
UNESCO World Heritage Site
Middle Alkali Lake U.S.A. 180 B4
Middle Andaman *i.* India 95 G3
Middle Atlas *mts* Morocco *see* **Moyen Atlas**
Middle Bay Canada 169 J3
Middleboro U.S.A. 177 O4
Middleburg *PA* U.S.A. 177 H5
Middleburg *VA* U.S.A. 176 H7
Middleburgh U.S.A. 177 K3
Middlebury *IN* U.S.A. 172 H9
Middlebury *VT* U.S.A. 177 L1
Middle Caicos *i.* Turks and Caicos Is 187 F2
Middle Concho *r.* U.S.A. 179 B6
Middle Congo *country* Africa *see* **Congo**
Middle Creek *r.* Australia 149 D3
Middle Island U.S.A. 177 M5
Middle Loup *r.* U.S.A. 178 C3
Middlemount Australia 149 F4
Middleport U.S.A. 176 C6
Middle Raccoon *r.* U.S.A. 178 D3
Middle Ridge Wildlife Reserve *nature res.* Canada 169 K3
Middle River U.S.A. 177 I6
Middlesboro U.S.A. 176 B9
Middlesbrough U.K. 47 K9
Middlesex U.S.A. 177 H3
Middle Strait India *see* **Andaman Strait**
Middleton Australia 149 D4
Middleton Canada 169 H4
Middleton S. Africa 133 J9
Middleton U.S.A. 172 D7
Middleton Reef *reef* Australia 145 E4
Middletown *CA* U.S.A. 182 B3
Middletown *CT* U.S.A. 177 M4
Middletown *DE* U.S.A. 177 J6
Middletown *MD* U.S.A. 176 H6
Middletown *NY* U.S.A. 177 K4
Middletown *OH* U.S.A. 176 A6
Middletown *PA* U.S.A. 177 I5
Middletown *VA* U.S.A. 176 G6
Middleville *MI* U.S.A. 172 H8
Middleville *NY* U.S.A. 177 K2
Midelt Morocco 122 D2
Midhisho *well* Somalia 128 E2
Midhurst U.K. 47 L13
Mīdī Yemen 104 C4
Midi, Canal du France 50 I9
UNESCO World Heritage Site
Midi de Bigorre, Pic du *mt.* France 50 G10
Midi-Pyrénées *admin. reg.* France 50 I8
Midland Canada 168 E4
Midland *CA* U.S.A. 183 J8
Midland *MI* U.S.A. 173 I7
Midland *TX* U.S.A. 179 B5
Midland Junction Australia 151 A6
Midlands *prov.* Zimbabwe 131 F3
Midleton Ireland 47 D12
Midlothian *TX* U.S.A. 179 C5
Midlothian *VA* U.S.A. 176 H8
Midmar Nature Reserve S. Africa 133 O6
Midmay Canada 173 L6
Midnapore India *see* **Medinipur**
Midongy Atsimo Madag. 131 [inset] J4
Midou *r.* France 50 F9
Midouze *r.* France 50 F9
Midsayap Phil. 74 C5
Midu China 86 B3
also known as Micheng
Midvale U.S.A. 183 M1
Midway Oman *see* **Thamarīt**
Midway *KY* U.S.A. 176 A7
Midway *UT* U.S.A. 183 M1

▶**Midway Islands** N. Pacific Ocean 220 H4
United States Unincorporated Territory.
▶▶**138–139 Oceania** Countries

Midway Well Australia 150 C4
Midwest U.S.A. 180 F4
Midwest City U.S.A. 179 C5
Midyan *reg.* Saudi Arabia 104 A2
Midyat Turkey 107 E3
Midye Turkey *see* **Kıyıköy**
Midzhur *mt.* Bulg./Serb. and Mont. 58 D5
Mie Japan 91 B8
Mie *pref.* Japan 91 E7
Miechów Poland 49 R5
Miedwie, Jezioro *l.* Poland 49 L2
Międzychód Poland 49 M3
Międzylesie Poland 49 N5
Międzyrzec Podlaski Poland 49 T4
Międzyrzecz Poland 49 M3
Międzyzdroje Poland 49 L2
Miehikkälä Fin. 42 I1
Miekojärvi *l.* Fin. 44 N2
Mielec Poland 49 S5
Miembwe Tanz. 129 C7
Mień *r.* Poland 49 P3
Mienga Angola 127 C9
Miengwe Zambia 127 F8
Mienhua Yü *i.* Taiwan 87 G3
Mieraslompolo Fin. 44 N1
also known as Mierašluoppal
Mierašluoppal Fin. *see* **Mieraslompolo**
Miercurea-Ciuc Romania 58 G2
Mieres Spain 54 F1
long form Mieres del Camín *or* Mieres del Camino
Mieres del Camín Spain *see* **Mieres**
Mieres del Camino Spain *see* **Mieres**
Mierojávri Norway 44 M1
Miesbach Germany 48 I8
Mī'ēso Eth. 128 D2
Mieste Germany 48 I3
Mieszkowice Poland 49 L3
Mietoinen Fin. 45 M3
Mīfah Saudi Arabia 104 C4
Mifflin U.S.A. 176 C5
Mifflinburg U.S.A. 177 H5
Mifflintown U.S.A. 176 H5
Migang Shan *mt.* China 85 E5
Migdol S. Africa 133 J3
Migennes France 51 J5
Mignone *r.* Italy 56 D6
Migriggyangzham Co *l.* China 89 E5
Miguasha, Parc de *nature res.* Canada 169 H3
UNESCO World Heritage Site
Miguel Alemán, Presa *resr* Mex. 185 F5
Miguel Alves Brazil 202 D3
Miguel Auza Mex. 184 E3
Miguel Calmon Brazil 202 D4
Miguel de la Borda Panama 186 C5
Miguel Hidalgo, Presa *resr* Mex. 184 C3
Migushino Rus. Fed. 43 K6
Migyaunye Myanmar 78 A4
Mihăilești Romania 58 G4
Mihalıççık Turkey 106 B3
Mihara Japan 91 C7
Mihara-yama *vol.* Japan 91 F7
Mi He *r.* China 85 H4
Mihidjan India *see* **Chittaranjan**
Mihijam India 97 E5
Mihumo Chini Tanz. 129 C7
Mijares *r.* Spain 55 K4
Mijas *mt.* Spain 54 G8
Mikasa Japan 90 G3
Mikashevichy Belarus 42 I9
Mikawa-wan *b.* Japan 91 E7
Mikhali Rus. Fed. 43 U6
Mikhalishki Belarus 42 H7
Mikhanavichy Belarus 42 I8
Mikha Tskhakaia Georgia *see* **Senaki**
Mikhaykovskiy Rus. Fed. *see* **Prozorovo**
Mikhaylov Rus. Fed. 43 U7
Mikhaylovgrad Bulg. *see* **Montana**
Mikhaylovka Kazakh. *see* **Sarykemer**
Mikhaylovka *Amurskaya Oblast'* Rus. Fed. 82 C2
Mikhaylovka *Chitinskaya Oblast'* Rus. Fed. 85 H1
Mikhaylovka *Kurskaya Oblast'* Rus. Fed. 43 Q9
Mikhaylovka *Primorskiy Kray* Rus. Fed. 82 D4
Mikhaylovka *Tul'skaya Oblast'* Rus. Fed. *see* **Kimovsk**
Mikhaylovka *Volgogradskaya Oblast'* Rus. Fed. 41 G6
Mikhaylovo Bulg. 58 E5
Mikhaylovskiy *Altayskiy Kray* Rus. Fed. 103 I2
Mikhaylovskiy *Altayskiy Kray* Rus. Fed. *see* **Malinovoye Ozero**
Mikhaylovskoye *Stavropol'skiy Kray* Rus. Fed. *see* **Shpakovskoye**
Mikhaylovskoye *Vologod. Obl.* Rus. Fed. 43 V2
Mikhaytov Island Antarctica 223 F2
Mikhnevo Rus. Fed. 43 S6
Miki Japan 91 D7
Mikínes *tourist site* Greece *see* **Mycenae**
Mikir Hills India 97 G4
Mikkeli Fin. 45 N3
Mikkelin mlk Fin. 45 N3
Mikkwa *r.* Canada 167 H3
Míkonos *i.* Greece *see* **Mykonos**
Mikoyan Armenia *see* **Yeghegnadzor**
Mikropoli Greece 58 E7
Mikulkin, Mys *c.* Rus. Fed. 40 H2
Mikulov Czech Rep. 49 N7
Mikumi Tanz. 129 C6
Mikumi National Park Tanz. 129 C6
Mikun' Rus. Fed. 40 I3
Mikuni Japan 91 E6
Mikuni-sanmyaku *mts* Japan 91 F6
Mikura-jima *i.* Japan 91 F8
Mila Alg. 123 G1
Milaca U.S.A. 174 A2
Miladhunmadulu Atoll Maldives 94 B5
Milagres Brazil 202 E3
Milagro Arg. 204 D3
Milagro Ecuador 198 B5
Milan Italy 56 B3
also spelt Milano; *historically known as* Mediolanum
UNESCO World Heritage Site
Milan *MI* U.S.A. 173 J8
Milan *MO* U.S.A. 174 A3
Milan *OH* U.S.A. 176 C4
Milando Angola 127 C7
Milando, Reserva Especial do *nature res.* Angola 127 C7
Milang Australia 146 C3
Milange Moz. 131 G3
Milano Italy *see* **Milan**
Milano (Malpensa) *airport* Italy 51 O7
Milaş Romania 58 F2
Milas Turkey 106 A3
historically known as Mylasa
Milavidy Belarus 42 G9
Milazzo *Sicily* Italy 57 H10
historically known as Mylae
Milazzo, Capo di *c. Sicily* Italy 57 H10
Milbank U.S.A. 178 C2
Milde *r.* Germany 48 I3
Mildura Australia 147 D3
Mile China 86 B3
also known as Miyang
Mīlē Eth. 128 D2
Miles Australia 149 F5
Milesburg U.S.A. 176 H5
Miles City U.S.A. 180 F3
Mīlē Serdo Reserve *nature res.* Eth. 128 D2
Miletin *r.* Romania 58 I1
Mileura Australia 151 B5
Mílevsko Czech Rep. 49 L6
Mileyevo Rus. Fed. 43 Q8
Milford *CT* U.S.A. 177 L4
Milford *DE* U.S.A. 177 J7
Milford *IL* U.S.A. 172 F10
Milford *NE* U.S.A. 178 C3
Milford *NH* U.S.A. 177 N3
Milford *PA* U.S.A. 177 K4
Milford *UT* U.S.A. 183 K3
Milford *VA* U.S.A. 176 H7
Milford Haven U.K. 47 G12
also known as Aberdaugleddau
Milford Lake U.S.A. 178 C4
Milford Sound N.Z. 153 B12
Milford Sound *inlet* N.Z. 153 B12
also known as Piopiotahi
Milgarra Australia 149 D3
Milgun Australia 151 B5
Milḩ, Baḩr al *l.* Iraq *see* **Razāzah, Buḩayrat ar**
Milḩ, Wādī al *watercourse* Iraq 109 P5
Milḩat Ashqar *salt l.* Iraq 109 N2
Miliana Alg. 55 N8
Milicz Poland 49 O4
Milid Turkey *see* **Malatya**
Milikapiti Australia 148 A1
Miling Australia 151 B6
Milingimbi Australia 148 B2
Milip Vanuatu 145 F3
Militello in Val di Catania *Sicily* Italy 57 G11
UNESCO World Heritage Site
Milk *r.* U.S.A. 180 F2
Milk, Wadi el *watercourse* Sudan 121 F5
Mil'kovo Rus. Fed. 39 P4
Milk River Canada 167 H5
Millaa Millaa Australia 149 E3
Millárs *r.* Spain 55 K4
Millau France 51 J8
Millboro U.S.A. 176 F8
Millbrook Canada 173 O6
Millbrook U.S.A. 177 L4
Mill City U.S.A. 180 B3
Mill Creek *r.* U.S.A. 182 B1
Milledgeville *GA* U.S.A. 175 D5
Milledgeville *IL* U.S.A. 172 D9
Mille Lacs *lakes* U.S.A. 174 A2
Mille Lacs, Lac des *l.* Canada 168 B3
Millen U.S.A. 175 D5
Millenium Island Kiribati *see* **Caroline Island**
Miller S. Africa 132 H10
Miller U.S.A. 178 C2
Miller Dam Flowage *resr* U.S.A. 172 C5
Miller Lake Canada 173 L5
Millerovo Rus. Fed. 41 G6
Millersburg *MI* U.S.A. 173 I5
Millersburg *OH* U.S.A. 176 D5
Millers Creek Australia 146 C2
Millers Creek U.S.A. 176 B8
Millers Falls U.S.A. 177 M3
Millers Flat N.Z. 153 D13
Millerton U.S.A. 177 L4
Millerton Lake U.S.A. 182 E4
Milleur Point U.K. 47 G8
Mill Glacier Antarctica 223 L1
Mill Hall U.S.A. 176 H4
Millicent Australia 146 D4
Millijiddie Aboriginal Reserve Australia 150 D3
Millington *MI* U.S.A. 173 J7
Millington *TN* U.S.A. 174 B5
Mill Inlet Antarctica 222 T2
Millinocket U.S.A. 174 G2
Milliri, Cerro *mt.* Bol. 200 C5
Mill Island Antarctica 223 G2
Mill Island Canada 165 L3
Millmerran Australia 147 F1
Millom U.K. 47 I9
Millsboro U.S.A. 177 J7
Mills Creek *watercourse* Australia 149 D4
Mills Lake Canada 167 G2
Millston U.S.A. 172 C6
Millstone U.S.A. 176 D7
Millstream Australia 150 B4
Millstream-Chichester National Park Australia 150 B4
Milltown U.S.A. 172 A5
Millungera Australia 149 D3
Millvale S. Africa 133 K2
Mill Valley U.S.A. 182 B4
Millville *CA* U.S.A. 182 B1
Millville *NJ* U.S.A. 177 J6
Millwood Lake U.S.A. 179 D5
Milly-la-Forêt France 51 I4
Milly Milly Australia 151 B5
Milne Bay P.N.G. 149 F1
Milne Land *i.* Greenland *see* **Ilimananngip Nunaa**
Milo *r.* Guinea 124 C4
Milo U.S.A. 174 G2
Milogradovo Rus. Fed. 82 D4
Miloli'i U.S.A. 181 [inset] Z2
Milos *i.* Greece 59 F12
Miloslavskoye Rus. Fed. 43 U8
Miłosław Poland 49 O3
Miloud *well* Alg. 122 D4
Milove Ukr. 41 G6
also spelt Melovoye
Milparinka Australia 146 D2
Milpitas U.S.A. 182 C4
Milroy U.S.A. 176 H5
Milton Canada 173 N7
Milton N.Z. 153 D14
Milton *DE* U.S.A. 177 J7
Milton *FL* U.S.A. 175 C6
Milton *VT* U.S.A. 177 L1
Milton *WV* U.S.A. 176 C7
Milton-Freewater U.S.A. 180 C3
Milton Keynes U.K. 47 L11
Miluo China 87 E2
Milverton Canada 173 M7
Milwaukee U.S.A. 172 F7

▶**Milwaukee Deep** *sea feature* Caribbean Sea 216 J4
Deepest point in the Atlantic Ocean (Puerto Rico Trench).
▶▶**208–209 Oceans and Poles**

Mily Kazakh. 103 E2
Milybulabk Kazakh. 103 H2
formerly spelt Myylybulak
Milyushino Rus. Fed. 43 T3
Milyutinskaya Rus. Fed. 41 G6
Mimbelly Congo 126 C4
Mimbres *watercourse* U.S.A. 181 F6
Mimili Australia 146 B1
Mimisal India 94 C4
Mimizan France 50 E8
Mimoň Czech Rep. 49 L5
Mimongo Gabon 126 A5
Mimosa Rocks National Park Australia 147 F4
Mimoso Brazil 206 E2
Mimoso do Sul Brazil 207 L8
Mina Mex. 185 E3
Mina U.S.A. 182 F3
Mina, Nevado *mt.* Peru 200 C3
Mina, Oued *watercourse* Alg. 55 L9
Mīnāb Iran 100 D5
Mīnāb *r.* Iran 100 D5
Minabe Japan 91 D8
Mina Clavero Arg. 204 D3
Minaçu Brazil 202 B5
Minago *r.* Canada 167 L4
Minahasa, Semenanjung *pen.* Indon. 75 B2
English form Minahassa Peninsula
Minahassa Peninsula Indon. *see* **Minahasa, Semenanjung**
Mina Jebel Ali U.A.E. 105 F2
short form Jebel Ali
Minaker Canada *see* **Prophet River**
Minaki Canada 167 M5
Minamata Japan 91 B8
Minamia Australia 148 B2
Minami Alps National Park Japan 91 F7
Minami-Daitō-jima *i.* Japan 81 M7
Minami-Iō-jima *vol.* Japan 73 J2
Min'an China *see* **Longshan**
Minaret Peaks N.Z. 153 D12
Minas Cuba 186 D2
Minas Indon. 76 C2
Minas Uruguay 204 G4
Minas, Sierra de las *mts* Guat. 185 H6
Mīnā' Sa'ūd Kuwait 107 G5
Minas Basin *b.* Canada 169 H4
Minas Channel Canada 169 H4
Minas de Matahambre Cuba 186 C2
Minas Gerais *state* Brazil 207 I5
Minas Novas Brazil 207 K4
Minatitlán Mex. 185 G5
Minbu Myanmar 78 A3
Minbya Myanmar 78 A3
Minchinabad Pak. 101 H4

Monastery of St Catherine tourist site Egypt 108 E9
UNESCO World Heritage Site
Monastery of St Anthony tourist site Egypt 108 D9
Monastery of St Paul tourist site Egypt 108 D9
Monastir Macedonia see Bitola
Monastir Tunisia 123 H2
Monastyrishche Ukr. see Monastyryshche
Monastyrshchina Rus. Fed. 43 M7
Monastyryshche Ukr. 41 D6
also spelt Monastyrishche
Monavale N.Z. 153 E12
Monbetsu Hokkaidō Japan 90 H2
also spelt Mombetsu
Monbetsu Hokkaidō Japan 90 H3
also spelt Mombetsu
Monboré Cameroon 125 I4
Moncalieri Italy 51 N7
Moncalvo mt. Spain 54 E2
Monchegorsk Rus. Fed. 44 P2
Mönchengladbach Germany 48 D4
formerly spelt München-Gladbach
Monchique Port. 54 C7
Monchique, Serra de mts Port. 54 C7
Moncks Corner U.S.A. 175 D5
Monclova Mex. 185 E3
Moncton Canada 169 H4
Mondai Brazil 203 A8
Mondego r. Port. 54 C4
Mondego, Cabo c. Port. 54 C4
Mondimbi Dem. Rep. Congo 126 D4
Mondim de Basto Port. 54 D3
Mondjamboli Dem. Rep. Congo 126 D4
Mondlo S. Africa 133 O4
Mondo Chad 120 B6
Mondolfo Italy 56 F5
Mondoñedo Spain 54 D1
Mondovì Italy 51 N8
Mondovi U.S.A. 172 B6
Mondragón Spain see Arrasate
Mondragone Italy 56 F7
Mondsee l. Austria 49 K8
Mondúver hill Spain 55 K5
Monee U.S.A. 172 F9
Monemvasia Greece 59 E12
also known as Malvasia
Moneron, Ostrov i. Rus. Fed. 82 F3
Monessen U.S.A. 176 F5
Monesterio Spain 54 E6
Monet Canada 173 R2
Moneta U.S.A. 176 F8
Monéteau France 51 J5
Monfalcone Italy 56 F3
Monflanquin France 50 G8
Monfort Col. 198 D4
Monforte Port. 54 D5
Monforte de Lemos Spain 54 D2
Monfurado hill Port. 54 C6
Monga Katanga Dem. Rep. Congo 127 E7
Monga Orientale Dem. Rep. Congo 126 D3
Mongaguá Brazil 206 G11
Mongala r. Dem. Rep. Congo 126 C4
Mongar Bhutan 97 F4
Mongbwalu Dem. Rep. Congo 126 F4
Mông Cai Vietnam 78 D3
Mongemputu Dem. Rep. Congo 126 D5
Mongers Lake salt flat Australia 151 B6
Mong Hang Myanmar 78 B3
Monghidoro Italy 56 D4
Mong Hpayak Myanmar 78 B3
Mong Hsat Myanmar 78 B3
Mong Hsu Myanmar 78 B3
Monghyr India see Munger
Mong Kung Myanmar 78 B3
Mong Kyawt Myanmar 78 B4
Mongla Bangl. 97 F5
Mong La Myanmar 78 C3
Mong Lin Myanmar 78 C3
Mong Loi Myanmar 78 C3
Mong Long Myanmar 78 B3
Mong Mit Myanmar 78 B3
also known as Momeik
Mong Nai Myanmar 78 B3
Mong Nawng Myanmar 78 B3
Mongo Chad 120 C6
►Mongolia country Asia 84 C2
known as Mongol Uls in Mongolian; formerly known as Outer Mongolia
►►64–65 Asia Countries
Mongolküre China see Zhaosu
Mongol Uls country Asia see Mongolia
Mongomo Equat. Guinea 125 H6
Mongonu Nigeria 125 I3
Mongora Pak. 101 H3
Mongororo Chad 120 D6
Mongoumba Cent. Afr. Rep. 126 C4
Mong Pan Myanmar 78 B3
Mong Pat Myanmar 78 B3
Mong Ping Myanmar 78 B3
Mongu Zambia 127 D8
Mongua Angola 127 B9
Mong Un Myanmar 78 C3
Mong Yai Myanmar 78 B3
Mong Yang Myanmar 78 B3
Mong Yawng Myanmar 78 C3
Mong Yu Myanmar 78 B3
Mönhbulag Mongolia 84 D2
Monhegan Island U.S.A. 177 P2
Mönh Hayrhan Uul mt. Mongolia 84 A2
Monico U.S.A. 172 D5
Moniquirá Col. 198 C3
Monistrol-sur-Loire France 51 K7
Monitor Mountain U.S.A. 183 H3
Monitor Range mts U.S.A. 183 H3
Moñitos Col. 198 B2
Monjolos Brazil 207 I5
Monjukly Turkm. 102 C5
Monkey Bay Malawi 129 B8
Monkey Mia Australia 151 A5
Mońki Poland 49 T2
Monkira Australia 149 D5
Monkman Provincial Park Canada 166 F4
Monkoto Dem. Rep. Congo 126 D5
Monkton Canada 173 L7
Monmouth U.K. 47 J12
also known as Trefynwy
Monmouth CA U.S.A. 182 E5
Monmouth IL U.S.A. 174 B3
Monmouth Mountain Canada 166 F5
Monnett U.S.A. 176 B5
Mono r. Togo 125 F5
Mono, Punta del pt Nicaragua 186 C5
Mono Lake U.S.A. 182 F3
Monolithos Greece 59 I12
Monon U.S.A. 172 G10
Monona U.S.A. 172 B7
Monongahela r. U.S.A. 176 F5
Monopoli Italy 56 J8
Monor Hungary 49 Q8
Monou Chad 120 D5
Monóvar Spain 55 K6
Monowai, Lake N.Z. 153 B13
Monreal del Campo Spain 55 J4
Monreale Sicily Italy 57 F10
Monroe GA U.S.A. 175 D5
Monroe IA U.S.A. 174 A3
Monroe LA U.S.A. 179 D5
Monroe MI U.S.A. 173 J9
Monroe NC U.S.A. 174 D5
Monroe NY U.S.A. 177 K4
Monroe UT U.S.A. 183 L3
Monroe VA U.S.A. 176 F8
Monroe WA U.S.A. 180 B3
Monroe WI U.S.A. 172 D8
Monroe Center U.S.A. 172 D6
Monroe City U.S.A. 174 B4
Monroe Lake U.S.A. 174 C4
Monroeton U.S.A. 177 I4
Monroeville AL U.S.A. 175 C6
Monroeville IN U.S.A. 176 A5
Monroeville OH U.S.A. 176 C4

►Monrovia Liberia 124 C5
Capital of Liberia.

Mons Belgium 51 J2
UNESCO World Heritage Site
Monsarás, Ponta de pt Brazil 207 N6
Monselice Italy 56 D3
Møns Klint cliff Denmark 49 J1
Mönsterås Sweden 45 L4
Montabaur Germany 48 E5
Montagne d'Ambre, Parc National de la nat. park Madag. 131 [inset] K2
Montagne de Reims, Parc Naturel Régional de la nature res. France 51 J3
Montagu S. Africa 132 E10
Montague Canada 169 I4
Montague U.S.A. 179 C5
Montague Island U.S.A. 164 E3
Montague Range hills Australia 151 B5
Montague Sound b. Australia 150 D2
Montaigu France 50 E6
Montaigu-de-Quercy France 50 H8
Montalat r. Indon. 77 F3
Montalto mt. Italy 57 H10
Montalto di Castro Italy 56 D6
Montalto Uffugo Italy 57 I9
Montalvo Ecuador 198 B5
Montana Bulg. 58 E5
formerly known as Mikhaylovgrad
Montana state U.S.A. 180 E3
Montaña de Comayagua, Parque Nacional nat. park Hond. 186 B4
Montaña de Cusuco, Parque Nacional nat. park Hond. 186 A4
Montaña de Yoro nat. park Hond. 186 B4
Montánchez hill Spain 54 E5
Montánchez, Sierra de mts Spain 54 E5
Montanha Brazil 207 M5
Montanhas do Tumucumaque, Parque Nacional nat. park Brazil 199 H4
Montargis France 51 I5
Montauban France 50 H8
Montauk U.S.A. 177 N4
Montauk Point U.S.A. 177 N4
Mont-aux-Sources mt. Lesotho 133 M5
Montbard France 51 K5
UNESCO World Heritage Site
Montbéliard France 51 M5

►Mont Blanc mt. France/Italy 51 M7
5th highest mountain in Europe.

Montblanc Spain 55 M3
also spelt Montblanch
Montblanch Spain see Montblanc
Montbrison France 51 K7
Montcalm U.S.A. 176 D8
Montceau-les-Mines France 51 K6
Montchanin France 51 K6
Montcuq France 50 H8
Mont-de-Marsan France 50 F9
Montdidier France 51 I3
Monte, Laguna del l. Arg. 204 E5
Monteagudo Bol. 201 D4
Monte Albán tourist site Mex. 185 F5
UNESCO World Heritage Site
Monte Alegre Brazil 199 H5
Monte Alegre r. Brazil 206 C4
Monte Alegre de Goiás Brazil 202 C5
Montealegre del Castillo Spain 55 J6
Monte Alegre de Minas Brazil 206 E5
Monte Aprazível Brazil 206 D7
Monte Azul Paulista Brazil 206 E7
Montebello Canada 169 F4
Montebello Islands Australia 150 A4
Montebelluna Italy 56 E3
Monte Buey Arg. 204 E4
Monte Carlo Monaco see Monte-Carlo
Monte-Carlo Monaco 51 N9
English form Monte Carlo
Monte Carmelo Brazil 206 F5
Monte Caseros Arg. 204 F3
Montecatini Terme Italy 56 C5
Montecchio Maggiore Italy 56 D3
Montech France 50 H9
Montecito U.S.A. 182 E7
Monte Cotugna, Lago di l. Italy 57 I8
Monte Cristi Dom. Rep. 187 F3
Monte Cristi nat. park Dom. Rep. 187 F3
Montecristi Ecuador 198 A5
Monte Cristo Bol. 201 E3
Monte Cristo S. Africa 131 E4
Montecristo, Isola di i. Italy 56 C6
Monte da Rocha, Barragem do resr Port. 54 C7
Monte Dinero Arg. 205 C9
Monte Dourado Brazil 199 H5
Monte Escobedo Mex. 184 E4
Monte Falterona, Campigna e delle Foreste Casentinesi, Parco Nazionale del nat. park Italy 56 D5
Montefiascone Italy 56 E6
Montegiorgio Italy 56 F5
Montego Bay Jamaica 186 D3
Monte Hermoso Arg. 204 E5
Montehermoso Spain 54 E4
Monteiro Brazil 202 E3
Montejinnie Australia 148 A3
Montejunto, Serra de hill Port. 54 B5
Monte León Arg. 205 C8
Monte Libano Col. 198 C2
Montélimar France 51 K8
historically known as Acunum Acusio
Monte Lindo r. Para. 201 F5
Montellano Spain 54 F7
Montello U.S.A. 172 D7
Montemayor, Meseta de plat. Arg. 205 D7
Montemorelos Mex. 185 F3
Montemor-o-Novo Port. 54 C6
Montendre France 50 F7
Montenegro aut. rep. Serb. and Mont. see Crna Gora
Monte Pascoal, Parque Nacional de nat. park Brazil 207 N4
Monte Patria Chile 204 C3
Montepuez Moz. 131 H1
Montepuez r. Moz. 129 D8
Monte Quemado Arg. 204 E2
Montereau-fault-Yonne France 51 I4
Monterey Mex. see Monterrey
Monterey CA U.S.A. 182 C5
Monterey KY U.S.A. 176 A7
Monterey VA U.S.A. 176 F7
Monterey Bay U.S.A. 182 B5
Monterey Bay National Marine Sanctuary nature res. U.S.A. 182 B5
Montería Col. 198 C2
Monteriggioni Italy 56 D5
Montero Bol. 201 E4
Monte Roraima, Parque Nacional do nat. park Brazil 199 F3
Monteros Arg. 204 D2
Monterotondo Italy 56 E6
Monterrey Baja California Norte Mex. 183 I9
Monterrey Nuevo León Mex. 185 E3
also spelt Monterey
Montes Altos Brazil 202 C3
Montesano U.S.A. 180 B3
Montesano sulla Marcellana Italy 57 H8
Monte Sant'Angelo Italy 56 H7
Monte Santo Brazil 202 E4
Monte Santo de Minas Brazil 206 G8
Monte Santu, Capo di c. Sardinia Italy 57 B8
Montes Claros Brazil 202 D6
Montesilvano Italy 56 G6
Montesquieu-Volvestre France 50 H9

►Montevideo Uruguay 204 F4
Capital of Uruguay.

Montevideo U.S.A. 178 D2
Monte Vista U.S.A. 181 F5
Montezinho, Parque Natural de nature res. Port. 54 E3
Montezuma U.S.A. 174 A3
Montezuma Creek U.S.A. 183 O4
Montezuma Creek r. U.S.A. 183 O4
Montezuma Peak U.S.A. 183 G4
Montfort-le-Gesnois France 50 G4
Montfragüe, Parque Natural de nature res. Spain 54 F5
Montgomery U.K. 47 I11
also known as Trefaldwyn

►Montgomery AL U.S.A. 175 C5
State capital of Alabama.

Montgomery PA U.S.A. 177 I4
Montgomery WV U.S.A. 176 D7
Montgomery City U.S.A. 174 B4
Montgomery Islands Australia 150 C2
Monthey Switz. 51 M6
Monti Sardinia Italy 57 B8
Monticello AR U.S.A. 175 B5
Monticello FL U.S.A. 175 D6
Monticello GA U.S.A. 175 D5
Monticello IA U.S.A. 172 B8
Monticello IL U.S.A. 174 B3
Monticello IN U.S.A. 174 C3
Monticello KY U.S.A. 176 A9
Monticello MO U.S.A. 174 B3
Monticello MS U.S.A. 175 B6
Monticello NY U.S.A. 177 K4
Monticello UT U.S.A. 183 O4
Monticello WI U.S.A. 172 D8
Montichiari Italy 56 C3
Montiel, Cuchilla de hills Arg. 204 F3
Montier-en-Der France 51 K4
Montignac France 50 H7
Montigny, Lac de l. Canada 173 P2
Montigny-le-Roi France 51 L4
Montijo Port. 54 C6
Montijo Spain 54 E6
Montilla Spain 54 G7
Monti Sibillini, Parco Nazionale dei nat. park Italy 56 F6
Montivilliers France 50 G3
Mont-Joli Canada 169 G3
Mont-Laurier Canada 168 F4
Mont Louis Canada 169 H3
Montluçon France 51 I6
Montmagny Canada 169 G4
Montmélian France 51 M7
Montmirail France 51 J4
Montmoreau-St-Cybard France 50 G7
Montmorillon France 50 G6
Monto Australia 149 F5
Montoire-sur-le-Loir France 50 G5
Montoro Spain 54 G6
Montour Falls U.S.A. 177 I3
Montoursville U.S.A. 177 I4
Mont Peko, Parc National du nat. park Côte d'Ivoire 124 D5
Montpelier ID U.S.A. 180 E4
Montpelier IN U.S.A. 172 H10
Montpelier OH U.S.A. 176 A4

►Montpelier VT U.S.A. 177 M1
State capital of Vermont.

Montpellier France 51 J9
Montpezat-de-Quercy France 50 H8
Montpon-Ménestérol France 50 G7
Montreal Canada see Montréal
Montréal Canada 169 F4
English form Montreal; historically known as Ville-Marie
Montreal r. Ont. Canada 168 C4
Montreal r. Ont. Canada 168 E4
Montreal U.S.A. 172 C4
Montreal Island Canada 173 I3
Montreal Lake Canada 167 J4
Montreal Lake l. Canada 167 J4
Montréal-Mirabel airport Canada 169 F4
Montreal River Canada 168 C4
Montréal-Trudeau airport Canada 169 F4
Montreuil France 50 H2
Montreux Switz. 51 M6
Montrose well S. Africa 132 E3
Montrose U.K. 46 J7
Montrose CO U.S.A. 181 F5
Montrose MI U.S.A. 173 J7
Montrose PA U.S.A. 177 J4
Montrose WV U.S.A. 176 F6
Monts France 50 G5
Mont-St-Aignan France 50 H3
Mont-St-Michel, Baie du b. France 50 E4
Montsalvy France 51 I8
Mont Sangbé, Parc National du nat. park Côte d'Ivoire 124 D5
Montseny, Parc Natural de nature res. Spain 55 N3

►Montserrat terr. West Indies 187 H3
United Kingdom Overseas Territory.
►►158–159 North America Countries

Mont St Michel tourist site France see Le Mont-St-Michel
Montuosa, Isla i. Panama 186 C6
Montvale U.S.A. 176 F8
Montviel, Lac l. Canada 169 G2
Monument Draw watercourse U.S.A. 179 B5
Monument Valley reg. U.S.A. 183 N5
Monveda Dem. Rep. Congo 126 D4
Monyakeng S. Africa 133 K4
Monywa Myanmar 78 A3
Monza Italy 56 B3
Monza r. Rus. Fed. 43 V3
Monze Zambia 127 E9
Monze, Cape pt Pak. see Muari, Ras
Monzón Peru 200 A2
Monzón Spain 55 L3
Mooi r. KwaZulu-Natal S. Africa 133 O5
Mooi r. North West S. Africa 133 K3
Mooifontein Namibia 132 A3
Mooirivier S. Africa 133 O6
Mookane Botswana 131 E4
Moolawatana Australia 146 C2
Moomba Australia 146 D2
Moomin Creek r. Australia 147 F2
Moonbi Range mts Australia 147 F2
Moonda Lake salt flat Australia 149 D5
Moonie Australia 147 F1
Moonie r. Australia 147 F2
Moonta Australia 146 C3
Moora Australia 151 B6
Mooraberree Australia 149 D5
Moorcroft U.S.A. 180 F3
Moordenaarsnek pass S. Africa 133 M7
Moordorf (Südbrookmerland) Germany 48 E2
Moore r. Australia 151 A6
Moore U.S.A. 180 E3
Moore, Lake salt flat Australia 151 B6
Moore Embayment b. Antarctica 223 K1
Moorefield U.S.A. 176 G6
Moore Haven U.S.A. 175 D7
Moore Reef reef Australia 149 F3
Moore Reservoir U.S.A. 177 N1
Moore River National Park Australia 151 A6
Moorfoot Hills U.K. 46 I8
Moorhead U.S.A. 178 C2
Moornanyah Lake imp. l. Australia 147 D3
Mooroopna Australia 147 E4
Moorpark U.S.A. 182 F7
Moorreesburg S. Africa 132 C10
Moorrinya National Park Australia 149 E4
Moosburg an der Isar Germany 48 I7
Moose r. Canada 168 D3
Moose Factory Canada 168 D3
Moosehead Lake U.S.A. 174 G2
Moose Jaw Canada 167 J5
Moose Jaw r. Canada 167 J5
Moose Lake U.S.A. 174 A2
Moose Mountain Creek r. Canada 167 K5
Moose River Canada 168 D3
Moosilauke, Mount U.S.A. 177 N1
Moosomin Canada 167 K5
Moosonee Canada 168 D3
Mootwingee National Park Australia 147 D2
Mopane S. Africa 131 F4
Mopeia Moz. 131 G3
Mopipi Botswana 131 E4
Mopti Mali 124 D3
Mopti admin. reg. Mali 124 E3
Moqatta Sudan 104 A5
Moquegua Peru 200 C4
Moquegua dept Peru 200 C4
Mór Hungary 49 P8
Mora Cameroon 125 I4
Mora Port. 54 C6
Mora Spain 54 H5
Mora Sweden 45 K3
Mora MN U.S.A. 174 A2
Mora NM U.S.A. 181 F6
Mora r. U.S.A. 181 F6
Mora, Cerro mt. Arg./Chile 204 C4
Morača r. Serb. and Mont. 58 A6
Morach r. Belarus 42 I9
Morad r. Pak. 101 F4
Moradabad India 96 C3
Morada Nova Amazonas Brazil 200 C1
Morada Nova Ceará Brazil 202 E3
Morada Nova de Minas Brazil 207 H5
Morafenobe Madag. 131 [inset] J3
Morąg Poland 49 Q2
Mórahalom Hungary 49 Q9
formerly known as Aslóközpont
Moraine Lake Canada 167 J1
Moraleda, Canal sea chan. Chile 205 B7
Moraleja Spain 54 E4
Morales Guat. 185 H6
Moram India 94 C2
Moramanga Madag. 131 [inset] K3
Moran MI U.S.A. 173 I5
Moran WY U.S.A. 180 E4
Moranbah Australia 149 F4
Morang Nepal see Biratnagar
Morangas Brazil 206 A6
Moranhat India 97 G4
Morant Cays is Jamaica 186 E3
Morant Point Jamaica 186 D3
Morappur India 94 C3
Morar, Loch l. U.K. 46 G7
Morari, Tso l. Jammu and Kashmir 96 C2
Moratalla Spain 55 J6
Moratuwa Sri Lanka 94 C5
Morava reg. Czech Rep. see Moravia
Morava r. Europe 49 N7
also known as March
Moravato Madag. 131 [inset] K2
Moraveh Tappeh Iran 100 C2
Moravia reg. Czech Rep. 49 O6
also known as Morava; formerly known as Mähren
Moravia U.S.A. 177 I3
Moravian Falls U.S.A. 176 D9
Moravica r. Serb. and Mont. 58 B5
Moravica r. Serb. and Mont. 58 C5
Moravice r. Czech Rep. 49 O6
Moravská Třebová Czech Rep. 49 N6
Moravské Budějovice Czech Rep. 49 M6
Moravskoslezské Beskydy mts Czech Rep. 49 P6
Morawa Australia 151 A6
Morawhanna Guyana 199 G2
Moray Firth b. U.K. 46 H6
Moray Range hills Australia 148 A2
Morbach Germany 48 E6
Morbegno Italy 56 B2
Morbi India 96 A5
formerly spelt Morvi
Mörbylånga Sweden 45 L4
Morcenx France 50 F8
Morcillo Mex. 184 D3
Mordaga China 85 I1
Mor Dağı mt. Turkey 107 F3
Mordelles France 50 E4
Morden Canada 167 L5
Mordovia aut. rep. Rus. Fed. see Mordoviya, Respublika
Mordoviya, Respublika aut. rep. Rus. Fed. 41 H5
English form Mordovia or Mordvinia; formerly known as Mordovskaya A.S.S.R.
Mordovo Rus. Fed. 41 G5
Mordovskaya A.S.S.R. aut. rep. Rus. Fed. see Mordoviya, Respublika
Mordves Rus. Fed. 43 T7
Mordvinia aut. rep. Rus. Fed. see Mordoviya, Respublika
Mordy Poland 49 T3
Moreau r. U.S.A. 178 B2
Moreau, South Fork r. U.S.A. 178 B2
Morecambe U.K. 47 J9
Morecambe Bay U.K. 47 I9
Moree Australia 147 F2
Morehead P.N.G. 73 J8
Morehead U.S.A. 176 B7
Morehead City U.S.A. 174 E5
Moreira Brazil 199 F5
More-Iz, Gora hill Rus. Fed. 40 L1
Morel r. India 96 C4
Moreland U.S.A. 176 A8
Morelia Col. 198 C4
Morelia Mex. 185 E5
UNESCO World Heritage Site
Morella Australia 149 D4
Morella Spain 55 K4
Morelos state Mex. 185 F5
Moremi Wildlife Reserve nature res. Botswana 130 D3
Morena India 96 C4
Morena, Sierra mts Spain 54 E7
formerly known as Mariánica, Cordillera
Morenci U.S.A. 183 O8
Moreni Romania 58 G4
Moreno Mex. 184 C2
Moreno Valley U.S.A. 183 G8
Møre og Romsdal county Norway 44 I3
Moreni r. Brazil 201 F2
Mores Sardinia Italy 57 A8
Moresby, Mount Canada 166 D4
Moresby Island Canada 166 C4
Moreton Bay Australia 147 G1
Moreton Island Australia 147 G1
Moreuil France 51 I3
Moreyu r. Rus. Fed. 40 K1
Morez France 51 M6
Morfou Cyprus 108 D2
also known as Güzelyurt; also spelt Morphou
Morfou Bay Cyprus 108 D2
Morgam-Viibus hill Fin. 44 N1
Morgan Australia 146 C3
Morgan U.S.A. 176 A7
Morgan, Mount U.S.A. 182 F4
Morgan City U.S.A. 175 B6
Morgan Hill U.S.A. 182 C4
Morgans Corner U.S.A. 177 I9
Morganton U.S.A. 174 D5
Morgantown KY U.S.A. 174 C4
Morgantown WV U.S.A. 176 F6
Morgenzon S. Africa 133 N3
Morges Switz. 51 M6
Morgex Italy 51 N7
Morhar r. India 97 E4
Mori China 88 E3
Mori Japan 90 G3
Moriah, Mount U.S.A. 183 J2
Moriarty U.S.A. 181 F6
Moriarty's Range hills Australia 147 E2
Moribaya Guinea 124 C4
Morice Lake Canada 166 E4
Moricetown Canada 166 E4
Morichal Col. 198 D4
Moricsalas rezervāts nature res. Latvia 42 D4
Morija Lesotho 133 L6
Moriki Nigeria 125 G3
Morin Dawa China see Nirji
Morine pass Bos.-Herz. 56 K5
Morino Rus. Fed. 43 L4
Morioka Japan 90 G5
Morire Moz. 131 G3
Morisset Australia 147 F3
Moriyama Japan 91 E7
Moriyoshi Japan 90 G4
Moriyoshi-zan vol. Japan 90 G5
Morjärv Sweden 44 M2
Morjen r. Pak. 101 E4
Morki Rus. Fed. 40 I4
Morkiny Gory Rus. Fed. 43 R4
Morlaix France 50 C4
Morley Canada 167 H5
Mormal' Belarus 43 K9
Mormant France 51 I4
Mormon Lake U.S.A. 183 M7
Mormugao India see Marmagao
Morne Trois Pitons National Park Dominica 187 H4
UNESCO World Heritage Site
Morney watercourse Australia 149 D5
Mornington, Isla i. Chile 205 B8
Mornington Island Australia 148 C3
Mornington Peninsula National Park Australia 147 E4
Mornos r. Greece 59 C10
Moro Pak. 101 F5
Moro U.S.A. 180 B3
Morobe P.N.G. 73 K8
►Morocco country Africa 122 C3
►►114–115 Africa Countries
Morocco U.S.A. 172 F10
Moro Creek r. U.S.A. 179 D5
Morogoro Tanz. 129 C6
Morogoro admin. reg. Tanz. 129 C7
Moro Gulf Phil. 74 B5
Morojaneng S. Africa 133 K6
Morokweng S. Africa 132 H3
Moroleón Mex. 185 E4
Moromaho i. Indon. 75 C4
Morombe Madag. 131 [inset] I4
Moromoro Bol. 201 D4
Morón Arg. 204 E6
Morón Cuba 186 D2
Mörön Mongolia 84 D1
Morona Ecuador 198 B5
Morona r. Peru 198 B6
Morona-Santiago prov. Ecuador 198 B5
Morondava Madag. 131 [inset] J4
Morón de la Frontera Spain 54 F7
Morondo Côte d'Ivoire 124 D4
Morongo Valley U.S.A. 183 H7

►Moroni Comoros 129 D7
Capital of the Comoros.

Moroni U.S.A. 183 M2
Moros r. Spain 54 G3
Morotai i. Indon. 75 D2
Morotai, Selat sea chan. Indon. 75 C2
Moroto Uganda 128 B4
Moroto, Mount Uganda 128 B4
Morotsuka Japan 91 B8
Morowai N.Z. 153 B13
Morowali Reserve nature res. Indon. 75 B3
Morozova Rus. Fed. 43 L2
Morozovo Rus. Fed. 43 V5
Morozovsk Rus. Fed. 41 G6
Morpara Brazil 202 D4
Morpeth Canada 173 L8
Morpeth U.K. 47 K8
Morphou Cyprus see Morfou
Morretes Brazil 203 B8
Morrill U.S.A. 176 A8
Morrilton U.S.A. 179 D5
Morrin Canada 167 H5
Morrinhos Brazil 206 D4
Morrinsville N.Z. 152 J5
Morris Canada 167 L5
Morris IL U.S.A. 174 B3
Morris MN U.S.A. 178 D2
Morris PA U.S.A. 177 H4
Morrisburg Canada 177 J1

►Morris Jesup, Kap c. Greenland 165 P1
Most northerly point of North America.
►►154–155 North America Landscapes

Morrison U.S.A. 174 B3
Morrisons N.Z. 153 E13
Morristown AZ U.S.A. 183 L8
Morristown NJ U.S.A. 177 K5
Morristown NY U.S.A. 177 J1
Morristown TN U.S.A. 176 B9
Morrisville NY U.S.A. 177 J3
Morrisville VT U.S.A. 177 M1
Morr Morr Aboriginal Holding res. Australia 149 D3
Morro Brazil 207 I3
Morro, Punta pt Chile 204 C2
Morro Agudo Brazil 206 E7
Morro Bay U.S.A. 182 D6
Morro d'Anta Brazil 203 E6
Morro de Papanoa hd Mex. 185 E5
Morro de Petatlán hd Mex. 185 E5
Morro do Chapéu Brazil 202 D4
Morro do Coco Brazil 207 L8
Morro do Sinal hills Brazil 201 G2
Morros Brazil 202 C2
Morrosquillo, Golfo de b. Col. 198 C2
Morrumbala Moz. 131 G3
Morrumbene Moz. 131 G4
Mors reg. Denmark 45 J4
Morse Canada 167 J5
Morse U.S.A. 172 C4
Morse, Cape Antarctica 223 I2
Morshanka Rus. Fed. 41 G5
formerly known as Morshansk
Morshansk Rus. Fed. see Morshanka
Morsi India 96 C5
Morsott Alg. 57 A13
Mørsvikbotn Norway 44 K2
Mort watercourse Australia 149 D4
Mortagne-au-Perche France 50 G4
Mortagne-sur-Sèvre France 50 F5
Mortain France 50 F4
Mortara Italy 56 A3
Morteau France 51 M5
Morteros Arg. 204 E3
Mortes, Rio das r. Minas Gerais Brazil 207 I8
Mortes, Rio das r. Tocantins Brazil 202 B4
also known as Manso
Mortimer's Bahamas 187 E2
Mortlach Canada 167 J5
Mortlake Australia 147 D4
Mortlock Islands Micronesia 220 F5
also known as Nomoi Islands
Mortlock Islands P.N.G. see Takuu Islands
Morton IL U.S.A. 174 B3
Morton TX U.S.A. 179 B5
Morton WA U.S.A. 180 B3
Morton National Park Australia 147 F3
Mortugaba Brazil 207 K1
Morundah Australia 147 E3
Moruroa atoll Fr. Polynesia see Mururoa
Moruya Australia 147 F3
Morvan, Parc Naturel Régional du nature res. France 51 K5
Morven Australia 149 E5
Morven N.Z. 153 F12
Morven hill U.K. 46 I5
Morvern reg. U.K. 46 G7
Morvi India see Morbi
Morwell Australia 147 E4
Mor'ye Rus. Fed. 43 M1
Morzhovets, Ostrov i. Rus. Fed. 40 G2
Mosal'sk Rus. Fed. 43 P7
Mosbach Germany 48 G6
Mosby U.S.A. 180 F3
Moscarter, Punta des pt Spain 55 M5

►Moscow Rus. Fed. 43 S6
Capital of the Russian Federation, and most populous city in Europe. Also known as Moskva.
UNESCO World Heritage Site
►►18–19 World Cities
►►24–25 World Terrorism

Moscow IA U.S.A. 172 B9
Moscow ID U.S.A. 180 C3
Moscow PA U.S.A. 177 J4
Moscow Oblast admin. div. Rus. Fed. see Moskovskaya Oblast'
Moscow University Ice Shelf Antarctica 223 I2
Mosel r. Germany 48 E5
Moselebe watercourse Botswana 130 D5
Moseley U.S.A. 176 H8
Moselle r. France 51 M3
Moses, Mount U.S.A. 183 G1
Moses Lake U.S.A. 180 C3
Mosgiel N.Z. 153 E13
Moshannon U.S.A. 176 G4
Moshaweng watercourse S. Africa 132 G3
Moshchnyy, Ostrov i. Rus. Fed. 42 I2
Moshenskoye Rus. Fed. 43 P3
Mosher Canada 173 I2
Moshi r. Nigeria 125 G4
Moshi Tanz. 128 C5
Mosina Poland 49 N3
Mosinee U.S.A. 172 D6
Mosi-oa-Tunya National Park Zimbabwe see Victoria Falls National Park
Mosita S. Africa 133 I3
Mosjøen Norway 44 K2
Moskal'vo Rus. Fed. 82 F1
Moskángáisi mt. Norway 44 M1
Moskenesøy i. Norway 44 K2
Moskenestraumen sea chan. Norway 44 K2
Moskosel Sweden 44 L2
Moskovskaya Oblast' admin. div. Rus. Fed. 43 T6
English form Moscow Oblast
Moskovskiy Uzbek. see Shahrihon
Moskva Rus. Fed. see Moscow
Moskva r. Rus. Fed. 43 T6
Moskva Tajik. 101 G2
Moskvy, Kanal imeni canal Rus. Fed. 43 S5
Moșna Romania 58 I2
Mosonmagyaróvár Hungary 49 O8
Mosopo Botswana 133 J1
Mosor mts Croatia 56 I5
Mosquera Col. 198 B4
Mosquero U.S.A. 181 F6
Mosquitia reg. Hond. 186 C4
UNESCO World Heritage Site
Mosquito Creek Lake U.S.A. 176 E4
Mosquito Lake Canada 167 K2
Mosquitos, Golfo de los b. Panama 186 C5
Moss Norway 45 J4
Mossaka Congo 126 C5
Mossâmedes Angola see Namibe
Mossâmedes Brazil 206 C3
Mossburn N.Z. 153 C13
Mosselbaai S. Africa see Mossel Bay
Mossel Bay S. Africa 132 G11
also spelt Mosselbaai
Mossel Bay b. S. Africa 132 G11
Mossendjo Congo 126 B5
Mossgiel Australia 147 E3
Mossman Australia 149 E3
Mossoró Brazil 202 E3
Moss Vale Australia 147 F3
Mossy r. Canada 167 K4
Most Bulg. 58 G7
Most Czech Rep. 49 K5
Mostaganem Alg. 123 F2
also spelt Mestghanem
Mostar Bos.-Herz. 56 J5
Mostardas Brazil 204 H3
Moșteni Romania 58 G4
Mostiștea r. Romania 58 H4
Móstoles Spain 54 H4
Mostoos Hills Canada 167 I4
Mostovskoy Rus. Fed. 41 G7
Mosty Belarus see Masty
Mosul Iraq 107 E3
also spelt Al Mawşil
Møsvatn Austfjell park Norway 45 J4
Møsvatnet l. Norway 45 J4
Mosvik Norway 44 J3
Mot'a Eth. 128 C2
Motaba r. Congo 126 C4
Mota del Cuervo Spain 55 I5
Motagua r. Guat. 185 H6
Motal' Belarus 42 G9
Motala Sweden 45 K4
Mota Lava i. Vanuatu 145 F3
also known as Saddle Island or Valua
Motaze Moz. 131 G5
Moțca Romania 58 H1
Motenge-Boma Dem. Rep. Congo 126 C4
Moteng Pass Lesotho 133 M5
Moth India 96 C4
Motherwell U.K. 46 I8
Mothibistad S. Africa 132 H4
Mothonaio, Akra pt Greece 59 E12
Motian Ling hill China 83 A4
Motihari India 97 E4
Motilla hill Spain 54 F6
Motilla del Palancar Spain 55 J5
Motiti Island N.Z. 152 K5
Motloutse r. Botswana 131 F4
Motokwe Botswana 130 D5
Motovskiy Zaliv sea chan. Rus. Fed. 44 P1
Motoyoshi Japan 90 G5
Motozintla Mex. 185 G6
Motril Spain 55 H8
Motru Romania 58 D4
Motru r. Romania 58 E4
Motshikiri S. Africa 133 L2
Mott U.S.A. 178 B2
Mottama Myanmar 78 B4
also known as Möktama
Mottama, Gulf of Myanmar 78 B4
Motueka N.Z. 152 H9
Motuhora Island N.Z. see Moutohora Island
Motu Ihupuku i. N.Z. see Campbell Island

Motukarara N.Z. **153** G11
Motul Mex. **185** H4
Motupipi N.Z. **152** G8
Mouali Gbangba Congo **126** C4
Mouan, Nam *r.* Laos **78** D4
Mouaskar Alg. *see* **Mascara**
Moubray Bay Antarctica **223** L2
Mouchalagane *r.* Canada **169** G3
Mouchet, Mont *mt.* France **51** J8
Mouchoir Bank *sea feature* Turks and Caicos Is **187** F2
Mouchoir Passage Turks and Caicos Is **187** F2
Mouding China **86** B3
also known as Gonghe
Moudjéria Mauritania **124** B2
Moudon Switz. **51** M6
Moudros Greece **59** G9
Mougalaba, Réserve de la *nature res.* Gabon **126** A5
Mougri *well* Mauritania **124** B2
Mouhijärvi Fin. **45** M3
Mouhoun *r.* Africa **124** E4 *see* **Black Volta**
Mouila Gabon **126** A5
Moul *well* Niger **125** I3
Moulamein Australia **147** E3
Moulamein Creek *r.* Australia **147** D3
also known as Billabong Creek
Moulavibazar Bangl. *see* **Moulvibazar**
Moulèngui Binza Gabon **126** A5
Moulentâr *well* Mali **124** D2
Moulhoulé Djibouti **128** D1
Moulins France **51** J6
Moulins-Engilbert France **51** J6
Moulle de Jaut, Pic du *mt.* France **50** F9
Moulmein Myanmar *see* **Mawlamyaing**
Moulouya, Oued *r.* Morocco **122** E2
Moulton U.S.A. **174** C5
Moulton, Mount Antarctica **222** P1
Moultonborough U.S.A. **177** N2
Moultrie U.S.A. **175** D6
Moultrie, Lake U.S.A. **175** E5
Moulvibazar Bangl. **97** F4
also spelt Moulavibazar
Mounana Gabon **126** B5
Mound City *KS* U.S.A. **178** D4
Mound City *MO* U.S.A. **178** D3
Mound City *SD* U.S.A. **178** B2
Moundou Chad **126** C2
Moundsville U.S.A. **176** E6
Mounta, Akra *pt* Greece **59** B10
Mount Abu India **96** B4
Mountainair U.S.A. **181** F6
Mountain Brook U.S.A. **175** C5
Mountain City U.S.A. **176** D9
Mountain Grove U.S.A. **178** D4
Mountain Home *AR* U.S.A. **179** D4
Mountain Home *ID* U.S.A. **180** D4
Mountain Home *UT* U.S.A. **183** N1
Mountain Iron U.S.A. **172** A3
Mountain Lake Park U.S.A. **176** F6
Mountain Pass U.S.A. **183** I6
Mountain View *AR* U.S.A. **179** D5
Mountain View *CA* U.S.A. **182** B4
Mountain View *HI* U.S.A. **181** [inset] Z2
Mountain Village U.S.A. **164** C3
Mountain Zebra National Park S. Africa **133** J9
Mount Airy *MD* U.S.A. **177** H6
Mount Airy *NC* U.S.A. **176** E9
Mount Anderson Aboriginal Reserve Australia **150** C3
Mount Arapiles-Tooan State Park *nature res.* Australia **146** D4
Mount Aspiring National Park N.Z. **153** C12
UNESCO World Heritage Site
Mount Assiniboine Provincial Park Canada **167** H5
UNESCO World Heritage Site
Mount Augustus Australia **150** B5
Mount Ayliff S. Africa **133** N7
Mount Ayr U.S.A. **178** D3
Mount Baldy U.S.A. **182** G7
Mount Barker *S.A.* Australia **146** C3
Mount Barker *W.A.* Australia **151** B7
Mount Barnett Australia **150** D3
Mount Barnett Aboriginal Reserve Australia **150** D3
Mount Beauty Australia **147** E4
Mount Bellew Ireland **47** D10
Mount Bruce N.Z. **152** J8
Mount Brydges Canada **173** L8
Mount Buffalo National Park Australia **147** E4
Mount Carmel *IL* U.S.A. **174** C4
Mount Carmel *TN* U.S.A. **176** C9
Mount Carmel Junction U.S.A. **183** L4
Mount Carroll U.S.A. **174** B3
Mount Clere Australia **151** B5
Mount Cook Australia **153** E11 *see* **Aoraki**
Mount Cook National Park N.Z. **153** E11
UNESCO World Heritage Site
Mount Coolon Australia **149** E4
Mount Currie Nature Reserve S. Africa **133** N7
Mount Darwin Zimbabwe **131** F3
Mount Denison Australia **148** B4
Mount Desert Island U.S.A. **177** Q1
Mount Eba Australia **146** B2
Mount Eccles National Park Australia **146** D4
Mount Edziza Provincial Park Canada **166** D3
Mount Etna U.S.A. **172** H10
Mount Field National Park Australia **147** E5
Mount Fletcher S. Africa **133** M7
Mount Forest Canada **168** D5
Mount Frankland National Park Australia **151** B7
Mount Frere S. Africa **133** M7
also known as Kwabhaca
Mount Gambier Australia **146** D4
Mount Garnet Australia **149** E3
Mount Hagen P.N.G. **73** J8
Mount Holly U.S.A. **177** K6
Mount Holly Springs U.S.A. **177** H5
Mount Hope *N.S.W.* Australia **147** E3
Mount Hope *S.A.* Australia **146** B3
Mount Hope U.S.A. **176** D8
Mount Horeb U.S.A. **172** D7
Mount House Australia **150** D3
Mount Howitt Australia **149** D5
Mount Hutt N.Z. **153** F11
Mount Ida U.S.A. **179** D5
Mount Isa Australia **148** C4
Mount Jackson U.S.A. **176** G7
Mount James Aboriginal Reserve Australia **151** B5
Mount Jewett U.S.A. **176** G4
Mount Kaputar National Park Australia **147** F2
Mount Keith Australia **151** C5
Mount Kenya National Park Kenya **128** C5
UNESCO World Heritage Site
Mount Lebanon U.S.A. **176** E5
Mount Lofty Range *mts* Australia **146** C3
Mount MacDonald Canada **173** M3
Mount Magnet Australia **151** B6
Mount Manara Australia **147** D3
Mount Manning Nature Reserve Australia **151** B6
Mount Maunganui N.Z. **152** K5
Mount McKinley National Park U.S.A. *see* **Denali National Park and Preserve**
Mount Meadows Reservoir U.S.A. **182** D1
Mount Molloy Australia **149** E3
Mount Moorosi Lesotho **133** L7
Mount Morgan Australia **149** F4
Mount Morris *IL* U.S.A. **172** D8
Mount Morris *MI* U.S.A. **173** J7
Mount Morris *NY* U.S.A. **176** H3
Mount Nebo U.S.A. **176** E7
Mount Olivet U.S.A. **176** A7
Mount Orab U.S.A. **176** B6
Mount Pearl Canada **169** K4
Mount Perry Australia **149** F5
Mount Pierre Aboriginal Reserve Australia **150** D3
Mount Pleasant Canada **169** H4
Mount Pleasant *IA* U.S.A. **174** B3
Mount Pleasant *MI* U.S.A. **173** I7
Mount Pleasant *PA* U.S.A. **176** F5
Mount Pleasant *SC* U.S.A. **175** E5
Mount Pleasant *TX* U.S.A. **179** D5
Mount Pleasant *UT* U.S.A. **183** M2
Mount Rainier National Park U.S.A. **180** B3
Mount Remarkable National Park Australia **146** C3
Mount Revelstoke National Park Canada **166** G5
Mount Richmond Forest Park *nature res.* N.Z. **152** H9
Mount Robson Provincial Park Canada **166** G4
UNESCO World Heritage Site
Mount Rogers National Recreation Area *park* U.S.A. **176** D9
Mount Rupert S. Africa **133** I5
Mount St Helens National Volcanic Monument *nat. park* U.S.A. **180** B3
Mount Sanford Australia **148** A3
Mount's Bay U.K. **47** G13
Mount Shasta U.S.A. **180** B4
Mount Somers N.Z. **153** F11
Mount Sterling *IL* U.S.A. **174** B4
Mount Sterling *KY* U.S.A. **176** B7
Mount Sterling *OH* U.S.A. **176** B6
Mount Stewart S. Africa **133** I10
Mount Storm U.S.A. **176** F6
Mount Surprise Australia **149** E3
Mount Upton U.S.A. **177** J3
Mount Vernon Australia **150** B5
Mount Vernon *GA* U.S.A. **175** D5
Mount Vernon *IA* U.S.A. **172** B9
Mount Vernon *IL* U.S.A. **174** B4
Mount Vernon *IN* U.S.A. **174** C4
Mount Vernon *KY* U.S.A. **176** A8
Mount Vernon *MO* U.S.A. **178** D4
Mount Vernon *OH* U.S.A. **176** C5
Mount Vernon *TX* U.S.A. **179** D5
Mount Vernon *WA* U.S.A. **180** B2
Mount Wedge Australia **148** B4
Mount Welcome Aboriginal Reserve Australia **150** B4
Mount William National Park Australia **147** F5
Mount Willoughby Australia **146** B1
Moura Australia **149** F5
Moura Brazil **199** F5
Moura *r.* Brazil **200** B1
Moura Port. **54** D6
Mourão Port. **54** D6
Mouraya Chad **126** D2
Mourdi, Dépression du *depr.* Chad **120** D5
Mourdiah Mali **124** D3
Mourenx France **50** F9
Mourne Mountains *hills* U.K. **47** F9
Mourre de Chanier *mt.* France **51** M9
Mourtzeflos, Akra *pt* Greece **59** G9
Mousa *i.* U.K. **46** K3
Mouscron Belgium **51** J2
Mousgougou Chad **126** C2
Mousie U.S.A. **176** C8
Moussafoyo Chad **126** C2
Moussoro Chad **120** C6
Moutamba Congo **126** B5
Mouth of Wilson U.S.A. **176** D9
Moûtiers France **51** M7
Moutohora Island N.Z. **152** K5
also known as Whale Island; *formerly known as* Motuhora Island
Moutong Indon. **75** B2
Moutourwa Cameroon **125** I4
Mouydir, Monts du *plat.* Alg. **123** F4
Mouyondzi Congo **126** B5
Mouzaki Greece **59** C9
Mouzarak Chad **120** B6
Mouzon France **51** L3
Movas Mex. **184** C2
Movila Miresii Romania **58** I3
Movileni Romania **58** F4
Mowanjum Aboriginal Reserve Australia **150** C3
Mowbullan, Mount Australia **149** F5
Mowchadz' Belarus **42** G8
Moxahala U.S.A. **176** C6
Moxey Town Bahamas **186** D1
Moxico *prov.* Angola **127** C8
Moy *r.* Ireland **47** C9
Moyahua Mex. **185** E4
Moyale Eth. **128** C4
Moyamba Sierra Leone **124** B4
Moyen Atlas *mts* Morocco **122** D2
English form Middle Atlas
Moyen-Chari *pref.* Chad **126** C2
Moyen Congo *country* Africa *see* **Congo**
Moyeni Lesotho **133** L7
also known as Quthing
Moyenne-Guinée *admin. reg.* Guinea **124** B4
Moyen-Ogooué *prov.* Gabon **126** A5
Moynalyk Rus. Fed. **88** F1
Moynaq Uzbek. *see* **Mo'ynoq**
Mo'ynoq Uzbek. **102** D4
also spelt Moynaq *or* Muynoq
Moyo *i.* Indon. **77** G5
Moyo Uganda **128** A4
Moyobamba Peru **198** B6
Moyowosi *r.* Tanz. **129** A6
Møysalen *mt.* Norway **44** K1
Moyto Chad **120** C6
Moyu China **89** B4
formerly known as Karakax
Moyum *waterhole* Kenya **128** C4
Moyynkum *Zhambylskaya Oblast'* Kazakh. **103** H3
formerly known as Furmanovka
Moyynkum *Zhambylskaya Oblast'* Kazakh. **103** H4
Moyynkum, Peski *des.* Kazakh. **103** F3
also known as Moinkum
Moyynkum, Peski *des.* Kazakh. **103** G3
Moyynty Kazakh. **103** H3
formerly spelt Mointy
►**Mozambique** *country* Africa **131** G4
spelt Moçambique in Portuguese; *historically known as* Portuguese East Africa
►►**114–115 Africa** Countries
Mozambique Channel *strait* Africa **131** I4
Mozarlândia Brazil **206** C1
Mozdok Rus. Fed. **41** H8
Mozdūrān Iran **101** E2
Mozelle U.S.A. **176** B8
Mozhaysk Rus. Fed. **43** R6
Mozhga Rus. Fed. **40** J4
Mozhong China **86** A1
Mozo Myanmar **78** A3
Mozyr' Belarus *see* **Mazyr**
Mpal Senegal **124** A3
formerly spelt Pal
Mpanda Tanz. **129** A6
Mpandamatenga Botswana **131** E3
Mpande Zambia **127** F7
Mpé Congo **126** B5
Mpemvana S. Africa **133** O4
Mpessoba Mali **124** D3
Mpigi Uganda **128** B4
Mpika Zambia **127** F7
Mpoko *r.* Cent. Afr. Rep. **126** C3
Mpolweni S. Africa **133** O6
Mpongwe Zambia **127** F8
Mporokoso Zambia **127** F7
Mposa S. Africa **133** Q5
Mpouya Congo **126** C5
Mpui Tanz. **129** A7
Mpulungu Zambia **127** F7
Mpumalanga S. Africa **133** O6
Mpumalanga *prov.* S. Africa **133** N3
formerly known as Eastern Transvaal
Mpwapwa Tanz. **129** C6
Mqanduli S. Africa **133** M8
Mqinvartsveri *mt.* Georgia/Rus. Fed. *see* **Kazbek**
Mrągowo Poland **49** S2
Mrauk-U Myanmar **78** A3
Mrewa Zimbabwe *see* **Murehwa**
Mrežnica *r.* Croatia **56** H3
Mrkonjić-Grad Bos.-Herz. **56** J4
Mrocza Poland **49** O2
Mroga *r.* Poland **49** Q4
M'Saken Tunisia **57** C13
Msambweni Kenya **129** C6
Msata Tanz. **129** C6
Mshinskaya Rus. Fed. **43** K2
M'Sila Alg. **123** G2
Msta Rus. Fed. **43** P4
Msta *r.* Rus. Fed. **43** M3
Mstinskiy Most Rus. Fed. **43** N3
Mstislavl' Belarus *see* **Mstsislaw**
Mstsislaw Belarus **43** M7
also spelt Mstislavl'
Msunduze *r.* S. Africa **133** Q4
Mszana Dolna Poland **49** R6
Mtama Tanz. **129** C7
Mt'at'ushet'is Nakrdzali *nature res.* Georgia **107** F2
Mtelo Kenya **128** B4
Mtera Reservoir Tanz. **129** B6
Mtoko Zimbabwe *see* **Mutoko**
Mtonjaneni S. Africa **133** P5
Mtorashanga Zimbabwe *see* **Mutorashanga**
Mtsensk Rus. Fed. **43** R8
Mts'khet'a Georgia **107** F2
UNESCO World Heritage Site
Mtukula Tanz. **129** C7
Mtunzini S. Africa **133** P5
Mtwara Tanz. **129** D7
Mtwara *admin. reg.* Tanz. **129** C7
Mu *r.* Myanmar **78** A3
Mu *hill* Port. **54** C7
Mu'āb, Jibāl *reg.* Jordan *see* **Moab**
Muaguide Moz. **129** C8
Mualama Moz. **131** H3
Muana Brazil **202** B2
Muanda Dem. Rep. Congo **127** B6
Muang Không Laos **79** D5
Muang Khôngxédôn Laos **79** D5
Muang Pakbeng Laos **78** C4
Muang Phin Laos **78** D4
Muang Phôn-Hông Laos **78** C4
Muang Sam Sip Thai. **79** D5
Muang Sing Laos **78** C3
Muang Thai *country* Asia *see* **Thailand**
Muang Vangviang Laos **78** C4
Muanza Moz. **131** G3
Muar Malaysia **76** C2
Muar *r.* Malaysia **76** C2
Muara Brunei **77** F1
Muaraancalong Indon. **77** G2
Muaraatap Indon. **77** G2
Muarabeliti Indon. **76** C3
Muarabungo Indon. **76** C3
Muaradua Indon. **76** D4
Muaraenim Indon. **76** C3
Muarainu Indon. **77** F3
Muarakaman Indon. **77** G3
Muaralesan Indon. **77** G2
Muararupit Indon. **76** C3
Muarasoma Indon. **76** B2
Muaras Reef *reef* Indon. **75** A2
Muaratebo Indon. **76** C3
Muaratembesi Indon. **76** C3
Muarateweh Indon. **77** F3
Muara Tuang *Sarawak* Malaysia *see* **Kota Samarahan**
Muarawahau Indon. **77** G2
Muari, Ras *pt* Pak. **101** F5
also known as Monze, Cape
Mu'aylā, Wādī al *watercourse* Iraq **109** M5
Mu'ayqil, Khashm al *hill* Saudi Arabia **105** E2
Muazzam India **96** B3
Mubārak, Jabal *mt.* Jordan/Saudi Arabia **108** G8
Mubarakpur India **97** D4
Mubarek Uzbek. *see* **Muborak**
Mubarraz *well* Saudi Arabia **107** E5
Mubende Uganda **128** A4
Mubi Nigeria **125** I4
Muborak Uzbek. **103** F5
also spelt Mubarek
Mubur *i.* Indon. **77** D2
Mucaba Angola **127** B6
Mucajá Brazil **199** G5
Mucajaí *r.* Brazil **199** F4
Mucajaí, Serra do *mts* Brazil **199** F4
Mucalic *r.* Canada **169** H1
Mučanj *mt.* Serb. and Mont. **58** B5
Mucheng China *see* **Wuzhi**
Muchinga Escarpment Zambia **127** F8
Muchiri Bol. **201** E4
Muchuan China **86** B2
also known as Muxi
Muck *i.* U.K. **46** F7
Muckadilla Australia **149** F5
Muckaty Aboriginal Land *res.* Australia **148** B3
Muco *r.* Col. **198** D3
Mucojo Moz. **129** D8
Muconda Angola **127** D7
formerly known as Nova Chaves
Mucope Angola **127** B9
Mucubela Moz. **131** H3
Mucucuaú *r.* Brazil **199** F5
Mucuim *r.* Brazil **199** E6
Mucumbura Moz. **131** F3
Mucundi Angola **127** C9
Mucunha Angola **127** C8
Mucupia Moz. **131** H3
Mucur Turkey **106** C3
Mucura Brazil **199** F5
Mucuri Brazil **203** E6
Mucuri *r.* Brazil **207** N5
Mucurici Brazil **207** M5
Mucuripe Brazil **198** D5
Mucuripe, Ponta de *pt* Brazil **202** E2
Mucusso, Coutada Pública do *nature res.* Angola **127** D9
Mucussueje Angola **127** D7
Muda *r.* Malaysia **76** C1
Mudabidri India **94** B3
Mudanjiang China **82** C3
Mudan Jiang *r.* China **82** C3
Mudan Ling *mts* China **82** B4
Mudanya Turkey **106** B2
Mudayrah Kuwait **107** F5
Mudaysīsāt, Jabal al *hill* Jordan **108** H6
Muddebihal India **94** C2
Muddus nationalpark *nat. park* Sweden **44** L2
Muddy *r.* U.S.A. **183** J5
Muddy Boggy Creek *r.* U.S.A. **179** D5
Muddy Creek *r.* U.S.A. **183** N3
Muddy Gap *pass* U.S.A. **180** F4
Muddy Peak U.S.A. **183** J5
Mūd-e Dahanāb Iran **101** D3
Muden S. Africa **133** O5
Mudgal India **94** C3
Mudgee Australia **147** F3
Mudhol India **94** B2
Mudigere India **94** B3
Mudjatik *r.* Canada **167** J3
Mudkhed India **94** C2
Mudki India **96** B3
Mud Lake U.S.A. **183** G4
Mudon Myanmar **78** B4
Mudraya *country* Africa *see* **Egypt**
Mudug *admin. reg.* Somalia **128** E3
Mudukani Tanz. **129** B5
Mudumu National Park Namibia **130** D3
Mudurnu Turkey **106** B2
Mud'yuga Rus. Fed. **40** F3
Muecate Moz. **131** H2
Mueda Moz. **129** C7
Mueller Range *hills* Australia **150** D3
Muende Moz. **131** G2
formerly known as Vila Caldas Xavier
Muerto, Mar *lag.* Mex. **185** G5
Muertos Cays *is* Bahamas **186** C1
Muftah *well* Sudan **121** G4
Muftyuga Rus. Fed. **40** H2
Mufulira Zambia **127** F8
Mufumbwe Zambia **127** E8
Mufu Shan *mts* China **87** E2
Muğan Düzü *lowland* Azer. **107** G3
Muge *r.* Port. **54** C5
Mugeba Moz. **131** H3
Mughalbhin Pak. *see* **Jati**
Mughal Sarai India **97** D4
Mūghār Iran **100** C3
Mughayrā' Saudi Arabia **107** D5
Mughayrā' *well* Saudi Arabia **105** D2
Mughshin Oman **105** F4
Mughsu *r.* Tajik. **101** G2
also spelt Muksu
Mugia Spain *see* **Muxía**
Mugila, Monts *mts* Dem. Rep. Congo **127** F6
Muğla Turkey **106** B3
Muğla *prov.* Turkey **59** J11
Mugodzharskoye Kazakh. **102** D2
Mugodzhary, Gory *mts* Kazakh. **102** D3
Mug Qu *r.* China **80** E6
Muguia Moz. **129** C8
Mugu Karnali *r.* Nepal **97** D3
Mugur-Aksy Rus. Fed. **84** A1
Mugxung China **89** F5
Mūḩ, Sabkhat *imp. l.* Syria **109** J3
Muhagiriya Sudan **126** E2
Muhala China *see* **Yutian**
Muhala Dem. Rep. Congo **127** F6
Muḩammad, Ra's *pt* Egypt **121** G3
Muhammadabad India **97** D4
Muhammad Qol Sudan **121** H4
Muhammarah Iran *see* **Khorramshahr**
Muhashsham, Wādī al *watercourse* Egypt **108** F7
Muḩayriqah Saudi Arabia **105** D3
Muḩaysh, Wādī al *watercourse* Jordan **108** H8
Muḩaywīr *tourist site* Iraq **109** M4
Muheza Tanz. **129** C6
Mühlacker Germany **48** F7
Mühlberg Germany **49** K4
Mühldorf am Inn Germany **49** J7
Mühlhausen (Thüringen) Germany **48** H4
Mühlig-Hofmann Mountains Antarctica **223** A2
Muhos Fin. **44** N2
Muḩradah Syria **109** H2
Muhu *i.* Estonia **42** E3
Muhukuru Tanz. **129** B7
Muhula Moz. **131** H2
Muhulu Dem. Rep. Congo **126** E5
Mui Eth. **128** B3
Mui Bai Bung *c.* Vietnam *see* **Ca Mau, Mui**
Muidumbe Moz. **129** C7
Muiliyk *i.* Indon. **75** D3
Muineachán Ireland *see* **Monaghan**
Muine Bheag Ireland **47** F11
Muir U.S.A. **173** I8
Muir Glacier Canada/U.S.A. **166** B3
Muirkirk U.K. **46** H8
Muisne Ecuador **198** B4
Muite Moz. **131** H2
Mūjān, Chāh-e *well* Iran **100** C3
Mujeres, Isla *i.* Mex. **186** B2
Muji China **88** B4
Mujong *r.* *Sarawak* Malaysia **77** F2
Muju S. Korea **83** B5
Mujuí Joboti Brazil **199** H5
Mukačevo Ukr. *see* **Mukacheve**
Mukacheve Ukr. **49** T7
also spelt Mukachevo *or* Mukačevo; *historically known as* Munkács
Mukachevo Ukr. *see* **Mukacheve**
Mukah *Sarawak* Malaysia **77** F2
Mukah *r.* *Sarawak* Malaysia **77** F2
Mukalla Yemen **105** E5
also spelt Al Mukallā
Mukandgarh India **96** B4
Mukandwara India **96** C4
also spelt Mokundurra
Mukanga Dem. Rep. Congo **127** D6
Mukassir, Banī *des.* Saudi Arabia **105** E3
Mukawa Japan **90** G3
Mu-kawa *r.* Japan **90** G3
Mukawwar, Gezirat *i.* Sudan **121** H4
Mukdahan Thai. **78** D4
Mukden China *see* **Shenyang**
Mukerian India **96** B3
Muketei *r.* Canada **168** C2
Mukhen Rus. Fed. **82** E2
Mukhino Rus. Fed. **82** B1
Mukhorshibir' Rus. Fed. **85** F1
Mukhtuya Rus. Fed. *see* **Lensk**
Mukinbudin Australia **151** B6
Mu Ko Chang Marine National Park Thai. **79** C6
Mukomuko Indon. **76** C3
Mukono Uganda **128** B4
Mukoshi Zambia **127** F7
Mukry Turkm. **103** F5
Muksu *r.* Tajik. *see* **Mughsu**
Muktinath Nepal **97** D3
Muktsar India **96** B3
Mukuku Zambia **127** F8
Mukumbura Zimbabwe **131** F3
formerly spelt Mkumvura
Mukunsa Zambia **127** F7
Mukur *Atyrauskaya Oblast'* Kazakh. **102** C3
also spelt Muqyr
Mukur *Vostochnyy Kazakhstan* Kazakh. **103** J2
Mukutawa *r.* Canada **167** L4
Mukwonago U.S.A. **172** E8
Mul India **94** C1
Mula *r.* India **94** B2
Mula *r.* Pak. **101** F4
Mula Spain **55** J6
Mulaku *atoll* Maldives *see* **Mulaku Atoll**
Mulaku Atoll Maldives **93** D10
formerly known as Mulaku
Mulaly Kazakh. **103** I3
also spelt Molaly
Mulan China **82** C3
Mulanay Phil. **74** B3
Mulanje Malawi **129** B9
Mulapula, Lake *salt flat* Australia **146** C2
Mula-tupo Panama **186** D5
Mulayḩ *salt pan* Saudi Arabia **109** J8
Mulayjah Saudi Arabia **105** E2
Mulayz, Wādī al *watercourse* Egypt **108** E7
Mulbagal India **94** C3
Mulbekh Jammu and Kashmir **96** C2
Mulberry *AR* U.S.A. **179** D5
Mulberry *NC* U.S.A. **176** D9
Mulchatna *r.* U.S.A. **164** D3
Mulchén Chile **204** B5
Mulde *r.* Germany **49** J4
Muleba Tanz. **128** A5
Mule Creek U.S.A. **180** F4
Mulegé Mex. **184** B3
Mulekatembo Zambia **129** B7
Mules *i.* Indon. **75** B5
Muleshoe U.S.A. **179** B5
Mulevala Moz. **131** H3
Mulga Park Australia **148** A5
Mulgathing Australia **146** B2
Mulhacén *mt.* Spain **55** H7
Mülhausen France *see* **Mulhouse**
Mülheim an der Ruhr Germany **48** D4
Mulhouse France **51** N5
also known as Mülhausen
Muli China **86** B3
also known as Qiaowa; *formerly known as* Bowa
Muli Rus. Fed. *see* **Vysokogorniy**
Mulilansolo Zambia **129** B7
Muling *Heilong.* China **82** C3
formerly known as Bamiantong
Muling *Heilong.* China **82** C3
Muling He *r.* China **82** D3
Mull *i.* U.K. **46** G7
Mulla Ali Iran **100** B2
Mullaaxe Beyle Somalia **128** E2
Mullaittivu Sri Lanka **94** D4
Muller *watercourse* Australia **148** B4
Muller, Pegunungan *mts* Indon. **77** F2
Mullett Lake U.S.A. **173** I5
Mullewa Australia **151** A6
Müllheim Germany **48** E8
Mullica *r.* U.S.A. **177** K6
Mulligan *watercourse* Australia **148** C5
Mullingar Ireland **47** E10
also known as An Muileann gCearr
Mullins U.S.A. **175** E5
Mull of Galloway *c.* U.K. **47** H9
Mull of Kintyre *hd* U.K. **47** G8
Mull of Oa *hd* U.K. **46** F8
Müllrose Germany **49** L3
Mullsjö Sweden **45** K4
Mullutu laht *l.* Estonia **42** D3
Mulobezi Zambia **127** E9
Mulondo Angola **127** B8
Mulonga Plain Zambia **127** D9
Mulongo Dem. Rep. Congo **127** E6
Mulsanne France **50** G5
Mulshi Lake India **94** B2
Multai India **96** C5
Mūltān Iran **101** E5
Multan Pak. **101** G4
Multia Fin. **44** N3
Mulu, Gunung *mt.* *Sarawak* Malaysia **77** F1
Mulug India **94** C2
Mulumbe, Monts *mts* Dem. Rep. Congo **127** E7
Mulurulu Lake Australia **147** D3
Mulūşī, Wādī al *watercourse* Iraq **109** K4
Muma Dem. Rep. Congo **126** D4
Mūmān Iran **101** E5

►**Mumbai** India **94** B2
2nd most populous city Asia, and 4th in the world. Formerly known as Bombay.
UNESCO World Heritage Site
►►**18–19 World** Cities

Mumbeji Zambia **127** D8
Mumbondo Angola **127** B7
Mumbwa Zambia **127** E8
Mumbwi Tanz. **129** C6
Mume Dem. Rep. Congo **127** E7
Muminabad Tajik. *see* **Leningrad**
Mŭ'minobod Tajik. *see* **Leningrad**
Mumoma Dem. Rep. Congo **127** D6
Mumra Rus. Fed. **102** A3
Mun, Mae Nam *r.* Thai. **79** D5
Muna *i.* Indon. **75** B4
Muna Mex. **185** H4
Muna *r.* Rus. Fed. **39** M3
Munabao Pak. **101** G5
Munaðarnes Iceland **44** [inset] B2
Munagala India **94** C2
Munakata Japan **91** B8
Munayjah, Jabal *mts* Egypt/Sudan **104** A3
Munayly Kazakh. **102** C3
Munayshy Kazakh. **102** C4
Münchberg Germany **48** I5
München Germany *see* **Munich**
München-Gladbach Germany *see* **Mönchengladbach**
Munchique, Parque Nacional *nat. park* Col. **198** B4
Muncho Lake Canada **166** E3
Muncho Lake Provincial Park Canada **166** E3
Munch'ŏn N. Korea **83** B5
Muncie U.S.A. **174** C3
Muncoonie West, Lake *salt flat* Australia **148** C5
Muncy U.S.A. **177** I4
Munda Solomon Is **145** E2
Mundel Lake Sri Lanka **94** C5
Mundemba Cameroon **125** H5
Mundiwindi Australia **150** C4
Mundjura Creek *r.* Australia **149** D3
Mundo *r.* Spain **55** J6
Mundo Novo Brazil **202** D4
Mundra India **96** A5
Mundrabilla Australia **151** D6
Munds Park U.S.A. **183** M7
Mundubbera Australia **149** F5
Mundwa India **96** B4
Muneru *r.* India **94** D2
Munfordville U.S.A. **174** C4
Mungallala Australia **149** E5
Mungallala Creek *r.* Australia **147** E2
Mungana Australia **149** E3
Mungaoli India **96** C4
Mungári Moz. **131** G3
Mungaroona Range Nature Reserve Australia **150** B4
Mungbere Dem. Rep. Congo **126** F4
Mungeli India **97** D5
Munger India **97** E4
formerly spelt Monghyr
Munger U.S.A. **173** J7
Mungeranie Australia **146** C2
Mu Nggava *i.* Solomon Is *see* **Rennell**
Mungguresak, Tanjung *pt* Indon. **77** E2
Mungilli Aboriginal Reserve Australia **151** D5
Mungindi Australia **147** F2
Mungkarta Aboriginal Land *res.* Australia **148** B4
Mungo Angola **127** C7
Mungo, Lake Australia **147** D3
Mungo National Park Australia **147** D3
Mungwi Zambia **127** F7
Mun'gyŏng S. Korea **83** B5
Munhango Angola **127** C8
Munhino Angola **127** B8
Munich Germany **48** I7
also known as München
Munising U.S.A. **172** G4
Muniz Freire Brazil **207** L7
Munkács Ukr. *see* **Mukacheve**
Munkedal Sweden **45** J4
Munkflohögen Sweden **44** K3
Munku-Sardyk, Gora *mt.* Mongolia/Rus. Fed. **84** D1
Munro, Mount Australia **147** F5
Munse Indon. **75** B4
Munshiganj Bangl. **97** F5
Münsingen Switz. **51** N6
Münster *Niedersachsen* Germany **48** H3
Münster *Nordrhein-Westfalen* Germany **48** E4
Munster *reg.* Ireland **47** D11
Münsterland *reg.* Germany **48** E4
Münster-Osnabrück *airport* Germany **48** E3
Muntadgin Australia **151** B6
Munte Indon. **75** A2
Muntele Mare, Vârful *mt.* Romania **58** E2
Munteni Romania **58** I3
Mununga Zambia **127** F7
Munyal-Par *sea feature* India *see* **Bassas de Pedro Padua Bank**
Munyati *r.* Zimbabwe **131** F3
Munyu S. Africa **133** M8
Munzur Vadisi Milli Parkı *nat. park* Turkey **107** D3
Muodoslompolo Sweden **44** M2
Muojärvi *l.* Fin. **44** O2
Muonio Fin. **44** M2
Muonioälven *r.* Fin./Sweden **44** M2
also known as Muonionjoki
Muonionjoki *r.* Fin./Sweden *see* **Muonioälven**
Mupa Angola **127** B9
Mupa, Parque Nacional da *nat. park* Angola **127** B8
Mupfure *r.* Zimbabwe **131** F3
formerly known as Umfuli
Muping China **85** I4
Muqaddam *watercourse* Sudan **121** F5
Muqaybirah Yemen **105** D5
Muqaynimah *well* Saudi Arabia **105** E3
Muqdisho Somalia *see* **Mogadishu**
Muqnīyāt Oman **105** G3
Muqshin, Wādī *r.* Oman **105** F4
Muquem Brazil **202** B5
Muqui Brazil **203** D7
Muqyr Kazakh. *see* **Mukur**
Mur *r.* Austria **49** N9
also spelt Mura
Mur *r.* Croatia/Slovenia **49** N9
also spelt Mur
Mu'r, Wādī *watercourse* Egypt **108** E9
Muradiye *Manisa* Turkey **59** I10
Muradiye *Van* Turkey **107** E3
also known as Bargıri
Murai, Tanjong *pt* Sing. **76** [inset]
Murai Reservoir Sing. **76** [inset]
Murakami Japan **90** F5
Murallón, Cerro *mt.* Chile **205** B8
Muramvya Burundi **126** F5
Muráň *r.* Slovakia **49** R7
Murang'a Kenya **128** C5
formerly known as Fort Hall
Muras Spain **54** D1
Murashi Rus. Fed. **40** I4
Murat France **51** I7
Murat *r.* Turkey **107** D3
Muratlı Turkey **106** A2
Murayama Japan **90** G5
Murayr, Jabal *hill* Saudi Arabia **104** C2
Muraysah, Ra's al *pt* Libya **120** E2
Murça Port. **54** D3
Murcheh Khvort Iran **100** B3
Murchison Australia **147** E4
Murchison *watercourse* Australia **151** A5
Murchison N.Z. **153** G9
Murchison, Mount Antarctica **223** L2
Murchison, Mount *hill* Australia **151** B5
Murchison Falls Uganda **128** A4
Murchison Falls National Park Uganda **128** A4
also known as Kabalega Falls National Park *or* Kabarega National Park
Murchison Island Canada **168** B3
Murchison Mountains N.Z. **153** B13
Murchison Range *hills* Australia **148** B4
Murcia Spain **55** J7
Murcia *aut. comm.* Spain **55** J7
Murcielagos Bay Phil. **74** B4
Mûr-de-Bretagne France **50** D4
Murdo U.S.A. **178** B3
Murdochville Canada **169** H3
Mürefte Turkey **106** A2
Muregi Nigeria **125** G4
Murehwa Zimbabwe **131** F3
formerly spelt Mrewa *or* Murewa
Mureşul *r.* Romania **58** B2
Muret France **50** H9
Murewa Zimbabwe *see* **Murehwa**
Murfjället *mt.* Norway **44** K2
Murfreesboro *AR* U.S.A. **179** D5
Murfreesboro *NC* U.S.A. **177** H9
Murfreesboro *TN* U.S.A. **174** C5
Murgab Tajik. *see* **Murghob**
Murgab Turkm. *see* **Murgap**
Murgab *r.* Turkm. *see* **Murgap**
Murgap Turkm. **103** E5
also spelt Murgab
Murgap *r.* Turkm. **103** E5
formerly spelt Murgab
Murgeni Romania **58** J2
Murge Tarantine *hills* Italy **57** J8
Murghab *r.* Afgh. **101** E3
Murghab *reg.* Afgh. **101** E3
Murgha Kibzai Pak. **101** G4
Murghob Tajik. **101** H2
also spelt Murgab
Murghob *r.* Tajik. **101** H2
Murgh Pass Afgh. **101** G3
Murgon Australia **149** F5
Murgoo Australia **151** B5
Muri *Qinghai* China **84** C4
Muri *Qinghai* China **84** D4
Muri India **97** E5
Mūrī Iran **100** D2
Muria, Gunung *mt.* Indon. **77** E4
Muriaé Brazil **203** D7
Muriege Angola **127** D7
Murih, Pulau *i.* Indon. **77** E2
Murii-dake *mt.* Japan **90** H3
Murillo Canada **172** D2
Müritz *l.* Germany **49** J2
Müritz, Nationalpark *nat. park* Germany **49** K2
Müritz-Elde-Wasserstraße *r.* Germany **48** I2
Muriwai N.Z. **152** L6
Murjek Sweden **44** M2
Murkong Selek India **97** G4
Murmansk Rus. Fed. **44** P1
Murmanskaya Oblast' *admin. div.* Rus. Fed. **44** P1
English form Murmansk Oblast
Murmanskiy Bereg *coastal area* Rus. Fed. **40** E1
Murmansk Oblast *admin. div.* Rus. Fed. *see* **Murmanskaya Oblast'**
Murmashi Rus. Fed. **44** P1
Murmino Rus. Fed. **43** V7
Muro, Capo di *c.* *Corsica* France **56** A7
Muro Lucano Italy **57** H8
Murom Rus. Fed. **40** G5
Murongo Tanz. **128** A5
Muroran Japan **90** G3
Muros Spain **54** B2
Muros e Noia, Ría de *est.* Spain **54** B2
Muroto Japan **91** D8
Muroto-zaki *pt* Japan **91** D8
Murowana Goślina Poland **49** O3
Murphy *ID* U.S.A. **180** C4
Murphy *NC* U.S.A. **174** D5
Murphys U.S.A. **182** D3
Murrah *reg.* Saudi Arabia **105** E3
Murrah, Wādī *watercourse* Egypt **108** F9
Murra Murra Australia **147** E2
Murranji Aboriginal Land *res.* Australia **148** B3
Murrat el Kubra, Buheirat *l.* Egypt *see* **Great Bitter Lake**
Murrat el Sughra, Buheirat *l.* Egypt *see* **Little Bitter Lake**

►**Murray** *r. S.A.* Australia **147** C3
3rd longest river in Oceania. Part of the longest (Murray-Darling).
►►**134–135 Oceania** Landscapes

Murray *r. W.A.* Australia **151** A7
Murray *r.* Canada **166** F3
Murray *KY* U.S.A. **174** B4
Murray *UT* U.S.A. **183** M1
Murray, Lake P.N.G. **73** J8
Murray, Lake U.S.A. **175** D5
Murray, Mount Canada **166** D2
Murray Bridge Australia **146** C3
Murray City U.S.A. **176** C6

►**Murray-Darling** *r.* Australia **144** D5
Longest river in Oceania.
►►**134–135 Oceania** Landscapes

Murray Downs Australia **148** B4
Murray Harbour Canada **169** I4
Murray Range *hills* Australia **151** E5
Murraysburg S. Africa **132** H8

Murray Sunset National Park Australia **146** D3
Murrayville Australia **146** D3
Murree Pak. **101** H3
Murrieta U.S.A. **183** G8
Murroa Moz. **131** H3

►**Murrumbidgee** *r.* Australia **147** D3
4th longest river in Oceania.
►►**134–135 Oceania** Landscapes

Murrupula Moz. **131** H2
Murrurundi Australia **147** F2
Murshidabad India **97** F4
Murska Sobota Slovenia **56** I2
Murtajapur India **94** C1
Murten Switz. **51** N6
Murter Croatia **56** H5
Murter *i.* Croatia **56** H5
Murtoa Australia **147** D4
Murtovaara Fin. **44** O2
Muru *r.* Brazil **200** C2
Murua *i.* P.N.G. *see* **Woodlark Island**
Murud India **94** B2
Murud, Gunung *mt.* Indon. **77** F2
Murui *r.* Indon. **77** F3
Muruin Sum Shuiku *resr* China **85** I3
Murung *r.* Indon. **77** F3
Murung *r.* Indon. **77** F3
Muruntov Uzbek. **103** F4
Murupara N.Z. **152** K6
Mururoa *atoll* Fr. Polynesia **221** J7
also spelt Moruroa; *historically known as* Osnaburg
Muruti, Ilha *i.* Brazil **199** I5
Murviedro Spain *see* **Sagunto**
Murwānī, Wādī *watercourse* Saudi Arabia **104** B3
Murwara India **96** D5
Murwillumbah Australia **147** G2
Murygino *Kirovskaya Oblast'* Rus. Fed. **40** I4
Murygino *Smolenskaya Oblast'* Rus. Fed. **43** N7
Mürz *r.* Austria **49** M8
Murzechirla Turkm. **102** E5
formerly spelt Mirzachirla
Murzūq Libya **120** B3
Murzuq, Ḥamādat *plat.* Libya **120** B3
Murzūq, Idhān *des.* Libya **120** B3
Mürzzuschlag Austria **49** M8
Muş Turkey **107** E3
Musa Dem. Rep. Congo **126** C4
Mūša *r.* Latvia/Lith. **42** F5
Mūsa *r.* Latvia/Lith. **42** F5
Mûsa, Gebel *mt.* Egypt *see* **Mūsá, Jabal**
Mūsá, Jabal *mt.* Egypt **108** E9
also known as Mûsa, Gebel; *English form* Sinai, Mount
Mūsā, Khowr-e *b.* Iran **100** B4
Musa Āli Terara *vol.* Africa **128** D1
Musabani India **97** E5
Musabeyli Turkey **109** H1
Muşabih Saudi Arabia **104** C4
Musa Khel Bazar Pak. **101** G4
Musala *mt.* Bulg. **58** E6
Musala *i.* Indon. **76** B2
Musalı Turkey **108** F1
Musan N. Korea **82** C4
Musandam *admin. reg.* Oman **105** G2
Musandam Peninsula Oman/U.A.E. **105** G2
Mūsá Qal'eh, Rūd-e *r.* Afgh. **101** F3
Musay'īd Qatar *see* **Umm Sa'id**
Musaymir Yemen **104** D5
Musbat *well* Sudan **120** E6

►**Muscat** Oman **105** G3
Capital of Oman. Also spelt Masqaţ.

Muscat *reg.* Oman *see* **Masqaţ**
Muscat and Oman *country* Asia *see* **Oman**
Muscatine U.S.A. **174** B3
Muscoda U.S.A. **172** C7
Muscongus Bay U.S.A. **177** P2
Musė *r.* Lith. **42** F7
Musgrave Australia **149** D2
Musgrave, Mount N.Z. **153** E11
Musgrave Harbour Canada **169** K3
Musgrave Ranges *mts* Australia **148** A5
Mūshakī Afgh. **101** G3
Mushandike Sanctuary *nature res.* Zimbabwe **127** F10
Mushāsh al Kabid *well* Jordan **109** H8
Mushash Dabl *well* Saudi Arabia **109** H9
Mushāsh Muḍayyān *well* Saudi Arabia **109** J9
Mushaynīqah *well* Yemen **105** D4
Mushayyish, Wādī al *watercourse* Jordan **108** H7
Mushenge Dem. Rep. Congo **126** D6
Mushie Dem. Rep. Congo **126** C5
Mushin Nigeria **125** F5
Musi *r.* India **94** C2
Musi *r.* Indon. **76** D3
Musica *mt.* Macedonia **58** C7
Music Mountain U.S.A. **183** K6
Musikot Nepal **97** D3
Musina S. Africa **131** F4
Musinia Peak U.S.A. **183** M2
Muskeg *r.* Canada **166** F2
Muskeget Channel U.S.A. **177** O4
Muskegon U.S.A. **172** G7
Muskegon *r.* U.S.A. **172** G7
Muskegon Heights U.S.A. **172** G7
Muskeg River Canada **166** G4
Muskingum *r.* U.S.A. **176** D6
Muskogee U.S.A. **179** D5
Muskoka Canada **173** N6
Muskoka, Lake Canada **168** E4
Muskrat Dam Lake Canada **168** B2
Muskwa *r.* Canada **166** F3
Muslimbagh Pak. **101** F4
Muslim-Croat Federation *aut. div.* Bos.-Herz. *see* **Federacija Bosna i Hercegovina**
Musmar Sudan **121** G5
Musoma Tanz. **128** B5
Musombe Tanz. **129** B6
Musquanousse, Lac *l.* Canada **169** I3
Musquaro Canada **169** I3
Musquaro, Lac *l.* Canada **169** I3
Mussau Island P.N.G. **145** D2
Musselburgh U.K. **46** I8
Musselshell *r.* U.S.A. **180** F3
Mussende Angola **127** C7
Musserra Angola **127** B6
Mussidan France **50** G7
Mussolo Angola **127** C7
Mussoorie India **96** C3
Mussuma Angola **127** D8
Mussuma *r.* Angola **127** D8
Mustafabad India **97** D4
Mustafakemalpaşa Turkey **106** B2
Mustahīl Eth. **128** E3
Müstair Switz. **48** H9
UNESCO World Heritage Site
Mustamaa *i.* Fin. **42** I1
Mustang Draw *watercourse* U.S.A. **179** B6
Mustau, Gora *mt.* China **88** D2
Mustayevo Rus. Fed. **102** C2
Musters, Lago *l.* Arg. **205** C7
Mustique *i.* St Vincent **187** H4
Mustjala Estonia **42** D3
Mustjõgi *r.* Estonia **42** H4
Mustla Estonia **42** G3
Mustvee Estonia **42** H3
Musu-dan *pt* N. Korea **83** C4
Muswellbrook Australia **147** F3
Mūţ Egypt **121** F3
Mut Turkey **106** C3
Mutá, Ponta do *pt* Brazil **202** E5
Mutanda Zambia **127** E8
Mutare Zimbabwe **131** G3
formerly spelt Umtali
Mutarjim, Khashm *hill* Saudi Arabia **105** D3
Mutayr *reg.* Saudi Arabia **105** D2
Mutina Italy *see* **Modena**
Mu'tiq, Jabal *mts* Egypt **104** A2
Mutis Col. **198** B3
Mutis, Gunung *mt.* Indon. **75** C5
Mutnyy Materik Rus. Fed. **40** J2
Mutoko Zimbabwe **131** G3
formerly spelt Mtoko
Mutombo Dem. Rep. Congo **127** D6
Mutooroo Australia **146** D3
Mutorashanga Zimbabwe **131** F3
formerly spelt Mtorashanga
Mutsamudu Comoros **129** E8
Mutshatsha Dem. Rep. Congo **127** E7
Mutsu Japan **90** G4
Mutsu-wan *b.* Japan **90** G4
Muttaburra Australia **149** E4
Muttukuru India **94** D3
Muttupet India **94** C4
Mutuali Moz. **131** H2
Mutum Brazil **207** L6
Mutum *r.* Brazil **198** D6
Mutum Biyu Nigeria **125** H4
Mutumparaná Brazil **200** D2
Mutungu-Tari Dem. Rep. Congo **127** C6
Mutunópolis Brazil **202** B5
Mutur Sri Lanka **94** D4
Muuga Estonia **42** H2
Muurame Fin. **45** N3
Muurla Fin. **42** E1
Muurola Fin. **44** N2
Mu Us Shamo *des.* China **85** F4
Muxaluando Angola **127** B7
formerly known as General Freire
Muxi China *see* **Muchuan**
Muxía Spain **54** B1
also spelt Mugia
Muxima Angola **127** B7
Muyezerskiy Rus. Fed. **44** P3
Muyinga Burundi **126** F5
Muynoq Uzbek. *see* **Mo'ynoq**
Muyombe Zambia **129** B7
Muyuka Cameroon **125** H5
Muyumba Dem. Rep. Congo **127** E6
Muyuping China **87** D2
Muzaffarabad Pak. **101** H3
Muzaffargarh Pak. **101** G4
Muzaffarnagar India **96** C3
Muzaffarpur India **97** E4
Muzamane Moz. **131** G4
Muzambinho Brazil **206** G8
Muzat He *r.* China **88** C3
Muzbel', Uval *hills* Kazakh. **102** C4
Muze Moz. **131** F2
Muzillac France **50** D5
Mūzīn Iran **101** E5
Muzon, Cape U.S.A. **166** C4
Múzquiz Mex. **185** E3
Muztag *mt.* China **89** C5
Muz Tag *mt.* China **89** D4
Muztagata *mt.* China **88** A4
Muztor Kyrg. *see* **Toktogul**
Mvadi Gabon **126** B4
Mvangan Cameroon **125** H6
Mvolo Sudan **126** F3
Mvomero Tanz. **129** C6
Mvoung *r.* Gabon **126** B4
Mvouti Congo **126** B6
Mvuma Zimbabwe **131** F3
formerly spelt Umvuma
Mwali *i.* Comoros **129** D8
also spelt Mohéli
Mwanisenga Tanz. **129** B6
Mwanya Zambia **129** B8
Mwanza Malawi **129** B8
Mwanza Tanz. **128** B5
Mwanza *admin. reg.* Tanz. **128** B5
Mwape Zambia **127** F8
Mweho Dem. Rep. Congo **126** E6
Mweka Dem. Rep. Congo **126** D6
Mwenda Zambia **127** F7
Mwene-Biji Dem. Rep. Congo **127** D7
Mwene-Ditu Dem. Rep. Congo **127** D6
Mwenezi Zimbabwe **131** F4
Mwenezi *r.* Zimbabwe **131** F4
formerly known as Nuanetsi
Mwenga Dem. Rep. Congo **126** F5
Mwereni Kenya **129** C6
Mweru, Lake Dem. Rep. Congo/Zambia **127** F7
formerly spelt Moero, Lake
Mweru Plateau Tanz. **129** C7
Mweru Wantipa, Lake Zambia **127** F7
Mweru Wantipa National Park Zambia **127** F7
Mwewa Zambia **129** A7
Mwimba Dem. Rep. Congo **127** D7
Mwingi Kenya **128** C5
Mwinilunga Zambia **127** E7
Mya, Oued *watercourse* Alg. **123** G3
Myadzyel Belarus **42** H7
Myadzyel, Vozyera *l.* Belarus **42** H7
Myaglo China **86** B2
Myaing Myanmar **78** A3
Myajlar India **96** A4
Myakishevo Rus. Fed. **43** J5
Myakit Rus. Fed. **39** P3
Myaksa Rus. Fed. **43** T3
Myall Lakes National Park Australia **147** G3
Myamoura-dake *mt.* Japan **91** B9
Myanaung Myanmar **78** A4
►**Myanmar** *country* Asia **78** A3
also known as Burma
►►**64–65 Asia** Countries
Myaretskiya Belarus **42** I6
Myatlevo Rus. Fed. **43** Q7
Myaundzha Rus. Fed. **39** O3
Myaungmya Myanmar **78** A4
Myawadi Thai. **78** B4
Mycenae *tourist site* Greece **59** D11
also known as Mikínes *or* Mykines
UNESCO World Heritage Site
Myeik Myanmar **79** B5
also known as Mergui
Myerkulavichy Belarus **43** L9
Myers U.S.A. **176** B7
Myingyan Myanmar **78** A3
Myinmoletkat *mt.* Myanmar **79** B5
Myinmu Myanmar **78** A3
Myitkyina Myanmar **78** B2
Myitson Myanmar **78** B3
Myitta Myanmar **79** B5
Myittha Myanmar **78** B3
Myittha *r.* Myanmar **95** G1
Myjava Slovakia **49** O7
Mykines *i.* Faroe Is **46** E1
Mykines *tourist site* Greece *see* **Mycenae**
Myklebostad Norway **44** K2
Mykolayiv Ukr. **41** E7
formerly spelt Nikolayev
Mykolayivka *Chernihivs'ka Oblast'* Ukr. **43** N9
Mykolayivka *Odes'ka Oblast'* Ukr. **58** L3
Mykolayivka-Novorosiys'ka Ukr. **58** K2
Mykonos Greece **59** G11
Mykonos *i.* Greece **59** G11
also spelt Míkonos
Myla Rus. Fed. **40** I2
Myla *r.* Rus. Fed. **40** I2
Mylae *Sicily* Italy *see* **Milazzo**
Mylasa Turkey *see* **Milas**
Myllykoski Fin. **42** H1
Mymensing Bangl. *see* **Mymensingh**
Mymensingh Bangl. **97** F4
also spelt Mymensing; *formerly known as* Nasirabad
Mynäjoki *r.* Fin. **42** C1
Mynämäki Fin. **45** M3
Mynaral Kazakh. **103** H3
also spelt Myngaral
Mynfontein S. Africa **132** H7
Myngaral Kazakh. *see* **Mynaral**
Myŏnggan N. Korea **82** C4
Myory Belarus **42** I6
Myotha Myanmar **78** A3
Myozin-sho *i.* Japan **91** G9
Mýrdalsjökull *ice cap* Iceland **44** [inset] C3
Mýrdalssandur *sand area* Iceland **44** [inset] C3
Myre Norway **44** K1
Myrheden Sweden **44** M2
Myrhorod Ukr. **41** E6
also spelt Mirgorod
Myrina Greece **59** G9
also spelt Mírina
Myrlandshaugen Norway **44** L1
Myrnam Canada **167** I4
Myrnopillya Ukr. **58** K2
Myronivka Ukr. **41** D6
also spelt Mironovka
Myrskylä Fin. **45** N3
Myrtle Beach U.S.A. **175** E5
Myrtle Creek U.S.A. **180** B4
Myrtleford Australia **147** E4
Myrtle Point U.S.A. **180** A4
Myrzakent Kazakh. **103** G4
formerly known as Slavyanka
Mysen Norway **45** J4
Myshanka *r.* Belarus **42** G9
Myshkin Rus. Fed. **43** T4
formerly known as Myshkino
Myshkino Rus. Fed. *see* **Myshkin**
Mys Lazareva Rus. Fed. *see* **Lazarev**
Myślenice Poland **49** Q6
Myślibórz Poland **49** L3
My Son *tourist site* Vietnam **78** E5
My Son Sanctuary *tourist site* Vietnam **78** E5
UNESCO World Heritage Site
Mysore India **94** C3
Mysore *state* India *see* **Karnataka**
Mysovsk Rus. Fed. *see* **Babushkin**
Mys Shmidta Rus. Fed. **39** S3
Myszków Poland **49** Q5
Myszyniec Poland **49** S2
Myt Rus. Fed. **40** G4
My Tho Vietnam **79** D6
Mytilene *i.* Greece *see* **Lesbos**
Mytilini Greece **59** H9
also spelt Mitilíni
Mytilinioi Greece **59** H11
Mytilini Strait Greece/Turkey **59** H9
Mytishchi Rus. Fed. **43** S6
Myton U.S.A. **183** N1
Mývatn *l.* Iceland **44** [inset] C2
Mývatn-Laxá *nature res.* Iceland **44** [inset] C2
Mývatnsöræfi *lava field* Iceland **44** [inset] C2
Myylybulak Kazakh. *see* **Milybulabk**
M'Zab Valley *tourist site* Alg. **123** F2
UNESCO World Heritage Site
Mzamomhle S. Africa **133** K8
Mže *r.* Czech Rep. **49** J6
Mziha Tanz. **129** C6
Mzimba Malawi **129** B7
Mzingwani *r.* Zimbabwe **131** F4
also spelt Umzingwani
Mzuzu Malawi **129** B7

N

Na, Nam *r.* China/Vietnam **86** B4
Naab *r.* Germany **48** J6
Nā'ālehu U.S.A. **181** [inset] Z2
Naam Sudan **126** F2
Naama Alg. **123** E2
Naantali Fin. **45** M3
also known as Nådendal
Naas Ireland **47** F10
also spelt An Nás
Näätämö Fin. **44** O1
Naba Myanmar **78** B2
Nababeep S. Africa **132** B6
Nabadwip India *see* **Navadwip**
Nabão *r.* Port. **54** C5
Nabarangapur India **95** D2
Nabas Phil. **74** B4
Nabatîyé et Tahta Lebanon **108** G4
Nabberu, Lake *salt flat* Australia **151** C5
Nabéré, Réserve Partielle de *nature res.* Burkina **124** E4
Naberera Tanz. **129** C6
Naberezhnyye Chelny Rus. Fed. **40** J5
formerly known as Brezhnev
Nabeul Tunisia **123** H1
Nabha India **96** C3
Nabileque *r.* Brazil **201** F5
Nabinagar India **97** E4
Nabire Indon. **73** I7
Nabi Younés, Ras en *pt* Lebanon **108** G4
Nāblus West Bank **108** G5
English form Nablus; *also known as* Shekhem; *also spelt* Nābulus
Nablus West Bank *see* **Nāblus**
Nabolo Ghana **125** E4
Naboomspruit S. Africa **131** F5
Nabule Myanmar **79** B5
Nābulus West Bank *see* **Nāblus**
Nacajuca Mex. **185** G5
Nacala Moz. **131** I2
formerly known as Maiaia
Nacaome Hond. **186** B4
Nacaroa Moz. **131** H2
Nacebe Bol. **200** D2
Nacha Belarus **42** F7
Nacha *r.* Belarus **43** J7
Nachalovo Rus. Fed. **102** B3
Nachingwea Tanz. **129** C7
Nachna India **96** A4
Náchod Czech Rep. **49** N5
Nachuge India **95** G4
Nacimiento Chile **204** B5
Nacimiento Reservoir U.S.A. **182** D6
Nacogdoches U.S.A. **179** D6
Nacozari de García Mex. **184** C2
Nada China *see* **Danzhou**
Nadaleen *r.* Canada **166** C2
Nadbai India **96** C4
Nådendal Fin. *see* **Naantali**
Nadezhdinka Kazakh. **103** E1
formerly known as Nadezhdinskiy
Nadezhdinskiy Kazakh. *see* **Nadezhdinka**
Nadi Fiji **145** G3
Nadiad India **96** B5
Nădlac Romania **58** B2
Nador Morocco **123** E2
Nadporozh'ye Rus. Fed. **43** P1
Nadqān, Qalamat *well* Saudi Arabia **105** E3
Nădrag Romania **58** D3
Nadūshan Iran **100** C3
Nadvirna Ukr. **41** C6
also spelt Nadvornaya
Nadvornaya Ukr. *see* **Nadvirna**
Nadym Rus. Fed. **38** H3
Naenwa India **96** B4
Næstved Denmark **45** J5
Naf *r.* Bangl./Myanmar **97** G5
Nafas, Ra's an *mt.* Egypt **108** F8
Nafāzah, 'Alam *hill* Egypt **108** A7
Nafḫa, Har *hill* Israel **108** F7
Nafpaktos Greece **59** C10
also spelt Návpaktos
Nafplio Greece **59** D11
also known as Návplion
Naft *r.* Iraq *see* **Nafţ, Āb**
Nafţ, Āb *r.* Iraq **107** F4
also known as Naft
Naftalan Azer. **100** A1
Naft-e Safīd Iran **100** B4
Naft-e Shāh Iran *see* **Naft Shahr**
Naft Shahr Iran **107** F4
formerly known as Naft-e Shāh
Nafūsah, Jabal *hills* Libya **120** A2
Nafy Saudi Arabia **104** C2
Nag, Co *l.* China **89** E5
Naga Phil. **74** B3
Nagagami *r.* Canada **168** C3
Nagagami Lake Canada **168** C3
Nagahama *Ehime* Japan **91** C8
Nagahama *Shiga* Japan **91** E7
Naga Hills India **97** G4
Naga Hills *state* India *see* **Nagaland**
Nagai Japan **90** G5
Nagaland *state* India **97** G4
formerly known as Naga Hills
Nagambie Australia **147** E4
Nagano Japan **91** F6
Nagano *pref.* Japan **91** E6
Nagaoka Japan **90** F6
Nagaon India **97** G4
also spelt Nowgong
Nagapatam India *see* **Nagapattinam**
Nagapattinam India **94** C4
formerly spelt Nagapatam
Nagar *r.* Bangl./India **97** F4
Nagar *Himachal Pradesh* India **96** C2
Nagar *Karnataka* India **94** B3
Nagar *Rajasthan* India **96** C4
Nagaram India **94** D2
Nagarjuna Sagar Reservoir India **94** C2
Nagar Karnul India **94** C2
Nagarote Nicaragua **186** B4
Nagarzê China **89** E6
Nagasaki Japan **91** A8
Nagasaki *pref.* Japan **91** A8
Naga-shima *i.* Japan **91** B8
Naga-shima *i.* Japan **91** C8
Nagato Japan **91** B7
Nagaur India **96** B4
Nagavali *r.* India **95** D2
Nagda India **96** B5
Nagercoil India **94** C4
Nagha Kalat Pak. **101** F5
Nagina India **96** C3
Nagineh Iran **100** D3
Nagma Nepal **97** D3
Nagod India **96** D4
Nagold Germany **48** F7
Nagong Chu *r.* China *see* **Parlung Zangbo**
Nagorno-Karabakh *aut. reg.* Azer. *see* **Dağlıq Qarabağ**
Nagornyy Rus. Fed. **81** K1
Nagornyy Karabakh *aut. reg.* Azer. *see* **Dağlıq Qarabağ**
Nagorsk Rus. Fed. **40** I4
Nagor'ye Rus. Fed. **43** T5
Nagoya Japan **91** E7
Nagpur India **96** C5
Nagqu China **89** F6
Nag Qu *r.* China **89** F6
Nagu Fin. **45** M3
also known as Hauvo
Nagua Dom. Rep. **187** F3
Nagurskoye Rus. Fed. **38** E1
Nagyatád Hungary **49** O9
Nagybecskerek *Vojvodina, Srbija* Serb. and Mont. *see* **Zrenjanin**
Nagyecsed Hungary **49** T8
Nagyenyed Romania *see* **Aiud**
Nagyhalász Hungary **49** S7
Nagykálló Hungary **49** S8
Nagykanizsa Hungary **49** N9
Nagykáta Hungary **49** Q8
Nagykőrös Hungary **49** Q8
Nagykunság *reg.* Hungary **49** R9
Nagyvárad Romania *see* **Oradea**
Naha Estonia **42** I3
Naha Japan **81** L7
Nahan India **96** C3
Nahang *r.* Iran/Pak. **101** E5
Nahanni Butte Canada **166** F2
also known as Tthenaagoo
Nahanni National Park Reserve Canada **166** E2
UNESCO World Heritage Site
Nahanni Range *mts* Canada **166** F2
Nahari Japan **91** D8
Nahariyya Israel **108** G4
Nahāvand Iran **100** B3
N'Ahnet, Adrar *mts* Alg. **123** F4
Nahr, Jabal *hill* Saudi Arabia **104** B2
Nahr Ouassel, Oued *watercourse* Alg. **55** N9
Nahr 'Umr Iraq **100** A4
Nahuel Huapí Arg. **204** C6
Nahuel Huapí, Parque Nacional *nat. park* Arg. **204** C6
Nahuel Mapá Arg. **204** D4
Nahuel Niyeu Arg. **204** D6
Nahunta U.S.A. **175** D6
Naic Phil. **74** B3
Naica Mex. **184** D3
Naidor *well* Tanz. **129** C6
Nā'ikah, Qarārat an *depr.* Libya **120** C3
Naikliu Indon. **75** B5
Nailung China **89** F6
Na'ima Sudan **121** G6
Naiman Qi China *see* **Daqin Tal**
Naimin Shuiquan *well* China **84** A2
Nain Canada **169** I1
Nā'īn Iran **100** C3
Naina India **97** D4
Nainital India **96** C3
Nainpur India **96** D5
Naiopué Moz. **131** H3
Nairn U.K. **46** I6
Nairn Centre Canada **173** L4

►**Nairobi** Kenya **128** C5
Capital of Kenya.

Naissaar *i.* Estonia **42** F2
Naissus *Srbija* Serb. and Mont. *see* **Niš**
Naivasha Kenya **128** C5
Naizishan China **82** B4
Najaf Iraq *see* **An Najaf**
Najaf, Baḩr an *l.* Iraq **109** P6
Najafābād Iran **100** B3
Najasa *r.* Cuba **186** D2
Najd *reg.* Saudi Arabia **104** C2
English form Nejd
Nájera Spain **55** I2
Najerilla *r.* Spain **55** I2
Naji China **85** I1
also known as Arun Qi; *formerly known as* Najitun
Najibabad India **96** C3
Najin N. Korea **82** C4
Najitun China *see* **Naji**
Najmah Saudi Arabia **105** E2
Najrān Saudi Arabia **104** D4
Najrān *prov.* Saudi Arabia **105** D4
Najrān, Wādī *watercourse* Saudi Arabia **104** D4
Nakadōri-shima *i.* Japan **91** A8
Naka-gawa *r.* Japan **91** D8
Nākālele Point U.S.A. **181** [inset] Z1
Nakama Japan **91** B8
Nakambé *watercourse* Burkina/Ghana **125** E3 *see* **White Volta**
Nakamura Japan **91** C8
Nakanbe *watercourse* Burkina/Ghana *see* **White Volta**
Nakanno Rus. Fed. **39** K3
Nakano Japan **91** F6
Nakanojō Japan **91** F6
Nakano-shima *i.* Japan **83** C7
Nakapanya Tanz. **129** C7
Nakapiripirit Uganda **128** B4
Nakasatsunai Japan **90** H3
Nakashibetsu Japan **90** I3
Nakasongola Uganda **128** B4
Nakatonbetsu-chō *hill* Japan **90** H2
Nakatsu Japan **91** B8
Nakatsugawa Japan **91** E7
Nakfa Eritrea **121** H5
Nakfa Wildlife Reserve *nature res.* Eritrea **121** H5
Nakhichevan' Azer. *see* **Naxçıvan**
Nakhl Egypt **121** G2
Nakhl-e Taqī Iran **100** C5
Nakhodka Rus. Fed. **82** D4
Nakhola India **97** G4
Nakhon Nayok Thai. **79** C5
Nakhon Pathom Thai. **79** C5
Nakhon Phanom Thai. **78** D4
Nakhon Ratchasima Thai. **79** C5
also known as Korat
Nakhon Sawan Thai. **79** C5
also known as Paknampho
Nakhon Si Thammarat Thai. **79** B6
Nakhrachi Rus. Fed. *see* **Kondinskoye**
Nakhtarana India **96** A5
Nakina *r.* Canada **166** C3
Nakło nad Notecią Poland **49** O2
Naknek U.S.A. **164** D4
Nakodar India **96** B3
Nakonde Zambia **129** B7
Nakop Namibia **132** D5
Nākotne Latvia **42** E5
Nakpanduri Ghana **125** E4
Nakskov Denmark **45** J5
Näkten *l.* Sweden **44** K3
Naktong-gang *r.* S. Korea **83** C6
Nakuru Kenya **128** C5
Nakusp Canada **166** G5
Na-lang Myanmar **78** B3
Nalayh Mongolia **85** E2
Nalázi Moz. **131** G5
Nalbari India **97** F4
Nal'chik Rus. Fed. **41** G8
Naldurg India **94** C2
Nałęczów Poland **49** T4
Nalerigu Ghana **125** E4
Nalgonda India **94** C2
Nalhati India **97** E4
Nalitabari Bangl. **97** F4
Nalkhera India **96** C5
Nallamala Hills India **94** C3
Nallıhan Turkey **106** B2
Nalolo Zambia **127** D8
Nalón *r.* Spain **50** A9
Nālūt Libya **120** A2
Namaa, Tanjung *pt* Indon. **75** D3
Namaacha Moz. **131** G5
Namacala Moz. **131** H2
Namacunde Angola **127** B9
Namacurra Moz. **131** H3
Namadgi National Park Australia **147** F3
Namahadi S. Africa **133** M4
Namak, Daryācheh-ye *salt flat* Iran **100** B3
Namak, Kavīr-e *salt flat* Iran **100** D3
Namak-e Mīqhān, Kavīr-e *salt flat* Iran **100** B3
Nāmakī *watercourse* Iran **100** C4
Namakkal India **94** C4
Namakzar-e Shadad *salt flat* Iran **100** D4
Namanga Kenya **128** C5
Namangan Uzbek. **103** G4
Namangan *admin. div.* Uzbek. **103** G4
English form Namangan Oblast; *also known as* Namangan Wiloyati
Namangan Oblast *admin. div.* Uzbek. *see* **Namangan**
Namangan Wiloyati *admin. div.* Uzbek. *see* **Namangan**
Namanyere Tanz. **129** A6
Namapa Moz. **131** H2
Namaponda Moz. **131** H2
Namaqualand *reg.* S. Africa **132** A6
Namarrói Moz. **131** H2
Namasale Uganda **128** B4
Namatanai P.N.G. **145** E2
Namba Angola **127** B7
Nambol India **97** G4
Nambour Australia **149** G5
Nambucca Heads Australia **147** G2
Nambung National Park Australia **151** A6
Năm Căn Vietnam **79** D6
Namcha Barwa *mt.* China *see* **Namjagbarwa Feng**
Namche Bazar Nepal **97** E4
Namco China **89** E6
Nam Co *salt l.* China **89** E6
Namdalen *valley* Norway **44** K2
Namdalseid Norway **44** J2
Nam Định Vietnam **78** D3
Nam Du, Quần Đao *i.* Vietnam **79** D6
Namekagon *r.* U.S.A. **172** B5
Namen Belgium *see* **Namur**
Námestovo Slovakia **49** Q6
Nametil Moz. **131** H2
Namew Lake Canada **167** K4
Nam-gang *r.* N. Korea **83** B5
Namhkan Myanmar **78** B3
Namhsan Myanmar **78** B3
Namialo Moz. **131** H2
Namib Desert Namibia **130** B5
Namibe Angola **127** B8
formerly known as Moçâmedes *or* Mossâmedes
Namibe *prov.* Angola **127** B8
Namibe, Reserva de *nature res.* Angola **127** B8
►**Namibia** *country* Africa **130** B4
formerly known as South-West Africa; *historically known as* German South-West Africa
►►**114–115 Africa** Countries
Namib-Naukluft Game Park *nature res.* Namibia **130** B5
Namichiga Tanz. **129** C7
Namicunde Moz. **131** H2
Namidobe Moz. **131** H3
Namie Japan **90** G6
Namies S. Africa **132** D6
Namīn Iran **100** B2
Namina Moz. **131** H2
Namitete Malawi **129** B8
Namjagbarwa Feng *mt.* China **80** E7
also known as Namcha Barwa
Namji S. Korea **91** A7
Namka China **89** E6
also known as Doilungdêqên
Namlan Myanmar **78** B3
Namlang *r.* Myanmar **78** B3
Namlea Indon. **75** C3
Namling China **89** E6
also known as Nanmulingzue
Nam Nao National Park Thai. **78** C4
Nam Ngum Reservoir Laos **78** C4
Namoi *r.* Australia **147** F2
Nampa Canada **167** G3
Nampa *mt.* Nepal **96** D3
Nampa U.S.A. **180** C4
Nampala Mali **124** D3
Nam Phung Reservoir Thai. **78** C4
Namp'o N. Korea **83** B5
formerly known as Chinnamp'o
UNESCO World Heritage Site
Nampuecha Moz. **131** I2
Nampula Moz. **131** H2
Nampula *prov.* Moz. **131** H2
Namrole Indon. **75** C3
Namrup India **97** G4
Namsai Myanmar **78** B2
Namsang Myanmar **78** B3
Nam She Tsim *hill Hong Kong* China *see* **Sharp Peak**
Namsos Norway **44** J2
Namsskogan Norway **44** K2
Namtari Nigeria **125** I4
Namtok Myanmar **78** B4
Nam Tok Thai. **79** B5
Namtok Chattakan National Park Thai. **78** C4
Namtok Mae Surin National Park Thai. **78** B4
Namton Myanmar **78** B3
Namtsy Rus. Fed. **39** M3
Namtu Myanmar **78** B3
Namu Canada **166** E5
Namuli, Monte *mt.* Moz. **131** H2
Namuno Moz. **131** H2
Namur Belgium **51** K2
also known as Namen
Namutoni Namibia **130** C3
Namwala Zambia **127** E8
Namwera Malawi **129** B8
Namwŏn S. Korea **83** B6
Namya Ra Myanmar **78** B2
Namyit Island S. China Sea **72** D4
Namysłów Poland **49** O4
Nan Thai. **78** C4
Nan, Mae Nam *r.* Thai. **78** C5
Nana *r.* Cent. Afr. Rep. **126** B3
Nana Bakassa Cent. Afr. Rep. **126** C3
Nana Barya *r.* Cent. Afr. Rep./Chad **126** C3
Nana-Grébizi *pref.* Cent. Afr. Rep. **126** C3
Nanaimo Canada **166** F5
Nana-Mambéré *pref.* Cent. Afr. Rep. **126** B3
Nan'an China **87** F3
Nanango Australia **149** G5
Nananib Plateau Namibia **130** C5
Nan'ao China *see* **Dayu**
Nanao Japan **91** E6
Nanatsu-shima *i.* Japan **90** E6
Nanay *r.* Peru **198** C5
Nanbai China *see* **Zunyi**
Nanbaxian China **84** B4
Nanbin China *see* **Shizhu**
Nanbu China **86** C2
also known as Nanlong
Nancha China **82** C3
Nanchang *Jiangxi* China **87** E2
also known as Liantang
Nanchang *Jiangxi* China **87** E2
Nanchangshan China *see* **Changdao**
Nancheng China **87** F3
also known as Jianchang
Nanchong China **86** C2
Nanchuan China **86** C2
Ñancorainza Bol. **201** E5
Nancowry *i.* India **95** G5
Nancut Canada **166** E4
Nancy France **51** M4
UNESCO World Heritage Site
Nancy U.S.A. **176** A8
Nanda Devi *mt.* India **96** D3
UNESCO World Heritage Site
Nanda Kot *mt.* India **96** D3
Nandan China **87** C3
Nanded India **94** C2
formerly known as Nander
Nander India *see* **Nanded**
Nandewar Range *mts* Australia **147** F2
Nandgaon India **94** B1
Nandi Zimbabwe **131** F4
Nandigama India **94** D2
Nandikotkur India **94** C3
Nanding He *r.* China **86** A4
Nandod India **96** B5
Nandu Jiang *r.* China **87** D4
Nandura India **94** C1
Nandurbar India **96** B5
Nandyal India **94** C3
Nănești Romania **58** I3
Nanfeng *Guangdong* China **87** D4
Nanfeng *Jiangxi* China **87** F3
also known as Qincheng
Nang China **89** F6
Nangade Moz. **129** C7
Nanga Eboko Cameroon **125** I5
Nangah Dedai Indon. **77** E3
Nangahembaloh Indon. **77** F2
Nangahkemangai Indon. **77** F3
Nangahmau Indon. **77** E3
Nangahpinoh Indon. **77** E3
Nangahsuruk Indon. **77** F2
Nangahtempuai Indon. **77** F2
Nangalala Australia **148** B2
Nanganga Tanz. **129** C7
Nangang Shan *mts* China **82** C4

►**Nanga Parbat** *mt.* Jammu and Kashmir **96** B2
9th highest mountain in the world and in Asia.
►►**6–7 World** Landscapes
►►**60–61 Asia** Landscapes

Nangarhār *prov.* Afgh. **101** G3
Nangatayap Indon. **77** E3
Nangbéto, Retenue de *resr* Togo **125** F5
Nangin Myanmar **79** B6
Nangis France **51** J4
Nangnim N. Korea **83** B4
Nangnim-sanmaek *mts* N. Korea **83** B4
Nangō Japan **90** F6
Nangong China **85** G4
Nangqên China **86** A1
also known as Xangda
Nangulangwa Tanz. **129** C7
Nanguneri India **94** C4
Nanhe China **85** G4
also known as Heyang
Nanhu China **84** B4
Nanhua *Gansu* China **84** C4
Nanhua *Yunnan* China **86** B3
also known as Longchuan
Nanhui China **87** G2
also known as Huinan
Nani Afgh. **101** G3
Nanisivik Canada **165** K2
Nanjangud India **94** C3
Nanjian China **86** B3
Nanjiang China **86** C1
Nanjie China *see* **Guangning**
Nanjing *Fujian* China **87** F3
also known as Shancheng
Nanjing *Jiangsu* China **87** F1
formerly spelt Nanking
UNESCO World Heritage Site
Nanji Shan *i.* China **87** G3
Nanka Jiang *r.* China **86** A4
Nankang *Jiangxi* China **87** E3
formerly known as Rongjiang
Nankang *Jiangxi* China *see* **Xingzi**
Nanking China *see* **Nanjing**
Nankoku Japan **91** C8
Nankova Angola **127** C9
Nanlan He *r.* China **86** A4
Nanle China **85** G4
Nanling China **87** F2
Nan Ling *mts* China **87** D3
Nanliu Jiang *r.* China **87** D4
Nanlong China *see* **Nanbu**
Nanma China *see* **Yiyuan**
Nanmulingzue China *see* **Namling**
Nannine Australia **151** B5
Nanning China **87** D4
Nannup Australia **151** A7
Na Noi Thai. **78** C4

Neuenkirchen-Seelscheid Germany 48 E5
Neufchâteau Belgium 51 L3
Neufchâteau France 51 L4
Neufchâtel-en-Bray France 50 H3
Neuhausen Rus. Fed. *see* Gur'yevsk
Neuhof Germany 48 G5
Neuillé-Pont-Pierre France 50 G5
Neukuhren Rus. Fed. *see* Pionerskiy
Neumarkt in der Oberpfalz Germany 48 I6
Neumayer *research station* Antarctica 223 X2 *long form* Georg von Neumayer
Neumünster Germany 48 G1
Neun, Nam *r.* Laos 78 D4
Neunkirchen Austria 49 N8
Neunkirchen Germany 48 E6
Neuquén Arg. 204 C5
Neuquén *prov.* Arg. 204 C5
Neuquén *r.* Arg. 204 D5
Neuruppin Germany 49 J3
Neu Sandez Poland *see* Nowy Sącz
Neuse *r.* U.S.A. 174 E5
Neusiedl am See Austria 49 N8
Neusiedler See *l.* Austria/Hungary 49 N8 *UNESCO World Heritage Site*
Neusiedler See Seewinkel, Nationalpark *nat. park* Austria 49 N8
Neuss Germany 48 D4
Neustadt (Wied) Germany 48 E5
Neustadt am Rübenberge Germany 48 G3
Neustadt an der Aisch Germany 48 H6
Neustadt an der Hardt Germany *see* Neustadt an der Weinstraße
Neustadt an der Weinstraße Germany 48 F6 *formerly known as* Neustadt an der Hardt
Neustadt in Holstein Germany 48 H1
Neustadt in Sachsen Germany 49 L4
Neustift im Stubaital Austria 56 D1
Neustrelitz Germany 49 K2
Neuves-Maisons France 51 M4
Neuville-aux-Bois France 51 I4
Neuville-lès-Dieppe France 50 H3
Neuwerk *i.* Germany 48 F2
Neuwied Germany 48 E5
Nevada *IA* U.S.A. 174 A3
Nevada *MO* U.S.A. 178 D4
Nevada *state* U.S.A. 183 G2
Nevada, Sierra *mt.* Arg. 204 C2
Nevada, Sierra *mts* Spain 55 H7
Nevada, Sierra *nature res.* Spain 55 H7
Nevada, Sierra *mts* U.S.A. 182 C1
Nevada City U.S.A. 182 C2
Nevado, Cerro *mt.* Arg. 204 C4
Nevado, Sierra del *mts* Arg. 204 C5
Nevado de Colima, Parque Nacional *nat. park* Mex. 184 E5
Nevado de Tolúca, Parque Nacional *nat. park* Mex. 185 F5
Nevasa India 94 B2
Nevdol'sk Rus. Fed. 43 P9
Nevdubstroy Rus. Fed. *see* Kirovsk
Neve, Serra da *mts* Angola 127 B8
Nevel' Rus. Fed. 43 K5
Nevel', Ozero *l.* Rus. Fed. 43 K6
Nevel'sk Rus. Fed. 82 F3
Neverkino Rus. Fed. 41 H5
Neveronys Lith. 42 F7
Nevers France 51 J5
Nevertire Australia 147 E2
Neves Brazil 207 J9
Nevesinje Bos.-Herz. 56 K5
Nevėžis *r.* Lith. 42 E7
Nevinnomyssk Rus. Fed. 41 G7
Nevis *i.* St Kitts and Nevis 187 H3
Nevşehir Turkey 106 C3
Nevskoye Rus. Fed. 90 C2
New *r.* *CA* U.S.A. 183 I8
New *r.* *WV* U.S.A. 176 D8
New Aiyansh Canada 166 D4
Newala Tanz. 129 C7
New Albany *IN* U.S.A. 174 C4
New Albany *MS* U.S.A. 174 B5
Newald U.S.A. 172 E5
New Amsterdam Guyana 199 G3
New Angledool Australia 147 E2
Newark *CA* U.S.A. 182 B4
Newark *DE* U.S.A. 177 J6
Newark *NJ* U.S.A. 177 K5
Newark *NY* U.S.A. 177 H2
Newark *OH* U.S.A. 176 C5
Newark *airport* U.S.A. 177 K5
Newark Lake U.S.A. 183 I2
Newark-on-Trent U.K. 47 L10
Newark Valley U.S.A. 177 I3
New Augusta U.S.A. 175 B6
Newaygo U.S.A. 172 H7
New Bedford U.S.A. 177 O4
Newberg U.S.A. 180 B3
New Berlin U.S.A. 177 J3
New Bern U.S.A. 174 E5
Newberry *MI* U.S.A. 172 H4
Newberry *SC* U.S.A. 175 D5
Newberry National Volcanic Monument *nat. park* U.S.A. 180 B4
Newberry Springs U.S.A. 183 H7
New Bethlehem U.S.A. 176 F4
New Bight Bahamas 187 E1
New Bloomfield U.S.A. 177 H5
Newboro Canada 168 E4
New Boston *IL* U.S.A. 172 C9
New Boston *OH* U.S.A. 176 C7
New Boston *TX* U.S.A. 179 D5
New Braunfels U.S.A. 179 C6
New Brighton U.S.A. 176 E5
New Britain *i.* P.N.G. 145 D2
New Brunswick *prov.* Canada 169 H4
New Brunswick U.S.A. 177 K5
New Buffalo U.S.A. 172 G9
Newburg U.S.A. 176 H5
Newburgh Canada 173 Q6
Newburgh U.K. 46 J6
Newburgh U.S.A. 177 K4
Newbury U.K. 47 K12
Newburyport U.S.A. 177 O3
New Caledonia *i.* S. Pacific Ocean *see* Nouvelle Calédonie

►New Caledonia *terr.* S. Pacific Ocean 145 F4
French Overseas Country. Also known as Nouvelle Calédonie.
►►138–139 Oceania Countries

New Carlisle Canada 169 H3
Newcastle Australia 147 F3
Newcastle *N.B.* Canada 169 H4
Newcastle *Ont.* Canada 168 E5
Newcastle S. Africa 133 N4
Newcastle U.K. 47 G9
Newcastle *CA* U.S.A. 182 C3
New Castle *DE* U.S.A. 177 J6
New Castle *IN* U.S.A. 174 C4
New Castle *KY* U.S.A. 174 C4
Newcastle *ME* U.S.A. 177 P1
New Castle *PA* U.S.A. 176 E4
Newcastle *UT* U.S.A. 183 K4
New Castle *VA* U.S.A. 176 E8
Newcastle *WY* U.S.A. 180 F4
Newcastle Creek *r.* Australia 148 B3
Newcastle Emlyn U.K. 47 H11 *also known as* Castell Newydd Emlyn
Newcastle Range *hills* Australia 149 D3
Newcastle-under-Lyme U.K. 47 J10
Newcastle upon Tyne U.K. 47 K9
New Church U.S.A. 177 J8
Newchwang China *see* Yingkou
New City U.S.A. 177 L4
Newcomerstown U.S.A. 176 D5
New Concord U.S.A. 176 D6
Newdegate Australia 151 B7

►New Delhi India 96 C3
Capital of India.

New Don Pedro Reservoir U.S.A. 182 D4
Newell, Lake *salt flat* Australia 151 D5
Newell, Lake Canada 167 I5
New England Range *mts* Australia 147 F2
Newenham, Cape U.S.A. 164 C4
New Era U.S.A. 172 G7
Newfane U.S.A. 176 G2
Newfound Lake U.S.A. 177 N2
►Newfoundland *i.* Canada 169 J3 *historically known as* Vinland
►►154–155 North America Landscapes
Newfoundland U.S.A. 177 J4
Newfoundland and Labrador *prov.* Canada 165 N4
Newfoundland Evaporation Basin *salt l.* U.S.A. 183 K1
New Freedom U.S.A. 177 I6
New Galloway U.K. 47 H8
New Georgia *i.* Solomon Is 145 E2
New Georgia Islands Solomon Is 145 E2
New Georgia Sound *sea chan.* Solomon Is 145 E2 *also known as* The Slot
New Glarus U.S.A. 172 D8
New Glasgow Canada 169 I4
Newgrange Tomb *tourist site* Ireland 47 F10

►New Guinea *i.* Indon./P.N.G. 73 J8
Largest island in Oceania and 2nd in the world.
►►6–7 World Landscapes
►►134–135 Oceania Landscapes

New Halfa Sudan 121 G6
Newhall U.S.A. 182 F7
New Hampshire *state* U.S.A. 177 N1
New Hanover *i.* P.N.G. 145 E2 *also known as* Lavongal
New Hanover S. Africa 133 O6
New Hartford U.S.A. 177 J2
New Haven *CT* U.S.A. 177 M4
New Haven *IN* U.S.A. 173 H9
New Haven *MI* U.S.A. 173 K8
New Haven *WV* U.S.A. 176 D7
New Hazelton Canada 166 E4
New Hebrides *country* S. Pacific Ocean *see* Vanuatu
New Hogan Reservoir U.S.A. 182 D3
New Holland *country* Oceania *see* Australia
New Holland U.S.A. 177 I5
New Holstein U.S.A. 172 E7
New Iberia U.S.A. 175 B6
Newington S. Africa 133 P1
New Ireland *i.* P.N.G. 145 E2
New Jersey *state* U.S.A. 177 K6
New Kandla India 96 A5
New Kensington U.S.A. 176 F5
New Kent U.S.A. 177 H8
Newkirk U.S.A. 178 C4
New Lanark U.K. 46 I8 *UNESCO World Heritage Site*
Newland Range *hills* Australia 151 C6
New Lexington U.S.A. 176 C6
New Lisbon U.S.A. 172 C7
New Liskeard Canada 168 E4
New London *CT* U.S.A. 177 M4
New London *IA* U.S.A. 172 B10
New London *OH* U.S.A. 176 C4
New London *WI* U.S.A. 172 E6
New Madrid U.S.A. 174 B4
Newman Australia 150 B4
Newman U.S.A. 182 C4
Newman, Mount Australia 150 B4
Newman Island Antarctica 222 O1
Newmarket Canada 168 E4
Newmarket Ireland 47 C11
Newmarket U.K. 47 M11
Newmarket U.S.A. 177 O2
New Market *TN* U.S.A. 176 B9
New Market *VA* U.S.A. 176 G7
Newmarket-on-Fergus Ireland 47 D11
New Martinsville U.S.A. 176 E6
New Meadows U.S.A. 180 C3
New Mexico *state* U.S.A. 181 F6
New Miami U.S.A. 176 A6
New Milford *CT* U.S.A. 177 L4
New Milford *PA* U.S.A. 177 J4
Newnan U.S.A. 175 C5
New Norcia Australia 151 B6
New Norfolk Australia 147 E5
New Orleans U.S.A. 175 B6
New Oxford U.S.A. 177 H6
New Paltz U.S.A. 177 K4
New Paris *IN* U.S.A. 172 H9
New Paris *OH* U.S.A. 176 A6
New Philadelphia U.S.A. 176 D5
New Plymouth N.Z. 152 I7
Newport *Isle of Wight, England* U.K. 47 K13
Newport *Newport, Wales* U.K. 47 I12 *also known as* Casnewydd
Newport *AR* U.S.A. 174 B5
Newport *DE* U.S.A. 177 J6
Newport *IN* U.S.A. 174 C4
Newport *ME* U.S.A. 177 P1
Newport *NH* U.S.A. 177 M2
Newport *NJ* U.S.A. 177 J6
Newport *OR* U.S.A. 180 A3
Newport *PA* U.S.A. 177 H5
Newport *RI* U.S.A. 177 N4
Newport *TN* U.S.A. 174 D5
Newport *VT* U.S.A. 177 M1
Newport *WA* U.S.A. 180 C2
Newport Beach U.S.A. 182 G8
Newport News U.S.A. 177 I8
New Port Richey U.S.A. 175 D6
New Providence *i.* Bahamas 186 D1
Newquay U.K. 47 G13
New Richmond Canada 169 H3
New Richmond U.S.A. 172 A5
New River U.S.A. 183 L8
New Roads U.S.A. 175 B6
New Rockford U.S.A. 178 C2
New Ross Canada 169 H4
New Ross Ireland 47 F11
Newry Australia 148 A3
Newry U.K. 47 F9
Newry U.S.A. 172 C7
New Sharon U.S.A. 174 A3
New Siberia Islands Rus. Fed. 39 O2 *also known as* Novosibirskiye Ostrova
New Smyrna Beach U.S.A. 175 D6
New South Wales *state* Australia 147 E3
New Stanton U.S.A. 176 F5
New Tazewell U.S.A. 176 B9
Newton *GA* U.S.A. 175 C6
Newton *IA* U.S.A. 174 A3
Newton *IL* U.S.A. 174 B4
Newton *KS* U.S.A. 178 C4
Newton *MA* U.S.A. 177 N3
Newton *MS* U.S.A. 175 B5
Newton *NJ* U.S.A. 177 K4
Newton *TX* U.S.A. 179 D6
Newton Abbot U.K. 47 I13
Newton Falls U.S.A. 177 K1
Newton Stewart U.K. 47 H9
Newtontoppen *mt.* Svalbard 38 B2
Newtown U.K. 47 I11 *also known as* Y Drenewydd
New Town U.S.A. 178 B1
Newtown U.S.A. 177 K5
Newtownabbey U.K. 47 G9
Newtownards U.K. 47 G9
Newtownbarry Ireland *see* Bunclody
Newtownbutler U.K. 47 E9
Newtown St Boswells U.K. 46 J8
Newtownstewart U.K. 47 E9
New Ulm U.S.A. 178 D2
New Vienna U.S.A. 176 B6
Newville U.S.A. 176 H5
New Vineyard U.S.A. 177 O1
New Woodstock U.S.A. 177 J3

►New York U.S.A. 177 L5
2nd most populous city in North America, and 3rd in the world.
►►18–19 World Cities
►►24–25 World Terrorism

New York *state* U.S.A. 177 J3
New York Mountains U.S.A. 183 I6

►New Zealand *country* Oceania 152 E7
3rd largest and 3rd most populous country in Oceania. Known as Aotearoa in Maori.
►►10–11 World Earthquakes and Volcanoes
►►138–139 Oceania Countries

Neya Rus. Fed. 40 G4
Neya *r.* Rus. Fed. 40 G4
Ney Bīd Iran 100 D4
Neyestānak Iran 100 C3
Neyrīz Iran 100 C4
Neyshābūr Iran 100 D2 *also spelt* Nîshāpūr; *historically known as* Abarshahr
Neyyattinkara India 94 C4
Nezahualcóyotl, Presa *resr* Mex. 185 G5
Nezhin Ukr. *see* Nizhyn
Nezperce U.S.A. 180 C3
Nez Perce Indian Reservation *res.* U.S.A. 180 C3
Ngabang Indon. 77 E2
Ngabé Congo 126 C5
Nga Chong, Khao *mt.* Myanmar/Thai. 79 B5
Ngadda *watercourse* Nigeria 125 I3
Ngagahtawng Myanmar 78 B2
Ngagli Rus. Fed. 82 B1
Ngaiotonga N.Z. 152 I3
Ngajira Tanz. 129 B6
Ngala Nigeria 125 I3
Ngalipaëng Indon. 75 C2
Ngalu Indon. 75 B5
Ngam Chad 126 C2
Ngama Chad 126 C2
Ngamaseri *watercourse* Botswana 130 D3
Ngamatapouri N.Z. 152 I7
Ngambé Cameroon 125 H5
Ngamda China 86 A2
Ngamring China 89 D6
Ngangala Sudan 128 A3
Ngangla Ringco *salt l.* China 89 C6
Nganglong Kangri *mt.* China 89 C5
Nganglong Kangri *mts* China 89 C5
N'gangula Angola 127 B7
Ngangzê Co *salt l.* China 89 D6
Ngangzê Shan *mts* China 89 D6
Ngan Hei Shui Tong *resr* *Hong Kong* China *see* Shing Mun Reservoir
Nganjuk Indon. 77 E4
Ngan Sâu, Sông *r.* Vietnam 86 C5
Ngân Sơn Vietnam 78 D3
Ngao Thai. 78 B4
Ngaoundal Cameroon 125 I5
Ngaoundéré Cameroon 125 I5
Ngapuke N.Z. 152 J6
Ngara Malawi 129 B7
Ngara Tanz. 128 A5
Ngarkat Conservation Park *nature res.* Australia 146 D3
Ngarrab China *see* Gyaca
Ngaruawahia N.Z. 152 J5
Ngaruroro *r.* N.Z. 152 K7
Ngatapa N.Z. 152 L6
Ngathainggyaung Myanmar 78 A4
Ngau Mei Hoi *b.* *Hong Kong* China *see* Port Shelter
Ngawa China *see* Aba
Ngawan Chaung *r.* Myanmar 79 B5
Ngawi Indon. 77 E4
Ngayok Bay Myanmar 78 A4
Ngcheangel *atoll* Palau *see* Kayangel Atoll
Ngeaur *i.* Palau *see* Angaur
Ngegera Tanz. 129 A6
Ngeruangel *i.* Palau 73 H5
Ngezi Zimbabwe 131 F4 *formerly spelt* Ingezi
Nggelelevu *i.* Fiji *see* Qele Levu
Nghabe *r.* Botswana 130 D4
Nghê, Hon *i.* Vietnam 79 D6
Ngiap *r.* Laos 78 C4
Ngilmina Indon. 75 C5
Ngimbang Indon. 77 F4
Ngiva Angola *see* Ondjiva
Ngo Congo 126 B5
Ngofakiaha Indon. 75 C2
Ngoïla Cameroon 125 I6
Ngoin, Co *salt l.* China 89 E6
Ngok Linh *mt.* Vietnam 79 D5
Ngoko *r.* Cameroon/Congo 125 J6
Ngola Shankou *pass* China 84 C5
Ngol Bembo Nigeria 125 H4
Ngoma Zambia 127 E8
Ngoma Bridge Botswana 131 E3
Ngoma Tsé-Tsé Congo 126 B6
Ngomba Tanz. 129 B7
Ngome S. Africa 133 P4
Ngong Cameroon 125 I4
Ngongola Angola 127 C8
Ngongotaha N.Z. 152 K6
Ngong Shuen Chau *pen.* *Hong Kong* China *see* Stonecutters' Island
Ngoqumaima China 89 D5
Ngoring China 86 A1
Ngoring Hu *l.* China 86 A1
Ngorongoro Conservation Area *nature res.* Tanz. 128 B5 *UNESCO World Heritage Site*
Ngorongoro Crater Tanz. 128 B5
Ngoumou Cameroon 125 H6
Ngounié *prov.* Gabon 126 A5
Ngounié *r.* Gabon 126 A5
Ngouoni Gabon 126 B5
Ngoura Chad 120 C6
Ngouri Chad 120 B6
Ngourti Niger 125 I3
Ngoutchey *well* Chad 120 C5
Ngozi Burundi 126 F5
Ngqeleni S. Africa 133 N8
Nguigmi Niger 125 I3
Nguini *well* Niger 125 H3
Nguiu Australia 148 A1
Ngukurr Australia 148 B2
Ngulu *atoll* Micronesia 73 I5 *also spelt* Goulou
Ngum, Nam *r.* Laos 78 C4
Ngundu Zimbabwe 131 F4
Ngunguru Bay N.Z. 152 I3
Ngunju, Tanjung *pt* Indon. 75 B5
Ngunza Angola *see* Sumbe
Ngunza-Kabolu Angola *see* Sumbe
Nguru Nigeria 125 H3
Nguru Mountains Tanz. 129 C6
Ngwako Pan *salt pan* Botswana 130 D4
Ngwane *country* Africa *see* Swaziland
Ngwathe S. Africa 133 L4
Ngwavuma *r.* Swaziland 133 Q3 *also spelt* Ingwavuma
Ngwelezana S. Africa 133 P5
Ngwempisi *r.* S. Africa 133 P3
Ngwezi *r.* Zambia 127 E9
Nhamatanda Moz. 131 G3
Nhamundá Brazil 199 G5
Nhamundá *r.* Brazil 199 G5
Nhandeara Brazil 206 C7
N'harea Angola 127 C7
Nha Trang Vietnam 79 E5
Nhecolândia Brazil 201 F4
Nhill Australia 146 D4
Nhlangano Swaziland 133 P4 *formerly known as* Goedgegun
Nhlazatshe S. Africa 133 P5
Nhoma Namibia 130 D3
Nho Quan Vietnam 78 D3
Nhulunbuy Australia 148 C2
Nhu Pora Brazil 203 A9
Niabembe Dem. Rep. Congo 126 E5
Niablé Ghana 124 E5
Niacam Canada 167 J4
Niafounké Mali 124 E3
Niagara U.S.A. 172 F5
Niagara Falls Canada 168 E5
Niagara Falls *waterfall* Canada/U.S.A. 176 G2
Niagara Falls U.S.A. 176 F2
Niagara-on-the-Lake Canada 173 N7
Niagassola Guinea 124 C3
Niagouelé, Mont du *hill* Guinea 124 C4
Niagzu Aksai Chin 89 B5
Niah *Sarawak* Malaysia 77 F2
Niak Nepal 97 E3
Niakaramandougou Côte d'Ivoire 124 D4

►Niamey Niger 125 F3
Capital of Niger.

Niamina Mali 124 D3
Nianbai China *see* Ledu
Niandan *r.* Guinea 124 C4
Niandankoro Guinea 124 C4
Niangandu Tanz. 129 C6
Niangara Dem. Rep. Congo 126 E4
Niangay, Lac *l.* Mali 124 E3
Niangoloko Burkina 124 D4
Niangua *r.* U.S.A. 178 D4
Niangxi China *see* Xinshao
Nia-Nia Dem. Rep. Congo 126 E4
Niankorodougou Burkina 124 D4
Niantic U.S.A. 177 M4
Nianzishan China 85 I2
Niari *admin. reg.* Congo 126 B5
Nias *i.* Indon. 76 B2
Niassa *prov.* Moz. 131 H2 *formerly known as* Lago
Niassa, Lago *l.* Africa *see* Nyasa, Lake
Niassa, Reserva do *nature res.* Moz. 129 C8
Niaur *i.* Palau *see* Angaur
Nibil Well Australia 150 D4
Nīca Latvia 42 C5
Nicaea Turkey *see* İznik

►Nicaragua *country* Central America 186 B4
5th largest country in North America.
►►158–159 North America Countries

Nicaragua, Lago de *l.* Nicaragua *see* Nicaragua, Lake
Nicaragua, Lake Nicaragua 186 B5 *also known as* Nicaragua, Lago de
Nicaro Cuba 187 E2
Nicastro Italy 57 I10
Nice France 51 N9 *also known as* Nizza
Nice U.S.A. 182 B2
Nicephorium Syria *see* Ar Raqqah
Niceville U.S.A. 175 C6
Nichicun, Lac *l.* Canada 169 G2
Nichihara Japan 91 B7
Nichinan Japan 91 B9
Nichlaul India 97 D4
Nicholas Channel Bahamas/Cuba 186 C2
Nicholasville U.S.A. 176 A8
Nicholl's Town Bahamas 186 D1
Nichols *IA* U.S.A. 172 B9
Nichols *NY* U.S.A. 177 I3
Nicholson Australia 150 E3
Nicholson *r.* Australia 148 C3
Nicholson Canada 173 J3
Nicholson U.S.A. 177 J4
Nicholson Lake Canada 167 K2
Nicholson Range *hills* Australia 151 B5
Nicholville U.S.A. 177 K1
Nickol Bay Australia 150 B4
Nicobar Islands India 95 G4
Nicolae Bălcescu Romania 58 J4
Nicolás Bravo Mex. 185 H5
Nicolaus U.S.A. 182 C3
Nicomedia Turkey *see* İzmit
Nico Pérez Uruguay 204 G4
Nicopolis Bulg. *see* Nikopol

►Nicosia Cyprus 108 E2
Capital of Cyprus. Also known as Lefkosia or Lefkoşa.

Nicosia *Sicily* Italy 57 G11
Nicotera Italy 57 H10
Nicoya Costa Rica 186 B5
Nicoya, Golfo de *b.* Costa Rica 186 B5
Nicoya, Península de *pen.* Costa Rica 186 B5
Nicuadala Moz. 131 H3
Niculiţel Romania 58 J3
Nida Lith. 42 B6
Nida *r.* Poland 49 R5
Nidadavole India 94 D2
Nidagunda India 94 C2
Nidym Rus. Fed. 39 J3
Nidže *mt.* Greece/Macedonia 58 C8
Nidzica Poland 49 R2
Nidzkie, Jezioro *l.* Poland 49 S2
Niebüll Germany 48 F1
Nied *r.* France 51 M3
Niederaula Germany 48 G5
Niederer Fläming *park* Germany 49 J3
Niedere Tauern *mts* Austria 49 K8
Niederlausitz *reg.* Germany 49 K4
Niedersachsen *land* Germany 48 F3 *English form* Lower Saxony
Niedersächsisches Wattenmeer, Nationalpark *nat. park* Germany 48 D2
Niefang Equat. Guinea 125 H6
Niekerkshoop S. Africa 132 G6
Niellé Côte d'Ivoire 124 D4
Niem Cent. Afr. Rep. 126 B3
Niemba Dem. Rep. Congo 127 F6
Niemegk Germany 49 J3
Niemisel Sweden 44 M2
Niéna Mali 124 D4
Nienburg (Weser) Germany 48 G3
Niéri Ko *watercourse* Senegal 124 B3
Niers *r.* Germany 48 C4
Niesky Germany 49 L4
Nietverdiend S. Africa 133 K2
Nieuw Amsterdam Suriname 199 H3
Nieuw Nickerie Suriname 199 G3
Nieuwoudtville S. Africa 132 D8
Nieuwpoort Belgium 51 I1
Nieves Spain *see* As Neves
Niğde Turkey 106 C3
Nigel S. Africa 133 M3
►Niger *country* Africa 125 G2
►►114–115 Africa Countries

►Niger *r.* Africa 124 G5
3rd longest river in Africa.
►►110–111 Africa Landscapes

Niger *state* Nigeria 125 G4
Niger, Mouths of the Nigeria 125 G5
Niger, Source of the *tourist site* Guinea 124 C4

►Nigeria *country* Africa 125 G4
Most populous country in Africa, and 9th in the world.
►►16–17 World Population
►►114–115 Africa Countries

Nighasan India 96 D3
Nightcaps N.Z. 153 C13
Nighthawk Lake Canada 168 D3
Nīgrande Latvia 42 D5
Nigrita Greece 58 E8
Nihing Pak. 101 F4
Nihommatsu Japan *see* Nihonmatsu
Nihon *country* Asia *see* Japan
Nihonmatsu Japan 90 G6 *also spelt* Nihommatsu
Niigata Japan 90 F6
Niigata *pref.* Japan 90 F6
Niigata-yake-yama *vol.* Japan 91 F6
Niihama Japan 91 C8
Ni'ihau *i.* U.S.A. 181 [inset] Y1
Nii-jima *i.* Japan 91 F7
Niikappu Japan 90 H3
Niimi Japan 91 C7
Niitsu Japan 90 F6
Níjar Spain 55 I8
Nijerâne *well* Mauritania 124 C2
Nijil, Wādī *watercourse* Jordan 108 G7
Nijmegen Neth. 48 C4 *formerly spelt* Nimwegen
Nijverdal Neth. 48 D3
Nikaia Greece 59 D9
Nikel' Rus. Fed. 44 O1
Nikel'tau Kazakh. 102 D2
Nikiniki Indon. 75 C5
Nikkaluokta Sweden 44 L2
Nikki Benin 125 F4
Nikkō Japan 91 F6
Nikkō National Park Japan 90 F6 *UNESCO World Heritage Site*
Nikola Rus. Fed. 40 H4
Nikolaevo Bulg. 58 G6
Nikolayev Ukr. *see* Mykolayiv
Nikolayevka *Chelyabinskaya Oblast'* Rus. Fed. 103 E1
Nikolayevka *Khabarovskiy Kray* Rus. Fed. 82 D2
Nikolayevka *Ul'yanovskaya Oblast'* Rus. Fed. 41 H5
Nikolayevo Rus. Fed. 43 K3
Nikolayevsk Rus. Fed. 41 H6 *formerly known as* Nikolayevskiy
Nikolayevskiy Rus. Fed. *see* Nikolayevsk
Nikolayevsk-na-Amure Rus. Fed. 82 F1
Nikol'sk *Penzenskaya Oblast'* Rus. Fed. 41 H5 *formerly known as* Nikol'skaya Pestravka
Nikol'sk *Vologod. Obl.* Rus. Fed. 40 H4
Nikol'skaya Pestravka Rus. Fed. *see* Nikol'sk
Nikol'skiy Kazakh. *see* Satpayev
Nikol'skiy Rus. Fed. 43 P1
Nikol'skiy Torzhok Rus. Fed. 43 T2
Nikol'skoye *Kamchatskaya Oblast'* Rus. Fed. 39 Q4
Nikol'skoye *Lipetskaya Oblast'* Rus. Fed. 43 U9
Nikol'skoye *Orenburgskaya Oblast'* Rus. Fed. 102 C1
Nikol'skoye *Vologod. Obl.* Rus. Fed. 43 S2
Nikol'skoye *Vologod. Obl.* Rus. Fed. *see* Sheksna
Nikopol Bulg. 58 F5 *historically known as* Nicopolis
Nikopol' Ukr. 41 E7
Nīk Pey Iran 100 B2
Niksar Turkey 107 D2
Nīkshahr Iran 101 E5 *also known as* Gey
Nikšić *Crna Gora* Serb. and Mont. 56 K6
Nikumaroro *i.* Kiribati 145 H2 *formerly known as* Gardner Island
Nikunau *i.* Kiribati 145 G2 *also spelt* Nukunau; *formerly known as* Byron Island
Nîl, Bahr el *r.* Africa *see* Nile
Nila *vol.* Indon. 75 D4
Nilagiri India 97 E5
Nilakka *l.* Fin. 44 N3
Nilakkottai India 94 C4
Nilambur India 94 C4
Niland U.S.A. 183 I8
Nilandhoo Atoll Maldives 93 D10
Nilanga India 94 C2
Nilaveli Sri Lanka 94 D4

►Nile *r.* Africa 121 F2
Longest river in the world and in Africa. Also known as Nîl, Bahr el.
►►6–7 World Landscapes
►►110–111 Africa Landscapes

Nile *state* Sudan 121 G5
►Nile Delta Egypt 108 C6
►►6–7 World Landscapes
Niles *MI* U.S.A. 172 G9
Niles *OH* U.S.A. 176 E4
Nileswaram India 94 B3
Nilgiri Hills India 94 C4
Nili *r.* Eth. 104 B5
Nilka China 88 C3
Nilópolis Brazil 207 J9
Nil Pass Afgh. 101 F3
Nilphamari Bangl. 97 F4
Nilsiä Fin. 44 O3
Niltepec Mex. 185 G5
Nilüfer *r.* Turkey 59 J8
Nimach India *see* Neemuch
Nimaj India 96 B4
Niman *r.* Rus. Fed. 82 D2
Nimba, Monts *mts* Africa *see* Nimba, Mount
Nimba, Mount *mts* Africa 124 C5 *also known as* Nimba, Monts *UNESCO World Heritage Site*
Nimbahera India 96 B4 *also spelt* Nimbhera
Nimbal India 94 B2
Nimberra Well Australia 150 C4
Nimbhera India *see* Nimbahera
Nimelen *r.* Rus. Fed. 82 E1
Nîmes France 51 K9 *historically known as* Nemausus
Nimka Thana India 96 B4
Nimmitabel Australia 147 F4
Nimos *i.* Greece 59 I12
Nimpkish *r.* Canada 166 E5
Nimrod Glacier Antarctica 223 K1
Nīmrūz *prov.* Afgh. 101 E4
Nimu Jammu and Kashmir 96 C2
Nimule Sudan 128 B4
Nimwegen Neth. *see* Nijmegen
Nina Estonia 42 I3
Nīnawá *governorate* Iraq 107 E4
Nīnawá *tourist site* Iraq 107 E3 *also spelt* Nineveh
Ninda Angola 127 D8
Nindai Tanz. 129 B7
Nindigully Australia 147 F2
Nine Degree Channel India 94 B4
Nine Islands P.N.G. *see* Kilinailau Islands
Nine Mile Lake *salt flat* Australia 147 D2
Ninemile Peak U.S.A. 183 H2
Ninepin Group *is* *Hong Kong* China 87 [inset] *also known as* Kwo Chau Kwan To
Ninety Mile Beach Australia 147 E4
Ninety Mile Beach N.Z. 152 G2
Nineveh *tourist site* Iraq *see* Nīnawá
Ninfas, Punta *pt* Arg. 205 D6
Ningaloo Marine Park *nature res.* Australia 150 A4
Ning'an China 82 C3
Ningbo China 87 G2 *also known as* Yinxian
Ningcheng China 85 H3 *also known as* Tianyi
Ningde China 87 F3
Ningdu China 87 E3 *also known as* Meijiang
Ning'er China *see* Pu'er
Ningguo China 87 F2 *also known as* Helixi
Ninghai China 87 G2
Ninghe China 85 H4 *also known as* Lutai
Ninghsia *aut. reg.* China *see* Ningxia Huizu Zizhiqu
Ninghsia Hui Autonomous Region *aut. reg.* China *see* Ningxia Huizu Zizhiqu
Ninghua China 87 F3 *also known as* Cuijiang
Ningi Nigeria 125 H4
Ninging India 97 G3
Ningjiang China *see* Songyuan
Ningjing Shan *mts* China 86 A2
Ninglang China 86 B3 *also known as* Daxing
Ningling China 87 E1
Ningming China 86 C4 *also known as* Chengzhong
Ningnan China 86 B3 *also known as* Pisha
Ningqiang China 86 C1
Ningshan China 87 D1
Ningwu China 85 G4
Ningxia *aut. reg.* China *see* Ningxia Huizu Zizhiqu
Ningxia Huizu Zizhiqu *aut. reg.* China 85 E4 *short form* Ningxia; *English form* Ninghsia *or* Ninghsia Hui Autonomous Region
Ningxian China 85 E5 *also known as* Xinning
Ningxiang China 87 E2
Ningyang China 85 H5
Ningyuan China 87 D3
Ningzhou China *see* Huaning
Ninh Binh Vietnam 78 D3
Ninh Hoa Vietnam 79 E5
Ninigo Group *is* P.N.G. 73 J7
Ninnis Glacier Antarctica 223 J2
Ninnis Glacier Tongue Antarctica 223 K2
Ninohe Japan 90 G4
Ninualac, Canal *sea chan.* Chile 205 B7
Nioaque Brazil 201 G5
Niobrara *r.* U.S.A. 178 C3
Nioghalvfjerdsfjorden *inlet* Greenland 165 R2
Nioki Dem. Rep. Congo 126 C5
Niokolo Koba, Parc National du *nat. park* Senegal 124 B3 *UNESCO World Heritage Site*
Niono Mali 124 D3
Nioro Mali 124 C3
Niort France 50 F6
Nioût *well* Mauritania 124 D3
Nipa P.N.G. 73 J8
Nipani India 94 B2
Nipanipa, Tanjung *pt* Indon. 75 B3
Nipawin Canada 167 J4
Niphad India 94 B1
Nipigon Canada 168 B3
Nipigon, Lake Canada 168 B3
Nipigon Bay Canada 172 F2
Nipiodi Moz. 131 H3
Nipishish Lake Canada 169 I2
Nipissing Canada 173 N4
Nipissing, Lake Canada 168 E4
Nipomo U.S.A. 182 D6
Nippon *country* Asia *see* Japan
Nippon Hai *sea* N. Pacific Ocean *see* Japan, Sea of
Nippur *tourist site* Iraq 107 F4
Niquelândia Brazil 202 B5
Niquero Cuba 186 D2
Nir *Ardabīl* Iran 100 A2
Nir *Yazd* Iran 100 C4
Nira *r.* India 94 B2
Nirasaki Japan 91 F7
Nirji China 85 J1 *also known as* Morin Dawa
Nirmal India 94 C2
Nirmali India 97 E4
Nirmal Range *hills* India 94 C2
Nirzas *l.* Latvia 42 I5
Niš *Srbija* Serb. and Mont. 58 C5 *historically known as* Naissus
Nisa Port. 54 D5
Nişāb Yemen 105 D5
Nisah, Wādī *watercourse* Saudi Arabia 105 D2
Nišava *r.* Serb. and Mont. 58 C5
Niscemi *Sicily* Italy 57 G11
Niseko Japan 90 G3
Nîshāpūr Iran *see* Neyshābūr
Nishcha *r.* Belarus 43 J6
Nishibetsu-gawa *r.* Japan 90 I3
Nishikawa Japan 90 G5
Nishinomiya Japan 91 D7
Nishino-omote Japan 91 B9
Nishino-shima *i.* Japan 91 C6
Nishino-shima *vol.* Japan 81 O7
Nishi-Sonogi-hantō *pen.* Japan 91 A8
Nishi-suidō *sea chan.* Japan/S. Korea 91 A7 *also known as* Chōsen-kaikyō
Nishiwaki Japan 91 D7
Nísia Floresta Brazil 202 F3
Nisibis Turkey *see* Nusaybin
Nisi-mera Japan 91 B8
Nísiros *i.* Greece *see* Nisyros
Niskanselkä *l.* Fin. 44 N2
Niskayuna U.S.A. 177 L3
Niskibi *r.* Canada 168 B1
Nisko Poland 49 T5
Nisling *r.* Canada 166 B2
Nisporeni Moldova 58 J1
Nissan *r.* Sweden 45 K4
Nisser *l.* Norway 45 J4
Nissum Bredning *b.* Denmark 45 J4
Nistru *r.* Moldova *see* Dniester
Nistrului Inferior, Cîmpia *lowland* Moldova 58 K1
Nisutlin *r.* Canada 166 C2
Nisyros *i.* Greece 59 I12 *also spelt* Nísiros
Nita Japan 91 C7
Nitchequon Canada 169 G2
Nitendi *i.* Solomon Is *see* Ndeni
Niterói Brazil 203 D7
Nith *r.* U.K. 47 I8
Niti Pass China 96 C3
Nitmiluk National Park Australia 148 B2 *formerly known as* Katherine Gorge National Park
Nitra Slovakia 49 P7
Nitra *r.* Slovakia 49 P8
Nitro U.S.A. 176 D7
Nittedal Norway 45 J3
Niuafo'ou *i.* Tonga 145 H3 *also spelt* Niuafu
Niuafu *i.* Tonga *see* Niuafo'ou
Niuatoputopu *i.* Tonga 145 H3 *formerly known as* Boscawen Island
Niubiziliang China 84 B4

►Niue *terr.* S. Pacific Ocean 145 I3
Self-governing New Zealand Overseas Territory.
►►138–139 Oceania Countries

Niujing China *see* Binchuan
Niulakita *i.* Tuvalu 145 G3 *formerly spelt* Nurakita
Niulan Jiang *r.* China 86 B3
Niur, Pulau *i.* Indon. 76 C3
Niushan China *see* Donghai

Niutao *i.* Tuvalu **145** G2
Niutoushan China **87** F2
Niuzhuang China **85** I3
Nivala Fin. **44** N3
Nivastroy Rus. Fed. **44** P2
Nive *watercourse* Australia **149** E5
Nive *r.* France **50** E9
Nive Downs Australia **149** E5
Nivelles Belgium **51** K2
Nivnoye Rus. Fed. **43** N8
Nivskiy Rus. Fed. **44** P2
Niwai India **96** B4
Niwari India **96** C4
Niwas India **96** D5
Nixia China *see* **Sêrxü**
Nixon U.S.A. **182** E2
Niya China *see* **Minfeng**
Niya He *r.* China **89** C4
Niyut, Gunung *mt.* Indon. **77** E2
Niz Rus. Fed. **43** Q2
Nizamabad India **94** C2
also known as Indur
Nizampatnam India **94** D3
Nizam Sagar *l.* India **94** C2
Nizh Aydere Turkm. **102** D5
Nizhegorodskaya Oblast' *admin. div.* Rus. Fed. **40** H4
English form Nizhniy Novgorod Oblast; *formerly known as* Gor'kovskaya Oblast'
Nizhneangarsk Rus. Fed. **81** H1
Nizhnedevitsk Rus. Fed. **41** F6
Nizhnekamsk Rus. Fed. **40** I5
Nizhnekamskoye Vodokhranilishche *resr* Rus. Fed. **40** J5
Nizhnekolymsk Rus. Fed. **39** Q3
Nizhne-Svirskiy Zapovednik *nature res.* Rus. Fed. **43** O1
Nizhneudinsk Rus. Fed. **80** F2
Nizhnevartovsk Rus. Fed. **38** H3
Nizhnevolzhsk Rus. Fed. *see* **Narimanov**
Nizhneyansk Rus. Fed. **39** N2
Nizhniy Kuyto, Ozero *l.* Rus. Fed. **44** O2
Nizhni Irginski Rus. Fed. **40** K4
Nizhniy Baskunchak Rus. Fed. **102** A2
Nizhniy Chir Rus. Fed. **41** G6
Nizhniye Kayrakty Kazakh. **103** H2
also spelt Qayraqty
Nizhniye Kresty Rus. Fed. *see* **Cherskiy**
Nizhniye Ustriki Poland *see* **Ustrzyki Dolne**
Nizhniy Lomov Rus. Fed. **41** G5
Nizhniy Novgorod Rus. Fed. **40** G4
formerly known as Gor'kiy
Nizhniy Novgorod Oblast *admin. div.* Rus. Fed. *see* **Nizhegorodskaya Oblast'**
Nizhniy Odes Rus. Fed. **40** J3
Nizhniy Pyandzh Tajik. *see* **Panji Poyon**
Nizhniy Tagil Rus. Fed. **38** F4
Nizhniy Yenangsk Rus. Fed. **40** H4
Nizhnyaya Mola Rus. Fed. **40** H2
Nizhnyaya Omra Rus. Fed. **40** J3
Nizhnyaya Pesha Rus. Fed. **40** H2
Nizhnyaya Pirenga, Ozero *l.* Rus. Fed. **44** P2
Nizhnyaya Poyma Rus. Fed. **80** F1
Nizhnyaya Suyetka Rus. Fed. **103** I1
Nizhnyaya Tunguska *r.* Rus. Fed. **39** I3
English form Lower Tunguska
Nizhnyaya Tura Rus. Fed. **38** F4
Nizhnyaya Zolotitsa Rus. Fed. **40** G2
Nizhyn Ukr. **41** D6
also spelt Nezhin
Nizip Turkey **107** D3
Nizkabor"ye Belarus **43** L6
Nízke Beskydy *hills* Slovakia **49** S6
Nízke Tatry *mts* Slovakia **49** Q7
Nízke Tatry *nat. park* Slovakia **49** Q7
Nizmennyy, Mys *pt* Rus. Fed. **90** D3
Nizwá Oman *see* **Nazwá**
Nizza France *see* **Nice**
Nizza Monferrato Italy **56** A4
Njavve Sweden **44** L2
Njazidja *i.* Comoros **129** D7
also known as Grande Comore
Njegoš *mts* Serb. and Mont. **56** K6
Njellim Fin. *see* **Nellim**
Njinjo Tanz. **129** C7
Njombe Tanz. **129** B7
Njombe *r.* Tanz. **129** B6
Njutånger Sweden **45** L3
Nkai Zimbabwe *see* **Nkayi**
Nkambe Cameroon **125** H5
Nkandla S. Africa **133** P5
Nkasi Tanz. **129** A6
Nkawkaw Ghana **125** E5
Nkayi Zimbabwe **131** F3
formerly spelt Nkai
Nkhailé *well* Mauritania **124** D2
Nkhata Bay Malawi **129** B7
Nkhotakota Malawi **129** B8
Nkhotakota Game Reserve *nature res.* Malawi **129** B8
Nkomfap Nigeria **125** H5
Nkomi, Lagune *lag.* Gabon **126** A5
Nkondwe Tanz. **129** A6
Nkongsamba Cameroon **125** H5
Nkoranza Ghana **125** E5
Nkoteng Cameroon **125** I5
Nkululeko S. Africa **133** L7
Nkundi Tanz. **129** A6
Nkungwi Tanz. **129** A6
Nkurenkuru Namibia **130** C3
Nkwalini S. Africa **133** P5
Nkwanta Ghana **125** F4
Nkwenkwezi S. Africa **133** K10
Nmai Hka *r.* Myanmar **78** B2
Noa Dihing *r.* India **97** H4
Noakhali Bangl. **97** F5
Noamundi India **97** E5
Noatak *r.* U.S.A. **164** C3
Noatak National Preserve *nature res.* U.S.A. **164** D3
Nobeoka Japan **91** B8
Noblesville U.S.A. **174** C3
Nobokwe S. Africa **133** L8
Noboribetsu Japan **90** G3
Nobres Brazil **201** F3
Noccundra Australia **147** D1
Noce *r.* Italy **56** D2
Nocera Terinese Italy **57** I9
Nochistlán Mex. **185** E4
Nochixtlán Mex. **185** F5
Noci Italy **57** J8
Nockatunga Australia **147** D1
Nocoleche Nature Reserve Australia **147** E2
Nocona U.S.A. **179** C5
Noda Japan **91** F7
Nodales, Bahía de los *b.* Arg. **205** D8
Nodaway *r.* U.S.A. **178** D4
Nodeland Norway **45** I4
Noel Kempff Mercado, Parque Nacional *nat. park* Bol. **201** E3
UNESCO World Heritage Site
Noelville Canada **173** M4
Noenieput S. Africa **132** E4
Nogales Mex. **184** C2
also known as Heroica Nogales
Nogales U.S.A. **181** E7
Nogaro France **50** F9
Nogat *r.* Poland **49** Q1
Nōgata Japan **91** B8
Nogayty Kazakh. **102** C2
Nogent-le-Rotrou France **50** G4
Nogent-sur-Oise France **51** I3
Nogent-sur-Seine France **51** J4
Noginsk *Evenkiyskiy Avtonomnyy Okrug* Rus. Fed. **39** J3
Noginsk *Moskovskaya Oblast'* Rus. Fed. **43** T6
Nogliki Rus. Fed. **82** F2
Nogo *r.* Australia **149** F5
Nogoa *r.* Australia **149** F4
Nōgōhaku-san *mt.* Japan **91** E7
Nogoyá Arg. **204** F4
Nohar India **96** B3
Noheji Japan **90** G4
Nohfelden Germany **48** E6
Nohili Point U.S.A. **181** [inset] Y1
Nohur Turkm. **102** D5
also spelt Nokhur
Noia Spain **54** C2
also spelt Noya
Noidore *r.* Brazil **206** A1
Noire *r.* Canada **173** Q5
Noire, Montagne *mts* France **51** I9
Noire, Pointe *pt* Morocco **55** H9
Noires, Montagnes *hills* France **50** C4
Noirmoutier, Île de *i.* France **50** D6
Noirmoutier-en-l'Île France **50** D5
Nojima-zaki *c.* Japan **91** F7
Nokesville U.S.A. **176** H7
Nokha India **96** B4
Nokhowch, Kūh-e *mt.* Iran **101** E5
Nokhur Turkm. *see* **Nohur**
Nokia Fin. **45** M3
Nōkis Uzbek. *see* **Nukus**
Nok Kundi Pak. **101** E4
Nokomis Canada **167** J5
Nokomis Lake Canada **167** K3
Nokou Chad **120** B6
Nokrek Peak India **97** F4
Nola Cent. Afr. Rep. **126** C4
Nolichuky *r.* U.S.A. **176** B9
Nolinsk Rus. Fed. **40** I4
formerly known as Molotovsk
Noll S. Africa **132** G10
Nólsoy *i.* Faroe Is **46** F1
Noma-misaki *pt* Japan **91** B9
Nome U.S.A. **164** C3
Nomgon Mongolia **85** E3
Nomhon China **84** C4
Nomin Gol *r.* China **85** J1
Nomoi Islands Micronesia *see* **Mortlock Islands**
Nomonde S. Africa **133** K8
Nomo-zaki *pt* Japan **91** A8
Nomto Rus. Fed. **84** E1
Nomuka Tonga **145** H4
Nomzha Rus. Fed. **40** G4
Nonacho Lake Canada **167** I2
Nong'an China **82** B3
Nong Hong Thai. **79** C5
Nonghui China *see* **Guang'an**
Nong Khai Thai. **78** C4
Nongoma S. Africa **133** P4
Nongstoin India **97** F4
Nonni *r.* China *see* **Nen Jiang**
Nonoai Brazil **203** A8
Nonoava Mex. **184** D3
Nonouti *atoll* Kiribati **145** G2
also spelt Nanouki *or* Nanouti; *formerly known as* Sydenham
Nonsan S. Korea **83** B5
Nonthaburi Thai. **79** C5
Nontron France **50** G7
Nonzwakazi S. Africa **132** I7
Nõo Estonia **42** H3
Nookawarra Australia **151** B5
Noolyeanna Lake *salt flat* Australia **146** C1
Noonamah Australia **148** A2
Noondie, Lake *salt flat* Australia **151** B6
Noonkanbah Australia **150** D3
Noonkanbah Aboriginal Reserve Australia **150** D3
Noonthorangee Range *hills* Australia **147** D2
Noorama Creek *watercourse* Australia **147** E1
Noordbeveland *i.* Neth. **48** A4
Noorderhaaks *i.* Neth. **48** B3
Noordkaap S. Africa **133** P2
Noordkuil S. Africa **132** C9
Noordoewer Namibia **132** B5
Noordoost Polder Neth. **48** C3
Noordpunt *pt* Neth. Antilles **187** F4
Noormarkku Fin. **45** M3
Noorvik U.S.A. **164** C3
Nootka Island Canada **166** E5
Nopiming Provincial Park Canada **167** M5
Nóqui Angola **127** B6
Nora *r.* Rus. Fed. **82** C2
Norak Tajik. **101** G2
also spelt Nurek
Norala Phil. **74** C5
Noranda Canada **168** E3
Nor-Bayazet Armenia *see* **Gavarr**
Norberg Sweden **45** K3
Nord *prov.* Cameroon **125** I4
Nord Greenland *see* **Station Nord**
Nord, Canal du France **48** A5
Nordaustlandet *i.* Svalbard **38** C2
Norddorf Germany **48** F1
Nordborg Denmark **48** G1
Nordbotn Norway **44** M1
Nordegg Canada **167** G4
Norden Germany **48** E2
Nordenshel'da, Arkhipelag *is* Rus. Fed. **39** J2
English form Nordenskjold Archipelago
Nordenskiold *r.* Canada **166** B2
Nordenskjold Archipelago *is* Rus. Fed. *see* **Nordenshel'da, Arkhipelag**
Norder Hever *sea chan.* Germany **48** F1
Norderney Germany **48** E2
Norderney *i.* Germany **48** E2
Norderstedt Germany **48** H2
Nordfjord Norway **44** O1
Nordfjord *inlet* Norway **44** I3
Nordfjordeid Norway **45** I3
Nordfold Norway **44** K2
Nordfriesische Inseln *is* Germany *see* **North Frisian Islands**
Nordhausen Germany **48** H4
Nordholz Germany **48** F2
Nordhorn Germany **48** E3
Nordhuglo Norway **45** I4
Nordingrå naturreservat *nature res.* Sweden **44** L3
Nord Kap *c.* Iceland *see* **Horn**
Nordkapp *c.* Norway *see* **North Cape**
Nordkinnhalvøya *i.* Norway **44** N1
Nord-Kivu *prov.* Dem. Rep. Congo **126** F5
Nordkvaløy *i.* Norway **44** L1
Nordland *county* Norway **44** K2
Nordli Norway **44** K2
Nördliches Harzvorland *park* Germany **48** H4
Nördlingen Germany **48** H7
Nordmaling Sweden **44** L3
Nordmannvik Norway **44** M1
▸**Nord- og Østgrønland, Nationalparken i** *nat. park* Greenland **165** P2
▸▸**14–15 World** Environmental Impacts
Nordostrundingen *c.* Greenland *see* **Northeast Foreland**
Nord-Ostsee-Kanal *canal* Germany *see* **Kiel Canal**
Nord-Ouest *prov.* Cameroon **125** H5
Nord-Pas-de-Calais *admin. reg.* France **51** I2
Nord-Pas-de-Calais, Parc Naturel Régional du *nature res.* France **51** J2
Nordre Strømfjord *inlet* Greenland *see* **Nassuttooq**
Nordrhein-Westfalen *land* Germany **48** E4
English form North Rhine - Westphalia
Nordstrand *i.* Germany **48** F1
Nord-Trøndelag *county* Norway **44** K2
Norðurland eystra *constituency* Iceland **44** [inset] C2
Norðurland vestra *constituency* Iceland **44** [inset] B2
Nordvik Rus. Fed. **39** L2
Nordvika Norway **44** J3
Nore *r.* Ireland **47** F11
Nore, Pic de *mt.* France **51** I9
Noreg *country* Europe *see* **Norway**
Noreikiškės Lith. **42** E7
Noresund Norway **45** J3
Norfolk *NE* U.S.A. **178** C3
Norfolk *NY* U.S.A. **177** K1
Norfolk *VA* U.S.A. **177** I9

▸**Norfolk Island** *terr.* S. Pacific Ocean **145** F4
Territory of Australia.
▸▸**138–139 Oceania** Countries

Norfork Lake U.S.A. **179** D4
Norge *country* Europe *see* **Norway**
Norheimsund Norway **45** I3
Noria Chile **200** C5
Norikura-dake *vol.* Japan **91** E6
Noril'sk Rus. Fed. **39** I3
Norkyung China **89** E6
also known as Bainang
Norland Canada **173** O6
Norlina U.S.A. **176** G9
Normal U.S.A. **174** B3
Norman *r.* Australia **149** D3
Norman U.S.A. **179** C5
Norman, Lake *resr* U.S.A. **174** D5
Normanby *r.* Australia **149** E2
Normanby N.Z. **152** I7
Normanby Island P.N.G. **145** E2
Normanby Range *hills* Australia **149** F4
Normandes, Îles *is* English Chan. *see* **Channel Islands**
Normandia Brazil **199** G4
Normandie *reg.* France *see* **Normandy**
Normandie, Collines de *hills* France **50** F4
Normandie-Maine, Parc Naturel Régional *nature res.* France **50** F4
Normandien S. Africa **133** N4
Normandy *reg.* France **50** F4
also spelt Normandie
Normanton Australia **149** D3
Norman Wells Canada **166** E1
also known as Legohli
Normétal Canada **173** N2
Norogachic Mex. **184** D3
Norquay Canada **167** K5
Ñorquinco Arg. **205** C6
Norråker Sweden **44** K2
Norra Kvarken *strait* Fin./Sweden **44** M3
Norrbotten *county* Sweden **44** L2
Nørre Nebel Denmark **45** J5
Norrent-Fontes France **51** I2
Norrfjärden Sweden **44** M2
Norrhult-Klavreström Sweden **45** K4
Norris U.S.A. **176** A9
Norris Lake U.S.A. **176** B9
Norristown U.S.A. **177** J5
Norrköping Sweden **45** L4
Norrsundet Sweden **45** L3
Norrtälje Sweden **45** L4
Norseman Australia **151** C7
Norsewood N.Z. **152** K8
Norsjö Sweden **44** L2
Norsk Rus. Fed. **82** C1
Norske Øer *is* Greenland **165** R2
Norsup Vanuatu **145** F3
Norte, Punta *pt Buenos Aires* Arg. **204** F5
Norte, Punta *pt* Arg. **205** C8
Norte, Punta *pt* Arg. **205** E6
Norte, Serra do *hills* Brazil **201** F2
Norte de Santander *dept* Col. **198** C2
Nortelândia Brazil **201** F3
North, Cape Antarctica **223** L2
North, Cape Canada **169** I4
North Adams U.S.A. **177** L3
Northallerton U.K. **47** K9
Northam Australia **151** B6
Northam S. Africa **133** L1
Northampton Australia **151** A6
Northampton U.K. **47** L11
Northampton *MA* U.S.A. **177** M3
Northampton *PA* U.S.A. **177** J5
Northampton Downs Australia **149** E5
North Andaman *i.* India **95** G3
North Anna *r.* U.S.A. **176** H8
North Anson U.S.A. **177** P1
North Arm *b.* Canada **167** H2
North Balabac Strait Phil. **74** A4
North Baltimore U.S.A. **176** B4
North Battleford Canada **167** I4
North Bay Canada **168** E4
North Bend *OR* U.S.A. **180** A4
North Bend *PA* U.S.A. **176** H4
North Bennington U.S.A. **177** L3
North Berwick U.K. **46** J7
North Berwick U.S.A. **177** O2
North Borneo *state* Malaysia *see* **Sabah**
North Bosque *r.* U.S.A. **179** C6
North Branch *MI* U.S.A. **173** J7
North Branch *MN* U.S.A. **172** A5
North Caicos *i.* Turks and Caicos Is **187** F2
North Canadian *r.* U.S.A. **179** D5
North Cape Canada **169** H4
North Cape Norway **44** N1
also known as Nordkapp
North Cape N.Z. **152** H2
North Cape S. Georgia **205** [inset]
North Caribou Lake Canada **168** B2
North Carolina *state* U.S.A. **176** F9
North Cascades National Park U.S.A. **180** B2
North Central Aboriginal Reserve Australia **150** D4
North Channel *lake channel* Canada **168** D4
North Channel *strait* U.K. **47** G9
North Charleston U.S.A. **175** E5
North Cheyenne Indian Reservation *res.* U.S.A. **180** F3
Northcliffe Australia **151** B7
Northcliffe Glacier Antarctica **223** G2
North Collins U.S.A. **176** G3
North Concho *r.* U.S.A. **179** B6
North Conway U.S.A. **177** N1
North Cowichan Canada **166** F5
North Creek U.S.A. **177** L2
North Dakota *state* U.S.A. **178** B2
North Downs *hills* U.K. **47** L12
North-East *admin. dist.* Botswana **131** E4
North East *MD* U.S.A. **177** J6
North East *PA* U.S.A. **176** F3
North East Cay *reef* Australia **149** G4
North Eastern *prov.* Kenya **128** D4

▸**Northeast Foreland** *c.* Greenland **165** R1
Most easterly point of North America. Also known as Nordostrundingen.
▸▸**154–155 North America** Landscapes

North-East Frontier Agency *state* India *see* **Arunachal Pradesh**
Northeast Point Bahamas **175** F8
Northeast Providence Channel Bahamas **186** D1
North Edwards U.S.A. **182** G6
Northeim Germany **48** G4
North End Point Bahamas **175** F7
Northern *admin. reg.* Ghana **125** E4
Northern *admin. reg.* Malawi **129** B7
Northern *prov.* Sierra Leone **124** C4
Northern *state* Sudan **121** F4
Northern *prov.* Zambia **127** F7
Northern Aegean *admin. reg.* Greece *see* **Voreio Aigaio**
Northern Areas *admin. div.* Pak. **101** H2
Northern Bahr el Ghazal *state* Sudan **126** E2
Northern Cape *prov.* S. Africa **132** D6
Northern Darfur *state* Sudan **121** E5
Northern Donets *r.* Rus. Fed./Ukr. *see* **Severskiy Donets**
Northern Dvina *r.* Rus. Fed. *see* **Severnaya Dvina**
Northern Indian Lake Canada **167** L3
Northern Ireland *prov.* U.K. **47** F9
Northern Kordofan *state* Sudan **121** F6
Northern Lau Group *is* Fiji **145** H3
Northern Light Lake Canada **168** B3

▸**Northern Mariana Islands** *terr.* N. Pacific Ocean **73** J3
United States Commonwealth. Historically known as Ladrones.
▸▸**138–139 Oceania** Countries

Northern Rhodesia *country* Africa *see* **Zambia**
Northern Rocky Mountains Provincial Park Canada **166** E3
Northern Sporades *is* Greece *see* **Voreioi Sporades**
Northern Territory *admin. div.* Australia **148** B3
Northern Transvaal *prov.* S. Africa *see* **Limpopo**
North Fabius *r.* U.S.A. **174** B4
Northfield *MA* U.S.A. **177** M3
Northfield *MN* U.S.A. **174** A2
Northfield *NJ* U.S.A. **171** H3
Northfield *VT* U.S.A. **177** M1
Northfield *WI* U.S.A. **172** B6
North Foreland *c.* U.K. **47** N12
North Fork U.S.A. **182** E4
North Fork Pass Canada **166** B1
North Fox Island U.S.A. **172** H5
North French *r.* Canada **168** D3
North Frisian Islands Germany **48** F1
also known as Nordfriesische Inseln
North Geomagnetic Pole Arctic Ocean **224** T1
North Haven U.S.A. **177** M4
North Head N.Z. **152** I4
North Henik Lake Canada **167** L2
North Hero U.S.A. **177** L1
North Highlands U.S.A. **182** C3
North Horr Kenya **128** C4
North Hudson U.S.A. **177** L2
North Island India **94** B4

▸**North Island** N.Z. **152** H6
3rd largest island in Oceania.
▸▸**134–135 Oceania** Landscapes

North Island Phil. **74** B1
North Islet *reef* Phil. **74** B4
North Jadito Canyon *gorge* U.S.A. **183** N6
North Judson U.S.A. **172** G9
North Kazakhstan Oblast *admin. div.* Kazakh. *see* **Severnyy Kazakhstan**
North Kingsville U.S.A. **176** E4
North Knife *r.* Canada **167** M3
North Knife Lake Canada **167** L3
North Koel *r.* India **97** D4
North Komelik U.S.A. **183** M9
▸**North Korea** *country* Asia **83** B4
▸▸**64–65 Asia** Countries
▸**North Korea** *country* Asia **83** B4
▸▸**64–65 Asia** Countries
North Lakhimpur India **97** G4
Northland *admin. reg.* N.Z. **152** I3
North Land *is* Rus. Fed. *see* **Severnaya Zemlya**
Northland Forest Park *nature res.* N.Z. **152** H3
North Las Vegas U.S.A. **183** I5
North Liberty U.S.A. **172** G9
North Little Rock U.S.A. **179** D5
North Loup *r.* U.S.A. **178** C3
North Luangwa National Park Zambia **129** B7
North Maalhosmadulu Atoll Maldives **94** B5
North Macmillan *r.* Canada **166** C2
North Magnetic Pole Canada **224** R1
North Mam Peak U.S.A. **180** F5
North Manchester U.S.A. **172** H10
North Middletown U.S.A. **176** A7
North Moose Lake Canada **167** K4
North Muiron Island Australia **150** A4
North Nahanni *r.* Canada **166** F2
North Ossetia *aut. rep.* Rus. Fed. *see* **Severnaya Osetiya-Alaniya, Respublika**
North Palisade *mt.* U.S.A. **182** F4
North Platte U.S.A. **178** B3
North Platte *r.* U.S.A. **178** B3
North Point Australia **151** A6
North Point *Hong Kong* China **87** [inset]
also known as Tsat Tsze Mui
North Pole Arctic Ocean **224** A1
Northport U.S.A. **175** C5
North Port U.S.A. **175** D7
North Reef Island India **95** G3
North Rhine - Westphalia *land* Germany *see* **Nordrhein-Westfalen**
North River Bridge Canada **169** I4
North Rona *i.* U.K. *see* **Rona**
North Ronaldsay *i.* U.K. **46** J4
North Saskatchewan *r.* Canada **167** J4
North Schell Peak U.S.A. **183** J2
North Sea Europe **46** N6
North Seal *r.* Canada **167** L3
North Sentinel Island India **95** G4
North Shoal Lake Canada **167** L5
North Shoshone Peak U.S.A. **183** G2
North Siberian Lowland Rus. Fed. **39** J2
also known as Severo-Sibirskaya Nizmennost'
North Similpal National Park India **97** E5
North Sinai *governorate* Egypt *see* **Shamāl Sīnā'**
North Slope *plain* U.S.A. **164** E3
North Spirit Lake Canada **167** M4
North Stradbroke Island Australia **147** G1
North Stratford U.S.A. **177** N1
North Taranaki Bight *b.* N.Z. **152** I6
North Thompson *r.* Canada **166** F5
North Tonawanda U.S.A. **176** G2
North Trap *reef* N.Z. **153** B15
North Troy U.S.A. **177** M1
North Truro U.S.A. **177** O3
North Tuas Basin *dock* Sing. **76** [inset]
North Twin Island Canada **168** E2
North Twin Lake Canada **169** K3
North Ubian *i.* Phil. **74** B5
North Uist *i.* U.K. **46** E6
also known as Uibhist a' Tuath
Northumberland Isles Australia **149** F4
Northumberland National Park U.K. **46** J8
Northumberland Strait Canada **169** H4
North Umpqua *r.* U.S.A. **180** B4
North Vancouver Canada **166** F5
Northville U.S.A. **177** K2
North Wabasca Lake Canada **167** H3
North Walsham U.K. **47** N11
North Waterford U.S.A. **177** O1
Northway U.S.A. **166** A2
Northway Junction U.S.A. **166** A2
North-West *admin. dist.* Botswana **130** D3
North West *prov.* S. Africa **133** J3
North West Cape Australia **150** A4
North-Western *prov.* Zambia **127** D8
North-West Frontier *prov.* Pak. **101** G3
North West Nelson Forest Park *nat. park* N.Z. *see* **Kahurangi National Park**
Northwest Providence Channel Bahamas **186** D1
North West River Canada **169** J2
Northwest Territories *admin. div.* Canada **167** J2
North Wilkesboro U.S.A. **176** D9
North Windham U.S.A. **177** O2
Northwood *IA* U.S.A. **174** A3
Northwood *ND* U.S.A. **178** C2
Northwood *NH* U.S.A. **177** N2
Northwoods Beach U.S.A. **172** B5
North York Canada **173** N7
North York Moors *moorland* U.K. **47** L9
North York Moors National Park U.K. **47** L9
Norton Canada **169** H4
Norton *KS* U.S.A. **178** C4
Norton *VT* U.S.A. **174** G2
Norton de Matos Angola *see* **Balombo**
Norton Shores U.S.A. **172** G7
Norton Sound *sea chan.* U.S.A. **164** C3
Nortorf Germany **48** G1
Nort-sur-Erdre France **50** E5
Norvegia, Cape Antarctica **223** X2
Norwalk *OH* U.S.A. **176** C4
Norwalk *WI* U.S.A. **172** C7
▸**Norway** *country* Europe **45** J3
known as Norge *or* Noreg *in Norwegian*
▸▸**32–33 Europe** Countries
Norway U.S.A. **177** O1
Norway Bay Canada **173** Q5
Norway House Canada **167** L4
Norwegian Bay Canada **165** J2
Norwegian Sea N. Atlantic Ocean **224** A2
Norwich Canada **173** M8
Norwich U.K. **47** N11
Norwich *CT* U.S.A. **177** M4
Norwich *NY* U.S.A. **177** J3
Norwood *MA* U.S.A. **177** N3
Norwood *NY* U.S.A. **177** K1
Norwood *OH* U.S.A. **176** A6
Norzagaray Phil. **74** B3
Nose Lake Canada **167** I1
Noshappu-misaki *hd* Japan **90** G2
Noshiro Japan **90** G4
Noshul' Rus. Fed. **40** I3
Nosivka Ukr. **41** D6
also spelt Nosovka
Nosop *watercourse* Africa *see* **Nossob**
Nosovaya Rus. Fed. **40** J1
Nosovka Ukr. *see* **Nosivka**
Noṣratābād Iran **101** D4
Nossa Senhora da Glória Brazil **200** B1
Nossa Senhora do Livramento Brazil **201** F3
Nossen Germany **49** K4
Nossob *watercourse* Africa **132** E3
also spelt Nosop
Nossob Camp S. Africa **132** E2
Nosy Varika Madag. **131** [inset] K4
Nota *r.* Fin./Rus. Fed. **44** O1
Notakwanon *r.* Canada **169** I1
Notch Peak U.S.A. **183** K2
Noteć *r.* Poland **49** M3
Notikewin *r.* Canada **166** G3
Notio Aigaio *admin. reg.* Greece **59** H12
English form Southern Aegean; *also spelt* Nótion Aiyaíon
Nótion Aiyaíon *admin. reg.* Greece *see* **Notio Aigaio**
Notios Evvoïkos Kolpos *sea chan.* Greece **59** E10
Notio Steno Kerkyras *sea chan.* Greece **59** B9
Noto *Sicily* Italy **57** H12
UNESCO World Heritage Site
Noto Japan **90** E6
Noto, Golfo di *g. Sicily* Italy **57** H12
Notodden Norway **45** J4
Noto-hantō *pen.* Japan **90** E6
Notre Dame, Monts *mts* Canada **169** G4
Notre Dame Bay Canada **169** K3
Notre-Dame-de-Koartac Canada *see* **Quaqtaq**
Notre-Dame-de-la-Salette Canada **173** R5
Notre-Dame-du-Laus Canada **173** R4
Notre-Dame-du-Nord Canada **173** N3
Notsé Togo **125** F5
Notsu Japan **91** B8
Notsuke-saki *pt* Japan **90** I3
Notsuke-suidō *sea chan.* Japan/Rus. Fed. **90** I3
also known as Izmeny, Proliv
Nottawasaga Bay Canada **173** M6
Nottaway *r.* Canada **168** E3
Nottingham U.K. **47** K11
Nottingham Island Canada **165** L3
Nottingham Road S. Africa **133** O6
Nottoway U.S.A. **176** G8
Nottoway *r.* U.S.A. **176** I9
Notukeu Creek *r.* Canada **167** J5
Nouabalé-Ndoki National Park Congo **126** C4
Nouâdhibou Mauritania **122** A5
formerly known as Port Étienne
Nouâdhibou, Râs *c.* Mauritania **122** A5

▸**Nouakchott** Mauritania **124** B2
Capital of Mauritania.

Noual *well* Mauritania **124** D2
Nouâmghâr Mauritania **124** A2
Nouei Vietnam **79** D5

▸**Nouméa** New Caledonia **145** F4
Capital of New Caledonia.

Noun *r.* Cameroon **125** H5
Nouna Burkina **124** E3
Noupoort S. Africa **133** I8
Noupoortsnek *pass* S. Africa **133** M5
Nousu Fin. **44** O2
Nouveau-Comptoir Canada *see* **Wemindji**
Nouvelle Anvers Dem. Rep. Congo *see* **Makanza**
Nouvelle Calédonie *i.* S. Pacific Ocean **145** F4
also known as New Caledonia
Nouvelle Calédonie *terr.* S. Pacific Ocean *see* **New Caledonia**
Nouvelles Hébrides *country* S. Pacific Ocean *see* **Vanuatu**
Nov Tajik. **101** G1
also spelt Nau
Nõva Estonia **42** E2
Nova Almeida Brazil **207** M7
Nova América Brazil **206** D2
Nova Aurora Brazil **206** E5
Novabad Tajik. *see* **Novobod**
Novabad Tajik. *see* **Novobod**
Nová Baňa Slovakia **49** P7
Nova Chaves Angola *see* **Muconda**
Novaci Romania **58** E3
Nova Crnja *Vojvodina, Srbija* Serb. and Mont. **58** B3
Nova Cruz Brazil **202** F3
Nova Era Brazil **207** J6
Nova Esperança Angola *see* **Buengas**
Nova Esperança Brazil **206** A10
Nova Freixa Moz. *see* **Cuamba**
Nova Friburgo Brazil **203** D7
Nova Gaia Angola *see* **Cambundi-Catembo**
Nova Goa India *see* **Panaji**
Nova Gorica Slovenia **56** F3
Nova Gradiška Croatia **56** J3
Nova Granada Brazil **206** D7
Nova Iguaçu Brazil **203** D7
Nova Kakhovka Ukr. **41** E7
also spelt Novaya Kakhovka
Nova Lima Brazil **203** D6
Nova Lisboa Angola *see* **Huambo**
Nova Londrina Brazil **201** G5
Novalukoml' Belarus **43** K7
also spelt Novolukoml'
Nova Mambone Moz. **131** G4
Nova Nabúri Moz. **131** H3
Nova Odesa Ukr. **41** D7
also spelt Novaya Odessa
Nová Paka Czech Rep. **49** M5
Nova Paraiso Brazil **199** F4
Nova Pazova *Vojvodina, Srbija* Serb. and Mont. **58** B4
Nova Pilão Arcado Brazil **202** D4
Nova Ponte Brazil **206** F6
Nova Ponte, Represa *resr Minas Gerais* Brazil **206** F6
Nova Ponte, Represa *resr* Brazil **203** C6
Novara Italy **56** A3
UNESCO World Heritage Site
Nova Remanso Brazil **202** D4
Nova Resende Brazil **206** G8
Nova Russas Brazil **202** D3
Nova Scotia *prov.* Canada **169** H5
historically known as Acadia
Nova Sento Sé Brazil **202** D4
Nova Serrana Brazil **207** I6
Nova Sintra Angola *see* **Catabola**
Nova Soure Brazil **202** E4
Novate Mezzola Italy **56** B2
Novato U.S.A. **182** B3
Nova Topola Bos.-Herz. **56** J3
Novator Rus. Fed. **40** H3
Nova Vandúzi Moz. **131** G3
Nova Varoš *Srbija* Serb. and Mont. **58** A5
Nova Venécia Brazil **203** D6
Nova Viçosa Brazil **207** N4
Nova Vida *Amazonas* Brazil **199** E5
Nova Vida *Rondônia* Brazil **201** E2
Nova Xavantino Brazil **206** A1
Novaya Kakhovka Ukr. *see* **Nova Kakhovka**
Novaya Kazanka Kazakh. **102** B2
also known as Zhanga Qazan
Novaya Ladoga Rus. Fed. **43** N1
Novaya Odessa Ukr. *see* **Nova Odesa**
Novaya Pismyanka Rus. Fed. *see* **Leninogorsk**
Novaya Sibir', Ostrov *i.* Rus. Fed. **39** O2

▸**Novaya Zemlya** *is* Rus. Fed. **40** J1
3rd largest island in Europe.
▸▸**28–29 Europe** Landscapes
▸▸**214–215 Arctic** Features

Novaya Zhizn Rus. Fed. *see* **Kazinka**
Nova Zagora Bulg. **58** H6
Novelda Spain **55** K6
Novellara Italy **56** C4
Nové Město nad Metují Czech Rep. **49** N5
Nové Mlýny, Vodní nádrž *resr* Czech Rep. **49** N7
Nové Zámky Slovakia **49** P8
Novgorod Rus. Fed. *see* **Velikiy Novgorod**
Novgorodka Rus. Fed. **43** J4
Novgorod Oblast *admin. div.* Rus. Fed. *see* **Novgorodskaya Oblast'**
Novgorod-Severskiy Ukr. *see* **Novhorod-Sivers'kyy**
Novgorodskaya Oblast' *admin. div.* Rus. Fed. **43** N3
English form Novgorod Oblast
Novgorod-Volynskiy Ukr. *see* **Novohrad-Volyns'kyy**
Novgradets Bulg. *see* **Suvorovo**
Novhorod-Sivers'kyy Ukr. **41** E6
also spelt Novgorod-Severskiy
Novi U.S.A. **173** J8
Novi Bečej *Vojvodina, Srbija* Serb. and Mont. **58** B3
Novichikha Rus. Fed. **103** J1
Novi Grad Bos.-Herz. *see* **Bosanski Novi**
Novi Iskŭr Bulg. **58** E6
Novikovo Rus. Fed. **82** F3
Novi Kozarci *Vojvodina, Srbija* Serb. and Mont. **58** B3
Novi Kritsim Bulg. *see* **Stamboliyski**
Novi Ligure Italy **56** A4
Novillero Mex. **184** D4
Novi Marof Croatia **56** I2
Novi Pazar Bulg. **58** I5
Novi Pazar *Srbija* Serb. and Mont. **58** B5
Novi Sad *Vojvodina, Srbija* Serb. and Mont. **58** A3
also known as Újvidék
Novi Travnik Bos.-Herz. **56** J4
formerly known as Pucarevo
Novi Vinodolski Croatia **56** G3
Novlenskoye Rus. Fed. **43** U2
Novoaleksandropov Rus. Fed. **82** F3
Novoaleksandrovsk Rus. Fed. **41** G7
Novoaleksandrovskiy Rus. Fed. **43** P7
Novoalekseyevka Kazakh. *see* **Khobda**
Novoaltaysk Rus. Fed. **80** C2
formerly known as Chesnokovka
Novoanninskiy Rus. Fed. **41** G6
Novo Aripuanã Brazil **199** F6
Novoazovs'k Ukr. **41** F7
Novo Beograd *Srbija* Serb. and Mont. **58** B4
Novobod Tajik. **101** G2
also spelt Novabad
Novobod Tajik. **101** G2
also spelt Navabad; *formerly known as* Shul'mak; *formerly spelt* Novabad
Novobogatinsk Kazakh. *see* **Khamit Yergaliyev**
Novobureyskiy Rus. Fed. **82** C2
formerly known as Bureya-Pristan'
Novocheboksarsk Rus. Fed. **40** H4
Novocherkassk Rus. Fed. **41** G7
Novo Cruzeiro Brazil **203** D6
Novodolinka Kazakh. **103** H2
Novodugino Rus. Fed. **43** P6
Novodvinsk Rus. Fed. **40** G2
formerly known as Pervomayskiy
Novogeorgiyevka Rus. Fed. **82** B2
Novognezdilovo Rus. Fed. **43** Q9
Novogrudok Belarus *see* **Navahrudak**
Novogurovskiy Rus. Fed. **43** S7
Novo Hamburgo Brazil **203** B9
Novo Horizonte Brazil **206** D8
Novohrad-Volyns'kyy Ukr. **41** C6
also spelt Novgorod-Volynskiy
Novoil'insk Rus. Fed. **85** F1
Novoishimskiy Kazakh. **103** F1
also known as Küybyshev; *formerly known as* Trudovoy
Novokazalinsk Kazakh. *see* **Ayteke Bi**
Novokhopersk Rus. Fed. **41** G6
Novokhovansk Rus. Fed. **43** K6
Novokiyevskiy Uval Rus. Fed. **82** C2
Novokizhinginsk Rus. Fed. **85** F1
Novokubansk Rus. Fed. **107** E1
formerly known as Novokubanskiy
Novokubanskiy Rus. Fed. *see* **Novokubansk**
Novokuybyshevsk Rus. Fed. **102** B1
Novokuznetsk Rus. Fed. **80** D2
formerly known as Stalinsk
Novolazarevskaya *research station* Antarctica **223** A2
Novolukoml' Belarus *see* **Novalukoml'**
Novol'vovsk Rus. Fed. **43** T8
Novo Marapi Brazil **199** E5
Novomarkovka Kazakh. **103** H2
Novo Mesto Slovenia **56** H3
Novomichurinsk Rus. Fed. **43** U7
Novomikhaylovskiy Rus. Fed. **41** F7
Novo Miloševo *Vojvodina, Srbija* Serb. and Mont. **58** B3
Novomirgorod Ukr. *see* **Novomyrhorod**
Novomoskovsk Rus. Fed. **43** T7
formerly known as Bobriki *or* Stalinogorsk
Novomoskovs'k Ukr. **41** E6
Novomyrhorod Ukr. **41** D6
also spelt Novomirgorod
Novonazyvayevka Rus. Fed. *see* **Nazyvayevsk**
Novonikolayevka Kazakh. **103** G4
Novonikolayevsk Rus. Fed. *see* **Novosibirsk**
Novonikolayevskiy Rus. Fed. **41** G6
Novooleksiyivka Ukr. **41** E7
Novo Olinda do Norte Brazil **199** G5
Novo Oriente Brazil **202** D3
Novoorsk Rus. Fed. **102** D2
Novo Parnarama Brazil **202** D3
Novopashiyskiy Rus. Fed. *see* **Gornozavodsk**
Novopavlovka Rus. Fed. **85** F1
Novopokrovka *Kustanayskaya Oblast'* Kazakh. **103** F1
Novopokrovka *Severnyy Kazakhstan* Kazakh. **103** F1
Novopokrovka *Vostochnyy Kazakhstan* Kazakh. **103** J2
Novopokrovka Rus. Fed. **82** D3
Novopokrovskaya Rus. Fed. **41** G7
Novopolotsk Belarus *see* **Navapolatsk**
Novopolyan'ye Rus. Fed. **43** U8
Novopskov Ukr. **41** F6
Novo Redondo Angola *see* **Sumbe**
Novorepnoye Rus. Fed. **102** B2
Novorossiysk Rus. Fed. **41** F7
Novorossiyskiy Kazakh. *see* **Akzhar**

Novorybnaya Rus. Fed. 39 K2
Novorzhev Rus. Fed. 43 K4
Novoselki *Moskovskaya Oblast'* Rus. Fed. 43 T7
Novoselki *Tverskaya Oblast'* Rus. Fed. 43 M6
Novoselovo Rus. Fed. 43 U5
Novoselskoye Rus. Fed. *see* **Achkhoy-Martan**
Novosel'ye Rus. Fed. 43 J3
Novosergiyevka Rus. Fed. 102 C1
Novoshakhtinsk Rus. Fed. 41 F7
Novoshakhtinskiy Rus. Fed. 82 D3
Novosheshminsk Rus. Fed. 40 I5
Novosibirsk Rus. Fed. 80 C1
formerly known as Novonikolayevsk
Novosibirskaya Oblast' *admin. div.* Rus. Fed. 80 C1
English form Novosibirsk Oblast
Novosibirskiye Ostrova *is* Rus. Fed. *see* **New Siberia Islands**
Novosibirsk Oblast *admin. div.* Rus. Fed. *see* **Novosibirskaya Oblast'**
Novosil' Rus. Fed. 43 S9
Novosokol'niki Rus. Fed. 43 L5
Novospasskoye Rus. Fed. 41 H5
Novotroitsk Rus. Fed. 102 D2
Novotroitskoye Kazakh. *see* **Tole Bi**
Novotroitskoye Rus. Fed. 43 O8
Novotroyits'ke Ukr. 41 E7
Novoukrainka Ukr. *see* **Novoukrayinka**
Novoukrayinka Ukr. 41 D6
also spelt Novoukrainka
Novoural'sk Rus. Fed. 102 D2
Novouzensk Rus. Fed. 102 B2
Novovasylivka Ukr. 43 O9
Novo Virje Croatia 56 J2
Novovolyns'k Ukr. 41 C6
Novovoronezh Rus. Fed. 41 F6
formerly known as Novovoronezhskiy
Novovoronezhskiy Rus. Fed. *see* **Novovoronezh**
Novo-Voskresenovka Rus. Fed. 82 B1
Novovoznesenovka Kyrg. 103 I4
Novoyamskoye Rus. Fed. 43 P9
Novoye Dubovoye Rus. Fed. 43 U9
Novoyegor'yevskoye Rus. Fed. 103 J2
Novoye Leushino Rus. Fed. 43 V5
Novozavidovskiy Rus. Fed. 43 R5
Novozhilovskaya Rus. Fed. 40 I2
Novozybkov Rus. Fed. 43 M9
Novska Croatia 56 I3
Novy Boletsk Belarus 43 L6
Nový Bor Czech Rep. 49 L5
Novy Bykhaw Belarus 43 L8
Novy Dvor Belarus 42 F9
Nový Jičín Czech Rep. 49 O6
Novyya Kruki Belarus 42 I6
Novyya Zhuravichy Belarus 43 L8
Novyy Bor Rus. Fed. 40 J2
Novyye Burasy Rus. Fed. 102 A1
Novyye Ivaytenki Rus. Fed. 43 O9
Novyye Petushki Rus. Fed. *see* **Petushki**
Novyy Izborsk Rus. Fed. 42 I4
Novyy Kholmogory Rus. Fed. *see* **Archangel**
Novyy Margelan Uzbek. *see* **Farg'ona**
Novyy Nekouz Rus. Fed. 43 T4
Novyy Oskol Rus. Fed. 41 F6
Novyy Port Rus. Fed. 38 H3
Novyy Ropsk Rus. Fed. 43 N9
Novyy Sinets Rus. Fed. 43 R8
Novyy Urengoy Rus. Fed. 38 H3
Novyy Urgal Rus. Fed. 82 D2
formerly known as Raz"yezd 3km
Novyy Uzen' Kazakh. *see* **Zhanaozen**
Novyy Zay Rus. Fed. 40 J5
Now Iran 100 C4
Nowa Dęba Poland 49 S5
Nowa Ruda Poland 49 N5
Nowa Sarzyna Poland 49 T5
Nowa Sól Poland 49 M4
Nowata U.S.A. 178 D4
Now Dezh Iran 100 B3
Nowdī Iran 100 B2
Nowe Poland 49 P2
Nowe Miasteczko Poland 49 M4
Nowe Miasto Lubawskie Poland 49 Q2
Nowe Miasto nad Pilicą Poland 49 R4
Nowe Skalmierzyce Poland 49 O4
Now Gombad Iran 100 C3
Nowgong *Assam* India *see* **Nagaon**
Nowgong *Madhya Pradesh* India 96 C4
Now Kharegan Iran 100 C2
Nowleye Lake Canada 167 K2
Nowogard Poland 49 M2
Nowogród Poland 49 S2
Nowogród Bobrzański Poland 49 M4
Nowood *r.* U.S.A. 180 F3
Noworadomsk Poland *see* **Radomsko**
Nowra Australia 147 F3
Nowshahr Iran 100 B2
Now Shahr Iran 100 B2
Nowshera Pak. 101 H3
Nowsūd Iran 100 A3
Nowy Dwór Gdański Poland 49 Q1
Nowy Dwór Mazowiecki Poland 49 R3
Nowy Sącz Poland 49 R6
historically known as Neu Sandez
Nowy Staw Poland 49 Q1
Nowy Targ Poland 49 R6
Nowy Tomyśl Poland 49 N3
Noxen U.S.A. 177 I4
Noxubee National Wildlife Refuge *nature res.* U.S.A. 175 B5
Noy, Xé *r.* Laos 78 D4
Noy, Xé *r.* Laos 78 D4
Noya Spain *see* **Noia**
Noyabr'sk Rus. Fed. 38 H3
Noyant France 50 G5
Noyes Island U.S.A. 166 C4
Noyil *r.* India 94 C4
Noyon France 51 I3
Nozay France 50 E5
Nozizwe S. Africa 133 J7
Npitamaiong *mt.* Kenya 128 B4
Nqabeni S. Africa 133 O7
Nqamakwe S. Africa 133 L9
Nqutu S. Africa 133 O5
Nsalamu Zambia 127 F8
Nsambi Dem. Rep. Congo 126 C5
Nsanje Malawi 129 B9
formerly known as Port Herald
Nsawam Ghana 125 E5
Nseluka Zambia 127 F7
Nsoc Equat. Guinea 125 H6
Nsoko Swaziland 133 P4
Nsombo Zambia 127 F7
Nsukka Nigeria 125 G5
Nsumbu National Park Zambia *see* **Sumbu National Park**
Ntalfa *well* Mauritania 122 B5
Ntambu Zambia 127 E8
Ntandembele Dem. Rep. Congo 126 C5
Ntcheu Malawi 129 B8
formerly spelt Ncheu
Ntchisi Malawi 129 B8
Ntem *r.* Cameroon 125 H6
formerly known as Campo
Ntha S. Africa 133 L4
Ntibane S. Africa 133 M8
Ntiona Chad 120 B6
Ntoroko Uganda 128 A4
Ntoum Gabon 126 A4
Ntshingwayo Dam S. Africa 133 N4
Ntui Cameroon 125 H5
Ntungamo Uganda 128 A5
Ntwetwe Pan *salt pan* Botswana 131 E4
Ntywenka S. Africa 133 M8
Nuakata Island P.N.G. 149 F1
Nuanetsi *r.* Zimbabwe *see* **Mwenezi**
Nuangan Indon. 75 C2
Nu'aym *reg.* Oman 105 F3
Nuba, Lake *resr* Sudan 121 F4
Nuba Mountains Sudan 128 A2
Nubian Desert Sudan 121 G4
Nubivarri *hill* Norway 44 M1
Nubra *r.* India 96 C2
Nucet Romania 58 D2
Nüden Mongolia 85 F3
Nudol' Rus. Fed. 43 R5
Nueces *r.* U.S.A. 179 C7
Nueltin Lake Canada 167 L2
Nueva, Isla *i.* Chile 205 D9
Nueva Alejandría Peru 198 C6
Nueva Arcadia Hond. 186 A4
Nueva Ciudad Guerrero Mex. 179 C7
Nueva Esparta *state* Venez. 199 E2
Nueva Florida Venez. 198 D2
Nueva Germania Para. 201 F5
Nueva Gerona Cuba 186 C2
Nueva Harberton Arg. 205 D9
Nueva Lubecka Arg. 205 C7
Nueva Ocotepeque Hond. 186 A4
Nueva Palmira Uruguay 204 F4
Nueva Rosita Mex. 185 E3
Nueva San Salvador El Salvador 185 H6
Nueva Villa de Padilla Mex. 185 F3
Nueve de Julio Arg. *see* **9 de Julio**
Nuevitas Cuba 186 D2
Nuevo, Cayo *i.* Mex. 185 H4
Nuevo, Golfo *g.* Arg. 205 D6
Nuevo Casas Grandes Mex. 184 D2
Nuevo Ideal Mex. 184 D3
Nuevo Laredo Mex. 185 F3
Nuevo León Mex. 183 I9
Nuevo León *state* Mex. 185 F3
Nuevo Mamo Venez. 187 H5
Nufayyid Şabḩah *des.* Saudi Arabia 104 D3
Nuga Mongolia 84 B1
Nugaal *admin. reg.* Somalia 128 F2
Nugaal *watercourse* Somalia 128 F3
Nuga Nuga, Lake Australia 149 F5
Nugget Point N.Z. 153 D14
Nugr' *r.* Rus. Fed. 43 R8
Nugu *r.* India 94 C3
Nuguria Islands P.N.G. 145 E2
also known as Fead Group
Nuh, Ras *pt* Pak. 101 E5
Nuhaka N.Z. 152 L7
Nui *i.* Tuvalu 145 G2
Nui Con Voi *r.* Vietnam *see* **Red River**
Nuijamaa Fin. 43 J1
Nui Ti On *mt.* Vietnam 79 D5
Nuits-St-Georges France 51 K5
Nu Jiang *r.* China 86 A3 *see* **Salween**
Nukey Bluff *hill* Australia 146 B3
Nukha Azer. *see* **Şäki**
Nūklok, Chāh-e *well* Iran 100 C3

▶Nuku'alofa Tonga 145 H4
Capital of Tonga.
▶▶8–9 World Countries

Nukufetau *i.* Tuvalu 145 G2
Nukulaelae *i.* Tuvalu 145 G2
also spelt Nukulailai; *formerly known as* Mitchell Island
Nukulailai *i.* Tuvalu *see* **Nukulaelae**
Nukumanu Islands P.N.G. 145 E2
Nukunau *i.* Kiribati *see* **Nikunau**
Nukunono *atoll* Tokelau *see* **Nukunonu**
Nukunonu *atoll* Tokelau 145 H2
also spelt Nukunono; *formerly known as* Duke of Clarence
Nukus Uzbek. 102 D4
also spelt Nökis
Nulato U.S.A. 164 D3
Nules Spain 55 K5
Nullagine Australia 150 C4
Nullagine *r.* Australia 150 C4
Nullarbor Australia 146 A2
Nullarbor National Park Australia 146 A2
Nullarbor Plain Australia 146 A2
Nullarbor Regional Reserve *park* Australia 146 A2
Nuluarniavik, Lac *l.* Canada 168 E1
Nulu'erhu Shan *mts* China 85 H3
Num *i.* Indon. 73 I7
Num Nepal 97 E4
Numalla, Lake *salt flat* Australia 147 E2
Numan Nigeria 125 I4
Nu'mān *i.* Saudi Arabia 104 A2
Numata *Gumma* Japan 91 F6
Numata *Hokkaidō* Japan 90 G3
Numazu Japan 91 F7
Numbi Gate S. Africa 133 P2
Numbulwar Australia 148 B2
Numfoor *i.* Indon. 73 H7
Numin He *r.* China 82 B3
Numkaub Namibia 130 C3
Nummi Fin. 45 M3
Numurkah Australia 147 E4
Nunaksaluk Island Canada 169 I2
Nunakuluut *i.* Greenland 165 O3
also known as Nunarsuit
Nunap Isua *c.* Greenland *see* **Farewell, Cape**
Nunarsuit *i.* Greenland *see* **Nunakuluut**
Nunavik *reg.* Canada 169 E1
Nunavut *admin. div.* Canada 167 L2
Nunda U.S.A. 176 H3
Nuneaton U.K. 47 K11
Nungatta National Park Australia 147 F4
Nungesser Lake Canada 167 M5
Nungnain Sum China 85 H2
Nungo Moz. 131 H2
Nunivak Island U.S.A. 164 C4
Nunkapasi India 95 E1
Nunkun *mt.* Jammu and Kashmir 96 C2
Nunligran Rus. Fed. 39 S3
Nuñoa Peru 200 C3
Nuñomoral Spain 54 E4
Nunukan *i.* Indon. 77 G2
Nuojiang China *see* **Tongjiang**
Nuoro *Sardinia* Italy 57 B8
Nupani *i.* Solomon Is 145 F3
Nuqayy, Jabal *mts* Libya 120 C4
Nuqrah Saudi Arabia 104 C2
Nuquş, Jabal *mt.* Egypt 121 G3
Nuquí Col. 198 B3
Nur *r.* Iran 100 C2
Nura Kazakh. 103 I4
Nura *r.* Kazakh. 103 G2
Nūrābād Iran 100 B4
Nurakita *i.* Tuvalu *see* **Niulakita**
Nurata Uzbek. *see* **Nurota**
Nur Dağları *mts* Turkey 107 C3
Nure *r.* Italy 56 B3
Nurek Tajik. *see* **Norak**
Nuremberg Germany 48 I6
also spelt Nürnberg
Nūrestān Afgh. 101 G3
Nūrestān *prov.* Afgh. 101 G3
Nūrestān *reg.* Afgh. 101 G3
Nūr Gal Afgh. 101 G3
Nuri Mex. 184 C2
Nuri Sudan 121 G5
Nuri, Teluk *b.* Indon. 77 E3
Nurla Jammu and Kashmir 96 C2
Nurlat Rus. Fed. 40 I5
Nurmes Fin. 44 O3
Nurmijärvi Fin. 45 N3
Nurmo Fin. 44 M3
Nürnberg Germany *see* **Nuremberg**
Nurota Uzbek. 103 F4
also spelt Nurata
Nurota tizmasi *mts* Uzbek. 103 F4
Nurpur Pak. 101 G4
Nurrai Lakes *salt flat* Australia 146 A2
Nurri, Mount *hill* Australia 147 E2
Nursfjellet *mt.* Norway 44 K2
Nurste Estonia 42 D3
Nürtingen Germany 48 G7
Nurzec *r.* Poland 49 T3
Nusa Tenggara Barat *prov.* Indon. 77 G5
English form Western Lesser Sunda Islands
Nusa Tenggara Timur *prov.* Indon. 75 B5
English form Eastern Lesser Sunda Islands
Nusaybin Turkey 107 E3
historically known as Nisibis
Nusela, Kepulauan *is* Indon. 75 D3
Nuşfalău Romania 58 D1
Nu Shan *mts* China 86 A3
Nushki Pak. 101 F4
Nutak Canada 169 I1
Nutarawit Lake Canada 167 L2
Nutrioso U.S.A. 183 O8
Nutwood Downs Australia 148 B2
Nuugaatsiaap Imaa *inlet* Greenland 165 N2
also known as Karrats Fjord
Nuugaatsiaq Greenland 165 N2

▶Nuuk Greenland 165 N3
Capital of Greenland. Also known as Godthåb.
▶▶8–9 World Countries

Nuuksion kansallispuisto *nat. park* Fin. 42 F1
Nuupas Fin. 44 N2
Nuussuaq Greenland 165 N2
also known as Kraulshavn
Nuussuaq *pen.* Greenland 165 N2
Nuwakot Nepal 97 D3
Nuwaybi' al Muzayyinah Egypt 121 G2
Nuwekloof *pass* S. Africa 132 H10
Nuwerus S. Africa 132 C8
Nuweveldberge *mts* S. Africa 132 F9
Nuyts, Point Australia 151 B7
Nuyts Archipelago *is* Australia 146 B3
Nuyts Archipelago Conservation Park *nature res.* Australia 146 B3
Nuytsland Nature Reserve Australia 151 D7
Nuzvid India 94 D2
Nxai Pan National Park Botswana 131 E3
Nxaunxau Botswana 130 D3
Nyaän, Bukit *hill* Indon. 77 F2
Nyabessan Cameroon 125 H6
Nyabing Australia 151 B7
Nyack U.S.A. 177 L4
Nyagan' Rus. Fed. 38 G3
formerly known as Nyakh
Nyagquka China *see* **Yajiang**
Nyagrong China *see* **Xinlong**
Nyahua Tanz. 129 B6
Nyahururu Kenya 128 C4
formerly known as Thompson's Falls
Nyainqêntanglha Feng *mt.* China 89 E6
Nyainqêntanglha Shan *mts* China 89 E6
English form Nyenchen Tanglha Range
Nyainrong China 89 F5
also known as Sêrkang
Nyakahura Tanz. 128 A5
Nyakaliro Tanz. 128 B5
Nyakallong S. Africa 133 K4
Nyakanazi Tanz. 128 A5
Nyåker Sweden 44 L3
Nyakh Rus. Fed. *see* **Nyagan'**
Nyakhachava Belarus 42 G9
Nyakrom Ghana 125 E5
Nyala Sudan 120 E6
Nyalam China *see* **Congdü**
Nyamandhlovu Zimbabwe 131 F3
Nyamapanda Zimbabwe 131 G3
Nyambiti Tanz. 128 B5
Nyamirembe Tanz. 128 A5
Nyamlell Sudan 126 E2
Nyamtumbo Tanz. 129 C7
Nyande Zimbabwe *see* **Masvingo**
Nyandoma Rus. Fed. 40 G3
Nyandomskiy Vozvyshennost' *hills* Rus. Fed. 40 F3
Nyanga Congo 126 A5
Nyanga Gabon 126 A5
Nyanga *prov.* Gabon 126 A5
Nyanga Zimbabwe 131 G3
formerly spelt Inyanga
Nyanga National Park Zimbabwe 131 G3
formerly known as Rhodes Inyanga National Park; *formerly spelt* Inyanga National Park
Nyang Qu *r.* China 89 E6
Nyang Qu *r.* China 89 F6
Nyankpala Ghana 125 E4
Nyanza *prov.* Kenya 128 B5
Nyapa, Gunung *mt.* Indon. 77 G2
Nyapongeth Sudan 128 B3
Nyar *r.* India 96 C3
Nyarling *r.* Canada 167 H2

▶Nyasa, Lake Africa 129 B7
3rd largest lake in Africa and 9th in the world. Also known as Malawi, Lake or Niassa, Lago.
▶▶6–7 World Landscapes
▶▶110–111 Africa Landscapes

Nyasaland *country* Africa *see* **Malawi**
Nyashabozh Rus. Fed. 40 J2
Nyasvizh Belarus 42 H8
also spelt Nesvizh
Nyathi Zimbabwe 131 F3
formerly spelt Inyati
Nyaunglebin Myanmar 78 B4
Nyaungu Myanmar 78 A3
Nyays *r.* Rus. Fed. 40 L3
Nyazura Zimbabwe 131 G3
formerly spelt Inyazura
Nyborg Denmark 45 J5
Nyborg Norway 44 O1
Nyborg Sweden 44 M2
Nybro Sweden 45 K4
Nyeboe Land *reg.* Greenland 165 N1
Nyeharelaye Belarus 42 I8
Nyêmo China 89 E6
also known as Tarrong
Nyenchen Tanglha Range *mts* China *see* **Nyainqêntanglha Shan**
Nyeri Kenya 128 C5
Nyeshcharda, Vozyera *l.* Belarus 43 K6
Nyhammar Sweden 45 K3
Nyi, Co *l.* China 89 D5
Nyika National Park Zambia 129 B7
also known as Malawi National Park
Nyika Plateau Malawi 129 B7
Nyima China 89 D6
Nyimba Zambia 127 F8
Nyingchi China 89 F6
also known as Pula
Nyinma China *see* **Maqu**
Nyiradony Hungary 49 S8
Nyiragongo *vol.* Dem. Rep. Congo 126 F5
Nyírbátor Hungary 49 T8
Nyírbéltek Hungary 49 T8
Nyíregyháza Hungary 49 S8
Nyiri Desert Kenya 128 C5
Nyiru, Mount Kenya 128 C4
Nykarleby Fin. 44 M3
also known as Uusikaarlepyy
Nykøbing Denmark 45 J5
Nykøbing Mors Denmark 45 J4
Nykøbing Sjælland Denmark 45 J5
Nyköping Sweden 45 L4
Nykvarn Sweden 45 L4
Nylsvley *nature res.* S. Africa 133 M1
Nymagee Australia 147 E3
Nymboida National Park Australia 147 G2
Nymburk Czech Rep. 49 M5
Nynäshamn Sweden 45 L4
Nyngan Australia 147 E2
Nyogzê China 89 C6
Nyoman *r.* Belarus/Lith. 42 E8
also spelt Neman
Nyomanskaya Nizina *lowland* Belarus 42 G8
Nyon Switz. 51 M6
Nyong *r.* Cameroon 125 H6
Nyons France 51 L8
Nýřany Czech Rep. 49 K6
Nyrob Rus. Fed. 40 K3
Nyrud Norway 44 O1
Nysa Poland 49 O5
Nysa Kłodzka *r.* Poland 49 O5
Nysa Łużycka *r.* Germany/Poland *see* **Neiße**
Nysäter Sweden 45 K4
Nysätern Sweden 44 K3
Nysh Rus. Fed. 82 F2
Nyssa U.S.A. 180 C4
Nystad Fin. *see* **Uusikaupunki**
Nyūdō-zaki *pt* Japan 90 F5
Nyuk, Ozero *l.* Rus. Fed. 44 O2
Nyuksenitsa Rus. Fed. 40 H3
Nyunzu Dem. Rep. Congo 127 F6
Nyurba Rus. Fed. 39 L3
Nyuvchim Rus. Fed. 40 I3
Nyuya Rus. Fed. 39 L3
Nyuya *r.* Rus. Fed. 39 L3
Nyyskiy Zaliv *lag.* Rus. Fed. 82 F1
Nyzhn'ohirs'kyy Ukr. 41 E7
Nzambi Congo 126 A5
Nzara Sudan 126 F3
Nzébéla Guinea 124 C4
Nzega Tanz. 129 B6
Nzérékoré Guinea 124 C5
N'zeto Angola 127 B6
formerly known as Ambrizete
Nzi *r.* Côte d'Ivoire 124 D5
Nzilo, Lac *l.* Dem. Rep. Congo 127 E7
Nzingu Dem. Rep. Congo 126 E5
Nzo *r.* Côte d'Ivoire 124 D5
N'Zo, Réserve de Faune du *nature res.* Côte d'Ivoire 124 D5
Nzobe Dem. Rep. Congo 127 B6
Nzoia *r.* Kenya 128 B4
Nzoro *r.* Dem. Rep. Congo 126 F4
Nzwani *i.* Comoros 129 E8
also known as Anjouan; *also spelt* Ndjouani

O

Oahe, Lake U.S.A. 178 B2
O'ahu *i.* U.S.A. 181 [inset] Y1
Oaitupu *i.* Tuvalu *see* **Vaitupu**
Oakbank Australia 146 D3
Oak Bluffs U.S.A. 177 O4
Oak City U.S.A. 183 L2
Oak Creek U.S.A. 172 F8
Oakdale *CA* U.S.A. 182 D4
Oakdale *LA* U.S.A. 179 D6
Oakes U.S.A. 178 C2
Oakey Australia 147 F1
Oakfield U.S.A. 176 G2
Oak Grove *LA* U.S.A. 175 B5
Oak Grove *MI* U.S.A. 173 I6
Oakham U.K. 47 L11
Oak Harbor *OH* U.S.A. 176 B4
Oak Harbor *WA* U.S.A. 180 B2
Oak Hill *OH* U.S.A. 176 C7
Oak Hill *WV* U.S.A. 176 D8
Oakhurst U.S.A. 182 E4
Oak Island U.S.A. 172 C4
Oak Knolls U.S.A. 182 D7
Oak Lake Canada 167 K5
Oakland *CA* U.S.A. 182 B4
Oakland *MD* U.S.A. 176 F6
Oakland *ME* U.S.A. 177 P1
Oakland *NE* U.S.A. 178 C3
Oakland *airport* U.S.A. 182 B4
Oakland City U.S.A. 174 C4
Oaklands Australia 147 E3
Oak Lawn U.S.A. 174 C3
Oakley *KS* U.S.A. 178 B4
Oakley *MI* U.S.A. 173 I7
Oakover *r.* Australia 150 C4
Oak Park U.S.A. 172 F9
Oakridge U.S.A. 180 B4
Oak Ridge U.S.A. 176 A9
Oakura N.Z. 152 H7
Oak View U.S.A. 182 E7
Oakville Canada 168 E5
Oamaru N.Z. 153 E13
Oaonui N.Z. 152 H7
Oaro N.Z. 153 H10
Oasis U.S.A. 182 G4
Oates Coast *reg.* Antarctica *see* **Oates Land**
Oates Land *reg.* Antarctica 223 K2
also known as Oates Coast
Oatlands Australia 147 E5
Oatlands S. Africa 133 I9
Oaxaca Mex. 185 F5
UNESCO World Heritage Site
Oaxaca *state* Mex. 185 F5
Ob' *r.* Rus. Fed. 38 G3
Ob, Gulf of *sea chan.* Rus. Fed. *see* **Obskaya Guba**
Oba Canada 168 C3
Oba *i.* Vanuatu *see* **Aoba**
Obaghan *r.* Kazakh. *see* **Ubagan**
Obal' Belarus 43 K6
Obal' *canal* Belarus 43 K6
Obala Cameroon 125 H5
Oba Lake Canada 173 I2
Obama Japan 91 D7
Oban Nigeria 125 H5
Oban U.K. 46 G7
Obanazawa Japan 90 G5
Oban Hills *mt.* Nigeria 125 H5
O Barco Spain 54 E2
also known as El Barco de Valdeorras
Obbia Somalia *see* **Hobyo**
Obbola Sweden 44 M3
Obdorsk Rus. Fed. *see* **Salekhard**
Óbecse *Vojvodina, Srbija* Serb. and Mont. *see* **Bečej**
Obed Canada 167 G4
Obeliai Lith. 42 G6
Obelisk *mt.* N.Z. 153 D13
Oberá Arg. 204 G2
Oberau Germany 48 I8
Obere Donau *park* Germany 48 F7
Obere Saale *park* Germany 48 I5
Oberes Westerzgebirge *park* Germany 49 J5
Oberlausitzer Bergland *park* Germany 49 L4
Oberlin *KS* U.S.A. 178 B4
Oberlin *LA* U.S.A. 179 D6
Obernai France 51 N4
Oberndorf am Neckar Germany 48 F7
Oberon Australia 147 F3
Oberpfälzer Wald *mts* Germany 49 J6
Oberpullendorf Austria 49 N8
Oberstdorf Germany 48 H8
Oberviechtach Germany 49 J6
Oberwart Austria 49 N8
Obi *i.* Indon. 75 C3
Obi, Kepulauan *is* Indon. 75 C3
Obi, Selat *sea chan.* Indon. 75 C3
Óbidos Brazil 199 H5
Obigarm Tajik. 101 G2
Obihiro Japan 90 H3
Obilatu *i.* Indon. 75 C3
Obilić *Kosovo, Srbija* Serb. and Mont. 58 C6
Obil'noye Rus. Fed. 41 H7
Obion *r.* U.S.A. 174 B4
Obira Japan 90 G2

▶Ob'-Irtysh *r.* Asia 38 G3
2nd longest river in Asia and 5th in the world.
▶▶6–7 World Landscapes
▶▶60–61 Asia Landscapes

Obispos Venez. 198 D2
Obluch'ye Rus. Fed. 82 C2
Obninsk Rus. Fed. 43 R6
Obnora *r.* Rus. Fed. 43 V3
Obo Cent. Afr. Rep. 126 E3
Obo China 84 D4
Obobogorap S. Africa 132 E4
Obock Djibouti 128 D2
Obokote Dem. Rep. Congo 126 E5
Obolo Nigeria 125 G5
Obong, Gunung *mt. Sarawak* Malaysia 77 F1
Oborniki Poland 49 N3
Obouya Congo 126 B5
Oboyan' Rus. Fed. 41 F6
Obozerskiy Rus. Fed. 40 G3
Obra India 97 D4
Obra *r.* Poland 49 M3
Obrage Arg. 204 F3
Obregón, Presa *resr* Mex. 184 C3
Obrenovac *Srbija* Serb. and Mont. 58 B4
O'Brien U.S.A. 180 B4
Obrochishte Bulg. 58 J5
Obruk Turkey 106 C3
Obrzycko Poland 49 N3
Observatory Hill Australia 146 B2
Observatory Inlet Canada 166 D4
Obsha *r.* Rus. Fed. 43 N6
Obshchiy Syrt *hills* Rus. Fed. 102 B2
Obskaya Guba *sea chan.* Rus. Fed. 38 H3
English form Ob, Gulf of
Obuasi Ghana 125 E5
Obubra Nigeria 125 H5
Obudovac Bos.-Herz. 56 K4
Obudu Nigeria 125 H5
Obukhovo Rus. Fed. 43 T6
Obva *r.* Rus. Fed. 40 J4
Ob"yachevo Rus. Fed. 40 I3
Ocala U.S.A. 175 D6
Ocampo Mex. 185 E3
Ocaña Col. 198 C2
Ocaña Peru 200 B3
Ocaña Spain 55 H5
O Carballiño Spain 54 C2
Occidental, Cordillera *mts* Chile 200 C4
Occidental, Cordillera *mts* Col. 198 B4
Occidental, Cordillera *mts* Peru 200 C4
Oceana U.S.A. 176 D8
Ocean Beach U.S.A. 177 L5
Ocean Cape U.S.A. 166 B3
Ocean Cay *i.* Bahamas 186 D1
Ocean City *MD* U.S.A. 177 J7
Ocean City *NJ* U.S.A. 177 K6
Ocean Falls Canada 166 E4
Ocean Island Kiribati *see* **Banaba**
Ocean Island *atoll* U.S.A. *see* **Kure Atoll**
Oceano U.S.A. 182 D6
Oceanside U.S.A. 183 G8
Ocean Springs U.S.A. 175 B6
Ochakiv Ukr. 41 D7
Och'amch'ire Georgia 107 E2
Ocher Rus. Fed. 40 J4
Ochi *mt.* Greece 59 F10
also known as Ókhi Óros
Ōchi Japan 91 C7
Ochiishi-misaki *pt* Japan 90 I3
Ochil Hills U.K. 46 I7
Ochkyne Ukr. 43 O9
Ochlockonee *r.* U.S.A. 175 C6
Ochrida, Lake Albania/Macedonia *see* **Ohrid, Lake**
Ochsenfurt Germany 48 H6
Ochthonia Greece 59 F10
also spelt Okhthonia
Ochthonia, Akra *pt* Greece 59 F10
Ocilla U.S.A. 175 D6
Ockelbo Sweden 45 L3
Ocland Romania 58 G2
Ocmulgee *r.* U.S.A. 175 D6
Ocna Mureş Romania 58 E2
Ocna Sibiului Romania 58 F3
Ocolaşul Mare, Vârful *mt.* Romania 58 G2
Ocoña Peru 200 B4
O'Connell Creek *r.* Australia 149 D4
Oconomowoc U.S.A. 172 E7
Oconto U.S.A. 172 F6
Oconto Falls U.S.A. 172 E6
O Corgo Spain 54 D2
Ocoruro Peru 200 C3
Ocos Guat. 185 G6
Ocosingo Mex. 185 G5
Ocotal Nicaragua 186 B4
Ocotlán Mex. 185 F5
Ocozocoautla Mex. 185 G5
October Revolution Island Rus. Fed. *see* **Oktyabr'skoy Revolyutsii, Ostrov**
Ocuri Bol. 200 D4
Ocussi East Timor *see* **Pante Macassar**
Ocussi *enclave* East Timor 75 C5
Oda Ghana 125 E5
Ōda Japan 91 C7
Oda, Jebel *mt.* Sudan 121 H4
Ódáðahraun *lava field* Iceland 44 [inset] C2
Ōdaejin N. Korea 82 C4
Odae-san National Park S. Korea 83 C5
Ōdaigahara-zan *mt.* Japan 91 E7
Odanah U.S.A. 172 C4
Ōdate Japan 90 G4
Odawara Japan 91 F7
Odda Norway 45 I3
Odder Denmark 45 J5
Odei *r.* Canada 167 L3
Odell U.S.A. 172 E9
Odem U.S.A. 179 C7
Odemira Port. 54 C7
Ödemiş Turkey 106 A3
Ödenburg Hungary *see* **Sopron**
Odendaalsrus S. Africa 133 K4
Odensbacken Sweden 45 K4
Odense Denmark 45 J5
Oder *r.* Germany 48 G4
also spelt Odra (Poland)
Oderbucht *b.* Germany 49 L1
Oderhaff *b.* Germany 49 L2
also known as Stettiner Haff
Oderzo Italy 56 E3
Odesa Ukr. 41 D7
also spelt Odessa
Ödeshog Sweden 45 K4
Odes'ka Oblast' *admin. div.* Ukr. 58 K1
English form Odessa Oblast; *also spelt* Odesskaya Oblast'
Odessa Ukr. *see* **Odesa**
Odessa U.S.A. 179 B6
Odessa Oblast *admin. div.* Ukr. *see* **Odes'ka Oblast'**
Odesskaya Oblast' *admin. div.* Ukr. *see* **Odes'ka Oblast'**
Odessus Bulg. *see* **Varna**
Odi *watercourse* Sudan 121 H5
Odiel *r.* Spain 54 E7
Odienné Côte d'Ivoire 124 D4
Odintsovo Rus. Fed. 43 S6
Odobeşti Romania 58 I3
Odobeştilor, Măgura *hill* Romania 58 H3
Odolanów Poland 49 O4
Odom Inlet Antarctica 222 T2
Odorheiu Secuiesc Romania 58 G2
Odoyev Rus. Fed. 43 R8
Odra *r.* Poland 49 P6
also spelt Oder (Germany)
Odra *r.* Spain 54 G2
Odžaci *Vojvodina, Srbija* Serb. and Mont. 58 A3
Odzala, Parc National d' *nat. park* Congo 126 B4
Odzi Zimbabwe 131 G3
Odzi *r.* Zimbabwe 131 G3
Oea Libya *see* **Tripoli**
Oedong S. Korea 91 A7
Oeiras Brazil 202 D3
Oelde Germany 48 F4
Oelixdorf Germany 48 G2
Oelrichs U.S.A. 178 B3
Oelsnitz Germany 49 J5
Oelwein U.S.A. 174 B3
Oenpelli Australia 148 B2
Oesel *i.* Estonia *see* **Hiiumaa**
Oeufs, Lac des *l.* Canada 169 F2
Oeversee Germany 48 G1
Of Turkey 107 E2
O'Fallon *r.* U.S.A. 180 F3
Ofanto *r.* Italy 57 I7
Offa Nigeria 125 G4
Offenbach am Main Germany 48 F5
Offenburg Germany 48 E7
Offerdal Sweden 44 K3
Ofidoussa *i.* Greece 59 H12
Ofotfjorden *sea chan.* Norway 44 L1
Ōfunato Japan 90 G5
Oga *r.* Indon. 77 F2
Oga Japan 90 F5
Ogachi Japan 90 G5
Ogadēn *reg.* Eth. 128 E3
Oga-hantō *pen.* Japan 90 F5
Ōgaki Japan 91 E7
Ogallala U.S.A. 178 B3
Ogan *r.* Indon. 76 D3
Ogasawara-shotō *is* N. Pacific Ocean *see* **Bonin Islands**
Ogascanane, Lac *l.* Canada 173 O3
Ōgawa Japan 90 G6
Ogawara-ko *l.* Japan 90 G4
Ogbomosho Nigeria 125 G4
also spelt Ogbomoso
Ogbomoso Nigeria *see* **Ogbomosho**
Ogden *IA* U.S.A. 178 D3
Ogden *UT* U.S.A. 180 E4
Ogden, Mount Canada 166 C3
Ogdensburg U.S.A. 177 J1
Ogeechee *r.* U.S.A. 175 D6
Ogema U.S.A. 172 C5
Ogi Japan 90 F6
Ogidaki Canada 168 C4
Ogilvie *r.* Canada 164 F3
Ogilvie Mountains Canada 166 A1
'Oglāt el Khnâchîch *well* Mali 122 E5
Oglat Sbot *well* Alg. 122 D4
Oglio *r.* Italy 56 C3
Ogmore Australia 149 F4
Ognon *r.* France 51 L5
Oğnut Turkey *see* **Göynük**
Ogoamas, Gunung *mt.* Indon. 75 B2
Ogoja Nigeria 125 H5
Ogoki *r.* Canada 168 C3
Ogoki Lake Canada 168 C3
Ogoki Reservoir Canada 168 B3
Ogooué *r.* Gabon 126 A5
Ogooué-Ivindo *prov.* Gabon 126 B5
Ogooué-Lolo *prov.* Gabon 126 B5
Ogooué-Maritime *prov.* Gabon 126 A5
Ogoron Rus. Fed. 82 C1
Ogosta *r.* Bulg. 58 E5
Ogou *r.* Togo 125 F5
O'Grady, Lake *salt flat* Australia 151 B6
Ograzhden *mts* Bulg./Macedonia 58 D7
also spelt Ograzhden
Ograzhden *mts* Bulg./Macedonia *see* **Ograzhden**
Ogre Latvia 42 F5
Ogre *r.* Latvia 42 F5
Ogudnevo Rus. Fed. 43 T5
Ogulin Croatia 56 H3
Ogun *state* Nigeria 125 F5
Ogurchinskiy, Ostrov *i.* Turkm. *see* **Ogurjaly Adasy**
Ogurjaly Adasy *i.* Turkm. 102 C5
also known as Ogurchinskiy, Ostrov; *also known as* Turkmen Adasy
Oğuz Azer. 107 F2
formerly known as Vartashen
Ohafia Nigeria 125 G5
Ohai N.Z. 153 B13
Ohakune N.Z. 152 J7
Ohanet Alg. 123 H3
Ohangwena *admin. reg.* Namibia 130 C3
Ōhara Japan 91 G7
Ōhata Japan 90 G4
Ohau N.Z. 152 J8
Ohau, Lake N.Z. 153 D12
Ohcejohka Fin. *see* **Utsjoki**
O'Higgins Chile 200 C5
O'Higgins *admin. reg.* Chile 204 C4
O'Higgins, Lago *l.* Chile 205 B8
Ohio U.S.A. 172 D9
Ohio *r.* U.S.A. 178 E4
Ohio *state* U.S.A. 176 C5
Ohio Range *mts* Antarctica 223 Q1
Ohm *r.* Germany 51 O2
Õhne *r.* Estonia 42 H3
'Ohonua Tonga 145 H4
Ohope N.Z. 152 L5
Ohrdruf Germany 48 H5
Ohře *r.* Czech Rep. 49 L5
Ohre *r.* Germany 48 I3
Ohrid Macedonia 58 B7
Ohrid, Lake Albania/Macedonia 58 B7
also known as Ochrida, Lake or Ohridsko Ezero or Ohrit, Liqeni i
UNESCO World Heritage Site
Ohridsko Ezero *l.* Albania/Macedonia *see* **Ohrid, Lake**
Ohrigstad S. Africa 133 O1
Ohrigstad Dam Nature Reserve S. Africa 133 O1
Öhringen Germany 48 G6
Ohrit, Liqeni i *l.* Albania/Macedonia *see* **Ohrid, Lake**
Ohura N.Z. 152 I6
Oiapoque Brazil 199 I4
Oiba Col. 198 C3
Oich *r.* U.K. 46 H6
Oik Kazakh. *see* **Uyuk**
Oil City U.S.A. 176 F4
Oildale U.S.A. 182 E6
Oi Qu *r.* China 86 A2
Oirase-gawa *r.* Japan 90 G4
Oise *r.* France 51 I4
Oiseaux du Djoudj, Parc National des *nat. park* Senegal 124 A2
UNESCO World Heritage Site
Ōita Japan 91 B8
Ōita *pref.* Japan 91 B8
Oiti *mt.* Greece 59 D10
Oiti *nat. park* Greece 59 D10
Oituz *r.* Romania 58 H2
Oiuru *well* Libya 120 C4
Oiwake Japan 90 G3
Ojai U.S.A. 182 E7
Ojailén *r.* Spain 54 H6
Ojalava *i.* Samoa *see* **'Upolu**
Ojamaa *r.* Estonia 42 I2
Ojcowski Park Narodowy *nat. park* Poland 49 Q5
Öje Sweden 45 K3
Ojika-jima *i.* Japan 91 A8
Ojinaga Mex. 184 D2
Ojitlán Mex. 185 F5

Ojiya Japan 90 F6
Ojobo Nigeria 125 G5
Ojo de Laguna Mex. 184 D2
Ojo de Liebre, Lago *b.* Mex. 184 B3
UNESCO World Heritage Site

►**Ojos del Salado, Nevado** *mt.* Arg./Chile 204 C2
2nd highest mountain in South America.
►►**188–189 South America** Landscapes

Ojuelos de Jalisco Mex. 185 E4
Öjung Sweden 45 K3
Oka Nigeria 125 G5
Oka *r.* Rus. Fed. 43 R9
Okahandja Namibia 130 C4
Okahu *b.* N.Z. *see* **Jackson Bay**
Okahukura N.Z. 152 J6
Okaihau N.Z. 152 H3
Okains Bay N.Z. 153 H11
Okains Bay *b.* N.Z. 153 H11
Okaka Nigeria 125 F4
Okakarara Namibia 130 C4
Okak Islands Canada 169 I1
Okanagan Falls Canada 166 G5
Okanagan Lake Canada 166 G5
Okanogan U.S.A. 180 C2
Okanogan *r.* U.S.A. 180 C2
Okanogan Range *mts* U.S.A. 180 B2
Okapi, Parc National de la *nat. park* Dem. Rep. Congo 126 E4
UNESCO World Heritage Site
Okaputa Namibia 130 C4
Okara Pak. 101 H4
Okarem Turkm. *see* **Ekerem**
Okarito Lagoon N.Z. 153 E11
Okaukuejo Namibia 130 B3
Okavango *r.* Botswana/Namibia 130 D3
Okavango *admin. reg.* Namibia 130 C3

►**Okavango Delta** *swamp* Botswana 130 D3
Largest oasis in the world.

Ōkawa Japan 91 B8
Okaya Japan 91 F6
Okayama Japan 91 C7
Okayama *pref.* Japan 91 C7
Okazaki Japan 91 E7
Okeechobee U.S.A. 175 D7
Okeechobee, Lake U.S.A. 175 D7
Okeene U.S.A. 179 C4
Okefenokee National Wildlife Refuge and Wilderness *nature res.* U.S.A. 175 D6
Okefenokee Swamp U.S.A. 175 D6
Okemah U.S.A. 179 C5
Okene Nigeria 125 G5
Oker *r.* Germany 48 H3
Oketo Japan 90 H3
Okha India 96 A5
Okha Rus. Fed. 82 F1
Okhadunga Nepal *see* **Okhaldhunga**
Okhaldhunga Nepal 97 E4
also spelt Okhadunga
Okhansk Rus. Fed. 40 J4
Ókhi Óros *mt.* Greece *see* **Ochi**
Okhotino Rus. Fed. 43 T4
Okhotka *r.* Rus. Fed. 39 O4
Okhotsk Rus. Fed. 39 O4
Okhotsk, Sea of Japan/Rus. Fed. 90 I2
also known as Okhotskoye More
Okhotskoye More *sea* Japan/Rus. Fed. *see* **Okhotsk, Sea of**
Okhthoniá Greece *see* **Ochthonia**
Okhtyrka Ukr. 41 E6
also spelt Akhtyrka
Okhvat Rus. Fed. 43 N5
Okiep S. Africa 132 B6
Okinawa *i.* Japan 81 L7
Okinawa-guntō *is* Japan *see* **Okinawa-shotō**
Okinawa-shotō *is* Japan 81 L7
also known as Okinawa-guntō
Okino-Daitō-jima *i.* Japan 81 M8
Okino-shima *i.* Japan 91 B7
Okino-shima *i.* Japan 91 C8
Okino-Tori-shima *i.* Japan 81 N8
also known as Parece Vela; *formerly known as* Douglas Reef
Oki-shotō *is* Japan 91 C6
Okitipupa Nigeria 125 G5
Okkan Myanmar 78 A4
Oklahoma *state* U.S.A. 179 C5

►**Oklahoma City** U.S.A. 179 C5
State capital of Oklahoma.

Oklawaha *r.* U.S.A. 175 D6
Okmulgee U.S.A. 179 C5
Oko, Wadi *watercourse* Sudan 121 H4
Okola Cameroon 125 H5
Okolona *MS* U.S.A. 174 B5
Okolona *OH* U.S.A. 176 A4
Okondja Gabon 126 B5
Okonek Poland 49 N2
Okor *r.* Hungary 56 J3
Okotoks Canada 167 H5
Okotusu *well* Namibia 130 A3
Okovskiy Les *for.* Rus. Fed. 43 N7
Okoyo Congo 126 B5
Okpety, Gora *mt.* Kazakh. 88 C2
Oksbøl Denmark 45 J5
Øksfjord Norway 44 M1
Oksovskiy Rus. Fed. 40 F3
Oksskolten *mt.* Norway 44 K2
Oktemberyan Armenia *see* **Armavir**
Oktumgum *des.* Turkm. 102 C4
Oktwin Myanmar 78 B4
Oktyabr' Kazakh. *see* **Kandyagash**
Oktyabr' Rus. Fed. 43 S4
Oktyabr'sk Kazakh. *see* **Kandyagash**
Oktyabr'sk Rus. Fed. 41 I5
Oktyabr'skaya Belarus *see* **Aktsyabrskaya**
Oktyabr'skiy Belarus *see* **Aktsyabrski**
Oktyabr'skiy Belarus *see* **Aktsyabrski**
Oktyabr'skiy Kazakh. 103 E1
Oktyabr'skiy *Amurskaya Oblast'* Rus. Fed. 82 C1
Oktyabr'skiy *Arkhangel'skaya Oblast'* Rus. Fed. 40 G3
Oktyabr'skiy *Ivanovskaya Oblast'* Rus. Fed. 43 V4
Oktyabr'skiy *Kaluzhskaya Oblast'* Rus. Fed. 43 R7
Oktyabr'skiy *Kamchatskaya Oblast'* Rus. Fed. 39 P4
Oktyabr'skiy *Murmanskaya Oblast'* Rus. Fed. 44 P2
Oktyabr'skiy *Respublika Bashkortostan* Rus. Fed. 40 J5
Oktyabr'skiy *Ryazanskaya Oblast'* Rus. Fed. 43 T7
Oktyabr'skiy *Ryazanskaya Oblast'* Rus. Fed. 43 U8
Oktyabr'skiy *Sverdlovskaya Oblast'* Rus. Fed. 40 K4
Oktyabr'skiy *Volgogradskaya Oblast'* Rus. Fed. 41 G7
formerly known as Kruglyakov
Oktyabr'skoye Kazakh. 103 F1
Oktyabr'skoye *Khanty-Mansiyskiy Avtonomnyy Okrug* Rus. Fed. 38 G3
formerly known as Kondinskoye
Oktyabr'skoye *Orenburgskaya Oblast'* Rus. Fed. 102 C1
Oktyabr'skoy Revolyutsii, Ostrov *i.* Rus. Fed. 39 J2
English form October Revolution Island
Okučani Croatia 56 J3
Ōkuchi Japan 91 B8
Okulovka Rus. Fed. 43 O3
Okuru N.Z. 153 C11
Okushiri-kaikyō *sea chan.* Japan 90 F3
Okushiri-tō *i.* Japan 90 F3
Okutango-hantō *pen.* Japan 91 D7

Okwa *watercourse* Botswana 130 E4
Ola Rus. Fed. 39 P4
Ola U.S.A. 179 D5
Ólafsvík Iceland 44 [inset] B2
Olaine Latvia 42 E5
Olan, Pic d' *mt.* France 51 M8
Olancha Peak U.S.A. 182 F5
Olanchito Hond. 186 B4
Öland *i.* Sweden 45 L4
UNESCO World Heritage Site
Olanga Rus. Fed. 44 O2
Olary Australia 146 D3
Olary *watercourse* Australia 146 D3
Olathe U.S.A. 178 D4
Olavakod India 94 C4
Olavarría Arg. 204 E5
Oława Poland 49 O5
Olbernhau Germany 49 K5
Olbia *Sardinia* Italy 56 B8
Olbia, Golfo di *b. Sardinia* Italy 56 B8
Ol'chan Rus. Fed. 39 O3
Olcott U.S.A. 176 G2
Old Bahama Channel Bahamas/Cuba 186 D2
Old Bastar India 94 D2
Old Cherrabun Australia 150 D3
Old Cork Australia 149 D4
Old Crow Canada 164 F3
Oldeide Norway 45 I3
Oldenburg Germany 48 F2
Oldenburg in Holstein Germany 48 H1
Oldenzaal Neth. 48 D3
Olderdalen Norway 44 M1
Oldfield *r.* Australia 151 C7
Old Forge U.S.A. 177 K2
Old Gidgee Australia 151 B5
Oldham U.K. 47 J10
Old Head of Kinsale Ireland 47 D12
Oldmeldrum U.K. 46 J6
Old Mkushi Zambia 127 F8
Old Morley S. Africa 133 N8
Old Orchard Beach U.S.A. 177 O2
Old Perlican Canada 169 K4
Old River U.S.A. 182 E6
Olds Canada 167 H5
Old Saybrook U.S.A. 177 M4
Old Speck Mountain U.S.A. 177 O1
Old Station U.S.A. 182 C1
Oldtown U.S.A. 176 C7
Old Town U.S.A. 174 G2
Olduvai Gorge *tourist site* Tanz. 128 B5
Old Washington U.S.A. 176 D5
Old Wives Lake Canada 167 J5
formerly known as Johnstone Lake
Old Woman Mountains U.S.A. 183 I7
Öldziyt *Arhangay* Mongolia 84 D1
Öldziyt *Dornogovĭ* Mongolia 85 F2
Olean U.S.A. 176 G3
Olecko Poland 49 T1
Oleggio Italy 56 A3
Olekma *r.* Rus. Fed. 39 M3
Olekminsk Rus. Fed. 39 M3
Oleksandrivs'k Ukr. *see* **Zaporizhzhya**
Oleksandriya Ukr. 41 E6
also spelt Aleksandriya
Ølen Norway 45 I4
Olenegorsk Rus. Fed. 44 P1
formerly known as Olenya
Olenek Rus. Fed. 39 L3
Olenek *r.* Rus. Fed. 39 L2
Olenek Bay Rus. Fed. *see* **Olenekskiy Zaliv**
Olenekskiy Zaliv *b.* Rus. Fed. 39 M2
English form Olenek Bay
Ölengti *r.* Kazakh. *see* **Olenti**
Olenino Rus. Fed. 43 O5
Olenitsa Rus. Fed. 40 E2
Olenivs'ki Kar"yery Ukr. *see* **Dokuchayevs'k**
Oleniy, Ostrov *i.* Rus. Fed. 39 H2
Olenti *r.* Kazakh. 102 C2
also spelt Ölengti
Olenti *r.* Kazakh. 103 H1
Olentuy Rus. Fed. 85 G1
Olenya Rus. Fed. *see* **Olenegorsk**
Oléron, Île d' *i.* France 50 E7
Oleshky Ukr. *see* **Tsyurupyns'k**
Oleśnica Poland 49 O4
Olesno Poland 49 P5
Olet Tongo *mt.* Indon. 77 G5
Olevs'k Ukr. 41 C6
Ølfjellet *mt.* Norway 44 K2
Ol'ga Rus. Fed. 82 D4
Olga, Lac *l.* Canada 168 E3
Olga, Mount Australia 148 A5
Ölgiy Mongolia 84 A1
Olhão Port. 54 D7
Olhava Fin. 44 N2
Olhos d'Agua Brazil 207 J4
Olia Chain *mts* Australia 148 A5
Oliana Spain 55 M2
Olib *i.* Croatia 56 G4
Oliena *Sardinia* Italy 57 B8
Olifants *watercourse* Namibia 130 C5
Olifants *r. W. Cape* S. Africa 132 C8
Olifants *r. W. Cape* S. Africa 132 F10
Olifants *r.* S. Africa 131 F4
Olifantshoek S. Africa 132 G4
Olifantsrivierberge *mts* S. Africa 132 C9
Olimarao *atoll* Micronesia 73 K5
Olimbos *hill* Cyprus *see* **Olympos**
Olimbos *mt.* Greece *see* **Olympus, Mount**
Olímpia Brazil 206 E7
Olimpos Beydağları Milli Parkı *nat. park* Turkey 106 B3
Olinalá Mex. 185 F5
Olinda Brazil 202 F3
UNESCO World Heritage Site
Olinda Entrance *sea chan.* Australia 149 E1
Olinga Moz. 131 H3
Olio Australia 149 D4
Öli Qoltyq Sory *dry lake* Kazakh. *see* **Mertvyy Kultuk, Sor**
Olisipo Port. *see* **Lisbon**
Olite Spain 55 J2
Oliva Arg. 204 E4
Oliva Spain 55 K6
Oliva *hill* Spain 54 E6
Oliva, Cordillera de *mts* Arg./Chile 204 C3
Oliva de la Frontera Spain 54 E6
Olivares, Cerro de *mt.* Arg./Chile 204 C3
Olive Hill U.S.A. 176 B7
Olivehurst U.S.A. 182 C2
Oliveira Brazil 203 C7
Oliveira do Douro Port. 54 C3
Oliveira dos Brejinhos Brazil 202 D5
Olivença Moz. *see* **Lupilichi**
Olivença-a-Nova Angola *see* **Capunda Cavilongo**
Olivenza *r.* Port./Spain 54 D6
Olivenza Spain 54 D6
Oliver Canada 166 G5
Oliver Lake Canada 167 K3
Oliver Springs U.S.A. 176 A9
Olivet France 51 H5
Olivet U.S.A. 178 C3
Olivia U.S.A. 178 D2
Oljoro Wells Tanz. 129 C6
Ölkeyek *r.* Kazakh. *see* **Ul'kayak**
Ol'khovatka Rus. Fed. 41 F6
Ol'khovets Rus. Fed. 43 U8
Olkusz Poland 49 Q5
Ollachea Peru 200 C3
Ollagüe Chile 200 C5
Ollioules France 51 L9
Ollita, Cordillera de *mts* Arg./Chile 204 C3
Ollitas *mt.* Arg. 204 C3
Öllölä Fin. 44 O3
Ollombo Congo 126 B5

Olmaliq Uzbek. 103 G4
also spelt Almalyk
Olmedo Spain 54 G3
Olmeto *Corsica* France 56 A7
Olmos Peru 198 B6
Olmütz Czech Rep. *see* **Olomouc**
Olney *IL* U.S.A. 174 B4
Olney *MD* U.S.A. 177 H6
Olney *TX* U.S.A. 179 C5
Olochi Rus. Fed. 85 H1
Olofström Sweden 45 K4
Ol'oinka Kazakh. 103 F1
Olomane *r.* Canada 169 I3
Olomouc Czech Rep. 49 O6
also known as Olmütz
UNESCO World Heritage Site
Olonets Rus. Fed. 43 N1
Olonetskaya Vozvyshennost' *hills* Rus. Fed. 43 O1
Olongapo Phil. 74 B3
Olongliko Indon. 77 F3
Olonne-sur-Mer France 50 E6
Oloron-Ste-Marie France 50 F9
Olosenga *i.* American Samoa *see* **Swains Island**
Olot Spain 55 N2
Olot Uzbek. 103 E5
also spelt Alat
Olovo Bos.-Herz. 56 K4
Olovyannaya Rus. Fed. 85 G1
Oloy, Qatorkŭhi *mts* Asia *see* **Alai Range**
Olpad India 96 B5
Olpe Germany 48 E4
Ol'sa *r.* Belarus 43 K8
Olše *r.* Czech Rep. 49 P6
Ol'sha Rus. Fed. 43 M7
Olsztyn Poland 49 R2
historically known as Allenstein
Olsztynek Poland 49 R2
Olt *r.* Romania 58 F5
Olta Arg. 204 D3
Olte, Sierra de *mts* Arg. 205 C6
Olten Switz. 51 N5
Oltenița Romania 58 H4
Olteț *r.* Romania 58 F4
Oltina Romania 58 I4
Oltinko'l Uzbek. 102 D4
also spelt Oltinkŭl
Oltinkŭl Uzbek. *see* **Oltinko'l**
Oltintopkan Tajik. 101 G1
also spelt Altyn-Topkan
Oltu Turkey 107 E2
Oluan Cape Taiwan *see* **Oluan Pi**
Oluan Pi *c.* Taiwan 87 G4
English form Oluan Cape
Olutanga *i.* Phil. 74 B5
Ólvega Spain 55 J3
Olvera Spain 54 F8
Ol'viopol' Ukr. *see* **Pervomays'k**
Olym *r.* Rus. Fed. 43 T9
Olymbos *hill* Cyprus *see* **Olympos**
Olympia *tourist site* Greece 59 C11
UNESCO World Heritage Site

►**Olympia** U.S.A. 180 B3
State capital of Washington.

Olympic National Park U.S.A. 180 B3
UNESCO World Heritage Site
Olympos *hill* Cyprus 108 E2
also spelt Olimbos *or* Olymbos
Olympos *mt.* Greece *see* **Olympus, Mount**
Olympos *nat. park* Greece 59 D8
Olympus, Mount Greece 59 D8
also spelt Olimbos *or* Olympos
Olympus, Mount U.S.A. 180 B3
Olyutorskiy Rus. Fed. 39 Q3
Olyutorskiy, Mys *c.* Rus. Fed. 39 R4
Olyutorskiy Zaliv *b.* Rus. Fed. 39 Q4
Olzheras Rus. Fed. *see* **Mezhdurechensk**
Oma China 89 C5
Ōma Japan 90 G4
Oma *r.* Rus. Fed. 40 H2
Ōmachi Japan 91 E6
Omae-zaki *pt* Japan 91 F7
Ōmagari Japan 90 G5
►**Omagh** U.K. 47 E9
►►**24–25 World** Terrorism
Omaguas Peru 198 C6
Omaha U.S.A. 178 D3
Omaha Indian Reservation *res.* U.S.A. 178 C3
Omaheke *admin. reg.* Namibia 130 C4
Omakere N.Z. 152 K8
Omal'skiy Khrebet *mts* Rus. Fed. 82 E1
Omalur India 94 C4
►**Oman** *country* Asia 105 F4
spelt 'Umān in Arabic; *formerly known as* Muscat and Oman
►►**64–65 Asia** Countries
Oman, Gulf of Asia 105 G2
Omangambo Namibia 130 B4
Omarama N.Z. 153 D12
Omarchevo Bulg. 58 H6
Omarska Bos.-Herz. 56 I4
Omaruru Namibia 130 B4
Omas Peru 200 A3
Omatako *watercourse* Namibia 130 D3
Omate Peru 200 C4
Omatjette Namibia 130 B4
Omaweneno Botswana 132 G2
Ōma-zaki *c.* Japan 90 G4
Omba *i.* Vanuatu *see* **Aoba**
Ombai, Selat *sea chan.* Indon. 75 C5
Ombalantu Namibia *see* **Uutapi**
Ombella-Mpoko *pref.* Cent. Afr. Rep. 126 C3
Ombika *waterhole* Namibia 130 B3
Omboué Gabon 126 A5
Ombrone *r.* Italy 56 D6
Ombu China 89 D6
Omdraaisvlei S. Africa 132 H7
Omdurman Sudan 121 G6
Ōme Japan 91 F7
Omedu Estonia 42 I3
Omegna Italy 56 A3
Omeo Australia 147 E4
Ömerler Turkey 59 K9
Ometepe, Isla de *i.* Nicaragua 186 B5
Ometepec Mex. 185 F5
Omgoy Wildlife Reserve *nature res.* Thai. 78 B4
Om Hajēr Eritrea 121 H6
Omīdīyeh Iran 100 B4
Ōmihachiman Japan 91 E7
Omihi N.Z. 153 G11
Omineca Mountains Canada 166 E3
Omineca Provincial Park Canada 166 E4
Omiš Croatia 56 I5
Omitara Namibia 130 C4
Ōmiya Japan 91 F7
Ommaney, Cape U.S.A. 166 C3
Ommen Neth. 48 D3
Ömnögovĭ *prov.* Mongolia 84 E3
Omodeo, Lago *l. Sardinia* Italy 57 B8
Omoku Nigeria 125 G5
Omolon Rus. Fed. 39 Q3
Omolon *r.* Rus. Fed. 39 P3
Omo National Park Eth. 128 B3
Omono-gawa *r.* Japan 90 G5
Omo Wenz *r.* Eth. 128 C3
UNESCO World Heritage Site
Omro U.S.A. 172 E6
Omsk Rus. Fed. 80 A1
Omskaya Oblast' *admin. div.* Rus. Fed. 80 A1
English form Omsk Oblast
Omsk Oblast *admin. div.* Rus. Fed. *see* **Omskaya Oblast'**
Omsukchan Rus. Fed. 39 P3
Ōmū Japan 90 H2
Omu, Vârful *mt.* Romania 58 G3

Omu-Aran Nigeria 125 G4
Omulew *r.* Poland 49 S2
Ōmura Japan 91 A8
Ōmura-wan *b.* Japan 91 A8
Omurtag Bulg. 58 H5
Omusati *admin. reg.* Namibia 130 B3
Omutninsk Rus. Fed. 40 J4
Onalaska U.S.A. 172 B7
Onaman Lake Canada 168 C3
Onancock U.S.A. 177 J8
Onang Indon. 75 A3
Onangué, Lac *l.* Gabon 126 A5
Onarga U.S.A. 172 E10
Onavas Mex. 184 C2
Onawa U.S.A. 178 C3
Onaway U.S.A. 173 I5
Onbingwin Myanmar 79 B5
Oncativo Arg. 204 E3
Oncócua Angola 127 B9
Öncül Turkey 109 K1
Onda Spain 55 K5
Ondal India *see* **Andal**
Ondangwa Namibia 130 B3
Ondarroa Spain 55 I1
Ondava *r.* Slovakia 49 S7
Onderstedorings S. Africa 132 E7
Ondjiva Angola 127 B9
also spelt Onjiva; *formerly known as* Pereira de Eça; *formerly spelt* Ngiva
Ondo Nigeria 125 G5
Ondo *state* Nigeria 125 G5
Öndörhaan Mongolia 85 F2
Öndörhushuu Mongolia 85 G1
Ondor Mod China 84 E3
Ondor Sum China 85 G3
One Botswana 130 D4
One and a Half Degree Channel Maldives 93 D10
One and a Half Mile Opening *sea chan.* Australia 149 E2
Onega Rus. Fed. 40 F3
Onega *r.* Rus. Fed. 40 F3

►**Onega, Lake** Rus. Fed. 40 E3
3rd largest lake in Europe. Also known as Onezhskoye Ozero.
►►**28–29 Europe** Landscapes

Onega Bay *g.* Rus. Fed. *see* **Onezhskaya Guba**
One Hundred and Fifty Mile House Canada *see* **150 Mile House**
One Hundred Mile House Canada *see* **100 Mile House**
Oneida *IL* U.S.A. 172 C9
Oneida *NY* U.S.A. 177 J2
Oneida *TN* U.S.A. 176 A9
Oneida Lake U.S.A. 177 J2
O'Neill U.S.A. 178 C3
Onekaka N.Z. 152 G8
Onekama U.S.A. 172 G6
Onekotan, Ostrov *i.* Rus. Fed. 39 P5
Oneonta *AL* U.S.A. 175 C5
Oneonta *NY* U.S.A. 177 J3
Oneroa N.Z. 152 J4
Onești Romania 58 H2
formerly known as Gheorghe Gheorghiu-Dej
Onet-le-Château France 51 I8
Onezhskaya Guba *g.* Rus. Fed. 40 E2
English form Onega Bay
Onezhskiy Kanal *canal* Rus. Fed. 43 Q1
Onezhskoye Ozero *l.* Rus. Fed. *see* **Onega, Lake**
Ong *r.* India 95 D1
Onga Gabon 126 B5
Ongaonga N.Z. 152 K7
Ông Đôc, Sông *r.* Vietnam 79 D6
Ongeri Dem. Rep. Congo 126 E6
Ongers *watercourse* S. Africa 132 H6
Ongerup Australia 151 B7
Ongi *Dundgovĭ* Mongolia 84 D2
Ongi *Övörhangay* Mongolia 84 D2
Ongiyn Gol *r.* Mongolia 84 D2
Ongjin N. Korea 83 B5
Ongniud Qi China *see* **Wudan**
Ongole India 94 D3
Ongon Mongolia 84 D2
Ongtüstik Qazaqstan Oblysy *admin. div.* Kazakh. *see* **Yuzhnyy Kazakhstan**
Onguday Rus. Fed. 88 D1
Oni Georgia 107 E2
Onida U.S.A. 178 B2
Onilahy *r.* Madag. 131 [inset] I4
Onistagane, Lac *l.* Canada 169 G3
Onitsha Nigeria 125 G5
Onjati Mountain Namibia 130 C4
Onjiva Angola *see* **Ondjiva**
Onkamo Fin. 44 O3
Onkivesi *l.* Fin. 44 N3
Onnes Rus. Fed. 39 N3
Ōno *Fukui* Japan 91 E7
Ōno *Hokkaidō* Japan 90 G4
Onoda Japan 91 B8
Ono-i-Lau *i.* Fiji 145 H4
Ōnojō Japan 91 B8
Onomichi Japan 91 C7
Onon Mongolia 85 F1
Onon *r.* Rus. Fed. 85 G1
Onon Gol *r.* Mongolia 85 G1
Onor, Gora *mt.* Rus. Fed. 82 F2
Onotoa *atoll* Kiribati 145 G2
also spelt Onutu
Ons, Illa de *i.* Spain 54 C2
Onsan S. Korea 91 A7
Onseepkans S. Africa 132 D5
Onslow Australia 150 A4
Onslow Bay U.S.A. 174 E5
Onsŏng N. Korea 82 C4
Ontake-san *vol.* Japan 83 E6
Ontaratue *r.* Canada 166 D1
Ontario *prov.* Canada 167 N5
Ontario *CA* U.S.A. 182 G7
Ontario *OR* U.S.A. 180 C3
Ontario *WI* U.S.A. 172 C7
►**Ontario, Lake** Canada/U.S.A. 173 P7
►►**154–155 North America** Landscapes
Onteniente Spain *see* **Ontinyent**
Ontinyent Spain 55 K6
also spelt Onteniente
Ontojärvi *l.* Fin. 44 O2
Ontong Java Atoll Solomon Is 145 E2
formerly known as Lord Howe Atoll
Ontur Spain 55 J6
Onutu *atoll* Kiribati *see* **Onotoa**
Onverwacht Suriname 199 H3
Onyx U.S.A. 182 F6
Oodnadatta Australia 146 B1
Oodweyne Somalia 128 E2
Ooldea Australia 146 A2
Ooldea Range *hills* Australia 146 A2
Oologah Lake *resr* U.S.A. 178 D4
Oombulg Aboriginal Reserve Australia 150 D2
Ooratippra *r.* Australia 148 C4
Oorindi Australia 149 D4
Oos-Londen S. Africa *see* **East London**
Oostanaula *r.* U.S.A. 174 C5
Oostende Belgium *see* **Ostend**
Oosterhout Neth. 48 B4
Oosterschelde *est.* Neth. 48 A4
Oost-Vlaanderen *prov.* Belgium 48 A4
UNESCO World Heritage Site
Oostvleteren Belgium 51 I2
Ootacamund India *see* **Udagamandalam**
Ootsa Lake Canada 166 E4
Ootsa Lake *l.* Canada 166 E4
Opalenica Poland 49 N3
Oparau N.Z. 152 I6
Opari N.Z. 152 J8
Opari Sudan 128 B4

Oparino Rus. Fed. 40 I4
Oparo *i.* Fr. Polynesia *see* **Rapa**
Opasatika *r.* Canada 168 D3
Opasatika Lake Canada 168 D3
Opasquia Canada 167 M4
Opasquia Provincial Park Canada 167 M4
Opataca, Lac *l.* Canada 169 F3
Opatija Croatia 56 G3
Opatów Poland 49 S5
Opava Czech Rep. 49 O6
Opava *r.* Czech Rep. 49 O5
Opechenskiy Posad Rus. Fed. 43 P3
Opelika U.S.A. 175 C5
Opelousas U.S.A. 179 D6
Opeongo Lake Canada 168 E4
Opheim U.S.A. 180 F2
Ophir Canada 173 J4
Ophir N.Z. 153 D13
Ophir, Gunung *vol.* Indon. 76 C2
Opihikao U.S.A. 181 [inset] Z2
Opinaca *r.* Canada 169 E2
Opinaca, Réservoir *resr* Canada 168 E2
Opinnagau *r.* Canada 168 D2
Opis *tourist site* Iraq 107 F4
Opiscotéo, Lac *l.* Canada 169 G2
Op Luang National Park Thai. 78 B4
Opobo Nigeria 125 G5
Opochka Rus. Fed. 43 J5
Opoco Bol. 200 D4
Opoczno Poland 49 R4
Opodepe Mex. 184 C2
Opole Poland 49 O5
historically known as Oppeln
Opole Lubelskie Poland 49 S4
Opononi N.Z. 152 H3
O Porriño Spain 54 C2
Oporto Port. 54 C3
also known as Porto
UNESCO World Heritage Site
Opotiki N.Z. 152 L6
Opovo *Vojvodina, Srbija* Serb. and Mont. 58 B3
Opp U.S.A. 175 C6
Oppdal Norway 44 J3
Oppedal Norway 45 I3
Oppeln Poland *see* **Opole**
Oppido Lucano Italy 57 H8
Oppland *county* Norway 45 J3
Opportunity U.S.A. 180 C3
Oprișor Romania 58 E4
Optași-Măgura Romania 58 F4
Opuatia N.Z. 152 I5
Opunake N.Z. 152 H7
Opuwo Namibia 130 B3
Opytnoye Kazakh. 102 B3
Oqqal'a Uzbek. 102 D4
also spelt Oqqal"a
Oqqal"a Uzbek. *see* **Oqqal'a**
Oqsu *r.* Tajik. 101 H2
also spelt Aksu
Oqtosh Uzbek. 103 F5
also spelt Aktash
Oquawka U.S.A. 174 B3
Or' *r.* Rus. Fed. 102 D2
Øra Norway 44 M1
Oracle U.S.A. 183 N9
Oradea Romania 58 C1
also known as Nagyvárad
Orahovac *Kosovo, Srbija* Serb. and Mont. 58 B6
Orahovica Croatia 56 J3
Orai India 96 C4
Oraibi U.S.A. 183 N6
Oraibi Wash *watercourse* U.S.A. 183 N6
Orain *r.* France 51 L6
Orajärvi Fin. 44 N2
Oral Kazakh. *see* **Ural'sk**
Oran Alg. 123 E2
also spelt Ouahran *or* Wahran
Orán Arg. 201 D5
Oran, Sebkha d' *salt pan* Alg. 55 K9
Ŏrang N. Korea 82 C4
Orange Australia 147 F3
Orange France 51 K8
UNESCO World Heritage Site
Orange *r.* Namibia/S. Africa 132 A5
also spelt Oranje
Orange *CA* U.S.A. 182 G8
Orange *TX* U.S.A. 179 D6
Orange *VA* U.S.A. 176 G7
Orange, Cabo *c.* Brazil 199 I3
Orangeburg U.S.A. 175 D5
Orange Cay *i.* Bahamas 186 D1
Orange City U.S.A. 178 C3
Orange Cove U.S.A. 182 E5
Orange Free State *prov.* S. Africa *see* **Free State**
Orange Park U.S.A. 175 D6
Orangerie Bay P.N.G. 149 F1
Orangevale U.S.A. 182 C3
Orangeville Canada 168 D5
Orangeville U.S.A. 183 M2
Orange Walk Belize 185 H5
Orani *Sardinia* Italy 57 B8
Orani Phil. 74 B3
Oranienburg Germany 49 K3
Oranje *r.* Namibia/S. Africa *see* **Orange**
Oranje Gebergte *hills* Suriname 199 H4
Oranjemund Namibia 130 C6
Oranjerivier S. Africa 133 I6

►**Oranjestad** Aruba 187 F4
Capital of Aruba.

Oranjestad Neth. Antilles 187 H3
Oranjeville S. Africa 133 M3
Orantjugurr, Lake *salt flat* Australia 150 E4
Oranzherei Rus. Fed. 102 A3
Orapa Botswana 131 E4
Oras Phil. 74 C3
Orašac Bos.-Herz. 56 I4
Oras Bay Phil. 74 C3
Orăștie Romania 58 E3
Orăștioara de Sus Romania 58 E3
UNESCO World Heritage Site
Orașul Stalin Romania *see* **Brașov**
Orava *r.* Slovakia 49 Q6
Orava, Vodná nádrž *resr* Slovakia 49 Q6
Oravais Fin. 44 M3
Oravița Romania 58 C3
Oravská Magura *mts* Slovakia 49 Q6
Orawia N.Z. 153 B14
Orba Co *l.* China 89 C5
Orbassano Italy 51 N7
Orbeasca Romania 58 G4
Orbec France 50 G3
Orbetello Italy 56 D6
Orbieu *r.* France 51 I9
Orbigo *r.* Spain 54 F3
Orbisonia U.S.A. 176 H5
Orbost Australia 147 F4
Orcadas *research station* S. Atlantic Ocean 222 V2
Orcera Spain 55 I6
Orchard Mesa U.S.A. 183 P2
Orchha India 96 C4
Orchila, Isla *i.* Venez. 199 E2
Orchomenos Greece 59 D10
also spelt Orkhomenós
Orchy *r.* U.K. 46 G7
Orcia *r.* Italy 56 D6
UNESCO World Heritage Site
Orco *r.* Italy 51 N7
Orcotuna Peru 200 B2
Orcutt U.S.A. 182 D7
Ord *r.* Australia 150 E2
Ord U.S.A. 178 C3
Ord, Mount *hill* Australia 150 D3
Orda Rus. Fed. 40 K4
Órdenes Spain *see* **Ordes**

Ordes Spain 54 C1
also known as Órdenes
Ordesa-Monte Perdido, Parque Nacional *nat. park* Spain 55 L2
Ord Mountain U.S.A. 183 H7
Ordos China 85 F4
Ord River Dam Australia 150 E3
Ord River Nature Reserve Australia 150 E2
Ordu *Hatay* Turkey *see* **Yayladağı**
Ordu *Ordu* Turkey 107 D2
Ordubad Azer. 107 F3
Ordway U.S.A. 178 B4
Ordzhonikidze Kazakh. *see* **Denisovka**
Ordzhonikidze Rus. Fed. *see* **Vladikavkaz**
Ordzhonikidze Ukr. 41 E7
Ordzhonikidzeabad Tajik. *see* **Kofarnihon**
Ordzhonikidzevskaya Rus. Fed. *see* **Sleptsovskaya**
Ore Nigeria 125 G5
O Real Spain 54 C1
Öreälven *r.* Sweden 44 L3
Oreälven *r.* Sweden 45 K3
Oreana U.S.A. 182 F1
Örebro Sweden 45 K4
Örebro *county* Sweden 45 K4
Oredezh *r.* Rus. Fed. 43 K3
Oregon *IL* U.S.A. 174 B3
Oregon *OH* U.S.A. 176 B4
Oregon *WI* U.S.A. 172 D8
Oregon *state* U.S.A. 180 B4
Oregon City U.S.A. 180 B3
Öregrund Sweden 45 L3
Orekhi-Vydritsa Belarus *see* **Arekhawsk**
Orekhov Ukr. *see* **Orikhiv**
Orekhovo-Zuyevo Rus. Fed. 43 T6
Orekhovsk Belarus *see* **Arekhawsk**
Orel *Orlovskaya Oblast'* Rus. Fed. 43 R9
also spelt Oryol
Orel *Permskaya Oblast'* Rus. Fed. 40 K4
Orel, Gora *mt.* Rus. Fed. 82 E1
Orel', Ozero *l.* Rus. Fed. 82 E1
Orelek *mt.* Bulg. 58 E7
Orellana *prov.* Ecuador 198 B5
Orellana Peru 198 C6
Orellana, Embalse de *resr* Spain 54 F5
Orel Oblast *admin. div.* Rus. Fed. *see* **Orlovskaya Oblast'**
Orem U.S.A. 183 M1
Ore Mountains Czech Rep./Germany *see* **Erzgebirge**
Ören *Muğla* Turkey 59 K12
Ören *Muğla* Turkey 106 A3
Orenburg Rus. Fed. 102 C2
formerly known as Chkalov
Orenburg Oblast *admin. div.* Rus. Fed. *see* **Orenburgskaya Oblast'**
Orenburgskaya Oblast' *admin. div.* Rus. Fed. 102 B2
English form Orenburg Oblast; *formerly known as* Chkalovskaya Oblast'
Orense Arg. 204 F5
Orense Spain *see* **Ourense**
Oreón, Dhíavlos *sea chan.* Greece *see* **Oreon, Diavlos**
Oreon, Diavlos *sea chan.* Greece 59 D10
also spelt Oreón, Dhíavlos
Oreor Palau *see* **Koror**
Orepuki N.Z. 153 B14
Oresh Bulg. 58 G5
Öreskilsälven *r.* Sweden 45 J4
Orestiada Greece 58 H7
also known as Orestiás
Orestiás Greece *see* **Orestiada**
Öresund *strait* Denmark/Sweden 45 K5
Oretana, Cordillera *mts* Spain *see* **Toledo, Montes de**
Oreti *r.* N.Z. 153 C14
Orewa N.Z. 152 I4
Orfane *well* Niger 125 G2
Orfanou, Kolpos *b.* Greece 58 E8
Orford Bay Australia 149 D1
Orford Ness *hd* U.K. 47 N11
Organabo Fr. Guiana 199 H3
Organos, Sierra de los *hills* Cuba 175 C8
Organ Pipe Cactus National Monument *nat. park* U.S.A. 183 L9
Orgeyev Moldova *see* **Orhei**
Orgil Mongolia 84 C1
Orgiva Spain 55 H8
Orgon Tal China 85 G3
Orgtrud Rus. Fed. 43 V5
Orgūn Afgh. 101 G3
Orhaneli Turkey 106 B3
also known as Beyce
Orhangazi Turkey 58 K8
Orhei Moldova 58 J1
formerly spelt Orgeyev *or* Orkhey
Orhon Gol *r.* Mongolia 84 E1
Orhontuul Mongolia 84 E1
Orhy, Pic d' *mt.* France/Spain 55 J2
Oria Spain 55 I7
Oribi Gorge Nature Reserve S. Africa 133 O7
Orichi Rus. Fed. 40 I4
Oriental, Cordillera *mts* Bol. 200 D4
Oriental, Cordillera *mts* Col. 198 C3
Oriental, Cordillera *mts* Peru 200 C3
Orientale *prov.* Dem. Rep. Congo 126 E4
formerly known as Haut-Congo *or* Haut-Zaïre
Oriente Brazil 201 D2
Orient Island U.S.A. 177 M4
Orihuela Spain 55 K6
Orikhiv Ukr. 41 E7
also spelt Orekhov
Orikum Albania 59 A8
Orillia Canada 168 E4
Orimattila Fin. 45 N3
Orin U.S.A. 180 F4
Orinoco *r.* Col./Venez. 199 F2
Orinoco Delta Venez. 199 F2
Orion U.S.A. 172 C9
Oripää Fin. 45 M3
Oriskany U.S.A. 177 J2
Orissa *state* India 95 E1
formerly known as Jajnagar
Orissaare Estonia 42 E3
Oristano *Sardinia* Italy 57 A9
Oristano, Golfo di *b. Sardinia* Italy 57 A9
Orivesi Fin. 45 N3
Orivesi *l.* Fin. 44 O3
Oriximiná Brazil 199 H5
Orizaba Mex. 185 F5

►**Orizaba, Pico de** *vol.* Mex. 185 F5
3rd highest mountain in North America. Also known as Citlaltépetl.
►►**154–155 North America** Landscapes

Orizona Brazil 206 E4
Orjonikidzeobod Tajik. *see* **Kofarnihon**
Örkelljunga Sweden 45 K4
Orkhey Moldova *see* **Orhei**
Orkhomenós Greece *see* **Orchomenos**
Orkhon Valley *tourist site* Mongolia 84 D2
UNESCO World Heritage Site
Orkney S. Africa 133 K3
Orkney Islands U.K. 46 I4
Orla *r.* Poland 49 N4
Orla *r.* Poland 49 O2
Orland U.S.A. 182 B2
Orlândia Brazil 206 F7
Orlando U.S.A. 175 D6
Orleaes Brazil 203 B9
Orléans France 51 H5
Orleans *MA* U.S.A. 177 P4
Orleans *VT* U.S.A. 177 M1
Orléans, Île d' *i.* Canada 169 G4
Orléansville Alg. *see* **Chlef**

Orlické hory mts Czech Rep. 49 N5
Orlik Rus. Fed. 80 F2
Orlik, Vodní nádrž resr Czech Rep. 49 L6
Orljava r. Croatia 56 J3
Orlov Rus. Fed. 40 I4
formerly known as Khalturin
Orlov Gay Rus. Fed. 102 B2
Orlovo Rus. Fed. 41 F6
Orlovskaya Oblast' admin. div. Rus. Fed. 43 R9
English form Orel Oblast
Orlovskiy Rus. Fed. 41 G7
Ormankalns hill Latvia 42 G5
Ormara Pak. 101 F5
Ormara, Ras hd Pak. 101 F5
Ormilia Greece see Ormylia
Ormoc Phil. 74 C4
Ormond N.Z. 152 L6
Ormond Beach U.S.A. 175 D6
Ormskirk U.K. 47 J10
Ormylia Greece 59 E8
also spelt Ormilia
Ornans France 51 M5
Orne r. France 50 F3
Orne r. France 50 G4
Ørnes Norway 44 K2
Orneta Poland 49 R1
Ornö i. Sweden 45 L4
Örnsköldsvik Sweden 44 L3
Örö i. Fin. 42 D2
Oro N. Korea 83 B4
Oro, Lac l. Mali 124 E2
Orobayaya Bol. 201 E3
Orobie, Alpi mts Italy 56 B2
Orocó Brazil 202 E4
Orocué Col. 198 D3
Orodara Burkina 124 D4
Oroel, Peña de mt. Spain 55 K2
Orofino U.S.A. 180 C3
Orog Nuur salt l. Mongolia 84 D2
Oro Grande U.S.A. 183 G7
Orol Dengizi salt l. Kazakh./Uzbek. see Aral Sea
Oromīya admin. reg. Eth. 128 C2
Oromocto Canada 169 H4
Oromocto Lake Canada 169 H4
Oron Israel 108 G7
Oron Nigeria 125 H5
Orona i. Kiribati 145 H2
formerly known as Hull Island
Orono U.S.A. 174 G2
Oronoque Guyana 199 G4
Oronoque r. Guyana 199 G4
Orontes r. Lebanon/Syria 109 H3
also known as 'Āşī or 'Āṣī, Nahr al
Orope Venez. 198 C2
Oropesa, Cabo de c. Spain 55 L4
Oroqen Zizhiqi China see Alihe
Oroquieta Phil. 74 B4
Ororbia Spain 55 J2
Orós Brazil 202 E3
Orós, Açude resr Brazil 202 E3
Orosei Sardinia Italy 57 B8
Orosei, Golfo di b. Sardinia Italy 57 B8
Orosháza Hungary 49 R9
Oroszlány Hungary 49 P8
Orotukan Rus. Fed. 39 P3
Oro Valley U.S.A. 183 N9
Oroville CA U.S.A. 182 C2
Oroville WA U.S.A. 180 C2
Oroville, Lake resr U.S.A. 182 C2
Orqohan China 85 I1
Orri, Monte hill Sardinia Italy 57 A9
Orri, Tossal de l' mt. Spain 55 M2
also spelt Tozal del Orri
Orrkjølen hill Norway 45 J3
Orroroo Australia 146 C3
Orsa Sweden 45 K3
Őrségi Tájvédelmi Körzet nature res. Hungary 49 N9
Orsha Belarus 43 L7
Orsha Rus. Fed. 43 R5
Orshanka Rus. Fed. 40 H4
Orsjön l. Sweden 45 L3
Orsk Rus. Fed. 102 D2
Orşova Romania 58 D4
Ørsta Norway 44 I3
Örsundsbro Sweden 45 L4
Ortaca Turkey 59 J12
Orta Nova Italy 56 H7
Orta Toroslar plat. Turkey 108 E1
Orte Italy 56 E6
Ortegal, Cabo c. Spain 54 D1
Orteguaza r. Col. 198 C4
Orthez France 50 F9
Ortholmen Sweden 45 K3
Ortigueira Brazil 206 C11
Ortigueira Spain 54 D1
Orţişoara Romania 58 C3
Ortiz Mex. 184 C2
Ortíz Venez. 199 E2
Ortles mt. Italy 56 C2
Ortona Italy 56 G6
Ortonville MI U.S.A. 173 J8
Ortonville MN U.S.A. 178 C2
Ortospana Afgh. see Kābul
Orträsk Sweden 44 L2
Örtülü Turkey see Şenkaya
Oru Estonia 42 I2
Orulgan, Khrebet mts Rus. Fed. 39 M3
Orumbo Namibia 130 C4
Orumbo Boka hill Côte d'Ivoire 124 D5
Orūmīyeh Iran see Urmia
Orūmīyeh, Daryācheh-ye salt l. Iran see Urmia, Lake
Oruro Bol. 200 D4
Oruro dept Bol. 200 D4
Orvault France 50 E5
Orvieto Italy 56 E6
historically known as Urbs Vetus or Velsuna or Volsinii
Orville Coast Antarctica 222 T1
Orwell OH U.S.A. 176 E4
Orwell VT U.S.A. 177 L2
Orxon Gol r. China 85 H1
Oryakhovo Bulg. 58 E5
Oryol Rus. Fed. see Orel
Orzinuovi Italy 56 B3
Orzyc r. Poland 49 S3
Orzysz Poland 49 S2
Orzysz, Jezioro l. Poland 49 T2
Os Norway 44 J3
Oša r. Latvia 42 H5
Osa r. Poland 49 P2
Osa Rus. Fed. 40 J4
Osa, Península de pen. Costa Rica 186 C5
Osage IA U.S.A. 174 A3
Osage WV U.S.A. 176 E6
Osage r. U.S.A. 178 D4
Osage City U.S.A. 178 D4
►Ōsaka Japan 91 D7
►►18–19 World Cities
Ōsaka pref. Japan 90 D7
Osakarovka Kazakh. 103 H2
Ōsaka-wan b. Japan 91 D7
Osasco Brazil 206 G10
Osawatomie U.S.A. 178 D4
Osborn S. Africa 133 P5
Osborne U.S.A. 178 C4
Oscar Fr. Guiana 199 H4
Oscar Range hills Australia 150 D3
Osceola AR U.S.A. 174 B5
Osceola IA U.S.A. 174 A3
Osceola MO U.S.A. 178 D4
Osceola NE U.S.A. 178 C3
Osceola WI U.S.A. 172 A5
Oschersleben (Bode) Germany 48 I3
Oschiri Sardinia Italy 57 B8
Oscoda U.S.A. 173 J6
Osečina Srbija Serb. and Mont. 58 A4
O Seixo Spain 54 C3
Ösel i. Estonia see Hiiumaa
Osensjøen l. Norway 45 J3
Osetr r. Rus. Fed. 43 T7
Ōse-zaki pt Japan 91 A8
Osgoode Canada 168 F4
Osgood Mountains U.S.A. 180 C4
Osh Kyrg. 103 H4
Osh admin. div. Kyrg. 103 H4
English form Osh Oblast; also known as Oshskaya Oblast'
Oshakati Namibia 130 B3
Oshamambe Japan see Oshamanbe
Oshamanbe Japan 90 G3
also spelt Oshamambe
Oshana admin. reg. Namibia 130 B3
Oshawa Canada 168 E5
Oshika Japan 90 G5
Oshika-hantō pen. Japan 90 G5
Oshikango Namibia 130 B3
Oshikoto admin. reg. Namibia 130 C3
Oshikuku Namibia 130 B3
Ō-shima i. Japan 90 F4
Ō-shima i. Japan 91 D8
Ō-shima i. Japan 91 F7
Oshima-hantō pen. Japan 90 F3
Oshin r. Nigeria 125 G4
Oshivelo Namibia 130 C3
Oshkosh NE U.S.A. 178 B3
Oshkosh WI U.S.A. 172 E6
Oshmyany Belarus see Ashmyany
Oshnovīyeh Iran 100 A2
Osh Oblast admin. div. Kyrg. see Osh
Oshogbo Nigeria 125 G5
also spelt Osogbo
Oshper Rus. Fed. 40 L2
Oshskaya Oblast' admin. div. Kyrg. see Osh
Oshtorān Kūh mt. Iran 100 B3
Oshun state Nigeria 125 G5
also spelt Osun
Oshwe Dem. Rep. Congo 126 C5
Osica de Sus Romania 58 F4
Osijek Croatia 56 K3
Osikovitsa Bulg. 58 F6
Osilinka r. Canada 166 E3
Osimo Italy 56 F5
Osipaonica Srbija Serb. and Mont. 58 C4
Osipenko Ukr. see Berdyans'k
Osipovichi Belarus see Asipovichy
Osire Namibia 130 C4
Osiyan India 96 B4
Osizweni S. Africa 133 O4
Osječenica mts Bos.-Herz. 56 I4
Oskaloosa IA U.S.A. 174 A3
Oskaloosa KS U.S.A. 178 D4
Oskarshamn Sweden 45 L4
Oskarström Sweden 45 K4
Oskélanéo Canada 173 R2
Öskemen Kazakh. see Ust'-Kamenogorsk
Oskil r. Rus. Fed. see Oskol
Oskol r. Rus. Fed. 41 F6
also known as Oskil
Oskuya r. Rus. Fed. 43 M2
Oslava r. Czech Rep. 49 N6
Osława r. Poland 49 T6

►Oslo Norway 45 J4
Capital of Norway. Historically known as Christiania or Kristiania.

Oslo airport Norway see Gardermoen
Oslob Phil. 74 B4
Oslofjorden sea chan. Norway 45 J4
Osmanabad India 94 C2
Osmancık Turkey 106 C2
Osmaneli Turkey 106 B2
Osmaniye Turkey 106 D3
Osmannagar India 94 C2
also known as Sultanabad
Os'mino Rus. Fed. 43 K2
Ösmo Sweden 45 L4
Osmussaar i. Estonia 42 E2
Osnabrück Germany 48 F3
Osnaburg atoll Fr. Polynesia see Mururoa
Osno Lubuskie Poland 49 L3
Oso r. Dem. Rep. Congo 126 E5
Osogbo Nigeria see Oshogbo
Osogovska Planina mts Bulg./Macedonia 58 D6
Osor hill Croatia 56 G4
Osório Brazil 203 B9
Osorno Chile 204 B6
Osorno Spain 54 G2
Osoyoos Canada 166 G5
Osøyri Norway 46 P3
Ospino Venez. 198 D2
Osprey Reef reef Australia 149 E2
Oss Neth. 48 C4
Ossa hill Port. 54 D6
Ossa, Mount Australia 147 E5
Osse r. Nigeria 125 G5
Osseo U.S.A. 172 B6
Ossi Sardinia Italy 57 A8
Ossineke U.S.A. 173 J6
Ossining U.S.A. 177 L4
Ossipee Lake U.S.A. 177 N2
Ossokmanuan Lake Canada 169 H2
Ossora Rus. Fed. 39 Q4
Ossu East Timor 75 C5
Ostashevo Rus. Fed. 43 Q6
Ostashkov Rus. Fed. 43 O4
Oste r. Germany 48 G2
Osten Germany 48 G2
Ostend Belgium 51 I1
also spelt Oostende or Ostende
Ostende Belgium see Ostend
Oster Rus. Fed. 43 N7
Oster r. Rus. Fed. 43 N8
Oster Ukr. 41 D6
Osterburg (Altmark) Germany 48 I3
Österbybruk Sweden 45 L3
Österbymo Sweden 45 K4
Österdalälven l. Sweden 45 K3
Østerfärnebo Sweden 45 L3
Östergotland county Sweden 45 K4
Osterholz-Scharmbeck Germany 48 F2
Ostermundigen Switz. 51 N6
Osterode am Harz Germany 48 H4
Österreich country Europe see Austria
Östersund Sweden 44 K3
Östervåla Sweden 45 L3
Osterzgebirge park Germany 49 K5
Østfold county Norway 45 J4
Ostfriesische Inseln is Germany see East Frisian Islands
Ostfriesland reg. Germany 48 E2
Östhammar Sweden 45 L3
Östra Kvarken strait Fin./Sweden 44 M3
Ostrava Czech Rep. 49 P6
Ostróda Poland 49 Q2
Ostrogozhsk Rus. Fed. 41 F6
Oštro Koplje mt. Serb. and Mont. 58 C5
Ostrołęka Poland 49 S3
Ostrov Czech Rep. 49 J5
Ostrov Romania 58 I4
Ostrov Romania 58 J4
Ostrov Rus. Fed. 43 J4
Ostrovets Poland see Ostrowiec Świętokrzyski
Ostrovskoye Rus. Fed. 40 G4
formerly known as Semyonovskoye
Ostrow Poland see Ostrów Wielkopolski
Ostrowiec Poland see Ostrowiec Świętokrzyski
Ostrowiec Świętokrzyski Poland 49 S5
formerly known as Ostrovets; short form Ostrowiec
Ostrów Lubelski Poland 49 T4
Ostrów Mazowiecka Poland 49 S3
Ostrowo Poland see Ostrów Wielkopolski
Ostrów Wielkopolski Poland 49 O4
formerly known as Ostrowo; short form Ostrow
Ostrzeszów Poland 49 O4
Ostuni Italy 57 J8
Osuga r. Rus. Fed. 43 P4
Osuga r. Rus. Fed. 43 P5
O'Sullivan, Lac l. Canada 173 R3
Osum r. Albania 59 A8
Osŭm r. Bulg. 58 F5
Ōsumi-hantō pen. Japan 91 B9
Ōsumi-kaikyō sea chan. Japan 91 B9
Ōsumi-shotō is Japan 91 B9
Osun state Nigeria see Oshun
Osuna Spain 54 F7
Osvaldo Cruz Brazil 206 C8
Oswego IL U.S.A. 172 E9
Oswego KS U.S.A. 178 D4
Oswego NY U.S.A. 177 I2
Oswego r. U.S.A. 177 I2
Oswestry U.K. 47 I11
Oświęcim Poland 49 Q5
historically known as Auschwitz
UNESCO World Heritage Site
Osyno Rus. Fed. 43 J5
Ōta Japan 91 F6
Otago admin. reg. N.Z. 153 D13
Otago Peninsula N.Z. 153 E13
Otahiti i. Fr. Polynesia see Tahiti
Otairi N.Z. 152 J7
Otaki N.Z. 152 J8
Otama N.Z. 153 C13
Otamauri N.Z. 152 K7
Otar Kazakh. 103 H4
Otaru Japan 90 G3
Otatara N.Z. 153 C14
Otautau N.Z. 153 B14
Otava r. Czech Rep. 49 L6
Otava Fin. 45 N3
Otavalo Ecuador 198 B4
Otavi Namibia 130 C3
Ōtawara Japan 90 G6
Otchinjau Angola 127 B9
Otdia atoll Marshall Is see Wotje
Otegen Batyr Kazakh. 103 I4
Otekaieke N.Z. 153 E12
Otelnuc, Lac l. Canada 169 G1
Oţelu Roşu Romania 58 D3
Otematata N.Z. 153 E12
Otepää Estonia 42 H3
Otepää kõrgustik hills Estonia 42 H3
Oteren Norway 44 L1
Oteros r. Mex. 181 E8
Otgon Tenger Uul mt. Mongolia 84 C2
Othe, Forêt d' for. France 51 J4
Othello U.S.A. 180 C3
Othonoi i. Greece 59 A9
Oti r. Ghana/Togo 125 F4
Oti Indon. 75 A3
Oti, Réserve de Faune de l' nature res. Togo 125 F4
Otimati S. Africa 133 P6
Otinapa Mex. 184 D3
Otira N.Z. 153 F10
Otisco Lake U.S.A. 177 I3
Otish, Monts hills Canada 169 G3
Otjikondo Namibia 130 B2
Otjinene Namibia 130 C4
Otjitambi Namibia 130 B3
Otjiwarongo Namibia 130 C4
Otjovasandu waterhole Namibia 130 B3
Otjozondjupa admin. reg. Namibia 130 C4
Otobe Japan 90 G4
Otobe-dake mt. Japan 90 G3
Otočac Croatia 56 H4
Otofuke Japan 90 H3
Otog Qi China see Ulan
Otoineppu Japan 90 H2
Otok Croatia 56 K3
Otoka Bos.-Herz. 56 I4
Otoko N.Z. 152 L6
Otonga N.Z. 152 I3
Otoro, Jebel mt. Sudan 121 F7
Otorohanga N.Z. 152 J6
also known as Harrodsville
Otoskwin r. Canada 168 B3
Ōtoyo Japan 91 C8
Otpan, Gora hill Kazakh. 102 B3
Otpor Rus. Fed. see Zabaykal'sk
Otradinskiy Rus. Fed. 43 R8
Otradnoye Leningradskaya Oblast' Rus. Fed. 43 L2
Otradnoye Samarskaya Oblast' Rus. Fed. see Otradnyy
Otradnoye, Ozero l. Rus. Fed. 43 L1
Otradnyy Rus. Fed. 41 I5
formerly known as Otradnoye
Otranto Italy 57 K8
Otranto, Strait of strait Albania/Italy 56 K7
Otrogovo Rus. Fed. see Stepnoye
Otrokovice Czech Rep. 49 O6
Otrozhnyy Rus. Fed. 39 R3
Ötscher-Tormäuer nature res. Austria 49 M8
Otsego U.S.A. 172 H8
Otsego Lake U.S.A. 177 K3
Ōtsu Japan 91 D7
UNESCO World Heritage Site
Otta Norway 45 J3

►Ottawa Canada 168 F4
Capital of Canada.

Ottawa r. Canada 168 F4
also known as Outaouais, Rivière des
Ottawa IL U.S.A. 174 B3
Ottawa KS U.S.A. 178 D4
Ottawa OH U.S.A. 176 A4
Ottawa Islands Canada 168 D1
Otter r. U.K. 47 I13
Otterburn U.K. 47 J8
Otter Creek U.S.A. 172 C8
Otterstad Sweden 45 K4
Ottignies Belgium 51 K2
Ottosdal S. Africa 133 J3
Ottoshoop S. Africa 133 J2
Ottumwa U.S.A. 174 A3
Otukpa Nigeria 125 G5
Otukpo Nigeria 125 H5
Otuyo Bol. 200 D4
Otway U.S.A. 176 B7
Otway, Bahía b. Chile 205 B9
Otway, Cape Australia 147 D4
Otway, Seno b. Chile 205 C9
Otway National Park Australia 147 D4
Otway Range mts Australia 147 D4
Otwock Poland 49 S3
Ötztaler Alpen mts Austria 48 H9
Ou, Nam r. Laos 78 C3
Ouacha Niger 125 H3
Ouachita r. U.S.A. 179 E6
Ouachita, Lake U.S.A. 179 D5
Ouachita Mountains U.S.A. 179 D5
Ouadâne Mauritania 122 C5
UNESCO World Heritage Site
Ouadda Cent. Afr. Rep. 126 D2
Ouaddaï pref. Chad 120 D6
Ouadjinkarem well Niger 125 G1
Ouâd Nâga Mauritania 124 B2
Ouadou watercourse Mauritania 124 C3

►Ouagadougou Burkina 125 E3
Capital of Burkina.

Ouahigouya Burkina 124 E3
Ouahran Alg. see Oran
Ouaka pref. Cent. Afr. Rep. 126 D3
Ouaka r. Cent. Afr. Rep. 126 C3
Oualâta Mauritania 124 D2
Oualé r. Burkina 125 F4
Oualia Mali 124 C3
Ouallam Niger 125 F3
Ouallene Alg. 123 F4
Ouanary Fr. Guiana 199 I3
Ouanazein well Chad 120 C5
Ouanda-Djailé Cent. Afr. Rep. 126 D2
Ouandago Cent. Afr. Rep. 126 C3
Ouandjia Haute-Kotto Cent. Afr. Rep. 126 D2
Ouandjia Vakaga Cent. Afr. Rep. 126 D2
Ouandjia-Vakaga, Réserve de Faune de la nature res. Cent. Afr. Rep. 126 D2
Ouando Cent. Afr. Rep. 126 E3
Ouango Cent. Afr. Rep. 126 D3
Ouangolodougou Côte d'Ivoire 124 D4
formerly spelt Wangolodougou
Ouani Kalaoua well Niger 125 G3
Ouaqui Fr. Guiana 199 H4
Ouara r. Cent. Afr. Rep. 126 E3
Ouarâne reg. Mauritania 122 C5
Ouargaye Burkina 125 F4
also known as Ouarogou
Ouargla Alg. 123 G3
also spelt Wargla
Ouarissibitil well Mali 125 F2
Ouaritoufoulout well Mali 125 F2
Ouarkziz, Jbel ridge Alg./Morocco 122 C3
Ouarogou Burkina see Ouargaye
Ouarsenis, Massif de l' Alg. 55 M9
Ouarzazate Morocco 122 D3
Ouatagouna Mali 125 F3
Oubangui r. Cent. Afr. Rep./Dem. Rep. Congo see Ubangi
Oubergpas pass S. Africa 133 I9
Oudenaarde Belgium 51 J2
also spelt Audenarde
Oudon r. France 50 F5
Oudtshoorn S. Africa 132 G10
Oued Laou Morocco 54 F9
Oued Rhiou Alg. 55 L9
Oued Tlélat Alg. 55 K9
Oued Zem Morocco 122 D2
Ouéléssébougou Mali 124 D4
Ouémé r. Benin 125 F5
Ouessa Burkina 124 E4
Ouessant, Île d' i. France 50 A4
historically known as Ushant
Ouesso Congo 126 C4
Ouest prov. Cameroon 125 H5
Ouest, Pointe de l' pt Canada 169 H3
Ouezzane Morocco 122 D2
Oughterard Ireland 47 C10
Ougnat, Jbel mt. Morocco 122 D3
Ouham pref. Cent. Afr. Rep. 126 C3
Ouham r. Cent. Afr. Rep./Chad 126 C2
Ouham-Pendé pref. Cent. Afr. Rep. 126 C3
Ouidah Benin 125 F5
historically known as Whydah
Ouinardene Mali 125 E2
Ouiriego Mex. 184 C3
Ouistreham France 50 F3
Oujâf well Mauritania 124 D2
Oujda Morocco 123 E2
Oujeft Mauritania 124 B2
Oulad Teïma Morocco 122 C3
Oulainen Fin. 44 N2
Oulangan kansallispuisto nat. park Fin. 44 O2
Ould Yenjé Mauritania 124 C3
Ouled Djellal Alg. 123 G2
Ouled Farès Alg. 55 M8
Ouled Naïl, Monts des mts Alg. 123 F2
Ouled Saïd well Alg. 123 F3
Ouli Cameroon 125 I5
Oullins France 51 K7
Oulu Fin. 44 N2
also known as Uleåborg
Oulu prov. Fin. 44 N2
Oulujärvi l. Fin. 44 N2
Oulujoki r. Fin. 44 N2
Oulunsalo Fin. 44 N2
Oulx Italy 51 M7
Oum-Chalouba Chad 120 D6
Oumé Côte d'Ivoire 124 D5
Oum el Bouaghi Alg. 123 G2
Oum-Hadjer Chad 120 C6
Oumm ed Droûs Guebli, Sebkhet salt flat Mauritania 122 C5
Oumm ed Droûs Telli, Sebkha salt flat Mauritania 122 C4
Oumm el A'sel well Mali 122 D5
Ounara Morocco 122 C3
Ounasjoki r. Fin. 44 N2
Oungre Canada 167 K5
Ounianga Kébir Chad 120 D5
Ounianga Sérir Chad 120 D5
Ounissoui well Niger 125 I2
Oupeye Belgium 51 L2
Our r. Lux. 51 M3
Ouray U.S.A. 181 F5
Ourcq r. France 51 J3
Ouré Kaba Guinea 124 C4
Ourém Brazil 202 C2
Ourense Spain 54 D2
also spelt Orense
Ouricurí Brazil 202 D3
Ourinhos Brazil 206 D9
Ourini Chad 120 D5
Ourique Port. 54 C7
Ouro Brazil 202 C4
Ouro Branco Brazil 207 J7
Ouro Fino Brazil 206 G9
Ouro Preto Brazil 203 D7
UNESCO World Heritage Site
Ourthe r. Belgium 51 L2
Ouse r. U.K. 47 L10
Oust r. France 50 D5
Outamba Kilimi National Park Sierra Leone 124 B4
Outaouais, Rivière des r. Canada see Ottawa
Outardes r. Canada 169 G3
Outardes Quatre, Réservoir resr Canada 169 G3
Outat Oulad el Haj Morocco 122 E2
Outeniekwaberge mts S. Africa 132 G10
Outer Hebrides is U.K. 46 E6
Outer Island U.S.A. 172 C3
Outer Mongolia country Asia see Mongolia
Outer Santa Barbara Channel U.S.A. 182 F8
Outjo Namibia 130 C4
Outlook Canada 167 J5
Outokumpu Fin. 40 D3
Outoul Alg. 123 G5
Outram N.Z. 153 E13
Out Skerries is U.K. 46 L3
Ouvéa i. New Caledonia 145 F4
also spelt Uéa or Uvéa
Ouyanghai Shuiku resr China 87 E3
Ouyen Australia 147 D3
Ova r. Turkey 58 I7
Ovace, Punta d' mt. Corsica France 56 B7
Ovacık Turkey 107 D3
Ovada Italy 56 A4
Ovaeymiri Turkey 59 I11
Ovalle Chile 204 C3
Ovamboland reg. Namibia 130 B3
Ovan Gabon 126 B4
Ovar Port. 54 C4
Ovejas Col. 187 E5
Oveng Cameroon 125 I6
Ovens r. Australia 147 E4
Øvergard Norway 44 L1
Overhalla Norway 44 J2
Överkalix Sweden 44 M2
Overlander Roadhouse Australia 151 A5
Overland Park U.S.A. 178 D4
Övermark Fin. 44 M3
Overo, Volcán vol. Arg. 204 C4
Overton NV U.S.A. 183 J5
Overton TX U.S.A. 179 D5
Övertorneå Sweden 44 M2
Överum Sweden 45 L4
Överuman l. Sweden 44 K2
Ovid MI U.S.A. 173 I7
Ovid NY U.S.A. 177 I3
Ovidiopol' Ukr. 58 L2
Ovidiu Romania 58 J4
Oviedo Spain 54 F1
UNESCO World Heritage Site
Ovinishchenskaya Vozvyshennost' hills Rus. Fed. 43 R3
Ovišrags hd Latvia 42 C4
Oviston Nature Reserve S. Africa 133 J7
Ovminzatov tog'lari hills Uzbek. 103 E4
also known as Ovminzatow Toghi
Övögdiy Mongolia 84 C1
Ovoot Mongolia 85 G2
Övörhangay prov. Mongolia 84 D2
Øvre Anárjohka Nasjonalpark nat. park Norway 44 N1
Øvre Årdal Norway 45 I3
Øvre Dividal Nasjonalpark nat. park Norway 44 L1
Øvre Forra nature res. Norway 44 J3
Øvre Pasvik Nasjonalpark nat. park Norway 44 O1
Øvre Rendal Norway 45 J3
Övre Soppero Sweden 44 M1
also known as Badje-Sohppar
Ovruch Ukr. 41 D6
Övt Mongolia 84 D2
Owahanga N.Z. 152 K8
Owaka N.Z. 153 D14
Owakonze Canada 172 C2
Owando Congo 126 B5
formerly known as Fort Rousset
Owasco Lake U.S.A. 177 I3
Owase Japan 91 E7
Owasso U.S.A. 179 D4
Owatonna U.S.A. 174 A2
Owbeh Afgh. 101 E3
Owego U.S.A. 177 I3
Owen, Mount N.Z. 153 G9
Owendale S. Africa 132 H5
Owen Falls Dam Uganda 128 B4
Owen Island Myanmar 79 B6
Owen River N.Z. 153 G9
Owens r. U.S.A. 182 G5
Owensboro U.S.A. 174 C4
Owens Lake U.S.A. 182 G5
Owen Sound Canada 168 D4
Owen Sound inlet Canada 173 M6
Owen Stanley Range mts P.N.G. 145 D2
Owensville MO U.S.A. 174 B4
Owensville OH U.S.A. 176 A6
Owenton U.S.A. 176 A7
Owerri Nigeria 125 G5
Owhango N.Z. 152 J7
Owikeno Lake Canada 166 E5
Owings U.S.A. 177 I7
Owingsville U.S.A. 176 B7
Owl r. Canada 167 M3
Owl Creek r. U.S.A. 180 E4
Owminzatow Toghi hills Uzbek. see Ovminzatov tog'lari
Owo Nigeria 125 G5
Owosso U.S.A. 173 I8
Owyhee r. U.S.A. 180 C4
Owyhee Mountains U.S.A. 180 C4
Owyhee North Fork r. U.S.A. 180 C4
Owyhee South Fork r. U.S.A. 180 C4
Oxapampa Peru 200 B2
Öxarfjörður b. Iceland 44 [inset] C2
Oxbow Canada 167 K5
Ox Creek r. U.S.A. 178 B1
Oxelösund Sweden 45 L4
Oxford N.Z. 153 G11
Oxford U.K. 47 K12
Oxford IA U.S.A. 172 B9
Oxford MA U.S.A. 177 N3
Oxford ME U.S.A. 177 O1
Oxford MI U.S.A. 173 J8
Oxford MS U.S.A. 174 B5
Oxford NC U.S.A. 176 G9
Oxford NY U.S.A. 177 J3
Oxford OH U.S.A. 176 A6
Oxford PA U.S.A. 177 J6
Oxford WI U.S.A. 172 D7
Oxford House Canada 167 M4
Oxford Junction U.S.A. 172 C9
Oxford Lake Canada 167 M4
Oxkutzcab Mex. 185 H4
Oxley Australia 147 E3
Oxleys Peak Australia 147 F2
Oxley Wild Rivers National Park Australia 147 G2
Ox Mountains hills Ireland see Slieve Gamph
Oxnard U.S.A. 182 E7
Oxtongue Lake Canada 173 O5
Oxus r. Asia see Amudar'ya
Oxylithos Greece 59 F10
Oya r. Sarawak Malaysia 77 E2
Øya Norway 44 K2
Oyabe Japan 91 E6
Oyama Japan 91 F6
Ō-yama mt. Japan 91 F7
Ō-yama vol. Japan 83 E6
Oyapock r. Brazil/Fr. Guiana 199 I3
Oyapock r. Brazil/Fr. Guiana 199 I3
Oyapock, Baie d' b. Fr. Guiana 199 I3
Oyem Gabon 126 A4
Oyen Canada 167 I5
Øyeren l. Norway 45 J4
Oygon Mongolia 84 C1
Oykel r. U.K. 46 H6
Oymapinar Turkey 108 C1
Oymyakon Rus. Fed. 39 O3
Oyo Congo 126 B5
Oyo Nigeria 125 F5
Oyo state Nigeria 125 F4
Oyo Sudan 121 H4
Oyón Peru 200 A2
Oyonnax France 51 L6
Oyoqquduq Uzbek. 103 F4
also spelt Ayakkuduk
Oyster Bay S. Africa 133 I11
Oytal Kazakh. 103 H4
Oy-Tal Kyrg. 103 H4
Oytograk China 89 C4
Oyukludağı mt. Turkey 108 D1
Oyyl Kazakh. see Uil
Oyyq Kazakh. see Uyuk
Özalp Turkey 107 F3
formerly known as Karakalli
Ozamiz Phil. 74 B4
Ozark AL U.S.A. 175 C6
Ozark AR U.S.A. 179 D5
Ozark MO U.S.A. 178 D4
Ozark Plateau U.S.A. 178 D4
Ozarks, Lake of the U.S.A. 178 D4
Ożarów Poland 49 S5
Özbaşı Turkey 59 I11
Ozbekiston country Asia see Uzbekistan
Özd Hungary 49 R7
Özdere Turkey 59 I11
Özen Kazakh. see Kyzylsay
Ozerevo Rus. Fed. 43 P2
Ozerishche Rus. Fed. 43 O7
Ozerne Ukr. 58 J3
Ozerninskoye Vodokhranilishche resr Rus. Fed. 43 R6
Ozernovskiy Rus. Fed. 39 P4
Ozernoye Kazakh. 103 E1
formerly known as Ozernyy
Ozernoye Rus. Fed. 102 B2
Ozernyy Karagandinskaya Oblast' Kazakh. see Shashubay
Ozernyy Kustanayskaya Oblast' Kazakh. see Ozernoye
Ozernyy Ivanovskaya Oblast' Rus. Fed. 43 V4
Ozernyy Orenburgskaya Oblast' Rus. Fed. 103 E2
Ozernyy Smolenskaya Oblast' Rus. Fed. 43 N6
Ozerpakh Rus. Fed. 82 F1
Ozersk Rus. Fed. 42 D7
Ozerskiy Rus. Fed. 82 F3
Ozery Rus. Fed. 43 T7
Ozeryane Rus. Fed. 82 C2
Özgön Kyrg. 103 H4
also spelt Uzgen
Ozherel'ye Rus. Fed. 43 T7
Ozhogina r. Rus. Fed. 39 P3
Ozieri Sardinia Italy 57 B8
Ozimek Poland 49 P5
Ozinki Rus. Fed. 102 B2
Ozolnieki Latvia 42 E5
Ozona U.S.A. 179 B6
Ozorków Poland 49 Q4
Ōzu Ehime Japan 91 C8
Ōzu Kumamoto Japan 91 B8
Ozuki Japan 91 B7
Ozuluama Mex. 185 F4
Ozurget'i Georgia 107 E2
formerly known as Makharadze

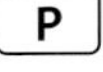

Pâ Burkina 124 E4
Paakkola Fin. 44 N2
Paamiut Greenland 165 O3
also known as Frederikshåb
Pa-an Myanmar see Hpa-an
Paanopa i. Kiribati see Banaba
Paarl S. Africa 132 C10
Paasvere Estonia 42 H2
Paatsjoki r. Europe see Patsoyoki
Pa'auilo U.S.A. 181 [inset] Z1
Pabaigh i. U.K. see Pabbay
Paballelo S. Africa 132 F5
P'abal-li N. Korea 83 C4
Pabbay i. Western Isles, Scotland U.K. 46 E6
Pabbay i. Western Isles, Scotland U.K. 46 E7
also spelt Pabaigh
Pabianice Poland 49 Q4
historically known as Pabianitz
Pabianitz Poland see Pabianice
Pabna Bangl. 97 F4
Pabradė Lith. 42 G7
Pab Range mts Pak. 101 F5
Pacaás, Serra dos hills Brazil 201 D2
Pacaás Novos, Parque Nacional nat. park Brazil 201 E2
Pacaembu Brazil 206 B8
Pacahuaras r. Bol. 200 D2
Pacajus Brazil 202 E3
Pacaraimã, Serra mts S. America see Pakaraima Mountains
Pacaraima Mountains S. America see Pakaraima Mountains
Pacarán Peru 200 B3
Pacasmayo Peru 200 A1
Pacatuba Brazil 202 E2
Pacaya r. Peru 198 C6
Pacaya, Volcán de vol. Guat. 185 H6
Pacaya Samiria, Reserva Nacional nature res. Peru 198 C6
Paceco Sicily Italy 57 E11
Pacheco Chihuahua Mex. 184 C2
Pacheco Zacatecas Mex. 185 E3
Pachia i. Greece 59 G12
also spelt Pakhiá
Pachía Peru 200 C4
Pachino Sicily Italy 57 H12
Pachitea r. Peru 200 B2
Pachiza Peru 200 A1
Pachmarhi India 96 C5
Pachor India 96 C5
Pachora India 94 B1
Pachpadra India 96 B4
Pachuca Mex. 185 F4
Pacifica U.S.A. 182 B4
Pacific Grove U.S.A. 182 C5

►Pacific Ocean 220
Largest ocean in the world.
►►208–209 Oceans and Poles

Pacific Rim National Park Canada 166 E5
Pacijan i. Phil. 74 C4
Pacinan, Tanjung pt Indon. 77 F4
Pačir Vojvodina, Srbija Serb. and Mont. 58 A3
Pacitan Indon. 77 E5
Packsaddle pass Australia 49 L9
Pacov Czech Rep. 49 M6
Pacoval Brazil 199 H5
Pacuí r. Brazil 207 I3
Paczków Poland 49 O5
Padada Phil. 74 C5
Padalere Indon. 75 B3
Padali Rus. Fed. see Amursk
Padamarang i. Indon. 75 B4
Padampur India 96 B3
Padang Kalimantan Barat Indon. 77 E3
Padang Sumatra Indon. 76 C3
Padang i. Indon. 76 C2
Padang Endau Malaysia 76 C2
Padangpanjang Indon. 76 C3
Padangsidimpuan Indon. 76 B2
Padangtikar Indon. 77 E3
Padangtikar i. Indon. 77 E3
Padany Rus. Fed. 40 E3
Padarosk Belarus 42 F9
Padas r. Sabah Malaysia 77 F1
Padasjoki Fin. 45 N3
Padatha, Kūh-e mt. Iran 100 B3
Padauiri r. Brazil 199 E5
Padaung Myanmar 78 A4
Padcaya Bol. 201 D5
Paddington Australia 147 E3
Paden City U.S.A. 176 E6
Paderborn Germany 48 F4
Pader Palwo Uganda 128 B4
Padeşu, Vârful mt. Romania 58 D3
Padilla Bol. 201 D4
Padina Romania 58 I4
Padina Vojvodina, Srbija Serb. and Mont. 58 B3
Padinska Skela Srbija Serb. and Mont. 58 B4
Padjelanta nationalpark nat. park Sweden 44 L2
Padluzhzha Belarus 43 M8
Padma r. Bangl. see Ganges
Padmanabhapuram India 94 C4
Padmapur India 96 D5
Padova Italy see Padua
Padra India 96 B5
Padrão, Ponta pt Angola 127 B6
Padrauna India 97 E4
Padre Bernardo Brazil 206 E2
Padre Caro hill Spain 54 F7
Padre Island U.S.A. 179 C7
Padre Island National Seashore nature res. U.S.A. 179 C7
Padre Paraíso Brazil 207 L4
Padrón Spain 54 C2

Pomona U.S.A. 182 G7
Pomorie Bulg. 58 I6
Pomorskie, Pojezierze reg. Poland 49 O2
Pomorskiy Bereg coastal area Rus. Fed. 40 E2
Pomorskiy Proliv sea chan. Rus. Fed. 40 I1
Pomos Point Cyprus 108 D2 also known as Pomou, Akra
Pomo Tso l. China see **Puma Yumco**
Pomou, Akra pt Cyprus see **Pomos Point**
Pompei Italy 57 G8 historically known as Pompeii UNESCO World Heritage Site
Pompéia Brazil 206 C9
Pompeii Italy see **Pompei**
Pompéu Brazil 203 C6
Pompton Lakes U.S.A. 177 K4
Ponape atoll Micronesia see **Pohnpei**
Ponask Lake Canada 167 M4
Ponazyrevo Rus. Fed. 40 H4
Ponca U.S.A. 178 C3
Ponca City U.S.A. 178 C4
Ponce Puerto Rico 187 G3
Ponce de Leon Bay U.S.A. 175 D7
Poncha Springs U.S.A. 181 F5
Ponda India 94 B3
Pondicherry India 94 C4 also spelt Pondichéry or Puduchcheri
Pondicherry union terr. India 95 C4
Pondichéry India see **Pondicherry**
Pond Inlet Canada 165 L2 also known as Mittimatalik; formerly known as Ponds Bay
Pondoland reg. S. Africa 133 N8
Ponds, Island of Canada 169 K2
Ponds Bay Canada see **Pond Inlet**
Pơ Ne, Đak r. Vietnam 79 D5
Poneloya Nicaragua 186 B4
Ponente, Riviera di coastal area Italy 56 A5
Ponferrada Spain 54 E2
Pongakawa N.Z. 152 K5
Pongara, Pointe pt Gabon 126 A4
Pongaroa N.Z. 152 K8
Pongo watercourse Sudan 126 E3
Pongo de Manseriche gorge Peru 198 B6
Pongola S. Africa 133 P4
Pongola r. S. Africa 133 Q3
Pongolapoort Dam l. S. Africa 133 P4
Pongolapoort Public Resort Nature Reserve S. Africa 133 P4
Poniatowa Poland 49 T4
Poniki, Gunung mt. Indon. 75 B2
Ponindilisa, Tanjung pt Indon. 75 B3
Ponizov'ye Rus. Fed. 43 M6
Ponnagyun Myanmar 78 A3
Ponnaivar r. India 94 C4
Ponnampet India 94 B3
Ponnani India 94 B4
Ponnani r. India 94 B4
Ponneri India 94 D3
Ponnyadaung Range mts Myanmar 78 A3
Ponoka Canada 167 H4
Ponomarevka Rus. Fed. 102 C1
Ponorogo Indon. 77 E4
Ponoy r. Rus. Fed. 40 G2
Pons r. Canada 169 G1
Pons France 50 F7
Pons Spain see **Ponts**
Ponsacco Italy 56 C5
Ponsul r. Port. 54 D5
Pontacq France 50 F9
Ponta Delgada Arquipélago dos Açores 54 [inset]

►**Ponta Delgada** Azores 216 M3 Capital of the Azores.

Ponta de Pedras Brazil 202 B2
Ponta dos Índios Brazil 199 I3
Ponta do Sol Cape Verde 124 [inset]
Ponta Grossa Brazil 203 B8
Pontal do Ipiranga Brazil 207 N6
Pontalina Brazil 206 D4
Pont-à-Mousson France 51 M4
Pontant Arg. 204 E5
Pontão Brazil 202 B3
Ponta Porã Brazil 201 G5
Pontarlier France 51 M6
Pontassieve Italy 56 D5
Pont-Audemer France 50 G3
Pont-Aven France 50 C5
Pontax r. Canada 168 E3
Pontchartrain, Lake U.S.A. 175 B6
Pontchâteau France 50 D5
Pont-d'Ain France 51 L6
Pont-de-Roide France 51 M5
Pont de Suert Spain 55 L2
Pont du Gard tourist site France 51 K9 UNESCO World Heritage Site
Ponte Alta do Norte Brazil 202 C4
Ponteareas Spain 54 C2 also spelt Puenteareas
Pontebba Italy 56 F2
Ponte Branca Brazil 206 A3
Ponteceso Spain 54 C1
Pontecorvo Italy 56 F7
Ponte de Pedra Brazil 201 F3
Pontedera Italy 56 C5
Ponte de Sor Port. 54 C5
Ponte do Rio Verde Brazil 203 A6
Ponte Firme Brazil 206 G5
Ponteix Canada 167 J5
Ponteland U.K. 47 K8
Ponte Nova Brazil 203 D7
Pontes-e-Lacerda Brazil 201 F3
Pontevedra Spain 54 C2
Pontevedra, Ría de est. Spain 54 C2
Ponthierville Dem. Rep. Congo see **Ubundu**
Pontiac IL U.S.A. 174 B3
Pontiac MI U.S.A. 173 J8
Pontiae is Italy see **Ponziane, Isole**
Pontianak Indon. 77 E3
Pontine Islands is Italy see **Ponziane, Isole**
Pontivy France 50 D4
Pont-l'Abbé France 50 B5
Pontões Capixabas, Parque Nacional dos nat. park Brazil 207 M5
Pontoetoe Suriname 199 H4
Pontoise France 51 I3
Ponton watercourse Australia 151 C6
Ponton Canada 167 L4
Pontotoc U.S.A. 174 B5
Pontremoli Italy 56 B4
Ponts Spain 55 M3 also spelt Pons
Pont-St-Esprit France 51 K8
Pont-sur-Yonne France 51 J4
Pontypool Canada 173 O6
Pontypool U.K. 47 I12
Pontypridd U.K. 47 I12
Ponui Island N.Z. 152 J4
Ponyatovka Rus. Fed. 43 N8
Ponyri Rus. Fed. 43 R9
Ponza Italy 57 E8
Ponza, Isola di i. Italy 56 E8
Ponziane, Isole is Italy 56 E8 English form Pontine Islands; historically known as Pontiae
Poochera Australia 146 B3
Pool admin. reg. Congo 126 B5
Poole U.K. 47 K13
Poolowanna Lake salt flat Australia 148 C5
Poona India see **Pune**
Pooncarie Australia 147 D3
Poopelloe Lake Australia 147 E2
Poopó Bol. 200 D4
Poopó, Lago de l. Bol. 200 D4
Poor Knights Islands N.Z. 152 I3
Pop Uzbek. 103 G4 also spelt Pap
Popa Mountain Myanmar 78 A3
Popayán Col. 198 B4
Pope Latvia 42 C4
Popes Creek U.S.A. 177 I7
Popigay r. Rus. Fed. 39 K2
Popilta Lake imp. l. Australia 146 D3
Popio Lake Australia 146 D3
Poplar r. Man. Canada 167 L4
Poplar r. N.W.T. Canada 166 G2
Poplar U.S.A. 172 B4
Poplar r. U.S.A. 180 F2
Poplar, West Fork r. U.S.A. 180 F2
Poplar Bluff U.S.A. 174 B4
Poplar Camp U.S.A. 176 E9
Poplar Plains U.S.A. 176 B7
Poplarville U.S.A. 175 B6
Poplevinskiy Rus. Fed. 43 U8

►**Popocatépetl, Volcán** vol. Mex. 185 F5 5th highest mountain in North America. UNESCO World Heritage Site ►►154–155 **North America** Landscapes

Popoh Indon. 77 E5
Popokabaka Dem. Rep. Congo 127 C6
Popoli Italy 56 F6
Popondetta P.N.G. 145 D2
Popovača Croatia 56 I3
Popovichskaya Rus. Fed. see **Kalininskaya**
Popovka Vologod. Obl. Rus. Fed. 43 S2
Popovka Vologod. Obl. Rus. Fed. 43 U1
Popovo Bulg. 58 H5
Popovo Polje plain Bos.-Herz. 56 J6
Popovska Reka r. Bulg. 58 H6
Poppberg hill Germany 48 I6
Poppenberg hill Germany 48 H4
Poprad r. Poland 49 R6
Poprad Slovakia 49 R6
Poquis, Nevado de mt. Chile 200 D5
Poquoson U.S.A. 177 I8
Por r. Poland 49 U5
Porali r. Pak. 101 F5
Porangahau N.Z. 152 K8
Porangatu Brazil 202 B5
Porazava Belarus 42 F9
Porbandar India 96 A5
Porcher Island Canada 166 D4
Porciúncula Brazil 207 K7
Porco Bol. 200 D4
Porcsalma Hungary 49 T8
Porcuna Spain 54 G7
Porcupine r. Canada/U.S.A. 164 E3
Porcupine, Cape Canada 169 J2
Porcupine Creek r. U.S.A. 180 F2
Porcupine Gorge National Park Australia 149 E4
Porcupine Hills Canada 167 K4
Porcupine Mountains U.S.A. 172 D4
Porcupine Plain Canada 167 K4
Porcupine Provincial Forest nature res. Canada 167 K4
Pordenone Italy 56 E3
Pordim Bulg. 58 F5
Pore Col. 198 D3
Poreč Croatia 56 F3 UNESCO World Heritage Site
Porecatu Brazil 206 B9
Porech'ye Moskovskaya Oblast' Rus. Fed. 43 Q6
Porech'ye Pskovskaya Oblast' Rus. Fed. 43 L5
Porech'ye Tverskaya Oblast' Rus. Fed. 43 R3
Poretskoye Rus. Fed. 40 H5
Porga Benin 125 F4
Pori Fin. 45 M3 also known as Björneborg
Porirua N.Z. 152 I9
Þórisvatn l. Iceland 44 [inset] C2
Porjus Sweden 44 L2
Porkhov Rus. Fed. 43 K4
Porkkalafjärden b. Fin. 42 F2
Porlamar Venez. 199 F2
Porma r. Spain 54 F2
Pormpuraaw Australia 149 D2
Pornainen Fin. 45 N3
Pornic France 50 D5
Poro i. Phil. 74 C4
Poro, Monte hill Italy 57 H10
Poronaysk Rus. Fed. 82 F2
Porong China 89 E6 also known as Baingoin
Pôrông, Stœng r. Cambodia 79 D5
Poros Greece 59 E11
Poros i. Greece 59 E11
Porosozero Rus. Fed. 40 E3
Porpoise Bay Antarctica 223 I2
Porquerolles, Île de i. France 51 M10
Porquis Junction Canada 173 M2
Porrentruy Switz. 51 N5
Porsangerfjorden sea chan. Norway 44 N1
Porsangerhalvøya pen. Norway 44 N1
Porsgrunn Norway 45 J4
Þórshöfn Iceland 44 [inset] D2
Porsuk r. Turkey 106 B3
Portadown U.K. 47 F9
Portaferry U.K. 47 G9
Portage IN U.S.A. 172 F9
Portage MI U.S.A. 172 H8
Portage PA U.S.A. 176 G5
Portage WI U.S.A. 172 D7
Portage Lakes U.S.A. 176 D5
Portage la Prairie Canada 167 L5
Portal U.S.A. 178 B1
Port Alberni Canada 166 E5
Port Albert Australia 147 E4
Portalegre Port. 54 D5
Portalegre admin. dist. Port. 54 D5
Portales U.S.A. 179 B5
Port-Alfred Canada see **La Baie**
Port Alfred S. Africa 133 K10
Port Alice Canada 166 E5
Port Allegany U.S.A. 176 G4
Port Alma Australia 149 F4
Port Angeles U.S.A. 180 B2
Port Antonio Jamaica 186 D3
Port-à-Piment Haiti 187 E3
Portarlington Ireland 47 E10
Port Arthur Australia 147 E5
Port Arthur China see **Lüshun**
Port Arthur U.S.A. 179 D6
Port Askaig U.K. 46 F8
Port Augusta Australia 146 C3
Port-au-Port Bay Canada 169 J3

►**Port-au-Prince** Haiti 187 E3 Capital of Haiti.

Port aux Choix Canada 169 J3
Port Beaufort S. Africa 132 E11
Port Blair India 95 G4
Port Bolster Canada 173 N6
Portbou Spain 55 O2
Port Bradshaw b. Australia 148 C2
Port Broughton Australia 146 C3
Port Burwell Canada 173 M8
Port Campbell Australia 147 D4
Port Campbell National Park Australia 147 D4
Port Canning India 97 F5
Port Carling Canada 173 N5
Port-Cartier Canada 169 H3 formerly known as Shelter Bay
Port Chalmers N.Z. 153 E13
Port Charles N.Z. 152 J4
Port Charlotte U.S.A. 175 D7
Port Clements Canada 166 C4
Port Clinton U.S.A. 176 C4
Port Clyde U.S.A. 177 P2
Port Colborne Canada 168 E5
Port Credit Canada 173 N7
Port Darwin b. Australia 148 A2
Port Davey b. Australia 147 E5
Port-de-Paix Haiti 187 E3
Port de Pollença Spain 55 O5 also spelt Puerto de Pollensa
Port Dickson Malaysia 76 C2
Port Douglas Australia 149 E3
Port Dover Canada 173 M8
Port Easington inlet Australia 148 A1
Porte des Morts lake channel U.S.A. 172 G5
Port Edward Canada 166 D4
Port Edward S. Africa 133 O8
Port Edwards U.S.A. 172 D6
Porteira Brazil 199 G5
Porteirinha Brazil 202 D5
Portel Brazil 202 B2
Portel Port. 54 D6
Portelândia Brazil 206 A4
Port Elgin N.B. Canada 169 H4
Port Elgin Ont. Canada 168 D4
Port Elizabeth S. Africa 133 J10
Port Ellen U.K. 46 F8
Port Erin Isle of Man 47 H9
Porter Lake N.W.T. Canada 167 J2
Porter Lake Sask. Canada 167 J3
Porter Landing Canada 166 D3
Porterville S. Africa 132 C10
Porterville U.S.A. 182 E5
Portes-lès-Valence France 51 K8
Port Étienne Mauritania see **Nouâdhibou**
Port Everglades U.S.A. see **Fort Lauderdale**
Port Fairy Australia 147 D4
Port Fitzroy N.Z. 152 J4
Port Francqui Dem. Rep. Congo see **Ilebo**
Port-Gentil Gabon 126 A5
Port Gibson U.S.A. 175 B6
Port Grosvenor S. Africa 133 N8
Port Harcourt Nigeria 125 G5
Port Hardy Canada 166 E5
Port Harrison Canada see **Inukjuak**
Port Hawkesbury Canada 169 I4
Porthcawl U.K. 47 I12
Port Hedland Australia 150 B4
Port Henry U.S.A. 177 L1
Port Herald Malawi see **Nsanje**
Porthmos Zakynthou sea chan. Greece 59 B11
Port Hope Canada 173 O7
Port Hope U.S.A. 173 K7
Port Hope Simpson Canada 169 K2
Port Hueneme U.S.A. 182 E7
Port Huron U.S.A. 173 K8
Port-İliç Azer. 107 G3
Portillo Cuba 186 D3
Portimão Port. 54 C7
Port Island Hong Kong China 87 [inset] also known as Chek Chau
Port Jackson Australia see **Sydney**
Port Jackson inlet Australia 147 F3
Port Jefferson U.S.A. 177 L5
Port Kaituma Guyana 199 G3
Port Keats Australia see **Wadeye**
Port Kent U.S.A. 177 L1
Port Klang Malaysia see **Pelabuhan Klang**
Port Láirge Ireland see **Waterford**
Portland Australia 146 D4
Portland IN U.S.A. 176 A5
Portland ME U.S.A. 177 O2
Portland MI U.S.A. 173 I8
Portland OR U.S.A. 180 B3
Portland, Isle of pen. U.K. 47 J13
Portland Bay Australia 146 D4
Portland Bill hd U.K. see **Bill of Portland**
Portland Canal inlet Canada 166 D4
Portland Creek Pond l. Canada 169 J3
Portland Inlet Canada 166 D4
Portland Point Jamaica 186 D3
Portland Roads Australia 149 D2
Portlaoise Ireland 47 E10
Port Lavaca U.S.A. 179 C6
Port Lincoln Australia 146 B3
Port Loko Sierra Leone 124 B4
Port-Louis Guadeloupe 187 H3

►**Port Louis** Mauritius 219 K7 Capital of Mauritius.

Port-Lyautrey Morocco see **Kénitra**
Port MacDonnell Australia 146 D4
Port Macquarie Australia 147 G2
Port Manvers inlet Canada 169 I1
Port McArthur b. Australia 148 C2
Port McNeill Canada 166 E5
Port-Menier Canada 169 H3
Port Moller b. U.S.A. 164 C4
Port Morant Jamaica 186 D3

►**Port Moresby** P.N.G. 73 K8 Capital of Papua New Guinea.

Port Musgrave b. Australia 149 D1
Portnacroish U.K. 46 G7
Portnahaven U.K. 46 F8
Port Neches U.S.A. 179 D6
Port Neill Australia 146 C3
Port Nelson Bahamas 187 E2
Portneuf r. Canada 169 G3
Portneuf, Réserve Faunique de nature res. Canada 169 F4
Port Nolloth S. Africa 132 A6
Port Norris U.S.A. 177 J6
Port-Nouveau-Québec Canada see **Kangiqsualujjuaq**
Porto Brazil 202 D2
Porto Port. see **Oporto**
Porto admin. dist. Port. 54 C3
Porto, Golfe de b. Corsica France 51 O10 UNESCO World Heritage Site
Porto Acre Brazil 200 D2
Porto Alegre Amazonas Brazil 200 D2
Porto Alegre Mato Grosso do Sul Brazil 203 A7
Porto Alegre Pará Brazil 199 H6
Porto Alegre Rio Grande do Sul Brazil 203 B9
Porto Alencastro Brazil 206 C6
Porto Alexandre Angola see **Tombua**
Porto Amarante Brazil 201 E3
Porto Amboim Angola 127 B7 also known as Gunza
Porto Amélia Moz. see **Pemba**
Porto Artur Brazil 201 G3
Porto Azzurro Italy 56 C6
Porto Belo Brazil 203 B8
Portobelo Panama 186 D5
Portobelo, Parque Nacional nat. park Panama 186 D5 UNESCO World Heritage Site
Porto Camargo Brazil 203 A7
Porto Cavlo Brazil 202 F4
Porto da Fôlha Brazil 202 E4
Porto da Lontra Brazil 199 H6
Porto de Meinacos Brazil 202 A5
Porto de Moz Brazil 199 H5
Porto de Santa Cruz Brazil 207 L2
Porto do Barka Brazil 199 H6
Porto do Massacas Brazil 201 E3
Porto dos Gaúchos Óbidos Brazil 201 F2
Porto do Son Spain 54 B2 also spelt Puerto del Son
Porto Empedocle Sicily Italy 57 F11
Porto Esperança Brazil 201 F4
Porto Esperidião Brazil 201 F3
Porto Estrêla Brazil 201 F3
Porto Feliz Brazil 206 F10
Portoferraio Italy 56 C6
Porto Ferreira Brazil 206 F8
Porto Firme Brazil 207 J7
Port of Ness U.K. 46 F5
Porto Franco Brazil 202 C3

►**Port of Spain** Trin. and Tob. 187 H5 Capital of Trinidad and Tobago.

Porto Grande Brazil 199 I4
Portogruaro Italy 56 E3
Porto Inglês Cape Verde 124 [inset]
Porto Jofre Brazil 201 F4
Portola U.S.A. 182 D2
Porto Luceno Brazil 203 A8
Portomaggiore Italy 56 D4
Porto Mauá Brazil 203 A8
Porto Murtinho Brazil 201 F5
Porto Nacional Brazil 202 B4

►**Porto-Novo** Benin 125 F5 Capital of Benin.

Porto Novo Cape Verde 124 [inset]
Porto Novo India see **Parangipettai**
Portopalo di Capo Passero Sicily Italy 57 H12
Porto Primavera, Represa resr Brazil 206 A8
Port Orange U.S.A. 175 D6
Port Orchard U.S.A. 180 B3
Port Orford U.S.A. 180 A4
Porto Rincão Cape Verde 124 [inset]
Porto San Giorgio Italy 56 F5
Porto Santana Brazil 199 I5
Porto Sant'Elpidio Italy 56 F5
Porto Santo, Ilha de i. Madeira 122 A2
Portoscuso Sardinia Italy 57 A9
Porto Seguro Brazil 202 E6
Porto Tolle Italy 56 E4
Porto Torres Sardinia Italy 56 A8 historically known as Turris Libisonis
Porto Triunfo Brazil 201 E3
Porto União Brazil 203 B8
Porto-Vecchio Corsica France 52 D3
Porto Velho Brazil 201 E2
Portovenere Italy 56 B4 UNESCO World Heritage Site
Portoviejo Ecuador 198 A5
Porto Wálter Brazil 200 B2
Portpatrick U.K. 47 G9
Port Pegasus b. N.Z. 153 B15 also known as Pikihatiti
Port Perry Canada 173 O6
Port Phillip Bay Australia 147 E4
Port Pirie Australia 146 C3
Portree U.K. 46 F6
Port Renfrew Canada 166 E5
Port Rexton Canada 169 K3
Port Roper b. Australia 148 B2
Port Rowan Canada 173 M8
Port Royal U.S.A. 177 H7
Port Royal Sound inlet U.S.A. 175 D5
Port Said Egypt 121 G2 also known as Bûr Sa'îd
Port St Joe U.S.A. 175 C6
Port St Johns S. Africa 133 N8
Port St-Louis Madag. see **Antsohimbondrona**
Port-St-Louis-du-Rhône France 51 K9
Port St Lucie City U.S.A. 175 D7
Port Salvador Falkland Is 205 F8
Ports de Beseit mts Spain 55 L4 also spelt Puertos de Beceite
Port Severn Canada 173 N6
Port Shelter b. Hong Kong China 87 [inset] also known as Ngau Mei Hoi
Port Shepstone S. Africa 133 O7
Port Simpson Canada see **Lax Kw'alaams**
Portsmouth Dominica 187 H4
Portsmouth U.K. 47 K13
Portsmouth NH U.S.A. 177 O2
Portsmouth OH U.S.A. 176 C7
Portsmouth VA U.S.A. 177 I9
Port Stanley Falkland Is see **Stanley**
Port Stephens Falkland Is 205 E9
Port Sudan Sudan 121 H5 also known as Būr Sudan
Port Sulphur U.S.A. 175 B6
Port-sur-Saône France 51 M5
Port Swettenham Malaysia see **Pelabuhan Klang**
Port Talbot U.K. 47 I12
Port Tambang b. Phil. 74 B3
Porttipahdan tekojärvi l. Fin. 44 N1
Port Townsend U.S.A. 180 B2
►**Portugal** country Europe 54 C7 ►►32–33 **Europe** Countries
Portugalete Spain 55 H1
Portugália Angola see **Chitato**
Portuguesa state Venez. 198 D2
Portuguese East Africa country Africa see **Mozambique**
Portuguese Guinea country Africa see **Guinea-Bissau**
Portuguese Timor country Asia see **East Timor**
Portuguese West Africa country Africa see **Angola**
Portumna Ireland 47 D10
Portus Herculis Monoeci country Europe see **Monaco**
Port-Vendres France 51 J10
Port Victoria Australia 146 C3

►**Port Vila** Vanuatu 145 F3 Capital of Vanuatu. Also known as Vila.

Portville U.S.A. 176 G3
Port Vladimir Rus. Fed. 44 P1
Port Waikato N.Z. 152 I5
Port Wakefield Australia 146 C3
Port Warrender Australia 150 D2
Port Washington U.S.A. 172 F7
Port Wing U.S.A. 172 B4
Porumamilla India 94 C3
Porus'ya r. Rus. Fed. 43 M4
Þorvaldsfell vol. Iceland 44 [inset] C2
Porvenir Pando Bol. 200 C2
Porvenir Santa Cruz Bol. 201 E3
Porvenir Chile 205 C9
Porvoo Fin. 45 N3 also known as Borgå
Porvoonjoki r. Fin. 42 G1
Por'ya Guba Rus. Fed. 44 P2
Poryŏng S. Korea 83 B5 formerly known as Taech'ŏn
Porzuna Spain 54 G5
Posada Sardinia Italy 57 B8
Posada r. Sardinia Italy 57 B8
Posada Spain 54 F1
Posadas Arg. 204 G2
Posadas Spain 54 F7
Posadowsky Bay Antarctica 223 G2
Posavina reg. Bos.-Herz./Croatia 56 I3
Poschiavo Switz. 51 Q6
Poseidonia Greece 59 F11
Poseidonia tourist site Italy see **Paestum**
Posen Poland see **Poznań**
Posen U.S.A. 173 J5
Poshekhon'ye Rus. Fed. 43 U3 formerly known as Poshekon'ye-Volodarsk
Poshekon'ye-Volodarsk Rus. Fed. see **Poshekhon'ye**
Posht watercourse Iran 100 D4
Posht-e Āsemān spring Iran 100 D3
Posht-e Badam Iran 100 C3
Poshteh-ye Chaqvīr hill Iran 100 D4
Posht-e Kūh mts Iran 100 A3
Posht Kūh hill Iran 100 B2
Posio Fin. 44 O2
Poskam China see **Zepu**
Poso Indon. 75 B3
Poso r. Indon. 75 B3
Poso, Danau l. Indon. 75 B3
Poso, Teluk b. Indon. 75 B3
Posof Turkey 107 E2
Posorja Ecuador 198 A5
Pospelikha Rus. Fed. 103 J1
Posse Brazil 202 C5
Possession Islands Antarctica 223 L2
Pößneck Germany 48 I5
Post U.S.A. 179 B5
Poșta Câlnău Romania 58 H3 formerly spelt Poșta Cîlnău
Poșta Cîlnău Romania see **Poșta Câlnău**
Postavy Belarus see **Pastavy**
Poste-de-la-Baleine Canada see **Kuujjuarapik**
Postmasburg S. Africa 132 H5
Postojna Slovenia 56 G3
Poston U.S.A. 183 J7
Postville Canada 169 J2
Postville U.S.A. 174 B3
Post Weygand Alg. 123 F4
Postysheve Ukr. see **Krasnoarmiys'k**
Posušje Bos.-Herz. 56 J5
Pos'yet Rus. Fed. 82 C4
Pota Indon. 75 B5
Potamia Greece 58 F8
Potamos Greece 59 D12
Potanino Rus. Fed. 43 N1
Potchefstroom S. Africa 133 L3
Potcoava Romania 58 F4
Poté Brazil 203 D6
Poteau U.S.A. 179 D5
Potegaon India 94 D2
Potentia Italy see **Potenza**
Potenza Italy 57 H8 historically known as Potentia
Potenza r. Italy 56 F5
Poteriteri, Lake N.Z. 153 B14
Potfontein S. Africa 132 I7
Poti r. Brazil 202 D3
P'ot'i Georgia 107 E2
Potikal India 94 D2
Potiraguá Brazil 202 E5
Potiskum Nigeria 125 H4
Potnarvin Vanuatu 145 F3
Poto Peru 200 C3
Po Toi i. Hong Kong China 87 [inset] also spelt Putoi
Potomac r. U.S.A. 177 I7
Potomac, South Branch r. U.S.A. 176 G6
Potomac, South Fork South Branch r. U.S.A. 176 F7
Potomana, Gunung mt. Indon. 75 C5
Potoru Sierra Leone 124 C5
Potosí Bol. 200 D4 UNESCO World Heritage Site
Potosí dept Bol. 200 D5
Potosi U.S.A. 174 B4
Potosi Mountain U.S.A. 183 I6
Pototan Phil. 74 B4
Potrerillos Chile 204 C2
Potrero del Llano Mex. 184 D2
Potro r. Peru 198 B6
Potsdam Germany 49 K3 UNESCO World Heritage Site
Potsdam U.S.A. 177 K1
Potsdamer Havelseengebiet park Germany 49 J3
Pottangi India 95 D2
Pottendorf Austria 49 N8
Potter U.S.A. 178 B3
Potter Valley U.S.A. 182 A2
Potterville U.S.A. 176 A3
Pottsville U.S.A. 177 I5
Potwar reg. Pak. 101 H3
Pouancé France 50 E5
Pouce Coupe Canada 166 F4
Pouch Cove Canada 169 K4
Poughkeepsie U.S.A. 177 L4
Poultney U.S.A. 177 L2
Pouma Cameroon 125 H6
Pound U.S.A. 176 C8
Poupan S. Africa 132 I7
Pourerere N.Z. 152 K8
Pouso Alegre Brazil 207 H9
Pouso Alegre, Serra mts Brazil 206 D2
Pouso Alto Brazil 206 A3
Poutasi Samoa 145 H3
Poŭthĭsăt Cambodia 79 C5 also spelt Pursat
Pouto N.Z. 152 I4
Pouzauges France 50 F6
Povarovo Rus. Fed. 43 S5
Považská Bystrica Slovakia 49 P6
Poved' r. Rus. Fed. 43 P4
Povenets Rus. Fed. 40 E3
Povlen mt. Serb. and Mont. 58 A4
Povoação Brazil 207 N6
Póvoa de Varzim Port. 54 C3
Povorino Rus. Fed. 41 G6
Povorotnyy, Mys hd Rus. Fed. 82 D4
Poway U.S.A. 183 G9
Powder r. MT U.S.A. 180 F3
Powder r. OR U.S.A. 180 C3
Powder, South Fork r. U.S.A. 180 F4
Powder River U.S.A. 180 F4
Powell U.S.A. 180 E3
Powell r. U.S.A. 176 B9
Powell, Lake resr U.S.A. 183 N4
Powell Creek watercourse Australia 149 D5
Powell Mountain U.S.A. 182 F3
Powell River Canada 166 E5
Powellsville U.S.A. 177 I9
Powers U.S.A. 172 F5
Powhatan U.S.A. 176 H8
Powhatan Point U.S.A. 176 E6
Powidzkie, Jezioro l. Poland 49 O3
Powo China 86 A1
Poxoréu Brazil 202 A5
Poyan, Sungai r. Sing. 76 [inset]
Poyang China see **Boyang**
Poyang Hu l. China 87 F2
Poyan Reservoir Sing. 76 [inset]
Poyarkovo Rus. Fed. 82 C2
Poygan, Lake U.S.A. 172 E6
Poynette U.S.A. 172 D7
Poyo, Cerro mt. Spain 55 I7
Poysdorf Austria 49 N7
Pöytyä Fin. 45 M3
Pozantı Turkey 106 C3
Požarevac Srbija Serb. and Mont. 58 C4
Poza Rica Mex. 185 F4
Požega Croatia 56 J3 formerly known as Slavonska Požega
Požega Srbija Serb. and Mont. 58 B5
Pozharskoye Rus. Fed. 90 D1
Pozhnya Rus. Fed. 43 M5
Pozhva Rus. Fed. 40 K4
Poznań Poland 49 N3 historically known as Posen
Pozo Alcón Spain 55 I7
Pozo Betbeder Arg. 204 D2
Pozoblanco Spain 54 G6
Pozo Colorado Para. 201 F5
Pozo del Tigre Arg. 201 E6
Pozo Hondo Arg. 204 D2
Pozohondo Spain 55 J6
Pozo Nuevo Mex. 184 C2
Pozos, Punta pt Arg. 205 D7
Pozo San Martin Arg. 204 E2
Pozsony Slovakia see **Bratislava**
Pozuzo Peru 200 B2
Pozzallo Sicily Italy 57 G12
Pozzuoli Italy 57 G8 historically known as Puteoli
Pra r. Ghana 125 E5
Prabumulih Indon. 76 D3
Prabuty Poland 49 Q2
Prachatice Czech Rep. 49 L6
Prachi r. India 95 E2
Prachin Buri Thai. 79 C5
Prachuap Khiri Khan Thai. 79 B6
Pradairo mt. Spain 54 D1
Praděd mt. Czech Rep. 49 O5
Pradera Col. 198 B4
Prades France 51 I10
Prado Brazil 203 E6
Pradópolis Brazil 206 E8

►**Prague** Czech Rep. 49 L5 Capital of the Czech Republic. Also known as Praha. UNESCO World Heritage Site

Praha Czech Rep. see **Prague**
Prahova r. Romania 58 H4

►**Praia** Cape Verde 124 [inset] Capital of Cape Verde.

Praia a Mare Italy 57 H9
Praia do Bilene Moz. 131 G5
Praia Grande Brazil 206 G11
Praia Rica Brazil 201 G3
Prainha Amazonas Brazil 201 E1
Prainha Pará Brazil 199 H5
Prairie Australia 149 E4
Prairie r. U.S.A. 174 A2
Prairie City U.S.A. 180 C3
Prairie Dog Town Fork r. U.S.A. 179 B5
Prairie du Chien U.S.A. 172 B7
Prairie River Canada 167 K4
Prakhon Chai Thai. 79 C5
Pram r. Austria 49 K7
Pramanta Greece 59 C9
Prambanan Indon. 77 E4 UNESCO World Heritage Site
Pran r. Thai. 79 C5
Pran Buri Thai. 79 B5
Prangli i. Estonia 42 G2
Pranhita r. India 94 C2
Prapat Indon. 76 B2
Praslin i. Seychelles 129 [inset] UNESCO World Heritage Site
Prasonisi, Akra pt Greece 59 I13
Praszka Poland 49 P4
Prat i. Chile 205 B8
Prata Brazil 206 E6
Prata r. Goiás Brazil 206 A5
Prata r. Minas Gerais Brazil 206 D5
Prata r. Minas Gerais Brazil 207 G4
Pratapgarh India 96 B4
Pratas Islands China see **Dongsha Qundao**
Prat de Llobregat Spain see **El Prat de Llobregat**
Prathes Thai country Asia see **Thailand**
Pratinha Brazil 206 G6
Prato Italy 56 D5
Pratt U.S.A. 178 C4
Prattville U.S.A. 175 C5
Pravara r. India 94 B2
Pravda Bulg. 58 I5
Pravdinsk Rus. Fed. 42 C7 historically known as Friedland
Pravia Spain 54 E1
Praya Indon. 77 G5
Prazaroki Belarus 45 O5
Preah, Prêk r. Cambodia 79 D5
Preăh Vihéar Cambodia 79 D5
Prechistoye Smolenskaya Oblast' Rus. Fed. 43 N6
Prechistoye Yaroslavskaya Oblast' Rus. Fed. 43 V3
Precipice National Park Australia 149 F5
Predazzo Italy 56 D2
Predeal Romania 58 G3
Preeceville Canada 167 K5
Pré-en-Pail France 50 F4
Preetz Germany 48 H1
Pregolya r. Rus. Fed. 42 B7
Preiļi Latvia 42 H5
Preissac, Lac l. Canada 173 O2
Prejmer Romania 58 G3 UNESCO World Heritage Site
Prekornica mts Serb. and Mont. 58 A6
Prelate Canada 167 I5
Prémery France 51 J5
Premnitz Germany 49 J3
Prenj mts Bos.-Herz. 56 J5
Prentiss U.S.A. 175 B6
Prenzlau Germany 49 K2
Preobrazheniye Rus. Fed. 82 D4
Preparis Island Cocos Is 79 A5
Preparis North Channel Cocos Is 79 A5
Preparis South Channel Cocos Is 79 A5
Přerov Czech Rep. 49 O6
Presa de la Amistad, Parque Natural nature res. Mex. 185 E2
Presanella, Cima mt. Italy 56 C2
Presa San Antonio Mex. 185 E3
Prescott Canada 168 F4
Prescott AR U.S.A. 179 D5
Prescott AZ U.S.A. 183 L7
Prescott Valley U.S.A. 183 L7
Preservation Inlet N.Z. 153 A14
Preševo Srbija Serb. and Mont. 58 C6
Presidencia Roca Arg. 204 F2
Presidencia Roque Sáenz Peña Arg. 204 E2
Presidente Bernardes Brazil 206 B9
Presidente de la Plaza Arg. 204 F2
Presidente Dutra Brazil 202 C3
Presidente Eduardo Frei research station Antarctica 222 U2
Presidente Epitácio Brazil 206 A8
Presidente Hermes Brazil 201 E2
Presidente Jânio Quadros Brazil 207 L1
Presidente Juan Perón prov. Arg. see **Chaco**
Presidente Juscelino Brazil 207 I5
Presidente Olegário Brazil 206 G5
Presidente Prudente Brazil 206 B9
Presidente Venceslau Brazil 206 B8
Presidio U.S.A. 181 F7
Preslav Bulg. see **Veliki Preslav**
Prešov Slovakia 49 S7
Prespa, Lake Europe 58 C8 also known as Prespansko Ezero or Prespës, Liqeni i
Prespansko Ezero l. Europe see **Prespa, Lake**
Prespes nat. park Greece 58 C8
Prespës, Liqeni i l. Europe see **Prespa, Lake**
Presque Isle ME U.S.A. 174 G2
Presque Isle MI U.S.A. 173 J5
Presque Isle WI U.S.A. 172 D4
Presque Isle Point U.S.A. 172 F4
Pressbaum Austria 49 N7
Pressburg Slovakia see **Bratislava**
Prestea Ghana 125 E5
Presteigne U.K. 47 I11
Přeštice Czech Rep. 49 K6
Preston U.K. 47 J10
Preston GA U.S.A. 175 C5
Preston IA U.S.A. 172 C8
Preston ID U.S.A. 180 E4
Preston MD U.S.A. 177 J7
Preston MN U.S.A. 174 A3
Preston, Cape Australia 150 B4
Prestonsburg U.S.A. 176 C8
Prestrud Inlet Antarctica 223 N1
Prestwick U.K. 46 H8
Preto r. Amazonas Brazil 199 F5
Preto r. Bahia Brazil 202 D4
Preto r. Goiás Brazil 206 C5
Preto r. Minas Gerais Brazil 206 G3
Preto r. Rondônia Brazil 201 E2
Preto r. São Paulo Brazil 206 D7

Qūz Saudi Arabia 104 C4
Quzhou *Hebei* China 85 G4
Quzhou *Zhejiang* China 87 F2
Quzi China 85 E4
Qvareli Georgia 107 F2
also spelt Kvareli
Qypshaq Köli *salt l.* Kazakh. *see* **Kypshak, Ozero**
Qyteti Stalin Albania *see* **Kuçovë**
Qyzan Kazakh. *see* **Kyzan**
Qyzylaghash Kazakh. *see* **Kyzylagash**
Qyzylkesek Kazakh. *see* **Kyzylkesek**
Qyzylkōl *l.* Kazakh. *see* **Kyzylkol', Ozero**
Qyzylorda Kazakh. *see* **Kyzylorda**
Qyzylorda Oblysy *admin. div.* Kazakh. *see* **Kzyl-Ordinskaya Oblast'**
Qyzyltaū Kazakh. *see* **Kyzyltau**
Qyzyltū Kazakh. *see* **Kishkenekol'**
Qyzylzhar Kazakh. *see* **Kyzylzhar**

R

Raab *r.* Austria 49 N9
Raab Hungary *see* **Győr**
Raahe Fin. 44 N2
Rääkkylä Fin. 44 O3
Raalte Neth. 48 D3
Ra'an, Khashm ar *hill* Saudi Arabia 104 C2
Raanujärvi Fin. 44 N2
Raas *i.* Indon. 77 F4
Raasay *i.* U.K. 46 F6
Raasiku Estonia 42 G2
Rab *i.* Croatia 56 G4
Rába *r.* Hungary 49 O8
Raba Indon. 77 G5
Raba *r.* Poland 49 R5
Rabaale Somalia 128 F2
Rabak Sudan 121 G6
Rabang China 89 C5
Rabat Gozo Malta *see* **Victoria**
Rabat Malta 53 E4

▸Rabat Morocco 122 D2
Capital of Morocco.

Rabatakbaytal Tajik. *see* **Rabotoqbaytal**
Rabāt-e Kamah Iran 100 D3
Rabaul P.N.G. 145 E2
Rabaul *vol.* P.N.G. 145 E2
Rabbath Ammon Jordan *see* **'Ammān**
Rabbi *r.* Italy 56 E4
Rabbit *r.* Canada 166 E3
Rabbit Flat Australia 148 A4
Rabbitskin *r.* Canada 166 F2
Rábca *r.* Hungary 49 O8
Rabezha Rus. Fed. 43 O4
Rabidine *well* Niger 125 G3
Rābigh Saudi Arabia 104 B3
Rabinal Guat. 185 H6
Rabka Poland 49 Q6
Rabkob India *see* **Dharmjaygarh**
Rabnabad Islands Bangl. 97 F5
Râbniţa Moldova *see* **Rîbniţa**
Rābor Iran 100 D4
Rabotoqbaytal Tajik. 101 H2
also known as Akbaytal *or* Rabatakbaytal
Rabt Sbayta *des.* W. Sahara 122 B5
Rabyānah *oasis* Libya 120 D3
Rača *Srbija* Serb. and Mont. 58 B4
Racaka China 86 A2
Racalmuto *Sicily* Italy 57 F11
Racconigi Italy 51 N8
Raccoon Cay *i.* Bahamas 186 E2
Raccoon Creek *r.* U.S.A. 176 C7
Raceland U.S.A. 175 B6
Race Point U.S.A. 177 O3
Rachaïya Lebanon 108 G4
Rachel U.S.A. 183 I4
Rachevo Rus. Fed. 43 S3
Rach Gia Vietnam 79 D6
Rach Gia, Vinh *b.* Vietnam 79 D6
Raciąż Poland 49 R3
Racibórz Poland 49 P5
historically known as Ratibor
Racine *WI* U.S.A. 172 F8
Racine *WV* U.S.A. 176 D7
Racine Lake Canada 173 J2
Răciu Romania 58 F2
Racoş Romania 58 G2
Racoviţa Romania 58 I3
Radā' Yemen 104 D5
Radashkovichy Belarus 42 I7
also spelt Radoshkovichi
Rădăuţi Romania 41 C7
Radbuza *r.* Czech Rep. 49 K6
Radchenko Rus. Fed. 43 R5
Radcliff U.S.A. 174 C4
Radd, Wādī ar *watercourse* Syria 109 M1
Radde Rus. Fed. 82 C2
Rade Norway 45 J4
Radebeul Germany 49 K4
Radenthein Austria 49 K9
Radew *r.* Poland 49 M1
Radford U.S.A. 176 E8
Radford Point Australia 148 A1
Radhanpur India 96 A5
Radili Ko Canada *see* **Fort Good Hope**
Radishchevo Rus. Fed. 102 A1
Radisson *Que.* Canada 168 E2
Radisson *Sask.* Canada 167 J4
Raditsa-Krylovka Rus. Fed. 43 P8
Radium S. Africa 133 M2
Radium Hot Springs Canada 167 G5
Radlinski, Mount Antarctica 222 R1
Radnevo Bulg. 58 G6
Rado de Tumaco *inlet* Col. 198 B4
Radogoshcha Rus. Fed. 43 P2
Radolfzell am Bodensee Germany 48 F8
Radom Poland 49 S4
Radom Sudan 126 E2
Radomir Bulg. 58 D6
Radomir *mt.* Bulg./Greece 58 E7
formerly known as Kalabak
Radomka *r.* Poland 49 S4
Radom National Park Sudan 126 D2
Radomsko Poland 49 Q4
formerly known as Noworadomsk
Radomyshl' Ukr. 41 D6
Radoshkovichi Belarus *see* **Radashkovichy**
Radovets Bulg. 58 H7
Radoviš Macedonia 58 D7
Radovitskiy Rus. Fed. 43 U6
formerly known as Tsentral'nyy
Radovljica Slovenia 56 G2
Radøy *i.* Norway 46 Q3
Radstock, Cape Australia 146 B3
Răducăneni Romania 58 I2
Radun' Belarus 42 F7
Radunia *r.* Poland 49 P1
Radviliškis Lith. 42 E6
Radwā, Jabal *mt.* Saudi Arabia 104 B2
Radymno Poland 49 T6
Radziejów Poland 49 P3
Radzyń Podlaski Poland 49 T4
Rae Bareli India 96 D4
Raecreek *r.* Canada 166 B1
Rae-Edzo Canada 167 G2
also known as Edzo
Raeford U.S.A. 174 E5
Rae Lakes Canada 167 G1
also known as Garneti
Raeside, Lake *salt flat* Australia 151 C6
Raetihi N.Z. 152 J7
Rāf *hill* Saudi Arabia 107 D5
Rafaela Arg. 204 E3
Rafaḥ Gaza *see* **Rafiaḥ**
Rafaï Cent. Afr. Rep. 126 D3
Raffadali *Sicily* Italy 57 F11
Rafḥā' Saudi Arabia 107 E5
Rafiaḥ Gaza 108 F6
also spelt Rafaḥ
Rafina Greece 59 F10
Rafsanjān Iran 100 C4
also known as Bahāmabād
Raft *r.* U.S.A. 180 D4
Raga Sudan 126 E2
Ragag Sudan 126 E2
Ragana Latvia 42 F4
Ragang, Mount *vol.* Phil. 74 C5
Ragay Gulf Phil. 74 B3
Ragged, Mount *hill* Australia 151 C7
Ragged Island Bahamas 186 E2
Ragged Island U.S.A. 177 Q2
Raghogarh India 96 C4
Raghwah *waterhole* Saudi Arabia 109 P9
Raghwān, Wādī *watercourse* Yemen 104 D5
Raglan N.Z. 152 I5
Rago Nasjonalpark *nat. park* Norway 44 L2
Ragueneau Canada 169 G3
Ragusa Croatia *see* **Dubrovnik**
Ragusa *Sicily* Italy 57 G12
UNESCO World Heritage Site
Raha India 97 G4
Raha Indon. 75 B4
Rahachow Belarus 43 L8
also spelt Rogachev
Rahad *r.* Sudan 121 G6
Rahad Canal Sudan 121 G6
Rahad el Berdi Sudan 126 D2
Rahad Wahal *well* Sudan 120 E6
Rahaeng Thai. *see* **Tak**
Rahaṭ, Ḥarrat *lava field* Saudi Arabia 104 C3
Rahatgaon India 96 C5
Rahimatpur India 94 B2
Rahimyar Khan Pak. 101 G4
Rāhjerd Iran 100 B3
Raḥmān, Chāh-e *well* Iran 101 D4
Rahotu N.Z. 152 H7
Rahouia Alg. 55 M9
Rahumäe Estonia 42 I3
Rahuri India 94 B2
Rahzanak Afgh. 101 E3
Rai, Hon *i.* Vietnam 79 D6
Raiatea *i.* Fr. Polynesia 221 I7
also known as Uliatea
Raibu *i.* Indon. *see* **Air**
Raichur India 94 C2
Raiganj India 97 F4
Raigarh *Chhattisgarh* India 97 D5
Raigarh *Orissa* India 94 D2
Raijua *i.* Indon. 75 B5
Raikot India 96 B3
Railroad Valley *valley* U.S.A. 183 I3
Raimangal *r.* Bangl. 97 F5
Raimbault, Lac *l.* Canada 169 G2
Rainbow Lake Canada 166 G3
Raine Entrance *sea chan.* Australia 149 E1
Raine Island Australia 149 E1
Rainelle U.S.A. 176 E8
Raini *r.* Pak. 101 G4
Rainier, Mount *vol.* U.S.A. 180 B3
Rainy *r.* U.S.A. 174 A1
Rainy Lake Canada 168 A3
Raippaluoto *i.* Fin. 44 M3
Raipur Bangl. 97 F5
Raipur *Chhattisgarh* India 97 D5
Raipur *Rajasthan* India 96 B4
Raipur *W. Bengal* India 97 E5
Rairangpur India 97 E5
Raisen India 96 C5
Raisinghnagar India 96 B3
Raisio Fin. 45 M3
Raistakka Fin. 44 O2
Raitalai India 96 C5
Raith Canada 172 D2
Rai Valley N.Z. 152 H9
Raivavae *i.* Fr. Polynesia 221 J7
also known as Vavitao
Raiwind Pak. 101 H4
Raja Estonia 42 H3
Raja, Ujung *pt* Indon. 76 B2
Rajaampat, Kepulauan *is* Indon. 75 D3
Rajabasa, Gunung *vol.* Indon. 77 D4
Rajagangapur India 97 E5
Rajahmundry India 94 D2
Raja-Joosepp Fin. 44 O1
also known as Rājijovsset
Rajaldesar India 96 B3
Rajamäki Fin. 42 F1
Rajampet India 94 C3
Rajang *r. Sarawak* Malaysia 77 E2
Rajanpur Pak. 101 G4
Rajapalaiyam India 94 C4
Rajapur India 94 B2
Rajasthan *state* India 96 B4
historically known as Rajputana Agency
Rajasthan Canal India 96 B3
Rajauli India 97 E4
Rajbari Bangl. 97 F5
Rajgarh *Madhya Pradesh* India 96 C4
Rajgarh *Maharashtra* India 94 B2
Rajgarh *Rajasthan* India 96 B3
Rajgarh *Rajasthan* India 96 C4
Rajgir India 97 E4
Rajgród Poland 49 T2
Rājijovsset Fin. *see* **Raja-Joosepp**
Rajim India 94 D1
Rajince *Srbija* Serb. and Mont. 58 C6
Rajkot India 96 A5
Rajmahal India 97 E4
Rajmahal Hills India 97 E4
Raj Nandgaon India 96 D5
Rajpipla India 96 B5
Rajpur India 96 B5
Rajpura India 96 C3
Rajputana Agency *state* India *see* **Rajasthan**
Rajsamand India 96 B4
Rajshahi Bangl. 97 F4
also known as Rampur Boalia
Rajshahi *admin. div.* Bangl. 97 F4
Rājū Syria 109 H1
Rajula India 96 A5
Rajur India 94 C1
Rajura *Maharashtra* India 94 C2
also known as Manikgarh
Rajura *Maharashtra* India *see* **Ahmadpur**
Raka China 89 D6
Rakabah, Qalamat ar *oasis* Saudi Arabia 105 F3
Rakahuri *r.* N.Z. *see* **Ashley**
Rakai Uganda 128 A5
Rakaia N.Z. 153 G11
Rakaia *r.* N.Z. 153 G11
Rakan, Ra's *pt* Qatar 105 E2
Rakaposhi *mt.* Jammu and Kashmir 96 B1
Raka Zangbo *r.* China *see* **Dogxung Zangbo**
Rakeahua, Mount *hill* N.Z. 153 B14
Rakhaing *state* Myanmar *see* **Arakan**
Rakhine *state* Myanmar *see* **Arakan**
Rakhiv Ukr. 53 G2
Rakhshan *r.* Pak. 101 E5
Rakiraki Fiji 145 G3
Rakit *i.* Indon. 77 E4
Rakitnitsa *r.* Bulg. 58 G6
Rakitnoye *Belgorodskaya Oblast'* Rus. Fed. 41 E6
Rakitnoye *Primorskiy Kray* Rus. Fed. 82 D3
Rakitu Island N.Z. 152 J4
formerly known as Arid Island
Rakiura *i.* N.Z. *see* **Stewart Island**
Rakke Estonia 42 H3
Rakkestad Norway 45 J4
Rakmanovskie Klyuchi Kazakh. 88 D1
Rakni *r.* Pak. 101 G4
Rakoniewice Poland 49 N3
Rakops Botswana 131 E4
Rakovitsa Bulg. 58 D5
Rakovník Czech Rep. 49 K5
Rakovski Bulg. 58 F6
Rakusheсhnyy, Mys *pt* Kazakh. 102 B4
Rakvere Estonia 42 H2
Ralebona Lesotho 133 M7
Raleigh *MS* U.S.A. 175 B5

▸Raleigh *NC* U.S.A. 174 E5
State capital of North Carolina.

Raleighvallen Voltsberg, Natuurreservaat *nature res.* Suriname 199 G3
Ralla Indon. 75 A4
Ralph U.S.A. 172 F4
Ralston Canada 167 I5
Ralston U.S.A. 177 I4
Ram *r.* Canada 166 F2
Rama Israel 108 G5
Rama Nicaragua 186 B4
Ramacca *Sicily* Italy 57 G11
Ramādī Iraq *see* **Ar Ramādī**
Ramādī, Saddat ar *dam* Iraq 109 O4
Ramaditas Chile 200 C5
Ramah Canada 169 I1
Ramales de la Victoria Spain 55 H1
Ramalho, Serra do *hills* Brazil 202 C5
Ramallah West Bank 108 G6
Ramallo Arg. 204 E4
Ramanagaram India 94 C3
Ramanathapuram India 94 C4
also known as Ramnad
Ramanuj Ganj India 97 D5
Ramas, Cape India 94 B3
Ramasukha Rus. Fed. 43 O9
Ramatlabama *watercourse* Botswana/S. Africa 133 J2
Ramatlabama S. Africa 133 J2
Ramban India 96 B2
Ramberg Norway 44 K1
Rambervillers France 51 M4
Rambouillet France 50 H4
Rambutyo Island P.N.G. 73 K7
historically known as Jesu Maria Island
Ramdurg India 94 B3
Ramechhap Nepal 97 E4
Rame Head S. Africa 133 N8
Rame Head U.K. 47 H13
Ramenskoye Rus. Fed. 43 T6
Rameshki Rus. Fed. 43 R4
Rameswaram India 94 C4
Ramezān Kalak Iran 101 E5
Ramgarh Bangl. 97 F5
Ramgarh *Jharkhand* India 97 E5
Ramgarh *Rajasthan* India 96 A4
Ramgarh *Rajasthan* India 96 C4
Ramgul *reg.* Afgh. 101 G3
Rāmhormoz Iran 100 B4
Ramingining Australia 148 B2
Ramit Tajik. *see* **Romit**
Ramitan Uzbek. *see* **Romiton**
Ramla Israel 108 F6
Ramlat Rabyānah *des.* Libya *see* **Rebiana Sand Sea**
Ramm, Jabal *mts* Jordan 108 G8
also spelt Rum, Jebel
Rammulotsi S. Africa 133 K4
Ramnad India *see* **Ramanathapuram**
Ramnagar *Madhya Pradesh* India 96 D4
Ramnagar *Uttaranchal* India 96 C3
Ramnagar Jammu and Kashmir 96 B2
Ramnäs Sweden 45 L4
Ramni Belarus 43 L6
Râmnicul Sărat *r.* Romania 58 I3
Râmnicu Sărat Romania 58 I3
formerly spelt Rîmnicu Sărat
Râmnicu Vâlcea Romania 58 F3
formerly spelt Rîmnicu Vîlcea
Ramo Eth. 128 D3
Ramokgwebane Botswana 131 E4
Ramona U.S.A. 183 H8
Ramón Lista Arg. 205 D7
Ramonville-St-Agne France 50 H9
Ramore Canada 173 M2
Ramos Arg. 201 D5
Ramos Arizpe Mex. 185 E3
Ramotswa Botswana 131 E5
Rampart of Genghis Khan *tourist site* Asia 85 G1
Ramparts *r.* Canada 166 D1
Rampur *Himachal Pradesh* India 89 B6
Rampur *Uttar Pradesh* India 96 C3
Rampur *Uttar Pradesh* India 96 C3
Rampura India 96 B4
Rampur Boalia Bangl. *see* **Rajshahi**
Rampur Hat India 97 E4
Ramree Myanmar 78 A4
Ramree Island Myanmar 78 A4
Rāmsar Iran 100 B2
Ramsele Sweden 44 L3
Ramsey Canada 173 K3
Ramsey Isle of Man 47 H9
Ramsey Lake Canada 168 D4
Ramsgate S. Africa 133 O7
Ramsgate U.K. 47 N12
Ramshai Hat India 97 F4
Rāmshir Iran 100 B4
Ramsing *mt.* India 97 G3
Ramsjö Sweden 45 K3
Ramtek India 96 C5
Ramu Bangl. 97 G5
Ramu *r.* P.N.G. 73 J7
Ramundberget Sweden 44 K3
Ramusio, Lac *l.* Canada 169 I2
Ramvik Sweden 44 L3
Ramygala Lith. 42 F6
Rana, Cerro *hill* Col. 199 D4
Rañadoiro, Puerto de *pass* Spain 54 E2
Rañadoiro, Sierra de *mts* Spain 54 E1
Ranaghat India 97 F5
Ranai *i.* U.S.A. *see* **Lāna'i**
Rana Pratap Sagar *resr* India 96 B4
Ranapur India 96 B5
Rånåsfoss Norway 45 J3
Ranau *Sabah* Malaysia 77 G1
Ranau, Danau *l.* Indon. 76 C4
Rancagua Chile 204 C4
Rance *r.* France 50 D4
Rancharia Brazil 206 C9
Rancheria Canada 166 D2
Rancheria *r.* Canada 166 D2
Ranchester U.S.A. 180 F3
Ranchi India 97 E5
Rancho Cordova U.S.A. 182 C3
Rancho de Caçados Tapiúnas Brazil 201 F2
Ranchos de Taos U.S.A. 181 F5
Rancho Veloz Cuba 175 D8
Ranco, Lago *l.* Chile 204 B6
Randallstown U.S.A. 177 I6
Randazzo *Sicily* Italy 57 G11
Randburg S. Africa 133 L3
Randers Denmark 45 J4
Randfontein S. Africa 133 L3
Randijaure *l.* Sweden 44 L2
Randolph *MA* U.S.A. 177 N3
Randolph *ME* U.S.A. 177 P1
Randolph *NY* U.S.A. 176 G3
Randolph *UT* U.S.A. 180 E4
Randolph *VT* U.S.A. 177 M2
Randow *r.* Germany 49 L2
Randsburg U.S.A. 182 G6
Randsfjorden *l.* Norway 45 J3
Randsjö Sweden 45 K3
Randsverk Norway 45 J3
Randvaal S. Africa 133 M3
Råneå Sweden 44 M2
Ranfurly N.Z. 153 E13
Ranga *r.* India 78 A2
Rangae Thai. 79 C7
Rangamati Bangl. 97 G5
Rangapara North India 97 G4
Rangas, Tanjung *pt* Indon. 75 A3
Rangasa, Tanjung *pt* Indon. 75 A3
Rangaunu Bay N.Z. 152 H2
Rangeley Lake U.S.A. 177 O1
Rangely U.S.A. 183 P1
Ranger Lake Canada 168 D4
Ranger Lake *l.* Canada 173 J4
Rangi India 94 D1
Rangia Patharughat India 97 F4
Rangiauria *i.* S. Pacific Ocean *see* **Pitt Island**
Rangiora N.Z. 153 G11
Rangipoua *mt.* N.Z. 152 L5
also known as Hardy, Mount
Rangitaiki N.Z. 152 K6
Rangitata N.Z. 153 F12
Rangitata *r.* N.Z. 153 F12
Rangitikei *r.* N.Z. 152 J8
Rangitoto Islands N.Z. 152 H8
Rangiwaea Junction N.Z. 152 J7
Rangiwahia N.Z. 152 J7
Rangkasbitung Indon. 77 D4
Rangke China *see* **Zamtang**
Rangkūl Tajik. 101 H2
Rangôn Myanmar *see* **Rangoon**
Rangôn *admin. div.* Myanmar *see* **Yangôn**

▸Rangoon Myanmar 78 B4
Capital of Myanmar. Also known as Yangôn; also spelt Rangôn; historically known as Dagon.

Rangoon *admin. div.* Myanmar *see* **Yangôn**
Rangoon *r.* Myanmar 78 B4
Rangpur Bangl. 97 F4
Rangsang *i.* Indon. 76 C2
Rangse Myanmar 78 A2
Rani India 96 B4
Rania India 96 B3
Ranibennur India 94 B3
Raniganj India 97 E5
Ranijula Peak India 97 D5
Ranikhet India 96 C3
Ranipur Pak. 101 G5
Raniwara India 96 B4
Ranken *watercourse* Australia 148 C4
Rankin U.S.A. 179 B6
Rankin Inlet Canada 167 M2
also known as Kangiqliniq
Rankin Inlet *inlet* Canada 167 M2
Rankin's Springs Australia 147 E3
Rankovićevo *Srbija* Serb. and Mont. *see* **Kraljevo**
Ranna Estonia 42 I3
Rannes Australia 149 F5
Ranneye Rus. Fed. 102 C2
Rannoch, Loch *l.* U.K. 46 H7
Rannu Estonia 42 H3
Rano Nigeria 125 H4
Ranobe *r.* Madag. 131 [inset] J3
Ranohira Madag. 131 [inset] J4
Ranomafana Madag. 131 [inset] K3
Ranomatana Madag. 131 [inset] J5
Ranong Thai. 79 B6
Ranongga *i.* Solomon Is 145 E2
Ranopiso Madag. 131 [inset] J5
Ranot Thai. 79 C7
Ranotsara Avaratra Madag. 131 [inset] J4
Ranova *r.* Rus. Fed. 43 V7
Ranpur India 96 A5
Ransiki Indon. 73 H7
Ransom U.S.A. 172 E9
Ranta Fin. 44 N1
Rantabe Madag. 131 [inset] K2
Rantasalmi Fin. 44 O3
Rantau Indon. 77 F3
Rantau *i.* Indon. 76 C2
Rantaukampar Indon. 76 C2
Rantaupanjang *Kalimantan Tengah* Indon. 77 F3
Rantaupanjang *Kalimantan Timur* Indon. 77 G2
Rantauprapat Indon. 76 B2
Rantaupulut Indon. 77 F3
Rantemario, Gunung *mt.* Indon. 75 B3
Rantepao Indon. 75 A3
Rantoul U.S.A. 174 B3
Rantsevo Rus. Fed. 43 P5
Rantsila Fin. 44 N2
Ranua Fin. 44 N2
Ranxë Albania 58 A7
Rānya Iraq 107 F3
Ranyah, Wādī *watercourse* Saudi Arabia 104 C3
Rao Go *mt.* Laos/Vietnam 78 D4
Raohe China 82 D3
Raon-l'Étape France 51 M4
Raoul Island N.Z. 145 H4
Rapa *i.* Fr. Polynesia 221 J7
also known as Oparo *or* Rapa-iti
Rapa-iti *i.* Fr. Polynesia *see* **Rapa**
Rapallo Italy 56 B4
Rapar India 96 A5
Rapch *watercourse* Iran 101 D5
Raper, Cape Canada 165 M3
Rapidan *r.* U.S.A. 176 H7
Rapid Bay Australia 146 C3
Rapid City U.S.A. 178 B2
Rapide-Deux Canada 173 O3
Rapide-Sept Canada 173 O3
Rāpina Estonia 42 I3
Rapirrān *r.* Brazil 200 D2
Rapla Estonia 42 F3
Rappahannock *r.* U.S.A. 177 I8
Rappang Indon. 75 A3
Rapti *r.* India 97 D4
Rapulo *r.* Bol. 200 D3
Rapur *Andhra Pradesh* India 94 C3
Rapur *Gujarat* India 96 A5
Rapurapu *i.* Phil. 74 C3
Raqqa Syria *see* **Ar Raqqah**
Raquette *r.* U.S.A. 177 K1
Raquette Lake U.S.A. 177 K2
Rara National Park Nepal 97 D3
Raritan Bay U.S.A. 177 K5
Raroia *atoll* Fr. Polynesia 221 J7
formerly known as Barclay de Tolly
Rarotonga *i.* Cook Is 221 I7
historically known as Armstrong Island *or* Roxburgh Island
Ras India 96 B4
Raša *r.* Croatia 56 G3
Rasa *i.* Phil. 74 A4
Rasa, Punta *pt* Arg. 204 E6
Ra's ad Daqm Oman 105 G4
Ra's al 'Ayn Syria 109 L1
Ra's al Ḥadd Oman 105 G3
Ra's al Ḥikmah Egypt 121 E2
Ras al Khaimah U.A.E. *see* **Ra's al Khaymah**
Ra's al Khaymah U.A.E. 105 F2
English form Ras al Khaimah
Ra's al Mish'āb Saudi Arabia 105 E1
Raşan, Jabal *hill* Saudi Arabia 104 C3
Ra's an Naqb Jordan 108 G7
Ra's ash Shaykh Humayd Saudi Arabia 104 A1

▸Ras Dejen *mt.* Eth. 128 C1
5th highest mountain in Africa.
▸▸110–111 **Africa** Landscapes

Raseiniai Lith. 42 E6
Ras el Ma Alg. 123 E2
formerly known as Bedeau
Râs el Mâ Mali 124 D2
Ra's Ghārib Egypt 121 G2
Rashaant *Bayan-Ölgiy* Mongolia 84 A2
Rashaant *Dundgovi* Mongolia 85 E2
Rashad Sudan 128 A2
Rashid Egypt 121 F2
historically known as Rosetta
Rāshid *reg.* Saudi Arabia 105 F3
Rashid Qala Afgh. 101 F4
Rashshah Yemen 105 D5
Rasht Iran 100 B2
Rasina Estonia 42 I3
Rasina *r.* Serb. and Mont. 58 C5
Råsjö Sweden 44 K3
Rāsk Iran 101 E5
also known as Firuzabad
Raška *Srbija* Serb. and Mont. 58 B5
Raskam *mts* China 89 A4
Ras Koh *mt.* Pak. 101 F4
Raskoh *mts* Pak. 101 F4
Ra's Muḥammad National Park Egypt 104 A2
Rasmussen Basin *sea feature* Canada 165 J3
Rasna Belarus 43 M7
Rasna Belarus 43 K7
Râşnov Romania 58 G3
formerly spelt Rîşnov
Raso *i.* Cape Verde 124 [inset]
Raso da Catarina *hills* Brazil 202 E4
Rason Lake *salt flat* Australia 151 D6
Rasony Belarus 43 J6
also spelt Rossony
Rasova Romania 58 I4
Rasovo Bulg. 58 E5
Rasra India 97 D4
Ra's Sāq, Jabal *hill* Saudi Arabia 104 B2
Ra's Sharwayn *c.* Yemen 105 E5
Rasshua, Ostrov *i.* Rus. Fed. 81 Q3
Ra's Şirāb Oman 105 G3
Rass Jebel Tunisia 57 C11
Rasskazovo Rus. Fed. 41 G5
Rast Romania 58 E5
Rasta *r.* Belarus 43 L8
Ras Tannūrah Saudi Arabia 105 E2
Rastatt Germany 48 F7
Rastede Germany 48 F2
Rastorguyevo Rus. Fed. *see* **Vidnoye**
Rata N.Z. 152 J7
Ratae U.K. *see* **Leicester**
Ratai, Gunung *mt.* Indon. 76 D4
Ratamka Belarus 42 I8
Ratanda S. Africa 133 M3
Ratangarh *Madhya Pradesh* India 96 B4
Ratangarh *Rajasthan* India 96 B3
Ratanpur *Chhattisgarh* India 97 D5
Ratanpur *Gujarat* India 96 B5
Rätansbyn Sweden 44 K3
Rat Buri Thai. 79 B5
Ratchino Rus. Fed. 102 C1
Ratelfontein S. Africa 132 C8
Rath India 96 C4
Rathbun Lake U.S.A. 174 A3
Rathedaung Myanmar 78 A3
Rathenow Germany 49 J3
Rathenower Wald- und Seengebiet *park* Germany 49 J3
Rathlin Island U.K. 47 F8
Rathluirc Ireland 47 D11
also known as Charleville
Ratibor Poland *see* **Racibórz**
Ratisbon Germany *see* **Regensburg**
Ratitovec *mt.* Slovenia 56 G2
Ratiya India 96 B3
Raţīyah, Wādī *watercourse* Jordan 108 H8
Rat Lake Canada 167 L3
Ratlam India 96 B5
Ratnagiri India 94 B2
Ratnapura Sri Lanka 94 D5
Ratne Ukr. 41 C6
also spelt Ratno
Ratno Ukr. *see* **Ratne**
Rato Dero Pak. 101 G5
Raton U.S.A. 181 F5
Ratqah, Wādī ar *watercourse* Iraq 109 L3
Rattray Head U.K. 46 K6
Rättvik Sweden 45 K3
Ratz, Mount Canada 166 C3
Ratzeburg Germany 48 H2
Rau *i.* Indon. 75 D2
Raub Malaysia 76 C2
Rauch Arg. 204 F5
Rauđamýri Iceland 44 [inset] B2
Raudanjoki *r.* Fin. 44 N2
Râu de Mori Romania 58 D3
Raudhatain Kuwait 107 F5
Raudna *r.* Estonia 42 G3
Raudondvaris Lith. 42 E7
Raufarhöfn Iceland 44 [inset] D2
Raukokore N.Z. 152 L5
Raukumara *mt.* N.Z. 152 M5
Raukumara Forest Park *nature res.* N.Z. 152 L5
Raukumara Range *mts* N.Z. 152 L6
Raul *r.* India 95 D1
Raul Soares Brazil 207 K7
Rauma Fin. 45 M3
UNESCO World Heritage Site
Rauna Latvia 42 G4
Raurimu N.Z. 152 J7
Raurkela India 97 E5
Rauschen Rus. Fed. *see* **Svetlogorsk**
Rausu Japan 90 I2
Rausu-dake *mt.* Japan 90 I2
Rautalampi Fin. 44 N3
Rautavaara Fin. 44 O3
Rautjärvi Fin. 45 O3
Rauza India *see* **Khuldabad**
Ravalli U.S.A. 180 D3
Ravānsar Iran 100 A3
Ravanusa *Sicily* Italy 57 F11
Rāvar Iran 100 D4
Ravat Kyrg. 101 G2
Ravello Italy 57 G8
UNESCO World Heritage Site
Ravena U.S.A. 177 L3
Ravenna Italy 56 E4
UNESCO World Heritage Site
Ravenna *NE* U.S.A. 178 C3
Ravenna *OH* U.S.A. 176 D4
Ravensburg Germany 48 G8
Ravenshoe Australia 149 E3
Ravensthorpe Australia 151 C7
Ravenswood Australia 149 E4
Ravenswood U.S.A. 176 D7
Raver India 96 C5
Ravi *r.* Pak. 101 G4
Ravna Gora Croatia 56 G3
Ravna Gora *hill* Croatia 56 J3
Ravnina Turkm. *see* **Rawnina**
Ravshan Uzbek. 102 D4
Rawa Aopa Watumohai National Park Indon. 75 B4
Rāwah Iraq 107 E4
Rawai *well* Sudan 104 A4
Rawaki *i.* Kiribati 145 H2
formerly known as Phoenix Island
Rawala Kot Pak. 101 H3
Rawalpindi Pak. 101 H3
Rawalpindi Lake Canada 167 H1
Rawa Mazowiecka Poland 49 R4
Ŗawāndiz Iraq 107 F3
Ŗawāndiz, Rūbār-i *r.* Iraq 109 P1
Rawas *r.* Indon. 76 C3
Rawatsar India 96 B3
Rawdah Yemen 104 D5
Rawdah, Sabkhat ar *salt flat* Syria 109 M2
Rawghah *watercourse* Saudi Arabia 109 I9
Rawhide Lake Canada 173 K4
Rawi, Ko *i.* Thai. 79 B7
Rawicz Poland 49 N4
Rawka *r.* Poland 49 R4
Rawlinna Australia 151 D6
Rawlins U.S.A. 180 F4
Rawlinson, Mount *hill* Australia 151 D5
Rawlinson Range *hills* Australia 151 E5
Rawnina Turkm. 103 E5
also spelt Ravnina
Rawson Arg. 205 D6
Rawson Mountains Antarctica 223 N1
Rawu China 86 A2
Raxaul India 97 E4
Ray, Cape Canada 169 J4
Raya, Bukit *mt. Kalimantan* Indon. 77 E3
Raya, Bukit *mt. Kalimantan* Indon. 77 F3
Rayachoti India 94 C3
Rayadurg India 94 C3
Rayagada India 95 D2
Rayak Lebanon 108 H4
Raychikhinsk Rus. Fed. 82 C2
Rayda Rus. Fed. 43 R3
Raydah Yemen 104 D5
Raydār Iraq 109 P2
Rāyen Iran 100 D4
Rayes Peak U.S.A. 182 E7
Rayevskiy Rus. Fed. 40 J5
Raymān *i.* Saudi Arabia 108 G9
Raymond Canada 167 H5
Raymond *NH* U.S.A. 177 N2
Raymond *WA* U.S.A. 180 B3
Raymond Terrace Australia 147 F3
Raymondville U.S.A. 179 C7
Raymore Canada 167 J5
Rayna India 97 E5
Rayner Glacier Antarctica 223 D2
Rayón Mex. 185 F4
Rayones Mex. 185 E3
Rayong Thai. 79 C5
Raystown Lake U.S.A. 176 G5
Raysūt Oman 105 F4
Rayth al Khayl *watercourse* Saudi Arabia 109 I9
Rayton S. Africa 133 M2
Rayville U.S.A. 175 B5
Rayyis Saudi Arabia 104 B3
Raz, Pointe du *pt* France 50 B4
Razam India 95 D2
Razan Iran 100 B3
Ražanj *Srbija* Serb. and Mont. 58 C5
Razāzah, Buḥayrat ar *l.* Iraq 107 E4
formerly known as Milḥ, Baḥr al
Razdan Armenia *see* **Hrazdan**
Razdel'naya Ukr. *see* **Rozdil'na**
Razdol'noye Rus. Fed. 82 C4
Razdzyalavichy Belarus 42 H9
Razeh Iran 100 B3
Razgrad Bulg. 58 H5
Razhêng Zangbo *r.* China 89 E6
Razim, Lacul *lag.* Romania 58 J4
Razlog Bulg. 58 E7
Rāznas *l.* Latvia 42 I5
Raz"yezd 3km Rus. Fed. *see* **Novyy Urgal**
R. D. Bailey Lake U.S.A. 176 D8
Ré, Île de *i.* France 50 E6
Reading U.K. 47 L12
Reading *MI* U.S.A. 173 I9
Reading *OH* U.S.A. 176 A6
Reading *PA* U.S.A. 177 J5
Readsboro U.S.A. 177 M3
Readstown U.S.A. 172 C7
Reagile S. Africa 133 K2
Real *r.* Brazil 202 E4
Reales *mt.* Spain 54 F8
Realicó Arg. 204 D4
Réalmont France 51 I9
Reăng Kesei Cambodia 79 C5
Reata Mex. 185 E3
Reate Italy *see* **Rieti**
Rebaa Alg. 123 G3
Rebbenesøya *i.* Norway 44 L1
Rebecca, Lake *salt flat* Australia 151 C6
Rebiana Sand Sea *des.* Libya 120 D3
also known as Ramlat Rabyānah
Rebollera *mt.* Spain 54 G6
Reboly Rus. Fed. 44 O3
Rebrebti Dhubo *well* Eth. 128 E3
Rebrikha Rus. Fed. 103 J1
Rebun-tō *i.* Japan 90 G2
Recanati Italy 56 F5
Recaş Romania 58 C3
Recco Italy 56 B4
Rechane Rus. Fed. 43 M5
Recherche, Archipelago of the *is* Australia 151 C7
Recherche Archipelago Nature Reserve Australia 151 C7
Rechitsa Belarus *see* **Rechytsa**
Rechna Doab *lowland* Pak. 101 H4
Rechytsa Belarus 43 L9
also spelt Rechitsa
Recife Brazil 202 F4
formerly known as Pernambuco
Recife, Cape S. Africa 133 J11
Recinto Chile 204 C5
Recklinghausen Germany 48 E4
Recknitz *r.* Germany 49 J1
Reconquista Arg. 204 F3
Recovery Glacier Antarctica 223 V1
Recreio *Mato Grosso* Brazil 201 F2
Recreio *Minas Gerais* Brazil 207 K8
Recreo Arg. 204 D3
Rectorville U.S.A. 176 B7
Recz Poland 49 M2
Red *r.* Australia 149 D3
Red *r.* Canada 166 E3
Red *r.* Canada/U.S.A. 167 L5
Red *r.* U.S.A. 179 E6
Red, North Fork *r.* U.S.A. 179 C5
Redang *i.* Malaysia 76 C1
Red Bank *NJ* U.S.A. 177 K5
Red Bank *TN* U.S.A. 174 C5
Red Basin China *see* **Sichuan Pendi**
Red Bay Canada 169 J3
Redberry Lake Canada 167 J4
Red Bluff *hill* Australia 151 B5
Red Bluff U.S.A. 182 B1
Red Bluff Lake U.S.A. 179 B6
Red Butte *mt.* U.S.A. 183 L6
Redcar U.K. 47 K9
Redcliff Canada 167 I5
Red Cliff U.S.A. 172 C4
Redcliff Zimbabwe 131 F3
Redcliffe, Mount *hill* Australia 151 C6
Red Cliffs Australia 147 D3
Red Cloud U.S.A. 178 C3
Red Deer Canada 167 H4
Red Deer *r. Alta./Sask.* Canada 167 I5
Red Deer *r. Man./Sask.* Canada 167 K4
Red Deer Lake Canada 167 K4
Reddersburg S. Africa 133 K6
Redding U.S.A. 182 B1
Redditch U.K. 47 K11
Red Earth Creek Canada 167 H3
Redelinghuys S. Africa 132 C9
Redenção *Pará* Brazil 202 B3
Redenção *Piauí* Brazil 202 C4
Redeyef Tunisia 123 H2
Redfield U.S.A. 178 C2
Red Granite Mountain Canada 166 B2
Redhill Australia 146 C3
Red Hills U.S.A. 178 C4
Red Hook U.S.A. 177 L4
Red Idol Gorge China 89 E6
Red Indian Lake Canada 169 J3
Redkino Rus. Fed. 43 R5
Redknife *r.* Canada 166 G2
Red Lake Canada 167 M5
Red Lake *l.* Canada 167 M5

Red Lake U.S.A. 183 L6
Red Lake r. U.S.A. 178 C2
Red Lake Falls U.S.A. 178 C2
Red Lake Indian Reservation res. U.S.A. 178 D1
Red Lakes U.S.A. 178 D1
Redlands U.S.A. 183 G7
Red Lion NJ U.S.A. 177 K6
Red Lion PA U.S.A. 177 I6
Red Lodge U.S.A. 180 E3
Red Mercury Island N.Z. 152 J4
Redmond OR U.S.A. 180 B3
Redmond UT U.S.A. 183 M2
Red Oak U.S.A. 178 D3
Redojari waterhole Kenya 128 C5
Redon France 50 D5
Redonda i. Antigua and Barbuda 187 H3
Redondela Spain 54 C2
Redondo Port. 54 D6
Redondo Beach U.S.A. 182 F8
Red Peak U.S.A. 180 D3
Red River r. Vietnam 78 D3
also known as Hồng, Sông or Nui Con Voi
Red Rock Canada 168 B3
Red Rock AZ U.S.A. 183 M9
Red Rock PA U.S.A. 177 I4
Red Rock r. U.S.A. 180 D3
Red Sea Africa/Asia 104 A2
Red Sea state Sudan 121 G5
Redstone Canada 166 F4
Redstone r. N.W.T. Canada 166 E1
Redstone r. Ont. Canada 173 L2
Red Volta r. Burkina/Ghana 125 E4
also known as Nazinon (Burkina)
Redwater r. U.S.A. 180 F2
Redway U.S.A. 182 A1
Red Willow Creek r. U.S.A. 178 B3
Red Wine r. Canada 169 J2
Red Wing U.S.A. 174 A2
Redwood City U.S.A. 182 B4
Redwood Falls U.S.A. 178 D2
Redwood National Park U.S.A. 180 A4
UNESCO World Heritage Site
Redwood Valley U.S.A. 182 A2
Ree, Lough l. Ireland 47 E10
Reed City U.S.A. 172 H7
Reed Lake Canada 167 K4
Reedley U.S.A. 182 E5
Reedsburg U.S.A. 172 D7
Reedsport U.S.A. 180 A4
Reedsville OH U.S.A. 176 D6
Reedsville PA U.S.A. 176 H5
Reedville U.S.A. 177 I8
Reedy U.S.A. 176 D7
Reedy Creek watercourse Australia 149 E4
Reedy Glacier Antarctica 223 P1
Reefton N.Z. 153 F10
Reese U.S.A. 173 J7
Reese r. U.S.A. 183 H1
Refahiye Turkey 107 D3
Reform U.S.A. 175 B5
Reforma Mex. 185 G5
Refugio U.S.A. 179 C6
Rega r. Poland 49 M1
Regen Germany 49 K7
Regência Brazil 207 N6
Regensburg Germany 48 J6
historically known as Castra Regina or Ratisbon
Regenstauf Germany 51 S3
Regente Feijó Brazil 206 B9
Reggane Alg. 123 F4
Reggio Calabria Italy see **Reggio di Calabria**
Reggio Emilia-Romagna Italy see **Reggio nell'Emilia**
Reggio di Calabria Italy 57 H10
historically known as Rhegium; short form Reggio
Reggio Emilia Italy see **Reggio nell'Emilia**
Reggio nell'Emilia Italy 56 C4
also known as Reggio Emilia; historically known as Regium Lepidum; short form Reggio
Reghin Romania 58 F2
Regi Afgh. 101 F3

▶**Regina** Canada 167 J5
Provincial capital of Saskatchewan.

Régina Fr. Guiana 199 H3
Registān reg. Afgh. 101 F4
Registro Brazil 206 F11
Registro do Araguaia Brazil 206 B2
Regium Lepidum Italy see **Reggio nell'Emilia**
Regozero Rus. Fed. 44 O2
Rehli India 96 C5
Rehoboth Namibia 130 C4
Rehoboth Bay U.S.A. 177 J7
Rehoboth Beach U.S.A. 177 J7
Rehovot Israel 108 F6
Reïbell Alg. see **Ksar Chellala**
Reichenau Germany 48 G8
UNESCO World Heritage Site
Reichenbach Germany 49 J5
Reichshoffen France 51 N4
Reid Australia 151 E6
Reidsville GA U.S.A. 175 D5
Reidsville NC U.S.A. 176 F9
Reigate U.K. 47 L12
Reiley Peak U.S.A. 183 N9
Reims France 51 K3
English form Rheims; historically known as Durocortorum or Remi
UNESCO World Heritage Site
Reinach Switz. 51 N5
Reinbek Germany 48 H2
Reindeer r. Canada 167 K4
Reindeer Island Canada 167 L4
Reindeer Lake Canada 167 K3
Reine Norway 44 K2
Reinersville U.S.A. 176 D6
Reineskarvet mt. Norway 45 J3
Reinga, Cape N.Z. 152 G2
Reinosa Spain 54 G2
Reinsfeld Germany 48 D6
Reipholsfjöll hill Iceland 44 [inset] B2
Reisa Nasjonalpark nat. park Norway 44 M1
Reisjärvi Fin. 44 N3
Reisterstown U.S.A. 177 I6
Reitz S. Africa 133 M4
Reitzburg S. Africa 133 L4
Reiu r. Estonia 42 F3
Reivilo S. Africa 132 I4
Rejowiec Fabryczny Poland 49 U4
Rekapalle India 94 D2
Rekohua i. S. Pacific Ocean see **Chatham Island**
Rekovac Srbija Serb. and Mont. 58 C5
Rėkyvos ežeras l. Lith. 42 E6
Reliance Canada 167 I2
Relizane Alg. 123 F2
Rellano Mex. 184 D3
Relli India 95 D2
Remada Tunisia 123 H2
Remarkable, Mount hill Australia 146 C3
Rembang Indon. 77 E4
Remedios Cuba 186 D2
Remedios, Punta pt El Salvador 185 H6
Remel el Abiod des. Tunisia 123 H3
Remennikovo Rus. Fed. 43 J5
Remeshk Iran 100 D5
Remeskylä Fin. 44 N3
Remi France see **Reims**
Remington U.S.A. 176 H7
Rémire Fr. Guiana 199 H3
Rémire i. Seychelles 129 [inset]
Remiremont France 51 M4
Remmel Mountain U.S.A. 180 B2
Remontnoye Rus. Fed. 41 G7
Rempang i. Indon. 76 D2
Remscheid Germany 48 E4
Remus U.S.A. 173 H7
Rena Norway 45 J3
Rena r. Norway 45 J3
Renabie Canada 173 J2
Renaix Belgium see **Ronse**
Renapur India 94 C2
Renard Islands P.N.G. 149 G1
Rende China see **Xundian**
Rende Italy 57 I9
Rend Lake U.S.A. 174 B4
Rendsburg Germany 48 G1
Renedo Spain 54 H1
René-Levasseur, Île i. Canada 169 G3
Renens Switz. 51 M6
Renews Canada 169 K4
Renfrew Canada 168 E4
Rengat Indon. 76 C3
Rengo Chile 204 C4
Ren He r. China 87 D1
Renheji China 87 E2
Renhou China see **Tangxian**
Renhua China 87 E3
Renhuai China 86 C3
Reni Ukr. 41 D7
Renick U.S.A. 176 E8
Renigunta India 94 C3
Renko Fin. 42 F1
Renland reg. Greenland see **Tuttut Nunaat**
Renmark Australia 146 D3
Rennell i. Solomon Is 145 F3
also known as Mu Nggava
UNESCO World Heritage Site
Rennell, Islas is Chile 205 B8
Rennerod Germany 48 F5
Renner Springs Australia 148 B3
Rennes France 50 E4
Rennes, Bassin de basin France 50 E4
Rennick Glacier Antarctica 223 K2
Rennie Canada 167 M5
Reno r. Italy 56 E4
Reno MN U.S.A. 172 B7
Reno NV U.S.A. 182 E2
Renoster r. S. Africa 133 K3
Renoster watercourse S. Africa 132 E8
Renosterkop S. Africa 132 G9
Renovo U.S.A. 176 H4
Renqiu China 85 H4
Renshou China 86 C2
also known as Wenlin
Rensselaer IN U.S.A. 174 C3
Rensselaer NY U.S.A. 177 L3
Rentjärn Sweden 44 L2
Renton U.S.A. 180 B3
Renukut India 97 D4
Renwick N.Z. 152 H9
Renya r. Rus. Fed. 43 S3
Réo Burkina 124 E3
Reo Indon. 75 B5
Repartimento Brazil 199 G5
Repembe r. Moz. 131 G4
Repetek Turkm. 103 E5
Repetek Döwlet Gorugy nature res. Turkm. 103 E5
Repino Rus. Fed. 43 N6
Repokaira reg. Fin. 44 N1
Repolka Rus. Fed. 43 K2
Reporoa N.Z. 152 K6
Reposaari Fin. 45 M3
Republic OH U.S.A. 176 B4
Republic WA U.S.A. 180 C2
Republican r. U.S.A. 178 C4
Republican, South Fork r. U.S.A. 178 B3
Republika Srpska aut. div. Bos.-Herz. 56 J4
Repulse Bay b. Australia 149 F4
Repulse Bay Canada 165 K3
also known as Naujaat
Repvåg Norway 44 N1
Requena Peru 198 C6
Requena Spain 55 J5
Réquista France 51 I8
Reriutaba Brazil 202 D3
Reşadiye Turkey 107 E3
also known as Sorp
Reşadiye Turkey 107 D2
Reşadiye Yarımadası pen. Turkey 59 I12
Resag, Gunung mt. Indon. 76 D4
Resava r. Serb. and Mont. 58 C4
Resavica Srbija Serb. and Mont. 58 C4
Resen Macedonia 58 C7
Resende Brazil 207 I9
Reserva Brazil 203 B8
Reserve U.S.A. 181 E6
Reshetnikovo Rus. Fed. 43 R5
Reshi China 87 D2
Resia, Passo di pass Austria/Italy 48 H9
Resistencia Arg. 204 F2
Reşiţa Romania 58 C3
Resko Poland 49 M2
Resolute Canada 165 J2
Resolution Island Canada 165 M3
Resolution Island N.Z. 153 A13
Resplendor Brazil 207 L6
Ressa r. Rus. Fed. 43 Q7
Ressango Garcia S. Africa 133 P2
Resseta r. Rus. Fed. 43 Q8
Restefond, Col de pass France 51 M8
Restelica Kosovo, Srbija Serb. and Mont. 58 B7
Restinga de Marambaia coastal area Brazil 207 I10
Restinga Seca Brazil 203 A9
Restrepo Col. 198 C3
Resülayn Turkey see **Ceylanpınar**
Retalhuleu Guat. 185 H6
Retem, Oued er watercourse Alg. 123 G2
Retén Llico Chile 204 B4
Retezat, Parcul Naţional nat. park Romania 58 D3
Retford U.K. 47 L10
also known as East Retford
Rethel France 51 K3
Réthimnon Greece see **Rethymno**
Rethymno Greece 59 F13
also known as Réthimnon
Retiers France 50 E5
Retortillo tourist site Spain 54 G2
Rettikhovka Rus. Fed. 90 C2
Retuerta mt. Spain 55 J4

▶**Réunion** terr. Indian Ocean 218 K7
French Overseas Department. Historically known as Bourbon.
▶▶114–115 Africa Countries

Reus Spain 55 M3
Reusam, Pulau i. Indon. 76 B2
Reutlingen Germany 48 G7
Reutov Rus. Fed. 43 S6
Reval Estonia see **Tallinn**
Revda Rus. Fed. 44 P2
Reveille Peak U.S.A. 183 H4
Revel Estonia see **Tallinn**
Revel France 51 I9
Revelganj India 97 E4
Revelstoke Canada 166 G5
Reventazón Peru 198 A6
Revermont reg. France 51 L7
Reviga Romania 58 I4
Reviga r. Romania 58 I4
Revigny-sur-Ornain France 51 K4
Revillagigedo, Islas is Mex. 184 B5
Revillagigedo Island U.S.A. 164 F4
Revna r. Rus. Fed. 43 P9
Revolyutsii, Pik mt. Tajik. see **Revolyutsiya, Qullai**
Revolyutsiya, Qullai mt. Tajik. 101 H2
also known as Revolyutsii, Pik
Revsnes Norway 44 L1
Revúca Slovakia 49 R7
Revuè r. Moz. 131 G3
Revyakino Rus. Fed. 43 S7
Rewa India 97 D4
Rewari India 96 C3
Rex, Mount Antarctica 222 S2
Rexburg U.S.A. 180 E4
Rexton Canada 169 H4
Rey, Isla del i. Panama 186 D5
Reyes Bol. 200 D3
Reyes, Point U.S.A. 182 A3
Reyes, Punta pt Col. 198 B4
Reyhanlı Turkey 109 H1
Reykir Iceland 44 [inset] B2
Reykjanes constituency Iceland 44 [inset] B3
Reykjanestá pt Iceland 44 [inset] B3

▶**Reykjavík** Iceland 44 [inset] B2
Capital of Iceland. English form Reykjavik.

Reykjavik Iceland see **Reykjavík**
Reynolds Range mts Australia 148 B4
Reynosa Mex. 185 F3
Reyssouze r. France 51 K6
Rezā, Kūh-e hill Iran 100 B3
Rezā'īyeh Iran see **Urmia**
Rezā'īyeh, Daryācheh-ye salt l. Iran see **Urmia, Lake**
Rēzekne Latvia 42 I5
Rēzekne r. Latvia 42 I5
Rezinjski vrh mt. Slovenia 56 G3
Rezovska Reka r. Bulg./Turkey 58 J7
Rezvāndeh Iran see **Rezvānshahr**
Rezvānshahr Iran 100 B2
formerly known as Rezvāndeh
R. F. Magón Mex. see **Ricardo Flores Magón**
Rgotina Srbija Serb. and Mont. 58 D4
Rharbi, Oued el watercourse Alg. 123 F3
Rhegium Italy see **Reggio di Calabria**
Rheims France see **Reims**
Rhein r. Germany 48 D4 see **Rhine**
Rheine Germany 48 E3
Rheinland-Pfalz land Germany 48 E6
English form Rhineland-Palatinate
UNESCO World Heritage Site
Rheinsberg Germany 49 J2
Rhein-Taunus, Naturpark nature res. Germany 48 F5
Rheinwaldhorn mt. Switz. 51 P6
Rhemilès well Alg. 122 D3
Rheris, Oued watercourse Morocco 122 D3
Rhin r. France 51 N4 see **Rhine**
Rhine r. Europe 48 D4
also spelt Rhein (Germany) or Rhin (France)
Rhinebeck U.S.A. 177 L4
Rhinelander U.S.A. 172 D5
Rhineland-Palatinate land Germany see **Rheinland-Pfalz**
Rhinluch marsh Germany 49 J3
Rhino Camp Uganda 128 A4
Rhinow Germany 49 J3
Rhir, Cap c. Morocco 122 C3
Rho Italy 56 B3
Rhode Island state U.S.A. 177 N4
Rhodes Greece 59 J12
also spelt Rodos
UNESCO World Heritage Site
Rhodes i. Greece 59 J12
also spelt Rodos or Ródhos; formerly known as Rodi; historically known as Rhodus
Rhodesia country Africa see **Zimbabwe**
Rhodes Inyanga National Park Zimbabwe see **Nyanga National Park**
Rhodes Matopos National Park Zimbabwe see **Matobo National Park**
Rhodes Peak U.S.A. 180 D3
Rhodope Mountains Bulg./Greece 58 E7
also known as Rodopi Planina
Rhodus i. Greece see **Rhodes**
Rhône r. France/Switz. 51 K9
Rhône-Alpes admin. reg. France 51 L7
Rhube, Oasis of Syria see **Ruḩbah**
Rhuthun U.K. see **Ruthin**
Rhyl U.K. 47 I10
Riaba Equat. Guinea 125 H6
Riachão Brazil 202 C3
Riachão das Neves Brazil 202 C4
Riacho de Santana Brazil 202 D5
Riacho dos Machados Brazil 207 J2
Riachos, Islas de los is Arg. 204 E6
Ri'al Fuhah hill Saudi Arabia 108 H9
Rialma Brazil 206 D2
Rialp, Pantà de resr Spain 55 M3
Rialto U.S.A. 183 G7
Riangnom Sudan 126 F2
Riaño, Embalse de resr Spain 54 F2
Rianópolis Brazil 206 D2
Riansáres r. Spain 55 H5
Riasi Jammu and Kashmir 96 B2
Riau prov. Indon. 76 C2
Riau, Kepulauan is Indon. 76 D2
Riaza r. Spain 55 H3
Ribadavia Spain 54 C2
Ribadeo Spain 54 D1
Ribadesella Spain 54 F1
Ribas de Fresser Spain see **Ribes de Freser**
Ribas do Rio Pardo Brazil 203 A7
Ribat Afgh. 101 G2
Ribat-i-Shur waterhole Iran 100 D3
Ribáuè Moz. 131 H2
Ribble r. U.K. 47 J10
Ribe Denmark 45 J5
Ribeirão Branco Brazil 206 E11
Ribeirão das Neves Brazil 207 I6
Ribeirão do Pinhal Brazil 206 C10
Ribeirão Preto Brazil 206 F8
Ribera Sicily Italy 57 F11
Ribérac France 50 G7
Riberalta Bol. 200 D2
Ribes de Freser Spain 55 N2
also spelt Ribas de Fresser
Ribnica Slovenia 56 G3
Rîbniţa Moldova 41 D7
formerly spelt Râbniţa or Rybnitsa
Ribnitz-Damgarten Germany 49 J1
Ribnovo Bulg. 58 E7
Rica Aventura Chile 200 C5
Říčany Czech Rep. 49 L6
Ricardo Flores Magón Mex. 184 D2
short form R. F. Magón
Riccione Italy 56 E4
Rice CA U.S.A. 183 J7
Rice VA U.S.A. 176 G8
Rice Lake Ont. Canada 168 E4
Rice Lake Ont. Canada 173 K3
Rice Lake U.S.A. 172 B5
Riceville U.S.A. 176 C8
Richards Bay S. Africa 133 Q5
Richards Inlet Antarctica 223 L1
Richards Island Canada 164 F3
Richardson r. Canada 167 I3
Richardson Island Canada 167 G1
Richardson Lakes U.S.A. 177 O1
Richardson Mountains Canada 164 F3
Richardson Mountains N.Z. 153 C12
Richard Toll Senegal 124 B2
Richelieu France 50 G5
Richfield U.S.A. 183 L3
Richfield Springs U.S.A. 177 K3
Richford NY U.S.A. 177 I3
Richford VT U.S.A. 177 M1
Richgrove U.S.A. 182 E6
Richibucto Canada 169 H4
Rich Lake Canada 167 I4
Richland U.S.A. 180 C3
Richland Center U.S.A. 172 C7
Richlands U.S.A. 176 D8
Richmond N.S.W. Australia 147 F3
Richmond Qld Australia 149 D4
Richmond Ont. Canada 173 R5
Richmond Que. Canada 169 F4
Richmond N.Z. 152 H9
Richmond Kwazulu-Natal S. Africa 133 O6
Richmond N. Cape S. Africa 132 H8
Richmond U.K. 47 K9
Richmond CA U.S.A. 182 B4
Richmond IL U.S.A. 172 E8
Richmond IN U.S.A. 176 A6
Richmond KY U.S.A. 176 A8
Richmond ME U.S.A. 177 P1
Richmond MI U.S.A. 173 K8
Richmond TX U.S.A. 179 D6

▶**Richmond** VA U.S.A. 176 H8
State capital of Virginia.

Richmond VT U.S.A. 177 M1
Richmond, Mount N.Z. 152 H9
Richmond Dale U.S.A. 176 C6
Richmond Hill Canada 168 E5
Richmond Hill U.S.A. 175 D6
Richmond Range hills Australia 147 G2
Richmond Range mts N.Z. 152 H9
Richmondville U.S.A. 177 K3
Rich Square U.S.A. 177 H9
Richtersveld National Park S. Africa 132 B5
Richvale U.S.A. 182 C2
Richwood OH U.S.A. 176 B5
Richwood WV U.S.A. 176 E7
Rickleån r. Sweden 44 M2
Ricobayo, Embalse de resr Spain 54 F3
also known as Esla, Embalse de
Ricomagus France see **Riom**
Riddell Nunataks nunataks Antarctica 223 E2
Ridder Kazakh. see **Leninogorsk**
Riddlesburg U.S.A. 176 G5
Rideau r. Canada 173 R5
Rideau Lakes Canada 168 E4
Ridge r. Canada 168 C3
Ridgecrest U.S.A. 182 G6
Ridgefield U.S.A. 177 L4
Ridgeland MS U.S.A. 175 B5
Ridgeland SC U.S.A. 175 D5
Ridgeland WI U.S.A. 172 B5
Ridgetown Canada 173 L8
Ridgeway U.S.A. 176 F9
Ridgway U.S.A. 176 G4
Riding Mountain National Park Canada 167 K5
Ridley r. Australia 150 B4
Riebeek-Kasteel S. Africa 132 C10
Riebeek-Oos S. Africa 133 K10
Riebeek-Wes S. Africa 132 C10
Riecito Venez. 198 D2
Ried im Innkreis Austria 49 K7
Riedlingen Germany 48 G7
Riekertsdam S. Africa 133 K2
Rieppesgai'sa mt. Norway 44 M1
Riesa Germany 49 K4
Riesco, Isla i. Chile 205 B9
Riesi Sicily Italy 57 G11
Rieste Germany 48 F3
Riet r. S. Africa 133 H6
Riet watercourse S. Africa 132 E8
Rietavas Lith. 42 C6
Rietberg Germany 48 F4
Rietbron S. Africa 132 H9
Rietfontein S. Africa 132 E3
Riethuiskraal S. Africa 132 F11
Rieti Italy 56 E6
historically known as Reate
Rietpoort S. Africa 132 C7
Rietschen Germany 49 L4
Riet se Vloer salt pan S. Africa 132 E7
Rietvlei S. Africa 133 O6
Rietvlei Nature Reserve S. Africa 133 M2
Rieumes France 50 H9
Rifā'ī, Tall mt. Jordan/Syria 109 H5
Rifaina Brazil 206 F7
Rifeng China see **Lichuan**
Rifle U.S.A. 180 F5
Rift Valley prov. Kenya 128 B4
Rift Valley Lakes National Park Eth. see **Abijatta-Shalla National Park**
Riga Latvia see **Rīga**

▶**Rīga** Latvia 42 F5
Capital of Latvia. English form Riga.
UNESCO World Heritage Site

Riga, Gulf of Estonia/Latvia 42 E4
also known as Liivi laht or Rīgas jūras līcis or Riia laht
Rigacikun Nigeria 125 G4
Rigaio Greece 59 D9
Rīgān Iran 100 D4
Rīgas jūras līcis b. Estonia/Latvia see **Riga, Gulf of**
Rigby U.S.A. 180 E4
Rig-Rig Chad 120 B6
Riguel r. Spain 55 J2
Riia laht b. Estonia/Latvia see **Riga, Gulf of**
Riihimäki Fin. 45 N3
Riiser-Larsen Ice Shelf Antarctica 223 W2
Riisipere Estonia 42 F2
Riisitunturin kansallispuisto nat. park Fin. 44 O2
Riito Mex. 184 B1
Rijau Nigeria 125 G4
Riječki Zaliv b. Croatia 56 G3
Rijeka Croatia 56 G3
formerly known as Fiume
Rijm al Mudhari hill Iraq 109 K5
Rikā, Wādī ar watercourse Saudi Arabia 104 D3
Rikubetsu Japan 90 H3
Rikuchū-kaigan National Park Japan 90 H5
Rikuzen-takata Japan 90 G5
Rila Bulg. 58 E6
Rila mts Bulg. 58 E6
UNESCO World Heritage Site
Rila China 89 D6
Riley U.S.A. 180 C4
Rileyville U.S.A. 176 G7
Rillieux-la-Pape France 51 K7
Rillito U.S.A. 183 M9
Rima watercourse Niger/Nigeria 125 G3
Rimah, Wādī al watercourse Saudi Arabia 104 C2
Rimau, Pulau i. Indon. 76 D3
Rimava r. Slovakia 49 R7
Rimavská Sobota Slovakia 49 R7
Rimbey Canada 167 H4
Rimbo Sweden 45 L4
Rimersburg U.S.A. 176 F4
Rimetea Romania 58 E2
Rimforsa Sweden 45 K4
Rimini Italy 56 E4
historically known as Ariminum
Rîmnicu Sărat Romania see **Râmnicu Sărat**
Rîmnicu Vîlcea Romania see **Râmnicu Vâlcea**
Rimo Glacier Jammu and Kashmir 96 C2
Rimouski Canada 169 G3
Rimouski, Réserve Faunique de nature res. Canada 169 G3
Rimutaka Forest Park nature res. N.Z. 152 J9
Rinbung China 89 E6
also known as Deji
Rinca i. Indon. 75 A5
Rincão Brazil 206 E8
Rincon Morocco see **Mdiq**
Rincón, Cerro del mt. Chile 200 D6
Rinconada Arg. 200 D5
Rincón del Bonete, Lago Artificial de resr Uruguay 204 F4
Rincón de los Sauces Arg. 204 C5
Rincón de Romos Mex. 185 E4
Rind r. India 96 D4
Rinda r. Latvia 42 C4
Rindal Norway 44 J3
Rineia i. Greece 59 G11
also spelt Rinía
Riner U.S.A. 176 E8
Ringarooma Bay Australia 147 E5
Ringas India 96 B4
Ringe Denmark 45 J5
Ringebu Norway 45 J3
Ringgold U.S.A. 174 C5
Ringim Nigeria 125 H3
Ringkøbing Denmark 45 J4
Ringkøbing Fjord lag. Denmark 45 J5
Ringsted Denmark 45 J5
Ringvassøya i. Norway 44 L1
Ringwood U.K. 47 K13
Ringwood U.S.A. 177 K4
Rinía i. Greece see **Rineia**
Rinópolis Brazil 206 C8
Rinteln Germany 48 G3
Rinya r. Romania 49 O9
Rio IL U.S.A. 172 C9
Rio WI U.S.A. 172 D7
Río Abiseo, Parque Nacional nat. park Peru 200 A1
UNESCO World Heritage Site
Rio Alegre Brazil 201 F4
Riobamba Ecuador 198 B5
Rio Bananal Brazil 207 M6
Rio Blanco U.S.A. 180 F5
Rio Bonito Brazil 207 K9
Rio Branco Brazil 200 D2
Rio Branco state Brazil see **Roraima**
Rio Branco, Parque Nacional do nat. park Brazil 199 F4
Río Bravo, Parque Internacional del nat. park Mex. 185 E2
Rio Brilhante Brazil 203 A7
Río Bueno Chile 204 B6
Río Caribe Venez. 199 F2
Rio Casca Brazil 203 D7
Río Chico Arg. 205 C8
Río Chico Venez. 199 E2
Rio Claro Rio de Janeiro Brazil 207 I9
Rio Claro São Paulo Brazil 206 F9
Rio Claro Trin. and Tob. 187 H5
Río Claro Venez. 187 F5
Río Colorado Arg. 204 D5
Río Corrientes Ecuador 198 B5
Río Cuarto Arg. 204 D4
Rio das Pedras Moz. 131 G4

▶**Rio de Janeiro** Brazil 203 D7
3rd most populous city in South America. Former capital of Brazil.
▶▶18–19 World Cities

Rio de Janeiro state Brazil 203 D7
Río de Jesús Panama 186 C6

▶**Río de la Plata - Paraná** r. S. America 204 F4
2nd longest river in South America and 9th in the world.
▶▶6–7 World Landscapes
▶▶188–189 South America Landscapes

Rio Dell U.S.A. 180 A4
Rio do Sul Brazil 203 B8
Rio Formoso Brazil 202 F4
Río Frío Costa Rica 186 C5
Río Gallegos Arg. 205 C8
Río Grande Arg. 205 D9
Río Grande Bol. 200 D5
Rio Grande Brazil 204 G4
Río Grande Mex. 185 E4
▶**Rio Grande** r. Mex./U.S.A. 185 F3
also known as Bravo del Norte, Río
▶▶154–155 North America Landscapes
Río Grande, Salar de salt flat Arg. 204 C2
Rio Grande City U.S.A. 179 C7
Rio Grande do Norte state Brazil 202 E3
Rio Grande do Sul state Brazil 203 A9
Ríohacha Col. 198 C2
Río Hato Panama 186 C5
Río Hondo, Embalse resr Arg. 204 D2
Rioja Peru 198 B6
Río Lagartos Mex. 185 H4
Rio Largo Brazil 202 F4
Riom France 51 J7
historically known as Ricomagus
Rio Maior Port. 54 C5
Riom-ès-Montagnes France 51 I7
Río Muerto Arg. 204 E2
Río Mulatos Bol. 200 D4
Río Muni reg. Equat. Guinea 125 H6
Río Negro prov. Arg. 204 D5
Rio Negro Brazil 203 B8
Río Negro Chile 204 B6
Rionero in Vulture Italy 56 H8
Rioni r. Georgia 107 E2
Rio Novo Brazil 207 J8
Rio Novo do Sul Brazil 207 M7
Rio Pardo de Minas Brazil 202 D5
Río Plátano, Reserva Biósfera del nature res. Hond. 186 B4
Rio Pomba Brazil 207 J8
Rio Preto Brazil 207 J9
Rio Preto, Serra do hills Brazil 206 G3
Rio Rancho U.S.A. 181 F6
Ríos Spain 54 D3
Ríosucio Col. 198 B3
Río Tercero Arg. 204 D4
Río Tigre Ecuador 198 B5
Rio Tinto Brazil 202 F3
Rio Tuba Phil. 74 A4
Riou, Oued watercourse Alg. 55 L9
Riou Lake Canada 167 J3
Rio Verde Brazil 206 C4
Río Verde Chile 205 C9
Rioverde Ecuador 198 B4
Río Verde Quintana Roo Mex. 185 H5
Río Verde San Luis Potosí Mex. 185 F4
Rio Verde de Mato Grosso Brazil 203 A6
Rio Vermelho Brazil 207 J5
Rio Vista U.S.A. 182 C3
Riozinho Brazil 200 D2
Riozinho r. Amazonas Brazil 199 E5
Riozinho r. Mato Grosso do Sul Brazil 201 F4
Ripanj Srbija Serb. and Mont. 58 B4
Ripats Sweden 44 M2
Ripky Ukr. 41 D6
Ripley MS U.S.A. 174 B5
Ripley NY U.S.A. 176 F3
Ripley OH U.S.A. 176 B7
Ripley TN U.S.A. 174 B5
Ripley WV U.S.A. 176 D7
Ripoll Spain 55 N2
Ripon U.K. 47 K9
Ripon CA U.S.A. 182 C4
Ripon WI U.S.A. 172 E7
Riposto Sicily Italy 57 H11
Risalpur Pak. 101 H3
Rīsān 'Unayzah hill Egypt 108 E7
Risaralda dept Col. 198 C3
Risasi Dem. Rep. Congo 126 E5
Risbäck Sweden 44 K2
Riscle France 50 F9
Risco Plateado mt. Arg. 204 C4
Rishā', Wādī ar watercourse Saudi Arabia 104 D2
Rishikesh India 96 C3
Rishiri-Rebun-Sarobetsu National Park Japan 90 G2
Rishiri-tō i. Japan 90 G2
Rishiri-zan vol. Japan 82 F3
Rishon Le Ẕiyyon Israel 108 F6
Rising Sun IN U.S.A. 176 A7
Rising Sun MD U.S.A. 177 I6
Risle r. France 50 G3
Risnjak nat. park Croatia 56 G3
Rîşnov Romania see **Râşnov**
Rison U.S.A. 179 D5
Risør Norway 45 J4
Rissa Norway 44 J3
Rissington N.Z. 152 K7
Rişşū, Jabal hill Egypt 108 B8
Ristiina Fin. 45 N3
Ristijärvi Fin. 44 O2
Ristikent Rus. Fed. 44 O1
Risum China 89 B5
Ritan r. Indon. 77 F2
Rītausma Latvia 42 F5
Ritchie S. Africa 133 I6
Ritchie's Archipelago is India 95 G3
Ritch Island Canada 167 G1
Ritscher Upland mts Antarctica 223 X2
Ritsem Sweden 44 L2
Ritsis Nakrdzali nature res. Georgia 107 E2
Ritter, Mount U.S.A. 182 E4
Ritupe r. Latvia 42 I5
Ritzville U.S.A. 180 C3
Riu, Mount hill P.N.G. 149 G1
Rīva r. Latvia 42 C5
Rivadavia Buenos Aires Arg. 204 E4
Rivadavia Mendoza Arg. 204 C4
Rivadavia Salta Arg. 201 E6
Rivadavia Chile 204 C3
Riva del Garda Italy 56 C3
Riva Palacio Mex. 181 F7
Rivarolo Canavese Italy 51 N7
Rivas Nicaragua 186 B5
Rivash Iran 100 D3
Rive-de-Gier France 51 K7
Rivera Arg. 204 E5
Rivera Uruguay 204 G3
River Cess Liberia 124 C5
Riverdale U.S.A. 182 E5
Riverhead U.S.A. 177 M5
Riverina Australia 151 C6
Riverina reg. Australia 147 E3
Rivero, Isla i. Chile 205 B7
Rivers state Nigeria 125 G5
Riversdale N.Z. 153 C13
Riversdale S. Africa 132 F11
Riversdale Beach N.Z. 152 K9
Riverside S. Africa 133 N7
Riverside CA U.S.A. 182 G8
Riverside IA U.S.A. 172 B9
Riversleigh Australia 148 C3
UNESCO World Heritage Site
Riverton Canada 167 L5
Riverton N.Z. 153 C14
also known as Aparima
Riverton S. Africa 133 I5
Riverton UT U.S.A. 183 M1
Riverton VA U.S.A. 176 G7
Riverton WY U.S.A. 180 E4
Riverview Canada 169 H4
River View S. Africa 133 Q5
Rives France 51 L7
Rivesaltes France 51 I10
Rivesville U.S.A. 176 E6
Rivière-au-Renard Canada 169 H3
Rivière Bleue Canada 169 G4
Rivière-du-Loup Canada 169 G4
Rivière-Pentecôte Canada 169 H3
Rivière-Pigou Canada 169 H3
Rivière-Pilote Martinique 187 H4
Riviersonderend S. Africa 132 D11
Riviersonderend Mountains S. Africa 132 D11
Rivne Ukr. 41 C6
also spelt Rovno; formerly spelt Równe
Rivoli Italy 51 N7
Rivulets S. Africa 133 O2
Rivungo Angola 127 D9
Riwaka N.Z. 152 G9

▶**Riyadh** Saudi Arabia 105 D2
Capital of Saudi Arabia. Also spelt Ar Riyāḑ.

Riyan Yemen 105 E5
Riyue Shankou pass China 84 D4
Riza well Iran 100 C3
Rizal Phil. 74 B3
Rize Turkey 107 E2
Rizhao China 85 H5
formerly known as Shijiusuo
Rizokarpaso Cyprus see **Rizokarpason**
Rizokarpason Cyprus 108 F2
also known as Dipkarpaz or Rizokarpaso
Rīzū well Iran 100 D3
Rīzū'īyeh Iran 100 D4
Rjukan Norway 45 J4
Rkîz, Lac l. Mauritania 124 B2
Roa Norway 45 J3
Roa Spain 54 H3
Roach Lake U.S.A. 183 I6
Roads U.S.A. 176 C6

▶**Road Town** Virgin Is (U.K.) 187 G3
Capital of the British Virgin Islands.

Roan Norway 44 J2
Roan Cliffs ridge U.S.A. 183 O2
Roan Fell hill U.K. 47 J8
Roan Mountain U.S.A. 176 C9
Roanne France 51 K6
Roanoke AL U.S.A. 175 C5
Roanoke IL U.S.A. 172 D10
Roanoke VA U.S.A. 176 F8
Roanoke r. U.S.A. 176 I9
Roanoke Rapids U.S.A. 176 H9
Roan Plateau U.S.A. 183 O2
Roaringwater Bay Ireland 47 C12
Roatán Hond. 186 B3
also known as Coxen Hole
Robat r. Afgh. 101 E4
Robāţ Iran 100 D4
Robāţ-e Khān Iran 100 D3
Robāţ-e Shahr-e Bābak Iran 100 C4
Robāţe Tork Iran 100 B3
Robāţ-e Ţoroq Iran 101 D2
Robāţ Karīm Iran 100 B3
Robāt-Sang Iran 101 D3
Robat Thana Pak. 101 E4
Robb Canada 167 G4
Robben Island S. Africa 132 C10
UNESCO World Heritage Site
Robbins U.S.A. 176 A9
Robbins Island Australia 147 E5
Robbinsville U.S.A. 174 D5
Robe r. Australia 150 A4
Robe, Mount hill Australia 146 D2
Röbel Germany 49 J2
Robe Noire, Lac de la l. Canada 169 I3
Robert Glacier Antarctica 223 D2
Robert Lee U.S.A. 179 B6
Roberts U.S.A. 180 D4
Roberts, Mount Australia 147 G2
Robertsburg U.S.A. 176 D7
Roberts Butte mt. Antarctica 223 K2
Roberts Creek Mountain U.S.A. 183 H2
Robertsfors Sweden 44 M2
Robertsganj India 97 D4
Robert S. Kerr Reservoir U.S.A. 179 D5
Robertson r. Australia 149 D3
Robertson S. Africa 132 D10
Robertson, Lac l. Canada 169 J3
Robertson Bay Antarctica 223 L2
Robertson Island Antarctica 222 U2
Robertson Point N.Z. 152 I9
Robertson Range hills Australia 150 C4
Robertsport Liberia 124 C5
Robertstown Australia 146 C3
Robert Williams Angola see **Caála**

Roberval Canada 169 F3
Robeson Channel Canada/Greenland 165 M1
Robhanais, Rubha hd U.K. see Butt of Lewis
Robin's Nest hill Hong Kong China 87 [inset]
also known as Hung Fa Leng
Robinson r. N.T. Australia 148 C3
Robinson r. W.A. Australia 150 D3
Robinson Canada 166 C2
Robinson IL U.S.A. 174 C4
Robinson KY U.S.A. 176 A7
Robinson Creek r. Australia 149 F5
Robinson Range hills Australia 151 B5
Robinvale Australia 147 D3
Robles La Paz Col. 198 C2
Roblin Canada 167 K5
Robore Bol. 201 F4
Robsart Canada 167 I5
Robson, Mount Canada 166 G4
Robstown U.S.A. 179 C7
Roby U.S.A. 179 B5
Roçadas Angola see Xangongo
Roca Partida, Isla i. Mex. 184 B5
Rocas, Atol das atoll Brazil 202 F2
UNESCO World Heritage Site
Rocas Alijos is Mex. 184 B3
Rocca Busambra mt. Sicily Italy 57 F11
Rocca Imperiale Italy 57 I8
Roccastrada Italy 56 D5
Roc de Montalet mt. France 51 I9
Roc d'Enfer mt. France 51 M6
Rocha Uruguay 204 G4
Rochdale U.K. 47 J10
Rochechouart France 50 G7
Rochedo Brazil 203 A6
Rochefort Belgium 51 L2
Rochefort France 50 F7
Rochefort, Lac l. Canada 169 F1
Rochegda Rus. Fed. 40 G3
Rochelle U.S.A. 172 D9
Rochester IN U.S.A. 174 C3
Rochester MN U.S.A. 174 A2
Rochester NH U.S.A. 177 O2
Rochester NY U.S.A. 176 H2
Roc'h Trévezel hill France 50 C4
Rocina r. Spain 54 E8
Rock r. Canada 166 E2
Rock U.S.A. 172 F4
Rock r. IA U.S.A. 178 C3
Rock r. IL U.S.A. 174 B3
Rock and Pillar Range mts N.Z. 153 D13
Rock Bay Canada 166 E5
Rock Creek Canada 166 B1
Rock Creek r. U.S.A. 180 F2
Rockdale U.S.A. 179 C6
Rockefeller National Wildlife Refuge nature res. U.S.A. 179 D6
Rockefeller Plateau Antarctica 222 O1
Rockford AL U.S.A. 175 C5
Rockford IL U.S.A. 174 B3
Rockford NC U.S.A. 176 E9
Rockford OH U.S.A. 176 A5
Rockglen Canada 167 J5
Rock Hall U.S.A. 177 I6
Rockhampton Australia 149 F4
Rockhampton Downs Australia 148 B3
Rock Hill U.S.A. 174 D5
Rockingham Australia 151 A7
Rockingham U.S.A. 174 E5
Rockingham Bay Australia 149 E3
Rockinghorse Lake Canada 167 H1
Rock Island U.S.A. 174 B3
Rockland MA U.S.A. 177 O3
Rockland ME U.S.A. 177 P1
Rocklands Reservoir Australia 147 D4
Rocklea Australia 150 B4
Rocklin U.S.A. 182 C3
Rocknest Lake Canada 167 H1
Rock Point U.S.A. 183 O5
Rockport IN U.S.A. 174 C4
Rockport MA U.S.A. 177 O3
Rockport TX U.S.A. 179 C7
Rockport WV U.S.A. 176 D6
Rock Rapids U.S.A. 178 C3
Rock River U.S.A. 180 F4
Rock Sound Bahamas 186 D1
Rock Springs MT U.S.A. 180 F3
Rocksprings U.S.A. 179 B6
Rock Springs WY U.S.A. 180 E4
Rockstone Guyana 199 G3
Rockton U.S.A. 172 D8
Rockville IN U.S.A. 174 C4
Rockville MD U.S.A. 177 H6
Rockwall U.S.A. 179 C5
Rockwell City U.S.A. 178 D3
Rockwood U.S.A. 173 J8
Rocky Boy's Indian Reservation res. U.S.A. 180 E2
Rockyford Canada 167 H5
Rocky Ford U.S.A. 178 B4
Rocky Fork U.S.A. 176 C9
Rocky Fork Lake U.S.A. 176 B6
Rocky Harbour Canada 169 J3
Rocky Hill U.S.A. 176 C7
Rocky Lane Canada 167 G3
Rocky Mount NC U.S.A. 174 E5
Rocky Mount VA U.S.A. 176 F9
Rocky Mountain House Canada 167 H4
Rocky Mountain National Park U.S.A. 180 F4
Rocky Mountains U.S.A. 170 E3
Rocky Mountains Forest Reserve nature res. Canada 167 G4
Rocroi France 51 K3
Rodberg Norway 45 J3
Rødbyhavn Denmark 45 J5
Roddickton Canada 169 K3
Rode S. Africa 133 N7
Rödeby Sweden 45 K4
Rodeo Mex. 184 D3
Roderick r. Australia 151 B5
Rodez France 51 I8
Rodholívos Greece see Rodolivos
Rodhópolis Greece see Rodopoli
Ródhos i. Greece see Rhodes
Rodi i. Greece see Rhodes
Roding Germany 49 J6
Rodino Rus. Fed. 103 J1
Rødlia Norway 44 K2
Rodna Romania 58 F1
Rodney, Cape N.Z. 152 I4
Rodnichek Rus. Fed. see Rodnichok
Rodnichok Rus. Fed. 41 G6
also spelt Rodnichek
Rodnikovka Kazakh. 102 D2
Rodnya Belarus 43 N8
Rodolfo Sanchez Toboada Mex. 184 A2
Rodolivos Greece 58 E8
also spelt Rodholívos
Rodonit, Kepi i pt Albania 58 A7
Rodopi Planina mts Bulg./Greece see Rhodope Mountains
Rodopoli Greece 58 E7
also known as Rodhópolis
Rodopos Greece 59 E13
Rodos Greece see Rhodes
Rodos i. Greece see Rhodes
Rodosto Turkey see Tekirdağ
Rodovoye Rus. Fed. 42 I4
Rodøya i. Norway 44 K2
Rodrigues Peru 198 C6
Rodrigues Island Mauritius 218 L7
Rødsand Norway 44 O1
Roe r. Australia 150 D2
Roebourne Australia 150 B4
Roebuck Bay Australia 150 C3
Roedtan S. Africa 131 F5
Roe Plains Australia 151 D6
Roermond Neth. 48 C4
Roeselare Belgium 51 J2
also known as Roulers
Roes Welcome Sound sea chan. Canada 167 O2
Rogachev Belarus see Rahachow
Rogachevo Rus. Fed. 43 S5
Rogagua, Laguna l. Bol. 200 D3
Rogaland county Norway 45 I4
Rogaška Slatina Slovenia 49 M9
Rogatica Bos.-Herz. 56 L5
Roger, Lac l. Canada 173 O3
Rogers Canada 167 G5
Rogers U.S.A. 179 D4
Rogers, Mount U.S.A. 176 D9
Rogers City U.S.A. 173 J5
Rogers Lake U.S.A. 182 G7
Rogersville U.S.A. 176 B9
Roggan r. Canada 168 E2
Roggan, Lac l. Canada 168 E2
Roggeveld plat. S. Africa 132 E9
Roggeveldberge esc. S. Africa 132 E9
Rogliano Italy 57 I9
Rognan Norway 44 K2
Rognedino Rus. Fed. 43 O8
Rögnitz r. Germany 48 H2
Rogoźno Poland 49 O3
Rogue r. U.S.A. 180 A4
Roha India 94 B2
Rohnert Park U.S.A. 182 B3
Rohrbach in Oberösterreich Austria 49 K7
Rohri Sangar Pak. 101 G5
Rohtak India 96 C3
Rohuküla Estonia 42 E3
Roi Et Thai. 78 C4
Roi Georges, Îles du is Fr. Polynesia 221 J6
English form King George Islands
Roine l. Fin. 45 N3
Roing India 97 G3
Roja Latvia 42 D4
Rojas Arg. 204 E4
Röjdåfors Sweden 45 K3
Rojhan Pak. 101 G4
Rojo, Cabo c. Mex. 185 F4
Rojo, Cabo c. Puerto Rico 187 G3
Rojo Aguado, Laguna l. Bol. 200 D3
Rokan r. Indon. 76 C2
Rokeby Australia 149 D2
Rokeby National Park Australia 149 D2
Rokiškis Lith. 42 G6
Rokkasho Japan 90 G4
Rokkō-zaki pt Japan 90 E6
Røkland Norway 44 K2
Roknäs Sweden 44 M2
Rokycany Czech Rep. 49 K6
Rokytne Ukr. 41 C6
Rola Kangri mt. China 89 E5
Rolândia Brazil 206 B10
Rolas, Ilha das i. São Tomé and Príncipe 125 G7
Rolim de Moura Brazil 201 E2
Roll U.S.A. 183 K9
Rolla MO U.S.A. 174 B4
Rolla ND U.S.A. 178 C1
Rollag Norway 45 J3
Rolleston Australia 149 F5
Rolleston N.Z. 153 G11
Rollet Canada 173 N3
Rolleville Bahamas 186 E2
Rolling Fork U.S.A. 175 B5
Rollinsford U.S.A. 177 O2
Rolphton Canada 173 P4
Rolvsøya i. Norway 44 N1
Rom mt. Uganda 128 B4
Roma Australia 149 F5
Roma Italy see Rome
Roma Lesotho 133 L6
Roma U.S.A. 179 C7
Romain, Cape U.S.A. 171 K5
Romaine r. Canada 169 I3
Roman Romania 58 H2
Romană, Câmpia plain Romania 58 E4
Romanaţilor, Câmpia plain Romania 58 E4
Romanet, Lac l. Canada 169 H1
Romang, Pulau i. Indon. 75 C4
►Romania country Europe 58 E3
also spelt Roumania or Rumania
►►32–33 Europe Countries
Roman-Kosh mt. Ukr. 41 E7
Romano, Cayo i. Cuba 186 D2
Romanovka Moldova see Basarabeasca
Romanovka Respublika Buryatiya Rus. Fed. 81 I2
Romanovka Saratovskaya Oblast' Rus. Fed. 41 G6
Romanovo Rus. Fed. 103 J1
Romans-sur-Isère France 51 L7
Romanzof, Cape U.S.A. 164 C3
Romão Brazil 199 F5
Rombas France 51 M3
Romblon Phil. 74 B3
Romblon i. Phil. 74 B3
Romblon Passage Phil. 74 B3
Rombo, Ilhéus do is Cape Verde see Secos, Ilhéus

►Rome Italy 56 E7
Capital of Italy. Also spelt Roma. UNESCO World Heritage Site

Rome GA U.S.A. 179 F5
Rome ME U.S.A. 177 P1
Rome NY U.S.A. 177 J2
Romeo U.S.A. 173 J8
Romford U.K. 47 M12
Romilly-sur-Seine France 51 J4
Romit Tajik. 101 G2
also spelt Ramit
Romiton Uzbek. 103 F5
formerly spelt Ramitan
Romney U.S.A. 176 G6
Romny Ukr. 41 E6
Rømø i. Denmark 45 J5
Romorantin-Lanthenay France 50 H5
Rompin r. Malaysia 76 C2
Romppala Fin. 44 O3
Romsey U.K. 47 K13
Romu mt. Indon. 77 G5
Romulus U.S.A. 173 J8
Ron India 94 B3
Ron, Mui hd Vietnam 78 D4
Rona i. U.K. 46 G4
also known as North Rona
Ronas Hill U.K. 46 K3
Roncador, Serra do hills Brazil 202 A5
Roncador Cay i. Caribbean Sea 186 C4
Roncador Reef reef Solomon Is 145 E2
Ronceverte U.S.A. 176 E8
Ronciglione Italy 56 E6
Ronco r. Italy 56 E4
Ronda Spain 54 F8
Ronda, Serranía de mts Spain 54 F8
Ronda, Serranía de nature res. Spain 54 G8
Ronda das Salinas Brazil 201 E3
Rondane Nasjonalpark nat. park Norway 45 J3
Ronde i. Grenada 187 H4
Rondon Brazil 201 G5
Rondón Col. 198 D3
Rondônia state Brazil 201 E2
formerly known as Guaporé
Rondonópolis Brazil 202 A6
Rondout Reservoir U.S.A. 177 K4
Rong'an China 87 D3
also known as Chang'an
Rongbaca China 86 A2
Rongchang China 86 C2
also known as Changyuan
Rongcheng Anhui China see Qingyang
Rongcheng Guangxi China see Rongxian
Rongcheng Hubei China see Jianli
Rongcheng Shandong China 85 I4
formerly known as Yatou
Rongcheng Wan b. China 85 I4
Rong Chu r. China 89 E6
Rongelap atoll Marshall Is 220 G6
also known as Kongelab; also spelt Rönlap
Rongjiang Guizhou China 87 D3
also known as Guzhou
Rongjiang Jiangxi China see Nankang
Rong Jiang r. China 87 D4
Rongjiawan China see Yueyang
Rongklang Range mts Myanmar 78 A3
Rongmei China see Hefeng
Rongshui China 87 D3
Rongwo China see Tongren
Rongxian Guangxi China 87 D4
also known as Rongcheng
Rongxian Sichuan China 86 C2
also known as Xuyang
Rongzhag China see Danba
Rönlap atoll Marshall Is see Rongelap
Rønne Denmark 45 K5
Ronneby Sweden 45 K4
Ronne Entrance strait Antarctica 222 S2
Ronne Ice Shelf Antarctica 222 T1
formerly known as Edith Ronne Land
Ronnenberg Germany 48 G3
Ronse Belgium 51 J2
also known as Renaix
Ronuro r. Brazil 202 A5
Roodebank S. Africa 133 N3
Rooiberg mt. Free State S. Africa 133 M5
Rooiberg mt. W. Cape S. Africa 132 F10
Rooikloof pass S. Africa 132 E9
Rooikraal S. Africa 133 N2
Rooke Island P.N.G. see Umboi
Rookh Aboriginal Reserve Australia 150 B4
Roorkee India 96 C3
Roosboom S. Africa 133 N5
Roosendaal Neth. 48 B4
Roosevelt AZ U.S.A. 183 M8
Roosevelt UT U.S.A. 183 O1
Roosevelt, Mount Canada 166 E3
Roosevelt Island Antarctica 223 N1
Roosna-Alliku Estonia 42 G2
Roossenekal S. Africa 133 N2
Root r. Canada 166 F2
Root r. U.S.A. 174 B3
Ropa r. Poland 49 S6
Ropaži Latvia 42 F5
Ropczyce Poland 49 S5
Roper r. Australia 148 B2
Roper Bar Australia 148 B2
Roper Bar Aboriginal Land res. Australia 148 B2
also known as Yutpundji Djindiniwirritj
Roper Creek r. Australia 149 F4
Ropinsalmi Fin. 44 M1
Roquebrune-sur-Argens France 51 M9
Roquefort France 50 F8
Roquetas de Mar Spain 55 I8
Roraima state Brazil 199 F4
formerly known as Rio Branco
Roraima, Mount Guyana 199 F3
Rorey Lake Canada 166 D1
Rori India 96 B3
Røros Norway 44 J3
UNESCO World Heritage Site
Rorschach Switz. 51 P5
Rørvik Norway 44 J2
Ros' r. Belarus 42 F8
Roś, Jezioro l. Poland 49 S2
Rosa, Lake Bahamas 187 E2
Rosa, Punta pt Mex. 184 C3
Rosal de la Frontera Spain 54 D7
Rosales Mex. 184 D2
Rosalia U.S.A. 180 C3
Rosalind Bank sea feature Caribbean Sea 186 C3
Rosamond U.S.A. 182 F7
Rosamond Lake U.S.A. 182 F7
Rosamorada Mex. 184 D4
Rosario Jujuy Arg. 200 D5
Rosario Santa Fé Arg. 204 E3
Rosário Brazil 202 C2
Rosario Baja California Norte Mex. 184 B2
Rosario Coahuila Mex. 185 E3
Rosario Sinaloa Mex. 184 D4
Rosario Sonora Mex. 184 C3
Rosario Para. 201 F6
Rosario Phil. 74 B2
Rosario Phil. 74 B3
Rosario Venez. 198 C2
Rosario, Cayo del i. Cuba 186 C2
Rosario, Sierra del hills Cuba 175 D8
Rosario de la Frontera Arg. 204 D2
Rosario de Lerma Arg. 200 D6
Rosário do Sul Brazil 203 A9
Rosário Oeste Brazil 201 F3
Rosarito Baja California Norte Mex. 184 A1
Rosarito Baja California Norte Mex. 184 B2
Rosarito Baja California Sur Mex. 184 C3
Rosarno Italy 57 H10
Rosas Spain see Roses
Rosas, Golfo de b. Spain see Roses, Golf de
Roscoff France 50 C4
Roscommon Ireland 47 D10
Roscommon U.S.A. 173 I6
Roscrea Ireland 47 E11
Rose r. Australia 148 B2
Rose, Mount U.S.A. 182 E2

►Roseau Dominica 187 H4
Capital of Dominica.

Roseau U.S.A. 178 D1
Roseau r. U.S.A. 178 C1
Roseberth Australia 148 C5
Rosebery Australia 147 E5
Rose Blanche Canada 169 J4
Rosebud r. Canada 167 H5
Rosebud Creek r. U.S.A. 180 F3
Rosebud Indian Reservation res. U.S.A. 178 B3
Roseburg U.S.A. 180 B4
Rose City U.S.A. 173 I6
Rosedale MS U.S.A. 174 B5
Rosedale TN U.S.A. 176 A9
Rosedene S. Africa 132 G9
Rosehall Guyana 199 G3
Roseires Reservoir Sudan 128 B2
Rosemary Island Australia 150 B4
Rosenberg U.S.A. 179 D6
Rosendal Norway 45 I4
Rosendal S. Africa 133 L5
Rosendale U.S.A. 172 E7
Rosengarten Germany 48 G2
Rosenheim Germany 48 J8
Rose Peak U.S.A. 183 O8
Rose Point Canada 166 D4
Roses Spain 55 O2
also spelt Rosas
Roses, Golf de b. Spain 55 O2
also spelt Rosas, Golfo de
Roseto degli Abruzzi Italy 56 G6
Rosetown Canada 167 J5
Rosetta Egypt see Rashîd
Rosetta Creek r. Australia 149 E4
Rose Valley Canada 167 K4
Roseville CA U.S.A. 182 C3
Roseville IL U.S.A. 174 B3
Roseville MI U.S.A. 173 K8
Roseville OH U.S.A. 176 C6
Roshal' Rus. Fed. 43 U6
Roshchino Leningradskaya Oblast' Rus. Fed. 43 K1
Roshchino Primorskiy Kray Rus. Fed. 90 D2
Roshkhvär Iran 101 D3
Rosholt U.S.A. 172 D6
Rosh Pinah Namibia 130 C5
Roshtkala Tajik. see Roshtqal'a
Roshtqal'a Tajik. 96 A1
also spelt Roshtkala
Rosignano Marittimo Italy 56 C5
Rosily Island Australia 150 A4
Roşiori Romania 58 I4
Roşiori de Vede Romania 58 G4
Rositsa Bulg. 58 I5
Rositsa r. Bulg. 58 G5
Roskilde Denmark 45 K5
UNESCO World Heritage Site
Roskovec Albania 58 A8
Roskruge Mountains U.S.A. 183 M9
Roslavl' Rus. Fed. 43 N8
Roslyakovo Rus. Fed. 44 P1
Roslyatino Rus. Fed. 40 H4
Rosmead S. Africa 133 J8
Rosolina Italy 56 E3
Rosolini Sicily Italy 57 G12
Rosporden France 50 C5
Ross Australia 147 E5
Ross r. Canada 166 C2
Ross N.Z. 153 E10
Ross, Mount hill N.Z. 152 J9
Rossano Italy 57 I9
Rossan Point Ireland 47 D9
Ross Barnett Reservoir U.S.A. 175 B5
Ross Bay Junction Canada 169 H2
Ross Dependency Antarctica 222 N2
Rosseau, Lake Canada 173 N5
Rossel Island P.N.G. 149 G1
Rossel Lagoon P.N.G. 149 G1
Ross Ice Shelf Antarctica 223 M1
Rossignol, Lac l. Canada 169 F2
Rössing Namibia 130 B4
Ross Island Antarctica 223 L1
Ross Island Myanmar see Daung Kyun
Rossiter Bay Australia 151 C7
Rossiyskaya Sovetskaya Federativnaya Sotsialisticheskaya Respublika country Asia/Europe see Russian Federation
Rossland Canada 166 G5
Rosslare Ireland 47 F11
Rosslare Harbour Ireland 47 F11
Rosso Mauritania 124 B2
Rossön Sweden 44 L3
Ross-on-Wye U.K. 47 J12
Rossony Belarus see Rasony
Rossosh' Rus. Fed. 41 F6
Rossouw S. Africa 133 L8
Rossport Canada 172 F2
Ross River Australia 148 B4
Ross River Canada 166 C2
Ross Sea Antarctica 223 L1
Røssvatnet l. Norway 44 K2
Rossville U.S.A. 172 B7
Rosswood Canada 166 D4
Röst Iraq 107 F3
Røst Norway 44 K2
Rostāq Afgh. 101 G2
Rostāq Fārs Iran 100 C4
Rostāq Hormozgan Iran 100 C5
Røsthavet sea chan. Norway 44 K2
Rosthern Canada 167 J4
Rostock Germany 49 J1
Rostonsölkä ridge Sweden 44 M1
Rostov Rus. Fed. 43 U4
Rostov-na-Donu Rus. Fed. 41 F7
English form Rostov-on-Don
Rostov Oblast admin. div. Rus. Fed. see Rostovskaya Oblast'
Rostov-on-Don Rus. Fed. see Rostov-na-Donu
Rostovskaya Oblast' admin. div. Rus. Fed. 41 G7
English form Rostov Oblast
Rostrenen France 50 C4
Rostujávri l. Sweden 44 M1
Røsvik Norway 44 K2
Rosvik Sweden 44 M2
Roswell GA U.S.A. 175 C5
Roswell NM U.S.A. 181 F6
Rota i. N. Mariana Is 73 K4
formerly known as Sarpan
Rotch Island Kiribati see Tamana
Rote i. Indon. 75 B5
also spelt Roti
Rotenburg (Wümme) Germany 48 G2
Rote Wand mt. Austria 48 G8
Roth Germany 48 I6
Rothenburg ob der Tauber Germany 48 H6
Rothera research station Antarctica 222 T2
Rotherham N.Z. 153 G10
Rotherham U.K. 47 K10
Rothes U.K. 46 I6
Rothesay U.K. 46 G8
Rothschild U.S.A. 172 D6
Rothschild Island Antarctica 222 T2
Roti Indon. 75 B5
Roti i. Indon. see Rote
Roti, Selat sea chan. Indon. 75 B5
Roto Australia 147 E3
Rotoaira, Lake N.Z. 152 J7
Rotomagus France see Rouen
Rotomanu N.Z. 153 F10
Rotondo, Monte mt. Corsica France 56 B6
Rotorua N.Z. 152 K6
Rotorua, Lake N.Z. 152 K6
Rott r. Germany 49 K7
Rottenburg am Neckar Germany 48 F7
Rottenmann Austria 49 L8
Rotterdam Neth. 48 B4
Rotterdam U.S.A. 177 L3
Rottnest Island Australia 151 A7
Rottweil Germany 48 F7
Rotuma i. Fiji 145 G3
formerly known as Grenville Island
Rotunda Romania 58 F5
Rötviken Sweden 44 K3
Rötz Germany 49 J6
Roubaix France 51 J2
Roudnice nad Labem Czech Rep. 49 L5
Rouen France 50 H3
historically known as Rotomagus
Rõuge Estonia 42 H4
Rouge-Matawin, Réserve Faunique nature res. Canada 169 F4
Rougemont U.S.A. 176 G9
Rough Ridge N.Z. 153 D13
Rouhia Tunisia 57 B13
Roui, Oued er watercourse Niger 125 H1
Roulers Belgium see Roeselare
Roulette U.S.A. 176 G4
Roulpmaulpma Aboriginal Land res. Australia 148 B4
Roumania country Europe see Romania
Roundeyed Lake Canada 169 G2
Roundhead U.S.A. 176 B5
Round Hill Nature Reserve Australia 147 E3
Round Lake Canada 168 E4
Round Mountain mt. Australia 147 G2
Round Mountain U.S.A. 183 G3
Round Rock AZ U.S.A. 183 O5
Round Rock TX U.S.A. 179 C6
Roundup U.S.A. 180 E3
Roura Fr. Guiana 199 H3
Rousay i. U.K. 46 I4
Rouses Point U.S.A. 177 L1
Roussillon France 51 K7
Routh Bank sea feature Phil. see Seahorse Bank
Rouxville S. Africa 133 K7
Rouyn-Noranda Canada 168 E3
Rouyuan China see Huachi
Rouyuanchengzi China see Huachi
Rovaniemi Fin. 44 N2
Rovato Italy 56 C3
Roven'ki Rus. Fed. 41 F6
Rovereto Italy 56 D3
Roversi Arg. 204 E2
Rovigo Italy 56 D3
Rovinari Romania 58 E4
Rovinj Croatia 56 F3
Rovkul'skoye, Ozero l. Rus. Fed. 44 O3
Rovno Ukr. see Rivne
Rovnoye Rus. Fed. 102 A2
Rowlesburg U.S.A. 176 F6
Rowley Island Canada 165 L3
Rowley Shoals sea feature Australia 150 B3
Rownaye Belarus 43 K6
Równe Ukr. see Rivne
Rów Polski r. Poland 49 N4
Rowsburg U.S.A. 176 C5
Roxas Phil. 74 B2
Roxas Phil. 74 B4
Roxas Phil. 74 B3
Roxas Phil. 74 A4
Roxas Phil. 74 B4
Roxboro U.S.A. 176 G9
Roxborough Downs Australia 148 C4
Roxburgh Island Cook Is see Rarotonga
Roxby Downs Australia 146 C2
Roxen l. Sweden 45 K4
Roxo r. Port. 54 C7
Roxo, Barragem do resr Port. 54 C7
Royal Canal Ireland 47 E10
Royal Center U.S.A. 172 G10
Royal Chitwan National Park Nepal 97 E4
UNESCO World Heritage Site
Royale, Île i. Canada see Cape Breton Island
Royale, Isle i. U.S.A. 172 E2
Royal Natal National Park S. Africa 133 M5
Royal Oak U.S.A. 173 J8
Royal Society Range mts Antarctica 223 K1
Royalton U.S.A. 172 E6
Royan France 50 E7
Roye France 51 I3
Roy Hill Australia 150 B4
Royston U.K. 47 L11
Röyttä Fin. 44 N2
Rožaje Crna Gora Serb. and Mont. 58 B6
Różan Poland 49 S3
Rožanj hill Serb. and Mont. 58 A4
Rozdil'na Ukr. 41 D7
also known as Razdel'naya
Rozdol'ne Ukr. 41 E7
Rozhdestvenka Kazakh. 103 G2
Rozhdestveno Tverskaya Oblast' Rus. Fed. 43 R5
Rozhdestveno Yaroslavskaya Oblast' Rus. Fed. 43 S4
Rozhdestvenskoye Rus. Fed. 40 H4
Rozhdestvo Rus. Fed. 43 O4
Rozhkovychi Rus. Fed. 43 P9
Rozino Bulg. 58 F6
Rozivka Ukr. 41 F7
Rožňava Slovakia 49 R7
Rozoy-sur-Serre France 51 K3
Roztoczański Park Narodowy nat. park Poland 49 U5
Rozveh Iran 100 B3
Rozzano Italy 56 B3
Rrëshen Albania 58 A7
Rrogozhinë Albania 58 A7
Rtishchevo Rus. Fed. 41 G5
Ruacana Namibia 130 B3
Ruaha National Park Tanz. 129 B6
Ruahine Forest Park nature res. N.Z. 152 K7
Ruahine Range mts N.Z. 152 K8
Ruakaka N.Z. 152 I3
Ruanda country Africa see Rwanda
Ruapehu, Mount vol. N.Z. 152 J7
Ruapuke Island N.Z. 153 C14
Ruarwe Malawi 129 B7
Ruatangata N.Z. 152 I3
Ruatapu N.Z. 153 E10
Ruatoria N.Z. 152 M5
Ruba Belarus 43 L6
formerly known as Vyarkhowye

►Rub' al Khālī des. Saudi Arabia 105 D4
Largest uninterrupted stretch of sand in the world. English form Empty Quarter.
►►14–15 World Environmental Impacts

Rubaydā reg. Saudi Arabia 105 E2
Rubeho Mountains Tanz. 129 C6
Rubelita Brazil 207 K3
Rubeshibe Japan 90 H3
Rubezhnoye Ukr. see Rubizhne
Rubi r. Dem. Rep. Congo 126 E4
Rubiácea Brazil 206 C8
Rubiataba Brazil 206 D2
Rubicon r. U.S.A. 182 C3
Rubim Brazil 207 M3
Rubinéia Brazil 206 C7
Rubio U.S.A. 172 B9
Rubizhne Ukr. 41 F6
also spelt Rubezhnoye
Rubondo National Park Tanz. 128 A5
Rubtsovsk Rus. Fed. 88 C1
Rubuga Tanz. 129 B6
Rubūţ, Jabal ar hill Saudi Arabia 104 C4
Ruby U.S.A. 164 D3
Ruby Dome mt. U.S.A. 183 I1
Ruby Lake U.S.A. 183 I1
Ruby Lake National Wildlife Refuge nature res. U.S.A. 180 D4
Ruby Mountains U.S.A. 183 I1
Rubyrock Lake Provincial Park Canada 166 E4
Rubys Inn U.S.A. 183 L4
Ruby Valley U.S.A. 183 I1
Rucăr Romania 58 G3
Ruchay Belarus 42 I6
Rucheng Guangdong China see Ruyuan
Rucheng Hunan China 87 E3
Ruciane-Nida Poland 49 S2
Ruckersville U.S.A. 176 G7
Rudall watercourse Australia 150 C4
Rudall River National Park Australia 150 C4
Rudarpur India 97 D4
Ruda Śląska Poland 49 P5
Rudauli India 97 D4
Rudbar Afgh. 101 E4
Rūdbār Iran 100 B2
Rüdersdorf Berlin Germany 49 K3
Rudhumatal Hiri hill Iraq 109 K4
Rudina pass Serb. and Mont. 58 A5
Rūdiškės Lith. 42 F7
Rudka r. Poland 49 U4
Rudkøbing Denmark 45 J5
Rudna Glava Srbija Serb. and Mont. 58 D4
Rudnaya Pristan' Primorskiy Kray Rus. Fed. 82 D3
formerly known as Tetyukhe-Pristan'
Rudnaya Pristan' Primorskiy Kray Rus. Fed. 82 D4
Rudnichnyy Rus. Fed. 40 J4
Rudnik Ingichka Uzbek. see Ingichka
Rudnik nad Sadem Poland 49 T5
Rudnya Smolenskaya Oblast' Rus. Fed. 43 M7
Rudnya Tverskaya Oblast' Rus. Fed. 43 M5
Rudnya Volgogradskaya Oblast' Rus. Fed. 41 H6
Rudnyy Kazakh. 103 E1
Rudnyy Rus. Fed. 82 D3
formerly known as Lifudzin
Rudolf, Lake salt l. Eth./Kenya see Turkana, Lake

►Rudol'fa, Ostrov i. Rus. Fed. 38 F1
Most northerly point of Europe. English form Rudolph Island.
►►28–29 Europe Landscapes

Rudolph Island Rus. Fed. see Rudol'fa, Ostrov
Rudolstadt Germany 48 I5
Rudong China 87 G1
also known as Juegang
Rudozem Bulg. 58 F7
Rūdsar Iran 100 B2
Rudzyensk Belarus 42 I8
Rue France 50 H2
Ruecas r. Spain 54 F5
Ruel Canada 173 L3
Ruen mt. Macedonia see Rujen
Ruenya r. Zimbabwe 131 G3
Rufa'a Sudan 121 G6
Ruffec France 50 G6
Rufiji r. Tanz. 129 C7
Rufino Arg. 204 E4
Rufisque Senegal 124 A3
Rufunsa Zambia 127 F8
Rugāji Latvia 42 I4
Rugao China 87 G1
Rugby U.K. 47 K11
Rugby ND U.S.A. 178 B1
Rugby TN U.S.A. 176 A9
Rügen i. Germany 49 K1
Rügen, Naturpark park Germany 49 K1
Rugged Mountain Canada 166 E5
Rugheiwa well Sudan 121 F5
Rugles France 50 G4
Ruhangino Tanz. 129 C7
Ruḩayyat al Ḩamr'ā' waterhole Saudi Arabia 105 D2
Ruḩbah oasis Syria 109 I4
English form Rhube, Oasis of
Ruhengeri Rwanda 126 F5
Ruhla Germany 48 H5
Ruhnu i. Estonia 42 E4
Ruhpolding Germany 49 J8
Ruhr r. Germany 48 D4
Ruhudji r. Tanz. 129 B7
Ruhuna National Park Sri Lanka 94 D5
also known as Yala National Park
Ru'ī, Chāh well Iran 101 D4
Rui'an China 87 G3
Ruichang China 87 E2
formerly known as Pencheng
Ruidoso U.S.A. 181 F6
Ruijin China 87 E3
Ruiz Mex. 184 D4
Ruiz, Nevado del vol. Col. 198 C3
Ruj mt. Bulg. 58 D6
Rūja r. Latvia 42 G4
Rujaylah, Ḩarrat ar lava field Jordan 109 I5
Rujen mt. Macedonia 58 D6
also spelt Ruen
Rūjiena Latvia 42 G4
Ruki r. Dem. Rep. Congo 126 C4
Rukumkot Nepal 97 D3
Rukungiri Uganda 128 A5
Rukuwa Indon. 75 C4
Rukwa admin. reg. Tanz. 129 A6
Rukwa, Lake Tanz. 129 B7
Rūl Dadnah U.A.E. 105 G2
Ruleville U.S.A. 175 B5
Rulin China see Chengbu
Rulong China see Xinlong
Rūm Iran 101 D3
Rum i. U.K. 46 F7
Rum r. U.S.A. 174 A2
Rum, Jebel mts Jordan see Ramm, Jabal
Ruma Nigeria 125 G3
Ruma Vojvodina, Srbija Serb. and Mont. 58 A3
Rumādah Yemen 104 C5
Rumāh Saudi Arabia 105 D2
Ruma National Park Kenya 128 B5
Rumania country Europe see Romania
Rumaylah waterhole Syria 109 O4
Rumaylah, Wādī watercourse Syria 109 M1
Rumayn i. Saudi Arabia 104 C4
Rumbek Sudan 126 F3
Rumblar r. Spain 54 H6
Rumburk Czech Rep. 49 L5
Rum Cay i. Bahamas 187 E2
Rumford U.S.A. 177 O1
Rumia Poland 49 P1
Rumilly France 51 L7
Rummān, Jabal ar mts Saudi Arabia 104 C2
Rummānā hill Syria 109 J4
Rumoi Japan 90 G3
Rumphi Malawi 129 B7
Runan China 87 E1
also known as Runing
Runanga N.Z. 153 F10
Runaway, Cape N.Z. 152 L5
Runcorn U.K. 47 J10
Runcu Romania 58 E3
Runde r. Zimbabwe 131 G4
formerly spelt Lundi
Rundu Namibia 130 C3
Rundvik Sweden 44 L3
Rŭng, Kaôh i. Cambodia 79 C6
Rungan r. Indon. 77 F3
Rungu Dem. Rep. Congo 126 E4
Rungwa Rukwa Tanz. 129 A6
Rungwa Singida Tanz. 129 B6
Rungwa r. Tanz. 129 A6
Rungwa Game Reserve nature res. Tanz. 129 B6
Runing China see Runan
Rūnīz-e Bālā Iran 100 C4
Runn l. Sweden 45 K3
Running Springs U.S.A. 183 G7
Running Water watercourse U.S.A. 179 B5
Runton Range hills Australia 150 C4
Ruokolahti Fin. 45 O3
Ruoqiang China 88 E4
formerly known as Charkhlik or Qarkilik
Ruoqiang He r. China 88 E4
Ruo Shui watercourse China 84 D3
Ruotsinpyhtää Fin. 42 H1
Ruovesi Fin. 45 N3
Rupa India 97 G4
Rupat i. Indon. 76 C2
Rupea Romania 58 G2
Rupert r. Canada 168 E3
Rupert ID U.S.A. 180 D4
Rupert WV U.S.A. 176 E8
Rupert Bay Canada 168 E3
Rupert Coast Antarctica 222 O1
Rupert Creek r. Australia 149 D4
Rupnagar Punjab India 96 C3
Rupnagar Rajasthan India 96 B4
Rupshu reg. Jammu and Kashmir 96 C2
Ruqayţah Saudi Arabia 104 C3
Ruqqād, Wādī ar watercourse Israel 108 G5
Rural Hall U.S.A. 176 E9
Rural Retreat U.S.A. 176 D9
Rurrenabaque Bol. 200 D3
Rus Romania 58 E1
Rusaddir N. Africa see Melilla
Rusape Zimbabwe 131 G3
Rusca Montană Romania 58 D3
Ruschuk Bulg. see Ruse
Ruse Bulg. 58 G5
historically known as Ruschuk
Rusenski Lom nat. park Bulg. 58 H5
Rusera India 97 E4
Ruşeţu Romania 58 I4
Rushan China 85 I4
formerly known as Xiacun
Rushan Tajik. see Rushon
Rushanskiy Khrebet mts Tajik. see Rushon, Qatorkŭhi
Rush Creek r. U.S.A. 178 B4
Rushford U.S.A. 174 B3
Rush Lake U.S.A. 172 E7
Rushmere U.S.A. 177 I8
Rushon Tajik. 101 G2
also spelt Rushan
Rushon, Qatorkŭhi mts Tajik. 101 G2
also known as Rushanskiy Khrebet
Rushui He r. China 85 E5
Rushville IL U.S.A. 174 B3

St Maries U.S.A. 180 C3
St Marks S. Africa 133 L9
St Mark's S. Africa see Cofimvaba
St Marks National Wildlife Refuge nature res. U.S.A. 175 C6

▶St-Martin i. West Indies 187 H3
Dependency of Guadeloupe (France). The southern part of the island is the Dutch territory of Sint Maarten.

St Martin, Lake Canada 167 L5
St-Martin-de-Crau France 51 K9
St-Martin-de-Ré France 50 E6
St-Martin-d'Hères France 51 L7
St Mary r. Canada 167 H5
St Mary, Mount N.Z. 153 D12
St Mary Peak Australia 146 C2
St Marys Australia 147 F5
St Mary's Canada 173 L7
St Mary's i. U.K. 47 F14
St Marys KS U.S.A. 178 C4
St Marys OH U.S.A. 176 A5
St Marys PA U.S.A. 176 G4
St Marys WV U.S.A. 176 D6
St Marys r. U.S.A. 176 A5
St Mary's, Cape Canada 169 K4
St Mary's Bay Canada 169 K4
St Marys City U.S.A. 177 I7
St-Mathieu Canada 173 O2
St-Mathieu, Pointe de pt France 50 B4
St Matthew Island U.S.A. 164 B3
St Matthews U.S.A. 175 D5
St Matthew's Island Myanmar see Zadetkyi Kyun
St Matthias Group is P.N.G. 145 D2
St-Maurice r. Canada 169 F4
St-Maurice, Réserve Faunique du nature res. Canada 169 F4
St-Maximin-la-Ste-Baume France 51 L9
St-Médard-en-Jalles France 50 F8
St Michaels U.S.A. 177 I7
St Michael's Bay Canada 169 K2
St Michael's Mount tourist site U.K. 47 G13
St-Michel-de-Maurienne France 51 M7
St-Michel-des-Saints Canada 169 F4
St-Mihiel France 51 L4
St-Nazaire France 50 D5
St Nicolas Belgium see Sint-Niklaas
St-Nicolas-de-Port France 51 M4
St-Omer France 51 I2
Saintonge reg. France 50 F7
St-Pacôme Canada 169 G4
St-Palais France 50 E9
St Paris U.S.A. 176 B5
St-Pascal Canada 169 G4
St-Patrice, Lac l. Canada 173 P4
St Paul Canada 167 I4
St Paul r. Canada 169 J3
St Paul r. Liberia 124 C5
St Paul IA U.S.A. 172 B10

▶St Paul MN U.S.A. 174 A2
State capital of Minnesota.

St Paul NE U.S.A. 178 C3
St Paul VA U.S.A. 176 C9
St Paul, Île i. Indian Ocean 219 M8
English form St Paul Island
St-Paul-de-Fenouillet France 51 I10
St Paul Island Canada 169 I4
St Paul Island Indian Ocean see St Paul, Île
St-Paul-lès-Dax France 50 E9
St Paul Subterranean River National Park Phil. 74 A4
UNESCO World Heritage Site
St Peter U.S.A. 174 A2
St Peter and St Paul Rocks is N. Atlantic Ocean see São Pedro e São Paulo

▶St Peter Port Channel Is 50 D3
Capital of Guernsey.

St Peter's Canada 169 I4
St Peters Canada 169 I4
▶St Petersburg Rus. Fed. 43 L2
also known as Sankt-Peterburg; *formerly known as* Leningrad; *historically known as* Petrograd.
UNESCO World Heritage Site
▶▶18–19 World Cities
St Petersburg U.S.A. 175 D7
St-Philbert-de-Grand-Lieu France 50 E5
St-Pierre mt. France 51 L9
St-Pierre Mauritius 129 F7

▶St-Pierre St Pierre and Miquelon 169 K4
Capital of St Pierre and Miquelon.

St-Pierre, Lac l. Canada 169 F4

▶St Pierre and Miquelon terr. N. America 169 J4
French Territorial Collectivity.
▶▶158–159 North America Countries

St-Pierre-des-Corps France 50 G5
St-Pierre-d'Oléron France 50 E7
St-Pierre-le-Moûtier France 51 J6
St-Pol-sur-Ternoise France 51 I2
St-Pons-de-Thomières France 51 I9
St-Pourçain-sur-Sioule France 51 J6
St-Quentin Canada 169 H4
St-Quentin France 51 J3
St-Raphaël France 51 M9
St Regis r. U.S.A. 177 K1
St Regis Falls U.S.A. 177 K1
St-Renan France 50 B4
St-Rigaud, Mont mt. France 51 K6
St-Sauveur-des-Monts Canada 169 F4
St-Savin France 50 F7
St-Savinien France 50 F7
St-Sébastien-sur-Loire France 50 E5
St-Siméon Canada 169 G4
St-Sorlin, Mont de mt. France 51 M6
St Stephen U.S.A. 175 E5
St-Symphorien France 50 F8
St Terese U.S.A. 166 C3
St Theresa Point Canada 167 M4
St Thomas Canada 168 D5
St Thomas i. Virgin Is (U.S.A.) 187 G3
St-Tite-des-Caps Canada 169 G4
St-Tropez France 51 M9
St-Tropez, Cap de c. France 51 M9
St-Valery-en-Caux France 50 G3
St-Valery-sur-Somme France 50 H2
St-Vallier Bourgogne France 51 K6
St-Vallier Rhône-Alpes France 51 K7
St-Vaury France 50 H6
St-Vincent Italy 51 N7
St Vincent i. West Indies 199 F1
St-Vincent, Cap pt Madag. see Ankaboa, Tanjona
St Vincent, Cape Australia 147 E5
St Vincent, Cape Port. see São Vicente, Cabo de
St Vincent, Gulf Australia 146 C3
▶St Vincent and the Grenadines i. West Indies 187 H4
▶▶158–159 North America Countries
St-Vincent-de-Tyrosse France 50 E9
St Vincent Island U.S.A. 175 C6
St Vincent Passage St Lucia/St Vincent 187 H4
St-Vith Belgium 51 M2
St Walburg Canada 167 I4
St-Yrieix-la-Perche France 50 H7
Sain Us China 85 E3
Saipal mt. Nepal 97 D3
Saipan i. N. Mariana Is 73 K3
also spelt Seypan
Saison r. France 50 F9
Saitama pref. Japan 90 F7
Saiteli Turkey see Kadınhanı
Saito Japan 91 B8
Saittanulkki hill Fin. 40 C2
Saivomuotka Sweden 44 M1
Sai Yok National Park Thai. 79 B5
Sajama, Nevado mt. Bol. 200 C4
Sajīd Saudi Arabia 104 C4
Sājir Saudi Arabia 104 D2
Sājir, Ra's c. Oman 105 F4
Sajó r. Hungary 49 R8
Sajóhidvég Hungary 49 R7
Sājūr, Nahr r. Syria/Turkey 109 J1
also known as Bağırsak Deresi *or* Sacirsuyu
Sajzī Iran 100 C3
Sak watercourse S. Africa 132 F6
Saka Eth. 128 C2
Sakai Japan 91 D7
Sakaide Japan 91 C7
Sakaiminato Japan 91 C7
Sakākah Saudi Arabia 107 E5
also known as Sikaka
Sakakawea, Lake U.S.A. 178 B2
Sakala i. Indon. 77 G4
Sakalile Tanz. 129 A7
Sakami Canada 168 F2
Sakami r. Canada 169 E2
Sakami Lake Canada 168 E2
Sakania Dem. Rep. Congo 127 F8
Sakar mts Bulg. 58 H7
Sakar Turkm. 103 E5
Sakaraha Madag. 131 [inset] J4
Sakarçäge Turkm. 103 E5
Sakartvelo country Asia see Georgia
Sakarya r. Turkey 106 B2
Sakassou Côte d'Ivoire 124 D5
Sakata Japan 90 F5
Sakawa Japan 91 C8
Sakchu N. Korea 83 B4
Saken Seyfullin Kazakh. 103 H2
formerly known as Zharyk
Sa Keo r. Thai. 79 C5
Sakété Benin 125 F5
▶Sakhalin i. Rus. Fed. 82 F2
▶▶60–61 Asia Landscapes
Sakhalin Oblast admin. div. Rus. Fed. see Sakhalinskaya Oblast'
Sakhalinskaya Oblast' admin. div. Rus. Fed. 82 F2
English form Sakhalin Oblast
Sakhalinskiy Zaliv b. Rus. Fed. 82 F1
Sakhanina, Mys c. Rus. Fed. 40 J1
Sakharovo Rus. Fed. 43 R5
Sakhelwe S. Africa 133 O2
Sakhile S. Africa 133 N3
Şäki Azer. 107 F2
also spelt Sheki; *formerly known as* Nukha
Saki Nigeria see Shaki
Saki Ukr. see Saky
Šakiai Lith. 42 E7
Sakiet Sidi Youssef Tunisia 57 A12
Sakir mt. Pak. 101 F4
Sakishima-shotō is Japan 81 K8
Sakleshpur India 94 B3
Sakmara Rus. Fed. 102 C2
Sa-koi Myanmar 78 B4
Sakoli India 96 C5
Sakon Nakhon Thai. 78 D4
Sakra, Pulau reg. Sing. 76 [inset]
Sakrand Pak. 101 G5
Sakrivier S. Africa 132 E7
Saksaul'skiy Kazakh. 103 E3
also known as Sekseüil; *formerly known as* Saksaul'skoye
Saksaul'skoye Kazakh. see Saksaul'skiy
Sakshaug Norway 44 J3
Sakti India 97 D5
Saku Estonia 42 F2
Saku Japan 91 F6
Sakura Japan 91 G7
Sakura-jima vol. Japan 91 B9
Saky Ukr. 41 E7
also spelt Saki
Säkylä Fin. 45 M3
Sal i. Cape Verde 124 [inset]
Sal r. Rus. Fed. 53 K2
Sal, Cerros de la mts Peru 200 B2
Sal, Punta pt Hond. 186 B4
Sala Latvia 42 G5
Sala Latvia 42 E5
Šal'a Slovakia 49 O7
Sala Sweden 45 L4
Salabangka, Kepulauan is Indon. 75 B3
Salaberry-de-Valleyfield Canada 169 F4
Salaca r. Latvia 42 F4
Sălacea Romania 58 D1
Salacgrīva Latvia 42 F4
Sala Consilina Italy 57 H8
Salada, Bahía b. Chile 204 C2
Salada, Laguna salt l. Mex. 184 B1
Saladas Arg. 204 F3
Salādiḥ, Wādī watercourse Jordan 108 G8
Saladillo Arg. 204 F4
Saladillo r. Córdoba Arg. 204 E4
Saladillo r. Santiago del Estero Arg. 204 E3
Salado r. Buenos Aires Arg. 204 F4
Salado r. Formosa Arg. 204 F2
Salado r. La Rioja Arg. 204 C3
Salado r. Río Negro Arg. 204 D6
Salado r. Santa Fé Arg. 204 E4
Salado r. Arg. 204 D5
Salado r. Arg. 204 D5
Salado r. Cuba 186 D2
Salado Ecuador 198 B5
Salado r. Mex. 185 F3
Salado r. Spain 54 F8
Salado watercourse U.S.A. 181 F6
Saladou Guinea 124 C4
Salaga Ghana 125 E4
Şalāḥ Saudi Arabia 104 C3
Şalāḥ, Tall hill Jordan 109 J4
Şalāḥ ad Dīn governorate Iraq 107 E4
Salahuddin Iraq 107 F3
Salajwe Botswana 131 E4
Salakh, Jabal mt. Oman 105 G3
Salal Chad 120 C6
Şalāla Sudan 121 H4
Şalālah Oman 105 F4
Salalé well Niger 125 I3
Salamá Guat. 185 H6
Salamá Hond. 186 B4
Salamajärven kansallispuisto nat. park Fin. 44 N3
Salamanca Chile 204 C3
Salamanca Mex. 185 E4
Salamanca Spain 54 F4
historically known as Helmantica *or* Salamantica
UNESCO World Heritage Site
Salamanca U.S.A. 176 G3
Salamanga Moz. 131 G5
Salamantica Spain see Salamanca
Salamat pref. Chad 126 D2
Salamat, Bahr r. Chad 126 C2
Salāmatābād Iran 100 A3
Salamban Indon. 77 F3
Salamina Greece 59 E11
Salamina i. Greece 59 E11
also known as Salamis
Salamis tourist site Cyprus 108 E2
also known as Constantia
Salamís i. Greece see Salamina
Salamīyah Syria 109 I2
Salamonie r. U.S.A. 172 H10
Salamonie Lake U.S.A. 172 H10
Salandi r. India 95 E1
Salantai Lith. 42 C5
Salaqi China 85 F3
also known as Tumd Youqi
Sălard Romania 58 D1
Salar de Pocitos Arg. 200 D6
Salas Spain 54 E1
Salas de los Infantes Spain 55 H2
Salaspils Latvia 42 F5
Salat r. France 50 G9
Salatiga Indon. 77 E4
Sălăuţa r. Romania 58 F1
Salavan Laos 79 D5
Salavat Rus. Fed. 102 C1
Salaverry Peru 200 A2
Salawati i. Indon. 73 H7
Salawin Wildlife Reserve nature res. Thai. 78 B4
Salay Phil. 74 C4
Salaya India 96 A5
Salayar i. Indon. 75 B4
Salayar, Selat sea chan. Indon. 75 B4
Sala y Gómez, Isla i. S. Pacific Ocean 221 L7
Salazar Angola see N'dalatando
Salazar Arg. 204 E5
Salbris France 51 I5
Salccantay, Cerro mt. Peru 200 B3
Salcedo Dom. Rep. 187 F3
Sălciile Romania 58 H4
Šalčininkai Lith. 42 G7
Sălcioara Romania 58 H4
Saldae Alg. see Bejaïa
Salda Gölü l. Turkey 59 K11
Saldana Col. 198 C4
Saldaña Spain 54 G2
Saldanha S. Africa 132 B10
Saldanha Bay S. Africa 132 B10
Saldus Latvia 42 D5
Sale Australia 147 E4
Sale Myanmar 78 A3
Salea Indon. 75 B3
Saleh, Teluk b. Indon. 77 G5
Şāleḩābād Hamadān Iran 100 B3
Şāleḩābād Khorāsan Iran 101 E3
Salekhard Rus. Fed. 38 G3
historically known as Obdorsk
Salem India 94 C4
Salem S. Africa 133 K10
Salem AR U.S.A. 174 B4
Salem IA U.S.A. 172 B10
Salem IL U.S.A. 174 B4
Salem IN U.S.A. 174 C4
Salem MA U.S.A. 177 O3
Salem MO U.S.A. 174 B4
Salem NJ U.S.A. 177 J6
Salem NY U.S.A. 177 L2

▶Salem OR U.S.A. 180 B3
State capital of Oregon.

Salem SD U.S.A. 178 C3
Salem UT U.S.A. 183 M1
Salem VA U.S.A. 176 E8
Salem WV U.S.A. 176 E6
Salemi Sicily Italy 57 E11
Sälen Sweden 45 K3
Salerno Italy 57 G8
historically known as Salernum
Salerno, Golfo di g. Italy 57 G8
Salernum Italy see Salerno
Sales Oliveira Brazil 206 F7
Salesópolis Brazil 207 H10
Salford U.K. 47 J10
Salgada Brazil 199 F5
Salgado Brazil 202 E4
Salgótarján Hungary 49 Q7
Salgueiro Brazil 202 E4
Sali Alg. 123 E4
Salian Afgh. 101 E4
Salibabu i. Indon. 75 C2
Salida U.S.A. 181 F5
Saliena Latvia 42 E5
Salignac-Eyvignes France 50 H8
Salihli Turkey 106 B3
Salihorsk Belarus 42 I9
also spelt Soligorsk
Salihorskaye Vodaskhovishcha resr Belarus 42 I9
Salikénié Senegal 124 B3
Salimbatu Indon. 77 G2
Salimi Dem. Rep. Congo 127 D7
Salimo Moz. 129 C8
Salina KS U.S.A. 178 C4
Salina UT U.S.A. 183 M3
Salina, Isola i. Isole Lipari Italy 57 G10
Salina Cruz Mex. 185 G5
Salinas Brazil 202 D6
Salinas Ecuador 198 A5
Salinas Mex. 185 E4
Salinas r. Mex. 179 C7
Salinas U.S.A. 182 C5
Salinas r. U.S.A. 182 C5
Salinas, Cabo de c. Spain see Salines, Cap de ses
Salinas, Pampa de las salt pan Arg. 204 D3
Salinas, Ponta das pt Angola 127 B8
Salinas, Punta pt Dom. Rep. 187 F3
Salinas de Garci Mendoza Bol. 200 D4
Salinas Peak U.S.A. 181 F6
Saline U.S.A. 173 J8
Saline r. AR U.S.A. 179 D5
Saline r. KS U.S.A. 178 C4
Salines, Cap de ses c. Spain 55 O5
also spelt Salinas, Cabo de
Saline Valley depr. U.S.A. 182 G5
Salineville U.S.A. 176 E5
Salingyi Myanmar 78 A3
Salinópolis Brazil 202 C2
Salinosó Lachay, Punta pt Peru 200 A2
Salisbury U.K. 47 K12
Salisbury MD U.S.A. 177 J7
Salisbury NC U.S.A. 174 D5
Salisbury PA U.S.A. 176 F6
Salisbury Zimbabwe see Harare
Salisbury Island Canada 165 L3
Salisbury Plain U.K. 47 J12
Săliştea Romania 58 E3
Salitre r. Brazil 202 D4
Şalkhad Syria 109 H5
Salki r. India 95 E1
Salla Fin. 44 O2
Salliq Canada see Coral Harbour
Salliqueló Arg. 204 E5
Sallisaw U.S.A. 179 D5
Sallom Sudan 104 B4
Salluit Canada 165 L3
formerly known as Saglouc
Sallyana Nepal 97 D3
Salmā Syria 108 H2
Salmās Iran 100 A2
also known as Shāhpūr
Salmi Rus. Fed. 40 D3
Salmivaara Fin. 44 O2
Salmo Canada 167 G5
Salmon U.S.A. 180 D3
Salmon r. U.S.A. 180 C3
Salmon, Middle Fork r. U.S.A. 180 D3
Salmon Arm Canada 166 G5
Salmon Falls Creek r. U.S.A. 180 D4
Salmon Gums Australia 151 C7
Salmon Reservoir U.S.A. 177 J2
Salmon River Mountains U.S.A. 180 D3
Salmonsdam Nature Reserve S. Africa 132 D11
Salmtal Germany 48 D6
Sal'nye Tundry, Khrebet mts Rus. Fed. 44 O1
Salo Cent. Afr. Rep. 126 C4
Salo Fin. 45 M3
Salò Italy 56 C3
Saloinen Fin. 44 N2
Salome U.S.A. 183 K8
Salon India 97 D4
Salon-de-Provence France 51 L9
Salonga r. Dem. Rep. Congo 126 D5
Salonga Nord, Parc National de la nat. park Dem. Rep. Congo 126 D5
UNESCO World Heritage Site
Salonga Sud, Parc National de la nat. park Dem. Rep. Congo 126 D5
UNESCO World Heritage Site
Salonica Greece see Thessaloniki
Salonika Greece see Thessaloniki
Salonta Romania 58 C2
Salor r. Spain 54 D5
Salou Spain 55 M3
Salou, Cap de c. Spain 55 M3
Saloum watercourse Senegal 124 A3
Salpausselkä reg. Fin. 45 N3
Sal Rei Cape Verde 124 [inset]
Salsacate Arg. 204 D3
Salsbruket Norway 44 J2
Salses, Étang de l. France see Leucate, Étang de
Sal'sk Rus. Fed. 41 G7
Salso r. Sicily Italy 57 F11
Salso r. Sicily Italy 57 G11
Salsomaggiore Terme Italy 56 B4
Salt Jordan see As Salţ
Salt watercourse S. Africa 132 H10
Salt Spain 55 N3
Salt r. AZ U.S.A. 183 L8
Salt r. MO U.S.A. 178 E4
Salt r. WY U.S.A. 180 E4
Salta Arg. 200 D6
Salta prov. Arg. 204 D2
Saltaire U.K. 47 K10
UNESCO World Heritage Site
Saltanovka Rus. Fed. 43 P9
Saltash U.K. 47 H13
Salt Creek r. U.S.A. 176 C6
Saltee Islands Ireland 47 F11
Saltery Bay Canada 166 E5
Saltfjellet Svartisen Nasjonalpark nat. park Norway 44 K2
Salt Fork r. U.S.A. 178 C4
Salt Fork Arkansas r. U.S.A. 178 C4
Salt Fork Brazos r. U.S.A. 179 B5
Salt Fork Lake U.S.A. 176 D5
Salt Fork Red r. U.S.A. 179 C5
Saltillo Mex. 185 E3
Salt Lake salt l. India 89 A7
Salt Lake S. Africa 132 I6

▶Salt Lake City U.S.A. 183 M1
State capital of Utah.

Salt Lick U.S.A. 176 B7
Salt Marsh Lake salt l. U.S.A. 183 K2
Salto Arg. 204 E4
Salto Brazil 206 F10
Salto r. Italy 56 E6
Salto Uruguay 204 F3
Salto da Divisa Brazil 202 E6
Salto de Agua Mex. 185 G5
Salto del Guairá Para. 201 G6
Salto Grande Brazil 206 D9
Salto Grande, Embalse de resr Uruguay 204 F3
Salton City U.S.A. 183 H8
Salton Sea salt l. U.S.A. 183 I8
Saltpond Ghana 125 E5
Salt River Canada 167 H2
Saltrou Haiti see Belle-Anse
Saltville U.S.A. 176 D9
Sal'tykí Rus. Fed. 43 U8
Saluda SC U.S.A. 175 D5
Saluda VA U.S.A. 177 I8
Saluda r. U.S.A. 174 D5
Saluebesar i. Indon. 75 B3
Salue Timpaus, Selat sea chan. Indon. 75 B3
Salûm, Gulf of Egypt 121 E2
Salumbar India 96 B4
Saluq, Kūh-e mt. Iran 100 D2
Salur India 95 D2
Saluzzo Italy 51 N8
Salvador Brazil 202 E5
formerly known as Bahia
UNESCO World Heritage Site
Salvador country Central America see El Salvador
Salvador, Lake U.S.A. 175 B6
Salvador Mazza Arg. 201 E5
Salvaterra Brazil 202 B2
Salvatierra Mex. 185 E4
Salvation Creek r. U.S.A. 183 N3
Salviac France 50 H8
Salwah Saudi Arabia 105 E2
Salwah, Dawḩat b. Qatar/Saudi Arabia 105 E2
Salween r. China/Myanmar 78 B4
also known as Khong, Mae Nam *or* Thanlwin (Myanmar) *or* Nu Jiang (China)
Salyan Azer. 107 G3
also spelt Sal'yany
Sal'yany Azer. see Salyan
Salyersville U.S.A. 176 B8
Salza r. Austria 49 L8
Salzach r. Austria/Germany 49 J7
Salzbrunn Namibia 130 C5
Salzburg Austria 49 K8
UNESCO World Heritage Site
Salzgitter Germany 48 H3
formerly known as Watenstadt-Salzgitter
Salzkammergut reg. Austria 49 K8
UNESCO World Heritage Site
Salzkotten Germany 48 F4
Salzwedel Germany 48 I3
Salzwedel-Diesdorf park Germany 48 H3
Sam Gabon 126 A4
Sam India 96 A4
Sam, Nam r. Laos/Vietnam 78 D4
Samá Cuba 186 E2
also known as Puerto Sama
Šamac Bos.-Herz. see Bosanski Šamac
Şamad Oman 105 G3
Samae San, Laem pt Thai. 79 C5
English form Liant, Cape
Samagaltay Rus. Fed. 84 B1
Samāh well Saudi Arabia 105 D1
Samaida Iran see Someydeh
Samaipata Bol. 201 E4
UNESCO World Heritage Site
Samak, Tanjung pt Indon. 77 D3
Samakoulou Mali 124 C3
Samal i. Phil. 74 C5
Samalayuca Mex. 184 D2
Samales Group is Phil. 74 B5
Samalkot India 95 D2
Samālūţ Egypt 121 F2
Samaná Dom. Rep. 187 F3
Samana India 96 C3
Samaná, Cabo c. Dom. Rep. 187 F3
Samana Cay i. Bahamas 187 E2
Samanala mt. Sri Lanka see Adam's Peak
Samandağı Turkey 106 C3
also known as Alevişik; *historically known as* Seleucia Pieria
Samangān prov. Afgh. 101 F2
Samangān Iran 101 E3
Samani Japan 90 H3
Samaniego Col. 198 B4
Samanlı Dağları mts Turkey 58 J8
Samannūd Egypt 108 C7
also spelt Sebennytos
Samaqua r. Canada 169 F3
Samar Kazakh. see Samarskoye
Samar i. Phil. 74 C4
Samara Rus. Fed. 102 B1
formerly known as Kuybyshev
Samara r. Rus. Fed. 102 B1
Samarahan Sarawak Malaysia see Sri Aman
Samarai P.N.G. 149 F1
Samara Oblast admin. div. Rus. Fed. see Samarskaya Oblast'
Samarga Rus. Fed. 82 E3
Samaria nat. park Greece 59 E13
Samariapo Venez. 199 E3
Samarinda Indon. 77 G3
Samarka Rus. Fed. 82 D3
Samarkand Uzbek. see Samarqand
Samarkand, Pik mt. Tajik. see Samarqand, Qullai
Samarkand Oblast admin. div. Uzbek. see Samarqand
Samarobriva France see Amiens
Samarqand Uzbek. 103 F5
also spelt Samarkand; *historically known as* Maracanda
UNESCO World Heritage Site
Samarqand admin. div. Uzbek. 103 F5
English form Samarkand Oblast; *also known as* Samarqand Wiloyati
Samarqand, Qullai mt. Tajik. 101 G2
also known as Samarkand, Pik
Samarqand Wiloyati admin. div. Uzbek. see Samarqand
Sāmarrā' Iraq 107 E4
Sāmarrā', Saddat dam Iraq 109 O3
Samar Sea g. Phil. 74 C4
Samarskaya Oblast' admin. div. Rus. Fed. 102 B1
English form Samara Oblast; *formerly known as* Kuybyshevskaya Oblast'
Samarskoye Kazakh. 88 C1
also known as Samar
Samasata Pak. 101 G4
Samassi Sardinia Italy 57 A9
Samastipur India 97 E4
Samaúma Brazil 199 F6
Şamaxı Azer. 107 G2
also spelt Shemakha
Samba Dem. Rep. Congo 126 E6
Samba r. Indon. 77 F3
Samba Jammu and Kashmir 96 B2
Samba Cajú Angola 127 B7
Sambaliung mts Indon. 77 G2
Sambalpur India 97 D5
Sambar, Tanjung pt Indon. 77 E3
Sambas Indon. 77 E2
Sambat Ukr. see Kiev
Sambava Madag. 131 [inset] K2
Sambhal India 96 C3
Sambhar India 96 B4
Sambhar Lake India 96 B4
Sambir Ukr. 53 G2
also spelt Sambor
Sambit i. Indon. 77 G2
Sambo Angola 127 C8
Sambo Indon. 75 A3
Samboja Indon. 77 G3
Sambor Ukr. see Sambir
Sambor Dam Cambodia 79 D5
Samborombón, Bahía b. Arg. 204 F4
Samch'ŏk S. Korea 83 C5
Samch'ŏnp'o S. Korea see Sach'on
Sameikkon Myanmar 78 A3
Samer France 50 H2
Samet' Rus. Fed. 43 V4
Samet, Ko i. Thai. 79 C5
Samfya Zambia 127 F7
Samḩah i. Yemen 105 F5
Samḩān, Jabal mts Oman 105 F4
Sami India 96 A5
Sami Pak. 101 E5
Samīrah Saudi Arabia 104 C2
Samiria r. Peru 198 C6
Samirum Iran see Yazd-e Khvāst
Şämkir Azer. 107 F2
also spelt Shamkhor
Samnah oasis Saudi Arabia 104 B2
Samnan va Damghan reg. Iran 100 C3
Sam Neua Laos see Xam Nua
Samnū Libya 120 B3
▶Samoa country S. Pacific Ocean 145 H3
formerly known as Western Samoa *or* Samoa i Sisifo
▶▶138–139 Oceania Countries
Samoa i Sisifo country S. Pacific Ocean see Samoa
Samobor Croatia 56 H3
Samoded Rus. Fed. 40 G3
Samokov Bulg. 58 E6
Šamorín Slovakia 49 O7
Samos Greece 59 H11
Samos i. Greece 59 H11
UNESCO World Heritage Site
Samosir i. Indon. 76 B2
Samothrace i. Greece see Samothraki
Samothraki Greece 58 G8
Samothraki i. Greece 59 G8
English form Samothrace
Samovodene Bulg. 58 G5
Samoylovka Rus. Fed. 41 G6
Sampa Côte d'Ivoire 124 E5
Sampacho Arg. 204 D4
Sampaga Indon. 75 A3
Sampang Indon. 77 F4
Sampit Indon. 77 F3
Sampit r. Indon. 77 F3
Sampit, Teluk b. Indon. 77 F3
Sampolawa Indon. 75 B4
Sampur Rus. Fed. 41 G5
Sampwe Dem. Rep. Congo 127 E7
Samr al 'Abd, Jabal mt. Egypt 108 D9
Samran, Huai r. Thai. 79 D5
Sam Rayburn Reservoir U.S.A. 179 D6
Samreboe Ghana 124 E5
Samro, Ozero l. Rus. Fed. 43 J3
Samrong Cambodia see Phumĭ Sâmraông
Samsang China 89 C6
Sam Sao, Phou mts Laos/Vietnam 78 C3
Samsø i. Denmark 45 J5
Samsø Bælt sea chan. Denmark 45 J5
Sâm Sơn Vietnam 78 D4
Samsun Turkey 107 D2
historically known as Amisus
Samsy Kazakh. 103 I4
Samtens Germany 49 K1
Samthar India 96 C4
Samtredia Georgia 107 E2
Samui, Ko i. Thai. 79 C6
Samulun, Pulau i. Sing. 76 [inset]
Samundri Pak. 101 H4
Samur r. Azer./Rus. Fed. 107 G2
Samutlu Turkey see Temelli
Samut Prakan Thai. 79 C5
Samut Sakhon Thai. 79 C5
Samut Songkhram Thai. 79 C5
San Mali 124 D3
San r. Poland 49 S5
San, Phou mt. Laos 78 C4
San, Tônlé r. Cambodia 79 D5
Sana r. Bos.-Herz. 56 I3

▶Şan'ā' Yemen 104 D5
Capital of Yemen.
UNESCO World Heritage Site

Şan'ā' governorate Yemen 104 D5
Sanaag admin. reg. Somalia 128 E2
San Adrián, Cabo c. Spain 54 C1
Sanae research station Antarctica 223 X2
Sanaga r. Cameroon 125 H6
San Agostín U.S.A. see St Augustine
San Agustín Col. 198 B4
San Agustin, Cape Phil. 74 C5
San Agustín, Parque Arqueológico tourist site Col. 198 B4
UNESCO World Heritage Site
Sanak Island U.S.A. 164 C4
Şān al Ḩajar al Qiblīyah Egypt 108 C7
Sanām Saudi Arabia 104 D3
San Ambrosio, Isla i. S. Pacific Ocean 200 A6
Sanana Indon. 75 C3
Sanandaj Iran 100 A3
also known as Sinneh
Sanando Mali 124 D3
San Andreas U.S.A. 182 D3
San Andrés Bol. 201 D3
San Andrés Col. 198 C3
San Andres Phil. 74 C3
San Andrés, Isla de i. Caribbean Sea 186 C4
San Andrés del Rabanedo Spain 54 F2
San Andres Mountains U.S.A. 181 F6
San Andrés Tuxtla Mex. 185 G5
San Angelo U.S.A. 179 B6
Sanankoroba Mali 124 D3
San Antolín Spain 54 E1
San Antonio Arg. 204 D3
San Antonio Belize 185 H5
San Antonio Bol. 201 D3
San Antonio Chile 204 C4
San Antonio Hond. 186 B4
San Antonio Peru 198 C5
San Antonio Phil. 74 B3
San Antonio NM U.S.A. 181 F6
San Antonio TX U.S.A. 179 C6
San Antonio r. CA U.S.A. 182 D6
San Antonio r. TX U.S.A. 179 C6
San Antonio Venez. 187 H5
San Antonio, Cabo c. Arg. 204 F5
San Antonio, Cabo c. Cuba 186 B2
San Antonio, Mount U.S.A. 182 G7
San Antonio Abad Spain 55 M6
San Antonio Bay Phil. 74 A4
San Antonio de Caparo Venez. 198 D3
San Antonio del Mar Mex. 184 A2
San Antonio de los Cobres Arg. 200 D6
San Antonio de Palé Equat. Guinea 125 G7
San Antonio de Tamanaco Venez. 199 E2
San Antonio Este Arg. 204 D6
San Antonio Oeste Arg. 204 D6
San Antonio Reservoir U.S.A. 182 D6
San Augustín Arg. 204 F5
San Augustín de Valle Fértil Arg. 204 D3
San Augustine U.S.A. 179 D6
Sanaw Yemen 105 E4
Sanawad India 96 C5
San Bartolo Mex. 185 E4
San Bartolomeo in Galdo Italy 56 H7
San Benedetto del Tronto Italy 56 F6
San Benedicto, Isla i. Mex. 184 C5
San Benito Guat. 185 H5
San Benito U.S.A. 179 C7
San Benito r. U.S.A. 182 C5
San Benito Mountain U.S.A. 182 D5
San Bernardino U.S.A. 183 G7
San Bernardino, Passo di pass Switz. 51 P6
San Bernardino Mountains U.S.A. 183 G7
San Bernardino Strait Phil. 74 C3
San Bernardo Chile 204 C4
San Bernardo Mex. 184 D3
San Blas Arg. 204 D3
San Blas Nayarit Mex. 184 D4
San Blas Sinaloa Mex. 184 C3
San Blas, Archipiélago de is Panama 186 D5
formerly known as Las Mulatas
San Blas, Cape U.S.A. 175 C6
San Blas, Cordillera de mts Panama 186 D5
San Borja Bol. 200 D3
Sanborn U.S.A. 178 D3
Sanbornville U.S.A. 177 N2
San Buenaventura Mex. 185 E3
Sança Moz. 131 G3
San Candido Italy 56 E2
historically known as Aguntum
San Caprasio hill Spain 55 K3
San Carlos Mendoza Arg. 204 C4
San Carlos Salta Arg. 204 D2
San Carlos Chile 204 C5
San Carlos Equat. Guinea see Luba
San Carlos Coahuila Mex. 185 E2
San Carlos Tamaulipas Mex. 185 F3
San Carlos Nicaragua 186 B5
San Carlos Para. 201 F5
San Carlos r. Para. 201 F5
San Carlos Phil. 74 B3
San Carlos Phil. 74 B4
San Carlos Uruguay 204 G4
San Carlos U.S.A. 183 N8
San Carlos Amazonas Venez. 199 E4
San Carlos Apure Venez. 199 E3
San Carlos Cojedes Venez. 198 D2
San Carlos de Bariloche Arg. 204 C6
San Carlos de Bolívar Arg. 204 E5
San Carlos de la Rápita Spain see Sant Carles de la Ràpita
San Carlos del Zulia Venez. 198 D2
San Carlos Indian Reservation U.S.A. 183 N8
San Carlos Lake U.S.A. 183 N8
San Cataldo Sicily Italy 57 F11
San Cayetano Arg. 204 F5
San Celoni Spain see Sant Celoni
Sancerre France 51 I5
Sancerrois, Collines du hills France 51 I5
San Cesario di Lecce Italy 57 K8
Sancha Gansu China 86 C1
Sancha Shanxi China 85 F4
Sanchahe China see Fuyu
Sancha He r. China 86 C3
Sanchakou China 88 B4
Sanchi India 96 C5
UNESCO World Heritage Site
San Chien Pau mt. Laos 78 C3
Sanchor India 96 A4
Sanchuan He r. China 85 F4
Sanchursk Rus. Fed. 40 H4
San Ciro de Acosta Mex. 185 F4
San Clemente Chile 204 C4
San Clemente Spain 55 I5
San Clemente U.S.A. 182 G8
San Clemente del Tuyú Arg. 204 F5
San Clemente Island U.S.A. 182 F9
Sancoins France 51 I6
Sanco Point Phil. 74 C4
San Cristóbal Arg. 204 E3
San Cristóbal Potosí Bol. 200 D5
San Cristóbal Santa Cruz Bol. 201 E3
San Cristóbal Col. 198 C5
San Cristóbal Dom. Rep. 187 F3
San Cristobal i. Solomon Is 145 F3
also known as Arossi, *or* Makira
San Cristóbal Venez. 198 C3
San Cristóbal, Volcán vol. Nicaragua 186 B4
San Cristóbal de las Casas Mex. 185 G5
San Cristobal Wash watercourse U.S.A. 183 K9
Sancti Spíritus Cuba 186 D2
Sand Norway 45 I4
Sand r. Free State S. Africa 133 K5
Sand r. Northern S. Africa 131 F4
Sanda Japan 91 D7
Sandagou Rus. Fed. 90 D3
Sandai Indon. 77 E3
Sandakan Sabah Malaysia 77 G1
Sandakan, Pelabuhan inlet Sabah Malaysia 77 G1
Sandakphu Peak India 97 F4
Sandane Norway 45 I3
Sandanski Bulg. 58 E7
Sandaohezi China see Shawan
Sandaré Mali 124 C3
Sanday i. U.K. 46 J4
Sandberg S. Africa 132 C9

Sand Cay reef India 94 B4
Sande Sogn og Fjordane Norway 45 I3
Sande Vestfold Norway 45 J4
Sandefjord Norway 45 J4
Sandefjord (Torp) airport Norway 45 J4
Sandelva Norway 44 M1
Sandercock Nunataks nunataks Antarctica 223 D2
Sanders U.S.A. 183 O6
Sanderson U.S.A. 179 B6
Sandersville U.S.A. 175 D5
Sandfire Roadhouse Australia 150 C3
Sandfloeggi mt. Norway 45 I4
Sand Hill r. U.S.A. 178 C2
Sand Hills U.S.A. 178 B3
Sandhornøy i. Norway 44 K2
Sandi India 96 D4
Sandia Peru 200 C3
San Diego Mex. 181 E7
San Diego CA U.S.A. 183 G9
San Diego TX U.S.A. 179 C7
San Diego, Cabo c. Arg. 205 D9
San Diego, Sierra mts Mex. 184 C2
San Diego de Cabrutica Venez. 199 E2
Sandıklı Turkey 106 B3
Sandila India 96 D4
Sanding i. Indon. 76 C3
Sand Island U.S.A. 172 C4
Sandivey r. Rus. Fed. 40 K2
Sand Lake Canada 168 C4
Sand Lake l. Canada 167 M5
Sandnes Norway 45 I4
Sandnessjøen Norway 44 K2
Sandø i. Faroe Is see Sandoy
Sandoa Dem. Rep. Congo 127 D7
Sandomierska, Kotlina basin Poland 49 S5
Sandomierz Poland 49 S5
Sândominic Romania 58 G2
formerly spelt Sîndominic
San Domino, Isola i. Italy 56 H6
Sandoná Col. 198 B4
San Donà di Piave Italy 56 E3
Sandover watercourse Australia 148 C4
Sandovo Rus. Fed. 43 R3
Sandow, Mount Antarctica 223 G2
Sandoway Myanmar see Thandwè
Sandoy i. Faroe Is 46 F2
also spelt Sandø
Sandpoint U.S.A. 180 C2
Sandray i. U.K. 46 E7
also spelt Sanndraigh
Sandringham Australia 148 C5
Sand River Reservoir Swaziland 133 P3
Sandsele Sweden 44 L2
Sandspit Canada 166 D4
Sand Springs IA U.S.A. 172 B8
Sand Springs OK U.S.A. 179 C4
Sand Springs Salt Flat U.S.A. 182 F2
Sandspruit r. S. Africa 133 K4
Sandstone Australia 151 B5
Sandstone U.S.A. 174 A2
Sandstone Peak hill U.S.A. 182 F7
Sand Tank Mountains U.S.A. 183 L9
Sandton S. Africa 133 M3
Sandu Guizhou China 87 C3
also known as Sanhe
Sandu Hunan China 87 E3
Sandur India 94 C3
Sandusky MI U.S.A. 173 K7
Sandusky OH U.S.A. 176 C4
Sandusky Bay U.S.A. 176 C4
Sandveld mts S. Africa 132 C8
Sandveld Nature Reserve S. Africa 133 J4
Sandverhaar Namibia 132 B3
Sandvika Akershus Norway 45 J4
Sandvika Nord-Trøndelag Norway 44 K3
Sandviken Sweden 45 L3
Sandvlakte S. Africa 133 I10
Sandwich U.S.A. 177 O4
Sandwich Bay Canada 169 J2
Sandwich Island Vanuatu see Éfaté
Sandwip Bangl. 97 F5
Sandwip Channel Bangl. 97 F5
Sandy U.S.A. 183 M1
Sandy r. U.S.A. 177 P1
Sandy Bay Canada 167 K4
Sandy Bight b. Australia 151 C7
Sandy Cape Qld Australia 149 G5
Sandy Cape Tas. Australia 147 E5
Sandy Creek r. Australia 148 C3
Sandy Island Australia 150 C2
Sandykgaçy Turkm. 103 E5
Sandykly Gumy des. Turkm. 103 E5
also known as Sundukli, Peski
Sandy Lake Alta Canada 167 H4
Sandy Lake Ont. Canada 167 M4
Sandy Lake l. Canada 167 M4
Sandy Springs U.S.A. 175 C5
Sandyville U.S.A. 176 D7
San Estanislao Para. 201 F6
San Esteban Hond. 186 B4
San Esteban, Isla i. Mex. 184 B2
San Fabián de Alico Chile 204 C5
San Felipe Chile 204 C4
San Felipe Baja California Norte Mex. 184 B2
San Felipe Chihuahua Mex. 184 D3
San Felipe Guanajuato Mex. 185 E4
San Felipe mt. Spain 55 J4
San Felipe Venez. 198 D2
San Felipe, Cayos de is Cuba 186 C2
San Felipe Creek watercourse U.S.A. 183 I8
San Feliú de Guíxols Spain see
Sant Feliu de Guíxols
San Félix, Isla i. S. Pacific Ocean 221 N7
San Fernando Arg. 204 F4
San Fernando Chile 204 C4
San Fernando Baja California Norte Mex. 184 B2
San Fernando Tamaulipas Mex. 185 F3
San Fernando Phil. 74 B2
San Fernando Phil. 74 B3
San Fernando Spain 54 E8
San Fernando Trin. and Tob. 187 H5
San Fernando U.S.A. 182 F7
San Fernando de Apure Venez. 199 E3
San Fernando de Atabapo Venez. 199 E3
Sånfjället nationalpark nat. park Sweden 45 K3
Sanford r. Australia 151 A5
Sanford FL U.S.A. 175 D6
Sanford ME U.S.A. 177 O2
Sanford MI U.S.A. 173 I7
Sanford NC U.S.A. 174 E5
San Francisco Arg. 204 E3
San Francisco Bol. 200 D3
San Francisco Mex. 184 B2
San Francisco U.S.A. 182 B4
San Francisco r. U.S.A. 181 E6
San Francisco, Paso de pass Arg. 204 C2
San Francisco, Sierra mts Mex. 184 B3
UNESCO World Heritage Site
San Francisco Bay inlet U.S.A. 182 B4
San Francisco del Oro Mex. 184 D3
San Francisco de Macorís Dom. Rep. 187 F3
San Francisco de Paula, Cabo c. Arg. 205 D8
San Francisco Gotera El Salvador 185 H6
San Francisco Javier Spain 55 M6
Sanga Dem. Rep. Congo 127 F6
San Gabriel Ecuador 198 B4
San Gabriel, Punta pt Mex. 184 B2
San Gabriel Mountains U.S.A. 182 F7
Sangachaly Azer. see Sanqaçal
Sangaigerong Indon. 76 D3
Sa'ngain China 86 A2
San Gallan, Isla i. Peru 200 A3
Sangam India 94 C3
Sangameshwar India 94 B2
Sangamner India 94 B2
Sangamon r. U.S.A. 174 B3
Sangān Iran 101 D3
Sangān, Kūh-e mt. Afgh. 101 F3
Sangar r. Pak. 101 G4
Sangar Rus. Fed. 39 M3
Sangaréa Guinea 124 B4
Sangareddi India 94 C2
Sangarédi Guinea 124 B4
Sangaria India 96 B3
Sangasanga Indon. 77 G3
Sanga Sanga i. Phil. 74 A5
Sangasso Mali see Zangasso
Sangaste Estonia 42 H4
San Gavino Monreale Sardinia Italy 57 A9
Sangay, Parque Nacional nat. park Ecuador 198 B5
UNESCO World Heritage Site
Sangay, Volcán vol. Ecuador 198 B5
Sang Bast Iran 101 D3
Sangbé Cameroon 125 I5
Sangboy Islands Phil. 74 B5
Sangbur Afgh. 101 E3
Sangeang i. Indon. 77 G5
Sangejing China 85 E3
Sângeorgiu de Pădure Romania 58 F2
formerly spelt Sîngeorgiu de Pădure
Sângeorz-Băi Romania 58 F1
formerly spelt Sîngeorz-Băi
Sangequanzi China 88 E3
Sânger Romania 58 F2
Sanger U.S.A. 182 E5
Sângera Moldova see Sîngera
Sangerfield U.S.A. 177 J3
Sangerhausen Germany 48 I4
San Germán Puerto Rico 187 G3
Sanggan He r. China 85 G3
Sanggar, Teluk b. Indon. 77 G5
Sanggarmai China 86 B1
Sanggau Indon. 77 E2
Sanggou Wan b. China 85 I4
Sangha admin. reg. Congo 126 B4
Sangha r. Congo 126 C5
Sangha-Mbaéré pref. Cent. Afr. Rep. 126 C4
Sanghar Pak. 101 G5
San Gil Col. 198 C3
Sangilen, Nagor'ye mts Rus. Fed. 84 B1
San Gimignano Italy 56 C5
UNESCO World Heritage Site
San Giovanni in Fiore Italy 57 I9
San Giovanni Rotondo Italy 56 H7
San Giovanni Suegiu Sardinia Italy 57 A9
Sangir India 96 B5
Sangir i. Indon. 75 C2
Sangir, Kepulauan is Indon. 75 C2
Sangiran tourist site Java Indon. 77 E4
Sangiran tourist site Indon. 77 E4
UNESCO World Heritage Site
San Giuliano Terme Italy 56 C5
San Giustino Italy 56 E5
Sangiyn Dalay Mongolia 84 E2
Sangiyn Dalay Nuur salt l. Mongolia 84 C1
Sangju S. Korea 83 C5
Sangkapura Indon. 77 F4
Sangkarang, Kepulauan is Indon. 75 A4
Sângke, Stœng r. Cambodia 79 C5
Sangkulirang Indon. 77 G2
Sangkulirang, Teluk b. Indon. 77 G2
Sangla Pak. 101 H4
Sangli India 94 B2
San Glorio, Puerto de pass Spain 54 G1
Sangmélima Cameroon 125 H6
Sango Zimbabwe 131 F4
formerly known as Vila Salazar or Villasalazar
Sangod India 96 C4
Sangole India 94 B2
San Gorgonio Mountain U.S.A. 183 H7
Sangowo Indon. 75 D2
Sangpi China see Xiangcheng
Sang Qu r. China 86 A2
Sangre de Cristo Range mts U.S.A. 181 F5
San Gregorio de Polanca Uruguay 204 G4
Sangre Grande Trin. and Tob. 187 H5
Sangri China see Xueba
Sangro r. Italy 56 G6
Sangrur India 96 B3
Sangsang China 89 D6
Sangu r. Bangl. 97 F5
Sangue r. Brazil 201 F2
Sangüesa Spain 55 J2
San Guiliano Milanese Italy 56 B3
San Guillermo, Parque Nacional nat. park Arg. 204 C3
Sangū'īyeh Iran 100 D4
also known as Isfandaqeh
Sangyuan China see Wuqiao
Sangzhi China 87 D2
also known as Liyuan
Sanhe Guizhou China see Sandu
Sanhe Nei Mongol China 85 I1
Sanhezhen China 87 F2
San Hilario Mex. 184 C3
San Hipólito, Punta pt Mex. 184 B3
Sanhūr Egypt 121 F2
San Ignacio Belize 185 H5
San Ignacio Beni Bol. 200 D3
San Ignacio Santa Cruz Bol. 201 E4
San Ignacio Santa Cruz Bol. 201 E4
San Ignacio Baja California Sur Mex. 184 B3
San Ignacio Sonora Mex. 184 C2
San Ignacio Para. 201 F6
San Ignacio Peru 198 B6
San Ignacio, Laguna l. Mex. 184 B3
UNESCO World Heritage Site
Sanikiluaq Canada 168 E1
San Ildefonso Peninsula Phil. 74 B2
Sanin-kaigan National Park Japan 91 D7
Sanipas pass S. Africa 133 N6
Sanirajak Canada see Hall Beach
Sanislău Romania 49 T8
Sanitz Germany 49 J1
Sāniyat al Fawākhir well Libya 120 C3
San Jacinto Col. 198 C2
San Jacinto Phil. 74 B3
San Jacinto U.S.A. 183 H8
San Jacinto Peak U.S.A. 183 H8
Sanjai r. India 97 E5
San Jaime Arg. 204 F3
San Javier Arg. 204 F3
San Javier Beni Bol. 200 D3
San Javier Santa Cruz Bol. 201 E4
San Javier Spain 55 K7
San Javier de Loncomilla Chile 204 C4
Sanjawi Pak. 101 G4
Sanjbod Iran 100 B2
San Jerónimo Mex. 185 E5
San Jerónimo Peru 200 B1
Sanjiang Guangdong China see Liannan
Sanjiang Guangxi China 87 D3
also known as Guyi
Sanjiang Guizhou China see Jinping
Sanjiaocheng China see Haiyan
Sanjiaoping China 87 D2
Sanjie China 87 G2
Sanjō Japan 90 F6
San Joaquín Bol. 200 D3
San Joaquín Para. 201 F6
San Joaquin U.S.A. 182 D5
San Joaquin r. U.S.A. 182 C3
San Joaquin Valley valley U.S.A. 182 D4
San Jon U.S.A. 178 B5
San Jorge Arg. 204 E3
San Jorge, Golfo de g. Arg. 205 D7
San Jorge, Golfo de g. Spain see Sant Jordi, Golf de
San José Col. 199 D4
►San José Costa Rica 186 B5
Capital of Costa Rica.
San José watercourse Mex. 181 D8
San Jose Phil. 74 B3
San Jose Phil. 74 B3
San Jose Phil. 74 B3
San Jose CA U.S.A. 182 C4
San Jose NM U.S.A. 181 F6
San Jose watercourse U.S.A. 181 F6
San José Venez. 199 E2
San José, Cabo c. Arg. 205 D7
San José, Cuchilla de hills Uruguay 204 F3
San José, Golfo g. Arg. 205 D6
San José, Isla i. Mex. 184 C3
San José, Volcán vol. Chile 204 C4
San José de Amacuro Venez. 199 F2
San José de Bavicora Mex. 184 D2
San Jose de Buenavista Phil. 74 B4
San José de Chiquitos Bol. 201 E4
San José de Comondú Mex. 184 C3
San José de Gracia Baja California Sur Mex. 184 B3
San José de Gracia Sonora Mex. 184 C2
San José de Guaribe Venez. 187 G5
San José de Jáchal Arg. 204 C3
San Joséde la Brecha Mex. 184 C3
San José de la Dormida Arg. 204 E3
San José de la Mariquina Chile 204 B5
San José del Boquerón Arg. 204 E2
San José del Cabo Mex. 184 C4
San José del Guaviare Col. 198 C4
San José de Mayo Uruguay 204 F4
San José de Ocuné Col. 198 D3
San José de Primas Mex. 181 E7
San José de Raíces Mex. 185 E3
San Juan Arg. 204 C3
San Juan prov. Arg. 204 C3
San Juan Bol. 201 E4
San Juan Col. 198 B2
San Juan r. Col. 198 B3
San Juan r. Costa Rica/Nicaragua 186 C5
San Juan mt. Cuba 186 C2
San Juan Dom. Rep. 187 F3
San Juan Chihuahua Mex. 184 D3
San Juan Coahuila Mex. 185 E3
San Juan Peru 200 B3
San Juan Phil. 74 C4
►San Juan Puerto Rico 187 G3
Capital of Puerto Rico.
UNESCO World Heritage Site
San Juan r. CA U.S.A. 182 D6
San Juan r. UT U.S.A. 183 N4
San Juan Venez. 199 E3
San Juan, Cabo c. Arg. 205 E9
San Juan, Cabo c. Equat. Guinea 125 H6
San Juan, Punta pt El Salvador 186 A4
San Juan Bautista Para. 201 F6
San Juan Bautista Spain 55 M5
San Juan Bautista U.S.A. 182 C5
San Juan Bautista Tuxtepec Mex. 185 F5
San Juan Capistrano U.S.A. 182 G8
San Juancito Hond. 186 B4
San Juan de Cesar Col. 198 C2
San Juan de Guadalupe Mex. 185 E3
San Juan dela Costa Chile 204 B6
San Juan de la Peña, Sierra de mts Spain 55 K2
San Juan del Norte Nicaragua 186 C5
San Juan del Norte, Bahía de b. Nicaragua 186 C5
San Juan de los Cayos Venez. 198 D2
San Juan de los Morros Venez. 199 E2
San Juan del Río Durango Mex. 184 D3
San Juan del Río Querétaro Mex. 185 F4
San Juan del Sur Nicaragua 186 B5
San Juan de Salvamento Arg. 205 E9
San Juan Evangelista Mex. 185 G5
San Juan Islands U.S.A. 180 B2
San Juanito Mex. 184 D3
San Juanito, Isla i. Mex. 184 D4
San Juan Mountains U.S.A. 181 F5
San Juan y Martínez Cuba 186 C2
San Julián Arg. 205 D8
San Just mt. Spain 55 K4
San Justo Arg. 204 E3
Sanka Myanmar 78 B3
Sankarani r. Côte d'Ivoire/Guinea 124 C4
Sankarankovil India 94 C4
Sankeshwar India 94 B2
Sankh r. India 97 E5
Sankosh r. Bhutan see Sunkosh Chhu
Sankra Chhattisgarh India 94 D1
Sankra Rajasthan India 96 A4
Sankt Andrä Austria 49 L9
Sankt Gallen Switz. 51 P5
UNESCO World Heritage Site
Sankt Gotthard Hungary see Szentgotthárd
Sankt Johann im Pongau Austria 49 K8
Sankt Moritz Switz. 51 P6
Sankt Niklaus Switz. 51 N6
Sankt-Peterburg Rus. Fed. see St Petersburg
Sankt Peter-Ording Germany 48 F1
Sankt Pölten Austria 49 M7
Sankt Veit an der Glan Austria 49 L9
Sankt Wendel Germany 48 E6
Sanku Jammu and Kashmir 96 C2
Sankuru r. Dem. Rep. Congo 126 D6
San Lázaro Para. 201 F5
San Lázaro, Cabo c. Mex. 184 B3
San Lázaro, Sierra de mts Mex. 184 C4
San Leandro U.S.A. 182 B4
San Leonardo in Passiria Italy 56 D2
Şanlıurfa Turkey 107 D3
formerly known as Urfa; historically known as Edessa
Şanlıurfa prov. Turkey 109 J1
San Lorenzo Corrientes Arg. 204 F3
San Lorenzo Santa Fé Arg. 204 E4
San Lorenzo Beni Bol. 200 D3
San Lorenzo Pando Bol. 200 D2
San Lorenzo Tarija Bol. 200 D5
San Lorenzo Ecuador 198 B4
San Lorenzo Hond. 186 B4
San Lorenzo Mex. 184 D2
San Lorenzo Peru 200 C2
San Lorenzo mt. Spain 55 I2
San Lorenzo, Cabo c. Ecuador 198 A5
San Lorenzo, Cerro mt. Arg./Chile 205 B7
San Lorenzo, Isla i. Mex. 184 B2
San Lorenzo, Isla i. Peru 200 A3
Sanlúcar de Barrameda Spain 54 E8
San Lucas Bol. 200 D5
San Lucas Baja California Sur Mex. 184 B3
San Lucas Baja California Sur Mex. 184 C4
San Lucas, Cabo c. Mex. 184 C4
San Lucas, Serranía de mts Col. 198 C3
San Luis Arg. 204 D4
San Luis prov. Arg. 204 D4
San Luis Brazil 200 D2
San Luis Cuba 186 E2
San Luis Guat. 185 H5
San Luis Mex. 185 E5
San Luis Peru 198 C5
San Luis AZ U.S.A. 183 J9
San Luis AZ U.S.A. 183 M9
San Luis CO U.S.A. 181 F5
San Luis Venez. 198 D2
San Luis, Isla i. Mex. 184 B2
San Luis, Sierra de mts Arg. 204 D4
San Luis de la Paz Mex. 185 E4
San Luis del Palmar Arg. 204 F2
San Luis Gonzaga Mex. 184 C3
San Luisito Mex. 184 B2
San Luis Obispo U.S.A. 182 D6
San Luis Obispo Bay U.S.A. 182 D6
San Luis Potosí Mex. 185 E4
San Luis Potosí state Mex. 185 E4
San Luis Reservoir U.S.A. 182 C4
San Luis Río Colorado Mex. 184 B1
Sanluri Sardinia Italy 57 A9
San Manuel U.S.A. 183 N9
San Marcello Pistoiese Italy 56 C4
San Marcial, Punta pt Mex. 184 C3
San Marco, Capo c. Sardinia Italy 57 A9
San Marco, Capo c. Sicily Italy 57 F11
San Marcos Chile 204 C3
San Marcos Col. 198 C2
San Marcos Guat. 185 H6
San Marcos Hond. 186 B4
San Marcos Mex. 185 F5
San Marcos Peru 200 A1
San Marcos U.S.A. 179 C6
San Marcos r. U.S.A. 179 C6
San Marcos, Isla i. Mex. 184 B3
►San Marino country Europe 56 E5
►►16–17 World Population
►►32–33 Europe Countries
►San Marino San Marino 56 E5
Capital of San Marino.
San Martín research station Antarctica 222 T2
long form General San Martín
San Martín Catamarca Arg. 204 D3
San Martín Mendoza Arg. 204 C4
San Martín r. Bol. 201 E3
San Martín dept Peru 200 A1
San Martín, Lago l. Arg./Chile 205 B8
San Martín, Volcán vol. Mex. 185 G5
San Martín de los Andes Arg. 204 C6
San Martín de Valdeiglesias Spain 54 G4
San-Martino-di-Lota Corsica France 51 P10
San Mateo Peru 198 D5
San Mateo U.S.A. 182 B4
San Mateo Venez. 199 E2
San Matías Bol. 201 F4
San Matías, Golfo g. Arg. 204 D6
San Mauricio Venez. 199 E2
Sanmen China 87 G2
also known as Haiyou
Sanmen Wan b. China 87 G2
Sanmenxia China 87 D1
San Miguel Arg. 204 F3
San Miguel Bol. 201 E4
San Miguel r. Bol. 201 E3
San Miguel r. Col. 198 C4
San Miguel El Salvador 185 H6
San Miguel Panama 186 D5
San Miguel Peru 200 B3
San Miguel U.S.A. 182 D6
San Miguel r. U.S.A. 181 E5
San Miguel Bay Phil. 74 B3
San Miguel de Allende Mex. 185 E4
San Miguel de Cruces Mex. 184 D3
San Miguel de Horcasitas r. Mex. 184 C2
San Miguel de Huachi Bol. 200 D3
San Miguel del Monte Arg. 204 F4
San Miguel de Tucumán Arg. 204 D2
short form Tucumán
San Miguel do Araguaia Brazil 202 B5
San Miguel el Alto Mex. 185 E4
San Miguel Island U.S.A. 182 D7
San Miguel Islands Phil. 74 A5
San Miguelito Panama 186 D5
San Miguel Sola de Vega Mex. 185 F5
Sanming China 87 F3
San Miniato Italy 56 C5
Sanna r. Poland 49 S5
San Narciso Phil. 74 B3
Sannaspos S. Africa 133 K6
Sanndatti India 94 B3
Sanndraigh i. U.K. see Sandray
Sannicandro Garganico Italy 56 H7
San Nicolás Mex. 185 F3
San Nicolas Phil. 74 B2
San Nicolás, Bahía b. Peru 200 B3
San Nicolás de los Arroyos Arg. 204 E4
San Nicolás del Presidio Mex. 184 D3
San Nicolas Island U.S.A. 182 E8
Sânnicolau Mare Romania 58 B2
formerly spelt Sînnicolau Mare
Sannieshof S. Africa 133 J3
Sanniquellie Liberia 124 C5
Sannohe Japan 90 G4
Sañogasta, Sierra de mts Arg. 204 D3
Sanok Poland 49 T6
San Onofre Col. 198 C2
San Pablo Arg. 205 D9
San Pablo Potosí Bol. 200 D5
San Pablo Santa Cruz Bol. 201 E3
San Pablo r. Bol. 201 E3
San Pablo Col. 198 D3
San Pablo Mex. 185 F4
San Pablo Phil. 74 B3
San Pablo U.S.A. 182 B4
San Pablo de Manta Ecuador see Manta
San Pedro Buenos Aires Arg. 204 F4
San Pedro Catamarca Arg. 204 D2
San Pedro Jujuy Arg. 200 D6
San Pedro Misiones Arg. 204 G2
San Pedro Belize 185 I5
San Pedro Beni Bol. 200 D3
San Pedro Santa Cruz Bol. 201 E4
San Pedro r. Bol. 200 D4
San-Pédro Côte d'Ivoire 124 D5
San Pedro r. Cuba 186 D2
San Pedro Mex. 184 C4
San Pedro r. Mex. 181 F7
San Pedro Peru 200 C2
San Pedro Phil. 74 B3
San Pedro watercourse U.S.A. 183 N9
San Pedro, Punta pt Costa Rica 186 C5
San Pedro, Sierra de mts Spain 54 D5
San Pedro Carchá Guat. 185 H6
San Pedro Channel U.S.A. 182 F8
San Pedro de Atacama Chile 200 C5
San Pedro de las Colonias Mex. 185 E3
San Pedro de Lloc Peru 200 A1
San Pedro del Pinatar Spain 55 K7
San Pedro de Macorís Dom. Rep. 187 F3
San Pedro de Ycuamandyyú Para. 201 F6
San Pedro el Saucito Mex. 184 C2
San Pedro Martir, Parque Nacional nat. park Mex. 184 B2
San Pedro Sula Hond. 186 A4
San Pietro, Isola di i. Sardinia Italy 57 A9
San Pietro in Cariano Italy 56 C3
San Pitch r. U.S.A. 183 M2
Sanqaçal Azer. 107 G2
also spelt Sangachaly
Sanquhar U.K. 46 I8
Sanquianga, Parque Nacional nat. park Col. 198 B4
San Quintín, Cabo c. Mex. 184 A2
San Rafael Arg. 204 C4
San Rafael Bol. 201 E4
San Rafael U.S.A. 182 B4
San Rafael r. U.S.A. 183 N3
San Rafael Venez. 198 D2
also known as San Rafael del Moján
San Rafael del Moján Venez. see San Rafael
San Rafael del Norte Nicaragua 186 B4
San Rafael del Yuma Dom. Rep. 187 F3
San Rafael Knob mt. U.S.A. 183 N3
San Rafael Mountains U.S.A. 182 D7
San Ramón Beni Bol. 200 D3
San Ramón Santa Cruz Bol. 201 E4
San Remo Italy 51 N9
San Rodrigo watercourse Mex. 179 B6
San Román, Cabo c. Venez. 198 D1
San Roque Andalucía Spain 54 F8
San Roque Galicia Spain 54 C1
San Roque Galicia Spain 54 C2
San Roque, Punta pt Mex. 184 B3
San Saba U.S.A. 179 C6
San Saba r. U.S.A. 179 C6
Sansalé Guinea 124 B4
San Salvador Arg. 204 F3
San Salvador i. Bahamas 187 E1
formerly known as Watling Island
►San Salvador El Salvador 185 H6
Capital of El Salvador.
San Salvador Peru 198 D5
San Salvador de Jujuy Arg. 200 D6
San Salvo Italy 56 G6
Sansané Haoussa Niger 125 F3
Sansanné-Mango Togo 125 F4
San Sebastián Arg. 205 C9
San Sebastián hill Spain 54 C2
San Sebastián, Bahía de b. Arg. 205 C9
San Sebastián de los Reyes Spain 55 H4
Sansepolcro Italy 56 E5
San Severino Marche Italy 56 F5
San Severo Italy 56 H7
Sansha China 87 G3
San Silvestre Bol. 200 C2
San Silvestre Venez. 198 D2
San Simon U.S.A. 183 O9
Sanski Most Bos.-Herz. 56 I4
Sanson N.Z. 152 J8
Sansoral Islands Palau see Sonsorol Islands
Sansui China 87 D3
also known as Bagong
Santa Peru 200 A2
Santa r. Peru 200 A2
Santa Adélia Brazil 206 E8
Santa Ana Arg. 204 D2
Santa Ana La Paz Bol. 200 D3
Santa Ana Santa Cruz Bol. 201 F4
Santa Ana El Salvador 185 H6
Santa Ana Mex. 184 C2
Santa Ana U.S.A. 182 G8
Santa Ana de Yacuma Bol. 200 D3
Santa Anita Mex. 184 C4
Santa Anna U.S.A. 179 C6
Santa Bárbara Brazil 201 F3
Santa Bárbara Cuba see La Demajagua
Santa Bárbara Hond. 186 A4
Santa Bárbara Mex. 184 D3
Santa Bárbara mt. Spain 55 I7
Santa Bárbara mt. Spain 55 J6
Santa Barbara U.S.A. 182 E7
Santa Bárbara Amazonas Venez. 199 E4
Santa Bárbara Barinas Venez. 198 D3
Santa Bárbara, Ilha i. Brazil 207 O4
Santa Bárbara, Parque Nacional nat. park Hond. 186 A4
Santa Bárbara, Serra de hills Brazil 203 A7
Santa Barbara Channel U.S.A. 182 D7
Santa Bárbara d'Oeste Brazil 206 F9
Santa Bárbara do Sul Brazil 203 A9
Santa Barbara Island U.S.A. 182 E8
Santa Catalina Chile 204 C2
Santa Catalina Panama 186 C5
Santa Catalina Venez. 199 F2
Santa Catalina, Gulf of U.S.A. 182 G8
Santa Catalina, Isla i. Mex. 184 C3
Santa Catalina de Armada Spain 54 C1
Santa Catalina Island U.S.A. 182 F8
Santa Catarina state Brazil 203 B8
Santa Catarina Baja California Norte Mex. 184 B2
Santa Catarina Nuevo León Mex. 185 E3
Santa Catarina Neth. Antilles 187 F4
also spelt Santa Catharina
Santa Catarina, Ilha de i. Brazil 203 B8
Santa Catharina Neth. Antilles see Santa Catarina
Santa Clara Col. 198 D5
Santa Clara Cuba 186 D2
Santa Clara r. Mex. 181 F7
Santa Clara CA U.S.A. 182 C4
Santa Clara UT U.S.A. 183 K4
Santa Clara r. U.S.A. 182 E7
Santa Clara, Barragem de resr Port. 54 C7
Santa Clarita U.S.A. 182 F7
Santa Clotilde Peru 198 C5
Santa Coloma de Farners Spain 55 N3
Santa Coloma de Gramanet Spain 55 N3
Santa Comba Angola see Waku-Kungo
Santa Comba Dão Port. 54 C4
Santa Croce Camerina Sicily Italy 57 G12
Santa Cruz prov. Arg. 205 C8
Santa Cruz r. Arg. 205 C8
Santa Cruz Bol. 201 E4
Santa Cruz dept Bol. 201 E4
Santa Cruz Espírito Santo Brazil 207 M6
Santa Cruz Pará Brazil 199 H5
Santa Cruz Pará Brazil 202 B2
Santa Cruz Costa Rica 186 B5
Santa Cruz Mex. 184 C2
Santa Cruz Peru 198 C6
Santa Cruz Phil. 74 A3
Santa Cruz Phil. 74 B2
Santa Cruz Phil. 74 B3
Santa Cruz mt. Spain 55 J3
Santa Cruz U.S.A. 182 B5
Santa Cruz watercourse U.S.A. 183 L8
Santa Cruz, Isla i. Mex. 184 C3
Santa Cruz, Puerto inlet Arg. 205 C8
Santa Cruz Barillas Guat. 185 H6
Santa Cruz Cabrália Brazil 202 E6
Santa Cruz das Palmeiras Brazil 206 F8
Santa Cruz de Goiás Brazil 206 E4
Santa Cruz de la Palma Canary Is 122 A3
Santa Cruz del Quiché Guat. 185 H6
Santa Cruz del Sur Cuba 186 D2
Santa Cruz de Mudela Spain 55 H6
►Santa Cruz de Tenerife Canary Is 122 A3
Joint capital of the Canary Islands.
Santa Cruz de Yojoa Hond. 186 B4
Santa Cruz do Rio Pardo Brazil 206 D9
Santa Cruz do Sul Brazil 203 A9
Santa Cruz Island U.S.A. 182 E7
Santa Cruz Islands Solomon Is 145 F3
Santa Efigênia de Minas Brazil 207 K5
Santa Elena Buenos Aires Arg. 204 E5
Santa Elena Entre Ríos Arg. 204 F3
Santa Elena Bol. 200 D5
Santa Elena Peru 198 C6
Santa Elena Venez. 199 F3
Santa Elena, Cabo c. Costa Rica 186 B5
Santa Elena, Punta pt Ecuador 198 A5
Santa Eufemia, Golfo di g. Italy 57 I10
Santa Eulalia del Río Spain 55 M6
Santa Fé Arg. 204 E3
Santa Fé prov. Arg. 204 E3
Santa Fé Cuba 186 C2
Santa Fé Panama 186 C5
Santa Fe Phil. 74 B3
Santa Fé Spain 54 H7
►Santa Fe U.S.A. 181 F6
State capital of New Mexico.
Santa Fé de Bogotá Col. see Bogotá
Santa Fé de Minas Brazil 202 C6
Santa Fé do Sul Brazil 206 C7
Santa Filomena Brazil 202 C4
Sant'Agata di Militello Sicily Italy 57 G10
Santa Helena Brazil 202 C2
Santa Helena de Goiás Brazil 206 C4
Santai Sichuan China 86 C2
also known as Tongchuan
Santai Xinjiang China 88 C2
Santa Inês Bahia Brazil 202 E5
Santa Inês Maranhão Brazil 202 C2
Santa Inés, Isla i. Chile 205 B9
Santa Isabel Arg. 204 D5
Santa Isabel Bol. 200 D5
Santa Isabel Brazil 201 E3
Santa Isabel Equat. Guinea see Malabo
Santa Isabel i. Solomon Is 145 E2
formerly spelt Santa Ysabel
Santa Isabel, Ilha Grande de i. Brazil 202 D2
Santa Isabel, Sierra mts Mex. 184 B2
Santa Isabel de Sihuas Peru 200 B4
Santa Isabel do Araguaia Brazil 201 H1
Santa Juliana Brazil 206 F6
Santalpur India 96 A5
Santa Lucia Chile 200 C5
Santa Lucía Ecuador 198 B5
Santa Lucia Guat. 185 H6
Santa Lucía, Cerro de mt. Spain 54 G7
Santa Lucia Range mts U.S.A. 182 C5
Santa Luzia Maranhão Brazil 202 C3
Santa Luzia Paraíba Brazil 202 E3
Santa Luzia i. Cape Verde 124 [inset]
Santa Magdalena Arg. 204 E4
Santa Margarita Arg. 204 E3
Santa Margarita Spain 55 O5
Santa Margarita U.S.A. 182 D6
Santa Margarita, Isla i. Mex. 184 C3
Santa Maria Arg. 204 D2
Santa Maria i. Arquipélago dos Açores 54 [inset]
Santa Maria Bol. 201 E3
Santa Maria Amazonas Brazil 199 F5
Santa Maria Amazonas Brazil 199 G5
Santa Maria Pará Brazil 199 H5
Santa Maria Rio Grande do Sul Brazil 203 A9
Santa Maria r. Brazil 203 A9
Santa Maria r. Brazil 206 G1
Santa Maria Cape Verde 124 [inset]
Santa María Mex. 185 H5
Santa María r. Mex. 184 D2
Santa Maria Phil. 74 B2
UNESCO World Heritage Site
Santa Maria U.S.A. 182 D7
Santa Maria r. U.S.A. 183 K7
Santa María Venez. 199 E3
Santa Maria, Cabo de c. Moz. 131 G5
Santa Maria, Cabo de c. Port. 54 D8
Santa Maria, Cape Bahamas 175 F8
Santa María, Cayo i. Cuba 186 D2
Santa Maria, Chapadão de hills Brazil 202 C5
Santa María, Isla i. Chile 204 B5
Santa María, Punta pt Peru 200 B3
Santa Maria, Serra de hills Brazil 206 G1
Santa Maria Capua Vetere Italy 56 G7
Santa Maria da Boa Vista Brazil 202 E4
Santa Maria das Barreiras Brazil 202 B4
Santa Maria da Vitória Brazil 202 C5
Santa María de Ipire Venez. 199 E2
Santa María del Oro Mex. 184 D3
Santa María del Río Mex. 185 E4
Santa Maria di Leuca, Capo c. Italy 57 K9
Santa Maria do Salto Brazil 207 M3
Santa Maria do Suaçuí Brazil 203 D6
Santa María Island Vanuatu 145 F3
Santa María Mountains U.S.A. 183 L7
Santa Marina Salina Isole Lipari Italy 57 G10
Santa Marinella Italy 56 D6
Santa Marta Col. 198 C2
Santa Marta, Cabo de c. Angola 127 B8
Santa Marta, Serra de mts Brazil see Divisões, Serra das
Santa Marta Grande, Cabo de c. Brazil 203 B9
Santa Martha, Cerro mt. Mex. 185 G5
Santa Maura i. Greece see Lefkada
Santa Monica U.S.A. 182 F7
Santa Monica Bay U.S.A. 182 F8
Santan Indon. 77 G3
Santana Amazonas Brazil 199 E4
Santana Bahia Brazil 202 D5
Santana r. Brazil 206 B6
Sântana Romania 58 C2
Santana da Boa Vista Brazil 203 A9
Santana do Acaraú Brazil 202 D2
Santana do Araguaia Brazil 202 B4
Santana do Cariri Brazil 202 E3
Santana do Livramento Brazil 204 G3
Santander Col. 198 B4
Santander dept Col. 198 C3
Santander Spain 54 H1
Santa Nella U.S.A. 182 C4
Sant'Angelo in Lizzola Italy 56 E5
Sant'Angelo Lodigiano Italy 56 B3
Santanghu China 84 B2
Santanilla, Islas is Caribbean Sea see Swan Islands
Santan Mountain hill U.S.A. 183 M8
Sant'Anna, Ilha de i. Brazil 207 L9
Sant'Antioco Sardinia Italy 57 A9
historically known as Sulci or Sulcis
Sant'Antioco, Isola di i. Sardinia Italy 57 A9
Santañy Spain see Santanyí
Santanyí Spain 55 O5
also spelt Santañy
Santa Paula U.S.A. 182 E7
Santapilly India 95 D2
Santa Pola Spain 55 K6
Santa Pola, Cabo de c. Spain 55 K6
Santaquin U.S.A. 183 M2
Santa Quitéria Brazil 202 D3
Sant'Arcangelo Italy 57 I8
Santarém Brazil 199 H5
Santarém Port. 54 C5
Santarém admin. dist. Port. 54 C5
Santa Rita Mato Grosso Brazil 201 F1
Santa Rita Paraíba Brazil 202 F3
Santa Rita Col. 198 C4
Santa Rita Mex. 185 E3
Santa Rita Guárico Venez. 199 E2
Santa Rita Zulia Venez. 198 D2
Santa Rita de Cassia Brazil 202 C4
Santa Rita do Araguaia Brazil 203 A6
Santa Rita do Pardo Brazil 206 A8
Santa Rita do Sapucaí Brazil 207 H9
Santa Rita do Weil Brazil 198 D5
Santa Rosa Corrientes Arg. 204 F3
Santa Rosa La Pampa Arg. 204 D5
Santa Rosa Río Negro Arg. 204 D6
Santa Rosa Salta Arg. 200 D6
Santa Rosa Bol. 200 D3
Santa Rosa Acre Brazil 200 C2
Santa Rosa Rio Grande do Sul Brazil 203 A8
Santa Rosa Col. 198 D4
Santa Rosa Ecuador 198 B5
Santa Rosa Mex. 185 H5
Santa Rosa Para. 201 F6
Santa Rosa Loreto Peru 198 C5
Santa Rosa Puno Peru 200 C3
Santa Rosa CA U.S.A. 182 B3
Santa Rosa NM U.S.A. 181 F6
Santa Rosa Venez. 199 E4
Santa Rosa and San Jacinto Mountains National Monument nat. park U.S.A. 181 C6
Santa Rosa de Copán Hond. 186 A4
Santa Rosa de la Roca Bol. 201 E4
Santa Rosa del Conlara Arg. 204 D4
Santa Rosa del Palmar Bol. 201 E4
Santa Rosa de Osos Col. 198 C3
Santa Rosa de Vigo Bol. 200 D3
Santa Rosa de Viterbo Brazil 206 F8
Santa Rosa Island U.S.A. 182 D8
Santa Rosalía Mex. 184 B3
Santa Rosa Mountains U.S.A. 183 H8
Santa Rosa Range mts U.S.A. 180 C4
Santa Rosa Wash watercourse U.S.A. 183 L8
Santa Sylvina Arg. 204 E2
Santa Teresa Australia 148 B5
Santa Teresa Brazil 207 M6
Santa Teresa r. Brazil 202 B4
Santa Teresa Mex. 185 F3
Santa Teresa, Embalse de resr Spain 54 F4

Santa Teresa Aboriginal Land res. Australia see Ltyentye Apurte Aboriginal Land
Santa Teresa di Gallura Sardinia Italy 56 B7
Santa Terezinha Brazil 202 B4
Santa Uxía de Ribeira Spain 54 C2
Santa Vitória Brazil 206 C5
Santa Vitória do Palmar Brazil 204 G4
Santa Vittoria, Monte mt. Sardinia Italy 57 B9
Santa Ynez r. U.S.A. 182 D7
Santa Ysabel i. Solomon Is see Santa Isabel
Sant Carles de la Ràpita Spain 55 L4
also spelt San Carlos de la Rápita
Sant Celoni Spain 55 N3
also spelt San Celoni
Santee U.S.A. 183 H9
Santee r. U.S.A. 175 E5
Santeramo in Colle Italy 57 I8
Santerno r. Italy 56 D4
Sant Feliu de Guíxols Spain 55 O3
also spelt San Feliú de Guíxols
Santiago Brazil 203 A9
Santiago i. Cape Verde 124 [inset]

►Santiago Chile 204 C4
Capital of Chile.
►►192–193 South America Countries

Santiago admin. reg. Chile 204 C4
Santiago Dom. Rep. 187 F3
long form Santiago de los Caballeros
Santiago Baja California Sur Mex. 184 C4
Santiago Nuevo León Mex. 185 E3
Santiago Panama 186 C5
Santiago Para. 201 F6
Santiago Peru 200 B3
Santiago r. Peru 198 B6
Santiago Phil. 74 B2
Santiago, Cabo c. Chile 205 B8
Santiago, Cerro mt. Panama 186 C5
Santiago, Río Grande de r. Mex. 184 D4
Santiago, Sierra de hills Bol. 201 F4
Santiago Astata Mex. 185 G5
Santiago de Cao Peru 200 A1
Santiago de Compostela Spain 54 C2
UNESCO World Heritage Site
Santiago de Cuba Cuba 186 E2
UNESCO World Heritage Site
Santiago de la Espada Spain 55 I6
Santiago del Estero Arg. 204 D2
Santiago del Estero prov. Arg. 204 E2
Santiago de los Caballeros Dom. Rep. see Santiago
Santiago de Méndez Ecuador 198 B5
Santiago de Pacaguaras Bol. 200 C3
Santiago do Cacém Port. 54 C6
Santiago Ixcuintla Mex. 184 D4
Santiago Peak U.S.A. 182 G8
Santiago Temple Arg. 204 E3
Santiago Vazquez Uruguay 204 F4
Santiaguillo, Laguna de l. Mex. 184 D3
Santillana Spain 54 G1
San Timoteo Venez. 198 D2
Santipur India see Shantipur
Santisteban del Puerto Spain 55 H6
Sant Jordi, Golf de g. Spain 55 L4
also spelt San Jorge, Golfo de
Sant Llorenç de Munt, Parc Natural del nature res. Spain 55 M3
Santo Amaro Brazil 202 E5
Santo Amaro de Campos Brazil 207 L8
Santo Anastácio r. Brazil 206 A8
Santo André Brazil 206 G10
Santo André Port. 54 C6
Santo Angelo Brazil 203 A9

►Santo Antão i. Cape Verde 124 [inset]
Most westerly point of Africa.
►►110–111 Africa Landscapes

Santo Antônio Amazonas Brazil 199 F5
Santo Antônio Maranhão Brazil 202 C3
Santo Antônio Rio Grande do Norte Brazil 202 F3
Santo Antônio r. Brazil 203 D6
Santo António São Tomé and Príncipe 125 G6
Santo Antônio, Ponta pt Brazil 207 O3
Santo Antônio da Barra Brazil 206 C4
Santo Antônio da Cachoeira Brazil 199 H5
Santo Antônio da Platina Brazil 206 C10
Santo Antônio de Jesus Brazil 202 E5
Santo Antônio de Leverger Brazil 201 F3
Santo Antônio de Pádua Brazil 207 K8
Santo Antônio do Amparo Brazil 207 I7
Santo Antônio do Içá Brazil 199 E5
Santo Antônio do Jacinto Brazil 207 M3
Santo Antônio do Monte Brazil 207 H7
Santo Antônio do Rio Verde Brazil 206 F4
Santo António dos Cavaleiros Port. 54 B6
Santo António do Zaire Angola see Soyo
Santo Corazón Bol. 201 F4
Santo Domíngo Cuba 186 C2

►Santo Domingo Dom. Rep. 187 F3
Capital of the Dominican Republic. Formerly known as Ciudad Trujillo.
UNESCO World Heritage Site

Santo Domingo Baja California Norte Mex. 184 B2
Santo Domingo San Luis Potosí Mex. 185 E4
Santo Domingo Nicaragua 186 B4
Santo Domingo Peru 200 C3
Santo Domingo country West Indies see Dominican Republic
Santo Domingo de la Calzada Spain 55 I2
Santo Domingo Pueblo U.S.A. 181 F6
Santo Domingo Tehuantepec Mex. 185 G5
Santo Eduardo Brazil 207 L8
Santo Hipólito Brazil 207 I5
Santo Inácio Brazil 206 B9
San Tomé Venez. 199 E2
Santoña Spain 55 H1
Santong He r. China 82 B4
Santo Niño i. Phil. 74 C4
Santorini i. Greece see Thira
Santos Brazil 207 G10
Santos Dumont Brazil 207 J8
Santos Mercado Bol. 200 D2
Santo Stefano di Camastra Sicily Italy 57 G10
Santo Tirso Port. 54 C3
Santo Tomás Chihuahua Mex. 181 F7
Santo Tomás Sonora Mex. 181 D7
Santo Tomás Nicaragua 186 B4
Santo Tomás Peru 200 B3
Santo Tomé Arg. 204 F3
Santrampur India 96 B5
Sanup Plateau U.S.A. 183 K5
San Valentín, Cerro mt. Chile 205 B7
San Vicente El Salvador 185 H6
San Vicente Mex. 184 A2
San Vicente Phil. 74 B2
San Vicente de Cañete Peru 200 A3
San Vicente de la Barquera Spain 54 G1
San Vicente del Caguán Col. 198 C4
San Vicente del Raspeig Spain 55 K6
San Vincenzo Italy 56 C5
San Vito, Capo c. Sicily Italy 57 E10
San Vito al Tagliamento Italy 56 E3
San Vito Chietino Italy 56 G6
San Vito dei Normanni Italy 57 J8
San Vito lo Capo Sicily Italy 57 E10
Sanwer India 96 B5
Sanya China 87 D5
formerly known as Yaxian
San Yanaro Col. 198 D4
Sanyati r. Zimbabwe 131 F3
Sanyuan China 87 D1
S. A. Nyýazow Adyndaky Turkm. 103 E5
formerly known as imeni Chapayevka

Sanza Pombo Angola 127 C6
Sao, Phou mt. Laos 78 C4
São Bartolomeu r. Brazil 206 F3
São Benedito Brazil 202 D3
São Bento Amazonas Brazil 200 D1
São Bento Maranhão Brazil 202 C2
São Bento Roraima Brazil 199 F4
São Bento do Norte Brazil 202 F3
São Bernardo Brazil 202 D2
São Bernardo do Campo Brazil 206 G10
São Borja Brazil 204 F3
São Carlos Rondônia Brazil 201 D2
São Carlos Rondônia Brazil 201 E2
São Carlos São Paulo Brazil 206 F9
São Desidério Brazil 202 C5
São Domingos Brazil 202 C5
São Domingos r. Mato Grosso do Sul Brazil 203 A7
São Domingos r. Minas Gerais Brazil 206 C6
São Domingos r. Brazil 206 G2
São Domingos do Norte Brazil 207 M6
São Felipe, Serra de hills Brazil 202 C5
São Félix Bahia Brazil 202 E5
São Félix Mato Grosso Brazil 202 B4
São Félix Pará Brazil 199 I6
São Fidélis Brazil 203 D7
São Filipe Cape Verde 124 [inset]
São Francisco Acre Brazil 200 C2
São Francisco Amazonas Brazil 199 F6
São Francisco Minas Gerais Brazil 202 C5
São Francisco r. Brazil 200 D2
also known as Espalha

►São Francisco r. Brazil 207 H4
5th longest river in South America.
►►188–189 South America Landscapes

São Francisco, Ilha de i. Brazil 203 B8
São Francisco de Assis Brazil 203 A9
São Francisco de Goiás Brazil 206 D2
São Francisco de Paula Brazil 203 B9
São Francisco de Sales Brazil 206 D6
São Francisco do Sul Brazil 203 B8
São Gabriel Brazil 203 A9
São Gabriel da Palha Brazil 207 M6
São Gabriel de Goiás Brazil 206 F2
São Gonçalo Brazil 203 D7
São Gonçalo do Abaeté Brazil 203 C6
São Gotardo Brazil 207 H6
Sao Hill Tanz. 129 B7
São Jerônimo da Serra Brazil 206 C10
São João Brazil 199 E5
São João, Ilhas de is Brazil 202 C2
São João, Serra de hills Brazil 201 E2
São João da Aliança Brazil 202 C5
São João da Barra Brazil 203 D7
São João da Boa Vista Brazil 206 G8
São João da Madeira Port. 54 C4
São João da Ponte Brazil 207 I2
São João das Duas Pontas Brazil 206 C7
São João del Rei Brazil 203 C7
São João de Meriti Brazil 207 J9
São João do Araguaia Brazil 202 B3
São João do Caiuá Brazil 206 A9
São João do Cariri Brazil 202 E3
São João do Paraíso Brazil 202 D5
São João do Piauí Brazil 202 D4
São João dos Patos Brazil 202 D3
São João do Sul Angola 127 B8
São João Evangelista Brazil 207 K5
São Joaquim Amazonas Brazil 199 E4
São Joaquim Santa Catarina Brazil 203 B9
São Jorge i. Arquipélago dos Açores 54 [inset]
São Jorge da Mina Ghana see Elmina
São José Amazonas Brazil 199 E5
São José Santa Catarina Brazil 203 B8
São José do Anauá Brazil 199 F4
São José do Belmonte Brazil 202 E3
São José do Divino Brazil 207 L5
São José do Egito Brazil 202 E3
São José do Jacurí Brazil 207 K5
São José do Norte Brazil 204 G4
São José do Peixe Brazil 202 D3
São José do Rio Pardo Brazil 206 G8
São José do Rio Preto Brazil 206 D7
São José dos Campos Brazil 207 H10
São José dos Dourados r. Brazil 206 B7
São José dos Pinhais Brazil 203 B8
São Lourenço Brazil 207 H9
São Lourenço r. Brazil 201 F4
São Lourenço, Pantanal de marsh Brazil 201 F4
São Lourenço do Sul Brazil 204 H3
São Lucas Angola 127 C7
São Luís Maranhão Brazil 202 C2
UNESCO World Heritage Site
São Luís Pará Brazil 199 G6
São Luís de Montes Belos Brazil 206 C3
São Luís do Paraitinga Brazil 207 H10
São Luís do Quitunde Brazil 202 F4
São Luís Gonzaga Brazil 203 A9
São Manuel Brazil 206 E9
São Marceline Brazil 199 E4
São Marcos r. Brazil 206 F5
São Marcos, Baía de b. Brazil 202 C2
São Martinho Brazil 199 G6
São Mateus Brazil 203 E6
São Mateus r. Brazil 207 N5
São Mateus do Sul Brazil 203 B8
São Miguel i. Azores 54 [inset]
São Miguel r. Brazil 206 G3
São Miguel Arcanjo Brazil 206 F10
São Miguel do Tapuio Brazil 202 D3
São Miguel Jesuit Missions tourist site Brazil 203 A9
UNESCO World Heritage Site
Saona, Isla i. Dom. Rep. 187 F3
Saône r. France 51 K7
São Nicolau Angola see Bentiaba
São Nicolau i. Cape Verde 124 [inset]

►São Paulo Brazil 206 G10
Most populous city in South America, and 5th in the world.
►►18–19 World Cities

São Paulo state Brazil 206 E9
UNESCO World Heritage Site
São Paulo de Olivença Brazil 198 D5
São Pedro Amazonas Brazil 199 G6
São Pedro Mato Grosso do Sul Brazil 206 B6
São Pedro Rondônia Brazil 201 E2
São Pedro São Paulo Brazil 206 F9
São Pedro da Aldeia Brazil 203 D7
São Pedro do Desterro Brazil 200 D2
São Pedro do Ivaí Brazil 206 B10
São Pedro do Sul Brazil 203 A9
São Pedro do Sul Port. 54 C4
São Pedro e São Paulo is N. Atlantic Ocean 216 M5
English form St Peter and St Paul Rocks
São Pires r. Brazil see Teles Pires
São Raimundo das Mangabeiras Brazil 202 C3
São Raimundo Nonato Brazil 202 D4
São Romão Amazonas Brazil 199 E6
São Romão Minas Gerais Brazil 202 C6
São Roque Brazil 206 F10
São Roque de Minas Brazil 206 G7
São Salvador Angola see M'banza Congo
São Salvador do Congo Angola see M'banza Congo
São Sebastião Amazonas Brazil 200 C1
São Sebastião Pará Brazil 199 H6
São Sebastião Rondônia Brazil 201 E2
São Sebastião São Paulo Brazil 203 C7
São Sebastião, Ilha do i. Brazil 203 C7
São Sebastião da Amoreira Brazil 206 C10
São Sebastião da Boa Vista Brazil 202 B2
São Sebastião do Paraíso Brazil 206 G7

São Simão Mato Grosso do Sul Brazil 201 F5
São Simão Minas Gerais Brazil 206 C5
São Simão, Barragem de resr Brazil 206 C6
São Simão, Represa de resr Brazil 206 D5
Sao-Siu Indon. 75 C2
São Tiago Brazil 207 I7

►São Tomé São Tomé and Príncipe 125 G6
Capital of São Tomé and Príncipe.

São Tomé i. São Tomé and Príncipe 125 G6
São Tomé, Cabo de c. Brazil 203 D7
São Tomé, Pico de mt. São Tomé and Príncipe 125 G6
►São Tomé and Príncipe country Africa 125 G6
►►114–115 Africa Countries
Saoura, Oued watercourse Alg. 123 E3
São Vicente Brazil 206 G10
São Vicente i. Cape Verde 124 [inset]
São Vicente, Cabo de c. Port. 54 C7
English form St Vincent, Cape
São Vicente Ferrer Brazil 202 C2
Sápai Greece see Sapes
Sapallanga Peru 200 B3
Sapanca Turkey 106 B2
Sapão r. Brazil 202 C4
Saparmyrat Türkmenbaşy Turkm. 102 D4
Saparua Indon. 75 D3
Saparua i. Indon. 75 D3
Sape, Selat sea chan. Indon. 75 A5
Sape, Teluk b. Indon. 77 G5
Sapele Nigeria 125 G5
Sapes Greece 58 G7
also known as Sápai
Şaphane Turkey 59 K9
Sapientza i. Greece 59 C12
Sapo, Serranía del mts Panama 186 D6
Sa Pobla Spain 55 O5
also spelt La Puebla
Sapo National Park Liberia 124 C5
Sapopema Brazil 206 C10
Sapotskin Belarus 42 E8
Sapouy Burkina 125 E4
Sapozhok Rus. Fed. 41 G5
Sappa Creek r. U.S.A. 178 C3
Sapporo Japan 90 G3
Saptamukhi r. India 97 F5
Sapucai r. Minas Gerais Brazil 207 H8
Sapucai r. São Paulo Brazil 206 E7
Sapucaia Brazil 199 G5
Sapudi i. Indon. 77 F4
Sapulpa U.S.A. 179 C4
Sapulut Sabah Malaysia 77 G1
Sāq, Jabal hill Saudi Arabia 104 C2
Sāqī Iran 101 D3
Saqqaq Greenland 165 N2
Saqqez Iran 100 A2
Sara Bangl. 97 F4
Sarā Iran 100 A2
Sarāb Iran 100 A2
Sarābīţ al Khādim tourist site Egypt 108 E8
Sarābiyūm Egypt 108 D7
Sara Buri Thai. 79 C5
Saracá, Lago l. Brazil 199 G5
Saraf Doungous Chad 120 C6
Saragossa Spain see Zaragoza
Saragt Turkm. 102 E5
Saraguro Ecuador 198 B5
Saraikela India 97 E5
Sarai Sidhu Pak. 101 H4
Säräisniemi Fin. 44 N2

►Sarajevo Bos.-Herz. 56 K5
Capital of Bosnia-Herzegovina. Historically known as Bosna Saray.

Sarakiniko, Akra pt Greece 59 E10
Sarakino i. Greece 59 F10
Saraktash Rus. Fed. 102 D2
Saraland U.S.A. 175 B6
Saralzhin Kazakh. 102 C2
Saramati mt. India/Myanmar 97 G4
Sarameriza Peru 198 B6
Saran France 51 H5
Saran' Kazakh. 103 H2
Saran, Gunung mt. Indon. 77 E3
Saranac r. U.S.A. 177 L1
Saranac Lake U.S.A. 177 K1
Sarandë Albania 59 B9
Sarandi Paraná Brazil 206 B10
Sarandi Rio Grande do Sul Brazil 203 A8
Sarandib country Asia see Sri Lanka
Sarandí del Yí Uruguay 204 G4
Sarandí Grande Uruguay 204 F4
Sarangani i. Phil. 74 C5
Sarangani Bay Phil. 74 C5
Sarangani Islands Phil. 74 C5
Sarangani Strait Phil. 74 C5
Sarangarh India 97 D5
Sarangpur India 96 C5
Saransk Rus. Fed. 41 H5
Sara Peak Nigeria 125 H4
Saraphi Thai. 78 B4
Sarapul Rus. Fed. 40 J4
Sarasota U.S.A. 175 D7
Saraswati r. India 96 A5
Sărata r. Moldova 58 J2
Sărata r. Romania 58 H4
Sarata Ukr. 41 D7
Sarata r. Ukr. 58 K3
Saratoga CA U.S.A. 182 B4
Saratoga WY U.S.A. 180 F4
Saratoga Springs U.S.A. 177 L2
Saratok Sarawak Malaysia 77 E2
Saratov Rus. Fed. 41 H6
Saratov Oblast admin. div. Rus. Fed. see Saratovskaya Oblast'
Saratovskaya Oblast' admin. div. Rus. Fed. 102 A2
English form Saratov Oblast
Saratovskoye Vodokhranilishche resr Rus. Fed. 102 A1
Saravan Iran 101 E5
Sarawa r. Myanmar 79 B5
Sarawak state Malaysia 77 E2
Saray Turkey 106 A2
Saraya Guinea 124 C4
Saraya Senegal 124 C3
Saraya, Pulau reg. Sing. 76 [inset]
Saraycık Turkey 59 K10
Sarayköy Turkey 106 B3
Saraylar Turkey 58 I8
Sarayönü Turkey 106 C3
Sarbāz Iran 101 E5
Sarbāz r. Iran 101 E5
Sarbāz reg. Iran 101 E5
Sârbeni Romania 58 G4
Sarbhang Bhutan 97 F4
Sarbīsheh Iran 101 D3
Sárbogárd Hungary 49 P9
Sarbulak China 84 A2
Sarcham Iran 100 B2
Sarco Chile 204 C3
Sarda r. India/Nepal 99 K4
Sardab Pass Afgh. 101 G2
Sardarpur India 96 B5
Sardarshahr India 96 B3
Sar Dasht Iran 100 A2
Sardasht Būshehr Iran 100 B4
Sardasht Khūzestān Iran 100 B3
Sardegna i. Italy see Sardinia
Sardica Bulg. see Sofia
Sardinata Col. 198 C2
Sardinia Costa Rica 186 B5
Sardinia admin. reg. Italy 57 B8
Sardinia i. Italy 57 A8
also spelt Sardegna

Sardis U.S.A. 174 B5
Sardis Lake resr U.S.A. 174 B5
Sardoal Port. 54 C5
Sareb, Rās as pt U.A.E. 105 E2
Sar-e Būm Afgh. 101 F3
Sareks nationalpark nat. park Sweden 44 L2
Sarektjåkkå mt. Sweden 44 L2
Sarempaka, Gunung mt. Indon. 77 F3
Sar-e Pol Sar-e Pol Afgh. 101 F2
Sar-e Pol Sar-e Pol Afgh. 101 F3
Sar-e Pol prov. Afgh. 101 F2
Sar Eskandar Iran see Hashtrud
Sare Yazd Iran 100 C4
Sarez, Kŭli l. Tajik. 101 H2
also known as Sarezskoye Ozero
Sarezskoye Ozero l. Tajik. see Sarez, Kŭli
Sargasso Sea Europe 216 J4
Sargentu Loros Peru 198 C5
Sargodha Pak. 101 H3
Sarh Chad 126 C2
formerly known as Fort Archambault
Sarhad reg. Iran 101 E4
Sarhro, Jbel mt. Morocco 122 D3
Sārī Iran 100 C2
Saria i. Greece 59 I13
Sáric Mex. 184 C2
Sarichioi Romania 58 J4
Sarigan i. N. Mariana Is 73 K3
Sarıgöl Turkey 106 B3
Sarıkamış Turkey 107 E2
Sarikei Sarawak Malaysia 77 E2
Sarıkemer Turkey 59 I11
Sarıköy Turkey 59 I8
Sarikŭl, Qatorkŭhi mts China/Tajik. see Sarykol Range
Sarila India 96 C4
Sarimbun Reservoir Sing. 76 [inset]
Sarina Australia 149 F4
Sariñena Spain 55 K3
Sarıoğlan Turkey see Belören
Sar-i Pīrān mt. Iraq 100 A2
Sāri Qamīsh Iran 100 C2
Sariqamish Kuli salt l. Turkm./Uzbek. see Sarykamyshskoye Ozero
Sarīr Tibesti des. Libya 120 C4
Sarir Water Wells Field Libya 120 D3
Sarishabari Bangl. 97 F4
Sarita U.S.A. 179 C7
Sarıveliler Turkey 108 D1
Sariwŏn N. Korea 83 B5
Sarıyer Turkey 106 B2
Sarız Turkey 107 D3
Sark i. Channel Is 50 D3
Sarkad Hungary 49 S9
Sarkand Kazakh. 103 I3
also spelt Sarqant
Sarkari Tala India 96 A4
Şarkikaraağaç Turkey 106 B3
Särkisalo Fin. 42 D1
Şarkışla Turkey 107 D3
Şarköy Turkey 106 A2
Sarlath Range mts Afgh./Pak. 101 F4
Sarlat-la-Canéda France 50 H8
Şarlawuk Turkm. 102 C5
also spelt Sharlawuk
Sarmanovo Rus. Fed. 40 J5
Şărmăşag Romania 58 D1
Sărmaşu Romania 58 F2
Sarmento r. Italy 57 I8
Sarmi Indon. 73 I7
Sarmiento Arg. 205 C7
Särna Sweden 45 K3
Sārnate Latvia 42 C4
Sarneh Iran 100 A3
Sarnen Switz. 51 O6
Sarni India see Amla
Sarnia Canada 168 D5
Sarny Ukr. 41 C6
Saroako Indon. 75 B3
Sarogozha r. Rus. Fed. 43 Q3
Sarolangun Indon. 76 C3
Saroma-ko l. Japan 90 H2
Sarona U.S.A. 172 B5
Saronikos Kolpos g. Greece 59 E11
Saros Körfezi b. Turkey 106 A2
Sárospatak Hungary 49 S7
Sarotra India 96 B4
Sarova Rus. Fed. 40 G5
Sarowbī Afgh. 101 G3
Sarpa, Ozero l. Rus. Fed. 41 H7
Sarpan i. N. Mariana Is see Rota
Šar Planina mts Macedonia/Serb. and Mont. 58 B7
Sarpsborg Norway 45 J4
Sarqant Kazakh. see Sarkand
Sarre r. France 51 N3
Sarrebourg France 51 N4
Sarreguemines France 51 N3
Sarre-Union France 51 N4
Sarria Spain 54 D2
Sarrión Spain 55 K4
Sarro Mali 124 D3
Sarròch Sardinia Italy 57 B9
Sars Rus. Fed. 40 K4
Sartana Ukr. 41 F7
formerly known as Prymors'ke
Sartène Corsica France 56 A7
Sarthe r. France 50 F5
Sarti Greece 59 E8
Sartininkai Lith. 42 C6
Sartu China see Daqing
Sarud, Rūdkhāneh-ye r. Iran 100 B3
Saruhanlı Turkey 59 I10
Saruna r. Pak. 101 F5
Sarupsar India 96 B3
Şärur Azer. 107 F3
also spelt Sharur; formerly known as Il'ichevsk
Saru Tara tourist site Afgh. 101 E4
Sarvābād Iran 100 A3
Sarvani Georgia see Marneuli
Sárvár Hungary 49 N8
Sarvestān Iran 100 C4
Sárvíz r. Romania 49 P9
Sarwar India 96 B4
Sarya r. India 94 B2
Saryagash Kazakh. 103 G4
Sary-Bulak Kyrg. 103 H4
Sarydhaz r. Kyrg. see Sary-Jaz
Sarydzhas Kazakh. see Saryzhaz
Sarygamysh Köli salt l. Turkm./Uzbek. see Sarykamyshskoye Ozero
Sary-Ishikotrau, Peski des. Kazakh. see Saryyesik-Atyrau, Peski
Sary-Jaz r. Kyrg. 103 I4
also spelt Sarydhaz
Sarykamys Kazakh. 102 C3
also spelt Saryqamys
Sarykamyshskoye Ozero salt l. Turkm./Uzbek. 102 D4
also known as Sariqamish Kul or Sarygamysh Köli
Sarykemer Kazakh. 103 G4
formerly known as Mikhaylovka
Sarykiyak Kazakh. 103 H2
Sarykol' Kazakh. 103 F1
Sarykol Range mts China/Tajik. 88 A4
also known as Sarikŭl, Qatorkŭhi
Sarymoyyn, Ozero salt l. Kazakh. 103 F2
Saryozek Kazakh. 103 I3
Saryqamys Kazakh. see Sarykamys
Saryshagan Kazakh. 103 H3
Sarysu watercourse Kazakh. 103 F3
formerly known as Zhaksy Sarysu
Sary-Tash Kyrg. 103 H5
Saryter, Gora mt. Kyrg. 103 I4
Saryumir Kazakh. 102 B2

Saryýazy Suw Howdany resr Turkm. 103 E5
Saryyesik-Atyrau, Peski des. Kazakh. 103 H3
formerly known as Sary-Ishikotrau, Peski
Saryzhal Kazakh. see Sarzhal
Saryzhaz Kazakh. 103 I4
also spelt Sarydzhas
Sarzana Italy 56 B4
Sarzeau France 50 D5
Sarzhal Kazakh. 103 I2
also spelt Saryzhal
Sasak Indon. 76 B2
Sasar, Tanjung pt Indon. 75 A5
Sasaram India 97 E4
Saschiz Romania 58 G3
UNESCO World Heritage Site
Sásd Hungary 49 P9
Sasebo Japan 91 A8
Saskatchewan prov. Canada 167 J4
Saskatchewan r. Canada 167 K4
Saskatchewan Landing Provincial Park Canada 180 F2
Saskatoon Canada 167 J4
Saskylakh Rus. Fed. 39 L2
Saslaya mt. Nicaragua 186 B4
Saslaya, Parque Nacional nat. park Nicaragua 186 B4
Sasnovy Bor Belarus 43 K9
also spelt Sosnovyy Bor; formerly known as Golyashi
Sasolburg S. Africa 133 L3
Sasovo Rus. Fed. 41 G5
Sass r. Canada 167 H2
Sassandra Côte d'Ivoire 124 D5
Sassandra r. Côte d'Ivoire 124 D5
Sassari Sardinia Italy 57 A8
Sassnitz Germany 49 K1
Sassoferrato Italy 56 E5
historically known as Sentinum
Sasso Marconi Italy 56 D4
Sass Rigais mt. Italy 56 D2
Sass Town Liberia 124 C5
Sassuolo Italy 56 C4
Sastobe Kazakh. 103 G4
also spelt Saztöbe
Sastre Arg. 204 E3
Sasvad India 94 B2
Sasykkol', Ozero l. Kazakh. 103 J3
also known as Sasyqköl
Sasyqköl l. Kazakh. see Sasykkol', Ozero
Satadougou Mali 124 C3
Satahual i. Micronesia see Satawal
Sata-misaki c. Japan 91 B9
Satana India 94 B1
Satara India 94 B2
Satara S. Africa 131 F5
Satawal i. Micronesia 73 K5
also spelt Satahual
Sätbaev Kazakh. see Satpayev
Satchinez Romania 58 C3
Satéma Cent. Afr. Rep. 126 D3
Satengar i. Indon. 77 G4
Säter Sweden 45 K3
Satevó Mex. 184 D3
Saticoy U.S.A. 182 E7
Satihaure l. Sweden 44 L2
Satilla r. U.S.A. 175 D6
Satipo Peru 200 B2
Satiri Burkina 124 D4
Satırlar Turkey see Yeşilova
Satka Rus. Fed. 38 F4
Satkania Bangl. 97 G5
Satkhira Bangl. 97 F5
Satluj r. India/Pak. see Sutlej
Satmala Range hills India 94 C2
Satna India 96 D4
Sátoraljaújhely Hungary 49 S7
Satorina mt. Croatia 56 H4
Satpayev Kazakh. 103 F3
also spelt Sätbaev; formerly known as Nikol'skiy
Satpura Range mts India 96 B5
Šatrijos kalnis hill Lith. 42 D6
Satsuma-hantō pen. Japan 91 B9
Satsunai-gawa r. Japan 90 H3
Sattahip Thai. 79 C5
Sattanen Fin. 44 N2
Sattenapalle India 94 D2
Satthwa Myanmar 78 A4
Satti Jammu and Kashmir 96 C2
Satu Mare Romania 53 G2
Satun Thai. 79 C7
Satwas India 96 C5
Saubi i. Indon. 77 F4
Sauce Arg. 204 F3
Sauceda Mountains U.S.A. 183 L9
Sauce de Luna Arg. 204 F3
Saucillo Mex. 184 D2
Sauda Norway 45 I4
Saudakent Kazakh. 103 G4
formerly known as Baykadam or Bayqadam
Sauðárkrókur Iceland 44 [inset] C2
►Saudi Arabia country Asia 104 C3
known as Al 'Arabīyah as Sa'ūdīyah in Arabic
►►64–65 Asia Countries
Saue Estonia 42 F2
Sauêruiná r. Brazil 201 F3
also known as Papagaio
Saug r. Phil. 74 C5
Sauga r. Estonia 42 F3
Saugeen r. Canada 168 D4
Saugerties U.S.A. 177 L3
Saugues France 51 J8
Sāūjbolāgh Iran see Mahābād
Saujil Arg. 204 D2
Saujon France 50 F7
Saukas ezers l. Latvia 42 G5
Sauk Center U.S.A. 178 D2
Sauk City U.S.A. 172 D7
Saül Fr. Guiana 199 H4
Sauland Norway 45 J4
Sauldre r. France 51 H5
Saulgau Germany 48 G7
Saulieu France 51 K5
Saulkrasti Latvia 42 F4
Sault Sainte Marie Canada 168 C4
Sault Sainte Marie U.S.A. 173 I4
Saumalkol' Kazakh. 103 G1
formerly known as Volodarskoye
Saumarez Reef reef Australia 149 G4
Saumlakki Indon. 73 H8
Saumur France 50 F5
Saunavaara Fin. 44 N2
Saunders, Mount hill Australia 148 A2
Saunders Coast Antarctica 222 O1
Saunders Island Falkland Is 205 E8
Saunemin U.S.A. 172 E10
Saungka Myanmar 78 B2
Sauquoit U.S.A. 177 J2
Saur, Khrebet mts China/Kazakh. 88 D2
Saurieši Latvia 42 F5
Saurimo Angola 127 D7
formerly known as Henrique de Carvalho
Sausalito U.S.A. 182 B4
Sausar India 96 C5
Sautar Angola 127 C7
Sava r. Europe 49 M9
Savá Hond. 186 B4
Sava Italy 57 J8
Savage U.S.A. 177 I6
Savage River Australia 147 E5
Savai'i i. Samoa 145 H3
historically known as Chatham Island
Savala r. Rus. Fed. 41 G6
Savalou Benin 125 F5
Savanat Iran see Eşţahbān
Savane r. Canada 169 G3

Savane Moz. 131 G3
Savanna U.S.A. 174 B3
Savannah GA U.S.A. 175 D5
Savannah MO U.S.A. 178 D4
Savannah OH U.S.A. 176 C5
Savannah TN U.S.A. 174 B5
Savannah r. U.S.A. 175 D5
Savannah Sound Bahamas 186 D1
Savannakhét Laos 78 D4
Savanna-la-Mar Jamaica 186 D3
Savanne Canada 172 C2
Savant Lake Canada 168 B3
Savantvadi India see Vadi
Savanur India 94 B3
Sävar Sweden 44 M3
Săvârşin Romania 58 D2
Sävast Sweden 44 M2
Savaştepe Turkey 106 A3
Savè Benin 125 F4
Save r. France 50 H9
Save Moz. 131 G4
Save r. Moz./Zimbabwe 131 G4
formerly spelt Sabi
Sāveh Iran 100 B3
Savelugu Ghana 125 E4
Savenay France 50 E5
Saveretik Guyana 199 G3
Saverne France 51 N4
Savigliano Italy 51 N8
Săvineşti Romania 58 H2
Savinja r. Slovenia 56 H2
Savino Rus. Fed. 40 G4
Savinskiy Rus. Fed. 40 G3
Savinskoye Rus. Fed. 43 U6
Savio r. Italy 56 E4
Savitaipale Fin. 45 N3
Savitri r. India 94 B2
Sävja Sweden 45 L4
Šavnik Crna Gora Serb. and Mont. 58 A6
Savoie reg. France see Savoy
Savona Italy 56 A4
Savonlinna Fin. 45 O3
Savonranta Fin. 44 O3
Savoonga U.S.A. 164 B3
Savoy reg. France 51 M6
also spelt Savoie
Savozero, Ozero l. Rus. Fed. 43 O1
Şavşat Turkey 107 E2
Sävsjö Sweden 45 K4
Savu i. Indon. 75 B5
also spelt Sawu
Savudrija, Rt pt Croatia 56 F3
Savukoski Fin. 44 O2
Savur Turkey 107 E3
Savute r. Botswana 130 E3
Savuti Botswana 131 E3
Saw Myanmar 78 A3
Şawab, Wādī aş watercourse Iraq 109 K4
Şawāb, Wādī aş watercourse Syria 109 L3
Sawahlunto Indon. 76 C3
Sawai, Teluk b. Indon. 75 D3
Sawai Madhopur India 96 C4
Sawan Indon. 77 F3
Sawan Myanmar 78 B2
Sawankhalok Thai. 78 B4
also known as Wang Mai Khon
Sawar India 96 B4
Sawara Japan 91 G7
Sawasaki-bana pt Japan 90 F6
Sawata Japan 90 F6
Sawatch Range mts U.S.A. 180 F5
Sawdā', Jabal as hills Libya 120 B2
Sawhāj Egypt 121 F3
also spelt Sūhāj
Sawi, Ao b. Thai. 79 B6
Şawl Egypt 108 C8
Sawla Ghana 124 E4
Sawmills Zimbabwe 131 F3
Sawn China 86 A4
Şawqirah, Dawḩat b. Oman 105 G4
English form Şawqirah Bay
Şawqirah, Ra's c. Oman 105 G4
Şawqirah Bay Oman see Şawqirah, Dawḩat
Sawtell Australia 147 G2
Sawtooth Mountains hills U.S.A. 174 B2
Sawtooth Range mts ID U.S.A. 180 D3
Sawtooth Range mts WA U.S.A. 180 B2
Sawu Indon. 75 B5
Sawu i. Indon. see Savu
Sawu Sea Indon. 75 B5
Saxby r. Australia 149 D3
Saxnäs Sweden 44 K2
Saxony land Germany see Sachsen
Saxony-Anhalt land Germany see Sachsen-Anhalt
Saxton KY U.S.A. 176 A9
Saxton PA U.S.A. 176 G5
Say Mali 124 D3
Say Niger 125 F3
Sayabouri Laos see Xaignabouli
Sayafi i. Indon. 75 D2
Sayak Kazakh. 103 I3
also spelt Sayaq
Sayalkudi India 94 C4
Sayam well Niger 125 I3
Sayán Peru 200 A2
Sayang i. Indon. 75 D2
Sayano-Shushenskoye Vodokhranilishche resr Rus. Fed. 80 E2
Sayaq Kazakh. see Sayak
Saýat Turkm. 103 E5
also spelt Sayot; formerly spelt Sayyod
Sayda Lebanon see Sidon
Sāyen Iran 100 C4
Sayer Island Thai. 79 B6
Sayghān Afgh. 101 F3
Şayḩ well Yemen 104 D4
Sayḩ al Aḩmar reg. Oman 105 G3
Sayḩūt Yemen 105 E5
Sayingpan China 86 B3
Saykhin Kazakh. 102 A2
also spelt Sayqyn
Saylac Somalia 128 D2
Saylan country Asia see Sri Lanka
Saynshand Mongolia 85 F2
Sayn-Ust Mongolia 84 B2
Sayot Turkm. see Saýat
Say-Ötesh Kazakh. see Say-Utes
Şayqal, Baḩr imp. l. Syria 109 I4
Sayqyn Kazakh. see Saykhin
Sayram Hu salt l. China 88 C2
Sayramskiy, Pik mt. Uzbek. 103 G4
Sayre OK U.S.A. 179 C5
Sayre PA U.S.A. 177 I4
Sayreville U.S.A. 177 K5
Sayula Jalisco Mex. 184 E5
Sayula Veracruz Mex. 185 G5
Say'ūn Yemen 105 E4
Say-Utes Kazakh. 102 C3
also spelt Say-Ötesh
Sayward Canada 166 E5
Sayy well Oman 105 G4
Sayyod Turkm. see Saýat
Sazan i. Albania 58 A8
Sázava r. Czech Rep. 49 L6
Sazonovo Rus. Fed. 43 Q2
Saztöbe Kazakh. see Sastobe
Sbaa Alg. 123 E3
Sbeitla Tunisia 123 H2
Sbiba Tunisia 57 B13
Scaddan Australia 151 C7
Scaër France 50 C4
Scafell Pike hill U.K. 47 I9
Scalea Italy 57 H9
Scaletta Zanclea Sicily Italy 57 H10
Scalloway U.K. 46 K3
Scalpaigh, Eilean i. U.K. see Scalpay

Scalpay i. U.K. 46 F6
also known as Scalpaigh, Eilean
Scandicci Italy 56 D5
Scansano Italy 56 D6
Scânteia Romania 58 I4
Scanzano Jonico Italy 57 I8
Scapa Flow *inlet* U.K. 46 I5
Scarba i. U.K. 46 G7
Scarborough Canada 168 E5
Scarborough Trin. and Tob. 187 H5
Scarborough U.K. 47 L9
Scarborough Shoal *sea feature* S. China Sea 73 E3
Scargill N.Z. 153 G10
Scarinish U.K. 46 F7
Scarp i. U.K. 46 E5
Scarpanto i. Greece *see* Karpathos
Scaterie Island Canada 169 J4
Scawfell Shoal *sea feature* S. China Sea 77 D1
Sceale Bay Australia 146 B3
Šćedro i. Croatia 56 I5
Schaale r. Germany 48 H2
Schaalsee l. Germany 48 H2
Schaalsee *park* Germany 48 H2
Schaffhausen Switz. 51 O5
Schagen Neth. 48 B3
Schakalskuppe Namibia 130 C5
Schao *watercourse* Afgh./Iran 101 E4
Scharbeutz Germany 48 H1
Schärding Austria 49 K7
Scharhörn *sea feature* Germany 48 F2
Schaumburg U.S.A. 172 E8
Scheeßel Germany 48 G2
Schefferville Canada 169 H2
formerly known as Knob Lake
Scheibbs Austria 49 M7
Schell Creek Range *mts* U.S.A. 183 J3
Schellsburg U.S.A. 176 G5
Schellville U.S.A. 182 B3
Schenectady U.S.A. 177 L3
Schenefeld Germany 48 G2
Schertz U.S.A. 179 C6
Schesaplana *mt.* Austria/Switz. 51 P5
Scheßlitz Germany 48 I6
Schierling Germany 48 J7
Schiermonnikoog i. Neth. 48 D2
Schiermonnikoog Nationaal Park *nat. park* Neth. 48 D2
Schiers Switz. 51 P6
Schimatari Greece 59 E10
also known as Skhimatárion
Schio Italy 56 D3
Schirmeck France 51 N4
Schitu Duca Romania 58 I1
Schiza i. Greece 59 C12
also spelt Skhíza
Schkeuditz Germany 49 J4
Schladen Germany 48 H3
Schladming Austria 49 K8
Schlei r. Germany 48 H1
Schleiz Germany 48 I5
Schleswig Germany 48 G1
Schleswig-Holstein *land* Germany 48 G1
Schleswig-Holsteinisches Wattenmeer, Nationalpark *nat. park* Germany 48 F1
Schlosshof *tourist site* Austria 49 N7
Schloss Holte-Stukenbrock Germany 48 F4
Schluchsee Germany 48 F8
Schlüchtern Germany 48 G5
Schlüsselburg Rus. Fed. *see* Shlissel'burg
Schmallenberg Germany 48 F4
Schmidt Island Rus. Fed. *see* Shmidta, Ostrov
Schmidt Peninsula Rus. Fed. *see* Shmidta, Poluostrov
Schmidtsdrif S. Africa 132 I5
Schneidemühl Poland *see* Piła
Schneverdingen Germany 48 G2
Schoemanskloof *pass* S. Africa 133 O2
Schoharie U.S.A. 177 K3
Schokland *tourist site* Neth. 48 C3
UNESCO World Heritage Site
Schombee S. Africa 133 J8
Schönebeck (Elbe) Germany 48 I3
Schönefeld *airport* Germany 49 K3
Schöningen Germany 48 H3
Schoodic Point U.S.A. 177 R1
Schoolcraft U.S.A. 172 H8
Schoonhoven Neth. 48 B4
Schöpfl *hill* Austria 49 M7
Schorfheide *reg.* Germany 49 K3
Schouten Island Australia 147 F5
Schouten Islands P.N.G. 73 J7
Schrankogel *mt.* Austria 48 I8
Schreiber Canada 168 C3
Schrems Austria 49 M7
Schrobenhausen Germany 48 I7
Schroon Lake U.S.A. 177 L2
Schröttersburg Poland *see* Płock
Schulenburg U.S.A. 179 C6
Schull Ireland 47 C12
Schultz Lake Canada 167 L1
Schuyler U.S.A. 178 C3
Schuyler Lake U.S.A. 177 J3
Schuylerville U.S.A. 177 L2
Schuylkill Haven U.S.A. 177 I5
Schwaan Germany 49 J2
Schwabach Germany 48 I6
Schwäbische Alb *mts* Germany 48 F8
Schwäbisch-Fränkischer Wald, Naturpark *nature res.* Germany 48 G7
Schwäbisch Hall Germany 48 G6
Schwabmünchen Germany 48 H7
Schwalm r. Germany 51 P1
Schwanden Switz. 51 P5
Schwandorf Germany 48 J6
Schwaner, Pegunungan *mts* Indon. 77 F3
Schwangau Germany 48 H8
Schwartz Range *mts* Antarctica 223 D2
Schwarzenbek Germany 48 H2
Schwarzenberg Germany 49 J5
Schwarzer Mann *hill* Germany 48 D5
Schwarzrand *mts* Namibia 130 C5
Schwarzwald *mts* Germany *see* Black Forest
Schwaz Austria 48 I8
Schwedeneck Germany 48 H1
Schwedt an der Oder Germany 49 L2
Schweinfurt Germany 48 H5
Schweiz *country* Europe *see* Switzerland
Schweizer-Reneke S. Africa 133 J4
Schwerin Germany 48 I2
Schweriner See l. Germany 48 I2
Schweriner Seenlandschaft *park* Germany 48 I2
Schwyz Switz. 51 O5
Sciacca *Sicily* Italy 57 F11
Scicli *Sicily* Italy 57 G12
UNESCO World Heritage Site
Science Hill U.S.A. 176 A8
Scilla Italy 57 H10
Scilly, Île *atoll* Fr. Polynesia *see* Manuae
Scilly, Isles of U.K. 47 F14
Scio U.S.A. 176 D5
Scioto r. U.S.A. 176 C7
Scipio U.S.A. 183 L2
Scobey U.S.A. 180 F2
Scodra Albania *see* Shkodër
Scofield Reservoir U.S.A. 183 M2
Scone Australia 147 F3
Scordia *Sicily* Italy 57 G11
Scoresby Land *reg.* Greenland 165 Q2
Scoresbysund Greenland *see* Ittoqqortoormiit
Scoresby Sund *sea chan.* Greenland *see* Kangertittivaq
Scorniceşti Romania 58 F4
Scorpion Bight b. Australia 151 D7
Scorzè Italy 56 E3
Scotia Sea S. Atlantic Ocean 217 K9
Scotland *admin. div.* U.K. 46 I6
historically known as Caledonia
Scotland U.S.A. 177 I7
Scotstown Canada 169 G4
Scott, Cape Australia 148 A2
Scott, Cape Canada 166 D5
Scott, Mount *hill* U.S.A. 179 C5
Scott Base *research station* Antarctica 223 L1
Scottburgh S. Africa 133 O7
Scott City U.S.A. 178 B4
Scott Coast Antarctica 223 K1
Scott Glacier Antarctica 223 G2
Scott Glacier Antarctica 223 N1
Scott Inlet Canada 165 L2
Scott Island Antarctica 223 L2
Scott Islands Canada 166 D5
Scott Mountains Antarctica 223 D2
Scott Reef *reef* Australia 150 C2
Scottsbluff U.S.A. 178 B3
Scottsboro U.S.A. 174 C5
Scottsburg U.S.A. 174 C4
Scottsdale Australia 147 E5
Scotts Head Dominica 187 H4
Scottsville *KY* U.S.A. 174 C4
Scottsville *VA* U.S.A. 176 G8
Scottville U.S.A. 172 G7
Scourie U.K. 46 G5
Scranton U.S.A. 177 J4
Scugog, Lake Canada 168 E4
Scunthorpe U.K. 47 L10
Scuol Switz. 51 Q6
Scupi Macedonia *see* Skopje
Scutari Albania *see* Shkodër
Scutari, Lake Albania/Serb. and Mont. 58 A6
also known as Shkodrës, Liqeni i *or* Skardarsko Jezero
Seaboard U.S.A. 176 H9
Seabrook, Lake *salt flat* Australia 151 B6
Seaca Romania 58 F4
Seaford U.K. 47 M13
Seaford U.S.A. 177 J7
Seaforth Canada 173 L7
Seahorse Bank *sea feature* Phil. 74 A4
also known as Routh Bank
Seal r. Canada 167 M3
Seal, Cape S. Africa 132 H11
Sea Lake Australia 147 D3
Seal Bay Antarctica 223 X2
Seal Cove Canada 169 J3
Seal Island U.S.A. 177 Q2
Seal Lake Canada 169 I2
Sealy U.S.A. 179 C6
Seaman U.S.A. 176 B7
Seaman Range *mts* U.S.A. 183 I4
Searcy U.S.A. 174 B5
Searles Lake U.S.A. 183 G6
Searsport U.S.A. 177 Q1
Seascale U.K. 47 I9
Seaside *CA* U.S.A. 182 C5
Seaside *OR* U.S.A. 180 B3
Seaside Park U.S.A. 177 K6
Seaton Glacier Antarctica 223 D2
Seattle U.S.A. 180 B3
Sea View S. Africa 133 J11
Seaview Range *mts* Australia 149 E3
Seaville U.S.A. 177 K6
Seaward Kaikoura Range *mts* N.Z. 153 H10
Seba Indon. 75 B5
Sebaco Nicaragua 186 B4
Sebago Lake U.S.A. 177 O2
Sebakwe Recreational Park Zimbabwe 127 F9
Sebangan, Teluk b. Indon. 77 F3
Sebangka i. Indon. 76 D2
Sebastea Turkey *see* Sivas
Sebastian U.S.A. 175 D7
Sebastián Vizcaíno, Bahía b. Mex. 184 B2
Sebasticook r. U.S.A. 177 P1
Sebastopol Ukr. *see* Sevastopol'
Sebastopol U.S.A. 182 B3
Sebatik i. Indon. 77 G1
Sebauh *Sarawak* Malaysia 77 F2
Sebayan, Bukit *mt.* Indon. 77 E3
Sebba Burkina 125 F3
Sebderat Eritrea 121 H6
Sebdou Alg. 123 E2
Sébékoro Mali 124 C3
Seben Turkey 106 B2
Sebenico Croatia *see* Šibenik
Sebennytos Egypt *see* Samannūd
Sebeş Romania 58 E3
Sebeş r. Romania 58 E2
Sebewaing U.S.A. 173 J7
Sebezh Rus. Fed. 43 J5
Şebinkarahisar Turkey 107 D2
Sebiş Romania 58 D2
Sebisseb, Oued r. Alg. 55 O9
Sebla r. Rus. Fed. 43 S3
Seblat, Gunung *mt.* Indon. 76 C3
Sebrell U.S.A. 177 H9
Sebring U.S.A. 175 D7
Sebuku i. Indon. 77 G3
Sebuku r. Indon. 77 G1
Sebuku, Teluk b. Indon. 77 G2
Sečanj *Vojvodina, Srbija* Serb. and Mont. 58 B3
Secaş r. Romania 58 E2
Secas, Islas is Panama 186 C6
Secchia r. Italy 56 D3
Seccia *mts* Eth. 128 C3
Sechelt Canada 166 F5
Sechenovo Rus. Fed. 40 H5
Sechura Peru 198 A6
Sechura, Bahía de b. Peru 198 A6
Second Cataract *rapids* Sudan *see* 2nd Cataract
Second Mesa U.S.A. 183 N6
Secos, Ilhéus is Cape Verde 124 [inset]
also known as Rombo, Ilhéus do
Sečovce Slovakia 49 S7
Secretary Island N.Z. 153 A13
Secunda S. Africa 133 N3
Secunderabad India 94 C2
Sécure r. Bol. 200 D3
Seda Latvia 42 G4
Seda r. Latvia 42 G4
Seda Lith. 42 D5
Seda r. Port. 54 C6
Sedalia U.S.A. 178 D4
Sedam India 94 C2
Sedan France 51 K3
Sedan U.S.A. 178 C4
Sedan Dip Australia 149 D3
Seddon N.Z. 153 I9
Seddonville N.Z. 153 F9
Sedeh *Fārs* Iran 100 C4
Sedeh *Khorāsan* Iran 101 D3
Sedgefield U.S.A. 176 F9
Sedgewick Canada 167 I4
Sedgwick U.S.A. 177 Q1
Sédhiou Senegal 124 B3
Sedico Italy 56 E2
Sedlčany Czech Rep. 49 L6
Sedlets Poland *see* Siedlce
Sedom Israel 108 G6
Sedona U.S.A. 183 M7
Sédrata Alg. 123 G1
Šeduva Lith. 42 E6
Sędziszów Poland 49 R5
Seeberg *pass* Austria/Slovenia 49 L9
Seehausen (Altmark) Germany 48 I3
Seeheim Namibia 130 C5
Seeheim-Jugenheim Germany 48 F6
Seekoegat S. Africa 132 G10
Seekoei r. S. Africa 133 I7
Seekoevlei Nature Reserve S. Africa 133 N4
Seela Pass Canada 166 B1
Seeley U.S.A. 183 I9
Seelig, Mount Antarctica 222 R1
Seelow Germany 49 L3
Seenu Atoll Maldives *see* Addu Atoll
Sées France 50 G4
Seesen Germany 48 H4
Seevetal Germany 48 H2
Sefadu Sierra Leone 124 C4
also known as Koidu
Seferihisar Turkey 59 H10
Sefid, Küh-e *mt.* Iran 100 B3
Sefid, Küh-e *mts* Iran 100 B4
Sefophe Botswana 131 E4
Ségala Mali 124 C3
Segalstad Norway 45 J3
Segama r. *Sabah* Malaysia 77 G1
Segamat Malaysia 76 C2
Segangane Morocco 55 H9
Şegarcea Romania 58 E4
Ségbana Benin 125 F4
Segen Wenz *watercourse* Eth. 128 C3
Segera Tanz. 129 C6
Segezha Rus. Fed. 40 E3
Seggeur, Oued *watercourse* Alg. 123 F2
Seghnān Afgh. 101 G2
Seghouane Alg. 55 N8
Segiz, Ozera *salt l.* Kazakh. 103 F3
Segontia U.K. *see* Caernarfon
Segontium U.K. *see* Caernarfon
Segonzac France 50 F7
Segorbe Spain 55 K5
Ségou Mali 124 D3
Ségou *admin. reg.* Mali 124 D3
Segovia Col. 198 C3
Segovia r. Hond./Nicaragua *see* Coco
Segovia Spain 54 G4
UNESCO World Heritage Site
Segozerskoye, Ozero *resr* Rus. Fed. 40 E3
Segré France 50 F5
Segre r. Spain 55 L3
Séguédine Niger 125 I1
Séguéla Côte d'Ivoire 124 D5
Séguéla Mali 124 D3
formerly spelt Sagala
Séguénéga Burkina 125 E3
Seguin U.S.A. 179 C6
Segura r. Spain 55 K6
Segura, Sierra de *mts* Spain 55 I7
Sehithwa Botswana 130 D4
Sehlabathebe Lesotho 133 N6
Sehlabathebe National Park Lesotho 133 N6
Seho i. Indon. 75 C3
Sehore India 96 C5
Sehwan Pak. 101 F5
Seiche r. France 50 E5
Seignelay r. Canada 169 G3
Seikphyu Myanmar 78 A3
Seiland i. Norway 44 M1
Seiling U.S.A. 179 C4
Seille r. France 51 K6
Seille r. France 51 M3
Šeimena r. Lith. 42 D7
Sein, Île de i. France 50 B4
Seinäjoki Fin. 44 M3
Seine r. Canada 168 B3
Seine r. France 51 G3
Seine, Baie de b. France 50 F3
Seine, Sources de la *tourist site* France 51 K5
Seine, Val de *valley* France 51 J4
Seipinang Indon. 77 F3
Seistan *reg.* Iran *see* Sīstān
Seitsemisen kansallispuisto *nat. park* Fin. 45 M3
Seival Brazil 204 G3
Sejny Poland 49 U1
Sekadau Indon. 77 E2
Sekanak, Teluk b. Indon. 76 D3
Sekatak Bengara Indon. 77 G2
Sekayu Indon. 76 C3
Sekčov r. Slovakia 49 S7
Seke China *see* Sêrtar
Seke-Banza Dem. Rep. Congo 127 B6
Sekhukhune S. Africa 133 O1
Seki Japan 91 E7
Seki Turkey 108 A1
Seki r. Turkey 108 A1
Sekicau, Gunung *vol.* Indon. 76 D4
Sekoma Botswana 131 D5
Sekondi Ghana 125 E5
Sek'ot'a Eth. 128 C1
Sękowa Poland 49 S6
UNESCO World Heritage Site
Sekseüil Kazakh. *see* Saksaul'skiy
Seküheh Iran 101 E4
Şela Rus. Fed. *see* Shali
Selagan r. Indon. 76 C3
Selah U.S.A. 180 B3
Selangor *state* Malaysia 76 C2
Selargius *Sardinia* Italy 57 B9
Selaru i. Indon. 73 H8
Selatan, Tanjung *pt* Indon. 77 F4
Selat Makassar *strait* Indon. 75 A2
also spelt Macassar Strait
Selatpanjang Indon. 76 C2
Selawik U.S.A. 164 C3
Selbjørnsfjorden *sea chan.* Norway 46 Q4
Selbu Norway 44 J3
Selby U.K. 47 K10
Selby U.S.A. 178 B2
Selbyville U.S.A. 177 J7
Selçuk Turkey 59 I11
also known as Akıncılar
Sele r. Italy 57 G8
Selebi-Phikwe Botswana 131 E4
formerly spelt Selebi-Pikwe
Selebi-Pikwe Botswana *see* Selebi-Phikwe
Selečka Planina *mts* Macedonia 58 C7
Selemdzha r. Rus. Fed. 82 C1
Selemdzhinskiy Khrebet *mts* Rus. Fed. 82 D1
Selendi Turkey 59 J10
Selenduma Rus. Fed. 85 E1

►Selenga r. Rus. Fed. 85 E1
Part of the Yenisey-Angara-Selenga, 3rd longest river in Asia.
►►60–61 Asia Landscapes

Selenge Dem. Rep. Congo 126 C5
Selenge Mongolia 84 D1
Selenge *prov.* Mongolia 85 E1
Selenge Mörön r. Mongolia 85 E1
Selenginsk Rus. Fed. 85 E1
Selenicë Albania 58 A8
Sélestat France 51 N4
Seletar Sing. 76 [inset]
Seletar, Pulau i. Sing. 76 [inset]
Seletar Reservoir Sing. 76 [inset]
Seletinskoye Kazakh. 103 H1
also known as Sileti
Selety r. Kazakh. *see* Sileti
Seletyteniz, Ozero *salt l.* Kazakh. *see* Siletiteniz, Ozero
Seleucia Turkey *see* Silifke
Seleucia Pieria Turkey *see* Samandağı
Seleznevo Rus. Fed. 43 J1
Selezni Rus. Fed. 43 M6
Selfoss Iceland 44 [inset] B3
Sel'gon Stantsiya Rus. Fed. 82 D2
Selib Rus. Fed. 40 I3
Sélibabi Mauritania 124 B3
Seligenstadt Germany 48 F5
Seliger, Ozero l. Rus. Fed. 43 O4
Seligman U.S.A. 183 L6
Selikhino Rus. Fed. 82 E2
Selîma Oasis Sudan 121 F4
Selimiye Turkey 59 I11
Sélingué, Lac de l. Mali 124 C4
Selinnkegni Mali 124 C3
Selinous r. Greece 59 D10
Selinsgrove U.S.A. 177 I5
Selinunte *tourist site Sicily* Italy 57 E11
Selishche Rus. Fed. 43 O5
Selishchi Rus. Fed. 41 G5
Selitrennoye Rus. Fed. 102 A3
Seliu i. Indon. 77 D3
Selizharovo Rus. Fed. 43 O5
Selje Norway 44 I3
Seljord Norway 45 J4
Selkirk Canada 167 L5
Selkirk U.K. 46 J8
Selkirk Mountains Canada 167 G4
Selkopp Norway 44 N1
Sellia Marina Italy 57 I10
Sellore Island Myanmar *see* Saganthit Kyun
Selma *AL* U.S.A. 175 C5
Selma *CA* U.S.A. 182 E5
Selmer U.S.A. 174 B5
Selmęt Wielki, Jezioro l. Poland 49 T2
Selong Indon. 77 G5
Selongey France 51 L5
Selonsrivier S. Africa 133 N2
Sélouma Guinea 124 C4
Selous, Mount Canada 166 C2
Selous Game Reserve *nature res.* Tanz. 129 C7
UNESCO World Heritage Site
Selseleh-ye Pīr Shūrān *mts* Iran 101 E4
Selsey Bill *hd* U.K. 47 L13
Sel'tso *Bryanskaya Oblast'* Rus. Fed. 43 P8
Sel'tso *Bryanskaya Oblast'* Rus. Fed. 43 P8
Selty Rus. Fed. 40 J4
Seluan i. Indon. 77 D1
Selukwe Zimbabwe *see* Shurugwi
Selvagens, Ilhas is Madeira 122 B3
Selvänä Iran 100 A2
Selvas *reg.* Brazil 199 D6
Selviria Brazil 206 B7
Selway r. U.S.A. 180 D3
Selwyn Lake Canada 167 J2
Selwyn Mountains Canada 166 D1
Selwyn Range *hills* Australia 149 C4
Seman r. Albania 58 A8
Semangka, Teluk b. Indon. 76 D4
Semarang Indon. 77 E4
Sematan *Sarawak* Malaysia 77 E2
Semau i. Indon. 75 B5
Semayang, Danau l. Indon. 77 G3
Sembakung r. Indon. 77 G2
Sembawang Sing. 76 [inset]
Sembawang, Sungai r. Sing. 76 [inset]
Sembé Congo 126 B4
Şemdinli Turkey 107 F3
also known as Navşar
Semendire *Srbija* Serb. and Mont. *see* Smederevo
Semendua Dem. Rep. Congo 126 C5
Semendyayevo Rus. Fed. 43 T4
Semenic, Vârful *mt.* Romania 58 D3
Semenivka Ukr. 41 E5
also spelt Semenovka
Semenov Rus. Fed. 40 H4
Semenovka Ukr. *see* Semenivka
Semenovskoye Rus. Fed. 43 U3
Semeru, Gunung *vol.* Indon. 77 F5
Semey Kazakh. *see* Semipalatinsk
Semibratovo Rus. Fed. 43 U4
Semidi Islands U.S.A. 164 D4
Semigorodnyaya Rus. Fed. 43 V2
Semikarakorsk Rus. Fed. 41 G7
Semiluki Rus. Fed. 41 F6
Semily Czech Rep. 49 M5
Seminoe Reservoir U.S.A. 180 F4
Seminole U.S.A. 179 B5
Seminole, Lake U.S.A. 175 C6
Semipalatinsk Kazakh. 103 J2
also known as Semey
Semirara i. Phil. 74 B3
Semirara Islands Phil. 74 B4
Semīrom Iran 100 B4
Semitau Indon. 77 E2
Semiyarka Kazakh. 103 I2
Semizbuga Kazakh. 103 H2
also known as Semizbughy
Semizbughy Kazakh. *see* Semizbuga
Semkhoz Rus. Fed. 43 T5
Sem Kolodezey Ukr. *see* Lenine
Semlac Romania 58 B2
Semlevo *Smolenskaya Oblast'* Rus. Fed. 43 O6
Semlevo *Smolenskaya Oblast'* Rus. Fed. 43 O6
Semmering *pass* Austria 49 M8
UNESCO World Heritage Site
Semnān Iran 100 C3
Semnān *prov.* Iran 100 B3
Sêmnyi China 84 D4
Semois r. Belgium 51 K3
Semonkong Lesotho 133 M6
Sempach Switz. 51 O5
Semporna *Sabah* Malaysia 77 G1
Sempu i. Indon. 77 F5
Sem Tripa Brazil 199 H6
Semtsy Rus. Fed. 43 O9
Semyonovskoye *Arkhangel'skaya Oblast'* Rus. Fed. *see* Bereznik
Semyonovskoye *Kostromskaya Oblast'* Rus. Fed. *see* Ostrovskoye
Sên, Stœng r. Cambodia 79 D5
Sena Bol. 200 D2
Senador Canedo Brazil 206 D3
Senador Pompeu Brazil 202 E3
Senafe Eritrea 104 B5
Senaki Georgia 107 E2
formerly known as Mikha Tskhakaia *or* Tskhakaia
Sena Madureira Brazil 200 C2
Senanayake Samudra l. Sri Lanka 94 D5
Senanga Zambia 127 D9
Sénas France 51 L9
Senatobia U.S.A. 174 B5
Sendai *Kagoshima* Japan 91 B9
Sendai *Miyagi* Japan 90 G5
Sendai-wan b. Japan 90 G5
Sendelingsfontein S. Africa 133 K3
Senden Germany 48 H7
Şendreni Romania 58 I3
Sene r. Ghana 125 E5
Senebui, Tanjung *pt* Indon. 76 C2
Seneca *IL* U.S.A. 172 E9
Seneca *KS* U.S.A. 178 C4
Seneca *OR* U.S.A. 180 C3
Seneca *PA* U.S.A. 176 F4
Seneca Lake U.S.A. 177 I3
Seneca Rocks U.S.A. 176 F7
Senecaville Lake U.S.A. 176 D6
►Senegal *country* Africa 124 B3
►►8–9 World Countries
►►114–115 Africa Countries
Sénégal r. Mauritania/Senegal 124 A2
Seneka, Mys *hd* Rus. Fed. 82 E1
Senekal S. Africa 133 L5
Seney National Wildlife Refuge *nature res.* U.S.A. 172 G4
Senftenberg Germany 49 L4
Senga Malawi 129 B8
Senga Hill Zambia 127 F7
Sengar r. India 96 C4
Sengata Indon. 77 G2
Sengerema Tanz. 128 B5
Sengés Brazil 206 D11
Sengeyskiy, Ostrov i. Rus. Fed. 40 I1
Sengiley Rus. Fed. 41 I5
Sengirli, Mys *pt* Kazakh. *see* Syngyrli, Mys
Sêngli Co l. China 89 D6
Senguerr r. Arg. 205 C7
Sengwa r. Zimbabwe 131 F3
Senhor do Bonfim Brazil 202 D4
Senica Slovakia 49 O7
Senigallia Italy 56 F5
Senj Croatia 56 G4
Senja i. Norway 44 L1
Senjehopen Norway 44 L1
Şenkaya Turkey 107 E2
also known as Örtülü
Senko Guinea 124 C4
Senkobo Zambia 127 E9
Sen'kove Ukr. 41 F6
Sen'kovo Rus. Fed. 43 L6
Şenköy Turkey 108 H1
Senlac S. Africa 132 H2
Senlin Shan *mt.* China 82 C4
Senlis France 51 I3
Senmonorom Cambodia 79 D5
Sennar Sudan 121 G6
Sennar *state* Sudan 121 G6
Senneterre Canada 168 E3
Senno Belarus *see* Syanno
Senonches France 50 H4
Senorbì *Sardinia* Italy 57 B9
Senqu r. Lesotho 133 L7
Sens France 51 J4
Sensuntepeque El Salvador 185 H6
Senta *Vojvodina, Srbija* Serb. and Mont. 58 B3
also spelt Zenta
Sentinel Peak Canada 166 F4
Sentinel Range *mts* Antarctica 222 S1
Sentinum Italy *see* Sassoferrato
Sentosa i. Sing. 76 [inset]
formerly known as Blakang Mati, Pulau
Şenyurt Turkey 107 E3
also known as Derbesiye
Seo de Urgell Spain *see* La Seu d'Urgell
Seonath r. India 97 D5
Seondha India 96 C4
Seoni India 96 C5
Seoni Chhapara India 96 C5
Seoni-Malwa India 96 C5

►Seoul S. Korea 83 B5
Capital of South Korea. Also spelt Sŏul.
UNESCO World Heritage Site
►►18–19 World Cities

Séoune r. France 50 G8
Sepanjang i. Indon. 77 F4
Separation Point N.Z. 152 G8
Separation Well Australia 150 C4
Separ Shāhābād Iran 100 A3
Sepasu Indon. 77 G2
Sepatini r. Brazil 200 D1
Sepetiba, Baía de b. Brazil 207 I10
Sepik r. P.N.G. 73 J7
Sepinang Indon. 77 G2
Sepino Italy 56 G7
Sep'o N. Korea 83 B5
Sępólno Krajeńskie Poland 49 O2
Sepotuba r. Brazil 201 F3
Seppa India 97 G4
Şepreuş Romania 58 C2
Septèmes-les-Vallons France 51 L9
Sept-Îles Canada 169 H3
also known as Seven Islands
Sept-Îles-Port-Cartier, Réserve Faunique de *nature res.* Canada 169 H3
Sepupa Botswana 130 D3
Seputih r. Indon. 77 D4
Sequillo r. Spain 54 F3
Sequoia National Park U.S.A. 182 F5
Serafimovich Rus. Fed. 41 G6
Sêraitang China *see* Baima
Seram i. Indon. 75 D3
English form Ceram
Seram Sea Indon. 75 D3
English form Ceram Sea
Serang Indon. 77 D4
Serangoon, Pulau i. Sing. 76 [inset]
also known as Coney Island
Serangoon, Sungai r. Sing. 76 [inset]
Serangoon Harbour b. Sing. 76 [inset]
Serapong, Mount *hill* Sing. 76 [inset]
Serasan i. Indon. 77 E2
Serasan, Selat *sea chan.* Indon. 77 E2
Seraya i. Indon. 77 E2
Serbia *aut. rep.* Serb. and Mont. *see* Srbija
►Serbia and Montenegro *country* Europe 58 B5
spelt Srbija i Crna Gora in Serbian. Formerly known as Yugoslavia.
►►32–33 Europe Countries
Sêrbug Co l. China 89 E5
Sêrca China 97 G3
Serdar Turkm. 102 D5
formerly spelt Kizyl-Arbat
Serdica Bulg. *see* Sofia
Serdo Eth. 128 D2
Serdoba r. Rus. Fed. 41 H5
Serdobsk Rus. Fed. 41 H5
Serebryanka Rus. Fed. 40 J3
Serebryansk Kazakh. 88 C1
Serebryanyye Prudy Rus. Fed. 43 T7
Sered' Slovakia 49 O7
Sereda *Moskovskaya Oblast'* Rus. Fed. 43 Q6
Sereda *Yaroslavskaya Oblast'* Rus. Fed. 43 V4
Seredeyskiy Rus. Fed. 43 Q7
Seredka Rus. Fed. 43 J3
Serednikovo Rus. Fed. 43 U6
Seredniy Kuyal'nyk r. Ukr. 58 L2
Seredyna-Buda Rus. Fed. 43 P9
Seredyne Ukr. 49 T7
Şereflikoçhisar Turkey 106 C3
Serein r. France 51 J5
Seremban Malaysia 76 C2
Serena, Embalse de la *resr* Spain 54 F6
Serengeti National Park Tanz. 128 B5
UNESCO World Heritage Site
Serengeti Plain Tanz. 128 B5
Serenje Zambia 127 F8
Serere Uganda 128 B4
Serezha r. Rus. Fed. 40 G5
Serezha r. Rus. Fed. 43 L5
Sergach Rus. Fed. 40 H5
Sergeikha Rus. Fed. 43 V5
Sergelen *Dornod* Mongolia 85 G1
Sergelen *Sühbaatar* Mongolia 85 F2
Sergen Turkey 58 I7
Sergeyevka Rus. Fed. 90 C3
Sergeyevka *Akmolinskaya Oblast'* Kazakh. 103 G2
Sergeyevka *Severnyy Kazakhstan* Kazakh. 103 F1
Sergino Rus. Fed. 38 G3
Sergipe *state* Brazil 202 E4
Sergiyev Posad Rus. Fed. 43 T5
formerly known as Zagorsk
UNESCO World Heritage Site
Sergiyevskiy Rus. Fed. *see* Fakel
Sergiyevskoye Rus. Fed. 43 S9
Sergo Ukr. *see* Stakhanov
Serhiyivka Ukr. 58 L2
Seria Brunei 77 F1
Serian *Sarawak* Malaysia 77 E2
Seribu, Kepulauan *is* Indon. 77 D4
Seribudolok Indon. 76 B2
Serifos Greece 59 F11
Serifos i. Greece 59 F11
Serifou, Steno *sea chan.* Greece 59 F11
Sérignan France 51 J9
Sérigny r. Canada 169 G2
Sérigny, Lac l. Canada 169 G2
Serik Turkey 106 B3
Serikbuya China 88 B4
Serikkembelo Indon. 75 C3
Sèrinama Madag. 131 [inset] J3
Seringa, Serra da *hills* Brazil 199 I6
Seringapatam Reef *reef* Australia 150 C2
Serinhisar Turkey 59 K11
Serio r. Italy 56 B3
Serio, Parco del *park* Italy 56 B3
Sêrkang China *see* Nyainrong
Sermata i. Indon. 75 D5
Sermata, Kepulauan *is* Indon. 75 D5
Sermersuaq *glacier* Greenland 165 M2
also known as Humboldt Gletscher
Sermersuaq *glacier* Greenland 165 N2
also known as Steenstrup Gletscher
Sērmūkši Latvia 42 G4
Sernovodsk Rus. Fed. 41 I5
Sernur Rus. Fed. 40 I4
Sernyy Zavod Turkm. *see* Kükürtli
Serón Spain 55 I7
Seronga Botswana 130 D3
Serouenout *well* Alg. 123 G4
Serov Rus. Fed. 38 G4
Serowe Botswana 131 E4
Serpa Port. 54 D7
Serpa Pinto Angola *see* Menongue
Serpent r. Canada 169 G3
Serpent, Vallée du *watercourse* Mali 124 C3
Serpentine r. Australia 151 A7
Serpentine Lakes *salt flat* Australia 146 A2
Serpent's Mouth *sea chan.* Trin. and Tob./Venez. 187 H5
Serpeysk Rus. Fed. 43 Q7
Serpis r. Spain 55 K6
Serpneve Ukr. 58 K2
Serpukhov Rus. Fed. 43 S7
Serra Brazil 203 D7
Serra Bonita Brazil 206 G2
Serra da Bocaina, Parque Nacional da *nat. park* Brazil 203 C7
Serra da Canastra, Parque Nacional da *nat. park* Brazil 206 G7
Serra da Capivara, Parque Nacional da *nat. park* Brazil 202 D4
UNESCO World Heritage Site
Serra da Estrela, Parque Natural da *nature res.* Port. 54 D4
Serra da Mesa, Represa *resr* Brazil 202 B5
Serra da Mociade, Parque Nacional da *nat. park* Brazil 199 F4
Serra das Araras Brazil 207 H2
Serra das Confusões, Parque Nacional da *nat. park* Brazil 202 D3
Serradilla Spain 54 E5
Serra do Divisor, Parque Nacional da *nat. park* Brazil 200 B2
Serra do Navio Brazil 199 H4
Serra dos Aimorés Brazil 207 M4
Serra do Salitre Brazil 206 G6
Sérrai Greece *see* Serres
Serramanna *Sardinia* Italy 57 A9
Serrana Brazil 206 F8
Serrana Bank *sea feature* Caribbean Sea 186 C4
Serranía de la Neblina, Parque Nacional *nat. park* Venez. 199 E4
Serranilla Bank *sea feature* Caribbean Sea 186 D4
Serrano i. Chile 205 B8
Serranópolis Brazil 206 A5
Serraria, Ilha i. Brazil *see* Queimada, Ilha
Serra San Bruno Italy 57 I10
Serras de Aire e Candeeiros, Parque Natural das *nature res.* Port. 54 C5
Serra Talhada Brazil 202 E3
Serravalle Scrivia Italy 56 A4
Serre r. France 51 J3
Serres Greece 58 E7
also known as Sérrai
Serrezuela Arg. 204 D3
Serrinha Brazil 202 E4
Serrita Brazil 202 E3
Sêrro Brazil 203 D6
Serrota *mt.* Spain 54 F4
Sers Tunisia 57 A12
Sersou, Plateau du Alg. 55 M9
Sertã Port. 54 C5
Sertânia Brazil 202 E4
Sertanópolis Brazil 206 B10
Sertão de Camapuã *reg.* Brazil 206 A6
Sertãozinho Brazil 206 F8
Sêrtar China 86 B1
also known as Seke
Sertavul Geçidi *pass* Turkey 108 E1
Sertolovo Rus. Fed. 43 L1
Serua *vol.* Indon. 75 D4
Serui Indon. 73 I7
Serule Botswana 131 E4
Serutu i. Indon. 77 E3
Seruyan r. Indon. 77 F3
Servach r. Belarus 42 I7
Servia Greece 59 D8
Serwaru Indon. 75 C5
Sêrwolungwa China 84 B5
also known as Yiggêtang
Sêrxü China 86 A1
also known as Nixia
Sesayap Indon. 77 G2
Sesayap r. Indon. 77 G2
Sese Dem. Rep. Congo 126 E4
Sesekinika Canada 173 M2
Sesel *country* Indian Ocean *see* Seychelles
Sesepe Indon. 75 C3
Sesfontein Namibia 130 B3
Seshachalam Hills India 94 C3
Seshcha Rus. Fed. 43 O8
Sesheke Zambia 127 E9
Sesia r. Italy 56 A3
Seskar Furö i. Sweden 44 M2
Seskio i. Greece 59 I12
Sesostris Bank *sea feature* India 94 A3
S'Espalmador i. Spain 55 M6
also known as Espalmador, Isla
Sessa Angola 127 D8
Sestra r. Rus. Fed. 43 S5
Sestri Levante Italy 56 B4
Sestroretsk Rus. Fed. 43 K1
Sestrunj i. Croatia 56 G4
Sestu *Sardinia* Italy 57 B9
Šešupė r. Lith./Rus. Fed. 42 D6
Sesvete Croatia 56 I3
Set r. Spain 55 L3
Set, Phou *mt.* Laos 79 D5
Sète France 51 J9
Sete Barras Brazil 206 F11
Šetekšna r. Lith. 42 G6
Sete Lagoas Brazil 203 C6
Setermoen Norway 44 L1
Setesdal *valley* Norway 45 I4
Seti r. Nepal 97 D3
Seti r. Nepal 97 E4
Setia Italy *see* Sezze
Sétif Alg. 123 G1
also spelt Stif
Setit r. Africa 121 H6
Seto Japan 91 E7
Seto-naikai *sea* Japan 91 C8
English form Inland Sea
Seto-naikai National Park Japan 91 C7
Setsan Myanmar 78 A4
Settat Morocco 122 D2
Setté Cama Gabon 126 A5
Settepani, Monte *mt.* Italy 56 A4
Settimo Torinese Italy 51 N7
Settle U.K. 47 J9
Settlement Creek r. Australia 148 C3
Settlers S. Africa 133 M1
Setúbal r. Brazil 207 K3
Setúbal Port. 54 C6
Setúbal *admin. dist.* Port. 54 C6
Setúbal, Baía de b. Port. 54 B6
Setubinha Brazil 207 K4
Seugne r. France 50 F7
Seul, Lac l. Canada 168 A3

Seurre France 51 L5
Sev r. Rus. Fed. 43 P9
Sevan Armenia 107 F2
Sevan, Lake Armenia 107 F2
also known as Sevan, Ozero or Sevana Lich
Sevan, Ozero l. Armenia see Sevan, Lake
Sevana Lich l. Armenia see Sevan, Lake
Sevaruyo Bol. 200 D4
Sevastopol' Ukr. 41 E7
English form Sebastopol
Seven Islands Canada see Sept-Îles
Sevenoaks S. Africa 133 O6
Sevenoaks U.K. 47 M12
Seventeen Seventy Australia 149 F5
Seventy Mile House Canada see 70 Mile House
Sévérac-le-Château France 51 J8
Severino Ribeiro Brazil 204 G3
Severka r. Rus. Fed. 43 T6
Severn r. Australia 147 F2
Severn r. Canada 168 C2
Severn mt. N.Z. 153 H10
Severn S. Africa 132 G3
Severn r. U.K. 47 J12
Severn U.S.A. 177 H9
Severnaya Dvina r. Rus. Fed. 40 G2
English form Northern Dvina
Severnaya Mylva r. Rus. Fed. 40 K3
Severnaya Osetiya-Alaniya, Respublika aut. rep. Rus. Fed. 41 H8
English form North Ossetia; formerly known as Severo-Osetinskaya A.S.S.R.
Severnaya Sos'va r. Rus. Fed. 38 G3
Severnaya Zemlya is Rus. Fed. 39 K2
English form North Land
Severn Lake Canada 168 B2
Severnoye Rus. Fed. 41 J5
formerly known as Sol-Karmala
Severn River Provincial Park Canada 168 B2
Severnyy Moskovskaya Oblast' Rus. Fed. 43 S5
Severnyy Nenetskiy Avtonomnyy Okrug Rus. Fed. 40 I1
Severnyy Respublika Komi Rus. Fed. 40 M2
Severnyy Anyuyskiy Khrebet mts Rus. Fed. 39 R3
Severnyy Berezovyy, Ostrov i. Rus. Fed. 43 J1
Severnyy Chink Ustyurta esc. Kazakh. 102 D3
Severnyy Kazakhstan admin. div. Kazakh. 103 G1
English form North Kazakhstan Oblast; also known as Soltüstik Qazaqstan Oblysy; long form Severo-Kazakhstanskaya Oblast'
Severnyy Kommunar Rus. Fed. 40 J4
Severnyy Suchan Rus. Fed. see Uglekamensk
Severnyy Ural mts Rus. Fed. 40 K3
Severobaykal'sk Rus. Fed. 81 H1
Severo-Baykal'skoye Nagor'ye mts Rus. Fed. 81 I1
Severodonetsk Ukr. see Syeverodonets'k
Severodvinsk Rus. Fed. 40 F2
formerly known as Molotovsk
Severo-Kazakhstanskaya Oblast' admin. div. Kazakh. see Severnyy Kazakhstan
Severo-Kuril'sk Rus. Fed. 39 P4
Severomorsk Rus. Fed. 44 P1
formerly known as Vayenga
Severoonezhsk Rus. Fed. 40 F3
Severo-Osetinskaya A.S.S.R. aut. rep. Rus. Fed. see Severnaya Osetiya-Alaniya, Respublika
Severo-Sibirskaya Nizmennost' lowland Rus. Fed. see North Siberian Lowland
Severoural'sk Rus. Fed. 40 K3
Severo-Yeniseyskiy Rus. Fed. 39 J3
Severo-Zadonsk Rus. Fed. 43 T7
Severskaya Rus. Fed. 107 D1
Severskiy Donets r. Rus. Fed./Ukr. 41 G7
English form Northern Donets; also spelt Sivers'kyy Donets'
Seveso Italy 56 B3
Sevettijärvi Fin. 44 O1
also spelt Čevetjävri
Sevier U.S.A. 183 L3
Sevier r. U.S.A. 183 L2
Sevier Bridge Reservoir U.S.A. 183 M2
Sevier Desert U.S.A. 183 L2
Sevier Lake U.S.A. 183 K3
Sevierville U.S.A. 174 D5
Sevilla Col. 198 C3
Sevilla Spain see Seville
Seville Spain 54 F7
also spelt Sevilla; historically known as Hispalis
UNESCO World Heritage Site
Sevlievo Bulg. 58 G5
Sevnica Slovenia 56 H2
Sevojno Srbija Serb. and Mont. 58 A5
Sèvre Nantaise r. France 50 E5
Sevsk Rus. Fed. 43 P9
Sewand r. India 94 B2
Sewani India 96 B3
Seward AK U.S.A. 164 E3
Seward IL U.S.A. 172 D8
Seward NE U.S.A. 178 C3
Seward PA U.S.A. 176 F5
Seward Mountains Antarctica 222 T2
Seward Peninsula U.S.A. 164 C3
Sewell Chile 204 C4
Sewell Inlet Canada 166 C4
Sexi Spain see Almuñécar
Sexsmith Canada 166 G4
Sextín Mex. 184 D3
Sextín r. Mex. 184 D3
Seyah Band Koh mts Afgh. 101 E3
Seyakha Rus. Fed. 38 H2
Seybaplaya Mex. 185 H5
►Seychelles country Indian Ocean 218 K6
also spelt Sesel
►►114–115 Africa Countries
Seydi Turkm. 103 E5
formerly known as Neftezavodsk
Seydişehir Turkey 106 B3
Seyðisfjörður Iceland 44 [inset] D2
Seyfe Gölü salt flat Turkey 106 C3
Seyhan Turkey see Adana
Seyhan r. Turkey 106 C3
Seyitgazi Turkey 106 B3
Seyitömer Turkey 59 K9
Seym r. Rus. Fed./Ukr. 41 E6
Seymchan Rus. Fed. 39 P3
Seymour Australia 147 E4
Seymour S. Africa 133 K9
Seymour IN U.S.A. 174 C4
Seymour TX U.S.A. 179 C5
Seymour Inlet Canada 166 E5
Seymour Range mts Australia 148 B5
Seynod France 51 M7
Seypan i. N. Mariana Is see Saipan
Seytan r. Turkey 58 I7
Seyyedābād Afgh. 101 G3
Sežana Slovenia 56 F3
Sézanne France 51 J4
Sezela S. Africa 133 O7
Sezha r. Rus. Fed. 43 P6
Sezze Italy 56 F7
historically known as Setia
Sfakia Greece 59 F13
Sfântu Gheorghe Romania 58 G3
formerly spelt Sfîntu Gheorghe
Sfântu Gheorghe Romania 58 K4
Sfântu Gheorghe, Brațul watercourse Romania 58 K3
Sfântu Gheorghe-Palade-Perișor nature res. Romania 58 K4
Sfax Tunisia 123 H2
also spelt Aş Şafāqis
Sfendami Greece 59 D8
Sfîntu Gheorghe Romania see Sfântu Gheorghe
Sfizef Alg. 55 K9
Sgiersch Poland see Zgierz
's-Gravenhage Neth. see The Hague
Sgurr Alasdair hill U.K. 46 F6
Sgurr Mòr mt. U.K. 46 G6
Sgurr na Ciche mt. U.K. 46 G6
Shaanxi prov. China 87 D1
English form Shensi
Shaartuz Tajik. see Shahrtuz
Shaba prov. Dem. Rep. Congo see Katanga
Shābah Egypt 108 B6
Shabani Zimbabwe see Zvishavane
Shabbaz Uzbek. see Beruniy
Shabeellaha Dhexe admin. reg. Somalia 128 E4
Shabeellaha Hoose admin. reg. Somalia 128 D4
Shabestar Iran 100 A2
Shabla Bulg. 58 J5
Shabla, Nos pt Bulg. 58 J5
Shablykino Rus. Fed. 43 Q9
Shabogamo Lake Canada 169 H2
Shabunda Dem. Rep. Congo 126 E5
Shabwah Yemen 105 D5
Shabwah governorate Yemen 105 D5
Shacha r. Rus. Fed. 43 V3
Shache China 88 B4
formerly known as Yarkand or Yarkant
Shacheng China see Huailai
Shackleton Coast Antarctica 223 L1
Shackleton Glacier Antarctica 223 M1
Shackleton Ice Shelf Antarctica 223 G2
Shackleton Range mts Antarctica 223 V1
Shadād Saudi Arabia 104 C3
Shadadkot Pak. 101 F5
Shadaogou China 87 D2
Shade U.S.A. 176 C6
Shādegān Iran 100 B4
Shādkām watercourse Iran 100 C4
Shadrinsk Rus. Fed. 38 G4
Shadwān Island Egypt see Shākir, Gezîret
Shadwell U.S.A. 176 G7
Shady Grove U.S.A. 180 B4
Shady Spring U.S.A. 176 D8
Sha'fāt al Bashīr hill Syria 109 K2
Shafer, Lake U.S.A. 172 G10
Shafer Peak Antarctica 223 K2
Shafi'abad Iran 100 D2
Shafirkan Uzbek. see Shofirkon
Shafranovo Rus. Fed. 40 J5
Shafrikan Uzbek. see Shofirkon
Shafter U.S.A. 182 E6
Shaftesbury U.K. 47 J12
Shag r. N.Z. 153 E13
Shagamu r. Canada 168 C2
Shagamu Nigeria 125 F5
also spelt Sagamu
Shagan watercourse Kazakh. 102 D3
Shagan watercourse Kazakh. 103 I2
Shagedu China 85 F4
also known as Jungar Qi
Shaghab oasis Saudi Arabia 104 B2
Shaghan Kazakh. see Chagan
Shaghyray Üstirti plat. Kazakh. see Shagyray, Plato
Shag'irlik Uzbek. 102 D4
Shagonar Respublika Tyva Rus. Fed. 84 B1
Shagonar Respublika Tyva Rus. Fed. 84 B1
Shag Point N.Z. 153 E13
Shag Rocks is S. Georgia 217 L9
Shagyray, Plato plat. Kazakh. 102 D3
also known as Shaghyray Üstirti; formerly known as Chagrayskoye Plato
Shahabad Andhra Pradesh India 94 C2
Shahabad Haryana India 96 C3
Shahabad Karnataka India 94 C2
Shahabad Rajasthan India 96 C4
Shahabad Uttar Pradesh India 96 D4
Shāhābād Iran see Eslāmābād-e Gharb
Shahada India 96 B5
Shah Alam Malaysia 76 C2
Shahana Pak. 101 E5
Shahapur Karnataka India 94 B3
Shahapur Maharashtra India 94 B2
Shahbā' Syria 109 H5
Shahbazpur sea chan. Bangl. 97 F5
Shahdād Iran 100 D4
also known as Khabis
Shahdadpur Pak. 101 G5
Shahdol India 97 D5
Shahe Chongqing China 87 D2
Shahe Shandong China 85 H4
Sha He r. China 85 G4
Shahejie China see Jiujiang
Shahepu China see Linze
Shahezhen Gansu China see Linze
Shahezhen Jiangxi China see Jiujiang
Shah Fuladi mt. Afgh. 101 F3
Shahganj India 97 D4
Shahgarh Madhya Pradesh India 96 C4
Shahgarh Rajasthan India 96 A4
Shaḥḥāt Libya 120 D1
Shāhīn Dezh Iran see Sa'īndezh
Shah Ismail Afgh. 101 F4
Shahjahanpur India 96 C4
Shāh Jehān, Kūh-e mts Iran 100 D2
Shāh Jūy Afgh. 101 F3
Shāh Kūh mt. Iran 101 D4
Shahpur Karnataka India 94 C2
Shahpur Madhya Pradesh India 96 C5
Shahpur Madhya Pradesh India 96 C5
Shahpur Madhya Pradesh India 96 C5
Shāhpūr Iran see Salmās
Shahpur Balochistān Pak. 101 G4
Shahpur Punjab Pak. 101 H3
Shahpur Sindh Pak. 101 G5
Shahpura Madhya Pradesh India 96 C5
Shahpura Madhya Pradesh India 96 D5
Shahpura Rajasthan India 96 B4
Shahr oasis Saudi Arabia 105 E4
Shahrak Afgh. 101 F3
Shāhrakht Iran 101 E3
Shahrān reg. Saudi Arabia 104 C4
Shahr-e Bābak Iran 100 C4
Shahr-e Kord Iran 100 B3
Shahr-e Now Iran 101 E3
Shahrezā Iran 100 B3
formerly known as Qomisheh
Shahrihon Uzbek. 103 H4
formerly known as Moskovskiy or Stalino
Shahrisabz Uzbek. 103 F5
also spelt Shakhrisabz
UNESCO World Heritage Site
Shahriston Tajik. 101 G2
also spelt Shakhristan
Shahr Rey Iran 100 B3
Shahr Sultan Pak. 101 G4
Shahrtuz Tajik. 101 G2
also spelt Shaartuz
Shāhrūd Iran see Emāmrūd
Shāhrūd, Rūdkhāneh-ye r. Iran 100 B2
Shahrud Bustam reg. Iran 100 C3
Shāh Savārān, Kūh-e mts Iran 100 D4
Shāh Taqī Iran see Emām Taqī
Shaikh Husain mt. Pak. 101 F4
Sha'īr, Jabal mts Syria 109 I3
Sha'irah, Jabal mt. Egypt 108 F8
Shaistaganj Bangl. 97 F4
Shaj'ah, Jabal hill Saudi Arabia 105 E2
Shajapur India 96 C5
Shakar Bolāghī Iran 100 A2
Shakaskraal S. Africa 133 P6
Shakaville S. Africa 133 P6
Shakawe Botswana 130 D3
Shakespeare Island Canada 168 B3
Shakh Tajik. see Shoh
Shakhbuz Azer. see Şahbuz
Shakhovskaya Rus. Fed. 43 Q5
Shakhrisabz Uzbek. see Shahrisabz
Shakhristan Tajik. see Shahriston
Shakhtars'k Ukr. 41 F6
also spelt Shakhtersk or Shakhtyorsk; formerly known as Katyk
Shakhtersk Ukr. see Shakhtars'k
Shakhtinsk Kazakh. 103 H2
Shakhty Respublika Buryatiya Rus. Fed. see Gusinoozersk
Shakhty Rostovskaya Oblast' Rus. Fed. 41 G7
Shakhtyorsk Ukr. see Shakhtars'k
Shakhun'ya Rus. Fed. 40 H4
Shaki Nigeria 125 F4
also spelt Saki
Shâkir, Gezîret i. Egypt 121 G3
English form Shadwān Island
Shakopee U.S.A. 178 D2
Shakotan-hantō pen. Japan 90 G3
Shakotan-misaki c. Japan 90 G3
Shakou China 87 E3
Shala Hāyk' l. Eth. 128 C3
Shalakusha Rus. Fed. 40 G3
Shālamzār Iran 100 B3
Shalday Kazakh. 103 I2
Shalginskiy Kazakh. 103 G3
also known as Shalqïya; formerly known as Shalgiya
Shalgiya Kazakh. see Shalginskiy
Shali Rus. Fed. 41 H8
also known as Şela; formerly known as Mezhdurechnye
Shalim Oman 105 F4
Shālimah Egypt 108 B6
Shaliuhe China see Gangca
Shalkar Kazakh. 102 D3
also spelt Shalqar
Shalkar, Ozero salt l. Kazakh. 102 B2
also known as Shalqar Köli; formerly spelt Chalkar, Ozero
Shalkar Karashatau salt l. Kazakh. 103 E2
Shalkar-Yega-Kara, Ozero l. Rus. Fed. 103 E2
Shalqar Kazakh. see Shalkar
Shalqar Köli salt l. Kazakh. see Shalkar, Ozero
Shalqïya Kazakh. see Shalginskiy
Shaluli Shan mts China 86 A2
Shaluni mt. India 97 H3
Shama r. Tanz. 129 B6
Shamāl Sīnā' governorate Egypt 108 D7
English form North Sinai; also known as Sinai ash Shamâlîya
Shamalzā'ī Afgh. 101 F4
Shamary Rus. Fed. 40 K4
Shāmat al Akbād des. Saudi Arabia 104 C1
Shamattawa Canada 167 M3
Shamattawa r. Canada 168 C2
Shamava Belarus 43 M7
Shambār Iran 100 B3
Shambe Sudan 128 A3
Shambu Eth. 128 C2
Shambuanda Dem. Rep. Congo 127 D6
Sham Chun r. China 87 [inset]
Shamgarh India 96 B4
Shamgong Bhutan see Shemgang
Shamis U.A.E. 105 F3
Shamkhal Rus. Fed. 102 A4
Shamkhor Azer. see Şəmkir
Shammar, Jabal reg. Saudi Arabia 104 C2
Shamoksha Rus. Fed. 43 O1
Shamrock U.S.A. 179 B5
Shamva Zimbabwe 131 F3
Shan state Myanmar 78 B3
Shancheng Fujian China see Nanjing
Shancheng Shandong China see Shanxian
Shand Afgh. 101 E4
Shandan China 84 D4
Shandian He r. China 85 H3
Shandiz Iran 101 D2
Shandong prov. China 85 H4
English form Shantung
Shandong Bandao pen. China 85 I4
Shandrūkh Iraq 107 F4
Shandur Pass Pak. 101 H2
Shangani r. Zimbabwe 131 E3
Shangcai China 87 E1
also known as Caidu
Shangcheng China 87 E2
Shang Chu r. China 89 E6
Shangchuan Dao i. China 87 E4
Shangchuankou China see Minhe
Shangdu China 85 G3
Shangganling China 82 C3
Shanggao China 87 E2
also known as Aoyang
►Shanghai China 87 G2
10th most populous city in the world.
►►18–19 World Cities
Shanghai municipality China 87 G2
Shanghang China 87 F3
also known as Linjiang
Shanghe China 85 H4
Shanghekou China 83 B4
Shangji China see Xichuan
Shangjie China see Yangbi
Shangjin China 87 D1
Shangkuli China 85 I1
Shangluo China 87 D1
Shangnan China 87 D1
Shangombo Zambia 127 D9
Shangpai China see Feixi
Shangpaihe China see Feixi
Shangqiu China 87 E1
also known as Zhuji
Shangrao China 87 F2
Shangshui China 87 E1
Shangsi China 87 D4
also known as Siyang
Shangtang China see Yongjia
Shangyou China 87 E3
also known as Dongshan
Shangyou Shuiku salt flat China 88 C3
Shangyu China 87 G2
also known as Baiguan
Shangzhi China 82 B3
Shanhaiguan China 85 H3
Shanhe China see Zhengning
Shanhetun China 82 B3
Shani Nigeria 125 I4
Shankou China 84 B3
Shannon airport Ireland 47 D11
Shannon est. Ireland 47 D11
Shannon r. Ireland 47 D11
Shannon N.Z. 152 J8
Shannon S. Africa 133 K6
Shannon U.S.A. 172 D8
Shannon, Mouth of the Ireland 47 C11
Shannon National Park Australia 151 B7
Shannon Ø i. Greenland 165 R2
Shan Plateau Myanmar 78 B3
Shanshan China 88 E3
also known as Piqan
Shanshanzhan China 88 E3
Shansi prov. China see Shanxi
Shantarskiye Ostrova is Rus. Fed. 39 N4
Shan Tei Tong hill Hong Kong China see Stenhouse, Mount
Shan Teng hill Hong Kong China see Victoria Peak
Shantipur India 97 F5
also spelt Santipur
Shantou China 87 F4
formerly known as Swatow
Shantung prov. China see Shandong
Shanwei China 87 E4
Shanxi prov. China 85 F4
English form Shansi
Shanxian China 87 F1
also known as Shancheng
Shanya r. Rus. Fed. 43 Q7
Shanyang China 87 D1
Shanyin China 85 G4
also known as Daiyue
Shaodong China 87 D3
also known as Liangshi
Shaoguan China 87 E3
Shaoshan China 87 E3
Shaowu China 87 F3
Shaoxing China 87 G2
Shaoyang China 87 D3
Shapa China 87 D4
Shapembe Dem. Rep. Congo 126 D6
Shaping China see Ebian
Shapinsay i. U.K. 46 J4
Shapki Rus. Fed. 43 M2
Shapkina r. Rus. Fed. 40 J2
Shapsha Rus. Fed. 43 P1
Shapyalyevichy Belarus 43 K7
Shaqlāwa Iraq 109 P1
Shaqq el Giefer, Wadi watercourse Sudan 121 E6
Shaqq el Khadir Sudan 121 E6
Shaqrā' Saudi Arabia 105 D2
Shar Kazakh. 103 J2
formerly known as Charsk
Shār, Jabal mt. Saudi Arabia 104 A2
Sharaf well Iraq 107 E5
Sharafa Sudan 121 E6
Sharalday Rus. Fed. 85 E1
Sharan Paktīkā Afgh. 101 G3
Sharanga Rus. Fed. 40 H4
Sharan Jogizai Pak. 101 G4
Sharashova Belarus 42 F9
Sharātib, Ra's pt Egypt 108 E9
Sharawrā, Jabal hills Saudi Arabia 109 H9
Sharawrā', Qa' salt pan Saudi Arabia 109 H9
Sharbaqty Kazakh. see Shcherbakty
Sharbithāt, Ra's c. Oman 105 G4
Sharbulag Mongolia 84 B1
Sharchino Rus. Fed. 103 J1
Shardara Kazakh. 103 F4
formerly spelt Chardara
Shardara Bögeni resr Kazakh./Uzbek. see Chardarinskoye Vodokhranilishche
Shardi Pak. 101 H3
Sharga Govĭ-Altay Mongolia 84 B2
Sharga Hövsgöl Mongolia 84 C1
formerly known as Tsagaan-Uul
Shargorod Ukr. see Sharhorod
Sharg'un Uzbek. 103 F5
also spelt Shorghun
Sharhorod Ukr. 41 D6
also spelt Shargorod
Sharhulsan Mongolia 84 E2
Shari r. Cameroon/Chad see Chari
Shari Japan 90 I3
Shārī, Buḥayrat imp. l. Iraq 107 F4
Shari-dake vol. Japan 90 I3
Sharīrah Pass Egypt 108 F9
Sharjah U.A.E. 105 F2
also known as Ash Shāriqah
Sharka-leb La pass China 89 E6
Sharkawshchyna Belarus 42 I6
Shark Bay Australia 151 A5
UNESCO World Heritage Site
Shark Fin Bay Phil. 74 A4
Sharkhāt Yemen 105 E5
Shark Reef reef Australia 149 E2
Sharlawuk Turkm. see Şarlawuk
Sharlyk Rus. Fed. 102 C1
Sharmah Saudi Arabia 104 A1
Sharm ash Shaykh Egypt 121 G3
Sharon PA U.S.A. 176 E4
Sharon WI U.S.A. 172 E8
Sharon, Plain of Israel 108 F5
also known as HaSharon
Sharon Springs U.S.A. 178 B4
Sharonville U.S.A. 176 A6
Sharpe, Lake salt flat Australia 151 C7
Sharpe Lake Canada 167 M4
Sharp Peak hill Hong Kong China 87 [inset]
also known as Nam She Tsim
Sharpsburg U.S.A. 176 D6
Sharqat Iraq see Ash Sharqāţ
Sharqī, Jabal ash mts Lebanon/Syria 108 G4
English form Anti Lebanon
Sharqiy Ustyurt Chink esc. Uzbek. 102 D4
Sharqpur Pak. 101 H4
Sharur Azer. see Şərur
Shar Us Gol r. Mongolia 84 C2
Shary well Saudi Arabia 104 C2
Shar'ya Rus. Fed. 40 H4
Shar'ya r. Rus. Fed. 43 N2
Sharyn Kazakh. see Charyn
Shashe r. Botswana/Zimbabwe 131 F4
Shashemenē Eth. 128 C3
Shashi China see Jingzhou
Shashubay Kazakh. 103 H3
formerly known as Ozernyy
Shasta U.S.A. 182 B1
Shasta, Mount vol. U.S.A. 180 E4
Shasta Dam U.S.A. 182 B1
Shasta Lake U.S.A. 182 B1
Shatalovo Rus. Fed. 43 N7
Sha Tau Kok Hoi inlet Hong Kong China see Starling Inlet
Shāţi', Wādī ash watercourse Libya 120 B3
Shatilki Belarus see Svyetlahorsk
Sha Tin Hong Kong China 87 [inset]
Shatki Rus. Fed. 40 H5
Shaţnat as Salmās, Wādī watercourse Syria 109 J2
Sha Tong Hau Shan i. Hong Kong China see Bluff Island
Shatoy Rus. Fed. 41 H8
formerly known as Sovetskoye
Shatsk Rus. Fed. 41 G5
Shats'k nat. park Ukr. 41 B6
Shaţţ, Ra's osh pt Iran 100 B4
Shaţţ al 'Arab r. Iran/Iraq 107 G5
Shaţţ al Gharrāf r. Iraq 107 F5
Shattuck U.S.A. 179 C4
Shatura Rus. Fed. 43 U6
Shaturtorf Rus. Fed. 43 U6
Shaubak Jordan see Ash Shawbak
Shaŭildir Kazakh. see Shaul'der
Shaul'der Kazakh. 103 G4
also spelt Shaŭildir
Shaunavon Canada 167 I5
Shaverki Rus. Fed. 44 O3
Shaver Lake U.S.A. 182 E4
Shavers Fork r. U.S.A. 176 F7
Shaw r. Australia 150 B4
Shawan China 88 D2
also known as Sandaohezi
Shawangunk Mountains hills U.S.A. 177 K4
Shawano U.S.A. 172 E6
Shawano Lake U.S.A. 172 E6
Shawāq well Saudi Arabia 104 B2
Shawnee U.S.A. 179 C5
Shawsville U.S.A. 176 E8
Sha Xi r. China 87 F3
Shaxian China 87 F3
also known as Fengggang
Shayan Kazakh. 103 G4
formerly spelt Chayan
Shayang China 87 E2
Shaybārā i. Saudi Arabia 104 B2
Shayboveyem r. Rus. Fed. 39 Q3
Shay Gap Australia 150 C4
Shaykh, Sha'ib ash watercourse Iraq 109 N5
Shaykh, Wādī ash watercourse Egypt 108 E9
Shaykh Jūwī Iraq 107 F4
Shaykh Sa'd Iraq 107 F4
Shaykovka Rus. Fed. 43 P7
Shāzand Iran 100 B3
Shazaoyuan China 84 B4
Shaţāz, Jabal mt. Saudi Arabia 104 C2
Shaţī Ḥāmir, Wādī watercourse Saudi Arabia 109 M6
Shazud Tajik. 101 H2
Shchara r. Belarus 42 F8
Shchekino Rus. Fed. 43 S7
Shchelkanovo Rus. Fed. 43 Q7
Shchelkovo Rus. Fed. 43 T6
Shchel'yayur Rus. Fed. 40 J2
Shcherbakov Rus. Fed. see Rybinsk
Shcherbakty Kazakh. 103 I1
also spelt Sharbaqty
Shchetinskoye Rus. Fed. 43 T3
Shchichengskoye, Ozero l. Rus. Fed. 43 V2
Shchigry Rus. Fed. 41 F6
Shcholkine Ukr. 41 E7
Shchomyslitsa Belarus 42 I8
Shchors Ukr. 41 D6
formerly known as Snovsk
Shchuchin Belarus see Shchuchyn
Shchuchinsk Kazakh. 103 G1
Shchuchyn Belarus 42 F8
also spelt Shchuchin
Shchuger r. Rus. Fed. 40 K2
Shchytkavichy Belarus 42 J8
Shea Guyana 199 G4
Shebalino Rus. Fed. 88 D1
Shebandowan Lakes Canada 172 C2
Shebekino Rus. Fed. 41 F6
Shebergān Afgh. 101 F2
Sheboygan U.S.A. 172 F7
Shebshi Mountains Nigeria 125 H4
Shebunino Rus. Fed. 82 F3
Shecheng China see Shexian
Shediac Canada 169 H4
Shedin Peak Canada 166 E4
Shedok Rus. Fed. 107 E1
Sheelin, Lough l. Ireland 47 E10
Sheepmoor S. Africa 133 O3
Sheep Peak U.S.A. 183 I5
Sheerness U.K. 47 M12
Sheet Harbour Canada 169 I4
Shefar'am Israel 108 G5
Sheffield N.Z. 153 G11
Sheffield U.K. 47 K10
Sheffield AL U.S.A. 174 C5
Sheffield IL U.S.A. 172 D9
Sheffield PA U.S.A. 176 F4
Sheffield TX U.S.A. 179 B6
Sheffield Lake Canada 169 J3
Shegaon India 94 C1
Sheguiandah Canada 173 L5
Shēh Husēn Eth. 128 D3
Shehong China 86 C2
also known as Taihe; formerly known as Taihezhen
Sheikh, Jebel esh mt. Lebanon/Syria see Hermon, Mount
Sheikh Othman Yemen see Ash Shaykh 'Uthman
Shekak r. Canada 168 C3
Shekhawati reg. India 96 B4
Shekhem West Bank see Nāblus
Shekhupura Pak. 101 H4
Sheki Azer. see Şəki
Shekka Ch'ün-Tao is Hong Kong China see Soko Islands
Shek Kwu Chau i. Hong Kong China 87 [inset]
Shekou China 87 [inset]
Shek Pik resr Hong Kong China see Shek Pik Reservoir
Shek Pik Reservoir Hong Kong China 87 [inset]
also known as Shek Pik
Sheksna Rus. Fed. 43 T2
formerly known as Nikol'skoye
Sheksna r. Rus. Fed. 43 T2
Sheksninskoye Vodokhranilishche resr Rus. Fed. 43 T2
Shek Uk Shan mt. Hong Kong China 87 [inset]
Shela China 89 F6
Shelag watercourse Afgh./Iran 101 E4
Shelagskiy, Mys pt Rus. Fed. 39 R2
Shelbiana U.S.A. 176 C8
Shelbina U.S.A. 178 D4
Shelburn U.S.A. 174 C4
Shelburne N.S. Canada 169 H5
Shelburne Ont. Canada 173 M6
Shelburne Bay Australia 149 D1
Shelburne Falls U.S.A. 177 M3
Shelby MS U.S.A. 174 B5
Shelby MT U.S.A. 180 E2
Shelby NC U.S.A. 174 D5
Shelby OH U.S.A. 176 C5
Shelbyville IL U.S.A. 174 B4
Shelbyville IN U.S.A. 174 C4
Shelbyville MO U.S.A. 178 D4
Shelbyville TN U.S.A. 174 C5
Shelbyville, Lake U.S.A. 174 B4
Sheldon S. Africa 133 J10
Sheldon IA U.S.A. 178 D3
Sheldon IL U.S.A. 172 F10
Sheldon WI U.S.A. 172 B5
Sheldon National Wildlife Refuge U.S.A. 180 C4
Sheldon Springs U.S.A. 177 M1
Sheldrake Canada 169 H3
Shelek Kazakh. see Chilik
Shelekhov Rus. Fed. 84 D1
Shelikhova, Zaliv g. Rus. Fed. 39 P3
Shelikof Strait U.S.A. 164 D4
Shellbrook Canada 167 J4
Shelley U.S.A. 180 D4
Shell Lake Canada 167 J4
Shell Lake U.S.A. 172 B5
Shell Lakes salt flat Australia 151 D6
Shell Mountain U.S.A. 182 A1
Shellsburg U.S.A. 172 B8
Shelon' r. Rus. Fed. 43 L3
Shelopugino Rus. Fed. 85 H1
Shelter Bay Canada see Port-Cartier
Shelter Island U.S.A. 177 M4
Shelter Point N.Z. 153 C15
Shelton U.S.A. 180 B3
Sheltozero Rus. Fed. 40 E3
Shemakha Azer. see Şamaxı
Shemankar r. Nigeria 125 H4
Shemenichi Rus. Fed. 43 P1
Shemgang Bhutan 97 F4
also spelt Shamgong
Shemonaikha Kazakh. 103 J2
Shemordan Rus. Fed. 40 I4
Shemursha Rus. Fed. 40 H5
Shenandoah IA U.S.A. 178 D3
Shenandoah PA U.S.A. 177 I5
Shenandoah VA U.S.A. 176 G7
Shenandoah r. U.S.A. 176 H6
Shenandoah Mountains U.S.A. 176 F7
Shenandoah National Park U.S.A. 176 G7
Shen'ao China 87 F4
also known as Houzhai
Shenbertal Kazakh. 103 E2
Shenchi China 85 G4
Shendam Nigeria 125 H4
Shendi Sudan 121 G5
Shending Shan hill China 82 D3
Shenge Sierra Leone 124 B5
Shengel'dy Kazakh. 103 I3
formerly spelt Chengel'dy
Shëngjin Albania 58 A7
Shengli China 87 E2
Shengli Daban pass China 88 D3
Shengli Feng mt. China/Kyrg. see Pobeda Peak
Shengrenjian China see Pinglu
Shengsi China 87 G2
also known as Caiyuanzhen
Shengsi Liedao is China 87 G2
Shengxian China see Shengzhou
Shengzhou China 87 G2
formerly known as Shengxian
Shënkoll Albania 58 A7
Shenkursk Rus. Fed. 40 G3
Shenmu China 85 F4
Shennongjia China 87 D2
also known as Songbai
Shenqiu China 87 E1
also known as Huaidian
Shenshu China 82 C3
Shensi prov. China see Shaanxi
Shentala Rus. Fed. 40 I5
Shenton, Mount hill Australia 151 C6
Shenxian Hebei China see Shenzhou
Shenxian Shandong China 85 G4
Shenyang China 85 I3
formerly known as Mukden
UNESCO World Heritage Site
Shenzhen China 87 [inset]
also known as Bao'an
Shenzhen Wan b. Hong Kong China see Deep Bay
Shenzhou China 85 G4
formerly known as Shenxian
Sheoganj India 96 B4
Sheopur India 96 C4
Shepard Island Antarctica 222 P2
Shepetivka Ukr. 41 C6
also spelt Shepetovka
Shepetovka Ukr. see Shepetivka
Shepherd Islands Vanuatu 145 F3
Shepparton Australia 147 E4
Sheptaky Ukr. 43 O9
Sheqi China 87 E1
Sherabad Uzbek. see Sherobod
Sherard, Cape Canada 165 K2
Sherborne S. Africa 133 I8
Sherborne U.K. 47 J13
Sherbro Island Sierra Leone 124 B5
Sherbrooke N.S. Canada 169 I4
Sherbrooke Que. Canada 169 G4
Sherburne U.S.A. 177 J3
Shercock Ireland 47 F10
Sherda well Chad 120 C4
Shereiq Sudan 121 G5
Shergarh India 96 B4
Sherghati India 97 E4
Sheridan AR U.S.A. 179 D5
Sheridan WY U.S.A. 180 F3
Sherkaly Rus. Fed. 38 G3
Sherlock r. Australia 150 B4
Sherlovaya Gora Rus. Fed. 85 H1
Sherman NY U.S.A. 176 F3
Sherman TX U.S.A. 179 C5
Sherman Mountain U.S.A. 183 I1
Sherobod Uzbek. 103 F5
also spelt Sherabad
Sherovichi Rus. Fed. 43 M7
Sherpur Dhaka Bangl. 97 F4
Sherpur Rajshahi Bangl. 97 F4
Sherridon Canada 167 K4
Shertally India 94 C4
also known as Cherthala
's-Hertogenbosch Neth. 48 C4
also known as Den Bosch
Sherwood U.S.A. 176 A4
Sherwood Downs N.Z. 153 E11
Sherwood Lake Canada 167 K2
Sheryshevo Rus. Fed. 82 C2
Sheshegwaning Canada 173 K5
Sheshtamad Iran 100 D2
Sheslay Canada 166 D3
Sheslay r. Canada 166 C3
Shestikhino Rus. Fed. 43 T4
Shethanei Lake Canada 167 L3
Shetland Islands U.K. 46 K3
Shetpe Kazakh. 102 C3
Sheung Shui Hong Kong China 87 [inset]
Sheung Sze Mun sea chan. Hong Kong China 87 [inset]
Sheung Yue Ho r. Hong Kong China 87 [inset]
Shevaroy Hills India 94 C4
Shevchenko Kazakh. see Aktau
Shevchenko, Zaliv l. Kazakh. 102 E3
formerly known as Paskevicha, Zaliv
Shevgaon India 94 B2
Shevli r. Rus. Fed. 82 D1
Shexian Anhui China 87 F2
also known as Huicheng
Shexian Hebei China 85 G4
also known as Shecheng
Sheya Rus. Fed. 39 L3
Sheyang China 87 G1
also known as Hede
Sheybukhta Rus. Fed. 43 V2
Sheyenne r. U.S.A. 178 C2
Sheykino Rus. Fed. 43 M5
Shey Phoksundo National Park Nepal 97 D3
Shiant Islands U.K. 46 F6
Shiashkotan, Ostrov i. Rus. Fed. 81 Q3
Shiawassee r. U.S.A. 173 J7
Shibām Yemen 105 E5
UNESCO World Heritage Site
Shibar Pass Afgh. 101 G3
Shibata Japan 90 F6
Shibazhan China 82 B1
Shibetsu Hokkaidō Japan 90 H2
Shibetsu Hokkaidō Japan 90 I3
Shibīn al Kawm Egypt 121 F2
Shibing China 87 D3
Shibogama Lake Canada 168 B2
Shibotsu-jima i. Rus. Fed. see Zelenyy, Ostrov
Shibukawa Japan 91 F6
Shibushi Japan 91 B9
Shibushi-wan b. Japan 91 B9
Shicheng Fujian China see Zhouning
Shicheng Jiangxi China 87 F3
also known as Qinjiang
Shicheng Bay Canada see Port-Cartier
Shichinohe Japan 90 G4
Shickshinny U.S.A. 177 I4
Shicun China see Xiangfen
Shidād al Mismā' hill Saudi Arabia 109 J6
Shidao China 85 I4
Shiderti r. Kazakh. 103 H1
Shidongsi China see Gaolan
Shiel, Loch l. U.K. 46 G7
Shield, Cape Australia 148 C2
Shīeli Kazakh. see Chiili
Shifa, Jabal ash mts Saudi Arabia 104 A1
Shifang China 86 C2
Shiga pref. Japan 91 D7
Shigatse China see Xigazê
Shiggaon India 94 B3
Shigong China 88 F3
Shigony Rus. Fed. 41 I5
Shiguai China 85 F3
formerly known as Shiguaigou
Shiguaigou China see Shiguai
Shiḥan Yemen 105 F4
Shiḥan, Wādī r. Oman 105 F4
Shihezi China 88 D2
Shiḥiyāt, Birkat ash waterhole Saudi Arabia 109 O8
Shihkiachwang China see Shijiazhuang
Shiikh Somalia 128 E2
Shijak Albania 58 A7
Shijiao China see Fogang
Shijiazhuang China 85 G4
formerly spelt Shihkiachwang
Shijiu Hu l. China 87 F2
Shijiusuo China see Rizhao
Shikabe Japan 90 G3
Shikag Lake Canada 168 B3
Shikar r. Pak. 101 E4
Shikarpur India 94 B3
Shikarpur Pak. 101 G5
Shikengkong mt. China 87 E3
Shikhany Rus. Fed. 102 A1

Simpson Island Canada **172** F2
Simpson Islands Canada **167** H2
Simpson Park Mountains U.S.A. **183** H2
Simpson Peninsula Canada **165** K3
Simpsonville U.S.A. **174** D5
Simra Nepal **97** E4
Simrishamn Sweden **45** K5
Simuk *i.* Indon. **76** B3
Simulubek Indon. **76** B3
Simunjan *Sarawak* Malaysia **77** E2
Simunul *i.* Phil. **74** A5
Simushir, Ostrov *i.* Rus. Fed. **81** Q3
Sina *r.* India **94** B2
Sīnā', Shibh Jazīrat *pen.* Egypt *see* **Sinai**
Sinabang Indon. **76** B2
Sinabung *vol.* Indon. **76** B2
Sina Dhaqa Somalia **128** E3
►**Sinai** *pen.* Egypt **121** G2
also known as Sīnā', Shibh Jazīrat
►►**6–7 World** Landscapes
Sinai, Mont *hill* France **51** K3
Sinai, Mount Egypt *see* **Mūsá, Jabal**
Sinaia Romania **58** G3
Sinai al Janūbīya *governorate* Egypt *see* **Janūb Sīnā'**
Sinai ash Shamālīya *governorate* Egypt *see* **Shamāl Sīnā'**
Si Nakarin Reservoir Thai. **79** B5
Sinaloa *state* Mex. **184** C3
Sinamaica Venez. **198** D2
Sinan China **87** D3
Sinancha Rus. Fed. *see* **Cheremshany**
Sinanju N. Korea **83** B5
Sinarades Greece **59** A9
Sīnāwin Libya **120** A2
Sinazongwe Zambia **127** E9
Sinbaungwe Myanmar **78** A4
Sinbo Myanmar **78** B2
Sinbyugyun Myanmar **78** A3
Sincan Turkey **107** D3
Sincé Col. **198** C2
Sincelejo Col. **198** C2
Sinchu Taiwan *see* **T'aoyüan**
Sinclair, Lake U.S.A. **175** D5
Sinclair Mills Canada **166** F4
Sincora, Serra do *hills* Brazil **202** D5
Sind *r.* India **96** C4
Sind *prov.* Pak. *see* **Sindh**
Sinda Rus. Fed. **82** E2
Sinda Zambia **127** F8
Sindal Denmark **45** J4
Sindañgan Phil. **74** B4
Sindangan Bay Phil. **74** B4
Sindangbarang Indon. **77** D4
Sindara Gabon **126** A5
Sindari India **96** A4
Sindeh, Teluk *b.* Indon. **75** B5
Sindelfingen Germany **48** F7
Sindgi India **94** C2
Sindh *prov.* Pak. **101** G5
formerly spelt Sind
Sindhnur India **94** C3
Sindhuli Garhi Nepal **97** E4
also known as Sindhulimadi
Sindhulimadi Nepal *see* **Sindhuli Garhi**
Sindi Estonia **42** F3
Sindi India **94** C1
Sındırgı Turkey **106** B3
Sindkhed India **94** C2
Sindkheda India **96** B5
Sîndominic Romania *see* **Sândominic**
Sindor Rus. Fed. **40** I3
Sindou Burkina **124** D4
Sindphana *r.* India **94** C2
Sindri India **97** E5
Sind Sagar Doab *lowland* Pak. **101** G4
Sinegor'ye Rus. Fed. **40** I4
Sinekçi Turkey **59** I8
Sinel'nikovo Ukr. *see* **Synel'nykove**
Sinendé Benin **125** F4
Sines Port. **54** C7
Sines, Cabo de *c.* Port. **54** C7
Sinettä Fin. **44** N2
Sinezerki Rus. Fed. **43** P8
Sinfra Côte d'Ivoire **124** D5
Sing Myanmar **78** B3
Singa Sudan **121** G6
Singahi India **96** D3
Singaing Myanmar **78** B3
►**Singapore** *country* Asia **76** C2
known as Hsin-chia-p'o *in Chinese; spelt* Singapura *in Malay*
►►**16–17 World** Population
►►**64–65 Asia** Countries

►**Singapore** Sing. **76** C2
Capital of Singapore. Also known as Hsin-chia-p'o; also spelt Singapura; historically known as Tumasik.

Singapore *r.* Sing. **76** [inset]
Singapore, Strait of Indon./Sing. **76** C2
Singapura *country* Asia *see* **Singapore**
Singapura Sing. *see* **Singapore**
Singaraja Indon. **77** F5
Singareni India **94** D2
Singatoka Fiji *see* **Sigatoka**
Singave Wallis and Futuna Is *see* **Sigave**
Sing Buri Thai. **79** C5
Singen (Hohentwiel) Germany **48** F8
Sîngeorgiu de Pădure Romania *see* **Sângeorgiu de Pădure**
Sîngeorz-Băi Romania *see* **Sângeorz-Băi**
Sîngera Moldova **58** J2
formerly spelt Sângera
Singgimtay China **88** E3
formerly known as Singim
Singh India **89** A6
Singhampton Canada **173** M6
Singida Tanz. **129** B6
Singida *admin. reg.* Tanz. **129** B6
Singidunum *Srbija* Serb. and Mont. *see* **Belgrade**
Singim China *see* **Singgimtay**
Singkaling Hkamti Myanmar **78** A2
Singkang Indon. **75** B4
Singkawang Indon. **77** E2
Singkep *i.* Indon. **76** D3
Singkil Indon. **76** B2
Singkuang Indon. **76** B2
Singleton Australia **147** F3
Singleton, Mount *hill N.T.* Australia **148** A4
Singleton, Mount *hill W.A.* Australia **151** B6
Singoli India **96** B4
Singon Myanmar **78** A3
Singora Thai. *see* **Songkhla**
Sin'gosan N. Korea *see* **Kosan**
Singou, Réserve Totale du *nature res.* Burkina **125** F4
Singra India **97** F4
Singu Myanmar **78** A3
Singureni Romania **58** G4
Sin'gye N. Korea **83** B5
Sinhala *country* Asia *see* **Sri Lanka**
Sinharaja Forest Reserve *nature res.* Sri Lanka **94** D5
UNESCO World Heritage Site
Sinhŭng N. Korea **83** B4
Siniloan Phil. **74** B3
Sining China *see* **Xining**
Sinio, Gunung *mt.* Indon. **75** A3
Siniscola *Sardinia* Italy **57** B8
Sini Vrŭkh *mt.* Bulg. **58** G7
Siniy-Shikhan Rus. Fed. **103** E2
Sinj Croatia **56** I5
Sinjai Indon. **75** B4
Sinjār Iraq **107** E3
Sinjār, Jabal *mt.* Iraq **107** E3
Sinkat Sudan **121** H5
Sinkiang *aut. reg.* China *see* **Xinjiang Uygur Zizhiqu**
Sinkiang Uighur Autonomous Region *aut. reg.* China *see* **Xinjiang Uygur Zizhiqu**
Sinking Spring U.S.A. **176** B6
Sinkyevichy Belarus **42** I9
Sinmi-do *i.* N. Korea **83** B5
Sinnamary Fr. Guiana **199** H3
Sinnar India **94** B2
Şinnār, Khashm *hill* Saudi Arabia **109** O8
Sinn Bishr, Jabal *hill* Egypt **108** D8
Sinneh Iran *see* **Sanandaj**
Sinnemahoning U.S.A. **176** G4
Sinni *r.* Italy **57** I8
Sînnicolau Mare Romania *see* **Sânnicolau Mare**
Sinnūris Egypt **108** B8
Sinoia Zimbabwe *see* **Chinhoyi**
Sinoie, Lacul *lag.* Romania **58** J4
Sinole Latvia **42** H4
Sinop Brazil **201** G2
Sinop Turkey **106** C2
historically known as Sinope
Sinope Turkey *see* **Sinop**
Sinoquipe Mex. **184** C2
Sinp'a N. Korea **82** B4
Sinp'o N. Korea **83** C4
Sinp'yŏng N. Korea **83** B5
Sinsang N. Korea **83** B5
Sinsheim Germany **48** F6
Sintang Indon. **77** E2
Sint Eustatius *i.* Neth. Antilles **187** H3
Sint-Laureins Belgium **51** J1

►**Sint Maarten** *i.* Neth. Antilles **187** H3
Part of the Netherlands Antilles. The northern part of the island is the French territory of St Martin.

Sint Nicolaas Aruba **187** F4
Sint-Niklaas Belgium **51** K1
also spelt St Nicolas
Sinton U.S.A. **179** C6
Sintra Brazil **199** F6
UNESCO World Heritage Site
Sintsovo Rus. Fed. **43** R5
Sinú *r.* Col. **198** C2
Sinŭiju N. Korea **83** B4
Sinujiif Somalia **128** F2
Sinyaya *r.* Rus. Fed. **43** J4
Siocon Phil. **74** B5
Siófok Hungary **49** P9
Sioma Zambia **127** D9
Sioma Ngwezi National Park Zambia **127** D9
Sion Switz. **51** N6
Siorapaluk Greenland **165** L2
Sioule *r.* France **51** J6
Sioux Center U.S.A. **178** C3
Sioux City U.S.A. **178** C3
Sioux Falls U.S.A. **178** C3
Sioux Lookout Canada **168** B3
Sipacate Guat. **185** H6
Sipadan, Pulau *i. Sabah* Malaysia **77** G1
Sipalay Phil. **74** B4
Šipan *i.* Croatia **56** J6
Sipang, Tanjung *pt Sarawak* Malaysia **77** E2
Siphaqeni S. Africa *see* **Flagstaff**
Siping China **82** B4
Sipiwesk Canada **167** L4
Sipiwesk Lake Canada **167** L4
Siple, Mount Antarctica **222** P2
Siple Coast Antarctica **223** N1
Siple Island Antarctica **222** P2
Sipolilo Zimbabwe *see* **Guruve**
Šipovo Bos.-Herz. **56** J4
Sipsey *r.* U.S.A. **175** B5
Sipura *i.* Indon. **76** B3
Sipura, Selat *sea chan.* Indon. **76** B3
Şīq, Wādī as *watercourse* Egypt **108** D8
Siqirah Yemen **105** F5
Siqueira Campos Brazil **206** D10
Siquijor Phil. **74** B4
Siquijor *i.* Phil. **74** B4
Siquisique Venez. **198** D2
Sir *r.* Pak. **101** G6
Sira India **94** C3
Sira Norway **45** I4
Şīr Abū Nu'āyr *i.* U.A.E. **105** F2
Si Racha Thai. **79** C5
Siracusa *Sicily* Italy *see* **Syracuse**
Siraha Nepal *see* **Sirha**
Sirajganj Bangl. **97** F4
Sir Alexander, Mount Canada **166** F4
Şiran Turkey **107** D2
Sirathu India **97** D4
Sirba *r.* Burkina/Niger **125** F3
Şirbāl, Jabal *mt.* Egypt **108** E9
Şīr Banī Yās *i.* U.A.E. **105** F2
Sircilla India *see* **Sirsilla**
Sirdaryo *r.* Asia *see* **Syrdar'ya**
Sirdaryo Uzbek. **103** G4
also spelt Syrdar'ya; *formerly known as* Syrdaryinskiy
Sirdaryo *admin. div.* Uzbek. **103** G4
English form Syrdarya Oblast; *also known as* Sirdaryo Wiloyati
Sirdaryo Wiloyati *admin. div.* Uzbek. *see* **Sirdaryo**
Sirdingka China *see* **Si'erdingka**
Sire Tanz. **129** A6
Sir Edward Pellew Group *is* Australia **148** C2
Siren U.S.A. **172** A5
Siret *r.* Romania **58** J3
Sir Graham Moore Islands Australia **150** D2
Sirha Nepal **97** E4
also spelt Siraha
Sirḥān, Wādī as *watercourse* Jordan/Saudi Arabia **109** I6
Sirhind India **96** C3
Siri, Cape P.N.G. **149** G1
Siria Romania **58** C2
Sīrīk Iran **100** D5
Sirik, Tanjung *pt Sarawak* Malaysia **77** E2
Siri Kit Reservoir *dam* Thai. **78** C4
Sirina *i.* Greece *see* **Syrna**
Siritoi *r.* Pak. **101** G4
Sīrjā Iran **101** E5
Sir James MacBrien, Mount Canada **166** E2
Sīrjān Iran **100** C4
Sīrjān *salt flat* Iran **100** C4
Sir Joseph Banks Group Conservation Park *nature res.* Australia **146** C3
Sirkka Fin. **44** N2
Sirmaur India **96** C3
formerly spelt Sirmur
Sirmilik National Park Canada **165** L2
Sirmium *Vojvodina, Srbija* Serb. and Mont. *see* **Sremska Mitrovica**
Sirmour India **97** D4
Sirmur India *see* **Sirmaur**
Şırnak Turkey **107** E3
Sirniö Fin. **44** O2
Sirohi India **96** B4
Siroko Uganda **128** B4
Sironcha India **94** D2
Sironj India **96** C4
Siros *i.* Greece *see* **Syros**
Sirotsina Belarus **43** K6
Siroua, Jbel *mt.* Morocco **122** D3
Sirpur India **94** C2
Sirr, Nafūd as *des.* Saudi Arabia **104** D2
Sirrayn Island Saudi Arabia **104** C4
Sirrei Eth. **128** D3
Sirretta Peak U.S.A. **182** F6
Sīrrī, Jazīreh-ye *i.* Iran **100** C5
Sirsa India **96** B3
Sirs al Layyānah Egypt **108** B7
Sir Sandford, Mount Canada **166** G5
Sirsi *Karnataka* India **94** B3
Sirsi *Uttar Pradesh* India **96** C3
Sirsilla India **94** C2
formerly spelt Sircilla
Sirte Libya **120** C2
also spelt Surt
Sirte, Gulf of Libya **120** C2
also known as Surt, Khalīj
Sir Thomas, Mount *hill* Australia **146** A1
Siruguppa India **94** C3
Sirupa *r.* Mex. **181** E7
Sirur *Karnataka* India **94** B2
Sirur *Maharashtra* India **94** B2
Sirutiškis Lith. **42** E6
Şirvan Turkey **107** E3
Sirvel India **94** C3
Širvintos Lith. **42** F6
Şirwāḥ Yemen **104** D5
Sīrwān *r.* Iraq **107** F4
Sir Wilfrid Laurier, Mount Canada **166** G4
Sir William Thompson Range *hills* Australia **149** D2
Siryan Iran **100** D3
Sis Turkey *see* **Kozan**
Sisak Croatia **56** I3
historically known as Siscia
Sisaket Thai. **79** D5
Sisal Mex. **185** H4
Sisante Spain **55** I5
Siscia Croatia *see* **Sisak**
Sishen S. Africa **132** H4
Sishilipu China **85** E5
Sisian Armenia **107** F3
Sisimiut Greenland **165** N3
also known as Holsteinsborg
Sisipuk Lake Canada **167** K4
Siskiwit Bay U.S.A. **172** E3
Sisogúichic Mex. **184** D3
Sisŏphŏn Cambodia **79** C5
Sisquoc *r.* U.S.A. **182** D7
Sissach Switz. **51** N5
Sisseton U.S.A. **178** C2
Sissili *r.* Burkina **125** E4
Sissonville U.S.A. **176** D7
Sistān *reg.* Iran **101** E4
also spelt Seistan
Sīstan, Daryācheh-ye *marsh* Afgh. **101** E4
Sīstān va Balūchestān *prov.* Iran **101** E5
Sister Bay U.S.A. **172** F5
Sisteron France **51** L8
Sisters U.S.A. **180** B3
Sistersville U.S.A. **176** E6
Sisto *r.* Italy **56** F7
Sit' *r.* Rus. Fed. **43** S3
Sitalike Tanz. **129** A6
Sitamarhi India **97** E4
Sitamau India **96** B5
Sitampiky Madag. **131** [inset] J3
Sitapur India **96** D4
Siteia Greece **59** H13
also spelt Sitía
Siteki Swaziland **133** P3
formerly spelt Stegi
Sithonia *pen.* Greece **59** E8
Sitía Greece *see* **Siteia**
Sitian China **84** B3
Sitila Moz. **131** G4
Siting China **87** C3
Sitio da Abadia Brazil **202** C5
Sitio do Mato Brazil **202** D5
Sitka U.S.A. **164** F4
Sitnica *r.* Serb. and Mont. **58** B6
Sitno *mt.* Slovakia **49** P7
Sitnya *r.* Rus. Fed. **43** K4
Sitrah *oasis* Egypt **121** E2
Sitsyenyets Belarus **43** K6
Sittang *r.* Myanmar *see* **Sittaung**
Sittard Neth. **48** C5
Sittaung Myanmar **78** A2
Sittaung *r.* Myanmar **78** B4
also spelt Sittang; *also spelt* Sittoung
Sittoung *r.* Myanmar *see* **Sittaung**
Sittwe Myanmar **78** A3
formerly known as Akyab
Situbondo Indon. **77** F4
Siu A Chau *i. Hong Kong* China **87** [inset]
Siumpain, Rubha an t- *hd* U.K. *see* **Tiumpan Head**
Siumpu *i.* Indon. **75** B4
Siuna Nicaragua **186** B4
Siuntio Fin. **42** F1
Siuri India **97** E5
formerly spelt Suri
Siva Rus. Fed. **40** J4
Sivaganga India **94** C4
Sivakasi India **94** C4
Sivaki Rus. Fed. **82** B1
Sivand Iran **100** C4
Sivas Turkey **107** D3
historically known as Sebastea
Sivaslı Turkey **106** B3
Siverek Turkey **107** D3
Sīvers *l.* Latvia **42** I5
Siverskiy Rus. Fed. **43** L2
Sivers'kyy Donets' *r.* Rus. Fed./Ukr. *see* **Severskiy Donets**
Sivomaskinskiy Rus. Fed. **40** L2
Sivrice Turkey **107** D3
Sivrihisar Turkey **106** B3
Sivukile S. Africa **133** N3
Siwa Indon. **75** B3
Sīwah Egypt **121** E2
Siwalik Range *mts* India/Nepal **96** C3
Siwan India **97** E4
Siwana India **96** B4
Siwa Oasis Egypt **121** E2
Six Cross Roads Barbados **187** I4
Six-Fours-les-Plages France **51** L9
Sixian China **87** F1
Six Lakes U.S.A. **173** H7
Sixtymile Canada **166** A1
Siyabuswa S. Africa **133** N2
Siyang *Guangxi* China *see* **Shangsi**
Siyang *Jiangsu* China **87** F1
also known as Zhongxing
Siyathemba S. Africa **133** M3
Siyathuthuka S. Africa **133** O2
Siyäzän Azer. **107** G2
also spelt Siazan'; *formerly known as* Kyzyl-Burun
Siyitang China **85** F3
Siyom *r.* India **78** A1
Siyunī Iran **100** C3
Siziwang Qi China *see* **Ulan Hua**
Sizyabsk Rus. Fed. **40** J2
Sjælland *i.* Denmark *see* **Zealand**
Sjaunja naturreservat *nature res.* Sweden **44** L2
Sjenica *Srbija* Serb. and Mont. **58** B5
Sjoa Norway **45** J3
Sjöbo Sweden **45** K5
Sjøholt Norway **44** I3
Sjona *sea chan.* Norway **44** K2
Sjoutnäset Sweden **44** K2
Sjøvegan Norway **44** L1
Sjulsmark Sweden **44** M2
Sjuøyane *is* Svalbard **38** C1
Skäckerfjällen *mts* Sweden **44** K3
Skadarsko Jezero *nat. park* Serb. and Mont. **58** A6
Skadovs'k Ukr. **41** E7
Skælsør Denmark **45** J5
Skærbæk Denmark **45** J5
Skærfjorden *inlet* Greenland **165** R2
Skaftafell *nat. park* Iceland **44** [inset] C2
Skaftárós *r. mouth* Iceland **44** [inset] C3
Skagafjörður *inlet* Iceland **44** [inset] C2
Skagaheiði *reg.* Iceland **44** [inset] B2
Skagen Denmark **45** J4
Skagern *l.* Sweden **45** K4
Skagerrak *strait* Denmark/Norway **45** J4
Skagit *r.* U.S.A. **180** B2
Skagit Mountain Canada **166** F5
Skagway U.S.A. **164** F4
Skaidi Norway **44** N1
Skaidiškės Lith. **42** G7
Skala *Notio Aigaio* Greece **59** H11
Skala *Peloponnisos* Greece **59** D12
Skala Kallonis Greece **59** H9
Skaland Norway **44** L1
Skalino Rus. Fed. **43** V3
Skallelv Norway **44** O1
Skalmodal Sweden **44** K2
Skanderborg Denmark **45** J4
Skåne *county* Sweden **45** K5
Skaneateles U.S.A. **177** I3
Skaneateles Lake U.S.A. **177** I3
Skånevik Norway **45** I4
Skansholm Sweden **44** L2
Skantzoura *i.* Greece **59** F9
Skara Sweden **45** K4
Skara Brae *tourist site* U.K. **46** I4
Skarberget Norway **44** L1
Skardarsko Jezero *l.* Albania/Serb. and Mont. *see* **Scutari, Lake**
Skardu Jammu and Kashmir **96** B2
Skare Norway **45** I4
Skärgårdshavets nationalpark *nat. park* Fin. **45** M4
also known as Saaristomeren Kansallispuisto
Skarnes Norway **45** J3
Skärplinge Sweden **45** L3
Skärsjövålen Sweden **45** K3
Skarstind *mt.* Norway **45** J3
Skarszewy Poland **49** P1
Skarvedalseggen *mt.* Norway **45** J3
Skarvsjöby Sweden **44** L2
Skaryszew Poland **49** S4
Skarżysko-Kamienna Poland **49** R4
Skaudvilė Lith. **42** D6
Skaulo Sweden **44** M2
Šķaune Belarus **45** N4
Skaupsjøen-Hardangerjøkulen *park* Norway **45** I3
Skawa *r.* Poland **49** Q5
Skawina Poland **49** Q6
Skaymat W. Sahara **122** B4
Skeena *r.* Canada **166** D4
Skeena Mountains Canada **166** D3
Skegness U.K. **47** M10
Skeiðarársandur *sand area* Iceland **44** [inset] C3
Skeleton Coast Game Park *nature res.* Namibia **130** B3
Skellefteå Sweden **44** M2
Skellefteälven *r.* Sweden **44** M2
Skelleftebukten *b.* Sweden **44** M2
Skelleftehamn Sweden **44** M2
Skellig Rocks *is* Ireland **47** B12
UNESCO World Heritage Site
Skeppshamn Sweden **44** L3
Skerries Ireland **47** F10
Skhimatárion Greece *see* **Schimatari**
Skhira Tunisia **123** H2
Skhíza *i.* Greece *see* **Schiza**
Ski Norway **45** J4
Skiathos Greece **59** E9
Skiathos *i.* Greece **59** E9
Skibbereen Ireland **47** C12
Skibotn Norway **44** M1
Skidal' Belarus **42** F8
also spelt Skidel'
Skiddaw *hill* U.K. **47** I9
Skidegate Mission Canada **166** D4
Skidel' Belarus *see* **Skidal'**
Skiemonys Lith. **42** G6
Skien Norway **45** J4
Skierniewice Poland **49** R4
Skikda Alg. **123** G1
formerly known as Philippeville
Šķilbēni Latvia **42** I4
Skinari, Akra *pt* Greece **59** B11
Skinnskatteberg Sweden **45** K4
Skio Jammu and Kashmir **96** C2
Skipskop S. Africa **132** E11
Skipton Australia **147** D4
Skipton U.K. **47** J10
Skiropoúla *i.* Greece *see* **Skyropoula**
Skíros *i.* Greece *see* **Skyros**
Skive Denmark **45** J4
Skjálfandafljót *r.* Iceland **44** [inset] C2
Skjálfandi *b.* Iceland **44** [inset] C2
Skjelatinden *mt.* Norway **44** K2
Skjellbreid Norway **44** K2
Skjellinhovde *hill* Norway **45** J3
Skjerkeknuten *hill* Norway **45** I4
Skjern Denmark **45** J5
Skjern Norway **44** J2
Skjerstadfjorden *inlet* Norway **44** K2
Skjervøy Norway **44** M1
Skjolden Norway **45** I3
Skhnyatino Rus. Fed. **43** S4
Skobelev Uzbek. *see* **Farg'ona**
Skobeleva, Pik *mt.* Kyrg. **103** H5
Škocjanske Jame *tourist site* Slovenia **56** F3
UNESCO World Heritage Site
Skoenmakerskop S. Africa **133** J11
Škofja Loka Slovenia **56** G2
Skog Sweden **45** L3
Skoganvarri Norway **44** N1
Skogfoss Norway **44** O1
Skoki Poland **49** O3
Skokie U.S.A. **172** F8
Skol' Kazakh. **103** E2
Sköllersta Sweden **45** K4
Skomvær *is* Norway **44** J2
Skoonspruit *r.* S. Africa **133** K4
Skopelos Greece **59** E9
Skopelos *i.* Greece **59** E9
Skopia *hill* Greece **59** G9
Skopin Rus. Fed. **43** U8

►**Skopje** Macedonia **58** C7
Capital of Macedonia. Also spelt Skopje; historically known as Scupi.

Skoplje Macedonia *see* **Skopje**
Skopunarfjørður *sea chan.* Faroe Is **46** F2
Skórcz Poland **49** P2
Skorodnoye Rus. Fed. **41** F6
Skørping Denmark **45** J4
Skotoussa Greece **58** E7
Skotterud Norway **45** K4
Skoutari Greece **58** E7
Skoutaros Greece **59** H9
Skövde Sweden **45** K4
Skovorodino Rus. Fed. **82** A1
Skowhegan U.S.A. **177** P1
Skrīveri Latvia **42** G5
Škrlatica *mt.* Slovenia **56** F2
Skröven Sweden **44** M2
Skrunda Latvia **42** D5
Skrwa *r.* Poland **49** Q3
Skrydlyeva Belarus **43** L6
Skukum, Mount Canada **166** C2
Skukuza S. Africa **133** P1
Skuleskogens nationalpark *nat. park* Sweden **44** L3
Skull Peak U.S.A. **183** H5
Skull Valley U.S.A. **183** L7
Skultuna Sweden **45** L4
Skunk *r.* U.S.A. **174** B3
Skuodas Lith. **42** C5
Skuratovskiy Rus. Fed. **43** S7
Skurup Sweden **45** K5
Skŭt *r.* Bulg. **58** E5
Skutskär Sweden **45** L3
Skúvoy *i.* Faroe Is **46** F2
Skvyra Ukr. **41** D6
Skwierzyna Poland **49** M3
Skye *i.* U.K. **46** F6
Skykula *hill* Norway **45** I4
Skyring, Seno *b.* Chile **205** B9
Skyropoula *i.* Greece **59** F10
also spelt Skiropoúla
Skyros Greece **59** F10
Skyros *i.* Greece **59** F10
also spelt Skíros
Skytrain Ice Rise Antarctica **222** S1
Slabodka Belarus **42** I6
Slættaratindur *hill* Faroe Is **46** E1
Slagelse Denmark **45** J5
Slagnäs Sweden **44** L2
Slamet, Gunung *vol.* Indon. **77** E4
Slaná *r.* Slovakia **49** R7
Slaney *r.* Ireland **47** F11
Slănic Romania **58** G3
Slănic *r.* Romania **58** H3
Slănic Moldova Romania **58** H2
Slanské vrchy *mts* Slovakia **49** S7
Slantsy Rus. Fed. **43** J2
Slaný Czech Rep. **49** L5
Šlapaberžė Lith. **42** E6
Slapovi Krke *nat. park* Croatia **56** H5
Slashers Reefs *reef* Australia **149** E3
Śląska, Wyżyna *hills* Poland **49** P5
Slate Islands Canada **168** C3
Slatina Croatia **56** J3
Slatina Romania **58** F4
Slatina *r.* Slovakia **49** Q7
Slatina-Timiş Romania **58** D3
Slaty Fork U.S.A. **176** E7
Slautnoye Rus. Fed. **39** Q3
Slave *r.* Canada **167** H2
Slave Coast Africa **125** F5
Slave Lake Canada **167** H4
Slave Point Canada **167** H2
Slavgorod Belarus *see* **Slawharad**
Slavgorod Rus. Fed. **103** I1
Slavkovichi Rus. Fed. **43** K4
Slavnoye Rus. Fed. **43** R5
Slavonia *reg.* Croatia **56** J3
also spelt Slavonija
Slavonija *reg.* Croatia *see* **Slavonia**
Slavonska Požega Croatia *see* **Požega**
Slavonski Brod Croatia **56** K3
Slavsk Rus. Fed. **42** C6
historically known as Heinrichswalde
Slavuta Ukr. **41** C6
Slavutych Ukr. **41** D6
Slavyanka Kazakh. *see* **Myrzakent**
Slavyanka Rus. Fed. **82** C4
Slavyanovo Bulg. **58** F5
Slavyansk Ukr. *see* **Slov"yans'k**
Slavyanskaya Rus. Fed. *see* **Slavyansk-na-Kubani**
Slavyansk-na-Kubani Rus. Fed. **41** F7
formerly known as Slavyanskaya
Sława Poland **49** N4
Slawharad Belarus **43** M8
also spelt Slavgorod
Sławno Poland **49** N1
Slayton U.S.A. **178** D3
Sleaford U.K. **47** L10
Sleaford Bay Australia **146** B3
Slea Head Ireland **47** B11
Sleat, Sound of *sea chan.* U.K. **46** G6
Sled Lake Canada **167** J4
Sleeper Islands Canada **168** E1
Sleeping Bear Dunes National Lakeshore *nature res.* U.S.A. **172** G6
Sleeping Bear Point U.S.A. **172** G6
Sleep Island *Hong Kong* China **87** [inset]
Sleman Indon. **77** E4
Sleptsovskaya Rus. Fed. **41** H8
formerly known as Ordzhonikidzevskaya
Slessor Glacier Antarctica **223** W1
Ślęża *hill* Poland **49** N5
Slick Rock U.S.A. **183** P3
Slidell U.S.A. **175** B6
Slide Mountain U.S.A. **177** K4
Slidre Norway **45** J3
Slieve Car *hill* Ireland **47** C9
Slieve Donard *hill* U.K. **47** G9
Slieve Gamph *hills* Ireland **47** C10
also known as Ox Mountains
Slieve Mish Mountains *hills* Ireland **47** B11
Sligachan U.K. **46** F6
Sligeach Ireland *see* **Sligo**
Sligo Ireland **47** D9
also spelt Sligeach
Sligo U.S.A. **176** F4
Sligo Bay Ireland **47** D9
Slipper Island N.Z. **152** J5
Slippery Rock U.S.A. **176** E4
Slīteres rezervāts *nature res.* Latvia **42** D4
Sliven Bulg. **58** H6
Slivnitsa Bulg. **58** E6
Slivo Pole Bulg. **58** H5
Sljeme *mt.* Croatia **56** H3
Sloan *r.* Canada **167** G1
Sloan U.S.A. **183** I6
Sloat U.S.A. **182** D2
Sloboda *Respublika Komi* Rus. Fed. *see* **Ezhva**
Sloboda *Smolenskaya Oblast'* Rus. Fed. *see* **Przheval'skoye**
Sloboda *Voronezhskaya Oblast'* Rus. Fed. **41** G6
Slobodchikovo Rus. Fed. **40** I3
Slobodka Rus. Fed. **43** P7
Slobodskoy Rus. Fed. **40** I4
Slobodzeya Moldova *see* **Slobozia**
Slobozia Moldova **58** K2
formerly spelt Slobodzeya
Slobozia Romania **58** I4
Slobozia Bradului Romania **58** I3
Słomniki Poland **49** R5
Slonim Belarus **42** G8
Slough U.K. **47** L12
►**Slovakia** *country* Europe **49** P7
also known as Slovensko *in Slovakian*
►►**32–33 Europe** Countries
►**Slovenia** *country* Europe **56** G2
spelt Slovenija *in Slovenian*
►►**32–33 Europe** Countries
Slovenija *country* Europe *see* **Slovenia**
Slovenj Gradec Slovenia **56** H2
Slovenska Bistrica Slovenia **56** H2
Slovenske Gorice *hills* Slovenia **56** H2
Slovenské Rudohorie *mts* Slovakia **49** Q7
Slovensko *country* Europe *see* **Slovakia**
Slovenský kras *mts* Slovakia **49** R7
Slovenský raj *nat. park* Slovakia **49** R7
Slov"yans'k Ukr. **41** F6
also spelt Slavyansk
Słowiński Park Narodowy *nat. park* Poland **49** O1
Słubice Poland **49** L3
Sluch *r.* Belarus **42** I9
Sluch *r.* Ukr. **53** H1
Sludka Rus. Fed. **40** I4
S'Lung, B'Nom *mt.* Vietnam **79** D6
Slunj Croatia **56** H3
Słupca Poland **49** O3
Słupia *r.* Poland **49** N1
Słupsk Poland **49** O1
historically known as Stolp
Slussfors Sweden **44** L2
Slutsk Belarus **42** I8
Šlyna *r.* Lith. **42** D6
Slyne Head Ireland **47** B10
Slyudyanka Rus. Fed. **84** D1
Smackover U.S.A. **179** D5
Smålandsstenar Sweden **45** K4
Small Point U.S.A. **177** P2
Smallwood Reservoir Canada **169** H2
Smalowka Belarus **43** L6
Smalyavichy Belarus **42** J7
also spelt Smolevichi
Smarhon' Belarus **42** H7
also spelt Smorgon'
Smartt Syndicate Dam *resr* S. Africa **132** H7
Smeaton Canada **167** J4
Smederevo *Srbija* Serb. and Mont. **58** B4
historically known as Semendire
Smederevska Palanka *Srbija* Serb. and Mont. **58** B4
Smeeni Romania **58** H3
Smela Ukr. *see* **Smila**
Smelror Norway **44** O1
Smethport U.S.A. **176** G4
Śmigiel Poland **49** N3
Smila Ukr. **41** D6
also spelt Smela
Smilavichy Belarus **42** J8
Smiltene Latvia **42** G4
Smiltiņu kalns *hill* Latvia **42** D5
Smines Norway **44** K1
Smirnykh Rus. Fed. **82** F2
Smith Canada **167** H4
Smith *r. MT* U.S.A. **180** E3
Smith *r. VA* U.S.A. **176** F9
Smith Arm *b.* Canada **166** F1
Smith Bay U.S.A. **164** D2
Smith Center U.S.A. **178** C4
Smithers Canada **166** E4
Smithers Landing Canada **166** E4
Smithfield S. Africa **133** K7
Smithfield *NC* U.S.A. **174** E5
Smithfield *UT* U.S.A. **180** E4
Smithfield *VA* U.S.A. **177** I9
Smith Glacier Antarctica **222** Q1
Smith Island Antarctica **222** T2
Smith Island India **95** G3
Smith Island *MD* U.S.A. **177** I7
Smith Island *VA* U.S.A. **177** J8
Smithland U.S.A. **174** B4
Smith Mountain Lake U.S.A. **176** F8
Smith River Canada **166** E3
Smithsburg U.S.A. **176** H6
Smiths Falls Canada **168** E4
Smith Sound *sea chan.* Canada/Greenland **165** L2
Smithton Australia **147** E5
Smithville *TN* U.S.A. **174** C5
Smithville *WV* U.S.A. **176** D6
Smitskraal S. Africa **133** I10
Smjörfjöll *mts* Iceland **44** [inset] D2
Smoke Creek Desert U.S.A. **182** E1
Smoky *r.* Canada **166** G3
Smoky Bay Australia **146** B3
Smoky Cape Australia **147** G2
Smoky Falls Canada **168** D3
Smoky Hill *r.* U.S.A. **178** B4
Smoky Hill, North Fork *r.* U.S.A. **178** B4
Smoky Hills U.S.A. **178** C4
Smoky Lake Canada **167** H4
Smoky Mountains U.S.A. **180** D4
Smøla *i.* Norway **44** I3
Smolenka Rus. Fed. **102** B2
Smolensk Rus. Fed. **43** N7
Smolenskaya Oblast' *admin. div.* Rus. Fed. **43** O7
English form Smolensk Oblast
Smolensk Oblast *admin. div.* Rus. Fed. *see* **Smolenskaya Oblast'**
Smolensko-Moskovskaya Vozvyshennost' *hills* Rus. Fed. **43** N7
Smolevichi Belarus *see* **Smalyavichy**
Smolikas *mt.* Greece **59** B8
Smolyan Bulg. **58** F7
Smolyoninovo Rus. Fed. **82** D4
Smooth Rock Falls Canada **168** D3
Smoothrock Lake Canada **168** B3
Smoothstone Lake Canada **167** J4
Smørfjord Norway **44** N1
Smorgon' Belarus *see* **Smarhon'**
Smotrova Buda Rus. Fed. **43** N9
Smyadovo Bulg. **58** I5
Smyley Island Antarctica **222** S2
Smyrna Turkey *see* **İzmir**
Smyrna *DE* U.S.A. **177** J6
Smyrna *GA* U.S.A. **175** C5
Smyrna *TN* U.S.A. **174** C5
Smyth, Canal *sea chan.* Chile **205** B8
Snæfell *mt.* Iceland **44** [inset] D2
Snaefell *hill* Isle of Man **47** H9
Snæfellsjökull *ice cap* Iceland **44** [inset] B2
Snæfellsnes *pen.* Iceland **44** [inset] B2
Snake *r.* Canada **166** C1
Snake *r. NE* U.S.A. **178** B3
Snake *r.* U.S.A. **180** C3
Snake Range *mts* U.S.A. **183** J2
Snake River Canada **166** F3
Snake River Plain U.S.A. **180** D4
Snare *r.* Canada **167** G2
Snare Lake Canada **167** J3
Snare Lakes Canada *see* **Wekweti**
Snares Islands N.Z. **145** F6
also known as Tini Heke
UNESCO World Heritage Site
Snåsa Norway **44** K2
Snåsvatn *l.* Norway **44** K2
Sneedville U.S.A. **176** B9
Sneek Neth. **48** C2
Sneem Ireland **47** C12
Sneeuberg *mt.* S. Africa **132** D9
Sneeuberge *mts* S. Africa **133** I8
Snegamook Lake Canada **169** I2
Snegurovka Ukr. *see* **Tetiyiv**
Snelling U.S.A. **182** D4
Snēpele Latvia **42** C5
Snezhed' *r.* Rus. Fed. **43** R8
Snezhnogorsk Rus. Fed. **39** I3
Sněžka *mt.* Czech Rep. **49** M5
also spelt Śnieżka
Snežnik *mt.* Slovenia **56** G3
Śniardwy, Jezioro *l.* Poland **49** S2
Sniečkus Lith. *see* **Visaginas**
Śnieżka *mt.* Czech Rep. *see* **Sněžka**
Śnieżnik *mt.* Poland **49** N5
Snihurivka Ukr. **41** E7
Snina Slovakia **49** T7
Snøhetta *mt.* Norway **44** J3
Snohomish U.S.A. **180** B3
Snønuten *mt.* Norway **45** I4
Snopot' *r.* Rus. Fed. **43** O8
Snov *r.* Ukr. **43** N9
Snova *r.* Rus. Fed. **43** R9
Snova *r.* Rus. Fed. **43** T9
Snovsk Ukr. *see* **Shchors**
Snow Belarus **42** H8
Snowbird Lake Canada **167** K2
Snowcrest Mountain Canada **167** G5
Snowdon *mt.* U.K. **47** H10
also known as Yr Wyddfa
Snowdonia National Park U.K. **47** I11
Snowdrift Canada *see* **Łutselk'e**
Snowdrift *r.* Canada **167** I2
Snowflake U.S.A. **183** N7
Snow Hill *MD* U.S.A. **177** J7
Snow Hill *NC* U.S.A. **174** E5
Snow Lake Canada **167** K4
Snowtown Australia **146** C3
Snow Water Lake U.S.A. **183** J1
Snowy *r.* Australia **147** F4
Snowy Mountain U.S.A. **177** K2
Snowy Mountains Australia **147** E4
Snudy, Vozyera *l.* Belarus **42** I6
Snug Corner Bahamas **187** E2
Snug Harbour *Nfld. and Lab.* Canada **169** K2
Snug Harbour *Ont.* Canada **173** M5
Snyder *OK* U.S.A. **179** C5
Snyder *TX* U.S.A. **179** B5
Snyderspoort *pass* S. Africa **132** E8
Snykhovo Rus. Fed. **43** R8

Soahany Madag. 131 [inset] J3
Soaigh i. U.K. see Soay
Soalala Madag. 131 [inset] J3
Soamanonga Madag. 131 [inset] J4
Soanierana-Ivongo Madag. 131 [inset] K3
Soan-kundo is S. Korea 83 B6
Soata Col. 198 C3
Soavinandriana Madag. 131 [inset] J3
Soay i. U.K. 46 D6
also spelt Soaigh
Sobaek-sanmaek mts S. Korea 83 B6
Sobaek-san National Park S. Korea 83 C5
Sobat r. Sudan 128 A2
Soběslav Czech Rep. 49 L6
Sobger r. Indon. 73 J7
Sobinka Rus. Fed. 43 V6
Sobolevo Rus. Fed. 43 T6
Sobo-san mt. Japan 91 B8
Sobradinho Brazil 206 F2
Sobradinho, Barragem de resr Brazil 202 D4
Sobrado Bahia Brazil 202 D4
Sobrado Pará Brazil 199 H6
Sobral Brazil 202 D2
Sobrance Slovakia 49 T7
Soča r. Italy see Isonzo
Soča r. Slovenia 56 F3
Sochaczew Poland 49 R3
Sochi Rus. Fed. 41 F8
Sŏch'ŏn S. Korea 83 B5
Sochos Greece 58 E8
also spelt Sokhós
Société, Archipel de la is Fr. Polynesia see Society Islands
Society Islands Fr. Polynesia 221 I7
also known as Société, Archipel de la
Socol Romania 58 C4
Socompa Chile 200 C6
Soconusco, Sierra de mts Mex. see Madre de Chiapas, Sierra
Socorro Brazil 206 G9
Socorro Col. 198 C3
Socorro U.S.A. 181 F6
Socorro, Isla i. Mex. 184 C5
Socota Peru 198 B6
Socotra i. Yemen 105 F5
also spelt Suquṭrā
Socovos Spain 55 J6
Soc Trăng Vietnam 79 D6
formerly known as Khan Hung
Socuéllamos Spain 55 I5
Soda Lake CA U.S.A. 182 E6
Soda Lake CA U.S.A. 183 H6
Sodankylä Fin. 44 N2
Soda Plains Aksai Chin 89 B5
Soda Springs U.S.A. 180 E4
Söderhamn Sweden 45 L3
Söderköping Sweden 45 L4
Södermanland county Sweden 45 L4
Södertälje Sweden 45 L4
Sodiri Sudan 121 F6
Sodium S. Africa 132 H7
Sodo Eth. 128 C3
Södra Kvarken strait Fin./Sweden 45 L3
Sodus U.S.A. 177 H2
Sodwana Bay National Park S. Africa 133 Q4
Soë Indon. 75 C5
Soekmekaar S. Africa 131 F4
Soela väin sea chan. Estonia 42 D3
Soerabaia Indon. see Surabaya
Soest Germany 48 F4
Soetdoring Nature Reserve S. Africa 133 K5
Soetendalsvlei l. S. Africa 132 D11
Sofades Greece 59 D9
Sofala Moz. 131 G4
Sofala prov. Moz. 131 G3
formerly known as Beira
Sofala, Baía de b. Moz. 131 G4

►Sofia Bulg. 58 E6
Capital of Bulgaria. Also spelt Sofiya; historically known as Sardica or Serdica or Sredets.

Sofia r. Madag. 131 [inset] J2
Sofiko Greece 59 E11
Sofiya Bulg. see Sofia
Sofiyevka Ukr. see Vil'nyans'k
Sofiysk Khabarovskiy Kray Rus. Fed. 82 D1
Sofiysk Khabarovskiy Kray Rus. Fed. 82 E2
Sofporog Rus. Fed. 44 O2
Sofrino Rus. Fed. 43 S5
Softa Kalesi tourist site Turkey 108 D1
Sōfu-gan i. Japan 81 O7
English form Lot's Wife
Sog China 89 F6
also known as Garqêntang
Sogamoso Col. 198 C3
Sogat China 88 D3
formerly spelt Süget
Sogda Rus. Fed. 82 D2
Sogma China 89 C5
Søgne Norway 45 I4
Sognefjorden inlet Norway 45 I3
Sogn og Fjordane county Norway 45 I3
Sogo Rus. Fed. 39 M2
Sogod Phil. 74 C4
Sogod Bay Phil. 74 C4
Sogo Hills Kenya 128 C4
Sogolle well Chad 120 B6
Sogo Nur l. China 84 D3
Sogozha r. Rus. Fed. 43 U3
Söğüt Turkey 106 B2
Söğüt Dağı mts Turkey 106 B3
Sŏgwip'o S. Korea 83 B6
Sohagpur India 96 C5
Sohan r. Pak. 101 G3
Sohano P.N.G. 145 E2
Sohar Oman see Şuḥār
Sohela India 97 D5
Sohna India 96 C3
Sohng Gwe, Khao hill Myanmar/Thai. 79 B5
Soignies Belgium 51 K2
Soila China 86 A2
Soini Fin. 44 N3
Soissons France 51 J3
Sōja Japan 91 C7
Sojat India 96 B4
Sojat Road India 96 B4
Sojoton Point Phil. 74 B4
Sok r. Rus. Fed. 41 I5
Sokch'o S. Korea 83 C5
Söke Turkey 106 A3
Sokele Dem. Rep. Congo 127 E7
Sokhondo, Gora mt. Rus. Fed. 85 F1
Sokhor, Gora mt. Rus. Fed. 85 E1
Sokhós Greece see Sochos
Sokhumi Georgia 107 E2
also known as Aq"a; also spelt Sukhumi; historically known as Dioscurias or Sukhum-Kale
Sokiryany Ukr. see Sokyryany
Sŏkkuram Grotto tourist site S. Korea 90 A7
Soknedal Norway 44 J3
Sokobanja Srbija Serb. and Mont. 58 C5
Sokodé Togo 125 F4
Soko Islands Hong Kong China 87 [inset]
also known as Shekka Ch'ün-Tao
Sokol Sakhalin Rus. Fed. 82 F3
Sokol Vologod. Obl. Rus. Fed. 43 V2
Sokolac Bos.-Herz. 56 K5
Sokółka Poland 49 U2
Sokol'niki Tul'skaya Oblast' Rus. Fed. 43 T7
Sokol'niki Tverskaya Oblast' Rus. Fed. 43 P5
Sokolo Mali 124 D3
Sokolov Czech Rep. 49 J5
Sokolovka Rus. Fed. 90 C3
Sokołów Małopolski Poland 49 T5
Sokołów Podlaski Poland 49 T3
Sokolozero, Ozero l. Rus. Fed. 44 O2
Sokone Senegal 124 A3
Sokosti hill Fin. 44 O1
Sokoto Nigeria 125 G3
Sokoto r. Nigeria 125 G4
Sokoto state Nigeria 125 G3
Sokourala Guinea 124 C4
Sokyryany Ukr. 41 C6
also spelt Sokiryany
Sola Cuba 186 D2
Sola r. Poland 49 Q6
Sola i. Tonga see Ata
Solan India 96 C3
Solana Beach U.S.A. 183 G9
Solander Island N.Z. 153 A14
Solanet Arg. 204 F5
Solano Phil. 74 B2
Solano Venez. 199 E4
Solapur India 94 B2
formerly spelt Sholapur
Soldado Bartra Peru 198 C5
Soldotna U.S.A. 164 D3
Solec Kujawski Poland 49 P2
Soledad Arg. 204 E3
Soledad U.S.A. 182 C5
Soledad Venez. 199 F2
Soledad de Doblado Mex. 185 F5
Soledade Brazil 198 D6
Sølen mt. Norway 45 J3
Solenoye Rus. Fed. 41 G7
Solenzo Burkina 124 D3
Solfjellsjøen Norway 44 K2
Solginskiy Rus. Fed. 40 G3
Solhan Turkey 107 E3
Soligalich Rus. Fed. 40 G4
Soligorsk Belarus see Salihorsk
Solihull U.K. 47 K11
Solikamsk Rus. Fed. 40 K4
Sol'-Iletsk Rus. Fed. 102 C2
Soliman Tunisia 57 C12
Solimón, Punta pt Mex. 185 I5
Solingen Germany 48 E4
Solita Col. 198 C4
Solita Venez. 187 F5
Sol-Karmala Rus. Fed. see Severnoye
Sölktäler nature res. Austria 49 K8
Sollefteå Sweden 44 L3
Sollentuna Sweden 45 L4
Sóller Spain 55 N5
Sollerön Sweden 45 K3
Solling hills Germany 48 G4
Solnechnogorsk Rus. Fed. 43 R5
Solnechnyy Khabarovskiy Kray Rus. Fed. see Gornyy
Solnechnyy Khabarovskiy Kray Rus. Fed. 82 E2
Solo r. Java Indon. 77 F4
Solo r. Sulawesi Indon. 75 B3
Solofra Italy 57 G8
Solok Indon. 76 C3
Sololá Guat. 185 H6
Solomon U.S.A. 183 O9
Solomon r. U.S.A. 178 C4
Solomon, North Fork r. U.S.A. 178 C4
Solomon, South Fork r. U.S.A. 178 C4

►Solomon Islands country S. Pacific Ocean 145 F2
4th largest and 5th most populous country in Oceania. Formerly known as British Solomon Islands.
►►138–139 Oceania Countries

Solomon Sea P.N.G./Solomon Is 145 E2
Solon China 85 I2
Solon U.S.A. 172 B9
Solor i. Indon. 75 B5
Solor, Kepulauan is Indon. 75 B5
Solotcha Rus. Fed. 43 U7
Solothurn Switz. 51 N5
Solovetskiy Rus. Fed. 40 E2
formerly known as Kreml'
Solovetskiye Ostrova is Rus. Fed. 40 E2
UNESCO World Heritage Site
Solovetskoye Rus. Fed. 40 H4
Solov'yevo Rus. Fed. 43 N7
Solov'yevsk Mongolia 85 G1
Solov'yevsk Rus. Fed. 82 B1
Solsona Spain 55 M3
Solt Hungary 49 Q9
Šolta i. Croatia 56 I5
Solṭānābād Khorāsan Iran 100 D2
Solṭānābād Iran 101 D3
Solṭānābād Tehrān Iran 100 B3
Soltān-e Bakva Afgh. 101 E3
Soltānī, Khowr-e b. Iran 100 B4
Solṭanqolī Iran 100 A3
Soltau Germany 48 G3
Sol'tsy Rus. Fed. 43 L3
Soltüstik Qazaqstan Oblysy admin. div. Kazakh. see Severnyy Kazakhstan
Soltvadkert Hungary 49 Q9
Solunska Glava mt. Macedonia 58 C7
Solvang U.S.A. 182 D7
Solvay U.S.A. 177 I2
Sölvesborg Sweden 45 K4
Sol'vychegodsk Rus. Fed. 40 H3
Solway Firth est. U.K. 47 I9
Solwezi Zambia 127 E8
Sōma Japan 90 G6
Soma Turkey 106 A3
Somabhula Zimbabwe 131 F3
formerly spelt Somabula
Somabula Zimbabwe see Somabhula
►Somalia country Africa 128 E4
spelt Soomaaliya in Somali; long form Somali Republic
►►114–115 Africa Countries
Somali Republic country Africa see Somalia
Somanga Tanz. 129 C7
Somanya Ghana 125 E5
Sombak'e Canada see Yellowknife
Sombang, Gunung mt. Indon. 77 G2
Sombo Angola 127 D7
Sombor Vojvodina, Srbija Serb. and Mont. 58 A3
also spelt Zombor
Sombrerete Mex. 184 E4
Sombrero i. Anguilla 187 H3
Sombrero Chile 205 C9
Sombrero Channel India 95 G5
Somdari India 96 B4
Somero Fin. 45 M3
Somerset KY U.S.A. 176 A8
Somerset MA U.S.A. 177 N4
Somerset MI U.S.A. 173 I8
Somerset OH U.S.A. 176 C6
Somerset PA U.S.A. 176 F6
Somerset East S. Africa 133 J9
Somerset Island Canada 165 J2
Somerset West S. Africa 132 C11
Somersworth U.S.A. 177 O2
Somerton U.S.A. 183 J9
Sõmeru Estonia 42 H2
Somerville NJ U.S.A. 177 K5
Somerville TN U.S.A. 174 B5
Somerville Reservoir U.S.A. 179 C6
Someşan, Podişul plat. Romania 58 E2
Someşu Cald r. Romania 58 E2
Someşul Mare r. Romania 58 E1
Someşu Mic r. Romania 58 E1
Somesville U.S.A. 177 Q1
Someydeh Iran 100 A3
also spelt Samaida
Somino Rus. Fed. 43 P2
Somkele S. Africa 133 Q5
Sommarøy Norway 44 L1
Somme r. France 50 H2
Sommen l. Sweden 45 K4
Sömmerda Germany 48 I4
Sommet, Lac du l. Canada 169 G2
Somnath India 94 A1
also known as Patan
Somogyszob Hungary 49 O9
Somosomo Fiji 145 H3
Somotillo Nicaragua 186 B4
Somoto Nicaragua 186 B4
Somovo Orlovskaya Oblast' Rus. Fed. 43 Q9
Somovo Tul'skaya Oblast' Rus. Fed. 43 R8
Sompeta India 95 E2
Sompolno Poland 49 P3
Somport, Col du pass France/Spain 55 K2
Šomrda hill Serb. and Mont. 58 C4
Somuncurá, Mesa Volcánica de plat. Arg. 204 D6
Somvarpet India 94 B3
Son r. India 96 E4
Soná Panama 186 C6
Sonag China see Zêkog
Sonai r. India 97 G4
Sonai r. India 97 G4
Sonala India 94 C1
Sonaly Karagandinskaya Oblast' Kazakh. 103 G2
Sonaly Karagandinskaya Oblast' Kazakh. 103 G2
Sonamukhi India 97 E5
Sonapur India 95 D1
Sonari India 97 G4
Sŏnch'ŏn N. Korea 83 B5
Sondalo Italy 56 C2
Sønderå r. Denmark 48 F1
Sønderborg Denmark 45 J5
Sondershausen Germany 48 H4
Sønderup Denmark 45 J4
Søndre Strømfjord Greenland see Kangerlussuaq
Søndre Strømfjord inlet Greenland see Kangerlussuaq
Søndre Upernavik Greenland see Upernavik Kujalleq
Sondrio Italy 56 B2
Sonepet India 94 C2
Song Nigeria 125 I4
Songa Indon. 75 C3
Songad India 96 A5
Songbai China see Shennongjia
Songbu China 87 E2
Sông Câu Vietnam 79 E5
Songcheng China see Xiapu
Sông Da, Hô resr Vietnam 78 D3
Songea Tanz. 129 B7
Sŏnggan N. Korea 83 B4
Songhua Hu resr China 82 B4
Songhua Jiang r. China 82 D3
English form Sungari
Songjiachuan China see Wubu
Songjiang Jilin China 82 C4
formerly known as Antu
Songjiang Shanghai China 87 G2
formerly known as Sungkiang
Songjianghe China 82 B4
Sŏngjin N. Korea see Kimch'aek
Sŏngju S. Korea 91 A7
Songkan China 86 C2
Songkhla Thai. 79 C7
also known as Singora
Songkhram, Mae Nam r. Thai. 78 D4
Songköl l. Kyrg. 103 H4
also known as Sonkël', Ozero
Song Ling mts China 85 H3
Songmai China see Dêrong
Songming China 86 B3
also known as Songyang
Sŏngnam S. Korea 83 B5
Songnim N. Korea 83 B5
Songni-san National Park S. Korea 83 B5
Songo Angola 127 B6
Songo Moz. 131 G2
Songololo Bas-Congo Dem. Rep. Congo 127 B6
Songololo Bas-Congo Dem. Rep. Congo see Mbanza-Ngungu
Songo Mnara Island Tanz. 129 C7
UNESCO World Heritage Site
Songpan China 86 B1
also known as Jin'an or Sungqu
Songsak India 97 F4
Sŏngsan S. Korea 83 B6
Songshan China see Ziyun
Song Shan mt. China 87 E1
Songtao China 87 D2
Songxi China 87 F3
also known as Songyuan
Songxian China 87 E1
Songyang China see Songming
Songyuan Fujian China see Songxi
Songyuan Jilin China 82 B3
also known as Ningjiang; formerly known as Fuyu
Songzi China 87 D2
formerly known as Xinjiangkou
Sonhat India 97 D5
Sonid Youqi China see Saihan Tal
Sonid Zuoqi China see Mandalt
Sonipat India 96 C3
Sonkach India 96 C5
Sonkajärvi Fin. 44 N3
Sonkël', Ozero l. Kyrg. see Songköl
Sonkovo Rus. Fed. 43 S4
Sơn La Vietnam 78 C3
Sonmiani Bay Pak. 101 F5
Sonneberg Germany 48 I5
Sonnenjoch mt. Austria 48 J8
Sono r. Minas Gerais Brazil 203 C6
Sono r. Tocantins Brazil 202 B4
Sonoita watercourse Mex. 181 D7
Sonoma U.S.A. 182 B3
Sonoma Peak U.S.A. 182 G1
Sonora r. Mex. 184 C2
Sonora state Mex. 184 C2
Sonora CA U.S.A. 182 D4
Sonora TX U.S.A. 179 B6
Sonora Peak U.S.A. 182 E3
Sonqor Iran 100 A3
Sonseca Spain 54 H5
Son Servera Spain 55 O5
Sonsón Col. 198 C3
Sonsonate El Salvador 185 H6
Sonsorol Islands Palau 73 H5
also spelt Sansoral Islands
Sonstraal S. Africa 132 G4
Sơn Tây Vietnam 78 D3
Sonthofen Germany 48 H8
Sonwabile S. Africa 133 M8
Soochow China see Suzhou
Soodla r. Estonia 42 G2
Sool admin. div. Somalia 128 E2
Soomaaliya country Africa see Somalia
Soperton U.S.A. 175 D5
Sopi, Tanjung pt Indon. 75 D2
Sopo watercourse Sudan 126 E2
Sopot Bulg. 58 F6
Sopot Poland 49 P1
Sopot Srbija Serb. and Mont. 58 B4
Sopron Hungary 49 N8
historically known as Ödenburg
Sopu-Korgon Kyrg. 88 A3
also known as Sufi-Kurgan
Sopur Jammu and Kashmir 96 B2
Soputan, Gunung vol. Indon. 75 C2
Sor r. France 51 I9
Sôr r. Port. 54 C6
Sor r. Spain 54 D1
Sora Italy 56 F7
Sorab India 94 B3
Söråker Sweden 44 L3
Sŏrak-san mt. S. Korea 83 C5
Sorak-san National Park S. Korea 83 C5
Sorata Bol. 200 C3
Sør-Audnedal Norway 45 I4
Sorbas Spain 55 I7
Sorbe r. Spain 55 H4
Sorel Canada 169 F4
Sorell Australia 147 E5
Soreq r. Israel 108 F6
Sørfjorden inlet Norway 45 I3
Sorgono Sardinia Italy 57 B8
Sorgues France 51 K8
Sorgues r. France 51 I9
Sorgun Turkey 106 C3
also known as Yeşilova
Sorgun r. Turkey 108 F1
Soria Spain 55 I3
Sorikmarapi vol. Indon. 76 B2
Sørkappøya i. Svalbard 38 B2
Sorkh, Kūh-e mts Iran 100 C3
Sorkheh Iran 100 C3
Sørland Norway 44 K2
Sørli Norway 44 K2
Sörmjöle Sweden 44 M3
Sorø Denmark 45 J5
Soro India 97 E5
Soro, Monte mt. Sicily Italy 57 G11
Soroca Moldova 41 D6
formerly spelt Soroki
Sorocaba Brazil 206 F10
Sorochinsk Rus. Fed. 102 C1
Soroki Moldova see Soroca
Sorokino Rus. Fed. 43 K4
Sorol atoll Micronesia 73 J5
formerly known as Philip Atoll
Sorong Indon. 73 H7
Sororó r. Brazil 202 B3
Soroti Uganda 128 B4
Sørøya i. Norway 44 M1
Sørøysundet sea chan. Norway 44 M1
Sorp Turkey see Reşadiye
Sorraia r. Port. 54 C5
Sørreisa Norway 44 L1
Sorrento Italy 57 G8
Sorsakoski Fin. 44 N3
Sorsatunturi hill Fin. 44 O2
Sorsele Sweden 44 L2
Sorso Sardinia Italy 57 A8
Sorsogon Phil. 74 C3
Sortavala Rus. Fed. 45 O3
Sortland Norway 44 K1
Sortot Sudan 121 F5
Sør-Trøndelag county Norway 44 J3
Sørvær Norway 44 M1
Sørvågen Norway 44 K2
Sõrve väin sea chan. Estonia/Latvia see Irbe Strait
Sŏsan S. Korea 83 B5
Sosedno Rus. Fed. 43 J3
Sosenskiy Rus. Fed. 43 Q7
Soshanguve S. Africa 133 M2
Soskovo Rus. Fed. 43 Q9
Sosna r. Rus. Fed. 43 T9
Sosnogorsk Rus. Fed. 40 J3
formerly known as Izhma
Sosnovka Kazakh. 103 I2
Sosnovka Arkhangel'skaya Oblast' Rus. Fed. 40 H3
Sosnovka Murmanskaya Oblast' Rus. Fed. 40 G2
Sosnovka Tambovskaya Oblast' Rus. Fed. 41 G5
Sosnovka Vologod. Obl. Rus. Fed. 43 S3
Sosnovka Vologod. Obl. Rus. Fed. 43 U2
Sosnovo Rus. Fed. 43 L1
Sosnovoborsk Rus. Fed. 41 H5
Sosnovo-Ozerskoye Rus. Fed. 81 I2
Sosnovyy Rus. Fed. 44 P2
Sosnovyy Bor Belarus see Sasnovy Bor
Sosnovyy Bor Rus. Fed. 43 K2
Sosnowiec Poland 49 Q5
historically known as Sosnowitz
Sosnowitz Poland see Sosnowiec
Sosny Belarus 42 I9
Sosso Cent. Afr. Rep. 126 B4
Sos'va Rus. Fed. 38 G4
Sot' r. Rus. Fed. 43 V4
Sota r. Benin 125 F4
Sotang China 97 G3
Sotério r. Brazil 201 D2
Sotillo r. Spain 54 F6
Sotkamo Fin. 44 O2
Soto Arg. 204 D3
Soto la Marina Mex. 185 F4
Sotouboua Togo 125 F4
Sotteville-lès-Rouen France 50 H3
Sottunga Fin. 45 M3
Sotuta Mex. 185 H4
Souanké Congo 126 B4
Soubré Côte d'Ivoire 124 D5
Soucis, Cape N.Z. 152 H9
Souda Greece 59 F13
also spelt Soúdha
Soudan Australia 148 C4
Soudas, Ormos b. Greece 59 F13
Soúdha Greece see Souda
Soufli Greece 58 H7
Soufrière vol. Guadeloupe 187 H3
Soufrière St Lucia 187 H4
Soufrière vol. St Vincent 199 F1
Soufrière Hills Montserrat 187 H3
Souguéta Guinea 124 B4
Sougueur Alg. 55 M9
Souillac France 50 H8
Souk Ahras Alg. 123 G1
Souk el Arbaâ du Rharb Morocco 122 D2
Souk el Had el Rharbia Morocco 54 F9
Souk el Kella Morocco 54 F9
Souk-Khémis-des-Anjra Morocco 54 F9
Souk Khemis du Sahel Morocco 54 E9
Soukoukoutane Niger 125 F3
Souk Tleta Taghramet Morocco 54 F9
Souk-Tnine-de-Sidi-el-Yamani Morocco 54 F9
Sŏul S. Korea see Seoul
Soulac-sur-Mer France 50 E7
Sounding Creek r. Canada 167 I4
Sounfat well Mali see Tessoûnfat
Sounio nat. park Greece 59 F11
Soûr Lebanon see Tyre
Sourdeval France 50 F4
Soure Brazil 202 B2
Sour el Ghozlane Alg. 55 O8
Souris Man. Canada 167 K5
Souris P.E.I. Canada 169 I4
Souris r. Canada 167 L5
Souriya country Asia see Syria
Souroumelli well Mauritania 124 C2
Sous, Oued watercourse Morocco 122 C3
Sousa Brazil 202 E3
Sousa Lara Angola see Bocoio
Sousel Port. 54 D6
Sousse Tunisia 123 H2
also spelt Susah; historically known as Hadrumetum
UNESCO World Heritage Site
Soussellem, Oued watercourse Alg. 55 N9
Soustons France 50 E9
Sout r. S. Africa 132 C8
Sout watercourse S. Africa 132 E5
South Africa country Africa see South Africa, Republic of

►South Africa, Republic of country Africa 130 D6
5th most populous country in Africa. Also known as Suid-Afrika in Afrikaans; short form South Africa
►►114–115 Africa Countries

South Alligator r. Australia 148 B2
Southampton Canada 168 D4
Southampton U.K. 47 K13
historically known as Hamwic
Southampton U.S.A. 177 M5
Southampton Island Canada 167 O1
South Andaman i. India 95 G4
South Anna r. U.S.A. 176 H8
South Aulatsivik Island Canada 169 I1
South Australia state Australia 146 B2
Southaven U.S.A. 174 B5
South Baldy mt. U.S.A. 181 F6
South Bay U.S.A. 175 D7
South Bend IN U.S.A. 174 C3
South Bend WA U.S.A. 180 B3
South Bluff pt Bahamas 187 E2
South Boston U.S.A. 176 G9
Southbridge N.Z. 153 G11
Southbridge U.S.A. 177 M3
South Brook Canada 169 J3
South Burlington U.S.A. 177 L1
Southburn N.Z. 153 F12
South Carolina state U.S.A. 175 D5
South Charleston OH U.S.A. 176 B6
South Charleston WV U.S.A. 176 D7
South China Sea N. Pacific Ocean 72 E4
South Coast Town Australia see Gold Coast
South Dakota state U.S.A. 178 B2
South Deerfield U.S.A. 177 M3
South Downs hills U.K. 47 L13
South-East admin. dist. Botswana 133 J2
South East Cape Australia 147 E5
South East Isles Australia 151 C7
Southend Canada 167 K3
Southend-on-Sea U.K. 47 M12
Southern admin. dist. Botswana 131 E5
Southern admin. reg. Malawi 129 B8
Southern prov. Sierra Leone 124 B5
Southern prov. Zambia 127 E9
Southern Aegean admin. reg. Greece see Notio Aigaio
Southern Alps mts N.Z. 153 E11
also known as Kā Tiritiri o te Moana
Southern Central Aboriginal Reserve Australia 151 D5
Southern Cross Australia 151 B6
Southern Darfur state Sudan 126 E2
Southern Indian Lake Canada 167 L3
Southern Kordofan state Sudan 128 A2
Southern Lau Group is Fiji 145 H3
Southern National Park Sudan 126 F3
Southern Ocean 222 F3
Southern Pines U.S.A. 174 E5
Southern Rhodesia country Africa see Zimbabwe
Southern Uplands hills U.K. 46 H8
Southern Urals mts Rus. Fed. see Yuzhnyy Ural
Southern Ute Indian Reservation res. U.S.A. 181 F5
South Esk Tableland reg. Australia 150 D3
Southey Canada 167 J5
Southeyville S. Africa 133 L8
South Fabius r. U.S.A. 178 E4
Southfield U.S.A. 173 J8
Southfields U.S.A. 177 K4
South Fork CA U.S.A. 182 A1
South Fork CO U.S.A. 181 F5
South Fork PA U.S.A. 176 G5
South Fox Island U.S.A. 172 H5
Southgate r. Canada 166 E5
South Geomagnetic Pole Antarctica 223 H1

►South Georgia and South Sandwich Islands terr. S. Atlantic Ocean 217 L9
United Kingdom Overseas Territory.
►►192–193 South America Countries

South Gillies Canada 172 D2
South Grand r. U.S.A. 178 D4
South Hatia Island Bangl. 97 F5
South Haven U.S.A. 172 G8
South Head N.Z. 152 I4
South Head hd N.Z. 152 I4
South Henik Lake Canada 167 L2
South Hero U.S.A. 177 L1
South Hill U.S.A. 176 G9
South Horr Kenya 128 C4
South Indian Lake Canada 167 L3
South Island India 94 B4

►South Island N.Z. 153 G12
2nd largest island in Oceania. Also known as Te Waipounamu.
►►134–135 Oceania Landscapes

South Island National Park Kenya 128 C4
UNESCO World Heritage Site
South Islet reef Phil. 74 A4
South Junction Canada 167 M5
South Kazakhstan Oblast admin. div. Kazakh. see Yuzhnyy Kazakhstan
South Kitui National Reserve Kenya 128 C5
South Koel r. India 97 E5
►South Korea country Asia 83 B5
►►16–17 World Population
►►64–65 Asia Countries
South Lake Tahoe U.S.A. 182 D3
Southland admin. reg. N.Z. 153 B13
South Loup r. U.S.A. 178 C3
South Luangwa National Park Zambia 127 F8
South Macmillan r. Canada 166 C2
South Magnetic Pole (2000) Antarctica 223 J2
South Manitou Island U.S.A. 173 G5
South Mills U.S.A. 177 I9
Southminster U.K. 47 M12
South Moose Lake Canada 167 K4
South Mountains hills U.S.A. 177 H6
South Muiron Island Australia 150 A4
South Nahanni r. Canada 166 D1
South Negril Point Jamaica 186 D3
South New Berlin U.S.A. 177 J3
South Orkney Islands S. Atlantic Ocean 222 V2
South Paris U.S.A. 177 O1
South Passage Australia 151 A5
South Patrick Shores U.S.A. 175 D6
South Platte r. U.S.A. 178 B3
South Point U.S.A. 181 [inset] Z2
South Pole Antarctica 223 T1
South Porcupine Canada 173 L2
Southport Australia 147 F5
Southport U.K. 47 I10
Southport NC U.S.A. 175 E5
Southport NY U.S.A. 177 I3
South Portland U.S.A. 177 O2
South River Canada 173 N5
South Ronaldsay i. U.K. 46 J5
South Royalton U.S.A. 177 M2
South Salt Lake U.S.A. 183 M1
South San Francisco U.S.A. 182 B4
South Saskatchewan r. Canada 167 J4
South Seal r. Canada 167 L3
South Shetland Islands Antarctica 222 U2
South Shields U.K. 47 K8
South Sinai governorate Egypt see Janūb Sīnā'
South Skunk r. U.S.A. 174 A3
South Taranaki Bight b. N.Z. 152 I7
South Tent mt. U.S.A. 183 M2
South Tons r. India 97 D4
South Tucson U.S.A. 183 N9
South Turkana Nature Reserve Kenya 128 B4
South Twin Island Canada 168 E2
South Twin Lake Canada 169 K3
South Uist i. U.K. 46 E6
also known as Uibhist a' Deas
South Umpqua r. U.S.A. 180 B4
South Wellesley Islands Australia 148 C3
South-West Africa country Africa see Namibia
South West Cape Australia 147 E5
South West Cape N.Z. 153 B15
also known as Puhiwaero
South West Cay reef Australia 149 G3
Southwest Conservation Area Australia 147 E5
South West Entrance sea chan. P.N.G. 149 F1
Southwest Harbor U.S.A. 177 Q1
South West Island Australia 149 F3
South West National Park Australia 147 E5
South West Rocks Australia 147 G2
South Whitley U.S.A. 172 H9
South Williamson U.S.A. 176 C8
South Williamsport U.S.A. 177 I4
South Windham U.S.A. 177 O2
Southwold U.K. 47 N11
Southwood National Park Australia 147 F1
South Zanesville U.S.A. 176 C6
Soutpansberg mts S. Africa 131 F4
Souttouf, Adrar mts W. Sahara 122 B5
Souvigny France 51 J6
Sovata Romania 58 G2
Soveja Romania 58 H2
Soverato Italy 57 I10
Sovet Tajik. 101 G2
also known as Sovetskiy
Sovetabad Uzbek. see Xonobod
Sovetsk Kaliningradskaya Oblast' Rus. Fed. 42 C6
historically known as Tilsit
Sovetsk Kirovskaya Oblast' Rus. Fed. 40 I4
Sovetsk Tul'skaya Oblast' Rus. Fed. 43 S8
Sovetskaya Rus. Fed. 107 F1
Sovetskaya Gavan' Rus. Fed. 82 F2
Sovetskiy Khanty-Mansiyskiy Avtonomnyy Okrug Rus. Fed. 38 G3
Sovetskiy Leningradskaya Oblast' Rus. Fed. 43 J1
Sovetskiy Respublika Mariy El Rus. Fed. 40 I4
Sovetskiy Tajik. see Sovet
Sovetskoye Chechenskaya Respublika Rus. Fed. see Shatoy
Sovetskoye Saratovskaya Oblast' Rus. Fed. 102 A2
Sovetskoye Stavropol'skiy Kray Rus. Fed. see Zelenokumsk
Sovići Bos.-Herz. 56 J5
Sowa Botswana 131 E4
Sowa China 86 A2
formerly known as Dagxoi
Sowa Pan salt pan Botswana 131 E4
Soweto S. Africa 133 L3
Sōya-kaikyō strait Japan/Rus. Fed. see La Pérouse Strait
Soyaló Mex. 185 G5
Sōya-misaki c. Japan 90 G2
Soyana r. Rus. Fed. 40 G2
Soyang-ho l. S. Korea 83 B5
Soyaux France 50 G7
Sōya-wan b. Japan 90 G2
Soylan Armenia see Vayk'
Soyma r. Rus. Fed. 40 I2
Soyo Angola 127 B6
formerly known as Santo António do Zaire
Sozaq Kazakh. see Suzak
Sozh r. Europe 43 L9
Sozimskiy Rus. Fed. 40 J4
Sozopol Bulg. 58 I6
historically known as Apollonia
Spaatz Island Antarctica 222 T2
Spadafora Sicily Italy 57 H10

►Spain country Europe 54 F4
4th largest country in Europe. Known as España in Spanish; historically known as Hispania.
►►32–33 Europe Countries

Spalato Croatia see Split
Spalatum Croatia see Split
Spalding Australia 146 C3
Spalding U.K. 47 L11
Spaniard's Bay Canada 169 K4
Spanish Canada 168 D4
Spanish r. Canada 168 D4
Spanish Fork U.S.A. 183 M1
Spanish Guinea country Africa see Equatorial Guinea
Spanish Netherlands country Europe see Belgium
Spanish Point Ireland 47 C11
Spanish Sahara terr. Africa see Western Sahara
Spanish Town Jamaica 186 D3
Spanish Wells Bahamas 175 E7
Sparagio, Monte mt. Sicily Italy 57 E10
Sparks U.S.A. 182 E2
Sparta Greece see Sparti
Sparta GA U.S.A. 175 D5
Sparta MI U.S.A. 172 H7
Sparta NC U.S.A. 176 D9
Sparta TN U.S.A. 174 C5
Sparta WI U.S.A. 172 C7
Spartanburg U.S.A. 174 D5
Spartansburg U.S.A. 176 F4
Spartel, Cap c. Morocco 54 F9
Sparti Greece 59 D11
historically known as Lacedaemon or Sparta
Spartivento, Capo c. Sardinia Italy 57 A10
Spartivento, Capo c. Italy 57 I11
Sparwood Canada 167 H5
Spas-Demensk Rus. Fed. 43 P7
Spas-Klepiki Rus. Fed. 43 V6
Spass Rus. Fed. 43 Q6
Spasskaya Polist' Rus. Fed. 43 M3
Spassk-Dal'niy Rus. Fed. 82 D3
Spasskoye Kazakh. 103 G1
Spasskoye-Lutovinovo Rus. Fed. 43 R8
Spas-Ugol Rus. Fed. 43 S5
Spatha, Akra pt Greece 59 E13
Spatsizi Plateau Wilderness Provincial Park Canada 166 D3
Spean Bridge U.K. 46 H7
Spearfish U.S.A. 178 B2
Spearman U.S.A. 179 B4
Speers Canada 167 J4
Speightstown Barbados 187 I4
Speikkogel mt. Austria 49 M8
Speke Gulf Tanz. 128 B5
Spence Bay Canada see Taloyoak
Spencer IA U.S.A. 178 D3
Spencer ID U.S.A. 180 D3
Spencer IN U.S.A. 174 C4
Spencer MA U.S.A. 177 N3
Spencer NY U.S.A. 177 I3
Spencer VA U.S.A. 176 E9
Spencer, Cape Australia 146 C3
Spencer, Cape U.S.A. 166 B3
Spencer, Point U.S.A. 39 T3
Spencer Gulf est. Australia 146 C3
Spencer Range hills N.T. Australia 148 A2
Spencer Range hills N.T. Australia 148 B2
Spences Bridge Canada 166 F5
Spenser Mountains N.Z. 153 G10
Spercheios r. Greece 59 D10
also spelt Sperkhiós
Sperkhiós r. Greece see Spercheios
Spermezeu Romania 58 F1
Sperrin Mountains hills U.K. 47 E9
Sperryville U.S.A. 176 G7
Spétsai i. Greece see Spetses
Spetses Greece 59 E11
Spetses i. Greece 59 E11
also known as Spétsai
Spey r. U.K. 46 I6
Speyer Germany 48 F6
UNESCO World Heritage Site
Spezand Pak. 101 F4
Spice Islands Indon. see Moluccas
Spiekeroog i. Germany 48 E2
Spiez Switz. 51 N6
Spijkenisse Neth. 48 B4
Spil Dağı Milli Parkı nat. park Turkey 59 I10
Spilimbergo Italy 56 E2
Spīn Būldak Afgh. 101 F4
Spioenkop Dam Nature Reserve S. Africa 133 N5
Spirit Lake U.S.A. 178 D3
Spiritwood Canada 167 J4
Spirovo Rus. Fed. 43 P4
Spišská Nová Ves Slovakia 49 R7

Subei China 84 B4
also known as Dangchengwan
Subeita tourist site Israel see **Shivta**
Subiaco Italy 56 F7
Subi Besar i. Indon. 77 E2
Subi Kecil i. Indon. 77 E2
Sublette U.S.A. 178 B4
Subotica Vojvodina, Srbija Serb. and Mont. 58 A2
also known as Szabadka
Subucle mt. Eritrea 121 I6
Subugo mt. Kenya 128 B5
Success, Lake U.S.A. 182 F5
Suceava Romania 53 H2
formerly spelt Suczawa
Sucevița Romania 41 C7
UNESCO World Heritage Site
Sucha Beskidzka Poland 49 Q6
Suchan Rus. Fed. see **Partizansk**
Suchan r. Rus. Fed. 82 D4
Suchedniów Poland 49 R4
Suchixtepec Mex. 185 F5
Sucio r. Col. 198 B3
Suciu de Sus Romania 58 F1
Suck r. Ireland 47 D10
Sucker Creek Landing Canada 173 M4

►**Sucre** Bol. 200 D4
Legislative capital of Bolivia.
UNESCO World Heritage Site
►►**8–9 World** Countries

Sucre dept Col. 198 C2
Sucre state Venez. 199 F2
Sucuaro Col. 198 D3
Sucumbíos prov. Ecuador 198 B5
Sucunduri r. Brazil 199 G6
Sucuriú r. Brazil 206 B7
Suczawa Romania see **Suceava**
Sud prov. Cameroon 125 H6
Sud, Grand Récif du reef New Caledonia 145 F4
Sud, Rivière du r. Canada 177 L1
Suda Rus. Fed. 43 S2
Suda r. Rus. Fed. 43 S2
Sudak Ukr. 41 E7

►**Sudan** country Africa 121 E5
Largest country in Africa and 10th largest in the world. Historically known as Anglo-Egyptian Sudan.
►►**8–9 World** Countries
►►**114–115 Africa** Countries

Suday Rus. Fed. 40 G4
Sudayr reg. Saudi Arabia 105 D2
Sudayr, Sha'īb watercourse Iraq 107 F5
Sudbishchi Rus. Fed. 43 S9
Sud'bodarovka Rus. Fed. 102 C1
Sudbury Canada 168 D4
Sudbury U.K. 47 M11
Sudd swamp Sudan 126 F3
Sudd an Na'ām, Jabal hill Egypt 108 C8
Suddie Guyana 199 G3
Sude r. Germany 48 H2
Sudest Island P.N.G. see **Tagula Island**
Sudetenland mts Czech Rep./Poland see **Sudety**
Sudety mts Czech Rep./Poland 49 M5
historically known as Sudetenland
Sudimir Rus. Fed. 43 P8
Sudislavl' Rus. Fed. 40 G4
Sud-Kivu prov. Dem. Rep. Congo 126 F5
Sudlersville U.S.A. 177 J6
Sudogda Rus. Fed. 40 G5
Sudomskiye Vysoty hills Rus. Fed. 43 K4
Sudost' r. Rus. Fed. 43 O9
Sud-Ouest prov. Cameroon 125 H5
Sudr Egypt 121 G2
Suðurland constituency Iceland 44 [inset] B2
Suðuroy i. Faroe Is 46 F2
Suðuroyarfjørður sea chan. Faroe Is 46 F2
Sue watercourse Sudan 126 F3
Sueca Spain 55 K5
Sŭedinenie Bulg. 58 F6
Suez Egypt 121 G2
also spelt El Suweis or As Suways
Suez, Gulf of Egypt 121 G2
also known as Suweis, Khalîg el or Suways, Khalīj as
Suez Bay Egypt 108 D8
also known as Qulzum, Baḩr el
Suez Canal Egypt 121 G2
also known as Suways, Qanāt as or Suweis, Qanâ el
Şufaynah Saudi Arabia 104 C3
Suffolk U.S.A. 177 I9
Sūfiān Iran 100 A2
Sufi-Kurgan Kyrg. see **Sopu-Korgon**
Sug-Aksy Rus. Fed. 88 E1
Sugar r. U.S.A. 172 D8
Sugarbush Hill U.S.A. 172 E5
Sugar Grove NC U.S.A. 176 D9
Sugar Grove OH U.S.A. 176 C6
Sugarloaf Mountain U.S.A. 174 G2
Sugarloaf Point Australia 147 G3
Sugar Notch U.S.A. 173 R9
Sugbuhan Point Phil. 74 C4
Süget China see **Sogat**
Sugi i. Indon. 76 C2
Sugun China 88 B4
Sugut r. Sabah Malaysia 77 G1
Sugut, Tanjung pt Sabah Malaysia 77 G1
Suhaia Romania 58 G5
Suhai Hu l. China 84 B4
Suhait China 84 E4
Sūhāj Egypt see **Sawhāj**
Şuḩār Oman 105 G2
English form Sohar
Suhaymī, Wādī as watercourse Egypt 108 E7
Sühbaatar Mongolia 85 E1
Sühbaatar prov. Mongolia 85 G2
Suheli Par i. India 94 B4
Suhl Germany 48 H5
Suhopolje Croatia 56 J3
Suhul reg. Saudi Arabia 105 D3
Suhūl al Kidan plain Saudi Arabia 105 F3
Suhum Ghana 125 E5
Şuhut Turkey 106 B3
Sui, Laem pt Thai. 79 B6
Suiá Missur r. Brazil 202 A4
Sui'an China see **Zhangpu**
Suibin China 82 C3
Suichang China 87 F2
also known as Miaogao
Suicheng Fujian China see **Jianning**
Suicheng Guangdong China see **Suixi**
Suichuan China 87 E3
also known as Quanjiang
Suid-Afrika country Africa see **South Africa, Republic of**
Suide China 85 F4
also known as Mingzhou
Suidzhikurmsy Turkm. see **Madaw**
Suifenhe China 82 C3
Suifen He r. China 82 C4
Suigam India 96 A4
Suihua China 82 B3
Suijiang China 86 B2
also known as Zhongcheng
Suileng China 82 B3
Suining Hunan China 87 D3
also known as Changpu
Suining Jiangsu China 87 F1
Suining Sichuan China 86 C2
Suiping China 87 E1
also known as Zhuoyang
Suippes France 51 K3
Suir r. Ireland 47 E11
Suisse country Europe see **Switzerland**
Suixi Anhui China 87 F1
Suixi Guangdong China 87 D4
also known as Suicheng
Suixian Henan China 87 E1
Suixian Hubei China see **Suizhou**
Suiyang Guizhou China 87 C3
also known as Yangchuan
Suiyang Henan China 87 E1
Suizhai China see **Xiangcheng**
Suizhong China 85 I3
Suizhou China 87 E2
formerly known as Suixian
Sujangarh India 96 B4
Sujawal Pak. 101 G5
Sukabumi Indon. 77 D4
Sukadana Kalimantan Barat Indon. 77 E3
Sukadana Sumatra Indon. 77 D4
Sukadana, Teluk b. Indon. 77 E3
Sukagawa Japan 90 G6
Sukaraja Indon. 77 E3
Sukaramai Indon. 77 E3
Sukarnapura Indon. see **Jayapura**
Sukarno, Puntjak mt. Indon. see **Jaya, Puncak**
Suket India 96 C4
Sukeva Fin. 44 N3
Sukhanovka Rus. Fed. 90 C1
Sukhary Belarus 43 L8
Sukhinichi Rus. Fed. 43 Q7
Sukhodol'skoye, Ozero l. Rus. Fed. 43 L1
Sukhodrev r. Rus. Fed. 43 Q7
Sukhona r. Rus. Fed. 43 V2
Sukhothai Thai. 78 B4
UNESCO World Heritage Site
Sukhoverkovo Rus. Fed. 43 Q5
Sukhumi Georgia see **Sokhumi**
Sukhum-Kale Georgia see **Sokhumi**
Sukkertoppen Greenland see **Maniitsoq**
Sukkozero Rus. Fed. 40 E3
Sukkur Pak. 101 G5
Sukkur Barrage Pak. 101 G5
Sukma India 94 D2
Sukpay Rus. Fed. 82 E3
Sukpay r. Rus. Fed. 82 E3
Sukri r. India 96 B4
Sukromlya Rus. Fed. 43 P5
Sukromny Rus. Fed. 43 R4
Sukses Namibia 130 C4
Suktel r. India 95 D1
Sukumo Japan 91 C8
Sukun i. Indon. 75 B5
Sul, Canal do sea chan. Brazil 202 B2
Sul, Pico do mt. Brazil 207 J7
Sula i. Norway 46 Q2
Sula r. Rus. Fed. 40 I2
Sula, Kepulauan is Indon. 75 C3
Sula, Ozero l. Rus. Fed. 44 O3
Sulabesi i. Indon. 75 C3
Sulaiman Range mts Pak. 101 G4
Sulak Rus. Fed. 102 A4
Sulak r. Rus. Fed. 102 A4
Sūlār Iran 100 B4
Sula Sgeir i. U.K. 46 F4
Sulasih, Gunung vol. Indon. 76 C3
Sulat Phil. 74 C4
Sulawesi i. Indon. see **Celebes**
Sulawesi Selatan prov. Indon. 75 A3
Sulawesi Tengah prov. Indon. 75 B3
Sulawesi Tenggara prov. Indon. 75 B4
Sulawesi Utara prov. Indon. 75 C2
Sulaymān Beg Iraq 107 F4
Sulaymānīyah Iraq see **As Sulaymānīyah**
Sulayyimah Saudi Arabia 105 D3
Sulci Sardinia Italy see **Sant'Antioco**
Sulcis Sardinia Italy see **Sant'Antioco**
Sulechów Poland 49 M3
Sulęcin Poland 49 M3
Suledeh Iran 100 B2
Sulejów Poland 49 Q4
Sulejowskie, Jezioro l. Poland 49 Q4
Suleman, Teluk b. Indon. 75 A2
Sule Skerry i. U.K. 46 H4
Sule Stack i. U.K. 46 H4
Süleymanlı Turkey 107 D3
Suliki Indon. 76 C3
Sulima Sierra Leone 124 C5
Sulina Romania 58 K3
Sulina, Braţul watercourse Romania 58 K3
Suliskongen mt. Norway 44 L2
Sulitjelma Norway 44 L2
Sulkava Fin. 45 O3
Sullana Peru 198 A6
Süller Turkey 59 K10
Sullivan IL U.S.A. 174 B4
Sullivan IN U.S.A. 174 C4
Sullivan Bay Canada 166 E5
Sullivan Island Myanmar see **Lanbi Kyun**
Sullivan Lake Canada 167 I5
Sully-sur-Loire France 51 I5
Sulmo Italy see **Sulmona**
Sulmona Italy 56 F6
historically known as Sulmo
Süloğlu Turkey 58 H7
Sulphur LA U.S.A. 179 D6
Sulphur OK U.S.A. 179 C5
Sulphur r. U.S.A. 179 D5
Sulphur Draw watercourse U.S.A. 179 B5
Sulphur Springs U.S.A. 179 D5
Sulphur Springs Draw watercourse U.S.A. 179 B5
Sultan Canada 168 D4
Sultan Libya 120 D2
Sultan, Koh-i- mts Pak. 101 E4
Sultanabad India see **Osmannagar**
Sultanabad Iran see **Arāk**
Sultanbeyli Turkey 58 K8
Sultanhanı Turkey 106 C3
Sultanhisar Turkey 59 J11
Sultaniça Turkey 58 H8
Sultanıye Turkey see **Karapınar**
Sultanpur India 97 D4
Sultansandzharskoye Vodokhranilishche resr Turkm. 103 E4
Sulu Dem. Rep. Congo 126 E6
Suluan i. Phil. 74 C4
Sulu Archipelago is Phil. 74 B5
Sülüklü Turkey 106 C3
Sülüktü Kyrg. 103 G5
also spelt Sulyukta
Sulunţah Libya 120 D1
Sulūq Libya 120 D2
Suluru India 94 D3
Sulu Sea N. Pacific Ocean 74 A4
Sulyukta Kyrg. see **Sülüktü**
Sulzbach-Rosenberg Germany 48 I6
Sulzberger Bay Antarctica 222 N1
Sumaco, Volcán vol. Ecuador 198 B5
Šumadija reg. Serb. and Mont. 58 B4
Sumāil Oman 105 G3
Sumalata Indon. 75 B2
Sumalē admin. reg. Eth. 128 D3
Sumampa Arg. 204 E3
Sumangat, Tanjung pt Sabah Malaysia 74 A5
Sumapaz, Parque Nacional nat. park Col. 198 C4
Sumatera i. Indon. see **Sumatra**
Sumatera Barat prov. Indon. 76 C3
Sumatera Selatan prov. Indon. 76 C3
Sumatera Utara prov. Indon. 76 B2

►**Sumatra** i. Indon. 76 B2
2nd largest island in Asia and 6th in the world. Also spelt Sumatera.
►►**6–7 World** Landscapes
►►**60–61 Asia** Landscapes
►►**66–67 Asia** Tsunami

Sumaúma Brazil 201 E1
Šumava mts Czech Rep. 49 K6
Šumava nat. park Czech Rep. 49 K6
Sumba i. Indon. 75 B5
Sumba, Île i. Dem. Rep. Congo 126 C4
Sumba, Selat sea chan. Indon. 75 A5
Sumbar r. Turkm. 102 C5
Sumbawa i. Indon. 77 G5
Sumbawabesar Indon. 77 G5
Sumbawanga Tanz. 129 A6
Sumbay Peru 200 C3
Sumbe Angola 127 B7
formerly known as Ngunza or Ngunza-Kabolu or Novo Redondo
Sumbing, Gunung vol. Indon. 76 C3
Sumbu Zambia 127 F7
Sumbu National Park Zambia 127 F7
also spelt Nsumbu National Park
Sumburgh U.K. 46 K4
Sumburgh Head U.K. 46 K4
Sumbuya Sierra Leone 124 C5
Sumdo Aksai Chin 89 B5
Sumdo China 86 B2
Sumdum, Mount U.S.A. 166 C3
Sumé Brazil 202 E3
Sumedang Indon. 77 D4
Sume'eh Sarā Iran 100 B2
Sümeg Hungary 49 O9
Sumeih Sudan 126 E2
Sumenep Indon. 77 F4
Sumerpur India 96 B4
Sumgait Azer. see **Sumqayıt**
Sumisu-jima i. Japan 91 G9
Sümiyn Bulag Mongolia 85 G1
Summēl Iraq 107 E3
Summer Beaver Canada 168 B2
Summerdown Namibia 130 C4
Summerford Canada 169 K3
Summer Island U.S.A. 172 G5
Summerland Canada 166 G5
Summerside Canada 169 I4
Summersville U.S.A. 176 E7
Summersville Lake U.S.A. 176 E7
Summerville GA U.S.A. 174 C5
Summerville SC U.S.A. 175 D5
Summit Lake B.C. Canada 166 E3
Summit Lake B.C. Canada 166 F4
Summit Mountain U.S.A. 183 H2
Summit Peak U.S.A. 181 F5
Sumnal Aksai Chin 89 B5
Sumner U.S.A. 174 B5
Sumner, Lake N.Z. 153 G10
Sumner Strait U.S.A. 166 C3
Sumon-dake mt. Japan 90 F6
Sumoto Japan 91 D7
Sumpangbinangae Indon. 75 A4
Šumperk Czech Rep. 49 N6
Sumprabum Myanmar 78 B2
Sumpu Japan see **Shizuoka**
Sumqayıt Azer. 107 G2
also spelt Sumgait
Sumqayıt r. Azer. 107 G2
Sumsar Kyrg. 103 G4
Sumskiy Posad Rus. Fed. 40 E2
Sumter U.S.A. 175 D5
Sumur Jammu and Kashmir 96 C2
Sumy Ukr. 41 E6
Sun r. U.S.A. 180 E3
Suna Rus. Fed. 40 I4
Sunagawa Japan 90 G3
Sunam India 96 B3
Sunamganj Bangl. 97 F4
Sunan China 84 C4
also known as Hongwansi
Sunan N. Korea 83 B5
Şunaynah Oman 105 F3
Sunaysilah salt l. Iraq 109 M2
Sunbright U.S.A. 176 A9
Sunbula Kuh mts Iran 100 A3
Sunbury Australia 147 E4
Sunbury NC U.S.A. 177 I9
Sunbury OH U.S.A. 176 C5
Sunbury PA U.S.A. 177 I5
Sunchales Arg. 204 E3
Suncho Corral Arg. 204 E2
Sunch'ŏn N. Korea 83 B5
Sunch'ŏn S. Korea 83 B6
Sun City S. Africa 133 L2
Sun City U.S.A. 183 L8
Suncook U.S.A. 177 N2
Sund Fin. 42 B1
Sunda, Selat strait Indon. 77 D4
English form Sunda Strait
Sunda Kalapa Indon. see **Jakarta**
Sundance U.S.A. 180 F3
Sundarbans reg. Bangl./India 97 F5
UNESCO World Heritage Site
Sundarbans National Park Bangl./India 97 F5
UNESCO World Heritage Site
Sundargarh India 97 E5
Sundarnagar India 96 C3
Sunda Strait Indon. see **Sunda, Selat**
Sundays r. E. Cape S. Africa 133 J10
Sundays r. Kwazulu-Natal S. Africa 133 O5
Sunday Strait Australia 150 C3
Sunderland U.K. 47 K9
Sündiken Dağları mts Turkey 106 B3
Sundre Canada 167 H5
Sundridge Canada 168 E4
Sundsvall Sweden 45 L3
Sundukli, Peski des. Turkm. see **Sandykly Gumy**
Sundumbili S. Africa 133 P6
Sunel India 96 C4
Sunga Tanz. 129 C6
Sungaiapit Indon. 76 C2
Sungaiguntung Indon. 76 C2
Sungailiat Indon. 77 D3
Sungaipenuh Indon. 76 C3
Sungai Petani Malaysia 76 C1
Sungaipinyuh Indon. 77 E2
Sungai Tuas Basin dock Sing. 76 [inset]
Sungari r. China see **Songhua Jiang**
Sungei Seletar Reservoir Sing. 76 [inset]
Sungguminasa Indon. 75 A4
Sungikai Sudan 121 F6
Sungkiang China see **Songjiang**
Sung Kong i. Hong Kong China 87 [inset]
Sungo Moz. 131 G3
Sungqu China see **Songpan**
Sungurlare Bulg. 58 H6
Sungurlu Turkey 106 C2
Sunja Croatia 56 I3
Sunkar, Gora mt. Kazakh. 103 H3
Sunkosh Chhu r. Bhutan 97 F4
also spelt Sankosh
Sun Kosi r. Nepal 97 E4
Sunndal Norway 45 I3
Sunndalsøra Norway 44 J3
Sunne Sweden 45 K4
Sunnyside UT U.S.A. 183 N2
Sunnyside WA U.S.A. 180 C3
Sunnyvale U.S.A. 182 B4
Sun Prairie U.S.A. 172 D7
Sunsas, Sierra de hills Bol. 201 F4
Sunset House Canada 167 G4
Sunset Peak hill Hong Kong China 87 [inset]
also known as Tai Tung Shan
Sunshine Island Hong Kong China 87 [inset]
also known as Chau Kung To
Suntar Rus. Fed. 39 L3
Suntsar Pak. 101 E5
Suntu Eth. 128 C2
Sunwi-do i. N. Korea 83 B5
Sunwu China 82 B2
Sunyani Ghana 124 E5
Suojanperä Fin. 44 O1
Suolahti Fin. 44 N3
Suolijärvet l. Fin. 40 D2
Suoločielgi Fin. see **Saariselkä**
Suoluvuobmi Norway 44 M1
Suomenniemi Fin. 45 N3
Suomi Canada 172 D2
Suomi country Europe see **Finland**
Suomusjärvi Fin. 42 E1
Suomussalmi Fin. 44 O2
Suō-nada b. Japan 91 B8
Suonenjoki Fin. 44 N3
Suŏng Cambodia 79 D6
Suong r. Laos 78 C4
Suontee Fin. 44 N3
Suontienselkä l. Fin. 44 N3
Suoyarvi Rus. Fed. 40 E3
Suozhen China see **Huantai**
Supa India 94 B3
Supai U.S.A. 183 L5
Supaul India 97 E4
Superfosfatnyy Uzbek. 103 F5
Superior AZ U.S.A. 183 M8
Superior MT U.S.A. 180 D3
Superior NE U.S.A. 178 C3
Superior WI U.S.A. 172 A4
Superior, Laguna lag. Mex. 185 G5

►**Superior, Lake** Canada/U.S.A. 172 F3
Largest lake in North America and 2nd in the world.
►►**6–7 World** Landscapes
►►**154–155 North America** Landscapes

Supetar Croatia 56 I5
Suphan Buri Thai. 79 C5
Süphan Dağı mt. Turkey 107 E3
Supiori i. Indon. 73 I7
Suponevo Rus. Fed. 43 P8
Support Force Glacier Antarctica 223 V1
Supraśl Poland 49 U2
Supraśl r. Poland 49 U2
Sup'sa r. Georgia 107 E2
Supung N. Korea 83 B4
Sūq al Inān Yemen 104 D4
Sūq ar Rubū' Saudi Arabia 104 C3
Sūq ash Shuyūkh Iraq 107 F5
Suqian China 87 F1
Sūq Suwayq Saudi Arabia 104 B2
Suquţrā i. Yemen see **Socotra**
Sur r. Ghana 125 E4
Súr Hungary 49 P8
Şūr Oman 105 G3
Sur, Point U.S.A. 182 C5
Sur, Punta pt Arg. 204 F5
Sura Rus. Fed. 41 H5
Sura r. Rus. Fed. 41 H4
Şuraabad Azer. 107 G2
Surab Pak. 101 F4
Surabaya Indon. 77 F4
formerly spelt Soerabaia
Surajpur India 97 D5
Sūrak Iran 100 D5
Surakarta Indon. 77 E4
Suramana Indon. 75 A3
Şura Mare Romania 58 F3
Sūran Iran 101 E5
Şūrān Syria 109 H2
Surára Brazil 199 F6
Surat Australia 147 F1
Surat India 96 B5
Suratgarh India 96 B3
Surat Thani Thai. 79 B6
also known as Ban Don
Suraż Poland 49 T3
Surazh Belarus 43 L6
Surazh Rus. Fed. 43 N8
Surbiton Australia 149 E4
Sūrdāsh Iraq 107 F4
Surdila-Greci Romania 58 I3
Surduc Romania 58 E1
Surdulica Srbija Serb. and Mont. 58 D6
Sûre r. Germany/Lux. 51 M3
Surendranagar India 96 A5
formerly known as Wadhwan
Suretka Costa Rica 186 C5
Surf U.S.A. 182 D7
Surgana India 94 B1
Surgères France 50 F6
Surgidero de Batabanó Cuba 186 C2
Surgut Rus. Fed. 38 H3
Suri India see **Siuri**
Suriapet India 94 C2
also spelt Suryapet
Surigao Phil. 74 C4
Surigao Strait Phil. 74 C4
Surimena Col. 198 C4
Surin Thai. 79 C5
Surinam country S. America see **Suriname**
►**Suriname** country S. America 199 G3
also spelt Surinam; formerly known as Dutch Guiana
►►**192–193 South America** Countries
Suriname r. Suriname 199 H3
Surin Nua, Ko i. Thai. 79 B6
Suripá Venez. 198 D3
Surkhābād Iran 100 C3
Surkhandar'ya r. Uzbek. 103 F5
also spelt Surkhondaryo
Surkhandarya Oblast admin. div. Uzbek. see **Surxondaryo**
Surkhet Nepal 97 D3
also known as Birendranagar
Surkhob r. Tajik. 101 G2
Surkhondaryo r. Uzbek. see **Surkhandar'ya**
Surkhondaryo Wiloyati admin. div. Uzbek. see **Surxondaryo**
Surmāq Iran 100 C4
Sürmene Turkey 107 E2
Surnadalsøra Norway 44 J3
Sŭrnevo Bulg. 58 G6
Surovikino Rus. Fed. 41 G6
Surprise Canada 166 C3
Surprise Lake Canada 166 C3
Surrah, Nafūd as des. Saudi Arabia 104 C3
Surrey Canada 166 F5
Surskoye Rus. Fed. 41 H5
Surt Libya see **Sirte**
Surt, Khalīj g. Libya see **Sirte, Gulf of**
Surtsey i. Iceland 44 [inset] B3
Sūrū Iran 100 D5
Suru, Vârful mt. Romania 58 F3
Surubiú r. Brazil 202 B2
Suruç Turkey 107 D3
Surud, Raas pt Somalia 128 E2
Surud Ad mt. Somalia see **Shimbiris**
Suruga-wan b. Japan 91 F7
Surulangun Indon. 76 C3
Surumú r. Brazil 199 F4
Surup Phil. 74 C5
Surxondaryo admin. div. Uzbek. 103 F5
English form Surkhandarya Oblast; also known as Surkhondaryo Wiloyati
Suryapet India see **Suriapet**
Şuşa Azer. 107 F3
also spelt Shusha
Susa Italy 51 N7
Susa Japan 91 B7
Sušac i. Croatia 56 I6
Susah Tunisia see **Sousse**
Susak i. Croatia 56 G4
Susaki Japan 91 C8
Susami Japan 91 D8
Susan U.S.A. 177 I8
Sūsangerd Iran 100 B4
Susanville U.S.A. 182 D1
Suşehri Turkey 107 D2
Sushitsa Bulg. 58 G5
Sushui He r. China 87 D1
Sušice Czech Rep. 49 K6
Šuškova Latvia 43 J5
Susner India 96 C5
Susong China 87 F2
Susquehanna U.S.A. 177 J4
Susquehanna r. U.S.A. 177 I6
Susquehanna, West Branch r. U.S.A. 176 I5
Susques Arg. 200 D5
Sussex Canada 169 H4
Sussex U.S.A. 177 K4
Sustut Provincial Park Canada 166 E3
Susua Indon. 75 B3
Susuman Rus. Fed. 39 O3
Susupu Indon. 75 C2
Susurluk Turkey 106 B3
Šušvė r. Lith. 42 E6
Susz Poland 49 Q2
Sutak Jammu and Kashmir 96 C2
Sutaşı Turkey 108 G1
Sutay Uul mt. Mongolia 84 B2
Sutherland Australia 147 F3
Sutherland S. Africa 132 E9
Sutherland NE U.S.A. 178 B3
Sutherland VA U.S.A. 176 H8
Sutherland Range hills Australia 151 D5
Sutjeska nat. park Bos.-Herz. 56 K5
Sutlej r. India/Pak. 96 A3
also spelt Satluj
Sutlepa meri l. Estonia 42 E2
Sütlüce İçel Turkey 108 E1
Sütlüce Kırklareli Turkey 58 I7
Sutter U.S.A. 182 C2
Sutter Creek U.S.A. 182 D3
Sutton r. Canada 168 D2
Sutton N.Z. 153 E13
Sutton NE U.S.A. 178 C3
Sutton WV U.S.A. 176 E7
Sutton Coldfield U.K. 47 K11
Sutton Lake Canada 168 C2
Sutton Lake U.S.A. 176 E7
Suttor r. Australia 149 E4
Suttsu Japan 90 G3
Sutwik Island U.S.A. 164 D4
Sutyr' r. Rus. Fed. 82 D2
Suugant Mongolia 85 E2
Suurberg mt. S. Africa 133 J8
Suurberg mts S. Africa 133 J10
Suurbraak S. Africa 132 E11
Suure-Jaani Estonia 42 G3
Suuremõisa Estonia 42 D3
Suur katel b. Estonia 42 D3
Suur-Pakri i. Estonia 42 E2
Suurpea Estonia 42 G2
Suur väin sea chan. Estonia 42 E3

►**Suva** Fiji 145 G3
Capital of Fiji.

Suvalki Poland see **Suwałki**
Suva Reka Kosovo, Srbija Serb. and Mont. 58 B6
Suvorov atoll Cook Is see **Suwarrow**
Suvorov Rus. Fed. 43 R7
Suvorove Ukr. 58 J3
Suvorovo Bulg. 58 I5
formerly known as Novgradets
Suvorovo Moldova see **Ştefan Vodă**
Suwa Japan 91 F6
Suwakong Indon. 77 F3
Suwałki Poland 49 T1
formerly spelt Suvalki
Suwannaphum Thai. 79 C5
Suwannee r. U.S.A. 175 D6
Suwanose-jima i. Japan 83 C7
Suwaran, Gunung mt. Indon. 77 G2
Suwarrow atoll Cook Is 221 I6
also known as Anchorage Island; also spelt Suvorov
Suwaylih Jordan 108 G5
also spelt Suweilih
Suwayqīyah, Hawr as imp. l. Iraq 107 F4
Suwayr well Saudi Arabia 107 E5
Suways, Khalīj as g. Egypt see **Suez, Gulf of**
Suways, Qanāt as canal Egypt see **Suez Canal**
also known as Suways, Qanāt as or Suweis, Qanâ el
Suweilih Jordan see **Suwaylih**
Suweis, Khalîg el g. Egypt see **Suez, Gulf of**
Suweis, Qanâ el canal Egypt see **Suez Canal**
Suwŏn S. Korea 83 B5
UNESCO World Heritage Site
Suxu China 87 D4
Suykbulak Kazakh. 103 J2
also spelt Sūyqbulaq
Suyo Peru 198 A6
Sūyqbulaq Kazakh. see **Suykbulak**
Suyūl Ḩanīsh i. Yemen 104 C5
Suz, Mys pt Kazakh. 102 C4
Sūzā Iran 100 D5
Suzak Kazakh. 103 G3
also spelt Sozaq
Suzaka Japan 91 F6
Suzdal' Rus. Fed. 43 V5
UNESCO World Heritage Site
Suzemka Rus. Fed. 43 P9
Suzhou Anhui China 87 F1
Suzhou Gansu China see **Jiuquan**
Suzhou Jiangsu China 87 G2
formerly spelt Soochow
UNESCO World Heritage Site
Suzi He r. China 82 B4
Suzu Japan 90 E6
Suzuka Japan 91 E7
Suzu-misaki pt Japan 83 E5
Suzzara Italy 56 C4
Sværholthalvøya pen. Norway 44 N1

►**Svalbard** terr. Arctic Ocean 38 A2
Part of Norway.

Svalenik Bulg. 58 H5
Svanet'is K'edi hills Georgia 107 E2
UNESCO World Heritage Site
Svanstein Sweden 44 M2
Svapa r. Rus. Fed. 43 Q9
Svappavaara Sweden 44 M2
also known as Veaikevárri
Svapushcha Rus. Fed. 43 N4
Svärdsjö Sweden 45 K3
Svarta r. Fin. 42 G1
Svartälven r. Sweden 45 K4
Svartbyn Sweden 44 M2
Svartenhuk Halvø pen. Greenland see **Sigguup Nunaa**
Svartlä Sweden 44 M2
Svatove Ukr. 41 F6
Svay Riĕng Cambodia 79 D6
Svecha Rus. Fed. 40 H4
Svėdasai Lith. 42 G6
Sveg Sweden 45 K3
Svegsjön l. Sweden 45 K3
Sveio Norway 45 I4
Sveķi Latvia 42 H4
Švėkšna Lith. 42 C6
Svelgen Norway 45 I3
Svellingen Norway 44 J3
Švenčionėliai Lith. 42 G6
Švenčionys Lith. 42 H6
Svendborg Denmark 45 J5
Svenljunga Sweden 45 K4
Svenstavik Sweden 44 K3
Šventoji r. Lith. 42 F6
Sverchkovo Rus. Fed. 43 Q6
Sverdlovsk Rus. Fed. see **Yekaterinburg**
Sverdlovs'k Ukr. 41 F6
Sverdlovskaya Oblast' admin. div. Rus. Fed. 40 L4
English form Sverdlovsk Oblast
Sverdlovsk Oblast admin. div. Rus. Fed. see **Sverdlovskaya Oblast'**
Sverdrup Channel Canada 165 J2
Sverdrup Islands Canada 165 J2
Sverige country Europe see **Sweden**
Sveshtari, Tomb of tourist site Bulg. 58 H5
UNESCO World Heritage Site
Sveta Andrija i. Croatia 56 H5
Švėtė r. Lith. 42 E5
Sveti Ivan Zelina Croatia see **Zelina**
Sveti Jure mt. Croatia 56 J5
Sveti Nikole Macedonia 58 C7
Svetlaya Rus. Fed. 82 E3
Svetlodarskoye Rus. Fed. 82 F2
Svetlogorsk Belarus see **Svyetlahorsk**
Svetlogorsk Kaliningradskaya Oblast' Rus. Fed. 42 B7
historically known as Rauschen
Svetlogorsk Krasnoyarskiy Kray Rus. Fed. 39 I3
Svetlograd Rus. Fed. 41 G7
formerly known as Petrovskoye
Svetlopolyansk Rus. Fed. 40 J4
Svetlovodsk Ukr. see **Svitlovods'k**
Svetlyy Kaliningradskaya Oblast' Rus. Fed. 42 B7
historically known as Zimmerbude
Svetlyy Orenburgskaya Oblast' Rus. Fed. 103 E2
Svetlyy Yar Rus. Fed. 41 H6
Svetogorsk Rus. Fed. 43 J1
Svetozarevo Srbija Serb. and Mont. see **Jagodina**
Svētupe r. Latvia 42 F4
Svíahnúkar vol. Iceland 44 [inset] C2
Svidník Slovakia 49 S6
Sviibi Estonia 42 E3
Svilaja mts Croatia 56 I5
Svilajnac Srbija Serb. and Mont. 58 C4
Svilengrad Bulg. 58 H7
Svinecea Mare, Vârful mt. Romania 58 D4
Svinø i. Faroe Is see **Svínoy**
Svínoy i. Faroe Is 46 F1
also spelt Svinø
Svir Belarus 42 H7
Svir' r. Rus. Fed. 43 P1
Svir, Vozyera l. Belarus 42 H7
Sviritsa Rus. Fed. 43 N1
Svirskaya Guba b. Rus. Fed. 43 N1
Svir'stroy Rus. Fed. 43 O1
Svishtov Bulg. 58 G5
Svislach Belarus 42 F8
Svislach Belarus 42 I8
Svislach r. Belarus 42 J8
also spelt Svisloch
Svislach r. Belarus/Poland 42 F8
also spelt Svisloch or Świstocz
Svisloch r. Belarus see **Svislach**
Svisloch r. Belarus see **Svislach**
Svit Slovakia 49 R6
Svitava r. Czech Rep. 49 N7
Svitavy Czech Rep. 49 N6
Svitlovods'k Ukr. 41 E6
also spelt Svetlovodsk; formerly known as Khrushchev or Kremges
Svizzera country Europe see **Switzerland**
Svoboda Rus. Fed. 42 C7
Svobodnyy Rus. Fed. 82 C2
Svoge Bulg. 58 E6
Svol'nya r. Belarus 43 J6
Svolvær Norway 44 K1
Svratka r. Czech Rep. 49 N6
Svrljig Srbija Serb. and Mont. 58 D5
Svrljiške Planine mts Serb. and Mont. 58 D5
Svyantsyanskiya Hrady hills Belarus 42 H7
Svyatoy Nos, Mys c. Rus. Fed. 40 I2
Svyatsk Rus. Fed. 43 M9
Svyetlahorsk Belarus 43 K9
also spelt Svetlogorsk; formerly known as Shatilki
Svyha r. Ukr. 43 O9
Swabi Pak. 101 H3
Swaershoek S. Africa 133 J9
Swaershoekpas pass S. Africa 133 J9
Swain Reefs reef Australia 149 G4
Swainsboro U.S.A. 175 D5
Swains Island American Samoa 145 H3
also known as Olosenga
Swakop watercourse Namibia 130 B4
Swakopmund Namibia 130 B4
Swale r. U.K. 47 K9
Swallow Islands Solomon Is 145 F3
Swampy r. Canada 169 G1
Swan r. Australia 151 A6
Swan r. Man./Sask. Canada 167 K4
Swan r. Ont. Canada 168 D2
Swanage U.K. 47 K13
Swana-Mume Dem. Rep. Congo 127 E7
Swandale U.S.A. 176 E7
Swanepoelspoort mt. S. Africa 132 H10
Swan Hill Australia 147 D3
Swan Hills Canada 167 H4
Swan Islands is Caribbean Sea 186 C3
also known as Santanilla, Islas
Swan Lake B.C. Canada 166 D4
Swan Lake Man. Canada 167 K4
Swan Lake U.S.A. 178 D2
Swanlinbar Ireland 47 E9
Swanquarter U.S.A. 174 E5
Swanquarter National Wildlife Refuge nature res. U.S.A. 174 E5
Swan Reach Australia 146 C3
Swan River Canada 167 K4
Swansea Australia 147 F5
Swansea U.K. 47 I12
also known as Abertawe
Swansea Bay U.K. 47 I12
Swans Island U.S.A. 177 Q1
Swanton CA U.S.A. 182 B4
Swanton VT U.S.A. 177 L1
Swartberg S. Africa 133 N7
Swartberg mt. S. Africa 132 D11
Swartbergpas pass S. Africa 132 F10
Swartdoorn r. S. Africa 132 B7
Swart Kei r. S. Africa 133 L9
Swartkolkvloer salt pan S. Africa 132 E7
Swartkops r. S. Africa 133 J10
Swart Nossob watercourse Namibia see **Black Nossob**
Swartplaas S. Africa 133 K3
Swartputs S. Africa 132 H5
Swartput se Pan salt pan Namibia 132 D3
Swartruggens S. Africa 133 K2
Swartruggens mts S. Africa 133 K2
Swartz Creek U.S.A. 173 J8
Swarzędz Poland 49 O3
Swasey Peak U.S.A. 183 K2
Swastika Canada 173 M2
Swat r. Pak. 101 G3
Swat Kohistan reg. Pak. 101 H3
Swatow China see **Shantou**
►**Swaziland** country Africa 133 P3
known as Ngwane in Swazi
►►**114–115 Africa** Countries

►**Sweden** country Europe 45 K4
5th largest country in Europe. Known as Sverige in Swedish.
►►**32–33 Europe** Countries

Swedesburg U.S.A. 172 B9
Sweet Briar U.S.A. 176 F8
Sweet Home U.S.A. 180 B3
Sweet Springs U.S.A. 176 E8
Sweetwater U.S.A. 179 B5
Sweetwater r. U.S.A. 180 F4
Swellendam S. Africa 132 E11
Swempoort S. Africa 133 L8
Świder r. Poland 49 S3
Świdnica Poland 49 N5
UNESCO World Heritage Site

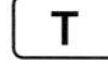

Ţāmīyah Egypt 121 F2
Tamīyah, Jabal *hill* Saudi Arabia 104 C2
Tamjit *well* Niger 125 H1
Tamkuhi India 97 E4
Tam Ky Vietnam 79 E5
Tamlelt, Plaine de *plain* Morocco 123 E2
Tamluk India 97 E5
Tammaro *r.* Italy 56 G7
Tammarvi *r.* Canada 167 K1
Tammela *Etelä-Suomi* Fin. 42 E1
Tammela *Oulu* Fin. 44 O2
Tammerfors Fin. *see* **Tampere**
Tammio *i.* Fin. 42 I1
Tammisaaren Saariston Kansallispuisto *nat. park* Fin. *see* **Ekenäskärgårds nationalpark**
Tammisaari Fin. *see* **Ekenäs**
Tammispää Estonia 42 I3
Tamnava *r.* Serb. and Mont. 58 B4
Tamou Niger 125 F3
Tamou, Réserve Totale de Faune de *nature res.* Niger 125 F3
Tampa U.S.A. 175 D7
Tampa Bay U.S.A. 175 D7
Tampang Indon. 76 D4
Tampere Fin. 45 M3
also known as Tammerfors
Tampico Mex. 185 F4
Tampines Sing. 76 [inset]
Tampines, Sungai *r.* Sing. 76 [inset]
Tampo Indon. 75 B4
Tamrah Saudi Arabia 105 D3
Tamsagbulag Mongolia 85 H2
Tamsalu Estonia 42 H2
Tamshiyacu Peru 198 C6
Tamsweg Austria 49 K8
Tamu Myanmar 78 A2
Tamuín Mex. 185 F4
Tamur *r.* Nepal 97 E4
Tamworth Australia 147 F2
Tamworth U.K. 47 K11
Tan Kazakh. 103 I2
Tana *r.* Fin./Norway *see* **Tenojoki**
Tana *r.* Kenya 128 D5
Tana Madag. *see* **Antananarivo**
Tana *i.* Vanuatu *see* **Tanna**
Tana, Lake Eth. 128 C2
also known as T'ana Hāyk'
Tanabe Japan 91 D8
Tanabi Brazil 206 D7
Tana Bru Norway 44 O1
Tanafjorden *inlet* Norway 44 O1
also known as Deanuvuotna
Tanagro *r.* Italy 57 H8
Tanah, Tanjung *pt* Indon. 77 E4
T'ana Hāyk' *l.* Eth. *see* **Tana, Lake**
Tanahbala *i.* Indon. 76 B3
Tanahgrogot Indon. 77 G3
Tanahjampea *i.* Indon. 75 B4
Tanahmasa *i.* Indon. 76 B3
Tanahmerah Indon. 77 G2
Tanahputih Indon. 76 C2
Tanah Rata Malaysia 76 C1
Tanakeke *i.* Indon. 75 A4
Tanakpur India 96 D3
Tanambung Indon. 75 A3
Tanami Australia 148 A3
Tanami Desert Australia 148 A3
Tanami Downs Aboriginal Land *res.* Australia 148 A4
Tân An Vietnam 79 D6
Tananarive Madag. *see* **Antananarivo**
Tanandava Madag. 131 [inset] I4
Tanāqīb, Ra's *pt* Saudi Arabia 105 E2
Tanaro *r.* Italy 56 A3
Tanauan Phil. 74 C4
Tanbar Australia 149 D5
Tancheng *Fujian* China *see* **Pingtan**
Tancheng *Shandong* China 87 F1
Tanch'ŏn N. Korea 83 C4
Tanda Côte d'Ivoire 124 E5
Tanda *Uttar Pradesh* India 96 C3
Tanda *Uttar Pradesh* India 97 D4
Tandag Phil. 74 C4
Ţăndărei Romania 58 I4
Tandaué Angola 127 C9
Tandek *Sabah* Malaysia 77 G1
formerly known as Taritipan
Tandi India 96 C2
Tandil Arg. 204 F5
Tandjilé *pref.* Chad 126 C2
Tando Adam Pak. 101 G5
Tando Alahyar Pak. 101 G5
Tando Bago Pak. 101 G5
Tando Muhammmad Khan Pak. 101 G5
Tandou Lake *imp. l.* Australia 147 D3
Tandsjöborg Sweden 45 K3
Tandubatu *i.* Phil. 74 B5
Tandula *r.* India 96 D5
Tandur *Andhra Pradesh* India 94 C2
Tandur *Andhra Pradesh* India 94 C2
Taneatua N.Z. 152 K6
Tanega-shima *i.* Japan 91 B9
Taneichi Japan 90 G4
Tanen Taunggyi *mts* Thai. 78 B4
Taneti *i.* Indon. 75 C3
Tanew *r.* Poland 49 T5
Taneytown U.S.A. 177 H6
Tanezrouft *reg.* Alg./Mali 123 E5
Tanezrouft Tan-Ahenet *reg.* Alg. 123 E5
Ţanf, Jabal aţ *hill* Syria 109 J4
Tang, Ra's-e *pt* Iran 101 D5
Tanga Rus. Fed. 85 F1
Tanga Tanz. 129 C6
Tanga *admin. reg.* Tanz. 129 C6
Tangaehe N.Z. 152 I4
Tangail Bangl. 97 F4
Tanga Islands P.N.G. 145 E2
Tangalla Sri Lanka 94 D5
Tanganyika *country* Africa *see* **Tanzania**

►**Tanganyika, Lake** Africa 127 F6
Deepest and 2nd largest lake in Africa and 6th largest in the world.
►►**6–7 World** Landscapes
►►**110–111 Africa** Landscapes

Tangar Iran 100 C2
Tangasseri India 94 C4
Tangdan China 86 B3
formerly known as Dongshuan
Tangeli Iran 100 C2
Tange Promontory *hd* Antarctica 223 D2
Tanger Morocco *see* **Tangier**
Tangerang Indon. 77 D4
Tangermünde Germany 48 I3
Tang-e Sarkheh Iran 101 D5
Tanggor China 86 B1
Tanggu China 85 H4
Tanggulashan China 84 B5
also known as Tuotuoheyan
Tanggula Shan *mt.* China 89 E5
Tanggula Shan *mts* China 89 E5
also known as Dangla Shan
Tanggula Shankou *pass* China 89 E5
Tangguo China 89 D6
Tanghe China 87 E1
Tang He *r.* China 87 E1
Tangi Pak. 101 G3
Tangier Morocco 122 D2
also spelt Tanger *or* Tanjah; *historically known as* Tingis
Tangimoana N.Z. 152 J8
Tangkittebak, Gunung *mt.* Indon. 76 D4
Tang La *pass* China 89 E7
Tanglag China 86 A1
Tanglin Sing. 76 [inset]
Tangmai China 97 G3
Tango Japan 91 D7
Tangorin Australia 149 E4
Tangra Yumco *salt l.* China 89 D6
Tangse Indon. 76 A1
Tangshan China 85 H4
Tangsyq Kazakh. *see* **Tansyk**
Tangte *mt.* Myanmar 78 B3
Tangub Phil. 74 B4
Tangub Phil. 74 B4
Tanguieta Benin 125 F4
Tangwan China 87 D3
Tangwanghe China 82 C2
Tangwang He *r.* China 82 C3
Tangxian China 85 G4
also known as Renhou
Tangxianzhen China 87 E2
Tang-yan Myanmar 78 B3
Tangyan He *r.* China 87 D2
Tangyin China 85 G5
Tangyuan China 82 C3
Tanhaçu Brazil 202 D5
Tanhua Fin. 44 N2
Taniantaweng Shan *mts* China 86 A2
Tanimbar, Kepulauan *is* Indon. 73 H8
Taninthari Myanmar *see* **Tenasserim**
Tanintharyi Myanmar *see* **Tenasserim**
Tanintharyi *admin. div.* Myanmar *see* **Tenasserim**
Taninthayi Myanmar *see* **Tenasserim**
Taniwel Indon. 75 D3
Tanjah Morocco *see* **Tangier**
Tanjay Phil. 74 B4
Tanjore India *see* **Thanjavur**
Tanjung *Kalimantan Selatan* Indon. 77 F3
Tanjung *Sumatra* Indon. 76 D3
Tanjungbalai *Sumatra* Indon. 76 B2
Tanjungbalai *Sumatra* Indon. 76 C2
Tanjungbaliha Indon. 75 C3
Tanjungbatu *Kalimantan Timur* Indon. 77 G2
Tanjungbatu *Sumatra* Indon. 76 C2
Tanjungbuayabuaya, Pulau *i.* Indon. 77 G2
Tanjunggaru Indon. 77 G3
Tanjungkarang-Telukbetung Indon. *see* **Bandar Lampung**
Tanjungpandan Indon. 77 D3
Tanjungpinang Indon. 76 D2
Tanjungpura Indon. 76 B2
Tanjung Puting National Park Indon. 77 F3
Tanjungraja Indon. 76 D3
Tanjungredeb Indon. 77 G2
Tanjungsaleh *i.* Indon. 77 E3
Tanjungsatai Indon. 77 E3
Tanjungselor Indon. 77 G2
Tank Pak. 101 G3
Tankara India 96 A5
Tankavaara Fin. 44 N1
Tankhala India 96 B5
Tankhoy Rus. Fed. 85 E1
Tanktse Jammu and Kashmir 96 C2
Tankwa *r.* S. Africa 132 D9
Tankwa-Karoo National Park S. Africa 132 D9
Tanlwe *r.* Myanmar 78 A4
Tanna *i.* Vanuatu 145 F3
also spelt Tana
Tännäs Sweden 44 K3
Tanner, Mount Canada 166 G5
Tannila Fin. 44 N2
Tannu-Ola, Khrebet *mts* Rus. Fed. 84 A1
Tannu Tuva *aut. rep.* Rus. Fed. *see* **Tyva, Respublika**
Tano Japan 91 B9
Tañon Strait Phil. 74 B4
Tanot India 96 A4
Tanout Niger 125 H3
Tanquian Mex. 185 F4
Tansen Nepal 97 D4
Tanshui Taiwan 87 G3
also spelt Danshui
Tansilla Burkina 124 D3
Tansyk Kazakh. 103 I3
also spelt Tangsyq
Ţanţā Egypt 121 F2
Tantabin *Pegu* Myanmar 78 B4
Tantabin *Sagaing* Myanmar 78 A3
Tan-Tan Morocco 122 C3
Tantoyuca Mex. 185 F4
Tantpur India 96 C4
Tantu China 85 I2
Tanuku India 94 D2
Tanums hällristningar *tourist site* Sweden 45 J4
UNESCO World Heritage Site
Tanumshede Sweden 45 J4
Tanwakka, Sabkhat *well* W. Sahara 122 B5
►**Tanzania** *country* Africa 129 B6
formerly known as Tanganyika
►►**114–115 Africa** Countries
Tanzilla *r.* Canada 166 D3
Tao, Ko *i.* Thai. 79 B6
Tao'an China *see* **Taonan**
Taocheng *Fujian* China *see* **Yongchun**
Taocheng *Guangdong* China *see* **Daxin**
Taodeni Mali *see* **Taoudenni**
Tao'er He *r.* China 85 I2
Tao He *r.* China 84 D5
also known as Lu Qu
Taohong China *see* **Longhui**
Taohuaping China *see* **Longhui**
Taojiang China 87 E2
Taolanaro Madag. *see* **Tôlañaro**
Taole China 85 E4
also known as Mataigou
Taonan China 85 I2
formerly known as Tao'an
Taongi *atoll* Marshall Is 220 G5
►**Taormina** *Sicily* Italy 57 H11
►►**34–35 Europe** Mediterranean Basin
Taos U.S.A. 181 F5
Taos Pueblo U.S.A. 181 F5
UNESCO World Heritage Site
Taouârdeï *well* Mali 125 F2
Taoudenni Mali 122 E5
also spelt Taodeni
Taounate Morocco 122 D2
Taounnant *well* Mali 123 E5
formerly known as Tin Tounnant
Taourirt Morocco 123 E2
Taoxi China 87 F3
Taoyang China *see* **Lintao**
Taoyuan China 87 D2
T'aoyüan Taiwan 87 G3
formerly known as Sinchu
Taozhou China *see* **Guangde**
Tapa Estonia 42 G2
Tapaan Passage Phil. 74 B5
Tapachula Mex. 185 G6
Tapajós *r.* Brazil 199 H5
Tapaktuan Indon. 76 B2
Tapalqué Arg. 204 E5
Tapan Indon. 76 C3
Tapan Turkey *see* **Mansurlu**
Tapanahoni *r.* Suriname 199 H3
Tapanatepec Mex. 185 G5
Tapanuli, Teluk *b.* Indon. 76 B2
Tapará, Ilha Grande do *i.* Brazil 199 H5
Tapara, Serra do *hills* Brazil 199 H5
Tapat *i.* Indon. 75 C3
Tapauá Brazil 199 E6
Tapauá *r.* Brazil 199 E6
Tapawera N.Z. 152 G9
Tapera *Rio Grande do Sul* Brazil 203 A9
Tapera *Roraima* Brazil 199 F5
Tapera Chile 205 C7
Taperoá Brazil 202 E5
Tapes Brazil 203 B9
Tapeta Liberia 124 C5
Tapi *r.* India 96 B5
Ta Pi, Mae Nam *r.* Thai. 79 B6
Tapia, Sierra de *hills* Bol. 201 F4
Tapi Aike Arg. 205 C8
Tapiantana *i.* Phil. 74 B5
Tapiau Rus. Fed. *see* **Gvardeysk**
Tapiche *r.* Peru 198 C6
Tápió *r.* Hungary 49 R8
Tapiocanga, Chapada do *hills* Brazil 206 F3
Tápiószecső Hungary 49 Q8
Tapira Brazil 206 G6
Tapiracanga Brazil 202 C5
Tapiraí Brazil 206 F10
Tapirapé *r.* Brazil 202 B4
Tapirapecó, Sierra *mts* Brazil/Venez. 199 E4
Tapirapuã Brazil 201 F3
Tapis, Gunung *mt.* Malaysia 76 C1
Tapisuelas Mex. 184 C3
Taplejung Nepal 97 E4
Tap Mun Chau *i. Hong Kong* China 87 [inset]
Tapoa *watercourse* Burkina 125 F3
Tapol Chad 126 B2
Tapolca Hungary 49 O9
Ta-pom Myanmar 78 B3
Tappahannock U.S.A. 177 I8
Tappal India 96 C3
Tappeh, Kūh-e *hill* Iran 100 B3
Tappi-zaki *pt* Japan 90 G4
Taprobane *country* Asia *see* **Sri Lanka**
Tapuaenuku *mt.* N.Z. 153 H9
Tapul Phil. 74 B5
Tapul Group *is* Phil. 74 B5
Tapulonanjing *mt.* Indon. 76 B2
Tapung *r.* Indon. 76 C2
Tapurú Brazil 199 F6
Tapurucuara Brazil 199 E5
Taputeouea *atoll* Kiribati *see* **Tabiteuea**
Taqar *mt.* Yemen 104 D5
Ţāqestān, Chāh-e *well* Iran 100 C4
Ţaqţaq Iraq 107 F4
Taquara Brazil 203 B9
Taquaral, Serra do *hills* Brazil 206 A2
Taquarí *r.* Brazil 201 F4
Taquarí, Pantanal do *marsh* Brazil 201 F4
Taquaritinga Brazil 206 E8
Taquarituba Brazil 206 D10
Taquaruçu *r.* Brazil 206 A8
Tara Australia 147 F1
Tara *r.* Bos.-Herz./Serb. and Mont. 56 K5
Tara *nat. park* Serb. and Mont. 58 A5
Taraba *r.* Nigeria 125 H4
Taraba *state* Nigeria 125 H4
Tarabaí Brazil 206 B9
Tarabuco Bol. 200 D4
Ţarābulus Libya *see* **Tripoli**
Taraclia Moldova 58 J3
formerly spelt Tarakliya
Taraco Peru 200 C3
Taracua Brazil 198 D4
Taradale N.Z. 152 K7
Tarāghin Libya 120 B3
Tarai *reg.* India 97 F4
Taraíra *r.* Brazil *see* **Traíra**
Tarairí Bol. 201 E5
Tarakan Indon. 77 G2
Tarakan *i.* Indon. 77 G2
Tarakki *reg.* Afgh. 101 F3
Taraklı Turkey 106 B2
Tarakliya Moldova *see* **Taraclia**
Tarakua Fiji 145 H3
Taran, Mys *pt* Rus. Fed. 42 A7
Tarana India 96 C5
Taranagar India 96 B3
Taranaki *admin. reg.* N.Z. 152 H7
Taranaki, Mount *vol.* N.Z. 152 I7
also known as Egmont, Mount
Tarancón Spain 55 H4
Tarangambadi India 94 C4
Tarangara Chad 126 C2
Tarangire National Park Tanz. 129 C6
Tarangul *l.* Kazakh. *see* **Tarankol', Ozero**
Tarankol', Ozero *l.* Kazakh. 103 G1
formerly known as Tarangul
Taranovskoye Kazakh. 103 E1
formerly known as Viktorovka
Taranto Italy 57 J8
historically known as Tarentum
Taranto, Golfo di *g.* Italy 57 J8
Tarapacá *admin. reg.* Chile 200 C4
Tarapacá Col. 198 D5
Tarapoto Peru 198 B6
Ţaraq an Na'jah *reg.* Syria 109 K3
Tarare France 51 K7
Tararua Forest Park *nature res.* N.Z. 152 J8
Tararua Range *mts* N.Z. 152 J8
Tarascon-sur-Ariège France 50 H10
Tarashcha Ukr. 41 D6
Tarasht Iran 100 D3
Tarasovskiy Rus. Fed. 41 G6
Tarat Alg. 123 H4
Tarata Peru 200 C4
Tarauacá Brazil 200 C2
Tarauacá *r.* Brazil 198 D6
Taravo *r. Corsica* France 56 A7
Tarawa *atoll* Kiribati 145 G1
formerly known as Cook Atoll *or* Knox Atoll
Tarawera N.Z. 152 K7
Tarawera, Lake N.Z. 152 K6
Tarawera, Mount N.Z. 152 K6
Taraz Kazakh. 103 G4
formerly known as Dzhambul *or* Zhambyl; *historically known as* Auliye Ata
Tarazona Spain 55 J3
Tarazona de la Mancha Spain 55 J5
Tarbagatay Kazakh. 103 J3
Tarbagatay Rus. Fed. 85 E1
Tarbagatay, Khrebet *mts* Kazakh. 88 C2
Tarbat Ness *pt* U.K. 46 I6
Tarbert Ireland 47 C11
Tarbert *Argyll and Bute, Scotland* U.K. 46 G8
Tarbert *Western Isles, Scotland* U.K. 46 F6
also spelt Tairbeart
Tarbes France 50 G9
Tarbet U.K. 46 H7
Tarboro U.S.A. 174 E5
Tarcoola Australia 146 B2
Tarcoon Australia 147 E2
Tarcoonyinna *watercourse* Australia 146 B1
Ţarcului, Munţii *mts* Romania 58 D3
Tardes *r.* France 51 I6
Tardoire *r.* France 50 G7
Tardoki-Yani, Gora *mt.* Rus. Fed. 82 E2
Taree Australia 147 G2
Tareifing Sudan 128 B2
Tärendö Sweden 44 M2
Tarentum Italy *see* **Taranto**
Tareya Rus. Fed. 39 J2
Ţarfā', Baţn aţ *depr.* Saudi Arabia 105 E3
Ţarfā, Ra's aţ *pt* Saudi Arabia 104 C4
Tarfaya Morocco 122 B4
formerly known as Cabo Yubi *or* Cape Juby *or* Villa Bens
Targa *well* Niger 125 G2
Targan Kazakh. *see* **Targyn**
Targhee Pass U.S.A. 180 E3
Târgovişte Romania 58 G4
formerly spelt Tîrgovişte
Târgu Bujor Romania 58 I3
formerly spelt Tîrgu Bujor
Târgu Cărbuneşti Romania 58 E4
formerly spelt Tîrgu Cărbuneşti
Târgu Frumos Romania 58 H1
formerly spelt Tîrgu Frumos
Targuist Morocco 122 D2
Târgu Jiu Romania 58 E3
formerly spelt Tîrgu Jiu
Târgu Lăpuş Romania 58 E1
formerly spelt Tîrgu Lăpuş
Târgu Mureş Romania 58 F2
also known as Marosvásárhely; *formerly spelt* Tîrgu Mureş
Târgu Neamţ Romania 58 H1
formerly spelt Tîrgu Neamţ
Târgu Ocna Romania 58 H2
formerly spelt Tîrgu Ocna
Târgu Secuiesc Romania 58 H2
formerly spelt Tîrgu Secuiesc
Targyailing China 89 D6
Targyn Kazakh. 88 C1
formerly spelt Targan
Tarhān Iran 100 A3
Tarhmanant *well* Mali *see* **Taghmanant**
Tarhūnah Libya 120 B1
Tari P.N.G. 73 J8
Tarian Gol China 85 F4
Tarib, Wādī *watercourse* Saudi Arabia 104 C4
Tarif U.A.E. 105 F2
Tarifa Spain 54 F8
Tarifa, Punta de *pt* Spain 54 F8
Tarigtig Point Phil. 74 B2
Tarija Bol. 201 D5
Tarija *dept* Bol. 201 D5
Tarikere India 94 B3
Tariku *r.* Indon. 73 I7
Tarīm Yemen 105 E4
Tarim Basin China 88 C4
also known as Tarim Pendi
Tarime Tanz. 128 B5
Tarim He *r.* China 88 D3
Tarim Liuchang China 88 D3
Tarim Pendi *basin* China *see* **Tarim Basin**
Taringuiti Bol. 201 E5
Tarīn Kowt Afgh. 101 F3
Taritatu *r.* Indon. 73 I7
Taritipan *Sabah* Malaysia *see* **Tandek**
Tarjīl Iraq 109 P2
Tarka *r.* S. Africa 133 J9
Tarka, Vallée de *watercourse* Niger 125 G3
Tarkastad S. Africa 133 K9
Tarkio U.S.A. 178 D3
Tarko-Sale Rus. Fed. 39 H3
Tarkwa Ghana 125 E5
Tarlac Phil. 74 B3
Tarlac *r.* Phil. 74 B2
Tarlo River National Park Australia 147 F3
Tarlton U.S.A. 176 C6
Tarma *Junín* Peru 200 B2
Tarma *Loreto* Peru 198 D5
Tarn *r.* France 51 H8
Tarna *r.* Hungary 49 Q8
Tärnaby Sweden 44 K2
Tarnak *r.* Afgh. 101 F4
Târnava Mare *r.* Romania 58 E2
Târnava Mică *r.* Romania 58 E2
Târnăveni Romania 58 F2
formerly spelt Tîrnăveni
Tarnica *mt.* Poland 49 T6
Tarnobrzeg Poland 49 S5
Tarnogród Poland 49 T5
Tarnogskiy Gorodok Rus. Fed. 40 G3
Tarnopol Ukr. *see* **Ternopil'**
Tarnos France 50 E9
Târnova Romania 58 D3
Tarnów Poland 49 R5
Tarnowitz Poland *see* **Tarnowskie Góry**
Tarnowskie Góry Poland 49 P5
historically known as Tarnowitz
Tårnvik Norway 44 K2
Taro *r.* Italy 56 C4
Tarō Japan 90 G5
Taro Co *salt l.* China 89 C6
Ţārom Iran 100 C4
Taroom Australia 149 F5
Taroudannt Morocco 122 C3
Tarpasa Bangl. 97 F5
Tarpaulin Swamp Australia 148 C3
Tarpon Springs U.S.A. 175 D6
Tarpum Bay Bahamas 175 E7
Tarq Iran 100 B3
Tarquinia Italy 56 D6
historically known as Corneto *or* Tarquinii
UNESCO World Heritage Site
Tarquinii Italy *see* **Tarquinia**
Tarrabool Lake *salt flat* Australia 148 B3
Tarracina Italy *see* **Terracina**
Tarraco Spain *see* **Tarragona**
Tarrafal Cape Verde 124 [inset]
Tarragona Spain 55 M3
historically known as Tarraco
UNESCO World Heritage Site
Tårrajaur Sweden 44 L2
Tarraleah Australia 147 E5
Tarrant Point Australia 148 C3
Tarras N.Z. 153 D12
Tarrasa Spain *see* **Terrassa**
Tàrrega Spain 55 M3
Tarrong China *see* **Nyêmo**
Tarso Ahon *mt.* Chad 120 C4
Tarso Emissi *mt.* Chad 120 C4
Tarso Kobour *mt.* Chad 120 C4
Tarsus Turkey 106 C3
Tarta Turkm. 102 C4
formerly known as Kianly; *formerly spelt* Darta
Tartagal *Salta* Arg. 201 E5
Tartagal *Santa Fé* Arg. 204 F3
Tärtär Azer. 107 F2
also spelt Terter; *formerly known as* Mir-Bashir
Tartas France 50 F9
Tartu Estonia 42 H3
formerly known as Yuryev; *historically known as* Dorpat
Ţarţūs Syria 108 G3
Ţarţūs *governorate* Syria 108 H2
Tarumae-san *vol.* Japan *see* **Shikotsu**
Tarumirim Brazil 207 L6
Tarumizu Japan 91 B9
Tarumovka Rus. Fed. 102 A3
Tarung Hka *r.* Myanmar 78 B2
Tarusa Rus. Fed. 43 S7
Tarusa *r.* Rus. Fed. 43 S7
Tārūt Saudi Arabia 105 E2
Tarutao, Ko *i.* Thai. 79 B7
Tarutao National Park Thai. 79 B7
Tarutung Indon. 76 B2
Tarutyne Ukr. 58 K2
Tarvisio Italy 56 F2
Tarvisium Italy *see* **Treviso**
Tarvo Bol. 201 E3
Tarz Iran 100 D4
Tasaral Kazakh. 88 A2
Tasbuget Kazakh. 103 F3
Taschereau Canada 173 O2
Taseko Mountain Canada 166 F5
Tasendjanet, Oued *watercourse* Alg. 123 F4
Tasgaon India 94 B2
Tashauz Turkm. *see* **Daşoguz**
Tashauzskaya Oblast' *admin. div.* Turkm. *see* **Dashkhovuzskaya Oblast'**
Tash-Bashat Kyrg. 103 I4
formerly known as imeni Voroshilova *or* Kalinin
Tashbunar *r.* Ukr. 58 J3
Tashi China 84 B3
Tashi Chho Bhutan *see* **Thimphu**
Tashigang Bhutan 97 F4
also spelt Trashigang
Tashino Rus. Fed. *see* **Pervomaysk**
Tashir Armenia 107 F2
formerly known as Kalinino
Tashk, Daryācheh-ye *l.* Iran 100 C4
Tashkent Uzbek. *see* **Toshkent**
Tashkent Oblast *admin. div.* Uzbek. *see* **Toshkent**
Tash-Kömür Kyrg. 103 H4
also spelt Tash-Kumyr
Tash-Kumyr Kyrg. *see* **Tash-Kömür**
Tashla Rus. Fed. 102 C2
Tāshqurghān Afgh. *see* **Kholm**
Tasialujjuaq, Lac *l.* Canada 169 F1
Tasiat, Lac *l.* Canada 169 F1
Tasiilap Karra *c.* Greenland 165 P3
also known as Gustav Holm, Kap
Tasiilaq Greenland *see* **Ammassalik**
Tasikmalaya Indon. 77 E4
Tasiujaq Canada 169 G1
formerly known as Baie-aux-Feuilles *or* Leaf Bay
Tasiusaq Greenland 165 N2
Tåsjö Sweden 44 K2
Task *well* Niger 125 H3
Tasker Niger 125 H3
Taskesken Kazakh. 103 J3
Taşköprü Turkey 106 C2
Taşlıçay Turkey 107 E3
Tasman N.Z. 152 H9
Tasman *admin. reg.* N.Z. 152 G9
Tasman *r.* N.Z. 153 E12
Tasman, Mount N.Z. 153 E11
Tasman Bay N.Z. 152 H9
Tasmania *i.* Australia 147 E5
UNESCO World Heritage Site

►**Tasmania** *state* Australia 147 E5
4th largest island in Oceania. Historically known as Van Diemen's Land.
►►**134–135 Oceania** Landscapes

Tasman Mountains N.Z. 152 G9
Tasman Peninsula Australia 147 F5
Tasman Sea S. Pacific Ocean 145 G6
Tăşnad Romania 58 D1
Taşova Turkey 107 D2
also known as Yemişenbükü
Tassara Niger 125 G2
Tassedjefit, Erg *des.* Alg. 123 F4
Tasselot, Mont *hill* France 51 K5
Tassi Gabon 126 A5
Tassialouc, Lac *l.* Canada 169 F1
Tassili du Hoggar *plat.* Alg. 123 G5
Tassili n'Ajjer *plat.* Alg. 123 G4
UNESCO World Heritage Site
Tassin-la-Demi-Lune France 51 K7
Tastavíns *r.* Spain 55 L3
Tas-Tumus Rus. Fed. 39 M3
Tasty Kazakh. 103 G3
Tasty-Taldy Kazakh. 103 F2
Tasu Canada 166 C4
Taşucu Turkey 108 E1
Tas-Yuryakh Rus. Fed. 39 L3
Tata Hungary 49 P8
Tata Morocco 122 D3
Tataba Indon. 75 B3
Tatabánya Hungary 49 P8
Tatamagouche Canada 169 I4
Tatamailau, Foho *mt.* East Timor 75 C5
Tatanagar India 97 E5
Tataouine Tunisia 123 H2
Tatarbunary Ukr. 41 D7
Tatarka Belarus 43 J8
Tatarpur India 96 C4
Tatarsk *Novosibirskaya Oblast'* Rus. Fed. 80 B1
Tatarsk *Smolenskaya Oblast'* Rus. Fed. 43 M7
Tatarskaya A.S.S.R. *aut. rep.* Rus. Fed. *see* **Tatarstan, Respublika**
Tatarskiy Proliv *strait* Rus. Fed. 82 F2
English form Tatar Strait
Tatarstan, Respublika *aut. rep.* Rus. Fed. 40 I5
formerly known as Tatarskaya A.S.S.R.
Tatar Strait Rus. Fed. *see* **Tatarskiy Proliv**
Tătăruşi Romania 58 H1
Tatau *Sarawak* Malaysia 77 F2
Tatavi *r.* Iran 100 A2
Tate *r.* Australia 149 D3
Tatebayashi Japan 91 F6
Tateyama Japan 91 F7
Tate-yama *vol.* Japan 91 E6
Tathlina Lake Canada 167 G2
Tathlīth Saudi Arabia 104 C4
Tathlīth, Wādī *watercourse* Saudi Arabia 104 D3
Tathra Australia 147 F4
Tati Botswana 131 E4
Tâtîlt *well* Mauritania 124 B2
Tatishchevo Rus. Fed. 41 H6
Tatkon Myanmar 78 B3
Tatla Lake Canada 166 E5
Tatlatui Provincial Park Canada 166 E3
Tatlayoko Lake Canada 166 E5
Tatlikbulak China 88 D4
Tatnam, Cape Canada 167 N3
Tatra Mountains Poland/Slovakia 49 Q6
also known as High Tatras *or* Tatry
Tatrang China 88 D4
Tatranský *nat. park* Slovakia 49 R6
Tatry *mts* Poland/Slovakia *see* **Tatra Mountains**
Tatrzański Park Narodowy *nat. park* Poland 49 Q6
Tatshenshini *r.* Canada 166 B3
Tatshenshini-Alsek Provincial Wilderness Park Canada 166 B3
UNESCO World Heritage Site
Tatsuno Japan 91 D7
Tatta Pak. 101 F5
UNESCO World Heritage Site
Tatti Kazakh. 103 H4
formerly spelt Tatty
Tatty Kazakh. *see* **Tatti**
Tatuí Brazil 206 F10
Tatuk Mountain Canada 166 E4
Tatula *r.* Lith. 42 F5
Tatum *NM* U.S.A. 178 B5
Tatum *TX* U.S.A. 179 D5
Tatvan Turkey 107 E3
Ta'u *i.* American Samoa 145 I3
Taua Brazil 202 D3
Tauapeçaçu Brazil 199 F5
Tauariã Brazil 199 F6
Taubaté Brazil 203 C7
Tauber *r.* Germany 48 G6
Tauberbischofsheim Germany 48 G6
Tauchik Kazakh. 102 B3
also spelt Taūshyq
Taufkirchen (Vils) Germany 48 J7
Tauhara *mt.* N.Z. 152 K6
Tauhoa N.Z. 152 I4
Tauini *r.* Brazil 199 G4
Taukum, Peski *des.* Kazakh. 103 H3
Taumarunui N.Z. 152 J6
Taumaturgo Brazil 200 B2
Taunay Brazil 201 G5
Taung S. Africa 133 I4
Taungbon Myanmar 79 B5
Taungdwingyi Myanmar 78 A3
Taunggyi Myanmar 78 B3
Taunglau Myanmar 78 B3
Taung-ngu Myanmar 78 B4
Taungnyo Range *mts* Myanmar 78 B4
Taungtha Myanmar 78 A3
Taungup Myanmar 78 A4
Taunsa Pak. 101 G4
Taunton U.K. 47 I12
Taunton U.S.A. 177 N4
Taunus *hills* Germany 48 E5
Taupiri N.Z. 152 J5
Taupo N.Z. 152 K6
Taupo, Lake N.Z. 152 J6
Tauragė Lith. 42 D6
Tauralaukis Lith. 42 C6
Tauramena Col. 198 C3
Tauranga N.Z. 152 K5
Taurasia Italy *see* **Turin**
Taureau, Réservoir *resr* Canada 169 F4
Taurianova Italy 57 I10
Taurikura N.Z. 152 I3
Taurion *r.* France 50 H7
Tauroa Point N.Z. 152 H3
Taurus Mountains Turkey 106 C3
also known as Toros Dağları
Taūshyq Kazakh. *see* **Tauchik**
Tauste Spain 55 J3
Tauwhareparae N.Z. 152 M6
Tauyskaya Guba *g.* Rus. Fed. 39 P4
Tauz Azer. *see* **Tovuz**
Tavagnacco Italy 56 F2
Tavankut *Vojvodina, Srbija* Serb. and Mont. 58 A2
Tavares U.S.A. 175 D6
Tavas Turkey 106 B3
also known as Yarangüme
Tavastehus Fin. *see* **Hämeenlinna**
Tavda Rus. Fed. 38 G4
Tavelsjö Sweden 44 M2
Tavernes de la Valldigna Spain 55 K5
also spelt Tabernes de Valldigna
Taveuni *i.* Fiji 145 H3
Tavgetos *mts* Greece 59 D11
also known as Taïyetos Óros
Taviano Italy 57 K9
Tavignano *r. Corsica* France 56 B6
Tavildara Tajik. 101 G2
also spelt Tovil'-Dora
Tavira Port. 54 D7
Tavistock Canada 173 M7
Tavistock U.K. 47 H13
Tavolara, Isola *i. Sardinia* Italy 56 B8
Tavolzhan Kazakh. 103 I1
also spelt Tobylzhan
Távora *r.* Spain 54 D3
Tavoy Myanmar 79 B5
also known as Dawei; *also spelt* Tawè
Tavoy *b.* Myanmar 79 B5
also known as Dawei
Tavoy Island Myanmar *see* **Mali Kyun**
Tavoy Point Myanmar 79 B5
Tavrichanka Rus. Fed. 90 B3
Tavricheskoye Kazakh. 103 J2
also known as Tavrīl
Tavrīl Kazakh. *see* **Tavricheskoye**
Tavşanlı Turkey 106 B3
Tavua Fiji 145 G3
Taw *r.* U.K. 47 H12
Tawai, Bukit *mt. Sabah* Malaysia 77 G1
also known as Melta, Mount
Tawakoni, Lake U.S.A. 179 D5
Tawallah Range *hills* Australia 148 B2
Tawang India 97 F4
Tawas Bay U.S.A. 173 J6
Tawas City U.S.A. 173 J6
Tawau *Sabah* Malaysia 77 G1
Tawau, Teluk *b. Sabah* Malaysia 77 G1
Tawè Myanmar *see* **Tavoy**
Taweisha Sudan 121 E6
Tawi *r.* India 96 B2
Ţawī Ḩafīr *well* U.A.E. 105 F2
Tawila Sudan 120 E6
Tawîla, Gezâ'ir *is* Egypt 104 A2
English form Tawîla Islands
Tawîla Islands Egypt *see* **Tawîla, Gezâ'ir**
Ţawī Murra *well* U.A.E. 105 F2
Tawitawi *i.* Phil. 74 A5
Tawmaw Myanmar 78 B2
Tawu Taiwan 87 G4
also spelt Dawu
Taxco Mex. 185 F5
Taxiatosh Uzbek. 102 D4
formerly known as Takhiatash
Taxila *tourist site* Pak. 101 H3
UNESCO World Heritage Site
Taxkorgan China 88 A4
Taxtako'pir Uzbek. 102 E4
Tay *r.* Canada 166 C2
Tay *r.* U.K. 46 I7
Tay, Firth of *est.* U.K. 46 I7
Tay, Lake *salt flat* Australia 151 C7
Tay, Loch *l.* U.K. 46 H7
Tayabamba Peru 200 A2
Tayabas Bay Phil. 74 B3
Tayan Indon. 77 E2
Tayeeglow Somalia 128 E3
Tayga Rus. Fed. 80 D1
Taygan Mongolia 84 C2
Taykanskiy Khrebet *mts* Rus. Fed. 82 D1
Taylor Canada 166 F3
Taylor *AZ* U.S.A. 183 N7
Taylor *NE* U.S.A. 178 C3
Taylor *TX* U.S.A. 179 C6
Taylor, Mount N.Z. 153 F11
Taylor, Mount U.S.A. 181 F6
Taylorsville U.S.A. 174 C4
Taylorville U.S.A. 174 B4
Taymā' Saudi Arabia 104 B2
Taymura *r.* Rus. Fed. 39 J3
Taymyr, Ozero *l.* Rus. Fed. 39 K2
Taymyr, Poluostrov *pen.* Rus. Fed. *see* **Taymyr Peninsula**
Taymyr Peninsula Rus. Fed. 39 J2
also known as Taymyr, Poluostrov
Tây Ninh Vietnam 79 D6
Taypak Kazakh. 102 B2
also spelt Taypaq; *formerly known as* Kalmykovo
Taypaq Kazakh. *see* **Taypak**
Tayport U.K. 46 J7
Tayshet Rus. Fed. 80 F1
Taysoygan, Peski *des.* Kazakh. 102 C2
Tayspun *tourist site* Iraq *see* **Ctesiphon**
Taytan Turkey 59 J10
Taytay Phil. 74 B3
Taytay Phil. 74 A4
Taytay Bay Phil. 74 A4
Tayu Indon. 77 E4
Tayuan China 82 B2
Tayyebād Iran 101 E3
Tayynsha Kazakh. 103 G1
formerly known as Krasnoarmeysk
Taz *r.* Rus. Fed. 39 H3
Taza Morocco 122 E2
Taza-Bazar Uzbek. *see* **Shumanay**
Tāza Khurmātū Iraq 107 F4
Taze Myanmar 78 A3
Tazeh Kand Azer. 107 F3
Tazenakht Morocco 122 D3
Tazewell *TN* U.S.A. 176 B9
Tazewell *VA* U.S.A. 176 D8
Tazin *r.* Canada 167 I2
Tāzirbū Libya 120 D3
Tazirbu Water Wells Field Libya 120 D3
Tazizilet *well* Niger 125 H2
Tazlău Romania 58 H2
Tazlău *r.* Romania 58 H2
Tazmalt Alg. 55 P8
Tazoghrane Tunisia 57 C12
Tazouikert *hill* Mali 123 E5
Tazovskaya Guba *sea chan.* Rus. Fed. 39 H3
Tazovskiy Rus. Fed. 39 H3
Tazrouk Alg. 123 G5
Tazzarine Morocco 122 D3
Tazzouguert Morocco 122 E2
Tbessa Alg. *see* **Tébessa**

►**T'bilisi** Georgia 107 F2
Capital of Georgia. English form Tbilisi; historically known as Tiflis.

Tbilisi Georgia *see* **T'bilisi**
Tchabal Mbabo *mt.* Cameroon 125 I5
Tchad *country* Africa *see* **Chad**
Tchamba Togo 125 F4
Tchaourou Benin 125 F4
Tchetti Benin 125 F5
Tchibanga Gabon 126 A5
Tchidoutene *watercourse* Niger 125 G2
Tchié *well* Chad 120 C5

Thingvallavatn (Þingvallavatn) l. Iceland 44 [inset] B2
Thingvellir (Þingvellir) Iceland 44 [inset] B2
Thingvellir (Þingvellir) nat. park Iceland 44 B2 UNESCO World Heritage Site
Thionville France 51 M3 formerly known as Diedenhofen
Thira Greece 59 G12
Thira i. Greece 59 G12 also known as Santorini; historically known as Thera
Thirasia i. Greece 59 G12
Third Cataract rapids Sudan see 3rd Cataract
Thirsk U.K. 47 K9
Thirty Mile Lake Canada 167 L2
Thiruvananthapuram India see Trivandrum
Thiruvarur India 94 C4
Thiruvattiyur India see Tiruvottiyur
Thissavros, Techniti Limni resr Greece 58 F7
Thisted Denmark 45 J4
Thistle Creek Canada 166 B2
Thistle Island Australia 146 C3
Thistle Lake Canada 167 I1
Thityabin Myanmar 78 A3
Thiva Greece 59 E10 also known as Thívai; historically known as Thebes
Thívai Greece see Thiva
Thiviers France 50 G7
Thlewiaza r. Canada 167 M2
Thoa r. Canada 167 I2
Thô Chu, Đao i. Vietnam 79 C6
Thoen Thai. 78 B4
Thoeng Thai. 78 C4
Thohoyandou S. Africa 131 F4
Tholen i. Neth. 48 B4
Thomas r. Australia 151 B5
Thomas, Lake salt flat Australia 148 C5
Thomas Hill Reservoir U.S.A. 178 D4
Thomas Hubbard, Cape Canada 165 J1
Thomas Mountain U.S.A. 183 H8
Thomaston CT U.S.A. 177 L4
Thomaston GA U.S.A. 175 C5
Thomaston ME U.S.A. 177 P1
Thomastown Ireland 47 E11
Thomasville AL U.S.A. 175 C6
Thomasville GA U.S.A. 175 D6
Thomasville NC U.S.A. 174 D5
Thomonde Haiti 187 F3
Thompson Canada 167 L4
Thompson r. Canada 166 F5
Thompson MI U.S.A. 172 G5
Thompson UT U.S.A. 183 O3
Thompson r. U.S.A. 174 A4
Thompson Falls U.S.A. 180 D3
Thompson Peak U.S.A. 181 F6
Thompson's Falls Kenya see Nyahururu
Thompson Sound Canada 166 E5
Thompson Sound inlet N.Z. 153 A13
Thompsonville U.S.A. 177 M4
Thomson watercourse Australia 149 D5
Thomson GA U.S.A. 175 D5
Thomson IL U.S.A. 172 C9
Thon Buri Thai. 79 C5
Thongwa Myanmar 78 B4
Thonon-les-Bains France 51 M6
Thoreau U.S.A. 181 E6
Thorhild Canada 167 H4
Thorn Poland see Toruń
Thornapple r. U.S.A. 173 H8
Thornbury N.Z. 153 C14
Thorne Canada 173 N4
Thorne U.K. 47 L10
Thorne U.S.A. 182 F3
Thornhill U.K. 47 I8
Thornton r. Australia 148 C3
Thornton U.S.A. 172 E6
Thorp U.S.A. 172 C6
Thorsby Canada 167 H4
Thorshavn Faroe Is see Tórshavn
Thorshavnfjella reg. Antarctica see Thorshavnheiane
Thorshavnheiane reg. Antarctica 223 B2 also known as Thorshavnfjella
Thota-ea-Moli Lesotho 133 L6
Thouars France 50 F6
Thoubal India 97 G4
Thouet r. France 50 F5
Thouin, Cape pt Australia 150 B4
Thourout Belgium see Torhout
Thousand Islands Canada/U.S.A. 173 Q6
Thousand Lake Mountain U.S.A. 183 M3
Thousand Oaks U.S.A. 182 F7
Thousand Palms U.S.A. 183 H8
Thousandsticks U.S.A. 176 B8
Thrace reg. Turkey 106 A2 also spelt Thraki or Trakiya or Trakya
Thraki reg. Turkey see Thrace
Thrakiko Pelagos sea Greece 58 F8
Thredbo Australia 147 F4
Three Fathoms Cove b. Hong Kong China 87 [inset] also known as Kei Ling Ha Hoi
Three Forks U.S.A. 180 E3
►Three Gorges Dam Project resr China 87 D2 ►►68–69 Asia Water
Three Hummock Island Australia 147 E5
Three Kings Islands N.Z. 152 G2
Three Oaks U.S.A. 172 G9
Three Pagodas Pass Myanmar/Thai. 79 B5
Three Points U.S.A. 183 M9
Three Points, Cape Ghana 125 E5
Three Rivers CA U.S.A. 182 F5
Three Rivers MI U.S.A. 172 H9
Three Rivers TX U.S.A. 179 C6
Three Sisters S. Africa 132 H8
Three Sisters mt. U.S.A. 180 B3
Three Springs Australia 151 A6
Thrissur India see Trichur
Throckmorton U.S.A. 179 C5
Throssell, Lake salt flat Australia 151 D5
Throssel Range hills Australia 150 C4
Thrushton National Park Australia 147 E1
Thu Bôn, Sông r. Vietnam 79 E4
Thubun Lakes Canada 167 I2
Thu Dâu Môt Vietnam 79 D6 formerly known as Phu Cuong
Thu Đuc Vietnam 79 D6
Thuin Belgium 51 K2
Thul Sudan 128 B2
Thul watercourse Sudan 128 A2
Thulaythawāt Gharbī, Jabal hill Syria 109 K2
Thule Greenland 165 M2 also known as Qaanaaq
Thuli Zimbabwe 131 F4
Thuli r. Zimbabwe 131 F4
Thumayl, Wādī watercourse Iraq 109 O4
Thun Switz. 51 N6
Thunda Australia 149 D5
Thundelarra Australia 151 B6
Thunder Bay Canada 168 B3
Thunder Bay b. Canada 168 B3
Thunder Bay b. U.S.A. 173 J5
Thunder Creek r. Canada 167 J5
Thunder Knoll sea feature Caribbean Sea 186 C3
Thuner See l. Switz. 51 N6
Thung Salaeng Luang National Park Thai. 78 C4
Thung Song Thai. 79 B6
Thung Wa Thai. 79 B7
Thung Yai Naresuan Wildlife Reserve nature res. Thai. 79 B5 UNESCO World Heritage Site
Thur r. Switz. 51 O5
Thüringen land Germany 48 H4 English form Thuringia
Thüringer Becken reg. Germany 48 I4
Thüringer Wald mts Germany 48 H5 English form Thuringian Forest
Thüringer Wald park Germany 48 H5
Thuringia land Germany see Thüringen
Thuringian Forest mts Germany see Thüringer Wald
Thurles Ireland 47 E11 also spelt Durlas
Thurmont U.S.A. 176 H6
Thursby U.K. 47 I9
Thursday Island Australia 149 D1
Thurso U.K. 46 I5
Thurso r. U.K. 46 I5
Thurston Island Antarctica 222 R2 formerly known as Thurston Peninsula
Thurston Peninsula i. Antarctica see Thurston Island
Thusis Switz. 51 P6
Thwaites Glacier Tongue Antarctica 222 Q1
Thy reg. Denmark 45 J4
Thyamis r. Greece 59 B9 also spelt Thíamis
Thyatira Turkey see Akhisar
Thyborøn Denmark 45 J4
Thylungra Australia 149 D5
Thymaina i. Greece 59 H11
Thyolo Malawi 129 B9
Thyou Burkina 125 E4
Thyou Burkina see Tiou
Thysville Dem. Rep. Congo see Mbanza-Ngungu
Tiāb Iran 100 D5
Tiahuanaco Bol. 200 C4
Tiancang China 84 C3
Tianchang China 87 F1
Tiancheng China see Chongyang
Tianchi China see Lezhi
Tiandeng China 87 C4
Tiandiba China see Jinyang
Tiandong China 86 C4 also known as Pingma
Tian'e China 87 C3 also known as Liupai
Tianfanjie China 87 F2
Tiângol Lougguéré watercourse Senegal 124 B3
Tianguá Brazil 202 D2
►Tianjin China 85 H4 English form Tientsin ►►18–19 World Cities
Tianjin municipality China 85 H4 English form Tientsin
Tianjun China 84 C4 also known as Xinyuan
Tiankoye Senegal 124 B3
Tianlin China 86 C3 also known as Leli
Tianmen China 87 E2
Tianmu Shan mts China 87 F2
Tianqiaoling China 82 C4
Tianquan China 86 B2 also known as Chengxiang
Tianshan China 85 I3 also known as Ar Horqin Qi
Tian Shan mts China/Kyrg. see Tien Shan
Tianshifu China 82 B4
Tianshui China 86 C1
Tianshuihai Aksai Chin 89 B5
Tianshuijing China 84 B3
Tiantai China 87 G2
Tiantaiyong China 85 H3
Tiantang China see Yuexi
Tianyang China 86 C4 also known as Tianzhou
Tianyi China see Ningcheng
Tianzhen Shandong China see Gaoqing
Tianzhen Shanxi China 85 G3
Tianzhou China see Tianyang
Tianzhu Gansu China 84 D4 also known as Huazangsi
Tianzhu Guizhou China 87 D3
Tiaret Alg. 123 F2 also known as Tagdempt
Tiaret well Tunisia 123 H3
Tiassalé Côte d'Ivoire 124 D5
Tibabar Sabah Malaysia see Tambunan
Tibagi Brazil 203 B8
Tibagi r. Brazil 206 C10 also spelt Tibaji
Tibaji r. Brazil see Tibagi
Tibal, Wādī watercourse Iraq 107 E4
Tibaná Col. 198 C3
Tibati Cameroon 125 I5
Tibba Pak. 101 G4
Tibé, Pic de mt. Guinea 124 C4
Tiber r. Italy 56 E7 also spelt Tevere
Tiberghamine Alg. 123 F3
Tiberias Israel 108 G5 also spelt Teverya
Tiberias, Lake Israel see Galilee, Sea of
Tiber Reservoir U.S.A. 180 E2
Tibesti mts Chad 120 C4
Tibet aut. reg. China see Xizang Zizhiqu
Tibet, Plateau of China 89 D5 also known as Qingzang Gaoyuan or Xizang Gaoyuan
Tibet Autonomous Region aut. reg. China see Xizang Zizhiqu
Tibiri Niger 125 G3
Țibleș, Vârful mt. Romania 58 F2
Tiboku Falls Guyana 199 G3
Tibooburra Australia 147 D2
Tibrikot Nepal 97 D3
Tibuga, Ensenada b. Col. 198 B3
Tibur Italy see Tivoli
Tiburón, Isla i. Mex. 184 B2
Ticao i. Phil. 74 B3
Ticha r. Bulg. 58 H5
Tichak mt. Bulg. 58 D6
Tichau Poland see Tychy
Tichborne Canada 173 Q6
Tichégami r. Canada 169 F3
Tichet well Mali 125 F2
Tîchît Mauritania 124 C2
Tichla W. Sahara 122 B5
Ticino r. Italy/Switz. 56 B3
Ticinum Italy see Pavia
Țicleni Romania 58 E4
Ticonderoga U.S.A. 177 L2 historically known as Fort Carillon
Ticul Mex. 185 H4
Ticumbia i. Fiji see Cikobia
Tiddim Myanmar 78 A3
Tideridjaounine, Adrar mts Alg. 123 F5
Tidikelt, Plaine du plain Alg. 123 F4
Tidioute U.S.A. 176 F4
Tidjerouene well Mali 125 F2
Tidjikja Mauritania 124 C2
Tidore i. Indon. 75 C2
Tiébissou Côte d'Ivoire 124 D5
Tiéboro Chad 120 C4
Tiefa China 85 I3 also known as Diaobingshan
Tiel Neth. 48 C4 formerly spelt Thiel
Tiel Senegal 124 B3
Tieli China 82 B3
Tieling China 82 A4
Tielongtan Aksai Chin 89 B5
Tielt Belgium 51 J2 also spelt Thielt
Tiémé Côte d'Ivoire 124 D4
Tiene Liberia 124 C5
Tienen Belgium 51 K2 also known as Tirlemont
Tien Shan mts China/Kyrg. 88 B3 also spelt Tian Shan or Tyan' Shan'
Tien Shan Oblast admin. div. Kyrg. see Naryn
Tientsin China see Tianjin
Tientsin municipality China see Tianjin
Tiên Yên Vietnam 78 D3
Tierfontein S. Africa 133 K5
Tierp Sweden 45 L3
Tierra Amarilla U.S.A. 181 F5
Tierra Blanca Mex. 185 F5
Tierra Blanca Peru 198 C6
Tierra Colorada Mex. 185 F5
Tierra del Fuego prov. Arg. 205 D9
►Tierra del Fuego, Isla Grande de i. Arg./Chile 205 C9 Largest island in South America. ►►188–189 South America Landscapes
Tierra del Fuego, Parque Nacional nat. park Arg. 205 D9
Tierradentro, Parque Arqueológico Nacional tourist site Col. 198 B4 UNESCO World Heritage Site
Tierralta Col. 198 B2
Tiétar r. Spain 54 F5
Tiétar, Valle de valley Spain 54 F4
Tietê Brazil 206 F10
Tietê r. Brazil 206 B7
Tieyon Australia 148 B5
Tiffin U.S.A. 176 B4
Tiflis Georgia see T'bilisi
Tifore i. Indon. 75 C2
Tifton U.S.A. 175 D6
Tifu Indon. 75 C3
Tiga i. Sabah Malaysia 77 F1
Tigane S. Africa 133 K3
Țigănești Romania 58 G5
Tigapuluh, Pegunungan mts Indon. 76 C3
Tigen Kazakh. 102 B3
Tīgh Āb Iran 101 E5
Tigheciului, Dealurile hills Moldova 58 J3
Tighina Moldova 58 K2 formerly known as Bender or Bendery
Tigiretskiy Khrebet mts Kazakh./Rus. Fed. 88 C1
Tigiria India 95 E1
Tignère Cameroon 125 I5
Tignish Canada 169 H4
Tigoda r. Rus. Fed. 43 M2
Tigranocerta Turkey see Siirt
Tigray admin. reg. Eth. 128 C1
Tigre r. Ecuador/Peru 198 C6
Tigre, Cerro del mt. Mex. 185 F4
►Tigris r. Asia 107 F4 also known as Dicle (Turkey) or Dijlah, Nahr (Iraq/Syria) ►►68–69 Asia Water
Tigrovaya Balka Zapovednik nature res. Tajik. 101 G2
Tiguent Mauritania 124 B2
Tiguesmat hills Mauritania 122 C4
Tiguidit, Falaise de esc. Niger 125 G2
Tiguir well Niger 125 H2
Tīh, Jabal at plat. Egypt 121 G2
Tihāmah reg. Saudi Arabia 104 C4
Tihuatlán Mex. 185 F4
Tijamuchi r. Bol. 200 D3
Tijara India 96 C4
Tiji Libya 120 A1
Tijirīt reg. Mauritania 122 B5
Tijuana Mex. 184 A1
Tijucas Brazil 203 B8
Tijucas, Baía de b. Brazil 203 B8
Tijuco r. Brazil 206 C5
Tikal tourist site Guat. 185 H5
Tikal, Parque Nacional nat. park Guat. 185 H5 UNESCO World Heritage Site
Tikamgarh India 96 C4 also known as Tehri
Tikanlik China 88 D3
Tikchik Lake U.S.A. 164 D4
Tikherón Greece see Tykhero
Tikhmenevo Rus. Fed. 43 T3
Tikhonova Pustyn' Rus. Fed. 43 R7
Tikhoretsk Rus. Fed. 41 G7
Tikhtozero Rus. Fed. 44 O2
Tikhvin Rus. Fed. 43 O2
Tikhvinka r. Rus. Fed. 43 O2
Tikhvinskaya Gryada ridge Rus. Fed. 43 O2
Tikiktene well Niger 125 G2
Tikirarjuaq Canada see Whale Cove
Tikitiki N.Z. 152 M5
Tikkakoski Fin. 44 N3
Tikkurila Fin. 42 G1
Tikokino N.Z. 152 K7
Tikrīt Iraq 107 E4
Tiksheozero, Ozero l. Rus. Fed. 44 P2
Tiksi Rus. Fed. 39 M2
Tikumbia i. Fiji see Cikobia
Tikveš Ezero l. Macedonia 58 C7
Tikwana S. Africa 133 J4
Tila r. Nepal 97 D3
Tilaiya Reservoir India 97 E4
Tilavar Iran 100 C2
Tilbeşar Ovasi plain Turkey 109 I1
Tilbooroo Australia 147 E1
Tilburg Neth. 48 C4
Tilbury Canada 173 K8
Tilbury U.K. 47 M12
Tilcara Arg. 200 D5
Tilcha Australia 146 D2
Tilden U.S.A. 179 C6
Tileagd Romania 58 D1
Tilemsès Niger 125 G3
Tilemsi, Vallée du watercourse Mali 125 F2
Tilghman U.S.A. 177 I7
Tilhar India 96 C4
Tilia, Oued watercourse Alg. 123 F4
Tilimsen Alg. see Tlemcen
Tilin Myanmar 78 A3
Tillabéri Niger 125 F3
Tillabéri dept Niger 125 F3
Tillamook U.S.A. 180 B3
Tillanchong Island India 95 G4
Tille r. France 51 L5
Tilley Canada 167 I5
Tillia Niger 125 G2
Tillsonburg Canada 168 D5
Tiloa Niger 125 F3
Tilogne Senegal see Thilogne
Tilomonte Chile 200 C5
Tilos i. Greece 59 I12
Tilpa Australia 147 E2
Tilsa r. Latvia 42 I5
Tilsit Rus. Fed. see Sovetsk
Tilton U.S.A. 177 N2
Tilža Latvia 42 I5
Tim Rus. Fed. 41 F6
Tim r. Rus. Fed. 43 S9
Ţimā Egypt 121 F3
Timah, Bukit hill Sing. 76 [inset]
Timakara i. India 94 B4
Timane r. Para. 201 F5
Timanskiy Kryazh ridge Rus. Fed. 40 I2
Timar Turkey 107 E3
Timaru N.Z. 153 F12
Timashevsk Rus. Fed. 41 F7 formerly known as Timashevskaya
Timashevskaya Rus. Fed. see Timashevsk
Timbákion Greece see Tympaki
Timbalier Bay U.S.A. 175 B6
Timbaúba Brazil 202 F3
Timbedgha Mauritania 124 C2
Timber Creek Australia 148 A2
Timber Lake U.S.A. 178 B2
Timber Mountain U.S.A. 183 H4
Timberville U.S.A. 176 G7
Timbiquí Col. 198 B4
Timbué, Ponta pt Moz. 131 H3
Timbuktu Mali 124 E2 also spelt Tombouctou UNESCO World Heritage Site
Timbun Mata i. Sabah Malaysia 77 G1
Timelkam Austria 49 K7
Timétrine Mali 125 E2
Timétrine reg. Mali 125 E2
Timgad tourist site Alg. 123 G2 also known as Thamugadi UNESCO World Heritage Site
Timia Niger 125 H2
Timiaouine Alg. 123 F5
Timimoun Alg. 123 F3
Timirist, Râs pt Mauritania 124 A2
Timiryazev Kazakh. 103 F1
Timiryazevo Kazakh. 103 F1
Timiș r. Romania 58 B3
Timiskaming, Lake Canada see Témiscamingue, Lac
Timișoara Romania 58 C3
Timișului, Câmpia plain Romania 58 B3
Timkovichi Belarus see Tsimkavichy
Ti-m-Meghsoi watercourse Niger 125 G2
Timmelsjoch pass Austria/Italy 48 I9
Timmins Canada 168 D3
Timms Hill U.S.A. 172 C5
Timok r. Serb. and Mont. 58 D4
Timokhino Rus. Fed. 43 R2
Timon Brazil 202 D3
Timor i. Indon. 75 C5
Timor Sea Australia/Indon. 144 B3
Timor Timur country Asia see East Timor
Timoshino Rus. Fed. 43 R1
Timóteo Brazil 207 K6
Timoudi Alg. 123 E3
Timperley Range hills Australia 151 C5
Timrå Sweden 44 L3
Timsāḩ, Buḩayrat at l. Egypt 108 D7
Tims Ford Lake U.S.A. 174 C5
Timshor r. Rus. Fed. 40 J3
Timur Kazakh. 103 G4 also spelt Temir; formerly spelt Tumur
Timurni Muafi India 96 C5
Tin, Jabal hill Saudi Arabia 104 C2
Tin, Ra's at pt Libya 120 D1
Tina r. S. Africa 133 N8
Tina, Khalīg el b. Egypt 108 D6 English form Pelusium, Bay of
Ti-n-Aba well Mali 125 E2
Tin Alkoum Alg. 120 A3
Tin Amzi, Oued watercourse Alg. 123 G5
Ti-n-Azabo well Mali 125 F2
Ti-n-Bessaïs well Mauritania 122 C5
Tin Can Bay Australia 149 G5
Tinchebray France 50 F4
Ti-n-Didine well Mali 123 E5
Tindivanam India 94 C3
Tindouf Alg. 122 C4
Tiné Chad 120 D6
Ti-n-Echeri well Mali 125 E2
Tinée r. France 51 N9
Tineo Spain 54 E1
Tinerhir Morocco 122 D3
Ti-n-Etissane well Mali 125 E2
Tinfouchy Alg. 122 D3
Tinggi i. Malaysia 76 D2
Tingharat, Hammādat des. Libya 120 A2
Tingi Mountains Sierra Leone 124 C4
Tingis Morocco see Tangier
Ting Jiang r. China 87 F3
Tingkawk Sakan Myanmar 78 B2
Tinglev Denmark 45 J5
Tingo Maria Peru 200 B2
Tingrela Côte d'Ivoire see Tengréla
Tingri China 89 D6
Tingsryd Sweden 45 K4
Tingstäde Sweden 45 L4
Tingvatn Norway 45 I4
Tingvoll Norway 44 J3
Tingzhou China see Changting
Tinharé, Ilha de i. Brazil 202 E5
Tinian i. N. Mariana Is 73 K4 formerly known as Buena Vista
Tiniéré well Mauritania 124 B2
Tinigua, Parque Nacional nat. park Col. 198 C4
Tini Heke is N.Z. see Snares Islands
Tiniroto N.Z. 152 L6
Tinja r. Bos.-Herz. 56 K4
Tinjar r. Sarawak Malaysia 77 F1
Tinkisso r. Guinea 124 C4
Tinline, Mount N.Z. 153 H10
Tinn Norway 45 J4
Tinnelvelly India see Tirunelveli
Tinnsjø l. Norway 45 J4
Tino, Isola del i. Italy 56 B4 UNESCO World Heritage Site
Tinogasta Arg. 204 D3
Tinompo Indon. 75 B2
Tinos Greece 59 G11
Tinos i. Greece 59 G11
Tiñosa mt. Spain 54 G7
Ti-n-Rerhoh well Alg. 123 G5
Tinrhert, Plateau du Alg. 123 G3
Tin Shui Wai Hong Kong China 87 [inset]
Ti-n-Srir well Mali 125 F2
Tinsukia India 97 G4
Tintagel Canada 166 E4
Tînțâne Mauritania 124 C2
Ti-n-Tarabine well Alg. 123 G5
Ti-n-Tarabine, Oued watercourse Alg. 123 G5
Ti-n-Tehoun well Mali 124 E2
Tintejert, Adrar mt. Alg. 123 F4
Ti-n-Tersi well Mali 125 F2
Tintina Arg. 204 E2
Tintinara Australia 146 D3
Tinto r. Spain 54 E7
Tin Tounnant well Mali see Taounnant
Tinui N.Z. 152 K8
Ti-n-Zaouâtene Mali 125 F2
Tioga ND U.S.A. 178 B1
Tioga PA U.S.A. 177 H4
Tioga r. U.S.A. 177 H3
Tioman i. Malaysia 76 D2
Tionaga Canada 173 K2
Tioribougou Mali 124 C3
Tiou Burkina 124 E3 formerly spelt Thyou
Tioughnioga r. U.S.A. 177 J3
Tipasa Alg. 123 F1 UNESCO World Heritage Site
Tipitapa Nicaragua 186 B4
Tiplet U.S.A. 172 E5
Tippecanoe r. U.S.A. 174 C3
Tipperary Ireland 47 D11
Tiptala Bhanjyang pass Nepal 97 E4
Tipton CA U.S.A. 182 E5
Tipton IA U.S.A. 174 B3
Tipton MO U.S.A. 178 D4
Tipton, Mount U.S.A. 183 J6
Tiptonville U.S.A. 174 B4
Tiptop U.S.A. 176 D8
Tip Top Hill Canada 168 C3
Tiptur India 94 C3
Tipuani Bol. 200 C3
Tiquié r. Brazil 198 D4
Tiquisate Guat. 185 H6
Tiracambu, Serra do hills Brazil 202 C3
Tirahart, Oued watercourse Alg. 123 F5
Tirān Iran 100 B3
Tirān i. Saudi Arabia 104 A2
►Tirana Albania 58 A7 Capital of Albania. Also spelt Tiranë.
Tiranë Albania see Tirana
Tirano Italy 56 C2
Tiraouene well Niger 125 G2
Tirap India 97 G4
Tiraraouine well Mali 125 E2
Tirari Desert Australia 146 C1
Tiraspol Moldova 58 K2
Tirau N.Z. 152 J5
Tiraumea N.Z. 152 K8
Tiraz Mountains Namibia 130 C5
Tire Turkey 59 I10
Tiree i. U.K. 46 F7
Tirek well Alg. 123 F5
Tirest well Mali 123 F5
Tîrgoviște Romania see Târgoviște
Tîrgu Bujor Romania see Târgu Bujor
Tîrgu Cărbunești Romania see Târgu Cărbunești
Tîrgu Frumos Romania see Târgu Frumos
Tîrgu Jiu Romania see Târgu Jiu
Tîrgu Lăpuș Romania see Târgu Lăpuș
Tîrgu Mureș Romania see Târgu Mureș
Tîrgu Neamț Romania see Târgu Neamț
Tîrgu Ocna Romania see Târgu Ocna
Tîrgu Secuiesc Romania see Târgu Secuiesc
Tirich Mir mt. Pak. 101 G2
Tiririne, Oued watercourse Alg. 123 H5
Tiris Zemmour admin. reg. Mauritania 122 C5
Tirkšliai Lith. 42 D5
Tirlemont Belgium see Tienen
Tirna r. India 94 C2
Tîrnăveni Romania see Târnăveni
Tîrnavos Greece see Tyrnavos
Tiro hill Spain 54 F6
Tirodi India 96 C5
Tiros Brazil 203 C6
Tiroungoulou Cent. Afr. Rep. 126 D2
Tirourda, Col de pass Alg. 55 P8
Tirreno, Mare sea France/Italy see Tyrrhenian Sea
Tirso r. Sardinia Italy 57 A9
Tirthahalli India 94 B3
Tiruchchendur India 94 C4
Tiruchchirappalli India 94 C4 formerly known as Trichinopoly
Tiruchengodu India 94 C4
Tirukkoyilur India 94 C3
Tirumangalam India 94 C4
Tirunelveli India 94 C4 formerly known as Tinnelvelly
Tiruntán Peru 200 B1
Tirupati India 94 C3
Tiruppattur Tamil Nadu India 94 C3
Tiruppattur Tamil Nadu India 94 C4
Tiruppur India 94 C4
Tiruttani India 94 C3
Tirutturaippundi India 94 C4
Tiruvallur India 94 C3
Tiruvannamalai India 94 C3
Tiruvettipuram India 94 C3
Tiruvottiyur India 94 D3 also spelt Thiruvattiyur
Tiru Well Australia 150 D4
Tiryns tourist site Peloponnisos Greece 59 D11 UNESCO World Heritage Site
Tiryns tourist site Greece 59 D11
Tirza r. Latvia 42 H4
Tisa r. Serb. and Mont. 58 B3 also known as Tisza
Tisa r. Serb. and Mont. 58 C5
Tisaiyanvilai India 94 C4
Tisău Romania 58 H3
Tisdale Canada 167 J4
Tishomingo U.S.A. 179 C5
Tiska, Mont mt. Alg. 123 H5
Tissemsilt Alg. 123 F2 formerly known as Vialar
Tista r. India 97 F4
Tisza r. Hungary see Tisa
Tiszabezdéd Hungary 49 T7
Tiszaföldvár Hungary 49 R9
Tiszafüred Hungary 49 R8
Tiszakécske Hungary 49 R9
Tiszaújváros Hungary 49 S8
Tiszavasvári Hungary 49 S8 formerly known as Bődszentmihály
Tit Alg. 123 F4
Tit Alg. 123 G5
Titabar India 97 G4
Titan Dome ice feature Antarctica 223 K1
Titao Burkina 125 E3
Titarisios r. Greece 59 D9
Tit-Ary Rus. Fed. 39 M2
Titawin Morocco see Tétouan
Titel Vojvodina, Srbija Serb. and Mont. 58 B3
Tithwal Pak. 101 H3
Titicaca, Lago l. Bol./Peru see Titicaca, Lake
►Titicaca, Lake Bol./Peru 200 C3 Largest lake in South America. Also known as Titicaca, Lago. ►►188–189 South America Landscapes
Titi Islands N.Z. 153 B15
Titiea mt. N.Z. see Aspiring, Mount
Titlagarh India 95 D1
Titlis mt. Switz. 51 O6
Titograd Crna Gora Serb. and Mont. see Podgorica
Titova Mitrovica Kosovo, Srbija Serb. and Mont. see Kosovska Mitrovica
Titov Drvar Bos.-Herz. 56 I4
Titovka r. Rus. Fed. 44 O1
Titovo Užice Srbija Serb. and Mont. see Užice
Titovo Velenje Slovenia see Velenje
Titov Veles Macedonia see Veles
Titov Vrbas Vojvodina, Srbija Serb. and Mont. see Vrbas
Ti Tree Australia 148 B4
Tittabawassee r. U.S.A. 173 J7
Titteri mts Alg. 55 O8
Tittmoning Germany 49 J7
Titu Romania 58 G4
Titule Dem. Rep. Congo 126 E4
Titusville FL U.S.A. 175 D6
Titusville PA U.S.A. 176 F4
Tiu Chung Chau i. Hong Kong China 87 [inset]
Tiumpan Head U.K. 46 F5 also known as Siumpain, Rubha an t-
Tiva watercourse Kenya 128 C5
Tivari India 96 B4
Tivat Crna Gora Serb. and Mont. 56 K6
Tiveden nationalpark nat. park Sweden 45 K4
Tiverton Canada 173 L6
Tiverton U.K. 47 I13
Tivoli Italy 56 E7 historically known as Tibur UNESCO World Heritage Site
Tiwal, Wadi watercourse Sudan 126 D2
Tiwāl al 'Abā reg. Syria 109 K1
Tiwanaku tourist site Bol. 200 C4 UNESCO World Heritage Site
Ţīwī Oman 105 G3
Tiwi Aboriginal Land res. Australia 148 A1
Tiworo, Selat sea chan. Indon. 75 B4
Tixkokob Mex. 185 H4
Tixtla Mex. 185 F5
Tiya tourist site Eth. 128 C2 UNESCO World Heritage Site
Tizi El Arba hill Alg. 55 O8
Tizi Mighert pass Morocco 122 C3
Tizimín Mex. 185 H4
Tizi-n-Test pass Morocco 122 C3
Tizi-n-Tichka pass Morocco 122 D3
Tizi Ouzou Alg. 123 G1
Tiznap He r. China 88 B4
Tiznit Morocco 122 C3
Tizoc Mex. 185 E3
Tjaktjajaure l. Sweden 44 L2
Tjåmotis Sweden 44 L2
Tjaneni Swaziland 133 P2
Tjappsåive Sweden 44 L2
Tjautas Sweden 44 M2
Tjeggelvas l. Sweden 44 L2
Tjirebon Indon. see Cirebon
Tjirrkarli Aboriginal Reserve Australia 151 D5
Tjolotjo Zimbabwe see Tsholotsho
Tjörn i. Sweden 45 J4
Tjörnes pen. Iceland 44 [inset] C2
Tjøtta Norway 44 K2
Tkibuli Georgia see Tqibuli
Tkvarcheli Georgia see Tqvarch'eli
Tlacolula Mex. 185 F5
Tlacotalpán Mex. 185 G5 UNESCO World Heritage Site
Tlacotepec, Cerro mt. Mex. 185 E5
Tlalnepantla Mex. 185 F5
Tlancualpican Mex. 185 F5
Tlapa Mex. 185 F5
Tlapacoyan Mex. 185 F5
Tlaxcala Mex. 185 F5
Tlaxcala state Mex. 185 F5
Tlaxco Mex. 185 F5
Tlaxcoapán Mex. 185 F4
Tlaxiaco Mex. 185 F5
Tl'ell Canada 166 D4
Tlemcen Alg. 123 E2 formerly spelt Tilimsen
Tleta Rissana Morocco 54 F9
Tlhabologang S. Africa 133 K3
Tlhakalatlou S. Africa 132 H5
Tlhakgameng S. Africa 133 I3
Tlholong S. Africa 133 M5
Tlokweng Botswana 131 E5
Tłuszcz Poland 49 S3
Tlyarata Rus. Fed. 107 F2
T'ma r. Rus. Fed. 43 Q5
Tmeïmîchât Mauritania 122 B5
Tnaôt, Prêk r. Cambodia 79 D6
To r. Myanmar 78 B4 also known as China Bakir
Toad r. Canada 166 E3
Toad River Canada 166 E3
Toamasina Madag. 131 [inset] K3 formerly known as Tamatave
Toamasina prov. Madag. 131 [inset] K3
Toana mts U.S.A. 183 J1
Toano U.S.A. 177 I8
Toa Payoh Sing. 76 [inset]
Toast U.S.A. 176 E9
Toatoa N.Z. 152 L6
To Awai well Sudan 121 G4
Toay Arg. 204 D5
Toba China 86 A2
Toba Japan 91 E7
Toba, Danau l. Indon. 76 B2 English form Toba, Lake
Toba, Lake Indon. see Toba, Danau
Toba and Kakar Ranges mts Pak. 101 F4
Tobago i. Trin. and Tob. 187 H5
Toba Inlet Canada 166 E5
Tobarra Spain 55 J6
Tobas Arg. 204 E3
Toba Tek Singh Pak. 101 H4
Tobelo Indon. 75 C2
Tobermorey Australia 148 C4
Tobermory Australia 147 D1
Tobermory Canada 168 D4
Tobermory U.K. 46 F7
Tōbetsu Japan 90 G3
Tobi i. Palau 73 H6
Tobias Barreto Brazil 202 E4
Tobin, Lake salt flat Australia 150 D4
Tobin, Mount U.S.A. 183 G1
Tobin Lake Canada 180 G1
Tobique r. Canada 169 H4
Tobi-shima i. Japan 90 F5
Toboali Indon. 77 D3
Tobol Kazakh. 103 E1 also spelt Tobyl
Tobol r. Kazakh./Rus. Fed. 103 E1 also spelt Tobyl
Tobol'sk Rus. Fed. 38 G4
Toboso Phil. 74 B4
Tobruk Libya see Tubruq
Tobyhanna U.S.A. 177 J4
Tobyl Kazakh. see Tobol
Tobyl r. Kazakh./Rus. Fed. see Tobol
Tobylzhan Kazakh. see Tavolzhan
Tobysh r. Rus. Fed. 40 I2
Tocache Nuevo Peru 200 A2
Tocantinópolis Brazil 202 C3
Tocantins r. Pará Brazil 199 G6
►Tocantins r. Brazil 202 B2 ►►188–189 South America Landscapes
Tocantins state Brazil 202 B4
Toccoa U.S.A. 174 D5
Toce r. Italy 56 A3
Tochi r. Pak. 101 G3
Tochigi Japan 91 F6
Tochigi pref. Japan 91 F6
Tochio Japan 90 F6
Töcksfors Sweden 45 J4
Tocoa Hond. 186 B4
Tocopilla Chile 200 C5
Tocorpuri, Cerros de mts Bol./Chile 200 D5
Tocumwal Australia 147 E3
Tod, Mount Canada 166 G5
Toda Bhim India 96 C4
Toda Rai Singh India 96 B4
Todd watercourse Australia 148 B5
Todd Range hills Australia 151 D5
Todi Italy 56 E6 historically known as Tuder
Todi mt. Switz. 51 O6
Todog China 88 C2 formerly spelt Todok
Todohokke Japan 90 G4
Todok China see Todog
Todos os Santos r. Brazil 207 M4
Todos Santos Bol. 200 D4
Todos Santos Mex. 184 C4
Todtmoos Germany 48 E8
Toe Jaga, Khao hill Thai. 79 B5
Toéni Burkina 124 E3
Tofield Canada 167 H4
Tofino Canada 166 E5
Toft U.K. 46 K3
Tofte U.S.A. 172 C3
Toftlund Denmark 45 J5
Tofua i. Tonga 145 H3
Toga U.S.A. 176 G8
Tōgane Japan 91 G7
Togdheer admin. reg. Somalia 128 E2
Togi Japan 91 E6
Togiak U.S.A. 164 C4
Togian i. Indon. 75 B3
Togian, Kepulauan is Indon. 75 B3
Togliatti Rus. Fed. see Tol'yatti
►Togo country Africa 125 F4 ►►114–115 Africa Countries
Tograsay He r. China 88 E4
Tögrög Mongolia 84 B2 formerly known as Manhan
Togrog Ul China 85 G3 also known as Qahar Youyi Qianqi
Togtoh China 85 F3
Togton He r. China 97 G2
Toguchin Rus. Fed. 80 C1
Toguz Kazakh. 103 E3
Tog Wajaale Somalia 128 D2
Tohamiyam Sudan 121 H5
Tohana India 96 B3
Tohenbatu mt. Sarawak Malaysia 77 F2
Tohmajärvi Fin. 44 O3
Tohmajärvi l. Fin. 44 O3
Toholampi Fin. 44 N3
Tohom China 85 E3

Tres Puentes Chile 204 C2
Tres Puntas, Cabo c. Arg. 205 D7
Três Ranchos Brazil 206 F5
Três Rios Brazil 203 D7
Třešť Czech Rep. 49 M6
Trestino Rus. Fed. 43 O4
Trestna Rus. Fed. 43 Q4
Três Unidos Brazil 198 D6
Tres Zapotes tourist site Mex. 185 G5
Tretten Norway 45 J3
Treuchtlingen Germany 48 H7
Treuenbrietzen Germany 49 J3
Treungen Norway 45 J4
Trevelín Arg. 205 C6
Treves Germany see Trier
Trevi Italy 56 E6
Treviglio Italy 56 B3
Treviso Italy 56 E3
historically known as Tarvisium
Trevose Head U.K. 47 G13
Trgovište Srbija Serb. and Mont. 58 D6
Triabunna Australia 147 E5
Tri An, Hô resr Vietnam 79 D6
Triánda Greece see Trianta
Triangle U.S.A. 177 H7
Tria Nisia i. Greece 59 H12
Trianta Greece 59 J12
also spelt Triánda
Tribal Areas admin. div. Pak. 101 G3
Tribeč mts Slovakia 49 P7
Tri Brata, Gora hill Rus. Fed. 82 F1
Tribune U.S.A. 178 B4
Tricarico Italy 57 I8
Tricase Italy 57 K9
Trichinopoly India see Tiruchchirappalli
Trichonida, Limni l. Greece 59 C10
Trichur India 94 C4
also known as Thrissur
Trida Australia 147 E3
Tridentum Italy see Trento
Trier Germany 48 D6
historically known as Augusta Treverorum or Treves
UNESCO World Heritage Site
Trieste Italy 56 F3
historically known as Tergeste
Trieste, Golfo di g. Europe see Trieste, Gulf of
Trieste, Gulf of Europe 56 F3
also known as Trieste, Golfo di
Trie-sur-Baïse France 50 G9
Trieux r. France 50 C4
Triggiano Italy 56 I7
Triglavski narodni park nat. park Slovenia 56 F2
Trigno r. Italy 56 G6
Trikala Greece 59 C9
also spelt Tríkkala
Tríkkala Greece see Trikala
Trikomo Cyprus see Trikomon
Trikomon Cyprus 108 E2
also known as Trikomo or İskele

►Trikora, Puncak mt. Indon. 73 I7
2nd highest mountain in Oceania.
►►134–135 Oceania Landscapes

Trikorfa mt. Greece 59 D10
Trilj Croatia 56 I5
Trim Ireland 47 F10
Trincheras Mex. 184 C2
Trincomalee Sri Lanka 94 D4
Trindade Brazil 206 D3
Trindade, Ilha da i. S. Atlantic Ocean 217 L7
Tringia mt. Greece 59 C9
Trinidad Bol. 200 D3
Trinidad Cuba 186 D2
UNESCO World Heritage Site
Trinidad i. Trin. and Tob. 187 H5
Trinidad Uruguay 204 F4
Trinidad U.S.A. 181 F5
Trinidad, Golfo b. Chile 205 B8
►Trinidad and Tobago country West Indies 187 H5
►►158–159 North America Countries
Trinitapoli Italy 56 I7
Trinity U.S.A. 179 D6
Trinity r. CA U.S.A. 182 A1
Trinity r. TX U.S.A. 179 D6
Trinity, West Fork r. U.S.A. 179 C5
Trinity Bay Australia 149 E3
Trinity Bay Canada 169 K4
Trinity Dam U.S.A. 182 B1
Trinity Islands U.S.A. 164 D4
Trinity Range mts U.S.A. 182 E1
Trinkat Island India 95 G4
Trinkitat Sudan 104 B4
Trino Italy 56 A3
Trinway U.S.A. 176 C5
Trionto, Capo c. Italy 57 I9
Tripa r. Indon. 76 B2
Tripoli Greece 59 D11
also known as Trípolis
Tripoli Lebanon 108 G3
also known as Trâblous; historically known as Tripolis

►Tripoli Libya 120 B1
Capital of Libya. Also known as Ţarābulus; historically known as Oea.

Trípolis Greece see Tripoli
Tripolis Lebanon see Tripoli
Tripolitania reg. Libya 120 B2
Tripunittura India 94 C4
Tripura state India 97 F5
Trischen i. Germany 48 F1

►Tristan da Cunha i. S. Atlantic Ocean 217 N8
Dependency of St Helena.

Tristao, Îles is Guinea 124 B4
Trisul mt. India 96 C3
Triton Canada 169 K3
Triton Island atoll Paracel Is 72 D3
Triunfo Pernambuco Brazil 202 E3
Triunfo Rondônia Brazil 200 D2
Triunfo Hond. 186 B4
Trivandrum India 94 C4
also spelt Thiruvananthapuram
Trivento Italy 56 G7
Trizina Greece 59 E11
Trnava Slovakia 49 O7
Trobriand Islands P.N.G. 145 E2
also known as Kiriwina Islands
Trofa Port. 54 C3
Trofaiach Austria 49 M8
Trofors Norway 44 K2
Trogir Croatia 56 I5
UNESCO World Heritage Site
Troglav mt. Croatia 56 I5
Troina Sicily Italy 57 G11
Troisdorf Germany 48 E5
Trois Fourches, Cap des c. Morocco 123 E2
also known as Tres Forcas, Cabo or Uarc, Ras
Trois-Pistoles Canada 169 G3
Trois-Rivières Canada 169 F4
Troitsa Rus. Fed. 38 G3
Troitsk Chelyabinskaya Oblast' Rus. Fed. 38 G4
Troitsk Moskovskaya Oblast' Rus. Fed. 43 S6
formerly known as Troitskiy
Troitskiy Rus. Fed. see Troitsk
Troitsko-Pechorsk Rus. Fed. 40 K3
Troitskoye Khabarovskiy Kray Rus. Fed. 82 E2
Troitskoye Orenburgskaya Oblast' Rus. Fed. 102 C1
Troitskoye Respublika Bashkortostan Rus. Fed. 102 D1
Troitskoye Respublika Kalmykiya - Khalm'g-Tangch Rus. Fed. 41 H7
Troll research stn Antarctica 223 X2
Trolla well Chad 120 B6
Trollhättan Sweden 45 K4
Trollheimen park Norway 44 J3
Trombetas r. Brazil 199 G5
Tromelin, Île i. Indian Ocean 218 K7
English form Tromelin Island
Tromelin Island Indian Ocean see Tromelin, Île
Tromelin Island Micronesia see Fais
Tromen, Volcán vol. Arg. 204 C5
Trompsburg S. Africa 133 J7
Troms county Norway 44 L1
Tromsø Norway 44 L1
Trona U.S.A. 183 G6
Tronador, Monte mt. Arg. 204 C6
Tronçais, Forêt de for. France 51 I6
Trondheim Norway 44 J3
Trondheimsfjorden sea chan. Norway 44 J3
Trondheimsleia sea chan. Norway 44 J3
Trongsa Bhutan see Tongsa
Trongsa Chhu r. Bhutan 97 F4
also known as Mangde Chhu
Tronto r. Italy 56 F6
Troödos, Mount Cyprus 108 D3
UNESCO World Heritage Site
Troödos Mountains Cyprus 108 D3
Troon U.K. 46 H8
Tropaia Greece 59 C11
Troparevo Rus. Fed. 43 Q6
Tropas r. Brazil 199 G6
Tropea Italy 57 H10
Tropeiros, Serra dos hills Brazil 202 C5
Tropic U.S.A. 183 L4
Trosh Rus. Fed. 40 J2
Trosna Rus. Fed. 43 Q9
Trostan' Rus. Fed. 43 N9
Trostan hill U.K. 47 F8
Trostberg Germany 49 J7
Trotuş r. Romania 58 H2
Trout r. B.C. Canada 166 E3
Trout r. N.W.T. Canada 166 G2
Trout Creek Canada 173 N5
Trout Creek U.S.A. 172 D4
Trout Dale U.S.A. 176 D9
Trout Lake Alta Canada 167 H3
Trout Lake N.W.T. Canada 166 F2
Trout Lake l. N.W.T. Canada 166 F2
Trout Lake l. Ont. Canada 167 M5
Trout Lake l. U.S.A. 172 D4
Trout Run U.S.A. 177 H4
Troutville U.S.A. 176 F8
Trowbridge U.K. 47 J12
Trowutta Australia 147 E5
Troy tourist site Turkey 106 A3
also known as Truva; historically known as Ilium
UNESCO World Heritage Site
Troy AL U.S.A. 175 C6
Troy KS U.S.A. 178 D4
Troy MI U.S.A. 173 J8
Troy MO U.S.A. 174 B4
Troy NC U.S.A. 174 E5
Troy NH U.S.A. 177 M3
Troy NY U.S.A. 177 L3
Troy OH U.S.A. 176 A5
Troy PA U.S.A. 177 I4
Troyan Bulg. 58 F6
Troyekurovo Lipetskaya Oblast' Rus. Fed. 43 T9
Troyekurovo Lipetskaya Oblast' Rus. Fed. 43 U8
Troyes France 51 K4
Troy Lake U.S.A. 183 H7
Troy Peak U.S.A. 183 I3
Trstenik Srbija Serb. and Mont. 58 C5
Trubchevsk Rus. Fed. 43 O9
Trubetchino Rus. Fed. 43 U9
Trubia r. Spain 54 F1
Truc Giang Vietnam see Bên Tre
Trucial Coast country Asia see United Arab Emirates
Trucial States country Asia see United Arab Emirates
Truckee U.S.A. 182 D2
Trud Rus. Fed. 43 O4
Trudovoy Kazakh. see Novoishimskiy
Trudovoy Rus. Fed. see Yusta
Trudovoye Rus. Fed. 82 D4
Trudy r. Rus. Fed. 43 S9
Truer Range hills Australia 148 A4
Trufanovo Rus. Fed. 40 H2
Truite, Lac à la l. Canada 173 O3
Trujillo Hond. 186 B4
Trujillo Peru 200 A2
Trujillo Spain 54 F5
Trujillo Venez. 198 D2
Trujillo state Venez. 198 D2
Trujillo, Monte mt. Dom. Rep. see Duarte, Pico
Trumann U.S.A. 174 B5
Trumansburg U.S.A. 177 I3
Trumbull U.S.A. 177 L4
Trumbull, Mount U.S.A. 183 K5
Trumon Indon. 76 B2
Trün Bulg. 58 D6
Trun France 50 G4
Trŭna mt. Bulg. 58 E6
Trung Khanh Vietnam 78 D3
Truong Sa is S. China Sea see Spratly Islands
Truro Canada 169 I4
Truro U.K. 47 G13
Trusan Sarawak Malaysia 77 F1
Trusan r. Sarawak Malaysia 77 F1
Truskmore hill Ireland 47 D9
Trus Madi, Gunung mt. Sabah Malaysia 77 G1
Trŭstenik Bulg. 58 F5
Trutch Canada 166 F3
Trutch Creek r. Canada 166 F3
Truth or Consequences U.S.A. 181 F6
formerly known as Hot Springs
Trutnov Czech Rep. 49 M5
Truva tourist site Turkey see Troy
Truyère r. France 51 I8
Truzhenik Rus. Fed. 43 Q3
Tryavna Bulg. 58 G6
Tryon U.S.A. 178 B3
Trypiti, Akra pt Kriti Greece 59 F13
Trypiti, Akra pt Greece 59 F9
Trysil Norway 45 K3
Trysilelva r. Norway 45 K3
Trysilfjellet mt. Norway 45 K3
Tryškiai Lith. 42 D5
Tržac Bos.-Herz. 56 H4
Trzcianka Poland 49 N2
Trzebiatów Poland 49 M1
Trzebinia Poland 49 Q5
Trzebnica Poland 49 O4
Trzemeszno Poland 49 O3
Tržič Slovenia 56 G2
Trzrcińsko-Zdrój Poland 49 L3
Tsagaannuur Bayan-Ölgiy Mongolia 84 A1
Tsagaannuur Dornod Mongolia 85 H2
Tsagaan Nuur salt l. Mongolia 84 B2
Tsagaan-Olom Mongolia 84 C2
Tsagaan Ovoo Mongolia 85 G1
Tsagaan-Ovoo Mongolia 84 D2
Tsagaan-Uul Mongolia see Sharga
Tsagan Aman Rus. Fed. 102 A3
formerly known as Burunniy
Tsagan Khurtey, Khrebet mts Rus. Fed. 85 F1
Tsagan-Nur Rus. Fed. 41 H7
Tsaidam Basin China see Qaidam Pendi
Tsäktso mt. Sweden 44 M1
Tsalenjikha Georgia 107 E2
Tsama I Congo 126 B5
Tsangatjåkkå mt. Sweden 44 K2
Tsao Botswana 130 D4
Tsaratanana, Massif du mts Madag. 131 [inset] K2
Tsarevo Bulg. 58 I6
formerly known as Michurin
Tsarevo-Zaymishche Rus. Fed. 43 P6
Tsaribrod Srbija Serb. and Mont. see Dimitrovgrad
Tsarimir Bulg. 58 F6
Tsaritsyn Rus. Fed. see Volgograd
Tsatsana mt. S. Africa 133 M7
Tsat Tsze Mui pt Hong Kong China see North Point
Tsaukaib Namibia 130 B5
Tsavo East National Park Kenya 128 C5
Tsavo West National Park Kenya 129 C5
Tsazo S. Africa 133 L8
Tsebanana Botswana 131 E3
Tseel Mongolia 84 B2
Tsefat Israel see Ẕefat
Tselina Rus. Fed. 41 G7
Tselinnyy Rus. Fed. 103 E2
Tselinograd Kazakh. see Astana
Tselinogradskaya Oblast' admin. div. Kazakh. see Akmolinskaya Oblast'
Tsementnyy Rus. Fed. see Fokino
Tsengel Mongolia 84 D1
Tsenogora Rus. Fed. 40 H2
Tsentralen Balkan nat. park Bulg. 58 F6
Tsentral'nyy Kirovskaya Oblast' Rus. Fed. 40 I4
Tsentral'nyy Moskovskaya Oblast' Rus. Fed. see Radovitskiy
Tsentral'nyy Ryazanskaya Oblast' Rus. Fed. 43 U8
Tserkovishche Rus. Fed. 43 L6
Tserovo Bulg. 58 E5
Tses Namibia 130 C5
Tsetsegnuur Mongolia 84 B2
Tsetseng Botswana 130 D4
Tsetserleg Arhangay Mongolia 84 D2
Tsetserleg Hövsgöl Mongolia see Halban
Tseung Kwan O Hong Kong China 87 [inset]
Tsévié Togo 125 F5
Tshabong Botswana 130 D5
Tshad country Africa see Chad
Tshchikskoye Vodokhranilishche resr Rus. Fed. 41 F7
Tshela Dem. Rep. Congo 126 B6
Tshene Dem. Rep. Congo 126 C6
Tshibala Dem. Rep. Congo 127 D6
Tshibuka Dem. Rep. Congo 127 D6
Tshibwika Dem. Rep. Congo 127 D7
Tshidilamolomo Botswana 133 I2
Tshikapa Dem. Rep. Congo 127 D6
Tshikapa r. Dem. Rep. Congo 127 D6
Tshilenge Dem. Rep. Congo 127 D6
Tshimbulu Dem. Rep. Congo 127 D6
Tshing S. Africa 133 K3
Tshipise S. Africa 131 F4
Tshiumbe r. Angola/Dem. Rep. Congo 127 D6
Tshofa Dem. Rep. Congo 127 E6
Tshokwane S. Africa 133 P1
Tsholotsho Zimbabwe 131 E3
formerly spelt Tjolotjo
Tshootsha Botswana 130 D4
Tshuapa r. Dem. Rep. Congo 126 D5
Tshumbiri Dem. Rep. Congo 126 C5
Tshwane S. Africa see Pretoria
Tsiazonano mt. Madag. 131 [inset] J3
Tsibritsa r. Bulg. 58 E5
Tsiigehtchic Canada 164 F3
formerly known as Arctic Red River
Tsil'ma r. Rus. Fed. 40 I2
Tsimkavichy Belarus 42 H8
also spelt Timkovichi
Tsimlyansk Rus. Fed. 41 G7
Tsimlyanskoye Vodokhranilishche resr Rus. Fed. 41 G7
Tsinan China see Jinan
Tsineng S. Africa 132 H4
Tsinghai prov. China see Qinghai
Tsing Shan hill Hong Kong China see Castle Peak
Tsing Shan Wan b. Hong Kong China see Castle Peak Bay
Tsing Shui Wan b. Hong Kong China see Clear Water Bay
Tsingtao China see Qingdao
Tsingy de Bemaraha, Réserve nature res. Madag. 131 [inset] J3
UNESCO World Heritage Site
Tsing Yi i. Hong Kong China 87 [inset]
Tsining China see Jining
Tsinjomay mt. Madag. 131 [inset] J3
Tsintsabis Namibia 130 C3
Tsiombe Madag. 131 [inset] J5
Tsiroanomandidy Madag. 131 [inset] J3
Tsiteli Tskaro Georgia see Dedop'listsqaro
Tsitondroina Madag. 131 [inset] J4
Tsitsihar China see Qiqihar
Tsitsikamma Forest and Coastal National Park S. Africa 132 H11
Tsitsutl Peak Canada 166 E4
Tsivil'sk Rus. Fed. 40 H5
Tskhakaia Georgia see Senaki
Tskhaltubo Georgia see Tsqaltubo
Ts'khinvali Georgia 107 E2
formerly known as Staliniri
Tsna r. Belarus 42 I9
Tsna r. Rus. Fed. 41 G5
Tsna r. Rus. Fed. 43 P4
Tsna r. Rus. Fed. 43 U6
Tsnori Georgia 107 F2
Tsodilo Hills Botswana 130 D3
UNESCO World Heritage Site
Tsolo S. Africa 133 M8
Tsomo S. Africa 133 L9
Tsomo r. S. Africa 133 L9
Tson r. Rus. Fed. 43 R9
Tsona China see Cona
Tsopan hill Greece 58 G8
Tsqaltubo Georgia 107 E2
also spelt Tskhaltubo
Tsu Japan 91 E7
Tsubame Japan 90 F6
Tsubata Japan 91 E6
Tsubetsu Japan 90 I3
Tsuchiura Japan 91 G6
Tsuen Wan Hong Kong China 87 [inset]
also known as Quanwan
Tsugarū-kaikyō strait Japan 90 G4
English form Tsugaru Strait
Tsugaru Strait Japan see Tsugarū-kaikyō
Tsukigata Japan 90 G3
Tsukuba Japan 91 G6
Tsukumi Japan 91 B8
Tsul-Ulaan Mongolia 84 E2
Tsumeb Namibia 130 C3
Tsumis Park Namibia 130 C4
Tsumkwe Namibia 130 D3
Tsuno-shima i. Japan 91 B7
Tsuru Japan 91 F7
Tsuruga Japan 91 E7
Tsurugi-san mt. Japan 91 D8
Tsurukhaytuy Rus. Fed. see Priargunsk
Tsuruoka Japan 90 F5
Tsushima Japan 91 E7
Tsushima is Japan 91 A7
Tsushima-kaikyō strait Japan/S. Korea see Korea Strait
Tsuyama Japan 91 D7
Tsvetino Bulg. 58 E7
Tswaane Botswana 130 D4
Tswaraganang S. Africa 133 J5
Tswelelang S. Africa 133 J4
Tsyelyakhany Belarus 42 G9
also spelt Telekhany
Tsyerakhowka Belarus 43 M9
Ts'yl-os Provincial Park Canada 166 E5
Tsyomny Lyes Belarus 43 M7
Tsyp-Navolok Rus. Fed. 44 P1
Tsyurupyns'k Ukr. 41 E7
formerly known as Aleshki or Oleshky
Tthedzehk'edeli Canada see Jean Marie River
Tthedzeh Koe Canada see Wrigley
Tthenaagoo Canada see Nahanni Butte
Tua r. Port. 54 D3
Tua, Tanjung pt Indon. 77 D4
Tuakau N.Z. 152 I5
Tual Indon. 73 H8
Tuam Ireland 47 D10
Tuamarina N.Z. 152 H9
Tuamotu, Archipel des is Fr. Polynesia see Tuamotu Islands
Tuamotu Archipelago is Fr. Polynesia see Tuamotu Islands
Tuamotu Islands Fr. Polynesia 221 J6
English form Tuamotu Archipelago; also known as Tuamotu, Archipel des; formerly known as Paumotu, Îles
Tuân Giao Vietnam 78 C3
Tuangku i. Indon. 76 B2
Tuapeka Mouth N.Z. 153 D14
Tuapse Rus. Fed. 41 F7
Tuaran Sabah Malaysia 77 G1
Tuas Sing. 76 [inset]
Tuatapere N.Z. 153 B14
Tuath, Loch a' b. U.K. 46 F5
also known as Broad Bay
Tuba City U.S.A. 183 M5
Tubalai i. Indon. 75 D3
Tuban Indon. 77 F4
Tubarão Brazil 203 B9
Tūbās West Bank 108 G5
Tubau Sarawak Malaysia 77 F2
Tubbataha Reefs reef Phil. 74 A4
UNESCO World Heritage Site
Tubeya Dem. Rep. Congo 127 D6
Tubigan i. Phil. 74 B5
Tübingen Germany 48 G7
Tubinskiy Rus. Fed. 102 D1
Tubmanburg Liberia 124 C5
Tubo r. Nigeria 125 G4
Tubod Phil. 74 B4
Tubou Fiji 145 H3
also spelt Tumbou
Tubruq Libya 120 D1
English form Tobruk
Tubu r. Indon. 77 G2
Tubuai i. Fr. Polynesia 221 J7
Tubuai Islands Fr. Polynesia 221 J7
also known as Australes, Îles
Tubutama Mex. 184 C2
Tucandera Brazil 199 F5
Tucannon r. U.S.A. 180 C3
Tucano Brazil 202 E4
Tucavaca Bol. 201 F4
Tucavaca r. Bol. 201 F4
Tuchitua Canada 166 D2
Tuchkovo Rus. Fed. 43 R6
Tuchodi r. Canada 166 F3
Tuchola Poland 49 O2
Tuchów Poland 49 S6
Tuckanarra Australia 151 B5
Tucker Glacier Antarctica 223 L2
Tuckerton U.S.A. 177 K6
Tucson U.S.A. 183 N9
Tucson Mountains U.S.A. 183 M9
Tuctuc r. Canada 169 H1
Tucumán Arg. see San Miguel de Tucumán
Tucumán prov. Arg. 204 D2
Tucumcari U.S.A. 179 B5
Tucunuco Arg. 204 C3
Tucuparé Brazil 199 H6
Tucupita Venez. 199 F2
Tucuracas Col. 198 C2
Tucuruí Brazil 202 B2
Tucuruí, Represa resr Brazil 202 B3
Tuczno Poland 49 N2
Tudela Spain 55 J2
also spelt Tutera
Tudela de Duero Spain 54 G3
Tuder Italy see Todi
Tudor Vladimirescu Romania 58 I3
Tudovka r. Rus. Fed. 43 O5
Tudu Estonia 42 H2
Tudulinna Estonia 42 I2
Tuen Mun Hong Kong China 87 [inset]
Tuensang India 97 G4
Tueré r. Brazil 199 I5
Tuerto r. Spain 50 A10
Tufanovo Rus. Fed. 43 V3
Ţufayḩ Saudi Arabia 105 E2
Tufi P.N.G. 145 D2
Tugela r. S. Africa 133 P6
Tugela Ferry S. Africa 133 O5
Tūghyl Kazakh. see Tugyl
Tuglung China 89 F6
Tugnug Point Phil. 74 C4
Tuguancun China 86 B3
Tuguegarao Phil. 74 B2
Tugur Rus. Fed. 82 E1
Tugurskiy Zaliv b. Rus. Fed. 82 E1
Tugwi r. Zimbabwe 131 F4
formerly spelt Tokwe
Tugyl Kazakh. 88 D2
also spelt Tūghyl; formerly known as Priozernyy
Tuhai He r. China 85 H4
Tuhemberua Indon. 76 B2
Tui Spain 54 C2
also spelt Túy
Tuichi r. Bol. 200 D3
Tuilianpui r. Bangl./India 97 G5
Tuinplaas S. Africa 133 M1
Tuins watercourse S. Africa 132 E6
Tūja Latvia 42 F4
Tujiabu China see Yongxiu
Tujuh, Kepulauan is Indon. 77 D3
Tukan Rus. Fed. 102 D1
Tukangbesi, Kepulauan is Indon. 75 B4
Tukarak Island Canada 168 E1
Tukayel Eth. 128 E2
Ţūkh Egypt 108 C7
Tukhavichy Belarus 42 G9
Ţukhmān, Banī reg. Saudi Arabia 105 E3
Tūkhtamish Tajik. 101 H2
also spelt Tokhtamysh
Tukituki r. N.Z. 152 K7
Tūkrah Libya 120 D1
Tuktoyaktuk Canada 164 F3
formerly known as Fort Brabant
Tuktut Nogait National Park Canada 164 G3
Tukums Latvia 42 E5
Tukung, Bukit mt. Indon. 77 E3
Tukuringra, Khrebet mts Rus. Fed. 82 B1
Tukuyu Tanz. 129 B7
Tula watercourse Kenya 128 C5
Tula Mex. 185 F4
Tula Rus. Fed. 43 S7
Tulach Mhór Ireland see Tullamore
Tulagt Ar Gol r. China 89 F4
Tulai China 84 C4
Tulai Nanshan mts China 84 C4
Tulai Shan mts China 84 C4
Tulak Afgh. 101 E3
Tula Mountains Antarctica 223 D2
Tulancingo Mex. 185 F4
Tulangbawang r. Indon. 76 D4
Tula Oblast admin. div. Rus. Fed. see Tul'skaya Oblast'
Tulare U.S.A. 182 E5
Tulare Lake Bed U.S.A. 182 E6
Tularosa U.S.A. 181 F6
Tulasi mt. India 94 D2
Tulcán Ecuador 198 B4
Tulcea Romania 58 J3
Tul'chin Ukr. see Tul'chyn
Tul'chyn Ukr. 41 D6
also spelt Tul'chin
Tule Venez. 187 E5
Tulé r. U.S.A. 182 E5
Tuléar Madag. see Toliara
Tulehu Indon. 75 D3
Tulelake U.S.A. 180 B4
Tule Mod China 85 I2
Tulgheș Romania 58 G2
Tulia U.S.A. 179 B5
Tulihe China 85 I1
Tuliszków Poland 49 P3
Tulita Canada 166 E1
formerly known as Fort Norman
Tuljapur India 94 C2
Ţūlkarm West Bank 108 G5
English form Tulkarm
Tulkarm West Bank see Ţūlkarm
Tullahoma U.S.A. 174 C5
Tullamore Australia 147 E3
Tullamore Ireland 47 E10
also spelt Tulach Mhór
Tulle France 50 H7
Tullibigeal Australia 147 E3
Tulln Austria 49 N7
Tullow Ireland 47 F11
Tully Australia 149 E3
Tully Falls Australia 149 E3
Tulnici Romania 58 H3
Tuloma r. Rus. Fed. 44 P1
Tulos Rus. Fed. 44 O3
Tulppio Fin. 44 O2
Tulsa U.S.A. 179 D4
Tulsequah Canada 166 C3
Tulsipur Nepal 97 D3
Tul'skaya Oblast' admin. div. Rus. Fed. 43 S8
English form Tula Oblast
Tul'skoye Kazakh. 103 H1
Tuluá Col. 198 B3
Tulucești Romania 58 J3
Tuluksak U.S.A. 164 C3
Tulūl al Ashāqif hills Jordan 109 I5
Tulūl al Bissah hills Saudi Arabia 109 K6
Tulum tourist site Mex. 185 I4
Tulun Rus. Fed. 80 G2
Tulungagung Indon. 77 E5
Tulu-Tuloi, Serra hills Brazil 199 F4
Tulu Welel mt. Eth. 128 B2
Tulva r. Rus. Fed. 40 J4
Tuma Rus. Fed. 40 G5
Tumaco Col. 198 B4
Tumahole S. Africa 133 L3
Tumain China 89 E5
Tumak Rus. Fed. 102 B3
Tūmān Āqā Iran 101 E3
Tuman-gang r. Asia see Tumen Jiang
Tumannaya r. Asia see Tumen Jiang
Tumannyy Rus. Fed. 40 E1
Tumanovo Rus. Fed. 43 P6
Tumanskiy Rus. Fed. 39 R3
Tumasik Sing. see Singapore
Tumatumari Guyana 199 G3
Tumazy Rus. Fed. 43 P1
Tumba Sweden 45 L4
Tumba, Lac l. Dem. Rep. Congo 126 C5
Tumbangmiri Indon. 77 F3
Tumbangsamba Indon. 77 F3
Tumbangtiti Indon. 77 E3
Tumbao Phil. 74 C5
Tumbarumba Australia 147 F3
Tumbes Peru 198 A5
Tumbes dept Peru 198 A5
Tumbiscatío Mex. 185 E5
Tumbler Ridge Canada 166 F4
Tumbou Fiji see Tubou
Tumby Bay Australia 146 C3
Tumcha r. Fin./Rus. Fed. 44 O2
Tumd Youqi China see Salaqi
Tumd Zuoqi China see Qasq
Tumen Jilin China 82 C4
Tumen Shaanxi China 87 D1
Tumen Jiang r. Asia 82 C4
also known as Tuman-gang or Tumannaya
Tumeremo Venez. 199 F3
Tumereng Guyana 199 F3
Tumindao i. Phil. 74 A5
Tumiritinga Brazil 203 D6
Tumkur India 94 C3
Tumlingtar Nepal 97 E4
Tummo, Mountains of Libya/Niger 120 B4
Tumnin r. Rus. Fed. 82 F2
Tump Pak. 101 E5
Tumpah Indon. 77 F3
Tumpôr, Phnum mt. Cambodia 79 C5
Tumpu, Gunung mt. Indon. 75 B3
Tumputiga, Gunung mt. Indon. 75 B3
Tumsar India 96 C5
Tumshuk Uzbek. 103 F5
Tumu Ghana 125 E4
Tumucumaque, Serra hills Brazil 199 G4
Tumudibandh India 95 D2
Tumupasa Bol. 200 D3
Tumur Kazakh. see Timur
Tumusla Bol. 200 D5
Tumut Australia 147 F3
Tumutuk Rus. Fed. 40 J5
Tumxuk China 88 C3
Tuna Ghana 124 E4
Tunapuna Trin. and Tob. 187 H5
Tunas de Zaza Cuba 186 D2
Ţunb al Kubrá i. The Gulf see Greater Tunb
Ţunb aş Şughrá i. The Gulf see Lesser Tunb
Tunbridge Wells, Royal U.K. 47 M12
Tunçbilek Turkey 59 K9
Tunceli Turkey 107 D3
Tuncurry Australia 147 G3
Tundla India 89 B7
Tundubai well Sudan 121 F5
Tunduma Tanz. 129 B7
Tundun-Wada Nigeria 125 H4
Tunduru Tanz. 129 C7
Tundzha r. Bulg. 58 H7
Tunes Tunisia see Tunis
Tunga Nigeria 125 H4
Tungabhadra r. India 94 C3
Tungabhadra Reservoir India 94 C3
Tungawan Phil. 74 B5
Tung Chung Hong Kong China 87 [inset]
Tungdor China see Mainling
Tungi Bangl. 97 F5
also spelt Tongi
Tungku Sabah Malaysia 77 G1
Tungla Nicaragua 186 B4
Tung Lung Chau i. Hong Kong China see Tung Lung Island
Tung Lung Island Hong Kong China 87 [inset]
also known as Tung Lung Chau
Tungnaá r. Iceland 44 [inset] C2
Tungor Rus. Fed. 82 F1
Tungozero Rus. Fed. 44 O2
Tung Pok Liu Hoi Hap sea chan. Hong Kong China see East Lamma Channel
Tungsten Canada 166 D2
Tungun, Bukit mt. Indon. 77 F2
Tungurahua prov. Ecuador 198 B5
Tung Wan b. Hong Kong China 87 [inset]
Tuni India 95 D2
Tūnī, Chāh-e well Iran 100 D3
Tunica U.S.A. 174 B5
Tunis Canada 173 M2

►Tunis Tunisia 123 H1
Capital of Tunisia. Historically known as Tunes.
UNESCO World Heritage Site

Tunis, Golfe de g. Tunisia 123 H1
►Tunisia country Africa 123 H2
spelt At Tūnisīyah in Arabic; historically known as Africa Nova
►►114–115 Africa Countries
Tunja Col. 198 C3
Tunkhannock U.S.A. 177 J4
Tunki Nicaragua 186 B4
Tunkinskiye Gol'tsy mts Rus. Fed. 84 D1
Tunliu China 85 G4
Tunnel City U.S.A. 172 C6
Tunnelton U.S.A. 176 F6
Tunnsjøen l. Norway 44 K2
Tunoshna Rus. Fed. 43 V4
Tuntsa Fin. 44 O2
Tunulic r. Canada 169 H1
Tununak U.S.A. 164 C3
Tunungayualok Island Canada 169 I1
Tunuyán Arg. 204 C4
Tunuyán r. Arg. 204 D4
Tunuyán, Travesía des. Arg. 204 D4
Tunxi China see Huangshan
Tuodian China see Shuangbai
Tuo He r. China 87 F1
Tuojiang Hunan China see Fenghuang
Tuojiang Hunan China see Shuikou
Tuo Jiang r. China 86 C2
Tuolumne U.S.A. 182 D4
Tuolumne r. U.S.A. 182 C4
Tuolumne Meadows U.S.A. 182 E4
Tuoniang Jiang r. China 86 C3
Tuotuoheyan China see Tanggulashan
Tüp Kyrg. 103 I4
also spelt Tyup
Tupã Brazil 206 C8
Tupaciguara Brazil 206 E5
Tupanaóca Brazil 199 F5
Tupanciretã Brazil 203 A9
Tupelo U.S.A. 174 B5
Tupinambarama, Ilha i. Brazil 199 G5
Tupi Paulista Brazil 206 B8
Tupiza Bol. 200 D5
Tupper Canada 166 F4
Tupper Lake U.S.A. 177 K1
Tupper Lake l. U.S.A. 177 K1
Tüpqaraghan Tübegi pen. Kazakh. see Mangyshlak, Poluostrov
Tupungato Arg. 204 C4

►Tupungato, Cerro mt. Arg./Chile 204 C4
5th highest mountain in South America.
►►188–189 South America Landscapes

Tuqayyid well Iraq 107 F5
Tuquan China 85 I2
Túquerres Col. 198 B4
Tura China 89 D4
Tura India 97 F4
Tura Rus. Fed. 39 K3
Turabah Ḩā'il Saudi Arabia 104 C1
Turabah Makkah Saudi Arabia 104 C3
Turabah, Wādī watercourse Saudi Arabia 104 C3
Turagua, Serranía mt. Venez. 199 E3
Turakina N.Z. 152 J8
Turakina r. N.Z. 152 J8
Turana, Khrebet mts Rus. Fed. 82 C2
Turangi N.Z. 152 J6
Turan Lowland Asia 101 D2
also known as Turanskaya Nizmennost'
Turanskaya Nizmennost' lowland Asia see Turan Lowland
Ţurāq al 'Ilab hills Syria 109 J4
Turar Ryskulov Kazakh. 103 G4
formerly known as Vannovka
Turaw Belarus 42 I9
Ţurayf Saudi Arabia 107 D5
Ţurayf well Saudi Arabia 105 E2
Ţurayf, Kutayfat vol. Saudi Arabia 109 J6
Ţurayf, Wādī watercourse Iraq 109 N4
Turba Estonia 42 F2
Turbaco Col. 198 C2
Turbacz mt. Poland 49 R6
Turbat Pak. 101 E5
Turbo Col. 198 B2
Turčianske Teplice Slovakia 49 P7
Turco Bol. 200 C4
Turda Romania 58 E2
Tūreh Iran 100 B3
Turek Poland 49 P3
Turfan China see Turpan
Turfan Depression China see Turpan Pendi
Turgay Akmolinskaya Oblast' Kazakh. 103 H2
Turgay Kustanayskaya Oblast' Kazakh. 103 E2
also spelt Torghay
Turgay r. Kazakh. 103 E3
Turgayskaya Dolina valley Kazakh. 103 E2
Turgayskaya Stolovaya Strana reg. Kazakh. 103 E2
Türgen Uul mt. Mongolia 84 A1
Türgen Uul mts Mongolia 84 A1
Turgeon r. Canada 168 E3
Türgovishte Bulg. 58 H5
Turgut Konya Turkey 106 B3
Turgut Muğla Turkey 59 J11
Turgutalp Turkey 59 I9
Turgutlu Turkey 106 A3
also known as Kasaba
Turgutreis Turkey 59 I12
Turhal Turkey 106 D2
Türi Estonia 42 G3
Turi Italy 56 J8
Turia r. Spain 55 K5
Turiaçu Brazil 202 C2
Turiaçu r. Brazil 202 C2
Turiaçu, Baía de b. Brazil 202 C2
Turiamo Venez. 199 E2
Turiec r. Slovakia 49 P6
Turin Canada 167 H5
Turin Italy 51 N7
also spelt Torino; historically known as Augusta Taurinorum or Taurasia
UNESCO World Heritage Site
Turinsk Rus. Fed. 38 G4
Turiy Rog Rus. Fed. 82 C3
Türje Hungary 49 O9
Turka Rus. Fed. 81 H2

►Turkana, Lake salt l. Eth./Kenya 128 B4
5th largest lake in Africa. Formerly known as Rudolf, Lake
►►110–111 Africa Landscapes

Türkeli Turkey 58 I8
Türkeli Adası i. Turkey 58 I8
Turkestan Kazakh. 103 G4
also spelt Türkistan
UNESCO World Heritage Site
Turkestan Range mts Asia 99 H2
Türkeve Hungary 49 R8
►Turkey country Asia 106 B3
►►16–17 World Population
►►64–65 Asia Countries
Turkey U.S.A. 176 B8
Turkey r. U.S.A. 174 B3
Turki Rus. Fed. 41 G6
Türkistan Kazakh. see Turkestan
Turkmenabat Turkm. see Türkmenabat
Türkmenabat Turkm. 103 E5
also known as Turkmenabat; also spelt Chärjew; formerly spelt Chardzhou
Turkmen Adasy i. Turkm. see Ogurjaly Adasy
Türkmen Aylagy b. Turkm. see Türkmen Aýlagy
Türkmen Aýlagy b. Turkm. 102 C5
also known as Türkmen Aylagy
Türkmenbaşy Turkm. 102 C4
formerly known as Krasnovodsk
Türkmenbaşy Aýlagy b. Turkm. 102 C5
Türkmenbaşy Döwlet Gorugy nature res. Turkm. 102 C5
Türkmen Dağı mt. Turkey 106 B3

Unije *i.* Croatia 56 G4
Unimak Island U.S.A. 164 C4
Unini *r.* Brazil 199 F5
Unini Peru 200 B2
Unión Arg. 204 D4
Unión Para. 201 F6
Union *ME* U.S.A. 177 P1
Union *MO* U.S.A. 174 B4
Union *OR* U.S.A. 180 C3
Union *WV* U.S.A. 176 E8
Unión, Bahía *b.* Arg. 204 E5
Union, Mount U.S.A. 183 L7
Union City *OH* U.S.A. 176 A5
Union City *PA* U.S.A. 176 F4
Union City *TN* U.S.A. 174 B4
Uniondale S. Africa 132 H10
Unión de Reyes Cuba 186 C2
Union Springs *AL* U.S.A. 175 C5
Union Springs *NY* U.S.A. 177 I3
Uniontown U.S.A. 176 F6
Union Valley Reservoir U.S.A. 182 D3
Unionville *MI* U.S.A. 173 J7
Unionville *MO* U.S.A. 174 A3
Unionville *NV* U.S.A. 182 F1
Unionville *VA* U.S.A. 176 H7
►**United Arab Emirates** *country* Asia 105 F3
known as Al Imārāt al 'Arabīyah at Muttaḥidah, in Arabic; *formerly known as* Trucial Coast *or* Trucial States
►►**64–65 Asia** Countries
United Arab Republic *country* Africa *see* **Egypt**

►**United Kingdom** *country* Europe 47 L8
4th most populous country in Europe.
►►**32–33 Europe** Countries

United Provinces *state* India *see* **Uttar Pradesh**

►**United States of America** *country* N. America 170 E3
Most populous country in North America and 3rd in the world. 2nd largest country in North America and 3rd in the world.
►►**8–9 World** Countries
►►**16–17 World** Population
►►**158–159 North America** Countries

United States Range *mts* Canada 165 M1
Unity Canada 167 I4
Unjab *watercourse* Namibia 130 B4
Unjha India 96 B5
Unnao India 96 D4
Ŭnp'a N. Korea 83 B5
Unsan N. Korea 83 B4
Ŭnsan N. Korea 83 B5
Unst *i.* U.K. 46 L3
Unstrut *r.* Germany 48 I4
Unstrut-Trias-Land *park* Germany 48 I4
Untari India 97 D4
Untere Havel *park* Germany 48 J3
Unteres Odertal, Nationalpark *nat. park* Germany 49 L3
Unterschleißheim Germany 48 I7
Unturán, Sierra de *mts* Venez. 199 E4
Unuk *r.* Canada/U.S.A. 166 D3
Unuli Horog China 97 F2
Un'ya *r.* Rus. Fed. 40 K3
Unzen-Amakusa National Park Japan 91 B8
Unzen-dake *vol.* Japan 91 B8
Unzha Rus. Fed. 40 H4
Uozu Japan 91 E6
Úpa *r.* Czech Rep. 49 M5
Upa *r.* Rus. Fed. 43 R7
Upalco U.S.A. 183 N1
Upar Ghat *reg.* India 97 E5
Upata Venez. 199 F2
Upemba, Lac *l.* Dem. Rep. Congo 127 E7
Upemba, Parc National de l' *nat. park* Dem. Rep. Congo 127 E7
Upernavik Greenland 165 N2
Upernavik Kujalleq Greenland 165 N2
also known as Søndre Upernavik
Upi Phil. 74 C5
Upía *r.* Col. 198 C3
Upington S. Africa 132 F5
Upinniemi Fin. 45 N3
Upland U.S.A. 182 G7
Upleta India 96 A5
Upokongaro N.Z. 152 J7
Upoloksha Rus. Fed. 44 O2
'Upolu *i.* Samoa 145 H3
formerly known as Ojalava
'Upolu Point U.S.A. 181 [inset] Z1
Upper Alkali Lake U.S.A. 180 B4
Upper Arlington U.S.A. 176 B5
Upper Arrow Lake Canada 166 G5
Upper Chindwin Myanmar *see* **Mawlaik**
Upper East *admin. reg.* Ghana 125 E4
Upper Fraser Canada 166 F4
Upper Garry Lake Canada 167 K1
Upper Hutt N.Z. 152 J9
Upper Iowa *r.* U.S.A. 174 B3
Upper Klamath Lake U.S.A. 180 B4
Upper Liard Canada 166 D2
Upper Lough Erne *l.* U.K. 47 E9
Upper Marlboro U.S.A. 177 I7
Upper Mazinaw Lake Canada 173 P6
Upper Missouri Breaks National Monument U.S.A. 180 F3
Upper Nile *state* Sudan 128 B2
Upper Peirce Reservoir Sing. 76 [inset]
Upper Preoria Lake U.S.A. 172 D10
Upper Red Lake U.S.A. 178 D1
Upper Sandusky U.S.A. 176 B5
Upper Saranac Lake U.S.A. 177 K1
Upper Seal Lake Canada *see* **Iberville, Lac d'**
Upper Takaka N.Z. 152 G9
Upper Tunguska *r.* Rus. Fed. *see* **Angara**
Upper Volta *country* Africa *see* **Burkina**
Upper West *admin. reg.* Ghana 125 E4
Uppinangadi India 94 B3
Upplands-Väsby Sweden 45 L4
Uppsala Sweden 45 L4
Uppsala *county* Sweden 45 L3
Upsala Canada 168 B3
Upshi Jammu and Kashmir 96 C2
Upson U.S.A. 172 C4
Upstart, Cape Australia 149 E3
Upstart Bay Australia 149 E3
Upton U.S.A. 177 N3
'Uqayqah, Wādī *watercourse* Jordan 108 G7
'Uqayribāt Syria 109 I2
Uqlat al 'Udhaybah *well* Iraq 107 F5
'Uqlat aş Şuqūr Saudi Arabia 104 C2
Uqsuqtuq Canada *see* **Gjoa Haven**
Uqturpan China *see* **Wushi**
Ur *tourist site* Iraq 107 F5
Urabá, Golfo de *b.* Col. 198 B2
Urad Qianqi China *see* **Xishanzui**
Urad Zhongqi China *see* **Haliut**
Ūrāf Iran 100 D4
Uraga-suidō *sea chan.* Japan 91 F7
Uragawara Japan 90 F6
Ura-Guba Rus. Fed. 44 P1
Urahoro Japan 90 H3
Urakam India 94 C4
Urakawa Japan 90 H3
Ural *hill* Australia 147 E3
Ural *r.* Kazakh./Rus. Fed. 102 B3
also known as Zhayyq
Uralla Australia 147 F2
Ural Mountains Rus. Fed. 40 K2
also known as Ural'skiye Gory *or* Ural'skiy Khrebet
Uralovka Rus. Fed. 82 C1
Ural'sk Kazakh. 102 B2
also known as Oral
Ural'skaya Oblast' *admin. div.* Kazakh. *see* **Zapadnyy Kazakhstan**
Ural'skiye Gory *mts* Rus. Fed. *see* **Ural Mountains**
Ural'skiy Khrebet *mts* Rus. Fed. *see* **Ural Mountains**
Urambo Tanz. 129 B6
Uran India 94 B2
Urana Australia 147 E3
Urana, Lake Australia 147 E3
Urandangi Australia 148 C4
Urandi Brazil 202 D5
Uranium City Canada 167 I3
Urapunga Australia 148 B2
Urapuntja Australia 148 B4
Uraricoera Brazil 199 F4
Uraricoera *r.* Brazil 199 F4
Urartu *country* Asia *see* **Armenia**
Uras *Sardinia* Italy 57 A9
Ura-Tyube Tajik. *see* **Ŭroteppa**
Uravakonda India 94 C3
Uravan U.S.A. 183 P3
Urawa Japan 91 F7
Uray Rus. Fed. 38 G3
'Urayf an Nāqah, Jabal *hill* Egypt 108 F7
Uray'irah Saudi Arabia 105 E2
Urayn Egypt 108 B7
'Urayq, Nafūd al *des.* Saudi Arabia 104 C2
'Urayq ad Duḩūl *des.* Saudi Arabia 105 D2
'Urayq Sāqān *des.* Saudi Arabia 105 D2
Urazovka Rus. Fed. 40 H5
Urazovo Rus. Fed. 41 F6
Urbana *IA* U.S.A. 172 B8
Urbana *IL* U.S.A. 174 B3
Urbana *IN* U.S.A. 172 H10
Urbana *OH* U.S.A. 176 B5
Urbania Italy 56 E5
Urbano Santos Brazil 202 D2
Urbel *r.* Spain 54 H2
Urbino Italy 56 E5
historically known as Urbinum
UNESCO World Heritage Site
Urbinum Italy *see* **Urbino**
Urbión *mt.* Spain 55 I2
Urbs Vetus Italy *see* **Orvieto**
Urcos Peru 200 C3
Urda Spain 54 H5
Ur'devarri *hill* Fin./Norway *see* **Urtivaara**
Urdoma Rus. Fed. 40 I3
Urd Tamir Gol *r.* Mongolia 84 D2
Urdyuzhskoye, Ozero *l.* Rus. Fed. 40 I2
Urdzhar Kazakh. 88 C2
also spelt Ürzhar
Ure *r.* U.K. 47 K9
Urechcha Belarus 42 I9
Urecheşti Romania 58 I2
Uren' Rus. Fed. 40 H4
Urengoy Rus. Fed. 39 H3
Urenosi *mt.* Norway 45 I4
Urenui N.Z. 152 I6
Uréparapara *i.* Vanuatu 145 F3
Urewera National Park N.Z. 152 L6
Urfa Turkey *see* **Şanlıurfa**
Urga Mongolia *see* **Ulan Bator**
Urgal *r.* Rus. Fed. 82 D2
Urganch Uzbek. 102 E4
also spelt Urgench
Urganlı Turkey 59 I10
Urgench Uzbek. *see* **Urganch**
Ürgüp Turkey 106 C3
Urgut Uzbek. 103 F5
Urho China 88 D2
Urho Kekkosen kansallispuisto *nat. park* Fin. 44 N1
Uri Jammu and Kashmir 96 B2
Uribia Col. 198 C2
Uripitijuata, Cerro *mt.* Mex. 185 E5
Urique *r.* Mex. 181 F8
Urisino Australia 147 D2
Uritskoye Rus. Fed. 43 T9
Urī Wenz *r.* Eth. 104 B5
Urjala Fin. 45 M3
Urk Neth. 48 C3
Urkan Rus. Fed. 82 B1
Urkan *r.* Rus. Fed. 82 B1
Urkut Somalia 128 D4
Urla Turkey 106 A3
Urlaţi Romania 58 H4
Urlui *r.* Romania 58 G5
Urluk Rus. Fed. 85 E1
Urmai China 89 D6
Urmary Rus. Fed. 40 H5
Urmetan Tajik. 101 G2
Urmi *r.* Rus. Fed. 82 D2
Urmia Iran 100 A2
also spelt Orūmīyeh; *formerly known as* Reẕā'īyeh
Urmia, Lake *salt l.* Iran 100 A2
also known as Orūmīyeh, Daryācheh-ye; *formerly known as* Reẕā'īyeh, Daryācheh-ye
Urmston Road *sea chan.* Hong Kong China 87 [inset]
Uromi Nigeria 125 G5
Uroševac *Kosovo, Srbija* Serb. and Mont. 58 C6
Urosozero Rus. Fed. 40 E3
Ŭroteppa Tajik. 101 G2
also spelt Ura-Tyube
Urru Co *salt l.* China 89 D6
also known as Jagok Tso
Ursat'yevskaya Uzbek. *see* **Xovos**
Urshel'skiy Rus. Fed. 43 V6
Urt Mongolia 84 D3
Urtivaara *hill* Fin./Norway 44 M1
also spelt Ur'devarri
Urt Moron China 84 B4
Uru *r.* Brazil 206 D2
Uruáchic Mex. 184 C3
Uruaçu Brazil 202 B5
Uruana Brazil 206 D2
Uruapan *Baja California Norte* Mex. 184 A2
Uruapan *Michoacán* Mex. 185 E5
Urubamba Peru 200 B3
Urubaxi *r.* Brazil 199 E5
Urubu *r.* Brazil 199 G5
Urubupungá, Salto do *waterfall* Brazil 206 B7
Urucara Brazil 199 G5
Uruch'ye Rus. Fed. 43 O9
Urucu *r.* Brazil 199 F6
Uruçuí Brazil 202 C3
Uruçuí, Serra do *hills* Brazil 202 C4
Urucuia Brazil 202 C6
Urucuia *r.* Brazil 202 C6
Uruçui Preto *r.* Brazil 202 C3
Urucum Brazil 201 F4
Urucurituba Brazil 199 G5
Uruguai *r.* Brazil 203 A8
also spelt Uruguay
Uruguaiana Brazil 204 F3
Uruguay *r.* Arg./Uruguay 204 F4
also spelt Uruguai
►**Uruguay** *country* S. America 204 F4
►►**192–193 South America** Countries
Uruk *tourist site* Iraq *see* **Erech**
Urukthapel *i.* Palau 73 H5
Urumchi China *see* **Ürümqi**
Ürümqi China 88 D3
English form Urumchi
Urundi *country* Africa *see* **Burundi**
Urunga Australia 147 G2
Urup *r.* Rus. Fed. 41 G7
Urup, Ostrov *i.* Rus. Fed. 81 Q3
Urup, Proliv *strait* Rus. Fed. 81 Q3
Urupá *r.* Brazil 201 E2
Uru Pass China/Kyrg. 88 B3
'Urūq al Awārik *des.* Saudi Arabia 105 D4
'Urūq ash Shaybah *des.* Saudi Arabia 105 F3
Urusha Rus. Fed. 82 A1
Urusha *r.* Rus. Fed. 82 A1
Urussu Rus. Fed. 40 J5
Uruti N.Z. 152 I6
Uruwira Tanz. 129 A6
Urūzgān *prov.* Afgh. 101 F3
Uryl' Kazakh. 88 D1
Uryū Japan 90 G3
Uryupinsk Rus. Fed. 41 G6
Ürzhar Kazakh. *see* **Urdzhar**
Urzhum Rus. Fed. 40 I4
Urziceni Romania 58 H4
Usa *r.* Belarus 43 J8
Usa Japan 91 B8
Usa *r.* Rus. Fed. 40 K2
Usada *i.* Phil. 74 B5
Uşak Turkey 106 B3
Uşak *prov.* Turkey 59 K10
Usakos Namibia 130 B4
Usambara Mountains Tanz. 129 C6
Usangu Flats *plain* Tanz. 129 B7
Usarp Mountains Antarctica 223 K2
'Usaylān Yemen 105 D5
Usborne, Mount *hill* Falkland Is 205 F8
Usedom Germany 49 K2
Usedom *i.* Germany 49 L2
Useless Loop Australia 151 A5
Usengi Kenya 128 B5
Usfān Saudi Arabia 104 B3
Usha *r.* Belarus 42 G8
Usha *r.* Belarus 43 J8
Ushachi Belarus *see* **Ushachy**
Ushachy Belarus 43 J6
also spelt Ushachi
Ushakova, Ostrov *i.* Rus. Fed. 39 H1
Ushanovo Kazakh. 88 C1
Ushant *i.* France *see* **Ouessant, Île d'**
Üsharal Kazakh. *see* **Ucharal**
Usharal Kazakh. 103 G4
Ushayqir Saudi Arabia 105 D2
'Ushayrah Saudi Arabia 104 C3
Ushcha *r.* Rus. Fed. 43 K6
Ushcherp'ye Rus. Fed. 43 M9
Ushibuka Japan 91 B8
Ushirombo Tanz. 128 A5
Ushtobe Kazakh. 103 I3
formerly spelt Ush-Tyube
Ush-Tyube Kazakh. *see* **Ushtobe**
Ushuaia Arg. 205 C9
Uši Latvia 42 D4
Usina Brazil 202 A3
Usinsk Rus. Fed. 40 K2
Usk *r.* U.K. 47 J12
Uska India 97 D4
Uskhodni Belarus 42 I8
Uskoplje Bos.-Herz. *see* **Gornji Vakuf**
Üsküdar Turkey 106 B2
Üsküp Turkey 58 I7
Usma Latvia 42 D4
Usman' Rus. Fed. 41 F5
Usmas ezers *l.* Latvia 42 D4
Usmat Uzbek. 103 F5
formerly spelt Usmet
Usmet Uzbek. *see* **Usmat**
Usmyn' Rus. Fed. 43 M6
Uso *r.* Spain 54 F5
Usogorsk Rus. Fed. 40 I3
Usoke Tanz. 129 B6
Usol'ye Rus. Fed. 40 K4
Usol'ye-Sibirskoye Rus. Fed. 80 G2
Usora *r.* Bos.-Herz. 56 K4
Usozha *r.* Rus. Fed. 43 P9
Usozha *r.* Rus. Fed. 43 Q9
Uspallata Arg. 204 C4
Uspenka Kazakh. 103 I1
Uspenskiy Kazakh. 103 H2
Uspenskoye Rus. Fed. 43 L5
Uspen'ye Rus. Fed. 40 G4
Ussel France 51 I7

►**U.S.S.R.**
Divided in 1991 into 15 independent nations: Armenia, Azerbaijan, Belarus, Estonia, Georgia, Kazakhstan, Kyrgyzstan, Latvia, Lithuania, Moldova, the Russian Federation, Tajikistan, Turkmenistan, Ukraine and Uzbekistan.

Ussuri *r.* Rus. Fed. 82 D2
also known as Wusuli Jiang
Ussuriysk Rus. Fed. 82 C4
formerly known as Voroshilov
Ust'-Abakanskoye Rus. Fed. *see* **Abakan**
Ust'-Alekseyevo Rus. Fed. 40 H3
Usta Muhammad Pak. 101 G4
Ust'-Balyk Rus. Fed. *see* **Nefteyugansk**
Ust'-Barguzin Rus. Fed. 81 H2
Ust'-Dolyssy Rus. Fed. 43 K5
Ust'-Donetskiy Rus. Fed. 41 G7
Ust'-Dzheguta Rus. Fed. 41 G7
formerly known as Ust'-Dzhegutinskaya
Ust'-Dzhegutinskaya Rus. Fed. *see* **Ust'-Dzheguta**
Uster Switz. 51 O5
Ustica, Isola di *i. Sicily* Italy 57 F10
Ust'-Ilimsk Rus. Fed. 39 K4
Ust'-Ilimskiy Vodokhranilishche *resr* Rus. Fed. 80 G1
Ust'-Ilya Rus. Fed. 85 G1
Ust'-Ilych Rus. Fed. 40 K3
Ústí nad Labem Czech Rep. 49 L5
Ústí nad Orlicí Czech Rep. 49 N6
Ustinov Rus. Fed. *see* **Izhevsk**
Ustirt *plat.* Kazakh./Uzbek. *see* **Ustyurt Plateau**
Ustka Poland 49 N1
Ust'-Kamchatsk Rus. Fed. 39 Q4
Ust'-Kamenogorsk Kazakh. 88 C1
also known as Öskemen
Ust'-Kan Rus. Fed. 88 D1
Ust'-Kara Rus. Fed. 40 M1
Ust'-Koksa Rus. Fed. 88 D1
Ust'-Kulom Rus. Fed. 40 J3
Ust'-Kut Rus. Fed. 80 H1
Ust'-Kuyga Rus. Fed. 39 N2
Ust'-Labinsk Rus. Fed. 41 F7
formerly known as Ust'-Labinskaya
Ust'-Labinskaya Rus. Fed. *see* **Ust'-Labinsk**
Ust'-Luga Rus. Fed. 43 J2
Ust'-Lyzha Rus. Fed. 40 K2
Ust'-Maya Rus. Fed. 39 N3
Ust'-Mongunay Rus. Fed. *see* **Primorskiy**
Ust'-Munduyka Rus. Fed. 39 I3
Ust'-Nem Rus. Fed. 40 J3
Ust'-Nera Rus. Fed. 39 O3
Ust'-Olenek Rus. Fed. 39 L2
Ust'-Omchug Rus. Fed. 39 O3
Ust-Orda Buryat Autonomous Okrug *admin. div.* Rus. Fed. *see* **Ust'-Ordynskiy Buryatskiy Avtonomnyy Okrug**
Ust'-Ordynskiy Rus. Fed. 80 G2
Ust'-Ordynskiy Buryatskiy Avtonomnyy Okrug *admin. div.* Rus. Fed. 80 G2
English form Ust-Orda Buryat Autonomous Okrug
Ust'-Port Rus. Fed. 39 I3
Ustrem Bulg. 58 H6
Ustrzyki Dolne Poland 49 T6
formerly known as Nizhniye Ustriki
Ust'-Sara Rus. Fed. 43 O1
Ust'-Shonosha Rus. Fed. 40 G3
Ust'-Tsil'ma Rus. Fed. 40 J2
Ust'-Ulagan Rus. Fed. 88 D1
Ust'-Umalta Rus. Fed. 82 D2
Ust'-Ura Rus. Fed. 40 H3
Ust'-Usa Rus. Fed. 40 K2
Ust'-Vayen'ga Rus. Fed. 40 G3
Ust'-Voya Rus. Fed. 40 K2
Ust'ya *r.* Rus. Fed. 40 G3
Ust'-Yansk Rus. Fed. 39 N2
Ust'ye *Tverskaya Oblast'* Rus. Fed. 43 M5
Ust'ye *Vologod. Obl.* Rus. Fed. 40 G4
Ust'ye *Vologod. Obl.* Rus. Fed. 43 U2
Ust'ye *Yaroslavskaya Oblast'* Rus. Fed. 43 U4
Ust'ye *r.* Rus. Fed. 43 U4
Ust'ye-Kirovskoye Rus. Fed. 43 Q3
Ustyurt, Plato *plat.* Kazakh./Uzbek. *see* **Ustyurt Plateau**
Ustyurt Plateau Kazakh./Uzbek. 102 D4
also known as Ustirt *or* Ustyurt, Plato *or* Ustyurt Platosi
Ustyurt Platosi *plat.* Kazakh./Uzbek. *see* **Ustyurt Plateau**
Ustyutskoye Rus. Fed. 43 Q3
Ustyuzhna Rus. Fed. 43 R3
Usu China 88 D2
Usuki Japan 91 B8
Usulután El Salvador 185 H6
Usumacinta *r.* Guat./Mex. 185 G5
Usumbura Burundi *see* **Bujumbura**
Usun Apau, Dataran Tinggi *plat. Sarawak* Malaysia 77 F2
Usutu *r.* Africa 133 Q3
also known as Great Usutu *or* Lusutufu
Usvyaty Rus. Fed. 43 L6
Usvyeyka *r.* Belarus 43 K7
Uta Indon. 73 I7
Utah *state* U.S.A. 183 M2
Utah Lake U.S.A. 183 M1
Utajärvi Fin. 44 N2
Utan Indon. 77 G5
Utashinai Rus. Fed. *see* **Yuzhno-Kuril'sk**
'Utaybah *reg.* Saudi Arabia 104 C3
'Utaybah, Buḩayrat al *imp. l.* Syria 109 H4
Utayrtīr ad Dahamī, Jabal *mt.* Egypt 108 E9
Utayyiq Saudi Arabia 105 E2
Utbjoa Norway 45 I4
Utebo Spain 55 K3
Ute Creek *r.* U.S.A. 179 B5
Utembo *r.* Angola 127 D9
Ute Mountain Indian Reservation *res.* U.S.A. 183 P4
Utena Lith. 42 G6
Utete Tanz. 129 C7
Uthai Thani Thai. 79 C5
Uthal Pak. 101 F5
Utiariti Brazil 201 F3
Utica *NY* U.S.A. 177 J2
Utica *OH* U.S.A. 176 C5
Utiel Spain 55 J5
Utikuma Lake Canada 167 H4
Utila Hond. 186 B3
Utinga *r.* Brazil 202 D5
Utladalen *park* Norway 45 I3
Utlwanang S. Africa 133 J4
Uto Japan 91 B8
Utrata *r.* Poland 49 R3
Utraula India 97 D4
Utrecht Neth. 48 C3
historically known as Trajectum
UNESCO World Heritage Site
Utrecht S. Africa 133 O4
Utrera Spain 54 F7
Utrera, Peña *hill* Spain 54 E6
Utroya *r.* Rus. Fed. 42 J4
Utsira Norway 46 Q4
Utsjoki Fin. 44 N1
also spelt Ohcejohka
Utsunomiya Japan 91 F6
Utta Rus. Fed. 102 A3
Uttaradit Thai. 78 C4
Uttaranchal *state* India 96 C3
Uttarkashi India 96 C3
Uttar Pradesh *state* India 96 C4
formerly known as United Provinces
Utu China *see* **Miao'ergou**
Utubulak China 88 D2
Utupua *i.* Solomon Is 145 F3
formerly known as Edgecumbe Island
Utva *r.* Kazakh. 102 C2
Uulu Estonia 42 F3
Uummannaq Greenland *see* **Dundas**
Uummannaq Greenland 165 N2
Uummannaq Fjord *inlet* Greenland 165 N2
Uummannarsuaq *c.* Greenland *see* **Farewell, Cape**
Uurainen Fin. 44 N3
Üüreg Nuur *salt l.* Mongolia 84 A1
Üür Gol *r.* Mongolia 84 D1
Uusikaarlepyy Fin. *see* **Nykarleby**
Uusikaupunki Fin. 45 M3
also known as Nystad
Uutapi Namibia 130 B3
also known as Ombalantu
Uva *r.* Col. 198 D4
Uva Rus. Fed. 40 J4
Uvac *r.* Bos.-Herz./Serb. and Mont. 58 A5
Uvalde U.S.A. 179 C6
Uvaravichy Belarus 43 L9
Uvarovka Rus. Fed. 43 Q6
Uvarovo Rus. Fed. 41 G6
Uvéa *i.* New Caledonia *see* **Ouvéa**
Uver' *r.* Rus. Fed. 43 P3
Uvinza Tanz. 129 A6
Uvira Dem. Rep. Congo 126 F5
Uvod' *r.* Rus. Fed. 43 V4
Uvongo S. Africa 133 O7
Uvs *prov.* Mongolia 84 B1
Uvs Nuur *salt l.* Mongolia 84 B1
UNESCO World Heritage Site
Uwa Japan 91 C8
Uwainid, Wādī al *watercourse* Saudi Arabia 109 H9
Uwajima Japan 91 C8
Uwa-kai *b.* Japan 91 C8
'Uwayfī Oman 105 G3
'Uwayja *well* Saudi Arabia 104 C2
'Uwaynāt Wannīn Libya 120 B2
'Uwayriḑ, Ḩarrat al *lava field* Saudi Arabia 104 B2
Uwaysiţ *well* Saudi Arabia 109 J7
Uweinat, Jebel *mt.* Sudan 120 E4
Uwemba Tanz. 129 B7
Uwi *i.* Indon. 77 D2
Uxin Ju China 85 F4
Uxin Qi China *see* **Dabqig**
Uxmal *tourist site* Mex. 185 H4
UNESCO World Heritage Site
Uxxaktal China 88 D3
Uyaly Kazakh. 103 E3
Uyaly, Ozero *l.* Kazakh. *see* **Koshkarkol', Ozero**
Uyar Rus. Fed. 80 E1
Üydzin Mongolia 85 E2
Uyo Nigeria 125 G5
Üyönch Mongolia 84 B2
Üyönch Gol *r.* China 84 A2
Uyu Chaung *r.* Myanmar 78 A2
Uyuk Kazakh. 103 G4
also spelt Oyyq; *formerly spelt* Oik
Uyun Saudi Arabia 105 E2
Uyuni Bol. 200 D5
Uyuni, Salar de *salt flat* Bol. 200 D5
Uza *r.* Rus. Fed. 41 H5
'Uẕaym, Nahr al *r.* Iraq 107 F4
►**Uzbekistan** *country* Asia 102 D4
spelt Ozbekiston *or* Ŭzbekiston in Uzbek; *formerly known as* Uzbekskaya S.S.R. *or* Uzbek S.S.R.
►►**64–65 Asia** Countries
Ŭzbekiston *country* Asia *see* **Uzbekistan**
Uzbekskaya S.S.R. *country* Asia *see* **Uzbekistan**
Uzbek S.S.R. *country* Asia *see* **Uzbekistan**
Uzboý Turkm. 102 C5
Uzda Belarus 42 I8
Uzen' Kazakh. *see* **Kyzylsay**
Uzerche France 50 H7
Uzès France 51 K8
Uzgen Kyrg. *see* **Özgön**
Uzh *r.* Ukr. 49 T7
Uzha *r.* Rus. Fed. 43 O7
Uzhgorod Ukr. *see* **Uzhhorod**
Uzhhorod Ukr. 49 T7
also spelt Uzhgorod; *formerly spelt* Užhorod; *historically known as* Ungvár
Uzhok Ukr. 49 T7
Užhorod Ukr. *see* **Uzhhorod**
Užice *Srbija* Serb. and Mont. 58 A5
formerly known as Titovo Užice
Uzlovaya Rus. Fed. 43 T8
Uzola *r.* Rus. Fed. 40 G4
Üzöngü Toosu *mt.* China/Kyrg. 88 B3
Üzümlü Turkey 59 K12
Uzun Uzbek. 103 G5
Uzun Ada *i.* Turkey 59 H10
Uzunagach *Almatinskaya Oblast'* Kazakh. 103 I4
also spelt Uzynaghash
Uzunagach *Almatinskaya Oblast'* Kazakh. 103 I4
Uzunbulak China 88 D2
Uzuncaburç Turkey 108 E1
Uzunköprü Turkey 106 A2
Užventis Lith. 42 D6
Uzvoz Rus. Fed. 43 M6
Uzyn Ukr. 41 D6
Uzynaghash Kazakh. *see* **Uzunagach**
Uzynkair Kazakh. 103 E3

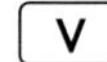

Vaajakoski Fin. 44 N3
Vaal *r.* S. Africa 132 H6
Vaala Fin. 44 N2
Vaalbos National Park S. Africa 133 I5
Vaal Dam S. Africa 133 M4
Vaal Dam Nature Reserve S. Africa 133 M3
Vaalplass S. Africa 133 M2
Vaalwater S. Africa 131 F5
Vaartsi Estonia 42 I4
Vaasa Fin. 44 M3
also spelt Vasa
Vabalninkas Lith. 42 F6
Vabich *r.* Belarus 43 K8
Vablya *r.* Rus. Fed. 43 O9
Vác Hungary 49 Q8
Vacaré *r.* Brazil 207 H8
Vacaria Brazil 203 B9
Vacaria *r. Mato Grosso do Sul* Brazil 203 A7
Vacaria *r. Minas Gerais* Brazil 202 D6
Vacaria, Campo da *plain* Brazil 203 B9
Vacaria, Serra *hills* Brazil 203 A7
Vacaville U.S.A. 182 C3
Väckelsång Sweden 45 K4
Vad Rus. Fed. 40 H5
Vad *r.* Rus. Fed. 41 G5
Vada India 94 B2
Vadakste *r.* Latvia/Lith. 42 D5
Vădăstriţa Romania 58 F5
Vadehavet *nature res.* Denmark 45 J5
Vădeni Romania 58 I3
Vadi India 94 B3
also known as Savantvadi
Vadodara India 96 B5
formerly known as Baroda
Vadsø Norway 44 O1
Vadstena Sweden 45 K4
Vadu Crişului Romania 58 D2

►**Vaduz** Liechtenstein 48 G8
Capital of Liechtenstein.

Værøy *i.* Norway 44 K2
Vaga *r.* Rus. Fed. 43 V1
Vågåmo Norway 45 J3
Vaganski Vrh *mt.* Croatia 56 H4
Vágar *i.* Faroe Is 46 E1
Vagavaram India 94 D2
Vagnhärad Sweden 45 L4
Vagos Port. 54 C4
Vägsele Sweden 44 L2
Vågsfjorden *sea chan.* Norway 44 L1
Váh *r.* Slovakia 49 P8
Vahhābī Iran 100 D4
Vahsel, Cape S. Georgia 205 [inset]
Vahto Fin. 45 M3

►**Vaiaku** Tuvalu 145 G2
Capital of Tuvalu, on Funafuti atoll.
►►**8–9 World** Countries

Vaida Estonia 42 F2
Vaiden U.S.A. 175 B5
Vaigai *r.* India 94 C4
Vaijapur India 94 B2
Vaikam India 94 C4
Väike Emajõgi *r.* Estonia 42 H3
Väike-Maarja Estonia 42 H2
Väike-Pakri *i.* Estonia 42 E2
Vaikijaur Sweden 44 L2
Väimela Estonia 42 I4
Vaiņode Latvia 42 C5
Vaippar *r.* India 94 C4
Vair *r.* France 51 L4
Vairowal India 96 B3
Vaison-la-Romaine France 51 L8
Vaitupu *i.* Tuvalu 145 G2
also spelt Oaitupu
Vajrakarur India *see* **Kanur**
Vajszló Hungary 56 J3
Vakaga *pref.* Cent. Afr. Rep. 126 D2
Vakaga *r.* Cent. Afr. Rep. 126 D2
Vakhan Tajik. 96 B1
Vakhsh Tajik. 101 G2
formerly known as Vakhstroy
Vakhsh *r.* Tajik. 101 G2
Vakhstroy Tajik. *see* **Vakhsh**
Vakīlābād Iran 100 D4
Vaksdal Norway 45 I3
Vålådalen naturreservat *nature res.* Sweden 44 K3
Valamaz Rus. Fed. 40 J4
Valandovo Macedonia 58 D7
Valassaaret-Björkögrund *nature res.* Fin. 44 M3
Valašské Klobouky Czech Rep. 49 P6
Valašské Meziříčí Czech Rep. 49 O6
Valaxa *i.* Greece 59 F10
Val-Barrette Canada 173 R4
Vâlcăneşti Romania 58 G3
Vâlcanului, Munţii *mts* Romania 58 D3
Valcheta Arg. 204 D6
Valdai Hills Rus. Fed. *see* **Valdayskaya Vozvyshennost'**
Valday Rus. Fed. 43 O4
Valdayskaya Vozvyshennost' *hills* Rus. Fed. 43 N5
English form Valdai Hills
Valdayskoye, Ozero *l.* Rus. Fed. 43 O3
Valdecañas, Embalse de *resr* Spain 54 F5
Val del Ticino, Parco della *park* Italy 56 A3
Valdemārpils Latvia 42 D4
Valdemarsvik Sweden 45 L4
Valdemoro Spain 54 H4
Valdepeñas Spain 55 H6
Valderaduey *r.* Spain 54 F3
Valderas Spain 54 F2
Val-de-Reuil France 50 H3
Valders U.S.A. 172 F6

►**Valdés, Península** *pen.* Arg. 205 E6
Lowest point in South America.
UNESCO World Heritage Site
►►**188–189 South America** Landscapes

Val-des-Bois Canada 173 R5
Valdez U.S.A. 164 E3
Valdivia Chile 204 B5
Valdivia Col. 198 C3
Valdobbiadene Italy 56 D3
Val-d'Or Canada 168 E3
Valdosa *mt.* Spain 55 H3
Valdosta U.S.A. 175 D6
Valdres *valley* Norway 45 J3
Vale Georgia 107 E2
Vale U.S.A. 180 C3
Valea lui Mihai Romania 49 T8
Valea Lungă Romania 58 F2
Valea Lungă Romania 58 G3
Valea Viilor Romania 58 F2
UNESCO World Heritage Site
Valemount Canada 166 G4
Valença Brazil 202 E5
Valença do Piauí Brazil 202 D3
Valençay France 50 H5
Valence *Midi-Pyrénées* France 50 G8
Valence *Rhône-Alpes* France 51 K8
Valencia Spain 55 K5
historically known as Valentia
UNESCO World Heritage Site
Valencia *aut. comm.* Spain 55 K5
also known as Valenciana, Comunidad
Valencia Venez. 199 E2
Valencia, Golfo de *g.* Spain 55 L5
Valencia de Alcántara Spain 54 D5
Valencia de Don Juan Spain 54 F2
Valencia Island Ireland 47 B12
Valenciana, Comunidad *aut. comm.* Spain *see* **Valencia**
Valenciennes France 51 J2
Vălenii de Munte Romania 58 H3
Valensole, Plateau de France 51 M9
Valentia Spain *see* **Valencia**
Valentin Rus. Fed. 82 D4
Valentine U.S.A. 178 B3
Valentine National Wildlife Refuge *nature res.* U.S.A. 178 B3
Valenza Italy 56 A3
Valenzuela Phil. 74 B3
Våler Norway 45 J3
Valera Venez. 198 D2
Vale Verde Brazil 207 N3
Valga Estonia 42 H4
Valgejõgi *r.* Estonia 42 G2
Valhalla Provincial Park Canada 166 G5
Valikhanovo Kazakh. 103 G1
also known as Ūālīkhanov
Valinco, Golfe de *b. Corsica* France 56 A7
Valinhos Brazil 206 G9
Valjevo *Srbija* Serb. and Mont. 58 A4
Valka Latvia 42 H4
Valkeakoski Fin. 45 N3
Valkenswaard Neth. 48 C4
Valkla Estonia 42 G2
Valko Fin. 42 H1
also spelt Valkoni
Valkoni Fin. *see* **Valko**
Valky Ukr. 41 E6
Valkyrie Dome *ice feature* Antarctica 223 C1
Vallabhipur India 96 A5
Valladolid Mex. 185 H4
Valladolid Spain 54 G3
Vallard, Lac *l.* Canada 169 G2
Valldal Norway 44 I3
Valle *dept* Col. 198 B4
Valle Norway 45 I4
Vallecito Arg. 204 D3
Valle d'Aosta *admin. reg.* Italy 51 N7
Valle de la Pascua Venez. 199 E2
Valle de Rosario Mex. 181 F8
Valle de Santiago Mex. 185 E4
Valle de Zaragoza Mex. 184 D3
Valledupar Col. 198 C2
Vallée-Jonction Canada 169 G4
Valle Fértil, Sierra de *mts* Arg. 204 C3
Valle Grande Bol. 201 D4
Valle Hermoso Mex. 185 F3
Vallejo U.S.A. 182 B3
Vallelunga Pratameno *Sicily* Italy 57 F11
Valle Nacional Mex. 185 F5
Vallenar Chile 204 C3
Vallentuna Sweden 45 L4

►**Valletta** Malta 57 G13
Capital of Malta.
UNESCO World Heritage Site

Valley *r.* Canada 167 L5
Valley Center U.S.A. 183 G8
Valley City U.S.A. 178 C2
Valley Falls U.S.A. 180 B4
Valley Head *hd* Phil. 74 B2
Valley Head U.S.A. 176 E7
Valley of the Kings *tourist site* Egypt 121 G3
UNESCO World Heritage Site
Valley Springs U.S.A. 182 D3
Valley Station U.S.A. 174 C4
Valley Stream U.S.A. 177 L5
Valleyview Canada 167 G4
Valley View U.S.A. 176 A8
Vallo della Lucania Italy 57 H8
Valls Spain 55 M3
Vallsta Sweden 45 L3
Val Marie Canada 167 J5
Valmaseda Spain *see* **Balmaseda**
Valmiera Latvia 42 G4
Valmy U.S.A. 183 G1
Valnera *mt.* Spain 55 H1
Valognes France 50 E3
Valona Albania *see* **Vlorë**
Valozhyn Belarus 42 H7
also spelt Volozhin
Valpaços Port. 54 D3
Val-Paradis Canada 168 E3
Valparai India 94 C4
Valparaíso Brazil 206 C8
Valparaíso Chile 204 C4
UNESCO World Heritage Site
Valparaíso *admin. reg.* Chile 204 C4
Valparaíso Mex. 184 E4
Valparaiso *FL* U.S.A. 185 I2
Valparaiso *IN* U.S.A. 174 C3
Valpelline *valley* Italy 51 N7
Valpoi India 94 B3
Valpovo Croatia 56 K3
Valronquillo *hill* Spain 54 G5
Vals *r.* S. Africa 133 K4
Vals, Tanjung *c.* Indon. 73 I8
Valsad India 94 B1
Valshui Wash *watercourse* U.S.A. 181 D7
Valspan S. Africa 131 E5
Valsrivier S. Africa 133 M5
Valtice Czech Rep. 49 N7
UNESCO World Heritage Site
Valtimo Fin. 44 O3
Valtou *mts* Greece 59 C9
Valua *i.* Vanuatu *see* **Mota Lava**
Valuyets Rus. Fed. 43 O9
Valuyevka Rus. Fed. 41 G7
Valuyki Rus. Fed. 41 F6
Valverde Dom. Rep. *see* **Mao**
Valverde del Camino Spain 54 E7
Valverde del Fresno Spain 54 E4
Vam Co Đông *r.* Vietnam 79 D6
Vam Co Tây *r.* Vietnam 79 D6
Vamizi, Ilha *i.* Moz. 129 D7
Vammala Fin. 45 M3
Vampula Fin. 45 M3
Vamsadhara *r.* India 95 E2
Vamvakas, Akra *pt* Greece 59 H10
Van Turkey 107 E3
Van, Lake *salt l.* Turkey 107 E3
also known as Van Gölü
Vanadzor Armenia 107 F2
formerly known as Karaklis *or* Kirovakan
Vanajavesi *l.* Fin. 45 N3

327

Voss Norway 45 I3
Vostochnaya Litsa Rus. Fed. 40 F1
Vostochno-Kazakhstanskaya Oblast' admin. div. Kazakh. see Vostochnyy Kazakhstan
Vostochno-Kounradskiy Kazakh. see Shygys Konyrat
Vostochno-Sakhalinskiy Gory mts Rus. Fed. 82 F2
Vostochno-Sibirskoye More sea Rus. Fed. see East Siberian Sea
Vostochnyy Rus. Fed. 40 J4
Vostochnyy Kazakhstan admin. div. Kazakh. 103 I2
English form East Kazakhstan Oblast; also known as Shyghys Qazaqstan Oblysy; long form Vostochno-Kazakhstanskaya Oblast'
Vostochnyy Sayan mts Rus. Fed. 80 E2
English form Eastern Sayan Mountains

►Vostok research station Antarctica
Lowest recorded screen temperature in the world.
►►12–13 World Climate and Weather

Vostok research stn Antarctica 223 H1
Vostok Primorskiy Kray Rus. Fed. 82 D3
Vostok Sakhalin Rus. Fed. see Neftegorsk
Vostok Island Kiribati 221 I6
Vostretsovo Rus. Fed. 82 D3
Vostroye Rus. Fed. 40 H3
Võsu Estonia 42 G2
Votkinsk Rus. Fed. 40 J4
Votkinskoye Vodokhranilishche resr Rus. Fed. 40 J4
Votorantim Brazil 206 F10
Votrya r. Rus. Fed. 43 N6
Votuporanga Brazil 206 D7
Voudi, Akra pt Greece 59 J12
Vouga Angola see Cunhinga
Vouga r. Port. 54 C4
Vouillé France 50 G6
Voula Greece 59 E11
Vourinos mt. Greece 59 C8
Vouziers France 51 K3
Voves France 50 H4
Vovodo r. Cent. Afr. Rep. 126 E3
Voxna Sweden 45 K3
Voxnan r. Sweden 45 L3
Voya r. Rus. Fed. 40 I4
Voyageurs National Park U.S.A. 174 A1
Voykar r. Rus. Fed. 40 M2
Voynitsa Rus. Fed. 44 O2
Vöyri Fin. see Vörå
Voyvozh Respublika Komi Rus. Fed. 40 J2
Voyvozh Respublika Komi Rus. Fed. 40 J3
Vozdvizhenskoye Moskovskaya Oblast' Rus. Fed. 43 R5
Vozdvizhenskoye Moskovskaya Oblast' Rus. Fed. 43 T5
Vozha r. Rus. Fed. 43 U7
Vozhayel' Rus. Fed. 40 I3
Vozhd' Proletariata Rus. Fed. 43 U6
Vozhe, Ozero l. Rus. Fed. 43 T1
Vozhega Rus. Fed. 43 V1
Vozhega r. Rus. Fed. 43 U1
Vozhgora Rus. Fed. 40 I2
Voznesenka Kazakh. 103 G1
Voznesens'k Ukr. 41 D7
Voznesen'ye Rus. Fed. 43 Q1
Vozrojdenie Uzbek. 102 D3
Vozrozhdenya Island Uzbek. 102 D3
also known as Wozrojdeniye Oroli
Vozzhayevka Rus. Fed. 82 C2
Vrå Denmark 45 J4
Vrabevo Bulg. 58 F6
Vrachionas hill Greece 59 B11
also known as Vrakhiónas Óros
Vrachnaiika Greece 59 C10
also spelt Vrakhnaíika
Vrådal Norway 45 J4
Vrakhiónas Óros hill Greece see Vrachionas
Vrakhnaíika Greece see Vrachnaiika
Vran mt. Bos.-Herz. 56 J5
Vrana r. Bulg. 58 H5
Vrangel' Rus. Fed. 82 D4
Vrangelya, Mys pt Rus. Fed. 82 E1
Vrangelya, Ostrov i. Rus. Fed. see Wrangel Island
Vranjak Bos.-Herz. 56 K4
Vranje Srbija Serb. and Mont. 58 C6
Vranjska Banja Srbija Serb. and Mont. 58 D6
Vranov, Vodní nádrž resr Czech Rep. 49 M7
Vranov nad Topľou Slovakia 49 S7
Vrapčište Macedonia 58 B7
Vrasidas, Akra pt Greece 58 F8
Vratnik pass Bulg. 58 H6
Vratsa Bulg. 58 E5
Vrbanja r. Bos.-Herz. 56 J4
Vrbas r. Bos.-Herz. 56 J3
Vrbas Vojvodina, Srbija Serb. and Mont. 58 A3
formerly known as Titov Vrbas
Vrbno pod Pradědem Czech Rep. 49 O5
Vrbovec Croatia 56 I3
Vrbovsko Croatia 56 H3
Vrchlabí Czech Rep. 49 M5
Vrede S. Africa 133 N4
Vredefort S. Africa 133 L3
Vredenburg S. Africa 132 B9
Vredendal S. Africa 132 C8
Vredeshoop Namibia 132 D4
Vreed-en-Hoop Guyana 199 G3
Vrela Kosovo, Srbija Serb. and Mont. 58 B6
Vrhnika Slovenia 56 G3
Vridhachalam India 94 C4
Vrigstad Sweden 45 K4
Vrindavan India 89 B7
Vrnjačka Banja Srbija Serb. and Mont. 58 B5
Vrolijkheid Nature Reserve S. Africa 132 D10
Vrrin Albania 58 A7
Vršac Vojvodina, Srbija Serb. and Mont. 58 C3
also known as Versec
Vryburg S. Africa 133 I3
Vryheid S. Africa 133 O4
Vsetín Czech Rep. 49 O6
Vsevolozhsk Rus. Fed. 43 L1
Vskhody Rus. Fed. 43 P7
Vtáčnik mt. Slovakia 49 P7
Vtáčnik mts Slovakia 49 P7
Vũcha r. Bulg. 58 F7
Vučica r. Croatia 56 K3
Vučitrn Kosovo, Srbija Serb. and Mont. 58 B6
Vučje Srbija Serb. and Mont. 58 C6
Vuka r. Croatia 56 L3
Vukovar Croatia 56 L3
Vuktyl' Rus. Fed. 40 K3
Vukuzakhe S. Africa 133 N4
Vulcan Canada 167 H5
Vulcan Romania 58 E3
Vulcăneşti Moldova 58 J3
formerly spelt Vulkaneshty
Vulcan Island P.N.G. see Manam Island
Vulcano, Isola i. Isole Lipari Italy 57 G10
Vŭlchedrŭm Bulg. 58 E5
Vŭlchidol Bulg. 58 I5
Vulkaneshty Moldova see Vulcăneşti
Vulture Mountains U.S.A. 183 K8
Vung Tau Vietnam 79 D6
formerly known as St Jacques, Cap
Vuntut National Park Canada 164 F3
Vuohijärvi Fin. 42 H1
Vuohijärvi l. Fin. 45 N3
Vuokatti Fin. 44 O2
Vuoksa r. Rus. Fed. 43 L1
Vuoksa, Ozero l. Rus. Fed. 43 K1
Vuolijoki Fin. 44 N2
Vuollerim Sweden 44 M2
Vuolvojaure l. Sweden 44 L2
Vuostimo Fin. 44 N2
Vuotso Fin. 44 N1
Vŭrbitsa Bulg. 58 H6
Vurpær Romania 58 F3
Vŭrshets Bulg. 58 E5
Vustsye Belarus 42 I6
Vutcani Romania 58 I2
Vuyyuru India 94 D2
Vuzlove Ukr. 49 T7
Vuzlyanka r. Belarus 42 H7
Vvedenka Kazakh. 103 E1
Vwaza Game Reserve nature res. Malawi 129 B7
Vyalikiya Bortniki Belarus 43 K8
Vyal'ye, Ozero l. Rus. Fed. 43 L2
Vyara India 96 B5
Vyarechcha Belarus 43 L6
Vyarkhovichy Belarus 42 E9
Vyarkhowye Belarus see Ruba
Vyatchyn Belarus 42 J9
Vyatka Rus. Fed. see Kirov
Vyatka r. Rus. Fed. 40 I5
Vyatskiye Polyany Rus. Fed. 40 I4
Vyatskoye Rus. Fed. 43 V4
Vyaz Rus. Fed. 43 K5
Vyazemskiy Rus. Fed. 82 D3
Vyaz'ma Rus. Fed. 43 P6
Vyaz'ma r. Rus. Fed. 43 O6
Vyazniki Rus. Fed. 40 G4
Vyazovka Saratovskaya Oblast' Rus. Fed. 102 A1
Vyazovka Volgogradskaya Oblast' Rus. Fed. 41 G6
Vyazovo Rus. Fed. 43 U8
Vyborg Rus. Fed. 43 J1
formerly known as Viipuri; formerly spelt Viborg
Vyborgskiy Zaliv b. Rus. Fed. 43 J1
Vychegda r. Rus. Fed. 40 H3
Vychegodskiy Rus. Fed. 40 H3
Vydrino Rus. Fed. 85 E1
Vyeramyeyki Belarus 43 M8
Vyerkhnyadzvinsk Belarus 42 I6
formerly known as Drissa
Vyetka Belarus 43 M9
Vyetryna Belarus 43 J6
Vygonichi Rus. Fed. 43 P8
Vygozero, Ozero l. Rus. Fed. 40 E3
Vyksa Rus. Fed. 40 G5
Vylkove Ukr. 41 D7
Vym' r. Rus. Fed. 40 I3
Vypolzovo Rus. Fed. 43 O4
Vyritsa Rus. Fed. 43 L2
Vyselki Rus. Fed. 41 F7
Vyshgorod Rus. Fed. 43 V7
Vyshgorodok Rus. Fed. 42 I4
Vyshhorod Ukr. 41 D6
Vyshkov Rus. Fed. 43 M9
Vyshkovo Rus. Fed. 43 Q4
Vyshnevolotskaya Gryada ridge Rus. Fed. 43 P5
Vyshnevolotskoye Vodokhranilishche resr Rus. Fed. 43 P4
Vyshneye-Ol'shanoye Rus. Fed. 43 S9
Vyshniy-Volochek Rus. Fed. 43 P4
Vyskod' Rus. Fed. 43 L4
Vyškov Czech Rep. 49 O6
Vysoká hill Slovakia 49 O7
Vysokaye Belarus 42 E9
also spelt Vysokoye
Vysokaye Belarus 43 L7
Vysoké Mýto Czech Rep. 49 N6
Vysokinichi Rus. Fed. 43 R7
Vysokogorniy Rus. Fed. 82 E2
formerly known as Muli
Vysokovo Rus. Fed. 43 T4
Vysokovsk Rus. Fed. 43 R5
Vysokoye Belarus see Vysokaye
Vysokoye Rus. Fed. 43 P5
Vysotsk Rus. Fed. 43 J1
Vystupovychi Ukr. 41 D6
Vytebet' r. Rus. Fed. 43 Q8
Vytegra Rus. Fed. 40 F3
Vyvenka Rus. Fed. 39 Q3
Vyya r. Rus. Fed. 40 H3
Vyžuona r. Lith. 42 G6

W

Wa Ghana 124 E4
Waajid Somalia 128 D4
Waal r. Neth. 48 B4
Waalwijk Neth. 48 C4
Waanyi/Garawa Aboriginal Land res. Australia 148 C3
Waat Sudan 128 B2
Wabag P.N.G. 73 J8
Wabakimi Lake Canada 168 B3
Wabal well Oman 105 G3
Wabamun Lake Canada 167 H4
Wabasca r. Canada 167 H3
Wabasca-Desmarais Canada 167 H4
Wabash IN U.S.A. 174 C3
Wabash OH U.S.A. 173 I10
Wabash r. U.S.A. 174 B4
Wabasha U.S.A. 174 A2
Wabassi r. Canada 168 C3
Wabatongushi Lake Canada 173 I2
Wabē Gestro r. Eth. 128 D3
Wabē Mena r. Eth. 128 D3
Wabeno U.S.A. 172 E5
Wabē Shebelē Wenz r. Eth. 128 E3
Wabigoon Lake Canada 168 A3
Wabikimi Provincial Park Canada 168 B3
Wabowden Canada 167 L4
Wabrah well Saudi Arabia 105 D2
Wąbrzeźno Poland 49 P2
Wabu China 87 F1
Wabuk Point Canada 168 C2
Wabush Canada 169 H2
Wabush Lake Canada 169 H2
Waccamaw r. U.S.A. 175 E5
Waccamaw, Lake U.S.A. 175 E5
Waccasassa Bay U.S.A. 175 D6
Wachapreague U.S.A. 177 J8
Wachau reg. Austria 49 M7
UNESCO World Heritage Site
Wächtersbach Germany 48 G5
Wachusett Reservoir U.S.A. 177 N3
Waco Canada 169 H3
Waco U.S.A. 179 C6
Waconda Lake U.S.A. 178 C4
Wad Pak. 101 F5
Wada'a Sudan 121 E6
Wada Wadalla Aboriginal Land res. Australia 148 C2
Wadayama Japan 91 D7
Wad Banda Sudan 121 E6
Wadbilliga National Park Australia 147 F4
Waddān Libya 120 C2
Waddān, Jabal hills Libya 120 B2
Waddell Dam U.S.A. 183 L8
Waddeneilanden is Neth. see West Frisian Islands
Wadden Islands Neth. see West Frisian Islands
Waddenzee sea chan. Neth. 48 B3
Waddikee Australia 146 C3
Waddington, Mount Canada 166 E5
Waddinxveen Neth. 48 B3
Wadena Canada 167 K5
Wadena U.S.A. 178 D2
Wad en Nail Sudan 121 G6
Wadesboro U.S.A. 174 D5
Wadeye Australia 148 A2
formerly known as Port Keats
Wadgaon Maharashtra India 94 B2
Wadgaon Maharashtra India 94 C1
Wad Hamid Sudan 121 G5
Wadhwan Gujarat India 96 A5
Wadhwan Gujarat India see Surendranagar
Wadi India 94 C2
Wadian China 87 E1
Wādī as Sīr Jordan 108 G6
Wādī Gimāl, Gezîret i. Egypt 104 A2
English form Wādī Gimāl Island
Wādī Gimāl Island Egypt see Wādī Gimāl, Gezîret
Wadi Halfa Sudan 121 F4
Wādī Ḥammah Saudi Arabia 104 C3
Wādī Mūsā Jordan 108 G7
Wad Medani Sudan 121 G6
Wadsworth NV U.S.A. 182 E2
Wadsworth OH U.S.A. 176 D4
Waegwan S. Korea 91 A7
Waenhuiskrans S. Africa 132 E11
Waesche, Mount Antarctica 222 P1
Wafangdian China 85 I4
formerly known as Fuxian
Wafra Kuwait see Al Wafrah
Wagah India 96 B3
Wagait Aboriginal Land res. Australia 148 A2
Wageningen Neth. 48 C4
Wageningen Suriname 199 G3
Wager Bay Canada 167 N1
Wagga Wagga Australia 147 E3
Wagiman Aboriginal Land res. Australia 148 A2
Wagin Australia 151 B7
Wagner Brazil 202 D5
Wagner U.S.A. 178 C3
Wagoner U.S.A. 179 D4
Wagon Mound U.S.A. 181 F5
Wągrowiec Poland 49 O3
Wah Pak. 101 H3
Wahai Indon. 75 D3
Wahda state Sudan 126 F2
Wahemen, Lac l. Canada 169 G2
Wahiawā U.S.A. 181 [inset] Y1
Wahibah, Ramlat al des. Oman 105 G3
Wahoo U.S.A. 178 C3
Wahpeton U.S.A. 178 C2
Wahran Alg. see Oran
Wah Wah Mountains U.S.A. 183 K3
Wai India 94 B2
Waiapu r. N.Z. 152 M5
Waiau N.Z. 153 H10
Waiau r. North I. N.Z. 152 L6
Waiau r. South I. N.Z. 153 B14
Waiau r. South I. N.Z. 153 H10
Waidhofen an der Thaya Austria 49 M7
Waidhofen an der Ybbs Austria 49 L8
Waigama Indon. 75 D3
Waigeo i. Indon. 73 H7
Waihao Downs N.Z. 153 E12
Waiharara N.Z. 152 H2
Waiharoa N.Z. 152 J5
Waiheke Island N.Z. 152 J4
Waihi N.Z. 152 J5
Waihi Beach N.Z. 152 J5
Waihou r. N.Z. 152 J5
Waihua N.Z. 152 L7
Waikabubak Indon. 75 A5
Waikaia N.Z. 153 C13
Waikaia r. N.Z. 153 C13
Waikaka N.Z. 153 D13
Waikanae N.Z. 152 J8
Waikare, Lake N.Z. 152 J5
Waikaremoana, Lake N.Z. 152 K6
Waikaretu N.Z. 152 I5
Waikari N.Z. 153 G10
Waikato admin. reg. N.Z. 152 I5
Waikato r. N.Z. 152 I5
Waikawa N.Z. 153 D14
Waikeria N.Z. 152 J6
Waikerie Australia 146 C3
Waiki'i U.S.A. 181 [inset] Z2
Waikirikiri N.Z. 152 K6
Waiklibang Indon. 75 B5
Waikoikoi N.Z. 153 D14
Waikokopa N.Z. 152 L7
Waikouaiti N.Z. 153 E13
Wailuku U.S.A. 181 [inset] Z1
Waimahake N.Z. 153 C14
Waimakariri r. N.Z. 153 G11
Waimangaroa N.Z. 153 F9
Waimarama N.Z. 152 K7
Waimarie N.Z. 153 F9
Waimate N.Z. 153 F12
Waimatenui N.Z. 152 H3
Waimauku N.Z. 152 I4
Waimea U.S.A. 181 [inset] Z1
Wainganga r. India 94 C2
Waingapu Indon. 75 B5
Waingawa N.Z. 152 J8
Waini Point Guyana 199 G2
Wainwright Canada 167 I4
Wainwright U.S.A. 164 D2
Waiotira N.Z. 152 I3
Waiouru N.Z. 152 J7
Waipa r. N.Z. 152 J5
Waipahi N.Z. 153 D14
Waipahu U.S.A. 181 [inset] Y1
Waipaoa r. N.Z. 152 L6
Waipapa Point N.Z. 153 C14
Waipara N.Z. 153 G11
Waipawa N.Z. 152 K7
Waipipi N.Z. 152 I5
Waipu N.Z. 152 I3
Waipukurau N.Z. 152 K7
Wairakei N.Z. 152 K6
Wairarapa, Lake N.Z. 152 J9
Wairau r. N.Z. 153 I9
Wairau Valley N.Z. 152 H9
Wairoa N.Z. 152 L7
Wairoa r. North I. N.Z. 152 I4
Wairoa r. North I. N.Z. 152 L7
Waishe China 87 F2
Waitahanui N.Z. 152 K6
Waitahuna N.Z. 153 D13
Waitakaruru N.Z. 152 J5
Waitaki N.Z. 153 F12
Waitaki r. N.Z. 153 F12
Waitangi S. Pacific Ocean 145 H6
Waitangitaona r. N.Z. 153 E11
Waitara N.Z. 152 I6
Waitati N.Z. 153 E13
Waite River Australia 148 B4
Waitomo Caves N.Z. 152 J6
Waitotara N.Z. 152 I7
Waitotari r. N.Z. 152 I7
Waitsburg U.S.A. 180 C3
Waiuku N.Z. 152 I5
Waiwera South N.Z. 153 D14
Waiya Indon. 75 D3
Waiyang China 87 F3
Waiyevo Fiji 145 H3
Wajid, Jabal al hills Saudi Arabia 104 D4
Wajiki Japan 91 D8
Wajima Japan 90 E6
Wajir Kenya 128 D4
Waka Dem. Rep. Congo 126 D5
Waka, Tanjung pt Indon. 75 C3
Wakami Lake Canada 173 K3
Wakapuaka N.Z. 152 H9
Wakasa-wan b. Japan 91 D7
Wakatipu, Lake N.Z. 153 C13
Wakatobi Marine National Park nature res. Indon. 75 B4
Wakatoma Lake Canada 173 J4
Wakaw Canada 167 J4
Wakaya Aboriginal Land res. Australia 148 C3
Wakayama Japan 91 D7
Wakayama pref. Japan 91 D8
Wake Atoll terr. N. Pacific Ocean see Wake Island
WaKeeney U.S.A. 178 C4
Wakefield Canada 173 R5
Wakefield N.Z. 152 H9
Wakefield U.K. 47 K10
Wakefield MI U.S.A. 172 D4
Wakefield OH U.S.A. 176 B7
Wakefield RI U.S.A. 177 N4
Wakefield VA U.S.A. 177 I9
Wakeham Canada see Kangiqsujuaq

►Wake Island terr. N. Pacific Ocean 220 G4
United States Unincorporated Territory. Also known as Āneen-Kio or EnenKio; also known as Wake Atoll.
►►138–139 Oceania Countries

Wakema Myanmar 78 A4
Wakhan reg. Afgh. 101 H2
Waki Japan 91 D7
Wakinosawa Japan 90 G4
Wakiro watercourse Eritrea 104 B5
Wakiso Uganda 128 B4
Wakkanai Japan 90 G2
Wakkerstroom S. Africa 133 O4
Wakool Australia 147 E3
Wakool r. Australia 147 D3
Wakuach, Lac l. Canada 169 H2
Waku-Kungo Angola 127 B7
formerly known as Santa Comba; formerly spelt Uaco Congo
Wakuya Japan 90 G5
Wakwayowkastic r. Canada 168 D3
Walagunya Aboriginal Reserve Australia 150 C4
Walajapet India 94 C3
Wałbrzych Poland 49 N5
historically known as Waldenburg
Walcha Australia 147 F2
Walcott U.S.A. 180 F4
Wałcz Poland 49 N2
Waldaist r. Austria 49 L7
Waldburg Range mts Australia 151 B5
Walden U.S.A. 177 K4
Waldenburg Poland see Wałbrzych
Waldkraiburg Germany 49 J7
Waldo U.S.A. 172 F7
Waldorf U.S.A. 177 I7
Waldport U.S.A. 180 A3
Waldron U.S.A. 179 D5
Waldron, Cape Antarctica 223 H2
Waldshut Germany 48 F8
Walea, Selat sea chan. Indon. 75 B3
Waleabahi i. Indon. 75 B3
Walêg China 86 B2
formerly known as Warli
Walej, Sha'īb al watercourse Iraq 109 K5
Wales admin. div. U.K. 47 I11
also known as Cymru; historically known as Cambria
Walewale Ghana 125 E4
Walford U.S.A. 172 B9
Walgett Australia 147 F2
Walgreen Coast Antarctica 222 Q1
Walhalla MI U.S.A. 172 G7
Walhalla ND U.S.A. 178 C1
Walhalla SC U.S.A. 174 D5
Walikale Dem. Rep. Congo 126 F5
Walker r. Australia 148 B2
Walker watercourse Australia 148 B3
Walker IA U.S.A. 172 B8
Walker MI U.S.A. 172 H7
Walker MN U.S.A. 178 D2
Walker r. U.S.A. 182 F3
Walker Bay S. Africa 132 D11
Walker Cay i. Bahamas 186 D1
Walker Creek r. Australia 149 D3
Walker Lake l. Canada 167 L4
Walker Lake U.S.A. 182 F3
Walker Lake l. U.S.A. 182 F3
Walker Mountains Antarctica 222 R2
Walker River Indian Reservation res. U.S.A. 182 F3
Walkersville MD U.S.A. 177 H6
Walkersville WV U.S.A. 176 E7
Walkerton U.S.A. 172 G9
Wall, Mount hill Australia 150 B4
Wallabi Group is Australia 151 A6
Wallaby Island Australia 149 D2
Wallace ID U.S.A. 180 C3
Wallace NC U.S.A. 174 E5
Wallace VA U.S.A. 176 C9
Wallaceburg Canada 168 D5
Wallal Downs Australia 150 C3
Wallambin, Lake salt flat Australia 151 B6
Wallangarra Australia 147 F2
Wallaroo Australia 146 C3
Walla Walla U.S.A. 180 C3
Walldürn Germany 48 G6
Wallekraal S. Africa 132 B7
Wallenpaupack, Lake U.S.A. 177 J4
Wallingford CT U.S.A. 177 M4
Wallingford VT U.S.A. 177 M2
Wallis, Îles is Wallis and Futuna Is see Wallis Islands

►Wallis and Futuna Islands terr. S. Pacific Ocean 145 H3
French Overseas Territory. Also known as Wallis et Futuna, Îles.
►►138–139 Oceania Countries

Wallis et Futuna, Îles terr. S. Pacific Ocean see Wallis and Futuna Islands
Wallis Islands Wallis and Futuna Is 145 H3
also known as Wallis, Îles
Wallis Lake inlet Australia 147 G3
Wallops Island U.S.A. 177 J8
Wallowa Mountains U.S.A. 180 C3
Walls U.K. 46 K3
Walls of Jerusalem National Park Australia 147 E5
Wallumbilla Australia 149 F5
Walmsley Lake Canada 167 I2
Walney, Isle of i. U.K. 47 I9
Walnut U.S.A. 176 H5
Walnut Bottom U.S.A. 176 H5
Walnut Cove U.S.A. 176 E9
Walnut Creek U.S.A. 182 B4
Walnut Creek r. U.S.A. 178 C4
Walnut Grove U.S.A. 182 C3
Walnut Ridge U.S.A. 174 B4
Walong India 97 H3
Walpole U.S.A. 177 M2
Walpole, Île i. New Caledonia 145 F4
Walsall U.K. 47 K11
Walsenburg U.S.A. 181 F5
Walsh r. Australia 149 D3
Walsrode Germany 48 G3
Waltair India 95 D2
Walterboro U.S.A. 175 D5
Walter F. George Reservoir U.S.A. 175 C6
Walters U.S.A. 179 C5
Walter's Range hills Australia 147 E2
Walthall U.S.A. 175 B5
Waltham Canada 173 Q5
Waltham MA U.S.A. 177 N3
Waltham ME U.S.A. 177 Q1
Walton IN U.S.A. 172 G10
Walton KY U.S.A. 176 A7
Walton NY U.S.A. 177 J3
Walton WV U.S.A. 176 D7
Walton on the Naze U.K. 47 N12
Walvisbaai Namibia see Walvis Bay
Walvis Bay Namibia 130 B4
also spelt Walvisbaai
Walvis Bay b. Namibia 130 B4
Wamala, Lake Uganda 128 A4
Wamba Dem. Rep. Congo 126 E4
Wamba r. Dem. Rep. Congo 126 C5
Wamba Nigeria 125 H4
Wambardi Aboriginal Land res. Australia 148 A2
Wamena Indon. 73 I7
Wami r. Tanz. 129 C6
Wamlana Indon. 75 C3
Wampaya Aboriginal Land res. Australia 148 B3
Wampsville U.S.A. 173 R7
Wampusirpi Hond. 186 B4
Wanaaring Australia 147 E2
Wanaka N.Z. 153 D12
Wanaka, Lake N.Z. 153 D12
Wan'an China 87 E3
also known as Furong
Wanapitei Lake Canada 173 M4
Wanaque Reservoir U.S.A. 177 K4
Wanasabari Indon. 75 B4
Wanbi Australia 146 D3
Wanbi China 86 B3
Wanci Indon. 75 B4
Wanda Arg. 204 G2
Wandana Nature Reserve Australia 151 A6
Wanda Shan mts China 82 D3
Wandering River Canada 167 H4
Wanding China 86 A3
formerly known as Wandingzhen
Wandingzhen China see Wanding
Wandiwash India see Vandavasi
Wandle Downs N.Z. 153 H10
Wandlitz Germany 49 K3
Wandoan Australia 149 F5
Wang, Mae Nam r. Thai. 78 B4
Wanganui N.Z. 152 J7
Wanganui r. North I. N.Z. 152 I7
Wanganui r. South I. N.Z. 153 E11
Wangaratta Australia 147 E4
Wangary Australia 146 B3
Wangcang China 86 C1
also known as Hongjiang; formerly known as Fengjiaba
Wangcheng China 87 E2
formerly known as Gaotangling
Wangda China see Zogang
Wangdi Phodrang Bhutan 97 F4
Wangdu China 85 G4
Wangerooge i. Germany 48 E2
Wanggamet, Gunung mt. Indon. 75 B5
Wang Gaxun China 84 C4
Wangezhuang China see Jiaonan
Wangguan China 86 C1
Wangiwangi i. Indon. 75 B4
Wangjiang China 87 F2
Wangkibila Hond. 186 B4
Wangkui China 82 B3
Wang Mai Khon Thai. see Sawankhalok
Wangmao China 86 C3
Wangmo China 86 C3
also known as Fuxing
Wangolodougou Côte d'Ivoire see Ouangolodougou
Wangqing China 82 C4
Wangying China see Huaiyin
Wanham Canada 166 G4
Wanhatti Suriname 199 H3
Wan Hsa-la Myanmar 78 B3
Wanie-Rukula Dem. Rep. Congo 126 E4
Wanimiyn Aboriginal Land res. Australia 148 A2
Wanjarri Nature Reserve Australia 151 C5
Wankaner India 96 A5
Wankie Zimbabwe see Hwange
Wanlaweyn Somalia 128 E4
Wanna Lakes salt flat Australia 151 E6
Wannian China 87 F2
also known as Chenying
Wanning China 87 D5
Wanrong China 85 F5
Wanshan China 87 D3
Wanshan Qundao is China 87 E4
English form Lima Islands
Wanstead N.Z. 152 K8
Wantage U.K. 47 K12
Wanup Canada 173 M4
Wanxian China 87 D2
Wanyuan China 87 D1
Wanzai China 87 E2
also known as Kangle
Wanzhi China see Wuhu
Wapakoneta U.S.A. 176 A5
Wapawekka Lake Canada 167 J4
Wapello U.S.A. 172 B9
Wapikopa Lake Canada 168 B2
Wapiti r. Canada 166 G4
Wapotih Indon. 75 C3
Wappingers Falls U.S.A. 177 L4
Wapsipinicon r. U.S.A. 174 B3
Wapusk National Park Canada 167 M3
Waqên China 86 B1
Wāqf aş Şawwān, Jibāl hills Jordan 109 H6
Wāqişah well Iraq 107 E5
Waqr well Saudi Arabia 105 E3
Waqr Maryamah well Yemen 105 D4
War U.S.A. 176 D8
Wa'r, Wādī al watercourse Syria 109 L3
Warab Sudan 126 F2
Warab state Sudan 126 F2
Waradi waterhole Kenya 128 D4
Warah Pak. 101 F5
Warakurna-Wingellina-Irrunytju Aboriginal Reserve Australia 151 E5
Warandab Eth. 128 E3
Warangal India 94 C2
Waraseoni India 96 D5
Waratah Australia 147 E5
Warbreccan Australia 149 D5
Warburg Germany 48 G4
Warburton Vic. Australia 147 E4
Warburton W.A. Australia 151 D5
Warburton watercourse Australia 146 C1
Warburton S. Africa 133 O3
Warburton Aboriginal Reserve Australia 151 D5
Warburton Bay Canada 167 I2
Warburton Range hills Australia 151 D5
Warche r. Belgium 51 L2
Ward watercourse Australia 149 E5
Ward N.Z. 153 I9
Ward, Mount Antarctica 222 T2
Ward, Mount South I. N.Z. 153 B13
Ward, Mount South I. N.Z. 153 D11
Wardag prov. Afgh. 101 G3
Wardang Island Australia 146 C3
Wardeglo waterhole Kenya 128 D4
Warden S. Africa 133 M4
Wardha India 94 C1
Wardha r. India 94 C2
Ward Hill U.K. 46 I5
Ware Canada 166 E3
also known as Fort Ware
Ware U.S.A. 177 M3
Wareham U.K. 47 J13
Waremme Belgium 51 L2
Waren Germany 49 J2
Warendorf Germany 48 E4
Warginburra Peninsula Australia 149 F4
Wargla Alg. see Ouargla
War Gunbi waterhole Somalia 128 E2
Warialda Australia 147 F2
Wari Island P.N.G. 149 F1
Warin Chamrap Thai. 79 D5
Warka Poland 49 S4
Warkworth N.Z. 152 I4
War Idaad Somalia 128 E2
Warli China see Walêg
Warman Canada 167 J4
Warmbad Namibia 130 C6
Warmbad S. Africa 133 M1
Warmfontein Namibia 132 D4
Warmia reg. Poland 49 R1
Warm Springs NV U.S.A. 183 H3
Warm Springs VA U.S.A. 176 F7
Warm Springs Indian Reservation res. U.S.A. 180 B3
Warmwaterberg S. Africa 132 E10
Warmwaterberg mts S. Africa 132 E10
Warner Canada 167 H5
Warner Lakes U.S.A. 180 C4
Warner Mountains U.S.A. 180 B4
Warner Robins U.S.A. 175 D5
Warner Springs U.S.A. 183 H8
Warnes Bol. 201 E4
Warnow r. Germany 49 J1
Waronda India 94 C2
Waroona Australia 151 A7
Warora India 94 C1
Warra Australia 149 F5
Warrabri Aboriginal Land res. Australia 148 B4
Warracknabeal Australia 147 D4
Warragamba Reservoir Australia 147 F3
Warragul Australia 147 E4
Warrakalanna, Lake salt flat Australia 146 C2
Warramboo hill Australia 151 B6
Warrambool r. Australia 147 E2
Warrandirinna, Lake salt flat Australia 146 C1
Warrāq al 'Arab Egypt 108 C7
Warrawagine Australia 150 C4
Warrego r. Australia 147 E2
Warrego Range hills Australia 149 E5
Warren Australia 147 E2
Warren r. Australia 151 A7
Warren Canada 173 M4
Warren AR U.S.A. 179 D5
Warren IL U.S.A. 172 D8
Warren IN U.S.A. 172 H10
Warren MI U.S.A. 173 J8
Warren MN U.S.A. 178 C1
Warren OH U.S.A. 176 E4
Warren PA U.S.A. 176 F4
Warren Hastings Island Palau see Merir
Warren Island U.S.A. 166 C4
Warrenpoint U.K. 47 F9
Warrens U.S.A. 172 C6
Warrensburg MO U.S.A. 178 D4
Warrensburg NY U.S.A. 177 L2
Warrenton S. Africa 133 I5
Warrenton GA U.S.A. 175 D5
Warrenton MO U.S.A. 174 B4
Warrenton NC U.S.A. 176 G9
Warrenton VA U.S.A. 176 H7
Warri Nigeria 125 G5
Warriedar hill Australia 151 B6
Warriners Creek watercourse Australia 146 C2
Warrington N.Z. 153 E13
Warrington U.K. 47 J10
Warrington U.S.A. 175 C6
Warrnambool Australia 147 D4
Warroad U.S.A. 178 D1
Warrumbungle National Park Australia 147 F2
Warrumbungle Range mts Australia 147 F2
Warruwi Australia 148 B1
Warry Warry watercourse Australia 146 D2

►Warsaw Poland 49 S3
Capital of Poland. Also spelt Warszawa.
UNESCO World Heritage Site

Warsaw IN U.S.A. 174 C3
Warsaw KY U.S.A. 176 A7
Warsaw MO U.S.A. 178 D4
Warsaw NY U.S.A. 176 G3
Warsaw VA U.S.A. 177 I8
Warsingsfehn Germany 48 E2
Warszawa Poland see Warsaw
Warta Poland 49 P4
Warta r. Poland 49 L3
Wartburg U.S.A. 176 A9
Wartburg, Schloss tourist site Germany 48 H5
UNESCO World Heritage Site
Wartburg, Schloß tourist site Germany 48 H4
Waru Indon. 77 G3
Warud India 96 C5
Warumungu Aboriginal Land res. Australia 148 B3
Warwick Australia 147 G2
Warwick U.K. 47 K11
Warwick NY U.S.A. 177 K4
Warwick RI U.S.A. 177 N4
Warwick Channel Australia 148 C2
Warzhong China 86 B2
Wasa Canada 167 H5
Wasaga Beach Canada 173 M6
Wasagu Nigeria 125 G4
Wasatch Range mts U.S.A. 183 M2
Wasbank S. Africa 133 O5
Wascana Creek r. Canada 167 J5
Wasco U.S.A. 182 E6
Wascott U.S.A. 172 B4
Waseca U.S.A. 174 A2
Wasekamio Lake Canada 167 I3
Washado Suriname 199 G3
Washap Pak. 101 E5
Washburn IL U.S.A. 172 D10
Washburn ND U.S.A. 178 B2
Washburn TN U.S.A. 176 B9
Washburn WI U.S.A. 172 C4
Washim India 94 C1
Washimeska r. Canada 169 F3

►Washington DC U.S.A. 177 H7
Capital of the United States of America.
►►8–9 World Countries

Washington GA U.S.A. 175 D5
Washington IA U.S.A. 172 B9
Washington IL U.S.A. 172 D10
Washington IN U.S.A. 174 C4
Washington KS U.S.A. 178 C4
Washington KY U.S.A. 176 B7
Washington NC U.S.A. 174 E5
Washington NH U.S.A. 177 M2
Washington NJ U.S.A. 177 K5
Washington PA U.S.A. 176 E5
Washington UT U.S.A. 183 K4
Washington state U.S.A. 180 B3
Washington, Cape Antarctica 223 L2
Washington, Mount U.S.A. 177 N1
Washington Court House U.S.A. 176 B6
Washington Island U.S.A. 172 G5
Washington Land reg. Greenland 165 M2
Washir Afgh. 101 E3
Washita r. U.S.A. 179 C5
Washpool National Park Australia 147 G2
Washtucna U.S.A. 180 C3
Wasī' Saudi Arabia 105 D2
Wasī' well Saudi Arabia 105 E3
Wasilków Poland 49 U2
Wasilla U.S.A. 164 E3
Wāsiţ governorate Iraq 107 F4
Wasit tourist site Iraq 107 F4
Wāsiţah Saudi Arabia 104 B3
Waskaganish Canada 168 E3
also known as Fort Rupert
Waskaiowaka Lake Canada 167 L3
Waskatenau Canada 167 H4
Wąsosz Poland 49 N4
Waspán Nicaragua 186 B4
Wassadou Senegal 124 B3
Wassamu Japan 90 H2
Wassenaar Neth. 48 B3
Wasser Namibia 130 C5
Wasserkuppe hill Germany 48 G5
Wassou Guinea 124 B4
Wassuk Range mts U.S.A. 182 F3
Wassy France 51 K4
Waswanipi, Lac l. Canada 168 E3
Watabeag Lake Canada 173 M2
Watambayoli Indon. 75 B3
Watampone Indon. 75 B4
Watansoppeng Indon. 75 A4
Watapi Lake Canada 167 I4
Watarrka National Park Australia 148 A5
Watauga r. U.S.A. 176 C9
Watauga Lake U.S.A. 176 C9
Watenstadt-Salzgitter Germany see Salzgitter

Yayva Rus. Fed. 40 K4
Yazagyo Myanmar 78 A3
Yazd Iran 100 C4
Yazd *prov.* Iran 100 C4
Yazdān Iran 101 E3
Yazd-e Khvāst Iran 100 C4
also known as Samirum
Yazgulemskiy Khrebet *mts* Tajik. *see* Yazgulom, Qatorkŭhi
Yazgulom, Qatorkŭhi *mts* Tajik. 101 G2
also known as Yazgulemskiy Khrebet
Yazhelbitsy Rus. Fed. 43 N3
Yazıhan Turkey 107 D3
also known as Fethiye
Yazıkent Turkey 59 J11
Yazoo *r.* U.S.A. 175 B5
Yazoo City U.S.A. 175 B5
Yaz'va *r.* Rus. Fed. 40 K3
Ybakoura *well* Chad 120 B4
Y Bala U.K. *see* Bala
Ybbs *r.* Austria 49 M7
Ybbs an der Donau Austria 49 M7
Ybycui Para. 201 F6
Yding Skovhøj *hill* Denmark 45 J5
Ydra Greece 59 E11
Ydra *i.* Greece 59 E11
English form Hydra; *also spelt* Idhra *or* Idra
Ydras, Kolpos *sea chan.* Greece 59 E11
also spelt Ídhras, Kólpos
Y Drenewydd U.K. *see* Newtown
Ye Myanmar 79 B5
Ye *r.* Myanmar 79 B5
Yebaishou China *see* Jianping
Yebawmi Myanmar 78 A2
Yebbi-Bou Chad 120 C4
Yecheng China 88 B4
formerly known as Karghalik *or* Kargilik
Yecla Spain 55 J6
Yécora Mex. 184 C2
Yedashe Myanmar 78 B4
Yedatore India 94 C3
YeDebub Bihēroch Bihēreseboch na Hizboch *admin. reg.* Eth. 128 C3
Yedi Burun Başı *pt* Turkey 59 K12
Yedoma Rus. Fed. 40 H3
Yedri *well* Chad 120 C4
Yedrovo Rus. Fed. 43 O4
Yedy Belarus 42 I6
Yeed Eth. 128 D3
Yeeda River Australia 150 C3
Yeelanna Australia 146 B3
Yefimovskiy Rus. Fed. 43 P2
Yefremov Rus. Fed. 43 T8
Yêgainnyin China *see* Henan
Yeggueba *well* Niger 125 I2
Yeghegnadzor Armenia 107 F3
formerly known as Mikoyan; *formerly spelt* Yekhegnadzor
Yegindybulak Kazakh. 103 I2
also spelt Egindibulaq
Yegindykol' Kazakh. 103 G2
formerly known as Krasnoznamenskiy
Yegorlyk *r.* Rus. Fed. 41 G7
Yegorlykskaya Rus. Fed. 41 G7
Yegorova, Mys *pt* Rus. Fed. 82 E3
Yegor'ye Rus. Fed. 43 O6
Yegor'yevsk Rus. Fed. 43 U6
Yégué Togo 125 F4
Yei Sudan 128 A3
Yei *r.* Sudan 128 A3
Yeina Island P.N.G. 149 G1
Yeji China 87 E2
formerly known as Yejiaji
Yeji Ghana 125 E4
Yejiaji China *see* Yeji
Yekaterinburg Rus. Fed. 38 G4
formerly known as Sverdlovsk
Yekaterinodar Rus. Fed. *see* Krasnodar
Yekaterinoslav Ukr. *see* Dnipropetrovs'k
Yekaterinoslavka Rus. Fed. 82 C2
Yekaterinovka *Lipetskaya Oblast'* Rus. Fed. 43 T9
Yekaterinovka *Saratovskaya Oblast'* Rus. Fed. 41 H5
Yekhegnadzor Armenia *see* Yeghegnadzor
Yekimovichi Rus. Fed. 43 O7
Yekokora *r.* Dem. Rep. Congo 126 D4
Yelabuga *Khabarovskiy Kray* Rus. Fed. 82 D2
Yelabuga *Respublika Tatarstan* Rus. Fed. 40 I5
Yelan' Rus. Fed. 41 G6
Yelbarsli Turkm. 102 E5
Yeleğen Turkey 59 J10
Yelenovskiye Kar'yery Ukr. *see* Dokuchayevs'k
Yelenskiy Rus. Fed. 43 Q8
Yelets Rus. Fed. 43 T9
Yeletskiy Rus. Fed. 40 M2
Yeligovo Rus. Fed. 43 O3
Yélimané Mali 124 C3
Yelino Rus. Fed. 43 U7
Yelizavetgrad Ukr. *see* Kirovohrad
Yelizavety, Mys *c.* Rus. Fed. 39 O4
Yelizovo Rus. Fed. 39 P4
Yelkhovka Rus. Fed. 41 I5
Yell *i.* U.K. 46 K3
Yellabina Regional Reserve *nature res.* Australia 146 B2
Yellandu India 94 D2
Yellapur India 94 B3
Yellareddi India 94 C2

►Yellow *r.* China 85 H4
4th longest river in Asia and 7th in the world. Also known as Huang He or Ma Qu; formerly spelt Hwang Ho.
►►6–7 World Landscapes
►►60–61 Asia Landscapes

Yellow *r.* U.S.A. 172 C7
Yellow Bluff *hd* Canada 167 O1
Yellowdine Australia 151 B6
Yellowhead Pass Canada 166 G4

►Yellowknife Canada 167 H2
Capital of Northwest Territories. Also known as Sombak'e

Yellowknife *r.* Canada 167 H2
Yellow Mountain *hill* Australia 147 E3
Yellow Sea N. Pacific Ocean 83 B6
Yellow Springs U.S.A. 176 B6
Yellowstone *r.* U.S.A. 178 B2
Yellowstone Lake U.S.A. 180 E3
►Yellowstone National Park U.S.A. 180 E3
UNESCO World Heritage Site
►►14–15 World Environmental Impacts
Yell Sound *strait* U.K. 46 K3
Yellville U.S.A. 179 D4
Yelm U.S.A. 180 B3
Yel'nya Rus. Fed. 43 O7
Yelovo Rus. Fed. 40 J4
Yel'sk Belarus 41 D6
Yel'tsy Rus. Fed. 43 O5
Yelva *r.* Rus. Fed. 40 I3
Yelverton Bay Canada 165 K1
Yelwa Nigeria 125 H4
Yema Nanshan *mts* China 84 B4
Yema Shan *mts* China 84 B4
Yematan China 84 C4
Yembo Eth. 128 C2
►Yemen *country* Asia 104 D5
►►64–65 Asia Countries
Yemetsk Rus. Fed. 40 G3
Yemişenbükü Turkey *see* Taşova
Yemmiganur India *see* Emmiganuru
Yemtsa Rus. Fed. 40 G3
Yemva Rus. Fed. 40 I3
formerly known as Zheleznodorozhnyy
Yena Rus. Fed. 44 O2
Yenagoa Nigeria 125 G5
Yenakiyeve Ukr. 41 F6
also spelt Yenakiyevo; *formerly known as* Rykovo
Yenakiyevo Ukr. *see* Yenakiyeve
Yenangyat Myanmar 78 A3
Yenangyaung Myanmar 78 A3
Yenanma Myanmar 78 A4
Yên Bai Vietnam 78 D3
Yenbekshi Kazakh. 103 G4
Yendi Ghana 125 E4
Yêndum China *see* Zhag'yab
Yénéganou Congo 126 B5
Yenge *r.* Dem. Rep. Congo 126 D5
Yengejeh Iran 100 A2
Yengema Sierra Leone 124 C4
Yengisar *Xinjiang* China 88 B4
Yengisar *Xinjiang* China 88 D3
Yengo Congo 126 B4
Yengo National Park Australia 147 F3
Yenice *Çanakkale* Turkey 59 I9
Yenice *İçel* Turkey 108 G1
Yeniceoba Turkey 106 C3
Yeniçiftlik Turkey 58 I7
Yenidere *r.* Turkey 59 J11
Yenifoça Turkey 59 H10
Yenıhan Turkey *see* Yıldızeli
Yenihisar Turkey 59 I11
Yenije-i-Vardar Greece *see* Giannitsa
Yeniköy *Kütahya* Turkey 59 J9
Yeniköy *Kütahya* Turkey 59 K10
Yenipazar Turkey 59 J11
Yenişakran Turkey 59 I10
Yeniséa Greece *see* Genisea
Yenişehir Greece *see* Larisa
Yenişehir Turkey 106 B2
Yenisey *r.* Rus. Fed. 84 B1

►Yenisey-Angara-Selenga *r.* Rus. Fed. 39 I2
3rd longest river in Asia and 6th in the world.
►►6–7 World Landscapes
►►60–61 Asia Landscapes

Yeniseysk Rus. Fed. 39 J4
Yeniseyskiy Kryazh *ridge* Rus. Fed. 39 J4
Yeniseyskiy Zaliv *inlet* Rus. Fed. 39 H2
Yeniugou China 86 A1
Yeniyol Turkey *see* Borçka
Yenotayevka Rus. Fed. 102 A3
Yeola India 94 B1
Yeo Lake *salt flat* Australia 151 D5
Yeo Lake Nature Reserve Australia 151 D6
Yeotmal India *see* Yavatmal
Yeovil U.K. 47 J13
Yeo Yeo *r.* Australia *see* Bland
Yepachi Mex. 184 C2
Yepifan' Rus. Fed. 43 T8
Yeppoon Australia 149 F4
Yerakaroú Greece *see* Gerakarou
Yerakhtur Rus. Fed. 41 G5
Yeráki, Ákra *pt* Greece *see* Geraki, Akra
Yerákion Greece *see* Geraki
Yeraliyev Kazakh. *see* Kuryk
Yerbent Turkm. 102 D5
Yerbogachen Rus. Fed. 39 K3
Yercaud India 94 C4
Yerementau, Gory *hills* Kazakh. 103 H2

►Yerevan Armenia 107 F2
Capital of Armenia. Also spelt Erevan.

Yereymentau Kazakh. 103 H2
also spelt Erementaū; *formerly spelt* Yermentau
Yergara India 94 C2
Yergeni *hills* Rus. Fed. 41 H7
Yergoğu Romania *see* Giurgiu
Yeriho West Bank *see* Jericho
Yerilla Australia 151 C6
Yerington U.S.A. 182 E3
Yerköy Turkey 106 C3
Yerla *r.* India 94 B2
Yermak Kazakh. *see* Aksu
Yermakovo Rus. Fed. 43 T3
Yermentau Kazakh. *see* Yereymentau
Yermo Mex. 184 D3
Yermo U.S.A. 183 H7
Yerofey Pavlovich Rus. Fed. 81 K2
Yeroham Israel 108 F7
Yersa *r.* Rus. Fed. 40 J2
Yershi Rus. Fed. 43 P7
Yershichi Rus. Fed. 43 N8
Yershov Rus. Fed. 102 B2
Yershovo Rus. Fed. 43 J4
Yertsevo Rus. Fed. 40 G3
Yerupaja *mt.* Peru 200 A2
Yerushalayim Israel/West Bank *see* Jerusalem
Yeruslan *r.* Rus. Fed. 102 A2
Yerzhar Uzbek. *see* Gagarin
Yesenovichi Rus. Fed. 43 P4
Yesik Kazakh. 103 I4
Yesil' Kazakh. 103 F2
also spelt Esil
Yeşil Turkey 108 H1
Yeşildere *Burdur* Turkey 59 K11
Yeşildere *Gaziantep* Turkey 109 I1
Yeşilhisar Turkey 106 C3
Yeşilırmak *r.* Turkey 107 D2
Yeşilkent Turkey 109 I1
Yeşilova Turkey 106 B3
also known as Satırlar
Yeşilova Turkey *see* Sorgun
Yesiplevo Rus. Fed. 43 U5
Yessentuki Rus. Fed. 41 G7
Yessey Rus. Fed. 39 K3
Yeste Spain 55 I6
Yes Tor *hill* U.K. 47 H13
Yêtatang China *see* Baqên
Ye-U Myanmar 78 A3
Yeu, Île d' *i.* France 50 D6
Yevdokimovskoye Rus. Fed. *see* Krasnogvardeyskoye
Yevlakh Azer. *see* Yevlax
Yevlax Azer. 107 F2
also spelt Yevlakh
Yevpatoriya Ukr. 41 E7
Yevreyskaya Avtonomnaya Oblast' *admin. div.* Rus. Fed. 82 D2
English form Jewish Autonomous Oblast
Yexian *Henan* China 87 E1
also known as Kunyang
Yexian *Shandong* China *see* Laizhou
Yeygen'yevka Kazakh. 103 I4
Yeyik China 89 C4
Yeysk Rus. Fed. 41 F7
Yeyungou China 88 D3
Yezerishche, Ozero *l.* Belarus/Rus. Fed. 43 L6
Yezhou China *see* Jianshi
Yezhuga *r.* Rus. Fed. 40 H2
Yezo *i.* Japan *see* Hokkaidō
Yezyaryshcha Belarus 43 K6
Y Fenni U.K. *see* Abergavenny
Y Fflint U.K. *see* Flint
Yí *r.* Uruguay 204 F4
Yialí *i.* Greece *see* Gyali
Yialousa Cyprus *see* Aigialousa
Yi'an China 82 B3
Yianisádha *i.* Greece *see* Gianysada
Yiannitsá Greece *see* Giannitsa
Yibā, Wādī *watercourse* Saudi Arabia 104 C4
Yibin *Sichuan* China 86 C2
also known as Baixi
Yibin *Sichuan* China 86 C2
Yibug Caka *salt l.* China 89 D5
Yichang China 87 D2
Yicheng *Hubei* China 87 E2
Yicheng *Shanxi* China 85 F5
Yichuan *Henan* China 87 E1
Yichuan *Shaanxi* China 85 F5
also known as Danzhou
Yichun *Heilong.* China 82 C3
Yichun *Jiangxi* China 87 E3
Yidu China *see* Qingzhou
Yidun China 86 A2
also known as Dagxoi
Yifeng China 87 E2
also known as Xinchang
Yiggêtang China *see* Sêrwolungwa
Yi He *r. Henan* China 87 E1
Yi He *r. Shandong* China 87 F1
Yihuang China 87 F3
also known as Fenggang
Yijiang China *see* Yiyang
Yijun China 85 F5
Yilaha China 85 J1
Yilan China 82 C3
Yilan Taiwan *see* Ilan
Yıldız Dağları *mts* Turkey 106 A2
Yıldızeli Turkey 107 D3
also known as Yenıhan
Yilehuli Shan *mts* China 85 I1
Yiliang *Yunnan* China 86 B3
also known as Kuangyuan
Yiliang *Yunnan* China 86 C3
also known as Jiaokui
Yiliping China 84 B4
Yilliminning Australia 151 B7
Yilong *Heilong.* China 82 B3
Yilong *Sichuan* China 86 C2
also known as Jincheng
Yilong *Yunnan* China *see* Shiping
Yilong Hu *l.* China 86 B4
Yimatu He *r.* China 85 H3
Yimianpo China 82 C3
Yimin He *r.* China 85 H1
Yinan China 85 H5
also known as Jiehu
Yincheng China *see* Dexing
Yinchuan China 85 E4
Yindarlgooda, Lake *salt flat* Australia 151 C6
Yingawunarri Aboriginal Land *res.* Australia 148 A3
Yingcheng China 87 E2
Yingde China 87 E3
Ying He *r.* China 87 F1
Yingjing China 86 B2
also known as Yandao
Yingkou *Liaoning* China 85 I3
historically known as Newchwang
Yingkou *Liaoning* China *see* Dashiqiao
Yingpanshui China 84 E4
Yingshan *Hubei* China 87 E2
also known as Wenquan
Yingshan *Sichuan* China 86 C2
also known as Chengshou
Yingshang China 87 F1
Yingtan China 87 F2
Yingtaoyuan China *see* Fanxian
Yingxian China 85 G4
Yining *Jiangxi* China *see* Xiushui
Yining *Xinjiang* China 88 C3
also known as Gulja; *formerly known as* Kuldja
Yiningarra Aboriginal Land *res.* Australia 148 A4
Yinjiang China 87 D3
Yinkengxu China 87 E3
Yinmabin Myanmar 78 A3
Yinma He *r.* China 82 B3
Yinnyein Myanmar 78 B4
Yin Shan *mts* China 85 F3
Yinxian China *see* Ningbo
Yi'ong Zangbo *r.* China 89 F6
Yioúra *i.* Greece *see* Gioura
Yipinglang China 86 B3
Yiquan China *see* Meitan
Yira Chapéu, Monte *mt.* Brazil 207 I9
Yirga Alem Eth. 128 C3
Yirol Sudan 128 A3
Yirrkala Australia 148 C2
Yirshi China 85 H2
formerly known as Yirxie
Yirxie China *see* Yirshi
Yisa China *see* Honghe
Yishan *Guangxi* China *see* Yizhou
Yishan *Jiangsu* China *see* Guanyun
Yi Shan *mt.* China 85 H4
Yi Shan *mts* China 85 H4
Yishui China 85 H5
Yishun Sing. 76 [inset]
Yi Tchouma *well* Niger 125 I1
Yíthion Greece *see* Gytheio
Yitiaoshan China *see* Jingtai
Yitong China 82 B4
Yitong He *r.* China 82 B3
Yi Tu, Nam *r.* Myanmar 78 B3
Yitulihe China 85 I1
Yiwanquan China 84 B3
Yiwu China 84 B3
also known as Aratürük
Yiwulü Shan *mts* China 85 I3
Yixian *Anhui* China 87 F2
also known as Biyang
UNESCO World Heritage Site
Yixian *Hebei* China 85 G4
also known as Yizhou
Yixian *Liaoning* China 85 I3
also known as Yizhou
Yixing China 87 F2
Yixun He *r.* China 85 H3
Yiyang *Hunan* China 87 E2
Yiyang *Jiangxi* China 87 F2
also known as Yijiang
Yiyuan China 85 H4
also known as Nanma
Yizhang China 87 E3
Yizheng China 87 F1
Yizhou *Guangxi* China 87 D3
formerly known as Qingyuan *or* Yishan
Yizhou *Hebei* China *see* Yixian
Yizhou *Liaoning* China *see* Yixian
Yizra'el *country* Asia *see* Israel
Ylä-Keitele *l.* Fin. 44 N3
Ylämaa Fin. 45 O3
Yläne Fin. 45 M3
Ylihärmä Fin. 44 M3
Yli-Ii Fin. 44 N2
Yli-Kärppä Fin. 44 N2
Ylikiiminki Fin. 44 N2
Yli-Kitka *l.* Fin. 44 O2
Ylistaro Fin. 44 M3
Ylitornio Fin. 44 M2
Ylivieska Fin. 44 N2
Ylläs *hill* Fin. 44 N2
Ylöjärvi Fin. 45 M3
Ymer Nunatak Greenland 165 Q2
Ymer Ø *i.* Greenland 165 Q2
Ynykchanskiy Rus. Fed. 39 N3
Ynys Môn *i.* U.K. *see* Anglesey
Yoakum U.S.A. 179 C6
Yobe *state* Nigeria 125 H4
Yobetsu-dake *vol.* Japan 90 G3
Yoboki Djibouti 128 D2
Yogan, Cerro *mt.* Chile 205 C9
Yogoum *well* Chad 120 C5
Yogyakarta Indon. 77 E4
formerly spelt Jogjakarta
Yogyakarta *admin. dist.* Indon. 77 E5
Yoho National Park Canada 167 G5
UNESCO World Heritage Site
Yoichi Japan 90 G3
Yoichi-dake *mt.* Japan 90 G3
Yojoa, Lago de *l.* Hond. 186 B4
Yŏju S. Korea 83 B5
Yōka Japan 91 D7
Yokadouma Cameroon 125 I6
Yōkaichi Japan 91 E7
Yōkaichiba Japan 91 G7
Yokkaichi Japan 91 E7
Yoko Cameroon 125 I5
Yokohama *Aomori* Japan 90 G4
Yokohama *Kanagawa* Japan 91 F7
Yokosuka Japan 91 F7
Yokote Japan 90 G5
Yokotsu-dake *mt.* Japan 90 G4
Yola Nigeria 125 I4
Yolo U.S.A. 182 C3
Yolombo Dem. Rep. Congo 126 D5
Ýolöten Turkm. 103 E5
also spelt Yolöten; *formerly spelt* Iolotan'
Yolöten Turkm. *see* Ýolöten
Yoluk Mex. 185 I4
Yom, Mae Nam *r.* Thai. 78 C5
Yomou Guinea 124 C5
Yonago Japan 91 C7
Yŏnan N. Korea 83 B5
Yoneshiro-gawa *r.* Japan 90 G4
Yonezawa Japan 90 G6
Yŏng-am S. Korea 83 B6
Yong'an *Chongqing* China *see* Fengjie
Yong'an *Fujian* China 87 F3
Yongbei China *see* Yongsheng
Yongchang China 84 D4
Yongcheng China 87 F1
Yŏngch'ŏn S. Korea 83 C6
Yongchuan China 86 C2
Yongchun China 87 F3
also known as Taocheng
Yongdeng China 84 D4
Yongding *Fujian* China 87 F3
also known as Fengcheng
Yongding *Yunnan* China *see* Yongren
Yongding *Yunnan* China *see* Fumin
Yongding He *r.* China 85 H4
Yongfeng *Jiangxi* China 87 E3
also known as Wenfeng; *formerly known as* Jishui
Yongfeng *Jiangxi* China *see* Guangfeng
Yongfengqu China 88 D3
Yongfu China 87 D3
Yŏnggwang S. Korea 83 B6
Yŏnghŭng N. Korea 83 B5
Yŏnghŭng-man *b.* N. Korea 83 B5
Yongji China 82 B4
also known as Kouqian
Yongjia China 87 G2
also known as Shangtang
Yongjing *Gansu* China 84 D5
also known as Liujiaxia
Yongjing *Guizhou* China *see* Xifeng
Yongjing *Liaoning* China *see* Xifeng
Yongjin Qu *r.* China 85 G4
Yŏngju S. Korea 83 C5
Yongkang China 87 G2
Yongle *Shaanxi* China *see* Zhen'an
Yongle *Sichuan* China *see* Jiuzhaigou
Yongling China 82 B4
Yongnian China 85 G4
also known as Linmingguan
Yongning *Guangxi* China 87 D4
also known as Pumiao
Yongning *Jiangxi* China *see* Tonggu
Yongning *Ningxia* China 85 E4
also known as Yanghe
Yongning *Sichuan* China *see* Xuyong
Yongqing China *see* Qingshui
Yongren China 86 B3
also known as Yongding
Yŏngsan-gang *r.* S. Korea 83 B6
Yongshan China 86 B2
also known as Jingxin
Yongsheng China 86 B3
also known as Yongbei
Yongshou China 87 D1
also known as Jianjun
Yongshun China 87 D2
also known as Lingxi
Yongtai China 87 F3
also known as Zhangcheng
Yŏngwol S. Korea 83 C5
Yongxi China *see* Nayong
Yongxing *Hunan* China 87 E3
Yongxing *Jiangxi* China 87 E3
also known as Hechuan
Yongxiu China 87 E2
also known as Tujiabu
Yongzhou China 87 D3
Yonkers U.S.A. 177 L5
Yonne *r.* France 51 I4
Yoo Baba *well* Niger 125 I2
Yopal Col. 198 C3
Yopurga China 88 B4
Yordon Uzbek. 101 G1
also spelt Iordan *or* Yardan
Yordu Jammu and Kashmir 96 B2
York Australia 151 B6
York Canada 173 N7
York *r.* Canada 167 M4
York U.K. 47 K10
historically known as Eburacum
York *AL* U.S.A. 175 B5
York *NE* U.S.A. 178 C3
York *PA* U.S.A. 177 I6
York, Cape Australia 149 D1
York, Kap *c.* Greenland *see* Innaanganeq
York Downs Australia 149 D2
Yorke Peninsula Australia 146 C3
Yorkshire Dales National Park U.K. 47 J9
Yorkshire Wolds *hills* U.K. 47 L10
York Springs U.S.A. 177 H5
Yorkton Canada 167 K5
Yorktown U.S.A. 177 I8
Yoro Hond. 186 B4
Yoronga *i.* Indon. 75 D3
Yöröö Gol *r.* Mongolia 85 E1
Yosemite U.S.A. 176 A8
Yosemite National Park U.S.A. 182 E4
UNESCO World Heritage Site
Yosemite Village U.S.A. 182 E4
Yoshino-gawa *r.* Japan 91 C7
Yoshino-Kumano National Park Japan 91 E8
Yoshkar-Ola Rus. Fed. 40 H4
Yos Sudarso *i.* Indon. *see* Dolak, Pulau
Yŏsu S. Korea 83 B6
Yotau Bol. 201 E4
Yōtei-zan *mt.* Japan 90 G3
Yotvata Israel 108 G8
Youbou Canada 166 E5
Youdunzi China 88 E4
Youghal Ireland 47 E12
also spelt Eochaill
You Jiang *r.* China 87 D4
Youlin China 85 H4
Young Australia 147 F3
Young *r.* Australia 151 C7
Young Uruguay 204 F4
Young U.S.A. 183 N7
Younghusband, Lake *salt flat* Australia 146 C2
Younghusband Peninsula Australia 146 C3
Young Island Antarctica 223 K2
Young Nicks Head N.Z. 152 L6
Young Range *mts* N.Z. 153 D12
Youngstown Canada 167 I5
Youngstown U.S.A. 176 E4
Youngsville *NC* U.S.A. 176 G9
Youngsville *PA* U.S.A. 176 F4
Yountville U.S.A. 182 B3
Youshashan China 88 E4
You Shui *r.* China 87 D2
Youssoufia Morocco 122 C2
formerly known as Louis-Gentil
Youvarou Mali 124 D3
Youxi China 87 F3
Youxian China 87 E3
Youyang China 87 D2
also known as Zhongduo
Youyi China 82 C3
Youyi Feng *mt.* China/Rus. Fed. 88 D1
Youyu China 85 G4
also known as Liangjiayoufang
Yovon Tajik. 101 G2
also spelt Yavan
Yowah *watercourse* Australia 147 E2
Yowereena Hill Australia 151 B5
Yozgat Turkey 106 C3
Ypé-Jhú Para. 201 G5
Yppäri Fin. 44 N2
Ypres Belgium *see* Ieper
Ypsilanti U.S.A. 173 J8
Yreka U.S.A. 180 B4
Yrghyz Kazakh. *see* Irgiz
Yr Wyddfa *mt.* U.K. *see* Snowdon
Yser *r.* Belgium 51 I2
also known as Yser (France)
Yser *r.* France 51 I2
also known as IJzer (Belgium)
Yssingeaux France 51 K7
Ystad Sweden 45 K5
Ysyk-Köl Kyrg. *see* Balykchy
Ysyk-Köl *admin. div.* Kyrg. 103 I4
English form Issyk-Kul Oblast; *also known as* Issyk-Kul'skaya Oblast'

►Ysyk-Köl *salt l.* Kyrg. 103 I4
5th largest lake in Asia. Also known as Issyk-Kul', Ozero.
►►60–61 Asia Landscapes

Y Trallwng U.K. *see* Welshpool
Ytre Vinje Norway *see* Åmot
Ytyk-Kyuyel' Rus. Fed. 39 N3
Yu *i.* Indon. 75 D3
Yu'alliq, Jabal *mt.* Egypt 108 E7
Yuan'an China 87 D2
also known as Mingfeng
Yuanbao Shan *mt.* China 87 D3
Yuanjiang *Hunan* China 87 E2
Yuanjiang *Yunnan* China 86 B4
also known as Lijiang
Yuan Jiang *r. Hunan* China 87 D2
Yuan Jiang *r. Yunnan* China 86 B4
Yuanjiazhuang China *see* Foping
Yüanli Taiwan 87 G3
Yuanlin China 85 I1
Yuanling China 87 D2
Yuanma China *see* Yuanmou
Yuanmou China 86 B3
also known as Yuanma
Yuanping China 85 G4
Yuanqu China 85 F5
also known as Xincheng; *formerly known as* Liuzhangzhen
Yuanquan China *see* Anxi
Yuanshan China *see* Lianping
Yuanshanzi China 84 C4
Yuanyang China *see* Xinjie
Yuba City U.S.A. 182 C2
Yūbari Japan 90 G3
Yūbari-dake *mt.* Japan 90 H3
Yūbari-sanchi *mts* Japan 90 H3
Yubei China 86 C2
formerly known as Jiangbei
Yūbetsu Japan 90 H2
Yūbetsu-gawa *r.* Japan 90 H2
Yubu Sudan 126 E3
Yucaipa U.S.A. 183 G7
Yucatán *pen.* Mex. 185 H5
Yucatán *state* Mex. 185 H4
Yucatan Channel *strait* Cuba/Mex. 171 I7
Yucca U.S.A. 183 J7
Yucca Lake U.S.A. 183 H5
Yucca Valley U.S.A. 183 H7
Yucheng *Guangdong* China *see* Yunan
Yucheng *Henan* China 87 E1
Yucheng *Shandong* China 85 H4
Yudino *Moskovskaya Oblast'* Rus. Fed. 43 S5
Yudino *Yaroslavskaya Oblast'* Rus. Fed. 43 U3
Yudoma *r.* Rus. Fed. 39 N4
Yudu China 87 E3
also known as Gongjiang
Yuecheng China *see* Yuexi
Yuechi China 86 C2
also known as Jiulong
Yuelai China *see* Huachuan
Yueliang Pao *l.* China 85 I2
Yuendumu Australia 148 A4
Yuendumu Aboriginal Land *res.* Australia 148 A4
Yuen Long *Hong Kong* China 87 [inset]
Yueqing China 87 G2
Yuexi *Anhui* China 87 F2
also known as Tiantang
Yuexi *Sichuan* China 86 B2
also known as Yuecheng
Yueyang *Hunan* China 87 E2
also known as Rongjiawan
Yueyang *Hunan* China 87 E2
Yueyang *Sichuan* China *see* Anyue
Yug Rus. Fed. 40 K4
Yug *r.* Rus. Fed. 40 H3
Yugan China 87 F2
Yuğluk Dağı *mts* Turkey 108 E1
Yugo-Kamskiy Rus. Fed. 40 J4
Yugorsk Rus. Fed. 38 G3
formerly known as Komsomol'skiy
Yugorskiy Poluostrov *pen.* Rus. Fed. 40 L1
Yugorskiy Shar Rus. Fed. 40 L1

►Yugoslavia
Former European country. Up to 1993 included Bosnia-Herzegovina, Croatia, Macedonia and Slovenia. Renamed as Serbia and Montenegro in 2003.

Yugud-Vayskiy Natsional'nyy Park *nat. park* Rus. Fed. 40 K2
UNESCO World Heritage Site
Yuhang China 87 G2
Yu He *r.* China 85 G4
Yuhu China *see* Eryuan
Yuhuan China 87 G2
also known as Huanshan
Yuhuang Ding *mt.* China 85 H4
Yuin Australia 151 B5
Yujiang China 87 F2
also known as Dengjiabu
Yu Jiang *r.* China 87 D4
Yujin China *see* Qianwei
Yukagirskoye Ploskogor'ye *plat.* Rus. Fed. 39 P3
Yukamenskoye Rus. Fed. 40 J4
Yukarı Sakarya Ovaları *plain* Turkey 106 B3
Yukarısarıkaya Turkey 106 C3
Yukhavichy Belarus 43 J5
Yukhmachi Rus. Fed. 40 I5
Yukhnov Rus. Fed. 43 Q7
Yukhovo Rus. Fed. 43 L5
Yuki Dem. Rep. Congo 126 C5
Yuki Japan 91 C7

►Yukon *r.* Canada/U.S.A. 164 C3
5th longest river in North America.
►►154–155 North America Landscapes

Yukon-Charley Rivers National Preserve *nature res.* U.S.A. 164 E3
Yukon Crossing Canada 166 B2
Yukon Territory *admin. div.* Canada 166 C2
Yüksekova Turkey 107 F3
also known as Dize
Yukuhashi Japan 91 B8
Yulara Australia 148 A5
Yuldybayevo Rus. Fed. 102 D1
Yule *r.* Australia 150 B4
Yuleba Australia 149 F5
Yuli China 88 D3
also known as Lopnur
Yüli Taiwan 87 G4
Yulin *Guangxi* China 87 D4
Yulin *Shaanxi* China 85 F4
Yulong Xueshan *mt.* China 86 B3
Yuma *AZ* U.S.A. 183 J9
Yuma *CO* U.S.A. 178 B3
Yuma Desert U.S.A. 183 J9
Yumaguzino Rus. Fed. 102 D1
Yumbarra Conservation Park *nature res.* Australia 146 B2
Yumbe Uganda 128 A4
Yumbi *Bandundu* Dem. Rep. Congo 126 C5
Yumbi *Maniema* Dem. Rep. Congo 126 E5
Yumbo Col. 198 B4
Yumen China 84 C4
also known as Laojunmiao
Yumendongzhan China 84 C4
Yumenguan China 84 B3
Yumenzhen China 84 C3
Yumin China 88 C2
also known as Karabura
Yumt Uul *mt.* Mongolia 84 C2
Yumurtalık Turkey 108 G1
Yuna Australia 151 A6
Yuna *r.* Dom. Rep. 187 F3
Yunak Turkey 106 B3
Yunan China 87 D4
also known as Yucheng
Yunchara Bol. 200 D5
Yuncheng *Shandong* China 85 G5
Yuncheng *Shanxi* China 87 D1
Yundamindera Australia 151 C6
Yunfu China 87 E4
Yungas *reg.* Bol. 200 D4
Yungay Chile 200 C6
Yungayo Peru 200 C4
Yungui Gaoyuan *plat.* China 86 B3
Yunhe *Jiangsu* China *see* Pizhou
Yunhe *Yunnan* China *see* Heqing
Yunhe *Zhejiang* China 87 F2
Yunjinghong China *see* Jinghong
Yunkai Dashan *mts* China 87 D4
Yunkanjini Aboriginal Land *res.* Australia 148 A4
Yunling China *see* Yunxiao
Yun Ling *mts* China 86 A3
Yunmeng China 87 E2
Yunnan *prov.* China 86 B3
UNESCO World Heritage Site
Yun Shui *r.* China 87 E2
Yunta Australia 146 C3
Yunt Dağı *mt.* Turkey 108 D1
Yunuslar Turkey 59 K9
Yunwu Shan *mts* China 87 D4
Yunxi *Hubei* China 87 D1
Yunxi *Sichuan* China *see* Yanting
Yunxian *Hubei* China 87 D1
Yunxian *Yunnan* China 86 B3
also known as Aihua
Yunxiao China 87 F4
also known as Yunling
Yun'yakha *r.* Rus. Fed. 40 L2
Yunyang *Chongqing* China 87 D2
Yunyang *Henan* China 87 E1
Yupin China *see* Pingbian
Yuping *Guizhou* China *see* Libo
Yuping *Guizhou* China 87 D3
also known as Pingxi
Yuqian China 87 F2
Yuqing China 87 C3
also known as Baini
Yura Bol. 200 D5
Yura *r.* Bol. 200 D5
Yura Peru 200 C4
Yuracyacu Peru 198 B6
Yura-gawa *r.* Japan 91 D7
Yūrappu-dake *mt.* Japan 90 G3
Yuratsishki Belarus 42 G7
Yuraygir National Park Australia 147 G2
Yurba Co *l.* China 89 D5
Yurga Rus. Fed. 80 C1
Yurimaguas Peru 198 B6
Yurino Rus. Fed. 40 H4
Yurla Rus. Fed. 40 J4
Yurungkax He *r.* China 89 C4
Yur'ya Rus. Fed. 40 I4
Yur'yakha *r.* Rus. Fed. 40 J2
Yuryev Estonia *see* Tartu
Yur'yevets *Ivanovskaya Oblast'* Rus. Fed. 40 G4
Yur'yevets *Vladimirskaya Oblast'* Rus. Fed. 43 V5
Yur'yev-Pol'skiy Rus. Fed. 43 U5
Yuscarán Hond. 186 B4
Yushan *Fujian* China 87 F3
Yushan *Jiangxi* China 87 F2
also known as Bingxi
Yü Shan *mt.* Taiwan 87 G4
Yushan Liedao *is* China 87 G2
Yushe China 85 G4
Yushino Rus. Fed. 40 J1
Yushkozero Rus. Fed. 40 E2
Yushu *Jilin* China 82 B3
Yushu *Qinghai* China 86 A1
also known as Gyêgu
Yushugou China 88 D3
Yushut *r.* Rus. Fed. 40 I4
Yushuwan China *see* Huaihua
Yusta Rus. Fed. 102 A3
formerly known as Trudovoy
Yusufeli Turkey 107 E2
Yusuhara Japan 91 C8
Yus'va Rus. Fed. 40 J4
Yuta West Bank *see* Yaṭṭa
Yutai China 87 F1
also known as Guting
Yutian *Hebei* China 85 H4
Yutian *Xinjiang* China 89 C4
also known as Keriya *or* Muhala
Yutpundji Djindiniwirritj *res.* Australia *see* Roper Bar Aboriginal Land
Yuty Para. 201 F6
Yuva Turkey 108 A1
Yuwang China 85 E4
Yuxi *Guizhou* China *see* Daozhen
Yuxi *Hubei* China 87 D2
Yuxi *Yunnan* China 86 B3
Yuxiakou China 87 D2
Yuxian *Hebei* China 85 G4
also known as Yuzhou
Yuxian *Shanxi* China 85 G4
Yuxikou China 87 F2
Yuyangguan China 87 D2
Yuyao China 87 G2
Yuyue China *see* Jiayu
Yuza Japan 90 F5
Yuzawa Japan 90 G5
Yuzha Rus. Fed. 40 G4
Yuzhno-Alichurskiy, Khrebet *mts* Tajik. *see* Alichuri Janubí, Qatorkŭhi
Yuzhno-Kamyshovyy Khrebet *ridge* Rus. Fed. 82 F3
Yuzhno-Kazakhstanskaya Oblast' *admin. div.* Kazakh. *see* Yuzhnyy Kazakhstan
Yuzhno-Kuril'sk Rus. Fed. 82 G3
also known as Utashinai
Yuzhno-Muyskiy Khrebet *mts* Rus. Fed. 81 I1
Yuzhno-Sakhalinsk Rus. Fed. 82 F3
Yuzhno-Sukhokumsk Rus. Fed. 41 H7
Yuzhnoukrayinsk Ukr. 41 D7
also spelt Južnoukrajinsk

Yuzhnyy Respublika Kalmykiya - Khalm'g-Tangch Rus. Fed. see Adyk
Yuzhnyy Rostovskaya Oblast' Rus. Fed. 41 G7
Yuzhnyy, Mys hd Rus. Fed. 39 P4
Yuzhnyy Altay, Khrebet mts Kazakh. 88 D1
Yuzhnyy Kazakhstan admin. div. Kazakh. 103 G4 English form South Kazakhstan Oblast; also known as Ongtüstik Qazaqstan Oblysy; formerly known as Chimkentskaya Oblast'; long form Yuzhno-Kazakhstanskaya Oblast'
Yuzhnyy Ural mts Rus. Fed. 102 D1 English form Southern Urals
Yuzhong China 84 E5
Yuzhou Hebei China see Yuxian
Yuzhou Henan China 87 E1
Yuzkuduk Uzbek. see Yuzquduq
Yuzovka Ukr. see Donets'k
Yuzquduq Uzbek. 103 E4 also spelt Yuzkuduk
Yverdon Switz. 51 M6
Yvetot France 50 G3
Ywamun Myanmar 78 A3
Ywathit Myanmar 78 B4
Ýylanly Turkm. 102 D4 formerly spelt Il'yaly
Yzerfonteinpunt pt S. Africa 132 C10
Yzeure France 51 J6

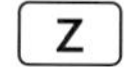

Za, Oued r. Morocco 123 E2
Zaaimansdal S. Africa 132 H10
Zaamin Uzbek. see Zomin
Zaandam Neth. 48 B3
Zăbala r. Romania 58 H3
Žabalj Vojvodina, Srbija Serb. and Mont. 58 B3
Zāb al Kabīr, Nahr az r. Iraq 107 E3 English form Great Zab
Zabalova Latvia 42 I4
Zāb aş Şaghīr, Nahr az r. Iraq 107 E4 English form Little Zab
Zabaykal'sk Rus. Fed. 85 H1 formerly known as Otpor
Zab-e Kuchek r. Iran 100 A3
Zabia Dem. Rep. Congo 126 E4
Zabīd Yemen 104 C5 UNESCO World Heritage Site
Zabīd, Wādī watercourse Yemen 104 C5
Ząbkowice Śląskie Poland 49 N5
Zabłudów Poland 49 U2
Żabno Poland 49 R5
Zabok Croatia 56 H2
Zābol Iran 101 E4 also known as Nasratabad
Zābolī Iran 101 E5 also known as Magas
Zabor'ye Rus. Fed. 43 Q2
Zabqung China 89 D6 also known as Gyêwa
Zăbrani Romania 58 C2
Zabré Burkina 125 E4
Zabrze Poland 49 P5 historically known as Hindenburg
Zābul prov. Afgh. 101 F3
Zaburun'ye Kazakh. 102 B3
Zacapa Guat. 185 H6
Zacapoaxtla Mex. 185 F5
Zacapu Mex. 185 E5
Zacatecas Mex. 185 E4 UNESCO World Heritage Site
Zacatecas state Mex. 185 E4
Zacatecoluca El Salvador 185 H6
Zacatepec Morelos Mex. 185 F5
Zacatepec Oaxaca Mex. 185 F5
Zacatlán Mex. 185 F5
Zachagansk Kazakh. 102 B2
Zacharo Greece 59 C11 also spelt Zakháro
Zacoalco Mex. 184 E4
Zacualtipán Mex. 185 F4
Zacynthus i. Greece see Zakynthos
Zad, Col du pass Morocco 122 D2
Zadar Croatia 56 H4 formerly known as Zara; historically known as Iadera
Zadarski Kanal sea chan. Croatia 56 H4
Zadetkale Kyun i. Myanmar 79 B6 also known as St Luke's Island
Zadetkyi Kyun i. Myanmar 79 B6 also known as St Matthew's Island
Zadi Myanmar 79 B5
Zadoi China 97 G2 also known as Sahu
Zadonsk Rus. Fed. 43 T9
Zadran reg. Afgh. 101 G3
Za'farānah Egypt 121 G2
Za'farānah, Ra's pt Egypt 108 D8
Zafarwal Pak. 101 H3
Zafer Adaları is Cyprus see Kleides Islands
Zafer Burnu c. Cyprus see Apostolos Andreas, Cape
Ẓafīrī, Birkat aẓ waterhole Saudi Arabia 109 O8
Zafora i. Greece 59 H12
Zafra Spain 54 E6
Zag Morocco 122 C3
Żagań Poland 49 M4
Žagarė Lith. 42 E5
Zagazig Egypt see Az Zaqāzīq
Zaghdeh well Iran 100 D3
Zāgheh Iran 100 B3
Zāgheh-ye Bālā Iran 100 A3
Zaghouan Tunisia 123 H1
Zagon Romania 58 H3
Zagora Greece 59 E9
Zagora Morocco 122 D3
Zagorje ob Savi Slovenia 56 G2
Zagorsk Rus. Fed. see Sergiyev Posad
Zagórz Poland 49 T6
Zagrazhden Bulg. 58 F7

►Zagreb Croatia 56 H3
Capital of Croatia. Historically known as Agram.

Zagros, Kūhhā-ye mts Iran see Zagros Mountains
Zagros Mountains Iran 100 A3 also known as Zagros, Kūhhā-ye
Žagubica Srbija Serb. and Mont. 58 C4
Zagunao China see Lixian
Za'gya Zangbo r. China 89 E6
Zahamena, Réserve de nature res. Madag. 131 [inset] K3
Ẓaḥawn, Wādī r. Yemen 105 E4
Zāhedān Balūchestān va Sīstān Iran 101 E4 also known as Duzdab
Zāhedān Fārs Iran 100 C4
Zahlé Lebanon 108 G4
Zähmet Turkm. 103 E5 also spelt Zakhmet
Ẓahrān Saudi Arabia 104 C4
Ẓahrat al Baṭn des. Iraq 109 N6
Zahrez Chergui salt pan Alg. 55 O9
Zaiceva Latvia 42 I4
Žaiginys Lith. 42 E6
Zaigrayevo Rus. Fed. 85 F1
Ẓā'in, Jabal hill Saudi Arabia 104 D3
Zaindeh r. Iran 100 C3
Zainlha China see Xiaojin
Zair Uzbek. see Zoir
Zaire country Africa see Congo, Democratic Republic of the
Zaire prov. Angola 127 B6
Zaïre r. Congo/Dem. Rep. Congo see Congo
Zaječar Srbija Serb. and Mont. 58 D5
Zaka Zimbabwe 131 F4
Zakamensk Rus. Fed. 84 D1 formerly known as Gorodok
Zakataly Azer. see Zaqatala
Zakháro Greece see Zacharo
Zakharovo Rus. Fed. 43 U7
Zakhmet Turkm. see Zähmet
Zākhō Iraq 107 E3
Zakhodnyaya Dzvina r. Europe see Zapadnaya Dvina
Zakhrebetnoye Rus. Fed. 38 D3
Zákinthos i. Greece see Zakynthos
Zakopane Poland 49 Q6
Zakouma Chad 126 C2
Zakouma, Parc National de nat. park Chad 126 C2
Zakros Greece 59 H13
Zakwaski, Mount Canada 166 F5
Zakynthos Greece 59 B11
Zakynthos i. Greece 59 B11 also spelt Zákinthos; historically known as Zacynthus
Zala Angola 127 B6
Zala r. Romania 49 O9
Zalābīyah tourist site Syria 109 K2
Zalaegerszeg Hungary 49 N9
Zalai-domsag hills Hungary 49 N9
Zalakomár Hungary 49 O9
Zalamea de la Serena Spain 54 F6
Zalanga Nigeria 125 H4
Zalantun China 85 I2 also known as Butha Qi
Zalaszentgrót Hungary 49 O9
Zalău Romania 58 E1
Zalavas Lith. 42 H7
Žalec Slovenia 56 H2
Zalegoshch' Rus. Fed. 43 R9
Zaleski U.S.A. 176 C6
Zales'ye Rus. Fed. 43 R3
Zalewo Poland 49 Q2
Ẓalim Saudi Arabia 104 C3
Zalingei Sudan 120 D6
Ẓalmā, Jabal aẓ mt. Saudi Arabia 104 B2
Zaltan, Jabal hills Libya 120 C2
Zaluch'ye Rus. Fed. 43 M4
Zama Japan 91 F7
Zama Niger 125 F3
Zama City Canada 166 G3
Zamakh Saudi Arabia 105 D4
Zamani S. Africa 133 N4
Zamanti r. Turkey 106 C3
Zambales Mountains Phil. 74 B3
Zambeze r. Africa see Zambezi

►Zambezi r. Africa 131 G2
4th longest river in Africa. Also spelt Zambeze.
►►110–111 Africa Landscapes

Zambezi Zambia 127 D8
Zambézia prov. Moz. 131 H3
Zambezi Escarpment Zambia/Zimbabwe 127 E9
Zambezi National Park Zimbabwe 131 E3
►Zambia country Africa 127 E8 formerly known as Northern Rhodesia
►►114–115 Africa Countries
►►116–117 Africa Aids
Zamboanga Phil. 74 B5
Zamboanga Peninsula Phil. 74 B5
Zamboanguita Phil. 74 B4
Zambrów Poland 49 T3
Zambue Moz. 131 F2
Zamfara state Nigeria 125 G3
Zamfara watercourse Nigeria 125 G3
Zamīndāvar reg. Afgh. 101 E4
Zamlat Amagraj hills W. Sahara 122 B4
Zamogil'ye Rus. Fed. 42 I3
Zamora Ecuador 198 B6
Zamora r. Ecuador 198 B5
Zamora Spain 54 F3
Zamora-Chinchipe prov. Ecuador 198 B5
Zamora de Hidalgo Mex. 185 E5
Zamość Poland 53 G1 formerly known as Zamost'ye UNESCO World Heritage Site
Zamost'ye Poland see Zamość
Zamtang China 86 B1 also known as Rangke; formerly known as Gamda
Zamuro, Punta pt Venez. 187 F5
Zamuro, Sierra del mts Venez. 199 F3
Zamzam, Wādī watercourse Libya 120 B2
Zanaga Congo 126 B5
Zanatepec Mex. 185 G5
Záncara r. Spain 55 H5
Zancle Sicily Italy see Messina
Zanda China 89 B6 also known as Toling
Zandamela Moz. 131 G5
Zanderij Suriname 199 H3
Zandvliet Belgium 51 K1
Zanesville U.S.A. 176 C6
Zangasso Mali 124 D3 formerly spelt Sangasso
Zangelan Azer. see Zängilan
Zängilan Azer. 107 F3 also spelt Zangelan; formerly known as Pirchevan
Zangla Jammu and Kashmir 96 C2
Zangsêr Kangri mt. China 89 D5
Zanhuang China 85 G4
Zanjān Iran 100 B2
Zanjān prov. Iran 100 B2
Zanjān Rūd r. Iran 107 F3
Ẓannah, Jabal aẓ hill U.A.E. 105 F2
Zanskar r. India 96 C2
Zanskar reg. Jammu and Kashmir 96 C2 also spelt Zaskar
Zanskar Mountains India 96 C2
Zanthus Australia 151 C6
Zantiébougou Mali 124 D4
Zanzibar Tanz. 129 C6 UNESCO World Heritage Site
Zanzibar Channel Tanz. 129 C6
Zanzibar Island Tanz. 129 C6
Zanzibar North admin. reg. Tanz. 129 C6 also known as Unguja North
Zanzibar South admin. reg. Tanz. 129 C6 also known as Unguja South
Zanzibar West admin. reg. Tanz. 129 C6 also known as Unguja West
Zaokskiy Rus. Fed. 43 S7
Zaonia Mornag Tunisia 57 C12
Zaoro-Songou Cent. Afr. Rep. 126 C3
Zaoshi Hubei China 87 E2
Zaoshi Hunan China 87 E3
Zaouatallaz Alg. 123 H4 formerly known as Fort Gardel
Zaouet el Kahla Alg. see Bordj Omer Driss
Zaouiet Kounta Alg. 123 E4
Zaoyang China 87 E1
Zaoyangzhan China 87 E1
Zaō-zan vol. Japan 90 G5
Zaozernyy Kazakh. 103 G1 formerly known as Aysarinskoye or Aysary
Zaozernyy Rus. Fed. 80 E1
Zaozer'ye Rus. Fed. 43 T4
Zaozhuang China 87 F1
Zap r. Turkey 107 E3
Zapadna Morava r. Serb. and Mont. 58 C5
Zapadnaya Dvina r. Europe 43 L6 English form Western Dvina; also known as Zakhodnyaya Dzvina
Zapadnaya Dvina Rus. Fed. 43 N5
Zapadni Rodopi mts Bulg. 58 E7
Zapadno-Kazakhstanskaya Oblast' admin. div. Kazakh. see Zapadnyy Kazakhstan
Zapadno-Sakhalinskiy Khrebet mts Rus. Fed. 82 F2
Zapadno-Sibirskaya Nizmennost' plain Rus. Fed. see West Siberian Plain
Zapadno-Sibirskaya Ravnina plain Rus. Fed. see West Siberian Plain
Zapadnyy Alamedin, Pik mt. Kyrg. 103 H4
Zapadnyy Berezovyy, Ostrov i. Rus. Fed. 43 J1
Zapadnyy Chink Ustyurta esc. Kazakh. 102 C4
Zapadnyy Kazakhstan admin. div. Kazakh. 102 B2 English form West Kazakhstan Oblast; also known as Batys Qazaqstan Oblysy; formerly known as Ural'skaya Oblast'; long form Zapadno-Kazakhstanskaya Oblast'
Zapadnyy Sayan reg. Rus. Fed. 80 D2 English form Western Sayan Mountains
Zapala Arg. 204 C5
Zapardiel r. Spain 54 F3
Zapata U.S.A. 179 C7
Zapata, Península de pen. Cuba 186 C2
Zapatoca Col. 198 C3
Zapatón r. Spain 54 E6
Zapatoza, Ciénaga de l. Col. 198 C2
Zapiga Chile 200 C4
Zaplyus'ye Rus. Fed. 43 K3
Zăpodeni Romania 58 I2
Zapolyarnyy Murmanskaya Oblast' Rus. Fed. 44 O1
Zapolyarnyy Respublika Komi Rus. Fed. 40 L2
Zapol'ye Pskovskaya Oblast' Rus. Fed. 43 K3
Zapol'ye Vologod. Obl. Rus. Fed. 43 R2
Zaporizhzhya Ukr. 41 E7 also spelt Zaporozh'ye; formerly known as Aleksandrovsk or Oleksandrivs'k
Zaporozhskoye Rus. Fed. 43 L1
Zaporozh'ye Ukr. see Zaporizhzhya
Zapponeta Italy 56 H7
Zaprešić Croatia 56 H3
Zaprudnya Rus. Fed. 43 S5
Zaprudy Belarus 42 F9
Zapug China 89 C5
Zaqatala Azer. 107 F2 also spelt Zakataly
Zaqāzīq Egypt see Az Zaqāzīq
Zaqên China 97 G2
Zaqqui Libya 120 C2
Za Qu r. China 86 A2
Zaqungngomar mt. China 89 E5
Zara China see Moinda
Zara Croatia see Zadar
Zara Turkey 107 D3
Zarafshan Uzbek. see Zarafshon
Zarafshon Tajik. 101 G2 also spelt Zeravshan
Zarafshon r. Tajik. 101 G2 also spelt Zeravshan
Zarafshon Uzbek. 103 F4 also spelt Zarafshan
Zarafshon r. Uzbek. 103 E5 also spelt Zeravshan
Zarafshon, Qatorkŭhi mts Tajik. 101 F2 also known as Zeravshanskiy Khrebet
Zaragoza Col. 198 C3
Zaragoza Mex. 185 E2
Zaragoza Spain 55 K3 English form Saragossa; historically known as Caesaraugusta
Zarand Kermān Iran 100 D4
Zarand Markazī Iran 100 B3
Zarandului, Munții hills Romania 58 D2
Zarang China 89 B6
Zaranj Afgh. 101 E4
Zarasai Lith. 42 H6
Zárate Arg. 204 F4
Zarautz Spain 55 I1
Zaraysk Rus. Fed. 43 T7
Zaraza Venez. 199 E2
Zarbdor Uzbek. 103 G4
Zärdab Azer. 107 F2
Zardak Iran 100 D3
Zard Kuh mts Iran 100 B3
Zarechensk Rus. Fed. 40 D2
Zarechka Belarus 42 G9
Zarechnyy Respublika Buryatiya Rus. Fed. 85 E1
Zarechnyy Ryazanskaya Oblast' Rus. Fed. 43 U8 formerly known as Pobedinskiy
Zāreh Iran 100 B3
Zarembo Island U.S.A. 166 C3
Žarėnai Lith. 42 D6
Zarghat Saudi Arabia 104 C2
Zarghūn Shahr Afgh. 101 G3
Zargun mt. Pak. 101 F4
Zari Afgh. 101 F3
Zaria Nigeria 125 G4
Zariaspa Afgh. see Balkh
Zarichne Ukr. 41 C6
Zarīneh Rūd r. Iran 100 A2
Zarmardan Afgh. 101 E3
Zărnești Romania 58 G3
Żarnowieckie, Jezioro l. Poland 49 P1
Zarqā' Jordan see Az Zarqā'
Zarqā', Nahr az r. Jordan 108 G5
Zarqā' Mā'īn, Wādī r. Jordan 108 G6
Zarqān Iran 100 C4
Zarubino Novgorodskaya Oblast' Rus. Fed. 43 O3
Zarubino Primorskiy Kray Rus. Fed. 82 C4
Żary Poland 49 M4
Zarzaïtine Alg. 123 H3
Zarzal Col. 198 B3
Zarzis Tunisia 123 H2
Zasa Latvia 42 G5
Zashchita Kazakh. 88 C1
Zasheyek Rus. Fed. 44 O2
Zaskar reg. Jammu and Kashmir see Zanskar
Zaskarki Belarus 43 J6
Zaslawkaye Vodaskhovishcha resr Belarus 42 I8
Zaslawye Belarus 42 I7
Zastron S. Africa 133 L7
Za'tarī, Wādī az watercourse Jordan 109 H5
Žatec Czech Rep. 49 K5
Zaterechnyy Rus. Fed. 107 F1
Zatobol'sk Kazakh. 103 E1
Zatoka Ukr. 58 L2 formerly known as Bugaz
Zatyshshya Ukr. 58 K1
Zaunguzskiye Karakumy des. Turkm. see Üngüz Angyrsyndaky Garagum
Zautla Mex. 185 F5
Zavadovskiy Island Antarctica 223 F2
Zavareh Iran 100 C3
Zavety Il'icha Rus. Fed. 82 F2
Zavidoviči Bos.-Herz. 56 K4
Zavidovskiy Zapovednik nature res. Rus. Fed. 43 R5
Zavitaya Rus. Fed. see Zavitinsk
Zavitinsk Rus. Fed. 82 C2 formerly known as Zavitaya
Zavodskoy Rus. Fed. see Komsomol'skiy
Zavolzhsk Rus. Fed. 40 G4 formerly known as Zavolzh'ye
Zavolzh'ye Rus. Fed. see Zavolzhsk
Závora, Ponta pt Moz. 131 G5
Zavutstsye Belarus 42 J6
Zavyachellye Belarus 43 J6
Zav'yalova, Ostrov i. Rus. Fed. 39 P4
Zav'yalovo Rus. Fed. 103 J1
Zawa Qinghai China 84 D4
Zawa Xinjiang China 96 C1
Zawadzkie Poland 49 P5
Zawgyi r. Myanmar 78 B3
Zawiercie Poland 49 Q5
Zawīlah Libya 120 B3
Zāwīyah, Jabal az hills Syria 109 H2
Zāwiyat Masūs Libya 120 D2
Zāwiyat Shammās pt Egypt 106 A5
Zāwiyat Sīdī Ghāzī Egypt 108 B6
Zawlīyah, Jiddat az plain Oman 105 F3
Zay r. Rus. Fed. 40 I5
Zaydī, Wādī az watercourse Syria 109 H5
Zaysan Kazakh. 88 D2
Zaysan, Lake Kazakh. 88 C1 also known as Zaysan, Ozero
Zaysan, Ozero l. Kazakh. see Zaysan, Lake
Zaytsevo Rus. Fed. 43 J4
Zayü Xizang China see Gyigang
Zayü Xizang China 86 A2
Zayü Qu r. China/India 86 A2 also known as Lohil or Luhit
Zayyr Uzbek. see Zoir
Zazafotsy Madag. 131 [inset] J4
Zazir, Oued watercourse Alg. 123 G6
Zbąszynek Poland 49 M3
Zborište mt. Serb. and Mont. 58 A5
Žďár nad Sázavou Czech Rep. 49 M6
Žďárské vrchy hills Czech Rep. 49 M6
Zdolbuniv Ukr. 41 C6 also spelt Zdolbunov
Zdolbunov Ukr. see Zdolbuniv
Zduńska Wola Poland 49 P4
Zealand i. Denmark 45 J5 also spelt Sjælland
Zēbāk Afgh. 101 G2
Zeballos mt. Arg. 205 C7
Zeballos Canada 166 E5
Zēbār Iraq 107 F3
Zebargad, Gezîret i. Egypt 104 B3 English form Zebirget Island
Zebirget Island Egypt see Zebargad, Gezîret
Žebrák Czech Rep. 49 K6
Zebulon GA U.S.A. 175 C5
Zebulon KY U.S.A. 176 C8
Zebulon NC U.S.A. 174 E5
Zeebrugge Belgium 51 J1
Zeehan Australia 147 E5
Zeeland U.S.A. 172 G8
Zeerust S. Africa 133 K2
Ẕefat Israel 108 G5 also known as Safad; also spelt Tsefat
Zegrzyńskie, Jezioro l. Poland 49 S3
Zehdenick Germany 49 K3
Zeil, Mount Australia 148 B4 formerly spelt Ziel, Mount
Žeimelis Lith. 42 F5
Zeitz Germany 48 J4
Zêkog China 86 B1 also known as Sonag
Zela Turkey see Zile
Żelechów Poland 49 S4
Zelena Gora mt. Bos.-Herz. 56 J5
Zelená hora tourist site Czech Rep. 49 N6 UNESCO World Heritage Site
Zelenaya Roshcha Kazakh. 103 H1
Zelengora mts Bos.-Herz. 56 K5
Zelennik Rus. Fed. 40 H3
Zelenoborskiy Rus. Fed. 44 P2
Zelenodol'sk Rus. Fed. 40 I5
Zelenogorsk Rus. Fed. 43 K1
Zelenograd Rus. Fed. 43 S5
Zelenogradsk Rus. Fed. 42 B7 historically known as Cranz
Zelenokumsk Rus. Fed. 41 G7 formerly known as Sovetskoye or Vorontsovo-Aleksandrovskoye
Zelentsovo Rus. Fed. 40 H4
Zelenyy, Ostrov i. Rus. Fed. 82 G4 also known as Shibotsu-jima
Zelenyy Gay Kazakh. 103 G2
Železné hory hills Czech Rep. 49 M6
Zelienople U.S.A. 176 E5
Želiezovce Slovakia 49 P7
Zelina Croatia 56 I3 formerly known as Sveti Ivan Zelina
Zelinggou China 84 C4
Želivka, Vodní nádrž resr Czech Rep. 49 L6
Željin mt. Serb. and Mont. 58 B5
Zell am See Austria 49 J8
Zellerrain pass Austria 49 M8
Zelów Poland 49 Q4
Zeltiņi Latvia 42 H4
Zel'va Belarus 42 F8
Žemaičių Naumiestis Lith. 42 C6
Žemaitijos nacionalinis parkas nat. park Lith. 42 C5
Zêmdasam China 86 B1
Zemen Bulg. 58 D6
Zemeș Romania 58 H2
Zemetchino Rus. Fed. 41 G5
Zémio Cent. Afr. Rep. 126 E3
Zemmora Alg. 55 L9
Zémongo, Réserve de Faune de nature res. Cent. Afr. Rep. 126 E3
Zempleni park Hungary 49 S7
Zemplínska šírava l. Slovakia 49 T7
Zempoaltépetl, Nudo de mt. Mex. 185 G5
Zemtsy Rus. Fed. 43 N5
Zemun Srbija Serb. and Mont. 58 B4
Zênda China 86 A1
Zengcheng China 87 E4
Zengfeng Shan mt. China 82 C4
Zenica Bos.-Herz. 56 J4
Ẕenifim watercourse Israel 108 F7
Zenta Vojvodina, Srbija Serb. and Mont. see Senta
Zentsūji Japan 91 C7
Zenyeh Afgh. 101 G3
Zenzach Alg. 55 O9
Žepče Bos.-Herz. 56 K4
Zephyr Cove U.S.A. 182 E2
Zepu China 88 B4 formerly known as Poskam
Zeraf, Bahr el r. Sudan 128 A2
Zeravshan Tajik. see Zarafshon
Zeravshan r. Tajik. see Zarafshon
Zeravshan r. Uzbek. see Zarafshon
Zeravshanskiy Khrebet mts Tajik. see Zarafshon, Qatorkŭhi
Zereh, Gowd-e depr. Afgh. 101 E4
Zereh, Gowd-e plain Afgh. 101 E4
Zerenda Kazakh. 103 G1
Zeribet el Oued Alg. 123 G2
Żerków Poland 49 O3
Zermatt Switz. 51 N6
Zernograd Rus. Fed. 41 G7 formerly known as Zernovoy
Zernovoy Rus. Fed. see Zernograd
Zestafoni Georgia see Zestap'oni
Zestap'oni Georgia 107 E2 also spelt Zestafoni
Zeta r. Serb. and Mont. 58 A6
Zêtang China 89 E6
Zetea Romania 58 G2
Zeulenroda Germany 48 I5
Zeven Germany 48 G2
Zevenaar Neth. 48 D4
Zevgolatio Greece 59 D11
Zeya Rus. Fed. 82 B1
Zeya r. Rus. Fed. 82 B2
Zeydābād Iran 100 C4
Zeydar Iran 100 D2
Zeynalābād Iran 100 D4
Zeyskiy Zapovednik nature res. Rus. Fed. 82 B1
Zeysko-Bureinskaya Vpadina depr. Rus. Fed. 82 C2
Zeyskoye Vodokhranilishche resr Rus. Fed. 82 B1
Zeytin Burnu c. Cyprus see Elaia, Cape
Zeytindağ Turkey 59 I10
Zêzere r. Port. 54 C5
Zgharta Lebanon 108 G3
Zgierz Poland 49 Q4 historically known as Sgiersch
Zhabinka Belarus 42 F9
Zhadove Ukr. 43 N9
Zhaggo China see Luhuo
Zhaglag China 86 A1
Zhag'yab China 86 A2 also known as Yêndum
Zhailma Kazakh. 103 E2 also spelt Zhayylma
Zhaksy Kazakh. 103 F2 also spelt Zhaqsy; formerly spelt Dzhaksy
Zhaksy-Kon watercourse Kazakh. 103 G2
Zhaksykylysh Kazakh. 103 E3
Zhaksykylysh, Ozero salt l. Kazakh. 103 E3
Zhaksy Sarysu watercourse Kazakh. see Sarysu
Zhalaghash Kazakh. see Dzhalagash
Zhalanash Almatinskaya Oblast' Kazakh. 103 I4
Zhalanash Kustanayskaya Oblast' Kazakh. see Damdy
Zhalgyztöbe Kazakh. see Zhangiztobe
Zhalpaktal Kazakh. 102 B2 also spelt Zhalpaqtal; formerly known as Furmanovo
Zhalpaqtal Kazakh. see Zhalpaktal
Zhaltyr Kazakh. 103 G2 formerly spelt Dzhaltyr
Zhaltyr, Ozero l. Kazakh. 102 B3
Zhaludok Belarus 42 F8
Zhamanakkol', Ozero salt l. Kazakh. 103 E2
Zhamansor Kazakh. 102 C3
Zhambyl Karagandinskaya Oblast' Kazakh. 103 G3
Zhambyl Zhambylskaya Oblast' Kazakh. see Taraz
Zhambyl Oblast admin. div. Kazakh. see Zhambylskaya Oblast'
Zhambylskaya Oblast' admin. div. Kazakh. 103 H3 English form Zhambyl Oblast; formerly known as Dzhambulskaya Oblast'
Zhameuka Kazakh. 103 J3
Zhamo China see Bomi
Zhanakorgan Kazakh. 103 F4 also spelt Zhangaqorghan; formerly known as Yany-Kurgan
Zhanakurylys Kazakh. 103 E3
Zhanang China 89 E6 also known as Chatang
Zhanaortalyk Kazakh. 103 H3
Zhanaozen Kazakh. 102 C4 also spelt Zhangaözen; formerly known as Novyy Uzen'
Zhanatalan Kazakh. 103 I4
Zhanatas Kazakh. 103 G4 also spelt Zhangatas
Zhanbay Kazakh. 102 B3
Zhanbei China 82 B2 formerly known as Zhanhe
Zhangaözen Kazakh. see Zhanaozen
Zhangaqazaly Kazakh. see Ayteke Bi
Zhanga Qazan Kazakh. see Novaya Kazanka
Zhangaqorghan Kazakh. see Zhanakorgan
Zhangatas Kazakh. see Zhanatas
Zhangbei China 85 G3
Zhangcheng China see Yongtai
Zhangcunpu China 87 F1
Zhangde China see Anyang
Zhangdian China see Zibo
Zhanggu China see Danba
Zhangguangcai Ling mts China 82 C3
Zhang He r. China 85 G4
Zhanghua Taiwan see Changhua
Zhangiztobe Kazakh. 103 J2 also known as Zhalgyztöbe
Zhangjiajie China 87 D2 formerly known as Dayong
Zhangjiakou China 85 G3 also known as Kalgan
Zhangjiapan China see Jingbian
Zhangla China 86 B1
Zhanglou China 87 F1
Zhangping China 87 F3
Zhangpu China 87 F3 also known as Sui'an
Zhangqiu China 85 H4
Zhangshu China 87 E2 formerly known as Qingjiang
Zhangwei Xinhe r. China 85 H4
Zhangwu China 85 I3
Zhangxian China 86 C1
Zhangye China 84 D4
Zhangzhou China 87 F3 formerly spelt Changchow
Zhangzi China 85 G4
Zhanhe China see Zhanbei
Zhan He r. China 82 C2
Zhanhua China 85 H4 also known as Fuguo
Zhanibek Kazakh. 102 A2 also known as Zhänibek
Zhänibek Kazakh. see Zhanibek
Zhanjiang China 87 D4 formerly spelt Changkiang
Zhansügirov Kazakh. see Dzhansugurov
Zhanterek Kazakh. 102 C3
Zhanti Koe Canada see Fort Providence
Zhanyi China 86 B3
Zhao'an China 87 F4 also known as Nanzhao
Zhaodong China 82 B3
Zhaoge China see Qixian
Zhaojue China 86 B2 also known as Xincheng
Zhaoliqiao China 87 E2
Zhaoping China 87 D3
Zhaoqing China 87 E4
Zhaoren China see Changwu
Zhaosu China 88 C3 also known as Mongolküre
Zhaosutai He r. China 85 I3
Zhaotong China 86 B3
Zhaoxian China 85 G4 also known as Zhaozhou
Zhaoyuan Heilong. China 82 B3
Zhaoyuan Shandong China 85 I4
Zhaozhen China see Jintang
Zhaozhou Hebei China see Zhaoxian
Zhaozhou Heilong. China 82 B3
Zhapo China 87 D4
Zhaqsy Kazakh. see Zhaksy
Zharbulak Almatinskaya Oblast' Kazakh. see Kabanbay
Zharbulak Vostochnyy Kazakhstan Kazakh. 88 C2
Zhardzyazhzha Belarus 42 I7
Zhari Namco salt l. China 89 D6
Zharkamys Kazakh. 102 D3
Zharkent Kazakh. 103 J3 formerly known as Panfilov; formerly spelt Dzharkent
Zharkovskiy Rus. Fed. 43 N6
Zharma Kazakh. 103 J2
Zharmysh-Ondy Kazakh. 102 C3
Zharsuat Kazakh. 103 J3
Zharyk Karagandinskaya Oblast' Kazakh. see Saken Seyfullin
Zharyk Vostochnyy Kazakhstan Kazakh. 103 J2
Zhashkiv Ukr. 41 D6 also spelt Zhashkov
Zhashkov Ukr. see Zhashkiv
Zhashui China 87 D1 also known as Qianyou
Zhaslyk Uzbek. see Jasliq
Zhastkovo Rus. Fed. 43 N8
Zhaxi China see Weixin
Zhaxi Co salt l. China 89 D5
Zhaxigang China 89 B5
Zhaxizê China 86 A2
Zhayrem Kazakh. 103 G2
Zhayü China 86 A2
Zhayylma Kazakh. see Zhailma
Zhayyq r. Kazakh./Rus. Fed. see Ural
Zhdanov Ukr. see Mariupol'
Zhdanovo Kazakh. 103 G4
Zhdanovo Rus. Fed. 43 O4
Zhdanovsk Azer. see Beyläqan
Zhecheng China 87 E1
Zhedao China see Lianghe
Zhêhor China 86 B2
Zhejiang prov. China 87 G2 English form Chekiang
Zhelang China 87 E4
Zhelaniya, Mys c. Rus. Fed. 39 G2
Zhelcha r. Rus. Fed. 42 I3
Zhelezinka Kazakh. 103 H1
Zheleznodorozhnyy Kaliningradskaya Oblast' Rus. Fed. 42 C7 historically known as Gerdauen
Zheleznodorozhnyy Respublika Komi Rus. Fed. see Yemva
Zheleznodorozhnyy Uzbek. see Qo'ng'irot
Zheleznogorsk Rus. Fed. 43 Q9
Zhelezny a Rus. Fed. 43 S7
Zhelou China see Ceheng
Zheltorangy Kazakh. 103 H3
Zheltyye Vody Ukr. see Zhovti Vody
Zhelyu Voyvoda Bulg. 58 H6
Zhem Kazakh. see Emba
Zhen'an China 87 D1 also known as Yongle
Zhenba China 87 C1
Zheng'an China 87 C2 also known as Fengyi
Zhengding China 85 G4
Zhenghe China 87 F3 also known as Xiongshan
Zhengjiakou China see Gucheng
Zhengjiatun China see Shuangliao
Zhengkou China see Gucheng
Zhenglan Qi China see Dund Hot
Zhengning China 85 F5 also known as Shanhe
Zhengxiangbai Qi China see Qagan Nur
Zhengyang China 87 E1 also known as Zhenyang
Zhengzhou China 87 E1 formerly spelt Chengchow
Zhenhai China 87 G2
Zhenjiang China see Dantu
Zhenjiangguan China 86 B1
Zhenlai China 85 I2
Zhenning China 86 C3
Zhenping China 87 D2
Zhenwudong China see Ansai
Zhenxi China 85 I2
Zhenxiong China 86 C3 also known as Wufeng
Zhenyang China see Zhengyang
Zhenyuan Gansu China 85 E5
Zhenyuan Guizhou China 87 D3 also known as Wuyang
Zhenyuan Yunnan China 86 B4 also known as Enle
Zhenziling China 87 D2
Zherdevka Rus. Fed. 41 G6 formerly known as Chibizovka
Zherdevo Rus. Fed. 43 R8
Zherong China 87 F3 also known as Shuangcheng
Zheshart Rus. Fed. 40 I3
Zhestylevo Rus. Fed. 43 S5
Zhetibay Kazakh. see Zhetybay
Zhetikara Kazakh. see Zhitikara
Zhetisay Kazakh. see Zhetysay
Zhetybay Kazakh. 102 C4 also spelt Zhetibay
Zhety-Kol', Ozero l. Rus. Fed. 103 E2
Zhetysay Kazakh. 103 G4 also spelt Zhetisay; formerly spelt Dzhetysay
Zhêxam China 89 D6
Zhexi Shuiku resr China 87 D2
Zhezdy Kazakh. 103 F2 formerly known as Marganets; formerly spelt Dzhezdy
Zhezkazgan Kazakh. 103 F3 also spelt Zhezqazghan; formerly spelt Dzhezkazgan
Zhezqazghan Kazakh. see Zhezkazgan
Zhicheng China see Changxing
Zhichitsy Rus. Fed. 43 M6
Zhidan China 85 F4 also known as Bao'an
Zhidoi China 97 G2 also known as Gyaijêpozhanggê
Zhigansk Rus. Fed. 39 M3
Zhigung China 89 E6
Zhijiang China 87 D3
Zhijin China 86 C3
Zhilevo Rus. Fed. 43 T7
Zhilino Rus. Fed. 43 R8
Zhilyanka Kazakh. see Kargalinskoye
Zhi Qu r. China see Yangtze Kiang
Zhi Qu r. China see Yangtze
Zhirnovsk Rus. Fed. 41 H6 formerly known as Zhirnovskiy or Zhirnoye
Zhirnovskiy Rus. Fed. see Zhirnovsk
Zhirnoye Rus. Fed. see Zhirnovsk
Zhiryatino Rus. Fed. 43 O8
Zhitarovo Bulg. see Vetren
Zhitikara Kazakh. 103 E1 also spelt Zhetikara; formerly known as Dzhetygara
Zhitkovichi Belarus see Zhytkavichy
Zhitkovo Rus. Fed. 43 K1
Zhitkur Rus. Fed. 102 A2
Zhitomir Ukr. see Zhytomyr
Zhizdra Rus. Fed. 43 P8
Zhizdra r. Rus. Fed. 43 R7
Zhizhitsa Rus. Fed. 43 M5
Zhizhitskoye, Ozero l. Rus. Fed. 43 M5
Zhlobin Belarus 43 L9
Zhmerinka Ukr. see Zhmerynka
Zhmerynka Ukr. 41 D6 also spelt Zhmerinka
Zhob Pak. 101 G4 formerly known as Fort Sandeman
Zhob r. Pak. 101 G3
Zhodzina Belarus 43 J7
Zhokhova, Ostrov i. Rus. Fed. 39 P2
Zholnuskay Kazakh. 88 C1
Zholymbet Kazakh. 103 G2
Zhong'an China see Fuyuan
Zhongba Guangdong China 87 E4
Zhongba Sichuan China see Jiangyou
Zhongba Xizang China 89 D6
Zhongcheng China see Suijiang
Zhongduo China see Youyang
Zhongguo country Asia see China
Zhongguo Renmin Gongheguo country Asia see China
Zhonghe China see Xiushan
Zhongmou China 87 E1
Zhongning China 85 E4
Zhongping China see Huize
Zhongshan research station Antarctica 223 F2
Zhongshan Guangdong China 87 E4 formerly known as Shiqizhen
Zhongshan Guangxi China 87 D3
Zhongshan Guizhou China see Lupanshui
Zhongsha Qundao sea feature S. China Sea see Macclesfield Bank
Zhongshu Yunnan China see Luxi
Zhongshu Yunnan China see Luliang
Zhongtai China see Lingtai
Zhongtiao Shan mts China 87 D1
Zhongwei China 84 E4
Zhongxian China 87 D2 also known as Zhongzhou
Zhongxiang China 87 E2 UNESCO World Heritage Site
Zhongxin Guangdong China 87 E3
Zhongxin Yunnan China see Xianggelila
Zhongxin Yunnan China see Huaping
Zhongxing China see Siyang
Zhongxingji China 87 F2

Geographical terms

This table contains the most commonly used geographical terms in this atlas. It explains the language and meaning of important non-English terms used on the maps and in the index. Generic terms such as these are commonly used within the names of places and geographical features to describe their nature or origin.

Afrikaans
Berg, -berg, -berge — mountain(s)
Groot — big
-punt — cape, point
-veld — field

Amharic (Ethiopia)
Hāyk' — lake
Ras — mountain
Shet' — river
Wenz — river

Arabic
Bahr — river
Buḥayrat — lake
Chott — impermanent lake, salt lake
Erg — sandy desert
Ghubbat — bay
Ḥadabat — plain
Hawr — lake
Jabal, Jebel — mountain(s)
Jazā'ir — islands
Jiddat — desert
Juzur — islands
Khalīj — gulf, bay
Nafūd — desert
Ra's — cape, point
Ramlat — sandy desert
Sebkha — impermanent lake, salt lake
Wāḥāt — oasis
Wādī — watercourse

Bulgarian
Nizina — lowland
Nos — cape, point
Planina — hills, mountains

Chinese
Bandao — peninsula
Feng — mountain
Gaoyuan — plateau
Hai — sea
He — river
Hu — lake
Jiang — river
Ling — mountain range
Nur — lake
Pendi — basin
Shamo — desert
Shan — mountain(s)
Tao — island
Wan — bay
Yunhe — canal

Dutch
Kanaal — canal
-meer — lake
-zee — sea

Farsi (Iran), Dari (Afghanistan)
Daryācheh — lake
Dasht — desert
Hāmūn — marsh, salt pan
Kūh, Kūhhā — mountain(s)
Reshteh — mountain range
Rūd — river

French
Baie — bay
Cap — cape, point
Chaîne — mountain range
Étang — lagoon, lake
Golfe — gulf, bay
Grande — big
Île, Îles — island; islands
Lac — lake
Massif — mountains,
Mont, Monts — mountain(s)
Petit — small
Pic — peak
Pointe (Pte) — cape, point

German
Alb — mountain range
-berg — hill, mountain
Bucht — gulf, bay
-gebirge — mountains
Heide — heath, moor
Inseln — islands
Kap — cape, point
Wald, -wald — forest (mountains)

Greek
Akra — cape, point
Kolpos — gulf, bay
Nisoi — islands
Pelagos — sea

Indonesian
Bukit — mountain
Gunung — mountain
Kepulauan — islands
Laut — sea
Pegunungan — mountain range
Pulau-pulau — islands
Puncak — mountain
Selat — strait
Semenanjung — peninsula
Tanjung — cape, point
Teluk — gulf, bay

Italian
Capo — cape, point
Golfo — gulf, bay
Isola, Isole — island; islands
Monte, Monti — mountain(s)

Japanese
-dake — mountain
-gang — river
-hantō — peninsula
-jima — island
-kaikyō — strait
-ko — lake
-misaki — cape, point
-nada — gulf, bay
-rettō — islands
-san — mountain
-sanmyaku — mountain range
-shima — island
-shotō — islands
-suidō — strait
-tō — island
-wan — bay
-zaki — cape, point

Korean
-bong — mountain
-do — island
-gang — river
-haehyŏp — strait
-ho — lake
-man — bay
-san — mountain

Malay
Banjaran — mountain range
Gunung — mountain

Norwegian
-dal — valley
-halvøya — peninsula
-kapp — cape, point

Portuguese
Baía — bay
Barragem — dam, reservoir
Cabo — cape, point
Chapada — hills, uplands

Ilha — island
Lago — lake
Lagoa — lagoon
Pico — peak
Planalto — plateau
Ponta — cape, point
Represa — reservoir
Rio — river
São, Santa, Santo — saint
Serra — mountain range

Romanian
Lacul — lake
Meridionali — southern
Pasul — pass
Podişul — plateau
Vârful — mountain

Russian
Bol'shoy — big
Gora — mountain
Gryada — ridge
Guba — gulf, bay
Khrebet — mountain range
Kryazh — hills, ridge
Les — forest
Malyy — small
More — sea
Mys — cape, point
Nizmennost' — lowland
Ostrov, Ostrova — island(s)
Ozero — lake
Peski — desert
Ploskogor'ye — plateau
Poluostrov — peninsula
Proliv — strait
Ravnina — plain
Vodokhranilishche — reservoir
Vozvyshennost' — upland
Zaliv — gulf, bay
Zemlya — land

Spanish
Bahía — bay
Cabo — cape, point
Cayos — islands
Cerro — mountain
Cordillera — mountain range
Costa — coastal area
Embalse — reservoir
Estrecho — strait
Golfo — gulf, bay
Gran, Grande — big
Isla, Islas — island; islands
Lago — lake
Laguna — lagoon
Mar — sea
Montes — mountains
Nevado, Nudo — snow-covered mountain
Picacho, Pico — peak
Presa — reservoir
Punta — cape, point
Río — river
Salar — salt pan
San, Santa, Santo — saint
Sierra — mountain range
Volcán — volcano

Turkish
Burun — cape, point
Dağ, Dağı — mountain
Dağları — mountain range
Denizi — sea
Gölü — lake
Körfezi — gulf, bay

Vietnamese
Cao Nguyên — plateau
Hô — lake
Mui — cape, point
Sông — river

Statistical definitions

The statistical tables on pages 36–37, 70–71, 118–119, 142–143, 162–163, 196–197, contain a series of indicators. The tables below define these indicators and give details of the main sources used.

Indicator	Definition
Population	
Total population	Estimated total population by country, 2005.
Population change	Percentage annual rate of change, 2000–2005.
Percentage urban	Urban population as a percentage of the total population, 2003.
Total fertility	Average number of children a woman will have during her child-bearing years, 2000-2005.
Population by age	Population in age groups 0–14 and 60 or over, 2005.
2050 projected population	Projected total population by country for the year 2050.
Economy	
Total Gross National Income (GNI)	The sum of value added to the economy by all resident producers plus taxes, less subsidies, plus net receipts of primary income from abroad. Data latest available, in U.S. dollars (millions). Formerly known as Gross National product, GNP.
GNI per capita	The gross national income, per person in U.S. dollars using the World Bank Atlas method, from latest available data.
Debt service ratio	Debt service as a percentage of GNI, from latest available data.
Total debt service	Sum of principal repayments and interest paid on long-term debt, interest paid on short-term debt and repayments to the IMF, 2002.
Aid receipts	Aid received as a percentage of GNI from the Development Assistance Committee (DAC) of the Organization for Economic Co-operation and Development (OECD), 2002.
Military spending	Military-related spending, including recruiting, training, construction, and the purchase of military supplies and equipment, as a percentage of GDP, from latest available data.
Social indicators	
Child mortality rate	Number of deaths of children aged under 5 per 1 000 live births, 2003.
Life expectancy	Average life expectancy at birth in years, male and female, 2000-05.
Literacy rate	Percentage of population aged 15–24 with at least a basic ability to read and write, 2002.
Access to safe water	Percentage of population with sustainable access to improved drinking water sources, from latest available data.
Doctors per 100 000 people	Number of trained doctors per 100 000 people. Latest figures in period 1990-2003.
Environment	
Forest area	Percentage of total land area covered by forest. 2000.
Annual change in forest area	Average annual percentage change in forest area. 1990–2000.
Protected land area	Percentage of total land area designated as protected land, 2004.
CO_2 emissions	Emissions of carbon, expressed in metric tonnes per capita, from the burning of fossil fuels and the manufacture of cement.
Communications	
Main telephone lines per 100 people	Main telephone lines per 100 inhabitants, from latest available data.
Cellular mobile subscribers per 100 people	Cellular mobile subscribers per 100 inhabitants, from latest available data.
Internet users per 10 000 people	Internet users per 10 000 inhabitants, from latest available data.
International dialling code	The country code prefix to be used when dialling from another country.
Time zone	Time difference in hours between local standard time and Greenwich Mean Time.

Main statistical sources

	Internet links
United Nations Statistics Division	unstats.un.org/unsd
World Population Prospects: The 2004 Revision and World Urbanization Prospects: The 2003 Revision, United Nations Population Division	www.un.org/esa/population/unpop
United Nations Population Information Network	www.un.org/popin
United Nations Development Programme	www.undp.org
Organisation for Economic Cooperation and Development	www.oecd.org
State of the World's Forests 2001, Food and Agriculture Organization of the United Nations	www.fao.org
World Development Indicators 2005, World Bank	www.worldbank.org/data
World Resources Institute Earth Trends Environmental Database online	earthtrends.wri.org
International Telecommunication Union	www.itu.int

Acknowledgements

Maps

Maps designed and created by HarperCollins Reference, Glasgow, UK

Continental perspective views (pp28–29, 60–61, 110–111, 134–135, 154–155, 188–189) and globes (pp 208–209, 214): Alan Collinson Design/GeoInnovations, Llandudno, UK, www.geoinnovations.co.uk

The publishers would like to thank all national survey departments, road, rail and national park authorities, statistical offices and national place name committees throughout the world for their valuable assistance, and in particular the following:

British Antarctic Survey, Cambridge, UK

Bureau of Rural Sciences, Barton, ACT, Australia, a scientific agency of the Department of Agriculture, Fisheries and Forestry, Australia

Tony Champion, Professor of Population Geography, University of Newcastle upon Tyne, UK

Mr P J M Geelan, London, UK

International Boundary Research Unit, University of Durham, UK

The Meteorological Office, Bracknell, Berkshire, UK

Permanent Committee on Geographical Names, London, UK

Data

Antarctica (pp222–223): Antarctic Digital Database (versions 1 and 2), © Scientific Committee on Antarctic Research (SCAR), Cambridge, UK (1993, 1998)

Bathymetric data: The GEBCO Digital Atlas published by the British Oceanographic Data Centre on behalf of IOC and IHO, 1994

Earthquakes data (pp10–11, 66): United States Geological Survey (USGS) National Earthquakes Information Center, Denver, USA

Coral reefs data (pp 14–15, 141): UNEP World Conservation Monitoring Centre (UNEP-WCMC), Cambridge, UK. 'Reefs at Risk', 1998 Washington, DC, USA from World Resources Institute (WRI), the International Center for Living Aquatic Resources Management (ICLARM) and UNEP-WCMC

Land cover data (pp30-31, 62–63, 112–113, 136–137, 156–157, 190–191): Global Land Cover 2000 Database. © Copyright European Communities, Joint Research Centre, European Commission. Digital data and more information available from http://www.gvm.jrc.it/glc2000/defaultGLC2000.htm Glc2000.info@jrc.it

Population data (pp16–17): Center for International Earth Science Information Network (CIESN), Columbia University; International Food Policy Research Institute (IFPRI); and World Resources Institute (WRI). 2000. Gridded Population of the World (GPW), Version 3. Palisades, NY: CIESN, Columbia University. Available at http://sedac.ciesn.columbia.edu/plue/gpw

Photographs and images

page	image	credit
6–7	Sinai	NASA
	Kamchatka	MODIS/NASA
8–9	Washington	US Geological Survey/Science Photo Library
	Mauretania/ Senegal	CNES/1986 Distribution Spot Image/ Science Photo Library
	Singapore	Courtesy of USGS EROS Data Center
10–11	Bam	© Fatih Saribas/Reuters/CORBIS
	Power station	© Robert Holmes/CORBIS
12–13	Aurora Borealis	NASA/Science Photo Library
14–15	Deforestation in Madagascar	© Wolfgang Kaehler/CORBIS
	Mt St Helens	© Roger Rossmeyer/CORBIS
	Ganges	© Amit Bhargava/CORBIS
	Yellowstone National Park	© Michael T. Sedam/CORBIS
	Greenland	© Galen Rowell/CORBIS
	Drought in Spain	© Despotovic Dusko/CORBIS Sygma
	Dust storm in north Africa	MODIS/NASA
	Desertification	Votchev-UNEP/Still Pictures
16–17	Tokyo	Cities Revealed ® Aeriel Photography © The Geoinformation ® Group 1998
	Village in Botswana	David Reed/Panos Pictures
18–19	Chengdu images	Annemarie Schneider, Boston University/ NASA
	Paris	IKONOS Space Imaging Europe/ Science Photo Library
20–21	Field hospital	Ron Giling/Still Pictures
	Unsafe water	Harmut Schwarzbach/Still Pictures
22–23	London	© London Aerial Photo Library/CORBIS
	Freetown	Edgar Cleijne/Still Pictures
24–25	Baghdad	© Ceerwan Aziz/Reuters/CORBIS
	Child soldier	© Patrick Robert/Sygma/CORBIS
	Gaza refugee	© Ahmed Rashad/Reuters/CORBIS
26–27	Sinai	NASA
	Vatican City	IKONOS satellite imagery provided by Space Imaging, Thornton, Colorado, www.spaceimaging.com
	Bora Bora	CNES/ Distribution SPOT Image/ Science Photo Library
	Global positioning system	David Vaughan/Science Photo Library
	Aral Sea	Data available from the U.S. Geological Survey, EROS Data Center, Sioux Falls, SD
28–29	Alps	NASA
	Consuegra, central Spain	© Royalty Free/CORBIS
	Iceland	MODIS/NASA
30–31	European vineyard	© Georgina Bowater/CORBIS
	Netherlands bulbfields	© Michael John Kielty/CORBIS
	Lakes in Finland	Geoslides Photography
	Italian fields	ESA, Eurimage/Science Photo Library
	Scotland	NRSC/Science Photo Library
	Corncrake	© Roger Tidman/CORBIS
32–33	Bosporus	CNES/1993 Distribution Spot Image/ Science Photo Library
	Berlin	CNES/1991Distribution Spot Image/ Science Photo Library
	Vatican City	IKONOS satellite imagery provided by Space Imaging, Thornton, Colorado, www.spaceimaging.com
34–35	Euro	© Matthias Kulka/CORBIS
	Taormina	© Wolfgang Kaehler/CORBIS
	Augusta	© Gianni Giansanti/Sygma/CORBIS
	EU building, Brussels	Wim Van Cappellen/Still Pictures
60–61	Yangtze	MODIS/NASA
	Himalaya	ImageState
	Aral Sea satellite images	1973, 1986, 2001: U.S. Geological Survey, EROS Data Center, Sioux Falls, SD; 2005: MODIS/NASA
62–63	Bali	Yann Arthus-Bertrand/CORBIS
	Zaskar	NASA/Science Photo Library
	Abu Dhabi images	1972 CNES/Science Photo Library; 1987 Distribution Spot Image/ Science Photo Library
	Red panda	Tim Davis/Science Photo Library
64–65	Great Wall of China	Georg Gerster/NGS Image Collection
66–67	Satellite images	Space Imaging/CRISP-Singapore
	Tsunami	Gemunu Amarasinghe/AP/EMPICS
	Map of earthquake activity	Data provided by USGS
68–69	West Bank Wall	© Gil Cohen Magen/Reuters/CORBIS
	Three Gorges Dam	© China Photos/Reuters/CORBIS
	Mesopotamian marshes images	NASA/EROS Data Center
110–111	Victoria Falls	Roger De La Harpe, Gallo Images/CORBIS
	Sahara desert	© Yann Arthus-Bertrand/CORBIS
	Congo river	© CORBIS
112–113	Gorilla	© Joe McDonald/CORBIS
	Okavango delta	NASA
	Nile	CNES/1994 Distribution Spot Image/ Science Photo Library
	Namib desert	John Beatty/Getty Images/Stone
	Lake Chad images	UNEP/GRID Sioux Falls, at the USGS National Center for Earth Resources Observation and Science.
114–115	Border post	Peter Hering
116–117	Refugees	© Radu Sigheti/Reuters/CORBIS
	AIDS sign	Friedrich Stark/Still Pictures
134–135	Lake Eyre	NASA
	Mount Cook	Mike Schroder/Still Pictures
	Kiritimati	NASA
136–137	Mangrove swamp	© Arne Hodalic/CORBIS
	Bilby	© Martin Harvey/CORBIS
	Rabbit damage	© Philip Perry, Frank Lane Picture Agency/ CORBIS
	Albatross	© Roger Tidman/CORBIS
	French Polynesia	ImageState
	Gibson desert	CNES/1986 Distribution Spot Image/ Science Photo Library
	Banks Peninsula	Institute of Geological and Nuclear Sciences, New Zealand
138–139	Ayers Rock	ImageState
	Canberra	Aerial photograph courtesy Geoscience Australia, Canberra. Crown Copyright ©. All rights reserved. www.ga.gov.au/nmd
140–141	Bora Bora	CNES/ Distribution Spot Image/ Science Photo Library
	Palau	© Jeffrey L. Rotman/CORBIS
	Mataiva	Gerard and Margi Moss/Still Pictures
	Bleached coral	Alexis Rosenfeld/Science Photo Library
	Salinity damage	Bill van Aken © CSIRO Land and Water
	Salinity hazard map	Bureau of Rural Sciences
142–143	Ghan train	© Tim Wimbourne/Reuters/CORBIS
	James Cook	© Hulton-Deutsch Collection/CORBIS
154–155	Grand Canyon	© Owen Franken/CORBIS
	Great Lakes	MODIS/NASA
156–157	St Lucia	© George H. H. Huey/CORBIS
	Arctic	© Lowell Georgia/CORBIS
	Monument valley	Pictures Colour Library Ltd
	Manatee	© Stephen Frinks/CORBIS
	Florida	Earth Satellite Corporation/ Science Photo Library
	Great Plains	Alex S. Maclean/Still Pictures
	Stockton, California	NRSC/Still Pictures
158–159	Panama Canal	Clifton-Campbell Imaging Inc. www.tmarchive.com
	USA-Mexico border	NASA
	USA-Canada border	Gregor Turk
160–161	Denver smog	© Ted Spiegel/CORBIS
	Pensacola images	IKONOS/Earth Observatory/NASA
	Hurricane Ivan	NASA
162–163	Mississippi	© Craig Aurness/CORBIS
188–189	Iguaçu Falls	© James Davis, Eye Ubiquitous/ CORBIS
	Atacama desert	© Ludovic Maisant/CORBIS
190–191	Nequen, Argentina	© Yann Artus-Bertrand/CORBIS
	Patagonia	© Francesc Muntada/CORBIS
	Macaw	© Royalty Free/CORBIS
	Amazon	Jacques Jangoux/Science Picture Library
	Atacama desert	CNES/1986 Distribution Spot Image/ Science Photo Library
	Mining in Rondônia, Brazil	Mark Edwards/Still Pictures
	Itaipu images	USGS Eros Data Center
192–193	Galapagos	CNES/1988 Distribution Spot Image/ Science Photo Library
	Santiago	Earth Satellite Corporation/ Science Photo Library
	Brasilia	CNES/1995 Distribution Spot Image/ Science Photo Library
	La Paz	© Wolfgang Kaehler/CORBIS
194–195	Deforestation images	NASA/Goddard Space Flight Center/ Science Photo Library
	Colombian soldiers	Getty Images
	Coca picking	© Gustavo Gilabert/CORBIS SABA
196–197	Machu Picchu	David Nunuk/Science Photo Library
	Jesuit mission	© Bojan Brecelj/CORBIS
208–209	Ocean floor globes	Geo-Innovations, Llandudno, UK. www.geoinnovations.co.uk
	Ice pressure ridge	Bryan and Cherry Alexander
	Mt Erebus	© Peter Johnson/CORBIS
210–211	Seafloor/trenches image	Geo-Innovations, Llandudno, UK. www.geoinnovations.co.uk
	Heat transport map	A. McDonald and C. Wunsch, USA
	Seafloor map	WHF Smith, US National Oceanic and Atmospheric Administration (NOAA), USA
	El Niño globe	NASA/Science Photo Library
212–213	Cruise ship	Bryan and Cherry Alexander
	Ozone Hole	Image courtesy of Scientific Visualization Studio, GSFC, NASA
	Antarctic image	NRSC Ltd/Science Photo Library
214–215	Arctic peoples' globe	Geo-Innovations, Llandudno, UK. www.geoinnovations.co.uk
	Nenets herders	Bryan and Cherry Alexander
	Sea ice maps	F. Fetterer and K. Knowles. 2002, updated 2004. Sea Ice Index. Boulder, CO: National Snow and Ice Data Center. Digital media.
	Novaya Zemlya	NASA
Cover	Sinai Peninsula	© 1996 CORBIS; Original image courtesy of NASA/CORBIS

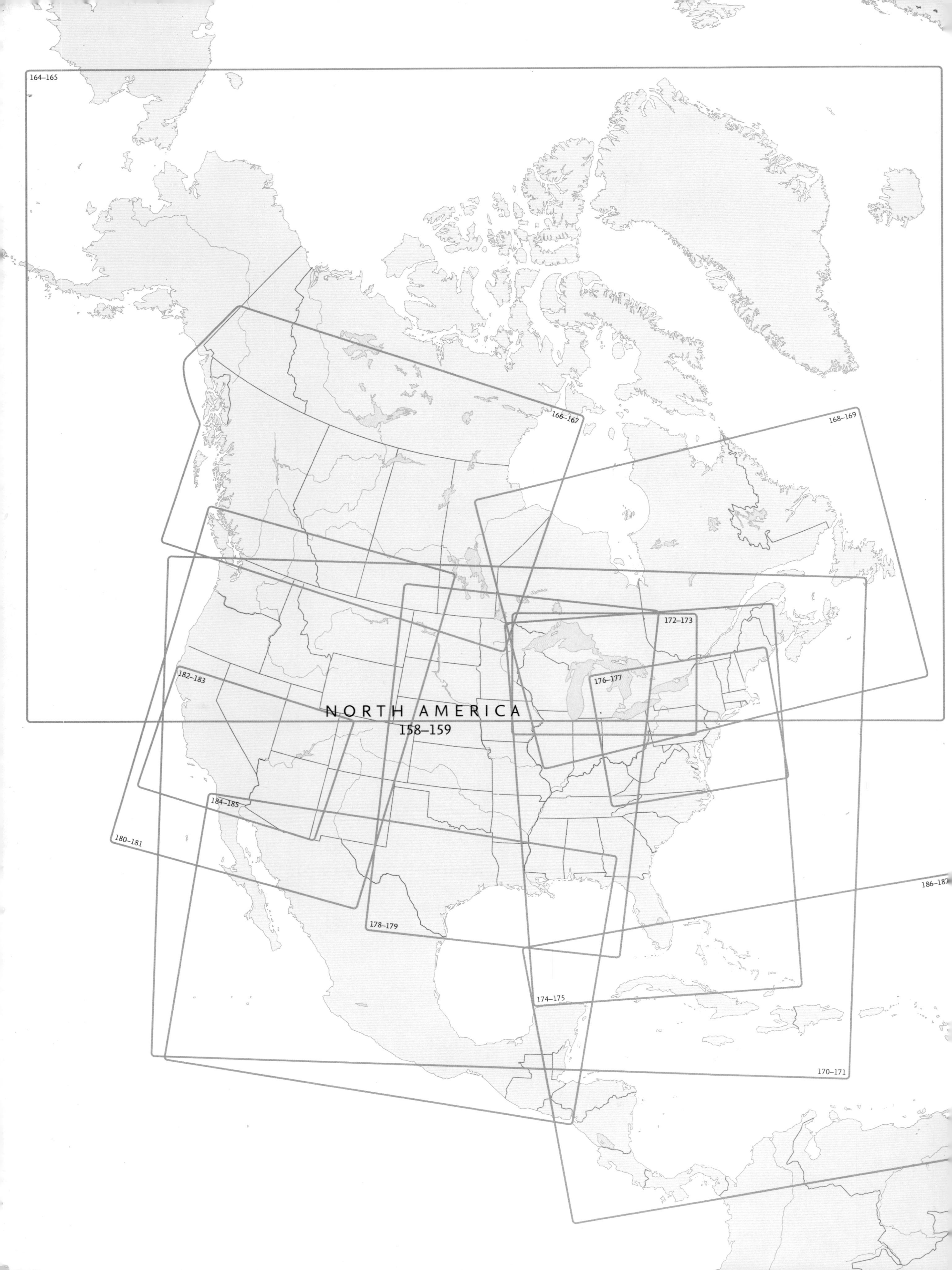

NORTH AMERICA
158–159

164–165

166–167

168–169

172–173

176–177

182–183

184–185

180–181

178–179

186–187

174–175

170–171